CHILTON'S GUIDE TO
FUEL INJECTION & ELECTRONIC ENGINE CONTROLS-1984-88

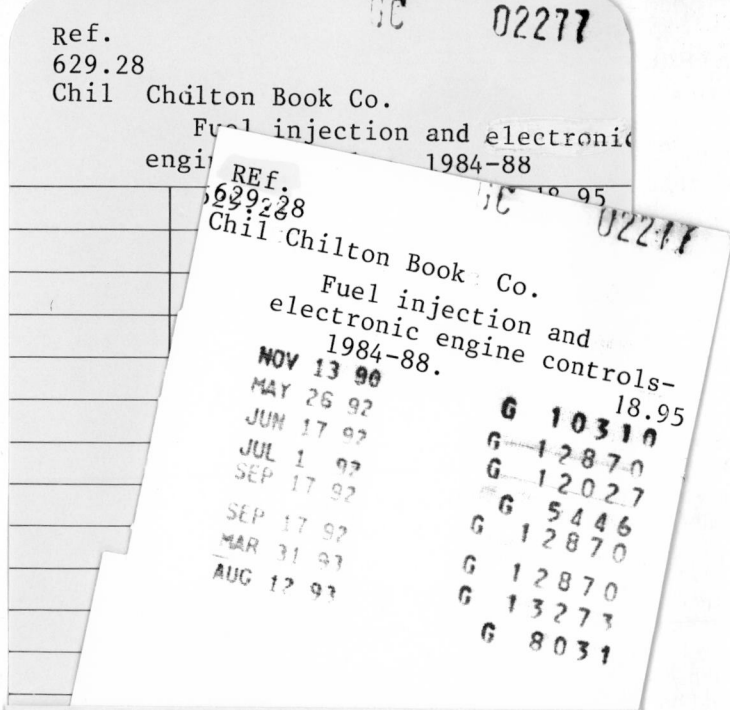

Vice Presi

MPANY
, PA 19089

86-47790

HOW TO USE THIS MANUAL

For ease of use, this manual is divided into sections as follows:

SECTION 1 Basic Electricity
SECTION 2 Troubleshooting and Diagnosis
SECTION 3 Self-Diagnostic Systems
SECTION 4 Electronic Ignition Systems
SECTION 5 Fuel Injection Systems

The **CONTENTS** summarize the subjects covered in each section.

To quickly locate the proper service section, use the application chart on the following pages. It references applicable **CAR AND TRUCK MODELS** and **SERVICE SECTIONS** for major electronic engine control systems.

It is recommended that the user be familiar with the applicable **GENERAL INFORMATION, SERVICE PRECAUTIONS** and **TROUBLESHOOTING AND DIAGNOSIS TECHNIQUES** before testing or servicing any engine control system.

Major service sections are grouped by vehicle manufacturer, with each engine control system subsection containing:

- **GENERAL INFORMATION** pertaining to the operation of the system, individual components and the overall logic by which components work together.

- **SERVICE PRECAUTIONS** (if any) of which the user should be aware to prevent injury or damage to the vehicle or components.

- **FAULT DIAGNOSIS** in the form of diagnostic charts or test procedures which lead the user through the various system circuit tests and explain the trouble codes stored in the computer memory.

SAFETY NOTICE

Proper service and repair procedures are vital to the safe, reliable operation of all motor vehicles, as well as the personal safety of those performing service or repairs. This manual outlines procedures for servicing and repairing vehicles using safe, effective methods. The procedures contain many NOTES and CAUTIONS which should be followed along with standard safety procedures to eliminate the possibility of personal injury or improper service which could damage the vehicle or compromise its safety.

It is important to note that repair procedures and techniques, tools and parts for servicing motor vehicles, as well as the skill and experience of the individual performing the work vary widely. It is not possible to anticipate all of the hazards that may result. Standard and accepted safety precautions and equipment should be used when handling toxic or flammable fluids and safety goggles or other protection should be used during cutting, grinding, chiseling, prying or any other process that that can cause material removal or projectiles. Similar protection against the high voltages generated in all electronic ignition systems should be employed during service procedures.

Some procedures require the use of tools or test equipment specially designed for a specific purpose. Before substituting another tool or procedure, you must be completely satisfied that neither your personal safety, nor the performance of the vehicle will be endangered.

PART NUMBERS

Part numbers listed in this reference are not recommendations by Chilton for any product by brand name. They are references that can be used with interchange manuals and aftermarket supplier catalogs to locate each brand supplier's discrete part number.

Although information in this manual is based on industry sources and is complete as possible at the time of publication, the possibilty exists that some car manufacturers made later changes which could not be included here. While striving for total accuracy, Chilton Book Company cannot assume responsibility for any errors, changes or omissions that may occur in the compilation of this data.

CONTENTS

COMPUTERIZED ENGINE CONTROL APPLICATIONS

Manufacturer	Year	Model	Engine cu. in. (liter)	VIN	SECTION 4 Electronic Ignition System	SECTION 5 Fuel Injection System
		GENERAL MOTORS CORPORATION				
Buick	1984	Skyhawk	110 (1.8)	O	HEI/EST	TBI
			110 (1.8)	J	HEI/EST	MPI-Turbo
			122 (2.0)	P	HEI/EST	TBI
		Century, Skylark	151 (2.5)	R	HEI/EST	TBI
		Regal, Riviera	231 (3.8)	9	C^3I	SFI-Turbo
	1985	Skyhawk	110 (1.8)	O	HEI/EST	TBI
			110 (1.8)	J	HEI/EST	MPI-Turbo
			122 (2.0)	P	HEI/EST	TBI
		Century, Skylark	151 (2.5)	R	HEI/EST	TBI
		Somerset Regal	151 (2.5)	U	HEI/EST	TBI
		Skylark	173 (2.8)	W	HEI/EST	MPI
		Somerset Regal	181 (3.0)	L	C^3I	MPI
		Century, Electra	231 (3.8)	3	HEI/EST	MPI
		Regal, Riviera	231 (3.8)	9	C^3I	SFI-Turbo
	1986	Skyhawk	110 (1.8)	O	HEI/EST	TBI
			110 (1.8)	J	HEI/EST	MPI-Turbo
			122 (2.0)	P	HEI/EST	TBI
		Century	151 (2.5)	R	HEI/EST	TBI
		Skylark, Somerset	151 (2.5)	U	HEI/EST	TBI
		LeSabre, Skylark, Somerset	181 (3.0)	L	C^3I	MPI
		Century, Electra, LeSabre, Riviera	231 (3.8)	B	C^3I	SFI
		Century, LeSabre	231 (3.8)	3	C^3I	SFI
		Regal	231 (3.8)	9	C^3I	SFI-Turbo
	1987-88	Skyhawk	122 (2.0)	K	HEI/EST	TBI
			122 (2.0)	M	HEI/EST	MPI
			122 (2.0) HO	1	HEI/EST	TBI
		Skylark, Somerset	151 (2.5)	U	HEI/EST	TBI
		Century	151 (2.5)	R	HEI/EST	TBI
		Skylark, Somerset	181 (3.0)	L	C^3I	MPI
		Electra, LeSabre, Riviera, Century	231 (3.8)	3	C^3I	SFI
		Regal	231 (3.8)	7	HEI/EST	SFI
Cadillac	1984	Cimarron	122 (2.0)	P	HEI/EST	TBI
		DeVille, Eldorado, Seville, Fleetwood	250 (4.1)	8	HEI/EST	DFI
	1985	Cimarron	122 (2.0)	P	HEI/EST	TBI

Refer to footnotes at the end of this chart

COMPUTERIZED ENGINE CONTROL APPLICATIONS

Manufacturer	Year	Model	Engine cu. in. (liter)	VIN	SECTION 4 Electronic Ignition System	SECTION 5 Fuel Injection System
AMERICAN MOTORS CORPORATION						
AMC/Jeep	1984	Wagoneer, Commanche, Cherokee	150 (2.5)	H	SSI	TBI
	1985	Commanche, Wagoneer, Cherokee	150 (2.5)	H	SSI	TBI
	1986	Commanche, Wagoneer, Cherokee	150 (2.5)	H	SSI	TBI
	1987–88	Cherokee, Wagoneer, Commanche, YJ, Wrangler	150 (2.5)	H	SSI	TBI
		Cherokee, Wagoneer, Commanche	242 (4.0)	M	SSI	MPI
CHRYSLER CORPORATION						
Chrysler	1984	All Models	135 (2.2)	D	HALL/ESA	SFI
			135 (2.2)	D	HALL/ESA	MFI Turbo
	1985	All Models	135 (2.2)	D	HALL/ESA	SFI
			135 (2.2)	E	HALL/ESA	MFI Turbo
	1986	All Models	135 (2.2)	D	HALL/ESA	SFI
			135 (2.2)	E	HALL/ESA	MFI Turbo
			153 (2.5)	K	HALL/ESA	SFI
	1987–88	All Models	135 (2.2)	D	HALL/ESA	SFI
			135 (2.2)	E	HALL/ESA	MFI Turbo
			153 (2.5)	K	HALL/ESA	SFI
			181 (3.0)	3	HALL/ESA	MFI
FORD MOTOR COMPANY						
Ford	1984	All Models	98 (1.6)	5	TFI-IV	EFI
		Federal Models	98 (1.6)	5	TFI-IV	EFI-Turbo
		All Models	140 (2.3)	W	TFI-IV	EFI-Turbo
		Thunderbird, Cougar, Mustang Capri, LTD, Marquis	230 (3.8)	3	TFI-IV	CFI
		Mustang, Capri, LTD, Lincoln, Mark VII, Crown Victoria, Grand Marquis, Continental, Cougar, Thunderbird	302 (5.0)	F	TFI-IV	CFI
	1985	Escort, Lynx, EXP	98 (1.6)	5	TFI-IV	EFI
			98 (1.6)	5	TFI-IV	EFI-Turbo
		Tempo, Topaz	140 (2.3)	X	TFI-IV	CFI
		Thunderbird, Cougar, Mustang SVO	140 (2.3)	W	TFI-IV	EFI
		Thunderbird, Cougar, LTD, Marquis, Capri, Mustang	230 (3.8)	3	TFI-IV	CFI
		Continental, Lincoln, Mark VII, Cougar, Thunderbird, Crown Victoria Crown Victoria, Grand Marquis	302 (5.0)	F	TFI-IV	CFI

Refer to footnotes at the end of this chart

COMPUTERIZED ENGINE CONTROL APPLICATIONS

Manufacturer	Year	Model	Engine cu. in. (liter)	VIN	SECTION 4 Electronic Ignition System	SECTION 5 Fuel Injection System
Ford	1985	Mustang, Capri, LTD, Marquis, Mark VII	302 (5.0) HO	M	TFI-IV	CFI
		Ranger, Aerostar	140 (2.3)	Z	TFI-IV	EFI
	1986	Escort, Lynx, EXP	113 (1.9)	J	TFI-IV	EFI
		Mustang SVO, Merkur, Thunderbird, Cougar	140 (2.3)	W, T	TFI-IV	EFI-Turbo
		Tempo, Topaz	140 (2.3)	R, S	TFI-IV	CFI
		Taurus, Sable	153 (2.5)	D	TFI-IV	CFI
			183 (3.0)	U	TFI-IV	EFI
		Mustang, Capri, LTD, Thunderbird, Cougar, Marquis	232 (3.8)	3	TFI-IV	CFI
		Thunderbird, Cougar, Continental, Mark VII, Lincoln, Mercury	302 (5.0)	F	TFI-IV	SEFI
		Mustang, Capri, Mark VII	302 (5.0) HO	M	TFI-IV	SEFI
		Ranger, Bronco II, Aerostar	140 (2.3)	A	TFI-IV	EFI
		Ranger, Bronco II	177 (2.9)	T	TFI-IV	EFI
		Aerostar	183 (3.0)	U	TFI-IV	EFI
		Bronco, E-Series, F-Series	302 (5.0)	F	TFI-IV	EFI
	1987-88	Escort, Lynx, EXP	113 (1.9)	9	TFI-IV	CFI
			113 (1.9)	J	TFI-IV	EFI
		Mustang	140 (2.3)	A	TFI-IV	EFI
		Thunderbird, Merkur	140 (2.3)	T, W	TFI-IV	EFI-Turbo
		Tempo, Topaz	140 (2.3)	X	TFI-IV	CFI
		Taurus, Sable	153 (2.5)	D	TFI-IV	CFI
			183 (3.0)	U	TFI-IV	EFI
		Thunderbird, Cougar, Taurus Police Models	232 (3.8)	3	TFI-IV	EFI
		Thunderbird, Cougar, Continental, Mark VII, Ford, Mercury	302 (5.0)	F	TFI-IV	SEFI
		Mustang, Mark VII	302 (5.0) HO	M	TFI-IV	SEFI
		Ranger, Aerostar	140 (2.3)	A	TFI-IV	EFI
		Ranger, Bronco II	177 (2.9)	T	TFI-IV	EFI
		Aerostar	183 (3.0)	U	TFI-IV	EFI
		Bronco, E-Series, F-Series	300 (4.9)	Y	TFI-IV	EFI
			302 (5.0)	N	TFI-IV	EFI
		E-Series, F-Series	460 (7.5)	L	TFI-IV	EFI

Refer to footnotes at the end of this chart

COMPUTERIZED ENGINE CONTROL APPLICATIONS

Manufacturer	Year	Model	Engine cu. in. (liter)	VIN	SECTION 4 Electronic Ignition System	SECTION 5 Fuel Injection System
Cadillac	1985	DeVille, Eldorado, Seville, Fleetwood	250 (4.1)	8	HEI/EST	DFI
	1986	Cimarron	122 (2.0)	P	HEI/EST	TBI
			173 (2.8)	W	HEI/EST	MPI
		DeVille, Eldorado, Seville, Fleetwood	250 (4.1)	8	HEI/EST	DFI
	1987-88	Allante	250 (4.1)	V	HEI/EST	SFI
		Cimarron	173 (2.8)	W	HEI/EST	MPI
		DeVille, Eldorado, Seville, Fleetwood	250 (4.1)	8	HEI/EST	DFI
Chevrolet	1984	Citation, Celebrity	151 (2.5)	R	HEI/EST	TBI
		Camaro, Cavalaier	151 (2.5)	2	HEI/EST	TBI
		Corvette	350 (5.7)	8	HEI/EST	TBI
	1985	Cavalier	122 (2.0)	P	HEI/EST	TBI
		Camaro, Citation, Celebrity	151 (2.5)	2, R	HEI/EST	TBI
		Camaro, Cavalier, Celebrity, Citation	173 (2.8)	S, W	HEI/EST	MPI
		Caprice, El Camino, Monte Carlo	265 (4.3)	Z	HEI/EST	TBI
		Camaro	305 (5.0)	F	HEI/EST	MPI
		Corvette	350 (5.7)	8	HEI/EST	TPI
	1986	Cavalier	122 (2.0)	P	HEI/EST	TBI
		Camaro, Celebrity	151 (2.5)	2, R	HEI/EST	TBI
		Camaro, Cavalier, Celebrity	173 (2.8)	S, W	HEI/EST	MPI
		Caprice, El Camino, Monte Carlo	265 (4.3)	Z	HEI/EST	TBI
		Camaro	305 (5.0)	F	HEI/EST	MPI
		Corvette	350 (5.7)	Y	HEI/EST	TPI
	1987-88	Beretta, Cavalier, Corsica	122 (2.0)	1	DIS	TBI
		Celebrity	151 (2.5)	R	DIS	TBI
		Camaro	173 (2.8)	S	HEI/EST	MPI
		Beretta, Cavalier, Celebrity, Corsica	173 (2.8)	W	DIS	MPI
		Caprice, El Camino, Monte Carlo	265 (4.3)	Z	HEI/EST	TBI
		Camaro	305 (5.0)	F	HEI/EST	MPI
			350 (5.7)	8	HEI/EST	MPI
		Corvette	350 (5.7)	8	HEI/EST	TPI
Oldsmobile	1984	Firenza	110 (1.8)	0	HEI/EST	TBI
			122 (2.0)	P	HEI/EST	TBI
		Cutlass Ciera, Omega	151 (2.5)	R	HEI/EST	TBI
		Cutlass Ciera, 98	231 (3.8)	3	HEI/EST	MPI
	1985	Firenza	110 (1.8)	0	HEI/EST	TBI
			122 (2.0)	P	HEI/EST	TBI

Refer to footnotes at the end of this chart

COMPUTERIZED ENGINE CONTROL APPLICATIONS

Manufacturer	Year	Model	Engine cu. in. (liter)	VIN	SECTION 4 Electronic Ignition System	SECTION 5 Fuel Injection System
Oldsmobile	1985	Calais, Firenza, Cutlass Ciera	151 (2.5)	R, U	HEI/EST	TBI
		Firenza	173 (2.8)	W	HEI/EST	MPI
		Calais, Firenza	181 (3.0)	L	HEI/EST	MPI
		Cutlass Ciera, 98	231 (3.8)	3	HEI/EST	MPI
	1986	Firenza	110 (1.8)	O	HEI/EST	TBI
			122 (2.0)	P	HEI/EST	TBI
		Cutlass Ciera, Calais	151 (2.5)	R, U	HEI/EST	TBI
		Cutlass Ciera, Firenza	173 (2.8)	W	HEI/EST	MPI
		Calais, Delta 88	181 (3.0)	L	C³I	MPI
		Toronado	231 (3.8)	B	C³I	MPI
		Cutlass Ciera, 88, 98	231 (3.8)	B, 3	C³I	SFI
	1987-88	Firenza	122 (2.0)	K	HEI/EST	TBI
			122 (2.0) HO	1	HEI/EST	TBI
		Cutlass Ciera, Calais	151 (2.5)	R, U	C³I	TBI
		Cutlass Ciera, Firenza	173 (2.8)	W	HEI/EST	MPI
		Calais	181 (3.0)	L	C³I	MPI
		Cutlass Ciera, 88, 98, Toronado, Trofeo	231 (3.8)	3	C³I	MPI
Pontiac	1984	2000 Sunbird	110 (1.8)	O	HEI/EST	TBI
			110 (1.8)	J	HEI/EST	MPI-Turbo
			122 (2.0)	P	HEI/EST	TBI
		6000, Fiero, Phoenix	151 (2.5)	R	HEI/EST	TBI
		Firebird	151 (2.5)	2	HEI/EST	TBI
	1985	Sunbird	110 (1.8)	O	HEI/EST	TBI
			110 (1.8)	J	HEI/EST	MPI-Turbo
		6000, Fiero	151 (2.5)	R	HEI/EST	TBI
		Firebird	151 (2.5)	2	HEI/EST	TBI
		Grand Am	151 (2.5)	U	HEI/EST	TBI
		6000, Firebird, Fiero	173 (2.8)	W,S,9	HEI/EST	MPI
		Grand Am	181 (3.0)	L	HEI/EST	MPI
		Bonneville, Grand Prix, Parisienne	265 (4.3)	Z	HEI/EST	TBI
		Firebird	305 (5.0)	F	HEI/EST	MPI
	1986	Sunbird	110 (1.8)	O	HEI/EST	TBI
			110 (1.8)	J	HEI/EST	MPI-Turbo
		6000, Firebird, Fiero, Grand AM	151 (2.5)	R,U,2	HEI/EST	TBI

Refer to footnotes at the end of this chart

COMPUTERIZED ENGINE CONTROL APPLICATIONS

Manufacturer	Year	Model	Engine cu. in. (liter)	VIN	SECTION 4 Electronic Ignition System	SECTION 5 Fuel Injection System
Pontiac	1986	6000, Fiero, Firebird	173 (2.8)	S,W,9	HEI/EST	MPI
		Grand Am	181 (3.0)	L	C³I	MPI
		Bonneville, Grand Prix, Parisienne	265 (4.3)	Z	HEI/EST	TBI
		Firebird	305 (5.0)	F	HEI/EST	MPI
			350 (5.7)	8	HEI/EST	MPI
	1987-88	Sunbird	122 (2.0)	K	HEI/EST	TBI
		Sunbird, Grand Am	122 (2.0)	M	HEI/EST	MPI-Turbo
		6000	151 (2.5)	R	DIS	TBI
		Fiero, Grand Am	151 (2.5)	R, U	HEI/EST	TBI
		Firebird	173 (2.8)	S	HEI/EST	MPI
		6000, Fiero	173 (2.8)	W, 9	DIS	MPI
		Grand Am	181 (3.0)	L	C³I	MPI
		Bonneville	231 (3.8)	3	C³I	MPI
		Grand Prix	265 (4.3)	Z	HEI/EST	TBI
		Firebird	305 (5.0)	F	HEI/EST	MPI
			350 (5.7)	8	HEI/EST	MPI
Light Trucks	1985	S-10, S-15, Astro	151 (2.5)	E	HEI	TBI
	1986	S-10, S-15, Astro, C, K, G	151 (2.5)	E	HEI	TBI
		S-10, S-15, C, K, G	173 (2.8)	R	HEI	TBI
		Astro, C, K, G	265 (4.3)	Z	HEI	TBI
	1987-88	S-10, S-15, Astro, C, K, G	151 (2.5)	E	HEI	TBI
		S-10, S-15, C, K, G	173 (2.8)	R	HEI	TBI
		Astro, C, K, G	265 (4.3)	Z	HEI	TBI
		C, K, G	305 (5.0)	H	HEI	TBI
			350 (5.7)	K	HEI	TBI
		C, K, P	454 (7.4)	N	HEI	TBI

NOTE: Refer to the underhood emission control decal to determine which electronic engine control system is used on a particular vehicle. The underhood decal also contains information on ignition timing and idle speed adjustment.

CFI — Central Fuel Injection (Ford)
C³I — Computer Controlled Coil Ignition
DFI — Digital Fuel Injection
DIS — Direct Ignition System
DS-II Ford Duraspark II Ignition System
EFI — Electronic Fuel Injection
EIS — Electronic Ignition System
ESA — Electronic Spark Advance
ESC — Electronic Spark Control
EST — Electronic Spark Timing
HALL — Hall Effect Distributor
HEI — High Energy Ignition
HO — High Output

MFI — Multi-point Fuel Injection
MPI — Multi-port Fuel Injection
SEFI — Sequential Fuel Injection (Ford)
SFI — Sequential Fuel Injection (GM)
SFI — Single Point Fuel Injection (Chrysler)
SSI — Solid State Ignition
TBI — Throttle Body Injection
TFI — Thick Film Integrated Ignition System
TPI — Tuned Port Injection
Turbo — Turbocharged Engine
UIC — Universal Integrated Circuit
Cross Fire Injection — dual TBI units

1 Basic Electricity

INDEX

FUNDAMENTALS OF ELECTRICITY

A good understanding of basic electrical theory and how circuits work is necessary to successfully perform the service and testing outlined in this manual. Therefore, this section should be read before attempting any diagnosis and repair.

All matter is made up of tiny particles called molecules. Each molecule is made up of two or more atoms. Atoms may be divided into even smaller particles called protons, neutrons and electrons. These particles are the same in all matter and differences in materials (hard or soft, conductive or non-conductive) occur only because of the number and arrangement of these particles. In other words, the protons, neutrons and electrons in a drop of water are the same as those in an ounce of lead, there are just more of them (arranged differently) in a lead molecule than in a water molecule. Protons and neutrons packed together form the nucleus of the atom, while electrons orbit around the nucleus much the same way as the planets of the solar system orbit around the sun.

The proton is a small positive natural charge of electricity, while the neutron has no electrical charge. The electron carries a negative charge equal to the positive charge of the proton. Every electrically neutral atom contains the same number of protons and electrons, the exact number of which determines the element. The only difference between a conductor and an insulator is that a conductor possesses free electrons in large quantities, while an insulator has only a few. An element must have very few free electrons to be a good insulator, and vice-versa. When we speak of electricity, we're talking about these free electrons.

In a conductor, the movement of the free electrons is hindered by collisions with the adjoining atoms of the element (matter). This hindrance to movement is called RESISTANCE and it varies with different materials and temperatures. As temperature increases, the movement of the free electrons increases, causing more frequent collisions and therefore increasing resistance to the movement of the electrons. The number of collisions (resistance) also increases with the number of electrons flowing (current). Current is defined as the movement of electrons through a conductor such as a wire. In a conductor (such as copper) electrons can be caused to leave their atoms and move to other atoms. This flow is continuous in that every time an atom gives up an electron, it collects another one to take its place. This movement of electrons is called electric current and is measured in amperes. When 6.28 billion, billion electrons pass a certain point in the circuit in one second, the amount of current flow is called one ampere.

The force or pressure which causes electrons to flow in any conductor (such as a wire) is called VOLTAGE. It is measured in volts and is similar to the pressure that causes water to flow in a pipe. Voltage is the difference in electrical pressure measured between two different points in a circuit. In a 12 volt system, for example, the force measured between the two battery posts is 12 volts. Two important concepts are voltage potential and polarity. Voltage potential is the amount of voltage or electrical pressure at a certain point in the circuit with respect to another point. For example, if the voltage potential at one post of the 12 volt battery is zero, the voltage potential at the other post is 12 volts with respect to the first post. One post of the battery is said to be positive (+); the other post is negative (-) and the conventional direction of current flow is from positive to negative in an electrical circuit. It should be noted that the electron flow in the wire is opposite the current flow. In other words, when the circuit is energized, the current flows from positive to negative, but the electrons actually move from negative to positive. The voltage or pressure needed to produce a current flow in a circuit must be greater than the resistance present in the circuit. In other words, if the voltage drop across the resistance is greater than or equal to the voltage input, the

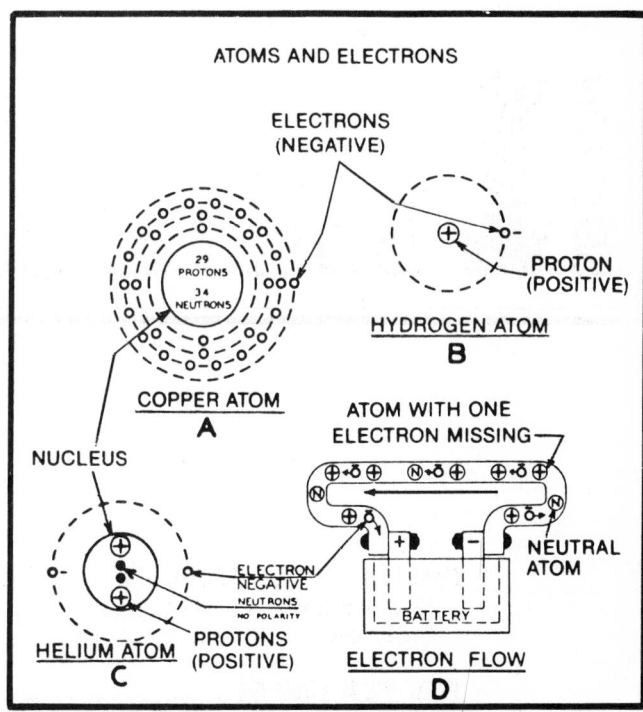

Typical atoms of copper (A), hydrogen (B) and helium (C). Electron flow in battery circuit (D)

voltage potential will be zero—no voltage will flow through the circuit. Resistance to the flow of electrons is measured in ohms. One volt will cause one ampere to flow through a resistance of one ohm.

Units Of Electrical Measurement

There are three fundamental characteristics of a direct-current electrical circuit: volts, amperes and ohms.

VOLTAGE in a circuit controls the intensity with which the loads in the circuit operate. The brightness of a lamp, the heat of an electrical defroster, the speed of a motor are all directly proportional to the voltage, if the resistance in the circuit and/

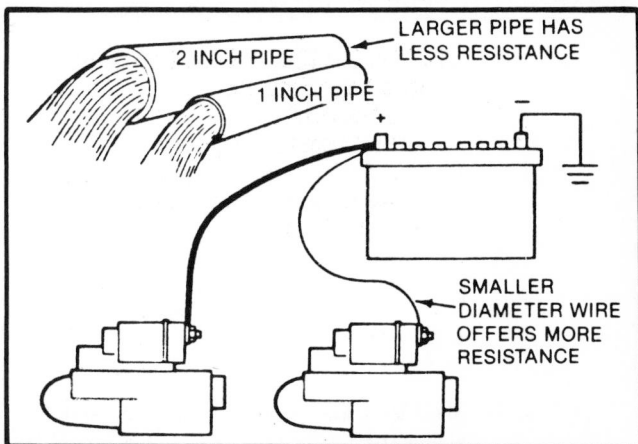

Electrical resistance can be compared to water flow through a pipe. The smaller the wire (pipe), the more resistance to the flow of electrons (water)

or mechanical load on electric motors remains constant. Voltage available from the battery is constant (normally 12 volts), but as it operates the various loads in the circuit, voltage decreases (drops).

AMPERE is the unit of measurement of current in an electrical circuit. One ampere is the quantity of current that will flow through a resistance of one ohm at a pressure of one volt. The amount of current that flows in a circuit is controlled by the voltage and the resistance in the circuit. Current flow is directly proportional to resistance. Thus, as voltage is increased or decreased, current is increased or decreased accordingly. Current is decreased as resistance is increased, however, and is increased as resistance is decreased. With little or no resistance in a circuit, current is high.

OHM is the unit of measurement of resistance, represented by the Greek letter Omega (Ω). One ohm is the resistance of a conductor through which a current of one ampere will flow at a pressure of one volt. Electrical resistance can be measured on an instrument called an ohmmeter. The loads (electrical devices) are the primary resistances in a circuit. Loads such as lamps, solenoids, and electric heaters have a resistance that is essentially fixed; at a normal fixed voltage, they will draw a fixed current. Motors, on the other hand, do not have a fixed resistance. Increasing the mechanical load on a motor (such as might be caused by a misadjusted track in a power window system) will decrease the motor speed. The drop in motor rpm has the effect of reducing the internal resistance of the motor because the current draw of the motor varies directly with the mechanical load on the motor, although its actual resistance is unchanged. Thus, as the motor load increases, the current draw of the motor increases, and may increase up to the point where the motor stalls (cannot move the mechanical load).

Circuits are designed with the total resistance of the circuit taken into account. Troubles can arise when unwanted resistances enter into a circuit. If corrosion, dirt, grease, or any other contaminant occurs in places like switches, connectors, and grounds, or if loose connections occur, resistances will develop in these areas. These resistances act like additional loads in the circuit and cause problems.

OHM'S LAW

Ohm's law is a statement of the relationship between the three fundamental characteristics of an electrical circuit. These rules apply to direct current (DC) only.

Ohm's law provides a means to make an accurate circuit analysis without actually seeing the circuit. If, for example, one wanted to check the condition of the rotor winding in a alternator whose specifications indicate that the field (rotor) current draw is normally 2.5 amperes at 12 volts, simply connect the rotor to a 12 volt battery and measure the current with an ammeter. If it measures about 2.5 amperes, the rotor winding can be assumed good.

$$I = \frac{E}{R} \quad \text{or} \quad \text{AMPERES} = \frac{\text{VOLTS}}{\text{OHMS}}$$

$$R = \frac{E}{I} \quad \text{or} \quad \text{OHMS} = \frac{\text{VOLTS}}{\text{AMPERES}}$$

$$E = I \times R \quad \text{or} \quad \text{VOLTS} = \text{AMPERES} \times \text{OHMS}$$

Ohms Law is the basis for all electrical measurements. By simply plugging in two values, the third can be calculated using the illustrated formula.

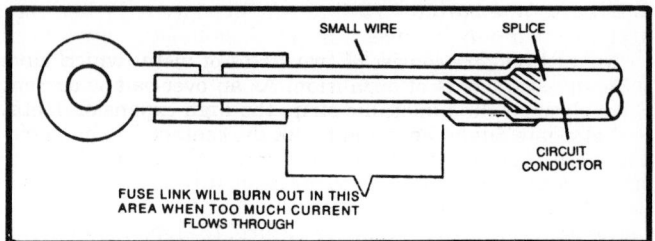

$$R = \frac{E}{I} \qquad \text{Where:} \quad E = 12 \text{ volts}$$
$$I = 2.5 \text{ amperes}$$
$$R = \frac{12 \text{ volts}}{2.5 \text{ amps}} = 4.8 \text{ ohms}$$

An example of calculating resistance (R) when the voltage (E) and amperage (I) is known.

Typical fusible link wire

An ohmmeter can be used to test components that have been removed from the vehicle in much the same manner as an ammeter. Since the voltage and the current of the rotor windings used as an earlier example are known, the resistance can be calculated using Ohms law. The formula would be:

If the rotor resistance measures about 4.8 ohms when checked with an ohmmeter, the winding can be assumed good. By plugging in different specifications, additional circuit information can be determined such as current draw, etc.

Electrical Circuits

An electrical circuit must start from a source of electrical supply and return to that source through a continuous path. Circuits are designed to handle a certain maximum current flow. The maximum allowable current flow is designed higher than the normal current requirements of all the loads in the circuit. Wire size, connections, insulation, etc., are designed to prevent undesirable voltage drop, overheating of conductors, arcing of contacts, and other adverse effects. If the safe maximum current flow level is exceeded, damage to the circuit components will result; it is this condition that circuit protection devices are designed to prevent.

Protection devices are fuses, fusible links or circuit breakers designed to open or break the circuit quickly whenever an overload, such as a short circuit, occurs. By opening the circuit quickly, the circuit protection device prevents damage to the wiring, battery, and other circuit components. Fuses and fusible links are designed to carry a preset maximum amount of current and to melt when that maximum is exceeded, while circuit breakers merely break the connection and may be manually reset. The maximum amperage rating of each fuse is marked on the fuse body and all contain a see-through portion that shows the break in the fuse element when blown. Fusible link maximum amperage rating is indicated by gauge or thickness of the wire. Never replace a blown fuse or fusible link with one of a higher amperage rating.

CAUTION

Resistance wires, like fusible links, are also spliced into conductors in some areas. Do not make the mistake of replacing a fusible link with a resistance wire. Resistance wires are longer than fusible links and are stamped "RESISTOR-DO NOT CUT OR SPLICE."

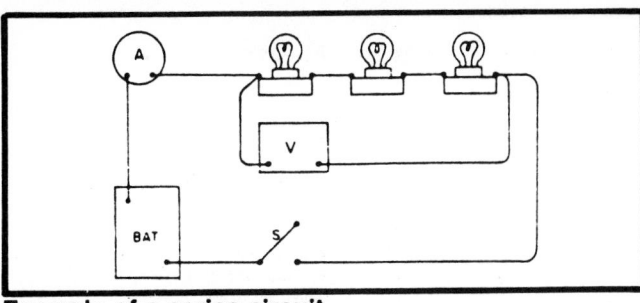

Example of a series circuit

Circuit breakers consist of two strips of metal which have different coefficients of expansion. As an overload or current flows through the bimetallic strip, the high-expansion metal will elongate due to heat and break the contact. With the circuit open, the bimetal strip cools and shrinks, drawing the strip down until contact is re-established and current flows once again. In actual operation, the contact is broken very quickly if the overload is continuous and the circuit will be repeatedly broken and remade until the source of the overload is corrected.

The self-resetting type of circuit breaker is the one most generally used in automotive electrical systems. On manually reset circuit breakers, a button will pop up on the circuit breaker case. This button must be pushed in to reset the circuit breaker and restore power to the circuit. Always repair the source of the overload before resetting a circuit breaker or replacing a fuse or fusible link. When searching for overloads, keep in mind that the circuit protection devices protect only against overloads between the protection device and ground.

There are two basic types of circuit; Series and Parallel. In a series circuit, all of the elements are connected in chain fashion with the same amount of current passing through each element or load. No matter where an ammeter is connected in a series circuit, it will always read the same. The most important fact to remember about a series circuit is that the sum of the voltages across each element equals the source voltage. The total resistance of a series circuit is equal to the sum of the individual resistances within each element of the circuit. Using ohms law, one can determine the voltage drop across each element in the circuit. If the total resistance and source voltage is known, the amount of current can be calculated. Once the amount of current (amperes) is known, values can be substituted in the Ohms law formula to calculate the voltage drop across each individual element in the series circuit. The individual voltage drops must add up to the same value as the source voltage.

A parallel circuit, unlike a series circuit, contains two or more branches, each branch a separate path independent of the others. The total current draw from the voltage source is the sum of all the currents drawn by each branch. Each branch of a parallel circuit can be analyzed separately. The individual branches can be either simple circuits, series circuits or combinations of series-parallel circuits. Ohms law applies to parallel

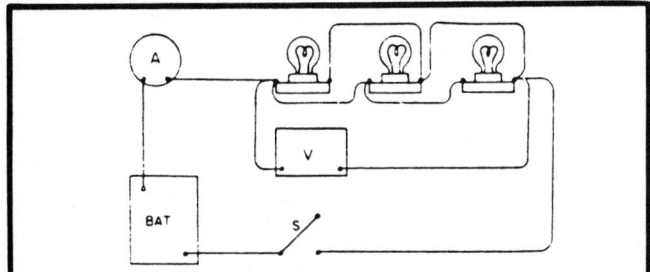

Example of a parallel circuit

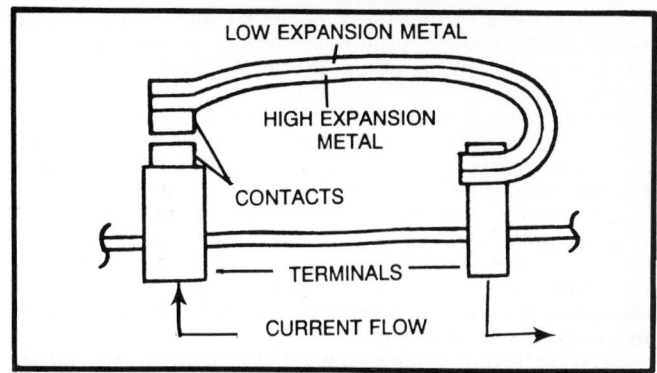

Typical circuit breaker construction

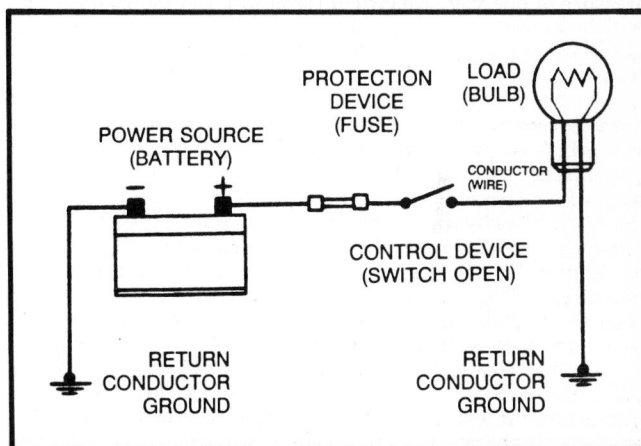

Typical circuit with all essential components

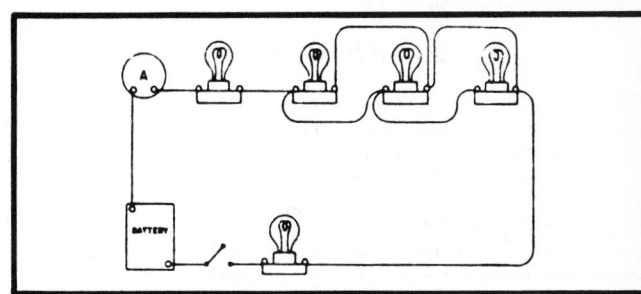

Example of a series-parallel circuit

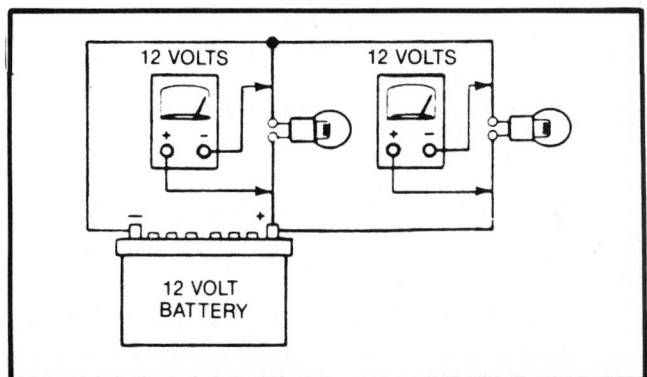

Voltage drop in a parallel circuit. Voltage drop across each lamp is 12 volts

circuits just as it applies to series circuits, by considering each branch independently of the others. The most important thing to remember is that the voltage across each branch is the same as the source voltage. The current in any branch is that voltage divided by the resistance of the branch. A practical method of determining the resistance of a parallel circuit is to divide the product of the two resistances by the sum of two resistances at a time. Amperes through a parallel circuit is the sum of the amperes through the separate branches. Voltage across a parallel circuit is the same as the voltage across each branch.

By measuring the voltage drops, you are in effect measuring the resistance of each element within the circuit. The greater the voltage drop, the greater the resistance. Voltage drop measurements are a common way of checking circuit resistances in automotive electrical systems. When part of a circuit developes excessive resistance (due to a bad connection) the element will show a higher than normal voltage drop. Normally, automotive wiring is selected to limit voltage drops to a few tenths of a volt. In parallel circuits, the total resistance is less than the sum of the individual resistances; because the current has two paths to take, the total resistance is lower.

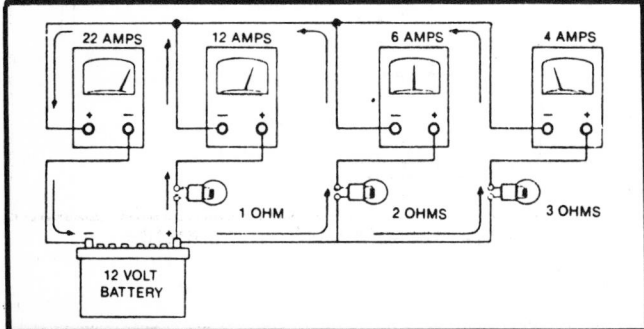

Total current in parallel circuit: 4 + 6 + 12 = 22 amps

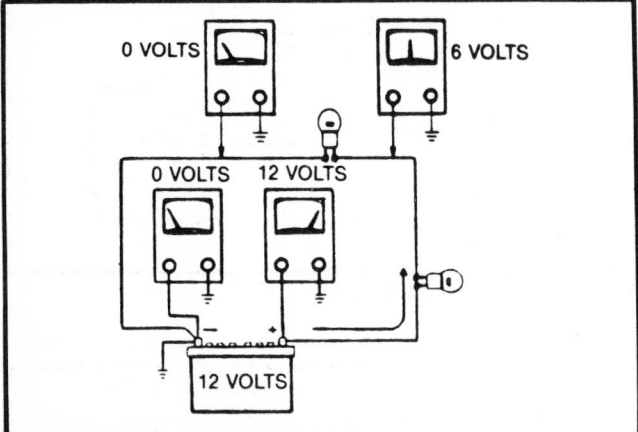

Voltage drop in a series circuit

Magnetism and Electromagnets

Electricity and magnetism are very closely associated because when electric current passes through a wire, a magnetic field is created around the wire. When a wire carrying electric current is wound into a coil, a magnetic field with North and South poles is created just like in a bar magnet. If an iron core is placed within the coil, the magnetic field becomes stronger because iron conducts magnetic lines much easier than air. This arrangement is called an electromagnet and is the basic princi-

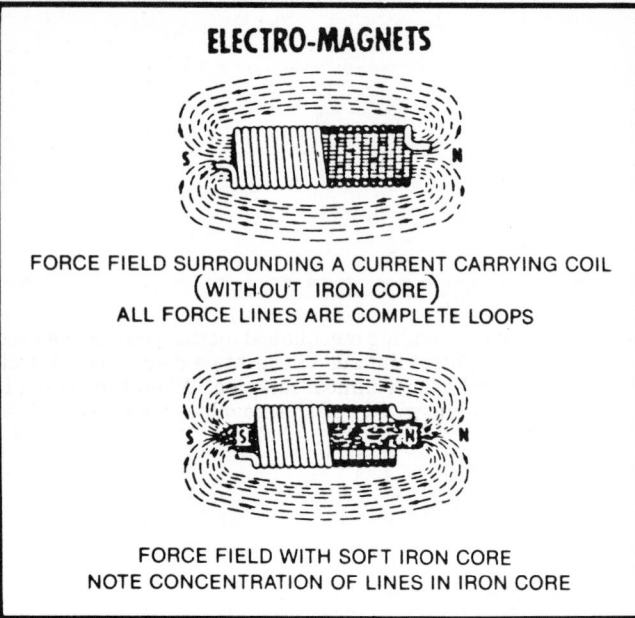

Magnetic field surrounding an electromagnet

ple behind the operation of such components as relays, buzzers and solenoids.

A relay is basically just a remote-controlled switch that uses a small amount of current to control the flow of a large amount of current. The simplest relay contains an electromagetic coil in series with a voltage source (battery) and a switch. A movable armature made of some magnetic material pivots at one end and is held a small distance away from the electromagnet by a spring or the spring steel of the armature itself. A contact point, made of a good conductor, is attached to the free end of the armature with another contact point a small distance away. When the relay is switched on (energized), the magnetic field created by the current flow attracts the armature, bending it until the contact points meet, closing a circuit and allowing current to flow in the second circuit through the relay to

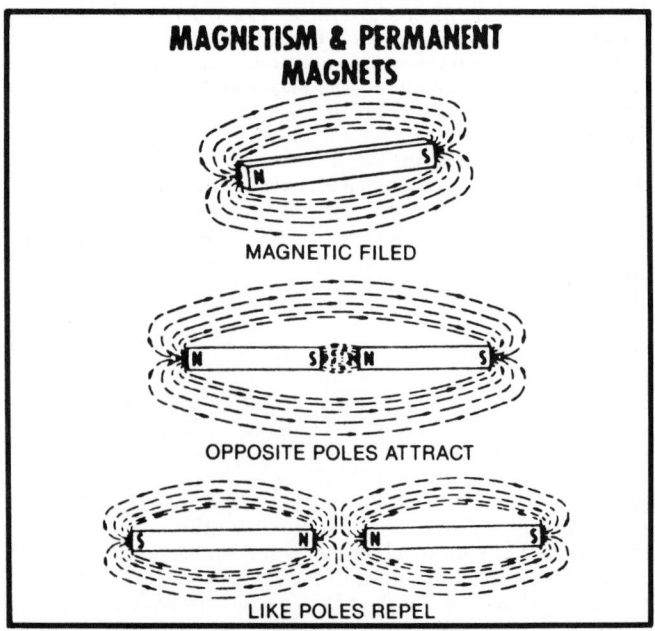

Magnetic field surrounding a bar magnet

the load the circuit operates. When the relay is switched off (de-energized), the armature springs back and opens the contact points, cutting off the current flow in the secondary, or controlled, circuit. Relays can be designed to be either open or closed when energized, depending on the type of circuit control a manufacturer requires.

A buzzer is similar to a relay, but its internal connections are different. When the switch is closed, the current flows through the normally closed contacts and energizes the coil. When the coil core becomes magnetized, it bends the armature down and breaks the circuit. As soon as the circuit is broken, the spring-loaded armature remakes the circuit and again energizes the coil. This cycle repeats rapidly to cause the buzzing sound.

A solenoid is constructed like a relay, except that its core is allowed to move, providing mechanical motion that can be used to actuate mechanical linkage to operate a door or trunk lock or control any other mechanical function. When the switch is closed, the coil is energized and the movable core is drawn into the coil. When the switch is opened, the coil is de-energized and spring pressure returns the core to its original position.

Basic Solid State

The term "solid state" refers to devices utilizing transistors, diodes and other components which are made from materials known as semiconductors. A semiconductor is a material that is neither a good insulator nor a good conductor; principally silicon and germanium. The semiconductor material is specially treated to give it certain qualities that enhance its function, therefore becoming either P-type (positive) or N-type (negative) material. Most semiconductors are constructed of silicon and can be designed to function either as an insulator or conductor.

Diodes

The simplest semiconductor function is that of the diode or rectifier (the two terms mean the same thing). A diode will pass current in one direction only, like a one-way valve, because it has low resistance in one direction and high resistance on the other. Whether the diode conducts or not depends on the polarity of the voltage applied to it. A diode has two electrodes, an anode and a cathode. When the anode receives positive (+) voltage and the cathode receives negative (-) voltage, current can flow easily through the diode. When the voltage is reversed, the diode becomes non-conducting and only allows a very slight amount of current to flow in the circuit. Because the semiconductor is not a perfect insulator, a small amount of reverse current leakage will occur, but the amount is usually too small to consider. The application of voltage to maintain the current flow described is called "forward bias."

A light-emitting diode (LED) is made of a particular type of crystal that glows when current is passed through it. LED's are used in display faces of many digital or electronic instrument clusters. LED's are usually arranged to display numbers (digital readout), but can be used to illuminate a variety of electronic graphic displays.

Like any other electrical device, diodes have certain ratings that must be observed and should not be exceeded. The forward current rating (or bias) indicates how much current can safely pass through the diode without causing damage or destroying it. Forward current rating is usually given in either amperes or milliamperes. The voltage drop across a diode remains constant regardless of the current flowing through it. Small diodes designed to carry low amounts of current need no special provision for dissipating the heat generated in any electrical device, but large current carrying diodes are usually mounted on heat sinks to keep the internal temperature from rising to the point where the silicon will melt and destroy the diode. When diodes are operated in a high ambient temperature environment, they must be de-rated to prevent failure.

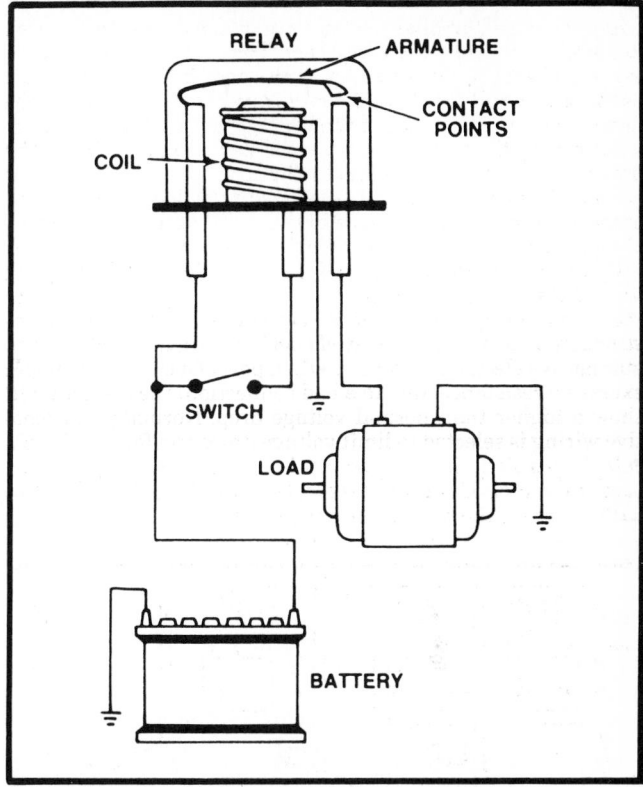

Typical relay circuit with basic components

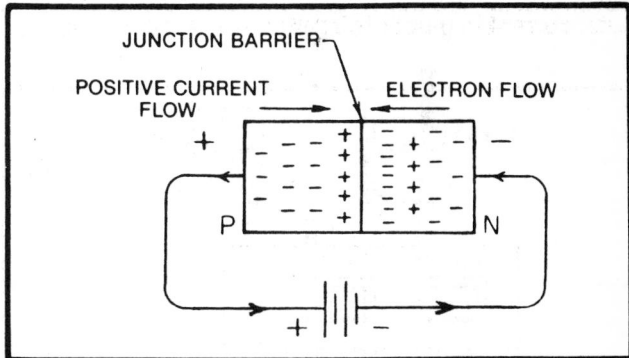

Diode with forward bias

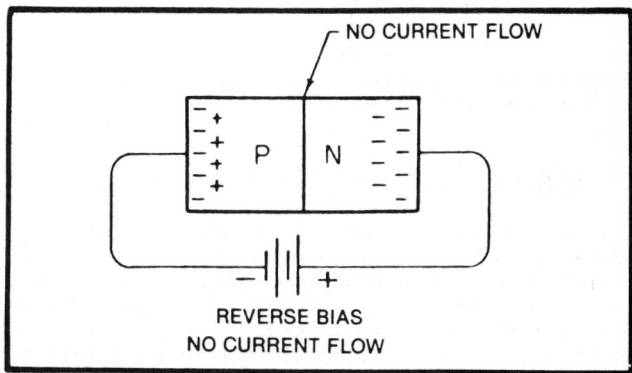

Diode with reverse bias

Another diode specification is its peak inverse voltage rating. This value is the maximum amount of voltage the diode can safely handle when operating in the blocking mode. This value can be anywhere from 50-1000 volts, depending on the diode, and if exceeded can damage the diode just as too much forward current will. Most semiconductor failures are caused by excessive voltage or internal heat.

One can test a diode with a small battery and a lamp with the same voltage rating. With this arrangement one can find a bad diode and determine the polarity of a good one. A diode can fail and cause either a short or open circuit, but in either case it fails to function as a diode. Testing is simply a matter of connecting the test bulb first in one direction and then the other and making sure that current flows in one direction only. If the diode is shorted, the test bulb will remain on no matter how the light is connected.

Transistors

The transistor is an electrical device used to control voltage within a circuit. A transistor can be considered a "controllable diode" in that, in addition to passing or blocking current, the transistor can control the amount of current passing through it. Simple transistors are composed of three pieces of semiconductor material, P and N type, joined together and enclosed in a container. If two sections of P material and one section of N material are used, it is known as a PNP transistor; if the reverse is true, then it is known as an NPN transistor. The two types cannot be interchanged.

Most modern transistors are made from silicon (earlier transistors were made from germanium) and contain three elements; the emitter, the collector and the base. In addition to passing or blocking current, the transistor can control the

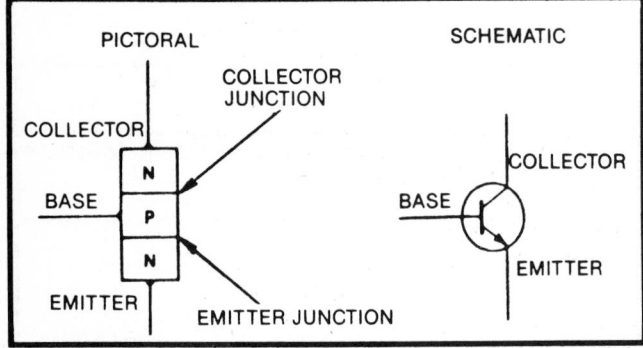

NPN transistor illustrations (pictorial and schematic)

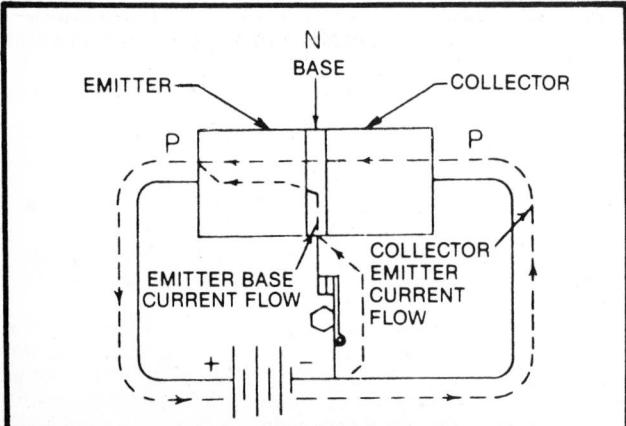

PNP transistor with base switch closed (base emitter and collector emitter current flow)

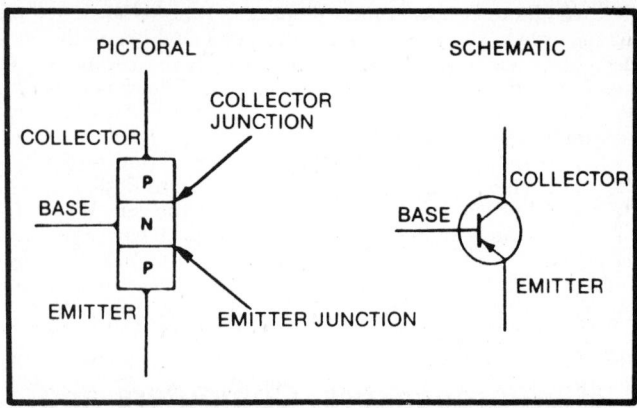

PNP transistor illustrations (pictorial and schematic)

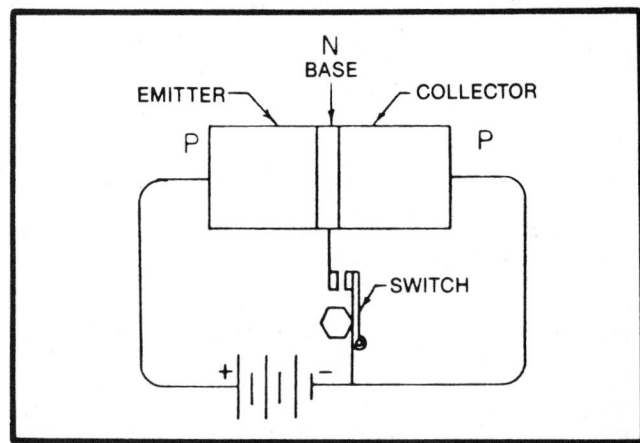

PNP transistor with base switch open (no current flow)

amount of current passing through it and because of this can function as an amplifier or a switch. The collector and emitter form the main current-carrying circuit of the transistor. The amount of current that flows through the collector-emitter junction is controlled by the amount of current in the base circuit. Only a small amount of base-emitter current is necessary to control a large amount of collector-emitter current (the amplifier effect). In automotive applications, however, the transistor is used primarily as a switch.

When no current flows in the base-emitter junction, the collector-emitter circuit has a high resistance, like to open contacts of a relay. Almost no current flows through the circuit and transistor is considered OFF. By bypassing a small amount of current into the base circuit, the resistance is low, allowing current to flow through the circuit and turning the transistor ON. This condition is known as "saturation" and is reached when the base current reaches the maximum value designed into the transistor that allows current to flow. Depending on various factors, the transistor can turn on and off (go from cutoff to saturation) in less than one millionth of a second.

Much of what was said about ratings for diodes applies to transistors, since they are constructed of the same materials. When transistors are required to handle relatively high currents, such as in voltage regulators or ignition systems, they are generally mounted on heat sinks in the same manner as diodes. They can be damaged or destroyed in the same manner if their voltage ratings are exceeded. A transistor can be checked for proper operation by measuring the resistance with an ohmmeter between the base-emitter terminals and then between the base-collector terminals. The forward resistance should be small, while the reverse resistance should be large. Compare the readings with those from a known good transistor. As a final check, measure the forward and reverse resistance between the collector and emitter terminals.

Integrated Circuits

The integrated circuit (IC) is an extremely sophisticated solid state device that consists of a silicone wafer (or chip) which has been doped, insulated and etched many times so that it contains an entire electrical circuit with transistors, diodes, conductors and capacitors miniaturized within each tiny chip. Integrated circuits are often referred to as "computers on a chip" and are largely responsible for the current boom in electronic control technology.

Microprocessors, Computers and Logic Systems

Mechanical or electromechanical control devices lack the precision necessary to meet the requirements of modern control standards, and the ability to respond to a variety of input conditions common to antilock brakes, climate control and electronic suspension operation. To meet these requirements, manufacturers have gone to solid state logic systems and microprocessors to control the basic functions of suspension, brake and temperature control, as well as other systems and accessories.

One of the more vital roles of microprocessor-based systems is their ability to perform logic functions and make decisions. Logic designers use a shorthand notation to indicate whether a voltage is present in a circuit (the number 1) or not present (the number 0), and their systems are designed to respond in different ways depending on the output signal (or the lack of it) from various control devices.

There are three basic logic functions or "gates" used to construct a microprocessor control system: the AND gate, the OR gate or the NOT gate. Stated simply, the AND gate works when voltage is present in two or more circuits which then energize a third (A and B energize C). The OR gate works when voltage is present at either circuit A or circuit B which then energizes circuit C. The NOT function is performed by a solid state device called an "inverter" which reverses the input from a circuit so that, if voltage is going in, no voltage comes out and vice versa. With these three basic building blocks, a logic designer can create complex systems easily. In actual use, a logic or decision making system may employ many logic gates and receive inputs from a number of sources (sensors), but for the most part, all utilize the basic logic gates discussed above.

Stripped to its bare essentials, a computerized decision-making system is made up of three subsystems:
    a. Input devices (sensors or switches)
    b. Logic circuits (computer control unit)
    c. Output devices (actuators or controls)

The input devices are usually nothing more than switches or sensors that provide a voltage signal to the control unit logic circuits that is read as a 1 or 0 (on or off) by the logic circuits. The output devices are anything from a warning light to solenoid-operated valves, motors, linkage, etc. In most cases, the

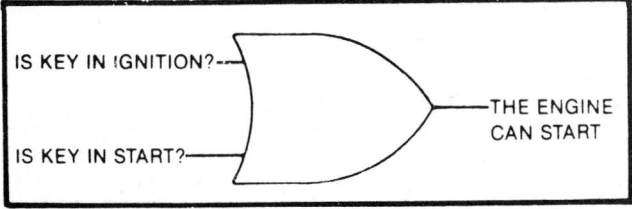

Typical two-input OR circuit operation

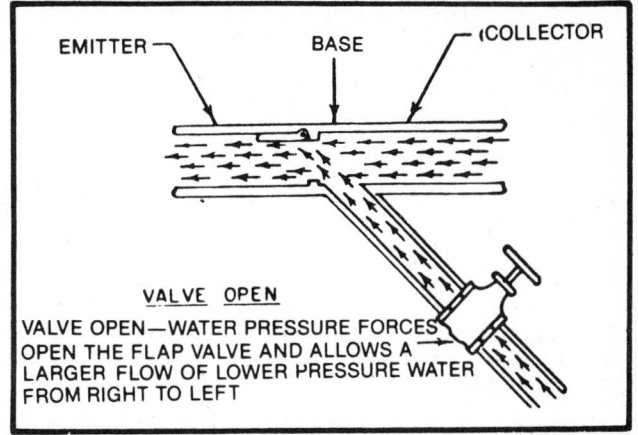

Hydraulic analogy to transistor function is shown with the base circuit energized

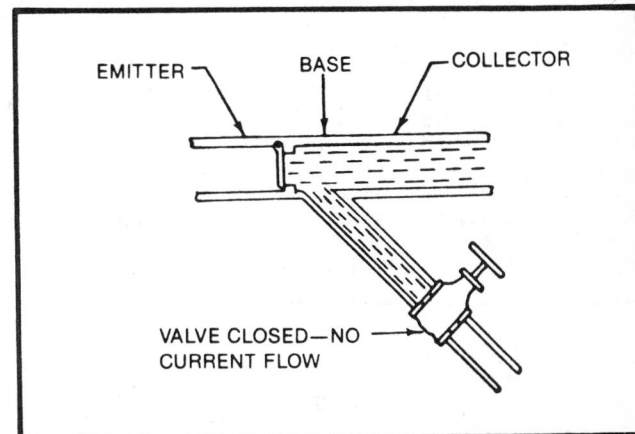

Hydraulic analogy to transistor function is shown with the base circuit shut off

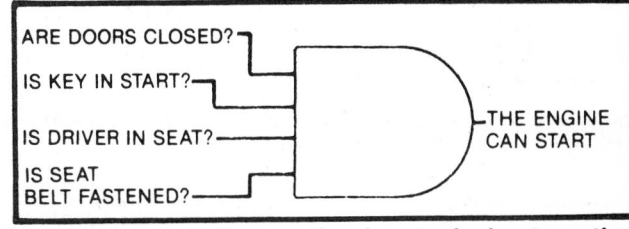

Multiple input AND operation in a typical automotive starting circuit

logic circuits themselves lack sufficient output power to operate these devices directly. Instead, they operate some intermediate device such as a relay or power transistor which in turn operates the appropriate device or control. Many problems diagnosed as computer failures are really the result of a malfunctioning intermediate device like a relay. This must be kept in mind whenever troubleshooting any microprocessor-based control system.

The logic systems discussed above are called "hardware" systems, because they consist only of the physical electronic components (gates, resistors, transistors, etc.). Hardware systems do not contain a program and are designed to perform specific or "dedicated" functions which cannot readily be changed. For many simple automotive control requirements, such dedicated logic systems are perfectly adequate. When more complex logic functions are required, or where it may be desirable to alter these functions (e.g. from one model car to another) a true computer system is used. A computer can be programmed through its software to perform many different functions and, if that program is stored on a separate integrated circuit chip called a ROM (Read Only Memory), it can be easily changed simply by plugging in a different ROM with the desired program. Most on-board automotive computers are designed with this capability. The on-board computer method of engine control offers the manufacturer a flexible method of responding to data from a variety of input devices and of controlling an equally large variety of output controls. The computer response can be changed quickly and easily by simply modifying its software program. The microprocessor is the heart of the microcomputer. It is the thinking part of the computer system through which all the data from the various sensors passes. Within the microprocessor, data is acted upon, compared, manipulated or stored for future use. A microprocessor is not necessarily a microcomputer, but the differences between the two are becoming very minor. Originally, a microprocessor was a major part of a microcomputer, but nowadays microprocessors are being called "single-chip microcomputers". They contain all the essential elements to make them behave as a computer, including the most important ingredient–the program.

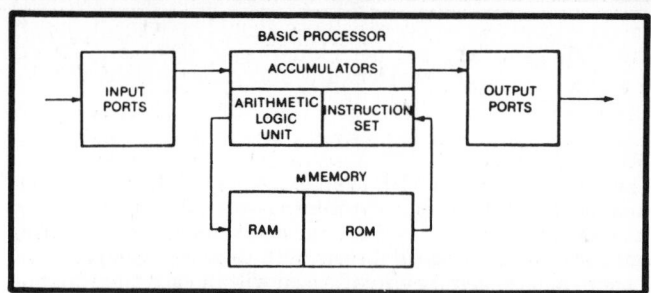

Schematic of typical microprocessor based on-board computer showing essential components

All computers require a program. In a general purpose computer, the program can be easily changed to allow different tasks to be performed. In a "dedicated" computer, such as most on-board automotive computers, the program isn't quite so easily altered. These automotive computers are designed to perform one or several specific tasks, such as maintaining the passenger compartment temperature at a specific, predetermined level. A program is what makes a computer smart; without a program a computer can do absolutely nothing. The term "software" refers to the program that makes the hardware do what you want it to do.

The software program is simply a listing in sequential order of the steps or commands necessary to make a computer perform the desired task. Before the computer can do anything at all, the program must be fed into it by one of several possible methods. A computer can never be "smarter" than the person programming it, but it is a lot faster. Although it cannot perform any calculation or operation that the programmer himself cannot perform, its processing time is measured in millionths of a second.

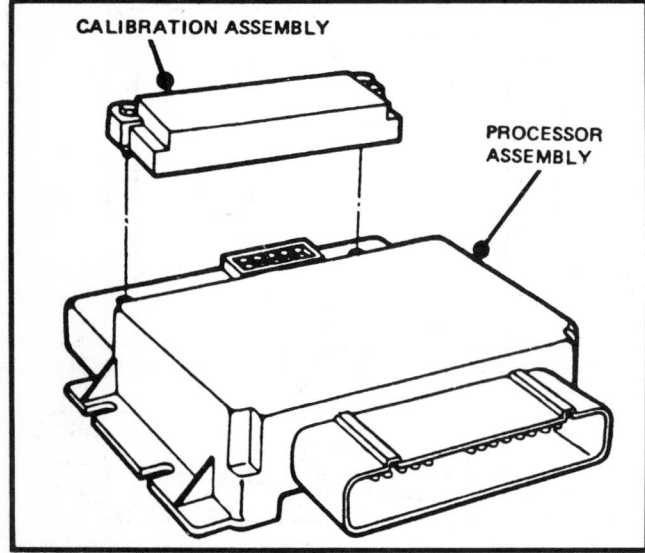

Electronic control assembly

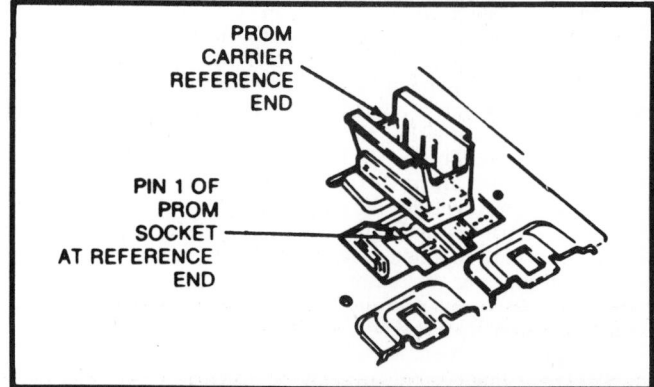

Installation of PROM unit in GM on-board computer

Because a computer is limited to performing only those operations (instructions) programmed into its memory, the program must be broken down into a large number of very simple steps. Two different programmers can come up with two different programs, since there is usually more than one way to perform any task or solve a problem. In any computer, however, there is only so much memory space available, so an overly long or inefficient program may not fit into the memory. In addition to performing arithmetic functions (such as with a trip computer), a computer can also store data, look up data in a table and perform the logic functions previously discussed. A Random Access Memory (RAM) allows the computer to store bits of data temporarily while waiting to be acted upon by the program. It may also be used to store output data that is to be sent to an output device. Whatever data is stored in a RAM is lost when power is removed from the system by turning off the ignition key, for example.

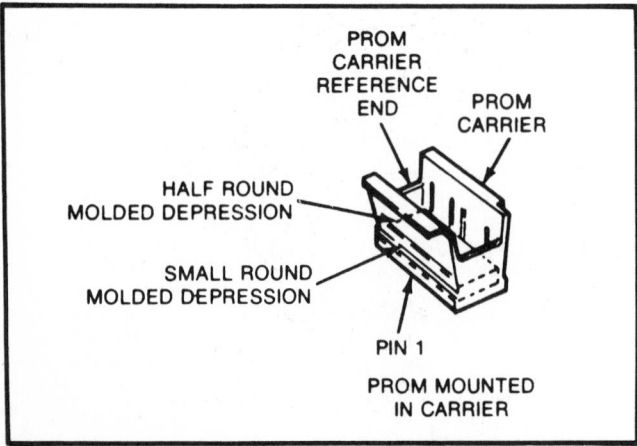

Typical PROM showing carrier refernce markings

Computers have another type of memory called a Read Only Memory (ROM) which is permanent. This memory is not lost when the power is removed from the system. Most programs for automotive computers are stored on a ROM memory chip. Data is usually in the form of a look-up table that saves computing time and program steps. For example, a computer designed to control the amount of distributor advance can have this information stored in a table. The information that determines distributor advance (engine rpm, manifold vacuum and temperature) is coded to produce the correct amount of distributor advance over a wide range of engine operating conditions. Instead of the computer computing the required advance, it simply looks it up in a pre-programmed table. However, not all electronic control functions can be handled in this manner; some must be computed. On an antilock brake system, for example, the computer must measure the rotation of each separate wheel and then calculate how much brake pressure to apply in order to prevent one wheel from locking up and causing a loss of control.

There are several ways of programming a ROM, but once programmed the ROM cannot be changed. If the ROM is made on the same chip that contains the microprocessor, the whole computer must be altered if a program change is needed. For this reason, a ROM is usually placed on a separate chip. Another type of memory is the Programmable Read Only Memory (PROM) that has the program "burned in" with the appropriate programming machine. Like the ROM, once a PROM has been programmed, it cannot be changed. The advantage of the PROM is that it can be produced in small quantities economi-

cally, since it is manufactured with a blank memory. Program changes for various vehicles can be made readily. There is still another type of memory called an EPROM (Erasable PROM) which can be erased and programmed many times. EPROM's are used only in research and development work, not on production vehicles.

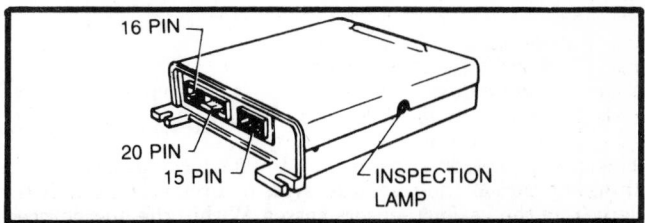

Typical automotive computer or electronic control unit (ECU). Except for pin connectors, all ECU assemblies look similar

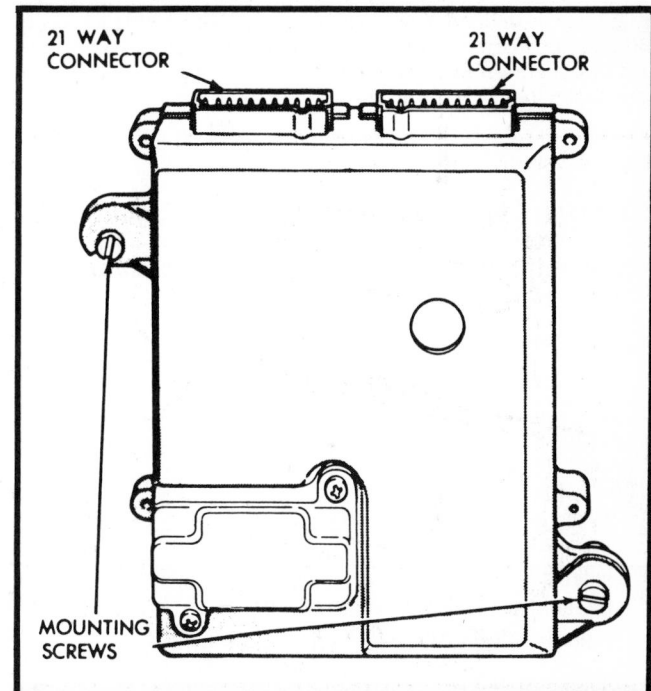

Chrysler MFI system logic module with pin connectors

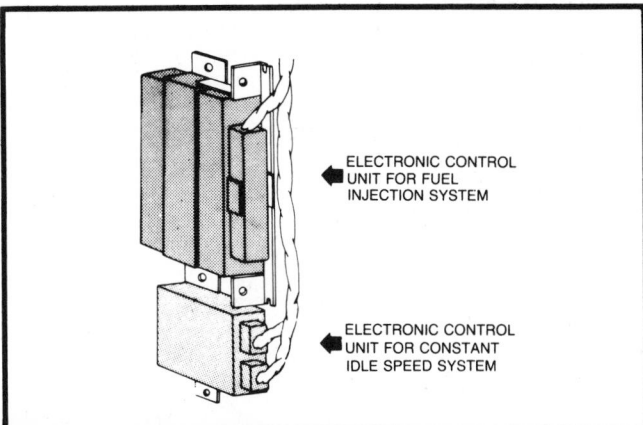

Typical control unit installations

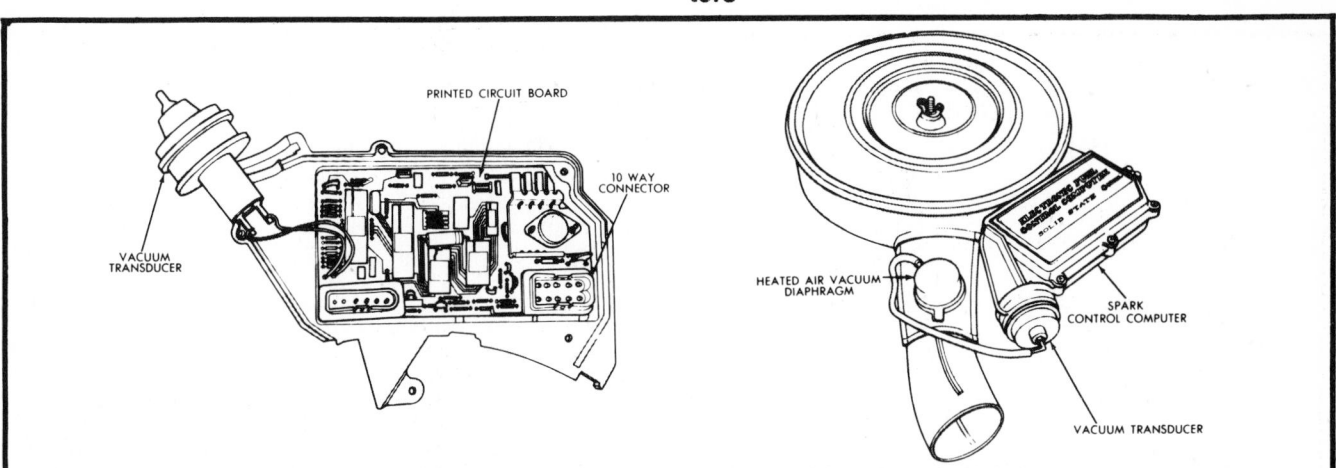

Typical Chrysler combustion assembly showing air cleaner mounting

INDEX

TROUBLESHOOTING AND DIAGNOSIS

Diagnostic Equipment and Special Tools

While we may think that with no moving parts, electronic components should never wear out, in the real world malfunctions do occur. The problem is that any computer-based system is extremely sensitive to electrical voltages and cannot tolerate careless or haphazard testing or service procedures. An inexperienced individual can literally do major damage looking for a minor problem by using the wrong kind of test equipment or connecting test leads or connectors with the ignition switch ON. Therefore, when selecting test equipment, make sure the manufacturers instructions state that the tester is compatible with whatever type of electronic control system is being serviced. Read all instructions carefully and double check all test points before installing probes or making any connections.

The following section outlines basic diagnosis techniques for dealing with computerized engine control systems. Along with a general explanation of the various types of test equipment available to aid in servicing modern electronic automotive systems, basic repair techniques for wiring harnesses and connectors is given. Read the basic information before attempting any repairs or testing on any computerized system, to provide the background of information necessary to avoid the most common and obvious mistakes that can cost both time and money. Likewise, the individual system sections for engine controls, fuel injection and feedback carburetors should be read from the beginning to the end before any repairs or diagnosis is attempted. Although the replacement and testing procedures are simple in themselves, the systems are not, and unless one has a thorough understanding of all components and their function within a particular fuel injection system (for example), the logical test sequence these systems demand cannot be followed. Minor malfunctions can make a big difference, so it is important to know how each component affects the operation of the overall electronic system to find the ultimate cause of a problem without replacing good components unnecessarily. It is not enough to use the correct test equipment; the test equipment must be used correctly.

Safety Precautions

--- CAUTION ---

Whenever working on or around any computer-based microprocessor control system, always observe these general precautions to prevent the possibility of personal injury or damage to electronic components:

• Never install or remove battery cables with the key ON or the engine running. Jumper cables should be connected with the key OFF to avoid power surges that can damage electronic control units. Engines equipped with computer controlled systems should avoid both giving and getting jump starts due to the possibility of serious damage to components from arcing in the engine compartment when connections are made with the ignition ON.

• Always remove the battery cables before charging the battery. Never use a high-output charger on an installed battery or attempt to use any type of "hot shot" (24 volt) starting aid.

• Exercise care when inserting test probes into connectors to insure good connections without damaging the connector or spreading the pins. Always probe connectors from the rear (wire) side, NOT the pin side, to avoid accidental shorting of terminals during test procedures.

• Never remove or attach wiring harness connectors with the ignition switch ON, especially to an electronic control unit.

• Do not drop any components during service procedures and never apply 12 volts directly to any component (like a solenoid or relay) unless instructed specifically to do so. Some component electrical windings are designed to safely handle only 4 or 5 volts and can be destroyed in seconds if 12 volts are applied directly to the connector.

• Remove the electronic control unit if the vehicle is to be placed in an environment where temperatures exceed approximately 176°F (80°C), such as a paint spray booth or when arc- or gas-welding near the control unit location in the car.

Organized Troubleshooting

When diagnosing a specific problem, organized troubleshooting is a must. The complexity of a modern automobile demands that you approach any problem in a logical, organized manner. There are certain troubleshooting techniques that are standard:

1. Establish when the problem occurs. Does the problem appear only under certain conditions? Were there any noises, odors, or other unusual symptoms? Make notes on any symptoms found, including warning lights and trouble codes, if applicable.

2. Isolate the problem area. To do this, make some simple tests and observations; then eliminate the systems that are working properly. Check for obvious problems such as broken wires or split or disconnected vacuum hoses. Always check the obvious before assuming something complicated is the cause.

3. Test for problems systematically to determine the cause once the problem area is isolated. Are all the components functioning properly? Is there power going to electrical switches and motors? Is there vacuum at vacuum switches and/or actuators? Is there a mechanical problem such as bent linkage or loose mounting screws? Doing careful, systematic checks will often turn up most causes on the first inspection without wasting time checking components that have little or no relationship to the problem.

4. Test all repairs after the work is done to make sure that the problem is fixed. Some causes can be traced to more than one component, so a careful verification of repair work is important to pick up additional malfunctions that may cause a problem to reappear or a different problem to arise. A blown fuse, for example, is a simple problem that may require more than just replacing a fuse. If you don't look for a problem that caused a fuse to blow, a shorted wire may go undetected.

The diagnostic tree charts are designed to help solve problems by leading the user through closely defined conditions and tests so that only the most likely components, vacuum and electrical circuits are checked for proper operation when troubleshooting a particular malfunction. By using the trouble trees to eliminate those systems and components which normally will not cause the condition described, a problem can be isolated within one or more systems or circuits without wasting time on unnecessary testing. Experience has shown that most problems tend to be the result of a fairly simple and obvious cause, such as loose or corroded connectors or air leaks in the intake system. A careful inspection of components during testing is essential to quick and accurate troubleshooting. Frequent references to special test equipment will be found in the text and in the diagnosis charts. These devices or compatible equivalents are necessary to perform some of the more complicated test procedures listed, but many components can be functionally tested with the quick checks outlined in the "On-Car Service" procedures. Aftermarket testers are available from a variety of sources, as well as from the vehicle manufacturer, but care should be taken that any test equipment being used is designed to diagnose that particular system accurately without damaging the control unit (ECU) or components being tested.

NOTE: Pinpointing the exact cause of trouble in an electrical system can sometimes only be done using special test equipment. The following describes commonly used test equipment and explains how to put it to best use in diagnosis. In addition to the information covered below, the manufacturer's instructions booklet provided with the tester should be read and clearly understood before attempting any test procedures.

Jumper Wires

Jumper wires are simple, yet extremely valuable pieces of test equipment. Jumper wires are merely wires that are used to bypass sections of a circuit. The simplest type of jumper wire is merely a length of multistrand wire with an alligator clip at each end. Jumper wires are usually fabricated from lengths of standard automotive wire and whatever type of connector (alligator clip, spade connector or pin connector) that is required for the particular vehicle being tested. The well-equipped tool box will have several different styles of jumper wires in several different lengths. Some jumper wires are made with three or more terminals coming from a common splice for special-purpose testing. In cramped, hard-to-reach areas it is advisable to have insulated boots over the jumper wire terminals in order to prevent accidental grounding, sparks, and possible fire, especially when testing fuel system components.

Jumper wires are used primarily to locate open electrical circuits, on either the ground (–) side of the circuit or on the hot (+) side. If an electrical component fails to operate, connect the jumper wire between the component and a good ground. If the component operates only with the jumper installed, the ground circuit is open. If the ground circuit is good, but the component does not operate, the circuit between the power feed and component is open. You can sometimes connect the jumper wire directly from the battery to the hot terminal of the component, but first make sure the component uses 12 volts in operation. Some electrical components, such as fuel injectors, are designed to operate on about 4 volts and running 12 volts directly to the injector terminals can burn out the wiring. By inserting an in-line fuseholder between a set of test leads, a fused jumper wire can be used for bypassing open circuits. Use a 5 amp fuse to provide protection against voltage spikes. When in doubt, use a voltmeter to check the voltage input to the component and measure how much voltage is being applied normally. By moving the jumper wire successively back from the lamp toward the power source, you can isolate the area of the circuit where the open is located. When the component stops functioning, or the power is cut off, the open is in the segment of wire between the jumper and the point previously tested.

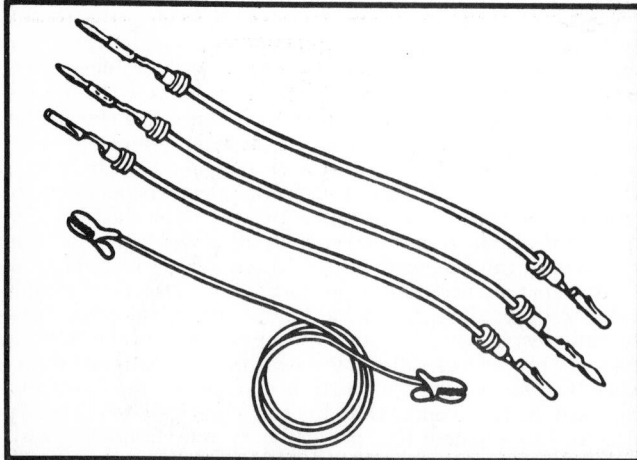

Typical jumper wires with various terminal ends

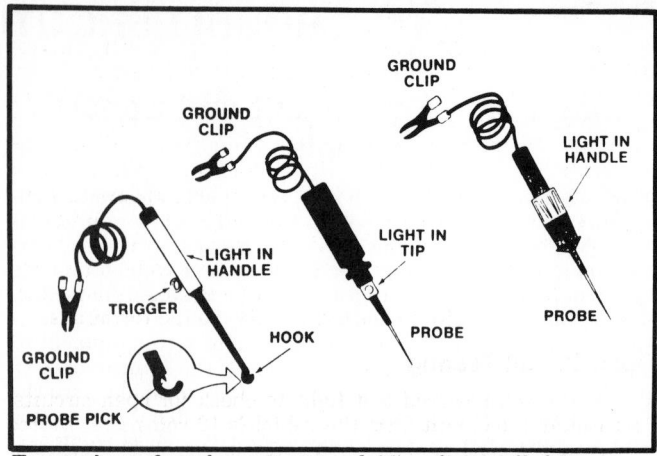

Examples of various types of 12 volt test lights

CAUTION

Never use jumpers made from wire that is of lighter gauge than used in the circuit under test. If the jumper wire is of too small gauge, it may overheat and possibly melt. Never use jumpers to bypass high-resistance loads (such as motors) in a circuit. Bypassing resistances, in effect, creates a short circuit which may, in turn, cause damage and fire. Never use a jumper for anything other than temporary bypassing of components in a circuit.

12 Volt Test Light

The 12 volt test light is used to check circuits and components while electrical current is flowing through them. It is used for voltage and ground tests. Twelve volt test lights come in different styles but all have three main parts; a ground clip, a probe, and a light. The most commonly used 12 volt test lights have pick-type probes. To use a 12 volt test light, connect the ground clip to a good ground and probe wherever necessary with the pick. The pick should be sharp so that it can penetrate wire insulation to make contact with the wire, without making a large hole in the insulation. The wrap-around light is handy in hard to reach areas or where it is difficult to support a wire to push a probe pick into it. To use the wrap around light, hook the wire to be probed with the hook and pull the trigger. A small pick will be forced through the wire insulation into the wire core.

CAUTION

Do not use a test light to probe electronic ignition spark plug or coil wires. Never use a pick-type test light to probe wiring on computer controlled systems unless specifically instructed to do so. Any wire insulation that is pierced by the test light probe should be taped and sealed with silicone after testing to weatherproof it.

Like the jumper wire, the 12 volt test light is used to isolate opens in circuits. But, whereas the jumper wire is used to bypass the open to operate the load, the 12 volt test light is used to locate the presence of voltage in a circuit. If the test light glows, you know that there is power up to that point; if the 12 volt test light does not glow when its probe is inserted into the wire or connector, you know that there is an open circuit (no power). Move the test light in successive steps back toward the power source until the light in the handle does glow. When it does glow, the open is between the probe and point previously probed.

NOTE: The test light does not detect that 12 volts (or any particular amount of voltage) is present; it only detects that some voltage is present. It is advisable before using the test light to touch its terminals across the battery posts to make sure the light is operating properly.

Self-Powered Test Light

The self-powered test light usually contains a 1.5 volt penlight battery. One type of self-powered test light is similar in design to the 12 volt test light. This type has both the battery and the light in the handle and pick-type probe tip. The second type has the light toward the open tip, so that the light illuminates the contact point. The self-powered test light is dual-purpose piece of test equipment. It can be used to test for either open or short circuits when power is isolated from the circuit (continuity test). A powered test light should not be used on any computer controlled system or component unless specifically instructed to do so. Many engine sensors can be destroyed by even this small amount of voltage applied directly to the terminals.

Open Circuit Testing

To use the self-powered test light to check for open circuits, first isolate the circuit from the vehicle's 12 volt power source by disconnecting the battery or wiring harness connector. Connect the test light ground clip to a good ground and probe sections of the circuit sequentially with the test light. (start from either end of the circuit). If the light is out, the open is between the probe and the circuit ground. If the light is on, the open is between the probe and end of the circuit toward the power source.

Short Circuit Testing

By isolating the circuit both from power and from ground, and using a self-powered test light, you can check for shorts to ground in the circuit. Isolate the circuit from power and ground. Connect the test light ground clip to a good ground and probe any easy-to-reach test point in the circuit. If the light comes on, there is a short somewhere in the circuit. To isolate the short, probe a test point at either end of the isolated circuit (the light should be on). Leave the test light probe connected and open connectors, switches, remove parts, etc., sequentially, until the light goes out. When the light goes out, the short is between the last circuit component opened and the previous circuit opened.

NOTE: The 1.5 volt battery in the test light does not provide much current. A weak battery may not provide enough power to illuminate the test light even when a complete circuit is made (especially if there are high resistances in the circuit). Always make sure that the test battery is strong. To check the battery, briefly touch the ground clip to the probe; if the light glows brightly the battery is strong enough for testing. Never use a self-powered test light to perform checks for opens or shorts when power is applied to the electrical system under test. The 12-volt vehicle power will quickly burn out the 1.5 volt light bulb in the test light.

Voltmeter

A voltmeter is used to measure voltage at any point in a circuit, or to measure the voltage drop across any part of a circuit. It can also be used to check continuity in a wire or circuit by indicating current flow from one end to the other. Voltmeters usually have various scales on the meter dial and a selector switch to allow the selection of different voltages. The voltmeter has a positive and a negative lead. To avoid damage to the meter, always connect the negative lead to the negative (–) side of circuit (to ground or nearest the ground side of the circuit) and connect the positive lead to the positive (+) side of the circuit (to the power source or the nearest power source). Note that the negative voltmeter lead will always be black and that the positive voltmeter will always be some color other than black (usually red). Depending on how the voltmeter is connected into the circuit, it has several uses.

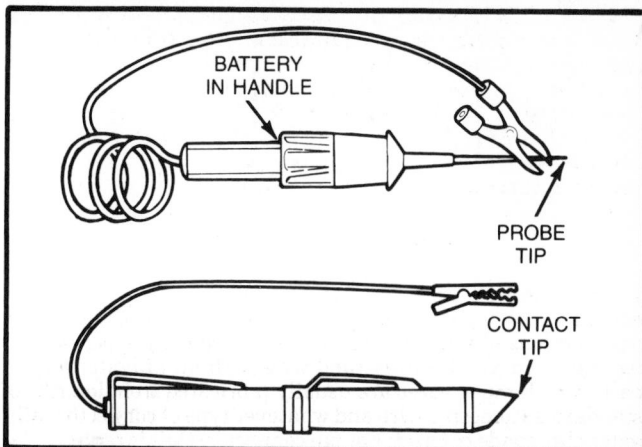

Two types of self-powered test lights

A voltmeter can be connected either in parallel or in series with a circuit and it has a very high resistance to current flow. When connected in parallel, only a small amount of current will flow through the voltmeter current path; the rest will flow through the normal circuit current path and the circuit will work normally. When the voltmeter is connected in series with a circuit, only a small amount of current can flow through the circuit. The circuit will not work properly, but the voltmeter reading will show if the circuit is complete or not.

Available Voltage Measurement

Set the voltmeter selector switch to the 20V position and connect the meter negative lead to the negative post of the battery. Connect the positive meter lead to the positive post of the battery and turn the ignition switch ON to provide a load. Read the voltage on the meter or digital display. A well-charged battery should register over 12 volts. If the meter reads below 11.5 volts, the battery power may be insufficient to operate the electrical system properly. This test determines voltage available from the battery and should be the first step in any electrical trouble diagnosis procedure. Many electrical problems, especially on computer controlled systems, can be caused by a low state of charge in the battery. Excessive corrosion at the battery cable terminals can cause a poor contact that will prevent proper charging and full battery current flow.

Normal battery voltage is 12 volts when fully charged. When the battery is supplying current to one or more circuits it is said to be "under load". When everything is off the electrical system is under a "no-load" condition. A fully charged battery

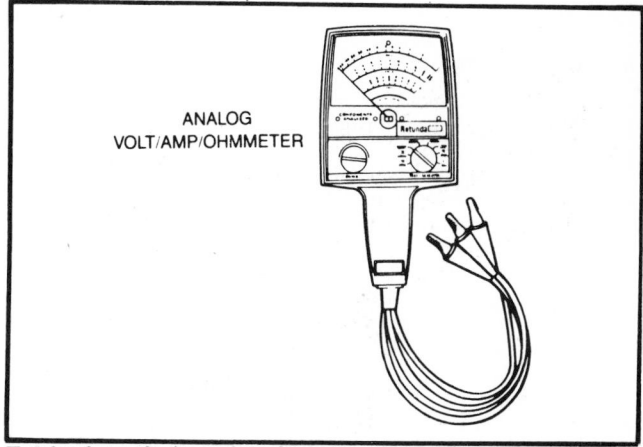

Typical analog-type voltmeter

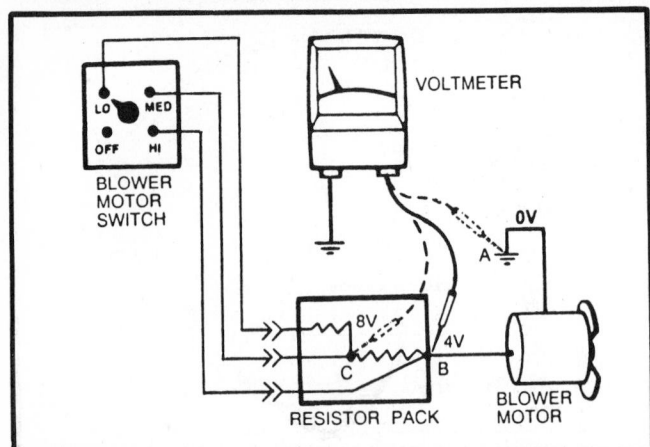

Measuring available voltage in a blower circuit

may show about 12.5 volts at no load; will drop to 12 volts under medium load; and will drop even lower under heavy load. If the battery is partially discharged the voltage decrease under heavy load may be excessive, even though the battery shows 12 volts or more at no load. When allowed to discharge further, the battery's available voltage under load will decrease more severely. For this reason, it is important that the battery be fully charged during all testing procedures to avoid errors in diagnosis and incorrect test results.

VOLTAGE DROP

When current flows through a resistance, the voltage beyond the resistance is reduced (the larger the current, the greater the reduction in voltage). When no current is flowing, there is no voltage drop because there is no current flow. All points in the circuit which are connected to the power source are at the same voltage as the power source. The total voltage drop always equals the total source voltage. In a long circuit with many connectors, a series of small, unwanted voltage drops due to corrosion at the connectors can add up to a total loss of voltage which impairs the operation of the normal loads in the circuit.

Indirect Computation of Voltage Drops

1. Set the voltmeter selector switch to the 20 volt position.
2. Connect the meter negative lead to a good ground.
3. Probe all resistances in the circuit with the positive meter lead.
4. Operate the circuit in all modes and observe the voltage readings.

Direct Measurement of Voltage Drops

1. Set the voltmeter switch to the 20 volt position.
2. Connect the voltmeter negative lead to the ground side of the resistance load to be measured.
3. Connect the positive lead to the positive side of the resistance or load to be measured.
4. Read the voltage drop directly on the 20 volt scale.

Too high a voltage indicates too high a resistance. If, for example, a blower motor runs too slowly, you can determine if there is too high a resistance in the resistor pack. By taking voltage drop readings in all parts of the circuit, you can isolate the problem. Too low a voltage drop indicates too low a resistance. If, for example, a blower motor runs too fast in the MED and/or LOW position, the problem can be isolated in the resistor pack by taking voltage drop readings in all parts of the circuit to locate a possibly shorted resistor. The maximum allowable voltage drop under load is critical, especially if there is

more than one high resistance problem in a circuit because all voltage drops are cumulative. A small drop is normal due to the resistance of the conductors.

High Resistance Testing

1. Set the voltmeter selector switch to the 4 volt position.
2. Connect the voltmeter positive lead to the positive post of the battery.
3. Turn on the headlights and heater blower to provide a load.
4. Probe various points in the circuit with the negative voltmeter lead.
5. Read the voltage drop on the 4 volt scale. Some average maximum allowable voltage drops are:
FUSE PANEL – 7 volts
IGNITION SWITCH – 5 volts
HEADLIGHT SWITCH – 7 volts
IGNITION COIL (+) – 5 volts
ANY OTHER LOAD – 1.3 volts

NOTE: Voltage drops are all measured while a load is operating; without current flow, there will be no voltage drop.

Ohmmeter

The ohmmeter is designed to read resistance (ohms) in a circuit or component. Although there are several different styles of ohmmeters, all will usually have a selector switch which permits the measurement of different ranges of resistance (usually the selector switch allows the multiplication of the meter reading by 10, 100, 1000, and 10,000). A calibration knob al-

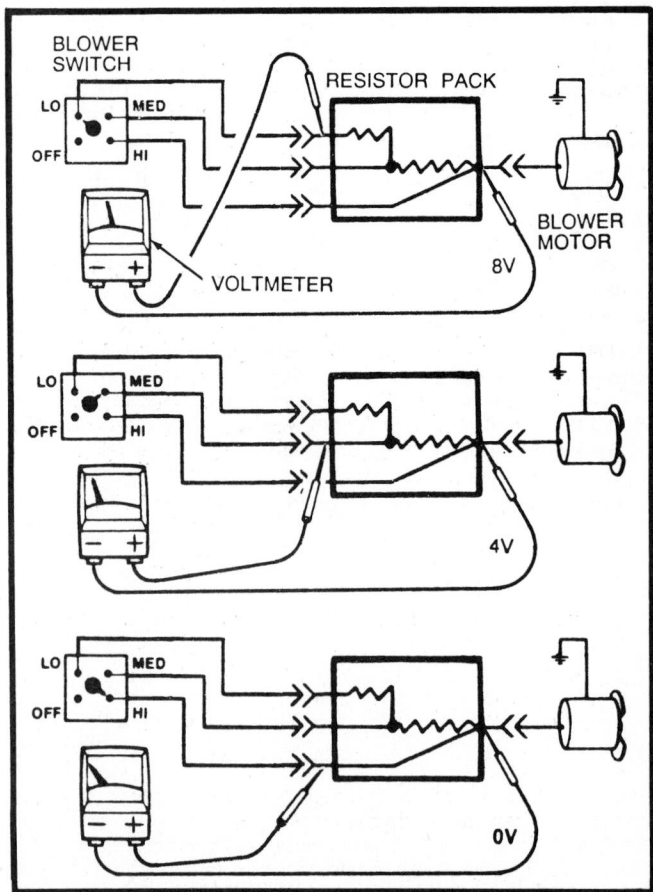

Direct measurement of voltage drops in a circuit

lows the meter to be set at zero for accurate measurement. Since all ohmmeters are powered by an internal battery (usually 9 volts), the ohmmeter can be used as a self-powered test light. When the ohmmeter is connected, current from the ohmmeter flows through the circuit or component being tested. Since the ohmmeter's internal resistance and voltage are known values, the amount of current flow through the meter depends on the resistance of the circuit or component being tested.

The ohmmeter can be used to perform continuity test for opens or shorts (either by observation of the meter needle or as a self-powered test light), and to read actual resistance in a circuit. It should be noted that the ohmmeter is used to check the resistance of a component or wire while there is no voltage applied to the circuit. Current flow from an outside voltage source (such as the vehicle battery) can damage the ohmmeter, so the circuit or component should be isolated from the vehicle electrical system before any testing is done. Since the ohmmeter uses its own voltage source, either lead can be connected to any test point.

NOTE: When checking diodes or other solid state components, the ohmmeter leads can only be connected one way in order to measure current flow in a single direction. Make sure the positive (+) and negative (-) terminal connections are as described in the test procedures to verify the one-way diode operation.

In using the meter for making continuity checks, do not be concerned with the actual resistance readings. Zero resistance, or any resistance readings, indicate continuity in the circuit. Infinite resistance indicates an open in the circuit. A high resistance reading where there should be none indicates a problem in the circuit. Checks for short circuits are made in the same manner as checks for open circuits except that the circuit must be isolated from both power and normal ground. Infinite resistance indicates no continuity to ground, while zero resistance indicates a dead short to ground.

Resistance Measurement

The batteries in an ohmmeter will weaken with age and temperature, so the ohmmeter must be calibrated or "zeroed" before taking measurements. To zero the meter, place the selector switch in its lowest range and touch the two ohmmeter leads together. Turn the calibration knob until the meter needle is exactly on zero.

NOTE: All analog (needle) type ohmmeters must be zeroed before use, but some digital ohmmeter models are automatically calibrated when the switch is turned on. Self-calibrating digital ohmmeters do not have an adjusting knob, but it's a good idea to check for a zero readout before use by touching the leads together. All computer controlled systems require the use of a digital ohmmeter with at least 10 megohms impedance for testing. Before any test procedures are attempted, make sure the ohmmeter used is compatible with the electrical system, or damage to the on-board computer could result.

To measure resistance, first isolate the circuit from the vehicle power source by disconnecting the battery cables or the harness connector. Make sure the key is OFF when disconnecting any components or the battery. Where necessary, also isolate at least one side of the circuit to be checked to avoid reading parallel resistances. Parallel circuit resistances will always give a lower reading than the actual resistance of either of the branches. When measuring the resistance of parallel circuits, the total resistance will always be lower than the smallest resistance in the circuit. Connect the meter leads to both sides of the circuit (wire or component) and read the actual measured ohms on the meter scale. Make sure the selector switch is set to

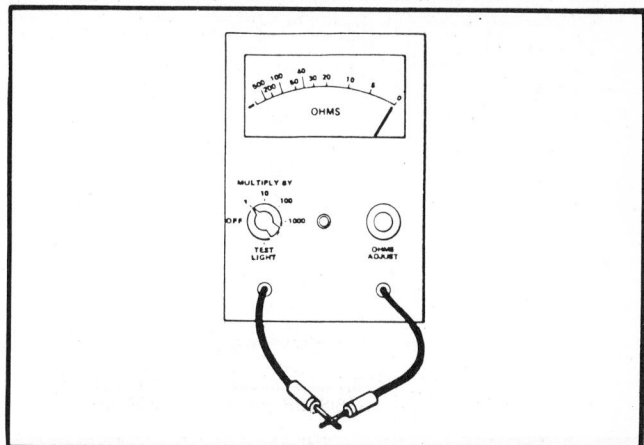

Analog ohmmeters must be calibrated before use by touching the probes together and adjusting the knob

the proper ohm scale for the circuit being tested to avoid misreading the ohmmeter test value.

CAUTION

Never use an ohmmeter with power applied to the circuit. Like the self-powered test light, the ohmmeter is designed to operate on its own power supply. The normal 12 volt automotive electrical system current could damage the meter.

Ammeters

An ammeter measures the amount of current flowing through a circuit in units called amperes or amps. Amperes are units of electron flow which indicate how fast the electrons are flowing through the circuit. Since Ohm's Law dictates that current flow in a circuit is equal to the circuit voltage divided by the total circuit resistance, increasing voltage also increases the current level (amps). Likewise, any decrease in resistance will increase the amount of amps in a circuit. At normal operating voltage, most circuits have a characteristic amount of amperes, called "current draw" which can be measured using an ammeter. By referring to a specified current draw rating, measuring the amperes, and comparing the two values, one can determine what is happening within the circuit to aid in diagnosis. An open circuit, for example, will not allow any current to flow so the ammeter reading will be zero. More current flows through a heavily loaded circuit or when the charging system is operating.

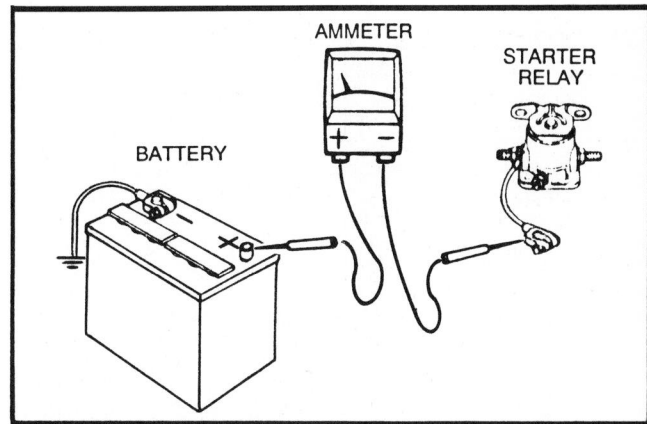

Battery current drain test

An ammeter is always connected in series with the circuit being tested. All of the current that normally flows through the circuit must also flow through the ammeter; if there is any other path for the current to follow, the ammeter reading will not be accurate. The ammeter itself has very little resistance to current flow and therefore will not affect the circuit, but it will measure current draw only when the circuit is closed and electricity is flowing. Excessive current draw can blow fuses and drain the battery, while a reduced current draw can cause motors to run slowly, lights to dim and other components not to operate properly. The ammeter can help diagnose these conditions by locating the cause of the high or low reading.

Multimeters

Different combinations of test meters can be built into a single unit designed for specific tests. Some of the more common combination test devices are known as Volt-Amp testers, Tach-Dwell meters, or Digital Multimeters. The Volt-Amp tester is used for charging system, starting system or battery tests and consists of a voltmeter, an ammeter and a variable resistance carbon pile. The voltmeter will usually have at least two ranges for use with 6, 12 and 24 volt systems. The ammeter also has more than one range for testing various levels of battery loads and starter current draw and the carbon pile can be adjusted to offer different amounts of resistance. The Volt-Amp tester has heavy leads to carry large amounts of current and many later models have an inductive ammeter pickup that clamps around the wire to simplify test connections. On some models, the ammeter also has a zero-center scale to allow test-

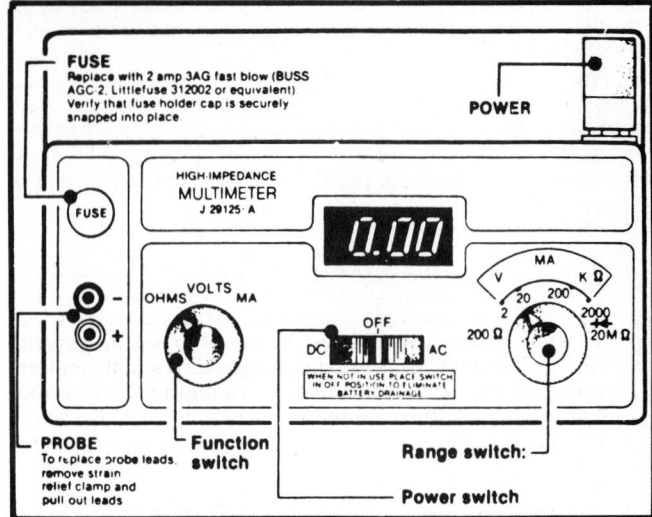

Typical multimeter used to test GM systems

ing of charging and starting systems without switching leads or polarity. A digital multimeter is a voltmeter, ammeter and ohmmeter combined in an instrument which gives a digital readout. These are often used when testing solid state circuits because of their high input impedence (usually 10 megohms or more).
UF9
The tach-dwell meter combines a tachometer and a dwell (cam angle) meter and is a specialized kind of voltmeter. The tachometer scale is marked to show engine speed in rpm and the dwell scale is marked to show degrees of distributor shaft rotation. In most electronic ignition systems, dwell is determined by the control unit, but the dwell meter can also be used to check the duty cycle (operation) of some electronic engine control systems. Some tach-dwell meters are powered by an internal battery, while others take their power from the car battery in use. The battery powered testers usually require calibration much like an ohmmeter before testing.

Special Test Equipment

A variety of diagnostic tools are available to help troubleshoot and repair computerized engine control systems. The most sophisticated of these devices are the console-type engine analyzers that usually occupy a garage service bay, but there are several types of aftermarket electronic testers available that will allow quick circuit tests of the engine control system by plugging directly into a special connector located in the engine compartment or under the dashboard. Several tool and equipment manufacturers offer simple, hand-held testers that measure various circuit voltage levels on command to check all system components for proper operation. Although these testers usually cost about $300–500, consider that the average computer control unit (or ECM) can cost just as much and the money saved by not replacing perfectly good sensors or components in an attempt to correct a problem could justify the purchase price of a special diagnostic tester the first time it's used.

These computerized testers can allow quick and easy test measurements while the engine is operating or while the car is being driven. In addition, the on-board computer memory can be read to access any stored trouble codes; in effect allowing the computer to tell you where it hurts and aid trouble diagnosis by pinpointing exactly which circuit or component is malfunctioning. In the same manner, repairs can be tested to make sure the problem has been corrected. The biggest advantage these special testers have is their relatively easy hookups that

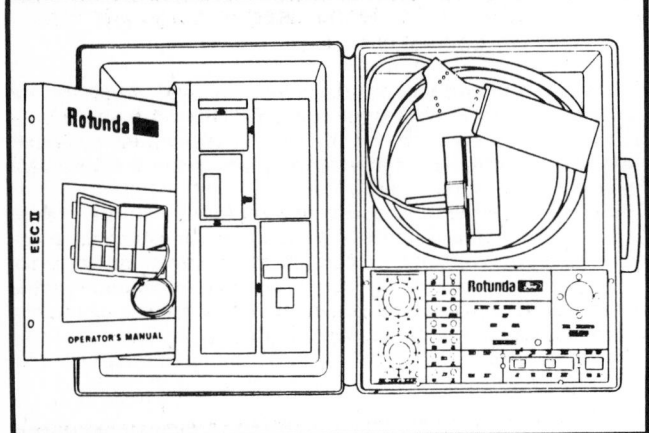

Typical electronic engine control tester used on Ford EEC systems

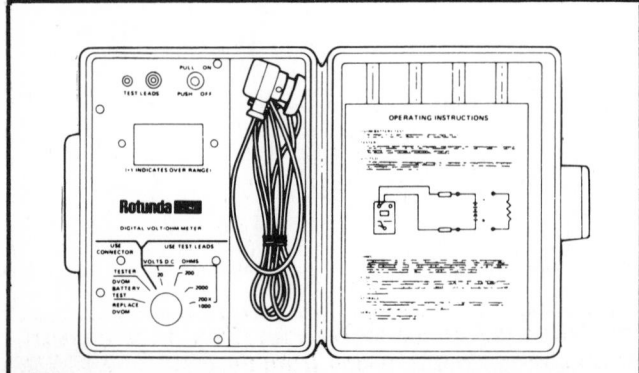

Digital volt-ohmmeter used to test Ford systems

minimize or eliminate the chances of making the wrong connections and getting false voltage readings or damaging the computer accidentally.

NOTE: It should be remembered that these testers check voltage levels in circuits; they don't detect mechanical problems or failed components if the circuit voltage falls within the preprogrammed limits stored in the tester PROM unit. Also, most of the hand-held testers are designed to work only on one or two systems made by a specific manufacturer.

A variety of aftermarket testers are available to help diagnose different computerized control systems. Owatonna Tool Company (OTC), for example, markets a device called the OTC Monitor which plugs directly into the assembly line diagnostic link (ALDL). The OTC tester makes diagnosis a simple matter of pressing the correct buttons and, by changing the internal PROM or inserting a different diagnosis cartridge, it will work on any model from full size to subcompact, over a wide range of years. An adapter is supplied with the tester to allow connection to all types of ALDL links, regardless of the number of pin terminals used. By inserting an updated PROM into the OTC tester, it can be easily updated to diagnose any new modifications of computerized control systems.

Hand-held aftermarket tester used to diagnosis electronic engine control systems

gle, they are organized into bundles, enclosed in plastic or taped together and called wire harnesses. Different wiring harnesses serve different parts of the vehicle. Individual wires are color-coded to help trace them through a harness where sections are hidden from view.

A loose or corroded connection or a replacement wire that is too small for the circuit will add extra resistance and an additional voltage drop to the circuit. A ten percent voltage drop can result in slow or erratic motor operation, for example, even though the circuit is complete. Automotive wiring or circuit conductors can be in any one of three forms:

1. Single strand wire
2. Multistrand wire

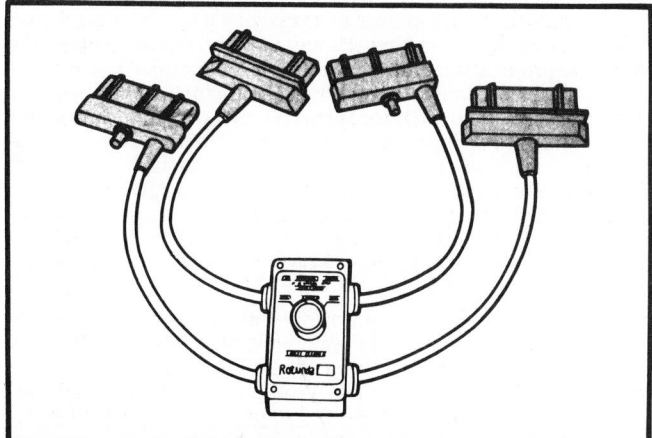

Typical adapter wiring harness for connecting tester to diagnostic terminal

Wiring Diagrams

The average automobile contains about ½ mile of wiring, with hundreds of individual connections. To protect the many wires from damage and to keep them from becoming a confusing tan-

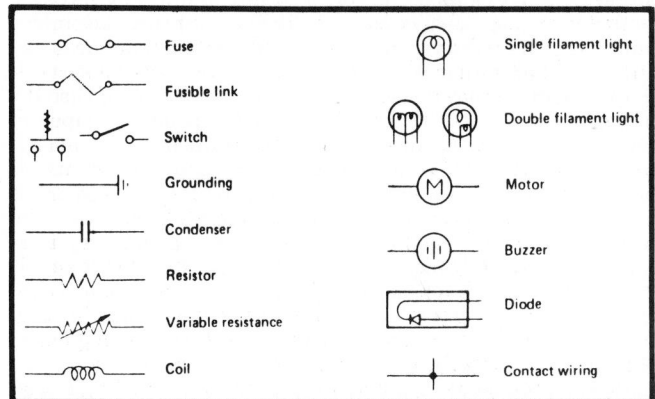

Fuse	Single filament light
Fusible link	
Switch	Double filament light
Grounding	Motor
Condenser	
Resistor	Buzzer
Variable resistance	Diode
Coil	Contact wiring

Typical electrical symbols found on wiring diagrams

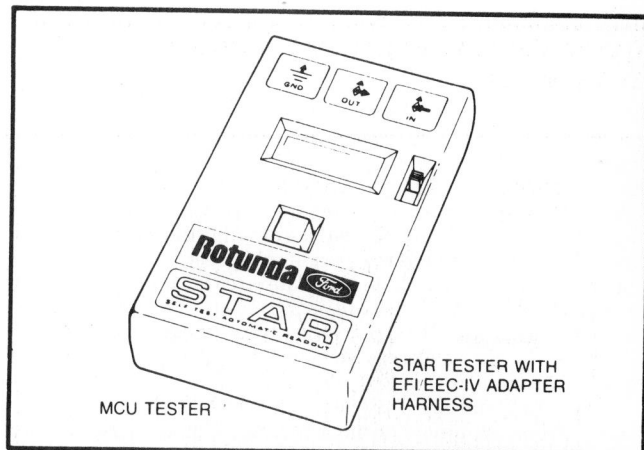

STAR TESTER WITH EFI EEC-IV ADAPTER HARNESS

MCU TESTER

Self-Test and Automatic Readout (STAR) tester used for obtaining trouble codes from Ford MCU and EEC IV systems

Typical diagnostic terminal locations on GM models. The diagnosis terminals are usually mounted under the dash or in the engine compartment

3. Printed circuitry

Single strand wire has a solid metal core and is usually used inside such components as alternators, motors, relays and other devices. Multistrand wire has a core made of many small strands of wire twisted together into a single conductor. Most of the wiring in an automotive electrical system is made up of multistrand wire, either as a single conductor or grouped together in a harness. All wiring is color-coded on the insulator, either as a solid color or as a colored wire with an identification stripe. A printed circuit is a thin film of copper or other conductor that is printed on an insulator backing. Occasionally, a printed circuit is sandwiched between two sheets of plastic for more protection and flexibility. A complete printed circuit, consisting of conductors, insulating material and connectors for lamps or other components is called a printed circuit board. Printed circuitry is used in place of individual wires or harnesses in places where space is limited, such as behind instrument panels.

Wire Gauge

Since computer-controlled automotive electrical systems are very sensitive to changes in resistance, the selection of properly sized wires is critical when systems are repaired. The wire gauge number is an expression of the cross section area of the conductor. The most common system for expressing wire size is the American Wire Gauge (AWG) system.

Wire cross section area is measured in circular mils. A mil is one-thousandth of an inch (0.001); a circular mil is the area of a circle one mil in diameter. For example, a conductor $\frac{1}{4}$ inch in diameter is 0.250 in. or 250 mils. The circular mil cross section area of the wire is 250 squared or 62,500 circular mils. Imported car models usually use metric wire gauge designations, which is simply the cross section area of the conductor in square millimeters (mm^2).

Gauge numbers are assigned to conductors of various cross section areas. As gauge number increases, area decreases and the conductor becomes smaller. A 5 gauge conductor is smaller than a 1 gauge conductor and a 10 gauge is smaller than a 5 gauge. As the cross section area of a conductor decreases, resistance increases and so does the gauge number. A conductor

with a higher gauge number will carry less current than a conductor with a lower gauge number.

NOTE: Gauge wire size refers to the size of the conductor, not the size of the complete wire. It is possible to have two wires of the same gauge with different diameters because one may have thicker insulation than the other.

12 volt automotive electrical systems generally use 10, 12, 14, 16 and 18 gauge wire. Main power distribution circuits and larger accessories usually use 10 and 12 gauge wire. Battery cables are usually 4 or 6 gauge, although 1 and 2 gauge wires are occasionally used. Wire length must also be considered when making repairs to a circuit. As conductor length increases, so does resistance. An 18 gauge wire, for example, can carry a 10 amp load for 10 feet without excessive voltage drop; however if a 15 foot wire is required for the same 10 amp load, a 16 gauge wire must be used.

An electrical schematic shows the electrical current paths when a circuit is operating properly. It is essential to understand how a circuit works before trying to figure out why it doesn't. Schematics break the entire electrical system down into individual circuits and show only one particular circuit. In a schematic, no attempt is made to represent wiring and components as they physically appear on the vehicle; switches and other components are shown as simply as possible. Face views of harness connectors show the cavity or terminal locations in all multi-pin connectors to help locate test points. The component locator in Chapter One will help in determining the exact location of various components in a particular model of vehicle.

If you need to backprobe a connector while it is on the component, the order of the terminals must be mentally reversed. The wire color code can help in this situation, as well as a keyway, lock tab or other reference mark.

Wiring Repairs

Soldering is a quick, efficient method of joining metals permanently. Everyone who has to make wiring repairs should know how to solder. Electrical connections that are soldered are far less likely to come apart and will conduct electricity much better than connections that are only "pig-tailed" together. The most popular (and preferred) method of soldering is with an electrical soldering gun. Soldering irons are available in many sizes and wattage ratings. Irons with higher wattage ratings deliver higher temperatures and recover lost heat faster. A small soldering iron rated for no more than 50 watts is recommended, especially on electrical systems where excess heat can damage the components being soldered.

There are three ingredients necessary for successful soldering; proper flux, good solder and sufficient heat. A soldering flux is necessary to clean the metal of tarnish, prepare it for soldering and to enable the solder to spread into tiny crevices. When soldering, always use a resin flux or resin core solder which is non-corrosive and will not attract moisture once the job is finished. Other types of flux (acid core) will leave a residue tht will attract moisture and cause the wires to corrode. Tin is a unique metal with a low melting point. In a molten state, it dissolves and alloys easily with many metals. Solder is made by mixing tin with lead. The most common proportions are 40/60, 50/50 and 60/40, with the percentage of tin listed first. Low priced solders usually contain less tin, making them very difficult for a beginner to use because more heat is required to melt the solder. A common solder is 40/60 which is well suited for general use, but 60/40 melts easier, has more tin for a better joint and is preferred for electrical work.

Soldering Techniques

Successful soldering requires that the metals to be joined be heated to a temperature that will melt the solder (usually 360-

COMMON SYMBOLS FOR AUTOMOTIVE COMPONENTS USED IN SCHEMATIC DIAGRAMS

Automotive service manuals use schematic diagrams to show how electrical and other types of components work, and how such components are connected to make circuits. Components that are shown whole are represented in full lines in a rectangular shape, and are identified by name; where only a part of a component is shown in a schematic diagram, the rectangular shape is outlined with a dashed line.

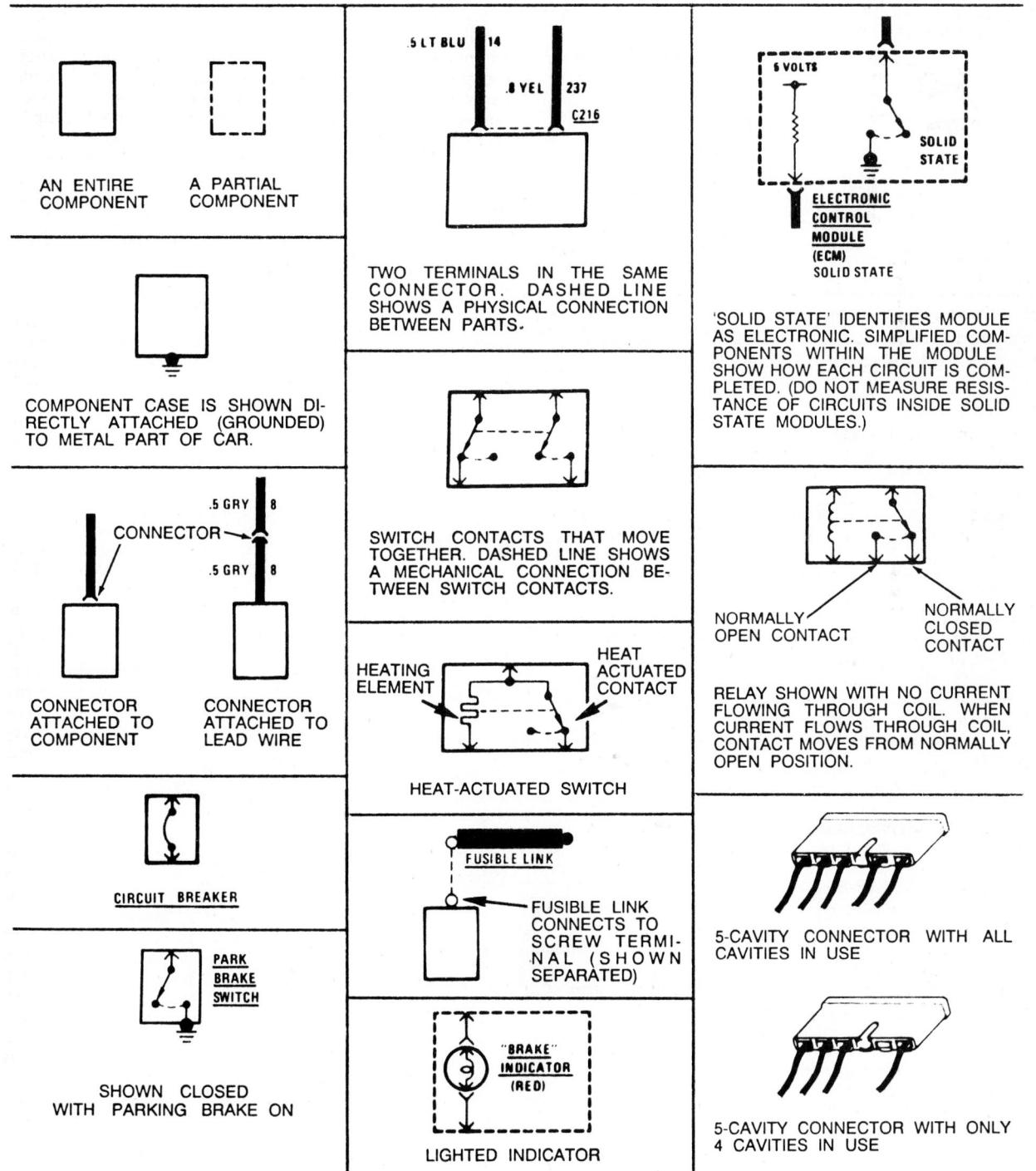

AN ENTIRE COMPONENT   A PARTIAL COMPONENT

COMPONENT CASE IS SHOWN DIRECTLY ATTACHED (GROUNDED) TO METAL PART OF CAR.

CONNECTOR ATTACHED TO COMPONENT   CONNECTOR ATTACHED TO LEAD WIRE

CIRCUIT BREAKER

PARK BRAKE SWITCH

SHOWN CLOSED WITH PARKING BRAKE ON

TWO TERMINALS IN THE SAME CONNECTOR. DASHED LINE SHOWS A PHYSICAL CONNECTION BETWEEN PARTS.

SWITCH CONTACTS THAT MOVE TOGETHER. DASHED LINE SHOWS A MECHANICAL CONNECTION BETWEEN SWITCH CONTACTS.

HEAT-ACTUATED SWITCH

FUSIBLE LINK CONNECTS TO SCREW TERMINAL (SHOWN SEPARATED)

LIGHTED INDICATOR

ELECTRONIC CONTROL MODULE (ECM) SOLID STATE

'SOLID STATE' IDENTIFIES MODULE AS ELECTRONIC. SIMPLIFIED COMPONENTS WITHIN THE MODULE SHOW HOW EACH CIRCUIT IS COMPLETED. (DO NOT MEASURE RESISTANCE OF CIRCUITS INSIDE SOLID STATE MODULES.)

NORMALLY OPEN CONTACT   NORMALLY CLOSED CONTACT

RELAY SHOWN WITH NO CURRENT FLOWING THROUGH COIL. WHEN CURRENT FLOWS THROUGH COIL, CONTACT MOVES FROM NORMALLY OPEN POSITION.

5-CAVITY CONNECTOR WITH ALL CAVITIES IN USE

5-CAVITY CONNECTOR WITH ONLY 4 CAVITIES IN USE

WIRE IS GROUNDED, AND GROUND IS NUMBERED FOR REFERENCE ON COMPONENT LOCATION TABLE.

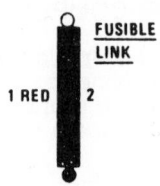

FUSIBLE LINK SHOWS WIRE SIZE AND INSULATION COLOR.

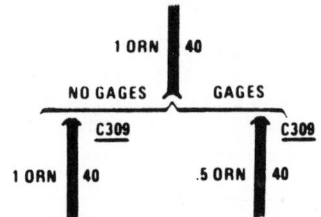

WIRE CHOICES FOR OPTIONS OR DIFFERENT MODELS ARE SHOWN AND LABLED.

WIRE IS INDIRECTLY CONNECTED TO GROUND. (WIRE MAY HAVE ONE OR MORE SPLICES BEFORE IT IS GROUNDED.)

CURRENT PATH IS CONTINUED AS LABLED. THE ARROW SHOWS THE DIRECTION OF CURRENT FLOW, AND IS REPEATED WHERE CURRENT PATH CONTINUES.

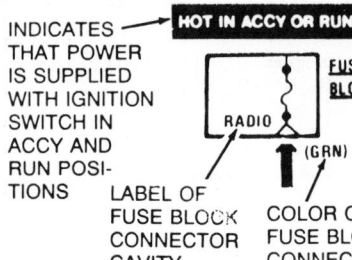

INDICATES THAT POWER IS SUPPLIED WITH IGNITION SWITCH IN ACCY AND RUN POSITIONS

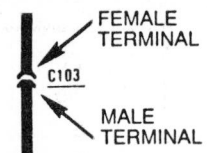

CONNECTOR REFERENCE NO. IS LISTED IN COMPONENT LOCATION TABLE, WHICH ALSO SHOWS TOTAL NO. OF TERMINALS POSSIBLE: C103 (6 CAVITIES).

A WIRE IS SHOWN WHICH CONNECTS TO ANOTHER CIRCUIT. THE WIRE IS SHOWN AGAIN ON THAT CIRCUIT.

DIODE

CURRENT CAN FLOW ONLY IN THE DIRECTION OF THE ARROW

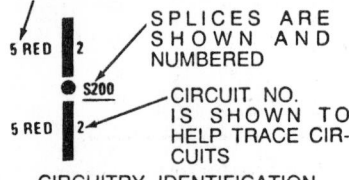

CIRCUITRY IDENTIFICATION

THE DASHED LINE INDICATES THAT THE CIRCUITRY IS NOT SHOWN IN COMPLETE DETAIL BUT IS COMPLETE ON THE INDICATED PAGE.

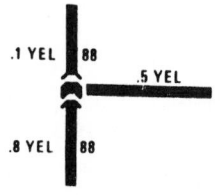

3 WIRES ARE SHOWN CONNECTED TOGETHER WITH A PIGGYBACK CONNECTOR

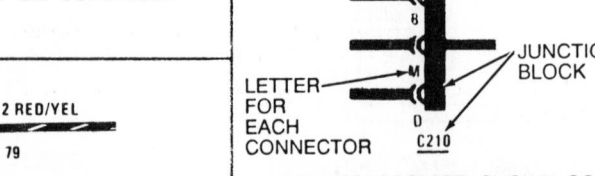

A WAVY LINE MEANS WIRE IS TO BE CONTINUED

WIRE INSULATION IS ONE COLOR, WITH ANOTHER COLOR STRIPE (EXAMPLE: RED COLOR, WITH YELLOW STRIPE).

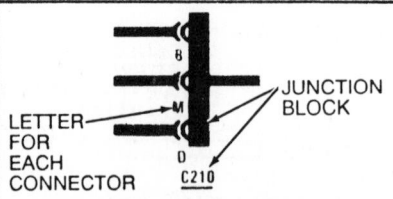

3 CONNECTORS ARE SHOWN CONNECTED TOGETHER AT A JUNCTION BLOCK. FOURTH WIRE IS SOLDERED TO COMMON CONNECTION ON BLOCK.

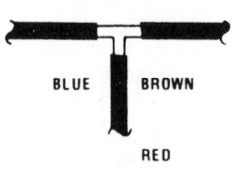

HOSE COLORS ARE SHOWN AT A VACUUM JUNCTION.

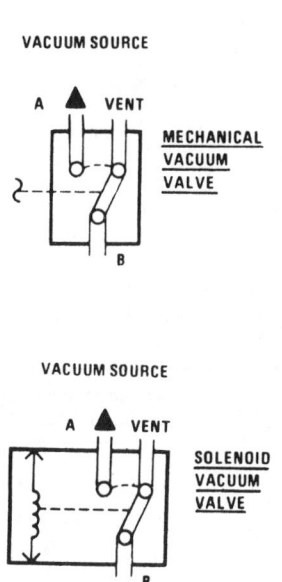

VACUUM SOURCE

MECHANICAL VACUUM VALVE

VACUUM SOURCE

SOLENOID VACUUM VALVE

2-POSITION VACUUM MOTORS

IN THE 'AT REST' POSITION SHOWN, THE VALVE SEALS PORT 'A' AND VENTS PORT 'B' TO THE ATMOSPHERE. WHEN THE VALVE IS MOVED TO THE 'OPERATED' POSITION, VACUUM FROM PORT 'A' IS CONNECTED TO PORT 'B'. THE SOLENOID VACUUM VALVE USES THE SOLENOID TO MOVE THE VALVE.

VACUUM MOTORS OPERATE LIKE ELECTRICAL SOLENOIDS, MECHANICALLY PUSHING OR PULLING A SHAFT BETWEEN TWO FIXED POSITIONS. WHEN VACUUM IS APPLIED, THE SHAFT IS PULLED IN. WHEN NO VACUUM IS APPLIED, THE SHAFT IS PUSHED ALL THE WAY OUT BY A SPRING.

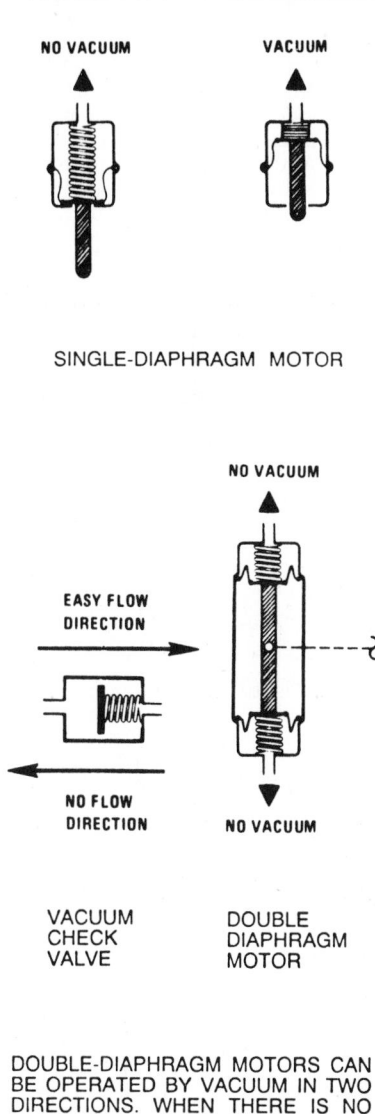

NO VACUUM   VACUUM

SINGLE-DIAPHRAGM MOTOR

EASY FLOW DIRECTION

NO FLOW DIRECTION

NO VACUUM

NO VACUUM

VACUUM CHECK VALVE

DOUBLE DIAPHRAGM MOTOR

DOUBLE-DIAPHRAGM MOTORS CAN BE OPERATED BY VACUUM IN TWO DIRECTIONS. WHEN THERE IS NO VACUUM, THE MOTOR IS IN THE CENTER 'AT REST' POSITION.

PARTIAL VACUUM

SERVO MOTOR

SOME VACUUM MOTORS, SUCH AS THE SERVO MOTOR IN THE CRUISE CONTROL, CAN POSITION THE ACTUATING ARM AT ANY POSITION BETWEEN FULLY EXTENDED AND FULLY RETRACTED. THE SERVO IS OPERATED BY A CONTROL VALVE THAT APPLIES VARYING AMOUNTS OF VACUUM TO THE MOTOR. THE HIGHER THE VACUUM LEVEL, THE GREATER THE RETRACTION OF THE MOTOR ARM. SERVO MOTORS WORK LIKE THE TWO-POSITION MOTORS; THE ONLY DIFFERENCE IS IN THE WAY THE VACUUM IS APPLIED. SERVO MOTORS ARE GENERALLY LARGER AND PROVIDE A CALIBRATED CONTROL.

METRIC SIZE	AWG SIZES
.22	24
.35	22
.5	20
.8	18
1.0	16
2.0	14
3.0	12
5.0	10
8.0	8
13.0	6
19.0	4
32.0	2

Wire Size Conversion Table

460°F). Contrary to popular belief, the purpose of the soldering iron is not to melt the solder itself, but to heat the parts being soldered to a temperature high enough to melt the solder when it touches the work. Melting flux-cored solder on the soldering iron will usually destroy the effectiveness of the flux.

NOTE: Soldering tips are made of copper for good heat conductivity, but must be "tinned" regularly for quick transfer of heat to the project and to prevent the solder from sticking to the iron. To "tin" the iron, simply heat it and touch the flux-cored solder to the tip; the solder will flow over the hot tip. Wipe the excess off with a clean rag, but be careful as the iron will be hot.

After some use, the tip may become pitted. If so, simply dress the tip smooth with a smooth file and "tin" the tip again. An old saying holds that "metals well cleaned are half soldered." Flux-cored solder will remove oxides but rust, bits of insulation and oil or grease must be removed with a wire brush or emery cloth.

For maximum strength in soldered parts, the joint must start off clean and tight. Weak joints will result if there are gaps too wide for the solder to bridge.

If a separate soldering flux is used, it should be brushed or swabbed only on areas that are to be soldered. Most solders

Proper soldering method. Allow the soldering iron to heat the wire first, then apply the solder as shown

contain a core of flux and separate fluxing is unnecessary. Hold the work to be soldered firmly. It is best to solder on a wooden board, because a metal vise will only rob the piece to be soldered of heat and make it difficult to melt the solder. Hold the soldering tip with the broadest face against the work to be soldered. Apply solder under the tip close to the work, using enough solder to give a heavy film between the iron and the piece being soldered, while moving slowly and making sure the solder melts properly. Keep the work level or the solder will run to the lowest part and favor the thicker parts, because these require more heat to melt the solder. If the soldering tip overheats (the solder coating on the face of the tip burns up), it should be retinned. Once the soldering is completed, let the soldered joint stand until cool. Tape and seal all soldered wire splices after the repair has cooled.

Wire Harness and Connectors

The on-board computer (ECM) wire harness electrically connects the control unit to the various solenoids, switches and sensors used by the control system. Most connectors in the engine compartment or otherwise exposed to the elements are protected against moisture and dirt which could create oxidation and deposits on the terminals. This protection is important because of the very low voltage and current levels used by the computer and sensors. All connectors have a lock which secures the male and female terminals together, with a secondary lock holding the seal and terminal into the connector. Both terminal locks must be released when disconnecting ECM connectors.

These special connectors are weather-proof and all repairs

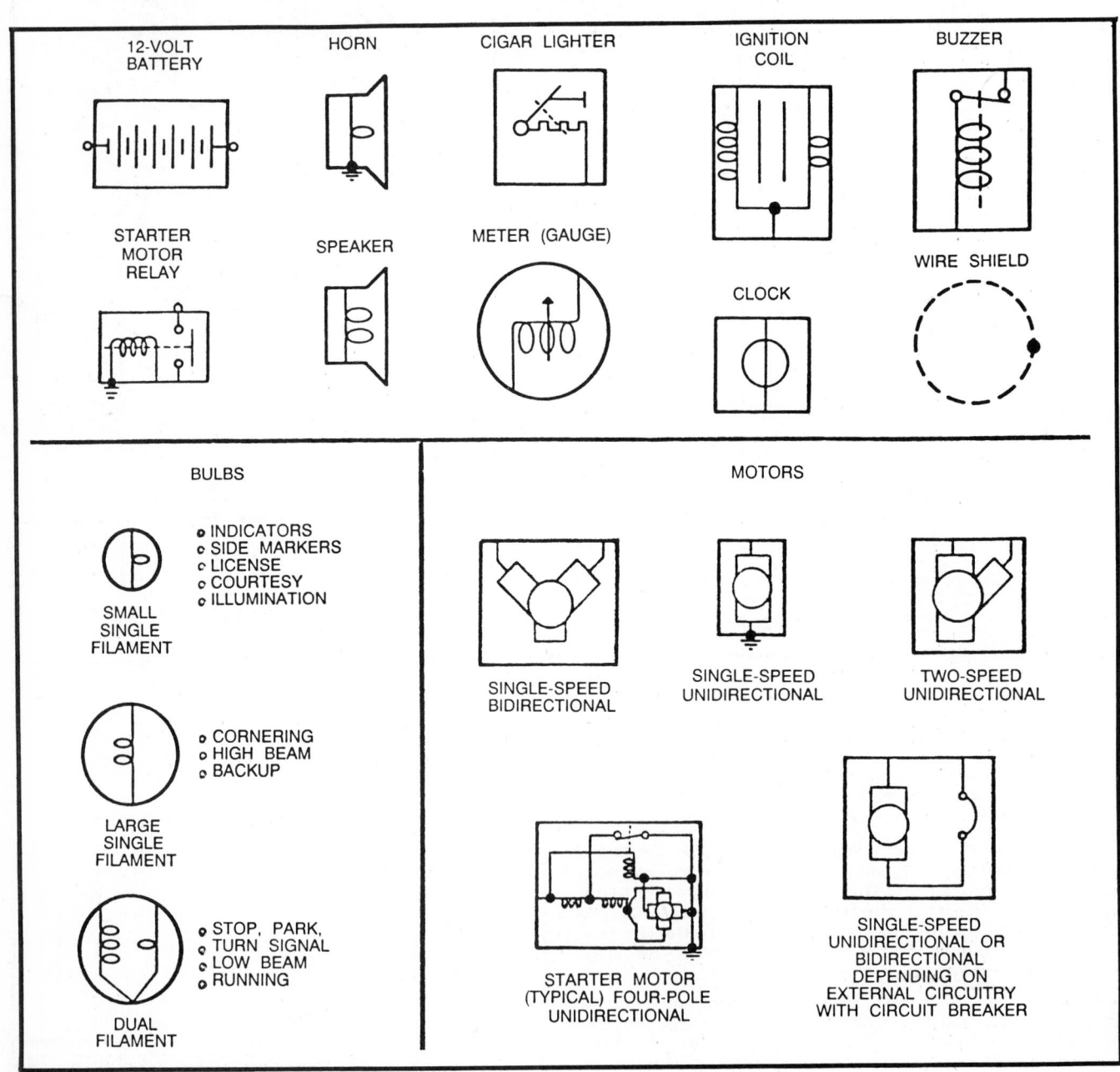

require the use of a special terminal and the tool required to service it. This tool is used to remove the pin and sleeve terminals. If removal is attempted with an ordinary pick, there is a good chance that the terminal will be bent or deformed. Unlike standard blade type terminals, these terminals cannot be straightened once they are bent. Make certain that the connectors are properly seated and all of the sealing rings in place when connecting leads. On some models, a hinge-type flap provides a backup or secondary locking feature for the terminals. Most secondary locks are used to improve the connector reliability by retaining the terminals if the small terminal lock tangs are not positioned properly.

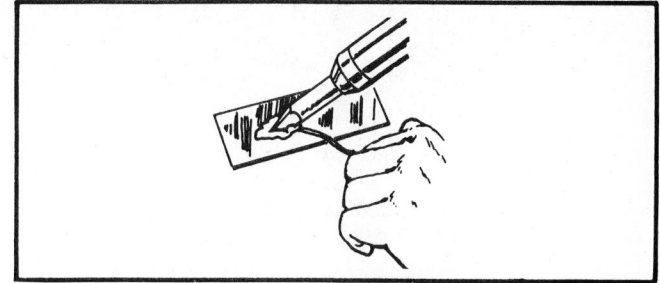

Tinning the soldering iron before use

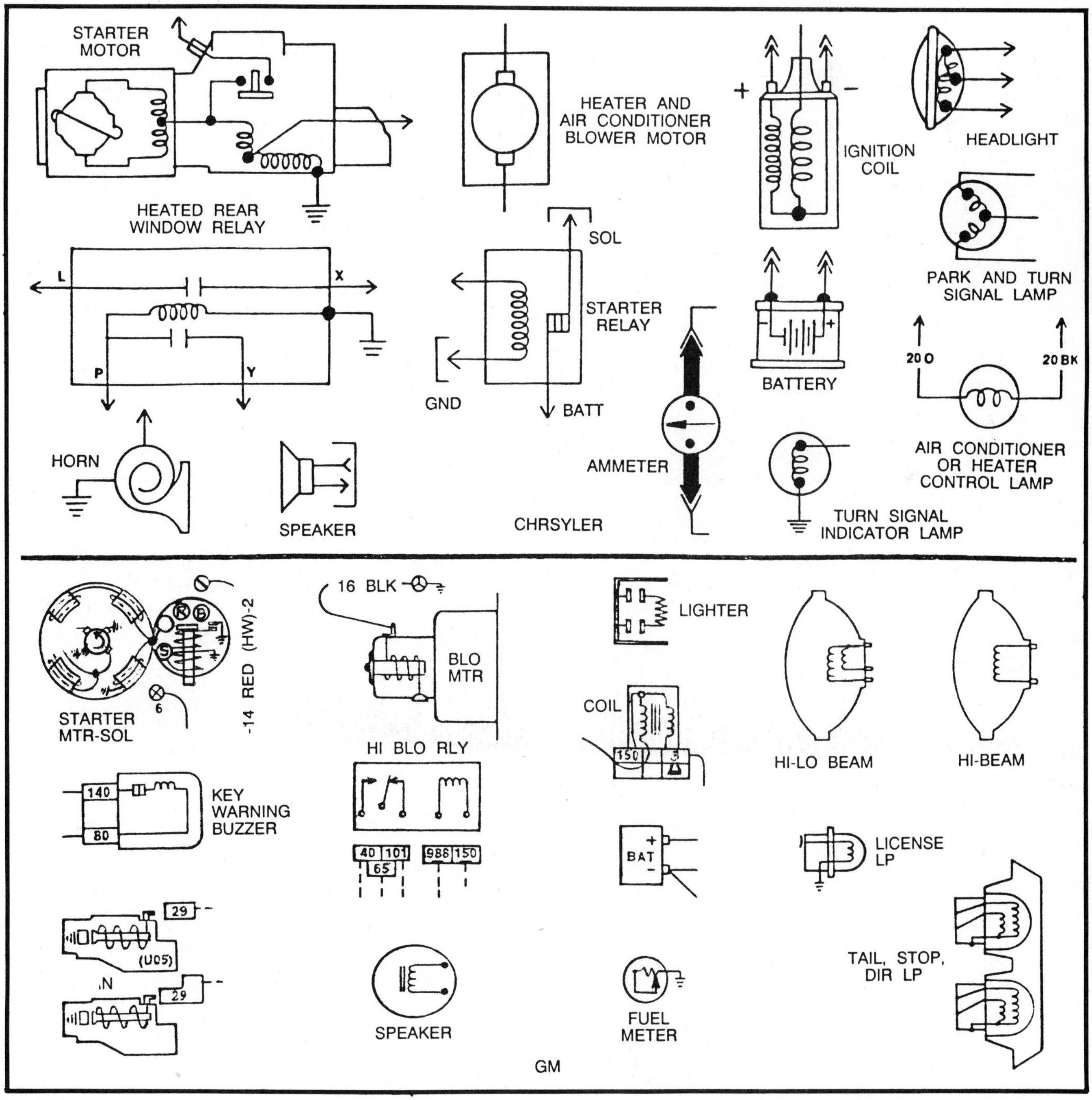

STARTER MOTOR

HEATED REAR WINDOW RELAY

HEATER AND AIR CONDITIONER BLOWER MOTOR

IGNITION COIL

HEADLIGHT

L

X

P

Y

SOL

STARTER RELAY

GND

BATT

BATTERY

AMMETER

PARK AND TURN SIGNAL LAMP

20 O

20 BK

AIR CONDITIONER OR HEATER CONTROL LAMP

HORN

SPEAKER

CHRSYLER

TURN SIGNAL INDICATOR LAMP

STARTER MTR-SOL

-14 RED (HW)-2

6

16 BLK

BLO MTR

LIGHTER

COIL

150

5

HI-LO BEAM

HI-BEAM

HI BLO RLY

40 | 101

65

988 | 150

140

80

KEY WARNING BUZZER

29

(U05)

.N

29

SPEAKER

BAT

+

−

FUEL METER

LICENSE LP

TAIL, STOP, DIR LP

GM

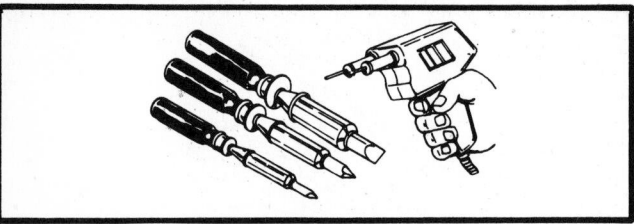

Various types of soldering guns

Molded-on connectors require complete replacement of the connection. This means splicing a new connector assembly into the harness. All splices in on-board computer systems should be soldered to insure proper contact. Use care when probing the connections or replacing terminals in them as it is possible to short between opposite terminals. If this happens to the wrong terminal pair, it is possible to damage certain components. Always use jumper wires between connectors for circuit checking and never probe through weatherproof seals.

Open circuits are often difficult to locate by sight because corrosion or terminal misalignment are hidden by the connectors. Merely wiggling a connector on a sensor or in the wiring harness may correct the open circuit condition. This should always be considered when an open circuit or a failed sensor is indicated. Intermittent problems may also be caused by oxidized or loose connections. When using a circuit tester for diagnosis, always probe connections from the wire side. Be careful not to damage sealed connectors with test probes.

All wiring harnesses should be replaced with identical parts, using the same gauge wire and connectors. When signal wires are spliced into a harness, use wire with high temperature insulation only. With the low voltage and current levels found in the system, it is important that the best possible connection at all wire splices be made by soldering the splices together. It is seldom necessary to replace a complete harness. If replacement is necessary, pay close attention to insure proper harness rout-

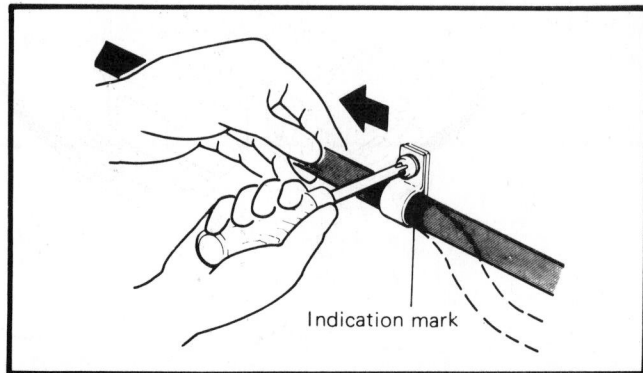

Indication mark

Secure the wiring harness at the indication marks, if used, to prevent vibrations from causing wear and a possible short

WIRE HARNESS REPAIR PROCEDURES

Condition	Location	Correction
Non-continuity	Using the electric wiring diagram and the wiring harness diagram as a guideline, check the continuity of the circuit in question by using a tester, and check for breaks, loose connector couplings, or loose terminal crimp contacts.	**Breaks**—Reconnect the point of the break by using solder. If the wire is too short and the connection is impossible, extend it by using a wire of the same or larger size. *Solder* *Be careful concerning the size of wire used for the extension* **Loose couplings**—Hold the connector securely, and insert it until there is a definite joining of the coupling. If the connector is equipped with a locking mechanism, insert the connector until it is locked securely. **Loose terminal crimp contacts**—Remove approximately 2 in. (5mm) of the insulation covering from the end of the wire, crimp the terminal contact by using a pair of pliers, and then, in addition, complete the repair by soldering. *Crimp by using pliers* *Solder*
Short-circuit	Using the electric wiring diagram and the wiring harness diagram as a guideline, check the entire circuit for pinched wires.	Remove the pinched portion, and then repair any breaks in the insulation covering with tape. Repair breaks of the wire by soldering.
Loose terminal	Pull the wiring lightly from the connector. A special terminal removal tool may be necessary for complete removal.	Raise the terminal catch pin, and then insert it until a definite clicking sound is heard. *Catch pin*

Note: There is the chance of short circuits being caused by insulation damage at soldered points. To avoid this possibility, wrap all splices with electrical tape and use a layer of silicone to seal the connection against moisture. Incorrect repairs can cause malfunctions by creating excessive resistance in a circuit.

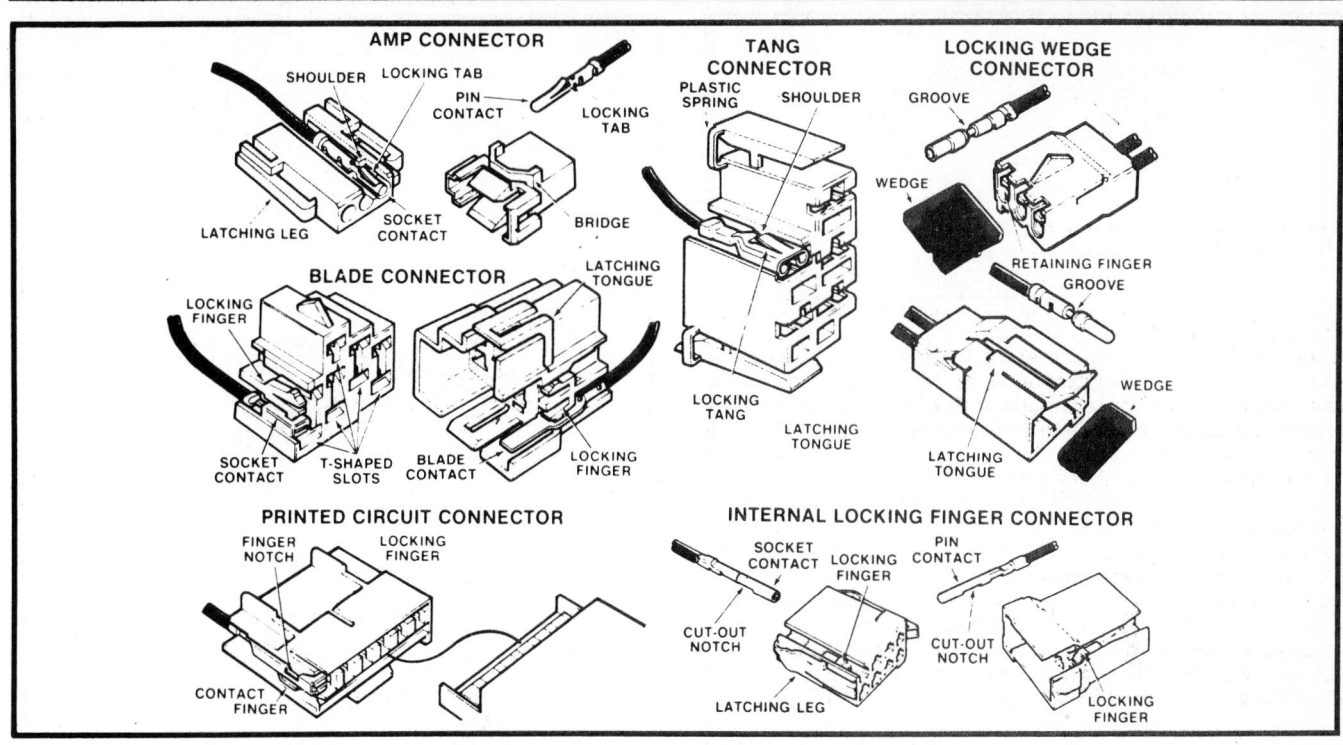

ing. Secure the harness with suitable plastic wire clamps to prevent vibrations from causing the harness to wear in spots or contact any hot components.

NOTE: Weatherproof connectors cannot be replaced with standard connectors. Instructions are provided with replacement connector and terminal packages.

Some wire harnesses have mounting indicators (usually pieces of colored tape) to mark where the harness is to be secured.

In making wiring repairs, it's important that you always replace damaged wires with wires that are the same gauge as the wire being replaced. The heavier the wire, the smaller the

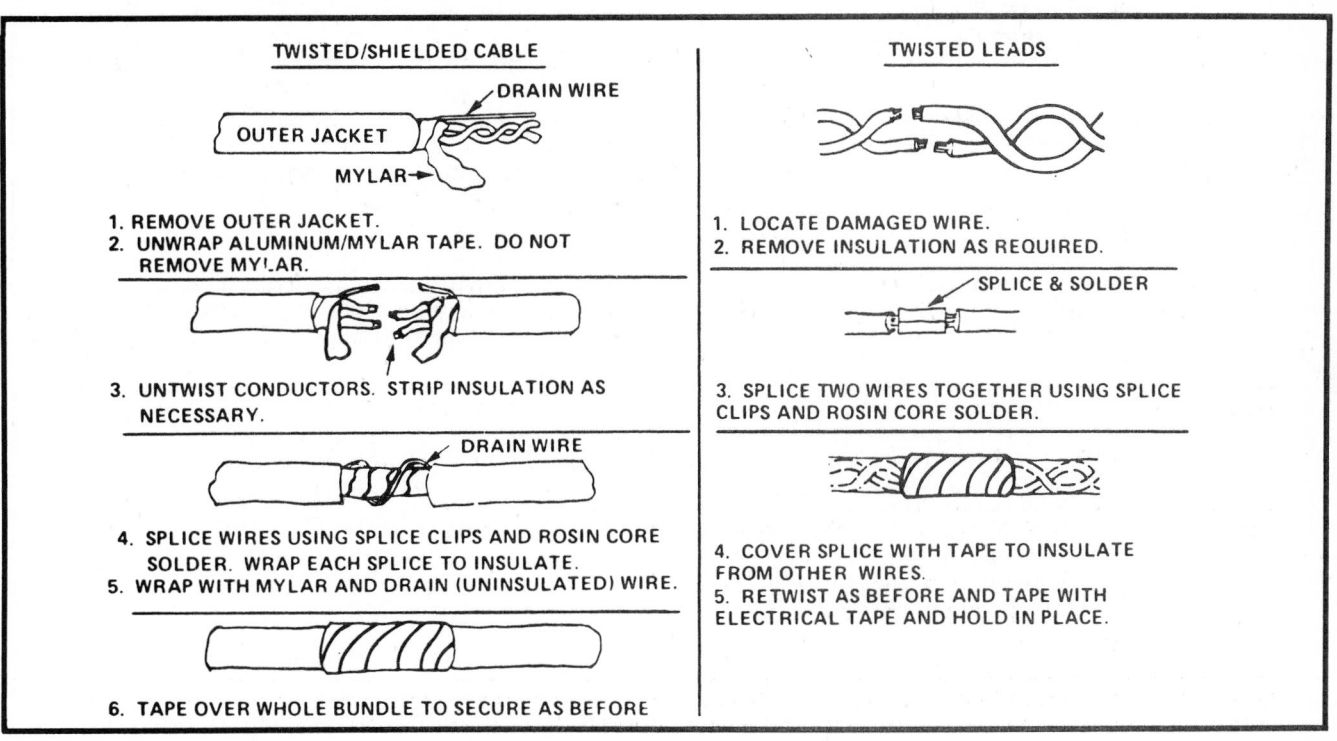

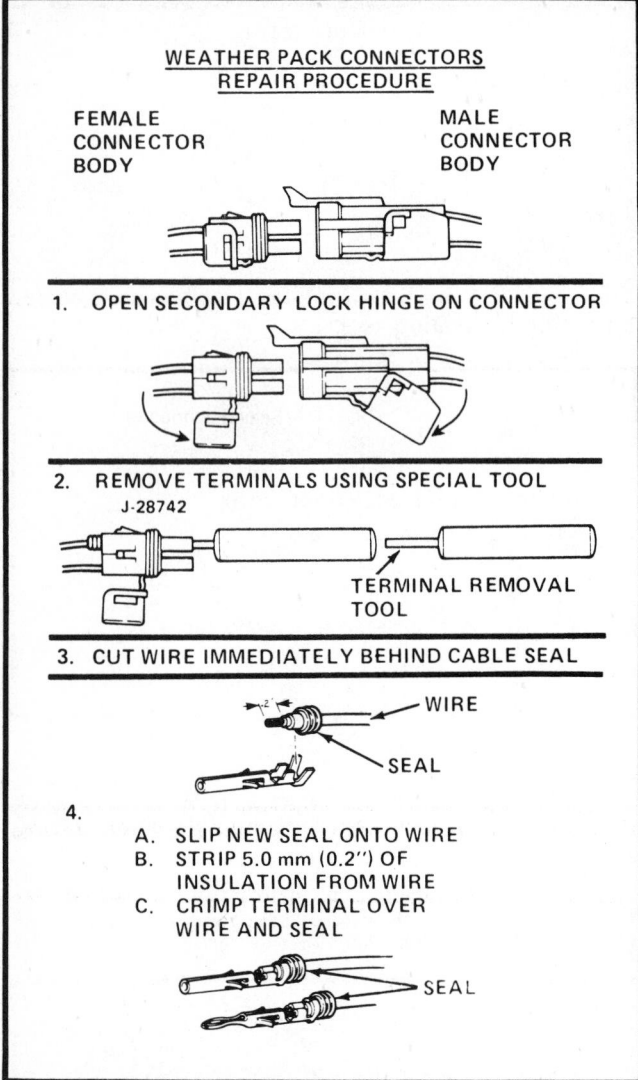

WEATHER PACK CONNECTORS REPAIR PROCEDURE

FEMALE CONNECTOR BODY

MALE CONNECTOR BODY

1. OPEN SECONDARY LOCK HINGE ON CONNECTOR

2. REMOVE TERMINALS USING SPECIAL TOOL
   J-28742
   TERMINAL REMOVAL TOOL

3. CUT WIRE IMMEDIATELY BEHIND CABLE SEAL
   WIRE
   SEAL

4.
   A. SLIP NEW SEAL ONTO WIRE
   B. STRIP 5.0 mm (0.2") OF INSULATION FROM WIRE
   C. CRIMP TERMINAL OVER WIRE AND SEAL
   SEAL

Repairing GM Weatherpak connectors. Note special terminal removal tools

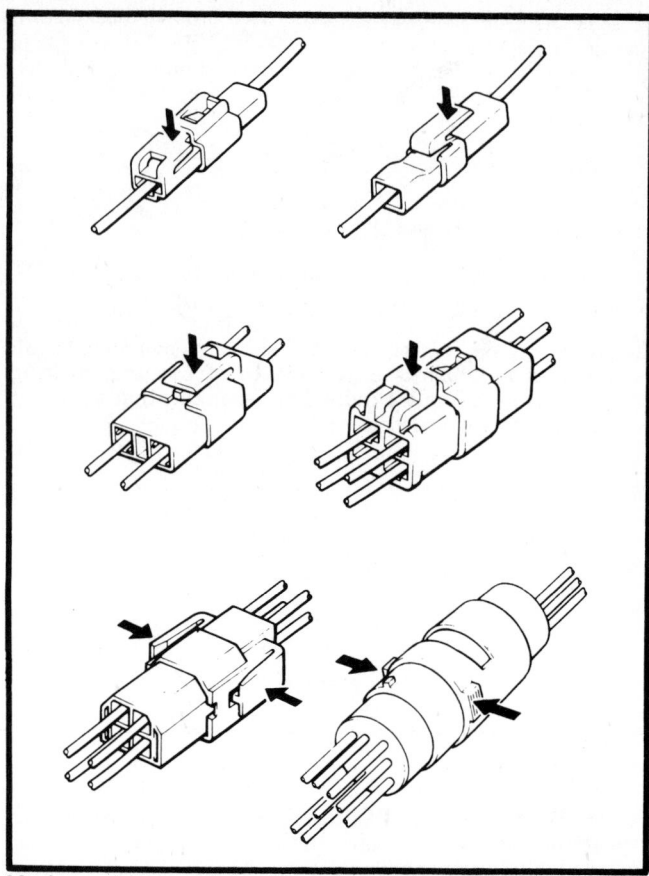

Various types of locking harness connectors. Depress the locks at the arrows to separate the connectors

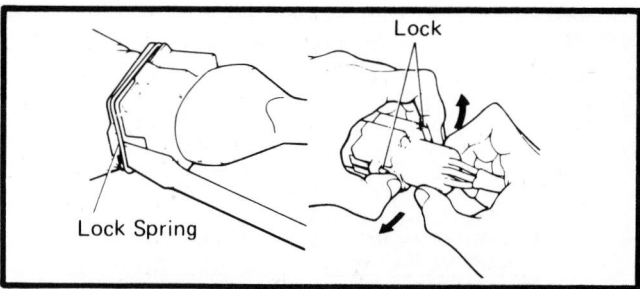

Lock

Lock Spring

Some electrical connectors use a lock spring instead of the molded locking tabs

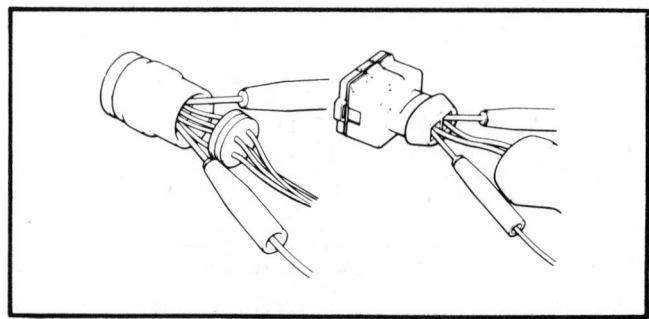

Correct method of testing weatherproof connectors. Do not pierce connector seals with test probes

gauge number. Wires are color-coded to aid in identification and whenever possible the same color coded wire should be used for replacement. A wire stripping and crimping tool is necessary to install solderless terminal connectors. Test all crimps by pulling on the wires; it should not be possible to pull the wires out of a good crimp.

Wires which are open, exposed or otherwise damaged are repaired by simple splicing. Where possible, if the wiring harness is accessible and the damaged place in the wire can be located, it is best to open the harness and check for all possible damage. In an inaccessible harness, the wire must be bypassed with a new insert, usually taped to the outside of the old harness.

When replacing fusible links, be sure to use fusible link wire, NOT ordinary automotive wire. Make sure the fusible segment is of the same gauge and construction as the one being replaced and double the stripped end when crimping the terminal connector for a good contact. The melted (open) fusible link segment of the wiring harness should be cut off as close to the harness as possible, then a new segment spliced in as described. In the case of a damaged fusible link that feeds two harness wires, the harness connections should be replaced with two fusible link wires so that each circuit will have its own separate protection.

Most of the problems caused in the wiring harness are due to bad ground connections. Always check all vehicle ground connections for corrosion or looseness before performing any power feed checks to eliminate the chance of a bad ground affecting the circuit.

Repairing Hard Shell Connectors

Unlike molded connectors, the terminal contacts in hard shell connectors can be replaced. Weatherproof hard-shell connectors with the leads molded into the shell have non-replaceable terminal ends. Replacement usually involves the use of a special terminal removal tool that depress the locking tangs (barbs) on the connector terminal and allow the connector to be removed from the rear of the shell. The connector shell should be replaced if it shows any evidence of burning, melting, cracks, or breaks. Replace individual terminals that are burnt, corroded, distorted or loose.

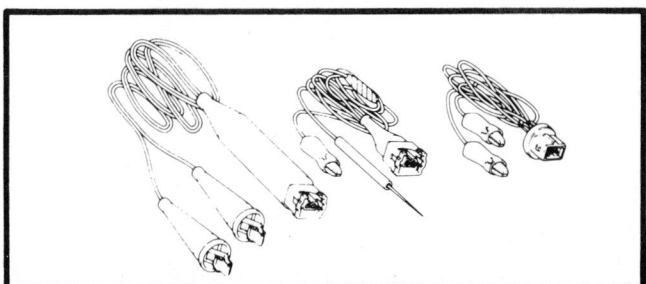

Special purpose test connections for use on some systems made up from factory connectors and jumper wires

NOTE: The insulation crimp must be tight to prevent the insulation from sliding back on the wire when the wire is pulled. The insulation must be visibly compressed under the crimp tabs, and the ends of the crimp should be turned in for a firm grip on the insulation.

The wire crimp must be made with all wire strands inside the crimp. The terminal must be fully compressed on the wire strands with the ends of the crimp tabs turned in to make a firm grip on the wire. Check all connections with an ohmmeter to insure a good contact. There should be no measurable resistance between the wire and the terminal when connected.

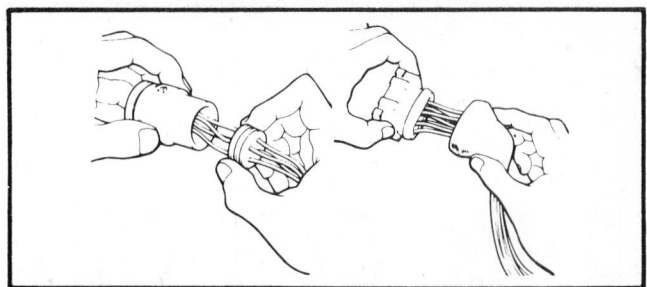

Slide back the weatherproof seals or boots on sealed terminals for testing

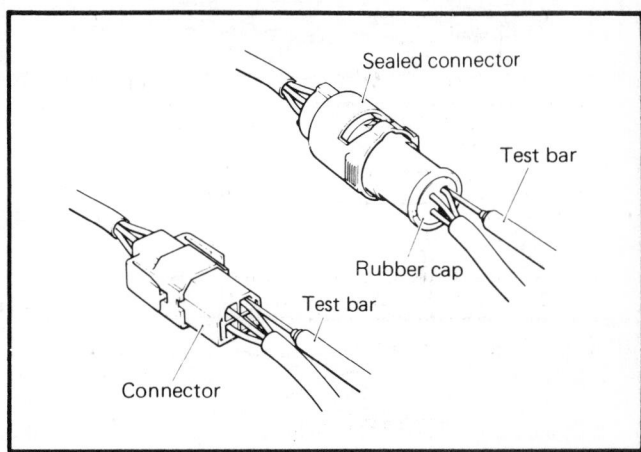

Probe all connectors from the wire side when testing

Mechanical Test Equipment
VACUUM GAUGE

Most gauges are graduated in inches of mercury (in. Hg), although a device called a manometer reads vacuum in inches of water (in. H_2O). The normal vacuum reading usually varies between 18 and 22 in. Hg at sea level. To test engine vacuum, the vacuum gauge must be connected to a source of manifold vacuum. Many engines have a plug in the intake manifold which can be removed and replaced with an adapter fitting. Connect the vacuum gauge to the fitting with a suitable rubber hose or, if no manifold plug is available, connect the vacuum gauge to any device using manifold vacuum, such as EGR valves, etc. The vacuum gauge can be used to determine if enough vacuum is reaching a component to allow its actuation.

HAND VACUUM PUMP

Small, hand-held vacuum pumps come in a variety of designs.

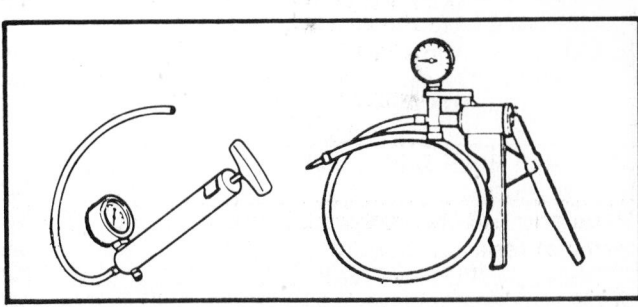

Typical hand vacuum pumps

Most have a built-in vacuum gauge and allow the component to be tested without removing it from the vehicle. Operate the pump lever or plunger to apply the correct amount of vacuum required for the test specified in the diagnosis routines. The level of vacuum in inches of Mercury (in. Hg) is indicated on the pump gauge. For some testing, an additional vacuum gauge may be necessary.

Intake manifold vacuum is used to operate various systems and devices on late model cars. To correctly diagnose and solve problems in vacuum control systems, a vacuum source is necessary for testing. In some cases, vacuum can be taken from the intake manifold when the engine is running, but vacuum is normally provided by a hand vacuum pump. These hand vacuum pumps have a built-in vacuum gauge that allow testing while the device is still attached to the car. For some tests, an additional vacuum gauge may be necessary.

INDEX

SELF-DIAGNOSTIC SYSTEMS

American Motors Corporation Computerized Emission Control (CEC) System

Both the four and the six cylinder CEC Fuel Feedback systems incorporate a diagnostic connector, located in the engine compartment near the distributor, to provide a means for systematic evaluation of each component that could cause an operational malfunction.

Electronic Fuel Feedback testers, ET–501–82 and ET–501–84 or equivalent, are available to aid in the system diagnosis. When a tester is not available, other test equipment can be substituted. Other test equipment required to perform the tests include:

1. Tachometer
2. Hand Vacuum Pump
3. Digital Volt-Ohmmeter (DVOM)
4. Dwell meter
5. Jumper wires

When performing the diagnostic tests, the following safety precautions must be followed:

1. Shape a sheet of clear acrylic plastic at least 0.250 in. thick and 15 in. by 15 in. square. Drill a ¼ in. hole in the center of the plastic and secure it to the top of the air cleaner with the wing nut, after the air cleaner assembly has been removed (six cylinder engine).
2. Wear eye protection whenever performing tests.
3. When operating the engine, keep hands and arms clear of the fan, drive pulleys and belts. Do not wear loose clothing.
4. Do not stand in direct line with the fan blades.

Preliminary Tests

The CEC system should be considered as a possible source of trouble for engine performance, fuel economy and exhaust emission complaints only after normal tests that would apply to an engine without the system have been performed.

Before performing any diagnostic tests, other engine associated components and systems that can effect the air/fuel mixture, combustion efficiency or exhaust gas composition should be tested for faults. These could include the following:

1. Basic carburetor adjustments.
2. Mechanical engine operation (i.e. spark plugs, valves, rings and etc.).
3. Ignition system.
4. Gasket sealing on induction system.
5. Loose vacuum hoses or fittings.

INITIALIZATION

When the ignition system is turned off, the MCU is also turned off. It has no long term memory circuit for prior operation or storing of fault codes. As a result, it has an initialization function that is activated when the ignition switch is turned On.

The MCU initialization function for the six cylinder engine moves the metering pins to a predetermined starting position by first driving them all the way to the rich end stop and then driving them in the lean direction by a predetermined number of steps. No matter where they were before initialization, they will be at the correct position at the end of every initialization period. Because each open loop operation metering pin position is dependent on the initialization function, this function is the first test in the diagnostic procedure.

During open loop operation, the air supplied by the mixture control solenoid is pre-programmed.

CAUTION

The use of a voltmeter with less than 10 megohms per volt input impedence can destroy the oxygen sensor. A digital volt-ohmmeter must be used.

The dwell meter, set for the six-cylinder engine scale and connected to a pigtail wire test connector leading from the mixture control (MC) solenoid, is used to determine the air/fuel

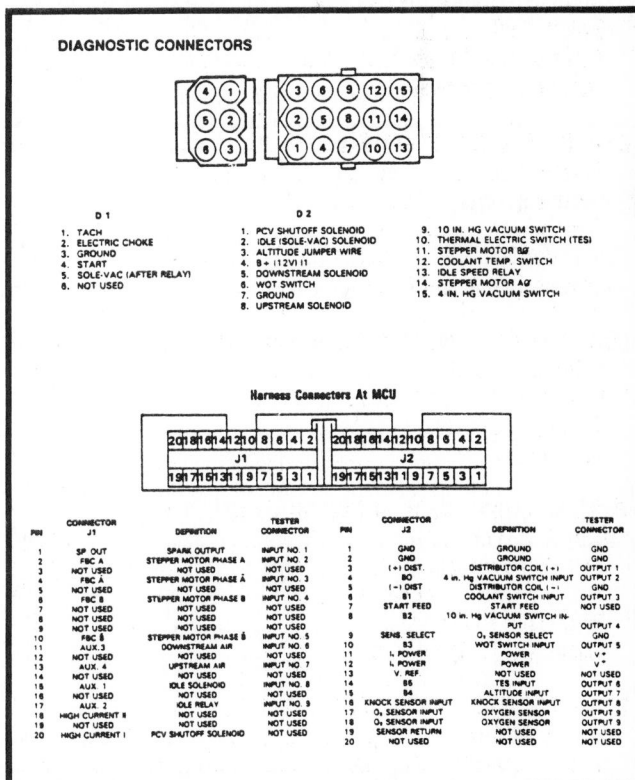

4 cylinder engine diagnostic connectors

6 cylinder engine diagnostic connectors

mixture dwell. When the dwell meter is connected, do not allow the connector terminal to contact any engine component that is connected to engine ground. This includes hoses because they may be electrically conductive. With a normally operating engine, the dwell at both idle speed and partial throttle will be between 10 degrees and 50 degrees and will be varying. Varying means the pointer continually moves back and forth across the scale. The amount it varies is not important, only the fact that it does vary.

The variance of the pointer indicates closed loop operation, indicating the mixture is being varied according to the input voltage to the MCU from the oxygen sensor. With wide open throttle (WOT) and/or cold engine operation, the air/fuel mixture ratio will be predetermined and the pointer will only vary slightly. This is open loop operation, indicating the oxygen sensor output has no effect on the air/fuel mixture.

If there is a question whether or not the system is in closed loop operation, richening or leaning the air/fuel mixture will cause the dwell to vary more if the system is in closed loop operation.

Chrysler Single Point Electronic Fuel Injection System

The Logic Module tests many of its own input and output circuits, If a fault is found in a major system, this information is stored in the Logic Module. Information on this fault can be displayed by a technician by means of the instrument panel power loss lamp or by connecting a diagnostic read-out tester and reading a numbered display code, which directly relates to a general fault.

The power loss lamp comes on each time the ignition key is turned on and stays on for a three seconds as a bulb test. If the logic module receives an incorrect signal or no signal from either the coolant temperature sensor, manifold absolute pressure sensor, or the throttle position sensor, the power loss lamp on the instrument panel is illuminated. This is a warning that the logic module has gone into LIMP-IN mode in an attempt to keep the system operational and a signal for immediate service.

The power loss lamp is also used to display fault codes. To enter the system, cycle the ignition switch ON, OFF, ON, OFF, ON within five seconds and any fault codes stored in the logic module will be displayed.

LIMP-IN MODE

The LIMP-IN mode is the attempt by the logic module to compensate for the failure of certain components by substituting information from other sources. If the logic module senses incorrect data or no data at all from the MAP sensor, throttle position sensor or coolant temperature sensor, the system is placed into LIMP-IN Mode and the power loss lamp on the instrument panel is activated.

SELF DIAGNOSTIC SYSTEM

The logic module has been programmed to monitor several different circuits of the fuel injection system. This monitoring is called On-Board Diagnosis. If a problem is sensed with a monitored circuit, often enough to indicate an actual problem, its fault code is stored in the logic module for eventual display to the service technician. If the problem is repaired or ceases to exist, the logic module cancels the fault code after 30 ignition key ON/OFF cycles for the 1984 models and 20 to 40 ignition key ON/OFF cycles for 1985 and later models

Trouble Codes

When a trouble code appears, either by flashes of the power loss lamp or by watching the diagnostic readout Tool C-4805 or equivalent, it indicates that the logic module has recognized an abnormal signal in the system. Trouble codes indicate the results of a failure but do not always identify the failed component.

CODE 88 – Start of test

CODE 11 – Engine not cranked since battery was disconnected.

CODE 12 – Memory standby power lost.

CODE 13 – MAP Sensor pneumatic circuit.*

CODE 14 – MAP sensor electrical system.*

CODE 15 – Vehicle Speed Sensor circuit.

CODE 16 – Lose of battery voltage sense.*

CODE 17 – Engine is running too cool (1986–88).

CODE 21 – Oxygen sensor (O_2) sensor circuit.

CODE 22 – Coolant temperature sensor circuit.*

CODE 23 – Throttle body temperature sensor circuit(1985 and later).

CODE 24 – Throttle position sensor circuit.*

CODE 25 – Automatic idle speed (AIS) control circuit.

CODE 26 – Peak injector current has not been reached.

CODE 27 – Fuel interface circuit (internal fuel circuit problem of logic module).

CODE 31 – Canister purge solenoid circuit.

CODE 32 – Power loss lamp circuit (1984–85 models only).

CODE 33 – Air conditioning wide open throttle cut out relay circuit.

CODE 34 – means a problem in the EGR solenoid circuit (1984 models), and indicates problem in spare driver circuit (1985–88 models).

CODE 35 – Fan control relay circuit.

CODE 36 – Problem in spare driver circuit (1985 models)

CODE 37 – Shift indicator lamp circuit (manual transmissions only).

CODE 41 – Charging system excess or no field circuit.

CODE 42 – Automatic shut down relay (ASD) circuit.

CODE 43 – Spark interface (internal) circuits.

CODE 44 – Logic module failure on 1984 models. Indicate battery temperature is out of range on 1985–88 models.

CODE 46 – Battery voltage too high.*

CODE 47 – Battery voltage too low.

CODE 51 – Closed loop fuel system problem. 1984 models have O_2 signal either too lean or too rich. 1985–88 models have the O_2 signal stuck at the lean position

CODE 52 – Logic module problem or failure in 1984 models. 1985–88 models have O_2 signal stuck at the rich position.

CODE 53 – Logic module problem or failure.

CODE 54 – Logic module problem or failure in 1984 models.

CODE 55 – means "end of message".

CODE 88 – means start of message. This code only appears on the diagnostic readout Tool C–4805 or equivalent, and means start of message.

NOTE: * indicates the power loss/limited lamp is on.

Obtaining Trouble Codes

1. Connect diagnostic readout box tool C–4805 or equivalent to the diagnostic connector located in the engine compartment near the passenger side strut tower.

2. Start the engine if possible, cycle the transmission selector and the A/C switch if applicable. Shut off the engine.

3. Turn the ignition switch ON, OFF, ON, OFF, ON. Within 5 seconds record all the diagnostic codes shown on the diagnostic readout box tool, observe the power loss lamp on the instrument panel the lamp should light for 2 seconds on 1984–85 models and 3 seconds on 1986–88 models, then go out (bulb check).

Switch Test

After all codes have been shown and has indicated Code 55 end of message, actuate the following component switches. The digital display must change its numbers when the following switches are activated and released:

    a. Brake pedal.
    b. Gear shift selector park, reverse, park.
    c. A/C switch (if applicable).
    d. Electric backlite switch (if applicable).

Actuator Test Mode (ATM)
1984 MODELS

1. Remove coil wire from cap and place ¼ in. from a ground.

—————————— CAUTION ——————————

Coil wire must be ¼ in. or less from ground or power module damage may result.

2. Remove air cleaner hose from throttle body.
3. Press the ATM button on the diagnostic readout box tool and observe the following:
    a. 3 sparks from the coil wire to ground.
    b. 2 AIS motor movements (1 open, 1 close), listen carefully for AIS operation.
    c. 1 fuel pulse from the injector into the throttle body.
4. The ATM capability is cancelled 5 minutes after the ignition switch is turned on. To reinstate this capability cycle the ignition ON and OFF three times ending in the ON position.
5. When the ATM button is pressed, fault code 42 is generated because the ASD relay is bypassed. Do not use this code for diagnostics after ATM operation.
6. The ATM test will check 3 categories of operation:
• When coil fires three times:
    a. Coil operational.
    b. Logic module portion operational.
    c. Power module portion operational.
    d. Interface between power module and logic module is working.
• AIS is operational
• Injector fuel pulse into Throttle Body:
    a. Fuel injector operational.
    b. Fuel pump operational.
    c. Fuel lines intact
7. The electronic fuel injection system must be evaluated using all the information found in the systems test:
• Start/no start
• Trouble codes
• Loss of power lamp on or off (limp in)
• ATM results:
    a. Spark yes/no.
    b. Fuel yes/no.
    c. AIS movement yes/no.
    Once this information is found, it will be easier to determine the circuit to consider for further testing.

Obtaining Circuit Actuation Test Mode (ATM Test)
1985–88 MODELS

1. Put the system into the Diagnostic Test Mode and wait for code 55 to appear on the display screen.
2. Press ATM button on the tool to activate the display. If a specific ATM test is desired, hold the ATM button down until the desired test code appears.
3. The computer will continue to turn the selected circuit on and off for as long as five minutes or until the ATM button is pressed again or the ignition switch is turned to the OFF position.
4. If the ATM button is not pressed again, the computer will continue to cycle the selected circuit for five minutes and then shut the system off. Turning the ignition to the OFF position will also turn the test mode off.

ACTUATOR TEST DISPLAY CODES

1. 01–Spark activation – once every two seconds.

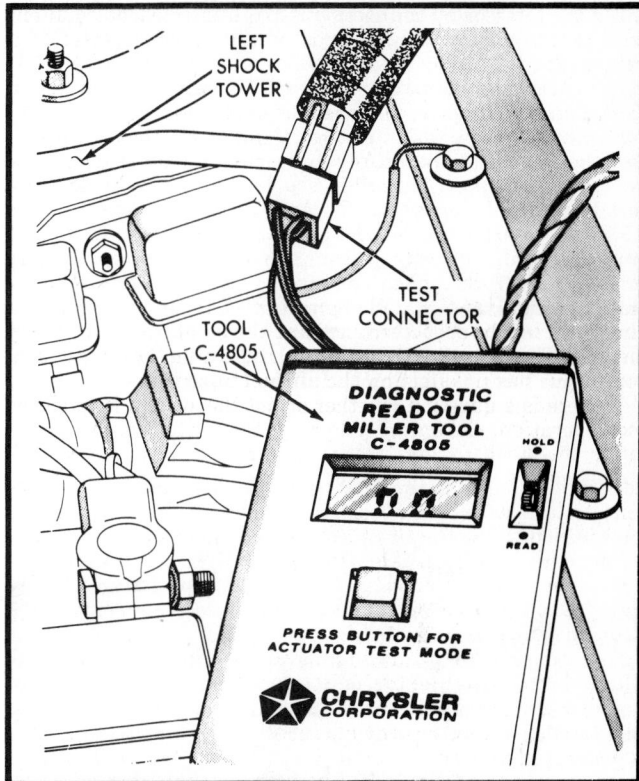

Diagnostic tester used on Chrysler vehicles

2. 02–Injector activation – once every two seconds.
3. 03–AIS activation – one step open, one step closed every four seconds.
4. 04–Radiator fan relay – once every two seconds.
5. 05–A/C WOT cutout relay – once every two seconds.
6. 06–ASD relay activation – once every two seconds.
7. 07–Purge solenoid activation – one toggle every two seconds.

Obtaining Sensor Read Test Mode Display Codes

With the Diagnostic Readout Box, Tool number C–4805 or its equivalent, sensor voltage, degrees F, vacuum, rpm and mileage reading can be determined with the vehicle's engine both off and on. Since each available diagnostic readout box may differ in its interpretation and display of the sensor results, refer to the instructional procedure that accompanies each tester unit.

Leaving Diagnostic Mode

By turning the ignition switch to the OFF position, the test mode system is turned off and exited. With a Diagnostic Readout Box attached to the system and the ATM control button not pressed, the computer will continue to cycle the selected circuits for five minutes and then automatically shut the system down.

Chrysler Multi-Point Electronic Fuel Injection System

The logic module tests many of its own inputs and output circuits. If a fault is found in a major circuit, this information is stored in the logic module. Information of this fault can be displayed to a technician by means of the instrument panel POW-

ER LOSS lamp or by connecting a diagnostic readout and observing a numbered display code which directly relates to a general fault.

The power loss lamp comes on each time the ignition key is turned on and stays on for three seconds as a bulb test. If the logic module receives an incorrect signal or no signal from either the coolant temperature sensor, charge temperature sensor (1985 and later), manifold absolute pressure sensor, the throttle position sensor, or the battery voltage sensor input (1985 and later), the power loss lamp on the instrument panel is illuminated. This is a warning that the logic module has gone into LIMP-IN mode in an attempt to keep the system operational and is a signal for immediate service.

The power loss lamp is also used to display fault codes. To enter the system, cycle the ignition switch ON, OFF, ON, OFF, ON within five seconds and any fault codes stored in the logic module will be displayed.

Limp–In Mode

The Limp-In mode is the attempt by the logic module to compensate for the failure of certain components by substituting information from other sources. If the logic module senses incorrect data or no data at all from the MAP sensor, throttle position sensor or coolant temperature sensor, the system is placed into Limp-In Mode and the power loss lamp on the instrument panel is activated.

The logic module has been programmed to monitor several different circuits of the fuel injection system. This monitoring is called On-Board Diagnosis. If a problem is sensed with a monitored circuit, often enough to indicate an actual problem, its fault code is stored in the logic module for eventual display to the service technician. If the problem is repaired or ceases to exist, the logic module cancels the fault code after 30 ignition key ON/OFF cycles.

When a fault code appears (either by flashes of the light emitting diode or by watching the diagnostic readout, Tool C–4805 or equivalent, it indicates that the logic module has recognized an abnormal signal in the system. Fault codes indicate the results of a failure but do not always identify the failed component.

CODE 88 – Start of test.

CODE 11 – 1984 models – indicates logic module has not recognized distributor signal since battery was reconnected.

1985–88 models – engine not cranked since battery was disconnected.

CODE 12 – Memory standby power lost.
CODE 13 – MAP Sensor pneumatic circuit.*
CODE 14 – MAP sensor electrical system.*
CODE 15 – Vehicle Speed Sensor circuit.
CODE 16 – Lose of battery voltage sense (1985 and later).*
CODE 17 – Engine is running too cool (1986 and later).
CODE 21 – Oxygen sensor (O_2) sensor circuit.
CODE 22 – Coolant temperature sensor circuit.*
CODE 23 – Charge temperature sensor circuit (1985 and later).
CODE 24 – Throttle position sensor circuit.*
CODE 25 – Automatic idle speed (AIS) control circuit.
CODE 26 – Number one injector circuit (1985 and later).
CODE 27 – Number two injector circuit (1985 and later).
CODE 31 – Canister purge solenoid circuit (1984–86) EGR/purge solenoid circuit (1987 and later).
CODE 32 – Power loss lamp circuit (1984–85 models only).
CODE 33 – A/C wide cut out relay circuit.
CODE 34 – Problem in the EGR solenoid circuit (1984–86 models). Speed control malfunction (1987 models) .
CODE 35 – Fan control relay circuit.
CODE 36 – Wastegate solenoid circuit (1985 and later)*
CODE 37 – Barometric read solenoid circuit (1985 and later).
CODE 41 – Charging system excess or no field circuit.
CODE 42 – Automatic shutdown relay driver (ASD) circuit.

CODE 43 – Spark interface (internal) circuits.
CODE 44 – Logic module failure on 1984 models. Indicate battery temperature is out of range on 1985 and later models.
CODE 45 – Overboost shut-off circuit.*
CODE 46 – Battery voltage too high.*
CODE 47 – Battery voltage too low.
CODE 51 – Closed loop fuel system problem. 1984 models have O_2 signal either too lean or too rich. 1985 and later models have the O_2 signal stuck at the lean position
CODE 52 – Logic module problem or failure in 1984 models. 1985 and later models have O_2 signal stuck at the rich position.
CODE 53 – Logic module problem or failure.
CODE 54 – Distributor sync pick-up circuit.
CODE 55 – means "end of message".

NOTE: * indicates the power loss/limited lamp is on.

SYSTEMS TEST

Obtaining Fault Codes

1. Connect diagnostic readout box tool C–4805 or equivalent, to the diagnostic connector located in the engine compartment near the passenger side strut tower.
2. Start the engine if possible, cycle the transmission selector and the A/C switch, if applicable. Shut off the engine.
3. Turn the ignition switch on, off, on, off, on within 5 seconds. Record all the diagnostic codes shown on the diagnostic readout box tool, observe the power loss lamp on the instrument panel the lamp should light for 2 seconds on 1984–85 models and 3 seconds on 1986–88 models, then go out (bulb check).

Switch Test

After all codes have been shown and has indicated Code 55 (end of message), actuate the following component switches. The digital display must change its numbers when the switch is activated and released:

1. Brake pedal.
2. Gear shift selector Park, Reverse, Park.
3. A/C switch (if applicable).
4. Electric Backlite switch (if applicable on 1984 models)

NOTE: On 1986–88 models, switch test No. 3 is valid only if the A/C dampened switch is closed and blower switch is on.

Obtaining Circuit Actuation Test Mode (ATM Test)
1985–88 MODELS

1. Put the system into the Diagnostic Test Mode and wait for code 55 to appear on the display screen.
2. Press ATM button on the tool to activate the display. If a specific ATM test is desired, hold the ATM button down until the desired test code appears.
3. The computer will continue to turn the selected circuit on and off for as long as five minutes or until the ATM button is pressed again or the ignition switch is turned to the OFF position.
4. If the ATM button is not pressed again, the computer will continue to cycle the selected circuit for five minutes and then shut the system off. Turning the ignition to the OFF position will also turn the test mode off.

Actuator Test Display Codes

1. CODE 01–Spark activation – once every two seconds.
2. CODE 02–Injector activation – once every two seconds.
3. CODE 03–AIS activation – one pulse open, one pulse closed every four seconds.
4. CODE 04–Radiator fan relay – one pulse every two seconds.

5. CODE 05–A/C WOT cutout relay – one pulse every two seconds.

6. CODE 06–ASD relay activation – one toggle every two seconds.

7. CODE 07–EGR/Purge solenoid activation – one toggle every two seconds.

8. CODE 08–Speed control switch ON, S/C vacuum and vent solenoid activation – every two seconds.

9. CODE 09–Wastegate solenoid activation – one toggle every two seconds.

10. CODE 10–Barometric read solenoid activation – one toggle every two seconds.

11. CODE 11–Alternator full field activation – one toggle every two seconds.

Obtaining Sensor Read Test Mode Display Codes

With the Diagnostic Readout Box, Tool number C–4805 or its equivalent, sensor voltage, degrees F, vacuum, rpm and mileage reading can be determined with the vehicle's engine both off and on.

Since each available diagnostic readout box may differ in its interpretation and display of the sensor results, refer to the instructional procedure that accompanies each tester unit.

Exiting Diagnostic Mode

By turning the ignition switch to the OFF position, the test mode system is turned off and exited.

With a Diagnostic Readout Box attached to the system and the ATM control button not pressed, the computer will continue to cycle the selected circuits for five minutes and then automatically shut the system down.

Ford Motor Company EEC–III System

The EEC–III system is equipped with a self-test feature to aid in diagnosis. The self-test is a set of instructions programmed in the computer memory of the calibration assembly. When the program is activated, the computer performs a system test. This verifies the proper connection and operation of the various sensors and actuators. The self-test program controls vehicle operation during the test sequence. Basically, the self-test program does the following.

1. Sends commands to the solenoids and checks for proper response.

2. Checks for reasonable readings from the sensors.

3. Produces numbered codes that inform the technician of a trouble area or of "all okay" operation.

To further test and service the EEC–III system, perform what is called a "Quick Test" first and if the vehicle passes these tests, the EEC–III system is functioning properly and the vehicle's problem exists somewhere other than in the EEC–III system. Should the "Quick Test" fail in one or more catagories, tests known as "Pin Tests" should be initiated to located the malfunction.

A Self Test is used in conjunction with the Quick Test, to perform proper diagnostics. The EEC–III system includes self test capabilities in the computer memory of the processor and when a Self Test is activated during a Quick Test, the ECA performs the EEC system test to verify that various sensors and actuators are connected and operating properly.

Before attempting any repairs or extensive diagnosis, visually examine the vehicle for obvious faults.

1. Remove air cleaner assembly. Check for dirt, foreign matter or other contamination in and around filter element.

2. Examine vacuum hose for proper routing and connection. Also check for broken, cracked or pinched hoses or fittings.

3. Examine each portion of the EEC–III wiring harness. Check for the following at each location.

   a. Proper connection to sensors and solenoids.

   b. Loose or disconnected connectors.

   c. Broken or disconnected wires.

   d. Partially seated connectors.

   e. Broken or frayed wires.

   f. Shorting between wires.

   g. Corrosion.

4. Inspect sensor for obvious physical damage.

5. Operate engine and inspect exhaust manifold and exhaust gas oxygen sensor for leaks.

6. Repair faults as necessary. Reinstall air cleaner. If the problem has not been corrected, proceed to self-test.

Self-Test Operation

The EEC diagnostic tester includes provisions for the self-test feature. In this case, the technician monitors the test panel for flashes of the thermactor solenoids operation. The series of light flashes represent a service code. The test can also be accomplished using a vacuum pump and gauges. In this case, the technician must actually monitor the solenoids for pulses or observe corresponding vacuum signals caused by the pulses. In all cases, the starting method for the self-test is the same.

The technician should activate the self-test only after proper engine preparation. The engine should be run until the radiator hose is hot and pressurized.

Displaying Service Codes With Test Meter

Service codes are displayed by a series of pulses on both the thermactor air lights (TAB and TAD) on the Test meter. The pulses form two-digit numbers. Each pulse is on for $1/2$ second then off for $1/2$ second for each count. A full second pause separates the digits, a 5 second pause separates service code numbers. A digital Volt/Ohmmeter can also be used and connected to the EEC–III tester.

NOTE: Complete connection and operational instructions accompany the tester and are located on the inside of the tester cover. Refer to the instructions before initiating test.

The begin the test, the test meter cables must be connected in the following manner:

1. With the ignition switch in the OFF position, disconnect the EEC–III harness from the ECA.

2. Connect the EFI adapter harness and tester harness as per the tester's instructions.

3. If the tester lamps are illuminated with the ignition in the OFF position, check for a short circuit between the vehicle battery and the ECA power circuit or an open circuit in the ECC–III ground circuits.

4. Turn the ignition switch to the ON position. Press and holds the "Test Light" button. All lights on the control panel of the tester should light up.

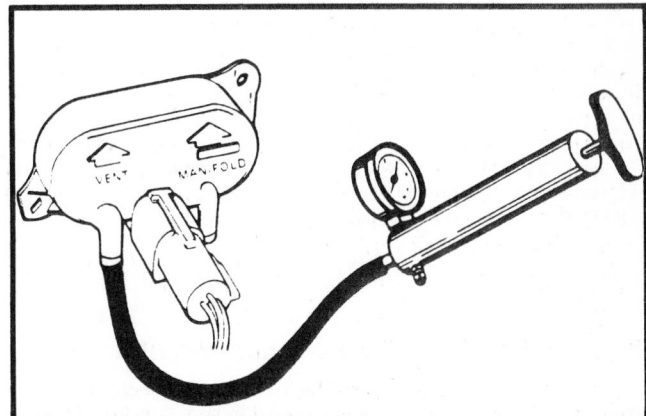

Triggering self-test on EEC III system

5. If the lights do not display, a problem exists within the tester.

Triggering Self–Test

1. Start the engine after observing all shop safety procedures.
2. Operate the engine at 1800 rpm for one or two minutes until the upper radiator hose is pressurized and hot or have the engine near normal operating temperature.
3. Set the tester switch to A-8 position.
4. Attach a vacuum pump to the B/MAP sensor vent port and apply vacuum (approximately 20 in. Hg.) until the DVOM reading is 2.85 volts and hold for for approximately 8 seconds.

NOTE: It maybe necessary to hold the vacuum for a longer time interval in order to trigger the system.

5. Release the vacuum on the vent port of the B/MAP sensor and observe the lights on the tester console.
6. The throttle kicker light (TKS) will blink the ON light, and then blink the OFF light. An interval of two seconds will elapse and the TKS ON light will blink.
7. The TKS light will stay on and the Throttle kicker actuator will extend for approximately 1½ minutes.

NOTE: The throttle kicker movement may be as small as ¹⁄₁₆ in.

8. When the TKS light goes from the ON light to the OFF light and the throttle kicker retracts, be prepared to read the service codes.

NOTE: The pulse indications can be observed on both the tester and the DVOM. The tester by lights and the DVOM by voltage pulse readings.

SERVICE CODES

The service codes are a series of pulses on both thermactor solenoids at the same time. Each pulse is on for one-half second and off for a one-half second. This sequence represents the number "one". The solenoids are off for a full second before starting the second digit of the code. In the case of the multiple service codes, the solenoids are off for five full seconds between two-digit codes.

As an example, service code 23 (throttle position sensor), would follow this pattern.
1. One-half second on; one-half second off.
2. One-half second on; indicates number two (2).
3. Off for a full second between numbers.
4. One-half second on; one-half second off.
5. One-half second on; one-half second off.
6. One-half second on; indicates number three (3).
7. Five full seconds off between codes.
8. Code indicated would be 23.

The vehicle remains in self-test for 15 seconds after completing the last code, with the tester's Canister Purge "ON" Light (CANP) illuminating for the 15 seconds. The system then returns to normal operation. When beginning diagnosis and repairs, consider the final code first. In the above case of 23, then 41, begin with diagnosis of code 41 (fuel control lean), and then continue with code 23 (throttle position sensor).

NOTE: On some engine calibrations, both the CANP lights (ON and OFF) could be illuminated during the test.

Displaying Service Codes Without Tester Unit

1. Tee a vacuum gauge into the hose that connects the air injection pump diverter valve and the Thermactor Air Diverter Solenoid valve.
2. Have the engine at normal operating temperature.

3. Attach the vacuum pump hose to the VENT port on the B/MAP sensor.
4. Apply 20 in. Hg of vacuum and hold for approximately 60 seconds.
5. The Throttle Kicker actuator (TKS) will extend and then retract when the vacuum is released.
6. The vacuum gauge needle will pulse twice on the EFI system to indicate the system is ready to check its self out.
7. If the needle doesn't move, either the diagnostic circuit inside the ECA is faulty, or the Thermactor pump is faulty.
8. The system will activate the Throttle Kicker Actuator again. As the system starts through its self examination, the vacuum gauge reading will rise and jump a few times and then the Throttle Kicker Actuator will pull in.
9. This operation means the diagnosis is completed and the system is ready to communicate the findings to the technician.
10. To translate the findings, count the pulses noted on the vacuum gauge.
11. As an example, two pulses, pause, three pulses represent code 23.
12. If there are more than malfunction, the system sends out trouble codes, one at a time, with a long pause between then.

Trouble Codes

1. CODE 11 – System is OK.
2. CODE 12 – No rpm signal to the ECA.
3. CODE 21 – ECT sensor wiring faulty.
4. CODE 22 – B/MAP faulty.
5. CODE 23 – TP sensor faulty.
6. CODE 31 – EVP sensor not moving to open position.
7. CODE 32 – EVP sensor not moving to closed position.
8. CODE 41 – Air/fuel mixture too lean.
9. CODE 42 – Air/fuel mixture too rich.
10. CODE 43 – Coolant temperature below 120° F.
11. CODE 44 – Thermactor system faulty.

Ford Microprocessor Control Unit (MCU) System

The MCU has the capability to diagnose a malfunction within its own system. However, it is not designed to diagnose malfunctions outside the MCU system.

Through the use of trouble code indications, the system will indicate to the technician where to look for MCU problems through the use of a self-test computer program, built into the MCU module. Standard test equipment, such as an analog voltmeter, can be used to check the system, or a special tester can be used to simplify the testing procedure on the MCU self-test connector.

When the analog voltmeter or the special tester is connected to the test connector and the system is triggered, the self-test simulates a variety of engine operating conditions and evaluates all the responses received from the various MCU components, so that any abnormal operating condition can be detected.

A routine inspection should be the first procedure the technician should use to begin the diagnosis of the MCU system. Broken or frayed wires, loose connections, obvious shorts, disconnected or damaged vacuum hoses are among the areas that should be inspected and corrected before any tests are done.

Self-Test Procedure

The MCU system incorporates a self-test connector, located near the MCU module in the engine compartment on one of the fender aprons, for isolating problems in the system.

A received response to the initiated self-test is reported, through the self-test connector to one of two testing devices, an analog voltmeter or a self-test automatic readout (STAR) test-

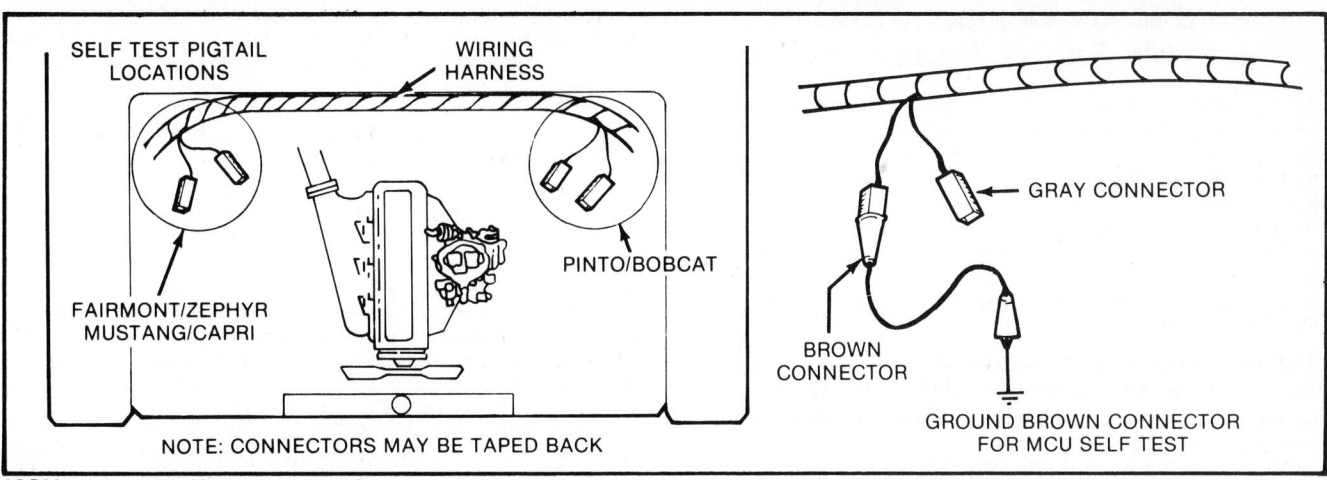

MCU system self-test connectors

er, which in turn indicate service codes as a pulsing series of electrical outputs, displayed on the meters of the testers.

The service codes are displayed by the series of electrical pulses which indicate a two digit number. This two digit service code indicates to the technician the nature of the MCU system's problem.

CONNECTION OF ANALOG VOLTMETER

1. With the ignition key in the OFF position, connect a jumper wire between circuits 60 and 201 on the self-test connector.
2. Connect an analog voltmeter from the battery positive post to the self-test output on the self-test connector.
3. Set the voltmeter on the DC volt range to read from 0–15 volts.

NOTE: One quick initialization pulse may occur on the voltmeter immediately after turning the ignition key to the ON position. The output service code will occur in approximately five seconds.

CONNECTION OF STAR TESTER

1. With the ignition key in the OFF position, connect the black negative lead to the battery's negative post.
2. Connect the red lead to the self-test output terminal on the self-test connector.
3. Connect the white lead to the self-test trigger on the self-test connector.

NOTE: Operating instructions for the STAR tester are located on the back panel of the tester.

DIAGNOSTIC PROCEDURE

Analog Voltmeter

With the analog voltmeter connected and the ignition switch turned to the ON position, without the engine operating, the MCU system is placed in its reporting service code mode.

When a service code is reported on the analog meter, it will represent itself as a pulsing or sweeping movement of the voltmeter scale's needle across the dial face of the meter. Therefore, a single digit number of three will be indicated by three pulses (sweeps) of the needle across the dial. Since the service codes are indicated by a two digit number, such as 32, the self-test's service code of 32 will be displayed as three pulses (sweeps) of the meter's needle with a one-half second pause between pulses (sweeps) and a two second pause between digits. When more than one service code is indicated, a five second pause between service codes will occur.

Self-Test Automatic Readout (STAR) Tester

After connecting the tester and turning on its power switch, the tester will run a display check with the numerals 88 beginning to flash in the display window. A steady 00 will then appear to signify that the tester is ready to start the self-test and receive the stored service codes.

In order to receive the service codes, press the pushbutton on the front of the tester. The button will latch down and a colon will appear in the display window in the front of the 00 numerals (:00). The colon MUST be displayed before the trouble codes can be received.

Follow the instructions accompanying the tester to complete the self-test procedure.

Other Circuit and Self-Test Units

Numerous other self-test units have been developed to aid the technician in obtaining the stored trouble codes. Should these units be used in determining malfunctions or to retrieve stored trouble codes from the system, the manufacturer's operating procedures must be followed to prevent damage to the MCU system and/or the test unit.

Exiting the MCU System

To exit the MCU system, turn the ignition key to the OFF position and disconnect the read-out meter from the self-test connnector.

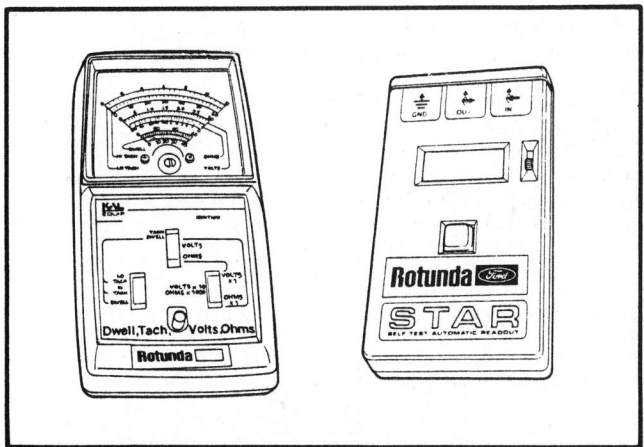

STAR tester and analog voltmeter used to diagnose Ford EEC systems

Ford Motor Company EEC–IV Electronic Engine Control System

The EEC–IV system has a "KEEP ALIVE MEMORY", which the other systems did not have. The "KEEP ALIVE MEMORY" was not used on the first release of the EEC–IV system on the 1.6L EFI engine in 1983. It simply goes to its normal strategy and continuous self-test.

The ECA retains any intermittent trouble codes stored within the last 20 engine restarts. With this system, the memory is not erased when the key is turned off. Trouble codes retained in the ECA are used by the technicians to evaluate and diagnose the EEC–IV system.

NOTE: In the EEC–IV system, the reference voltage is five volts, instead of the nine volts used with the other EEC systems and a power relay is used to provide all necessary power required for the EEC–IV system.
A short learning period will occur on new vehicles, when the battery has been disconnected during normal service and when an EEC–IV component is disconnected or replaced.

If, due to age or damage, an EEC–IV component is replaced, the memory may need to be cleared to eliminate the adjustments that were made to correct for the replaced component. It is possible for the engine operation to actually deteriorate because the new component will be controlled as if it were still the replaced aged or damaged component.

During the adjustment or learning period, usually under five miles of driving, some vehicles could exhibit abnormal drive symptoms, such as surge, hesitation, high idle speed, etc., which should clear up after the learning period.

Beginning with the 1986 model year, improvements have been made on the EEC–IV system to provide better driveability when one or more sensors fail. The basic improvement within the ECA is that each sensor now has an input operating range. The ECA monitors whether the sensor is operating within it operating limits. When an out of limit condition occurs, the ECA will store a diagnostic code in its memory and will substitute an in-limit signal.

By substituting an in-limit signal, an alternate system strategy comes into operation, which allows the vehicle to continue running. Prior to this change, the engine may have stalled or may not have run at all. With the addition of the Failure Mode Effects Management, the vehicle can now be started and operated. It may not run well, but it will allow the operator to drive the vehicle to a service center.

EEC–IV SELF TEST

The EEC–IV system has the capability of checking the electronic components in the system. This self-test, often referred to as a "QUICK TEST", is an internal function performed by the electronic control assembly (ECA), in which the ECA checks the operational status of every circuit and component in the EEC–IV system.

NOTE: The EEC–IV self-test only checks the system components, such as sensors, relays, switches and solenoids. It cannot provide information on driveability/engine performance problems, unless related to one of the system's components.

During the self-test, the ECA reads and evaluates signals received from the system input components. The input components are checked by the ECA during a KEY ON/ENGINE OFF and during the ENGINE RUNNING portion of the test.

This self-test also allows the technician to determine if the ECA is capable of controlling the ignition timing of the engine, since different engine operating modes require the timing be advanced or retarded. The ECA must do this automatically or the engine will not perform properly.

NOTE: EEC–IV system engines have an in-line base timing connector that must be disconnected to check the base ignition timing. The connector is part of the SPOUT circuit and when disconnected, interrupts the electronic timing signal and locks the system into a fixed timing base. The SPOUT connector is located within six inches of the distributor on all EEC–IV applications.

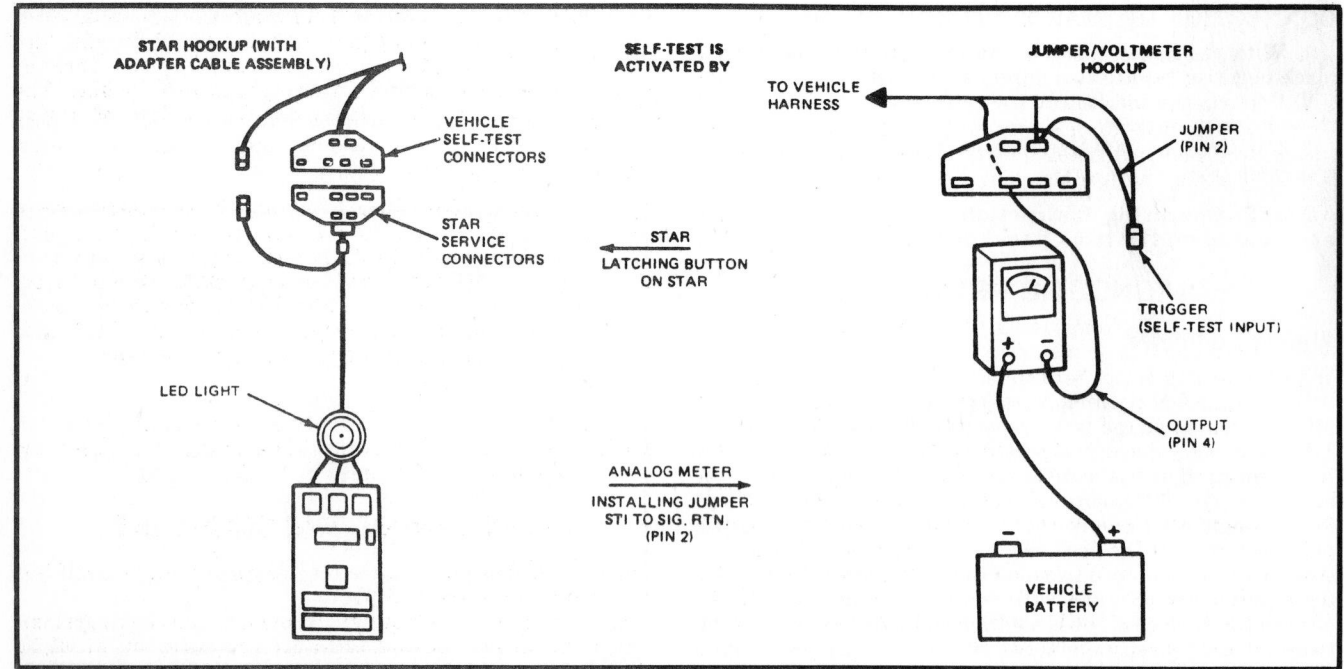

Making the self test equipment hookups

Self-Test Procedure

The EEC–IV system self-test can be performed by either an analog voltmeter or by the Self-Test Automatic Readout (STAR) tester or its equivalent. Other types of automatic testers are marketed and are available to the technicians. With each of the automatic testers, it is imperative that the technician follows the manufacturer's instructions on hook-up and display procedures.

KEY ON/ENGINE OFF (KOEO)

In this segment of the test, the system inputs and outputs are checked for existing faults. These type of faults are referred to as HARD FAULTS in this test procedure because they represent a failure that is always present. Also, the system is checked for INTERMEDIATE FAULTS, which indicate that a problem did exist recently somewhere in the system. The fault is not now present, but it did occur some time recently. This usually indicates a loose wire, a bad connection, a broken wire that opens periodically, or some failure similar to these. Some times, recent work that may have been done to the vehicle is good place to start when trying to determine the root of an intermediate problem.

KEY ON/ENGINE RUNNING (KOER)

In this portion of the test, the system is checked under all operating conditions. The output devices are all activated to check for proper operation. Only HARD FAULTS are noted during this test.

INTERMITTENT FAULT CONFIRMATION CHECK

This test is also referred to as the WIGGLE TEST because connectors, wires and components are wiggled during the check. This test is performed if intermittent faults are indicated during the KEY ON/ENGINE OFF segment of the self-test.

Connection of Analog Voltmeter

1. Set the analog voltmeter on a DC voltage range to read from 0 to 15 volts. Insert one end of a jumper wire into the number four pin on the self-test output connector. Clamp the negative lead from the analog voltmeter to the other end of the jumper wire.
2. Clamp the positive lead from the voltmeter to the positive terminal of the battery.
3. Insert the end of a second jumper wire into the number two terminal of the self-test output connector. Insert the other end of the jumper wire into the self-test input wire connector.

NOTE: The final connection to the self-test input wire connector also activates the self-test sequence inside the ECA when the ignition switch is turned on.

SERVICE CODES

After the EEC–IV system completes its self-test, it communicates with the service technician by way of the analog voltmeter needle and scale.

When a service code is reported on the analog meter, it will represent itself as a pulsing or sweeping movement of the voltmeter scale's needle across the dial face of the meter. Therefore, a single digit number of three will be indicated by three pulses (sweeps) of the needle across the dial. Since the service codes are indicated by a two digit number, such as 32, the self-test's service code of 32 will be displayed as three pulses (sweeps) of the meter's needle with a one-half second pause between pulses (sweeps) and a two second pause between digits. When more than one service code is indicated, a four second pause between service codes will occur.

Separator and dynamic response codes (numeral 10 in both cases), are represented by a single pulse or sweep of the needle.

There are no pulses or sweeps generated for the digit "0". There will be a six second pause before each one of these.

The key to sorting out the service codes on the voltmeter is to keep the pulses and the pauses straight.

1. Each digit is separated by a two second pause.
2. Each code is separated by a four second pause.
3. Separator and dynamic response codes are separated from previous and subsequent codes by six second (or longer) pauses. The self-test consists of two segments: Key On/Engine Off and the Engine Running. Each segment displays its own set of service codes.

Key ON/Engine OFF Sequence

FAST CODES

At the very beginning of the Key On/Engine Off self-test sequence, the ECA generates standard service codes at a rate of approximately 100 times faster than a voltmeter can respond. These fast codes are read by special computer type machines in the assembly plants and maybe observed on the voltmeter by a slight deflection of the needle. They have no practical application in the service field.

ON–DEMAND CODES

The On–Demand Codes indicate there is something wrong somewhere in the EEC–IV system at the time of the self-test. This type of malfunction is considered to be a HARD FAULT.

SEPARATOR CODES

The Separator Codes or pulses, cause the voltmeter needle to sweep once, indicating that on-demand codes have ceased and memory codes are about to begin.

MEMORY CODES

Memory Codes indicate there was a recent problem, somewhere in the EEC–IV system, such as an open or short circuit, though it is not present at the time of the self-test. These codes are often referred to as intermediate faults.

Engine Running Segment

ENGINE IDENTIFICATION CODES

The engine identification codes have no practical application in the service field, but are part of the assembly process. When the self-test is initiated at the beginning of the Engine Running Segment, the voltmeter needle will sweep two, three or four times to denote a four, six or eight cylinder engine. The I.D. code multiplied by two equals the number of engine cylinders.

DYNAMIC RESPONSE CODE

The Dynamic Response Code is indicated by the needle sweeping once, signals the operator to perform a brief wide open throttle. This allows the ECA to check for proper movement of the throttle position sensor and operation of the manifold absolute pressure sensor, The operator has 15 seconds to "goose" the engine after the dynamic response code appears. Otherwise a code 77 (operator did not do goose test) will appear.

ON–DEMAND CODES

The On–Demand Codes indicate there is something wrong in the EEC–IV system at this time. These faults or malfunctions are referred to as hard faults.

PERFORMING THE SELF-TEST

Three conditions must be met before performing the self-test procedures. They are as follows:

1. Preliminary check out of the engine, associated systems and vehicle systems and engine preparation must be performed.
2. Voltmeter must be connected and functioning properly.

3. The technician performing the self-test must know what to expect when the self-test is activated and what to do when the service codes begin being read out.

Key ON/Engine OFF Test

1. Set the voltmeter to a range that covers 0 to 15 volts DC and connected as previously explained.
2. Connect a jumper wire from the number two pin on the self-test connector to the self-test input connector.
3. Turn the ignition switch to the ON position.
4. Assuming the system inputs check out OK for hard and intermediate faults, service codes should be registering as follows:
    a. The needle will fluctuate from zero to approximately three volts for fast codes.
    b. Next the needle will sweep twice, with a two second pause in between, representing a code 11 (system pass). The code 11 will be repeated once (in case it was missed the first time). There is a four second pause in between the codes.
    c. A six second pause is next, followed by a single sweep of the needle (representing the separator code). Another six second pause follows the separator pulse.
    d. Finally, the code 11 is repeated twice, again with a four second pause in between.

Engine Running Test

1. Start the engine and run at approximately 1500 rpm for two minutes to warm the EGO sensor.
2. Turn the engine off and insert the jumper wire from the number two pin on the self-test output connector to the self-test input wire connector.
3. Wait ten seconds and then start the engine.
4. Assuming the system checks out OK for hard faults, the service codes should register as follows:
    a. The needle will sweep two, three or four times without a pause, depending upon the number of cylinders in the engine.
    b. The needle will then sweep once after a six second to twenty second pause. This is the dynamic response code and the technician has 15 seconds to "goose" the throttle.
    c. A four to fifteen second pause follows the "goose test", after which the needle will fluctuate from zero to three volts for the fast codes.
    d. Finally, the needle will sweep twice with a two second pause in between sweeps, representing another code 11. After four seconds, the code will be repeated.

Intermittent Fault Confirmation Check (Wiggle Test)

The ECA is continually looking for shorts, open circuits and other problems within the EEC–IV system and when noted, stores them in the memory, when they occur. Memory codes obtained during the KEY ON/ENGINE OFF segment of the self test, recalls intermittent faults from the ECA memory. To make final diagnosis and repair as easy as possible, it is recommended that the technician do two things before proceeding to further diagnostics.
1. Repeat the self-test segment when any code other than "SYSTEM PASS" (code 11), is generated by the ECA.
2. Attempt to re-create intermittent faults while the test equipment is still connected to the system. This is called an intermittent fault confirmation check.
3. During the KEY ON/ENGINE OFF segment, perform this check with self-test sequence de-activated (ECA not in the self-test mode). A fault is indicated when the VOM deflection is 10.5 volts or greater.
4. During the KEY ON/ENGINE RUNNING mode, perform this check with self-test sequence activated (ECA in self-test mode). A fault will be indicated in the same way as it is with the KEY ON/ENGINE OFF mode.

RECREATING INTERMITTENT FAULTS

Intermittent faults can generally be recreated by the following methods:
1. Wiggling connectors and harnesses.
2. Manipulating moveable sensors and actuators.
3. Heating thermistor-type sensors with a heat gun.
Suspected components, such as the sensors, actuators and harnesses, are identified by matching service codes obtained during the KEY ON/ENGINE OFF segment of the self-test.

When an intermittent fault is re-created, the voltmeter needle will sweep back and forth across the scale or sweep to the right and stay there.

Malfunctioning components identified with this procedure can be repaired or replaced without further diagnostic testing. Further testing must be done for hard faults and for intermittent faults that can not be re-created by the above method.

Output Cycling Test

This test is performed during the KEY ON/ENGINE OFF test segment, after the memory codes have been generated. Without deactivating the self-test sequence, momentarily depress the throttle to the floor, then release it. Most of the EEC–IV actuators will be energized and the solenoid armatures should move (open or close) accordingly. Another throttle depression will de-energize the actuators. This cycle can be repeated as many times as necessary.

Malfunctiuoning actuators identified in this fashion, should be repaired or replaced. Further diagnostics are required for faults that cannot be isolated by the above method.

NOTE: After completing the self-test and repairing the EEC–IV system, always repeat the self-test to verify that the problem has been repaired.

Cadillac Digital Electronic Fuel Injection (DEFI) System

1984–85 REAR WHEEL DRIVE MODELS

The ECM is designed to withstand normal current draws associated with the vehicle operation. However, care must be exercised to avoid overloading any of these circuits. In testing for opens or shorts, do not ground or apply voltage to any of the ECM circuits, unless instructed to do so by a diagnostic procedure. These circuits should only be tested using a high impedance Mulimeter, should they remain connected to the ECM.

Power should never be applied to the ECM with the ignition in the ON position. Before removing or connecting battery cables, ECM fuses or ECM connectors, always turn the ignition to the OFF position.

The ECM has a learning ability that allows the fuel control calibration to be tailored to account for minor differences in the fuel control system and the engine mechanical system. This allows the ECM to better adapt the vehicle to changing environmental conditions. If the battery is disconnected or if an ECM is replaced, the ECM in the vehicle will have to begin the learning process all over again. A change in vehicle driveability may be noted after a battery disconnect or ECM replacement. To teach the ECM, operate the vehicle at normal operating temperature, at part throttle and at idle until driveability and performance returns

Trouble Codes

The dash mounted SERVICE NOW and SERVICE SOON indicator lamps are used to inform the technician of detected system malfunctions or system abnormalities. These malfunctions may be related to the various operating sensors or to the ECM itself. The light that comes on will automatically go out if the fault clears, such as an intermediate malfunction. However, the ECM stores the trouble code associated with the detected failure until the diagnostic system is cleared or until 50 OFF/ON ignition switch cycles have occurred without any fault reappearing.

Proper operation of SERVICE NOW or the SERVICE SOON indicator lamps are as follows:

1. Both lamps are normally off.

2. A bulb check is performed with both bulbs on, when the ignition switch is in the CRANK position only. When the engine starts, both lamps go out.

3. Depending upon the trouble code set, either the SERVICE SOON or the SERVICE NOW lamps will come on and stay on when a constant malfunction is detected.

4. If the malfunction is intermittent, the lamp that came on previously, will go out when the malfunction is no longer detected. The lamp will come on each time the malfunction is again detected and will either be on bright or flickering.

5. When a SERVICE SOON malfunction is detected at the same time a SERVICE NOW malfunction is detected, only the SERVICE NOW lamp will be on.

6. Both lamps will stay on when the system is displaying the diagnostic routines.

The dash mounted digital display panel, normally used for the ECC system, can be temporarily directed to display trouble codes stored in the ECM.

INTERMITTENT AND HARD FAILURE CODES

For codes 12 through 51, the service indicator lamp will go out automatically if the malfunction clears. However, the ECM stores the trouble code associated with the detected failure until the diagnostic system is cleared or until 50 ignition cycles have occurred without any fault reappearing. This condition is known as an intermediate failure.

Therefore, the ECM may have two types of trouble codes stored in its memory. These two codes types are:

1. A code for malfunction which is a hard failure. A hard failure turns on the appropriate service indicator lamp and keeps it on as long as the malfunction is present.

2. A code for intermediate malfunction which has occurred within the last 50 ignition cycles. An intermediate failure turns off the service lamp when the malfunction clears up.

For codes 52 through 67, the service indicator lamp will never come on. These codes indicate that a specific condition occurred of which the technician should be aware. Since these codes can be operator induced, a judgement must be made whether or not the code requires investigation. These codes will also be stored until the diagnostic system is cleared or until 50 ignition cycles have occurred without any faults reappearing.

INTERMITTENT PROBLEM DIAGNOSIS

It should be noted that diagnostic charts cannot be used to diagnose intermittent failures. The testing required at various points of the chart depends upon the fault to be present in order to locate its source in order to correct it.

If the fault is intermittent, an unnecessary ECM replacement could be indicated and the problem could remain. Exceptions to this rule includes trouble codes 13, 20, 30, 33, 39, 44 and 45. The nature of these codes or the design of their charts allow them to be treated as hard failures.

Since many of the intermittent problems are caused at electrical connections, diagnosis of intermittent problems should start with a visual and physical inspection of the connectors involved in the circuit. Disconnect the connectors, examine and reconnect before replacing any component of the system.

Some causes of connector problems are:

1. Improperly formed terminals or connector bodies.

2. Damaged terminals or connector bodies.

3. Corrosion, body sealer, or other foreign matter on the terminal mating surfaces which could insulate the terminals.

4. Incomplete mating of the connector halves.

5. Connectors not fully seated in the connector body.

6. Terminals not tightly crimped to the wire.

If an affected circuit is one that may be checked by the status light on the ECC, the switch tests, the output cycling tests, or the engine data displays, make the check on the appropriate circuit. Some of the trouble codes include a "Note On Intermittents" describing a suggested procedure for isolating the location of intermittent malfunctions.

ENTERING DIAGNOSTIC MODE

To enter diagnostics, proceed as follows.

1. Turn ignition ON.

2. Depress OFF and WARMER buttons on the ECC panel simultaneously and hold until ".." appears. "–1.8.8" will then be displayed, which indicates the beginning of the diagnostic readout.

3. If "–1.8.8" does not display or is partically displayed, a malfunction is indicated and a misdiagnose of codes could occur due to segments of the display inoperative. The display head would then have to be replaced.

NOTE: Some vehicles may not display one or both of the decimal points. This is a normal condition and the control head should not be replaced because of it.

4. Trouble codes will be displayed on the digital ECC panel beginning with the lowest numbered code. Note that the Fuel Data panel goes blank when the system is in the diagnostic mode.

5. The lowest numbered code will be displayed for approximately two seconds. Progressively higher numbered codes, if present, will be displayed consecutively for two seconds until all stored codes have been displayed.

6. The code "–1.8.8" will be displayed again.

7. A second pass will be repeated of the first pass.

8. On the third pass, only HARD trouble codes will be displayed. These are the codes which indicate a malfunction and keep the indicator lamp on.

NOTE: Codes which were displayed on the first and second pass, but not the third, are intermittent codes.

9. The "–1.8.8" will be displayed again. When the trouble codes are displayed again, code .7.0 will then be displayed. Code .7.0 indicates that the ECM is ready for the next diagnostic feature to be selected.

10. If a code 51 (PROM error) is present, it will be displayed continuously until the diagnostic mode is exited. During the display of code 51, none of the other diagnostic features will be possible.

11. If a code 16 (alternator voltage out of range) is present, this must be diagnosed first, since this malfunction can affect the setting of other codes.

12. If no trouble codes are present, "–1.8.8" will be displayed for two seconds and then the ECM will display the code .7.0, which indicates the ECM is ready for the next diagnostic feature to be selected.

Display Of Code .7.0

Code .7.0 is a decision point for the technician. When code .7.0 is displayed, the technician should select the diagnostic feature that he wants to display. The following choices are available:

1. Switch tests.

2. Engine data display.

3. Output cycling tests.

4. Fixed spark mode.

5. Exit diagnostics or clear codes and then exit.

SWITCH TEST PROCEDURE

Code .7.0 must be displayed on the ECC control head before the switch tests can begin. To start the switch tests sequence, depress and release the brake pedal. The switch tests begin as the display switches from code .7.0 to code .7.1. If the display codes do not advance, the ECM is not processing the brake signal.

As each code is displayed, the associated switch must be cycled within 10 seconds or the code will be recorded in the ECM's memory as a failure.

After the ECM recognizes a test as passings or after the 10 second time-out elapses without the proper cycling being recognized, the display will automatically advance to the next switch test code.

1. With code .7.0 displayed to start the test sequence, depress and release the brake pedal.

2. With code .7.1 displayed, depress the throttle from the idle position to an open throttle position and slowly release the throttle.

3. With code .7.3 displayed, shift the transmission lever into DRIVE and then the NEUTRAL position.

4. On vehicles without Cruise Control, codes .7.5, .7.6. and .7.7 will be displayed, but cannot be performed during the switch tests.

5. On vehicles with Cruise Control, code .7.5 will be displayed. With the cruise instrument panel switch in the ON position, depress and release the SET/COAST button.

5. With code .7.6 displayed and with the cruise instrument panel switch in the ON position, depress and release the RESUME/ACCELERATION switch.

6. With code .7.8 displayed, depress and release the INSTANT/AVERAGE button on the fuel data panel.

7. With code .7.9 displayed, depress and release the RESET button on the fuel data panel.

8. With code .8.0 displayed, depress and release the outside temperature button TWICE. This operation works in conjunction with the air conditioning compressor clutch.

9. When all the tests are completed, the ECM will then go back to display the switch codes that did not test properly, from the lowest number to the highest. The switch codes will not disappear until the affected switch circuit has been repaired and retested.

10. After the switch tests are completed and all circuits pass, the ECC panel will display ".0.0" and then return to code .7.0.

NOTE: "0.0" indicates that all switch circuits are operating properly.

ENGINE DATA DISPLAY PROCEDURE

The code .7.0 must be displayed on the ECC control head before the engine data can be displayed. To begin the display procedure, proceed as follows:

1. Depress and release the RESET button on the fuel data panel. The engine data series begins as the display switches from code .7.0 to code 9.0.

2. To advance the display, depress the INSTANT/AVERAGE button on the fuel data panel.

3. It is possible to leave the engine data series at any time and return to code .7.0 by simultaneously depressing the OFF and the HI buttons on the ECC control panel.

4. After the last parameter is displayed, the system advances to code .9.5 and waits for the next command.

5. When the engine data display is initiated, the ECC will display .0.1 for one second to indicate the first parameter check and then a number will be displayed for nine seconds to indicate the first parameter value. The ECC will continue to repeat this sequence of event until the technician decides to move to the next parameter.

OUTPUT CYCLING TEST PROCEDURE

This series of tests can be initiated after .9.5 is displayed on the ECC panel. The display of .9.5 can be reached by either of the following methods:

1. Depress the INSTANT/AVERAGE button while code .7.0 is displayed on the ECC control head.

2. Depress the INSTANT/AVERAGE button while parameter .1.3 of the engine data series is being displayed.

3. The output cycling test, code .9.6, turns the ECM's outputs on and off. To enter the output cycling test, proceed as follows:

   a. The engine must be operating.

   b. Turn the engine OFF and within two seconds, turn the ignition switch to the ON position.

   c. Enter the diagnostics and display code .9.5.

   d. Depress the accelerator pedal the open the throttle switch and release it to close it. Code .9.6 will appear on the display.

   e. Turn the Cruise Control instrument panel switch to the ON position so that the Cruise Control outputs will cycle.

   f. The output cycling test will end automatically after two minutes of cycling and display will switch from code .9.6 to code .9.5.

4. The outputs will cycle ON and OFF every three seconds until the two minute automatic shut-off occurs. The only exception to this three second cycle is the cruise control power valve which cycles continuously. If additional output cycling is desired, recycle the throttle switch.

FIXED SPARK MODE PROCEDURE

To verify proper adjustment of the spark timing, the ECM will command a fixed $20°$ of spark advance and disable the EGR valve operation when ever the following conditions are met:

1. The engine must be operating and to normal operating temperature.

2. Code .9.5 must be displayed on the ECC control head.

3. Engine speed must be under 900 rpm.

4. The transmission must be in the PARK position.

The display of code .9.5 can be reached by either to the following methods:

1. Depress the INSTANT/AVERAGE button while the .7.0 is displayed on the ECC control head.

2. Depress the INSTANT/AVERAGE BUTTON while the parameter .1.3. of the engine data series is being displayed.

As long as these conditions are met, codes 23 and 25 are not set and the HEI system is operating correctly, a timing light can be used to verify that the engine timing is adjusted correctly. If the engine timing is not at $20° \pm 2°$ BTDC under the above conditions, the base timing of $10°$ BTDC should be adjusted.

Status Display

While in the diagnostic mode, the mode indicators on the CCP are used to indicate the status of certain operating systems. These different modes of operation are indicated by the status light either being turned OFF or ON.

1985–88 FWD DEVILLE AND FLEETWOOD DEFI SYSTEM

At the center of the self-diagnostic system is the Body Computer Module (BCM), located behind the glove compartment opening. An internal microprocessor is used to control various vehicle function, based on monitored sensor and switch inputs. The ECM is located on the right side of the instrument panel and is the major factor in providing self-diagnostic capabilities for those subsection which it controls.

When both the BCM and ECM are used, a communication process has been incorporated which allows the two modules to share information and thereby provide for additional control capability. In a method similar to a telegraph key operator, each module's internal circuitry rapidly switches a circuit between 0 and 5 volts. This process is used to convert information into a series of pulses which represent coded data messages understood by the other components.

One of the data messages transferred from the BCM is a request for specific ECM diagnostic action. This action may affect

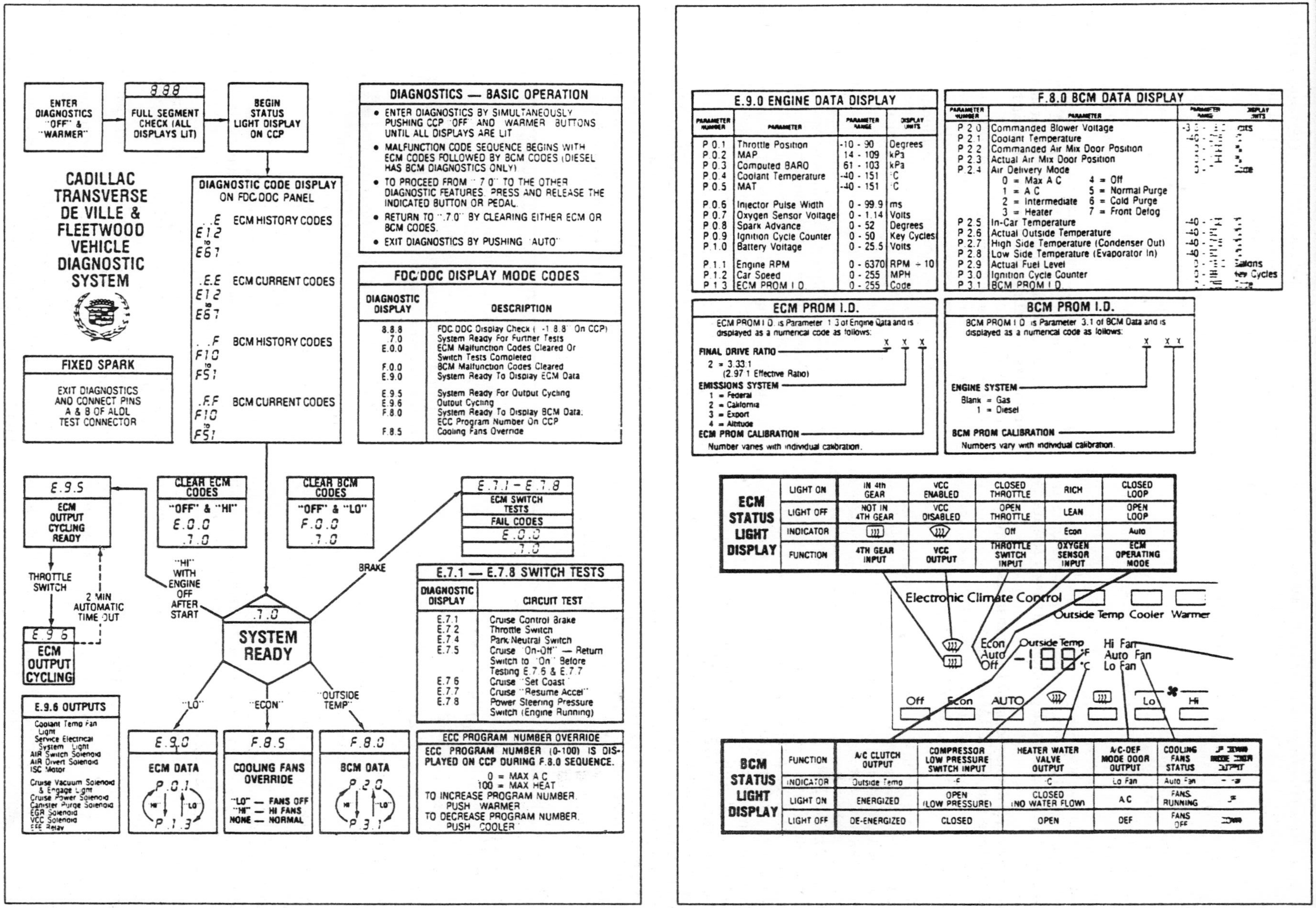

E.9.0 ENGINE DATA DISPLAY

PARAMETER NUMBER	PARAMETER	PARAMETER RANGE	DISPLAY UNITS
P.0.1	Throttle Position	-10 - 90	Degrees
P.0.2	MAP	14 - 109	kPa
P.0.3	Computed BARO	61 - 103	kPa
P.0.4	Coolant Temperature	-40 - 151	C
P.0.5	MAT	-40 - 151	C
P.0.6	Injector Pulse Width	0 - 99.9	ms
P.0.7	Oxygen Sensor Voltage	0 - 1.14	Volts
P.0.8	Spark Advance	0 - 52	Degrees
P.0.9	Ignition Cycle Counter	0 - 50	Key Cycles
P.1.0	Battery Voltage	0 - 25.5	Volts
P.1.1	Engine RPM	0 - 6370	RPM
P.1.2	Car Speed	0 - 255	MPH ÷ 10
P.1.3	ECM PROM I.D.	0 - 255	Code

ECM PROM I.D.
ECM PROM I.D. is Parameter 13 of Engine Data and is displayed as a numerical code as follows:

FINAL DRIVE RATIO —
2 = 3.33:1
3 = 2.97:1 (Effective Ratio)

EMISSIONS SYSTEM —
1 = Federal
2 = California
3 = Export
4 = Altitude

ECM PROM CALIBRATION —
Number varies with individual calibration.

F.8.0 BCM DATA DISPLAY

PARAMETER NUMBER	PARAMETER		DISPLAY UNITS
P.2.0	Commanded Blower Voltage		Volts
P.2.1	Coolant Temperature		kPa
P.2.2	Commanded Air Mix Door Position		C
P.2.3	Actual Air Mix Door Position		C
P.2.4	Air Delivery Mode	0 = Max A/C 4 = Off	
		1 = A/C 5 = Normal Purge	
		2 = Intermediate 6 = Cold Purge	
		3 = Heater 7 = Front Defog	
P.2.5	In-Car Temperature		C
P.2.6	Actual Outside Temperature		C
P.2.7	High Side Temperature (Condenser Out)		C
P.2.8	Low Side Temperature (Evaporator In)		C
P.2.9	Actual Fuel Level		Gallons
P.3.0	Ignition Cycle Counter		Key Cycles
P.3.1	BCM PROM I.D.		

BCM PROM I.D.
BCM PROM I.D. is Parameter 3.1 of BCM Data and is displayed as a numerical code as follows:

ENGINE SYSTEM —
Blank = Gas
1 = Diesel

BCM PROM CALIBRATION —
Numbers vary with individual calibration.

ECM STATUS LIGHT DISPLAY

FUNCTION							
LIGHT ON	IN 4th GEAR	VCC ENABLED	CLOSED THROTTLE	RICH	CLOSED LOOP		
LIGHT OFF	NOT IN 4TH GEAR	VCC DISABLED	OPEN THROTTLE	LEAN	OPEN LOOP		
INDICATOR				Econ	Auto		
FUNCTION	4TH GEAR INPUT	VCC OUTPUT	THROTTLE SWITCH INPUT	OXYGEN SENSOR INPUT	ECM OPERATING MODE		

BCM STATUS LIGHT DISPLAY

FUNCTION	INDICATOR		COMPRESSOR LOW PRESSURE SWITCH INPUT	HEATER WATER VALVE OUTPUT	A/C-DEF MODE DOOR OUTPUT	COOLING FANS STATUS	
A/C CLUTCH OUTPUT	Outside Temp						
LIGHT ON	ENERGIZED		ENERGIZED (LOW PRESSURE)	CLOSED (NO WATER FLOW)	A/C	FANS RUNNING	
LIGHT OFF	DE-ENERGIZED		OPEN (LOW PRESSURE)	OPEN	DEF	FANS OFF	

DIAGNOSTICS — BASIC OPERATION

- Enter diagnostics by simultaneously pushing CCP "OFF" and "WARMER" buttons until all displays are lit.
- Malfunction code sequence begins with ECM codes followed by BCM codes (diesel has BCM diagnostics only)
- To proceed from "7.0" to the other diagnostic features press and release the indicated button or pedal.
- Return to "7.0" by clearing either ECM or BCM codes.
- Exit diagnostics by pushing "AUTO"

FDC/DDC DISPLAY MODE CODES

DIAGNOSTIC DISPLAY	DESCRIPTION
8.8.8	FDC/DDC Display Check (·1·8.8· On CCP)
7.0	System Ready For Further Tests
E.0.0	ECM Malfunction Codes Cleared Or
F.0.0	Switch Tests Completed
	BCM Malfunction Codes Cleared
E.9.0	System Ready To Display ECM Data
E.9.5	System Ready For Output Cycling
E.9.6	Output Cycling
F.8.0	System Ready To Display BCM Data.
	ECC Program Number On CCP
F.8.5	Cooling Fans Override

E.7.1 — E.7.8 SWITCH TESTS

DIAGNOSTIC DISPLAY	CIRCUIT TEST
E.7.1	Cruise Control Brake
E.7.2	Throttle Switch
E.7.4	Park/Neutral Switch
E.7.5	Cruise "On-Off" Before
	Switch "On-Off" Return
	Testing E.7.5 & E.7.7
E.7.6	Cruise "Set Coast"
E.7.7	Cruise "Resume Accel"
E.7.8	Power Steering Pressure Switch (Engine Running)

ECM SWITCH TESTS: E.7.1 - E.7.8
FAIL CODES: E.9.0

ECC PROGRAM NUMBER OVERRIDE
ECC PROGRAM NUMBER (0-100) IS DISPLAYED ON CCP DURING F.8.0 SEQUENCE.
0 = MAX A/C
100 = MAX HEAT
TO INCREASE PROGRAM NUMBER PUSH WARMER
TO DECREASE PROGRAM NUMBER PUSH COOLER

CADILLAC TRANSVERSE DE VILLE & FLEETWOOD VEHICLE DIAGNOSTIC SYSTEM

ENTER DIAGNOSTICS "OFF" & "WARMER"

8.8.8 FULL SEGMENT CHECK (ALL DISPLAYS LIT)

BEGIN STATUS LIGHT DISPLAY ON CCP

DIAGNOSTIC CODE DISPLAY ON FDC/DDC PANEL

E.1.2 to E.6.7	ECM HISTORY CODES	
.E.E to .E.6.7	ECM CURRENT CODES	
.F.1.0 to F.5.1	BCM HISTORY CODES	
.F.F to F.5.1	BCM CURRENT CODES	

CLEAR ECM CODES "OFF" & "HI" E.0.0 7.0

CLEAR BCM CODES "OFF" & "LO" F.0.0 7.0

SYSTEM READY 7.0

FIXED SPARK — EXIT DIAGNOSTICS AND CONNECT PINS A & B OF ALDL TEST CONNECTOR

E.9.5 ECM OUTPUT CYCLING READY

THROTTLE SWITCH — 2 MIN AUTOMATIC TIME OUT

E.9.6 ECM OUTPUT CYCLING

E.9.6 OUTPUTS
Coolant Temp Fan
Service Electrical
Light
A/C Switch Solenoid
Air Switch Solenoid
ISC Motor
Cruise Vacuum Solenoid
& Engage Light
Canister Purge Solenoid
EGR Solenoid
VCC Solenoid
Fuel Relay

"HI" WITH ENGINE OFF AFTER START

"LO" — E.9.0 ECM DATA P.0.1 / P.1.3

ECCN — F.8.5 COOLING FANS OVERRIDE
"LO" = FANS OFF
"HI" = HI FANS
NONE = NORMAL

OUTSIDE TEMP — F.8.0 BCM DATA P.2.0 / P.3.1

BRAKE

Climate control panel operation for diagnostics on 1985 front wheel drive Cadillac models

ELECTRONIC CLIMATE CONTROL

SECTION 3

the ECM controlled output or require the ECM to transfer some information back to the BCM. This communication gives the BCM control over the ECM's self-diagnostic capabilities in addition to its own.

In order to access and control the self-diagnostic features, available to the BCM, two additional electronic components are utilized by the service technician. Located to the right of the steering column is the Climate Control Panel (CCP) and located to the left of the steering column is either the Fuel Data Center (FDC), used with DFI equipped vehicles, or the Diesel Data Center (DDC), used with diesel engines.

These devices provide displays and keyboard switches used with several BCM controlled subsystems. This display and keyboard information is transferred over the single wire data circuits which carry coded data back and forth between the BCM and the display panels. This communication process allows the BCM to transfer any of its available diagnostic information to the instrument panel for display during service. By depressing the appropriate buttons on the CCP, data messages can be sent to the BCM, requesting the specific diagnostic features required.

The ECM/BCMs are designed to withstand normal current draws associated with the vehicle operation. However, care must be exercised to avoid overloading any of these circuits. In testing for opens or shorts, do not ground or apply voltage to any of the ECM/BCM circuits, unless instructed to do so by a diagnostic procedure. These circuits should only be tested using a high impedance multimeter (10 megohms minimum), should they remain connected to the ECM/BCM.

Power should never be applied to the ECM with the ignition in the ON position. Before removing or connecting battery cables, ECM/BCM fuses or ECM/BCM connectors, always turn the ignition to the OFF position.

Trouble Codes

In the process of controlling its various subsystems, the ECM and BCM continually monitor the operating conditions for possible system malfunctions. By comparing system conditions against standard operating limits, certain circuit and component malfunctions can be detected. A two digit numerical trouble code is stored in the computer's memory when a problem is detected by this self-diagnostic system. These trouble codes can later be displayed by the service technician as an aid in system repair.

If a particular malfunction would result in unacceptable system operation, the self-diagnostics will attempt to minimize the effect by taking FAIL–SAFE action. FAIL–SAFE action refers to any specific attempt by the computer system to compensate for the detected problem. A typical FAIL–SAFE action would be the substitution of a fixed input value when a sensor/circuit is detected to be open or shorted.

INTERMITTENT AND HARD FAILURE CODES

For codes 12 through 51, the SERVICE SOON or SERVICE NOW indicator will go out automatically if the malfunction clears. However, the ECM stores the trouble code associated with the detected failure until the diagnostic system is cleared or until 50 ignition cycles have occurred without any fault reappearing. This condition is known as an intermediate failure.

Therefore, the ECM may have two types of trouble codes stored in its memory. These two codes types are:

1. A code for malfunction which is a hard failure. A hard failure turns on the appropriate service indicator lamp and keeps it on as long as the malfunction is present.

2. A code for intermediate malfunction which has occurred within the last 50 ignition cycles. An intermediate failure is one that was previously present, but was not detected the last time the ECM tested the circuit. The service indicator lamp turns out after the ECM tests the circuit without the defect being detected.

The first pass of the diagnostic codes, preceded by "..E", will contain all history codes, both hard and intermittent. The second pass contains only the hard codes that are present and will be preceded by ".E.E".

For codes 52 through 67, the service indicator lamp will never come on. These codes indicate that a specific condition occurred of which the technician should be aware. Since these codes can be operator induced, a judgement must be made whether or not the code requires investigation. These codes will also be stored until the diagnostic system is cleared or until 50 ignition cycles have occurred without any faults reappearing.

INTERMITTENT PROBLEM DIAGNOSIS

It should be noted that diagnostic charts cannot be used to diagnose intermittent failures. The testing required at various points of the chart depends upon the fault to be present in order to locate its source in order to correct it.

If the fault is intermittent, an unnecessary ECM replacement could be indicated and the problem could remain.

Since many of the intermittent problems are caused at electrical connections, diagnosis of intermittent problems should start with a visual and physical inspection of the connectors involved in the circuit. Disconnect the connectors, examine and reconnect before replacing any component of the system.

Some causes of connector problems are:

1. Improperly formed terminals or connector bodies.
2. Damaged terminals or connector bodies.
3. Corrosion, body sealer, or other foreign matter on the terminal mating surfaces which could insulate the terminals.
4. Incomplete mating of the connector halves.
5. Connectors not fully seated in the connector body.
6. Terminals not tightly crimped to the wire.

If an affected circuit is one that may be checked by the status light on the ECC, the switch tests, the output cycling tests, or the engine data displays, make the check on the appropriate circuit. Some of the trouble codes include a "Note On Intermittents" describing a suggested procedure for isolating the location of intermittent malfunctions.

ENTERING DIAGNOSTIC MODE

To enter the diagnostic mode, proceed as follows:

1. Turn the ignition switch to the ON position.
2. Depress the OFF and the WARMER buttons on the CCP, simultaneously and hold them in until all display segments illuminate, which indicated the beginning of the diagnostic readout.

NOTE: If any of the segments are inoperative, the diagnosis should not be attempted, as this could lead to misdiagnosis. The display in question would have to be replaced before the diagnosis procedure is initiated.

Trouble Code Display

After the display segment check is completed, any trouble codes stored in the computer memory will be displayed on the Data Center panel as follows:

1. Display of the trouble codes will begin with an "8.8.8" on the data center panel for approximately one second. "..E" will then be displayed which indicates the beginning of the ECM stored trouble codes.

2. This first pass of ECM codes includes all detected malfunctions whether they are currently present or not. If no ECM trouble codes are stored, the "..E" display will be bypassed.

3. Following the display of "..E", the lowest numbered ECM trouble code will be displayed for approximately two seconds. All ECM trouble codes will be prefixed with the letter "E". (i.e. E12, E13, etc.).

4. Progressively higher numbered trouble codes will be displayed, until the highest code present has been displayed.

5. ".E.E" will then be displayed, which indicates the beginning of the second pass of the ECM trouble codes.

6. On the second pass, only "HARD" trouble codes will be displayed. These are the codes which indicate a currently present malfunction.

7. Codes which are displayed during the first pass, but not on the second, are classified as "intermittent" trouble codes. If all the ECM codes are considered "intermittent", the ".E.E" display will be bypassed.

8. When all the ECM trouble codes have been displayed, the BCM codes will then displayed in a similar fashion. The only exceptions during the BCM code display are as follows:

    a. "..F" precedes the first display pass.

    b. The BCM codes are prefixed by an "F".

    c. ".F.F" precedes the second display pass.

9. After all the ECM and BCM trouble codes have been displayed or if no codes are present, code ".7.0" will be displayed. This code indicates that the system is ready for the next diagnostic feature to be selected.

NOTE: If a code E51 is detected, it will be displayed continuously until the diagnostic mode is exited. During this display of code E51, none of the other diagnostic features will be possible.

Clearing Trouble Codes

Trouble codes stored in the ECM's memory may be cleared (erased) by entering the diagnostic mode and then depressing the OFF and HI buttons on the CCP simultaneously. Hold the buttons in until "E.0.0"appears on the display. Trouble codes stored in the BCM's memory may be cleared by depressing the OFF and LO buttons simultaneously until "F.0.0" appears. After "E.0.0" or "F.0.0" is displayed, ".7.0." will appear. With the ".7.0"displayed, turn the ignition off for at least ten seconds before re-entering the diagnostic mode.

Exiting Diagnostic Mode

To get out of the diagnostic mode, depress the AUTO button or turn the ignition switch OFF for ten seconds. Trouble codes are not erased when this is done. The temperature setting will reappear in the display panel.

NOTE: The Climate Control system will operate in whatever mode was commanded prior to depressing the necessary buttons to enter the diagnostic system. The prior operating mode will be remembered and will resume after the diagnostic mode is entered.

Status Display

While in the diagnostic mode, the mode indicators on the CCP are used to indicate the status of certain operating systems. These different modes of operation are indicated by the status light either being turned OFF or ON.

EEC Program Override

During the BCM display of data, a manual override of the system can be accomplished by the technician, for different levels of heating and cooling effort. Since this is not in the realm of this diagnostic coverage, no procedural explanation is given.

1986–88 ELDORADO AND SEVILLE DEFI SYSTEM

The Electronic Control Module (ECM) is located under the instrument panel and is the control center of the engine control and fuel injection systems. It constantly examines the information from the various sensors and controls the systems that af-

fect the vehicle performance. The ECM performs the diagnostic function of the system by recognizing operational problems, alert the operator through an ENGINE CONTROL SYSTEM lamp and will store a code or codes which identify the problem areas to aid the technician in determining what repairs are to be made.

The ECM consists of three parts; a controller, (the ECM without the PROM), A separate calibrator (PROM-Programmable Read Only Memory) and a resistor network (CALPAK) which provides the calibrated backup fuel calibrations and ECM/BCM communication instructions.

In addition to the ECM, the vehicle contains a Body Computer Module (BCM), which is used to control various vehicle functions, based on data sensors and switch inputs.

Both the ECM and BCM have the capability to diagnose faults with the various inputs and systems they control. When the ECM recognizes a problem, an ENGINE CONTROL SYSTEMS indicator lamp is illuminated on the instrument panel to alert the operator that a malfunction has occurred.

The ECM supplies either 5 or 12 volts to power the various sensors or switched. This is done through resistances in the ECM which are so high in value that a conventional test lamp will not illuminate when connected to a circuit. In some cases, a conventional shop voltmeter will not give accurate readings because its resistance is to low. Therefore, a 10 megohm input impedance digital voltmeter is required to assure accurate voltage readings.

The ECM has a learning ability that allows the fuel control calibration to be tailored to account for minor differences in fuel control systems and engine mechanical systems and to better adapt the vehicle to changing environmental conditions.

If the battery is disconnected or if an ECM is replaced, the ECM in the vehicle will have to begin the learning process all over again. A change in vehicle driveability may be noted after a battery disconnect or ECM replacement. To teach the ECM, operate the vehicle at normal operating temperature, at part throttle and at idle, until the driveability and performance returns.

ECM/BCM Service Precautions

The ECM/BCMs are designed to withstand normal current draws associated with vehicle operation. However, care must be taken to avoid overloading any of these circuits. In testing for open or short circuits, do not ground or apply voltage to any of the circuits, unless instructed to do so by diagnostic procedures. These circuits should only be tested using a high impedance multimeter, such as Kent Moore tool Number J–29125A or its equivalent, if they are to remain connected to any of the computers. Power should never be remove or applied to one of the computers with the key in the ON position. Before removing or connecting battery cables, fuses or connectors, always turn the ignition to the LOCK position.

Trouble Codes

NOTE: Should a problem exist in a vehicle that has a history of body repair work, the area of repairs should be scrutinzed very carefully for damages to the wiring, connectors, vacuum hoses or other sub-components that could contribute to component problems. After being satisfied that the concerned area appears trouble free, expand the diagnosis as required.

In the process of controlling the various subsystems, the ECM and BCM continually monitor operating conditions for possible system malfunctions. By comparing system conditions against standard operating limits, certain circuit and component malfunctions can be detected.

A three digit numerical trouble code is stored in the computer memory when a problem is detected by this self diagnostic system. These trouble codes can be displayed by the technician as an aid in the system repairs.

DIAGNOSTICS — BASIC OPERATION

- ENTER DIAGNOSTICS BY SIMULTANEOUSLY PRESSING CCP **"OFF"** AND **"WARMER"** BUTTONS UNTIL ALL DISPLAYS ARE LIT.
- MALFUNCTION CODES ARE DISPLAYED IN THE FOLLOWING SEQUENCE:
  - ..E—DESIGNATES ECM HISTORY CODES
  - .E.E—DESIGNATES ECM CURRENT CODES
  - ..F—DESIGNATES BCM HISTORY CODES
  - .F.F—DESIGNATES BCM CURRENT CODES
- TO PROCEED FROM **SYSTEM READY**, "..7.0", TO THE DESIRED **TEST TYPE**, PRESS AND RELEASE THE INDICATED BUTTON OR PEDAL.
- RETURN TO **SYSTEM READY**, ".7.0", BY CLEARING EITHER ECM OR BCM CODES
- TO CLEAR **ECM** CODES AND RESET DISPLAY TO ".7.0", SIMULTANEOUSLY PRESS CCP **"OFF"** AND **"HI"** BUTTONS UNTIL "E.0.0" IS DISPLAYED.
- TO CLEAR **BCM** CODES AND RESET DISPLAY TO ".7.0", SIMULTANEOUSLY PRESS CCP **"OFF"** AND **"LO"** BUTTONS UNTIL "F.0.0" IS DISPLAYED.
- EXIT DIAGNOSTICS BY PRESSING **"AUTO"** BUTTON.

STATUS LIGHTS

ECM STATUS LIGHT DISPLAY					
LIGHT ON	IN 4TH GEAR	VCC ENABLED	CLOSED THROTTLE	RICH	CLOSED LOOP
LIGHT OFF	NOT IN 4TH GEAR	VCC DISABLED	OPEN THROTTLE	LEAN	OPEN LOOP
INDICATOR	[icon]	[icon]	OFF	ECON	AUTO
FUNCTION	4TH GEAR INPUT	VCC OUTPUT	THROTTLE SWITCH INPUT	OXYGEN SENSOR INPUT	ECM OPERATING MODE

BCM STATUS LIGHT DISPLAY						
FUNCTION	A/C CLUTCH OUTPUT	COMPRESSOR LOW PRESSURE SWITCH INPUT	HEATER WATER VALVE OUTPUT	A/C-DEF MODE DOOR OUTPUT	COOLING FANS STATUS	UP/DOWN MODE DOOR OUTPUT
INDICATOR	OUTSIDE TEMP	°F	°C	LO FAN	AUTO FAN	HI FAN
LIGHT ON	ENERGIZED	OPEN (LOW PRESSURE)	CLOSED (NO WATER FLOW)	A/C	FANS RUNNING	UP
LIGHT OFF	DE-ENERGIZED	CLOSED	OPEN	DEF	FANS OFF	DOWN

ECM SWITCH TESTS

DIAGNOSTIC DISPLAY	CIRCUIT TEST
E.7.1	Brake Switch
E.7.2	Throttle Switch
E.7.4	Park/Neutral Switch
E.7.5	Cruise "ON-OFF"
E.7.6	Cruise "SET/COAST" †
E.7.7	Cruise "RESUME/ACCEL." †
E.7.8	Power Steering Pressure Switch (Engine Running)

† Switch Cruise "ON" Before Testing

ECM OUTPUT CYCLING

- "COOLANT TEMP FAN" Light
- "SERVICE ELECTRICAL SYSTEM" Light
- Air Switch Solenoid
- Air Divert Solenoid
- ISC Motor
- Cruise Vacuum Solenoid & Engage Light*
- Cruise Power Solenoid*
- Canister Purge Solenoid
- EGR Solenoid
- VCC Solenoid
- EFE Relay

**To Activate These Outputs, The Following Must Occur:*
A) Engine Running
B) Cruise Switch "ON"
C) Key OFF And ON Within 2 Seconds Prior To Entering Diagnostics.

KEY

To Select Another Test Press:
"HI" — To Increment
"LO" — To Decrement

ECM DATA
P.1.6
"LO" ↓↑ "HI"
P.0.1

ECM DATA

PARAMETER NUMBER	PARAMETER	DISPLAY RANGE	DISPLAY UNITS
P.0.1	Throttle Position	– 10.0 - 90.0	Degrees
P.0.2	MAP	14 - 109	kPa
P.0.3	Computed BARO	61 - 103	kPa
P.0.4	Coolant Temperature	– 40 - 151	°C
P.0.5	MAT	– 40 - 151	°C
P.0.6	Injector Pulse Width	0 - 99.9	ms
P.0.7	Oxygen Sensor Voltage	0 - 1.14	Volts
P.0.8	Spark Advance	– 30 - 60	Degrees
P.0.9	Ignition Cycle Counter	0 - 50	Key Cycles
P.1.0	Battery Voltage	0 - 25.5	Volts
P.1.1	Engine RPM	0 - 6370	RPM – 10
P.1.2	Car Speed	0 - 255	MPH
P.1.3	Oxygen Sensor Cross Cts.	0 - 255	Number
P.1.4	Fuel Integrator	0 - 255	Counts
P.1.5	VCC Volts	0 - 5.12	Volts
P.1.6	ECM PROM ID	0 - 999	Code •

FIXED SPARK

Exit Diagnostics And Connect Pins A&B Of ALDL Test Connector. Vehicle Will Be In Fixed Spark Mode If At Curb Idle With Transmission In Park.

• PROM ID

PROM ID Code Number Identifies An Individual Calibration And Is Periodically Updated; Refer To Latest Service Publication For Correct ID Number.

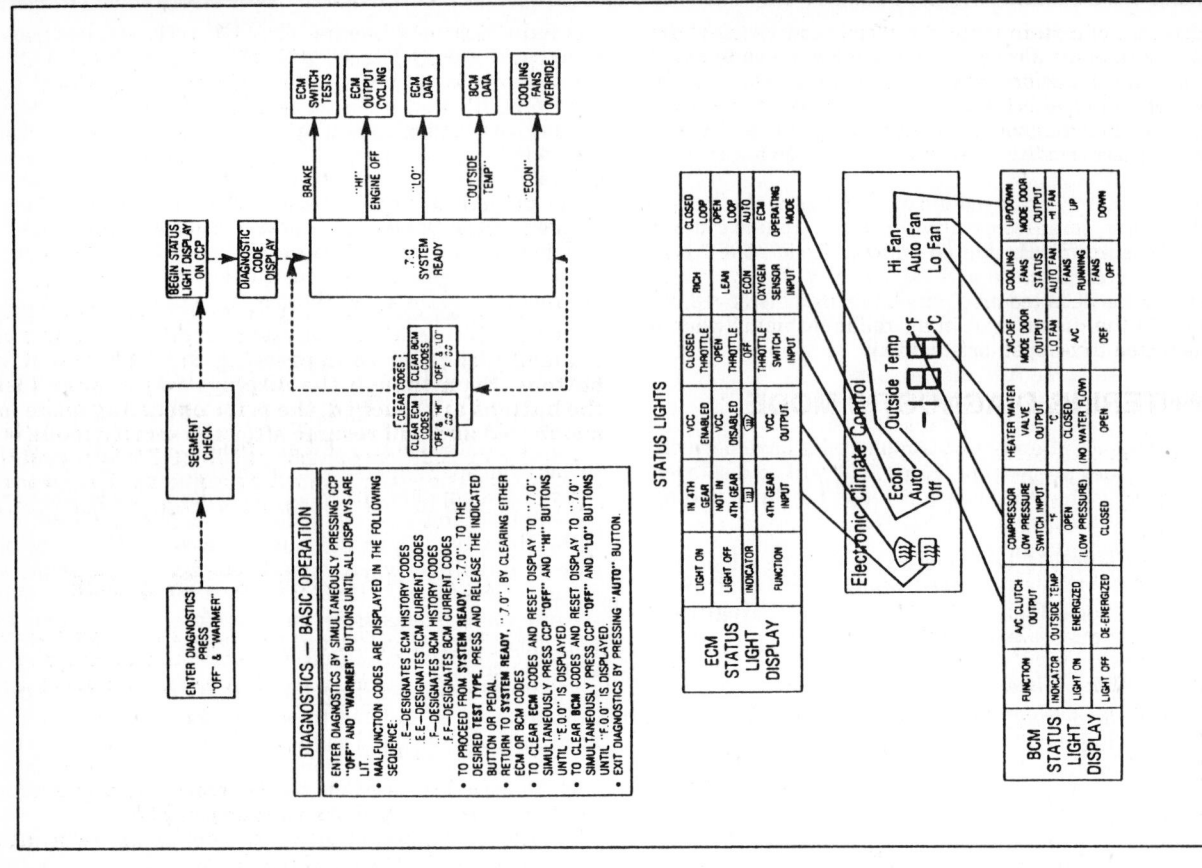

Climate control panel operation for diagnostics on 1986-88 front wheel drive Cadillac models

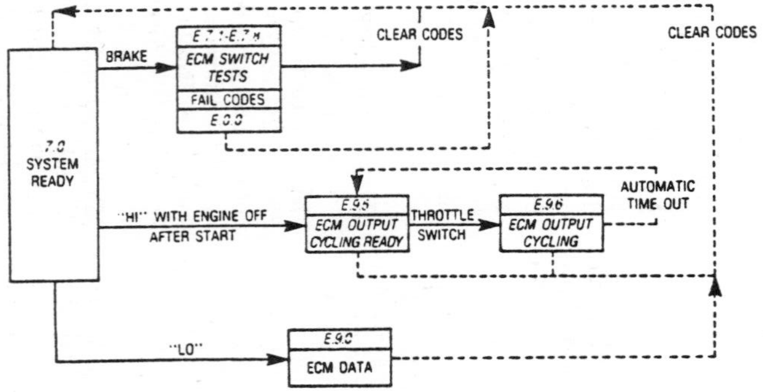

The occurrence of certain system malfunctions require that the vehicle operator be alerted to the problem so as to avoid prolonged vehicle operation under the downgraded system operation, which could affect other systems and components. Computer controlled diagnostic messages and/or telltales will appear under these conditions which indicate that service is required.

If a particular malfunction would result in unacceptable system operation, the self diagnostics will attempt to minimize the effect by taking "FAIL-SOFT" action. "FAIL-SOFT" action refers to any specific attempt by the computer system to compensate for the detected problem. A typical "FAIL-SAFE" action would be the substitution of a fixed input value when a sensor is detected to be open or shorted.

ENTERING DIAGNOSTIC MODE

To enter the diagnostic mode, proceed as follows:
1. Turn the ignition switch to the ON position.
2. Touch the OFF and the WARM buttons on the Climate Control panel simultaneously and hold until a segment check is displayed on the Instrument Panel Cluster (IPC) and Climate Control Driver Information Center, usually around three (3) seconds.

———————— CAUTION ————————
Operating the vehicle in the "SERVICE MODE" for extended time periods (exceeding $\frac{1}{2}$ hour) without the engine operating or without a "Trickle" type charger connected to the battery, can cause the the battery to discharge, resulting in possible relaying of false diagnostic information or causing a no-start condition.

Segment Check

The purpose of illuminating the Instrument Panel Cluster (IPC) and the Climate Control Driver Information Center (CCDIC), is to check that all segments of the vacuum fluorescent displays are working. On the IPC, however, the turnsignal indicators do not light during this check. Diagnosis should not be attempted unless all CCDIC segments appear, as this could lead to misdiagnosis, If any portions or segments of the CCDIC display are inoperative, it must be replaced.

Status Lamps

While in the diagnostic service mode, the mode indicator lamps on the Climate Control Panel of the CCDIC are used to indicate the status of the certain operating modes. The different modes of operation are indicated by the status lamp being turned on or off.

Trouble Code Display

After the service mode is entered, any trouble codes stored in the computer memory will be displayed. ECM codes will be displayed first. If no ECM trouble codes are stored, a "NO ECM CODES" message will be displayed. All ECM codes will be prefixed with a "E". Examples are E013, E014 and etc.

The lowest numbered ECM code will be displayed first, followed by progressively higher numbered codes present in the system. Following the highest ECM code present or the "NO ECM CODES" message, the BCM codes will be displayed. All BCM codes will be prefixed with a letter "B". Examples are B110, B111 and etc.

Progressively higher numbered BCM codes, if present, will be displayed consecutively for two (2) second intervals until the highest code present has been displayed. If no BCM trouble codes are stored, "NO BCM CODES" message will be displayed.

Any BCM and ECM codes displayed will also be accompanied by "CURRENT" or "HISTORY". "HISTORY" indicates the failure was not present the last time the code was tested and "CURRENT" indicates the fault still exists.

At any time during the display of ECM or BCM codes, if the "LO" fan button on the ECC is depressed, the display of codes will be bypassed.

At any time during the display of trouble codes, if the "RESET/RECALL" button on the DIC is depressed, the system will exit the service mode and go back to normal vehicle operation.

NOTE: Upon entering the service mode, the climate control will operate in whatever mode was being commanded just prior to depressing the OFF and WARM buttons. Even though the displays may change just as the buttons are touched, the prior operating mode is remembered and will resume after the service mode is entered. Extended Compressor at Idle (ECI) is not allowed while in the diagnostic mode. This allows observation of system parameters during normal compressor cycles.

SERVICE DIAGNOSTICS MODE

After the trouble codes have been displayed, the service mode can be used to perform several tests on the different systems, one at a time. Upon completion of code display, a specific system may be selected for testing.

Selecting The System

Following the display of the trouble codes, the first available system will be displayed. As an example, ECM.

While selecting the system to test, any of the following actions may be taken to control the display.
1. Pressing the OFF button, the Climate Control Panel (CCP) will stop the system selection process and return the display to the beginning of the trouble code sequence.
2. Pressing the LO fan button on the CCP will display the next available system selection. This allows the display to be stepped through all system choices. The list of systems can be repeated following the display of the last system.
3. Pressing the HI fan button on the CCP will select the system for testing.

Selecting The Test Type

Having selected a system, the first available test type will be displayed, such as "ECM DATA?". While selecting a specific test type, any of the following actions may be taken to control the display.
1. Pressing the OFF button on the CCP will stop the test type selection process and return the display to the next available system selection.
2. Pressing the LO fan button on the CCP will display the next available test type for the selected system. This allows the display to be stepped through all available test type choices. The list of test types can be repeated following the display of the last test type.
3. Pressing the HI fan button on the CCP will select the displayed test type.
4. At this point, the first of several specific tests will appear.

Selecting The Test

Selection of the "DATA", "INPUTS?", "OUTPUTS?" or "OVERRIDE" test types will result in the first available test being displayed.

ECM DATA			
PARAMETER NUMBER	PARAMETER	DISPLAY RANGE	DISPLAY UNITS
ED01	THROTTLE POSITION	−10.0 - 90.0	DEGREES
ED02	MAP	14 - 109	kPa
ED03	COMPUTED BARO	61 - 103	kPa
ED04	COOLANT TEMPERATURE	−40 - 151	°C
ED05	MAT	−40 - 151	°C
ED08	SPARK ADVANCE	0 - 52	DEGREES
ED10	BATTERY VOLTAGE	0 - 25.5	VOLTS
ED11	ENGINE RPM	0 - 637	RPM ÷ 10
ED12	CAR SPEED	0 - 255	MPH
ED19	POWER STEERING SENSOR	0 - 999	kPa ÷ 10
ED26	TRANS. TEMPERATURE SENSOR	−40 - 151	°C
ED30	LEFT INJECTOR PULSE WIDTH	0 - 99.9	mS
ED31	RT. INJECTOR PULSE WIDTH	0 - 99.9	mS
ED32	LEFT OXYGEN SENSOR VOLTAGE	0 - 1.14	VOLTS
ED33	RT. OXYGEN SENSOR VOLTAGE	0 - 1.14	VOLTS
ED34	LEFT OXYGEN SENSOR CROSS COUNTS	0 - 255	NUMBER/SECOND
ED35	RT. OXYGEN SENSOR CROSS COUNTS	0 - 255	NUMBER/SECOND
ED36	LEFT FUEL INTEGRATOR	0 - 255	COUNTS
ED37	RT. FUEL INTEGRATOR	0 - 255	COUNTS
ED70	CRUISE FEEDBACK	0 - 100	%
ED98	IGNITION CYCLE COUNTER	0 - 50	KEY CYCLES
ED99	ECM PROM ID	0 - 999	CODE ●

ECM INPUTS ▼	
INPUT NUMBER	INPUT
EI71	BRAKE SWITCH †
EI72	THROTTLE SWITCH
EI74	PARK/NEUTRAL SWITCH
EI80	THIRD GEAR
EI81	FOURTH GEAR
EI82	CRUISE ENABLE
EI83	CRUISE SET/COAST †
EI84	CRUISE RESUME/ACCELERATE †

† SWITCH CRUISE ON BEFORE TESTING

KEY
TO SELECT ANOTHER TEST WITHIN A PARTICULAR TEST TYPE PRESS: HI – TO INCREMENT LO – TO DECREMENT

● PROM ID CODE NUMBER IDENTIFIES AN INDIVIDUAL CALIBRATION AND IS PERIODICALLY UPDATED. REFER TO LATEST SERVICE PUBLICATION FOR CORRECT ID NUMBER.

ECM OUTPUTS ■	
OUTPUT NUMBER	OUTPUT
EO00	NO OUTPUTS
EO01	CANISTER PURGE SOLENOID
EO02	VCC SOLENOID
EO04	EGR SOLENOID
EO05	AIR SWITCH SOLENOID
EO06	AIR DIVERT SOLENOID
EO07	ISC MOTOR
EO08	CRUISE VENT SOLENOID †
EO09	CRUISE VACUUM SOLENOID †
EO10	2-3 SHIFT SOLENOID
EO11	3-4 SHIFT SOLENOID
EO99	CYCLE ALL OUTPUTS

† SWITCH CRUISE ON BEFORE TESTING

▼"O" = INPUT SAME SINCE DISPLAYED
▼"X" = INPUT CHANGED SINCE DISPLAYED

ECM OVERRIDE**			
OUTPUT OVERRIDE NUMBER	OUTPUT OVERRIDE	OVERRIDE VALUE 0	99
ES00	NO OVERRIDES	—	—
ES01	VCC SOLENOID	OFF	ON
ES02	EGR FLOW	OFF	FULL
ES03	ISC MOTOR CONTROL	RETRACT	ENABLE
ES04	INJECTOR CONTROL	OFF/CYL. 1-8	
ES05	FUEL PUMP RELAY (ENGINE RUNNING)	OFF	ON
ES06	TRANSMISSION SHIFT CONTROL	2ND/3RD/4TH	
ES07	CRUISE FEEDBACK	OFF	FULL

**WARMER INCREASES OVERRIDE VALUE: COOLER DECREASES OVERRIDE VALUE

■ IF "☰☰☰☰" OR "☰☰" MESSAGE APPEARS YOU ARE TRYING TO TEST A DEVICE UNDER THE WRONG CONDITIONS.

DIAGNOSTICS — BASIC OPERATION

- ENTER DIAGNOSTICS BY SIMULTANEOUSLY PRESSING CCP "OFF" AND "WARMER" BUTTONS UNTIL ALL DISPLAYS ARE LIT.
- DIAGNOSTIC CODE LEVEL DISPLAYS ECM CODES FOLLOWED BY BCM CODES FOLLOWED BY LIGHTING CODES.
- TO PROCEED TO THE DESIRED TEST LEVEL PRESS AND RELEASE THE INDICATED BUTTON.
- PRESS "**OFF**" TO RETURN TO THE **NEXT SELECTION** IN THE **PREVIOUS** TEST LEVEL.
- EXIT DIAGNOSTICS BY PRESSING "**RESET**" ON THE DRIVER INFORMATION CENTER.

STATUS LIGHTS

ECM STATUS LIGHT DISPLAY											
LIGHT ON	RICH	RICH	CLOSED LOOP	ENERGIZED	3RD GEAR	4TH & 3RD	4TH W/O 3RD	ENABLED	CLOSED	P/N
LIGHT OFF	LEAN	LEAN	OPEN LOOP	DE-ENERGIZED	NOT IN 3RD OR 4TH GEAR			DISABLED	OPEN	NOT P/N
INDICATOR	OFF	ECON	AUTO	FRONT DEF	°C	°F	°E	REAR DEF.	LOW FAN	NORM FAN
FUNCTION	LEFT OXYGEN SENSOR INPUT	RT. OXYGEN SENSOR INPUT	ECM OPERATING MODE	A/C CLUTCH OUTPUT	4TH & 3RD GEAR INPUT			VCC OUTPUT	THROTTLE SWITCH	PARK/NEUT. SWITCH

BCM STATUS LIGHT DISPLAY							
LIGHT ON	RECIRC	NORM	ENERGIZED	OPEN (LOW PRESSURE)	A/C	SET
LIGHT OFF	OAT	MANUAL	DE-ENERGIZED	CLOSED	DEFROST	RELEASED
INDICATOR	OFF	AUTO	FRONT DEF	REAR DEF.	LOW FAN	HI FAN
FUNCTION	RECIRC./OAT MODE DOOR	NORM/MANUAL SWITCH	A/C CLUTCH OUTPUT	COMPRESSOR LOW PRESSURE	DEF/AC MODE DOOR	PARK BRAKE RELEASE

ECM STATUS LIGHTS ARE DISPLAYED DURING ECM OPTIONS AND BCM STATUS LIGHTS ARE DISPLAYED DURING BCM OPTIONS.

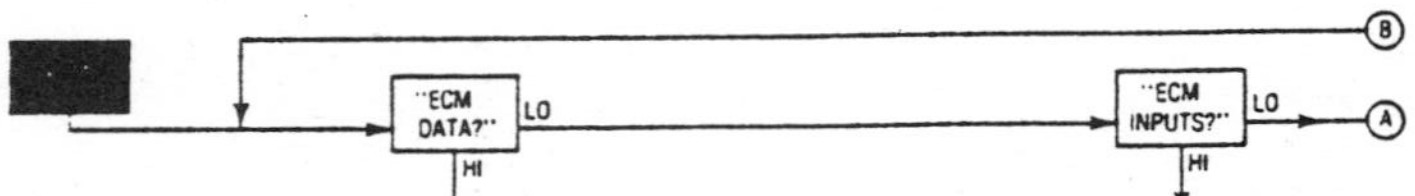

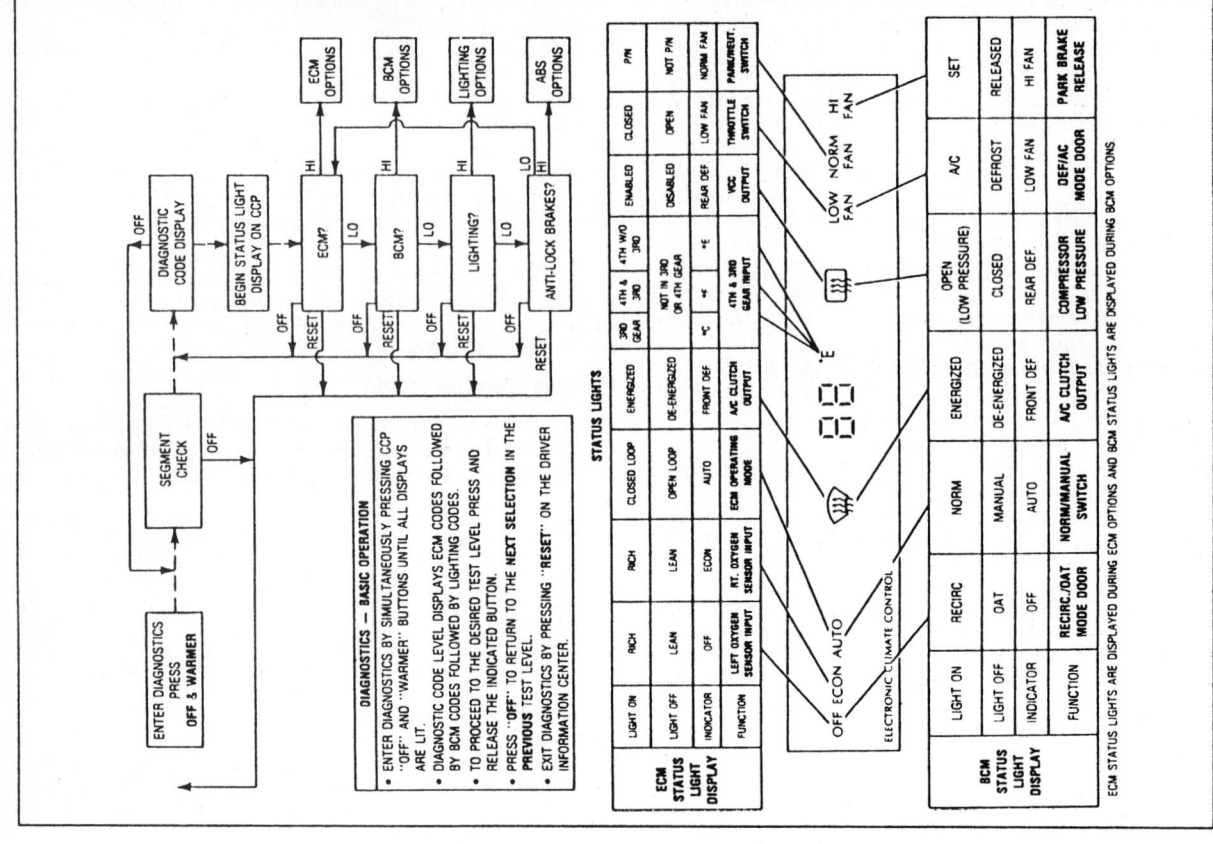

Climate control panel operation for diagnostics on 1988 Allante models

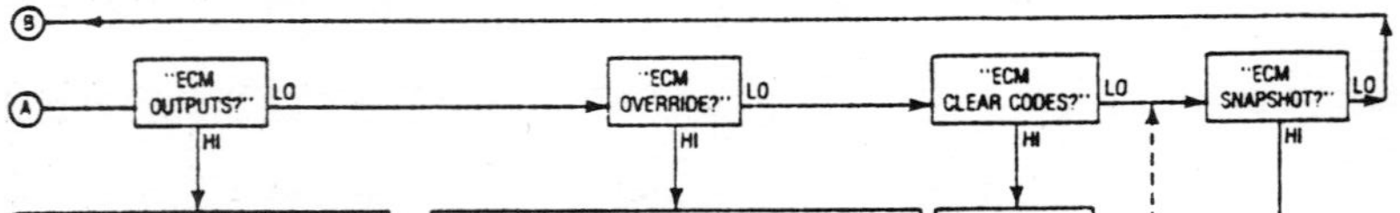

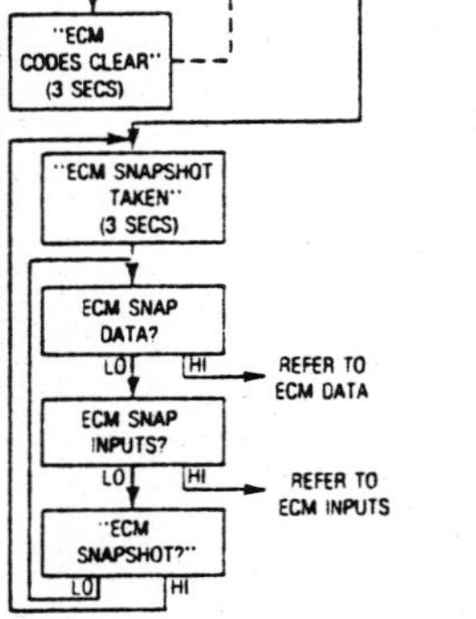

If dashes ever appears, this test is not allowed with the engine running. Turn the engine off and try again. Four characters of the display will contain a test code to identify the selection. The first two characters are letters which identify the system and test type, such as "ED" for ECM DATA and the last two characters are letters which identify the test, such as ED01 for Throttle Position. While selecting a specific test, any of the following actions may be taken to control the display.

1. Pressing the OFF button on the CCP will stop the test selection process and return the display to the next available test type for the selected system.

2. Pressing the LO fan button on the CCP will display the next smaller test number for the selected test type. If this button is pressed with the lowest test number displayed, the highest test number will then appear.

3. Pressing the HI fan button on the CCP will display the next larger test number for the selected test type. If this pad is touched with the highest test number displayed, the lowest test number will then appear.

Upon selecting an "OVERRIDE" test function, current operation will be represented as a percentage of its full range and this value will be displayed on the ECC panel. This display will alternate between "—" and the normal program value. This alternating display is a reminder that the function is not currently being overridden.

Pressing the WARM or COOL buttons on the ECC panel begins the override at which time the display will no longer alternate to "—". Pressing the WARM button increases the value while the COOL button decreases the value. Normal program control can be resumed in one of three ways.

1. Selection of another override test will cancel the current override.

2. Selection of another system (ECM, BCM or IPC) will cancel the current overide.

3. Overriding the value beyond either extreme (0 or 99) will display "—" momentarily and then jump to the opposite extreme. If the button is released while "—" is displayed, normal program control will resume and the display will again alternate.

The override test type is unique in that any other test type within the selected system may be active at the same time. After selecting an override test, pressing the OFF button will allow selection of another test type, "DATA", "INPUTS" or "OUTPUTS". The ECC panel will continue to display the selected override. By selecting another test type and test, while at the same time pressing the WARM or COOL button, it is possible to monitor the effects of the override on different vehicle parameters.

Selecting "CLEAR CODES?"

Selection of the "CLEAR CODES?" test type will result in the message "CODES CLEAR" being displayed along with the selected system name. This message will appear for three (3) seconds to indicate that all stored trouble codes have been erased from that system's memory. After three (3) seconds, the display will automatically return to the next available test type for the selected system

Selecting "SNAPSHOT?"

Selection of "SNAPSHOT?" test type will result in the message "SNAPSHOT TAKEN" being displayed with the selected system name proceeding it. This message will appear for three (3) seconds to indicate that all system data and inputs have been stored in memory. After three (3) seconds, the display will automatically proceed to the first available snapshot test type, for example "SNAP DATA". While selecting a snapshot test type, any of the following actions can be taken to control the display;

1. Pressing the OFF button on the CCP will stop the test type selection process and return the display to the next available system selection.

2. Pressing the LO button on the CCP will display the next available snapshot test type.

3. This allows the display to be stepped through all available choices. This list of snapshot test types can be repeated following the display of the last choice.

4. Pressing the HI button with "SNAP DATA?" or "SNAP INPUT?" displayed, will select that test type. At this point, the display is controlled as it would be for non-snapshot data and inputs displays. However, all values and status information represents memorized vehicle conditions.

5. Pressing the HI button on the CCP with "SNAPSHOT?" displayed will again display the "SNAPSHOT TAKEN" message to indicate that new information has been stored in the memory. Access to this information is obtained the same as previously outlined.

Exiting Service Mode

To exit the service mode, press the RESET/RECALL button on the DIC or turn the ignition switch to the OFF position. Trouble codes are not erased when this is done.

1986–88 Buick Riveria Electronic Engine Control System

The Electronic Control Module (ECM) is the controlling unit of the electronic engine control system. Though it communicates with the other vehicle computers, it alone has the primary responsibility of maintaining proper emissions while delivering optimum driveability characteristics.

The ECM monitors inputs from the engine as well as other vehicle sensors. It then correlates this information with data stored in the PROM. After all the information is evaluated, the ECM caluclates the necessary changes to compensate for all driving conditions.

The ECM is able to detect malfunctions in most of the systems it monitors. It will turn on the SERVICE ENGINE SOON indicator lamp, set a trouble code, or both if it detects a fault.

NOTE: Always repair all code malfunctions before any driveability or emission problem repairs are attempted. If more than one code is set, always repair the lowest numbered code first.

The ECM trouble codes are displayed on the Cathode Ray Tube (CRT) when in the diagnostic mode. Other service related information that can be displayed are as follows:

1. ECM data.
2. ECM Discrete inputs.
3. ECM output cycling.
4. ECM trouble codes

All displays except for the output mode cycling can be viewed under the following conditions:

1. The ignition switch in the ON position.
2. The engine NOT operating.
3. The engine at idle.
4. The vehicle being driven.

The output mode cycling function is only operational with the ignition switch in the ON position and the engine NOT operating.

Accessing The BCM Self Diagnostics

In order to access and control the BCM self-diagnostic features, two additional electronic components are necessary, the CRTC and the CRT picture tube. As part of the CRT's SERVICE MODE page, a 22 character display area is used to display diagnostic information. When a malfunction is sensed by the computer system, one of the driver warning messages is displayed on the CRT under the "DIAGNOSTIC" category. When the Service Mode is entered, the various BCM, ECM, or IPC parameters, fault codes, inputs, outputs as well as override com-

ECM OUTPUT CYCLING

Output Number	Description	Message	Status
EO00	No Outputs	None	
EO01	Canister Purge Solenoid	Purge	HI/LO
EO02	TCC Solenoid	TCC	HI/LO
EO04	EGR Solenoid	EGR	HI/LO
EO07	IAC Motor Set	IAC	Pintle Fully Extended*
EO08	A/C Clutch	A/C Clutch	HI/LO
EO09	Coolant Fan Relay	Fan	HI/LO

*Minimum air adjustment can be made when pintle is fully extended.

ECM DIAGNOSTIC CODES

CODE	DESCRIPTION	COMMENTS
E013	OpenOxygen Sensor Circuit *Canister Purge	A – B
E014	Coolant Sensor High Temp. Indicated	A – B
E015	Coolant Sensor Low Temp. Indicated	A
E016	System Voltage Out of Range *All Solenoids	A
E021	TPS Signal Voltage High *TCC	A
E022	TPS Signal Voltage Low *TCC	A
E024	Vehicle Speed Sensor Circuit Failure *TCC	A
E029	Fourth Gear Switch Circuit Open	A
E032	EGR Vacuum Control System Fault	A
E033	MAF Sensor Signal Frequency High	A
E034	MAF Sensor Signal Frequency Low	A
E037	MAT Sensor High Temperature Indicated	A
E038	MAT Sensor Low Temperature Indicated	A
E040	Power Steering Pressure Switch Circuit Open - *A/C Clutch and Cruise	A
E041	CAM Sensor Circuit Failure (C3I Module to ECM)	A – D
E042	C3I-EST or Bypass Circuit Failure	A – D
E043	ESC System Failure	A – C
E044	Lean Exhaust Indication	A – C
E045	Rich Exhaust Indication	A
E047	ECM-BCM Data *A/C Clutch and Cruise	A – D – E
E051	ECM PROM Error	A
E052	Calpak Error	A
E055	ECM Error	A

DIAGNOSTIC CODE COMMENTS

"A"	"Service Engine Soon" Message Displayed
"B"	Forces Cooling Fans "ON"
"C"	Forces Open Loop Operation
"D"	Causes System to Operate in Bypass Spark Mode (Module Timing)
"E"	Causes System to Operate in Back up Fuel Mode

*These functions are disengaged while specified malfunctions remains current.

ECM DATA

Data Number	Description	Message	Range	Units
ED01	Throttle Position	TPS	0 – 5100	mv
ED04	Coolant Temperature	COOLANT	–40 – 306/152	°F/°C*
ED05	Air Temperature	MAT	–40 – 306/152	°F/°C*
ED06	Injector Pulse Width	MS INJ PW	0 – 1002	ms
ED07	Oxygen Sensor Voltage	OXY SENSOR	0 – 1128	mv
ED08	Spark Avance	DEG SPARK	0 – 70	Degrees
ED09	Transaxle Convertor Clutch	TCC SOL	0 – 1	0 = OFF 1 = ON
ED10	Battery Voltage	BATT VOLTS	0 – 25.5	VOLTS
ED11	Engine RPM	RPM	0 – 6375	RPM
ED12	Vehicle Speed	MPH	0 – 159	MPH
ED15	Closed or Open Loop	OPER MODE	0 – 1	0 = OL 1 = CL
ED16	ESC (Knock Retard)	ESC	0 – 20	Degrees
ED17	OLDPA3 (Knock Signal)	OLD PA3	0 – 255	Counts
ED18	Cross Counts 02	CROSS CTS	0 – 255	Counts
ED19	Fuel Integrator	INT FUEL	0 – 255	Counts
ED20	Block Learn Memory (Fuel)	BLM FUEL	0 – 255	Counts
ED21	Air Flow	AIR FLOW	0 – 255	Grams Per Sec.
ED22	Idle Air Control	IAC MOTOR	0 – 255	Steps
ED23	LV8 (Engine Load)	LV8	0 – 255	Counts
ED98	Ignition Cycle Counter	IGN CYCLES	0 – 50	Key Cycles
ED99	ECM PROM ID	PROM ID	0 – 9999	CODE**

*F or °C selectable with the E/M button on the Left Switch Assy.

**PROM ID code number identifies an individual OEM ECM and PROM (last digits).If a service package # has been installed, the displayed value represents the last digits of the service package # (not stamped on PROM). Refer to the latest Service Publications for the correct ID number.

ECM DISCRETE INPUTS

Input Number	Description	Message	Status	Ign. "ON"* Display
EI60	EVRV EGR Vac. Switch	EVRV	HI/LO	HI
EI74	Park/Neutral Switch	P/N	HI/LO	LO
EI78	Power Steering Press. Switch	PS	HI/LO	HI
EI82	Fourth Gear Switch	4TH	HI/LO	LO

* In park, engine not running.

In the Input mode, four switches can be monitored relative to their "HI" and "LO" status.

Trouble code interpretation on Riviera and Toronado models

mands and clearing code capability are displayed when commanded through the CRT.

The CRT becomes the device to enter the diagnostics and access the Service Diagnostic routines. The CRTC is the device which controls the display on the CRT and interprets the switches touched on the CRT and passes this information along to the BCM. This communication process allows the BCM to transfer any of its available diagnostic information to the CRT for display during SERVICE MODE.

By touching the appropriate pads on the CRT, data messages can be sent to the BCM from the CRTC over the data line, requesting the specific diagnostic feature required.

SERVICE ENGINE SOON INDICATOR

The "SERVICE ENGINE SOON" indicator lamp warns that an engine problem has occurred and the vehicle needs service. With the ignition switch in the RUN position, but the engine not operating, the lamp will turn on as a bulb test. When the engine is started, the lamp should turn off. If the Electronic Control Module (ECM) detects an engine problem, the amber "SERVICE ENGINE SOON" lamp is turned on. If the lamp turns off in approximately ten seconds, the engine problem has disappeared, but the ECM stores a trouble code. The trouble code will stay in the ECM memory until the battery is disconnected from the ECM or until the memory is cleared, using the service mode.

CRT TESTER

A cathode ray tube tester (Kent Moore J–34914 or its equivalent) is available to help isolate faults that may occur during the CRT operation. Substituting the tool in place of the CRTC will verify the integrity of the picture tube and switching the circuitry that make up the CRT. By connecting the tester directly to the CRT, the CRT can be checked as a unit. Connecting the tester to the vehicle harness, after the CRT has been independently checked out, will determine if the fault is in the wiring or the CRTC. The tester will run automatic tests and then allow individual switch tests.

Should the service facility obtain this type of tester to be used with the CRT system, instructions on its use will be included with the tester. Follow the manufacturer's recommended operating procedures to obtain the tester's maximum potential.

ALDL CONNECTOR

The Assembly Line Diagnostic Link (ALDL) is a diagnostic connector located in the passenger compartment. Along with the assembly plant usage for proper engine operation before leaving the plant, it may also be used to access the SERIAL DATA circuit, using a service diagnostic tool, specifically designed and calibrated for that purpose.

The ALDL cover contains a jumper, which is part of the redundant SERIAL DATA CKT "800" and if removed for any reason, must be replaced before returning the vehicle to service. The missing ALDL cover could create a loss of SERIAL DATA communication if CKT "800" was already open elsewhere. This would result in the message "ELECTRICAL PROBLEM", accompanied by a "SERIAL DATA" loss code and potential driveability complaints.

Service Precautions

The computer system is designed to withstand normal current draws associated with vehicle operation. However, care must be taken to avoid overloading any of these circuits. In testing for open or short circuits, do not ground or apply voltage to any of the circuits unless instructed to do so by the diagnosis procedures. These circuits should only be tested by using a High Impedance Mulimeter (Kent Moore J–29125A or its equivalent), if the tester remains connected to one of the computers. Power should never be applied or removed to one of the computers

with the key in the ON position. Before removing or connecting battery cables, fuses or connectors, always turn the ignition switch to the OFF position.

Trouble Codes

In the process of controlling the various subsystems, the ECM and the BCM continually monitor operating conditions for possible malfunctions. By comparing systems conditions against standard operating limits, certain circuit and component malfunctions can be detected. A three digit numerical trouble code is stored in the computer memory when a problem is detected by this self-diagnostic system. These trouble codes can later be displayed by the service technician as an aid in system repair.

The occurrence of certain system malfunctions require that the vehicle operator be alerted to the problem so as to avoid prolonged operation of the vehicle under degrading system operations. The computer controlled diagnostic messages and/or telltales will appear under these conditions which indicate that service or repairs are required.

If a particular malfunction would result in unacceptable system operation, the self-diagnostics will attempt to minimize the effect by taking a "FAIL–SOFT" action. "FAIL–SOFT" action refers to any specific attempt by the computer system to compensate for the detected problem. A typical "FAIL–SOFT" action would be the substitution of a fixed input value when a sensor is detected to have an open or shorted circuit.

ENTERING DIAGNOSTIC SERVICE MODE

To enter the diagnostic service mode, proceed as follows:
1. Turn the ignition switch to the ON position.
2. Touch the OFF and the WARM pads on the CRT's climate control page, simultaneously and hold until a double "BEEP" is heard or a page entitled "SERVICE MODE" appears on the CRT.

NOTE: Operating the vehicle in the SERVICE MODE for an extended time period without the engine operating or without a trickle battery charger attached to the battery, can cause the battery to become discharged and possibly relate false diagnostic information or cause an engine no-start. Avoid lengthy (over $\frac{1}{2}$ hour) SERVICE MODE operation.

Trouble Code Display

After the SERVICE MODE is entered, any trouble codes stored in the computer memory will be displayed. ECM codes will be displayed first. If no ECM codes are stored, the CRT will display a "NO ECM CODES" message for approximately two seconds. All ECM codes will be prefixed with an "E" (Example – EO13, EO23, etc.).

The lowest numbered ECM code will be displayed first, followed by progressively higher numbered codes present. Codes will be displayed consecutively for two second intervals until the highest code present has been displayed. When all ECM codes have been displayed, BCM codes will be displayed. Following the highest ECM code present or the "NO ECM CODES" message, the lowest numbered BCM code will be displayed for approximately two seconds. BCM codes displayed will also be accompanied by "CURRENT" or "HISTORY". "HISTORY" indicates the failure was not present the last time the code was tested and "CURRENT" indicates the fault still exists. Since the ECM is not capable of making this determination, these messages do not appear when the ECM codes are being displayed.

All BCM codes will be prefixed with the letter "B" (Example – B110 and etc.). Progressively higher numbered BCM codes, if present, will be displayed for approximately two second intervals until the highest code present has been displayed. If no BCM trouble codes are stored, "NO BCM CODES" message will be displayed. At any time during the display of the ECM or BCM codes, if the "NO" pad is touched, the display will bypass the codes. At any time during the display of trouble codes, if the "EXIT" pad is touched, the CRT will exit the "SERVICE MODE" and go back to normal vehicle operation.

Climate Control Operation

Upon entering the service mode, the climate control will operate in whatever setting was being commanded just prior to depressing the OFF and WARM pads. Even though the display may change just as the pads are touched, the prior operating setting is remembered and will resume after the service mode is entered.

During the service mode, the climate control can be operated the same as normally by touching the climate control border pad and calling up climate control page. To get back to service mode page, simply touch the border pad marked "DIAGNOSTICS". This will take the system back to the exact same spot in the service mode as what it was before the climate control border pad was touched. The climate control and the diagnostic border pads are the only two border pads that will operate while in the service mode.

Operating The Service Mode

After trouble codes have been displayed, the service mode can be used to perform several tests on different systems one at a time. Upon completion of code display, a specific system may be selected for testing or a segment check can be performed.

SELECTING THE SYSTEM

Following the display of trouble codes, the first available system will be displayed (i.e. ECM?). While selecting a system to test, any of the following actions may be taken to control the display.

1. Touching the "EXIT" pad will stop the system selection process and return the display to the beginning of the trouble code sequence.

2. Touching the "NO" pad will display the next available system selection. This allows the display to be stepped through all systems choices. This list of systems can be repeated following the display of the last system.

3. Touching the "YES" pad will select the displayed system for testing. At this point, the first available test type will appear with the selected name above it.

SELECTING THE TEST TYPE

Having selected a system, the first available test type will be displayed (i.e. ECM data?). While selecting a specific test type, any of the following actions may be taken to control the display.

1. Touching the "EXIT" pad will stop the test type selection process and return the display to the next available system selection.

2. Touching the "NO" pad will display the next available test type for the selected system. This allows the display to be stepped through all available test type choices. The list of test types can be repeated following the display of the last test type.

3. Touching the "YES" pad will select the displayed test type. At this point, the display will either indicate the at the selected test type is in progress or the first of several specific tests will appear. If "NO DEVICES" is displayed, no tests are available.

SELECTING THE TEST

Selection of the "DATA", "INPUTS?", "OUTPUTS?" or "OVERRIDE?" test types will result in the first available test being displayed. If a "SELECT ERR" message ever appears, this test is not allowed with the engine operating. Turn the engine off and try again. Four characters of the display will contain a test code to identify the selection. The first two charac-

ters are letters which identify the system and the test type (i.e. ED01 for throttle position). While selecting a specific test, any of the following actions may be taken to control the display.

1. Touching the "EXIT" pad will stop the test selection process and return the display to the next available test type for the selected system.

2. Touching the "NO" pad will display the next smaller test number for the selected test type. If this pad is touched with the lowest test number displayed, the highest test number will then appear.

3. Touching the "YES" pad will display the next larger test number for the selected test type. If this pad is touched with the highest test number displayed, the lowest test number will then appear.

SELECTING "CODE RESET?"

Selection of "CODE RESET?" test type will result in the message "CODES CLEAR" being displayed with the selected system name above it after the "YES" pad has been touched. This message will appear for three seconds to indicate all stored trouble codes have been erased from that system's memory. After three seconds, the display will automatically return to the next available test type for the selected system

IPC SEGMENT CHECK

Whenever the key is on and the vehicle is in the PARK position, pressing the "TEST" button on the instrument panel cluster, will cause the IPC to sequentially illuminate and blank all segments and telltales in the cluster. This is helpful in determining if any bulbs or segments or the cluster's vacuum fluorescent display are out or always on. To provide more time to study the various segments, whenever in the SERVICE MODE and not in the middle of running a test, such as when the CRT displays "ECM?", if the "TEST" button on the ICP is depressed, the segment check will run ten times slower than when not in the SERVICE MODE.

Exiting Service Mode

To exit the service mode, repeatedly touch the "EXIT" pad until the SERVICE MODE page disappears or turn the ignition switch to the OFF position. Trouble codes are not erased when this is done.

Input Displays

Input displays are operated as outlined under the heading of Service Diagnostic Mode. When troubleshooting a malfunction, the ECM, BCM or IPC input display can be used to determine if the switched inputs can be used to determine if the switched inputs can be properly interpreted. When one of the various input tests is selected, the state of that device is displayed as "HI" or "LO". In general, the "HI" and "LO" refer to the input terminal voltage for that circuit. The display also indicates if the input changed state so that the technician could activate or deactivate any listed device and return to the display to see if it changed state. If a change of state occurred, an "X" will appear next to the "HI/LO" indicator, otherwise, an "O" will remain displayed. The "X" will only appear once per selected input, although the "HI/LO" indication will continue to change as the input changes. Some tests are momentary and the "X" can be used as an indication of a change. The following is a list of the ECM, BCM and IPC inputs:

1986–88 Oldsmobile Toronado Electronic Engine Control System

The Electronic Control Module (ECM) is the controlling unit of the Electronic Engine Control System. Though it communicates with the other vehicle computers, it alone has the primary responsibility of maintaining proper emissions while delivering optimum driveability characteristics.

The ECM monitors inputs from the engine as well as other vehicle sensors. It then correlates this information with data stored in the PROM. After all the information is evaluated, the ECM calculates the necessary changes to compensate for all driving conditions. The ECM is able to detect malfunctions in most of the systems it monitors. It will turn on the SERVICE ENGINE SOON indicator lamp, set a trouble code, or both if it detects a fault.

NOTE: Always repair all code malfunctions before any driveability or emission problem repairs are attempted. If more than one code is set, always repair the lowest numbered code first.

The ECM trouble codes are displayed on the Instrument Panel Cluster (IPC) when in the diagnostic mode. Other service related information that can be displayed are as follows:
1. ECM data.
2. ECM Discrete inputs.
3. ECM output cycling.
4. ECM trouble codes

All displays, except for the output mode cycling, can be viewed under the following conditions:
1. The ignition switch in the ON position.
2. The engine NOT operating.
3. The engine at idle.
4. The vehicle being driven.

The output mode cycling function is only operational with the ignition ON and the engine NOT operating. While in the ECM Data mode, the display will show twenty-one data messages and the data value of each. This information assists in tracing down emission and driveability problems, since the displays can be viewed while the vehicle is being driven.

Body Computer Module (BCM)

The Body Computer Module (BCM) is located behind the glove box. The BCM has an internal microprocessor, which is the center for communication with all other components in the system. All sensors and switches are monitored by the BCM or one of the five other major components that complete the computer system. The five components are as follows:
1. Electronic Control Module (ECM)
2. Instrument Panel Cluster (IPC)
3. Electronic Climate Control Panel (ECC)
4. Programmer/Heating/Ventilation/AC
5. Chime/Voice module

Between the BCM and the other five major components of the computer system, a communication process has been incorporated which allows the devices to share information and thereby provide additional control capabilities.

In order to access and control the self diagnostic features, two additional electronic components are necessary, the Instrument Panel Cluster (IPC) and the Electronic Climate Control panel (ECC). As part of the IPC, a 20 character display area called the Information Center is used. During normal engine operation, this area displays "Toronado" or is a Tachometer, displaying the engine rpm. When a malfunction is sensed by the ECM/BCM, one of the driver warning messages is displayed in this area. When the diagnostic mode is entered, the various BCM or ECM diagnostic codes are displayed. In addition to the codes of the ECM/BCM data parameters, discrete inputs and outputs, as well as output override messages are also displayed when commanded for, through the ECC.

The Electronic Comfort Control Panel (ECC) provides the controls for the heating and air conditioning systems. It also becomes the controller to enter the diagnostics and access the BCM self-diagnostics. This communication process allows the BCM to transfer any of its available diagnostic information top the instrument panel for display during service. By pressing the appropriate buttons on the ECC, data messages can be sent to the BCM over the serial data line requesting the specific diagnostic features desired. When in the Override mode of the BCM diagnostics, the amount of Override is displayed at the ECC where the outside and set temperatures are normally displayed.

Service Precautions

The computer control system is designed to withstand normal current draws associated with vehicle operation. However, care must be taken to avoid overloading any of these circuits. In testing for open or short circuits, do not ground or apply voltage to any of the circuits, unless instructed to do so by diagnostic procedures. These circuits should only be tested using a high impedance Multimeter, such as Kent Moore tool Number J–29125A or its equivalent, if they are to remain connected to any of the computers. Power should never be remove or applied to one of the computers with the key in the ON position. Before removing or connecting battery cables, fuses or connectors, always turn the ignition to the LOCK position.

A systematic approach is needed to begin the vehicle's self diagnostic capabilities along with an understanding of the basic operation and procedures, necessary to determine external or internal malfunctions of the computer operated circuits and systems. A systematic beginning is to determine if the "SERVICE ENGINE SOON" telltale lamp is illuminated when the ignition key is in the ON position and the engine not operating. If the lamp is off, a problem could be in the power supply circuits of the systems.

If the lamp is illuminated, can the "SERVICE MODE" be accessed? If the Electronic Climate Control panel is not operating, the self diagnostics cannot be used.

Is there a trouble code displayed? If a trouble code is identified, using the self diagnostics mode, a malfunction or problem has been detected by the system.

Trouble Codes

In the process of controlling the various subsystems, the ECM and BCM continually monitor operating conditions for possible system malfunctions. By comparing system conditions against standard operating limits, certain circuit and component malfunctions can be detected. A three digit numerical TROUBLE CODE is stored in the computer memory when a problem is detected by this self diagnostic system. These trouble codes can be displayed by the technician as an aid in the system repairs.

The occurrence of certain system malfunctions require that the vehicle operator be alerted to the problem so as to avoid prolonged vehicle operation under the downgraded system operation, which could affect other systems and components. Computer Controlled diagnostic messages and/or telltales will appear under these conditions which indicate that service is required.

If a particular malfunction would result in unacceptable system operation, the self diagnostics will attempt to minimize the effect by taking "FAIL–SOFT" action. "FAIL–SOFT" action refers to any specific attempt by the computer system to compensate for the detected problem. A typical "FAIL–SAFE" action would be the substitution of a fixed input value when a sensor is detected to be open or shorted.

ENTERING DIAGNOSTIC MODE

To enter the diagnostic mode, proceed as follows:
1. Turn the ignition switch to the ON position.
2. Touch the OFF and the WARM buttons on the Electronic Climate Control (ECC) panel simultaneously and hold until a segment check is displayed on the Instrument Panel Cluster (IPC) and Electronic Climate Control (ECC), usually around three (3) seconds.

— CAUTION —

Operating the vehicle in the service mode for extended time periods (exceeding $\frac{1}{2}$ hour) without the engine operating or without a trickle-type charger connected to the battery, can cause the the battery to discharge, resulting in possible relaying of false diagnostic information or causing a no-start condition.

Trouble Code Display

After the service mode is entered, any trouble codes stored in the computer memory will be displayed. ECM codes will be displayed first. If no ECM trouble codes are stored, the IPC will display a "NO ECM CODES" message for approximately two (2) seconds. All ECM codes will be prefixed with a "E". Examples are E013, E014 and etc. The lowest numbered ECM code will be displayed first, followed by progressively higher numbered codes present in the system.

The codes will be displayed consecutively for two (2) second intervals until the highest code present has been displayed. When all ECM codes have been displayed, the BCM codes will be displayed. The lowest numbered BCM code will be displayed for appropriately two (2) seconds. BCM codes accompanied by "CURRENT" indicates the fault still exits. Since the ECM is not capable of making this determination, this message does not appear when the ECM codes are being displayed. All BCM codes will be prefixed with a letter "B". Examples are B110, B111 and etc.

Progressively higher numbered BCM codes, if present, will be displayed consecutively for two (2) second intervals until the highest code present has been displayed. If no BCM trouble codes are stored, "NO BCM CODES" message will be displayed. At any time during the display of ECM or BCM codes, if the "LO" fan button on the ECC is depressed, the display of codes will be bypassed. At any time during the display of trouble codes, if the "BI–LEV" button is depressed, the BCM will exit the service mode and go back to normal vehicle operation.

NOTE: Upon entering the service mode, the climate control will operate in whatever mode was being commanded just prior to depressing the OFF and WARM buttons. Even though the displays may change just as the buttons are touched, the prior operating mode is remembered and will resume after the service mode is entered.

Operation of the Service Diagnostics

After the trouble codes have been displayed, the SERVICE MODE can be used to perform several tests on the different systems, one at a time. Upon completion of code display, a specific system may be selected for testing.

SELECTING THE SYSTEM

Following the display of the trouble codes, the first available system will be displayed. As an example, ECM. While selecting the system to test, any of the following actions may be taken to control the display.

1. Pressing the OFF button will stop the system selection process and return the display to the beginning of the trouble code sequence.
2. Pressing the LO fan button will display the next available system selection. This allows the display to be stepped through all system choices. The list of systems can be repeated following the display of the last system.
3. Pressing the HI fan button will select the displaced system for testing. At this point, the first available test type will appear with the selected system name above it.
4. Pressing the BI–LEV button will exit diagnostics and return to normal IPC and ECC operation.

SELECTING THE TEST TYPE

Having selected a system, the first available test type will be displayed, such as "ECM DATA?". While selecting a specific test type, any of the following actions may be taken to control the display.

1. Pressing the OFF button will stop the test type selection process and return the display to the next available system selection.
2. Pressing the LO fan button will display the next available test type for the selected system. This allows the display to be stepped through all available test type choices. The list of test types can be repeated following the display of the last test type.
3. Pressing the HI fan button will select the displayed test type. At this point, the display will either indicate that the selected test type is in progress or the first of several specific tests will appear.
4. Pressing the BI–LEVEL button will exit the diagnostics.

SELECTING THE TEST

Selection of the "DATA", "INPUTS?", or "OUTPUTS?" test types will result in the first available test being displayed. If a "EEEE" message ever appears, this test is not allowed with the engine running. Turn the engine off and try again. The last four characters of the display will contain a test code to identify the selection. The first two characters are letters which identify the system and test type, such as "ED" for ECM DATA. and the last two characters are letters which identify the test, such as ED01 for Throttle Position. While selecting a specific test, any of the following actions may be taken to control the display.

1. Pressing the OFF button will stop the test selection process and return the display to the next available test type for the selected system.
2. Pressing the LO fan button will display the next smaller test number for the selected test type. If this button is touched with the lowest test number displayed, the highest test number will then appear.
3. Pressing the HI fan button will display the next larger test number for the selected test type. If this pad is touched with the highest test number displayed, the lowest test number will then appear.

Upon selecting an "OVERRIDE" test function, current operation will be represented as a percentage of its full range and this value will be displayed on the ECC panel. This display will alternate between "—" and the normal program value. This alternating display is a reminder that the function is not currently being overridden.

Pressing the WARM or COOL buttons on the ECC panel begins the override at which time the display will no longer alternate to "—". Pressing the WARM button increases the value while the COOL button decreases the value. Normal program control can be resumed in one of three ways.

1. Selection of another override test will cancel the current override.
2. Selection of another system (ECM, BCM or IPC) will cancel the current overide.
3. Overriding the value beyond either extreme (0 or 99) will display "—" momentarily and then jump to the opposite extreme. If the button is released while "—" is displayed, normal program control will resume and the display will again alternate.

The override test type is unique in that any other test type within the selected system may be active at the same time. After selecting an override test, pressing the OFF button will allow selection of another test type, "DATA", "INPUTS" or "OUTPUTS". The ECC panel will continue to display the selected override. By selecting another test type and test, while at the same time pressing the WARM or COOL button, it is possible to monitor the effects of the override on different vehicle parameters.

SELECTING CLEAR CODES

Selecting reset codes will result in the message "CLEAR ECM

CODES?" or "CLEAR BCM CODES?" depending which system was being tested. At this point, the following action may be taken:

1. Pressing the OFF button will stop the test selection process and return the display to the next available test type for the selected system.

2. Pressing the LO fan button will display the next test type available.

3. Pressing the HI fan button will select "CLEAR CODES". A message "ECM CODES CLEARED" or "BCM CODES CLEARED" will appear to indicate those codes have been cleared from memory.

4. Pressing BI–LEV will exit diagnostics.

IPC SEGMENT CHECK

Whenever the key is on, pressing the SYSTEM MONITOR button on the left switch assembly will cause the IPC and the ECC to sequentially illuminate and darken all segments and telltales in the clusters. This is helpful in determining if any bulbs or segments or the clusters vacuum fluorescent display are out or always on. To provide more time to study the various segments, whenever service diagnostics are entered, a total illumination of all segments and bulbs on the IPC and ECC will also occur.

Exiting Service Mode

To exit the service mode, press the BI–LEV button. Trouble codes are not erased when this is done. Any mode button will exit diagnostics, however, BI–LEV was chosen for procedural consistency.

Battery Electrical Drain

If the vehicle is equipped with both the Body Control Module (BCM) and the Electronic Control Module (ECM) and exhibits a low or dead battery after being parked overnight, or the battery goes down over a period of two or three days, the electrical system should be checked for excessive electrical drain.

General Motors Computer Command Control (CCC) System

The ECM is equipped with a self-diagnostic capability which can detect system failures and aids the technician by identifying the fault via a trouble code system and a dash mounted indicator lamp, marked either SERVICE ENGINE SOON or CHECK ENGINE. The lamp is mounted on the instrument panel and has two functions:

1. It is used to inform the operator that a problem has occurred and the vehicle should be taken in for service as soon as reasonably possible.

2. It is used by the technician to read out stored trouble codes in order to localize malfunction areas during the diagnosis and repair phases.

As a bulb and system check, the light will come on with the ignition key in the ON position and the engine not operating. When the engine is started, the light will turn off. If the light does not turn off, the self diagnostic system has detected a problem in the system. If the problem goes away, the light will go out, in most cases after ten second, but a trouble code will be set in the ECM's memory.

Intermittent or Hard Trouble Codes

An intermittent code is one which does not reset itself and is not present when initiating the trouble codes. It is often be caused by a loose connection which, with vehicle movement, can possibly cure its self but intermittently reappear. A hard code is an operational malfunction which remains in the ECM memory and will be presented when calling for the trouble code display.

The Electronic Control Module (ECM) is actually a computer. It uses numerous sensors to look at many engine operating conditions. It has been programmed to know what certain sensor readings should be under most all operating conditions and if the sensor readings are not what the ECM thinks it should be, the ECM will turn on the SERVICE ENGINE SOON or CHECK ENGINE indicator light and will store a trouble code in its memory. When called up, the trouble code directs the technician to examine a particular circuit in order to locate and repair the trouble code setting defect.

Assembly Line Communication Link (ALCL)

In order to access the ECM to provide the trouble codes stored in its memory, the Assembly Line Communication Link (also known as the Assembly Line Diagnostic Link or ALDL) is used.

NOTE: This connector is utilized at the assembly plant to insure the engine is operating properly before the vehicle is shipped.

Terminal **B** of the diagnostic connnector is the diagnostic terminal and it can be connected to terminal **A**, or ground, to enter the diagnostic mode, or the field service mode on fuel injection models.

ENTERING DIAGNOSTIC MODE

If the diagnostic terminal is grounded with the ignition in the ON position and the engine stopped, the system will enter the diagnostic mode. In this mode, the ECM will accomplish the following:

1. The ECM will display a code 12 by flashing the SERVICE ENGINE SOON or CHECK ENGINE light, which indicates the system is working. A code 12 consists of one flash, followed by a short pause, then two flashes in quick succession.

a. This code will be flashed three times. If no other codes are stored, code 12 will continue to flash until the diagnostic terminal is disconnected from the ground circuit.

b. On a carbureted engine, the engine should not be started with the diagnostic terminal grounded, because it may continue to flash a code 12 with the engine running. Also, if the test terminal is grounded after the engine is running any stored codes will flash, but code 12 will flash only if there is a problem with the distributor reference signal.

c. On fuel injected engines, codes can only be obtained with the engine stopped. Grounding the diagnostic terminal with the engine running activates the FIELD SERVICE MODE.

2. The ECM will display any stored codes by flashing the SERVICE ENGINE SOON or CHECK ENGINE light. Each code will be flashed three times, then code 12 will be flashed again.

a. On carbureted engines, if a trouble code is displayed, the memory is cleared, then the engine is operated to see if the code is a hard or intermittent failure.

b. If the code represents a hard failure, a diagnostic code chart is used to locate the area of the failure.

c. If an intermittent failure is determined, the problem circuits can be examined physically for reasons of failure.

d. On fuel injected engines, if a trouble code is displayed, a diagnostic code chart is used to locate the area of failure.

3. The ECM will energize all controlled relays and solenoids that are involved in the current engine operation.

a. On carbureted engines, the ISC motor, if equipped, will move back and forth and the mixture control solenoid will be pulsed for 25 seconds or until the engine is started, which ever occurs first.

b. On fuel injected engines, the IAC valve is moved back and forth or is fully extended, depending upon the engine family.

Field Service Mode

FUEL INJECTION MODELS

If the diagnostic terminal is grounded with the engine operating, the system will enter the Field Service Mode. In this mode, the SERVICE ENGINE SOON or CHECK ENGINE indicator light will show whether the system is in Open or Closed Loop operation.

When in the Open Loop mode, the indicator light will flash two and one half times per second.

When in the Closed Loop Mode, the indicator light will flash once every second. Also, in Closed Loop, the light will stay out most of the time if the system is too lean. The light will stay on most of the time is the system is too rich. In either case, the Field Service Mode Check, which is part of the diagnostic circuit check, will direct the technician to the fault area.

While in the Field Service Mode, the ECM will be in the following mode:
1. The distributor will have a fixed spark advance.
2. New trouble codes cannot be stored in the ECM.
3. The closed loop timer is bypassed.

Trouble Codes

The trouble codes indicate problems in the following areas:
1. CODE 12 – No Distributor Reference Signal to the ECM. This code is not stored in the memory and will only flash while the fault is present. Normal code with the ignition switch in the ON position and the engine not operating.
2. CODE 13 – Oxygen Sensor circuit. The engine must be operated up to four minutes at part throttle, under road conditions, before this code will set.
3. CODE 14 – Shorted Coolant Sensor circuit. The engine must run five minutes before this code will set.
4. CODE 15 – Open Coolant Sensor circuit. The engine must run five minutes before this code will set.
5. CODE 21 – Throttle Position Sensor (TPS) circuit voltage high (open circuit or misadjusted TPS). The engine must operate ten seconds, at specified curb idle speed before this code will set.
6. CODE 22 – Throttle Position Sensor (TPS) circuit voltage low (grounded circuit or misadjusted TPS). The engine must run twenty seconds at specified curb idle speed.
7. CODE 23 – Mixture Control Solenoid circuit open or grounded.
8. CODE 24 – Vehicle Speed Sensor (VSS) circuit. The vehicle must operate up to two minutes, at road speed before this code will set.
9. CODE 32 – Barometric Pressure Sensor (BARO) circuit low.
10. CODE 34 – Vacuum Sensor or Manifold Absolute Pressure (MAP) circuit. The engine must be operated up to two minutes, at the specified curb idle before this code will set.
11. CODE 35 – Idle Speed Control (ISC) switch circuit shorted. Up to 70% TPS for over five seconds.
12. CODE 41 – No Distributor Reference Signal to the ECM at specified engine vacuum. This code will store in the memory.
13. CODE 42 – Electronic Spark Timing (EST) bypass circuit or EST circuit grounded or open.
14. CODE 43 – Electronic Spark Control (ESC) retard signal for too long of a time. Will cause retard in EST signal.

15. CODE 44 – Lean Exhaust Indication. The engine must operate for two minutes, in the closed loop mode and at part throttle before this code will set.
16. CODE 45 – Rich Exhaust Indication. The engine must operate for two minutes, in closed loop mode and at part throttle before this code will set.
17. CODE 51 – Faulty or improperly installed calibration unit (PROM). It takes up to 30 seconds before this code will set.
18. CODE 53 – Exhaust Gas Recirculation (EGR) valve vacuum sensor has noted improper EGR control vacuum.
19. CODE 54 – Mixture Control Solenoid voltage high at the ECM as a result of a shorted M/C solenoid circuit and/or a faulty ECM.

NOTE: Any codes will be erased if no problem re-occurs within 50 engine starts. All available codes may not be used on all engines.

Clearing the Trouble Codes

When the ECM sets a trouble code, the SERVICE ENGINE SOON or CHECK ENGINE lamp will be illuminated and a trouble code will be stored in the ECM's memory. If the problem is intermittent, the light will go out after ten seconds when the fault goes away, however, the trouble code will stay in the ECM memory until the battery voltage to the ECM is removed. Removing the battery voltage for ten seconds will clear all stored trouble codes.

To prevent damage to the ECM, the ignition key must be in the OFF position when disconnecting or reconnecting the power to the ECM through the battery cable, ECM pigtail, ECM fuse, jumper cables, etc.

All trouble codes should be cleared after repairs have been accomplished. In some cases, such as through a diagnoistic routine, the codes may have to be cleared first to allow the ECM to set a trouble code during the test, should a malfunction be present.

NOTE: The ECM has a learning ability to perform after the battery power has been disconnected to it. A change may be noted in the vehicle's performance. To teach the vehicle, make sure the engine is at normal operating temperature and drive it at part throttle, at moderate acceleration and idle conditions, until normal performance returns.

ALDL Scan Tools

The ALDL connector, located under the dash, has a variety of information available on terminals **E** and **M** (depending upon the engine used). There are several tools on the market, called "SCAN" units for reading the available information.

The use of the SCAN tools do not make the diagnostics unnecessary. They do not tell exactly where a problem is in a given circuit. However, with an understanding of what each position on the instrument measures and the knowledge of the circuit involved, the tool can be very useful in getting information which could be more time consuming to get with outer test equipment. It must be emphasized that each type scanner instrument must be used in accordance with the manufacturers instructions.

CODE 14

COOLANT TEMPERATURE SENSOR CIRCUIT
(HIGH TEMPERATURE INDICATED)
2.0L TURBO "N" SERIES (PORT)

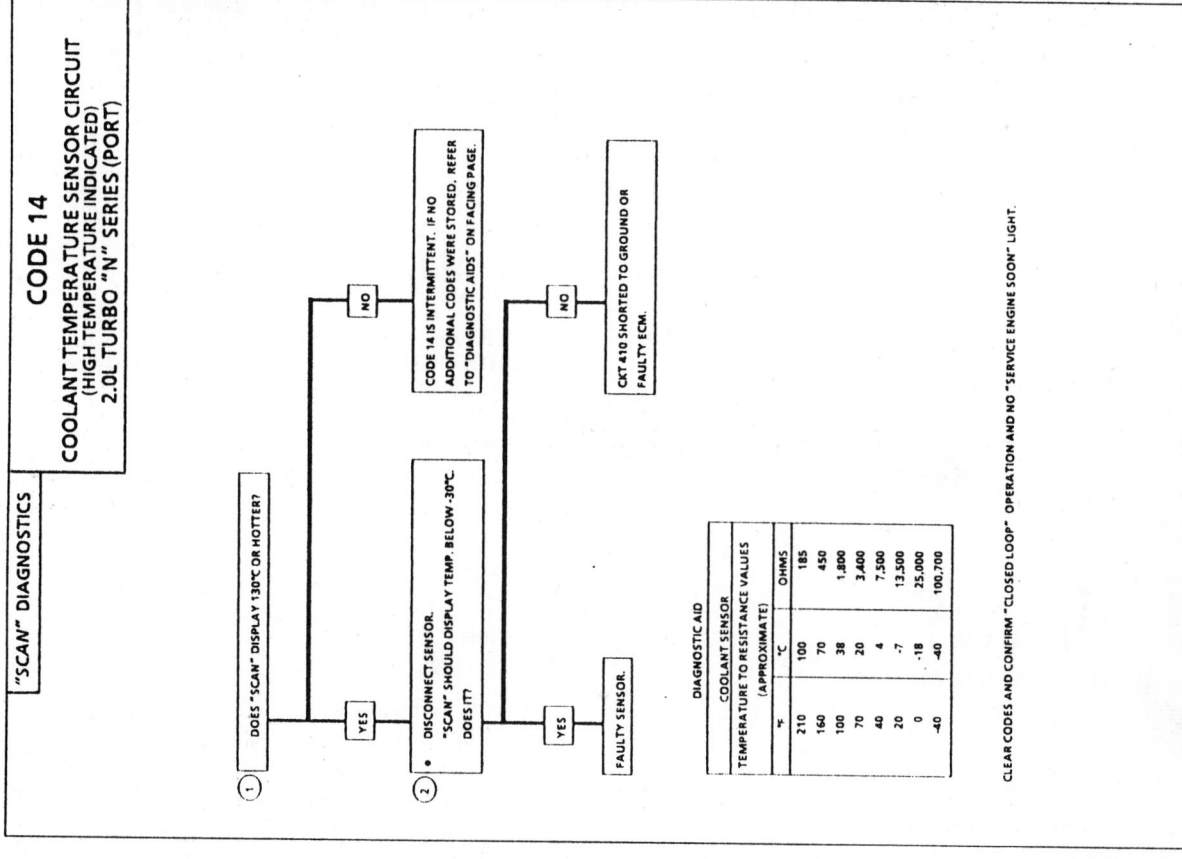

"SCAN" DIAGNOSTICS

(1) DOES "SCAN" DISPLAY 130°C OR HOTTER?

- YES
- NO → CODE 14 IS INTERMITTENT. IF NO ADDITIONAL CODES WERE STORED, REFER TO "DIAGNOSTIC AIDS" ON FACING PAGE.

(2) • DISCONNECT SENSOR.
"SCAN" SHOULD DISPLAY TEMP. BELOW -30°C. DOES IT?

- YES → FAULTY SENSOR.
- NO → CKT 410 SHORTED TO GROUND OR FAULTY ECM.

DIAGNOSTIC AID

COOLANT SENSOR TEMPERATURE TO RESISTANCE VALUES (APPROXIMATE)		
°F	°C	OHMS
210	100	185
160	70	450
100	38	1,800
70	20	3,400
40	4	7,500
20	-7	13,500
0	-18	25,000
-40	-40	100,700

CLEAR CODES AND CONFIRM "CLOSED LOOP" OPERATION AND NO "SERVICE ENGINE SOON" LIGHT.

CODE 14

COOLANT TEMPERATURE SENSOR CIRCUIT
(HIGH TEMPERATURE INDICATED)
2.0L TURBO "N" SERIES (PORT)

ECM

COOLANT SENSOR SIGNAL — 5 V

COOLANT TEMPERATURE SENSOR

410 YEL — E16

452 BLK — B6

TO MAP SENSOR

A | B

A

B

Circuit Description:

The Coolant Temperature Sensor uses a thermistor to control the signal voltage to the ECM. The ECM applies a voltage on CKT 410 to the sensor. When the engine is cold, the sensor (thermistor) resistance is high, therefore, the ECM will see high signal voltage.

As the engine warms, the sensor resistance becomes less, and the voltage drops. At normal engine operating temperature, the voltage will measure about 1.5 to 2.0 volts at the ECM terminal E16.

Coolant temperature is one of the inputs used to control:

- Fuel delivery
- Electronic Spark Timing (EST)
- Cooling Fan
- Convertor Clutch (TCC)
- Idle (IAC)

Test Description: Step numbers refer to step numbers on diagnostic chart.

1. Checks to see if code was set as result of hard failure or intermittent condition.
   Code 14 will set if:
   - Engine has been running for more than 10 seconds.
   - Signal Voltage indicates a coolant temperature above 135°C (275°F) for 3 seconds.

2. This test simulates conditions for a Code 15. If the ECM recognizes the open circuit (high voltage), and displays a low temperature, the ECM and wiring are ok.

Diagnostic Aids:

A "Scan" tool reads engine temperature in degrees centigrade.

After the engine is started, the temperature should rise steadily to about 90°, then stabilize, when the thermostat opens.

If the engine has been allowed to cool to an ambient temperature (overnight). Coolant and MAT temperature may be checked with a "Scan" tool and should read close to each other.

When a Code 14 is set, the ECM will turn on the Engine Cooling Fan.

A Code 14 will result if CKT 410 is shorted to ground.

If Code 14 is intermittent refer to Section "B".

Typical diagnostic charts using SCAN tool

INDEX

ELECTRONIC IGNITION SYSTEMS

General Service Precautions

• Always turn the ignition switch OFF when disconnecting or connecting any electrical connectors or components.

• Never reverse the battery polarity or disconnect the battery with the engine running.

• Do not pierce spark plug or wiring harness wires with test probes for any reason. Due to their more pliable construction, it is important to route spark plug wires properly to avoid chafing or cutting.

• Disconnect the ignition switch feed wire at the distributor when making compression tests to avoid arcing that may damage components, especially on computer-based ignition systems.

• Do not remove grease or dielectric compound from components or connectors when installing. Some manufacturers use grease to prevent corrosion and dielectric compound to dissipate heat generated during normal module operation.

• Check all replacement part numbers carefully. Installing the wrong components for a specific application can damage the system.

• All manufacturers instructions included with any testing equipment must be read carefully to insure proper capability and test results. Inaccurate readings and/or damage to ignition system components may result due to the use of improper test equipment.

ELECTRONIC IGNITION QUICK CHECK CHART
(Non-computer controlled systems only)

Condition	Possible Cause	Correction
Abrupt backfire	Control unit or ignition module malfunction. Incorrect timing. Bad cap or rotor	Check ignition timing. Replace control unit or module. Replace cap or rotor
Intermittent running	Magnetic pick-up or stator malfunction. Bad trigger wheel, reluctor or armature. Control unit or ignition module failure	Replace defective components after testing as described under appropriate system in this unit repair section
Does not fire on one or more cylinders	Defective pick-up, stator, trigger wheel, reluctor or armature. Bad spark plugs or ignition wires	Replace components as necessary
Cuts off suddenly	Malfunction in control unit of module. Damaged pick-up or stator	Check operation of pick-up and stator. Replace control unit or module
Won't start	Control unit or module failure. Defective cap, rotor, pick-up or stator ①	Replace control unit or module after testing. Replace distributor components as necessary
Poor performance, no power under load	Defective pick-up, stator, or ignition coil. Worn or fouled spark plugs. Bad plug wires	Check distributor components for signs of wear or damage. Replace spark plugs and wires
Arcing or excessive burning on rotor or distributor cap	Worn or fouled spark plugs. Bad plug wires	Replace spark plugs and wires

NOTE: This chart assumes the described conditions are problems in the electronic ignition system and not the result of another malfunction. Always perform basic checks for fuel, spark and compression first. See the individual system sections for all test procedures.
① Check ballast resistor on Chrysler models

AMC SOLID STATE IGNITION (SSI) SYSTEM

General Information

American Motors Solid State Ignition (SSI) is standard equipment on all 1984 and later 6 cylinder 258 CID engines and 4 cylinder 150 CID engines and is of the Ford Motor Company design.

The system consists of a sensor and toothed trigger wheel inside the distributor, and a permanently sealed electronic control unit which determines dwell, in addition to the coil, ignition wires, and spark plugs.

The trigger wheel rotates on the distributor shaft. As one of its teeth nears the sensor magnet, the magnetic field shifts toward the tooth. When the tooth and sensor are aligned, the magnetic field is shifted to its maximum, signaling the elec-tronic control unit to switch off the coil primary current. This starts an electronic timer inside the control unit, which allows the primary current to remain off only long enough for the spark plug to fire. The timer adjusts the amount of time primary current is off according to conditions, thus automatically adjusting dwell. There is also a special circuit within the control unit to detect and ignore spurious (false) signals. Spark timing is adjusted by both mechanical (centrifugal) and vacuum advance.

A wire of 1.35 ohms resistance is spliced into the ignition feed to reduce voltage to the coil during running conditions. The resistance wire is by-passed when the engine is being started so that full battery voltage may be supplied to the coil. Bypass is accomplished by the I-terminal on the solenoid.

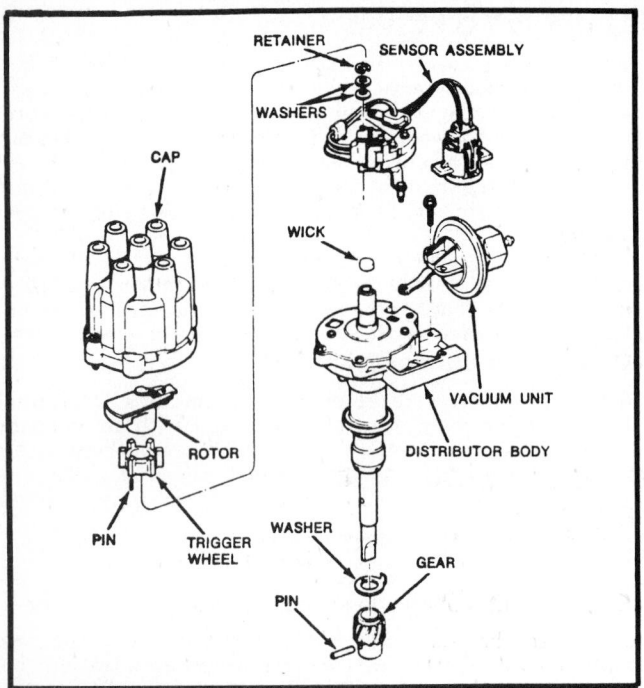

Six cylinder SSI distributor

The remainder of the system includes a pointless distributor, standard construction ignition coil, ignition switch, resistance wire and bypass, secondary spark plug wires and spark plugs. The electronic control unit (module) is a solid state, nonserviceable, sealed unit. This unit has reverse polarity and voltage surge circuit protection built in. Two weatherproof connectors attach the control unit to the ignition circuit.

NOTE: All system electrical connectors use lock tabs that must be released to disconnect the various components.

Troubleshooting

SECONDARY CIRCUIT TEST

1. Disconnect the coil wire from the center of the distributor cap.

NOTE: Twist the rubber boot slightly in either direction, then grasp the boot and pull straight up. Do not pull on the wire and do not use pliers.

2. Hold the wire $\frac{1}{2}$ in. from a ground with a pair of insulated pliers and a heavy glove. As the engine is cranked, watch for a spark.

3. If a spark appears, reconnect the coil wire. Remove the wire from one spark plug, and test for a spark as above.

--- CAUTION ---

Do not remove the spark plug wires from cylinder 1 or 5 (1984 and later) on a 6 cylinder engine when performing this test, as sensor damage could occur.

4. If a spark occurs, the problem is in the fuel system or ignition timing. If no spark occurs, check for a defective rotor, cap, or spark plug wires.

5. If no spark occurs from the coil wire in Step 2, test the coil wire resistance with an ohmmeter. It must not exceed 10,000 ohms.

COIL PRIMARY CIRCUIT TEST

1. Turn the ignition On. Connect a voltmeter to the coil positive (+) terminal and a ground. If the voltage is 5.5–6.5 volts, go to Step 2. If above 7 volts, go to Step 4. If below 5.5 volts, disconnect the condenser lead and measure. If the voltage is now

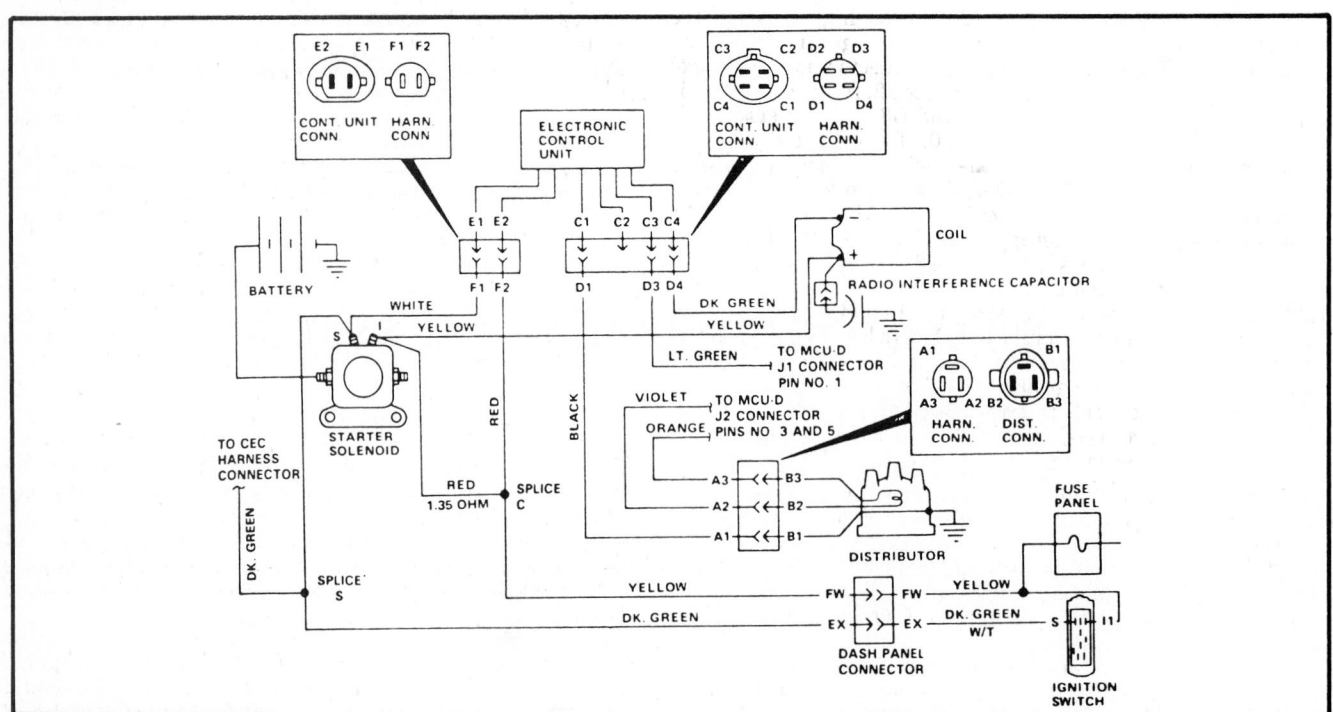

SSI system schematic

5.5–6.5 volts, replace the condenser. If not, go to Step 6.

2. With the voltmeter connected as in Step 1, read the voltage with the engine cranking. If battery voltage is indicated, the circuit is okay. If not, go to Step 3.

3. Check for a short or open in the starter solenoid I-terminal wire. Check the solenoid for proper operation.

4. Disconnect the wire from the starter solenoid I-terminal, with the ignition On and the voltmeter connected as in Step 1.

5. If the voltage drops to 5.5–6.5 volts, replace the solenoid. If not, connect a jumper between the coil negative (-) terminal and a ground. If the voltage drops to 5.5–6.5 volts, go to Step 5, and if the voltage does not drop, repair the resistance wire.

6. Check for continuity between the coil (-) terminal and D4, and D1 to ground. If the continuity is okay, replace the control unit. If not, check for an open wire and go back to Step 2 to recheck.

7. Turn ignition Off. Connect an ohmmeter between the + coil terminal and dash connector AV. If above 1.40 ohms, repair the resistance wire.

8. With the ignition Off, connect the ohmmeter between connector AV and ignition switch terminal 11. If less than 0.1 ohm, replace the ignition switch or repair the wire, whichever is the cause. If above 0.1 ohm, check connections, and check for defective wiring.

COIL TEST

1. Check the coil for cracks, carbon tracks, etc. and replace as necessary.

2. Connect an ohmmeter across the coil (+) and (-) terminals, with the coil connector removed. If 1.13–1.23 ohms/75°F, go to Step 3. If not, replace the coil.

3. Measure the resistance across the coil center tower and either the + or - terminal. If 7700–9300 ohms at 75°F, the coil is okay. If not, replace the coil.

CONTROL UNIT AND SENSOR TEST

1. With the ignition On, remove the coil high tension wire from the distributor cap and hold ½ in. from ground with insulated pliers. Disconnect the 4 wire connector at the control unit. If a spark occurs (normal), go to Step 2. If not, go to Step 5.

2. Connect an ohmmeter to D2 and D3. If the resistance is 400–800 ohms (normal), go to Step 6. If not, go to Step 3.

3. Disconnect and reconnect the 3 wire connector at distributor. If the reading is now 400–800 ohms, go to Step 6. If not, disconnect the 3 wire connector and go to Step 4.

4. Connect the ohmmeter across B2 and B3. If 400–800 ohms, repair the harness between the 3 wire and 4 wire connectors. If not, replace the sensor.

5. Connect the ohmmeter between D1 and the battery negative terminal. If the reading is 0 (0.002 or less), go to Step 2. If above 0.002 ohms, there is a bad ground in the cable or at the distributor. Repair the ground and retest.

6. Connect a voltmeter across D2 and D3. Crank the engine. If the needle fluctuates, the system is okay. If not, either the trigger wheel is defective, or the distributor is not turning. Repair or replace as required.

IGNITION FEED TO CONTROL UNIT TEST

NOTE: Do not perform this test without first performing the Coil Primary Circuit Test.

1. With the ignition ON, unplug the 2 wire connector at the module. Connect a voltmeter between F2 and ground. If the reading is battery voltage, replace the control unit and go to Step 3. If not, go to Step 2.

2. Repair the cause of the voltage reduction: either the ignition switch or a corroded dash connector. Check for a spark at the coil wire. If okay, stop. If not, replace the control unit and check for proper operation.

3. Reconnect the 2 wire connector at the control unit, and unplug the 4 wire connector at the control unit. Connect an ammeter between C1 and ground. If it reads 0.9–1.1 amps, the system is okay. If not, replace the module.

Control Unit Current Draw Test

If 11 volts or more were present at the connector's F2 terminal, measure the current draw of control unit with an ammeter. Disconnect 4-wire connector and connect ammeter between the connector terminal C1 and ground. With the ignition ON, current draw should be 0.9–1.1 amps; if it is not, replace the control unit.

Control Unit Voltage Test

Disconnect the 2-wire connector at the control unit and measure the voltage between the connector terminal F2 and ground, with the ignition ON. The voltage should be above 11 volts. If it is not, check the ignition switch and the wiring for an open circuit, or a loose or corroded connector. If, after obtaining the proper voltage at F2 terminal, a spark is not produced at the coil wire when the engine is cranked and the coil and sensor check are OK, replace the control unit.

Sensor Tests

1. Connect an ohmmeter (R x 100 scale) to D2 and D3 connector terminals. The resistance should be 400–800 ohms.

2. If the resistance is not within 400–800 ohms, check the voltage output of the sensor. Connect a voltmeter, 2–3 volt scale, to D2 and D3 connector terminals. Crank the engine and observe the voltmeter. A fluctuating voltmeter indicates proper sensor and trigger wheel operation. If not fluctuations are noted, check for a defective trigger wheel, distributor not turning, or a missing trigger wheel pin.

3. If the resistance in Step 1 was not 400–800 ohms, disconnect and reconnect 3–wire connector at the distributor. If the resistance is now 400–800 ohms, check sensor voltage output, Step 2.

4. If the sensor circuit resistance is still not within specification, disconnect 3–wire connector at the distributor and connect an ohmmeter to B2 and B3 terminals. If the resistance is 400–800 ohms, repair or replace the harness between 3–wire and 4–wire connector. If the resistance is still incorrect, replace the sensor.

Rotor Test

The rotor has silicone dielectric compound applied to the blade to reduce the radio interference. After a few thousand miles, the dielectric compound will become charred by the high voltage, which is normal. Do not scrape the residue off. When installing a new rotor, apply a thin coat (0.03–0.12 in.) of Silicone Dielectric Compound to the rotor blade.

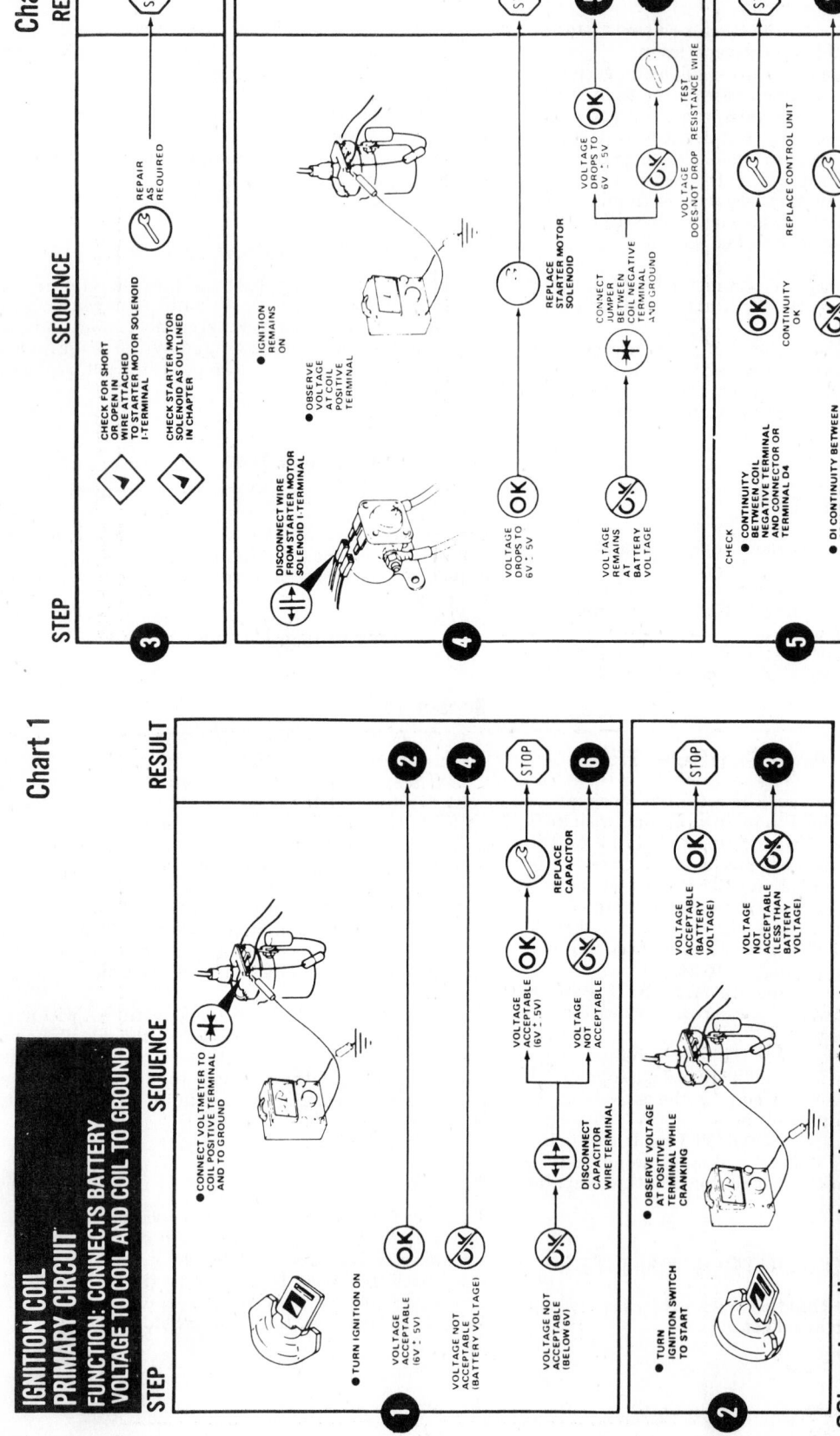

SSI system diagnosis and repair, Chart 1 (cont.)

SSI system diagnosis and repair, Chart 1

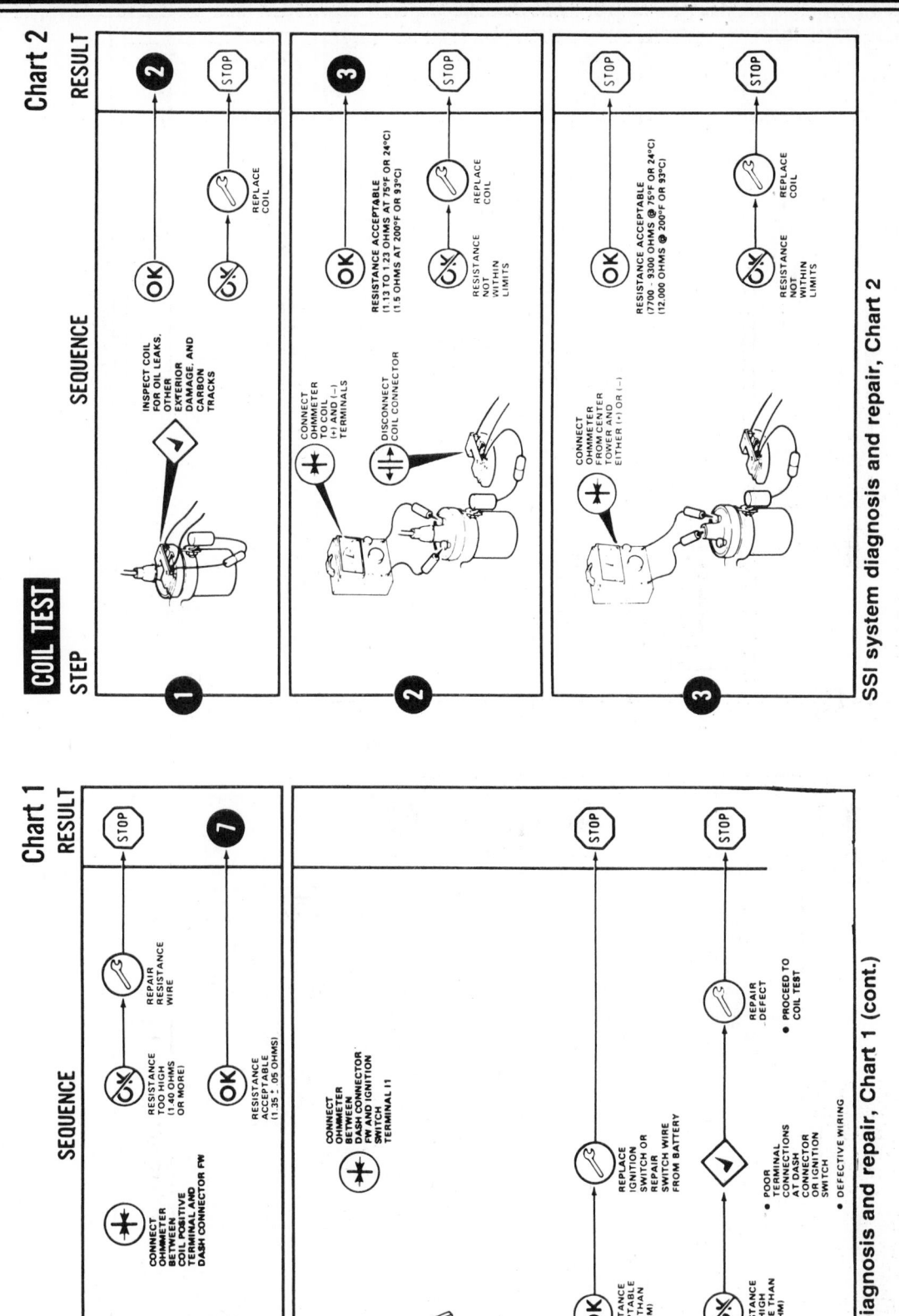

Chart 2

COIL TEST

RESULT / SEQUENCE / STEP

Step 1 — INSPECT COIL FOR OIL LEAKS, OTHER EXTERIOR DAMAGE, AND CARBON TRACKS → OK → 2 / NOT OK → REPLACE COIL → STOP

Step 2 — CONNECT OHMMETER TO COIL (+) AND (−) TERMINALS / DISCONNECT COIL CONNECTOR → OK RESISTANCE ACCEPTABLE (1.13 TO 1.23 OHMS AT 75°F OR 24°C) (1.5 OHMS AT 200°F OR 93°C) → 3 / RESISTANCE NOT WITHIN LIMITS → REPLACE COIL → STOP

Step 3 — CONNECT OHMMETER FROM CENTER TOWER AND EITHER (+) OR (−) → OK RESISTANCE ACCEPTABLE (7700–9300 OHMS @ 75°F OR 24°C) (12,000 OHMS @ 200°F OR 93°C) → STOP / RESISTANCE NOT WITHIN LIMITS → REPLACE COIL → STOP

SSI system diagnosis and repair, Chart 2

Chart 1

RESULT / SEQUENCE / STEP

Step 6 — TURN IGNITION OFF / CONNECT OHMMETER BETWEEN COIL POSITIVE TERMINAL AND DASH CONNECTOR FW → RESISTANCE TOO HIGH (1.40 OHMS OR MORE) → REPAIR RESISTANCE WIRE → STOP / RESISTANCE ACCEPTABLE (1.35–1.05 OHMS) OK → 7

Step 7 — IGNITION REMAINS OFF / CONNECT OHMMETER BETWEEN DASH CONNECTOR FW AND IGNITION SWITCH TERMINAL I1 → RESISTANCE ACCEPTABLE (LESS THAN 0.1 OHM) OK → REPLACE IGNITION SWITCH OR REPAIR SWITCH WIRE FROM BATTERY → STOP / RESISTANCE TOO HIGH (MORE THAN 0.1 OHM) → • POOR TERMINAL CONNECTIONS AT DASH CONNECTOR OR IGNITION SWITCH • DEFECTIVE WIRING → REPAIR DEFECT → • PROCEED TO COIL TEST → STOP

SSI system diagnosis and repair, Chart 1 (cont.)

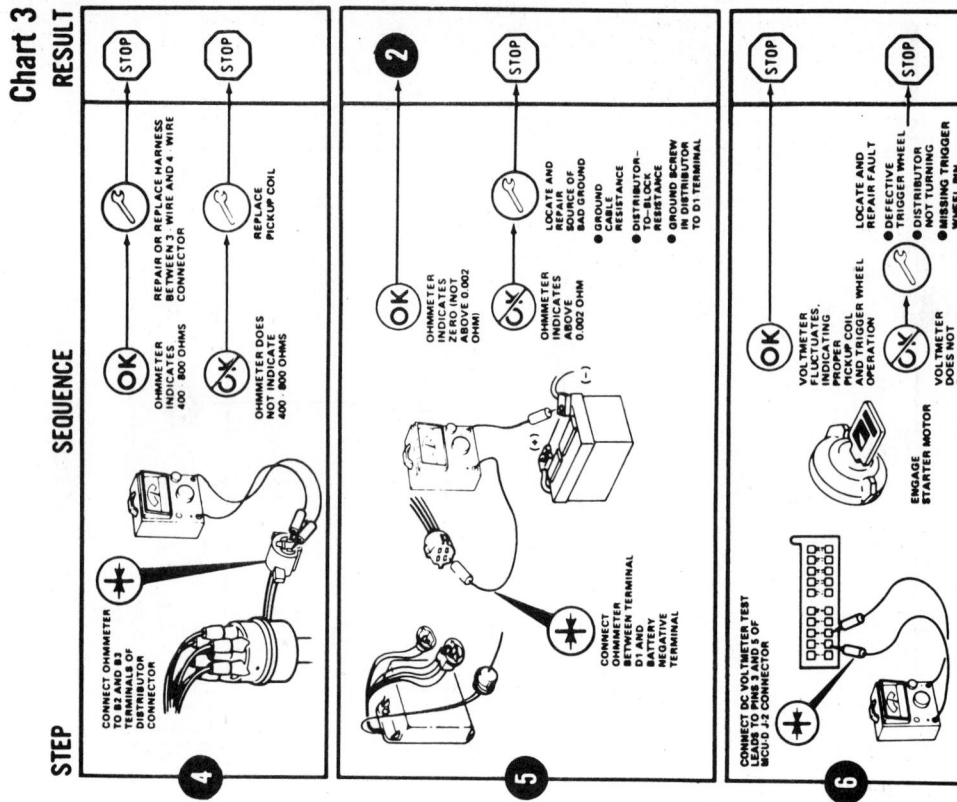

Chart 3

STEP / SEQUENCE / RESULT

4 CONNECT OHMMETER TO B2 AND B3 TERMINALS OF DISTRIBUTOR CONNECTOR

OK OHMMETER INDICATES 400 - 800 OHMS → STOP

OHMMETER DOES NOT INDICATE 400 - 800 OHMS → REPAIR OR REPLACE HARNESS BETWEEN 3 - WIRE AND 4 - WIRE CONNECTOR → STOP

REPLACE PICKUP COIL

5 CONNECT OHMMETER BETWEEN TERMINAL D1 AND BATTERY NEGATIVE TERMINAL

2 OHMMETER INDICATES ZERO (NOT ABOVE 0.002 OHM) → STOP

OHMMETER INDICATES ABOVE 0.002 OHM → LOCATE AND REPAIR SOURCE OF BAD GROUND
- GROUND CABLE RESISTANCE
- DISTRIBUTOR-TO-BLOCK RESISTANCE
- GROUND SCREW IN DISTRIBUTOR TO D1 TERMINAL

6 CONNECT DC VOLTMETER TEST LEADS TO PINS 3 AND 5 OF MCU-D J2 CONNECTOR — ENGAGE STARTER MOTOR

OK VOLTMETER FLUCTUATES, INDICATING PROPER PICKUP COIL AND TRIGGER WHEEL OPERATION → STOP

VOLTMETER DOES NOT FLUCTUATE → LOCATE AND REPAIR FAULT
- DEFECTIVE TRIGGER WHEEL
- DISTRIBUTOR NOT TURNING
- MISSING TRIGGER WHEEL PIN → STOP

SSI system diagnosis and repair, Chart 3 (cont.)

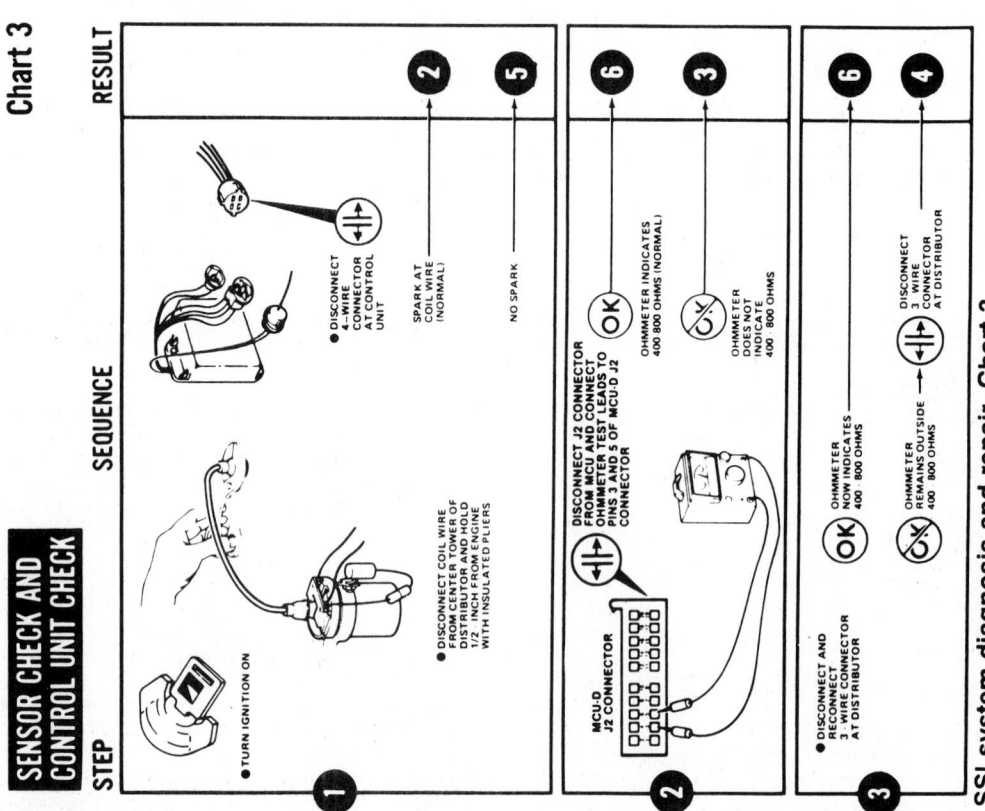

Chart 3

STEP / SEQUENCE / RESULT

SENSOR CHECK AND CONTROL UNIT CHECK

1
- TURN IGNITION ON
- DISCONNECT COIL WIRE FROM CENTER TOWER OF DISTRIBUTOR AND HOLD 1/2 - INCH FROM ENGINE WITH INSULATED PLIERS
- DISCONNECT 4-WIRE CONNECTOR AT CONTROL UNIT

SPARK AT COIL WIRE (NORMAL) → **2**

NO SPARK → **5**

2 MCU-D J2 CONNECTOR — DISCONNECT J2 CONNECTOR FROM MCU AND CONNECT OHMMETER TEST LEADS TO PINS 3 AND 5 OF MCU-D J2 CONNECTOR

OK OHMMETER INDICATES 400 - 800 OHMS (NORMAL) → **6**

OHMMETER DOES NOT INDICATE 400 - 800 OHMS → **3**

3
- DISCONNECT AND RECONNECT 3 - WIRE CONNECTOR AT DISTRIBUTOR

OK OHMMETER NOW INDICATES 400 - 800 OHMS → **6**

OHMMETER REMAINS OUTSIDE 400 - 800 OHMS → DISCONNECT 3 - WIRE CONNECTOR AT DISTRIBUTOR → **4**

SSI system diagnosis and repair, Chart 3

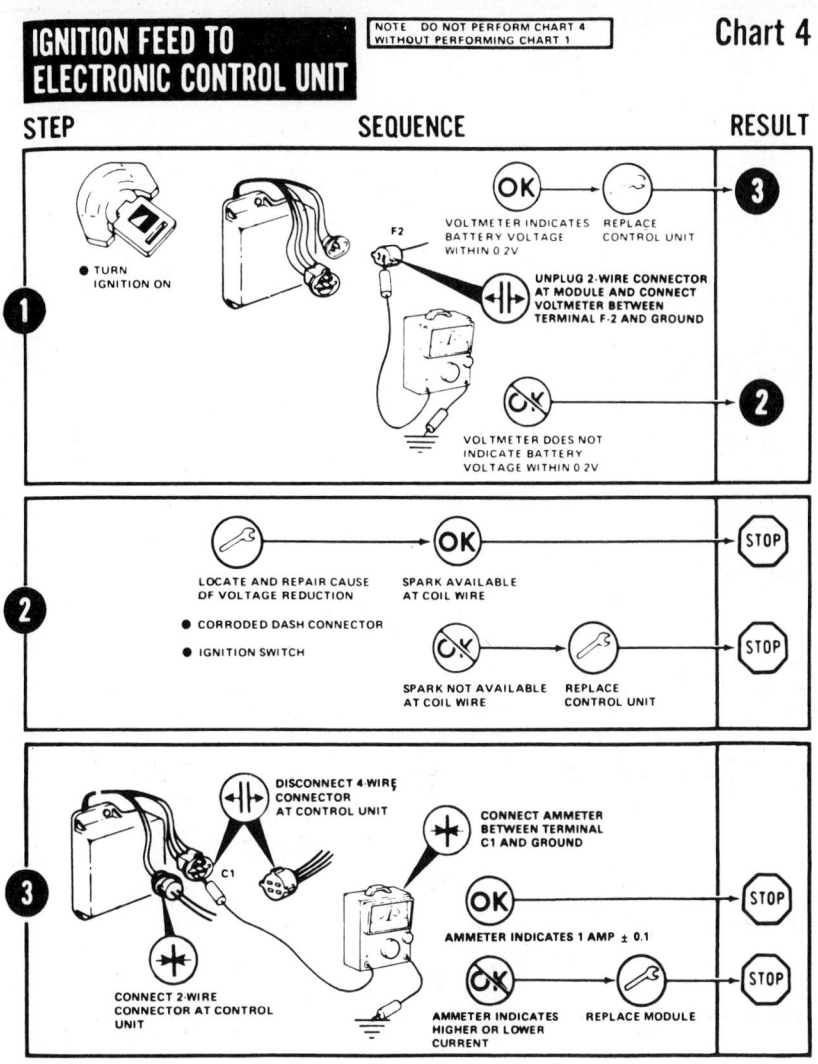

SSI system diagnosis and repair, Chart 4

CHRYSLER CORPORATION HALL EFFECT ELECTRONIC IGNITION

General Information

1984-88 1.6L, 2.2L CARBURETED ENGINES WITH HALL EFFECT DISTRIBUTORS

The Hall Effect electronic ignition is used in conjunction with the Chrysler Electronic Spark Control System used on the above noted engines. It consists of a sealed Spark Control Computer, specially calibrated carburetor and various engine sensors, such as the vacuum transducer, coolant switch, Hall Effect pickup assembly, oxygen sensor and carburetor switch.

SPARK CONTROL COMPUTER

During cranking, an electrical signal is sent from the distributor to the computer. This signal will cause the computer to fire the spark plugs at a fixed amount of advance. Once the engine starts, the timing will then be controlled by the computer based on the information received from the various sensors.

There are essentially two modes of operation of the Spark Control computer: the start mode and the run mode. The start mode is only used during engine cranking. During cranking, only the Hall Effect pickup signals the computer. These signals are interpreted to provide a fixed number of degrees of spark advance.

After the engine starts and during normal engine operation, the computer functions in the run mode. In this mode, the Hall Effect pickup serves as only one of the signals to the computer. It is a reference signal of maximum possible spark advance. The computer then determines, from information provided by the other engine sensors, how much of this advance is necessary and delays the coil saturation accordingly, to fire the spark plug at the exact moment when this advance (crankshaft position) is reached.

There is a third mode of operation which only becomes functional when the computer fails. This is the limp-in mode. This mode functions on signals from the pickup only and results in very poor engine performance. However, it does allow the car to be driven to a repair shop. If a failure occurs in the pickup assembly or the start mode of the computer, the engine will neither start nor run.

HALL EFFECT SWITCH

The distributor contains the Hall Effect pickup assembly. The pickup assembly supplies the computer with the basic information on engine speed and crankshaft position.

COOLANT SENSOR

The coolant sensor supplies a signal to the computer to assist it in controlling the air/fuel ratio and the spark advance during periods of warm-up.

VACUUM SENSOR

The vacuum transducer is located on the Spark Control Computer and it informs the computer as to the vacuum condition of the engine as it is operating. The engine vacuum is one of the factors that will determine how the computer will advance/retard ignition timing and with the feedback carburetor, how the air/fuel ratio will be changed.

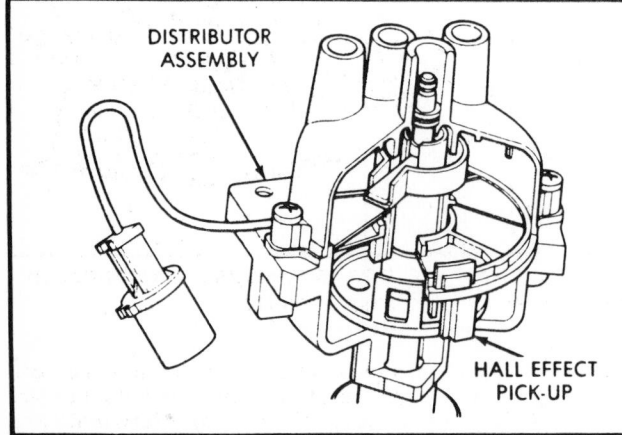

Hall Effect distributor for EFI/Carbureted models

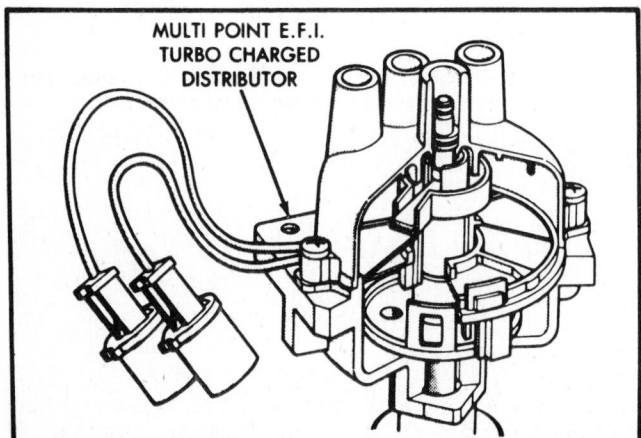

Hall Effect distributor for Turbo Multi-point EFI models

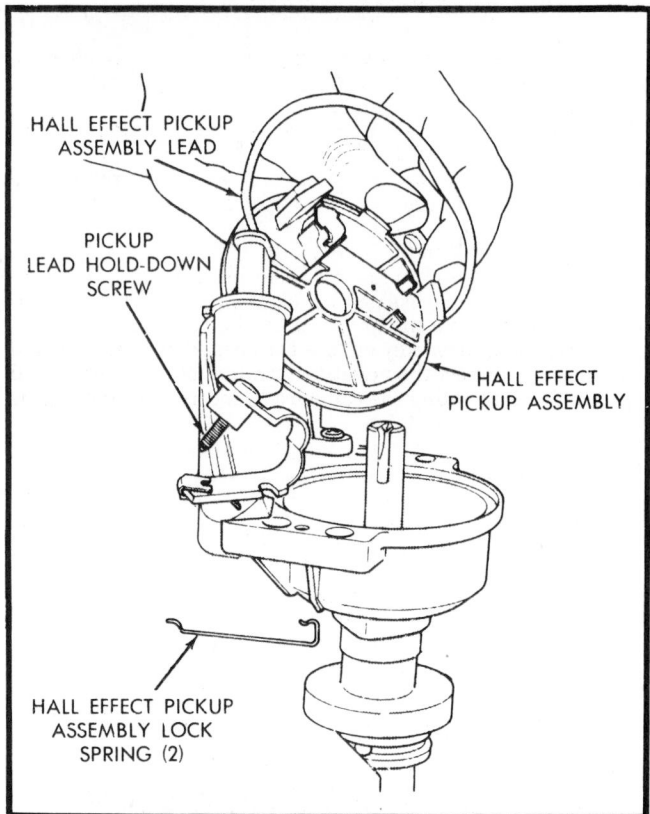

Hall Effect pickup installation

CARBURETOR SWITCH

The carburetor switch is used to signal the computer that the engine is at idle and is located at the end of the idle stop.

OXYGEN SENSOR

The Oxygen sensor (used with feedback carburetors) is located in the exhaust manifold and signals the computer how much oxygen is present in the exhaust gases. Since this amount is proportional to rich and lean mixtures, the computer will adjust the air/fuel ratio to a level which will maintain operating efficiency of the three-way catalyst system and engine

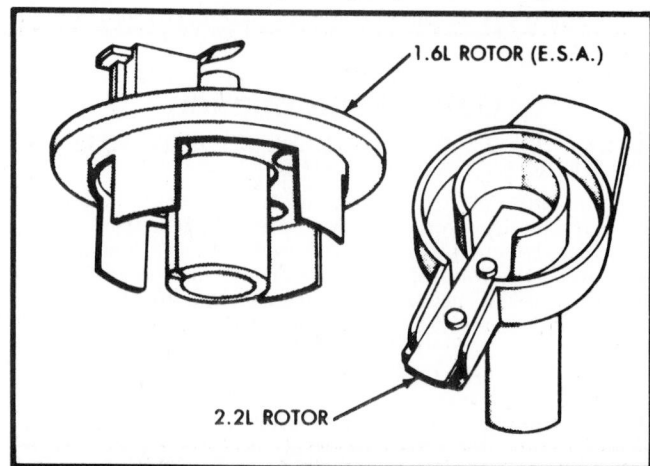

Types of rotors used with the 1.6L and 2.2L engine distributors

SYSTEM TESTS

1. Perform the "Troubleshooting" test before proceeding with the following. Make sure the battery is fully charged.

2. Remove the coil secondary wire from the distributor cap.

3. With the key on, use the special jumper wire and momentarily connect the negative terminal of the ignition coil to ground while holding the coil secondary wire (using insulated pliers and heavy gloves) about ¼ in. from a good ground. A spark should fire.

4. If spark was obtained, go to Step 9.

5. If no spark was obtained, turn off the ignition and disconnect the 10–wire harness going into the Spark Control Computer. Do not remove the grease from the connector.

6. With the ignition key on, use the special jumper wire and momentarily connect the negative terminal of the ignition coil to ground while holding the coil wire ¼ in. from a good engine ground. A spark should fire.

7. If a spark is present, the computer output is shorted; replace the computer.

8. If no spark is obtained, measure the voltage at the coil positive terminal. It should be within 1 volt of battery voltage. If voltage is present but no spark is available when shorting negative terminal, replace the coil. If no voltage is present, replace the coil or check the primary wiring.

9. If voltage was obtained but the engine will not start, hold the carburetor switch open with a thin cardboard insulator and measure the voltage at the switch. It should be at within 1 volt of battery voltage. If voltage is present, go to Step 16.

10. If no voltage is present, turn the ignition switch off and if not disconnected, disconnect the 10–wire harness going into the computer.

11. Turn the ignition switch on and measure the voltage at terminal 2 of the connector. It should be within 1 volt of battery voltage.

12. If no battery voltage is present, check for continuity between the battery and terminal 2 of the connector. If no continuity, repair fault and repeat Step 11.

13. If voltage is present turn ignition switch off and check for continuity between the carburetor switch and terminal 7 on the connector. If no continuity is present, check for open wire between terminal 7 and the carburetor switch.

14. If continuity is present, check continuity between terminal 10 and ground. If continuity is present here, replace the computer. (Correct voltage is going in, but not coming out). Repeat Step 9.

15. If no continuity is present, check for an open wire. If wiring is OK, but the engine still won't start, go to next step.

16. Plug the 10 terminal dual connector back into the com-

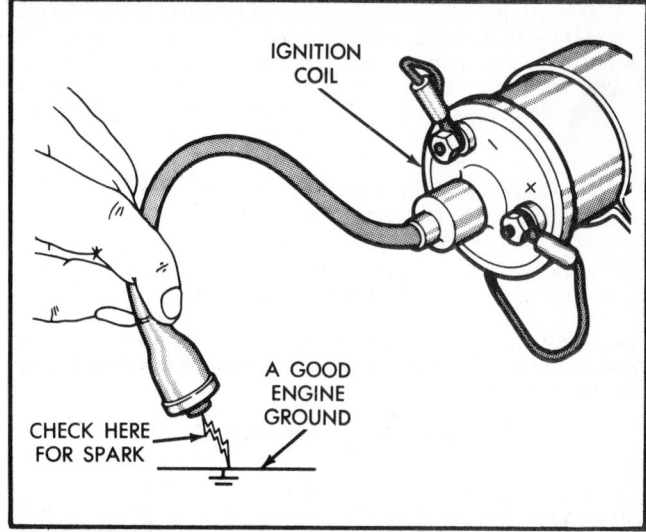

Testing for spark during engine cranking. Use insulated pliers and heavy gloves to handle coil wire

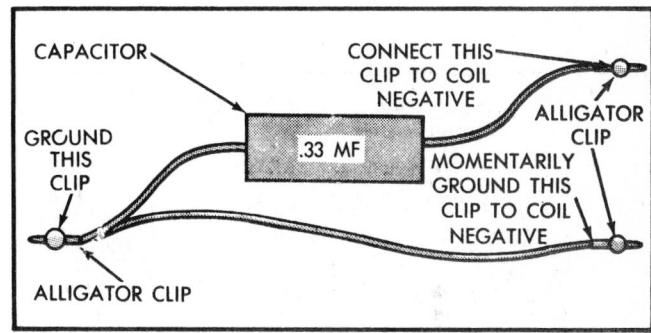

Special jumper wire from coil negative terminal to ground — front wheel drive vehicles.

puter and turn the ignition switch on, hold the secondary coil wire near a good ground and disconnect the distributor harness connector. Using a regular jumper wire, jumper terminal 2 and terminal 3, making and breaking the connection at either terminal of the connector and a spark should fire at the coil wire.

17. If spark is present at the coil wire but is not present when the when the distributor lead is re-connected, replace the Hall Effect pick-up.

NOTE: When replacing a pick-up, always make sure rotor blades are grounded using an ohmmeter.

18. If no spark is present at the coil wire, measure the voltage at terminal 1 of the distributor harness connector; it should be within 1 volt of battery voltage.

19. If correct, turn the ignition switch to the OFF position. Disconnect the dual connector from the computer and check for continuity between terminal 2 of distributor harness and terminal 9 of the dual connector. Repeat test on terminal 3 of distributor harness and terminal 5 of dual connector. If no continuity, repair the harness. If continuity is present, replace the computer and repeat Step 16.

20. If no battery voltage is present in Step 18, turn off the ignition switch, disconnect the 10 terminal dual connector from the computer and check for continuity between terminal 1 of distributor harness and terminal 3 of dual connector. If no continuity, repair wire and repeat Step 16.

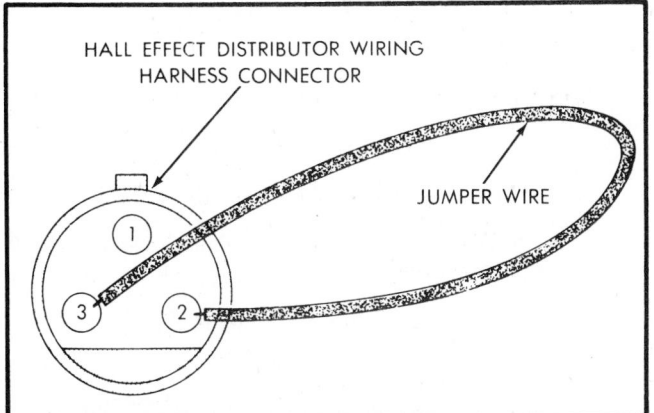

Use of jumper wire at terminals "2" and "3" — front wheel drive vehicles

21. If continuity is present, turn the ignition switch on and check for battery voltage between terminal 2 and terminal 10 of the dual connector. If voltage is present, replace the computer and repeat Step 16. If no battery voltage is present, the computer is not grounded. Check and repair the ground wire and repeat Step 16.

TESTING FOR POOR ENGINE PERFORMANCE

Correct basic engine timing is essential for optimum vehicle performance and must be checked before any of the following testing procedures are performed. Refer to the individual vehicle section for ignition timing procedures and/or refer to the Vehicle Information label, located in the engine compartment.

CARBURETOR SWITCH

Testing

NOTE: Grounding the carburetor switch on most systems with a feedback carburetor will give a fixed air/fuel ratio.

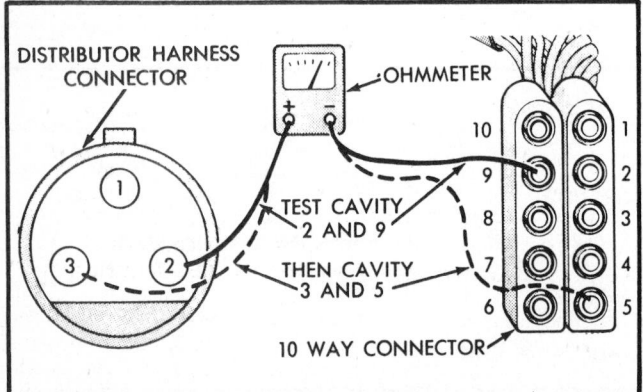

Testing cavities "2" and "9" and then cavities "3" and "5" for continuity — front wheel drive vehicles

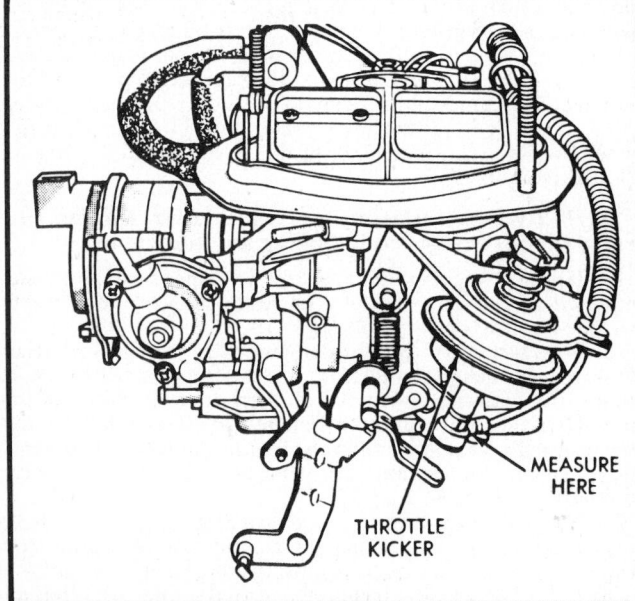

Measuring points for carburetor switch

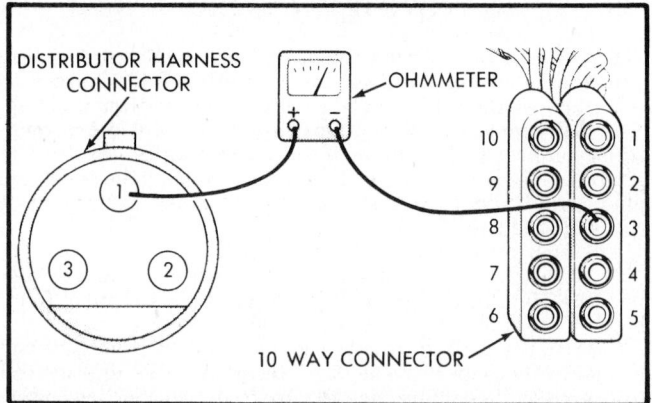

Testing for continuity between cavities "1" and "3" — front wheel drive vehicles

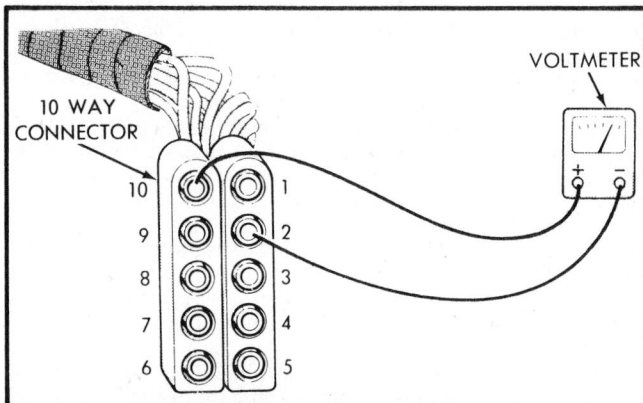

Testing for voltage between cavities "2" and "10" — front wheel drive vehicles

1. With the key off, disconnect the dual connector from the computer.
2. With the throttle completely closed, check the continuity between terminal 7 of the connector and a good ground. If there is no continuity, check the wire and the carburetor switch.
3. With the throttle open, check the continuity between terminal 7 of the connector and a good ground. There should be no continuity.

COOLANT SWITCH

Testing

1. With the key in the OFF position, disconnect the wire connector from the coolant sensor.
2. Connect one lead of the ohmmeter to one terminal of the coolant sensor.
3. Connect the other lead of the ohmmeter to the remaining connector of the coolant sensor.
4. With the engine/sensor at room temperature around 70° F., the reading should be 5000 to 6000 ohms.

DETONATION SENSOR Test

Testing

1. Connect an adjustable timing light to the engine.
2. Place the fast idle screw on the second highest step of the fast idle cam. Start the engine and allow it to idle. The engine should be running at 1200 rpm or more.

3. Use an open end wrench to tap lightly on the intake manifold next to the detonation sensor. As this is done, watch the timing marks; a decrease in timing advance should be seen. The amount of decrease should be directly proportional to the strength and frequency of tapping. Maximum retard is 11°.

4. If the sensor is not working correctly, install a new sensor and retest.

ELECTRONIC THROTTLE CONTROL SYSTEM

Incorporated within the spark control computer is the electronic throttle system. A solenoid, which regulates a vacuum dashpot is energized when the air conditioner or electronic timers are activated. The two timers which are incorporated within the ignition electronics operate when the throttle is closed, plus a time delay of 2 seconds or after an engine start condition.

Testing

1. Connect a tachometer to the engine.

2. Start the engine and bring to normal operating temperature.

3. Depress the accelerator and release it. A higher than curb engine idle should be seen for a specified time.

4. On vehicles equipped with/and turning on the A/C, a slight decrease in the idle speed will be noted. Turning off the A/C will produce the normal idle speed.

NOTE: The A/C clutch will cycle on and off as the system is in operation. This should not be mistaken as part of the electronic control system.

5. As the A/C compressor clutch cycles on and off, the solekicker plunger should extend and retract.

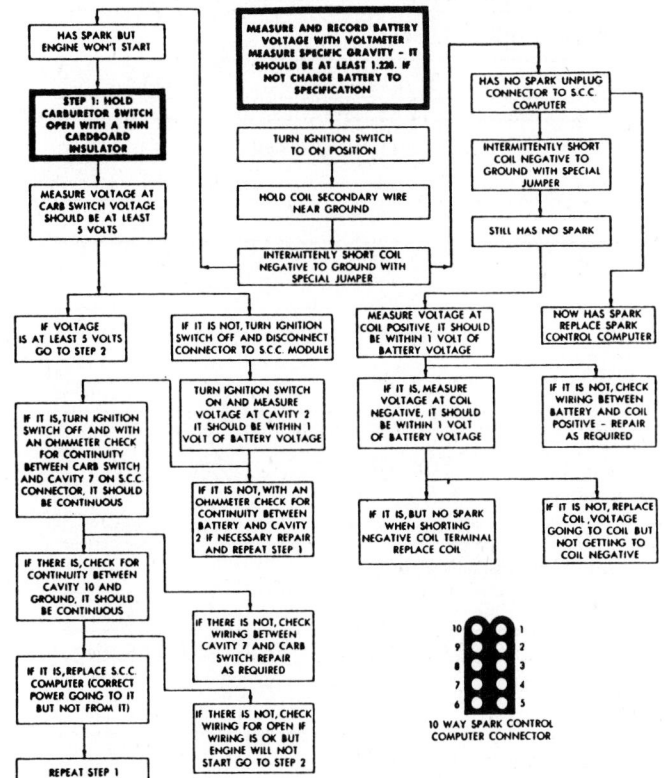

Hall Effect Electronic Spark Advance system diagnosis

Hall Effect Electronic Spark Advance system diagnosis (cont.), with step three for 1984 models

6. If the plunger does not move with the A/C clutch cycling or after a start-up, check the kicker system for vacuum leaks.

7. If the speed increases do not occur, disconnect the six way connector at the carburetor.

8. Check the solenoid with an ohmmeter by measuring the resistance across the terminal that contains the black wire to ground. The resistance should be between 20 and 100 ohms. If not within specifications, replace the solenoid.

9. Start the vehicle and before the time delay has timed out, measure the voltage across vacuum solenoid terminals. The voltage should be within 2 volts of charging system voltage. If not within specifications, replace the computer.

10. Turning the A/C on should also produce charging system voltage after the time delay has timed out. If not, check the wiring back to the instrument panel for an open circuit.

SPARK ADVANCE OF SPARK CONTROL COMPUTER

Incorporated in the digital microprocessor electronics are some unique spark advance schedules, which occur during cold weather operation. These commands have been added to reduce engine emissions and improve driveability. Because they will be changing at different engine operating temperatures during the engine warm-up, all spark advance testing should be done with the engine at normal operating temperature.

Testing

1. Adjust the basic timing to specifications.

2. Have the engine at normal operating temperature and the temperature sensor operating correctly.

3. Remove and plug the vacuum hose athe the vacuum transducer.

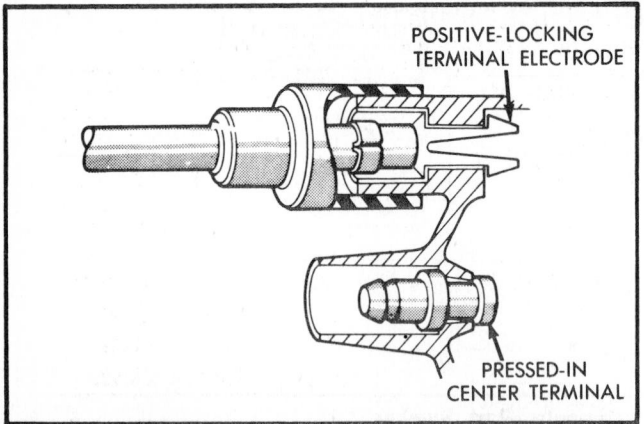

POSITIVE-LOCKING
TERMINAL ELECTRODE

PRESSED-IN
CENTER TERMINAL

Positive locking secondary ignition wire terminal. To remove, press lock together and push wire out of distributor cap—front wheel drive vehicles

4. Connect an auxillary vacuum supply to the vacuum transducer and adjust the vacuum to 16 in.Hg.

5. Start and raise the engine speed to 2000 rpm. Wait one minute and check the specifications.

6. The advance specifications are in addition to basic advance.

HALL EFFECT PICKUP

Removal and Installation

1. Loosen the distributor cap retaining screws and remove the cap.

2. Pull straight up on the rotor and remove it from the shaft.

3. Disconnect the pickup assembly lead.

4. Remove the pickup lead hold down screw, if equipped.

5. Remove the pickup assembly lock springs, if present and lift off the pickup.

6. Install the new pickup assembly onto the distributor housing and fasten it into place with the lock springs.

7. Fasten the pickup lead to the housing with the hold down screw, if equipped.

8. Reconnect the lead to the harness.

9. Press the rotor back into place on the shaft. Do not wipe off the silicone grease on the metal portion of the rotor.

10. Replace the distributor cap and tighten the retaining screws.

——————— CAUTION ———————

Care must be exercised during pick-up installation. The Hall Effect pick-up assembly leads may be damaged if not properly installed. Make sure that the lead retainer is properly seated in the locating hole before attaching the distributor cap.

SECONDARY WIRE RETENTION

The spark plug wires do not pull from the distributor cap, but are retained with positive locking terminal electrodes and must be released from inside the distributor cap. The coil secondary lead is retained in the cap in the conventional manner.

ELECTRONIC SPARK CONTROL SYSTEM
1984 1.6L, 2.2L Carbureted Engines

	Computer Part Number			
	5226106	5226162	5226164	5226118
Engine Application	1.6L E82 ECA Fed., Cal., (M) P.V.	1.6L E82 ECA Fed. (A) P.V.	1.6L E82 ECA Can. (M-A) P.V.	2.2L E62 EDE Fed., (M) P.V. T110 Hi-Alt. (M) TR
Basic Timing	12° BTDC**	12° BTDC**	12° BTDC**	10° BTDC**
Curb Idle Speed RPM***	(M) 850–875	(A) 1025	(M) 850–875(A) 1025	(M) 800
Spark Advance Test 2000 RPM 16 in. Vacuum Including Basic Timing	33° ±4°	33° 4°±	33° ±4°	42°±4°
Electronic Throttle Control	No	90 Sec. After Start 2 Sec. Off Idle 1 Sec. After Throttle Closes	90 Sec. After Start 2 Sec. Off Idle 1 Sec. After Throttle Closes	90 Sec. After Start

	Computer Part Number			
	5226122	5226158	5226160	5226166
Engine Application	2.2L E62 EDE Cal. (M) P.V. T110 Tr	2.2L E68 EDJ Fed. (M) P.V. Shelby ①	2.2L E68 EDJ Cal. (M) P.V. Shelby ①	2.2L E62 EDE Fed. (A) P.V. T110 Hi-Alt.* (A) TR
Basic Timing	10° BTDC**	15° BTDC**	15° BTDC**	10° BTDC**
Curb Idle Speed RPM***	(M) 800	(M) 850	(M) 850	(A) 900

ELECTRONIC SPARK CONTROL SYSTEM
1984 1.6L, 2.2L Carbureted Engines

	Computer Part Number			
	5226122	5226158	5226160	5226166
Spark Advance Test 2000 RPM 16 in. Vacuum Including Basic Timing	40° ±4°	43° ±4°	43° ±4°	38° ±4°
Electronic Throttle Control	90 Sec. After Start	90 Sec. After Start	90 Sec. After Start	90 Sec. After Start 2 Sec. Off Idle 1 Sec. After Throttle Closes

	Computer Part Number		
	5226168	5226174	5226180
Engine Application	2.2L E62 EDE Cal. (A) P.V. & T110 TR	2.2L E62 EDE Fed. (M-A) T110 TR	2.2L E62 EDE Can. (M-A) P.V. & T110 TR
Basic Timing	10° BTDC**	10° BTDC**	10° BTDC**
Curb Idle Speed RPM***	(A) 900	(M) 850 (A) 1000	(M-A) 900
Spark Advance Test 2000 RPM 16 in. Vacuum Including Basic Timing	40° ±4°	40° ±4°	40° ±4°
Electronic Throttle Control	90 Sec. After Start 2 Sec. Off Idle 1 Sec. After Throttle Closes	90 Sec. After Start 2 Sec. Off Idle 1 Sec. After Throttle Closes	90 Sec. After Start 2 Sec. Off Idle 1 Sec. After Throttle Closes

Should the listed specifications differ from those on the Emission Control Information Label, use the specifications on the label

(A) — Automatic Transmission
(M) — Manual Transmission
Can. — Canada
Fed. — Federal
Cal. — California
BTDC — Before Top Dead Center

P.V. — Passenger Vehicle
TR — Truck
* High Altitude
**Basic Timing set with vacuum line disconnected. Do not readjust curb idle

*** Curb Idle set with vacuum line connected
① Has denotation suppression

ELECTRONIC SPARK CONTROL SYSTEM
1985 1.6L, 2.2L Carbureted Engines

	Computer Part Number			
	5226411	5226429	5226433	5226439
Engine Application	1.6L E82 ECA Fed., Cal. (M) P.V.	1.6L E82 ECA Can. (M-A) P.V.	2.2L E62 EDE Fed. (A) P.V. Cal., Hi-Alt. T110 (A) TR	2.2L E62 EDE Fed. (M) P.V. Cal., Hi-Alt. T110 (M) TR
Basic Timing	12° BTDC**	12° BTDC**	10° BTDC**	10° BTDC**
Curb Idle Speed RPM***	(M) 850-875	(M) 850–875 (A) 1025	(A) 900	(M) 800
Spark Advance Test 2000 RPM 16 in. Vacuum Including Basic Timing	33° ±4°	33° ±4°	41° ±4°	42° ±4°

ELECTRONIC SPARK CONTROL SYSTEM
1985 1.6L, 2.2L Carbureted Engines

	Computer Part Number			
	5226411	5226429	5226433	5226439
Electronic Throttle Control	No	90 Sec. After Start 2 Sec. Off Idle 1 Sec. After Throttle Closes	30 Sec. Hot 300 Sec. Cold 2 Sec. Off Idle 2 Sec. After Throttle Closes	30 Sec. Hot 300 Sec. Cold After Start

	Computer Part Number			
	5226449	5226451	5226455	5226505
Engine Application	2.2L E68 EDJ Fed. (M) P.V. Shelby	2.2L E62 EDE Cal. (A) P.V.	2.2L E62 EDE Cal. (M) P.V.	2.2L E62 EDE Can. (A) Can., T110 (A) TR
Basic Timing	15° BTDC**	10° BTDC**	10° BTDC**	10° BTDC**
Curb Idle Speed RPM*	(M) 800	(A) 900	(M) 850	(M) 850
Spark Advance Test 2000 RPM 16 in. Vacuum Including Basic Timing	38° ±4°	37° ±4°	42° ±4°	41° ±4°
Electronic Throttle Control	30 Sec. Hot 300 Sec. Cold After Start	30 Sec. Hot 300 Sec. Cold 2 Sec. Off Idle 2 Sec. After Throttle Closes	30 Sec. Hot 300 Sec. Cold After Start	120 Sec. Hot 300 Sec Cold 2 Sec. Off Idle 2 Sec. After Throttle Closes

	Computer Part Number	
	5226507	5226645
Engine Application	2.2L E62 EDE Can. (M) P.V. and T110 TR	2.2L E68 EDJ Cal. (M) P.V. Shelby ①
Basic Timing	10° BTDC**	15° BTDC**
Curb Idle Speed RPM*	(M) 900	(M) 850
Spark Advance Test 2000 RPM 16 in. Vacuum Including Basic Timing	41° ±4°	36° ±4°
Electronic Throttle Control	90 Sec. Hot After Start 300 Sec. Cold After Start	30 Sec. Hot After Start 300 Sec. Cold After Start

Should the listed specifications differ from those on the Emission Control Information Label, use the specifications on the label

(A)—Automatic Transmission
(M)—Manual Transmission
Can.—Canada
Fed.—Federal
Cal.—California
BTDC—Before Top Dead Center
P.V.—Passenger Vehicle
TR—Truck
* High Altitude
**Basic Timing set with vacuum line disconnected. Do not readjust curb idle
*** Curb Idle set with vacuum line connected
① Has denotation suppression

ELECTRONIC SPARK CONTROL SYSTEM
1986 1.6L, 2.2L Carbureted Engines

	Computer Part Number			
	5226411	**5226429**	**5226433**	**5226439**
Engine Application	1.6L E82 ECA Fed., Cal., (M) P.V.	1.6L E82 ECA Can., (M) P.V.	2.2L E62 EDE Fed. (A) P.V. Cal., Hi-Alt	2.2L E62 EDE Fed. (M) P.V. Cal. Hi-Alt
Basic Timing	12° BTDC**	12° BTDC**	10° BTDC**	10° BTDC**
Curb Idle Speed RPM*	(M) 850	(M) 850	(A) 900	(M) 800
Spark Advance Test 2000 RPM 16 in. Vacuum Including Basic Timing	33° ±4°	33° ± 4°	41° ±4°	42° ± 4°
Electronic Throttle Control	No	90 Sec. After Start 2 Sec. Off Idle 1 Sec. After Throttle Closes Throttle Closes	30 Sec. Hot. 30 Sec. Cold 2 Sec. Off Idle 2 Sec. After Throttle Closes	30 Sec. Hot 300 Sec. Cold After Start

	Computer Part Number			
	5226451	**5226455**	**5226505**	**5226507**
Engine Application	2.2L E62 EDE Cal. (A) P.V.	2.2L E62 EDE Cal. (M) P.V.	2.2L E62 EDE Can. (A) Can.	2.2L E62 EDE Can. (M) P.V.
Basic Timing	10° BTDC**	10° BTDC**	10° BTDC**	10° BTDC**
Curb Idle Speed RPM*	(A) 900	(M) 800	(A) 900	(M) 900
Spark Advance Test 2000 RPM 16 in. Vacuum Including Basic Timing	37° ±4°	42° ±4°	41° ±4°	41° ±4°
Electronic Throttle Control	30 Sec. Hot. 30 Sec. Cold 2 Sec. Off Idle 2 Sec. After Throttle Closes	30 Sec. Hot 300 Sec. Cold After Start	120 Sec. Hot. 2 Sec Cold 2 Sec. Off Idle 2 Sec. After Throttle Closes	90 Sec. Hot After Start 300 Sec. Cold After Start

	Computer Part Number	
	5226645	**5227097**
Engine Application	2.2L E68 EDJ Cal. (M) P.V. Shelby ①	2.2L E68 EDJ Fed. (M) P.V. Shelby ①
Basic Timing	15° BTDC**	15° BTDC**
Curb Idle Speed RPM*	(M) 850	(M) 850
Spark Advance Test 2000 RPM 16 in. Vacuum Including Basic Timing	36° ±4°	43° ±4°
Electronic Throttle Control	30 Sec. Hot After Start 300 Sec. Cold After Start	30 Sec. Hot 300 Sec. Cold After Start

Should the listed specifications differ from those on the Emission Control Information Label, use the specifications on the label

(A) — Automatic Transmission
(M) — Manual Transmission
Can. — Canada
Fed. — Federal
Cal. — California
BTDC — Before Top Dead Center
P.V. — Passenger Vehicle

TR — Truck
* High Altitude
**Basic Timing set with vacuum line disconnected. Do not readjust curb idle
*** Curb Idle set with vacuum line connected
① Has denotation suppression

ELECTRONIC SPARK CONTROL SYSTEM
1984 1.6L, 2.2L Carbureted Engines

	Computer Part Number		
	5227614	5227608	5227612
Engine Application	2.2L E62 EDA Can. (A) Cal.	2.2L E62 EDE Fed. (A) P.V. Can., Hi-Alt*	2.2L E62 EDE Fed. (M) P.V. Cal., Can., Hi-Alt.
Basic Timing	10° BTDC**	10° BTDC**	10° BTDC**
Curb Idle Speed RPM***	(A) 900	(A) 900	(M) 800
Spark Advance Test 2000 RPM 16 in. Vacuum Including Basic Timing	36° ±4°	40° ±4°	40° ±4°
Electronic Throttle Control	60 Sec. Hot, 535 Sec. Cold 2 Sec. Off Idle 2 Sec. After Throttle Closes	60 Sec. Hot, 535 Cold 2 Sec. Off Idle 2 Sec. After Throttle Closes	535 Sec. Cold After Start

Should the listed specifications differ from those on the Emission Control Information Label, use the specifications on the label

(A)—Automatic Transmission
(M)—Manual Transmission
Can.—Canada
Fed.—Federal
Cal.—California

BTDC—Before Top Dead Center
P.V.—Passenger Vehicle
TR—Truck
* High Altitude

**Basic Timing set with vacuum line disconnected. Do not readjust curb idle
*** Curb Idle set with vacuum line connected

CHRYSLER ELECTRONIC IGNITION (EIS) SYSTEM

General Information

1984-85 2.6L ENGINE

This system consists of the battery, ignition coil, IC igniter (electronic control unit) which is built into the distributor, spark plugs, primary and secondary wiring. Primary current to the coil is switched on and off by the IC igniter in response to timing signals produced by the distributor magnetic pick-up.

The distributor consists of a power distributing section, IC igniter, advance mechanism, drive section and the signal generator. The signal generator, which houses a small magneto, produces a signal for driving the IC igniter. The signal is produced in exact synchronism with distributor shaft rotation. It is produced at equal intervals four times distributor shaft rotation. The distributor uses this signal as an ignition timing signal during its operation. The distributor is equipped with vacuum and centrifugal advance mechanisms.

The centrifugal advance mechanism is located below the rotor assembly. It is equipped with governor weights that move outward and inward depending on engine speed. As engine speed increases, the weights move outward which causes the reluctor to rotate ahead of the distributor shaft. This causes the ignition timing to advance.

The vacuum advance incorporates a spring loaded diaphragm which is connected to the breaker assembly. The diaphragm moves against the spring pressure by carburetor vacuum pressure. When the vacuum increases, the diaphragm causes the movable breaker assembly to pivot in direction opposite to distributor rotation. This action advances the ignition timing.

Troubleshooting

COIL SPARK

Test

1. Remove the coil wire from the center of the distributor cap.
2. Using heavy gloves and insulated pliers, hold the end of the wire 3/16 – 3/8 in. away from a good engine ground and crank the engine.

NOTE: Make sure there are no fuel leaks before performing this test.

3. If there is a spark at the coil wire, it must be bright blue in color and fire consistently. If it is, continue to crank the engine while slowly moving the coil wire away from ground. Look for arcing at the coil tower. If arcing occurs, replace coil. If there is no spark, or spark is weak or not consistent, proceed to the next step.
4. If a good spark is present, check the condition of the distributor cap, rotor, plug wires and spark plugs. If these check out, the ignition system is working; check the fuel system and engine mechanical systems.
5. With the ignition on, measure the voltage at the negative coil terminal. It should be the same as battery voltage. If it is 3 volts or less, the IC distributor is defective. If there is no voltage, check for an open circuit in the coil or wiring.
6. With the ignition on, hold the coil wire as instructed in Step 2 and using a jumper wire, momentarily connect the nega-

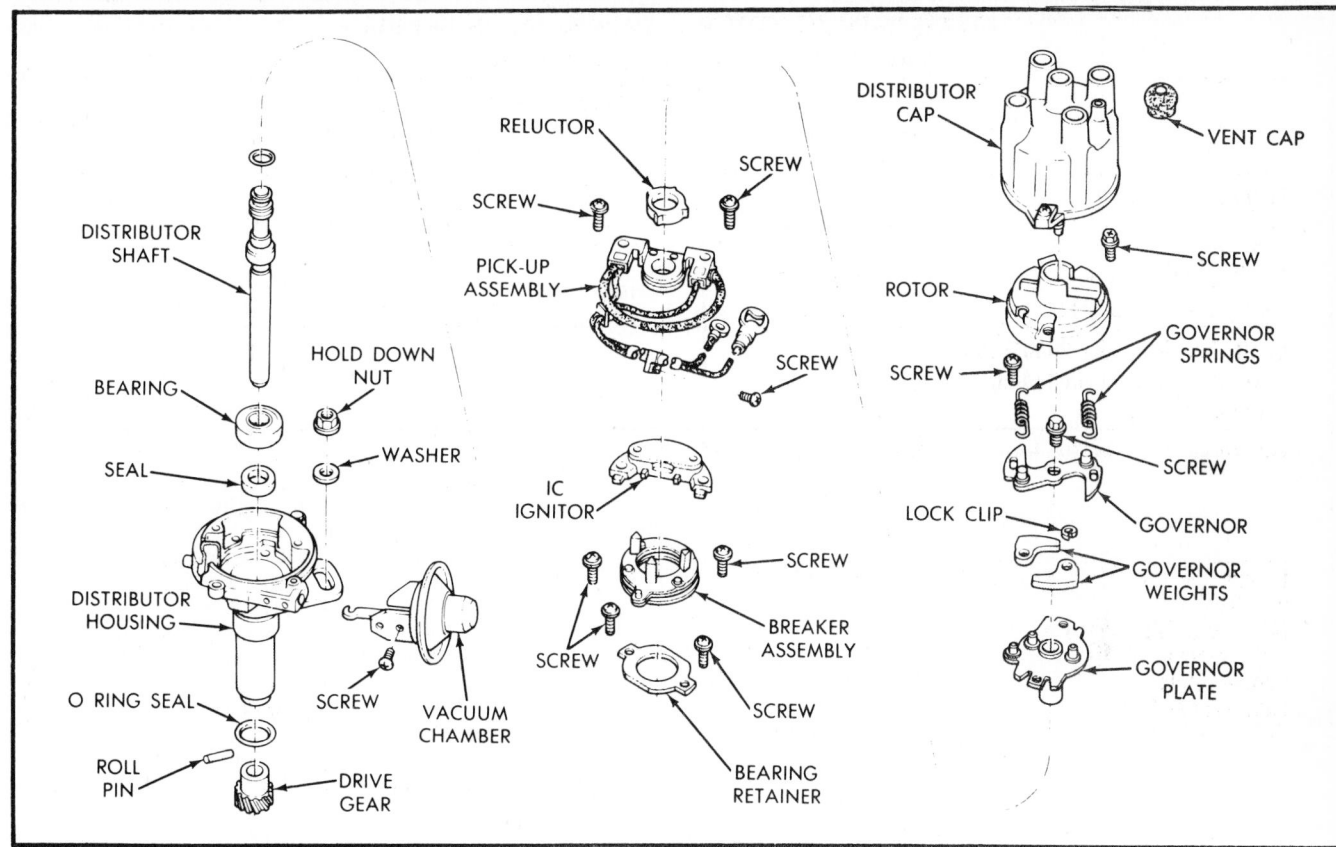

Exploded view of distributor

tive coil terminal to ground. There should be a spark at the coil wire.

7. If there is no spark, check for voltage at the positive coil terminal with the key on. Voltage should be at least 9 volts. If proper voltage is obtained, the coil is defective and should be replaced. If proper voltage is not obtained, check the wiring and connections.

CENTRIFUGAL ADVANCE

Test

1. Run the engine at idle and remove the vacuum hose from the vacuum controller.
2. Slowly accelerate the engine to check for advance.
3. Excessive advance indicates a damaged governor spring (a broken spring will result in abrupt advance).
4. Insufficient advance is usually caused by a broken governor weight or a malfunction in cam operation. Correct as needed.

VACUUM ADVANCE

Test

1. Connect a timing light and adjust the engine speed to 2500 rpm.
2. Check for advance by disconnecting and then reconnecting the vacuum hose at the distributor and watching the advance or retard at the crankshaft indicator.
3. For a more accurate determination of whether the vacuum advance mechanism is operating properly, remove the vacuum hose from the distributor and connect a hand vacuum pump.

4. Run the engine at idle and slowly apply vacuum pressure to check for advance.
5. If excessive advance is noted, look for a deteriorated vacuum controller spring.
6. If insufficient advance or no advance is noted, this could be caused by linkages problems or a ruptured vacuum diaphragm. Correct as necessary.

IGNITION COIL

Test

1. Clean the ignition coil.
2. Check the coil terminals for cleanliness and exterior of body for cracks. Replace if necessary.
3. Check for carbon deposit or corrosion in the high tension cable inserting hole. Repair or replace if necessary.
4. Measure the resistance of the primary coil, secondary coil and external resistor.
5. If the reading is not within 1.3–1.8 ohms on the primary coil and 9000–12000 ohms on the secondary coil windings, replace the coil.

IGNITION WIRE RESISTANCE

Test

— CAUTION —
When removing the high voltage cable at the ignition coil, grasp the cable rubber cap. Twist and pull slowly. Do not bend the cable. This could result in breaking the conductor.

1. Check the cable terminals.
2. A corroded terminal should be cleaned or replaced.

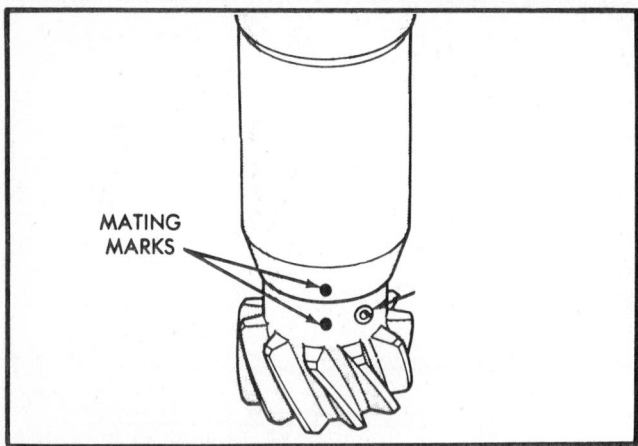

Timing mating marks

3. A broken or severely distorted cable should be replaced.

4. Check the resistance of each cable between both ends. If it exceeds 22 kilo-ohms, replace the wire.

5. Use silicone lubricant when installing wires on spark plugs.

DISTRIBUTOR

Removal

1. Disconnect the negative battery cable.
2. Disconnect the wiring harness from the distributor and the wires from the distributor cap. Note their location for ease of reassembly.

3. Disconnect the vacuum hose from the vacuum advance unit.

4. Rotate the engine crankshaft (in the direction of normal rotation) until the number one cylinder is at top dead center (TDC) on the compression stroke. Make a mark on the block where the rotor points to act as a reference for installation.

5. Remove the distributor hold-down nut and lift the distributor assembly away from the engine.

Installation
ENGINE CRANKED

1. If the engine has been cranked over while the distributor was removed, rotate the crankshaft until the No. 1 piston is at TDC on the compression stroke. Align the timing marks on the crankshaft to TDC mark on the timing plate.

2. Align the mating mark on the distributor housing with the mating mark on the distributor driven gear.

3. Lower the distributor into the engine. Tighten the hold-down nut and connect the wires.

4. Check and if necessary, adjust the ignition timing.

ENGINE NOT CRANKED

1. If the engine was not disturbed while the distributor was out, lower the distributor into the engine.

2. Make sure that the distributor gears are properly engaged with the engine.

3. Tighten the hold-down nut and connect the wires.

4. Check the ignition timing. Adjust if necessary.

CHRYSLER ELECTRONIC IGNITION SYSTEMS

GENERAL INFORMATION

1984 V-8 MODELS WITH DUAL PICK–UP AND VACUUM ADVANCE

The system consists of the battery, ignition switch, ignition resistor control unit, coil, dual pick-up distributor with vacuum advance mechanism, dual pick-up start/run relay, spark plugs and the necessary components for the routing of primary and secondary current.

During engine cranking, the dual pick-up start-run relay is energized through the starter solenoid circuit, which allows the start pick-up to adjust the timing for starting purposes only. As soon as the starter solenoid is de-energized, the start-run relay switches the sensing function back to the run pick-up.

The pick-up circuit is used to sense the proper timing for the control unit switch transistor. The reluctor rotating with the distributor shaft produces a voltage pulse in the magnetic pick-up each time a spark plug should be fired. This pulse is transmitted through the pick-up coil to the power switching transistor in the control unit and causes the transistor to interupt the current flow through the primary circuit. This break in the primary circuit induces a high voltage in the secondary coil circuit and fires the appropriate spark plug.

The length of time the switching transistor allows the current to flow in the primary circuit is determined by the electronic circuitry in the control unit. This determines "DWELL".

NOTE: Dwell is not adjustable and there is no means to change it because changes are not required.

ELECTRONIC IGNITION TEST

NOTE: To properly test the Electronic Ignition System, special testers should be used. But, in the event they are not available, the system may be tested using a voltmeter with a 20,000 ohm/volt rating and an ohmmeter which uses a 9 volt battery for its operation. Both meters should be in calibration.

Electronic Ignition system schematic, 1984 V8 models with dual pick-up and vacuum advance

Testing

1. Visually inspect all secondary cables at the coil, distributor and spark plugs for cracks and tightness.

2. Check the primary wire at the coil and ballast resistor for tightness.

CAUTION

Whenever removing or installing the wiring harness connector to the control unit, the ignition switch must be in the OFF position.

3. With a voltmeter, measure the voltage at the battery and to ascertain that enough current is available to operate the cranking and ignition systems.

4. Remove the coil secondary wire from the distributor cap.

5. With the key on, use a jumper wire and momentarily touch the negative terminal of the coil to ground while holding the coil secondary wire approximately $\frac{1}{4}$ in. from a good engine ground. A spark should be observed.

6. If no spark is obtained, turn the ignition key to the OFF position and disconnect the four wire harness going to the ECU control unit.

7. With the ignition key in the ON position, again use the jumper wire and ground the negative terminal of the coil to ground while holding the coil secondary wire approximately $\frac{1}{4}$ in. from a good engine ground. If a spark is observed, replace the ECU.

8. If no spark is observed, measure the voltage at the coil positive terminal. The voltage should be within one volt of battery voltage.

9. If battery voltage is not present, check wiring between battery positive terminal and the coil. Replace the starter relay if the wiring is correct.

10. If the current is not continuous between the battery and the coil positive terminal, replace the ignition resistor and repeat the test.

11. Check the battery voltage at the coil negative terminal. It should be within one volt of battery voltage.

12. If battery voltage is present at the negative coil terminal, but no spark is obtained when shorting the terminal with a jumper wire, replace the ignition coil.

13. If spark is obtained, but the engine will not start, turn the ignition switch to the OFF position and pull the ECU harness connector off, turn the ignition switch to the ON position cnd check for battery voltage at cavity No. 2 of the ECU harness connector. The voltage should be within one volt of battery voltage.

14. If no battery voltage is present, turn the ignition switch to the OFF position and check for continuity betrween cavity No. 2 and the coil negative terminal. If no continity is obtained, find the wiring fault, repair it and retest.

15. Check for continity between cavity No. 1 of the ECU connector and the ignition switch. If none exists, find the fault, repair it and retest.

16. If voltage is obtained at cavity No. 2 of the ECU connector, Turn the ignition switch to the OFFG position and with an ohmmeter, check the resistance between cavities No.4 and No. 5 of the ECU connector. The reading should range between 150 and 900 ohms.

17. If the resistance is not between 150 and 900 ohms, Disconnect the distributor pick-up leads. Measure the resistance at the pick-up 'leads. The resistance should be bewtween 150 and 900 ohms. If the resistance is not within the accepted range, the pick-up coils are bad and must be replaced.

18. If the resistance at the pick-up leads is within specifications, thei would indicate the wiring between cavities No. 4 and No. 5 are open or shorted, or the dual pick-up start/run relay is defective. Repair and retest as required.

19. Check pin No. 5 of the ECU for ground. If no ground is obtained, check the ECU for poor or dirty connections and tight mounting screws.

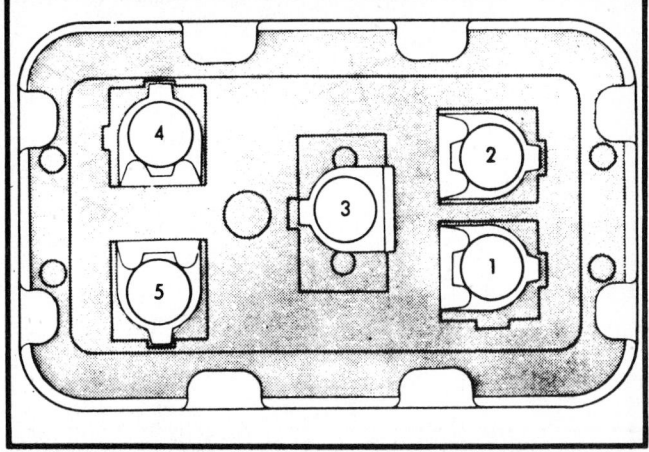

Dual pick-up start/run relay, 1984 V8 models

20. Reinstall all connections and check for spark. If no spark occurs, replace the ECU.

DUAL PICK–UP START/RUN RELAY TEST

Testing

1. Remove the two way connector from pins No. 4 and No. 5 of the dual pick-up start/run relay.

2. Using an ohmmeter, touch pins No. 4 and No.5. The meter should read 20-30 ohms. If not, replace the relay.

PICK–UP COIL AIR GAP

Adjustment

In the dual pick-up distributor, the start pick-up is identified by a two prong male connector and the run pick-up is identified by a male and female plug.

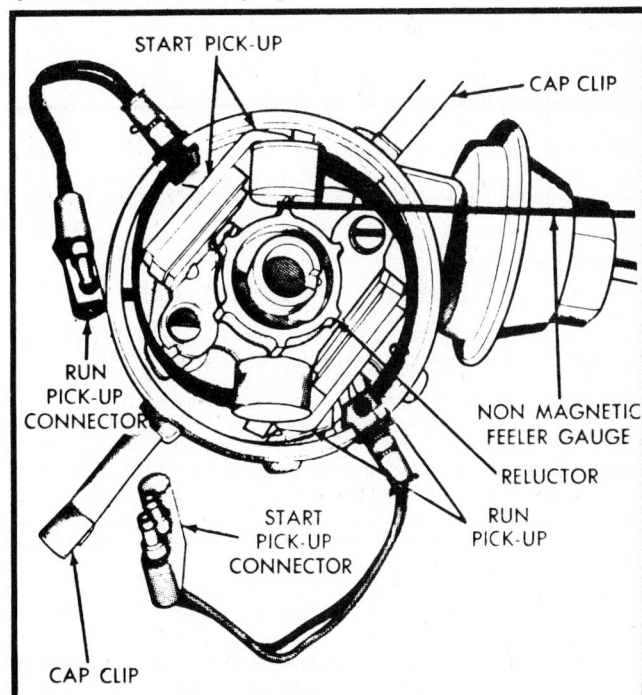

Dual pick-up distributor with vacuum advance, 1984 V8 models

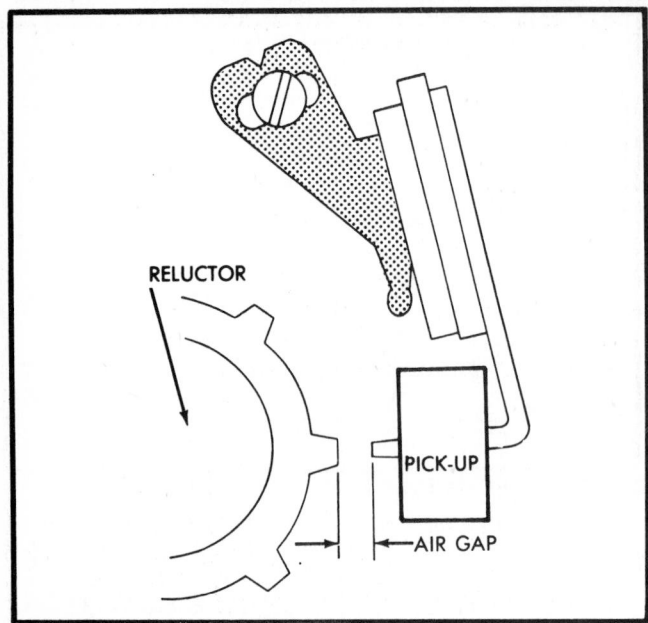

Air adjustment

START PICK–UP

1. Align one reluctor tooth with the pick-up coil tooth.
2. Loosen the pick-up coil holddown screw.
3. Insert a 0.006 in. non-magnetic feeler gauge between the reluctor tooth and the pick-up coil tooth.
4. Adjust the air gap so that contact is made between the reluctor tooth, the feeler gauge and the pick-up tooth.
5. Carefully tighten the holddown screw.
6. Remove the feeler gauge. There should be no force needed to remove the gauge.
7. Check the air gap with a NO-GO 0.008 in. feeler gauge. Do not force the gauge in the air gap.

RUN PICK–UP

1. Align on reluctor tooth with the pick-up coil tooth.

2. Loosen the pick-up coil holddown screw.
3. Insert a 0.012 in. non-magnetic feeler gauge beteeen the reluctor tooth and the pick-up tooth.
4. Adjust the air gap so that contact is made between the reluctor tooth, feeler gauge and the pick-up coil tooth.
5. Carefully tighten the holddown screw.
6. Remove the feeler gauge. There should be no force required to remove it.
7. Check the air gap with a NO-GO 0.014 in. feeler gauge. Do not force the gauge in the air gap.

CENTRIFUGAL ADVANCE

Test

1. With a timing light connected, operate the engine at idle and remove the vacuum hose from the vacuum controller.
2. Slowly accelerate the engine to check for advance.
3. Excessive advance indicates a damaged governor spring (a broken spring will result in abrupt advance).
4. Insufficient advance is usually caused by a broken governor weight or a malfunction in cam operation. Correct as needed.

VACUUM ADVANCE

Test

1. Connect a timing light and adjust the engine speed to 2500 rpm.
2. Check for advance by disconnecting and then reconnecting the vacuum hose at the distributor and watching the advance or retard at the crankshaft indicator.
3. For a more accurate determination of whether the vacuum advance mechanism is operating properly, remove the vacuum hose from the distributor and connect a hand vacuum pump.
4. Run the engine at idle and slowly apply vacuum pressure to check for advance.
5. If excessive advance is noted, look for a deteriorated vacuum controller spring.
6. If insufficient advance or no advance is noted, this could be caused by linkages problems or a ruptured vacuum diaphragm. Correct as necessary.

CHRYSLER CORPORATION ELECTRONIC SPARK CONTROL SYSTEM

GENERAL INFORMATION

1984-88 V–8 ENGINES WITH DUAL PICK–UP DISTRIBUTORS LESS VACUUM ADVANCE

The computer provides the engine with Ignition Spark Control during starting and during engine operation, providing an infinitely variable spark advance curve. Input data is fed instantaneously to the computer by a series of sensors located in the engine compartment which monitor timing, water temperature, air temperature, idle/off-idle operation and intake manifold vacuum. The program schedule module of the Spark Control Computer receives the information from the sensors, processes it and then directs the ignition control module to advance or retard the timing as necessary. This whole process is going on continuously as the engine is running, taking only milliseconds to complete a circuit from sensor to distributor. The main components of the system are a modified carburetor and Spark Control Computer, which is responsible for translating input data and which transmits data to the distributor to advance or retard the timing.

There are two functional modes of the computer, start and run. The start mode will only function during engine cranking and starting. The run mode only functions after the engine start and during engine operation. The two will never operate together.

Should a failure of the run mode of the computer occur, the system will go into a limp-in mode. This will enable the operator to continue to drive the vehicle until it can be repaired. However, while in this mode, very poor engine operation will result. Should failure of the pick-up coils or the start mode of the computer occur, the engine will not start.

The pick-up coil signal is a reference signal. When the signal is received by the computer the maximum amount of timing advance is made available. Based on the data from all the sensors, the computer determines how much of this maximum advance is needed at that instant.

The amount of spark advance is determined by two factors, enginbe speed and engine vacuum. However, when it happens depends on the following conditions:

1. Advance from the vacuum will ge given by the computer

when the carbutetor switch is open. The amount is programmed into the computer and is proportional to the amount of vacuum and engine rpm.

2. Advance from speed is given by the computer when the carburetor switch is open and is programmed to engine rpm.

IGNITION COMPUTER

The computer consists of one electronic printed circuit board which simultaneously receives signals from all the sensors and within milliseconds, analyzes them to determine how the engine is operating and then advances or retards the ignition timing by signaling the ignition coil to produce the electrical impulses to fire the spark plugs at the exact instant when ignition is required

MICROPROCESSOR ELECTRONIC SPARK CONTROL

The microprocessor is an electronic module located within the computer that processes the signals from the engine sensor for accurate engine spark timing. Its digital electronic circuitry offers more operating precision and programming flexibility than the voltage dependent analog system used previously.

MAGNETIC PICK–UP ASSEMBLIES

The start and the run pick-up sensors are located inside the distributor, suppling a signal to the computer to provide a fixed timing point that is used for starting (start pick-up) and the second for normal engine operation (run pick-up). The start pick-up also has a back-up function of taking over engine timing in case the run pick-up fails. Since the timing in this pick-

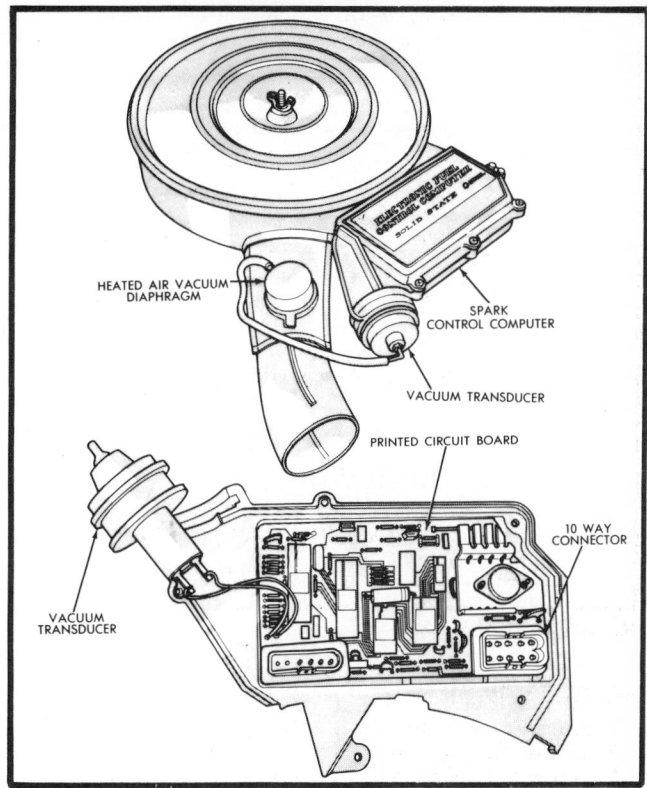

Combustion Computer assembly – typical

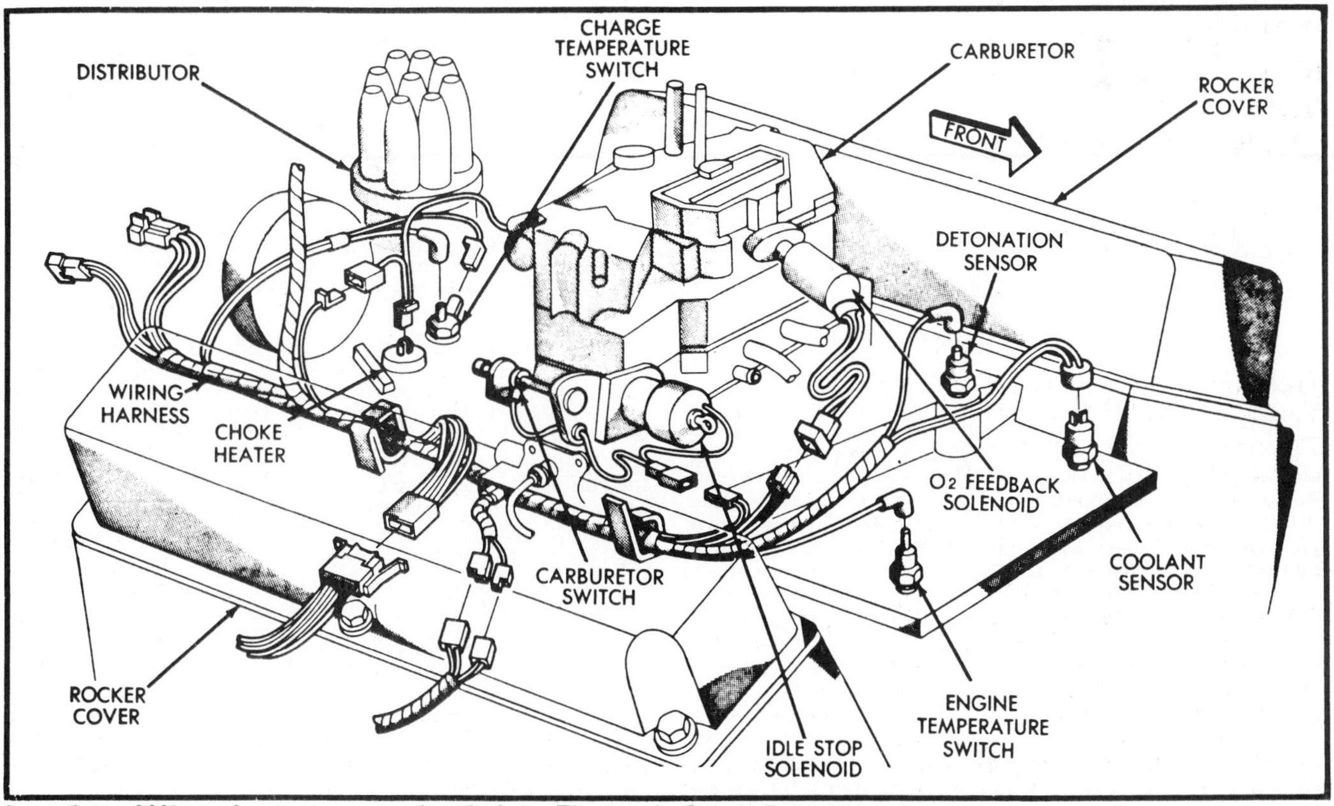

Location of V8 engine sensors and switches, Electronic Spark Control system

up is fixed at one point, the car will be able to run, but not very well. The run pick-up sensor also monitors engine speed and helps the computer decide when the piston is reaching the top of its compression stroke.

NOTE: The two systems will not operate at the same time.

COOLANT SENSOR

The coolant temperature sensor, located in the intake manifold, informs the computer when the coolant temperature reaches a predetermined operating level. This information is required when the engine is equipped with a feedback carburetor, to prevent changing of the air/fuel ratio with the engine in a non-operating temperature mode. Its signals to the computer also help to control the amount of spark advance with a cold engine.

CARBURETOR SWITCH

The carburetor switch sensor is located on the end of the idle stop solenoid and tells the computer when the engine is at idle or off-idle. With the carburetor switch grounding out at idle, the computer cancels the spark advance and the idle control of the air/fuel ratio at the carburetor.

VACUUM TRANSDUCER

The vacuum transducer, located on the computer, monitors the amount of intake manifold vacuum present in the engine.The engine vacuum is one of the factors that will determine how the computer will advance/retard the ignition timing and with a feedback carburetor, change the air/fuel ratio.

DETONATION SENSOR

The detonation sensor is mounted in the number two branch of the intake manifold and is tuned to the frequency characteristic of engine knocking. When detonation (knocking) occurs, the sensor sends a low voltage signal to the computer, which retards ignition timing in proportion to the strength and frequency of the signal. The maximum amount of retard is 11° for 1984 models and 20° for 1985 and later models. When the detonation has ceased, the computer advances timing to the original value.

OXYGEN SENSOR

The oxygen sensor is used when the engine is equipped with a feedback carburetor. The sensor is located in the exhaust manifold and through the use of a self-produced electrical current, signals the computer as to the oxygen content within the exhaust gases flowing past it. Since the electrical output of the oxygen sensor reflects the amount of oxygen in the exhaust, the results are proportional to the rich and lean mixture of the air/fuel ratio. The computer then adjusts the air/fuel ratio to a level that maintains the operating efficiency of the three-way catalytic converter and the engine.

CHARGE TEMPERATURE SWITCH

The charge temperature switch is located in the No. 8 runner of the intake manifold. When the intake air temperature is below approximately 60° F., the CTS will be closed , allowing no EGR timer function or valve operation. The air injection air is switched to the exhaust manifold (upstream). The CTS opens when the intake air temperature is above approximatelay 60° F., thus allowing the EGR timer to time out, the EGR valve to

operate and switches the air injection air to the catalytic converter (downstream).

Troubleshooting

NOTE: The electronic ignition system can be tested with either special ignition testers or a voltmeter with a 20,000 ohm/volt rating and an ohmmeter using a 9 volt battery as a power source. Since the special ignition system testers have manufacturer's instructions accompanying the units, the technician can refer to the procedural steps necessary to operate them. The following outline will cover the ohm/volt meter unit.

SECONDARY CIRCUIT

Test

1. Remove the coil wire from the distributor cap and hold it cautiously about ¼ in. away from an engine ground, then crank the engine while checking for spark.
2. If a good spark is present, slowly move the coil wire away from the engine and check for arcing at the coil while cranking.
3. If good spark is present and it is not arcing at the coil, check the rest of the parts of the ignition system.

IGNITION SYSTEM STARTING TEST

Testing

1. Visually inspect all secondary cables at the coil, distributor and spark plugs for cracks and tightness.
2. Check the primary wire at the coil and ballast resistor for tightness.

--- **CAUTION** ---

Whenever removing or installing the wiring harness connector to the control unit, the ignition switch must be in the OFF position.

3. With a voltmeter, measure the voltage at the battery and to ascertain that enough current is available to operate the cranking and ignition systems.
4. Remove the coil secondary wire from the distributor cap.
5. With the key on, use a jumper wire and momentarily touch the negative terminal of the coil to ground while holding the coil secondary wire approximately ¼ in. from a good engine ground. A spark should be observed.
6. Verify the the spark is getting to the spark plugs. If the spark plugs are being fired, the ignition system is not responsibile for the engine not starting.
7. If no spark is observed at the ignition coil wire, turn the ignition switch to the off position and disconnect the 10 way connector from the bottom of the spark control computer. Turn the ignition switch to the ON position and hold the ignition coil wire approximately ¼ in. away from a good engine ground.
8. With battery current to the coil negative terminal, intermittantly short the terminal to ground. If spark now occurs, replace the spark control computer.
9. If the voltage is incorrect, check the continuity of the wiring between the battery and the coil positive terminal. Repair the wiring as required and retest.
10. Should battery voltage (within one volt) not be present at the coil negative terminal with the ignition key on, replace the ignition coil.
11. Should battery voltage (within one volt) be present, but no spark is obtained when shorting the negative terminal, replace the ignition coil.
12. If spark is obrtained, but the engine will still not start, turn the ignition switch to the RUBN positon and with the positive lead of the voltmeter, measure the voltage from cavity No. 1 to the ground lead of the disconnecxted lead from the comput-

er. The voltage should be within 1 volt of the battery voltage noted earlier.

13. If battery voltage is not present, check the wire for an open circuit and repair. Retest as required.

14. Place a thin insulator between the curb idle adjusting screw and the carburetor switch or, make sure the curb idle adjusting screw is not touching the carburetor switch.

15. Connect the negative voltmeter lead to a good engine ground. Turn the ignition switch to the RUN position and measure the voltage at the carburetor switch terminal. The voltage should be approximately 5 volts.

16. If the voltage is not 5 volts, turn the ignition switch to the OFF position and disconnect the 10 way connector from the bottom of the spark control computer. Turn the ignition switch back to the RUN position and measure the voltage at terminal 2 of the connector.

17. Voltage should be within 1 volt of battery voltage. If the correct voltage is not present, check the wiring between terminal 2 of the connector and the ignition switch for open or shorted circuits or poor connections.

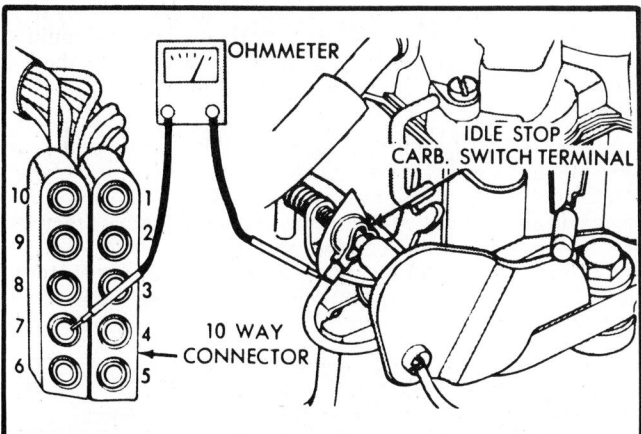

Checking continuity between terminal one and carburetor switch

18. Turn the ignition switch to the OFF position and disconnect the connector from the bottom of the spark computer, if not already done. With an ohmmeter, check the continuity between terminal 7 of the connector and the carburetor switch terminal. Continuity should exist between these two points. If not, check for opens or poor connections.

19. Check for continuity between terminal 10 of the connector and engine ground. If continuity exists, replace the Spark Control Computer assembly. If continuity does not exist, check the wiring for open circuits or poor connections. Repeat Step 18.

20. If the engine still fails to start, turn the ignition switch to the OFF position and with an ohmmeter, measure the resistance between terminal 5 and terminal 9 for the start pick-up coil of the 10 way connector. The resistance should be between 150-900 ohms.

21. If the resistance is not within the specified range, disconnect the Pick-up coil leads from the distributor. Measure the resistance at the lead going into the distributor. If the reading is now between 150-900 ohms, an open circuit or faulty connections exists between the distributor connector and terminals 5 and terminal 9 of of the 10 way connector. If the resistance is not within specifications, the pick-up coil is bad. Replace it and set the air gap to specifications.

22. Connect one lead of the ohmmeter to the engine ground and with the other lead, check for continuity at each terminal of the leads going to the distributor. There should be no continuity.

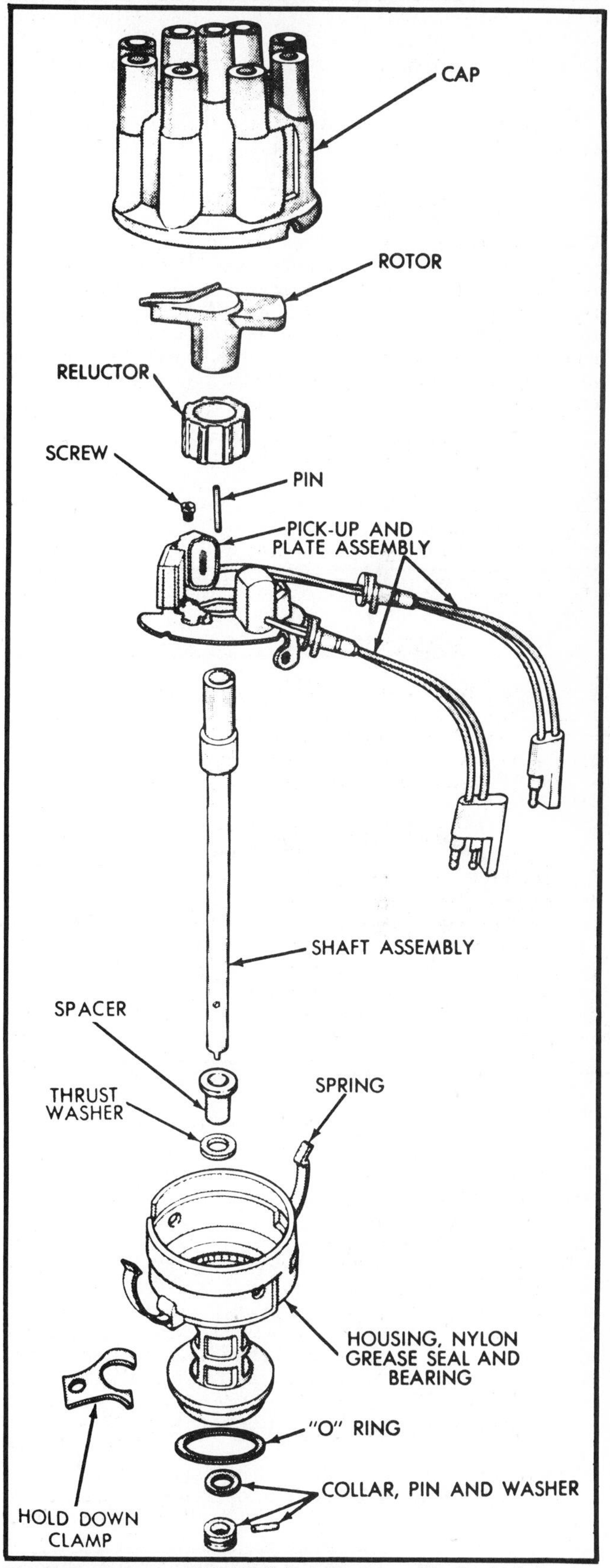

Exploded view of V8 ESC distributor with dual pick-up

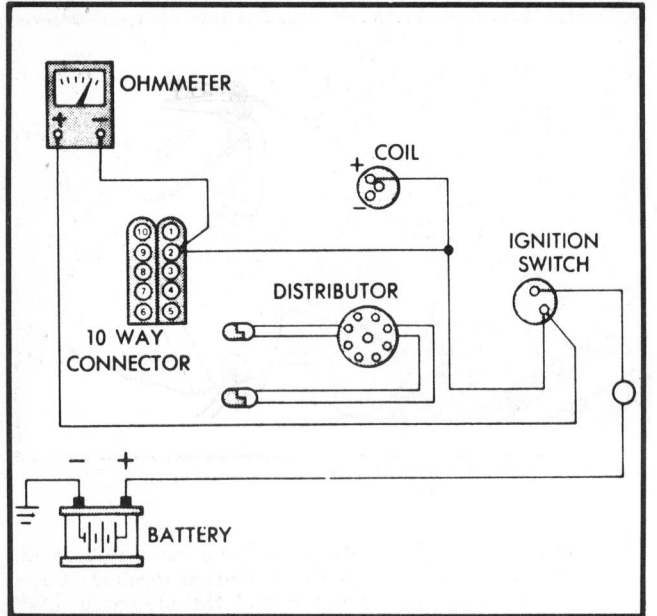

Checking continuity between terminal two and ignition switch

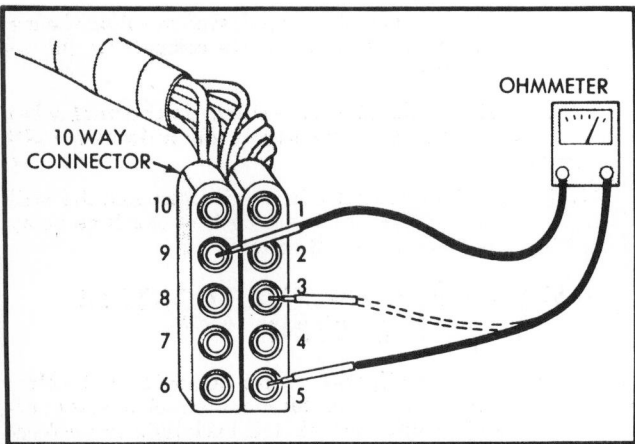

Checking resistance between terminal five and nine, then three and nine

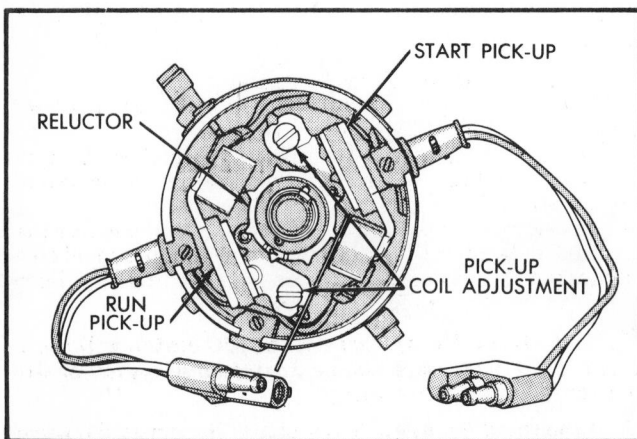

Air gap adjustment locations, dual pick-up illustrated

23. If there is continuity, replace the pick-up coils. Adjust the air gap to specifications.

24. Attempt to start the engine. If it fails to start, repeat the tests. If the engine still fails to start, replace the Spark Control Computer.

NOTE: Should the engine still fail to start with the replaced Spark Control Computer, Chrysler Corp. suggests reinstalling the original Spark Control Computer and repeating the tests. However, proper testing of the circuits and pick-up should result in the engine starting, unless unrelated problems exist in the systems.

TESTING FOR POOR PERFORMANCE

BASIC TIMING

Correct basic timing is essential for optimum engine performance. Before any testing and service is begun on a poor performance complaint, the basic timing must be checked and adjusted as required. Refer to the underhood specifications label and to the vehicle section for timing adjustment procedures.

SPARK COMPUTER ADVANCE OF SPARK CONTROL COMPUTER

Testing

Incorporated within the digital microprocessor electronics are programmed spark advance schedules which occur during cold engine operation. These programmed advance schedules have been added to reduce engine emissions and improve driveability. Because they will be changing at different engine operating temperatures during warm-up, all spark advance testing should be done with the engine at normal operating temperature and a temperature sensor that is connected and operating correctly.

1. With an attached timing light, be sure basic timing is correctly adjusted.

2. Place an insulator between the curb idle addjusting screw and the carburetor switch, or be sure the screw is not touching the switch.

3. Remove tand plug the vacuum line at vacuum transducer.

4. Connect an auxiliary vacuum source to the vacuum transducer and set the vacuum at 16 in. Hg. (318 CID engines).

5. Increase the engine speed to 2,000 rpm. Wait for approximately one minute or specified accumulator clock-up time and check the specifications. On certain systems with an accumulator, the specified time must be reached with the carburetor switch ungrounded before checking the specified spark advance schedule. This would be noted on the information specification label.

NOTE: Advance specifications are in addition to basic timing.

6. Should the computer fail to obtain specified specifications, the Spark Control Computer should be replaced. Perform the same test on the replacement computer.

CARBURETOR SWITCH

Testing

NOTE: Grounding the carburetor switch eliminates all spark advance on mosts systems.

1. With the ignition key in the OFF position, disconnect the 10 way connector from the Spark Control Computer.

2. With the throttle completely closed, check the continuity between pin 7 of the disconnected 10 way connector and a good engine ground.

3. If no continuity exists, check the wires and the carburetor switch. Recheck the basic timing.

4. With the throttle open, check the continuity between pin 7 of the disconnected 10 way connector harness connector and a good engine ground. There should be no continuity.

ENGINE TEMPERATURE SENSOR

Testing

**ENGINE TEMPERATURE SWITCH
(CHARGE TEMPERATURE AND COOLANT)**

1. Turn the ignition switch to the OFF position and disconnect the wire from the temperature switch.
2. Connect one lead of an ohmmeter to a good ground on the engine, or in the case of the charge temperature switch, to its ground terminal.
3. Connect the other lead of the ohmmeter to the center terminal of the coolant switch.
4. Check for continuity using the following ohmmeter readings:
   a. Cold engine—The continuity should be present with a resistance less than 100 ohms. If not, replace the switch. The charge temperature switch must be cooler than 60° F. in order to achieve this reading.
   b. Hot engine at normal operating temperature—The terminal reading should show no continuity. If it does, replace the coolant switch or the charge temperature switch.

COOLANT SENSOR

1. Connect the leads of an ohmmeter to the terminals of the sensor.
2. With the engine cold and the ambient temperature less than 90° F., the resistance should be between 500–1100 ohms.
3. With the engine at normal operating temperature, the resistance should be greater than 1300 ohms.
4. If the resistance is not within the specified range, replace the sensor. the sensor will continually change its resistance with a change in engine operating temperature.

DETONATION SENSOR

Testing

1. Connect an adjustable timing light to the engine.
2. Start the enmgine and run it on the second highest step of the fast idle cam (at least 1200 rpm).
3. Connect an auxiliary vacuum supply to the vacuum transducer and set on 16 in. Hg.
4. Tap lightly on the intake manifold near the sensor with a small metal object.
5. Using the timing light, look for a decrease in the spark advance. The amount of decrease in the timing is directly proportional to the strength and frequency of the tapping. The most decrease in timing will be 11° for 1984 models and 20° for 1985 and later models.
6. Turn the ignition switch to the OFF position. With the engine stopped, disconnect the timing light.

ELECTRONIC EXHAUST GAS RECIRCULATION SYSTEM

Testing

NOTE: The Electronic EGR control is located within the electronic circuitry of the Spark Control Computer and its testing procedure is outlined.

1. All the engine temperature sensors must be operating properly before the tests can be done.
2. With the engine temperature cold and the ignition switch turned to the OFF position, connect one voltmeter lead to the gray wire on the EGR solenoid and the second to a good engine ground.

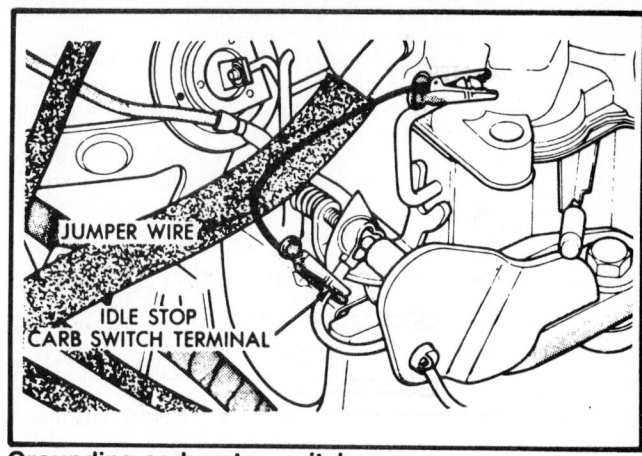

Grounding carburetor switch

3. Start the engine. The voltage should be less than one volt. It will remain at this level until the engine has reached its normal operating temperature range and the electronic EGR schedule has timed out. The solenoid will then de-energize and the voltmeter will read charging system voltage.
4. If the charging system voltage is not obtained, replace the solenoid and repeat the test.
5. If the voltmeter indicates charging system voltage before the EGR schedule is complete, replace the computer or the externally mounted timer.

NOTE: The 318-2 Federal engines have no thermal delay below 60° F. ambient temperature. It will follow the EGR time delay schedule only.

6. If an engine is started with the temperature hot, the EGR solenoid will be energized for the length of the time delay schedule only. It will then de-energize.

ELECTRONIC THROTTLE CONTROL SYSTEM

Incorporated within the Spark Control Computer is the electronic throttle system. A carburetor mounted solenoid is energized when the air conditioner, electric back light or the electric timers are activated. The two timers which are incorporated in the ignition electronics, operate when the throttle is closed, plus a time delay (2 seconds), or after an engine start condition.

Testing

1. Connect a tachometer to the engine.
2. Start the engine and run it until normal operating temperature is reached.
3. Depress the accelerator and release it. A higherthan curb idle speed should be seen on the tachometer for the length of the EGR schedule.
4. On vehicles equipped with/and turning on the A/C or the back light, depressing the accelerator for a moment should give a higher than curb idle speed. Turning the A/C and Back light off will produce the normal idle speed.

NOTE: With the A/C system on, the A/C clutch will cycle on and off. This should not be mistaken as a part of the electronic control system.

5. If the speed increases do not occur, disconnect the three way connector at the carburetor.
6. Check the solenoid with an ohmmeter by measuring the resistance from the terminal that contains the black wire to

ground. The resistance should be between 15–35 ohms. If not within specifications, replace the solenoid.

7. Start the engine and before the delay has timed out, measure the voltage of the black wire of the three way connector, The voltmeter should read charging system voltage. If it does not, replace the computer.

8. Turning the A/C or the back light on should also produce charging system voltage after the time delay has timed out. If not, check the wiring back to the instrument panel for open circuits.

DUAL PICK–UP START/RUN RELAY TEST

Testing

1. Remove the two way connector from pins No. 4 and No. 5 of the dual pick-up start/run relay.

2. Using an ohmmeter, touch pins No. 4 and No.5. The meter should read 20-30 ohms. If not, replace the relay.

PICK–UP COIL AIR GAP

Adjustment

In the dual pick-up distributor, the start pick-up is identified by a two prong male connector and the run pick-up is identified by a male and female plug.

START PICK–UP

1. Align one reluctor tooth with the pick-up coil tooth.
2. Loosen the pick-up coil holddown screw.
3. Insert a 0.006 in. non-magnetic feeler gauge between the reluctor tooth and the pick-up coil tooth.

4. Adjust the air gap so that contact is made between the reluctor tooth, the feeler gauge and the pick-up tooth.
5. Carefully tighten the holddown screw.
6. Remove the feeler gauge. There should be no force needed to remove the gauge.
7. Check the air gap with a NO-GO 0.008 in. feeler gauge. Do not force the gauge in the air gap.

RUN PICK–UP

1. Align on reluctor tooth with the pick-up coil tooth.
2. Loosen the pick-up coil holddown screw.
3. Insert a 0.012 in. non-magnetic feeler gauge beteeen the reluctor tooth and the pick-up tooth.
4. Adjust the air gap so that contact is made between the reluctor tooth, feeler gauge and the pick-up coil tooth.
5. Carefully tighten the holddown screw.
6. Remove the feeler gauge. There should be no force required to remove it.
7. Check the air gap with a NO-GO 0.014 in. feeler gauge. Do not force the gauge in the air gap.

CENTRIFUGAL ADVANCE

Test

1. With a timing light connected, operate the engine at idle and remove the vacuum hose from the vacuum controller.
2. Slowly accelerate the engine to check for advance.
3. Excessive advance indicates a damaged governor spring (a broken spring will result in abrupt advance).
4. Insufficient advance is usually caused by a broken governor weight or a malfunction in cam operation. Correct as needed.

CHRYSLER CORPORATION ELECTRONIC SPARK CONTROL SYSTEM

GENERAL INFORMATION

1987-88 V–8 ENGINES WITH SINGLE PICK–UP DISTRIBUTORS LESS VACUUM ADVANCE
1984-88 V–8 ENGINES WITH DUAL PICK–UP DISTRIBUTORS LESS VACUUM ADVANCE

The computer provides the engine with Ignition Spark Control during starting and during engine operation, providing an infinitely variable spark advance curve. Input data is fed instantaneously to the computer by a series of sensors located in the engine compartment which monitor timing, water temperature, air temperature, idle/off-idle operation and intake manifold vacuum. The program schedule module of the Spark Control Computer receives the information from the sensors, processes it and then directs the ignition control module to advance or retard the timing as necessary. This whole process is going on continuously as the engine is running, taking only milliseconds to complete a circuit from sensor to distributor. The main components of the system are a modified carburetor and Spark Control Computer, which is responsible for translating input data and which transmits data to the distributor to advance or retard the timing.

There are two functional modes of the computer, start and run. The start mode will only function during engine cranking and starting. The run mode only functions after the engine start and during engine operation. The two will never operate together.

Should a failure of the run mode of the computer occur, the system will go into a limp-in mode. This will enable the operator to continue to drive the vehicle until it can be repaired. However, while in this mode, very poor engine operation will result. Should failure of the pick-up coils or the start mode of the computer occur, the engine will not start.

The pick-up coil signal is a reference signal. When the signal is received by the computer the maximum amount of timing advance is made available. Based on the data from all the sensors, the computer determines how much of this maximum advance is needed at that instant.

The amount of spark advance is determined by two factors, engine speed and engine vacuum. However, when it happens depends on the following conditions:

1. Advance from the vacuum will ge given by the computer when the carburetor switch is open. The amount is programmed into the computer and is proportional to the amount of vacuum and engine rpm.

2. Advance from speed is given by the computer when the carburetor switch is open and is programmed to engine rpm.

IGNITION COMPUTER

The computer consists of one electronic printed circuit board which simultaneously receives signals from all the sensors and within milliseconds, analyzes them to determine how the engine is operating and then advances or retards the ignition timing by signaling the ignition coil to produce the electrical impulses to fire the spark plugs at the exact instant when ignition is required

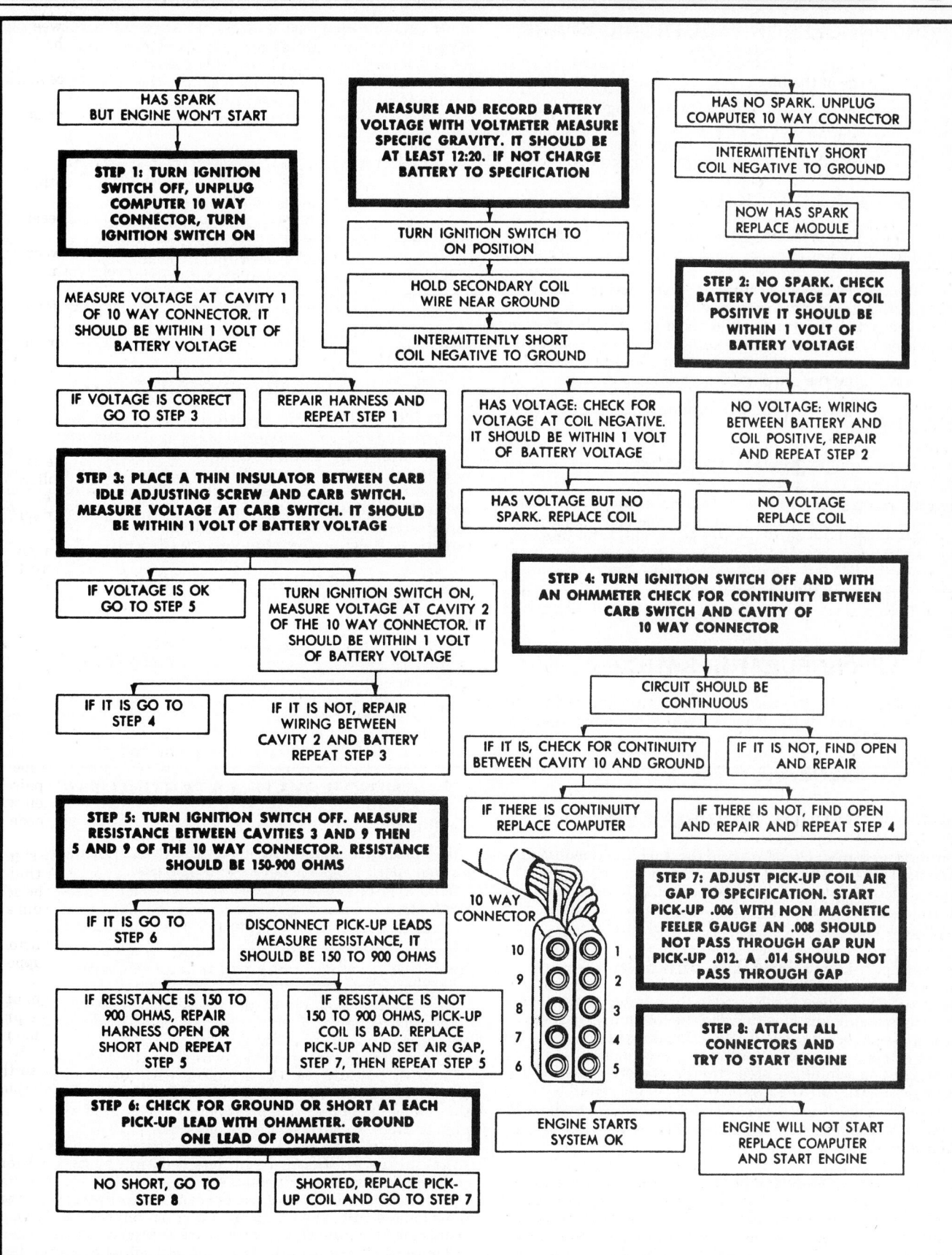

Electronic Spark Control system diagnosis, with dual pick-up distributors

MICROPROCESSOR ELECTRONIC SPARK CONTROL

The microprocessor is an electronic module located within the computer that processes the signals from the engine sensor for accurate engine spark timing. Its digital electronic circuitry offers more operating precision and programming flexibility than the voltage dependent analog system used previously.

MAGNETIC PICK–UP ASSEMBLY

The pick-up sensor is located inside the distributor, supplying a signal to the computer to provide a fixed timing point that is used for starting and the second for normal engine operation. The computer also has a back-up function of fixing the engine timing in the start-up mode in case the run mode fails. Since the timing in the start-up mode is fixed at one point, the car will be able to run, but not very well. The pick-up sensor also monitors engine speed and helps the computer decide when the piston is reaching the top of its compression stroke.

NOTE: **The start-up and run modes will not operate at the same time.**

COOLANT SENSOR

The coolant temperature sensor, located in the intake manifold, informs the computer when the coolant temperature reaches a predetermined operating level. This information is required when the engine is equipped with a feedback carburetor, to prevent changing of the air/fuel ratio with the engine in a non-operating temperature mode. Its signals to the computer also help to control the amount of spark advance with a cold engine.

CARBURETOR SWITCH

The carburetor switch sensor is located on the end of the idle stop solenoid and tells the computer when the engine is at idle or off-idle. With the carburetor switch grounding out at idle, the computer cancels the spark advance and the idle control of the air/fuel ratio at the carburetor.

VACUUM TRANSDUCER

The vacuum transducer, located on the computer, monitors the amount of intake manifold vacuum present in the engine. The engine vacuum is one of the factors that will determine how the computer will advance/retard the ignition timing and with a feedback carburetor, change the air/fuel ratio.

DETONATION SENSOR

The detonation sensor is mounted in the number two branch of the intake manifold and is tuned to the frequency characteristic of engine knocking. When detonation (knocking) occurs, the sensor sends a low voltage signal to the computer, which retards ignition timing in proportion to the strength and frequency of the signal. The maximum amount of retard is 11° for 1984 models and 20° for 1985 and later models. When the detonation has ceased, the computer advances timing to the original value.

OXYGEN SENSOR

The oxygen sensor is used when the engine is equipped with a feedback carburetor. The sensor is located in the exhaust manifold and through the use of a self-produced electrical current, signals the computer as to the oxygen content within the exhaust gases flowing past it. Since the electrical output of the oxygen sensor reflects the amount of oxygen in the exhaust, the results are proportional to the rich and lean mixture of the air/fuel ratio. The computer then adjusts the air/fuel ratio to a level that maintains the operating efficiency of the three-way catalytic converter and the engine.

CHARGE TEMPERATURE SWITCH

The charge temperature switch is located in the No. 8 runner of the intake manifold. When the intake air temperature is below approximately 60° F., the CTS will be closed , allowing no EGR timer function or valve operation. The air injection air is switched to the exhaust manifold (upstream). The CTS opens when the intake air temperature is above approximatelay 60° F., thus allowing the EGR timer to time out, the EGR valve to operate and switches the air injection air to the catalytic converter (downstream).

Troubleshooting

NOTE: **The electronic ignition system can be tested with either special ignition testers or a voltmeter with a 20,000 ohm/volt rating and an ohmmeter using a 9 volt battery as a power source. Since the special ignition system testers have manufacturer's instructions accompanying the units, the technician can refer to the procedural steps necessary to operate them. The following outline will cover the ohm/volt meter unit.**

SECONDARY CIRCUIT

Test

1. Remove the coil wire from the distributor cap and hold it cautiously about $\frac{1}{4}$ in. away from an engine ground, then crank the engine while checking for spark.
2. If a good spark is present, slowly move the coil wire away from the engine and check for arcing at the coil while cranking.
3. If good spark is present and it is not arcing at the coil, check the rest of the parts of the ignition system.

IGNITION SYSTEM STARTING TEST

Testing

1. Visually inspect all secondary cables at the coil, distributor and spark plugs for cracks and tightness.
2. Check the primary wire at the coil and ballast resistor for tightness.

— CAUTION —

Whenever removing or installing the wiring harness connector to the control unit, the ignition switch must be in the OFF position.

3. With a voltmeter, measure the voltage at the battery and to ascertain that enough current is available to operate the cranking and ignition systems.
4. Remove the coil secondary wire from the distributor cap.
5. With the key on, use a jumper wire and momentarily touch the negative terminal of the coil to ground while holding the coil secondary wire approximately $\frac{1}{4}$ in. from a good engine ground. A spark should be observed.
6. Verify the the spark is getting to the spark plugs. If the spark plugs are being fired, the ignition system is not responsibile for the engine not starting.
7. If no spark is observed at the ignition coil wire, turn the ignition switch to the off position and disconnect the 10 way connector from the bottom of the spark control computer. Turn the ignition switch to the ON position and hold the ignition coil wire approximately $\frac{1}{4}$ in. away from a good engine ground.

8. With battery current to the coil negative terminal, intermittantly short the terminal to ground. If spark now occurs, replace the spark control computer.

9. If the voltage is incorrect, check the continuity of the wiring between the battery and the coil positive terminal. Repair the wiring as required and retest.

10. Should battery voltage (within one volt) not be present at the coil negative terminal with the ignition key on, replace the ignition coil.

11. Should battery voltage (within one volt) be present, but no spark is obtained when shorting the negative terminal, replace the ignition coil.

12. If spark is obtained, but the engine will still not start, turn the ignition switch to the RUN positon and with the positive lead of the voltmeter, measure the voltage from cavity No. 1 to the ground lead of the disconnected lead from the computer. The voltage should be within 1 volt of the battery voltage noted earlier.

13. If battery voltage is not present, check the wire for an open circuit and repair. Retest as required.

14. Place a thin insulator between the curb idle adjusting screw and the carburetor switch or, make sure the curb idle adjusting screw is not touching the carburetor switch.

15. Connect the negative voltmeter lead to a good engine ground. Turn the ignition switch to the RUN position and measure the voltage at the carburetor switch terminal. The voltage should be approximately 5 volts.

16. If the voltage is not 5 volts, turn the ignition switch to the OFF position and disconnect the 10 way connector from the bottom of the spark control computer. Turn the ignition switch back to the RUN position and measure the voltage at terminal 2 of the connector.

17. Voltage should be within 1 volt of battery voltage. If the correct voltage is not present, check the wiring between terminal 2 of the connector and the ignition switch for open or shorted circuits or poor connections.

18. Turn the ignition switch to the OFF position and disconnect the connector from the bottom of the spark computer, if not already done. With an ohmmeter, check the continuity between terminal 7 of the connector and the carburetor switch terminal. Continuity should exist between these two points. If not, check for opens or poor connections.

19. Check for continuity between terminal 10 of the connector and engine ground. If continuity exists, replace the Spark Control Computer assembly. If continuity does not exist, check the wiring for open circuits or poor connections. Repeat Step 18.

20. If the engine still fails to start, turn the ignition switch to the OFF position and with an ohmmeter, measure the resistance between terminal 5 and terminal 9 for the pick-up coil of the 10 way connector. The resistance should be between 150-900 ohms.

21. If the resistance is not within the specified range, disconnect the Pick-up coil leads from the distributor. Measure the resistance at the lead going into the distributor. If the reading is now between 150-900 ohms, an open circuit or faulty connections exists between the distributor connector and terminals 5 and terminal 9 of of the 10 way connector. If the resistance is not within specifications, the pick-up coil is bad. Replace it and set the air gap to specifications.

22. Connect one lead of the ohmmeter to the engine ground and with the other lead, check for continuity at each terminal

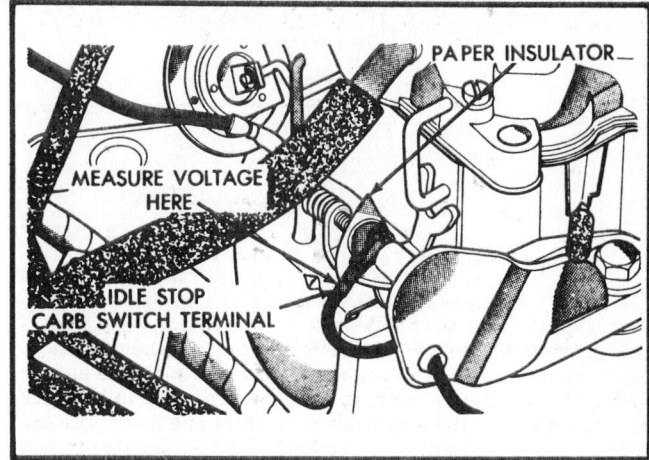

Checking voltage at carburetor switch

of the leads going to the distributor. There should be no continuity.

23. If there is continuity, replace the pick-up coil. Adjust the air gap to specifications.

24. Attempt to start the engine. If it fails to start, repeat the tests. If the engine still fails to start, replace the Spark Control Computer.

NOTE: Should the engine still fail to start with the replaced Spark Control Computer, Chrysler Corp. suggests reinstalling the original Spark Control Computer and repeating the tests. However, proper testing of the circuits and pick-up should result in the engine starting, unless unrelated problems exist in the systems.

POOR ENGINE PERFORMANCE

NOTE: When testing for Poor Engine Performance, refer to the 1984-88 Electronic Spark Control system with Dual Pick-up Distributor.

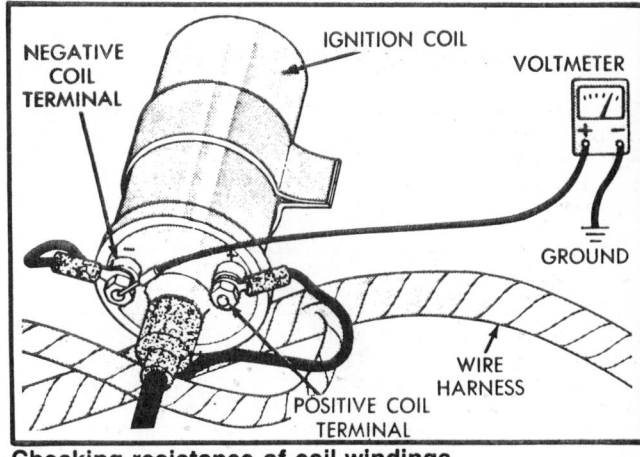

Checking resistance of coil windings

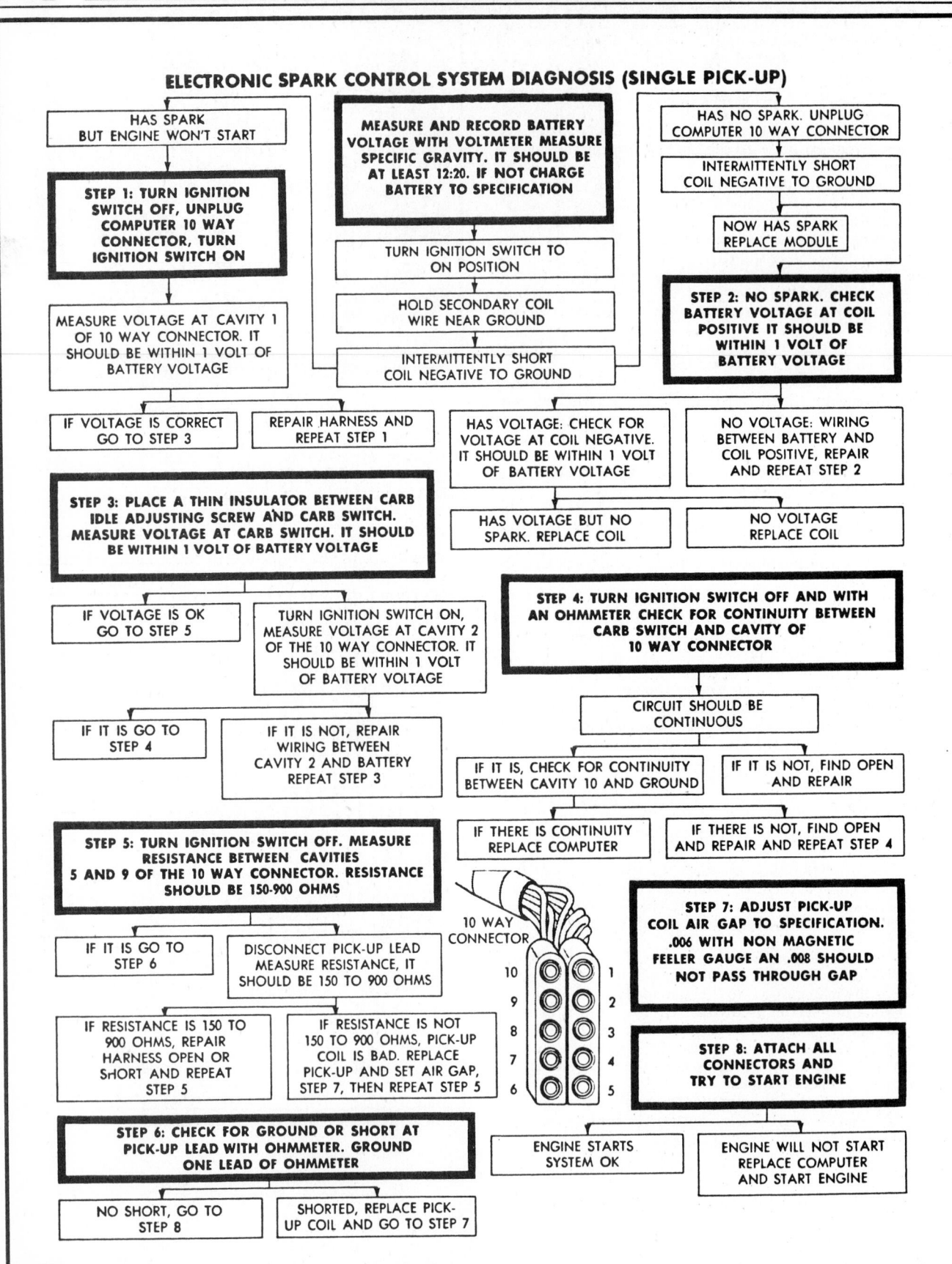

Electronic Spark Control system diagnosis with single pick-up distributor

ELECTRONIC SPARK CONTROL SYSTEM
1984 318 CID Engines

	Computer Part Number		
	4145452	**4289340**	**4289344**
Engine Application	318-2-Can.	318-2 Fed., Cal.	318-2 Cal.
Basic Timing	16° BTDC	16° BTDC	16° BTDC
Curb Idle Speed RPM*	730	700	700
Spark Advance Test 2000 RPM 16 in. Vacuum Including Basic Timing	39° ±4°	51° ±4°	51° ±4°
Electronic EGR	35 Sec.	20 Sec.	20 Sec.
Electronic Throttle Control	No	20 Sec. After Start 1 Sec. After Throttle Closes	20 Sec. After Start 1 Sec. After Throttle Closes
Detonation Supression	No	Yes	Yes
O₂ Feedback Air Switching (Electronic)	No	Yes	Yes
Temperature Sensor	Switch	Sensor	Sensor

	Computer Part Number	
	4289348	**4289354**
Engine Application	318-2 Fed., Cal., Can.	318-4 Fed., Cal., Can.
Basic Timing	16° BTDC	16° BTDC
Curb Idle Speed RPM*	700	700
Spark Advance Test 2000 RPM 16 in. Vacuum Including Basic Timing	41° ±4°	41° ±4°
Electronic EGR	30 Sec.	30 Sec.
Electronic Throttle Control	30 Sec. After Start 1 Sec. After Throttle Closes	30 Sec. After Start 1 Sec. After Throttle Closes
Detonation Supression	Yes	Yes
O₂ Feedback Air Switching (Electronic)	Yes	Yes
Temperature Sensor	Sensor	Sensor

Should the listed specifications differ from those on the Emission Control Information Label, use the specifications on the label
(A)—Automatic Transmission
(M)—Manual Transmission
Can.—Canada
Fed.—Federal
Cal.—California
BTDC—Before Top Dead Center
P.V.—Passenger Vehicle
TR—Truck
* High Altitude
**Basic Timing set with vacuum line disconnected. Do not readjust curb idle
*** Curb Idle set with vacuum line connected

ELECTRONIC SPARK CONTROL SYSTEM
1985 318 CID Engines

	Computer Part Number		
	4289677	**4289673**	**4289811**
Engine Application	318-2-Can.	318-2 Fed., Cal. (A)	318-2 Cal. (A)
Basic Timing	7° BTDC	7° BTDC	7° BTDC
Curb Idle Speed RPM***	730	680	680
Spark Advance Test 2000 RPM 16 in. Vacuum Including Basic Timing	46° ±4°	46° ±4°	46° ±4°
Electronic EGR	35 Sec.	20 Sec.	20 Sec.
Electronic Throttle Control	90 Sec. Cold 90 Sec. Hot 5 Sec. Off Idle 3 Sec After Throttle Closes	20 Sec. Cold 30 Sec After Start Hot 2 Sec. Off Idle 1 Sec. After Throttle Closes	20 Sec After Start 2 Sec. Off Idle 1 Sec After Throttle Closes
Detonation Supression	No	Yes	Yes
O₂ Feedback Air Switching (Electronic)	No	Yes	Yes
Temperature Sensor	Switch	Sensor	Sensor

	Computer Part Number	
	4289819	**4289821**
Engine Application	318-4 Fed., Cal., Can. (A)	318-4 Fed., Cal., Can. (A)
Basic Timing	16° BTDC	16° BTDC
Curb Idle Speed RPM***	750	750
Spark Advance Test 2000 RPM 16 in. Vacuum Including Basic Timing	38° ±4°	38° ±4°
Electronic EGR	50 Sec.	30 Sec.
Electronic Throttle Control	120 Sec. After Start Hot 3 Sec. Off Idle 1 Sec. After Throttle Closes	120 Sec. After Start Hot 3 Sec. Off Idle 1 Sec. After Throttle Closes
Detonation Supression	Yes	Yes
O₂ Feedback Air Switching (Electronic)	Yes	Yes
Temperature Sensor	Sensor	Sensor

Should the listed specifications differ from those on the Emission Control Information Label, use the specifications on the label

(A) — Automatic Transmission
(M) — Manual Transmission
Can. — Canada
Fed. — Federal
Cal. — California
BTDC — Before Top Dead Center
P.V. — Passenger Vehicle
TR — Truck
* High Altitude
**Basic Timing set with vacuum line disconnected. Do not readjust curb idle
*** Curb Idle set with vacuum line connected

ELECTRONIC SPARK CONTROL SYSTEM
1986 318 CID Engines

	Computer Part Number		
	4289813	**4289881**	**4289913**
Engine Application	318-2 Fed.,Can. (A)	318-2 Can. (A)	318-2 Cal. (A)
Basic Timing	7° BTDC	12° BTDC	7° BTDC
Curb Idle Speed RPM▲	630	730	630
Spark Advance Test 2000 RPM 16 in. Vacuum including Basic Timing	46° ±4°	42° ±4°	46° ±4°
Electronic EGR	40 Sec.	40 Sec.	40 Sec.
Electronic Throttle Control	20 Sec. Cold 60 Sec. After Start Hot 2 Sec. Off Idle 1 Sec After Throttle Closes	90 Sec. Cold 90 Sec After Start Hot 5 Sec. Off Idle 3 Sec. After Throttle Closes	20 Sec. Cold 60 Sec. After Start Hot 2 Sec. Off Idle 1 Sec. After Throttle Closes
Detonation Supression	Yes	No	Yes
O₂ Feedback Air Switching (Electronic)	Yes	No	Yes
Temperature Sensor	Switch	Sensor	Sensor

	Computer Part Number	
	4289919	**4289921**
Engine Application	318-2 Fed., Cal., Can. (A)	318-4 Fed., Cal., Can. (A)
Basic Timing	16° BTDC	16° BTDC
Curb Idle Speed RPM***	750	750
Spark Advance Test 2000 RPM 16 in. Vacuum Including Basic Timing	38° ±4°	38° ±4°
Electronic EGR	40 Sec.	40 Sec.
Electronic Throttle Control	200 Sec. After Start Hot 3 Sec. Off Idle 1 Sec. After Throttle Closes	200 Sec. After Start Hot 3 Sec. Off Idle 1 Sec. After Throttle Closes
Detonation Suppression	Yes	Yes
O₂ Feedback Air Switching (Electronic)	Yes	Yes
Temperature Sensor	Sensor	Sensor

Should the listed specifications differ from those on the Emission Control Information Label, use the specifications on the label

(A) — Automatic Transmission
(M) — Manual Transmission
(OD) — Overdrive
Can. — Canada
Fed. — Federal
Cal. — California
BTDC — Before Top Dead Center
P.V. — Passenger Vehicle
TR — Truck
* High Altitude

**Basic Timing set with vacuum line disconnected. Do not readjust curb idle
▲Curb Idle RPM ±100 RPM, set with vacuum line connected

ELECTRONIC SPARK CONTROL SYSTEM
1987 318 CID Engines

	Computer Part Number		
	4289813	**4289881**	**4289913**
Engine Application	318-2 Fed., Can. (A)	318-2 Can. (A)	318-2 Cal. (A)
Basic Timing	7° BTDC	12° BTDC	7° BTDC
Curb Idle Speed RPM▲	630	730	630
Spark Advance Test 2000 RPM 16 in. Vacuum including Basic Timing	46° ±4°	42° ±4°	46° ±4°
Electronic EGR	40 Sec.	40 Sec.	40 Sec.
Electronic Throttle Control	20 Sec. Cold 60 Sec. After Start Hot 2 Sec. Off Idle 1 Sec After Throttle Closes	90 Sec. Cold 90 Sec After Start Hot 5 Sec. Off Idle 3 Sec. After Throttle Closes	20 Sec. Cold 60 Sec. After Start Hot 2 Sec. Off Idle 1 Sec. After Throttle Closes
Detonation Supression	Yes	No	Yes
O₂ Feedback Air Switching (Electronic)	Yes	No	Yes
Temperature Sensor	Switch	Sensor	Sensor

	Computer Part Number	
	4379228	**4379228**
Engine Application	318-4 Fed., Cal., Can. (A)	318-4 Fed., Cal., Can. (A)
Basic Timing	16° BTDC	16° BTDC
Curb Idle Speed RPM▲	750	750
Spark Advance Test 2000 RPM 16 in. Vacuum Including Basic Timing	38° ±4°	38° ±4°
Electronic EGR	40 Sec.	40 Sec.
Electronic Throttle Control	200 Sec. After Start Hot 3 Sec. Off Idle 1 Sec. After Throttle Closes	200 Sec. After Start Hot 3 Sec. Off Idle 1 Sec. After Throttle Closes
Detonation Suppression	Yes	Yes
O₂ Feedback Air Switching (Electronic)	Yes	Yes
Temperature Sensor	Sensor	Sensor

Should the listed specifications differ from those on the Emission Control Information Label, use the specifications on the label

(A) — Automatic Transmission
(M) — Manual Transmission
(OD) — Overdrive
Can. — Canada
Fed. — Federal
Cal. — California
BTDC — Before Top Dead Center
P.V. — Passenger Vehicle
TR — Truck
* High Altitude
**Basic Timing set with vacuum line disconnected. Do not readjust curb idle

FORD MOTOR COMPANY
SOLID STATE IGNITION SYSTEMS

GENERAL INFORMATION

Two basic electronic ignition systems are being used in the 1984 and later Ford Motor Company vehicles.
1. Dura Spark II
2. TFI-I and TFI-IV (Thick Film Integrated)

NOTE: Dura Spark III was used until 1983 and can be identified by having a distributor that is used only for the distribution of the secondary spark. The distributor was stripped of the pick-up coil, armature, vacuum and centrifugal advances The primary pick-up coil and ar-mature were re-located to the front of the engine and the crankshaft, while the vacuum and centrifugal advance curves were controlled by the ECA. Crankshaft position signals were sent to the Electronic Control Assembly, which in turn controlled the operation of the spark control module and the timing of the secondary spark.

The following charts outline the Engine Control Systems, Ignition Systems and Fuel Systems used with Ford Motor Company passenger vehicles from 1984 and later, with the information available at time of publication. For further diagnostics, refer to the appropriate sections or manuals.

FORD MOTOR COMPANY ENGINE CONTROLS SYSTEMS, IGNITION SYSTEMS AND FUEL SYSTEMS
1984 Passenger Cars—50 States

Engine	Vehicle Application	Ignition System	Electronic Engine Control	Fuel System Mfg.	Type
1.6L	Escort, Lynx, EXP	TFI-I	None	Holley Carter	740-2V Carburetor
1.6L HO	Escort, Lynx, EXP	TFI-I	None	Holley Carter	740-2V Carburetor
1.6L	Escort, Lynx, EXP	TFI-IV	EEC-IV	Bosch/Ford	EFI
1.6L Turbo	Escort, Lynx, EXP	TFI-IV	ECC-IV	Bosch/Ford	EFI
1.9L	Escort, Lynx	TFI-I	None	Holley Carter	740-2V Carburetor
2.3L HSC	Tempo, Topaz	TFI-IV	EEC-IV	Bosch/Ford	CFI
2.3L OHC	Mustang, Capri, LTD, Marquis	TFI-IV	EEC-IV	Carter	YFA-IV, FBC Carb.
2.3L OHC Turbo	Thunderbird, Cougar, Mustang, S.V.O.	TFI-IV	EEC-IV	Bosch/Ford	EFI
3.8L	Thunderbird, Cougar, LTD, Marquis, Mustang, Capri	TFI-IV	EEC-IV	Ford	CFI
5.0L	Continental, Mark VII, Lincoln, Thunderbird, Cougar, Crown Victoria Grand Marquis	TFI-IV	EEC-VI	Ford	CFI
5.0L HO	Mustang, Capri (M/T)	DS-II	None	Holley	4180C-4V Carburetor
	Mustang, Capri, LTD, Marquis (A/T)	TFI-IV	EEC-IV	Ford	CFI
	Mark VII (A/T)	TFI-VI	EEC-IV	Ford	CFI
5.8L HO	Crown Victoria (Police Only)	UIC	MCU	Ford	7200-VV

S.V.O.—Special Vehicle Operation
EEC-III—Electronic Engine Control (System III)
FBC—Feedback Carburetor
EFI—Electronic Fuel Injection
MCU—Microprocessor Control Unit
M/T—Manual Transmission
A/T—Automatic Transmission
Mfg.—Manufacturer

DS-II—Duraspark II
DS-III—Duraspark III
TFI—Thick Film Ignition
UIC—Universal Integrated Circuit
ATX—Automatic Transaxle
MTX—Manual Transaxle

FORD MOTOR COMPANY ENGINE CONTROLS SYSTEMS, IGNITION SYSTEMS AND FUEL SYSTEMS
1984 Passenger Cars – Canada

Engine	Vehicle Application	Ignition System	Electronic Engine Control	Fuel System Mfg.	Fuel System Type
1.6L	Escort, Lynx, EXP	TFI-I MTX, TFI-I ATX	None	Holley Carter	740-2V Carburetor
1.6L Turbo	S.V.O. EXP, (Escort, Lynx 1984¼)	TFI-IV	EEC-IV	Bosch/Ford	EFI
1.6L	50 States	TFI-IV	EEC-IV	Bosch/Ford	EFI
2.3L	Mustang, Capri LTD, Marquis	DS-II	None	Carter	YFA-IV
2.3L HSC	Tempo, Topaz	DS-II	None	Holley	1949-IV
2.3L Turbo	Capri, Thunderbird, Cougar, Mustang (Turbo & S.V.O.)	TFI-IV	EEC-IV	Bosch/Ford	EFI
3.8L	Thunderbird, Cougar, LTD, Marquis, Mustang, Capri	DS-II	None	Ford	2150-2V
5.0L (302) CID	Continental, Mark VII, Lincoln, Thunderbird, Cougar	TFI-IV	EEC-VI	Ford	CFI Fuel Charging Assy.
	Ford Mercury	DS-II	None	Ford	2150-4V Carburetor
	Mustang, Capri HO T50D M/T	DS-II	None	Holley	4180-4V Carburetor
	Mustang, Capri HO AOD M/T	TFI-IV	EEC-IV	Ford	CFI Fuel Charging Assy.
	LTD-AOD A/T	TFI-VI	EEC-IV	Ford	CFI Fuel Charging Assy.
5.8L (351W CID)	Ford/ Mercury	UIC	MCU	Ford	7200-VV Carburetor

S.V.O.—Special Vehicle Operation	DS-II—Duraspark II
EEC-III—Electronic Engine Control (System III)	TFI—Thick Intregrated Film
FBC—Feedback Carburetor	UIC—Universal Integrated Circuit
EFI—Electronic Fuel Injection	HO—High Output
MCU—Microprocessor Control Unit	MTX—Manual Transaxle
M/T—Manual Transmission	ATX—Automatic Transaxle
A/T—Automatic Transmission	EEC-IV—Electronic Engine Control (System IV)
Mfg.—Manufacturer	CFI—Central Fuel Injection

FORD MOTOR COMPANY ENGINE CONTROLS SYSTEMS, IGNITION SYSTEMS AND FUEL SYSTEMS
1985 Passenger Cars – 50 States

Engine	Vehicle Application	Ignition System	Electronic Engine Control	Fuel System Mfg.	Fuel System Type
1.6L	50 States	TFI-I	None	Holley Carter	740-2V Carburetor
1.6L	50 States	TFI-IV	EEC-IV	Bosch/Ford	EFI
1.6L Turbo	49 States, M/T	TFI-IV	EEC-IV	Bosch/Ford	EFI
2.3L	50 States	TFI-IV	EEC-IV	Carter	YFA-IV, FB

FORD MOTOR COMPANY ENGINE CONTROLS SYSTEMS, IGNITION SYSTEMS AND FUEL SYSTEMS
1985 Passenger Cars—50 States

Engine	Vehicle Application	Ignition System	Electronic Engine Control	Fuel System Mfg.	Fuel System Type
2.3L HSC	50 States	TFI-IV	EEC-IV	Holley	6149-IV, FB
2.3L Turbo S.V.O.	50 States A/T & M/T,	TFI-IV	EEC-IV	Bosch/Ford	EFI
3.8L (230 CID)	50 States, Thunderbird, Cougar, LTD, Marquis, Mustang, Capri	TFI-IV	EEC-IV	Ford	CFI Fuel Charging Assy.
5.0L	Mustang, Capri A/T, AOD, HO	TFI-IV	EEC-VI	Ford	CFI Fuel Charging Assy.
	LTD A/T AOD H.O.	TFI-IV	EEC-VI	Ford	CFI Fuel Charging Assy.
	Mustang, Capri T50D M/T HO	DS-II	No	Holley	4180C-4V
	50 States, Lincoln, Mark VII*, Crown Victoria, Grand Marquis, Cougar*, Continental*, Thunderbird*	TFI-VI	EEC-IV	Ford	CFI Fuel Charging Assy.
5.8L HO (351 CID)	50 States Ford, Mercury (Police Only)	UIC	MCU	Ford	7200-VV

*EEC-III for California Job #1 (Duration 120 days) on Continental, Mark & Thunderbird, Cougar
S.V.O.—Special Vehicle Operation
EEC-III—Electronic Engine Control (System III)
EEC-IV—Electronic Engine Control (System IIV)
FBC—Feedback Carburetor
EFI—Electronic Fuel Injection
MCU—Microprocessor Control Unit
M/T—Manual Transmission
A/T—Automatic Transmission

Mfg.—Manufacturer
CFI—Central Fuel Injection
DS-II—Duraspark II
DS-III—Duraspark III
TFI—Thick Integrtaed Film
UIC—Universal Integrated Circuit
HO—High Output

FORD MOTOR COMPANY ENGINE CONTROLS SYSTEMS, IGNITION SYSTEMS AND FUEL SYSTEMS
1984 Passenger Cars—50 States

Engine	Vehicle Application	Ignition System	Electronic Engine Control	Fuel System Mfg.	Fuel System Type
1.6L	Escort, Lynx, EXP	TFI-I	None	Holley Carter	740-2V Carburetor
1.6L HO	Escort, Lynx, EXP	TFI-I	None	Holley Carter	740-2V Carburetor
1.6L	Escort, Lynx, EXP	TFI-IV	EEC-IV	Bosch/Ford	EFI
1.6L Turbo	Escort, Lynx, EXP	TFI-IV	EEC-IV	Bosch/Ford	EFI
1.9L	Escort, Lynx	TFI-I	None	Holley Carter	740-2V Carburetor
2.3L HSC	Tempo, Topaz	DS-II	None	Holley	1949-IV Carburetor
2.3L OHC	Mustang, Capri, LTD, Marquis	DS-II	None	Carter	YFA-IV
2.3L OHC Turbo	Thunderbird, Cougar, Mustang, S.V.O., XR4Ti	TFI-IV	EEC-IV	Bosch/Ford	EFI

FORD MOTOR COMPANY ENGINE CONTROLS SYSTEMS, IGNITION SYSTEMS AND FUEL SYSTEMS
1984 Passenger Cars—50 States

Engine	Vehicle Application	Ignition System	Electronic Engine Control	Fuel System Mfg.	Fuel System Type
3.8L	Thunderbird, Cougar, LTD, Marquis, Mustang, Capri	DS-II	None	Ford	2150-2V Carburetor
5.0L	Continental, Mark VII, Lincoln, Thunderbird, Cougar	TFI-IV	EEC-VI	Ford	CFI
	Crown Victoria Grand Marquis	DS-II	None	Ford	2150-2V Carburetor
5.0L HO	Mustang, Capri (M/T)	DS-II	None	Holley	4180-4V Carburetor
	Mustang, Capri, LTD, Marquis (A/T)	TFI-IV	EEC-IV	Ford	CFI
	Mark VII (A/T)	TFI-VI	EEC-IV	Ford	CFI
5.8L HO	Crown Victoria	UIC	MCU	Ford	7200-VV

S.V.O.—Special Vehicle Operation
EEC-IV—Electronic Engine Control (System IV)
FBC—Feedback Carburetor
EFI—Electronic Fuel Injection
MCU—Microprocessor Control Unit
M/T—Manual Transmission
A/T—Automatic Transmission

Mfg.—Manufacturer
DS-II—Duraspark II
TFI—Thick Integrated Film
UIC—Universal Integrated Circuit
HO—High Output
ATX—Automatic Transaxle
MTX—Manual Transaxle

FORD MOTOR COMPANY ENGINE CONTROLS SYSTEMS, IGNITION SYSTEMS AND FUEL SYSTEMS
1986 Passenger Cars—50 States & Canada

Engine	Vehicle Application	Ignition System	Electronic Engine Control	Fuel System Mfg.	Fuel System Type
1.9L	Escort, Lynx, EXP	TFI-I	None	Holley	740-2V Carburetor
		TFI-IV	EEC-IV	Bosch/Ford	EFI
2.3L OHC	Mustang, Capri, LTD, Marquis	TFI-IV	EEC-IV	Carter	YFA-1V, FBC Carb.
2.3L OHC Turbo	Thunderbird, Cougar, S.V.O., Mustang, Merkur	TFI-IV	EEC-IV	Bosch/Ford	EFI
2.3L HSC 50 States	Tempo, Topaz	TFI-IV	EEC-IV	Ford	CFI
2.3L HSC Canada	Tempo, Topaz	DS-II	None	Holley	1949-IV
2.5L HSC	Taurus, Sable	TFI-IV	EEC-IV	Ford	CFI
3.0L	Taurus, Sable	TFI-IV	EEC-IV	Bosch/Ford	EFI
3.8L 50 States	Thunderbird, Cougar, LTD, Marquis, Mustang, Capri Mustang, Capri (Canada)	TFI-IV	EEC-IV	Ford	CFI

FORD MOTOR COMPANY ENGINE CONTROLS SYSTEMS, IGNITION SYSTEMS AND FUEL SYSTEMS
1986 Passenger Cars — 50 States & Canada

Engine	Vehicle Application	Ignition System	Electronic Engine Control	Fuel System Mfg.	Type
3.8L Canada	Thunderbird, Cougar, LTD, Marquis	DS-II	None	Ford	2150A-2V NFB Carburetor
5.0L	Continental, Mark VII, Thunderbird, Cougar	TFI-IV	EEC-IV	—	SEFI
	Ford, Mercury, Lincoln	TFI-IV	EEC-IV	—	SEFI
5.0L HO	Mustang, Capri Mark VII	TFI-IV	EEC-IV	—	SEFI
5.8L	Ford/ Mercury (Police) Canada Trailer Tow	UIC	MCU	Ford	7200-VV FBC Carburetor

S.V.O.—Special Vehicle Operation
EEC-IV—Electronic Engine Control (System IV)
FBC—Feedback Carburetor
EFI—Electronic Fuel Injection
MCU—Microprocessor Control Unit
M/T—Manual Transmission
A/T—Automatic Transmission
Mfg.—Manufacturer
DS-II—Duraspark II
TFI—Thick Integrated Film

UIC—Universal Integrated Circuit
HO—High Output
ATX—Automatic Transaxle
MTX—Manual Transaxle
NFB—Non-Feedback Carburetor
SEFI—Sequential Feedback Carburetor
OHC—Overhead Cam
HSC—High Swirl Combustion
CFI—Central Fuel Injection

Diagnosis of Electronic Ignition systems

Many times a quick test can locate the cause of a problem without going into full system checkout. Included are tests which may isolate the cause of the problem. The first step is to verify that a problem exists and then to make some preliminary tests to determine if the problem is in the ignition system, a related system or a completely unrelated system. The following procedures are intended to provide tests to identify and locate some of the more frequently encountered problems.

Intermittant faults may be the result of corroded terminals, cracked or broken wires, voltage leakage, heat related failures, etc. Verify the mode of the ignition system and engine when the malfunction occurs and relate to this mode for failure indications. (examples = engine hot or cold, acceleration or deceleration, etc).

PRELIMINARY CHECKS

1. Check battery for state of charge and for clean, tight battery terminal connections.
2. Inspect all wires and connectors for breaks, cuts, abrasions or burned spots. Repair or replace as necessary. Make sure all wires are connected correctly.
3. Unplug all connectors and inspect for corroded or burned contacts. Repair as necessary and plug connectors back together. Do not remove the lubricant compound in connectors.
4. Check for loose or damaged spark plug or coil wires. If boots or nipples are removed on 8mm ignition wires, reline inside of each with new silicone dielectric compound.

GENERAL SPARK PLUG WIRE RESISTANCE TEST

Procedure

1. Remove the distributor cap from the distributor assembly.
2. Inspect the spark plug wires to insure that they are firmly seated on the distributor cap.
3. Disconnect the spark plug wire(s) thought to be defective at the spark plug.
4. Using an ohmmeter, measure the resistance between the distributor cap terminal and the spark plug terminal.

NOTE: Make certain that a good connection is made between the distributor cap and the spark terminal. Never, under any circumstances, measure resistance by puncturing the spark plug wire.

5. If the measured resistance is less than 7000 ohms per foot of wire, the wire is good. If the measured resistance is greater than 7000 ohms per foot, the wire is defective and should be replaced.

NOTE: The following outline is a general explanation of the electronic ignition systems and the tests that can be performed when the engine will not start, should the fault be determined to be in the electronic ignition system of the Dura Spark II, TFI-I or TFI-IV systems.

DURA SPARK II SYSTEM

The Dura Spark II ignition system consists of the typical elec-

...nventional secondary circuits, designed ...voltages. The primary and secondary circuits consists of the following components:

PRIMARY CIRCUIT

1. Battery.
2. Ignition switch.
3. Ballast resistor start bypass (wire).
4. Ignition coil primary winding.
5. Ignition module.
6. Distributor stator assembly.

SECONDARY CIRCUIT

1. Battery.
2. Ignition coil secondary winding.
3. Distributor rotor.
4. Distributor cap.
5. Ignition wires.
6. Spark plugs.

Operation

With the ignition switch in the RUN position, the primary circuit current is directed from the battery, through the ignition switch, the ballast resistor, the ignition coil (in the positive side, out the negative side), the ignition module and back to the battery through the ignition system ground in the distributor. This current flow causes a magnetic field to be built up in the ignition coil. When the poles on the armature and the stator assembly align, the ignition module turns the primary current flow off, collapsing the magnetic field in the ignition coil. The collapsing field induces a high voltage in the ignition coil secondary windings. The ignition coil wire then conducts the high voltage to the distributor where the cap and rotor distributes it to the appropriate spark plug.

A timing device in the ignition module turns the primary current back on after a very short period of time. High voltage is produced each time the magnetic field is built up and collapsed.

The Dura Spark II system has had several versions of control modules since its conception. They are as follows:

1. The Dual Mode module.
2. The Cranking Retard module.
3. The Universal Ignition module.

DUAL MODE, CRANKING RETARD AND UNIVERSAL IGNITION MODULES

The Cranking Retard modules were used before the 1984 model year on specific engines equipped with automatic transmissions. The Dual Mode and the Universal Ignition module are still being used with the Dura Spark II system, with continual updating from year to year, as required.

The Dual Mode ignition control module is equipped with an altitude sensor, an economy modulator, or pressure switches (turbocharged engines only). This module, when combined with the additional switches and sensor, varies the base engine timing according to altitude and engine load conditions. The Dual Mode Ignition Control modules use three wiring harness connectors, while the Cranking Retard module uses only two connectors.

Both ignition modules perform the function of turning off current flow through the ignition coil in response to a control signal. In the Dura Spark II ignition system, this signal comes from the distributor stator assembly. Additionally, the Universal Ignition Module (UIM), which is similar to the Cranking Retard Module, can respond to another control signal from either an ignition barometeric pressure switch or the Microprocessor Control Unit (MCU), depending upon the engine's calibration. In responding to this second control signal, the UIM provides additional spark timing control for certain operating conditions by turning off the ignition coil current flow at a different time than what would happen from just the distributor signal.

The Universal Ignition module has a programmable run/retard feature in a smaller, more compact module. This programmable run/retard function can be programmed as a step change by an external programming switch/resistor combination for altitude and some economy calibrations or as a variable controlled element in the closed loop system, such as with the spark control mode system. The switch/resistor combinations change resistance inside the module to determine the amount of compensation the module will make.

CENTRIFUGAL SPARK ADVANCE MECHANISM

The movement of the centrifugal weights change the initial relationship of the armature to the stator assembly ahead of its static position on the distributor shaft. This results in spark

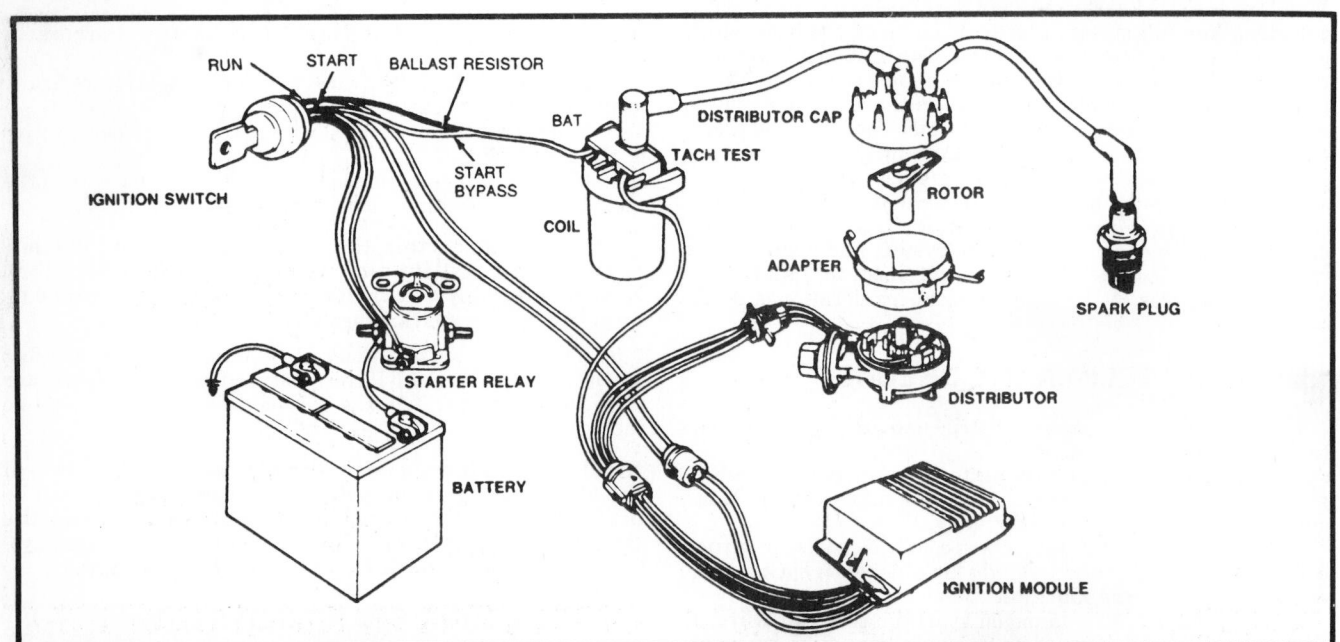

Dura Spark II component arrangement

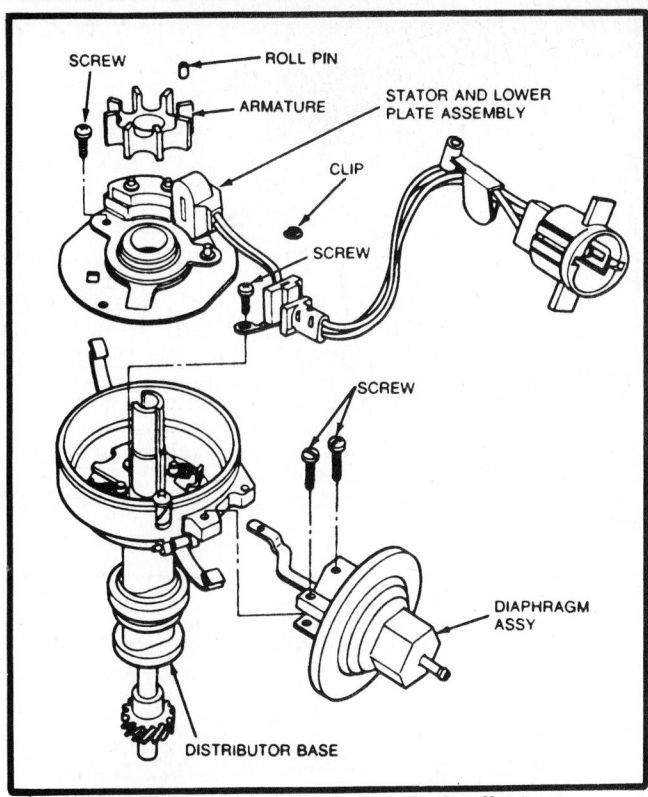

Exploded view of V8 Dura Spark II distributor

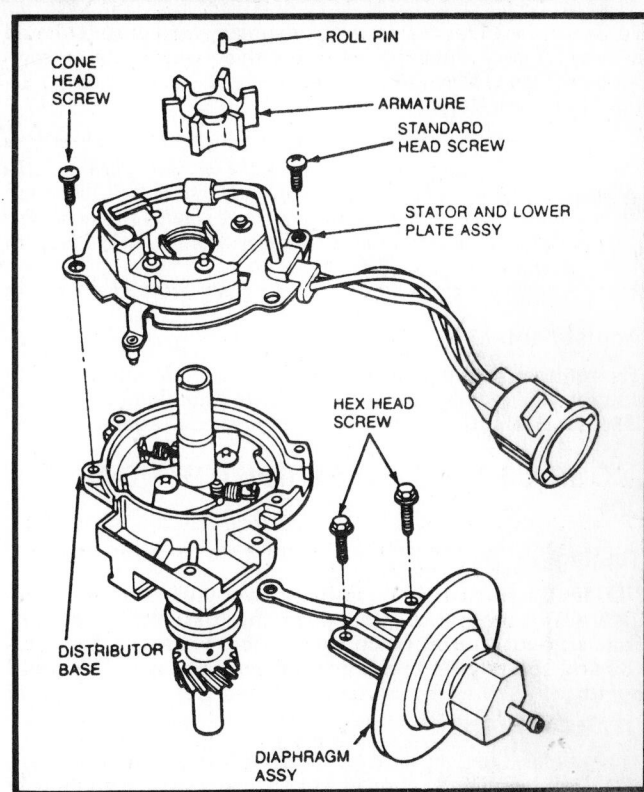

Exploded view of V6 Dura Spark II distributor

advance. The rate of movement of the centrifugal weights is controlled by calibrated springs.

VACUUM SPARK ADVANCE

The vacuum advance is controlled by either a single diaphragm or a dual diaphragm assembly, the use of which is controlled by engine operating and emission calibrations. The

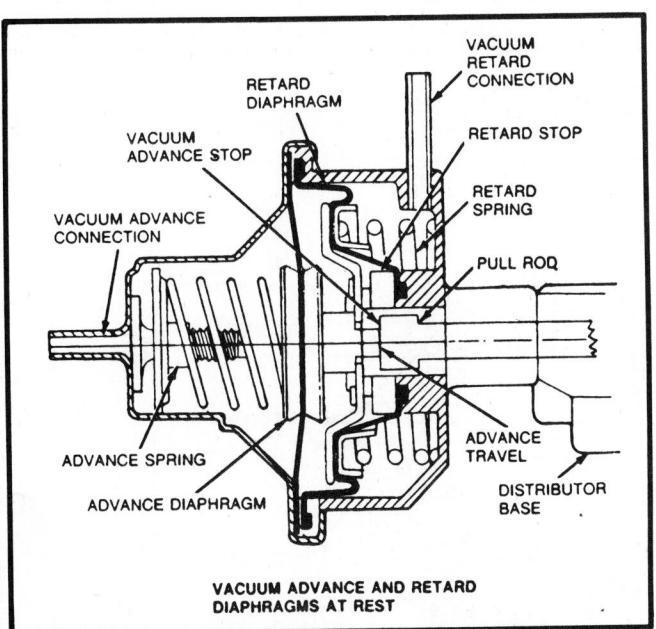

Cross section of dual diaphragm vacuum advance/retard assembly

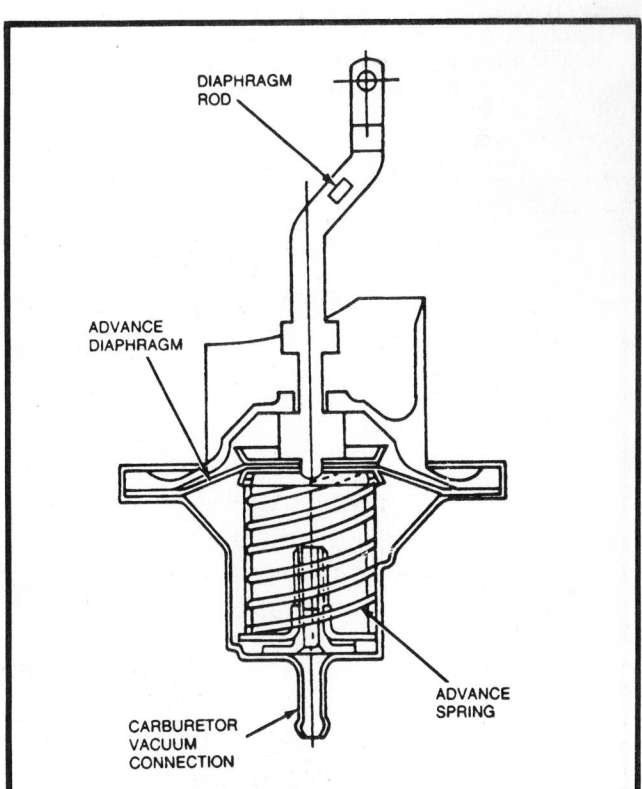

Cross section of single diaphragm vacuum advance assembly

dual vacuum advance unit is an advance/retard unit. It should be noted that vacuum applied to the advance port of the assembly overrides any spark retard caused by the application of vacuum to the retard port.

── CAUTION ──

The Dura Spark II coil is energized when the ignition switch is in the ON position. When servicing the Dura Spark II system, the ignition system could inadvertently "fire" while performing ignition system services (such as distributor cap removal or rotor movement) if the ignition is in the ON position.

Adjustments

The ignition system adjustments are limited to initial timing and spark plug gap. Refer to the Vehicle Emission Information label for initial timing and spark plug specifications.

DURA SPARK II DISTRIBUTOR/MODULE TESTS

Testing

NOTE: When testing circuits with a voltmeter and the grounding lead is to placed on the distributor, ensure that a good ground circuit exists between the distributor and the engine block or an erroneous reading could occur.

START CIRCUITS

1. Remove distributor cap and rotor from distributor.
2. Crank engine to align one tooth of armature with magnet in pick-up coil (ignition Off).
3. Remove coil wire from distributor cap, install a modified spark tester in the coil wire terminal and ground the spark tester shell against the engine block.
4. Turn the ignition switch and crank the engine. There should be a spark at the spark tester.
5. If there is a spark, the primary circuit is okay in the cranking mode.
6. Turn the ignition switch from the OFF to RUN to OFF positions several times.

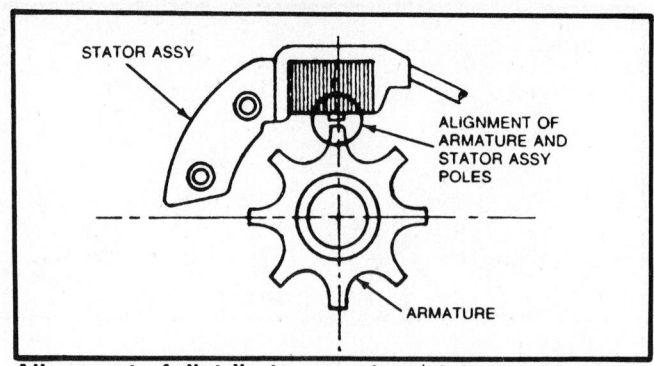

Alignment of distributor armature/stator assembly

7. Spark should occur each time the ignition switch goes from the RUN position to the OFF position.
8. If spark occurs as outlined, reassembly the coil wire, rotor and distributor cap.

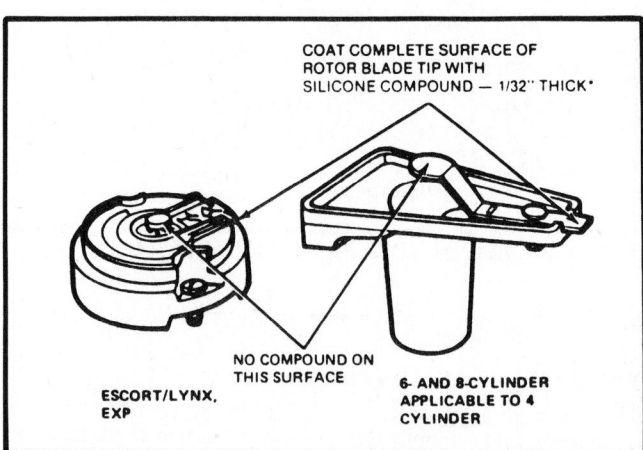

Coating of single blade rotor with silicone compound

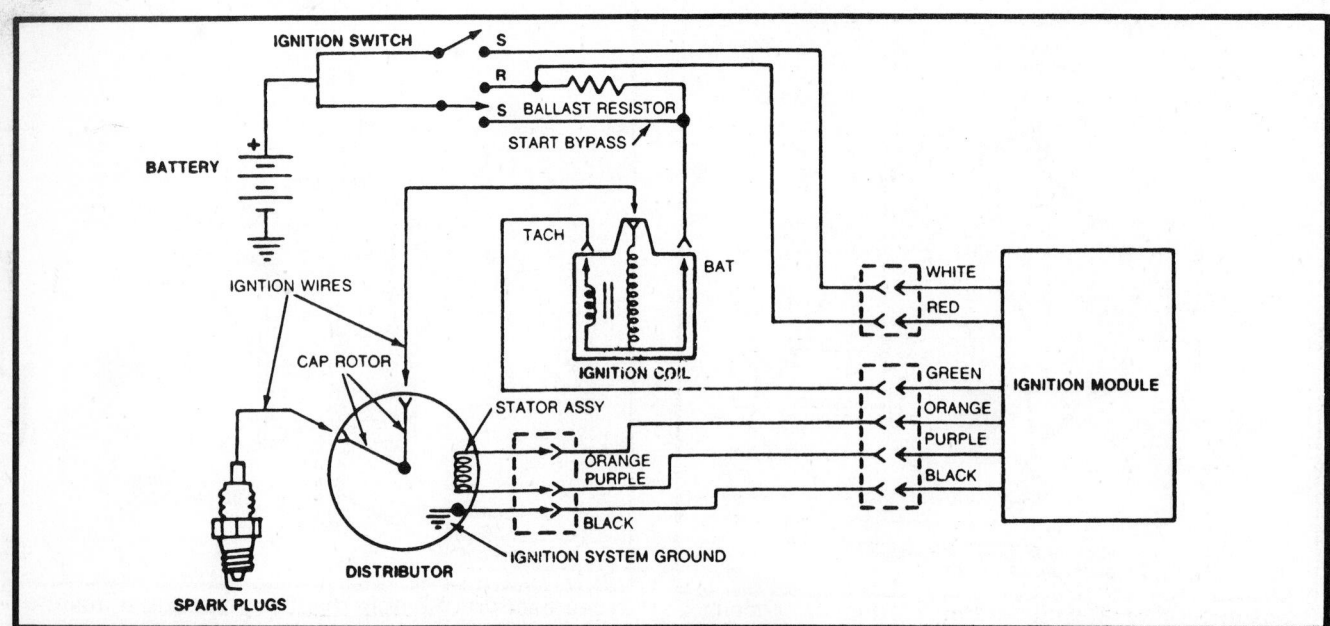

Wiring schematic of Dura Spark II Electronic Ignition system

Note: If the rotor has a wide single blade, coat the entire surface of the blade with silicone compound, 1/32 in. thick. If the rotor has a multipoint blade, do not use the silicone compound on the blade.

Testing

RUN CIRCUITS
NOTE: After performing any test which requires piercing a wire with a straight pin, remove the straight pin and seal the holes in the wire with silicone sealer.

1. If the secondary circuit sparks, but the engine will not start, continue testing. Check for roll pin securing the armature to the sleeve in the distributor.
2. Check that the ORANGE and the PURPLE wires are not crossed between the distributor and the ignition module.
3. If no spark was observed during the start or run tests by the ignition switch, be sure the ignition switch is turned OFF.
4. Carefully insert a straight pin in the RED module wire, being careful not to contact an electrical ground.
5. Attach the negative voltmeter cable to the distributor base.

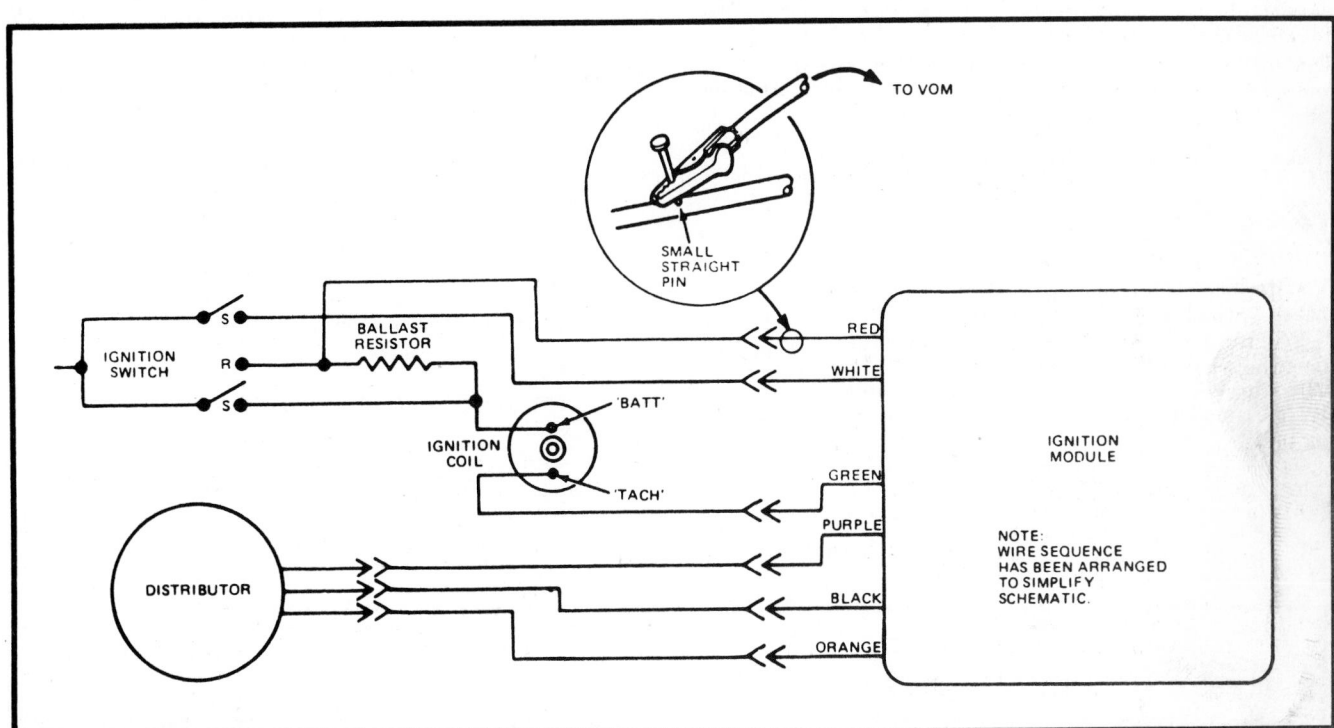

Testing module voltage-Dura Spark II system

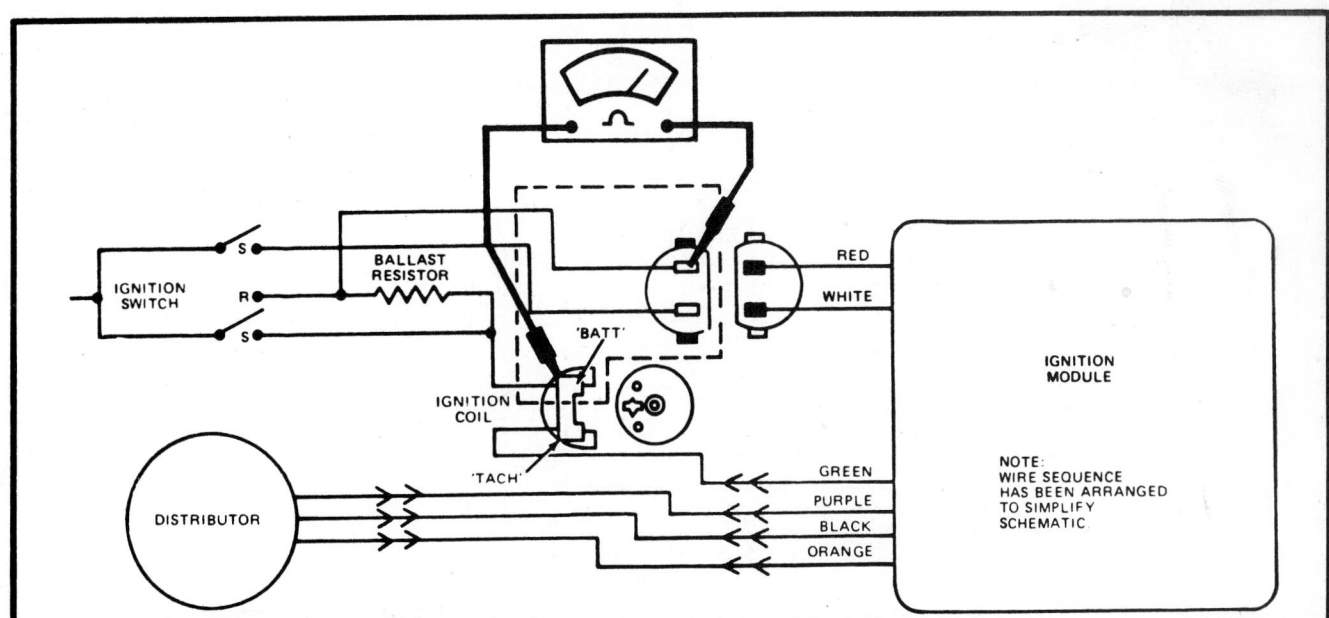

Testing ballast resistor-Dura Spark II system

6. With the positive voltmeter cable, measure the available voltage at the straight pin/RED wire with the ignition switch in the RUN position.

7. The voltage should not be less than 90% of battery voltage.

8. If the voltage is less than 90% of battery voltage, inspect the wiring harness between the module and the ignition switch. Inspect the ignition switch for being worn or defective.

9. If the voltage is within the OK range, separate and inspect the ignition module two wire connector with the RED and WHITE wires.

10. Disconnect the ignition coil connector and inspect. Measure the ballast resistor with an ohmmeter between the battery terminal of the ignition coil connector and the wiring harness connector mating with the RED module wire.

11. If a reading of between 0.8–1.6 ohms is obtained, an intermittent problem could exist.

12. If a reading of less than 0.8 or greater than 1.6 ohms is obtained, replace the ballast resistor

Testing

SUPPLY VOLTAGE CIRCUITS

1. If the starter relay has an "I"terminal, disconnect the cable from the starter relay to starter motor.

2. If the starter relay does not have the "I" terminal, disconnect the wire to the "S "terminal of the starter relay.

3. Carefully insert small straight pins into the RED and WHITE module wires. Do not allow the pins to contact a ground.

4. With a voltmeter, measure the available voltage at each wire. The available voltage should be 90% of battery voltage.

5. Have the ignition switch in the RUN position when testing the voltage at the RED wire.

6. Have the ignition switch in the START position when testing the White wire and the "BATT" terminal of the ignition coil.

7. While the voltmeter is attached to each circuit, wiggle each wire in the wiring harness while observing the voltmeter scale.

8. If the available voltage is less than 90% of battery voltage, inspect the wiring harness and connectors in the faulty circuits. Check for a defective or worn ignition switch.

NOTE: If the circuits and connections are good, check the radio interference capacitor mounted on the ignition coil.

9. Turn the ignition switch to the OFF position, remove the straight pins and reconnect any disconnected cables.

Testing

IGNITION COIL SUPPLY VOLTAGE

1. Attach the negative lead of the voltmeter to the distributor base.

2. Turn the ignition switch to the RUN position.

3. Measure the voltage at the "BATT" terminal of the ignition coil.

4. The voltage should be 6–8 volts. If less than 6 volts or more than 8 volts, refer to testing ignition coil.

5. Turn the ignition switch to the OFF position.

Testing

DISTRIBUTOR STATOR ASSEMBLY AND WIRING HARNESS

1. Separate the ignition module four wire connector. Examine it for dirt, corrosion and damage.

2. Measure the stator assembly and wiring harness resistance between the wiring harness terminals mating with the ORANGE and PURPLE module wires

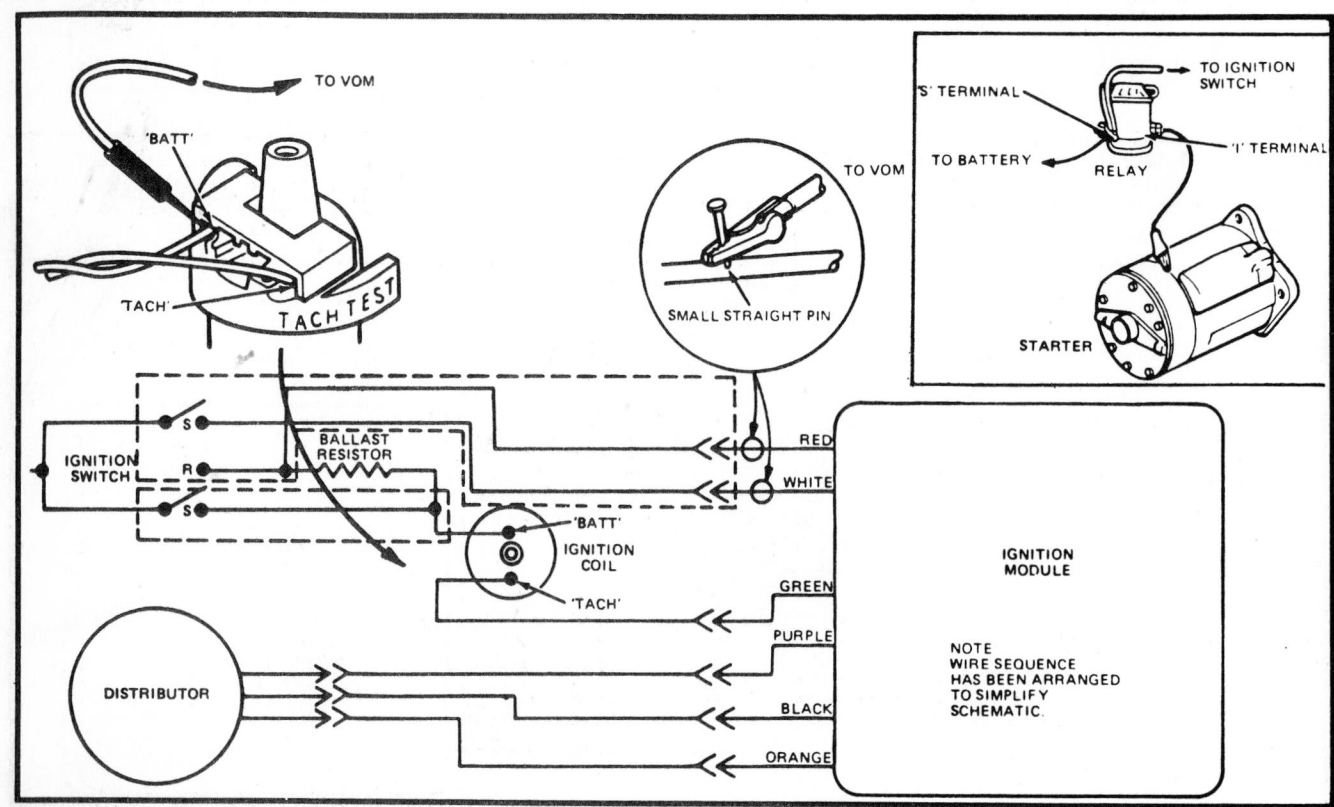

Testing Dura Spark II voltage supply circuits

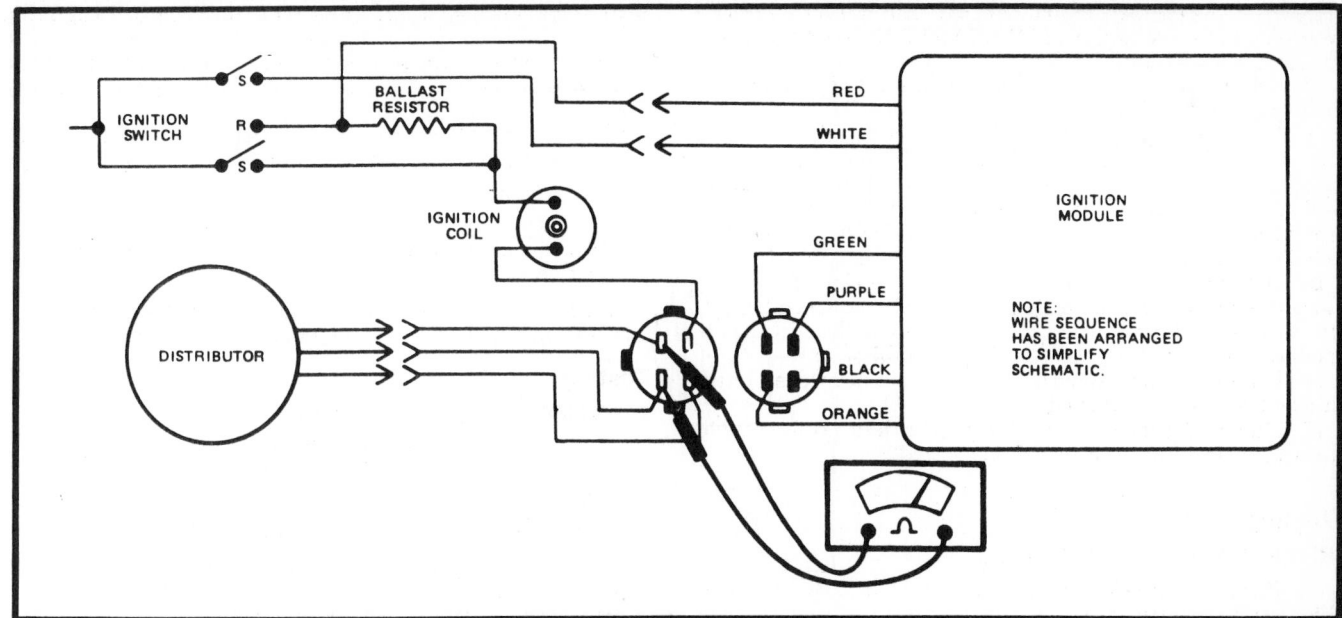

Testing Dura Spark II distributor stator assembly and wiring harness

3. The resistance should be 400–1300 ohms. Wiggle the wires in the wiring harness when taking the resistance reading.

4. If the reading is less than 400 ohms or greater than 1300 ohms, refer to testing the distributor stator assembly.

Testing
IGNITION MODULE TO DISTRIBUTOR STATOR ASSEMBLY WIRING HARNESS

1. Attach one lead of the ohmmeter to the distributor base.

2. Alternately measure the resistance between the wiring harness terminals mating with the ORANGE and PURPLE module wires and ground.

3. The resistance reading should be greater than 70,000 ohms.

4. If the resistance reading is less than 70,000 ohms, inspect the wiring harness between the module connector and distributor, including the distributor grommet.

Testing
IGNITION COIL SECONDARY RESISTANCE

1. Disconnect and inspect the ignition coil connector and the coil wire.

2. Measure the secondary resistance from the "BATT" terminal to the high voltage terminal.

3. The resistance should be 7,700–10,500 ohms.

4. If the resistance reading is less than 7,700 ohms or greater than 10,500 ohms, replace the ignition coil.

Testing
MODULE TO COIL WIRE

1. Separate and inspect the ignition module four wire connector and the ignition coil connector from the ignition coil.

2. Connect one lead of the ohmmeter to the distributor base.

3. Measure the resistance between the "TACH" terminal of the ignition coil connector and ground.

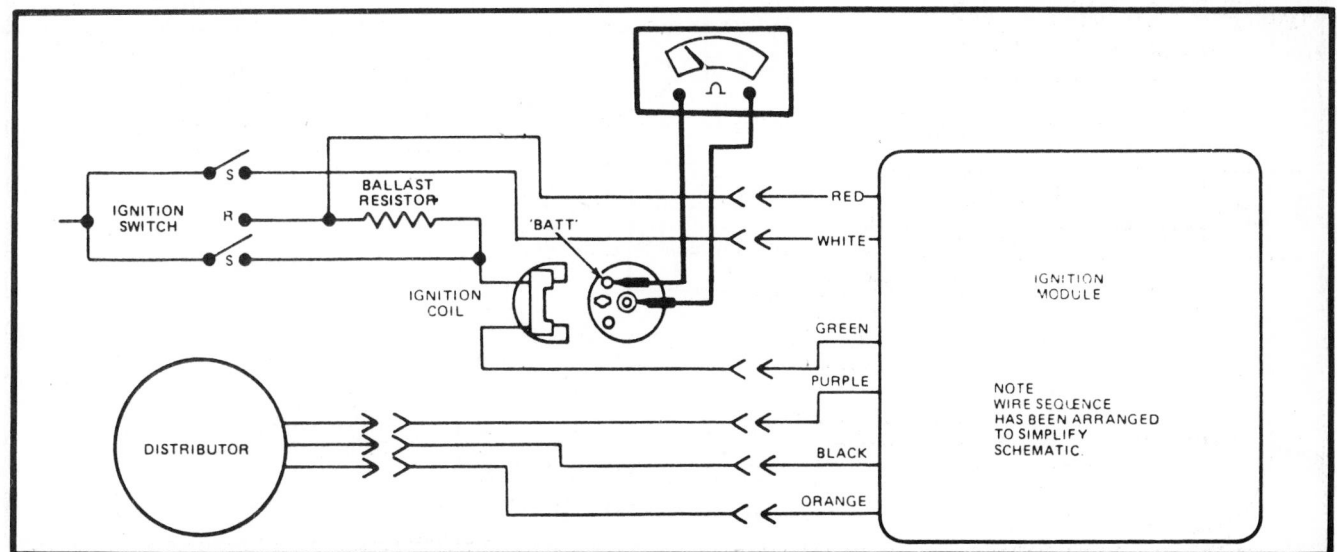

Testing ignition coil secondary resistance-Dura Spark II system

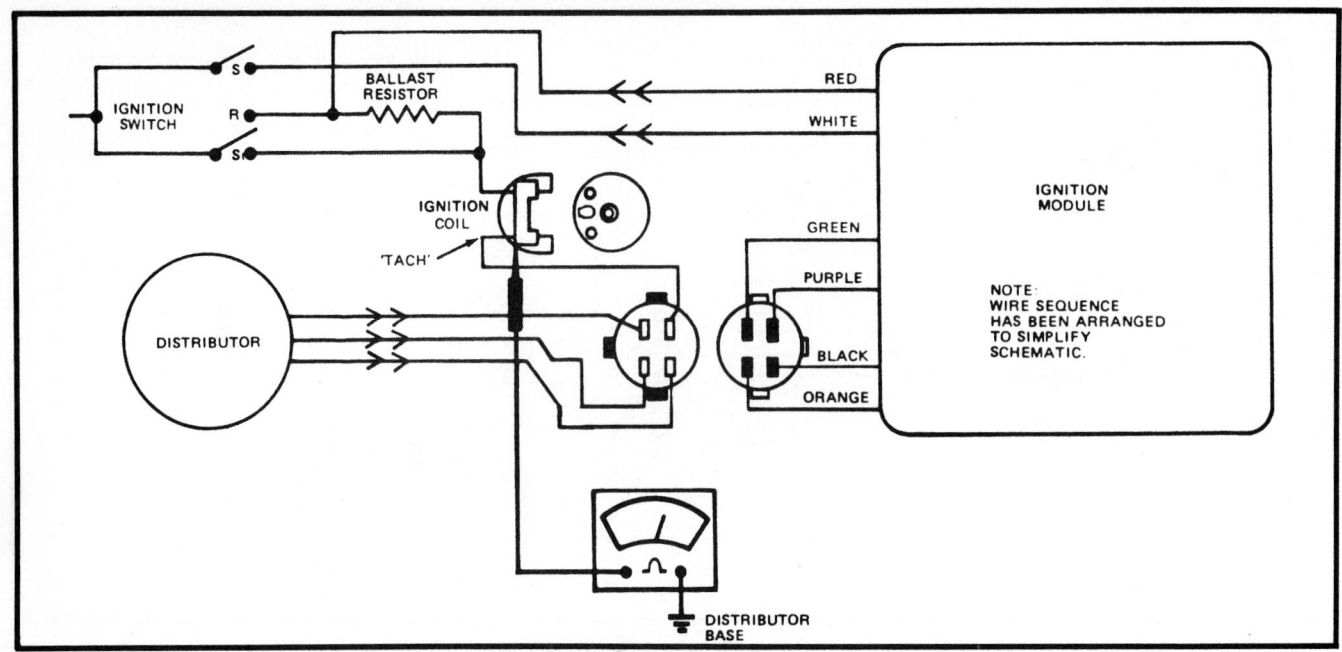

Testing module to ignition coil.primary wire-Dura Spark II system

4. The resistance should be greater than 100 ohms.
5. If the resistance is less than 100 ohms, inspect the wiring harness between the ignition module and the ignition coil.

Testing

DISTRIBUTOR STATOR ASSEMBLY

1. Separate the distributor connector from the wiring harness. Inspect the connector for dirt, corrosion and damage.
2. Measure the stator assembly resistance across the OR-ANGE and PURPLE wires at the distributor connector.
3. The resistance should be 400–1,000 ohms.
4. If the resistance is less than 400 ohms or greater than 1,000 ohms, replace the stator assembly.
5. Reconnect the distributor and module connectors.

Testing

IGNITION COIL PRIMARY RESISTANCE

1. Disconnect the ignition coil connector.
2. Measure the primary resistance from the "BATT" to the "TACH" terminal.
3. The resistance should be 0.8–1.6 ohms.
4. If the resistance is less than 0.8 ohm or greater than 1.6 ohms, replace the ignition coil.
5. Reconnect the ignition coil connector.

Testing

PRIMARY CIRCUIT CONTINUITY

1. Carefully insert a straight pin into the GREEN wire of

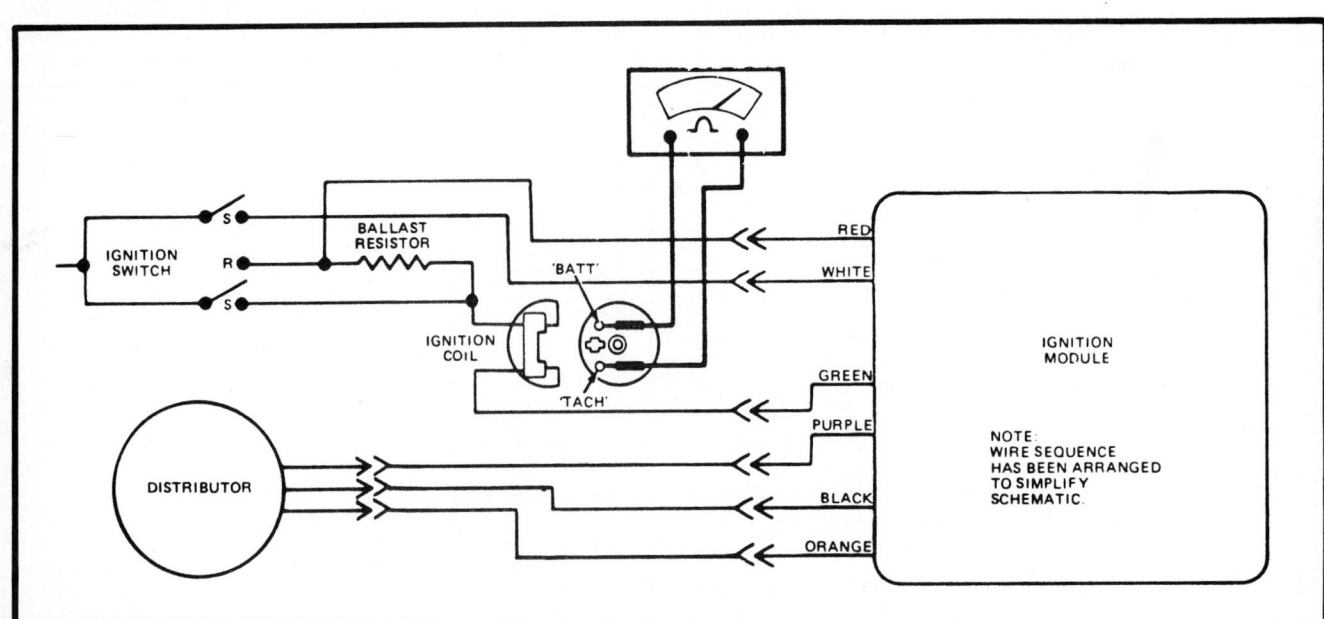

Testing ignition coil primary resistance-Dura Spark II system

the ignition module. Do not allow the pin to touch a grounding point.

2. Attach the negative voltmeter cable to the distributor base and turn the ignition switch to the ON position.

3. Measure the voltage at the GREEN module wire.

4. The voltage should be greater than 1.5 volts.

5. If the voltage is 1.5 or less, inspect the wiring harness and connectors between the ignition module and the ignition coil.

Testing

GROUND CIRCUIT CONTINUITY

1. Carefully insert a straight pin in the module BLACK wire.

2. Attach the negative voltmeter lead to the distributor base.

3. Turn the ignition switch to the RUN position.

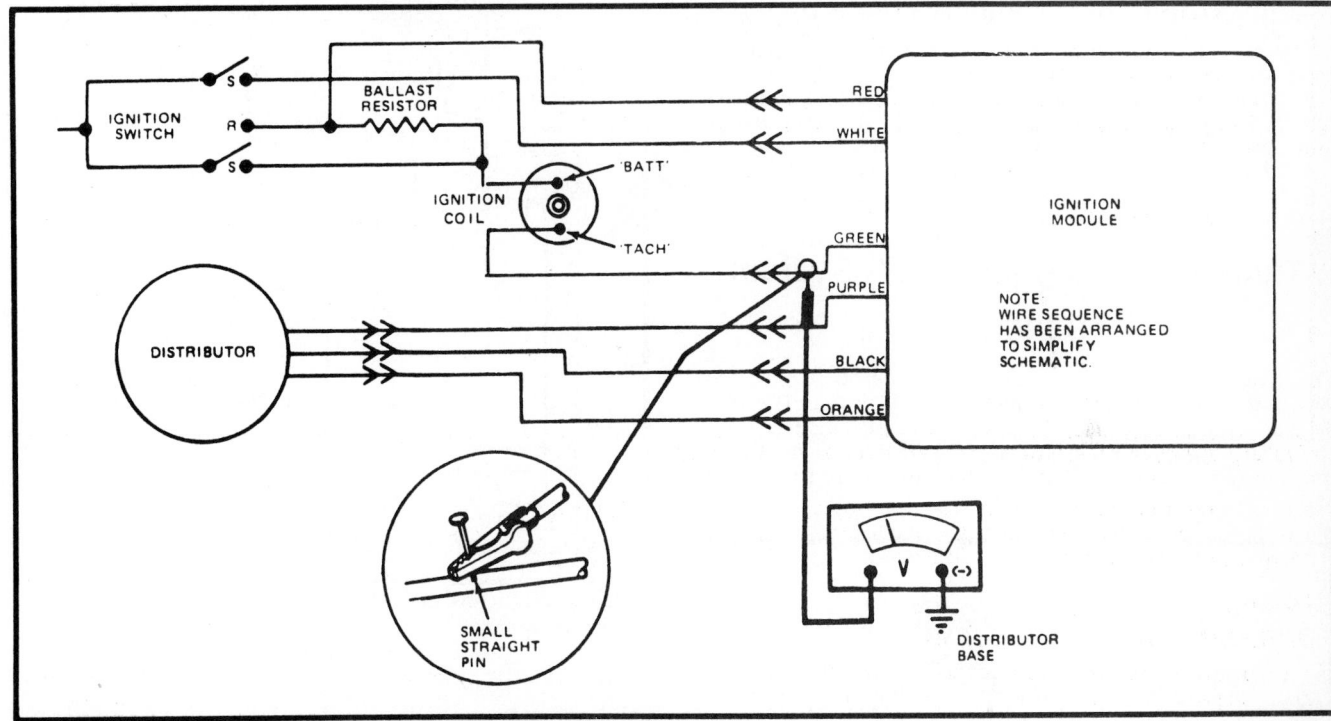

Testing Primary circuit continuity-Dura Spark II system

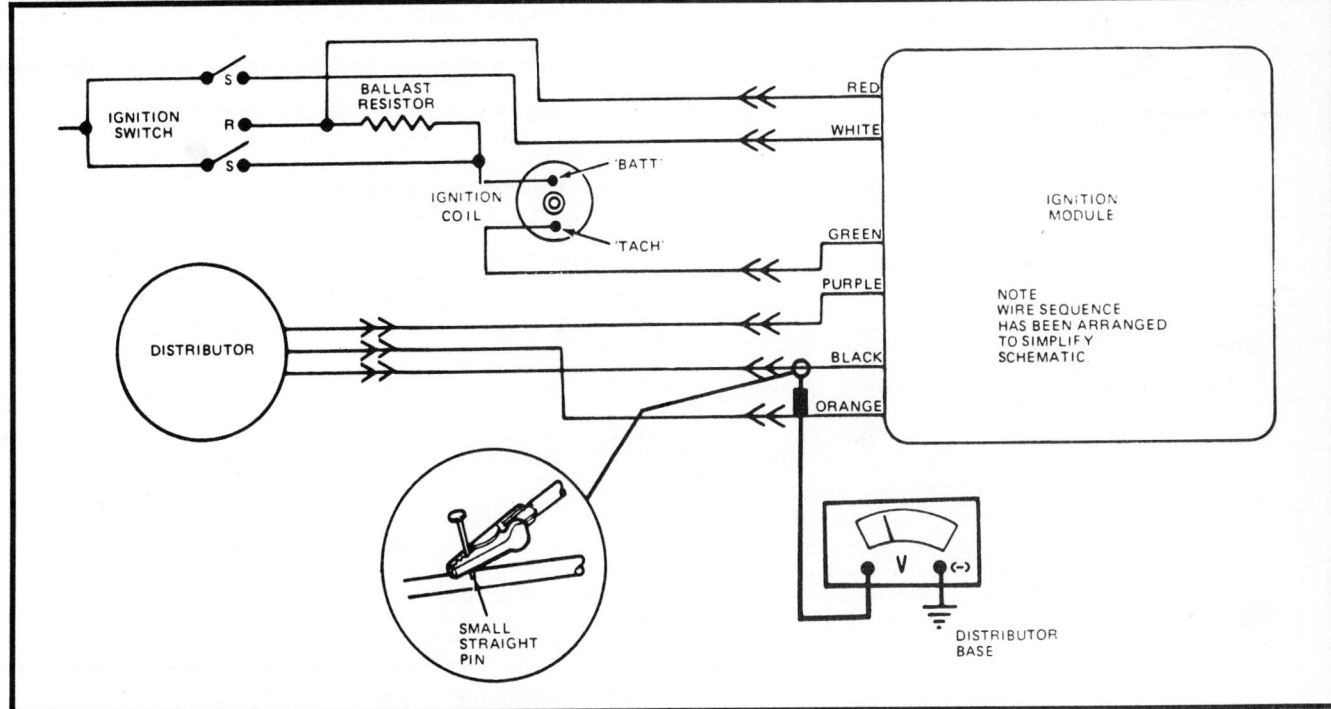

Testing ground circuit continuity-Dura Spark II system

4. Measure the voltage at the BLACK wire.

5. The voltage should be greater than 1.5 volts.

6. If the voltage is less than 1.5 volts, replace the ignition module.

7. Turn the ignition switch to the OFF position and remove the straight pin.

Testing

DISTRIBUTOR GROUND CIRCUIT CONTINUITY

1. Separate the distributor connector from the harness. Inspect for dirt, corrosion and damage.

2. Attach one lead of the ohmmeter to the distributor base.

3. Measure the resistance at the BLACK wire in the distributor connector.

4. The resistance should be less than one ohm.

5. If the resistance is greater than one ohm, inspect the ground screw in the distributor assembly.

Thick Film Integrated (TFI) System

GENERAL

The Thick Film Integrated (TFI) ignition system comprises two system, the TFI-I system and the TFI-IV system. The TFI-I system is used for non-electronic fuel controlled models, while the TFI-IV system is used for all EEC-IV/EFI models. The TFI ignition system uses a new style distributor, called the Univer-

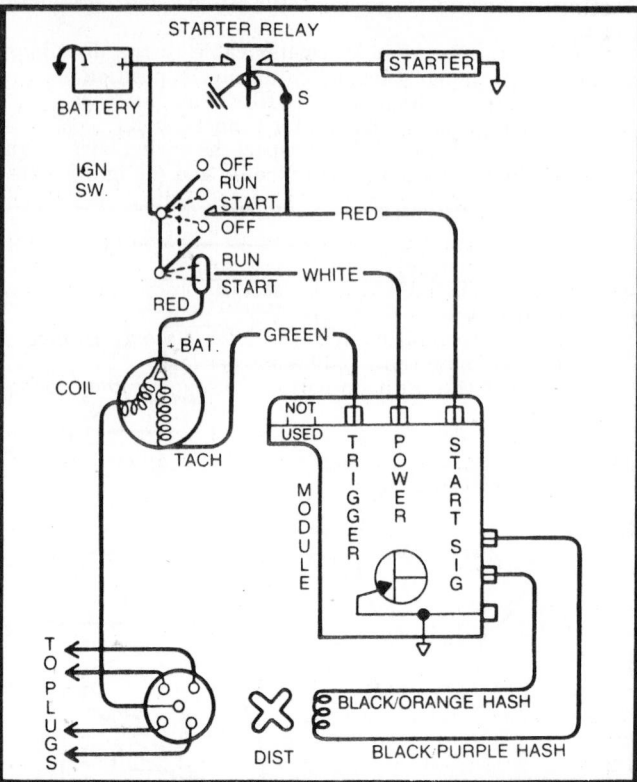

Typical electrical schematic for TFI-I Electronic Ignition system

sal distributor and is equipped with centrifugal and vacuum advance units when used with the TFI-I system and no centrifugal and vacuum advance units when used with the TFI-IV system. It has a distributor base mounted TFI ignition module, which is self-contained in a moulded thermo-plastic unit. The TFI-I system module can be identified by having three pins, while the TFI-IV system module has six pins. Also, both TFI systems use an E-Core ignition coil, named after the shape of the laminations making up the core.

The Universal distributor used with the TFI-IV system, contains a provision to change the basic distributor calibration with the use of a replaceable "Octane" rod, from the standard of zero degrees to either three or six degree retard rods. No other calibration changes are possible.

NOTE: Do not change the ignition timing by the use of a different octane rod without having the proper authority to do so as Federal Emission requirements will be effected.

The TFI system was designed for use with non-EFI systems and is known as the TFI-I system. The second design is used for all EEC-IV/EFI systems and is known as the TFI-IV system.

TFI-I SYSTEM

The basic operation of the distributor is the same as that of the Dura Spark system with the separate module. The rotating armature induces a signal in the stator assembly causing the ignition module to turn the ignition coil current ON and OFF, generating the high voltage to fire the spark plugs.

The TFI-I distributor contains vacuum and centrifugal advance units

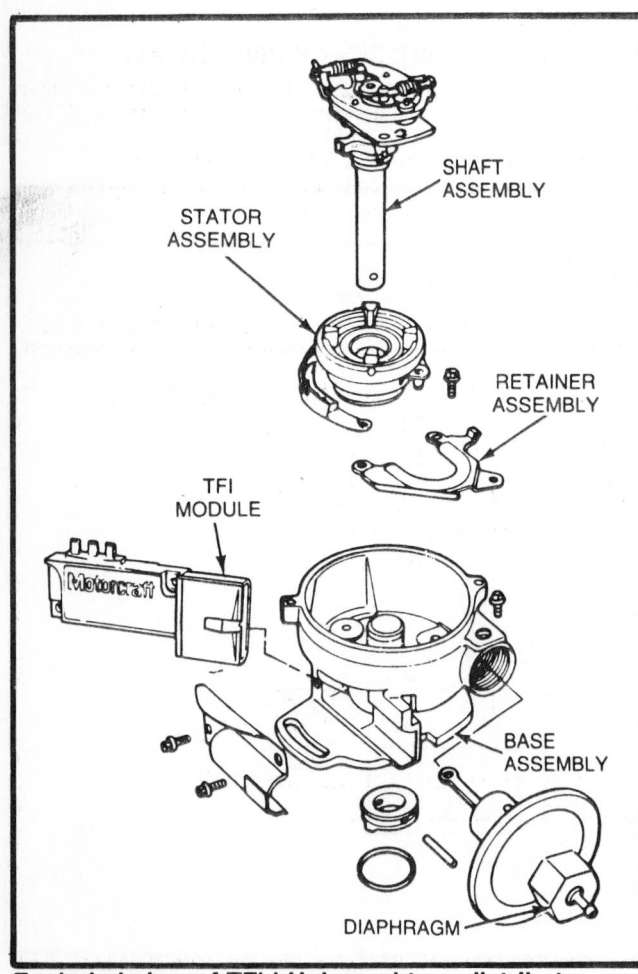

Exploded view of TFI-I Universal type distributor

Testing

IGNITION COIL SECONDARY VOLTAGE

NOTE: After performing any test which requires piercing a wire with a straight pin, remove the straight pin and seal the holes in the wire with silicone sealer.

1. Disconnect the secondary (high voltage) coil wire from the distributor cap and install a spark tester between the coil wire and ground.
2. Crank the engine. A spark should be noted at the spark tester. If spark is noted, but the engine will not start, check the spark plugs, spark plug wiring, and fuel system. If there is no spark at the tester:
    a. Check the ignition coil secondary wire resistance; it should be no more than 7000 ohms per foot.
    b. Inspect the ignition coil for damage and/or carbon tracking.
    c. With the distributor cap removed, verify that the distributor shaft turns with the engine; if it does not, repair the engine as required.

Testing

IGNITION COIL PRIMARY CIRCUIT SWITCHING

1. Insert a small straight pin in the wire which runs from the coil negative terminal to the TFI-I module, about one inch from the module.

——————— **CAUTION** ———————

The pin must not touch ground.
————————————————————————

2. Connect a 12V test lamp between the straight pin and an engine ground.
3. Crank the engine, noting the operation of the test lamp. If the test lamp flashes, proceed to the next test. If the test lamp lights but does not flash, proceed to the Wiring Harness test. If the test lamp does not light at all, proceed to the Primary Circuit continuity test.
4. Remove pin and seal wire with silicone sealer.

Testing

IGNITION COIL RESISTANCE

1. Have the ignition switch in the OFF position.

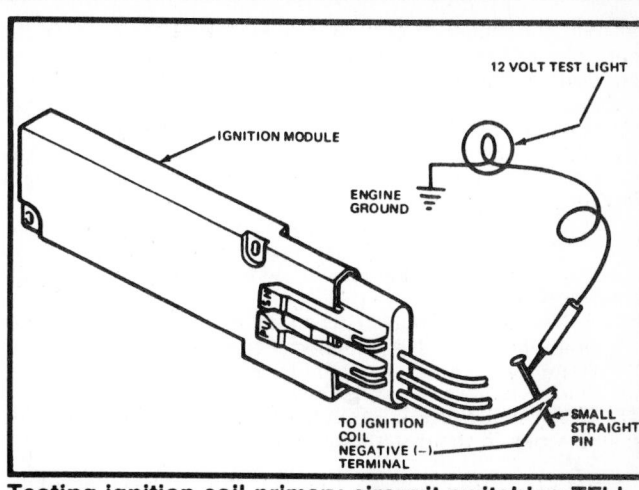

Testing ignition coil primary circuyit switching-TFI-I system

2. Disconnect the ignition coil connector. Inspect it for dirt, corrosion and damage.
3. Using an ohmmeter, measure the resistance from the positive to the negative terminals of the ignition coil.
4. The resistance should be 0.3–1.0 ohm.
5. If the resistance is less than 0.3 ohm or greater than 1.0 ohm, replace the ignition coil.

Testing

IGNITION COIL SECONDARY RESISTANCE

1. With the ignition coil wiring harness connector off, measure the resistance from the negative terminal to the high voltage terminal of the ignition coil connector.
2. The resistance should be 6,500–11,500 ohms.
3. If the resistance is less than 6,500 ohms or greater than 11,500 ohms, replace the ignition coil.

Testing

WIRING HARNESS

1. Disconnect the wiring harness connector from the TFI-I

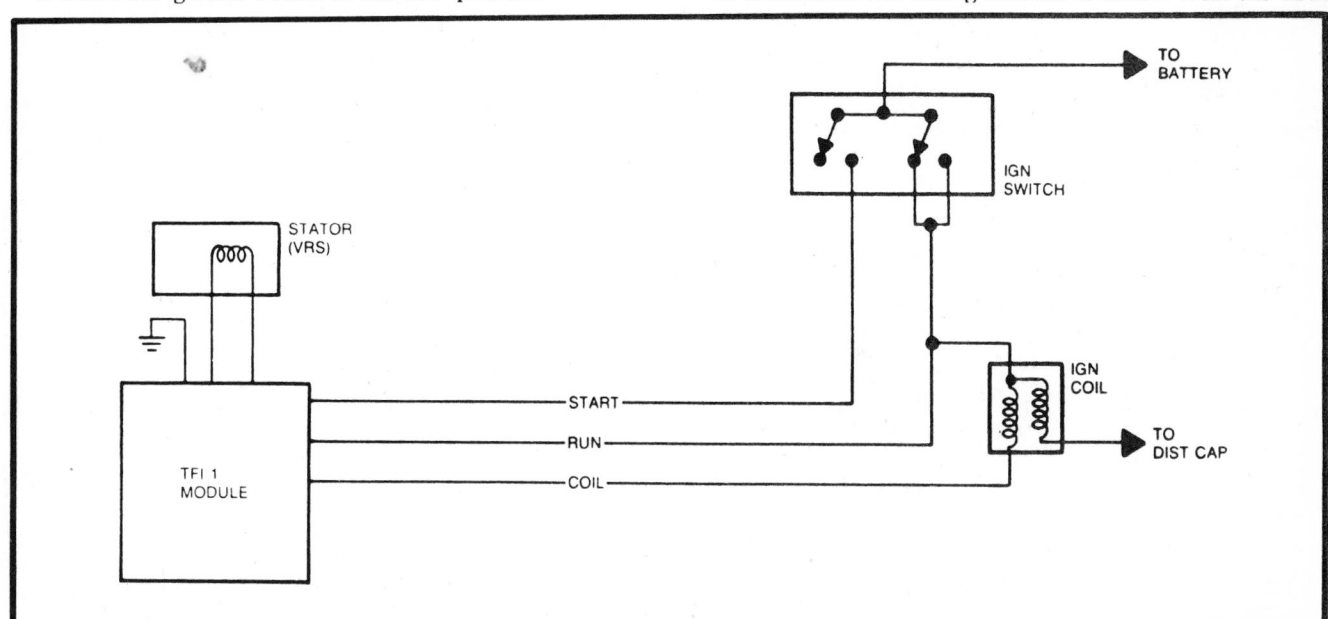

TFI-I system primary wire schematic for testing purposes

module; the connector tabs must be PUSHED to disengage the connector. Inspect the connector for damage, dirt, and corrosion.

2. Disconnect the wire at the "S" terminal of the starter relay.

3. Attach the negative lead of a voltmeter to the base of the distributor. Attach the other voltmeter lead to a small straight pin.

   a. With the ignition switch in the RUN position, insert the straight pin into the No. 1 terminal of the TFI-I module connector. Note the voltage reading, which should be 90% of battery voltage.

   b. With the ignition switch in the RUN position, move the straight pin to the No. 2 connector terminal. Again, note the voltage reading, which should be 90% of battery voltage.

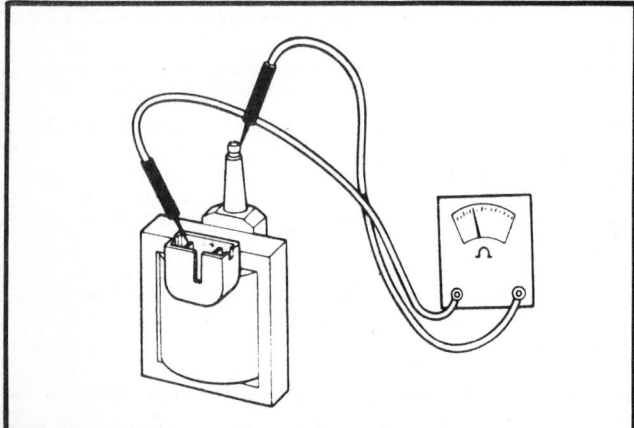

Testing ignition coil secondary resistance-TFI-I system

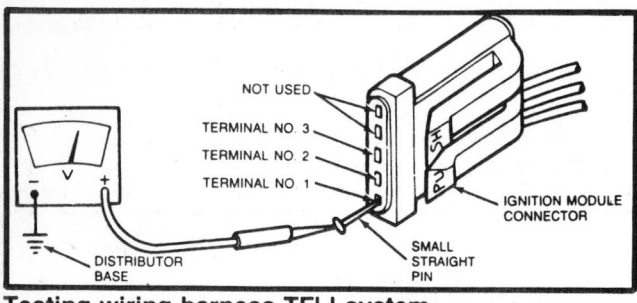

Testing wiring harness-TFI-I system

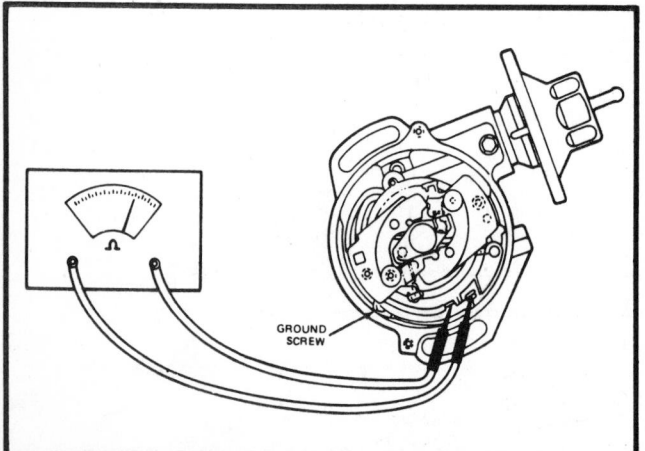

Testing module and stator assembly-TFI-I system

   c. Move the straight pin to the No. 3 connector terminal, then turn the ignition switch to the START position. Note the voltage reading, which should be 90% of battery voltage.

4. If any reading is less than 90% of the battery voltage, inspect the wiring, connectors and/or ignition switch for defects.

5. Turn the ignition switch to the OFF position. Remove the straight pin and reconnect the wire at the starter relay.

Testing

STATOR ASSEMBLY AND MODULE

1. Remove the distributor from the engine according to the procedure outlined in the appropriate car section.

2. Remove the TFI-I module from the distributor.

3. Inspect the distributor terminals, ground screw and stator wiring for damage. Repair as necessary.

4. Measure the resistance of the stator assembly, using an ohmmeter. If the ohmmeter reading is 650–1,300 ohms, the stator is okay, but the TFI-I module should be replaced. If the ohmmeter reading is less than 650 ohms or more than 1,300 ohms, the TFI-I module is okay, but the stator assembly should be replaced.

5. Reinstall the TFI-I module and the distributor.

Testing

PRIMARY CIRCUIT CONTINUITY

1. Separate the wiring harness from the ignition module by pushing the connector tabs to remove the connector.

2. Attach the negative voltmeter cable to the distributor base and measure the battery voltage.

3. Attach the positive voltmeter cable to a straight pin, inserted into the connector terminal No. 1.

4. Turn the ignition switch to the RUN position and measure the voltage at terminal No. 1.

5. The voltage should not be less then 90% of battery voltage.

6. If the voltage is less than 90% of battery voltage, proceed to the Ignition Coil Primary Voltage test.

7. Turn the ignition switch to the OFF position and remove the straight pin.

Testing

IGNITION COIL PRIMARY VOLTAGE

1. Attach the negative lead of a voltmeter to the distributor base and measure the battery voltage.

2. Turn the ignition switch to the RUN position and connect the positive voltmeter lead to the negative ignition coil terminal. Note the voltage reading and turn the ignition to the OFF position.

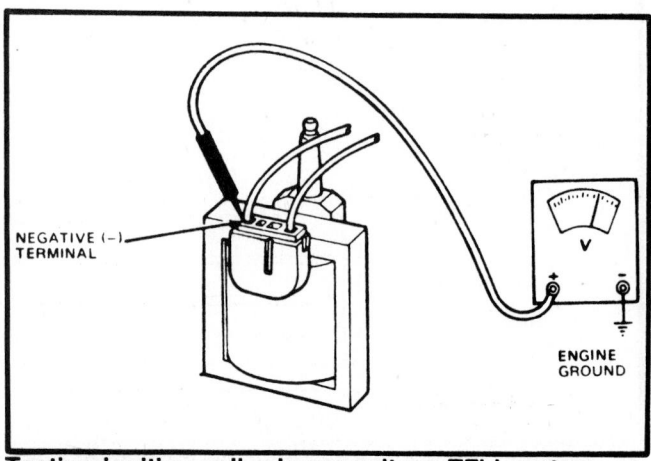

Testing ignition coil primary voltage-TFI-I system

3. If the voltmeter reading is less than 90% of the available battery voltage, inspect the wiring between the ignition module and the negative coil terminal.

Testing

IGNITION COIL SUPPLY VOLTAGE

1. Attach the negative lead of a voltmeter to the distributor base.

2. Turn the ignition switch to the ON position and connect the positive voltmeter lead to the positive (+) ignition coil terminal. Note the voltage reading, then turn the ignition to the OFF position.

3. If the voltage reading is at least 90% of the battery voltage, yet the engine will still not run; first, check the ignition coil connector and terminals for corrosion, dirt, and/or damage; second, replace the ignition switch if the connectors and terminals are damaged or corroded.

4. If the voltage reading is less than 90% of battery voltage, inspect and repair as necessary, the wiring between the ignition coil and the ignition switch. Check for a worn or damaged ignition switch.

5. Reconnect the ignition module connector.

Testing

STATOR ASSEMBLY AND MODULE

1. Remove the distributor from the engine according to the procedure outlined in the appropriate car section.

2. Remove the TFI-I module from the distributor.

3. Inspect the distributor ground screw, stator assembly wires and terminals.

4. Measure the resistance of the stator assembly. The resistance should be 650–1,300 ohms.

5. If the resistance of the stator is correct, replace the ignition module.

6. If the resistance is less than 650 ohms or greater than 1,300 ohms, the ignition module is good, but the ignition module must be replaced.

7. Reinstall the ignition module (new or original) to the distributor and re-install the distributor in the engine.

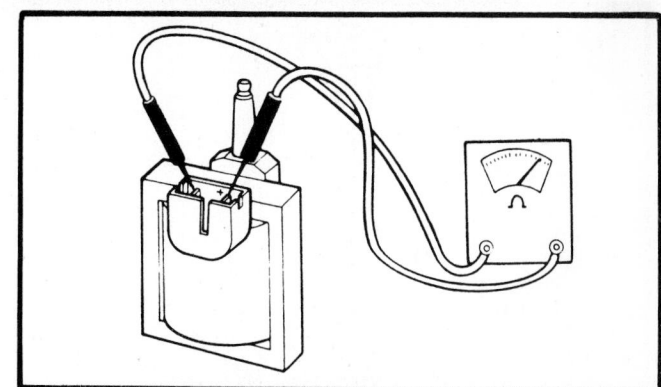

Testing ignition coil primary resistance-TFI-I system

TFI-IV SYSTEM

The major addition to the TFI-IV system is the Hall Effect Switch, used to signal the EEC-IV system as to the position of the crankshaft, allowing the ECA to compute the desired spark advance, based on the engine demand and calibration. This conditioned spark advance then pulses the TFI-IV module to turn the ignition coil current OFF and ON, generating the high voltage necessary to fire the spark plugs. The high voltage distribution is accomplished through the conventional rotor, distributor cap and ignition wires.

In addition to the Hall Effect switch, the ignition module contains the Profile Ignition Pick-up (PIP) sensor, which sends an electronically oriented crankshaft position signal to the ECA and the TFI module circuitry. The ECA, after taking all the sensors information, produces a new signal called the Spout. This Spout signal is then sent back to the TFI module for comparison with the PIP signal. The TFI-IV module then uses both of these signals to fire the ignition coil at the proper timing interval.

A modification to the circuitry allows for a Push-Start mode for manual transmission equipped vehicles.

The TFI-IV distributor contains no vacuum or centrifugal advance components, with all adjustment of timing and dwell adjusted electronically.

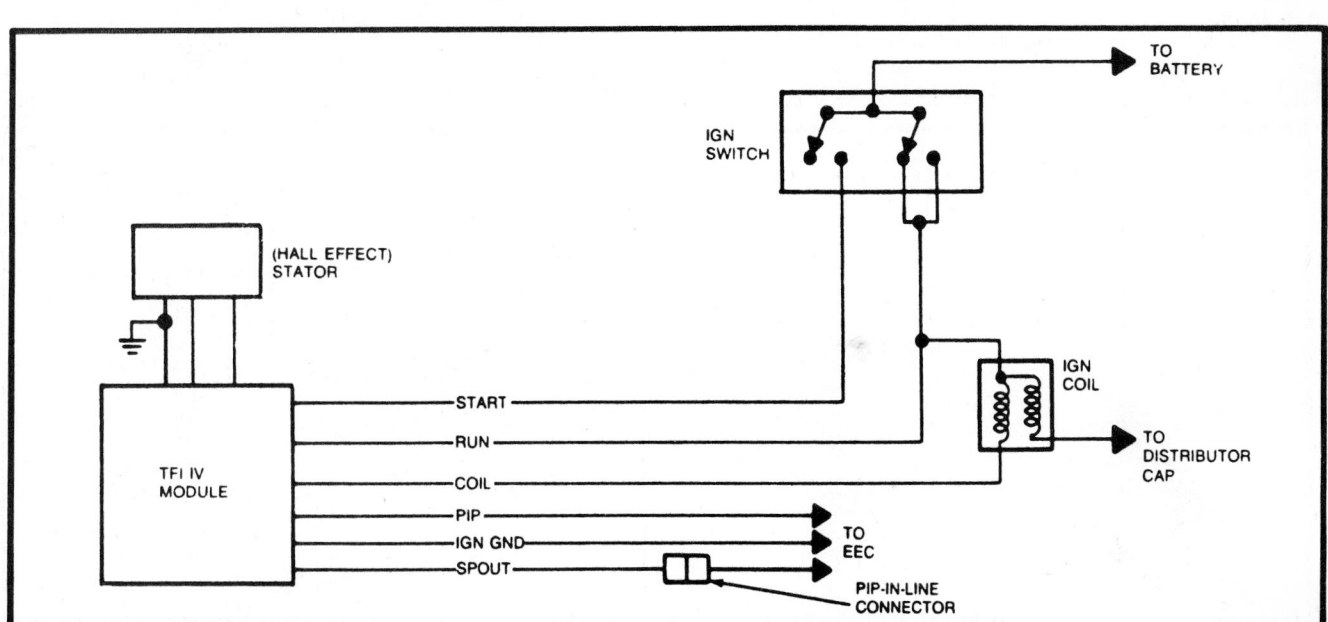

TFI-IV system primary circyuit electrical schematic

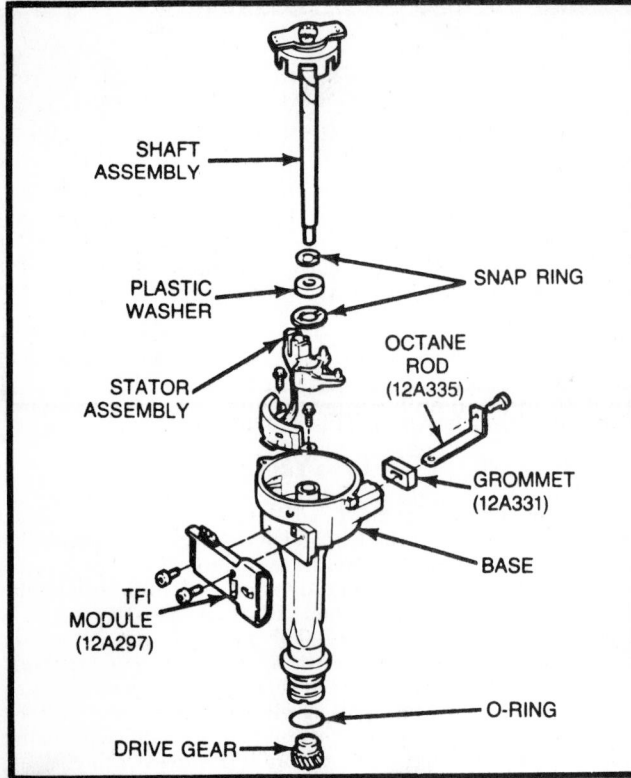

Hall Effect equipped universal distributor-TFI-IV system

Testing

IGNITION COIL SECONDARY VOLTAGE

NOTE: After performing any test which requires piercing a wire with a straight pin, remove the straight pin and seal the holes in the wire with silicone sealer.

1. Disconnect the secondary (high voltage) coil wire from the distributor cap and install a spark tester between the coil wire and ground.
2. Crank the engine. A spark should be noted at the spark tester. If spark is noted, but the engine will not start, check the spark plugs, spark plug wiring, and fuel system.

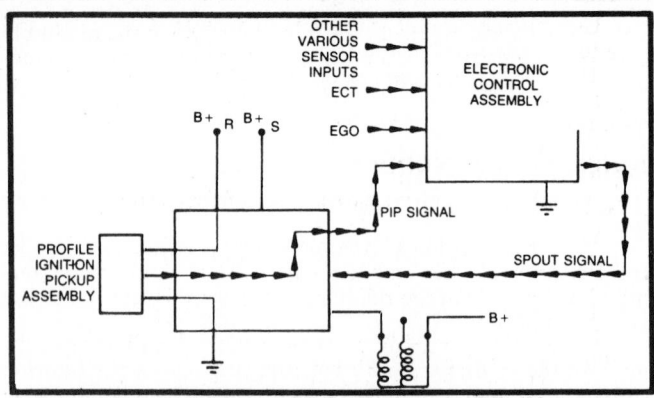

Current flow of PIP and SPOUT signals-TFI-IV system

3. If there is no spark at the tester:
   a. Check the ignition coil secondary wire resistance; it should be no more than 7000 ohms per foot.
   b. Inspect the ignition coil for damage and/or carbon tracking.
   c. With the distributor cap removed, verify that the distributor shaft turns with the engine; if it does not, repair the engine as required.
   d. Be sure the rotor single blade is coated with silicone compound, approximately $1/32$ in. thick. Do not coat the multipoint rotor.

Testing

IGNITION COIL PRIMARY CIRCUIT SWITCHING

1. Separate the wiring harness connector from the ignition module. Inspect for dirt, corrosion and damage. Re-connect the harness connector.
2. Attach a 12V test lamp between the ignition coil tach terminal and engine ground.
3. Crank the engine and observe the light.
4. If the lamp flashes or lights but will not flash, proceed to the Ignition Coil Primary Resistance test.
5. If the lamp does not light or is very dim, go to the Primary Circuit Continuity test.

Testing

IGNITION COIL PRIMARY RESISTANCE

1. Have the ignition switch in the OFF position.
2. Disconnect the ignition coil connector. Inspect it for dirt, corrosion and damage.

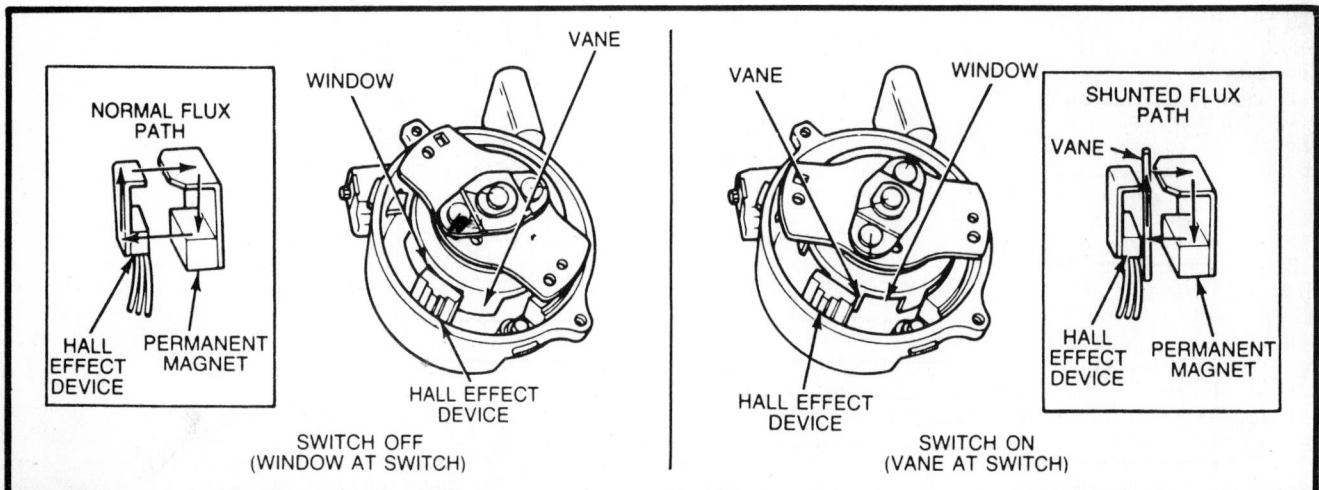

Hall Effect pick-up operation TFI-IV system

3. Using an ohmmeter, measure the resistance from the positive to the negative terminals of the ignition coil.

4. The resistance should be 0.3–1.0 ohm.

5. If the resistance is less than 0.3 ohm or greater than 1.0 ohm, replace the ignition coil.

Testing

IGNITION COIL SECONDARY RESISTANCE

1. With the ignition coil wiring harness connector off, measure the resistance from the negative terminal to the high voltage terminal of the ignition coil connector.

2. The resistance should be 6,500–11,500 ohms.

3. If the resistance is less than 6,500 ohms or greater than 11,500 ohms, replace the ignition coil.

Testing

WIRING HARNESS

1. Disconnect the wiring harness connector from the TFI-IV module; the connector tabs must be PUSHED to disengage the connector. Inspect the connector for damage, dirt, and corrosion.

2. Disconnect the wire at the "S" terminal of the starter relay.

3. Attach the negative lead of a voltmeter to the base of the distributor. Attach the other voltmeter lead to a small straight pin.

    a. With the ignition switch in the RUN position, insert the straight pin into the No. 2 terminal of the TFI-IV module connector. Note the voltage reading, which should be 90% of battery voltage.

    b. With the ignition switch in the RUN position, move the straight pin to the No. 3 connector terminal. Again, note the voltage reading, which should be 90% of battery voltage.

    c. Move the straight pin to the No. 4 connector terminal, then turn the ignition switch to the START position. Note the voltage reading, which should be 90% of battery voltage.

4. If any reading is less than 90% of the battery voltage, inspect the wiring, connectors, and/or ignition switch for defects.

5. Turn the ignition switch to the OFF position. Remove the straight pin and reconnect the wire at the starter relay.

Testing

STATOR

1. Turn the ignition switch to the OFF position.

2. Remove the coil wire and ground it.

3. Attach the negative voltmeter lead to the distributor base.

4. Disconnect the pin-in-line connector near the distributor and attach the positive voltmeter lead to the TFI-IV module side of the connector.

5. Turn the ignition switch to the ON position.

6. "Bump" the starter with the ignition switch and measure the voltage levels with the engine not operating. Record all measurements.

7. If the highest value is less than 90% of battery voltage, replace the stator assembly.

8. If the lowest value is greater than .5 volts, remove the distributor from the engine, remove the TFI-IV module from the distributor and inspect the stator connector terminals and the TFI terminals for misalignment. If OK, replace the stator.

9. If the values are between .5 volts and 90% of battery voltage, replace the stator assembly.

10. If there are no values between .5 volts and 90% of battery voltage, connect a spark tester between the ignition coil wire and the engine ground.

11. Crank the engine. If a spark occurs, check the PIP and ignition ground wires for continuity. Repair as required. If no fault is found, refer to EEC-IV diagnostics.

12. If no spark occurs, replace the TFI-IV module.

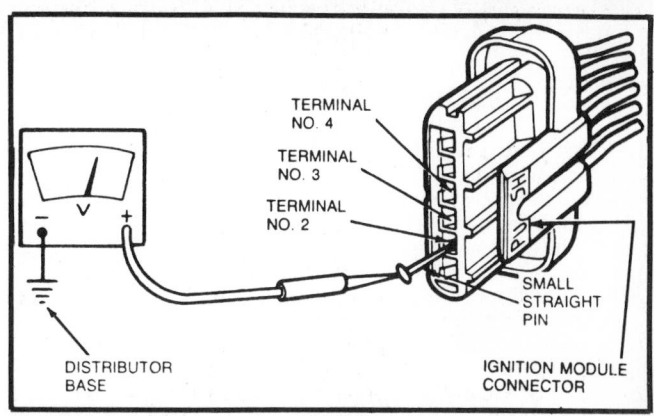

Testing wiring harness-TFI-IV system

Testing

PRIMARY CIRCUIT CONTINUITY

1. Separate the wiring harness connector from the ignition module. Inspect for dirt, corrosion and damage.

2. Attach the negative voltmeter lead to the distributor base.

3. Measure the battery voltage.

4. Attach the voltmeter lead to a straight pin and insert the pin into the connector terminal No. 2.

5. Turn the ignition switch to the RUN position and measure the voltage at terminal No. 2.

6. The voltage should be no less than 90% of battery voltage.

7. If less than 90% of battery voltage, perform the Ignition Coil Primary Voltage test.

8. Turn the ignition switch to the OFF position and remove the pin.

Testing

IGNITION COIL PRIMARY VOLTAGE

1. Attach the negative voltmeter lead to the distributor base.

2. Measure the battery voltage.

3. Turn the ignition switch to the RUN position.

4. Measure the voltage at the negative terminal of the ignition coil.

5. If the voltage is 90% of battery voltage, inspect the wiring harness between the ignition module and the coil negative terminal.

6. If the voltage is less the 90% of battery voltage, inspect the wiring harness between the ignition module and the coil negative terminal.

7. Turn the ignition switch to the OFF position.

Testing

IGNITION COIL SUPPLY VOLTAGE

1. Remove the coil connector.

2. Attach the negative voltmeter lead to the distributor base.

3. Measure the battery voltage.

4. Turn the ignition switch to the RUN psoition.

5. Measure the voltage at the positive terminal of the ignition coil.

6. The voltage should be 90% of battery voltage. Inspect the ignition coil and connector for dirt, corrosion and damage. If required, replace the ignition coil.

7. If the voltage is less than 90% of battery voltage, inspect and repair, as required, the wiring between the ignition coil and the ignition switch. Check for a worn or damaged ignition switch.

8. Turn the ignition switch to the OFF position. Reconnect the ignition module connector.

GM DELCO—REMY HIGH ENERGY IGNITION (HEI)

General Information

The High Energy Ignition distributor is used on all engines. The ignition coil is either mounted to the top of the distributor cap or is externally mounted on the engine, having a secondary circuit high tension wire connecting the coil to the distributor cap and interconnecting primary wiring as part of the engine harness.

The High Energy Ignition distributor is equipped to aid in spark timing changes, necessary for Emissions, Economy and performance. This system is called the Electronic Spark Timing Control (EST). The HEI distributors use a magnetic pickup assembly, located inside the distributor containing a permanent magnet, a pole piece with internal teethand a pick-up coil. When the teeth of the rotating timer core and pole piece align, an induced voltage in the pick-up coil signals the electronic module to open the coil primary circuit. As the primary current decreases, a high voltage is induced in the secondary windings of the ignition coil, directing a spark through the rotor and high voltage leads to fire the spark plugs. The dwell period is automatically controlled by the electronic module and is increased with increasing engine rpm. The HEI System features a longer spark duration which is instrumental in firing lean and EGR (Exhaust Gas Recirculation) diluted fuel/air mixtures. The condenser (capacitor) located within the HEI distributor is provided for noise (static) suppression purposes only and is not a regularly replaced ignition system component.

All spark timing changes in the HEI (EST) distributors are done electronically by the Electronic Control Module (ECM), which monitors information from the various engine sensors, computes the desired spark timing and signals the distributor to change the timeing accordingly. With this distributor, no vacuum or centrifugal advances are used.

Troubleshooting

NOTE: **An accurate diagnosis is the first step to problem solution and repair. For several of the following steps, a HEI spark tester, tool ST 125, which has a spring clip to attach it to ground. Use of this tool is recommended, as there is more control of the high energy spark and less chance of being shocked. If a tachometer is connected to the TACH terminal on the distributor, disconnect it before proceeding with this test.**

SECONDARY CIRCUIT

Testing

SECONDARY SPARK

1. Check for spark at the spark plugs by attaching the HEI spark tester, tool ST 125, to one of the plug wires, grounding the HEI spark tester on the engine and cranking the starter.
2. If no spark occurs on one wire, check a second. If spark is present, the HEI system is good.
3. Check fuel system, plug wires, and spark plugs. 4. If no spark occurs from EST distributor, disconnect the 4 terminal EST connector and recheck for spark. If spark is present, EST system service check should be performed.

NOTE: **Before making any circuit checks with test meters, be sure that all primary circuit connectors are properly installed and that spark plug cables are secure at the distributor and at the plugs.**

Distributor Component Testing
COIL IN CAP DISTRIBUTOR

Testing

IGNITION COIL

1. Remove the cap from the distributor.
2. With coil attached to cap, Connect an ohmmeter to the distributor cap terminals C and Ground. The reading should be zero or nearly zero. If not, replace the ignition coil.
3. Position the ohmmeter leads to terminal B + and the high tension rotor contact in the center of the cap.
4. Using the ohmmeter high scale, measure the resistance. Reverse the ohmmeter leads and again measure the resistance.
5. Replace the coil ONLY if BOTH readings are infinite.

Testing

PICK-UP COIL

1. Disconnect the rotor and pick-up coil leads from the module.
2. Using an ohmmeter, connect one lead to the distributor houing and the second lead to one of the pick-up terminals in the connector.
3. The reading should be infinite.

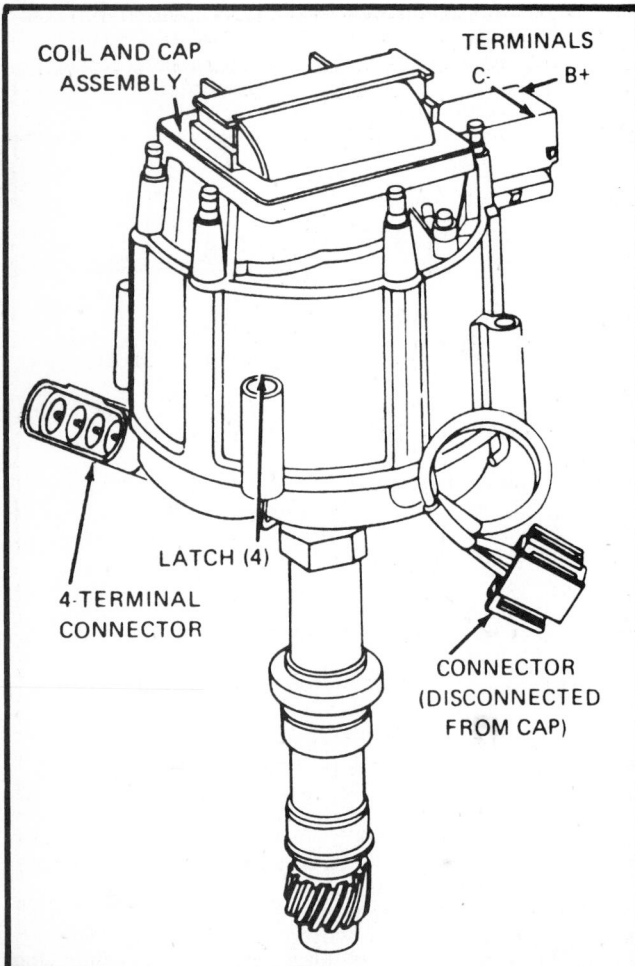

V6 engine coil-in-cap distributor, typical of V8 engine distributors

COIL AND CAP ASSEMBLY

TERMINALS

C-   B+

LATCH (4)

4-TERMINAL CONNECTOR

CONNECTOR (DISCONNECTED FROM CAP)

NOTE: While testing, flex the leads to determine if wire breaks are present under the wiring insulation.

4. Place the ohmmeter leads into both the pick-up terminals of the connector and measure the resistance.

5. The reading should be steady at one value, between 500-1500 ohms.

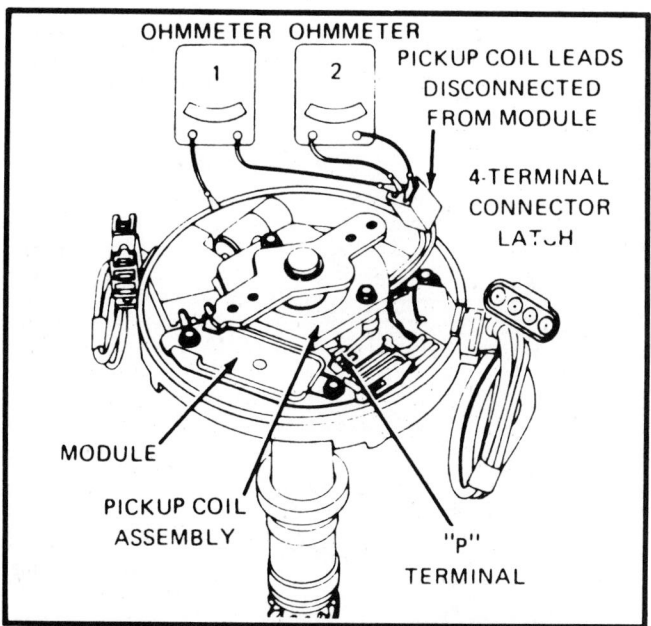

Testing pick-up coil used in coil-in-cap distributor

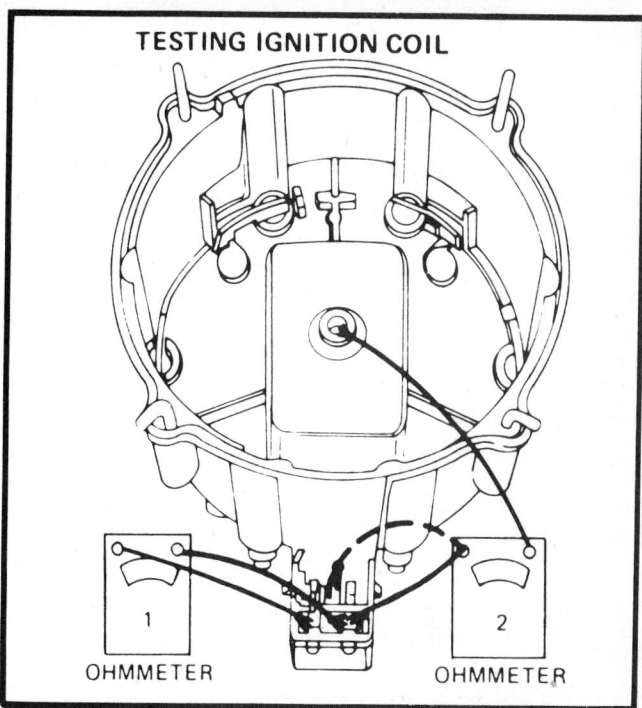

Testing ignition coil used in coil-in-cap distributor

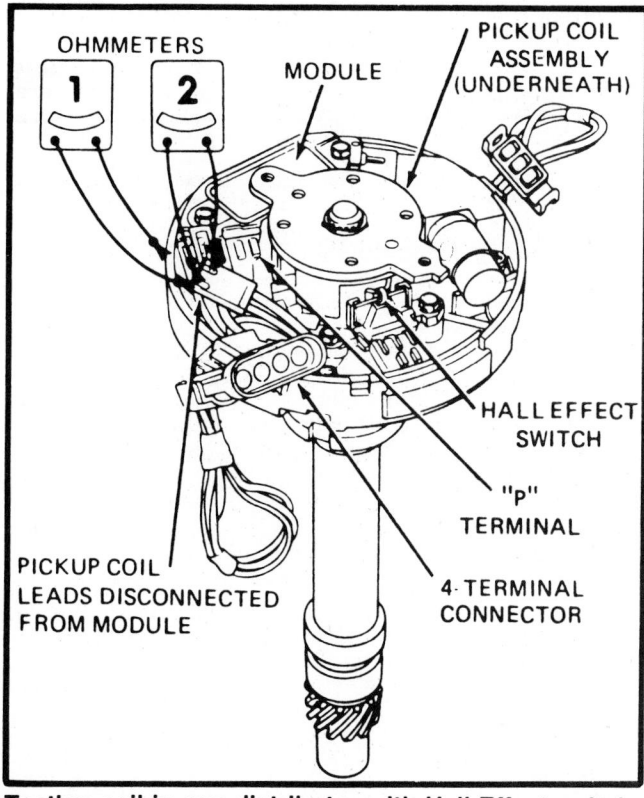

Testing coil-in-cap distributor with Hall Effect switch

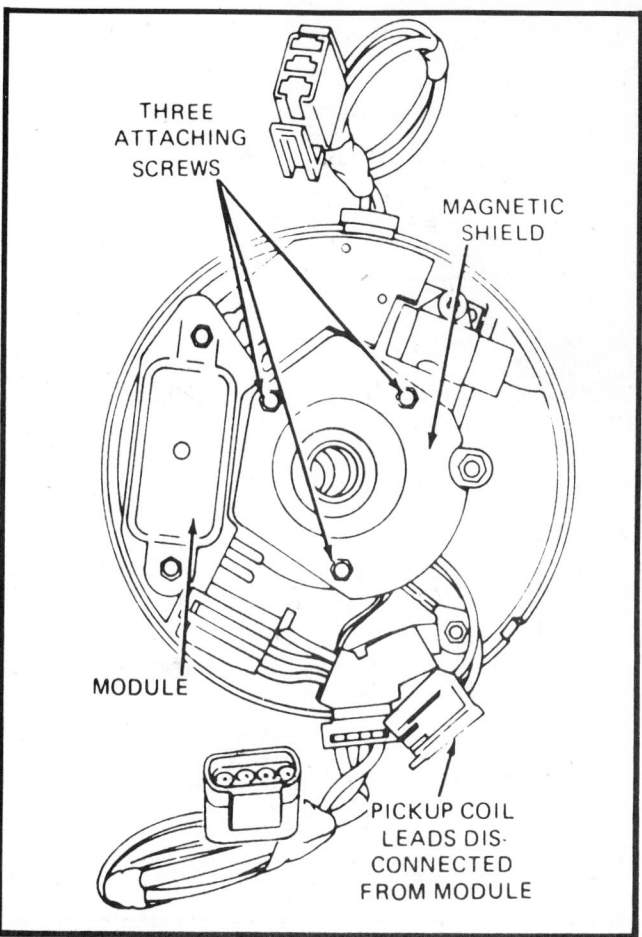

Magnetic shield used on selected coil-in-cap distributors

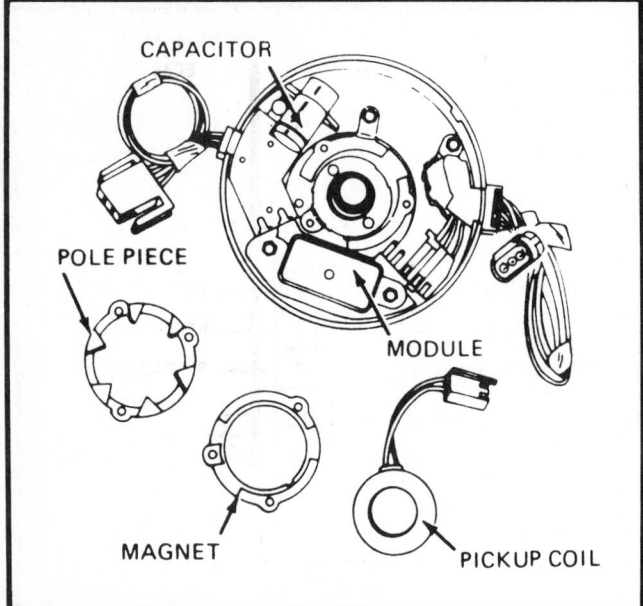

Pick-up coil components, coil-in-cap distributor

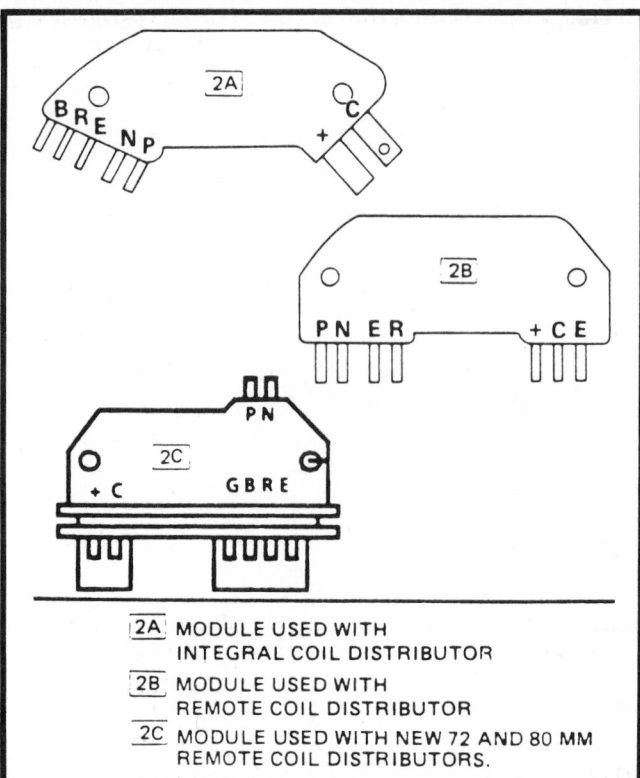

2A MODULE USED WITH
INTEGRAL COIL DISTRIBUTOR

2B MODULE USED WITH
REMOTE COIL DISTRIBUTOR

2C MODULE USED WITH NEW 72 AND 80 MM
REMOTE COIL DISTRIBUTORS.

Electronic distributor modules used with General Motors Electronic Ignition systems

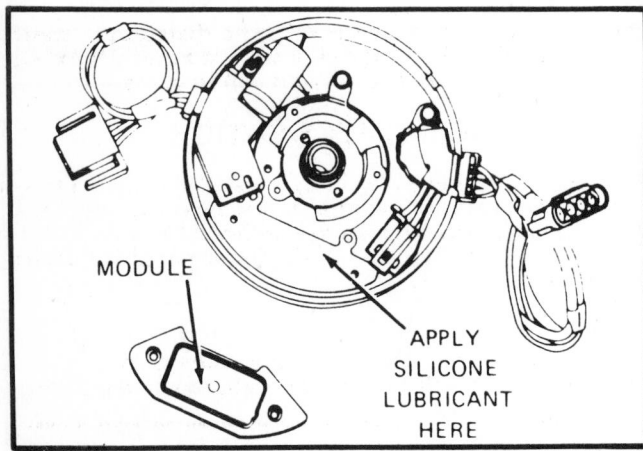

Module replacement and use of silicone lubricant, coil-in-cap distributor

Testing

IGNITION MODULE

Because of the complexity of the internal circuitry of the HEI/EST module, it is recommended the module be tested with an accurate module tester.

It is imperative that silicone lubricant be used under the module when it is installed, to prevent module failure due to overheating.

NOTE: The module can be replaced without distributor disassembly. However, the distributor must be disassembled to replace the pick-up coil, magnet and pole piece

DISTRIBUTOR WITH SEPARATE COIL TYPE ONE

NOTE: This type distributor has no vacuum or centrifugal advance mechanism and has the pick-up coil mount-ed above the module. This distributor is used with the EST system.

Testing

IGNITION COIL

1. Disconnect the primary wiring connectors and secondary coil wire from the ignition coil.

2. Using an ohmmeter on the high scale, connect one lead to a grounding screw and the second lead to one of the primary coil terminals.

3. The reading should be infinite. If not, replace the ignition coil.

4. Using the low scale, place the ohmmeter leads on both the primary coil terminals.

5. The reading should be very low or zero. If not, replace the signition coil.

6. Using the high scale, place one ohmmeter lead on the high tension output terminal and the other lead on a primary coil terminal.

7. The reading should NOT be infinite. If it is, replace the ignition coil.

Testing

PICK-UP COIL

1. Remove the rotor and pick-up coil leads from the module.

2. Using an ohmmeter, attach one lead to the distributor base and the second lead to one of the pick-up coil terminals of the connector.

3. The reading should be infinite at all times.

4. Position both leads of the ohmmeter to the pick-up terminal ends of the connector.

5. The reading should be a steady value between 500-1500 ohms.

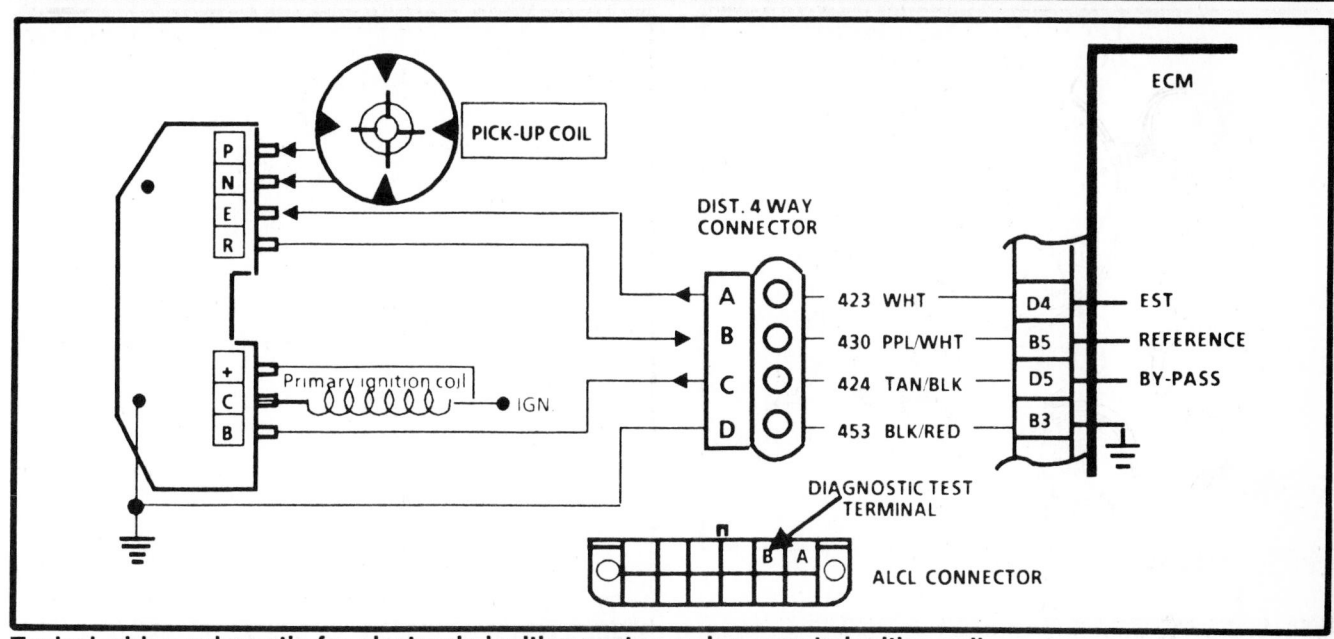

Typical wiring schematic for electronic ignition system using remote ignition coil

6. If not within the specification value, the pick-up coil is defective.

NOTE: While testing, flex the leads to determine if wire breaks are present under the wiring insulation.

IGNITION MODULE

Because of the complexity of the internal circuitry of the HEI/EST module, it is recommended the module be tested with an accurate module tester.

It is imperative that silicone lubricant be used under the module when it is installed, to prevent module failure due to overheating.

NOTE: The module and the Hall Effect switch (if used) can be removed from the distributor without disassem- bly. **To remove the pick-up coil, the distributor shaft must be removed to expose a waved retaining ring ("C"washer) holding the pick-up coil in place.**

HALL EFFECT SWITCH

The Hall Effect Switch, when used, is installed in the HEI distributor. The purpose of the switch is to sense engine speed and send the information to the Electronic Control Module (ECM). To remove the Hall Effect Switch, the distributor shaft must be removed from the distributor.

Testing

1. Remove the switch connectors from the switch.
2. Connect a 12 volt battery and voltmeter to the switch.

Testing ignition coil, type one distributor

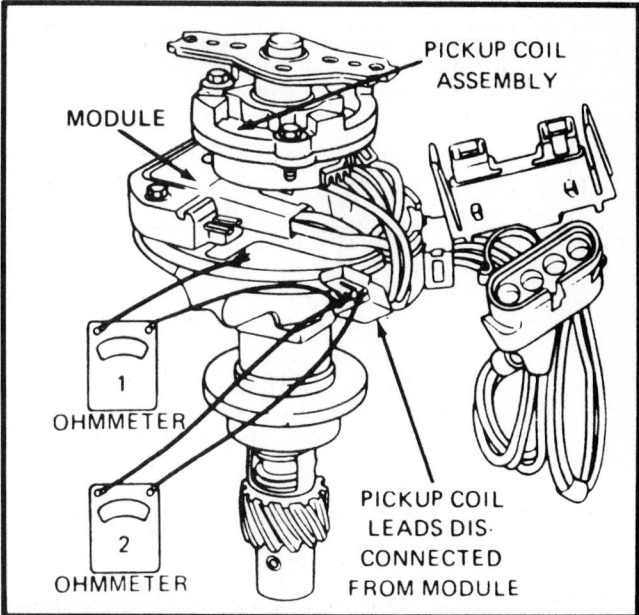

Testing pick-up coil, type one distributor

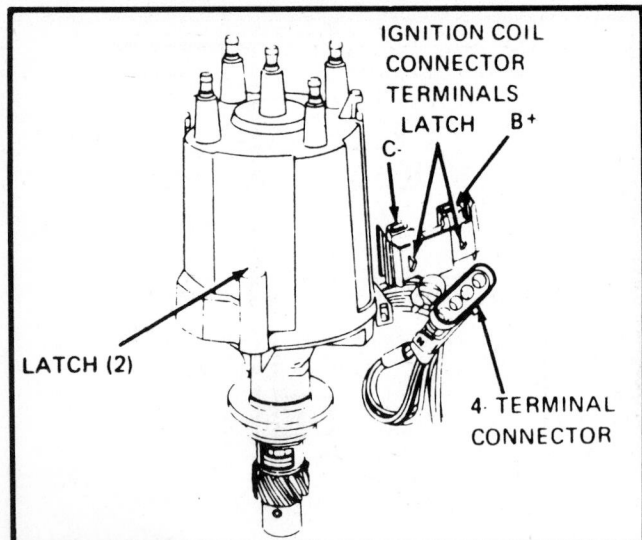

HEI/EST distributor, type one

Note and follow the polarity markings.

3. With a knife blade inserted straight down and against the magnet, the voltmeter should read within 0.5 volts of battery voltage. If not, the switch is defective.

4. Without the knife blade inserted against the magnet, the voltmeter should read less than 0.5 volts. If not, the switch is defective.

DISTRIBUTOR WITH SEPARATE COIL TYPE TWO

NOTE: This type distributor has no vacuum or centrifugal advance mechanisms and the module has two outside terminal connections for the wiring harness. This distributor is used with the EST system.

Testing
IGNITION COIL

1. Using an ohmmeter set on the high scale, place one lead on a ground of the ignition coil.

2. Place the second lead into one of the rearward terminals of the ignition coil primary connector.

3. The ohmmeter scale should read infinite. If not, replace the ignition coil.

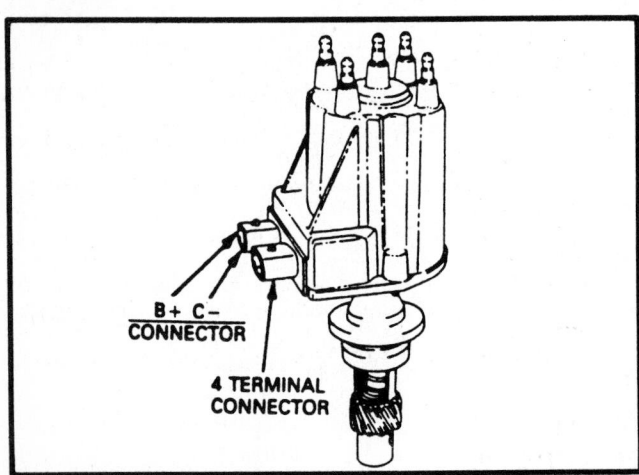

HEI/EST distributor, type two

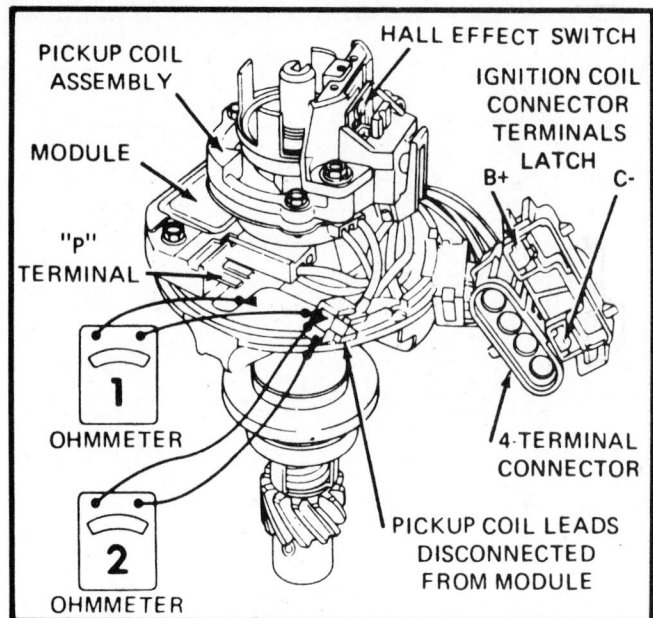

Testing Hall Effect switch, type one distributor

4. Using the low scale, place the ohmmeter leads into each of the outer terminals of the coil connector.

5. The reading should be zero or very low. If not, replace the ignition coil.

6. Using the high scale, place one ohmmeter lead on the coil secondary terminal and the second lead into the rearward terminal of the ignition coil primary connector.

7. The reading should not be infinite. If so, replace the ignition coil.

Testing
PICK-UP COIL

1. Remove the rotor and pick-up leads from the module.

2. Using an ohmmeter, connect one of the leads to the distributor base.

3. Connect the second lead to one of the pick-up coil lead terminals

4. The reading should be infinite. If not, the pick-up coil is defective.

During the ohmmeter tests, flex the leads by hand to check for intermediate opens in the wiring.

5. Connect both ohmmeter lead to the pick-up coil terminals at the connector.

6. The reading should be of one steady value, between 500-1500 ohms.

7. If the reading is not within specifications, the pick-up coil must is defective.

Testing
IGNITION MODULE

Because of the complexity of the internal circuitry of the HEI/EST module, it is recommended the module be tested with an accurate module tester.

It is imperative that silicone lubricant be used under the module when it is installed, to prevent module failure due to overheating.

NOTE: The module can be removed without distributor disassembly. To remove the pick-up coil, the distributor shaft must be removed. A retainer can then be removed from the top of the pole piece and the pick-up coil removed.

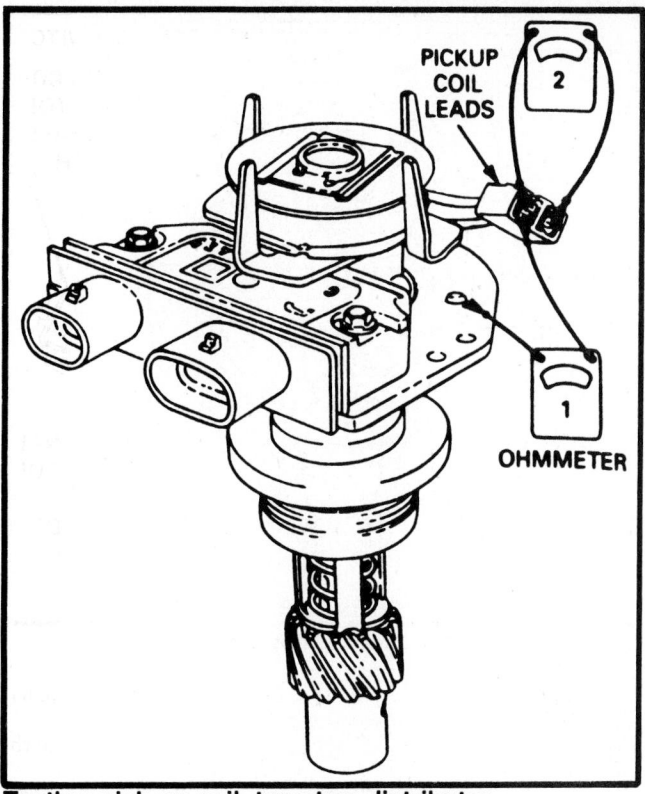

Testing pick-up coil, type two distributor

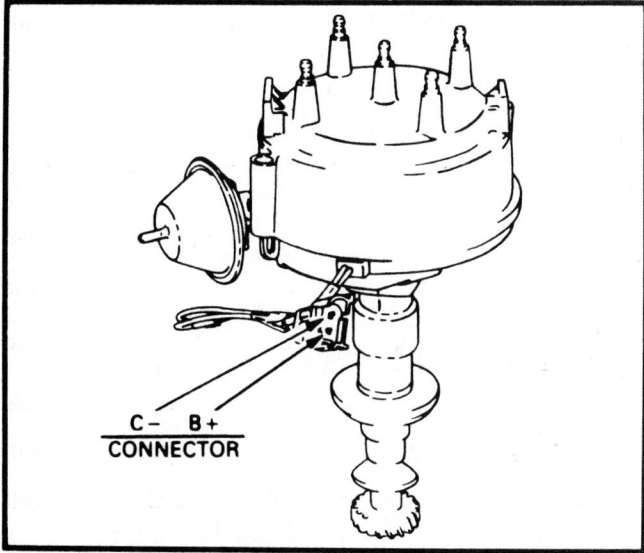

HEI distributor, type three

DISTRIBUTOR WITH SEPARATE COIL TYPE THREE

NOTE: This distributor uses vacuum and centrifugal advance units and does not have the EST system.

Testing

IGNITION COIL

1. Disconnect the primary wiring connectors and secondary coil wire from the ignition coil.

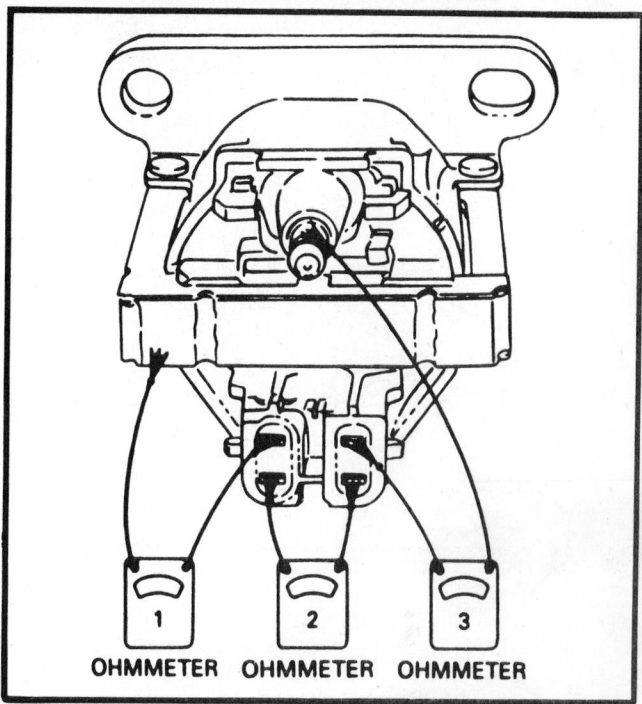

Testing ignition coil, type two distributor

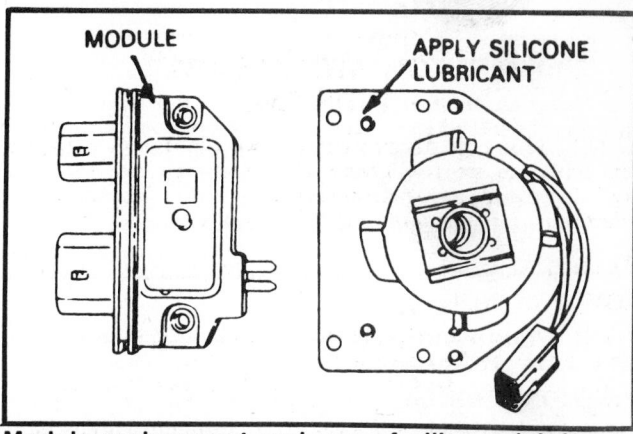

Module replacement and use of silicone lubricant, type two distributor

2. Using an ohmmeter on the high scale, connect one lead to a grounding screw and the second lead to one of the primary coil terminals.

3. The reading should be infinite. If not, replace the ignition coil.

4. Using the low scale, place the ohmmeter leads on both the primary coil terminals.

5. The reading should be very low or zero. If not, replace the signition coil.

6. Using the high scale, place one ohmmeter lead on the high tension output terminal and the other lead on a primary coil terminal.

7. The reading should NOT be infinite. If it is, replace the ignition coil.

Testing

PICK-UP COIL

1. Remove the rotor and pick-up coil leads from the module.

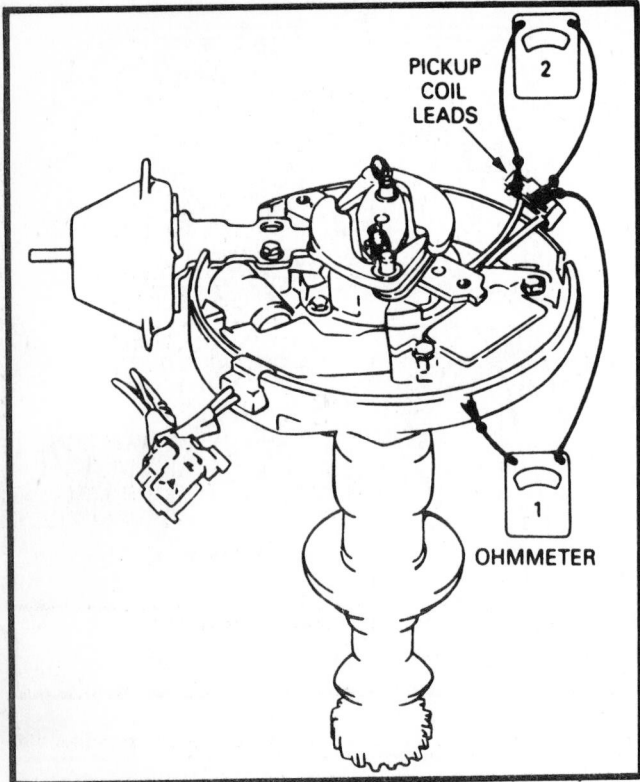

Testing pick-up coil, type three distributor

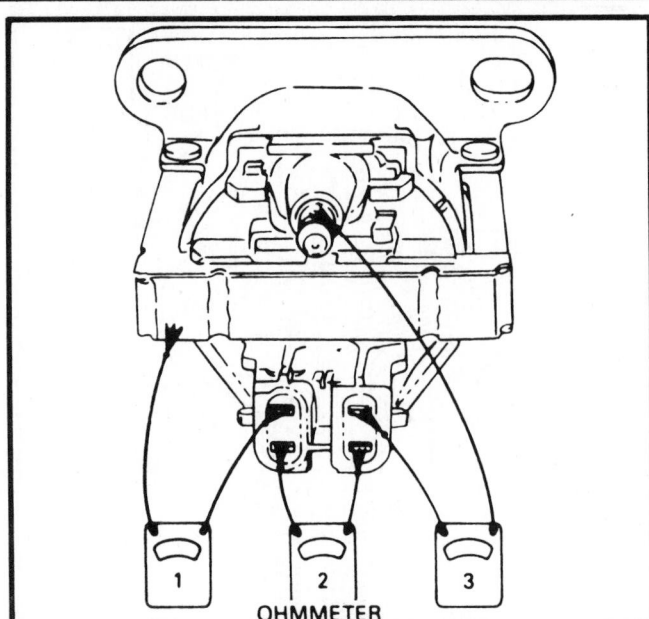

Testing ignition coil, type three distributor

2. Using an ohmmeter, attach one lead to the distributor base and the second lead to one of the pick-up coil terminals of the connector.3. The reading should be infinite at all times.

4. Position both leads of the ohmmeter to the pick-up terminal ends of the connector.

5. The reading should be a steady value between 500-1500 ohms.

6. If not within the specification value, the pick-up coil is defective.

NOTE: While testing, flex the leads to determine if wire breaks are present under the wiring insulation.

IGNITION MODULE

Because of the complexity of the internal circuitry of the HEI/EST module, it is recommended the module be tested with an accurate module tester.

It is imperative that silicone lubricant be used under the module when it is installed, to prevent module failure due to overheating.

NOTE: The module can be removed without distributor disassembly. The distributor shaft and "C" clip must be removed before the pick-up coil can be removed.

DISTRIBUTOR WITH SEPARATE COIL TYPE FOUR–TANG DRIVE

NOTE: This distributor is used with the EST system. The unit is mounted horizontally to the valve cover housing and is driven by the camshaft, through a tang on the distributor shaft.

Testing

IGNITION COIL

1. Using an ohmmeter set on the high scale, place one lead on a ground of the ignition coil.

2. Place the second lead into one of the rearward terminals of the ignition coil primary connector.

3. The ohmmeter scale should read infinite. If not, replace the ignition coil.

4. Using the low scale, place the ohmmeter leads into each of the outer terminals of the coil connector.

5. The reading should be zero or very low. If not, replace the ignition coil.

6. Using the high scale, place one ohmmeter lead on the coil secondary terminal and the second lead into the rearward terminal of the ignition coil primary connector.

7. The reading should not be infinite. If so, replace the ignition coil.

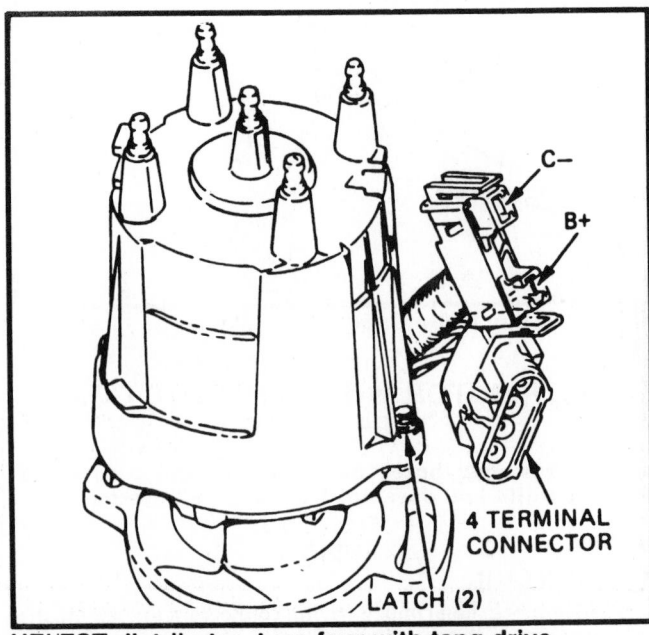

HEI/EST distributor, type four with tang drive

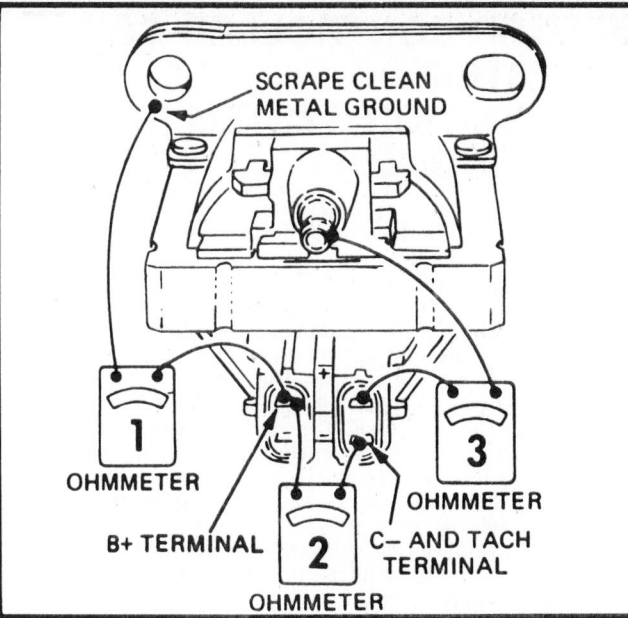

Testing ignition coil, type four distributor

Testing

PICK-UP COIL

1. Remove the rotor and pick-up leads from the module.
2. Using an ohmmeter, connect one of the leads to the distributor base.
3. Connect the second lead to one of the pick-up coil lead terminals
4. The reading should be infinite. If not, the pick-up coil is defective.

During the ohmmeter tests, flex the leads by hand to check for intermediate opens in the wiring.

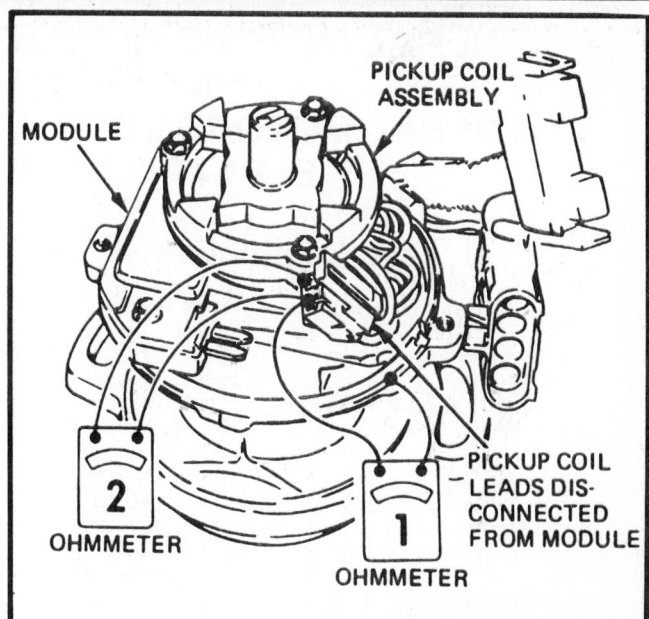

Testing pick-up coil, type four distributor

5. Connect both ohmmeter lead to the pick-up coil terminals at the connector.
6. The reading should be of one steady value, between 500-1500 ohms.
7. If the reading is not within specifications, the pick-up coil must is defective.

Testing

IGNITION MODULE

Because of the complexity of the internal circuitry of the HEI/EST module, it is recommended the module be tested with an accurate module tester.

It is imperative that silicone lubricant be used under the module when it is installed, to prevent module failure due to overheating.

NOTE: The module can be removed without distributor disassembly. The distributor shaft and "C" clip must be removed before the pick-up coil can be removed. Before removing the roll pin from the distributor tang drive to shaft, a spring must first be removed.

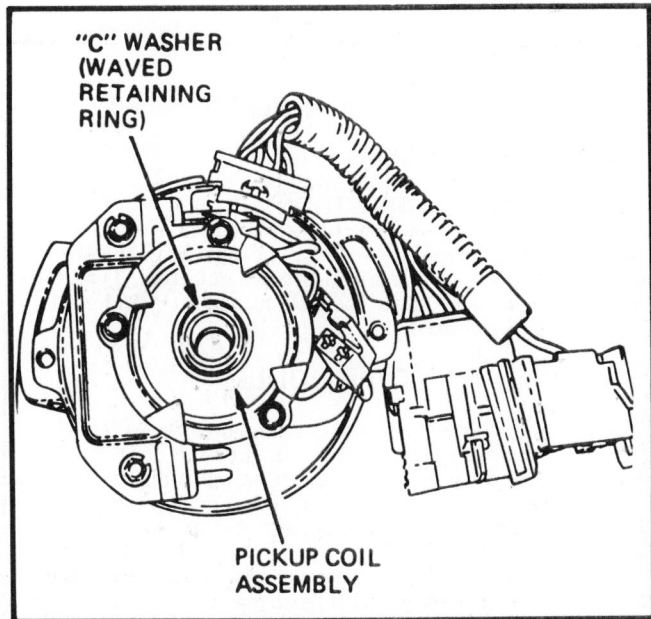

Replacement of pick-up coil with distributor shaft removed, type four distributor

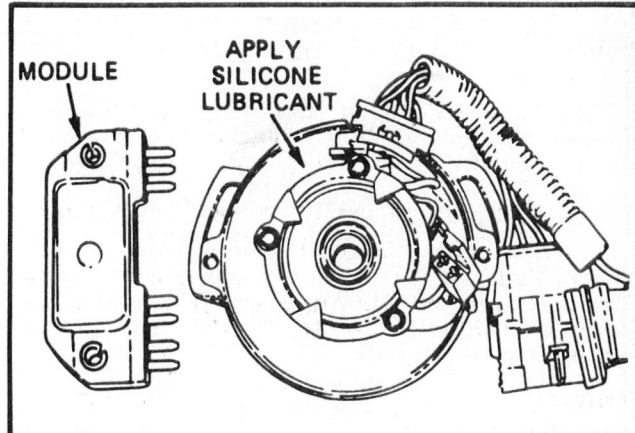

Replacement of module and use of silicone lubricant, type four distributor

GENERAL MOTORS CORP. COMPUTER CONTROLLED COIL IGNITION (C³1) SYSTEM
GENERAL MOTORS CORP. DIRECT IGNITION SYSTEM (DIS)/ ELECTRONIC SPARK TIMING (EST)

General Information

The C³I System and Direct Ignition System (DIS) do not use the conventional distributor and ignition coil. These systems consists of separate ignition coils, "C³I" or "DIS" ignition module, crankshaft sensor or combination sensor, camshaft sensor (C³I), along with the related connecting wires and Electronic Spark Timing (EST) portion of the Electronic Control Module (ECM).

The C³I and DIS systems use a "waste spark" method of spark distribution. Companion cylinders are paired and the spark occurs simultaneously in the cylinder with the piston coming up on the compression stroke and in the companion cylinder with the piston coming up on the exhaust stroke.

1. Example of firing order and companion cylinders–1–2–3–4–5–6: 1/4, 2/5, 3/6.

2. Example of firing order and companion cylinders–1–6–5–4–3–2: 1/4, 6/3, 5/2.

3. Example of firing order and companion cylinders–1–3–4–2: 1/4, 2/3

NOTE: Notice the companion cylinders in the V6 engine firing order remain the same, but the cylinder firing order sequence differs.

The cylinder on the exhaust stroke requires very little of the available voltage to arc, so the remaining high voltage is used by the cylinder in the firing position (TDC compression). This same process is repeated when the companion cylinders reverse roles.

It is possible in an engine no-load condition, for one plug to fire, even though the spark plug lead from the same coil is disconnected from the other spark plug. The disconnected spark plug lead acts as one plate of a capacitor, with the engine being the other plate. These two capacitors plates are charged as a current surge (spark) jumps across the gap of the connected spark plug.

These "plates" are then discharged as the secondary energy is dissipated in an oscillating current across the gap of the spark plug still connected. Because of the direction of current flow in the primary windings and thus in the secondary windings, one spark plug will fire from the center electrode to the side electrode, while the other will fire from the side electrode to the center electrode.

These systems utilize the EST signal from the ECM, as do the convention distributor type ignition systems equipped with the EST system to control timing.

In the Direct Ignition system and while under 400 rpm, the "DIS" ignition module controls the spark timing through a module timing mode. Over 400 rpm, the ECM controls the spark timing through the EST mode and in the C³I system, the injectors operate in the Sequential Fuel Injection mode (SFI). In the Direct Ignition system, to properly control the ignition timing, the ECM relies on the the following information from the various sensors.

1. Engine load (manifold pressure or vacuum).
2. Atmospheric (barometric) pressure.
3. Engine temperature.
4. Manifold air temperature.
5. Crankshaft position.
6. Engine speed (rpm).

In the C³I system, to properly control the ignition timing, the ECM relies on the following information from the various sensors.

1. Crankshaft position.
2. Camshaft position.
3. Engine speed (rpm).
4. Engine coolant (CTS) and induction air temperature (MAT).
5. Amount of air entering the throttle body (MAF).
6. Throttle position (TPS)
7. ESC signal (knock retard).
8. Park/Neutral position (P/N).
9. Vehicle speed.

C³I System Components

NOTE: The C³I system is used with the Sequential Fuel Injection system.

IGNITION COILS

Three separate coils are mounted to the module assembly. Each coil provides spark for two plugs simultaneously, called "WASTE SPARK DISTRIBUTION".

The ignition coils on Type I ignition coil and module assembly cannot be serviced separately, but must have the entire assembly replaced, should a coil become defective. Type II provides separate servicing of the coils or module by individual replacement, if required.

C³I MODULE

The Ignition module monitors the cam and crankshaft signals. This information is passed on to the ECM so that the correct spark and fuel injector timing can be maintained during all driving conditions. During the cranking mode, it monitors the camshaft signal to begin the ignition firing sequence and the fuel injection timing (SFI).

Below 400 rpm, the module controls the spark advance by triggering each of the three coils at a predetermined interval, based on engine speed only. Above 400 rpm, the C³I module relays the crankshaft signal to the ECM as a reference signal. The ECM then controls the spark timing and compensates for

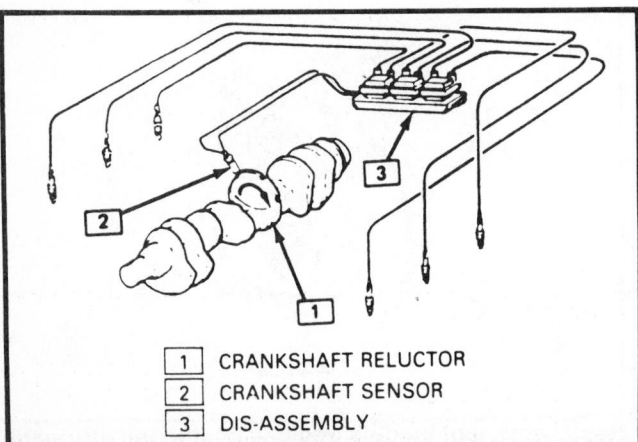

1	CRANKSHAFT RELUCTOR
2	CRANKSHAFT SENSOR
3	DIS-ASSEMBLY

Crankshaft sensor to crankshaft reluctor relationship

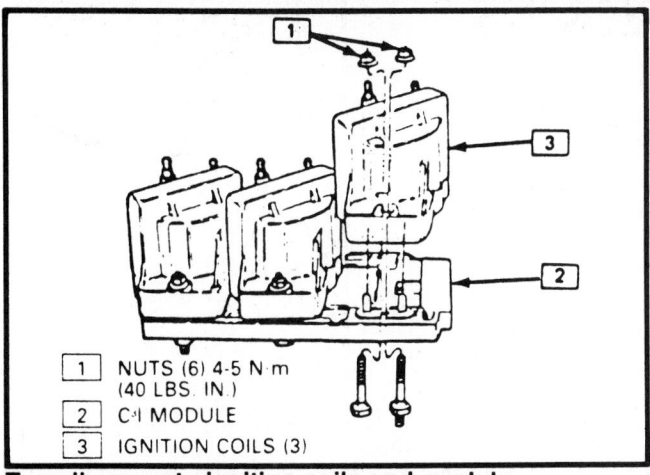

1	NUTS (6) 4-5 N·m (40 LBS. IN.)
2	C³I MODULE
3	IGNITION COILS (3)

Type II separate ignition coils and module

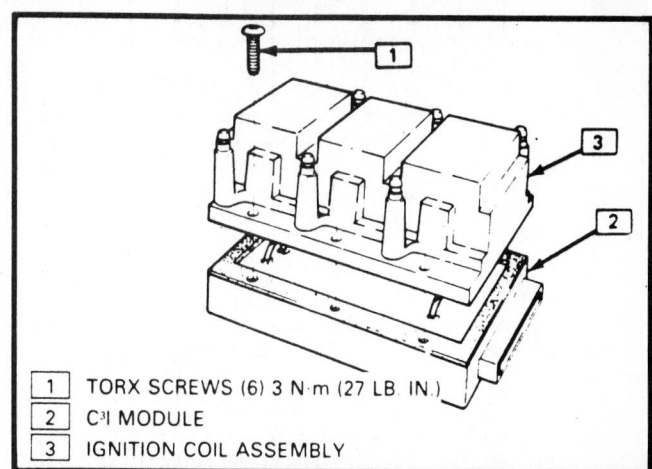

1	TORX SCREWS (6) 3 N·m (27 LB. IN.)
2	C³I MODULE
3	IGNITION COIL ASSEMBLY

Type I ignition coil assembly and module

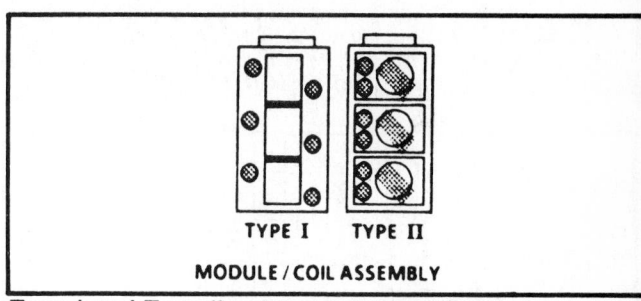

TYPE I   TYPE II

MODULE / COIL ASSEMBLY

Type I and Type II coil/module identification

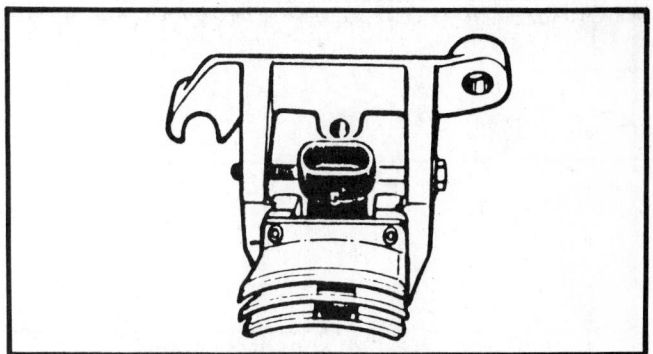

Crankshaft sensor

Camshaft sensor

all driving conditions. The C³I module must receive a camshaft and then a crankshaft signal, in that order, to enable the engine to start.

The C³I module is not repairable. When a module is replaced, the three coils must be transferred to the new module.

CAMSHAFT SENSOR

The camshaft sensor is located on the timing cover, behind the water pump, near the camshaft sprocket. As the camshaft sprocket turns, a magnet mounted on it, activates the Hall Effect switch in the cam sensor. This grounds the signal line to the C³I module, pulling the crankshaft signal line's applied voltage low. This is interpreted as a Cam Signal (Sync. Pulse). Because the way the signal is created by the crankshaft sensor, the signal circuit is always either at a high or a low voltage, known as a square voltage signal. While the camshaft sprocket continues to turn, the Hall Effect switch turns off as the magnetic field passes the cam sensor, resulting in one signal each time the camshaft makes one revolution. The cam signal is created as piston No.1 and No.4 reach approximately 25° after top dead center. It is then used by the C³I module to begin the ignition coil firing sequence, starting with the No.3/6 ignition coil because the No.6 piston is now at the correct position in its compression stroke for the spark plug to be fired.

This camshaft signal, which actually represents camshaft position due to the sensors mounting location, is also used by the ECM to properly time its Sequential fuel injection operation.

Both the crankshaft and camshaft sensor signals must be received by the ignition module for the engine to start. When the cam signal is not received by the ECM, such as during cranking, fuel injection is simultaneous, rather than sequenstially timed and a code (E041) will be set.

If the code (E041) is set and the engine will start and run, the fault is in circuit for the Cam signal (cirk.630), the C³I module or the ECM. Under these conditions, the C³I module will determine the ignition timing.

If the fault is in the camshaft sensor circuit, the cam sensor or the cam signal portion of the C³I module, code E041 may also be present, but the engine will not start, since the C³I module can not determine the position of the No. 1 piston.

CRANKSHAFT SENSOR

A magnetic crankshaft sensor (Hall Effect switch) is used and is mounted in a pedestal on the front of the engine near the harmonic balancer. The sensor is a "Hall Effect" switch which depends on metal interrupter ring, mounted on the balancer, to activate it. Windows in the interrupter activates the Hall Effect switch as they provide a a path for the magnetic field between the switch's transducer and its magnet.

When the Hall Effect switch is activated, it grounds the signal line to the C³I module, pulling the crankshaft signal line's applied voltage low, which is interperted as a crankshaft signal. Because of the way the signal by the crank sensor is created, the signal circuit is always either at a high or low voltage (square wave signal) and three signal pulses are created during each crankshaft revolution. This signal is used by the C³I module to create a reference signal, whic is also a "square wave" signal, similar to the crank signal. The reference signal is used to calculate engine rpm and crankshaft position by the ECM. A misadjusted sensor or bent interrupter ring could cause rubbing of the sensor resulting in potential driveability problems, such as rough idle, poor engine performance, or a no-start condition.

NOTE: Failure to have the correct clearance between the sensor and the interrupter ring could damage the sensor.

The Crankshaft sensor is not adjustable for ignition timing but positioning of the interrupter ring is very important. A clearance of 0.025 in. is required on either side of the interrupter ring.

A crankshaft sensor that is damaged due to mispositioning, or a bent interrupter ring can result in an engine hesitation, sag stumble or dieseling condition. To determine if the crankshaft sensor is at fault, observe the diagnostic display ECM data, ED11 (engine rpm), while driving the vehicle. An erratic

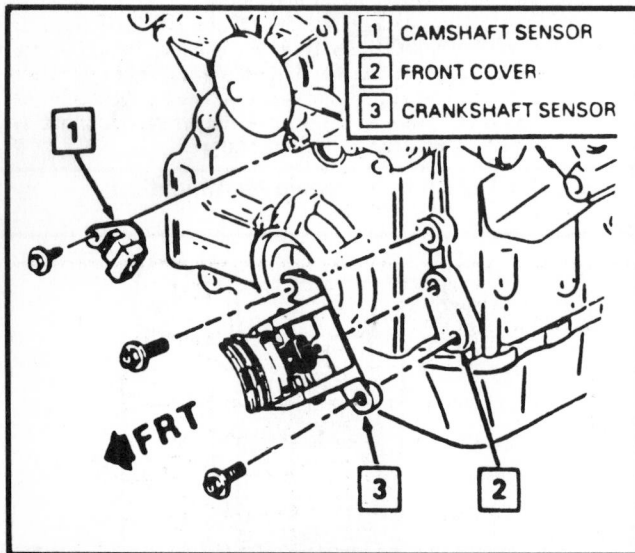

1	CAMSHAFT SENSOR
2	FRONT COVER
3	CRANKSHAFT SENSOR

Crankshaft and camshaft sensor locations

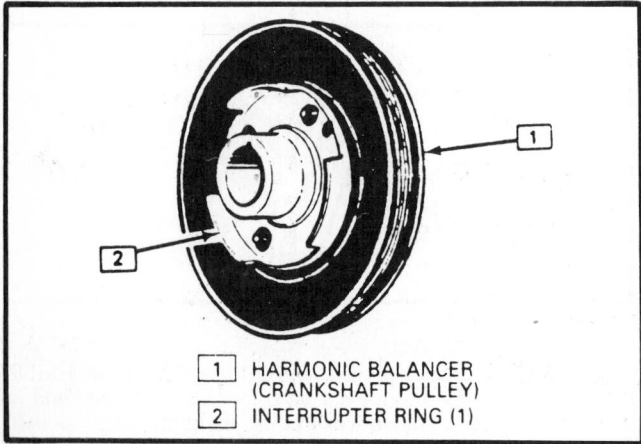

1	HARMONIC BALANCER (CRANKSHAFT PULLEY)
2	INTERRUPTER RING (1)

Harmonic balancer and interrupter ring

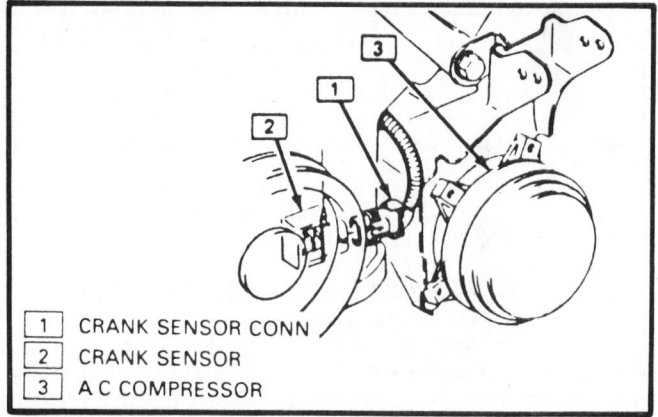

1	CRANK SENSOR CONN
2	CRANK SENSOR
3	A C COMPRESSOR

Combination sensor

display indicates that a proper reference pulse has not been received by the ECM, which may be the result of a malfunctioning crankshaft sensor.

COMBINATION SENSOR

On certain engine applications, such as the 3.0L engine, the crankshaft and camshaft functions are combined into one dual sensor, called a combination sensor, which is mounted at the harmonic balancer. It functions the same as though both camshaft and crankshaft sensors are used.

The reason this type of sensor can be used is the fact that the 3.0L engine is a simultaneously injected engine, which does not require the actual camshaft signal. Instead, it uses a "sync Pulse" signal from the combination sensor. at the rate of one per each revolution of the crankshaft. The combination sensor is activated and controls its signal lines in the same way the crankshaft sensor does on the other engines. The only difference is the "sync Pulse" portion of the sensor, which serves the same purpose as the cam sensor on the other engines, relative to ignition operation. That is , it starts the ignition coil firing sequence, starting with the 3–6 ignition coil.

ELECTRONIC CONTROL MODULE (ECM)

The ECM is responsible for maintaining the proper spark and fuel injection timing for all driving conditions.

To provide optimum driveability and emissions, the ECM monitors input signals from the following components in calculating Electronic Spark Timing (EST).
1. Ignition module.
2. Coolant temperature.
3. Manifold air temperature sensor.
4. Mass air flow sensor.
5. Park/neutral switch.
6. ESC module.
7. Throttle position sensor (TPS).
8. Vehicle speed sensor.

Under 400 rpm, the ECM will start injector timing (simultaneous) as soon as the C³I module receives a camshaft signal, syncronizes the spark and produces a reference signal for the ECM to calculate the fuel ignition timing sequence. The C³I module controls the spark timing during this period. Over 400 rpm, the ECM controls timing (EST) and also changes the mode of fuel injection to sequential, providing a camshaft signal is received.

ELECTRONIC SPARK CONTROL (ESC)

The ESC systems is comprised of a knock sensor and an ESC module. The ECM monitors the ESC signal to determine when engine detonation occurs.

As long as the ESC module is sending a voltage signal of 8-10 volts to the ECM, indicating that no detonation is detected by the ESC sensor, the ECM provides normal spark advance. When the knock sensor detects detonation, the ESC module turns "OFF" the circuit to the ECM and the voltage at the ECM terminal B7 drops to 0 volts. The ECM then retards EST to reduce detonation.

NOTE: Retarded timing can be the result of excessive engine noise, caused by valve lifters, pushrods or other mechanical engine or transmission noise.

C³I ELECTRONIC SPARK TIMING (EST) CIRCUITS

This system uses the same EST to ECM circuits that the distributor type systems with EST use. However, a difference does exist between the C³I system and the Direct Ignition system.

The following is a brief description for the EST circuits and the camshaft signal circuit (CIRK 630).

REFERENCE SIGNAL, CIRCUIT 430

This circuit provides the ECM with the rpm and crankshaft position information from the C³I module. The C³I module receives the signal from the crankshaft sensor's Hall Effect switch.

This signal will either be high or low, depending upon the position of the interrupter ring. This high-low signal is used to trigger the C³I module for ignition operation and by the ECM to calculate fuel injection timing. Both the camshaft and crankshaft sensor signals must be received by the C³I module in order for a reference signal to be produced on circuit 430. A loss of the reference signal would prevent the engine from running.

BY-PASS SIGNAL, CIRCUIT 424

At approximately 400 rpm, the ECM applies 5 volts to this circuit to switch spark timing control from the C³I module to the ECM.

An open or grounded by-pass circuit will set a code E042 and result in the engine operating in a back-up ignition timing mode (module timing) at a calculated timing value. This may cause poor performance and reduced fuel economy.

EST SIGNAL, CIRCUIT 423

The C³I module sends a reference signal to the ECM when the engine is cranking. While the engine is under 400 rpm, the C³I module controls the ignition timing. When the engine speed exceeds 400 rpm, the ECM applies 5 volts to the by-pass line to switch the timing to the ECM control (EST).

An open or ground in the EST circuit will stall the engine and set a code E042. The engine can be restarted, but will operate in a back-up ignition timing mode (module timing) at a calculated timing value. This may cause poor performance and reduced fuel economy.

CAM SIGNAL, CIRCUIT 630

The ECM uses this signal to determine the position of the No. 1 piston in its compression stroke. This signal is used by the ECM to calculate the sequential fuel injection (SFI) mode of operation. A loss of this signal will set a Code E041. If the cam signal is lost while the engine is running, the fuel injection system will shift to the simultaneous injection mode of operation and the engine will continue to operate. The engine can be restarted, but will continue to run in the simultaneous mode as long as the fault is present.

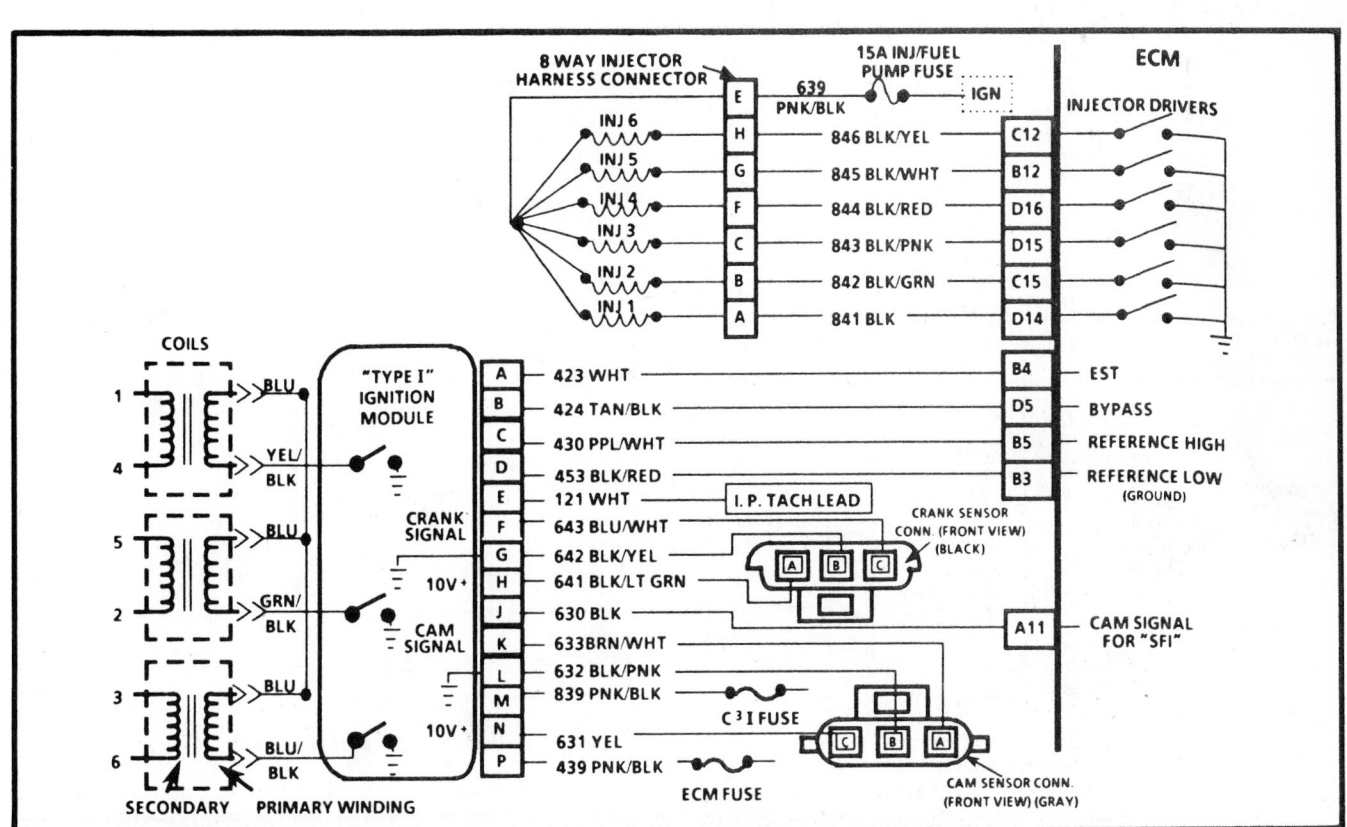

Type I C³I Ignition system electrical schematic, 3.8L engine with Sequential Fuel Injection

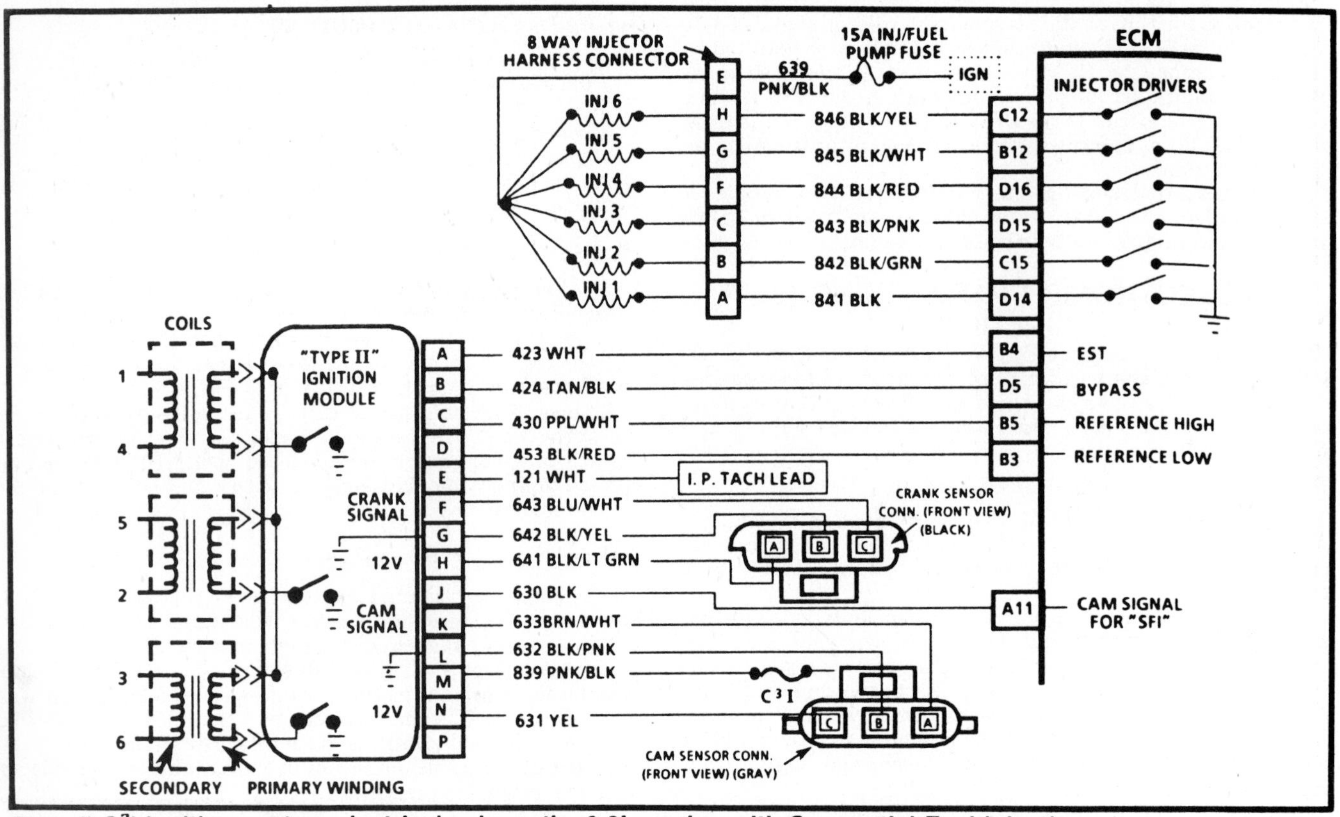

Type II C^{3}I Ignition system electrical schematic, 3.8L engine with Sequential Fuel Injection

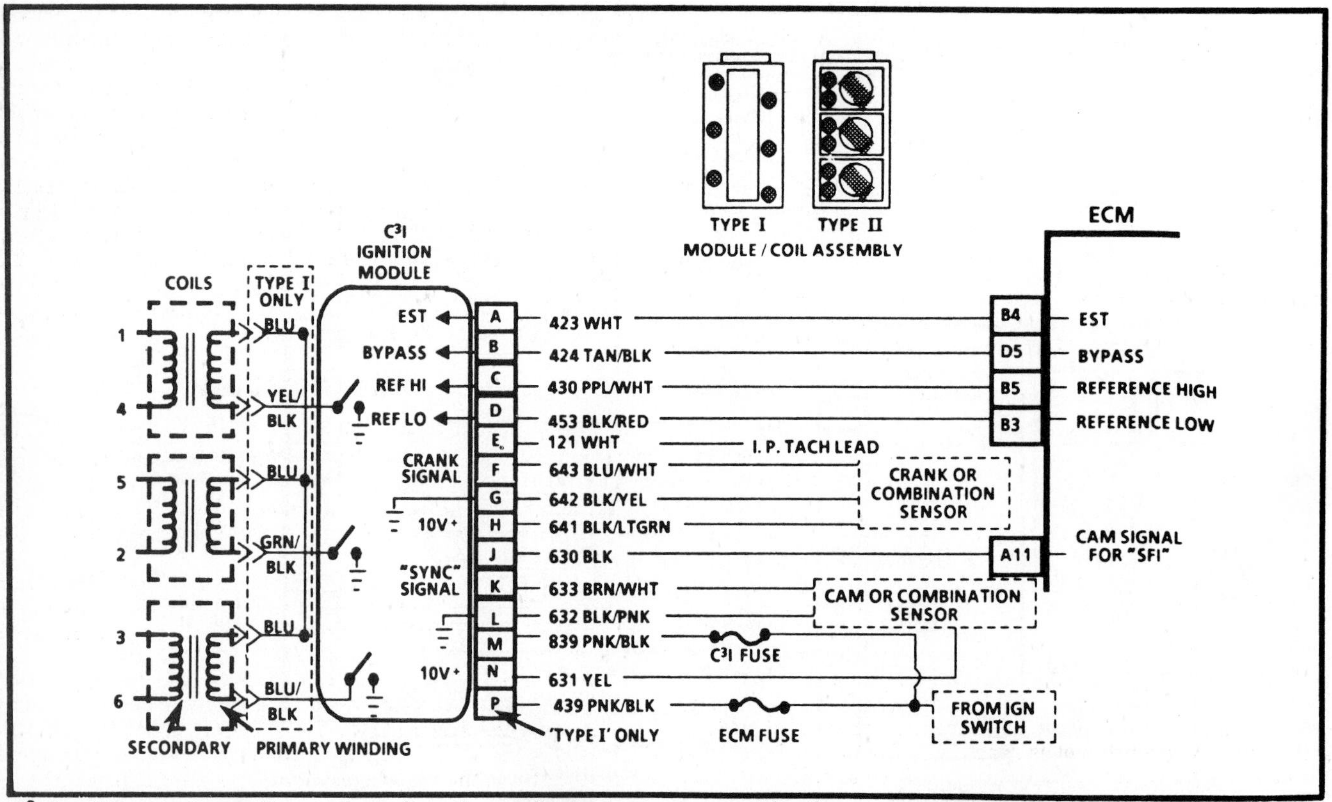

C^{3}I Ignition system with crankshaft and camshaft sensor or combination sensor in the electrical system

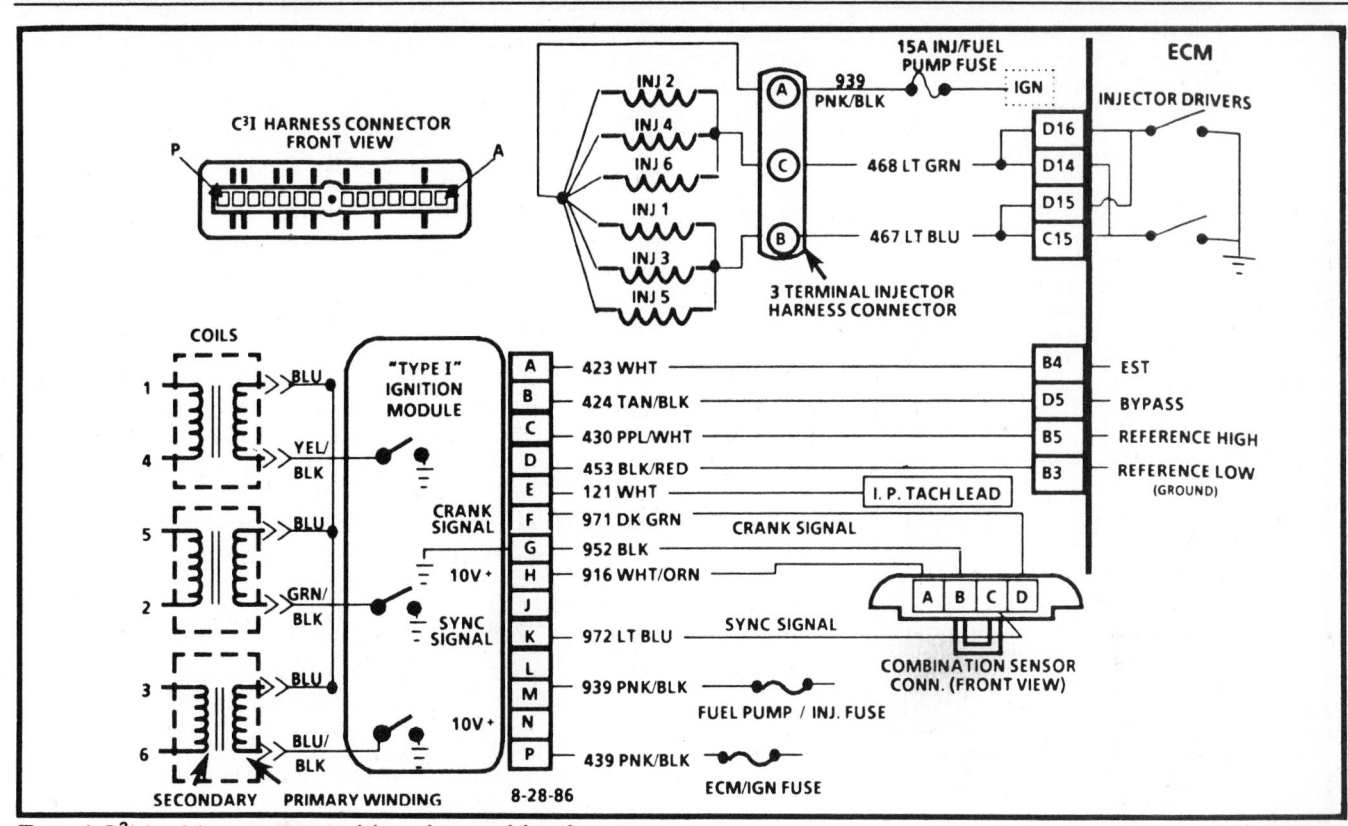

Type I C³I Ignition system with only combination sensor

Diagnostics

C³I IGNITION SYSTEM/EST

NOTE: Verification of Type I or Type II systems is very important, because the diagnostics are not the same for both types.

If the engine cranks, but will not operate, or starts and immediately stalls, further diagnosis must be made to determine if the failure is in the ignition system or the fuel system.

NOTE: If codes EO41 or EO42 are set, further electronic engine control system diagnosis is required. Refer to the appropriate diagnostic charts in Section 5 for complete C³I system performance check.

Direct Ignition System Components

NOTE: The Direct Ignition System/EST is used with TBI and Ported fuel injection systems.

CRANKSHAFT SENSOR

A magnetic crankshaft sensor (Hall Effect switch) is used and is remotely mounted on the opposite side of the engine from the "DIS" module. The sensor protrudes in to the engine block, within 0.050 in. of the crankshaft reluctor.

The reluctor is a special wheel cast into the crankshaft with seven slots machined into it, six of them being evenly spaced at 60° apart. A seventh slot is spaced 10° from one of the other slots and serves as a generator of a "sync-pulse". As the reluctor rotates as part of the crankshaft, the slots change the magnetic field of the sensor, creating an induced voltage pulse.

Based on the crankshaft sensor pulses, the "DIS" module sends reference signals to the ECM, which are used to indicate crankshaft position and engine speed. The "DIS" module will continue to send these reference pulses to the ECM at a rate of one per each 120° of crankshaft rotation. The ECM actvates the fuel injectors, based on the recognition of every other reaference pulse, beginning at a crankshaft position 120° after piston top dead center (TDC). By comparing the time between the pulses, the "DIS" module can recognize the pulse representing the seventh slot (sync pulse) which starts the calculation of ignition coil sequencing. The second crankshaft pulse following the "sync pulse" signals the "DIS" module to fire the No.2-5 ignition coil, the fourth crankshaft pulse signals the module to fire No.3-6 ignition coil and the sixth crankshaft pulse signals the module to fire the 1-4 ignition coil.

IGNITION COILS

There are two separate coils for the four cylinder engines and three separate coils for the V6 engines, mounted to the coil/module assembly. Spark distribution is synchronized by a signal from the crankshaft sensor which the ignition module uses to trigger each coil at the proper time. Each coil provides the spark for two spark plugs.

Two types of ignition coil assemblies are used, "Type I" and "Type II" During the diagnosis of the systems, the correct type of ignition coil assembly must be identified and the diagnosis directed to that system.

Type I module/coil assembly has three twin tower ignition coils, combined into a single coil pack unit. This unit is mounted to the DIS module. ALL THREE COILS MUST BE REPLACED AS A UNIT. A separate current source through a fused circuit to the module terminal "P" is used to power the ignition coils.

Type II coil/module assembly has three separate coils that

are mounted to the DIS module. EACH COIL CAN BE RE-PLACED SEPARATELY. A fused low current source to the module terminal "M", provides power for the sensors, ignition coils and internal module circuitry.

"DIS" MODULE

The "DIS" module monitors the crankshaft sensor signal and based on these signals, sends a reference signal to the ECM so that correct spark and fuel injector control can be maintained during all driving conditions. During cranking, the "DIS" module monitors the "sync-pulse" to begin the ignition firing sequence. Below 400 rpm, the module controls the spark advance by triggering each of the ignition coils at a predetermined interval, based on engine speed only. Above 400 rpm, the ECM controls the spark timing (EST) and compensates for all driving conditions. The "DIS" module must receive a "sync-pulse" and then a crank signal, in that order, to enable the engine to start.

The "DIS" module is not repairable. When a module is replaced, the remaining "DIS" components must be transferred to the new module.

DIRECT IGNITION ELECTRONIC SPARK TIMING (EST) CIRCUITS

This system uses the same EST to ECM circuits that the distributor type systems with EST use. However, a difference does exist between the C³I system and the Direct Ignition system.

The following is a brief description for the EST circuits.

"DIS"REFERENCE, CIRCUIT 430

The crankshaft sensor generates a signal to the ignition module, which results in a reference pulse being sent to the ECM.

The ECM uses this signal to calculate crankshaft position and engine speed for injector pulse width.

The crankshaft sensor is mounted to the base of the DIS module on the 2.5L four cylinder engines and is mounted directly into the side of the engine block.

REFERENCE GROUND, CIRCUIT 453

This wire is grounded through the module and insures that the ground circuit has no voltage drop between the ignition module and the ECM, which can affect performance.

BY-PASS, CIRCUIT 424

At approximately 400 rpm, the ECM applies 5 volts to this circuit to switch spark timing control from the "DIS" module to the ECM. An open or grounded by pass circuit will set a code 42 and result in the engine operating in a back-up ignition timing mode (module timing) at a calculated timing value. This may cause poor performance and reduced fuel economy.

ELECTRONIC SPARK TIMING (EST), CIRCUIT 423

The "DIS" module sends a reference signal to the ECM when the engine is cranking. While the engine is under 400 rpm, the "DIS" module controls the ignition timing. When the engine speed exceeds 400 rpm, the ECM applies 5 volts to the By-pass line to switch the timing to the ECM control (EST).

An open or ground in the EST circuit will result in the engine continuing to run, but in a back-up ignition timing mode (module timing mode) at a calculated timing value and the "SERVICE ENGINE SOON" light will not be on. If the EST fault is still present, the next time the engine is restarted, a code 42 will be set and the engine will operate in the module timing mode. This may cause poor performance and reduced fuel economy.

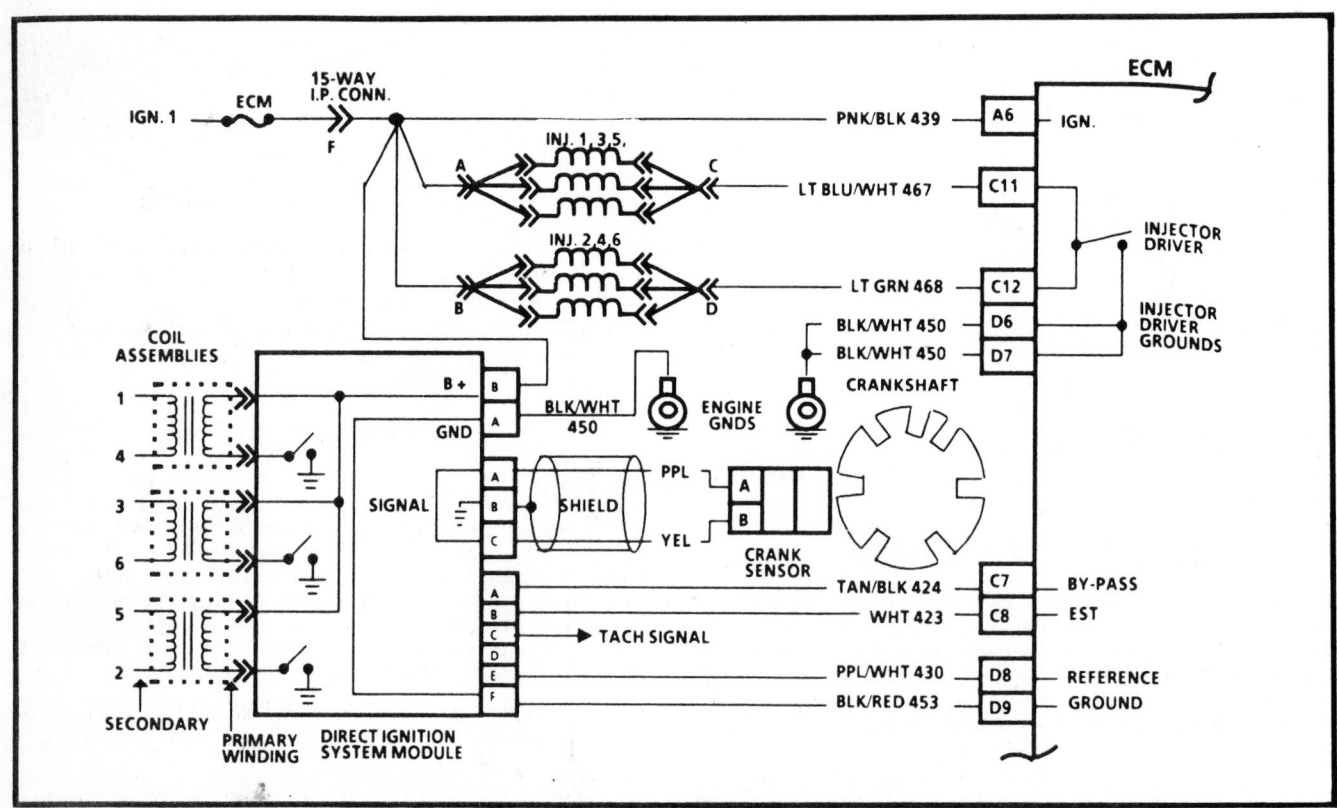

Direct Ignition system electrical schematic, 2.8L engine with port fuel injection

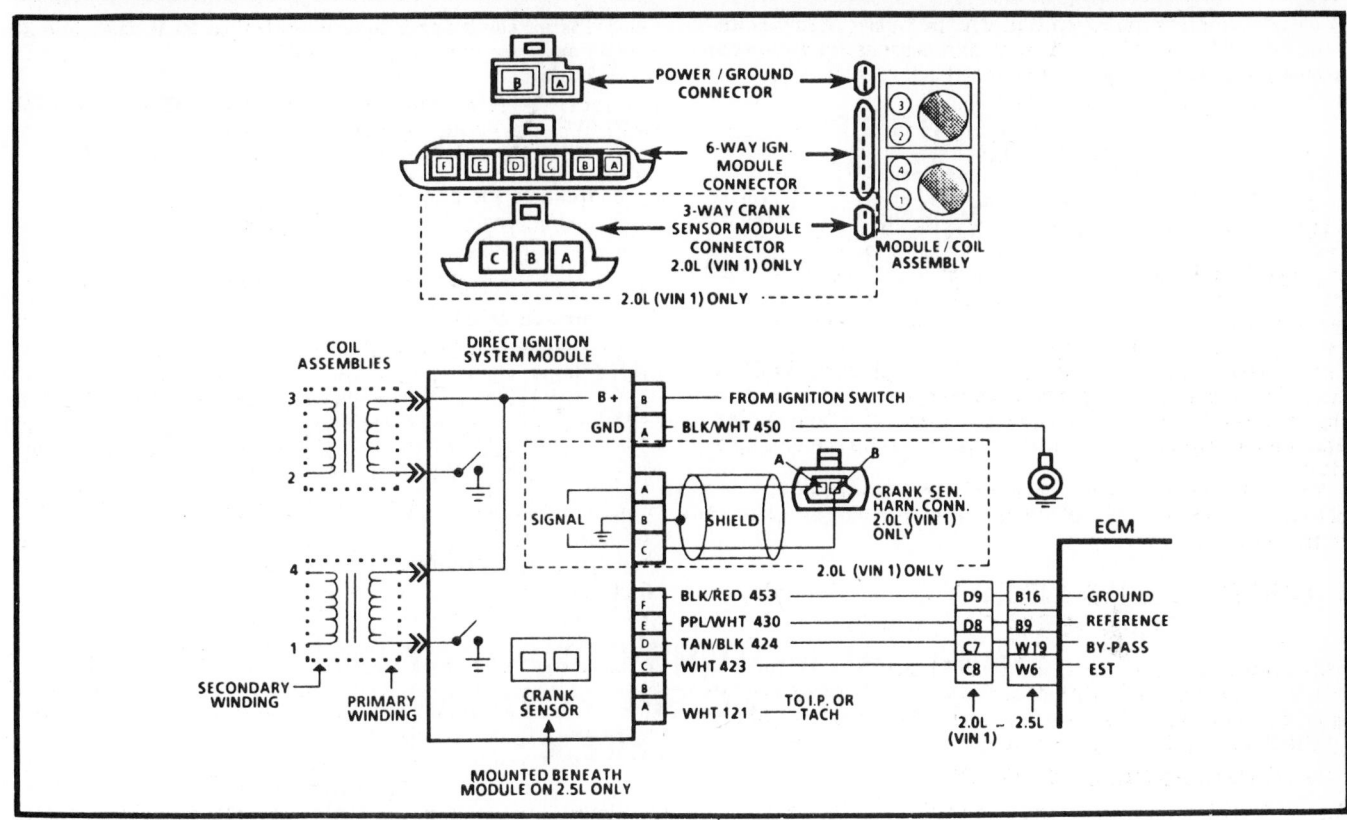

Typical Direct Ignition system electrical schematic

Diagnosis

DIRECT IGNITION SYSTEM

NOTE: For further diagnostic explanations and procedures, refer to the appropriate diagnostic charts in Section 5.

The ECM uses information from the MAP and Coolant sensors, in addition to rpm to calculate spark advance as follows;
1. Low MAP output voltage–More spark advance.
2. Cold engine–More spark advance.
3. High MAP output voltage–Less spark advance.
4. Hot engine–Less spark advance.

Therefore, detonation could be caused by low MAP output or high resistance in the coolant sensor circuit.

Poor performance could be caused by high MAP output or low resistance in the coolant sensor circuit.

If the engine cranks but will not operate, or starts, then immediately stalls, diagnosis must be accomplished to determine if the failure is in the "DIS" system or the fuel system.

CHECKING EST PERFORMANCE

The ECM will set timing at a specified value when the diagnostic "TEST" terminal in the ALDL connector is grounded. To check for EST operation, run the engine at 1500 rpm with the terminal ungrounded. Then ground the "TEST" terminal. If the EST is operating, there should be a noticeable engine rpm change. A fault in the EST system will set a trouble code 42.

CODE 42

If the code 42 is set, refer to the diagnosis procedures for code 42 in Chilton's Electronic Engine Control Manual.

CODE 12

Code 12 is used during the diagnostic circuit check procedure to test the diagnostic and code display ability of the ECM. This code indicates that the ECM is not receiving the engine rpm (reference) signal. This occurs with the ignition key in the ON position and the engine not operating.

SETTING IGNITION TIMING

Because the reluctor wheel is an integral part of the crankshaft and the crankshaft sensor is mounted in a fixed position, timing adjustment is not possible.

NOTE: For further diagnostic explanations and procedures, refer to the appropriate diagnostic charts in Section 5.

CRANKSHAFT SENSOR

Adjustment

1. Rotate the harmonic balancer until the interrupter ring fills the sensor slot and the edge of the interrupter window is aligned with the edge of the deflector on the pedestal.
2. Adjust the sensor so that there is an equal distance on each side of the disc.
3. There should be approximately 0.025 in. clearance between the disc and the sensor.

NOTE: Special tools are available for the measurement of the clearance through Kent Moore Tool Company.

4. Tighten the retaining bolt and recheck the clearance at approximately 120° apart.

5. If the interrupter ring contacts the sensor at any point of the 360° circle, the interrupter ring has excessive runout and must be replaced.

CAMSHAFT POSITION SENSOR

Removal, Installation and Adjustment

1. If only the camshaft sensor is being replaced, it is not necessary to remove the entire assembly.
2. The sensor is replaceable separately and into one position.

CAMSHAFT POSITION SENSOR DRIVE ASSEMBLY

Removal, Installation and Adjustment

1. Note the position of the slot in the rotating vane.
2. Remove the bolt securing the drive assembly to the engine.
3. Remove the drive assembly.

4. Install the drive assembly with the slot in the vane. Install mounting bolt.
5. Install the camshaft sensor.
6. Rotate the engine to set the No. 1 cylinder at TDC compression.
7. Mark the harmonic balancer and rotate the engine to 25° after TDC.
8. Remove the plug wires from the coil assembly.
9. Using weatherpack removal tool J–28742–A, or equivalent, remove terminal B of the sensor 3–way connector on the module side.
10. Probe terminal B by installing a jumper and reconnecting the wire removed to the jumper wire.
11. Connect a voltmeter between the jumper wire and ground.
12. With the key On and the engine stopped, rotate the camshaft sensor counterclockwise until the sensor switch just closes. This is indicated by the voltage reading going from a high 5–12 volts to a low 0–2 volts. The low voltage indicates the switch is closed.
13. Tighten the retaining bolt and reinstall the wire into terminal B.
14. Install remaining components.

GENERAL MOTORS CORPORATION
ELECTRONIC SPARK TIMING
(EST) SYSTEM

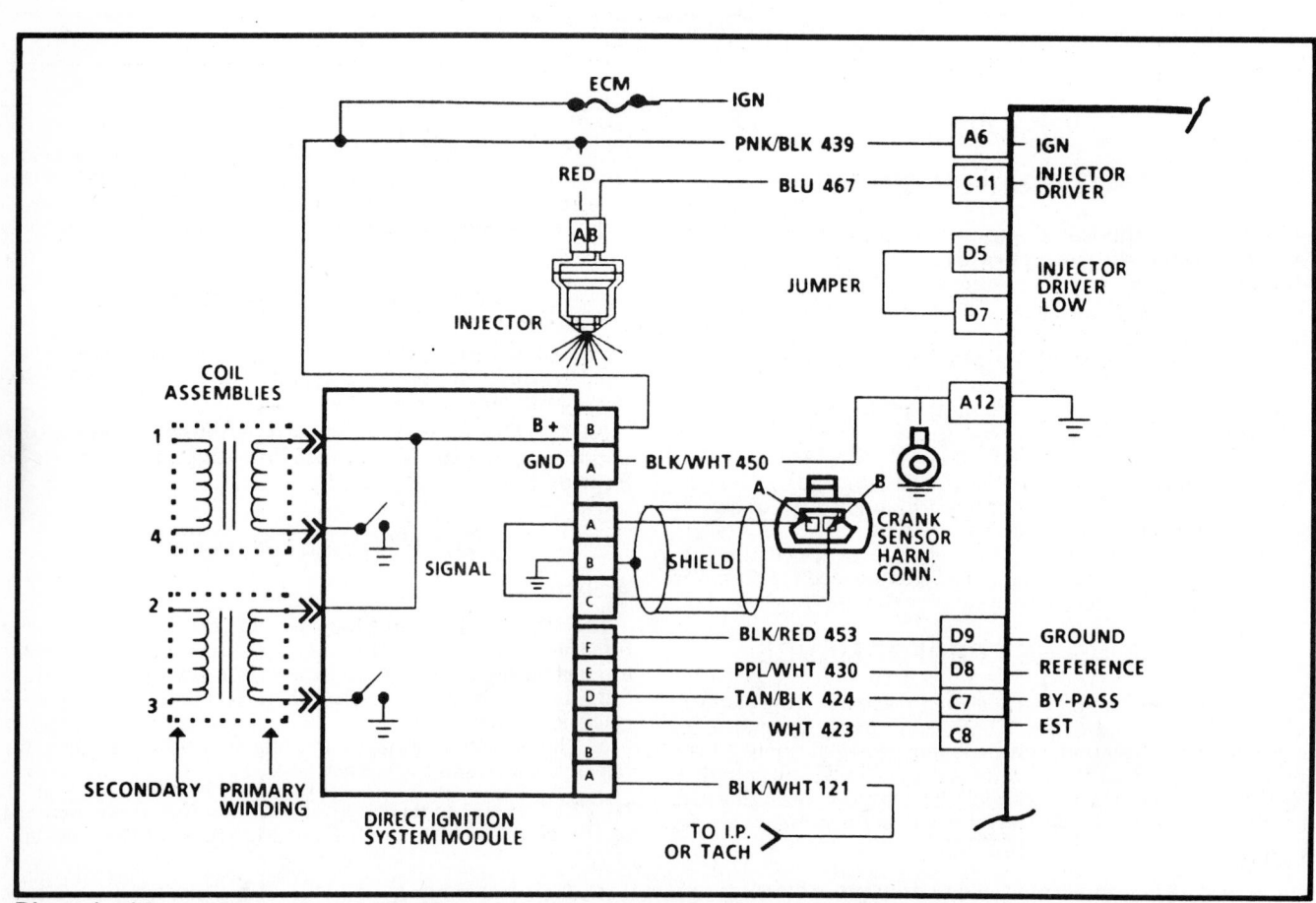

Direct Ignition system electrical schematic and charts for "Engine cranks but won't run", 2.0L engine

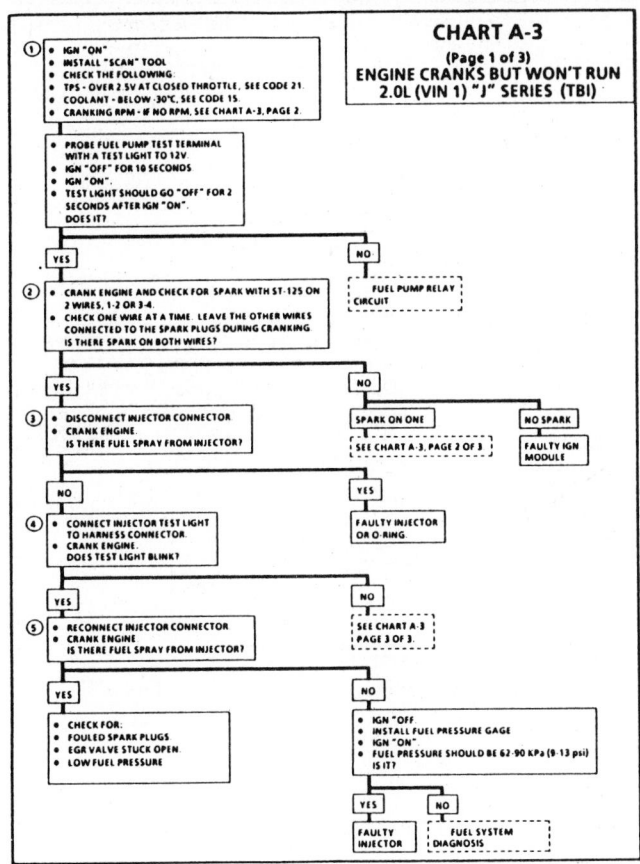

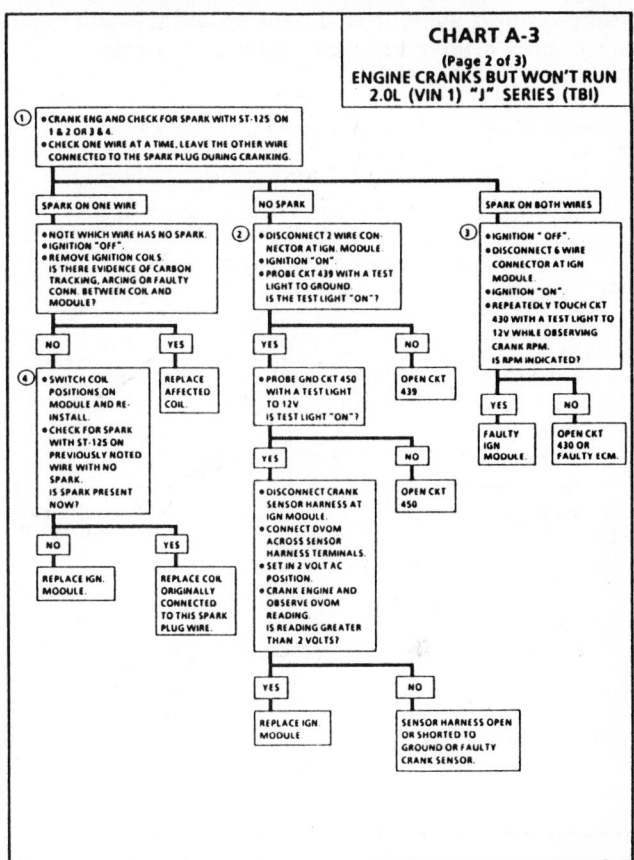

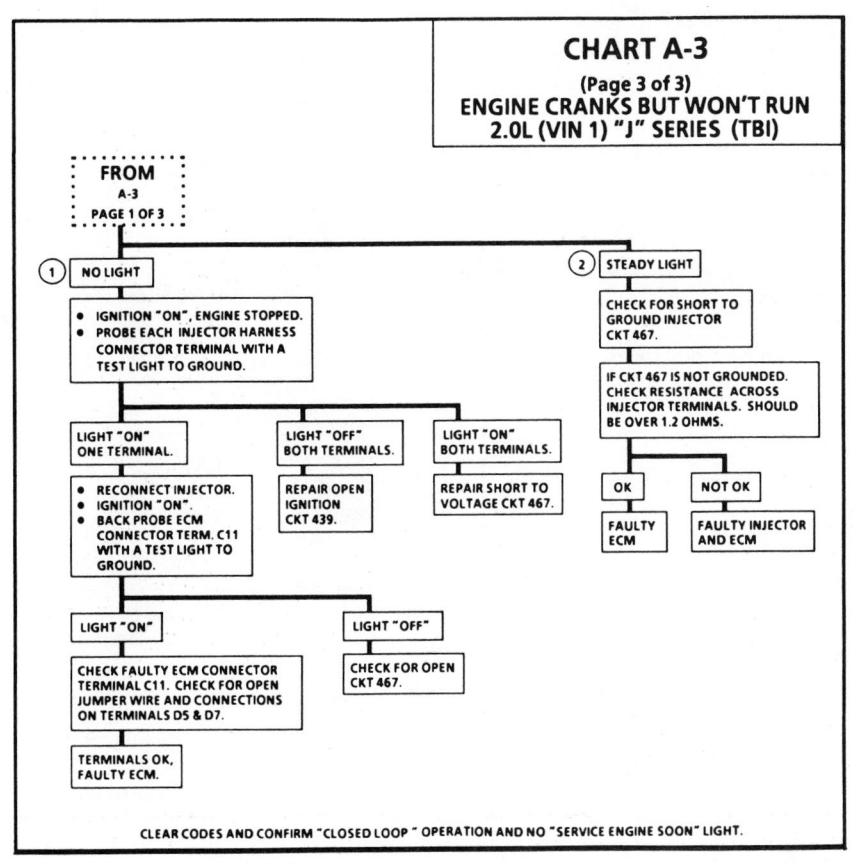

Direct Ignition system electrical schematic and charts for "Engine cranks but won't run", 2.5L engine

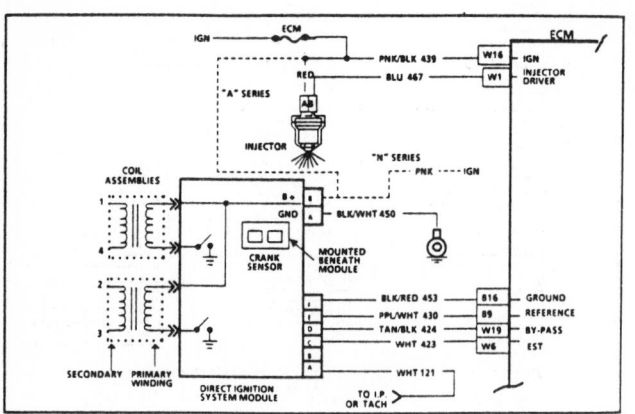

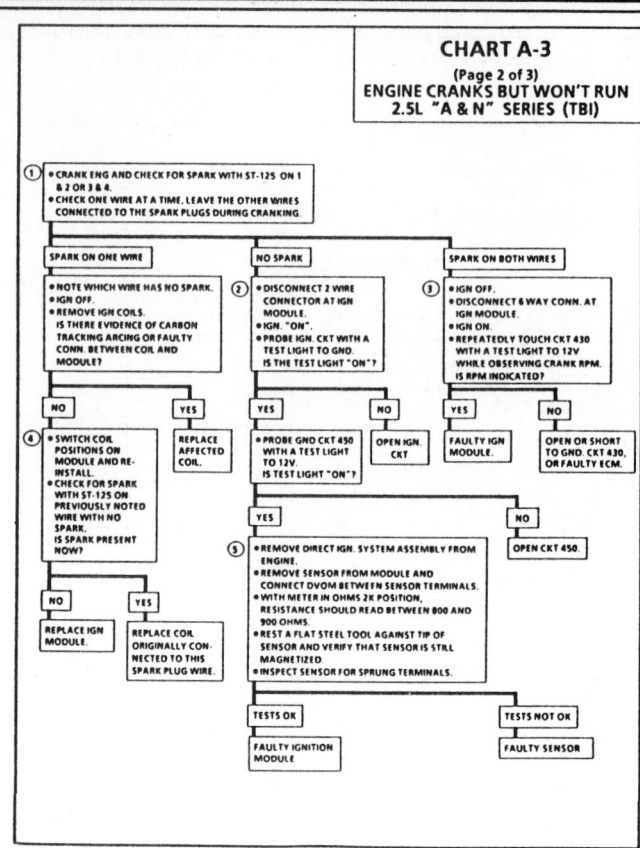

CHART A-3
(Page 2 of 3)
ENGINE CRANKS BUT WON'T RUN
2.5L "A & N" SERIES (TBI)

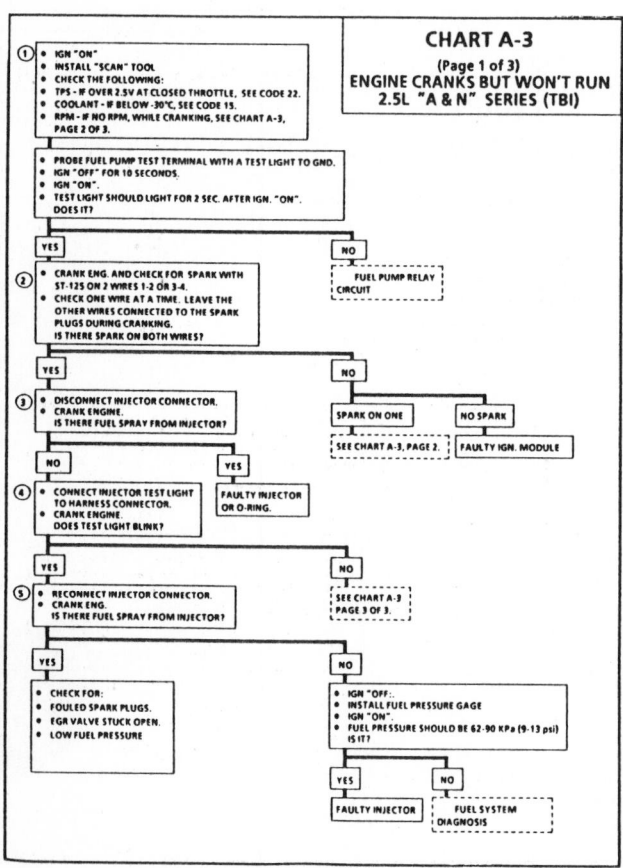

CHART A-3
(Page 1 of 3)
ENGINE CRANKS BUT WON'T RUN
2.5L "A & N" SERIES (TBI)

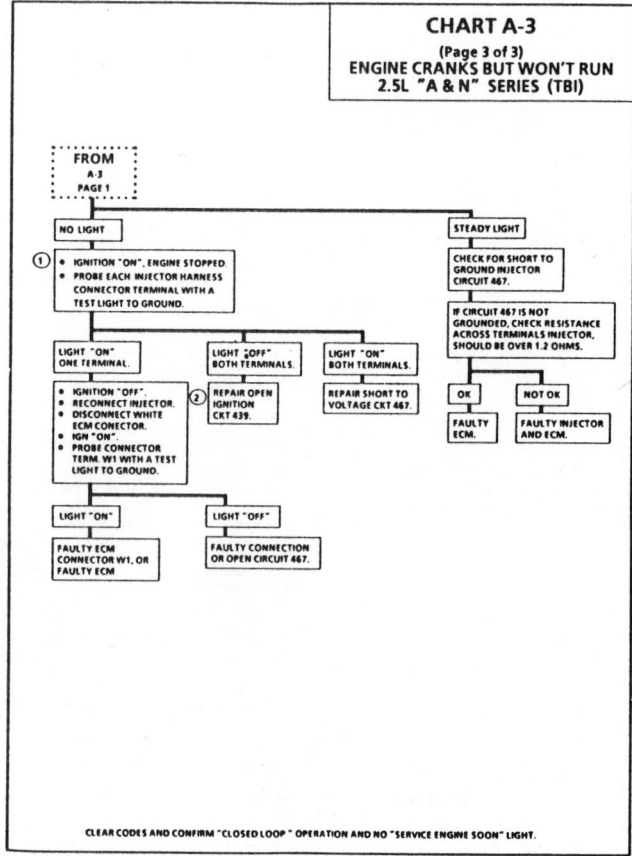

CHART A-3
(Page 3 of 3)
ENGINE CRANKS BUT WON'T RUN
2.5L "A & N" SERIES (TBI)

CLEAR CODES AND CONFIRM "CLOSED LOOP" OPERATION AND NO "SERVICE ENGINE SOON" LIGHT.

Direct Ignition system electrical schematic and charts for "Engine cranks but won't run", 2.8L engine

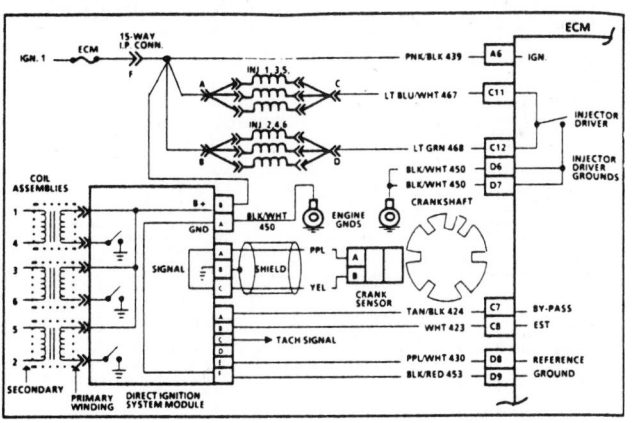

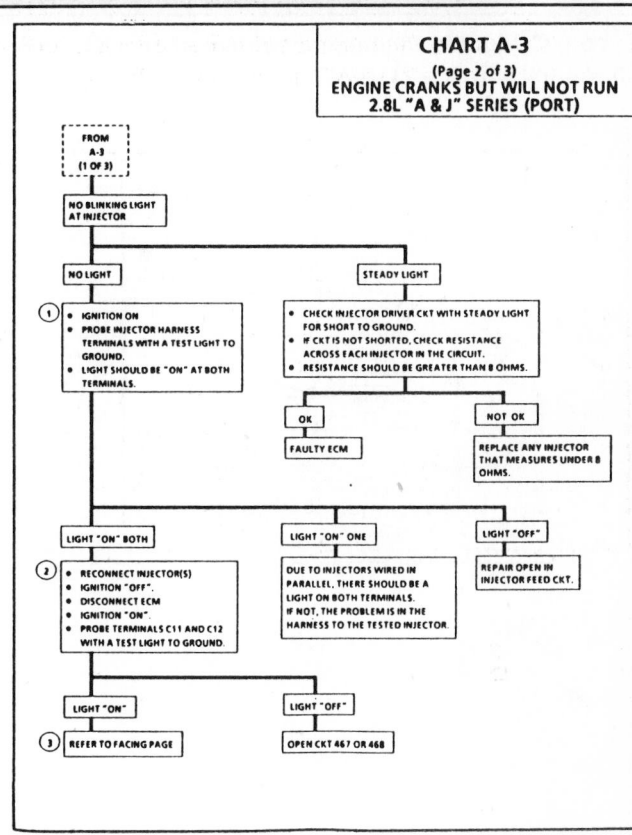

CHART A-3
(Page 2 of 3)
ENGINE CRANKS BUT WILL NOT RUN 2.8L "A & J" SERIES (PORT)

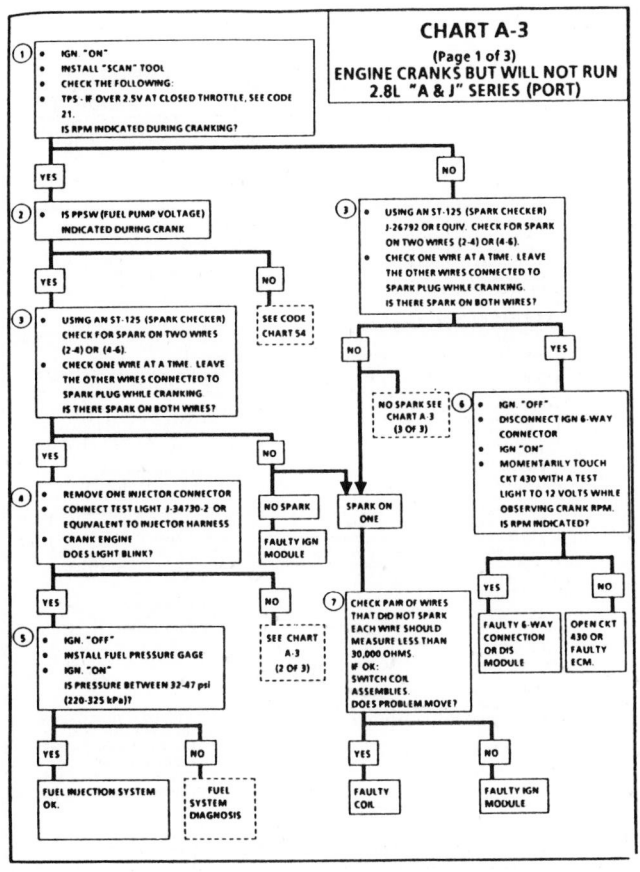

CHART A-3
(Page 1 of 3)
ENGINE CRANKS BUT WILL NOT RUN 2.8L "A & J" SERIES (PORT)

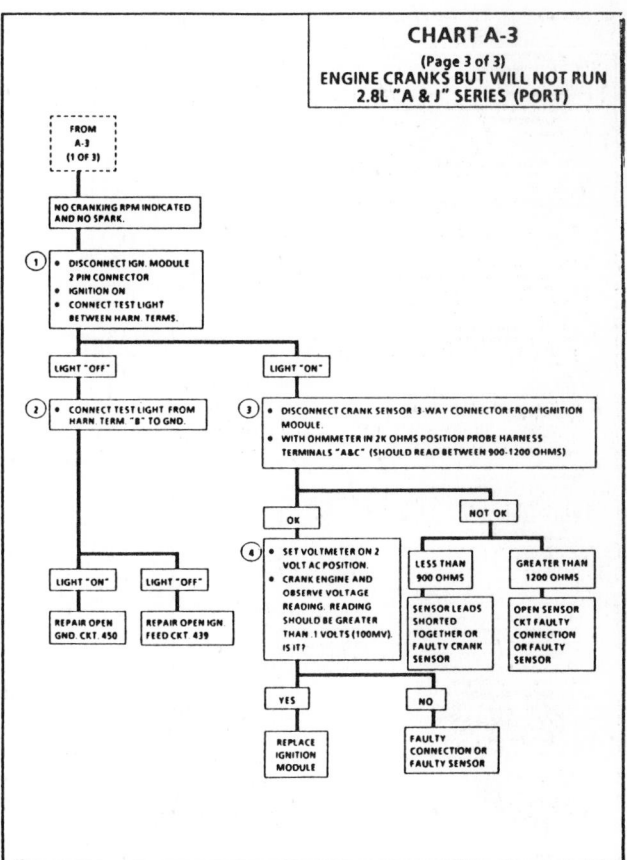

CHART A-3
(Page 3 of 3)
ENGINE CRANKS BUT WILL NOT RUN 2.8L "A & J" SERIES (PORT)

Type I, C³I Ignition system electrical schematic and charts for "Engine cranks but won't run

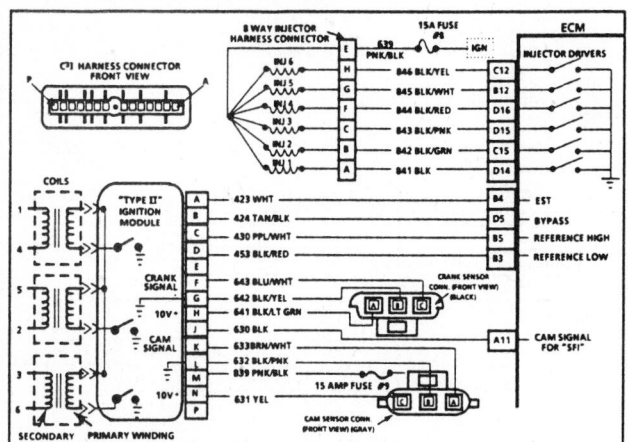

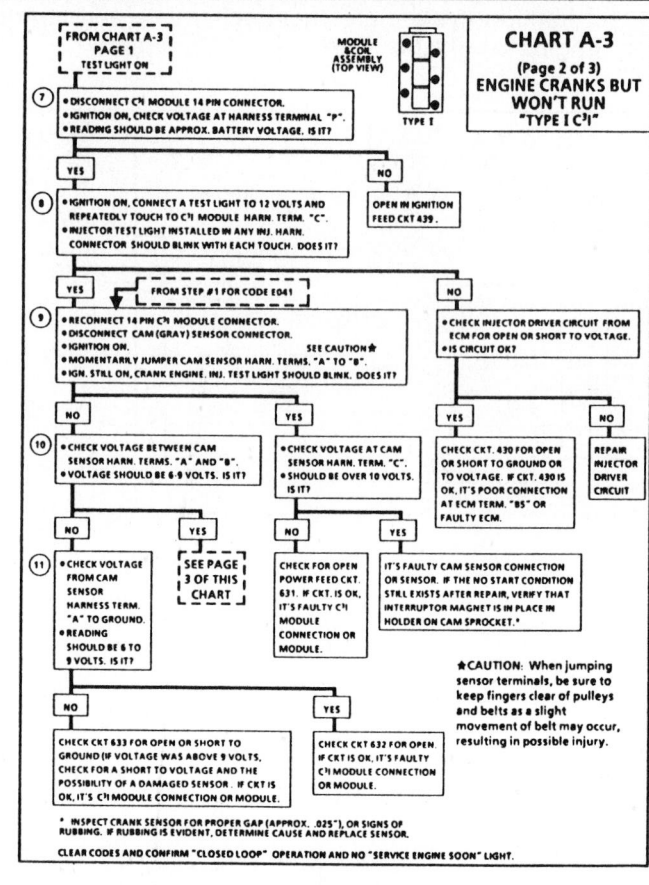

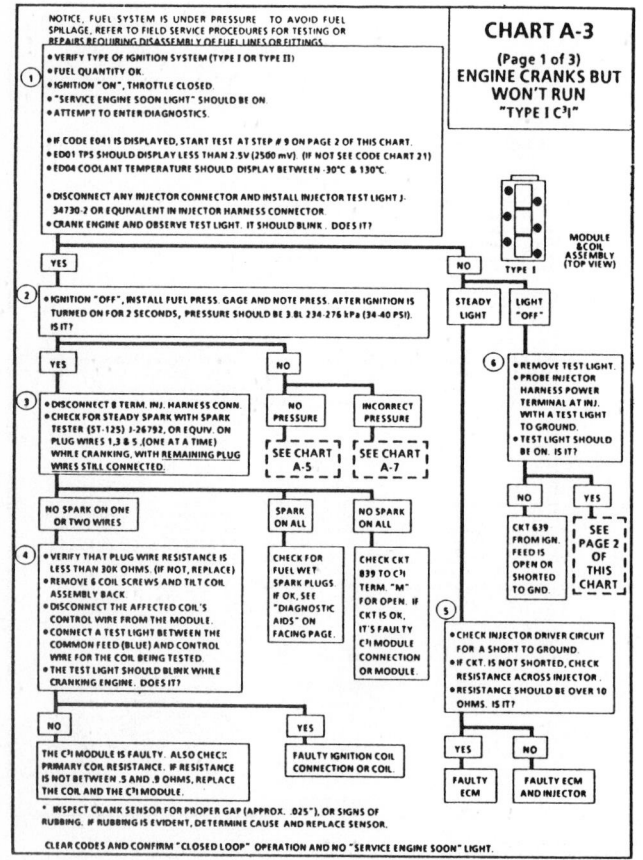

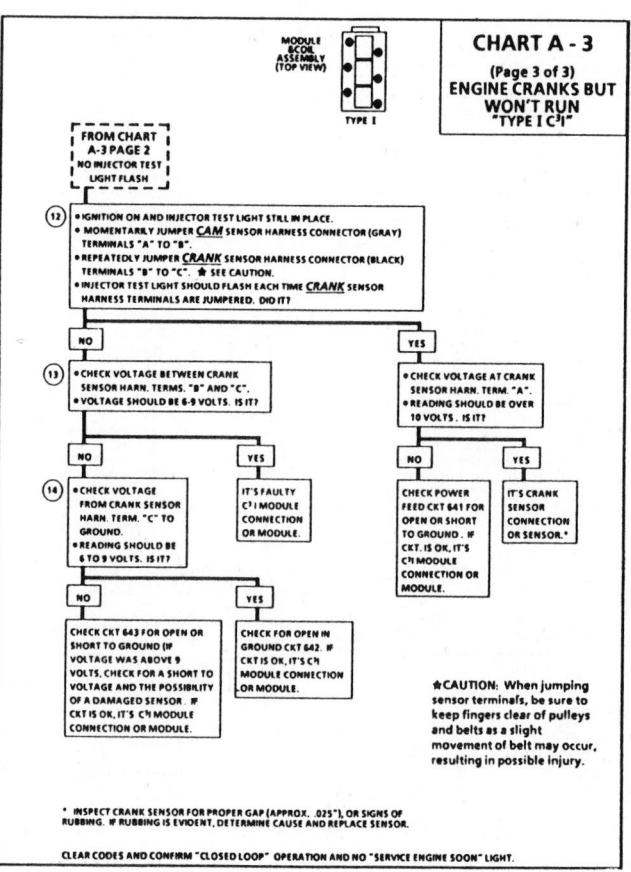

Type II, C³I Ignition system electrical schematic and charts for "Engine cranks but won't run"

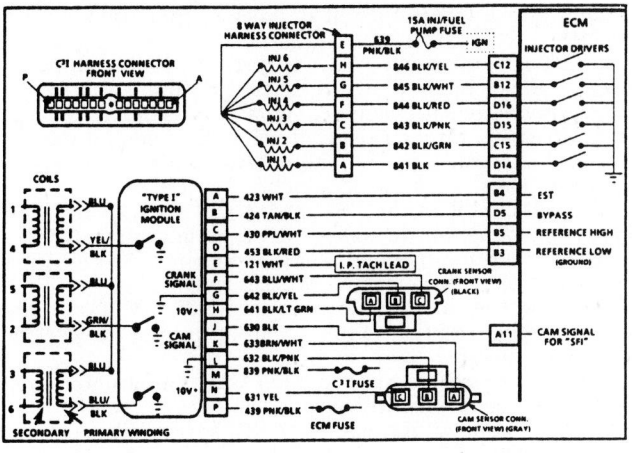

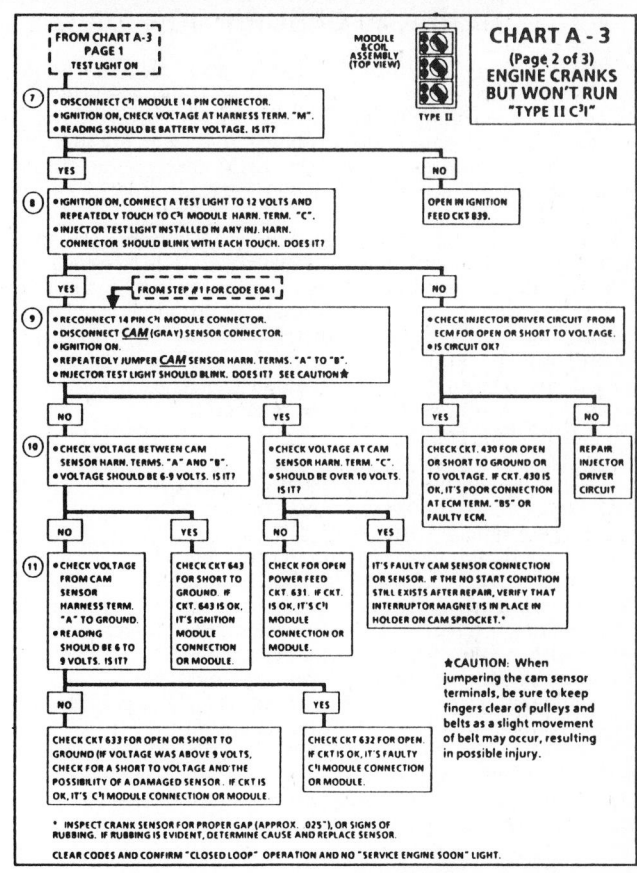

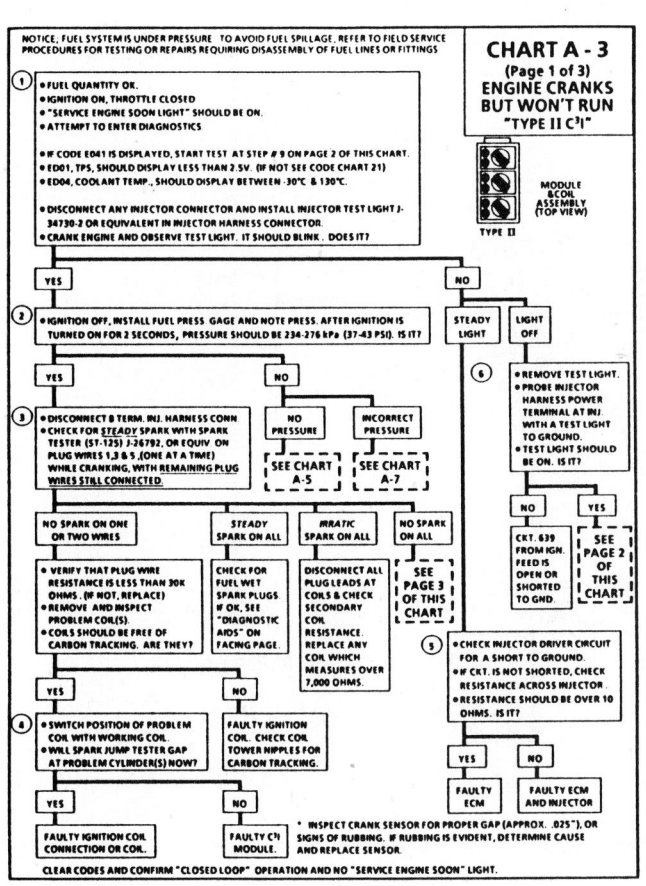

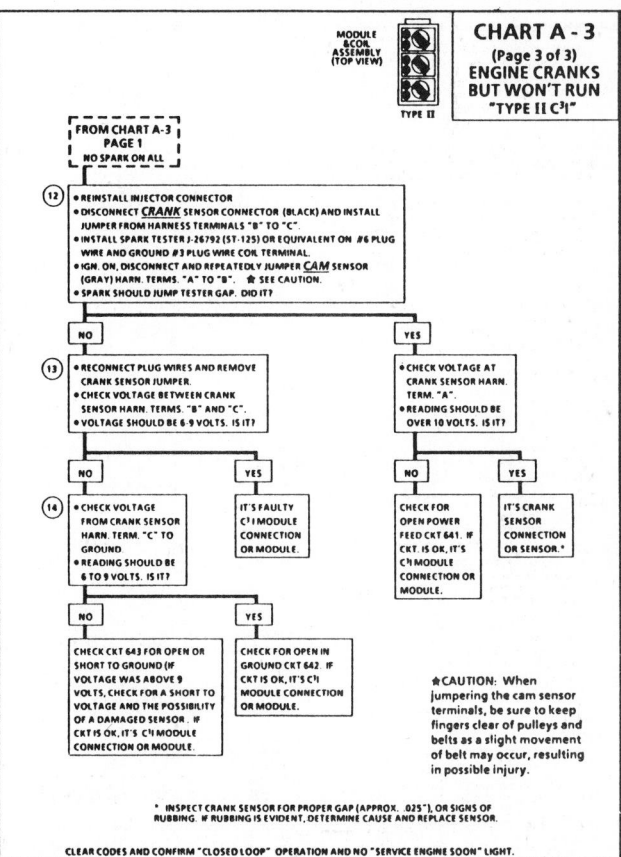

GENERAL DESCRIPTION

The High Energy Ignition (HEI) system controls fuel combustion by providing the spark to ignite the compressed air/fuel mixture, in the combustiuon chamber, at the correct time. To provide improved engine performance, fuel economy and control of the exhaust emissions, the ECM controls distributor spark advance (timing) with the Electronic Spark Timing (EST) system.

The standard High Energy Ignition (HEI) system has a modified distributor module which is used in conjunction with the EST system. The module has seven terminals instead of the four used without EST. Two different terminal arrangements are used, depending upon the distributor used with a particular engine application.

To properly control ignition/combustion timing, the ECM needs to know the following information:
1. Crankshaft position.
2. Engine speed (rpm).
3. Engine load (manifold pressure or vacuum).
4. Atmospheric (barometric) pressure.
5. Engine temperature.
6. Transmission gear position (certain models)

The EST system consists of the distributor module, ECM and its connecting wires. The distributor has four wires from the HEI module connected to a four terminal connector, which mates with a four wire connector from the ECM.

These circuits perform the following functions:
1. Distributor reference at terminal B – This provides the ECM with rpm and crankshaft position information.
2. Reference ground at terminal D – This wire is grounded in the distributor and makes sure the ground circuit has no voltage drop, which could affect performance. If this circusit is open, it could cause poor performance.

3. By-pass at terminal C – At approximately 400 rpm, the ECM applies 5 volts to this circuit to switch the spark timing control from the HEI module to the ECM. An open or grounded bypass circuit will set a Code 42 and the engine will run at base timing, plus a small amount of advance built into the HEI module.

4. EST at terminal A – This triggers the HEI module. The ECM does not know what the acrtual timing is, but it does know when it gets its reference signal. It then advances or retards the spark timing from that point. Therefore, if the base timing is set incorrectly, the entire spark curve will be incorrect.

An open circuit in the EST circuit will set a Code 42 and cause the engine to run on the HEI module timing. This will cause poor performance and poor fuel economy. A ground may set a Code 42, but the engine will not run.

The ECM uses information from the MAP or VAC and coolant sensors, in addition to rpm, in order to calulate spark advance as follows:
1. Low MAP output voltage (high VAC sensor output voltage) would require MORE spark advance.
2. Cold engine would require MORE spark advance.
3. High MAP output voltage (low VAC sensor output voltage) would require LESS spark advance.
4. Hot engine would require LESS spark advance.

RESULTS OF INCORRECT EST OPERATION

Detonation could be caused by low MAP output (high VAC sensor output), or high resistance in the coolant sensor circuit.

Poor performance could be caused by high MAP output (low VAC sensor output) or low resistance in the coolant sensor circuit.

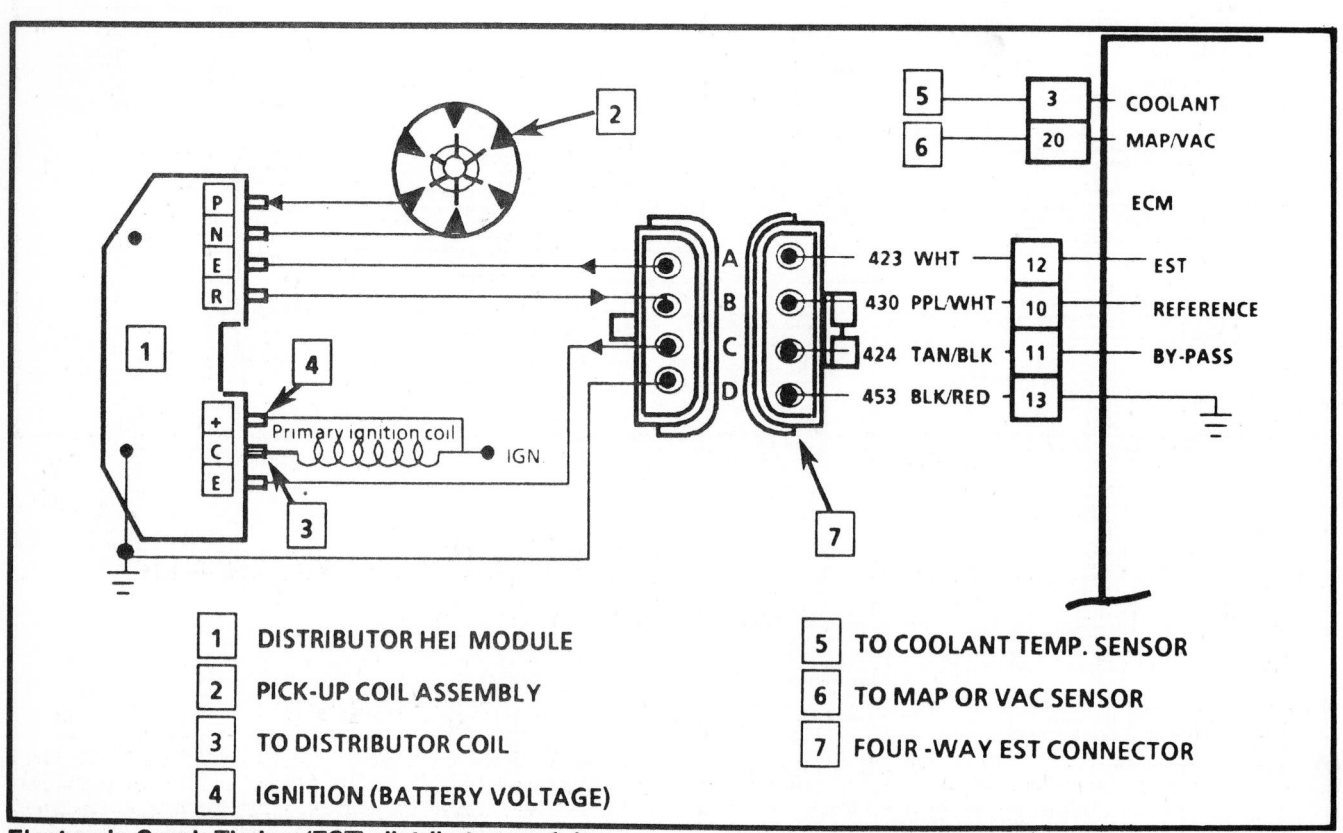

1	DISTRIBUTOR HEI MODULE
2	PICK-UP COIL ASSEMBLY
3	TO DISTRIBUTOR COIL
4	IGNITION (BATTERY VOLTAGE)
5	TO COOLANT TEMP. SENSOR
6	TO MAP OR VAC SENSOR
7	FOUR-WAY EST CONNECTOR

Electronic Spark Timing (EST) distributor modules

HOW CODE 42 IS DETERMINED

When the systems is operating on the HEI module with no voltage in the by-pass line, the HEI module grounds the EST signal. The ECM expects to sense no voltage on the EST line during this condition. If it senses voltage, it sets Code 42 and will not go into the EST mode.

When the rpm for EST is reached (approximately 400 rpm), the ECM applies 5 volts to the by-pass line and the EST should no longer be grounded in the HEI module, so the EST voltage should be varying.

If the by-pass line is open, the HEI module will not switch to the EST mode, so the EST voltage will be low and Code 42 will be set.

If the EST line is grounded, the HEI module will switch to the EST, but because the line is grounded, there will be no EST signal and the engine will not operate. A Code 42 may or may not be set.

NOTE: For further diagnostic explanations and procedures, refer to the appropriate diagnostic charts in Section 5.

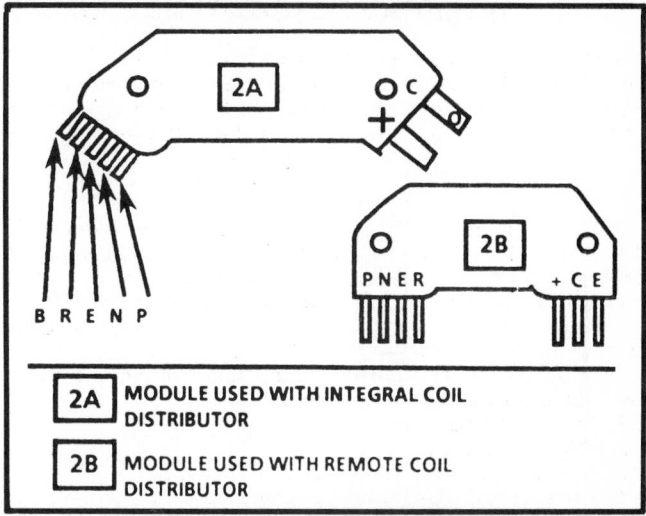

2A	MODULE USED WITH INTEGRAL COIL DISTRIBUTOR
2B	MODULE USED WITH REMOTE COIL DISTRIBUTOR

Typical Electronic Spark Timing (EST) system wiring schematic. Used with remote ignition coil

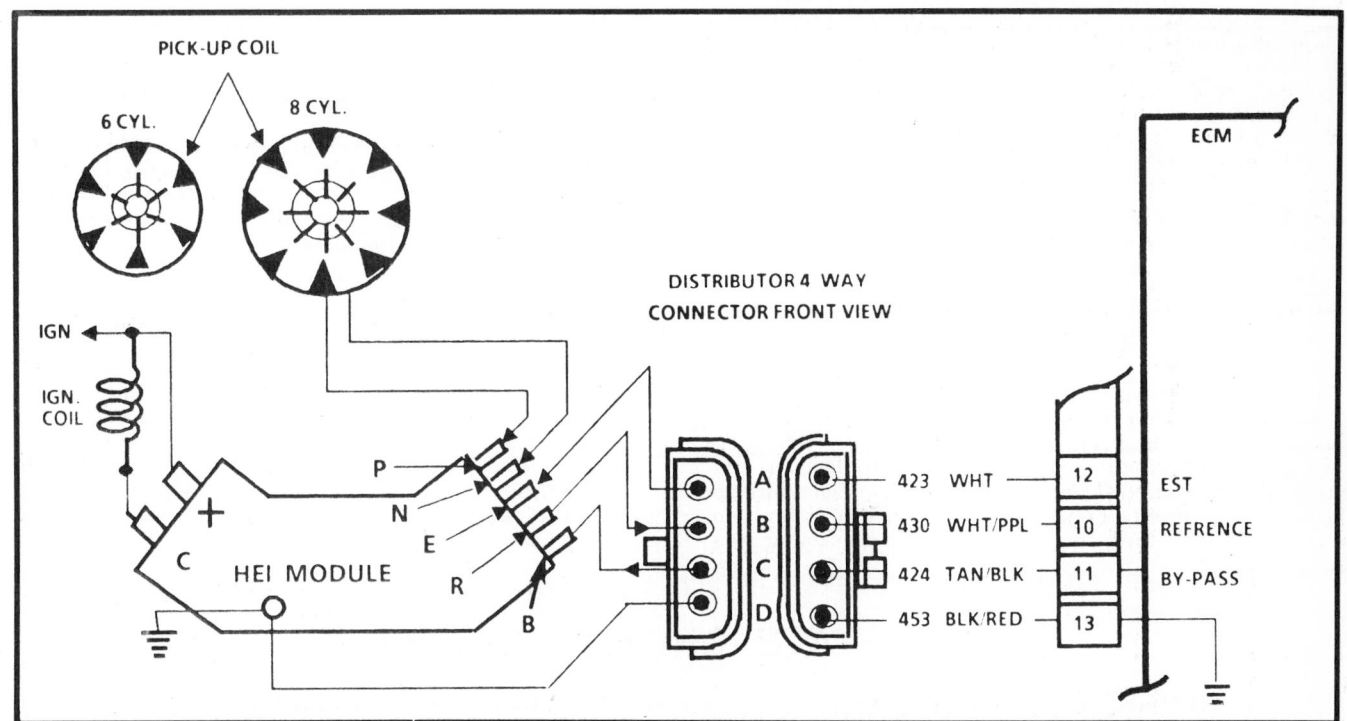

Typical Electronic Spark Timing (EST) system wiring schematic. Used with coil-in-cap distributor

GENERAL MOTORS CORPORATION ELECTRONIC SPARK CONTROL (ESC) SYSTEM

GENERAL DESCRIPTION

The Electronic Spark Control (ESC) operates in conjunction with the Electronic Spark Timing (EST) system and modifies (retards) the spark advance when detonation occurs. The retard mode is held for approximatelay 20 seconds after which the spark control will again revert to the Electronic Spark Timing (EST) system. There are three basic components of the Electronic Spark Control (ESC) system.

SENSOR

The Electronic Spark Control (ESC) sensor detects the presence (or absence) and intensity of the detonation by the vibration characteristics of the engine. The output is an electrical signal that goes to the controller. A sensor failure would allow no spark retard.

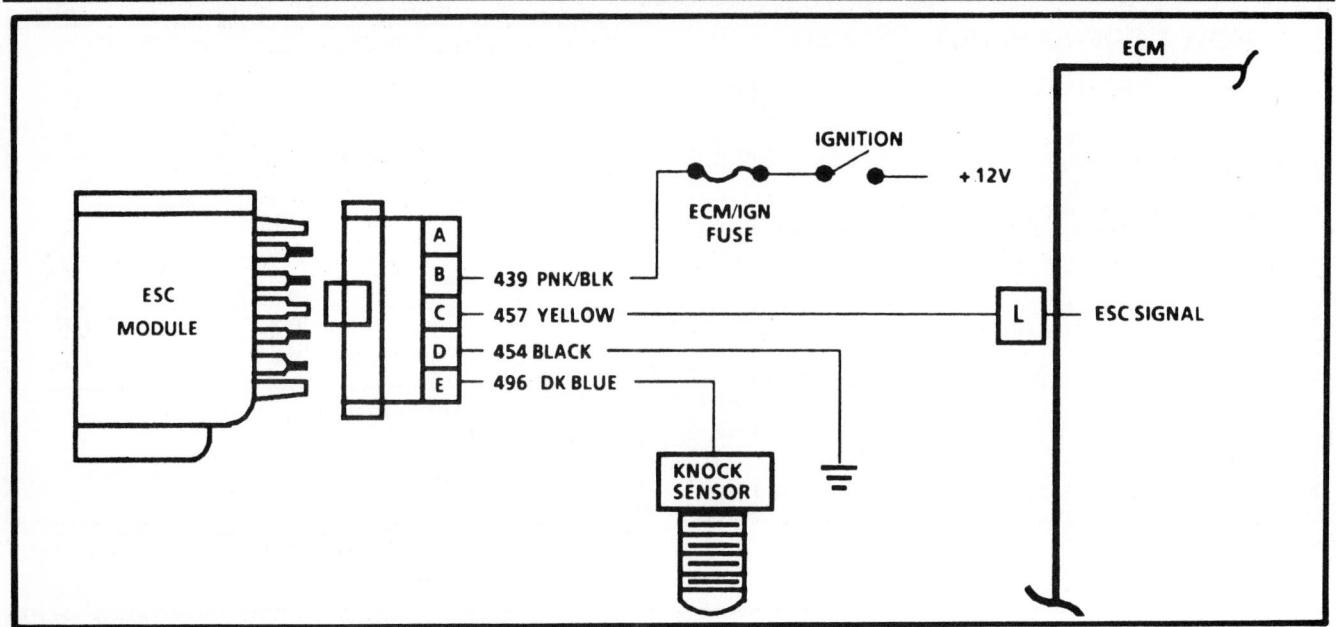

Typical wiring schematic for Electronic Spark Control (ESC) system

DISTRIBUTOR

The distributor is an HEI/EST unit with an electronic module, modified so it can respond to the ESC controller signal. This command is delayed when detonation is occurring, thus providing the level of spark retard required. The amount of spark retard is a function of the degree of detonation.

CONTROLLER

The Electronic Spark Control (ESC) controller processes the sensor signal into a command signal to the distributor, to adjust the spark timing. The process is continuous, so that the presence of detonation is monitored and controlled. The controller is a hard wired signal processor and amplifier which operates from 6-16 volts. Controller failure would be no ignition, no retard or full retard. The controller has no memory storage.

CODE 43

Should a Code 43 be set in the ECM memory, it would indicate that the ESC system retard signal has been sensed by the ECM for too long a period of time. When voltage at terminal L of the ECM is low, spark timing is retarded. Normal voltage in the non-retarded mode is approximately 7.5 volts or more.

BASIC IGNITION TIMING

Basic ignition timing is critical to the proper operation of the ESC system. Always follow the Vehicle Emission Control Information label procedures when adjusting ignition timing.

Some engines will incorporate a magnetic timing probe hole for use with special electronic timing equipment. Consult the manufacturer's instructions for the use of this electronic timing equipment.

SOLID STATE IGNITION SYSTEM

1985-88 Chevrolet Nova

GENERAL INFORMATION

The principal components of the ignition system are the ignition coil, spark plugs and ignition coil. The distributor has a rotor, pole piece, module, centrifugal advance and vacuum advance.

The signal generator (pick-up coil) is used to generate the ignition signal and consists of a signal rotor, signal generator and a magnet. The pole piece is attached to the distributor shaft and the magnet and the pick-up coil are attached to the pick-up coil base plate.

As the distributor shaft rotates, the magnetic flux passing through the pick-up coil varies due to the change of the air gap between the pick-up coil and the pole piece. Due to this action, the alternating current voltage is induced in the pick-up coil. The induced voltage turns the module on and off which in turn

switches off the ignition coil primary voltage. The high voltage is induced in the secondary winding of the ignition coil and ignition sparks are generated at the spark plugs.

Troubleshooting
IGNITION COIL

Testing

1. Disconnect the wiring, ignition coil and the high tension cable at the connector.

2. Measure the resistance between the positive and negative terminals. Primary coil resistance (cold) should be 0.4–0.5 ohms.

3. Measure the resistance between the positive terminal and the high tension terminal. Secondary coil resistance should be 7500–10400 ohms.

4. If the measured resistance varies from the above specifications, replace defective components as necessary.

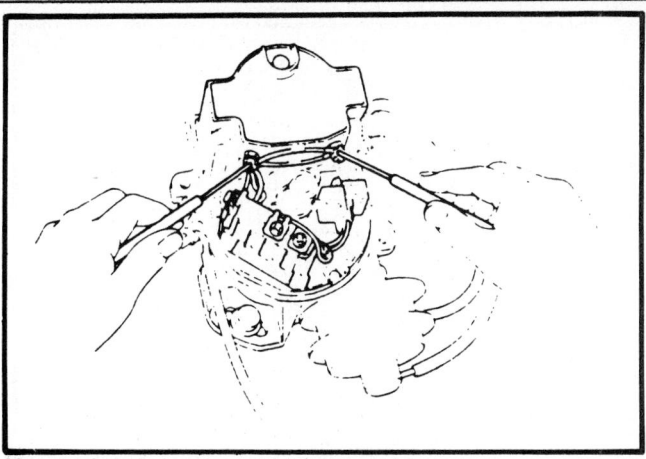

Measuring primary coil resistance

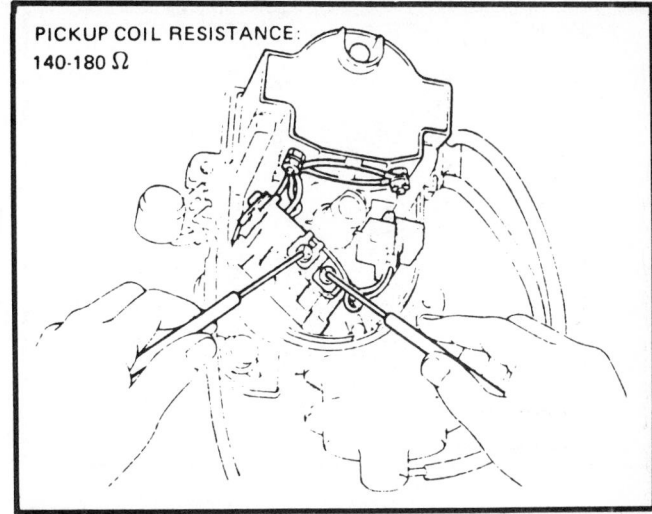

PICKUP COIL RESISTANCE:
140-180 Ω

Measuring pick-up coil resistance

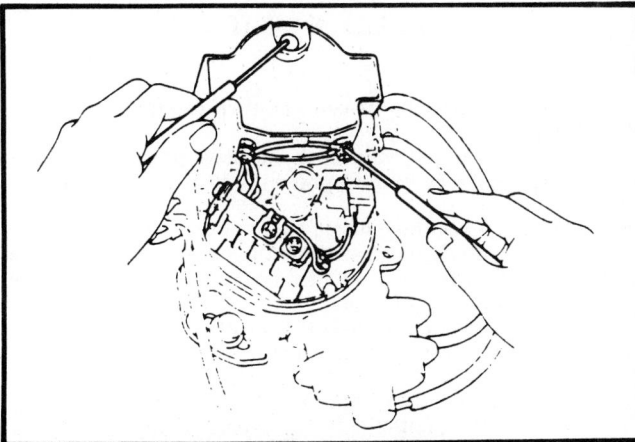

Measuring secondary coil resistance

PICK-UP COIL

Testing

1. Place the ignition switch in the OFF position.
2. Remove the distributor cap.
3. disconnect the pick-up wire from the module.
4. Measure the resistance with an ohmmeter across the pick-up coil.
5. The resistance should be 140-180 ohms.

AIR GAP

Adjustment

1. With the distributor cap off, position a reluctor lobe next to the pick-up coil projection.
2. Using a feeler gauge, measure the gap between the reluctor lobe and the pick-up coil projection.
3. The air gap should be 0.2–0.4mm (0.008–0.016 in.).

POWER SOURCE LINE VOLTAGE

Testing

1. Using a voltmeter, connect the positive probe to the ignition coil positive terminal and the negative probe to the body ground.
2. The voltage reading should be approximately 12 volts.

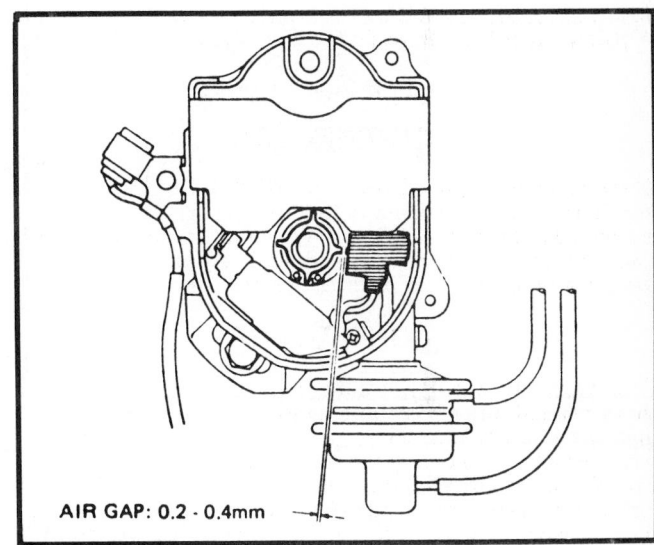

AIR GAP: 0.2 - 0.4mm

Measuring air gap

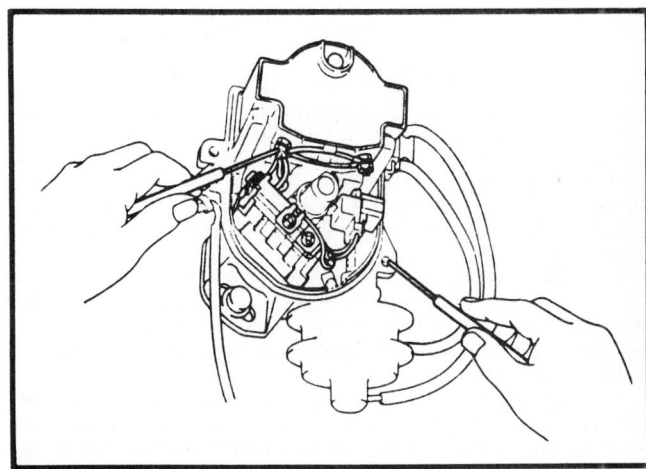

Measuring power transistor voltage

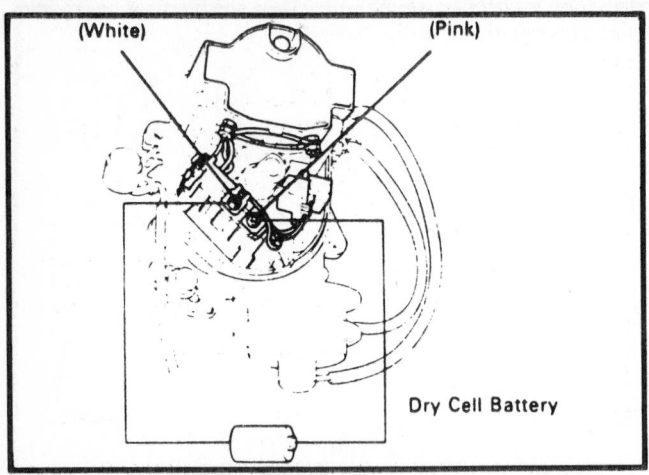

Attaching 1.5 volt battery

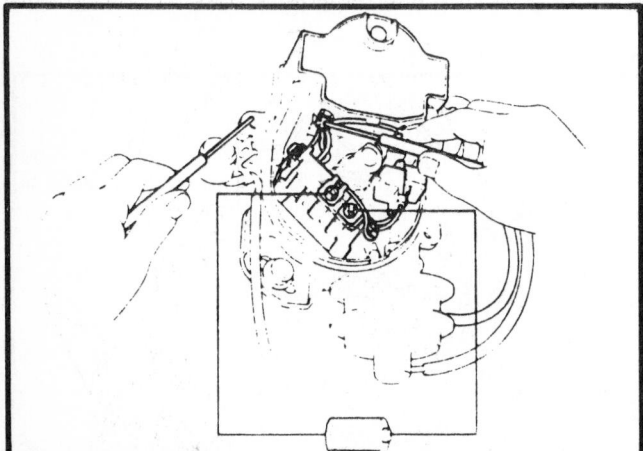

Measuring module voltage with 1.5 volt battery attached

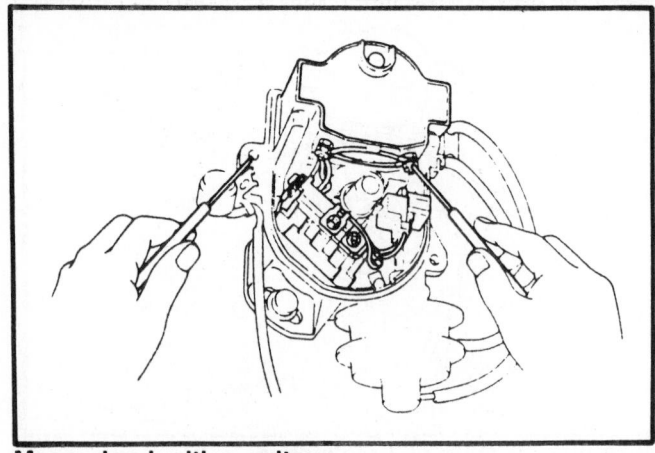

Measuring ignition voltage

MODULE UNIT

Testing

1. Remove the distributor cap and turn the ignition switch to the ON position.
2. Using a voltmeter, connect the positive probe to the ignition coil negative terminal. Connect the negative probe to the body ground.
3. The voltage reading should be 12 volts.
4. Using a dry cell battery (1.5 volts), connect the positive pole of the battery to the pink wire terminal and the negative pole to the white wire terminal.
5. Using a voltmeter, connect the positive probe to the ignition coil negativce terminal and the negative probe to the body ground.
6. The voltage should be approximately 0–3 volts.
7. If the voltage is out of specifications, replace the module.

—————————— **CAUTION** ——————————

Do not apply voltage for more than 5 seconds to avoid destroying the power transistor in the module.

CHERVOLET SPECTRUM

IGNITION SYSTEM

The Chevrolet Spectrum uses a solid state ignition system. It is comprised of the spark plugs, ignition coil, and distributor. The 1985 distributor has a rotor, a module, a pole piece, a vacuum advance and a centrifugal advance. The 1986 and later distributor has a rotor, module, pole piece, vacuum advance, centrifical advance. The ignition coil is not separate, but mounted to the side of the distributor, with internal secondary current routings.

The signal generator is used to generate the ignition signal and consists of a pole piece, a magnet and a pick-up coil. The pole piece is attached to the distributor shaft, and the magnet and pick-up coil are attached to the pick-up coil base plate.

When the distributor shaft rotates, the magnetic flux passing through the pick up coil varies due to the change in the air gap between the pick-up coil and the pole piece. Because of this, the alternating current voltage is induced in the pick-up coil. The induced voltage turns the module on and off which switches off the ignition coil primary current. The high voltage

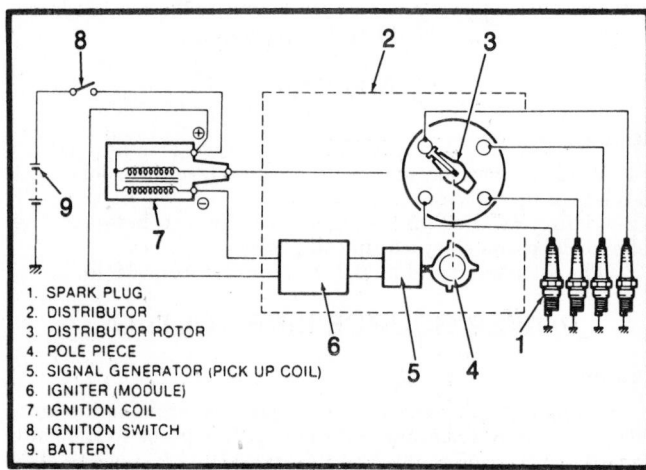

1. SPARK PLUG
2. DISTRIBUTOR
3. DISTRIBUTOR ROTOR
4. POLE PIECE
5. SIGNAL GENERATOR (PICK UP COIL)
6. IGNITER (MODULE)
7. IGNITION COIL
8. IGNITION SWITCH
9. BATTERY

1985 Spectrum ignition circuit schematic

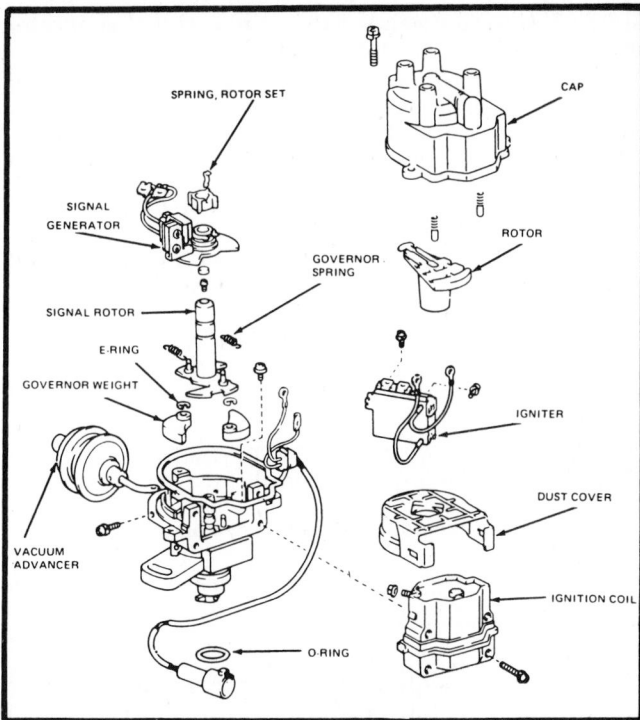

Exploded view of 1986-88 distributor

is induced in the secondary winding of the ignition coil and ignition sparks are generated at the spark plugs.

CENTRIFUGAL ADVANCE

Testing

1. Disconnect the negative battery cable.
2. Remove the distributor cap.
3. Turn the rotor counterclockwise and release it.
4. The rotor should return smoothly by spring force. If not, replace the defective components as required.

VACUUM ADVANCE

The vacuum advance unit is controlled by vacuum from the vacuum advance port on the two barrel carburetor. During normal operation, vacuum exerted on the "A" section of the ad-

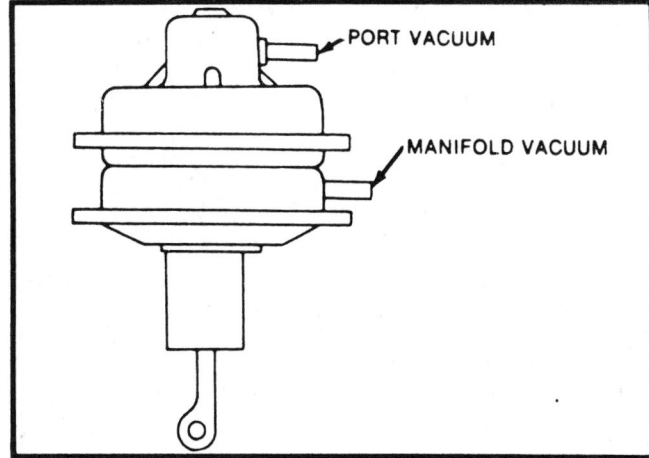

Vacuum nipple identification on vacuum advance unit

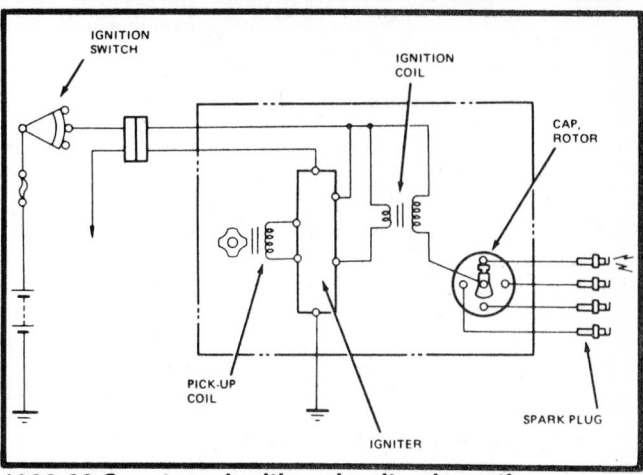

1986-88 Spectrum ignition circuit schematic

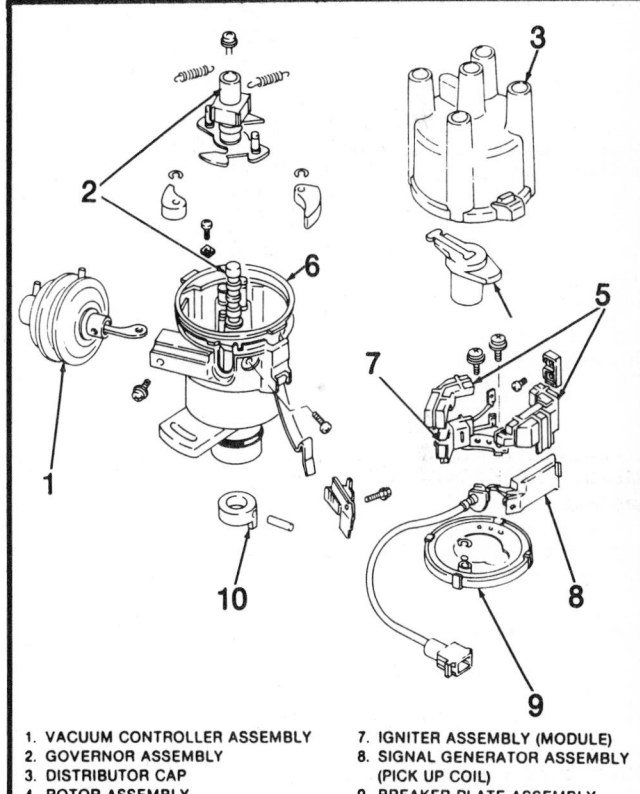

1. VACUUM CONTROLLER ASSEMBLY
2. GOVERNOR ASSEMBLY
3. DISTRIBUTOR CAP
4. ROTOR ASSEMBLY
5. DUST PROOF COVERS
6. PACKING
7. IGNITER ASSEMBLY (MODULE)
8. SIGNAL GENERATOR ASSEMBLY (PICK UP COIL)
9. BREAKER PLATE ASSEMBLY
10. PIN AND COUPLING LUG

Exploded view of 1985 distributor

vance unit from the carburetor port is sufficient to regulate the vacuum advance.

When the vehicle is idling, the advance unit "B" will operate with vacuum from the intake manifold. When the carburetor throttle is again opened, the "A" advance will return to its operating position.

Testing

1. Disconnect the negative battery cable. Remove the distributor cap.

2. Disconnect the vacuum hose from the vacuum advance unit.

3. Connect a vacuum tester to the advance unit.

4. Apply approximately 16 in. Hg. of vacuum and release it. Check to see that the pick-up base plate moves smoothly. Check both "A" and "B" sides.

5. If the base plate does not move smoothly, inspect the plate and vacuum advance unit. Repair or replace as required.

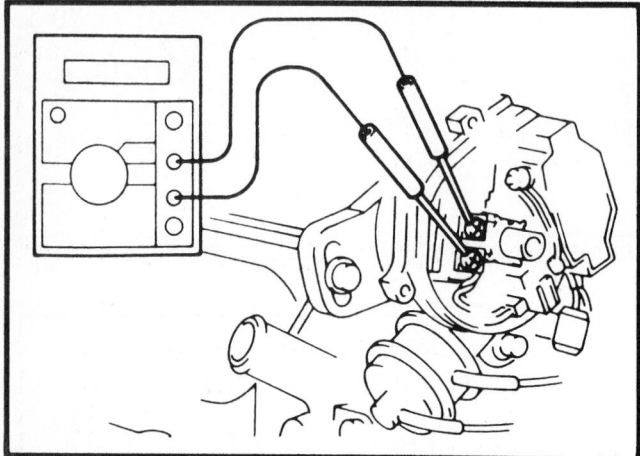

Measuring pick-up coil resistance

PICK—UP COIL

Testing

1. Measure the resistance of the pick-up coil by connecting the probes of the ohmmeter on each terminal.

2. The resistance should be 140–180 ohms.

AIR GAP

Adjustment

1. Use a non-magnetic feeler gauge to measure the air gap.

2. If the measurement is out of specifications of 0.008–0.016 in., adjustment of the air gap is required.

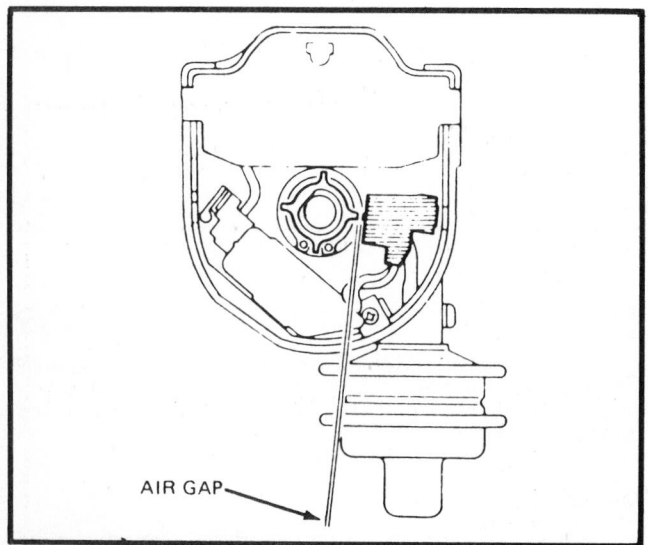

AIR GAP

Air gap measurement

NOTE: It is recommended that a new signal generator be installed if the air gap is out of specifications.

3. If the siganl generator assembly magnet holding screw is loosened for adjustment or replacement of the signal generator, it must be cleaned of all oil or grease with a solvent.

4. A sealing agent must be installed on the screw and after the air gap adjustment is made, the sealing agent must be allowed to properly cure before engine start-up is attempted.

NOTE: Replace the rotor spring set with new springs if the signal generator assembly is replaced.

IGNITION COIL

Testing

INPUT VOLTAGE

1. With the ignition switch in the ON position, measure the voltage between the positive terminal of the ignition coil and ground.

2. The voltage should equal battery voltage.

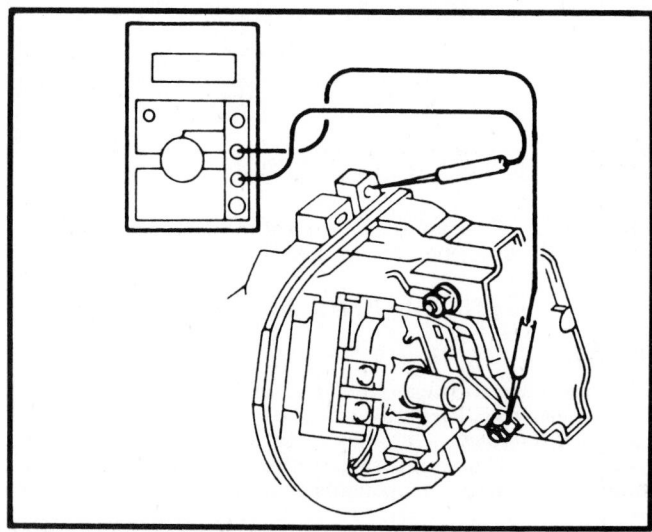

Measuring coil input voltage

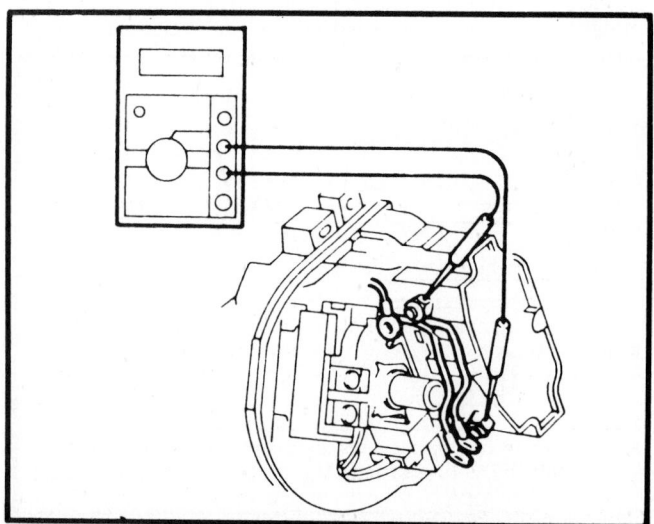

Measuring primary resistance of ignition coil

PRIMARY COIL RESISTANCE

1. The ignition switch must be in the OFF position.
2. Disconnect the terminal of the ignition coil.
3. Measure the resistance between the positive and the negative terminals of the ignition coil.
4. The resistance should be 1.2-1.5 ohms.

SECONDARY COIL RESISTANCE

1. The ignition switch must be in the OFF position.
2. Disconnect the positive terminal of the ignition coil.
3. Measure the resistance between the primary positive terminal and the high voltage terminal.
4. The resistance value should be 10.2–13.8 ohms.

INSULATION RESISTANCE

Testing

1. Have the ignition switch in the OFF position.
2. Disconnect the positive terminal of the ignition switch.
3. Measure the resistance between the positive terminal of the coil and ground.
4. The resistance should be more than 10 ohms.

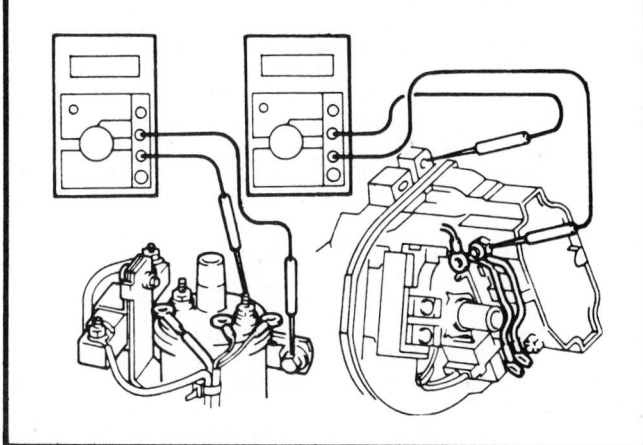

Measuring insulation resistance of remote and on-distributor coils

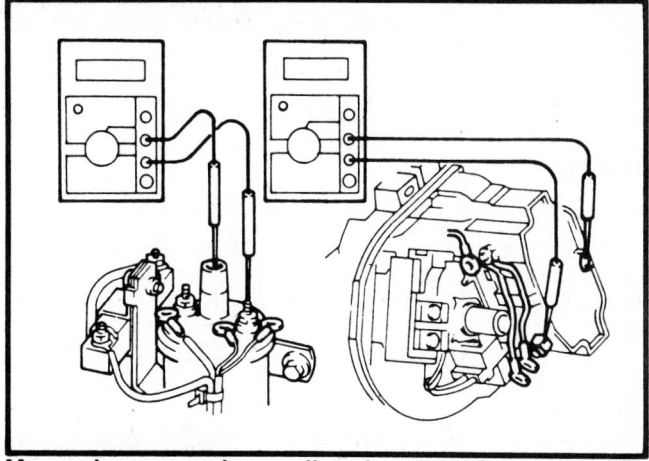

Measuring secondary coil resistance of remote and on-distributor coils

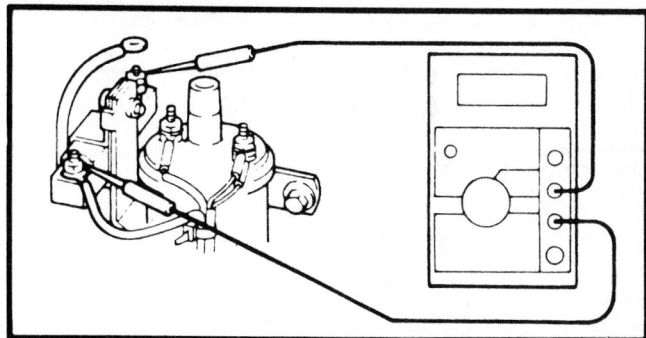

Measuring resistance of resistor unit

RESISTOR RESISTANCE

Testing

1. Disconnect the terminal of the resistor.
2. Measure the resistance of the resistor.
3. The resistance value should be 1.3–1.5 ohms.

CHERVOLET SPRINT

IGNITION SYSTEM

The Chevrolet Sprint 3 cylinder engine uses a solid state ignition system. It is comprised of the spark plugs, ignition coil and distributor. The distributor has a rotor, module, pole piece, vacuum advance and centrifugal advance.

The signal generator is used to generate the ignition signal and consists of a pole piece, a magnet and a pick-up coil. The pole piece is attached to the distributor shaft. The magnet and pick-up coil are attached to the pick-up coil base plate.

When the distributor shaft rotates, the magnetic flux passing through the pick-up coil varies due to the change in the air gap between the pick-up coil and the pole piece. Because of this, the alternating current voltage is induced in the pick-up coil. The induced voltage turns the module on and off which switches off the ignition coil primary current. The high voltage is induced in the secondary winding of the ignition coil and ignition sparks are generated at the spark plugs.

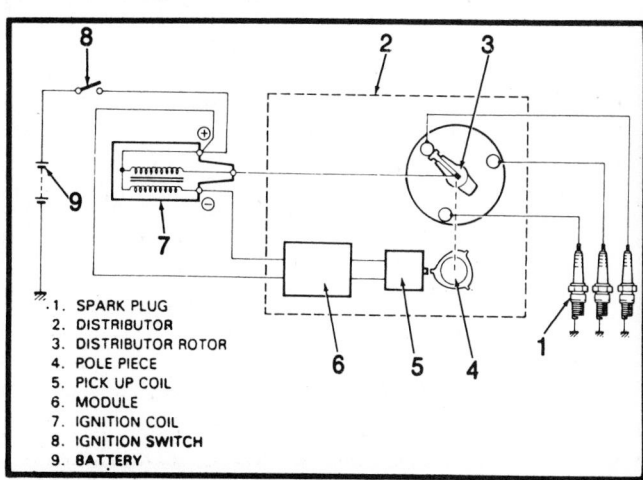

1. SPARK PLUG
2. DISTRIBUTOR
3. DISTRIBUTOR ROTOR
4. POLE PIECE
5. PICK UP COIL
6. MODULE
7. IGNITION COIL
8. IGNITION SWITCH
9. BATTERY

1985-88 Sprint ignition circuit schematic

NOTE: The engine firing order is 1-3-2 with number one cylinder at the front of the engine (right side of vehicle).

CENTRIFUGAL ADVANCE

Testing

1. Disconnect the negative battery cable.
2. Remove the distributor cap.
3. Turn the rotor counterclockwise and release it.
4. The rotor should return smoothly by spring force. If not, replace the defective components as required.

VACUUM ADVANCE

Testing

1. Disconnect the negative battery cable. Remove the distributor cap.
2. Disconnect the vacuum hose from the vacuum advance unit.
3. Connect a vacuum tester to the advance unit.

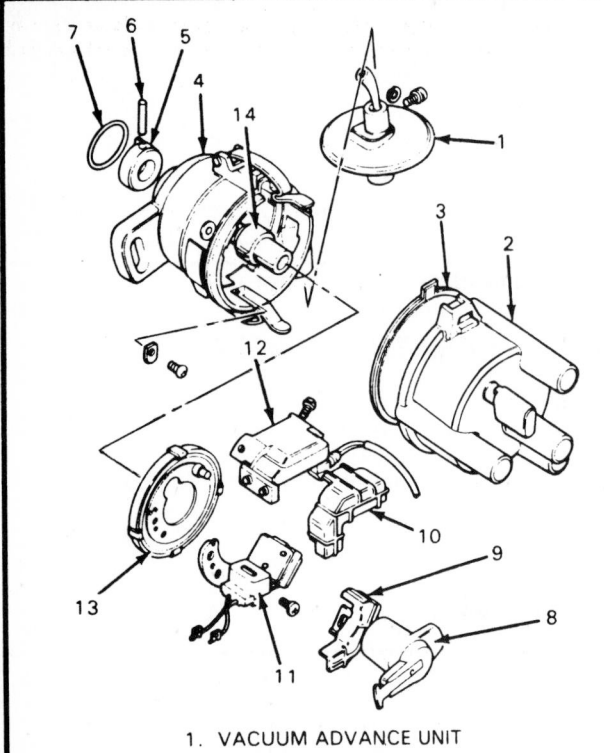

1. VACUUM ADVANCE UNIT
2. DISTRIBUTOR CAP
3. SEAL
4. DISTRIBUTOR HOUSING
5. DISTRIBUTOR COUPLING
6. PIN
7. SEAL
8. ROTOR
9. PICK UP COIL DUST COVER
10. MODULE DUST COVER
11. PICK UP COIL
12. MODULE
13. PICK UP COIL BASE PLATE
14. POLE PIECE

Exploded view of Sprint distributor

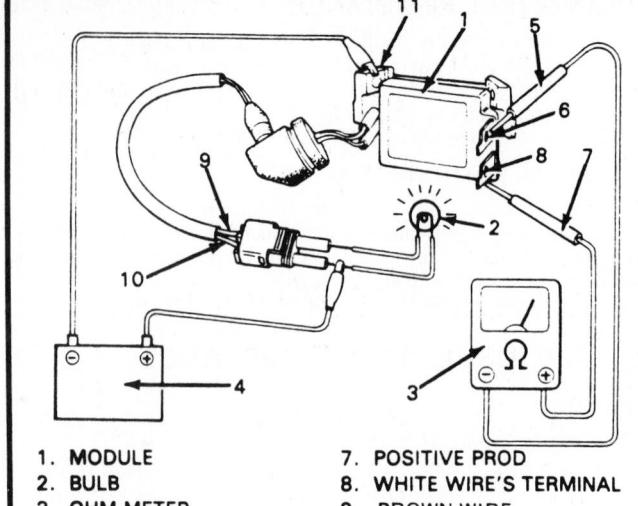

1. MODULE	7. POSITIVE PROD
2. BULB	8. WHITE WIRE'S TERMINAL
3. OHM METER	9. BROWN WIRE
4. BATTERY (12V)	10. WHITE/BLACK WIRE
5. NEGATIVE PROD	11. GROUND
6. RED WIRE'S TERMINAL	

Module test wiring schematic

4. Apply approximately 16 in. Hg. of vacuum and release it. Check to see that the pick-up base plate moves smoothly.
5. If the plate does not move smoothly, inspect the plate and vacuum advance unit. Repair or replace as required.

MODULE

Testing

1. Remove the dust cover from the module. Tag and disconnect the white and red wires from the module.
2. Connect a light bulb, an ohmmeter and a 12 volt battery to the module.
3. Set the ohmmeter to the 1–10 ohm range. Allow the ohmmeter negative probe to touch the red wire terminal of the module and the positive lead to touch the white wire terminal.
4. If the light bulb begins to light, the module is good. If not, replace the module. Repair or replace as required.

NOTE: Failure to connect the ohmmeter in the described manner can result in damage to the ohmmeter and/or module.

RELUCTOR AIR GAP

Testing

NOTE: The reluctor is also known as the "pole piece".

1. Using a non-magnetic feeler gauge, measure the air gap between the reluctor tooth and the pick-up coil.
2. The air gap should be 0.008–0.015 in.
3. If the air gap is out of specifications, adjust it by loosening two screws securing the pick-up coil.
4. Move the pick-up coil and adjust the gap to specifications.
5. After making the correct adjustment, tighten the two screws and recheck the air gap.

IGNITION COIL

Testing

1. Disconnect the negative battery cable and the coil primary/secondary leads.

2. Using an ohmmeter, measure the resistance between the positive and negative terminals.

3. The resistance reading should be 1.06–1.43 with the coil at room temperature.

4. Using an ohmmeter, measure the resistance between the positive coil terminal and the high voltage terminal.

5. The secondary resistance with the coil at room temperature should be 10.8–16.2 ohms.

PICK–UP COIL

Testing

1. Remove the dust cover from the module.

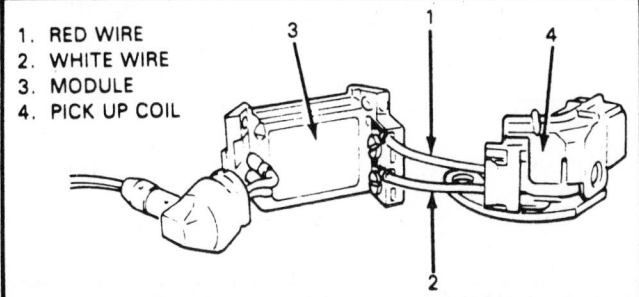

1. RED WIRE
2. WHITE WIRE
3. MODULE
4. PICK UP COIL

Proper connection of red and white wires between module and pick-up coil

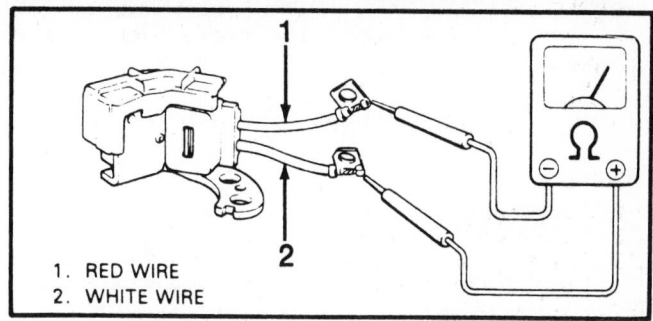

1. RED WIRE
2. WHITE WIRE

Testing pick-up coil

2. Disconnect the red and white wires from the module. Note where they were connected.

3. Connect an ohmmeter to the red and white wires and measure the resistance.

4. The pick-up coil resistance should be 130–190 ohms.

5. Reconnect the red and white wires in their proper positions on the module.

NOTE: Never connect the red and white wires in a reverse position. Damage to the pick-up coil and module may occur.

INDEX

AMC/JEEP THROTTLE BODY FUEL INJECTION (TBI) SYSTEM

Components and Operation

The Renix throttle body fuel injection is a "pulse time" system that uses a single solenoid-type injector to meter fuel into the throttle body above the throttle blade. Fuel is metered to the engine by an electronic control unit (ECU), which controls the amount of fuel delivery according to input from various engine sensors that monitor exhaust gas oxygen content, coolant temperature, manifold absolute pressure, crankshaft position and throttle position. These sensors provide an electronic signal by varying resistance within the sensor itself. By reading the difference in resistance, the ECU can determine engine operating conditions and calculate the correct air/fuel mixture, and ignition timing under varying engine loads and temperatures. In addition, the ECU controls idle speed, emission control and fuel pump operation, the upshift indicator lamp and the A/C compressor clutch.

Renix TBI fuel injection has two main subsystems; a fuel subsystem and a control subsystem. The fuel subsystem consists of an electric fuel pump (mounted in the fuel tank), a fuel filter, a pressure regulator and the fuel injector. The control subsystem consists of a manifold air/fuel mixture temperature sensor (MAT), a coolant temperature sensor (CTS), a manifold absolute pressure sensor (MAP), a knock sensor, an exhaust gas oxygen (O$_2$) sensor, an electronic control unit (ECU), a gear position indicator (automatic transmission only), a throttle position sensor and power steering pressure switch with a load swap relay. In addition to these sensors which send signals to the ECU, there are various devices which receive signals from the ECU to control different functions such as exhaust gas recirculation, idle speed control, air conditioner operation, etc.

Electronic Control Unit (ECU)

The electronic control unit (ECU) is a sealed microprocessor unit located above the accelerator pedal under the instrument panel or below the glove box, next to the fuse panel, and is the heart of the electronic engine control system. The throttle position sensor (or wide open throttle switch) is mounted on the throttle body assembly and provides the ECU with an input signal of up to 5 volts to indicate throttle position. At minimum throttle opening (idle speed), a signal input of approximately one volt is transmitted to the ECU. As the throttle opening increases, the signal voltage to the ECU increases.

Manifold Absolute Pressure (MAP) Sensor

The manifold absolute pressure (MAP) sensor is attached to the plenum chamber near the hood latch. It reacts to absolute pressure in the intake manifold and provides an input voltage to the ECU. Manifold pressure is used to supply mixture density information and ambient barometric pressure information that is necessary for computing the air/fuel mixture. A vacuum line from the throttle body attaches to the MAP sensor to provide its input pressure. The manifold air temperature (MAT) sensor is located in the intake manifold and measures the air/fuel mixture temperature to allow the ECU to compensate for air density changes during high temperature operation.

Coolant Temperature Sensor

The coolant temperature sensor (CTS) is located in the intake manifold coolant jacket and provides an engine coolant temperature signal to the ECU. The ECU uses the coolant temperature signal to enrich the air fuel mixture when the engine is cold, compensate for fuel condensation in the intake manifold, control engine warm-up speed, increase the ignition advance when the engine is cold and to cut off the EGR system when the engine is cold.

Knock Sensor

The knock sensor is located in the cylinder head and provides a signal to the ECU to detect detonation (spark knock) during engine operation. When detonation occurs, the ECU retards the ignition timing to elimintate it. On automatic transmission models, a transmission gear position indicator provides an input to the ECU to determine whether the transaxle is in a driving gear and not in Park or Neutral.

Pressure Sensing Switch

A pressure sensing switch is included in the power steering system to increase the idle speed during periods of high pump load and low engine rpm. Input signals from the pressure switch to the ECU are routed through the A/C request and A/C select input circuits. When pump pressure exceeds 250–300 psi, the switch contacts close and transmit an input signal to the ECU. The ECU raises engine idle speed immediately after receiving the pressure switch input signal.

Load Swap Relay

The load swap relay is used on models with air conditioning and power steering. The relay works in conjunction with the power steering pressure switch to disengage the A/C compressor clutch. If the A/C compressor clutch is engaged when the power steering pressure switch contacts close, the input signal from the switch to the ECU also activates the load swap relay. The relay contacts then open, cutting off electrical feed to the compressor clutch. The clutch remains disengaged until the pressure switch contacts open and the engine returns to normal idle speed. The load swap relay does not reengage the compressor clutch immediately. The relay has a timer that delays energizing the clutch for 0.5 seconds to permit smooth engagement.

System Power Relay

The system power relay is located on the right strut tower and is initially energized when starting the engine. The relay remains energized for 3–5 seconds after the engine stops to enable the ECU to extend the idle speed actuator (ISA) for the next start-up. The fuel pump control relay is also located on the front of the right strut tower. Battery voltage is applied to the fuel pump control relay through the ignition switch and is energized when a ground is provided by the ECU. In this manner, the ECU controls fuel pump operation.

EGR/Canister Purge Solenoid

The vacuum for both the EGR valve and the vapor canister purge function is controlled by the EGR/Canister Purge Solenoid. When energized by the ECU, it cuts off vacuum to the EGR valve and canister. The solenoid is energized during engine warm-up, closed throttle (idle), wide open throttle (WOT) and rapid acceleration/deceleraton. If the solenoid wire connector is disconnected, the EGR valve and canister purge function will be operational at all times.

Idle Speed Actuator

The idle speed actuator (ISA) is mounted on the throttle body and controls idle speed and engine deceleration throttle stop angle. The actuator changes the throttle stop angle by being a movable throttle stop. The ECU controls the ISA motor by providing the appropriate voltage outputs to produce the idle speed or throttle stop angle required for the particular engine operating condition. There is no idle speed adjustment.

Speed Sensor

The speed sensor is attached to the flywheel drive plate housing. This sensor detects the flywheel/drive plate teeth as they pass during engine operation and provides engine speed and crankshaft angle information to the ECU. The flywheel/drive plate has a large trigger tooth and notch located every 90 degrees and 12 smaller teeth before each top dead center (TDC) position. When a small tooth and notch pass the magnet core in the sensor, the concentration and then collapse of the magnetic flux induces a small voltage spike into the sensor pickup coil winding. The higher voltage spike indicates to the ECU that a piston will be at TDC position 12 teeth later. The ignition timing for the cylinder is either advanced or retarded as necessary by the ECU according to the sensor inputs.

DIAGNOSIS AND TESTING

Before performing any system tests, first determine that the problem is not being caused by a component other than the fuel injection system, such as spark plugs, distributor, ignition timing, etc. Also make sure that no air is entering the intake and exhaust system above the catalytic converter and that fuel is reaching the injector under normal pressure.

NOTE: The diagnostic connectors D1 and D2 are located on the dash panel in the engine compartment.

Oxygen Sensor Heating Element

The oxygen sensor heating element can be tested by connecting an ohmmeter test leads to terminals **A** and **B** of the sensor connector. Resistance should be between 5–7 ohms. Replace the sensor if an infinite reading is obtained.

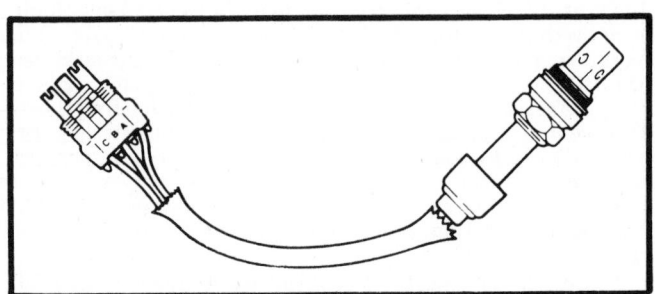

Oxygen sensor showing connector with terminal identification

DIAGNOSTIC CONNECTOR – THROTTLE BODY INJECTION

DASH PANEL

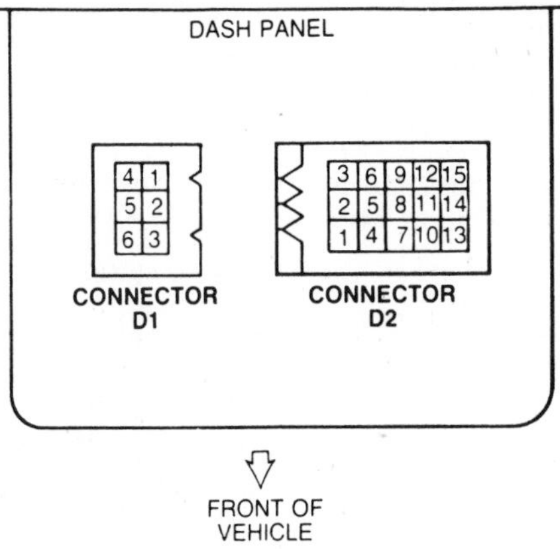

Connector D1
1. Tach Input
2. Ignition
3. Ground
4. Start Solenoid
5. Battery
6. Fuel Pump

CONNECTOR D1

4	1
5	2
6	3

CONNECTOR D2

3	6	9	12	15
2	5	8	11	14
1	4	7	10	13

Connector D2
1. Shift Lamp
2. Power Latch Relay
3. Park Neutral
4. Power Latched Relay (B+)
5. Air Conditioning Clutch Relay
6. Wide-Open Throttle Switch
7. Ground
8. Air Mixture Temperature
9. M.P.A. (Ignition Output)
10. EGR/Canister Purge Solenoid
11. Idle Speed Control Motor Forward
12. Coolant Temperature Sensor
13. Closed Throttle Switch
14. Idle Speed Control Motor Reverse
15. Not Used

FRONT OF VEHICLE

ECU CONNECTOR – THROTTLE BODY INJECTION

| 1 | 2 | 3 | 4 | 5 | 6 | 7 | 8 | 9 | 10 | 11 | 12 | 13 | 14 | 15 | 16 | 17 | 18 |
| 19 | 20 | 21 | 22 | 23 | 24 | 25 | 26 | 27 | 28 | 29 | 30 | 31 | 32 | 33 | 34 | 35 |

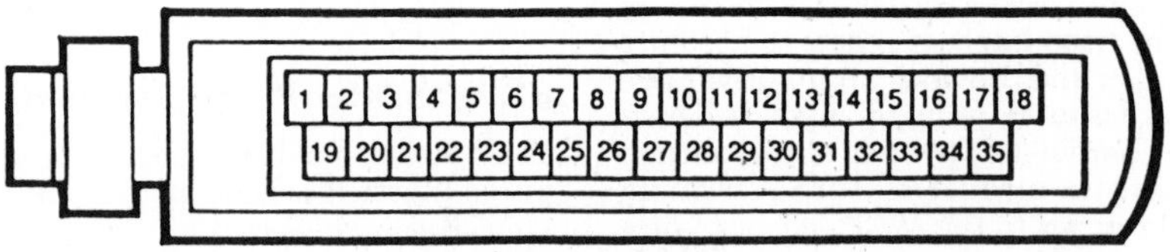

1. Ground
2. Ground
3. Ignition Switch
4. Battery
5. EGR Valve/Canister Purge
6. Fuel Pump Relay
7. System Power Relay (Latch Relay)
8. WOT Switch
9. Not Used
10. System Ground
11. Speed Sensor
12. Park/Neutral Switch (A/T Only)
13. Throttle Position Sensor (TPS) Ground

14. Manifold Air/Fuel Temperature Sensor
15. Coolant Temperature Sensor
16. Manifold Absolute Pressure (Supply Voltage)
17. Manifold Absolute Pressure (Ground)
18. Shift Lamp
19. System Power (B+)
20. Not Used
21. Injector
22. A/C Compressor Clutch
23. ISA Motor Retract (Reverse)
24. ISA Motor Extend (Forward)
25. Closed Throttle (Idle) Switch

26. Not Used
27. Ignition (Output)
28. Speed Sensor
29. Start
30. A/C Select
31. Throttle Position Sensor (TPS)
32. Sensor Ground
33. Manifold Absolute Pressure (Output Voltage)
34. A/C Temperature Control (Request)
35. Oxygen Sensor

Connector and pin number locations

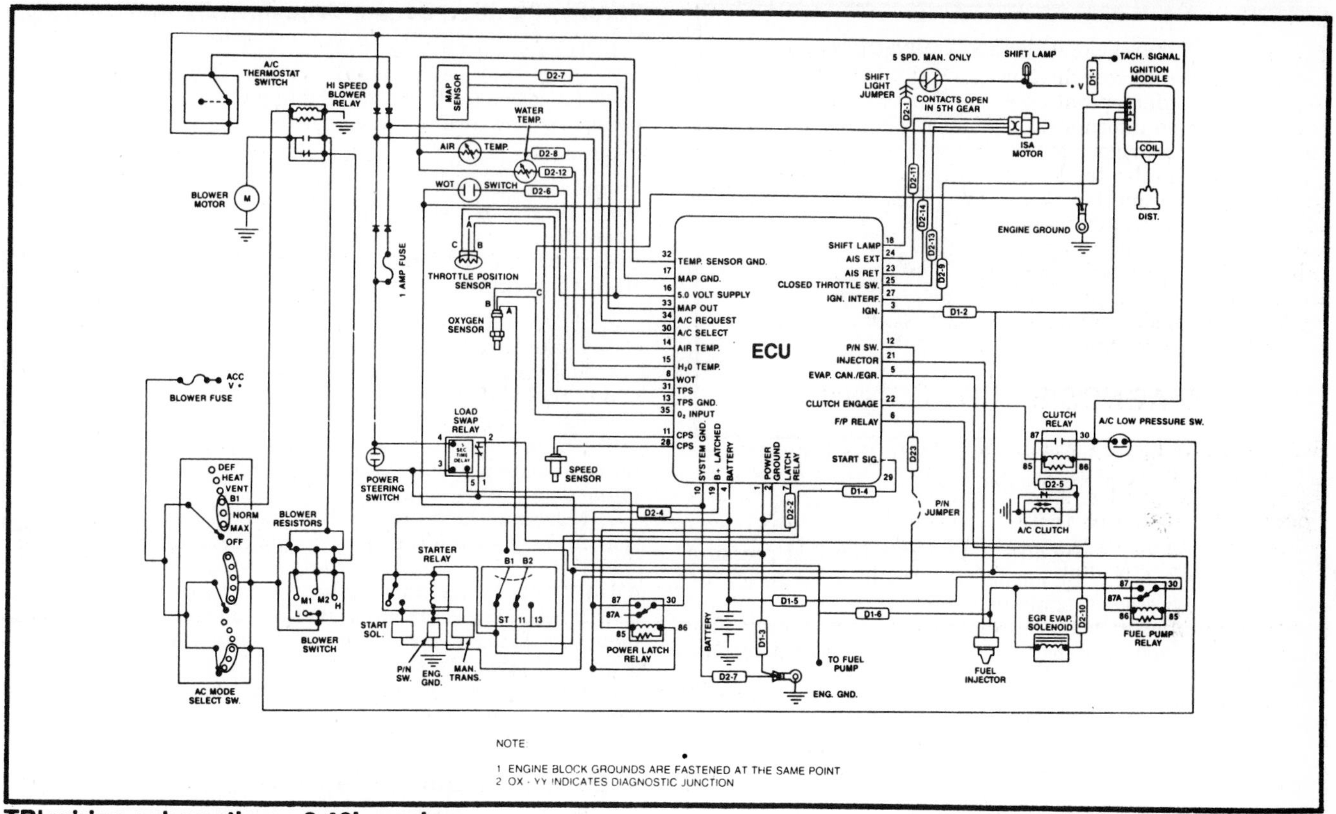

TBI wiring schematic on 2.46L engine

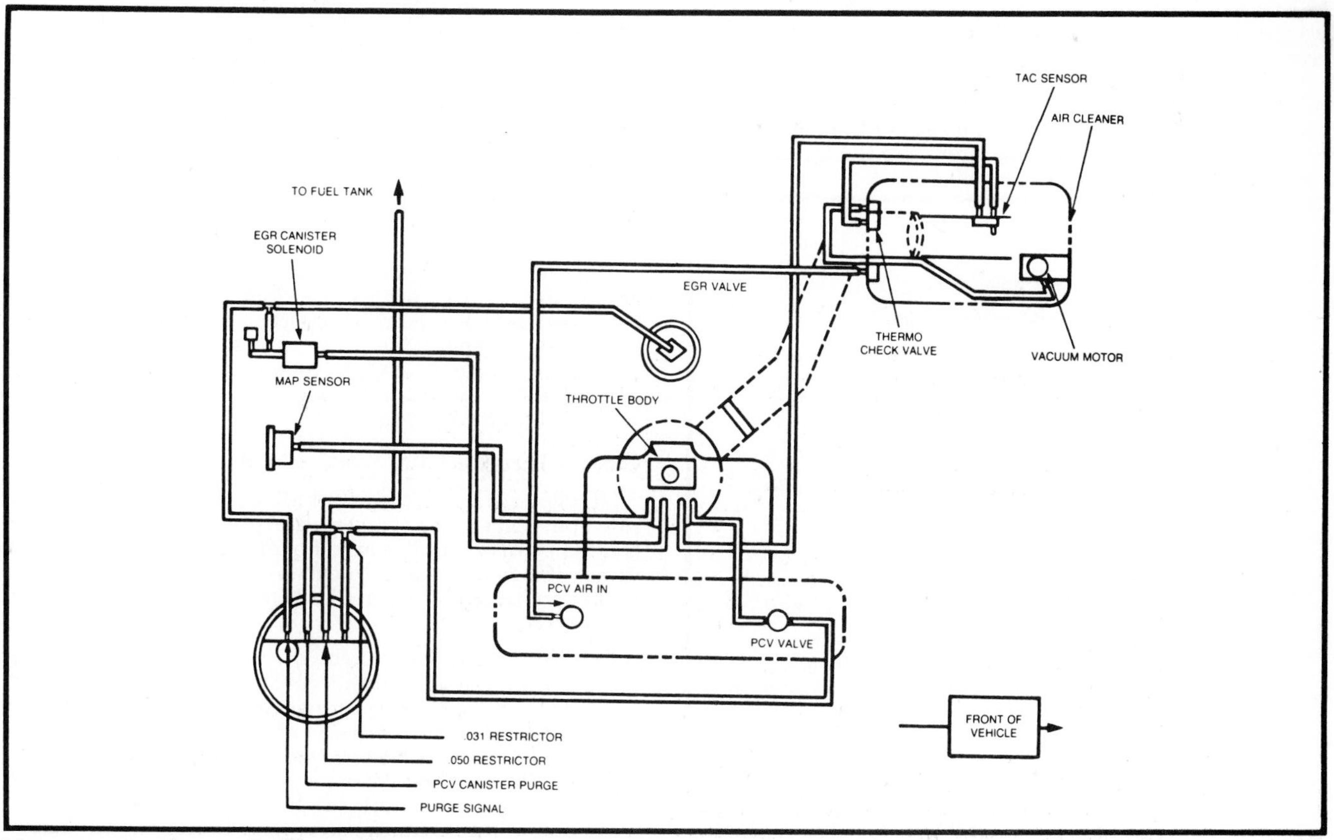

Vacuum circuits on 2.46L engine

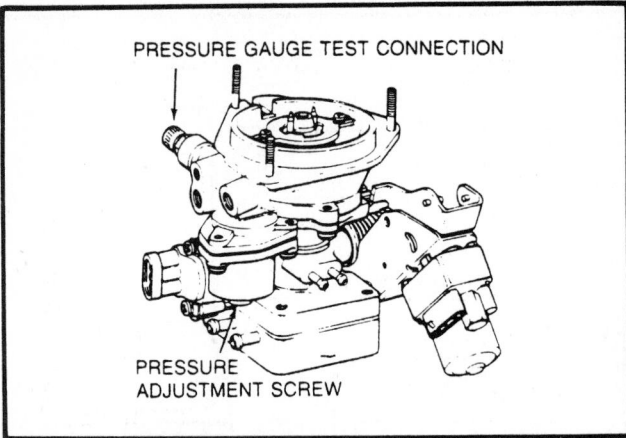

Typical throttle body assembly. Note the adjustment and test points for fuel pressure

Fuel Pump Pressure Test

Fuel pump operating pressure is 14.5 psi. The fuel pressure regulator is adjustable by means of a torx head screw on the bottom of the pressure regulator.

1. Remove the air cleaner assembly. Remove the screw plug on the throttle body and install a fuel pressure test fitting (No. 8983 501 572).
2. Connect an accurate pressure test gauge to the test fitting.
3. Connect a tachometer to diagnostic connector terminals D1-1 and D1-3, then start the engine and accelerate it to 2000 rpm.
4. Read the fuel pressure on the gauge. If necessary, turn the adjustment screw on the bottom of the fuel pressure regulator to obtain 14.5 psi (1 bar) of fuel pressure. Turning the screw inward increases the pressure and turning the screw outward decreases the pressure.
5. Once all adjustments are complete, install a lead seal ball to cover the regulator adjusting screw. Turn the ignition OFF, then disconnect the tachometer and remove the fuel pressure gauge. Install the original plug screw into the throttle body, then install the air cleaner assembly.

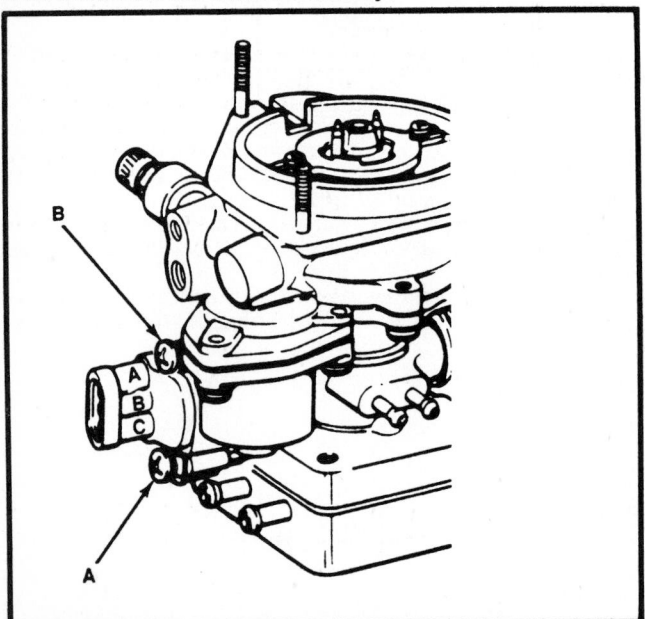

Throttle position sensor showing connetor pin identification and mounting screws (A & B)

Throttle Position Sensor Adjustment

1. Turn the ignition key ON.
2. Check the sensor input voltage. Connect the negative lead of a voltmeter to sensor terminal **B**, then connect the voltmeter positive lead to sensor terminal **C**.

NOTE: Do not disconnect the sensor wire harness connector. Insert the voltmeter test leads through the back of the wire harness connector to make contact with the sensor terminals during testing. It may be necessary to remove the throttle body from the intake manifold to gain access to the wire harness connector.

3. Move and hold the throttle plate in the wide open position. Make sure the throttle linkage contacts the stop.
4. Note the voltmeter reading. Input voltage at terminals **B** and **C** should be 5.0 volts at wide open throttle.
5. Return the throttle plate to the closed position.
6. Check the sensor output voltage. Disconnect the voltmeter positive lead from sensor terminal **C** and connect it to terminal **A**.
7. Move and hold the throttle plate in the wide open position. Make sure the throttle linkage contacts the stop.
8. Note the voltmeter reading. Output voltage should be 4.6–4.7 volts. Adjust the output voltage by loosening the lower sensor retaining screw and pivoting the sensor in the adjustment slot for coarse adjustment. Loosen the other retaining screw and pivot the sensor for fine adjustment.
9. Remove the voltmeter and return the throttle plate to the closed position. Make sure the sensor retaining screws are tightened securely.

Wide-Open Throttle (WOT) Switch Test

1. Disconnect the harness terminal connector from the WOT switch.
2. Test the on-off operation of the switch with a digital voltohmmeter while operating the switch manually.
3. The resistance should be infinite when the throttle is closed and a low resistance should be indicated when the throttle is wide open. Test the switch operation several times and replace the WOT switch is defective.
4. Connect the wire harness connector. With the ignition switch ON, test the WOT switch voltage at the diagnostic connector terminals D2-6 (+) and D2-7 (–). The voltage should be zero at the WOT position and greater than 2 volts if not at the WOT position.
5. If the voltage is always zero, test for a short circuit to ground in the wire harness or switch, or an open circuit between terminal 8 of the ECU connector and the switch connector. Repair or replace the wire harness as necessary.
6. If the voltage is always greater than 2 volts, test for an open circuit in the wire or connector between the switch and ground. Repair as necessary.

Closed Throttle (Idle) Switch Test

NOTE: It is important that all testing be done with the idle speed actuator (ISA) motor plunger in the fully extended position, as it would be after normal engine shutdown. If it is necessary to extend the ISA motor plunger to test the switch, an ISA motor failure can be suspected.

1. With the ignition switch ON, test the switch voltage at the diagnostic connector terminals D2-13 (+) and D2-7 (–). The voltage should be close to zero at closed throttle and greater than 2 volts when off the closed throttle position.
2. If the voltage is always zero, test for a short circuit to ground in the wire harness or switch, or for an open circuit between ECU connector terminal 25 and the switch.
3. If the voltage is always more than 2 volts, test for an open circuit in the wire harness between the ECU and the switch

Idle switch showing ground (A) and closed throttle switch (B) connectors

connector, and between the switch connector and ground. Repair or replace the wire harness as necessary.

Manifold Absolute Pressure (MAP) Sensor Test

1. Inspect the MAP sensor vacuum hose connections at the throttle body and sensor and repair as necessary.

2. Test the MAP sensor output voltage at the MAP sensor connector terminal **B** as marked on the sensor body, with the ignition switch ON (engine OFF). The output voltage should be 4–5 volts.

3. Test ECU terminal 33 for the same voltage described above to verify the wire harness condition. Repair as necessary.

4. Test the MAP sensor supply voltage at the sensor connector terminal **C** with the ignition ON. It should be 4.5–5.5 volts. This voltage should also be at terminal 16 of the ECU wire harness connector. Repair or replace the wire harness as necessary. Test the ECU with Diagnostic Tester MS 1700, if necessary.

5. Test the MAP sensor ground circuit at sensor connector terminal **A** and ECU connector terminal 17. Repair the wire harness, if necessary.

6. Test the MAP sensor ground circuit at the ECU connector between terminal 17 and terminal 2 with an ohmmeter. If the ohmmeter indicates an open circuit, inspect for a defective sensor ground connection on the flywheel/drive plate housing near the starter motor. If the ground connection is good, replace the ECU. If terminal 17 has a short circuit to 12 volts, correct this condition before replacing the ECU.

Manifold Air Temperature (MAT) Sensor and Coolant Temperature Sensor (CTS) Test

These two sensors are tested in the same manner and should yield the same results. The only difference is the pin number of the test points. Disconnect the wire harness connector from the sensor, then test the resistance with a digital volt-ohmmeter. The resistance should be less than 1000 ohms with the engine warm. Refer to the chart to check the temperature-to-resistance values and replace the sensor if the resistance is not within the specified range. If the MAT sensor is being tested, check the resistance between ECU harness connector termi-

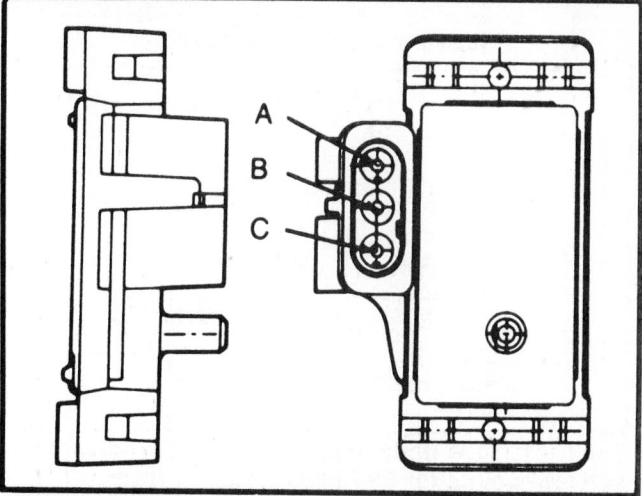

MAP sensor showing ground (A), output voltage (B) and 5 volt reference (C) connectors

nals 14 and 32 and the sensor connector terminals. If the CTS sensor is being tested, check the resistance between ECU harness connector terminals 15 and 32 and the sensor terminals. In either case, repair the wire harness if an open circuit is indicated.

DIAGNOSTIC CHARTS

There are six different diagnostic test flowcharts that are used to thoroughly evaluate the Renix fuel injection system:

1. The ignition switch OFF test checks the system power for the ECU memory keep-alive voltage.

2. The ignition switch ON power test checks the system power function and the fuel pump power function.

3. The ignition switch ON input test checks the closed throttle (idle) switch and circuit, the wide-open throttle (WOT) switch and circuit, the MAP sensor and circuit, the Park/Neutral switch and circuit (automatic trans only), the coolant temperature sensor and circuit and the manifold air/fuel temperature sensor and circuit (cold).

4. The system operational test checks the engine startup circuit, the fuel injector and circuit, the closed loop air/fuel mixture function, coolant temperature sensor function, manifold air/fuel temperature sensor function, knock sensor and closed loop ignition retard/advance function, EGR and canister purge solenoid function, idle speed control function and the A/C control function.

5. The basic engine test indicates possible failures within other engine related components (non fuel injection system components).

6. The manual transmission upshift test checks the upshift indicator lamp function on manual transmission equipped vehicles only.

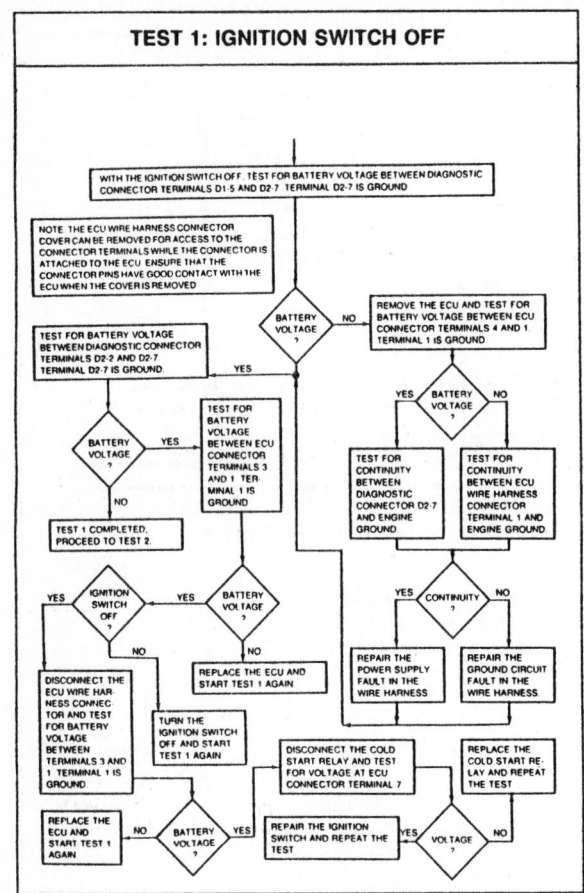

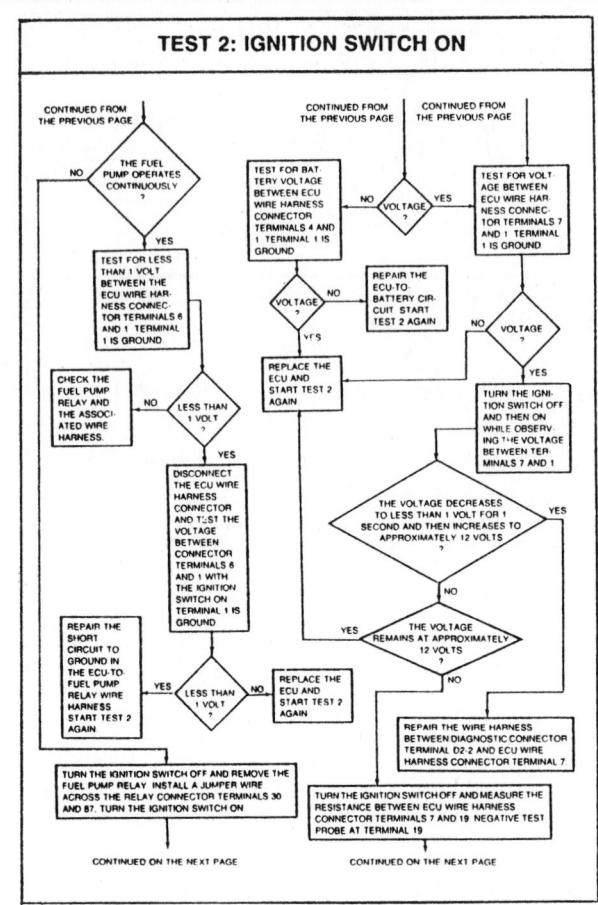

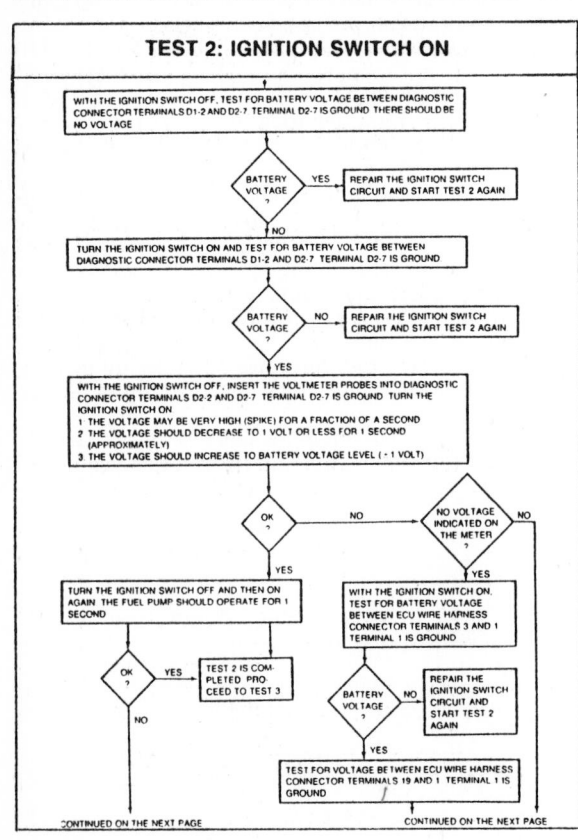

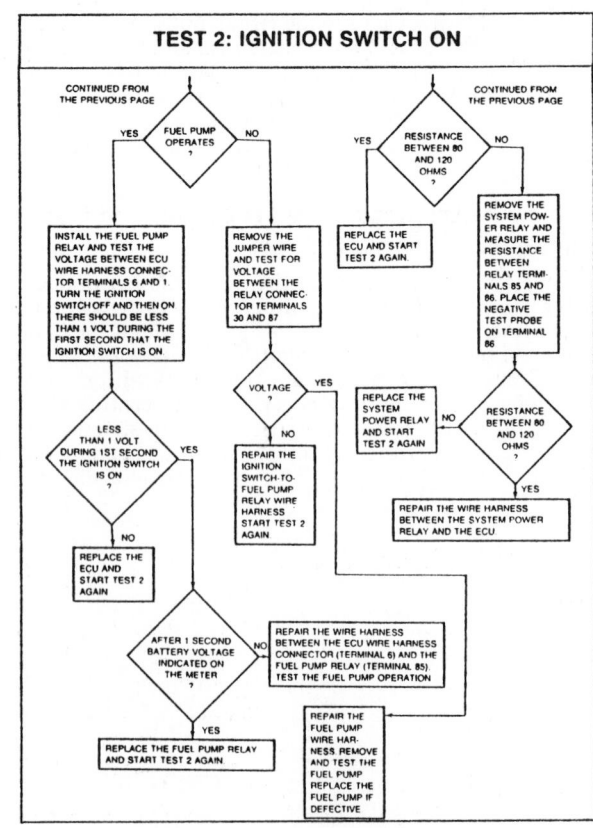

TEST 3: CLOSED THROTTLE SWITCH, WOT SWITCH AND SENSOR TEST

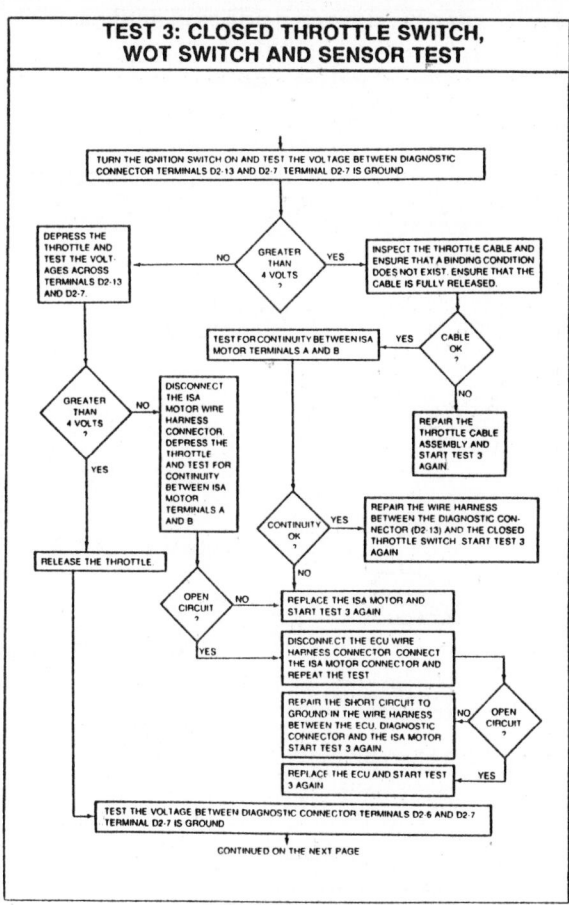

TEST 3: CLOSED THROTTLE SWITCH, WOT SWITCH AND SENSOR TEST

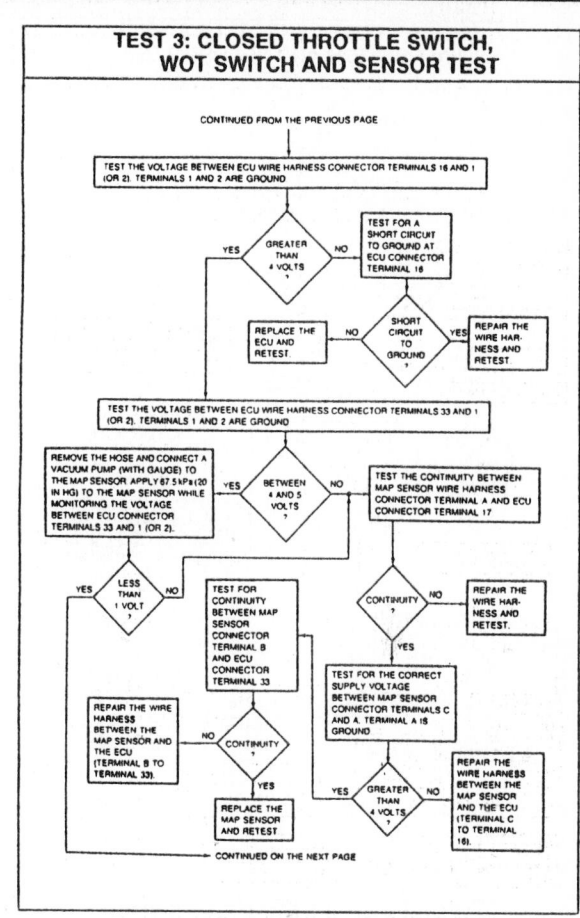

TEST 3: CLOSED THROTTLE SWITCH, WOT SWITCH AND SENSOR TEST

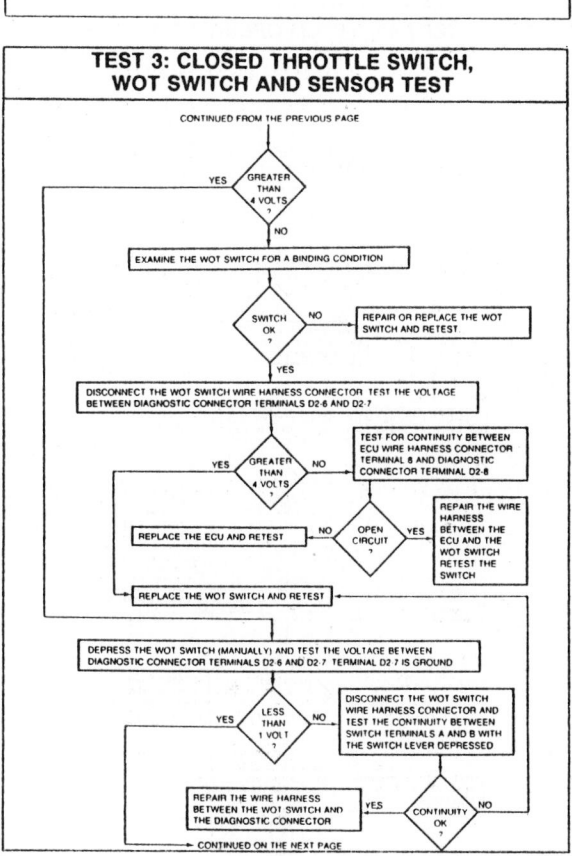

TEST 3: CLOSED THROTTLE SWITCH, WOT SWITCH AND SENSOR TEST

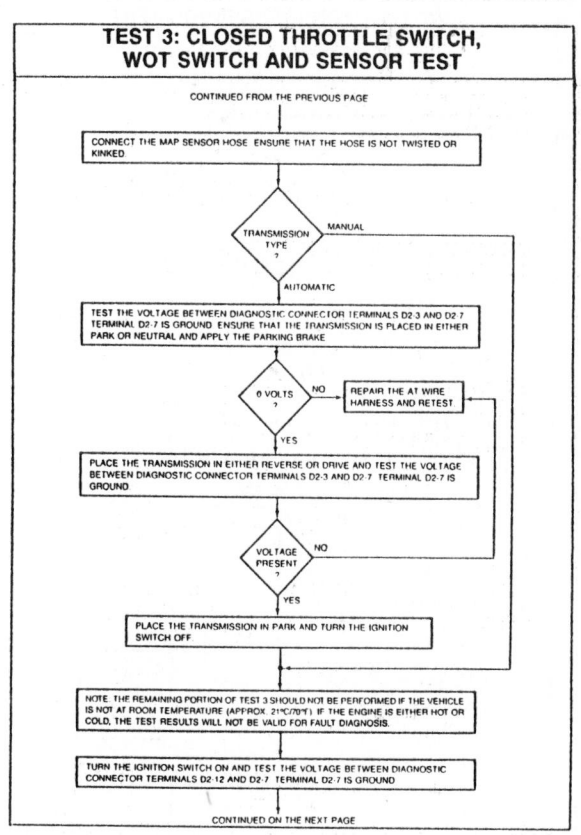

TEST 3: CLOSED THROTTLE SWITCH, WOT SWITCH AND SENSOR TEST

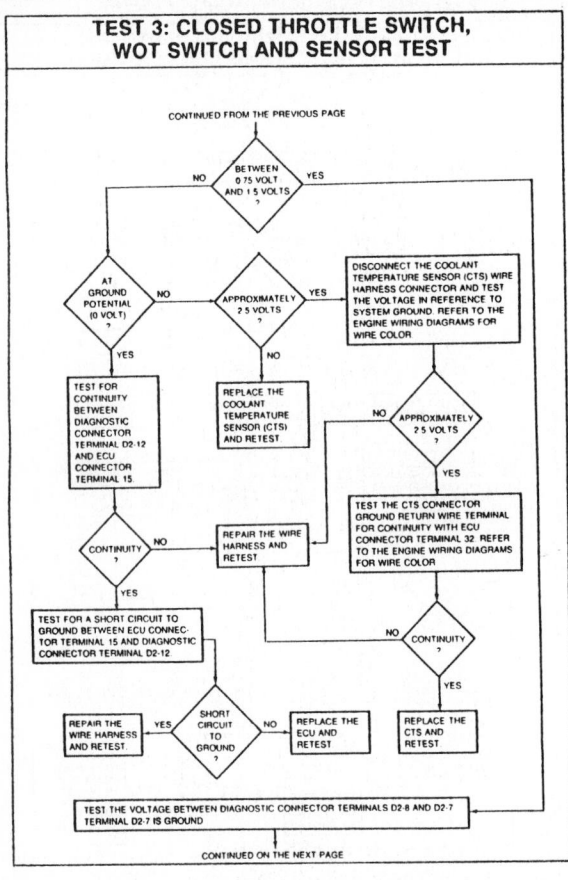

TEST 3A: THROTTLE POSITION SENSOR TEST

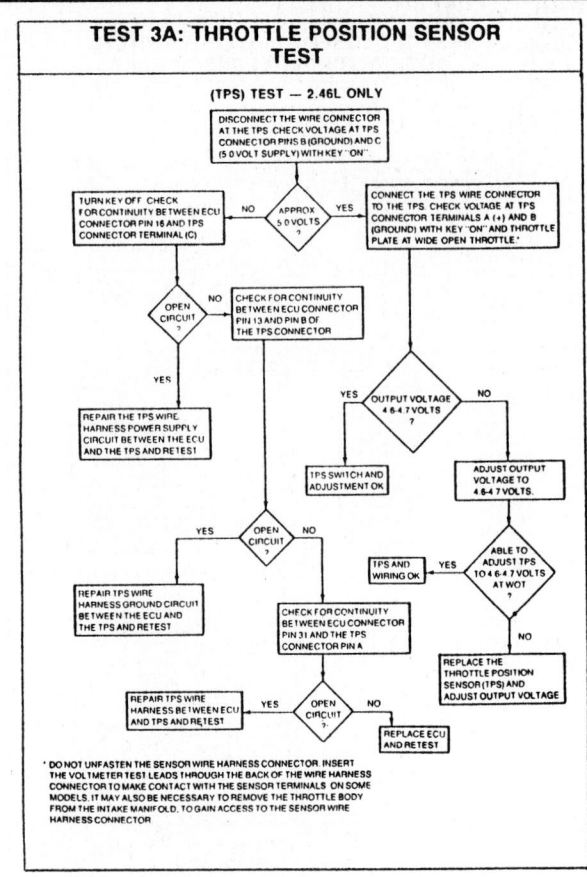

TEST 3: CLOSED THROTTLE SWITCH, WOT SWITCH AND SENSOR TEST

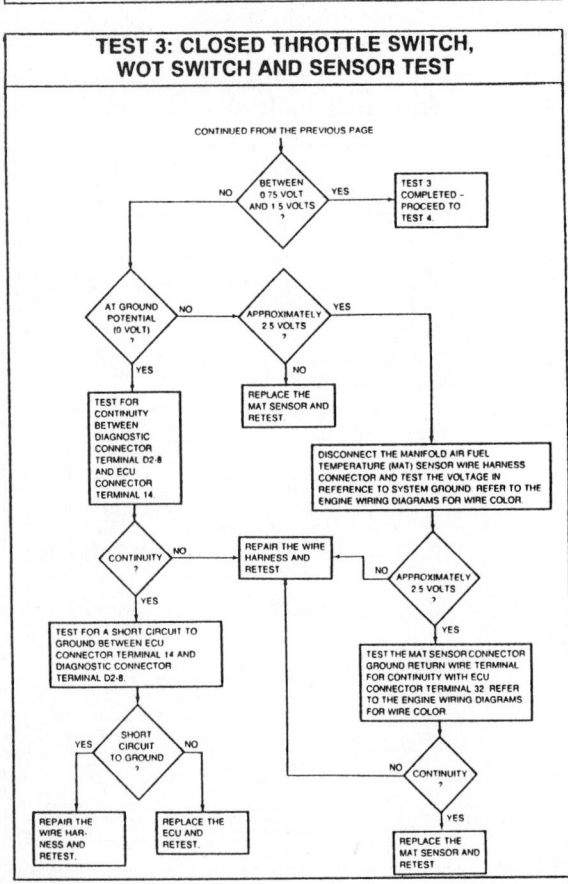

TEST 4: SYSTEM OPERATIONAL TEST

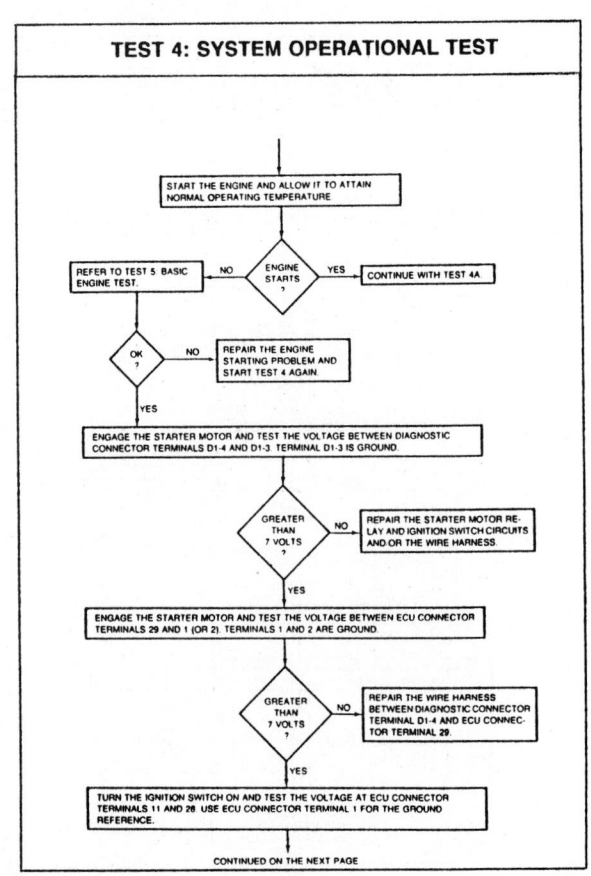

TEST 4: SYSTEM OPERATIONAL TEST

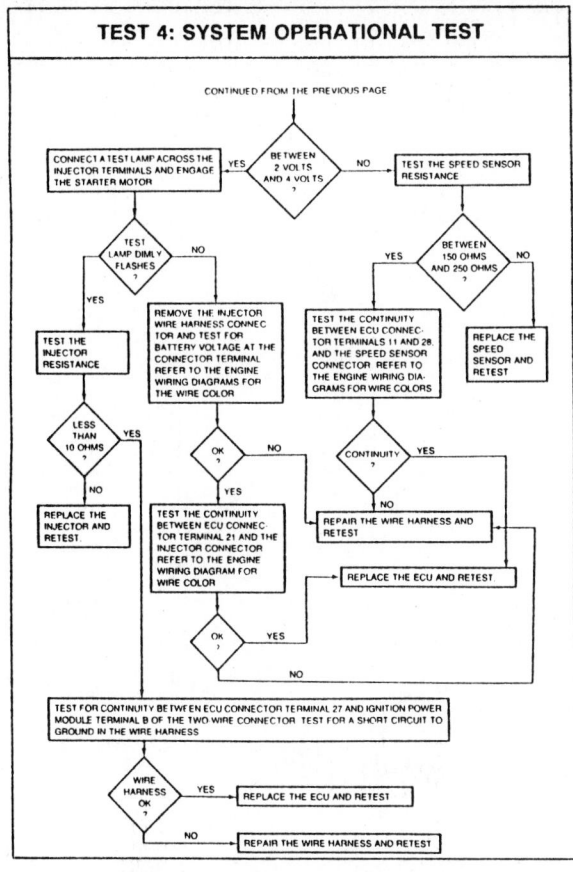

TEST 4A: SYSTEM OPERATIONAL TEST

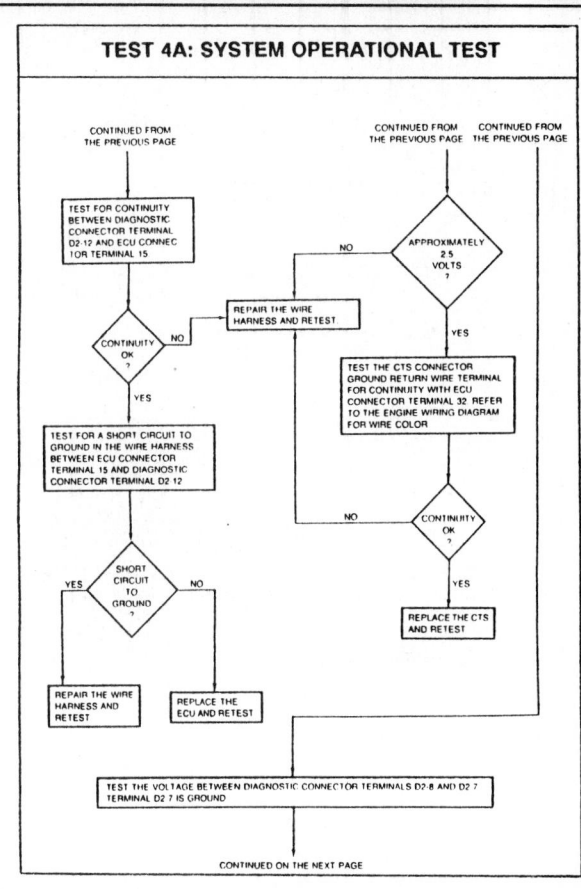

TEST 4A: SYSTEM OPERATIONAL TEST

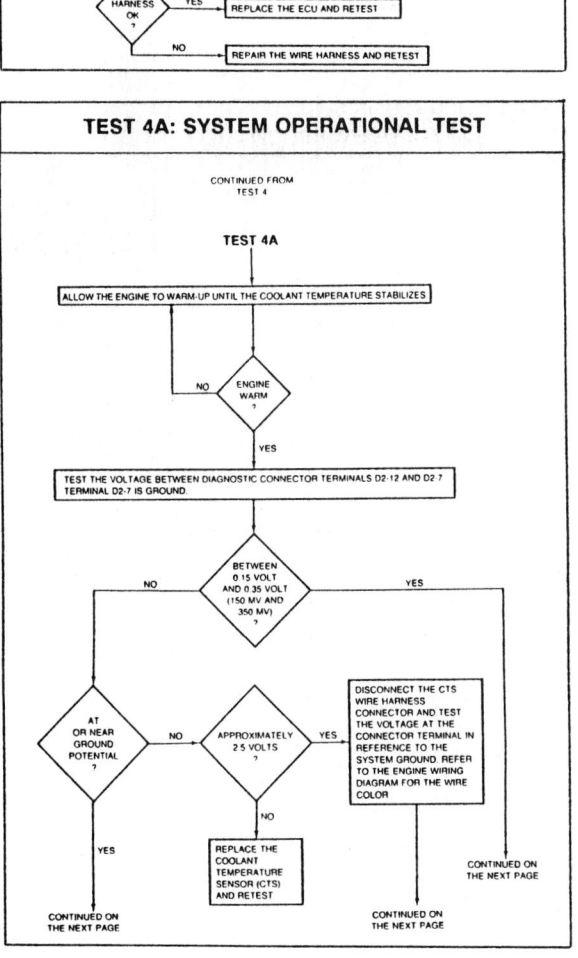

TEST 4A: SYSTEM OPERATIONAL TEST

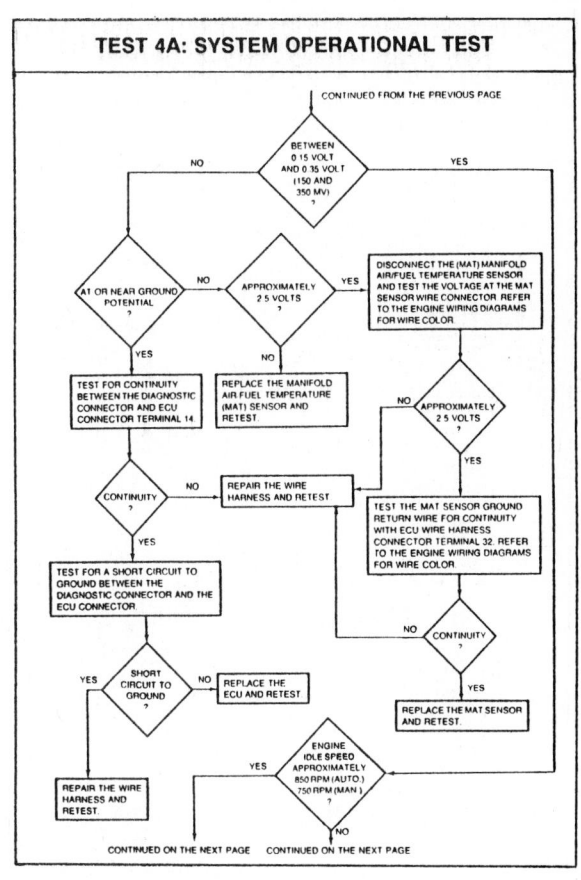

TEST 4A: SYSTEM OPERATIONAL TEST

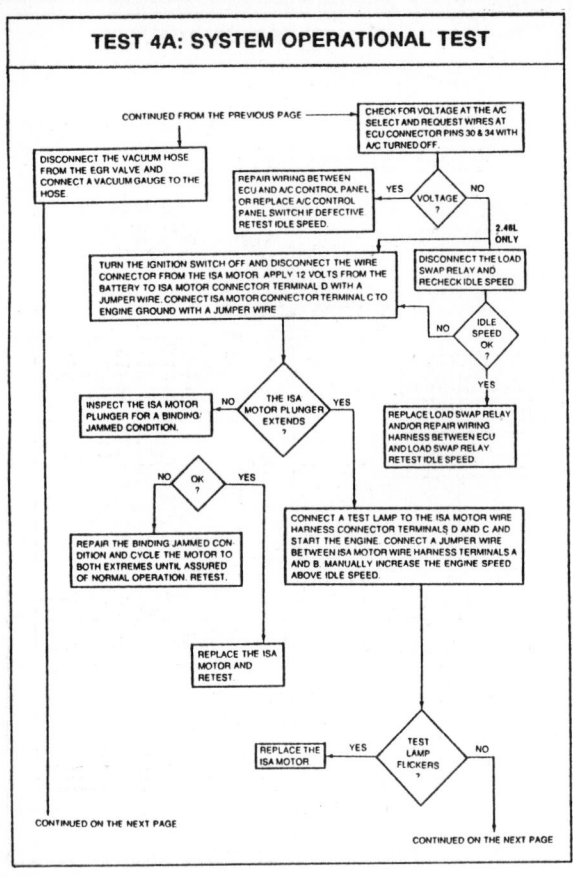

TEST 4A: SYSTEM OPERATIONAL TEST

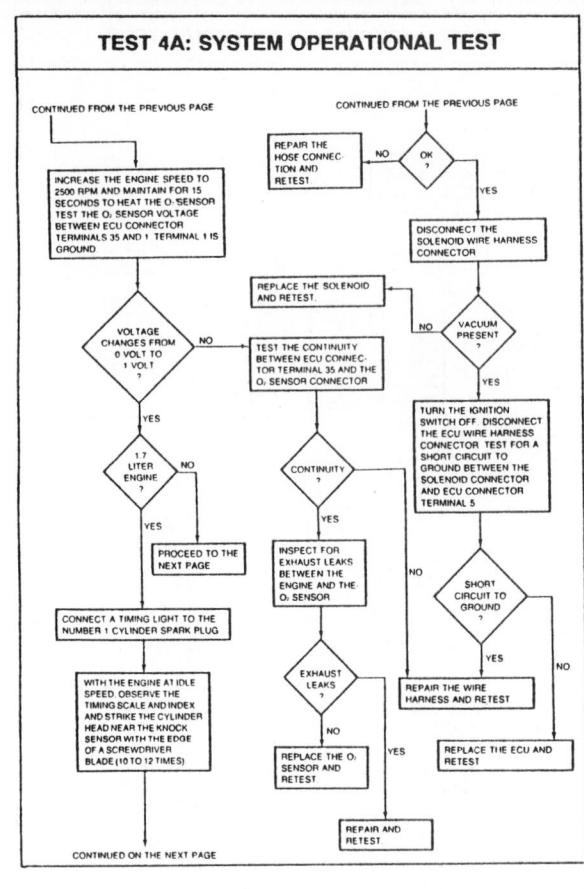

TEST 4A: SYSTEM OPERATIONAL TEST

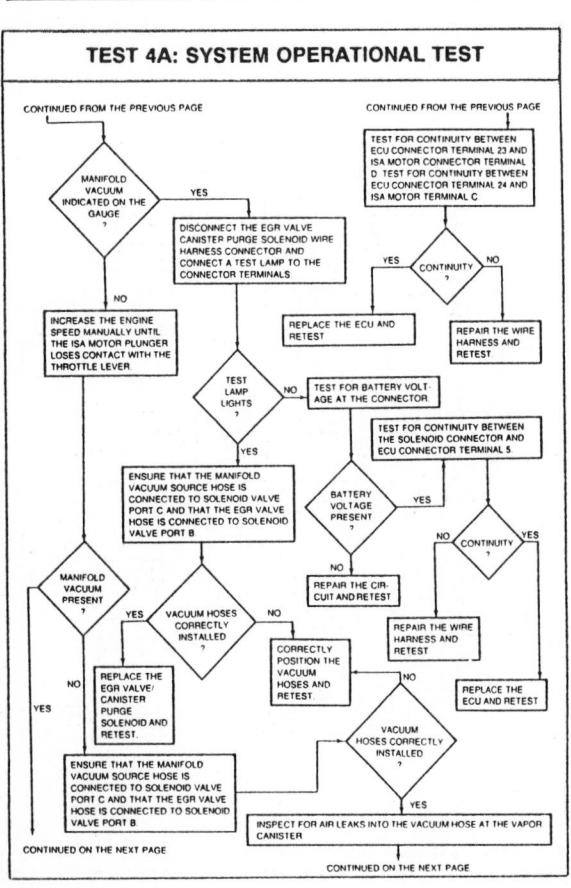

TEST 4A: SYSTEM OPERATIONAL TEST

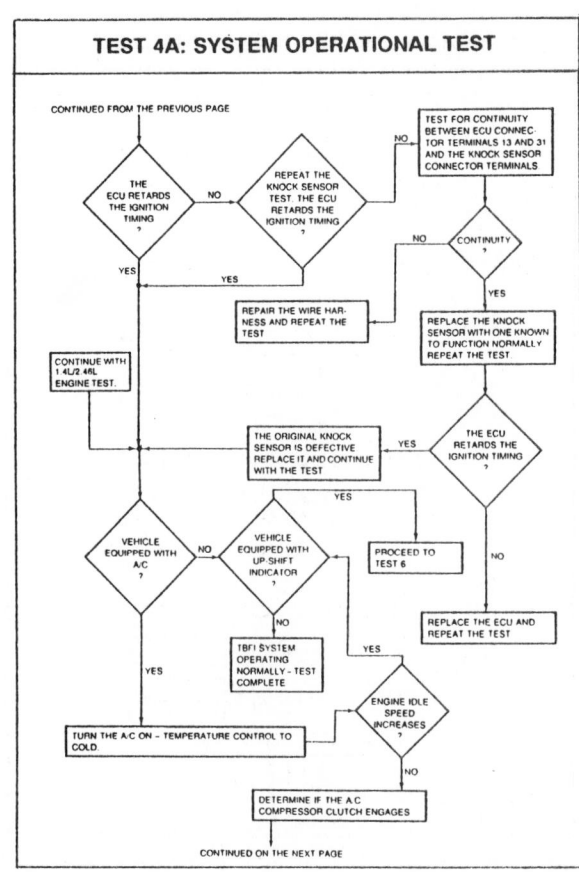

TEST 4A: SYSTEM OPERATIONAL TEST

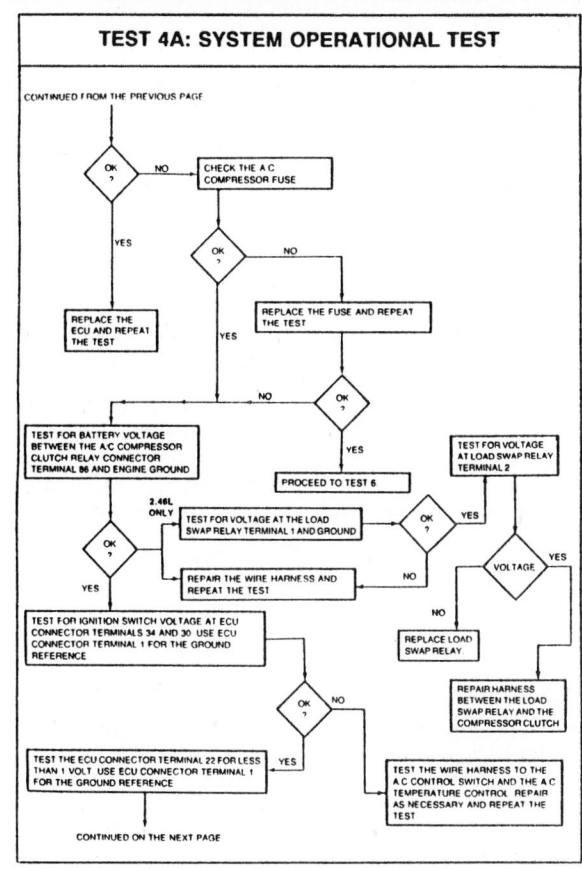

TEST 6: M/T UPSHIFT TEST

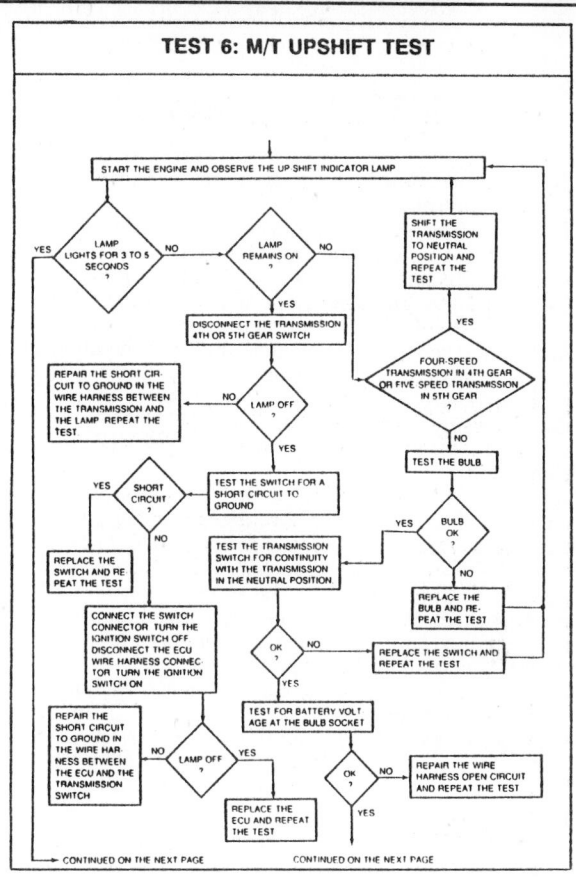

TEST 4A: SYSTEM OPERATIONAL TEST

TEST 5: BASIC ENGINE TEST

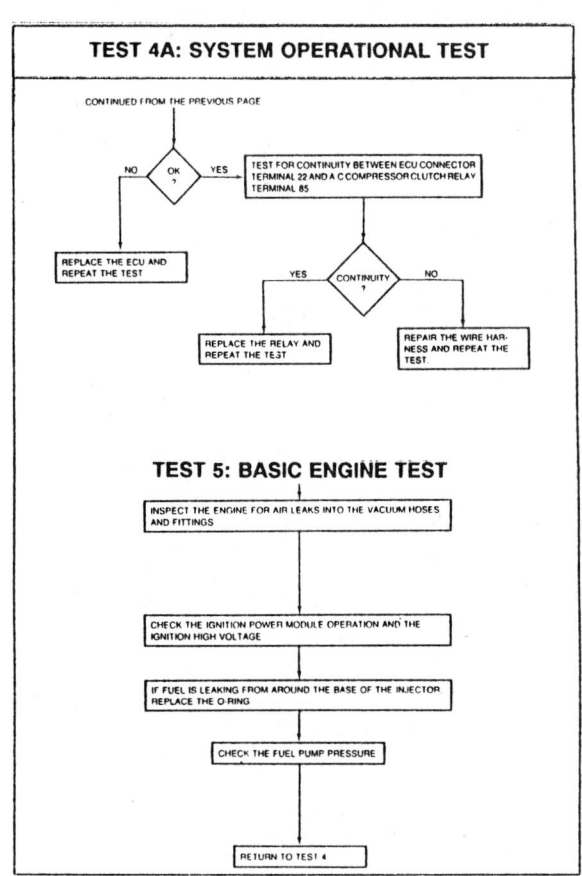

TEST 6: M/T UPSHIFT TEST

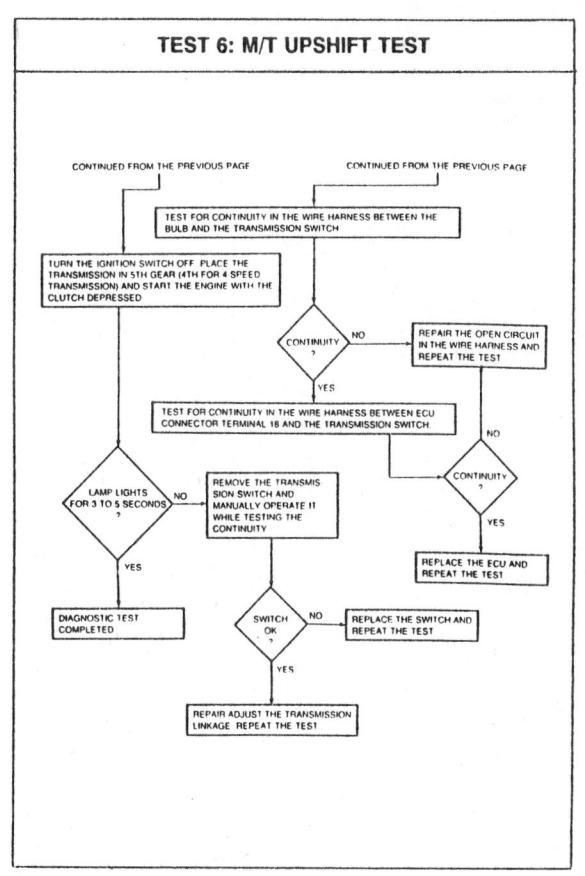

AMC/JEEP MULTI-POINT FUEL INJECTION SYSTEM

The Renix multi-point fuel injection system is controlled by a digital microprocessor called the electronic control unit, or ECU. The ECU receives information from various input sensors. Based on this information, the ECU is programmed to provide a precise amount of fuel and the correct ignition timing to meet existing engine speed and load conditions.

The ECU also calculates ignition timing and operates the ignition power module. The ignition timing is modified by the ECU to meet any engine operating condition. Information such as air temperature, engine coolant temperature, engine speed, absolute pressure in the intake manifold, or the presense of spark knock is used by the ECU when calculating the correct ignition timing.

The ECU controls the engine by receiving input signals from the manifold absolute pressure (MAP) sensor, the engine speed sensor, knock sensor, exhaust oxygen sensor, throttle position switch, coolant temperature sensor, air temperature sensor and battery voltage. Based on the information received from the input sensors, the ECU then sends control (output) signals to the fuel pump relay, fuel injectors, idle speed regulator, ignition power module and the EGR valve.

As input signals to the ECU change, the ECU adjusts its signals to the output devices. For example, the ECU must calculate a different injector pulse width and ignition timing for idle than it calculates for wide open throttle (WOT). There are eight different modes of operation that determine how and why the ECU responds to various input signals. The modes are:

1. Key ON mode
2. Crank mode
3. Warmup mode
4. Idle mode—operating temperature
5. Cruise mode—operating temperature
6. Deceleration mode
7. Wide open throttle (WOT) mode
8. Key OFF mode

Modes of operation exist as two different types. Crank, Warmup, Deceleration and WOT modes are Open Loop modes, while the Idle and Cruise modes at operating temperature are Closed Loop modes. In the Open Loop modes, the ECU receives input signals and responds only according to the preset ECU programming. In the Closed Loop modes, the ECU also receives a signal from the exhaust gas oxygen sensor which indicates whether or not the calculated injector pulse width results in the ideal air/fuel mixture of 14.7:1. By monitoring the exhaust oxygen content with the O_2 sensor, the ECU can fine tune the injector pulse width and achieve the optimum fuel mixture for all operating conditions.

System Operation

Key ON Mode

When the ignition switch is turned to the ON position (engine OFF), the ECU responds to inputs from the MAP sensor, air temperature sensor, coolant temperature sensor, throttle position switch and the battery voltage signal. The ignition switch supplies voltage to the B+ (fuel system power) relay and the ECU provides a ground path for the B+ relay to be energized. The ECU receives and stores a barometric pressure value from the MAP sensor in preparation for engine starting.

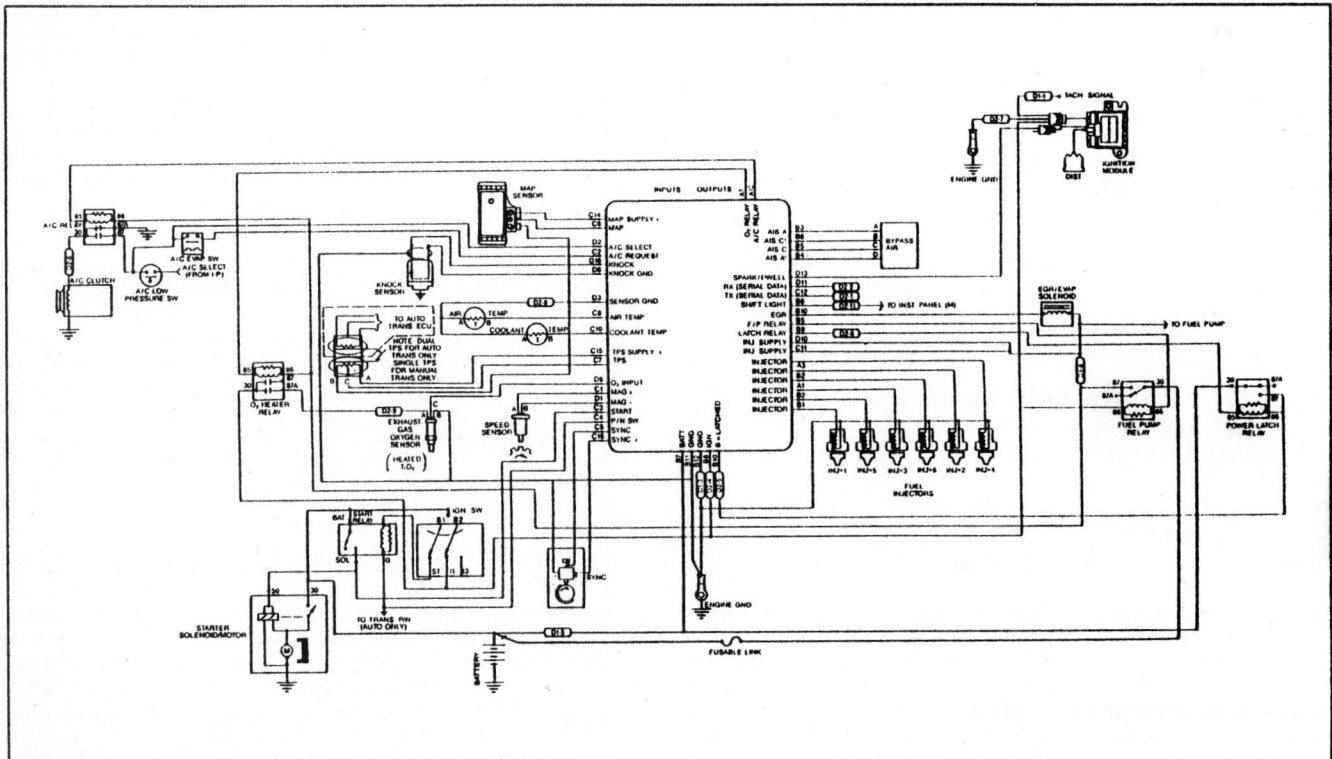

Multiport Fuel Injection wiring diagram on 4.0L engine

Voltage is supplied to the fuel pump relay from the B+ relay and the ECU provides a ground path for 1–3 seconds. During this period, the fuel pump relay is energized and the fuel pump pressurizes the fuel supply system. Voltage is supplied to the injectors via the fuel pump relay, but the ECU does not provide a ground path for the injector circuits. The idle regulating valve opens fully.

Crank Mode

During engine cranking, the ECU responds to inputs from the MAP sensor, engine speed sensor, air temperature sensor, throttle position switch, starter relay (automatic transmission only) and the battery voltage signal. The ballast resistor is by-passed during engine cranking. The ECU provides a ground path for the fuel pump relay and the fuel pump is energized.

The ECU restricts EGR and canister purge operation by energizing the EGR/canister purge solenoid. Voltage is supplied to the injectors and the ECU controls the injector pulse width (ON time) by controlling the length of time that the injector circuit ground path remains completed. Based on signals received from the engine speed sensor, the ECU determines the correct ignition timing and triggers the ignition coil.

All fuel injectors are energized simultaneously, once per engine revolution, except during cold start conditions when the injectors are energized twice per engine revolution. This extra fuel delivery continues for a few seconds after the engine starts. To eliminate the possibility of the engine flooding, the ECU limits the number of times that the injectors can be energized twice per engine revolution. This limit is calculated solely on the basis of engine coolant temperature. If the coolant temperature is extremely low, the ECU increases the number of times that the double injection sequence is possible during engine start.

When the ignition switch is turned to the START position, a crank signal is sent to the ECU. If the vehicle is equipped with an automatic transmission, the starter relay prevents the signal from reaching the ECU if the transmission is not in Park or Neutral.

Warmup Mode

During engine warmup, the ECU responds to input signals from the MAP sensor, engine speed sensor, air temperature sensor, coolant temperature sensor, throttle position switch, gear indicator (automatic transmission only), air conditioning select signal (if equipped) and the knock sensor. The ECU restricts EGR and canister purge operation by energizing the EGR/canister purge solenoid.

Voltage is supplied to the injectors and the ECU controls the injector pulse width by controlling the length of time that the injector circuit ground path remains closed. All fuel injectors are energized simultaneously once per engine revolution. The ECU also establishes the correct idle speed by providing the ground to the idle regulating valve. If necessary, the idle speed is also adjusted to compensate for increased engine load during the A/C compressor operation, if equipped.

In addition to the above, the ECU determines the correct ignition timing and triggers the ignition power module. The shift indicator light is actuated if the engine speed and load conditions warrant a change to a higher gear.

Idle Mode

During engine idle, the ECU responds to input signals from the MAP sensor, engine speed sensor, air temperature sensor, coolant temperature sensor, throttle position switch, battery voltage signal, oxygen sensor, knock sensor and air conditioning select signal (if equipped). The ECU restricts EGR and canister purge operation by energizing the EGR/canister purge solenoid.

Voltage is supplied to the injectors and the ECU controls the

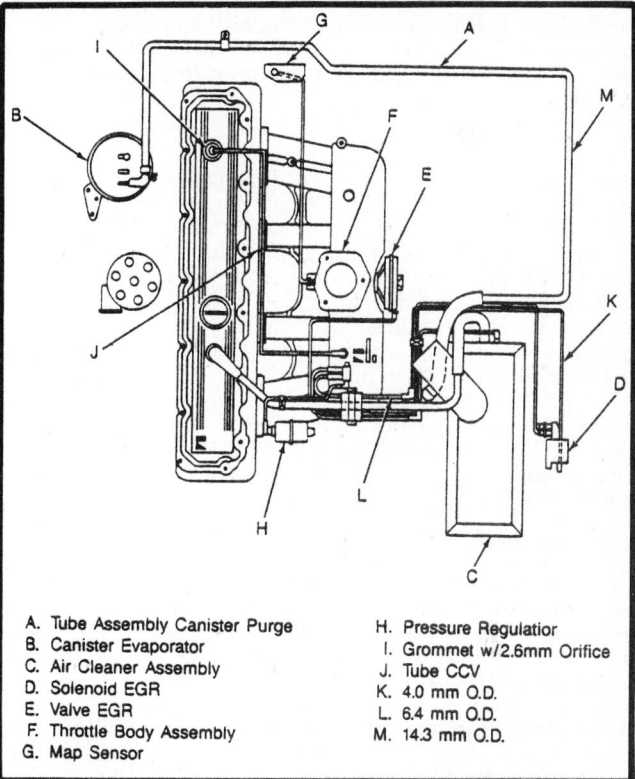

A. Tube Assembly Canister Purge
B. Canister Evaporator
C. Air Cleaner Assembly
D. Solenoid EGR
E. Valve EGR
F. Throttle Body Assembly
G. Map Sensor
H. Pressure Regulatior
I. Grommet w/2.6mm Orifice
J. Tube CCV
K. 4.0 mm O.D.
L. 6.4 mm O.D.
M. 14.3 mm O.D.

Multiport Fuel Injection vacuum circuits on 4.0L engine

injector pulse width by controlling the length of time that the injector circuit ground path remains closed. All fuel injectors are energized simultaneously once per engine revolution. The ECU also establishes the correct idle speed by providing the ground to the idle regulating valve. If necessary, the idle speed is also adjusted to compensate for increased engine load during the A/C compressor operation, if equipped.

In addition to the above, the ECU determines the correct ignition timing and triggers the ignition power module. By monitoring the oxygen sensor signal, the ECU can fine tune the fuel delivery by adjusting the injector pulse width (ON time), until the ideal 14.7:1 air/fuel mixture is achieved.

Cruise Mode

When the vehicle is moving at road speed, the ECU responds to input signals from the MAP sensor, engine speed sensor, air temperature sensor, coolant temperature sensor, throttle position switch, battery voltage signal, oxygen sensor, knock sensor and air contitioner select signal (if equipped). The ECU opens the ground path for the EGR/canister purge solenoid, allowing the EGR transducer and the evaporative vapor canister to receive manifold vacuum. Fuel delivery and timing control are as described under the Idle Mode.

Wide Open Throttle (WOT) Mode

During WOT operation, the ECU responds to input signals from the MAP sensor, engine speed sensor, air temperature sensor, coolant temperature sensor, battery voltage signal and the knock sensor. The barometric pressure is also updated in the computer. The ECU restricts EGR and canister purge operation by energizing the EGR/canister purge solenoid. The ECU controls fuel injector pulse width by controlling the time that the injector circuit ground remains closed.

The ECU also determines the correct ignition timing and triggers the ignition power module. If spark knock is detected, the ECU retards the ignition timing at the cylinder which is knocking until the knock is eliminated, with ignition timing progressively returning to its value prior to when the knock was detected.

Deceleration Mode

During engine deceleration, the ECU responds to input signals from the MAP sensor, engine speed sensor, air temperature sensor, coolant temperature sensor, throttle position switch and air conditioner select signal (if equipped). The ECU restricts EGR and canister purge operation by energizing the EGR/canister purge solenoid. The ECU controls fuel injector pulse width by controlling the time that the injector circuit ground remains closed, and determines correct ignition timing and triggers the ignition power module.

If the ECU receives a closed throttle signal and engine speed is over 1500 rpm, the ECU determines that the engine is in a hard deceleration condition and responds by completely shutting off fuel injection. Injection is resumed when the engine speed decreases to 1500 rpm.

Key OFF Mode

When the ignition switch is moved to the OFF position, the ECU breaks the injector ground circuit and all fuel injection stops. The ignition power module is deactivated and the ECU opens the ground circuit for the B+ relay, cutting off the voltage supply to the fuel injection circuitry.

SPECIAL OPERATING CONDITIONS

Full Load Altitude Correction

When the pressure in the intake manifold is around atmospheric pressure, the computer will modify the mixture fed to the engine to pass gradually from the minimum specific consumption point to the power point. The atmospheric pressure is stored in the ECU. It is measured each time the key is turned to the ON position and brought up to date each time the throttle is fully opened or each time the pressure noted is higher than atmospheric pressure. At higher altitude, the air is less dense and therefore has less oxygen per unit volume. To maintain a constant manifold pressure, the fuel mixture must be leaner at low load and when idling. The atmospheric pressure reading provides a basis for altitude correction.

Operation In Defect Mode

The injection system can remain operative when some of its sensors are defective. The ECU diagnoses its sensors by comparing their values to preset limits. If the value sensed does not lie between these limits, the sensor is treated as defective and the system operates in a defect mode.

If the coolant sensor is inoperative, air temperature is used in determining injection pulse width and ignition timing values. The air temperature value is then increased as a function of engine rpm to simulate coolant sensor output. If the oxygen sensor fails, open loop operation is forced.

System Components
ECU INPUTS

Coolant Temperature Sensor (CTS)

The coolant temperature sensor is located on the left side of the cylinder block, just below the exhaust manifold. The CTS provides an engine coolant temperature input to the ECU, which will then enrich the air/fuel mixture delivered by the injectors when the engine coolant is cold. Based on the CTS signal, the ECU will also control engine warmup idle speed, increase ignition advance and inhibit EGR operation when the coolant is cold.

Manifold Air Temperature (MAT) Sensor

The manifold air temperature sensor is located in the intake manifold. The MAT sensor reacts to the temperature of the air in the intake manifold and provides an input to the ECU to allow it to compensate for air density changes during high temperature operation.

Manifold Absolute Pressure (MAP) Sensor

The manifold absolute pressure sensor is mounted on the dash panel behind the engine. The MAP sensor reacts to absolute pressure in the intake manifold and provides an input voltage to the ECU. Manifold pressure is used to supply mixture density information and ambient barometric pressure information to the ECU. A hose from the intake manifold provides the input pressure.

Oxygen (O₂) Sensor

The oxygens sensor is located in the exhaust manifold. The voltage output from this sensor, which varies with the oxygen content in the exhaust gas, is supplied to the ECU. The O_2 sensor is equipped with a heating element that keeps the sensor at the proper operating temperature during all engine operating modes. Maintaining correct sensor temperature at all times allows the system to enter closed loop operation sooner and to remain in closed loop during periods of extended idle. Electrical feed to the O_2 sensor is through the ignition switch.

Knock Sensor

The knock sensor is located on the lower left side of the cylinder block, just above the oil pan. The knock sensor provides and input to the ECU that indicates detonation (knock) during engine operation. When detonation occurs, the ECU retards the ignition timing advance to eliminate the detonation at the applicable cylinder(s).

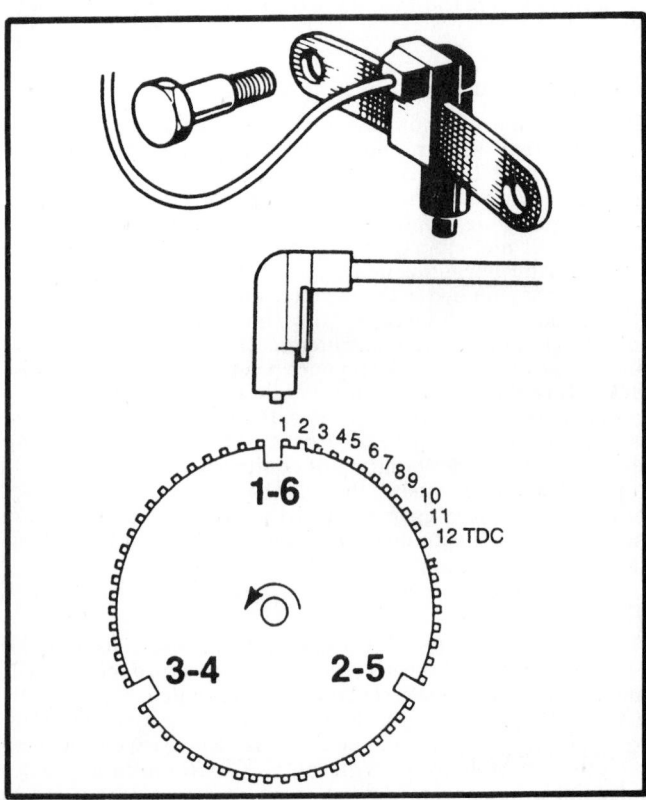

Speed sensor and flywheel teeth. See text for details

Speed Sensor

The speed sensor is secured by special shouldered bolts to the flywheel/drive plate housing. It is preset in its mounting at the factory and is non-adjustable in the field. The speed sensor senses TDC and engine speed by detecting the flywheel teeth as they pass during engine operation.

The flylwheel has a large trigger tooth and notch located 12 small teeth before each top dead center (TDC) position. When a small tooth and notch pass the magnet core in the sensor, the concentration and then collapse of the magnetic flux induces a small voltage spike into the sensor pickup coil winding. These small voltage spikes enable the ECU to count the teeth as they pass the sensor.

When a large trigger tooth and notch pass the magnet core in the sensor, the increased concentration/collapse of the magnetic flux induces a higher voltage spike into the pickup coil winding. This higher voltage spike indicates to the ECU that a piston will soon be at the TDC position 12 teeth later. The ignition timing for the cylinder is either advanced or retarded as necessary by the ECU according to the sensor inputs.

Starter Motor Relay

The engine starter motor relay provides an input to the ECU that indicates the starter motor is engaged.

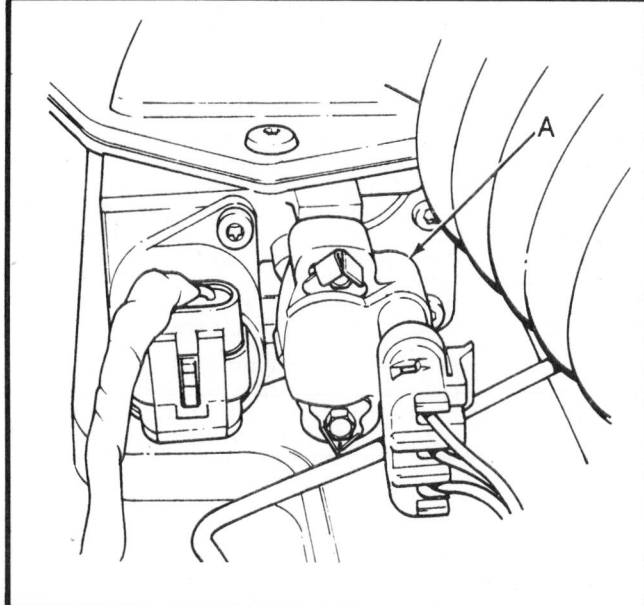

Throttle position switch (A) used on manual transmission models

Throttle Position Sensor (TPS)

The throttle position sensor is mounted on the throttle plate assembly and provides the ECU with an input signal of up to 5 volts to indicate throttle position. At minimum throttle opening (idle speed), a signal input of approximately 1 volt is transmitted to the ECU. As the throttle opening increases, voltage increases to a maximum of approximately 5 volts at the wide open throttle position.

A dual TPS is used on models equipped with automatic transmission. This dual TPS not only provides the ECU with input voltages, but also supplies the automatic transmission TCU with an input of throttle position.

Battery Voltage

The battery voltage input to the ECU is monitored so that the injector is energized for the proper amount of time. As the bat-

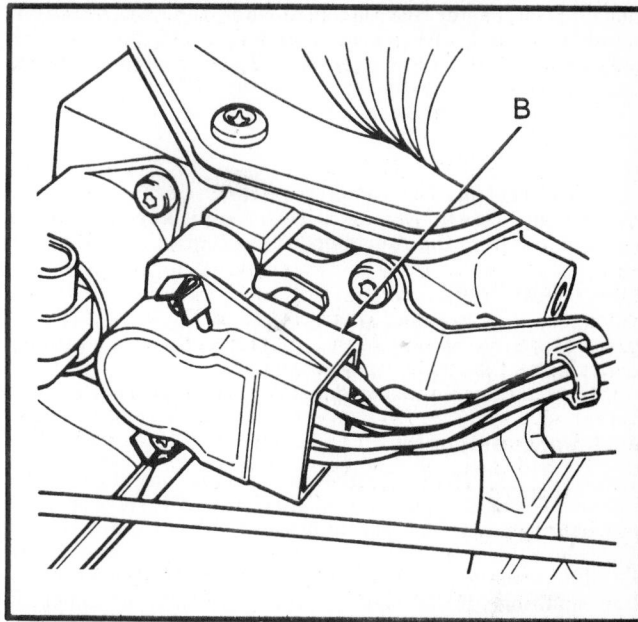

Throttle position switch (B) used on automatic transmission models

tery voltage input to the ECU varies, as during engine cranking, the ECU varies the injector pulse width to compensate.

In addition to the above inputs, the ECU also receives signals from the Park/Neutral switch on automatic transmission models; an A/C input signal to tell the ECU when the compressor is engaged so it can raise the idle speed to compensate for the load; and a sync pulse (stator) signal generated within the distributor to properly synchronize injector opening with intake valve closing.

ECU OUTPUTS
Oxygen Sensor Heater Relay

The oxygen sensor heater relay is normally closed, supplying voltage to the O_2 sensor heater under warmup and idle condi-

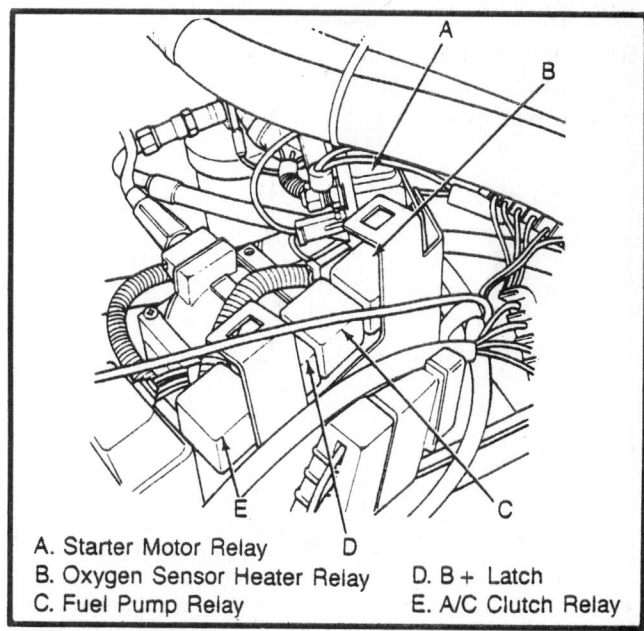

A. Starter Motor Relay
B. Oxygen Sensor Heater Relay
C. Fuel Pump Relay
D. B + Latch
E. A/C Clutch Relay

Relay locations on multiport fuel injection models

tions. The O_2 heater relay is controlled by the ECU. When the speed sensor and MAP sensor reach a predetermined input, it tells the ECU that the O_2 sensor will stay heated by the exhaust gas under those conditions, and the ECU can open the O_2 sensor heater relay and cut off the voltage supply to the heater.

A/C Clutch Relay

The ECU controls the compressor clutch through the A/C clutch relay. This allows the ECU to receive a request for air conditioning from the A/C temperature control thermostat.

Fuel Pump Relay

The fuel pump relay is located on the right inner fender panel. Battery voltage is supplied to the relay from the ignition switch and is energized when a ground is provided by the ECU. When energized, voltage is supplied to the fuel pump.

EGR Valve Solenoid

The vacuum for the EGR valve operation is controlled by this solenoid. When energized by the ECU, the EGR valve solenoid prevents vacuum from reaching the EGR valve diaphragm. The solenoid is energized during engine warmup, closed throttle (idle), wide open throttle and rapid acceleration/deceleration conditions. If the solenoid wire connector is disconnected, the EGR valve will be operative at all times and cause driveability problems.

Upshift Indicator Lamp

The indicator lamp is normally illuminated when the ignition switch is turned to the ON position and goes out when the engine is started. The indicator will be illuminated during engine operation according to engine speed and load conditions. A switch located on the transmission prevents the lamp from being illuminated when the transmission is shifted into its highest gear. The ECU will turn off the upshift indicator if the gear change is not performed within 3–5 seconds.

Ignition Control Module

Based on inputs, the ECU triggers the ignition coil to fire via the ignition control module. In this manner, the ECU can control spark timing according to engine operating conditions as reported by the various engine sensors.

Fuel Injectors

The fuel injectors are located in the intake manifold. The injectors are electronically and exclusively controlled by the ECU. The injection time duration, or pulse width, is based on engine operating conditions as reported by the various engine sensors. The ECU controls the injectors by supplying the ground; the longer the ground is supplied, the more fuel delivered to the engine.

Latch Relay

The latch relay is located on the right inner fender panel. This relay is initially energized during engine startup and remains energized until 3-5 seconds after the engine is stopped. This enables the ECU to extend the idle speed stepper motor for the next startup, then cease operation.

Idle Speed Stepper Motor

The idle speed stepper motor is located on the throttle plate assembly. The ECU controls the idle speed by providing the appropriate voltage outputs to mofe the stepper motor pin inward or outward to maintain a predetermined idle speed. There is no idle speed adjustment.

Component Testing and Diagnosis

Coolant Temperature Sensor (CTS) Test

Disconnect the wire harness connector from the CTS and measure the resistance of the sensor with a high input impedence (digital) volt-ohmmeter. The resistance should be less than 1000 ohms with the engine warm. Refer to the resistance chart and replace the sensor if it is not within the range of resistance specified in the chart. Measure the resistance of the wire harness between ECU wire harness connector terminal D-3 and the sensor connector terminal, and terminal C-10 to the sensor connector terminal and repair the wire harness if an open circuit is indicated.

Manifold Air Temperature (MAT) Sensor Test

Disconnect the wire harness connector from the CTS and measure the resistance of the sensor with a high input impedence (digital) volt-ohmmeter. The resistance should be less than

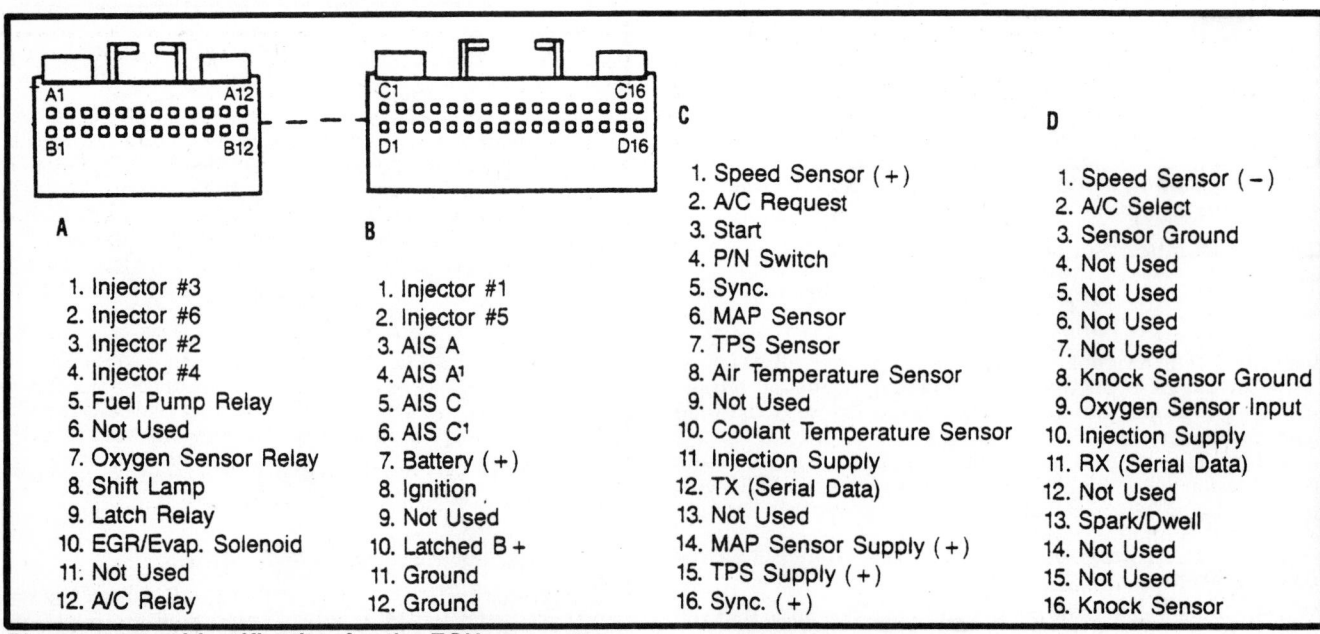

A

1. Injector #3
2. Injector #6
3. Injector #2
4. Injector #4
5. Fuel Pump Relay
6. Not Used
7. Oxygen Sensor Relay
8. Shift Lamp
9. Latch Relay
10. EGR/Evap. Solenoid
11. Not Used
12. A/C Relay

B

1. Injector #1
2. Injector #5
3. AIS A
4. AIS A^1
5. AIS C
6. AIS C^1
7. Battery (+)
8. Ignition
9. Not Used
10. Latched B +
11. Ground
12. Ground

C

1. Speed Sensor (+)
2. A/C Request
3. Start
4. P/N Switch
5. Sync.
6. MAP Sensor
7. TPS Sensor
8. Air Temperature Sensor
9. Not Used
10. Coolant Temperature Sensor
11. Injection Supply
12. TX (Serial Data)
13. Not Used
14. MAP Sensor Supply (+)
15. TPS Supply (+)
16. Sync. (+)

D

1. Speed Sensor (–)
2. A/C Select
3. Sensor Ground
4. Not Used
5. Not Used
6. Not Used
7. Not Used
8. Knock Sensor Ground
9. Oxygen Sensor Input
10. Injection Supply
11. RX (Serial Data)
12. Not Used
13. Spark/Dwell
14. Not Used
15. Not Used
16. Knock Sensor

Pin connector identification for the ECU connectors

1000 ohms with the engine warm. Refer to the resistance chart and replace the sensor if it is not within the range of resistance specified in the chart. Measure the resistance of the wire harness between ECU wire harness connector terminal D-3 and the sensor connector terminal, and terminal C-8 to the sensor connector terminal and repair the wire harness if the resistance is greater than 1 ohm.

Temperature-to-Resistance Values (Approximate)		
°F	°C	Ohms
212	100	185
160	70	450
100	38	1,600
70	20	3,400
40	4	7,500
20	-7	13,500
0	-18	25,000
-40	-40	100,700

CTS and MAT sensor resistance test chart

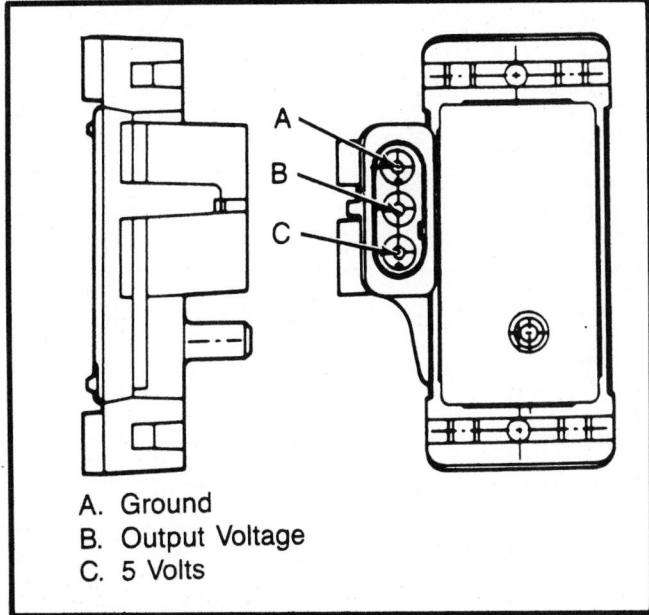

A. Ground
B. Output Voltage
C. 5 Volts

MAP sensor terminal Identification

Manifold Absolute Pressure (MAP) Sensor Test

1. Inspect the MAP sensor vacuum hose connection at the throttle body and sensor and repair as necessary.
2. Test the MAP sensor output voltage at the MAP sensor connector terminal B (as marked on the sensor body) with the ignition switch ON and the engine OFF. The output voltage should be 4–5 volts.

NOTE: The voltage should drop to 0.5–1.5 volts with a hot, neutral idle speed condition.

3. Test ECU terminal C-6 for the same voltage as in Step 2 to verify the wire harness condition and repair as necessary.

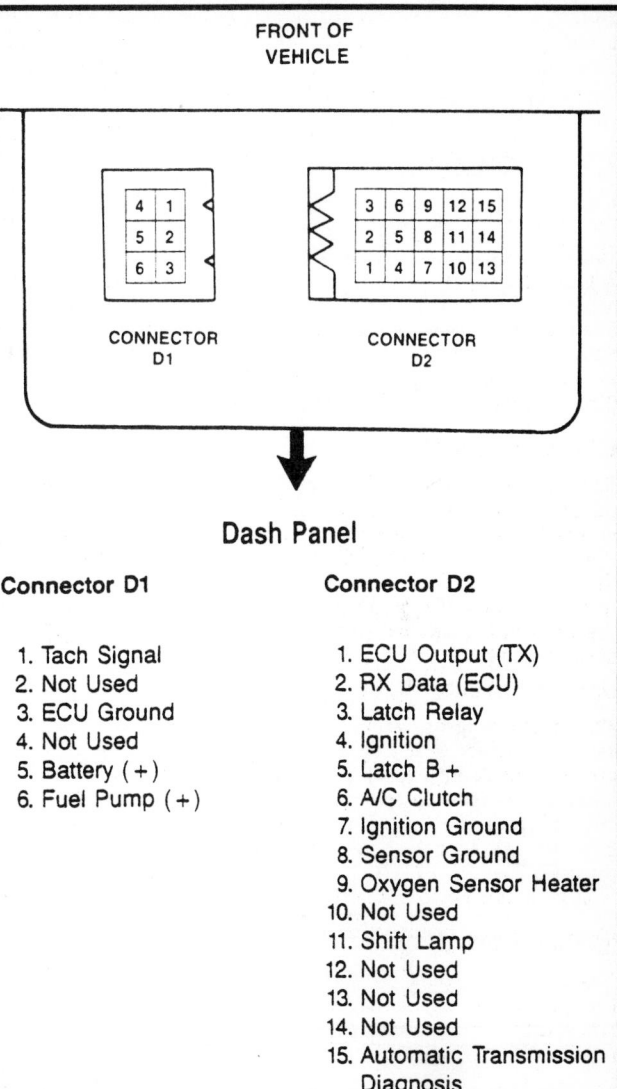

FRONT OF VEHICLE

CONNECTOR D1

CONNECTOR D2

Dash Panel

Connector D1

1. Tach Signal
2. Not Used
3. ECU Ground
4. Not Used
5. Battery (+)
6. Fuel Pump (+)

Connector D2

1. ECU Output (TX)
2. RX Data (ECU)
3. Latch Relay
4. Ignition
5. Latch B +
6. A/C Clutch
7. Ignition Ground
8. Sensor Ground
9. Oxygen Sensor Heater
10. Not Used
11. Shift Lamp
12. Not Used
13. Not Used
14. Not Used
15. Automatic Transmission Diagnosis

Diagnostic connector terminal locations on 4.0L engine

4. Test the MAP sensor supply voltage at the sensor connector terminal C with the ignition ON. The voltage should be 4.5–5.5 volts. The same voltage should be present at terminal C-14 of the ECU wire harness connector. Repair or replace the wire harness as necessary. If the ECU is suspect, use Diagnostic Tester M.S.1700, or equivalent, to test ECU function.

5. Test the MAP sensor ground circuit at the sensor connector terminal A and ECU connector terminal D-3. Repair the wire harness as necessary.

6. Test the MAP sensor ground circuit at the ECU connector between terminal D-3 and terminal B-11 with an ohmmeter. If the ohmmeter indicates an open circuit, check for a defective sensor ground connection located on the right side of the cylinder block. If the ground connection is good, replace the ECU.

NOTE: If terminal D-3 has a short circuit to 12 volts, correct this condition before replacing the ECU.

Oxygen Sensor Heating Element Test

Disconnect the O_2 sensor connector and connect ohmmeter test leads to terminals **A** and **B** of the sensor connector. The resistance should be 5–7 ohms. Replace the O_2 sensor if the ohmme-

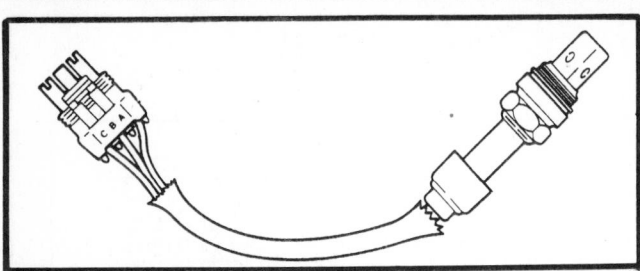

Typical oxygen sensor showing terminal identification on connector body

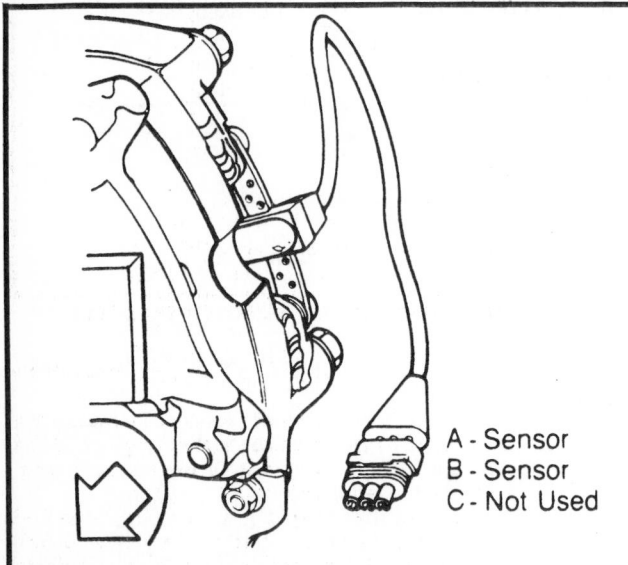

A - Sensor
B - Sensor
C - Not Used

Speed sensor connector showing terminal identification

ter displays an infinity reading. Oxygen sensor operational testing requires the use of a special tester M.S.1700, or equivalent.

Knock Sensor Test

NOTE: This procedure requires the use of a special tester M.S.1700, or equivalent.

1. Connect diagnostic tester M.S.1700, or equivalent, to the vehicle according to the manufacturer's instructions.
2. Proceed to state display mode.
3. Start the engine.
4. Observe and note the knock unit value.
5. Using the tip of a screwdriver or a small hammer, gently tap on the cylinder block near the knock sensor and watch the knock value. The knock value should increase while tapping on the block.
6. If the knock value does not increase while tapping on the block, check the sensor connector. If the connection is good, replace the knock sensor.

Speed Sensor Test

Disconnect the speed sensor connector from the ignition control module and connect an ohmmeter between terminals **A** and **B** as marked on the connector. The ohmmeter should read 125–275 ohms on a hot engine. Replace the sensor if the readings are not as stated.

Relay Testing

A relay in the de-energized position should have continuity between terminals 87A and 30. Resistance values between terminals 85 and 86 is 70–80 ohms for resistor relays and 81–91 ohms for diode relays. Not all relays have battery voltage connected to terminal 30. Some may have battery voltage connected to terminals 87 or 87A.

Starter Motor Relay Test

1. Disconnect the wire connectors from the **I** and **G** terminals.

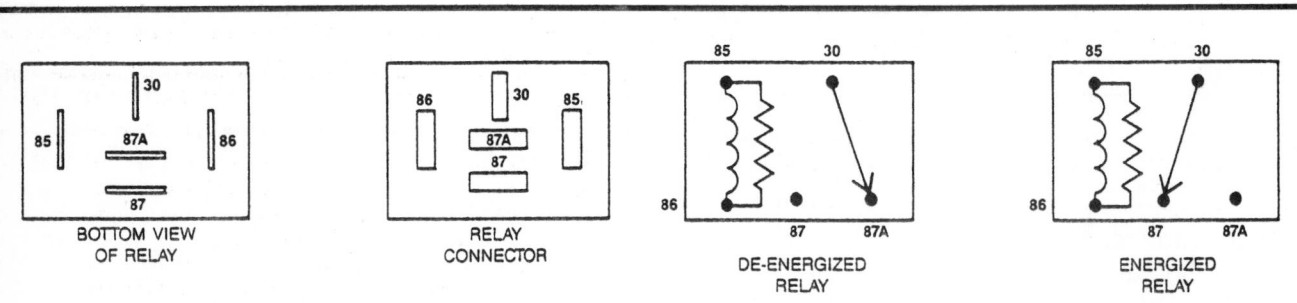

BOTTOM VIEW OF RELAY

RELAY CONNECTOR

DE-ENERGIZED RELAY

ENERGIZED RELAY

TERMINAL NUMBER

30   =   usually connected to battery voltage — can be switched or B+ at all times.
87A =   connected to 30 in the de-energized position.
87   =   connected to 30 in the energized position which supplies battery voltage to the operated device.

86   =   connected to the electromagnet and usually connected to a switched power source.
85   =   also is connected to the electromagnet and is usually grounded by a switch or ECU.

Relay operation and connector identification

2. Measure the resistance between the terminals with an ohmmeter. It should be approximately 22 ohms.

3. Measure the resistance between either terminal and the battery negative post. Reading should be infinite. If defective, replace the relay.

4. Remove the SOL terminal wire connector and connect a voltmeter between the terminal and the battery negative post. With the ignition switch in the START position, the voltmeter should indicate battery voltage (12 volts).

5. If battery voltage is not present, check the related wiring, bulkhead connector and ignition switch adjustment.

6. If battery voltage is present but the relay isn't working, make sure the transmission is in Park or Neutral and connect terminal **I** wire harness connector, then jumper terminal **G** to ground. If the relay doesn't click, replace the relay. If the starter relay does click, repair the ground circuit.

Sync Pulse (Stator) Test

1. Insert the positive (+) lead of a voltmeter into the blue wire at the distributor connector and the negative (–) lead into the gray/white wire at the distributor connector.

NOTE: Do not disconnect the distributor connector from the distributor. Insert the voltmeter leads into the back side of the connector to make contact with the terminals.

2. Set the voltmeter on the 15 volt AC scale and turn the ignition switch ON. The voltmeter should read approximately 5 volts. If there is no voltage, check the voltmeter leads for a good connection.

3. If there is still no voltage, remove the ECU and check for voltage at pin C-16 and ground with the harness connected. If there is still no voltage present, perform a vehicle test using tester M.S.1700, or equivalent.

4. If voltage is present, check for continuity between the blue wire at the distributor connector and pin C-16 at the ECU. If there is no continuity, repair the wire harness as necessary.

5. Check for continuity between the gray/white wire at the distributor connector and pin C-5 at the ECU. If there is no continuity, repair the wire harness as necessary.

6. Check for continuity between the black wire at the distributor connector and ground. If there is no continuity, repair the wire harness as necessary.

7. Crank the engine while observing the voltmeter; the needle should fluctuate back and forth while the engine is cranking. This verifies that the stator in the distributor is operating properly. If there is no sync pulse, stator replacement is necessary.

EGR Solenoid Test

1. Verify that source vacuum is present at port **C**.

2. Remove vacuum connector at ports **A** and **B** and connect a hand vacuum pump with a gauge at port **B**.

3. Start the engine and read the vacuum level on the gauge. There should be no vacuum at port **B**.

4. Disconnect the electrical connector from the solenoid and again note the reading on the vacuum gauge. There should now be vacuum at port **B**.

5. Reconnect the electrical connector to the solenoid and remove the vacuum gauge. Reconnect all vacuum lines.

Fuel Injector Test

Disconnect the wire connector from the fuel injector and connect an ohmmeter to the injector terminals. The resistance reading should be approximately 16 ohms at 68°F (20°C).

Fuel Pressure Test

1. Remove the cap from the pressure test connection on the fuel rail.

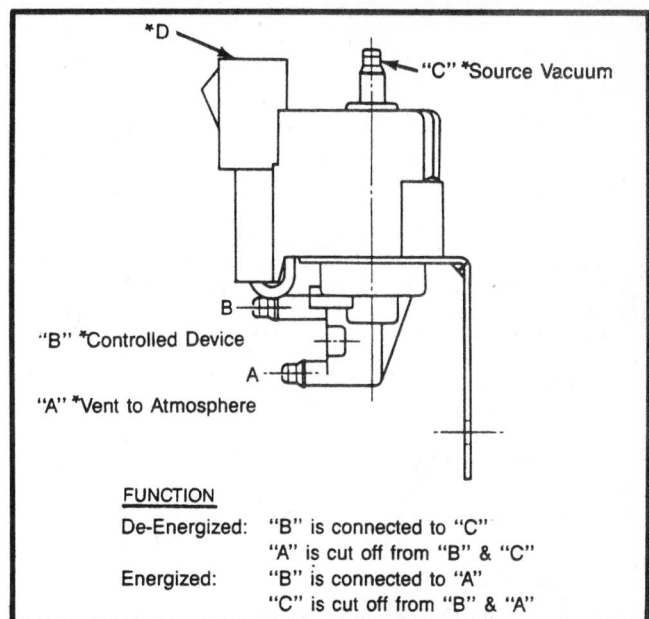

FUNCTION

De-Energized:	"B" is connected to "C"
	"A" is cut off from "B" & "C"
Energized:	"B" is connected to "A"
	"C" is cut off from "B" & "A"

Vacuum port identification for EGR solenoid test

2. Connect a fuel pressure gauge (J-34730-1 or equivalent) to the pressure fitting.

3. Start the engine and read the fuel pressure. Normal pressure should be 31 psi with the vacuum hose connected to the pressure regulator and 39 psi with the vacuum hose disconnected from the pressure regulator.

4. If the fuel pressure is not to specifications, check the fuel supply and return lines for kinks or restricting bends. Before replacing the pressure regulator, check the fuel pump flow rate by connecting one end of an old A/C gauge hose to the fuel test port on the fuel rail and inserting the other end into a container of at least 1 liter capacity. A good fuel pump will deliver at least 1 liter of fuel per minute with the return line pinched off. Run the pump by installing a jumper wire into diagnostic connector terminals D1-5 and D1-6.

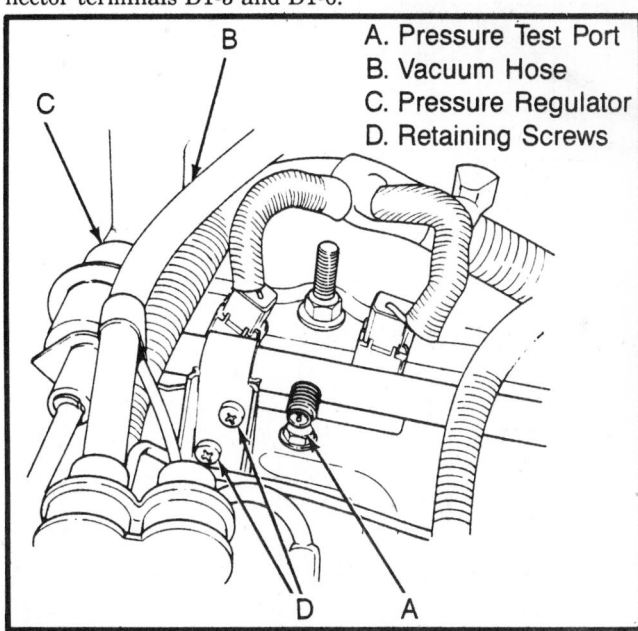

A. Pressure Test Port
B. Vacuum Hose
C. Pressure Regulator
D. Retaining Screws

Location of fuel pressure test connection and pressue regulator

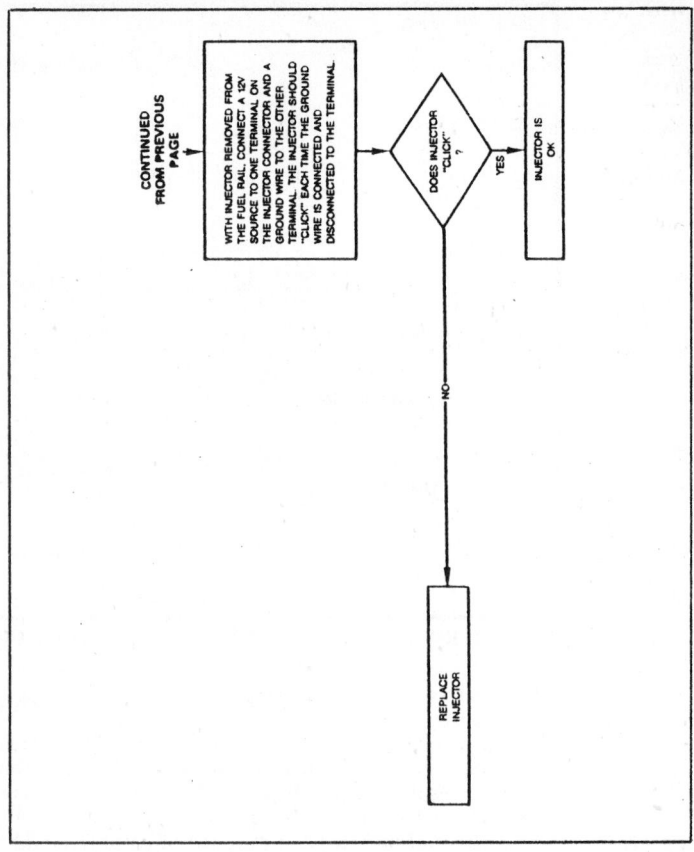

NOTE: Be sure to pinch off the return line or most of the fuel will be returned to the fuel tank. The fuel pressure regulator is not adjustable and must be replaced if found to be defective.

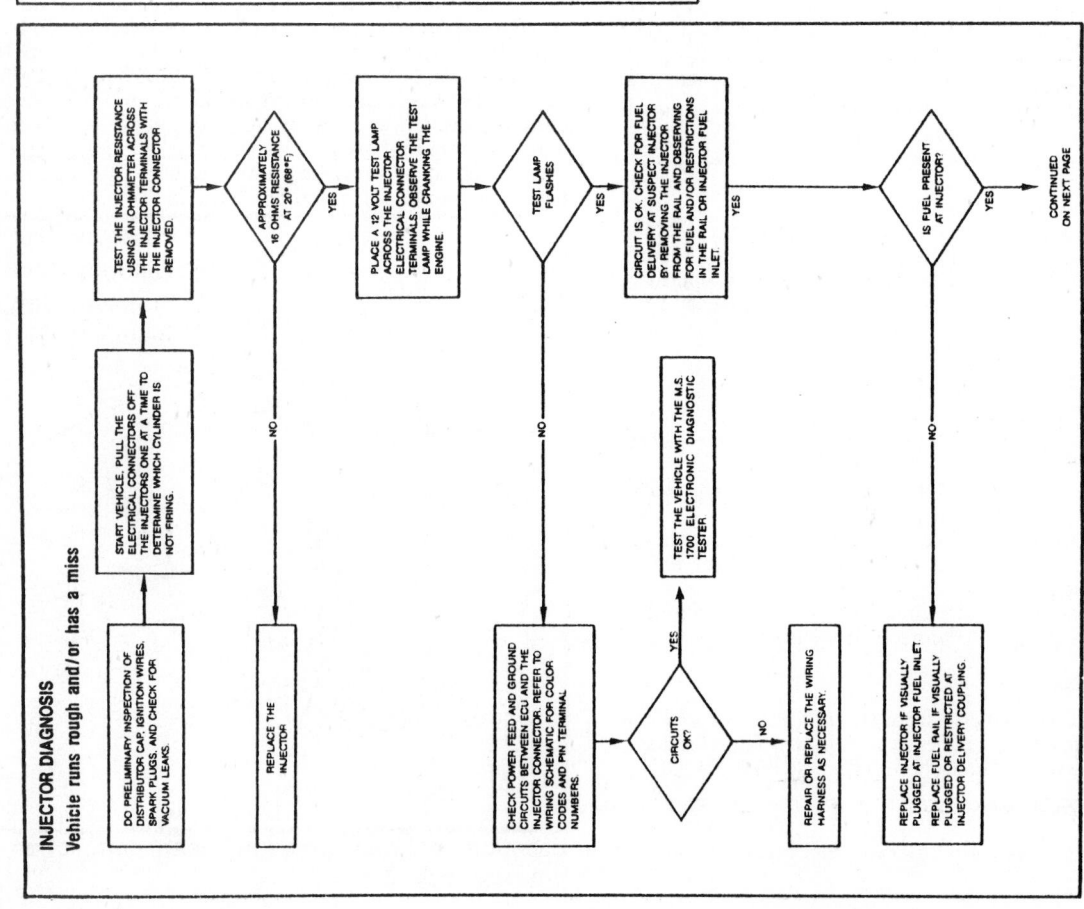

INJECTOR DIAGNOSIS

Vehicle runs rough and/or has a miss

THROTTLE POSITION SENSOR (TPS) TEST

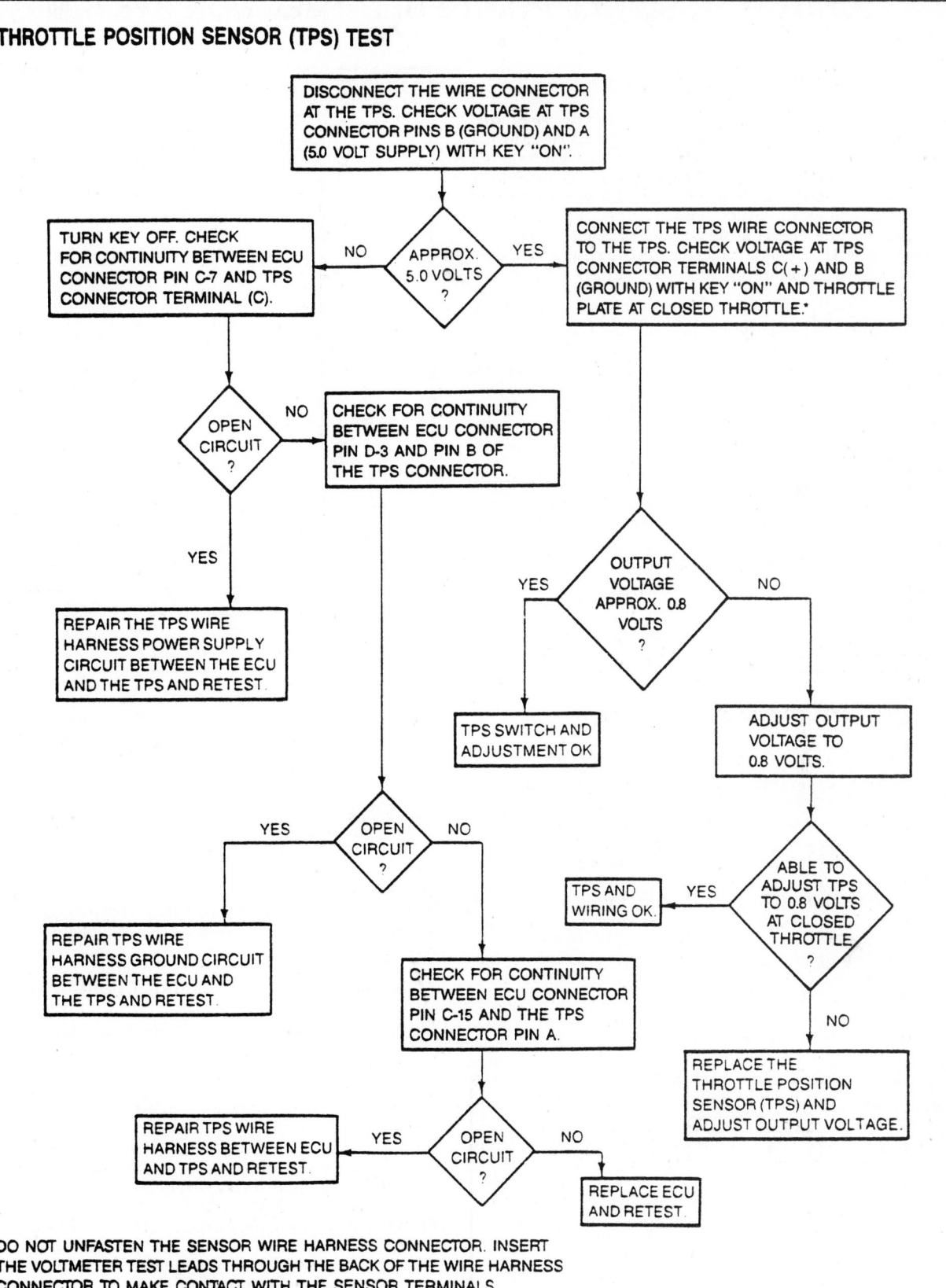

DISCONNECT THE WIRE CONNECTOR AT THE TPS. CHECK VOLTAGE AT TPS CONNECTOR PINS B (GROUND) AND A (5.0 VOLT SUPPLY) WITH KEY "ON".

APPROX. 5.0 VOLTS ?

NO → TURN KEY OFF. CHECK FOR CONTINUITY BETWEEN ECU CONNECTOR PIN C-7 AND TPS CONNECTOR TERMINAL (C).

YES → CONNECT THE TPS WIRE CONNECTOR TO THE TPS. CHECK VOLTAGE AT TPS CONNECTOR TERMINALS C(+) AND B (GROUND) WITH KEY "ON" AND THROTTLE PLATE AT CLOSED THROTTLE.*

OPEN CIRCUIT ?

NO → CHECK FOR CONTINUITY BETWEEN ECU CONNECTOR PIN D-3 AND PIN B OF THE TPS CONNECTOR.

YES → REPAIR THE TPS WIRE HARNESS POWER SUPPLY CIRCUIT BETWEEN THE ECU AND THE TPS AND RETEST.

OUTPUT VOLTAGE APPROX. 0.8 VOLTS ?

YES → TPS SWITCH AND ADJUSTMENT OK

NO → ADJUST OUTPUT VOLTAGE TO 0.8 VOLTS.

OPEN CIRCUIT ?

YES → REPAIR TPS WIRE HARNESS GROUND CIRCUIT BETWEEN THE ECU AND THE TPS AND RETEST.

NO → CHECK FOR CONTINUITY BETWEEN ECU CONNECTOR PIN C-15 AND THE TPS CONNECTOR PIN A.

ABLE TO ADJUST TPS TO 0.8 VOLTS AT CLOSED THROTTLE ?

YES → TPS AND WIRING OK.

NO → REPLACE THE THROTTLE POSITION SENSOR (TPS) AND ADJUST OUTPUT VOLTAGE.

OPEN CIRCUIT ?

YES → REPAIR TPS WIRE HARNESS BETWEEN ECU AND TPS AND RETEST.

NO → REPLACE ECU AND RETEST.

DO NOT UNFASTEN THE SENSOR WIRE HARNESS CONNECTOR. INSERT THE VOLTMETER TEST LEADS THROUGH THE BACK OF THE WIRE HARNESS CONNECTOR TO MAKE CONTACT WITH THE SENSOR TERMINALS.

CHRYSLER SINGLE POINT FUEL INJECTION SYSTEM

General Information

The Electronic Fuel Injection System is a computer regulated single point fuel injection system that provides precise air/fuel ratio for all driving conditions. At the center of this system is a digital pre-programmed computer known as a logic module or (on 1987½–88 models) a Single Module Engine Controller (SMEC) that regulates ignition timing, air/fuel ratio, emission control devices, idle speed and (on 1985–88 models) cooling fan and charging system. This component has the ability to update and revise its programming to meet changing operating conditions.

Various sensors provide the input necessary for the logic module or SMEC to correctly regulate the fuel flow at the fuel injector. These include the manifold absolute pressure, throttle position, oxygen sensor, coolant temperature, charge temperature, vehicle speed (distance) sensors and (on 1986–88 models) throttle body temperature. In addition to the sensors, various switches also provide important information. These include the neutral-safety, heated backlite, air conditioning, air conditioning clutch switches, and an electronic idle switch.

All inputs to the logic module or SMEC are converted into signals sent to the power module. These signals cause the power module to change either the fuel flow at the injector or ignition timing or both.

The logic module or SMEC tests many of its own input and output circuits. If a fault is found in a major system this information is stored in the logic module or SMEC. Information on this fault can be displayed to a technician by means of the instrument panel power loss (check engine) lamp or by connecting a diagnostic read out and reading a numbered display code which directly relates to a specific fault.

COMPONENTS AND OPERATION

Power Module

The power module contains the circuits necessary to power the ignition coil and the fuel injector. These are high current devices and their power supply has been isolated to minimize any "electrical noise" reaching the logic module. The power module also energizes the Automatic Shut Down (ASD) relay which activates the fuel pump, ignition coil, and the power module itself. The module also receives a signal from the distributor and sends this signal to the logic module. In the event of no distributor signal, the ASD relay is not activated and power is shut off from the fuel pump and ignition coil. The power module contains a voltage converter which reduces battery voltage to a regulated 8.0 volt output. This 8.0 volt output powers the distributor and also powers the logic module.

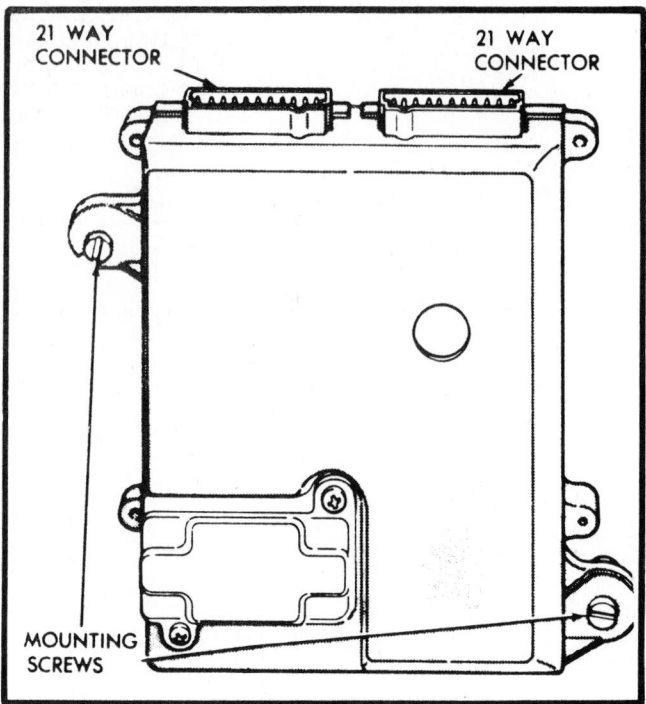

Logic module

Logic Module

The logic module is a digital computer containing a microprocessor. The module receives input signals from various switches, sensors, and components. It then computes the fuel injector pulse width, spark advance, ignition coil dwell, automatic idle speed actuation, and purge, EGR control solenoid cycles and (on 1985–88 models) cooling fan and alternator.

The logic module tests many of its own input and output circuits. If a fault is found in a major system, this information is stored in the logic module. Information on this fault can be displayed to a technician by means of the instrument panel power loss (check engine) lamp or by connecting a diagnostic read out and reading a numbered display code which directly relates to a general fault.

Single Module Engine Controller (SMEC) — 1987½–88

The SMEC contains the circuits necessary to drive the ignition coil, fuel injector, and the alternator field. These are high current devices and have been isolated to minimize any electrical noise in the passenger compartment.

The Automatic Shut Down (ASD) relay is mounted externally, but is turned on and off by the SMEC. Distributor pick-up signal goes to the SMEC. In the event of no distributor signal, the ASD relay is not activated and power is shut off from the fuel injector and ignition coil. The SMEC contains a voltage convertor which converts battery voltage to a regulated 8.0 volt output. This 8.0 volt output powers the distributor pick-up. The internal 5 volt supply which, in turn, powers the MAP sensor and TPS.

The SMEC is a digital computer containing a microprocessor. The module receives input signals from various switches and sensors. It then computes the fuel injector pulse width, spark advance, ignition coil dwell, idle speed, purge and cooling fan turn on and alternator charge rate.

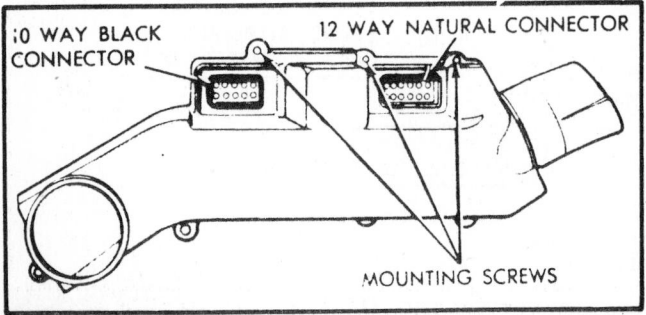

Power module

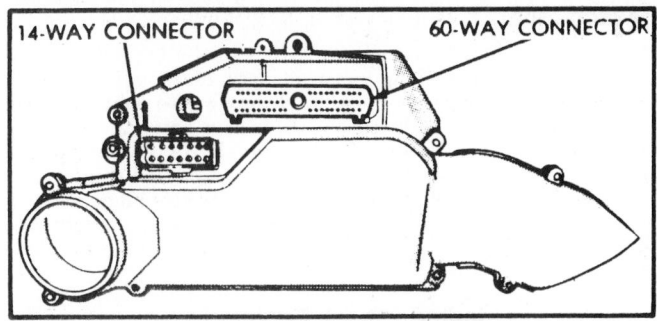

Single Module Engine Controller (SMEC)

The SMEC tests many of its own input and output circuits. If a fault is found in a major system, this information is stored in the SMEC. Information on this fault can be displayed to a technician by means of the instrument panel check engine lamp or by connecting the diagnostic read out tool C–4805 and reading a numbered display code which directly relates to a general fault.

Automatic Shutdown (ASD) Relay (1984)

The Automatic Shutdown Relay (ASD) is powered and controlled through the power module. When the module senses a distributor signal during cranking, it grounds the ASD closing its contacts. This completes the circuit for the electric fuel pump and ignition coil. If the distributor signal is lost for any reason the ASD interrupts this circuit in less than one second preventing fuel, spark, and engine operations. This fast shut down serves as a safety feature in the event of an accident.

Manifold Absolute Pressure (MAP) Sensor

The manifold absolute pressure (MAP) sensor is a device which monitors manifold vacuum. It is connected to a vacuum nipple on the throttle body and electrically to the logic module or SMEC. The sensor transmits information on manifold vacuum conditions and barometric pressure to the logic module or SMEC. The MAP sensor data on engine load is used with data from other sensors to determine the correct air/fuel mixture. It is located as follows:
  • 1984 – Mounted in the right side passenger compartment
  • 1985–86 – Mounted on the logic module
  • 1987–88 Front Wheel Drive Cars – Mounted underhood on the right shock tower
  • 1987½–88 – Front Wheel Drive Van/Wagon – Mounted underhood on the front of dash

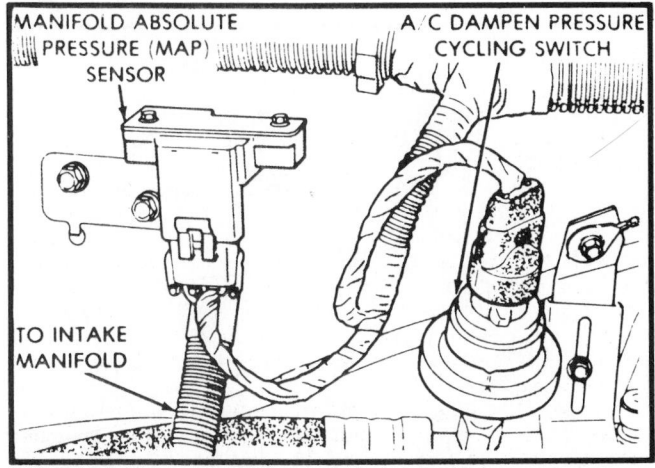

Manifold Air Pressure (MAP) sensor location – 1987½–88

Oxygen Sensor (O$_2$ Sensor)

The oxygen sensor (O$_2$ sensor) is a device which produces an electrical voltage when exposed to the oxygen present in the exhaust gases. The sensor is mounted in the exhaust manifold and, on 1984–86 models, must be heated by the exhaust gases before producing the voltage. On most 1987–88 models, the oxygen sensor is electrically heated internally for faster switch-

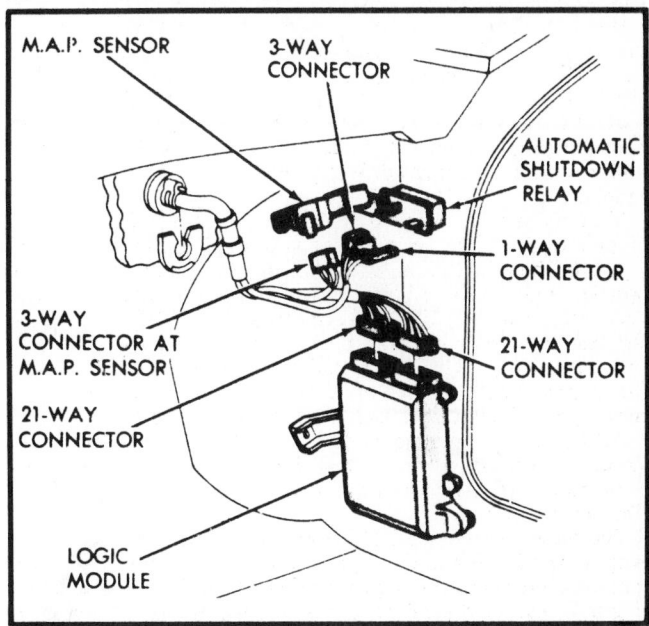

Logic module, MAP sensor and ASD relay location – 1984

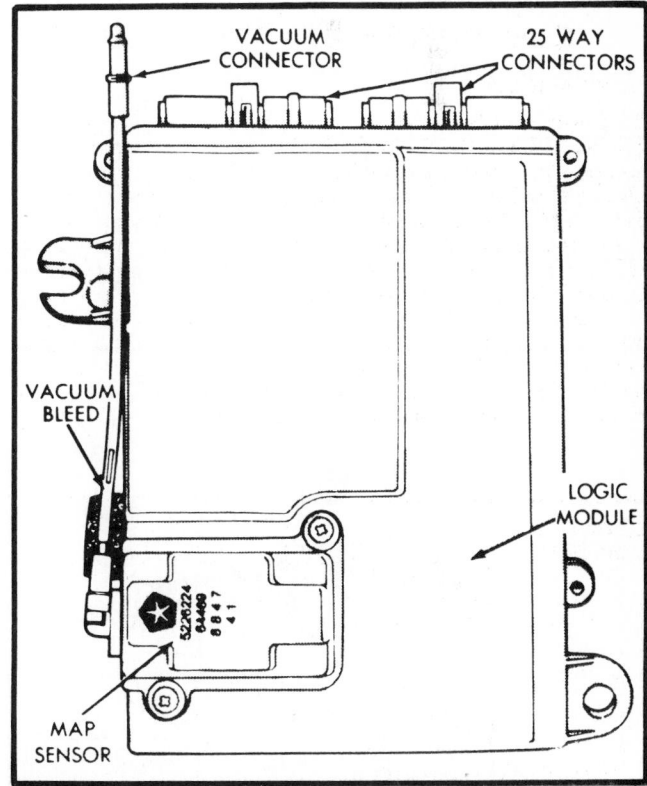

Manifold Air Pressure (MAP) sensor location – 1985–86

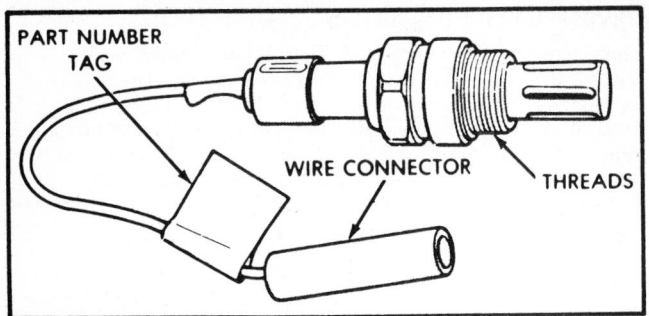

Oxygen (O₂) sensor

ing when the engine is running. When there is a large amount of oxygen present (lean mixture), the sensor produces a low voltage. When there is a lesser amount present (rich mixture) it produces a higher voltage. By monitoring the oxygen content and converting it to electrical voltage, the sensor acts as a rich-lean switch. The voltage is transmitted to the logic module. The logic module signals the power module to trigger the fuel injector. The injector changes the mixture.

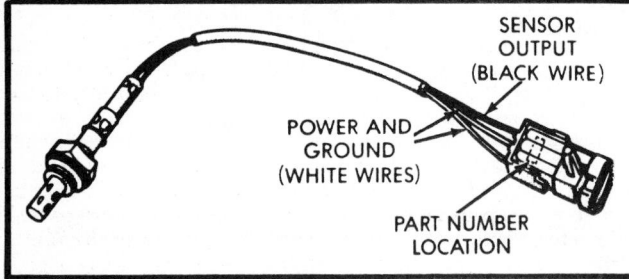

Oxygen (O₂) sensor (heated)

Coolant Temperature Sensor

The coolant temperature sensor is a device that monitors coolant temperature (which is the same as engine operating temperature). It is mounted in the thermostat housing. This sensor provides data on engine operating temperature to the logic module or SMEC. This allows the logic module or SMEC to demand slightly richer air/fuel mixtures and higher idle speeds until normal operating temperatures are reached. On 1985–88 models, this sensor is also used for cooling fan control.

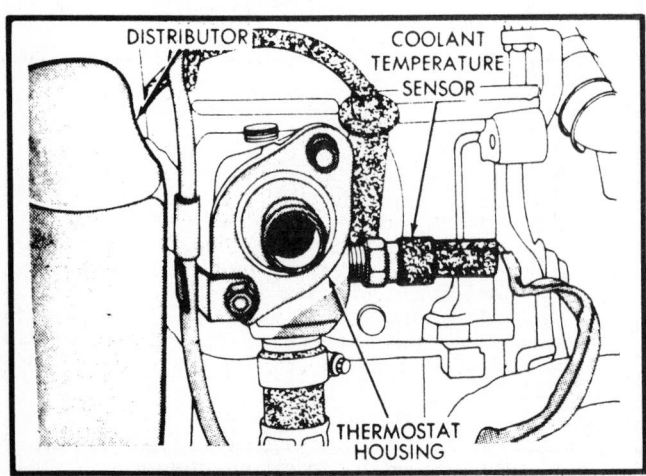

Coolant temperature sensor location

Switch Input

Various switches provide information to the logic module or SMEC. These include the neutral safety, electric backlite, air conditioning, air conditioning clutch, and brake light switches. If one or more of these switches is sensed as being in the on position, the logic module or SMEC signals the automatic idle speed motor to increase idle speed to a scheduled rpm.

With the air conditioning on and the throttle blade above a specific angle, the wide open throttle cut-out relay prevents the air conditioning clutch from engaging until the throttle blade is below this angle.

Power Loss/Limited (Check Engine) Lamp

The power loss (check engine) lamp comes on each time the ignition key is turned on and stays on for a few seconds as a bulb test. If the logic module or SMEC receives an incorrect signal or no signal from either the coolant temperature sensor, manifold absolute pressure sensor, or the throttle position sensor, the lamp on the instrument panel is illuminated. This is a warning that the logic module or SMEC has gone into limp-in mode in an attempt to keep the system operational.

The lamp can also be used to display fault codes. Cycle the ignition switch on, off, on, off, on, within five seconds and any fault code stored in the memory will be displayed.

Exhaust Gas Recirculation Solenoid

The EGR solenoid is operated by the logic module or SMEC.

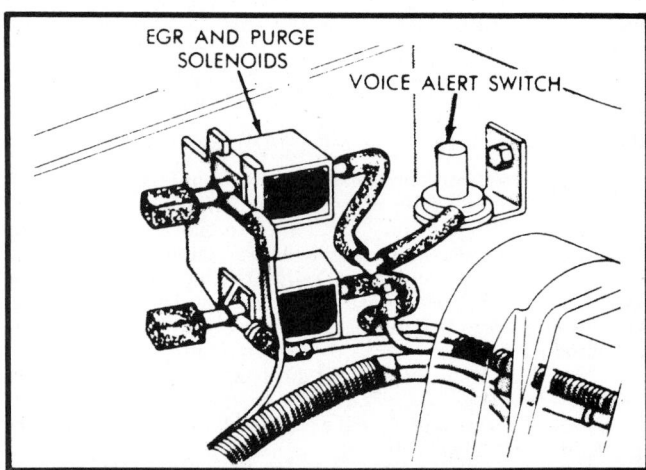

EGR and purge solenoid location – 1984

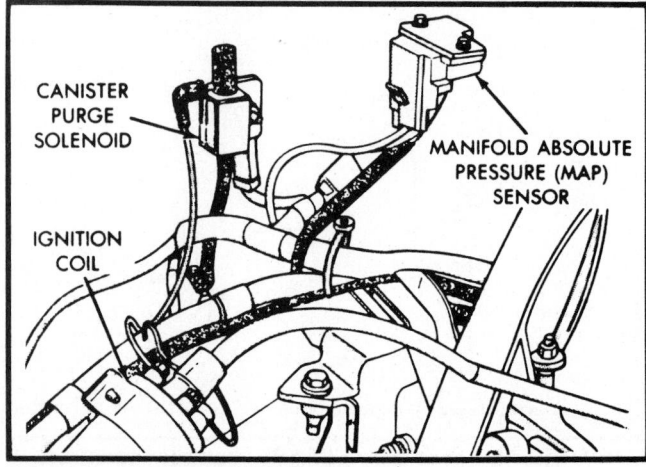

Purge solenoid and MAP sensor location – 1987

When engine temperature is below 70°F (21°C), the module energizes the solenoid by grounding it. This closes the solenoid and prevents ported vacuum from reaching the EGR valve. When the prescribed temperature is reached, the module will turn off the ground for the solenoid deenergizing it. Once the solenoid is deenergized, ported vacuum from the throttle body will pass through to the EGR valve. At idle and wide open throttle the solenoid is energized which prevents EGR operation.

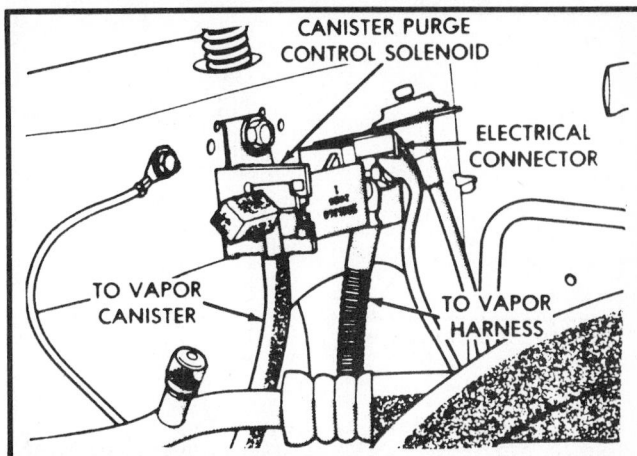

Purge solenoid location—1987½–88

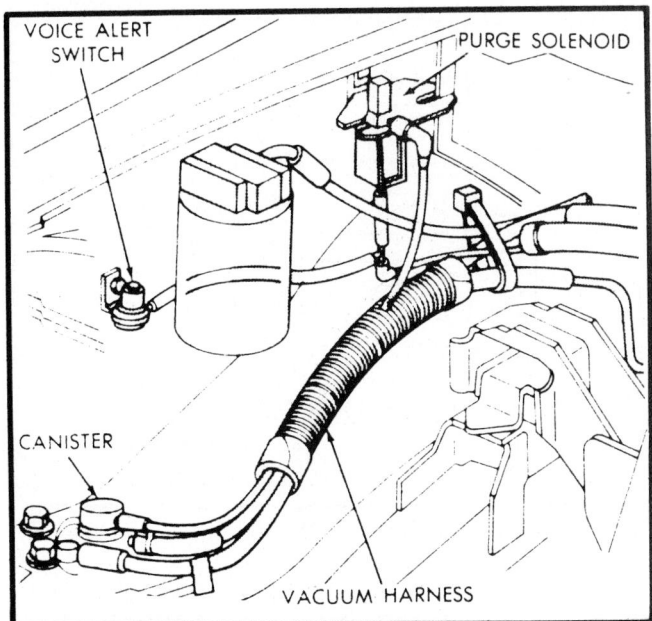

Purge solenoid location—1985–86

Purge Solenoid

The purge solenoid is controlled by the logic module or SMEC. When engine temperature is below 145°F (61°C) the module grounds the purge solenoid, energizing it. This prevents vacuum from reaching the charcoal canister valve. When this temperature is reached, the module deenergizes the solenoid by turning the ground off. Once this occurs, vacuum will flow to the canister purge valve and purge fuel vapors through the throttle body.

Air Conditioning Cutout Relay

The air conditioning cutout relay is connected, in series, electrically with the A/C damped pressure switch, the A/C switch and, on some models, the A/C fan relay. This relay is in the energized, closed (on), position during engine operation. When the module senses low idle speeds and wide open throttle through the throttle position sensor, it will deenergize the relay, open its contacts and prevent air conditioning clutch engagement.

Throttle Body

The throttle body assembly replaces a conventional carburetor and is mounted on top of the intake manifold. The throttle body houses the fuel injector, pressure regulator, throttle position sensor, automatic idle speed motor and (on 1986–88 models) throttle body temperature sensor. Air flow through the throttle body is controlled by a cable operated throttle blade located in the base of the throttle body. The throttle body itself provides the chamber for metering atomizing and distributing fuel throughout the air entering the engine.

Fuel Injector (1984–85)

The fuel injector is an electric solenoid powered by the power module, but controlled by the logic module. The logic module, based on ambient, mechanical, and sensor input, determines when and how long the power module should operate the injector. When an electric current is supplied to the injector the armature and pintle move a short distance against a spring, opening a small orifice. Fuel is supplied to the inlet of the injector by the fuel pump, then passes through the injector, around the pintle, and out the orifice. Since the fuel is under high pressure a fine spray is developed in the shape of a hollow cone. The injector, through this spraying action, atomizes the fuel and distributes it into the air entering the throttle body.

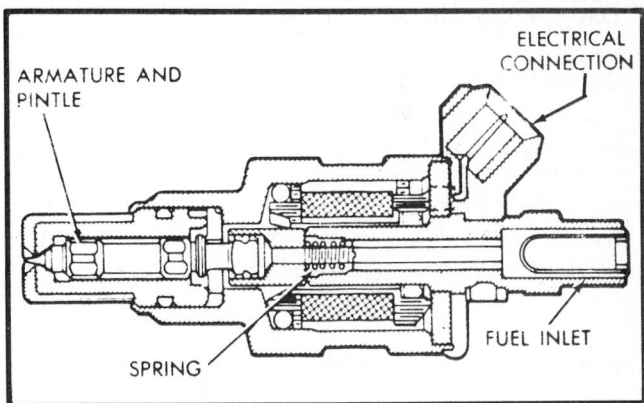

Fuel injector—1984–85

Fuel Injector (1986–88)

The fuel injector is an electric solenoid driven by the power module, but controlled by the logic module. The logic module, based on ambient, mechanical, and sensor input, determines when and how long the power module should operate the injector. When an electric current is supplied to the injector, a spring loaded ball is lifted from its seat. This allows fuel to flow through six spray orifices and deflects off the sharp edge of the injector nozzle. This action causes the fuel to form a 45° cone shaped spray pattern before entering the air stream in the throttle body.

NOTE: On models equipped with Single Module Engine Controller (SMEC), the fuel injector is controlled and driven solely by the SMEC.

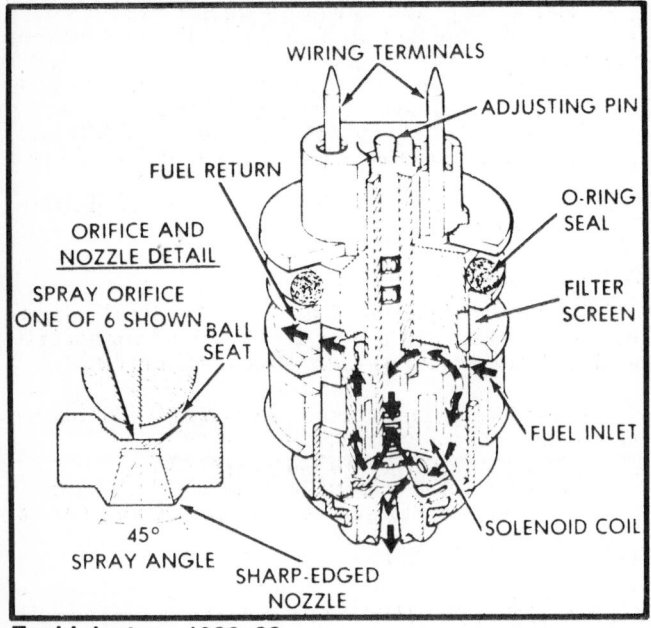

Fuel Injector—1986—88

Fuel Pressure Regulator

The pressure regulator is a mechanical device located downstream of the fuel injector on the throttle body. Its function is to maintain a constant 36 psi (250 kPa) on 1984–85 models and 14.5 psi (100 kPa) on 1986–88 models, across the fuel injector tip. The regulator uses a spring loaded rubber diaphragm to uncover a fuel return port. When the fuel pump becomes operational, fuel flows past the injector into the regulator, and is restricted from flowing any further by the blocked return port. When fuel pressure reaches the predetermined setting, it pushes on the diaphragm, compressing the spring, and uncovers the fuel return port. The diaphragm and spring will constantly move from an open to closed position to keep the fuel pressure constant. On 1984–85 models, an assist to the spring

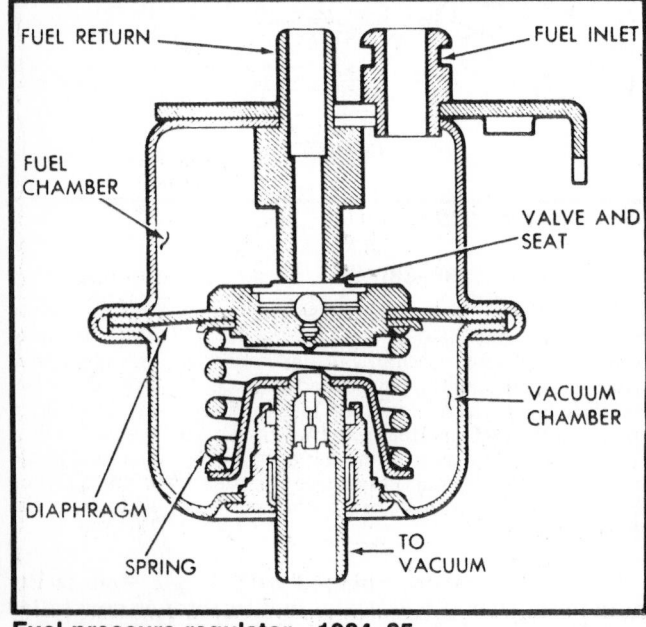

Fuel pressure regulator—1984—85

loaded diaphragm comes from vacuum in the throttle body above the throttle blade. As venturi vacuum increases less pressure is required to supply the same amount of fuel into the air flow. The vacuum assists in opening the fuel port during high vacuum conditions. This fine tunes the fuel pressure for all operating conditions.

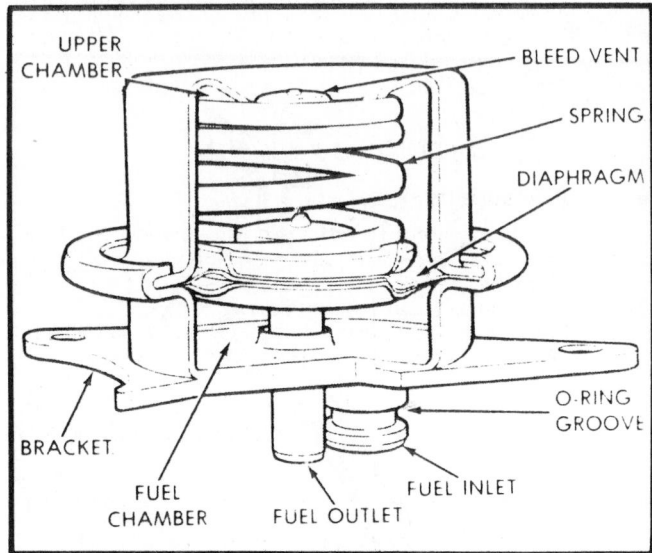

Fuel pressure regulator—1986—88

Throttle Position Sensor (TPS)

The throttle position sensor (TPS) is an electric resistor which is activated by the movement of the throttle shaft. It is mounted on the throttle body and senses the angle of the throttle blade opening. The voltage that the sensor produces increases or decreases according to the throttle blade opening. This voltage is transmitted to the logic module or SMEC, where it is used along with data from other sensors to adjust the air/fuel ratio to varying conditions and during acceleration, deceleration, idle, and wide open throttle operations.

Automatic Idle Speed (AIS) Motor

The automatic idle speed motor (AIS) is operated by the logic module or SMEC. Data from the throttle position sensor, speed sensor, coolant temperature sensor, and various switch operations, (electric backlite, air conditioning, safety/neutral, brake) are used by the module to adjust engine idle to an optimum during all idle conditions. The AIS adjusts the air portion of the air/fuel mixture through an air bypass on the back of the throttle body. Basic (no load) idle is determined by the minimum air flow through the throttle body. The AIS opens or closes off the air bypass as an increase or decrease is needed due to engine loads or ambient conditions. The module senses an air/fuel change and increases or decreases fuel proportionally to change engine idle. Deceleration die out is also prevented by increasing engine idle when the throttle is closed quickly after a driving (speed) condition.

Throttle Body Temperature Sensor (1986–88)

The throttle body temperature sensor is a device that monitors throttle body temperature which is the same as fuel temperature. It is mounted in the throttle body. This sensor provides information on fuel temperature which allows the logic module or SMEC, to provide the correct air fuel mixture for a hot restart condition.

Fuel Pump

The fuel pump used in this system is a positive displacement, roller vane immersible pump with a permanent magnet electric motor. The fuel is drawn in through a filter sock and pushed through the electric motor to the outlet. The pump contains two check valves. One valve is used to relieve internal fuel pump pressure and regulate maximum pump output. The other check valve, located near the pump outlet, restricts fuel movement in either direction when the pump is not operational. Voltage to operate the pump is supplied through the auto shutdown relay (ASD).

System Servicing

Service Precautions

1. When working around any part of the fuel system, take precautionary steps to prevent possible fire and/or explosion:
   a. Disconnect the negative battery terminal, except when testing with battery voltage is required.
   b. Whenever possible, use a flashlight instead of a drop light to inspect fuel system components or connections.
   c. Keep all open flames and smoking material out of the area and make sure there is adequate ventilation to remove fuel vapors.
   d. Use a clean shop cloth to catch fuel when opening a fuel system. Dispose of gasoline-soaked rags properly.
   e. Relieve the fuel system pressure before any service procedures are attempted that require disconnecting a fuel line.
   f. Use eye protection.
   g. Always keep a dry chemical (class B) fire extinguisher near the area.

Minimum Idle Speed Adjustment

NOTE: Normal idle speed is controlled by the logic module or SMEC. This adjustment is the minimum idle speed with the Automatic Idle Speed (AIS) closed.

1. Before adjusting the idle on an electronic fuel injected vehicle the following items must be checked.
   a. AIS motor has been checked for operation.
   b. Engine has been checked for vacuum or EGR leaks.
   c. Engine timing has been checked and set to specifications.

System and Component Identification

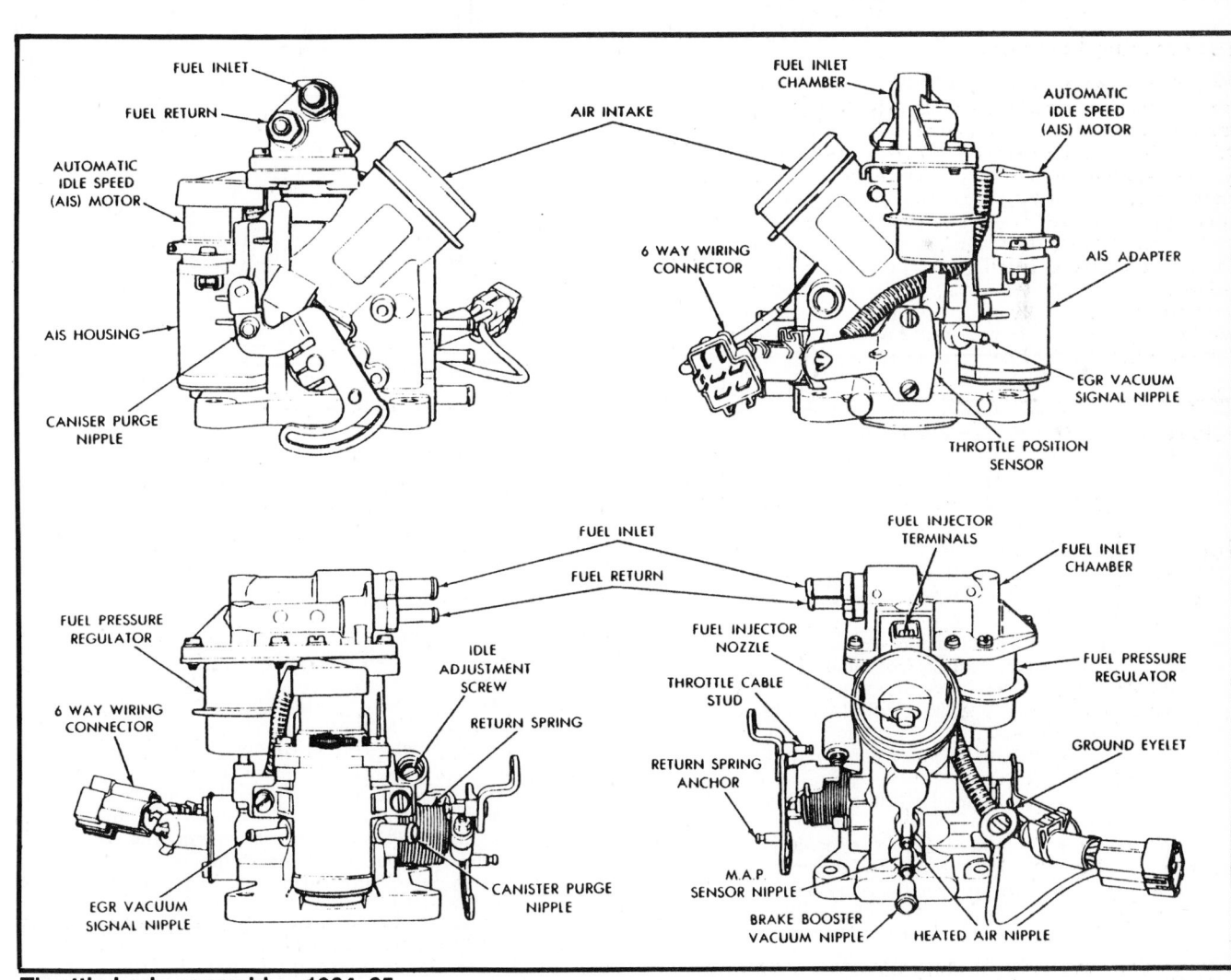

Throttle body assembly—1984–85

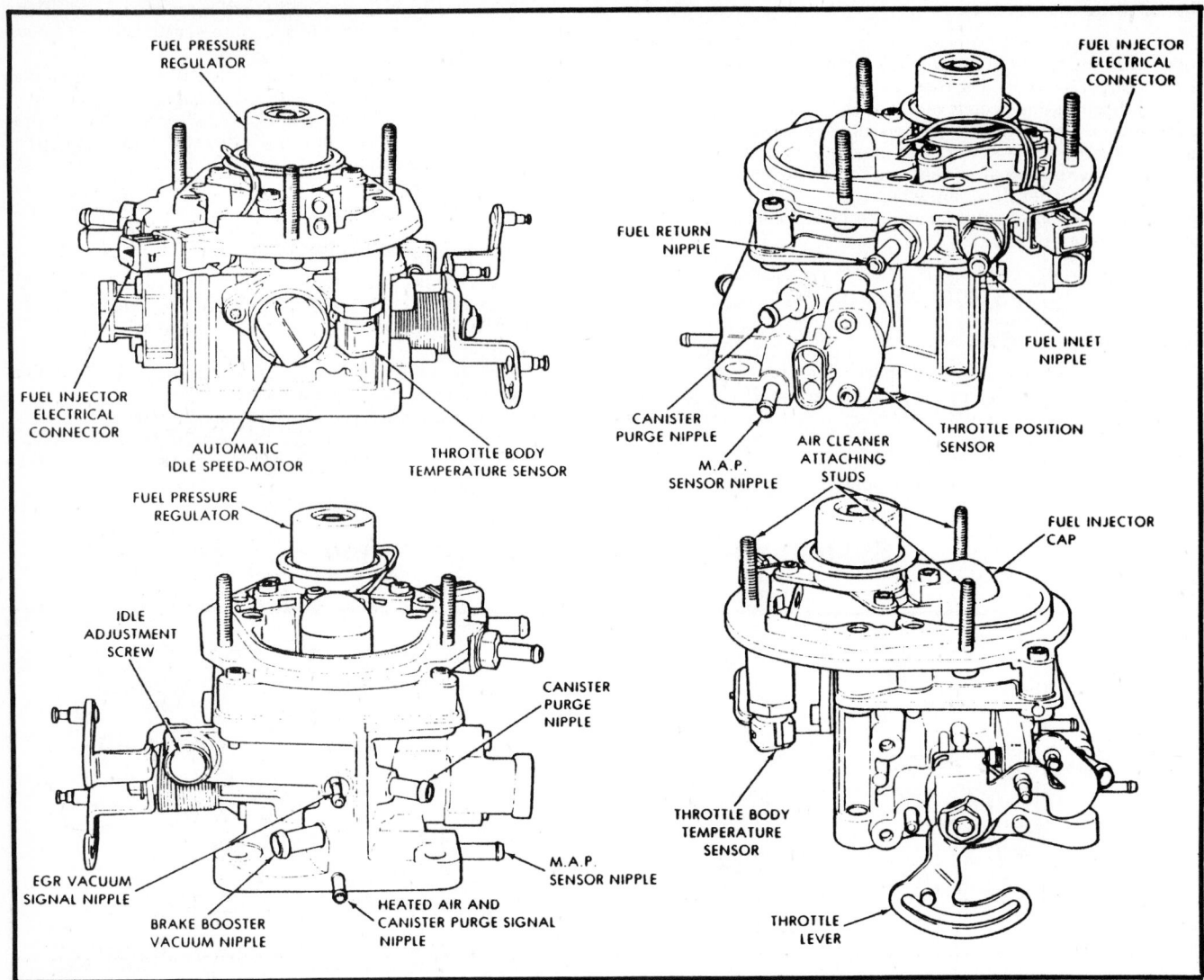

Throttle body assembly – 1986–87

d. Coolant temperature sensor has been checked for operation.

2. Connect a tachometer and timing light to engine.

3. On 1984–85 models:

a. Disconnect throttle body 6-way connector. Remove brown with white tracer AIS wire from connector and rejoin connector.

b. Connect one end of a jumper wire to AIS wire and other end to battery positive post for 5 seconds.

4. On 1986–88 models:

a. Close AIS by using ATM tester C–4805 or equivalent, ATM test code #03.

5. Connect a jumper to radiator fan so that it will run continuously.

6. Start and run the engine for 3 minutes to allow the idle speed to stabilize.

7. Check engine rpm and compare the result with the specifications listed on the underhood emission control sticker.

8. If idle rpm is not within specifications, use tool C–4804 or equivalent to turn the idle speed adjusting screw to obtain 800 ± 10 rpm. If the underhood emission sticker specifications are different, use those values for adjustment.

NOTE: If idle will not adjust down check for binding

linkage, speed control servo cable adjustment or throttle shaft binding.

9. Turn off the engine, disconnect tachometer, reinstall AIS wire and remove jumper wire from fan motor.

Ignition Timing Adjustment

1. Connect a power timing light to the number one cylinder, or a magnetic timing unit to the engine. Use a 10 degree offset when required.

2. Connect a tachometer to the engine and turn selector to the proper cylinder position.

3. Start engine and run until operating temperature is reached.

4. On 1984–86 models, disconnect and reconnect the coolant temperature sensor connector on the thermostat housing. The loss of power lamp on the dash must come on and stay on. On 1987–88 models, disconnect coolant temperature sensor connector. Engine rpm should be within emission label specifications.

5. Aim power timing light at timing hole in bell housing or read the magnetic timing unit.

6. Loosen distributor and adjust timing to emission label specifications if necessary.

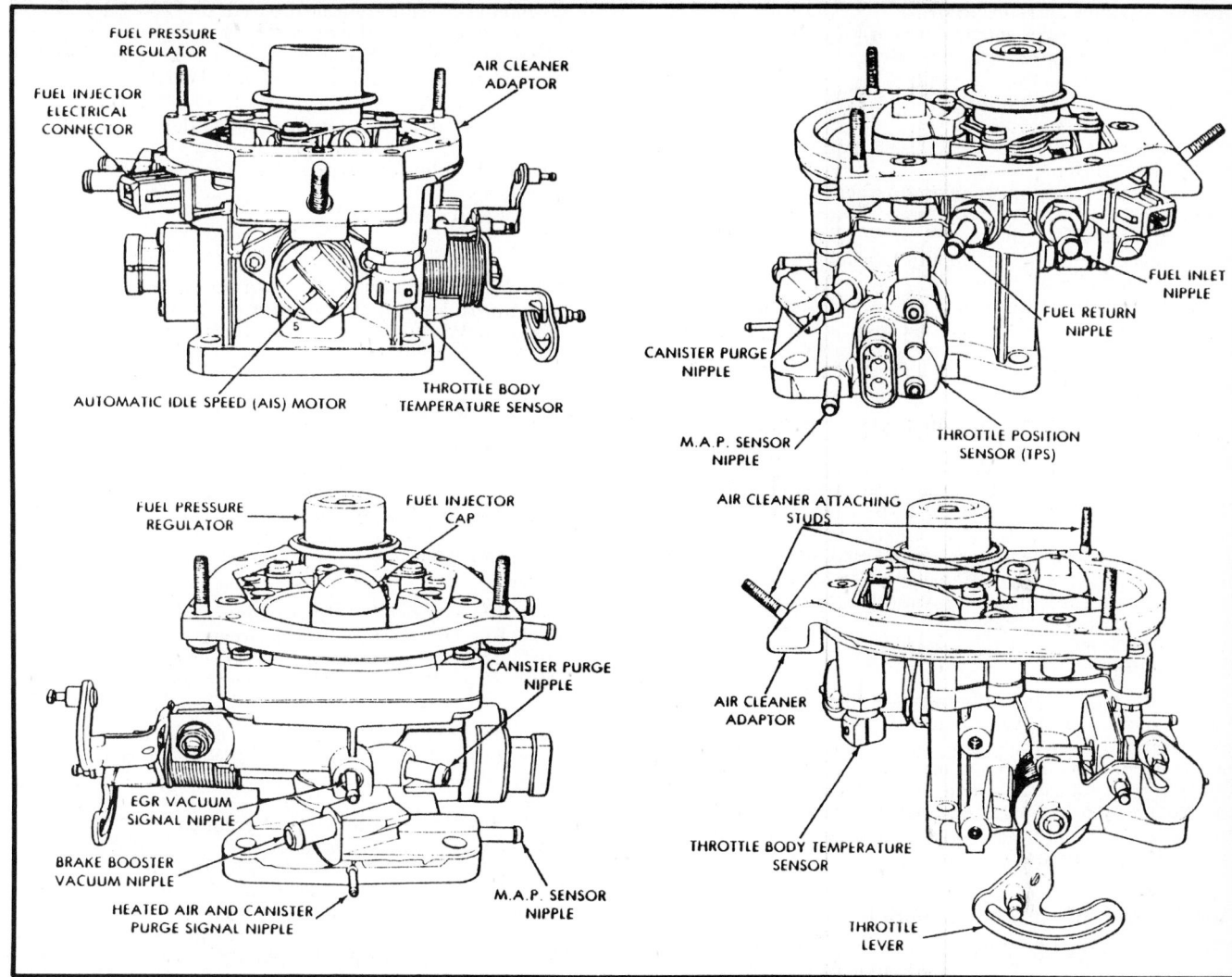

Throttle body assembly — 1987½—88

7. Shut the engine off. On 1987–88 models, reconnect coolant temperature sensor. Disconnect and reconnect positive battery quick disconnect (or erase the fault codes with sensor test #10 on 1987½–88 models), then start the vehicle. The loss of power (check engine) lamp should be off.

8. Shut engine off, then turn ignition on, off, on, off, on. Fault codes should be clear with 88-51-55 shown.

Diagnosis and Testing

NOTE: Mechanical malfunctions are more difficult to diagnose with the EFI system. The logic module has been programmed to compensate for some mechanical malfunctions such as incorrect cam timing, vacuum leaks, etc. If engine performance problems are encountered, and no fault codes are displayed, the problem may be mechanical rather than electronic.

VISUAL INSPECTION

A visual inspection for loose, disconnected or misrouted wires and hoses should be made before attempting to diagnose or service the fuel injection system. A visual check will help spot these faults and save unnecessary test and diagnostic time. A thorough visual inspection will include the following checks:

1. Check that vacuum connections on rear and/or front of throttle body are secure and not leaking.

2. Check that vacuum connection(s) at EGR and/or purge solenoid is secure and not leaking.

3. Check that hoses are securely attached to vapor canister.

4. Check that hose from PCV valve is securely attached to the intake manifold vacuum port.

5. Check that hoses are attached to back pressure transducer.

6. Check that alternator wiring and belt are correctly installed and tight.

7. On 1984–85, check connections from air heater to throttle body.

8. On 1986–88, check that heated air door vacuum connection is connected and not leaking.

9. Check vacuum connections at MAP sensor.

10. Check that hose and wiring connections at the fuel pump are tight and wires are making contact with the terminals on pump.

11. Check power brake and speed control vacuum connections are tight.

12. Check that the following electrical connections are clean, tight and have good contact:
• Both connectors to the logic and power module or Single

Module Engine Controller (SMEC)
  • Connector at EGR solenoid and/or purge solenoid
  • Connector at speed (distance) sensor
  • Connector at cooling fan relay
  • Connector to oxygen sensor
  • Connector at fuel injector
  • Connector at automatic idle speed (AIS) and throttle position sensor (TPS)
  • Connector at coolant temperature sensor
  • Connector at throttle body temperature sensor (1986–88)
  • Connector to distributor
  • Connectors for engine-to-main harness
  • Connectors for all relays
  • Connector to neutral safety switch (automatic only)
  • All ignition cables are in order and seated
  • Ground straps to engine and dash panel
  • Connection to battery

ON-BOARD DIAGNOSTICS

The logic module or SMEC has been programmed to monitor several different circuits of the fuel injection system. This monitoring is called On Board Diagnosis. If a problem is sensed with a monitored circuit, often enough to indicate an actual problem, its fault code is stored in the module for eventual display to the service technician. If the problem is repaired or ceases to exist, the logic module cancels the fault code after 20–40 ignition key on/off cycles.

Fault Codes

Fault codes are two digit numbers that identify which circuit is bad. In most cases, they do not identify which component is bad in a circuit. When a fault code appears (either by flashes of the power loss/limited (check engine) lamp or by watching the diagnostic read out Tool C–4805, or equivalent, it indicates that the logic module or SMEC has recognized an abnormal signal in the system. Fault codes indicate the results of a failure but do not always identify the failed component directly.

Accessing Trouble Code Memory

There are two methods used in accessing trouble codes. The first method is the use of a diagnostic readout box Tool C–4805 or equivalent, the second method is observing the power loss/limited (check engine) lamp.

The diagnostic readout box is used to put the system into a Diagnostic Test Mode, Circuit Actuation Test Mode, Switch Test Mode, Engine Running Test Mode and, on 1986–88 models, Sensor Test Mode. Three (four) of these modes of testing are called for at certain points of the driveability test procedure. A fourth (fifth) test mode is available with the engine running. The following is a description of each test mode:
  • Diagnostic Test Mode – This mode is used to see is there are any fault codes stored in the on-board diagnostic system memory.
  • Circuit Actuation Test Mode (ATM Test) – This mode is used to turn a specific circuit on and off in order to check it. ATM test codes are used in this mode.
  • Switch Test Mode – This mode is used to determine if specific switch inputs are being received by the logic module.
  • Sensor Test Mode (1986–88) – This mode is used to see the output signals of certain sensors as received by the logic module.
  • Engine Running Test Mode – This mode is used to determine if the oxygen feedback system is switching from rich to lean and lean to rich.

DIAGNOSIS USING READOUT BOX

The diagnostic readout box is used to put the on-board diagnos-

tic system in three different modes (four on 1986–88 models) of testing as called for in the driveability test procedure.
  1. Connect Tool C–4805 or equivalent, to the mating connector located in the wiring harness by the right front shock tower.
  2. Place the read/hold switch on the readout box in the read position.
  3. Turn the ignition switch ON-OFF-ON-OFF-ON within five seconds.
  4. Record all codes.

NOTE:The display of codes can be stopped by moving the read/hold switch to the hold position. Returning to the read position will continue the displaying of codes.

Fault Code Description

  CODE 11 - Distributor signal circuit
  CODE 12 - Battery feed to logic module
  CODE 13 - MAP Sensor vacuum circuit
  CODE 14 - MAP Sensor electrical circuit
  CODE 15 - Vehicle speed (distance) sensor
  CODE 16 - (1985–88) Loss of battery voltage signal (charging system)
  CODE 17 - (1986–88) Engine running cool
  CODE 21 - Oxygen (O_2) sensor circuit
  CODE 22 - Coolant temperature sensor circuit
  CODE 23 - (1986–88) Throttle body temperature sensor circuit
  CODE 24 - Throttle position sensor (TPS) circuit
  CODE 25 - Automatic idle speed (AIS) motor driver circuit
  CODE 26 - (1985–88) Peak injector current has not been reached
  CODE 27 - Fuel injector control problem
  CODE 31 - Purge solenoid circuit
  CODE 32 - (1984–85) Power loss/limit lamp circuit
  CODE 33 - A/C cutout relay circuit
  CODE 34 - (1984) EGR solenoid circuit
  CODE 34 - (1987–88) Speed control solenoid driver circuit
  CODE 35 - Fan control relay circuit
  CODE 37 - (1985–86) Shift indicator lamp circuit (manual transmission only)
  CODE 37 - (1987–88) Part throttle unlock (PTU) circuit (automatic only)
  CODE 41 - Charging system excess or no field circuit
  CODE 42 - Auto shutdown (ASD) relay driver circuit
  CODE 43 - Spark interface circuit
  CODE 44 - (1984) Internal logic module problem
  CODE 44 - (1986–87) Battery temperature sensor circuit
  CODE 44 - (1987½–88) Loss of FJ2 to logic board
  CODE 46 - (1985–88) Battery voltage too high
  CODE 47 - (1985–88) Battery voltage too low
  CODE 51 - (1984) Lean or rich condition indicated
  CODE 51 - (1985–88) Lean condition indicated
  CODE 52 - (1984) Internal logic module problem
  CODE 52 - (1985–88) Rich condition indicated
  CODE 53 - Internal module problem
  CODE 54 - (1984) Internal logic module problem
  CODE 55 - End of message
  CODE 88 - Start of test

Circuit Actuation Test Mode (ATM Test)

Put the system into the diagnostic test mode and wait for 55 to appear on the readout box display. Press and hold the ATM button on the readout box until the desired ATM test code appears on the display and then release the button. The logic module will turn the selected circuit on and off at two second intervals for five minutes and then turn the test off. To stop thew test before the five minute period, turn the ignition switch off.

Actuator Test Display Codes

CODE 01 - Spark activation—once every 2 seconds
CODE 02 - Injector activation—once every 2 seconds
CODE 03 - Automatic idle speed (AIS) activation—one step open/one step closed every 4 seconds
CODE 04 - Radiator fan relay—once every 2 seconds
CODE 05 - A/C WOT cutout relay—once every 2 seconds

NOTE: A/C switch must be in the on position to allow actuation. A/C fan will run continually.

CODE 06 - Automatic shutdown (ASD) relay—once every 2 seconds
CODE 07 - Purge solenoid activation—one toggle every 2 seconds
CODE 08 - (1986) Shift indicator lamp activation—one toggle every 2 seconds
CODE 08 - (1987–88) Speed control activation—speed control vent and vacuum every 2 seconds

NOTE: Speed control switch must be in the on position to allow actuation

CODE 09 - (1986–88) Alternator field control activation—one toggle every 2 seconds
CODE 10 - (1987–88) Shift indicator lamp activation—one toggle every 2 seconds

Sensor Test Mode (1986–88 Models)

1. Put the system into the actuation test mode (ATM test).
2. Press and hold the ATM button until the desired sensor access code appears on the display and then release the button.
3. Move the read/hold switch to the "HOLD" position.

NOTE: Since sensor access codes are the same as some ATM test codes, the ATM test circuit will turn on before moving the read/hold switch to the "HOLD" position.

4. The logic module will now use the readout box to display the output of the selected sensor. All readings displayed are to be divided by 10, except the coolant sensor which is to be multiplied by 10. Battery voltage is actual and no correction is required.

SENSOR READ TEST DISPLAY CODES

CODE 01 - Battery temperature sensor—display number divided by 10 equals sensor temperature
CODE 02 - Oxygen sensor voltage—display number divided by 10 equals sensor voltage
CODE 03 - Throttle body temperature sensor voltage—display number divided by 10 equals sensor voltage
CODE 04 - Engine coolant temperature sensor voltage—display number multiply by 10 equals degrees of engine coolant sensor
CODE 05 - Throttle position sensor voltage—display number divided by 10 equals sensor voltage
CODE 07 - Battery voltage—display number is voltage
CODE 08 - MAP sensor voltage—display number divided by 10 equals sensor voltage
CODE 09 - Cruise control switches: cruise off—display is blank, cruise on—display shows 00, cruise set—display shows 10, cruise resume—display shows 01
CODE 10 - (1987½–88) Fault code erase routine—display will flash zeros (0) for 4 seconds

Switch Test Mode

1. Make sure all the switches that send an input to the logic module are turned off.
2. Put the system into the diagnostic test mode and wait for 55 to appear on the readout box display.
3. Turn on the desired switch for input into the logic module. If the input is received by the logic module the display will change from "00" to "88" when the switch is activated and released.
   - Brake pedal
   - Gear shift selector: park, reverse, park
   - A/C switch (valid only if A/C dampened pressure switch is closed and blower switch on)

Engine Running Test Mode (1986–88 Models)

The Engine Running Test Mode monitors the sensors on the vehicle which check operating conditions while the engine is running. The engine running test mode can be performed with the engine idling in neutral and with parking brake on or actual driving conditions. With the diagnostic readout box read/hold switch in the "READ" position, the engine running test mode is initiated after the engine is started.

Select a test code by switching the read/hold switch to the "READ" position and the actuator button depressed until the desired code appears. Release actuator button and switch read/hold switch to "HOLD" position. The logic module will monitor that system test and results will be displayed.

ENGINE RUNNING TEST DISPLAY CODES

CODE 61 - Battery temperature sensor—display number divided by 10 equals voltage
CODE 62 - Oxygen sensor—display number divided by 10 equals voltage
CODE 63 - Fuel injector temperature sensor—display number divided by 10 equals voltage
CODE 64 - Engine coolant temperature sensor—display number multiplied by 10 equals degrees F
CODE 65 - Throttle position sensor—display number divided by 10 equals voltage
CODE 67 - Battery voltage sensor—display is voltage
CODE 68 - Manifold vacuum sensor—display is in. Hg.
CODE 69 - Minimum throttle position sensor—display number divided by 10 equals voltage
CODE 70 - Minimum airflow idle speed sensor—display number multiplied by 10 equals rpm (see minimum air flow check procedure)
CODE 71 - Vehicle speed sensor—display is mph
CODE 72 - Engine speed sensor—display number multiplied by 10 equals rpm

Throttle Body Minimum Air Flow Check Procedure— ATM #70

1. Connect diagnostic readout box Tool C–4805 or equivalent.
2. Remove air cleaner assembly. Plug heated air door vacuum hose.
3. While in PARK or NEUTRAL, start and run engine until cooling fan has cycled on and off at least once.
4. Connect timing light and tachometer.
5. Disconnect coolant temperature sensor and set basic timing to 12 degrees BTDC ± 2 degrees BTDC.
6. Turn engine off and reconnect coolant temperature sensor.
7. Disconnect PCV valve hose from intake manifold nipple and attach Miller Tool C–5004 or equivalent (0.125 in. orifice in attached hose) to intake manifold PCV nipple.

8. Restart and run engine at idle for at least one minute.

9. With readout box, press and hold ATM button with read/hold switch in READ position. Proceed to actuation test mode (ATM) #70.

10. Move read/hold switch to HOLD position. The following will then occur:
- AIS motor will fully close
- Idle spark advance will become fixed
- Idle fuel will become enriched
- Engine rpm will be displayed on readout box in units of rpm multiplied by 10.

11. Check idle rpm. Correct rpm should be within 1100–1300 rpm for 2.2L engine and 1050–1250 rpm for 2.5L engine. If rpm is not within specifications, replace throttle body.

12. Turn off engine and remove all diagnostic equipment.

13. Install PCV valve hose, air cleaner and heated air door vacuum hose.

DIAGNOSIS USING POWER LOSS/LIMIT (CHECK ENGINE) LAMP

If for some reason the diagnostic readout box is not available, the logic module can show fault codes by means of flashing the power loss (check engine) lamp on the instrument panel.

To activate this function, turn the ignition key ON-OFF-ON-OFF-ON within five seconds. The power loss (check engine) lamp will then come on for two seconds as a bulb check. Immediately following this it will display a fault code by flashing on and off. There is a short pause between flashes and a longer pause between digits. All codes displayed are two digit numbers with a four second pause between codes.

1. Lamp on for two seconds, then turns off.
2. Lamp flashes five pauses and then flashes once.
3. Lamp pauses for four seconds, flashes five times, pauses and then flashes five times.

The two codes are 51 and 55. Any number of codes can be displayed as long as they are in memory. The lamp will flash until all of them are displayed.

NOTE: In some cases proper diagnostic cannot be determined by only using fault codes. Remember they are only the result, not necessarily the reason for the problem. This driveability test procedure is designed for use with the Diagnostic Readout Box not the flashing power loss (check engine) lamp.

Additional Information From Power Loss (Check Engine) Lamp

Switch Test—After all codes are displayed, switch function can be verified. The lamp will turn on or off when a switch is turned on or off.

Unlike the diagnostic readout box, the power loss lamp cannot do the following:

1. Once the lamp begins to display fault codes, it can not be stopped. If code count is forgotten or lost, it is necessary to start over.

2. The lamp can not display any codes related to 88 diagnostic or blank displays.

3. The lamp can not show if the oxygen feedback system is switching (lean/rich).

4. The lamp can not perform the actuation test, sensor read test or engine running test modes.

DIAGNOSTIC PROCEDURE CHARTS

When using the Test Procedure some guidelines should be followed:
- Start from Test 1 of the catagory. Starting from any other test will give incorrect results.
- Tests are made up of many steps. Only perform the steps

which are required. Performing all steps will give incorrect results.
- Some steps within a test have reminders. These are to inform that previous instructions are still required.
- At the end of each test reconnect all wires and hoses, turn engine off if required and reinstall any components that were removed for testing.
- The vehicle being tested must have a fully charged battery, specific gravity 1.220 temperature corrected.
- To perform the cold test, the engine must not be started for at least 7 hours.
- To perform the warm test, the engine must be at normal operating temperature.

TOOLS AND EQUIPMENT

Make sure the following equipment is on hand:
1. Volt/ohmmeter
2. Jumper wires
3. Auxiliary vacuum supply (hand-held vacuum pump)
4. Fuel pressure gauge
5. Tachometer
6. Timing light
7. Oscilloscope
8. Vacuum gauge
9. High pressure gauge (Tool C–3292 or equivalent)
10. High pressure gauge adapter hoses (Tool C–4799 or equivalent)
11. Two gallon gasoline can
12. Diagnostic readout box (Tool C–4805 or equivalent)

1984-86 EFI DRIVEABILITY TEST PROCEDURES

Code	Type	Power Loss/Limit Lamp	Circuit	When Monitored By The Logic Module	When Put Into Memory	ATM Test Code	Sensor Access Code
11	Fault	No	Distributor Signal	During cranking.	If no distributor signal is present since the battery was disconnected.	None	None
12	Indication	No	Battery Feed to the Logic Module	All the time when the ignition switch is on.	If the battery feed to the logic module has been disconnected within the last 20-40 engine starts.	None	None
13	Fault	Yes	M.A.P. Sensor (Vacuum)	When the throttle is closed during cranking and after the engine starts.	If the M.A.P. sensor vacuum level does not change between cranking and when the engine starts.	None	None
14	Fault	Yes	M.A.P. Sensor (Electrical)	All the time when the ignition switch is on.	If the M.A.P. sensor signal is below .02 or above 4.9 volts.	None	08
15	Fault	No	Vehicle Speed Sensor	Over a 7 second period during decel from highway speeds when the throttle is closed.	If the speed sensor signal indicates less than 2 mph when the vehicle is moving.	None	None
16	Fault	Yes	Battery Voltage Sensing (Charging System)	All the time after one minute from when the engine starts.	If the battery sensing voltage drops below 4 or between 7½ and 8½ volts for more than 20 seconds.	None	07
17	Fault	No	Engine Cooling System	During cranking when engine coolant temperature is between −20 and 212°F.	If engine coolant temperature does not reach 160°F within 20 minutes after the engine is started.	None	None
21	Fault	No	Oxygen Sensor	All the time after 12 minutes from when the engine starts.	If there is no oxygen sensor signal for more than 22 seconds when in closed loop.	None	02
22	Fault	Yes	Engine Coolant Sensor	All the time when the ignition switch is on.	If the coolant sensor voltage is above 4.96 volts when the engine is cold or below .51 volts when the engine is warm.	None	04
23	Fault	No	Throttle Body Temperature Sensor	During cranking.	If the throttle body temperature sensor voltage is below .04 or above 4.96 when engine coolant temperature is above 77°F.	None	03
24	Fault	Yes	Throttle Position Sensor	All the time when the ignition switch is on.	If the throttle position sensor signal is below .16 or above 4.7 volts.	None	05
25	Fault	No	Automatic Idle Speed Motor (AIS)	Only when the AIS system is required to control the engine speed.	If proper voltage in the AIS system is not present. NOTE: Open circuit will not activate code.	03	None
26	Fault	No	Fuel Injector Driver	During cranking.	If the current through the fuel injector does not reach its proper peak level.	02	None
27	Fault	No	Fuel Control	All the time when the ignition switch is on.	If the fuel control interface fails to switch properly.	None	None
31	Fault	No	Canister Purge Solenoid	All the time when the ignition switch is on.	If the solenoid does not turn on and off when it should.	07	None
32	Fault	No	Power Loss/Power Limit Lamp	All the time when the ignition switch is on.	If the lamp does not turn on and off when it should.	None	None
33	Fault	No	A/C Cutout Relay	All the time when the ignition switch is on.	If the relay does not turn on and off when it should.	05	None

1984-86 EFI DRIVEABILITY TEST PROCEDURES

Code	Type	Power Loss/ Limit Lamp	Circuit	When Monitored By The Logic Module	When Put Into Memory	ATM Test Code	Sensor Access Code
35	Fault	No	Radiator Fan Relay Circuit	All the time when the ignition switch is on.	If the relay does not turn on and off when it should.	04	None
37	Fault	No	Shift Indicator Lamp (Manual Trans Only)	All the time when the ignition switch is on.	If the lamp does not turn on and off when it should.	08	None
41	Fault	No	Alternator Field Control (Charging System)	All the time when the ignition switch is on.	If the field control fails to switch properly.	09	None
42	Fault	No	Auto Shutdown	All the time when the ignition switch is on.	If the relay does not turn on and off when it should.	06	None
43	Fault	No	Spark Control	All the time when the ignition switch is on.	If the spark control interface fails to switch properly.	01	None
44	Fault	No	Battery Temperature Sensor (Charging System)	All the time when the ignition switch is on.	If the battery temperature sensor signal is below .04 or above 4.9 volts.	None	01
46	Fault	Yes	Battery Voltage Sensing (Charging System)	All the time when the engine is running.	If the battery sense voltage is more than 1 volt above the desired control voltage for more than 20 seconds.	None	None
47	Fault	No	Battery Voltage Sensing (Charging System)	When the engine has been running for more than 6 minutes, engine temperature above 160°F and engine rpm above 1,500 rpm.	If the battery sense voltage is less than 1 volt below the desired control voltage for more than 20 seconds.	None	None
51	Fault	No	Oxygen Feedback System	During all closed loop conditions.	If the system stays lean for more than 2 minutes.	None	None
52	Fault	No	Oxygen Feedback System	During all closed loop conditions.	If the system stays rich for more than 2 minutes.	None	None
53	Fault	No	Logic Module	All the time in the diagnostic mode.	If the logic module fails.	None	None
55	Indication	No			Indicates end of diagnostic mode.		
88	Indication	No			Indicates start of diagnostic mode. NOTE: This code must appear first in the diagnostic mode or fault codes will be inaccurate.		
0	Indication	No			Indicates oxygen feedback system is lean with the engine running.		
1	Indication	No			Indicates oxygen feedback system is rich with the engine running.		

TEST 1	STEP A	CHECKING FOR SPARK AT SPARK PLUGS
PROCEDURE	**TEST INDICATION**	**ACTION REQUIRED**
• Disconnect any spark plug wire. • Insert an insulated screwdriver in terminal. • Hold screwdriver shaft (¼") near a good engine ground. • Have someone crank the engine.	• There should be a good spark between screwdriver and ground as long as the engine is cranking. **NOTE:** Handle 1 or 2 sparks as no spark.	• Spark okay, **Perform TEST NO. 2.**
		• No spark at all, **Perform STEP B.**

TEST 1	STEP B	CHECKING FOR SPARK AT IGNITION COIL WIRE
PROCEDURE	**TEST INDICATION**	**ACTION REQUIRED**
• Disconnect ignition coil wire from distributor cap. • Hold coil wire (¼") near a good engine ground. • Have someone crank the engine.	• There should be a good spark between ignition coil wire and ground conditions. **NOTE:** Handle 1 or 2 sparks as no spark.	• Spark okay, repair secondary ignition system (distributor cap and/or rotor).
		• No spark, check ignition coil wire. If okay **Perform STEP C.**

IGNITION COIL WIRE

TEST 1	STEP C	CHECKING FOR FUEL FROM INJECTOR
PROCEDURE	**TEST INDICATION**	**ACTION REQUIRED**
• Remove the air cleaner cover. • Have someone crank the engine while you look for a fuel spray from the injector.	• There should be fuel spraying from the injector.	• Fuel spray okay. Perform **TEST NO. 6.**
		• No fuel spray. Perform **TEST NO. 14.**

TEST 2	STEP A	CHECKING FOR FUEL FROM INJECTOR
PROCEDURE	**TEST INDICATION**	**ACTION REQUIRED**
• Remove the air cleaner cover. • Have someone crank the engine while you look for a fuel spray from the injector.	• There should be a slow steady stream of fuel from the injector. **NOTE:** If injector is flooding. Perform **TEST NO. 13.**	• Fuel spray okay. **Perform TEST NO. 3.**
		• No fuel spray. Perform **TEST NO. 9.**

TEST 3	STEP A	CHECKING LOGIC MODULE
PROCEDURE	**TEST INDICATION**	**ACTION REQUIRED**
• Connect diagnostic readout box to engine harness connector. • Turn ignition switch on-off-on-off-on within 5 seconds.	• Code 88 should appear on the readout box display.	• Code 88 appears. Perform **TEST NO. 4.**
		• Code 88 does not appear, replace the logic module. **CAUTION:** Before replacing the logic module make sure your diagnostic readout box is operational and that there is not an open circuit in the wires between the logic module and diagnostic connector.

DIAGNOSTIC READOUT BOX

TEST 4	STEP A	CHECKING FOR FUEL FOULED SPARK PLUGS
PROCEDURE	**TEST INDICATION**	**ACTION REQUIRED**
• Remove spark plugs. • Look at tips for wet fuel.	• Spark plug tips should not be wet with fuel. **NOTE:** It is normal for spark plugs to be black after engine is started cold.	• Spark plugs are dry. Perform **TEST NO. 5.**
		• Spark plugs are wet with fuel, clean and reinstall. Do not replace spark plugs. • Attempt restart.

1984-86 EFI DRIVEABILITY TEST PROCEDURES

TEST 5	STEP A	CHECKING ENGINE TIMING
PROCEDURE	**TEST INDICATION**	**ACTION REQUIRED**
• Connect timing device to engine. • Have someone crank engine while you look at the timing marks.	• Timing should be within 0°-16° BTC.	• Timing okay, check compression and valve timing. • Timing not okay, **Perform Step B.**

TEST 5	STEP B	CHECKING ENGINE TIMING
PROCEDURE	**TEST INDICATION**	**ACTION REQUIRED**
REMINDERS • Timing device connected to engine. • Set timing to 10° BTC during cranking.	• Engine should start.	• Engine starts reset to specifications. • Engine does not start, check compression and valve timing.

TEST 6	STEP A	CHECKING IGNITION CONTROL SYSTEM FOR FAULT CODES
PROCEDURE	**TEST INDICATION**	**ACTION REQUIRED**
• Connect diagnostic readout box to the engine harness connector. • Disconnect and reconnect the battery connector. • Crank the engine for 5 seconds and then turn the ignition switch off. • Put the system in the Diagnostic Mode. (Refer to introduction) • **Record all codes**	88-12-55 No fault codes	Perform TEST NO. 7.
	88-12-43-55 Spark control circuit	Perform TEST NO. 8.

DIAGNOSTIC READOUT BOX
BATTERY CONNECTOR

TEST 7	STEP A	CHECKING FOR THE VOLTAGE SUPPLY TO THE IGNITION COIL POSITIVE TERMINAL FROM THE POWER MODULE
PROCEDURE	**TEST INDICATION**	**ACTION REQUIRED**
REMINDERS • Diagnostic readout box connected to the engine harness connector. • System in the diagnostic mode. • Connect an analog voltmeter to the positive terminal of the ignition coil and ground. • Put the system in the **ATM Test Mode — Code 01.** (Refer to introduction)	• Voltmeter should read within one volt of battery voltage.	• Voltage okay, **Perform STEP B.** • 0 volts, repair wire of coil positive terminal for open circuit to the power module

DIAGNOSTIC READOUT BOX
POSITIVE TERMINAL
IGNITION COIL

TEST 7	STEP B	CHECKING THE IGNITION SYSTEM PRIMARY CONTROL CIRCUIT VOLTAGE AT THE IGNITION COIL (−) TERMINAL
PROCEDURE	**TEST INDICATION**	**ACTION REQUIRED**
REMINDERS • Diagnostic readout box connected to the engine harness connector. • System in ATM Test Mode — Code 01. • Connect an analog voltmeter to the negative terminal of the ignition coil and ground.	• Voltmeter should be pulsating between 1 and 3 volts.	• Voltage okay, replace the ignition coil.
		• Voltmeter not pulsating but reads above 10 volts. **Perform STEP C.**
		• Voltmeter pulsating between 0 and 1 volt, replace the ignition coil.
		• Voltmeter not pulsating but reads between 0 and 1 volt. **Perform STEP D.**

DIAGNOSTIC READOUT BOX
ANALOG VOLTMETER
NEGATIVE TERMINAL
IGNITION COIL

TEST 7	STEP C	CHECKING THE IGNITION SYSTEM PRIMARY CONTROL CIRCUIT FOR AN OPEN CIRCUIT
PROCEDURE	**TEST INDICATION**	**ACTION REQUIRED**
• Turn the ignition switch off. • Disconnect the 10-way connector from the power module. • Connect an ohmmeter between the negative (−) terminal of the ignition coil and cavity No. 1 of the power module 10-way connector.	• Ohmmeter should show continuity.	• Continuity, replace the power module. CAUTION: Before replacing the power module check the terminal in cavity No. 1 of the 10-way connector to make sure that it is not spread apart causing a poor connection. • No continuity repair the wire of cavity No. 1 for an open circuit

IGNITION COIL
OHMMETER
POWER MODULE 10-WAY CONNECTOR

TEST 7	STEP D	CHECKING THE IGNITION COIL PRIMARY WINDINGS FOR AN OPEN CIRCUIT
PROCEDURE	**TEST INDICATION**	**ACTION REQUIRED**
REMINDERS • Diagnostic readout box connected to the engine harness connector. • Turn the ignition switch off. • Disconnect the wire from the negative side (−) of the ignition coil. • Connect the voltmeter to the negative (−) terminal of the ignition coil and ground. • Put the system in the **ATM Test Mode – Code 01.**	• Voltmeter should above 10 volts.	• Voltage okay, **Perform STEP E.** • 0 volts replace the ignition coil.

DIAGNOSTIC READOUT BOX
VOLTMETER
IGNITION COIL

TEST 7	STEP E	CHECKING THE IGNITION SYSTEM PRIMARY CIRCUIT FOR A SHORT CIRCUIT TO GROUND
PROCEDURE	**TEST INDICATION**	**ACTION REQUIRED**
REMINDERS • Ignition coil negative (−) wire disconnected. • Turn the ignition switch off. • Disconnect the 10-way connector from the power module. • Connect an ohmmeter between cavity No. 1 of the power module 10-way connector and ground.	• Ohmmeter should not show continuity.	• No continuity, replace the power module. • Continuity, repair wire of cavity No. 10 for a short circuit to ground.

OHMMETER
POWER MODULE 10-WAY CONNECTOR

1984-86 EFI DRIVEABILITY TEST PROCEDURES

TEST 8	STEP A	CHECKING FOR FAULT CODE 43 – SPARK CONTROL CIRCUIT
PROCEDURE	TEST INDICATION	ACTION REQUIRED

PROCEDURE		TEST INDICATION	ACTION REQUIRED
REMINDERS • Diagnostic readout box connected to the engine harness connector. • Turn the ignition switch off. • Disconnect the ignition coil wire at the distributor and place it on the thermostat housing so there is a ¼ inch gap. • Disconnect the white connector from the logic module and connect one end of a jumper wire to cavity No. 6. • Turn the ignition switch on and press the ATM button on the readout box.	• Touch the other end of the jumper to a good ground. Make and break this connection several times while looking at the ignition coil wire. DIAGNOSTIC READOUT BOX JUMPER LOGIC MODULE WHITE CONNECTOR	• There should be spark at the ignition coil wire as you make and break the connection.	• Spark okay, replace the logic module. CAUTION: Before replacing the logic module check the terminal in cavity No. 6 of the white connector to make sure it is not crushed causing a poor connection. • No spark, Perform STEP B.

TEST 8	STEP B	CHECKING THE SPARK CONTROL WIRE BETWEEN THE LOGIC AND POWER MODULES FOR AN OPEN CIRCUIT
PROCEDURE	TEST INDICATION	ACTION REQUIRED

PROCEDURE		TEST INDICATION	ACTION REQUIRED
REMINDERS • Logic module white connector disconnected. • Turn the ignition switch off. • Remove the jumper wire from cavity No. 6 of the white connector. • Disconnect the power module 12-way connector. • Connect an ohmmeter between cavity No. 6 of the white and cavity No. 10 of the 12-way connectors.	LOGIC MODULE WHITE CONNECTOR OHMMETER POWER MODULE 12-WAY CONNECTOR	• Ohmmeter should show continuity.	• Continuity, replace the power module. CAUTION: Before replacing the power module check the terminal in cavity No. 10 of the 12-way connector to make sure it is not spread apart causing a poor connection. • No continuity, repair wire for an open circuit.

TEST 9	STEP A	CHECKING FUEL CONTROL SYSTEM FOR FAULT CODES
PROCEDURE	TEST INDICATION	ACTION REQUIRED

PROCEDURE		TEST INDICATION	ACTION REQUIRED
• Connect the diagnostic readout box to the engine harness connector. • Disconnect and reconnect the battery connector. • Crank the engine for 5 seconds and then turn the ignition switch off. • Put the system in the Diagnostic Mode. (Refer to introduction)	DIAGNOSTIC READOUT BOX BATTERY CONNECTOR	88-12-55 No fault codes	Perform TEST NO. 10.
		88-12-26-55 Fuel injector driver circuit	Perform TEST NO. 11.
		88-12-27-55 Fuel control circuit	Perform TEST NO. 12.

TEST 10	STEP A	CHECKING FOR PRESSURE IN FUEL SUPPLY SYSTEM
PROCEDURE	TEST INDICATION	ACTION REQUIRED

PROCEDURE		TEST INDICATION	ACTION REQUIRED
REMINDERS • Diagnostic readout box connected to engine harness connector. • Turn the ignition switch off. • Install fuel pressure gauge in fuel supply hose at the throttle body. CAUTION: Fuel may be under high pressure in the supply hose. Refer to the service manual for instructions on how to bleed down the system. • Turn ignition switch to the run position. • Press the ATM button on the readout box.	DIAGNOSTIC READOUT BOX RETURN LINE SUPPLY LINE FUEL PRESSURE SUPPLY LINE	• Fuel pressure should read 14½ psi ± 1. 1986-88 • Fuel pressure should read 36 psi ± 2. 1985	• Fuel pressure okay, Perform STEP B. • No fuel pressure Perform STEP C.

TEST 10	STEP B	CHECKING THE THROTTLE POSITION SENSOR	1985
PROCEDURE	TEST INDICATION	ACTION REQUIRED	

PROCEDURE		TEST INDICATION	ACTION REQUIRED
• Connect a voltmeter to the orange with dark blue tracer wire of the throttle body 6-way connector and ground. • Turn ignition switch to the run position.	WIRE END THROTTLE BODY 6-WAY CONNECTOR	• Voltmeter should read 1 volt ± 1/2 volt.	• Voltage okay, replace the injector. • Voltage not okay, replace the throttle position sensor.

TEST 10	STEP B	CHECKING THE THROTTLE POSITION SENSOR	1986-88
PROCEDURE	TEST INDICATION	ACTION REQUIRED	

PROCEDURE		TEST INDICATION	ACTION REQUIRED
• Put the system into the **Sensor Test Mode — Access Code 05.** (Refer to introduction)		• Display on readout box should be 1 volt ± 1/2 volt NOTE: Don't forget to divide display reading by 10 for actual reading.	• Voltage okay, replace the injector. • Voltage not okay, replace the throttle position sensor.

TEST 10	STEP C	CHECKING INTANK FUEL PUMP
PROCEDURE	TEST INDICATION	ACTION REQUIRED

PROCEDURE		TEST INDICATION	ACTION REQUIRED
REMINDERS • Ignition key in the run position. • Diagnostic readout box connected to engine harness connector. • Press ATM button readout box. • Listen for intake fuel pump noise at rear of car.	DIAGNOSTIC READOUT BOX	• You should be able to hear fuel pump operate.	• Fuel pump operates: • Check fuel supply line and hoses between fuel tank and throttle body for restrictions. • Check for a plugged fuel filter. • Check for a plugged intank fuel filter. • Fuel pump does not operate, Perform STEP D.

TEST 10	STEP D	CHECKING VOLTAGE SUPPLY TO INTANK PUMP
PROCEDURE	TEST INDICATION	ACTION REQUIRED

PROCEDURE		TEST INDICATION	ACTION REQUIRED
REMINDERS • Ignition key in the run position. • Diagnostic readout box connected to the engine harness connector. • Raise car on hoist. • Disconnect the intank fuel pump connector. • Connect voltmeter to dark green with black tracer wire of connector and ground. • Press ATM button on readout box.	FUEL TANK CONNECTOR 1985 DIAGNOSTIC READOUT BOX VOLTMETER GY DG/BK IN TANK FUEL PUMP CONNECTOR 1986-88	• Voltmeter should read within one volt of battery voltage	• Voltage okay, Perform STEP E. • Voltage not okay, repair wire for open circuit to wiring harness splice.

1984-86 EFI DRIVEABILITY TEST PROCEDURES

TEST 10	STEP E	CHECKING INTANK PUMP GROUND CIRCUIT
PROCEDURE	**TEST INDICATION**	**ACTION REQUIRED**

PROCEDURE	TEST INDICATION	ACTION REQUIRED
REMINDERS • Car raised on hoist. • Intank fuel pump connector disconnected. • Connect ohmmeter between gray wire of fuel pump connector and ground. FUEL TANK CONNECTOR 1985 GY · DG/BK IN TANK FUEL PUMP CONNECTOR 1986-88	• Ohmmeter should show continuity with no resistance.	• Continuity okay, replace intank fuel pump.
	• No continuity, repair wire for open circuit to body ground connection.	

TEST 11	STEP A	CHECKING FOR FAULT CODE 26 – FUEL INJECTOR DRIVER CIRCUIT
PROCEDURE	**TEST INDICATION**	**ACTION REQUIRED**

PROCEDURE	TEST INDICATION	ACTION REQUIRED
REMINDERS • Diagnostic readout box connected to engine harness connector. • System in the Diagnostic Test Mode. DIAGNOSTIC READOUT BOX ANALOG VOLTMETER TN WT FUEL INJECTOR CONNECTOR • Disconnect the fuel injector connector. • Connect an analog voltmeter between the terminals of the fuel injector connector. • **Select the lowest voltage scale available on your voltmeter.** • Put the system in the **ATM Test Mode — Code 02.**	• Voltmeter should pulsate between 0 and 1 volt. **NOTE:** If voltmeter is showing a negative voltage, reverse its leads at the injector connector, and repeat the test.	• Voltmeter pulsates, replace the fuel injector.
	• **Voltmeter does not pulsate. Perform STEP B.**	

TEST 11	STEP B	CHECKING FUEL INJECTOR CONTROL WIRE TO THE POWER MODULE FOR AN OPEN CIRCUIT
PROCEDURE	**TEST INDICATION**	**ACTION REQUIRED**

PROCEDURE	TEST INDICATION	ACTION REQUIRED
REMINDERS • Injector connector disconnected. • Turn ignition switch off. • Disconnect the power module 10-way connector. • Connect ohmmeter between cavity No. 7 of 10-way connector and white wire of injector connector. TN WT FUEL INJECTOR CONNECTOR OHMMETER POWER MODULE 10-WAY CONNECTOR	• Ohmmeter should show continuity.	• Continuity, **Perform STEP C.**
	• No continuity, repair wire of cavity No. 7 for open circuit to injector.	

TEST 11	STEP C	CHECKING FUEL INJECTOR CONTROL WIRE TO THE POWER MODULE FOR AN OPEN CIRCUIT
PROCEDURE	**TEST INDICATION**	**ACTION REQUIRED**

PROCEDURE	TEST INDICATION	ACTION REQUIRED
REMINDERS • Power module 10-way connector disconnected. • Injector connector disconnected. • Connect ohmmeter between cavity No. 5 of 10-way connector and tan wire of injector connector. OHMMETER TN WT FUEL INJECTOR CONNECTOR POWER MODULE 10-WAY CONNECTOR	• Ohmmeter should show continuity.	• Continuity, replace the power module. **CAUTION:** Before replacing the power module check the terminals in cavities 5 and 7 of the 10-way connector to make sure they are not spread apart causing a poor connection.
	• No continuity, repair wire of cavity No. 5 for open circuit to injector.	

TEST 12	STEP A	CHECKING FOR FAULT CODE 27 – FUEL CONTROL CIRCUIT
PROCEDURE	**TEST INDICATION**	**ACTION REQUIRED**

PROCEDURE	TEST INDICATION	ACTION REQUIRED
REMINDERS • Diagnostic readout box connected to the engine harness connector. • Turn the ignition switch off. • Disconnect the injector connector. • Connect a voltmeter between the terminals of the injector connector. • Disconnect the logic module white connector. • Connect a jumper wire between cavity No. 2 of the white connector and ground. • Turn the ignition switch to the run position. • Press the ATM button on the readout box. VOLTMETER TN WT FUEL INJECTOR CONNECTOR JUMPER LOGIC MODULE WHITE CONNECTOR	• Voltmeter should show voltage. **NOTE:** The amount of voltage is not important. Just make sure there is some. Also if voltmeter is showing a negative voltage, reverse its leads at the injector connector and repeat the test.	• Some voltage, replace the logic module. **CAUTION:** Before replacing the logic module check the terminal in cavity No. 2 of the white connector to make sure it is not crushed causing a poor connection.
	• No voltage, **Perform STEP B.**	

TEST 12	STEP B	CHECKING THE FUEL CONTROL WIRE BETWEEN THE LOGIC AND POWER MODULE FOR AN OPEN CIRCUIT
PROCEDURE	**TEST INDICATION**	**ACTION REQUIRED**

PROCEDURE	TEST INDICATION	ACTION REQUIRED
REMINDERS • Logic module white connector disconnected. • Turn the ignition switch off. • Remove the jumper wire from cavity No. 2 of the white connector. • Disconnect the power module 12-way connector. • Connect an ohmmeter between cavity No. 2 of the white and cavity No. 1 of the 12-way connectors. OHMMETER POWER MODULE 12-WAY CONNECTOR LOGIC MODULE WHITE CONNECTOR	• Ohmmeter should show continuity.	• Continuity, replace the power module. **CAUTION:** Before replacing the power module check the terminal in cavity No. 1 of the 12-way connector to make sure it is not spread apart causing a poor connection.
	• No continuity repair wire for an open circuit.	

TEST 13	STEP A	CHECKING FOR A FLOODING INJECTOR
PROCEDURE	**TEST INDICATION**	**ACTION REQUIRED**

PROCEDURE	TEST INDICATION	ACTION REQUIRED
REMINDERS • Throttle body air intake hose removed. • Remove air cleaner assembly. • Disconnect injector electrical connector. • Have someone crank engine while you look for a fuel spray from injector. DISCONNECT TN □□ WT FUEL INJECTOR CONNECTOR	• There should be no fuel spraying from injector	• Fuel spraying replace injector.
	• No fuel spraying **Perform STEP B.**	

TEST 13	STEP B	CHECKING THE FUEL CONTROL CIRCUIT TO THE POWER MODULE
PROCEDURE	**TEST INDICATION**	**ACTION REQUIRED**

PROCEDURE	TEST INDICATION	ACTION REQUIRED
REMINDERS • Air cleaner removed. • Diagnostic readout box connected to the wiring harness connector. • Turn the ignition switch off. • Disconnect the logic module white connector. • Reconnect the injector connector. • Turn the ignition switch to the run position. • Press the ATM button. DIAGNOSTIC READOUT BOX DISCONNECT LOGIC MODULE WHITE CONNECTOR	• There should be no fuel spraying from injector	• Fuel spraying from injector Perform STEP C.
		• No fuel spraying, replace the logic module.

1984-86 EFI DRIVEABILITY TEST PROCEDURES

TEST 13	STEP C	CHECKING THE FUEL CONTROL WIRE BETWEEN THE LOGIC AND POWER MODULE FOR A SHORT TO GROUND

PROCEDURE	TEST INDICATION	ACTION REQUIRED
REMINDERS • Logic module white connector, disconnected. • Turn the ignition switch off. • Disconnect the power module 12-way connector. • Connect an ohmmeter between cavity No. 1 of the 12-way connector and ground.	• Ohmmeter should not show continuity.	• No continuity replace the power module.
		• Continuity repair wire for short to ground

POWER MODULE
12-WAY CONNECTOR

TEST 14	STEP A	CHECKING SYSTEM FOR FAULT CODES

PROCEDURE	TEST INDICATION	ACTION REQUIRED
• Connect diagnostic read-out box to engine harness connector. • Disconnect and reconnect the battery connector. • Crank the engine for 5 seconds, and then turn the ignition switch to the run position for 5 seconds before turning to off. • Put the system in the Diagnostic Mode. (Refer to introduction) • Record all codes.	88-12-55 No fault codes	Repair wire in cavity No. 6 of the power module 10-way connector for an open circuit to ignition coil and fuel pump.
	No Code 88 System power circuits	Perform TEST NO. 15.
	88-11-12-55 Distributor pickup circuit	Perform TEST NO. 16.
	88-26-42-55 Auto shutdown relay pull in coil circuit.	Perform TEST NO. 17.
	88-11-12-22-23-24-55 Sensor ground circuit	Repair wire in cavity No. 25 of the logic module white connector for an open circuit.
	88-12-26-55 Auto shutdown relay output circuit.	Replace power module.

DIAGNOSTIC READOUT BOX

BATTERY CONNECTOR

TEST 15	STEP A	CHECKING FOR NO CODE 88 – SYSTEM POWER CIRCUIT FOR THE 5 VOLT SUPPLY

PROCEDURE	TEST INDICATION	ACTION REQUIRED
• Turn ignition switch off. • Connect a digital voltmeter to cavity No. 1 of the logic module white connector and ground. • Turn the ignition switch to the run position.	• Voltmeter should read at least 4½ volts.	• Voltage okay, Perform STEP B.
		• 0 volts. Perform STEP F.

DIGITAL VOLTMETER

LOGIC MODULE
WHITE CONNECTOR

TEST 15	STEP B	CHECKING BATTERY VOLTAGE TO THE LOGIC MODULE

PROCEDURE	TEST INDICATION	ACTION REQUIRED
• Turn the ignition switch off. • Connect a voltmeter to cavity No. 2 of the logic module black connector and ground.	• Voltmeter should read within one volt of battery voltage.	• Voltage okay, replace the logic module. **CAUTION:** Before replacing the logic module, check the terminal in cavity No. 2 of the black connector to make sure it is not crushed causing a poor connection. Also make sure your diagnostic readout box is operational and that there is not an open circuit in the wires between the logic module and diagnostic connector.
		• 0-Volts. Perform STEP C.

VOLTMETER

LOGIC MODULE
BLACK CONNECTOR

TEST 15	STEP C	CHECKING THE BATTEY VOLTAGE SUPPLY FROM THE POWER MODULE

PROCEDURE	TEST INDICATION	ACTION REQUIRED
• Disconnect the power module 12-way connector. • Connect a voltmeter to pin No. 6 of the power module and ground.	• Voltmeter should read within one volt of battery voltage.	• Voltage okay, repair wire to cavity No. 2 of the logic module black connector for an open circuit.
		• 0-volts Perform STEP D.

VOLTMETER

POWER MODULE
12-WAY PIN CONNECTOR

TEST 15	STEP D	CHECKING THE BATTERY VOLTAGE SUPPLY TO THE POWER MODULE

PROCEDURE	TEST INDICATION	ACTION REQUIRED
• Disconnect the 10-way connector from the power module. • Connect a voltmeter to cavity No. 4 of the 10-way connector and ground.	• Voltmeter should read within one volt of battery voltage.	• Voltage okay. Perform STEP E.
		• 0 volts, repair the wire in cavity No. 4 for an open circuit to the battery. **NOTE:** This wire has a fusable link in it. If it is blown, circuit must be repaired for a short to ground.

VOLTMETER

POWER MODULE
10-WAY CONNECTOR

TEST 15	STEP E	CHECKING THE AUTO SHUTDOWN RELAY OUTPUT CIRCUIT FOR A SHORT CIRCUIT TO GROUND

PROCEDURE	TEST INDICATION	ACTION REQUIRED
REMINDERS • Power module 10-way connector disconnected. • Disconnect the wire from the ignition coil positive (+) terminal. • Disconnect the intank fuel pump connector. • Connect an ohmmeter between cavity No. 6 of the power module 10-way connector and ground.	• Ohmmeter should not show continuity.	• No continuity, replace the power module. **CAUTION:** Before replacing the power module check the terminal in cavity No. 4 of the 10-way connector to make sure it is not spread apart causing a poor connection.
		• Continuity, repair wire of cavity No. 6 for a short circuit to ground. • Replace power module

OHMMETER

POWER MODULE
10-WAY CONNECTOR

TEST 15	STEP F	CHECKING LOGIC MODULE GROUND CIRCUIT	1985

PROCEDURE	TEST INDICATION	ACTION REQUIRED
• Turn the ignition switch off. • Disconnect the white connector from the logic module. • Connect an ohmmeter between cavity No. 24 of the logic module white connector and ground.	• Ohmmeter should show continuity	• Continuity. Perform STEP G.
		• No continuity, repair wire of cavity No. 24 for an open circuit

LOGIC MODULE
WHITE CONNECTOR
VIEW FROM WIRE END

5–39

1984-86 EFI DRIVEABILITY TEST PROCEDURES

TEST 15	STEP F	CHECKING THE LOGIC MODULE GROUND CIRCUIT 1986–88

PROCEDURE	TEST INDICATION	ACTION REQUIRED
• Turn the ignition switch off. • Disconnect the black connector from the logic module. • Connect an ohmmeter between cavity No. 7 or 8 of the logic module black connector and ground.	• Ohmmeter should show continuity.	• Continuity. Perform **STEP G.**
		• Open circuit, repair wires of cavity 7 and 8 for an open circuit to the wiring harness splice.

LOGIC MODULE BLACK CONNECTOR

TEST 15	STEP G	CHECKING THE SYSTEM POWER CIRCUIT FOR THE 8 VOLT SUPPLY TO THE LOGIC MODULE

PROCEDURE	TEST INDICATION	ACTION REQUIRED
REMINDERS • Ignition switch in the run position. • Connect a digital voltmeter to cavity No. 23 of the logic module white connector and ground.	• Voltmeter should read at least 7 volts.	• Voltage okay. Perform **STEP H.**
		• Voltage not okay. Perform **STEP I.**

DIGITAL VOLTMETER

LOGIC MODULE WHITE CONNECTOR

TEST 15	STEP H	CHECKING FOR NO 5 VOLTS IN SYSTEM POWER CIRCUIT CAUSED BY A SHORTED M.A.P. SENSOR

PROCEDURE	TEST INDICATION	ACTION REQUIRED
• Turn the ignition switch off. • Disconnect both connectors from logic module. • Remove logic module from cowl side. • Remove cover plate of logic module to gain access to M.A.P. sensor connector. • Disconnect M.A.P. sensor connector. • Reconnect logic module connectors. • Connect a voltmeter to cavity No. 1 of logic module black connector and ground. • Turn ignition switch to the run position.	• Voltmeter should read at least 4½ volts.	• Voltage okay, replace the M.A.P. sensor.
		• 0 volts, replace the logic module.

VOLTMETER

LOGIC MODULE BLACK CONNECTOR

TEST 15	STEP I	CHECKING FOR NO 8 VOLTS IN SYSTEM POWER CIRCUIT CAUSED BY A SHORTED DISTRIBUTOR PICKUP

PROCEDURE	TEST INDICATION	ACTION REQUIRED
REMINDERS • Voltmeter connected to cavity No. 23 of logic module white connector and ground. • Ignition switch in the run position. • Disconnect the distributor connector.	• Voltmeter should read at least 7 volts.	• Voltage okay, replace distributor pickup coil.
		• 0 volts, Perform **STEP J.**

VOLTMETER

LOGIC MODULE WHITE CONNECTOR

TEST 15	STEP J	CHECKING THE SYSTEM POWER CIRCUIT FOR THE 8 VOLT OUTPUT FROM THE POWER MODULE

PROCEDURE	TEST INDICATION	ACTION REQUIRED
• Turn the ignition switch off. • Disconnect the 12-way connector from the power module. • Connect a voltmeter to pin No. 12 of the power module and ground. • Turn the ignition switch to the run position.	• Voltmeter should read at least 7 volts.	• Voltage okay, repair the wire in cavity No. 12 of the power module 12-way connector for an open circuit to the logic module. **NOTE:** Check the terminal in cavity No. 12 to make sure it is not spread apart causing a poor connection.
		• 0 volts. Perform **STEP K.**

VOLTMETER

POWER MODULE 12-WAY PIN CONNECTOR

TEST 15	STEP K	CHECKING FOR IGNITION SWITCH VOLTAGE SUPPLY TO THE POWER MODULE

PROCEDURE	TEST INDICATION	ACTION REQUIRED
• Turn the ignition switch off. • Disconnect the 10-way connector from the power module. • Connect the positive lead of a voltmeter to cavity No. 2 of the 10-way connector. • Connect the negative lead of the voltmeter to either cavity No. 9 or 10 of the 10-way connector. • Turn the ignition switch to the run position.	• Voltmeter should read within one volt battery voltage.	• Voltage okay, replace the power module. **CAUTION:** Before replacing the power module, check the terminals in cavities 2, 9 and 10 of the 10-way connector to make sure they are not spread apart causing a poor connection.
		• 0 volts, move voltmeter negative lead to a good engine ground and if — • Voltmeter now reads within one volt of battery voltage, repair power module ground for an open circuit. • Voltmeter still reads 0 volts repair wire in cavity No. 2 for an open circuit to the ignition switch.

POWER MODULE 10-WAY CONNECTOR

TEST 16	STEP A	CHECKING FOR FAULT CODE 11 – DISTRIBUTOR PICKUP CIRCUIT

PROCEDURE	TEST INDICATION	ACTION REQUIRED
• Turn ignition switch off. • Disconnect distributor pick up coil connector. • Remove coil wire from distributor and place it (⅛ inch) near a good engine ground. • Turn ignition switch to the run position. • Connect a jumper wire to the pickup coil harness connector cavity No. 2 and 3. • Make and break this connection several times while looking at coil wire.	• There should be spark at the coil wire.	• Spark okay, **Perform STEP B.**
		• No spark, Perform **STEP C.**

JUMPER

DISTRIBUTOR PICKUP COIL HARNESS CONNECTOR

TEST 16	STEP B	CHECKING FOR THE 8 VOLT POWER SUPPLY TO THE DISTRIBUTOR PICKUP FROM THE POWER MODULE

PROCEDURE	TEST INDICATION	ACTION REQUIRED
REMINDERS • Distributor pick up coil connector disconnected. • Ignition switch in the run position. • Connect a voltmeter to cavity No. 1 of the pickup coil harness connector and ground.	• Voltmeter should read at least 7 volts.	• Voltage not okay, replace the distributor pick up coil. **CAUTION:** Before replacing the pick up check the terminals in the distributor harness connector to make sure they are not spread apart causing a poor connection.
		• Voltage not okay, repair wire of cavity No. 1 for open circuit to wiring harness splice.

DISTRIBUTOR PICKUP COIL HARNESS CONNECTOR

1984-86 EFI DRIVEABILITY TEST PROCEDURES

TEST 16	STEP C	CHECKING FOR THE PICKUP COIL SIGNAL VOLTAGE FROM THE LOGIC MODULE
PROCEDURE	**TEST INDICATION**	**ACTION REQUIRED**

REMINDERS

- Distributor pick up coil connector disconnected.
- Ignition switch in the run position.
- Connect the positive lead of the voltmeter to cavity No. 3 of the pickup coil harness connector.
- Connect the negative lead of the voltmeter to cavity No. 2 of the pickup coil harness connector.

- Voltmeter should read at least 4 volts. → Voltage okay, replace the logic module.

- 0 volts. **Perform STEP D.**

DISTRIBUTOR PICKUP COIL HARNESS CONNECTOR

TEST 16	STEP D	CHECKING THE DISTRIBUTOR PICKUP HARNESS GROUND CIRCUIT
PROCEDURE	**TEST INDICATION**	**ACTION REQUIRED**

REMINDERS

- Distributor pick up coil connector disconnected.
- Ignition switch in the run position.
- Positive lead of a voltmeter connected to cavity No. 3 of the pickup coil harness connector.
- Connect the negative lead of the voltmeter to a good engine ground.

- Voltmeter should read at least 4 volts. → Voltage okay, repair wire in cavity No. 2 of the distributor harness connector for an open circuit to the wiring harness splice.

- 0 volts. **Perform STEP E.**

DISTRIBUTOR PICKUP COIL HARNESS CONNECTOR

TEST 16	STEP E	CHECKING FOR THE PICKUP COIL SIGNAL VOLTAGE AT THE LOGIC MODULE
PROCEDURE	**TEST INDICATION**	**ACTION REQUIRED**

REMINDERS

- Ignition switch in the run position.
- Connect a voltmeter to cavity No. 10 of the logic module white connector and ground.

- Voltmeter should read at least 4 volts. → Voltage okay, repair wire in cavity No. 10 for an open circuit to distributor wiring harness connector.

- 0 volts replace the logic module.

CAUTION: Before replacing the logic module, check the terminal in cavity No. 10 of the white connector to make sure it is not crushed causing a poor connection.

LOGIC MODULE WHITE CONNECTOR

TEST 17	STEP A	CHECKING FOR FAULT CODES 26-42 – AUTO SHUTDOWN RELAY PULL IN COIL CIRCUIT
PROCEDURE	**TEST INDICATION**	**ACTION REQUIRED**

- Turn the ignition switch off.
- Disconnect the white connector from the logic module.
- Connect a voltmeter to cavity No. 17 of the white connector and ground.
- Turn the ignition switch to the run position.

- Voltmeter should read within one volt of battery voltage. → Voltage okay, replace the logic module.

CAUTION: Before replacing the logic module, check the terminal in cavity No. 17 of the white connector to make sure it is not crushed causing a poor connection.

- 0-1 volts, **Perform STEP B.**

LOGIC MODULE WHITE CONNECTOR

TEST 17	STEP B	CHECKING THE AUTO SHUTDOWN RELAY PULL IN COIL CIRCUIT AT THE POWER MODULE
PROCEDURE	**TEST INDICATION**	**ACTION REQUIRED**

- Turn the ignition switch off.
- Disconnect the 12-way connector from the power module.
- Turn the ignition switch to the run position.
- Connect a voltmeter to Pin No. 5 of the power module and ground.

- Voltmeter should read within one volt of battery voltage. → Voltage okay, repair wire in cavity No. 5 of the power mode 12-way connector for an open or shorted circuit.

CAUTION: Check the terminal in cavity No. 12 of the 12-way to make sure it is not spread apart causing a poor connection.

- 0-1 volts, replace the power module.

POWER MODULE 12-WAY PIN CONNECTOR

NOTES

TEST 1	STEP A	CHECKING SYSTEM FOR FAULT CODES		
PROCEDURE	**TEST INDICATION**	**CIRCUIT**	**ACTION REQUIRED**

PROCEDURE	TEST INDICATION	CIRCUIT	ACTION REQUIRED
• Connect diagnostic read-out box to engine harness connector	88-12-55	No fault codes	Perform STEP B
	88-12-13-55 88-12-14-55 88-12-13-14-55	M.A.P. sensor	Perform TEST No. 2
• Turn ignition switch on-off-on-off-on within 5 seconds.	88-12-15-55	Speed sensor	Perform TEST No. 3
	88-12-16-55	Battery voltage for charging system	Perform TEST No. 4
• RECORD ALL CODES	88-12-17-55	Engine running too cool	Check engine cooling system for a possible bad thermostat.
NOTE: If fault codes 15-17-21-47-51 or 52 appear at this time proceed to test indication.	88-12-21-55	Oxygen sensor	Perform TEST No. 5
	88-12-22-55	Engine coolant sensor	Perform TEST No. 6
	88-12-17-22-55		
• Turn ignition switch off and disconnect and re-connect the battery connector.	88-12-23-55	Throttle body temperature sensor	Perform TEST No. 7
	88-12-24-55	Throttle position sensor	Perform TEST No. 8
	88-12-25-55	Idle motor	Perform TEST No. 9
• Start engine.	88-12-31-55	Purge solenoid	Perform TEST No. 10
CAUTION: Do not depress accelerator to start engine.	88-12-33-55	A/C cut off relay	Perform TEST No. 11
	88-12-35-55	Radiator fan relay	Perform TEST No. 12
	88-12-37-55	Shift indicator lamp	Perform TEST No. 13
• Let engine run for 2 minutes.	88-12-41-46-55 88-12-46-55	Alternator field (charging system output to high)	Perform TEST No. 14
	88-12-41-55 88-12-41-47-55	Alternator field (charging system output to low)	Perform TEST No. 15
• Cycle transmission gear selector (auto trans only).	88-12-44-55	Battery temperature sensor	Perform TEST No. 16
	88-12-51-55	Oxygen feedback system locked lean	Perform TEST No. 17
• If so equipped press A/C button on and off.	88-12-52-55	Oxygen feedback system locked rich	
• Turn engine off.	88-12-53-55		Replace logic module
• Turn ignition switch on-off-on-off-on within 5 seconds.	88-12-47-55	Alternator output	Check for a loose fan belt. If okay, check the battery or alternator using the service manual procedure.
• RECORD ALL CODES	No code 88	Battery voltage for logic module standby memory	Repair battery feed wire to cavity No. 2 of the logic module black connector for an open circuit.

If the same code appears before and after the engine is started, the problem still exists. Proceed to test indications.

NOTE: Make sure your diagnostic readout box is operational and that there is not an open circuit in the wires between the logic module and diagnostic connector.

If a code does not reappear after the engine is started, the problem no longer exists. **Perform STEP L.**

DIAGNOSTIC READOUT BOX

1984-86 EFI DRIVEABILITY TEST PROCEDURES

TEST 1	STEP B	CHECKING THE OUTPUT CIRCUITS OF THE LOGIC MODULE CONTROLLED COMPONENTS

PROCEDURE	TEST INDICATION	ACTION REQUIRED
REMINDERS • Diagnostic readout box connected to the engine harness connector. • Put the system into the **ATM Test Mode — Code 04**. (Refer to the introduction)	**Test Code 04** • The radiator fan should be turning on and off every two seconds.	• Radiator fan is turning on and off press and hold the ATM button as follows: **Without A/C** until Test Code 07 appears. **With A/C** until Test Code 05 appears
		• If fan does not turn on and off, is the relay clicking? If it is, repair the circuit to the radiator fan motor as required. • If the relay does not click, replace it.
	Test Code 05 • You should hear the A/C cutout relay clicking every two seconds.	• A/C relay clicking, press and hold the ATM button until test code 07 appears.
		• If the A/C relay is not clicking replace it.
	Test Code 07 • You should hear the canister purge solenoid clicking.	• Canister purge solenoid clicking, **Perform STEP C.**
		• If the canister purge solenoid is not clicking replace it.

DIAGNOSTIC
READOUT BOX

TEST 1	STEP C	CHECKING SWITCH INPUTS TO THE LOGIC MODULE

PROCEDURE	TEST INDICATION	ACTION REQUIRED
REMINDERS • Diagnostic readout box connected to the engine harness connector • Put the system into the **Switch Test Mode.** (Refer to introduction) • Check switch inputs as follows: a) press down on brake pedal b) with auto trans. move gear selector from park to reverse c) with A/C, move blower switch to an on position and then press the A/C button	• Display on the readout box should change as each switch is activated. **NOTE:** It is not important what display changes to. Just make sure it changes.	• Display changes for all switches. **Perform STEP G.**
		• One or more switch inputs do not change the display, **Perform STEPS** as follows: Brake Switch **STEP D.** Park/Neutral Switch **STEP E.** A/C Button **STEP F.**

DIAGNOSTIC
READOUT BOX

TEST 1	STEP D	CHECKING BRAKE SWITCH INPUT CIRCUIT TO THE LOGIC MODULE

PROCEDURE	TEST INDICATION	ACTION REQUIRED
• Turn ignition switch off. • Disconnect black connector from logic module. • Connect voltmeter to cavity No. 13 of black connector and ground. • Turn ignition switch to the run position. • Press brake pedal down.	• Voltmeter should read within one volt of battery voltage.	• Voltage okay, replace logic module. **CAUTION:** Before replacing the logic module check terminal in cavity No. 13 of the blue connector to make sure it is not crushed causing a poor connection.
		• Voltage not okay, repair wire of cavity No. 13 for open circuit to brake switch.

VOLTMETER

LOGIC MODULE
BLACK CONNECTOR

TEST 1	STEP E	CHECKING PARK/NEUTRAL SWITCH INPUT CIRCUIT TO THE LOGIC MODULE

PROCEDURE	TEST INDICATION	ACTION REQUIRED
• Turn ignition switch off. • Disconnect black connector from logic module. • Connect an ohmmeter to cavity No. 12 of black connector and ground. • Put gear selector in park, reverse, neutral, and drive and observe ohmmeter in each position.	• Ohmmeter should read as follows: **Park** – Continuity **Reverse** – No continuity **Neutral** – Continuity **Drive** – No continuity **NOTE:** Disregard any resistance readings. Just make sure there is continuity.	• Ohmmeter readings not okay, repair wire of cavity No. 12 for open circuit to safety neutral switch.
		• Ohmmeter readings okay, replace logic module. **CAUTION:** Before replacing the logic module check the terminal in cavity No. 12 of the black connector to make sure it is not crushed causing a poor connection.

OHMMETER

LOGIC MODULE
BLACK CONNECTOR

TEST 1	STEP F	CHECKING A/C PUSH BUTTON SWITCH INPUT CIRCUIT TO THE LOGIC MODULE

PROCEDURE	TEST INDICATION	ACTION REQUIRED
• Turn ignition switch off. • Connect voltmeter to cavity No. 11 of the logic module black connector and ground. • Start the engine and wait 10 seconds.	• Voltmeter should read within one volt of battery voltage.	• Voltage okay, replace logic module. **CAUTION:** Before replacing the logic module check the terminal in cavity No. 11 of the blue connector to make sure it is not crushed causing a poor connection.
		• Voltage not okay, repair wire of cavity No. 11 for open circuit to A/C switch circuit.

VOLTMETER

LOGIC MODULE
BLACK CONNECTOR

TEST 1	STEP G	CHECKING AUTOMATIC IDLE SPEED MOTOR OPERATION

PROCEDURE	TEST INDICATION	ACTION REQUIRED
• Connect the diagnostic readout box to the engine harness connector. **NOTE:** Make sure read/hold switch is in the read position. • Connect a tachometer to the engine. • Start the engine. • Move the read/hold switch to the **hold** position.	• Engine speed should increase to approximately 1500 rpm.	• Speed increase okay, **Perform TEST** as follows: If a cold problem TEST NO. 17 If a warm problem TEST NO. 20
		• No speed increase Perform STEP H.

DIAGNOSTIC
READOUT BOX

TEST 1	STEP H	CHECKING THE AUTOMATIC IDLE SPEED MOTOR FOR AN OPEN FIELD WINDING

PROCEDURE	TEST INDICATION	ACTION REQUIRED
• Turn the ignition switch off. • Disconnect the throttle body 6-way connector. (round one). • Connect an ohmmeter between terminals 4 and 6 of the throttle body connector.	• Ohmmeter should show resistance. **NOTE:** The amount of resistance is not important. Just make sure there is some.	• Some resistance, Perform STEP I.
		• Open circuit replace the A.I.S. motor.

OHMMETER

THROTTLE BODY
6-WAY CONNECTOR

1984-86 EFI DRIVEABILITY TEST PROCEDURES

TEST 1	STEP I	CHECKING THE AUTOMATIC IDLE SPEED MOTOR FOR AN OPEN FIELD WINDING
PROCEDURE	**TEST INDICATION**	**ACTION REQUIRED**
REMINDERS • Ignition switch off. • Throttle body 6-way connector disconnected. • Connect an ohmmeter between terminals 3 and 5 of the throttle body connector.	• Ohmmeter should show resistance. **NOTE:** The amount of resistance is not important. Just make sure there is some.	• Some resistance. **Perform STEP J.**
		• Open circuit, replace the A.I.S. motor.

TEST 1	STEP J	CHECKING THE AUTOMATIC IDLE SPEED MOTOR CONTROL WIRES FOR OPEN CIRCUIT
PROCEDURE	**TEST INDICATION**	**ACTION REQUIRED**
REMINDERS • Ignition switch off. • Reconnect the throttle body connector. • Disconnect the logic module white connector. • Connect an ohmmeter between cavities No. 18 and 20.	• Ohmmeter should show resistance higher than 0. **NOTE:** The amount of resistance is not important. Just make sure there is some.	• Some resistance. **Perform STEP K.**
		• Open circuit, repair wires of cavities 18 and 20 for an open circuit to the throttle body connector.

TEST 1	STEP K	CHECKING THE AUTOMATIC IDLE SPEED MOTOR CONTROL WIRES FOR AN OPEN CIRCUIT
PROCEDURE	**TEST INDICATION**	**ACTION REQUIRED**
REMINDERS • Ignition switch off. • Throttle body connector connected. • Logic module white connector disconnected. • Connect an ohmmeter between cavities 16 and 22.	• Ohmmeter should show resistance. **NOTE:** The amount of resistance is not important. Just make sure there is some.	• Some resistance, replace the logic module. **CAUTION:** Before replacing the logic module check the terminals in cavities 16, 18, 20, and 22 of the white connector to make sure they are not crushed causing a poor connection.
		• Open circuit, repair wires of cavities 16 and 22 for an open circuit to the throttle body connector.

NOTES

_____

_____

_____

_____

_____

_____

_____

_____

_____

_____

_____

_____

TEST 1	STEP L	CHECKING FOR INTERMITTENT FAILURES

The majority of intermittent failures are caused by wiring and connections. The only way to find them is to try and duplicate the problem. Since the logic module can remember where they are, the ATM and sensor test modes can be used in an attempt to locate them. If a fault code does not reappear in **TEST 1A**, the following procedure should be used to determine if the wiring and connections are the cause of the problem.

• If the following fault codes do not reappear use the **ATM Test Mode** as indicated.

Fault Code	ATM Test Mode
25	03
26	02
27	02
31	07
33	05
35	04
37	08
41*	09
42	06
43	01

* Connect a voltmeter to the F2 terminal of the alternator and watch pulsations of meter.

Once in the correct test mode, wiggle all the connectors and wires in the circuit. When the bad connection or wire is located the ATM test will stop.

• If the following fault codes do not reappear use the **Sensor Test Mode** as indicated.

Fault Code	Sensor Test Mode
14**	08
16	07
21***	02
22	04
23	03
24	05
44	01

** When checking the M.A.P. sensor circuit, (fault code 14) apply 10 inches of vacuum to the M.A.P. sensor before testing.

*** Disconnect the oxygen sensor connector and ground the harness end with a jumper wire before testing.

Once in the correct test mode, wiggle all the connectors and wires in the circuit. When the bad connection or wire is located the display on the readout box will change.

TEST 2	STEP A	CHECKING FOR FAULT CODES 13 AND/OR 14 – M.A.P. SENSOR CIRCUIT
PROCEDURE	**TEST INDICATION**	**ACTION REQUIRED**
• Turn ignition switch off. • Tee a vacuum gauge into the M.A.P. sensor vacuum line at the logic module. • Start the engine and look at the vacuum gauge with the engine idling. • Look at the vacuum gauge while snapping the throttle open and close.	• Vacuum gauge should read manifold vacuum with the engine idling. • Vacuum gauge should immediately drop to 0 when the throttle is snapped open and closed.	• Vacuum gauge reads manifold vacuum and drops to 0 when the throttle is snapped **Perform STEP B.**
		• 0 vacuum, repair vacuum line to throttle body.
		• Vacuum drops slowly, repair restriction in vacuum supply line.

TEST 2	STEP B	CHECKING THE M.A.P. SENSOR CIRCUIT FROM THE LOGIC MODULE PRINTED CIRCUIT BOARD
PROCEDURE	**TEST INDICATION**	**ACTION REQUIRED**
• Turn the engine off. • Remove the M.A.P. sensor from the logic module. • Disconnect the M.A.P. sensor from the logic module. • Connect the negative lead of a digital voltmeter to the black wire of the logic module M.A.P. sensor connector. • Turn the ignition switch to the run position. • Touch the positive lead of the voltmeter to the white and red wires of the logic module M.A.P. sensor connector.	• Voltmeter should read at least 4 volts at the white and red wires.	• Voltage okay, at red and white wires, replace the M.A.P. sensor.
		• 0 volts at red, white or both, replace the logic module.

1984-86 EFI DRIVEABILITY TEST PROCEDURES

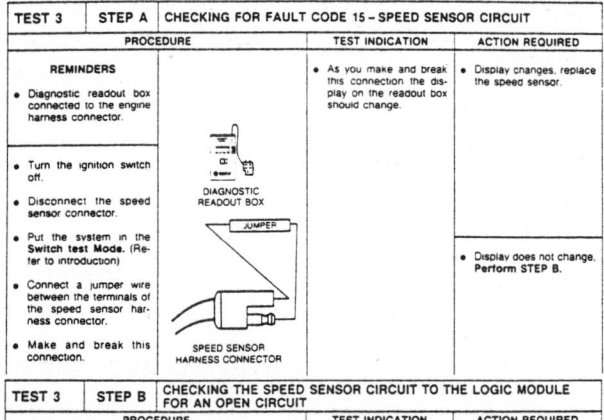
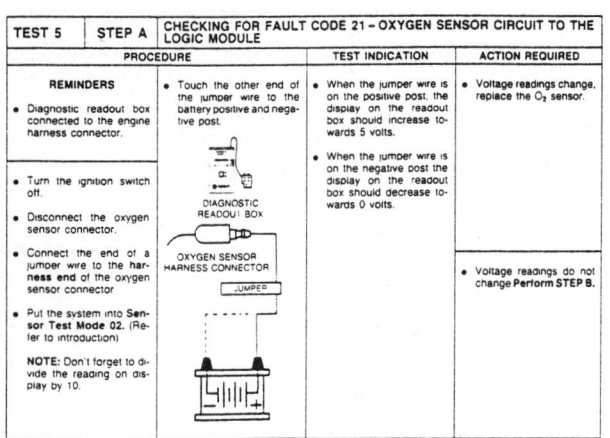

TEST 3	STEP A	CHECKING FOR FAULT CODE 15 – SPEED SENSOR CIRCUIT	
	PROCEDURE	TEST INDICATION	ACTION REQUIRED
REMINDERS • Diagnostic readout box connected to the engine harness connector. • Turn the ignition switch off. • Disconnect the speed sensor connector. • Put the system in the **Switch test Mode.** (Refer to introduction) • Connect a jumper wire between the terminals of the speed sensor harness connector. • Make and break this connection.		• As you make and break this connection the display on the readout box should change.	• Display changes, replace the speed sensor.
			• Display does not change, **Perform STEP B.**

TEST 3	STEP B	CHECKING THE SPEED SENSOR CIRCUIT TO THE LOGIC MODULE FOR AN OPEN CIRCUIT	
	PROCEDURE	TEST INDICATION	ACTION REQUIRED
REMINDERS • Diagnostic readout box connected to the engine harness connector. • System in the switch test mode. • Speed sensor connector disconnected. • Connect a jumper wire between cavity No. 24 of the white and cavity No. 14 of the black connectors of the logic module. • Make and break this connection.		• As you make and break this connection the display on the readout box should change.	• Display changes, repair the wires to the speed sensor for an open circuit.
			• Display does not change, replace the logic module. CAUTION: Before replacing the logic module check the terminal of cavity No. 14 of the black connector to make sure it is not crushed causing a poor connection.

TEST 4	STEP A	CHECKING FOR FAULT CODE 16 – BATTERY VOLTAGE SENSING CIRCUIT FOR CHARGING SYSTEM	
	PROCEDURE	TEST INDICATION	ACTION REQUIRED
REMINDERS • Diagnostic readout box connected to the engine harness connector. • Put the system in **Sensor Test Mode 07.** (Refer to introduction) NOTE: Reading on display is actual. • Connect a jumper wire between cavities No. 2 and 22 of the logic module black connector.		• Display on the readout box should read within one volt of battery voltage.	• Display reads within one of battery, repair wire in cavity No. 22 of the logic module black connector for an open circuit to the wiring harness splice.
			• Display reads 0 volts replace the logic module. CAUTION: Before replacing the logic module check the terminal in cavity No. 22 of the black connector to make sure it is not crushed causing a poor connection.

TEST 5	STEP A	CHECKING FOR FAULT CODE 21 – OXYGEN SENSOR CIRCUIT TO THE LOGIC MODULE	
	PROCEDURE	TEST INDICATION	ACTION REQUIRED
REMINDERS • Diagnostic readout box connected to the engine harness connector. • Turn the ignition switch off. • Disconnect the oxygen sensor connector. • Connect the end of a jumper wire to the harness end of the oxygen sensor connector. • Put the system into **Sensor Test Mode 02.** (Refer to introduction) NOTE: Don't forget to divide the reading on display by 10.	• Touch the other end of the jumper wire to the battery positive and negative post.	• When the jumper wire is on the positive post, the display on the readout box should increase towards 5 volts. • When the jumper wire is on the negative post the display on the readout box should decrease towards 0 volts.	• Voltage changes change, replace the O₂ sensor.
			• Voltage readings do not change Perform STEP B.

TEST 5	STEP B	CHECKING THE OXYGEN SENSOR CIRCUIT AT THE LOGIC MODULE	
	PROCEDURE	TEST INDICATION	ACTION REQUIRED
REMINDERS • Oxygen sensor connector disconnected. • Turn the ignition switch off. • Connect a digital voltmeter to cavity No. 18 of the logic module black connector and ground. • Turn the ignition switch to the run position.		• Voltmeter should read at least .3 (3 tenths) of a volt.	• Voltage okay, repair the wire of cavity No. 18 for an open circuit to the oxygen sensor.
			• 0 volts, replace the logic module. CAUTION: Before replacing the logic module check the terminal in cavity No. 18 of the black connector to make sure it is not crushed causing a poor connection.

TEST 6	STEP A	CHECKING FOR FAULT CODE 22 – COOLANT SENSOR CIRCUIT	
	PROCEDURE	TEST INDICATION	ACTION REQUIRED
REMINDERS • Diagnostic readout box connected to the engine harness connector. • Turn the ignition switch off. • Disconnect the connector from the coolant sensor. • Put the system in **Sensor Test Mode 04.** (Refer to introduction)		• Display on the readout box should read 00°.	• Display reads 00° Perform STEP B.
			• Display reads 260°, replace the logic module.

TEST 6	STEP B	CHECKING THE COOLANT SENSOR CIRCUIT TO THE LOGIC MODULE	
	PROCEDURE	TEST INDICATION	ACTION REQUIRED
REMINDERS • Diagnostic readout box connected to the engine harness connector. • System in Sensor Test Mode 04. NOTE: Don't forget to multiply the reading on display by 10. • Coolant sensor connector disconnected. • Connect a jumper wire between the terminals of the coolant sensor connector.		• Display on the readout box should read 260°.	• Display reads 260°, replace the coolant sensor.
			• Display reads 00°, Perform STEP C.

TEST 6	STEP C	CHECKING THE COOLANT SENSOR WIRES TO THE LOGIC MODULE FOR AN OPEN CIRCUIT	
	PROCEDURE	TEST INDICATION	ACTION REQUIRED
REMINDERS • Diagnostic readout box connected to the engine harness connector. • System in Sensor Test Mode 04. NOTE: Don't forget to multiply the reading on display by 10. • Coolant sensor connector disconnected. • Connect one end of a jumper wire to the negative terminal of the battery. • Connect the other end of the jumper wire to the tan wire terminal of the coolant sensor harness connector		• Display on the readout box should read 260°.	• Display reads 260° repair the black with light blue tracer wire of the coolant sensor harness connector for an open circuit to the wiring harness splice. • Display reads 00°, repair the tan wire of the coolant sensor harness connector for an open circuit to the logic module.

1984-86 EFI DRIVEABILITY TEST PROCEDURES

TEST 7	STEP A	CHECKING FOR FAULT CODE 23 – THROTTLE BODY TEMPERATURE SENSOR
PROCEDURE		TEST INDICATION	ACTION REQUIRED

PROCEDURE	TEST INDICATION	ACTION REQUIRED
REMINDERS • Diagnostic readout box connected to the engine harness connector. • Disconnect the throttle body temperature sensor connector. • Put the system in **Sensor Test Mode 03.** (Refer to introduction) NOTE: Don't forget to divide the reading on the display by 10.	• Display on the the readout box should read 5 volts.	• Display reads 5 volts, **Perform STEP B.**
	• Display reads 0 volts or 0 volts and then increases, replace the logic module.	

TEST 7	STEP B	CHECKING THE THROTTLE BODY TEMPERATURE SENSOR SIGNAL CIRCUIT TO THE LOGIC MODULE

PROCEDURE	TEST INDICATION	ACTION REQUIRED
REMINDERS • Diagnostic readout box connected to the engine harness connector. • System in **Sensor Test Mode 03.** NOTE: Don't forget to divide the reading on the display box by 10. • Throttle body temperature sensor connector disconnected. • Connect a jumper wire between the terminals of the throttle body temperature sensor connector.	• Display on the readout box should read 0 volts.	• Display reads 0 volts, replace the throttle body temperature sensor.
	• Display reads 5 volts. **Perform STEP C.**	

TEST 7	STEP C	CHECKING THE THROTTLE BODY TEMPERATURE SENSOR WIRES TO THE LOGIC MODULE FOR AN OPEN CIRCUIT

PROCEDURE	TEST INDICATION	ACTION REQUIRED
REMINDERS • Diagnostic readout box connected to the engine harness connector. • System in **Sensor Test Mode 03.** NOTE: Don't forget to divide the reading on the display box by 10. • Throttle body temperature sensor connector disconnected. • Connect one end of a jumper wire to the negative terminal of the battery.	• Connect the other end of the jumper wire to the black with red tracer wire terminal of the throttle body temperature sensor connector. • Display on the readout box should read 0 volts.	• Display reads 0 volts, repair the black with light blue tracer wire of the throttle position sensor connector for an open circuit to the wiring harness splice.
		• Display reads 5 volts repair the black with red tracer wire of the throttle body temperature sensor connector for an open circuit to the logic module.

TEST 8	STEP A	CHECKING FOR FAULT CODE 24 – THROTTLE POSITION SENSOR CIRCUIT

PROCEDURE	TEST INDICATION	ACTION REQUIRED
REMINDERS • Diagnostic readout box connected to the engine harness connector. • Disconnect the connector from the throttle position sensor. • Put the system in **Sensor Test Mode 05.** (Refer to introduction) NOTE: Don't forget to divide the reading on the display by 10.	• Display on the readout box should read 5 volts.	• Display reads 5 volts, **Perform STEP B.**
	• Display reads 0 volts, replace the logic module.	

TEST 8	STEP B	CHECKING THE THROTTLE POSITION SENSOR SIGNAL CIRCUIT TO THE LOGIC MODULE

PROCEDURE	TEST INDICATION	ACTION REQUIRED
REMINDERS • Diagnostic readout box connected to the engine harness connector. • System in Sensor Test Mode 05. NOTE: Don't forget to divide the reading on the display box by 10. • Throttle position sensor connector disconnected. • Connect a jumper wire between the orange with blue and black with blue wires of the throttle position sensor harness connector.	• Display on the readout box should read 0 volts.	• Display reads 0 volts. **Perform STEP D.**
		• Display reads 5 volts. **Perform STEP C.**

TEST 8	STEP C	CHECKING THE THROTTLE POSITION SENSOR WIRES TO THE LOGIC MODULE FOR AN OPEN CIRCUIT

PROCEDURE	TEST INDICATION	ACTION REQUIRED
REMINDERS • Diagnostic readout box connected to the engine harness connector. • System in Sensor Test Mode 05. NOTE: Don't forget to divide the reading on the display box by 10. • Throttle position sensor disconnected. • Connect one end of a jumper wire to the negative terminal of the battery. • Connect the other end of the jumper wire to the orange with blue tracer wire terminal of the throttle position sensor harness connector	• Display on the readout box should read 0 volts.	• Display reads 0 volts, repair the black with light blue tracer wire of the throttle position sensor connector for an open circuit to the wiring harness splice. • Display reads 5 volts, repair the orange with blue tracer wire of the throttle position sensor connector for an open circuit to the logic module.

TEST 8	STEP D	CHECKING THE 5 VOLT SUPPLY TO THE THROTTLE POSITION SENSOR

PROCEDURE	TEST INDICATION	ACTION REQUIRED
REMINDERS • Ignition switch in the run position. • Throttle position sensor connector disconnected. • Connect a digital voltmeter to the orange with white tracer wire of the throttle position sensor harness connector and ground.	• Voltmeter should read at least 4 volts.	• Voltage okay, replace the throttle position sensor. NOTE: Before replacing the throttle pot, make sure it is installed correctly on the throttle body. Connector facing rear of vehicle. • 0 volts repair the orange with white tracer wire for an open circuit to the logic module.

TEST 9	STEP A	CHECKING FOR FAULT CODE 25 – AUTOMATIC IDLE SPEED MOTOR CIRCUIT

PROCEDURE	TEST INDICATION	ACTION REQUIRED
• Turn the ignition switch off. • Disconnect the throttle body 6-way connector. (round one). • Connect an ohmmeter between terminals 4 and 6 of the throttle body connector.	• Ohmmeter should show resistance. NOTE: The amount of resistance is not important. Just make sure there is some.	• Some resistance, Perform STEP B. • 0 resistance, replace the A.I.S. motor.

1984-86 EFI DRIVEABILITY TEST PROCEDURES

TEST 9	STEP B	CHECKING THE AUTOMATIC IDLE SPEED MOTOR FOR A SHORTED FIELD WINDING		
	PROCEDURE		TEST INDICATION	ACTION REQUIRED
REMINDERS • Ignition switch off. • Throttle body 6-way connector disconnected • Connect an ohmmeter between terminals 3 and 5 of the throttle body connector.	 THROTTLE BODY 6-WAY CONNECTOR		• Ohmmeter should show resistance. NOTE: The amount of resistance is not important. Just make sure there is some.	• Some resistance. Perform STEP C.
			• 0 resistance, replace the A.I.S. motor.	

TEST 9	STEP C	CHECKING THE AUTOMATIC IDLE SPEED MOTOR CONTROL WIRES FOR A SHORT CIRCUIT		
	PROCEDURE		TEST INDICATION	ACTION REQUIRED
REMINDERS • Ignition switch off. • Throttle body 6-way connector disconnected. • Disconnect the logic module white connector. • Connect an ohmmeter between cavities No. 18 and 20.	 LOGIC MODULE WHITE CONNECTOR		• Ohmmeter should show an open circuit.	• Ohmmeter reading okay. Perform STEP D.
			• Ohmmeter shows 0 resistance, repair wires of cavities 18 and 20 for short to each other.	

TEST 9	STEP D	CHECKING THE AUTOMATIC IDLE SPEED MOTOR CONTROL WIRES FOR A SHORT CIRCUIT		
	PROCEDURE		TEST INDICATION	ACTION REQUIRED
REMINDERS • Ignition switch off. • Logic module white connector disconnected. • Connect an ohmmeter between cavities 16 and 22.	 LOGIC MODULE WHITE CONNECTOR		• Ohmmeter should show an open circuit.	• Ohmmeter reading okay. Perform STEP E.
			• Ohmmeter shows 0 resistance, repair wires of cavities 16 and 22 for short to each other.	

TEST 9	STEP E	CHECKING THE FJ2 WIRE FROM THE POWER MODULE FOR AN OPEN CIRCUIT		
	PROCEDURE		TEST INDICATION	ACTION REQUIRED
REMINDERS • Logic module white connector disconnected. • Connect a voltmeter to cavity No. 7 or 8 of the white connector and ground. • Turn the ignition switch to the run position.	 LOGIC MODULE WHITE CONNECTOR		• Voltmeter should read within one volt of the battery voltage.	• Voltage okay, replace the logic module. CAUTION: Before replacing the logic module check the terminal in cavities 7 and 8 of the white connector to make sure they are not crushed causing a poor connection.
				• 0 volts repair fused J2 wire to the power module for an open circuit.

TEST 10	STEP A	CHECKING FOR FAULT CODE 31 – CANISTER PURGE SOLENOID CIRCUIT		
	PROCEDURE		TEST INDICATION	ACTION REQUIRED
REMINDERS • Diagnostic readout box connected to the engine harness connector. • Connect a voltmeter to the pink with white tracer wire of the canister purge solenoid connector and ground. • Put the system in the ATM Test Mode — Code 07. (Refer to introduction)	 DIAGNOSTIC READOUT BOX VOLTMETER DB — PK* CANISTER PURGE SOLENOID CONNECTOR		• Voltmeter reading should be pulsating between 0 and 14 volts.	• Voltmeter is not pulsating but reads within one volt of battery voltage. Perform STEP B. • Voltmeter pulsates between 0 and 3 volts. Perform STEP C. • Voltmeter is not pulsating but reads 0-1 volt, disconnect the logic module black connector. If voltage is now within one volt of battery, replace the logic module. If not repair pink with white tracer wire for a short to ground.

TEST 10	STEP B	CHECKING THE CANISTER PURGE SOLENOID CONTROL WIRE FOR AN OPEN CIRCUIT TO THE LOGIC MODULE		
	PROCEDURE		TEST INDICATION	ACTION REQUIRED
REMINDERS • Turn the ignition switch off. • Connect a voltmeter to cavity No. 5 of the black connector and ground. • Turn the ignition switch to the run position.	 LOGIC MODULE BLACK CONNECTOR		• Voltmeter should read within one volt of battery voltage.	• Voltage okay, replace the logic module. CAUTION: Before replacing the logic module check the terminal in cavity No. 5 of the black connector to make sure it is not crushed causing a poor connection. • 0 volts repair wire of cavity No. 5 for an open circuit to the canister purge solenoid.

TEST 10	STEP C	CHECKING THE CANISTER PURGE SOLENOID WINDINGS FOR AN OPEN CIRCUIT		
	PROCEDURE		TEST INDICATION	ACTION REQUIRED
REMINDERS • Turn the ignition switch off. • Disconnect the canister purge solenoid connector. • Connect an ohmmeter between the terminals of the solenoid.	 CANISTER PURGE SOLENOID		• Ohmmeter should show resistance. NOTE: The amount of resistance is not important. Just make sure there is some.	• Some resistance, repair the blue wire of the solenoid connector for an open circuit to the ignition switch. • Open circuit, replace the solenoid.

TEST 11	STEP A	CHECKING FOR FAULT CODE 33 – A/C CUTOUT RELAY		
	PROCEDURE		TEST INDICATION	ACTION REQUIRED
REMINDERS • Diagnostic readout box connected to the engine harness connector. • Connect a voltmeter to the dark blue with orange tracer wire of the A/C cut-out relay and ground. • Put the system in the ATM Test Mode — Code 05. (Refer to the introduction)	 DIAGNOSTIC READOUT BOX VOLTMETER DB/OR* DB/BK* BR WIRE END A/C CUT-OUT RELAY 3-WAY CONNECTOR		• Voltmeter reading should be pulsating between 0 and 14 volts.	• Voltmeter is not pulsating but reads within one volt of battery voltage. Perform STEP B. • Voltmeter pulsates between 0 and 3 volts. Perform STEP C. • Voltmeter is not pulsating but read 0-1 volts, disconnect the logic module black connector. If voltage is now within one volt of battery, replace the logic module. If not repair dark blue with orange tracer wire for a short to ground.

1984-86 EFI DRIVEABILITY TEST PROCEDURES

TEST 11	STEP B	CHECKING THE A/C CUTOUT RELAY CONTROL WIRE FOR AN OPEN CIRCUIT TO THE LOGIC MODULE	
PROCEDURE		TEST INDICATION	ACTION REQUIRED
• Turn the ignition switch off. • Connect a voltmeter to cavity No. 3 of the logic module black connector and ground. • Turn the ignition switch to the run position.		• Voltmeter should read within one volt of battery voltage.	• Voltage okay, replace the logic module. CAUTION: Before replacing the logic module check the terminal in cavity No. 3 of the black connector to make sure it is not crushed causing a poor connection.
			• 0 volts repair the wire of cavity No. 3 for an open circuit to the A/C cutout relay.

LOGIC MODULE
BLACK CONNECTOR

TEST 11	STEP C	CHECKING A/C CUTOUT RELAY PULL IN COIL WINDINGS FOR AN OPEN CIRCUIT	
PROCEDURE		TEST INDICATION	ACTION REQUIRED
• Turn the ignition switch off. • Disconnect the connectors from the A/C cutout relay. • Connect an ohmmeter between terminals 1 and 4 of the relay.		• Ohmmeter should show resistance. NOTE: The amount of resistance is not important. Just make sure there is some.	• Some resistance, repair the dark blue with orange tracer wire of the relay 3-way connector for an open circuit to the ignition switch.
			• Open circuit, replace the relay.

A/C CUT-OUT RELAY

TEST 12	STEP A	CHECKING FOR FAULT CODE 35 – RADIATOR FAN RELAY CONTROL CIRCUIT	
PROCEDURE		TEST INDICATION	ACTION REQUIRED
REMINDERS • Diagnostic readout box connected to the engine harness connector. • Connect a voltmeter to the dark blue with pink tracer wire of the radiator fan relay and ground. • Put the system in the ATM Test Mode — Code 04. (Refer to the introduction)		• Voltmeter should be pulsating between 0 and 14 volts.	• Voltmeter is not pulsating but reads within one volt of battery voltage. Perform STEP B.
		• Voltmeter pulsates between 0 and 3 volts. Perform STEP C.	
		• Voltmeter is not pulsating but reads 0-1 volts, disconnect the logic module white connector. If voltage is now within one of battery, replace the logic module. If not repair dark blue with pink tracer wire for a short to ground.	

DIAGNOSTIC READOUT BOX

RADIATOR FAN RELAY CONNECTORS

TEST 12	STEP B	CHECKING THE RADIATOR FAN RELAY CONTROL WIRE FOR AN OPEN CIRCUIT TO THE LOGIC MODULE	
PROCEDURE		TEST INDICATION	ACTION REQUIRED
• Turn the ignition switch off. • Connect a voltmeter to cavity No. 21 of the logic module white connector and ground. • Turn the ignition switch to the run position.		• Voltmeter should read within one volt of battery voltage.	• Voltage okay, replace the logic module. CAUTION: Before replacing the logic module check the terminal in cavity No. 21 of the white connector to make sure it is not crushed causing a poor connection.
			• 0 volts, repair the wire of cavity No. 21 for an open circuit to the radiator fan relay.

LOGIC MODULE
WHITE CONNECTOR

TEST 12	STEP C	CHECKING RADIATOR FAN RELAY PULL IN COIL WINDINGS FOR AN OPEN CIRCUIT	
PROCEDURE		TEST INDICATION	ACTION REQUIRED
• Turn the ignition switch off. • Disconnect the smaller of the two 3-way connectors from the relay. • Connect an ohmmeter between terminals 1 and 2 of the relay.		• Ohmmeter should show resistance. NOTE: The amount of resistance is not important. Just make sure there is some.	• Some resistance repair the white wire of the relay 3-way connector for an open circuit to the fuse box.
			• Open circuit, replace the relay.

RADIATOR FAN RELAY

TEST 13	STEP A	CHECKING FOR FAULT CODE 37 – SHIFT INDICATOR LAMP	
PROCEDURE		TEST INDICATION	ACTION REQUIRED
• Turn the ignition switch off. • Disconnect the logic module white connector. • Turn the ignition switch to the run position. • Ground cavity No. 15 of the logic module white connector with a jumper wire.		• Shift indicator lamp should be on.	• Lamp on, replace the logic module. CAUTION: Before replacing the logic module check the terminal in cavity No. 15 of the white connector to make sure it is not crushed causing a poor connection.
			• Lamp off, repair wire of cavity No. 15 for an open circuit, check for a burned out bulb or check for ignition feed voltage to lamp.

LOGIC MODULE
WHITE CONNECTOR

TEST 14	STEP A	CHECKING FOR FAULT CODES 46 OR 41-46 ALTERNATOR FIELD (CHARGING SYSTEM OUTPUT TOO HIGH)	
PROCEDURE		TEST INDICATION	ACTION REQUIRED
• Disconnect the power module 10-way connector. • Connect a voltmeter between cavity No. 8 of the 10-way connector and ground. • Turn the ignition switch to the run position.		• Voltmeter should read within one volt of the battery voltage.	• Voltage okay, Perform STEP B.
			• 0-1 volts, repair alternator field circuit for short to ground.

POWER MODULE
10-WAY CONNECTOR

TEST 14	STEP B	CHECKING THE ALTERNATOR FIELD CONTROL TO THE POWER MODULE FOR A SHORT CIRCUIT	
PROCEDURE		TEST INDICATION	ACTION REQUIRED
• Turn the ignition switch off. • Reconnect the power module 10-way connector. • Disconnect the power module 12-way connector. • Connect a voltmeter between the F2 terminal on the alternator and ground. • Turn the ignition switch to the run position.		• Voltmeter should read within one volt of the battery voltage.	• Voltage okay, Perform STEP C.
			• 0-1 volt replace the power module.

ALTERNATOR F2 TERMINAL

1984-86 EFI DRIVEABILITY TEST PROCEDURES

TEST 14	STEP C	CHECKING THE ALTERNATOR FIELD CONTROL TO THE LOGIC MODULE FOR A SHORT CIRCUIT		
	PROCEDURE		TEST INDICATION	ACTION REQUIRED
REMINDERS • Power module 12-way connector disconnected. • Turn the ignition switch off. • Disconnect the logic module white connector. • Connect an ohmmeter between cavity No. 11 of the power module 12-way connector and ground.			• Ohmmeter should **not** show continuity.	• No continuity, replace the logic module.
			• Continuity repair wire of cavity No. 11 for a short circuit to ground.

TEST 15	STEP A	CHECKING FOR FAULT CODES 47 OR 41-47 ALTERNATOR FIELD (CHARGING SYSTEM OUTPUT TOO LOW)		
	PROCEDURE		TEST INDICATION	ACTION REQUIRED
• Connect a voltmeter to the battery. • Connect one end of a jumper wire to a good engine ground. • Start the engine and note the reading of the voltmeter. • Very quickly touch the other end of the jumper wire to the F2 terminal on the alternator and watch the voltmeter.			• Voltmeter should show an increase in voltage.	• Voltage increases, Perform **STEP B.**
			• Voltage does not increase. **Perform STEP F.**

TEST 15	STEP B	CHECKING CHARGING SYSTEM FIELD CONTROL CIRCUIT AT THE LOGIC MODULE		
	PROCEDURE		TEST INDICATION	ACTION REQUIRED
REMINDERS • Engine running. • Connect a voltmeter between cavity No. 2 of the logic module black connector and ground. • Connect one end of a jumper wire to cavity No. 5 of the logic module white connector. • Very quickly touch the other end of the jumper wire to the logic module mounting stud and watch the voltmeter.			• Voltmeter should show an increase in voltage.	• Voltage increase, replace the logic module. **CAUTION:** Before replacing the logic module check the terminal in cavity No. 5 of the white connector to make sure it is not crushed causing a poor connection.
			• Voltage does not increase. **Perform STEP C.**

TEST 15	STEP C	CHECKING ALTERNATOR FIELD CONTROL WIRE TO THE POWER MODULE FOR AN OPEN CIRCUIT		
	PROCEDURE		TEST INDICATION	ACTION REQUIRED
• Turn the engine off. • Disconnect the logic module white connector. • Connect a voltmeter between cavity No. 5 of the logic module white connector and ground. • Turn the ignition switch to the run position.			• Voltmeter should read within one volt of the battery voltage.	• Voltage okay, **Perform STEP E.**
			• 0 volts **Perform STEP D.**

TEST 15	STEP D	CHECKING ALTERNATOR FIELD CONTROL CIRCUIT OF THE POWER MODULE		
	PROCEDURE		TEST INDICATION	ACTION REQUIRED
• Turn the ignition switch off. • Disconnect the power module 12-way connector. • Connect a voltmeter to Pin No. 11 of the power module and ground. • Turn the ignition switch to the run position.			• Voltmeter should read within one volt of battery voltage.	• Voltage okay, repair wire to cavity No. 5 of the logic module white connector for an open circuit.
			• 0 volts, replace the power module.

TEST 15	STEP E	CHECKING THE ALTERNATOR FIELD CONTROL TO THE POWER MODULE FOR AN OPEN CIRCUIT		
	PROCEDURE		TEST INDICATION	ACTION REQUIRED
• Turn the ignition switch off. • Disconnect the 10-way connector from the power module. • Connect a voltmeter between cavity No. 8 of the 10-way connector and ground. • Turn the ignition switch to the run position.			• Voltmeter should read within one volt of battery voltage.	• Voltage okay, replace the power module. **CAUTION:** Before replacing the power module check the terminal tabs in cavity No. 8 of the 10-way connector to make sure it is not spread apart causing a poor connection.
			• 0 volts repair wire of cavity No. 8 for an open circuit to the alternator.

TEST 15	STEP F	CHECKING FOR VOLTAGE TO ALTERNATOR FIELD CIRCUIT		
	PROCEDURE		TEST INDICATION	ACTION REQUIRED
• Turn the engine off. • Connect a voltmeter between the F1 terminal of the alternator and ground. • Turn the ignition switch to the run position.			• Voltmeter should read within one volt of the battery voltage.	• Voltage okay, repair the alternator.
			• 0 volts repair the wire of F1 terminal for an open circuit to the ignition switch.

TEST 16	STEP A	CHECKING FOR FAULT CODE 44 – BATTERY TEMPERATURE SENSOR CIRCUIT		
	PROCEDURE		TEST INDICATION	ACTION REQUIRED
• Turn the ignition switch off. • Disconnect the logic module black connector. • Connect an ohmmeter between cavity No. 20 of the logic module black connector and ground.			• Ohmmeter should show resistance. **NOTE:** The amount of resistance is not important. Just make sure there is some.	• Some resistance, replace the logic module. **CAUTION:** Before replacing the logic module check the terminal in cavity No. 20 of the black connector to make sure it is not crushed causing a poor connection.
			• 0 resistance, **Perform STEP B.**
			• Open circuit. **Perform STEP C.**

1984-86 EFI DRIVEABILITY TEST PROCEDURES

TEST 16	STEP B	CHECKING BATTERY TEMPERATURE SENSOR WIRE FOR SHORT CIRCUIT
PROCEDURE	**TEST INDICATION**	**ACTION REQUIRED**

PROCEDURE	TEST INDICATION	ACTION REQUIRED
REMINDERS • Logic module black connector disconnected. • Ohmmeter connected between cavity No. 20 of the logic module black connector and ground. • Disconnect the power module 12-way connector.	• Ohmmeter should show an open circuit.	• Open circuit, replace the power module.
		• 0 resistance, repair wire of cavity No. 20 for short circuit to ground.

TEST 16	STEP C	CHECKING BATTERY TEMPERATURE SENSOR WIRE FOR OPEN CIRCUIT
PROCEDURE	**TEST INDICATION**	**ACTION REQUIRED**

PROCEDURE	TEST INDICATION	ACTION REQUIRED
• Disconnect the power module 12-way connector. • Connect an ohmmeter between pin 3 and 12 of the power module.	• Ohmmeter should show resistance. NOTE: The amount of resistance is not important. Just make sure there is some.	• Some resistance, repair wire in cavity No. 3 of power module 12-way connector for an open circuit.
		• 0 resistance or open circuit, replace the power module.

TEST 17	STEP A	CHECKING SENSOR CALIBRATIONS (ENGINE COOLANT TEMPERATURE SENSOR)
PROCEDURE	**TEST INDICATION**	**ACTION REQUIRED**

PROCEDURE	TEST INDICATION	ACTION REQUIRED
REMINDERS • Diagnostic readout box connected to the engine harness connector. • Put the system in **Sensor TEST Mode 04.** (Refer to introduction) NOTE: Don't forget to multiply the reading on display by 10.	• Display on the readout box should read approximately ambient temperature ± 10°F.	• Temperature okay, **Perform STEP B.**
		• Temperature not okay, replace the coolant sensor.

TEST 17	STEP B	CHECKING SENSOR CALIBRATIONS (THROTTLE POSITION SENSOR)
PROCEDURE	**TEST INDICATION**	**ACTION REQUIRED**

PROCEDURE	TEST INDICATION	ACTION REQUIRED
REMINDERS • Diagnostic readout box connected to the engine harness connector. • Engine cold. • Put the system in **Sensor TEST Mode 05.** (Refer to introduction) NOTE: Don't forget to divide the reading on display by 10	• Display on readout box should read as follows: **Throttle Fully Closed** 1 volt ± ½ volt NOTE: Make sure none of the cables that are attached to the throttle body are not misadjusted and are holding the throttle open. **In Between Closed and Open** You should see an uninterrupted change of voltage between closed and open throttle. **Throttle Wide Open** at least 3½ volts	• Voltage okay, **Perform STEP C.** • Voltage not okay, replace throttle sensor.

TEST 17	STEP C	CHECKING SENSOR CALIBRATION (M.A.P. SENSOR)
PROCEDURE	**TEST INDICATION**	**ACTION REQUIRED**

PROCEDURE	TEST INDICATION	ACTION REQUIRED
REMINDERS • Diagnostic readout box connected to the engine harness connector. • Engine cold. • Put the system in **Sensor TEST Mode 08.** (Refer to introduction) NOTE: Don't forget to divide the reading on display by 10. • Disconnect the vacuum hose from the M.A.P. sensor. • Connect an auxiliary vacuum supply to the M.A.P. sensor. • Apply 5 inches of vacuum and record the voltage displayed on the readout box.	• Slowly apply vacuum to 20 inches and watch display on readout box. • Record the voltage displayed on the readout box at 20 inches. • Subtract the voltage recorded at 20 inches from the voltage recorded at 5 inches. **Example** Voltage at 5" 3.8 Voltage at 20" − 1.1 Difference 2.7	• You should see an uninterrupted change of voltage between 5 and 20 inches of vacuum. • The voltage difference should be between 2.3 and 2.9 volts. • Voltage okay, **Perform STEP D.** • Voltage not okay, replace the M.A.P. sensor.

TEST 17	STEP D	CHECKING SENSOR CALIBRATION (THROTTLE BODY TEMPERATURE SENSOR)
PROCEDURE	**TEST INDICATION**	**ACTION REQUIRED**

PROCEDURE	TEST INDICATION	ACTION REQUIRED
REMINDERS • Diagnostic readout box connected to the engine harness connector. • Engine cold. • Put the system in **Sensor TEST Mode 03.** (Refer to introduction) NOTE: Don't forget to divide the reading on display by 10.	• Display on the readout box should be between 4.9 and 2.6 volts.	• Voltage okay, **Perform STEP E.** • Voltage not okay, replace the throttle body temperature sensor.

TEST 17	STEP E	CHECKING SENSOR CALIBRATION (BATTERY TEMPERATURE SENSOR)
PROCEDURE	**TEST INDICATION**	**ACTION REQUIRED**

PROCEDURE	TEST INDICATION	ACTION REQUIRED
REMINDERS • Diagnostic readout box connected to the engine harness connector. • Engine cold. • Put the system in **Sensor TEST Mode 01.** (Refer to introduction) NOTE: Don't forget to divide the reading on display by 10.	• Display on the readout box should be between 5 and 2 volts.	• Voltage okay, **Perform TEST No. 18.** • Voltage not okay, replace the power module.

TEST 18	STEP A	CHECKING HEATED AIR INTAKE SYSTEM
PROCEDURE	**TEST INDICATION**	**ACTION REQUIRED**

PROCEDURE	TEST INDICATION	ACTION REQUIRED
REMINDERS • Engine cold. • Disconnect the air duct from the air cleaner snorkel. • Disconnect the vacuum supply hose to the heated air intake system air temperature sensor. • Connect an auxiliary vacuum supply to the air temperature sensor. • Apply at least 15 inches of vacuum.	• Vacuum should build up to 15 inches and close the heated air door when air temperature is below 76°F and then slowly bleed down opening the heated air door.	• Vacuum builds up, closes heated air door and then bleeds down opening the heated door. **Perform TEST No. 19.** • Vacuum builds up but heated air door does not close, repair or replace door as required. • Vacuum does not build up or does not bleed down, replace air temperature sensor. • Vacuum builds up, bleeds down, but heated air door does not open, repair or replace door as required.

1984-86 EFI DRIVEABILITY TEST PROCEDURES

TEST 19	STEP A	CHECKING FOR FUEL FOULED SPARK PLUGS	
PROCEDURE		TEST INDICATION	ACTION REQUIRED
• Remove the spark plugs.		• Spark plugs should be dry. NOTE: It is normal for spark plugs to be black after an engine has been started cold	• Spark plugs are dry. Perform TEST NO. 22.
		• Spark plugs are wet with fuel. clean and reinstall. **Do not install new spark plugs.** • Check for gas in the crankcase. Change oil and filter if required.	

TEST 20	STEP A	CHECKING SENSOR CALIBRATIONS (ENGINE COOLANT TEMPERATURE SENSOR)	
PROCEDURE		TEST INDICATION	ACTION REQUIRED
REMINDERS • Diagnostic readout box connected to the engine harness connector. • Put the system in **Sensor Test Mode 04.** (Refer to introduction) NOTE: Don't forget to multiply the reading on display by 10.		• Display on the readout box should read between 180° and 250°F.	• Temperature okay, **Perform STEP B.**
	DIAGNOSTIC READOUT BOX		• Temperature not okay, replace the coolant sensor.

TEST 20	STEP B	CHECKING SENSOR CALIBRATIONS (THROTTLE POSITION SENSOR)	
PROCEDURE		TEST INDICATION	ACTION REQUIRED
REMINDERS • Diagnostic readout box connected to the engine harness connector. • Engine warm. • Put the system in **Sensor Test Mode 05.** (Refer to introduction) NOTE: Don't forget to divide the reading on display by 10.		• Display on readout box should read as follows: **Throttle Fully Closed** 1 volt ± ½ volt NOTE: Make sure none of the cables that are attached to the throttle body are not misadjusted and are holding the throttle open. **In Between Closed and Open** You should see an uninterrupted change of voltage between closed and open throttle. **Throttle Wide Open** at least 3 volts	• Voltage okay, **Perform STEP C.** • Voltage not okay, replace throttle position sensor.
	DIAGNOSTIC READOUT BOX		

TEST 20	STEP C	CHECKING SENSOR CALIBRATION (M.A.P. SENSOR)	
PROCEDURE		TEST INDICATION	ACTION REQUIRED
REMINDERS • Diagnostic readout box connected to the engine harness connector. • Engine warm. • Put the system in **Sensor TEST Mode 06.** (Refer to introduction) NOTE: Don't forget to divide the reading on display by 10. • Disconnect the vacuum hose from the M.A.P. sensor. • Connect an auxiliary vacuum supply to the M.A.P. sensor. • Apply 5 inches of vacuum and record the voltage displayed on the readout box.		• Slowly apply vacuum to 20 inches and watch display on readout box. • Record the voltage displayed on the readout box at 20 inches. • Subtract the voltage recorded at 20 inches from the voltage recorded at 5 inches. **Example** Voltage at 5" 3.8 Voltage at 20" −1.1 Difference 2.7	• You should see an uninterrupted change of voltage between 5 and 20 inches of vacuum. • The voltage difference should be between 2.3 and 2.9 volts. • Voltage okay, **Perform STEP D.** • Voltage not okay, replace the M.A.P. sensor.

TEST 20	STEP D	CHECKING SENSOR CALIBRATION (THROTTLE BODY TEMPERATURE SENSOR)	
PROCEDURE		TEST INDICATION	ACTION REQUIRED
REMINDERS • Diagnostic readout box connected to the engine harness connector. • Engine warm. • Put the system in **Sensor Test Mode 03.** (Refer to introduction) NOTE: Don't forget to divide the reading on display by 10.		• Display on the readout box should be between 1.4 and 3.9 volts.	• Voltage okay, **Perform STEP E.** • Voltage not okay, replace the throttle body temperature sensor.
	DIAGNOSTIC READOUT BOX		

TEST 20	STEP E	CHECKING SENSOR CALIBRATION (BATTERY TEMPERATURE SENSOR)	
PROCEDURE		TEST INDICATION	ACTION REQUIRED
REMINDERS • Diagnostic readout box connected to the engine harness connector. • Engine warm. • Put the system in **Sensor Test Mode 01.** (Refer to introduction) NOTE: Don't forget to divide the reading on display by 10.		• Display on the readout box should be between .2 and 2.5 volts.	• Voltage okay, **Perform TEST NO. 21.** • Voltage not okay, replace the power module.
	DIAGNOSTIC READOUT BOX		

TEST 21	STEP A	CHECKING HEATED AIR INTAKE SYSTEM	
PROCEDURE		TEST INDICATION	ACTION REQUIRED
REMINDERS • Engine warm. • Disconnect the air duct from the air cleaner snorkel. • Disconnect the vacuum supply hose to the heated air intake system air temperature sensor. • Connect an auxiliary vacuum supply to the air temperature sensor. • Try to apply vacuum.	REMOVE THIS HOSE AIR TEMPERATURE SENSOR	• Vacuum should not hold and heated air door should be open.	• Vacuum does not hold and heated air door is open. Perform TEST NO. 22. • Vacuum holds. replace air temperature sensor. • Heated air door not open repair or replace as required.

TEST 22	STEP A	CHECKING THE EGR SYSTEM – VACUUM SUPPLY FROM THE THROTTLE BODY TO THE EGR BACKPRESSURE VALVE	
PROCEDURE		TEST INDICATION	ACTION REQUIRED
• Disconnect the vacuum line at the EGR backpressure valve that comes from the throttle body. • Connect a vacuum gauge to this line. • Start the engine. • Raise engine speed to 2000 rpm's.	CONNECT VACUUM GAUGE BACK PRESSURE VALVE EGR VALVE	• Vacuum gauge should read at least 5 inches.	• Vacuum okay, remember what it is and **Perform STEP B.** • Vacuum below 5 inches. repair vacuum supply from throttle body.

1984-86 EFI DRIVEABILITY TEST PROCEDURES

TEST 22	STEP B	CHECKING THE VACUUM SUPPLY FROM THE BACKPRESSURE VALVE TO THE EGR VALVE

PROCEDURE	TEST INDICATION	ACTION REQUIRED
REMINDERS • Engine running. • Disconnect the vacuum gauge from the vacuum line and reconnect the vacuum line to the backpressure valve. • Disconnect the vacuum line from the EGR valve and connect a vacuum gauge to it. • Raise the engine speed to 2000 rpm's.	• Vacuum gauge should read the same or near the same as seen in STEP A.	• Vacuum okay, **Perform STEP C.**
		• Vacuum not okay, replace EGR/backpressure valve assembly.

TEST 22	STEP C	CHECKING THE EGR VALVE OPERATION

PROCEDURE	TEST INDICATION	ACTION REQUIRED
REMINDERS • Vacuum line disconnected from the EGR valve. • Engine running. • Connect an auxiliary vacuum supply to the EGR valve. • With engine running at idle speed slowly apply vacuum.	• Engine speed should begin to drop when applied vacuum reaches 2½ to 3½ inches. NOTE: The automatic idle speed motor will attempt to compensate for drop in engine speed from EGR, so idle speed drop may only be momentary at lower applied vacuum level.	• Engine speed drops, **Perform STEP D.**
		• Engine speed does not drop, replace EGR/backpressure valve assembly. NOTE: After valve is removed, make sure supply tube from manifold is not plugged before replacing EGR valve assembly.

TEST 22	STEP D	CHECKING THE EGR VALVE VACUUM CHAMBER FOR LEAKS

PROCEDURE	TEST INDICATION	ACTION REQUIRED
REMINDERS • Vacuum line disconnected from the EGR valve. • Auxiliary vacuum supply connected to the EGR valve. • Engine running at idle speed. • Apply 10 inches of vacuum to EGR valve.	• Vacuum should hold for at least 10 seconds before bleeding down.	• Vacuum holds, **Perform TEST NO. 23.**
		• Vacuum does not hold, replace EGR, EGR/backpressure valve assembly.

TEST 23	STEP A	CHECKING SECONDARY IGNITION SYSTEM

PROCEDURE	TEST INDICATION	ACTION REQUIRED
• Connect suitable engine analyzer to engine. • Start engine and let engine speed stabilize for two minutes.	• Follow equipment manufacturer's procedure for secondary ignition testing and pattern analysis. CAUTION: Make sure ignition coil output is checked in this testing. Open circuit secondary voltage should be at least 25,000 volts.	• Secondary ignition system okay, **Perform TEST NO. 24.**
		• Secondary ignition not to specs, repair as required.

TEST 24	STEP A	CHECKING BASIC IGNITION TIMING

PROCEDURE	TEST INDICATION	ACTION REQUIRED
• Connect a tachometer to engine. • Connect a power timing light to engine. NOTE: If a mag timer is not used, it will be necessary to remove air cleaner assembly to see timing marks. • Start and run engine until operating temperature is reached. • Disconnect and reconnect engine coolant sensor connector. NOTE: The power loss lamp on the instrument panel must come on.	• Basic timing should be within 2° of specification as shown on the emission label.	• Basic timing okay, **Perform STEP B.**
		• Basic timing not okay, adjust following basic ignition timing procedure.

TEST 24	STEP B	CHECKING SPARK ADVANCE

PROCEDURE	TEST INDICATION	ACTION REQUIRED
REMINDERS • Tachometer connected to engine. • Timing light connected to engine. • Air cleaner removed (if necessary). • Engine at operating temperature. • Turn engine off and then restart. NOTE: Power loss lamp on instrument panel must go off. • Raise engine speed to 2,000 rpm's.	• Timing should be as follows: All but 2.5L manual trans- 27° BTDC minimum 2.5L manual trans- 19° BTDC minimum	• Timing okay, **Perform TEST NO. 25.**
		• Timing not okay, replace logic module.

TEST 25	STEP A	CHECKING FUEL SUPPLY AND RETURN SYSTEM

PROCEDURE	TEST INDICATION	ACTION REQUIRED
• Install pressure gauge (Tool C-3292) with (C-4799 adapter) in fuel supply hose at throttle body. CAUTION: Fuel is under high pressure. Refer to service manual for pressure release procedure. • Start engine.	• Fuel pressure must be 14½ psi ± 1.	• Fuel pressure okay, **Perform TEST NO. 26.**
		• Fuel pressure below 13½ record what it is and **Perform STEP B.**
		• Fuel pressure above 15½ **Perform STEP D.**

TEST 25	STEP B	CHECKING FOR LOW FUEL PRESSURE

PROCEDURE	TEST INDICATION	ACTION REQUIRED
• Turn engine off. • Release pressure. • Remove pressure gauge. • Reinstall hose to throttle body. • Install pressure gauge before fuel filter. • Start engine.	• Fuel pressure should not be higher than 5 psi of previously recorded pressure.	• Fuel pressure higher than 5 psi, replace fuel filter.
		• Fuel pressure still below 13½ psi, **Perform STEP C.**

1984-86 EFI DRIVEABILITY TEST PROCEDURES

TEST 25	STEP C	CHECKING FOR LOW FUEL PRESSURE

PROCEDURE	TEST INDICATION	ACTION REQUIRED
• Turn engine off. • Release pressure. • Remove pressure gauge from before filter and reinstall it after filter. • Start engine. • Very gently, squeeze fuel return line at throttle body and immediately let go. INSTALL PRESSURE GAUGE FUEL FILTER	• Fuel pressure should increase above operating pressure.	• Fuel pressure increases, replace pressure regulator valve.
	• Fuel pressure does not increase, replace intank fuel pump. **NOTE:** Before replacing pump look for contamination in the fuel tank that may be plugging pump filter. Also make sure electrical connections are not corroded.

TEST 25	STEP D	CHECKING FOR HIGH FUEL PRESSURE

PROCEDURE	TEST INDICATION	ACTION REQUIRED
REMINDERS • Pressure gauge connected. • Turn engine off. • Remove fuel return hose (small one) from throttle body. • Connect a 3 foot piece of fuel hose to throttle body and put open end into an approved gasoline container. (2-gallon size.) • Have someone start engine, look at pressure gauge, and then immediately turn engine off. **CAUTION:** Do not let engine run for more than 10 seconds. REMOVE HOSE RETURN HOSE FUEL PRESSURE RETURN HOSE	• Fuel pressure should be 14½ psi ±.	• Fuel pressure okay, check fuel return lines for kinks or restrictions, including lines and return line check valve inside fuel tank.
	• Fuel pressure above 15½ psi, replace pressure regulator valve.

TEST 26	STEP A	CHECKING THE OXYGEN SENSOR OPERATION

PROCEDURE	TEST INDICATION	ACTION REQUIRED
• Connect the diagnostic readout box to the engine harness connector. **NOTE:** Make sure the read/hold switch is in the read position. • Start the engine • Move the read/hold switch to the hold position to increase engine speed DIAGNOSTIC READOUT BOX	• Display on the readout box should be switching between 0 and 1	• 0-1 switching. **Perform TEST NO. 27.**
	• No 0-1 switching, replace the oxygen sensor.

NOTES

_____
_____
_____
_____
_____
_____
_____
_____
_____
_____

CHRYSLER MULTI—POINT ELECTRONIC FUEL INJECTION
General Information

The turbocharged and non-turbocharged Multi-point Electronic Fuel Injection system combines an electronic fuel and spark advance control system with a turbocharged intake system (if equipped). At the center of this system is a digital pre-programmed computer known as a Logic Module or (on 1987½–88 models) a Single Module Engine Controller (SMEC) that regulates ignition timing, air/fuel ratio, emission control devices, idle speed, (on 1986–88 models) cooling fan, charging system, turbocharger wastegate (on turbo models) and (on 1987½–88) speed control. This component has the ability to update and revise its programming to meet changing operating conditions.

Various sensors provide the input necessary for the Logic Module or SMEC to correctly regulate fuel flow at the fuel injectors. These include the Manifold Absolute Pressure, Throttle Position, Oxygen Feedback, Coolant Temperature, Charge Temperature, Vehicle Speed (Distance) Sensors and (on 1986–88 models) throttle body temperature. In addition to the sensors, various switches also provide important information. These include the Transmission Neutral-Safety, Heated Backlite, Air Conditioning Clutch Switch, Brake Switch (on 1986–88) and Speed Control Switch (on 1987½–88).

Inputs to the Logic Module or SMEC are converted into signals sent to the Power Module. These signals cause the Power Module to change either the fuel flow at the injector or ignition timing or both.

The Logic Module or SMEC tests many of its own input and output circuits. If a fault is found in a major circuit, this information is stored in the Logic Module or SMEC. Information on this fault can be displayed to a technician by means of the instrument panel power loss (check engine) lamp or by connecting a diagnostic readout and observing a numbered display code which directly relates to a specific fault.

COMPONENTS AND OPERATION

Power Module

The Power Module contains the circuits necessary to power the ignition coil and the fuel injector. These are high current devices and their power supply has been isolated to minimize any "electrical noise" reaching the Logic Module. The Power Module also energizes the Automatic Shut Down (ASD) Relay which activates the fuel pump, ignition coil, and the Power Module itself. The module also receives a signal from the distributor and sends this signal to the logic module. In the event

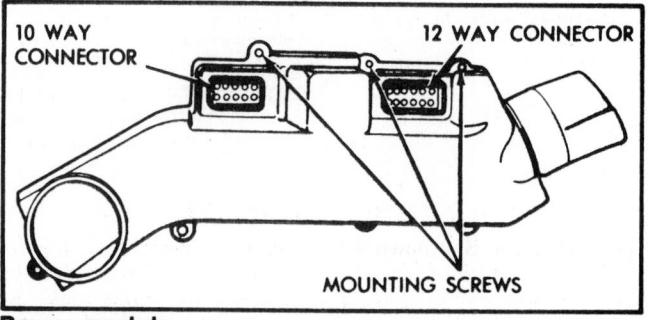

Power module

of no distributor signal, the ASD relay is not activated and power is shut off from the fuel pump and ignition coil. The Power Module contains a voltage converter which reduces battery voltage to a regulated 8.0 volt output. This 8.0 volt output powers the distributor and also powers the Logic Module.

Logic Module

The Logic Module is a digital computer containing a microprocessor. The module receives input signals from various switches, sensors, and components. It then computes the fuel injector pulse width, spark advance, ignition coil dwell, idle speed, purge and EGR solenoid cycles and (on 1985–88 models) cooling fan and alternator.

The Logic Module tests many of its own input and output circuits. If a fault is found in a major system, this information is stored in the Logic Module. Information on this fault can be displayed to a technician by means of flashing lamp on the instrument panel or by connecting a diagnostic readout tool and reading a numbered display code which relates to a general fault.

Single Module Engine Controller (SMEC)

On 1987½–88 models, the SMEC contains the circuits necessary to drive the ignition coil, fuel injector, and the alternator field. These are high current devices and have been isolated to minumize any electrical noise in the passenger compartment.

The Automatic Shut Down (ASD) relay is mounted externally, but is turned on and off by the SMEC. Distributor pick-up signal goes to the SMEC. In the event of no distributor signal, the ASD relay is not activated and power is shut off from the

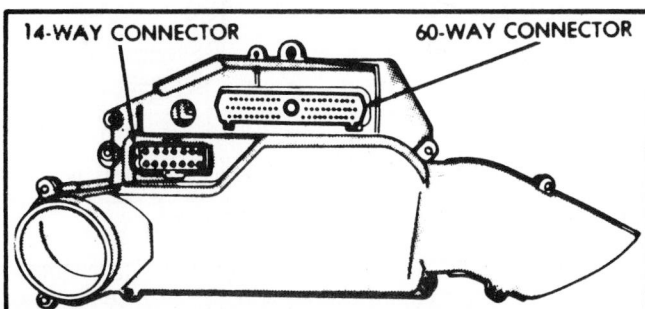

Single Module Engine Controller (SMEC)

14-WAY CONNECTOR   60-WAY CONNECTOR

fuel injector and ignition coil. The SMEC contains a voltage convertor which converts battery voltage to a regulated 8.0 volt output. This 8.0 volt output powers the distributor pick-up. The internal 5 volt supply which, in turn, powers the MAP sensor and TPS.

The SMEC is a digital computer containing a microprocessor. The module receives input signals from various switches and sensors. It then computes the fuel injector pulse width, spark advance, ignition coil dwell, idle speed, purge and cooling fan turn on and alternator charge rate.

The SMEC tests many of its own input and ouput circuits. If a fault is found in a major system, this information is stored in the SMEC. Information on this fault can be displayed to a technician by means of the instrument panel check engine lamp or by connecting the diagnostic read out tool C–4805 and reading a numbered display code which directly relates to a general fault.

Automatic Shutdown (ASD) Relay (1984)

The Automatic Shutdown Relay (ASD) is powered and controlled through the Power Module. When the Power Module senses a distributor signal during cranking, it grounds the ASD closing its contacts. This completes the circuit for the elec-

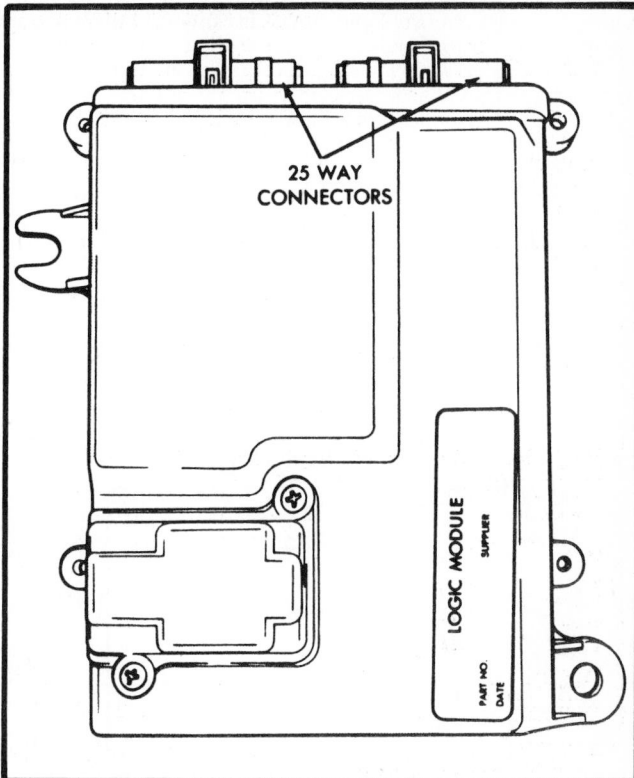

Logic module

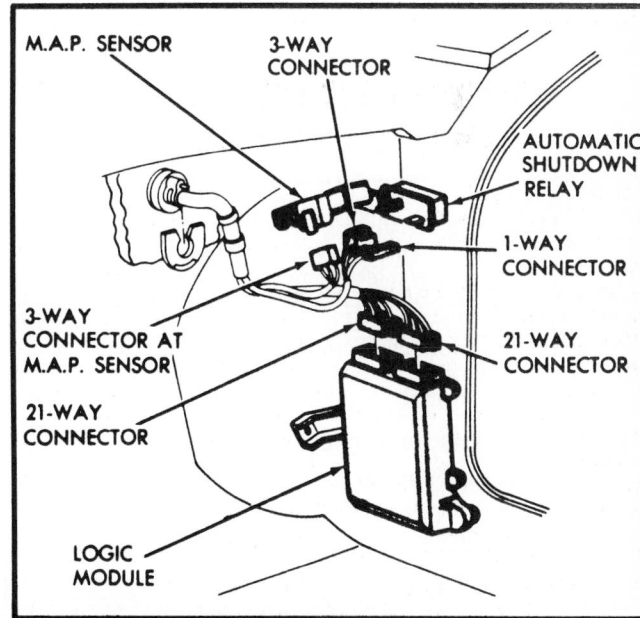

M.A.P. SENSOR   3-WAY CONNECTOR   AUTOMATIC SHUTDOWN RELAY   1-WAY CONNECTOR   3-WAY CONNECTOR AT M.A.P. SENSOR   21-WAY CONNECTOR   21-WAY CONNECTOR   LOGIC MODULE

Automatic Shutdown (ASD) relay–1984

tric fuel pump, Power Module, and ignition coil. If the distributor signal is lost for any reason the ASD interrupts this circuit in less than one second preventing fuel, spark, and engine operations. This fast shut down serves as a safety feature in the event of an accident.

Manifold Absolute Pressure (MAP) Sensor

The Manifold Absolute Pressure (MAP) sensor is a device

which monitors manifold vacuum. It is connected to a vacuum nipple on the throttle body and, electrically to the logic module or SMEC. The sensor transmits information on manifold vacuum conditions and barometric pressure to the Logic Module or SMEC. The MAP sensor data on engine load is used with data from other sensors to determine the correct air/fuel mixture. It is located as follows:
- 1984—Mounted in the right side passenger compartment
- 1985–86—Mounted on the logic module
- 1987–88 Front Wheel Drive Cars—Mounted underhood on the right shock tower
- 1987½–88—Front Wheel Drive Van/Wagon—Mounted underhood on the front of dash

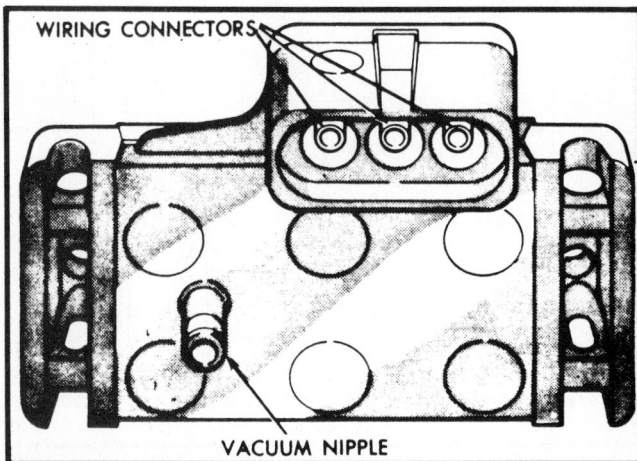

Manifold Air Pressure (MAP) sensor

Oxygen Sensor (O₂ Sensor)

The Oxygen Sensor (O₂ Sensor) is a device which produces an electrical voltage when exposed to the oxygen present in the exhaust gases. The sensor is mounted in the exhaust manifold and, on 1984–86 models, must be heated by the exhaust gases before producing the voltage. On most 1987–88 models, the oxygen sensor is electrically heated internally for faster switching when the engine is running. When there is a large amount of oxygen present (lean mixture), the sensor produces a low voltage. When there is a lesser amount present (rich mixture) it produces a higher voltage. By monitoring the oxygen content and converting it to electrical voltage, the sensor acts as a rich-lean switch. The voltage is transmitted to the Logic Module. The Logic Module signals the Power Module to trigger the fuel injector. The injector changes the mixture.

Charge Temperature Sensor

The Charge Temperature Sensor is a device mounted in the intake manifold which measures the temperature of the air/

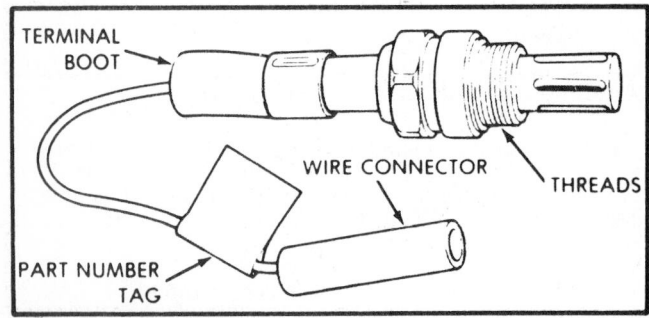

Oxygen (O₂) sensor

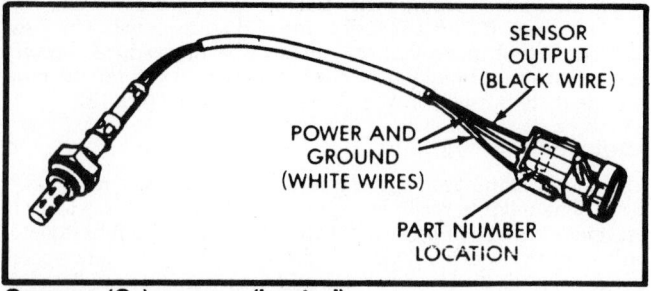

Oxygen (O₂) sensor (heated)

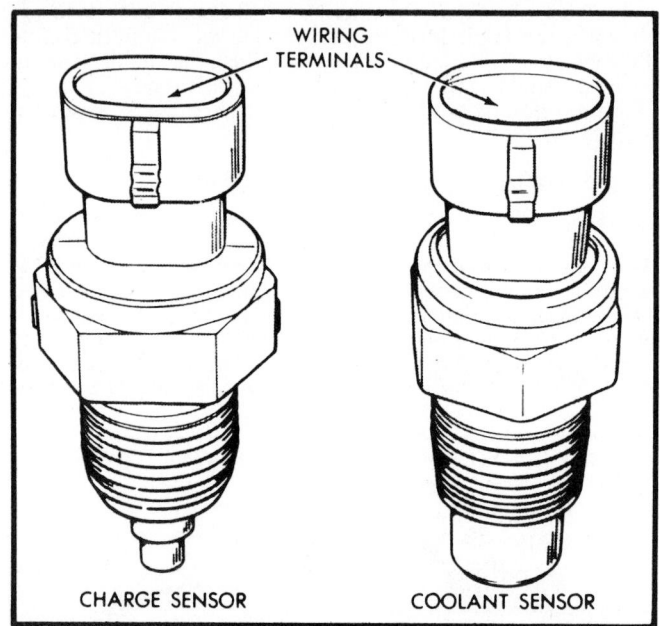

Charge and coolant temperature sensors

fuel mixture. This information is used by the Logic Module or SMEC to determine engine operating temperature and engine warm-up cycles in the event of a Coolant Temperature Sensor failure.

Coolant Temperature Sensor

The Coolant Temperature Sensor is a device which monitors coolant temperature (which is the same as engine operating temperature). It is mounted in the thermostat housing. This sensor provides data on engine operating temperature to the Logic Module or SMEC. This data along with data provided by the Charge Temperature Switch allows the Logic Module or SMEC to demand slightly richer air/fuel mixtures and higher idle speeds until normal operating temperatures are reached. The sensor is a variable resistor with a range of -60°F to 300°F. On 1985–88 models, this sensor is also used for cooling fan control.

Switch Input

Various switches provide information to the Logic Module or SMEC. These include the Neutral Safety, Air Conditioning Clutch, and Brake Light switches. If one or more of these switches is sensed as being in the on position, the Logic Module or SMEC signals the Automatic Idle Speed Motor to increase idle speed to a scheduled rpm.

With the air conditioning on and the throttle blade above a specific angle, the wide open throttle cut-out relay prevents the air conditioning clutch from engaging until the throttle blade is below this angle.

Power Loss Lamp (Check Engine)

The Power Loss (Check Engine) Lamp comes on each time the ignition key is turned on and stays on for a few seconds as a bulb test. If the Logic Module or SMEC receives an incorrect signal or no signal from either the Coolant Temperature Sensor, Manifold Absolute Pressure Sensor, or the Throttle Position Sensor, the lamp on the instrument panel is illuminated. This is a warning that the Logic Module or SMEC has gone into Limp In Mode in an attempt to keep the system operational.

The lamp can also be used to display fault codes. Cycle the ignition switch on, off, on, off, on within five seconds and any fault codes stored in the memory will be displayed.

Limp In Mode is the attempt by the Logic Module or SMEC to compensate for the failure of certain components by substituting information from other sources. If the module senses incorrect data or not data at all from the MAP Sensor, Throttle Position Sensor, Charge Temperature Sensor, Coolant Temperature Sensor, or (on 1987½–88 models) the system is placed into Limp In Mode and lamp on the instrument panel is activated.

Purge Solenoid (1984–86 and 1987 L Body with Black Dot)

The Purge Solenoid works in the same fashion as the EGR solenoid. When engine temperature is below 61°C (145°F) the Logic Module grounds the Purge Solenoid energizing it. This prevents vacuum from reaching the charcoal canister valve. Then this temperature is reached the Logic Module de-energizes the solenoid by turning the ground off. Once this occurs vacuum will flow to the canister purge valve and purge fuel vapors through the throttle body.

Purge Solenoid (1987½–88)

The Purge Solenoid controls both canister purge and fuel pressure regulator. When energized, it blocks the flow of fuel vapor and increases fuel pressure. Depending upon data supplied by the coolant temperature sensor and charge temperature at start up, the solenoid will be energized for a controlled time.

Exhaust Gas Recirculation Solenoid (1984–85, 1986–87 with White Dot)

The EGR solenoid is operated by the Logic Module. When engine temperature is below 21°C (70°F), the Logic Module energizes the solenoid by grounding it. This closes the solenoid and prevents ported vacuum from reaching the EGR valve. When the prescribed temperature is reached, the logic module will turn off the ground for the solenoid de-energizing it. Once the solenoid is de-energized, ported vacuum from the throttle body will pass through to the EGR valve. At idle and wide open throttle the solenoid is energized which prevents EGR operation.

Exhaust Gas Recirculation EGR/Purge Solenoid (1987 Turbo I and II)

The purge/EGR solenoid is operated by the Logic Module. When engine temperature is below 80°F or is above 80°F for less than seven seconds, the module energizes the solenoid by grounding it. This closes the solenoid and prevents manifold vacuum or pressure from reaching the EGR valve. When the prescribed time and temperature conditions are reached, the module will turn off the ground for the solenoid, de-enerizing it. Once the solenoid is de-energized, manifold vacuum from the throttle body will actuate canister purge and pass through to the EGR valve. When in boost, the solenoid is energized, which prevents EGR operation.

Wastegate Control Solenoid (1985–88 Turbo)

The Wastegate Control Solenoid is controlled by the Logic

EGR/purge solenoid—1984

Module. The module adjusts maximum boost to varying engine conditions by varying the duty cycle of the wastegate solenoid. Green dot on 1986–88 models.

Barometric Read Solenoid (1985–88 Turbo)

The Barometric Read Solenoid is controlled by the Logic Module. The solenoid is in the MAP sensor vacuum line. The solenoid controls whether manifold pressure or atmospheric pressure is supplied to the MAP sensor. Atmospheric pressure is periodically supplied to the MAP sensor to measure barometric pressure. This occurs at closed throttle, once per throttle closure but no more often than once every 30 seconds (3 minutes on 1987–88) and below a specified rpm. The barometric information is used primarily for boost control. Blue dot on 1986–88 models.

Air Conditioning Cutout Relay (1984–85)

The Air Conditioning Cutout Relay is electrically connected in series with the cycling clutch switch and low pressure cut out switch. This relay is in the normally closed (on) position during engine operation. When the Logic Module sense wide open throttle through the Throttle Position Sensor, it will energize the relay, open its contracts, and prevent air conditioning clutch engagement.

Air Conditioning Cutout Relay (1986–88)

The Air Conditioning Cutout Relay is electrically connected in series with the A/C Damped Pressure Switch and the A/C Switch. This relay is in the energized closed (on) position during engine operation. When the Logic Module or SMEC senses wide open throttle through the Throttle Position Sensor it will deenergize the relay, open its contacts and prevent air conditioning clutch engagement.

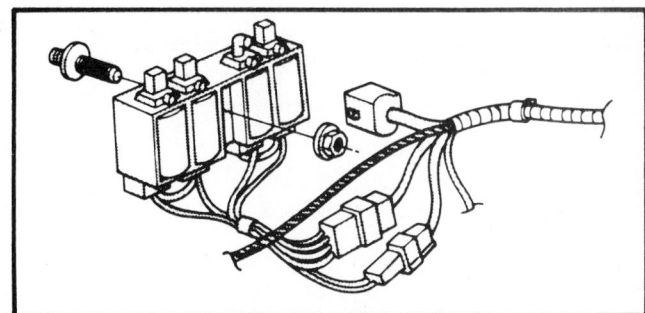

EGR/purge/wastegate/barometric read solenoids

Detonation (Knock) Sensor (1986–88 Turbo)

The Detonation Sensor is a device that generates a signal when spark knock occurs in the combustion chamber(s). It is mounted at a position on the intake manifold where detonation in each cylinder can be detected. The sensor provides information used by the Logic Module to modify spark advance and boost schedules in order to eliminate detonation.

Throttle Body

The throttle body assembly replaces a conventional carburetor air intake system and is connected to both the turbocharger and the intake manifold. The throttle body houses the Throttle Position Sensor and the Automatic Idle Speed Motor. Air flow through the throttle body is controlled by a cable operated throttle blade located in the base of the throttle body.

Fuel Supply Circuit

Fuel is pumped to the fuel rail by an electrical pump which is mounted in the fuel tank. The pump inlet is fitted with filter to prevent water and other contaminents from entering the fuel supply circuit.

Fuel pressure is controlled to a preset level above intake manifold pressure by a pressure regulator which is mounted near the fuel rail. The regulator uses intake manifold pressure at the vacuum tee as a reference.

Fuel Injectors and Fuel Rail Assembly

The fuel injectors are retained in the fuel rail by lock rings. The rail and injector assembly is then bolted in position with the injectors inserted in the recessed holes in the intake manifold.

Fuel Injector

The Fuel Injector is an electric solenoid powered by the Power Module, but controlled by the Logic Module. On 1987½–88 models, the injectors are controlled by the Single Module Engine Controller (SMEC). The module determines when and how long the injector should operate. When an electric current is supplied to the injector, the armature and pintle move a short distance against a spring, opening a small orifice. Fuel is supplied to the inlet of the injector by the fuel pump, then passes through the injector, around the pintle, and out the orifice. Since the fuel is under high pressure a fine spray id developed in the shape of a hollow cone. The injector, through this spraying action, atomizes the fuel and distributes it into the air entering the combustion chamber.

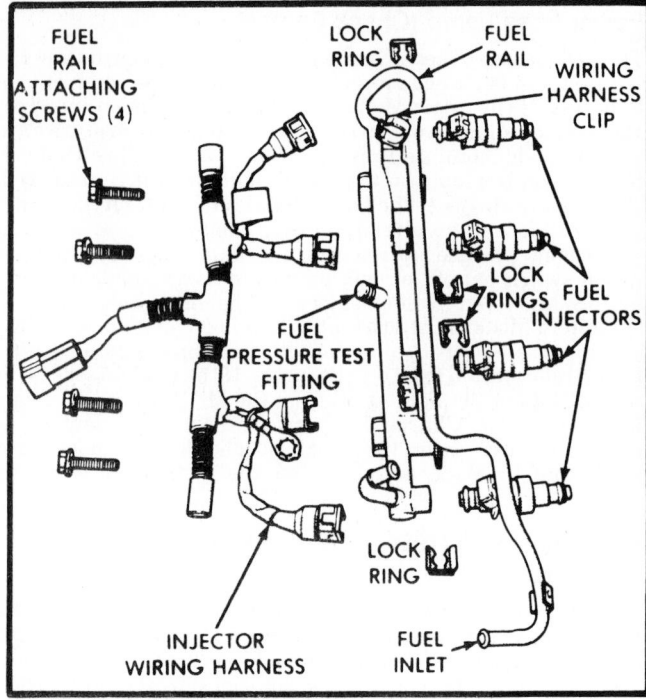

Fuel rail and injector assembly

Fuel Pressure Regulator

The pressure regulator is a mechanical device located downstream of the fuel injector on the throttle body. Its function is to maintain constant fuel pressure across the fuel injector tip: 55 psi (380 kPa) for turbo models and 36 psi (248 kPa) for non-turbo models. The regulator uses a spring loaded rubber diaphragm to uncover a fuel return port. When the fuel pump becomes operational, fuel flows past the injector into the regula-

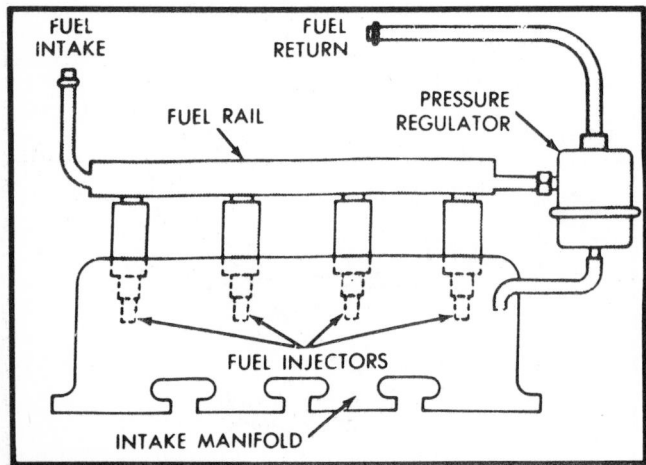

Fuel supply system

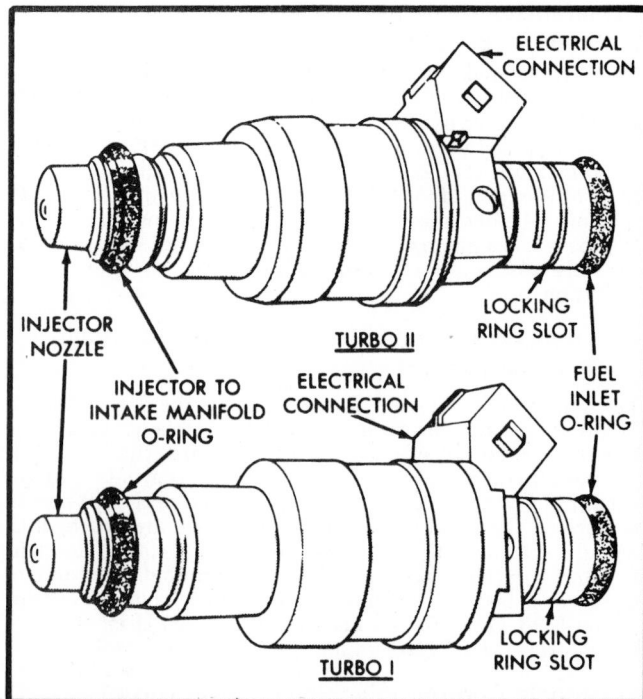

Fuel injector

tor and is restricted from flowing any further by the blocked return port. When the specified operating fuel pressure reached it pushes on the diaphragm, compressing the spring and uncovers the fuel return port. The diaphragm and spring will constantly move from an open to closed position to keep the fuel pressure constant. An assist to the spring loaded diaphragm comes from vacuum in the throttle body above the throttle blade. As venturi vacuum increases less pressure is required to supply the same amount of fuel into the air flow. The vacuum assists in opening the fuel port during high vacuum conditions. This fine tunes the fuel pressure for all operating conditions.

Throttle Position Sensor (TPS)

The Throttle Position Sensor (TPS) is an electric resistor which is activated by the movement of the throttle shaft. It is mounted on the throttle body and senses the angle of the throttle blade opening. The voltage that the sensor produces increases or decreases according to the throttle blade opening. This voltage is transmitted to the Logic Module or SMEC where it is used along with data from other sensors to adjust the air/fuel ratio to varying conditions and during acceleration, deceleration, idle, and wide open throttle operations.

Automatic Idle Speed (AIS) Motor

The Automatic Idle Speed Motor (AIS) is operated by the Logic Module or SMEC. Data from the Throttle Position Sensor, Speed Sensor, Coolant Temperature Sensor, and various switch operations, (Safety/Neutral, Brake) are used by the module to adjust engine idle to an optimum during all idle conditions. The AIS adjust the air portion of the air/fuel mixture through an air bypass in the throttle body. Basic (no load) idle is determined by the minimum air flow through the throttle body. The AIS opens or closes off the air bypass as an increase or decrease is needed due to engine loads or ambient conditions. The Logic Module senses an air/fuel change and increases or decreases fuel proportionally to change engine idle. Deceleration die out is also prevented by increasing engine idle when the throttle is closed quickly after a driving (speed) condition.

Fuel Pump

The fuel pump used in this system is a positive displacement, roller vane immersible pump with a permanent magnet elec-

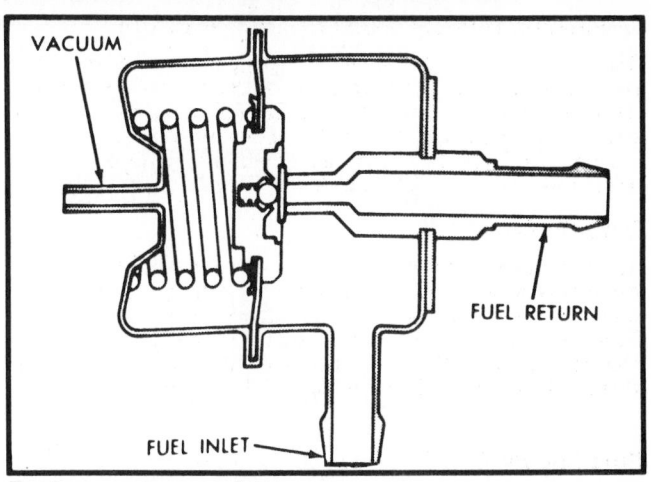

Fuel pressure regulator

tric motor. The fuel is drawn in through a filter sock and pushed through the electric motor to the outlet. The pump contains two check valves. One valve is used to relieve internal fuel pump pressure and regulate maximum pump output. The other check valve, located near the pump outlet, restricts fuel movement in either direction when the pump is not operational. Voltage to operate the pump is supplied through the Auto Shutdown (ASD) relay.

Some turbocharged models (like Shelby) feature two electric fuel pumps. One pump is mounted in the fuel tank called the secondary pump. The other pump, primary pump, is mounted outside the tank.

Fuel Reservoir

The fuel pump is mounted within a fuel reservoir in the fuel tank. The purpose of the reservoir is to provide fuel at the pump intake during all driving conditions, especially those when low fuel levels are present. The fuel return line directs fuel into a cup on the side of the reservoir. The stream of fuel coming into this cup creates a low pressure area and causes additional fuel from the main tank to flow into the reservoir. This combination of return fuel and fuel from the main tank keeps the reservoir full even when the fuel level is below the reservoir walls.

System and Component Identification

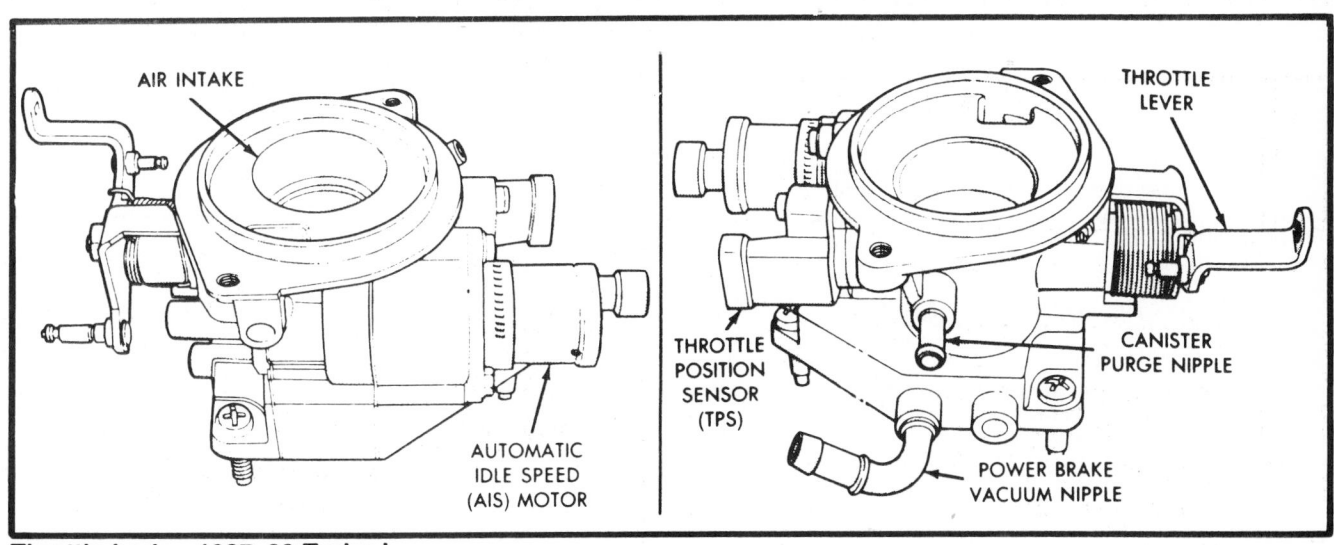

Throttle body—1987–88 Turbo I

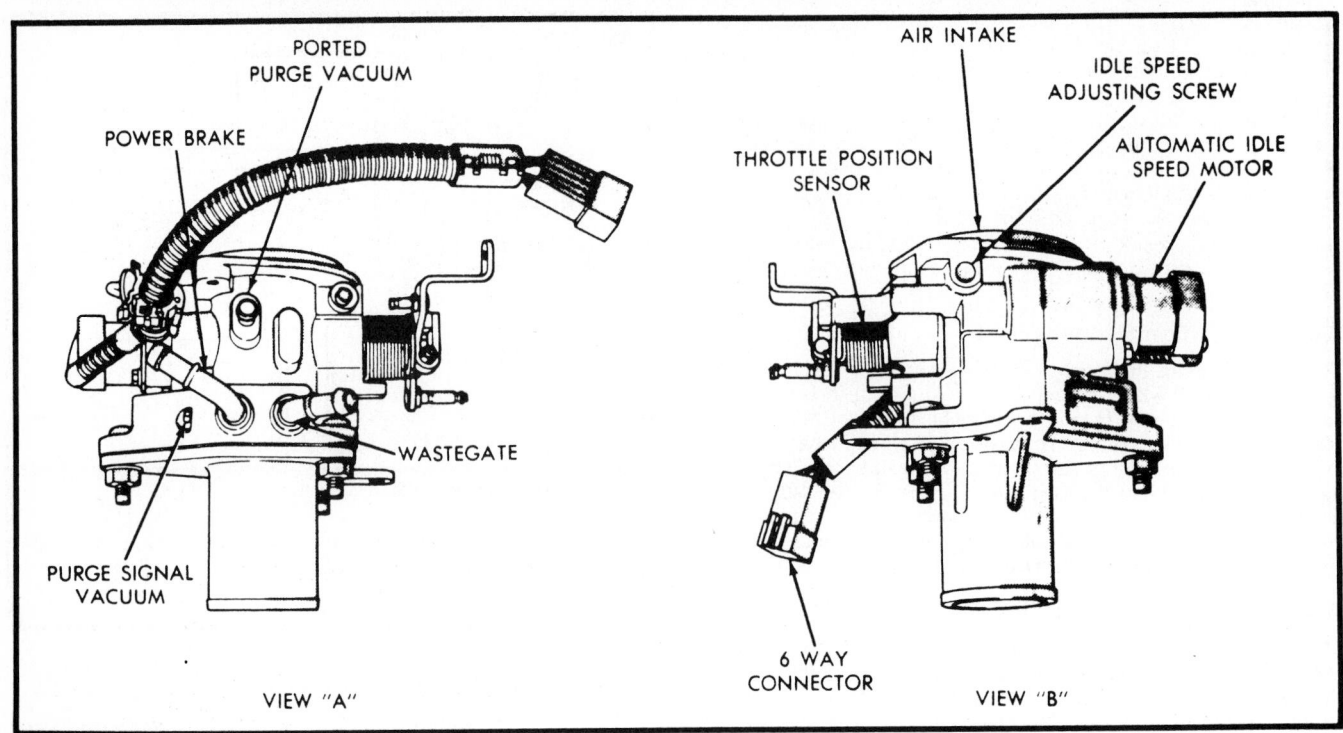

Throttle body—1984–86 and 1987 L-Body

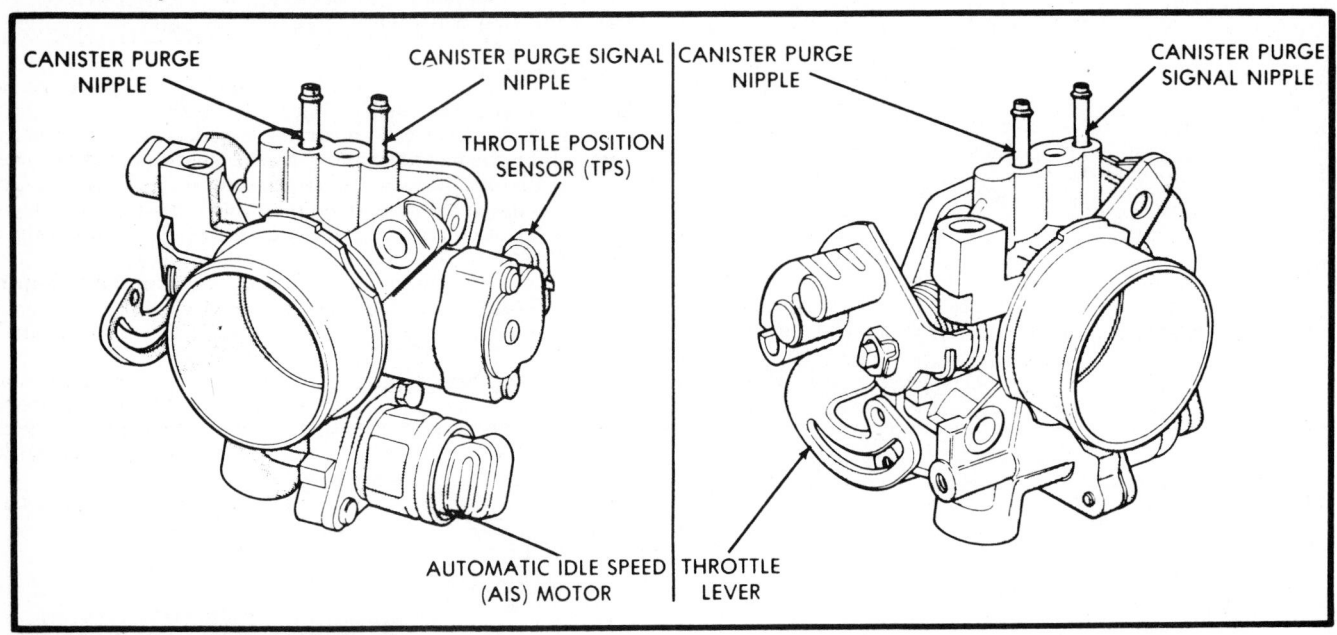

Throttle body—1987–88 Turbo II

System Servicing

Service Precautions

1. When working around any part of the fuel system, take precautionary steps to prevent fire and/or explosion:

a. Disconnect negative terminal from battery (except when testing with battery voltage is required).

b. When ever possible, use a flashlight instead of a drop light.

c. Keep all open flame and smoking material out of the area.

d. Use a shop cloth or similar to catch fuel when opening a fuel system.

e. Relieve fuel system pressure before servicing.

f. Use eye protection.

g. Always keep a dry chemical (class B) fire extinguisher near the area.

Minimum Idle Speed Adjustment

Before adjusting the idle on an electronic fuel injected vehicle the following items must be checked:

a. AIS motor has been checked for operation.

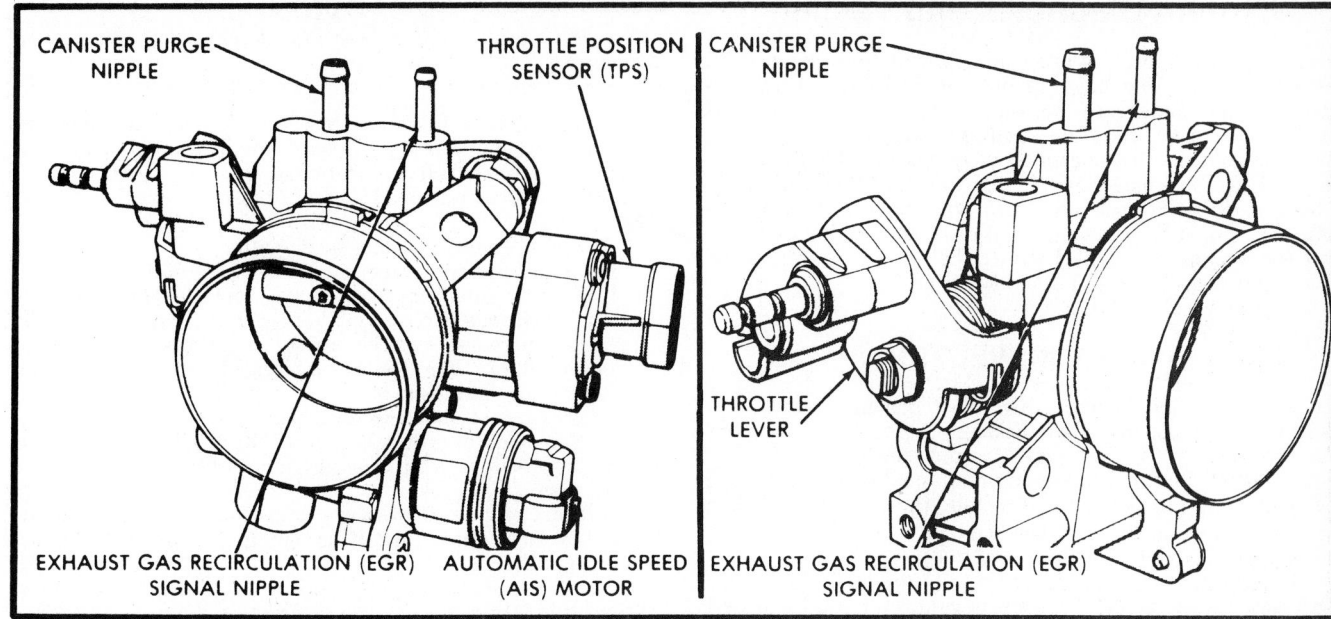

Throttle body—3.0L V6 engine

b. Engine has been checked for vacuum or EGR leaks.

c. Engine timing has been checked and set to specifications.

d. Coolant temperature sensor has been checked for operation.

1. Install a tachometer.

2. Warm up engine to normal operating temperature (accessories off).

3. Shut engine off and disconnect radiator fan.

4. Disconnect Throttle Body 6-way connector. Remove the brown with white tracer AIS wire from the connector and reconnect connector.

5. Start engine with transaxle selector in PARK or NEUTRAL.

6. Apply 12 volts to AIS brown with white tracer wire. This will drive the AIS fully closed and the idle should drop.

7. Disconnect then reconnect coolant temperature sensor.

8. With transaxle in NEUTRAL, idle speed should be 775 ± 25 (700 ± 25 green engine).

9. If idle is not to specifications adjust idle air bypass screws.

10. If idle will not adjust down, check for vacuum leaks, AIS motor damage, throttle body damage, or speed control cable adjustment.

Ignition Timing Adjustment

1. Connect a power timing light to the number one cylinder, or a magnetic timing unit to the engine. Use a 10 degree offset when required.

2. Connect a tachometer to the engine and turn selector to the proper cylinder position.

3. Start engine and run until operating temperature is reached.

4. On 1984–86 models, disconnect and reconnect the coolant temperature sensor connector on the thermostat housing. The loss of power lamp on the dash must come on and stay on. On 1987–88 models, disconnect coolant temperature sensor connector. Engine rpm should be within emission label specifications.

5. Aim power timing light at timing hole in bell housing or read the magnetic timing unit.

6. Loosen distributor and adjust timing to emission label specifications if necessary.

7. Shut engine off. On 1987–88 models, reconnect coolant temperature sensor. Disconnect and reconnect positive battery quick disconnect (or use erase fault codes with sensor test #10 on 1987½–88 models). Start vehicle, the loss of power (check engine) lamp should be off.

8. Shut engine off, then turn ignition on, off, on, off, on. Fault codes should be clear with 88-51-55 shown.

System Diagnosis and Testing

Mechanical malfunctions are more difficult to diagnose with the EFI system. The Logic Module or SMEC has been programmed to compensate for some mechanical malfunctions such as incorrect cam timing, vacuum leaks, etc. If engine performance problems are encountered, and no fault codes are displayed, the problem may be mechanical rather than electronic.

Most complaints that may occur with turbocharged multipoint Electronic Fuel Injection can be traced to poor wiring or hose connections. A visual check will help spot these faults and save unnecessary test and diagnosis time.

VISUAL INSPECTION

A visual inspection for loose, disconnected or misrouted wires and hoses should be made before attempting to diagnose or service the fuel injection system. A visual check will help spot these faults and save unnecessary test and diagnostic time. A thorough visual inspection will include the following checks:

- Hose connections at throttle body.
- Throttle body electrical connector(s).
- Harness ground eyelet mounting to intake manifold.
- 2 way charge temperature sensor connector and 1 way detonation sensor connection.
- 2 way connector attachment at each fuel injector. Check vacuum tee hose connection.
- Both 3 way distributor connectors. (4 way connector on models with SMEC.)
- O₂ sensor connector.
- 2 way distance sensor and starter relay ground connector (manual only).
- Both connectors at power module or SMEC.
- Electrical connections at EGR and/or purge solenoids.
- 2 way connector at coolant temperature sensor and battery cable ground at engine.
- Engine temperature sensor electrical connections.
- Vacuum hose connection between vacuum source and fuel pressure regulator.
- Vacuum hose connections between vacuum source and EGR, purge, wastegate and barometric read solenoids.
- Vacuum connection between purge solenoid and charcoal canister..
- Oil pressure sending unit electrical connection.
- Ignition cable routing and attachment.
- Ignition coil electrical connection.
- Fuel pressure regulator hoses.
- Radiator fan electrical connection.
- Alternator wiring connections and belt tension.
- MAP sensor hose at dash panel grommet.
- Engine ground mounting at dash panel.
- EGR system vacuum hose connection.
- Power brake booster and speed connections.
- Air conditioning, starter, radiator fan relay connections.
- Battery cable connections.
- Engine harness to main harness connections.
- Neutral safety switch wiring connection.
- Logic module wiring connections (if equipped).
- Hose and wiring connections at fuel pump. Check that wiring connector is making contact with terminals on pump.
- MAP sensor vacuum connection.

FUEL SYSTEM PRESSURE TEST
1984 Models

———————— CAUTION ————————
Fuel system pressure must be released each time a fuel hose is to be disconnected. Take precautions to avoid the risk of fire.
——————————————————————

———————— CAUTION ————————
Fuel system pressure must be released each time a fuel hose is to be disconnected.
——————————————————————

1. Remove fuel intake hose from throttle body and connect fuel system pressure testers C–3292 and hose adaptor C–4749 or equivalent, between fuel filter hose and throttle body.
2. Start engine and read gauge. Pressure should be 55 psi (380 kPa).
3. If fuel pressure is below specifications:
   a. Install tester between fuel filter hose and fuel line.
   b. Start engine. If pressure is now correct, replace fuel filter. If no change is observed, gently squeeze return hose. If pressure increases, replace pressure regulator. If no change is observed, problem is either a plugged pump filter sock or defective fuel pump.
5. If pressure is above specifications:
   a. Remove fuel return hose from throttle body. Connect a substitute hose and place other end of hose in clean container.
   b. Start engine. If pressure is now correct, check for restricted fuel return line. If no change is observed, replace fuel regulator.

1985–88 Models

1. Perform fuel system release.
2. Remove protective cover from service valve on fuel rail.
3. Connect fuel pressure gauge C–3292 and hose adaptor C–4749 or equivalent to fuel rail service valve.
4. On 1985 models, start engine and read gauge. On 1986–88 models, use ATM tester C–4805 or equivalent, with ignition key in RUN position, depress ATM button. This will activate fuel pump and pressurize the system. Fuel pressure should be 55 psi (380 kPa) for turbo models and 36 psi (240 kPa) for nonturbo models

ON BOARD DIAGNOSTICS

The Logic Module or SMEC has been programmed to monitor several different circuits of the fuel injection system. This monitoring is called On Board Diagnosis. If a problem is sensed with a monitored circuit, often enough to indicate an actual problem, its fault code is stored in the module for eventual display to the service technician. If the problem is repaired or ceases to exist, the Logic Module cancels the fault code after 20–40 ignition key on/off cycles.

Fault Codes

Fault codes are two digit numbers that identify which circuit is bad. In most cases, they do not identify which component is bad in a circuit. When a fault code appears (either by flashes of the power loss/limited (check engine) lamp or by watching the diagnostic read out Tool C–4805, or equivalent, it indicates that the logic module or SMEC has recognized an abnormal signal in the system. Fault codes indicate the results of a failure but do not always identify the failed component directly.

Accessing Trouble Code Memory

There are two methods used in accessing trouble codes. The first method is the use of a diagnostic readout box Tool C–4805 or equivalent, the second method is observing the power loss/limited (check engine) lamp.

The diagnostic readout box is used to put the system into a Diagnostic Test Mode, Circuit Actuation Test Mode, Switch Test Mode, Engine Running Test Mode and, on 1986–88 models, Sensor Test Mode. Three (four) of these modes of testing are called for at certain points of the driveability test procedure. A fourth (fifth) test mode is available with the engine running. The following is a description of each test mode:

• Diagnostic Test Mode—This mode is used to see is there are any fault codes stored in the on-board diagnostic system memory.

• Circuit Actuation Test Mode (ATM Test)—This mode is used to turn a specific circuit on and off in order to check it. ATM test codes are used in this mode.

• Switch Test Mode—This mode is used to determine if specific switch inputs are being received by the logic module.

• Sensor Test Mode (1986–88)—This mode is used to see the output signals of certain sensors as received by the logic module.

• Engine Running Test Mode—This mode is used to determine if the oxygen feedback system is switching from rich to lean and lean to rich.

DIAGNOSIS USING READOUT BOX

The diagnostic readout box is used to put the on-board diagnostic system in three different modes (four on 1986–88 models) of testing as called for in the driveability test procedure.

1. Connect Tool C–4805 or equivalent, to the mating connector located in the wiring harness by the right front shock tower.

2. Place the read/hold switch on the readout box in the read position.

3. Turn the ignition switch ON-OFF-ON-OFF-ON within five seconds.

4. Record all codes.

NOTE:The display of codes can be stopped by moving the read/hold switch to the hold position. Returning to the read position will continue the displaying of codes.

Fault Code Description

CODE 11 - Distributor signal circuit
CODE 12 - Battery feed to logic module
CODE 13 - MAP Sensor vacuum circuit
CODE 14 - MAP Sensor electrical circuit
CODE 15 - Vehicle speed (distance) sensor
CODE 16 - (1985–88) Loss of battery voltage sense (charging system)
CODE 17 - (1985) Detonation (knock) sensor circuit
CODE 17 - (1986–88) Engine running cool
CODE 21 - Oxygen (O_2) sensor circuit
CODE 22 - Coolant temperature sensor circuit
CODE 23 - Charge temperature sensor circuit
CODE 24 - Throttle position sensor (TPS) circuit
CODE 25 - Automatic idle speed (AIS) motor driver circuit
CODE 26 - (1985–87) Number one injector circuit
CODE 26 - (1987½–88) Injector currect limit not achieved
CODE 27 - (1985–87) Number two injector circuit
CODE 27 - (1987½–88) Injector driver interface circuit
CODE 31 - Purge (1987 EGR/purge) solenoid circuit
CODE 32 - (1984–85) Power loss/limit lamp circuit
CODE 33 - A/C cutout relay circuit
CODE 34 - (1984–86) EGR solenoid circuit
CODE 34 - (1987–88) Speed control solenoid driver circuit
CODE 35 - Fan control relay circuit
CODE 37 - (1985–88 Turbo) Barometric read solenoid circuit
CODE 37 - (1987½–88 Non-turbo) Part throttle unlock (PTU) circuit
CODE 41 - Charging system excess or no field circuit
CODE 42 - Auto shutdown (ASD) relay driver circuit
CODE 43 - (1984–87) Spark interface circuit
CODE 43 - (1987½–88) Ignition coil control circuit
CODE 44 - (1984) Internal logic module problem
CODE 44 - (1986–87) Battery temperature sensor circuit

CODE 44 - (1987½–88) Loss of FJ2 to logic board
CODE 45 - (Turbo only) Overboost shutoff circuit
CODE 46 - (1985–88) Battery voltage too high
CODE 47 - (1985–88) Battery voltage too low
CODE 51 - (1984–85) Lean or rich condition indicated
CODE 51 - (1986–88) Lean condition indicated
CODE 52 - (1984) Internal logic module problem
CODE 52 - (1985) Battery temperature circuit
CODE 52 - (1986–88) Rich condition indicated
CODE 53 - Internal module problem
CODE 54 - Distributor sync (high data rate) pickup circuit
CODE 55 - End of message
CODE 88 - Start of test

Circuit Actuation Test Mode (ATM Test)

1. Put the system into the diagnostic test mode and wait for 55 to appear on the readout box display.

2. Press and hold the ATM button on the readout box until the desired ATM test code appears on the display and then release the button. The logic module will turn the selected circuit on and off at two second intervals for five minutes and then turn the test off. To stop thew test before the five minute period, turn the ignition switch off.

ACTUATOR TEST DISPLAY CODES

CODE 01 - Spark activation—once every 2 seconds
CODE 02 - Injector activation—once every 2 seconds
CODE 03 - Automatic idle speed (AIS) activation—one step open/one step closed every 4 seconds
CODE 04 - Radiator fan relay—once every 2 seconds
CODE 05 - A/C WOT cutout relay—once every 2 seconds
CODE 06 - Automatic shutdown (ASD) relay—once every 2 seconds
CODE 07 - Purge solenoid activation—one toggle every 2 seconds
CODE 08 - (1986) EGR solenoid activation—one toggle every 2 seconds
CODE 08 - (1987–88) Speed control activation—speed control vent and vacuum every 2 seconds

NOTE: Speed control switch must be in the on position to allow actuation

CODE 09 - (1986–88 Turbo) Wastegate solenoid activation—one toggle every 2 seconds
CODE 09 - (1987½–88 Non-turbo) Alternator field control activation—one toggle every 2 seconds
CODE 10 - (1986–88 Turbo) Barometric read solenoid activation—one toggle every 2 seconds
CODE 10 - (1987½–88 Non-turbo) Shift indicator lamp (manual transmission) or part throttle unlock solenoid activation—one toggle every 2 seconds

Sensor Test Mode (1986–88)

1. Put the system into the actuation test mode (ATM test).

2. Press and hold the ATM button until the desired sensor access code appears on the display and then release the button.

3. Move the read/hold switch to the "HOLD" position.

NOTE: Since sensor access codes are the same as some ATM test codes, the ATM test circuit will turn on before moving the read/hold switch to the "HOLD" position.

4. The logic module will now use the readout box to display the output of the selected sensor. All readings displayed are to be divided by 10, except the coolant sensor which is to be multiplied by 10. Battery voltage is actual and no correction is required.

SENSOR READ TEST DISPLAY CODES

CODE 01 - Battery temperature sensor—display number divided by 10 equals sensor temperature

CODE 02 - Oxygen sensor voltage – display number divided by 10 equals sensor voltage

CODE 03 - Throttle body temperature sensor voltage – display number divided by 10 equals sensor voltage

CODE 04 - Engine coolant temperature sensor voltage – display number multiply by 10 equals degrees of engine coolant sensor

CODE 05 - Throttle position sensor voltage – display number divided by 10 equals sensor voltage

CODE 06 - (Turbo only) Peak knock sensor voltage – display number is sensor voltage

CODE 07 - Battery voltage – display number is voltage

CODE 08 - MAP sensor voltage – display number divided by 10 equals sensor voltage

CODE 09 - Cruise control switches: cruise off – display is blank, cruise on – display shows 00, cruise set – display shows 10, cruise resume – display shows 01

CODE 10 - (1987½–88) Fault code erase routine – display will flash 0s for 4 seconds

Switch Test Mode

1. Make sure all the switches that send an input to the logic module are turned off.
2. Put the system into the diagnostic test mode and wait for 55 to appear on the readout box display.
3. Turn on the desired switch for input into the logic module. If the input is received by the logic module the display will change from "00" to "88" when the switch is activated and released.
   - Brake pedal
   - Gear shift selector: park, reverse, park
   - A/C switch (valid only if A/C dampened pressure switch is closed and blower switch on)

Engine Running Test Mode

The Engine Running Test Mode monitors the sensors on the vehicle which check operating conditions while the engine is running. The engine running test mode can be performed with the engine idling in neutral and with parking brake on or actual driving conditions. With the diagnostic readout box read/hold switch in the "READ" position, the engine running test mode is initiated after the engine is started.

Select a test code by switching the read/hold switch to the "READ" position and the actuator button depressed until the desired code appears. Release actuator button and switch read/hold switch to "HOLD" position. The logic module will monitor that system test and results will be displayed.

ENGINE RUNNING TEST DISPLAY CODES

CODE 61 - Battery temperature sensor – display number divided by 10 equals voltage

CODE 62 - Oxygen sensor – display number divided by 10 equals voltage

CODE 63 - Fuel injector temperature sensor – display number divided by 10 equals voltage

CODE 64 - Engine coolant temperature sensor – display number multiplied by 10 equals degrees F

CODE 65 - Throttle position sensor – display number divided by 10 equals voltage

CODE 67 - Battery voltage sensor – display is voltage

CODE 68 - Manifold vacuum sensor – display is in. Hg.

CODE 69 - Minimum throttle position sensor – display number divided by 10 equals voltage

CODE 70 - Minimum airflow idle speed sensor – display number multiplied by 10 equals rpm (see minimum air flow check procedure)

CODE 71 - Vehicle speed sensor – display is mph

CODE 72 - Engine speed sensor – display number multiplied by 10 equals rpm

Throttle Body Minimum Air Flow Check Procedure – ATM #70

1987–88 Turbo

1. While in PARK or NEUTRAL, start and run engine until cooling fan has cycled on and off at least once.
2. Connect timing light and tachometer.
3. Disconnect and reconnect coolant temperature sensor and set basic timing to 12 degrees BTDC ± 2 degrees BTDC.
4. Turn engine off.
5. Connect diagnostic readout box Tool C–4805 or equivalent.
6. Restart and run engine at idle for at least one minute.
7. With readout box, press and hold ATM button with read/hold switch in READ position. Proceed to actuation test mode (ATM) #70.
8. Move read/hold switch to HOLD position. The following will then occur:
   - AIS motor will fully close
   - Idle spark advance will become fixed
   - Idle fuel will become enriched
   - Engine rpm will be displayed on readout box in units of rpm multiplied by 10.
9. Check idle rpm. Correct rpm should be within 700–900 rpm. If rpm is not within specifications, replace throttle body.
10. Turn off engine and remove all diagnostic equipment.

1987½–88 Non-Turbo

1. While in PARK or NEUTRAL, start and run engine until cooling fan has cycled on and off at least once.
2. Connect timing light and tachometer.
3. Disconnect coolant temperature sensor and set basic timing to 12 degrees BTDC ± 2 degrees BTDC.
4. Turn engine off and reconnect coolant temperature sensor.
5. Disconnect PCV valve hose from intake manifold nipple and attach Miller Tool C–5004 or equivalent (0.125 in. orifice in attached hose) to intake manifold PCV nipple.
6. Connect diagnostic readout box Tool C–4805 or equivalent.
7. Restart and run engine at idle for at least one minute.
8. With readout box, press and hold ATM button with read/hold switch in READ position. Proceed to actuation test mode (ATM) #70.
9. Move read/hold switch to HOLD position. The following will then occur:
   - AIS motor will fully close
   - Idle spark advance will become fixed
   - Idle fuel will become enriched
   - Engine rpm will be displayed on readout box in units of rpm multiplied by 10.
10. Check idle rpm. Correct rpm should be within 850–1050 rpm. If rpm is not within specifications, replace throttle body.
11. Turn off engine and remove all diagnostic equipment.
12. Install PCV valve hose.

DIAGNOSIS USING POWER LOSS/LIMIT (CHECK ENGINE) LAMP

The power loss/limit (check engine) lamp has two modes of operation. If for some reason the diagnostic readout box is not available, the logic module can show fault codes by means of flashing the power loss (check engine) lamp on the instrument panel

NOTE: In some cases proper diagnostic cannot be determined by only using fault codes. Remember they are only the result, not necessarily the reason for the problem. This driveability test procedure is designed for use with the Diagnostic Readout Box not the flashing power loss (check engine) lamp.

To activate this function, turn the ignition key ON-OFF-ON-OFF-ON within five seconds. The power loss (check engine) lamp will then come on for two seconds as a bulb check. Immediately following this it will display a fault code by flashing on and off. There is a short pause between flashes and a longer pause between digits. All codes displayed are two digit numbers with a four second pause between codes.

1. Lamp on for two seconds, then turns off.
2. Lamp flashes five pauses and then flashes once.
3. Lamp pauses for four seconds, flashes five times, pauses and then flashes five times.

The two codes are 51 and 55. Any number of codes can be displayed as long as they are in memory. The lamp will flash until all of them are displayed.

Additional Information From Power Loss (Check Engine) Lamp

Switch Test – After all codes are displayed, switch function can be verified. The lamp will turn on or off when a switch is turned on or off.

Unlike the diagnostic readout box, the power loss lamp can not do the following:

1. Once the lamp begins to display fault codes, it can not be stopped. If code count is forgotten or lost, it is necessary to start over.
2. The lamp can not display any codes related to 88 diagnostic or blank displays.
3. The lamp can not show if the oxygen feedback system is switching (lean/rich).
4. The lamp can not perform the actuation test, sensor read test or engine running test modes.

DIAGNOSTIC PROCEDURE CHARTS

When using the Test Procedure some guidelines should be followed:

• Start from test 1 of the catagory. Starting from any other test will give incorrect results.

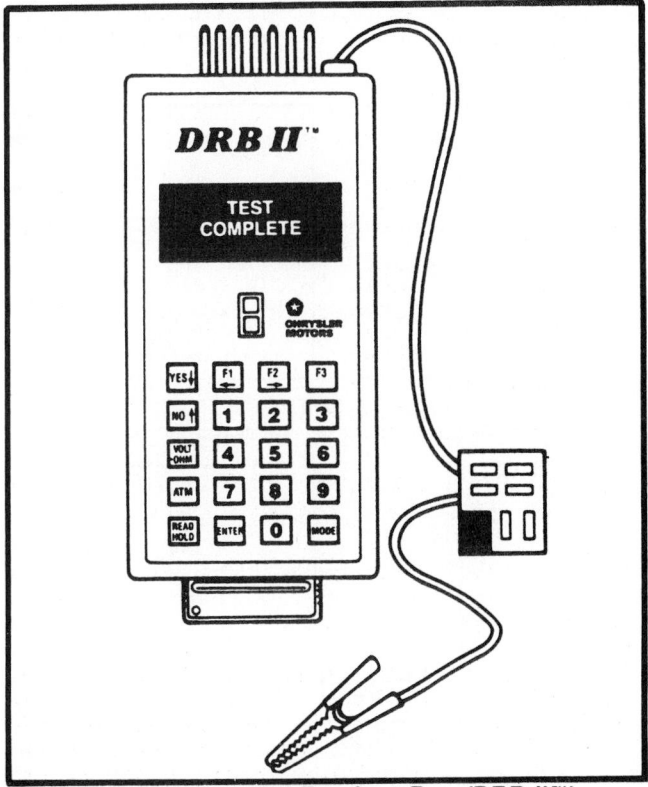

Diagnostic tool – Digital Readout Box (DRB II™)

• Tests are made up of many steps. Only perform the steps which are required. Performing all steps will give incorrect results.

• Some steps within a test have reminders. These are to inform that previous instructions are still required.

• At the end of each test reconnect all wires and hoses, turn engine off if required and reinstall any components that were removed for testing.

• The vehicle being tested must have a fully charged battery, specific gravity 1.220 temperature corrected.

• To perform the cold test, the engine must not be started for at least 7 hours.

• To perform the warm test, the engine must be at normal operating temperature.

Tools and Equipment

Make sure the following equipment is on hand.

1. Volt/ohm meter
2. Jumper wires
3. Auxiliary vacuum supply (hand held vacuum pump)
4. Fuel pressure gauge
5. Tachometer
6. Timing light
7. Oscilloscope
8. Vacuum gauge
9. High pressure gauge (Tool C–3292 or equivalent)
10. High pressure gauge adapter hoses (Tool C–4799 or equivalent)
11. Two gallon gasoline can
12. Diagnostic readout box (Tool C–4805 or equivalent)

1986–88 TURBO DRIVEABILITY TEST PROCEDURES

Code	Type	Power Loss/ Limit Lamp	Circuit	When Monitored By The Logic Module	When Put Into Memory	ATM Test Code	Sensor Access Code
11	Fault	No	Distributor Signal	During cranking.	If no distributor signal is present since the battery was disconnected.	None	None
12	Indication	No	Battery Feed to the Logic Module	All the time when the ignition switch is on.	If the battery feed to the logic module has been disconnected within the last 20-40 engine starts.	None	None
13	Fault	Yes	M.A.P. Sensor (Vacuum)	When the throttle is closed during cranking and after the engine starts.	If the M.A.P. sensor vacuum level does not change between cranking and when the engine starts.	None	None
14	Fault	Yes	M.A.P. Sensor (Electrical)	All the time when the ignition switch is on.	If the M.A.P. sensor signal is below .02 or above 4.9 volts.	None	08
15	Fault	No	Vehicle Speed Sensor	Over a 7 second period during decel from highway speeds when the throttle is closed.	If the speed sensor signal indicates less than 2 mph when the vehicle is moving.	None	None
16	Fault	Yes	Battery Voltage Sensing (Charging System)	All the time after one minute from when the engine starts.	If the battery sensing voltage drops below 4 or between 7½ and 8½ volts for more than 20 seconds.	None	07
17	Fault	No	Engine Cooling System	During cranking when engine coolant temperature is between –20 and 212°F.	If engine coolant temperature does not reach 160°F within 20 minutes after the engine is started.	None	None
21	Fault	No	Oxygen Sensor	All the time after 12 minutes from when the engine starts.	If there is no oxygen sensor signal for more than 22 seconds when in closed loop.	None	02
22	Fault	Yes	Engine Coolant Sensor	All the time when the ignition switch is on.	If the coolant sensor voltage is above 4.96 volts when the engine is cold or below .51 volts when the engine is warm.	None	04
23	Fault	Yes	Charge Temperature Sensor	All the time when the ignition switch is on.	If the charge temperature sensor voltage is above 4.98 or below .06.	None	03
24	Fault	Yes	Throttle Position Sensor	All the time when the ignition switch is on.	If the throttle position sensor signal is below .16 or above 4.7 volts.	None	05
25	Fault	No	Automatic Idle Speed Motor (AIS)	Only when the AIS system is required to control the engine speed.	If proper voltage in the AIS system is not present. NOTE: Open circuit will not activate code.	03	None
26	Fault	No	Injector 1 and 2	During cranking.	If injectors 1 and 2 do not fire correctly.	02	None
27	Fault	No	Injectors 3 and 4	During cranking.	If injectors 3 and 4 do not fire correctly.	02	None
31	Fault	No	Canister Purge Solenoid	All the time when the ignition switch is on.	If the solenoid does not turn on and off when it should.	07	None
33	Fault	No	A/C Cutout Relay	All the time when the ignition switch is on.	If the relay does not turn on and off when it should.	05	None
34	Fault	No	E.G.R. Solenoid	All the time when the ignition switch is on.	If the solenoid does not turn on and off when it should.	08	None
35	Fault	No	Radiator Fan Relay Circuit	All the time when the ignition switch is on.	If the relay does not turn on and off when it should.	04	None

1986–88 TURBO DRIVEABILITY TEST PROCEDURES

Code	Type	Power Loss/ Limit Lamp	Circuit	When Monitored By The Logic Module	When Put Into Memory	ATM Test Code	Sensor Access Code
36	Fault	Yes	Wastegate Control Solenoid	All the time when the ignition switch is on.	If the solenoid does not turn on and off when it should.	09	None
37	Fault	No	Baro Read Solenoid	All the time when the ignition switch is on.	If the solenoid does not turn on and off when it should.	10	None
41	Fault	No	Alternator Field Control (Charging System)	All the time when the ignition switch is on.	If the field control fails to switch properly.	None	None
42	Fault	No	Auto Shutdown	All the time when the ignition switch is on.	If the control voltage of the relay pull in coil in the power module is not correct.	06	None
43	Fault	No	Spark Control	All the time when the ignition switch is on.	If the spark control interface fails to switch properly.	01	None
44	Fault	No	Battery Temperature Sensor (Charging System)	All the time when the ignition switch is on.	If the battery temperature sensor signal is below .04 or above 4.9 volts.	None	01
45	Fault	Yes	Overboost Monitor	All the time when the engine is running.	When M.A.P. sensor signal exceed a predetermine amount of boost indication.	None	None
46	Fault	Yes	Battery Voltage Sensing (Charging System)	All the time when the engine is running.	If the battery sense voltage is more than 1 volt above the desired control voltage for more than 20 seconds.	None	None
47	Fault	No	Battery Voltage Sensing (Charging System)	When the engine has been running for more than 6 minutes, engine temperature above 160°F and engine rpm above 1,500 rpm.	If the battery sense voltage is less than 1 volt below the desired control voltage for more than 20 seconds.	None	None
51	Fault	No	Oxygen Feedback System	During all closed loop conditions.	If the system stays lean for more than 12 minutes.	None	None
52	Fault	No	Oxygen Feedback System	During all closed loop conditions.	If the system stays rich for more than 12 minutes.	None	None
53	Fault	No	Logic Module	All the time in the diagnostic mode.	If the logic module fails.	None	None
54	Fault	No	Distributor Sync. Pickup	All the time when the engine is running.	If there is no distributor sync. pickup signal.	None	None
55	Indication	No			Indicates end of diagnostic mode.	None	None
88	Indication	No			Indicates start of diagnostic mode. NOTE: This code must appear first in the diagnostic mode or fault codes will be inaccurate.	None	None
0	Indication	No			Indicates oxygen feedback system is lean with the engine running.	None	None
1	Indication	No			Indicates oxygen feedback system is rich with the engine running.	None	None
8	Indication	No	Knock Circuit		Indicates knock sensor system is detecting knock.	None	06

TEST 1	STEP C	CHECKING VOLTAGE SUPPLY FROM POWER MODULE	
PROCEDURE		TEST INDICATION	ACTION REQUIRED
• Connect a voltmeter the green with black tracer wire of the injector 6-way connector and ground. • Crank the engine for at least 7 seconds.		• Voltmeter should read within one volt of cranking voltage as long as the engine is cranking.	• Voltage okay, Perform TEST NO. 7.
			• No voltage or voltage for about 1 second, Perform TEST NO. 14.

VOLTMETER

DG-BK

INJECTOR 6-WAY CONNECTOR

TEST 2	STEP A	CHECKING FUEL SUPPLY PRESSURE	
PROCEDURE		TEST INDICATION	ACTION REQUIRED
• Install high pressure gauge to fitting on the fuel rail. • Crank the engine for at least 7 seconds.		• Fuel pressure should be at least 40 psi.	• Fuel pressure okay, Perform STEP B.
			• No fuel pressure, Perform TEST NO. 6.

TEST 1	STEP A	CHECKING FOR SPARK AT SPARK PLUGS	
PROCEDURE		TEST INDICATION	ACTION REQUIRED
• Disconnect any spark plug wire. • Insert an insulated screw driver in terminal. • Hold screwdriver shaft (¼") near a good engine ground. • Have someone crank the engine for at least 7 seconds.		• There should be a good spark between screwdriver and ground as long as the engine is cranking. NOTE: Handle 1 or 2 sparks as no spark.	• Spark okay, Perform TEST NO. 2.
			• No spark at all, Perform STEP B.
			• Spark for about 5 seconds and then stops, Perform TEST NO. 10.

TEST 2	STEP B	CHECKING THROTTLE POSITION SENSOR	
PROCEDURE		TEST INDICATION	ACTION REQUIRED
• Connect a voltmeter to the orange with dark blue tracer wire of the throttle body 6-way connector and ground. • Turn ignition switch to the run position.		• Voltmeter should read 1 volt ± ½ volt.	• Voltage okay, Perform TEST NO. 3.
			• Voltage not okay, replace the throttle position sensor.

VOLTMETER

OR/DB

THROTTLE BODY 6-WAY HARNESS CONNECTOR

TEST 1	STEP B	CHECKING FOR SPARK AT IGNITION COIL WIRE	
PROCEDURE		TEST INDICATION	ACTION REQUIRED
• Disconnect ignition coil wire from distributor cap. • Hold coil wire (¼") near a good engine ground. • Have someone crank the engine.		• There should be a good spark between ignition coil wire and ground. NOTE: Handle 1 or 2 sparks as no spark.	• Spark okay, repair secondary ignition system (distributor cap and/or rotor).
			• No spark, Perform STEP C.

IGNITION COIL WIRE

TEST 3	STEP A	CHECKING LOGIC MODULE	
PROCEDURE		TEST INDICATION	ACTION REQUIRED
• Connect diagnostic read-out box to engine harness connector. • Turn ignition switch on-off-on-off-on within 5 seconds.		• Code 88 should appear on readout box display.	• Code 88 appears, Perform TEST NO. 4.
			• Code 88 does not appear, replace the logic module. CAUTION: Before replacing the logic module make sure your diagnostic readout box is operational and that there is not an open circuit in the wires between the logic module and diagnostic connector.

DIAGNOSTIC READOUT BOX

1986–88 TURBO DRIVEABILITY TEST PROCEDURES

TEST 4	STEP A	CHECKING FOR FUEL FOULED SPARK PLUGS	
PROCEDURE		TEST INDICATION	ACTION REQUIRED
• Remove spark plugs. • Look at tips for wet fuel.		• Spark plug tips should not be wet with fuel. NOTE: It is normal for spark plug tips to be black after engine is started cold.	• Spark plugs are dry, Perform TEST NO. 5.
		• Spark plugs are wet with fuel, clean and reinstall. Do not replace spark plugs. • Attempt restart.	

TEST 5	STEP A	CHECKING ENGINE TIMING	
PROCEDURE		TEST INDICATION	ACTION REQUIRED
• Connect timing device to engine. • Have someone crank engine while you look at the timing marks.		• Timing should be within 0°-16° BTC.	• Timing okay, check compression and valve timing.
		• Timing not okay, Perform STEP B.	

TEST 5	STEP B	CHECKING ENGINE TIMING	
PROCEDURE		TEST INDICATION	ACTION REQUIRED
REMINDERS • Timing device connected to engine. • Set timing to 10° BTC during cranking.		• Engine should start.	• Engine starts reset to specifications.
			• Engine does not start, check compression and valve timing.

TEST 6	STEP A	CHECKING FUEL PUMP	
PROCEDURE		TEST INDICATION	ACTION REQUIRED
• Connect the diagnostic readout box to the engine harness connector. • Turn the ignition switch to the run position. NOTE: If a Shelby Charger or GLH disconnect the harness connector from the secondary fuel pump (intank pump). • Press the ATM button on the readout box.	DIAGNOSTIC READOUT BOX DISCONNECT INTANK FUEL PUMP CONNECTOR SHELBY CHARGER & GLH	• You should be able to hear the fuel pump running.	• Fuel pump running check the following: ALL EXCEPT SHELBY OR GLH a) all fuel lines for kicks, restrictions, or leaks b) a plugged fuel filter If all okay remove the pump for inspection. SHELBY OR GLH Perform STEP C. • Fuel pump not running Perform STEP B.

TEST 6	STEP B	CHECKING FUEL PUMP WIRES	
PROCEDURE		TEST INDICATION	ACTION REQUIRED
REMINDERS • Diagnostic readout box connected to the engine harness connector. • Ignition switch in the run position. • Raise the car on a hoist. • Disconnect the intank fuel pump connector. • Connect the positive lead of a voltmeter to the green with white tracer wire of the connector. • Connect the negative lead of the voltmeter to the gray wire of the connector. • Press the ATM button.	DIAGNOSTIC READOUT BOX VOLTMETER GY — DG/BK IN TANK FUEL PUMP CONNECTOR	• Voltmeter should read within one volt of battery voltage.	• Voltage okay, replace the fuel pump. • Voltage not okay, move negative lead of voltmeter to a good engine ground and press the ATM button. • If voltage is now okay repair gray wire of connector for an open circuit. • If voltage is still 0, repair the green with white tracer wire for an open circuit.

TEST 6	STEP C	CHECKING SECONDARY FUEL PUMP	
PROCEDURE		TEST INDICATION	ACTION REQUIRED
REMINDERS • Diagnostic readout box connected to the engine harness connector. • Ignition switch in the run position. • Reconnect the electrical connector to the secondary fuel pump (intake pump). • Disconnect the harness connector from the primary fuel pump. (Frame rail pump) • Press the ATM button on the readout box.	DIAGNOSTIC READOUT BOX	• You should be able to hear the secondary fuel pump running.	• Secondary fuel pump running check the following: a) all fuel lines for kicks, restrictions, or leaks b) a plugged fuel filter If all okay, remove the pump for inspection. • Secondary fuel pump not running, check voltage supply and ground circuits to pump. If okay, replace the secondary fuel pump.

TEST 7	STEP A	CHECKING IGNITION CONTROL SYSTEM FOR FAULT CODES	
PROCEDURE		TEST INDICATION	ACTION REQUIRED
• Connect diagnostic readout box to the engine harness connector. • Disconnect and reconnect the battery connector. • Crank the engine for 5 seconds and then turn the ignition switch off. • Put the system in the Diagnostic Mode. (Refer to Introduction) • Record all codes	DIAGNOSTIC READOUT BOX BATTERY CONNECTOR	88-12-55 No Fault Codes	Perform TEST NO. 8.
		88-12-43-55 Spark Control Circuit	Perform TEST NO. 9.

TEST 8	STEP A	CHECKING FOR THE VOLTAGE SUPPLY TO THE IGNITION COIL POSITIVE TERMINAL FROM THE POWER MODULE	
PROCEDURE		TEST INDICATION	ACTION REQUIRED
REMINDERS • Diagnostic readout box connected to the engine harness connector. • System in the diagnostic mode. • Connect an analoge voltmeter to the positive terminal of the ignition coil and ground. • Put the system in the ATM Test Mode — Code 01. (Refer to Introduction)	DIAGNOSTIC READOUT BOX ANALOGE VOLTMETER POSITIVE TERMINAL IGNITION COIL	• Voltmeter should read within one volt of battery voltage.	• Voltage okay, Perform STEP B. • 0 volts, repair wire of coil positive terminal for open circuit to the power module.

FUEL INJECTION SYSTEMS
CHRYSLER CORPORATION

1986–88 TURBO DRIVEABILITY TEST PROCEDURES

TEST 8	STEP B	CHECKING THE IGNITION SYSTEM PRIMARY CONTROL CIRCUIT VOLTAGE AT THE IGNITION COIL (–) TERMINAL		
	PROCEDURE		TEST INDICATION	ACTION REQUIRED
REMINDERS			• Voltmeter should be pulsating between 1 and 3 volts.	• Voltage okay, replace the ignition coil.
• Diagnostic readout box connected to the engine harness connector.				
• System in ATM Test Mode — Code 01.			• Voltmeter not pulsating but reads above 10 volts, Perform STEP C.	
• Connect an analoge voltmeter to the negative terminal of the ignition coil and ground.			• Voltmeter pulsating between 0 and 1 volt, replace the ignition coil.	
			• Voltmeter not pulsating but reads between 0 and 1 volt, Perform STEP D.	

TEST 8	STEP C	CHECKING THE IGNITION SYSTEM PRIMARY CONTROL CIRCUIT FOR AN OPEN CIRCUIT		
	PROCEDURE		TEST INDICATION	ACTION REQUIRED
• Turn the ignition switch off.			• Ohmmeter should show continuity	• Continuity, replace the power module. CAUTION: Before replacing the power module check the terminal in cavity No. 1 of the 10-way connector to make sure it is not spread apart causing a poor connection.
• Disconnect the 10-way connector from the power module.				
• Connect an ohmmeter between the negative (–) terminal of the ignition coil and cavity. No. 1 of the power module 10-way connector.			• No continuity repair the wire of cavity No. 1 for an open circuit.	

TEST 8	STEP D	CHECKING THE IGNITION COIL PRIMARY WINDINGS FOR AN OPEN CIRCUIT		
	PROCEDURE		TEST INDICATION	ACTION REQUIRED
REMINDERS			• Voltmeter should be above 10 volts	• Voltage okay, Perform STEP E.
• Diagnostic readout box connected to the engine harness connector.				
• Turn the ignition switch off.				
• Disconnect the wire from the negative side (–) of the ignition coil.			• 0 volts replace the ignition coil.	
• Connect the voltmeter to the negative (–) terminal of the ignition coil and ground.				
• Put the system in the ATM Test Mode — Code 01.				

TEST 8	STEP E	CHECKING THE IGNITION SYSTEM PRIMARY CIRCUIT FOR A SHORT CIRCUIT TO GROUND		
	PROCEDURE		TEST INDICATION	ACTION REQUIRED
REMINDERS			• Ohmmeter should not show continuity.	• No continuity, replace the power module.
• Ignition coil negative (–) wire disconnected				
• Turn the ignition switch off.				
• Disconnect the 10-way connector from the power module.				
• Connect an ohmmeter between cavity No. 1 of the power module 10-way connector and ground			• Continuity, repair wire of cavity No. 10 for a short circuit to ground.	

TEST 9	STEP A	CHECKING FOR FAULT CODE 43 – SPARK CONTROL CIRCUIT		
	PROCEDURE		TEST INDICATION	ACTION REQUIRED
REMINDERS			• Touch the other end of the jumper to a good ground make and break this connection several times while looking at the ignition coil wire	• There should be spark at the ignition coil wire as you make and break the connection.	• Spark okay, replace the logic module. CAUTION: Before replacing the logic module check the terminal in cavity No. 6 of the red connector to make sure it is not crushed causing a poor connection.
• Diagnostic readout box connected to the engine harness connector.				
• Turn the ignition switch to off.				
• Disconnect the ignition coil wire at the distributor and place it on the thermostat housing so there is a ¼ inch gap.				• No spark, Perform STEP B.
• Disconnect the red connector from the logic module and connect one end of a jumper wire to cavity No. 6				
• Turn the ignition switch on and press the ATM button on the readout box.				

TEST 9	STEP B	CHECKING THE SPARK CONTROL WIRE BETWEEN THE LOGIC AND POWER MODULES FOR AN OPEN CIRCUIT		
	PROCEDURE		TEST INDICATION	ACTION REQUIRED
REMINDERS			• Ohmmeter should show continuity	• Continuity, replace the power module. CAUTION: Before replacing the power module check the terminal in cavity No. 10 of the 12-way connector to make sure it is not spread apart causing a poor con-nection.
• Logic module red connector disconnected.				
• Turn the ignition switch off.				
• Remove the jumper wire from cavity No. 6 of the white connector.				
• Disconnect the power module 12-way connector.				• No continuity, repair wire for an open circuit.
• Connect an ohmmeter between cavity No. 6 of the red and cavity No. 10 of the 12-way connectors.				

TEST 10	STEP A	CHECKING INJECTOR CONTROL SYSTEM FOR FAULT CODES		
	PROCEDURE		TEST INDICATION	ACTION REQUIRED
• Connect the diagnostic readout box to the engine harness connector.			88-12-26-55 Injector 1 and 2 circuit	• Perform TEST NO. 11.
• Disconnect and reconnect the battery connector.			88-12-27-55 Injector 3 and 4 circuit	• Perform TEST NO. 12.
• Crank the engine for 7 seconds and then turn the ignition switch off.			88-12-54-55 Distributor sync pickup circuit	• Perform TEST NO. 13.
• Put the system in the Diagnostic Mode. (Refer to introduction)				
• Record all codes.				

TEST 11	STEP A	CHECKING INJECTOR 1 AND 2 CONTROL CIRCUIT		
	PROCEDURE		TEST INDICATION	ACTION REQUIRED
REMINDERS			• Press the ATM button on the readout box.	• Voltmeter should pulsate as you make and break the connection.	• Voltmeter pulsates, replace the logic module. CAUTION: Before replacing the logic module check the terminal in cavity No. 2 of the red connector to make sure it is not crushed causing a poor connection.
• Diagnostic readout box connected to the engine harness connector.			• Touch the other end of the jumper wire to a good ground. Make and break this connection several times.		
• Turn the ignition switch off.				
• Connect a voltmeter to the white wire of the injector 6-way connector and ground.				
• Disconnect the electrical leads from injectors 3 and 4.				• Voltmeter does not pulsate, Perform STEP B.
• Disconnect the red connector from the logic module.				
• Connect one end of a jumper wire to cavity No. 2 of the red connector.				
• Turn the ignition switch to the run position.				

1986–88 TURBO DRIVEABILITY TEST PROCEDURES

TEST 11	STEP B	CHECKING INJECTOR 1 AND 2 CONTROL WIRE BETWEEN THE POWER AND LOGIC MODULE FOR AN OPEN CIRCUIT		
		PROCEDURE	TEST INDICATION	ACTION REQUIRED
REMINDERS			• Ohmmeter should show continuity.	• Continuity, **Perform STEP C.**
• Logic module red connector disconnected.				
• Turn the ignition switch off.		POWER MODULE 12-WAY CONNECTOR		
• Disconnect the power module 12-way connector.				
• Connect an ohmmeter between cavity No. 2 of the logic module red and cavity No. 1 of the power module 12-way connectors.			• No continuity, repair wire for an open circuit.	
		LOGIC MODULE RED CONNECTOR		

TEST 11	STEP C	CHECKING INJECTOR 1 AND 2 WIRES TO THE POWER MODULE FOR AN OPEN CIRCUIT		
		PROCEDURE	TEST INDICATION	ACTION REQUIRED
REMINDERS			• Ohmmeter should show continuity.	• Continuity, **Perform STEP D.**
• Power module 10-way connector disconnected.			NOTE: Disregard any resistance value. Just make sure there is continuity.	
• Ignition switch off.				
• Connect an ohmmeter between cavities 5 and 6 of the power module 10-way connector.		POWER MODULE 10-WAY CONNECTOR	• No continuity, repair wire in cavity No. 5 or 6 for an open circuit. NOTE: If wire in cavity No. 6 is the open one the problem is between the injector harness and where it splices into the main harness.	

TEST 11	STEP D	CHECKING FOR A SHORTED INJECTOR		
		PROCEDURE	TEST INDICATION	ACTION REQUIRED
• Disconnect the injector 6-way connector.			• Ohmmeter should not show continuity.	• No continuity replace the power module.
• Connect an ohmmeter between the white wire of the 6-way connector and ground.				
		INJECTOR 6-WAY CONNECTOR		• Continuity, disconnect injector No. 1. If short goes away, replace injector No. 1. If short does not go away replace injector No. 2.

TEST 12	STEP A	CHECKING INJECTOR 3 AND 4 CONTROL CIRCUIT		
		PROCEDURE	TEST INDICATION	ACTION REQUIRED
REMINDERS		• Turn the ignition switch to the run position.	• Voltmeter should pulsate as you make and break the connection.	• Voltmeter pulsates, replace the logic module.
• Diagnostic readout box connected to the engine harness connector.		• Press the ATM button on the readout box.		CAUTION: Before replacing the logic module check the terminal in cavity No. 3 of the red connector to make sure it is not crushed causing a poor connection.
• Turn the ignition switch off.		• Touch the other end of the jumper wire to a good ground. Make and break this connection several times.		
• Connect a voltmeter to the tan wire of the injector 6-way connector and ground.		DIAGNOSTIC READOUT BOX		
• Disconnect the electrical leads from injectors 1 and 2.				
• Disconnect the red connector from the logic module.		VOLTMETER		• Voltmeter does not pulsate, **Perform STEP B.**
• Connect one end of a jumper wire to cavity No. 3 of the red connector.		INJECTOR 6 WAY CONNECTOR		

TEST 12	STEP B	CHECKING INJECTOR 3 AND 4 CONTROL WIRE BETWEEN THE POWER AND LOGIC MODULE FOR AN OPEN CIRCUIT		
		PROCEDURE	TEST INDICATION	ACTION REQUIRED
REMINDERS			• Ohmmeter should show continuity.	• Continuity, **Perform STEP C.**
• Logic module red connector disconnected.		POWER MODULE 12-WAY CONNECTOR		
• Turn the ignition switch off.		OHMMETER		
• Disconnect the power module 12-way connector.				
• Connect an ohmmeter between cavity No. 3 of the logic module red and cavity No. 8 of the power module 12-way connectors.			• No continuity, repair wire for an open circuit.	
		LOGIC MODULE RED CONNECTOR		

TEST 12	STEP C	CHECKING INJECTOR 3 AND 4 WIRES TO THE POWER MODULE FOR AN OPEN CIRCUIT		
		PROCEDURE	TEST INDICATION	ACTION REQUIRED
REMINDERS			• Ohmmeter should show continuity.	• Continuity, **Perform STEP D.**
• Power module 10-way connector disconnected.			NOTE: Disregard any resistance value. Just make sure there is continuity.	
• Ignition switch off.				
• Connect an ohmmeter between cavities 6 and 7 of the power module 10-way connector.		POWER MODULE 10-WAY CONNECTOR	• No continuity, repair wire in cavity No. 6 or 7 for an open circuit. NOTE: If wire in cavity No. 6 is the open one the problem is between the injector harness and where it splices into the main harness.	

TEST 12	STEP D	CHECKING FOR A SHORTED INJECTOR		
		PROCEDURE	TEST INDICATION	ACTION REQUIRED
• Disconnect the injector 6-way connector.			• Ohmmeter should not show continuity.	• No continuity replace the power module.
• Connect an ohmmeter between the tan wire of the 6-way connector and ground.				
		INJECTOR 6-WAY CONNECTOR		• Continuity, disconnect injector No. 3. If short goes away, replace injector No. 3. If short does not go away replace injector No. 4.

TEST 13	STEP A	CHECKING FOR FAULT CODE 54 – DISTRIBUTOR SYNC PICKUP		
		PROCEDURE	TEST INDICATION	ACTION REQUIRED
• Turn the ignition switch off.			• Voltmeter should read at least 7 volts at both terminals.	• Voltage okay, replace the distributor sync pickup.
• Disconnect the distributor sync pickup connector.				CAUTION: Before replacing the pickup check the terminals in the harness connector to make sure they are not spread apart causing a poor connection.
• Turn the ignition switch to the run position.				
• Connect the negative lead of a digital voltmeter to cavity No. 3 of the harness connector.				• 0 volts at cavity No. 1 repair wire for open circuit to wiring harness splice.
• Connect the positive lead of a digital voltmeter to cavities 1 and 2 of the harness connector.		DISTRIBUTOR SYNC PICKUP HARNESS CONNECTOR		• 0 volts at cavity No. 2, **Perform STEP B.**

1986–88 TURBO DRIVEABILITY TEST PROCEDURES

TEST 13	STEP B	CHECKING THE DISTRIBUTOR SYNC PICKUP SIGNAL WIRE FOR AN OPEN CIRCUIT TO THE LOGIC MODULE	
PROCEDURE		TEST INDICATION	ACTION REQUIRED
REMINDERS • Ignition switch in the run position • Connect a digital voltmeter to cavity No. 17 of the logic module blue connector and ground.		• Voltmeter should read at least 7 volts	• Voltage okay, repair wire in cavity No. 17 for an open circuit to the sync pickup.
	DIGITAL VOLTMETER / LOGIC MODULE BLUE CONNECTOR		• 0 volts, check for a crushed terminal in cavity No. 17. If it is not crushed replace the logic module.

TEST 14	STEP A	CHECKING SYSTEM FOR FAULT CODES	
PROCEDURE		TEST INDICATION	ACTION REQUIRED
• Connect the diagnostic readout box to the engine harness connector. • Disconnect and reconnect the battery connector • Crank the engine for 5 seconds and then turn the ignition switch to the run position for 5 seconds before turning it off. • Put the system in the Diagnostic Mode. (Refer to introduction) • Record all codes	DIAGNOSTIC READOUT BOX / BATTERY CONNECTOR	88-12-55 No fault codes	Repair wire in cavity No. 6 of the power module 10-way connector for an open circuit to ignition coil fuel pump and injectors.
		No Code 88 System Power Circuits	**Perform TEST NO. 15**
		88-11-12-55 Distributor pickup circuit	**Perform TEST NO. 16**
		88-26-42-55 88-27-42-55 Auto shutdown relay pull in coil circuit	**Perform TEST NO. 17**
		88-11-12-22-23-24-55 Sensor Ground Circuit	Repair wire in cavity No. 25 of the logic module red connector for an open circuit.
		88-12-26-55 88-12-27-55 Auto shutdown relay output circuit	Replace Power Module

TEST 15	STEP A	CHECKING FOR NO CODE 88 – SYSTEM POWER CIRCUIT FOR THE 5 VOLT SUPPLY	
PROCEDURE		TEST INDICATION	ACTION REQUIRED
• Turn ignition switch off. • Connect a digital voltmeter to cavity No. 1 of the logic module red connector and ground. • Turn the ignition switch to the run position.		• Voltmeter should read at least 4½ volts	• Voltage okay, **Perform STEP B.**
	DIGITAL VOLTMETER / LOGIC MODULE RED CONNECTOR		• 0 volts, **Perform STEP F.**

TEST 15	STEP B	CHECKING BATTERY VOLTAGE TO THE LOGIC MODULE	
PROCEDURE		TEST INDICATION	ACTION REQUIRED
• Turn the ignition switch off. • Connect a voltmeter to cavity No. 2 of the logic module blue connector and ground.		• Voltmeter should read within one volt of battery voltage.	• Voltage okay, replace the logic module. CAUTION: Before replacing the logic module, check the terminal in cavity No. 2 of the blue connector to make sure it is not crushed causing a poor connection. Also make sure your diagnostic readout box is operational and that there is not an open circuit in the wires between the logic module and diagnostic connector.
	VOLTMETER / LOGIC MODULE BLUE CONNECTOR		• 0 volts, **Perform STEP C.**

TEST 15	STEP C	CHECKING THE BATTERY VOLTAGE SUPPLY FROM THE POWER MODULE	
PROCEDURE		TEST INDICATION	ACTION REQUIRED
• Disconnect the power module 12-way connector. • Connect a voltmeter to pin No. 6 of the power module and ground.		• Voltmeter should read within one volt of battery voltage.	• Voltage okay, repair wire to cavity No. 2 of the logic module blue connector for an open circuit.
	VOLTMETER / POWER MODULE 12 WAY PIN CONNECTOR		• 0 volts Perform STEP D.

TEST 15	STEP D	CHECKING THE BATTERY VOLTAGE SUPPLY TO THE POWER MODULE	
PROCEDURE		TEST INDICATION	ACTION REQUIRED
• Disconnect the 10-way connector from the power module. • Connect a voltmeter to cavity No. 4 of the 10-way connector and ground.		• Voltmeter should read within one volt of battery voltage.	• Voltage okay, **Perform STEP E.**
	VOLTMETER / POWER MODULE 10-WAY CONNECTOR		• 0 volts, repair the wire in cavity No. 4 for an open circuit to the battery. NOTE: This wire has a fusible link in it. If it is blown, circuit must be repaired for a short circuit to ground.

TEST 15	STEP E	CHECKING THE AUTO SHUTDOWN RELAY OUTPUT CIRCUIT FOR A SHORT CIRCUIT TO GROUND	
PROCEDURE		TEST INDICATION	ACTION REQUIRED
REMINDERS • Power module 10-way connector disconnected. • Disconnect the wire from the ignition coil positive (+) terminal. • Disconnect the intank fuel pump connector. NOTE: GLH and Shelby models: disconnect primary fuel pump on frame rail. • Disconnect the injector 6-way connector. • Connect an ohmmeter between cavity No. 6 of the power module 10-way connector and ground.	OHMMETER / POWER MODULE 10-WAY CONNECTOR	• Ohmmeter should not show continuity.	• No continuity, replace the power module. CAUTION: Before replacing the power module make sure the terminal in cavity No. 4 of the 10-way connector are not spread apart so they cannot touch the power module pin • Continuity, repair wire of cavity No. 6 for a short circuit to ground. • Replace power module

TEST 15	STEP F	CHECKING THE LOGIC MODULE GROUND CIRCUIT	
PROCEDURE		TEST INDICATION	ACTION REQUIRED
• Turn the ignition switch off. • Disconnect the blue connector from the logic module. • Connect an ohmmeter between cavity No. 7 or 8 of the logic module blue connector and ground.		• Ohmmeter should show continuity.	• Continuity, **Perform STEP G.**
	OHMMETER / LOGIC MODULE BLUE CONNECTOR		• Open circuit, repair wires of cavity 7 and 8 for an open circuit to the wiring harness splice.

1986–88 TURBO DRIVEABILITY TEST PROCEDURES

TEST 15	STEP G	CHECKING THE SYSTEM POWER CIRCUIT FOR THE 8 VOLT SUPPLY TO THE LOGIC MODULE		
PROCEDURE			TEST INDICATION	ACTION REQUIRED

REMINDERS

- Ignition switch in the run position.
- Connect a digital voltmeter to cavity No. 23 of the logic module red connector and ground.

DIGITAL VOLTMETER

LOGIC MODULE RED CONNECTOR

- Voltmeter should read at least 7 volts.

- Voltage okay, **Perform STEP H.**

- Voltage not okay, **Perform STEP I.**

TEST 15	STEP H	CHECKING FOR NO 5 VOLTS IN SYSTEM POWER CIRCUIT CAUSED BY A SHORTED M.A.P. SENSOR		
PROCEDURE			TEST INDICATION	ACTION REQUIRED

- Turn the ignition switch off.
- Disconnect both connectors from logic module.
- Remove logic module from cowl side.
- Remove cover plate of logic module to gain access to M.A.P. sensor connector.
- Disconnect M.A.P. sensor connector.
- Reconnect logic module connectors.
- Connect a voltmeter to cavity No. 1 of logic module blue connector and ground.
- Turn ignition switch to the run position.

CONNECTORS

M.A.P. SENSOR COVER

LOGIC MODULE

VOLTMETER

LOGIC MODULE BLUE CONNECTOR

- Voltmeter should read at least 4½ volts.

- Voltage okay, replace the M.A.P. sensor.

- 0 volts, replace the logic module.

TEST 15	STEP I	CHECKING FOR NO 8 VOLTS IN SYSTEM POWER CIRCUIT CAUSED BY A SHORTED DISTRIBUTOR REFERENCE PICKUP		
PROCEDURE			TEST INDICATION	ACTION REQUIRED

REMINDERS

- Voltmeter connected to cavity No. 23 of logic module red connector and ground.
- Ignition switch in the run position.
- Disconnect the distributor reference pickup connector, (black one).

VOLTMETER

LOGIC MODULE RED CONNECTOR

DISCONNECT

DISTRIBUTOR SYNC PICKUP HARNESS CONNECTOR

- Voltmeter should read at least 7 volts.

- Voltage okay, replace distributor pickup coil.

- 0 volts, Perform STEP J.

TEST 15	STEP J	CHECKING THE SYSTEM POWER CIRCUIT FOR THE 8 VOLT OUTPUT FROM THE POWER MODULE		
PROCEDURE			TEST INDICATION	ACTION REQUIRED

- Turn the ignition switch off.
- Disconnect the 12-way connector from the power module.
- Connect a voltmeter to pin No. 12 of the power module and ground.
- Turn the ignition switch to the run position.

VOLTMETER

POWER MODULE 12-WAY PIN CONNECTOR

- Voltmeter should read at least 7 volts.

- Voltage okay, repair the wire in cavity No. 12 of the power module 12-way connector for an open circuit to the logic module.

  NOTE: Check the terminal in cavity No. 12 to make sure it is not spread apart causing a poor connection.

- 0 volts, Perform STEP H.

TEST 15	STEP K	CHECKING FOR IGNITION SWITCH VOLTAGE SUPPLY TO THE POWER MODULE		
PROCEDURE			TEST INDICATION	ACTION REQUIRED

- Turn the ignition switch off.
- Disconnect the 10-way connector from the power module.
- Connect the positive lead of a voltmeter to cavity No. 2 of the 10-way connector.
- Connect the negative lead of the voltmeter to either cavity No. 9 or 10 of the 10-way connector.
- Turn the ignition switch to the run position.

VOLTMETER

POWER MODULE 10-WAY CONNECTOR

- Voltmeter should read within one volt of battery voltage.

- Voltage okay, replace the power module.

  CAUTION: Before replacing the power module, check the terminals in cavities 2, 9, and 10 of the 10-way connector to make sure they are not spread apart causing a poor connection.

- 0 volts, move voltmeter negative lead to a good engine ground and if —

- Voltmeter now reads within one volt of battery voltage, repair power module ground for an open circuit.

- Voltmeter still reads 0 volts repair wire in cavity No. 2 for an open circuit.

TEST 16	STEP A	CHECKING FOR FAULT CODE 11 – DISTRIBUTOR REFERENCE PICKUP CIRCUIT		
PROCEDURE			TEST INDICATION	ACTION REQUIRED

REMINDERS

- Diagnostic readout box connected to the engine harness connector.
- Turn ignition switch off.
- Disconnect distributor reference pickup coil connector, black one.
- Turn ignition switch to the run position
- Connect a jumper wire to reference pickup coil harness connector cavity No. 2 and 3
- Make and break this connection several times

- Put the system into the **Diagnostic Mode** (Refer to introduction)
- Record all codes.

DIAGNOSTIC READOUT BOX

JUMPER

DISTRIBUTOR SYNC PICKUP HARNESS CONNECTOR

- There should be no fault code 11

- No fault code 11, Perform **STEP B.**

  NOTE: Disregard fault code 54.

- Fault code 11 still present. **Perform STEP C.**

TEST 16	STEP B	CHECKING FOR THE 8 VOLT POWER SUPPLY TO THE DISTRIBUTOR REFERENCE PICKUP FROM THE POWER MODULE		
PROCEDURE			TEST INDICATION	ACTION REQUIRED

REMINDERS

- Distributor reference pickup coil connector disconnected.
- Ignition switch in the run position.
- Connect a voltmeter to cavity No. 1 of reference pickup coil harness connector and ground.

VOLTMETER

DISTRIBUTOR SYNC PICKUP HARNESS CONNECTOR

- Voltmeter should read at least 7 volts.

- Voltage okay, replace the distributor pick up coil.

  CAUTION: Before replacing the pick up check the terminals in the distributor harness connector to make sure they are not spread apart causing a poor connection.

- Voltage not okay, repair wire of cavity No. 1 for open circuit to wiring harness splice.

TEST 16	STEP C	CHECKING FOR THE REFERENCE PICKUP COIL SIGNAL VOLTAGE FROM THE LOGIC MODULE		
PROCEDURE			TEST INDICATION	ACTION REQUIRED

REMINDERS

- Distributor reference pickup coil connector disconnected.
- Ignition switch in the run position.
- Connect the positive lead of a voltmeter to cavity No. 3 of the reference pickup coil harness connector
- Connect the negative lead of the voltmeter to cavity No. 2 of the reference pickup coil harness connector.

VOLTMETER

DISTRIBUTOR SYNC PICKUP HARNESS CONNECTOR

- Voltmeter should read at least 4 volts.

- Voltage okay, replace the logic module.

- 0 volts, **Perform STEP D.**

1986–88 TURBO DRIVEABILITY TEST PROCEDURES

TEST 16	STEP D	CHECKING THE DISTRIBUTOR REFERENCE PICKUP HARNESS GROUND CIRCUIT	
PROCEDURE		TEST INDICATION	ACTION REQUIRED
REMINDERS • Distributor reference pickup coil connector disconnected • Ignition switch in the run position. • Positive lead of a voltmeter connected to cavity No 3 of the distributor harness connector. • Connect the negative lead of the voltmeter to a good engine ground.		• Voltmeter should read at least 4 volts.	• Voltage okay, repair wire in cavity No. 2 of the distributor harness connector for an open circuit to the wiring harness splice. • 0 volts, **Perform STEP E.**

TEST 16	STEP E	CHECKING FOR THE REFERENCE PICKUP COIL SIGNAL VOLTAGE AT THE LOGIC MODULE	
PROCEDURE		TEST INDICATION	ACTION REQUIRED
REMINDERS • Ignition switch in the run position. • Connect a voltmeter to cavity No. 10 of the logic module red connector and ground.		• Voltmeter should read at least 4 volts.	• Voltage okay, repair wire in cavity No. 10 for an open circuit to distributor wiring harness connector. • 0 volts replace the logic module. **CAUTION:** Before replacing the logic module, check the terminal in cavity No. 10 of the red connector to make sure it is not crushed causing a poor connection.

TEST 17	STEP A	CHECKING FOR FAULT CODES 26-42-AUTO SHUTDOWN RELAY PULL IN COIL CIRCUIT	
PROCEDURE		TEST INDICATION	ACTION REQUIRED
• Turn the ignition switch off. • Disconnect the red connector from the logic module. • Connect a voltmeter to cavity No. 17 of the red connector and ground. • Turn the ignition switch to the run position.		• Voltmeter should read within one volt of battery voltage.	• Voltage okay, replace the logic module. **CAUTION:** Before replacing the logic module, check the terminal in cavity No. 17 of the red connector to make sure it is not crushed causing a poor connection. • 0-1 volts, **Perform STEP B.**

TEST 17	STEP B	CHECKING THE AUTO SHUTDOWN RELAY PULL IN COIL CIRCUIT AT THE POWER MODULE	
PROCEDURE		TEST INDICATION	ACTION REQUIRED
• Turn the ignition switch off. • Disconnect the 12-way connector from the power module. • Turn the ignition switch to the run position. • Connect a voltmeter to Pin No. 5 of the power module and ground.		• Voltmeter should read within one volt of battery voltage.	• Voltage okay, repair wire in cavity No. 5 of the power mode 12-way connector for an open or shorted circuit. **CAUTION:** Check the terminal in cavity No. 12 of the 12-way to make sure it is not spread apart causing a poor connection. • 0-1 volts, replace the power module.

TEST 1	STEP A	CHECKING SYSTEM FOR FAULT CODES		
PROCEDURE		TEST INDICATION	CIRCUIT	ACTION REQUIRED
• Connect diagnostic readout box to engine harness connector.		88-12-55	No fault codes	Perform STEP B
		88-12-13-55 88-12-14-55 88-12-13-14-55	M.A.P. sensor	Perform TEST No. 2
• Turn ignition switch on-off-on-off-on within 5 seconds.		88-12-15-55	Speed sensor	Perform TEST No. 3
		88-12-16-55	Battery voltage for charging system	Perform TEST No. 4
• **RECORD ALL CODES**		88-12-17-55	Engine running too cool	Check engine cooling system for a possible bad thermostat.
NOTE: If fault codes 15-21-47-51 or 52 appear at this time proceed to test indication.		88-12-21-55	Oxygen sensor	Perform TEST No. 5
		88-12-22-55 88-12-17-22-55	Engine coolant sensor	Perform TEST No. 6
• Turn ignition switch off and disconnect and reconnect the battery connector.		88-12-23-55	Charge temperature sensor	Perform TEST No. 7
		88-12-24-55	Throttle position sensor	Perform TEST No. 8
		88-12-25-55	Idle motor	Perform TEST No. 9
• Start engine.		88-12-31-55	Purge solenoid	Perform TEST No. 10
CAUTION: Do not depress accelerator to start engine.		88-12-33-55	A/C cut off relay	Perform TEST No. 11
		88-12-34-55	EGR Solenoid	Perform TEST No. 12
		88-12-35-55	Radiator fan relay	Perform TEST No. 13
• Let engine run for 2 minutes.		88-12-36-55 88-12-36-45-55	Wastegate solenoid	Perform TEST No. 14
		88-12-37-55	Baro read solenoid	Perform TEST No. 15
• Cycle transmission gear selector (auto trans only)		88-12-41-46-55 88-12-46-55	Alternator field (charging system output to high)	Perform TEST No. 16
		88-12-41-55 88-12-41-47-55	Alternator field (charging system output to low)	Perform TEST No. 17
• If so equipped press A/C button on and off.		88-12-44-55	Battery temperature sensor	Perform TEST No. 18
		88-12-45-55	Overboost shutoff	Perform TEST No. 19
• Turn engine off.		88-12-51-55	Oxygen feedback system locked lean	Perform TEST No. 26
• Turn ignition switch on-off-on-off-on within 5 seconds.		88-12-52-55 88-12-31-34-36-37-55	Oxygen feedback system locked rich	Check ignition switch supply voltage wire to solenoid assembly for an open circuit
• **RECORD ALL CODES**		88-12-53-55		Replace logic module.
If the same code appears before and after the engine is started, the problem still exists. Proceed to test indications. If a code does not reappear after the engine is started, the problem no longer exists **Perform STEP K.** **NOTE:** Make sure your diagnostic readout box is operational and that there is not an open circuit in the wires between the logic module and diagnostic connector.		88-12-47-55	Alternator output	Check for a loose belt. If okay, check the battery or alternator using the service manual procedure.
		No code 88	Battery voltage for logic module standby memory	Repair battery feed wire to cavity No. 2 of the logic module black connector for an open circuit

TEST 1	STEP B	CHECKING LOGIC MODULE CONTROLLED COMPONENTS	
PROCEDURE		TEST INDICATION	ACTION REQUIRED
REMINDERS • Diagnostic readout box connected to the engine harness connector. • Put the system into the **ATM Mode Code 04.** (Refer to the introduction)		**Test Code 04** • The radiator fan should be turning on and off every two seconds.	• Radiator fan is turning on and off press and hold the ATM button as follows: **without A/C** until test code 07 appears. **with A/C** until test code 05 appears. • If fan does not turn on and off, is the relay clicking? If it is repair the circuit to the radiator fan motor as required. • If the relay does not click, replace it.
		Test Code 05 • You should hear the A/C cutout relay clicking every two seconds.	• A/C relay clicking, press and hold the ATM button until test code 07 appears. • If the A/C relay is not clicking replace it.
		Test Code 07 • You should hear the canister purge solenoid clicking.	• Canister purge solenoid clicking, press and hold the ATM button until test code 08 appears. • If the canister purge solenoid is not clicking replace it.
		Test Code 08 • You should hear the EGR solenoid clicking.	• EGR solenoid clicking, press and hold the ATM button until test code 09 appears. • If the EGR solenoid is not clicking, replace it
		Test Code 09 • You should hear the wastegate solenoid clicking.	• Wastegate solenoid clicking, press and hold ATM button until test code 10 appears. • If the wastegate solenoid is not clicking replace it.
		Test Code 10 • You should hear the baro read solenoid clicking.	• Baro read solenoid clicking **Perform STEP C.** • If the baro read solenoid is not clicking, replace it.

1986–88 TURBO DRIVEABILITY TEST PROCEDURES

TEST 1	STEP C	CHECKING SWITCH INPUTS TO LOGIC MODULE

PROCEDURE	TEST INDICATION	ACTION REQUIRED
REMINDERS • Diagnostic readout box connected to the engine harness connector	• Display on the readout box should change as each switch is activated. NOTE: It is not important what display changes to Just make sure it changes	• Display changes for all switches, Perform STEP G.
• Put the system into the switch test mode. • Check switch inputs as follows: a) press down on brake pedal b) with auto trans, move gear selector from park to reverse c) with A/C move blower switch to an on position and then press the A/C button	DIAGNOSTIC READOUT BOX	• One or more switch inputs do not change the display Perform STEPS as follows Brake Switch STEP D Park/Neutral Switch STEP E A/C Button STEP F

TEST 1	STEP D	CHECKING BRAKE SWITCH INPUT CIRCUIT TO THE LOGIC MODULE

PROCEDURE	TEST INDICATION	ACTION REQUIRED
• Turn ignition switch off • Disconnect blue connector from logic module. • Connect voltmeter to cavity No. 13 of blue connector and ground. • Turn ignition switch to the run position. • Press brake pedal down	• Voltmeter should read within one volt of battery voltage.	• Voltage okay, replace logic module. CAUTION: Before replacing the logic module check terminal in cavity No. 13 of the blue connector to make sure it is not crushed causing a poor connection.
LOGIC MODULE BLUE CONNECTOR		• Voltage not okay, repair wire of cavity No. 13 for open circuit to brake switch.

TEST 1	STEP E	CHECKING PARK/NEUTRAL SWITCH INPUT CIRCUIT TO THE LOGIC MODULE

PROCEDURE	TEST INDICATION	ACTION REQUIRED
• Turn ignition switch off • Disconnect blue connector from logic module. • Connect an ohmmeter to cavity No. 12 of blue connector and ground. • Put gear selector in park, reverse, neutral, and drive and observe ohmmeter in each position.	• Ohmmeter should read as follows Park – Continuity Reverse – No continuity Neutral – Continuity Drive – No continuity NOTE: Disregard any resistance readings. Just make sure there is continuity.	• Ohmmeter readings not okay, repair wire of cavity No. 12 for open circuit to safety neutral switch.
LOGIC MODULE BLUE CONNECTOR		• Ohmmeter readings okay replace logic module. CAUTION: Before replacing the logic module check the terminal in cavity No. 12 of the blue connector to make sure it is not crushed causing a poor connection.

TEST 1	STEP F	CHECKING A/C PUSH BUTTON SWITCH INPUT CIRCUIT TO THE LOGIC MODULE

PROCEDURE	TEST INDICATION	ACTION REQUIRED
• Turn ignition switch off. • Connect voltmeter to cavity No. 11 of the logic module blue connector and ground. • Start the engine and wait 10 seconds.	• Voltmeter should read within one volt of battery voltage.	• Voltage okay, replace logic module. CAUTION: Before replacing the logic module check the terminal in cavity No. 11 of the blue connector to make sure it is not crushed causing a poor connection.
LOGIC MODULE BLUE CONNECTOR		• Voltage not okay, repair wire of cavity No. 11 for open circuit to A/C switch circuit.

TEST 1	STEP G	CHECKING FUEL INJECTORS

PROCEDURE	TEST INDICATION	ACTION REQUIRED
• Connect the diagnostic readout box to the engine harness connector • Disconnect all four injector connectors • Put the system into the ATM Test Mode Code 02 (Refer to the introduction) • Connect and disconnect each injector one at a time.	DIAGNOSTIC READOUT BOX WT / DG BK DISCONNECT TN / DG BK INJECTOR CONNECTORS	• When the injector is connected you should hear it click	• All injectors click, Perform STEP H.
		• If any injector does not click, replace it.

TEST 1	STEP H	CHECKING AUTOMATIC IDLE SPEED MOTOR OPERATION

PROCEDURE	TEST INDICATION	ACTION REQUIRED
• Connect the diagnostic readout box to the engine harness connector • Put the system in the ATM Test Code 03. (Refer to the introduction)	• You should hear the automatic idle speed motor move two times every four seconds	• Motor movement okay, Perform TESTS as follows If a cold problem TEST NO. 20 If a warm problem TEST NO. 23
DIAGNOSTIC READOUT BOX		• No motor movement. Perform STEP I.

TEST 1	STEP I	CHECKING AUTOMATIC IDLE SPEED MOTOR FOR AN OPEN CIRCUIT

PROCEDURE	TEST INDICATION	ACTION REQUIRED
• Turn the ignition switch off • Disconnect the throttle body 6-way connector. • Connect an ohmmeter between the terminals of the 6-way connector that go to the idle motor.	• Ohmmeter should show resistance. NOTE: The amount of resistance is not important. Just make sure there is some.	• Some resistance, Perform STEP J.
OHMMETER GY/RD BR THROTTLE BODY 6-WAY CONNECTOR		• Open circuit, replace the idle motor.

TEST 1	STEP J	CHECKING AUTOMATIC IDLE SPEED MOTOR CONTROL WIRES TO LOGIC MODULE FOR AN OPEN CIRCUIT

PROCEDURE	TEST INDICATION	ACTION REQUIRED
• Reconnect the throttle body 6-way connector. • Disconnect the logic module red connector. • Connect an ohmmeter between cavities 18 and 22 of the red connector.	• Ohmmeter should show resistance. NOTE: The amount of resistance is not important. Just make sure there is some.	• Some resistance, replace the logic module. CAUTION: Before replacing the logic module check the terminals in cavities 18 to 22 of the red connector to make sure they are not crushed causing a poor connection.
LOGIC MODULE RED CONNECTOR		• Open circuit, repair the wires to the throttle body 6-way connector.

1986–88 TURBO DRIVEABILITY TEST PROCEDURES

TEST 1	STEP K	CHECKING FOR INTERMITTENT FAILURES

The majority of intermittent failures are caused by wiring and connections. The only way to find them is to try and duplicate the problem. Since the logic module can remember where they are, the ATM and sensor test modes can be used in an attempt to locate them. If a fault code does not reappear in TEST 1A, the following procedure should be used to determine if the wiring and connections are the cause of the problem.

- If the following fault codes do not reappear use the ATM Test Mode as indicated.

Fault Code	ATM TEST Mode
25	03
26	02
27	02
31	07
34	08
33	05
35	04
36	09
37	10
41	11
42	06
43	01

* Connect a voltmeter to the F2 terminal of the alternator and watch pulsations of meter.

Once in the correct test mode, wiggle all the connectors and wires in the circuit. When the bad connection or wire is located the ATM test will stop.

- If the following fault codes do not reappear use the Sensor Test Mode as indicated.

Fault Code	Sensor Test Mode
14**	06
16	07
21***	02
22	04
23	03
24	05
44	01

** When checking the M.A.P. sensor circuit, (Fault Code 14) apply 10 inches of vacuum to the M.A.P. sensor before testing.

*** Disconnect the oxygen sensor connector and ground the harness end with a jumper wire before testing.

Once in the correct test mode, wiggle all the connectors and wires in the circuit. When the bad connection or wire is located the display on the readout box will change.

TEST 2	STEP A	CHECKING FOR FAULT CODES 13 AND/OR 14 – M.A.P. SENSOR CIRCUIT

PROCEDURE	TEST INDICATION	ACTION REQUIRED
• Turn ignition switch off. • Tee a vacuum gauge into the M.A.P. sensor vacuum line at the logic module. • Start the engine and look at the vacuum gauge with the engine idling. • Look at the vacuum gauge while snapping the throttle open and close.	• Vacuum gauge should read manifold vacuum with the engine idling. • Vacuum gauge should immediately drop to 0 then the throttle is snapped open and closed.	• Vacuum gauge reads manifold vacuum and drops to 0 when the throttle is snapped open. Perform STEP B.
	• 0 vacuum, repair vacuum supply line.	
	• Vacuum drops slowly, repair restriction in vacuum supply line.	

CONNECT VACUUM GAUGE

LOGIC MODULE

TEST 2	STEP B	CHECKING THE M.A.P. SENSOR CIRCUIT FROM THE LOGIC MODULE PRINTED CIRCUIT BOARD

PROCEDURE	TEST INDICATION	ACTION REQUIRED
• Turn the engine off. • Remove the M.A.P. sensor from the logic module. • Disconnect the M.A.P. sensor from the logic module. • Connect the negative lead of a digital voltmeter to the black wire of the logic module M.A.P. sensor connector. • Turn the ignition switch to the run position. • Touch the positive lead of the voltmeter to the white and red wires of the logic module M.A.P. sensor connector.	• Voltmeter should read at least 4 volts at the whites and red wires.	• Voltage okay at red and whites wires, replace the M.A.P. sensor.
	• 0 volts at red, white or both, replace the logic module.	

DIGITAL VOLTMETER

BK WT RD

LOGIC MODULE M.A.P. SENSOR CONNECTOR

TEST 3	STEP A	CHECKING FOR FAULT CODE 15 – SPEED SENSOR CIRCUIT

PROCEDURE		TEST INDICATION	ACTION REQUIRED
REMINDERS		• As you make and break this connection the display on the readout box should change	• Display changes, replace the speed sensor.
• Diagnostic readout box connected to the engine harness connector. • Turn the ignition switch off. • Disconnect the speed sensor connector. • Put the system in the Switch Test Mode. (Refer to Introduction) • Connect a jumper wire between the terminals of the speed sensor harness connector. • Make and break this connection.	DIAGNOSTIC READOUT BOX JUMPER SPEED SENSOR HARNESS CONNECTOR		• Display does not change, Perform STEP B.

TEST 3	STEP B	CHECKING THE SPEED SENSOR CIRCUIT TO THE LOGIC MODULE FOR AN OPEN CIRCUIT

PROCEDURE		TEST INDICATION	ACTION REQUIRED
REMINDERS		• As you make and break this connection the display on the readout box should change	• Display changes, repair the wires to the speed sensor for an open circuit.
• Diagnostic readout box connected to the engine harness connector. • System in the Switch Test Mode. • Speed sensor connector disconnected. • Connect a jumper wire between cavity No. 24 of the red and cavity No. 14 of the blue connectors of the logic module • Make and break this connection.	DIAGNOSTIC READOUT BOX JUMPER LOGIC MODULE RED CONNECTOR LOGIC MODULE BLUE CONNECTOR		• Display does not change, replace the logic module. CAUTION: Before replacing the logic module check the terminal of cavity No. 14 of the blue connector to make sure it is not crushed causing a poor connection.

TEST 4	STEP A	CHECKING FOR FAULT CODE 16 – BATTERY VOLTAGE SENSING CIRCUIT FOR CHARGING SYSTEM

PROCEDURE		TEST INDICATION	ACTION REQUIRED
REMINDERS		• Display on the readout box should read within one volt of battery voltage.	• Display reads within one of battery, repair wire in cavity No. 22 of the logic module blue connector for an open circuit to the wiring harness splice.
• Diagnostic readout box connected to the engine harness connector. • Put the system in Sensor Test Mode 07 (Refer to Introduction) NOTE: Reading on display is actual. • Connect a jumper wire between cavities No. 2 and 22 of the logic module blue connector.	DIAGNOSTIC READOUT BOX JUMPER LOGIC MODULE BLUE CONNECTOR		• Display reads 0 volts, replace the logic module. CAUTION: Before replacing the logic module check the terminal in cavity No. 22 of the blue connector to make sure it is not crushed causing a poor connection.

TEST 5	STEP A	CHECKING FOR FAULT CODE 21 – OXYGEN SENSOR CIRCUIT TO THE LOGIC MODULE

PROCEDURE		TEST INDICATION	ACTION REQUIRED
REMINDERS		• When the jumper wire is on the positive post the display on the readout box should increase towards 5 volts. • When the jumper wire is on the negative post the display on the readout box should decrease towards 0 volts.	• Voltage readings change, replace the O₂ sensor
• Diagnostic readout box connected to the engine harness connector. • Turn the ignition switch off. • Disconnect the oxygen sensor connector. • Connect the end of a jumper wire to the harness end of the oxygen sensor connector. • Put the system into Sensor Test Mode 02 (Refer to introduction) NOTE: Don't forget to divide the reading on display by 10. • Touch the other end of the jumper wire to the battery positive and negative post	DIAGNOSTIC READOUT BOX OXYGEN SENSOR HARNESS CONNECTOR JUMPER BATTERY		• Voltage readings do not change, Perform STEP B.

1986–88 TURBO DRIVEABILITY TEST PROCEDURES

TEST 5	STEP B	CHECKING THE OXYGEN SENSOR CIRCUIT AT THE LOGIC MODULE

PROCEDURE		TEST INDICATION	ACTION REQUIRED
REMINDERS • Oxygen sensor connector disconnected. • Turn the ignition switch off. • Connect a digital voltmeter to cavity No. 18 of the logic module blue connector and ground. • Turn the ignition switch to the run position.		• Voltmeter should read at least .3 (3 tenths) of a volt.	• Voltage okay, repair the wire of cavity No. 18 for an open circuit to the oxygen sensor.
	DIGITAL VOLTMETER LOGIC MODULE BLUE CONNECTOR	• 0 volts, replace the logic module. **CAUTION:** Before replacing the logic module check the terminal in cavity No. 18 of the blue connector to make sure it is not crushed causing a poor connection.	

TEST 6	STEP A	CHECKING FOR FAULT CODE 22 – COOLANT SENSOR CIRCUIT

PROCEDURE		TEST INDICATION	ACTION REQUIRED
REMINDERS • Diagnostic readout box connected to the engine harness connector. • Turn the ignition switch off. • Disconnect the connector from the coolant sensor. • Put the system in **Sensor Test Mode 04.** (Refer to introduction)		• Display on the readout box should read 00°.	• Display reads 00° Perform Step B.
	DIAGNOSTIC READOUT BOX	• Display reads 260°, replace the logic module.	

TEST 6	STEP B	CHECKING THE COOLANT SENSOR CIRCUIT TO THE LOGIC MODULE

PROCEDURE		TEST INDICATION	ACTION REQUIRED
REMINDERS • Diagnostic readout box connected to the engine harness connector. System in **Sensor Test Mode 04.** **NOTE:** Don't forget to multiply the reading on display by 10. • Coolant sensor connector disconnected. • Connect a jumper wire between the terminals of the coolant sensor connector.	DIAGNOSTIC READOUT BOX JUMPER TN — BK LB COOLANT SENSOR CONNECTOR	• Display on the readout box should read 260°.	• Display reads 260°, replace the coolant sensor. • Display reads 00°, Perform STEP C.

TEST 6	STEP C	CHECKING THE COOLANT SENSOR WIRES TO THE LOGIC MODULE FOR AN OPEN CIRCUIT

PROCEDURE		TEST INDICATION	ACTION REQUIRED
REMINDERS • Diagnostic readout box connected to the engine harness connector. • System in **Sensor Test Mode 04.** **NOTE:** Don't forget to multiply the reading on display by 10. • Coolant sensor connector disconnected. • Connect one end of a jumper wire to the negative terminal of the battery. • Connect the other end of the jumper wire to the tan wire terminal of the coolant sensor harness connector.	DIAGNOSTIC READOUT BOX JUMPER TN — BK LB COOLANT SENSOR HARNESS CONNECTOR	• Display on the readout box should read 260°.	• Display reads 260° repair the black with light blue tracer wire of the coolant sensor harness connector for an open circuit to the wiring harness splice. • Display reads 00°, repair the tan wire of the coolant sensor harness connector for an open circuit to the logic module.

TEST 7	STEP A	CHECKING FOR FAULT CODE 23 – CHARGE TEMPERATURE SENSOR

PROCEDURE		TEST INDICATION	ACTION REQUIRED
REMINDERS • Diagnostic readout box connected to the engine harness connector. • Disconnect the charge temperature sensor connector. • Put the system in **Sensor Test Mode 03.** (Refer to introduction) **NOTE:** Don't forget to divide the reading on the display by 10.		• Display on the readout box should read 5 volts.	• Display reads 5 volts, **Perform STEP B.**
	DIAGNOSTIC READOUT BOX	• Display reads 0 volts or 0 volts and then increases, replace the logic module.	

TEST 7	STEP B	CHECKING THE CHARGE TEMPERATURE SENSOR SIGNAL CIRCUIT TO THE LOGIC MODULE

PROCEDURE		TEST INDICATION	ACTION REQUIRED
REMINDERS • Diagnostic readout box connected to the engine harness connector. • System in **Sensor Test Mode 03.** **NOTE:** Don't forget to divide the reading on the display box by 10. • Charge temperature sensor connector disconnected. • Connect a jumper wire between the terminals of the charge temperature sensor connector	DIAGNOSTIC READOUT BOX JUMPER BK LB — BK RD CHARGE TEMPERATURE SENSOR HARNESS CONNECTOR	• Display on the readout box should read 0 volts.	• Display reads 0 volts, replace the charge temperature sensor. • Display reads 5 volts, **Perform STEP C.**

TEST 7	STEP C	CHECKING THE CHARGE TEMPERATURE SENSOR WIRES TO THE LOGIC MODULE FOR AN OPEN CIRCUIT

PROCEDURE		TEST INDICATION	ACTION REQUIRED
REMINDERS • Diagnostic readout box connected to the engine harness connector. • System in **Sensor Test Mode 03.** **NOTE:** Don't forget to divide the reading on the display box by 10. • Charge temperature sensor connector disconnected. • Connect one end of a jumper wire to the negative terminal of the battery.	• Connect the other end of the jumper wire to the black with red tracer wire terminal of the charge temperature sensor connector. JUMPER BK/LB — BK/RD CHARGE TEMPERATURE SENSOR HARNESS CONNECTOR	• Display on the readout box should read 0 volts.	• Display reads 0 volts, repair the black with light blue tracer wire of the charge temperature sensor connector for an open circuit to the wiring harness splice. • Display reads 5 volts repair the black with red tracer wire of the charge temperature sensor connector for an open circuit to the logic module.

TEST 8	STEP A	CHECKING FOR FAULT CODE 24 – THROTTLE POSITION SENSOR CIRCUIT

PROCEDURE		TEST INDICATION	ACTION REQUIRED
REMINDERS • Diagnostic readout box connected to the engine harness connector. • Disconnect the throttle body 6-way connector. • Put the system in **Sensor Test Mode 05.** (Refer to introduction) **NOTE:** Don't forget to divide the reading on the display by 10.		• Display on the readout box should read 5 volts.	• Display reads 5 volts, **Perform STEP B.**
	DIAGNOSTIC READOUT BOX	• Display reads 0 volts, replace the logic module.	

1986–88 TURBO DRIVEABILITY TEST PROCEDURES

TEST 8	STEP B	CHECKING THE THROTTLE POSITION SENSOR SIGNAL CIRCUIT TO THE LOGIC MODULE		
		PROCEDURE	TEST INDICATION	ACTION REQUIRED
REMINDERS • Diagnostic readout box connected to the engine harness connector. • System in **Sensor Test Mode 05**. NOTE: Don't forget to divide the reading on the display box by 10. • Throttle body 6-way connector disconnected. • Connect a jumper wire between the orange with blue and black with blue wires of the throttle body 6-way harness connector.		DIAGNOSTIC READOUT BOX JUMPER BK/LB OR/DB THROTTLE BODY 6-WAY HARNESS CONNECTOR	• Display on the readout box should read 0 volts.	• Display reads 0 volts, **Perform STEP D.** • Display reads 5 volts, **Perform STEP C.**

TEST 8	STEP C	CHECKING THE THROTTLE POSITION SENSOR WIRES TO THE LOGIC MODULE FOR AN OPEN CIRCUIT		
		PROCEDURE	TEST INDICATION	ACTION REQUIRED
REMINDERS • Diagnostic readout box connected to the engine harness connector. • System in **Sensor Test Mode 05**. NOTE: Don't forget to divide the reading on the readout box by 10. • Throttle position sensor disconnected. • Connect one end of a jumper wire to the negative terminal of the battery. • Connect the other end of the jumper wire to the orange with blue tracer wire terminal of the throttle position sensor harness connector.		DIAGNOSTIC READOUT BOX OR/DB THROTTLE BODY 6-WAY HARNESS CONNECTOR	• Display on the readout box should read 0 volts.	• Display reads 0 volts, repair the black with light blue tracer wire of the throttle position sensor connector for an open circuit to the wiring harness splice. • Display reads 5 volts, repair the orange with blue tracer wire of the throttle position sensor connector for an open circuit to the logic module.

TEST 8	STEP D	CHECKING THE 5 VOLT SUPPLY TO THE THROTTLE POSITION SENSOR		
		PROCEDURE	TEST INDICATION	ACTION REQUIRED
REMINDERS • Ignition switch in the run position. • Throttle body 6-way connector disconnected. • Connect a voltmeter to the orange with white tracer wire of the throttle body 6-way harness connector and ground.		VOLTMETER OR/WT THROTTLE BODY 6-WAY HARNESS CONNECTOR	• Voltmeter should read at least 4 volts.	• Voltmeter okay, replace the throttle position sensor. • 0 volts repair the orange with white tracer wire for an open circuit to the logic module.

TEST 9	STEP A	CHECKING FOR FAULT CODE 25 – AUTOMATIC IDLE SPEED MOTOR CIRCUIT		
		PROCEDURE	TEST INDICATION	ACTION REQUIRED
• Turn the ignition switch off. • Disconnect the throttle body 6-way connector. • Connect an ohmmeter between the brown with white and gray with red tracer wires of the throttle body connector.		OHMMETER GY/RD BR THROTTLE BODY 6-WAY HARNESS CONNECTOR	• Ohmmeter should show resistance. NOTE: The amount of resistance is not important. Just make sure there is some.	• Some resistance. Perform STEP B. • 0 resistance, replace the A.I.S. motor.

TEST 9	STEP B	CHECKING A.I.S. MOTOR FOR SHORT TO GROUND		
		PROCEDURE	TEST INDICATION	ACTION REQUIRED
REMINDERS • Ignition switch off. • Throttle body 6-way connector disconnected. • Connect an ohmmeter between the brown with white tracer wire of the throttle body 6-way connector and ground.		OHMMETER BR THROTTLE BODY 6-WAY HARNESS CONNECTOR	• Ohmmeter should show an open circuit.	• Ohmmeter reading okay, **Perform STEP C.** • Ohmmeter shows 0 resistance, replace the A.I.S. motor.

TEST 9	STEP C	CHECKING A.I.S. CONTROL WIRES FOR A SHORT CIRCUIT		
		PROCEDURE	TEST INDICATION	ACTION REQUIRED
REMINDERS • Ignition switch off. • Throttle body 6-way connector disconnected. • Disconnect the logic module red connector. • Connect an ohmmeter between cavities No. 18 and 22.		OHMMETER LOGIC MODULE RED CONNECTOR	• Ohmmeter should show an open circuit.	• Ohmmeter reading okay, **Perform STEP D.** • Ohmmeter shows 0 resistance, repair wires of cavities 18 and 22 for short to each other.

TEST 9	STEP D	CHECKING THE FJ2 WIRE FROM THE POWER MODULE FOR AN OPEN CIRCUIT		
		PROCEDURE	TEST INDICATION	ACTION REQUIRED
REMINDERS • Logic module red connector disconnected. • Connect a voltmeter to cavity No. 7 or 8 of the red connector and ground. • Turn the ignition switch to the run position.		VOLTMETER LOGIC MODULE RED CONNECTOR	• Voltmeter should read within one volt of the battery voltage.	• Voltage okay, replace the logic module. CAUTION: Before replacing the logic module check the terminal in cavities 7 and 8 of the red connector to make sure they are not crushed causing a poor connection. • 0 volts repair fused J2 wire to the power module for an open circuit.

TEST 10	STEP A	CHECKING FOR FAULT CODE 31 – CANISTER PURGE SOLENOID CIRCUIT		
		PROCEDURE	TEST INDICATION	ACTION REQUIRED
REMINDERS • Diagnostic readout box connected to the engine harness connector. • Connect a voltmeter to the pink wire of the solenoid assembly 4-way connector and ground. • Put the system in the **ATM Test Mode – Code 07.** (Refer to introduction)		DIAGNOSTIC READOUT BOX VOLTMETER PK WIRE END SOLENOID ASSEMBLY 4-WAY CONNECTOR	• Voltmeter reading should be pulsating between 0 and 14 volts.	• Voltmeter is not pulsating but reads within one volt of battery voltage. **Perform STEP B.** • Voltmeter pulsates between 1 and 3 volts, replace solenoid assembly. • Voltmeter is not pulsating but reads 0-1 volt, disconnect the logic module blue connector. If voltage is now within one of battery, replace the logic module. If not, repair pink wire for a short to ground.

1986–88 TURBO DRIVEABILITY TEST PROCEDURES

TEST 10	STEP B	CHECKING THE CANISTER PURGE SOLENOID CONTROL WIRE FOR AN OPEN CIRCUIT TO THE LOGIC MODULE
PROCEDURE	**TEST INDICATION**	**ACTION REQUIRED**

PROCEDURE	TEST INDICATION	ACTION REQUIRED
• Turn the ignition switch off. • Connect a voltmeter to cavity No. 5 of the logic module blue connector and ground. • Turn the ignition switch to the run position.	• Voltmeter should read within one volt of battery voltage	• Voltage okay, replace the logic module. CAUTION: Before replacing the logic module check the terminal in cavity No. 3 of the blue connector to make sure it is not crushed causing a poor connection. • 0 volts repair wire of cavity No. 3 for and open circuit to the solenoid assembly.

VOLTMETER

LOGIC MODULE BLUE CONNECTOR

TEST 11	STEP A	CHECKING FOR FAULT CODE 33 – A/C CUTOUT RELAY
PROCEDURE	**TEST INDICATION**	**ACTION REQUIRED**

PROCEDURE	TEST INDICATION	ACTION REQUIRED
REMINDERS • Diagnostic readout box connected to the engine harness connector. • Connect a voltmeter to the dark blue with orange tracer wire of the A/C cut out relay and ground. • Put the system in the **ATM Test Mode – Code 05.** (Refer to the Introduction)	• Voltmeter reading should be pulsating between 0 and 14 volts	• Voltmeter is not pulsating but reads within one volt of battery voltage. Perform STEP B. • Voltmeter pulsates between 0 and 3 volts. Perform STEP C. • Voltmeter is not pulsating but reads 0-1 volts, disconnect the logic module blue connector. If voltage is now within one of battery, replace the logic module. If not repair dark blue with orange tracer wire for a short to ground.

DIAGNOSTIC READOUT BOX

VOLTMETER

DB OR

DB BK

BR WIRE END

A.C CUT-OUT RELAY 3-WAY CONNECTOR

TEST 11	STEP B	CHECKING THE A/C CUTOUT RELAY CONTROL WIRE FOR AN OPEN CIRCUIT TO THE LOGIC MODULE
PROCEDURE	**TEST INDICATION**	**ACTION REQUIRED**

PROCEDURE	TEST INDICATION	ACTION REQUIRED
• Turn the ignition switch off. • Connect a voltmeter to cavity No. 3 of the logic module blue connector and ground. • Turn the ignition switch to the run position.	• Voltmeter should read within one volt of battery voltage	• Voltage okay, replace the logic module. CAUTION: Before replacing the logic module check the terminal in cavity No. 3 of the blue connector to make sure it is not crushed causing a poor connection. • 0 volts repair the wire of cavity No. 3 for an open circuit to the A/C cutout relay.

VOLTMETER

LOGIC MODULE BLUE CONNECTOR

TEST 11	STEP C	CHECKING A/C CUTOUT RELAY PULL IN COIL WINDINGS FOR AN OPEN CIRCUIT
PROCEDURE	**TEST INDICATION**	**ACTION REQUIRED**

PROCEDURE	TEST INDICATION	ACTION REQUIRED
• Turn the ignition switch off. • Disconnect the connectors from the A/C cutout relay. • Connect an ohmmeter between terminals 1 and 4 of the relay.	• Ohmmeter should show resistance. NOTE: The amount of resistance is not important. Just make sure there is some	• Some resistance repair the dark blue with orange tracer wire of the relay 3-way connector for an open circuit to the ignition switch. • Open circuit, replace the relay.

OHMMETER

1   2

3

4

A.C CUT-OUT RELAY

TEST 12	STEP A	CHECKING FOR FAULT CODE 34 – EGR SOLENOID CIRCUIT
PROCEDURE	**TEST INDICATION**	**ACTION REQUIRED**

PROCEDURE	TEST INDICATION	ACTION REQUIRED
REMINDERS • Diagnostic readout box connected to the engine harness connector. • Connect a voltmeter to the gray wire of the solenoid assembly 4-way connector and ground. • Put the system in the **ATM Test Mode – Code 08.** (Refer to the introduction)	• Voltmeter reading should be pulsating between 0 and 14 volts.	• Voltmeter is not pulsating but reads within one volt of battery voltage. Perform STEP B. • Voltmeter pulsates between 0 and 3 volts, replace the solenoid assembly • Voltmeter is not pulsating but reads 0-1 volt, disconnect the logic module blue connector. If voltage is now within one of battery, replace the logic module. If not repair gray wire for a short to ground.

DIAGNOSTIC READOUT BOX

VOLTMETER

GY   WIRE END

SOLENOID ASSEMBLY 4-WAY CONNECTOR

TEST 12	STEP B	CHECKING THE EGR SOLENOID CONTROL WIRE FOR AN OPEN CIRCUIT TO THE LOGIC MODULE
PROCEDURE	**TEST INDICATION**	**ACTION REQUIRED**

PROCEDURE	TEST INDICATION	ACTION REQUIRED
• Turn the ignition switch off. • Connect a voltmeter to cavity No. 6 of the logic module blue connector and ground. • Turn the ignition switch to the run position.	• Voltmeter should read within one volt of battery voltage	• Voltage okay, replace the logic module. CAUTION: Before replacing the logic module check the terminal in cavity No. 6 of the blue connector to make sure it is not crushed causing a poor connection. • 0 volts repair wire of cavity No. 6 for an open circuit to the solenoid assembly.

VOLTMETER

LOGIC MODULE BLUE CONNECTOR

TEST 13	STEP A	CHECKING FOR FAULT CODE 35 – RADIATOR FAN RELAY CONTROL CIRCUIT
PROCEDURE	**TEST INDICATION**	**ACTION REQUIRED**

PROCEDURE	TEST INDICATION	ACTION REQUIRED
REMINDERS • Diagnostic readout box connected to the engine harness connector. • Connect a voltmeter to the dark blue with pink tracer wire of the radiator fan relay and ground. • Put the system in the **ATM Test Mode – Code 04.** (Refer to the Introduction)	• Voltmeter should be pulsating between 0 and 14 volts.	• Voltmeter is not pulsating but reads within one volt of battery voltage. Perform STEP B. • Voltmeter pulsates between 0 and 3 volts. Perform STEP C. • Voltmeter is not pulsating but reads 0-1 volts, disconnect the logic module red connector. If voltage is now within one of battery, replace the logic module. If not repair dark blue with pink tracer wire for a short to ground.

DIAGNOSTIC READOUT BOX

VOLTMETER

DB PK

DB BK

WT   WIRE END

RADIATOR FAN RELAY CONNECTORS

TEST 13	STEP B	CHECKING THE RADIATOR FAN RELAY CONTROL WIRE FOR AN OPEN CIRCUIT TO THE LOGIC MODULE
PROCEDURE	**TEST INDICATION**	**ACTION REQUIRED**

PROCEDURE	TEST INDICATION	ACTION REQUIRED
• Turn the ignition switch off. • Connect a voltmeter to cavity No. 21 of the logic module red connector and ground. • Turn the ignition switch to the run position.	• Voltmeter should read within one volt of battery voltage	• Voltage okay, replace the logic module. CAUTION: Before replacing the logic module check the terminal in cavity No. 21 of the red connector to make sure it is not crushed causing a poor connection. • 0 volts, repair the wire of cavity No. 21 for an open circuit to the radiator fan relay.

VOLTMETER

LOGIC MODULE RED CONNECTOR

1986–88 TURBO DRIVEABILITY TEST PROCEDURES

TEST 13	STEP C	CHECKING RADIATOR FAN RELAY PULL IN COIL WINDINGS FOR AN OPEN CIRCUIT	
PROCEDURE		TEST INDICATION	ACTION REQUIRED
• Turn the ignition switch off. • Disconnect the smaller of the two 3-way connectors from the radiator fan relay. • Connect an ohmmeter between terminals 1 and 2 of the relay.		• Ohmmeter should show resistance. NOTE: The amount of resistance is not important. Just make sure there is some.	• Some resistance, repair the dark blue with pink tracer wire of the relay 3-way connector for an open circuit to the fuse box.
			• Open circuit, replace the relay.

OHMMETER

RADIATOR FAN RELAY

TEST 14	STEP A	CHECKING FOR FAULT CODE 36/36-45 – WASTEGATE SOLENOID CIRCUIT	
PROCEDURE		TEST INDICATION	ACTION REQUIRED
REMINDERS • Diagnostic readout box connected to the engine harness connector. • Connect a voltmeter to the green wire of the solenoid assembly 4-way connector and ground. • Put the system in the ATM Test Mode – Code 09. (Refer to the introduction)		• Voltmeter reading should be pulsating between 0 and 14 volts.	• Voltmeter is not pulsating but reads within one volt of battery voltage, Perform STEP B.
			• Voltmeter pulsates between 0 and 3 volts, replace solenoid assembly.
			• Voltmeter is not pulsating but reads 0-1 volt, disconnect the logic module red connector. If voltage is now within one of battery, replace the logic module. If not repair green wire for a short to ground.

DIAGNOSTIC READOUT BOX

VOLTMETER

LB
LG PK
GY WIRE END

SOLENOID ASSEMBLY 4-WAY CONNECTOR

TEST 14	STEP B	CHECKING THE WASTEGATE SOLENOID CONTROL WIRE FOR AN OPEN CIRCUIT TO THE LOGIC MODULE	
PROCEDURE		TEST INDICATION	ACTION REQUIRED
• Turn the ignition switch off. • Connect a voltmeter to cavity No. 19 of the logic module red connector and ground. • Turn the ignition switch to the run position.		• Voltmeter should read within one volt of battery voltage.	• Voltage okay, replace the logic module. CAUTION: Before replacing the logic module check the terminal in cavity No. 19 of the red connector is not crushed causing a poor connection.
			• 0 volts repair wire of cavity No. 19 for an open circuit to the solenoid assembly.

VOLTMETER

LOGIC MODULE RED CONNECTOR

TEST 15	STEP A	CHECKING FOR FAULT CODE 37 – BARO READ SOLENOID CIRCUIT	
PROCEDURE		TEST INDICATION	ACTION REQUIRED
REMINDERS • Diagnostic readout box connected to the engine harness connector. • Connect a voltmeter to the blue wire of the solenoid assembly 4-way connector and ground. • Put the system in the ATM Test Mode – Code 10. (Refer to the introduction)		• Voltmeter reading should be pulsating between 0 and 14 volts.	• Voltmeter is not pulsating but reads within one volt of battery voltage, Perform STEP B.
			• Voltmeter pulsates between 0 and 3 volts, replace the solenoid assembly.
			• Voltmeter is not pulsating but reads 0-1 volt, disconnect the logic module red connector. If voltage is now within one of battery, replace the logic module. If not repair blue wire for a short to ground.

DIAGNOSTIC READOUT BOX

VOLTMETER

LB PK
LG
GY WIRE END

SOLENOID ASSEMBLY 4-WAY CONNECTOR

TEST 15	STEP B	CHECKING THE BARO READ SOLENOID CONTROL WIRE FOR AN OPEN CIRCUIT TO THE LOGIC MODULE	
PROCEDURE		TEST INDICATION	ACTION REQUIRED
• Turn the ignition switch off. • Connect a voltmeter to cavity No. 15 of the logic module red connector and ground. • Turn the ignition switch to the run position.		• Voltmeter should read within one volt of battery voltage.	• Voltage okay, replace the logic module. CAUTION: Before replacing the logic module check the terminal in cavity No. 15 of the red connector to make sure it is not crushed causing a poor connection.
			• 0 volts repair wire of cavity No. 15 for an open circuit to the solenoid assembly.

VOLTMETER

LOGIC MODULE RED CONNECTOR

TEST 16	STEP A	CHECKING FOR FAULT CODES 46 OR 41-46 ALTERNATOR FIELD (CHARGING SYSTEM OUTPUT TOO HIGH)	
PROCEDURE		TEST INDICATION	ACTION REQUIRED
• Disconnect the power module 10-way connector. • Connect a voltmeter between cavity No. 8 of the 10-way connector and ground. • Turn the ignition switch to the run position.		• Voltmeter should read within one volt of the battery voltage.	• Voltage okay, Perform STEP B.
			• 0-1 volts, repair alternator field circuit for short to ground.

VOLTMETER

POWER MODULE 10-WAY CONNECTOR

TEST 16	STEP B	CHECKING THE ALTERNATOR FIELD CONTROL TO THE POWER MODULE FOR A SHORT CIRCUIT	
PROCEDURE		TEST INDICATION	ACTION REQUIRED
NOTE: The alternator field terminals (F1 and F2) of the engine wiring harness on Shelby Chargers and GLH models are interchangeable. Therefore, it will be necessary to identify which one is F1 (ignition switch feed) and which one is F2 (field control to the power module) before performing the test. • Turn the ignition switch off. • Reconnect the power module 10-way connector. • Disconnect the power module 12-way connector. • Connect a voltmeter between the F2 terminal on the alternator and ground. • Turn the ignition switch to the run position.		• Voltmeter should read within one volt of the battery voltage.	• Voltage okay, Perform STEP C.
			• 0-1 volt replace the power module.

F2

VOLTMETER

ALTERNATOR F2 TERMINAL

TEST 16	STEP C	CHECKING THE ALTERNATOR FIELD CONTROL TO THE LOGIC MODULE FOR A SHORT CIRCUIT	
PROCEDURE		TEST INDICATION	ACTION REQUIRED
REMINDERS • Power module 12-way connector disconnected. • Turn the ignition switch off. • Disconnect the logic module red connector. • Connect an ohmmeter between cavity No. 11 of the power module 12-way connector and ground.		• Ohmmeter should not show continuity.	• No continuity, replace the logic module.
			• Continuity repair wire of cavity No. 11 for a short circuit to ground.

OHMMETER

POWER MODULE 12-WAY CONNECTOR

DISCONNECT

LOGIC MODULE RED CONNECTOR

1986–88 TURBO DRIVEABILITY TEST PROCEDURES

TEST 17	STEP A	CHECKING FOR FAULT CODES 47 OR 41-47 ALTERNATOR FIELD (CHARGING SYSTEM OUTPUT TOO LOW)		
		PROCEDURE	**TEST INDICATION**	**ACTION REQUIRED**

• Connect a voltmeter to the battery. • Connect one end of a jumper wire to a good engine ground. • Start the engine and note the reading of the voltmeter. • Very quickly touch the other end of the jumper wire to the F2 terminal on the alternator and watch the voltmeter.	NOTE: The alternator field terminals of the engine wiring harness (F1 and F2) on the Shelby Charger are interchangeable. Therefore, it will be necessary to identify which one is F1 (ignition switch feed) and which one is F2 (field control to power module) before performing the tests.

- Voltmeter should show an increase in voltage.

- **Voltage increases, Perform STEP B.**

- Voltage does not increase, **Perform STEP F.**

ALTERNATOR F2 TERMINAL

TEST 17	STEP B	CHECKING CHARGING SYSTEM FIELD CONTROL CIRCUIT AT THE LOGIC MODULE		
		PROCEDURE	**TEST INDICATION**	**ACTION REQUIRED**

REMINDERS
- Engine running.
- Connect a voltmeter between cavity No. 2 of the logic module blue connector and ground.
- Connect one end of a jumper wire to cavity No. 5 of the logic module red connector.
- Very quickly touch the other end of the jumper wire to the logic module mounting stud and watch the voltmeter.

- Voltmeter should show an increase in voltage.

- Voltage increases, replace the logic module.

  CAUTION: Before replacing the logic module check the terminal in cavity No. 5 of the blue connector to make sure it is not crushed causing a poor connection.

- Voltage does not increase, **Perform STEP C.**

LOGIC MODULE BLUE CONNECTOR

LOGIC MODULE RED CONNECTOR

TEST 17	STEP C	CHECK ALTERNATOR FIELD CONTROL WIRE TO THE POWER MODULE FOR AN OPEN CIRCUIT		
		PROCEDURE	**TEST INDICATION**	**ACTION REQUIRED**

- Turn the engine off.
- Disconnect the logic module red connector.
- Connect a voltmeter between cavity No. 5 of the logic module red connector and ground.
- Turn the ignition switch to the run position.

- Voltmeter should read within one volt of the battery voltage.

- **Voltage okay, Perform STEP E.**

- 0 volts, **Perform STEP D.**

LOGIC MODULE RED CONNECTOR

TEST 17	STEP D	CHECKING ALTERNATOR FIELD CONTROL CIRCUIT OF THE POWER MODULE		
		PROCEDURE	**TEST INDICATION**	**ACTION REQUIRED**

- Turn the ignition switch off.
- Disconnect the power module 12-way connector.
- Connect a voltmeter to pin No. 11 of the power module and ground.
- Turn the ignition switch to the run position.

- Voltmeter should read within one volt of battery voltage

- Voltage okay, repair wire to cavity No. 5 of the logic module white connector for an open circuit.

- 0 volts, replace the power module

POWER MODULE 12-WAY PIN CONNECTOR

TEST 17	STEP E	CHECKING THE ALTERNATOR FIELD CONTROL TO THE POWER MODULE FOR AN OPEN CIRCUIT		
		PROCEDURE	**TEST INDICATION**	**ACTION REQUIRED**

- Turn the ignition switch off.
- Disconnect the 10-way connector from the power module.
- Connect a voltmeter between cavity No. 8 of the 10-way connector and ground.
- Turn the ignition switch to the run position.

- Voltmeter should read within one volt of battery voltage.

- Voltage okay, replace the power module.

  CAUTION: Before replacing the power module check the terminal in cavity No. 8 of the 10-way connector to make sure it is not spread apart causing a poor connection.

- 0 volts repair wire of cavity No. 8 for an open circuit to the alternator.

POWER MODULE 10-WAY CONNECTOR

TEST 17	STEP F	CHECKING FOR VOLTAGE TO ALTERNATOR FIELD CIRCUIT		
		PROCEDURE	**TEST INDICATION**	**ACTION REQUIRED**

- Turn the engine off.
- Connect a voltmeter between the F1 terminal of the alternator and ground.
- Turn the ignition switch to the run position.

- Voltmeter should read within one volt of the battery voltage.

- Voltage okay, repair the alternator.

- 0 volts repair the wire of F1 terminal for an open circuit to the ignition switch

ALTERNATOR F1 TERMINAL

TEST 18	STEP A	CHECKING FOR FAULT CODE 44 – BATTERY TEMPERATURE SENSOR CIRCUIT		
		PROCEDURE	**TEST INDICATION**	**ACTION REQUIRED**

- Turn the ignition switch off.
- Disconnect the logic module blue connector.
- Connect an ohmmeter between cavity No. 20 of the logic module blue connector and ground.

- Ohmmeter should show resistance.

  NOTE: The amount of resistance is not important. Just make sure there is some.

- Some resistance replace the logic module.

  CAUTION: Before replacing the logic module check the terminal in cavity No. 20 of the blue connector to make sure it is not crushed causing a poor connection.

- 0 resistance, **Perform STEP B.**

- Open circuit, **Perform STEP C.**

LOGIC MODULE BLUE CONNECTOR

TEST 18	STEP B	CHECKING BATTERY TEMPERATURE SENSOR WIRE FOR SHORT CIRCUIT		
		PROCEDURE	**TEST INDICATION**	**ACTION REQUIRED**

REMINDERS
- Logic module blue connector disconnected.
- Ohmmeter connected between cavity No. 20 of the logic module blue connector and ground.
- Disconnect the power module 12-way connector.

- Ohmmeter should show an open circuit.

- Open circuit, replace the power module.

- 0 resistance, repair wire of cavity No. 20 for short circuit to ground.

LOGIC MODULE BLUE CONNECTOR

DISCONNECT

POWER MODULE 12-WAY CONNECTOR

1986–88 TURBO DRIVEABILITY TEST PROCEDURES

TEST 18	STEP C	CHECKING BATTERY TEMPERATURE SENSOR WIRE FOR OPEN CIRCUIT
PROCEDURE	TEST INDICATION	ACTION REQUIRED

PROCEDURE	TEST INDICATION	ACTION REQUIRED
• Disconnect the power module 12-way connector. • Connect an ohmmeter between pin 3 and 12 of the power module.	• Ohmmeter should show resistance. NOTE: The amount of resistance is not important. Just make sure there is some.	• Some resistance, repair wire in cavity No. 3 of power module 12-way connector for an open circuit.
	• 0 resistance or open circuit, replace the power module.	

OHMMETER
12 11 10 9 8 7
1 2 3 4 5 6
POWER MODULE
12-WAY PIN CONNECTOR

TEST 19	STEP A	CHECKING FOR FAULT CODE 45 – OVERBOOST SHUTOFF

PROCEDURE	TEST INDICATION	ACTION REQUIRED
• Disconnect vacuum line connector from wastegate diaphragm and connect a vacuum gauge to it. • Disconnect vacuum line connector from the side of the wastegate solenoid and connect an auxiliary vacuum supply to it. • Apply 15 inches of vacuum. • Release vacuum.	• Vacuum gauge should read within two inches of the applied vacuum and then immediately drop to 0 when released.	• Vacuum gauge reads within two inches and drops to 0, Perform STEP B.
		• Vacuum gauge does not read within one inch or drops slowly towards 0, repair vacuum line for a restriction or break.

CONNECT VACUUM GAUGE
WASTEGATE
TURBOCHARGER
CONNECT AN AUXILIARY VACUUM SUPPLY
WASTEGATE SOLENOID
WASTEGATE SYSTEM

TEST 19	STEP B	CHECKING VACUUM SUPPLY TO THE WASTEGATE SOLENOID

PROCEDURE	TEST INDICATION	ACTION REQUIRED
• Disconnect the vacuum line connector from the top of the wastegate solenoid and connect a vacuum gauge to it. • Start the engine.	• Vacuum gauge should read manifold vacuum.	• Vacuum okay, check wastegate calibration.
		• 0 vacuum, repair vacuum line to manifold nipple for a restriction or break.

TO WASTEGATE
MANIFOLD VACUUM/ PRESSURE SOURCE
CONNECT A VACUUM GAUGE
WASTEGATE SOLENOID
WASTEGATE SOLENOID

THE FOLLOWING TEST MUST BEGIN WITH A COLD ENGINE

TEST 20	STEP A	CHECKING SENSOR CALIBRATIONS (ENGINE COOLANT TEMPERATURE SENSOR)

PROCEDURE	TEST INDICATION	ACTION REQUIRED
REMINDERS • Diagnostic readout box connected to the engine harness connector. • Put the system in Sensor Test Mode 04. (Refer to introduction) NOTE: Don't forget to multiply the reading on display by 10.	• Display on the readout box should read approximately ambient temperature ± 10°F.	• Temperature okay, Perform STEP B.
	• Temperature not okay, replace the coolant sensor.	

DIAGNOSTIC READOUT BOX

TEST 20	STEP B	CHECKING SENSOR CALIBRATIONS (THROTTLE POSITION SENSOR)

PROCEDURE	TEST INDICATION	ACTION REQUIRED
REMINDERS • Diagnostic readout box connected to the engine harness connector. • Engine cold • Put the system in Sensor Test Mode 05. (Refer to introduction) NOTE: Don't forget to divide the reading on display by 10.	• Voltage on readout box should read as follows **Throttle Fully Closed** 1 volt ± ½ volt NOTE: Make sure none of the cables that are attached to the throttle body are not misadjusted and are holding the throttle open. **In Between Closed and Open** You should see an uninterrupted change of voltage between closed and open throttle. **Throttle Wide Open** at least 3½ volts	• Voltage okay, Perform STEP C.
		• Voltage not okay, replace throttle sensor.

DIAGNOSTIC READOUT BOX

TEST 20	STEP C	CHECKING SENSOR CALIBRATION (M.A.P. SENSOR)

PROCEDURE	TEST INDICATION	ACTION REQUIRED
REMINDERS • Diagnostic readout box connected to the engine harness connector. • Engine cold. • Put the system in Sensor Test Mode 08. (Refer to introduction) NOTE: Don't forget to divide the reading on display by 10. • Disconnect the vacuum hose from the M.A.P. sensor. • Connect an auxiliary vacuum supply to the M.A.P. sensor. • Apply 5 inches of vacuum and record the voltage displayed on the readout box	• Slowly apply vacuum to 20 inches and watch display on readout box. • Record the voltage displayed on the readout box at 20 inches • Subtract the voltage recorded at 20 inches from the voltage recorded at 5 inches. **Example** Voltage at 5" 1.9 Voltage at 20" 6 Difference 1.3	• You should see an uninterrupted change of voltage between 5 and 20 inches of vacuum • The voltage difference should be between 1.1 and 1.4 volts
		• Voltage okay, Perform STEP D.
		• Voltage not okay, replace the M.A.P. sensor

TEST 20	STEP D	CHECKING SENSOR CALIBRATION (CHARGE TEMPERATURE SENSOR)

PROCEDURE	TEST INDICATION	ACTION REQUIRED
REMINDERS • Diagnostic readout box connected to the engine harness connector. • Engine cold. • Put the system in Sensor Test Mode 03. (Refer to introduction) NOTE: Don't forget to divide the reading on display by 10.	• Display on the readout box should be between 3 and 5 volts.	• Voltage okay, Perform STEP E.
		• Voltage not okay, replace the charge temperature sensor.

DIAGNOSTIC READOUT BOX

TEST 20	STEP E	CHECKING SENSOR CALIBRATION (BATTERY TEMPERATURE SENSOR)

PROCEDURE	TEST INDICATION	ACTION REQUIRED
REMINDERS • Diagnostic readout box connected to the engine harness connector. • Engine cold. • Put the system in Sensor Test Mode 01. (Refer to introduction) NOTE: Don't forget to divide the reading on display by 10.	• Display on the readout box should be between 5 and 2 volts.	• Voltage okay, Perform TEST NO. 21.
		• Voltage not okay, replace the power module.

DIAGNOSTIC READOUT BOX

1986–88 TURBO DRIVEABILITY TEST PROCEDURES

TEST 21 — STEP A — CHECKING EGR SYSTEM

PROCEDURE		TEST INDICATION	ACTION REQUIRED
• Disconnect the vacuum hose from the EGR valve and connect a vacuum gauge to it. • Start the engine and raise engine speed to 2000 rpm.	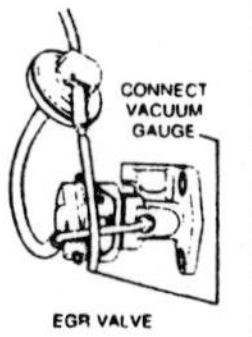	• Vacuum gauge should show a steady reading of 0. (Engine temperature below 90°F)	• Vacuum okay. **Perform TEST NO. 22.**
			• **Vacuum gauge shows an unsteady reading above 0, replace the EGR solenoid.**

TEST 22 — STEP A — CHECKING FOR FUEL FOULED SPARK PLUGS

PROCEDURE		TEST INDICATION	ACTION REQUIRED
• Remove the spark plugs.		• Spark plugs should be dry. **NOTE: It is normal for spark plugs to be black after an engine has been started cold.**	• **Spark plugs are dry, Perform TEST NO. 25.**
			• **Spark plugs are wet with fuel, clean and reinstall. Do not install new spark plugs.** • **Check for gas in the crankcase. Change oil and filter if required.**

TEST 23 — STEP A — CHECKING SENSOR CALIBRATIONS (ENGINE COOLANT TEMPERATURE SENSOR)

PROCEDURE		TEST INDICATION	ACTION REQUIRED
REMINDERS • Diagnostic readout box connected to the engine harness connector.	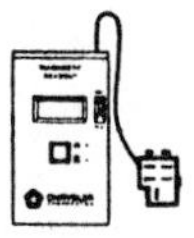 DIAGNOSTIC READOUT BOX	• Display on the readout box should read between 180° and 250° F.	• Temperature okay. **Perform STEP B.**
• Put the system in **Sensor Test Mode 04.** (Refer to introduction) **NOTE:** Don't forget to multiply the reading on display by 10.			• Temperature not okay, replace the coolant sensor.

TEST 23 — STEP B — CHECKING SENSOR CALIBRATIONS (THROTTLE POSITION SENSOR)

PROCEDURE		TEST INDICATION	ACTION REQUIRED
REMINDERS • Diagnostic readout box connected to the engine harness connector. • Engine warm.	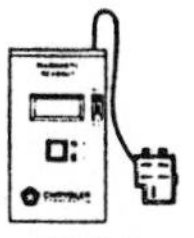 DIAGNOSTIC READOUT BOX	• Display on readout box should read as follows: **Throttle Fully Closed** 1 volt ± ½ volt **NOTE:** Make sure none of the cables that are attached to the throttle body are not misadjusted and are holding the throttle open. **In Between Closed and Open** You should see an uninterrupted change of voltage between closed and open throttle. **Throttle Wide Open** at least 3 volts	• Voltage okay. **Perform STEP C.**
• Put the system in **Sensor Test Mode 05.** (Refer to introduction) **NOTE:** Don't forget to divide the reading on display by 10.			• Voltage not okay, replace throttle position sensor.

TEST 23 — STEP C — CHECKING SENSOR CALIBRATION (M.A.P. SENSOR)

PROCEDURE		TEST INDICATION	ACTION REQUIRED
REMINDERS • Diagnostic readout box connected to the engine harness connector. • Engine warm.	• Apply 5 inches of vacuum and record the voltage displayed on the readout box. • Slowly apply vacuum to 20 inches and watch display on readout box. • Record the voltage displayed on the readout box at 20 inches. • Subtract the voltage recorded at 20 inches from the voltage recorded at 5 inches. **Example** Voltage at 5" 1.9 Voltage at 20" − .6 Difference 1.3	• You should see an uninterrupted change of voltage between 5 and 20 inches of vacuum. • The voltage difference should be between 1.1 and 1.4 volts.	• Voltage okay. **Perform STEP D.**
• Put the system in **Sensor Test Mode 08.** (Refer to introduction) **NOTE:** Don't forget to divide the reading on display by 10. • Disconnect the vacuum hose from the M.A.P. sensor. • Connect an auxiliary vacuum supply to the M.A.P. sensor.			• Voltage not okay, replace the M.A.P. sensor.

TEST 23 — STEP D — CHECKING SENSOR CALIBRATION (CHARGE TEMPERATURE SENSOR)

PROCEDURE		TEST INDICATION	ACTION REQUIRED
REMINDERS • Diagnostic readout box connected to the engine harness connector. • Engine warm.	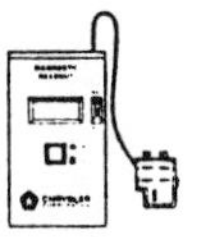 DIAGNOSTIC READOUT BOX	• Display on the readout box should be between ½ and 3 volts.	• Voltage okay. **Perform STEP E.**
• Put the system in **Sensor Test Mode 03.** (Refer to introduction) **NOTE:** Don't forget to divide the reading on display by 10.			• Voltage not okay, replace the charge temperature sensor.

TEST 23 — STEP E — CHECKING SENSOR CALIBRATION (BATTERY TEMPERATURE SENSOR)

PROCEDURE		TEST INDICATION	ACTION REQUIRED
REMINDERS • Diagnostic readout box connected to the engine harness connector. • Engine warm.	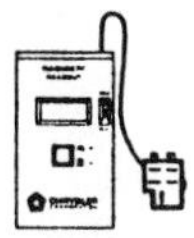 DIAGNOSTIC READOUT BOX	• Display on the readout box should be between .2 and 2.5 volts.	• Voltage okay. **Perform TEST NO. 24.**
• Put the system in **Sensor Test Mode 01.** (Refer to introduction) **NOTE:** Don't forget to divide the reading on display by 10.			• Voltage not okay, replace the power module.

TEST 24 — STEP A — CHECKING THE EGR SYSTEM - VACUUM SUPPLY FROM THE THROTTLE BODY TO THE EGR BACKPRESSURE VALVE

PROCEDURE		TEST INDICATION	ACTION REQUIRED
REMINDERS • Engine warm.	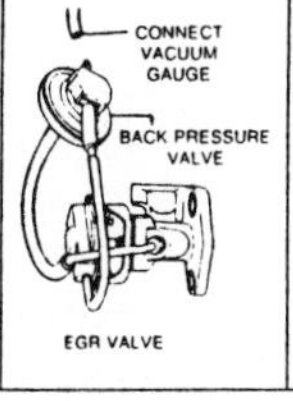	• Vacuum gauge should read at least 5 inches.	• Vacuum okay, remember what it is and **Perform STEP B.**
• Disconnect the vacuum line at the EGR back-pressure valve that comes from the EGR solenoid. • Connect a vacuum gauge to this line. • Start the engine. **NOTE:** Engine must be at operating temperature. • Raise engine speed to 2000 rpm's.			• Vacuum below 5 inches, repair vacuum supply from solenoid or throttle body to solenoid.

FUEL INJECTION SYSTEMS
CHRYSLER CORPORATION

1986–88 TURBO DRIVEABILITY TEST PROCEDURES

TEST 24	STEP B	CHECKING THE VACUUM SUPPLY FROM THE BACKPRESSURE VALVE TO THE EGR VALVE	
PROCEDURE		**TEST INDICATION**	**ACTION REQUIRED**
REMINDERS • Engine running. • Disconnect the vacuum gauge from the vacuum line and reconnect the vacuum line to the backpressure valve. • Disconnect the vacuum line from the EGR valve and connect a vacuum gauge to it. • Raise the engine speed to 2000 rpm's.	CONNECT VACUUM GAUGE EGR VALVE	• Vacuum gauge should read the same or near the same as seen in Step A. • Vacuum not okay, replace EGR/backpressure valve assembly.	• Vacuum okay. Perform STEP C.

TEST 24	STEP C	CHECKING THE EGR VALVE OPERATION	
PROCEDURE		**TEST INDICATION**	**ACTION REQUIRED**
REMINDERS • Vacuum line disconnected from the EGR valve. • Engine running. • Connect an auxiliary vacuum supply to the EGR valve. • With engine running at idle speed slowly apply vacuum.	CONNECT AUXILIARY VACUUM SUPPLY EGR VALVE	• Engine speed should begin to drop when applied vacuum reaches 2 to 3½ inches. **NOTE:** The automatic idle speed motor will attempt to compensate for drop in engine speed from EGR, so idle speed drop may only be momentary at lower applied vacuum level. • Engine speed does not drop, replace EGR/backpressure valve assembly. **NOTE:** After valve is removed, make sure supply tube from manifold is not plugged before replacing EGR valve assembly.	• Engine speed drops, Perform STEP D.

TEST 24	STEP D	CHECKING THE EGR VALVE VACUUM CHAMBER FOR LEAKS	
PROCEDURE		**TEST INDICATION**	**ACTION REQUIRED**
REMINDERS • Vacuum line disconnected from the EGR valve. • Auxiliary vacuum supply connected to the EGR valve. • Engine running at idle speed. • Apply 10 inches of vacuum to EGR valve.		• Vacuum should hold for at least 10 seconds before bleeding down. • Vacuum does not hold, replace EGR/backpressure valve assembly.	• Vacuum holds, Perform Test NO. 25.

TEST 25	STEP A	CHECKING SECONDARY IGNITION SYSTEM	
PROCEDURE		**TEST INDICATION**	**ACTION REQUIRED**
• Connect suitable engine analyzer to engine. • Start engine and let engine speed stabilize for two minutes.		• Follow equipment manufacturer's procedure for secondary ignition testing and pattern analysis. **CAUTION:** Make sure ignition coil output is checked in this testing. Open circuit secondary voltage should be at least 25,000 volts. • Secondary ignition not to specs, repair as required.	• Secondary ignition system okay, Perform TEST NO. 26.

TEST 26	STEP A	CHECKING BASIC IGNITION TIMING	
PROCEDURE		**TEST INDICATION**	**ACTION REQUIRED**
• Connect a tachometer to engine. • Connect a power timing light to engine. **NOTE:** If a mag timer is not used, it will be necessary to remove air cleaner assembly to see timing marks. • Start and run engine until operating temperature is reached. • Disconnect and reconnect engine coolant sensor connector. **NOTE:** The power loss lamp on the instrument panel must come on.		• Basic timing should be within 2° of specification as shown on the emission label. • Basic timing not okay, adjust following basic ignition timing procedure.	• Basic timing okay. Perform STEP B.

TEST 26	STEP B	CHECKING SPARK ADVANCE	
PROCEDURE		**TEST INDICATION**	**ACTION REQUIRED**
REMINDERS • Tachometer connected to engine. • Timing light connected to engine. • Air cleaner removed (if necessary). • Engine fully warmed up. • Turn engine off and then restart. **NOTE:** Power loss lamp on instrument panel must go off. • Raise engine speed to 2,000 rpm's.		• Timing should be as follows: 37° ± 4° • Timing not okay, replace logic module.	• Timing okay, Perform TEST NO. 27.

TEST 27	STEP A	CHECKING FUEL SUPPLY AND RETURN SYSTEM	
PROCEDURE		**TEST INDICATION**	**ACTION REQUIRED**
• Install pressure gauge (Tool C-3292) to fitting on fuel rail. • Connect diagnostic readout box to engine harness connector. • Press ATM button.	DIAGNOSTIC READOUT BOX INSTALL PRESSURE GAUGE FUEL RAIL FUEL RAIL	• Fuel pressure must be 55 psi ± 2.	• Fuel pressure okay, Perform TEST NO. 26. • Fuel pressure below 53, record what it is and Perform STEP B. • Fuel pressure above 57, Perform STEP D.

TEST 27	STEP B	CHECKING FOR LOW FUEL PRESSURE	
PROCEDURE		**TEST INDICATION**	**ACTION REQUIRED**
• Turn ignition switch off. • Install pressure gauge before fuel filter. Use adapter C-4799. • Turn ignition to run position. • Press ATM button.	INSTALL PRESSURE GAUGE FUEL FILTER	• Fuel pressure should not be higher than 5 psi of previously recorded pressure. • Fuel pressure still below 53 psi, Perform STEP C.	• Fuel pressure higher than 5 psi, replace fuel filter.

1986–88 TURBO DRIVEABILITY TEST PROCEDURES

TEST 27	STEP C	CHECKING FOR LOW FUEL PRESSURE
PROCEDURE	**TEST INDICATION**	**ACTION REQUIRED**
• Turn ignition switch off. • Release pressure in fuel lines. • Remove pressure gauge from before filter and reinstall it on fuel rail. • Turn ignition to run position. • Press ATM button. • Very gently, squeeze fuel return line at the pressure regulator valve and immediately let go.	• Fuel pressure should increase above 55 psi.	• Fuel pressure increases, replace pressure regulator valve.
	• Fuel pressure does not increase, replace intank fuel pump. **NOTE:** Before replacing pump look for contamination in the fuel tank that may be plugging pump filter. Also make sure electrical connections are not corroded.

TEST 27	STEP D	CHECKING FOR HIGH FUEL PRESSURE
PROCEDURE	**TEST INDICATION**	**ACTION REQUIRED**
REMINDERS • Pressure gauge connected. • Turn ignition switch off. • Remove fuel return hose (small one) from pressure regulator. • Connect a 3 foot piece of fuel hose to pressure regulator and put open end into an approved gasoline container. (2 gallon size) • Turn ignition to run position. • Press ATM button, look at pressure gauge, and then immediately release button.	**CAUTION:** Do not hold button down for more than 10 seconds. • Fuel pressure should be 55 psi ±2.	• Fuel pressure okay, check fuel return lines for kinks or restrictions, including lines and return line check valve inside fuel tank.
	• Fuel pressure above 57 psi, replace pressure regulator valve.

TEST 28	STEP A	CHECKING THE OXYGEN SENSOR OPERATION
PROCEDURE	**TEST INDICATION**	**ACTION REQUIRED**
• Connect the diagnostic readout box to the engine harness connector. **NOTE:** Make sure the read/hold switch is in the read position. • Start the engine. • Move the read/hold switch to the hold position to increase engine speed.	• Display on the readout box should be switching between 0 and 1.	• 0-1 switching, **Perform TEST NO. 29.**
	• No 0-1 switching, replace the oxygen sensor.

NOTES

1987–88 EFI DRIVEABILITY TEST PROCEDURES

Code	Type	Power Loss/ Limit Lamp	Circuit	When Monitored By The Logic Module	When Put Into Memory	ATM Test Code	Sensor Access Code	Engine Running Test Code
11	Fault	No	Distributor Signal	During cranking	If no distributor signal is present since the battery was disconnected	None	None	None
12	Indication	No	Battery Feed to the Logic Module	All the time when the ignition switch is on	If the battery feed to the logic module has been disconnected within the last 20-40 engine starts.	None	None	None
13	Fault	Yes	M.A.P. Sensor (Vacuum)	When the throttle is closed during cranking and after the engine starts.	If the M.A.P. sensor vacuum level does not change between cranking and when the engine starts.	None	None	68
14	Fault	Yes	M.A.P. Sensor (Electrical)	All the time when the ignition switch is on.	If the M.A.P. sensor signal is below .02 or above 4.9 volts.	None	08	None
15	Fault	No	Vehicle Speed Sensor	Over a .7 second period during decel from highway speeds when the throttle is closed.	If the speed sensor signal indicates less than 2 mph when the vehicle is moving.	None	None	71
16	Fault	Yes	Battery Voltage Sensing (Charging System)	All the time after one minute from when the engine starts.	If the battery sensing voltage drops below 4 or between 7½ and 8½ volts for more than 20 seconds.	None	07	67
17	Fault	No	Engine Cooling System	After 12 minutes from when the engine starts.	If engine coolant temperature does not reach 160°F within 8 minutes of vehicle speeds greater than 28 mph.	None	None	None
21	Fault	No	Oxygen Sensor	All the time after 12 minutes from when the engine starts.	If there is no oxygen sensor signal for more than 22 seconds when in closed loop.	None	02	62
22	Fault	Yes	Engine Coolant Sensor	All the time when the ignition switch is on.	If the coolant sensor voltage is above 4.96 volts when the engine is cold or below .51 volts when the engine is warm.	None	04	64
23	Fault	No	Throttle Body Temperature Sensor	During cranking.	If the throttle body temperature sensor voltage is below .04 or above 4.96 when engine coolant temperature is above 77°F	None	03	63
24	Fault	Yes	Throttle Position Sensor	All the time when the ignition switch is on.	If the throttle position sensor signal is below .16 or above 4.7 volts.	None	05	65 59
25	Fault	No	Automatic Idle Speed Motor (AIS)	Only when the AIS system is required to control the engine speed.	If proper voltage in the AIS system is not present. **NOTE:** Open circuit will not activate code.	03	None	None
26	Fault	No	Fuel Injector Driver	During cranking.	If the current through the fuel injector does not reach its proper peak level.	02	None	None
27	Fault	No	Fuel Control	All the time when the ignition switch is on.	If the fuel control interface fails to switch properly.	None	None	None
31	Fault	No	Canister Purge Solenoid	All the time when the ignition switch is on.	If the solenoid does not turn on and off when it should.	07	None	None
33	Fault	No	A/C Cutout Relay	All the time when the ignition switch is on	If the relay does not turn on and off when it should	05	None	None
34	Fault	No	Speed Control Servo Circuit	All the time when the speed control switch is on	If the servo does not turn on and off when it should.	08	None	None
35	Fault	No	Radiator Fan Relay Circuit	All the time when the ignition switch is on.	If the relay does not turn on and off when it should	04	None	None

Code	Type	Power Loss/ Limit Lamp	Circuit	When Monitored By The Logic Module	When Put Into Memory	ATM Test Code	Sensor Access Code	Engine Running Test Code
37	Fault	No	Transmission Lockup Solenoid (2.5L Auto Trans)	All the time when the ignition switch is on	If the lockup solenoid does not turn on and off when it should	10	None	None
41	Fault	No	Alternator Field Control (Charging System)	All the time when the ignition switch is on	If the field control fails to switch properly	09	None	None
42	Fault	No	Auto Shutdown	All the time when the ignition switch is on	If the relay does not turn on and off when it should	06	None	None
43	Fault	No	Spark Control	During cranking only	If the spark control interface fails to switch properly	01	None	None
44	Fault	No	Battery Temperature Sensor (Charging System)	During cranking only	If the battery temperature sensor signal is below .04 or above 4.9 volts.	None	01	61
46	Fault	Yes	Battery Voltage Sensing (Charging System)	All the time when the engine is running	If the battery sense voltage is more than 1 volt above the desired control voltage for more than 20 seconds	None	07	67
47	Fault	No	Battery Voltage Sensing (Charging System)	All the time when the engine has been running for more than 6 minutes, engine temperature above 160°F and engine rpm above 1,500 rpm.	If the battery sense voltage is less than 1 volt below the desired control voltage for more than 20 seconds	None	07	67
51	Fault	No	Oxygen Feedback System	During all closed loop conditions.	If the O₂ sensor indicates a lean condition for more than 2 minutes	None	None	0-1 Switching
52	Fault	No	Oxygen Feedback System	During all closed loop conditions.	If the O₂ sensor indicates a rich condition for more than 2 minutes	None	None	0-1 Switching
53	Fault	No	Logic Module	All the time in the diagnostic mode.	If the logic module fails.	None	None	None
55	Indication	No			Indicates end of diagnostic mode.			
88	Indication	No			Indicates start of diagnostic mode. **NOTE:** This code must appear first in the diagnostic mode or fault codes will be inaccurate.			
0	Indication	No	Indicates oxygen feedback system is lean with the engine running					
1	Indication	No			Indicates oxygen feedback system is rich with the engine running			

1987–88 EFI DRIVEABILITY TEST PROCEDURES

TEST 1	STEP A	CHECKING FOR SPARK AT SPARK PLUGS	
PROCEDURE		**TEST INDICATION**	**ACTION REQUIRED**
• Disconnect any spark plug wire. • Insert an insulated screwdriver in terminal. • Hold screwdriver shaft (¼") near a good engine ground. • Have someone crank the engine.		• There is a good spark between screwdriver and ground as long as the engine is cranking.	• Spark okay. **Perform TEST NO. 2**
		• There is no spark. **NOTE:** Handle 1 or 2 sparks as no spark.	• **Perform STEP B.**

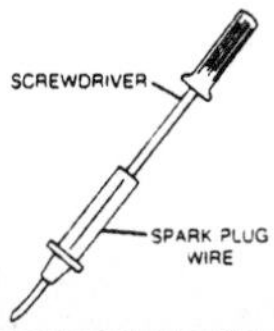

SCREWDRIVER
SPARK PLUG WIRE

TEST 1	STEP B	CHECKING FOR SPARK AT IGNITION COIL WIRE	
PROCEDURE		**TEST INDICATION**	**ACTION REQUIRED**
• Disconnect ignition coil wire from distributor cap. • Hold coil wire (¼") near a good engine ground. • Have someone crank the engine.		• There is a good spark between ignition coil wire and ground.	• Repair secondary ignition system (distributor cap and/or rotor).
		• There is no spark. **NOTE:** Handle 1 or 2 sparks as no spark.	• Check ignition coil wire. If okay, **Perform STEP C.**

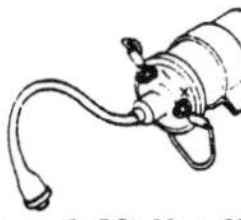

IGNITION COIL WIRE

TEST 1	STEP C	CHECKING FOR FUEL FROM INJECTOR	
PROCEDURE		**TEST INDICATION**	**ACTION REQUIRED**
• Remove the air cleaner cover. • Have someone crank the engine while you look for a fuel spray from the injector.		• There is fuel spraying from the injector.	• **Perform TEST NO. 6.**
		• There is no fuel spraying from the injector.	• **Perform TEST NO. 14.**

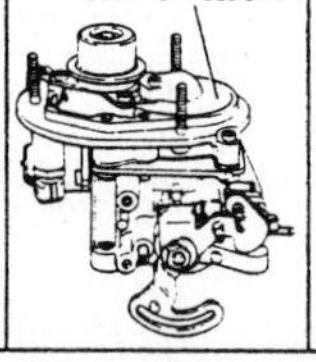

LOOK FOR FUEL SPRAY

TEST 2	STEP A	CHECKING FOR FUEL FROM INJECTOR	
PROCEDURE		**TEST INDICATION**	**ACTION REQUIRED**
• Remove the air cleaner cover. • Have someone crank the engine while you look for a fuel spray from the injector.		• There is a slow steady stream of fuel from the injector.	• **Perform TEST NO. 3.**
		• There is no fuel spray.	• **Perform TEST NO. 9.**
		• Injector is spraying an excessive amount of fuel.	• **Perform TEST NO. 13**

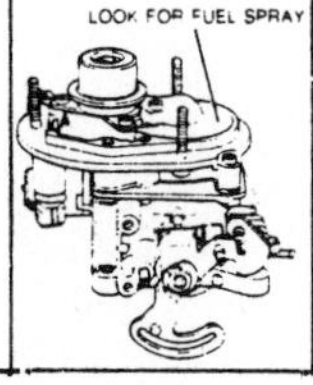

LOOK FOR FUEL SPRAY

TEST 3	STEP A	CHECKING LOGIC MODULE	
PROCEDURE		**TEST INDICATION**	**ACTION REQUIRED**
• Connect diagnostic readout box to engine harness connector. • Turn ignition switch on-off-on-off-on within 5 seconds.		• Code 88 appears on the readout box display.	• **Perform TEST NO. 4.**
		• Code 88 does not appear on the readout box display.	• Replace the logic module. **CAUTION:** Before replacing the logic module make sure your diagnostic readout box is operational and that there is not an open circuit in the wires between the logic module and diagnostic connector.

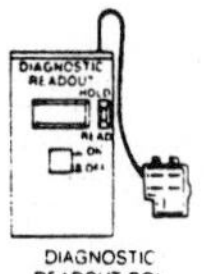

DIAGNOSTIC READOUT
DIAGNOSTIC READOUT BOX

TEST 4	STEP A	CHECKING FOR FUEL FOULED SPARK PLUGS	
PROCEDURE		**TEST INDICATION**	**ACTION REQUIRED**
• Remove spark plugs. • Look at tips for wet fuel.		• Spark plug tips are not wet with fuel. **NOTE:** It is normal for spark plugs to be black after engine is started cold.	• **Perform TEST NO. 5.**
		• Spark plugs are wet with fuel.	• Clean and reinstall. **Do not replace spark plugs.** • Attempt restart.

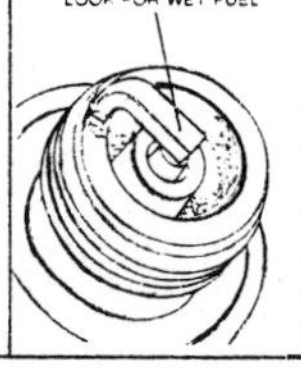

LOOK FOR WET FUEL

TEST 5	STEP A	CHECKING ENGINE TIMING	
PROCEDURE		**TEST INDICATION**	**ACTION REQUIRED**
• Connect timing device to engine. • Have someone crank engine while you look at the timing marks.		• Timing is between 0°–16° BTC.	• Remove distributor cap, crank engine to make sure rotor is turning and is indexed correctly. • Check compression and valve timing.
		• Timing is not between 0°–16° BTC.	• **Perform STEP B.**

TEST 5	STEP B	CHECKING ENGINE TIMING	
PROCEDURE		**TEST INDICATION**	**ACTION REQUIRED**
REMINDERS • Timing device connected to engine. • Set timing to 10° BTC during cranking.		• Engine starts.	• Reset timing to specifications.
		• Engine does not start.	• Remove distributor cap, crank engine to make sure rotor is turning and is indexed correctly. • Check compression and valve timing.

1987–88 EFI DRIVEABILITY TEST PROCEDURES

TEST 6	STEP A	CHECKING IGNITION CONTROL SYSTEM FOR FAULT CODES	
PROCEDURE		TEST INDICATION	ACTION REQUIRED
• Connect diagnostic read-out box to the engine harness connector. • Disconnect and reconnect the battery connector. • Crank the engine for 5 seconds and then turn the ignition switch off. • Put the system in the Diagnostic Mode. (Refer to introduction) • Record all codes.		88-12-55 No fault codes 88-12-43-55 Spark control circuit	Perform TEST NO. 7. Perform TEST NO. 8.

BATTERY CONNECTOR

TEST 7	STEP A	CHECKING FOR THE VOLTAGE SUPPLY TO THE IGNITION COIL POSITIVE TERMINAL FROM THE POWER MODULE	
PROCEDURE		TEST INDICATION	ACTION REQUIRED
REMINDERS • Diagnostic readout box connected to the engine harness connector. • System in the diagnostic mode. • Disconnect the wire from the negative (−) terminal of the ignition coil. • Connect an analog voltmeter to the positive terminal of the ignition coil and ground. • Put the system in the ATM Test Mode - Code 01. (Refer to introduction)		• Voltmeter is reading within one volt of battery voltage. • Voltmeter reads 0.	• Perform STEP B. • Repair wire of coil positive terminal for open circuit to the power module.

ANALOG VOLTMETER
 POSITIVE TERMINAL
 IGNITION COIL

TEST 7	STEP B	CHECKING THE IGNITION SYSTEM PRIMARY CONTROL CIRCUIT VOLTAGE AT THE IGNITION COIL (−) TERMINAL	
PROCEDURE		TEST INDICATION	ACTION REQUIRED
REMINDERS • Diagnostic readout box connected to the engine harness connector. • System in ATM Test Mode - Code 01. • Reconnect wire to the negative (−) terminal of the ignition coil. • Connect an analog voltmeter to the negative terminal of the ignition coil and ground.		• Voltmeter reading is pulsating between 10 and 14 volts. • Voltmeter not pulsating but reads above 10 volts. • Voltmeter pulsating between 0 and 10 volts. • Voltmeter pulsating between 0 and 2 volts.	• Replace the ignition coil. • Perform STEP C. • Replace the ignition coil. • Perform STEP D.

ANALOG VOLTMETER
 NEGATIVE TERMINAL
 IGNITION COIL

TEST 7	STEP C	CHECKING THE IGNITION SYSTEM PRIMARY CONTROL CIRCUIT FOR AN OPEN CIRCUIT	
PROCEDURE		TEST INDICATION	ACTION REQUIRED
• Turn the ignition switch off. • Disconnect the 10-way connector from the power module. • Connect an ohmmeter between the negative (−) terminal of the ignition coil and cavity No. 1 of the power module 10-way connector.		• Ohmmeter is showing continuity. • Ohmmeter is showing no continuity.	• Replace the power module. CAUTION: Before replacing the power module check the terminal in cavity No. 1 of the 10-way connector to make sure that it is not spread apart causing a poor connection. • Repair wire of cavity No. 1 for an open circuit.

IGNITION COIL
 OHMMETER
 POWER MODULE 10-WAY CONNECTOR

TEST 7	STEP D	CHECKING THE IGNITION COIL PRIMARY WINDINGS FOR A SHORT CIRCUIT	
PROCEDURE		TEST INDICATION	ACTION REQUIRED
REMINDERS • Diagnostic readout box connected to the engine harness connector. • Turn the ignition switch off. • Disconnect the wire from the negative side (−) of the ignition coil. • Connect the voltmeter to the negative (−) terminal of the ignition coil and ground. • Put the system in the ATM Test Mode - Code 01.		• Voltmeter is reading above 10 volts. • Voltmeter reads between 0 and 2 volts.	• Perform STEP E. • Replace the ignition coil.

VOLTMETER
 IGNITION COIL

TEST 7	STEP E	CHECKING THE IGNITION SYSTEM PRIMARY CIRCUIT FOR A SHORT CIRCUIT TO GROUND	
PROCEDURE		TEST INDICATION	ACTION REQUIRED
REMINDERS • Ignition coil negative (−) wire disconnected. • Turn the ignition switch off. • Disconnect the 10-way connector from the power module. • Connect an ohmmeter between cavity No. 1 of the power module 10-way connector and ground.		• Ohmmeter is not showing continuity. • Ohmmeter is showing continuity.	• Replace the power module. • Repair wire of cavity No. 10 for a short circuit to ground.

OHMMETER

TEST 8	STEP A	CHECKING FOR FAULT CODE 43 — SPARK CONTROL CIRCUIT	
PROCEDURE		TEST INDICATION	ACTION REQUIRED
REMINDERS • Diagnostic readout box connected to the engine harness connector. • Turn the ignition switch off. • Disconnect the ignition coil wire at the distributor and place it on the thermostat housing so there is a ¼ inch gap. • Disconnect the white connector from the logic module and connect one end of a jumper wire to cavity No. 6. • Turn the ignition switch on and press and hold the ATM button on the readout box.		• Touch the other end of the jumper to a good ground. Make and break this connection several times while looking at the ignition coil wire. • There is spark at the ignition coil wire as you make and break the connection. • There is no spark at the ignition coil wire as you make and break the connection.	• Replace the logic module. CAUTION: Before replacing the logic module check the terminal in cavity No. 6 of the white connector to make sure it is not crushed causing a poor connection. • Perform STEP B.

JUMPER
 LOGIC MODULE WHITE CONNECTOR

TEST 8	STEP B	CHECKING THE SPARK CONTROL WIRE BETWEEN THE LOGIC AND POWER MODULES FOR AN OPEN CIRCUIT	
PROCEDURE		TEST INDICATION	ACTION REQUIRED
REMINDERS • Logic module white connector disconnected. • Turn the ignition switch off. • Remove the jumper wire from cavity No. 6 of the logic module white connector. • Disconnect the power module 12-way connector. • Connect an ohmmeter between cavity No. 6 of the white and cavity No. 10 of the 12-way connectors.		• Ohmmeter is showing continuity. • Ohmmeter is not showing continuity.	• Replace the power module. CAUTION: Before replacing the power module check the terminal in cavity No. 10 of the 12-way connector to make sure it is not spread apart causing a poor connection. Also make sure the wire of cavity No. 10 is not shorted to ground. • Repair wire for an open circuit.

LOGIC MODULE WHITE CONNECTOR
 OHMMETER
 POWER MODULE 12-WAY CONNECTOR

FUEL INJECTION SYSTEMS
CHRYSLER CORPORATION

1987–88 EFI DRIVEABILITY TEST PROCEDURES

TEST 9	STEP A	CHECKING FUEL CONTROL SYSTEM FOR FAULT CODES	
	PROCEDURE	TEST INDICATION	ACTION REQUIRED
• Connect the diagnostic readout box to the engine harness connector.		88-12-55 No fault codes	Perform TEST NO. 10.
• Disconnect and reconnect the battery connector.		88-12-26-55 Fuel injector driver circuit	Perform TEST NO. 11.
• Crank the engine for 5 seconds and then turn the ignition switch off.		88-12-27-55 Fuel control circuit	Perform TEST NO. 12.
• Put the system in the Diagnostic Mode (Refer to introduction)			

BATTERY CONNECTOR

TEST 10	STEP A	CHECKING FOR PRESSURE IN FUEL SUPPLY SYSTEM	
	PROCEDURE	TEST INDICATION	ACTION REQUIRED
REMINDERS		• Fuel gauge is reading 14½ psi ± 1.	• Perform STEP B.
• Diagnostic readout box connected to engine harness connector.			
• Turn the ignition switch off.			
• Install fuel pressure gauge in fuel supply hose at the throttle body.			
CAUTION: Fuel may be under high pressure in the supply hose. Refer to the service manual for instructions on how to bleed down the system.		• Fuel gauge is reading 0.	• Perform STEP C.
• Turn ignition switch to the run position.			
• Press the ATM button on the readout box.			

RETURN LINE / SUPPLY LINE

FUEL PRESSURE SUPPLY LINE

TEST 10	STEP B	CHECKING THE THROTTLE POSITION SENSOR	
	PROCEDURE	TEST INDICATION	ACTION REQUIRED
REMINDERS		• Display on readout box is reading between ½ and 1½ volts	• Replace the injector
• Diagnostic readout box connected to the engine harness connector			
• Put the system into the Sensor Test Mode 05. (Refer to introduction)			
NOTE: Don't forget to divide display reading by 10 for actual reading		• Display on the readout box reads more than 1½ volts.	• Replace the throttle position sensor

DIAGNOSTIC READOUT BOX

TEST 10	STEP C	CHECKING INTANK FUEL PUMP	
	PROCEDURE	TEST INDICATION	ACTION REQUIRED
REMINDERS		• The fuel pump is running.	• Check fuel supply line and hoses between fuel tank and throttle body for restrictions.
• Ignition key in the run position.			• Check for a plugged fuel filter
• Diagnostic readout box connected to engine harness connector			• Check for a plugged intank fuel filter
• Press ATM button readout box.			
• Listen for intake fuel pump noise at rear of car.		• The fuel pump is not running.	• Perform STEP D.

DIAGNOSTIC READOUT BOX

TEST 10	STEP D	CHECKING VOLTAGE SUPPLY TO INTANK PUMP	
	PROCEDURE	TEST INDICATION	ACTION REQUIRED
REMINDERS		• Voltmeter is reading within one volt of battery voltage.	• Perform STEP E.
• Ignition key in the run position.			
• Diagnostic readout box connected to the engine harness connector.			
• Raise car on hoist.			
• Disconnect the intank fuel pump connector.			
• Connect voltmeter to dark green with black tracer wire of connector and ground.	VOLTMETER	• Voltmeter is reading 0.	• Repair wire for open circuit to wiring harness splice.
• Press ATM button on readout box.			

G Y / DG/BK

IN TANK FUEL PUMP CONNECTOR

TEST 10	STEP E	CHECKING INTANK PUMP GROUND CIRCUIT	
	PROCEDURE	TEST INDICATION	ACTION REQUIRED
REMINDERS		• Ohmmeter is showing continuity.	• Replace the intank fuel pump.
• Car raised on hoist.			
• Intank fuel pump connector disconnected			
• Connect ohmmeter between gray wire of fuel pump connector and ground.	OHMMETER	• Ohmmeter is not showing continuity.	• Repair wire for open circuit to body ground connection.

G Y / DG/BK

IN TANK FUEL PUMP CONNECTOR

TEST 11	STEP A	CHECKING FOR FAULT CODE 26 — FUEL INJECTOR DRIVER CIRCUIT	
	PROCEDURE	TEST INDICATION	ACTION REQUIRED
REMINDERS		• Voltmeter reading is pulsating between 0 and 1 volt	• Replace the fuel injector
• Diagnostic readout box connected to engine harness connector		NOTE: If voltmeter is showing a negative voltage, reverse its leads at the injector connector and repeat the test	
• System in the Diagnostic Test Mode			
• Disconnect the fuel injector connector.			
• Connect an analog voltmeter between the terminals of the fuel injector connector			
• Select the lowest voltage scale available on your voltmeter.	ANALOG VOLTMETER	• Voltmeter reading is not pulsating.	• Perform STEP B.
• Put the system in the ATM Test Mode - Code 02.	TN / WT		

FUEL INJECTOR CONNECTOR

TEST 11	STEP B	CHECKING FUEL INJECTOR CONTROL WIRE TO THE POWER MODULE FOR AN OPEN CIRCUIT	
	PROCEDURE	TEST INDICATION	ACTION REQUIRED
REMINDERS		• Ohmmeter is showing continuity	• Perform STEP C.
• Injector connector disconnected	TN / WT FUEL INJECTOR CONNECTOR		
• Turn ignition switch off.			
• Disconnect the power module 10-way connector.	OHMMETER		
• Connect ohmmeter between cavity No. 7 of 10-way connector and white wire of injector connector		• Ohmmeter is not showing continuity	• Repair wire of cavity No. 7 for open circuit to injector

POWER MODULE 10-WAY CONNECTOR

1987–88 EFI DRIVEABILITY TEST PROCEDURES

TEST 11	STEP C	CHECKING FUEL INJECTOR CONTROL WIRE TO THE POWER MODULE FOR AN OPEN CIRCUIT

PROCEDURE		TEST INDICATION	ACTION REQUIRED
REMINDERS • Power module 10-way connector disconnected. • Injector connector disconnected. • Connect ohmmeter between cavity No. 5 of 10-way connector and tan wire of injector connector.		• Ohmmeter is showing continuity.	• Replace the power module. **CAUTION:** Before replacing the power module check the terminals in cavities 5 and 7 of the 10-way connector to make sure they are not spread apart causing a poor connection.
		• Ohmmeter is not showing continuity.	• Repair wire of cavity No. 5 for open circuit to injector.

TEST 12	STEP A	CHECKING FOR FAULT CODE 27 — FUEL CONTROL CIRCUIT

PROCEDURE		TEST INDICATION	ACTION REQUIRED
REMINDERS • Diagnostic readout box connected to the engine harness connector. • Turn the ignition switch off. • Disconnect the injector connector. • Connect a voltmeter between the terminals of the injector connector. • Disconnect the logic module white connector. • Connect a jumper wire between cavity No. 2 of the white connector and ground. • Turn the ignition switch to the run position.	• Press the ATM button on the readout box.	• Voltmeter reads voltage. **NOTE:** The amount of voltage is not important. Just make sure there is some. Also if voltmeter is showing a negative voltage, reverse its leads at the injector connector and repeat the test.	• Replace the logic module. **CAUTION:** Before replacing the logic module check the terminal in cavity No. 2 of the white connector to make sure it is not crushed causing a poor connection.
		• Voltmeter reads 0.	• Perform STEP B.

TEST 12	STEP B	CHECKING THE FUEL CONTROL WIRE BETWEEN THE LOGIC AND POWER MODULE FOR AN OPEN CIRCUIT

PROCEDURE		TEST INDICATION	ACTION REQUIRED
REMINDERS • Logic module white connector disconnected. • Turn the ignition switch off. • Remove the jumper wire from cavity No. 2 of the white connector. • Disconnect the power module 12-way connector. • Connect an ohmmeter between cavity No. 2 of the white and cavity No. 1 of the 12-way connectors.		• Ohmmeter is showing continuity.	• Perform STEP C.
		• Ohmmeter is not showing continuity.	• Repair wire for an open circuit.

TEST 12	STEP C	CHECKING THE FUEL CONTROL WIRE BETWEEN THE LOGIC AND POWER MODULE FOR A SHORT TO GROUND

PROCEDURE		TEST INDICATION	ACTION REQUIRED
REMINDERS • Logic module white connector disconnected. • Turn the ignition switch off. • Disconnect the power module 12-way connector. • Connect an ohmmeter between cavity No. 1 of the 12-way connector and ground.		• Ohmmeter is not showing continuity.	• Replace the power module. **CAUTION:** Before replacing the power module check the terminal in cavity No. 1 of the 12-way connector to make sure it is not spread apart causing a poor connection.
		• Ohmmeter is showing continuity.	• Repair wire for short to ground.

TEST 13	STEP A	CHECKING FOR A FLOODING INJECTOR

PROCEDURE		TEST INDICATION	ACTION REQUIRED
REMINDERS • Throttle body air intake hose removed. • Remove air cleaner assembly. • Disconnect injector electrical connector. • Have someone crank engine while you look for a fuel spray from injector.		• There is fuel spraying from injector.	• Replace the injector. **NOTE:** Before replacing the injector make sure the lower O ring is not split or rolled over.
		• There is no fuel spraying from injector.	• Perform STEP B.

TEST 13	STEP B	CHECKING THE FUEL CONTROL CIRCUIT TO THE POWER MODULE

PROCEDURE		TEST INDICATION	ACTION REQUIRED
REMINDERS • Air cleaner removed. • Diagnostic readout box connected to the wiring harness connector. • Turn the ignition switch off. • Disconnect the logic module white connector. • Reconnect the injector connector. • Turn the ignition switch to the run position. • Press the ATM button		• There is fuel spraying from injector.	• Replace the power module.
		• There is no fuel spraying from injector.	• Replace the logic module. **NOTE:** Before replacing the logic module check for excessive fuel pressure.

TEST 14	STEP A	CHECKING SYSTEM FOR FAULT CODES

PROCEDURE		TEST INDICATION	ACTION REQUIRED
• Connect diagnostic readout box to engine harness connector. • Disconnect and reconnect the battery connector. • Crank the engine for 7 seconds and then turn the ignition switch to the run position for 5 seconds before turning to off. • Put the system in the Diagnostic Mode. (Refer to introduction) • Record all codes.		No Code 88 or 00 System power circuits	Perform TEST NO. 15.
		88-11-12-55 Distributor pickup circuit	Perform TEST NO. 16.
		88-12-42-55 88-12-26-42-55 Auto shutdown relay pull in coil circuit	Perform TEST NO. 17.
		88-11-12-22-23-24-55 Sensor ground circuit	Repair wire in cavity No. 25 of the logic module white connector for an open circuit
		88-12-26-55 Auto shutdown relay output circuit	Replace Power Module
		88-12-55 No fault codes	Repair wire in cavity No. 6 of the power module 10-way connector for an open circuit to ignition coil and fuel pump

TEST 15	STEP A	CHECKING FOR NO CODE 88 - SYSTEM POWER CIRCUIT FOR THE 5 VOLT SUPPLY

PROCEDURE		TEST INDICATION	ACTION REQUIRED
• Turn ignition switch off. • Connect a digital voltmeter to cavity No. 1 of the logic module white connector and ground. • Turn the ignition switch to the run position.		• Voltmeter is reading at least 4½ volts.	• Perform STEP B.
		• Voltmeter reads 0.	• Perform STEP E.

1987–88 EFI DRIVEABILITY TEST PROCEDURES

TEST 15 | STEP B | CHECKING THE LOGIC MODULE GROUND CIRCUIT

PROCEDURE	TEST INDICATION	ACTION REQUIRED
• Turn the ignition switch off. • Disconnect the black connector from the logic module. • Connect a digital ohmmeter between cavity No. 7 or 8 or the logic module black connector and ground.	• Ohmmeter is showing continuity with less than ½ ohm of resistance.	• **Perform STEP C.**
	• Ohmmeter is not showing continuity.	• Repair wires of cavity 7 and 8 for an open circuit to the wiring harness splice. • Replace the logic module.
	• Ohmmeter is showing more than ½ ohm of resistance at either cavity of the logic module.	• Repair circuit for high resistance.

LOGIC MODULE BLACK CONNECTOR

TEST 15 | STEP C | CHECKING THE BATTERY VOLTAGE SUPPLY TO THE POWER MODULE

PROCEDURE	TEST INDICATION	ACTION REQUIRED
• Turn the ignition switch off. • Disconnect the 10-way connector from the power module. • Connect a voltmeter to cavity No. 4 of the 10-way connector and ground.	• Voltmeter is reading within one volt of battery voltage.	• **Perform STEP D.**
	• Voltmeter reads 0.	• Repair the wire in cavity No. 4 for an open circuit to the battery. **NOTE:** This wire has a fusable link in it. If it is blown, circuit must be repaired for a short to ground.

POWER MODULE 10-WAY CONNECTOR

TEST 15 | STEP D | CHECKING THE AUTO SHUTDOWN RELAY OUTPUT CIRCUIT FOR A SHORT CIRCUIT TO GROUND

PROCEDURE	TEST INDICATION	ACTION REQUIRED
REMINDERS • Power module 10-way connector disconnected. • Disconnect the wire from the ignition coil positive (+) terminal. • Disconnect the intank fuel pump connector. • Connect an ohmmeter between cavity No. 6 of the power module 10-way connector and ground.	• Ohmmeter is not showing continuity.	• Replace the power module. **CAUTION:** Before replacing the power module check the terminal in cavity No. 4 of the 10-way connector to make sure it is not spread apart causing a poor connection.
	• Ohmmeter is showing continuity.	• Repair wire of cavity No. 6 for a short circuit to ground. • Replace power module.

POWER MODULE 10-WAY CONNECTOR

TEST 15 | STEP E | CHECKING THE SYSTEM POWER CIRCUIT FOR THE 8 VOLT SUPPLY TO THE LOGIC MODULE

PROCEDURE	TEST INDICATION	ACTION REQUIRED
REMINDERS • Ignition switch in the run position. • Connect a digital voltmeter to cavity No. 23 of the logic module white connector and ground.	• Voltmeter is reading at least 7 volts.	• **Perform STEP F.**
	• Voltmeter reads 0.	• Voltage not okay. **Perform STEP G.**

LOGIC MODULE WHITE CONNECTOR

TEST 15 | STEP F | CHECKING FOR NO 5 VOLTS IN SYSTEM POWER CIRCUIT CAUSED BY A SHORTED M.A.P. SENSOR

PROCEDURE	TEST INDICATION	ACTION REQUIRED
• Turn the ignition switch off. • Disconnect M.A.P. sensor connector. • Connect a voltmeter to cavity No. 1 of logic module black connector and ground. • Turn ignition switch to the run position.	• Voltmeter is reading at least 4½ volts.	• Replace the M.A.P. sensor.
	• Voltmeter reads 0.	• Replace the logic module. **NOTE:** Before replacing the logic module check the wire of cavity No. 1 of the logic module black connector for a short to ground.

LOGIC MODULE BLACK CONNECTOR

TEST 15 | STEP G | CHECKING FOR NO 8 VOLTS IN SYSTEM POWER CIRCUIT CAUSED BY A SHORTED DISTRIBUTOR PICKUP

PROCEDURE	TEST INDICATION	ACTION REQUIRED
REMINDERS • Voltmeter connected to cavity No. 23 of logic module white connector and ground. • Ignition switch in the run position. • Disconnect the distributor connector.	• Voltmeter is reading at least 7 volts.	• Replace distributor pickup coil.
	• Voltmeter reads 0.	• **Perform STEP H.**

LOGIC MODULE WHITE CONNECTOR

TEST 15 | STEP H | CHECKING THE SYSTEM POWER CIRCUIT FOR THE 8 VOLT OUTPUT FROM THE POWER MODULE

PROCEDURE	TEST INDICATION	ACTION REQUIRED
• Turn the ignition switch off. • Disconnect the 12-way connector from the power module. • Connect a voltmeter to PIN No. 12 of the power module and ground. • Turn the ignition switch to the run position.	• Voltmeter is reading at least 7 volts.	• Repair the wire in cavity No. 12 of the power module 12-way connector for an open or short circuit to the logic module. **NOTE:** Check the terminal in cavity No. 12 to make sure it is not spread apart causing a poor connection.
	• Voltmeter reads 0.	• **Perform STEP I.**

POWER MODULE 12-WAY PIN CONNECTOR

TEST 15 | STEP I | CHECKING FOR IGNITION SWITCH VOLTAGE SUPPLY TO THE POWER MODULE

PROCEDURE	TEST INDICATION	ACTION REQUIRED
• Turn the ignition switch off. • Disconnect the 10-way connector from the power module. • Connect the positive lead of a voltmeter to cavity No. 2 of the 10-way connector. • Connect the negative lead of the voltmeter to either cavity No. 9 or 10 of the 10-way connector. • Turn the ignition switch to the run position.	• Voltmeter is reading within one volt of battery voltage.	• Replace the power module. **CAUTION:** Before replacing the power module, check the terminals in cavities 2, 9, and 10 of the 10-way connector to make sure they are not spread apart causing a poor connection. • Move voltmeter negative lead to a good engine ground and if — a or b.
	• Voltmeter reads 0.	a. Voltmeter now reads within one volt of battery voltage, repair power module ground for an open circuit. b. Voltmeter still reads 0 volts repair wire in cavity No. 2 for an open circuit to the ignition switch.

POWER MODULE 10-WAY CONNECTOR

1987–88 EFI DRIVEABILITY TEST PROCEDURES

TEST 16	STEP A	CHECKING FOR FAULT CODE 11 — DISTRIBUTOR PICKUP CIRCUIT	
PROCEDURE		**TEST INDICATION**	**ACTION REQUIRED**

PROCEDURE	TEST INDICATION	ACTION REQUIRED
• Turn ignition switch off. • Disconnect distributor pick up coil connector. • Remove coil wire from distributor and place it (¼ inch) near a good engine ground. • Turn ignition switch to the run position. • Connect a jumper wire to the pickup coil harness connector cavity No. 2 and 3. • Make and break this connection several times while looking at coil wire.	• There is spark at the coil wire	• Perform STEP B.
	• There is no spark at the coil wire.	• Perform STEP C.

DISTRIBUTOR PICKUP COIL CONNECTOR

TEST 16	STEP B	CHECKING FOR THE 8 VOLT POWER SUPPLY TO THE DISTRIBUTOR PICKUP FROM THE POWER MODULE	
PROCEDURE		**TEST INDICATION**	**ACTION REQUIRED**

PROCEDURE	TEST INDICATION	ACTION REQUIRED
REMINDERS • Distributor pick up coil connector disconnected. • Ignition switch in the run position. • Connect a voltmeter to cavity No. 1 of the pickup coil harness connector and ground.	• Voltmeter is reading at least 7 volts	• Replace the distributor pick up coil. **CAUTION:** Before replacing the pick up check the terminals in the distributor harness connector to make sure they are not spread apart causing a poor connection. Also make sure distributor rotor turns while cranking the engine.
	• Voltmeter reads 0.	• Repair wire of cavity No. 1 for open circuit to wiring harness splice.

DISTRIBUTOR PICKUP COIL CONNECTOR

TEST 16	STEP C	CHECKING FOR THE PICKUP COIL SIGNAL VOLTAGE FROM THE LOGIC MODULE	
PROCEDURE		**TEST INDICATION**	**ACTION REQUIRED**

PROCEDURE	TEST INDICATION	ACTION REQUIRED
REMINDERS • Distributor pick up coil connector disconnected. • Ignition switch in the run position. • Connect the positive lead of the voltmeter to cavity No. 3 of the pickup coil harness connector. • Connect the negative lead of the voltmeter to cavity No. 2 of the pickup coil harness connector.	• Voltmeter is reading at least 4 volts	• Replace the logic module
	• Voltmeter reads 0.	• Perform STEP D.

DISTRIBUTOR PICKUP COIL CONNECTOR

TEST 16	STEP D	CHECKING THE DISTRIBUTOR PICKUP HARNESS GROUND CIRCUIT	
PROCEDURE		**TEST INDICATION**	**ACTION REQUIRED**

PROCEDURE	TEST INDICATION	ACTION REQUIRED
REMINDERS • Distributor pick up coil connector disconnected. • Ignition switch in the run position. • Positive lead of voltmeter connected to cavity No. 3 of the pickup coil harness connector • Connect the negative lead of the voltmeter to a good engine ground.	• Voltmeter is reading at least 4 volts.	• Repair wire in cavity No. 2 of the distributor harness connector for an open circuit to the wiring harness splice
	• Voltmeter reads 0	• Perform STEP E.

DISTRIBUTOR PICKUP COIL CONNECTOR

TEST 16	STEP E	CHECKING FOR THE PICKUP COIL SIGNAL VOLTAGE AT THE LOGIC MODULE	
PROCEDURE		**TEST INDICATION**	**ACTION REQUIRED**

PROCEDURE	TEST INDICATION	ACTION REQUIRED
REMINDERS • Ignition switch in the run position. • Connect a voltmeter to cavity No. 10 of the logic module white connector and ground.	• Voltmeter is reading at least 4 volts	• Repair wire in cavity No. 10 for an open circuit to distributor wiring harness connector
	• Voltmeter reads 0	• Replace the logic module. **CAUTION:** Before replacing the logic module, check the terminal in cavity No. 10 of the white connector to make sure it is not crushed causing a poor connection.

LOGIC MODULE WHITE CONNECTOR

TEST 17	STEP A	CHECKING FOR FAULT CODE 42 OR 26 AND 42 — AUTO SHUTDOWN RELAY PULL IN COIL CIRCUIT	
PROCEDURE		**TEST INDICATION**	**ACTION REQUIRED**

PROCEDURE	TEST INDICATION	ACTION REQUIRED
• Turn the ignition switch off. • Disconnect the white connector from the logic module. • Connect a voltmeter to cavity No. 17 of the white connector and ground. • Turn the ignition switch to the run position.	• Voltmeter is reading within one volt of battery voltage	• Replace the logic module. **CAUTION:** Before replacing the logic module check the terminal in cavity No. 17 of the white connector to make sure it is not crushed causing a poor connection.
	• Voltmeter reads 0 volts	• Perform STEP B.

LOGIC MODULE WHITE CONNECTOR

TEST 1	STEP A	CHECKING SYSTEM FOR FAULT CODES		
PROCEDURE		**TEST INDICATION**	**CIRCUIT**	**ACTION REQUIRED**

PROCEDURE	TEST INDICATION	CIRCUIT	ACTION REQUIRED
• Connect diagnostic readout box to engine harness connector	88-12-55	No fault codes	Perform STEP B
	88-12-13-55 88-12-14-55 88-12-13-14-55	M.A.P. sensor	Perform TEST No. 2
• Turn ignition switch on-off-on-off-on within 5 seconds	88-12-15-55	Speed sensor	Perform TEST No. 3
	88-12-17-55	Engine running too cool	Check engine cooling system for a possible bad thermostat.
• **RECORD ALL CODES**	88-12-21-55	Oxygen sensor	Perform TEST No. 4
NOTE: If fault codes 15-17-21-51 or 52 appear at this time proceed to test indication	88-12-22-55 88-12-17-22-55	Engine coolant sensor	Perform TEST No. 5
	88-12-23-55	Throttle body temperature sensor	Perform TEST No. 6
• Turn ignition switch off and disconnect and reconnect the battery connector	88-12-24-55	Throttle position sensor	Perform TEST No. 7
	88-12-25-55	Idle motor	Perform TEST No. 8
	88-12-31-55	Purge solenoid	Perform TEST No. 9
• Start engine	88-12-33-55	A/C cut off relay	Perform TEST No. 10
CAUTION: Do not depress accelerator to start engine.	88-12-35-55	Radiator fan relay	Perform TEST No. 11
	88-12-37-55 (2.5L Auto Trans)	Transmission lock-up solenoid circuit	Perform TEST No. 12
• Let engine run for 5 minutes	88-12-51-55	Oxygen feedback system locked lean	Perform TEST No. 16
	88-12-52-55	Oxygen feedback system locked rich	
• Raise engine speed to 2,000 rpm for 10 seconds and then return to idle	88-12-53-55		Replace logic module
	No code 88	Battery voltage for logic module standby memory	Repair battery feed wire to cavity No. 2 of the logic module black connector for an open circuit.
• Cycle transmission gear selector (auto trans only)	**NOTE:** Make sure your diagnostic readout box is operational and that there is not an open circuit in the wires between th logic module and diagnostic connector		
• If so equipped press A/C button on and off.			
• Turn engine off.			
• Turn ignition switch on-off-on-off-on within 5 seconds.			
• **RECORD ALL CODES**			
If the same code appears before and after the engine is started, the problem still exists. Proceed to test indications.			
If a code does not reappear after the engine is started the problem no longer exists. **Perform STEP D.**			

DIAGNOSTIC READOUT BOX

1987–88 EFI DRIVEABILITY TEST PROCEDURES

TEST 17	STEP B	CHECKING THE AUTO SHUTDOWN RELAY PULL IN COIL CIRCUIT AT THE POWER MODULE		
PROCEDURE			TEST INDICATION	ACTION REQUIRED
• Turn the ignition switch off. • Disconnect the 12-way connector from the power module. • Turn the ignition switch to the run position. • Connect a voltmeter to PIN No. 5 of the power module and ground			• Voltmeter is reading within one volt of battery voltage.	• Voltage okay, repair wire in cavity No. 5 of the power module 12-way connector for an open or shorted circuit. CAUTION: Check the terminal in cavity No. 12 of the 12-way to make sure it is not spread apart causing a poor connection.
			• Voltmeter reads between 0 and 1 volt.	• 0-1 volts replace the power module.

POWER MODULE 12-WAY PIN CONNECTOR

TEST 1	STEP C	CHECKING SHIFT INDICATOR LAMP		
PROCEDURE			TEST INDICATION	ACTION REQUIRED
• Turn the ignition switch off. • Disconnect the logic module white connector. • Turn the ignition switch to the run position. • Ground cavity No. 15 of the logic module white connector with a jumper wire.			• Shift indicator lamp is on.	• Replace the logic module. CAUTION: Before replacing the logic module check the terminal in cavity No. 15 of the white connector to make sure it is not crushed causing a poor connection.
			• Shift indicator lamp is off.	• Repair wire of cavity No. 15 for an open circuit, check for a burned out bulb, or check for ignition feed voltage to lamp.

JUMPER

LOGIC MODULE WHITE CONNECTOR

TEST 1	STEP D	CHECKING SWITCH INPUTS TO THE LOGIC MODULE		
PROCEDURE			TEST INDICATION	ACTION REQUIRED
REMINDERS • Diagnostic readout box connected to the engine harness connector. • Put the system into the Switch Test Mode. (Refer to introduction) • Check switch inputs as follows: a) press down on brake pedal b) with auto trans, move gear selector from park to reverse c) with A/C, move blower switch to an on position and then press the A/C button			• Display on the readout box changes as each switch is activated. NOTE: It is not important what display changes to. Just make sure it changes.	• Perform STEP I.
			• Display on the readout box does not change when one or more of the switches are activated.	• Perform STEPS as follows. Brake Switch Without Speed Control STEP E. With Speed Control STEP F. Park/Neutral Switch STEP G. A/C Button STEP H.

DIAGNOSTIC READOUT BOX

TEST 1	STEP B	CHECKING THE OUTPUT CIRCUITS OF THE LOGIC MODULE CONTROLLED COMPONENTS		
PROCEDURE			TEST INDICATION	ACTION REQUIRED
REMINDERS • Diagnostic readout box connected to the engine harness connector. • Put the system into the ATM Test Mode — Code 04. (Refer to the introduction)			Test Code 04 • The radiator fan should be turning on and off every two seconds.	• Radiator fan is turning on and off press and hold the ATM button as follows. Without A/C until Test Code 07 appears. With A/C until Test Code 05 appears.
				• If fan does not turn on and off; is the relay clicking? If it is, repair the circuit to the radiator fan motor as required. • If the relay does not click, replace it.
			Test Code 05 • You should hear the A/C cutout relay clicking every two seconds.	• A/C relay clicking, press and hold the ATM button until test code 07 appears. • If the A/C relay is not clicking replace it.
			Test Code 07 • You should hear the canister purge solenoid clicking.	• Canister purge solenoid clicking. • With manual trans or 2.5L auto trans, press and hold ATM button until test code 10 appears. • With 2.2L auto trans, Perform STEP D. • If the canister purge solenoid is not clicking replace it.
			TEST CODE 10 Manual Trans • You should see the shift indicator lamp on the instrument panel turning on and off. TEST CODE 10 2.5L Auto Trans • You should hear the transmission lockup solenoid clicking.	• If the shift indicator lamp is turning on and off Perform STEP D. • If the shift indicator lamp is not turning on and off Perform STEP C. • Transmission lockup solenoid clicking Perform STEP D. • If the transmission lockup solenoid is not clicking replace it

DIAGNOSTIC READOUT BOX

TEST 1	STEP E	CHECKING BRAKE SWITCH INPUT CIRCUIT TO THE LOGIC MODULE — WITHOUT SPEED CONTROL		
PROCEDURE			TEST INDICATION	ACTION REQUIRED
• Turn ignition switch off. • Disconnect black connector from logic module. • Connect voltmeter to cavity No. 13 of black connector and ground. • Turn ignition switch to the run position. • Press brake pedal down.			• Voltmeter is reading within one volt of battery voltage.	• Replace logic module CAUTION: Before replacing the logic module check terminal in cavity No. 13 of the black connector to make sure it is not crushed causing a poor connection.
			• Voltmeter reads 0.	• Check wire of cavity No. 13 for an open circuit to brake switch. • Check for a bad brake switch. • Check for an open voltage supply circuit to the brake switch.

LOGIC MODULE BLACK CONNECTOR

TEST 1	STEP F	CHECKING BRAKE SWITCH INPUT CIRCUIT TO THE LOGIC MODULE — WITH SPEED CONTROL		
PROCEDURE			TEST INDICATION	ACTION REQUIRED
• Turn the ignition switch off. • Connect voltmeter to cavity No. 13 of the logic module black connector and ground. • Turn the ignition switch to the run position.			• Voltmeter is reading greater than 5 volts.	• Check wire of cavity No. 13 for an open circuit to the brake switch. • Check for a bad brake switch. • Check for an open circuit to the tail lamps.
				• Replace the logic module
			• Voltmeter reads 0 volts.	CAUTION: Before replacing the logic module check terminal in cavity No. 13 of the black connector to make sure it is not crushed causing a poor connection.

LOGIC MODULE BLACK CONNECTOR

1987–88 EFI DRIVEABILITY TEST PROCEDURES

TEST 1	STEP G	CHECKING PARK/NEUTRAL SWITCH INPUT CIRCUIT TO THE LOGIC MODULE	
PROCEDURE		TEST INDICATION	ACTION REQUIRED
• Turn ignition switch off. • Disconnect black connector from logic module. • Connect an ohmmeter to cavity No. 12 of black connector and ground. • Put gear selector in park, reverse neutral, and drive and observe ohmmeter in each position.		• Ohmmeter shows continuity in all positions of the gear selector.	• Check wire of cavity No. 12 for a short circuit to ground. • Check for a bad safety neutral switch.
		• Ohmmeter shows no continuity in all positions of the gear selector.	• Repair wire of cavity No. 12 for an open circuit to the safety neutral switch.
		• Ohmmeter reads as follows. **Park** - Continuity **Reverse** - No continuity **Neutral** - Continuity **Drive** - No continuity NOTE: Disregard any resistance readings. Just make sure there is continuity.	• Replace the logic module CAUTION: Before replacing the logic module check the terminal in cavity No. 12 of the black connector to make sure it is not crushed causing a poor connection.

LOGIC MODULE
BLACK CONNECTOR

TEST 1	STEP H	CHECKING A/C PUSH BUTTON SWITCH INPUT CIRCUIT TO THE LOGIC MODULE	
PROCEDURE		TEST INDICATION	ACTION REQUIRED
• Turn ignition switch off. • Connect voltmeter to cavity No. 11 of the logic module black connector and ground. • Start the engine. • Move blower switch to an on position and then press the A/C button. • Wait for the A/C clutch to engage.		• Voltmeter is reading between 7 and 9 volt when the A/C clutch is engaged.	• Repair wire of cavity No. 11 for an open circuit to the wiring harness splice.
		• Voltmeter is reading between 0 and 1 volt when the A/C clutch is engaged.	• Replace the logic module CAUTION: Before replacing the logic module check cavity No. 11 of the black connector to make sure it is not crushed causing a poor connection.

LOGIC MODULE
BLACK CONNECTOR

TEST 1	STEP I	CHECKING AUTOMATIC IDLE SPEED MOTOR OPERATION	
PROCEDURE		TEST INDICATION	ACTION REQUIRED
• Connect the diagnostic readout box to the engine harness connector. NOTE: Make sure read/hold switch is in the **read** position. • Connect a tachometer to the engine. • Start the engine. • Disconnect and reconnect the coolant sensor. • Move the read/hold switch to the **hold** position.		• Engine speed increases to approximately 1500 rpm.	• Perform STEP N.
		• Engine speed does not increase	• Perform STEP J.

DIAGNOSTIC
READOUT BOX

TEST 1	STEP J	CHECKING AUTOMATIC IDLE SPEED MOTOR SIGNAL FROM THE LOGIC MODULE	
PROCEDURE		TEST INDICATION	ACTION REQUIRED
REMINDERS • Diagnostic readout box connected to the engine harness connector • Turn the engine off. • Disconnect the automatic idle speed motor connector. • Connect a digital voltmeter between terminals 1 and 4 of the idle speed motor connector • Set the digital voltmeter to the **AC voltage** position. • Put the system into ATM Test Mode 03. (Refer to introduction.)		• Voltmeter is pulsating between 0 and 6 volts every two seconds.	• Perform STEP K.
		• Voltmeter does not pulsate	• Perform STEP L.

DIGITAL VOLTMETER
SET TO AC POSITION
1 2 3 4

TEST 1	STEP K	CHECKING AUTOMATIC IDLE SPEED MOTOR SIGNAL FROM THE LOGIC MODULE	
PROCEDURE		TEST INDICATION	ACTION REQUIRED
REMINDERS • Diagnostic readout box connected to the engine harness connector. • Automatic idle speed motor disconnected. • Digital voltmeter set to the AC voltage position. • System in ATM test mode 03. • Connect voltmeter between terminals 2 and 3 of the idle speed motor connector.		• Voltmeter is pulsating between 0 and 6 volts every two seconds	• Replace the automatic idle speed motor CAUTION: Before replacing the idle motor check terminals of the connector to make sure they are not crushed causing a poor connection.
		• Voltmeter does not pulsate.	• Perform STEP M.

DIGITAL VOLTMETER
SET TO A.C. POSITION
1 2 3 4

TEST 1	STEP L	CHECKING AUTOMATIC IDLE SPEED MOTOR SIGNAL AT THE LOGIC MODULE	
PROCEDURE		TEST INDICATION	ACTION REQUIRED
REMINDERS • Diagnostic readout box connected to the engine harness connector • Digital voltmeter set to the AC voltage position. • System in ATM test mode 03. • Connect voltmeter between cavities 18 and 20 of the logic module white connector		• Voltmeter is pulsating between 0 and 6 volts.	• Repair wire of cavity 18 or 20 for an open circuit to the automatic idle speed motor connector
		• Voltmeter does not pulsate.	• Replace the logic module. CAUTION: Before replacing the logic module check the terminals in cavities 18 and 20 of the logic module white connector to make sure they are not crushed causing a poor connection.

LOGIC MODULE
WHITE CONNECTOR

DIGITAL VOLTMETER
SET TO A.C. POSITION

TEST 1	STEP M	CHECKING AUTOMATIC IDLE SPEED MOTOR SIGNAL AT THE LOGIC MODULE	
PROCEDURE		TEST INDICATION	ACTION REQUIRED
REMINDERS • Diagnostic readout box connected to the engine harness connector • Digital voltmeter set to the AC voltage position • System in ATM test mode 03 • Connect voltmeter between cavities 16 and 22 of the logic module white connector		• Voltmeter is pulsating between 0 and 6 volts	• Repair wire of cavity 16 or 22 for an open circuit to the automatic idle speed motor
		• Voltmeter does not pulsate.	• Replace the logic module. CAUTION: Before replacing the logic module check the terminals in cavities 16 and 22 of the white logic module connector to make sure they are not crushed causing a poor connection.

DIGITAL VOLTMETER
SET TO A.C. POSITION

LOGIC MODULE
WHITE CONNECTOR

TEST 1	STEP N	CHECKING THE COMPUTER GROUND CIRCUITS	
PROCEDURE		TEST INDICATION	ACTION REQUIRED
• Turn the ignition switch off. • Disconnect the logic module connectors. • Connect one lead of a digital ohmmeter to a good vehicle ground. • Connect the other lead of ohmmeter as follows: White connector — cavity No. 24 Black connector — cavities No. 7 and 8		• Ohmmeter is showing continuity with less than ½ ohm of resistance at all three cavities of the logic module connectors.	• Perform TESTS as follows: If a cold problem **TEST NO. 13**. If a warm problem **TEST NO. 16**.
		• Ohmmeter is not showing continuity at one or more cavities of the logic module connectors	• Repair the wire for an open circuit to the wiring harness connector
		• Ohmmeter is showing more than ½ ohm of resistance at one or more cavities of the logic module connectors.	• Repair circuit for high resistance

LOGIC MODULE
WHITE CONNECTOR

OHMMETER

LOGIC MODULE
BLACK CONNECTOR

1987–88 EFI DRIVEABILITY TEST PROCEDURES

TEST 1	STEP 0	CHECKING FOR INTERMITTENT FAILURES CAUSED BY WIRING AND/OR CONNECTORS

The majority of intermittent failures are caused by wiring and connections. The only way to find them is to try and duplicate the problem. Since the logic module can remember where they are, the ATM and Sensor Test Modes can be used in an attempt to locate them.

• If the following fault codes do not reappear use the **ATM Test Mode** as indicated.

Fault Code	ATM Test Mode
25	03
26	02
27	02
31	07
33	05
35	04
37	08
42	06
43	01

Once in the correct test mode, wiggle all the connectors and wires in the circuit. When the bad connection or wire is located the ATM test will be interrupted.

• If the following fault codes do not reappear use the **Sensor Test Mode** as indicated.

Fault Code	Sensor Test Mode
14**	08
22	04
23	03
24	05

** When checking the M.A.P. sensor circuit, (fault code 14) apply 10 inches of vacuum to the M.A.P. sensor before testing.

Once in the correct test mode, wiggle all the connectors and wires in the circuit. When the bad connection or wire is located the display on the readout box will change.

TEST 2	STEP A	CHECKING FOR FAULT CODES 13 AND/OR 14 — M.A.P. SENSOR CIRCUIT

PROCEDURE	TEST INDICATION	ACTION REQUIRED
• Turn ignition switch off. • Tee a vacuum gauge into the vacuum line at the M.A.P. sensor. • Start the engine and look at the vacuum gauge with the engine idling. • Look at the vacuum gauge while snapping the throttle open and close.	• Vacuum gauge is reading manifold vacuum with the engine idling. • Vacuum gauge reading immediately drops to 0 when the throttle is snapped open and closed.	• Perform STEP B.
	• Vacuum gauge reads 0 at idle.	• Repair vacuum line to throttle body.
VACUUM GAUGE	• Vacuum gauge reading slowly drops to 0 when the throttle is snapped open and closed.	• Repair restriction in vacuum supply line to M.A.P. sensor.

TEST 2	STEP B	CHECKING THE M.A.P. SENSOR CIRCUIT IN THE LOGIC MODULE

PROCEDURE	TEST INDICATION	ACTION REQUIRED
REMINDERS • Diagnostic readout box connected to the engine harness connector. • Disconnect the connector from the M.A.P. sensor. • Put the system in **Sensor Test Mode 08**. (Refer to introduction) NOTE: Don't forget to divide the reading on the display by 10.	• Display on the readout box is reading 5 volts.	• Perform STEP C.
DISCONNECT	• Display on the readout box is reading 0 volts.	• Replace the logic module. NOTE: Before replacing the logic module make sure the wire of cavity No. 19 of the logic module black connector is not shorted to ground.

TEST 2	STEP C	CHECKING THE M.A.P. SENSOR SIGNAL CIRCUIT TO THE LOGIC MODULE

PROCEDURE	TEST INDICATION	ACTION REQUIRED
REMINDERS • Diagnostic readout box connected to the engine harness connector. • System in Sensor Test Mode 08. NOTE: Don't forget to divide the reading on the display box by 10. • M.A.P. sensor connector disconnected.	• Display on the readout box is reading 0 volts.	• Perform STEP E.
• Connect a jumper wire between the dark green with red and black with light blue wires of the M.A.P. sensor harness connector. 	• Display on the readout box is not reading 0 volts.	• Perform STEP D.

TEST 2	STEP D	CHECKING THE M.A.P. SENSOR WIRE TO THE LOGIC MODULE FOR AN OPEN CIRCUIT

PROCEDURE	TEST INDICATION	ACTION REQUIRED
REMINDERS • Diagnostic readout box connected to the engine harness connector. • System in Sensor Test Mode 08. NOTE: Don't forget to divide the reading on the display box by 10. • M.A.P. sensor disconnected.	• Display on the readout box is reading 0 volts.	• Repair the black with light blue trace wire of the M.A.P. sensor connector for an open circuit to the wiring harness splice.
• Connect one end of a jumper wire to the negative terminal of the battery. • Connect the other end of the jumper wire to the dark green with red tracer wire terminal of the M.A.P. sensor harness connector. 	• Display on the readout box is reading 5 volts.	• Repair the dark green with red tracer wire of the M.A.P. sensor connector for an open circuit to the logic module.

TEST 2	STEP E	CHECKING THE 5 VOLT SUPPLY TO THE M.A.P. SENSOR

PROCEDURE	TEST INDICATION	ACTION REQUIRED
REMINDERS • Ignition switch in the run position. • M.A.P. sensor connector disconnected. • Connect a digital voltmeter to the violet with white tracer wire of the M.A.P. sensor harness connector and ground.	• Voltmeter is reading at least 4 volts.	• Replace the M.A.P. sensor. NOTE: Before replacing the M.A.P. sensor, check the terminals in the harness connector to make sure they are not spread apart causing a poor connection.
	• Voltmeter is reading 0 volts.	• Repair the dark green with white tracer wire for an open circuit to the logic module. Also check the terminal in cavity No. 1 of the logic module white connector to make sure it is not crushed causing a poor connection.

TEST 3	STEP A	CHECKING FOR FAULT CODE 15 — SPEED SENSOR CIRCUIT

PROCEDURE	TEST INDICATION	ACTION REQUIRED
REMINDERS • Diagnostic readout box connected to the engine harness connector. • Start the engine. • Disconnect the speed sensor connector. • Put the system in the **Engine Running Test Mode 71**. (Refer to introduction) • Connect a jumper wire between the terminals of the speed sensor harness connector. • Make and break this connection.	• As you make and break this connection the display on the readout box changes.	• Replace the speed sensor.
	• As you make and break this connection the display on the readout box does not change.	• Perform STEP B.

1987–88 EFI DRIVEABILITY TEST PROCEDURES

TEST 3	STEP B	CHECKING THE SPEED SENSOR CIRCUIT TO THE LOGIC MODULE FOR AN OPEN CIRCUIT	
PROCEDURE		TEST INDICATION	ACTION REQUIRED
REMINDERS		• As you make and break the connection the display on the readout box changes	• Repair the wires to the speed sensor for an open circuit
• Diagnostic readout box connected to the engine harness connector			
• Engine running			
• System in engine running test mode 71			
• Speed sensor connector disconnected			
• Connect a jumper wire between cavity No. 25 and cavity No. 9 of the white connector of the logic module		• As you make and break the connection the display on the readout box does not change	• Replace the logic module **CAUTION:** Before replacing the logic module check the terminal of cavity No. 9 of the white connector to make sure it is not crushed causing a poor connection.
• Make and break this connection			

LOGIC MODULE WHITE CONNECTOR

TEST 4	STEP A	CHECKING FOR FAULT CODE 21 — OXYGEN SENSOR CIRCUIT TO THE LOGIC MODULE	
PROCEDURE		TEST INDICATION	ACTION REQUIRED
REMINDERS	• Touch the other end of the jumper wire to the battery positive and negative post	• When the jumper wire is on the positive post the display on the readout box increases towards 5 volts	• Replace the O₂ sensor.
• Diagnostic readout box connected to the engine harness connector		• When the jumper wire is on the negative post the display on the readout box decreases towards 0 volts	
• Turn the ignition switch off			
• Disconnect the oxygen sensor connector			
• Connect the end of a jumper wire to the black wire of harness end of the oxygen sensor 3-way connector	HEATED OXYGEN SENSOR HARNESS CONNECTOR 	• When the jumper wires are touched to the battery post the display on the readout box does not increase or decrease	• Perform STEP B.
• Put the system into Sensor Test Mode 02. (Refer to introduction)			
NOTE: Don't forget to divide the reading on display by 10	BATTERY		

TEST 4	STEP B	CHECKING THE OXYGEN SENSOR CIRCUIT AT THE LOGIC MODULE	
PROCEDURE		TEST INDICATION	ACTION REQUIRED
REMINDERS		• Voltmeter reading is at least 4 volts	• Repair the wire of cavity No. 18 for an open circuit to the oxygen sensor.
• Oxygen sensor connector disconnected			
• Turn the ignition switch off			
• Connect a digital voltmeter to cavity No. 18 of the logic module black connector and ground	DIGITAL VOLTMETER 	• Voltmeter reading is 0	• Replace the logic module **CAUTION:** Before replacing the logic module check the terminal in cavity No. 18 of the black connector to make sure it is not crushed causing a poor connection.
• Turn the ignition switch to the run position			

LOGIC MODULE BLACK CONNECTOR

TEST 5	STEP A	CHECKING FOR FAULT CODE 22 — COOLANT SENSOR CIRCUIT	
PROCEDURE		TEST INDICATION	ACTION REQUIRED
REMINDERS		• Display on the readout box is reading 00°	• Perform STEP B.
• Diagnostic readout box connected to the engine harness connector			
• Turn the ignition switch off			
• Disconnect the coolant sensor connector	DISCONNECT 		
• Put the system in Sensor Test Mode 04. (Refer to introduction) **NOTE:** Don't forget to multiply the reading on the display by 10.		• Display on the readout box is reading 260°	• Replace the logic module **NOTE:** Before replacing the logic module make sure the wire of cavity No. 23 of the logic module black connector is not shorted to ground.

TEST 5	STEP B	CHECKING THE COOLANT SENSOR CIRCUIT TO THE LOGIC MODULE	
PROCEDURE		TEST INDICATION	ACTION REQUIRED
REMINDERS		• Display on the readout box is reading 260°	• Replace the coolant sensor
• Diagnostic readout box connected to the engine harness connector			
• System in Sensor Test Mode 04			
NOTE: Don't forget to multiply the reading on display by 10	JUMPER 	• Display on the readout box is reading 00°	• Perform STEP C.
• Coolant sensor connector disconnected			
• Connect a jumper wire between the terminals of the coolant sensor connector	TN BK/LB		

COOLANT SENSOR HARNESS CONNECTOR

TEST 5	STEP C	CHECKING THE COOLANT SENSOR WIRES TO THE LOGIC MODULE FOR AN OPEN CIRCUIT	
PROCEDURE		TEST INDICATION	ACTION REQUIRED
REMINDERS		• Display on the readout box is reading 260°	• Repair the black with light blue tracer wire of the coolant sensor harness connector for an open circuit to the wiring harness splice
• Diagnostic readout box connected to the engine harness connector			
• System in Sensor Test Mode 04			
NOTE: Don't forget to multiply the reading on display by 10	JUMPER 	• Display on the readout box is reading 00°	• Repair the tan wire of the coolant sensor harness connector for an open circuit to the logic module
• Coolant sensor connector disconnected			
• Connect one end of a jumper wire to the negative terminal of the battery			
• Connect the other end of the jumper wire to the tan wire terminal of the coolant sensor harness connector	TN BK/LB		

COOLANT SENSOR HARNESS CONNECTOR

TEST 6	STEP A	CHECKING FOR FAULT CODE 23 — THROTTLE BODY TEMPERATURE SENSOR	
PROCEDURE		TEST INDICATION	ACTION REQUIRED
REMINDERS		• Display on the readout box is reading 5 volts	• Perform STEP B.
• Diagnostic readout box connected to the engine harness connector			
• Disconnect the throttle body temperature sensor connector	THROTTLE BODY 		
• Put the system in Sensor Test Mode 03. (Refer to introduction) **NOTE:** Don't forget to divide the reading on the display by 10		• Display on the readout box is reading 0 volts or 0 volts and then increases	• Replace the logic module **NOTE:** Before replacing the logic module make sure the wire of cavity No. 25 of the logic module black connector is not shorted to ground.
	DISCONNECT		

TEST 6	STEP B	CHECKING THE THROTTLE BODY TEMPERATURE SENSOR SIGNAL CIRCUIT TO THE LOGIC MODULE	
PROCEDURE		TEST INDICATION	ACTION REQUIRED
REMINDERS		• Display on the readout box is reading 0 volts	• Replace the throttle body temperature sensor
• Diagnostic readout box connected to the engine harness connector			
• System in Sensor Test Mode 03. **NOTE:** Don't forget to divide the reading on the display box by 10.	JUMPER 		
• Throttle body temperature sensor connector disconnected			
• Connect a jumper wire between the terminals of the throttle body temperature sensor connector	BK/RD BK/LB	• Display on the readout box is reading 5 volts	• Perform STEP C.

THROTTLE BODY TEMPERATURE SENSOR CONNECTOR

FUEL INJECTION SYSTEMS
CHRYSLER CORPORATION

1987–88 EFI DRIVEABILITY TEST PROCEDURES

TEST 6	STEP C	CHECKING THE THROTTLE BODY TEMPERATURE SENSOR WIRES TO THE LOGIC MODULE FOR AN OPEN CIRCUIT	
PROCEDURE		**TEST INDICATION**	**ACTION REQUIRED**
REMINDERS • Diagnostic readout box connected to the engine harness connector. • System in **Sensor Test Mode 03**. NOTE: Don't forget to divide the reading on the display box by 10. • Throttle body temperature sensor connector disconnected. • Connect one end of a jumper wire to the negative terminal of the battery.	• Connect the other end of the jumper wire to the black with red tracer wire terminal of the throttle body temperature sensor connector.	• Display on the readout box is reading 0 volts. • Display on the readout box is reading 5 volts.	• Display reads 0 volts, repair the black with light blue tracer wire of the throttle body temperature sensor connector for an open circuit to the wiring harness splice. • Repair the black with red tracer wire of the throttle body temperature sensor connector for an open circuit to the logic module.

BK/RD*   BK/LB*

THROTTLE BODY TEMPERATURE SENSOR CONNECTOR

TEST 7	STEP D	CHECKING THE 5 VOLT SUPPLY TO THE THROTTLE POSITION SENSOR	
PROCEDURE		**TEST INDICATION**	**ACTION REQUIRED**
REMINDERS • Ignition switch in the run position. • Throttle position sensor connector disconnected. • Connect a digital voltmeter to the orange with white tracer wire of the throttle position sensor harness connector and ground.		• Voltmeter is reading at least 4 volts. • Voltmeter reads 0.	• Replace the throttle position sensor. NOTE: Before replacing the throttle pot, make sure it is installed correctly on the throttle body. Connector facing rear of vehicle. • Repair the orange with white tracer wire for an open circuit to the logic module. Also check the terminal in cavity No. 1 of the logic module black connector to make sure it is not crushed causing a poor connection.

DIGITAL VOLTMETER

OR/WT*   BK/LB*
OR/DB*

THROTTLE POSITION SENSOR HARNESS CONNECTOR

TEST 7	STEP A	CHECKING FOR FAULT CODE 24 — THROTTLE POSITION SENSOR CIRCUIT	
PROCEDURE		**TEST INDICATION**	**ACTION REQUIRED**
REMINDERS • Diagnostic readout box connected to the engine harness connector. • Disconnect the connector from the throttle position sensor. • Put the system in **Sensor Test Mode 05**. (Refer to introduction) NOTE: Don't forget to divide the reading on the display by 10.		• Display on the readout box is reading 5 volts. • Display on the readout box is reading 0 volts.	• Perform STEP B. • Replace the logic module. NOTE: Before replacing the logic module make sure the wire of cavity No. 21 of the logic module black connector is not shorted to ground.

THROTTLE BODY

DISCONNECT

TEST 8	STEP A	CHECKING FOR FAULT CODE 25 — AUTOMATIC IDLE SPEED MOTOR CIRCUIT FOR A SHORT	
PROCEDURE		**TEST INDICATION**	**ACTION REQUIRED**
• Turn the ignition switch off. • Disconnect the white logic module connector. • Connect an ohmmeter between cavities 18 and 20 of the logic module white connector.		• Ohmmeter is showing some resistance. NOTE: The amount of resistance is not important. Just make sure there is some. • Ohmmeter is showing 0 resistance.	• Some resistance, Perform STEP B. • Perform STEP C.

OHMMETER

LOGIC MODULE WHITE CONNECTOR

TEST 7	STEP B	CHECKING THE THROTTLE POSITION SENSOR SIGNAL CIRCUIT TO THE LOGIC MODULE	
PROCEDURE		**TEST INDICATION**	**ACTION REQUIRED**
REMINDERS • Diagnostic readout box connected to the engine harness connector. • System in **Sensor Test Mode 05**. NOTE: Don't forget to divide the reading on the display box by 10. • Throttle position sensor connector disconnected. • Connect a jumper wire between the orange with dark blue and black with blue wires of the throttle position sensor harness connector.		• Display on the readout box is reading 0 volts. • Display on the readout box is reading 5 volts.	• Perform STEP D. • Perform STEP C.

JUMPER

OR/WT*   BK/LB*
OR/DB*

THROTTLE POSITION SENSOR HARNESS CONNECTOR

TEST 8	STEP B	CHECKING AUTOMATIC IDLE SPEED MOTOR CIRCUIT FOR A SHORT	
PROCEDURE		**TEST INDICATION**	**ACTION REQUIRED**
REMINDERS • Ignition switch off. • Disconnect the white logic module connector. • Connect an ohmmeter between cavities 16 and 22 of the logic module white connector.		• Ohmmeter is showing some resistance. NOTE: The amount of resistance is not important. Just make sure there is some. • Ohmmeter is showing 0 resistance.	• Some resistance, Perform STEP D. • Perform STEP C.

OHMMETER

LOGIC MODULE WHITE CONNECTOR

TEST 7	STEP C	CHECKING THE THROTTLE POSITION SENSOR WIRES TO THE LOGIC MODULE FOR AN OPEN CIRCUIT	
PROCEDURE		**TEST INDICATION**	**ACTION REQUIRED**
REMINDERS • Diagnostic readout box connected to the engine harness connector. • System in **Sensor Test Mode 05**. NOTE: Don't forget to divide the reading on the display box by 10. • Throttle position sensor connector disconnected. • Connect one end of a jumper wire to the negative terminal of the battery. • Connect the other end of the jumper wire to the orange with dark blue tracer wire terminal of the throttle position sensor harness connector.		• Display on the readout box is reading 0 volts. • Display on the readout box is reading 5 volts.	• Repair the black with light blue tracer wire of the throttle position sensor connector for an open circuit to the wiring harness splice. • Repair the orange with blue tracer wire of the throttle position sensor connector for an open circuit to the logic module.

JUMPER

OR/WT*   BK/LB*
OR/DB*

THROTTLE POSITION SENSOR HARNESS CONNECTOR

TEST 8	STEP C	CHECKING AUTOMATIC IDLE SPEED MOTOR CONTROL WIRES FOR A SHORT	
PROCEDURE		**TEST INDICATION**	**ACTION REQUIRED**
REMINDERS • Ignition switch off. • Logic module white connector disconnected. • Ohmmeter connected to the white logic module connector. • Disconnect the idle motor connector.		• Ohmmeter is showing an open circuit. • Ohmmeter is showing 0 resistance.	• Replace the idle motor. • Repair the wires to the idle motor for a short circuit to each other.

THROTTLE BODY

DISCONNECT

1987–88 EFI DRIVEABILITY TEST PROCEDURES

TEST 8	STEP D	CHECKING THE FJ2 WIRE FROM THE POWER MODULE FOR AN OPEN CIRCUIT	
PROCEDURE		TEST INDICATION	ACTION REQUIRED
REMINDERS • Logic module white connector disconnected • Connect a voltmeter to cavity No. 7 or 8 of the white connector and ground • Turn the ignition switch to the run position.		• Voltmeter is reading within one volt of the battery voltage	• Voltage okay, replace the logic module. **CAUTION:** Before replacing the logic module check the terminal in cavities 7 and 8 of the white connector to make sure they are not crushed causing a poor connection.
		• Voltmeter reads 0 volts.	• Repair fused J2 wire to the power module for an open circuit.

LOGIC MODULE WHITE CONNECTOR

TEST 9	STEP A	CHECKING FOR FAULT CODE 31 — CANISTER PURGE SOLENOID CIRCUIT	
PROCEDURE		TEST INDICATION	ACTION REQUIRED
REMINDERS • Diagnostic readout box connected to the engine harness connector. • Connect a voltmeter to the pink with white tracer wire of the canister purge solenoid connector and ground • Put the system in the **ATM Test Mode - Code 07.** (Refer to introduction)		• Voltmeter is not pulsating but reads within one volt of battery voltage.	• Perform STEP B.
		• Voltmeter pulsates between 0 and 5 volts	• Perform STEP C.
		• Voltmeter is not pulsating but reads 0-1 volt.	• Disconnect the logic module black connector. If voltage is now within one of battery, replace the logic module. If not repair pink with white tracer wire for a short to ground.

CONNECT VOLTMETER

TEST 9	STEP B	CHECKING THE CANISTER PURGE SOLENOID CONTROL WIRE FOR AN OPEN CIRCUIT TO THE LOGIC MODULE	
PROCEDURE		TEST INDICATION	ACTION REQUIRED
• Turn the ignition switch off • Connect a voltmeter to cavity No. 5 of the black connector and ground • Turn the ignition switch to the run position.		• Voltmeter is reading within one volt of battery voltage	• Replace the logic module **CAUTION:** Before replacing the logic module check the terminal in cavity No. 5 of the black connector to make sure it is not crushed causing a poor connection.
		• Voltmeter reads between 0 and 7 volts.	• Repair wire of cavity No. 5 for an open circuit to the canister purge solenoid

LOGIC MODULE BLACK CONNECTOR

TEST 9	STEP C	CHECKING THE CANISTER PURGE SOLENOID WINDINGS FOR AN OPEN CIRCUIT	
PROCEDURE		TEST INDICATION	ACTION REQUIRED
• Turn the ignition switch off • Disconnect the canister purge solenoid connector • Connect an ohmmeter between the terminals of the solenoid		• Ohmmeter is showing some resistance. **NOTE:** The amount of resistance is not important. Just make sure there is some	• Repair the blue wire of the solenoid connector for an open circuit to the ignition switch.
		• Ohmmeter is showing an open circuit	• Replace the solenoid

CANISTER PURGE SOLENOID

TEST 10	STEP A	CHECKING FOR FAULT CODE 33 — A/C CUTOUT RELAY	
PROCEDURE		TEST INDICATION	ACTION REQUIRED
REMINDERS • Diagnostic readout box connected to the engine harness connector. • Connect a voltmeter to the dark blue with orange tracer wire of the A/C cut-out relay 3-way connector and ground • Put the system in the **ATM Test Mode - Code 05.** (Refer to the introduction)		• Voltmeter is not pulsating but reads within one volt of battery voltage.	• Perform STEP B.
		• Voltmeter pulsates between 0 and 5 volts.	• Perform STEP C.
		• Voltmeter is not pulsating but read 0-1 volts.	• Disconnect the logic module black connector. If voltage is now within one of battery, replace the logic module. If not repair dark blue with orange tracer wire for a short to ground

DB/OR, DB/BK, BK, WIRE END
A/C CUT-OUT RELAY 3-WAY CONNECTOR

TEST 10	STEP B	CHECKING THE A/C CUTOUT RELAY CONTROL WIRE FOR AN OPEN CIRCUIT TO THE LOGIC MODULE	
PROCEDURE		TEST INDICATION	ACTION REQUIRED
• Turn the ignition switch off. • Connect a voltmeter to cavity No. 3 of the logic module black connector and ground. • Turn the ignition switch to the run position.		• Voltmeter is reading within one volt of battery voltage	• Replace the logic module. **CAUTION:** Before replacing the logic module check the terminal in cavity No. 3 of the black connector to make sure it is not crushed causing a poor connection.
		• Voltmeter is reading between 0 and 7 volts.	• Repair the wire of cavity No. 3 for an open circuit to the A/C cutout relay

LOGIC MODULE BLACK CONNECTOR

TEST 10	STEP C	CHECKING A/C CUTOUT RELAY PULL IN COIL WINDINGS FOR AN OPEN CIRCUIT	
PROCEDURE		TEST INDICATION	ACTION REQUIRED
• Turn the ignition switch off • Disconnect the connectors from the A/C cutout relay • Connect an ohmmeter between terminals 2 and 4 of the relay		• Ohmmeter is showing some resistance **NOTE:** The amount of resistance is not important. Just make sure there is some	• Repair the dark blue with orange tracer wire of the relay 3-way connector for an open circuit to the ignition switch
		• Ohmmeter is showing an open circuit.	• Replace the relay.

A/C CUT-OUT RELAY

TEST 11	STEP A	CHECKING FOR FAULT CODE 35 — RADIATOR FAN RELAY CONTROL CIRCUIT	
PROCEDURE		TEST INDICATION	ACTION REQUIRED
REMINDERS • Diagnostic readout box connected to the engine harness connector. • Connect a voltmeter to the dark blue with pink tracer wire of the radiator fan relay small 3-way connector and ground • Put the system in the **ATM Test Mode - Code 04.** (Refer to the introduction)		• Voltmeter is not pulsating but reads within one volt of battery voltage.	• Perform STEP B.
		• Voltmeter pulsates between 0 and 5 volts.	• Perform STEP C.
		• Voltmeter is not pulsating but reads 0-1 volts.	• Disconnect the logic module white connector. If voltage is now within one of battery, replace the logic module. If not repair dark blue with pink tracer wire for a short to ground.

DB/PK, DB/BK, W, WIRE END
RADIATOR FAN RELAY CONNECTORS

1987–88 EFI DRIVEABILITY TEST PROCEDURES

TEST 11	STEP B	CHECKING THE RADIATOR FAN RELAY CONTROL WIRE FOR AN OPEN CIRCUIT TO THE LOGIC MODULE	
PROCEDURE		TEST INDICATION	ACTION REQUIRED
• Turn the ignition switch off • Connect a voltmeter to cavity No. 21 of the logic module white connector and ground • Turn the ignition switch to the run position		• Voltmeter is reading within one volt of battery voltage	• Replace the logic module CAUTION: Before replacing the logic module check the terminal in cavity No. 21 of the white connector to make sure it is not crushed causing a poor connection.
		• Voltmeter reads between 0 and 7 volts	• Repair the wire of cavity No. 21 for an open circuit to the radiator fan relay

VOLTMETER

LOGIC MODULE
WHITE CONNECTOR

TEST 11	STEP C	CHECKING RADIATOR FAN RELAY PULL IN COIL WINDINGS FOR AN OPEN CIRCUIT	
PROCEDURE		TEST INDICATION	ACTION REQUIRED
• Turn the ignition switch off • Disconnect the smaller of the two 3-way connectors from the relay • Connect an ohmmeter between terminals 4 and 5 of the relay		• Ohmmeter is showing some resistance NOTE: The amount of resistance is not important. Just make sure there is some	• Repair the white wire of the relay 3-way connector for an open circuit to the fuse box.
		• Ohmmeter is showing an open circuit	• Replace the relay

OHMMETER

RADIATOR FAN RELAY

TEST 12	STEP A	CHECKING FOR FAULT CODE 37 — TRANSMISSION LOCK UP SOLENOID CIRCUIT	
PROCEDURE		TEST INDICATION	ACTION REQUIRED
REMINDERS • Diagnostic readout box connected to the engine harness connector • Disconnect the transmission lock up solenoid wiring harness connector • Connect the positive lead of a voltmeter to the white wire of the solenoid connector • Connect the negative lead of the voltmeter to the orange with light green wire of the solenoid connector	• Put the system into ATM Test Mode 10. (Refer to introduction)	• Voltmeter is pulsating somewhere between 0 and 12 volts	• Replace the transmission lockup solenoid
		• Voltmeter is reading 0 volts	• Perform STEP B.

VOLTMETER

OR/LG   WT

TEST 12	STEP B	CHECKING THE POWER SUPPLY TO THE TRANSMISSION LOCKUP SOLENOID	
PROCEDURE		TEST INDICATION	ACTION REQUIRED
REMINDERS • Positive lead of voltmeter connected to the white wire of the transmission lockup solenoid connector. • Ignition switch in the run position. • Connect the negative lead of the voltmeter to a good engine ground.		• Voltmeter is reading within one volt of battery voltage	• Perform STEP C.
		• Voltmeter is reading 0 volts	• Repair the white wire of the transmission lockup solenoid for an open circuit to the fuse box.

VOLTMETER

OR/LG   WT

TEST 12	STEP C	CHECKING THE TRANSMISSION LOCKUP SOLENOID CONTROL WIRE TO THE LOGIC MODULE	
PROCEDURE		TEST INDICATION	ACTION REQUIRED
• Turn the ignition switch off • Connect a voltmeter to cavity No. 15 of the logic module white connector and ground • Put the system into ATM Test Mode 10. (Refer to introduction)		• Voltmeter is pulsating between 0 and 5 volts	• Repair the wire of cavity No. 15 of the logic module white connector for an open circuit to the transmission lockup solenoid connector
		• Voltmeter is reading 0 volts	• Replace the logic module CAUTION: Before replacing the logic module check the terminal in cavity No. 15 of the white connector to make sure it is not crushed causing a poor connection.

VOLTMETER

LOGIC MODULE
WHITE CONNECTOR

THE FOLLOWING TEST MUST BEGIN WITH A COLD ENGINE

TEST 13	STEP A	CHECKING SENSOR CALIBRATIONS (ENGINE COOLANT TEMPERATURE SENSOR)	
PROCEDURE		TEST INDICATION	ACTION REQUIRED
REMINDERS • Diagnostic readout box connected to the engine harness connector. • Start the engine. • Put the system in Engine Running Test Mode 64. (Refer to introduction) NOTE: Don't forget to multiply the reading on display by 10.		• Display on the readout box is reading approximately ambient temperature ± 10°F.	• Perform STEP B.
		• Display on the readout box is reading above or below ambient temperature ± 10°F.	• Replace the coolant sensor.

DIAGNOSTIC
READOUT

DIAGNOSTIC
READOUT BOX

TEST 13	STEP B	CHECKING SENSOR CALIBRATIONS (THROTTLE POSITION SENSOR)	
PROCEDURE		TEST INDICATION	ACTION REQUIRED
REMINDERS • Diagnostic readout box connected to the engine harness connector. • Engine cold • Turn the engine off • Put the system in Sensor TEST Mode 05. (Refer to introduction) NOTE: Don't forget to divide the reading on display by 10.		• Display on readout box reads as follows Throttle Fully Closed 1 volt ± ½ volt NOTE: Make sure none of the cables that are attached to the throttle body are not misadjusted and are holding the throttle open. In Between Closed and Open You should see an uninterrupted change of voltage between closed and open throttle Throttle Wide Open at least 3½ volts	• If the voltage readings are within specifications. Perform STEP C. • If the voltage readings are not within specifications replace the throttle position sensor.

DIAGNOSTIC
READOUT

DIAGNOSTIC
READOUT BOX

TEST 13	STEP C	CHECKING SENSOR CALIBRATION (THROTTLE POSITION SENSOR)	
PROCEDURE		TEST INDICATION	ACTION REQUIRED
REMINDERS • Diagnostic readout box connected to the engine harness connector. • Start the engine. • Put the system into Engine Running Test Mode 65. (Refer to introduction) NOTE: Don't forget to divide the reading on display by 10. • Slowly increase engine speed to 2,000 rpm.		• As engine speed increases the voltage displayed on the readout box also increases.	• Perform STEP D.
		• As engine speed increases the voltage displayed on the readout box is not increasing.	• Replace the throttle position sensor.

DIAGNOSTIC
READOUT

DIAGNOSTIC
READOUT BOX

1987–88 EFI DRIVEABILITY TEST PROCEDURES

TEST 13 | STEP D | CHECKING SENSOR CALIBRATION (THROTTLE POSITION SENSOR)

PROCEDURE	TEST INDICATION	ACTION REQUIRED
REMINDERS • Diagnostic readout box connected to the engine harness connector. • Engine running at idle • Put the system into Engine Running Test Mode 69. (Refer to introduction) NOTE: Don't forget to divide the reading on display by 10	• Display on the readout box is between 0 and .1 (one tenth) volt.	• Perform STEP E.
	• Display on the readout box is reading more than .1 (one tenth) volt.	• Replace the throttle position sensor.

DIAGNOSTIC READOUT BOX

TEST 13 | STEP E | CHECKING SENSOR CALIBRATION (M.A.P. SENSOR)

PROCEDURE	TEST INDICATION	ACTION REQUIRED
REMINDERS • Diagnostic readout box connected to the engine harness connector. • Tee a vacuum gauge into the vacuum line at the M.A.P. sensor. • Start the engine. • Put the system into Engine Running Test Mode 68. (Refer to introduction)	• Vacuum displayed on the readout box is within 1 inch of vacuum shown on the vacuum gauge.	• Perform STEP G.
	• Vacuum displayed on the readout box is not within 1 inch of vacuum shown on the vacuum gauge.	• Perform STEP F.

VACUUM GAUGE

TEST 13 | STEP F | CHECKING SENSOR CALIBRATION (M.A.P. SENSOR)

PROCEDURE	TEST INDICATION	ACTION REQUIRED
REMINDERS • Diagnostic readout box connected to the engine harness connector. • Engine cold. • Put the system in Sensor TEST Mode 08. (Refer to introduction) NOTE: Don't forget to divide the reading on display by 10. • Disconnect the vacuum hose from the M.A.P. sensor. • Connect an auxiliary vacuum supply to the M.A.P. sensor. • Apply 5 inches of vacuum and record the voltage displayed on the readout box.	• Slowly apply vacuum to 20 inches and watch display on readout box • Record the voltage displayed on the readout box at 20 inches. • Subtract the voltage recorded at 20 inches from the voltage recorded at 5 inches. **Example** Voltage at 5' 3.8 Voltage at 20' −1.1 Difference 2.7	• The readout box is showing an uninterrupted change of voltage between 5 and 20 inches of vacuum. • The voltage difference is between 2.3 and 2.9 volts.	• Repair vacuum line to the M.A.P. sensor for a restriction.
	• The readout box is showing an interrupted change of voltage between 5 and 20 inches of vacuum. • The voltage difference is not between 2.3 and 2.9 volts.	• Replace the M.A.P. sensor.

TEST 13 | STEP G | CHECKING SENSOR CALIBRATION (THROTTLE BODY TEMPERATURE SENSOR)

PROCEDURE	TEST INDICATION	ACTION REQUIRED
REMINDERS • Diagnostic readout box connected to the engine harness connector. • Engine cold. • Start the engine. • Put the system in Engine Running TEST Mode 63. (Refer to introduction) NOTE: Don't forget to divide the reading on display by 10.	• Display on the readout box is reading between 2 and 5 volts	• Perform TEST NO. 14.
	• Display on the readout box is not reading between 2 and 5 volts.	• Replace the throttle body temperature sensor.

DIAGNOSTIC READOUT BOX

TEST 14 | STEP A | CHECKING HEATED AIR INTAKE SYSTEM

PROCEDURE	TEST INDICATION	ACTION REQUIRED
REMINDERS • Engine cold • Disconnect the air duct from the air cleaner snorkel. • Disconnect the vacuum supply hose to the heated air intake system air temperature sensor. • Connect an auxiliary vacuum supply to the air temperature sensor. • Apply at least 15 inches of vacuum.	• Vacuum builds up, closes heated air door and then bleeds down opening the heated door. NOTE: With air temperature below 76°F.	• Perform TEST NO. 15
	• Vacuum builds up but heated air door does not close	• Repair or replace door as required
	• Vacuum does not build up or does not bleed down	• Replace air temperature sensor
	• Vacuum builds up, bleeds down, but heated air door does not open	• Repair or replace door as required.

DISCONNECT THIS HOSE
AIR CLEANER BASE
SENSOR

TEST 15 | STEP A | CHECKING FOR FUEL FOULED SPARK PLUGS

PROCEDURE	TEST INDICATION	ACTION REQUIRED
• Remove the spark plugs	• Spark plugs are dry NOTE: It is normal for spark plugs to be black after an engine has been started cold	• Perform TEST NO. 18.
	• Spark plugs are wet with fuel	• Clean and reinstall. Do not install new spark plugs. • Check for gas in the crankcase. Change oil and filter if required.

THE FOLLOWING TEST MUST BEGIN WITH A WARM ENGINE

TEST 16 | STEP A | CHECKING SENSOR CALIBRATION (ENGINE COOLANT TEMPERATURE SENSOR)

PROCEDURE	TEST INDICATION	ACTION REQUIRED
REMINDERS • Diagnostic readout box connected to the engine harness connector. • Start the engine. • Put the system in Engine Running Test Mode 64. (Refer to introduction). NOTE: Don't forget to multiply the reading on display by 10	• Display on the readout box is reading between 180° and 250°.	• Perform STEP B.
	• Display on the readout box is not reading between 180° and 250°.	• Replace the coolant sensor.

DIAGNOSTIC READOUT BOX

TEST 16 | STEP B | CHECKING SENSOR CALIBRATIONS (THROTTLE POSITION SENSOR)

PROCEDURE	TEST INDICATION	ACTION REQUIRED
REMINDERS • Diagnostic readout box connected to the engine harness connector. • Engine warm. • Turn the engine off. • Put the system in Sensor Test Mode 05. (Refer to introduction) NOTE: Don't forget to divide the reading on display by 10.	• Display on readout box should read as follows. **Throttle Fully Closed** 1 volt = ½ volt NOTE: Make sure none of the cables that are attached to the throttle body are not misadjusted and are holding the throttle open. **In Between Closed and Open** You should see an uninterrupted change of voltage between closed and open throttle **Throttle Wide Open** at least 3 volts	• If the voltage readings are within specifications. Perform STEP C. • If the voltage readings are not within specifications, replace the throttle position sensor.

DIAGNOSTIC READOUT BOX

1987–88 EFI DRIVEABILITY TEST PROCEDURES

TEST 16	STEP C	CHECKING SENSOR CALIBRATION (THROTTLE POSITION SENSOR)	
PROCEDURE		**TEST INDICATION**	**ACTION REQUIRED**
REMINDERS • Diagnostic readout box connected to the engine harness connector.		• As engine speed increases the voltage displayed on the readout box also increases	• **Perform STEP D.**
• Start the engine. • Put the system into **Engine Running Test Mode 65.** (Refer to introduction) NOTE: Don't forget to divide the reading on display by 10. • Slowly increase engine speed to 2000 rpm.		• As engine speed increases the voltage displayed on the readout box is not increasing.	• Replace the throttle position sensor.

DIAGNOSTIC READOUT BOX

TEST 16	STEP D	CHECKING SENSOR CALIBRATION (THROTTLE POSITION SENSOR)	
PROCEDURE		**TEST INDICATION**	**ACTION REQUIRED**
REMINDERS • Diagnostic readout box connected to the engine harness connector. • Engine running at idle.		• Display on the readout box is reading between 0 and .1 (one tenth) volt.	• **Perform STEP E.**
• Put the system into **Engine Running Test Mode 69.** (Refer to introduction) NOTE: Don't forget to divide the reading on display by 10.		• Display on the readout box is reading more than .1 (one tenth) volt.	• Replace the throttle position sensor.

DIAGNOSTIC READOUT BOX

TEST 16	STEP E	CHECKING SENSOR CALIBRATION (M.A.P. SENSOR)	
PROCEDURE		**TEST INDICATION**	**ACTION REQUIRED**
REMINDERS • Diagnostic readout box connected to the engine harness connector.		• Vacuum displayed on the readout box is within 1 inch of vacuum shown on the vacuum gauge.	• **Perform STEP G.**
• Tee a vacuum gauge into the vacuum line at the M.A.F. sensor. • Start the engine. • Put the system into **Engine Running Test Mode 68.** (Refer to introduction)		• Vacuum displayed on the readout box is not within 1 inch of vacuum shown on the vacuum gauge.	• **Perform STEP F.**

VACUUM GAUGE

TEST 16	STEP F	CHECKING SENSOR CALIBRATION (M.A.P. SENSOR)	
PROCEDURE		**TEST INDICATION**	**ACTION REQUIRED**
REMINDERS • Diagnostic readout box connected to the engine harness connector. • Engine warm.	• Slowly apply vacuum to 20 inches and watch display on readout box. • Record the voltage displayed on the readout box at 20 inches.	• The readout box is showing an uninterrupted change of voltage between 5 and 20 inches of vacuum. • The voltage difference is between 2.3 and 2.9 volts.	• Repair vacuum line to the M.A.P. sensor for a restriction.
• Put the system in **Sensor TEST Mode 08.** (Refer to introduction) NOTE: Don't forget to divide the reading on display by 10. • Disconnect the vacuum hose from the M.A.P. sensor.	• Subtract the voltage recorded at 20 inches from the voltage recorded at 5 inches. **Example**		
• Connect an auxiliary vacuum supply to the M.A.P. sensor. • Apply 5 inches of vacuum and record the voltage displayed on the readout box.	Voltage at 5' 3.8 Voltage at 20' 1.1 Difference 2.7	• The readout box is showing an interrupted change of voltage between 5 and 20 inches of vacuum. • The voltage difference is not between 2.3 and 2.9 volts.	• Replace the M.A.P. sensor.

TEST 16	STEP G	CHECKING SENSOR CALIBRATION (THROTTLE BODY TEMPERATURE SENSOR)	
PROCEDURE		**TEST INDICATION**	**ACTION REQUIRED**
REMINDERS • Diagnostic readout box connected to the engine harness connector.		• Display on the readout box is reading between 1 and 4 volts.	• **Perform TEST NO. 17.**
• Start the engine. • Put the system in **Engine Running Test Mode 63.** (Refer to introduction) NOTE: Don't forget to divide the reading on display by 10.		• Display on the readout box is not reading between 1 and 4 volts.	• Replace the throttle body temperature sensor.

DIAGNOSTIC READOUT BOX

TEST 17	STEP A	CHECKING HEATED AIR INTAKE SYSTEM	
PROCEDURE		**TEST INDICATION**	**ACTION REQUIRED**
REMINDERS • Engine warm.		• Vacuum does not hold and heated air door is open.	• **Perform TEST NO. 18.**
• Disconnect the air duct from the air cleaner snorkel. • Disconnect the vacuum supply hose to the heated air intake system air temperature sensor.		• Vacuum holds.	• Replace air temperature sensor.
• Connect an auxiliary vacuum supply to the air temperature sensor. • Try to apply vacuum.	DISCONNECT THIS HOSE AIR CLEANER BASE SENSOR	• Heated air door not open.	• Repair or replace as required.

TEST 18	STEP A	CHECKING THE EGR SYSTEM — VACUUM SUPPLY FROM THE THROTTLE BODY TO THE EGR BACKPRESSURE VALVE	
PROCEDURE		**TEST INDICATION**	**ACTION REQUIRED**
• Disconnect the vacuum line at the EGR backpressure valve that comes from the throttle body.		• Vacuum gauge is reading at least 5 inches.	• Remember what it is and **Perform STEP B.**
• Connect a vacuum gauge to this line. • Start the engine. • Raise engine speed to 2,000 rpm's.	CONNECT VACUUM GAUGE BACK PRESSURE VALVE EGR VALVE	• No vacuum or vacuum below 5 inches.	• Repair vacuum supply of vacuum from throttle body.

TEST 18	STEP B	CHECKING THE VACUUM SUPPLY FROM THE BACKPRESSURE VALVE TO THE EGR VALVE	
PROCEDURE		**TEST INDICATION**	**ACTION REQUIRED**
REMINDERS • Engine running		• Vacuum gauge is reading the same or near the same as seen in STEP A.	• **Perform STEP C.**
• Disconnect the vacuum gauge from the vacuum line and reconnect the vacuum line to the backpressure valve. • Disconnect the vacuum line from the EGR valve and connect a vacuum gauge to it. • Raise the engine speed to 2,000 rpm's.	CONNECT VACUUM GAUGE EGR VALVE	• Vacuum gauge is not reading the same or near the same as seen in STEP A.	• Replace EGR/backpressure valve assembly.

1987–88 EFI DRIVEABILITY TEST PROCEDURES

TEST 18	STEP C	CHECKING THE EGR VALVE OPERATION

PROCEDURE		TEST INDICATION	ACTION REQUIRED
REMINDERS • Vacuum line disconnected from the EGR valve. • Engine running. • Connect an auxiliary vacuum supply to the EGR valve. • Disconnect the idle motor harness connector. • With engine running at idle speed slowly apply vacuum.	CONNECT AUXILIARY VACUUM SUPPLY EGR VALVE	• Engine speed begins to drop when applied vacuum reaches 2½ to 3½ inches.	• Perform STEP D.
		• Engine speed does not drop.	• Replace EGR/back pressure valve assembly. **NOTE:** After valve is removed. make sure supply tube to the manifold is not plugged before replacing EGR valve assembly.

TEST 18	STEP D	CHECKING THE EGR VALVE VACUUM CHAMBER FOR LEAKS

PROCEDURE		TEST INDICATION	ACTION REQUIRED
REMINDERS • Vacuum line disconnected from the EGR valve. • Auxiliary vacuum supply connected to the EGR valve. • Engine running at idle speed. • Apply 10 inches of vacuum to EGR valve	CONNECT AUXILIARY VACUUM SUPPLY EGR VALVE	• Vacuum should hold without bleeding for at least 10 seconds.	• Perform TEST NO. 19.
		• Vacuum does not hold or bleeds down before 10 seconds	• Replace EGR, EGR/back pressure valve assembly.

TEST 19	STEP A	CHECKING SECONDARY IGNITION SYSTEM

PROCEDURE		TEST INDICATION	ACTION REQUIRED
• Connect suitable engine analyzer to engine • Start engine and let engine speed stabilize for **two minutes.**		• Follow equipment manufacturer's procedure for secondary ignition testing and pattern analysis **CAUTION:** Make sure ignition coil output is checked in this testing. Open circuit secondary voltage should be at least 25,000 volts. • Secondary ignition system okay.	• Perform TEST NO. 20.
		• Secondary ignition not to specs	• Repair as required

TEST 20	STEP A	CHECKING BASIC IGNITION TIMING

PROCEDURE		TEST INDICATION	ACTION REQUIRED
• Connect a tachometer to engine • Connect a power timing light to engine • Start and run engine until operating temperature is reached. • Disconnect and reconnect engine coolant sensor connector **NOTE:** The power loss lamp on the instrument panel must come on	DISCONNECT	• Basic timing is within 2° of specification as shown on the emission label.	• Perform STEP B.
		• Basic timing is not within 2° of specification as shown on the emission label	• Adjust following basic ignition timing procedure

TEST 20	STEP B	CHECKING SPARK ADVANCE

PROCEDURE		TEST INDICATION	ACTION REQUIRED
REMINDERS • Tachometer connected to engine • Timing light connected to engine • Air cleaner removed (if necessary). • Engine at operating temperature. • Turn engine off and then restart. **NOTE:** Power loss lamp on instrument panel must go off. • Raise engine speed to 2,000 rpm's.		• Timing is as follows: All but 2.5L manual trans-27° BTDC minimum 2.5L manual trans-19° BTDC minimum	• Timing okay, **Perform TEST NO. 21.**
		• Spark advance not within minimum specification.	• Replace logic module.

TEST 21	STEP A	CHECKING FUEL SUPPLY AND RETURN SYSTEM

PROCEDURE		TEST INDICATION	ACTION REQUIRED
• Install pressure gauge (Tool C-3292) with (C-4799 adapter) in fuel supply hose at throttle body. **CAUTION:** Fuel is under high pressure. Refer to service manual for pressure release procedure. • Start engine	PRESSURE GAUGE SUPPLY HOSE FUEL PRESSURE SUPPLY HOSE	• Fuel pressure is 14½ psi ± 1.	• Perform TEST NO. 22.
		• Fuel pressure below 13½ record what it is.	• Perform STEP B.
		• Fuel pressure above 15½.	• Perform STEP D.

TEST 21	STEP B	CHECKING FOR LOW FUEL PRESSURE

PROCEDURE		TEST INDICATION	ACTION REQUIRED
• Turn engine off. • Release pressure • Remove pressure gauge • Reinstall hose to throttle body • Install pressure gauge before fuel filter. • Start engine	INSTALL PRESSURE GAUGE FUEL FILTER	• Fuel pressure is not higher than 5 psi of previously recorded pressure	• Replace fuel filter
		• Fuel pressure still below 13½ psi.	• Perform STEP C.

TEST 21	STEP C	CHECKING FOR LOW FUEL PRESSURE

PROCEDURE		TEST INDICATION	ACTION REQUIRED
• Turn engine off. • Release pressure • Remove pressure gauge from before filter and reinstall it after filter • Start engine • **Very gently,** squeeze fuel return line at throttle body and **immediately** let go	INSTALL PRESSURE GAUGE FUEL FILTER	• Fuel pressure increases above operating pressure	• Replace pressure regulator valve
		• Fuel pressure does not increase	• Replace intank fuel pump. **NOTE:** Before replacing pump look for contamination in the fuel tank that may be plugging pump filter. Also make sure electrical connections are not corroded

1987–88 EFI DRIVEABILITY TEST PROCEDURES

TEST 21	STEP D	CHECKING FOR HIGH FUEL PRESSURE		
		PROCEDURE	TEST INDICATION	ACTION REQUIRED
REMINDERS • Pressure gauge connected • Turn engine off • Remove fuel return hose (small one) from throttle body • Connect a 3 foot piece of fuel hose to throttle body and put open end into an approved gasoline container (2-gallon size) • Have someone start engine, look at pressure gauge and then immediately turn engine off **CAUTION:** Do not let engine run for more than 10 seconds			• Fuel pressure is 14½ psi ± ½ • Fuel pressure is above 15½ psi	• Check fuel return lines for kinks or restrictions including return line check valve inside fuel tank • Replace pressure regulator valve

TEST 22	STEP A	CHECKING THE OXYGEN SENSOR OPERATION		
		PROCEDURE	TEST INDICATION	ACTION REQUIRED
• Connect the diagnostic readout box to the engine harness connector. **NOTE:** Make sure the read/hold switch is in the Read position. • Start the engine and wait 2 minutes • Move the read/hold switch to the hold position to increase engine speed			• Display on the readout box is switching between 0 and 1. • Display on the readout box is 0 • Display on the readout box is 1.	• **Perform TEST NO. 23.** • Check for a engine vacuum leak. • Check for a grounded oxygen sensor wire. • Check for a plugged fuel injector • **Perform STEP B.**

TEST 22	STEP B	CHECKING FOR A RICH ENGINE OPERATING CONDITION		
		PROCEDURE	TEST INDICATION	ACTION REQUIRED
REMINDERS • Diagnostic readout box connected to the engine harness connector • Turn the engine off • Disconnect the distributor pickup connector. • Make sure the read/hold switch of the readout box is in the read position • Crank the engine at wide open throttle for 10 seconds while looking at the display on the readout box • Crank engine again for 10 seconds at wide open throttle while looking at the display on the readout box			• Display on the readout box changes to 0 • Display on the readout box does not change to 0.	• Replace the fuel injector. **NOTE:** Before replacing the fuel injector make sure the lower O ring is not split or rolled over • **Perform TEST NO. 24.**

TEST 23	STEP A	CHECKING THROTTLE BODY MINIMUM AIR FLOW		
		PROCEDURE	TEST INDICATION	ACTION REQUIRED
• Connect diagnostic readout box to the engine harness connector. • Disconnect and plug the vacuum supply hose to the heated air temperature sensor. • Remove the air cleaner assembly. • Connect a tachometer to the engine • Disconnect the tee connector in the PCV valve vacuum supply hose. • Install Tool C-5004 (.125" orifice) into the PCV vacuum supply hose. • Start the engine and let it idle for one minute. • Put the system into Engine Running Test Mode 70. (Refer to introduction)			• Tachometer is reading as follow: 2.2L 1100 to 1300 rpm 2.5L 1050 to 1250 rpm • Tachometer is not reading within above specifications.	• **Perform TEST NO. 24.** • Replace the throttle body.

TEST NO. 24

AT THIS POINT IN THE DRIVEABILITY TEST PROCEDURE YOU HAVE DETERMINED THAT ALL OF THE ENGINE CONTROL SYSTEMS ARE OPERATING AS THEY WERE DESIGNED TO THEREFORE THEY ARE **NOT THE CAUSE OF THE DRIVEABILITY PROBLEM. THIS INCLUDES THE LOGIC AND POWER MODULES.**

THE FOLLOWING ADDITIONAL ITEMS SHOULD BE CHECKED AS POSSIBLE CAUSES:

1. **ENGINE VACUUM** – MUST BE AT LEAST 13 INCHES IN NEUTRAL.

2. **ENGINE VALVE TIMING** – TO SPECIFICATIONS.

3. **ENGINE COMPRESSION** – TO SPECIFICATIONS.

4. **ENGINE EXHAUST SYSTEM** – MUST BE FREE OF ANY RESTRICTIONS.

5. **ENGINE PCV SYSTEM** – MUST FLOW FREELY.

6. **ENGINE DRIVE SPROCKETS** – CAM, CRANK, AND INTERMEDIATE SHAFTS.

7. **TORQUE CONVERTOR STALL SPEED** – TO SPECIFICATIONS.

8. **POWER BRAKE BOOSTER** – NO INTERNAL VACUUM LEAKS.

9. **FUEL CONTAMINATION** – HIGH ALCOHOL AND WATER CONTENT.

10. **TECHNICAL SERVICE BULLETINS** – ANY THAT MAY APPLY TO VEHICLE.

ANY ONE OR MORE OF THESE ITEMS CAN GIVE A DRIVEABILITY RELATED PROBLEM. THEY CANNOT BE OVERLOOKED AS POSSIBLE CAUSES.

TEST 1	STEP A	CHECKING CHARGING SYSTEM FOR FAULT CODES			
		PROCEDURE	TEST INDICATION	CIRCUIT	ACTION REQUIRED
• Connect diagnostic readout box to engine harness connector • Turn ignition switch on-off-on-off-on within 5 seconds • **RECORD ALL CODES** **NOTE:** If fault code 47 appears at this time proceed to test indication. • Turn ignition switch off and disconnect and reconnect the battery connector. • Start engine • Let engine run for 2 minutes • Turn engine off • Turn ignition switch on-off-on-off-on within 5 seconds. • **RECORD ALL CODES** If the same code appears before and after the engine is started, the problem still exists. Proceed to test indications. If a code does not reappear after the engine is started, the problem no longer exists **Perform STEP B.**			88-12-55 88-12-16-55 88-12-41-46-55 88-12-46-55 88-12-41-55 88-12-41-47-55 88-12-44-55 88-12-47-55 No code 88	No fault codes Battery voltage for charging system Alternator field (charging system output to high) Alternator field (charging system output to low) Battery temperature sensor Alternator output Battery voltage for logic module standby memory	Perform TEST NO. 2 Perform TEST NO. 3 Perform TEST NO. 4 Perform TEST NO. 5 Perform TEST NO. 6 Check for a loose fan belt. If okay, check the battery or alternator using the service manual procedure Repair battery feed wire to cavity No. 2 of the logic module black connector for an open circuit. **NOTE:** Make sure your diagnostic readout box is operational and that there is not an open circuit in the wires between the logic module and diagnostic connector.

1987–88 EFI DRIVEABILITY TEST PROCEDURES

TEST 1	STEP B	CHECKING CHARGING SYSTEM FOR INTERMITTENT FAILURES

The majority of intermittent failures are caused by wiring and connections. The only way to find them is to try and duplicate the problem. Since the logic module can remember where they are. the ATM and sensor test modes can be used in an attempt to locate them.

- If the following fault codes do not reappear use the **ATM Test Mode** as indicated.

Fault Code	ATM Test Mode
41*	09

* Connect a voltmeter to the dark green wire of the headlamp to dash harness 8-way connector terminal and watch pulsations of meter.

Once in the correct test mode, wiggle all the connectors and wires in the circuit. When the bad connection or wire is located the ATM test will be interrupted.

- If the following fault codes do not reappear use the **Sensor Test Mode** as indicated.

Fault Code	Sensor Test Mode
16	07
44	01

Once in the correct test mode, wiggle all the connectors and wires in the circuit. When the bad connection or wire is located the display on the readout box will change.

TEST 2	STEP A	CHECKING SENSOR CALIBRATION (BATTERY TEMPERATURE SENSOR)

PROCEDURE	TEST INDICATION	ACTION REQUIRED
REMINDERS • Diagnostic readout box connected to the engine harness connector • Put the system in **Engine Running TEST Mode 61.** (Refer to introduction) NOTE: Don't forget to divide the reading on display by 10	• Display on the readout box is reading between .2 (two tenths) and 3 volts	• Check for a battery drain down condition
	• Display on the readout box is not reading between .2 (two tenths) and 3 volts	• Replace the power module

DIAGNOSTIC READOUT BOX

TEST 3	STEP A	CHECKING FOR FAULT CODE 16 — BATTERY VOLTAGE SENSING CIRCUIT FOR CHARGING SYSTEM

PROCEDURE	TEST INDICATION	ACTION REQUIRED
REMINDERS • Diagnostic readout box connected to the engine harness connector • Put the system in **Sensor Test Mode 07.** (Refer to introduction) NOTE: Reading on display actual. • Connect a jumper wire between cavities No. 2 and 22 of the logic module black connector.	• Display on the readout box is reading within one volt of battery voltage	• Repair wire in cavity No. 22 of the logic module black connector for an open circuit to the wiring harness splice.
	• Display on the readout box is reading 0 volts	• Replace the logic module CAUTION: Before replacing the logic module check the terminal in cavity No. 22 of the black connector to make sure it is not crushed causing a poor connection.

JUMPER
LOGIC MODULE BLACK CONNECTOR

TEST 4	STEP A	CHECKING FOR FAULT CODES 46 OR 41-46 ALTERNATOR FIELD (CHARGING SYSTEM OUTPUT TOO HIGH)

PROCEDURE	TEST INDICATION	ACTION REQUIRED
• Disconnect the power module 10-way connector. • Connect a voltmeter between cavity No. 8 of the 10-way connector and ground. • Turn the ignition switch to the run position	• Voltmeter is reading within one volt of the battery voltage	• **Perform STEP B.**
	• Voltmeter is reading between 0 and 1 volt.	• Repair alternator field circuit for short to ground

VOLTMETER
POWER MODULE 10-WAY CONNECTOR

TEST 4	STEP B	CHECKING THE ALTERNATOR FIELD CONTROL TO THE POWER MODULE FOR A SHORT CIRCUIT

PROCEDURE	TEST INDICATION	ACTION REQUIRED
• Turn the ignition switch off • Reconnect the power module 10-way connector. • Disconnect the power module 12-way connector • Connect a voltmeter to the dark green wire of the headlamp to dash harness 8-way connector and ground • Turn the ignition switch to the run position	• Voltmeter is reading within one volt of the battery voltage	• **Perform STEP C.**
	• Voltmeter is reading between 0 and 1 volt.	• Replace the power module NOTE: Before replacing the power module make sure the dark green wire is not shorted to the power module connector or the alternator connector

DG
VOLTMETER

TEST 4	STEP C	CHECKING THE ALTERNATOR FIELD CONTROL TO THE LOGIC MODULE FOR A SHORT CIRCUIT

PROCEDURE	TEST INDICATION	ACTION REQUIRED
REMINDERS • Power module 12-way connector disconnected • Turn the ignition switch off • Disconnect the logic module white connector. • Connect an ohmmeter between cavity No. 11 of the power module 12-way connector and ground	• Ohmmeter is not showing continuity	• Replace the logic module
	• Ohmmeter is showing continuity.	• Repair wire of cavity No. 11 for a short circuit to ground

OHMMETER
POWER MODULE 12-WAY CONNECTOR

TEST 5	STEP A	CHECKING FOR FAULT CODES 41 OR 41-47 ALTERNATOR FIELD (CHARGING SYSTEM OUTPUT TOO LOW)

PROCEDURE	TEST INDICATION	ACTION REQUIRED
• Connect one end of a jumper wire to a good engine ground. • Start the engine. • Put the system into **Engine Running Test Mode 67.** (Refer to introduction) NOTE: The voltage reading displayed is actual. • Very quickly touch the other end of the jumper wire to the dark green wire of the headlamp to dash harness 8-way connector.	• Voltmeter is showing an increase in voltage.	• **Perform STEP B.**
	• Voltmeter is not showing an increase in voltage.	• Perform STEP F.

DG
JUMPER

1987–88 EFI DRIVEABILITY TEST PROCEDURES

TEST 5	STEP B	CHECKING CHARGING SYSTEM FIELD CONTROL CIRCUIT AT THE LOGIC MODULE
PROCEDURE	**TEST INDICATION**	**ACTION REQUIRED**

PROCEDURE	TEST INDICATION	ACTION REQUIRED
REMINDERS • Engine running • System in Engine Running Test Mode 67 • Connect a voltmeter between cavity No. 2 of the logic module black connector and ground. • Connect one end of a jumper wire to cavity No. 5 of the logic module white connector. • Very quickly touch the other end of the jumper wire to the logic module mounting stud and watch the voltmeter. LOGIC MODULE BLACK CONNECTOR JUMPER LOGIC MODULE WHITE CONNECTOR	• Voltmeter is showing an increase in voltage.	• Replace the logic module. **CAUTION:** Before replacing the logic module check the terminal in cavity No. 2 of the white connector to make sure it is not crushed causing a poor connection.
	• Voltmeter is not showing an increase in voltage.	• Perform STEP C.

TEST 5	STEP C	CHECKING ALTERNATOR FIELD CONTROL WIRE TO THE POWER MODULE FOR AN OPEN CIRCUIT
PROCEDURE	**TEST INDICATION**	**ACTION REQUIRED**

PROCEDURE	TEST INDICATION	ACTION REQUIRED
• Turn the engine off. • Disconnect the logic module white connector. • Connect a voltmeter between cavity No. 5 of the logic module white connector and ground. • Turn the ignition switch to the run position. LOGIC MODULE WHITE CONNECTOR	• Voltmeter is reading within one volt of the battery voltage.	• Perform STEP E.
	• Voltage reads 0 volts.	• Perform STEP D.

TEST 5	STEP D	CHECKING ALTERNATOR FIELD CONTROL CIRCUIT OF THE POWER MODULE
PROCEDURE	**TEST INDICATION**	**ACTION REQUIRED**

PROCEDURE	TEST INDICATION	ACTION REQUIRED
• Turn the ignition switch off. • Disconnect the power module 12-way connector. • Connect a voltmeter to PIN No. 11 of the power module and ground. • Turn the ignition switch to the run position. POWER MODULE 12-WAY PIN CONNECTOR	• Voltmeter is reading within one volt of battery voltage.	• Repair wire to cavity No. 5 of the logic module white connector for an open circuit.
	• Voltmeter reads 0 volts.	• Replace the power module.

TEST 5	STEP E	CHECKING THE ALTERNATOR FIELD CONTROL TO THE POWER MODULE FOR AN OPEN CIRCUIT
PROCEDURE	**TEST INDICATION**	**ACTION REQUIRED**

PROCEDURE	TEST INDICATION	ACTION REQUIRED
• Turn the ignition switch off. • Disconnect the 10-way connector from the power module. • Connect a voltmeter between cavity No. 8 of the 10-way connector and ground. • Turn the ignition switch to the run position. POWER MODULE 10-WAY CONNECTOR	• Voltmeter is reading within one volt of battery voltage.	• Replace the power module. **CAUTION:** Before replacing the power module check the terminal tabs in cavity No. 8 of the 10-way connector to make sure it is not spread apart causing a poor connection.
	• Voltmeter reads 0 volts.	• Repair wire of cavity No. 8 for an open circuit to the alternator.

TEST 5	STEP F	CHECKING FOR VOLTAGE TO ALTERNATOR FIELD CIRCUIT
PROCEDURE	**TEST INDICATION**	**ACTION REQUIRED**

PROCEDURE	TEST INDICATION	ACTION REQUIRED
• Turn the engine off. • Connect a voltmeter to the dark blue wire of the headlamp to dash harness 6-way connector and ground. • Turn the ignition switch to the run position.	• Voltmeter is reading within one volt of the battery voltage.	• Repair the alternator or field wires of the engine harness for an open circuit to the alternator.
	• Voltmeter reads 0 volts.	• Repair the dark blue wire for an open circuit to the wiring harness splice.

TEST 6	STEP A	CHECKING FOR FAULT CODE 44 — BATTERY TEMPERATURE SENSOR CIRCUIT
PROCEDURE	**TEST INDICATION**	**ACTION REQUIRED**

PROCEDURE	TEST INDICATION	ACTION REQUIRED
• Turn the ignition switch off. • Disconnect the logic module black connector. • Connect an ohmmeter between cavity No. 20 of the logic module black connector and ground. LOGIC MODULE BLACK CONNECTOR	• Ohmmeter is showing some resistance. NOTE: The amount of resistance is not important. Just make sure there is some.	• Replace the logic module. **CAUTION:** Before replacing the logic module check the terminal in cavity No. 20 of the black connector to make sure it is not crushed causing a poor connection.
	• Ohmmeter is showing 0 resistance.	• Perform STEP B.
	• Ohmmeter is showing an open circuit.	• Perform STEP C.

TEST 6	STEP B	CHECKING BATTERY TEMPERATURE SENSOR WIRE FOR SHORT CIRCUIT
PROCEDURE	**TEST INDICATION**	**ACTION REQUIRED**

PROCEDURE	TEST INDICATION	ACTION REQUIRED
REMINDERS • Logic module black connector disconnected. • Ohmmeter connected between cavity No. 20 of the logic module black connector and ground. • Disconnect the power module 12-way connector. DISCONNECT	• Ohmmeter is showing an open circuit.	• Replace the power module.
	• Ohmmeter is showing 0 resistance.	• Repair wire of cavity No. 20 for short circuit to ground.

TEST 6	STEP C	CHECKING BATTERY TEMPERATURE SENSOR WIRE FOR OPEN CIRCUIT
PROCEDURE	**TEST INDICATION**	**ACTION REQUIRED**

PROCEDURE	TEST INDICATION	ACTION REQUIRED
• Disconnect the power module 12-way connector. • Connect an ohmmeter between PIN 3 and 12 of the power module. POWER MODULE 12-WAY PIN CONNECTOR	• Ohmmeter is showing some resistance. NOTE: The amount of resistance is not important. Just make sure there is some.	• Repair wire in cavity No. 3 of power module 12-way connector for an open circuit.
	• Ohmmeter is showing 0 resistance or an open circuit.	• Replace the power module.

1987–88 EFI DRIVEABILITY TEST PROCEDURES

TEST 1	STEP A	CHECKING SPEED CONTROL SYSTEM FOR FAULT CODES		
PROCEDURE		**TEST INDICATION**	**CIRCUIT**	**ACTION REQUIRED**
• Connect diagnostic read-out box to the engine harness connector.		88-55 88-12-55	No fault codes	**Perform STEP B.**
		86-34-55 88-12-34-55	Speed control servo	**Perform TEST NO. 2.**
• Put the system into the **Diagnostic Test Mode.** (Refer to introduction.)		88-15-55 88-12-15-55	Speed sensor	**Perform Driveability TEST NO. 3, Page 36.**
• **RECORD ALL CODES**				

DIAGNOSTIC READOUT BOX

TEST 1	STEP B	CHECKING SPEED CONTROL SWITCH INPUTS TO THE LOGIC MODULE		
PROCEDURE		**TEST INDICATION**		**ACTION REQUIRED**
REMINDERS		On 00	Set 10	Resume 01	• Speed control switch okay, **Perform TEST NO. 3.**
• Diagnostic readout box connected to the engine harness connector.		On Blank	Set Blank	Resume Blank	• **Perform TEST NO. 4.**
• Put the system into **Sensor Test Mode 09.** (Refer to introduction.)		On Blank	Set 10	Resume 10	• **Perform TEST NO. 5.**
NOTE: Make sure speed control switch is in the off position.		On 00	Set 00	Resume 00	• **Perform TEST NO. 6.**
• While looking at the read-out box display a) move on/off switch to the on position. b) press the **set** button c) press the **resume** button • Record display readings.					

OFF / ON / SET / RESUME

TEST 2	STEP A	CHECKING FOR FAULT CODE 34, SPEED CONTROL SERVO (VACUUM SOLENOID)		
PROCEDURE		**TEST INDICATION**		**ACTION REQUIRED**
REMINDERS		• Voltmeter is pulsating between 0 and 12 volts.		• Vacuum solenoid okay. **Perform STEP B.**
• Diagnostic readout box connected to the engine harness connector.		• Voltmeter is pulsating between 0 and 5 volts.		• Replace the speed control servo.
• Connect a voltmeter to the tan with red tracer wire of the speed control servo harness connector and ground. • Put the system into **ATM Test Mode 08.** (Refer to introduction.) • Turn the speed control switch to the **on** position.		• Voltmeter is reading within one volt of battery voltage		• **Perform STEP E.**
		• Voltmeter is reading between 0 and one volt.		• **Perform STEP F.**

VOLTMETER

TEST 2	STEP B	CHECKING FOR FAULT CODE 34, SPEED CONTROL (VENT SOLENOID)		
PROCEDURE		**TEST INDICATION**		**ACTION REQUIRED**
REMINDERS		• Voltmeter is pulsating between 0 and 5 volts.		• Replace the speed control servo.
• Diagnostic readout box connected to the engine harness connector. • System in ATM Test Mode 08				
• Speed control switch in the on position		• Voltmeter is reading within one volt of battery voltage.		• **Perform STEP C.**
• Connect a voltmeter to the light green with red tracer wire of the speed control servo harness connector and ground.		• Voltmeter is reading between 0 and 1 volt.		• **Perform STEP D.**

VOLTMETER

TEST 2	STEP C	CHECKING THE SPEED CONTROL (VENT SOLENOID) CONTROL WIRE FOR AN OPEN CIRCUIT TO THE LOGIC MODULE		
PROCEDURE		**TEST INDICATION**		**ACTION REQUIRED**
REMINDERS		• Voltmeter is reading within 1 volt of battery voltage.		• Replace the logic module **CAUTION:** Before replacing the logic module check the terminal of cavity No. 6 of the black connector to make sure it is not crushed causing a poor connection.
• Speed control switch in the on position • Turn the ignition switch off • Connect a voltmeter to cavity No. 6 of the logic module black connector and ground. • Turn the ignition switch to the run position.		• Voltmeter reads between 0 and 7 volts.		• Repair the light green with red tracer for an open circuit to the speed control servo.

VOLTMETER

LOGIC MODULE BLACK CONNECTOR

TEST 2	STEP D	CHECKING THE SPEED CONTROL (VENT SOLENOID) CONTROL WIRE FOR A SHORT CIRCUIT TO THE LOGIC MODULE		
PROCEDURE		**TEST INDICATION**		**ACTION REQUIRED**
REMINDERS		• Voltmeter is reading within 1 volt of battery voltage		• Replace the logic module
• Speed control switch in the on position • Voltmeter connected to the light green with red tracer wire of the speed control servo harness connector and ground. • System in ATM Test Mode 08				
• Disconnect the logic module black connector.		• Voltmeter is still reading between 0 and 1 volt.		• Repair the light green with red tracer wire for a short to ground

TEST 2	STEP E	CHECKING THE SPEED CONTROL (VACUUM SOLENOID) WIRE FOR AN OPEN CIRCUIT TO THE LOGIC MODULE		
PROCEDURE		**TEST INDICATION**		**ACTION REQUIRED**
REMINDERS		• Voltmeter is reading within 1 volt of battery voltage.		• Replace the logic module **CAUTION:** Before replacing the logic module check the terminal of cavity No. 4 of the black connector to make sure it is not crushed causing a poor connection.
• Speed control switch in the on position • Turn the ignition switch off • Connect a voltmeter to cavity No. 4 of the logic module black connector and ground. • Turn the ignition switch to the run position.		• Voltmeter reads between 0 and 7 volts.		• Repair the tan with red tracer wire for an open circuit to the speed control servo.

VOLTMETER

LOGIC MODULE BLACK CONNECTOR

TEST 2	STEP F	CHECKING THE SPEED CONTROL (VACUUM SOLENOID) WIRE FOR A SHORT CIRCUIT TO THE LOGIC MODULE		
PROCEDURE		**TEST INDICATION**		**ACTION REQUIRED**
REMINDERS		• Voltmeter is reading within 1 volt of battery voltage.		• Replace the logic module.
• Speed control switch in the on position • Voltmeter connected to the tan with red tracer wire of the speed control servo harness connector and ground. • System in ATM Test Mode 08				
• Disconnect the logic module black connector.		• Voltmeter is still reading between 0 and 1 volt.		• **Perform STEP G.**

1987–88 EFI DRIVEABILITY TEST PROCEDURES

TEST 2	STEP G	CHECKING THE POWER SUPPLY TO THE SPEED CONTROL SERVO

PROCEDURE	TEST INDICATION	ACTION REQUIRED
REMINDERS • Speed control switch in the on position. • Turn the ignition off. • Connect a voltmeter to the dark blue with red tracer wire of the speed control servo harness connector and ground. • Turn the ignition switch to the run position.	• Voltmeter is reading within one volt of battery voltage.	• Replace the speed control servo.
	• Voltmeter is still reading between 0 and 1 volt.	• Perform STEP H.

TEST 2	STEP H	CHECKING SPEED CONTROL POWER SUPPLY THROUGH THE BRAKE SWITCH

PROCEDURE	TEST INDICATION	ACTION REQUIRED
REMINDERS • Speed control switch in the on position. • Ignition switch in the run position. • Connect a voltmeter to the dark blue with red tracer wire of the brake switch harness connector and ground.	• Voltmeter is reading within one volt of battery voltage.	• Repair the dark blue with red tracer wire for an open circuit to the speed control servo.
	• Voltmeter is still reading between 0 and 1 volt.	• Perform STEP I.

TEST 2	STEP I	CHECKING SPEED CONTROL POWER SUPPLY TO THE BRAKE SWITCH

PROCEDURE	TEST INDICATION	ACTION REQUIRED
REMINDERS • Speed control switch in the on position. • Ignition switch in the run position. • Connect a voltmeter to the yellow with red tracer wire of the brake switch harness connector and ground.	• Voltmeter is reading within one volt of battery voltage.	• Replace the brake switch.
	• Voltmeter still reads 0.	• Repair the yellow with red tracer wire for an open circuit to the wiring harness splice.

TEST 3	STEP A	CHECKING THE SPEED CONTROL SERVO GROUND CIRCUIT

PROCEDURE	TEST INDICATION	ACTION REQUIRED
• Turn the ignition switch off. • Disconnect the speed control servo connector. • Connect an ohmmeter between the black wire of the speed control servo harness connector and ground.	• Ohmmeter is showing continuity.	• Perform STEP B.
	• Ohmmeter is not showing continuity.	• Repair the black wire for an open circuit to the wiring harness splice.

WIRE END

BK

OHMMETER

TEST 3	STEP B	CHECKING THE SPEED CONTROL SERVO OPERATION

PROCEDURE	TEST INDICATION	ACTION REQUIRED
• Reconnect the speed control servo connector. • Connect diagnostic readout box to the engine harness connector. • Remove the air cleaner in order to see throttle linkage. • Disconnect the speed control servo vacuum supply hose from the power brake booster and connect an auxiliary vacuum supply to it. • Put the system into ATM **Test Mode 08.** (Refer to introduction) • Continuously apply vacuum to servo.	• As the system turns on and off while vacuum is continuously being applied the throttle is opening and closing.	• Repair vacuum supply to the speed control servo.
DISCONNECT & CONNECT AN AUXILIARY VACUUM SUPPLY	• As the system turns on and off while vacuum is continuously being applied the throttle is not opening and closing.	• Replace the speed control servo. NOTE: Before replacing the servo, make sure the speed control cable is properly adjusted or is not broken or make sure there are no leaks or restrictions in the vacuum supply hose.

TEST 4	STEP A	CHECKING SPEED CONTROL SYSTEM ON/OFF FUNCTION IN THE LOGIC MODULE

PROCEDURE	TEST INDICATION	ACTION REQUIRED
REMINDERS • Diagnostic readout box connected to the engine harness connector. • System in sensor Test Mode 09. • Move speed control on/off switch to the on position. • Connect a jumper wire between cavities No. 2 and 15 of the logic module black connector.	• 00 is displayed on the readout box.	• Perform STEP B.
JUMPER LOGIC MODULE BLACK CONNECTOR	• Display on the readout box is blank.	• Replace the logic module. CAUTION: Before replacing the logic module check the terminal in cavity No. 15 of the black connector to make sure it is not crushed causing a poor connection.

TEST 4	STEP B	CHECKING THE SPEED CONTROL SYSTEM POWER SUPPLY CIRCUIT

PROCEDURE	TEST INDICATION	ACTION REQUIRED
REMINDERS • Diagnostic readout box connected to the engine harness connector. • System in Sensor Test Mode 09. • Speed control switch in the on position. • Connect a jumper wire between the dark blue with white tracer and yellow with red tracer wires of the speed control switch harness connector. NOTE: Do not disconnect the speed control switch connector.	• 00 is displayed on the readout box.	• Replace the speed control switch.
JUMPER	• Display on the readout box is blank.	• Perform STEP C.

TEST 4	STEP C	CHECKING THE SPEED CONTROL SYSTEM POWER SUPPLY CIRCUIT

PROCEDURE	TEST INDICATION	ACTION REQUIRED
REMINDERS • Diagnostic readout box connected to the engine harness connector. • System in Sensor Test Mode 09. • Speed control switch in the on position. • Connect one end of a jumper wire to the dark blue with white tracer wire of the speed control switch harness connector. NOTE: Do not disconnect the speed control switch connector. • Connect the other end of the jumper wire to cavity No. 15 of the logic module black connector.	• 00 is displayed on the readout box.	• Repair the yellow with red tracer wire of cavity No. 15 for an open circuit to the speed control switch.
JUMPER LOGIC MODULE BLACK CONNECTOR	• Display on the readout box is blank.	• Repair the dark blue with white tracer wire for an open circuit to the fuse box.

1987–88 EFI DRIVEABILITY TEST PROCEDURES

TEST 5	STEP A	CHECKING SPEED CONTROL SYSTEM SET FUNCTION IN THE LOGIC MODULE
PROCEDURE		TEST INDICATION	ACTION REQUIRED

REMINDERS
- Diagnostic readout box connected to the engine harness connector.
- System in Sensor Test Mode 09.
- Move speed control on/off switch to the on position.
- Connect a jumper wire between cavities 2 and 9 of the logic module black connector.

- 00 is displayed on the readout box.
  - Perform STEP B.

- 10 is displayed on the readout box.
  - Replace the logic module.

  CAUTION: Before replacing the logic module check the terminals in cavity No. 9 of the black connector to make sure it is not crushed causing a poor connection.

LOGIC MODULE BLACK CONNECTOR

TEST 5	STEP B	CHECKING THE SPEED CONTROL SYSTEM SET CIRCUIT
PROCEDURE		TEST INDICATION	ACTION REQUIRED

REMINDERS
- Diagnostic readout box connected to the engine harness connector.
- System in Sensor Test Mode 09.
- Speed control switch in the on position.
- Connect a jumper wire between the dark blue with white tracer and brown with red tracer wires of the speed control switch harness connector.

NOTE: Do not disconnect the speed control switch connector.

- 00 is displayed on the readout box.
  - Replace the speed control switch.

- 10 is displayed on the readout box.
  - Repair the brown with red tracer wire for an open circuit to cavity No. 9 of the logic module black connector.

TEST 6	STEP A	CHECKING SPEED CONTROL SYSTEM RESUME FUNCTION IN THE LOGIC MODULE
PROCEDURE		TEST INDICATION	ACTION REQUIRED

REMINDERS
- Diagnostic readout box connected to the engine harness connector.
- System in Sensor Test Mode 09.
- Move speed control on/off switch to the on position.
- Connect a jumper wire between cavities 2 and 10 of the logic module black connector.

- 01 is displayed on the readout box.
  - Perform STEP B.

- 00 is displayed on the readout box.
  - Replace the logic module.

  CAUTION: Before replacing the logic module check the terminal in cavity No. 10 of the black connector to make sure it is not crushed causing a poor connection.

LOGIC MODULE BLACK CONNECTOR

TEST 6	STEP B	CHECKING THE SPEED CONTROL SYSTEM RESUME CIRCUIT
PROCEDURE		TEST INDICATION	ACTION REQUIRED

REMINDERS
- Diagnostic readout box connected to the engine harness connector.
- System in Sensor Test Mode 09.
- Speed control switch in the on position.
- Connect a jumper wire between the dark blue with white tracer and white wires of the speed control switch harness connector.

NOTE: Do not disconnect the speed control switch connector.

- 01 is displayed on the readout box.
  - Replace the speed control switch.

- 00 is displayed on the readout box.
  - Repair the white wire for an open circuit to cavity No. 10 of the logic module black connector.

Code	Type	Power Loss/Limit Lamp	Circuit	When Monitored By The Engine Control Module	When Put Into Memory	ATM Test Code	Sensor Access Code	Engine Running Test Code
11	Fault	No	Distributor Reference Pickup Control	During cranking.	If no distributor reference pickup signal is present since the engine control module memory was cleared.	None	None	None
12	Indication		Battery Feed to the Engine Control Module	All the time when the ignition switch is on.	If the memory of the engine control module has been cleared within the last 20-40 engine starts.	None	None	None
13	Fault	Yes	M.A.P. Sensor (Vacuum)	During engine running between 600 and 1600 rpm and M.A.P. signal within electrical range.	If no variance in the M.A.P. signal is detected between ignition pulses.	None	None	68
14	Fault	Yes	M.A.P. Sensor (Electrical)	All the time when the ignition switch is on.	If the M.A.P. sensor signal is below .02 or above 4.9 volts.	None	08	None
15	Fault	No	Vehicle Speed Sensor	At engine speeds greater than 1800 rpm and vacuum less than 10 inches.	If no speed sensor signal is detected over an 11 second period.	None	None	71
16	Fault	Yes	Battery Voltage Sensing (Charging System)	All the time after one minute from when the engine starts.	If the battery sensing voltage drops below 4 volts for more than 4 seconds.	None	07	67
17	Fault	No	Engine Cooling System	After 12 minutes from when the engine starts.	If engine coolant temperature does not reach 160°F within 8 minutes of vehicle speeds greater than 28 mph.	None	None	None
21	Fault	No	Oxygen Sensor	Engine temperature above 170°F and engine rpm above 1500.	If no lean or rich condition is indicated for a 2 minute time period.	None	02	52
22	Fault	Yes	Engine Coolant Sensor	All the time when the ignition switch is on.	If the coolant sensor voltage is above 4.96 volts when the engine is cold or below .51 volts when the engine is warm.	None	04	64
23	Fault	No	Charge Temperature Sensor	During cranking.	If the charge temperature sensor voltage is below .04 or above 4.96 when engine coolant temperature is above 77°F.	None	03	63
24	Fault	Yes	Throttle Position Sensor	All the time when the ignition switch is on.	If the throttle position sensor signal is below .16 or above 4.7 volts.	None	05	65, 59
25	Fault	No	Automatic Idle Speed Motor (AIS)	Only when the AIS system is required to control the engine speed.	If proper voltage in the AIS system is not present. NOTE: Open circuit will not activate code.	03	None	None
26	Fault	No	Fuel Injector Driver	During cranking.	If the current through any of the fuel injector pairs does not reach its proper peak level.	02	None	None
27	Fault	No	Fuel Control	All the time when the ignition switch is on.	If the fuel control interface fails to switch properly.	None	None	None
31	Fault	No	Canister Purge Solenoid	All the time when the ignition switch is on.	If the solenoid does not turn on and off when it should.	07	None	None
33	Fault	No	A/C Cutout Relay	All the time when the A/C condensor fan relay is energized.	If the relay does not turn on and off when it should.	05	None	None
34	Fault	No	Speed Control Servo Circuit	All the time when the speed control switch is on and the brake is not applied.	If the servo does not turn on and off when it should.	08	None	None
35	Fault	No	Radiator Fan Relay Circuit	All the time when the ignition switch is on.	If the relay does not turn on and off when it should.	04	None	None

Code	Type	Power Loss/Limit Lamp	Circuit	When Monitored By The Engine Control Module	When Put Into Memory	ATM Test Code	Sensor Access Code	Engine Running Test Code
37	Fault	No	Transmission Lockup Solenoid	All the time when the ignition switch is on.	If the lockup solenoid does not turn on and off when it should.	10	None	None
41	Fault	No	Alternator Field Control (Charging System)	All the time when the ignition switch is on.	If the field control fails to switch properly.	09	None	None
42	Fault	No	Auto Shutdown	All the time when the ignition switch is on.	If the relay does not turn on and off when it should.	06	None	None
43	Fault	No	Spark Control	During cranking only.	If the spark control interface fails to switch properly.	01	None	None
44	Fault	No	Fused J2	All the time when the ignition key is on.	If fused J2 is not present in the logic board of the engine control module.	None	None	None
46	Fault	Yes	Battery Voltage Sensing (Charging System)	All the time when the engine is running.	If the battery sense voltage is more than 1 volt above the desired control voltage for more than 20 seconds.	None	07	67
47	Fault	No	Battery Voltage Sensing (Charging System)	When the engine has been running for more than 6 minutes, engine temperature above 160°F and engine rpm above 1,500.	If the battery sense voltage is less than 1 volt below the desired control voltage for more than 20 seconds.	None	07	67
51	Fault	No	Oxygen Feedback System	During all closed loop conditions.	If the O₂ sensor indicates a lean condition for more than 2 minutes.	None	None	01 Switching
52	Fault	No	Oxygen Feedback System	During all closed loop conditions.	If the O₂ sensor indicates a rich condition for more than 2 minutes.	None	None	01 Switching
53	Fault	No	Engine control module	When the ignition key is initially turned to the on position.	If the logic board fails.	None	None	None
54	Fault	No	Distributor Sync. Pickup	All the time when the engine is running.	If there is not a distributor sync. pickup signal.	None	None	None
55	Indication	No			Indicates end of diagnostic mode.			
88	Indication	No			Indicates start of diagnostic mode. NOTE: This code must appear first in the diagnostic mode or fault codes will be inaccurate.			
0	Indication	No	Indicates oxygen feedback system is lean with the engine running					
1	Indication	No			Indicates oxygen feedback system is rich with the engine running.			

1987–88 EFI DRIVEABILITY TEST PROCEDURES

TEST 1	STEP A	CHECKING FOR SPARK AT SPARK PLUGS	
PROCEDURE		**TEST INDICATION**	**ACTION REQUIRED**
• Disconnect any spark plug wire. • Insert an insulated screw driver in terminal. • Hold screwdriver shaft (¼") near a good engine ground. • Have someone crank the engine for at least 7 seconds.		• There is a good spark between screwdriver and ground as long as the engine is cranking.	• Perform TEST NO. 2.
		• There is no spark. NOTE: Handle 1 or 2 sparks as no spark.	• Perform STEP B.
		• There is spark for about 5 seconds and then stops and/or engine starts, runs for a few seconds and then stalls.	• Perform TEST NO. 9.

TEST 1	STEP B	CHECKING FOR SPARK AT IGNITION COIL WIRE	
PROCEDURE		**TEST INDICATION**	**ACTION REQUIRED**
• Disconnect ignition coil wire from distributor cap. • Hold coil wire (¼") near a good engine ground. • Have someone crank the engine.		• There is a good spark between ignition coil wire and ground.	• Repair secondary ignition system (distributor cap and/or rotor).
		• There is no spark. NOTE: Handle 1 or 2 sparks as no spark.	• Perform STEP C.

TEST 1	STEP C	CHECKING VOLTAGE SUPPLY FROM POWER MODULE	
PROCEDURE		**TEST INDICATION**	**ACTION REQUIRED**
• Connect a voltmeter to the dark green with black tracer wire of the injector 4-way connector and ground. • Crank the engine for at least 7 seconds.		• Voltmeter is reading within one volt of cranking voltage as long as the engine is cranking.	• Perform TEST NO. 6.
		• Voltmeter is reading 0 volts or cranking voltage for about 1 second.	• Perform TEST NO. 12.

TEST 2	STEP A	CHECKING FUEL SUPPLY PRESSURE	
PROCEDURE		**TEST INDICATION**	**ACTION REQUIRED**
• Install pressure gauge (Tool C3292) with (C4799 adapter) in fuel supply hose at throttle body. CAUTION: Fuel is under high pressure. Refer to service manual for pressure release procedure. • Crank the engine for at least 7 seconds.		• Fuel pressure is reading at least 30 psi.	• Perform STEP B.
		• Fuel pressure is 0.	• Perform TEST NO. 5.

TEST 2	STEP B	CHECKING THROTTLE POSITION SENSOR	
PROCEDURE		**TEST INDICATION**	**ACTION REQUIRED**
• Connect diagnostic readout box to the engine harness connector. • Put the system into Sensor Test Mode 05, Refer to introduction. NOTE: Don't forget to divide display reading by 10 for actual reading.		• Display on the readout box is reading between ½ and 1½ volts.	• Perform STEP C.
		• Display on the readout box reads more than 1½ volts.	• Replace the throttle position sensor.
		• System will not go into the sensor test mode (no code 88).	• Replace the engine control module.

TEST 2	STEP C	CHECKING VOLTAGE SUPPLY TO THE IGNITION COIL FROM THE AUTO SHUTDOWN RELAY	
PROCEDURE		**TEST INDICATION**	**ACTION REQUIRED**
REMINDERS • Diagnostic readout box connected to the engine harness connector. • Connect a voltmeter to the dark green with black tracer wire of the injector harness 4-way connector and ground. • Turn the ignition switch to the run position. • Put the system in ATM Test Mode 02, (Refer to introduction)		• Voltmeter is reading within one volt of battery voltage.	• Perform TEST NO. 3.
		• Voltmeter is reading 0 volts.	• Repair the dark green with black tracer wire of the injector harness connector for an open circuit to the wiring harness splice.

TEST 3	STEP A	CHECKING FOR FUEL FOULED SPARK PLUGS	
PROCEDURE		**TEST INDICATION**	**ACTION REQUIRED**
• Remove spark plugs. • Look at tips for wet fuel.		• Spark plug tips are not wet with fuel. NOTE: It is normal for spark plugs to be black after engine is started cold.	• Perform TEST NO. 4.
		• Spark plugs are wet with fuel.	• Clean and reinstall. Do not replace spark plugs. • Attempt restart.

TEST 4	STEP A	CHECKING ENGINE TIMING	
PROCEDURE		**TEST INDICATION**	**ACTION REQUIRED**
• Connect timing device to engine. • Have someone crank engine while you look at the timing marks.		• Timing is between 0°-16° BTC.	• Remove distributor cap, crank engine to make sure rotor is turning and is indexed correctly. • Check compression and valve timing.
		• Timing is not between 0°-16° BTC.	• Perform STEP B.

1987–88 EFI DRIVEABILITY TEST PROCEDURES

TEST 4	STEP B	CHECKING ENGINE TIMING
PROCEDURE	TEST INDICATION	ACTION REQUIRED

PROCEDURE	TEST INDICATION	ACTION REQUIRED
REMINDERS • Timing device connected to engine. • Set timing to 10° BTC during cranking.	• Engine starts.	• Reset timing to specifications.
	• Engine does not start.	• Remove distributor cap, crank engine to make sure rotor is turning and is indexed correctly. • Check compression and valve timing.

TEST 5	STEP A	CHECKING FUEL PUMP
PROCEDURE	TEST INDICATION	ACTION REQUIRED

PROCEDURE	TEST INDICATION	ACTION REQUIRED
• Connect the diagnostic readout box to the engine harness connector. • Turn the ignition switch to the run position. • Press the ATM button on the readout box.	• The fuel pump is running.	• Check the following: a) all fuel lines for kinks, restrictions, or leaks b) a plugged fuel filter. If all okay remove the pump for inspection and for fuel contamination.
	• The fuel pump is not running.	• Perform STEP B.

DIAGNOSTIC READOUT BOX

TEST 5	STEP B	CHECKING FUEL PUMP WIRES
PROCEDURE	TEST INDICATION	ACTION REQUIRED

PROCEDURE	TEST INDICATION	ACTION REQUIRED
REMINDERS • Diagnostic readout box connected to the engine harness connector. • Ignition switch in the run position. • Raise the car on a hoist. • Disconnect the intank fuel pump connector. • Connect the positive lead of a voltmeter to the dark green with black tracer wire of the connector. • Connect the negative lead of the voltmeter to the gray wire of the connector. • Press the ATM button.	• Voltmeter is reading within one volt of battery voltage.	• Replace the fuel pump.
	• Voltmeter reads 0.	• Move negative lead of voltmeter to a good engine ground and press the ATM button. • If voltage is now okay repair gray wire of connector for an open circuit. • If voltage is still 0, repair the dark green with black tracer wire for an open circuit.

IN TANK FUEL PUMP CONNECTOR

TEST 6	STEP A	CHECKING IGNITION CONTROL SYSTEM FOR FAULT CODES
PROCEDURE	TEST INDICATION	ACTION REQUIRED

PROCEDURE	TEST INDICATION	ACTION REQUIRED
• Connect diagnostic readout box to the engine harness connector. • Erase fault codes. (Refer to introduction) • Crank the engine for 5 seconds and then turn the ignition switch off. • Put the system in the Diagnostic Mode. (Refer to introduction) • Record all codes	88-12-55 No fault codes	Perform TEST NO. 7.
	88-12-43-55 Spark control circuit	Perform TEST NO. 8.

DIAGNOSTIC READOUT BOX

TEST 7	STEP A	CHECKING FOR THE VOLTAGE SUPPLY TO THE IGNITION COIL POSITIVE TERMINAL FROM THE AUTO SHUTDOWN RELAY
PROCEDURE	TEST INDICATION	ACTION REQUIRED

PROCEDURE	TEST INDICATION	ACTION REQUIRED
REMINDERS • Diagnostic readout box connected to the engine harness connector. • Connect an analog voltmeter to the positive terminal of the ignition coil and ground. • Put the system in the ATM Test Mode - Code 01. (Refer to Introduction)	• Voltmeter is reading within one volt of battery voltage.	• Perform STEP B.
	• Voltmeter reads 0.	• Repair the dark green with black tracer wire of coil positive terminal for open circuit to the wiring harness splice.

IGNITION COIL

TEST 7	STEP B	CHECKING THE IGNITION SYSTEM PRIMARY CONTROL CIRCUIT VOLTAGE AT THE IGNITION COIL (−) TERMINAL
PROCEDURE	TEST INDICATION	ACTION REQUIRED

PROCEDURE	TEST INDICATION	ACTION REQUIRED
REMINDERS • Diagnostic readout box connected to the engine harness connector. • System in ATM Test Mode - Code 01. • Connect an analog voltmeter to the negative terminal of the ignition coil and ground.	• Voltmeter reading is pulsating between 10 and 14 volts.	• Replace the ignition coil.
	• Voltmeter not pulsating but reads above 10 volts.	• Perform STEP C.
	• Voltmeter pulsating between 5 and 10 volts.	• Replace the ignition coil.
	• Voltmeter pulsating between 0 and 2 volts.	• Perform STEP D.

IGNITION COIL

TEST 7	STEP C	CHECKING THE IGNITION SYSTEM PRIMARY CONTROL CIRCUIT FOR AN OPEN CIRCUIT
PROCEDURE	TEST INDICATION	ACTION REQUIRED

PROCEDURE	TEST INDICATION	ACTION REQUIRED
• Turn the ignition switch off. • Disconnect the 14-way connector from the engine control module. • Connect an ohmmeter between the negative (−) terminal of the ignition coil and cavity No. 12 of the 14-way connector.	• Ohmmeter is showing continuity.	• Defective power board. Replace the engine control module. CAUTION: Before replacing the engine control module check the terminal in cavity No. 12 of the 14-way connector to make sure that it is not spread apart causing a poor connection.
	• Ohmmeter is showing no continuity.	• Repair the black with yellow tracer wire of cavity No. 12 for an open circuit.

IGNITION COIL
OHMMETER
14-WAY CONNECTOR

TEST 7	STEP D	CHECKING THE IGNITION COIL PRIMARY WINDINGS FOR A SHORT CIRCUIT
PROCEDURE	TEST INDICATION	ACTION REQUIRED

PROCEDURE	TEST INDICATION	ACTION REQUIRED
REMINDERS • Diagnostic readout box connected to the engine harness connector. • Turn the ignition switch off. • Disconnect the wire from the negative side (−) of the ignition coil. • Connect the voltmeter to the negative (−) terminal of the ignition coil and ground. • Put the system in the ATM Test Mode - Code 01.	• Voltmeter is reading above 10 volts.	• Perform STEP E.
	• Voltmeter reads between 0 and 2 volts.	• Replace the ignition coil.

IGNITION COIL

1987–88 EFI DRIVEABILITY TEST PROCEDURES

TEST 7 | STEP E | CHECKING THE IGNITION SYSTEM PRIMARY CIRCUIT FOR A SHORT CIRCUIT TO GROUND

PROCEDURE	TEST INDICATION	ACTION REQUIRED
REMINDERS • Ignition coil negative (−) wire disconnected. • Turn the ignition switch off. • Disconnect the 14-way connector from the engine control module. • Connect an ohmmeter between cavity No. 12 of the 14-way connector and ground.	• Ohmmeter is not showing continuity.	• Defective power board. Replace the engine control module.
	• Ohmmeter is showing continuity.	• Repair the black with yellow tracer wire of cavity No. 12 for a short circuit to ground.

14-WAY CONNECTOR

TEST 8 | STEP A | CHECKING FOR FAULT CODE 43 — SPARK CONTROL CIRCUIT

PROCEDURE	TEST INDICATION	ACTION REQUIRED
REMINDERS • Diagnostic readout box connected to the engine harness connector. • Turn the ignition switch off. • Disconnect the ignition coil wire at the distributor and place it near a good engine ground so there is a ¼ inch gap. • Disconnect the 60-way connector from the engine control module and connect one end of a jumper wire to cavity No. 34. • Turn the ignition switch on and press and hold the ATM button on the readout box.	• Touch the other end of the jumper to a good ground. Make and break this connection several times while looking at the ignition coil wire. • There is spark at the ignition coil wire as you make and break the connection.	• Defective logic board. Replace the engine control module. CAUTION: Before replacing the engine control module check the terminal in cavity No. 34 of the 60-way connector to make sure it is not damaged causing a poor connection.
VIEW FROM TERMINAL END	• There is no spark at the ignition coil wire as you make and break the connection.	• Perform STEP B.

34 / JUMPER

TEST 8 | STEP B | CHECKING THE SPARK CONTROL WIRE BETWEEN THE LOGIC AND POWER BOARDS FOR AN OPEN CIRCUIT

PROCEDURE	TEST INDICATION	ACTION REQUIRED
REMINDERS • Engine control module 60-way connector disconnected. • Turn the ignition switch off. • Remove the jumper wire from cavity No. 34 of the engine control module 60-way connector. • Disconnect the engine control module 14-way connector. • Connect one lead of an ohmmeter to cavity No. 34 of the engine control module 60-way connector. • Connect the other lead of the ohmmeter to cavity No. 13 the engine control module 14-way connector.	• Ohmmeter is showing continuity.	• Defective power board. Replace the engine control module. CAUTION: Before replacing the engine control module check the terminal in cavity No. 13 of the 14-way connector to make sure it is not spread apart causing a poor connection.
VIEW FROM TERMINAL END 34 / OHMMETER	• Ohmmeter is not showing continuity.	• Repair wire for an open circuit.

14-WAY CONNECTOR

TEST 9 | STEP A | CHECKING INJECTOR CONTROL SYSTEM FOR FAULT CODES

PROCEDURE	TEST INDICATION	ACTION REQUIRED
• Connect diagnostic readout box to the engine harness connector. • Erase fault codes. (Refer to introduction.) • Crank engine for 7 seconds and then turn the ignition switch off. NOTE: In some cases engine may start and run for a few seconds and then stall. • Put the system into the **Diagnostic Mode** (Refer to introduction). • Record all codes.	86-12-26-55 Injector driver circuits	• Perform TEST NO. 10.
	88-12-27-55 Injector control circuits.	• Perform TEST NO. 11.

DIAGNOSTIC READOUT BOX

TEST 10 | STEP A | CHECKING THE VOLTAGE SUPPLY CIRCUIT TO EACH INJECTOR

PROCEDURE	TEST INDICATION	ACTION REQUIRED
REMINDERS • Diagnostic readout box connected to the engine harness connector. • Remove air intake plenum. • Disconnect all injectors. • Put the system in the ATM Test Mode - Code 02. (Refer to introduction) • Connect the negative lead of a voltmeter to ground and touch the positive lead to the dark green with black tracer wire of each injector connector.	• Voltmeter shows within one volt of battery voltage at each connector.	• Perform STEP B.
DISCONNECT ALL INJECTORS	• Voltmeter shows 0 volts at one or more of the connectors.	• Repair the injector harness for an open circuit to the injector connector.

TEST 10 | STEP B | CHECKING INJECTOR NO. 1 CIRCUIT

PROCEDURE	TEST INDICATION	ACTION REQUIRED
REMINDERS • Diagnostic readout box connected to the engine harness connector. • Air intake plenum removed. • All injectors disconnected. • System in ATM Test Mode - Code 02. • Connect injector connector number 1 to injector number 1. • Leave connected for 10 seconds and listen for a click.	• Injector number 1 clicks.	• Perform STEP H.
DIAGNOSTIC READOUT	• Injector number 1 does not click.	• Perform STEP C. NOTE: Make sure ATM Test 02 has not timed out before proceeding to STEP C.

DIAGNOSTIC READOUT BOX

TEST 10 | STEP C | CHECKING INJECTOR NO. 6 CIRCUIT

PROCEDURE	TEST INDICATION	ACTION REQUIRED
REMINDERS • Diagnostic readout box connected to the engine harness connector. • Air intake plenum removed. • All injectors, except injector for cylinder number 1, disconnected. • System in ATM Test Mode - Code 02. • Disconnect injector connector number 1 from injector. • Connect injector connector number 6 to injector number 6. • Leave connected for 10 seconds and listen for a click.	• Injector number 6 clicks.	• Perform STEP G.
	• Injector number 6 does not click.	• Perform STEP D.

TEST 10 | STEP D | CHECKING INJECTORS 1 AND 6

PROCEDURE	TEST INDICATION	ACTION REQUIRED
REMINDERS • Diagnostic readout box connected to the engine harness connector. • Air intake plenum removed. • All injectors, except injector for cylinder number 6, disconnected. • System in ATM Test Mode - Code 02. • Disconnect injector connector number 6 from injector. • Connect injector connector number 2 to injector number 1. • Leave connected for 10 seconds and listen for a click.	• Disconnect injector connector number 2 from injector number 1. • Connect injector connector number 4 to injector number 6. • Leave connected for 10 seconds and listen for a click. • Injectors 1 and 6 do not click.	• Replace injectors number 1 and 6.
	• One injector, either 1 or 6, clicks and the other doesn't.	• Replace injector which failed to click.
DIAGNOSTIC READOUT	• Both injector 1 and 6 click.	• Perform STEP E.

DIAGNOSTIC READOUT BOX

1987–88 EFI DRIVEABILITY TEST PROCEDURES

TEST 10	STEP E	CHECKING 1 AND 6 CONTROL WIRE FOR A SHORT TO GROUND	
PROCEDURE		**TEST INDICATION**	**ACTION REQUIRED**
• Turn the ignition switch off. • Disconnect the 14-way connector from the engine control module. • Connect an ohmmeter between cavity No. 5 of the 14-way connector and ground.		• Ohmmeter is showing continuity.	• Repair the yellow with white tracer wire of cavity No. 5 of the 14-way connector for a short to ground.
		• Ohmmeter is showing no continuity.	• Perform STEP F.

14-WAY CONNECTOR

TEST 10	STEP F	CHECKING 1 AND 6 CONTROL WIRE FOR AN OPEN CIRCUIT TO THE ENGINE CONTROL MODULE	
PROCEDURE		**TEST INDICATION**	**ACTION REQUIRED**
REMINDERS • Ignition switch turned off. • 14-way connector disconnected from the engine control module. • Connect an ohmmeter between cavity No. 5 of the 14-way connector and the yellow with white tracer wire of injector connectors 1 and 6.		• Ohmmeter is showing continuity.	• Defective power board. Replace the engine control module. CAUTION: Before replacing the engine control module check the terminal in cavity No. 5 of the 14-way connector to make sure it is not spread apart causing a poor connection.
		• Ohmmeter is not showing continuity.	• Repair the yellow with white tracer wire of cavity No. 5 of the 14-way connector for an open circuit to the injector connector.

14-WAY CONNECTOR

TEST 10	STEP G	CHECKING INJECTOR NUMBER 1 CONTROL WIRE FOR AN OPEN CIRCUIT IN INJECTOR HARNESS	
PROCEDURE		**TEST INDICATION**	**ACTION REQUIRED**
• Turn the ignition switch off. • Disconnect injector connector No. 6 from injector. • Disconnect injector harness 4-way connector from the engine harness connector. • Connect an ohmmeter between the yellow with white tracer wire at injector No. 1 connector and the yellow with white tracer wire at the injector harness 4-way connector.		• Ohmmeter is showing continuity.	• Replace injector No. 1.
		• Ohmmeter is not showing continuity.	• Repair the yellow with white tracer wire for an open circuit in the injector harness.

TEST 10	STEP H	CHECKING INJECTOR NO. 6 CIRCUIT	
PROCEDURE		**TEST INDICATION**	**ACTION REQUIRED**
REMINDERS • Diagnostic readout box connected to the engine harness connector. • Air intake plenum removed. • All injectors, except injector No. 1, disconnected. • System in ATM Test Mode - Code 02. • Disconnect injector connector No. 1 from injector. • Connect injector connector No. 6 to injector No. 6. • Leave connected for 10 seconds and listen for a click.		• Injector No. 6 clicks.	• Perform STEP J.
		• Injector No. 6 does not click.	• Perform STEP I.

DIAGNOSTIC READOUT BOX

TEST 10	STEP I	CHECKING INJECTOR NUMBER 6 CONTROL WIRE FOR AN OPEN CIRCUIT IN INJECTOR HARNESS.	
PROCEDURE		**TEST INDICATION**	**ACTION REQUIRED**
• Turn the ignition switch off. • Disconnect injector connector No. 6 from injector. • Disconnect injector harness 4-way connector from the engine harness. • Connect an ohmmeter between the yellow with white tracer wire at injector No. 6 connector and the yellow with white tracer wire at the 4-way injector harness connector.		• Ohmmeter is showing continuity.	• Replace injector No. 6.
		• Ohmmeter is not showing continuity.	• Repair the yellow with white tracer wire for an open circuit in the injector harness.

TEST 10	STEP J	CHECKING INJECTOR NO. 2 CIRCUIT	
PROCEDURE		**TEST INDICATION**	**ACTION REQUIRED**
REMINDERS • Diagnostic readout box connected to the engine harness connector. • Air intake plenum removed. • All injectors, except injector for cylinder No. 6, disconnected. • System in ATM Test Mode - Code 02. • Disconnect injector connector No. 6 from injector. • Connect injector connector No. 2 to injector No. 2. • Leave connected for 10 seconds and listen for a click.		• Injector No. 2 clicks.	• Perform STEP P.
		• Injector No. 2 does not click.	• Perform STEP K. NOTE: Make sure ATM Test 02 has not timed out before proceeding to STEP K.

DIAGNOSTIC READOUT BOX

TEST 10	STEP K	CHECKING INJECTOR CIRCUIT NO. 3	
PROCEDURE		**TEST INDICATION**	**ACTION REQUIRED**
REMINDERS • Diagnostic readout box connected to the engine harness connector. • Air intake plenum removed. • All injectors, except injector for cylinder No. 2, disconnected. • System in ATM Test Mode - Code 02. • Disconnect injector connector No. 2 from injector. • Connect injector connector No. 3 to injector No. 3. • Leave connected for 10 seconds and listen for a click.		• Injector No. 3 clicks.	• Perform STEP O.
		• Injector No. 3 does not click.	• Perform STEP L.

TEST 10	STEP L	CHECKING INJECTORS 2 AND 3	
PROCEDURE		**TEST INDICATION**	**ACTION REQUIRED**
REMINDERS • Diagnostic readout box connected to the engine harness connector. • Air intake plenum removed. • All injectors, except injector for cylinder No. 3, disconnected. • System in ATM Test Mode - Code 02. • Disconnect injector connector No. 3 from injector. • Connect injector connector No. 1 to injector No. 2. • Leave connected for 10 seconds and listen for a click.	• Disconnect injector connector No. 1 from injector No. 2. • Connect injector connector No. 1 to injector No. 3. • Leave connected for 10 seconds and listen for a click.	• Injectors No. 2 and 3 do not click.	• Replace injectors No. 2 and 3.
		• One injector, either 2 or 3, clicks and the other doesn't.	• Replace injector which failed to click.
		• Both injectors 2 and 3 click.	• Perform STEP M.

DIAGNOSTIC READOUT BOX

1987–88 EFI DRIVEABILITY TEST PROCEDURES

TEST 10	STEP M	CHECKING 2 AND 3 CONTROL WIRE FOR A SHORT TO GROUND

PROCEDURE	TEST INDICATION	ACTION REQUIRED
• Turn the ignition switch off. • Disconnect the 14-way connector from the engine control module. • Connect an ohmmeter between cavity No. 10 of the 14-way connector and ground.	• Ohmmeter is showing continuity.	• Repair the tan wire at cavity No. 10 of the 14-way connector for a short to ground.
	• Ohmmeter is showing no continuity.	• Perform STEP N.

14-WAY CONNECTOR

TEST 10	STEP N	CHECKING 2 AND 3 CONTROL WIRE FOR AN OPEN CIRCUIT TO THE ENGINE CONTROL MODULE

PROCEDURE	TEST INDICATION	ACTION REQUIRED
REMINDERS • Ignition switch turned off. • 14-way connector disconnected from the engine control module. • Connect an ohmmeter between cavity No. 10 of the 14-way connector and tan wire of injector connectors 2 and then 3.	• Ohmmeter is showing continuity.	• Defective power board. Replace the engine control module. CAUTION: Before replacing the engine control module check the terminal in cavity No. 10 of the 14-way connector to make sure it is not spread apart causing a poor connection.
	• Ohmmeter is not showing continuity.	• Repair the tan wire of cavity No. 10 of the 14-way connector for an open circuit to the injector harness connector.

14-WAY CONNECTOR

TEST 10	STEP O	CHECKING INJECTOR NO. 2 CONTROL WIRE FOR AN OPEN CIRCUIT IN INJECTOR HARNESS

PROCEDURE	TEST INDICATION	ACTION REQUIRED
• Turn the ignition switch off. • Disconnect injector connector for cylinder No. 3 from injector. • Disconnect injector harness 4-way connector from the engine harness connector. • Connect an ohmmeter between the tan wire at injector No. 2 connector and the tan wire at injector harness 4-way connector.	• Ohmmeter is showing continuity.	• Replace injector No. 2.
	• Ohmmeter is not showing continuity.	• Repair the tan wire for an open circuit in the injector harness.

TEST 10	STEP P	CHECKING INJECTOR NO. 3 CIRCUIT

PROCEDURE	TEST INDICATION	ACTION REQUIRED
REMINDERS • Diagnostic readout box connected to the engine harness connector. • Air intake plenum removed. • All injectors, except injector No. 2, disconnected. • System in ATM Test Mode - Code 02.	• Injector No. 3 clicks.	• Perform STEP R.
• Disconnect injector connector No. 2. • Connect injector connector No. 3 to injector No. 3. • Leave connected for 10 seconds and listen for a click.	• Injector No. 3 does not click.	• Perform STEP Q.

DIAGNOSTIC READOUT BOX

TEST 10	STEP Q	CHECKING INJECTOR NO. 3 CONTROL WIRE FOR AN OPEN CIRCUIT IN INJECTOR HARNESS

PROCEDURE	TEST INDICATION	ACTION REQUIRED
• Turn the ignition switch off. • Disconnect injector connector No. 3 from injector. • Disconnect injector harness 4-way connector from the engine harness. • Connect an ohmmeter between the tan wire at injector No. 3 connector and the tan wire at the injector harness 4-way connector.	• Ohmmeter is showing continuity.	• Replace injector No. 3.
	• Ohmmeter is not showing continuity.	• Repair the tan wire for an open circuit in the injector harness.

TEST 10	STEP R	CHECKING INJECTOR NO. 4 CIRCUIT

PROCEDURE	TEST INDICATION	ACTION REQUIRED
REMINDERS • Diagnostic readout box connected to the engine harness connector. • Air intake plenum removed. • All injectors, except injector for cylinder No. 3, disconnected. • System in ATM Test Mode - Code 02.	• Injector No. 4 clicks.	• Perform STEP X.
• Disconnect injector connector No. 3 from injector. • Connect injector connector No. 4 to injector for cylinder No. 4 • Leave connected for 10 seconds and listen for a click.	• Injector No. 4 does not click.	• Perform STEP S. NOTE: Make sure ATM test 02 has not timed out before proceeding to Step S.

DIAGNOSTIC READOUT BOX

TEST 10	STEP S	CHECKING INJECTOR NO. 5 CIRCUIT

PROCEDURE	TEST INDICATION	ACTION REQUIRED
REMINDERS • Diagnostic readout box connected to the engine harness connector. • Air intake plenum removed. • All injectors, except injector for cylinder No. 4, disconnected. • System in ATM Test Mode - Code 02.	• Injector No. 5 clicks.	• Perform STEP W.
• Disconnect injector connector No. 4 from injector. • Connect injector connector No. 5 to injector for cylinder No. 5. • Leave connected for 10 seconds and listen for a click.	• Injector No. 5 does not click.	• Perform STEP T.

TEST 10	STEP T	CHECKING INJECTORS 4 AND 5

PROCEDURE	TEST INDICATION	ACTION REQUIRED
REMINDERS • Diagnostic readout box connected to the engine harness connector. • Air intake plenum removed. • All injectors, except injector for cylinder No. 5, disconnected. • System in ATM Test Mode - Code 02.	• Disconnect injector connector No. 6 from injector No. 4. • Connect injector connector No. 6 to injector No. 5. • Leave connected for 10 seconds and listen for a click.	• Injectors No. 4 and 5 do not click.	• Replace injectors No. 4 and 5.
		• One injector, either 4 or 5, clicks and the other doesn't.	• Replace injector which failed to click.
• Disconnect injector connector No. 5 from injector. • Connect injector connector No. 6 to injector No. 4 • Leave connected for 10 seconds and listen for a click.		• Both injectors 4 and 5 click.	• Perform STEP U.

DIAGNOSTIC READOUT BOX

1987–88 EFI DRIVEABILITY TEST PROCEDURES

TEST 10	STEP U	CHECKING 4 AND 5 CONTROL WIRE FOR A SHORT TO GROUND

PROCEDURE	TEST INDICATION	ACTION REQUIRED
• Turn the ignition switch off. • Disconnect the 14-way connector from the engine control module. • Connect an ohmmeter between cavity No. 9 of the 14-way connector and ground.	• Ohmmeter is showing continuity.	• Repair the white wire of cavity No. 9 of the 14-way connector for a short to ground.
	• Ohmmeter is showing no continuity.	• Perform STEP V.

14-WAY CONNECTOR

OHMMETER

TEST 10	STEP V	CHECKING INJECTOR NO. 5 CONTROL WIRE FOR AN OPEN CIRCUIT

PROCEDURE	TEST INDICATION	ACTION REQUIRED
REMINDERS • Ignition switch turned off. • 14-way connector disconnected from the engine control module. • Connect an ohmmeter between cavity 9 of the 14-way connector and the white wire of injector connectors 4 and 5.	• Ohmmeter is showing continuity.	• Defective power board. Replace the engine control module. **CAUTION:** Before replacing the engine control module check the terminal in cavity No. 9 of the 14-way connector to make sure it is not spread apart causing a poor connection.
	• Ohmmeter is not showing continuity.	• Repair the white wire of cavity No. 9 of the 14-way connector for an open circuit to the injector connectors.

OHMMETER

14-WAY CONNECTOR

TEST 10	STEP W	CHECKING INJECTOR NO. 4 CONTROL WIRE FOR AN OPEN CIRCUIT IN INJECTOR HARNESS

PROCEDURE	TEST INDICATION	ACTION REQUIRED
• Turn the ignition switch off. • Disconnect injector connector No. 5 from injector. • Disconnect injector harness 4-way connector from the engine harness connector. • Connect an ohmmeter between the white wire at injector No. 4 and the white wire at the injector harness 4-way connector.	• Ohmmeter is showing continuity.	• Replace injector No. 4.
	• Ohmmeter is not showing continuity.	• Repair the white wire for an open circuit in the injector harness.

OHMMETER

TEST 10	STEP X	CHECKING INJECTOR NO. 5 CONTROL WIRE FOR AN OPEN CIRCUIT IN INJECTOR HARNESS

PROCEDURE	TEST INDICATION	ACTION REQUIRED
• Turn the ignition switch off. • Disconnect injector connector No. 4 from injector. • Disconnect injector harness 4-way connector from engine harness connector. • Connect an ohmmeter between the white wire at injector No. 5 and the white wire at the injector harness 4-way connector.	• Ohmmeter is showing continuity.	• Replace injector No. 5.
	• Ohmmeter is not showing continuity.	• Repair the white wire for an open circuit in the injector harness.

OHMMETER

TEST 11	STEP A	CHECKING FOR FAULT CODE 27 - FUEL CONTROL CIRCUIT (INJECTORS 4 AND 5 CONTROL CIRCUIT)

PROCEDURE	TEST INDICATION	ACTION REQUIRED
REMINDERS • Diagnostic readout box connect to the engine harness connector. • Turn the ignition switch off. • Disconnect the 60-way connector from the engine control module. • Connect one end of a jumper wire to cavity No. 33 of the 60-way connector. • Turn ignition switch on. • Press the ATM button on diagnostic readout box and touch the other end of the jumper wire to the positive post of the battery.	• Injectors 4 and 5 click.	• Perform STEP C.
	• Injectors 4 and 5 do not click.	• Perform STEP B.

VIEW FROM TERMINAL END

33

JUMPER

BATTERY POSITIVE

TEST 11	STEP B	CHECKING INJECTORS 4 AND 5 CONTROL WIRE FOR AN OPEN CIRCUIT

PROCEDURE	TEST INDICATION	ACTION REQUIRED
REMINDERS • 60-way connector disconnected from engine control module. • Turn the ignition switch off. • Disconnect the 14-way connector from the engine control module. • Connect an ohmmeter between cavity No. 33 of the 60-way connector and cavity No. 8 of the 14-way connector.	• Ohmmeter is showing continuity.	• Defective power board. Replace the engine control module. **CAUTION:** Before replacing the engine control module check the terminal in cavity No. 8 of the 14-way connector to make sure it is not spread apart causing a poor connection.
	• Ohmmeter is not showing continuity.	• Repair the violet with yellow tracer wire for an open circuit between the 14 and 60-way connectors.

VIEW FROM TERMINAL END

33

OHMMETER

14-WAY CONNECTOR

TEST 11	STEP C	CHECKING INJECTORS 2 AND 3 CONTROL CIRCUIT

PROCEDURE	TEST INDICATION	ACTION REQUIRED
REMINDERS • Diagnostic readout box connected to the engine harness connector. • 60-way connector disconnected from the engine control module. • Turn the ignition switch off. • Disconnect the 14-way connector from the engine control module. • Remove the engine control module. • Remove the cover from the engine control module. • Disconnect the 2-way connector located between the logic and power boards.	• Connect the 14-way connector to the power board. • Connect one end of a jumper wire to the male terminal of the 2-way connector of the power board. • Turn the ignition switch on. • Press the ATM button on the diagnostic readout box and touch the other end of the jumper wire to the positive post of the battery.	• Injectors 2 and 3 click.	• Perform STEP D.
		• Injectors 2 and 3 do not click.	• Defective power board. Replace the engine control module.

JUMPER

BATTERY POSITIVE

POWER BOARD INTERNAL CONNECTOR

TEST 11	STEP D	CHECKING INJECTORS 1 AND 6 CONTROL CIRCUIT

PROCEDURE	TEST INDICATION	ACTION REQUIRED
REMINDERS • Diagnostic readout box connected to the engine harness connector. • 60-way connector disconnected from the engine control module. • Engine control module removed, opened, and the 2-way connector located between the logic and power board disconnected. • 14-way connector connected to the engine control module. • Ignition switch on. • Connect one end of a jumper wire to the female terminal of the 2-way connector of the power board.	• Press and hold the ATM button on the diagnostic readout box and touch the other end of the jumper wire to the positive post of the battery.	• Injectors 1 and 6 clicking.	• Defective logic board. Replace the engine control module.
		• Injectors 1 and 6 not clicking.	• Defective power board. Replace the engine control module.

JUMPER

BATTERY POSITIVE

POWER BOARD INTERNAL CONNECTOR

1987–88 EFI DRIVEABILITY TEST PROCEDURES

TEST 12 | STEP A | CHECKING SYSTEM FOR FAULT CODES

PROCEDURE	TEST INDICATION	ACTION REQUIRED
• Connect the diagnostic readout box to the engine harness connector. • Erase fault codes. (Refer to introduction.) • Crank the engine for 7 seconds and then turn the ignition switch to the run position for 5 seconds before turning to off. • Put the system in the Diagnostic Mode. (Refer to introduction.) • Record all codes.	No Code 88 or 00 System Power Circuits	Perform TEST NO. 13.
	88-11-12-55 Distributor pickup circuit.	Perform TEST NO. 14.
	88-42-55 Auto shutdown relay pull in coil circuit.	Perform TEST NO. 15.
	88-12-14-22-24-55 88-12-14-22-23-24-55	Repair wire in cavity No. 4 of the engine control module 60-way connector for an open circuit.

DIAGNOSTIC READOUT BOX

TEST 13 | STEP A | CHECKING FOR NO CODE 88 — 5 VOLT SUPPLY

PROCEDURE	TEST INDICATION	ACTION REQUIRED
• Turn the ignition switch off. • Disconnect the throttle position sensor connector. • Turn the ignition switch on. • Connect a voltmeter to the violet with white tracer wire at the throttle position sensor connector and ground.	• Voltmeter is reading at least 4.5 volts.	• Perform STEP B.
	• Voltmeter is reading 0 volts.	• Perform STEP C.

THROTTLE POSITION SENSOR CONNECTOR

TEST 13 | STEP B | CHECKING THE ENGINE CONTROL MODULE GROUND CIRCUIT

PROCEDURE	TEST INDICATION	ACTION REQUIRED
• Turn the ignition switch off. • Disconnect the 60-way connector from the engine control module. • Connect one lead of an ohmmeter to the system ground eyelet. • Touch the other end of the ohmmeter to cavity No. 15 and 16 of the 60-way connector.	• Ohmmeter is showing continuity with less than ½ ohm of resistance in both wires.	• Defective logic board. Replace the engine control module.
	• Ohmmeter is not showing continuity.	• Repair wires for an open circuit in the wiring harness splice. • Replace the engine control module.
	• Ohmmeter is showing more than ½ ohm of resistance at one or both wires.	• Repair ground circuit for high resistance to system ground eyelet.

VIEW FROM TERMINAL END

TEST 13 | STEP C | CHECKING FOR A SHORTED MAP SENSOR

PROCEDURE	TEST INDICATION	ACTION REQUIRED
REMINDERS • Ignition switch turned on. • Throttle position sensor connector disconnected. • Negative lead of a voltmeter connected to ground. • Disconnect the MAP sensor connector. • Touch the positive lead of a voltmeter to the violet with white tracer wire at the throttle position sensor connector.	• Voltmeter is reading at least 4.5 volts.	• Replace the MAP sensor.
	• Voltmeter is reading 0 volts.	• Perform STEP D.

THROTTLE POSITION SENSOR CONNECTOR

TEST 13 | STEP D | CHECKING FOR THE 8 VOLT SUPPLY

PROCEDURE	TEST INDICATION	ACTION REQUIRED
• Turn the ignition switch off. • Disconnect the 60-way connector from the engine control module. • Connect the negative lead of a voltmeter to ground. • Turn the ignition switch on. • Touch the positive lead of the voltmeter to cavity No. 52 of the engine control module 60-way connector.	• Voltmeter is reading at least 8 volts.	• Defective logic board. Replace the engine control module. CAUTION: Before replacing the engine control module check the terminal in cavity No. 52 to make sure it is not damaged causing a poor connection.
	• Voltmeter is reading 0 volts.	• Perform STEP E.

VIEW FROM TERMINAL END

TEST 13 | STEP E | CHECKING FOR A SHORTED DISTRIBUTOR PICKUP

PROCEDURE	TEST INDICATION	ACTION REQUIRED
REMINDERS • 60-way connector disconnected. • Ignition switch turned on. • The negative lead of a voltmeter connected to ground. • Disconnect the distributor pickup harness connector. • Touch the positive lead of the voltmeter to cavity No. 52 of the engine control module 60-way connector.	• Voltmeter is reading at least 8 volts.	• Replace the distributor pickup.
	• Voltmeter is reading 0 volts.	• Perform STEP F.

VIEW FROM TERMINAL END

TEST 13 | STEP F | CHECKING THE 8 VOLT SUPPLY WIRE FOR AN OPEN CIRCUIT BETWEEN THE LOGIC BOARD AND THE SPLICE

PROCEDURE	TEST INDICATION	ACTION REQUIRED
REMINDERS • 60-way connector disconnected. • Distributor pickup connector disconnected. • Turn the ignition switch off. • Touch one lead of an ohmmeter to cavity No. 52 of the 60-way connector and the other lead to the orange wire terminal of the distributor harness connector.	• Ohmmeter is showing continuity.	• Perform STEP G.
	• Ohmmeter is not showing continuity.	• Repair the orange wire of cavity No. 52 of the 60-way connector for an open circuit to the wiring harness splice.

VIEW FROM TERMINAL END

DISTRIBUTOR HARNESS CONNECTOR

TEST 13 | STEP G | CHECKING THE IGNITION SWITCH SUPPLY VOLTAGE TO THE ENGINE CONTROL MODULE

PROCEDURE	TEST INDICATION	ACTION REQUIRED
REMINDERS • Ignition switch off. • Disconnect the 14-way connector from the engine control module. • Connect the negative lead of a voltmeter to ground. • Turn the ignition switch on. • Touch the positive lead of a voltmeter to cavity No. 4 of the engine control module 14-way connector.	• Voltmeter is reading within one volt of battery voltage.	• Perform STEP H.
	• Voltmeter is not reading within one volt of battery voltage.	• Repair the blue wire in cavity No. 4 of the 14-way connector for an open circuit to the wiring harness splice.

14-WAY CONNECTOR

1987–88 EFI DRIVEABILITY TEST PROCEDURES

TEST 13	STEP H	CHECKING POWER MODULE GROUND WIRES FOR AN OPEN CIRCUIT	
PROCEDURE		TEST INDICATION	ACTION REQUIRED
REMINDERS • 14-way connector disconnected. • Turn the ignition switch off. • Connect one lead of an ohmmeter to the system ground eyelet. • Connect the other lead of the ohmmeter to the cavities 6 and 7 of the 14-way connector.		• Ohmmeter is showing continuity at both cavities with less than ½ ohm of resistance.	• Defective power board. Replace the engine control module. CAUTION: Before replacing the engine control module check the terminals in cavities 6 and 7 to make sure they are not spread apart causing a poor connection.
		• Ohmmeter is not showing continuity at cavities 6 and 7.	• Repair the black wires in cavities 6 and 7 of the 14-way connector for an open circuit to the wiring harness splice. • Replace the engine control module.
		• Ohmmeter is showing continuity with resistance higher than ½ ohm.	• Repair ground circuit for high resistance to system ground eyelet.

TEST 14	STEP A	CHECKING FOR FAULT CODE 11 - DISTRIBUTOR REFERENCE PICKUP CIRCUIT	
PROCEDURE		TEST INDICATION	ACTION REQUIRED
• Turn ignition switch off. • Disconnect distributor pickup coil connector. • Remove coil wire from distributor and place it (¼ inch) near a good engine ground. • Turn ignition switch to the run position. • Connect a jumper wire between the gray wire and the black with blue tracer wire of the distributor harness connector. • Make and break this connection several times while looking at the coil wire.		• There is spark at the coil wire.	• Perform STEP B.
		• There is no spark at the coil wire.	• Perform STEP D.

TEST 14	STEP B	CHECKING THE 8 VOLT POWER SUPPLY TO THE DISTRIBUTOR PICKUP	
PROCEDURE		TEST INDICATION	ACTION REQUIRED
REMINDERS • Ignition switch in the run position. • Distributor pickup coil connector disconnected. • Connect a voltmeter to the orange wire of the distributor harness connector and ground.		• Voltmeter is reading at least 7 volts.	• Perform STEP C.
		• Voltmeter reads 0 volts.	• Repair the orange wire of the distributor harness connector for an open circuit to the wiring harness splice.

TEST 14	STEP C	CHECKING DISTRIBUTOR MECHANICAL OPERATION	
PROCEDURE		TEST INDICATION	ACTION REQUIRED
• Turn the ignition switch off. • Remove the distributor cap. • Crank engine while watching rotor.		• The rotor is turning as the engine is cranked.	• Replace the distributor pickup coil. NOTE: Before replacing the pickup coil, check the terminals in the distributor harness connector to make sure they are not damaged causing a poor connection.
		• The rotor is not turning as the engine is cranked.	• Determine cause and repair engine or distributor as required.

TEST 14	STEP D	CHECKING THE DISTRIBUTOR PICKUP SIGNAL GROUND FOR AN OPEN CIRCUIT AT THE DISTRIBUTOR	
PROCEDURE		TEST INDICATION	ACTION REQUIRED
REMINDERS • Ignition switch in the run position. • Distributor pickup connector disconnected. • Coil wire removed from distributor and placed (¼ inch) near a good engine ground. • Connect a jumper wire between the gray wire of the distributor harness connector and a good engine ground.		• There is spark at the coil wire.	• Repair the black with blue tracer wire of the distributor harness connector for an open circuit to the wiring harness splice.
		• There is no spark at the coil wire.	• Perform STEP E.

TEST 14	STEP E	CHECKING REFERENCE PICKUP SIGNAL WIRE FOR AN OPEN CIRCUIT TO THE ENGINE CONTROL MODULE	
PROCEDURE		TEST INDICATION	ACTION REQUIRED
REMINDERS • Distributor pickup coil connector disconnected. • Disconnect the 60-way connector from the engine control module. • Connect one lead of an ohmmeter to cavity No. 47 of the 60-way connector and the other lead to the gray wire of the distributor harness connector.		• Ohmmeter is showing continuity.	• Defective logic board. Replace the engine control module. CAUTION: Before replacing the engine control module check the terminal in cavity No. 47 to make sure it is not damaged causing a poor connection.
		• Ohmmeter is not showing continuity.	NOTE: Repair the gray wire in cavity No. 47 of the 60-way connector for an open circuit to the distributor.

TEST 15	STEP A	CHECKING FOR FAULT CODE 42 - AUTO SHUTDOWN RELAY	
PROCEDURE		TEST INDICATION	ACTION REQUIRED
REMINDERS • Diagnostic readout box connected to the engine harness connector. • Connect a voltmeter to the dark blue with yellow tracer wire of the auto shutdown relay 3-way connector and ground. • Put the system in ATM Test Mode, Code 06 (Refer to the introduction). NOTE: Diagnostic readout box may go directly from indication code 55 to ATM test 01 and continue to cycle through all ATM tests without pressing the ATM button.		• The voltmeter pulsates between 0 and 12 volts while system is in ATM Test 06.	• Perform STEP B.
		• The voltmeter reading is within 1 volt of battery voltage and the system cannot be put into ATM Test 06.	• Perform STEP F.
		• The voltmeter reading is 0-1 volt steady and the system cannot be put into ATM Test 06.	• Perform STEP D.

TEST 15	STEP B	CHECKING FOR BATTERY SUPPLY VOLTAGE TO THE AUTO SHUTDOWN RELAY CONTACT POINTS (INPUT SIDE)	
PROCEDURE		TEST INDICATION	ACTION REQUIRED
• Connect a voltmeter to the red wire in the auto shutdown relay 3-way connector and ground.		• The voltmeter reading is within 1 volt of battery voltage.	• Perform STEP C.
		• The voltmeter reading is 0 volts.	• Repair the red wire of the 3-way connector for an open circuit to the wiring harness splice.

1987–88 EFI DRIVEABILITY TEST PROCEDURES

TEST 15 | STEP C | CHECKING THE AUTO SHUTDOWN RELAY CONTACTS (OUTPUT SIDE)

PROCEDURE	TEST INDICATION	ACTION REQUIRED
• Turn the ignition switch off. • Connect one lead of a jumper wire to the dark green with black tracer wire of the auto shutdown relay 3-way connector. • Touch the other end of the jumper wire to the red wire of the auto shutdown relay 3-way connector.	• The fuel pump turns on.	• Replace the auto shutdown relay.
	• The fuel pump does not turn on.	• Repair the dark green with black tracer wire of the 3-way connector for an open circuit to the wiring harness splice.

JUMPER
DG/BK
DB/YL   RD
AUTO SHUTDOWN RELAY CONNECTOR

TEST 15 | STEP D | CHECKING FOR SUPPLY VOLTAGE TO THE AUTO SHUTDOWN RELAY PULL IN COIL

PROCEDURE	TEST INDICATION	ACTION REQUIRED
REMINDERS • Negative lead of a voltmeter connected to ground. • Turn the ignition switch off. • Disconnect the single wire connector from the auto shutdown relay. • Connect a voltmeter to the dark blue with white tracer wire of the auto shutdown relay single wire connector and ground. • Turn the ignition switch on.	• The voltmeter reading is within one volt of battery voltage.	• Replace the auto shutdown relay.
	• The voltmeter is reading 0 volts.	• Perform STEP E.

VOLTMETER
DB/WT
DG/BK
DB/YL   RD
AUTO SHUTDOWN RELAY CONNECTORS

TEST 15 | STEP E | CHECKING THE VOLTAGE SUPPLY WIRE FOR AN OPEN CIRCUIT TO THE ENGINE CONTROL MODULE

PROCEDURE	TEST INDICATION	ACTION REQUIRED
• Turn the ignition switch off. • Disconnect the 14-way connector from the engine control module. • Connect an ohmmeter between cavity No. 3 of the 14-way connector and the dark blue with white tracer of the auto shutdown relay single wire connector.	• Ohmmeter does not show continuity.	• Repair the dark blue with white tracer wire in cavity No. 3 of the 14-way connector for an open circuit to the auto shutdown relay.
	• Ohmmeter shows continuity.	• Defective power board. Replace the engine control module. CAUTION: Before replacing the engine control module checking the terminal in cavity No. 3 to make sure it is not spread apart causing a poor connection.

1 2 3 4 5 6 7
14 13 12 11 10 9 8
OHMMETER
DB/WT
DG/BK
DB/YL   RD

TEST 15 | STEP F | CHECKING THE AUTO SHUTDOWN RELAY CONTROL WIRE FOR AN OPEN CIRCUIT TO THE ENGINE CONTROL MODULE

PROCEDURE	TEST INDICATION	ACTION REQUIRED
REMINDERS • Diagnostic readout box connected to the engine harness connector. • Turn the ignition switch off. • Disconnect the 60-way connector from the engine control module. • Connect a voltmeter to cavity No. 58 of the 60-way connector and ground. • Turn the ignition switch on.	• Voltmeter is reading within 1 volt of battery voltage.	• Defective logic board. Replace engine control module. CAUTION: Before replacing the engine control module check the terminal in cavity No. 58 of the 60-way connector to make sure it is not damaged causing a poor connection.
	• Voltmeter is reading 0 volts.	• Repair the dark blue with yellow tracer wire in cavity No. 58 of the 60-way connector for an open circuit to the auto shutdown relay.

VIEW FROM TERMINAL END
58
VOLTMETER

TEST 1 | STEP A | CHECKING SYSTEM FOR FAULT CODES

PROCEDURE	TEST INDICATION	CIRCUIT	ACTION REQUIRED
• Connect diagnostic readout box to engine harness connector.	88-12-55	No fault codes	Perform STEP B
	88-12-13-55 88-12-14-55 88-12-13-14-55	M.A.P. sensor	Perform TEST NO. 2
• Turn ignition switch on-off-on-off-on within 5 seconds.	88-12-15-55	Speed sensor	Perform TEST NO. 3
	88-12-17-55	Engine running too cool	Check engine cooling system for a possible bad thermostat
• RECORD ALL CODES NOTE: If fault codes 15-17-21-33-51 or 52 appear at this time proceed to test indication.	88-12-21-55	Oxygen sensor	Perform TEST NO. 4
	88-12-22-55 88-12-17-22-55	Engine coolant sensor	Perform TEST NO. 5
	88-12-23-55	Charge temperature sensor	Perform TEST NO. 6
	88-12-24-55	Throttle position sensor	Perform TEST NO. 7
• Turn ignition switch off and erase fault codes, (refer to introduction).	88-12-25-55	Idle motor	Perform TEST NO. 8
	88-12-31-55	Purge solenoid	Perform TEST NO. 9
	88-12-33-55 With A/C only	A/C cut out relay	Put system into ATM Test Mode 05. (Refer to introduction) Press the A/C button to the on position. If A/C cut out relay is clicking, disregard fault code 33. If the relay is not clicking, Perform TEST NO. 10.
• Start engine. CAUTION: Do not depress accelerator to start engine. • Let engine run for 5 minutes.			
	88-12-35-55	Radiator fan relay	Perform TEST NO. 11
• Raise engine speed to 2000 rpm for 10 seconds and then return to idle.	88-12-37-55	Transmission lock-up solenoid circuit	Perform TEST NO. 12.
	88-12-42-55	Auto shutdown relay	Repair dark green with black tracer wire in cavity No. 10 of the engine control module 60-way connector for an open circuit to the wiring harness splice.
• Cycle transmission gear selector. • If so equipped press A/C button on and off.	88-12-44-55	Fused J2	Perform TEST NO. 13
• Turn engine off.	88-12-51-55	Oxygen feedback system locked lean	Perform TEST NO. 16
• Turn ignition switch on-off-on-off-on within 5 seconds.	88-12-52-55	Oxygen feedback system locked rich	
	88-12-53-55		Replace the engine control module.
• RECORD ALL CODES If the same code appears before and after the engine is started, the problem still exists. Proceed to test indications. If a code does not reappear after the engine is started, the problem no longer exists. Perform STEP N.	88-12-54-55	Distributor sync. pickup circuit	Perform TEST NO. 14

DIAGNOSTIC READOUT BOX

DIAGNOSTIC READOUT BOX

TEST 1 | STEP B | CHECKING THE OUTPUT CIRCUITS OF THE ENGINE CONTROL MODULE CONTROLLED COMPONENTS

PROCEDURE		TEST INDICATION	ACTION REQUIRED
REMINDERS • Diagnostic readout box connected to the engine harness connector. • Put the system into the ATM Test Mode, Code 04. (Refer to the introduction)		Test Code 04 • The radiator fan should be turning on and off every two seconds.	• Radiator fan is turning on and off press and hold the ATM button as follows: Without A/C until Test Code 07 appears. With A/C until Test Code 05 appears.
			• If fan does not turn on and off, is the relay clicking? If it is, repair the circuit to the radiator fan motor as required. • If the relay does not click, replace it.
		Test Code 05 • You should hear the A/C cutout relay clicking every two seconds. • Press the A/C button on. CAUTION: A/C compressor clutch will also cycle every two seconds and A/C condenser fan will run continuously.	• A/C relay clicking, press and hold the ATM button until Test Code 07 appears. • If the A/C relay is not clicking replace it.
		Test Code 07 • You should hear the canister purge solenoid clicking.	• Canister purge solenoid clicking. • Press and hold the ATM button until Test Code 10 appears. • If the canister purge solenoid is not clicking replace it.
		Test Code 10 • You should hear the transmission lockup solenoid clicking.	• Transmission lockup solenoid clicking Perform STEP C. • If the transmission lockup solenoid is not clicking replace it.

DIAGNOSTIC READOUT BOX

DIAGNOSTIC READOUT BOX

1987–88 EFI DRIVEABILITY TEST PROCEDURES

TEST 1 | STEP C | CHECKING SWITCH INPUTS TO THE ENGINE CONTROL MODULE

PROCEDURE	TEST INDICATION	ACTION REQUIRED
REMINDERS • Diagnostic readout box connected to the engine harness connector. • Put the system into the **Switch Test Mode**. (Refer to introduction) • Check switch inputs as follows: a) press down on brake pedal b) move gear selector from park to reverse c) with A/C, press the A/C button	• Display on the readout box changes as each switch is activated. **NOTE:** It is not important what display changes to. Just make sure it changes.	• Perform STEP H.
	• Display on the readout box does not change when one or more of the switches are activated.	• Perform STEPS as follows: Brake Switch Without Speed Control **STEP D** With Speed Control **STEP E** Park/Neutral Switch **STEP F** A/C Button **STEP G**

TEST 1 | STEP D | CHECKING BRAKE SWITCH INPUT CIRCUIT TO THE ENGINE CONTROL MODULE - WITHOUT SPEED CONTROL

PROCEDURE	TEST INDICATION	ACTION REQUIRED
• Turn ignition switch off. • Disconnect the 60-way connector from the engine control module. • Connect voltmeter to cavity No. 29 of the 60-way connector and ground. • Turn ignition switch to the run position. • Press brake pedal down.	• Voltmeter is reading within one volt of battery voltage.	• Defective logic board. Replace engine control module. **CAUTION:** Before replacing the engine control module check terminal in cavity No. 29 of the 60-way connector to make sure it is not damaged causing a poor connection.
VIEW FROM TERMINAL END	• Voltmeter reads 0.	• Check wire of cavity No. 29 for open circuit to brake switch. • Check for a bad brake switch. • Check voltage supply circuit to the brake switch.

TEST 1 | STEP E | CHECKING BRAKE SWITCH INPUT CIRCUIT TO THE ENGINE CONTROL MODULE - WITH SPEED CONTROL

PROCEDURE	TEST INDICATION	ACTION REQUIRED
• Turn the ignition switch off. • Disconnect the 60-way connector from the engine control module. • Connect an ohmmeter between cavity No. 29 of the 60-way connector and ground. • Press down on brake pedal and then release.	• Ohmmeter shows no continuity when brake pedal is pressed down and continuity when released.	• Defective logic board. Replace engine control module. **CAUTION:** Before replacing the engine control module check terminal in cavity No. 29 of the 60-way connector to make sure it is not damaged causing a poor connection.
VIEW FROM TERMINAL END	• Ohmmeter does not read as above.	• Check wire of cavity of No. 29 for an open circuit to the brake switch. • Check for a bad brake switch. • Check for an open circuit to the tail lamps.

TEST 1 | STEP F | CHECKING PARK/NEUTRAL SWITCH INPUT CIRCUIT TO THE ENGINE CONTROL MODULE

PROCEDURE	TEST INDICATION	ACTION REQUIRED
• Turn ignition switch off. • Disconnect the 60-way connector from the engine control module. • Connect an ohmmeter to cavity No. 30 of the 60-way connector and ground. • Disconnect the battery quick disconnect. • Turn the ignition switch to the run position. • Put gear selector in park, reverse, neutral, and drive and observe ohmmeter in each position.	• Ohmmeter shows continuity in all positions of the gear selector.	• Check wire of cavity No. 30 for a short circuit to ground. • Check for a bad safety neutral switch.
	• Ohmmeter shows no continuity in all positions of the gear selector.	• Repair wire of cavity No. 30 for an open circuit to the safety neutral switch.
VIEW FROM TERMINAL END	• Ohmmeter reads as follows: **Park** - Continuity **Reverse** - No Continuity **Neutral** - Continuity **Drive** - No Continuity	• Defective logic board. Replace engine control module. **CAUTION:** Before replacing the engine control module check the terminal in cavity No. 30 of the 60-way connector to make sure it is not damaged causing a poor connection. **NOTE:** Disregard any resistance readings. Just make sure there is continuity.

TEST 1 | STEP G | CHECKING A/C PUSH BUTTON SWITCH INPUT CIRCUIT TO THE ENGINE CONTROL MODULE

PROCEDURE	TEST INDICATION	ACTION REQUIRED
• Turn ignition switch off. • Disconnect the 60-way connector from the engine control module. • Connect a voltmeter to cavity No. 45 of the 60-way connector and ground. • Turn the ignition switch to the run position. • Press the A/C button and then the off button.	• Voltmeter is reading 0-1 when A/C button is pressed and within one volt off battery when off button is pressed.	• Defective logic board. Replace engine control module. **CAUTION:** Before replacing the engine control module check terminal in cavity No. 45 of the black 60-way connector to make sure it is not damaged causing a poor connection.
VIEW FROM TERMINAL END	• Voltmeter reading is not as described above.	• Repair the wire of cavity No. 45 for an open or short circuit to the wiring harness splice.

TEST 1 | STEP H | CHECKING AUTOMATIC IDLE SPEED MOTOR OPERATION

PROCEDURE	TEST INDICATION	ACTION REQUIRED
• Connect the diagnostic readout box to the engine harness connector. **NOTE:** Make sure read/hold switch is in the read position. • Connect a tachometer to the engine. • Start the engine. • Disconnect the coolant sensor. • Move the read/hold switch to the hold position.	• Engine speed increases to approximately 1500 rpm.	• Perform STEP M.
	• Engine speed does not increase.	• Perform STEP I.

TEST 1 | STEP I | CHECKING AUTOMATIC IDLE SPEED MOTOR SIGNAL FROM THE ENGINE CONTROL MODULE

PROCEDURE	TEST INDICATION	ACTION REQUIRED
REMINDERS • Diagnostic readout box connected to the engine harness connector. • Turn the engine off. • Disconnect the automatic idle speed motor connector. • Connect a digital voltmeter between terminals 1 and 4 of the idle speed motor connector. • Set the digital voltmeter to the AC voltage position. • Put the system into ATM Test Mode 03. (Refer to introduction)	• Voltmeter is pulsating between 0 and 12 volts every two seconds.	• Perform STEP J.
DIGITAL VOLTMETER SET TO AC POSITION	• Voltmeter does not pulsate.	• Perform STEP K.

TEST 1 | STEP J | CHECKING AUTOMATIC IDLE SPEED MOTOR SIGNAL AT THE ENGINE CONTROL MODULE

PROCEDURE	TEST INDICATION	ACTION REQUIRED
REMINDERS • Diagnostic readout box connected to the engine harness connector. • Automatic idle speed motor disconnected. • Digital voltmeter set to the AC voltage position. • System in ATM Test Mode 03. • Connect voltmeter between terminals 2 and 3 of the idle speed motor connector.	• Voltmeter is pulsating between 0 and 12 volts every two seconds.	• Replace the automatic idle speed motor. **CAUTION:** Before replacing the idle motor check terminals of the connector to make sure they are not damaged causing a poor connection.
DIGITAL VOLTMETER SET TO AC POSITION	• Voltmeter does not pulsate.	• Perform STEP L.

1987–88 EFI DRIVEABILITY TEST PROCEDURES

TEST 1	STEP K	CHECKING AUTOMATIC IDLE SPEED CIRCUIT AT THE ENGINE CONTROL MODULE 60-WAY CONNECTOR.
PROCEDURE	TEST INDICATION	ACTION REQUIRED

PROCEDURE	TEST INDICATION	ACTION REQUIRED
• Turn the ignition switch off. • Disconnect the 60-way connector from the engine control module. • Connect an ohmmeter between cavities 19 and 20 of the 60-way connector.	• Ohmmeter is not showing continuity.	• Repair wire of cavity 19 or 20 for an open circuit to the automatic idle speed motor connector.
VIEW FROM TERMINAL END 19 20 OHMMETER	• Ohmmeter is showing continuity.	• Defective logic board. Replace engine control module. CAUTION: Before replacing the engine control module check the terminals in cavity 19 and 20 of the 60-way connector to make sure they are not damaged causing a poor connection.

TEST 1	STEP L	CHECKING AUTOMATIC IDLE SPEED MOTOR CIRCUIT AT THE ENGINE CONTROL MODULE 60-WAY CONNECTOR
PROCEDURE	TEST INDICATION	ACTION REQUIRED

PROCEDURE	TEST INDICATION	ACTION REQUIRED
• Turn the ignition switch off. • Disconnect the 60-way connector from the engine control module. • Connect an ohmmeter between cavities 17 and 18 of the 60-way connector.	• Ohmmeter is not showing continuity.	• Repair wire of cavity 17 or 18 for an open circuit to the automatic idle speed motor.
VIEW FROM TERMINAL END 17 18 OHMMETER	• Ohmmeter is showing continuity.	• Defective logic board. Replace engine control module. CAUTION: Before replacing the engine control module check the terminals in cavities 17 and 18 of the 60-way connector to make sure they are not damaged causing a poor connection.

TEST 1	STEP M	CHECKING THE ENGINE CONTROL MODULE GROUND CIRCUITS
PROCEDURE	TEST INDICATION	ACTION REQUIRED

PROCEDURE	TEST INDICATION	ACTION REQUIRED
• Turn the ignition switch off. • Disconnect both engine control module connectors. • Connect one lead of a digital ohmmeter to the system ground eyelet on cylinder head. • Connect the other lead of ohmmeter as follows: 14-way connector cavities No. 2, 6, and 7. 60-way connector cavities 15, 16, and 5.	• Ohmmeter is showing continuity with less than ½ ohm of resistance at all cavities of the connectors.	• Perform TESTS as follows: If a cold problem TEST NO. 15. If a warm problem TEST NO. 16.
VIEW FROM TERMINAL END 5 15 16 OHMMETER 14 13 12 11 10 9 8 14-WAY CONNECTOR GROUND EYELET ON CYLINDER HEAD	• Ohmmeter is not showing continuity at one or more cavities of the connectors. • Ohmmeter is showing more than ½ ohm of resistance at one or more cavities of the connectors.	• Repair the wire for an open circuit to the wiring harness connector. • Repair circuit for high resistance to system ground eyelet.

NOTES

_____
_____
_____
_____
_____
_____
_____
_____
_____
_____
_____
_____
_____
_____
_____

TEST 1	STEP N	CHECKING FOR INTERMITTENT FAILURES CAUSED BY WIRING AND/OR CONNECTORS

The majority of intermittent failures are caused by wiring and connections. The only way to find them is to try and duplicate the problem. Since the engine control module can remember where they are, the ATM and Sensor Test Modes can be used in an attempt to locate them.

• If the following fault codes do not reappear use the ATM Test Mode as indicated.

Fault Code	ATM Test Mode
25	03
26	02
27	02
31	07
35	04
37	10
42	06
43	01

Once in the correct test mode, wiggle all the connectors and wires in the circuit. When the bad connection or wire is located the ATM test will be interrupted.

• If the following fault codes do not reappear use the Sensor Test Mode as indicated.

Fault Code	Sensor Test Mode
14**	08
22	04
23	03
24	05

** When checking the M.A.P. sensor circuit, (fault code 14) apply 10 inches of vacuum to the M.A.P. sensor before testing.

Once in the correct test mode, wiggle all the connectors and wires in the circuit. When the bad connection or wire is located the display on the readout box will change.

TEST 2	STEP A	CHECKING FOR FAULT CODES 13 AND/OR 14 — M.A.P. SENSOR CIRCUIT
PROCEDURE	TEST INDICATION	ACTION REQUIRED

PROCEDURE	TEST INDICATION	ACTION REQUIRED
• Turn ignition switch off. • Tee a vacuum gauge into the vacuum line at the M.A.P. sensor. • Start the engine and look at the vacuum gauge with the engine idling. • Look at the vacuum gauge while snapping the throttle open and closed.	• Vacuum gauge is reading manifold vacuum with the engine idling. • Vacuum gauge reading immediately drops to 0 when the throttle is snapped open and closed.	• Perform STEP B.
	• Vacuum gauge reads 0 at idle.	• Repair vacuum line to throttle body.
VACUUM GAUGE	• Vacuum gauge reading slowly drops to 0 when the throttle is snapped open and closed.	• Repair restriction in vacuum supply line to M.A.P. sensor.

TEST 2	STEP B	CHECKING THE M.A.P. SENSOR CIRCUIT IN THE ENGINE CONTROL MODULE
PROCEDURE	TEST INDICATION	ACTION REQUIRED

PROCEDURE	TEST INDICATION	ACTION REQUIRED
REMINDERS • Diagnostic readout box connected to the engine harness connector. • Disconnect the connector from the M.A.P. sensor. • Put the system in Sensor Test Mode 08. (Refer to introduction) NOTE: Don't forget to divide the reading on the display by 10.	• Display on the readout box is reading 4 volts.	• Perform STEP C.
DISCONNECT	• Display on the readout box is reading 0 volts.	• Defective logic board. Replace engine control module. NOTE: Before replacing the engine control module make sure the wire of cavity No. 11 of the 60-way connector is not shorted to ground.

1987–88 EFI DRIVEABILITY TEST PROCEDURES

TEST 2	STEP C	CHECKING THE M.A.P. SENSOR SIGNAL CIRCUIT TO THE ENGINE CONTROL MODULE
PROCEDURE	**TEST INDICATION**	**ACTION REQUIRED**

REMINDERS

- Diagnostic readout box connected to the engine harness connector.
- System in Sensor Test Mode 08.
  NOTE: Don't forget to divide the reading on the display box by 10.
- M.A.P. sensor connector disconnected.
- Connect a jumper wire between the dark green with red and black with light blue wires of the M.A.P. sensor harness connector.

- Display on the readout box is reading 0 volts. → Perform STEP E.
- Display on the readout box is not reading 0 volts. → Perform STEP D.

TEST 2	STEP D	CHECKING THE M.A.P. SENSOR WIRE TO THE ENGINE CONTROL MODULE FOR AN OPEN CIRCUIT
PROCEDURE	**TEST INDICATION**	**ACTION REQUIRED**

REMINDERS

- Diagnostic readout box connected to the engine harness connector.
- System in Sensor Test Mode 08.
  NOTE: Don't forget to divide the reading on the display box by 10.
- M.A.P. sensor disconnected.
- Connect one end of a jumper wire to the negative terminal of the battery.
- Connect the other end of the jumper wire to the dark green with red tracer wire terminal of the M.A.P. sensor harness connector.

- Display on the readout box is reading 0 volts. → Repair the black with light blue tracer wire of the M.A.P. sensor connector for an open circuit to the wiring harness splice.
- Display on the readout box is reading 5 volts. → Repair the dark green with red tracer wire of the M.A.P. sensor connector for an open circuit to the engine control module.

TEST 2	STEP E	CHECKING THE 5 VOLT SUPPLY TO THE M.A.P. SENSOR
PROCEDURE	**TEST INDICATION**	**ACTION REQUIRED**

REMINDERS

- Ignition switch in the run position.
- M.A.P. sensor connector disconnected.
- Connect a digital voltmeter to the violet with white tracer wire of the M.A.P. sensor harness connector and ground.

- Voltmeter is reading at least 4 volts. → Replace the M.A.P. sensor.
  NOTE: Before replacing the M.A.P. sensor, check the terminals in the harness connector to make sure they are not spread apart causing a poor connection.
- Voltmeter is reading 0 volts. → Repair the violet with white tracer wire for an open circuit to the wiring harness splice.

TEST 3	STEP A	CHECKING FOR FAULT CODE 15 — SPEED SENSOR CIRCUIT
PROCEDURE	**TEST INDICATION**	**ACTION REQUIRED**

REMINDERS

- Diagnostic readout box connected to the engine harness connector.
- Start the engine.
- Disconnect the speed sensor connector.
- Put the system in the Engine Running Test Mode 71. (Refer to introduction.)
- Connect a jumper wire between the terminals of the speed sensor harness connector.
- Make and break this connection.

- As you make and break this connection the display on the readout box changes. → Replace the speed sensor.
- As you make and break this connection the display on the readout box does not change. → Perform STEP B.

TEST 3	STEP B	CHECKING THE SPEED SENSOR SIGNAL WIRE TO THE ENGINE CONTROL MODULE FOR AN OPEN CIRCUIT
PROCEDURE	**TEST INDICATION**	**ACTION REQUIRED**

REMINDERS

- Speed sensor connector disconnected.
- Turn the engine off.
- Disconnect the 60-way connector from the engine control module.
- Connect an ohmmeter between cavity No. 48 of the 60-way connector and the white with orange tracer wire terminal of the speed sensor harness connector.

VIEW FROM TERMINAL END

- Ohmmeter is showing continuity. → Perform STEP C.
- Ohmmeter is not showing continuity. → Repair the wire in cavity No. 48 of the 60-way connector for an open circuit to the speed sensor harness connector.

TEST 3	STEP C	CHECKING THE SPEED SENSOR GROUND WIRE TO THE ENGINE CONTROL MODULE FOR AN OPEN CIRCUIT
PROCEDURE	**TEST INDICATION**	**ACTION REQUIRED**

REMINDERS

- Engine off.
- Speed sensor connector disconnected.
- Engine control module 60-way connector disconnected.
- Connect an ohmmeter between cavity No. 4 of the 60-way connector and the black wire terminal of the speed sensor harness connector.

VIEW FROM TERMINAL END

- Ohmmeter is showing continuity. → Defective logic board. Replace engine control module.
  CAUTION: Before replacing the engine control module check the terminal in cavity No. 48 of the 60-way connector to make sure it is not damaged causing a poor connection.
- Ohmmeter is not showing continuity. → Repair the black wire of the speed sensor connector for an open circuit to the wiring harness splice.

TEST 4	STEP A	CHECKING FOR FAULT CODE 21 — OXYGEN SENSOR CIRCUIT
PROCEDURE	**TEST INDICATION**	**ACTION REQUIRED**

REMINDERS

- Diagnostic readout box connected to the engine harness connector.
- Turn the ignition switch off.
- Disconnect the oxygen sensor connector.
- Put the system into Sensor Test Mode 02. (Refer to introduction.)
  NOTE: Don't forget to divide the reading on display by 10.

- Display on the readout box is reading at least .4 volts. (4 tenths). → Perform STEP B.
- Display on the readout box is reading 0. → Defective logic board. Replace engine control module.
  NOTE: Before replacing the engine control module make sure the wire of cavity No. 23 of the engine control module 60-way connector is not shorted to ground.

HEATED OXYGEN SENSOR 3-WAY CONNECTOR

TEST 4	STEP B	CHECKING THE OXYGEN SENSOR CIRCUIT TO THE ENGINE CONTROL MODULE FOR AN OPEN CIRCUIT
PROCEDURE	**TEST INDICATION**	**ACTION REQUIRED**

REMINDERS

- System in Sensor Test Mode 02.
  NOTE: Don't forget to divide the reading on display by 10.
- Oxygen sensor connector disconnected.
- Connect one end of a jumper wire to the black wire of the oxygen sensor harness connector as shown in the illustration.
  CAUTION: Not the black wire in the center terminal of the connector. This wire goes to ground.
- Connect the other end of the jumper wire to the battery positive post.

- Display on readout box is reading at least 5 volts. → Replace the oxygen sensor.
- Display on readout box is reading .4 volts. (4 tenths). → Repair the black wire of the oxygen sensor connector for an open circuit to the engine control module.

HEATED OXYGEN SENSOR HARNESS CONNECTOR

BATTERY

5–115

1987–88 EFI DRIVEABILITY TEST PROCEDURES

TEST 5	STEP A	CHECKING FOR FAULT CODE 22 — COOLANT SENSOR CIRCUIT		
	PROCEDURE		TEST INDICATION	ACTION REQUIRED
REMINDERS • Diagnostic readout box connected to the engine harness connector. • Turn the ignition switch off. • Disconnect the coolant sensor connector. • Put the system in **Sensor Test Mode 04.** (Refer to introduction) NOTE: Don't forget to multiply the reading on the display by 10.	COOLANT TEMPERATURE SENSOR		• Display on the readout box is reading 00".	• Perform STEP B.
			• Display on the readout box is reading 260".	• Defective logic board. Replace engine control module. NOTE: Before replacing the engine control module make sure the wire of cavity No. 3 of the engine control module 60-way connector is not shorted to ground.

TEST 5	STEP B	CHECKING THE COOLANT SENSOR CIRCUIT TO THE ENGINE CONTROL MODULE		
	PROCEDURE		TEST INDICATION	ACTION REQUIRED
REMINDERS • Diagnostic readout box connected to the engine harness connector. • System in Sensor Test Mode 04. NOTE: Don't forget to multiply the reading on display by 10. • Coolant sensor connector disconnected. • Connect a jumper wire between the terminals of the coolant sensor connector.	JUMPER TN/WT BK/LB COOLANT SENSOR CONNECTOR		• Display on the readout box is reading 260".	• Replace the coolant sensor.
			• Display on the readout box is reading 00".	• Perform STEP C.

TEST 5	STEP C	CHECKING THE COOLANT SENSOR WIRES TO THE ENGINE CONTROL MODULE FOR AN OPEN CIRCUIT		
	PROCEDURE		TEST INDICATION	ACTION REQUIRED
REMINDERS • Diagnostic readout box connected to the engine harness connector. • System in Sensor Test Mode 04. NOTE: Don't forget to multiply the reading on display by 10. • Coolant sensor connector disconnected. • Connect one end of a jumper wire to the negative terminal of the battery. • Connect the other end of the jumper wire to the tan with white tracer wire terminal of the coolant sensor harness connector.	JUMPER TN/WT BK/LB COOLANT SENSOR CONNECTOR		• Display on the readout box is reading 260".	• Repair the black with light blue tracer wire of the coolant sensor harness connector for an open circuit to the wiring harness splice.
			• Display on the readout box is reading 00".	• Repair the tan with white tracer wire of the coolant sensor harness connector for an open circuit to the engine control module.

TEST 6	STEP A	CHECKING FOR FAULT CODE 23 — CHARGE TEMPERATURE SENSOR		
	PROCEDURE		TEST INDICATION	ACTION REQUIRED
REMINDERS • Diagnostic readout box connected to the engine harness connector. • Disconnect the charge temperature sensor connector. • Put the system in **Sensor Test Mode 03.** (Refer to introduction) NOTE: Don't forget to divide the reading on the display by 10.	CHARGE TEMPERATURE SENSOR		• Display on the readout box is reading 5 volts.	• Perform STEP B.
			• Display on the readout box is reading 0 volts or 0 volts and then increases.	• Defective logic board. Replace engine control module. NOTE: Before replacing the engine control module make sure the wire of cavity No. 21 of the 60-way connector is not shorted to ground.

TEST 6	STEP B	CHECKING THE CHARGE TEMPERATURE SENSOR SIGNAL CIRCUIT TO THE ENGINE CONTROL MODULE		
	PROCEDURE		TEST INDICATION	ACTION REQUIRED
REMINDERS • Diagnostic readout box connected to the engine harness connector. • System in Sensor Test Mode 03. NOTE: Don't forget to divide the reading on the display box by 10. • Charge temperature sensor connector disconnected. • Connect a jumper wire between the terminals of the charge temperature sensor connector.	JUMPER BK/LB BK/RD CHARGE TEMP SENSOR CONNECTOR		• Display on the readout box is reading 0 volts.	• Replace the charge temperature sensor.
			• Display on the readout box is reading 5 volts.	• Perform STEP C.

TEST 6	STEP C	CHECKING THE CHARGE TEMPERATURE SENSOR WIRES TO THE ENGINE CONTROL MODULE FOR AN OPEN CIRCUIT		
	PROCEDURE		TEST INDICATION	ACTION REQUIRED
REMINDERS • Diagnostic readout box connected to the engine harness connector. • System in Sensor Test Mode 03. NOTE: Don't forget to divide the reading on display by 10. • Charge temperature sensor connector disconnected. • Connect one end of a jumper wire to the negative terminal of the battery. • Connect the other end of the jumper wire to the black with red tracer wire terminal of the charge temperature sensor connector.	JUMPER BK/LB BK/RD CHARGE TEMP SENSOR CONNECTOR		• Display reads 0 volts.	• Repair the black with light blue tracer wire of the charge temperature sensor connector for an open circuit to the wiring harness splice.
			• Display on the readout box is reading 5 volts.	• Repair the black with red tracer wire of the charge temperature sensor connector for an open circuit to the engine control module.

TEST 7	STEP A	CHECKING FOR FAULT CODE 24 — THROTTLE POSITION SENSOR CIRCUIT		
	PROCEDURE		TEST INDICATION	ACTION REQUIRED
REMINDERS • Diagnostic readout box connected to the engine harness connector. • Disconnect the connector from the throttle position sensor. • Put the system in **Sensor Test Mode 05.** (Refer to introduction) NOTE: Don't forget to divide the reading on the display by 10.	DISCONNECT		• Display on the readout box is reading 5 volts.	• Perform STEP B.
			• Display on the readout box is reading 0 volts.	• Defective logic board. Replace engine control module. NOTE: Before replacing the engine control module make sure the wire of cavity No. 22 of the engine control module 60-way connector is not shorted to ground.

TEST 7	STEP B	CHECKING THE THROTTLE POSITION SENSOR SIGNAL CIRCUIT TO THE ENGINE CONTROL MODULE		
	PROCEDURE		TEST INDICATION	ACTION REQUIRED
REMINDERS • Diagnostic readout box connected to the engine harness connector. • System in Sensor Test Mode 05. NOTE: Don't forget to divide the reading on the display box by 10. • Throttle position sensor connector disconnected. • Connect a jumper wire between the orange with dark blue and black with blue wires of the throttle position sensor harness connector.	JUMPER VT/WT BK/LB OR/DB THROTTLE POSITION SENSOR		• Display on the readout box is reading 0 volts.	• Perform STEP D.
			• Display on the readout box is reading 5 volts.	• Perform STEP C.

1987–88 EFI DRIVEABILITY TEST PROCEDURES

TEST 7	STEP C	CHECKING THE THROTTLE POSITION SENSOR WIRES TO THE ENGINE CONTROL MODULE FOR AN OPEN CIRCUIT	
PROCEDURE		TEST INDICATION	ACTION REQUIRED
REMINDERS • Diagnostic readout box connected to the engine harness connector. • System in Sensor Test Mode 05. NOTE: Don't forget to divide the reading on the display box by 10. • Throttle position sensor connector disconnected.		• Display on the readout box is reading 0 volts.	• Repair the black with light blue tracer wire of the throttle position sensor connector for an open circuit to the wiring harness splice.
• Connect one end of a jumper wire to the negative terminal of the battery. • Connect the other end of the jumper wire to the orange with dark blue tracer wire terminal of the throttle position sensor harness connector.		• Display on the readout box is reading 5 volts.	• Repair the orange with blue tracer wire of the throttle position sensor connector for an open circuit to the engine control module.

THROTTLE POSITION SENSOR

TEST 7	STEP D	CHECKING THE 5 VOLT SUPPLY TO THE THROTTLE POSITION SENSOR	
PROCEDURE		TEST INDICATION	ACTION REQUIRED
REMINDERS • Ignition switch in the run position. • Throttle position sensor connector disconnected. • Connect a digital voltmeter to the violet with white tracer wire of the throttle position sensor harness connector and ground.		• Voltmeter is reading at least 4 volts.	• Replace the throttle position sensor.
		• Voltmeter reads 0.	• Repair the violet with white tracer wire for an open circuit to the wiring harness splice.

THROTTLE POSITION SENSOR

TEST 8	STEP A	CHECKING FOR FAULT CODE 25 — AUTOMATIC IDLE SPEED MOTOR CIRCUIT FOR A SHORT	
PROCEDURE		TEST INDICATION	ACTION REQUIRED
• Turn the ignition switch off. • Disconnect the 60-way connector from the engine control module. • Connect an ohmmeter between cavities 17 and 18 of the 60-way connector.		• Ohmmeter is showing some resistance. NOTE: The amount of resistance is not important. Just make sure there is some.	• Some resistance. Perform STEP B.
		• Ohmmeter is showing 0 resistance.	• Perform STEP C.

VIEW FROM TERMINAL END

TEST 8	STEP B	CHECKING AUTOMATIC IDLE SPEED MOTOR CIRCUIT FOR A SHORT	
PROCEDURE		TEST INDICATION	ACTION REQUIRED
REMINDERS • Ignition switch off. • Disconnect the 60-way connector from the engine control module. • Connect an ohmmeter between cavities 19 and 20 of the 60-way connector.		• Ohmmeter is showing some resistance. NOTE: The amount of resistance is not important. Just make sure there is some.	• Defective logic board. Replace engine control module.
		• Ohmmeter is showing 0 resistance.	• Perform STEP C.

VIEW FROM TERMINAL END

TEST 8	STEP C	CHECKING AUTOMATIC IDLE SPEED MOTOR CONTROL WIRES FOR A SHORT	
PROCEDURE		TEST INDICATION	ACTION REQUIRED
REMINDERS • Ignition switch off. • Engine control module 60-way connector disconnected. • Ohmmeter connected to the 60-way connector as instructed in STEP A or B. • Disconnect the idle motor connector.		• Ohmmeter is showing an open circuit.	• Replace the idle motor.
		• Ohmmeter is showing 0 resistance.	• Repair the wires to the idle motor for a short circuit to each other.

VIEW FROM TERMINAL END

VIEW FROM TERMINAL END

TEST 9	STEP A	CHECKING FOR FAULT CODE 31 — CANISTER PURGE SOLENOID CIRCUIT	
PROCEDURE		TEST INDICATION	ACTION REQUIRED
• Connect a voltmeter to the pink with white tracer wire of the canister purge solenoid connector and ground. • Turn the ignition switch to the run position.		• Voltmeter reads within one volt of battery voltage.	• Perform STEP B.
		• Voltage reads 0-1 volt.	• Perform STEP C.

CONNECT VOLTMETER

TEST 9	STEP B	CHECKING THE CANISTER PURGE SOLENOID CONTROL WIRE FOR AN OPEN CIRCUIT TO THE ENGINE CONTROL MODULE	
PROCEDURE		TEST INDICATION	ACTION REQUIRED
• Turn the ignition switch off. • Disconnect the 60-way connector from the engine control module. • Connect a voltmeter to cavity No. 54 of the 60-way connector and ground. • Turn the ignition switch to the run position.		• Voltmeter is reading within one volt of battery voltage.	• Defective logic board. Replace engine control module. CAUTION: Before replacing the engine control module check the terminal in cavity No. 54 of the 60-way connector to make sure it is not damaged causing a poor connection.
		• Voltmeter reads 0.	• Repair wire of cavity No. 54 for an open circuit to the canister purge solenoid.

VIEW FROM TERMINAL END

VOLTMETER

TEST 9	STEP C	CHECKING THE CANISTER PURGE SOLENOID CIRCUIT FOR A SHORT IN THE ENGINE CONTROL MODULE	
PROCEDURE		TEST INDICATION	ACTION REQUIRED
REMINDERS • Voltmeter connected to the pink with white tracer wire of the canister purge solenoid connector. • Disconnect the 60-way connector from the engine control module. • Turn the ignition switch to the run position.		• Voltmeter reads within one volt of battery voltage.	• Defective logic board, replace the engine control module.
		• Voltmeter reads 0.	• Perform STEP D.

CONNECT VOLTMETER

1987–88 EFI DRIVEABILITY TEST PROCEDURES

TEST 9	STEP D	CHECKING FOR VOLTAGE SUPPLY TO THE CANISTER PURGE SOLENOID	
		PROCEDURE	TEST INDICATION	ACTION REQUIRED

REMINDERS		TEST INDICATION	ACTION REQUIRED
• Ignition switch in the run position.		• Voltmeter reads within one volt of battery voltage.	• Replace the canister purge solenoid.
• Connect a voltmeter to the dark blue wire of the canister solenoid harness connector and ground.		• Voltmeter reads 0.	• Repair the dark blue wire of the canister purge solenoid harness for an open circuit to the wiring harness splice.

TEST 10	STEP D	CHECKING FOR VOLTAGE SUPPLY TO THE A/C CUTOUT RELAY PULL IN COIL	
		PROCEDURE	TEST INDICATION	ACTION REQUIRED

REMINDERS		TEST INDICATION	ACTION REQUIRED
• Ignition switch in the run position.		• Voltmeter reads within one volt of battery voltage.	• Replace the A/C cutout relay.
• A/C button in the on position.			
• Connect a voltmeter to the dark green wire of the A/C cut-out relay 3-way connector and ground.		• Voltmeter reads 0.	• Repair the dark green wire to the A/C condensor fan relay 3-way connector for an open circuit.

A/C CUTOUT RELAY CONNECTOR

TEST 10	STEP A	CHECKING FOR FAULT CODE 33 — A/C CUTOUT RELAY	
		PROCEDURE	TEST INDICATION	ACTION REQUIRED

	TEST INDICATION	ACTION REQUIRED
• Connect a voltmeter to the dark blue with orange tracer wire of the A/C cut-out relay single connector, and ground.	• Voltmeter reads within one volt of battery voltage.	• Perform STEP B.
• Turn ignition switch to the run position.		
• Press the A/C button to the on position.	• Voltmeter reads 0-1 volts.	• Perform STEP C.

A/C CUT-OUT RELAY

TEST 11	STEP A	CHECKING FOR FAULT CODE 35 — RADIATOR FAN RELAY CONTROL CIRCUIT	
		PROCEDURE	TEST INDICATION	ACTION REQUIRED

	TEST INDICATION	ACTION REQUIRED
• Connect a voltmeter to the dark blue with pink tracer wire of the radiator fan single connector and ground.	• Voltmeter reads within one volt of battery voltage.	• Perform STEP B.
• Turn the ignition switch to the run position.		
	• Voltmeter reads 0-1 volts.	• Perform STEP C.

RADIATOR FAN RELAY

TEST 10	STEP B	CHECKING THE A/C CUTOUT RELAY CONTROL WIRE FOR AN OPEN CIRCUIT TO THE ENGINE CONTROL MODULE	
		PROCEDURE	TEST INDICATION	ACTION REQUIRED

REMINDERS		TEST INDICATION	ACTION REQUIRED
• A/C button in the on position.		• Voltmeter is reading within one volt of battery voltage.	• Defective logic board. Replace engine control module. CAUTION: Before replacing the engine control module check the terminal in cavity No. 56 of the 60-way connector to make sure it is not damaged causing a poor connection.
• Turn the ignition switch off.			
• Disconnect the 60-way connector from the engine control module.			
• Connect a voltmeter to cavity No. 56 of the 60-way connector and ground.		• Voltmeter reads 0.	• Repair the wire of cavity No. 56 for an open circuit to the A/C cutout relay. NOTE: This wire has a diode in it.
• Turn the ignition switch to the run position.			

VIEW FROM TERMINAL END

56

TEST 11	STEP B	CHECKING THE RADIATOR FAN RELAY CONTROL WIRE FOR AN OPEN CIRCUIT TO THE ENGINE CONTROL MODULE	
		PROCEDURE	TEST INDICATION	ACTION REQUIRED

	TEST INDICATION	ACTION REQUIRED
• Turn the ignition switch off.	• Voltmeter is reading within one volt of battery voltage.	• Defective logic board. Replace engine control module. CAUTION: Before replacing the engine control module check the terminal in cavity No. 57 of the 60-way connector to make sure it is not damaged causing a poor connection.
• Disconnect the 60-way connector from the engine control module.		
• Connect a voltmeter to cavity No. 57 of the 60-way connector and ground.		
• Turn the ignition switch to the run position.	• Voltmeter reads 0 volts.	• Repair the wire of cavity No. 57 for an open circuit to the radiator fan relay.

VIEW FROM TERMINAL END

57

TEST 10	STEP C	CHECKING A/C CUTOUT RELAY PULL IN COIL CIRCUIT FOR A SHORT IN THE ENGINE CONTROL MODULE	
		PROCEDURE	TEST INDICATION	ACTION REQUIRED

REMINDERS		TEST INDICATION	ACTION REQUIRED
• Voltmeter connected to the dark blue with orange tracer wire of the A/C cutout relay single connector.		• Voltmeter reads within one volt of battery voltage.	• Defective logic board. Replace engine control module.
• Turn the ignition switch off.			
• A/C button in the on position.			
• Disconnect the 60-way connector from the engine control module.		• Voltmeter reads 0.	• Perform STEP D.
• Turn the ignition switch to the run position.			

A/C CUT-OUT RELAY

TEST 11	STEP C	CHECKING RADIATOR FAN RELAY PULL IN COIL CIRCUIT FOR A SHORT CIRCUIT IN THE ENGINE CONTROL MODULE	
		PROCEDURE	TEST INDICATION	ACTION REQUIRED

REMINDERS		TEST INDICATION	ACTION REQUIRED
• Voltmeter connected to the dark blue with pink tracer wire of the radiator fan relay single connector.		• Voltmeter reads within one volt of battery voltage.	• Defective logic board. Replace the engine control module.
• Turn the ignition switch off.			
• Disconnect the 60-way connector from the engine control module.		• Voltmeter reads 0 volts.	• Perform STEP D.
• Turn the ignition switch to the run position.			

RADIATOR FAN RELAY

1987-88 EFI DRIVEABILITY TEST PROCEDURES

TEST 11	STEP D	CHECKING FOR VOLTAGE SUPPLY TO THE RADIATOR FAN RELAY PULL IN COIL
PROCEDURE		TEST INDICATION	ACTION REQUIRED

PROCEDURE	TEST INDICATION	ACTION REQUIRED
REMINDERS • Ignition switch in the run position. • Connect a voltmeter to the dark blue wire of the radiator fan relay 3-way connector and ground.	• Voltmeter reads within one volt of battery voltage.	• Replace the radiator fan relay.
	• Voltmeter reads 0.	• Repair the dark blue wire of the 3-way connector for an open circuit to the wiring harness splice.

GY
DB — LG
VOLTMETER
RADIATOR FAN RELAY CONNECTOR

TEST 12	STEP A	CHECKING FOR FAULT CODE 37 — TRANSMISSION LOCKUP SOLENOID

PROCEDURE	TEST INDICATION	ACTION REQUIRED
• Turn the ignition switch off. • Disconnect the 60-way connector from the engine control module. • Connect a voltmeter to cavity No. 55 of the 60-way connector and ground. • Turn the ignition switch to the run position.	• Voltmeter is reading within one volt of battery voltage.	• Defective logic board. Replace engine control module. CAUTION: Before replacing the engine control module check the terminal in cavity No. 55 of the 60-way connector to make sure it is not damaged causing a poor connection.
	• Voltmeter reads 0 volts.	• Perform STEP B.

VIEW FROM TERMINAL END
55
VOLTMETER

TEST 12	STEP B	CHECKING THE TRANSMISSION LOCKUP SOLENOID CONTROL WIRE FOR AN OPEN CIRCUIT TO THE ENGINE CONTROL MODULE

PROCEDURE	TEST INDICATION	ACTION REQUIRED
REMINDERS • Engine control module 60-way connector disconnected. • Voltmeter connected to cavity No. 55 and ground. • Ignition switch in the run position. • Disconnect the transmission lockup solenoid connector. • Connect a jumper wire between the terminals of the transmission lockup solenoid connector.	• Voltmeter is reading within one volt of battery voltage.	• Replace the transmission lockup solenoid.
	• Voltmeter reads 0 volts.	• Perform STEP C.

JUMPER
DB — OR/BK
TRANSMISSION LOCK-UP SOLENOID CONNECTOR

TEST 12	STEP C	CHECKING FOR VOLTAGE SUPPLY TO THE TRANSMISSION LOCKUP SOLENOID

PROCEDURE	TEST INDICATION	ACTION REQUIRED
REMINDERS • Transmission lockup solenoid connector disconnected. • Ignition switch in the run position. • Connect a voltmeter to the dark blue wire terminal of the transmission lockup solenoid connector and ground.	• Voltmeter is reading within one volt of battery voltage.	• Repair the orange with black tracer wire of the transmission lockup solenoid connector for an open circuit to the engine control module.
	• Voltmeter reads 0 volts.	• Repair the dark blue wire of the transmission lockup solenoid connector for an open circuit to the wiring harness splice.

VOLTMETER
DB — OR/BK
TRANSMISSION LOCK-UP SOLENOID CONNECTOR

TEST 13	STEP A	CHECKING FOR FAULT CODE 44 — FUSED J2 CIRCUIT TO THE ENGINE CONTROL MODULE

PROCEDURE	TEST INDICATION	ACTION REQUIRED
• Turn the ignition switch off. • Disconnect the 60-way connector from the engine control module. • Connect a voltmeter to cavity No. 12 of the 60-way connector and ground. • Turn the ignition switch to the run position.	• Voltmeter is reading within one volt of battery voltage.	• Defective logic board. Replace engine control module. CAUTION: Before replacing the engine control module make sure the terminal in cavity No. 12 of the 60-way connector is not damaged causing a poor connection.
	• Voltmeter reads 0 volts.	• Repair the dark blue with white tracer wire of cavity No. 12 for an open circuit to the auto shutdown relay single connector.

VIEW FROM TERMINAL END
12
VOLTMETER

TEST 14	STEP A	CHECKING FOR FAULT CODE 54 — DISTRIBUTOR SYNC PICKUP

PROCEDURE	TEST INDICATION	ACTION REQUIRED
• Turn the ignition switch off. • Disconnect the distributor connector. • Connect a voltmeter to the tan with yellow tracer wire of the distributor harness connector and ground. • Turn the ignition switch to the run position.	• Voltmeter is reading at least 4 volts.	• Replace the distributor pickup assembly.
	• Voltmeter is reading 0.	• Perform STEP B.

OR — BK/LB
TN/YL — GY
VOLTMETER
DISTRIBUTOR HARNESS CONNECTOR

TEST 14	STEP B	CHECKING THE DISTRIBUTOR SYNC PICKUP SIGNAL WIRE FOR AN OPEN CIRCUIT TO THE ENGINE CONTROL MODULE

PROCEDURE	TEST INDICATION	ACTION REQUIRED
REMINDERS • Distributor pickup connector disconnected. • Turn the ignition switch off. • Disconnect the 60-way connector from the engine control module. • Connect an ohmmeter between cavity No. 49 of the 60-way connector and the tan with yellow tracer wire of the distributor harness connector.	• Ohmmeter is showing continuity.	• Defective logic board, replace the engine control module. CAUTION: Before replacing the engine control module, check the terminal in cavity No. 49 of the 60-way connector to make sure it is not damaged causing a poor connection.
	• Ohmmeter is not showing continuity.	• Repair the tan with yellow tracer wire in cavity No. 49 of the 60-way connector for an open circuit to the distributor harness connector.

VIEW FROM TERMINAL END
49
OHMMETER
OR — BK/LB
TN/YL — GY
DISTRIBUTOR HARNESS CONNECTOR

THE FOLLOWING TEST MUST BEGIN WITH A COLD ENGINE

TEST 15	STEP A	CHECKING SENSOR CALIBRATIONS (ENGINE COOLANT TEMPERATURE SENSOR)

PROCEDURE	TEST INDICATION	ACTION REQUIRED
REMINDERS • Diagnostic readout box connected to the engine harness connector. • Start the engine. • Put the system in Engine Running Test Mode 64. (Refer to introduction) NOTE: Don't forget to multiply the reading on display by 10.	• Display on the readout box is reading approximately ambient temperature ± 10°F.	• Perform STEP B.
	• Display on the readout box is reading above or below ambient temperature ± 10°F.	• Replace the coolant sensor.

DIAGNOSTIC READOUT
DIAGNOSTIC READOUT BOX

1987–88 EFI DRIVEABILITY TEST PROCEDURES

TEST 15	STEP B	CHECKING SENSOR CALIBRATIONS (THROTTLE POSITION SENSOR)
PROCEDURE	**TEST INDICATION**	**ACTION REQUIRED**
REMINDERS • Diagnostic readout box connected to the engine harness connector. • Engine cold. • Turn the engine off. • Put the system in Sensor Test Mode 05. (Refer to introduction) NOTE: Don't forget to divide the reading on display by 10. DIAGNOSTIC READOUT BOX	• Display on readout box reads as follows: **Throttle Fully Closed** 1 volt ± ½ volt NOTE: Make sure none of the cables that are attached to the throttle body are not misadjusted and are holding the throttle open. **In Between Closed and Open** You should see an uninterrupted change of voltage between closed and open throttle. **Throttle Wide Open** at least 3½ volts	• If the voltage readings are within specifications. Perform STEP C. • If the voltage readings are not within specifications, replace the throttle position sensor.

TEST 15	STEP C	CHECKING SENSOR CALIBRATION (THROTTLE POSITION SENSOR)
PROCEDURE	**TEST INDICATION**	**ACTION REQUIRED**
REMINDERS • Diagnostic readout box connected to the engine harness connector. • Start the engine. • Put the system into Engine Running Test Mode 65. (Refer to introduction) NOTE: Don't forget to divide the reading on display by 10. • Slowly increase engine speed to 2,000 rpm. DIAGNOSTIC READOUT BOX	• As engine speed increases the voltage displayed on the readout box also increases. • As engine speed increases the voltage displayed on the readout box is not increasing.	• Perform STEP D. • Replace the throttle position sensor.

TEST 15	STEP D	CHECKING SENSOR CALIBRATION (THROTTLE POSITION SENSOR)
PROCEDURE	**TEST INDICATION**	**ACTION REQUIRED**
REMINDERS • Diagnostic readout box connected to the engine harness connector. • Engine running at idle. • Put the system into Engine Running Test Mode 69. (Refer to introduction) NOTE: Don't forget to divide the reading on display by 10. DIAGNOSTIC READOUT BOX	• Display on the readout box is between 0 and .1 (one tenth) volt. • Display on the readout box is reading more than .1 (one tenth) volt.	• Perform STEP E. • Replace the throttle position sensor

TEST 15	STEP E	CHECKING SENSOR CALIBRATION (M.A.P. SENSOR)
PROCEDURE	**TEST INDICATION**	**ACTION REQUIRED**
REMINDERS • Diagnostic readout box connected to the engine harness connector. • Tee a vacuum gauge into the vacuum line at the M.A.P. sensor. • Start the engine. • Put the system into Engine Running Test Mode 68. (Refer to introduction) VACUUM GAUGE	• Vacuum displayed on the readout box is within .1 inch of vacuum shown on the vacuum gauge. • Vacuum displayed on the readout box is not within 1 inch of vacuum shown on the vacuum gauge.	• Perform STEP G. • Perform STEP F.

TEST 15	STEP F	CHECKING SENSOR CALIBRATION (M.A.P. SENSOR)
PROCEDURE	**TEST INDICATION**	**ACTION REQUIRED**
REMINDERS • Diagnostic readout box connected to the engine harness connector. • Engine cold. • Put the system in Sensor Test Mode 08. (Refer to introduction) NOTE: Don't forget to divide the reading on display by 10. • Disconnect the vacuum hose from the M.A.P. sensor. • Connect an auxiliary vacuum supply to the M.A.P. sensor. • Apply 5 inches of vacuum and record the voltage displayed on the readout box.	• Slowly apply vacuum to 20 inches and watch display on readout box. • Record the voltage displayed on the readout box at 20 inches. • Subtract the voltage recorded at 20 inches from the voltage recorded at 5 inches. Example Voltage at 5 inches 3.8 Voltage at 20 inches −1.1 Difference 2.7 • The readout box is showing an interrupted change of voltage between 5 and 20 inches of vacuum.	• The readout box is showing an uninterrupted change of voltage between 5 and 20 inches of vacuum. • The voltage difference is between 2.3 and 2.9 volts. • Repair vacuum line to the M.A.P. sensor for a restriction. • The voltage difference is not between 2.3 and 2.9 volts. • Replace the M.A.P. sensor.

TEST 15	STEP G	CHECKING SENSOR CALIBRATION (CHARGE TEMPERATURE SENSOR)
PROCEDURE	**TEST INDICATION**	**ACTION REQUIRED**
REMINDERS • Diagnostic readout box connected to the engine harness connector. • Engine cold. • Start the engine. • Put the system in Engine Running Test Mode 63. (Refer to introduction) NOTE: Don't forget to divide the reading on display by 10. DIAGNOSTIC READOUT BOX	• Display on the readout box is reading between 3 and 5 volts. • Display on the readout box is not reading between 3 and 5 volts.	• Perform STEP H. • Replace the charge temperature sensor.

TEST 15	STEP H	CHECKING FOR FUEL FOULED SPARK PLUGS
PROCEDURE	**TEST INDICATION**	**ACTION REQUIRED**
• Remove the spark plugs. LOOK FOR WET FUEL	• Spark plugs are dry. NOTE: It is normal for spark plugs to be black after an engine has been started cold. • Spark plugs are wet with fuel.	• Perform TEST NO. 17. • Clean and reinstall. Do not install new spark plugs. • Check for gas in the crankcase. Change oil and filter if required.

THE FOLLOWING TEST MUST BEGIN WITH A WARM ENGINE

TEST 16	STEP A	CHECKING SENSOR CALIBRATION (ENGINE COOLANT TEMPERATURE SENSOR)
PROCEDURE	**TEST INDICATION**	**ACTION REQUIRED**
REMINDERS • Diagnostic readout box connected to the engine harness connector. • Start the engine. • Put the system in Engine Running Test Mode 64. (Refer to introduction) NOTE: Don't forget to multiply the reading on display by 10. DIAGNOSTIC READOUT BOX	• Display on the readout box is reading between 180° and 250°. • Display on the readout box is not reading between 180° and 250°.	• Perform STEP B. • Replace the coolant sensor.

1987–88 EFI DRIVEABILITY TEST PROCEDURES

TEST 16 | STEP B | CHECKING SENSOR CALIBRATIONS (THROTTLE POSITION SENSOR)

PROCEDURE	TEST INDICATION	ACTION REQUIRED
REMINDERS • Diagnostic readout box connected to the engine harness connector. • Engine warm. • Turn the engine off. • Put the system in Sensor Test Mode 05. (Refer to introduction) NOTE: Don't forget to divide the reading on display by 10.	• Display on readout box should read as follows: **Throttle Fully Closed** 1 volt ± ½ volt NOTE: Make sure none of the cables that are attached to the throttle body are not misadjusted and are holding the throttle open. **In Between Closed and Open** You should see an uninterrupted change of voltage between closed and open throttle. **Throttle Wide Open** at least 3 volts	• If the voltage readings are within specifications. Perform STEP C. • If the voltage readings are not within specifications. replace the throttle position sensor.

DIAGNOSTIC READOUT BOX

TEST 16 | STEP C | CHECKING SENSOR CALIBRATION (THROTTLE POSITION SENSOR)

PROCEDURE	TEST INDICATION	ACTION REQUIRED
REMINDERS • Diagnostic readout box connected to the engine harness connector. • Start the engine. • Put the system into Engine Running Test Mode 65. (Refer to introduction) NOTE: Don't forget to divide the reading on display by 10. • Slowly increase engine speed to 2000 rpm.	• As engine speed increases the voltage displayed on the readout box also increases.	• Perform STEP D.
	• As engine speed increases the voltage displayed on the readout box is not increasing.	• Replace the throttle position sensor.

DIAGNOSTIC READOUT BOX

TEST 16 | STEP D | CHECKING SENSOR CALIBRATION (THROTTLE POSITION SENSOR)

PROCEDURE	TEST INDICATION	ACTION REQUIRED
REMINDERS • Diagnostic readout box connected to the engine harness connector. • Engine running at idle. • Put the system into Engine Running Test Mode 69. (Refer to introduction) NOTE: Don't forget to divide the reading on display by 10.	• Display on the readout box is reading between 0 and .1 (one tenth) volt.	• Perform STEP E.
	• Display on the readout box is reading more than .1 (one tenth) volt.	• Replace the throttle position sensor.

DIAGNOSTIC READOUT BOX

TEST 16 | STEP E | CHECKING SENSOR CALIBRATION (M.A.P. SENSOR)

PROCEDURE	TEST INDICATION	ACTION REQUIRED
REMINDERS • Diagnostic readout box connected to the engine harness connector. • Tee a vacuum gauge into the vacuum line at the M.A.P. sensor. • Start the engine. • Put the system into Engine Running Test Mode 69. (Refer to introduction)	• Vacuum displayed on the readout box is within 1 inch of vacuum shown on the vacuum gauge.	• Perform STEP G.
	• Vacuum displayed on the readout box is not within 1 inch of vacuum shown on the vacuum gauge.	• Perform STEP F.

VACUUM GAUGE

TEST 16 | STEP F | CHECKING SENSOR CALIBRATION (M.A.P. SENSOR)

PROCEDURE	TEST INDICATION	ACTION REQUIRED
REMINDERS • Diagnostic readout box connected to the engine harness connector. • Engine warm. • Put the system in Sensor Test Mode 08. (Refer to introduction) NOTE: Don't forget to divide the reading on display by 10. • Disconnect the vacuum hose from the M.A.P. sensor. • Connect an auxiliary vacuum supply to the M.A.P. sensor. • Apply 5 inches of vacuum and record the voltage displayed on the readout box.	• Slowly apply vacuum to 20 inches and watch display on readout box. • Record the voltage displayed on the readout box at 20 inches. • Subtract the voltage recorded at 20 inches from the voltage recorded at 5 inches. **Example** Voltage at 5 inches 3.8 Voltage at 20 inches −1.1 Difference 2.7 • The voltage difference is between 2.3 and 2.9 volts.	• Repair vacuum line to the M.A.P. sensor for a restriction.
	• The readout box is showing an uninterrupted change of voltage between 5 and 20 inches of vacuum. • The voltage difference is not between 2.3 and 2.9 volts.	• Replace the M.A.P. sensor.

TEST 16 | STEP G | CHECKING SENSOR CALIBRATION (CHARGE TEMPERATURE SENSOR)

PROCEDURE	TEST INDICATION	ACTION REQUIRED
REMINDERS • Diagnostic readout box connected to the engine harness connector. • Start the engine. • Put the system in Engine Running Test Mode 63. (Refer to introduction) NOTE: Don't forget to divide the reading on display by 10.	• Display on the readout box is reading between 1 and 4 volts.	• Perform TEST NO. 17.
	• Display on the readout box is not reading between 1 and 4 volts.	• Replace the charge temperature sensor.

DIAGNOSTIC READOUT BOX

TEST 17 | STEP A | CHECKING THE EGR SYSTEM — VACUUM SUPPLY FROM THE THROTTLE BODY TO THE EGR BACKPRESSURE VALVE

PROCEDURE	TEST INDICATION	ACTION REQUIRED
• Disconnect the vacuum line at the EGR backpressure valve that comes from the throttle body. • Connect a vacuum gauge to this line. • Start the engine. • Raise engine speed to 2,000 rpm's.	• Vacuum gauge is reading at least 5 inches.	• Remember what it is and Perform STEP B.
	• No vacuum or vacuum below 5 inches.	• Repair vacuum supply or vacuum from throttle body.

CONNECT VACUUM GAUGE
BACK PRESSURE VALVE
EGR VALVE

TEST 17 | STEP B | CHECKING THE VACUUM SUPPLY FROM THE BACKPRESSURE VALVE TO THE EGR VALVE

PROCEDURE	TEST INDICATION	ACTION REQUIRED
REMINDERS • Engine running. • Disconnect the vacuum gauge from the vacuum line and reconnect the vacuum line to the backpressure valve. • Disconnect the vacuum line from the EGR valve and connect a vacuum gauge to it. • Raise the engine speed to 2,000 rpm's.	• Vacuum gauge is reading the same or near the same as seen in STEP A.	• Perform STEP C.
	• Vacuum gauge is not reading the same or near the same as seen in STEP A.	• Replace EGR/backpressure valve assembly.

CONNECT VACUUM GAUGE
EGR VALVE

1987–88 EFI DRIVEABILITY TEST PROCEDURES

TEST 17	STEP C	CHECKING THE EGR VALVE OPERATION

PROCEDURE	TEST INDICATION	ACTION REQUIRED
REMINDERS • Vacuum line discon-nected from the EGR valve. • Engine running. • Connect an auxiliary vac-uum supply to the EGR valve. • Disconnect the idle motor harness connector. • With engine running at idle speed slowly apply vacuum.	• Engine speed begins to drop when applied vacuum reaches 2½ to 3½ inches.	• Perform STEP D.
 CONNECT AUXILIARY VACUUM SUPPLY EGR VALVE	• Engine speed does not drop.	• Replace EGR/back pressure valve assembly. NOTE: After valve is re-moved, make sure supply tube to the manifold is not plugged before replacing EGR valve assembly.

TEST 17	STEP D	CHECKING THE EGR VALVE VACUUM CHAMBER FOR LEAKS

PROCEDURE	TEST INDICATION	ACTION REQUIRED
REMINDERS • Vacuum line discon-nected from the EGR valve. • Auxiliary vacuum supply connected to the EGR valve. • Engine running at idle speed. • Reconnect the idle motor. • Apply 10 inches of vac-uum to EGR valve.	• Vacuum should hold without bleeding for at least 10 seconds.	• Perform TEST NO. 18.
 CONNECT AUXILIARY VACUUM SUPPLY EGR VALVE	• Vacuum does not hold or bleeds down before 10 seconds.	• Replace EGR/backpre-ssure valve assembly.

TEST 18	STEP A	CHECKING SECONDARY IGNITION SYSTEM

PROCEDURE	TEST INDICATION	ACTION REQUIRED
• Connect suitable engine analyzer to engine. • Start engine and let en-gine speed stabilize for two minutes.	• Follow equipment manu-facturer's procedure for secondary ignition testing and pattern analysis. CAUTION: Make sure ig-nition coil output is checked in this testing. Open circuit secondary voltage should be at least 25,000 volts. • Secondary ignition sys-tem okay.	• Perform TEST NO. 19.
	• Secondary ignition not to specs.	• Repair as required.

TEST 19	STEP A	CHECKING BASIC IGNITION TIMING

PROCEDURE	TEST INDICATION	ACTION REQUIRED
• Connect a tachometer to engine. • Connect a power timing light to engine. • Start and run engine until operating temperature is reached. • Disconnect the engine coolant sensor connec-tor and do not reconnect it. NOTE: The power loss lamp on the instrument panel must come on.	• Basic timing is within 2° of specification as shown on the emission label.	• Perform STEP B.
 COOLANT TEMPERATURE SENSOR	• Basic timing is not within 2° of specification as shown on the emission label.	• Adjust following basic ig-nition timing procedure.

TEST 19	STEP B	CHECKING SPARK ADVANCE

PROCEDURE	TEST INDICATION	ACTION REQUIRED
REMINDERS • Tachometer connected to engine. • Timing light connected to engine. • Air cleaner removed (if necessary). • Engine at operating tem-perature.	• Timing is 30° ± 4° before top dead center.	• Timing okay. **Perform TEST NO. 20.**
• Reconnect the coolant sensor connector. NOTE: Power loss lamp on instrument panel must go off. • Raise engine speed to 2,000 rpm s.	• Spark advance not within minimum specification.	• Defective logic board. Replace engine control module.

TEST 20	STEP A	CHECKING FUEL SUPPLY AND RETURN SYSTEM

PROCEDURE	TEST INDICATION	ACTION REQUIRED
• Connect diagnostic read-out box to the engine harness connector. • Install pressure gauge (Tool C3292) with (C4799 adapter) in fuel supply hose at throttle body. CAUTION: Fuel is under high pressure. Refer to service manual for pres-sure release procedure. • Turn the ignition switch to the run position. • Press the ATM button.	• Fuel pressure is 36 psi ± 1.	• Perform TEST NO. 21.
 RETURN LINE SUPPLY LINE	• Fuel pressure below 35 record what it is.	• Perform STEP B.
	• Fuel pressure above 37.	• Perform STEP D.

TEST 20	STEP B	CHECKING FOR LOW FUEL PRESSURE

PROCEDURE	TEST INDICATION	ACTION REQUIRED
REMINDERS • Diagnostic readout box connected to the engine harness connector. • Turn the ignition switch off. • Release pressure.	• Fuel pressure is higher than 5 psi of previously recorded pressure.	• Replace fuel filter.
• Remove pressure gauge. • Reinstall hose to throttle body. • Install pressure gage be-fore fuel filter. • Turn the ignition switch to the run position. • Press the ATM button.	 INSTALL PRESSURE GAUGE FUEL FILTER	• Fuel pressure still below 35 psi. • Perform STEP C.

TEST 20	STEP C	CHECKING FOR LOW FUEL PRESSURE

PROCEDURE	TEST INDICATION	ACTION REQUIRED
REMINDERS • Diagnostic readout box connected to the engine harness connector. • Turn the ignition switch off. • Release pressure.	• Fuel pressure increases above operating pres-sure.	• Replace pressure regula-tor valve.
• Remove pressure gauge from before filter and reinstall it after filter. • Turn the ignition switch to the run position. • Press the ATM button. • Very gently, squeeze fuel return line at fuel rail and immediately let go.	 INSTALL PRESSURE GAUGE FUEL FILTER	• Fuel pressure does not increase.	• Replace intank fuel pump. NOTE: Before replacing pump look for contamina-tion in the fuel tank that may be plugging pump filter. Also make sure electrical connections are not corroded.

1987–88 EFI DRIVEABILITY TEST PROCEDURES

TEST 20	STEP D	CHECKING FOR HIGH FUEL PRESSURE	
PROCEDURE		TEST INDICATION	ACTION REQUIRED
REMINDERS • Pressure gauge connected. • Diagnostic readout box connected to the engine harness connector. • Turn the ignition switch off. • Remove fuel return hose (small one) from fuel rail. • Connect a 3 foot piece of fuel hose to throttle body and put open end into an approved gasoline container. (2-gallon size.) • Turn the ignition switch to the run position.	• Press the ATM button. CAUTION: Do not hold button down for more than 10 seconds.	• Fuel pressure is 36 psi ± 1.	• Check fuel return lines for kinks or restrictions, including return line check valve inside fuel tank.
		• Fuel pressure is above 37 psi.	• Replace pressure regulator valve.

RETURN LINE   SUPPLY LINE

TEST 21	STEP A	CHECKING THE OXYGEN SENSOR OPERATION	
PROCEDURE		TEST INDICATION	ACTION REQUIRED
• Connect the diagnostic readout box to the engine harness connector. NOTE: Make sure the read/hold switch is in the Read position. • Start the engine and wait 2 minutes. • Move the read/hold switch to the hold position to increase engine speed.		• Display on the readout box is switching between 0 and 1 or stays on 1.	• Perform TEST NO. 22.
		• Display on the readout box is 0.	• Check for a grounded oxygen sensor wire. • Check for plugged fuel injectors.

DIAGNOSTIC READOUT BOX

TEST 22	STEP A	CHECKING THROTTLE BODY MINIMUM AIR FLOW	
PROCEDURE		TEST INDICATION	ACTION REQUIRED
• Connect diagnostic readout box to the engine harness connector. • Connect a tachometer to the engine. • Disconnect the hose from the PCV valve. • Install Tool C5004 (.125" orifice) into the PCV vacuum supply hose. • Start the engine and let it run until the radiator cooling fan cycles on then off. • With the radiator fan not running, put the system into Engine Running Test Mode 70. (Refer to introduction)		• Tachometer is reading between 850 and 1050 rpm. NOTE: If vehicle has less than 300 miles specification is between 725 and 925 rpm.	• Perform TEST NO. 23.
		• Tachometer is not reading within above specifications.	• Replace the throttle body.

CONNECT TOOL C5004
DISCONNECT

NOTES

TEST NO. 23

AT THIS POINT IN THE DRIVEABILITY TEST PROCEDURE YOU HAVE DETERMINED THAT ALL OF THE ENGINE CONTROL SYSTEMS ARE OPERATING AS THEY WERE DESIGNED TO. THEREFORE THEY ARE **NOT THE CAUSE** OF THE DRIVEABILITY PROBLEM.

THE FOLLOWING ADDITIONAL ITEMS SHOULD BE CHECKED AS POSSIBLE CAUSES:

1. ENGINE VACUUM – MUST BE AT LEAST 13 INCHES IN NEUTRAL.
2. ENGINE VALVE TIMING – TO SPECIFICATIONS.
3. ENGINE COMPRESSION – TO SPECIFICATIONS.
4. ENGINE EXHAUST SYSTEM – MUST BE FREE OF ANY RESTRICTIONS.
5. ENGINE PCV SYSTEM – MUST FLOW FREELY.
6. ENGINE DRIVE SPROCKETS – CAM AND CRANK SHAFTS.
7. TORQUE CONVERTOR STALL SPEED – TO SPECIFICATIONS.
8. POWER BRAKE BOOSTER – NO INTERNAL VACUUM LEAKS.
9. FUEL CONTAMINATION – HIGH ALCOHOL AND WATER CONTENT.
10. FUEL INJECTORS – ROUGH IDLE MAY BE CAUSED BY INJECTOR CONTROL WIRES NOT CONNECTED TO THE CORRECT INJECTOR.
11. TECHNICAL SERVICE BULLETINS – ANY THAT MAY APPLY TO VEHICLE.

ANY ONE OR MORE OF THESE ITEMS CAN GIVE A DRIVEABILITY RELATED PROBLEM. THEY CANNOT BE OVERLOOKED AS POSSIBLE CAUSES.

TEST 1	STEP A	CHECKING CHARGING SYSTEM FOR FAULT CODES		
PROCEDURE		TEST INDICATION	CIRCUIT	ACTION REQUIRED
• Connect diagnostic readout box to engine harness connector. • Turn ignition switch on-off-on-off-on within 5 seconds. • RECORD ALL CODES • Erase fault codes, (refer to introduction). • Start engine. • Let engine run for 7 minutes at idle rpm. • Raise engine speed above 1500 rpm for 30 seconds. • Turn engine off. • Turn ignition switch on-off-on-off-on within 5 seconds. • RECORD ALL CODES If the same code appears before and after the engine is started, the problem still exists. Proceed to test indications. If a code does not reappear after the engine is started, the problem no longer exists. Perform STEP B.		88-12-55	No fault codes	Perform TEST NO. 2
		88-11-12-16-55	Battery voltage sense	Perform TEST NO. 3
		88-12-41-46-55 88-12-46-55	Alternator field (charging system output to high)	Perform TEST NO. 4
		88-12-41-55 88-12-41-47-55 88-12-47-55	Alternator field (charging system output to low)	Perform TEST NO. 5

DIAGNOSTIC READOUT BOX

1987–88 EFI DRIVEABILITY TEST PROCEDURES

TEST 1	STEP B	CHECKING CHARGING SYSTEM FOR INTERMITTENT FAILURES

The majority of intermittent failures are caused by wiring and connections. The only way to find them is to try and duplicate the problem. Since the engine control module can remember where they are, the ATM and sensor test modes can be used in an attempt to locate them.

- If the following fault codes do not reappear use the ATM Test Mode as indicated.

Fault Code	ATM Test Mode
41*	09

* Connect a voltmeter to the field control wire terminal of the alternator and watch pulsations of meter.

Once in the correct test mode, wiggle all the connectors and wires in the circuit. When the bad connection or wire is located the ATM test will be interrupted.

- If the following fault codes do not reappear use the Sensor Test Mode as indicated.

Fault Code	Sensor Test Mode
16	07

Once in the correct test mode, wiggle all the connectors and wires in the circuit. When the bad connection or wire is located the display on the readout box will change.

TEST 2	STEP A	CHECKING SENSOR CALIBRATION (BATTERY TEMPERATURE SENSOR)

PROCEDURE		TEST INDICATION	ACTION REQUIRED
REMINDERS • Diagnostic readout box connected to the engine harness connector. • Put the system in Engine Running TEST Mode 61. (Refer to introduction) NOTE: Don't forget to divide the reading on display by 10.		• Display on the readout box is reading between .2 (two tenths) and 3 volts.	• Perform STEP B.
		• Display on the readout box is not reading between .2 (two tenths) and 3 volts.	• Defective logic board. Replace engine control module.

TEST 2	STEP B	CHECKING CHARGING SYSTEM OPERATING VOLTAGE

PROCEDURE		TEST INDICATION	ACTION REQUIRED
REMINDERS • Diagnostic readout box connected to the engine harness connector. • Put the system in Engine Running Test Mode 67. (Refer to introduction). NOTE: Reading on display is actual.		• Display on the readout box is reading between 13 and 15 volts.	• Check battery per service manual procedure. • Check for a battery drain down condition.
		• Display on the readout box is not reading between 13 and 15 volts.	• Check alternator per service manual procedure.

TEST 3	STEP A	CHECKING FOR FAULT CODE 16 — BATTERY VOLTAGE SENSING CIRCUIT

PROCEDURE		TEST INDICATION	ACTION REQUIRED
• Turn the ignition switch off. • Disconnect the 60-way connector from the engine control module. • Connect a voltmeter to cavity No. 41 of the 60-way connector and ground.		• Voltmeter reads within one volt of battery voltage.	• Defective engine control module. Replace engine control module. CAUTION: Before replacing the engine control module make sure the terminal in cavity No. 41 of the 60-way connector is not crushed causing a poor connection.
VIEW FROM TERMINAL END		• Voltmeter reads 0.	• Repair the red wire of cavity No. 41 for an open circuit to the wiring harness splice.

TEST 4	STEP A	CHECKING FOR FAULT CODE 46 OR 41-46 ALTERNATOR FIELD CIRCUIT (CHARGING SYSTEM OUTPUT TOO HIGH)

PROCEDURE		TEST INDICATION	ACTION REQUIRED
REMINDERS • Diagnostic readout box connected to the engine harness connector. • Turn the ignition switch off. • Disconnect the 14-way connector from the engine control module. • Separate the 14-way connector. • Reconnect the half of the connector that contains cavities 1 thru 7 to the engine control module.	• Connect the positive lead of an analog voltmeter to cavity No. 14 in the half of the 14-way connector that is not connected to the engine control module. • Connect the negative lead of the voltmeter to cavity No. 11 of the same connector. • Put the system in ATM Test Mode 09. (Refer to introduction).	• Voltmeter is pulsating between 0 and 12 volts.	• Defective power board. Replace engine control module.
	14-WAY CONNECTOR	• Voltmeter reads 0 volts.	• Perform STEP B.

TEST 4	STEP B	CHECKING ALTERNATOR FIELD CONTROL WIRE FOR A SHORT TO GROUND

PROCEDURE		TEST INDICATION	ACTION REQUIRED
REMINDERS • Half of 14-way connector with cavities 8-14 disconnected from the engine control module. • Ignition switch in the run position. • Positive lead of the voltmeter connected to cavity No. 14 of the 14-way engine control module connector. • Move the negative lead of the voltmeter from cavity No. 11 of the engine control module 14-way connector to the negative battery terminal.		• Voltmeter reads within one volt of battery voltage.	• Perform STEP C.
	14-WAY CONNECTOR	• Voltmeter reads 0-1 volts.	• Repair alternator field circuit for a short to ground.

TEST 4	STEP C	CHECKING THE CHARGING SYSTEM CONTROL CIRCUIT OF THE ENGINE CONTROL MODULE FOR A SHORT CIRCUIT

PROCEDURE		TEST INDICATION	ACTION REQUIRED
REMINDERS • Half of 14-way connector with cavities 8-14 disconnected from the engine control module. • Turn the ignition switch off. • Disconnect the 60-way connector from the engine control module. • Connect an ohmmeter between No. 14 of the 60-way connector and ground.		• Ohmmeter is not showing continuity.	• Defective logic board. Replace engine control module.
VIEW FROM TERMINAL END		• Ohmmeter is showing continuity.	• Repair the dark green with orange tracer wire of cavity No. 14 in the 60-way connector for a short to ground.

1987–88 EFI DRIVEABILITY TEST PROCEDURES

TEST 5	STEP A	CHECKING FOR FAULT CODE 41 OR 41-47 OR 47 ALTERNATOR FIELD (CHARGING SYSTEM OUTPUT TOO LOW)		
PROCEDURE			**TEST INDICATION**	**ACTION REQUIRED**
REMINDERS • Diagnostic readout box connected to the engine harness connector. • Connect the negative lead of a voltmeter to the battery negative post. • Put the system ATM Test Mode 09. (Refer to introduction). • Touch the positive lead of the voltmeter to each of the alternator field terminals.		 DIAGNOSTIC READOUT DIAGNOSTIC READOUT BOX	• Voltmeter reads 0 volts at both alternator field terminals.	• Repair the J2 circuit to the alternator field for an open circuit to the wiring harness splice.
			• Voltmeter reads battery voltage at one alternator field terminal and is pulsating between 0 and battery voltage at the other terminal.	• Check for a loose alternator drive belt, check the battery or alternator following the service manual procedure.
			• Voltmeter reads battery voltage at both alternator field terminals.	• Perform STEP B.

TEST 5	STEP C	CHECKING THE CHARGING SYSTEM CONTROL CIRCUIT IN THE ENGINE CONTROL MODULE		
PROCEDURE			**TEST INDICATION**	**ACTION REQUIRED**
REMINDERS • Diagnostic readout box connected to the engine harness connector. • Engine control module 14-way connector disconnected. • Turn the ignition switch off. • Separate the engine control module 14-way connector. • Reconnect the half of the connector that contains cavities 1 thru 7 to the engine control module.		• Connect the positive lead of an analog voltmeter to cavity No. 14 in the half of the 14-way connector that is not connected to the engine control module. • Connect the negative lead of the voltmeter to cavity No. 11 of the same connector. • Put the system in ATM Test Mode 09. (Refer to introduction). LEAD LEAD VOLTMETER 14 13 12 11 10 9 8 14-WAY CONNECTOR	• Voltmeter is pulsating between 0 and 12 volts.	• Defective power board. Replace engine control module. CAUTION: Before replacing the engine control module check the terminals in cavities 11 and 14 to make sure they are not spread apart causing a poor connection.
			• Voltmeter reads 0 volts.	• Perform STEP D.

TEST 5	STEP B	CHECKING THE ALTERNATOR FIELD CONTROL WIRE FOR AN OPEN CIRCUIT TO THE ENGINE CONTROL MODULE		
PROCEDURE			**TEST INDICATION**	**ACTION REQUIRED**
REMINDERS • Diagnostic readout box connected to the engine harness connector. • Turn the ignition switch off. • Disconnect the 14-way connector from the engine control module. • Connect a voltmeter to cavity No. 14 of the 14-way connector and ground. • Turn the ignition switch to the run position.		 VOLTMETER 14 13 12 11 10 9 8 14-WAY CONNECTOR	• Voltmeter reads within one volt of battery voltage.	• Perform STEP C.
			• Voltmeter reads 0 volts.	• Repair the dark green wire of cavity No. 14 of the 14-way connector for an open circuit to the alternator.

TEST 5	STEP D	CHECKING THE CHARGING SYSTEM CONTROL WIRE FOR AN OPEN CIRCUIT TO THE ENGINE CONTROL MODULE		
PROCEDURE			**TEST INDICATION**	**ACTION REQUIRED**
REMINDERS • Engine control module 14-way connector disconnected. • Turn the ignition switch off. • Disconnect the 60-way connector from the engine control module. • Connect an ohmmeter between cavity No. 14 of the 14-way connector and cavity No. 14 of the 60-way connector.		VIEW FROM TERMINAL END 14 OHMMETER 14 13 12 11 10 9 8 14-WAY CONNECTOR	• Ohmmeter shows continuity.	• Defective logic board. Replace engine control module. CAUTION: Before replacing the engine control module check the terminal in cavity No. 14 of the 60-way connector to make sure it is not crushed causing a poor connection.
			• Ohmmeter is not showing continuity.	• Repair the dark green with orange tracer wire of the 60-way connector for an open circuit to the 14-way connector.

TEST 1	STEP A	CHECKING SPEED CONTROL SYSTEM FOR FAULT CODES		
PROCEDURE		**TEST INDICATION**	**CIRCUIT**	**ACTION REQUIRED**
• Connect diagnostic readout box to the engine harness connector. • Put the system into the Diagnostic Test Mode. (Refer to introduction). • RECORD ALL CODES		88-55 88-12-55	No fault codes	Perform STEP B.
		88-34-55 88-12-34-55	Speed control servo	Perform TEST NO. 2.
		88-15-55 88-12-15-55	Speed sensor	Perform Driveability TEST NO. 3, Page 46.
	 DIAGNOSTIC READOUT DIAGNOSTIC READOUT BOX			

TEST 2	STEP A	CHECKING FOR FAULT CODE 34, SPEED CONTROL SERVO (VACUUM SOLENOID)		
PROCEDURE			**TEST INDICATION**	**ACTION REQUIRED**
REMINDERS • Diagnostic readout box connected to the engine harness connector. • Connect a voltmeter to the tan with red tracer wire of the speed control servo harness connector and ground. • Put the system into ATM Test Mode 08. (Refer to introduction). • Turn the speed control switch to the on position.		 VOLTMETER	• Voltmeter is pulsating between 0 and 12 volts.	• Vacuum solenoid okay. Perform STEP B.
			• Voltmeter is reading within one volt of battery voltage.	• Perform STEP E.
			• Voltmeter is reading between 0 and 1 volt.	• Perform STEP F.

TEST 1	STEP B	CHECKING SPEED CONTROL SWITCH INPUTS TO THE LOGIC MODULE			
PROCEDURE		**TEST INDICATION**			**ACTION REQUIRED**
REMINDERS • Diagnostic readout box connected to the engine harness connector. • Put the system into Sensor Test Mode 09. (Refer to introduction). NOTE: Make sure speed control switch is in the off position. • While looking at the readout box display a) move on/off switch to the on position. b) press the set button c) press the resume button • Record display readings.		On 00	Set 10	Resume 01	• Speed control switch okay. Perform TEST NO. 3.
		On Blank	Set Blank	Resume Blank	• Perform TEST NO. 4.
		On Blank	Set 10	Resume 10	• Perform TEST NO. 5.
		On 00	Set 00	Resume 00	• Perform TEST NO. 6.
	 OFF ON SET RESUME				

TEST 2	STEP B	CHECKING FOR FAULT CODE 34, SPEED CONTROL (VENT SOLENOID)		
PROCEDURE			**TEST INDICATION**	**ACTION REQUIRED**
• Turn ignition switch off. • Connect a voltmeter to the light green with red tracer wire of the speed control servo harness connector and ground. • Turn the ignition switch to the run position. • Turn the speed control switch on.		 VOLTMETER	• Voltmeter is reading within one volt of battery voltage.	• Perform STEP C.
			• Voltmeter is reading between 0 and 1 volt.	• Perform STEP D.

1987–88 EFI DRIVEABILITY TEST PROCEDURES

TEST 2	STEP C	CHECKING THE VENT SOLENOID WIRE FOR AN OPEN CIRCUIT TO THE ENGINE CONTROL MODULE

PROCEDURE		TEST INDICATION	ACTION REQUIRED
• Turn the ignition switch off. • Disconnect the 60-way connector from the engine control module. • Connect a voltmeter to cavity No. 60 of the 60-way connector and ground. • Turn the ignition switch to the run position.		• Voltmeter is reading within one volt of battery voltage.	• Defective logic board. Replace engine control module. CAUTION: Before replacing the engine control module, check the terminal in cavity No. 60 of the 60-way connector to make sure it is not damaged causing a poor connection.
	VIEW FROM TERMINAL END 60 VOLTMETER	• Voltmeter is reading between 0 and 1 volt.	• Repair wire of cavity No. 60 for an open circuit to the speed control servo connector.

TEST 2	STEP D	CHECKING THE VENT SOLENOID CIRCUIT FOR A SHORT IN THE ENGINE CONTROL MODULE

PROCEDURE		TEST INDICATION	ACTION REQUIRED
REMINDERS • Voltmeter connected to the light green with red tracer wire of the speed control servo harness and ground. • Disconnect the 60-way connector from the engine control module. • Turn the ignition to the run position.		• Voltmeter reading is within one volt of battery voltage.	• Defective logic board. Replace engine control module.
	VOLTMETER	• Voltmeter is reading between 0 and 1 volt.	• Repair wire of cavity No. 60 for a short circuit to ground from the logic board to the speed control servo connector.

TEST 2	STEP E	CHECKING THE VACUUM SOLENOID CONTROL WIRE FOR AN OPEN CIRCUIT TO THE ENGINE CONTROL MODULE

PROCEDURE		TEST INDICATION	ACTION REQUIRED
• Turn the ignition switch off. • Disconnect the 60-way connector from the engine control module. • Connect a voltmeter to cavity No. 53 of the 60-way connector and ground. • Turn the ignition switch to the run position.		• Voltmeter is reading within one volt of battery voltage.	• Defective logic board. Replace engine control module. CAUTION: Before replacing engine control module check cavity 53 of the 60-way connector to make sure it is not damaged causing a poor connection.
	VIEW FROM TERMINAL END 53 VOLTMETER	• Voltmeter is reading between 0 and 1 volt.	• Repair wire of cavity No. 53 for an open circuit to the speed control servo connector.

TEST 2	STEP F	CHECKING THE VACUUM SOLENOID CIRCUIT FOR A SHORT IN THE ENGINE CONTROL MODULE

PROCEDURE		TEST INDICATION	ACTION REQUIRED
REMINDERS • Voltmeter connected to the tan with red tracer wire of the speed control servo harness and ground. • Disconnect the 60-way connector from the engine control module. • Turn the ignition to the run position.		• Voltmeter reading is within one volt of battery voltage.	• Defective logic board. Replace engine control module.
	VOLTMETER	• Voltmeter is reading between 0 and 1 volt.	• Perform STEP G.

TEST 2	STEP G	CHECKING THE POWER SUPPLY TO THE SPEED CONTROL SERVO

PROCEDURE		TEST INDICATION	ACTION REQUIRED
REMINDERS • Speed control switch in the on position. • Turn the ignition off. • Connect a voltmeter to the dark blue with red tracer wire of the speed control servo harness connector and ground. • Turn the ignition switch to the run position.		• Voltmeter is reading within one volt of battery voltage.	• Replace the speed control servo.
	VOLTMETER	• Voltmeter is still reading between 0 and 1 volt.	• Perform STEP H.

TEST 2	STEP H	CHECKING SPEED CONTROL POWER SUPPLY THROUGH THE BRAKE SWITCH

PROCEDURE		TEST INDICATION	ACTION REQUIRED
REMINDERS • Speed control switch in the on position. • Ignition switch in the run position. • Connect a voltmeter to the dark blue with red tracer wire of the brake switch harness connector and ground.		• Voltmeter is reading within one volt of battery voltage.	• Repair the dark blue with red tracer wire for an open circuit to the speed control servo.
	VOLTMETER	• Voltmeter is still reading between 0 and 1 volt.	• Perform STEP I.

TEST 2	STEP I	CHECKING SPEED CONTROL POWER SUPPLY TO THE BRAKE SWITCH

PROCEDURE		TEST INDICATION	ACTION REQUIRED
REMINDERS • Speed control switch in the on position. • Ignition switch in the run position. • Connect a voltmeter to the yellow with red tracer wire of the brake switch harness connector and ground.		• Voltmeter is reading within one volt of battery voltage.	• Replace the brake switch.
	VOLTMETER	• Voltmeter still reads 0.	• Repair the yellow with red tracer wire for an open circuit to the wiring harness splice.

TEST 3	STEP A	CHECKING THE SPEED CONTROL SERVO GROUND CIRCUIT

PROCEDURE		TEST INDICATION	ACTION REQUIRED
• Turn the ignition switch off. • Disconnect the speed control servo connector. • Connect an ohmmeter between the black wire of the speed control servo harness connector and ground.		• Ohmmeter is showing continuity.	• Perform STEP B.
	WIRE END BK OHMMETER	• Ohmmeter is not showing continuity.	• Repair the black wire for an open circuit to the wiring harness splice.

1987–88 EFI DRIVEABILITY TEST PROCEDURES

TEST 3	STEP B	CHECKING BRAKE SWITCH INPUT TO THE ENGINE CONTROL MODULE
PROCEDURE	**TEST INDICATION**	**ACTION REQUIRED**
• Diagnostic readout box connected to the engine harness connector. • Put the system into the Switch Test Mode. (Refer to Introduction.) Press down on brake pedal.	• Display on the readout box changes as brake pedal is depressed. NOTE: It is not important what display changes to. Just make sure it changes.	• Perform STEP D.
	• Display on the readout box does not change when brake pedal is depressed.	• Perform STEP C.

TEST 3	STEP C	CHECKING BRAKE SWITCH INPUT CIRCUIT TO THE ENGINE CONTROL MODULE
PROCEDURE	**TEST INDICATION**	**ACTION REQUIRED**
• Turn the ignition switch off. • Disconnect the 60-way connector from the engine control module. • Connect an ohmmeter between cavity No. 29 of the 60-way connector and ground. • Press down on brake pedal and then release.	• Ohmmeter shows no continuity when brake pedal is pressed down and continuity when released.	• Defective logic board. Replace engine control module. CAUTION: Before replacing the engine control module check terminal in cavity No. 29 of the 60-way connector to make sure it is not damaged causing a poor connection.
	• Ohmmeter does not read as above.	• Refer to the wiring diagram and check the wire of cavity No. 29 of the 60-way connector for an open circuit to the stop lamp ground eyelet.

VIEW FROM TERMINAL END — 29 — OHMMETER

TEST 3	STEP D	CHECKING PARK/NEUTRAL SWITCH INPUT TO THE ENGINE CONTROL MODULE
PROCEDURE	**TEST INDICATION**	**ACTION REQUIRED**
REMINDERS • Diagnostic readout box connected to the engine harness connector. • System in the Switch Test Mode (Refer to Introduction). • Put gear selector in park, reverse, neutral, and drive and observe diagnostic readout box.	• Display on the readout box changes as the gear selector is moved from park to reverse, from reverse to neutral, from neutral to drive, and back to park. NOTE: It is not important what display changes to. Just make sure it changes.	• Perform STEP F.
	• Display on the readout box does not change when gear selector is moved.	• Perform STEP E.

TEST 3	STEP E	CHECKING PARK/NEUTRAL SWITCH INPUT CIRCUIT TO THE ENGINE CONTROL MODULE
PROCEDURE	**TEST INDICATION**	**ACTION REQUIRED**
• Turn ignition switch off. • Disconnect the 60-way connector from the engine control module. • Connect an ohmmeter to cavity No. 30 of the 60-way connector and ground. • Disconnect the battery quick disconnect. • Turn the ignition switch to the run position. • Put gear selector in park, reverse, neutral, and drive and observe position.	• Ohmmeter shows continuity in all positions of the gear selector.	• Check wire of cavity No. 30 for a short to ground. • Check for a bad safety neutral switch.
	• Ohmmeter shows no continuity in all positions of the gear selector.	• Repair wire of cavity No. 30 for an open circuit to the safety neutral switch.
	• Ohmmeter reads as follows: Park - continuity Reverse - no continuity Neutral - continuity Drive - no continuity NOTE: Disregard any resistance readings. Just make sure there is continuity.	• Defective logic board. Replace engine control module. NOTE: Before replacing the engine control module check the terminal in cavity No. 30 of the 60-way connector to make sure it is not damaged causing a poor connection.

VIEW FROM TERMINAL END — 30 — OHMMETER — BATTERY CONNECTOR

TEST 3	STEP F	CHECKING THE SPEED CONTROL SERVO OPERATION
PROCEDURE	**TEST INDICATION**	**ACTION REQUIRED**
• Reconnect the speed control servo connector. • Connect diagnostic readout box to the engine harness connector. • Disconnect the speed control servo vacuum supply hose from the power brake booster and connect an auxiliary vacuum supply to it. • Put the system into ATM Test Mode 08. (Refer to Introduction.) • Continuously apply vacuum to servo.	• As the system turns on and off while vacuum is continuously being applied the throttle is opening and closing.	• Check vacuum supply to the speed control servo. • Check speed sensor operation using Engine Running Test Mode 71, (refer to Introduction). Miles per hour shown on the readout box must be stable at all times. If not replace the speed sensor.
	• As the system turns on and off while vacuum is continuously being applied the throttle is not opening and closing.	• Replace the speed control servo. NOTE: Before replacing the servo, make sure the speed control cable is properly adjusted or is not broken or make sure there are no leaks or restrictions in the vacuum supply hose.

DISCONNECT & CONNECT AN AUXILIARY VACUUM SUPPLY

TEST 4	STEP A	CHECKING SPEED CONTROL SYSTEM POWER SUPPLY CIRCUIT
PROCEDURE	**TEST INDICATION**	**ACTION REQUIRED**
REMINDERS • Diagnostic readout box connected to the engine harness connector. • System in Sensor Test Mode 09. • Speed control switch in the on position. • Connect a jumper wire between the dark blue with white tracer and yellow with red tracer wires of the speed control switch harness connector. NOTE: Do not disconnect the speed control switch connector.	• 00 is displayed on the readout box.	• Replace the speed control switch.
	• Display on the readout box is blank.	• Perform STEP B.

JUMPER

TEST 4	STEP B	CHECKING THE SPEED CONTROL SYSTEM POWER SUPPLY CIRCUIT
PROCEDURE	**TEST INDICATION**	**ACTION REQUIRED**
• Turn the ignition switch off. • Connect the negative lead of a voltmeter to ground and the positive lead to the dark blue with white tracer wire of the speed control switch harness connector. NOTE: Do not disconnect the speed control switch connector. • Turn the ignition switch on.	• Voltmeter reading is within one volt of battery voltage.	• Perform STEP C.
	• Voltmeter reading is 0.	• Repair the dark blue with white tracer wire for an open circuit to the fuse box.

VOLTMETER

TEST 4	STEP C	CHECKING THE SPEED CONTROL SYSTEM POWER SUPPLY CIRCUIT
PROCEDURE	**TEST INDICATION**	**ACTION REQUIRED**
• Turn the ignition switch off. • Disconnect the 60-way connector from the engine control module. • Connect the negative lead of a voltmeter to ground and the positive lead to cavity No. 8 of the 60-way connector. NOTE: Do not disconnect the speed control switch connector. • Turn the ignition switch on.	• Voltmeter reading is within one volt of battery voltage.	• Defective logic board. Replace engine control module. NOTE: Before replacing the engine control module, check the terminal in cavity No. 8 of the 60-way connector to make sure it is not damaged causing a poor connection.
	• Voltmeter reading is 0.	NOTE: Repair the yellow with red tracer wire of cavity No. 8 of the 60-way for an open circuit to the speed control switch.

VIEW FROM TERMINAL END — 8 — VOLTMETER

1987–88 EFI DRIVEABILITY TEST PROCEDURES

TEST 5	STEP A	CHECKING SPEED CONTROL SYSTEM SET CIRCUIT	
PROCEDURE		**TEST INDICATION**	**ACTION REQUIRED**
REMINDERS • Diagnostic readout box connected to the engine harness connector. • System in Sensor Test Mode 09. • Speed control switch in the on position. • Connect a jumper wire between the dark blue with white tracer and brown with red tracer wires of the speed control switch harness connector. **NOTE:** do not disconnect the speed control switch connector.		• 00 is displayed on the readout box.	• Replace the speed control switch.
		• 10 is displayed on the readout box.	• Perform STEP B.

TEST 5	STEP B	CHECKING SPEED CONTROL SYSTEM SET CIRCUIT	
PROCEDURE		**TEST INDICATION**	**ACTION REQUIRED**
• Turn the ignition switch off. • Disconnect the 60-way connector from the engine control module. • Connect the negative lead of a voltmeter to ground and the positive lead to cavity No. 9 of the 60-way connector. **NOTE:** Do not disconnect the speed control switch connector. • Turn the ignition switch on.	VIEW FROM TERMINAL END	• Voltmeter reading is within one volt of battery voltage.	• Defective logic board. Replace engine control module. **NOTE:** Before replacing the engine control module, check the terminal in cavity No. 9 of the 60-way for an open circuit to the speed control switch.
		• Voltmeter reading is 0.	• Repair the brown with red tracer wire of cavity No. 9 of the 60-way for an open circuit to the speed control switch.

TEST 6	STEP A	CHECKING THE SPEED CONTROL SYSTEM RESUME CIRCUIT	
PROCEDURE		**TEST INDICATION**	**ACTION REQUIRED**
REMINDERS • Diagnostic readout box connected to the engine harness connector. • System in Sensor Test Mode 09. • Speed control switch in the on position. • Connect a jumper wire between the white wire and the dark blue with white tracer wire of the speed control switch harness connector. **NOTE:** do not disconnect the speed control switch connector.		• 01 is displayed on the readout box.	• Replace the speed control switch.
		• 00 is displayed on the readout box.	• Perform STEP B.

TEST 6	STEP B	CHECK THE SPEED CONTROL SYSTEM RESUME CIRCUIT	
PROCEDURE		**TEST INDICATION**	**ACTION REQUIRED**
• Turn the ignition switch off. • Disconnect the 60-way connector from the engine control module. • Connect the negative lead of a voltmeter to ground and the positive lead to cavity No. 7 of the 60-way connector. **NOTE:** do not disconnect the speed control switch connector. • Turn the ignition switch on. • Press resume switch.	VIEW FROM TERMINAL END	• Voltmeter reading is within one volt of battery voltage.	• Defective logic board. Replace engine control module. **NOTE:** Before replacing the engine control module, check the terminal in cavity No. 7 of the 60-way for an open circuit to the speed control switch.
		• Voltmeter reading is 0.	• Repair the white wire of cavity No. 7 of the 60-way for an open circuit to the speed control switch.

FORD EEC IV ENGINE CONTROL SYSTEM

General Information

The Ford Electronic Engine Control (EEC) IV system is the fifth generation of engine control systems used on Ford passenger cars and light trucks. EEC IV is similar to previous Ford engine control systems in that the heart of the system is a microcomputer called an Electronic Control Assembly (ECA). The ECA receives data (system inputs) from sensors, switches, relays and other electronic components and issues command signals (system outputs) to various devices in order to control engine operation under a variety of loads and ambient conditions. The ECA is calibrated according to the powertrain, axle ratio and gross vehicle weight (GVW) to optimize fuel economy and driveability while minimizing harmful emissions.

The ECA in the EEC IV system is similar in appearance to earlier control units, except that the calibration module is located within the ECA assembly instead of being attached to the outside as on earlier systems. The harness connectors are edge-card type contacts which provide a more positive connection and allow probing with volt/ohmmeter leads from the rear while connected to simplify diagnosis and testing. The ECA is usually mounted in the passenger compartment, under the front section of the center console, but the location will vary on different models. The ECA could also be located under the right (passenger) seat, or behind the right front (passenger) kick panel, for example.

The EEC IV engine control system is used in conjunction with either a throttle body (CFI) injection, multiport (EFI and SEFI) injection, or feedback carburetor (FBC) fuel delivery system depending on the year, model and powertrain. Although the individual system components vary, the electronic control system operation is basically the same. The major difference is the number and type of output devices being controlled by the ECA.

The EEC IV system electronically controls the fuel injectors or carburetor feedback and mixture control solenoids to maintain a 14.7:1 air/fuel ratio under all driving conditions. This 14.7:1 air/fuel mixture allows the three-way catalytic converter to operate at peak efficiency while getting the most performance and economy from the engine. Ignition spark timing, deceleration fuel cut-off, EGR function (on or off), curb and fast idle speed, evaporative emissions purge, A/C cut-off during wide open throttle, cold engine start and enrichment, electric fuel pump and self-test engine diagnostics are also controlled by the ECA to maintain consistent driveability across a wide range of operating conditions, temperatures and altitudes. The EEC IV system is self-adjusting for operation at high altitude elevations (over 4,000 ft. above sea level) and can actually compensate for engine component wear (a worn timing chain, for example).

The EEC IV engine control system is divided into three major subsystems:

• **Fuel Delivery Subsystem** – which includes the fuel tank and lines, fuel pump and fuel injection or feedback carburetor components. On fuel injected models, this includes the fuel supply manifold, fuel pressure regulator, injectors and fuel filter. On models with feedback carburetors, it includes the carburetor metering circuits, choke assembly and the carburetor body itself.

• **Air Induction Subsystem** – which includes the air cleaner and ducts, intake manifold, carburetor or fuel injection throttle body, throttle air bypass valve, vane airflow meter, turbocharger (if equipped) and related vacuum hoses and air ducts.

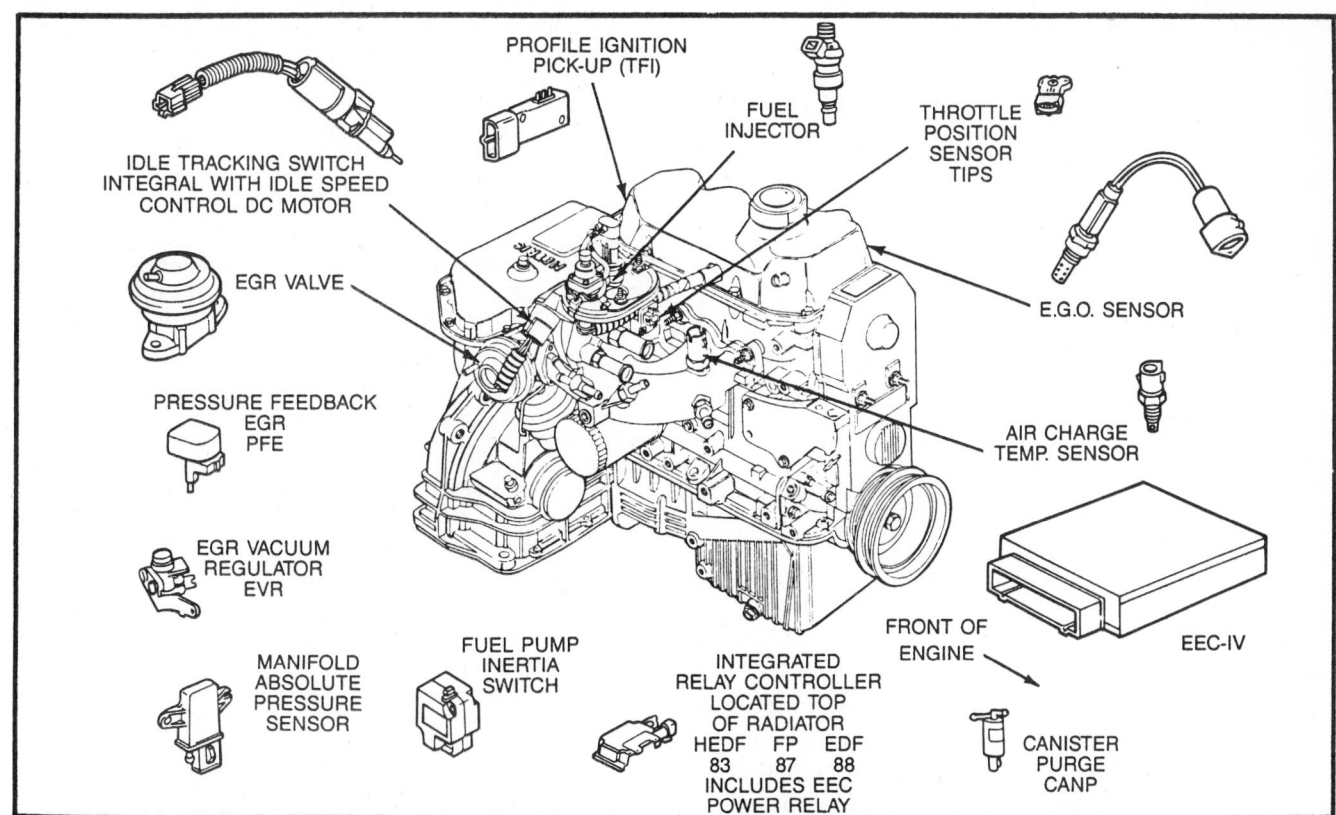

EEC IV fuel injection system components – 1.9L CFI engine shown

• **Electronic Control Subsystem** – which consists of the ECA and its various engine sensors (such as the oxygen sensor and coolant temperature sensor, etc.), along with the wiring harness, relays, fuses, battery and self-diagnostic system. On feedback carburetor models, it would include the throttle position sensor and mixture control solenoid (Carter YFA-1V), duty cycle/feedback solenoid (Motorcraft 2150A), or variable venturi feedback actuator motor (Motorcraft 7200VV). On fuel injected models, it would include the throttle position switch and the wire harness to the fuel injectors, but not the fuel injectors themselves. On turbocharged models, it would include the same multiport fuel injection components, along with such items like overboost pressure switches that are peculiar to turbocharged engines.

EEC IV SYSTEM OPERATION

Crank Mode

The crank mode is entered after initial engine starting, or after engine stall when key is in START. A special operation program is used in the crank mode to aid engine starting. After engine start, one of the run modes is entered and normal engine operation is performed. If the engine stumbles during a run mode, the underspeed mode is entered to help it recover from the stumble and prevent stalling. When cranking the engine, the fuel control is in the open loop mode (no feedback to the ECA) of operation and the ECA sets engine timing at 10–15 degrees BTDC (for the correct timing specification, refer to the Engine Emissions Decal under the hood.

On fuel injected (EFI and SEFI) models, the injectors fire either in a simultaneous, double-fire manner (fires twice every crankshaft revolution), or once per engine revolution in the normal engine firing order, to provide the base crank air/fuel control. The throttle air bypass valve solenoid is set to open the bypass valve to provide the fast idle/no-touch start.

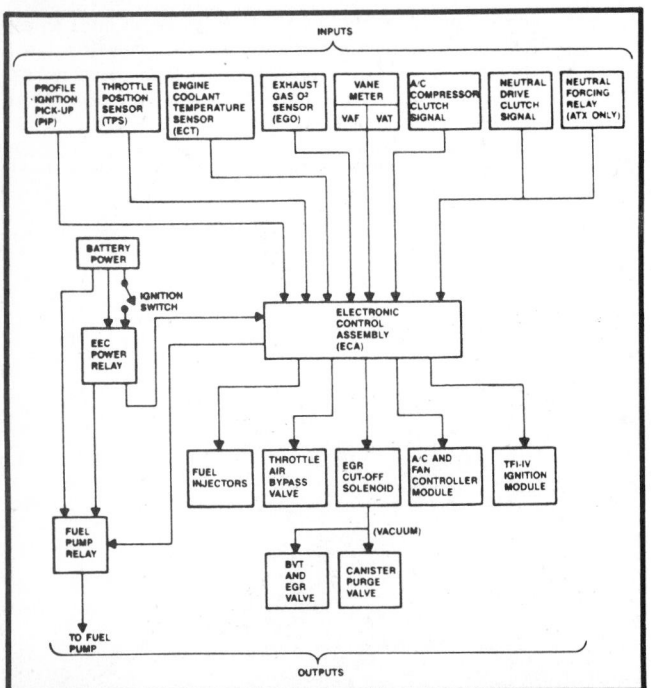

Schematic of EEC IV system operation. The ECA uses the voltage signals from the sensors (inputs) to control various components (outputs) that regulate the operation of the fuel, ignition and emission control systems

On models with a feedback carburetor, the air/fuel ratio is controlled through the feedback solenoid. The EGR cut-off solenoid is not energized, so EGR valve if Off.

NOTE: On some engines, the vapor canister purge solenoid is teed with the Thermactor Air Divert (TAD) solenoid, so when thermactor air is upstream, the canister purge if off.

At start-up, the throttle position sensor (TPS) keeps the ECA informed on the position of the throttle plate. When the throttle is kicked after start-up, the ECA will bring the engine down from fast idle by changing the signal to the throttle air bypass valve.

Underspeed Mode

Operation in the underspeed mode (under 500 rpm) is similar to that previously described for the crank mode. The system switches from the underspeed mode to the normal run mode when the required rpm is reached. The underspeed mode is used to provide a good pulse width to the injectors and ignores any signal from the vane meter. During this mode, the vane meter used on fuel injection models flutters and the signal generated would vary with the flutter. Therefore, the vane meter signal is ignored by the ECA in the underspeed mode.

Closed Throttle Mode (Idle or Deceleration)

In the closed throttle mode, the air/fuel ratio is trimmed by either varying the pulse width of the output from the ECA to the injectors, or by varying the duty cycle of the feedback solenoid on carbureted models, to obtain the desired mixture. To calculate what this output signal should be, the ECA evaluates inputs from the ECT sensor, the vane meter, the TPS, the EGO sensor, the PIP senso.· and the A/C clutch. These sensors inform the ECA of the various conditions that must be evaluated in order for the ECA to determine the correct air/fuel ratio for the closed-throttle condition present. Therefore, with the input from the EGO sensor, the system is maintained in closed-loop operation at idle. If the EGO sensor fails to switch rich/lean, the ECA programming assumes the EGO sensor has cooled off, and the system goes to open-loop fuel control. Under a deceleration condition, the TPS signal indicates closed throttle and the ECA shut-off fuel for improved fuel economy and emissions. The injectors are turned back on, as required, to prevent engine stalling.

NOTE: The point at which the injectors are turned back on will occur at different rpm's, depending on calibration factors and engine temperature, although the injectors are turned back on if the throttle is opened.

Ignition timing is also determined by ECA using these same inputs. The ECA has a series of tables programmed into the assembly at the factory. These tables provide the ECA with a reference of desired ignition timing for the various operating conditions reflected by the sensor inputs. The throttle air bypass valve position is determined by the ECA as a function of RPM, ECT, A/C On or Off, throttle mode and time since start-up inputs. The signal from the TPS to the ECA indicates that the throttle plate is closed, and the ECA de-energizes the EGR shut-off solenoid to close the EGR valve.

Part Throttle Mode (Cruise)

The air/fuel mixture ratio and ignition timing are calculated in the same manner as previously described for the closed throttle mode. The fuel control system remains in closed-loop during part throttle operation, as long as the EGO sensor is operational. In part throttle operation, the throttle air bypass valve is positioned to provide an electronic dashpot function in the event the throttle is closed. Again, as in the closed throttle mode, the ECA makes this determination based on the inputs from the applicable sensors. The TPS provides the throttle plate position signal to the ECA. With the throttle plate being in a partial open position, the ECA energizes the EGR shut-off solenoid to open the EGR valve.

Wide Open Throttle Mode (WOT)

Control of the air/fuel ratio in WOT mode is the same as in part, or closed throttle situations, except that fuel control switches to open-loop, and the fuel injector pulse width is increased to provide additional fuel enrichment. This pulse width increase is applied as a result of the WOT signal from the TPS to the ECA. This signal from the TPS also causes the ECA to remove the energizing signal from the EGR shut-off solenoid (if present). More spark advance is added in WOT for improved performance.

Cold or Hot Engine Operation

This modified operation changes the normal engine operation output signals, as required, to adjust for uncommon engine operating conditions. These include cold or excessively hot engine.

Limited Operation Strategy (LOS)

In this operation, the ECA provides the necessary output signals to allow the vehicle to "limp home" when an electronic malfunction occurs. The EGR valve is shut-off, the air bypass valve goes to a fixed voltage, timing is locked at the fixed timing (depends on calibration, refer to Engine Emissions Decal on the vehicle), and the injector pulse width is constant.

Central Fuel Injection (CFI) System

The Ford Central Fuel Injection (CFI) System is a single point, pulse time modulated injection system. Fuel is metered into the air intake stream according to engine demands by one or two solenoid injection valves, mounted in a throttle body on the intake manifold. Fuel is supplied from the fuel tank by a high-pressure electric fuel pump (either by itself or in addition to a low-pressure pump) on all except 2.3L HSC engines, which use a single low-pressure pump. The fuel is filtered, and sent to the air throttle body where a regulator keeps the fuel delivery

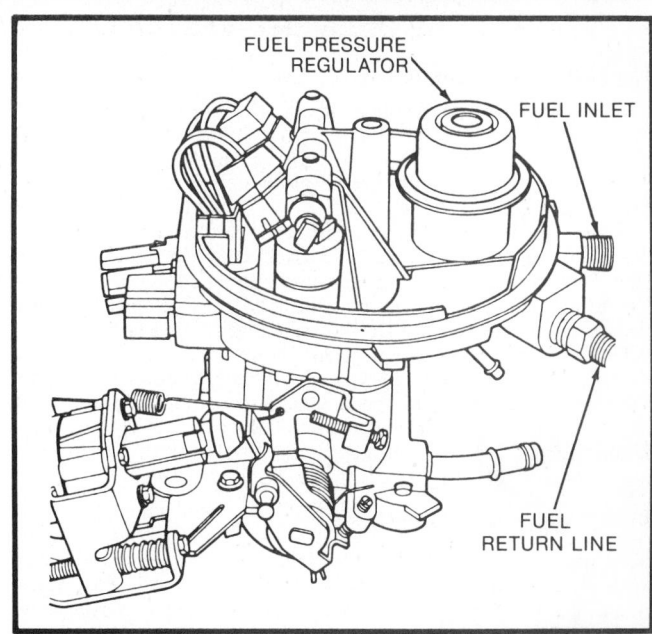

Central Fuel Injection (CFI) fuel charging assembly—left side

pressure at a constant 39 psi (269 kPa) on high-pressure systems, or 14.5 psi (100kPa) on low-pressure systems. One or two injector nozzles are mounted vertically above the throttle plates and connected in parallel with the fuel pressure regulator. Excess fuel supplied by the pump but not needed by the engine is returned to the fuel tank by a steel fuel return line.

NOTE: 1984–85 CFI models use a pintle-type fuel injector, while 1986-88 models with a single injector use a new design that incorporates a ball and seat to meter the fuel. Although both injectors are solenoid-operated, they are physically different and not interchangeable.

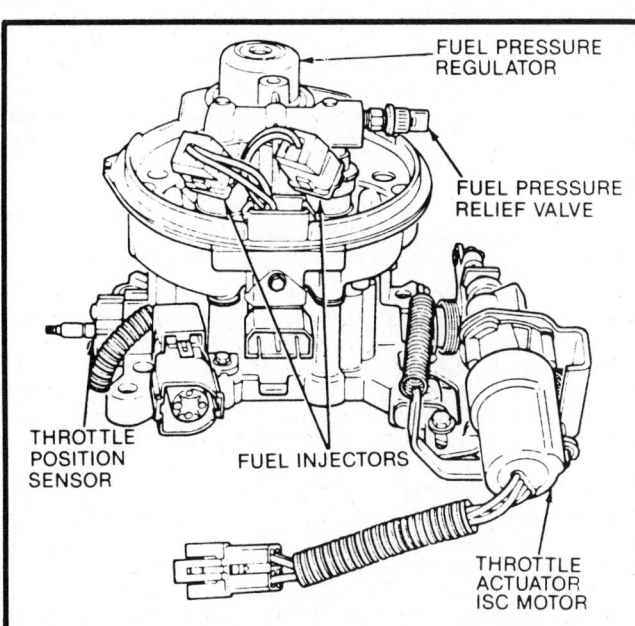

Central Fuel Injection (CFI) fuel charging assembly—right side view

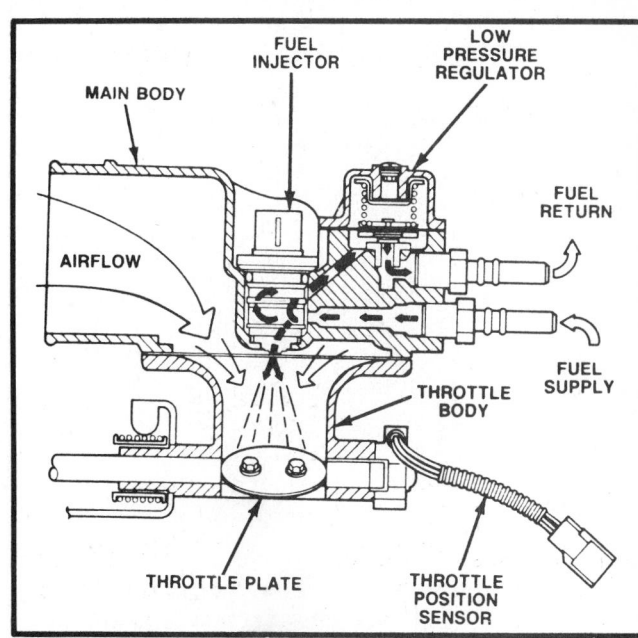

Cross section of single-injector throttle body used on low pressure CFI fuel delivery subsystem

CFI FUEL DELIVERY SYSTEM

Fuel Charging Assembly

The fuel charging assembly controls air/fuel ratio. It consists of a typical carburetor throttle body. It has two bores without venturis. The throttle shaft and valves control engine air flow based on driver demand. The throttle body attaches to the intake manifold mounting pad.

A throttle position sensor is attached to the throttle shaft. It includes a potentiometer (or rheostat) that electrically senses throttle opening A throttle kicker solenoid fastens opposite the throttle position sensor. During air conditioning operation, the solenoid extends to slightly increase engine idle speed.

Cold engine speed is controlled by an automatic kick-down vacuum motor. There is also an all-electric, bimetal coil spring which controls cold idle speed. The bimetal electric coil operates like a conventional carburetor choke coil, but the electronic fuel injection system uses no choke. Fuel enrichment for cold starts is controlled by the computer and injectors.

Fuel Pressure Regulator

The fuel pressure regulator controls critical injector fuel pressure. The regulator receives fuel from the electric fuel pump and then adjusts the fuel pressure for uniform fuel injection. The regulator sets fuel pressure at 39 psi on high pressure systems, or 14.5 psi on low pressure systems.

Fuel Manifold

The fuel manifold (or fuel rail) evenly distributes fuel to each injector. Its main purpose is to equalize the fuel flow. One end of the fuel rail contains a relief valve for testing fuel pressure during engine operation.

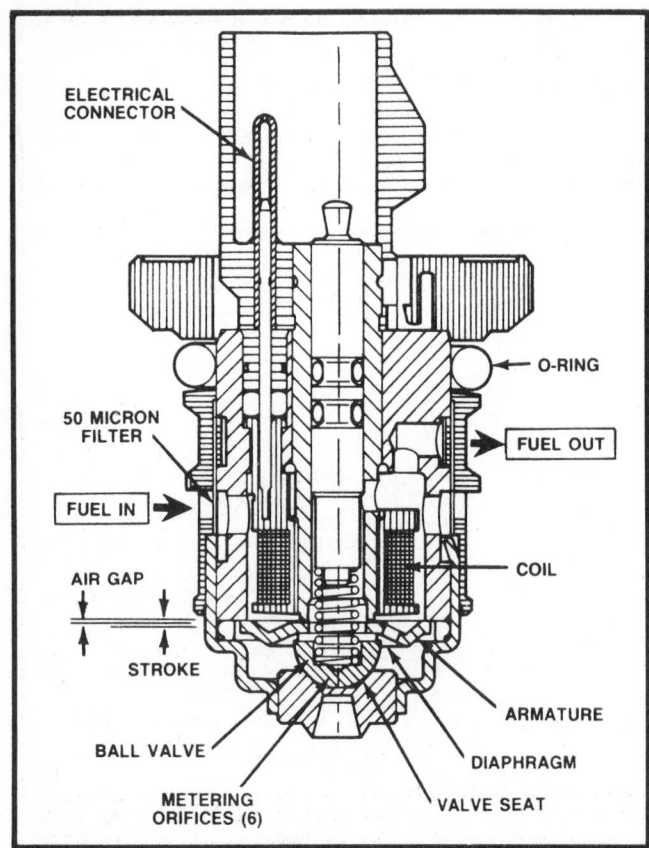

Cross section of solenoid-operated ball-type fuel injector used on low pressure CFI fuel system

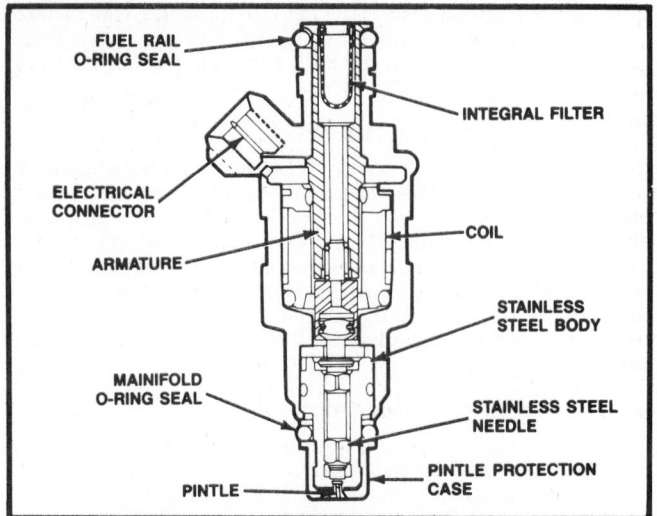

Cross section of typical solenoid-operated, pintle-type fuel injector used on high pressure CFI, EFI and SEFI systems

Fuel Injectors

The fuel injectors are electromechanical devices. The electrical solenoid operates a pintle or ball metering valve which always travels the same distance from closed to open to closed. Injection is controlled by varying the length of time the valve is open.

The computer, based on voltage inputs from the crank position sensor, operates each injector solenoid two times per engine revolution. When the injector metering valve unseats, fuel is sprayed in a fine mist into the intake manifold. The computer varies fuel enrichment based on voltage inputs from the exhaust gas oxygen sensor, barometric pressure sensor, manifold absolute pressure sensor, etc., by calculating how long to hold the injectors open. The longer the injectors remain open, the richer the mixture. This injector ON time is called pulse duration.

Fuel Pump

The fuel delivery system uses either a high or low-pressure in-line or in-tank electric fuel pump, with some models equipped with both. It is a recirculating system that delivers fuel to a pressure regulating valve in the throttle body and returns excess fuel from the throttle body regulator back to the fuel tank. The electrical system uses two types of control relays, one controlled by a vacuum switch and the other controlled by the electronic control assembly (ECA) to provide power to the fuel pump under various operating conditions.

─── **CAUTION** ───
Fuel supply lines on vehicles equipped with a high pressure fuel system will remain pressurized for long periods of time after engine shutdown. The fuel pressure must be relieved before servicing the fuel system.

An inertia switch is used as a safety device in the fuel system. The inertia switch is located in the trunk, near the left rear wheel well. It is designed to open the fuel pump power circuit in the event of a collision. The switch is reset by pushing each of 2 buttons on the switch simultaneously (some models use switches with only 1 reset button). The inertia switch should not be reset until the fuel system has been inspected for damage or leaks.

With the ignition switch OFF, the vacuum switch controlled relay is closed and the EEC controlled relay is open. Then the ignition switch is first turned to ignition ON position, the vacuum switch controlled relay remains closed and the EEC controlled relay also closes. This provides power to the fuel pump to pre-pressurize the fuel system. If the ignition switch is not turned to the CRANK position, the EEC module will open its relay after approximately two seconds and shut off power to the pump. Then the ignition switch is turned to the CRANK position, both the vacuum switch controlled relay and the EEC controlled relay are closed. This provides full battery power to the pump. When the engine starts, manifold vacuum increases and causes the vacuum switch to close and the vacuum controlled relay to open. This provides reduced normal operating voltage to the fuel pump through the resistor which by-passes the vacuum controlled relay. Under heavy engine load conditions, manifold vacuum will reduce, causing the vacuum switch to open. This causes the vacuum controlled relay to close, thus providing the return of full battery power to the pump. The EEC module senses engine speed and shuts off the pump by opening the EEC controlled relay when the engine stops.

ELECTRONIC CONTROL SYSTEM

Electronic Control Assembly (ECA)

The Electronic Control Assembly (ECA) is located under the instrument panel or passenger's seat and is usually covered by

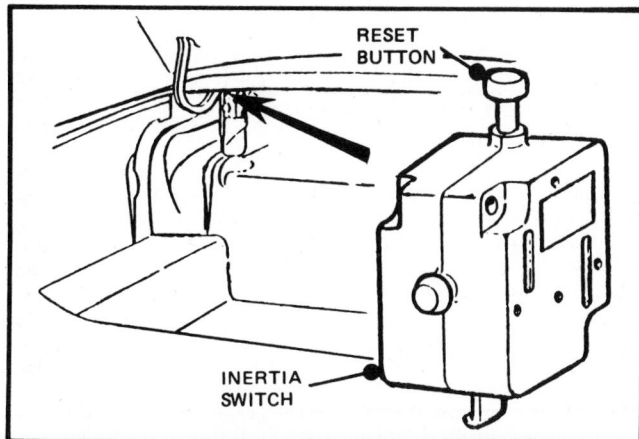

The fuel pump inertia switch is located in the trunk, usually fastened to a bracket. Press the reset button to restore power to the fuel pump when the switch is tripped. Some inertia switches have two reset buttons

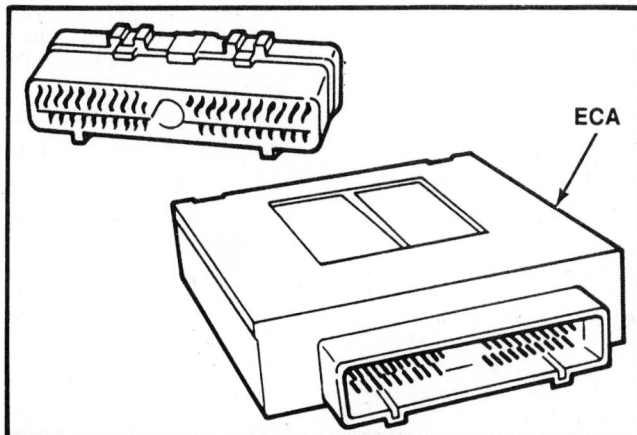

Electronic Control Assembly (ECA) showing multipin wire harness connector. The pin numbers are diagramed in the diagnostic charts

a kick panel. A multi-pin connector links the ECA with all system components. The processor provides a continuous reference voltage to the B/MAP, EVP and TPS sensors. EEC IV systems use a 5 volt reference signal. On early models, the calibration assembly is contained in a black plastic housing which

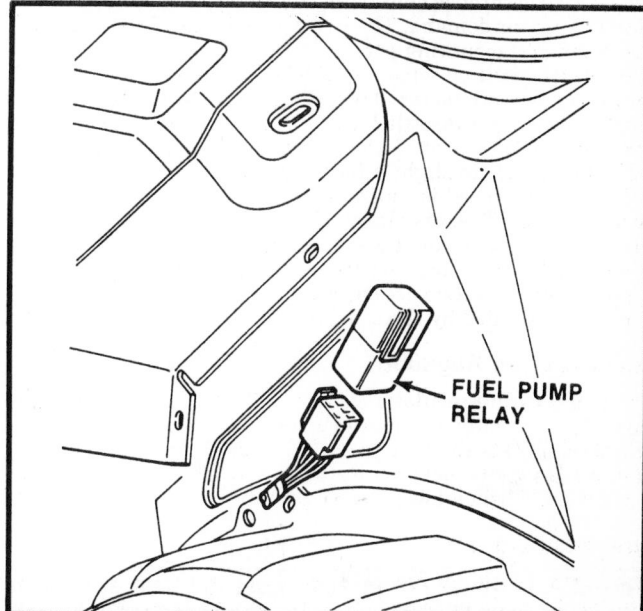

Fuel pump relay location on harness connector in the trunk on Thunderbird models

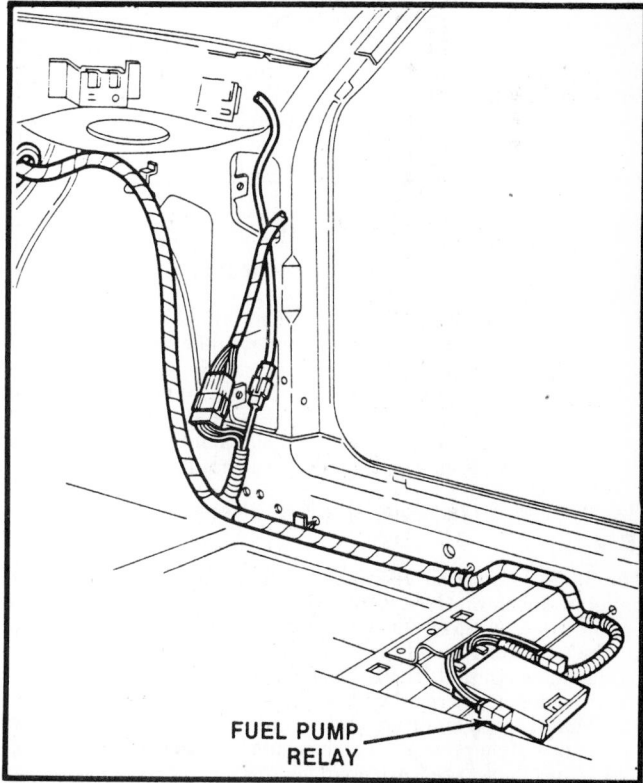

Fuel pump relay location next to ECA showing wire harness routing for Mustang/Capri models. The ECA controls the operation of the relay by opening and closing the ground path to the relay coil

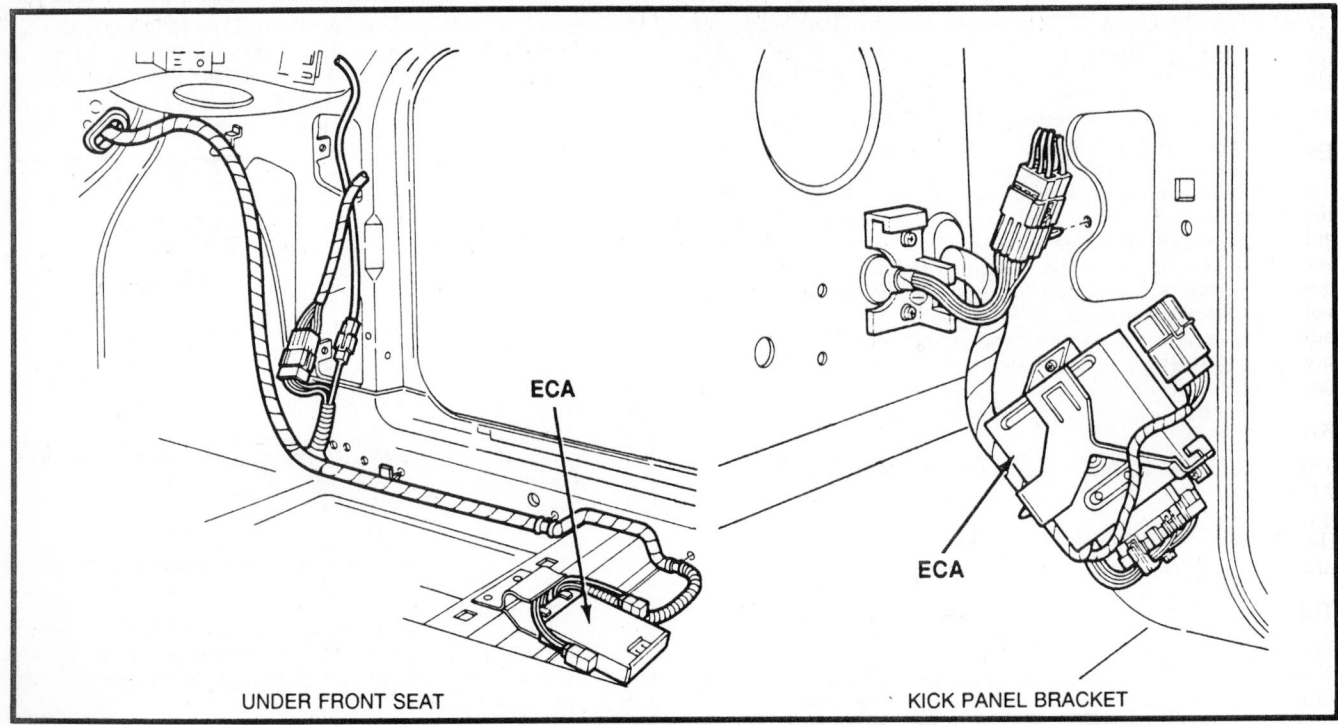

UNDER FRONT SEAT   KICK PANEL BRACKET

The ECA is usually mounted under the seat or attached to a bracket on the kick panel under the dash. Never attempt to connect or disconnect the ECA with the Ignition switch on

plugs into the top of the processor assembly, while later model ECA's have the calibration module mounted internally. The calibration module contains the memory and programming information used by the processor to determine optimum operating conditions. Different calibration information is used in different vehicle applications, such as California or Federal models. For this reason, careful identification of the engine, year, model and type of electronic control system is essential to insure correct component replacement.

CFI ENGINE SENSORS

Air Charge Temperature Sensor (ACT)

The ACT is threaded into the intake manifold air runner. It is located next to the throttle body on 4 cylinder engines, behind the distributor on V6 engines and directly below the accelerator linkage on V8 engines. The ACT monitors air/fuel charge temperature and sends an appropriate signal to the ECA. This information is used to correct fuel enrichment for variations in intake air density due to temperature changes.

Barometric & Manifold Absolute Pressure Sensors (B/MAP)

The B/MAP sensor on V8 engines is located on the right fender panel in the engine compartment. The MAP sensor used on V6 engines is separate from the barometric sensor and is located on the left finder panel in the engine compartment. The barometric sensor signals the ECA of changes in atmospheric pressure and density to regulate calculated air flow into the engine. The MAP sensor monitors and signals the ECA of changes in intake manifold pressure which result from engine load, speed and atmospheric pressure changes.

Crankshaft Position (CP) Sensor

The CP sensor is mounted on the right front of some 5.0L V8 engines. Its purpose is to provide the ECA with an accurate ig-

nition timing reference (when the piston reaches 10 degrees BTDC) and injector operation information (twice each crankshaft revolution). The crankshaft vibration damper is fitted with a 4 lobe "pulse ring". As the crankshaft rotates, the pulse ring lobes interrupt the magnetic field at the tip of the CP sensor.

EGR Valve Position Sensor (EVP)

This sensor, mounted on EGR valve, signals the computer of EGR opening so that it may subtract EGR flow from total air flow into the manifold. In this way, EGR flow is excluded from air flow information used to determine mixture requirements.

Engine Coolant Temperature Sensor (ECT)

The ECT is threaded into the intake manifold water jacket directly above the water pump by-pass hose. The ECT monitors

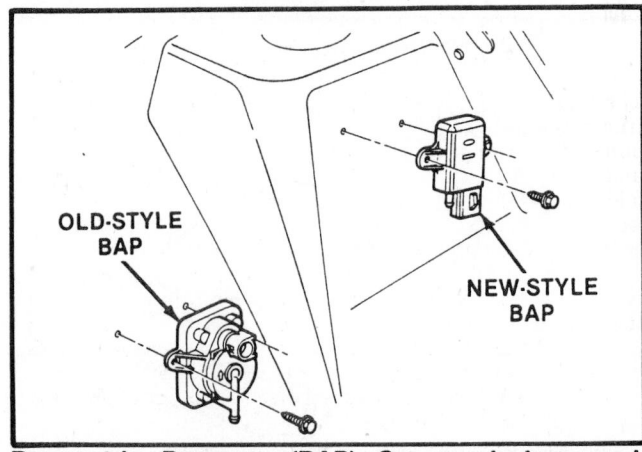

OLD-STYLE BAP

NEW-STYLE BAP

Barometric Pressure (BAP) Sensor designs and mounting on fender apron. The sensor is used to compensate for altitude variations

coolant temperature and signals the ECA, which then uses these signals for mixture enrichment (during cool operation), ignition timing and EGR operation. The resistance value of the ECT increases with temperature, causing a voltage signal drop as the engine warms up.

Exhaust Gas Oxygen Sensor (EGO)

An exhaust gas oxygen sensor, mounted in the exhaust manifold, is used on all engines. The EGO is mounted in the right side exhaust manifold on V8 engines, while V6 engines use two sensors, one in each exhaust manifold. The EGO monitors oxygen content of exhaust gases and sends a constantly changing voltage signal to the ECA. The ECA analyzes this signal and adjusts the air/fuel mixture to obtain the optimum (stoichiometric) ratio for combustion and three-way catalyst performance.

Knock Sensor (KS)

This sensor is attached to the intake manifold in front of the ACT sensor. The KS detects engine vibrations caused by pre-ignition (or detonation) and provides signals to the ECA, which then retards the ignition timing to eliminate detonation in the affected cylinder(s).

Thick Film Integrated Module Sensor (TFI)

The TFI module sensor plugs into the distributor just below the distributor cap and replaces the CP sensor for some engines. Its function is to provide the ECA with ignition timing information, similar to what the CP sensor provides. On manual transmission models, the TFI module allows the vehicle to be push-started if necessary.

Throttle Position Sensor (TPS)

The rotary-type TPS is mounted on the side of the throttle body, directly connected to the throttle shaft. The TPS senses throttle movement and position and transmits an appropriate electrical signal to the ECA. These signals are used by the ECA to adjust the air/fuel mixture, spark timing and EGR operation according to engine load at idle, part throttle, or full throttle. There are two types of throttle position sensors used, rotary and linear. The linear TPS is used on feedback carburetors and is adjustable. The rotary TPS has two versions, one adjustable and one non-adjustable; the difference being elongated mounting holes that allow the rotary sensor to be turned slightly to adjust the output voltage. The rotary TPS with round mounting holes are not adjustable.

Multiport (EFI) and Sequential (SEFI) Fuel Injection Systems

The EFI and SEFI fuel subsystems include a high pressure in-line electric fuel pump, a low-pressure tank-mouned fuel pump, fuel charging manifold, pressure regulator, fuel filter and both solid and flexible fuel lines. The fuel charging manifold includes four, six or eight electronically controlled fuel injectors, each mounted directly above an intake port in the lower intake manifold. On the 4 cylinder EFI system, all injectors are energized simultaneously and spray once every crankshaft revolution, delivering a predetermined quantity of fuel into the intake air stream. On 6 cylinder and V8 EFI engines, the injectors are energized in two banks of three (6 cyl) or four (V8) once each crankshaft revolution. On the SEFI system, each injector fires once every crankshaft revolution, in sequence with the engine firing order.

The fuel pressure regulator maintains a constant pressure drop across the injector nozzles. The regulator is referenced to intake manifold vacuum and is connected parallel to the fuel injectors and positioned on the far end of the fuel rail. Any excess fuel supplied by the pump passes through the regulator and is returned to the fuel tank via a return line.

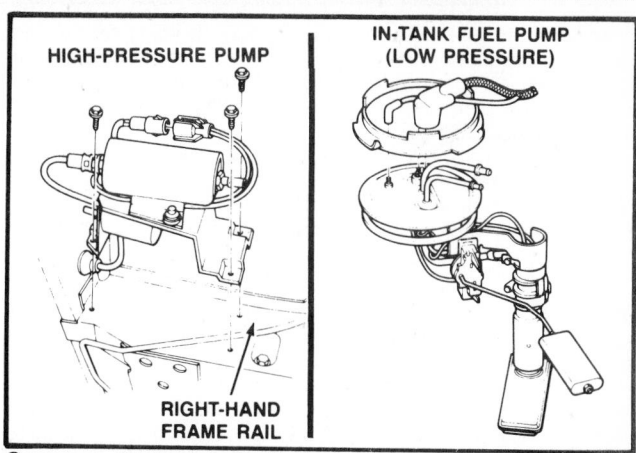

Some systems use both a chassis and tank-mounted electric fuel pumps

NOTE: The pressure regulator reduces fuel pressure to 39–40 psi under normal operating conditions. At idle or high manifold vacuum condition, fuel pressure is reduced to about 30 psi.

The fuel pressure regulator is a diaphragm operated relief valve in which one side of the diaphragm senses fuel pressure and the other side senses manifold vacuum. Normal fuel pressure is established by a spring preload applied to the diaphragm. Control of the fuel system is maintained through the EEC power relay and the EEC IV control unit, although electrical power is routed through the fuel pump relay and an inertia switch. The fuel pump relay is normally located on a bracket somewhere above the Electronic Control Assembly (ECA) and the Inertia Switch is located in the trunk. The in-line fuel pump is usually mounted on a bracket at the fuel tank, or on a frame rail. Tank-mounted pumps can be either high or low-pressure, depending on the model.

The inertia switch opens the power circuit to the fuel pump in the event of a collision. Once tripped, the switch must be reset manually by pushing the reset button on the assembly. Check that the inertia switch is reset before diagnosing power supply problems to the fuel pump circuit.

Fuel Injectors

The fuel injectors used with the EFI and SEFI system are electromechanical (solenoid) type designed to meter and atomize fuel delivered to the intake ports of the engine. The injectors are mounted in the lower intake manifold and positioned so that their spray nozzles direct the fuel charge in front of the intake valves. The injector body consists of a solenoid actuated pintle and needle valve assembly. The control unit sends an electrical impulse that activates the solenoid, causing the pintle to move inward off the seat and allow the fuel to flow. The amount of fuel delivered is controlled by the length of time the injector is energized (pulse width), since the fuel flow orifice is fixed and the fuel pressure drop across the injector tip is constant. Correct atomization is achieved by contouring the pintle at the point where the fuel enters the pintle chamber.

NOTE: Exercise care when handling fuel injectors during service. Be careful not to lose the pintle cap and replace O-rings to assure a tight seal. Never apply direct battery voltage to test a fuel injector.

The injectors receive high pressure fuel from the fuel manifold (fuel rail) assembly. The complete assembly includes a single, preformed tube with four, six, or eight injector connectors, mounting flange for the pressure regulator, mounting attachments to locate the manifold and provide the fuel injector retainers and a Schrader® quick-disconnect fitting used to perform fuel pressure tests.

The fuel manifold is normally removed with fuel injectors and pressure regulator attached. Fuel injector electrical connectors are plastic and have locking tabs that must be released when disconnecting when disconnecting the wiring harness.

AIR SUBSYSTEM

The air subsystem components include the air cleaner assembly, air flow (vane) meter, throttle air bypass valve and air ducts that connect the air system to the throttle body assembly. The throttle body regulates the air flow to the engine through a single butterfly-type throttle plate controlled by conventional accelerator linkage. The throttle body has an idle adjustment screw (throttle air bypass valve) to set the throttle plate position, a PCV fresh air source upstream of the throttle plate, individual vacuum taps for PCV and control signals and a throttle position sensor that provides a voltage signal for the EEC IV control unit.

The hot air intake system uses a thermostatic flap valve assembly whose components and operation are similar to previous hot air intake systems. Intake air volume and temperature are measured by the vane meter assembly which is mounted between the air cleaner and throttle body. The vane meter consists two separate devices; the van air flow sensor (VAF) uses a counter-balanced L-shaped flap valve mounted on a pivot pin and connected to a variable resistor (potentiometer). The control unit measures the amount of deflection of the flap vane by measuring the voltage signal from the potentiometer mounted on top of the meter body; larger air volume moves the vane further and produces a higher voltage signal. The vane air temperature (VAT) sensor is mounted in the middle of the air stream just before the flap valve. Since the mass (weight) of a specific volume of air varies with pressure and temperature, the control unit uses the voltage signal from the air temperature sensor to compensate for these variables and provide a more exact measurement of actual air mass that is necessary to calculate the fuel required to obtain the optimum air/fuel ratio under a wide range of operating conditions. On the EEC IV system, the VAT sensor affects spark timing as a function of air temperature.

NOTE: Make sure all air intake connections are tight before testing. Air leaking into the engine through a loose bellows connection can result in abnormal engine operation or idle speed and affect the air/fuel mixture ratio.

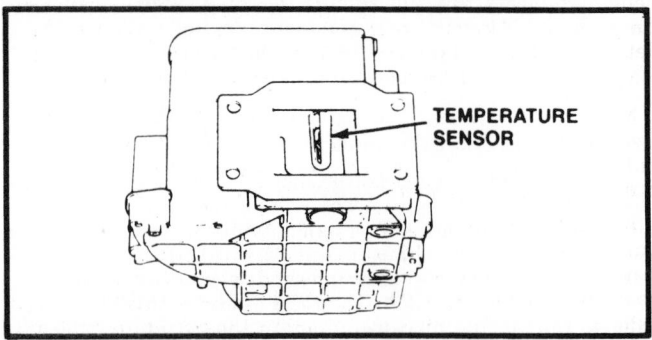

Location of Vane Air Temperature (VAT) sensor in the air flow meter

Throttle Air Bypass Valve

The throttle air bypass valve is an electro-mechanical (solenoid) device whose operation is controlled by the EEC IV control unit. A variable air metering valve controls both cold and warm idle air flow in response to commands from the control unit. The valve operates by bypassing a regulated amount of air around the throttle plate; the higher the voltage signal from the control unit, the more air is bypassed through the valve. In this manner, additional air can be added to the fuel mixture without moving the throttle plate. At curb idle, the valve provides smooth idle for various engine coolant temperatures, compensates for A/C load and compensates for transaxle load and no-load conditions. The valve also provides fast idle for start-up, replacing the fast idle cam, throttle kicker and anti-dieseling solenoid common to previous models.

There are no curb idle or fast idle adjustments. As in curb idle operation, the fast idle speed is proportional to engine coolant temperature. Fast idle kick-down will occur when the throttle is kicked. A time-out feature in the ECA will also automatically kick-down fast idle to curb idle after a time period of approximately 15–25 seconds; after coolant has reached approximately 71°C (160°F). The signal duty cycle from the ECA to the valve will be at 100% (maximum current) during the crank to provide maximum air flow to allow no touch starting at any time (engine cold or hot).

ELECTRONIC ENGINE CONTROL SUBSYSTEM

The electronic engine control subsystem consists of the ECA and various sensors and actuators. The ECA reads inputs from engine sensors, then outputs a voltage signal to various compo-

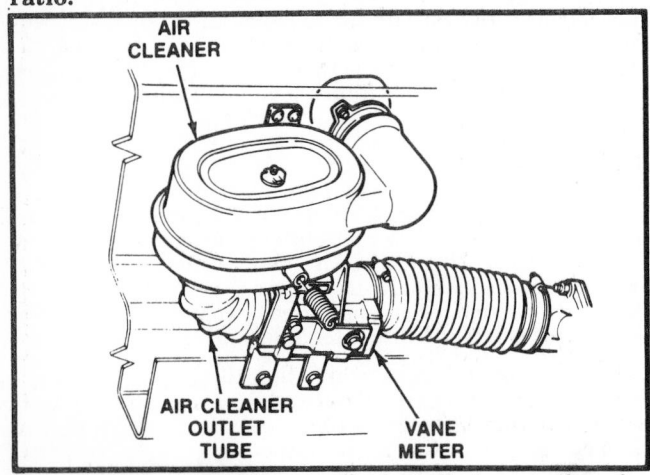

The air flow meter is usually installed near the air cleaner—2.3L shown

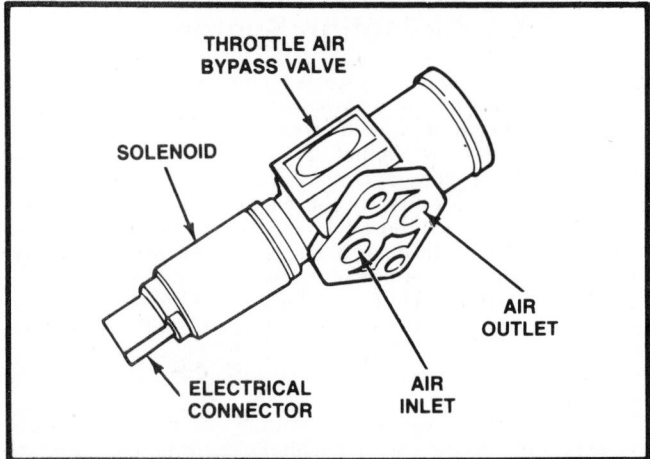

Throttle air bypass valve used on CFI, EFI and SEFI systems

nents (actuators) to control engine functions. The period of time that the injectors are energized (on-time or "pulse width") determines the amount of fuel delivered to each cylinder. The longer the pulse width, the richer the fuel mixture.

NOTE: The operating reference voltage (Vref) between the ECA and its sensors and actuators is five volts. This allows these components to work during the crank operation even though the battery voltage drops.

In order for the ECA to properly control engine operation, it must first receive current status reports on various operating conditions. The control unit constantly monitors crankshaft position, throttle plate position, engine coolant temperature, exhaust gas oxygen level, air intake volume and temperature, A/C (On/Off), spark knock and barometric pressure.

Universal Distributor

The primary function of the TFI-IV ignition system universal distributor is to direct the high secondary voltage to the spark plugs. In addition, the universal distributor supplies crankshaft position and frequency information to the ECA using a profile ignition pick-up (PIP) sensor in place of the magnetic pick-up or the crankshaft position sensor used on other models. This distributor does not have any mechanical or vacuum advance. The universal distributor assembly is adjustable for resetting base timing, if required, bu disconnecting the spout connector.

NOTE: The PIP replaces the crankshaft position sensor found on other EEC IV models.

The PIP sensor has an armature with four windows and four metal tabs that rotates past the stator assembly (Hall effect switch). When a metal tab enters the stator assembly, a positive signal (approximately 10 volts) is sent to the ECA, indicat-

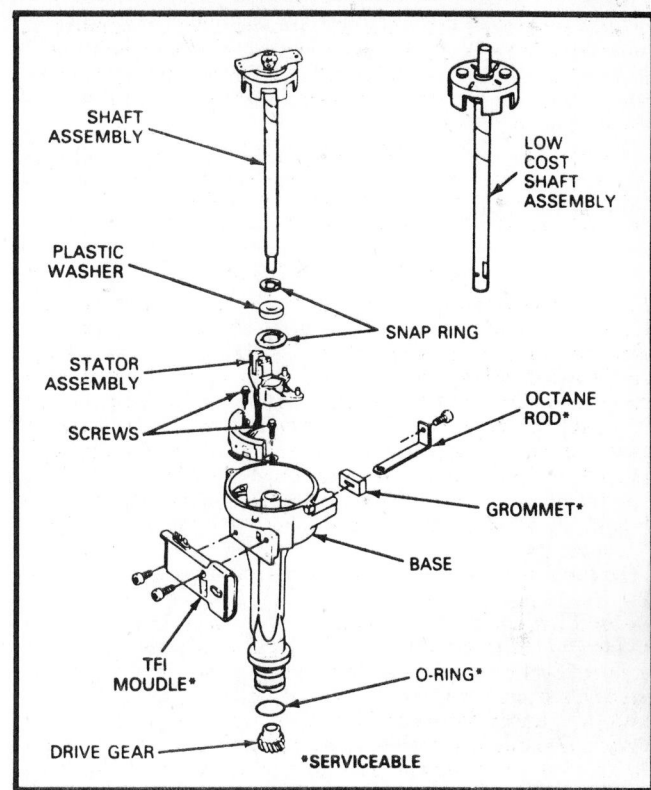

Exploded view of universal distributor

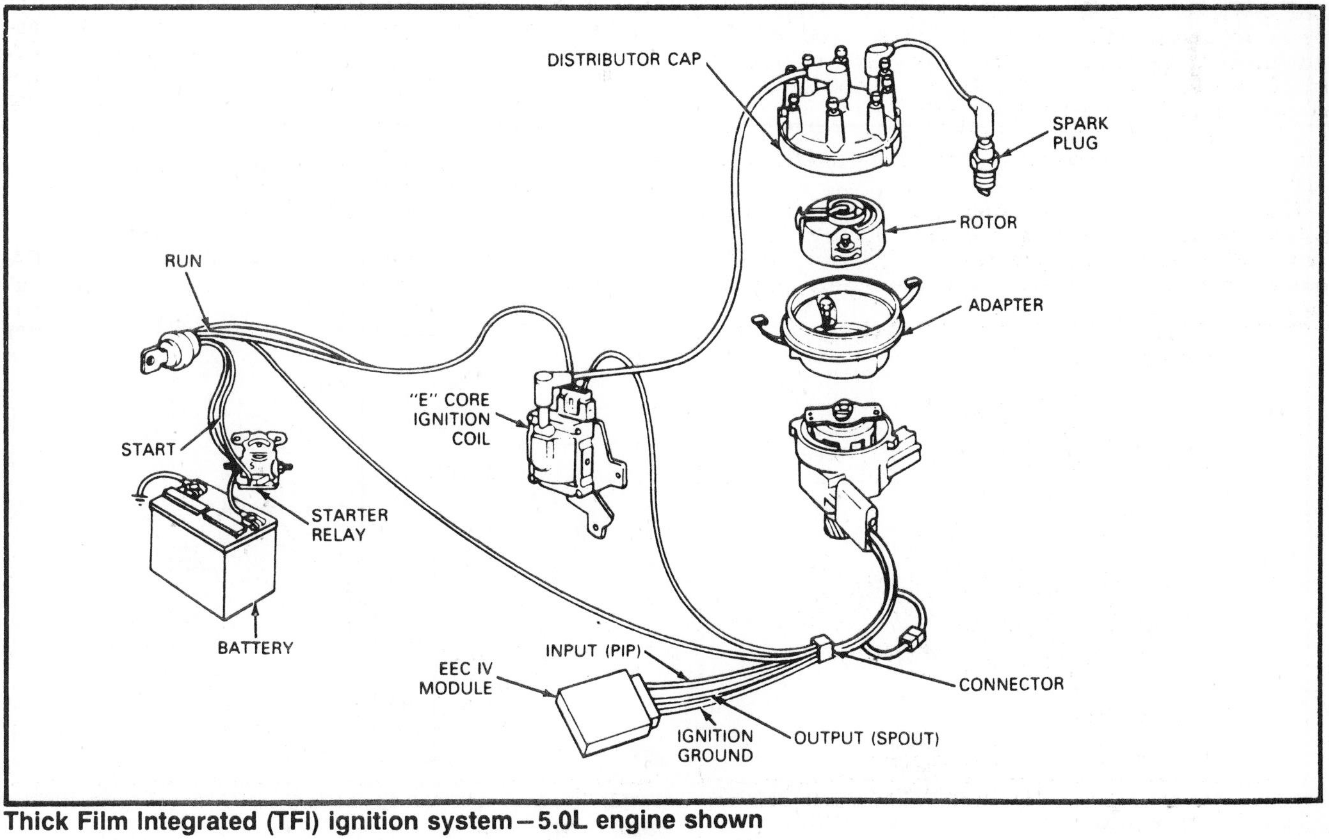

Thick Film Integrated (TFI) ignition system—5.0L engine shown

ing the 10 degrees BTDC crankshaft position. The ECA calculates the precise time to energize the spark output signal to the TFI module. When the TFI module receives the spark output signal, it shuts off the coil primary current and the collapsing field energizes the secondary output.

NOTE: Misadjustment of the base timing affects the spark advance in the same manner as a conventional solid-state ignition system.

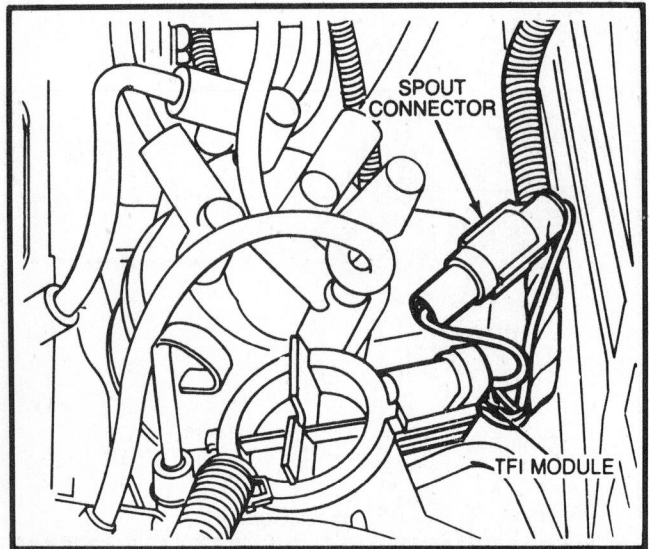

Location of inline base timing (SPOUT) connector near the distributor

Thick Film Ignition (TFI-IV) Module

The TFI-IV ignition module has six connector pins at the engine wiring harness that supply the following signals:
- Ignition switch in RUN position
- Engine cranking
- Tachometer
- PIP (crankshaft position to ECA)
- Spark advance (from ECA)
- Internal ground from the ECA to the distributor

The TFI-IV module supplies the spark to the distributor through the ignition coil and calculates the duration. It receives its control signal from the ECA (spark output).

Throttle Position Sensor (TPS)

The TPS is mounted on the throttle body. This sensor provides the ECA with a signal that indicates the opening angle of the throttle plate. The sensor output signal uses the 5 volt reference voltage (Vref) previously described. From this input, the ECA controls:

1. Operating modes, which are wide-open throttle (WOT), part throttle (PT) and closed throttle (CT).
2. Fuel enrichment at WOT.
3. Additional spark advance at WOT.
4. EGR cut off during WOT, deceleration and idle.
5. A/C cut off during WOT (30 seconds maximum).
6. Cold start kick-down.
7. Fuel cut off during deceleration.
8. WOT dechoke during crank mode (starting).

On the EEC IV system, the TPS signal to the ECA only changes the spark timing during the WOT mode. As the throttle plate rotates, the TPS varies its voltage output. As the throttle plate moves from a closed throttle position to a WOT Position, the voltage output of the TPS will change from a low voltage (approximately 1.0 volt) to a high voltage (approxi-

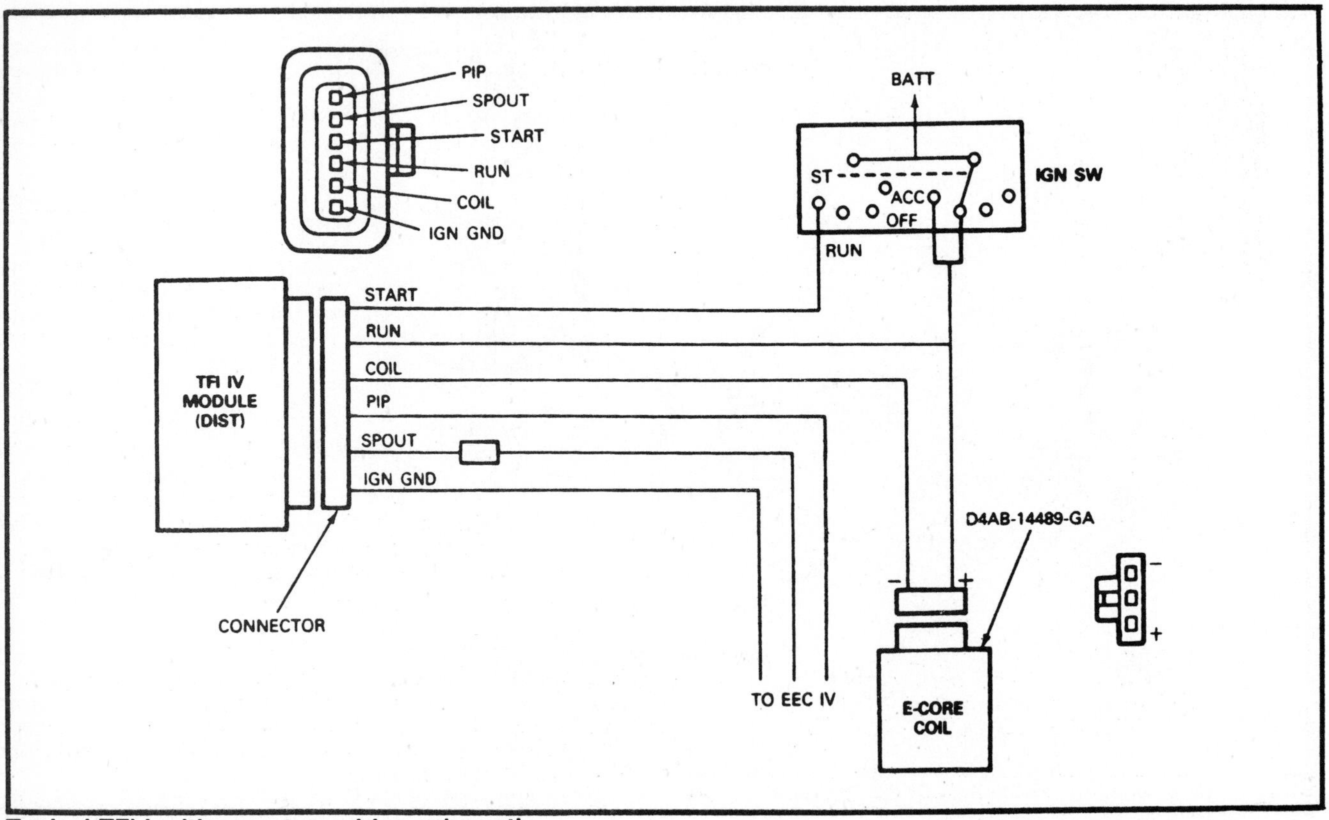

Typical TFI ignition system wiring schematic

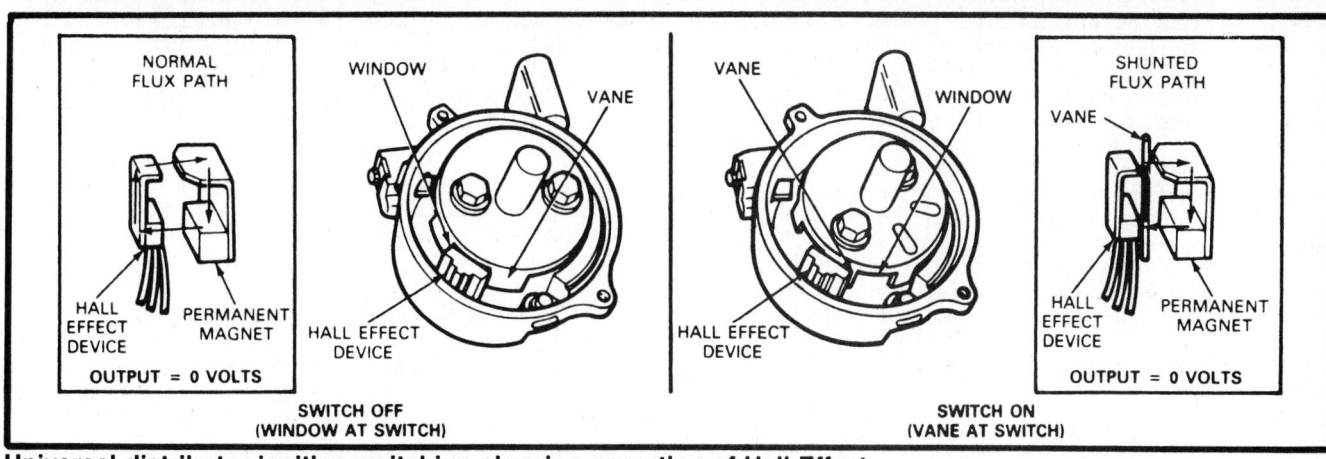

Universal distributor ignition switching showing operation of Hall Effect

mately 4.75 volts). The TPS used is not adjustable and must be replaced if it is out of specification. The EEC IV programming compensates for differences between sensors.

Engine Coolant Temperature (ECT) Sensor

The ECT sensor is located either in the heater supply tube at the rear of the engine, or in the lower intake manifold. The ECT is a thermistor (changes resistance as temperature changes). The sensor detects the temperature of engine coolant and provides a corresponding signal to the ECA. From this signal, the ECA will modify the air/fuel ratio (mixture), idle speed, spark advance, EGR and Canister purge control. When the engine coolant is cold, the ECT signal causes the ECA to provide enrichment to the air/fuel ratio for good cold drive away as engine coolant warms up, the voltage will drop.

Exhaust Gas Oxygen (EGO) Sensor

The EGO sensor on the EEC IV system is a little different from others used and is mounted in its own mounting boss, located between the two downstream tubes in the header near the exhaust system. On turbocharged models, the EGO sensor is

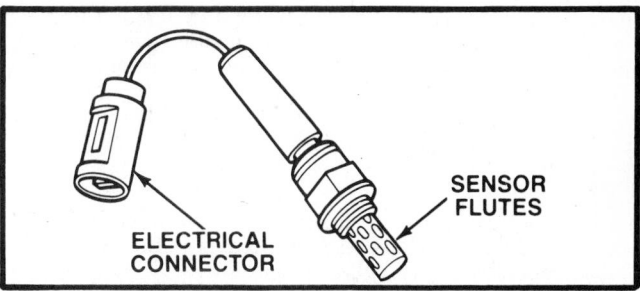

The oxygen sensor is mounted in the exhaust manifold. Do not allow grease, oil or anti-seize to contaminate the sensor flutes during service. Sensors with a heater have a two-wire connector

mounted in the turbocharger exhaust elbow. The EGO sensor works between zero and one volt output, depending on the presence (lean) or absence (rich) of oxygen in the exhaust gas. A voltage reading greater than 0.6 volts indicates a rich air/fuel ratio, while a reading of less than 0.4 volts indicates a lean ratio.

--- CAUTION ---

Never apply voltage to the EGO sensor because it could destroy the sensor's calibration. This includes the use of an ohmmeter. Before connecting and using a voltmeter, make sure it has a high-input impedance (at least 10 megohms) and is set on the proper resistance range. Any attempt to use a powered voltmeter to measure the EGO voltage output directly will damage or destroy the sensor.

Operation of the sensor is the same as previous models. One difference that should be noted is that the rubber protective cap used on top of the sensor on the earlier models has been replaced with a metal cap. In addition, later model sensors incorporate a heating element to bring the sensor up to operating temperature more quickly and keep it there during extended idle periods to prevent the sensor from cooling off and placing the system into open loop operation.

Vane Meter

The vane meter is actually two sensors in one assembly-a vane air flow (VAF) sensor and vane air temperature (VAT) sensor. This meter measures air flow to the engine and the temperature of the air stream. The vane meter is located either behind or under the air cleaner.

Air flow through the body moves a vane mounted on a pivot pin. The more air flowing through the meter, the further the

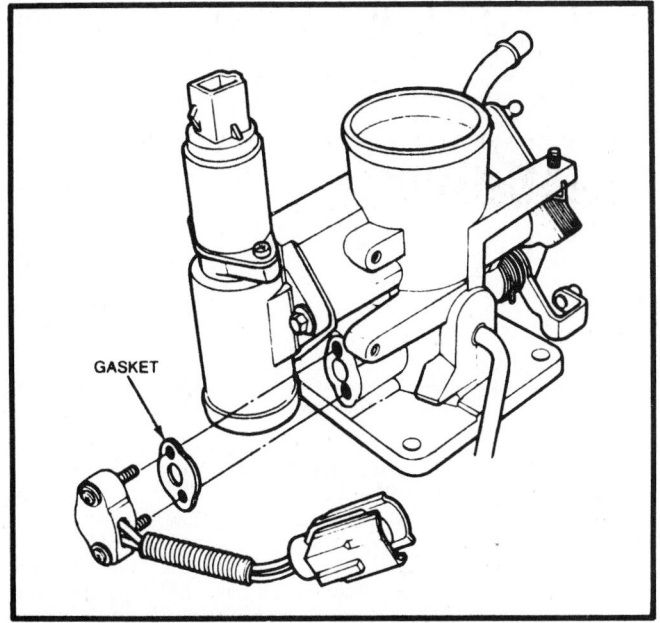

Rotary Throttle Position Switch (TPS) installation on 2.3L EFI throttle body

vane rotates about the pivot pin. The air vane pivot pin is connected to a variable resistor (potentiometer) on top of the assembly. The vane meter uses the 5 volt reference voltage. The output of the potentiometer to the ECA varies between zero and Vref (5 volts), depending on the volume of air flowing through the sensor. A higher volume of air will produce a higher voltage output.

The volume of air measured through the meter has to be converted into an air mass value. The mass (weight) of a specific volume of air varies with pressure and temperature. To compensate for these variables, a temperature sensor in front of the vane measures incoming air temperature. The ECA uses the air temperature and a programmed pressure value to convert the VAF signal into a mass air flow value. This value is used to calculate the fuel flow necessary for the optimum air/fuel ratio. The VAT also affects spark timing as a function of air temperature.

A/C Clutch Compressor (ACC) Signal

Anytime battery voltage is applied to the A/C clutch, the same signal is also applied to the ECA. The ECA then maintains the engine idle speed with the throttle air bypass valve control solenoid (fuel injection), or throttle kicker (carburetor), to compensate for the added load created by the A/C clutch operation. Shutting down the A/C clutch will have a reverse effect. The ECA will maintain the engine idle speed at 850–950 rpm.

Knock Sensor (KS)

The knock sensor is used to detect detonation. In situations of excessive knock the ECA receives a signal from this sensor and retards the spark accordingly. The operation of the knock sensor during boost on turbocharged models improves the engine's durability. It is mounted in the lower intake manifold at the rear of the engine.

Barometric (BAP) Sensor

The barometric sensor is used to compensate for altitude variations. From this signal, the ECA modifies the air/fuel ratio, spark timing, idle speed, and EGR flow. The barometric sensor is a design that produces a frequency based on atmospheric pressure (altitude). The barometric sensor is mounted on the right-hand fender apron.

EGR Shut-Off Solenoid

The electrical signal to the EGR shut-off solenoid is controlled by the ECA. The signal is either ON or OFF. It is OFF during cold start, closed throttle or WOT. It is ON at all other times.

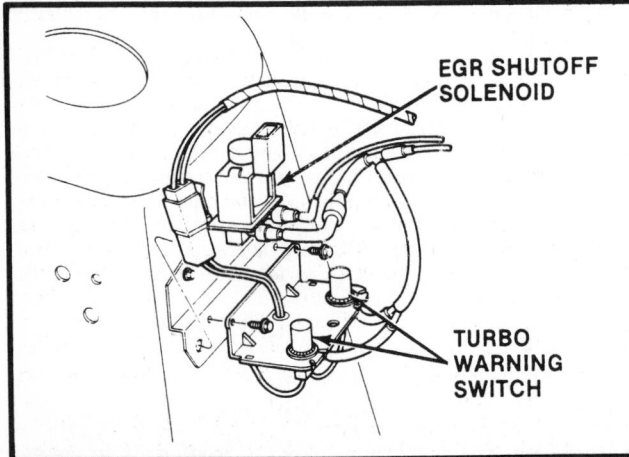

Location of EGR shutoff solenoid and overboost warning switches on shock tower in the engine compartment on 2.3L turbocharged models

The solenoid is the same as the EGR control solenoid used on previous EEC systems. It is usually mounted on the LH side of the dash panel in the engine compartment, or on the RH shock tower in the engine compartment. The solenoid is normally closed, and the control vacuum from the solenoid is applied to the EGR valve.

NOTE: The canister purge valve is controlled by vacuum from the EGR solenoid. The purge valve is a standard-type valve and operates the same as in previous systems.

Fuel System Testing

CAUTION
Fuel pressue must be relieved by disconnecting the inertia switch and cranking the engine for at least 15 seconds before attempting to disconnect any fuel lines.

PRESSURE TESTS

The diagnostic pressure valve (Schrader type) is located at the top of the Fuel charging main body on CFI systems, or on the fuel rail on multiport systems. This valve provides a convenient point for service personnel to monitor fuel pressure, bleed down the system pressure prior to maintenance, and to bleed out air which may become trapped in the system during filter replacement. A pressure gauge with an adapter is required to perform pressure tests.

If the pressure tap is not installed or an adapter is not available, use a T-fitting to install the pressure gauge between the fuel filter line and the throttle body fuel inlet or fuel rail.

System Pressure Test

Testing fuel pressure requires the use of a special pressure gauge (T80L–9974–A or equivalent) that attaches to the diagnostic pressure tap fitting. Depressurize the fuel system before disconnecting any lines.

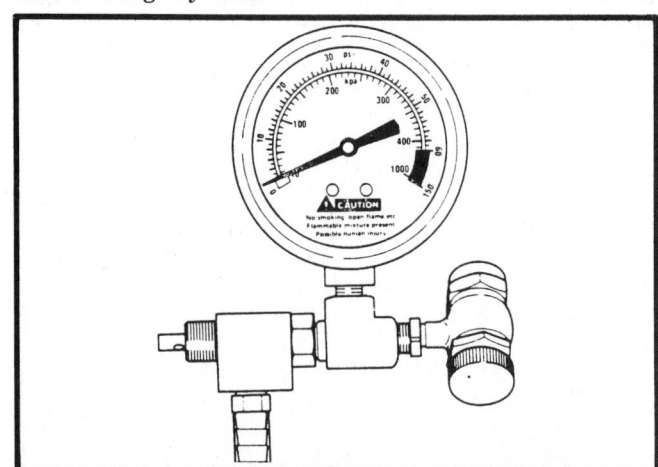

Fuel injection pressure gauge

1. Disconnect fuel return line at throttle body (in-tank high pressure pump) or at fuel rail (in-line high pressure and in-tank low pressure pumps) and connect the hose to a one-quart calibrated container. Connect pressure gauge.

2. Disconnect the electrical connector to the fuel pump. The connector is located ahead of fuel tank (in-tank high pressure pump) or just forward of pump outlet (in-line high pressure pump). Connect auxiliary wiring harness to connector of fuel pump. Energize the pump for 10 seconds by applying 12 volts to

the auxiliary harness connector, allowing the fuel to drain into the calibrated container. Note the fuel volume and pressure gauge reading.

3. Correct fuel pressure for high pressure fuel systems should be 35–45 psi (241–310 kPa). Fuel volume should be 10 ozs. in 10 seconds (minimum) and fuel pressure should maintain minimum 30 psi (206 kPa) immediately after pump cutoff. 2.3L HSC engines with a single CFI injector use a low pressure fuel system that maintains fuel pressure at 14.5 psi (100 kPa).

If pressure condition is met, but fuel flow is not, check for blocked filter(s) and fuel supply lines. After correcting problem, repeat test procedure. If fuel flow is still inadequate, replace high pressure pump. If flow specification is met but pressure is not, check for worn or damaged pressure regulator valve on throttle body. If both pressure and fuel flow specifications are met, but pressure drops excessively after de-energization, check for leaking injector valve(s) and/or pressure regulator valve. If injector valves and pressure regulator valve are okay, replace high pressure pump. If no pressure or flow is seen in fuel system, check for blocked filters and fuel lines. If no trouble is found, replace in-line fuel pump, in-tank fuel pump and the fuel filter inside the tank.

Fuel Injector Pressure Test

HIGH PRESSURE CFI FUEL SYSTEM ONLY

1. Connect pressure gauge T80L–9974–A, or equivalent, to fuel pressure test fitting. Disconnect coil connector from coil. Disconnect electrical lead from one injector and pressurize fuel system. Disable fuel pump by disconnecting inertia switch or fuel pump relay and observe pressure gauge reading.

2. Crank engine for 2 seconds. Turn ignition OFF and wait 5 seconds, then observe pressure drop. If pressure drop is 2–16 psi (14–110 kPa), the injector is operating properly. Reconnect injector, activate fuel pump, then repeat the procedure for other injector.

3. If pressure drop is less than 2 psi (14 kPa) or more than 16 psi (110 kPa), switch electrical connectors on injectors and repeat test. If pressure drop is still incorrect, replace disconnected injector with one of the same color code, then reconnect both injectors properly and repeat test.

4. Disconnect and plug vacuum hose to EGR valve. It may be necessary to disconnect the idle speed control (3.8L V6) or throttle kicker solenoid (5.0L V8) and use the throttle body stop screw to set engine speed. Start and run the engine at 2000 rpm. Disconnect left injector electrical connector. Note rpm after engine stabilizes (around 1200 rpm). Reconnect injector and allow engine to return to high idle.

5. Perform same procedure for right injector. Note difference between rpm readings of left and right injectors. If difference is 100 rpm or less, check the oxygen sensor. If difference is more than 100 rpm, replace both injectors.

COMPONENT TESTS

Before beginning any EEC IV component testing, always check the ignition and fuel systems to make sure there is fuel and spark. Check the distributor cap, rotor and internal components for damage, corrosion or signs of excessive wear.

• Remove air cleaner assembly and inspect all vacuum and pressure hoses for proper connection to fittings. Check for damaged or pinched hoses.

• Inspect all sub-system wiring harnesses for proper connections to the EGR solenoid valves, injectors, sensors, etc.

• Check for loose or detached connectors and broken or detached wires. Check that all terminals are seated firmly and are not corroded. Look for partially broken or grayed wires or any shorting between wires.

• Inspect sensors for physical damage. Inspect vehicle electrical system. Check battery for full charge and cable connections for tightness.

• Inspect the relay connector and make sure the ECA power relay is securely attached and making a good ground connection.

• Twist the oil filler cap on turbocharged engines to make sure it is tight. A loose oil filler cap will cause turbocharged engines to run rough at idle.

Fuel Pump Circuit Test

HIGH PRESSURE IN-TANK PUMP

Disconnect electrical connector just forward of the fuel tank. Connect voltmeter to body wiring harness connector. Turn key ON while watching voltmeter. Voltage should rise to battery voltage, then return to zero after about 1 second. Momentarily turn key to START position. Voltage should rise to about 8 volts while cranking. If voltage is not as specified, check electrical system.

HIGH PRESSURE IN-LINE AND LOW PRESSURE IN-TANK PUMPS

Disconnect electrical connector at fuel pumps. Connect voltmeter to body wiring harness connector. Turn key ON while watching voltmeter. Voltage should rise to battery voltage, then return to zero after about 1 second. If voltage is not as specified, check inertia switch and electrical system. Connect ohmmeter to in-line pump wiring harness connector. If no continuity is present, check continuity directly at in-line pump terminals. If no continuity at in-line pump terminals, replace in-line pump. If continuity is present, service or replace wiring harness.

Connect ohmmeter across body wiring harness connector. If continuity is present (about 5 ohms), low pressure pump circuit is okay. If no continuity is present, remove fuel tank and check for continuity at in-tank pump flange terminals on top of tank. If continuity is absent at in-tank pump flange terminals, replace assembly. If continuity is present at in-tank pump but not in harness connector, service or replace wiring harness to in-tank pump.

Solenoid and Sensor Resistance Tests

All CFI components must be disconnected form the circuit before testing resistance with a suitable ohmmeter. Replace any component whose measure resistance does not agree with the specifications chart. Shorting the wiring harness across a solenoid valve can burn out the circuitry in the ECA that controls the solenoid valve actuator. Exercise caution when testing solenoid valves to avoid accidental damage to ECA.

EEC IV SYSTEM TESTING

As in any service procedure, a routine inspection of the EEC IV system for loose connections, broken wires or obvious damage is the best way to start. Perform the system Quick Test outlined below before going any further. Check all vacuum connections and secondary ignition wiring before assuming that the problem lies with the EEC IV system. A self-diagnosis capability is built into the EEC IV system to aid in troubleshooting. The primary tool necessary to read the trouble codes stored in the system is an analog voltmeter or special Self Test Automatic Readout (STAR) tester (Motorcraft No. 007–0M004, or equivalent). While the self-test is not conclusive by itself, when activated it checks the EEC IV system by testing its memory integrity and processing capability. The self-test also verifies that all sensors and actuators are connected and working properly.

When a service code is displayed on an analog voltmeter, each code number is represented by pulses or sweeps of the meter needle. A code 3, for example, will be read as three needle pulses followed by a six-second delay. If a two digit code is stored, there will be a two second delay between the pulses for each digit of the number. Code 23, for example, will be dis-

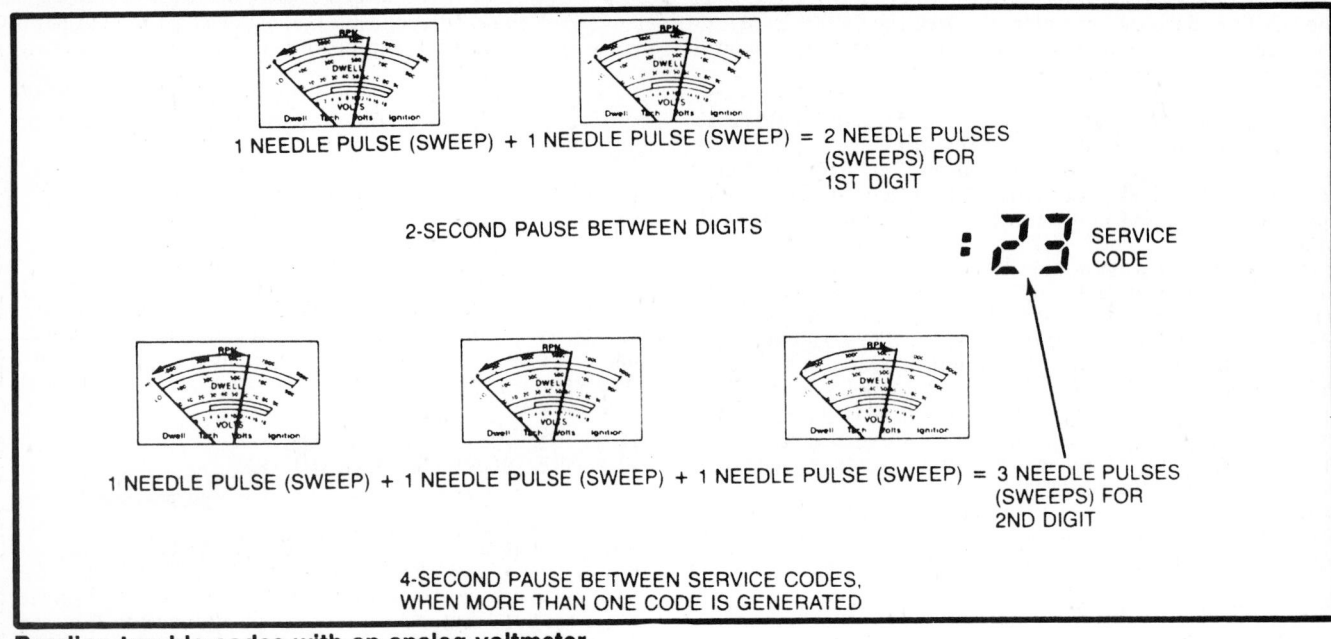

1 NEEDLE PULSE (SWEEP) + 1 NEEDLE PULSE (SWEEP) = 2 NEEDLE PULSES (SWEEPS) FOR 1ST DIGIT

2-SECOND PAUSE BETWEEN DIGITS

:23 SERVICE CODE

1 NEEDLE PULSE (SWEEP) + 1 NEEDLE PULSE (SWEEP) + 1 NEEDLE PULSE (SWEEP) = 3 NEEDLE PULSES (SWEEPS) FOR 2ND DIGIT

4-SECOND PAUSE BETWEEN SERVICE CODES, WHEN MORE THAN ONE CODE IS GENERATED

Reading trouble codes with an analog voltmeter

played as two needle pulses, a two second pause, then three more pulses followed by a four second pause. All testing is complete when the codes have been repeated once. The pulse format is ½ second ON-time for each digit, 2 seconds OFF-time between digits, 4 seconds OFF-time between codes and 6-10 seconds OFF-time before and after the half-second separator pulse.

NOTE: If using the STAR tester, or equivalent, consult the manufacturers instructions included with the unit for correct hook-up and trouble code interpretation.

In addition to the service codes, two other types of coded information are outputed during the self-test; engine identification and fast codes. Engine ID codes are one digit numbers equal to one-half the number of engine cylinders (e.g. 4 cylinder is code 2; 8 cylinder is code 4, etc.). Fast codes are simply the service codes transmitted at 100 times the normal rate in a short burst of information. Some meters may detect these codes and register a slight meter deflection just before the trouble codes are flashed. Both the ID and fast codes serve no purpose in the field and this meter deflection should be ignored.

Activating Self-Test Mode on EEC IV

Turn the ignition key OFF, then connect a jumper wire from the self-test input (STI) to pin 2 (signal return) on the self-test connector. Set the analog voltmeter on a DC voltage range to read from 0–15 volts, then connect the voltmeter from the battery positive (+) terminal to pin 4 self-test output in the self-test connector. Turn the ignition switch ON (engine off) and read the trouble codes on the meter needle as previously described. A code 11 means that the EEC IV system is operating properly and no faults are detected by the computer.

NOTE: This test will only detect "hard" failures that are present when the self-test is activated. For intermittent problems, remove the voltmeter clip from the self-test trigger terminal and wiggle the wiring harness. With the voltmeter still attached to the self-test output, watch for a needle deflection that signals an intermittent condition has occurred. The meter will deflect each time the fault is induced and a trouble code will be stored. Reconnect the self-test trigger terminal to the voltmeter to retrieve the code.

Output Cycling Test

This test is performed with the key ON and the engine OFF after the self-test codes have been sent and recorded. Without disconnecting the voltmeter or turning the key OFF, momentarily depress the accelerator pedal to the floor and then release it. All auxiliary EEC IV codes (including the self-test) will be activated and can be read on the voltmeter as before. Another pedal depression will turn them off. This cycle may be repeated as necessary, but if activated for more than 10 minutes, the cycle will automatically cancel. This feature forces the processor to activate these outputs for additional diagnosis.

EEV IV System Quick Test

Correct test results for the quick test are dependent on the correct operation of related non-EEC components, such as ignition wires, battery, etc. It may be necessary to correct defects in

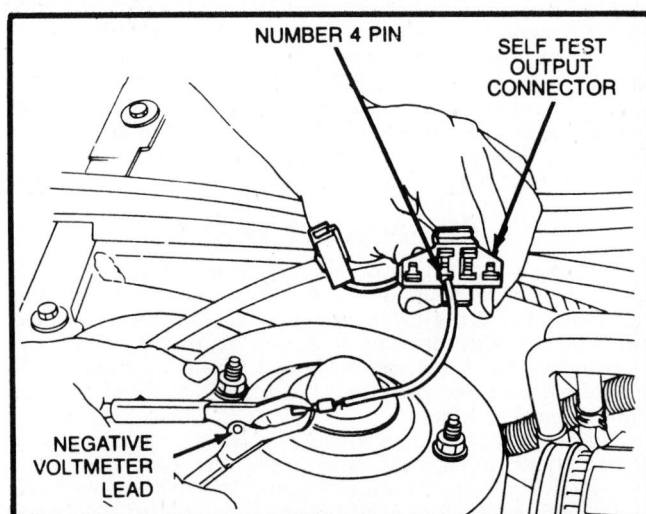

NUMBER 4 PIN
SELF TEST OUTPUT CONNECTOR
NEGATIVE VOLTMETER LEAD

To access the EEC IV trouble code memory, first connect a jumper wire from pin No. 4 on the self-test output connector to the negative lead of the analog voltmeter as shown

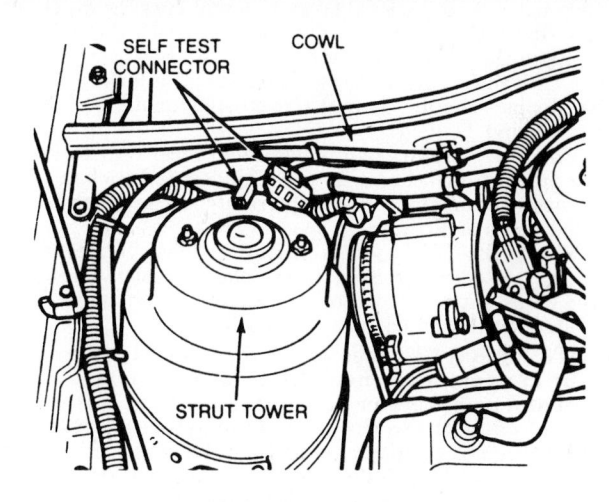

FRONT-WHEEL DRIVE CARS
(ESCORT/LYNX, EXP, TEMPO/TOPAZ)

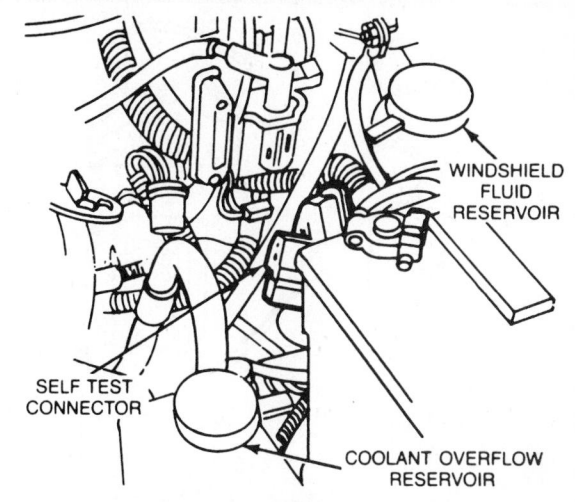

UNI-BODY REAR-WHEEL DRIVE-CARS
(THUNDERBIRD/COUGAR, LTD/MARQUIS, MUSTANG/CAPRI)

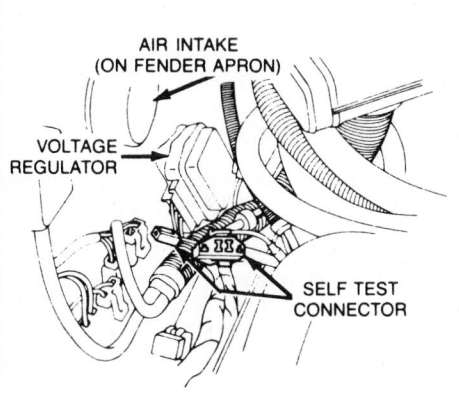

CONTINENTAL/MARK VII

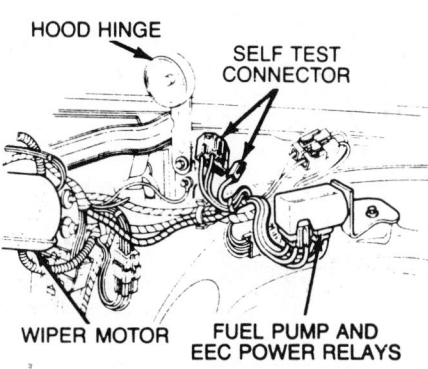

CONVENTIONAL FRAME, REAR-WHEEL
DRIVE CARS
(LINCOLN,
FORD CROWN VICTORIA/GRAND MARQUIS)

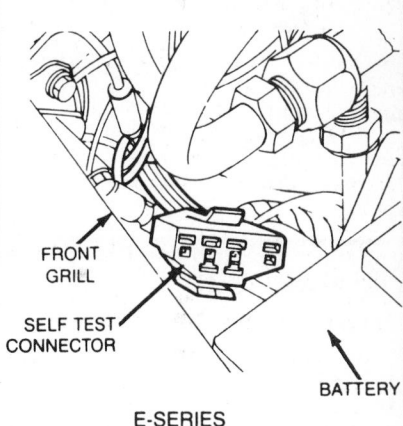

E-SERIES

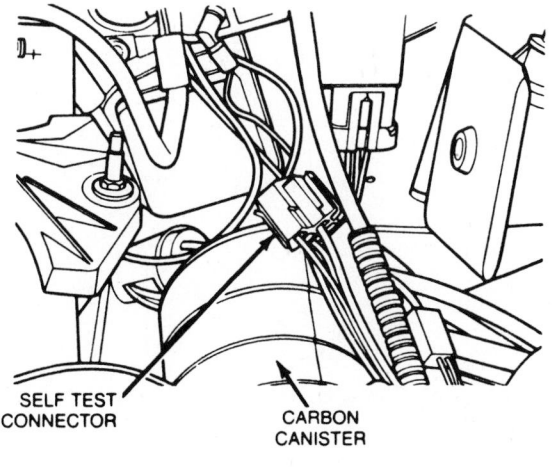

F-SERIES

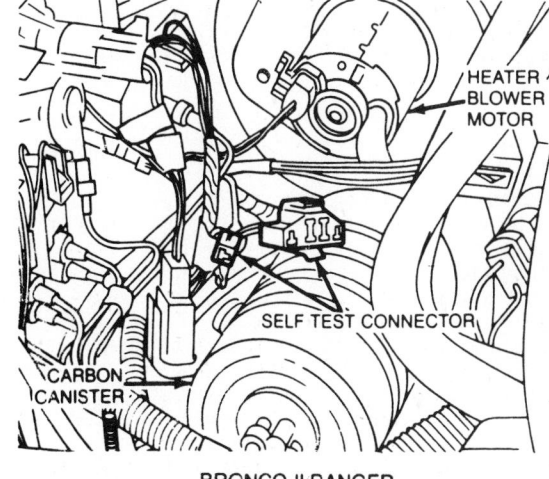

BRONCO II/RANGER

Self-Test connector locations

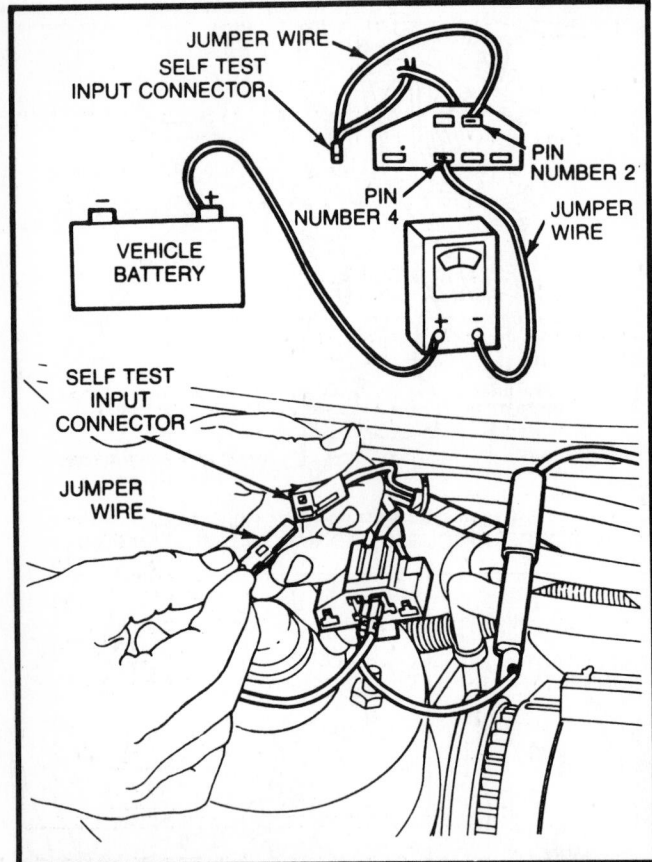

Voltmeter hookup and final connection for triggering EEC IV Self-Test

these areas before the EEC IV system will pass the quick test. Before connecting any test equipment to check the EEC system, make the following checks:

1. Check the air cleaner and intake ducts for leaks or restrictions. Replace the air cleaner if excessive amounts of dust or dirt are found.

2. Check all engine vacuum hoses for proper routing according to the vacuum schematic on the underhood sticker. Check for proper connections and repair any broken, cracked or pinched hoses or fittings.

3. Check the EEC system wiring harness connectors for tight fit, loose or detached terminals, corrosion, broken or frayed wires, short circuits to metal in the engine compartment or melted insulation exposing bare wire.

NOTE: It may be necessary to disconnect or disassemble the connector to check for terminal damage or corrosion and perform some of the inspections. Note the location of each pin in the connector before disassembly. When doing continuity checks to make sure there are no breaks in the wire, shake or wiggle the harness and connector during testing to check for looseness or intermittent contact.

4. Check the control module, sensors and actuators for obvious physical damage.

5. Turn off all electrical loads when testing and make sure the doors are closed whenever readings are made. DO NOT disconnect any electrical connector with key ON. Turn the key off to disconnect or reconnect the wiring harness to any sensor or the control unit.

6. Make sure the engine coolant and oil are at the proper level.

7. Check for leaks around the exhaust manifold, oxygen sensor and vacuum hoses connections with the engine idling at normal operating temperature.

8. Only after all the above checks have been performed should the voltmeter be connected to read the trouble codes. If not, the self-diagnosis system may indicate a failed component when all that is wrong is a loose or broken connection.

QUICK TEST: Test Description

SPECIAL NOTES:

- This diagnostic procedure is used ONLY on vehicles equipped with the fourth generation of Electronic Engine controls (EEC-IV).

- The QUICK TEST procedure should be used ONLY when the Diagnostic Routines, Section 2 direct you here.

- If all phases of the Quick Test, including the Diagnostic by Symptom found in the proper Engine Supplement Section, result in a PASS, it is likely that the problem is non-EEC-IV related and will be found elsewhere. You should return to the Diagnostic Routines in Section 2.

- When directed to a Pinpoint Test, look carefully at the schematic on the first page of the pinpoint test and read the STOP-WARNING below the schematic.

- Any time a repair is made, Steps 3.0, 5.0, and 6.0 should be repeated to ensure that the repair was effective.

QUICK TEST STEPS

1. Visual Check and Vehicle Preparation

2. Equipment Hookup

3. Key On Engine Off Self-Test

4. Computed Timing Check

5. Engine Running Self-Test

6. Continuous Self-Test

The Key On Engine Off and Engine Running Self-Tests detect faults that are present at the time of testing. Intermittent faults that have occurred in the last forty (40) warm-up cycles are detected during Continuous Self-Test and stored in the EEC-IV memory.

QUICK TEST: Visual Check Vehicle Preparation — 1.0

SPECIAL NOTES:

- Correct results of the QUICK TEST are dependent on the proper operation of related non-EEC-IV components.

- It may be necessary to disconnect or disassemble harness connector assemblies to do some of the inspections. Pin locations should be noted before disassembly.

- If the engine will not start, starts but stalls, idles rough, or runs rough; continue through QUICK TEST STEP 3.0 and follow the instructions in Step 3.0B.

VISUAL CHECK

1. Inspect the air cleaner and inlet ducting.

2. Check all engine vacuum hoses for damage, leaks, cracks, blockage, proper routing, etc.

3. Check EEC-IV system wiring harness for proper connections, bent or broken pins, corrosion, loose wires, proper routing, etc.

4. Check the processor, sensors, and actuators for physical damage.

5. Check the engine coolant for proper level.

6. Make all necessary repairs before continuing with QUICK TEST.

VEHICLE PREPARATION

1. Perform ALL safety steps required to start and run vehicle tests - apply parking brake, place shift lever firmly into PARK position (NEUTRAL on manual transmission), block drive wheels, etc.

2. Turn off ALL electrical loads — radios, lights, A/C-heater blower fans, etc.

3. Start engine and run until at operating temperature.

4. Turn engine off and proceed to QUICK TEST STEP 2.0.

QUICK TEST: Equipment Hookup — 2.0

SPECIAL NOTES:

- Refer to the illustration at the bottom of this page for Self-Test connector pin orientation and VOM and STAR hookup.

- After the equipment is properly hooked up proceed to QUICK TEST STEP 3.0A.

USING THE STAR TESTER

- Turn the ignition key off.
- Connect the color coded adapter cable to the STAR tester.
- Connect the adapter cable leads to the proper Self-Test connectors.
- Connect the timing light.

USING AN ANALOG VOLT/OHM METER (VOM)

1. Turn the ignition key off.

2. Connect a jumper wire from the Self-Test Input connector to the Signal Return pin of the large Self-Test connector. DO NOT connect jumper to Signal Return unless directed to do so.

3. Set the VOM on a DC voltage range to read from 0 to 15 volts.

4. Connect the VOM from the Battery + terminal to the Self-Test Output pin of the large Self-Test connector.

5. Connect the timing light.

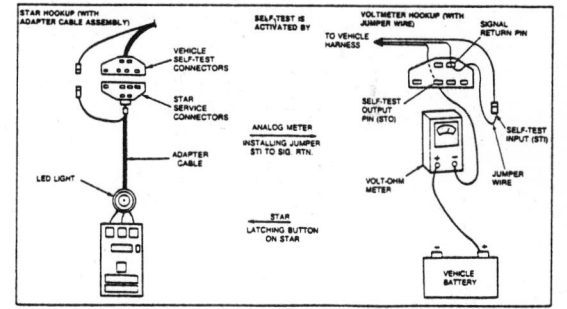

QUICK TEST: Key On Engine Off Self-Test — 3.0

| A | PERFORMING THE KEY ON ENGINE OFF SELF-TEST |

SPECIAL NOTES:

- It may be necessary to repair Non-EEC-IV faults before running Quick Test. Refer to Section 2.

- Continuous Memory Codes recorded in this step will be used for diagnosis after a PASS code 11 is received in both the Key On Engine Off and the Engine Running Self-Tests.

- On all vehicles equipped with a 4.9L ENGINE the clutch must be depressed during the Key On Engine Off Self-Test.

HOW TO RUN THE KEY ON ENGINE OFF SELF-TEST

DO

- Verify that the vehicle has been properly prepared per QUICK TEST STEPS 1.0 and 2.0.

- Place ignition key in the ON position.

- Activate Self-Test

—STAR Tester: Latch the center button in the down position.

—Analog VOM: Jumper STI to SIG RTN at the Self-Test connectors.

- Record all service codes displayed.

- Go to PART B of Key On Engine Off Self-Test.

DON'T

- Depress throttle during Key On Engine Off Self-Test.

QUICK TEST: Key On Engine Off Self-Test — 3.0

B   CODE OUTPUT

Key On Engine Off	Separator	Continuous Memory	ACTION TO TAKE
11	— 1(0) —	11	• Both tests indicate a PASS. — If engine idles or runs rough. Go to DIAGNOSTIC BY SYMPTOM in the proper Engine Supplement Section. If above condition is not present, Go to Quick TEST STEP 4.0. — If engine is a no start. Go directly to Pinpoint Test Step A1.
ANY CODE(S)	— 1(0) —	11	• Key On Engine Off Self-Test indicates a FAULT. — Go to **PART C** of Key On Engine Off Self-Test. — Always start with the first code displayed.
ANY CODE(S)	— 1(0) —	ANY CODE(S)	• Both tests indicate a FAULT. — DO NOT SERVICE CONTINUOUS MEMORY CODES AT THIS TIME! — Go to **PART C** of Key On Engine Off Self-Test. — Always start with the first code displayed.
11	— 1(0) —	ANY CODE(S) EXCEPT 15	• Continuous Memory indicates a FAULT. — DO NOT SERVICE CONTINUOUS MEMORY CODES AT THIS TIME! — If engine idles or runs rough. Go to DIAGNOSTIC BY SYMPTOM in the proper Engine Supplement Section. If above condition is not present, Go to Quick TEST STEP 4.0.
11	— 1(0) —	15	• Go To Pinpoint Test Step Q10.
NO CODES OUTPUTTED CODES NOT LISTED			• Self-Test did not activate or unlisted codes displayed. — Repeat Key On Engine Off Self-Test to verify the above condition. — If condition still exists Go to Pinpoint Test Step Q1.

QUICK TEST: Key On Engine Off Self-Test — 3.0

C   PASSENGER CAR SERVICE CODE CHART

Key On Engine Off Service Code		1.9L EFI	1.9L CFI	2.3L EFI	2.3L TC	2.3L CFI	2.5L CFI	3.0L EFI	3.8L CFI	5.0L SEFI
13 GO to	▶	—	KB1	—	—	KB1	—	—	—	—
15 GO to	▶	Q12	Q12	Q12	Q12	Q12	Q12	Q12	Q12	Q12
19 GO to	▶	—	—	Q50	—	—	—	Q50 •	—	Q50
21 GO to	▶	DE1	DE1	DE1	DE1	DE1	DE1	DE1	DE1	DE1
22 GO to	▶	DF1	DF1	DF1	DF1	DF1	DF1	DF1	DF1	DF1
23 GO to	▶	DH1	KB12	DH1	DH1	KB12	DH1	DH1	DH1	DH1
24 GO to	▶	DB1	DB1	DB1	DB1	DB1	DB1	DB1	DB1	DB1
26 GO to	▶	DK1	—	—	DK1	—	—	—	—	—
28 GO to	▶	DA1	—	—	DA1	—	—	—	—	—
31 GO to	▶	—	DL1	DD2	—	DN1	DN1	DL1	DD2	DN1
32 GO to	▶	—	—	—	—	DN25	DN25	—	—	DN25
34 GO to	▶	—	DL8	—	—	DN20	DN20	DL8	—	DN20
35 GO to	▶	—	DL5	—	—	DN5	DN5	DL5	—	DN5
51 GO to	▶	DE10	DE10	DE10	DE10	DE10	DE10	DE10	DE10	DE10
52 GO to	▶	—	—	FF1	—	FF1	FF1	FF1	—	—
53 GO to	▶	DH3	KB15	DH3	DH3	KB15	DH3	DH3	DH3	DH3
54 GO to	▶	—	DB10	DB10	DB10	DB10	DB10	DB10	DB10	DB10
56 GO to	▶	DK10	—	—	DK10	—	—	—	—	—
58 GO to	▶	DA10	KB5	—	DA10	KB5	—	—	—	—
61 GO to	▶	DE20	DE20	DE20	DE20	DE20	DE20	DE20	DE20	DE20
82 GO to	▶	—	—	—	—	—	—	T61	—	—
63 GO to	▶	DH10	KB18	DH10	DH10	KB18	DH10	DH10	DH10	DH10
64 GO to	▶	—	DB20	DB20	DB20	DB20	DB20	DB20	DB20	DB20
66 GO to	▶	DK20	—	—	DK20	—	—	—	—	—
67 GO to	▶	FA1	FA1	FA1	FA1	FA1	FA1	T81	FA1	FA1
68 GO to	▶	DA20	KB9	—	DA20	KB9	—	KF1	—	KF1
73 GO to	▶	—	KB22	—	—	KB22	—	—	—	—
79 GO to	▶	—	—	—	—	—	—	—	—	FA4
81 GO to	▶	—	—	KN1	—	KN1	—	—	KC8	KC8
82 GO to	▶	—	—	X80	—	—	—	—	KC8	KC8
83 GO to	▶	—	—	DD17	X30	—	X30	X30	DD17	—
84 GO to	▶	—	DL11	DD17	KA5	DN10	DN10	DL11	DD17	DN10
85 GO to	▶	—	KD6	—	KS10	KD6	KD6	—	—	KD6
87 GO to	▶	—	J7	J7	X15	J7	X15	X15	J7	J7
88 GO to	▶	—	—	—	KS1	—	X80	—	—	—
89 GO to	▶	—	KR1	—	—	—	—	—	—	—
93 GO to	▶	—	KB11	—	—	KB11	—	—	T51	KP5
NO CODES CODES NOT LISTED	▶				GO to Pinpoint Test Step Q1					

QUICK TEST: Key On Engine Off Self-Test — 3.0

C   LIGHT TRUCK SERVICE CODE CHART

Key On Engine Off Service Code		2.3L EFI	2.9L EFI	3.0L EFI	4.9L EFI	5.0L EFI	7.5L EFI
15 GO to	▶	Q12	Q12	Q12	Q12	Q12	Q12
19 GO to	▶	Q50	Q50	Q50	Q50	Q50	Q50
21 GO to	▶	DE1	DE1	DE1	DE1	DE1	DE1
22 GO to	▶	DF1	DF1	DF1	DF1	DF1	DF1
23 GO to	▶	DH1	DH1	DH1	DH1	DH1	DH1
24 GO to	▶	DB1	DB1	DB1	DB1	DB1	DB1
31 GO to	▶	DD2	DL1	—	DN1	DN1	DN1
32 GO to	▶	—	—	—	DN25	DN25	DN25
34 GO to	▶	—	DL8	—	DN20	DN20	DN20
35 GO to	▶	—	DL5	—	DN5	DN5	DN5
51 GO to	▶	DE10	DE10	DE10	DE10	DE10	DE10
52 GO to	▶	FF1	—	FF1	FF1	FF1	—
53 GO to	▶	DH3	DH3	DH3	DH3	DH3	DH3
54 GO to	▶	DB10	DB10	DB10	DB10	DB10	DB10
61 GO to	▶	DE20	DE20	DE20	DE20	DE20	DE20
63 GO to	▶	DH10	DH10	DH10	DH10	DH10	DH10
64 GO to	▶	DB20	DB20	DB20	DB20	DB20	DB20
67 GO to	▶	FA1	FA1	FA1	FA1	FA1	FA1
81 GO to	▶	—	—	—	KC8	KC8	KC8
82 GO to	▶	—	—	—	KC8	KC8	KC8
83 GO to	▶	DD17	—	—	—	—	—
84 GO to	▶	DD17	DL11	—	DN10	DN10	DN10
85 GO to	▶	—	—	KD6	KD6	KD6	KD6
87 GO to	▶	J7	J7	J7	J7	J7	J7
89 GO to	▶	KR1	KR1	KR1	—	—	—
NO CODES CODES NOT LISTED	▶			GO to Pinpoint Test Step Q1			

QUICK TEST: Computed Timing Check — 4.0

SPECIAL NOTES:

- If engine is a NO START, go directly to Pinpoint Test Step A1.

- If engine starts but stalls, or stalls during timing check go directly to DIAGNOSTICS BY SYMPTOM in the proper Engine Supplement Section.

- Self-Test timing is equal to Base Timing plus 20 degrees BTDC ± 3 degrees (see VECI decal for correct base timing).

Example

If base timing is 10 degrees BTDC, Self-Test timing is equal to: 10 degrees + 20 degrees = 30 degrees BTDC ± 3 degrees or 27 degrees to 33 degrees BTDC.

HOW TO RUN QUICK TEST TIMING CHECK

DO

- Turn the key off and wait 10 seconds.

- Start engine.

- Activate Self-Test per Quick Test Step 3.0 A.

- Check timing after the last service code has been displayed. The timing will remain fixed for 2 minutes. unless Self-Test is deactivated.

Is Self-Test Timing within specification?

YES   Go To QUICK TEST STEP 5.0.

NO   Go To Pinpoint Test Step P 1.

QUICK TEST: Engine Running Self-Test	5.0

A | PERFORMING THE ENGINE RUNNING SELF TEST

SPECIAL NOTES:

- If the engine starts but stalls, or stalls during Self-Test, go directly to DIAGNOSTICS BY SYMPTOM in the proper Engine Supplement Section.
- On vehicles equipped with 2.3L TC, 2.3L EFI (Car and Truck), 2.5L CFI, 2.9L EFI, and 3.0L EFI (Car and Truck), the brake pedal MUST be depressed and released AFTER the ID Code.
- On vehicles equipped with 2.3L CFI (Car), 4.9L and 5.0L EFI (Truck), the steering wheel must be turned one-half turn and released after the ID Code.

HOW TO RUN THE ENGINE RUNNING SELF-TEST

DO

- Deactivate Self-Test.
- Start and run engine at 2,000 rpm for 2 minutes. This action warms up the EGO sensor.
- Turn engine off, wait 10 seconds.
- Start engine.
- Activate Self-Test per Quick Test Step 3.0 A.
- After the ID code, depress and release the brake pedal if appropriate. See Special Note above.
- After the ID code, turn the steering wheel one-half turn and release it, if appropriate. See Special Note above.
- If a dynamic response code occurs, perform a brief wide open throttle (WOT).
- Record all service codes displayed.
- Go to **Part B** of Engine Running Self-Test.

DON'T

- Depress the throttle unless a Dynamic Response Code is displayed.

QUICK TEST: Engine Running Self-Test	5.0

B | CODE OUTPUT

Engine ID	Dynamic Response	Engine Running	ACTION TO TAKE
2(0), 3(0) or 4(0)	1(0) or no display	11	• Engine Running Self-Test indicates a PASS. — If Continuous Memory Codes were present, Go to QUICK TEST STEP 6.0. — If Continuous Memory is a PASS Code 11 and a symptom is present, Go to DIAGNOSTIC BY SYMPTOM in the proper Engine Supplement Section.
2(0), 3(0) or 4(0)	1(0) or no display	ANY CODE(S)	• Engine Running Self-Test indicates a FAULT. — Go to PART C of Engine Running Self-Test. — Always start with the first code displayed.
98	NO DISPLAY	ANY CODE(S)	• Code 98 in place of the I.D. code indicates that the vehicle DID NOT PASS Key On Engine Off Self-Test. Engine Running Self-Test will not initiate until a PASS Code 11 is obtained in Key On Engine Off Self-Test. — Run Key On Engine Off Self-Test and address all codes displayed.
NO CODE DISPLAYED CODES NOT LISTED			• Self-Test did not activate. — Rerun Engine Running Self-Test to verify the above condition. — If condition is still present, Go to Pinpoint Test Step Q1.

QUICK TEST: Engine Running Self-Test	5.0

C | PASSENGER CAR SERVICE CODE CHART

Engine Running Service Code	1.9L EFI	1.9L CFI	2.3L EFI	2.3L TC	2.3L CFI	2.5L CFI	3.0L EFI	3.8L CFI	5.0L SEFI
12 GO to	KE1	KB23	KE1	KE1	KB23	KF16	KE1	KF16	KE1
13 GO to	KE4	KB26	KE15	KE11	KB26	KF19	KE11	KF19	KE11
16 GO to	KE*	KB26	KE1	—	KB26	KF19	KE1	KF1*	KE1
17 GO to	KE12	—	—	KE12	—	—	—	—	—
18 GO to	—	—	—	—	—	—	—	—	—
19 GO to	—	KB26	—	—	—	—	—	—	—
21 GO to	DE1	DE1	DE1	DE1	DE1	DE1	DE1	DE1	DE1
22 GO to	DF1	DF7	DF7	DF1	DF7	DF7	DF7	DF7	DF7
23 GO to	DH1	KB12	DH1	DH1	KB12	DH1	DH1	DH1	DH1
24 GO to	—	DB1	DB1	DB1	DB1	DB1	DB1	DB1	DB1
25 GO to	—	—	DG1	DG1	—	—	DG1	—	—
26 GO to	DK1	—	DK1	DK1	—	—	—	—	—
28 GO to	DA1	—	—	DA1	—	—	—	—	—
31 GO to	—	DL21	DD1	—	DN1	DN1	DL21	DD1	DN1
32 GO to	—	DL20	DD11	—	DN25	DN25	DL20	DD11	DN25
33 GO to	—	DL30	DD11	—	DN40	DN40	DL30	DD11	DN40
34 GO to	—	DL25	DD11	KA1	DN50	DN50	DL25	DD11	DN50
35 GO to	—	DL25	DD30	—	DN5	DN5	DL25	DD30	DN5
41 GO to	HA14	HF6	HE14	HA14	HF6	HF6	HG15	HD7	HC9
42 GO to	HA8	HF13	HE8	HA8	HF13	HF13	HG8	HD14	HC15
44 GO to	—	—	—	—	—	—	—	KC1	KC1
45 GO to	—	—	—	—	—	—	—	KC1	KC1
46 GO to	—	—	—	—	—	—	—	KC1	KC1
47 GO to	KE11	—	—	—	—	—	—	—	—
48 GO to	KE20	—	—	—	—	—	—	—	—
52 GO to	—	—	—	—	FF5	—	FF5	—	—
55 GO to	—	FC3	—	—	FC3	—	FC3	HD1	—
58 GO to	—	KB5	—	—	KB5	KF12	—	KF12	—
62 GO to	—	—	—	—	—	—	T71	—	—
67 GO to	—	FA1	—	—	—	—	—	—	—
72 GO to	—	—	DF10	—	—	DF10	—	—	—
73 GO to	DH20	—	DH20	DH20	—	DH20	—	—	—
74 GO to	—	—	FD1	—	FD1	FD1	—	—	—
75 GO to	—	—	FD4	FD4	—	FD4	FD4	—	—
76 GO to	DK30	—	—	DK30	—	—	—	—	—
77 GO to	M1	—	M1	M1	—	M1	—	—	—
84 GO to	—	DL11	—	—	—	—	—	—	—
85 GO to	—	KD6	—	—	—	—	—	—	—
91 GO to	—	—	—	—	—	—	—	HD7	HC9
92 GO to	—	—	—	—	—	—	—	HD14	HC15
94 GO to	—	—	—	—	—	—	—	KC1	KC1
98 GO to	GO TO QUICK TEST STEP 5.0B								
99 GO to	ISC HAS NOT LEARNED YET. RERUN QUICK TEST STEPS 3 THRU 5								
NO CODES	GO to Pinpoint Test Step Q1								
CODES NOT LISTED									

QUICK TEST: Engine Running Self-Test	5.0

C | LIGHT TRUCK SERVICE CODE CHART

Engine Running Service Code	2.3L EFI	2.9L EFI	3.0L EFI	4.9L EFI	5.0L EFI	7.5L EFI
12 GO to	KE1	KE1	KE1	KE1	KE1	KE1
13 GO to	KE15	KE11	KE11	KE11	KE11	KE11
16 GO to	KE1	KE1	KE1	KE1	KE1	KE1
21 GO to	DE1	DE1	DE1	DE1	DE1	DE1
22 GO to	DF7	DF7	DF7	DF7	DF7	DF7
23 GO to	DH1	DH1	DH1	DH1	DH1	DH1
24 GO to	DB1	DB1	DB1	DB1	DB1	DB1
25 GO to	DG1	DG1	DG1	DG1	—	—
31 GO to	DD1	DL21	—	DN1	DN1	DN1
32 GO to	DD11	DL20	—	DN25	DN25	DN25
33 GO to	DD11	DL30	—	DN40	DN40	DN40
34 GO to	DD11	DL25	—	DN50	DN50	DN50
35 GO to	DD30	DL25	—	DN5	DN5	DN5
38 GO to	—	—	—	DN55	DN55	DN55
41 GO to	HE14	HG15	HG15	HG15	HH15	HH15
42 GO to	HE8	HG8	HG8	HG8	HH8	HH8
44 GO to	—	—	—	KC1	KC1	KC1
45 GO to	—	—	—	KC1	KC1	KC1
46 GO to	—	—	—	KC1	KC1	—
52 GO to	—	—	—	FF5	FF5	—
72 GO to	DF10	DF10	DF10	DF10	DF10	DF10
73 GO to	DH20	DH20	DH20	DH20	DH20	DH20
74 GO to	FD1	FD1	FD1	—	—	—
75 GO to	FD4	FD4	FD4	—	—	—
77 GO to	M1	M1	M1	M1	M1	M1
98 GO to	GO TO QUICK TEST STEP 5.0B					
NO CODES	GO to Pinpoint Test Step Q1					
CODES NOT LISTED						

QUICK TEST: Continuous Self-Test | 6.0

A CONTINUOUS MEMORY CODES

SPECIAL NOTES:

- Verify that a **Pass Code 11** was received in both Key On Engine Off and Engine Running Self-Tests before continuing with this test.

- It is necessary to clear the codes in Continuous Memory before continuing with this test.

- Refer to the Appendix for a detailed description of how to use the Continuous Monitor Mode.

HOW TO CLEAR THE CONTINUOUS MEMORY CODES

- Run the Key On Engine Off Self-Test per Quick Test Step 3.0 A.

- When the Service Codes begin to be displayed, deactivate Self-Test:
  - —STAR Tester: Unlatching the center button (up position).
  - —Analog VOM: Remove the jumper wire from between Self-Test Input (STI) connector and the Signal Return Pin of the Self-Test connector.

DETERMINING THE CONTINOUS MEMORY CODES TO BE TESTED

- Refer to the Continuous Memory Codes recorded in Quick Test Step 3.0 A.

- The cause of some of the Continuous Memory Codes may have been eliminated during either Key On Engine Off or Engine Running Self-Test repairs.

- Address only those Continuous Memory Codes for which a similar code has not been previously serviced.

- Go to **Part B** of Continuous Self-Test.

QUICK TEST: Continuous Self-Test | 6.0

B HOW TO USE THE CONTINUOUS MONITOR MODE (WIGGLE TEST)

SPECIAL NOTES:

- The Continuous Monitor Modes allow the technician to **ATTEMPT** to recreate an intermittent fault.

- The STAR Tester will flash the LED or sound an alert when a fault is recreated.

- The needle of the VOM will sweep across the face of the meter when a fault is recreated.

KEY ON ENGINE OFF

- Hook up a STAR Tester or VOM as shown in Quick Test Step 2.0.

- Turn the ignition key to the ON position.

- Activate, de-activate, and re-activate Self-Test. **DO NOT** turn the ignition key off.

- You are now in the Continuous Monitor Mode.

- Tap, move, and wiggle the suspect sensor and/or harness. If a fault is detected a Service Code will be stored in memory and will be indicated as explained above depending on the type of equipment being used.

- Go To **PART C** of Continuous Self-Test.

ENGINE RUNNING

- Hook up a STAR Tester or VOM as shown in Quick Test Step 2.0.

- Start the engine.

- Activate Self-Test, wait 10 seconds, deactivate and reactivate Self-Test. **DO NOT** shut the engine off.

- You are now in the Engine Running Continuous Monitor Mode.

- Tap, move and wiggle the suspect sensor and/or harness. If a fault is detected a Service Code will be stored in memory and will be indicated as explained above depending on the type of equipment being used.

- Go to **PART C** of Continuous Self-Test.

QUICK TEST: Continuous Self-Test | 6.0

C PASSENGER CAR SERVICE CODE CHART

Continuous Memory Service Code		Pinpoint Test Step Direction								
		1.9L EFI	1.9L CFI	2.3L EFI	2.3L TC	2.3L CFI	2.5L CFI	3.0L EFI	3.8L CFI	5.0L SEFI
13 GO to	▶	—	KB90	—	—	KB90	—	—	—	—
14 GO to	▶	Y1	Y1	Y1	Y1	Y1	Y1	Y1	Y1	Y1
15 GO to	▶	Q10	Q10	Q10	Q10	Q10	Q10	Q10	Q10	Q10
18 GO to	▶	N1	N1	N1	N1	N1	N1	N1	—	N1
21 GO to	▶	—	—	—	—	DE90	DE90	—	—	—
22 GO to	▶	DF90	DF90	DF90	DF90	DF90	DF90	DF90	DF90	DF90
23 GO to	▶	—	KB97	—	KB97	—	—	—	—	—
27 GO to	▶	—	—	—	DP1	—	—	T2	—	DP1
29 GO to	▶	—	—	—	—	—	—	—	—	DP1
31 GO to	▶	—	DL90	DD90	—	DN92	DN92	DL90	DD90	DN92
32 GO to	▶	—	DL94	—	—	DN90	DN90	DL94	—	DN90
33 GO to	▶	—	DL97	—	—	DN95	DN95	DL97	—	DN95
34 GO to	▶	—	DL93	—	—	DN98	DN98	DL93	—	DN98
35 GO to	▶	—	DL90	—	—	DN92	DN92	DL90	—	DN92
38 GO to	▶	—	KB91	—	—	KB91	—	—	—	—
39 GO to	▶	—	—	—	—	—	—	T31	—	—
41 GO to	▶	HA30	HF90	—	—	HF90	—	HG90	—	HC90
42 GO to	▶	HA30	—	—	—	—	—	—	—	—
43 GO to	▶	HA30	—	—	HA30	—	—	—	—	—
51 GO to	▶	DE91	DE91	DE91	DE91	DE91	DE91	DE91	DE91	DE91
53 GO to	▶	DH90	KB93	DH90	DH90	KB93	DH90	DH90	DH90	DH90
54 GO to	▶	—	DB90	DB90	—	DB90	DB90	DB90	DB90	DB90
56 GO to	▶	DK90	—	—	DK90	—	—	—	—	—
57 GO to	▶	—	—	—	—	—	T41	—	—	—
58 GO to	▶	DA90	—	—	DA90	—	—	—	—	—
59 GO to	▶	—	—	—	—	—	T21	—	—	—
61 GO to	▶	DE94	DE94	DE94	DE94	DE94	DE94	DE94	DE94	DE94
63 GO to	▶	DH94	KB97	DH94	DH94	KB97	DH94	DH94	DH94	DH94
64 GO to	▶	—	DB93	DB93	DB93	DB93	DB93	DB93	DB93	DB93
66 GO to	▶	DK93	—	—	DK93	—	—	—	—	—
67 GO to	▶	FA1	—	—	FA1	—	—	—	—	—
68 GO to	▶	DA93	—	—	DA93	—	—	—	—	—
69 GO to	▶	—	—	—	—	—	T11	—	—	—
71 GO to	▶	Q60	KB92	—	—	KB92	—	—	—	—
72 GO to	▶	B10	—	—	B10	—	—	—	—	—
78 GO to	▶	—	—	—	—	B10	X10	—	—	—
87 GO to	▶	—	J7	—	—	J7	—	J7	—	—
91 GO to	▶	—	—	—	—	—	—	—	—	HC90
NO CODES	▶	GO to Pinpoint Test Step Q1								
CODES NOT LISTED	▶									

C LIGHT TRUCK SERVICE CODE CHART

Continuous Memory Service Code		Pinpoint Test Step Direction					
		2.3L EFI	2.9L EFI	3.0L EFI	4.9L EFI	5.0L EFI	7.5l EFI
14 GO to	▶	Y1	Y1	Y1	Y1	Y1	Y1
15 GO to	▶	Q10	Q10	Q10	Q10	Q10	Q10
18 GO to	▶	N1	N1	N1	N1	N1	N1
21 GO to	▶	—	—	—	—	—	—
22 GO to	▶	DF90	DF90	DF90	DF90	DF90	DF90
29 GO to	▶	—	DP1	—	DP1	DP1	—
31 GO to	▶	DD90	DL90	—	DN92	DN92	DN92
32 GO to	▶	—	DL94	—	DN90	DN90	DN90
33 GO to	▶	—	DL97	—	DN95	DN95	DN95
34 GO to	▶	—	DL93	—	DN98	DN98	DN98
35 GO to	▶	—	DL90	—	DN92	DN92	DN92
41 GO to	▶	—	HG90	—	HH90	HH90	HH90
51 GO to	▶	DE91	DE91	DE91	DE91	DE91	DE91
53 GO to	▶	DH90	DH90	HD90	DH90	DH90	DH90
54 GO to	▶	DB90	DB90	DB90	DB90	DB90	DB90
61 GO to	▶	DE94	DE94	DE94	DE94	DE94	DE94
63 GO to	▶	DH94	DH94	DH94	DH94	DH94	DH94
64 GO to	▶	DB93	DB93	DB93	DB93	DB93	DB93
87 GO to	▶	—	J7	—	J7	J7	J7
NO CODES	▶	GO to Pinpoint Test Step Q1					
CODES NOT LISTED	▶						

Self-Test Description

The Self-Test is divided into three specialized tests: Key On Engine Off Self-Test, Engine Running Self-Test, and Continuous Self-Test. The Self-Test is not a conclusive test by itself, but is used as a part of the functional Quick-Test diagnostic procedure. The processor stores the Self-Test program in its permanent memory. When activated, it checks the EEC-IV system by testing its memory integrity and processing capability, and verifies that various sensors and actuators are connected and operating properly.

The Key On Engine Off and Engine Running Self-Tests are functional tests which only detect faults present at the time of the Self-Test. Continuous Self-Test is an ongoing test that stores fault information for retrieval at a later time.

KEY ON ENGINE OFF SELF-TEST

At this time, a test of the EEC-IV system is conducted with power applied and engine at rest.

For Self-Test to detect errors in the Key On Engine Off Self-Test mode, the fault must be present at the time of testing. For intermittents, refer to Continuous Memory Codes.

SEPARATOR PULSE

A single 1/2 second separator pulse is issued 6-9 seconds after the last Key On Engine Off Test code. Then 6-9 seconds after the single 1/2 second separator pulse, the continuous memory codes will be issued.

NOTE: The separator code and continuous memory codes follow Key On Engine Off Testing codes ONLY.

CONTINUOUS MEMORY CODES

Continuous memory codes are issued as a result of information stored during continuous Self-Test, while the vehicle was in normal operation. These codes are displayed only during Key On Engine Off testing and after the separator code. These codes should be used for diagnosis only when Key On Engine Off and Engine Running Self-Tests result in code 11 and all Quick Test Steps 1.0 through 5.0 have been successfully completed.

ENGINE RUNNING SELF-TEST

At this time, a test of the EEC-IV system is conducted with the engine running. The sensors are checked under actual operating conditions and at normal operating temperatures. The actuators are exercised and checked for corresponding results.

ENGINE IDENTIFICATION CODES (ID CODES)

Engine ID codes are issued at the beginning of the Engine Running Self-Test and are one-digit numbers represented by the number of pulses sent out. The engine ID code is equal to 1/2 the number of engine cylinder (i.e. 2 pulses = 4 cylinders). These codes are used to verify the proper processor is installed and that the Self-Test has been entered.

DYNAMIC RESPONSE CHECK

The dynamic response check verifies the movement of the TP, VAF, and MAP sensors during the brief Wide Open Throttle (WOT) performed during the Engine Running Self-Test. The signal for the operator to perform the brief WOT is a single pulse or 10 code on the STAR Tester.

Self-Test Description

POWER STEERING PRESSURE SWITCH TEST

On vehicles equipped with 2.3L CFI (Car), 4.9L and 5.0L EFI (Truck), the steering wheel must be turned one-half turn and released AFTER the ID Code. This tests the ability of the EEC-IV system to detect a change of state in the Power Steering Pressure Switch.

BRAKE ON/OFF SWITCH TEST

On vehicles equipped with 2.3L TC, 2.3L EFI (Car and Truck), 2.5L CFI, 2.9L EFI, and 3.0L EFI (Car and Truck), the brake pedal MUST be depressed and released AFTER the ID Code. This tests the ability of the EEC-IV system to detect a change of state in the Brake ON/OFF Switch.

Code Output Format

SERVICE CODES

The EEC-IV system communicates service information to the outside world by way of the Self-Test service codes. These service codes are two-digit numbers representing the results of Self-Test.

The service codes are transmitted on the Self-Test output (STO) line found in the vehicle Self-Test connector. They are in the form of timed pulses, and read by the technician on a voltmeter or on the STAR tester.

SELF-TEST OUTPUT CODE FORMAT
KEY ON ENGINE OFF AND CONTINUOUS MEMORY CODES

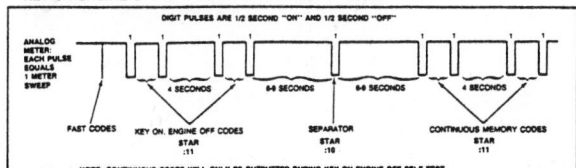

Figure 1 Key On Engine Off and Continuous Memory Code Format

SELF-TEST OUTPUT CODE FORMAT
ENGINE RUNNING CODES

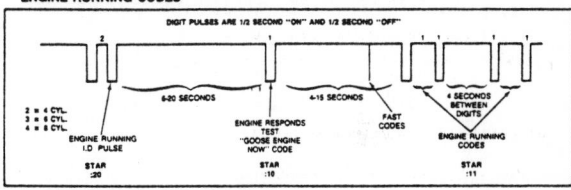

Figure 2 Engine Running Self-Test Code Format

Fast Codes

Fast codes are issued prior to regular service codes. These codes contain the identical information as the regular service codes but are transmitted at 100 times the normal rate. These codes are interpreted by special equipment at the end of the assembly line by the Body and Assembly Division.

Some meters in service detect these codes as a short burst of information (slight meter deflection).

Continuous Self-Test

The Continuous Memory service codes are separated from the Quick Test Key On Engine Off codes by a single separator pulse, Figure 3.

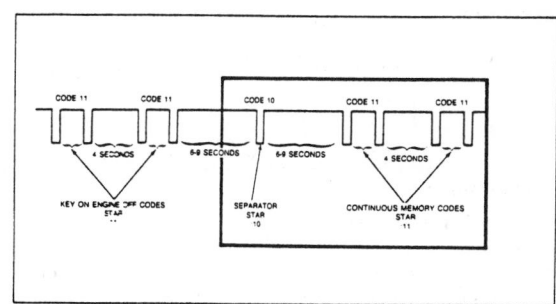

Figure 3 Continuous Memory Code Format

The Continuous Memory codes should never be used for Diagnosis until the Key On Engine Off and Engine Running Self-Tests result in a pass code 11.

During this mode of testing the EEC-IV Processor continuously monitors inputs for opens and shorts. The continuous memory codes must be retrieved within forty engine temperature warm up cycles. On the forty-first Engine Temperature cycle the service code will be automatically erased. The continuous memory codes can also be erased by deactivating Self-Test while the service codes are being outputted.

Self-Test With STAR Tester

READING CODES—SELF-TEST AUTOMATIC READOUT (STAR) TESTER

After hooking up the STAR tester and turning on its power switch, the tester will run a display check and the numerals 88 will begin to flash in the display window (Figure 4). A steady 00 will then appear to signify that the STAR tester is ready to start the Self-Test and receive the test's service codes.

To receive the service codes, press the pushbutton at the front of the STAR tester. The button will latch down, and a colon will appear in the display window in front of the 00 numerals. The colon must be displayed to receive the service codes.

If for any reason the technician wishes to clear the display window during the Self-Test, he must turn off the vehicle's engine, press the tester's pushbutton once to unlatch it (colon will disappear), then press the button again to latch down the button (colon will appear again). Every time the STAR tester is turned off, the low battery indicator (LO BAT) should show briefly at the upper left corner of the tester's display window. If the LO BAT indicator shows steadily at any other time during the operation of the STAR tester with any service code, turn its power switch to Off and replace the 9-volt battery in the tester.

The STAR tester will display the last service code received, even after disconnecting it from the vehicle. It will hold the service code on the display until the power is turned off or the pushbutton is unlatched and relatched.

WARNING: Anyone who departs from the instructions provided in this publication must first establish that he compromises neither his personal safety nor the vehicle integrity by his choice of methods, tools, or parts.

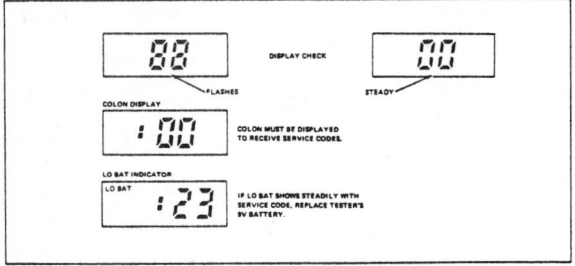

Figure 4   Star Tester Output Code Format

Self-Test With Analog Voltmeter

READING CODES—ANALOG VOLTMETER

When a service code is reported on the analog voltmeter for a function test, it will represent itself as a pulsing or sweeping movement of the voltmeter's needle across the dial face of the voltmeter (Figure 5). Therefore, a single-digit number of three will be reported by three needle pulses (sweeps). However, as previously stated, a service code is represented by a two-digit number, such as 2-3. As a result, the Self-Tests service code of 2-3 will appear on the voltmeter as two needle pulses (sweeps), then, after a two-second pause, the needle will pulse (sweep) three times.

The continuous memory codes are separated from the Key On Engine Off codes by a six-second delay, a single half-second sweep, and another six-second delay. They are produced on the voltmeter in the same manner as the Key On Engine Off codes.

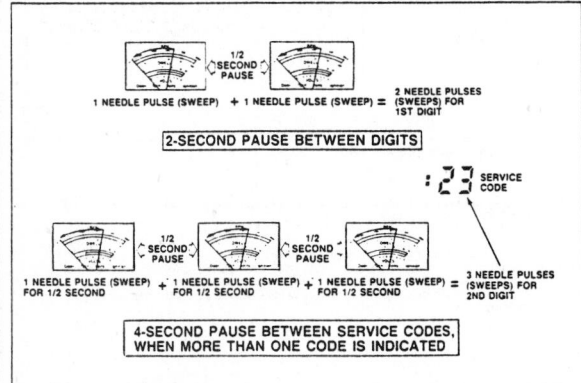

Figure 5 Analog Voltmeter Output Code Format

Diagnostic Aids

CONTINUOUS MONITOR TEST (WIGGLE TEST)

This test is intended as an aid in diagnosing intermittent failures in the sensor input circuits. The Self-Test output is energized whenever the continuous memory mode senses a fault and de-energized when the system is OK.

- Connect a VOM/STAR to the Self-Test output.

- Key On Engine Off/Engine Running Continuous Monitor Test, (Wiggle Test).

  Continuous Monitor Test is entered by activating, de-activating, and re-activating Self-Test (DO NOT turn key off). This will put you into Continuous Monitor ("Wiggle") Test. The Engine Running Continuous Monitor Test can also be entered by waiting approximately two minutes after the last service codes are received.

  The Continuous Monitor (Wiggle) Test will allow the technician to attempt to re-create the intermittent failure (tap, move, wiggle the harness and/or the suspected sensor). The Self-Test output will be activated whenever a continuous fault is detected. If the duration is long enough, a fault code will be stored.

  Now with the knowledge of the affected circuits, a close check of the harness and associated connectors can be made.

  NOTE: Remember to keep your eyes on the VOM/STAR for any change which will indicate where the intermittent is located.

EXAMPLE: How to Use the Continuous Monitor Test (Systematically)

If a service code 51 was displayed: Engine Coolant Temperature Sensor:

- Visually inspect the sensor very closely.
- Enter Continuous Monitor test.
- Lightly TAP on the sensor.
- Push/pull on the sensor harness connector (do not disconnect, yet).
- Test and Wiggle (shake) harness vigorously working from the sensor connector toward the dash panel and from the dash panel to the processor in short sections.
- If VOM has not given a positive indication of an intermittent, disconnect the sensor from the harness as carefully as possible. Remove terminals from the connector. Visually inspect terminals at both ends for corrosion, bad crimps, improperly seated terminals, etc.
- Reconnect after inspection.
- Disconnect processor from harness as carefully as possible.
- Inspect terminals.
- Only remove terminals associated with the sensor being inspected.
- If the VOM does not give a positive intermittent indication, reconnect the connector and erase the Continuous Test service codes.
- To erase the continuous memory service codes:
  — Initiate Key On Engine Off Self-Test.
  — Unlatch the push-button on the Star Tester as soon as the first service code is received (even if an "11" is the first code).
  — Rerun Self-Test to verify services have been erased.

Diagnostic Aids

OUTPUT STATE CHECK

The output state check aids in servicing output actuators associated with the EEC-IV system. It enables the technician to energize and de-energize most of the system output actuators on command. This mode is entered after all codes have been received from Key On Engine Off and Continuous Testing. At this time, leave Self-Test activated and depress the throttle. Each time the throttle is depressed the output actuators will change state from energized to de-energized or from de-energized to energized.

1. Enter Self-Test.
2. Code Output Ends.
3. Do Brief WOT.
4. EEC-IV Output To Actuators Energized.
5. Do Brief WOT.
6. EEC-IV Output To Actuators De-Energized.

CYLINDER BALANCE TEST

All Applications Except Mark VII/Lincoln Town Car Calibration 8-22

The Cylinder Balance Test on the 5.0L SEFI is designed to separately check each injector and injector circuit. By switching each injector off and on, one at a time, Self-Test will verify that an rpm drop of greater than 80 rpm results.

To enter the Cylinder Balance Test:

1. Perform Engine Running Self-Test.

2. After the last REPEATED service code is received wait approximately 10 seconds. (The test must be entered within 2 minutes of the last repeated service code.)

3. Lightly depress throttle. (A two to three degree throttle angle shaft movement is required, NOT wide open throttle.)

4. Test time is approximately 90 seconds.

5. The Cylinder Balance Test can be repeated (entered) as many times as necessary, by lightly depressing the throttle within two minutes after the last repeated service code has been displayed.

The Cylinder Balance Test service codes are listed in Pinpoint Test Step HC4.

The Cylinder Balance Test is designed to aid in the detection of a non-contributing cylinder. The Cylinder Balance Pinpoint Test Steps are designed to isolate only EEC related problems

CYLINDER BALANCE TEST (Continued)
Mark VII/Lincoln Town Car Calibration 8-22

The Cylinder Balance Test on the Mark VII/Lincoln Town Car calibration 8-22 has been modified to test rpm drop at three levels, allowing a more precise check of each cylinder. During first level testing, Cylinder Balance Test will verify that when each injector is separately turned "off and on", an rpm drop of greater than 80 rpm results. When a second test level is requested, an rpm drop of greater than 90 rpm must result. When a third test level is requested, a drop of greater than 100 rpm must result. Any additional tests (ie. fourth test, fifth test, etc.) that are requested will be run at the third level (100 rpm).

The Cylinder Balance Test service codes are listed in Pinpoint Test Step HC4.

1. Perform Engine Running Self-Test.

2. After the last repeated service code is received, wait 5-10 seconds.

3. Lightly depress and release throttle (not wide-open throttle) within two minutes of the last repeated service code.

4. Cylinder Balance Test will be performed at the first test level (80 rpm). Test time is approximately three minutes.

5. After the last repeated Cylinder Balance Test pass code 90, re-enter test within two minutes by lightly depressing and releasing the throttle. The second test level of the Cylinder Balance Test will now be performed (90 rpm).

6. After the last repeated Cylinder Balance Test pass code 90, re-enter test within two minutes by lightly depressing and releasing the throttle. Cylinder Balance Test will now be tested at the third test level (100 rpm).

7. Cylinder Balance Test may be repeated as many times as necessary by repeating Step 6. All additional testing will be performed at the third test level (100 rpm).

The Cylinder Balance Test is designed to aid in the detection of a non-contributing or partially contributing cylinder. The Cylinder Balance Pinpoint Test Steps are designed to isolate only EEC related problems.

Failure Mode Effects Management (FMEM)

DESCRIPTION

FMEM is an alternate system strategy in the ECA designed to allow improved vehicle drive should one or more sensor inputs fail.

When a sensor input is perceived to be out-of-limits by the ECA, an alternative strategy will be initiated.

The ECA will substitute a fixed in-limit sensor value and will continue to monitor the faulty sensor input. If the faulty sensor operates within limits, the ECA will return to the normal engine running strategy.

98 — Code 98 will be displayed when FMEM is in effect.

MIL — MIL "Check Engine" Light will remain on when FMEM is in effect.

"Check Engine" Light (Malfunction Indicator Light)

DESCRIPTION

The "Check Engine" light is intended to alert the driver of certain malfunctions in the engine control system.

If such a fault occurs, the EEC-IV processor will substitute a value or values and continue operating. This process is called Failure Mode Effects Management (FMEM). In some cases this action may result in a slight change in driveability.

HOW THE "CHECK ENGINE" LIGHT OPERATES

System OK

The "Check Engine" light will remain on while the key is in the RUN position.

Once the vehicle has started the "Check Engine" light will go out.

System Not OK

If the "Check Engine" light should remain on after the vehicle has started, run Key On Engine Off Self-Test to completion. If the light continues to remain on, go to EEC-IV Diagnostic By Symptom.

If the "Check Engine" light never comes on, go to EEC-IV Diagnostic By Symptom.

If the vehicle is a no start, go to Pinpoint Test Step A1.

NOTE: When in Self-Test the "Check Engine" light will also flash the service codes.

Test Equipment

EQUIPMENT REQUIRED:

- Rotunda Self-Test Automatic Readout (STAR), No. 007-00004 with cable assembly No. 007-00010. Refer to STAR Tester operation.
- Analog volt-ohmmeter, 0 to 20v DC, (alternate to STAR).

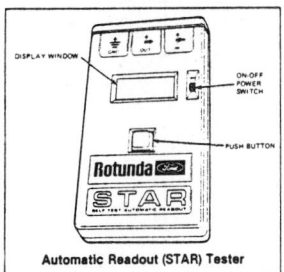 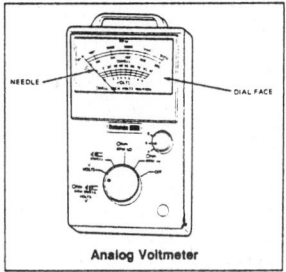

Automatic Readout (STAR) Tester   **Analog Voltmeter**

- Jumper wire.
- Vacuum gauge, Rotunda 059-00008 or equivalent. Range 0-30 in. Hg. Resolution 1 in. Hg.

 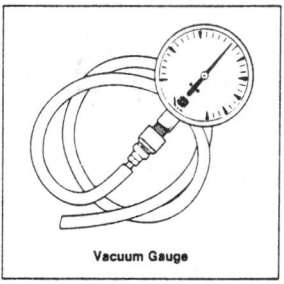

Jumper Wire   **Vacuum Gauge**

Test Equipment (Continued)

- Tachometer, Rotunda No. 059-00010 or equivalent. Range 0-6,000 rpm. Accuracy ± 40 rpm. Resolution 20 rpm.
- Breakout Box, Rotunda 014-00322. Special Service Tool T83L-50-EEC-IV or equivalent.

 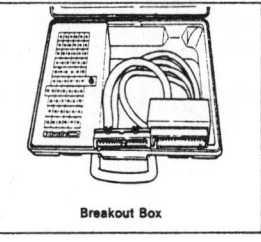

Tachometer   **Breakout Box**

- Vacuum pump, Rotunda No. 021-00014 or equivalent. Range 0-30 in. Hg.
- Digital volt-ohmmeter, Rotunda No. 014-00407 or equivalent. Input impedance 10 Megaohm minimum.

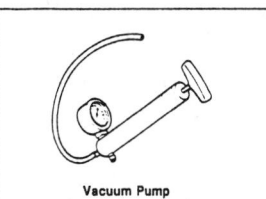 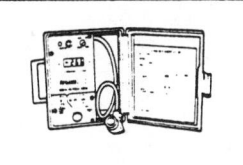

Vacuum Pump   **Digital Volt-Ohmmeter**

FUEL INJECTION SYSTEMS
FORD MOTOR COMPANY

Electrical Schematic	1.9L CFI

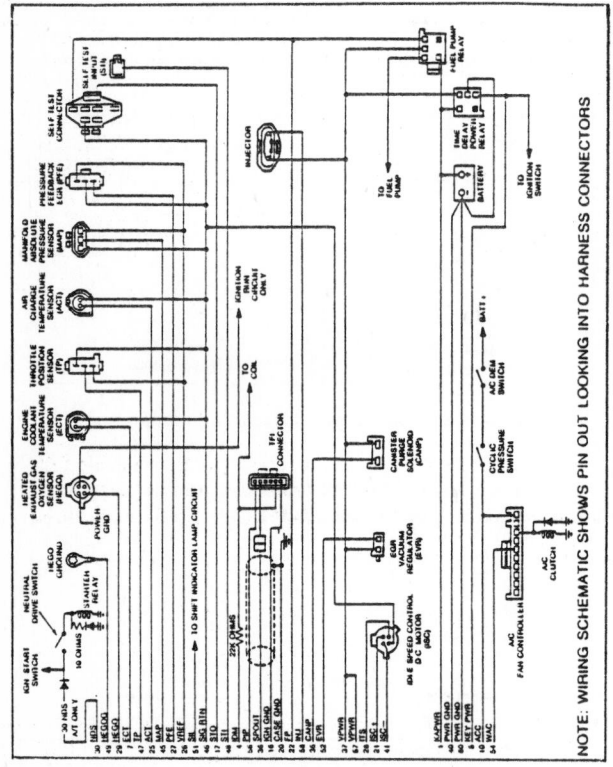

NOTE: WIRING SCHEMATIC SHOWS PIN OUT LOOKING INTO HARNESS CONNECTORS

Electrical Schematic	1.9L EFI

NOTE: WIRING SCHEMATIC SHOWS PIN OUT LOOKING INTO HARNESS CONNECTORS

EEC-IV Module Connector Pin Usage	1.9L CFI

Pin	Circuit	Wire Color	Application	Abbreviations
1	37	Y	Keep Alive Power	KAPWR
4	11	DG Y	Ignition Diagnostic Monitor	IDM
5	16	R LG	Key Power	VPWR
7	354	LG Y	Engine Coolant Temperature Sensor	ECT
10	347	BK Y	A C Clutch Compressor Signal	ACCS
16	259	BK O	Ignition Ground	IGN GND
17	201	T R	Self-Test Output Shift Indicator Light	STO SIL
20	57	BK	Case Ground	CSE GND
21	376	BR W	Idle Speed Control	ISC -
22	97	T LG	Fuel Pump Relay	FP
25	357	LG P	Air Charge Temperature Sensor	ACT
26	351	O W	Reference Voltage	VREF
27	352	BR LG	Pressure Feedback EGR	PFE
28	265	LG W	Idle Tracking Switch	ITS
29	94	DG P	Heated Exhaust Gas Oxygen Sensor	HEGO
30	614	GY O	Neutral Drive Switch (A.T Only)	NDS
35	101	GY Y	Canister Purge Solenoid	CANP
36	324	Y LG	Spark Output	SPOUT
37	361	R	Vehicle Power	VPWR
40	60	BK LG	Power Ground	PWR GND
41	264	W LB	Idle Speed Control	ISC -
45	358	LG BK	Manifold Absolute Pressure Sensor	MAP
46	359	BK W	Signal Return (Ground)	SIG RTN
47	355	DG LG	Throttle Position Sensor	TP
48	100	W R	Self-Test Input	STI
49	89	O	Heated Exhaust Gas Oxygen Ground	HEGOG
51	224	T LB	Shift Indicator Light (M T Only)	SIL
52	362	Y	EGR Valve Regulator Solenoid	EVR
54	73	O LB	WOT A C Cutoff	WAC
56	349	DB	Profile Ignition Pick-Up	PIP
57	361	R	Vehicle Power	VPWR
58	95	T R	Fuel Injector	INJ
60	60	BK LG	Power Ground	PWR GND

Pin locations given for reference only. Probing 60 pin connector with DVOM probe will result in permanent damage to the pin connectors. Always probe as directed using the Breakout Box.

EEC-IV Module Connector Pin Usage	1.9L EFI

Pin	Circuit	Wire Color	Application	Abbreviations
1	37A	Y	Keep Alive Power	KAPWR
4	11B	DG Y	Ignition Diagnostic Monitor	IDM
7	354	LG Y	Engine Coolant Temperature	ECT
10	347	BK Y	A C Clutch	ACCS
16	259	BK O	Ignition Ground	IGN GND
17	201	T R	Self-Test Output Shift Indicator Light	STO SIL
20	57	BK	Case Ground	CSE GND
21	68	O BK	Idle Speed Control	ISC
22	97	T LG	Fuel Pump	FP
25	357	LG P	Vane Air Temperature	VAT
26	351	O W	Reference Voltage	VREF
29	94	DG P	Heated Exhaust Gas Oxygen Sensor	HEGO
30	614	GY O	Neutral Drive Switch (A.T Only)	NDS
32	101	GY Y	Canister Purge Solenoid	CANP
35	362	Y	Exhaust Gas Recirculation Shut Off	EGR S.O
36	324A	Y LG	Spark Output	SPOUT
37	361	R	Vehicle Power	VPWR
40	60A	BK LG	Power Ground	PWR GND
43	200	W BK	Vane Air Flow	VAF
45	358	LG BK	Barometric Pressure	BP
46	359	BK W	Signal Return	SIG RTN
47	355	DG LG	Throttle Position Sensor	TP
48	100	W R	Self-Test Input	STI
49	89	O	Heated Exhaust Gas Oxygen Ground	HEGOG
54	73	O LB	Wide Open Throttle A C Cut-Off	WAC
56	349	DB	Profile Ignition Pickup	PIP
57	361A	R	Vehicle Power	VPWR
58	95	T R	Injector 1 (Bank 1)	INJ 1
59	96	T O	Injector 2 (Bank 2)	INJ 2
60	60B	BK LG	Power Ground	PWR GND

Pin locations given for reference only. Probing 60 pin connector with DVOM probe will result in permanent damage to the pin connectors. Always probe as directed using the Breakout Box.

EEC-IV Diagnostic By Symptom — 1.9L CFI

SYMPTOM	RESULT	ACTION TO TAKE
• Engine runs rough or misfires. • Engine stalls. • Lack of power. • Rough idle.		• GO to Pinpoint Test Step `S2`. • GO to Pinpoint Test Step `DF20`. • EGR Valve Function. • Ignition system distributor cap, rotor, wires, coil, plugs. • Base engine valves, cam timing, compression etc. • Poor power ground connections.
• Low idle with A/C on.		For A.T.: • Place A/C switch to A/C. • Perform KOEO Quick Test. • If code 67 is present GO to `FA1`. • If code 67 is not present GO to Pinpoint Test Step `FA20`. For M.T.: • GO to Pinpoint Test Step `FA20`.
• Stumble after hot restart (HEGO).		• GO to Pinpoint Test Step `HF20`.
• Shift indicator light always on or off.		GO to Pinpoint Test Step `KL1`.
• Gasoline fumes under hood		GO to Pinpoint Test Step `KD1`.
• Stall during parking maneuvers.		GO to Pinpoint Test Step `FF3`.

EEC-IV Diagnostic By Symptom — 1.9L EFI

SYMPTOM	RESULT	ACTION TO TAKE
• Engine stalls. • Stalls in Self-Test. • Runs rough. • Misses. • Always Rich/Lean.		• GO to Pinpoint Test Step `S1`. • GO to Pinpoint Test Step `DF20`. • Poor power ground connections. • Ignition system distributor cap, rotor, wires, coil, plugs. • Base engine valves, cam timing, compression etc.
• Stumble after hot restart.		GO to Pinpoint Test Step `HA20`.
• Fuel pump always runs.		GO to Pinpoint Test Step `J15`.
• Detonation/spark knock.		GO to Pinpoint Test Step `KA1`.
• High idle speeds on each restart may be accompanied by detonation for up to 3-5 minutes after a restart.		GO to Pinpoint Test Step `KA1`.
• Low engine rpm with A/C On.		GO to Pinpoint Test Step `FA20`.
• Gasoline fumes under hood.		GO to Pinpoint Test Step `KD1`.
• Shift indicator light always On or Off.		GO to Pinpoint Test Step `KL1`.
• A/C does not cut-off under WOT conditions.		GO to Pinpoint Test Step `KM1`.

EEC-IV Diagnostic By Symptom-Continued — 1.9L CFI

SYMPTOM	RESULT	ACTION TO TAKE
• High idle in Drive, automatic transmission only.		• Place transmission in Drive with engine off. Test neutral drive circuit (test Pin 30) for short to ground. SERVICE as necessary. NOTE: Circuit should NOT have continuity to ground in DRIVE.
• Fuel pump always runs.		GO to Pinpoint Test Step `J15`.
• A/C does not cut off under WOT conditions.		GO to Pinpoint Test Step `KM1`.

Note: Pin locations given for reference only. Probing 60 pin connector with DVOM probe can result in permanent damage to the pin connectors. Always probe as directed using Breakout Box.

EEC-IV Diagnostic By Symptom — 2.3L EFI

SYMPTOM	RESULT	ACTION TO TAKE
• Engine stalls. • Stalls in Self-Test. • Runs rough. • Misses. • Always Rich/lean.		• GO to Pinpoint Test Step `S1`. • MAP test. GO to Pinpoint Test Step `DF20`. • Idle speed control. GO to Pinpoint Test Step `KE1`. • Poor power ground connections. • Ignition system distributor cap, rotor, wires, coil, plugs. • Base engine valves, cam timing, compression etc.
• Detonation spark knock		GO to Pinpoint Test Step `DG1`, or EGR Diagnostic Section 6 of Volume H
• A/C compressor runs continuously.		GO to Pinpoint Test Step `FA4`.
• Low idle during A/C On.		GO to Pinpoint Test Step `FA20`.
• "CHECK ENGINE" light always on.		GO to Pinpoint Test `ML1`
• "CHECK ENGINE" light never on.		GO to Pinpoint Test `ML5`
• A/C does not cut-off under WOT conditions. • A/C not functioning		GO to Pinpoint Test Step `KM1`
• Surges with A/C on at idle		GO to Pinpoint Test Step `KM20`
• Stumble after hot re-start (HEGO).		GO to Pinpoint Test Step `HE21`
• Stall during parking maneuvers		GO to Pinpoint Test Step `FF3`
• Fuel pump runs with key off		GO to Pinpoint Test Step `J15`

FUEL INJECTION SYSTEMS
FORD MOTOR COMPANY

Electrical Schematic	2.3L EFI

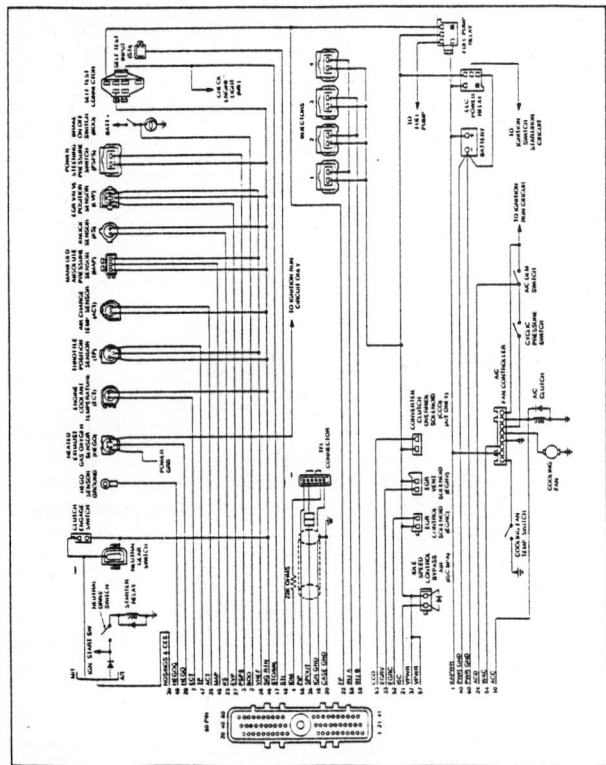

EEC-IV Diagnostic By Symptom	2.3L EFI TURBO

SYMPTOM	RESULT	ACTION TO TAKE
• Engine stalls. • Stalls in Self-Test. • Runs rough. • Misses.	• Always Rich Lean ►	GO to Pinpoint Test Step S1. • GO to Pinpoint Test Step DF20. • GO to Pinpoint Test Step KE1. • Poor power/ground connections. • Ignition system distributor cap, rotor, wires, coil, plugs. • Short to Ground. Go to Pinpoint Test Step J9. • Base engine valves cam timing, compression etc.
• Stumble after hot restart.		GO to Pinpoint Test Step HA20.
• "CHECK ENGINE" Light always on.		GO to Pinpoint Test Step ML1.
• "CHECK ENGINE" Light never on.		GO to Pinpoint Test Step ML5.
• Detonation/spark knock.		GO to Pinpoint Test Step DG1.
• High idle speeds on each restart may be accompanied by detonation for up to 3-5 minutes after a restart.		GO to Pinpoint Test Step DG1.
• Low engine rpm with A.C. On.		GO to Pinpoint Test Step FA20.
• Gasoline fumes under hood.		GO to Pinpoint Test Step KD1.
• Shift indicator light always On or Off.		GO to Pinpoint Test Step KL1.
• Poor performance, sluggish detonation	Boost control not functioning properly ►	GO to Pinpoint Test Step KN1.

EEC-IV Module Connector Pin Usage	2.3L EFI

MUSTANG/CAPRI

Pin	Circuit	Wire Color	Application	Abbreviations
1	38	BK-O	Keep Alive Power	KAPWR
2	810	R-LG	Brake On Off	BOO
3	330	Y-LG	Power Steering Pressure Switch	PSPS
4	11	DG-Y	Ignition Diagnostic Monitor	IDM
7	354	LG-Y	Engine Coolant Temperature	ECT
10	347	BK-Y	A.C Clutch	ACC
16	259	BK-O	Ignition Ground	IGN GND
17	657	T	Self-Test Output "CHECK ENGINE" Light	STO MIL
20	57	BK	Case Ground	CSE GND
21	264	W-LB	Idle Speed Control	ISC
22	97	T-LG	Fuel Pump	FP
23	310	Y-R	Knock Sensor	KS
24	348	LG-P	A.C Demand	ACD
25	357	LG-P	Air Charge Temperature	ACT
26	351	O-W	Reference Voltage	VREF
27	354	LG-Y	EGR Valve Position	EVP
29	94	DG-P	Heated Exhaust Gas Oxygen Sensor	HEGO
30	771	P-Y	Neutral Drive Switch (A.T Only)	NDS
30	771	P-Y	Neutral Gear Switch and Clutch Engage Switch (M.T)	NGS & CES
33	360	DG	Exhaust Gas Recirculation Vent	EGRV
36	324	Y-LG	Spark Output	SPOUT
37	361	R	Vehicle Power	VPWR
40	60	BK-LG	Power Ground	PWR GND
45	358	LG-BK	Manifold Absolute Pressure	MAP
46	359	BK-W	Signal Return	SIG RTN
47	355	DG-LG	Throttle Position Sensor	TP
48	209	W-R	Self-Test Input	STI
49	89	O	Heated Exhaust Gas Oxygen Sensor Ground	HEGOG
52	362	Y	Exhaust Gas Recirculation Control	EGRC
53	237	O-Y	Clutch Converter Override (A.T only)	CCO
54	73	O-LB	W.O.T A.C Cut Off	WAC
56	349	DB	Profile Ignition Pick-Up	PIP
57	361	R	Vehicle Power	VPWR
58	96	T-O	Injector 1 (Bank 1)	INJ 1
59	95	T-R	Injector 2 (Bank 2)	INJ 2
60	60	BK-LG	Power Ground	PWR GRD

Pin locations given for reference only. Probing 60 pin connector with DVOM probe will result in permanent damage to the pin connectors. Always probe as directed using the Breakout Box.

```
60  O O O O O O O O O 51    50 O O O O O O O O O O  41
40  O O O O O O O O O 31    30 O O O O O O O O O O  21
20  O O O O O O O O O 11    10 O O O O O O O O O O   1
```

EEC-IV Diagnostic By Symptom-Continued	2.3L EFI TURBO

SYMPTOM	RESULT	ACTION TO TAKE
• Fuel pump always runs.		GO to Pinpoint Test Step X14
• Primary fan or secondary fan always on.		GO to Pinpoint Test Step X35
• No A.C.		GO to Pinpoint Test Step X50
• No A.C cutout at WOT.		GO to Pinpoint Test Step X52
• No primary or secondary fan.		GO to Pinpoint Test Step X70

Note: Pin locations given for reference only. Probing 60 pin connector with DVOM probe can result in permanent damage to the pin connectors. Always probe as directed using Breakout Box.

Electrical Schematic	2.3L EFI TURBO

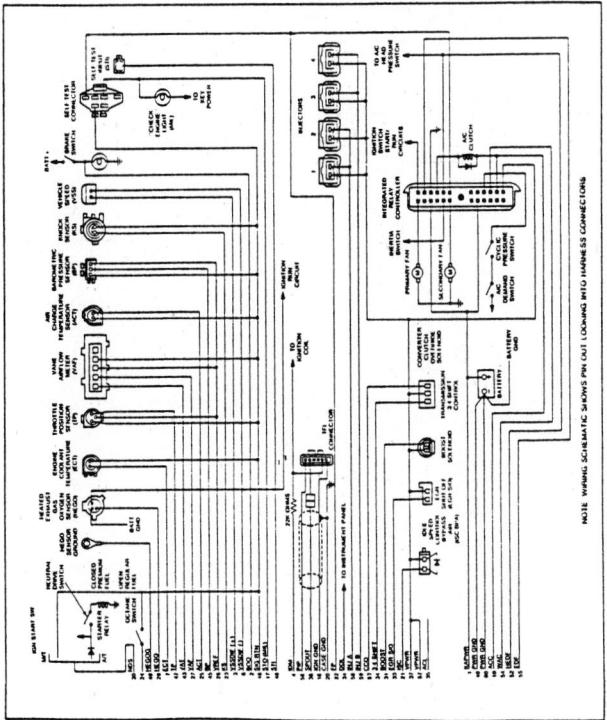

Integrated Controller Usage Pin	2.3L EFI TURBO

Pin	Circuit	Wire Color	Applications	Abbreviations
	229A	BR Y	Power to Primary Fan	PTPF
2	229B	BR Y	Power to Primary Fan	PTPF
3	374	Y	Power to Primary and Secondary Relays	PTPSR
4	37B	Y	Power to Primary and Secondary Relays	PTPSR
5	787	PK BK	Power to Fuel Pump	PTP
6	181A	BR O	Power to Secondary Fan	PTSF
7	181B	BR O	Power to Secondary Fan	PTSF
8	3°C	Y	Battery to EEC Relay	BATT
13	16C	R LG	Key Power	KEY PWR
14	197	T O	EDF Circuit (Primary)	EDF
15	60	BK LG	Power Ground	PWR GRD
16	321	GY W	A C Clutch Ground	PWR GRD
17	539	PK	HEDF Circuit (Secondary)	HEDF
18	97A	T LG	Fuel Pump Circuit	FP
21	883	PK LB	A C Cyclic Switch	ACC
22	331	R	WOT A C Cut Off Circuit	WAC
23	347B	BK Y	Power to A C	PTAC
24	361	R	Vehicle Power	VPWR

Note: Pin locations given for reference only. Probing 60 pin connector with DVOM probe can result in permanent damage to the pin connectors. Always probe as directed using Breakout Box.

Integrated Controller Schematic	2.3L EFI TURBO

EEC-IV Module Connector Pin Usage	2.3L EFI TURBO

THUNDERBIRD

Pin	Circuit	Wire Color	Application	Abbreviations
1	37	Y	Keep Alive Power	KAPWR
2	511	LG	Brake On Off	BOO
3	150	DG W	Vehicle Speed Sensor -	VSS DIF -
4		DG Y	Ignition Diagnostic Monitor	IDM
6	563	O Y	Vehicle Speed Sensor +	VSS DIF
7	354	LG Y	Engine Coolant Temperature	ECT
10	347	BK Y	A C Clutch	ACC
16	259	BK O	Ignition Ground	IGN GND
17	382	Y BK	Self-Test Output "CHECK ENGINE" Light	STO (MIL)
20	60	BK LG	Case Ground	CSE GND
21	68	O BK	Idle Speed Control	ISC
22	97	T LG	Fuel Pump Control	FP
23	310	Y R	Knock Sensor	KS
24	670	R Y	Octane Switch	OCTANE SW
25	470	P BK	Air Charge Temperature Sensor	ACT
26	351	O W	Voltage Reference	VREF
27	200	W BK	Vane Air Flow	VAF
29	94	DG P	Heated Exhaust Gas Oxygen Sensor	HEGO
30	376	BR W	Neutral Drive Switch (A T)	NDS
30	359	BK W	Neutral Gear Switch and Clutch Engage Switch (M T)	NGS and CES
31	464	BK P	Boost Control	BOOST
33	362	Y	Exhaust Gas Recirculation Shut Off	EGR S O
34	305	LB P	Data Output Link	DOL
35	836	O W	Automatic Adjustable Shock Controller	ACL
36	324	Y LG	Spark Output	SPOUT
37	361	R	Vehicle Power	VPWR
40	60	BK LG	Battery Ground	PWR GND
43	357	LG P	Vane Air Temperature	VAT
45	358	LG BK	Barometric Pressure	BP
46	359	BK W	Signal Return	SIG RTN
47	355	DG LG	Throttle Position Sensor	TP
48	209	W R	Self-Test Input	STI
49	89	O	Heated Exhaust Gas Oxygen Ground	HEGOG
52	539	P	High Electric Drive Fan	HEDF
54	331	R	W O T A C Cut-Off	WAC
55	197	T O	Electric Drive Fan	EDF
56	349	DB	Profile Ignition Pick-Up	PIP
57	361	R	Vehicle Power	VPWR
58	95	T R	Injector Bank A	INJ A
59	96	T O	Injector Bank B	INJ B
60	60	BK LG	Battery Ground	PWR GNC

Pin locations given for reference only. Probing 60 pin connector with DVOM probe will result in permanent damage to the pin connectors. Always probe as directed using the Breakout Box.

EEC-IV Diagnostic By Symptom	2.3L HSC-CFI

SYMPTOM	RESULT	ACTION TO TAKE
• Engine runs rough or misfires. • Engine stalls. • Lack of power. • Rough idle.		• GO to Pinpoint Test Step S2. • GO to Pinpoint Test Step DF20. • EGR Valve Function. • Ignition system distributor cap, rotor, wires, coil, plugs. • Base engine valves, cam timing, compression etc. • Poor power/ground connections.
• Low idle with A.C On.		• GO to Pinpoint Test Step FA20.
• Stumble after hot restart (HEGO).		• GO to Pinpoint Test Step HF20.
• Shift indicator light always on or off.		• GO to Pinpoint Test Step KL1.
• Stall during parking maneuvers.		• GO to Pinpoint Test Step FF3.
• High idle in Drive, automatic transmission only.		• Place transmission in Drive with engine Off. Test neutral drive circuit (test Pin 30) for short to ground. SERVICE as necessary. NOTE: Circuit should NOT have continuity to ground in Drive.
• Fuel pump always runs.		• GO to Pinpoint Test Step J15.
• A/C does not cutoff under WOT conditions. • No A/C.		• GO to Pinpoint Test Step KM1.

EEC-IV Module Connector Pin Usage	2.3L HSC-CFI

Pin	Circuit	Wire Color	Application	Abbreviations
1	37	Y	Keep Alive Power	KAPWR
4	11	DG Y	Ignition Diagnostic Monitor	IDM
5	20	W LB	Key Power	KPWR
7	354	LG Y	Engine Coolant Temperature Sensor	ECT
12	347	BK Y	A C Clutch Compressor Signal	ACC
18	259	BK O	Ignition Ground	IGN GND
19	201	T R	Self-Test Output Shift Indicator Light	STO SIL
20	57	BK	Case Ground	CASE GND
21	376	BR W	Idle Speed Control -	ISC -
22	238	O LB	Fuel Pump Relay	FP
24	330	Y LG	Power Steering Pressure Switch	PSPS
25	357	LG P	Air Charge Temperature Sensor	ACT
26	351	O W	Reference Voltage	VREF
27	352	BR LG	EGR Valve Position Sensor	EVP
28	265	LG W	Idle Tracking Switch	ITS
29	94	DG P	Heated Exhaust Gas Oxygen Sensor	HEGO
30	614	GY O	Neutral Drive Switch (A.T Drive)	NDS
36	324	Y LG	Spark Output	SPOUT
37	361	R	Vehicle Power	VPWR
40	60	BK LG	Power Ground	PWR GND
41	264	W LB	Idle Speed Control -	ISC -
45	358	LG-BK	Manifold Absolute Pressure Sensor	MAP
46	359	BK W	Signal Return (Ground)	SIG RTN
47	355	DG LG	Throttle Position Sensor	TP
48	209	W R	Self-Test Input	STI
49	89	O	Heated Exhaust Gas Oxygen Ground	HEGOG
52	362	Y	EGR Vacuum Regulator Solenoid	EVR
54	73	O LB	WOT A C Cutoff	WAC
56	349	DB	Profile Ignition Pick-Up	PIP
57	361	R	Vehicle Power	VPWR
58	95	T R	Fuel Injector	INJ
60	60	BK LG	Power Ground	PWR GND

* = Locations given for reference only. Probing 60 pin connector with DVOM probe
# = result in permanent damage to the pin connectors. Always probe as directed using the Breakout Box.

Electrical Schematic	2.3L HSC-CFI

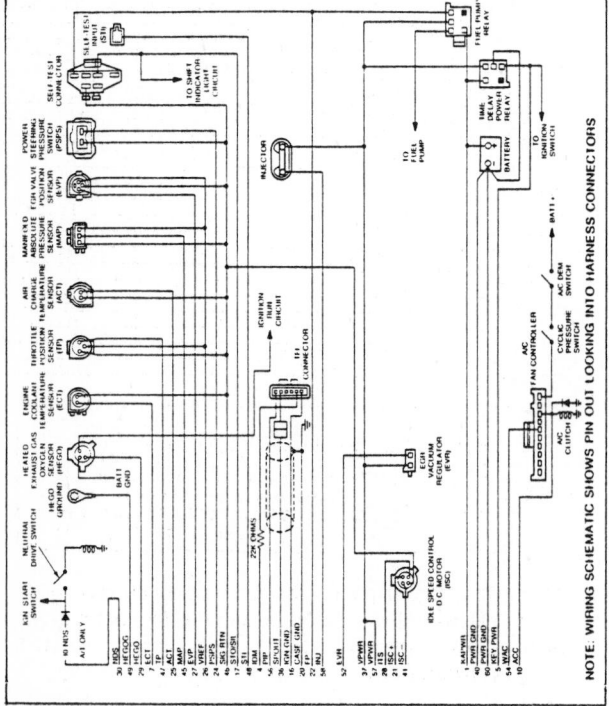

NOTE: WIRING SCHEMATIC SHOWS PIN OUT LOOKING INTO HARNESS CONNECTORS

EEC-IV Diagnostic By Symptom	2.5L CFI CLC, MTX

SYMPTOM	RESULT	ACTION TO TAKE
• Engine runs rough or miss-fires. • Engine stalls. • Lack of power. • Rough idle.		• GO to Pinpoint Test Step S2. • GO to map Pinpoint Test Step DF20. • EGR value function. • Ignition system distributor cap, rotor, wires, coil, plugs. • Base engine valves, cam timing, compression etc. • Poor power ground connections.
• Low idle with A.C On.		• Place A/C switch to A/C. • Perform KOEO Self Test • If code 67 is present GO to KF9. • If code 67 is not present GO to FA20.
• Gasoline fumes under hood.		• GO to Pinpoint Test Step KD1.
• Stalls during parking maneuvers.		• GO to Pinpoint Test Step FF3.
• High idle in Drive, automatic transmission only.		• Place transmission in Drive with engine Off. Test neutral drive circuit (test Pin 30) for short to ground. SERVICE as necessary. NOTE: Circuit should NOT have continuity to ground in Drive.
• Stumble after hot restart (HEGO).		• GO to Pinpoint Test Step HF20.

EEC-IV Diagnostic By Symptom-Continued	2.5L CFI CLC, MTX

SYMPTOM	RESULT	ACTION TO TAKE
• Shift indicator light always on or off.		• GO to Pinpoint Test Step KL1
• "CHECK ENGINE" light always on.		• GO to Pinpoint Test Step ML1
• "CHECK ENGINE" light never on.		• GO to Pinpoint Test Step ML5
• Fuel pump always runs.		• Go to Pinpoint Test X-14
• No cooling fan (MTX only).		• GO to Pinpoint Test X-40
• No engine cooling fan (CLC only). • No low speed engine cooling fan (CLC only). • No high speed engine cooling fan (CLC only).		• GO to Pinpoint Test X-20
• Low speed or high speed engine cooling fan on all the time (CLC only).		• GO to Pinpoint Test X-35
• No A/C.		• GO to Pinpoint Test X-50
• No A/C cut out at WOT.		• GO to Pinpoint Test X-52

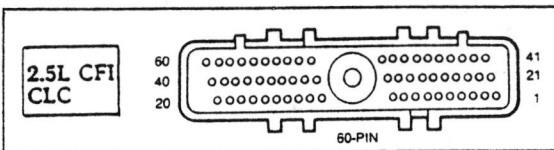

| 2.5L CFI CLC | 60 40 20 ... 41 21 1 |

60-PIN

Integrated Controller Schematic	2.5L CFI CLC

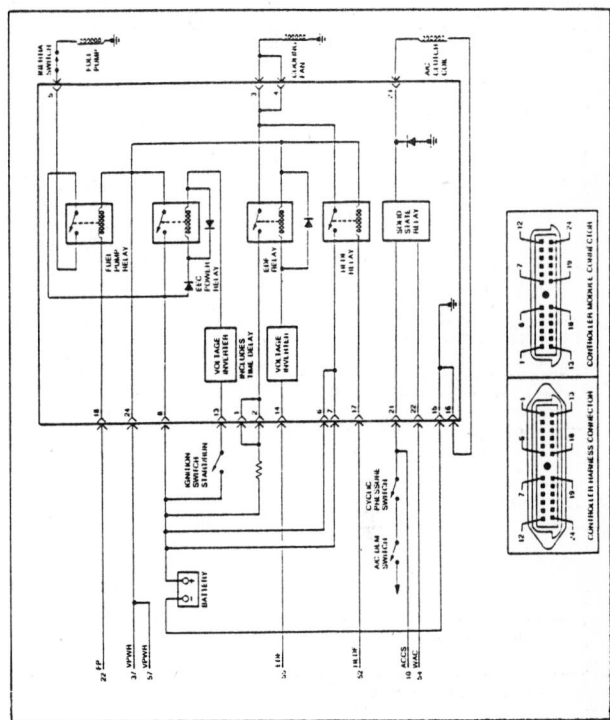

Electrical Schematic	2.5L CFI CLC

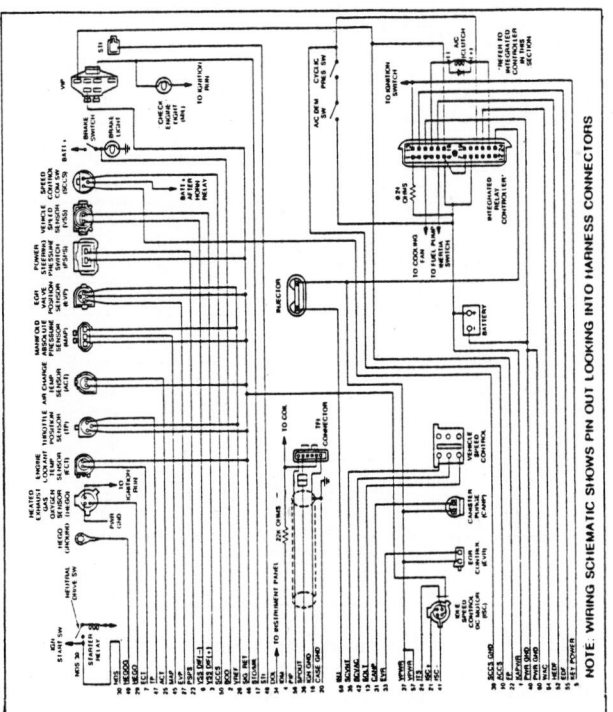

NOTE: WIRING SCHEMATIC SHOWS PIN OUT LOOKING INTO HARNESS CONNECTORS

Integrated Controller Usage Pin	2.5L CFI CLC

Pin	Circuit	Color	Application	Abbreviations
1	181	BR-O	EDF Power Into Controller	Batt -
2	181	BR-O	EDF Power Into Controller	Batt -
3	228	BR-Y	H EDF Power to Fan	PTF
4	228	BR-Y	H EDF Power to Fan	PTF
5	787	PK-BK	Power to the Pump	PTP
6	38	BK-O	HEDF Power Into Controller	Batt -
7	38	BK-O	HEDF Power Into Controller	Batt -
8	37	V	Battery Voltage (Power Relay)	Batt -
9	—	—	Not Used	—
10	—	—	Not Used	—
11	—	—	Not Used	—
12	—	—	Not Used	—
13	16	R-LG	Keypower	KPWR
14	197	T-O	EDF Ground	EDF
15	60	BK-LG	Vehicle Ground	PWR GND
16	57	BK	A C Ground	A C GND
17	639	PK	HEDF Ground	HEDF
18	97	T-LG	Fuel Pump Relay Ground	FP
19	—	—	Not Used	—
20	—	—	Not Used	—
21	883	PK-LB	A C Power In	ACCS
22	331	R	WOT A C Cutoff	WAC
23	347	BK-Y	A C Power to Clutch Coil	PTAC
24	361	R	EEC IV Power Out	VPWR

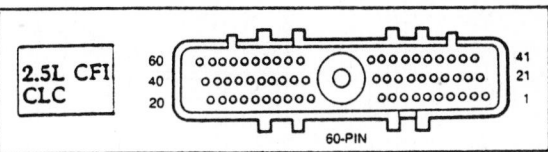

| 2.5L CFI CLC | 60 40 20 ... 41 21 1 |

60-PIN

Note: Pin locations given for reference only. Probing 60 pin connector with DVOM probe can result in permanent damage to the pin connectors. Always probe as directed using Breakout Box.

FUEL INJECTION SYSTEMS
FORD MOTOR COMPANY

EEC-IV Module Connector Pin Usage	2.5L CFI CLC

Pin	Circuit	Wire Color	Application	Abbreviations
1	37	Y	Keep Alive Power	KAPWR
2	810	R LG	Brake On Off	BOO
3	150	DG W	Vehicle Speed Sensor -	VSS DIF -
4	11	DG Y	Ignition Diagnostic Monitor	IDM
5	16	R LG	Key Power	KPWR
6	563	O Y	Vehicle Speed Sensor —	VSS DIF -
"	354	LG Y	Engine Coolant Temperature	ECT
10	883	PK LB	A C Cycling Switch	ACCS
13	144	O Y	Vehicle Speed Control Solenoid	SOL -
16	259	BK O	Ignition Ground	IGN GND
17	201	T R	Self-Test Out 'CHECK ENGINE' Light	STO MIL
20	57	BK	Case Ground	CSE GND
21	382	Y BK	Idle Speed Control (DC Motor)	ISC -
22	97	T LG	Fuel Pump	FP
23	330	Y LG	Power Steering Pressure Switch	PSPS
24	209	W R	Idle Tracking Switch	ITS
25	357	LG P	Air Charge Temperature	ACT
26	351	O W	Reference Voltage	VREF
27	352	BR LG	EGR Valve Position	EVP
29	94	DG P	Heated Exhaust Gas Oxygen (Sensor)	HEGO
30	199	LB Y	Neutral Drive Switch	NDS
31	101	GY Y	Canister Purge Solenoid	CANP
33	360	DG	EGR Vacuum Regulator (Solenoid)	EVR
34	305	LB PK	Data Output Link	DOL
35	146	W PK	Speed Control Vent (Solenoid)	SCVNT
36	324	Y LG	Spark Out	SPOUT
37	361	R	Vehicle Power	VPWR
39	461	O	Speed Control Command Switch Ground	SCCS GND
40	60	BK LG	Power Ground	PWR GND
41	37"	W	Idle Speed Control — (DC Motor)	ISC -
42	145	GY BK	Speed Control Vacuum (Solenoid)	SCVAC
45	358	LG BK	Manifold Absolute Pressure (Sensor)	MAP
46	359	BK W	Signal Return (Ground)	SIG RTN
47	355	DG LG	Throttle Position (Sensor)	TP
48	200	W BK	Self-Test Input	STI
49	89	O	Heated Exhaust Gas Oxygen (Sensor) Ground	HEGO GND
50	151	LB BK	Speed Control Command Switch	SCCS
52	639	PK	High Electric Drive Fan	HEDF
54	331	R	Wide Open Throttle (WOT) A C Cutoff	WAC
55	197	T O	Electro Drive Fan (Low)	EDF
56	349	DB	Profile Ignition Pick-up	PIP
57	361	R	Vehicle Power	VPWR
58	95	T R	Injector	INJ
60	60	BK LG	Power Ground	PWR GND

Electrical Schematic	2.5L CFI MTX

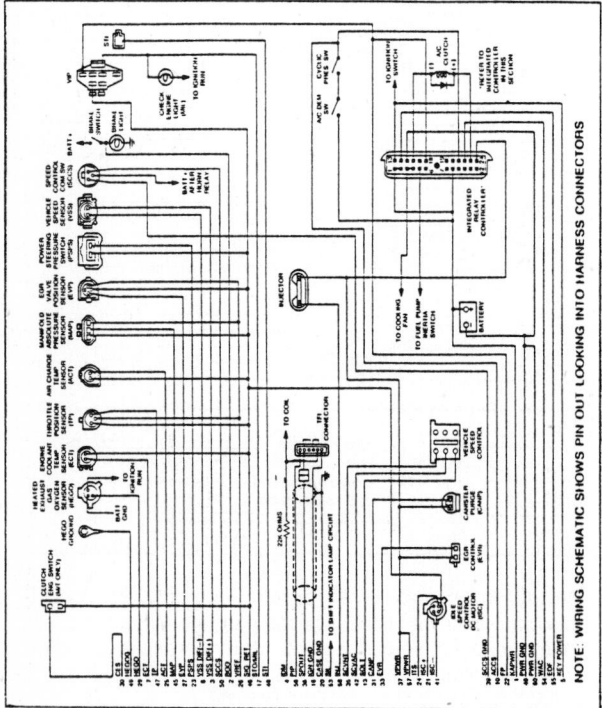

Integrated Controller Schematic	2.5L CFI MTX

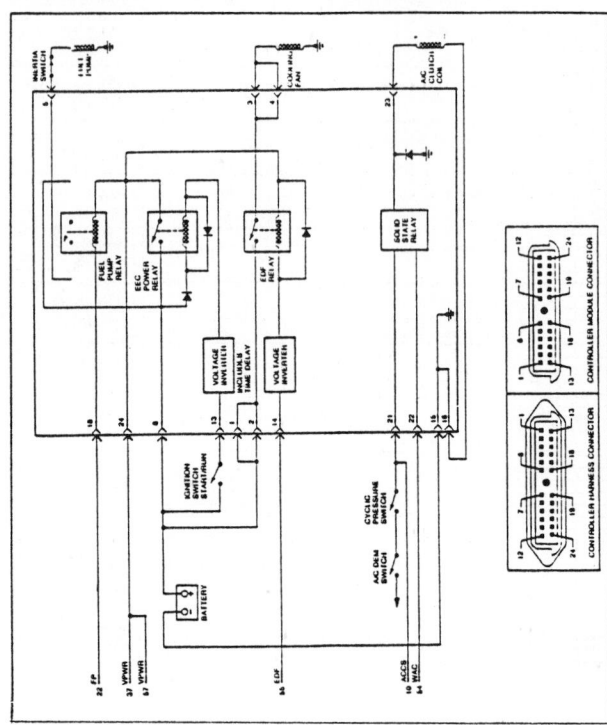

Integrated Controller Usage Pin	2.5L CFI MTX

Pin	Circuit	Color	Application	Abbreviations
1	181	BR-O	EDF Power Into Controller	Batt -
2	181	BR-O	EDF Power Into Controller	Batt -
3	228	BR-Y	H EDF Power to Fan	PTF
4	228	BR-Y	H EDF Power to Fan	PTF
5	787	PK-BK	Power to the Pump	PTP
6	—	—	Not Used	—
7	—	—	Not Used	—
8	37	Y	Battery Voltage (Power Relay)	Batt -
9	—	—	Not Used	—
10	—	—	Not Used	—
11	—	—	Not Used	—
12	—	—	Not Used	—
13	16	R-LG	Keypower	KPWR
14	197	T-O	EDF Ground	EDF
15	60	BK-LG	Vehicle Ground	PWR GND
16	57	BK	A C Ground	A C GND
17	—	—	Not Used	—
18	97	T-LG	Fuel Pump Relay Ground	FP
19	—	—	Not Used	—
20	—	—	Not Used	—
21	883	PK-LB	A C Power In	ACCS
22	331	R	WOT A C Cutoff	WAC
23	347	BK-Y	A C Power to Clutch Coil	PTAC
24	361	R	EEC IV Power Out	VPWR

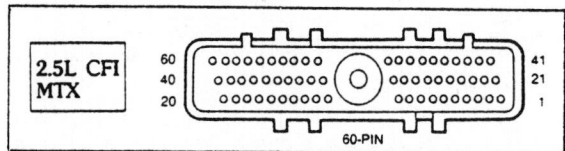

2.5L CFI MTX	60-PIN

Note: Pin locations given for reference only. Probing 60 pin connector with DVOM probe can result in permanent damage to the pin connectors. Always probe as directed using Breakout Box.

EEC-IV Module Connector Pin Usage | 2.5L CFI MTX

Pin	Circuit	Wire Color	Application	Abbreviations
1	37	Y	Keep Alive Power	KA PWR
2	510	R/LG	Brake On Off	BOO
3	150	DG/W	Vehicle Speed Sensor -	VSS DIF
4	11	DG/Y	Ignition Diagnostic Monitor	IDM
5	6	R/LG	Key Power	KPWR
6	563	GY	Vehicle Speed Sensor —	VSS DIF
7	354	LG/Y	Engine Coolant Temperature	ECT
10	383	PK/LB	A/C Cycling Switch	ACCS
13	44	GY	Vehicle Speed Control Solenoid	SOL -
16	259	BK/O	Ignition Ground	GN GND
17	201	T/R	Self-Test Out "CHECK ENGINE" Light	STO MIL
20	57	BK	Case Ground	CSE GND
21	382	Y/BK	Idle Speed Control (DC Motor)	ISC -
22	97	T/LG	Fuel Pump	FP
23	330	Y/LG	Power Steering Pressure Switch	PSPS
24	209	W/R	Idle Tracking Switch	ITS
25	357	LG/P	Air Charge Temperature	ACT
26	351	O/W	Reference Voltage	VREF
27	352	BR/LG	EGR Valve Position	EVP
29	94	DG/P	Heated Exhaust Gas Oxygen (Sensor)	HEGO
30	480	P/Y	Clutch Engage Switch	CES
31	101	GY/Y	Canister Purge Solenoid	CANP
33	360	DG	EGR Vacuum Regulator (Solenoid)	EVR
35	146	W PK	Speed Control Vent (Solenoid)	SCVNT
36	324	Y/LG	Spark Out	SPOUT
37	461	R	Vehicle Power	VPWR
38	461	O	Speed Control Command Switch Ground	SCCS GND
40	60	BK/LG	Power Ground	PWR GND
41	377	W	Idle Speed Control - (DC Motor)	ISC -
42	145	GY/BK	Speed Control Vacuum (Solenoid)	SCVAC
45	358	LG/BK	Manifold Absolute Pressure (Sensor)	MAP
46	359	BK/W	Signal Return (Ground)	SIG RTN
47	355	OG/LG	Throttle Position (Sensor)	TP
48	200	W/BK	Self-Test Input	STI
49	59	O	Heated Exhaust Gas Oxygen (Sensor) Ground	HEGO GND
50	151	LB/BK	Speed Control Command Switch	SCCS
53	462	R	Shift Indicator Light	SIL
54	331	R	Wide Open Throttle (WOT) A/C cutoff	WAC
55	197	T/O	Electro Drive Fan	EDF
56	349	OB	Probe Ignition Pick-Up	PIP
57	361	R	Vehicle Power	VPWR
58	95	T/R	Injector	INJ
60	60	BK/LG	Power Ground	PWR GND

Pin locations given for reference only. Probing 60 pin connector with DVOM probe will result in permanent damage to the pin connectors. Always probe as directed, using the Breakout Box.

EEC-IV Diagnostic By Symptom | 3.0L EFI

SYMPTOM	RESULT	ACTION TO TAKE
• Engine runs rough or miss-fires. • Engine stalls. • Rough idle.		• GO to Pinpoint Test Step S1. • GO to map Pinpoint Test Step DF20. • EGR valve function. • Ignition system distributor cap, rotor, wires, coil, plugs. • Base engine valves, cam timing, compression etc. • Fuel delivery. • Poor power ground connections.
• Detonation/spark knock.		GO to Pinpoint Test Step DG1.
• Stalls during parking maneuvers.		GO to Pinpoint Test Step FF3.
• Gasoline fumes under hood.		GO to Pinpoint Test Step KD1.
• Noise emitting from rear of vehicle with Key Off.	Fuel pump always on.	GO to Pinpoint Test Step X-14.
• No engine cooling fan. • No low speed engine cooling fan. • No high speed engine cooling fan.		GO to Pinpoint Test Step X-20.
• Low speed or high speed engine cooling fan on all the time.		GO to Pinpoint Test Step X-35.
• Stumble after hot restart (HEGO).		GO to Pinpoint Test Step HG-21.
• No A/C.		GO to Pinpoint Test Step X-50.

EEC-IV Diagnostic By Symptom-Continued | 3.0L EFI

SYMPTOM	RESULT	ACTION TO TAKE
• No A/C cut out at WOT.		GO to Pinpoint Test X-52.
• Low idle rpm during A/C On.		GO to Pinpoint Test Step FA20.
• "CHECK ENGINE" light always on.		• GO to Pinpoint Test Step ML1.
• "CHECK ENGINE" light never on.		• GO to Pinpoint Test ML5.

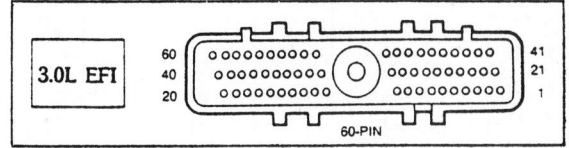

3.0L EFI — 60-PIN

Note: Pin locations given for reference only. Probing 60 pin connector with DVOM probe can result in permanent damage to the pin connectors. Always probe as directed using Breakout Box.

Electrical Schematic | 3.0L EFI

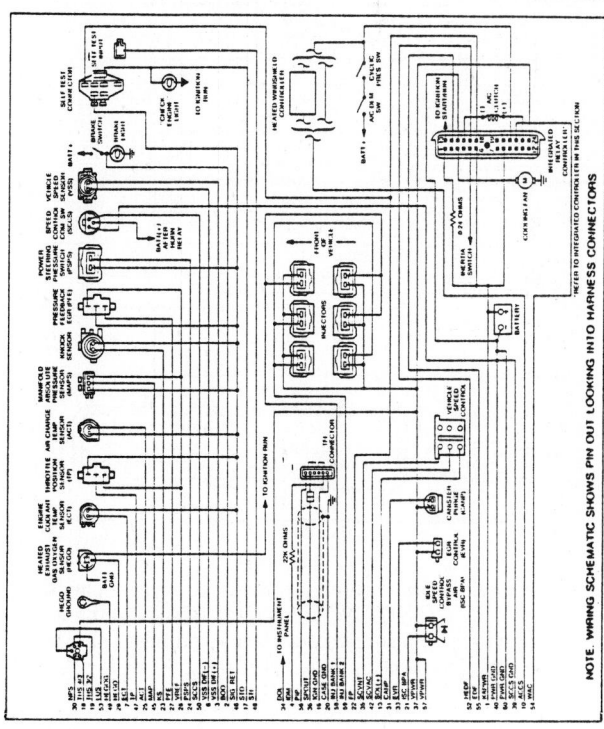

NOTE: WIRING SCHEMATIC SHOWS PIN OUT LOOKING INTO HARNESS CONNECTORS

Integrated Controller Schematic	3.0L EFI

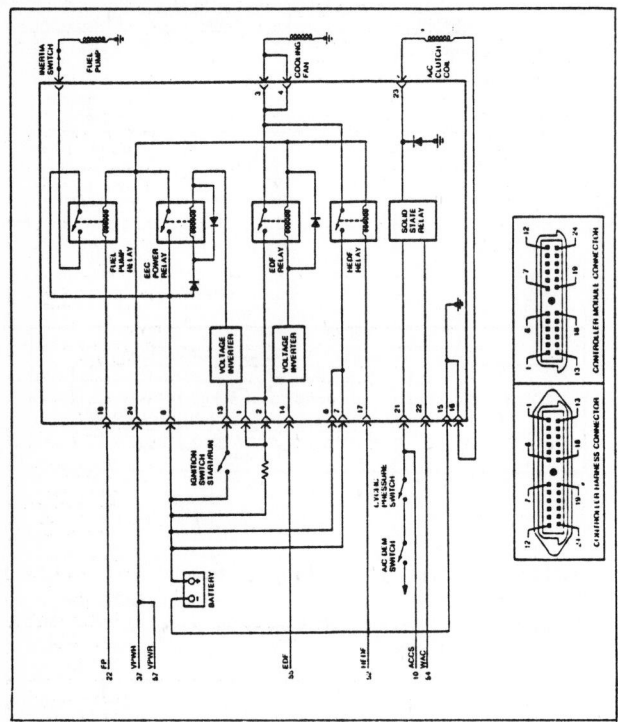

EEC-IV Module Connector Pin Usage	3.0L EFI

Pin	Circuit	Wire Color	Application	Abbreviations
1	37	Y	Keep Alive Power	KA PWR
2	810	R LG	Brake On On	BOO
3	150	DG W	Vehicle Speed Sensor +	VSS DIF +
4	11	DG Y	Ignition Diagnostic Monitor	IDM
6	563	O Y	Vehicle Speed Sensor —	VSS DIF −
7	354	LG Y	Engine Coolant Temperature	ECT
10	883	PR LB	A C Cycling Switch	ACCS
13	144	O Y	Vehicle Speed Control Solenoid	SOL −
16	259	BK O	Ignition Ground	IGN GND
17	201	T R	Self-Test Output "CHECK ENGINE" Light	STO MIL
18	315	DG P	Transmission 4/3 Switch	THS 4 3
19	237	O Y	Transmission 3 2 Switch	THS 3 2
20	57	BK	Case Ground	CSE GND
21	66	O BK	Idle Speed Control (Bypass Air)	ISC-BPA
22	97	T LG	Fuel Pump	EP
23	310	Y R	Knock Sensor	KS
24	330	Y LG	Power Steering Pressure Switch	PSPS
25	357	LG P	Air Charge Temperature	ACT
26	351	O W	Reference Voltage	VREF
27	352	BR LG	Pressure Feedback EGR	PFE
29	94	DG P	Heated Exhaust Gas Oxygen (Sensor)	HEGO
30	480	P Y	Neutral Pressure Switch	NPS
31	101	GY Y	Canister Purge Solenoid	CANP
33	360	DG	EGR Vacuum Regulator (Solenoid)	EVR
34	305	LB PK	Data Output Link	DOL
35	146	W PK	Speed Control Vent (Solenoid)	SCVNT
36	324	Y LG	Spark Output	SPOUT
37	361	R	Vehicle Power	VPWR
39	461	O	Speed Control Command Switch Ground	SCCS GND
40	60	BK LG	Power Ground	PWR GND
42	145	GY BK	Speed Control Vacuum (Solenoid)	SCVAC
45	358	LG BK	Manifold Absolute Pressure (Sensor)	MAP
46	359	BK W	Signal Return (Ground)	SIG RTN
47	355	DG LG	Throttle Position (Sensor)	TP
48	200	W BK	Self Test Input	STI
49	89	O	Heat Exhaust Gas Oxygen Sensor Ground	HEGO GND
50	151	LB BK	Speed Control Command Switch	SCCS
51	639	PK	High Electro Drive Fan	HEDF
52	224	T LB	Lock-Up Solenoid (Transmission)	LUS
54	331	R	Wide Open Throttle (WOT) A C Cutoff	WAC
55	197	T O	Electro Drive Fan (Low)	EDF
56	349	DB	Profile Ignition Pick-Up	PIP
57	361	R	Vehicle Power	VPWR
58	95	T R	Injector Bank 1	INJ 1
59	96	T O	Injector Bank 2	INJ 2
60	60	BK LG	Power Ground	PWR GND

Pin locations given for reference only. Probing 60 pin connector with DVOM probe will result in permanent damage to the pin connectors. Always probe as directed using the Breakout Box.

Integrated Controller Usage Pin	3.0L EFI

Pin	Circuit	Color	Applications	Abbreviations
1	181	BR O	Power to EDF Relay	PT EDF
2	181	BR O	Power to EDF Relay	PT EDF
3	228	BR Y	Power to Cooling Fan	PTF
4	228	BR Y	Power to Cooling Fan	PTF
5	787	PK BK	Power to Fuel Pump	PTP
6	38	BK O	Power to HEDF Relay	PT HEDF
7	38	BK O	Power to HEDF Relay	PT HEDF
8	37	Y	Battery to EEC Relay	BATT −
13	16	R LG	Key Power	KEY PWR
14	197	T O	EDF Circuit	EDF
15	60	BK LG	Power Ground	PWR GRD
16	57	BK	A C Clutch Ground	PWR GRD
17	639	PK	HEDF Circuit	HEDF
18	97	T LG	Fuel Pump	FP
21	883		A C Cyclic Switch	ACCS
22	331	R	WOT A C Cut Off	WAC
23	347	BK Y	Power to A C	PTAC
24	361	R	Vehicle Power	VPWR

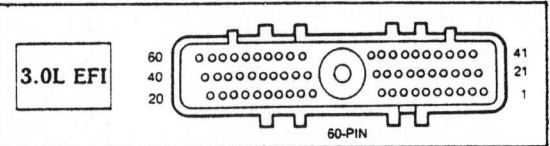

3.0L EFI	60 40 20	41 21 1

60-PIN

Note: Pin locations given for reference only. Probing 60 pin connector with DVOM probe can result in permanent damage to the pin connectors. Always probe as directed using Breakout Box.

EEC-IV Diagnostic By Symptom	3.8L CFI

SYMPTOM	RESULT	ACTION TO TAKE
• Engine runs rough or miss-fires. • Engine stalls. • Rough idle.		• GO to Pinpoint Test Step **S2**. • GO to Pinpoint Test Step **DF20**. • EGR valve function. • Ignition system distributor cap, rotor, wires, coil, plugs. • Base engine valves, cam timing, compression etc. • Fuel delivery. • Poor power ground connections.
• Detonation spark knock (Mustang Capri only).		• GO to Pinpoint Test Step **DG1**.
• Low engine rpm with A C On.		• GO to Pinpoint Test Step **FA20**. and or **KF1**
• Gasoline fumes under hood.		• GO to Pinpoint Test Step **KD1**
• Low idle on cold start-up. • High idle on hot start-up. • Engine diesels.		• GO to Pinpoint Test Step **KF16**
• High idle in Drive, automatic transmission only.		• Place transmission in Drive with engine Off. Test neutral drive circuit (test Pin 30) for short to ground. SERVICE as necessary. NOTE: Circuit should NOT have continuity to ground in Drive.
• Fuel pump always runs.		• GO to Pinpoint Test Step **J15**.
• "CHECK ENGINE" light always on.		• GO to Pinpoint Test Step **ML1**.
• "CHECK ENGINE" light never on.		• GO to Pinpoint Test Step **ML5**.

Electrical Schematic	3.8L CFI

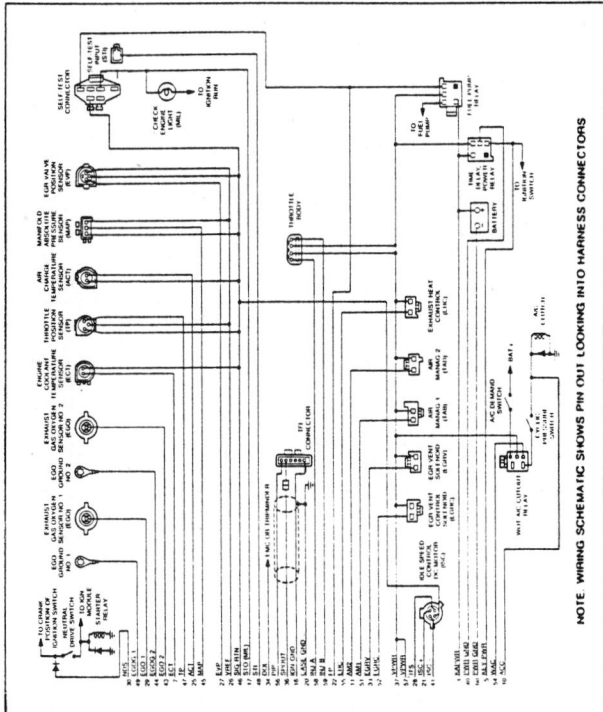

NOTE: WIRING SCHEMATIC SHOWS PIN OUT LOOKING INTO HARNESS CONNECTORS

EEC-IV Diagnostic By Symptom	5.0L SEFI

	SYMPTOM	RESULT COULD BE	ACTION TO TAKE
7.0	DIAGNOSTICS BY SYMPTOM		
•	Noise emitting from rear of vehicle with key-off.	Fuel pump always on	GO to Pinpoint Test Step J15.
•	Shift indicator light always on or. off.		GO to Pinpoint Test Step KL1.
•	Low idle rpm with A/C ON.		GO to Pinpoint Test Step FA20.
•	A.C does not cutoff during W.O.T.		GO to Pinpoint Test Step KM1.
•	Detonation and, or spark knock.	EGR valve function	GO to EGR Diagnostic Section 6 of Volume "H"
•	Engine stalls during quick test.	Idle speed control	GO to Pinpoint Test Step KE4.
•	Gasoline fumes under hood.		GO to Canister Purge Pinpoint Test Step KD1.
	• Misses. • Engine runs rough. • Engine stalls. • Lack of power. • Erratic RPM. • Surges		• Poor power ground connections. • Ignitions system distributor cap. rotor. wires. coil, plugs. • Base engine valves. cam timing. compression etc. • GO to Pinpoint Test Step S1 for ISC, MAP, EGR. and Cylinder Balance Test.
•	"CHECK ENGINE" light always on.		• GO to Pinpoint Test Step ML1.
•	"CHECK ENGINE" light never on.		• GO to Pinpoint Test Step ML5.

EEC-IV Module Connector Pin Usage	3.8L CFI

Pin	Circuit	Wire Color	Application	Abbreviations
1	38	BK O	Keep Alive Power	KAPWR
5	16	R LG	Key Power	KPWR
7	354	LG Y	Engine Coolant Temperature	ECT
10	347	BK Y	A C Clutch	ACC
11	99	LG BK	Air Management — TAD	AM2
16	259	BK O	Ignition Ground	IGN GND
17	382	Y B	Self-Test Output "CHECK ENGINE" Light	STO MIL
20	57	BK	Case Ground	CSE GND
21	382	Y BK	Idle Speed Control (T X)	ISC -
22	97	T LG	Fuel Pump	FP
25	357	LG P	Air Charge Temperature	ACT
26	351	O W	Reference Voltage	VREF
27	352	BR LG	EGR Valve Position	EVP
28	265	LG W	Idle Tracking Switch	ITS
29	94	DG P	Exhaust Gas Oxygen Sensor — Left	EGO 1(L)
30	32	R LB	Neutral Drive Switch (T X)	NDS
33	360	DG	Exhaust Gas Recirculation Vent	EGRv
34	305	LB P	Data Output Line	DOL
36	324	Y LG	Spark Output	SPOUT
37	175	BK Y	Vehicle Power (T X)	VPWR
40	60	BK LG	Battery Ground	BATT GND
41	264	W LB	Idle Speed Control	ISC -
43	90	DB LG	Exhaust Gas Oxygen Sensor — Right	EGO 2(R)
44	91	GY R	Exhaust Gas Oxygen Ground — Right	EGOG 2(R)
45	358	LG BK	Manifold Absolute Pressure (T X)	MAP
46	359	BK W	Signal Return	SIG RTN
47	355	DG LG	Throttle Position Sensor	TP
48	209	W R	Self-Test Input	STI
49	89	O	Exhaust Gas Oxygen Ground — Left	EGOG 1(L)
51	100	W R	Air Management — 1	AM1
52	362	Y	Exhaust Gas Recirculation Control	EGRC
54	73	O LB	W.O.T A.C Cut Off	WAC
55	377	W	Exhaust Heat Control	EHC
56	349	DB	Profile Ignition Pick-Up	PIP
57	175	BK Y	Vehicle Power (T X)	VPWR
58	95	T R	Injector 1	INJ 1
59	96	T O	Injector 2	INJ 2
60	60	BL LG	Battery Ground	BATT GND

Pin locations given for reference only. Probing 60 pin connector with DVOM probe will result in permanent damage to the pin connectors. Always probe as directed using the Breakout Box.

```
60 oooooooooo 51   500ooooooo 41
40 oooooooooo31    30ooooooooo
20 oooooooooo      10oooooooo  1
```

Electrical Schematic	5.0L SEFI

ALL EXCEPT 1987½ Mark VII/LINCOLN TOWN CAR CALIBRATION 8-22

FUEL INJECTION SYSTEMS
FORD MOTOR COMPANY

EEC-IV Module Connector Pin Usage | 5.0L SEFI

ALL EXCEPT 1987½ MARK VII/LINCOLN TOWN CAR CALIBRATION 8-22

Pin	Ford, Mercury, Town Car Crt.#	Wire Color	Thunderbird, Cougar Crt.#	Wire Color	Application	Abbreviations
1	37	Y	38	BK O	Keep Alive Power	KAPWR
4	11	DG Y	189	LB-PK	Ignition Diagnostic Monitor	IDM
7	354	LG Y	354	LG Y	Engine Coolant Temperature	ECT
10	683	PK LB	883	PK LB	A C Clutch Signal	ACCS
11	99	LG BK	99	LG BK	Air Management	AM2
12	557	BR Y	557	BR Y	Injector #3	INJ 3
13	558	BR LB	558	BR LB	Injector #4	INJ 4
14	559	T LB	559	T LB	Injector #5	INJ 5
15	560	LG	560	LG	Injector #6	INJ 6
16	259	BK O	259	BK O	Ignition Ground	IGN GND
17	201	T R	382	Y BK	Self-Test Output	STO
20	57	BK	57	BK	Case Ground	CASE GND
21	264	W LB	264	W LB	Idle Speed Control	ISC
22	37	T LG	97	T LG	Fuel Pump	FP
25	357	LG P	357	LG P	Air Charge Temperature Sensor	ACT
26	351	O W	351	O W	Reference Voltage	VREF
27	352	BR LG	352	BR LG	EGR Valve Position Sensor	EVP
29	94	DG P	94	DG P	Heated Exhaust Gas Oxygen Sensor	HEGO-R
30	33	W-PK	376	BR W	Neutral Drive Switch	NDS
31	101	GY Y	101	GY Y	Canister Purge	CANP
33	360	DG	360	DG	EGR Valve Regulator	EVR
34	305	LB-PK	305	LB PK	Data Output Line	DOL
36	324	Y-LG	324	Y LG	Spark Output	SPOUT
37	361	BK Y	174	BK Y	Vehicle Power	VPWR
40	60	BK LG	60	BK LG	Power Ground	PWR GND
42	561	T O	561	T O	Injector #7	INJ 7
43	90	DB LG	90	DB LG	Heated Exhaust Gas Oxygen Sensor	HEGO-L
45	358	DB LG	358	DB LG	Manifold Absolute Pressure Sensor	MAP
46	359	BK W	359	BK W	Signal Return	SIG RTN
47	355	DG LG	355	DG LG	Throttle Position Sensor	TP
48	200	W BK	209	W R	Self-Test Input	STI
49	89	O	89	O	Heated EGO Ground	HEGO GND
51	100	W R	100	W R	Air Management	AM1
52	562	LB	562	LB	Injector #8	INJ 8
54	73	O LB	73	O LB	Wide Open Throttle A-C Cut Off	WAC
56	349	DB	349	DB	Profile Ignition Pick-Up	PIP
57	361	R	175	BK Y	Vehicle Power	VPWR
58	555	T	555	T	Injector #1	INJ 1
59	556	W	556	W	Injector #2	INJ 2
60	50	BK LG	60	BK LG	Power Ground	PWR GND

Pin locations given for reference only. Probing 60 pin connector with DVOM probe will result in permanent damage to the pin connectors. Always probe as directed, using the Breakout Box.

Electrical Schematic | 5.0L SEFI

1987½ MARK VII/LINCOLN TOWN CAR CALIBRATION 8-22

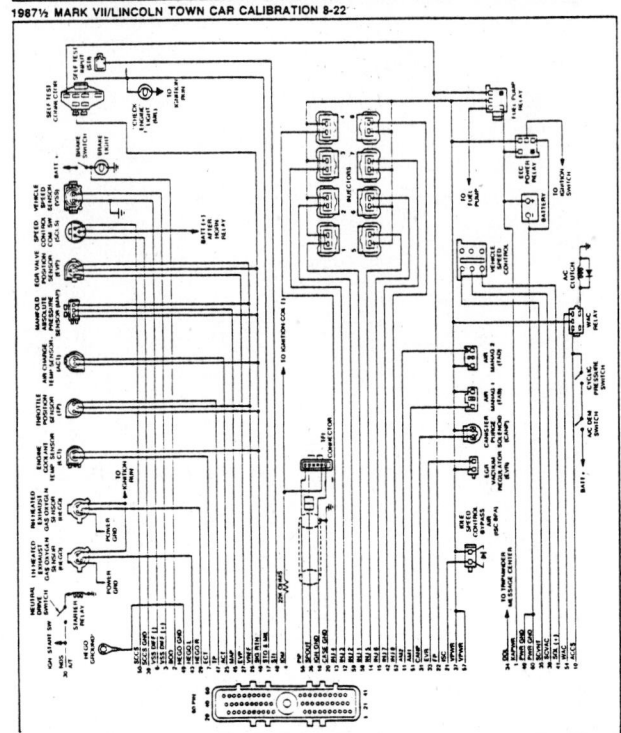

EEC-IV Module Connector Pin Usage | 5.0L SEFI

ALL EXCEPT 1987½ MARK VII/LINCOLN TOWN CAR CALIBRATION 8-22

Pin	Mark VII, Continental Crt.#	Wire Color	Mustang, Capri Crt.#	Wire Color	Application	Abbreviations
1	38	BK O	38	BK O	Keep Alive Power	KAPWR
4	11	DG Y	11	DG Y	Ignition Diagnostic Monitor	IDM
7	354	LG Y	354	LG Y	Engine Coolant Temperature	ECT
10	348	LG P	883	PK LB	A C Clutch Signal	ACCS
11	99	LG BK	99	LG BK	Air Management	AM2
12	557	BR Y	557	BR Y	Injector #3	INJ 3
13	558	BR LB	558	BR LB	Injector #4	INJ 4
14	559	T LB	559	T LB	Injector #5	INJ 5
15	560	LG	560	LG	Injector #6	INJ 6
16	259	BK O	259	BK O	Ignition Ground	IGN GND
17	382	Y BK	382	Y BK	Self-Test Output	STO
20	57	BK	57	BK	Case Ground	CASE GND
21	264	W LB	264	W LB	Idle Speed Control	ISC
22	97	T LG	97	T LG	Fuel Pump	FP
25	357	LG P	357	LG P	Air Charge Temperature	ACT
26	351	O W	351	O W	Reference Voltage	VREF
27	352	BR LG	352	BR LG	EGR Valve Position Sensor	EVP
29	94	DG P	94	DG P	Heated Exhaust Gas Oxygen Sensor	HEGO-R
30	—	—	199	LB Y	Clutch Neutral Gear Switches (M/T)	NGS and CES
30	33	W-PK	33	W PK	Neutral Drive Switch (A/T)	NDS
31	101	GY Y	101	GY Y	Canister Purge	CANP
33	360	DG	360	DG	EGR Valve Regulator	EVR
34	305	LB-PK	—	—	Data Output Line	DOL
36	324	Y-LG	324	Y LG	Spark Output	SPOUT
37	361	R	361	R	Vehicle Power	VPWR
40	60	BK LG	60	BK LG	Power Ground	PWR GND
42	561	T O	561	T O	Injector #7	INJ 7
43	90	DB LG	90	DB LG	Heated Exhaust Gas Oxygen Sensor	HEGO-L
45	356	DB LG	358	LG BK	Manifold Absolute Pressure	MAP
46	359	BW W	359	BK W	Signal Return	SIG RTN
47	355	DG LG	355	DG LG	Throttle Position Sensor	TP
48	209	W R	201	T R	Self-Test Input	STI
49	89	O	89	O	Heated EGO Ground	HEGO GND
51	100	W R	100	W R	Air Management	AM1
52	562	LB	562	LB	Injector #8	INJ 8
54	73	O LB	73	O LB	Wide Open Throttle A-C Cut Off	WAC
56	349	DB	349	DB	Profile Ignition Pick-Up	PIP
57	361	R	361	R	Vehicle Power	VPWR
58	555	T	555	T	Injector #1	INJ 1
59	556	W	556	W	Injector #2	INJ 2
60	60	BK LG	60	BK LG	Power Ground	PWR GND

Pin locations given for reference only. Probing 60 pin connector with DVOM probe will result in permanent damage to the pin connectors. Always probe as directed, using the Breakout Box.

EEC-IV Module Connector Pin Usage | 5.0L SEFI

1987½ MARK VII/LINCOLN TOWN CAR CALIBRATION 8-22

Pin	Mark VII Crt.#	Wire Color	Town Car Crt.#	Wire Color	Application	Abbreviations
1	38	BK O	37	Y	Keep Alive Power	KAPWR
2	511		511		Brake On-Off	BOO
3	150	DG W	150	DG W	Vehicle Speed Sensor +	VSS DIF +
4	11	DG Y	11	DG Y	Ignition Diagnostic Monitor	IDM
6	683	P LB	359	BK W	Vehicle Speed Sensor -	VSS DIF -
7	354	LG Y	354	LG Y	Engine Coolant Temperature	ECT
10	348	LG P	883	PK LB	A C Clutch Signal	ACCS
11	99	LG BK	99	LG BK	Air Management	AM2
12	557	BR Y	557	BR Y	Injector #3	INJ 3
13	558	BR LB	558	BR LB	Injector #4	INJ 4
14	559	T LB	559	T LB	Injector #5	INJ 5
15	560	LG	560	LG	Injector #6	INJ 6
16	259	BK O	259	BK O	Ignition Ground	IGN GND
17	382	T R	201	T R	Self-Test Output (Check Engine Light)	STO & MIL
20	57	BK	57	BK	Case Ground	CASE GND
21	264	W LB	264	W LB	Idle Speed Control	SC
22	97	T LG	97	T LG	Fuel Pump	FP
25	357	LG P	357	LG P	Air Charge Temperature	ACT
26	351	O W	351	O W	Reference Voltage	VREF
27	352	BR LG	352	BR LG	EGR Valve Position Sensor	EVP
29	94	DG P	94	DG P	Heated Exhaust Gas Oxygen Sensor	HEGO-R
30	33	W-PK	33	W PK	Neutral Drive Switch	NDS
31	101	GY Y	101	GY Y	Canister Purge	CANP
33	360	DG	360	DG	EGR Valve Regulator	EVR
34	305	LB-PK	305	LB PK	Data Output Line	DOL
35	146	W-PK	146	W PK	Speed Control Vent (Solenoid)	SCVNT
36	324	Y-LG	324	Y LG	Spark Output	SPOUT
37	361	R	361	R	Vehicle Power	VPWR
38	145	GY BK	145	GY BK	Speed Control Vacuum (Solenoid)	SCVAC
39	199	LB Y	879	GY BK	Speed Control Command Switch Ground	SCCS GND
40	60	BK LG	60	BK LG	Power Ground	PWR GND
41	144	O Y	144	O Y	Vehicle Speed Control Solenoid	SOL - +
42	561	T O	561	T O	Injector #7	INJ 7
43	90	DB LG	90	DB LG	Heated Exhaust Gas Oxygen Sensor	HEGO-L
45	356	DB LG	358	LG BK	Manifold Absolute Pressure	MAP
46	359	BK W	359	BK W	Signal Return	SIG RTN
47	355	DG LG	355	DG LG	Throttle Position Sensor	TP
48	209	W R	200	W BK	Self-Test Input	STI
49	89	O	89	O	Heated EGO Ground	HEGO GND
50	151	LB PK	151	LB PK	Speed Control Command Switch	SCCS
51	100	W R	100	W R	Air Management	AM1
52	562	LB	562	LB	Injector #8	INJ 8
54	73	O LB	73	O LB	Wide Open Throttle A-C Cut Off	WAC
56	349	DB	349	DB	Profile Ignition Pick-Up	PIP
57	361	R	361	R	Vehicle Power	VPWR
58	555	T	555	T	Injector #1	INJ 1
59	556	W	556	W	Injector #2	INJ 2
60	60	BK LG	60	BK LG	Power Ground	PWR GND

Pin locations given for reference only. Probing 60 pin connector with DVOM probe will result in permanent damage to the pin connectors. Always probe as directed, using the Breakout Box.

EEC-IV Diagnostic By Symptom — 2.3L EFI

SYMPTOM	RESULT	ACTION TO TAKE
• Engine stalls. • Stalls in Self-Test. • Runs rough. • Misses. • Always rich/lean.		• GO to Pinpoint Test Step [S1]. • Map test. GO to Pinpoint Test Step [DF20]. • Idle speed control. GO to Pinpoint Test Step [KE1]. • Poor power/ground connections. • Ignition system distributor cap. rotor. wires. coil. plugs. • Base engine valves. cam timing. compression etc.
• Detonation/spark knock.		GO to Pinpoint Test Step [DG1] .or EGR Diagnostic Section 5 of Volume H
• A/C compressor runs continuously.		GO to Pinpoint Test Step [FA4].
• Low idle during A/C On.		GO to Pinpoint Test Step [FA20].
• Shift indicator light always On or Off.		GO to Pinpoint Test Step [KL1].
• A/C does not cut-off under WOT conditions. • A/C not functioning.		GO to Pinpoint Test Step [KM1].
• Surges with A/C on at idle.		GO to Pinpoint Test Step [KM20].
• Stumble after hot re-start (HEGO).		GO to Pinpoint Test Step [HE21].
• Stalls during parking maneuvers.		GO to Pinpoint Test Step [FF3].
• Fuel pump runs with Key Off.		GO to Pinpoint Test Step [J15].

Electrical Schematic — 2.3L EFI

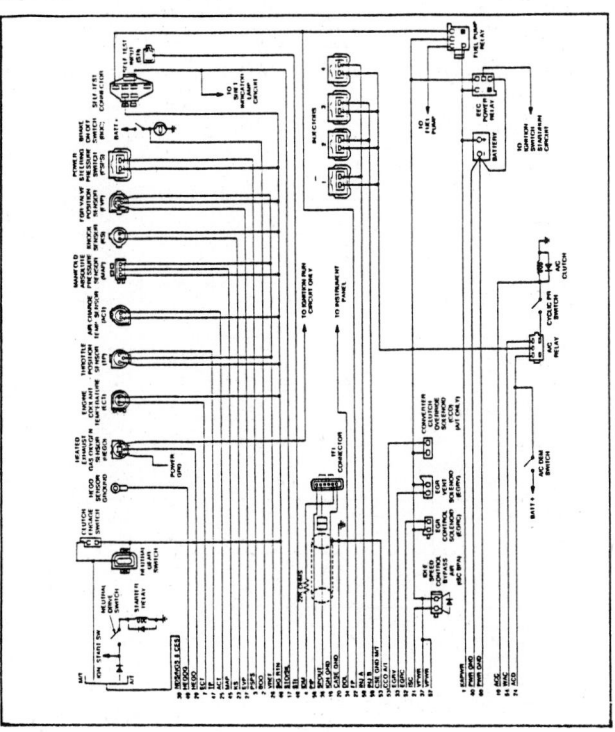

EEC-IV Module Connector Pin Usage — 2.3L EFI

RANGER/BRONCO II

Pin	Circuit	Wire Color	Application	Abbreviations
1	37	Y	Keep Alive Power	KAPWR
2	511	LG	Brake On/Off	BOO
3	330	Y-LG	Power Steering Pressure Switch	PSPS
4	11	DG-Y	Ignition Diagnostic Monitor	IDM
7	354	LG-Y	Engine Coolant Temperature	ECT
10	347	BK-Y	A C Clutch	ACC
16	57	BK	Ignition Ground	IGN GND
17	201	T-R	Self-Test Output/Shift Indicator Light	STO/SIL
20	57	BK	Case Ground	CSE GND
21	67	GY-W	Idle Speed Control	ISC
22	97	T-LG	Fuel Pump	FP
23	99	LG-BK	Knock Sensor	KS
24	348	LG-P	A C Demand	ACD
25	310	Y-R	Air Charge Temperature	ACT
26	351	O-W	Reference Voltage	VREF
27	352	BR-LG	EGR Valve Position	EVP
29	94	DG-P	Heated Exhaust Gas Oxygen Sensor	HEGO
30	150	DG-W	Neutral Drive Switch (A/T)	NDS
30	200	W-BK	Neutral Gear Switch and Clutch Engage Switch (M/T)	NGS/CES
33	360	DG	Exhaust Gas Recirculation Vent	EGRV
36	324	Y-LG	Spark Output	SPOUT
37	361	R	Vehicle Power	VPWR
40	60	BK-LG	Power Ground	PWR GND
45	356	DB-LG	Manifold Absolute Pressure	MAP
46	359	BK-W	Signal Return	SIG RTN
47	355	DG-LG	Throttle Position Sensor	TP
48	100	W-R	Self-Test Input	STI
49	89	O	Heated Exhaust Gas Oxygen Sensor Ground	HEGOG
52	362	Y	Exhaust Gas Recirculation Control	EGRC
53	237	O-Y	Clutch Converter Override (A/T only)	CCO
54	331	R	W.O.T. A/C Cut-Off	WAC
56	349	DB	Profile Ignition Pick-Up	PIP
57	361	R	Vehicle Power	VPWR
58	96	T-O	Injector 1 (Bank 1)	INJ 1
59	95	T-R	Injector 2 (Bank 2)	INJ 2
60	60	BK-LG	Power Ground	PWR GRD

Pin locations given for reference only. Probing 60 pin connector with DVOM probe will result in permanent damage to the pin connectors. Always probe as directed. using the Breakout Box.

EEC-IV Module Connector Pin Usage — 2.3L EFI

AEROSTAR

Pin	Circuit	Wire Color	Application	Abbreviations
1	37	Y	Keep Alive Power	KAPWR
2	810	R-LG	Brake On-Off	BOO
3	330	Y-LG	Power Steering Pressure Switch	PSPS
4	11	DG-Y	Ignition Diagnostic Monitor	IDM
7	354	LG-Y	Engine Coolant Temperature	ECT
10	347	BK-Y	A C Clutch	ACC
16	259	BK-O	Ignition Ground	IGN GND
17	201	T-R	Self-Test Output Shift Indicator Light	STO SIL
20	57	BK	Case Ground	CSE GND
21	67	GY-W	Idle Speed Control	ISC
22	97	T-LG	Fuel Pump	FP
23	99	LG-BK	Knock Sensor	KS
24	348	LG-P	A C Demand	ACD
25	357	LG-P	Air Charge Temperature	ACT
26	351	O-W	Reference Voltage	VREF
27	352	BR-LG	EGR Valve Position	EVP
29	94	DG-P	Heated Exhaust Gas Oxygen Sensor	HEGO
30	150	DG-W	Neutral Drive Switch (A/T)	NDS
30	200	W-BK	Neutral Gear Switch and Clutch Engage Switch (M/T)	NGS CES
33	360	DG	Exhaust Gas Recirculation Vent	EGRV
34	305	LB-PK	Data Output Link	DOL
36	324	Y-LG	Spark Output	SPOUT
37	361	R	Vehicle Power	VPWR
40	60	BK-LG	Power Ground	PWR GND
45	356	DB-LG	Manifold Absolute Pressure	MAP
46	359	BK-W	Signal Return	SIG RTN
47	355	DG-LG	Throttle Position Sensor	TP
48	100	W-R	Self-Test Input	STI
49	89	O	Heated Exhaust Gas Oxygen Sensor Ground	HEGOG
52	362	Y	Exhaust Gas Recirculation Control	EGRC
53	237	O-Y	Clutch Converter Override (A/T only)	CCO
53	48	Uninsulated	Case Ground (M/T)	CSE GND
54	331	R	W.O.T. A/C Cut-Off	WAC
56	349	DB	Profile Ignition Pick-Up	PIP
57	361	R	Vehicle Power	VPWR
58	96	T-O	Injector 1 (Bank 1)	INJ 1
59	95	T-R	Injector 2 (Bank 2)	INJ 2
60	60	BK-LG	Power Ground	PWR GRD

Pin locations given for reference only. Probing 60 pin connector with DVOM probe will result in permanent damage to the pin connectors. Always probe as directed. using the Breakout Box.

EEC-IV Diagnostic By Symptom | 2.9L EFI

SYMPTOM	RESULT	ACTION TO TAKE
• Engine stalls. • Stalls in Self-Test. • Runs rough. • Misses.	Always rich/lean.	▶ GO to Pinpoint Test Step S1. • Map test GO to Pinpoint Test Step DF-20. • Poor power/ground connections. • Ignition system distributor cap, rotor, wires, coil, plugs. • Base engine valves cam timing, compression etc.
• Detonation/spark knock.		GO to Pinpoint Test Step DG1.
• Low idle rpm with A/C On.		GO to Pinpoint Test Step FA20.
• A/C does not cut-off under WOT conditions. • A/C not functioning.		GO to Pinpoint Test Step KM1.
• Stumble after hot re-start (HEGO).		GO to Pinpoint Test Step HG21.
• Stalls during parking maneuvers.		GO to Pinpoint Test Step FF3.
• Fuel pump runs with Key Off.		GO to Pinpoint Test Step J15.

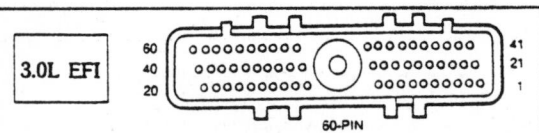

3.0L EFI

60 40 20   41 21 1

60-PIN

Electrical Schematic | 2.9L EFI

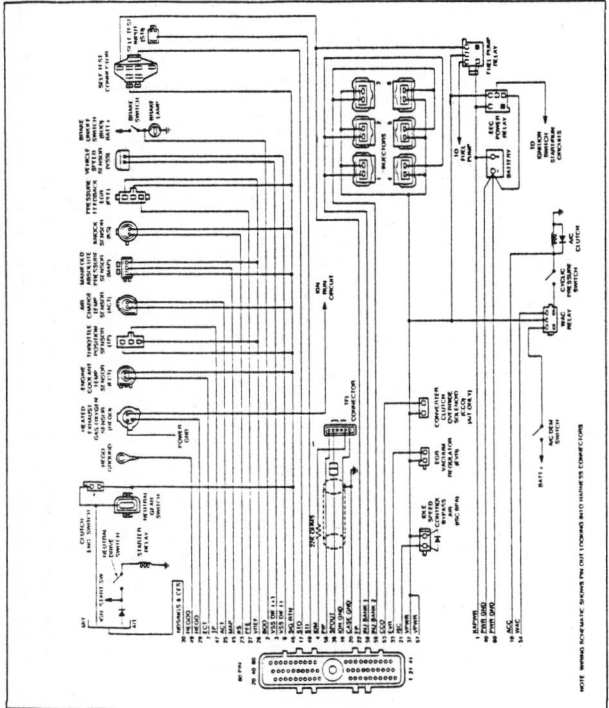

EEC-IV Module Connector PIN Usage | 2.9L EFI

Pin	Circuit	Wire Color	Application	Abbreviations
1	37	Y	Keep Alive Power	KAPWR
2	511	LG	Brake On-Off	BOO
3	150	DG/W	Vehicle Speed Sensor –	VSS DIF –
4	11	DG/Y	Ignition Diagnostic Monitor	IDM
6	397	BK/W	Vehicle Speed Sensor –	VSS DIF –
7	354	LG/Y	Engine Coolant Temp. Sensor	ECT
10	347	BK/Y	A/C Clutch	ACC
16	57	BK	Ignition Ground	IGN GND
17	201	T/R	Self-Test Output	STO
20	60	B/LG	Case Ground	CASE GND
21	67	GY/W	Idle Speed Control	ISC
22	97	T/LG	Fuel Pump	FP
23	310	Y/R	Knock Sensor	KS
25	357	LG/P	Air Charge Temp. Sensor	ACT
26	351	O/W	Reference Voltage	VREF
27	352	BR/LG	Pressure Feedback Electronic Sensor (EGR)	PFE
29	94	DG/P	Heated Exhaust Gas Oxygen Sensor	HEGO
30	33	W/PK	Neutral Drive Switch (A/T Only)	NDS
30	200	W/BK	Neutral Gear Switch and Clutch Engage Switch (M/T)	NGS/CES
33	362	Y	EGR Vacuum Regulator	EVR
36	324	Y/LG	Spark Output	SPOUT
37	361	R	Vehicle Power	VPWR
40	60	BK/LG	Power Ground	PWR GND
45	356	DB LG	Manifold Absolute Pressure Sensor	MAP
46	359	BK/W	Signal Return	SIG RTN
47	355	DG/LG	Throttle Position Sensor	TP
48	100	W/R	Self-Test Input	ST
49	89	O	Heated Exhaust Gas Oxygen Sensor Ground	HEGOG
53	237	O/Y	Clutch Converter Override (Not used on M/T)	CCO
54	331	R	W/C T A/C Cut-Off	WAC
56	349	DB	Profile Ignition Pick-up	PIP
57	361	R	Vehicle Power	VPWR
58	265	LG/W	Injector Bank 1 (Controls Engine Cylinder Numbers 1, 2 and 4)	INJ 1
59	95	T/R	Injector Bank 2 (Controls Engine Cylinder Numbers 3, 5 and 6)	INJ 2
60	60	BK/LG	Power Ground	PWR GND

Pin locations given for reference only. Probing 60 pin connector with DVOM probe will result in permanent damage to the pin connectors. Always probe as directed using the Breakout Box.

60 40 20   51 31 11   500 300 100   41 21 1

EEC-IV Diagnostic By Symptom | 3.0L EFI

SYMPTOM	RESULT	ACTION TO TAKE
• Engine stalls. • Stalls in Self-Test. • Runs rough. • Misses.	Always rich/lean.	▶ GO to Pinpoint Test Step S1. • Map test GO to Pinpoint Test Step DF-20. • Poor power/ground connections. • Ignition system distributor cap, rotor, wires, coil, plugs. • Base engine valves cam timing, compression etc.
• Detonation/spark knock.		GO to Pinpoint Test Step DG1.
• Lack of fast idle assist with A/C On.		GO to Pinpoint Test Step FA1.
• Shift indicator light always On or Off.		GO to Pinpoint Test Step KL1.
• A/C does not cut-off under WOT conditions.		GO to Pinpoint Test Step KM1.
• Stumble after hot re-start (HEGO).		GO to Pinpoint Test Step HG21.
• Stalls during parking maneuvers.		GO to Pinpoint Test Step FF3.
• Poor idle quality. • Rolling idle. • Shifts harshly. • Poor fuel economy.		GO to Pinpoint Test Step T90.
• Noise emitting from rear of vehicle with Key Off.	Fuel pump always on.	GO to Pinpoint Test Step J15.

Electrical Schematic	3.0L EFI

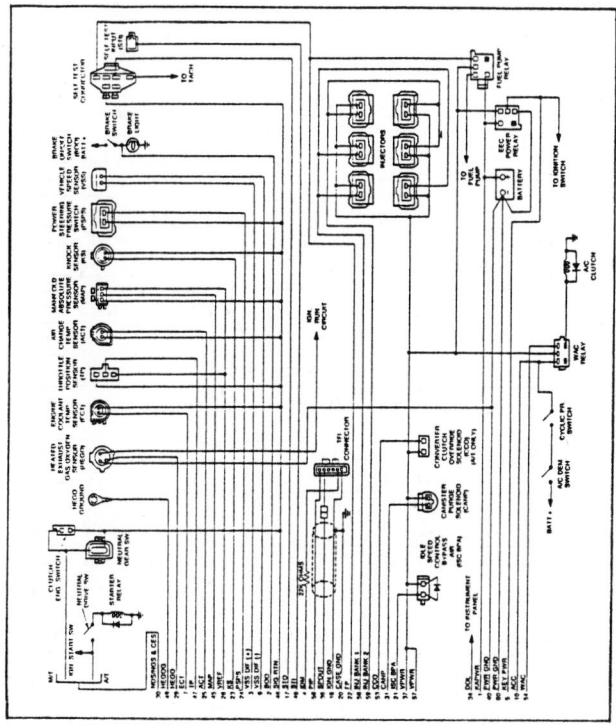

EEC-IV Diagnostic By Symptom	4.9L EFI

SYMPTOM	RESULT	ACTION TO TAKE
• Engine stalls. • Stalls in Self Test. • Runs rough. • Misses.	Always rich/lean	• GO to Pinpoint Test Step S1. • Map test. GO to Pinpoint Test Step DF20. • Idle Speed Control. GO to Pinpoint Test Step KE1. • Poor power/ground connections. • Ignition system distributor cap, rotor, wires, coil, plugs. • Base engine valves, cam timing, compression etc.
• Detonation/spark knock.		• GO to Pinpoint Test Step DG1.
• Low idle rpm with A/C On.		• GO to Pinpoint Test Step FA20.
• Shift indicator light always On or always Off.		• GO to Pinpoint Test Step KL1.
• Stumble after hot re-start (HEGO).		• GO to Pinpoint Test • Step HG21.
• Stalls during parking maneuvers.		• GO to Pinpoint Test Step FF3.
• Fuel pump runs with Key Off.		• GO to Pinpoint Test Step J15.

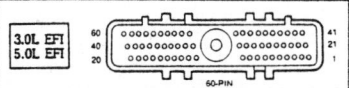

| 3.0L EFI
5.0L EFI | 60-PIN |

EEC-IV Module Connector Pin Usage	3.0L EFI

Pin	Circuit	Wire Color	Application	Abbreviations
1	37	Y	Keep Alive Power	KAPWR
2	810	R LG	Brake On-Off	BOO
3	150	DG W	Vehicle Speed Sensor Differential Positive	VSSDIF +
4	11	DG Y	Ignition Diagnostic Monitor	IDM
6	397	BK W	Vehicle Speed Sensor Differential Negative	VSSDIF −
7	354	LG Y	Engine Coolant Temperature Sensor	ECT
10	347	BK Y	A C Cycling Pressure Switch	ACCS
16	259	BK O	Ignition Ground	IGN GND
17	201	T R	Self-Test Output	STO
20	57	BK	Case Ground	CASE GND
21	58	O BK	Idle Speed Control (Bypass Air)	ISC-BPA
22	97	T LG	Fuel Pump	FP
23	310	Y R	Knock Sensor	KS
24	330	Y LG	Power Steering Pressure Switch	PSPS
25	357	LG P	Air Charge Temperature Sensor	ACT
26	351	O W	Reference Voltage	VREF
29	94	DG P	Heated Exhaust Gas Oxygen Sensor	HEGO
30	200	W BK	Neutral Gear Switch and Clutch Engage Switch M T	NGS and CES
30	151	LB BK	Neutral Drive Switch A T Only	NDS
31	101	GY Y	Canister Purge	CANP
34	305	LB P	Data Output Link	DOL
36	324	Y-LG	Spark Output	SPOUT
37	361	R	Vehicle Power	VPWR
40	60	BK LG	Power Ground	PWR GND
45	356	DB LG	Manifold Absolute Pressure Sensor	MAP
46	359	BK W	Signal Return	SIG RTN
47	355	DG LG	Throttle Position Sensor	TP
48	100	W R	Self-Test Input	STI
49	89	O	Heated Exhaust Gas Oxygen Sensor Ground	HEGO GND
53	237	O Y	Converter Clutch Override (Not used on M T)	CCD
54	331	P	W O T A C Cut-Off	WAC
56	349	DB	Profile Ignition Pick-up	PIP
57	361	R	Vehicle Power	VPWR
58	96	T O	Injector Bank 1	INJ 1
59	95	T R	Injector Bank 2	INJ 2
60	60	BL LG	Power Ground	PWR GND

Pin locations given for reference only. Probing 60 pin connector with DVOM probe will result in permanent damage to the pin connectors. Always probe as directed using the Breakout Box.

Electrical Schematic	4.9L EFI

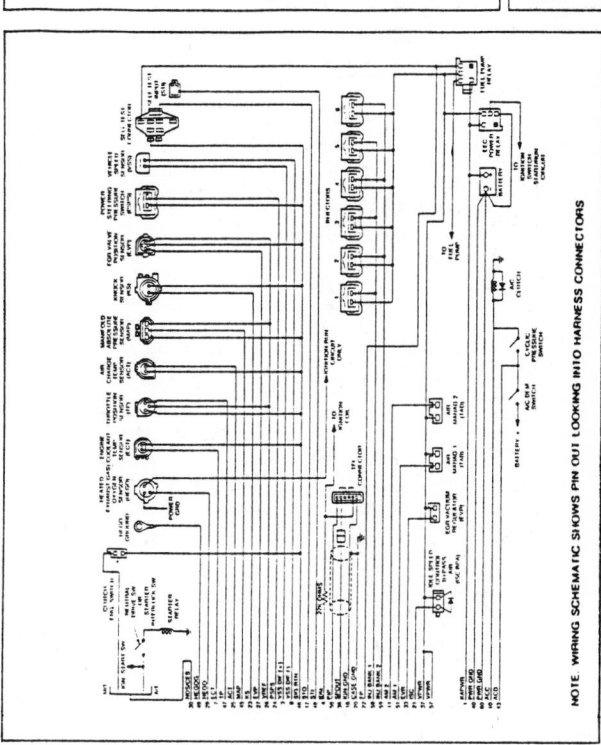

NOTE: WIRING SCHEMATIC SHOWS PIN OUT LOOKING INTO HARNESS CONNECTORS

EEC-IV Module Connector Pin Usage	4.9L EFI

ECONOLINE

Pin	Circuit	Wire Color	Application	Abbreviations
1	37	BK/Y	Keep Alive Power	KAPWR
3	145	BK	Vehicle Speed Sensor –	VSS DIF –
4	11	BK/Y	Ignition Diagnostic Module	IDM
6	146	BK	Vehicle Speed Sensor –	VSS DIF –
7	354	GR/Y	Engine Coolant Temperature Sensor	ECT
10	347	BK	A/C Clutch	ACC
11	200	BL	Air Management 2 (TAD)	AM2
16	259	BK/R	Ignition Ground	IGN GND
17	201	BL/Y	Self-Test Output	STO
20	57	BK	Case Ground	CASE GND
21	264	BL	Idle Speed Control — Bypass Air	ISC – BPA
22	97	O	Fuel Pump	FP
23	99	BK	Knock Sensor	KS
24	330	Y/G	Power Steering Pressure Switch	PSPS
25	310	R/BK	Air Charge Temperature Sensor	ACT
26	351	R	Reference Voltage	VREF
27	352	BR/GR	EGR Valve Position Sensor	EVP
29	94	GR/P	Heated Exhaust Gas Oxygen Sensor	HEGO
30	33	Y	Neutral Drive Switch (A/T)	NDS
30	199	BK/O	Clutch Engage Switch (M/T)	CES
33	360	W/BL	EGR Vacuum Regulator (Solenoid)	EVR
36	324	Y/GR	Spark Output	SPOUT
37	361	R	Vehicle Power	VPWR
40	60	BK/W	Power Ground	PWR GND
43	348	GR/W	A/C Demand	ACD
45	356	BL/GR	Manifold Absolute Pressure	MAP
46	359	BK/W	Signal Return	SIG RTN
47	355	GR	Throttle Position Sensor	TP
48	100	BK/R	Self-Test Input	STI
49	89	O	Heated Exhaust Gas Oxygen Ground	HEGOG
51	190	Y	Air Management 1 (TAB)	AM1
56	349	BR	Profile Ignition Pick-Up	PIP
57	361	R	Vehicle Power	VPWR
58	96	O/BK	Injector Bank 1 (Controls Engine Cylinder Numbers 1, 3 and 5)	INJ BANK 1
59	95	W	Injector Bank 2 (Controls Engine Cylinder Numbers 2, 4 and 6)	INJ BANK 2
60	60	BK/W	Power Ground	PWR GND

Pin locations given for reference only. Probing 60 pin connector with DVOM probe will result in permanent damage to the pin connectors. Always probe as directed, using the Breakout Box.

EEC-IV Module Connector Pin Usage	4.9L EFI

F-SERIES/BRONCO

Pin	Circuit	Wire Color	Application	Abbreviations
1	37	Y	Keep Alive Power	KAPWR
3	150	DG/W	Vehicle Speed Sensor –	VSS DIF –
4	11	DG/Y	Ignition Diagnostic Module	IDM
6	57	BK	Vehicle Speed Sensor –	VSS DIF –
7	354	LG/Y	Engine Coolant Temperature Sensor	ECT
10	347	BK/Y	A/C Clutch	ACC
11	200	W/BK	Air Management 2 (TAD)	AM 2
16	259	BK/O	Ignition Ground	IGN GND
17	201	T/R	Self-Test Output	STO
20	57	BK	Case Ground	CASE GND
21	67	GY/W	Idle Speed Control — Bypass Air	ISC-BPA
22	97	T/LG	Fuel Pump	FS
23	99	LG/BK	Knock Sensor	KS
24	330	Y/LG	Power Steering Pressure Switch	PSPS
25	310	Y/R	Air Charge Temperature Sensor	ACT
26	350	O/W	Reference Voltage	VREF
27	352	BR/LG	EGR Valve Position Sensor	EVP
29	94	DG/P	Heated Exhaust Gas Oxygen Sensor	HEGO
30	481	GY/Y	Neutral Drive Switch	NDS
33	360	DG	EGR Vacuum Regulator (Solenoid)	EVR
36	324	Y/LG	Spark Output	SPOUT
37	361	R	Vehicle Power	VPWR
40	60	BK/LG	Power Ground	PWR GND
43	348	LG/P	A/C Demand	ACD
45	356	DB/LG	Manifold Absolute Pressure	MAP
46	359	BK/W	Signal Return	SIG RTN
47	355	DG/LB	Throttle Position Sensor	TP
48	100	W/R	Self-Test Input	STI
49	89	O	Heated Exhaust Gas Oxygen Ground	HEGOG
51	190	W/R	Air Management 1	AM 1
56	349	DB	Profile Ignition Pick-Up	PIP
57	361	R	Vehicle Power	VPWR
58	96	T/O	Injector Bank 1 (Controls Engine Cylinder Numbers 1, 3 and 5)	INJ BANK 1
59	95	T/R	Injector Bank 2 (Controls Engine Cylinder Numbers 2, 4 and 6)	INJ BANK 2
60	60	BK/LG	Power Ground	PWR GND

Pin locations given for reference only. Probing 60 pin connector with DVOM probe will result in permanent damage to the pin connectors. Always probe as directed, using the Breakout Box.

EEC-IV Diagnostic By Symptom	5.0L EFI

SYMPTOM	RESULT	ACTION TO TAKE
• Engine stalls. • Stalls in Self-Test. • Runs rough. • Misses.	Always rich/lean.	• GO to Pinpoint Test Step S1. • Map test. GO to Pinpoint Test Step DF20. • Idle Speed Control, GO to Pinpoint Test Step KE1. • Poor power/ground connections. • Ignition system distributor cap, rotor, wires, coil, plugs. • Base engine valves, cam timing, compression etc.
• Detonation/spark knock.		GO to Pinpoint Test Step DG1.
• Low idle rpm with A/C On.		GO to Pinpoint Test Step FA20.
• Shift indicator light always On or Off.		GO to Pinpoint Test Step KL1.
• A/C does not cut-off under WOT conditions.		GO to Pinpoint Test Step KM1.
• Surges with A/C on at idle.		GO to Pinpoint Test Step KM20.
• Stumble after hot re-start (HEGO).		GO to Pinpoint Test Step HH21.
• Stalls during parking maneuvers.		GO to Pinpoint Test Step FF3.
• Fuel pump runs with Key Off.		GO to Pinpoint Test Step J15.

Electrical Schematic	5.0L EFI

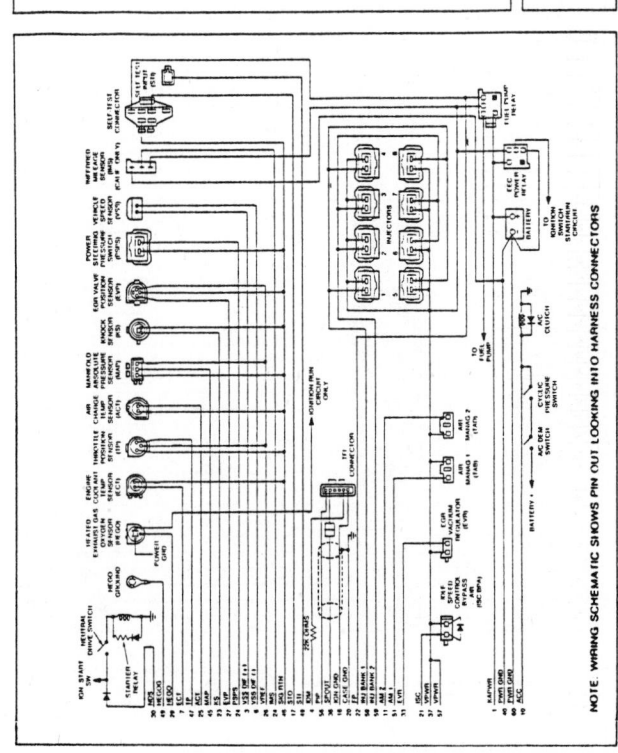

EEC-IV Module Connector Pin Usage — 5.0L EFI

F-SERIES/BRONCO

Pin	Circuit	Wire Color	Application	Abbreviations
1	37	Y	Keep Alive Power	KAPWR
3	150	DG-W	Vehicle Speed Sensor +	VSS DIF +
4	11	DG-Y	Ignition Diagnostic Monitor	IDM
6	57	BK	Vehicle Speed Sensor -	VSS DIF -
7	354	LG-Y	Engine Coolant Temperature Sensor	ECT
10	347	BK-Y	A/C Cycling Switch	ACCS
11	200	W/BK	Air Management 2 (TAD)	AM-2
16	259	BK-O	Ignition Ground	IGN GND
17	201	T-R	Self-Test Output	STO
18	223	T-LG	Inferred Mileage Sensor	IMS
20	57	BK	Case Ground	CASE GND
21	67	GY-W	Idle Speed Control — Bypass Air	ISC — BPA
22	97	T-LG	Fuel Pump	FP
23	99	LG-BK	Knock Sensor	KS
24	330	Y-LG	Power Steering Pressure Switch	PSPS
25	310	Y-R	Air Charge Temperature Sensor	ACT
26	351	O-W	Reference Voltage	VREF
27	352	BR-LG	EGR Valve Position Sensor	EVP
29	94	DG-P	Heated Exhaust Oxygen Sensor	HEGO
30	481	GY-Y	Neutral Drive Switch	NDS
33	360	DG	EGR Vacuum Regulator (Solenoid)	EVR
36	324	Y-LG	Spark Output	SPOUT
37	361	R	Vehicle Power	VPWR
40	60	BK-LG	Power Ground	PWR GND
45	356	DB-LG	Manifold Absolute Pressure	MAP
46	359	BK-W	Signal Return	SIG RTN
47	355	DG-LG	Throttle Position Sensor	TP
48	100	W-R	Self-Test Input	STI
49	89	O	Heated Exhaust Oxygen Ground	HEGOG
51	190	W-R	Air Management 1 (TAB)	AM-1
56	349	DB	Profile Ignition Pick-Up	PIP
57	361	R	Vehicle Power	VPWR
58	96	T-O	Injector Bank 1 (Controls Engine Cylinder Numbers 1, 4, 5 and 8)	INJ BANK 1
59	95	T-R	Injector Bank 2 (Controls Engine Cylinder Numbers 2, 3, 6 and 7)	INJ BANK 2
60	60	BK-LG	Power Ground	PWR GND

Pin locations given for reference only. Probing 60 pin connector with DVOM probe will result in permanent damage to the pin connectors. Always probe as directed, using the Breakout Box.

EEC-IV Module Connector Pin Usage — 5.0L EFI

ECONOLINE

Pin	Circuit	Wire Color	Application	Abbreviations
1	38	BK-R	Keep Alive Power	KAPWR
3	145	BK	Vehicle Speed Sensor -	VSS DIF -
4	11	BK-Y	Ignition Diagnostic Monitor	IDM
6	146	BK	Vehicle Speed Sensor -	VSS DIF -
7	354	GR-Y	Engine Coolant Temperature Sensor	ECT
10	347	BK	A/C Cycling Switch	ACCS
11	200	BL	Air Management 2 (TAD)	AM-2
16	57	BK	Ignition Ground	IGN GND
17	201	BL-Y	Self-Test Output	STO
20	60	BK-W	Case Ground	CASE GND
21	67	GR-W	Idle Speed Control — Bypass Air	ISC-BPA
22	97	O	Fuel Pump	FP
23	99	BK	Knock Sensor	KS
24	331	R	Power Steering Pressure Switch	PSPS
25	310	R-BK	Air Charge Temperature Sensor	ACT
26	351	R	Reference Voltage	VREF
27	352	BR-GR	EGR Valve Position Sensor	EVP
29	94	GR-P	Heated Exhaust Gas Oxygen Sensor	HEGO
30	150	R	Neutral Drive Switch	NDS
33	360	Y-BL	EGR Vacuum Regulator (Solenoid)	EVR
36	324	Y-GR	Spark Output	SPOUT
37	361	R	Vehicle Power	VPWR
40	60	BK-W	Power Ground	PWR GND
45	356	BL-GR	Manifold Absolute Pressure	MAP
46	359	BK-W	Signal Return	SIG RTN
47	355	GR	Throttle Position Sensor	TP
48	100	BK-R	Self-Test Input	STI
49	89	O	Heated Exhaust Gas Oxygen Ground	HEGOG
51	190	Y	Air Management 1 (TAB)	AM-1
56	349	BR	Profile Ignition Pick-Up	PIP
57	361	R	Vehicle Power	VPWR
58	96	O/BK	Injector Bank 1 (Controls Engine Cyl. Nos. 1, 4, 5, and 8)	INJ BANK 1
59	95	W	Injector Bank 2 (Controls Engine Cyl. Nos. 2, 3, 6, and 7)	INJ BANK 2
60	60	BK-W	Power Ground	PWR GND

Pin locations given for reference only. Probing 60 pin connector with DVOM probe will result in permanent damage to the pin connectors. Always probe as directed, using the Breakout Box.

EEC-IV Diagnostic By Symptom — 7.5L EFI

SYMPTOM	RESULT	ACTION TO TAKE
• Engine stalls. • Stalls in Self-Test. • Runs rough. • Misses.	Always rich/lean.	• GO to Pinpoint Test Step S1. • Map test, GO to Pinpoint Test Step DF20. • Idle Speed Control, GO to Pinpoint Test Step KE1. • Poor power/ground connections. • Ignition system distributor cap, rotor, wires, coil, plugs. • Ease engine valves, cam timing, compression etc.
• Low idle rpm with A/C On.		GO to Pinpoint Test Step FA20
• Shift indicator light always On or Off.		GO to Pinpoint Test Step KL1
• A/C does not cut-off under WOT conditions.		GO to Pinpoint Test Step KM1
• Surges with A/C on at idle.		GO to Pinpoint Test Step KM20
• Stumble after hot re-start (HEGO).		GO to Pinpoint Test Step HH21
• Fuel pump runs with Key Off.		GO to Pinpoint Test Step J15
• Gasoline fumes under hood.		GO to Pinpoint Test Step KD1

Electrical Schematic — 7.5L EFI

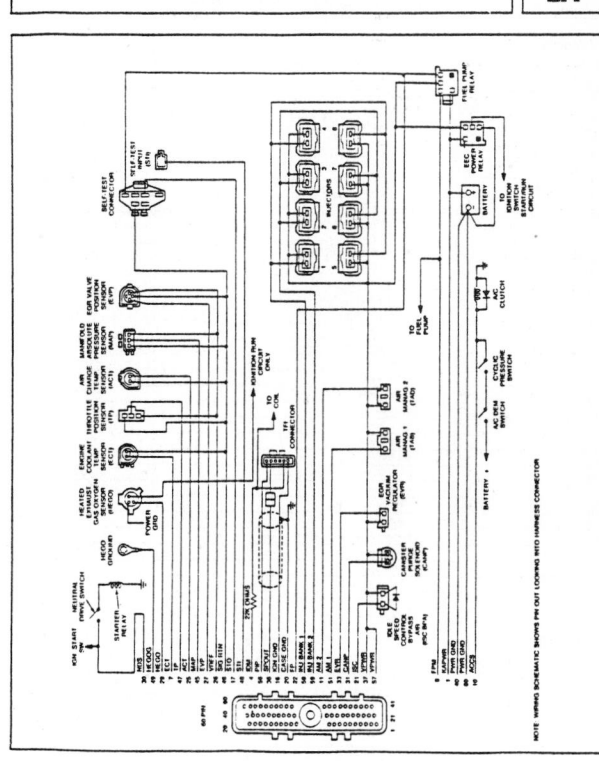

EEC-IV Module Connector Pin Usage | 7.5L EFI

F-SERIES/BRONCO

Pin	Circuit	Wire Color	Application	Abbreviations
1	37	Y	Keep Alive Power	KAPWR
4	11	DG/Y	Ignition Diagnostic Monitor	IDM
7	354	LG/Y	Engine Coolant Temperature Sensor	ECT
8	276	BR	Fuel Pump Monitor	FPM
10	347	BK/Y	A/C Cycling Switch	ACCS
11	200	W/BK	Air Management 2 (TAD)	AM-2
16	259	BK/O	Ignition Ground	IGN GND
17	201	T/R	Self-Test Output	STO
20	57	BK	Case Ground	CASE GND
21	67	GY/W	Idle Speed Control — Bypass Air	ISC — BPA
22	97	T/LG	Fuel Pump	FP
25	310	Y/R	Air Charge Temperature Sensor	ACT
26	351	O/W	Reference Voltage	VREF
27	352	BR/LG	EGR Valve Position Sensor	EVP
29	94	DG/P	Heated Exhaust Oxygen Sensor	HEGO
30	481	GY/Y	Neutral Drive Switch	NDS
31	101	GY/Y	Canister Purge	CANP
33	360	DG	EGR Vacuum Regulator (Solenoid)	EVR
36	324	Y/LG	Spark Output	SPOUT
37	361	R	Vehicle Power	VPWR
40	60	BK/LG	Power Ground	PWR GND
45	356	DB/LG	Manifold Absolute Pressure	MAP
46	359	BK/W	Signal Return	SIG RTN
47	355	DG/LG	Throttle Position Sensor	TP
48	100	W/R	Self-Test Input	STI
49	89	O	Heated Exhaust Oxygen Ground	HEGOG
51	190	W/R	Air Management 1 (TAB)	AM-1
56	349	DB	Profile Ignition Pick-Up	PIP
57	361	R	Vehicle Power	VPWR
58	96	T/O	Injector Bank 1 (Controls Engine Cylinder Numbers 1, 4, 5 and 8)	INJ BANK 1
59	95	T/R	Injector Bank 2 (Controls Engine Cylinder Numbers 2, 3, 6 and 7)	INJ BANK 2
60	60	BK/LG	Power Ground	PWR GND

Pin locations given for reference only. Probing 60 pin connector with DVOM probe will result in permanent damage to the pin connectors. Always probe as directed, using the Breakout Box.

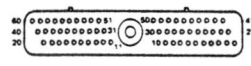

EEC-IV Module Connector Pin Usage | 7.5L EFI

ECONOLINE

Pin	Circuit	Wire Color	Application	Abbreviations
1	38	BK/R	Keep Alive Power	KAPWR
4	11	BK/Y	Ignition Diagnostic Monitor	IDM
7	354	GR/Y	Engine Coolant Temperature Sensor	ECT
8	787	R/BR	Fuel Pump Monitor	FPM
10	347	BK	A/C Cycling Switch	ACCS
11	200	BL	Air Management 2 (TAD)	AM 2
16	57	BK	Ignition Ground	IGN GND
17	201	BL/Y	Self-Test Output	STO
20	60	BK/W	Case Ground	CASE GND
21	67	GR/W	Idle Speed Control — Bypass Air	ISC-BPA
22	97	O	Fuel Pump	FP
25	310	R/BK	Air Charge Temperature Sensor	ACT
26	351	R	Reference Voltage	VREF
27	352	BR/GR	EGR Valve Position Sensor	EVP
29	94	GR/P	Heated Exhaust Gas Oxygen Sensor	HEGO
30	150	R	Neutral Drive Switch	NDS
31	101	GY	Canister Purge	CANP
33	360	Y/BL	EGR Vacuum Regulator (Solenoid)	EVR
36	324	Y/GR	Spark Output	SPOUT
37	361	R	Vehicle Power	VPWR
40	60	BK/W	Power Ground	PWR GND
45	356	BL/GR	Manifold Absolute Pressure	MAP
46	359	BK/W	Signal Return	SIG RTN
47	355	GR	Throttle Position Sensor	TP
48	100	BK/R	Self-Test Input	STI
49	89	O	Heated Exhaust Gas Oxygen Ground	HEGOG
51	190	Y	Air Management 1 (TAB)	AM 1
56	349	BR	Profile Ignition Pick-Up	PIP
57	361	R	Vehicle Power	VPWR
58	96	O/BK	Injector Bank 1 (Controls Engine Cyl. Nos. 1, 4, 5, and 8)	INJ BANK 1
59	95	W	Injector Bank 2 (Controls Engine Cyl. Nos. 2, 3, 6, and 7)	INJ BANK 2
60	60	BK/W	Power Ground	PWR GND

Pin locations given for reference only. Probing 60 pin connector with DVOM probe will result in permanent damage to the pin connectors. Always probe as directed, using the Breakout Box.

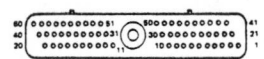

Pinpoint Tests

INSTRUCTIONS FOR USING THE PINPOINT TESTS

- Do not run any of the following Pinpoint Tests unless you are so instructed by the Quick Test. Each Pinpoint Test assumes that a fault has been detected in the system with direction to enter a specific repair routine. Doing any Pinpoint Test without direction from Quick Test may produce incorrect results and replacement of Non-Defective components.
- Correct test results for Quick Test are dependent on the proper operation of related non-EEC components/systems. It may be necessary to correct any defects in these areas before EEC will pass the Quick Test. Refer to the Diagnostic Routines, Section 2 for service.
- Do not replace any parts unless the test result indicates they should be replaced.
- When more than one service code is received, always start service with the first code received.
- Do not measure voltage or resistance at the processor or connect any test lights to it, unless otherwise specified.
- Isolate both ends of a circuit, and turn key Off whenever checking for shorts or continuity, unless specified.
- Disconnect solenoids and switches from the harness before measuring for continuity, resistance, or energizing by way of 12-volt source.
- In using the Pinpoint Tests, follow each Step in order, starting from the first Step in the appropriate test. Follow each Step until the fault is found.
- After completing any repairs to the EEC system, verify all components are properly reconnected and repeat the functional test (Retest).
- An open is defined as any resistance reading greater than 5 ohms unless otherwise specified.
- A short is defined as any resistance reading less than 10,000 ohms to ground, unless otherwise specified.

The standard Ford color abbreviations are:

BK	Black	N	Natural
BL	Blue	O	Orange
BR	Brown	PK	Pink
DB	Dark Blue	P	Purple
DG	Dark Green	R	Red
GY	Gray	T	Tan
GR	Green	W	White
LB	Light Blue	Y	Yellow
LG	Light Green		

Where two colors are shown for a wire, the first color is the basic color of the wire. The second color is the dot, hash, or stripe marking. If D or H is given, the second color is dots or hash marks. If there is no letter after the second color, the wire has a stripe.

For example:

BR/O is a brown wire with an orange stripe.

R/Y D is a red wire with yellow dots.

BK/W H is a black wire with white hash marks.

EEC-IV No Start | Pinpoint Test | A

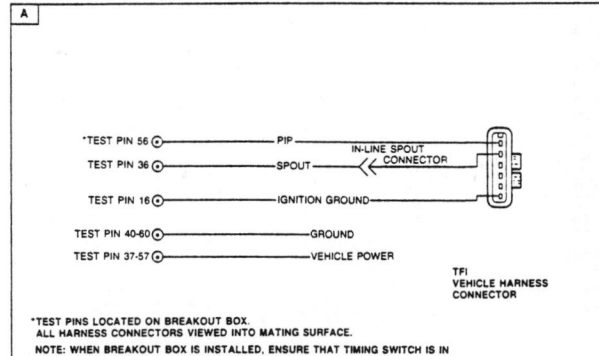

*TEST PIN 56 — PIP
TEST PIN 36 — SPOUT — IN-LINE SPOUT CONNECTOR
TEST PIN 16 — IGNITION GROUND
TEST PIN 40-60 — GROUND
TEST PIN 37-57 — VEHICLE POWER

TFI VEHICLE HARNESS CONNECTOR

*TEST PINS LOCATED ON BREAKOUT BOX.
ALL HARNESS CONNECTORS VIEWED INTO MATING SURFACE.
NOTE: WHEN BREAKOUT BOX IS INSTALLED, ENSURE THAT TIMING SWITCH IS IN "COMPUTED" POSITION UNLESS OTHERWISE NOTED.

STOP-WARNING

You should enter this Pinpoint Test only when Steps 1.0 through 3.0 have been successfully completed and the engine is still a no start, or when directed here from Pinpoint Test P. This Pinpoint Test will not diagnose ignition system problems.

To prevent the replacement of good components, be aware that the following non-EEC areas may be at fault:

- Fuel: quantity and quality
- Ignition: general condition, moisture, cracks, damage, etc.
- Engine: internal, valves, timing belt, camshaft
- Starter and battery circuit

This Pinpoint Test is intended to diagnose only the following:

- Spark (as related to EEC-IV).
- Circuits: pip, spout, ignition ground, vehicle power.

EEC-IV No Start		Pinpoint Test	A

WARNING: Stop this test at the first sign of a fuel leak and service as required.
CAUTION: No open flame — No smoking during fuel delivery checks.

TEST STEP	RESULT ▶	ACTION TO TAKE
A1 ATTEMPT TO START ENGINE		
	Engine cranks, but does not start, or stalls out ▶	GO to A2 .
	Engine does not crank ▶	REFER to Shop Manual, Group 28.
A2 CHECK FOR VREF AT THROTTLE POSITION SENSOR		
• Key Off, wait 10 seconds. • DVOM on 20V scale. • Disconnect TP sensor. • Key On, Engine Off. • Measure voltage at the TP vehicle harness connector between VREF and signal return. NOTE: Refer to electrical schematic in appropriate engine supplement section for connector pin orientation.	Less than 4.0V or greater than 6.0V ▶	GO to Pinpoint Test Step C1 .
	4.0V to 6.0V ▶	RECONNECT TP sensor. GO to A3 .
A3 CHECK FOR SPARK AT PLUGS		
• Disconnect the spark plug wire to any accessible cylinder. • Connect spark tester between spark plug wire and engine ground. • Crank engine and check for spark. • Reconnect the spark plug wire to the spark plug.	Spark ▶	GO to A13 .
	No spark ▶	GO to A4 .
A4 CHECK FOR SPARK AT COIL		
• Remove high tension coil wire from distributor and install spark tester. • Check for spark while cranking. • Reconnect high tension coil wire to distributor.	Spark ▶	REFER to Section 15, Part 2 for TFI Diagnosis for cap, rotor, wires.
	No spark ▶	GO to A5 .

EEC-IV No Start		Pinpoint Test	A

TEST STEP	RESULT ▶	ACTION TO TAKE
A5 HARNESS CHECK (IGNITION GROUND)		
• Key Off, wait 10 seconds. • Install Breakout box. Leave processor disconnected. • DVOM on 200 ohm scale. • Disconnect TFI. • Measure resistance between test Pin 16 at the Breakout box and TFI harness connector ignition ground.	Less than 5 ohms ▶	GO to A6 .
	5 ohms or greater ▶	SERVICE harness as necessary. RERUN Quick Test.
A6 ISOLATION OF PROBLEM TO SPOUT CIRCUIT		
• Breakout box installed. • Connect TFI. • Connect processor. • Timing switch to "Dist" position on Breakout box. • Attempt to start vehicle. • Does the vehicle start?	Yes ▶	GO to A10 .
	No ▶	GO to A7 .
A7 SPOUT SIGNAL CHECK		
• Breakout box installed. • Timing switch to "Computed" position on Breakout box. • DVOM on 20V scale. • Measure voltage between test Pin 36 at the Breakout box and chassis ground, during crank.	Less than 3.0V or greater than 6.0V ▶	GO to A8 .
	Between 3.0V and 6.0V ▶	EEC OK. REFER to Section 15, for TFI diagnosis.
A8 CHECK SPOUT FOR SHORTS		
• Key Off, wait 10 seconds. • Breakout box installed. • Disconnect processor. • Disconnect TFI. • DVOM on 200,000 ohm scale. • Measure resistance between test Pin 36 and test Pins 16, 20, 26, 40, 60 (short to ground), 37, 57 (short to power) and 56 (short to pip) at the Breakout box.	All readings 10,000 ohms or greater ▶	GO to A9 .
	Any reading less than 10,000 ohms ▶	SERVICE short in harness. RERUN Quick Test if vehicle does not start. GO to A9 .

EEC-IV No Start		Pinpoint Test	A

TEST STEP	RESULT ▶	ACTION TO TAKE
A9 ISOLATE SHORT(S) IN PROCESSOR		
• Key Off, wait 10 seconds. • Breakout box installed. • Reconnect processor. • TFI disconnected. • DVOM on 200 ohm scale. • Measure resistance between test Pin 36 and test Pins 37 and 57 (short to power) also, test Pins 40 and 60 (short to ground) at the Breakout box.	All readings 5.0 ohms or greater. ▶	Connect TFI. GO to A10 .
	Any reading less than 5.0 ohms ▶	REPLACE processor. RERUN Quick Test.
A10 PIP SIGNAL CHECK		
• Breakout box installed. • DVOM to 20V scale. • Measure voltage between test Pin 56 and test Pin 16 at the Breakout box. • Crank engine, record reading.	Between 3.0V and 6.0V ▶	REMOVE Breakout box. REPLACE processor. RERUN Quick Test.
	Less than 3.0V or greater than 6.0V ▶	GO to A11 .
A11 CONTINUITY OF PIP CIRCUIT CHECK		
• Breakout box installed. • Key Off, wait 10 seconds. • DVOM on 200 ohm scale. • Disconnect TFI. • Disconnect processor. • Measure resistance between test Pin 56 at the Breakout box and TFI harness connector PIP circuit.	Less than 5 ohms ▶	GO to A12 .
	5 ohms or greater ▶	SERVICE open PIP circuit. RERUN Quick Test.

EEC-IV No Start		Pinpoint Test	A

TEST STEP	RESULT ▶	ACTION TO TAKE
A12 CHECK PIP CIRCUIT FOR SHORTS		
• Breakout box installed. • Processor disconnected. • Key Off. • Disconnect TFI connector. • DVOM on 200,000 ohm scale. • Measure resistance between test Pin 56 and test Pins 16, 20, 26, 40, 60 (shorts to ground) and test Pins 37 and 57 (shorts to power) and test Pin 36 (short to spout) at the Breakout box.	Any resistance less than 10,000 ohms ▶	SERVICE PIP circuit. RERUN Quick Test.
	All resistance greater than 10,000 ohms ▶	REFER to Section 15 for TFI diagnosis.
A13 SPOUT SIGNAL VERIFICATION		
• Key Off, wait 10 seconds. • Disconnect processors 60 pin connector and inspect for damaged pins, corrosion, loose wires. Service as necessary. • Install Breakout box. • Processor connected. • DVOM on 20V scale. • Measure voltage between test Pin 36 at the Breakout box and chassis ground, during crank. • Ensure timing switch is in "Computed" position on Breakout box.	Between 3.0V and 6.0V ▶	GO to A21 .
	Less than 3.0V or greater than 6.0V ▶	GO to A10 .

EEC-IV No Start	Pinpoint Test	A

TEST STEP	RESULT ▶	ACTION TO TAKE
A21 FUEL PUMP CHECK • No smoking nearby. • Connect pressure gauge. • Note initial pressure reading. • Observe pressure gauge as you pressurize fuel system. (Turn key to RUN for 1 second, then turn key to OFF. Wait 10 seconds. Repeat 5 times.) WARNING: If fuel starts leaking, turn key OFF immediately. No smoking.	PRESSURE GAUGE READING: Increased ▶ Did not increase ▶	All EFI Go to Pinpoint Test Step S1. All CFI Go to Pinpoint Test Step S2. TURN key Off. and CONTINUE to A22.
A22 INERTIA SWITCH CHECK • Key Off. • Fuel pressure gauge installed. • Locate fuel pump inertia switch. Refer to Owner's Manual for location. • Push the button of inertia switch to reset to ON. NOTE: If switch will not reset to ON, replace inertia Switch and repeat Step A21. If switch button was on, go to Step J1, except 2.5L HSC CFI and 3.0L EFI passenger car, GO to Step X-11. • Observe pressure gauge as you pressurize fuel system. (Turn key to RUN for 1 second, then turn key to OFF. Wait 10 seconds.) Repeat 5 times.	PRESSURE GAUGE READING: Increase ▶ No increase ▶	RERUN Quick Test. • 2.3L EFI TC 2.5L HSC-CFI and 3.0L EFI passenger car go to X-11. • All others. GO to J1.

Vehicle Battery	Pinpoint Test	B

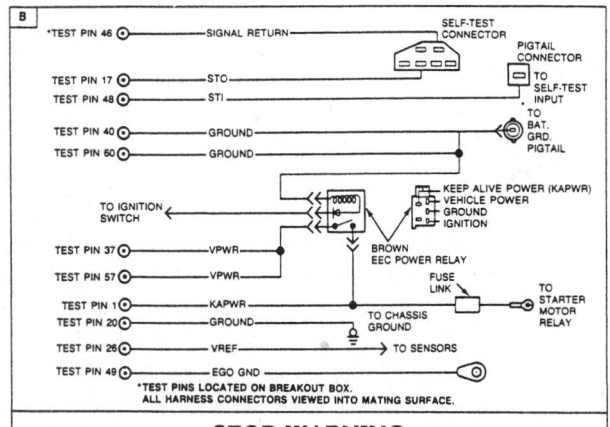

STOP-WARNING

You should enter this Pinpoint Test only when directed here from Pinpoint Tests C, J or P or when a continuous memory code 72 or 78 is received in Quick Test Step 6.0C.

To prevent the replacement of good components, be aware that the following non-EEC areas may be at fault:

• Ignition switch.
• Battery Cables.
• Alternator.
• Voltage Regulator.
• Ground Straps.

This pinpoint test is intended to diagnose only the following:

• Processor.
• Harness circuits: Signal Return, STO, STI, Ground, VPWR, KAPWR, VREF, Ignition.
• Battery Voltage.
• Power Relay.

Vehicle Battery	Pinpoint Test	B

TEST STEP	RESULT ▶	ACTION TO TAKE
B1 BATTERY VOLTAGE CHECK • Key On, Engine Off. • DVOM on 20V scale. • Measure voltage across battery terminals. • Is voltage reading 10.5 volts or greater?	Yes ▶ No ▶	GO to B2. SERVICE discharged battery. REFER to Shop Manual, Group 31.
B2 EEC GROUND TO BATTERY GROUND CHECK • Key Off, wait 10 seconds. • Install Breakout box. • Processor connected. • DVOM on 200 ohm scale. • Measure resistance between test Pin 40 and negative post of the battery and test Pin 60 and negative post of the battery. • Are both resistance readings less than 5 ohms?	Yes ▶ No ▶	GO to B3. CORRECT cause of resistance between negative side and Pin 40, or 60 of the EEC system. RERUN Quick Test.
B3 PROCESSOR GROUND FAULT ISOLATION • Breakout box installed. • Key Off, wait 10 seconds. • Processor connected. • DVOM on 200 ohm scale. • Measure resistance between test Pin 46 and test Pin 40 and between test Pin 46 and test Pin 60 both at the Breakout box. • Are both resistance readings 5 ohms or less?	Yes ▶ No ▶	GO to B4. DISCONNECT processor connector and INSPECT for corrosion, damaged pins, etc. SERVICE as necessary and RETEST. If fault is still present, REPLACE processor. RERUN Quick Test.
B4 HARNESS CHECK (SIGNAL RETURN) • Breakout box installed. • Key Off, wait 10 seconds. • Processor connected. • DVOM on 200 ohm scale. • Measure resistance between test Pin 46 at the Breakout box and Signal Return in the Self-Test connector. • Is resistance reading less than 5.0 ohms?	Yes ▶ No ▶	GO to B5. CORRECT cause of resistance in the harness Signal Return circuit. RERUN Quick Test.

Vehicle Battery	Pinpoint Test	B

TEST STEP	RESULT ▶	ACTION TO TAKE
B5 12 VOLT BATTERY POWER FAULT ISOLATION • Key On, Engine Off. • Processor connected. • DVOM on 20V scale. • Measure voltage between the battery negative post and KAPWR circuit (Test Pin 1) at EEC power relay. • Is voltage reading 10.5V or greater?	Yes ▶ No ▶	GO to B6. CHECK KAPWR and VPWR circuits for shorts to ground and KAPWR circuit from power relay to battery positive post for opens. SERVICE as necessary. RERUN Quick Test.
B6 12 VOLT BATTERY POWER FAULT ISOLATION • Key On, Engine Off. • Processor connected. • DVOM on 20V scale. • Measure voltage between the battery negative post and Ignition circuit at EEC power relay. • Is the reading 10.5 volts or greater?	Yes ▶ No ▶	GO to B7. CHECK for open in ignition switch circuits. SERVICE as necessary. RERUN Quick Test.
B7 12 VOLT BATTERY POWER FAULT ISOLATION • Key Off, wait 10 seconds. • Processor connected. • DVOM on 200 ohm scale. • Measure resistance between ground at the EEC power relay and negative post of battery. • Is the resistance reading 5 ohms or less?	Yes ▶ No ▶	GO to B8. SERVICE open or ground in Ground Circuit. RERUN Quick Test.
B8 12 VOLT BATTERY POWER FAULT ISOLATION • Key On, Engine Off. • Processor connected. • DVOM on 20V scale. • Measure voltage between the battery negative post and VPWR circuit at EEC power relay. • Is the voltage reading 10.5 volts or greater?	Yes ▶ No ▶	SERVICE open in VPWR circuit, if OK, SERVICE short to ground in VPWR circuit. REPLACE power relay. RERUN Quick Test.

Vehicle Battery		Pinpoint Test	B

TEST STEP	RESULT ▶	ACTION TO TAKE
B10 | WIGGLE TEST VPWR CIRCUITS		
• Key On, Engine Off. • STAR tester or VOM hooked up to Self-Test connector. • Self-Test deactivated. • Observe STAR/VOM for fault indication as explained in Quick Test Step 6.0D. • Shake, bend and twist the EEC-IV harness from the EEC time delay power relay to the processor. • Is a fault indicated or does code 72 or 78 reappear in continuous memory if Quick Test is rerun?	Yes ▶ No ▶	SERVICE intermittent VPWR circuit. RERUN Quick Test. INSPECT EEC-IV time delay power relay and harness connectors for damaged pins, corrosion. etc. SERVICE as necessary. If OK, REPLACE EEC-IV time delay relay. RERUN Quick Test.

Reference Voltage		Pinpoint Test	C

TEST STEP	RESULT ▶	ACTION TO TAKE
C1 | VEHICLE BATTERY POWER CIRCUIT CHECK		
• Disconnect 60 Pin connector. Inspect for damaged pins, corrosion, loose wires, etc. Service as necessary. • Breakout box installed. • Processor connected. • Key On, Engine Off. • DVOM on 20V scale. • Measure voltage between test Pin 37 at the Breakout box and Signal Return in Self-Test connector. • Is voltage 10.5 volts or greater?	Yes ▶ No ▶	GO to C2. 2.3L EFI TC. 2.5L HSC CFI and 3.0L EFI passenger car go to X-1. All others, GO to B1.
C2 | VREF VOLTAGE CHECK		
• Breakout box installed. • Key On, Engine Off. • Processor connected. • DVOM on 20V scale. • Measure voltage between test Pin 26 and test Pin 46 at the Breakout box.	6.0V or greater ▶ 4.0V or less ▶ Greater than 4.0V, less than 6.0V ▶	GO to C4. GO to C5. GO to C3.
C3 | CHECK VREF AND SIGNAL RETURN FOR CONTINUITY		
• Breakout box installed. • Processor disconnected. • Sensor that sent you here disconnected. • Key Off. • DVOM on 200 ohm scale. • Measure resistance from test Pin 26 at Breakout box to VREF at vehicle harness connector of the sensor that sent you here. • Measure resistance from test Pin 46 at Breakout box to signal return at vehicle harness connector of the sensor that sent you here. • Are both resistance readings less than 5.0 ohms?	Yes ▶ No ▶	RECONNECT sensors. Reference voltage OK. RERUN Quick Test. SERVICE open in Vref or Signal Return. RERUN Quick Test.

Reference Voltage		Pinpoint Test	C

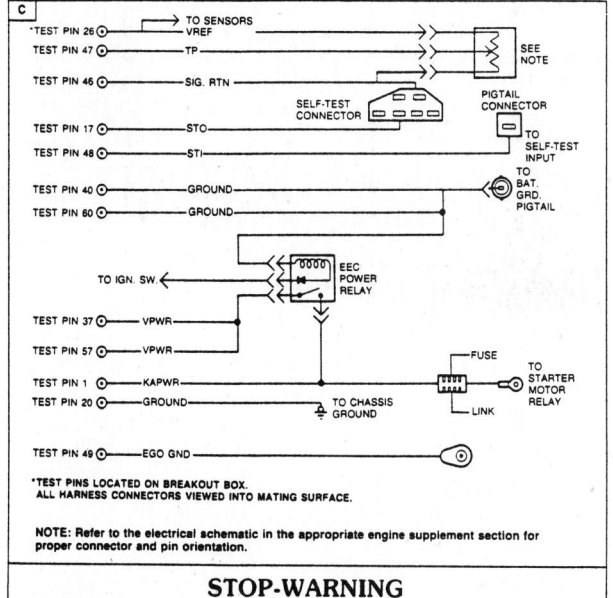

```
C
*TEST PIN 26 ⊙──── TO SENSORS
                   VREF
TEST PIN 47 ⊙──── TP
TEST PIN 45 ⊙──── SIG. RTN
                              SELF-TEST
TEST PIN 17 ⊙──── STO        CONNECTOR
TEST PIN 48 ⊙──── STI
TEST PIN 40 ⊙──── GROUND
TEST PIN 60 ⊙──── GROUND
          TO IGN. SW.
                              EEC
TEST PIN 37 ⊙──── VPWR       POWER
TEST PIN 57 ⊙──── VPWR       RELAY
TEST PIN 1 ⊙──── KAPWR
TEST PIN 20 ⊙──── GROUND
TEST PIN 49 ⊙──── EGO GND
```

SEE NOTE

PIGTAIL CONNECTOR — TO SELF-TEST INPUT

TO BAT. GRD. PIGTAIL

FUSE — TO STARTER MOTOR RELAY

LINK

TO CHASSIS GROUND

*TEST PINS LOCATED ON BREAKOUT BOX.
ALL HARNESS CONNECTORS VIEWED INTO MATING SURFACE.

NOTE: Refer to the electrical schematic in the appropriate engine supplement section for proper connector and pin orientation.

STOP-WARNING

You should enter this Pinpoint Test only when a check for Vref has failed in the sensor Pinpoint Tests (D-Series) or Pinpoint Tests A or Q.

This pinpoint test is intended to diagnose only the following:
• Processor.
• Sensor harness circuits: Signal Return, STO, STI, Ground, VPWR, KAPWR, VREF, Ignition.

Reference Voltage		Pinpoint Test	C

TEST STEP	RESULT ▶	ACTION TO TAKE
C4 | CHECK FOR SHORT FROM VREF TO VPWR		
• Key Off, wait 10 seconds. • Breakout box installed. • Disconnect processor. • Key On, Engine Off. • DVOM on 20V scale. • Measure voltage between test Pin 26 at the Breakout box and battery ground. • Is voltage less than 0.5 volts?	Yes ▶ No ▶	REPLACE processor. RERUN Quick Test. SERVICE short to battery power in EEC harness. RERUN Quick Test. If condition persists, REPLACE processor.
C5 | CHECK FOR SHORTED THROTTLE POSITION SENSOR		
• Key Off, wait 10 seconds. • Breakout box installed. • Processor connected. • Disconnect Throttle Position (TP) sensor from vehicle harness. • Key On, Engine Off. • DVOM on 20V scale. • Measure voltage between test Pin 26 and test Pin 46 at the Breakout box. • Is voltage less than 4.0 volts?	Yes ▶ No ▶	Vehicles equipped with EVP/PFE sensor, GO to C6. All other vehicles, GO to C7. REPLACE TP sensor. RERUN Quick Test.
C6 | CHECK FOR SHORTED EVP/PFE SENSOR		
• Key Off, wait 10 seconds. • Breakout box installed. • Processor connected. • Disconnect EVP/PFE sensor. • Key On, Engine Off. • DVOM on 20V scale. • Measure voltage between test Pin 26 and test Pin 46 at the Breakout box. • Is voltage less than 4.0 volts?	Yes ▶ No ▶	GO to C7. REPLACE EVP/PFE sensor. RERUN Quick Test.

| Reference Voltage | | Pinpoint Test | | C |

	TEST STEP	RESULT	▶	ACTION TO TAKE
C7	CHECK FOR SHORTED MAP/BP SENSOR			
	• Key Off, wait 10 seconds. • Breakout box installed. • Processor connected. • Disconnect MAP/BP sensor. • Key On, Engine Off. • DVOM on 20V scale. • Measure voltage between test Pin 26 and test Pin 46 at the Breakout box. • Is reading less than 4.0 volts?	Yes	▶	Vehicles equipped with VAF sensor. GO to C8 . All other vehicles. GO to C9 .
		No	▶	REPLACE MAP/BP sensor. RERUN Quick Test.
C8	CHECK FOR SHORTED VANE AIR METER (VAF) SENSOR			
	• Key Off, wait 10 seconds. • Breakout box installed. • Processor connected. • Disconnect vane air meter (VAF) sensor. • Key On, Engine Off. • DVOM on 20V scale. • Measure voltage between test Pin 26 and test Pin 46 at the Breakout box. • Is voltage less than 4.0 volts?	Yes	▶	GO to C9 .
		No	▶	REPLACE VAF sensor and RERUN Quick Test.
C9	SHORT TO GROUND IN VREF			
	• Breakout box installed. • Processor disconnected. • Key Off, wait 10 seconds. • Disconnect TP and MAP/BP, EVP/PFE and VAF, if so equipped. • DVOM on 200 ohm scale. • Measure resistance between test Pin 26 and test Pins 20, 40, 46 and 60 at the Breakout box. • Is any resistance less than 5 ohms?	Yes	▶	SERVICE short to ground. CONNECT all sensors. RERUN Quick Test. If original condition still exists, REPLACE processor.
		No	▶	RECONNECT sensors. REPLACE processor. RERUN Quick Test.

| Vane Air Temperature Sensor (VAT) | | Pinpoint Test | | DA |

	TEST STEP	RESULT	▶	ACTION TO TAKE
DA1	SERVICE CODE 28: CHECK AMBIENT TEMPERATURE			
	• Is ambient temperature greater than 50°F?	Yes	▶	GO to DA2 .
		No	▶	RERUN Quick Test.
DA2	CHECK FOR V REF AT THROTTLE POSITION SENSOR			
	• Refer to illustration Q. • Key Off, wait 10 seconds. • DVOM on 20V scale. • Disconnect TP sensor. • Key On, Engine Off. • Measure voltage at the TP vehicle harness connector between VREF and signal return. • Is voltage between 4.0 volts and 6.0 volts?	Yes	▶	RECONNECT TP sensor, GO to DA3 .
		No	▶	GO to Pinpoint Test Step C1 .
DA3	VAT SENSOR CHECK			
	NOTE: Ambient temperature must be greater than 50°F for this test. • Key Off, wait 10 seconds. • Harness disconnected from the vane meter. • DVOM on 200,000 ohm scale. • Measure resistance at the VAT sensor between VAT signal and Signal Return. • Is resistance from 125 ohms (240°F) to 3700 ohms (50°F)?	Yes	▶	REPLACE processor. RECONNECT harness to vane meter. RERUN Quick Test.
		No	▶	REPLACE vane meter. RERUN Quick Test.

| Vane Air Temperature Sensor (VAT) | | Pinpoint Test | | DA |

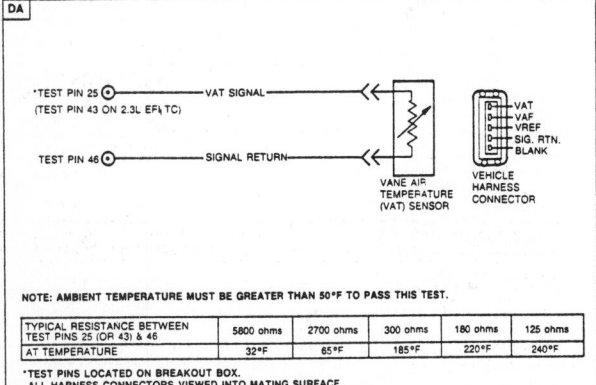

DA

*TEST PIN 25 — VAT SIGNAL
(TEST PIN 43 ON 2.3L EFI TC)

TEST PIN 46 — SIGNAL RETURN

VAT
VAF
VREF
SIG. RTN.
BLANK

VANE AIR TEMPERATURE (VAT) SENSOR

VEHICLE HARNESS CONNECTOR

NOTE: AMBIENT TEMPERATURE MUST BE GREATER THAN 50°F TO PASS THIS TEST.

TYPICAL RESISTANCE BETWEEN TEST PINS 25 (OR 43) & 46	5800 ohms	2700 ohms	300 ohms	180 ohms	125 ohms
AT TEMPERATURE	32°F	65°F	185°F	220°F	240°F

*TEST PINS LOCATED ON BREAKOUT BOX.
ALL HARNESS CONNECTORS VIEWED INTO MATING SURFACE.

STOP-WARNING

You should enter this Pinpoint Test only when a service code 28, 58 or 68 is received in Quick Test Step 3.0, 5.0 or 6.0.

To prevent the replacement of good components, be aware that the following non-EEC areas may be at fault:
• Test performed in unusually low (cold) or high (hot) ambient conditions.
• Ambient temperature greater than 50°F for this test.

This pinpoint test is intended to diagnose only the following:
• VAT sensor.
• Circuits: VAT, and Signal Return.
• Vehicle harness.
• Processor assembly.

| Vane Air Temperature Sensor (VAT) | | Pinpoint Test | | DA |

	TEST STEP	RESULT	▶	ACTION TO TAKE
DA10	SERVICE CODE 58: INDUCE OPPOSITE CODE			
	• Key Off, wait 10 seconds. • Disconnect vehicle harness from vane meter. Inspect for damaged pins, corrosion, loose wires, etc. Service as necessary. • Insert a jumper wire (paper clip) at the vane meter vehicle harness connector between VAT Signal and Signal Return. • Run Key On Engine Off Quick Test. • Is Code 68 present?	Yes	▶	REPLACE vane meter. REMOVE jumper wire. CONNECT harness to vane meter. RERUN Quick Test.
		No	▶	REMOVE jumper wire. GO to DA11 .
DA11	CHECK CONTINUITY OF VAT SIGNAL AND SIGNAL RETURN			
	• Key Off, wait 10 seconds. • Harness disconnected from vane meter, jumper wire removed. • Disconnect processor 60 pin connector. Inspect for damaged pins, corrosion, loose wires, etc. Service as necessary. • Install Breakout box leaving processor disconnected. • DVOM on 200 ohm scale. • Measure resistance between VAT signal at the vane meter vehicle harness connector, and test Pin 25 at the Breakout box. • Measure resistance between VAT signal at the vane meter vehicle harness connector, and test Pin 25 (test Pin 43 on 2.3L EFI TC) at the Breakout box. • Measure resistance between signal return at the vane meter vehicle harness connector, and test Pin 46 at the Breakout box. • Are both resistances less than 5 ohms?	Yes	▶	REPLACE processor. REMOVE Breakout box. RECONNECT harness to vane meter and processor. RERUN Quick Test.
		No	▶	CORRECT open circuit. REMOVE Breakout box. RECONNECT harness to vane meter and processor. RERUN Quick Test.

Vane Air Temperature Sensor (VAT)	Pinpoint Test	DA

TEST STEP	RESULT	▶	ACTION TO TAKE
DA20 SERVICE CODE 68: INDUCE OPPOSITE CODE			
• Key off, wait 10 seconds. • Disconnect vehicle harness from vane meter. Inspect for damaged pins, corrosion, loose wires, etc. Service as necessary. • Run Key On Engine Off Quick Test. • Is code 58 present?	Yes	▶	REPLACE vane meter. RECONNECT harness to vane meter. RERUN Quick Test.
	No	▶	GO to DA21.
DA21 CHECK FOR V REF AT THROTTLE POSITION SENSOR			
• Refer to illustration Q. • Key Off, wait 10 seconds. • DVOM on 20V scale. • Disconnect TP sensor. • Key On, Engine Off. • Measure voltage at the TP vehicle harness connector between VREF and signal return. • Is voltage between 4.0 volts and 6.0 volts?	Yes	▶	RECONNECT TP sensor, GO to DA22.
	No	▶	GO to Pinpoint Test Step C1.
DA22 CHECK VAT SIGNAL FOR SHORTS			
• Key Off, wait 10 seconds. • Harness disconnected from vane meter. • Disconnect processor 60 pin connector. Inspect for damaged pins, corrosion, loose wires, etc. Service as necessary. • Install Breakout box leaving processor disconnected. • DVOM on 200,000 ohm scale. • Measure resistance between test Pin 25 (test Pin 43 on 2.3L EFI TC) and test Pins 40, 46 and 60 at the Breakout box. • Are all resistances greater than 10,000 ohms?	Yes	▶	REPLACE processor. REMOVE Breakout box. RECONNECT processor. RERUN Quick Test.
	No	▶	CORRECT circuit shorts. REMOVE Breakout box. RECONNECT processor and vane meter. RERUN Quick Test.

Vane Air Temperature Sensor (VAT)	Pinpoint Test	DA

TEST STEP	RESULT	▶	ACTION TO TAKE
DA90 SERVICE CODE 58: CONTINUOUS TEST: CHECK VAT SENSOR			
• Using continuous monitor mode, observe VOM or STAR LED for indication of a fault while performing the following: • Lightly tap on VAT sensor (simulate road shock). • Wiggle VAT connector. • Is a fault indicated?	Yes	▶	DISCONNECT and INSPECT connectors. If connector and terminals are good, REPLACE VAT sensor. RERUN Quick Test.
	No	▶	GO to DA91.
DA91 CHECK EEC-IV HARNESS			
• Observe VOM or STAR LED for a fault indication while performing the following: • Referring to the illustration in Step DA90, grasp the harness closest to the sensor connector. Wiggle, shake or bend a small section of the EEC-IV system harness while working your way to the dash panel. Also wiggle, shake or bend the EEC-IV harness from the dash panel to the processor. • Is fault indicated?	Yes	▶	ISOLATE fault and make necessary repairs. RERUN Quick Test.
	No	▶	GO to DA92.
DA92 CHECK PROCESSOR AND HARNESS CONNECTORS			
• Key Off, wait 10 seconds. • Disconnect processor 60 pin connector. • Inspect both connectors and connector terminals for obvious damage or faults. • Are connectors and terminals OK?	No	▶	SERVICE as necessary. RERUN Quick Test.
	Yes	▶	Unable to duplicate fault at this time. Continuous code 58 testing complete.

Vane Air Temperature Sensor (VAT)	Pinpoint Test	DA

TEST STEP	RESULT	▶	ACTION TO TAKE
DA93 SERVICE CODE 68: CONTINUOUS TEST: CHECK VAT SENSOR			
• Using continuous monitor mode, observe VOM or STAR LED for indication of a fault while performing the following: • Lightly tap on VAT sensor (simulate road shock). • Wiggle VAT connector. • Is fault indicated?	Yes	▶	DISCONNECT and INSPECT connectors. If connector and terminals are good, REPLACE VAT sensor. RERUN Quick Test.
	No	▶	GO to DA94.
DA94 CHECK EEC-IV HARNESS			
• Observe VOM or STAR LED for a fault indication while performing the following: • Referring to the illustration in Step DA93, grasp the harness closest to the sensor connector. Wiggle, shake or bend a small section of the EEC-IV system harness while working your way to the dash panel. Also wiggle, shake or bend the EEC-IV harness from the dash panel to the processor. • Is fault indicated?	Yes	▶	ISOLATE fault and make necessary service. RERUN Quick Test.
	No	▶	GO to DA95.
DA95 CHECK PROCESSOR AND HARNESS CONNECTORS			
• Key Off, wait 10 seconds. • Disconnect processor 60 pin connector. • Inspect both connectors and connector terminals for obvious damage or faults. • Are connectors and terminals OK?	No	▶	SERVICE as necessary. RERUN Quick Test.
	Yes	▶	Unable to duplicate fault at this time. Continuous code 68 testing complete.

Air Charge Temperature Sensor (ACT)	Pinpoint Test	DB

DB

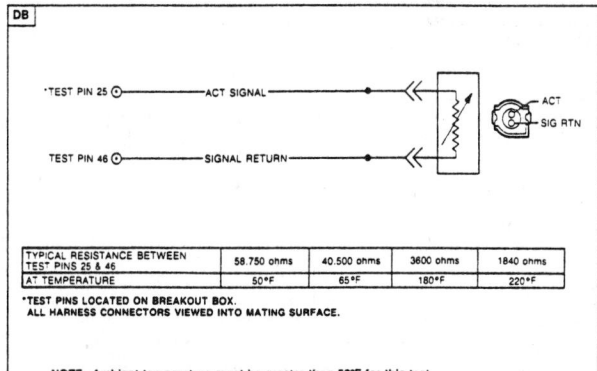

TYPICAL RESISTANCE BETWEEN TEST PINS 25 & 46	58,750 ohms	40,500 ohms	3600 ohms	1840 ohms
AT TEMPERATURE	50°F	65°F	180°F	220°F

*TEST PINS LOCATED ON BREAKOUT BOX.
ALL HARNESS CONNECTORS VIEWED INTO MATING SURFACE.

NOTE: Ambient temperature must be greater than 50°F for this test.

STOP-WARNING

You should enter this Pinpoint Test only when a service code 24, 54 or 64 is received in Quick Test Step 3.0, 5.0 or 6.0.

To prevent the replacement of good components, be aware that the following non-EEC areas may be at fault:

• Cooling system.
• Air cleaner duct problems.
• Improper engine oil level.

This pinpoint test is intended to diagnose only the following:

• ACT sensor.
• Harness circuits: ACT Signal and Signal Return.
• Processor assembly.

Air Charge Temperature Sensor (ACT) — Pinpoint Test — DB

TEST STEP	RESULT ▶	ACTION TO TAKE
DB1 SERVICE CODE 24: CHECK PROPER INSTALLATION		
• For vehicle with ACT mounted in intake manifold, GO to step DB2. • Is ACT mounted properly in air cleaner?	Yes ▶ No ▶	GO to DB2. INSTALL ACT properly. RERUN Quick Test.
DB2 CHECK FOR VREF AT THROTTLE POSITION SENSOR		
• Key Off, wait 10 seconds. • DVOM on 20V scale. • Disconnect TP sensor. • Key On, Engine Off. • Measure voltage at the TP vehicle harness connector between VREF and signal return.	Less than 4.0V or greater than 6.0V ▶ 4.0V to 6.0V ▶	GO to Pinpoint Test Step C1. RECONNECT TP sensor, GO to DB3.
DB3 CHECK ACT SENSOR — ENGINE OFF		
• Key Off, wait 10 seconds. • Harness disconnected from ACT sensor. • DVOM on 200,000 ohm scale. • Measure resistance of ACT sensor. **NOTE: Make sure engine is warmed up prior to this test.**	Reading is between 1,100 and 58,000 ohms (approximately 50°F) ▶ Reading is less than 1,100 ohms or greater than 58,000 ▶	GO to DB4. CHECK heat stove duct valve operation. If OK, REPLACE ACT sensor. RECONNECT harness to ACT sensor. RERUN Quick Test.
DB4 CHECK ACT SENSOR — ENGINE RUNNING		
• Key Off. Harness disconnected from ACT sensor. • DVOM on 200,000 ohm scale. • Run engine for 2 minutes. • Measure resistance of ACT sensor with engine running.	Reading is between 2,400 and 29,000 ohms ▶ Reading is less than 2,400 ohms or greater than 29,000 ohms ▶	REPLACE processor. RECONNECT harness to ACT sensor. RERUN Quick Test. CHECK heat stove duct valve operation. If OK, REPLACE ACT sensor. RERUN Quick Test.

Air Charge Temperature Sensor (ACT) — Pinpoint Test — DB

TEST STEP	RESULT ▶	ACTION TO TAKE
DB20 SERVICE CODE 64: INDUCE OPPOSITE CODE		
• Key Off, wait 10 seconds. • Disconnect vehicle harness from ACT sensor. Inspect for damaged pins, corrosion, loose wires, etc. Service as necessary. • Run Key On, Engine Off Quick Test. • Is code 54 present?	Yes ▶ No ▶	REPLACE ACT sensor. RECONNECT harness to ACT sensor. RERUN Quick Test. GO to DB21.
DB21 CHECK FOR VREF AT THROTTLE POSITION SENSOR		
• Key Off, wait 10 seconds. • DVOM on 20V scale. • Disconnect TP sensor. • Key On, Engine Off. • Measure voltage at the TP vehicle harness connector between VREF and Signal Return.	Less than 4.0V or greater than 6.0V ▶ 4.0V to 6.0V ▶	GO to Pinpoint Test Step C1. RECONNECT TP sensor, GO to DB22.
DB22 CHECK ACT SIGNAL FOR SHORTS TO GROUND		
• Key Off, wait 10 seconds. • Harness disconnected from ACT sensor. • Disconnect processor 60 pin connector. Inspect for damaged pins, corrosion, loose wires, etc. Service as necessary. • DVOM on 200,000 ohm scale. • Measure resistance between test Pin 25 and test Pins 40, 46 and 60 at the Breakout box.	Any reading less than 10,000 ohms ▶ All readings are 10,000 ohms or greater ▶	CORRECT circuit shorts. REMOVE Breakout box. RECONNECT processor and ACT sensor. RERUN Quick Test. REPLACE processor. REMOVE Breakout box. RECONNECT processor and ACT sensor. RERUN Quick Test.

Air Charge Temperature Sensor (ACT) — Pinpoint Test — DB

TEST STEP	RESULT ▶	ACTION TO TAKE
DB10 SERVICE CODE 54: INDUCE OPPOSITE CODE		
• Key Off, wait 10 seconds. • Disconnect vehicle harness from ACT sensor. Inspect for damaged pins, corrosion, loose wires, etc. Service as necessary. • Insert a jumper wire at the ACT vehicle harness connector between ACT Signal and Signal Return. • Run Key On, Engine Off Quick Test. • Is code 64 present?	Yes ▶ No ▶	REPLACE ACT sensor. REMOVE jumper wire. RECONNECT harness to ACT sensor. RERUN Quick Test. REMOVE jumper wire. GO to DB11.
DB11 CONTINUITY CHECK ACT SIGNAL AND SIGNAL RETURN		
• Key Off, wait 10 seconds. • Harness disconnected from ACT sensor. • Disconnect processor 60 pin connector. Inspect for damaged pins, corrosion, loose wires, etc. Service as necessary. • Install Breakout box. Leave processor disconnected. • DVOM on 200 ohm scale. • Measure resistance between ACT signal, at the ACT vehicle harness connector, and test Pin 25 at the Breakout box. • Measure resistance between Signal Return, at the ACT vehicle harness connector, and test Pin 46 at the Breakout box.	Both readings are less than 5 ohms ▶ Either reading is 5 ohms or greater ▶	REPLACE processor. REMOVE Breakout box. RECONNECT processor and ACT sensor. RERUN Quick Test. CORRECT circuit opens. REMOVE Breakout box. RECONNECT processor and ACT sensor. RERUN Quick Test.

Air Charge Temperature (ACT) — Pinpoint Test — DB

TEST STEP	RESULT ▶	ACTION TO TAKE
DB90 SERVICE CODE 54: CONTINUOUS TEST: CHECK ACT SENSOR		
• Using continuous monitor mode, observe VOM or STAR LED for indication of a fault while performing the following: • Lightly tap on ACT sensor (simulate road shock). • Wiggle ACT connector. • Is a fault indicated?	Yes ▶ No ▶	DISCONNECT and INSPECT connectors. If connector and terminals are good, REPLACE ACT sensor. RERUN Quick Test. GO to DB91.

POWER OR VREF CIRCUIT — ACT SIG. — SIG. RTN. — PROCESSOR — HARNESS — ACT SENSOR

TEST STEP	RESULT ▶	ACTION TO TAKE
DB91 CHECK EEC-IV HARNESS		
• Observe VOM or STAR LED for a fault indication while performing the following: • Referring to the illustration in Step DB90, grasp the harness closest to the sensor connector. Wiggle, shake or bend a small section of the EEC-IV system harness while working your way to the dash panel. Also wiggle, shake or bend the EEC-IV harness from the dash panel to the processor. • Is fault indicated?	Yes ▶ No ▶	ISOLATE fault and make necessary repairs. RERUN Quick Test. GO to DB92.
DB92 CHECK PROCESSOR AND HARNESS CONNECTORS		
• Key Off, wait 10 seconds. • Disconnect processor 60 pin connector. • Inspect both connectors and connector terminals for obvious damage or faults. • Connectors and terminals are OK.	No ▶ Yes ▶	SERVICE as necessary. RERUN Quick Test. Unable to duplicate fault at this time. Continuous code 54 testing complete.

Air Charge Temperature (ACT)	Pinpoint Test	DB

TEST STEP	RESULT ▶	ACTION TO TAKE
DB93 SERVICE CODE 64: CONTINUOUS TEST: CHECK ACT SENSOR		
• Using continuous monitor mode, observe VOM or STAR LED for fault while performing the following: • Lightly tap on ACT sensor (simulate road shock). • Wiggle ACT connector. • Is fault indicated?	Yes ▶	DISCONNECT and INSPECT connectors. If connector and terminals are good, REPLACE ACT sensor. RERUN Quick Test.
	No ▶	GO to DB94 .
DB94 CHECK EEC-IV HARNESS		
• Observe VOM or STAR LED for a fault indication while performing the following: • Referring to the illustration in Step DB93, grasp the harness closest to the sensor connector. Wiggle, shake or bend a small section of the EEC-IV system harness while working your way to the dash panel. Also wiggle, shake or bend the EEC-IV harness from the dash panel to the processor. • Is fault indicated?	Yes ▶	ISOLATE fault and make necessary repairs. RERUN Quick Test.
	No ▶	GO to DB95 .
DB95 CHECK PROCESSOR AND HARNESS CONNECTORS		
• Key Off, wait 10 seconds. • Disconnect processor 60 pin connector. • Inspect both connectors and connector terminals for obvious damage or faults.	No ▶	SERVICE as necessary. RERUN Quick Test.
• Connectors and terminals are OK.	Yes ▶	Unable to duplicate fault at this time. Continuous code 64 testing complete.

POWER OR VREF CIRCUIT

PROCESSOR — ACT SIG — SIG. RTN. — HARNESS — ACT SENSOR

EGR Valve Position Sensor (EVP) Control/Vent (EGRC/EGRV)	Pinpoint Test	DD

TEST STEP	RESULT ▶	ACTION TO TAKE
FAULT CODE 31		
DD1 RUN ENGINE RUNNING QUICK TEST WITH EGR VACUUM SIGNAL LINE DISCONNECTED AT EGR VALVE	Code 31 present ▶	GO to DD2 .
• Key Off, wait 10 seconds. • Disconnect EGR vacuum line at EGR valve and cap EGR vacuum line. • Run Engine Running Quick Test. • Check for code 31.	No code 31 present, but codes 32, 34 are present ▶	GO to DD11 .
DD2 CHECK EVP RESISTANCE WHILE APPLYING VACUUM TO EGR VALVE	Reading gradually decreases from no greater than 5500 ohms to no less than 100 ohms ▶	GO to DD3 .
• Key Off, wait 10 seconds. • Vacuum signal line disconnected. • Disconnect vehicle harness at EVP sensor. • DVOM on 200,000 ohm scale. • Connect vacuum pump to EGR valve. • Measure resistance at the EVP sensor between EVP SIG and Vref while gradually increasing vacuum to 33 kPa (10 in.-Hg.). • Observe resistance as vacuum increases.	Reading is less than 100 ohms or greater than 5500 ohms ▶	REPLACE EVP sensor. RECONNECT signal line and harness. RERUN Quick Test.
	Reading does not decrease or unable to hold vacuum ▶	GO to DD16 .
DD3 MEASURE VREF TO SIGNAL RETURN VOLTAGE		
• Key On, Engine Off. • Vacuum signal line disconnected and capped, harness disconnected from EVP sensor. • DVOM on 20V scale. • Measure voltage at the EVP vehicle harness connector between VREF and Signal Return. • Is voltage reading between 4.0 and 6.0 volts?	Yes ▶	GO to DD4 .
	No ▶	GO to Pinpoint Test Step C1 .

EGR Valve Position Sensor (EVP) Control/Vent (EGRC/EGRV)	Pinpoint Test	DD

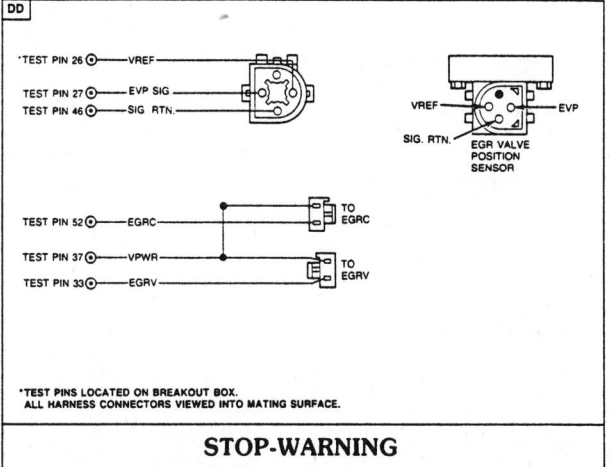

DD

*TEST PIN 26 — VREF

*TEST PIN 27 — EVP SIG

*TEST PIN 46 — SIG. RTN.

VREF — EVP

SIG. RTN. — EGR VALVE POSITION SENSOR

*TEST PIN 52 — EGRC — TO EGRC

*TEST PIN 37 — VPWR

*TEST PIN 33 — EGRV — TO EGRV

*TEST PINS LOCATED ON BREAKOUT BOX.
 ALL HARNESS CONNECTORS VIEWED INTO MATING SURFACE.

STOP-WARNING

You should enter this Pinpoint Test only when a Service Code 31, 32, 33, 34, 35, 83 or 84 is received in Quick Test Step 3.0, 5.0 or 6.0.

To prevent the replacement of good components, be aware that the following non-EEC area may be at fault:

• Damaged EGR valve.

This Pinpoint Test is intended to diagnose only the following:

• EVP sensor.
• Harness circuits: EVP, Signal Return, VREF, EGRV, EGRC, VPWR.
• EGR solenoids.
• EGR Valve assembly.
• Processor assembly.

EGR Valve Position Sensor (EVP) Control/Vent (EGRC/EGRV)	Pinpoint Test	DD

TEST STEP	RESULT ▶	ACTION TO TAKE
DD4 MEASURE CONTINUITY OF EVP SIGNAL CIRCUIT	Yes ▶	GO to DD5 .
• Key Off, wait 10 seconds. • Harness disconnected from EVP sensor. • Disconnect processor 60 Pin connector and inspect for damaged pins, corrosion, loose wires. Service as necessary. • Install Breakout box leaving processor disconnected. • DVOM on 200 ohm scale. • Measure resistance between test Pin 27 at the Breakout box and EVP signal at the EVP vehicle harness connector. • Is resistance less than 5 ohms?	No ▶	SERVICE open circuit. REMOVE Breakout box. RECONNECT processor and EVP sensor. RERUN Quick Test.
DD5 CHECK EVP SIGNAL FOR SHORTS TO VREF AND SIGNAL RETURN	Yes ▶	GO to DD6 .
• Key Off, harness disconnected from EVP sensor. Breakout box installed with processor not connected. • DVOM on 200,000 ohm scale. • Measure resistance between test Pin 27 and test Pins 26, 40, 46 and 60 at Breakout box. • Are all readings 10,000 ohms or greater?	No ▶	SERVICE short circuit. REMOVE Breakout box. RECONNECT processor and EVP sensor. RERUN Quick Test.
DD6 SUBSTITUTE EVP SENSOR AND EGR VALVE	Yes ▶	REPLACE processor. CONNECT original EVP sensor and EGR valve assembly. RERUN Quick Test.
• Key Off, wait 10 seconds. • Electrically connect known good EVP sensor and EGR valve assembly. • Remove Breakout box. • Reconnect processor. • Perform Key On, Engine Off Quick Test. • Is code 31 present?	No ▶	GO to DD7 .

EGR Valve Position Sensor (EVP) Control/Vent (EGRC/EGRV)	Pinpoint Test	DD

TEST STEP	RESULT	▶	ACTION TO TAKE
DD7 EVP SENSOR CHECK			
• Key Off, wait 10 seconds. • Install original EVP sensor on known good EGR valve. • EVP sensor connected. • Rerun Key On, Engine Off Quick Test. • Is code 31 present?	Yes No	▶ ▶	INSTALL new EVP sensor. RERUN Quick Test. REFER to EGR System, Section 6.
FAULT CODES 32, 33 AND 34			
DD11 OUTPUT STATE CHECK (REFER TO APPENDIX)			
NOTE: Do not use STAR tester for this test step. Use VOM/DVOM. • Key Off, wait 10 seconds. • DVOM on 20V scale. • Connect DVOM negative test lead to STO and positive test lead to battery positive. • Jumper STI to signal return. • Perform Key On, Engine Off Self-Test until the completion of the Continuous Test Codes. • DVOM will indicate zero volts. • Depress and release the throttle. • Did DVOM reading change to a high voltage reading?	No Yes	▶ ▶	DEPRESS throttle to WOT and RELEASE. If STO voltage does not go high, GO to Pinpoint Test Step ⬛Q40⬛. Remain in output state check and GO to ⬛DD12⬛.
DD12 CHECK EGR SOLENOIDS FOR ELECTRICAL CYCLING			
• Key On, Engine Off. • DVOM on 20V scale. • Reconnect DVOM to EGRV solenoid, between VPWR and EGRV signal. • While observing DVOM, depress and release the throttle several times to cycle output on and off. • Repeat for EGRC solenoid, between VPWR and EGRC signal. • Do both solenoid outputs cycle on and off?	Yes No	▶ ▶	REMAIN in output state check. GO to ⬛DD13⬛. Exit output state check. GO to ⬛DD17⬛.

EGR Valve Position Sensor (EVP) Control/Vent (EGRC/EGRV)	Pinpoint Test	DD

TEST STEP	RESULT	▶	ACTION TO TAKE
DD13 CHECK EGR SOLENOIDS FOR VACUUM CYCLING			
• Key On, Engine Off. • Still in output state check. • Disconnect and cap vacuum line from bottom port of EGRC solenoid and connect a vacuum pump. • Connect a vacuum gauge in the common output (top) vacuum line to EGR valve. • Disconnect but do not cap vacuum vent line from EGRV solenoid or remove filter from the top of the EGRV solenoid. • Apply vacuum. • While cycling outputs on and off (by depressing and releasing throttle), observe vacuum gauge at the output. Maintain vacuum at source. • Does the vacuum cycle on and off in less than 2 seconds?	Yes No	▶ ▶	RECONNECT all vacuum lines. GO to ⬛DD14⬛. CHECK filter and common output vacuum line for obstructions. REPLACE as necessary. If OK, REPLACE solenoid assembly. RECONNECT all vacuum lines. RERUN Quick Test.
DD14 CHECK VACUUM LINES			
• Key Off, wait 10 seconds. • Vacuum lines reconnected. • Check entire EEC vacuum line system per VECI emission schematic decal for kinks, cracks, obstructions or leaks. • Are vacuum lines OK? **NOTE FOR 3.8L CFI (ONLY): Special attention should be given to the canister purge valve. A canister purge valve that is stuck open will apply vacuum to the EGR valve.**	Yes No	▶ ▶	GO to ⬛DD15⬛. SERVICE as necessary. RERUN Quick Test.

EGR Valve Position Sensor (EVP) Control/Vent (EGRC/EGRV)	Pinpoint Test	DD

TEST STEP	RESULT	▶	ACTION TO TAKE
DD15 CHECK EVP RESISTANCE WHILE APPLYING VACUUM TO EGR VALVE			
• Key Off. • Disconnect vehicle harness from EVP sensor. Inspect for damaged pins, corrosion, and pins pushed out. Service as necessary. • DVOM on 200,000 ohm scale. • Disconnect vacuum line at EGR valve. • Connect vacuum pump to EGR valve. • Measure resistance of the EVP sensor between EVP Signal Pin and VREF Pin while increasing vacuum to 33 kPa (10 in.-Hg.). • Observe resistance as vacuum increases. • Does the resistance gradually change between 5500 and 100 ohms?	Yes No	▶ ▶	REPLACE processor. RECONNECT EVP sensor and EGR vacuum line. RERUN Quick Test. GO to ⬛DD16⬛.
DD16 MANUALLY EXERCISE EVP SENSOR			
• Key Off, harness disconnected from EVP sensor. • Remove EVP sensor from EGR valve. • Measure resistance of the EVP sensor between EVP Signal Pin and VREF Pin while gradually applying pressure to EVP sensor shaft. • Observe resistance as shaft is slowly pushed in and slowly released. • Do either of the readings change suddenly between 5500 and 100 ohms?	Yes No	▶ ▶	REPLACE EVP sensor. RECONNECT harness and EGR supply vacuum line. RERUN Quick Test. REFER to EGR System, Section 6. RECONNECT EVP sensor and EGR supply vacuum line. RERUN Quick Test.
NOTE: It is normal for the EVP sensor total resistance to drop below 100 ohms when disconnected from the EGR valve. A defective part will change resistance suddenly between 5500 and 100 ohms.			
DD17 MEASURE EGRV/EGRC SOLENOID RESISTANCE			
• Key Off, wait 10 seconds. • DVOM on 200 ohm scale. • Disconnect EGRV solenoid connector and measure solenoid resistance. Inspect for damaged pins, corrosion and pins pushed out. Service as necessary. • Disconnect EGRC solenoid connector and measure solenoid resistance. Inspect for damaged pins, corrosion and pins pushed out. Service as necessary. • Are both resistances between 30 and 70 ohms?	Yes No	▶ ▶	CONNECT EGRC/ EGRV solenoids. GO to ⬛DD18⬛. REPLACE EGRC/ EGRV solenoid assembly. RERUN Quick Test.

EGR Valve Position Sensor (EVP) Control/Vent (EGRC/EGRV)	Pinpoint Test	DD

TEST STEP	RESULT	▶	ACTION TO TAKE
DD18 CHECK FOR VOLTAGE ON VEHICLE POWER CIRCUIT			
• Disconnect EGR vent and EGR control solenoids from harness. • Key On, Engine Off. • DVOM on 20V scale. • Measure voltage between battery negative terminal and VPWR circuit on both EGR solenoids. • Are both readings 10.5 volts or greater?	Yes No	▶ ▶	GO to ⬛DD19⬛. SERVICE harness circuit open. RERUN Quick Test.
DD19 CHECK CONTINUITY OF EGRV AND EGRC CIRCUITS			
• Key Off, wait 10 seconds. • EGR vent and EGR control solenoid disconnected from harness. • Disconnect processor 60 Pin connector and inspect for damaged pins, corrosion, loose wires. Service as necessary. • Install Breakout box to processor harness connector. Leave processor disconnected. • DVOM on 200 ohm scale. • Measure resistance between test Pin 33 at the Breakout box and EGRV signal at the EGRV solenoid vehicle harness connector. • Measure resistance between test Pin 52 at the Breakout box and EGRC signal at the EGRC solenoid vehicle harness connector. • Are both readings less than 5 ohms?	Yes No	▶ ▶	GO to ⬛DD20⬛. SERVICE open circuit. REMOVE Breakout box. RECONNECT harness to processor. RERUN Quick Test.
DD20 CHECK FOR SHORT TO GROUND			
• Key Off, wait 10 seconds. • DVOM on 200,000 ohm scale. • Leave Breakout box installed and processor disconnected. • EGRV/EGRC solenoids disconnected. • Measure resistance between test Pins 33 and/or 52 and test Pins 40, 46 and 60 at the Breakout box. • Is resistance less than 10,000 ohms?	Yes No	▶ ▶	SERVICE short to ground. RERUN Quick Test. GO to ⬛DD21⬛.

EGR Valve Position Sensor (EVP) Control/Vent (EGRC/EGRV)	Pinpoint Test	DD

TEST STEP	RESULT	▶	ACTION TO TAKE
DD21 CHECK EGRV AND EGRC SIGNALS FOR SHORTS TO POWER • EGR vent and EGR control solenoids disconnected from harness. • Key Off, Breakout box installed. Processor disconnected. • DVOM on 200,000 ohm scale. • Measure resistance between test Pin 33 and test Pins 37 and 57 at the Breakout box. • Measure resistance between test Pin 52 and test Pins 37 and 57 at the Breakout box. • Are all readings 10,000 ohms or greater?	Yes No	▶ ▶	REPLACE processor. REMOVE Breakout box. RECONNECT harness to processor. RERUN Quick Test. SERVICE circuit short. REMOVE Breakout box. RECONNECT harness to processor. RERUN Quick Test. If code is repeated, REPLACE processor.
FAULT CODE 35 **DD30** RPM TOO LOW FOR EGR TEST • Is code 12 also present?	Yes No	▶ ▶	Vehicles equipped with air bypass (EFI), GO to KE1. Vehicles equipped with DC motor control, GO to KF1. GO to DD31.
DD31 RETEST AT 1,500 RPM • Key Off, wait 10 seconds. • Install tachometer. • Perform Key On, Engine Running Quick Test while maintaining 1,500 rpm. • Record Engine Running service codes. • Is code 35 still present?	Yes No	▶ ▶	REPLACE processor. RERUN Quick Test. RERUN Quick Test. SERVICE codes as necessary.

EGR Valve Position Sensor (EVP) Control/Vent (EGRC/EGRV)	Pinpoint Test	DD

TEST STEP	RESULT	▶	ACTION TO TAKE
DD90 SERVICE CODE 31 CONTINUOUS TEST: EXERCISE EVP SENSOR • Using continuous monitor mode, observe VOM or STAR LED for indication of a fault while performing the following: • Connect a vacuum pump to the EGR valve. • Very slowly apply 20 kPa (6 in.-Hg.) vacuum to the EGR valve. • Slowly bleed vacuum off the EGR valve and lightly tap on EVP sensor (simulate road shock). • Wiggle EVP sensor connector. • Is a fault indicated?	Yes No	▶ ▶	GO to DD91. GO to DD92.
PROCESSOR HARNESS EVP SENSOR VREF EVP SIG. SIG. RTN.			
DD91 MEASURE EVP SIGNAL VOLTAGE WHILE EXERCISING EVP SENSOR • Key Off, wait 10 seconds. • Disconnect processor 60 Pin connector and inspect for damaged pins, corrosion, loose wires. Service as necessary. • Install Breakout box and reconnect processor. • VOM or STAR LED still connected to STO as in previous Step. • Connect a DVOM from test Pin 27 to test Pin 46. • DVOM on 20V scale. • Key On, Engine Off. • While observing DVOM, repeat Step DD90. • Does the fault occur below 4.25V?	Yes No	▶ ▶	DISCONNECT and INSPECT connector. If connector and terminals are good, REPLACE EVP sensor. RERUN Quick Test. EGR valve overshoot may have caused continuous code 31. Sensor service is not required. To verify harness integrity, GO to DD92.

EGR Valve Position Sensor (EVP) Control/Vent (EGRC/EGRV)	Pinpoint Test	DD

TEST STEP	RESULT	▶	ACTION TO TAKE
DD92 CHECK EEC-IV HARNESS • Observe VOM or STAR LED for a fault indication while performing the following: • Referring to the illustration in Step DD90, grasp the harness closest to the sensor connector. Wiggle, shake or bend a small section of the EEC-IV system harness while working your way to the dash panel. Also wiggle, shake or bend the EEC-IV harness from the dash panel to the processor. • Is a fault indicated?	Yes No	▶ ▶	ISOLATE fault and SERVICE as necessary. REFER to appropriate figure. RERUN Quick Test. GO to DD93.
DD93 CHECK PROCESSOR AND HARNESS CONNECTORS • Key Off, wait 10 seconds. • Disconnect processor 60 Pin connector. • Inspect both connectors and connector terminals for obvious damage or faults. • Are connectors and terminals OK?	No Yes	▶ ▶	SERVICE as necessary. RERUN Quick Test. Unable to duplicate fault at this time. Continuous code 31 testing complete.

Engine Coolant Temperature Sensor (ECT)	Pinpoint Test	DE

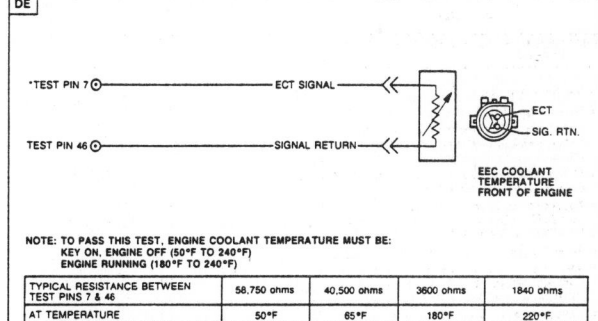

DE

*TEST PIN 7 —— ECT SIGNAL
TEST PIN 46 —— SIGNAL RETURN

ECT SIG. RTN.
EEC COOLANT TEMPERATURE FRONT OF ENGINE

NOTE: TO PASS THIS TEST, ENGINE COOLANT TEMPERATURE MUST BE:
KEY ON, ENGINE OFF (50°F TO 240°F)
ENGINE RUNNING (180°F TO 240°F)

TYPICAL RESISTANCE BETWEEN TEST PINS 7 & 46	58,750 ohms	40,500 ohms	3600 ohms	1840 ohms
AT TEMPERATURE	50°F	65°F	180°F	220°F

*TEST PINS LOCATED ON BREAKOUT BOX.
ALL HARNESS CONNECTORS VIEWED INTO MATING SURFACE.

STOP-WARNING

You should enter this Pinpoint Test only when a service code 21, 51 or 61 is received in Quick Test Step 3.0, 5.0 or 6.0.

To prevent the replacement of good components, be aware that the following non-EEC areas may be at fault:
• Coolant level.
• Oil level.
• Blocked or obstructed air flow.
• Engine not at normal operating temperature.
• Electro drive cooling fan.
• Open thermostat.
This pinpoint test is intended to diagnose only the following:
• ECT sensor.
• Harness sensor circuits: ECT and Signal Return.
• Processor assembly.

Engine Coolant Temperature Sensor (ECT)	Pinpoint Test	DE

TEST STEP	RESULT ▶	ACTION TO TAKE
DE1 SERVICE CODE 21: CHECK ENGINE OPERATING TEMPERATURE • Run engine for 2 minutes at 2,000 rpm. • Check that upper radiator hose is hot and pressurized. • Rerun Quick Test. • Is code 21 present?	Vehicle stalls ▶ Yes ▶ No ▶	Do not service code 21 at this time. REFER to diagnosis by symptoms. GO to DE2. SERVICE other codes as necessary.
DE2 CHECK FOR VREF AT THROTTLE POSITION SENSOR • Refer to illustration Q. • Key Off, wait 10 seconds. • DVOM on 20V scale. • Disconnect TP sensor. • Key On, Engine Off. • Measure voltage at the TP vehicle harness connector between VREF and signal return. • Is voltage reading between 4.0 and 6.0 volts?	Yes ▶ No ▶	RECONNECT TP sensor, GO to DE3. GO to Pinpoint Test Step C1.
DE3 ECT SENSOR CHECK NOTE: Engine may have cooled down. Always warm engine before taking ECT resistance measurement. Check for open thermostat. • Key Off, wait 10 seconds. • Harness disconnected from ECT sensor. • DVOM on 200,000 ohm scale. • Measure resistance of the ECT sensor. • Is the resistance reading: — 1300 ohms (240°F) to 7700 ohms (140°F) for engine off? — 1550 ohms (230°F) to 4550 ohms (180°F) for engine running?	Yes ▶ No ▶	REPLACE processor. RECONNECT harness to ECT sensor. RERUN Quick Test. REPLACE ECT sensor. RECONNECT harness to ECT sensor. RERUN Quick Test.

Engine Coolant Temperature Sensor (ECT)	Pinpoint Test	DE

TEST STEP	RESULT ▶	ACTION TO TAKE
DE10 SERVICE CODE 51: INDUCE OPPOSITE CODE • Key Off, wait 10 seconds. • Disconnect vehicle harness from ECT sensor. Inspect for damaged pins, corrosion, loose wires, etc. Service as necessary. • Insert a jumper wire at the ECT sensor vehicle harness connector between ECT Signal and Signal Return. • Run Key On, Engine Off Quick Test. • Is code 61 present?	Yes ▶ No ▶	REPLACE ECT sensor. REMOVE jumper wire. RECONNECT ECT sensor. RERUN Quick Test. GO to DE11.
DE11 CHECK CONTINUITY OF ECT SIGNAL AND SIGNAL RETURN • Key Off, wait 10 seconds. • Harness disconnected from ECT sensor, jumper wire removed. • Disconnect processor 60 pin connector. Inspect for damaged pins, corrosion, loose wires, etc. Service as necessary. • Install Breakout box to harness leaving processor disconnected. • DVOM on 200 ohm scale. • Measure resistance between ECT signal at the ECT vehicle harness connector and test Pin 7 at the Breakout box. • Measure resistance between Signal Return at the ECT sensor vehicle harness connector, and test Pin 46 at the Breakout box. • Are both readings less than 5 ohms?	Yes ▶ No ▶	REPLACE processor. REMOVE Breakout box. RECONNECT processor and ECT sensor. RERUN Quick Test. SERVICE open circuit(s). REMOVE Breakout box. RECONNECT processor and ECT sensor. RERUN Quick Test.

Engine Coolant Temperature Sensor (ECT)	Pinpoint Test	DE

TEST STEP	RESULT ▶	ACTION TO TAKE
DE20 SERVICE CODE 61: INDUCE OPPOSITE CODE • Key Off, wait 10 seconds. • Disconnect vehicle harness from ECT sensor. Inspect for damaged pins, corrosion, loose wires, etc. Service as necessary. • Run Key On, Engine Off Quick Test. • Is code 51 present?	Yes ▶ No ▶	REPLACE ECT sensor. RECONNECT ECT sensor. RERUN Quick Test. GO to DE21.
DE21 CHECK FOR VREF AT THROTTLE POSITION SENSOR • Refer to illustration Q. • Key Off, wait 10 seconds. • DVOM on 20V scale. • Disconnect TP sensor. • Key On, Engine Off. • Measure voltage at the TP vehicle harness connector between VREF and signal return. • Is voltage reading between 4.0 and 6.0 volts?	Yes ▶ No ▶	RECONNECT TP sensor, GO to DE22. GO to Pinpoint Test Step C1.
DE22 CHECK ECT SIGNAL FOR SHORT • Key Off, wait 10 seconds. • Harness disconnected from ECT sensor. • Disconnect processor 60 pin connector. Inspect for damaged pins, corrosion, loose wires, etc. Service as necessary. • Install Breakout box, leave processor disconnected. • DVOM on 200,000 ohm scale. • Measure resistance between test Pin 7 and test Pins 40, 46 and 60 at the Breakout box. • Are resistance readings 10,000 ohms or greater?	Yes ▶ No ▶	REPLACE processor. REMOVE Breakout box. RECONNECT processor and ECT harness. RERUN Quick Test. SERVICE circuit shorts. REMOVE Breakout box. RECONNECT processor and ECT sensor. RERUN Quick Test.

Engine Coolant Temperature Sensor (ECT)	Pinpoint Test	DE

TEST STEP	RESULT ▶	ACTION TO TAKE
DE90 SERVICE CODE 21: CONTINUOUS TEST: TEST DRIVE VEHICLE • Key Off and wait 10 seconds. • Disconnect all Self-Test equipment and prepare vehicle for test drive. • Drive vehicle. Try to simulate different drive modes or mode in which drive complaint is noticed. Attempt to maintain drive complaint mode for one minute or more, if possible. • Upon completion of drive evaluation, repeat Key On, Engine Off Self-Test. • Is code 21 present in the continuous test results?	Yes ▶ No ▶	VERIFY thermostat operating properly. If OK. REPLACE ECT sensor. RERUN Quick Test. Unable to duplicate fault. Code 21 testing complete.

Engine Coolant Temperature (ECT)	Pinpoint Test	DE

TEST STEP	RESULT ▶	ACTION TO TAKE
DE91 SERVICE CODE 51: CONTINUOUS TEST: CHECK ECT SENSOR		
• Using continuous monitor mode, observe VOM or STAR LED for indication of a fault while performing the following: • Lightly tap on ECT sensor (simulate road shock). • Wiggle ECT connector. • Is a fault indicated?	Yes ▶	DISCONNECT and INSPECT connectors. If connector and terminals are good, REPLACE ECT sensor. RERUN Quick Test.
	No ▶	GO to DE92 .
DE92 CHECK EEC-IV HARNESS		
• Observe VOM or STAR LED for a fault indication while performing the following: • Referring to the illustration in Step DE91, grasp the harness closest to the sensor connector. Wiggle, shake or bend a small section of the EEC-IV system harness while working your way to the dash panel. Also wiggle, shake or bend the EEC-IV harness from the dash panel to the processor. • Is fault indicated?	Yes ▶	ISOLATE fault and make necessary repairs. RERUN Quick Test.
	No ▶	GO to DE93 .
DE93 CHECK PROCESSOR AND HARNESS CONNECTORS		
• Key Off, wait 10 seconds. • Disconnect processor 60 pin connector. • Inspect both connectors and connector terminals for obvious damage or faults. • Connectors and terminals are OK.	No ▶	SERVICE as necessary. RERUN Quick Test.
	Yes ▶	Unable to duplicate fault at this time. Continuous code 51 testing complete.

Engine Coolant Temperature (ECT)	Pinpoint Test	DE

TEST STEP	RESULT ▶	ACTION TO TAKE
DE94 SERVICE CODE 61: CONTINUOUS TEST: CHECK ECT SENSOR		
• Using continuous monitor mode, observe VOM or STAR LED for indication of a fault while performing the following. • Lightly tap on ECT sensor (simulate road shock). • Wiggle ECT connector. Voltage greater than 5 volts or STAR LED Off. • Is fault indicated?	Yes ▶	DISCONNECT and INSPECT connectors. If connector and terminals are good, REPLACE ECT sensor. RERUN Quick Test.
	No ▶	GO to DE95 .
DE95 CHECK EEC-IV HARNESS		
• Observe VOM or STAR LED for a fault indication while performing the following: • Referring to the illustration in Step DE94, grasp the harness closest to the sensor connector. Wiggle, shake or bend a small section of the EEC-IV system harness while working your way to the dash panel. Also wiggle, shake or bend the EEC-IV harness from the dash panel to the processor. • Is fault indicated?	Yes ▶	ISOLATE fault and make necessary repairs. RERUN Quick Test.
	No ▶	GO to DE96 .
DE96 CHECK PROCESSOR AND HARNESS CONNECTORS		
• Key Off, wait 10 seconds. • Disconnect processor 60 pin connector. • Inspect both connectors and connector terminals for obvious damage or faults. • Connectors and terminals are OK.	No ▶	SERVICE as necessary. RERUN Quick Test.
	Yes ▶	Unable to duplicate fault at this time. Continuous code 61 testing complete.

Manifold Absolute Pressure (MAP)/ Barometric Pressure (BP) Sensor	Pinpoint Test	DF

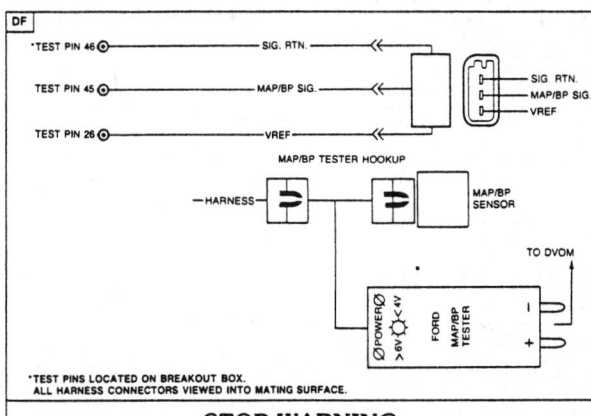

*TEST PINS LOCATED ON BREAKOUT BOX.
ALL HARNESS CONNECTORS VIEWED INTO MATING SURFACE.

STOP-WARNING

You should enter this Pinpoint Test only when a Service Code 22 or 72 is received in Quick Test Step 3.0, 5.0 or 6.0 or when directed here from Pinpoint Test S or Diagnostics by Symptom in the Engine Supplement Section.

To prevent the replacement of good components, be aware that the following non-EEC areas may be at fault:

• Unusually high/low atmospheric barometer reading (MAP/BP).
• Kinked or obstructed vacuum lines (MAP).
• Basic engine (valves, vacuum leaks, timing, EGR valve (MAP), etc.).
• Key On, Engine Off — MAP sensor must not see vacuum.
• Engine Running — MAP sensor must see actual manifold vacuum.

This Pinpoint Test is intended to diagnose only the following:

• MAP/BP sensor.
• Harness circuits: VREF, MAP/BP Signal, and Signal Return.
• Processor assembly.
• MAP vacuum line.

Manifold Absolute Pressure (MAP)/ Barometric Pressure (BP) Sensor	Pinpoint Test	DF

TEST STEP	RESULT ▶	ACTION TO TAKE
FAULT CODE 22, ENGINE OFF		
DF1 CONNECTING MAP/BP TESTER		
• Key Off. • Disconnect the MAP/BP sensor from the vehicle harness. • Connect the MAP/BP tester between the vehicle harness and the MAP/BP sensor. • Insert tester banana plugs into DVOM. • Set DVOM to 20V scale. • Refer to illustration DF.	Tester properly hooked up ▶	GO to DF2 .
DF2 POWER TO MAP/BP SENSOR TEST		
• MAP/BP tester connected. • Key On. • Observe red and green lights.	(ONLY) Green light, Vref is OK ▶	GO to DF4 .
	"Less than 4V" light (RED) or no lights, Vref is too low ▶ OR "Greater than 6V" light (Red), Vref is too high	GO to DF3 .
DF3 VREF ISOLATION		
• MAP/BP tester connected. • Key On. • Disconnect MAP/BP • Observe red and green lights.	(ONLY) Green light, Vref is OK ▶	REPLACE MAP/BP sensor. RERUN Quick Test.
	"Less than 4V" light (RED) or no lights, Vref is too low ▶ OR "Greater than 6V" light (Red), Vref is too high	REMOVE MAP/BP tester. GO to Pinpoint Test Step C1 .

Manifold Absolute Pressure (MAP)/ Barometric Pressure (BP) Sensor	Pinpoint Test	DF

TEST STEP	RESULT ▶	ACTION TO TAKE
DF4 MAP/BP TESTER OUTPUT READING		
• MAP tester connected, refer to Note. • Key On. • Approximate Altitude (Ft.) Voltage Output (+/−.04 Volts) 0 1.59 1000 1.56 2000 1.53 3000 1.50 4000 1.47 5000 1.44 6000 1.41 7000 1.39 • Is reading in range for your altitude?	Yes ▶ No (Sensor output is out-of-range) ▶	REMOVE MAP/BP Tester. GO to DF5. REMOVE MAP/BP Tester. GO to DF6. **NOTE: Measure several known good MAP sensors on available vehicles. The measured voltage will be typical for your location on the day of testing.**
DF5 CHECK CONTINUITY OF MAP/BP SIGNAL		
• Key Off, wait 10 seconds. • Harness disconnected from MAP/BP sensor. • Disconnect processor 60 Pin connector. Inspect for damaged pins, corrosion, loose wires, etc. Service as necessary. • Install Breakout box. Leave processor disconnected. • DVOM on 200 ohm scale. • Measure resistance between MAP/BP signal at the MAP/BP sensor vehicle harness connector and test Pin 45 at the Breakout box. • Is resistance reading 5.0 ohms or less?	Yes ▶ No ▶	REPLACE processor. CONNECT harness and MAP/BP sensor. RERUN Quick Test. SERVICE circuit opens. REMOVE Breakout box. RECONNECT processor and MAP/BP sensor. RERUN Quick Test.
DF6 CHECK MAP/BP SIGNAL FOR SHORTS TO VREF; SIGNAL RETURN AND GROUND		
• Key Off, wait 10 seconds. • Disconnect processor 60 Pin connector and inspect for damaged pins, corrosion, loose wires. Service as necessary. • Install Breakout box, leave processor disconnected. • Harness disconnected from MAP/BP sensor. • DVOM on 200,000 ohm scale. • Measure resistance between test Pin 45 and test Pins 26, 46, 40 and 60 at the Breakout box. • Are all resistance readings 10,000 ohms or greater?	Yes ▶ No ▶	REPLACE MAP/BP sensor. REMOVE Breakout box. RECONNECT, electrical connections. RERUN Quick Test. SERVICE circuit shorts. REMOVE Breakout box. RECONNECT processor and MAP/BP Sensor. RERUN Quick Test.

Manifold Absolute Pressure (MAP)/ Barometric Pressure (BP) Sensor	Pinpoint Test	DF

TEST STEP	RESULT ▶	ACTION TO TAKE
FAULT CODE 72		
DF10 CHECK THAT VACUUM TO MAP SENSOR DECREASES DURING DYNAMIC RESPONSE		
• Key Off, wait 10 seconds. • Tee a vacuum gauge in the intake manifold vacuum line at the MAP sensor. • Perform Engine Running Quick Test while observing vacuum. • Record engine service codes. • Did vacuum decrease by more than 30 kPa (10 in.-Hg.) during dynamic response test? • Is code 72 present?	Vacuum decrease is 30 kPa (10 in.-Hg.) or greater and code 72 is not present ▶ Vacuum decrease is 30 kPa (10 in.-Hg.) or greater and code 72 is present ▶ Vacuum decrease is less than 30 kPa (10 in.-Hg.) ▶	DISCONNECT vacuum equipment and SERVICE other codes as necessary. REPLACE MAP sensor and RERUN Quick Test. GO to DF11.
DF11 CHECK VACUUM LINES		
• Check vacuum line for proper routing. Refer to VECI decal. Check MAP sensor vacuum line for kinks or blockage. • Vacuum lines are OK.	Yes ▶ No ▶	EEC-IV system OK. REFER to Shop Manual, Group 21 for probable subjects affecting engine vacuum. SERVICE as necessary and REPEAT DF10.
DF20 CONNECTING MAP/BP TESTER		
• Key Off. • Disconnect the MAP/BP sensor from the vehicle harness. • Connect the MAP/BP Tester between the vehicle harness and the MAP/BP sensor. • Plug tester banana plugs into DVOM. • Set DVOM to 20V scale. • Refer to illustration DF.	Tester properly hooked up ▶	GO to DF21.

Manifold Absolute Pressure (MAP)/ Barometric Pressure (BP) Sensor	Pinpoint Test	DF

TEST STEP	RESULT ▶	ACTION TO TAKE
CODE 22 ENGINE RUNNING		
DF7 CHECK FOR EGR CODES		
• Are service codes 31, 32, 33, 34 or 35 present?	Yes ▶ No ▶	GO to Quick Test Step 5.0 for appropriate Pinpoint Test. GO to DF8.
DF8 CHECK MAP SENSOR		
• Key Off, wait 10 seconds. • Disconnect vacuum line from MAP sensor. • Install vacuum pump to MAP sensor. • Apply 18 in.-Hg. vacuum to MAP sensor. • Does MAP sensor hold vacuum?	Yes ▶ No ▶	RELEASE vacuum. GO to DF9. REPLACE MAP sensor. CONNECT vacuum line to MAP sensor. RERUN Quick Test.
DF9 ATTEMPT TO ELIMINATE CODE 22 (ENGINE RUNNING)		
• Key Off, wait 10 seconds. • Plug MAP vacuum supply hose. • Start engine and maintain 1500 ± 100 engine rpm. • Slowly apply 15 in.-Hg. vacuum to MAP sensor. • While maintaining rpm, perform Engine Running Quick Test. • Is code 22 still present? **NOTE: Disregard any other codes at this time.**	Yes ▶ No ▶	REPLACE MAP sensor. CONNECT vacuum line to MAP sensor. RERUN Quick Test. INSPECT vacuum supply hose to MAP sensor. SERVICE as necessary. If OK, SERVICE other engine running codes. If none, GO to Diagnostic Routines, Section 2 for a low vacuum problem.

Manifold Absolute Pressure (MAP)/ Barometric Pressure (BP) Sensor	Pinpoint Test	DF

TEST STEP	RESULT ▶	ACTION TO TAKE
DF21 MAP/BP TESTER OUTPUT READING		
• MAP Tester connected, refer to Note. • Key On. • Approximate Altitude (Ft.) Voltage Output (+/−.04 Volts) 0 1.59 1000 1.56 2000 1.53 3000 1.50 4000 1.47 5000 1.44 6000 1.41 7000 1.39 **NOTE: Measure several known good MAP sensors on available vehicles. The measured voltage will be typical for your location on the day of testing.** • Is reading in range for your altitude?	Yes ▶ No (Sensor output is out-of-range) ▶	For 1.9L EFI and 2.3L EFI TC engines GO to Diagnostic by Symptom in the Engine Supplement Section. For all others, GO to DF22. REPLACE MAP/BP sensor.
DF22 VACUUM LINE CHECK		
• Check MAP sensor vacuum line for holes, disconnections, kinks or blockage. • Are vacuum lines OK?	Yes ▶ No ▶	GO to Diagnostics by Symptom in the Engine Supplement Section. SERVICE vacuum lines to MAP sensor. RERUN Quick Test.

Manifold Absolute Pressure (MAP)/ Barometric Pressure (BP) Sensor	Pinpoint Test	DF

TEST STEP	RESULT ▶	ACTION TO TAKE
DF90 SERVICE CODE 22: CONTINUOUS TEST: EXERCISE MAP SENSOR		
• Using continuous monitor mode, observe VOM or STAR LED for indication of a fault while performing the following: • Connect a vacuum pump to the MAP sensor. • Slowly apply 84 kPa (25 in.-Hg.) vacuum to the sensor. • Slowly bleed vacuum off the MAP sensor. • Lightly tap on MAP sensor (simulate road shock). • Wiggle MAP connector. • Is fault indicated?	Yes ▶ No ▶	DISCONNECT and INSPECT connectors. If connector and terminals are good, REPLACE sensor. RERUN Quick Test. GO to DF91.
DF91 CHECK EEC-IV HARNESS		
• Observe VOM or STAR LED for a fault indication while performing the following: • Referring to the illustration in Step DF90, grasp the harness closest to the sensor connector. Wiggle, shake or bend a small section of the EEC-IV system harness while working your way to the dash panel. Also wiggle, shake or bend the EEC-IV harness from the dash panel to the processor. • Is a fault indicated?	Yes ▶ No ▶	ISOLATE fault and SERVICE as necessary. RERUN Quick Test. GO to DF92.
DF92 CHECK PROCESSOR AND HARNESS CONNECTORS		
• Key Off, wait 10 seconds. • Disconnect processor 60 Pin connector. • Inspect both connectors and connector terminals for obvious damage or faults. • Are connectors and terminals OK?	No ▶ Yes ▶	SERVICE as necessary. RERUN Quick Test. Unable to duplicate fault at this time. Continuous code 22 testing complete.

Knock Sensor	Pinpoint Test	DG

TEST STEP	RESULT ▶	ACTION TO TAKE
DG1 SERVICE CODE 25: GENERATE KNOCK MANUALLY		
NOTE: With knock conditions sensitive to fuel, altitude and weather, perform Step DG1 before servicing any components. • Prepare vehicle to run (Engine Running Self-Test). • Equipment needed: 4 oz. hammer. • Prepare to rap-tap on exhaust manifold. directly above the knock sensor, when the Dynamic Response Signal is given. NOTE: There is no need to actually depress throttle at this point. • Perform Engine Running Self-Test. • Rap moderately on exhaust manifold when meter indicates Dynamic Response Test is ready. • 15 seconds later a code will be generated. • Check for code 25. NOTE: Ignore all other codes at this point.	No ▶ Yes ▶ NOTE: Service code 25 may be received whenever the engine is not tapped	Knock system OK. REPEAT Engine Running Self-Test and SERVICE any other codes from that test. GO to DG2.
DG2 TEST KNOCK CIRCUIT FOR VOLTAGE		
• Key Off, wait 10 seconds. • Disconnect knock sensor connector and inspect. • Set DVOM on 20V scale. • Key On, Engine Off. • Measure voltage at the vehicle harness connector between KS and signal return.	Voltage is between 1 and 4V ▶ Voltage is less than 1V ▶ Voltage is greater than 4V ▶	GO to DG6. GO to DG3. GO to DG5.
DG3 CHECK CONTINUITY OF KS AND SIGNAL RETURN CIRCUITS		
• Key Off, wait 10 seconds. • Disconnect processor 60 Pin connector and inspect for damaged pins, corrosion, loose wires. Service as necessary. • Connect Breakout box to harness. Leave processor disconnected. • Knock sensor disconnected. • DVOM on 200 ohm scale. • Measure resistance between Signal Return at the vehicle harness and test Pin 46 at the Breakout box and between KS at the vehicle harness and test Pin 23 at the Breakout box.	Both resistances less than 5 ohms ▶ Either resistance 5 ohms or greater ▶	GO to DG4. SERVICE open circuit. RERUN Quick Test.

Knock Sensor	Pinpoint Test	DG

DG

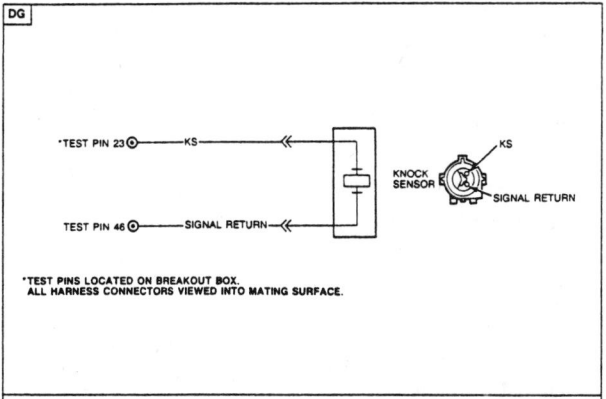

*TEST PIN 23 —— KS
TEST PIN 46 —— SIGNAL RETURN

KNOCK SENSOR
KS
SIGNAL RETURN

*TEST PINS LOCATED ON BREAKOUT BOX.
ALL HARNESS CONNECTORS VIEWED INTO MATING SURFACE.

STOP-WARNING

You should enter this Pinpoint Test only when a service code 25 is received in Quick Test Step 5.0 or you are directed here from Diagnostics by Symptom in the Engine Supplement Section.

To prevent the replacement of good components, be aware that the following non-EEC areas may be at fault:
• Fuel (quality).
• Basic engine.
• Spark timing.

This Pinpoint Test is intended to diagnose only the following:
• Knock sensor.
• Harness circuits: KS and Signal Return.
• Processor assembly.

TEST STEP	RESULT ▶	ACTION TO TAKE
DG4 CHECK KS CIRCUIT FOR SHORT TO GROUND		
• Key Off, wait 10 seconds. • Breakout box installed. • Processor disconnected. • Knock sensor disconnected. • DVOM on 200,000 ohm scale. • Measure resistance between KS at the vehicle harness and test Pins 40, 46 and 60 at the Breakout box.	All resistances 10,000 ohms or greater ▶ Any resistance less than 10,000 ohms ▶	GO to DG6. SERVICE harness short. RERUN Quick Test.
DG5 CHECK KS CIRCUIT FOR SHORT TO VOLTAGE		
• Key Off, wait 10 seconds. • Disconnect processor 60 Pin connector and inspect for damaged pins, corrosion, loose wires. Service as necessary. • Connect Breakout box to harness. Leave processor disconnected. • Knock sensor disconnected. • Key On, Engine Off. • DVOM on 20V scale. • Measure voltage between test Pin 23 and test Pin 40 at the Breakout box.	0.5V or greater ▶ Less than 0.5V ▶	SERVICE harness short to power. RERUN Quick Test. GO to DG6.
DG6 TEST PROCESSOR WITH SUBSTITUTE KNOCK SENSOR		
• Key Off, wait 10 seconds. • Remove Breakout box and reconnect processor. • Equipment Required: — Equivalent knock sensor (same part number). — 4 oz. hammer. • Plug substitute sensor in harness (do not install). • Perform Engine Running Self-Test. • Lightly tap knock sensor when Dynamic Test Ready Signal is given. • 15 seconds later, a code will be generated. • Check for code 25. NOTE: Ignore all other codes at this time.	No ▶ Yes ▶	INSTALL new knock sensor. RERUN Quick Test. REPLACE processor and REMOVE substitute sensor. RERUN Quick Test with original sensor.

Throttle Position Sensor (TPS) | Pinpoint Test | DH

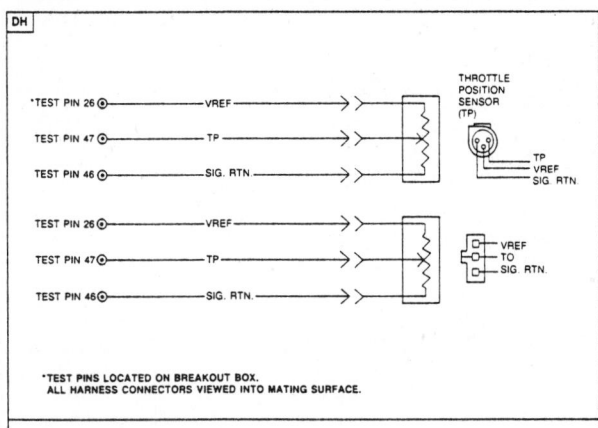

DH

*TEST PIN 26 — VREF — THROTTLE POSITION SENSOR (TP)
TEST PIN 47 — TP
TEST PIN 46 — SIG. RTN.

TP
VREF
SIG. RTN.

TEST PIN 26 — VREF
TEST PIN 47 — TP
TEST PIN 46 — SIG. RTN.

VREF
TO
SIG. RTN.

*TEST PINS LOCATED ON BREAKOUT BOX.
ALL HARNESS CONNECTORS VIEWED INTO MATING SURFACE.

STOP-WARNING

You should enter this Pinpoint Test only when a Service Code 23, 53, 63 or 73 is received in Quick Test Step 3.0, 5.0 or 6.0.

To prevent the replacement of good components, be aware that the following non-EEC areas may be at fault:
- Idle speeds/throttle stop adjustment.
- Binding throttle shaft/linkage or speed control linkage.
- Choke/high cam system, if equipped.

This Pinpoint Test is intended to diagnose only the following:
- TP sensor.
- Sensor harness circuits: VREF, TP Signal, and Signal Return.
- Processor assembly.

Throttle Position Sensor (TPS) | Pinpoint Test | DH

TEST STEP	RESULT ▶	ACTION TO TAKE
DH5 CHECK TP SIGNAL FOR SHORT TO POWER		
• Key Off, wait 10 seconds. TP harness disconnected. • DVOM on 200,000 ohm scale. • Disconnect processor 60 Pin connector and inspect for damaged pins, corrosion, loose wires. Service as necessary. • Install Breakout box, leave processor disconnected. • Measure resistance between test Pin 47 and test Pins 26 and 57 at the Breakout box.	Either resistance is less than 10,000 ohms ▶	SERVICE harness short. RERUN Quick Test.
	Both resistances are 10,000 ohms or greater ▶	REPLACE processor. RERUN Quick Test.
DH10 SERVICE CODE 63: GENERATE CODE 53		
• Key Off, wait 10 seconds, TP harness disconnected. • Jumper VREF to TP signal at TP vehicle harness connector. • Perform Key On, Engine Off self-test. **NOTE: If no codes are generated, immediately remove jumper and go directly to DH13.** • Check for Code 53 (Code 23) **NOTE: Ignore all other codes at this time.**	Code 53 present (Code 23 present) ▶	REPLACE TP sensor, REFER to Section 3 before replacement for adjustment procedures for EFI applications and RERUN Quick Test.
	Code 53 not present (Code 23 not present) ▶	GO to DH11 .
DH11 SERVICE CODE 63: CHECK VOLTAGE VREF TO SIGNAL RETURN		
• Refer to illustration DH. • Key Off, wait 10 seconds. • Disconnect TP vehicle harness connector at throttle body. Inspect for damaged pins, corrosion, and pins pushed out. Service as necessary. • DVOM on 20V scale. • Key On, Engine Off. • Measure voltage at the TP vehicle harness connector between VREF and Signal Return.	Voltage reading between 4V and 6V ▶	GO to DH12 .
	Voltage reading less than 4V or greater than 6V ▶	GO to Pinpoint Test Step C1 .

Throttle Position Sensor (TPS) | Pinpoint Test | DH

TEST STEP	RESULT ▶	ACTION TO TAKE
DH1 SERVICE CODE 23: THE FOLLOWING CHECK MUST BE MADE BEFORE SERVICING THIS CODE		
• Check for code 68: Key On, Engine Off or codes 58, 31 or 41 Engine Running.	Code(s) present	DISREGARD Code 23 at this time and RETURN to Quick Test Step 3.0B for code 68 or Step 5.0B for code 31, 41 or 58. PROCEED as directed.
	No codes present	GO to DH2 .
DH2 CHECK FOR STUCK THROTTLE PLATE		
• Visually inspect carburetor/throttle body and throttle linkage for binding or sticking. • Verify the throttle linkage is at mechanical/closed throttle. Check for: binding throttle linkage, speed control linkage, vacuum line/electrical harness interference, etc.	Throttle not stuck ▶	GO to DH3 .
	Throttle stuck ▶	CORRECT faults. RERUN Quick Test.
DH3 GENERATE CODE 63		
• Refer to illustration DH. • Key Off, wait 10 seconds. • Disconnect TP sensor vehicle harness connector at the throttle body. Inspect for damaged pins, corrosion, loose wires, etc. Service as necessary. • Perform Key On, Engine Off self-test and record codes. **NOTE: Ignore all other codes at this time.**	Code 63 present ▶	GO to DH4 .
	Code 63 not present ▶	GO to DH5 .
DH4 CHECK VOLTAGE VREF TO SIGNAL RETURN		
• Refer to illustration DH. • Key Off, wait 10 seconds. • Disconnect TP vehicle harness connector at throttle body. Inspect for damaged pins, corrosion, and pins pushed out. Service as necessary. • DVOM on 20V scale. • Key On, Engine Off. • Measure voltage at the TP vehicle harness connector between VREF and Signal Return.	Voltage reading between 4V and 6V ▶	REPLACE TP sensor. REFER to Section 3 before replacement for adjustment procedures for EFI applications. RERUN Quick Test.
	Voltage reading less than 4V or greater than 6V ▶	GO to Pinpoint Test Step C1 .

Throttle Position Sensor (TPS) | Pinpoint Test | DH

TEST STEP	RESULT ▶	ACTION TO TAKE
DH12 CHECK CONTINUITY OF TP CIRCUIT		
• Key Off, wait 10 seconds. TP harness disconnected. • DVOM on 200 ohm scale. • Disconnect processor 60 Pin connector and inspect for damaged pins, corrosion, loose wires. Service as necessary. • Connect Breakout box. Processor connected to Breakout box. • Measure resistance between TP Signal at the vehicle harness connector and test Pin 47 at the Breakout box.	Reading 5 ohms or greater ▶	SERVICE faulty circuit. CONNECT throttle position sensor. REMOVE Breakout box and RERUN Quick Test.
	Readings less than 5 ohms ▶	GO to DH13 .
DH13 CHECK RESISTANCE OF TP CIRCUIT TO GROUND/SIGNAL RETURN		
• Key Off, wait 10 seconds. TP harness disconnected. • Disconnect processor 60 Pin connector and inspect for damaged pins, corrosion, loose wires. Service as necessary. • DVOM on 200,000 ohm scale. • Measure resistance between TP signal at TP vehicle harness connector and test Pin 46 at the Breakout box and between TP signal at TP vehicle harness connector and ground.	Either reading is less than 10,000 ohms ▶	SERVICE circuit short and RERUN Quick Test.
	Both readings are 10,000 ohms or greater ▶	REPLACE processor. CONNECT throttle position sensor. REMOVE Breakout box and RERUN Quick Test.
DH20 SERVICE CODE 73: TP SENSOR MOVES IN ENGINE RESPONSE TEST		
NOTE: Code 73 indicates the TP Sensor did not exceed 25 percent of its rotation in the Engine Response Check. • Key Off. • Install Breakout box. • DVOM on 20V scale. • Connect DVOM to test Pins 47 and 46 at the Breakout box. • Perform Engine Running Quick Test, Step 5.0. • Verify DVOM reading exceeds 3.5V during brief WOT at Engine Response Check.	Reading exceeds 3.5V during Engine Response Check ▶	REPLACE processor. RERUN Quick Test.
	Reading does not exceed 3.5V during Engine Response Check ▶	VERIFY TP Sensor is properly attached to throttle body. If OK, REPLACE TP Sensor. Refer to Section 3 before replacement for adjustment procedures for EFI applications. RERUN Quick Test.

Throttle Position Sensor (TPS)	Pinpoint Test	DH

TEST STEP	RESULT	▶	ACTION TO TAKE
DH90 CONTINUOUS TEST SERVICE CODE 53: EXERCISE TP SENSOR • Using continuous monitor mode, observe VOM or STAR LED for indication of a fault while performing the following: • Move throttle slowly to WOT position. • Release throttle slowly to closed position and lightly tap on TP sensor (simulate road shock). • Wiggle TP harness connector. • Is a fault indicated?	Yes No	▶ ▶	GO to DH91. GO to DH92.
DH91 MEASURE THROTTLE POSITION SIGNAL VOLTAGE WHILE EXERCISING TP SENSOR • Key Off, wait 10 seconds. • Disconnect processor 60 Pin connector and inspect for damaged pins, corrosion, loose wires. Service as necessary. • Install Breakout box and reconnect processor. • VOM or STAR LED still connected to STO as in previous step. • Connect a DVOM from test Pin 47 to test Pin 46. • DVOM on 20V scale. • Key On engine Off. • While observing DVOM, repeat Step DH90. • Does the fault occur below 4.25V?	Yes No	▶ ▶	DISCONNECT and INSPECT connectors. If connector and terminals are good, REPLACE TP sensor, REFER to Shop Manual Group 24 and RERUN Quick Test. Throttle position sensor overtravel may have caused the continuous code 53. Sensor service is not required. To verify harness integrity, GO to DH92.

Throttle Position Sensor (TPS)	Pinpoint Test	DH

TEST STEP	RESULT	▶	ACTION TO TAKE
DH92 CHECK EEC-IV HARNESS • Observe VOM or STAR LED for a fault indication while performing the following: • Referring to the illustration in Step DH90, grasp the harness close to the sensor connector. Wiggle, shake or bend a small section of the EEC-IV system harness while working your way to the dash panel. Also wiggle, shake or bend the EEC-IV harness from the dash panel to the processor. • Is a fault indicated?	Yes No	▶ ▶	ISOLATE fault and make necessary repairs. REFER to appropriate figure. RERUN Quick Test. GO to DH93.
DH93 CHECK PROCESSOR AND HARNESS CONNECTORS • Key Off, wait 10 seconds. • Disconnect processor 60 Pin connector. • Inspect both connectors and connector terminals for obvious damage or faults. • Are connectors and terminals OK?	No Yes	▶ ▶	SERVICE as necessary. REPEAT Quick Test. Unable to duplicate fault at this time. Continuous code 53 testing complete.
DH94 CONTINUOUS TEST SERVICE CODE 63: EXERCISE TP SENSOR • Using continuous monitor mode, observe VOM or STAR LED for indication of a fault while performing the following: • Move throttle slowly to WOT position. • Release throttle slowly to closed condition. • Lightly tap on TP sensor (simulate road shock). • Wiggle TP harness connector. • Is a fault indicated?	Yes No	▶ ▶	DISCONNECT and INSPECT connectors. If connector and terminals are good, REPLACE TP sensor, REFER to Shop Manual Group 24 and RERUN Quick Test. GO to DH95.

Throttle Position Sensor (TPS)	Pinpoint Test	DH

TEST STEP	RESULT	▶	ACTION TO TAKE
DH95 CHECK EEC-IV HARNESS • Observe VOM or STAR LED for a fault indication while performing the following: • Referring to the illustration in Step DH94 grasp the harness close to the sensor connector. Wiggle, shake or bend a small section of the EEC-IV system harness while working your way to the dash panel. Also wiggle, shake or bend the EEC-IV harness from the dash panel to the processor. • Is a fault indicated?	Yes No	▶ ▶	ISOLATE fault and make necessary repairs. REFER to appropriate figure. RERUN Quick Test. Go to DH96.
DH96 CHECK PROCESSOR AND HARNESS CONNECTORS • Key Off, wait 10 seconds. • Disconnect processor 60 Pin connector. • Inspect both connectors and connector terminals for obvious damage or faults. • Are connectors and terminals OK?	No Yes	▶ ▶	SERVICE as necessary. RERUN Quick Test. Unable to duplicate fault at this time. Continuous code 63 testing complete.

Vane Airflow Sensor (VAF)	Pinpoint Test	DK

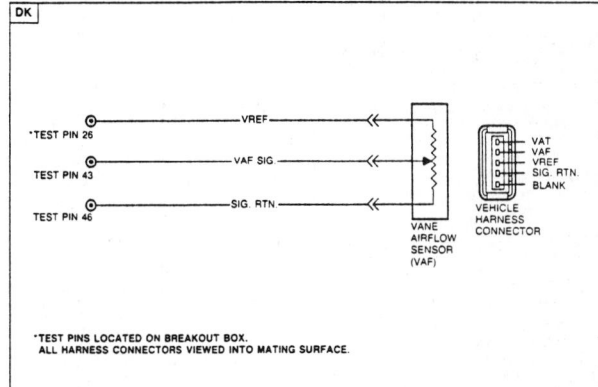

*TEST PINS LOCATED ON BREAKOUT BOX.
ALL HARNESS CONNECTORS VIEWED INTO MATING SURFACE.

STOP-WARNING

You should enter this Pinpoint Test only when a service code 26, 56, 66 or 76 is received in Quick Test Step 3.0, 5.0 or 6.0.

To prevent the replacement of good components, be aware that the following non-EEC areas may be at fault:

• Check for unmetered air (air leaks) between VAF meter and throttle body.
• Vacuum leaks.
• Engine sealing (PCV sealing, CANP, valve cover seal dipstick seated).

This Pinpoint Test is intended to diagnose only the following:

• VAF meter.
• Processor.
• Harness circuits: VREF, VAF Sig. and Signal Return.

Vane Airflow Sensor (VAF)	Pinpoint Test	DK

TEST STEP	RESULT ▶	ACTION TO TAKE
FAULT CODE 26		
DK1 CHECK FOR CONTAMINATION		
NOTE: Code 26 indicates the vane airflow input to the processor is out of engine off or engine idle limits (engine off 0.15-0.50V/engine idle 1.50-2.70V). There have been no opens or shorts in the VAF circuit or a code 56 (signal always high) or 66 (signal always low) would have been generated.		
• Key Off, wait 10 seconds. • Remove air cleaner element and check for contamination (oil residue, foreign material, etc.) that may impede VAF sensor vane movement and service as necessary.	Yes ▶	REPLACE vane meter. RERUN Quick Test.
• Is service code 26 present in the Key On Engine Off portion of Quick Test?	No ▶	GO to DK2.
DK2 VAF SENSOR CHECK		
• Key Off, air cleaner element reinstalled. • Check for unmetered air leaks between vane meter and throttle body. • Disconnect processor 60 Pin connector. Inspect for damaged pins, corrosion, loose wires, etc. Service as necessary. • Install Breakout box. Connect processor to Breakout box harness. • DVOM on 20V scale. • Key On, engine off. • Place new unsharpened pencil as shown below.	Yes ▶	Vane meter is capable of outputting an acceptable signal. The VAF code 26 has been caused by incorrect engine speed or an unmetered air leak (vacuum leak). SERVICE as necessary. REMOVE Breakout box. RERUN Quick Test.
• Measure voltage between test Pins 43 (test Pin 27 on 2.3L EFI TC) and 46 at the Breakout box. • Is voltage between 2.8V and 3.7V?	No ▶	REMOVE Breakout box. REPLACE processor. RERUN Quick Test.

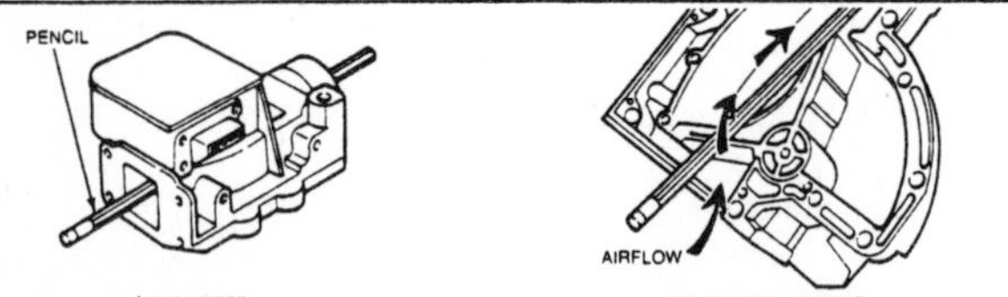

PENCIL

VANE METER

AIRFLOW

VAF SENSOR AIR VANE

Vane Airflow Sensor (VAF)	Pinpoint Test	DK

TEST STEP	RESULT ▶	ACTION TO TAKE
FAULT CODE 56		
DK10 INDUCE OPPOSITE CODE		
• Key Off, wait 10 seconds.	Yes ▶	GO to DK11.
• Disconnect vehicle harness from vane meter. Inspect for damaged pins, corrosion, loose wires, etc. Service as necessary.	No ▶	GO to DK12.
• Run Key On Engine Off Quick Test. • Is code 66 present?		
NOTE: Disconnecting vane meter disconnects both VAF and VAT sensors. A code 58 should also be present. Disregard all codes except VAF codes at this time.		
DK11 CHECK VAF TO SIGNAL RETURN VOLTAGE		
• Key Off, wait 10 seconds. • Harness disconnected from vane meter. • Key On, Engine Off. • DVOM on 20V scale.	Yes ▶	REPLACE vane meter. RECONNECT harness. RERUN Quick Test.
• Measure voltage at the vane meter vehicle harness connector between VREF and Signal Return. • Is voltage between 4.0 and 6.0 volts?	No ▶	GO to Pinpoint Test Step C1.
DK12 CHECK VAF SIGNAL FOR SHORT		
• Key Off, wait 10 seconds. • Harness disconnected from vane meter. • Disconnect processor 60 Pin connector. Inspect for damaged pins, corrosion, loose wires, etc. Service as necessary. • Install Breakout box, leave processor disconnected. • DVOM on 200,000 ohm scale.	Yes ▶	REPLACE processor. REMOVE Breakout box. RECONNECT processor and vane meter. RERUN Quick Test.
• Measure resistance between test Pin 43 (test Pin 27 on 2.3L EFI TC) and test Pins 26 and 57 at the Breakout box. • Are both resistances greater than 10,000 ohms?	No ▶	SERVICE circuit shorts. REMOVE Breakout box. RECONNECT processor and vane meter. RERUN Quick Test.

Vane Airflow Sensor (VAF)	Pinpoint Test	DK

TEST STEP	RESULT ▶	ACTION TO TAKE
FAULT CODE 66		
DK20 INDUCE OPPOSITE CODE		
• Key Off, wait 10 seconds. • Disconnect vehicle harness from vane meter. • Install jumper wire in vane meter vehicle harness connector between VREF and VAF signal. • Perform Key On Engine Off Self-Test.	Yes ▶	REPLACE vane meter. REMOVE jumper wire. RECONNECT vane meter. RERUN Quick Test.
NOTE: If no codes are generated, immediately remove jumper and go directly to DK23.	No ▶	REMOVE jumper wire and GO to DK21.
• Is code 56 present?		
NOTE: Disconnecting vane meter disconnects both VAF and VAT sensors. Code 58 should also be present. Disregard all codes except VAF codes at this time.		
DK21 CHECK VREF TO SIGNAL RETURN VOLTAGE		
• Key off, wait 10 seconds. • Harness disconnected from vane meter. • Key On, Engine Off. • DVOM on 20V scale.	Yes ▶	GO to DK22.
• Measure voltage at the vane meter vehicle harness connector between VREF and Signal Return. • Is voltage between 4.0 and 6.0 volts?	No ▶	GO to Pinpoint Test Step C1.
DK22 CHECK CONTINUITY OF VAF SIGNAL		
• Key Off, harness disconnected from vane meter. • Disconnect processor 60 Pin connector. Inspect for damaged pins, corrosion, loose wires, etc. Service as necessary. • Install Breakout box; leave processor disconnected. • DVOM on 200 ohm scale.	Yes ▶	SERVICE circuit open. REMOVE Breakout box. RECONNECT processor and vane meter. RERUN Quick Test.
• Measure resistance between VAF signal, at the vane meter vehicle harness connector, and test Pin 43 (test Pin 27 on 2.3L EFI TC) at the Breakout box. • Is resistance greater than 5 ohms?	No ▶	GO to DK23.

Vane Airflow Sensor (VAF)	Pinpoint Test	DK

TEST STEP	RESULT ▶	ACTION TO TAKE
DK23 CHECK VAF SIGNAL FOR SHORT		
• Key Off, wait 10 seconds. • Processor disconnected. • Harness disconnected from vane meter. • DVOM on 200,000 ohm scale.	Yes ▶	REPLACE processor. REMOVE Breakout box. RECONNECT processor and vane meter. RERUN Quick Test.
• Measure resistance at the vane meter vehicle harness between VAF signal and signal return and between VAF signal and negative battery terminal. • Are both resistances greater than 10,000 ohms?	No ▶	SERVICE circuit shorts. RECONNECT vane meter. RERUN Quick Test.
FAULT CODE 76		
DK30 CHECK FOR VOLTAGE INCREASE IN VAF SIGNAL TO SIGNAL RETURN		
NOTE: A sharp snap of the throttle may not be sufficient to pass this test. Be sure to move throttle to WOT and return.		
• Key Off, wait 10 seconds. • Disconnect processor 60 Pin connector. Inspect for damaged pins, corrosion, loose wires, etc. Service as necessary. • Install Breakout box. Connect processor to Breakout box harness. • DVOM on 20V scale.	Yes ▶	GO to DK31.
• Connect DVOM to test Pins 43 (test Pin 27 on 2.3L EFI TC) and 46. • Perform Engine Running Quick Test while monitoring DVOM.	No ▶	CHECK air cleaner duct for obstruction. If OK, REPLACE vane meter.
• After dynamic response prompt code 1(0) operator does a brief WOT. DVOM should increase more than 2.0V from reading before WOT.	• Observe service codes at end of test. • Did voltage increase more than 2.0 volts?	
DK31 CHECK PROCESSOR		
• Observe Key On Engine Running service codes at end of Pinpoint Test DK30. • Is code 76 present?	Yes ▶	REPLACE processor. REMOVE Breakout box. RERUN Quick Test.
	No ▶	Vane meter is OK. SERVICE other codes as necessary.

Vane Airflow Sensor (VAF)	Pinpoint Test	DK

TEST STEP	RESULT ▶	ACTION TO TAKE
DK90 SERVICE CODE 56 CONTINUOUS TEST: CHECK VAF SENSOR		
• Using continuous monitor mode, observe VOM or STAR LED for indication of a fault while performing the following: • Lightly tap on VAF sensor (simulate road shock). • Wiggle VAF connector. • Is a fault indicated?	Yes ▶	DISCONNECT and INSPECT connectors. If connector and terminals are good, REPLACE VAF sensor. RERUN Quick Test.
	No ▶	GO to DK91 .
DK91 CHECK EEC-IV HARNESS		
• Observe VOM or STAR LED for a fault indication while performing the following: • Referring to the illustration in Step DK90, grasp the harness close to the sensor connector. Wiggle, shake or bend a small section of the EEC-IV system harness while working your way to the dash panel. Also wiggle, shake or bend the EEC-IV harness from the dash panel to the processor. • Is a fault indicated?	Yes ▶	ISOLATE fault and make necessary repairs. REFER to appropriate figure. RERUN Quick Test.
	No ▶	GO to DK92 .
DK92 CHECK PROCESSOR AND HARNESS CONNECTORS		
• Key Off, wait 10 seconds. • Disconnect processor 60 Pin connector. • Inspect both connectors and connector terminals for obvious damage or faults. • Are connectors and terminals OK?	Yes ▶	Unable to duplicate fault at this time. Continuous code 56 testing complete.
	No ▶	SERVICE as necessary. RERUN Quick Test.

Vane Airflow Sensor (VAF)	Pinpoint Test	DK

TEST STEP	RESULT ▶	ACTION TO TAKE
DK93 SERVICE CODE 66 CONTINUOUS TEST: CHECK VAF SENSOR		
• Using continuous monitor mode, observe VOM or STAR LED for indication of a fault while performing the following: • Lightly tap on VAF sensor (simulate road shock). • Wiggle VAF connector. • Is a fault indicated?	Yes ▶	DISCONNECT and INSPECT connectors. If connector and terminals are good, REPLACE sensor. RERUN Quick Test.
	No ▶	GO to DK94 .
DK94 CHECK EEC-IV HARNESS		
• Observe VOM or STAR LED for a fault indication while performing the following: • Referring to the illustration in Step DK93 grasp the harness close to the sensor connector. Wiggle, shake or bend a small section of the EEC-IV system harness while working your way to the dash panel. Also wiggle, shake or bend the EEC-IV harness from the dash panel to the processor. • Is a fault indicated?	Yes ▶	ISOLATE fault and make necessary repairs. REFER to appropriate figure. RERUN Quick Test.
	No ▶	Go to DK95 .
DK95 CHECK PROCESSOR AND HARNESS CONNECTORS		
• Key Off, wait 10 seconds. • Disconnect processor 60 Pin connector. • Inspect both connectors and connector terminals for obvious damage or faults. • Are connectors and terminals OK?	No ▶	SERVICE as necessary. RERUN Quick Test.
	Yes ▶	Unable to duplicate fault at this time. Continuous code 66 testing complete.

Pressure Feedback EGR (PFE) EGR Valve Regulator (EVR)	Pinpoint Test	DL

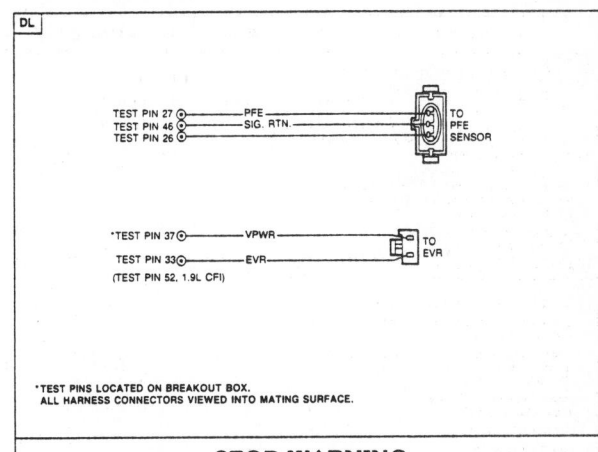

DL

TEST PIN 27 —— PFE
TEST PIN 46 —— SIG. RTN.
TEST PIN 26
TO PFE SENSOR

*TEST PIN 37 —— VPWR
TEST PIN 33 —— EVR
(TEST PIN 52, 1.9L CFI)
TO EVR

*TEST PINS LOCATED ON BREAKOUT BOX.
ALL HARNESS CONNECTORS VIEWED INTO MATING SURFACE.

STOP-WARNING

You should enter this Pinpoint Test only when a Service Code 31, 32, 33, 34, 35 or 84 is received in Quick Test Step 3.0, 5.0 or 6.0.

To prevent the replacement of good components, be aware that the following non-EEC area may be at fault:

• Damaged EGR valve.

This Pinpoint Test is intended to diagnose only the following:

• PFE sensor.
• Harness circuits: VREF, PFE, Signal Return, EVR, VPWR.
• EVR (EGR valve regulator).
• EGR valve assembly.
• Processor assembly.

Pressure Feedback EGR (PFE) EGR Valve Regulator (EVR)	Pinpoint Test	DL

TEST STEP	RESULT ▶	ACTION TO TAKE
SERVICE CODE 31		
DL1 ATTEMPT TO GENERATE OPPOSITE CODE (35)		
• Key Off. • Disconnect PFE vehicle harness at sensor. • Jumper VREF to PFE signal at vehicle harness sensor connector. • Perform Key On Engine Off Self-Test. **NOTE: If no codes are generated, immediately remove jumper and GO directly to Step DL4.** • Is code 35 present? **NOTE: Ignore all other codes at this time.**	Yes ▶	REMOVE Jumper. REPLACE PFE sensor. RERUN Quick Test.
	No ▶	REMOVE jumper. GO to DL2 .
DL2 MEASURE VREF TO SIGNAL RETURN VOLTAGE		
• Key Off. • PFE harness disconnected. • DVOM on 20V scale. • Key On Engine Off. • Measure voltage at PFE vehicle harness connector between VREF and Signal Return. • Is voltage reading between 4 and 6 volts? • Refer to illustration DL.	Yes ▶	GO to DL3 .
	No ▶	GO to C1 .
DL3 CHECK CONTINUITY OF PFE SIGNAL		
• Key Off. • PFE harness disconnected. • DVOM on 200 ohm scale. • Disconnect processor 60 Pin connector and inspect for damaged pins, corrosion, loose wires, etc. Service as necessary. • Connect Breakout box to harness. Processor connected to Breakout box. • Measure resistance between PFE signal at vehicle harness sensor connector and test Pin 27 at the Breakout box. • Is resistance reading 5 ohms or greater?	Yes ▶	SERVICE faulty circuit. CONNECT PFE sensor. REMOVE Breakout box. RERUN Quick Test.
	No ▶	GO to DL4 .

Pressure Feedback EGR (PFE) EGR Valve Regulator (EVR)	Pinpoint Test	DL

TEST STEP	RESULT	▶	ACTION TO TAKE
DL4 CHECK RESISTANCE OF PFE SIGNAL TO GROUND AND SIGNAL RETURN			
• Key Off. • PFE harness disconnected. • Breakout box installed. • Processor disconnected. • DVOM on 200,000 ohm scale. • Measure resistance between PFE signal at PFE vehicle harness connector and ground. • Measure resistance between PFE signal at the PFE vehicle harness connector and test Pin 46 (Signal Return) at the Breakout box. • Is either resistance reading less than 10,000 ohms?	Yes No	▶ ▶	SERVICE short circuit. CONNECT PFE. REMOVE Breakout box. RERUN Quick Test. REPLACE processor. CONNECT PFE sensor. REMOVE Breakout box. RERUN Quick Test.
SERVICE CODE 35			
DL5 ATTEMPT TO GENERATE OPPOSITE CODE (31)			
• Key Off. • Disconnect PFE vehicle harness at sensor. Inspect for damaged pins, corrosion, loose wires, etc. Service as necessary. • Perform Key On Engine Off Self-Test, and record codes. • Is code 31 present? **NOTE: Ignore all other codes at this time.**	Yes No	▶ ▶	GO to DL6 . GO to DL7 .
DL6 MEASURE VREF TO SIGNAL RETURN VOLTAGE			
• Key Off. • PFE harness disconnected. • DVOM on 20V scale. • Key On Engine Off. • Measure voltage at PFE vehicle harness connector between VREF and Signal Return. • Is voltage reading between 4 and 6 volts? • Refer to illustration DL.	Yes No	▶ ▶	REPLACE PFE sensor. RERUN Quick Test. GO to C1 .

Pressure Feedback EGR (PFE) EGR Valve Regulator (EVR)	Pinpoint Test	DL

TEST STEP	RESULT	▶	ACTION TO TAKE
DL10 MEASURE VREF TO SIGNAL RETURN VOLTAGE			
• Key Off. • Disconnect PFE sensor and inspect for damaged pins, corrosion, loose wires, etc. Service as necessary. • DVOM on 20V scale. • Key On Engine Off. • Measure voltage at PFE vehicle harness connector between VREF and Signal Return. • Is voltage reading between 4 and 6 volts? • Refer to illustration DL.	Yes No	▶ ▶	REPLACE PFE sensor. RERUN Quick Test. GO to Pinpoint Test C1 .
SERVICE CODE 84			
DL11 MEASURE EVR SOLENOID RESISTANCE			
• Key Off. • DVOM on 200 ohms scale. • Disconnect EVR solenoid connector and measure solenoid resistance. • Is resistance reading between 30 and 70 ohms?	Yes No	▶ ▶	GO to DL12 . REPLACE EVR solenoid assembly. RERUN Quick Test.
DL12 CHECK FOR VPWR AT EVR SOLENOID			
• EVR solenoid disconnected from harness. • DVOM on 20V scale. • Key on Engine Off. • Measure voltage between battery negative terminal and VPWR circuit at EVR solenoid vehicle harness connector. • Is voltage reading less than 10.5 volts?	Yes No	▶ ▶	SERVICE VPWR open circuit. RERUN Quick Test. GO to DL13 .
DL13 CHECK CONTINUITY OF EVR CIRCUIT			
• Key Off. • EVR solenoid disconnected from harness. • Disconnect processor 60 Pin connector and inspect for damaged pins, corrosion, loose wires, etc. Service as necessary. • Install Breakout box to processor harness connector. Leave processor disconnected. • DVOM on 200 ohm scale. • Measure resistance between test Pin 33 at the Breakout box and EVR signal at the EVR solenoid vehicle harness connector. • Is resistance reading less than 5 ohms?	Yes No	▶ ▶	GO to DL14 . SERVICE open circuit. REMOVE Breakout box. CONNECT process EVR solenoid. RERUN Quick Test.

Pressure Feedback EGR (PFE) EGR Valve Regulator (EVR)	Pinpoint Test	DL

TEST STEP	RESULT	▶	ACTION TO TAKE
DL7 CHECK PFE CIRCUIT FOR SHORT TO POWER			
• Key Off. • PFE harness disconnected. • Disconnect processor 60 Pin connector and inspect for damaged pins, corrosion, loose wires, etc. Service as necessary. • Install Breakout box, leave processor disconnected. • DVOM on 200,000 ohm scale. • Measure the resistance between test Pin 27 and test Pins 26 and 57 at the Breakout box. • Is either resistance reading less than 10,000 ohms?	Yes No	▶ ▶	SERVICE harness short. REMOVE Breakout box. CONNECT PFE sensor. RERUN Quick Test. REPLACE processor. REMOVE Breakout box. CONNECT PFE sensor. RERUN Quick Test.
SERVICE CODE: 34			
DL8 PFE SENSOR OUT OF RANGE			
• PFE system can sense a lack of pressure in the vehicle exhaust system. An efficient garage exhaust ventilation system, installed during Key On Engine Off Quick Test, may deflect the PFE sensor and generate a code 34. Remove the ventilation system and retest. • Is code 34 present?	Yes No	▶ ▶	GO to DL9 . ADDRESS any other codes in Key On Engine Off, if none CONTINUE with remaining Quick Test.
DL9 CHECK PRESSURE FEED TUBE TO PFE SENSOR			
• Remove the pressure feed tube from PFE sensor. • Inspect complete tube, including PFE inlet for blockage. • Is blockage present?	Yes No	▶ ▶	SERVICE as necessary. RERUN Quick Test. GO to DL10 .

Pressure Feedback EGR (PFE) EGR Valve Regulator (EVR)	Pinpoint Test	DL

TEST STEP	RESULT	▶	ACTION TO TAKE
DL14 CHECK EVR CIRCUIT FOR SHORT TO POWER AND GROUND			
• Key Off. • Breakout box installed, processor disconnected. • EVR solenoid disconnected. • DVOM on 200,000 ohm scale. • Measure resistance between test Pin 33 (EVR) and test Pins 37 and 57 (VPWR) and 40, 46 and 60 (GRD) at the Breakout box. • Are any readings less than 10,000 ohms?	Yes No	▶ ▶	SERVICE short circuit. REMOVE Breakout box. RECONNECT harness to processor and EVR solenoid. RERUN Quick Test. If code is repeated, REPLACE processor. REPLACE processor. REMOVE Breakout box. RECONNECT harness to processor and EVR solenoid. RERUN Quick Test.
SERVICE CODE 32			
DL20 VERIFY ENGINE RUNNING CODES			
The PFE system can sense a lack of pressure in the vehicle exhaust system. An efficient garage exhaust ventilation system installed during Key On Engine Run Quick Test may, on some calibrations, deflect the PFE sensor and generate a code 32. Temporarily, remove garage forced ventilation system and properly vent to atmosphere. • RERUN Engine Running Quick Test. • Is code 32 present?	Yes No	▶ ▶	GO to DL21 . ADDRESS any other codes in Engine Running. If none, CONTINUE with remaining Quick Test.

Pressure Feedback EGR (PFE) EGR Valve Regulator (EVR)	Pinpoint Test	DL

TEST STEP	RESULT ▶	ACTION TO TAKE
DL21 ATTEMPT TO SEPARATE EVR FROM PFE		
• Key Off. • Disconnect EGR valve vacuum line at valve and plug line. • Perform Engine Running Quick Test. • Is code 31 or 32 present?	Yes ▶ No ▶	GO to DL22. GO to DL23.
DL22 CHECK PFE SENSOR SUPPLY TUBE		
• Key Off. • Check PFE sensor supply tube for obstructions and/or leaks. • Are there any obstructions or leaks?	Yes ▶ No ▶	SERVICE as necessary. RECONNECT all lines and RERUN Quick Test. GO to EGR Diagnostic, Section 6.
DL23 CHECK EVR FILTER		
• Key Off. • Remove and inspect EVR filter for contamination. **NOTE: Blockage of filter will cause vacuum to be applied to EGR valve prematurely.** • Is filter contaminated?	Yes ▶ No ▶	REPLACE filter. RECONNECT all lines. RERUN Quick Test. REPLACE EVR solenoid. RERUN Quick Test.
ENGINE RUNNING SERVICE CODE 34 AND 35		
DL25 CHECK FOR EXCESSIVE EXHAUST BACK PRESSURE		
• Service codes 34 and 35 in Engine Running Self-Test indicate excessive exhaust back pressure; There are two possible causes: (A). The exhaust system is restricted, and (B). PFE sensor has shifted high. • Key Off. • Substitute known good PFE sensor in place of original. • Rerun Key On Engine Running Quick Test. • Is code 34 or 35 present?	Yes ▶ No ▶	GO to Section 5, Catalyst and Exhaust Systems Restricted Exhaust System Diagnosis. Original PFE was the cause of the original 34 or 35. REPLACE PFE sensor. RERUN Quick Test.

Pressure Feedback EGR (PFE) EGR Valve Regulator (EVR)	Pinpoint Test	DL

TEST STEP	RESULT ▶	ACTION TO TAKE
SERVICE CODE 33		
DL30 VERIFY VACUUM IS PRESENT AT VALVE		
• Key Off. • Standard vacuum gauge in. Hg (Mercury). • Tee in vacuum gauge at EGR valve. • Perform Engine Running Quick Test while observing vacuum gauge. • Is vacuum reading 1 in.-Hg. or less? **NOTE: Disregard code output.**	Yes ▶ No ▶	GO to DL31. GO to DL34.
DL31 VACUUM SUPPLY VERIFICATION		
• Key Off. • Do vacuum lines from EVR solenoid to EGR valve and source to EVR solenoid have loose connections, cracks or obstructions?	Yes ▶ No ▶	SERVICE as necessary. RERUN Quick Test. GO to DL32.
DL32 VERIFY VACUUM TO EVR		
• Key On Engine Running. • Attach vacuum gauge to source line from manifold. • Is vacuum present?	Yes ▶ No ▶	REPLACE EVR solenoid. RERUN Quick Test. REPLACE vacuum line to EVR. RERUN Quick Test.
DL34 CHECK EGR CONTROL PFE SENSOR TUBE		
• Key Off. • Is control pressure input tube to PFE sensor cracked, disconnected or obstructed?	Yes ▶ No ▶	SERVICE as necessary. RERUN Quick Test. REPLACE PFE Sensor. RERUN Quick Test.

Pressure Feedback EGR (PFE) EGR Valve Regulator (EVR)	Pinpoint Test	DL

TEST STEP	RESULT ▶	ACTION TO TAKE
DL90 SERVICE CODE 31 OR 35 CONTINUOUS TEST: EXERCISE PFE SENSOR		
• Using continuous monitor mode, observe VOM or STAR LED for indication of a fault while performing the following: • Connect a vacuum pump to the PFE sensor. • Slowly apply 5 in.-Hg. to the sensor. • Slowly bleed vacuum off the PFE sensor. • Lightly tap on PFE sensor (simulate road shock). • Wiggle PFE connector. • Is fault indicated?	Yes ▶ No ▶	DISCONNECT and INSPECT connectors. If connector and terminals are good, REPLACE sensor. RERUN Quick Test. GO to DL91.

Pressure Feedback EGR (PFE) EGR Valve Regulator (EVR)	Pinpoint Test	DL

TEST STEP	RESULT ▶	ACTION TO TAKE
DL91 CHECK EEC-IV HARNESS		
• Observe VOM or STAR LED for a fault indication while performing the following: • Referring to the illustration in Step DL90 grasp the harness closest to the sensor connector. Wiggle, shake or bend a small section of the EEC-IV system harness while working your way to the dash panel. Also wiggle, shake or bend the EEC-IV harness from the dash panel to the processor. • Is a fault indicated?	Yes ▶ No ▶	ISOLATE fault and SERVICE as necessary. RERUN Quick Test. GO to DL92.
DL92 CHECK PROCESSOR AND HARNESS CONNECTORS		
• Key Off, wait 10 seconds. • Disconnect processor 60 Pin connector. • Inspect both connectors and connector terminals for obvious damage or faults. • Are connectors and terminals OK?	Yes ▶ No ▶	Unable to duplicate and/or identify fault at this time. Continuous code 31 or 35 testing complete. SERVICE as necessary. RERUN Quick Test.
DL93 SERVICE CODE 34: CONTINUOUS TEST — INSPECT PFE SUPPLY TUBE FOR BLOCKAGE		
• Key Off. • Remove PFE sensor and inspect sensor supply inlet for liquids and/or any type of blockage. • Inspect PFE supply tube to EGR valve base for liquids and/or blockage. • Is supply tube free of any blockage?	Yes ▶ No ▶	Unable to duplicate and/or identify fault at this time. Continuous code 34 testing complete. CLEAN and/or SERVICE as necessary. RERUN Quick Test.

Pressure Feedback EGR (PFE) EGR Valve Regulator (EVR)	Pinpoint Test	DL

TEST STEP	RESULT ▶	ACTION TO TAKE
DL94 SERVICE CODE 32: CONTINUOUS TEST — INSPECT EGR VALVE FOR SMOOTH OPERATION.		
• Key Off. • Connect a vacuum pump to the EGR valve. • Apply 10 in.-Hg. of vacuum to EGR valve. • While observing EGR valve, release vacuum. • Does EGR valve function in a smooth manner? NOTE: Repeat test if necessary to ensure accurate result.	Yes ▶ No ▶	GO to DL95. GO to EGR Valve Diagnostic Section 6.
DL95 INSPECT VACUUM LINES BETWEEN EVR SOLENOID AND EGR VALVE		
• Inspect EGR valve vacuum supply line from EVR solenoid for kinks and/or obstructions. • Is vacuum supply line to EGR valve free of any obstructions?	Yes ▶ No ▶	GO to DL96. SERVICE as necessary. RERUN Quick Test.
DL96 EVR REGULATOR FILTER INSPECTION		
• Carefully check EVR filter for contamination and/or obstructions. • Is EVR filter condition acceptable?	Yes ▶ No ▶	Unable to duplicate and/or identify fault at this time. Continuous code 34 testing complete. REPLACE EVR filter. RERUN Quick Test.
DL97 SERVICE CODE 33: CONTINUOUS TEST — INSPECT EGR VALVE FOR FREE OPERATION.		
• Key Off. • Connect a vacuum pump to the EGR valve. • While observing the EGR valve, slowly apply 10 in.-Hg. vacuum. NOTE: EGR valve should begin to open with a very small amount of vacuum, approximately 1 to 1.5 in.-Hg. and be fully open with about 4 in.-Hg. vacuum. • Does EGR valve move freely and smoothly?	Yes ▶ No ▶	GO to DL98. GO to EGR Valve Diagnostic Section 6.

EGR Valve Position Sensor (EVP) EGR Valve Regulator (EVR)	Pinpoint Test	DN

DN

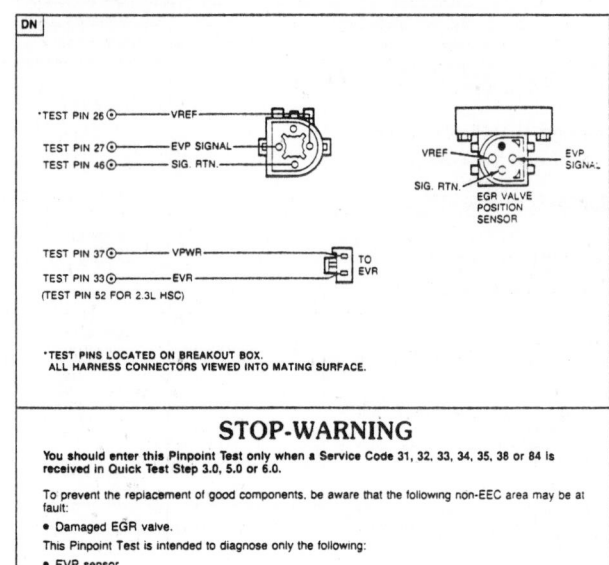

*TEST PIN 26 — VREF
TEST PIN 27 — EVP SIGNAL
TEST PIN 46 — SIG. RTN.

TEST PIN 37 — VPWR
TEST PIN 33 — EVR   TO EVR
(TEST PIN 52 FOR 2.3L HSC)

*TEST PINS LOCATED ON BREAKOUT BOX.
ALL HARNESS CONNECTORS VIEWED INTO MATING SURFACE.

STOP-WARNING

You should enter this Pinpoint Test only when a Service Code 31, 32, 33, 34, 35, 38 or 84 is received in Quick Test Step 3.0, 5.0 or 6.0.

To prevent the replacement of good components, be aware that the following non-EEC area may be at fault:
• Damaged EGR valve.
This Pinpoint Test is intended to diagnose only the following:
• EVP sensor.
• Harness circuits: VREF, EVP, Signal Return, EVR, VPWR.
• EVR (EGR valve regulator).
• EGR valve assembly.
• Processor assembly.
• EGR and EVR vacuum lines.

Pressure Feedback EGR (PFE) EGR Valve Regulator (EVR)	Pinpoint Test	DL

TEST STEP	RESULT ▶	ACTION TO TAKE
DL98 EVR HARNESS CHECK		
• Key Off. • Disconnect processor 60 Pin connector and inspect for damaged pins, corrosion, loose wires, etc. Service as necessary. • Connect Breakout box to harness. Processor connected to Breakout box. • Enter output state check. • DVOM on 20 V scale. • Connect DVOM negative test lead to test Pin 40 at the Breakout box and DVOM positive test lead to test Pin 33. • Cycle throttle if necessary to indicate 10.5 V or greater. • Remain at this position. • While observing DVOM, grasp the harness closest to the EVR connector. Wiggle, shake or bend a small section of the EEC-IV system harness while working your way to the dash panel. Lightly tap EVR solenoid to simulate road vibration. • Does DVOM indicate less than 10.5 V?	Yes ▶ No ▶	SERVICE as necessary. RERUN Quick Test. Unable to duplicate and/or identify fault at this time. Continuous code 33 testing complete.

EGR Valve Position Sensor (EVP) EGR Valve Regulator (EVR)	Pinpoint Test	DN

TEST STEP	RESULT ▶	ACTION TO TAKE
SERVICE CODE: 31		
DN1 ATTEMPT TO GENERATE CODE (35)		
• Key Off. • Disconnect EVP vehicle harness at sensor. • Jumper VREF to EVP signal at vehicle harness sensor connector. • Perform Key On Engine Off Self-Test. • Is code 35 present? NOTE: Ignore all other codes at this time.	Yes ▶ No ▶	REPLACE EVP sensor. RERUN Quick Test. REMOVE jumper. GO to DN2.
DN2 MEASURE VOLTAGE BETWEEN VREF AND SIGNAL RETURN		
• Key Off. • EVP disconnected from harness. • DVOM on 20 V scale. • Key on, engine off. • Measure voltage at EVP vehicle harness connector between VREF and Signal Return. • Is voltage between 4 and 6 volts?	Yes ▶ No ▶	GO to DN3. GO to C1.
DN3 CHECK CONTINUITY OF EVP SIGNAL		
• Key Off, EVP harness disconnected. • DVOM on 200 ohm scale. • Disconnect processor 60 Pin connector and inspect for damaged pins, corrosion, loose wires, etc. Service as necessary. • Connect Breakout box to harness. Processor connected to Breakout box. • Measure resistance between EVP signal at vehicle harness connector and test Pin 27 at the Breakout box. • Is resistance 5 ohms or less?	Yes ▶ No ▶	GO to DN4. SERVICE open circuit. CONNECT EVP sensor. REMOVE Breakout box. RERUN Quick Test.

EGR Valve Position Sensor (EVP) EGR Valve Regulator (EVR)	Pinpoint Test	DN

TEST STEP	RESULT	▶	ACTION TO TAKE
DN4 CHECK RESISTANCE OF EVP SIGNAL TO GROUND AND SIGNAL RETURN			
• Key Off. • EVP harness disconnected. • Breakout box installed. • Processor disconnected. • DVOM on 200,000 ohm scale. • Measure resistance between EVP signal at EVP vehicle harness connector and ground. • Measure resistance between EVP signal at EVP vehicle harness connector and test Pin 46 (Signal Return) at the Breakout box. • Are both resistances greater than 10,000 ohms?	Yes	▶	REPLACE processor. CONNECT EVP sensor. REMOVE Breakout box. RERUN Quick Test.
	No	▶	SERVICE short circuit. CONNECT EVP. REMOVE Breakout box. RERUN Quick Test.
SERVICE CODE: 35			
DN5 ATTEMPT TO GENERATE CODE 31			
• Key Off. • Disconnect EVP vehicle harness at sensor. inspect for damaged pins, corrosion, loose wires, etc. Service as necessary. Leave EVP sensor disconnected. • Perform Key On Engine Off Self-Test, and record codes. • Is code 31 present? NOTE: Ignore all other codes at this time.	Yes	▶	GO to DN6.
	No	▶	GO to DN7.
DN6 MEASURE VREF TO SIGNAL RETURN VOLTAGE			
• Key Off. • EVP harness disconnected. • DVOM on 20V scale. • Key on, engine off. • Measure voltage at EVP vehicle harness connector between VREF and Signal Return. • Is voltage between 4.0 and 6.0 volts?	Yes	▶	REPLACE EVP sensor. RERUN Quick Test.
	No	▶	GO to C1.

EGR Valve Position Sensor (EVP) EGR Valve Regulator (EVR)	Pinpoint Test	DN

TEST STEP	RESULT	▶	ACTION TO TAKE
DN7 CHECK EVP CIRCUIT FOR SHORT TO POWER			
• Key Off. • EVP disconnected from harness. • Disconnect processor 60 Pin connector and inspect for damaged pins, corrosion, loose wires, etc. Service as necessary. • Install Breakout box, leave processor disconnected. • DVOM on 200,000 ohm scale. • Measure the resistance between test Pin 27 and test Pins 26 and 57 at the Breakout box. • Are both resistances greater than 10,000 ohms?	Yes	▶	REPLACE processor. REMOVE Breakout box. CONNECT EVP sensor. RERUN Quick Test.
	No	▶	SERVICE harness short. REMOVE Breakout box, CONNECT EVP sensor. RERUN Quick Test.
SERVICE CODE: 84			
DN10 MEASURE EVR SOLENOID RESISTANCE			
• Key Off. • DVOM on 200 ohm scale. • Disconnect EVR solenoid connector and measure solenoid resistance. • Is resistance between 30 and 70 ohms?	Yes	▶	GO to DN11.
	No	▶	REPLACE EVR solenoid assembly. RERUN Quick Test.
DN11 CHECK FOR VPWR AT EVR SOLENOID			
• EVR solenoid disconnected from harness. • DVOM on 20V scale. • Key on, engine off. • Measure voltage between battery negative terminal and VPWR circuit at EVR solenoid vehicle harness connector. • Is voltage greater than 10.5 V?	Yes	▶	GO to DN12.
	No	▶	SERVICE VPWR open circuit. RERUN Quick Test.

EGR Valve Position Sensor (EVP) EGR Valve Regulator (EVR)	Pinpoint Test	DN

TEST STEP	RESULT	▶	ACTION TO TAKE
DN12 CHECK CONTINUITY OF EVR CIRCUIT			
• Key Off. • EVR solenoid disconnected from harness. • Disconnect processor 60 Pin connector and inspect for damaged pins, corrosion, loose wires, etc. Service as necessary. • Install Breakout box to processor harness connector. Leave processor disconnected. • DVOM on 200 ohm scale. • Measure resistance between test Pin 33 (test Pin 52 for 2.3L HSC) at the Breakout box and EVR signal at the EVR solenoid vehicle harness connector. • Is resistance less than 5 ohms?	Yes	▶	GO to DN13.
	No	▶	SERVICE open circuit. REMOVE Breakout box. CONNECT process EVR solenoid. RERUN Quick Test.
DN13 CHECK EVR CIRCUIT FOR SHORT TO POWER AND GROUND			
• Key Off. • Breakout box installed, processor disconnected. • EVR solenoid disconnected. • DVOM on 200,000 ohm scale. • Measure resistance between test Pin 33 (test Pin 52 for 2.3L HSC) EVR signal and test Pins 37 and 57 (VPWR) and 40, 46 and 60 (GRD) at the Breakout box. • Are all resistances greater than 10,000 ohms?	Yes	▶	REPLACE processor. REMOVE Breakout box. RECONNECT processor and EVR solenoid. RERUN Quick Test.
	No	▶	SERVICE short circuit. REMOVE Breakout box. RECONNECT processor and EVR solenoid. RERUN Quick Test. If code is repeated. REPLACE processor.

EGR Valve Position Sensor (EVP) EGR Valve Regulator (EVR)	Pinpoint Test	DN

TEST STEP	RESULT	▶	ACTION TO TAKE
DN20			
Code 34 Key On Engine Off, indicates that the EGR valve and/or EVP sensor is not fully seated in the closed position. NOTE: Because of the preload on the installed EVP sensor, it is very difficult to determine whether the problem cause is that the EGR valve is not seated, or that the EVP sensor is not in contact with the EGR valve stem.			
SUBSTITUTE EVP SENSOR ON ORIGINAL EGR VALVE			
• Key Off, wait 10 seconds. • Install a known good EVP sensor on original EGR valve. • Perform Key On Engine Off Self-Test. • Is code 34 present?	Yes	▶	GO to EGR Valve Diagnostic Section 6.
	No	▶	The original code 34 was the result of the original EVP sensor. SERVICE EVP sensor as necessary. RERUN Quick Test.
DN25			
Code 32 Key On Engine Off or Engine Running: indicates that the EGR valve and/or EVP sensor is lower than normal in the closed position. NOTE: Because of the preload of the EVP sensor, it is difficult to determine whether the EGR valve has malfunctioned or if the EVP sensor has abnormally high resistance.			
SUBSTITUTE EVP SENSOR ON ORIGINAL EGR VALVE			
• Key Off, wait 10 seconds. • Install a known good EVP sensor on original EGR valve. • Perform Key On Engine Off Self-Test. • Is code 32 present?	Yes	▶	GO to EGR Valve Diagnostic Section 6.
	No	▶	The original code 32 was the result of the original EVP sensor. SERVICE EVP sensor as necessary. RERUN Quick Test.

EGR Valve Position Sensor (EVP) EGR Valve Regulator (EVR)	Pinpoint Test	DN

TEST STEP	RESULT ▶	ACTION TO TAKE
DN40		
NOTE: Code 33 Key On Engine Running indicates that the EVP sensor reading did not change after the EVR solenoid was instructed by the processor to open the EGR valve. Items that are known: • EVR solenoid is electrically capable (indicated by a pass code 11 in Key On Engine Off). • EVP sensor was in its expected range when the EGR valve was closed.		
VERIFY VACUUM IS PRESENT AT EGR VALVE • Key Off. • Standard vacuum gauge in.-Hg. • Tee in vacuum gauge at EGR valve. • Perform Engine Running Self-Test while observing vacuum gauge. • Is vacuum greater than 1.5 in.-Hg. (5 kPa)?	Yes ▶ No ▶	GO to DN43. GO to DN41.
DN41 VERIFY VACUUM SUPPLY TO EVR SOLENOID • Key Off. • Disconnect the vacuum source to the EVR solenoid. • Install a vacuum gauge at source vacuum line. • Start engine. • Is vacuum greater than 10 in.-Hg. (33 kPa)?	Yes ▶ No ▶	GO to DN42. CHECK source vacuum line to EVR solenoid. SERVICE as necessary. RERUN Quick Test.
DN42 CHECK VACUUM LINE FROM EVR SOLENOID TO EGR VALVE • Carefully check vacuum line for cracks, loose connector, blockage, kinks and leaks. • Is vacuum line good?	Yes ▶ No ▶	CHECK EVR solenoid filter for obstructions. REPLACE as necessary. If OK, REPLACE EVR solenoid assembly. RECONNECT all vacuum lines. RERUN Quick Test. SERVICE vacuum lines as necessary. RECONNECT vacuum lines and RERUN Quick Test.

EGR Valve Position Sensor (EVP) EGR Valve Regulator (EVR)	Pinpoint Test	DN

TEST STEP	RESULT ▶	ACTION TO TAKE
DN55		
Code 38 Engine Running indicates that after opening the EGR valve (during the Engine Running Self Test) the EGR vacuum system was unable to maintain a specific opening (EVP position).		
VERIFY EGR VALVES VACUUM HOLDING CAPABILITY • Key Off. • Disconnect vacuum line at EGR valve. • With a hand vacuum pump, apply 10 in.-Hg. (33 kPa) to EGR valve. • Does vacuum hold for 10 seconds?	Yes ▶ No ▶	GO to DN56. GO to EGR Valve Diagnostic Section 6.
DN56 EVR SOLENOID TO EGR VALVE VACUUM LINE VERIFICATION • Key off. • Closely inspect the vacuum line from the EVR solenoid to the EGR valve for any source of leakage, which would include cracks, holes, loose connections etc. • Is the vacuum line good?	Yes ▶ No ▶	REPLACE the EVR solenoid. RERUN Quick Test. SERVICE vacuum line as necessary. RERUN Quick Test.
DN60 CHECK VACUUM LINE • Key Off, wait 10 seconds. • Vacuum lines reconnected. • Carefully check EGR vacuum line system from EGR valve to EVR for obstructions, kinks, leaks, etc. • Is vacuum line in good condition?	Yes ▶ No ▶	CHECK EVR filter for obstructions. REPLACE as necessary. If OK, REPLACE EVR solenoid. RECONNECT all vacuum lines. RERUN Quick Test. SERVICE as necessary. RERUN Quick Test.

EGR Valve Position Sensor (EVP) EGR Valve Regulator (EVR)	Pinpoint Test	DN

TEST STEP	RESULT ▶	ACTION TO TAKE
DN43 SUBSTITUTE EVP SENSOR ON ORIGINAL EGR VALVE • Key Off, wait 10 seconds. • Install a known good EVP sensor on original EGR valve. • Perform Engine Running Self-Test. • Is code 33 present?	Yes ▶ No ▶	GO to EGR Valve Diagnostic Section 6. The original code 33 was the result of the original EVP sensor. SERVICE EVP sensor as necessary. RERUN Quick Test.
DN50 SERVICE CODE 34: EGR VALVE OPERATION, ENGINE RUNNING SELF-TEST • Key Off. • Disconnect vacuum hose from EGR valve and plug hose. • Perform Engine Running Self-Test. • Is code 34 present?	Yes ▶ No ▶	GO to DN51. CHECK EVR filter for obstructions. REPLACE as necessary. If OK, REPLACE solenoid assembly. RECONNECT all vacuum lines. RERUN Quick Test.
DN51 CHECK EVP RESISTANCE WHILE APPLYING VACUUM TO EGR VALVE • Key Off. • Disconnect harness from EVP sensor. Inspect for damaged pins, corrosion, and pins pushed out. Service as necessary. • DVOM on 200,000 ohm scale. • Disconnect vacuum line at EGR valve. • Connect vacuum pump to EGR valve. • Measure resistance at the EVP sensor between EVP signal and VREF while increasing vacuum to 10 in. Hg. (33 kPa). • Observe resistance as vacuum increases. • Does resistance decrease gradually from no more than 5,500 ohms to no less than 100 ohms?	Yes ▶ No ▶	GO to EGR Valve Diagnostic Section 6. REPLACE EVP sensor. RECONNECT vacuum lines.

EGR Valve Position Sensor (EVP) EGR Valve Regulator (EVR)	Pinpoint Test	DN

TEST STEP	RESULT ▶	ACTION TO TAKE
DN90 CODE 32 CONTINUOUS TEST		
• **Code 32: The EVP circuit indicated that the EGR valve was closed further than normal with the engine at stabilized operating temperature and at idle.**		
MEASURE EVP SIGNAL VOLTAGE WHILE EXERCISING EVP SENSOR • Key Off, wait 10 seconds. • Disconnect processor 60 Pin connector and inspect for damaged pins, corrosion, loose wires, etc. Service as necessary. • Install Breakout box and reconnect processor. • Connect a vacuum pump to the EGR valve. • Connect a DVOM from test Pin 27 to test Pin 46. • DVOM on 20V scale. • Key on, engine off. • Observe DVOM. • Very slowly apply 6 in.-Hg. (20 kPa) vacuum to the EGR valve. • Slowly bleed vacuum off the EGR valve and lightly tap on EVP sensor (simulate road shock). • Are any voltage readings less than 0.29 volts?	Yes ▶ No ▶	EGR valve may have caused continuous code 32. Sensor service is not required. GO to EGR Valve Diagnostic Section 6. Unable to duplicate code 32 fault at this time. Test completed.

EGR Valve Position Sensor (EVP) EGR Valve Regulator (EVR)	Pinpoint Test	DN

TEST STEP	RESULT	►	ACTION TO TAKE
DN92 CODE 31 AND/OR 35 CONTINUOUS TEST			
• Code 31: The EVP circuit indicated an open in the EVP signal or VREF, or a short to signal return with the engine at stabilized operating temperature and at idle. • Code 35: The EVP circuit indicated a short to VREF and/or V Power, or an open in signal return with the engine at stabilized operating temperature and at idle. CHECK EEC-IV HARNESS			
• Observe VOM or STAR LED for a fault indication while performing the following: • Refer to illustration below by code for possible circuit faults. • Grasp the harness close to the sensor connector. Wiggle, shake or bend a small section of the EEV-IV system harness while working your way to the dash panel. Also wiggle, shake or bend the EEC-IV harness from the dash panel to the processor. • Is a fault indicated?	Yes No	► ►	ISOLATE fault and SERVICE as necessary. REFER to appropriate figure. RERUN Quick Test. GO to DN93 .

CODE 31

```
VREF
EVP SIG
SIG RTN
PROCESSOR    HARNESS    EVP SENSOR
```

CODE 35

```
VREF
EVP SIG
SIG RTN
PROCESSOR    HARNESS    EVP SENSOR
```

EGR Valve Position Sensor (EVP) EGR Valve Regulator (EVR)	Pinpoint Test	DN

TEST STEP	RESULT	►	ACTION TO TAKE
DN93 CHECK PROCESSOR AND HARNESS CONNECTORS			
• Key Off, wait 10 seconds. • Disconnect processor 60 Pin connector. • Inspect both connectors and connector terminals for obvious damage or faults. • Are connectors and terminals OK?	Yes No	► ►	Unable to duplicate fault at this time. Continuous Code 31 or 35 testing complete. SERVICE as necessary. RERUN Quick Test.
DN95 CODE 33 CONTINUOUS TEST			
• Code 33: The EVP circuit indicated that the EGR valve did not open with the engine at stabilized temperature and with an EVR solenoid duty cycle present. LEAK TEST			
• Key Off. • Connect a vacuum pump to EGR valve. • Apply 20 in. Hg (66 kPa) to EGR valve. • Does EGR valve open and maintain vacuum?	Yes No	► ►	GO to DN96 . GO to EGR diagnostic, Section 6.
DN96 EVR CHECK			
• Using continuous monitor mode, observe VOM or STAR LED for indication of a fault while performing the following: • Grasp the harness close to the EVR solenoid connector, wiggle, shake or bend a small section of the harness while working your way to the processor. • Inspect connectors, terminals for obvious damage or faults. • Are any faults detected or indicated?	Yes No	► ►	ISOLATE fault and SERVICE as necessary. RERUN Quick Test. Unable to duplicate fault at this time, testing complete.

EGR Valve Position Sensor (EVP) EGR Valve Regulator (EVR)	Pinpoint Test	DN

TEST STEP	RESULT	►	ACTION TO TAKE
DN98 CODE 34 CONTINUOUS TEST			
• Code 34: The EVP circuit indicated that the EGR valve was open with the engine at stabilized operating temperature and at idle. CHECK EVP RESISTANCE WHILE APPLYING VACUUM TO EGR VALVE			
• Key Off. • Disconnect harness from EVP sensor. • Inspect for damaged pins, corrosion, and pins pushed out. Service as necessary. • DVOM on 200,000 ohm scale. • Disconnect vacuum line at EGR valve. • Connect vacuum pump to EGR valve. • Measure resistance at the EVP sensor between EVP signal Pin and VREF Pin while increasing vacuum to 10 in. Hg (33 kPa). • Observe resistance as vacuum increases. • Does resistance gradually change from no more than 5,500 ohms to no less than 100 ohms as the vacuum increases?	Yes No	► ►	GO to DN99 . GO to EGR Diagnostic Section 6.
DN99 EVR CHECK			
• Key Off. • Disconnect vacuum hose from EGR valve and plug hose. • Perform Engine Running Self-Test. • Is code 34 present?	Yes No	► ►	CHECK EVR filter for obstructions. REPLACE as necessary. If OK, REPLACE EVR solenoid. RECONNECT all vacuum lines. RERUN Quick Test. Unable to duplicate fault at this time.

Vehicle Speed Sensor	Pinpoint Test	DP

DP

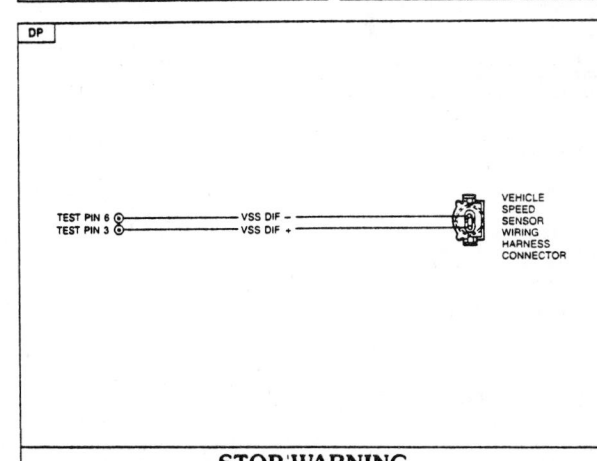

```
TEST PIN 6    VSS DIF −       VEHICLE
TEST PIN 3    VSS DIF +       SPEED
                              SENSOR
                              WIRING
                              HARNESS
                              CONNECTOR
```

STOP-WARNING

You should enter this Pinpoint Test only when service codes 27 or 29 are received in Quick Test Step 6.0.

This Pinpoint Test is intended to diagnose only the following:

• VSS Harness Circuit
• Vehicle Speed Sensor
• Processor Assembly

Vehicle Speed Sensor	Pinpoint Test	DP

TEST STEP	RESULT ▶	ACTION TO TAKE
DP1 DRIVE CYCLE FOR CHECKING VSS		
AUTOMATIC TRANSMISSION • Record and clear EEC-IV Self-Test continuous codes. • Warm engine to operating temperature. **NOTE: For 2.3L EFI T.C. automatic applications, engine must run without interruption for 5 minutes to enter VSS test.** • With PRNDL selector in 1st gear (low) position, accelerate moderately to 25 mph and coast down to idle and stop. Shut engine off. • Run Key On Engine Off Self-Test. Is code 29 present in continuous? (2.3L EFI T.C. uses code 27.) **MANUAL TRANSMISSION** • Record and clear EEC-IV Self-Test continuous codes. • Warm engine to operating temperature. • Starting in first gear, shift to second gear accelerate moderately to 40 mph, coast down to idle and stop. Shut engine off. • Run Key On Engine Off Self-Test. Is code 29 present in continuous? (2.3L EFI T.C. uses code 27.)	Yes ▶ No ▶	GO to DP2. Unable to duplicate fault at this time. If any other codes are present, return to Quick Test for directions. If codes are not present, test is completed.
DP2 SENSOR CHECK		
• Key Off, wait 10 seconds. • Locate and disconnect vehicle speed sensor. • DVOM on 200.000 ohm scale. • Measure resistance across vehicle speed sensor. • Is resistance between 190 and 240 ohms?	Yes ▶ No ▶	GO to DP3. REPLACE sensor. RERUN Test Step DP1.

Vehicle Speed Sensor	Pinpoint Test	DP

TEST STEP	RESULT ▶	ACTION TO TAKE
DP5 SUBSTITUTE VEHICLE SPEED SENSOR (VSS)		
• Substitute VSS with known good sensor. • Processor and VSS connected. • Perform Drive Cycle outlined in Test Step DP1 then return to this Step. • Is code 29 (for 2.3L EFI T.C. vehicles code 27) present in continuous?	Yes ▶ No ▶	REPLACE processor. RERUN Test Step DP1. The original continuous code 29 or 27 was the result of the original VSS. SERVICE VSS as necessary.

Vehicle Speed Sensor	Pinpoint Test	DP

TEST STEP	RESULT ▶	ACTION TO TAKE
DP3 CONTINUITY OF VEHICLE SPEED SENSOR (VSS) HARNESS		
• Key Off, wait 10 seconds. • Disconnect processor 60 Pin connector and inspect for damaged pins, corrosion, loose wires. Service as necessary. • Install Breakout box. • Processor and VSS disconnected. • DVOM on 200 ohm scale. • Measure resistance between test Pin 3 at the Breakout box and the VSS vehicle harness connector as shown below. • Measure resistance between test Pin 6 at the Breakout box and the VSS vehicle harness connector, as shown below. 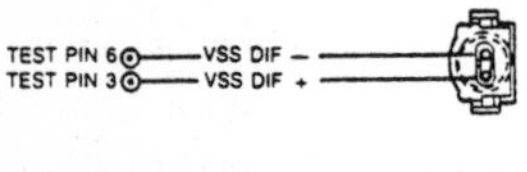 TEST PIN 6 ⊙ — VSS DIF − TEST PIN 3 ⊙ — VSS DIF + • Are both resistances 5 ohms or less?	Yes ▶ No ▶	GO to DP4. SERVICE open(s) in VSS harness. RERUN Test Step DP1.
DP4 CHECK VSS HARNESS FOR SHORTS TO POWER OR GROUND		
• Key Off. • Processor disconnected. • VSS disconnected. • DVOM on 200.000 ohm scale. • Measure resistance between test Pin 3 and test Pins 37, 40 and 6 at the Breakout box. Then measure resistance between test Pin 6 and test Pins 37 and 40 (except 2.3L EFI T.C.) at the Breakout box. • Are all readings greater than 10,000 ohms?	Yes ▶ No ▶	GO to DP5. SERVICE short(s) in VSS harness. RERUN Test Step DP1.

Neutral Drive Switch A/C Input	Pinpoint Test	FA

TEST STEP	RESULT ▶	ACTION TO TAKE
FA1 CODE 67 SYSTEM IDENTIFICATION		
2.5L CFI M/T, 5.0L M/T TK		GO to FA4.
2.9L M/T TK, 3.0L M/T TK, 5.0L M/T SEFI		GO to FA10.
1.9L M/T, 2.3L EFI M/T Car and Truck, 2.3L CFI M/T		GO to FA10.
2.3L Turbo		GO to FA15.
2.3L Turbo Octane Switch		GO to FA30.
4.9L M/T, Truck		GO to FA18.
All other systems		GO to FA2.
FA2 NEUTRAL DRIVE INPUT CHECK		
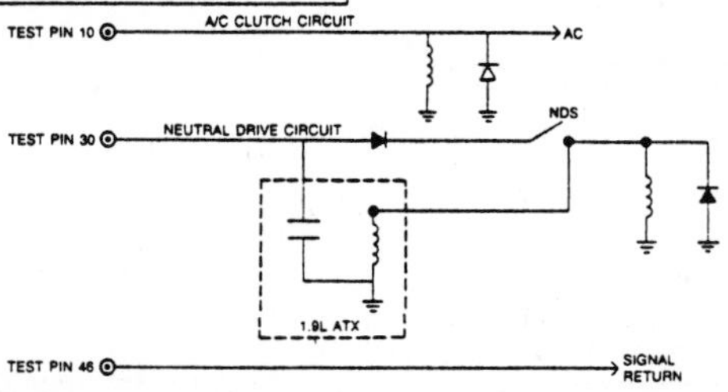		
• Key Off, wait 10 seconds. • Verify heater control is in OFF position, if so equipped. • Verify transmission is in NEUTRAL or PARK. • Disconnect processor 60 Pin connector and inspect for damaged pins, corrosion, loose wires. Service as necessary. • Install Breakout box. • Processor connected. • Key On, Engine Off. • DVOM on 20V scale. • Measure voltage between test Pin 30 (Neutral Drive circuit) at the Breakout box and chassis ground. • Is reading less than 1.0 volt?	Yes ▶ No ▶	GO to FA4. GO to FA3.

Neutral Drive Switch A/C Input	Pinpoint Test	FA

TEST STEP	RESULT	▶	ACTION TO TAKE
FA3 NEUTRAL DRIVE SWITCH CHECK			
• Key Off, wait 10 seconds. • Breakout box installed. • DVOM on 200 ohm scale. • Locate the Neutral Drive switch. • Disconnect vehicle harness from the Neutral Drive switch and measure resistance across the switch. • Is resistance reading less than 5 ohms?	Yes	▶	SERVICE open in vehicle harness Neutral Drive circuit. RERUN Quick Test.
	No	▶	REPLACE Neutral Drive switch. RERUN Quick Test
FA4 A/C INPUT CHECK			
NOTE: Before entering this test, verify A/C is off. If A/C was on, rerun Quick Test. If code 67 or code 79 is present, continue with this test. • Breakout box installed. • Processor disconnected. • Key on, engine off. • DVOM on 20V scale. • Measure voltage between test Pin 10 at the Breakout box and chassis ground. • Is voltage reading 1.0 volt or greater?	Yes	▶	SERVICE short to power in A/C clutch circuit. RERUN Quick Test.
	No	▶	REPLACE processor. RERUN Quick Test.

Neutral Drive Switch A/C Input	Pinpoint Test	FA

TEST STEP	RESULT	▶	ACTION TO TAKE
FA12 NEUTRAL CLUTCH HARNESS CHECK			
• Key Off. • DVOM on 200 ohm scale. • Breakout box installed. • Vehicle harness disconnected at the Neutral switch and Clutch switch. • Measure resistance between test Pin 30 and the Neutral switch harness connector and between test Pin 30 and the Clutch switch harness connector. • Measure resistance between test Pin 46 and the Neutral switch harness connector and between test Pin 46 and the Clutch switch harness connector. • Are all resistance readings less then 5 ohms?	Yes	▶	GO to FA4.
	No	▶	SERVICE the harness connector. RERUN Quick Test.
FA15 NEUTRAL INPUT CHECK — 2.3L TC M/T			
⊙———— NEUTRAL INPUT CIRCUIT ———— TEST PIN 30 ⊙———— SIGNAL RETURN ———— TEST PIN 46 A9654-A • Key Off, wait 10 seconds. • Verify A/C is off, if so equipped. • Disconnect processor 60 Pin connector and inspect for damaged pins, corrosion, loose wires. Service as necessary. • Install Breakout box. • Leave processor disconnected. • DVOM on 200 ohm scale. • Measure resistance between test Pin 30 (Neutral Input circuit) and test Pin 46 (Signal Return circuit) at the Breakout box. • Is resistance reading less than 5 ohms?	Yes	▶	GO to FA4.
	No	▶	SERVICE open in Neutral Input or Signal Return circuit. RERUN Quick Test.

Neutral Drive Switch A/C Input	Pinpoint Test	FA

TEST STEP	RESULT	▶	ACTION TO TAKE
FA10 NEUTRAL CLUTCH INPUT CHECK			

TEST PIN 10 ⊙—— A/C CLUTCH CIRCUIT ——→AC
 NEUTRAL DRIVE CIRCUIT   NEUTRAL SWITCH OPEN IN ANY GEAR
 TEST PIN 30 ⊙——   ——→ SIGNAL RETURN
 CLUTCH SWITCH OPEN WHEN CLUTCH PEDAL IS UP
 TEST PIN 46⊙——   —— SIG. RTN.
 	
 • Key Off, wait 10 seconds.
 • Verify A/C is off, if so equipped.
 • Disconnect processor 60 Pin connector and inspect for damaged pins, corrosion, loose wires. Service as necessary.
 • Install Breakout box.
 • Connect processor.
 • DVOM on 200 ohm scale.
 • Measure resistance between test Pin 30 and test Pin 46.
   1. With transmission in NEUTRAL and clutch up.
   2. With transmission in GEAR and clutch down.
 • Are both resistance readings less than 5 ohms?
	Yes	▶	GO to FA4.

	No	▶	GO to FA11.
FA11 NEUTRAL/CLUTCH SWITCH CHECK			
• Key Off. • DVOM on 200 ohm scale. • Breakout box installed. • Locate Neutral switch (on transmission) and Clutch switch (under dash). • Disconnect vehicle harness at both switches and inspect connectors for pushed back pins. • Measure resistance across the Neutral switch terminals with transmission in NEUTRAL and across the Clutch switch terminals with the clutch pedal down. • Are both resistance readings less than 5 ohms?	Yes	▶	GO to FA12.
	No	▶	REPLACE open switch(es). RECONNECT harness and RERUN Quick Test.

Neutral Drive Switch A/C Input	Pinpoint Test	FA

TEST STEP	RESULT	▶	ACTION TO TAKE
FA18 CLUTCH PEDAL SWITCH CHECK 4.9L M/T			
NOTE: The clutch pedal must be down during KOEO test; if not, a code 67 will result. • Key Off. • Disconnect processor 60 Pin connector and inspect for damaged pins, corrosion, loose wires. Service as necessary. • Install Breakout box. • DVOM on 200 ohm scale. • Clutch pedal down. • Measure resistance between test Pin 30 and test Pin 46, between test Pin 30 and test Pin 40. • Is resistance reading less than 5 ohms?	Yes	▶	REPAIR open in clutch circuit.
	No	▶	GO to FA4.
FA20 A/C INPUT CIRCUIT CHECK			
NOTE: A low idle with A/C could be the result of the processor not receiving, or recognizing the A/C input on Pin 10. • Key Off, wait 10 seconds. • Disconnect processor 60 Pin connector and inspect for damage, corrosion or loose wires. Service as necessary. • Install Breakout box. • Leave processor disconnected. • DVOM on 20 volt scale. • Key On. • A/C on. • Check voltage between Pin 10 and Pin 40. • Is voltage reading greater than 10.5 volts?	Yes	▶	REPLACE processor. RERUN Quick Test.
	No	▶	SERVICE open in A/C circuit. Refer to the appropriate engine schematic in Section 17 or 18. RERUN Quick Test.

Neutral Drive Switch A/C Input		Pinpoint Test	FA

TEST STEP	RESULT	▶	ACTION TO TAKE
FA30 CHECK OCTANE SWITCH INPUT FOR INPUT CHANGE • Key Off, wait 10 seconds. • Disconnect processor 60 Pin connector and inspect for damaged pins, corrosion, loose wires. Service as necessary. • Install Breakout box. Reconnect processor. • DVOM to 20V scale. • Connect positive test lead to test Pin 30 and negative test lead to test Pin 46 at the Breakout box. • Key On, Engine Off. • Cycle octane switch several times while observing DVOM. • Does voltage change from zero volts to 5V?	Yes No	▶ ▶	REPLACE processor. RERUN Quick Test. EEC-IV system OK. REFER to Shop Manual for boost diagnostics

Key Power Check		Pinpoint Test	FC

TEST STEP	RESULT	▶	ACTION TO TAKE
FC1 BATTERY VOLTAGE GREATER THAN 17.5V • Key Off, wait 10 seconds. • Install Breakout box with processor connected. • DVOM at 20V range and connected to test Pins 5 and 60 at the Breakout box. • Perform Engine Running Quick Test. Observe DVOM during test and record service codes.	Reading exceeds 17.5V during Quick Test Reading remains below 17.5V and code 65 is present Reading remains below 17.5V and code 65 is not present	▶ ▶ ▶	CORRECT charging system for over-voltage condition. REPLACE processor and RERUN Quick Test. GO to FC2
FC2 CODE 65 IN CONTINUOUS MEMORY • Perform Key On, Engine Off Quick Test and record continuous codes.	Code 65 not present Code 65 present	▶ ▶	TESTING complete. CHARGING system OK at this time. CHECK charging system. REFER to Shop Manual, Group 31 for cause of intermittent overcharging (greater than 17.5V).
FC3 BATTERY VOLTAGE LESS THAN 7.5V • Key Off, wait 10 seconds. • Disconnect processor 60 Pin connector and inspect for damaged pins, corrosion, loose wires. Service as necessary. • Install Breakout box to processor harness connector. • Processor connected. • DVOM on 20V scale. • Measure voltage between test Pin 5 and test Pin 60 at the Breakout box. • Perform Engine Running Quick Test.	Voltage below 7.5V during Quick Test Voltage remains above 7.5V and code 55 is present Voltage remains above 7.5V and code 55 is not present	▶ ▶ ▶	GO to FC4. REPLACE processor. RERUN Quick Test. GO to FC5

Key Power Check		Pinpoint Test	FC

FC

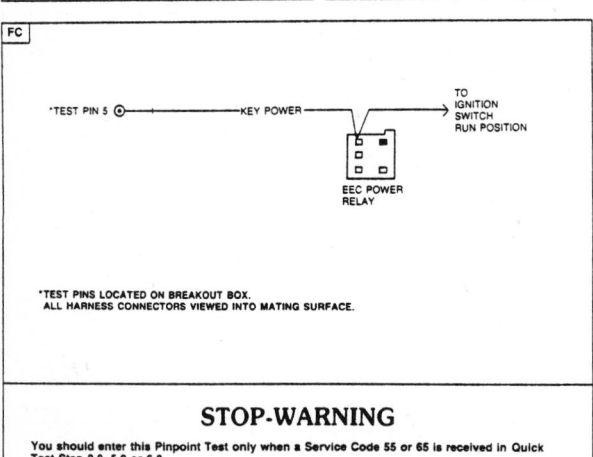

```
*TEST PIN 5 ○——————KEY POWER————                    TO
                                   ⌐        IGNITION
                                   │        SWITCH
                                   │        RUN POSITION
                              □  □
                              □  □
                              □  □
                            EEC POWER
                            RELAY
```

*TEST PINS LOCATED ON BREAKOUT BOX.
ALL HARNESS CONNECTORS VIEWED INTO MATING SURFACE.

STOP-WARNING

You should enter this Pinpoint Test only when a **Service Code 55 or 65** is received in Quick Test Step 3.0, 5.0 or 6.0.

To prevent the replacement of good components, be aware that the following non-EEC areas may be at fault:
• Charging system overvoltage.
• Battery charger connected with engine running.
• Jump starting.

This Pinpoint Test is intended to diagnose only the following:
• Harness circuit: key power.
• Processor.

Key Power Check		Pinpoint Test	FC

TEST STEP	RESULT	▶	ACTION TO TAKE
FC4 KEY POWER CIRCUIT CHECK • Key Off. • Breakout box installed, processor connected. • DVOM at 200 ohm scale. • Measure resistance between test Pin 5 at the Breakout box and key power terminal of EEC power relay.	5 ohms or less Greater than 5 ohms	▶ ▶	CORRECT charging system for under-voltage condition. SERVICE open in key power circuit. RERUN Quick Test.
FC5 CODE 55 IN CONTINUOUS MEMORY • Perform Key On, Engine Off Quick Test and record continuous codes.	Code 55 not present Code 55 present	▶ ▶	TESTING complete. CHARGING system OK at this time. CHECK charging system per Shop Manual, Group 31 for cause of intermittent overcharging (greater than 17.5V).

Brake On/Off (BOO)	Pinpoint Test	FD

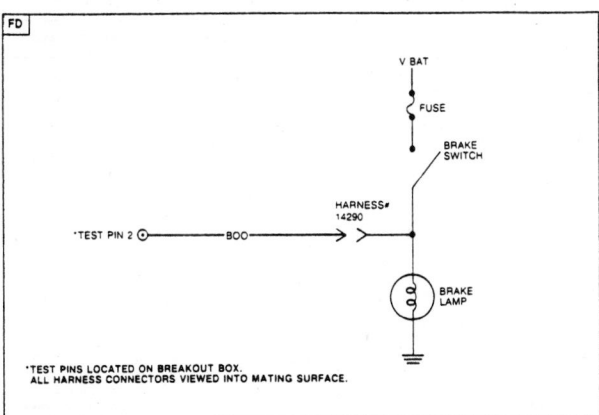

V BAT

FUSE

BRAKE SWITCH

HARNESS# 14290

*TEST PIN 2 ⊙——BOO——▷

BRAKE LAMP

*TEST PINS LOCATED ON BREAKOUT BOX.
ALL HARNESS CONNECTORS VIEWED INTO MATING SURFACE.

STOP-WARNING

You should enter this Pinpoint Test only when a Service Code 74 or 75 is received in Quick Test Step 5.0.

To prevent the replacement of good components, be aware that the following non-EEC areas may be at fault:

- Brake lamp, brake switch, and fuse.

This pinpoint test is intended to diagnose only the following:

- BOO circuit.
- Processor assembly.

Brake On/Off (BOO)	Pinpoint Test	FD

TEST STEP	RESULT	▶	ACTION TO TAKE
FD1 SERVICE CODE 74			
• Did you press brake during the Engine Running Quick Test? **NOTE: On some vehicles it is necessary to depress and release the brake after the dynamic response code 1(0) but before the brief WOT.**	Yes No	▶ ▶	GO to FD2. RERUN Engine Running Quick Test. PRESS brake once during test.
FD2 BOO CIRCUIT CYCLING			
• Key Off, wait 10 seconds. • Disconnect processor 60 Pin connector. Inspect for damaged pins, corrosion, loose wires, etc. Service as necessary. • Install Breakout box, leave processor disconnected. • DVOM on 20V scale. • Measure voltage between test Pin 2 and test Pin 40 at the Breakout box while depressing and releasing brake. • Does the voltage cycle?	Yes No	▶ ▶	REPLACE processor. RERUN Quick Test. GO to FD3.
FD3 BOO CIRCUIT SHORT TO GROUND			
• Key Off. • Breakout box installed. • Processor disconnected. • DVOM on 200 Ohm scale. • Disconnect BOO circuit from 14290 harness (12 pin connector). • Measure resistance between test Pin 2 at the Breakout box and ground. • Is resistance reading greater than 5 ohms?	Yes No	▶ ▶	GO to FD6. SERVICE BOO circuit short to ground. RERUN Engine Running Quick Test.

Brake On/Off (BOO)	Pinpoint Test	FD

TEST STEP	RESULT	▶	ACTION TO TAKE
FD4 BOO CIRCUIT CYCLING CODE 75			
• Key Off, wait 10 seconds. • Disconnect processor 60 Pin connector. Inspect for damaged pins, corrosion, loose wires, etc. Service as necessary. • Install Breakout box, leave processor disconnected. • DVOM on 20V scale. • Measure voltage between test Pin 2 and test Pin 40 at the Breakout box while depressing and releasing brake. • Does the voltage cycle?	Yes No	▶ ▶	REPLACE processor. RERUN Quick Test. GO to FD5.
FD5 BOO CIRCUIT SHORT TO POWER			
• Key Off. • Breakout box installed. • Processor disconnected. • DVOM on 20V scale. • Disconnect BOO circuit from 14290 harness (12 Pin connector). • Measure voltage between test Pin 2 at the Breakout box and engine block ground. • Is voltage reading greater than 10.5 volts?	Yes No	▶ ▶	SERVICE BOO circuit short to power. BOO circuit OK. GO to Shop Manual, Group 32 to SERVICE stoplamp circuit.
FD6 BOO HARNESS CONTINUITY CHECK			
• Key Off. • Breakout box installed. • Processor disconnected. • DVOM on 200 Ohm scale. • Disconnect BOO circuit from 14290 harness (12 pin connector). • Measure resistance between test Pin 2 at the Breakout box and BOO circuit at the 14290 harness connector. • Is resistance reading greater than 5 ohms?	Yes No	▶ ▶	SERVICE BOO circuit for open. RERUN Engine Running Self Test. GO to Shop Manual, Group 32.

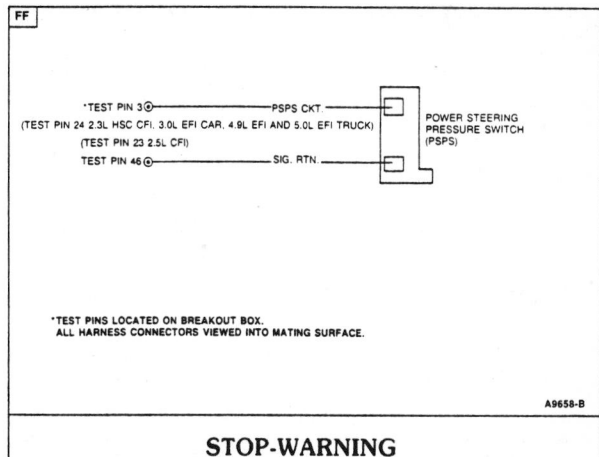

TEST PIN 2 ⊙——BOO——

14290 HARNESS CONNECTOR

Power Steering Pressure Switch (PSPS)	Pinpoint Test	FF

FF

*TEST PIN 3 ⊙————PSPS CKT————
(TEST PIN 24 2.3L HSC CFI, 3.0L EFI CAR, 4.9L EFI AND 5.0L EFI TRUCK)
(TEST PIN 23 2.5L CFI)
TEST PIN 46 ⊙————SIG. RTN.————

POWER STEERING PRESSURE SWITCH (PSPS)

*TEST PINS LOCATED ON BREAKOUT BOX.
ALL HARNESS CONNECTORS VIEWED INTO MATING SURFACE.

A9658-B

STOP-WARNING

You should enter this Pinpoint Test only when a Service Code 52 is received in Quick Test Steps 3.0, 5.0 or if you are directed here from Diagnostics by Symptom in the Engine Supplement Section.

To prevent the replacement of good components, be aware that the following non-EEC areas may be at fault:

- Idle speeds/throttle stop adjustment.
- Binding throttle shaft/linkage or speed control linkage.

This Pinpoint Test is intended to diagnose only the following:

- Power steering pressure switch.
- Switch harness circuits: PSPS Signal, and Signal Return.
- Processor assembly.

Power Steering Pressure Switch (PSPS)	Pinpoint Test	FF

TEST STEP	RESULT ▶	ACTION TO TAKE
FF1 ATTEMPT TO ELIMINATE CODE 52 • Key Off, wait 10 seconds. • Disconnect PSPS. • Jumper PSPS circuit to Signal Return at vehicle harness connector. • Rerun Key On, Engine Off Quick Test. • Is code 52 still present?	Yes ▶ No ▶	GO to FF2 . REPLACE PSPS. RERUN Quick Test.
FF2 PSPS HARNESS CHECK • Key Off, wait 10 seconds. • Disconnect harness from processor 60 Pin connector and inspect for damaged pins, corrosion, loose wires. Service as necessary. • PSPS disconnected. • Processor disconnected. • Breakout box installed. • DVOM on 200 ohm scale. • Measure resistance between test Pin 46 at the Breakout box and Signal Return at the PSPS connector and between test Pin 3 (2.3L OHC EFI), test Pin 23 (2.5L CFI), test Pin 24 (2.3L HSC, 3.0L EFI, 4.9L EFI and 5.0L EFI) at the Breakout box and PSPS circuit at the PSPS harness connector. • Are both readings less than 5 ohms?	Yes ▶ No ▶	REPLACE processor. RERUN Quick Test. SERVICE open in circuit. RERUN Quick Test.
FF3 SWITCH INTEGRITY • Install tachometer. • Start engine, allow to idle in Neutral/Park. • Disconnect PSPS at switch. • Does rpm increase?	Yes ▶ No ▶	REPLACE PSPS. GO to FF4 .

Power Steering Pressure Switch (PSPS)	Pinpoint Test	FF

TEST STEP	RESULT ▶	ACTION TO TAKE
FF4 PSPS HARNESS CHECK • Key Off, wait 10 seconds. • Disconnect harness from processor 60 Pin connector and inspect for damaged pins, corrosion, loose wires. Service as necessary. • PSPS disconnected. • Processor disconnected. • Breakout box installed. • DVOM on 200,000 ohm scale. • Measure resistance between test Pin 3 (2.3L OHC EFI), test Pin 23 (2.5L CFI), test Pin 24 (2.3L HSC CFI, 3.0L EFI, 4.9L EFI and 5.0L EFI) and test Pin 46 at the Breakout box. • Is reading less than 10,000 ohms?	Yes ▶ No ▶	SERVICE short in harness. REPLACE processor.
FF5 SERVICE CODE 52 ENGINE RUNNING SELF-TEST • Did you turn the steering wheel one-half turn any time after engine ID code, but before the dynamic response code? NOTE: Make sure the front wheels are centered (no load condition).	Yes ▶ No ▶	GO to FF6 . RERUN Quick Test.
FF6 DETERMINE WHETHER THE PROCESS CAN IDENTIFY AN OPEN CIRCUIT • Key Off, wait 10 seconds. • Disconnect PSPS. • Run Key On Engine Off Self-Test. • Is code 52 present?	Yes ▶ No ▶	GO to FF8 . GO to FF7 .
FF7 PSPS HARNESS CHECK • Key Off, wait 10 seconds. • Disconnect harness from processor 60 Pin connector and inspect for damaged pins, corrosion or loose wires. Service as necessary. • PSPS disconnected. • Processor disconnected. • Breakout box installed. • DVOM on 200,000 ohm scale. • Measure resistance between test Pin 46 and test Pin 24 at the Breakout box. • Is resistance reading 10,000 ohms or less?	Yes ▶ No ▶	SERVICE PSPS circuit short to signal return. RERUN Quick Test. REPLACE processor. RERUN Quick Test.

Power Steering Pressure Switch (PSPS)	Pinpoint Test	FF

TEST STEP	RESULT ▶	ACTION TO TAKE
FF8 PSPS POSITION KEY ON ENGINE NOT RUNNING VS. RUNNING • Key Off, wait 10 seconds. • Breakout box installed. • Processor connected. • PSPS connected. • DVOM on 200 ohm scale. • Key On. • Measure resistance from test Pin 24 to test Pin 46. • Start engine. • Does resistance remain less than 10 ohms between Key On Engine Off and Engine Running?	Yes ▶ No ▶	GO to FF9 . GO to FF11 .
FF9 PSPS POSITION ENGINE RUNNING NO LOAD VS. LOAD • Breakout box installed. • Processor connected. • PSPS connected. • DVOM on 200 ohm scale. • Engine idling. • Measure the resistance from test Pin 24 to test Pin 46. • Turn the steering wheel at least one-half turn then return. • Does resistance change from less than 10 ohms to infinity (indicating PSPS opening), then returning to 10 ohms or less when steering wheel is returned to center position?	Yes ▶ No ▶	PSPS system OK. REMOVE Breakout box and RETURN to Quick Test Step 5.0 to continue Diagnostics. GO to FF10 .

Power Steering Pressure Switch (PSPS)	Pinpoint Test	FF

TEST STEP	RESULT ▶	ACTION TO TAKE
FF10 PSPS VS. POWER STEERING HYDRAULIC PRESSURE (ENGINE RUNNING ALWAYS CLOSED) • At this point in the Diagnostics there are only two possible causes for the original code 52 Engine Running: — PSPS (switch) that will not open. — Low available hydraulic pressure. • Key Off, wait 10 seconds. • Substitute original PSPS with a known good PSPS. • Run Engine Running Self Test. (Turn steering wheel one-half turn during test.) • Is code 52 still present?	Yes ▶ No ▶	GO to Power Steering Pressure Diagnostics, Shop Manual, Group 13. looking for low pressure. Original code 52 Engine Running was a result of a bad PSPS (switch). REMOVE all equipment and continue, if necessary, with any other Diagnostics.
FF11 PSPS VS. POWER STEERING HYDRAULIC PRESSURE (ENGINE RUNNING ALWAYS OPEN) • At this point in the Diagnostics there are two possible causes for the original code 52 Engine Running: — PSPS (switch) that always remains open during Engine Running. — Excessively high hydraulic pressure. • Key Off, wait 10 seconds. • Substitute original PSPS with a known good PSPS. • Run Engine Running Self Test. (Turn steering wheel one-half turn during test.) • Is code 52 still present?	Yes ▶ No ▶	GO to Power Steering Pressure Diagnostics in Shop Manual, Group 13. looking for high pressure. Original code 52 Engine Running was a result of a bad PSPS (switch). REMOVE all equipment and continue, if necessary, with any other Diagnostics.

Fuel Control — 1.9L EFI and 2.3L EFI TC	Pinpoint Test	HA

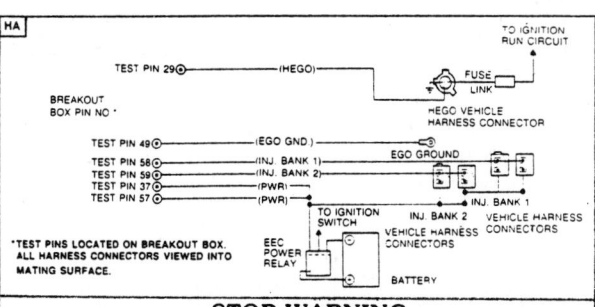

HA

TO IGNITION RUN CIRCUIT

TEST PIN 29 ⊕ ——— (HEGO) ———

FUSE LINK

BREAKOUT BOX PIN NO.

HEGO VEHICLE HARNESS CONNECTOR

TEST PIN 49 ⊕ ——— (EGO GND) ———
EGO GROUND

TEST PIN 58 ⊕ ——— (INJ. BANK 1) ———
TEST PIN 59 ⊕ ——— (INJ. BANK 2) ———
TEST PIN 37 ⊕ ——— (PWR) ———
TEST PIN 57 ⊕ ——— (PWR) ———

INJ. BANK 1

TO IGNITION SWITCH

INJ. BANK 2 VEHICLE HARNESS CONNECTORS
VEHICLE HARNESS CONNECTORS

*TEST PINS LOCATED ON BREAKOUT BOX. ALL HARNESS CONNECTORS VIEWED INTO MATING SURFACE.

EEC POWER RELAY

BATTERY

STOP-WARNING

You should enter this Pinpoint Test Only when a Service Code 41, 42 or 43 is received in Quick Test Step 5.0 or 6.0 or when directed here from Pinpoint Test A or Diagnostics by Symptom in the Engine Supplement Section.

To prevent the replacement of good components, be aware that the following non-EEC areas may be at fault:

- Ignition Coil
- Distributor Cap
- Distributor Rotor
- Fouled Spark Plugs
- Spark Plug Wires
- CANP Problems
- PCV Valves (see note below)

- EGR Valve and Gasket
- Air Filter
- Fuel Contamination, Engine Oil
- Poor Power Ground
- Fuel Pressure
- Manifold Leaks, Intake Exhaust
- Engine Not at Normal Operating Temperatures

This Pinpoint Test is intended to diagnose only the following:

- HEGO Sensor
- Harness Circuits HEGO Grd., HEGO, INJ BANK 1, INJ BANK 2, V PWR
- HEGO Sensor Connection
  — Code 42 start at HA8
  — Code 41 start HA14
  — Code 43 start at HA30

- Vacuum Systems
- Fuel Injectors
- Processor Assembly

NOTE: Fuel contaminated engine oil may affect 41, 42 Service Codes. If this is suspected, remove the PCV from the valve cover and repeat the Quick Test. If the problem is corrected, then change the engine oil and filter.

Fuel Control — 1.9L EFI and 2.3L EFI TC	Pinpoint Test	HA

TEST STEP	RESULT	▶	ACTION TO TAKE
HA1 FUEL PRESSURE CHECK 1			
• Key Off, wait 10 seconds.	Yes	▶	GO to HA2.
• Install fuel pressure gauge.	No	▶	REFER to the Shop Manual Group 24 for electric fuel pump and Section 11 for fuel pressure regulator check.
• Start and run engine. Is fuel pressure between 35 and 45 psi (241-310 kPa)?			
For No Starts:			
• If engine will not run, cycle the key from Off to On several times to increase fuel pressure.			
HA2 FUEL PRESSURE CHECK 2			
• Does fuel pressure remain between 35 and 45 psi (241-310 kPa) for 60 seconds or longer after final Key Off?	Yes	▶	GO to HA3.
	No	▶	GO to HA7.
HA3 FUEL DELIVERY TEST			
• Key Off.	Yes	▶	The EEC system is not the fault of the No Start. Fuel and spark are present. REFER to Section 2 for other No Start Routines. If complaint was runs rough/ misses or fuel code GO to HA4.
• Fuel pressure gauge installed.			
• Pressurize fuel system as per Step HA1.			
• Locate and disconnect the fuel pump relay.			
• Crank engine for 5 seconds.			
• Take pressure reading at the end of 5 second crank.			
• Is pressure between 10 and 20 psi?			
	No	▶	GO to HA4.

NOTE: The colder the engine, the greater the pressure drop (i.e., an engine coolant temperature of 200°F equals approximately a 10 psi drop in 5 seconds. 60°F equals approximately a 20 psi drop in 5 seconds).

Verify fuel quality; air and/or water will also pressurize and look like acceptable fuel delivery.

Fuel Control — 1.9L EFI and 2.3L EFI TC	Pinpoint Test	HA

TEST STEP	RESULT	▶	ACTION TO TAKE
HA4 INJECTOR HARNESS RESISTANCE CHECK			
• Key Off, wait 10 seconds.	Yes	▶	GO to HA6
• Disconnect processor 60 Pin connector and inspect for damaged pins, corrosion, loose wires. Service as necessary.	No	▶	GO to HA5.
• Connect Breakout box to harness. Leave processor disconnected.			
• DVOM on 200 ohm scale.			
• Measure the resistance of injector Bank 1 between test Pin 37 and test Pin 58 at the Breakout box. Record resistance.			
• Measure the resistance of injector Bank 2 between test Pin 37 and test Pin 59 at the Breakout box. Record resistance.			
• Are both resistances between 1.2 ohms and 1.8 ohms?			
HA5 ISOLATE FAULTY INJECTOR CIRCUIT			
• Key Off.	Yes	▶	GO to HA6.
• Breakout box installed.	No	▶	SERVICE the harness/connectors on the suspect injector for opens or shorts. If OK, REPLACE injector. RERUN Quick Test.
• Leave processor disconnected.			
• DVOM on 200 ohm scale.			
• Disconnect all injectors on suspect Bank. Measure resistance of each injector by connecting one injector at a time, and reading the resistance between test Pins 37 and 58 at the Breakout box for Bank 1 or test Pins 37 and 59 at the Breakout box for Bank 2.			
• Are all resistances between 2.0 and 2.7 ohms?			

Fuel Control — 1.9L EFI and 2.3L EFI TC	Pinpoint Test	HA

TEST STEP	RESULT	▶	ACTION TO TAKE
HA6 INJECTOR DRIVE SIGNAL CHECK			
Requires standard non-powered 12 volt test lamp.	Dim glow at light on both tests	▶	GO to HA7.
• Key Off.	No light on one or both tests	▶	VERIFY 12-volt battery power at Pins 37 and 57. If OK, REPLACE processor. RERUN Quick Test.
• Breakout box installed.			
• Connect processor to Breakout box.			
• Connect test lamp between test Pin 37 and test Pin 58 at the Breakout box.	Bright light on one or both tests	▶	CHECK circuits Bank 1 and Bank 2 for shorts to ground. If OK, REPLACE processor. RERUN Quick Test.
• Crank or start engine.			
• Repeat above test between test Pin 37 and test Pin 59 at the Breakout box.			
HA7 INJECTOR BALANCE TEST			
• Connect tachometer to engine. Disconnect ISC. Run engine at 2000 rpm. Use throttle body stop screw to set engine speed.	Yes	▶	Fuel delivery OK. Problem is with area common to all cylinders, i.e.: Air/ vacuum leak, fuel contamination, EGR.
• Disconnect and reconnect the injectors one at a time; note rpm drop for each injector.			
• Does each injector produce at least a 150 rpm drop?	No	▶	REPLACE faulty injector. RERUN Quick Test.
• Reconnect ISC. Reset curb idle. Refer to VECI decal and Section 4.			

Fuel Control — 1.9L EFI and 2.3L EFI TC	Pinpoint Test	HA

TEST STEP	RESULT	▶	ACTION TO TAKE
HA8 FUEL CONTROL — ALWAYS RICH: CODE 42. CHECK HEGO HARNESS FOR SHORT TO POWER • Key Off, wait 10 seconds. • Disconnect the HEGO sensor from the vehicle harness. • DVOM on 20 volt scale. • Key On. • Measure voltage between HEGO signal and ground at the HEGO harness connector. • Is voltage less than .5 volt?	Yes No	▶ ▶	GO to HA9. SERVICE short to power in HEGO signal circuit. RERUN Quick Test.
HA9 CHECK HEGO FOR SHORT TO KEY POWER • Key Off. • HEGO disconnected. • DVOM on 200,000 ohm scale. • Measure resistance between Key Power input and HEGO signal at the HEGO. • Is resistance greater than 10,000 ohms?	Yes No	▶ ▶	GO to HA10. REPLACE HEGO sensor. RERUN Quick Test.

Fuel Control — 1.9L EFI and 2.3L EFI TC	Pinpoint Test	HA

TEST STEP	RESULT	▶	ACTION TO TAKE

HA10 ATTEMPT TO GENERATE CODE 41
 	
• Key Off, wait 10 seconds.
• NOTE: Non-EEC areas could cause a code 42.
  Check for:
  — Fuel contaminated engine oil
  — Ignition caused misfire
  — CANP problems
• Disconnect vehicle harness at the HEGO sensor. Ground the HEGO circuit at the HEGO vehicle harness connector to the engine block.
• Repeat Engine Running Self-Test.
• Is service code 41 present?
	Yes
	
	No
		▶
		
		▶
			GO to HA12.
			
			GO to HA11.

HA11 HARNESS CHECK • Key Off, wait 10 seconds. • Install Breakout box. • Measure resistance of HEGO ground circuit between test Pin 49 at the Breakout box and HEGO ground at engine block. • Measure resistance of HEGO circuit between test Pin 29 at the Breakout box and HEGO harness connector. • Are both circuits less than 5 ohms?	Yes No	▶ ▶	DISCONNECT processor connector. INSPECT for damage or corrosion. If OK, REPLACE processor. RERUN Quick Test. CORRECT harness circuit with resistance greater than 5 ohms. RERUN Quick Test.

Fuel Control — 1.9L EFI and 2.3L EFI TC	Pinpoint Test	HA

TEST STEP	RESULT	▶	ACTION TO TAKE
HA12 EGO CHECK • DVOM on 20V scale. • With HEGO sensor disconnected from the vehicle harness, connect a DVOM from HEGO sensor to engine ground. • Run the engine at 2000 rpm for 1 minute. While observing DVOM, disconnect the manifold vacuum hose indicated below. • Is voltage less than 0.4V?	Yes No	▶ ▶	HEGO sensor OK. GO to HA1. REPLACE HEGO sensor. RERUN Quick Test.
HA13 FUEL CONTROL — ALWAYS LEAN: CODE 41 VERIFICATION • Run vehicle at 2000 rpm for two minutes. • Key Off, wait 10 seconds. • Perform Engine Running Self-Test. • Is code 41 present?	Yes No	▶ ▶	GO to HA14. GO to HA20.

Fuel Control — 1.9L EFI and 2.3L EFI TC	Pinpoint Test	HA

TEST STEP	RESULT	▶	ACTION TO TAKE

HA14 FUEL CONTROL — ALWAYS LEAN: CODE 41
 	
NOTE: Vacuum/air leaks in non-EEC areas could cause a code 41. Check for:
  — Leaking vacuum actuator (eg: A/C control motor)
  — Engine sealing
  — EGR system
  — PCV system
  — Unmetered air leak between air meter and throttle body
  — Lead contaminated HEGO sensor
• Key Off. DVOM on 20V scale. Disconnect HEGO sensor from vehicle harness. Connect DVOM between HEGO signal at HEGO sensor and engine ground. Remove air cleaner to gain access to air meter inlet. Using a standard wood lead pencil, prop the air meter door partway open.
• Start the engine and run at approximately 2000 rpm for 2 minutes.
• Does the DVOM read greater than 0.5V at the end of 1 minute?
	Yes
	
	No
		▶
		
		▶
			GO to HA15.
			
			REPLACE HEGO sensor. RERUN Quick Test.

HA15 HARNESS CHECK EGO CIRCUITS • Key Off. • Install Breakout box. Processor disconnected. • Measure resistance of HEGO circuit between test Pin 49 at the Breakout box and engine block ground. Also HEGO circuit between HEGO connector and test Pin 29 at the Breakout box. • Are both circuits less than 5 ohms?	Yes No	▶ ▶	GO to HA16. SERVICE/CORRECT as necessary any circuit greater than 5 ohms. RERUN Quick Test.

Fuel Control — 1.9L EFI and 2.3L EFI TC	Pinpoint Test	HA

TEST STEP	RESULT ▶	ACTION TO TAKE
HA16 CHECK HEGO CIRCUIT FOR SHORT TO GROUND • Key Off. • Breakout box installed. Processor disconnected. • DVOM to 200.000 ohms scale. • Measure the resistance between test Pin 29 and test Pin 40 at the Breakout box. • Is resistance greater than 10.000 ohms?	Yes ▶ No ▶	GO to **HA17**. CORRECT cause of resistance to ground. RERUN Quick Test.
HA17 CHECK HEGO SENSOR FOR SHORT TO GROUND • Key Off. • HEGO disconnected. • DVOM on 200.000 ohm scale. • Measure resistance between ground and HEGO signal at HEGO sensor. • Is resistance greater than 10.000 ohms?	Yes ▶ No ▶	GO to **HA18**. REPLACE HEGO sensor. RERUN Quick Test.
HA18 ATTEMPT TO ELIMINATE CODE 41 • Key Off. • Reconnect HEGO sensor. Remove air cleaner to gain access to air meter inlet. Using a standard wood lead pencil, prop the air meter door part-way open. • Start the engine and run at approximately 2000 rpm for 2 minutes. • Perform Engine Running Self-Test. • Is code 41 present?	Yes ▶ No ▶	INSPECT for corrosion or damaged pins. If OK, REPLACE processor. RERUN Quick Test. HEGO input circuit OK. GO to **HA1**.

Fuel Control — 1.9L EFI and 2.3L EFI TC	Pinpoint Test	HA

HA30	CONTINUOUS TESTING. CODE 41, 42 OR 43

41 — HEGO indicated the fuel system was lean for more than 15 seconds when the system should have been in closed loop fuel control.

42 — HEGO indicated the fuel system was rich for more than 15 seconds when the system should have been in closed loop fuel control.

43 — HEGO indicated the fuel system was lean at WOT for more than 3 seconds.

CLOSED LOOP — Fuel control under the influence of the HEGO sensor.

OPEN LOOP — Fuel control NOT under the influence of the HEGO sensor.

Before attempting to correct a continuous fuel control code 41, 42 or 43, diagnose all other drive complaints first, eg., rough idle, misses, etc.

NOTE: The fuel control code may help in this diagnosis.

Using the fuel control service code, isolate the cause of the fuel control problem.

Some areas to check are:

• Unmetered Air:	Vacuum leaks/intake air leaks. — Canister Purge System. — PCV System. — Engine sealing. — Air leaks between VAF meter and throttle body. — Crimped fuel line. — Plugged fuel filter. — Fouled injectors.
• HEGO Fuel Fouled:	Whenever an over-rich fuel condition has been experienced (fuel fouled spark plugs), make a thorough check of the ignition system. In the event the HEGO sensor is suspected of being fuel fouled (low output, slow response), run the vehicle at sustained high speeds (within legal limits) followed by a few hard accelerations. This will burn off HEGO contamination and restore proper HEGO operation.
• Fuel Pressure:	Perform Pinpoint Test Step **HA1**
• Ignition System:	Always in default spark (10 degrees). Refer to Quick Test Step **4.0**
• Improper Fueling:	Lead fouled HEGO sensor.
• TP Sensor:	Not moving (mechanical damage). Connect DVOM to test Pin 47 and to test Pin 46. Key to Run. Observe DVOM while moving the throttle. Reading must increase with increase in throttle opening. If not correct, REPLACE as necessary.

• If at this point, the drive concern is still present, perform Steps **HA3** through **HA6** only.

Fuel Control — 1.9L EFI and 2.3L EFI TC	Pinpoint Test	HA

TEST STEP	RESULT ▶	ACTION TO TAKE
HA20 CHECK HEATER ELEMENT RESISTANCE ON HEGO • Key Off. • DVOM on 200 ohm scale. • HEGO disconnected. • Measure resistance between ignition run circuit and power ground at HEGO sensor. • Hot to warm resistance specification is 5 to 20 ohms. • Is resistance within specification? **NOTE: Room temperature resistance specification is 2 to 5 ohms.** IGN. RUN POWER / HEGO SENSOR CONNECTOR HEGO SIGNAL / PWR GND.	Yes ▶ No ▶	GO to **HA21**. REPLACE HEGO sensor.
HA21 CHECK FOR POWER AT HEGO HARNESS CONNECTOR • Key On. Engine Off. • DVOM on 20V scale. • Measure voltage between ignition run power and power ground at HEGO vehicle harness. • Is voltage greater than 10.5 volts?	Yes ▶ No ▶	HEGO sensor system OK. RECONNECT HEGO and GO to **HA14**. GO to **HA22**.
HA22 CHECK CONTINUITY OF GROUND TO HEGO CONNECTOR • Key Off, wait 10 seconds. • DVOM on 200 ohm scale. • Measure resistance between battery ground and HEGO ground at HEGO vehicle harness. • Is resistance 5.0 ohms or less?	Yes ▶ No ▶	SERVICE open in ignition run power circuit. SERVICE open in ground circuit.

Fuel Control — 5.0L SEFI	Pinpoint Test	HC

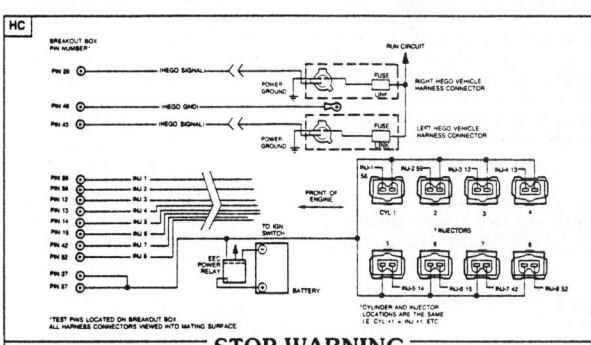

STOP-WARNING

You should enter this Pinpoint Test only when a Service Code 41, 91 or 42, 92 is received in Quick Test Step 5.0 or 6.0 or when directed here from Pinpoint Test S.

To prevent the replacement of good components, be aware that the following non-EEC areas may be at fault:

• Ignition Coil	• Valve Problem
• Distributor Cap	• EGR Valve and Gasket
• Distributor Rotor	• Air Filter
• Fouled Spark Plugs	• Fuel Contamination, Engine Oil
• Spark Plug Wires	• Poor Power Ground
• CANP Problems	• Fuel Pressure
• PCV Valves (see note below)	• Manifold Leaks, Intake/Exhaust
• Compression Level	• Engine Not at Normal Operating Temperatures
	• Cracked Piston

This Pinpoint Test is intended to diagnose only the following:

• HEGO Sensor	• Fuel Injectors
• HEGO Sensor Connection	• Processor Assembly
• Vacuum Systems	• Harness Circuits: HEGO GRD, HEGO, INJ 1-8 and VPWR

NOTE: Fuel-contaminated engine oil may affect 41, 91 and 42, 92 Service Codes, so if it is suspected, remove the PCV from the valve cover, and rerun the Quick Test. If the problem is corrected, then change the engine oil and filter.

Fuel Control — 5.0L SEFI	Pinpoint Test	HC

TEST STEP	RESULT ▶	ACTION TO TAKE
HC1 FUEL PRESSURE CHECK 1 • Key Off. wait 10 seconds. • Install fuel pressure gauge. • Start and run engine. RUNNING FUEL PRESSURE SPECIFICATION 5.0L SEFI = 27-37 psi (186-254 kPa) • Is fuel pressure within specification? **For No Starts:** • If engine will not run. cycle the key from Off to On several times to increase fuel pressure. ENGINE OFF FUEL PRESSURE SPECIFICATION 5.0L SEFI = 35-45 psi (241-310 kPa)	Yes ▶ No ▶	GO to HC2. REFER to the Shop Manual. Group 24 for electric fuel pump and Section 11 for fuel pressure regulator check.
HC2 FUEL PRESSURE CHECK 2 • Key On. • Does fuel pressure drop more than 5 psi within 60 seconds after Key Off?	Yes ▶ No ▶	GO to HC4. GO to HC3.
HC3 FUEL DELIVERY TEST • Key Off. • Fuel pressure gauge installed. • Pressurize fuel system as per Step HC1. • Locate and disconnect inertia switch (which disables fuel pump). • Crank engine for 5 seconds. • Take pressure reading at the end of 5 second crank. • Does pressure drop 5 psi or greater at end of 5 second crank cycle? **NOTE:** Verify fuel quality; air and/or water will also pressurize and look like acceptable fuel delivery. **NOTE:** The colder the engine. the greater the pressure drop (i.e., an engine coolant temperature of 200°F equals approximately a 10 psi drop in 5 seconds. 60°F equals approximately a 20 psi drop in 5 seconds).	Yes ▶ No ▶	RECONNECT inertia switch. The EEC system is not the fault of the No Start. Fuel and spark are present. REFER to Section 2 for other No Start Routines. If complaint was runs rough, misses or fuel code. GO to HC4. RECONNECT inertia switch. GO to HC7.

Fuel Control — 5.0L SEFI	Pinpoint Test	HC

TEST STEP	RESULT ▶	ACTION TO TAKE
HC5 PERFORM 2ND/3RD LEVEL CYLINDER BALANCE TEST **NOTE:** Mark VII/Lincoln Town Car calibration 8-22 only. a Cylinder Balance Test service code 90 received in the first test level indicates that the injector harness is not open or shorted and the processor is sending a drive signal to all injectors. The 2nd/3rd level Cylinder Balance Test is intended to aid in the detection of any partially contributing injectors. • Within 2 minutes after the previous Cylinder Balance Test. lightly depress and release throttle to enter 2nd or 3rd level Cylinder Balance Test. • Is service code 90 present for both levels? Refer to appendix for Cylinder Balance Test definition.	Yes ▶ No ▶	GO to Diagnostic By Symptom in the appropriate engine supplement section. Remember to use conventional Diagnostic methods such as engine compression checks and scoping. GO to HC8.
HC6 INJECTOR HARNESS SHORT CHECK • Key Off. • Disconnect processor 60 Pin connector and inspect for damaged Pins, corrosion, loose wires. Service as necessary. • Connect Breakout box to harness. Leave processor disconnected. • Suspect injector disconnected. • DVOM to 200,000 ohm scale. • Measure the resistance of the suspect injector circuit between the injector circuit test Pin at the Breakout box and test Pins 40 and 60 at the Breakout box. • Is resistance greater than 10,000 ohms?	Yes ▶ No ▶	RECONNECT injector. GO to HC7. Service short to ground. RECONNECT injector RERUN Quick Test and Cylinder Balance Test.

Fuel Control — 5.0L SEFI	Pinpoint Test	HC

TEST STEP	RESULT ▶	ACTION TO TAKE
HC4 CYLINDER BALANCE TEST • Perform the Engine Running Self-Test. • After the last repeated code. wait 5-10 seconds. • "Goose" throttle very lightly (not wide-open throttle). • Time of test approximately 90 seconds. • Use table below to interpret codes. • Is service code 90 present? **NOTE:** • See Appendix for cylinder balance test definition. • Mark VII/Lincoln Town Car calibration 8-22 has added Cylinder Balance Test capability.	Yes ▶ No ▶	Mark VII/Lincoln Town Car calibration 8-22, GO to HC5. ALL OTHERS, GO to Diagnostic By Symptom in the appropriate engine supplement section. Remember to use conventional diagnostic methods such as compression checks and scoping. GO to HC6.

The cylinder balance test switches each injector "OFF" and "ON," one at a time. Service codes correspond to cylinder number, e.g., service code 30 indicates a problem with cylinder number 3. The cylinder balance test is designed to aid in the detection of a non-contributing cylinder. The Cylinder Balance Pinpoint Test Steps are designed to isolate only EEC related problems.

SERVICE CODE	90	10	20	30	40	50	60	70	80	77*
Cylinder/Injector Number	Pass	1	2	3	4	5	6	7	8	Rerun Test
Breakout Box Pin Number		58	59	12	13	14	15	42	52	

Fuel Control — 5.0L SEFI	Pinpoint Test	HC

TEST STEP	RESULT ▶	ACTION TO TAKE
HC7 INJECTOR DRIVER SIGNAL CHECK Requires standard non-powered 12-volt test lamp. • Key Off. • Breakout box installed. • Connect processor to Breakout box. • Connect test lamp between test Pin 37 and the suspect injector(s) circuit test Pin at the Breakout box. • Crank or start engine. • Is glow on light dim?	Yes ▶ No (Bright light or no light) ▶	GO to HC8. Replace processor. Rerun Quick Test and Cylinder Balance Test.
HC8 HARNESS AND INJECTOR RESISTANCE CHECK • Key Off, wait 10 seconds. • Breakout box installed. • Disconnect processor. • DVOM on 200 ohm scale. • Measure the resistance of the suspect injector circuit between the injector circuit test Pin at the Breakout box and test Pins 37 and 57 at the Breakout box. • Is resistance between 13.0 and 19.0 ohms? **For No Starts:** Pick any injector to read resistance.	Yes ▶ No ▶	CHECK for dirty/clogged injector(s), CLEAN as necessary. If OK, REPLACE injector. RERUN Quick-Test and Cylinder Balance Test. SERVICE the harness/connectors on the suspect injector for OPENS or cause of high resistance. If OK, replace the injector. RERUN Quick Test and Cylinder Balance Test. FOR NO STARTS: SERVICE harness for open in VPWR circuit. RERUN Quick Test.

Fuel Control — 5.0L SEFI	Pinpoint Test	HC

TEST STEP	RESULT ▶	ACTION TO TAKE
HC9 FUEL CONTROL — ALWAYS LEAN: CODE 41, 91 VERIFICATION		
• Run vehicle at 2000 rpm for two minutes. • Key Off, wait 10 seconds. • Perform Engine Running Self-Test. • Is code 41 or 91 present?	Yes ▶ No ▶	GO to HC10. GO to HC21.
HC10 FUEL CONTROL — ALWAYS LEAN: CODE 91 LEFT HEGO, OR 41 RIGHT HEGO		
NOTE: Vacuum/air leaks in non-EEC areas could also cause code 41, or 91. Check for: — Leaking vacuum actuator (e.g.: A/C control motor) — Engine sealing — EGR system — PCV system — Unmetered air leak between air meter and throttle body — Lead contaminated HEGO sensor • Key Off. DVOM on 20V scale. Disconnect appropriate HEGO sensor from vehicle harness. Connect DVOM to HEGO sensor and engine ground. • Disconnect and plug vacuum line to MAP sensor. • Apply 14 in.-Hg. to MAP. • Start the engine. Does the DVOM read greater than 0.5V?	Yes ▶ No ▶	GO to HC11. REPLACE HEGO sensor. RECONNECT MAP vacuum line. RERUN Quick Test.
HC11 LEFT HEGO, OR RIGHT HEGO AND HEGO GROUND CONTINUITY CHECK		
• Key Off. • Install Breakout box. Processor disconnected. • DVOM on 200 ohm scale. • Measure resistance between test Pin 49 at Breakout box and engine block ground. • Measure resistance between test Pin 29 at Breakout box and HEGO signal at vehicle harness connector and/or measure resistance between test Pin 43 at Breakout box and HEGO signal at vehicle harness connector. • Are all resistances less than 5 ohms?	Yes ▶ No ▶	GO to HC12. SERVICE open in appropriate circuit. RERUN Quick Test.

Fuel Control — 5.0L SEFI	Pinpoint Test	HC

TEST STEP	RESULT ▶	ACTION TO TAKE
HC12 HEGO CIRCUIT SHORT TO GROUND		
• Key Off. processor disconnected. • Disconnect appropriate HEGO. • DVOM on 200.000 ohm scale. • Measure resistance between test Pin 29 or test Pin 43 to test Pin 40 at the Breakout box. • Is resistance 10.000 ohms or less?	Yes ▶ No ▶	CORRECT cause of resistance to ground. RERUN Quick Test. GO to HC13.
HC13 CHECK HEGO SENSOR TO GROUND		
• Key Off. • HEGO disconnected. • DVOM on 200.000 ohm scale. • Measure resistance from HEGO power ground to HEGO signal at HEGO sensor. • Is resistance 10.000 ohms or less?	Yes ▶ No ▶	REPLACE HEGO sensor. RECONNECT MAP vacuum line. RERUN Quick Test. GO to HC14.
HEGO SIGNAL POWER GROUND KEY POWER HEGO SENSOR CONNECTOR		
HC14 ATTEMPT TO ELIMINATE CODE 41		
• Key Off. • Processor connected. • Reconnect HEGO sensor. • MAP vacuum line still disconnected and plugged. • Apply 10 in.-Hg. (33 kPa) vacuum to MAP sensor. • Start the engine and run at approximately 2000 rpm for one minute. Allow engine to return to idle. • Perform Engine Running Self-Test. • Is code 41 still present? NOTE: Disregard any other code input at this time.	Yes ▶ No ▶	INSPECT for corrosion or damaged pins. If OK. REPLACE processor. RECONNECT MAP vacuum line. RERUN Quick Test. RECONNECT MAP vacuum line. HEGO input circuit OK. GO to HC1 (Basic Fuel Delivery).

Fuel Control — 5.0L SEFI	Pinpoint Test	HC

TEST STEP	RESULT ▶	ACTION TO TAKE
HC15 CHECK HEGO HARNESS FOR SHORT TO POWER		
• Key Off, wait 10 seconds. • Disconnect appropriate HEGO for code 42 or 92. • DVOM on 20 volt scale. • Key On. • Measure voltage between HEGO signal and HEGO power ground at the HEGO harness connector. • Is voltage less than 0.5 volts?	Yes ▶ No ▶	GO to HC16. REPAIR short to power in HEGO circuit. RERUN Quick Test.
		HEGO SIGNAL POWER GROUND KEY POWER HEGO VEHICLE HARNESS CONNECTOR
HC16 CHECK HEGO SENSOR FOR SHORT TO KEY POWER		
• Key Off. • HEGO disconnected. • DVOM on 200,000 ohm scale. • Measure resistance from Key Power input to HEGO circuit at the HEGO sensor. • Is reading less than 10,000 ohms?	Yes ▶ No ▶	REPLACE HEGO sensor. RERUN Quick Test. GO to HC17.
HC17 ATTEMPT TO GENERATE CODE 41 or 91		
• Key Off, wait 10 seconds. NOTE: Non-EEC areas could cause a code 42 or 92. Check for: — Fuel contaminated engine oil. — Ignition caused misfire (fouled spark plug) — CANP problems • Refer to Illustration HC. • Disconnect vehicle harness at the appropriate HEGO sensor. Jumper (ground) the HEGO circuit at the HEGO sensor vehicle harness connector to the engine block. • Repeat Engine Running Self Test. • Is service code 41 or 91 present?	Yes ▶ No ▶	REMOVE jumper. GO to HC18. REMOVE jumper. DISCONNECT processor connector. INSPECT for damage or corrosion. If OK, REPLACE processor. RERUN Quick Test.

Fuel Control — 5.0L SEFI	Pinpoint Test	HC

TEST STEP	RESULT ▶	ACTION TO TAKE
HC18 CHECK MAP SENSOR		
NOTE: Due to the MAP sensor's large influence on fuel control. there is a possibility that a code 42 could be a result of a MAP problem. even though a code 22 is not present. Therefore the next two Pinpoint Tests Steps will verify proper vacuum to the MAP sensor and its ability to hold vacuum. • Key Off. wait 10 seconds. • Disconnect vacuum line from MAP sensor. • Install vacuum pump to MAP sensor. • Apply 18 in.-Hg. (59 kPa) vacuum to MAP sensor. • Does MAP sensor hold vacuum?	Yes ▶ No ▶	RELEASE vacuum. GO to HC19. REPLACE MAP sensor. RECONNECT vacuum line to MAP sensor. RERUN Quick Test.
HC19 CHECK FOR LOSS OF MAP VACUUM		
• Tee a vacuum gauge in the intake manifold vacuum line at the MAP sensor. • Start engine and note vacuum reading. • Key Off. wait 10 seconds. • Remove vacuum gauge and tee and reconnect vacuum line to MAP. • Tee in vacuum gauge at a different source of intake manifold vacuum. • Start engine and note vacuum reading. • Do vacuum readings differ greater than 1 in.-Hg. (3.3 kPa)?	Yes ▶ No ▶	INSPECT vacuum lines for leaks, holes, disconnections, kinks, blockage and proper routing. SERVICE as necessary. GO to HC20.
HC20 HEGO CHECK		
• Refer to Illustration HC. • DVOM on 20 volt scale. • With HEGO sensor disconnected from the harness, connect a DVOM from HEGO sensor to engine ground. • Disconnect PCV hose. • Start engine and run at approximately 2000 rpm. Does the DVOM read less than 0.4 volts within 30 seconds?	Yes ▶ No ▶	HEGO sensor OK. GO to HC1. REPLACE HEGO sensor. RERUN Quick Test.

Fuel Control — 5.0L SEFI	Pinpoint Test	HC

TEST STEP	RESULT ▶	ACTION TO TAKE
HC21 CHECK HEATER ELEMENT RESISTANCE ON HEGO • Key off, engine off. • DVOM on 200 ohm scale. • HEGO disconnected. • Measure resistance between run circuit and ground at HEGO harness connector. — Refer to Pinpoint Test HC wiring schematic. • Hot to warm resistance specification is 5 to 20 ohms. **NOTE: At room temperature, resistance specification is 2 to 5 ohms.** • Is resistance within specification?	Yes ▶ No ▶	GO to **HC22**. REPLACE HEGO sensor.
HC22 CHECK FOR POWER AT HEGO HARNESS CONNECTOR • Key on, engine off. • DVOM on 20V scale. • Connect positive lead to run circuit and negative lead to ground at HEGO vehicle harness connector. • Is voltage greater than 10.5 volts?	Yes ▶ No ▶	HEGO's sensor system OK. RECONNECT HEGO and GO to **HC2**. GO to **HC23**.
HC23 CHECK CONTINUITY OF GROUND TO HEGO CONNECTOR • Key off, wait 10 seconds. • DVOM on 200 ohm scale. • Measure resistance of ground circuit from HEGO vehicle harness connector to battery ground. • Is resistance less than 5.0 ohms?	Yes ▶ No ▶	SERVICE open in run circuit. SERVICE open in ground circuit.

Fuel Control — 5.0L SEFI	Pinpoint Test	HC

HC90 CONTINUOUS TESTING: CODE 41 RIGHT HEGO/91 LEFT HEGO

CODE 41/91 — Indicates that a HEGO circuit has not switched during closed loop fuel control.

NOTE: In this situation, code 41/91 does not necessarily indicate a lean condition.

CLOSED LOOP —Fuel control under the influence of the HEGO sensors.

OPEN LOOP —Fuel control NOT under the influence of the HEGO sensors.

Before attempting to correct a continuous fuel control code 41/91, diagnose all other drive complaints first.. eg., rough idle, misses, etc. in EEC Diagnostic By Symptom in the appropriate engine supplement.

NOTE: The fuel control code may help in this diagnosis.

Using the fuel control service code, isolate the cause of the fuel control problem.

Some areas to check are:

• Vacuum Circuits: Vacuum leaks/intake air leaks.
—Canister Purge System.
—PCV System.
—Engine sealing.

• HEGO Fuel Fouled: Whenever an over-rich fuel condition has been experienced (fuel fouled spark plugs), make a thorough check of the ignition system. In the event a HEGO sensor is suspected of being fuel fouled (low output, slow response), run the vehicle at sustained high speeds (within legal limits) followed by a few hard accelerations. This will burn off HEGO contamination and restore proper HEGO operation.

• Ignition System: Always in default spark (10 degrees). Refer to Quick Test Step **4.0**.

• Improper Fueling: Lead fouled HEGO sensor.

• Fuel Pressure: Perform Pinpoint Test Step **HC1** and **HC2**.

• If at this point, the drive concern (if any) is still present, perform Steps **HC4** through **HC8** only.

Fuel Control — 3.8L CFI	Pinpoint Test	HD

HD REFERENCE DRAWING

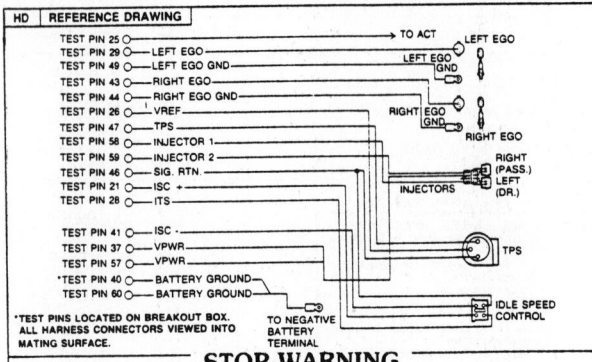

STOP-WARNING

You should enter this Pinpoint Test only when a Service Code 41, 91, 42 or 92 is received in Quick Test Step 5.0 or 6.0 or when directed here from Pinpoint Test A or by Diagnostics by Symptom in the Engine Supplement Section.

To prevent the replacement of good components, be aware that the following non-EEC areas may be at fault:

• Ignition Coil
• Distributor Cap
• Distributor Rotor
• Fouled Spark Plugs
• Spark Plug Wires
• CANP Problems
• PCV Valves (see note below)

• EGR Valve and Gasket
• Air Filter
• Fuel Contamination, Engine Oil
• Poor Power Ground
• Fuel Pressure
• Manifold Leaks, Intake/Exhaust
• Engine Not at Normal Operating Temperatures

This Pinpoint Test is intended to diagnose only the following:

• EGO Sensors
• EGO Signals and Ground Circuits
• EGO Sensor Connections

• Fuel Injectors
• Processor Assembly

NOTE: Fuel-contaminated engine oil may affect 41, 91, 42 and 92 Service Codes, so if it is suspected, remove the PCV from the valve cover, and rerun the Quick Test. If the problem is corrected, then change the engine oil and filter.

Fuel Control — 3.8L CFI	Pinpoint Test	HD

TEST STEP	RESULT ▶	ACTION TO TAKE
HD1 KEY POWER VOLTAGE CHECK • Key On. • Processor connected. • DVOM on 20V scale. • Measure voltage between test Pins 5 and 60 at the Breakout box.	Reading is less than 10.5V ▶ Reading is 10.5V or greater ▶	SERVICE open in key power circuit. RERUN Quick Test. GO to **HD2**.
HD2 FUEL PRESSURE CHECK • Install fuel pressure gauge. • Start and run engine. Fuel pressure must be 172-310 kPa (25-45 psi). • Fuel pressure must remain at 276 ± 34 kPa (40 psi ± 5 psi) for 60 seconds after final Key Off. **For No Starts:** • If engine will not run cycle the key from OFF to ON several times to increase fuel pressure.	Fuel pressure is within specifications ▶ Fuel pressure is not 172-310 kPa (25-45 psi) ▶ Fuel pressure does not remain at 276 ± 34 kPa (40 psi ± 5 psi) for 60 seconds or longer ▶	GO to **HD3**. REFER to Shop Manual, Group 24 for electric fuel pump. GO to **HD6**.
HD3 FUEL DELIVERY TEST • Key Off. • Fuel pressure gauge installed. • Pressurize fuel system as per Step HD2. • Locate and disconnect the fuel pump relay. • Crank engine for 5 seconds. • Take pressure reading at the end of 5-second crank. **NOTE: Verify fuel quality; air and/or water will also pressurize and look like acceptable fuel delivery.**	Pressure Gauge Reading: Pressure is approximately 10-20 psi at the end of 5-second crank cycle. Refer to Note below. Pressure is greater or less than specified ▶	The EEC system is not the fault of the No Start. Fuel and spark are present. REFER to Section 2 for other No Start Routines. If complaint was runs rough, misses or fuel code, GO to **HD4**. GO to **HD4**.

NOTE: The colder the engine, the greater the pressure drop (i.e., an engine coolant temperature of 200°F equals approximately a 10 psi drop in 5 seconds. 60°F equals approximately a 20 psi drop in 5 seconds).

Fuel Control — 3.8L CFI	Pinpoint Test	HD

TEST STEP	RESULT ▶	ACTION TO TAKE
HD4 HARNESS INJECTOR RESISTANCE CHECK • Key Off. • DVOM on 200 ohm range. • Disconnect processor 60 Pin connector and inspect for damaged pins, corrosion, loose wires. Service as necessary. • Install Breakout box, processor disconnected. • Measure resistance between test Pins 57 and 58 at the Breakout box and between test Pins 57 and 59 at the Breakout box.	Either resistance is less than 1.5 ohms ▶ Either resistance is greater than 3.5 ohms ▶ Both resistances are 1.5-3.5 ohms ▶	SERVICE the harness and/or connectors on the suspect injector for shorts. IF OK, REPLACE injector. SERVICE the harness and/or connectors on the suspect injector for opens. If OK, REPLACE injector. GO to HD5.
HD5 INJECTOR DRIVE SIGNAL CHECK **Requires standard non-powered 12V test lamp.** • Key Off. • Breakout box installed. • Connect processor to Breakout box. • Refer to illustration HD. • Connect test lamp between test Pin 37 and Pin 58 at the Breakout box. • Crank or start engine. • Repeat above test between test Pin 37 and Pin 59 at the Breakout box.	Dim glow at light on both tests ▶ No light on one or both tests ▶ Bright light on one or both tests ▶	GO to HD6. VERIFY 12V battery power at Pins 37 and 57. If OK, REPLACE processor. RERUN Quick Test. CHECK injector circuits 1 and 2 for shorts to ground. If OK, REPLACE processor. RERUN Quick Test.
HD6 INJECTOR BALANCE TEST • Connect tachometer to engine. Run engine at idle. • Disconnect and reconnect the injectors one at a time; note rpm drop for each injector. • Does each injector produce at least a 100 rpm momentary drop?	Yes ▶ No ▶	Fuel delivery OK. Problem in area common to all cylinders, i.e.: Air/ vacuum leak, fuel contamination, EGR. REPLACE faulty injector. RERUN Quick Test.

Fuel Control — 3.8L CFI	Pinpoint Test	HD

TEST STEP	RESULT ▶	ACTION TO TAKE
HD7 CODE 41 AND/OR 91 PRESENT • Verify codes received during Quick Test. • Are both code 41 and 91 present?	Yes ▶ No ▶	GO to HD9. GO to HD8.
HD8 SWAP INJECTOR CONNECTORS • Key Off. • Swap injector connections. • Start engine, run engine, run Quick Test. • Does the original code(s) repeat?	Yes ▶ No ▶	RECONNECT injector harness to original production state. GO to HD9. RECONNECT injector harness to original production state. GO to HD4.
HD9 FUEL CONTROL — ALWAYS LEAN CODES: 41 LEFT EGO, 91 RIGHT EGO **NOTE: Vacuum/air leaks in non-EEC areas could cause a code. Check for:** — **Leaking vacuum actuator (eg: A/C control motor)** — **Engine sealing** — **EGR system** — **PCV system** — **Lead contaminated EGO sensor** • Refer to illustration HD. • Key Off. DVOM on 20V scale. Disconnect appropriate EGO sensor from vehicle harness. Connect DVOM to EGO sensor and engine ground. • Apply 14 in.-Hg. of vacuum to MAP sensor. • Start the engine and run at approximately 2000 rpm. Does the DVOM read greater than 0.5V within 1 minute?	Yes ▶ No ▶	GO to HD10. REPLACE EGO sensor. RERUN Quick Test.

Fuel Control — 3.8L CFI	Pinpoint Test	HD

TEST STEP	RESULT ▶	ACTION TO TAKE
HD10 HARNESS CHECK EGO CIRCUITS • Key Off. wait 10 seconds. • Disconnect processor 60 Pin connector and inspect for damaged pins, corrosion, loose wires. Service as necessary. • Install Breakout box. Processor disconnected. • Disconnect appropriate EGO. • For left EGO code 41, measure resistance between test Pin 49 at the Breakout box and engine block ground and between left EGO connector and test Pin 29 at the Breakout box. • For right EGO code 91 measure resistance between test Pin 44 and engine block ground and also between right EGO harness connector and test Pin 43 at the Breakout box. • Are both resistances less than 5 ohms?	Yes ▶ No ▶	GO to HD11. SERVICE CORRECT open circuit as necessary. RERUN Quick Test
HD11 CHECK EGO CIRCUIT FOR SHORT TO GROUND • Key Off. • Breakout box installed. Processor disconnected. • DVOM to 200,000 ohms range. • Disconnect appropriate EGO sensor at harness. • Measure resistance between test Pin 29 (left EGO) or test Pin 43 (right EGO) to test Pin 40 at the Breakout box.	Reading is 10,000 ohms or greater ▶ Reading is less than 10,000 ohms ▶	GO to HD12. CORRECT cause of resistance to ground. RERUN Quick Test.
HD12 ATTEMPT TO ELIMINATE EGO LEAN CODE • Key Off. • Reconnect appropriate EGO sensor. • Reconnect processor. • Apply 14 in.-Hg. vacuum to MAP sensor. • Start the engine and run at approximately 2000 rpm for 1 minute. Allow engine to return to idle. • Enter Engine Running Quick Test. • Is code 41 or 91 still present? **NOTE: Disregard any other code output at this time.**	Yes ▶ No ▶	INSPECT for corrosion or damaged pins. If OK, REPLACE processor. RERUN Quick Test. EGO input circuit OK. GO to HD13.

Fuel Control — 3.8L CFI	Pinpoint Test	HD

TEST STEP	RESULT ▶	ACTION TO TAKE
HD13 CHECK FOR CODES WITH ACT RECONNECTED • Reconnect ACT sensor. • Repeat Quick Test. • Is code 41 or 91 present?	Yes ▶ No ▶	REPLACE processor. RERUN Quick Test. GO to HD2.

HD14 FUEL CONTROL — ALWAYS RICH CODES: 42 LEFT EGO, 92 RIGHT EGO
• Key Off, wait 10 seconds.
• **NOTE: Non-EEC areas could cause a code 42.**
    Check for:
    — **Fuel contaminated engine oil**
    — **Ignition caused misfire**
    — **CANP problems**
    — **Mechanical portion of EGR system**
• Refer to illustration HD.
• Disconnect vehicle harness at the appropriate EGO sensor. Using a jumper wire, ground vehicle harness EGO circuit at the EGO sensor to the engine block.
• Repeat Engine Running Self-Test.
• Is service code 41 or 91 present?
	Yes ▶
	No ▶
		GO to HD16.
		GO to HD15.

HD15 HARNESS CHECK • Key Off, wait 10 seconds. • Refer to illustration HD. • Disconnect processor 60 Pin connector and inspect for damaged pins, corrosion, loose wires. Service as necessary. • Install Breakout box. • Measure resistance between test Pin 49 at the Breakout box and left EGO ground at engine block or Pin 44 and right EGO ground at engine block. • Measure resistance between test Pin 29 and left EGO harness connector or test Pin 43 and right EGO harness connector. • Are both circuits less than 5 ohms?	Yes ▶ No ▶	DISCONNECT processor connector. INSPECT for damage or corrosion. If OK, REPLACE processor. RERUN Quick Test. CORRECT harness circuit with resistance greater than 5 ohms. RERUN Quick Test.

Fuel Control — 3.8L CFI	Pinpoint Test	HD

TEST STEP	RESULT	▶	ACTION TO TAKE
HD16 CHECK MAP SENSOR			
NOTE: Because the MAP sensor influences fuel control, it is possible for a code 42 to occur as a result of a MAP problem even though code 22 is not present. The next 2 steps will verify proper vacuum to the MAP sensor and its ability to hold vacuum.			
• Key Off, wait 10 seconds. • Disconnect vacuum line from MAP sensor. • Install vacuum pump to MAP sensor. • Apply 18 in.-Hg. vacuum to MAP sensor. • Does MAP sensor hold vacuum?	Yes No	▶ ▶	RELEASE vacuum. GO to HD17. REPLACE MAP sensor. CONNECT vacuum line to MAP sensor. RERUN Quick Test.
HD17 CHECK FOR LOSS OF MAP VACUUM			
• Tee a vacuum gauge in the intake manifold vacuum line at the MAP sensor. • Start engine and note vacuum reading. • Key Off, wait 10 seconds. • Remove vacuum gauge and tee and reconnect line to MAP. • Tee in vacuum gauge at a different source of intake manifold vacuum. • Start engine and note vacuum reading. • Do vacuum readings differ greater than 1 in.-Hg.?	Yes No	▶ ▶	INSPECT vacuum lines for leaks, holes, disconnections. kinks, blockage and proper routing. SERVICE as necessary. GO to HD18.
HD18 EGO CHECK			
• Refer to illustration HD. • DVOM on 20V scale. • With appropriate EGO sensor disconnected from the vehicle harness, connect a DVOM from EGO sensor to engine ground. • Disconnect PCV hose. • Start engine and run at approximately 2000 rpm. Does the DVOM read less than 0.4V within 1 minute?	Yes No	▶ ▶	EGO sensor OK. GO to HD2. REPLACE EGO sensor. RERUN Quick Test.

Fuel Control — 3.8L CFI	Pinpoint Test	HD

HD19   CONTINUOUS TESTING: CODE 41/42

41 — EGO indicated the fuel system was lean for more than 15 seconds when the system should have been in closed loop fuel control.

42 — EGO indicated the fuel system was rich for more than 15 seconds when the system should have been in closed loop fuel control.

*CLOSED LOOP — Fuel control under the influence of the EGO sensor.

*OPEN LOOP — Fuel control NOT under the influence of the EGO sensor.

Before attempting to correct a fuel control code,' 41/42, diagnose all other drive complaints first, eg., rough idle, misses, etc.

NOTE: The fuel control code may help in this diagnosis.

Using the fuel control service code, isolate the cause of the fuel control problem.

Some areas to check are:

• Vacuum Circuits:	Vacuum leaks/intake air leaks. — Canister Purge System. — PCV System. — Engine sealing.
• EGO Fuel Fouled:	Whenever an over-rich fuel condition has been experienced (fuel fouled spark plugs), make a thorough check of the ignition system. In the event the EGO sensor is suspected of being fuel fouled (low output, slow response), run the vehicle at sustained high speeds (within legal limits) followed by a few hard accelerations. This will burn off EGO contamination and restore proper EGO operation.
• Fuel Pressure:	Perform Pinpoint Test Step HD2.
• Ignition System:	Always in default spark (10 degrees). Refer to Quick Test Step 4.0.
• Improper Fueling:	Lead fouled EGO sensor.
• TP Sensor:	Not moving (mechanical damage). Connect DVOM to test Pin 47 and to test Pin 46. Key to Run. Observe DVOM while moving the throttle. Reading must increase with increase in throttle opening. If not correct, SERVICE as necessary.

• If at this point, the drive concern is still present, perform Steps HD3 through HD6 only.

Fuel Control — 2.3L EFI Car/Truck	Pinpoint Test	HE

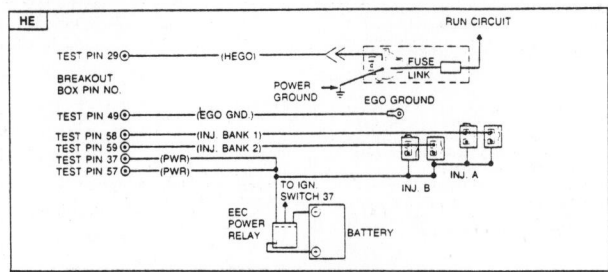

STOP-WARNING

You should enter this Pinpoint Test only when a Service Code 41 or 42 is received in Quick Test Step 5.0 or 6.0 or when directed here from Pinpoint Test A or Diagnostics by Symptom in the Engine Supplement Section.

To prevent the replacement of good components, be aware that the following non-EEC areas may be at fault:

• Ignition Coil	• EGR Valve and Gasket
• Distributor Cap	• Air Filter
• Distributor Rotor	• Fuel Contamination. Engine Oil
• Fouled Spark Plugs	• Poor Power Ground
• Spark Plug Wires	• Fuel Pressure
• CANP Problems	• Manifold Leaks. Intake Exhaust
• PCV Valves (see note below)	• Engine Not at Normal Operating Temperatures

This Pinpoint Test is intended to diagnose only the following:

• HEGO Sensor	• Vacuum Systems
• Harness Circuits HEGO Grd., HEGO. Inj. Bank 1. Inj. Bank 2. V PWR	• Fuel Injectors

• HEGO Sensor Connection
    — Code 42 start at HE8
    — Code 41 start at HE14
	• Processor Assembly

NOTE: Fuel contaminated engine oil may affect 41 and 42 Service Codes. If this is suspected, remove the PCV from the valve cover and repeat the Quick Test. If the problem is corrected, then change the engine oil and filter.

Fuel Control — 2.3L EFI Car/Truck	Pinpoint Test	HE

TEST STEP	RESULT	▶	ACTION TO TAKE
HE1 FUEL PRESSURE CHECK 1			
• Key Off, wait 10 seconds. • Install fuel pressure gauge. • Start and run engine. Fuel pressure must be 206 ± 35 kPa (30 ± 5 psi). **For No Starts:** • If engine will not run, cycle the key from Off to On several times to increase fuel pressure.	Yes No	▶ ▶	GO to HE2. REFER to the Shop Manual, Group 24 for electric fuel pump and Section 11 for fuel pressure regulator check.
HE2 FUEL PRESSURE CHECK 2			
• Fuel pressure must remain at 276 ± 34 kPa (40 ± 5 psi) for 60 seconds or longer after final key Off.	Yes No	▶ ▶	GO to HE3. GO to HE7.
HE3 FUEL DELIVERY TEST			
• Key Off. • Fuel pressure gauge installed. • Pressurize fuel system as per Step HE1. • Locate and disconnect the fuel pump relay. • Crank engine for 5 seconds. • Take pressure reading at the end of 5 second crank.	PRESSURE GAUGE READING: Pressure is approximately 10-20 psi at the end of 5 second crank cycle. Refer to note below Pressure is greater or less than specified	▶ ▶	The EEC system is not the fault of the No Start. Fuel and spark are present. REFER to Section 2 for other No Start Routines. If complaint was runs rough, misses or fuel code, GO to HE4. GO to HE4.

NOTE: The colder the engine, the greater the pressure drop (i.e., an engine coolant temperature of 200°F equals approximately a 10 psi drop in 5 seconds. 60°F equals approximately a 20 psi drop in 5 seconds).

Fuel Control — 2.3L EFI Car/Truck	Pinpoint Test	HE

TEST STEP	RESULT ▶	ACTION TO TAKE
HE4 HARNESS INJECTOR RESISTANCE CHECK • Key Off, wait 10 seconds. • Disconnect processor 60 pin connector and inspect for damaged pins, corrosion, loose wires. Service as necessary. • Connect Breakout box to harness. Leave processor disconnected. • DVOM on 200 ohm scale. • Measure the resistance of injector Bank 1 between test Pin 37 and test Pin 58 at the Breakout box. Record reading.	Yes ▶ No ▶ • Measure the resistance of injector Bank 2 between test Pin 37 and test Pin 59 at the Breakout box. Record reading. • Are both resistance readings between 7.0 ohms and 9.5 ohms?	GO to HE6 . GO to HE5 .
HE5 ISOLATE FAULTY INJECTOR CIRCUIT • Key Off. • Breakout box installed. • Leave processor disconnected. • DVOM on 200 ohm scale. • Disconnect all injectors on suspect Bank. Measure the resistance of each injector by connecting one injector at a time, and reading resistance between test Pin 37 and 58 at the Breakout box for Bank 1 or test Pin 37 and 59 at the Breakout box for Bank 2. • Are all resistance readings between 15.0 and 19.0 ohms?	Yes ▶ No ▶	GO to HE6 . SERVICE the harness connectors on the suspect injector for opens or shorts. If OK, REPLACE injector. RERUN Quick Test.
HE6 INJECTOR DRIVE SIGNAL CHECK **Requires standard non-powered 12-volt test lamp.** • Key Off. • Breakout box installed. • Connect processor to Breakout box. • Connect test lamp between test Pin 37 and test Pin 58 at the Breakout box. • Crank or start engine. • Repeat above test between test Pin 37 and test Pin 59 at the Breakout box.	Dim glow at light on both tests ▶ No light on one or both tests ▶ Bright light on one or both tests ▶	GO to HE7 . VERIFY 12-volt battery power at Pins 37 and 57. If OK, REPLACE processor. RERUN Quick Test. CHECK circuits Bank 1 and Bank 2 for shorts to ground. If OK, REPLACE processor. RERUN Quick Test.

Fuel Control — 2.3L EFI Car/Truck	Pinpoint Test	HE

TEST STEP	RESULT ▶	ACTION TO TAKE

HE10 ATTEMPT TO GENERATE CODE 41
 	
• Key Off, wait 10 seconds.
NOTE: Non-EEC areas could cause a code 42.
 	
   Check for:
   — Fuel contaminated engine oil
   — Ignition caused misfire
   — CANP problems
• Refer to Illustration HE.
• Disconnect vehicle harness at the HEGO sensor.
• Jumper (ground) the HEGO circuit at the HEGO sensor vehicle harness connector to the engine block.
• Repeat Engine Running Self-Test.
• Is service code 41 present?
	Yes ▶
	
	No ▶
		REMOVE jumper. GO to HE11 .
		
		REMOVE jumper. DISCONNECT the processor and INSPECT pins for damage or corrosion. If OK, REPLACE processor. RERUN Quick Test.

HE11 CHECK MAP SENSOR • Key Off, wait 10 seconds. • Disconnect vacuum line from MAP sensor. • Install vacuum pump to MAP sensor. • Apply 18 in.-Hg. vacuum to MAP sensor. • Does MAP sensor hold vacuum?	Yes ▶ No ▶	RELEASE vacuum. GO to HE12 . REPLACE MAP sensor. CONNECT vacuum line to MAP sensor. RERUN Quick Test.
HE12 CHECK FOR LOSS OF MAP VACUUM • Install vacuum gauge at the MAP sensor and the manifold source. • Start and run engine. • Compare vacuum readings between the MAP sensor and engine manifold. • Are the vacuum readings the same?	Yes ▶ No ▶	GO to HE13 . INSPECT vacuum lines for leaks, holes, disconnects, kinks, blockage and proper routings. SERVICE as necessary.

Fuel Control — 2.3L EFI Car/Truck	Pinpoint Test	HE

TEST STEP	RESULT ▶	ACTION TO TAKE
HE7 INJECTOR BALANCE TEST • Connect tachometer to engine. Run engine at idle. • Disconnect and reconnect the injectors one at a time; note rpm drop for each injector. • Does each injector produce at least a 100 rpm momentary drop, as ISC will attempt to re-establish rpm?.	Yes ▶ No ▶	Fuel delivery OK. Problem is with area common to all cylinders, i.e.: Air vacuum leak, fuel contamination, EGR. REPLACE faulty injector. RERUN Quick Test.
HE8 FUEL CONTROL — ALWAYS RICH: CODE 42. CHECK HEGO HARNESS FOR SHORT TO POWER • Key Off, wait 10 seconds. • Disconnect the HEGO sensor from the vehicle harness. • DVOM on 20 volt scale. • Key On. • Measure voltage between HEGO signal and ground at the HEGO connector. • Is voltage reading less than 0.5 volts?	Yes ▶ No ▶	GO to HE9 . SERVICE short to power in HEGO circuit. RERUN Quick Test.
HE9 CHECK HEGO FOR SHORT TO KEY POWER • Key Off. • HEGO disconnected. • DVOM on 200,000 ohm scale. • Measure resistance from key power input to HEGO circuit at the HEGO. • Is the resistance reading 10,000 ohms or greater?	Yes ▶ No ▶	GO to HE10 . REPLACE HEGO sensor. RERUN Quick Test.

HEGO SIGNAL
POWER GRD
TO IGNITION RUN CIRCUIT ONLY

Fuel Control — 2.3L EFI Car/Truck	Pinpoint Test	HE

TEST STEP	RESULT ▶	ACTION TO TAKE
HE13 HEGO CHECK • Refer to Illustration HE. • DVOM on 20V scale. • With HEGO sensor disconnected from the harness, connect a DVOM from HEGO sensor to engine ground. • Disconnect PCV hose. • Start engine and run at approximately 2000 rpm. • Does the DVOM read less than 0.4V within 1 minute?	Yes ▶ No ▶	HEGO sensor OK. GO to HE1 . REPLACE HEGO sensor. RERUN Quick Test.
HE14 FUEL CONTROL — ALWAYS LEAN: CODE 41 VERIFICATION • Run vehicle at 2000 rpm for 2 minutes. • Key Off, wait 10 seconds. • Perform Engine Running Quick Test. • Is code 41 present?	Yes ▶ No ▶	GO to HE15 . GO to HE21 .

HE15 FUEL CONTROL — ALWAYS LEAN
 	
NOTE: Vacuum/air leaks in non-EEC areas could cause a code 41. Check for:
   — Leaking vacuum actuator (eg: A/C control motor)
   — Engine sealing
   — EGR system
   — PCV system
   — Unmetered air leak between air meter and throttle body
   — Lead contaminated HEGO sensor
• Key Off. DVOM on 20V scale. Disconnect HEGO sensor from vehicle harness. Connect DVOM to HEGO sensor and engine ground.
• Apply 14 in.-Hg. vacuum to MAP.
• Start the engine and run at approximately 2000 rpm. Does the DVOM read greater than 0.5V within 1 minute?
	Yes ▶
	
	No ▶
		GO to HE16 .
		
		REPLACE HEGO sensor. RERUN Quick Test.

Fuel Control — 2.3L EFI Car/Truck	Pinpoint Test	HE

TEST STEP	RESULT ▶	ACTION TO TAKE
HE16 HARNESS CHECK HEGO CIRCUITS • Key Off. • Install Breakout box. Processor disconnected. • Measure resistance between test Pin 49 at the Breakout box and engine block ground and between HEGO circuit at the HEGO vehicle harness connector and test Pin 29 at the Breakout box. • Are both resistance readings less than 5 ohms?	Yes ▶ No ▶	GO to HE17. SERVICE/CORRECT as necessary. circuit with greater than 5 ohms resistance. RERUN Quick Test.
HE17 CHECK HEGO CIRCUIT FOR SHORT TO GROUND • Key Off. • HEGO disconnected. • Breakout box installed. Processor disconnected. • DVOM to 200,000 ohms range. • Measure resistance between test Pin 29 and test Pin 40 at the Breakout box. • Is the resistance reading 10.000 ohms or greater?	Yes ▶ No ▶	GO to HE18. CORRECT cause of resistance to ground. RERUN Quick Test.
HE18 CHECK HEGO SENSOR FOR SHORT TO GROUND • Key Off. • HEGO disconnected. • DVOM on 200,000 ohm scale. • Measure resistance from ground to HEGO signal at the HEGO sensor. • Is resistance reading 10.000 ohms or greater?	Yes ▶ No ▶	GO to HE19. REPLACE HEGO sensor. RERUN Quick Test.
HE19 ATTEMPT TO ELIMINATE CODE 41 • Key Off. • Reconnect HEGO sensor. • Apply 14 in.-Hg. vacuum to MAP sensor. • Start the engine and run at approximately 2000 rpm for 1 minute. Allow engine to return to idle. • Perform Engine Running Self-Test. • Is code 41 still present? NOTE: Disregard any other code output at this time.	Yes ▶ No ▶	INSPECT for corrosion or damaged pins. If OK. REPLACE processor. RERUN Quick Test. HEGO input circuit OK. GO to HE1.

Fuel Control — 2.3L EFI Car/Truck	Pinpoint Test	HE

TEST STEP	RESULT ▶	ACTION TO TAKE
HE21 CHECK HEATER ELEMENT RESISTANCE ON HEATED EGO • Key Off, Engine Off. • DVOM on 200 ohm scale. • HEGO disconnected. • Measure resistance between run circuit and ground at HEGO sensor. Refer to Pinpoint Test HE for wiring schematic. • Hot to warm resistance specification is 5 to 20 ohms. NOTE: At room temperature, resistance specification is 2 to 5 ohms. • Is resistance within specification?	Yes ▶ No ▶	GO to HE22. REPLACE HEGO sensor.
HE22 CHECK FOR POWER AT HEGO HARNESS CONNECTOR • Key On, Engine Off. • DVOM on 20V scale. • Connect positive lead to run circuit and negative lead to ground at HEGO vehicle harness connector. • Is voltage reading 10.5 volts or greater?	Yes ▶ No ▶	HEGO system OK. RECONNECT HEGO and GO to HE1. GO to HE23.
HE23 CHECK CONTINUITY OF GROUND TO HEGO CONNECTOR • Key Off, wait 10 seconds. • DVOM on 200 ohm scale. • Measure resistance of ground circuit from HEGO vehicle harness connector to battery ground. • Is resistance reading less than 5.0 ohms?	Yes ▶ No ▶	SERVICE open in run circuit. SERVICE open in ground circuit.

Fuel Control — 1.9L CFI and 2.3L/2.5L (HSC) CFI	Pinpoint Test	HF

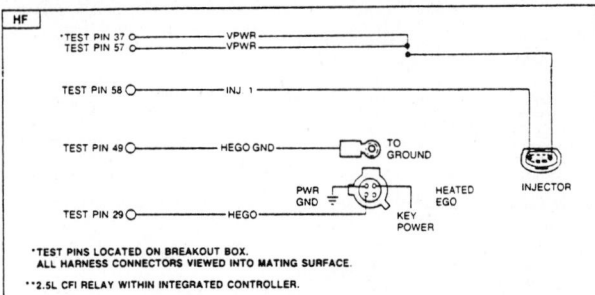

HF

*TEST PIN 37 — VPWR
TEST PIN 57 — VPWR

TEST PIN 58 — INJ 1

TEST PIN 49 — HEGO GND — TO GROUND

TEST PIN 29 — HEGO

PWR GND — HEATED EGO — KEY POWER — INJECTOR

*TEST PINS LOCATED ON BREAKOUT BOX.
ALL HARNESS CONNECTORS VIEWED INTO MATING SURFACE.
**2.5L CFI RELAY WITHIN INTEGRATED CONTROLLER.

STOP-WARNING

You should enter this Pinpoint Test only when a Service Code 41 or 42 is received in Quick Test Step 5.0 or 6.0 or when directed here from Pinpoint Test S.

To prevent the replacement of good components. be aware that the following non-EEC areas may be at fault:

- Ignition Coil
- Distributor Cap
- Distributor Rotor
- Fouled Spark Plugs
- Spark Plug Wires
- CANP Problems
- PCV Valves (see note below)

- EGR Valve and Gasket
- Air Filter
- Fuel Contamination. Engine Oil
- Poor Power Ground
- Fuel Pressure
- Manifold Leaks. Intake/Exhaust
- Engine Not at Normal Operating Temperatures

This Pinpoint Test is intended to diagnose only the following:

- EGO Sensor
- EGO Signal and Ground Circuit
- EGO Sensor Connection

- Fuel Injector
- Processor Assembly

NOTE: Fuel contaminated engine oil may affect 41 and 42 Service Codes, so if it is suspected, remove the PCV from the valve cover, and rerun the Quick Test. If the problem is corrected, then change the engine oil and filter.

Fuel Control — 1.9L CFI and 2.3L/2.5L (HSC) CFI	Pinpoint Test	HF

TEST STEP	RESULT ▶	ACTION TO TAKE
HF1 FUEL PRESSURE CHECK 1 • Key Off, wait 10 seconds. • Install fuel gauge. • Start and run engine.* FUEL PRESSURE SPECIFICATION 1.9L and 2.5L CFI = 13-16 psi (14.5 ± 1.5) 2.3L CFI = 14.5-17.5 psi (16 ± 1.5) *For No Starts: • If engine will not run, cycle the key from off to on several times. • Is fuel pressure within specification?	Yes ▶ No ▶	GO to HF2. REFER to Shop Manual, Group 24 for electric fuel pump and Section 11 for fuel pressure regulator check.
HF2 FUEL PRESSURE CHECK 2 • Key On. • Does fuel pressure remain at specification for 60 seconds?	Yes ▶ No ▶	GO to HF3. GO to HF25.
HF3 FUEL DELIVERY TEST • Key Off. • Fuel pressure gauge installed. • Pressurize fuel system as per Step HF1. • Locate and disconnect the inertia switch. • Crank engine for 5 seconds. • Take pressure reading at the end of 5-second crank. • Does pressure drop approximately 5-8 psi at the end of 5 second crank cycle. Refer to Note below. NOTE: Verify fuel quality; air and/or water will also pressurize and look like acceptable fuel delivery. NOTE: The colder the engine, the greater the pressure drop (i.e., an engine coolant temperature of 200°F equals approximately a 5 psi drop in 5 seconds. 60°F equals approximately a 8 psi drop in 5 seconds).	Yes ▶ No ▶	The EEC system is not the fault of the No Start. Fuel and spark are present. REFER to Section 2 for other No Start Routines. If complaint was runs rough, misses or fuel code, CONTINUE to HF4. GO to HF4.

Fuel Control — 1.9L CFI and 2.3L/2.5L (HSC) CFI	Pinpoint Test	HF

TEST STEP	RESULT	▶	ACTION TO TAKE
HF4 HARNESS INJECTOR RESISTANCE CHECK			
• Key Off. • DVOM on 200 ohm range. • Disconnect processor 60 Pin connector and inspect for damaged pins, corrosion, loose wires. Service as necessary. • Install Breakout box, processor disconnected. • Measure resistance between test Pins 57 and 58 at the Breakout box. • Is resistance between 1.0 and 2.0 ohms?	Yes No	▶ ▶	GO to HF5. SERVICE the harness and/or connectors on the injector for opens or shorts. If OK, REPLACE injector.
HF5 INJECTOR DRIVE SIGNAL CHECK			
Requires standard non-powered 12-volt test lamp. • Key Off. • Breakout box installed. • Connect processor to Breakout box. • Refer to illustration HF. • Connect test lamp between test Pin 37 and test Pin 58 at the Breakout box. • Crank or start engine.	Very dim glow at light ▶ No light Bright light	▶ ▶ ▶	Fuel delivery OK. Problem is with area common to all cylinders, i.e., air/vacuum leak, fuel contamination, EGR. VERIFY 12-volt battery power at Pins 37 and 57. If OK, REPLACE processor. RERUN Quick Test. CHECK injector circuit for shorts to ground. If OK, REPLACE processor. RERUN Quick Test.
HF6 FUEL CONTROL — ALWAYS LEAN: CODE 41 VERIFICATION			
• Run vehicle at 2000 rpm for 2 minutes. • Key Off, wait 10 seconds. • Perform Engine Running Quick Test. • Is code 41 present?	Yes No	▶ ▶	GO to HF7. GO to HF20.

Fuel Control — 1.9L CFI and 2.3L/2.5L (HSC) CFI	Pinpoint Test	HF

TEST STEP	RESULT	▶	ACTION TO TAKE
HF7 FUEL CONTROL — INDICATES LEAN: CODE 41			
NOTE: Vacuum/air leaks in non-EEC areas could cause a code 41. Check for: — Leaking vacuum actuator (eg: A/C control motor) — Engine sealing — EGR system — PCV system — Lead contaminated HEGO sensor • Refer to illustration HF. • Key Off. DVOM on 20V scale. Disconnect HEGO sensor from vehicle harness. Connect DVOM to EGO signal at HEGO sensor and engine ground. • Apply 14 in.-Hg. vacuum to MAP. • Start the engine and run at approximately 2000 rpm. Does the DVOM read greater than 0.5V within 60 seconds?	Yes No	▶ ▶	GO to HF8. REPLACE HEGO sensor. RERUN Quick Test.
HF8 HARNESS CHECK HEGO CIRCUITS			
• Key Off. • Install Breakout box. Processor disconnected. • HEGO disconnected. • Measure resistance between test Pin 49 at the Breakout box and engine block ground and between EGO circuit at the HEGO vehicle harness connector and test Pin 29 at the Breakout box. • Are both resistance readings less than 5 ohms?	Yes No	▶ ▶	GO to HF9. SERVICE/CORRECT circuit with resistance greater than 5 ohms, as necessary. RERUN Quick Test.
HF9 CHECK HEGO CIRCUIT FOR SHORT TO GROUND			
• Key Off. • HEGO disconnected. • Breakout box installed. Processor disconnected. • DVOM to 200,000 ohms range. • Measure resistance between test Pin 29 and test Pin 40 at the Breakout box. • Is resistance 10,000 ohms or greater?	Yes No	▶ ▶	GO to HF10. CORRECT cause of resistance to ground. RERUN Quick Test.

Fuel Control — 1.9L CFI and 2.3L/2.5L (HSC) CFI	Pinpoint Test	HF

TEST STEP	RESULT	▶	ACTION TO TAKE
HF10 CHECK HEGO SENSOR TO GROUND			
• Key Off. • HEGO disconnected. • DVOM on 200,000 ohm scale. • Measure resistance between power ground and EGO signal at HEGO sensor. • Is resistance 10,000 ohms or greater?	Yes No	▶ ▶	GO to HF11. REPLACE HEGO sensor. RERUN Quick Test.
HF11 ATTEMPT TO ELIMINATE CODE 41			
• Key Off. • Reconnect HEGO sensor. • Apply 14 in.-Hg. vacuum to MAP. • Start the engine and run at approximately 2000 rpm for 1 minute, allow engine to return to idle. • Perform Engine Running Self-Test. • Is code 41 still present? **NOTE: Disregard any other code output at this time.**	Yes No	▶ ▶	INSPECT for corrosion or damaged pins. If OK, REPLACE processor. RERUN Quick Test. HEGO input circuit OK. GO to HF1.
HF13 FUEL CONTROL — ALWAYS RICH: CODE 42 CHECK HEGO HARNESS FOR SHORT TO POWER			
• Key Off, wait 10 seconds. • Disconnect vehicle harness at the HEGO sensor. • DVOM on 20 volt scale. • Key On. • Measure voltage between EGO signal and power ground at the HEGO harness connector.	Yes No	▶ ▶	GO to HF14. REPAIR short to power in EGO circuit. RERUN Quick Test. If code 41 is now present, REPLACE HEGO.

HEGO — KEY POWER
 — EGO SIGNAL
 — POWER GROUND

• Is voltage less than .5 volts?

Fuel Control — 1.9L CFI and 2.3L/2.5L (HSC) CFI	Pinpoint Test	HF

TEST STEP	RESULT	▶	ACTION TO TAKE
HF14 CHECK HEGO FOR SHORT TO KEY POWER			
• Key Off. • HEGO disconnected. • DVOM on 200,000 ohm scale. • Measure resistance between key power input and EGO circuit at the HEGO sensor. • Is resistance 10,000 ohms or greater.	Yes No	▶ ▶	GO to HF15. REPLACE HEGO sensor. RERUN Quick Test.
HF15 ATTEMPT TO GENERATE CODE 41			
• Key Off, wait 10 seconds. • **NOTE: Non-EEC areas could cause code 42. Check for:** — Fuel contaminated engine oil — Ignition caused misfire (fouled spark plug) — CANP problems — Mechanical portion EGR system • Refer to illustration HF. • Disconnect vehicle harness at the HEGO sensor. Jumper (ground) the EGO circuit at the HEGO sensor vehicle harness connector to the engine block. • Repeat Engine Running Self-Test. • Service code 41 results.	Yes No	▶ ▶	DISCONNECT jumper to ground. GO to HF16. DISCONNECT processor connector. INSPECT for damage or corrosion. If OK, REPLACE Processor. RERUN Quick Test.
HF16 CHECK MAP SENSOR			
NOTE: Due to the MAP sensors large influence on fuel control, there is a possibility that a code 42 could be a result of a MAP problem, even though a code 22 is not present. Therefore, in the next two Pinpoint Test Steps we will verify proper vacuum to MAP, and its ability to hold it. • Key Off, wait 10 seconds. • Disconnect vacuum line from MAP sensor. • Install vacuum pump to MAP sensor. • Apply 18 in.-Hg. vacuum to MAP sensor. • Does MAP sensor hold vacuum?	Yes No	▶ ▶	RELEASE vacuum. GO to HF17. REPLACE MAP sensor. CONNECT vacuum line to MAP sensor. RERUN Quick Test.

Fuel Control — 1.9L CFI and 2.3L/2.5L (HSC) CFI	Pinpoint Test	HF

TEST STEP	RESULT	▶	ACTION TO TAKE
HF17 CHECK FOR LOSS OF VACUUM TO MAP			
• Tee a vacuum gauge in the intake manifold vacuum hose at the MAP sensor. • Start engine and let RPM stabilize. NOTE vacuum reading. • Key Off, wait 10 seconds. • Remove vacuum gauge and tee and reconnect vacuum line to MAP. • Tee in vacuum gauge at a different source of intake manifold vacuum. • Start engine and let RPM stabilize. NOTE vacuum reading. • Do the vacuum readings differ greater than 1 in.-Hg.?	Yes No	▶ ▶	INSPECT vacuum lines for leaks, holes, disconnections, kinks, blockage and proper routing. SERVICE as necessary. REMOVE vacuum gauge and tee. GO to **HF18** .
HF18 HEGO CHECK			
• Refer to illustration HF. • DVOM on 20V scale. • HEGO sensor disconnected. • Connect a DVOM from EGO circuit on sensor to engine ground. • Disconnect PCV hose. • Start engine and run at approximately 2000 rpm. Does the DVOM read less than 0.4V within 30 seconds?	Yes No	▶ ▶	HEGO sensor OK. GO to **HF1** REPLACE HEGO sensor. RERUN Quick Test.
HF20 CHECK HEATER ELEMENT RESISTANCE ON HEATED EGO			
• Key Off Engine Off. • DVOM on 200 ohm scale. • HEGO disconnected. • Measure resistance between run circuit and ground at HEGO sensor. — Refer to pinpoint test HF wiring schematic. • Hot to warm resistance specification is 5 to 20 ohms. NOTE: At room temperature, resistance specification is 2 to 5 ohms. • Is resistance within specification?	Yes No	▶ ▶	GO to **HF21** . REPLACE HEGO sensor.

Fuel Control — 1.9L CFI and 2.3L/2.5L (HSC) CFI	Pinpoint Test	HF

TEST STEP	RESULT	▶	ACTION TO TAKE
HF21 CHECK FOR POWER AT HEGO HARNESS CONNECTOR			
• Key On Engine Off. • DVOM on 20V scale. • Connect positive lead to run circuit and negative lead to ground at HEGO vehicle harness connector. • Is voltage 10.5V or greater?	Yes No	▶ ▶	HEGO sensor system OK. RECONNECT HEGO. GO to **HF1** . GO to **HF22** .
HF22 CHECK CONTINUITY OF GROUND TO HEGO CONNECTOR			
• Key Off, wait 10 seconds. • DVOM on 200 ohm scale. • Measure resistance of ground circuit from HEGO vehicle harness connector to battery ground. • Is resistance less than 5.0 ohms?	Yes No	▶ ▶	SERVICE open in run circuit. SERVICE open in ground circuit.
HF25 LEAKING INJECTOR			
• Remove air inlet tube at fuel charging assembly. • Pressurize fuel system as per Test Step HF1. • Key Off. • Observe throughout the air horn inlet for fuel leaking and/or weeping at the fuel injector discharge area. • Is there a visible leak?	Yes No	▶ ▶	SERVICE injector and/or O-rings as necessary. REFER to Shop Manual. Section 24-03 for service procedure. NOTE: After having completed service, RERUN Quick Test. GO to **HF26** .
HF26 EXTERNAL FUEL LEAKS			
• Pressurized fuel system as per Test Step HF1. • Key Off. • Look for fuel leak external to fuel charging assembly fuel line, fitting, etc. • Is there a visible leak?	Yes No	▶ ▶	SERVICE as necessary. RERUN Quick Test. SERVICE fuel pressure regulator as necessary. REFER to Shop Manual. Section 24-03 for service procedure.
			NOTE: After having completed service, RERUN Quick Test.

Fuel Control — 1.9L CFI and 2.3L/2.5L (HSC) CFI	Pinpoint Test	HF

HF90 CONTINUOUS TESTING: CODE 41

CODE 41 — Indicates that the EGO circuit has not switched during closed loop fuel control.

NOTE: In this situation, code 41 does not necessarily indicate a lean condition.

CLOSED LOOP — Fuel control under the influence of the HEGO sensor.

OPEN LOOP — Fuel control NOT under the influence of the HEGO sensor.

Before attempting to correct a continuous fuel control code 41, diagnose all other drive complaints first, eg., rough idle, misses, etc. in EEC Diagnostic By Symptom in the appropriate engine supplement.

NOTE: The fuel control code may help in this diagnosis.

Using the fuel control service code, isolate the cause of the fuel control problem.

Some areas to check are:

• Vacuum Circuits:	Vacuum leaks/intake air leaks. — Canister Purge System. — PCV System. — Engine sealing.
• EGO Fuel Fouled:	Whenever an over-rich fuel condition has been experienced (fuel fouled spark plugs), make a thorough check of the ignition system. In the event the HEGO sensor is suspected of being fuel fouled (low output, slow response), run the vehicle at sustained high speeds (within legal limits) followed by a few hard accelerations. This will burn off HEGO contamination and restore proper HEGO operation.
• Ignition System:	Always in default spark (10 degrees). Refer to Quick Test Step **4.0** .
• Improper Fueling:	Lead fouled HEGO sensor.
• Fuel Pressure:	Perform Pinpoint Test Step **HF1** and **HF2** .

• If at this point, the drive concern (if any) is still present, perform Steps **HF3** through **HF5** only.

Fuel Control — 2.9L, 3.0L and 4.9L EFI 6-Cylinder Engines	Pinpoint Test	HG

HG

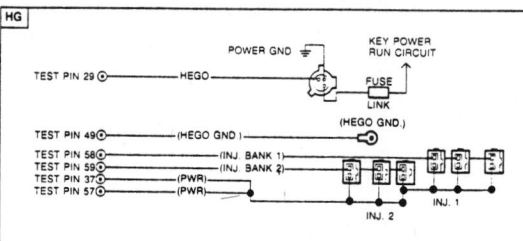

NOTE: REFER TO APPROPRIATE ENGINE SUPPLEMENT FOR PROPER INJECTOR BANK-TO-INJECTOR RELATIONSHIP.

STOP-WARNING

You should enter this Pinpoint Test only when a Service Code 41 or 42 is received in Quick Test Step 5.0 or 6.0 or when directed here from Pinpoint Test S or Diagnostics by Symptom in the Engine Supplement Section.

To prevent the replacement of good components, be aware that the following non-EEC areas may be at fault:

• Ignition Coil	• EGR Valve and Gasket
• Distributor Cap	• Air Filter
• Distributor Rotor	• Fuel Contamination, Engine Oil
• Fouled Spark Plugs	• Poor Power Ground
• Spark Plug Wires	• Fuel Pressure
• CANP Problems	• Manifold Leaks, Intake/Exhaust
• PCV Valves (see note below)	• Engine Not at Normal Operating Temperatures

This Pinpoint Test is intended to diagnose only the following:

• HEGO Sensor	• Vacuum Systems
• Harness Circuits EGO Grd., HEGO, Inj. Bank 1, Inj. Bank 2, VPWR.	• Fuel Injectors
• HEGO Sensor Connection	• Processor Assembly

NOTE: Fuel contaminated engine oil may affect 41 and 42 Service Codes. If this is suspected, remove the PCV from the valve cover and repeat the Quick Test. If the problem is corrected, then change the engine oil and filter.

Fuel Control — 2.9L, 3.0L and 4.9L EFI 6-Cylinder Engines	Pinpoint Test	HG

TEST STEP	RESULT ▶	ACTION TO TAKE
HG1 FUEL PRESSURE CHECK 1		
• Key Off, wait 10 seconds. • Install fuel pressure gauge. • Start and run engine. RUNNING FUEL PRESSURE SPECIFICATION 2.9L and 3.0L = 28-38 psi (33 ± 5) 4.9L = 42-52 psi (47 ± 5) ENGINE OFF FUEL PRESSURE SPECIFICATION 2.9L and 3.0L = 35-45 psi (40 ± 5) 4.9L = 50-60 psi (55 ± 5) • Is fuel pressure within specification? **For No Starts:** • If engine will not run, cycle the key from Off to On several times to increase fuel pressure.	Yes ▶ No ▶	GO to **HG2**. REFER to the Shop Manual, Group 24 for electric fuel pump and Section 11 for fuel pressure regulator check.
HG2 FUEL PRESSURE CHECK 2		
• Key On. • Does fuel pressure remain at specification for 60 seconds?	Yes ▶ No ▶	GO to **HG3**. GO to **HG7**.
HG3 FUEL DELIVERY TEST		
• Key Off. • Fuel pressure gauge installed. • Pressurize fuel system as per Step HG1. • Locate and disconnect the inertia switch which disables fuel pump. • Crank engine for 5 seconds. • Take pressure reading at the end of 5 second crank. • Does pressure drop approximately 5-8 psi at the end of crank cycle? Refer to Notes below. NOTE: Verify fuel quality: air and/or water will also pressurize and look like acceptable fuel delivery. NOTE: The colder the engine, the greater the pressure drop (for example, an engine coolant temperature of 200°F equals approximately a 69 kPa [10 psi] drop in 5 seconds. 60°F equals approximately a 138 kPa [20 psi] drop in 5 seconds).	Yes ▶ No ▶	The EEC system is not the fault of the No Start. Fuel and spark are present. REFER to Section 2 for other No Start Routines. If complaint was runs rough, misses or fuel code, GO to **HG4**. GO to **HG4**.

Fuel Control — 2.9L, 3.0L and 4.9L EFI 6-Cylinder Engines	Pinpoint Test	HG

TEST STEP	RESULT ▶	ACTION TO TAKE
HG4 HARNESS INJECTOR RESISTANCE CHECK		
• Key Off, wait 10 seconds. • Disconnect processor 60 Pin connector and inspect for damaged pins, corrosion, loose wires. Service as necessary. • Connect Breakout box to harness. Leave processor disconnected. • DVOM on 200 ohm scale. • Measure the resistance of injector Bank 1 between test Pin 37 and test Pin 58 at the Breakout box. • Measure the resistance of injector Bank 2 between test Pin 37 and test Pin 59 at the Breakout box. • Are both readings between 5.0 and 6.5 ohms?	Yes ▶ No ▶	GO to **HG6**. GO to **HG5**.
HG5 ISOLATE FAULTY INJECTOR CIRCUIT		
• Key Off. • Breakout box installed. • Leave processor disconnected. • DVOM on 200 ohm scale. • Disconnect all injectors on suspect Bank. Measure the resistance of each injector by connecting one injector at a time, and reading resistance between test Pin 37 and 58, for Bank 1, or test Pin 37 and 59, for Bank 2, at the Breakout box. • Are all readings between 16.0 and 18.0 ohms?	Yes ▶ No ▶	GO to **HG6**. SERVICE the harness and/or connectors on the suspect injector for opens or shorts. If OK, REPLACE injector. RERUN Quick Test.
HG6 INJECTOR DRIVE SIGNAL CHECK		
Requires standard non-powered 12-volt test lamp. • Key Off. • Breakout box installed. • Connect processor to Breakout box. • Connect test lamp between test Pin 37 and test Pin 58 at the Breakout box. • Crank or start engine. • Repeat above test between test Pin 37 and test Pin 59 at the Breakout box.	Dim glow at light on both tests ▶ No light on one or both tests ▶ Bright light on one or both tests ▶	GO to **HG7**. VERIFY 12V battery power at Pins 37 and 57. If OK, REPLACE processor. RERUN Quick Test. CHECK circuits Bank 1 and Bank 2 for shorts to ground. If OK, REPLACE processor. RERUN Quick Test.

Fuel Control — 2.9L, 3.0L and 4.9L EFI 6-Cylinder Engines	Pinpoint Test	HG

TEST STEP	RESULT ▶	ACTION TO TAKE
HG7 INJECTOR BALANCE TEST		
• Connect tachometer to engine. Run engine at idle. • Disconnect and reconnect the injectors one at a time; note rpm drop for each injector. • Does each injector produce at least a 100 rpm momentary drop? ISC will attempt to reestablish rpm.	Yes ▶ No ▶	Fuel delivery OK. Problem is with area common to all cylinders, i.e.: Air, vacuum leak, fuel contamination, EGR. REPLACE faulty injector. RERUN Quick Test.
HG8 FUEL CONTROL — ALWAYS RICH: CODE 42. CHECK HEGO HARNESS FOR SHORT TO POWER		
• Key Off, wait 10 seconds. • Disconnect vehicle harness at the HEGO sensor. • DVOM on 20 volt scale. • Key On. • Measure voltage between EGO signal and power ground at the HEGO harness connector. HEGO SIGNAL POWER GROUND KEY POWER RUN CIRCUIT • Is voltage less than .5 volts?	Yes ▶ No ▶	GO to **HG9**. REPAIR short to power in EGO circuit. RERUN Quick Test.
HG9 CHECK HEGO FOR SHORT TO KEY POWER		
• Key Off. • HEGO sensor disconnected. • DVOM on 200,000 ohm scale. • Measure resistance between key power input to EGO circuit at the HEGO sensor. • Is reading 10,000 ohms or less?	Yes ▶ No ▶	REPLACE HEGO sensor. RERUN Quick Test. GO to **HG10**.

Fuel Control — 2.9L, 3.0L and 4.9L EFI 6-Cylinder Engines	Pinpoint Test	HG

TEST STEP	RESULT ▶	ACTION TO TAKE
HG10 ATTEMPT TO GENERATE CODE 41		
• Key Off, wait 10 seconds. • NOTE: Non-EEC areas could cause a code 42. Check for: — Fuel contaminated engine oil — Ignition caused misfire (fouled spark plug) — CANP problems • Refer to illustration HF. • Disconnect vehicle harness at the EGO sensor. Jumper (ground) the EGO circuit at the EGO sensor vehicle harness connector to the engine block. • Repeat Engine Running Self-Test. • Service code 41 results.	Yes ▶ No ▶	REMOVE jumper. GO to **HG11**. REMOVE jumper. DISCONNECT processor connector. INSPECT for damage or corrosion. If OK, REPLACE processor. RERUN Quick Test.
HG11 CHECK MAP SENSOR		
NOTE: Due to the MAP sensor influence on fuel control, there is a possibility that a code 42 could be a result of a MAP problem even though a code 22 is not present. The next two Pinpoint Test steps will verify proper vacuum to the MAP sensor and the ability to hold vacuum. • Key Off, wait 10 seconds. • Disconnect vacuum line from MAP sensor. • Install vacuum pump to MAP sensor. • Apply 18 in.-Hg. vacuum to MAP sensor. • Does MAP sensor hold vacuum?	Yes ▶ No ▶	RELEASE vacuum. GO to **HG12**. REPLACE MAP sensor. CONNECT vacuum line to MAP sensor. RERUN Quick Test.

Fuel Control — 2.9L, 3.0L and 4.9L EFI 6-Cylinder Engines	Pinpoint Test	HG

TEST STEP	RESULT ▶	ACTION TO TAKE
HG12 CHECK FOR LOSS OF MAP VACUUM		
• Tee a vacuum gauge in the intake manifold vacuum line at the MAP sensor. • Start engine and note vacuum reading. • Key Off, wait 10 seconds. • Remove vacuum gauge and tee and reconnect vacuum line to MAP. • Tee in vacuum gauge at a different source of intake manifold vacuum. • Start engine and note vacuum reading. • Do vacuum readings differ by greater than 1 in.-Hg.?	Yes ▶ No ▶	INSPECT vacuum lines for leaks, holes, disconnections, kinks, blockage and proper routing. SERVICE as necessary. GO to HG13.
HG13 EGO CHECK		
• Refer to Illustration HG. • DVOM on 20V scale. • With EGO sensor disconnected from the harness, connect a DVOM from EGO sensor to engine ground. • Disconnect PCV hose. • Start engine and run at approximately 2000 rpm. Does the DVOM read less than 0.4V within 30 seconds?	Yes ▶ No ▶	EGO sensor OK. GO to HG1. REPLACE EGO sensor. RERUN Quick Test.
HG15 FUEL CONTROL — ALWAYS LEAN: CODE 41 VERIFICATION		
• Run vehicle at 2000 rpm for 2 minutes. • Key Off, wait 10 seconds. • Perform Engine Running Quick Test. • Is code 41 still present?	Yes ▶ No ▶	GO to HG16. GO to HG21.

Fuel Control — 2.9L, 3.0L and 4.9L EFI 6-Cylinder Engines	Pinpoint Test	HG

TEST STEP	RESULT ▶	ACTION TO TAKE
HG19 CHECK HEGO SENSOR TO GROUND		
• Key Off. • HEGO disconnected. • DVOM on 200.000 ohm scale. • Measure resistance from power ground to HEGO signal at HEGO sensor. • Is reading 10.000 ohms or less?	Yes ▶ No ▶	REPLACE HEGO sensor. RECONNECT MAP vacuum line. RERUN Quick Test. GO to HG20.
HG20 ATTEMPT TO ELIMINATE CODE 41		
• Key Off. • Processor connected. • Reconnect HEGO sensor. • MAP vacuum line still disconnected and plugged. • Apply 10 in.-Hg. vacuum to MAP sensor. • Start the engine and run at approximately 2000 rpm for 1 minute. Allow engine to return to idle. • Perform Engine Running Self-Test. • Is code 41 still present? **NOTE: Disregard any other code input at this time.**	Yes ▶ No ▶	INSPECT for corrosion or damaged pins. If OK, REPLACE processor. RECONNECT MAP vacuum line. RERUN Quick Test. RECONNECT MAP vacuum line. HEGO input circuit OK. GO to HG1 (Basic Fuel Delivery).
HG21 CHECK HEATER ELEMENT RESISTANCE ON HEATED EGO		
• Key Off. Engine Off. • DVOM on 200 ohm scale. • HEGO sensor disconnected. • Measure resistance between run circuit and power ground at the heated EGO sensor. Refer to Pinpoint Test HG wiring schematic. • Hot to warm resistance is 5-20 ohms. **NOTE: At room temperature, resistance specification is 2-5 ohms.** • Is resistance within specification?	Yes ▶ No ▶	GO to HG22. REPLACE HEGO sensor.

Fuel Control — 2.9L, 3.0L and 4.9L EFI 6-Cylinder Engines	Pinpoint Test	HG

TEST STEP	RESULT ▶	ACTION TO TAKE
HG16 FUEL CONTROL — INDICATES LEAN 41		
NOTE: Vacuum/air leaks in non-EEC areas could cause a code 41. **Check for:** — Leaking vacuum actuator (e.g.: A/C control motor) — Engine sealing — EGR system — PCV system — Lead contaminated HEGO sensor • Key Off. DVOM on 20V scale. Disconnect HEGO sensor from vehicle harness. Connect DVOM to HEGO sensor and engine ground. • Disconnect and plug vacuum line to MAP sensor. • Apply 10 in.-Hg. vacuum to MAP sensor. • Start the engine and run at approximately 2000 rpm. Does the DVOM read greater than 0.5V within 1 minute?	Yes ▶ No ▶	GO to HG17. REPLACE HEGO sensor. RECONNECT MAP vacuum line. RERUN Quick Test.
HG17 HARNESS CHECK HEGO CIRCUITS		
• Key Off. • Install Breakout box. Processor disconnected. • Measure resistance between test Pin 49 at the Breakout box and engine block ground and between HEGO circuit at the HEGO vehicle harness connector and test Pin 29 at the Breakout box. • Are both circuits less than 5 ohms?	Yes ▶ No ▶	GO to HG18. SERVICE/CORRECT as necessary circuit with greater than 5 ohms resistance. RECONNECT MAP vacuum line. RERUN Quick Test.
HG18 CHECK HEGO CIRCUIT FOR SHORT TO GROUND		
• Key Off. • EGO disconnected. • Breakout box installed. Processor disconnected. • DVOM to 200.000 ohms range. • Measure resistance between test Pin 29 and test Pin 40 at the Breakout box. • Is resistance 10.000 ohms or greater?	Yes ▶ No ▶	GO to HG19. CORRECT cause of resistance to ground. RECONNECT MAP vacuum line RERUN Quick Test.

Fuel Control — 2.9L, 3.0L and 4.9L EFI 6-Cylinder Engines	Pinpoint Test	HG

TEST STEP	RESULT ▶	ACTION TO TAKE
HG22 CHECK FOR POWER AT HEGO HARNESS CONNECTOR		
• Key On, Engine Off. • DVOM on 20V scale. • Connect positive lead to run circuit and negative lead to ground at HEGO vehicle harness connector. • Is voltage reading 10.5 volts or greater?	Yes ▶ No ▶	HEGO sensor system OK. RECONNECT HEGO and GO to HG1. GO to HG23.
HG23 CHECK CONTINUITY OF GROUND TO HEGO CONNECTOR		
• Key Off, wait 10 seconds. • DVOM on 200 ohm scale. • Measure resistance of power ground circuit from HEGO vehicle harness connector to battery ground. • Is resistance reading 5.0 ohms or less?	Yes ▶ No ▶	SERVICE open in run circuit. SERVICE open in power ground circuit.

Fuel Control — 2.9L, 3.0L and 4.9L EFI 6-Cylinder Engines	EFI Pinpoint Test	HG

HG90 | CONTINUOUS TESTING: CODE 41

Code 41: Indicates that the EGO circuit has not switched during closed loop fuel control.

NOTE: In this situation code 41 does not necessarily indicate a lean condition.

CLOSED LOOP — Fuel control under the influence of the EGO sensor.

OPEN LOOP — Fuel control NOT under the influence of the EGO sensor.

Before attempting to correct continuous code 41, diagnose all other drive complaints first, eg., rough idle, misses, etc. in EEC Diagnostic By Symptom in the appropriate engine supplement.

NOTE: The fuel control code may help in this diagnosis.

Using the fuel control service code, isolate the cause of the fuel control problem.

Some areas to check are:

- Vacuum Circuits: — Vacuum leaks/intake air leaks.
     — PCV System.
     — Engine sealing.

- EGO Fuel Fouled: Whenever an over-rich fuel condition has been experienced (fuel fouled spark plugs), make a thorough check of the ignition system. In the event the EGO sensor is suspected of being fuel fouled (low output, slow response), run the vehicle at sustained high speeds (within legal limits) followed by a few hard accelerations. This will burn off EGO contamination and restore proper EGO operation.

- Ignition System: Always in default spark (10 degrees). Refer to Quick Test Step 4.0.

- Improper Fueling: Lead fouled EGO sensor.

- Fuel Pressure: Perform Pinpoint Test Step HG1 and HG2.

- If at this point, the drive concern (if any) is still present, perform Steps HG3 and HG7 only.

Fuel Control — 5.0L/7.5L EFI Truck	Pinpoint Test	HH

TEST STEP	RESULT ▶	ACTION TO TAKE
HH1	FUEL PRESSURE CHECK 1		
• Key Off, wait 10 seconds. • Install fuel pressure gauge. • Start and run engine. Fuel pressure must be 28-38 psi (193-262 kPa). **For No Starts:** • If engine will not run, cycle the key from Off to On several times to increase fuel pressure. • Is fuel pressure 35-45 psi (241-310 kPa)?	Yes ▶ No ▶	GO to HH2. REFER to the Shop Manual, Group 24 for electric fuel pump and Section 11 for fuel pressure regulator check.
HH2	FUEL PRESSURE CHECK 2		
• Key On. • Does fuel pressure remain at 35-45 psi (241-310 kPa) for 60 seconds or longer after final key off?	Yes ▶ No ▶	GO to HH3. GO to HH7.
HH3	FUEL DELIVERY TEST		
• Key Off. • Fuel pressure gauge installed. • Pressurize fuel system as per Step HH1. • Locate and disconnect the fuel pump inertia switch (disables pump). • Crank engine for 5 seconds. • Take pressure reading at the end of 5 second crank. **NOTE: Verify fuel quality; air and/or water will also pressurize and look like acceptable fuel delivery.**	PRESSURE GAUGE READING: Pressure is approximately 10-20 psi at the end of 5 second crank cycle. Refer to note below ▶ Pressure is greater or less than specified ▶	The EEC system is not the fault of the No Start. Fuel and spark are present. REFER to Section 2 for other No Start Routines. If complaint was runs rough, misses or fuel code, GO to HH4. GO to HH4.

NOTE: The colder the engine, the greater the pressure drop (i.e., an engine coolant temperature of 200°F equals approximately a 10 psi drop in 5 seconds. 60°F equals approximately a 20 psi drop in 5 seconds).

Fuel Control — 5.0L/7.5L EFI Truck	Pinpoint Test	HH

HH

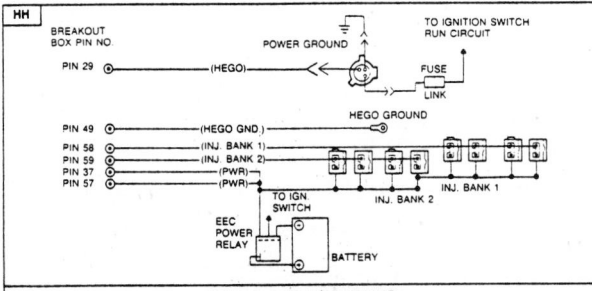

STOP-WARNING

You should enter this Pinpoint Test only when a Service Code 41 or 42 is received in Quick Test Step 5.0 or 6.0 or when directed here from Pinpoint Test S.

To prevent the replacement of good components, be aware that the following non-EEC areas may be at fault:

- Ignition Coil
- Distributor Cap
- Distributor Rotor
- Fouled Spark Plugs
- Spark Plug Wires
- CANP Problems
- PCV Valves (see note below)

- EGR Valve and Gasket
- Air Filter
- Fuel Contamination, Engine Oil
- Poor Power Ground
- Fuel Pressure
- Manifold Leaks, Intake/Exhaust
- Engine Not at Normal Operating Temperatures

This Pinpoint Test is intended to diagnose only the following:

- HEGO Sensor
- Harness Circuits HEGO Grd., HEGO, Inj. Bank 1, Inj. Bank 2, VPWR
- HEGO Sensor Connection
   — Code 42 start at HH8
   — Code 41 start at HH15

- Vacuum Systems
- Fuel Injectors
- Processor Assembly
- MAP Sensor (generating fuel codes)

NOTE: Fuel contaminated engine oil may affect 41 and 42 Service Codes. If this is suspected, remove the PCV from the valve cover and repeat the Quick Test. If the problem is corrected, then change the engine oil and filter.

Fuel Control — 5.0L/7.5L EFI Truck	Pinpoint Test	HH

TEST STEP	RESULT ▶	ACTION TO TAKE
HH4	HARNESS AND INJECTOR RESISTANCE CHECK		
• Key Off, wait 10 seconds. • Disconnect processor 60 pin connector and inspect for damaged pins, corrosion, loose wires. Service as necessary. • Connect Breakout box to harness. Leave processor disconnected. • DVOM on 200 ohm scale. • Measure and record the resistance of injector Bank 1 between test Pin 37 and test Pin 58 at the Breakout box. • Measure and record the resistance of injector Bank 2 between test Pin 37 and test Pin 59 at the Breakout box. • Are both resistances between 3.5 and 5.0 ohms?	Yes ▶ No ▶	GO to HH6. GO to HH5.
HH5	ISOLATE FAULTY INJECTOR CIRCUIT		
• Key Off. • Breakout box installed. • Leave processor disconnected. • DVOM on 200 ohm scale. • Disconnect all injectors on suspect Bank. Measure the resistance of each injector by connecting one injector at a time, and reading resistance between test Pin 37 and 58 at the Breakout box for Bank 1 or test Pin 37 and 59 at the Breakout box for Bank 2. • Are all resistances between 15.0 and 19.0 ohms?	Yes ▶ No ▶	GO to HH6. SERVICE the harness/connectors on the suspect injector for opens or shorts. If OK, REPLACE injector. REPEAT Quick Test.

Fuel Control — 5.0L/7.5L EFI Truck	Pinpoint Test	HH

TEST STEP	RESULT	▶	ACTION TO TAKE
HH6 INJECTOR DRIVER SIGNAL CHECK			
Requires standard non-powered 12-volt test lamp. • Key Off. • Breakout box installed. • Connect processor to Breakout box. • Connect test lamp between test Pin 37 and test Pin 58 at the Breakout box. • Crank or start engine. • Repeat above test between test Pin 37 and test Pin 59 at the Breakout box.	Dim glow at light on both tests	▶	GO to **HH7**.
	No light on one or both tests	▶	VERIFY 12-volt battery power at Pins 37 and 57. If OK, REPLACE processor. REPEAT Quick Test.
	Bright light on one or both tests	▶	CHECK circuits Bank 1 and Bank 2 for shorts to ground. If OK, REPLACE processor. REPEAT Quick Test.
HH7 INJECTOR BALANCE TEST			
• Connect tachometer to engine. Run engine at idle. • Disconnect and reconnect the injectors one at a time; note rpm drop for each injector. • Does each injector produce at least a 100 rpm momentary drop? **NOTE:** ISC will attempt to reestablish rpm.	Yes	▶	Fuel delivery OK. Problem is with area common to all cylinders, i.e.: Air/vacuum leak, fuel contamination, EGR.
	No	▶	REPLACE faulty injector. REPEAT Quick Test.

Fuel Control — 5.0L/7.5L EFI Truck	Pinpoint Test	HH

TEST STEP	RESULT	▶	ACTION TO TAKE
HH8 FUEL CONTROL — ALWAYS RICH: CODE 42 CHECK HEGO HARNESS FOR SHORT TO POWER			
• Key Off, wait 10 seconds. • Disconnect vehicle harness at the HEGO sensor. • DVOM on 20 volt scale. • Key On. • Measure voltage between HEGO signal and ground at the HEGO harness connector. HEGO SIGNAL POWER GROUND KEY POWER RUN CIRCUIT • Is voltage less than 0.5 volts?	Yes	▶	GO to **HH9**.
	No	▶	REPAIR short to key power in HEGO circuit. RERUN Quick Test.
HH9 CHECK HEGO FOR SHORT TO KEY POWER			
• Key Off. • HEGO disconnected. • DVOM on 200,000 ohm scale. • Measure resistance between key power input and HEGO circuit at the HEGO sensor. • Is resistance less than 10,000 ohms?	Yes	▶	REPLACE HEGO sensor. RERUN Quick Test.
	No	▶	GO to **HH10**.

Fuel Control — 5.0L/7.5L EFI Truck	Pinpoint Test	HH

TEST STEP	RESULT	▶	ACTION TO TAKE
HH10 ATTEMPT TO GENERATE CODE 41			
• Key Off, wait 10 seconds. • **NOTE:** Non-EEC areas could cause a code 42. Check for: — Fuel contaminated engine oil — Ignition caused misfire (fouled spark plug) — CANP problems • Refer to illustration HH. • Disconnect vehicle harness at the HEGO sensor. Jumper (ground) the HEGO circuit at the HEGO sensor vehicle harness connector to the engine block. • Repeat Engine Running Self-Test. • Is service code 41 present?	Yes	▶	REMOVE jumper. GO to **HH11**.
	No	▶	REMOVE jumper. DISCONNECT processor connector. INSPECT for damage or corrosion. If OK, REPLACE processor. RERUN Quick Test.
HH11 CHECK MAP SENSOR			
NOTE: Due to the MAP sensor's influence on fuel control, there is a possibility that a code 42 could be a result of a MAP problem even though a code 22 is not present. The next 2 Pinpoint Test Steps will verify proper vacuum to the MAP sensor and the ability to hold vacuum. • Key Off, wait 10 seconds. • Disconnect vacuum line from MAP sensor. • Install vacuum pump to MAP sensor. • Apply 18 in.-Hg. (59 kPa) vacuum to MAP sensor. • Does MAP sensor hold vacuum?	Yes	▶	RELEASE vacuum. GO to **HH12**.
	No	▶	REPLACE MAP sensor. CONNECT vacuum line to MAP sensor. RERUN Quick Test.

Fuel Control — 5.0L/7.5L EFI Truck	Pinpoint Test	HH

TEST STEP	RESULT	▶	ACTION TO TAKE
HH12 CHECK FOR LOSS OF MAP VACUUM			
• Tee a vacuum gauge in the intake manifold vacuum line at the MAP sensor. • Start engine and note vacuum reading. • Key Off, wait 10 seconds. • Remove vacuum gauge and tee and reconnect vacuum line to MAP. • Tee in vacuum gauge at a different source of intake manifold vacuum. • Start engine and note vacuum reading. • Are vacuum readings within 1 in.-Hg. (3 kPa) of each other?	Yes	▶	GO to **HH13**.
	No	▶	INSPECT vacuum lines for leaks, holes, disconnections, kinks, blockage and proper routing. SERVICE as necessary.
HH13 EGO CHECK			
• Refer to illustration HH. • DVOM on 20V scale. • With HEGO sensor disconnected from the harness, connect a DVOM from HEGO sensor to engine ground. • Disconnect PCV hose. • Start engine and run at approximately 2000 rpm. Does the DVOM read less than 0.4V within 30 seconds?	Yes	▶	HEGO sensor OK. GO to **HH1**.
	No	▶	REPLACE HEGO sensor. RERUN Quick Test.
HH15 FUEL CONTROL — ALWAYS LEAN: CODE 41 VERIFICATION			
• Run vehicle at 2000 rpm for 2 minutes. • Key Off, wait 10 seconds. • Perform Engine Running Self-Test. • Is code 41 present?	Yes	▶	GO to **HH16**.
	No	▶	GO to **HH21**.

Fuel Control — 5.0L/7.5L EFI Truck	Pinpoint Test	HH

TEST STEP	RESULT	▶	ACTION TO TAKE
HH16 FUEL CONTROL — INDICATES LEAN 41			
NOTE: Vaccum/air leaks in non-EEC areas could cause a code 41. Check for: — Leaking vacuum actuator (e.g.: A/C control motor) — Engine sealing — EGR system — PCV system — Lead contaminated HEGO sensor • Key Off. DVOM on 20V scale. Disconnect HEGO sensor from vehicle harness. Connect DVOM to HEGO sensor and engine ground. • Disconnect and plug vacuum line to MAP sensor. • Apply 10 in.-Hg. (33 kPa) vacuum to MAP sensor. • Start the engine and run at approximately 2000 rpm. Does the DVOM read greater than 0.5V within 1 minute?	Yes No	▶ ▶	GO to HH17. REPLACE HEGO sensor. RECONNECT MAP vacuum line. RERUN Quick Test.
HH17 HARNESS CHECK HEGO CIRCUITS			
• Key Off. • Install Breakout box. Processor disconnected. • Measure resistance between test Pin 49 at the Breakout box and engine block ground and between HEGO circuit at the HEGO vehicle harness connector and test Pin 29 at the Breakout box. • Are both circuits less than 5 ohms?	Yes No	▶ ▶	GO to HH18. SERVICE/CORRECT as necessary circuit with greater than 5 ohms resistance. RECONNECT MAP vacuum line. RERUN Quick Test.
HH18 CHECK HEGO CIRCUIT FOR SHORT TO GROUND			
• Key Off. • HEGO disconnected. • Breakout box installed. Processor disconnected. • DVOM to 200,000 ohms range. • Measure resistance between test Pin 29 and test Pin 40 at the Breakout box. • Is resistance greater than 10,000 ohms?	Yes No	▶ ▶	GO to HH19. CORRECT cause of resistance to ground. RECONNECT MAP vacuum line. RERUN Quick Test.

Fuel Control — 5.0L/7.5L EFI Truck	Pinpoint Test	HH

TEST STEP	RESULT	▶	ACTION TO TAKE
HH22 CHECK FOR POWER AT HEGO HARNESS CONNECTOR			
• Key on, engine off. • DVOM on 20V scale. • Connect positive lead to run circuit and negative lead to ground at HEGO vehicle harness connector. • Is voltage greater than 10.5V?	Yes No	▶ ▶	HEGO sensor system OK. RECONNECT HEGO and GO to HH1. GO to HH23.
HH23 CHECK CONTINUITY OF GROUND TO HEGO CONNECTOR			
• Key Off, wait 10 seconds. • DVOM on 200 ohm scale. • Measure resistance of power ground circuit from HEGO vehicle harness connector to battery ground. • Is resistance less than 5.0 ohms?	Yes No	▶ ▶	SERVICE open in run circuit. SERVICE open in power ground circuit.

Fuel Control — 5.0L/7.5L EFI Truck	Pinpoint Test	HH

TEST STEP	RESULT	▶	ACTION TO TAKE
HH19 CHECK HEGO SENSOR TO GROUND			
• Key Off. • HEGO disconnected. • DVOM on 200,000 ohm scale. • Measure resistance from power ground to HEGO signal at HEGO sensor. • Is resistance less than 10,000 ohms?	Yes No	▶ ▶	REPLACE HEGO sensor. RECONNECT MAP vacuum line. RERUN Quick Test. GO to HH20.
HH20 ATTEMPT TO ELIMINATE CODE 41			
• Key Off. • Processor connected. • Reconnect HEGO sensor. • MAP vacuum line still disconnected and plugged. • Apply 10 in.-Hg. (33 kPa) vacuum to MAP sensor. • Start the engine and run at approximately 2000 rpm for 1 minute. Allow engine to return to idle. • Perform Engine Running Self-Test. • Is code 41 still present? NOTE: Disregard any other code input at this time.	Yes No	▶ ▶	INSPECT for corrosion or damaged pins. If OK, REPLACE processor. RECONNECT MAP vacuum line. RERUN Quick Test. RECONNECT MAP vacuum line. HEGO input circuit OK. GO to HH1 (basic fuel delivery).
HH21 CHECK HEATER ELEMENT RESISTANCE ON HEATED EGO			
• Key off, engine off. • DVOM on 200 ohm scale. • HEGO disconnected. • Measure resistance between run circuit and ground at the HEGO sensor. Refer to illustration HH. • Hot to warm resistance specification is 5 to 20 ohms. NOTE: At room temperature, resistance specification is 2 to 5 ohms. • Is resistance within specification?	Yes No	▶ ▶	GO to HH22. REPLACE HEGO sensor.

Fuel Control – 5.0L/7.5L EFI Truck	Pinpoint Test	HH

HH90 CONTINUOUS TESTING: CODE 41

Code 41: Indicates that the HEGO circuit has not switched during closed loop fuel control.

NOTE: In this situation code 41 does not necessarily indicate a lean condition.

CLOSED LOOP — Fuel control under the influence of the HEGO sensor.

OPEN LOOP — Fuel control NOT under the influence of the HEGO sensor.

Before attempting to correct a continuous fuel control code 41, diagnose all other drive complaints first, eg., rough idle, misses, etc. in EEC Diagnostic By Symptom in the appropriate engine supplement.

NOTE: The fuel control code may help in this diagnosis.

Using the fuel control service code, isolate the cause of the fuel control problem.

Some areas to check are:

- Vacuum Circuits: — Vacuum leaks/intake air leaks.
— PCV System.
— Engine sealing.

- HEGO Fuel Fouled: Whenever an over-rich fuel condition has been experienced (fuel fouled spark plugs), make a thorough check of the ignition system. In the event the HEGO sensor is suspected of being fuel fouled (low output, slow response), run the vehicle at sustained high speeds (within legal limits) followed by a few hard accelerations. This will burn off HEGO contamination and restore proper HEGO operation.

- Ignition System: Always in default spark (10 degrees). Refer to Quick Test Step 4.0.

- Improper Fueling: Lead fouled HEGO sensor.

- Fuel Pressure: Perform Pinpoint Test Step HH1 and HH2.

- If at this point, the drive concern (if any) is still present, perform Steps HH3 and HH7 only.

Fuel Pump Circuit — (Inertia Switch)	Pinpoint Test	J

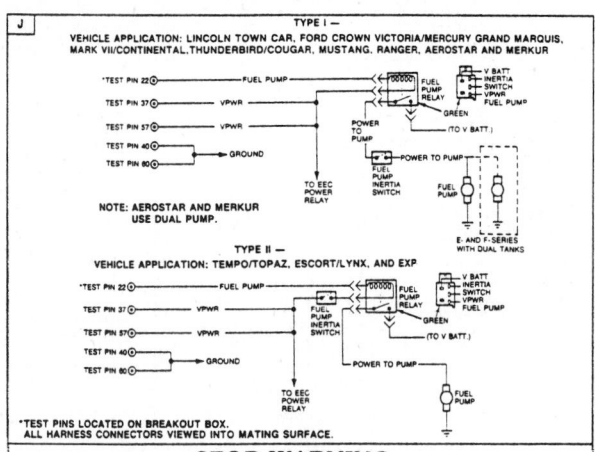

TYPE I —
VEHICLE APPLICATION: LINCOLN TOWN CAR, FORD CROWN VICTORIA/MERCURY GRAND MARQUIS, MARK VII/CONTINENTAL,THUNDERBIRD/COUGAR, MUSTANG, RANGER, AEROSTAR AND MERKUR

*TEST PIN 22 — FUEL PUMP
TEST PIN 37 — VPWR
TEST PIN 57 — VPWR
TEST PIN 40 — GROUND
TEST PIN 60 —

NOTE: AEROSTAR AND MERKUR USE DUAL PUMP.

TYPE II —
VEHICLE APPLICATION: TEMPO/TOPAZ, ESCORT/LYNX, AND EXP

*TEST PINS LOCATED ON BREAKOUT BOX.
ALL HARNESS CONNECTORS VIEWED INTO MATING SURFACE.

STOP-WARNING

You should enter this Pinpoint Test only when a service code 87 is received in Quick Test Step 3.0 or you are directed here from Pinpoint Test Step A22 or Diagnostics by Symptom in the Engine Supplement Section.

To prevent the replacement of good components, be aware that the following non-EEC areas may be at fault:
- Fuel Lines
- Fuel Filters
- Throttle Body
- Contaminated Fuel
- Fuel Pump
- Inertia Switch

This Pinpoint Test is intended to diagnose only the following:
- Fuel Pump Relay
- Harness Circuits: V Batt., V Power, F.P., Ground and Power to Pump(s)
- Processor Assembly

Fuel Pump Circuit — (Inertia Switch)	Pinpoint Test	J

TEST STEP	RESULT	▶	ACTION TO TAKE
J1 NO FUEL PUMP PRESSURE			
• Fuel pressure gauge installed. • To check if fuel pump runs, cycle key from Off to Run, repeat several times. (Do not enter start mode.) Fuel pump should run briefly each time the key enters Run.	Yes ▶		GO to Shop Manual, Group 24 electric fuel pump.
	No ▶		GO to J2.
J2 CHECK FOR V POWER TO PROCESSOR			
• Key Off, wait 10 seconds. • Disconnect processor 60 Pin connector and inspect for damaged pins, corrosion, loose wires. Service as necessary. • Install Breakout box and reconnect processor. • Key On, engine Off. • DVOM on 20V scale. • Measure voltage between test Pin 37 and test Pin 40 at the Breakout box and between test Pin 57 and test Pin 60 at the breakout box.	Either voltage reading is less than 10.5V ▶		GO to B1.
	Both voltage readings are 10.5V or greater ▶		GO to J3.
J3 RESISTANCE CHECK OF FUEL PUMP INERTIA SWITCH			
• Key Off, wait 10 seconds. • Leave Breakout box installed and processor connected. • Locate and disconnect fuel pump inertia switch. • DVOM on 200 ohm scale. • Measure the resistance of the fuel pump inertia switch.	Less than 5.0 ohms ▶		RECONNECT inertia switch and GO to J4.
	5.0 ohms or greater ▶		REPLACE or reset fuel pump inertia switch. RERUN Quick Test.
J4 POWER TO PUMP(S) CHECK			
• Key On, engine Off. • Leave Breakout box installed and processor connected. • Locate fuel pump relay. • DVOM on 20V scale. • Measure voltage between chassis ground and power-to-pump(s) circuit at fuel pump relay during crank mode.	8.0V or greater during crank ▶		GO to J5.
	Less than 8.0V during crank ▶		GO to J6.

Fuel Pump Circuit — (Inertia Switch)	Pinpoint Test	J

TEST STEP	RESULT	▶	ACTION TO TAKE
J5 POWER AT FUEL PUMP(S) CHECK			
• Key On, engine Off. • Leave Breakout box installed and processor connected. • Locate fuel pump(s). • DVOM on 20V scale. • Measure voltage between chassis ground and power-to-pump(s) circuit at fuel pump during crank mode.	8.0V or greater during crank ▶		GO to Shop Manual, Group 24 electric fuel pump.
	Less than 8.0V during crank ▶		SERVICE open in power to the pump(s) circuit. RERUN Quick Test.
J6 FUEL PUMP CIRCUIT CHECK TO V BATT.			
• Key On, engine Off. • Leave Breakout box installed and processor connected. • Locate fuel pump relay. • DVOM on 20V scale. • Measure voltage between chassis ground and V Batt. at the fuel pump relay.	10.5V or greater ▶		GO to J7.
	Less than 10.5V ▶		SERVICE open in V Batt. between fuel pump relay and vehicle battery positive post. RERUN Quick Test.
J7 V POWER TO FUEL PUMP RELAY CHECK			
• Key On, engine Off. • Leave Breakout box installed and processor connected. • Locate fuel pump relay. • DVOM on 20V scale. • Measure voltage between chassis ground and V Power circuit at the fuel pump relay.	10.5V or greater ▶		GO to J8.
	Less than 10.5V ▶		VERIFY inertia switch is reset to On. If switch will not reset, REPLACE switch. If OK, SERVICE open in V Power circuit between the processor and the fuel pump relay. RERUN Quick Test.
J8 FUEL PUMP CIRCUIT CHECK CONTINUITY			
• Leave Breakout box installed and processor connected. • Key Off, wait 10 seconds. • DVOM on 200 ohm scale. • Measure resistance between fuel pump circuit at the pump relay and test Pin 22 at the Breakout box.	Less than 5 ohms ▶		GO to J9.
	5 ohms or greater ▶		SERVICE open in fuel pump circuit and RERUN Quick Test.

Fuel Pump Circuit — (Inertia Switch)	Pinpoint Test	J

TEST STEP	RESULT	▶	ACTION TO TAKE
J9 CHECK FOR SHORT TO GROUND			
• Key Off. • Leave Breakout box installed and processor disconnected. • Fuel pump relay disconnected. • DVOM on 200,000 ohm scale. • Measure resistance between test Pin 22 and test Pins 40 and 60 at the Breakout box.	10,000 ohms or greater ▶		GO to J10.
	Less than 10,000 ohms ▶		SERVICE short in the fuel pump circuit. RERUN Quick Test.
J10 CHECK FOR SHORT TO POWER			
• Key Off, wait 10 seconds. • Leave Breakout box installed and disconnect processor. • Fuel pump relay disconnected. • DVOM on 200,000 ohm scale. • Measure resistance between test Pin 22 and test Pins 37 and 57 at the Breakout box.	10,000 ohms or greater ▶		RECONNECT fuel pump relay. GO to J11.
	Less than 10,000 ohms ▶		SERVICE short to power in the fuel pump circuit. RECONNECT processor, ATTEMPT to start vehicle. If vehicle fails to start, REPLACE processor. RERUN Quick Test.
J11 FINAL SYSTEM CHECK			
• Leave Breakout box installed and processor disconnected. • Connect jumper wire from test Pin 22 to test Pin 40 or 60 at the Breakout box. • DVOM on 20V scale. • Key On, engine Off. • Measure voltage between chassis ground and power-to-pump(s) circuit at fuel pump relay.	10.5V or greater ▶		REPLACE processor. RERUN Quick Test.
	Less than 10.5V ▶		REPLACE fuel pump relay. RECONNECT processor and RERUN Quick Test.
J15 FUEL PUMP RELAY CHECK			
• Key-Off. • Remove fuel pump relay. • Does fuel pump turn off?	Yes ▶		REPLACE fuel pump relay. RERUN Quick Test.
	No ▶		SERVICE short to power to pumps circuit.

EGR On/Off Control	Pinpoint Test	KA

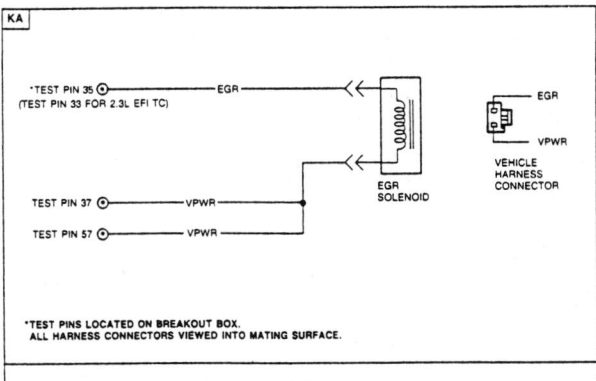

```
KA

*TEST PIN 35 ⊙ ── EGR ──
(TEST PIN 33 FOR 2.3L EFI TC)

                                        ── EGR
                                        ── VPWR
                                   VEHICLE
                                   HARNESS
                                   CONNECTOR
                           EGR
                           SOLENOID
TEST PIN 37 ⊙ ── VPWR ──
TEST PIN 57 ⊙ ── VPWR ──

*TEST PINS LOCATED ON BREAKOUT BOX.
ALL HARNESS CONNECTORS VIEWED INTO MATING SURFACE.
```

STOP-WARNING

You should enter this Pinpoint Test only when a service code 34 or 84 is received in Quick Test Step 3.0, 5.0 or when directed here from Diagnostic by Symptom in the Engine Supplement Section.

To prevent the replacement of good components, be aware that the following non-EEC areas may be at fault:

- Air or Vacuum Leaks
- EGR Flow Restrictions
- EGR Value

NOTE: Code 34 may be the result of high volume exhaust vent system (reduces backpressure). If this is suspected, perform the test in a well-ventilated area without exhaust vent connected.

This Pinpoint Test is intended to diagnose only the following:

- Circuits: EGR and VPWR
- EGR Solenoid
- Presence of Manifold Vacuum
- Processor Assembly

EGR On/Off Control	Pinpoint Test	KA

TEST STEP	RESULT	▶	ACTION TO TAKE
KA1 ENTER OUTPUT STATE CHECK (REFER TO APPENDIX) NOTE: Do not use STAR tester for this step, use a VOM/DVOM. • Key Off, wait 10 seconds. • DVOM on 20V scale. • Connect DVOM negative test lead to STO at the Self-Test connector and positive test lead to battery positive. • Jumper STI to signal return at the Self-Test connector. • Perform Key On Engine Off Self-Test until the completion of the Continuous Test Codes. • DVOM will indicate zero volts. • Depress and release the throttle. • Did DVOM reading change to a high voltage reading?	Yes No	▶ ▶	REMAIN in Output State Check. GO to `KA2`. DEPRESS throttle to WOT and release. If STO voltage does not go high, GO to Pinpoint Test Step `Q40`. Leave equipment hooked up.
KA2 CHECK EGR ON/OFF CONTROL SOLENOID ELECTRICAL OPERATION • DVOM on 20V scale. • Connect DVOM positive test lead to VPWR circuit on EGR solenoid and negative test lead to EGR output circuit. • While observing DVOM, depress and release the throttle several times to cycle output On and Off. • Does EGR output cycle On and Off?	Yes No	▶ ▶	GO to `KA3`. REMOVE STI jumper. GO to `KA5`.
KA3 CHECK SOLENOID FOR VACUUM CYCLING • Install vacuum pump to the solenoid vacuum supply port and install a vacuum gauge to the output port. Apply 6 in. Hg minimum. • While cycling outputs On and Off (by depressing and releasing throttle) observe the vacuum gauge at the output. NOTE: Maintain vacuum at source. • Does output port vacuum cycle On and Off?	Yes No	▶ ▶	GO to `KA4`. REPLACE solenoid. RERUN Quick Test.

EGR On/Off Control	Pinpoint Test	KA

TEST STEP	RESULT	▶	ACTION TO TAKE
KA4 CHECK MANIFOLD VACUUM LINES FOR BLOCKAGE OR LEAKS • Vacuum lines disconnected at solenoid. • Start engine. • Check for vacuum. • Is vacuum present?	Yes No	▶ ▶	EEC-IV system OK. REFER to Section 6. SERVICE vacuum source blockage or leak. RERUN Quick Test.
KA5 MEASURE EGR SOLENOID RESISTANCE • Key Off, wait 10 seconds. • DVOM on 200 ohm scale. • Disconnect EGR solenoid connector and measure solenoid resistance. • Is resistance between 65 and 110 ohms?	Yes No	▶ ▶	GO to `KA6`. REPLACE EGR solenoid. RERUN Quick Test.
KA6 CHECK VOLTAGE OF VPWR CIRCUIT • Key On, Engine Off. • DVOM on 20V scale. • Measure voltage between VPWR circuit at the EGR solenoid vehicle harness connector and battery ground. • Is voltage greater than 10.5 volts?	Yes No	▶ ▶	GO to `KA7`. SERVICE harness open circuit. RERUN Quick Test.
KA7 CHECK CONTINUITY OF EGR CIRCUIT • Key Off, wait 10 seconds. • Disconnect processor 60 Pin connector and inspect for damaged pins, corrosion, loose wires. Service as necessary. • Connect Breakout box to harness. Leave processor disconnected. • DVOM on 200 ohm scale. • Measure resistance between test Pin 35 (test Pin 33 for 2.3L EFI TC) at the Breakout box and EGR circuit at vehicle harness connector. • Is resistance less than 5 ohms?	Yes No	▶ ▶	GO to `KA8`. SERVICE open circuit. RERUN Quick Test.

EGR On/Off Control	Pinpoint Test	KA

TEST STEP	RESULT	▶	ACTION TO TAKE
KA8 CHECK FOR SHORT TO GROUND • Key Off, wait 10 seconds. • Leave Breakout box installed and processor disconnected. • Disconnect EGR solenoid. • DVOM on 200,000 ohm scale. • Measure resistance between test Pin 35 (test Pin 33 for 2.3L EFI TC) and test Pins 40, 46 and 60 at the Breakout box. • Is resistance greater than 10,000 ohms?	Yes No	▶ ▶	GO to `KA9`. SERVICE short to ground. RERUN Quick Test.
KA9 CHECK FOR SHORT TO POWER • Key Off, wait 10 seconds. • DVOM on 200,000 ohm scale. • Leave Breakout box installed and processor disconnected. • EGR solenoid disconnected. • Measure resistance between test Pin 35 (test Pin 33 for 2.3L EFI TC) and test Pins 37 and 57 at the Breakout box. • Is resistance greater than 10,000 ohms?	Yes No	▶ ▶	REPLACE Processor. RERUN Quick Test. SERVICE short to power. RERUN Quick Test. If code is repeated, REPLACE processor.

DC Motor Idle Speed Control/Idle Tracking Switch and Throttle Position Sensor — 1.9L CFI and 2.3L (HSC) CFI	Pinpoint Test	KB

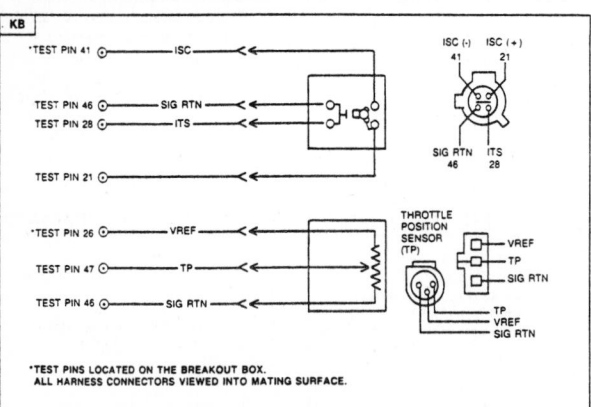

KB

*TEST PIN 41 — ISC
TEST PIN 46 — SIG RTN
TEST PIN 28 — ITS
TEST PIN 21

ISC (-)   ISC (+)
41   21

SIG RTN   ITS
46   28

*TEST PIN 26 — VREF
TEST PIN 47 — TP
TEST PIN 46 — SIG RTN

THROTTLE POSITION SENSOR (TP)
VREF
TP
SIG RTN

TP
VREF
SIG RTN

*TEST PINS LOCATED ON THE BREAKOUT BOX.
ALL HARNESS CONNECTORS VIEWED INTO MATING SURFACE.

STOP-WARNING

You should enter this Pinpoint Test only when a Service Code 12, 13, 23, 38, 53, 58, 63, 68, 71, 73 or 93 is received in Quick Test Step 3.0, 5.0, or 6.0 or when directed here from Diagnostics by Symptom in the Engine Supplement Section.

To prevent the replacement of good components, be aware that the following non-EEC areas may be at fault:

- Anti-diesel speed set too high
- Basic engine
- Vacuum leaks
- Throttle sticking

This Pinpoint Test is intended to diagnose only the following:

- DC motor
- Idle Tracking Switch
- Harness circuits ISC+, ISC –, ITS, TP, VREF, and, SIG RTN
- Throttle position sensor
- EEC-IV processor assembly

DC Motor Idle Speed Control/Idle Tracking Switch and Throttle Position Sensor — 1.9L CFI and 2.3L (HSC) CFI	Pinpoint Test	KB

TEST STEP	RESULT	▶	ACTION TO TAKE
KB1 CHECK DC MOTOR FOR PROPER OPERATION			
• Key Off, wait 10 seconds. • Disconnect harness from DC motor. • Jumper ISC + circuit of DC motor to battery positive and ISC – circuit of DC motor to battery ground for 4 seconds. • Jumper ISC + circuit of DC motor to battery ground and ISC – circuit of DC motor to battery positive for 4 seconds. • Does the DC motor shaft extend to greater than 2 inches (5 cm) and retract to less than 1.75 inches (4.4 cm) from mounting bracket (see below)?	Yes No	▶ ▶	GO to KB2. REPLACE DC MOTOR. RERUN Quick Test.
1.75 INCHES 4.4 cm 2 INCHES 5 cm			
KB2 CHECK CONTINUITY OF ISC + AND ISC – CIRCUITS			
• Key Off, wait 10 seconds. • Harness disconnected from DC motor. • Disconnect processor 60 pin connector and inspect for damaged pins, corrosion, loose wires. Service as necessary. • Connect Breakout box. Leave processor disconnected. • DVOM on 200 ohm scale. • Measure resistance between test Pin 41 at the Breakout box and ISC – circuit at the vehicle harness connector and between test Pin 21 at the Breakout box and ISC + circuit at the vehicle harness connector. • Are both resistances less than 5 ohms?	Yes No	▶ ▶	GO to KB3. SERVICE faulty circuit(s). RERUN Quick Test.

DC Motor Idle Speed Control/Idle Tracking Switch and Throttle Position Sensor — 1.9L CFI and 2.3L (HSC) CFI	Pinpoint Test	KB

TEST STEP	RESULT	▶	ACTION TO TAKE
KB3 CHECK FOR SHORTS TO GRND OF ISC + AND ISC – CIRCUITS			
• Key Off, wait 10 seconds. • Breakout box installed and processor disconnected. • Harness disconnected from DC motor. • DVOM on 200,000 ohm scale. • Measure resistance between test Pin 41 and test Pins 40, 46 and 60 at the Breakout box. • Measure resistance between test Pin 21 and test Pins 40, 46 and 60 at the Breakout box. • Are all resistances greater than 10,000 ohms?	Yes No	▶ ▶	GO to KB4. SERVICE faulty circuit(s). RERUN Quick Test.
KB4 CHECK FOR SHORTS TO PWR. OF ISC + AND ISC – CIRCUITS			
• Key On engine off. • Breakout box installed and processor disconnected. • Harness disconnected from DC motor. • DVOM on 20V scale. • Measure voltage between test Pin 41 and test Pin 40 and 60 at the Breakout box. • Measure voltage between test Pin 21 and test Pins 40 and 60 at the Breakout box. • Are all voltages less than 1 volt?	Yes No	▶ ▶	REPLACE processor. RERUN Quick Test. SERVICE faulty circuit(s). RERUN Quick Test.
KB5 CHECK FOR FULL DC MOTOR RETRACTION			
• Key Off, wait 10 seconds. • Disconnect harness from DC motor. • Jumper, at the DC motor connector, ISC – circuit to battery positive and the ISC + circuit to battery negative for 4 seconds. • Does the DC motor shaft retract away from the throttle lever as shown?	Yes No	▶ ▶	GO to KB7. GO to KB6.
MOVE THROTTLE AWAY FROM DC MOTOR SHAFT			

DC Motor Idle Speed Control/Idle Tracking Switch and Throttle Position Sensor — 1.9L CFI and 2.3L (HSC) CFI	Pinpoint Test	KB

TEST STEP	RESULT	▶	ACTION TO TAKE
KB6 MEASURE DC MOTOR RETRACTION			
• Key Off, wait 10 seconds. • Harness disconnected from DC motor. • DC motor fully retracted. • Measure the distance from the tip of the DC motor shaft to the mounting bracket. Refer to figure in step KB1. • Is the distance less than 1.75 inches (4.4 cm)?	Yes No	▶ ▶	RECONNECT DC motor. GO to Section 4 for throttle stop adjustment procedure. REPLACE DC motor. RERUN Quick Test.
KB7 CHECK IDLE TRACKING SWITCH STATE			
• Key Off, wait 10 seconds. • Harness disconnected from DC motor. • DC motor fully retracted. • DC motor shaft NOT touching the throttle lever. • DVOM on 200 ohm scale. • Measure resistance between ITS circuit and SIG RTN at the DC motor connector. • Is the resistance less than 5 ohms?	Yes No	▶ ▶	GO to KB8. REPLACE DC motor. RERUN Quick Test.
KB8 CHECK CONTINUITY OF ITS AND SIG RTN CIRCUITS			
• Key Off, wait 10 seconds. • Harness disconnected from DC motor. • Disconnect processor 60 pin connector and inspect for damaged pins, corrosion or loose wires. Service as necessary. • Connect Breakout box. Leave processor disconnected. • DVOM on 200 ohm scale. • Measure resistance between test Pin 46 at the Breakout box and SIG RTN circuit at the DC motor vehicle harness connector. • Measure resistance between test Pin 28 at the Breakout box and ITS circuit at the DC motor vehicle harness connector. • Are both resistances less than 5 ohms?	Yes No	▶ ▶	RECONNECT DC motor. REPLACE processor. RERUN Quick Test. RECONNECT DC motor. SERVICE faulty circuit(s) RERUN Quick Test.

DC Motor Idle Speed Control/Idle Tracking Switch and Throttle Position Sensor — 1.9L CFI and 2.3L (HSC) CFI	Pinpoint Test	KB

TEST STEP	RESULT ▶	ACTION TO TAKE
KB9 CHECK IDLE TRACKING SWITCH STATE • Key Off, wait 10 seconds. • Disconnect harness from DC motor. • DVOM on 200 ohm scale. • Measure resistance between ITS circuit and SIG RTN circuit at the DC motor connector. • Is the resistance greater than 5 ohms?	Yes ▶ No ▶	GO to KB10. REPLACE DC motor. RERUN Quick Test.
KB10 CHECK FOR SHORTS TO GRND OF THE ITS CIRCUIT • Key Off, wait 10 seconds. • Harness disconnected from DC motor. • Disconnect processor 60 pin connector and inspect for damaged pins, corrosion loose wires. Service as necessary. • Connect Breakout box. Leave processor disconnected. • Measure resistance between test Pin 28 and test Pins 40, 46 and 60 at the Breakout box. • Are all resistances greater than 10,000 ohms?	Yes ▶ No ▶	RECONNECT DC motor. REPLACE processor. RERUN Quick Test. RECONNECT DC motor. SERVICE faulty circuit(s). RERUN Quick Test.
KB11 CHECK THROTTLE LEVER AND LINKAGE • Key Off, wait 10 seconds. • Inspect throttle for freedom of movement to wide open throttle and for damaged or bent throttle lever. • Is throttle/throttle linkage functioning properly?	Yes ▶ No ▶	REPLACE DC motor. RERUN Quick Test. SERVICE as necessary. RERUN Quick Test.
KB12 CHECK THROTTLE PLATE FOR CLOSING • Run Key On Engine Off Self Test and disconnect DC motor after it is fully retracted. • Key Off, wait 10 seconds. • Remove air cleaner from throttle body. • Inspect throttle for freedom of movement and proper closure. • Does throttle move freely and close without obstruction?	Yes ▶ No ▶	RECONNECT DC motor. GO to KB13. SERVICE as necessary. RERUN Quick Test

DC Motor Idle Speed Control/Idle Tracking Switch and Throttle Position Sensor — 1.9L CFI and 2.3L (HSC) CFI	Pinpoint Test	KB

TEST STEP	RESULT ▶	ACTION TO TAKE
KB13 CHECK VOLTAGE OF VREF TO SIGNAL RETURN • Key Off, wait 10 seconds. • Disconnect TP vehicle harness connector at the throttle body. Inspect for damaged pins, corrosion, loose wires, etc. Service as necessary. • DVOM on 20V scale. • Key On Engine Off. • Measure voltage between VREF and SIG RTN at the vehicle harness connector. • Is the voltage between 4 and 6 volts?	Yes ▶ No ▶	RECONNECT TP sensor. GO to KB14. GO to Pinpoint Test Step C1.
KB14 CHECK THROTTLE STOP RPM • Run Key On Engine Off Self Test and disconnect the DC motor after it has fully retracted and exit Self Test. • Start engine and verify that the throttle stop rpm is less than curb idle rpm. • Is the throttle stop set below the curb idle? • Reconnect DC motor.	Yes ▶ No ▶	REPLACE the TP sensor. RERUN Quick Test. GO to the adjustment procedure in Section 4. ADJUST throttle stop rpm. RERUN Quick Test.
KB15 GENERATE CODE 63 • Key Off, wait 10 seconds. • Disconnect harness from the TP sensor at the throttle body. Inspect for damaged pins, corrosion and loose wires. Service as necessary. • Run Key On Engine Off Self Test and record codes. • Is code 63 present? • Ignore all other codes.	Yes ▶ No ▶	GO to KB16. GO to KB17.

DC Motor Idle Speed Control/Idle Tracking Switch and Throttle Position Sensor — 1.9L CFI and 2.3L (HSC) CFI	Pinpoint Test	KB

TEST STEP	RESULT ▶	ACTION TO TAKE
KB16 CHECK VOLTAGE VREF TO SIG RTN • Key Off, wait 10 seconds. • Harness disconnected from TP sensor at throttle body. • DVOM on 20V scale. • Key On Engine Off. • Measure voltage between VREF and SIG RTN at the TP vehicle harness connector. • Is the voltage between 4 and 6 volts?	Yes ▶ No ▶	REPLACE the TP sensor. RERUN Quick Test. GO to Pinpoint Test Step C1.
KB17 CHECK TP SIGNAL FOR SHORT TO POWER • Key Off, wait 10 seconds. • Harness disconnected from TP sensor. • DVOM on 200,000 ohm scale. • Disconnect the processor 60 pin connector and inspect for damaged pins, corrosion and loose wires. Service as necessary. • Install Breakout box. Leave processor disconnected. • Measure resistance between test Pin 47 and test Pins 26 and 57 at the Breakout box. • Are both resistances 10,000 ohms or greater?	Yes ▶ No ▶	REPLACE processor. RERUN Quick Test. SERVICE faulty circuit(s). RERUN Quick Test.
KB18 GENERATE CODE 53 • Key Off, wait 10 seconds. • Disconnect harness from the TP sensor at the throttle body. Inspect for damaged pins, corrosion and loose wires. Service as necessary. • Jumper VREF to TP signal at the vehicle harness connector. • Run Key On Engine Off Self Test. NOTE: If no codes are generated, immediately remove jumper and go directly to KB21. • Is code 53 present? • Ignore all other codes at this time.	Yes ▶ No ▶	REPLACE TP sensor. RERUN Quick Test. GO to KB19.

DC Motor Idle Speed Control/Idle Tracking Switch and Throttle Position Sensor — 1.9L CFI and 2.3L (HSC) CFI	Pinpoint Test	KB

TEST STEP	RESULT ▶	ACTION TO TAKE
KB19 CHECK VOLTAGE VREF TO SIG RTN • Key Off, wait 10 seconds. • Harness disconnected from TP sensor at throttle body. • DVOM on 20V scale. • Key On Engine Off. • Measure voltage between VREF and SIG RTN at the TP vehicle harness connector. • Is the voltage between 4 and 6 volts?	Yes ▶ No ▶	GO to KB20 GO to Pinpoint Test Step C1.
KB20 CHECK CONTINUITY OF TP CIRCUIT • Key Off, wait 10 seconds. • Harness disconnected from TP sensor at throttle body. • DVOM on 200 ohm scale. • Disconnect the processor 60 pin connector and inspect for damaged pins, corrosion and loose wires. Service as necessary. • Install Breakout box. Leave processor disconnected. • Measure resistance between TP signal at the vehicle harness connector and test Pin 47 at the Breakout box. • Is resistance less than 5 ohms?	Yes ▶ No ▶	GO to KB21. SERVICE faulty circuit(s). RECONNECT harness to TP sensor. RERUN Quick Test.
KB21 CHECK TP SIGNAL FOR SHORTS TO GROUND • Key Off, wait 10 seconds. • Harness disconnected from TP sensor at throttle body. • Breakout box installed. • DVOM on 200,000 ohm scale. • Measure resistance between TP signal at TP vehicle harness connector and test Pins 40, 46 and 60 at the Breakout box. • Are all resistances greater than 10,000 ohms?	Yes ▶ No ▶	REPLACE processor. RECONNECT TP sensor. RERUN Quick Test. SERVICE faulty circuit(s). RERUN Quick Test.

DC Motor Idle Speed Control/Idle Tracking Switch and Throttle Position Sensor — 1.9L CFI and 2.3L (HSC) CFI	Pinpoint Test	KB

TEST STEP	RESULT ▶	ACTION TO TAKE
KB22 SERVICE CODE 73		
• RERUN Key On Engine Off Self Test. • Is code 73 still present?	Yes ▶	REPLACE TP sensor. RERUN Quick Test.
	No ▶	SERVICE other codes.
KB23 CHECK FOR CODES THAT COULD CAUSE CODE 12		
• Are service codes 31, 32, 34, 35, 41, or 58 present in Engine Running Self Test?	Yes ▶	SERVICE these codes first. GO to Quick Test Step 5.0C for direction.
	No ▶	GO to KB24.
KB24 CHECK FOR STICKING THROTTLE LINKAGE		
• Check the throttle plates and/or linkage for sticking or binding. • Check speed control linkage for proper adjustment. • Does throttle open and close properly?	Yes ▶	GO to KB25.
	No ▶	SERVICE as necessary. RERUN Quick Test.
KB25 CHECK DC MOTOR FOR PROPER OPERATION		
• Key Off, wait 10 seconds. • Disconnect harness from DC motor. • Jumper ISC + circuit of DC motor to battery positive and ISC − circuit of DC motor to battery ground for 4 seconds. • Jumper ISC + circuit of DC motor to battery ground and ISC − circuit of DC motor to battery positive for 4 seconds. • Does the DC motor shaft extend to greater than 2 inches (5 cm) and retract to less than 1.75 inches (4.4 cm) from mounting bracket (see below)?	Yes ▶	REPLACE processor. RERUN Quick Test.
	No ▶	REPLACE DC MOTOR. RERUN Quick Test.

1.75 INCHES 4.4 cm
2 INCHES 5 cm

DC Motor Idle Speed Control/Idle Tracking Switch and Throttle Position Sensor — 1.9L CFI and 2.3L (HSC) CFI	Pinpoint Test	KB

TEST STEP	RESULT ▶	ACTION TO TAKE
KB26 CHECK FOR ERRATIC IDLE		
• Prepare system for normal engine operation. • Deactivate Self Test. • A/C off. • Run engine for 3 minutes alternating between 30 second idles and 5 second part throttle modes. • Is the idle erratic at the end of the three minute idle/part throttle test?	Yes ▶	CHECK for • Vacuum leaks • Code 22 • Code 31, 32, 34 or 35 • Code 41 • Code 58 SERVICE above codes before continuing.
	No ▶	GO to KB27.
KB27 CHECK FOR PROPER OPERATION OF THROTTLE		
• Inspect the throttle plates and/or linkage for proper function. • Does the throttle open and close properly?	Yes ▶	REPLACE DC motor. RERUN Quick Test.
	No ▶	SERVICE as necessary. RERUN Quick Test.

DC Motor Idle Speed Control/Idle Tracking Switch and Throttle Position Sensor — 1.9L CFI and 2.3L (HSC) CFI	Pinpoint Test	KB

KB90 | CONTINUOUS MEMORY CODE 13

A Continuous Memory Code 13 indicates that sometime in the last 40 warm-up cycles the TP sensor rotation did not follow the reaction of the DC motor when idle speed control was in a dashpot mode. This condition may be caused by:

• The DC motor sticking at part throttle.
• An open in the ITS circuit which, when coupled with other inputs to the processor, causes the EEC-IV system to falsely enter 'dashpot mode'.
• The TP sensor sticking at part throttle.

Each of these areas may generate Key On Engine Off (KOEO) or other continuous memory codes. Therefore, if a repair has been made for KOEO code 13 or 58, the continuous memory code 13 can be considered serviced and erased from memory. If a Continuous Memory Code 38 is present along with the Continuous Memory Code 13, service the 38 first.

If these other codes were not present make the following checks:

• Refer to KB1 and check for FULL travel of the DC motor shaft. Replace the DC motor if full travel is not possible. Leave the motor fully retracted.
• With the DC motor fully retracted and the ITS not touching the throttle lever (ITS closed circuit) check for an intermittent open in the ITS circuit. Turn the ignition key off and install the Breakout box. Make the necessary connector/pin inspections. With the DVOM on the 200 ohm scale, monitor between test Pins 28 and 46 while tapping, wiggling, bending, etc. the DC motor connector and harness.
DO NOT PUSH IN THE IDLE TRACKING SWITCH.
The DVOM will change from less than 5 ohms to greater than 5 ohms if an open circuit is created. Service as necessary.
• Check for a sticking TP sensor by monitoring TP voltage while moving the throttle from a wide open position to a closed throttle position. To do this it is necessary to install the Breakout box. Make the necessary connector/pin inspections. It is also necessary to fully retract the shaft of the DC motor by placing a jumper between test Pins 41 and 57. When the motor has fully retracted, disconnect it at the harness and remove the jumper wire from the Breakout box. With the ignition key on and the DVOM on the 20 volt scale, slowly move the throttle wide open to closed throttle. The voltage should move from more than 4 volts to less than 1.5 volts. If the TP sensor hangs up in midrange replace it, otherwise no service should be made.

KB91 | CONTINUOUS MEMORY CODE 38

A Continuous Memory Code 38 indicates that in the last 40 warm-up cycles the Idle Tracking Switch was open (ITS touching the throttle) when the throttle angle was greater than the MAX extension of the DC motor shaft. This could be caused by:

• An open (either intermittent or hard fault) in the ITS circuit.
• Idle Tracking Switch stuck open (pushed in position).

Either of these conditions may cause a code 58 to appear in Key On Engine Off (KOEO). If a repair has been made for a KOEO code 58, the Continuous Memory Code 38 can be considered serviced and erased from memory.

If KOEO code 58 was not present the following checks can be made:

• With the DC motor fully retracted and the ITS not touching the throttle lever (ITS closed circuit) check for an intermittent open in the ITS circuit. Turn the ignition key off and install the Breakout box. Make the necessary connector/pin inspections. With the DVOM on the 200 ohm scale, monitor between Test Pins 28 and 46 while tapping, wiggling, bending, etc. the DC motor connector and harness.
DO NOT PUSH IN THE IDLE TRACKING SWITCH.
The DVOM will change from less than 5 ohms to greater than 5 ohms if an open circuit is created. Service as necessary. If an open circuit cannot be created, no repair should be made.

KB92 | CONTINUOUS MEMORY CODE 71

A Continuous Memory Code 71 indicates that sometime in the last 40 warm-up cycles the Idle Tracking Switch was closed (ITS not touching the throttle lever) when the DC motor was in "preposition" — [after the engine has been running and the ignition key is turned off the DC motor fully retracts and then extends to a predetermined position for the next start-up]. This can be caused by:

• The ITS circuit shorted to ground or Signal Return (intermittent or hard fault).
• ITS stuck closed (ITS NOT in the pushed in position).

Either of these conditions may cause a Key On Engine Off (KOEO) code 68. If a repair has been made for KOEO code 68, the Continuous Memory Code 71 can be considered serviced and erased from memory.

If KOEO 68 was not present make the following checks:

• Check the ITS circuit for an intermittent short to ground or Signal Return. Turn the ignition key off. Enter the KOEO Continuous Monitor Mode per Quick Test Step 6.0B. Systematically tap, wiggle, or bend the harness while looking for an indication of a fault. If a fault is created, service as necessary, otherwise no repair should be made.

NOTE: Due to the nature of this Test Step, Code 71 will not reappear in memory if a fault is found.

DC Motor Idle Speed Control/Idle Tracking Switch and Throttle Position Sensor — 1.9L CFI and 2.3L (HSC)	Pinpoint Test	KB

TEST STEP	RESULT ▶	ACTION TO TAKE
KB93 CONTINUOUS TEST SERVICE CODE 53: EXERCISE TP SENSOR • Using continuous monitor mode, observe VOM or STAR LED for indication of a fault while performing the following: • Move throttle slowly to WOT position. • Release throttle slowly to closed position and lightly tap on TP sensor (simulate road shock). • Wiggle TP harness connector. • Is a fault indicated?	Yes ▶ No ▶	GO to KB94. GO to KB95.

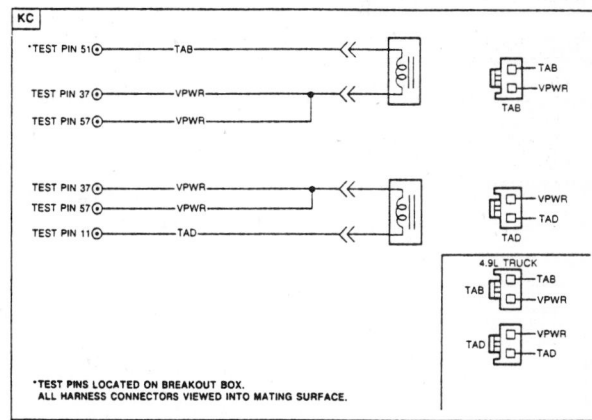

| **KB94** MEASURE THROTTLE POSITION SIGNAL VOLTAGE WHILE EXERCISING TP SENSOR

• Key Off, wait 10 seconds.
• Disconnect processor 60 Pin connector and inspect for damaged pins, corrosion, loose wires. Service as necessary.
• Install Breakout box and reconnect processor.
• VOM or STAR LED still connected to STO as in previous step.
• Connect a DVOM from test Pin 47 to test Pin 46.
• DVOM on 20V scale.
• Key On Engine Off.
• While observing DVOM, repeat Step KB93.
• Does the fault occur below 4.25V? | Yes ▶

No ▶ | DISCONNECT and INSPECT connectors. If connector and terminals are good, REPLACE TP sensor, REFER to Shop Manual Group 24 and RERUN Quick Test.

Throttle position sensor overtravel may have caused the continuous code 53. Sensor service is not required. To verify harness integrity, GO to KB95. |

DC Motor Idle Speed Control/Idle Tracking Switch and Throttle Position Sensor — 1.9L CFI and 2.3L (HSC)	Pinpoint Test	KB

TEST STEP	RESULT ▶	ACTION TO TAKE
KB95 CHECK EEC-IV HARNESS • Observe VOM or STAR LED for a fault indication while performing the following: • Referring to the illustration in Step DH90, grasp the harness close to the sensor connector. Wiggle, shake or bend a small section of the EEC-IV system harness while working your way to the dash panel. Also wiggle, shake or bend the EEC-IV harness from the dash panel to the processor. • Is a fault indicated?	Yes ▶ No ▶	ISOLATE fault and make necessary repairs. REFER to appropriate figure. RERUN Quick Test. GO to KB96.
KB96 CHECK PROCESSOR AND HARNESS CONNECTORS • Key Off, wait 10 seconds. • Disconnect processor 60 Pin connector. • Inspect both connectors and connector terminals for obvious damage or faults. • Are connectors and terminals OK?	Yes ▶ No ▶	Unable to duplicate fault at this time. Continuous code 53 testing complete. SERVICE as necessary. REPEAT Quick Test.
KB97 CONTINUOUS TEST SERVICE CODES 23 OR 63 EXERCISE TP SENSOR • Using continuous monitor mode, observe VOM or STAR LED for indication of a fault while performing the following: • Move throttle slowly to WOT position. • Release throttle slowly to closed condition. • Lightly tap on TP sensor (simulate road shock). • Wiggle TP harness connector. • Is a fault indicated?	Yes ▶ No ▶	DISCONNECT and INSPECT connectors. If connector and terminals are good, REPLACE TP sensor, REFER to Shop Manual Group 24 and RERUN Quick Test. GO to KB98.

DC Motor Idle Speed Control/Idle Tracking Switch and Throttle Position Sensor — 1.9L CFI and 2.3L (HSC)	Pinpoint Test	KB

TEST STEP	RESULT ▶	ACTION TO TAKE
KB98 CHECK EEC-IV HARNESS • Observe VOM or STAR LED for a fault indication while performing the following: • Referring to the illustration in Step DH94, grasp the harness close to the sensor connector. Wiggle, shake or bend a small section of the EEC-IV system harness while working your way to the dash panel. Also wiggle, shake or bend the EEC-IV harness from the dash panel to the processor. • Is a fault indicated?	Yes ▶ No ▶	ISOLATE fault and make necessary repairs. REFER to appropriate figure. RERUN Quick Test. GO to KB99.
KB99 CHECK PROCESSOR AND HARNESS CONNECTORS • Key Off, wait 10 seconds. • Disconnect processor 60 Pin connector. • Inspect both connectors and connector terminals for obvious damage or faults. • Are connectors and terminals OK?	Yes ▶ No ▶	Unable to duplicate fault at this time. Continuous code 63 testing complete. SERVICE as necessary. REPEAT Quick Test.

Air Management System	Pinpoint Test	KC

KC

*TEST PINS LOCATED ON BREAKOUT BOX.
ALL HARNESS CONNECTORS VIEWED INTO MATING SURFACE.

STOP-WARNING

You should enter this Pinpoint Test only when a service code 44, 45, 46, 94, 95, 96, 81 or 82 is received in Quick Test Step 3.0 or 5.0.

To prevent the replacement of good components, be aware that the following non-EEC areas may be at fault:

• Thermactor System
   — Belt
   — Pump
   — Valve

This Pinpoint Test is intended to diagnose only the following:

• TAB and TAD Solenoid Valve Assemblies
• Harness Circuits: TAB, TAD and VPWR
• Vacuum Supply
• Processor Assembly

Air Management System		Pinpoint Test	KC

TEST STEP	RESULT	▶	ACTION TO TAKE
KC1 SERVICE CODES 44 (94), 45 (95) AND 46 (96): VERIFY VACUUM LINE ROUTING			
• Verify proper vacuum line routing to the TAB/TAD solenoids and to the bypass diverter valve. Refer to VECI decal. • Check for kinked or blocked vacuum hoses. • Check for kinked or blocked air hoses. • Check for disconnected vacuum lines. • Are visual checks satisfactory?	No	▶	SERVICE routing or faults. RERUN Quick Test.
	Yes	▶	Service code 44 (94), GO to KC4. Service code 45 (95), GO to KC2. Service code 46 (96), GO to KC3.
KC2 ATTEMPT TO ELIMINATE SERVICE CODE 45 (95) (TAD ONLY)			
• Disconnect vacuum line on diverter valve and cap vacuum line. • Key Off, wait 10 seconds. • Repeat Engine Running Self-Test and record service codes. • Is code 45 (95) present?	Yes	▶	EEC-IV system OK. REFER to Section 3 for diverter valve or check valve diagnostics.
	No	▶	GO to KC4.
KC3 ATTEMPT TO ELIMINATE SERVICE CODE 46 (96) (TAB ONLY)			
• Disconnect vacuum line on bypass valve and cap vacuum line. • Key Off, wait 10 seconds. • Repeat Engine Running Self-Test and record codes. • Is code 46 (96) present?	Yes	▶	EEC-IV system OK. REFER to Section 3 for bypass valve diagnostics.
	No	▶	GO to KC4.

Air Management System		Pinpoint Test	KC

TEST STEP	RESULT	▶	ACTION TO TAKE
KC7 CHECK MANIFOLD VACUUM LINES FOR BLOCKAGE OR LEAKS			
• Vacuum lines disconnected at TAD/TAB solenoids. • Start engine. • Check for vacuum. • Is vacuum present at the solenoid?	Yes	▶	EEC-IV system OK. REFER to Section 3 for Thermactor valve and air pump diagnostics.
	No	▶	SERVICE vacuum source blockage or leak. RERUN Quick Test.
KC8 MEASURE TAB/TAD SOLENOID RESISTANCE			
• Key Off, wait 10 seconds. • DVOM on 200 ohm scale. • Disconnect TAB solenoid connector and measure solenoid resistance. • Disconnect TAD solenoid connector and measure solenoid resistance. • Are both solenoid resistances between 50 and 100 ohms?	Yes	▶	CONNECT TAB/TAD solenoids. GO to KC9.
	No	▶	REPLACE TAB/TAD solenoid assembly. RERUN Quick Test.
KC9 CHECK VOLTAGE OF VPWR CIRCUIT			
• Key On, engine Off. • DVOM on 20V scale. • Measure voltage between TAB solenoid VPWR circuit and battery ground. • Repeat for TAD solenoid. • Are both voltage readings 10.5 volts or greater?	Yes	▶	GO to KC10.
	No	▶	SERVICE harness circuit open. RERUN Quick Test.

Air Management System		Pinpoint Test	KC

TEST STEP	RESULT	▶	ACTION TO TAKE
KC4 ENTER OUTPUT STATE CHECK (REFER TO APPENDIX)			
NOTE: Do not use STAR tester for this Step, use a VOM/DVOM. • Key Off, wait 10 seconds. • DVOM on 20V scale. • Connect DVOM negative test lead to STO circuit at the Self-Test connector and positive test lead to battery positive. • Jumper STI circuit to signal return at the Self-Test connector. • Perform Key On, Engine Off Self-Test until the completion of the Continuous Test Codes. • DVOM will indicate zero volts when Test is complete. • Depress and release the throttle. • Did DVOM reading change to a high voltage reading?	Yes	▶	REMAIN in Output State Check. GO to KC5.
	No	▶	DEPRESS throttle to WOT and RELEASE. If STO voltage does not go high. GO to Pinpoint Test Step Q40. Leave equipment hooked up.
KC5 CHECK TAB/TAD SOLENOID ELECTRICAL OPERATION			
• DVOM on 20V scale. • Reconnect DVOM positive test lead to VPWR circuit on TAB solenoid and negative test lead to TAB circuit on TAB solenoid. • While observing DVOM depress and release the throttle several times (to cycle output On and Off). • Repeat for TAD solenoid. Connect positive test lead to VPWR circuit on TAD solenoid and negative test lead to TAD circuit on TAD solenoid. • Solenoids cycle On and Off.	Both outputs cycle On and Off	▶	GO to KC6.
	Either output does not cycle On and Off	▶	REMOVE jumper. GO to KC8.
KC6 CHECK TAB/TAD SOLENOID FOR VACUUM CYCLING			
• Install vacuum pump to the TAB solenoid vacuum supply port and install a vacuum gauge to the output port. • While cycling outputs On and Off (by depressing and releasing throttle), observe the vacuum gauge at the output. **NOTE: Maintain vacuum at source.** • Repeat for TAD solenoid. Connect vacuum pump to the TAD solenoid vacuum supply port and connect a vacuum gauge to the output port. • Cycle output On and Off.	Both vacuum outputs cycle On and Off	▶	GO to KC7.
	Either vacuum output does not cycle On and Off	▶	REPLACE solenoid assembly. RERUN Quick Test.

Air Management System		Pinpoint Test	KC

TEST STEP	RESULT	▶	ACTION TO TAKE
KC10 CHECK CONTINUITY OF TAB AND TAD CIRCUITS			
• Key Off, wait 10 seconds. • Disconnect processor 60 Pin connector and inspect for damaged pins, corrosion, loose wires. Service as necessary. • Connect Breakout box to harness. Leave processor disconnected. • DVOM on 200 ohm scale. • Measure resistance between test Pin 51 at Breakout box and TAB circuit at vehicle harness connector. • Measure resistance between test Pin 11 at the Breakout box and TAD circuit at vehicle harness connector. • Are both TAD and TAB circuits resistance 5 ohms or less?	Yes	▶	GO to KC11.
	No	▶	SERVICE harness open circuit. RERUN Quick Test.
KC11 CHECK FOR SHORT TO GROUND			
• Key Off, wait 10 seconds. • DVOM on 200,000 ohm. • Leave Breakout box installed and processor disconnected. • Disconnect TAB/TAD solenoids. • Measure resistance between test Pin 51 and test Pins 40, 46 and 60 and between test Pin 11 and test Pins 40, 46 and 60 at the Breakout box. • Are all resistance readings 10,000 ohms or greater?	Yes	▶	GO to KC12.
	No	▶	SERVICE short to ground. REMOVE Breakout box. RECONNECT harness to processor. RERUN Quick Test.
KC12 CHECK FOR SHORT TO POWER			
• Key Off, wait 10 seconds. • DVOM on 200,000 ohm scale. • Leave Breakout box installed and processor disconnected. • TAB/TAD solenoids disconnected. • Measure resistance between test Pin 51 and test Pins 37 and 57, and between test Pin 11 and test Pins 37 and 57 at the Breakout box. • Are all resistance readings 10,000 ohms or greater?	Yes	▶	REPLACE processor. RERUN Quick Test.
	No	▶	SERVICE short to power. RERUN Quick Test. If code is present. REPLACE processor.

Canister Purge (CANP)	Pinpoint Test	KD

KD

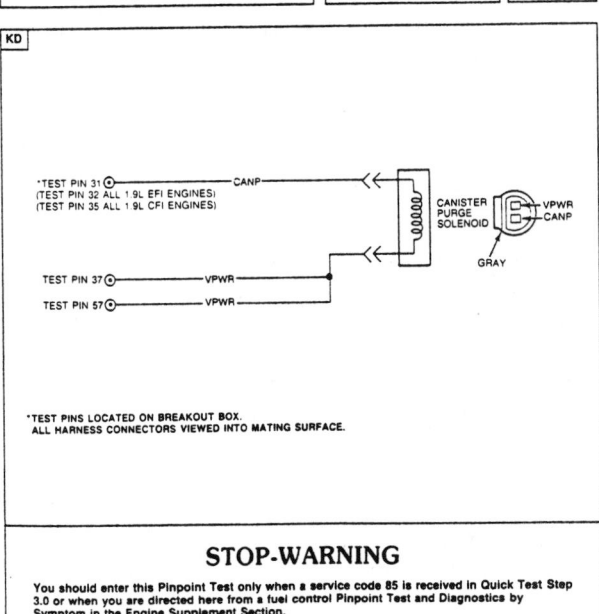

```
*TEST PIN 31 ─────────── CANP
(TEST PIN 32 ALL 1.9L EFI ENGINES)
(TEST PIN 35 ALL 1.9L CFI ENGINES)

                            CANISTER       VPWR
                            PURGE          CANP
                            SOLENOID
TEST PIN 37 ─────── VPWR
TEST PIN 57 ─────── VPWR          GRAY
```

*TEST PINS LOCATED ON BREAKOUT BOX.
ALL HARNESS CONNECTORS VIEWED INTO MATING SURFACE.

STOP-WARNING

You should enter this Pinpoint Test only when a service code 85 is received in Quick Test Step 3.0 or when you are directed here from a fuel control Pinpoint Test and Diagnostics by Symptom in the Engine Supplement Section.

This Pinpoint Test is intended to diagnose only the following:

- Harness Circuits: CANP and VPWR
- Processor Assembly

Canister Purge (CANP)	Pinpoint Test	KD

TEST STEP	RESULT	▶	ACTION TO TAKE
KD4 CHECK CANISTER PURGE SOLENOID FOR MECHANICAL OPERATION			
• Still in Output State Check. • CANP circuit Off (no voltage). • Reconnect CANP solenoid connector. • Apply 16 in.-Hg. to CANP solenoid as in KD3. • Depress and release throttle. • Is vacuum released?	Yes	▶	REMOVE Jumper from STI to signal return. GO to KD5.
	No	▶	REPLACE CANP solenoid. REPEAT Quick Test.
KD5 CHECK FOR VACUUM TO CANISTER PURGE SOLENOID			
• Disconnect vacuum hose at canister purge solenoid at PCV side. • Start engine. • Is vacuum present at engine vacuum hose?	Yes	▶	EEC-IV system OK. REFER to Shop Manual, Group 24.
	No	▶	CHECK vacuum line for proper routing, kinks or blockage. If OK, REFER to Shop Manual, Group 21 for probable subjects affecting engine vacuum.
KD6 MEASURE CANP SOLENOID RESISTANCE			
• Key Off, wait 10 seconds. • DVOM on 200 ohm scale. • Disconnect CANP solenoid connector and measure solenoid resistance. • Is resistance between 40 and 90 ohms?	Yes	▶	GO to KD7.
	No	▶	REPLACE CANP solenoid. RERUN Quick Test.
KD7 CHECK VOLTAGE OF VPWR CIRCUIT			
• Key On, engine Off. • DVOM on 20V scale. • Measure voltage between VPWR at the CANP solenoid vehicle harness connector and battery ground. • Is voltage reading 10.5 volts or greater?	Yes	▶	GO to KD8.
	No	▶	SERVICE harness open circuit. RERUN Quick Test.

Canister Purge (CANP)	Pinpoint Test	KD

TEST STEP	RESULT	▶	ACTION TO TAKE
KD1 ENTER OUTPUT STATE CHECK (REFER TO APPENDIX)			
NOTE: Do not use STAR tester for this step, use VOM/DVOM. • Key Off, wait 10 seconds. • DVOM on 20V scale. • Connect DVOM negative test lead to STO circuit at Self-Test connector and positive test lead to battery positive. • Jumper STI circuit to signal return at the Self-Test connector. • Perform Key On, Engine Off Self-Test until the completion of the Continuous Test Codes. • DVOM will indicate zero volts when test is completed. • Depress and release the throttle. • Did DVOM reading change to a high voltage reading?	Yes	▶	REMAIN in Output State Check. GO to KD2.
	No	▶	DEPRESS throttle to WOT and release. If STO voltage does not go high, GO to Pinpoint Test Step Q40. Leave equipment hooked up.
KD2 CHECK CANISTER PURGE (CANP) SOLENOID ELECTRICAL OPERATION			
• DVOM on 20V scale. • Disconnect CANP solenoid. • Connect DVOM positive test lead to VPWR circuit and negative test lead to CANP output circuit on the vehicle harness connector. • While observing DVOM depress and release the throttle several times (to cycle output On and Off). • CANP circuit cycles On and Off?	Yes	▶	GO to KD3.
	No	▶	REMOVE jumper. GO to KD6.
KD3 CHECK CANISTER PURGE SOLENOID FOR HOLDING VACUUM			
• Key On. • CANP solenoid disconnected. • Disconnect vacuum hose at canister purge solenoid on PCV side. • Apply 16 in. Hg to CANP solenoid. • Does CANP solenoid hold vacuum for 20 seconds?	Yes	▶	Leave vacuum pump setup in place. GO to KD4.
	No	▶	REPLACE CANP solenoid. RERUN Quick Test. If symptom is still present, GO to Section 3, Carbon Canister.

Canister Purge (CANP)	Pinpoint Test	KD

TEST STEP	RESULT	▶	ACTION TO TAKE
KD8 CHECK CONTINUITY OF CANP CIRCUIT			
• Key Off, wait 10 seconds. • Disconnect processor and inspect both 60 Pin connectors and inspect for damaged pins, corrosion, loose wires. Service as necessary. • Connect Breakout box to harness. Leave processor disconnected. • DVOM on 200 ohm scale. • Measure resistance between test Pin 31 (test Pin 35 for 1.9L CFI engines, test Pin 32 for 1.9L EFI engines) at the Breakout box and CANP on the vehicle harness connector. • Is resistance reading less than 5 ohms?	Yes	▶	GO to KD9.
	No	▶	SERVICE open circuit. RERUN Quick Test.
KD9 CHECK FOR SHORT TO GROUND			
• Key Off, wait 10 seconds. • Leave Breakout box to harness. Leave processor disconnected. • Disconnect CANP solenoid. • DVOM on 200,000 ohm scale. • Measure resistance between test Pin 31 (test Pin 35 for 1.9L CFI engines, test Pin 32 for 1.9L EFI engines) and test Pins 40, 46 and 60 at the Breakout box. • Are all resistance readings 10,000 ohms or greater?	Yes	▶	GO to KD10.
	No	▶	SERVICE short to ground. RERUN Quick Test.
KD10 CHECK FOR SHORT TO POWER			
• Key Off, wait 10 seconds. • DVOM on 200,000 ohm scale. • Leave Breakout box installed and processor disconnected. • CANP solenoid disconnected. • Measure resistance between test Pin 31 (test Pin 35 for 1.9L CFI engines, test Pin 32 for 1.9L EFI engines) and test Pins 37 and 57 at the Breakout box. • Are both resistance readings 10,000 ohms or greater?	Yes	▶	REMOVE Breakout box. REPLACE processor. RERUN Quick Test.
	No	▶	SERVICE short to power. REPEAT Quick Test. If code is repeated, REPLACE processor. RERUN Quick Test.

Idle Speed Control (Bypass Air)	Pinpoint Test	KE

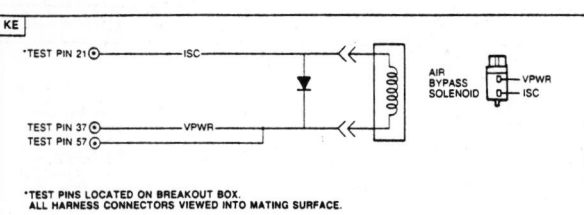

*TEST PINS LOCATED ON BREAKOUT BOX.
ALL HARNESS CONNECTORS VIEWED INTO MATING SURFACE.

STOP-WARNING

You should enter this Pinpoint Test only when a service code 12, 13, 16 and 17 is received in Quick Test Step 5.0 or when directed here from Diagnostic by Symptom in the Engine Supplement Section.

CAUTION: If the engine exhibits rough running and/or idle, correct these conditions before diagnosing Idle Speed Control (ISC). Rough running/misses may be caused by:

- Ignition System
  Refer to Section 15
- Fuel System
  Refer to Pinpoint Test Steps HA1 through HA7.
  Refer to Pinpoint Test Steps HE1 through HE7.
  Refer to Pinpoint Test Steps HG1 through HG6.
  Refer to Pinpoint Test Steps HC2 through HC9.
- EGR System, Section 6

To prevent the replacement of good components, be aware that the following non-EEC areas may be at fault:

- Engine not up to operating temperature
- Engine over operating temperature
- Improper Idle Speed Throttle Stop Adjustment
- A/C input (electrical problem)
- Throttle Speed Control Linkage
- Throttle Sticking or Linkage Binding.

This Pinpoint Test is intended to diagnose only the following:

- RPM in Self-Test only
- ISC Actuator
- Harness Circuits ISC and VPWR
- Processor Assembly

Idle Speed Control (Bypass Air)	Pinpoint Test	KE

TEST STEP	RESULT	▶	ACTION TO TAKE
KE1 RPM DROP			
• Key Off. • Connect engine tachometer. • Start engine. • Disconnect ISC harness connector. • Does rpm drop or stall?	Yes No	▶ ▶	GO to KE2. GO to KE3.
KE2 CHECK FOR EGR CODES			
• Are service codes 31, 32, 33 or 34 present?	Yes No	▶ ▶	GO to Quick Test Step 5.0 for appropriate Pinpoint Test. GO to KE3.
KE3 CHECK FOR OTHER EEC CODES			
• Are service codes 22, 41, 42, 91 or 92 present?	Yes No	▶ ▶	GO to Quick Test Step 5.0 for appropriate Pinpoint Test. GO to KE4.
KE4 MEASURE ISC SOLENOID RESISTANCE			
• Key Off. • DVOM on 200 ohm scale. • Disconnect ISC solenoid connector and measure solenoid resistance. • Is resistance between 7 and 13 ohms?	Yes No	▶ ▶	GO to KE5. REPLACE ISC solenoid. RERUN Quick Test.
KE5 ISC SHORT TO CASE (GROUND) CHECK			
• Key Off. • DVOM on 200.00 ohm scale. • ISC solenoid disconnected. • Measure resistance from either ISC pin to ISC housing. • Is resistance greater than 10.000 ohms?	Yes No	▶ ▶	GO to KE6. REPLACE ISC solenoid. RERUN Quick Test.

Idle Speed Control (Bypass Air)	Pinpoint Test	KE

TEST STEP	RESULT	▶	ACTION TO TAKE
KE6 CHECK VOLTAGE OF VPWR CIRCUIT			
• Key On, Engine Off. • DVOM on 20V scale. • ISC solenoid disconnected. • Measure voltage between VPWR at the ISC solenoid harness connector and battery ground. • Is voltage less than 10.5 volts?	Yes No	▶ ▶	SERVICE harness open circuit. RERUN Quick Test. GO to KE7.
KE7 CHECK CONTINUITY OF ISC CIRCUIT			
• Key Off, wait 10 seconds. • ISC solenoid disconnected. • Disconnect processor and inspect both 60 Pin connectors for damaged pins, corrosion, loose wires. Service as necessary. • Connect Breakout box to harness. Leave processor disconnected. • DVOM on 200 ohm scale. • Measure resistance between test Pin 21 at the Breakout box and ISC circuit at vehicle harness connector. • Is resistance greater than 5 ohms?	Yes No	▶ ▶	SERVICE open circuit. RERUN Quick Test. GO to KE8.
KE8 CHECK FOR SHORT TO GROUND			
• Key Off, wait 10 seconds. • Leave Breakout box installed and processor disconnected. • ISC solenoid disconnected. • DVOM on 200,000 ohm scale. • Measure resistance between test Pin 21 and test Pins 40, 46 and 60 at the Breakout box. • Is any resistance less than 10,000 ohms?	Yes No	▶ ▶	SERVICE short to ground. RERUN Quick Test. GO to KE9.

Idle Speed Control (Bypass Air)	Pinpoint Test	KE

TEST STEP	RESULT	▶	ACTION TO TAKE
KE9 CHECK FOR SHORT TO POWER			
• Key Off, wait 10 seconds. • DVOM on 200,000 ohm scale. • ISC solenoid disconnected. • Leave Breakout box connected to harness. Leave processor disconnected. • Place positive test lead to test Pin 37 and negative test lead to test Pin 21 to measure resistance. • Is resistance greater than 10,000 ohms?	Yes No	▶ ▶	GO to KE10. SERVICE short to power. RERUN Quick Test. If code or symptom is present, REPLACE processor.
KE10 CHECK FOR ISC SIGNAL FROM THE PROCESSOR			
• Key Off. • Connect processor and ISC actuator. • DVOM on a 20V scale. • Breakout box installed. • Connect DVOM between test Pin 21 and test Pin 40. • Start engine. • Slowly increase and decrease rpm. Does DVOM voltage vary?	Yes No	▶ ▶	GO to KE11. REPLACE processor. RERUN Quick Test.
KE11 VERIFY CURB IDLE			
• Go to Section 4 to verify curb idle. • Is curb idle within specification?	Yes No	▶ ▶	REPLACE ISC actuator. RERUN Quick Test. CHECK engine vacuum hoses. REFER to VECI decal. CHECK that throttle plates are fully closed, CHECK throttle linkage and/or speed control linkage for binding. If OK, REPLACE ISC actuator. RERUN Quick Test.

Idle Speed Control (Bypass Air)	Pinpoint Test	KE

TEST STEP	RESULT	▶	ACTION TO TAKE
KE12 CURB IDLE CHECK			
• Key Off, wait 10 seconds. • Deactivate Self-Test. • Run engine at 2000 rpm for 2 minutes or until inlet radiator hose is hot and pressurized. • Key Off, wait 10 seconds. • Run Engine Running Self-Test. • Is code 17 still present?	Yes	▶	INSPECT throttle body and air inlet for contamination. SERVICE as necessary. If OK, ADJUST curb idle (REFER to Section 4 for procedure). RERUN Quick Test.
	No	▶	SERVICE other codes as necessary.
KE15 CODE 13 HIGH RPM CHECK			
• Key Off. • Connect tachometer. • Start engine. • Disconnect ISC harness connector. • Does rpm drop or engine stall?	Yes	▶	REPLACE processor. RERUN Quick Test.
	No	▶	CHECK engine vacuum hoses. REFER to VECI decal. VERIFY curb idle. CHECK that throttle plates are fully closed. CHECK throttle linkage and/or speed control linkage for binding. If OK, REPLACE ISC actuator. RERUN Quick Test.
KE20 SERVICE CODE: 48			
• SERVICE holes, cracks, and/or disconnections to air cleaner outlet tube (between vane airflow meter and fuel charging assembly). • Perform Engine Running Self-Test. • Is code 48 present?	Yes	▶	CHECK for other source of excessive unmetered airflow.
	No	▶	EEC system OK for metered air. GO to Quick Test Step **5.0B** to service other code if necessary.

Idle Speed Control (DC Motor/Idle Tracking Switch Assembly) — 2.5L CFI, 3.8L CFI	Pinpoint Test	KF

TEST STEP	RESULT	▶	ACTION TO TAKE
KF1 SERVICE CODE 68: SIMULATE NO THROTTLE CONTACT TO FORCE A CODE 11 IN KEY ON — ENGINE OFF TEST			
• Key Off, wait 10 seconds. • Move throttle away from ISC DC motor shaft. • Perform Key On Engine Off Self-Test. • Is code 68 present? **NOTE: Ignore all other codes at this point.**	Yes	▶	RELEASE throttle and GO to **KF3**.
	No	▶	RELEASE throttle and GO to Pinpoint Test Step **KF2**.

MOVE THROTTLE AWAY FROM DC MOTOR SHAFT

KF2 RETRACT ISC DC MOTOR			
• Key Off, wait 10 seconds. • Connect Breakout box to harness. Leave processor disconnected. • Jumper test Pin 41 to test Pin 1 at the Breakout box and test Pin 21 at the Breakout box to battery ground (to retract DC motor). • Observe DC motor. **NOTE: Do not leave jumper wire in test pins if the motor will not move; it will damage Breakout box wiring.**	Motor does not retract ▶		REMOVE jumper and GO to **KF5**.
	Motor retracts and still contacts throttle lever ▶		GO to ISC Adjustments, Section 4.
	Motor retracts and does not contact throttle lever ▶		REMOVE jumper and GO to **KF25**.

Idle Speed Control (DC Motor/Idle Tracking Switch Assembly) — 2.5L CFI, 3.8L CFI	Pinpoint Test	KF

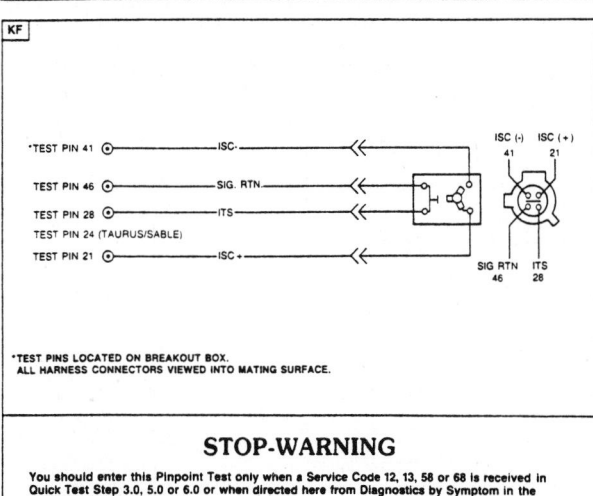

KF

*TEST PIN 41 —— ISC-
TEST PIN 46 —— SIG. RTN
TEST PIN 28 —— ITS-
TEST PIN 24 (TAURUS/SABLE)
TEST PIN 21 —— ISC+

ISC (-) ISC (+)
41 21

SIG RTN ITS
46 28

*TEST PINS LOCATED ON BREAKOUT BOX.
ALL HARNESS CONNECTORS VIEWED INTO MATING SURFACE.

STOP-WARNING

You should enter this Pinpoint Test only when a Service Code 12, 13, 58 or 68 is received in Quick Test Step 3.0, 5.0 or 6.0 or when directed here from Diagnostics by Symptom in the Engine Supplement Section.

To prevent the replacement of good components, be aware that the following non-EEC areas may be at fault:

• Anti-Diesel Speed too High
• Basic Engine
• Vacuum Leaks
• Throttle Sticking or on High Cam

This Pinpoint Test is intended to diagnose only the following:

• DC Motor
• Idle Tracking Switch
• Harness circuits: ISC +, ISC –, Signal Return and ITS
• Processor Assembly

TEST STEP	RESULT	▶	ACTION TO TAKE
KF3 SIMULATE A CLOSED CONTACT CONDITION IN KEY ON — ENGINE OFF TEST			
• Key Off, wait 10 seconds. • Disconnect harness from ISC. • Connect jumper between ISC vehicle harness connector Pins 3 and 4. • Install jumper as shown. • Perform Key On Engine Off Self-Test. • Is code 68 present?	Yes	▶	GO to **KF4**.
	No	▶	REPLACE ISC DC motor. RERUN Quick Test.

ISC HARNESS CONNECTOR

PIN 3 PIN 4
JUMPER WIRE

CAUTION: Do not short any other pins.

KF4 CHECK ITS AND SIGNAL RETURN CIRCUITS FOR CONTINUITY			
• Key Off, wait 10 seconds. • Disconnect processor 60 Pin connector and inspect for damaged pins, corrosion, loose wires. Service as necessary. • Leave Breakout box installed. Leave processor disconnected. • DVOM on 200 ohm scale. • Measure resistance between test Pin 46 at the Breakout box and Signal Return circuit at ISC vehicle harness connector and between test Pin 28* at the Breakout box and ITS circuit at ISC vehicle harness connector. *Test Pin 24 on Taurus/Sable vehicles.	Either resistance 5 ohms or greater	▶	SERVICE faulty circuit. RERUN Quick Test.
	Both resistances less than 5 ohms	▶	REPLACE processor. RERUN Quick Test.

Idle Speed Control (DC Motor/Idle Tracking Switch Assembly) — 2.5L CFI, 3.8L CFI	Pinpoint Test	KF

TEST STEP	RESULT ▶	ACTION TO TAKE
KF5 CHECK ISC CIRCUITS FOR CONTINUITY		
• Key Off, wait 10 seconds. • Disconnect processor 60 Pin connector and inspect for damaged pins, corrosion, loose wires. Service as necessary. • Connect Breakout box. Leave processor disconnected. • Disconnect harness connector for ISC motor. • DVOM on 200 ohm scale. • Measure resistance between test Pin 41 at the Breakout box and ISC – circuit at vehicle harness connector and between test Pin 21 at the Breakout box and ISC + circuit at vehicle harness connector.	Both resistance readings are less than 5 ohms ▶ Either resistance reading is 5 ohms or greater ▶	GO to KF6 . SERVICE faulty circuits. RERUN Quick Test.
KF6 CHECK ISC + AND ISC – CIRCUITS FOR SHORTS TO POWER		
• Key On Engine Off. • Leave Breakout box installed. Leave processor disconnected. • Harness disconnected from ISC motor. • DVOM on 20V scale. • Measure voltage between test Pin 41 and test Pins 40 and 60 at the Breakout box. Measure voltage between test Pin 21 and test Pins 40 and 60 at the Breakout box.	All voltage readings are less than 1V ▶ Any voltage reading is 1V or more ▶	GO to KF7 . SERVICE circuit short to power. RERUN Quick Test. If code 12 is still present, REPLACE processor.
KF7 CHECK ISC + AND ISC – CIRCUITS FOR SHORTS TO GROUND		
• Key Off, wait 10 seconds. • Leave Breakout box installed. Leave processor disconnected. • Harness disconnected from ISC motor. • DVOM on 200,000 ohm scale. • Measure resistance between test Pin 41 and test Pins 40, 46 and 60 at the Breakout box. Measure resistance between test Pin 21 and test Pins 40, 46 and 60 at the Breakout box.	All resistance readings greater than 10,000 ohms ▶ Any resistance reading is 10,000 ohms or less ▶	GO to KF8 . SERVICE faulty circuit. RERUN Quick Test. If code 12 is still present, REPLACE processor.

Idle Speed Control (DC Motor/Idle Tracking Switch Assembly) — 2.5L CFI, 3.8L CFI	Pinpoint Test	KF

TEST STEP	RESULT ▶	ACTION TO TAKE
KF8 PREPARE IDLE SPEED CONTROL DC MOTOR FOR OPERATION		
• Key Off, wait 10 seconds. • Leave Breakout box installed. Leave processor disconnected. • Harness disconnected from ISC motor. • DVOM on 20V scale. • Connect DVOM positive test lead to test Pin 1 at the Breakout box and negative test lead to ground.	Voltage reading is 10.5V or greater ▶ Voltage reading is less than 10.5V ▶	GO to KF9 . SERVICE open in KAPWR circuit. RERUN Quick Test. If code 12 is still present, GO to KF9 .
KF9 ISC DC MOTOR OPERATION CHECK		
• Key Off, wait 10 seconds. • Leave Breakout box installed. Leave processor disconnected. • Connect ISC DC motor to harness connector. • Jumper test Pin 21 to test Pin 1 at the Breakout box and test Pin 41 at the Breakout box to ground (to extend DC motor).' • Does DC motor shaft extend 5 cm (2 inches) or more?	Yes ▶ No ▶	GO to KF10 . REPLACE DC motor. RERUN Quick Test.
KF10 RETRACT ISC DC MOTOR		
• Key Off, wait 10 seconds. • Leave Breakout box installed. Leave processor disconnected. • Jumper test Pin 41 to test Pin 1 at the Breakout box and test Pin 21 at the Breakout box to ground (to retract DC motor). • Does ISC DC motor retract?	Yes ▶ No ▶	GO to KF11 . REPLACE DC motor. RERUN Quick Test.

Idle Speed Control (DC Motor/Idle Tracking Switch Assembly) — 2.5L CFI, 3.8L CFI	Pinpoint Test	KF

TEST STEP	RESULT ▶	ACTION TO TAKE
KF11 EXTEND ISC DC MOTOR		
• Key Off, wait 10 seconds. • Leave Breakout box installed. Leave processor disconnected. • Jumper test Pin 21 to test Pin 1 at the Breakout box and test Pin 41 at the Breakout box to ground (to extend DC motor). • Does ISC DC motor extend?	No ▶ Yes ▶	REPLACE DC motor. RERUN Quick Test. REPLACE processor. RERUN Quick Test.
KF12 SERVICE CODE 58: SIMULATE THROTTLE CONTACT TO FORCE A SERVICE CODE 68 IN KEY ON — ENGINE OFF TEST		
• Key Off, wait 10 seconds. • Press on ISC DC motor shaft to simulate throttle contact. • With a force pushing on DC motor shaft, perform Key On Engine Off Self-Test. NOTE: Ignore all other codes at this point. • Is code 68 present?	Yes ▶ No ▶	GO to Pinpoint Test Step KF5 . GO to KF13 .
KF13 RETRACT ISC DC MOTOR		
• Key Off, wait 10 seconds. • Leave Breakout box installed. Leave processor disconnected. • Jumper test Pin 41 to test Pin 1 at the Breakout box and test Pin 21 at the Breakout box to ground (to retract DC motor). • Does ISC DC motor retract?	Yes ▶ No ▶	GO to ISC Adjustments, Section 4. GO to KF14 .
KF14 IDLE TRACKING SWITCH ALWAYS "NOT TRACKING" (CLOSED)		
• Key Off, wait 10 seconds. • Reconnect processor. • Disconnect vehicle harness from ISC. • Perform Key On Engine Off Self-Test. NOTE: Ignore all other codes at this point. • Is code 68 present?	Yes ▶ No ▶	REPLACE DC motor. RERUN Quick Test. GO to KF15 .

Idle Speed Control (DC Motor/Idle Tracking Switch ·Assembly) — 2.5L CFI, 3.8L CFI	Pinpoint Test	KF

TEST STEP	RESULT ▶	ACTION TO TAKE
KF15 CHECK ITS CIRCUIT FOR SHORT TO GROUND		
• Key Off, wait 10 seconds. • Disconnect processor 60 Pin connector and inspect for damaged pins, corrosion, loose wires. Service as necessary. • Connect Breakout box. Disconnect processor. • Harness disconnected at ISC. • DVOM on 200,000 ohm scale. • Measure resistance between test Pin 28* and test Pins 40, 46 and 60 at the Breakout box. *Test Pin 24 Taurus/Sable.	Any resistance less than 10,000 ohms ▶ All resistances 10,000 ohms or more ▶	SERVICE short to ground. RERUN Quick Test. REPLACE processor. RERUN Quick Test.
KF16 DC MOTOR CONTROL FAULT ISOLATION: SERVICE CODE 12		
• Are service codes 58, 68, 31 or 41 present?	Yes ▶ No ▶	GO to Quick Test Step 5.0 B for next appropriate Pinpoint Code. GO to KF17 .
KF17 CHECK FOR THROTTLE STICKING		
• Check throttle plates and linkages for binding.' • Check speed control for binding (if so equipped).	Yes ▶ No ▶	SERVICE as necessary. RERUN Quick Test. GO to KF18 .
KF18 EXTEND ISC DC MOTOR		
• Key Off, wait 10 seconds. • Leave Breakout box installed. Leave processor disconnected. • Jumper test Pin 21 to test Pin 1 at the Breakout box and test Pin 41 at the Breakout box to ground (to extend DC motor). • Does ISC DC motor extend?	No ▶ Yes ▶	REPLACE DC motor. RERUN Quick Test. REPLACE processor. RERUN Quick Test.

Idle Speed Control (DC Motor/Idle Tracking Switch Assembly) — 2.5L CFI, 3.8L CFI	Pinpoint Test	KF

TEST STEP	RESULT ▶	ACTION TO TAKE
KF19 ENGINE RUNNING CODES 13 AND/OR 16 • Prepare system for normal engine operation. • Deactivate Self-Test. • Air conditioner Off. • Run engine. Alternate between 30 seconds at idle and 5 seconds at part throttle modes for 3 minutes. • Is idle speed erratic?	No ▶ Yes ▶	GO to KF20 . CHECK for: • Vacuum leaks • Code 22 • Code 31 • Code 41 • Code 58 SERVICE above codes as necessary before continuing.
KF20 CHECK FOR THROTTLE STICKING OR CHOKE POSITION • Inspect throttle mechanisms (plate linkage) for sticking or binding. • Are above inspections satisfactory?	No ▶ Yes ▶	SERVICE fault. RERUN Quick Test. GO to KF21 .
KF21 PERFORM KEY ON — ENGINE OFF TEST. OBSERVE ON DEMAND CODES • Perform Key On Engine Off Test. Record On Demand codes. • Key On Engine Off. • Is code 68 present?	Yes ▶ No ▶	GO to Pinpoint Test Step KF1 . REFER to Section 4 for anti-diesel speed adjustment.
KF25 CHECK ISC – AND ISC – CIRCUITS FOR SHORTS TO GROUND • Key Off, wait 10 seconds. • Leave Breakout box installed. Leave processor disconnected. • Harness disconnected from ISC motor. • DVOM on 200.000 ohm scale. • Measure resistance between test Pin 41 and test Pins 40, 46 and 60 at the Breakout box. Measure resistance between test Pin 21 and test Pins 40, 46 and 60 at the Breakout box.	All resistance readings greater than 10,000 ohms ▶ Any resistance reading is 10,000 ohms or less ▶	GO to KF26 . SERVICE faulty circuit. RERUN Quick Test. If code 12 is still present, REPLACE processor.

Idle Speed Control (DC Motor/Idle Tracking Switch Assembly) — 2.5L CFI, 3.8L CFI	Pinpoint Test	KF

TEST STEP	RESULT ▶	ACTION TO TAKE
KF26 CHECK ISC – AND ISC – CIRCUITS FOR SHORTS TO POWER • Key On Engine Off. • Leave Breakout box installed. Leave processor disconnected. • Harness disconnected from ISC motor. • DVOM on 20V scale. • Measure voltage between test Pin 41 and test Pins 40 and 60 at the Breakout box. Measure voltage between test Pin 21 and test Pins 40 and 60 at the Breakout box.	All voltage readings are less than 1V ▶ Any voltage reading is 1V or more ▶	RECONNECT DC motor. GO to KF27 . SERVICE circuit short to power. RERUN Quick Test. If code 12 is still present, REPLACE processor.
KF27 EXTEND ISC DC MOTOR • Key Off, wait 10 seconds. • Leave Breakout box installed. Leave processor disconnected. • Jumper test Pin 21 to test Pin 1 at the Breakout box and test Pin 41 at the Breakout box to ground (to extend DC motor). • Does ISC DC motor extend?	No ▶ Yes ▶	REPLACE DC motor. RERUN Quick Test. REPLACE processor. RERUN Quick Test.

Shift Indicator Light (SIL)	Pinpoint Test	KL

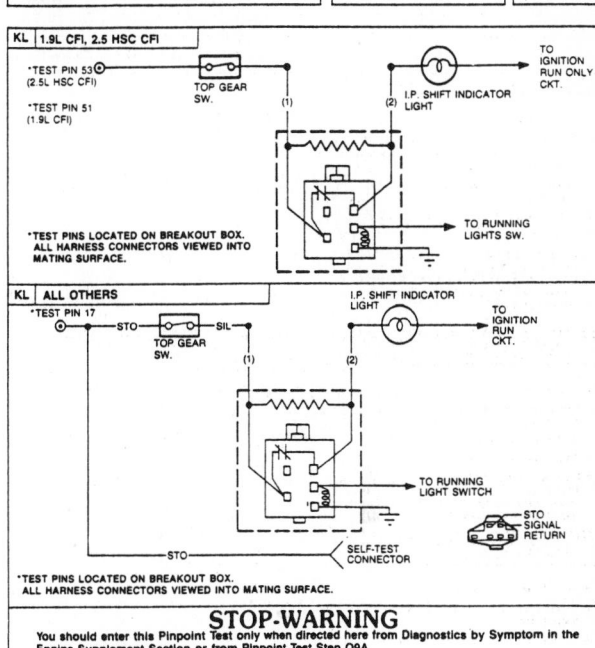

KL	1.9L CFI, 2.5 HSC CFI

*TEST PIN 53 (2.5L HSC CFI)
*TEST PIN 51 (1.9L CFI)
TOP GEAR SW.
I.P. SHIFT INDICATOR LIGHT
TO IGNITION RUN ONLY CKT.
TO RUNNING LIGHTS SW.

*TEST PINS LOCATED ON BREAKOUT BOX. ALL HARNESS CONNECTORS VIEWED INTO MATING SURFACE.

KL	ALL OTHERS

*TEST PIN 17 — STO
TOP GEAR SW. — SIL
I.P. SHIFT INDICATOR LIGHT
TO IGNITION RUN CKT.
TO RUNNING LIGHT SWITCH
STO SIGNAL RETURN
STO
SELF-TEST CONNECTOR

*TEST PINS LOCATED ON BREAKOUT BOX. ALL HARNESS CONNECTORS VIEWED INTO MATING SURFACE.

STOP-WARNING

You should enter this Pinpoint Test only when directed here from Diagnostics by Symptom in the Engine Supplement Section or from Pinpoint Test Step Q9A.

This Pinpoint Test is intended to diagnose only the following:

• Top Gear Switch
• Shift Indicator Light Bulb and Fuse
• Harness Circuits: SIL and STO

Shift Indicator Light (SIL)	Pinpoint Test	KL

TEST STEP	RESULT ▶	ACTION TO TAKE
KL1 ENTER OUTPUT STATE CHECK IN NEUTRAL (REFER TO APPENDIX) **NOTE:** Do not use STAR tester for this Step, use VOM/DVOM. • Key Off, wait 10 seconds. • Transmission in neutral. • DVOM on 20V scale. • Connect DVOM negative test lead to STO at the Self-Test connector and positive test lead to battery positive. • Jumper STI to signal return at the Self-Test connector. • Perform Key On, Engine Off Self-Test until the completion of the Continuous Test Codes. • DVOM will indicate zero volts when test is complete. • Depress and release the throttle. • Did DVOM reading change to a high voltage reading?	Yes ▶ No ▶	REMAIN in output state check. Go to KL2 . DEPRESS throttle to WOT and release. If STO voltage does not go high, GO to Pinpoint Test Step KL7 . Leave equipment hooked up.
KL2 CHECK FOR ELECTRICAL CYCLING AT DIMMER RELAY INPUT • DVOM on 20V scale. • Reconnect DVOM positive test lead to battery positive terminal and negative test lead to Pin 1 on dimmer relay. • While observing DVOM, depress and release the throttle several times to cycle Pin 1 On and Off. • Does Pin 1 cycle On and Off?	Yes ▶ No ▶	GO to KL3 . GO to KL5 .
KL3 CHECK FOR ELECTRICAL CYCLING AT DIMMER RELAY OUTPUT • DVOM on 20V scale. • Reconnect DVOM positive test lead to battery positive terminal and negative test lead to Pin 2 on dimmer relay. • While observing DVOM, depress and release the throttle several times to cycle Pin 2 On and Off. • Does Pin 2 cycle On and Off?	Yes ▶ No ▶	REMOVE jumper. GO to KL4 . REMOVE jumper. REPLACE dimmer relay.

Shift Indicator Light (SIL)		Pinpoint Test	KL

TEST STEP	RESULT	▶	ACTION TO TAKE
KL4 CHECK CONTINUITY BETWEEN DIMMER RELAY OUTPUT AND SIL BULB • Key Off, wait 10 seconds. • DVOM on 200 ohm scale. • Measure resistance between Pin 2 of dimmer relay connector and SIL bulb. • Is resistance reading 5 ohms or greater?	Yes ▶ No ▶		SERVICE harness open circuit. RERUN Quick Test. REPLACE SIL bulb.
KL5 CHECK FOR ELECTRICAL CYCLING AT SIL SIDE OF TOP GEAR SWITCH • DVOM on 20V scale. • Reconnect DVOM positive lead to battery positive terminal and negative test lead to SIL circuit of top gear switch. • While observing DVOM, depress and release the throttle several times to cycle SIL circuit On and Off. • Does SIL circuit cycle On and Off?	Yes ▶ No ▶		SERVICE harness open circuit. RERUN Quick Test. 4.9L only, change SIL bulb. GO to KL6 .
KL6 CHECK FOR ELECTRICAL CYCLING AT STO SIDE OF TOP GEAR SWITCH • DVOM on 20V scale. • Reconnect DVOM positive lead to battery positive terminal and negative test lead to STO circuit of top gear switch. • While observing DVOM, depress and release the throttle several times to cycle STO circuit On and Off. • Does STO circuit cycle On and Off?	Yes ▶ No ▶		CHANGE top gear switch. SERVICE harness open circuit. RERUN Quick Test.

Shift Indicator Light (SIL)		Pinpoint Test	KL

TEST STEP	RESULT	▶	ACTION TO TAKE
KL7 ENTER OUTPUT STATE CHECK IN TOP GEAR (REFER TO APPENDIX) **NOTE:** Do not use STAR tester for this Step, use VOM/DVOM. • Key Off, wait 10 seconds. • Transmission in top gear. • DVOM on 20V scale. • Reconnect DVOM negative test lead to STO at the Self-Test connector and positive test lead to battery positive. • Jumper STI to signal return at the Self-Test connector. • Perform Key On, Engine Off Self-Test until the completion of the Continuous Test Codes. • DVOM will indicate zero volts when test is complete. • Depress and release the throttle. • Did DVOM reading change to a high voltage reading?	Yes ▶ No ▶		CHECK SIL bulb and fuse 15. If OK, SERVICE short to ground in SIL circuit. GO to Pinpoint Test Step Q40 .

WOT A/C Cutoff (WAC) A/C Demand		Pinpoint Test	KM

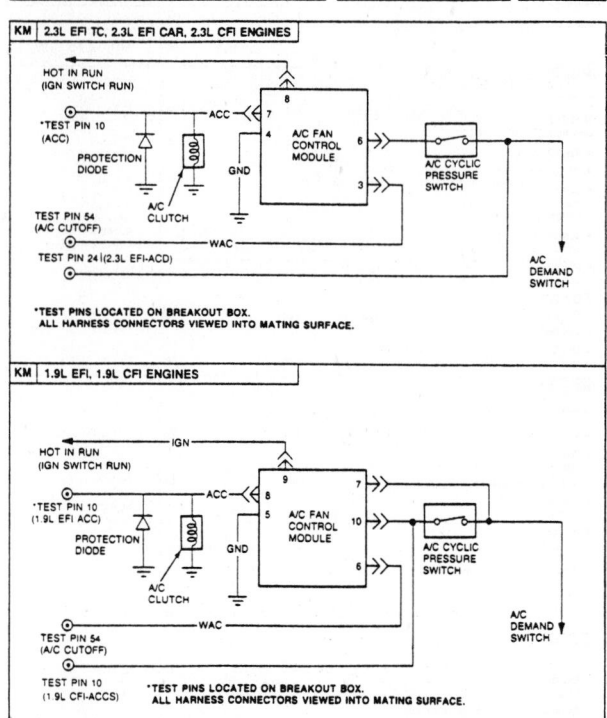

WOT A/C Cutoff (WAC) A/C Demand		Pinpoint Test	KM

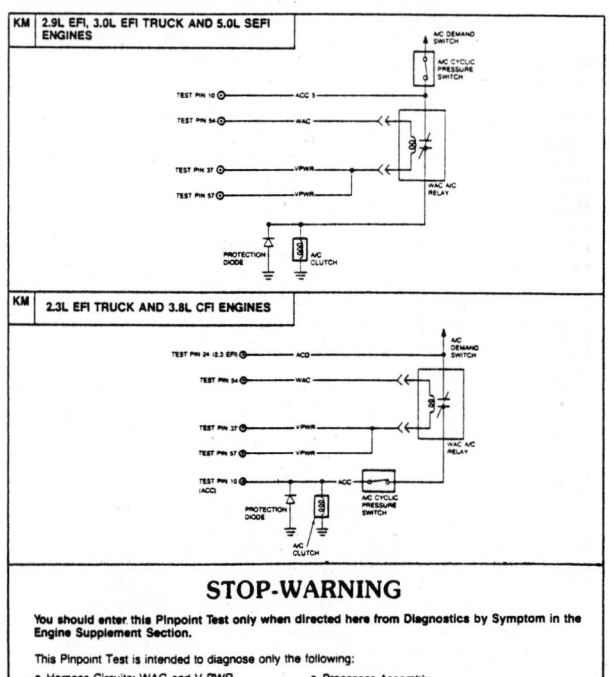

STOP-WARNING

You should enter this Pinpoint Test only when directed here from Diagnostics by Symptom in the Engine Supplement Section.

This Pinpoint Test is intended to diagnose only the following:

• Harness Circuits: WAC and V PWR • Processor Assembly
• WOT A/C Cut-Off Relay • A/C Demand Switch

WOT A/C Cutoff (WAC) A/C Demand — Pinpoint Test — KM

TEST STEP	RESULT ▶	ACTION TO TAKE
KM1 ENTER OUTPUT STATE CHECK (REFER TO APPENDIX) **NOTE: Do not use STAR tester for this Step, use VOM/DVOM.** • Key Off, wait 10 seconds. • DVOM on 20V scale. • Connect DVOM negative test lead to STO at the Self-Test connector and positive test lead to battery positive. • Jumper STI to signal return at the Self-Test connector. • Perform Key On, Engine Off Self-Test until the completion of the Continuous Test Codes. • DVOM will indicate zero volts when test complete. • Depress and release the throttle. • Did DVOM reading change to a high voltage reading?	Yes ▶ No ▶	REMAIN in Output State Check. GO to KM2. DEPRESS throttle to WOT and RELEASE. If STO voltage does not go high, GO to Pinpoint Test Step Q40. Leave equipment hooked up.
KM2 CHECK A/C CLUTCH ELECTRICAL OPERATION • Key On, engine Off. • Disconnect processor 60 Pin connector and inspect for damaged pins, corrosion, loose wires. Service as necessary. • Connect Breakout box to harness. Reconnect processor. • A/C switch to A/C. • DVOM on 20V scale. • Reconnect DVOM positive test lead to test Pin 37 and negative test lead to test Pin 54 at the Breakout box.	Yes ▶ No ▶	EEC-IV system OK. Refer to Shop Manual, Group 36. REMOVE jumper. GO to KM3.
	• While observing DVOM, depress and release the throttle several times (to cycle output On and Off). • Does A/C clutch output cycle On and Off?	
KM3 FAN CONTROL MODULE OR WAC RELAY • A/C fan/control module applications 1.9L EFI, 1.9L CFI, 2.3L EFI, 2.3L CFi engines. • All other systems with WAC relay.	A/C fan control ▶ WAC relay ▶	GO to KM4. GO to KM10.

WOT A/C Cutoff (WAC) A/C Demand — Pinpoint Test — KM

TEST STEP	RESULT ▶	ACTION TO TAKE
KM4 CHECK CONTINUITY OF GROUND CIRCUIT TO FAN CONTROL MODULE • Key Off, wait 10 seconds. • DVOM on 200 ohm scale. • Measure resistance of ground circuit between fan control module connector and battery ground. • Is resistance reading 5 ohms or greater?	Yes ▶ No ▶	SERVICE harness circuit. RERUN Quick Test. GO to KM5.
KM5 CHECK FOR IGN. CIRCUIT VOLTAGE • Key On, engine Off. • DVOM on 20V scale. • Measure voltage between ignition circuit and ground circuit on the fan control module connector. • Is voltage reading 10.5 volts or greater?	Yes ▶ No ▶	GO to KM6. SERVICE open in ign. circuit. RERUN Quick Test.
KM6 CHECK CONTINUITY OF WAC CIRCUIT • Key Off, wait 10 seconds. • Disconnect processor 60 Pin connector and inspect for damaged pins, corrosion, loose wires. Service as necessary. • Connect Breakout box to harness. Leave processor disconnected. • DVOM on 200 ohm scale. • Measure resistance between test Pin 54 at the Breakout box and WAC circuit at fan control module connector. • Is resistance reading 5 ohms or greater?	Yes ▶ No ▶	SERVICE harness WAC circuit. RERUN Quick Test. GO to KM7.
KM7 CHECK FOR SHORT TO GROUND ON WAC CIRCUIT • Key Off, wait 10 seconds. • Leave Breakout box installed and processor disconnected. • DVOM on 200,000 ohm scale. • Measure resistance between test Pin 54 and test Pins 40, 46 and 60 at the Breakout box. • Are resistance readings 10,000 ohms or greater?	Yes ▶ No ▶	REPLACE processor. RERUN Quick Test. GO to KM8.

WOT A/C Cutoff (WAC) A/C Demand — Pinpoint Test — KM

TEST STEP	RESULT ▶	ACTION TO TAKE
KM8 CHECK FOR SHORT TO GROUND WITH FAN CONTROL MODULE DISCONNECTED • Key Off, wait 10 seconds. • Leave Breakout box installed and processor disconnected. • DVOM on 200,000 ohm scale. • Disconnect fan control module. • Measure resistance between test Pin 54 and test Pins 40, 46 and 60 at the Breakout box. • Are resistance readings 10,000 ohms or greater?	Yes ▶ No ▶	REPLACE fan control module. RERUN Quick Test. SERVICE harness short. RERUN Quick Test.
KM10 MEASURE WAC RELAY RESISTANCE • Key Off, wait 10 seconds. • DVOM on 200 ohm scale. • Disconnect WAC relay connector and measure relay resistance. • Is resistance reading less than 50 ohms or greater than 70 ohms?	Yes ▶ No ▶	REPLACE WAC relay. RERUN Quick Test. CONNECT WAC solenoid. GO to KM11.
KM11 CHECK VOLTAGE OF V PWR CIRCUIT • Key On, Engine Off. • DVOM on 20V scale. • Connect DVOM positive test lead to V PWR circuit and negative test lead to ground. • Measure voltage on WAC relay V PWR circuit. • Is voltage reading 10.5 volts or greater?	Yes ▶ No ▶	GO to KM12. SERVICE harness open circuit. RERUN Quick Test.
KM12 CHECK CONTINUITY OF WAC CIRCUIT • Key Off, wait 10 seconds. • Disconnect processor 60 Pin connector and inspect for damaged pins, corrosion, loose wires. Service as necessary. • Connect Breakout box to harness. Leave processor disconnected. • DVOM on 200 ohm scale. • Measure resistance between test Pin 54 at the Breakout box and WAC circuit at harness connector. • Is resistance reading 5 ohms or greater?	Yes ▶ No ▶	SERVICE harness open circuit. RERUN Quick Test. GO to KM13.

WOT A/C Cutoff (WAC) A/C Demand — Pinpoint Test — KM

TEST STEP	RESULT ▶	ACTION TO TAKE
KM13 CHECK FOR SHORT TO GROUND • Key Off, wait 10 seconds. • Leave Breakout box installed and processor disconnected. • DVOM on 200,000 ohm scale. • Measure resistance between test Pin 54 and test Pins 40, 46 and 60 at Breakout box. • Are all resistance readings greater than 10,000 ohms?	Yes ▶ No ▶	GO to KM14. SERVICE short to ground. RERUN Quick Test.
KM14 CHECK FOR SHORT TO POWER • Key Off, wait 10 seconds. • DVOM on 200,000 ohm scale. • Leave Breakout box installed and processor disconnected. • WAC solenoid disconnected. • Measure resistance between test Pin 54 and test Pins 37 and 57 at Breakout box. • Are all resistance readings greater than 10,000 ohms?	Yes ▶ No ▶	GO to KM15. SERVICE short to power. RERUN Quick Test. If symptom is still present REPLACE processor.
KM15 CYCLE A/C DEMAND SWITCH • Key Off, wait 10 seconds. • Processor disconnected. • DVOM on 20V scale. • Measure voltage between test Pin 10 and test Pin 40 at the Breakout box. • Does output cycle low to high (high being 10.5 volts or greater) when A/C switch is cycled?	Yes ▶ No ▶	REPLACE processor. RERUN Quick Test. REPAIR open in A/C input to test Pin 10. RERUN Quick Test.

WOT A/C Cutoff (WAC) A/C Demand	Pinpoint Test	KM

TEST STEP	RESULT ▶	ACTION TO TAKE
KM20 CYCLE A/C DEMAND SWITCH		
• Key Off, wait 10 seconds. • Disconnect processor 60 Pin connector and inspect for damaged pins, corrosion, loose wires. Service as necessary. • Connect Breakout box to harness. Leave processor disconnected. • DVOM on 20V scale. • Measure voltage between test Pin 10 (Pin 24 for 2.3L EFI) and test Pin 40 at the Breakout box. • Does output cycle 4.0-10.5V when A/C switch is cycled?	Yes ▶ No ▶	REPLACE processor. RERUN Quick Test. GO to KM21 .
KM21 CHECK CONTINUITY OF ACC/ACD CIRCUIT		
• Key Off, wait 10 seconds. • DVOM on 200 ohm scale. • Measure resistance between ACC test Pin 10 at the Breakout box and A/C clutch. For 2.3L EFI, also measure resistance between ACD test Pin 24 at the Breakout box and A/C demand switch. • Is resistance reading 5 ohms or greater?	Yes ▶ No ▶	SERVICE harness circuit. RERUN Quick Test. EEC-IV system OK. REFER to Shop Manual, Group 36.

Turbo Boost	Pinpoint Test	KN

TEST STEP	RESULT ▶	ACTION TO TAKE
KN1 ENTER OUPUT STATE CHECK (REFER TO APPENDIX)		
NOTE: Do not use STAR tester for this Step, use VOM/DVOM. • Key Off, wait 10 seconds. • DVOM on 20V scale. • Connect DVOM negative test lead to STO at the Self-Test connector and positive test lead to battery positive. • Jumper STI to signal return at the Self-Test connector. • Perform Key On Engine Off Self-Test through the completion of the Continuous Test Codes. • DVOM will indicate zero volts when test is complete. • Depress and release the throttle. • Did DVOM reading change to a high voltage reading?	Yes ▶ No ▶	REMAIN in Output State Check. GO to KN2 . DEPRESS throttle to WOT and release. If STO voltage does not go high, GO to Pinpoint Test Step Q40 . Leave equipment hooked up.
KN2 CHECK BOOST OUTPUT ELECTRICAL OPERATION		
• Key On, Engine Off. • DVOM on 20V scale. • Connect DVOM positive test lead to circuit VPWR on boost solenoid connector and negative test lead to boost output on boost solenoid connector. • While observing DVOM, depress and release the throttle several times to cycle output On and Off. • Does boost output solenoid cycle On and Off?	Yes ▶ No ▶	GO to KN3 . REMOVE jumper. GO to KN4 .

Turbo Boost	Pinpoint Test	KN

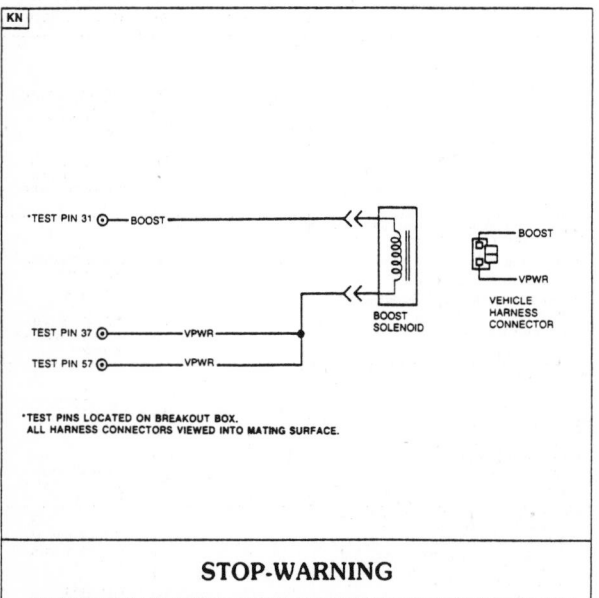

*TEST PIN 31 ○— BOOST ——————⟨⟨—— ——— BOOST
——— VPWR
TEST PIN 37 ○— VPWR ——
TEST PIN 57 ○— VPWR ——
BOOST SOLENOID
VEHICLE HARNESS CONNECTOR

*TEST PINS LOCATED ON BREAKOUT BOX.
ALL HARNESS CONNECTORS VIEWED INTO MATING SURFACE.

STOP-WARNING

You should enter this Pinpoint Test only when a service code 81 is received in Quick Test Step 3.0 or when directed here from Diagnostics by Symptom in the Engine Supplement Section.

This Pinpoint Test is intended to diagnose only the following:
• Harness circuits: VPWR, Boost

Turbo Boost	Pinpoint Test	KN

TEST STEP	RESULT ▶	ACTION TO TAKE
KN3 CHECK BOOST SOLENOID FUNCTION		
• Remain in output state check. • Disconnect turbo boost control solenoid vacuum hose at the turbocharger inlet end. • Attach a vacuum pump to the hose. • Depress the throttle once to cycle the solenoid closed. • Apply vacuum to the solenoid. • Depress the throttle once again to cycle the solenoid open and release trapped vacuum. • Did the solenoid hold and then release vacuum? TURBO BOOST CONTROL SOLENOID TO WASTE GATE — TO TURBO INLET — FLOW	Yes ▶ No ▶	EEC-IV system OK. REFER to Shop Manual for boost diagnostics. REPLACE solenoid. RERUN Quick Test.
KN4 MEASURE BOOST SOLENOID RESISTANCE		
• Key Off, wait 10 seconds. • DVOM on 200 ohm scale. • Disconnect boost solenoid connector and measure the solenoid resistance. • Is resistance between 65 and 110 ohms?	Yes ▶ No ▶	CONNECT BOOST solenoid. GO to KN5 . REPLACE BOOST solenoid. RERUN Quick Test.
KN5 CHECK VOLTAGE OF VPWR CIRCUIT		
• Key On, Engine Off. • DVOM on 20V scale. • Measure voltage between VPWR circuit of boost solenoid vehicle harness connector and battery ground. • Is voltage greater than 10.5 volts?	Yes ▶ No ▶	GO to KN6 . SERVICE harness open circuit. RERUN Quick Test.

Turbo Boost	Pinpoint Test	KN

TEST STEP	RESULT ▶	ACTION TO TAKE
KN6 CHECK CONTINUITY OF BOOST CIRCUIT		
• Key Off, wait 10 seconds. • Disconnect processor 60 Pin connector and inspect for damaged pins, corrosion, loose wires. Service as necessary. • Connect Breakout box to harness. Leave processor disconnected. • DVOM on 200 ohm scale. • Measure resistance between test Pin 31 at the Breakout box and boost circuit at vehicle harness connector. • Is resistance less than 5 ohms?	Yes ▶ No ▶	GO to KN7. SERVICE open circuit. RERUN Quick Test.
KN7 CHECK FOR SHORT TO GROUND		
• Key Off, wait 10 seconds. • Leave Breakout box installed and processor disconnected. • Disconnect boost solenoid. • DVOM on 200,000 ohm scale. • Measure resistance between test Pin 31 and test Pins 40, 46 and 60 at the Breakout box. • Is resistance greater than 10,000 ohms?	Yes ▶ No ▶	GO to KN8. SERVICE short to ground, RERUN Quick Test.
KN8 CHECK FOR SHORT TO POWER		
• Key Off, wait 10 seconds. • DVOM on 200,000 ohm scale. • Leave Breakout box installed and processor disconnected. • Boost solenoid disconnected. • Measure resistance between Pin 31 and test Pins 37 and 57 at the Breakout Box. • Is resistance greater than 10.000 ohms?	Yes ▶ No ▶	REPLACE processor. RERUN Quick Test. SERVICE short to power. RERUN Quick Test. If symptom is still present, REPLACE processor.

Exhaust Heat Control (EHC)	Pinpoint Test	KP

TEST STEP	RESULT ▶	ACTION TO TAKE
KP1 ENTER OUTPUT STATE CHECK (REFER TO APPENDIX)		
NOTE: Do not use STAR tester for this Step, use VOM/DVOM. • Key Off, wait 10 seconds. • DVOM on 20V scale. • Connect DVOM negative test lead to STO at the Self-Test connector and positive test lead to battery positive. • Jumper STI to signal return at the Self-Test connector. • Perform Key On, Engine Off Self-Test until the completion of the Continuous Test Codes. • DVOM will indicate zero volts when test is complete. • Depress and release the throttle. • Did DVOM reading change to a high voltage reading?	Yes ▶ No ▶	REMAIN in Output State Check. GO to KP2. DEPRESS throttle to WOT and release. If STO voltage does not go high, GO to Pinpoint Test Step Q40. Leave equipment hooked up.
KP2 CHECK EHC SOLENOID ELECTRICAL OPERATION		
• DVOM on 20V scale. • Measure voltage between VPWR and EHC circuit at EHC solenoid. • While observing DVOM, depress throttle several times to cycle output on and off. • Does EHC output cycle on and off?	Yes ▶ No ▶	GO to KP3. GO to KP5.
KP3 CHECK EXHAUST HEAT SOLENOID FOR VACUUM CYCLING		
• Install vacuum pump to the exhaust heat solenoid vacuum supply port and install a vacuum gauge to the output port. Apply 6 in. Hg minimum. • Does the vacuum output cycle On and Off while depressing and releasing the throttle?	Yes ▶ No ▶	GO to KP4. REPLACE solenoid. RERUN Quick Test.
NOTE: Maintain vacuum at source.		

Exhaust Heat Control (EHC)	Pinpoint Test	KP

KP

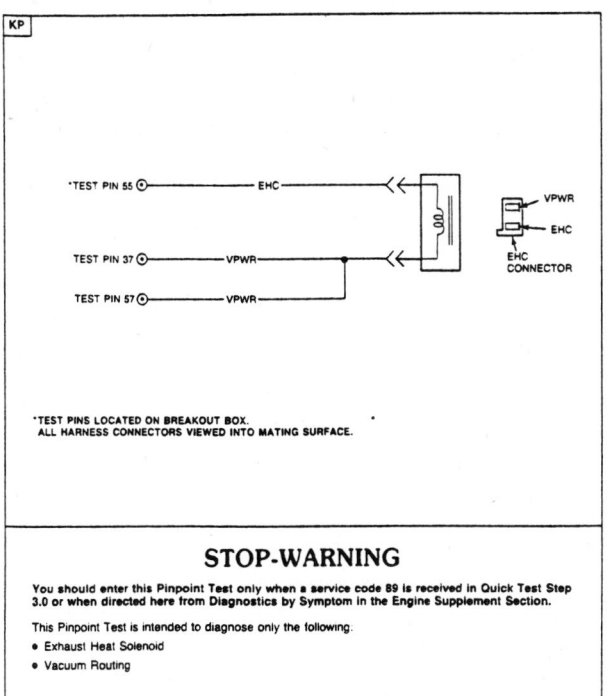

```
*TEST PIN 55 ⊙————— EHC ———————⧸⧹                    VPWR
                                 |‾‾|
TEST PIN 37 ⊙————— VPWR ——————⧸⧹  |  |              EHC
                                 |__|              EHC
TEST PIN 57 ⊙————— VPWR —————————————              CONNECTOR
```

*TEST PINS LOCATED ON BREAKOUT BOX.
ALL HARNESS CONNECTORS VIEWED INTO MATING SURFACE.

STOP-WARNING

You should enter this Pinpoint Test only when a service code 89 is received in Quick Test Step 3.0 or when directed here from Diagnostics by Symptom in the Engine Supplement Section.

This Pinpoint Test is intended to diagnose only the following:
• Exhaust Heat Solenoid
• Vacuum Routing

Exhaust Heat Control (EHC)	Pinpoint Test	KP

TEST STEP	RESULT ▶	ACTION TO TAKE
KP4 CHECK MANIFOLD VACUUM LINES FOR BLOCKAGE OR LEAKS		
• With vacuum lines disconnected at exhaust heat solenoid, check for vacuum. • Start engine. • Is vacuum present?	Yes ▶ No ▶	EEC-IV system OK. REFER to Section 3 for exhaust heat diagnostics. SERVICE vacuum source blockage or leak. RERUN Quick Test.
KP5 MEASURE EHC SOLENOID RESISTANCE		
• Key Off, wait 10 seconds. • DVOM on 200 ohm scale. • Disconnect exhaust heat solenoid connector and measure solenoid resistance. • Is resistance between 50 and 100 ohms?	Yes ▶ No ▶	CONNECT exhaust heat solenoid. Go to KP6. REPLACE exhaust heat solenoid. RERUN Quick Test.
KP6 CHECK VOLTAGE OF VPWR CIRCUIT		
• Key On, Engine Off. • DVOM on 20V scale. • Measure voltage between VPWR at the EHC solenoid vehicle harness connector circuit and ground. • Is voltage reading 10.5 volts or greater?	Yes ▶ No ▶	GO to KP7. SERVICE harness open circuit. RERUN Quick Test.
KP7 CHECK CONTINUITY OF EHC CIRCUIT		
• Key Off, wait 10 seconds. • Disconnect processor 60 Pin connector and inspect for damaged pins, corrosion, loose wires. Service as necessary. • Connect Breakout box to harness. Leave processor disconnected. • DVOM on 200 ohm scale. • Measure resistance between test Pin 55 at the Breakout box and EHC circuit at vehicle harness connector. • Is resistance reading 5 ohms or greater?	Yes ▶ No ▶	SERVICE harness open circuit. RERUN Quick Test. GO to KP8.

Exhaust Heat Control (EHC)	Pinpoint Test	KP

TEST STEP	RESULT ▶	ACTION TO TAKE
KP8 CHECK FOR SHORT TO GROUND		
• Key Off, wait 10 seconds. • Leave Breakout box installed and processor disconnected. • Disconnect EHC solenoid. • DVOM on 200,000 ohm scale. • Measure resistance between test Pin 55 and test Pins 40, 46 and 60 at Breakout box. • Are resistance readings 10.000 ohms or greater?	Yes ▶ No ▶	GO to KP9. SERVICE short to ground. RERUN Quick Test.
KP9 CHECK FOR SHORT TO POWER		
• Key Off, wait 10 seconds. • DVOM on 200,000 ohm scale. • Leave Breakout box installed and processor disconnected. • EHC solenoid disconnected. • Measure resistance between test Pin 55 and test Pins 37 and 57 at Breakout box. • Is the resistance reading 10.000 ohms or greater?	Yes ▶ No ▶	REPLACE processor. RERUN Quick Test. SERVICE short to power. RERUN Quick Test. If code is repeated, REPLACE processor.

Converter Clutch Override (CCO)	Pinpoint Test	KR

TEST STEP	RESULT ▶	ACTION TO TAKE
KR2 CHECK VOLTAGE OF VPWR CIRCUIT		
• Key On, Engine Off. • DVOM on 20V scale. • Measure voltage at the CCO solenoid connector between VPWR circuit and battery ground. • Is voltage reading less than 10.5 volts?	Yes ▶ No ▶	SERVICE harness open circuit. RERUN Quick Test. GO to KR3.
KR3 CHECK CONTINUITY OF CCO CIRCUIT		
• Key Off, wait 10 seconds. • Disconnect processor 60 Pin connector and inspect for damaged pins, corrosion, loose wires. Service as necessary. • Connect Breakout box to harness. Leave processor disconnected. • DVOM on 200 ohm scale. • Measure resistance between test Pin 53 at the Breakout box and CCO circuit at the solenoid vehicle harness connector. • Is resistance reading less 5 ohms?	Yes ▶ No ▶	GO to KR4. SERVICE harness open circuit. RERUN Quick Test.
KR4 CHECK FOR SHORT TO GROUND		
• Key Off, wait 10 seconds. • Leave Breakout box installed and processor disconnected. • Disconnect CCO solenoid. • DVOM on 200.000 ohm scale. • Measure resistance between test Pin 53 and test Pins 40, 46 and 60 at Breakout box. • Are all resistance readings 10.000 ohms or greater?	Yes ▶ No ▶	GO to KR5. SERVICE short to ground. RERUN Quick Test.
KR5 CHECK FOR SHORT TO POWER		
• Key Off, wait 10 seconds. • DVOM on 200.000 ohm scale. • Leave Breakout box installed and processor disconnected. • CCO solenoid disconnected. • Measure resistance between test Pin 53 and test Pins 37 and 57 at Breakout box. • Are all resistance readings 10.000 ohms or greater?	Yes ▶ No ▶	REPLACE processor. RERUN Quick Test. SERVICE short to power. RERUN Quick Test. If code is still present, REPLACE processor.

Converter Clutch Override (CCO)	Pinpoint Test	KR

KR

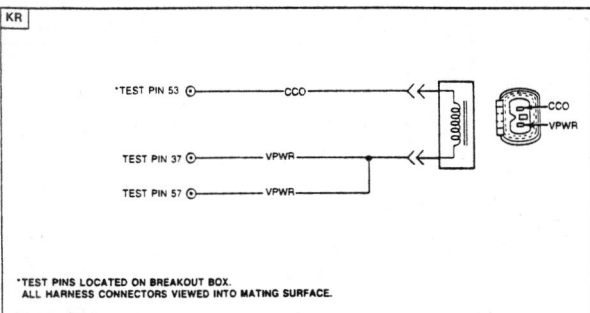

*TEST PINS LOCATED ON BREAKOUT BOX.
ALL HARNESS CONNECTORS VIEWED INTO MATING SURFACE.

STOP-WARNING

You should enter this Pinpoint Test only when a service code 88 or 89 is received in Quick Test Step 3.0.

This Pinpoint Test is intended to diagnose only the following:
• Harness Circuits: CCO and V PWR.
• CCO Solenoid.
• Processor Assembly.

TEST STEP	RESULT ▶	ACTION TO TAKE
CODE 89 PRESENT		
KR1 MEASURE CCO SOLENOID RESISTANCE		
• Key Off, wait 10 seconds. • DVOM on 200 ohm scale. • Disconnect CCO solenoid connector and measure solenoid resistance. • Is resistance reading between 26 and 40 ohms?	Yes ▶ No ▶	CONNECT CCO solenoid. GO to KR2. REPLACE CCO solenoid. RERUN Quick Test.

Converter Clutch Override (CCO) and Shift Solenoid 3/4-4/3 (SS 3/4-4/3)	Pinpoint Test	KS

KS

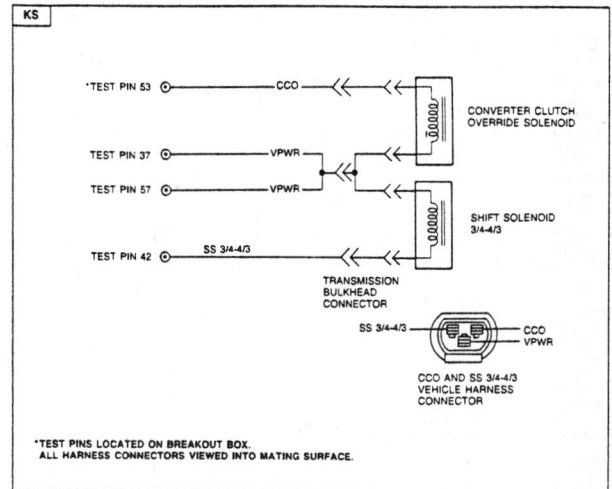

*TEST PINS LOCATED ON BREAKOUT BOX.
ALL HARNESS CONNECTORS VIEWED INTO MATING SURFACE.

STOP-WARNING

You should enter this Pinpoint Test only when a service code 85 or 88 are received in Quick Test Step 3.0.

This Pinpoint Test is intended to diagnose only the following:
• Harness Circuits: CCO SS 3/4-4/3 and V PWR.
• CCO Solenoid.
• Shift Solenoid 3/4-4/3.
• Processor Assembly.

Converter Clutch Override (CCO) and Shift Solenoid 3/4-4/3 (SS 3/4-4/3)	Pinpoint Test	KS

TEST STEP	RESULT ▶	ACTION TO TAKE
CODE 88 PRESENT		
KS1 MEASURE CCO SOLENOID RESISTANCE		
• Key Off, wait 10 seconds.	Yes ▶	CONNECT CCO solenoid. GO to KS2.
• DVOM on 200 ohm scale.		
• Disconnect CCO solenoid vehicle harness connector and measure solenoid resistance at transmission bulkhead connector.	No ▶	GO to Car Shop Manual Volume D, Section 17-08, A4LD transmission diagnosis.
• Is resistance between 26 and 40 ohms.		
SS 3/4-4/3 — CCO / VPWR CCO AND SS 3/4-4/3 TRANSMISSION BULKHEAD CONNECTOR		
KS2 CHECK VOLTAGE OF VPWR CIRCUIT		
• Key On Engine Off.	Yes ▶	GO to KS3.
• DVOM on 20V scale.		
• Measure voltage at the CCO solenoid vehicle harness connector between VPWR circuit and battery ground.	No ▶	SERVICE harness open circuit. RERUN Quick Test.
• Is voltage greater than 10.5V?		
KS3 CHECK CONTINUITY OF CCO CIRCUIT		
• Key Off, wait 10 seconds.	Yes ▶	GO to KS4.
• Disconnect processor 60 Pin connector and inspect for damaged pins, corrosion, loose wires. Service as necessary.	No ▶	SERVICE harness open circuit. RERUN Quick Test.
• Connect Breakout box to harness. Leave processor disconnected.		
• CCO solenoid vehicle harness connector disconnected at transmission bulkhead connector.	• Measure resistance between test Pin 53 and the Breakout box and CCO circuit at the solenoid vehicle harness connector.	
• DVOM on 200 ohm scale.	• Is resistance less than 5 ohms?	

Converter Clutch Override (CCO) and Shift Solenoid 3/4-4/3 (SS 3/4-4/3)	Pinpoint Test	KS

TEST STEP	RESULT ▶	ACTION TO TAKE
KS4 CHECK FOR SHORT TO GROUND		
• Key Off, wait 10 seconds.	Yes ▶	GO to KS5.
• Leave Breakout box installed and processor disconnected.	No ▶	SERVICE short to ground. RERUN Quick Test.
• CCO solenoid vehicle harness connector disconnected at transmission bulkhead connector.		
• DVOM on 200,000 ohm scale.		
• Measure resistance between test Pin 53 and test Pins 40, 46 and 60 at Breakout box.		
• Is resistance greater than 100,000 ohms?		
KS5 CHECK FOR SHORT TO POWER		
• Key Off, wait 10 seconds.	Yes ▶	REPLACE processor. RERUN Quick Test.
• DVOM on 200,000 ohm scale.		
• Leave Breakout box installed and processor disconnected.	No ▶	SERVICE short to power. RERUN Quick Test. If code is still present, REPLACE processor.
• CCO solenoid vehicle harness connector disconnected at transmission bulkhead connector.		
• Measure resistance between test Pin 53 and test Pins 37 and 57 at Breakout box.		
• Are all resistances greater than 10,000 ohms?		
CODE 85 PRESENT		
KS10 MEASURE SS 3/4-4/3 RESISTANCE		
• Key Off, wait 10 seconds.	Yes ▶	CONNECT SS 3/4-4/3. GO to KS11.
• DVOM on 200 ohm scale.		
• Disconnect SS 3/4-4/3 vehicle harness connector and measure solenoid resistance at transmission bulkhead connector.	No ▶	GO to Car Shop Manual Volume D, Section 17-08, A4LD transmission diagnosis.
• Is resistance between 26 and 40 ohms?		
CCO AND SS 3/4-4/3 TRANSMISSION BULKHEAD CONNECTOR SS 3/4-4/3 — CCO / VPWR		

Converter Clutch Override (CCO) and Shift Solenoid 3/4-4/3 (SS 3/4-4/3)	Pinpoint Test	KS

TEST STEP	RESULT ▶	ACTION TO TAKE
KS11 CHECK VOLTAGE OF VPWR CIRCUIT		
• Key On Engine Off.	Yes ▶	GO to KS12.
• DVOM on 20V scale.		
• Measure voltage at the SS 3/4-4/3 vehicle harness connector between VPWR circuit and battery ground.	No ▶	SERVICE harness open circuit. RERUN Quick Test.
• Is voltage greater than 10.5V?		
KS12 CHECK CONTINUITY OF SS 3/4-4/3 CIRCUIT		
• Key Off, wait 10 seconds.	Yes ▶	GO to KS13.
• Disconnect processor 60 Pin connector and inspect for damaged pins, corrosion, loose wires. Service as necessary.	No ▶	SERVICE harness open circuit. RERUN Quick Test.
• Connect Breakout box to harness. Leave processor disconnected.		
• SS 3/4-4/3 vehicle harness connector disconnected at transmission bulkhead connector.		
• DVOM on 200 ohm scale.		
• Measure resistance between test Pin 53 at the Breakout box and SS 3/4-4/3 circuit at the solenoid vehicle harness connector.		
• Is resistance less than 5 ohms?		
KS13 CHECK FOR SHORT TO GROUND		
• Key Off, wait 10 seconds.	Yes ▶	GO to KS14.
• Leave Breakout box installed and processor disconnected.	No ▶	SERVICE short to ground. RERUN Quick Test.
• SS 3/4-4/3 vehicle harness connector disconnected at transmission bulkhead connector.		
• DVOM on 200,000 ohm scale.		
• Measure resistance between test Pin 53 and test Pins 40, 46 and 60 at Breakout box.		
• Is resistance greater than 100,000 ohms?		

Converter Clutch Override (CCO) and Shift Solenoid 3/4-4/3 (SS 3/4-4/3)	Pinpoint Test	KS

TEST STEP	RESULT ▶	ACTION TO TAKE
KS14 CHECK FOR SHORT TO POWER		
• Key Off, wait 10 seconds.	Yes ▶	REPLACE processor. RERUN Quick Test.
• DVOM on 200,000 ohm scale.		
• Leave Breakout box installed and processor disconnected.	No ▶	SERVICE short to power. RERUN Quick Test. If code is still present, REPLACE processor.
• SS 3/4-4/3 vehicle harness connector disconnected at transmission bulkhead connector.		
• Measure resistance between Pin 53 and test Pins 37 and 57 at Breakout box.		
• Are all resistances greater than 10,000 ohms?		

Dynamic Response Test	Pinpoint Test	M

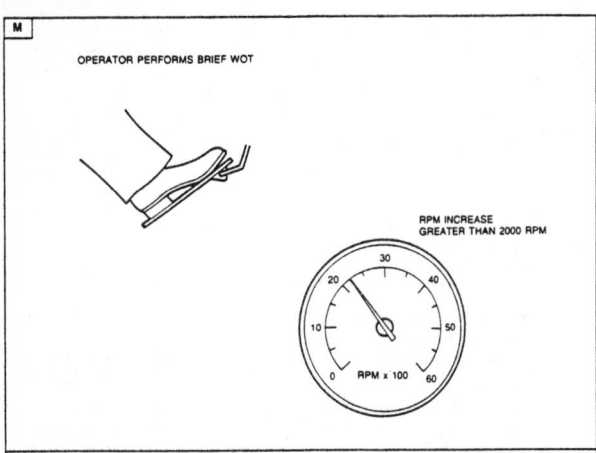

OPERATOR PERFORMS BRIEF WOT

RPM INCREASE GREATER THAN 2000 RPM

RPM x 100

STOP-WARNING

You should enter this Pinpoint Test only when a service code 77 is received in Quick Test Step 5.0.

To prevent the replacement of good components, be aware that the following non-EEC areas may be at fault:

- Operator did not perform a brief WOT after dynamic response code.
- Mechanical engine problems; engine did not achieve greater than 2000 rpm.

This Pinpoint Test is intended to diagnose only the following:

- Throttle movement (greater than 3/4 throttle).
- Vane Air Flow (greater than 50% open).
- RPM increase (greater than 2000 rpm).

Dynamic Response Test	Pinpoint Test	M

TEST STEP	RESULT	▶	ACTION TO TAKE
M1 CODE 77: SYSTEM FAILED TO RECOGNIZE BRIEF WOT			
NOTE: A brief snap of the throttle may not be sufficient to pass this test. Be sure to go to WOT and return.			
(If engine is a 5.0L SEFI, Go to Pinpoint Test HC.)			
• Repeat Engine Running Test of Quick Test. Be sure operator is familiar with the engine running format which proceeds as follows:	Yes	▶	REPLACE processor. RERUN Quick Test.
— With Self-Test activated restart the engine. — ID Code 2 (0) start of test. — Dynamic response Code 1 (0) perform brief WOT. — Testing over. — Service code output begins.	No	▶	Dynamic Response Test passed. SERVICE any other service code(s) received as necessary.
• Is code 77 still present?			

"CHECK ENGINE" Light (Malfunction Indicator Light)	Pinpoint Test	ML

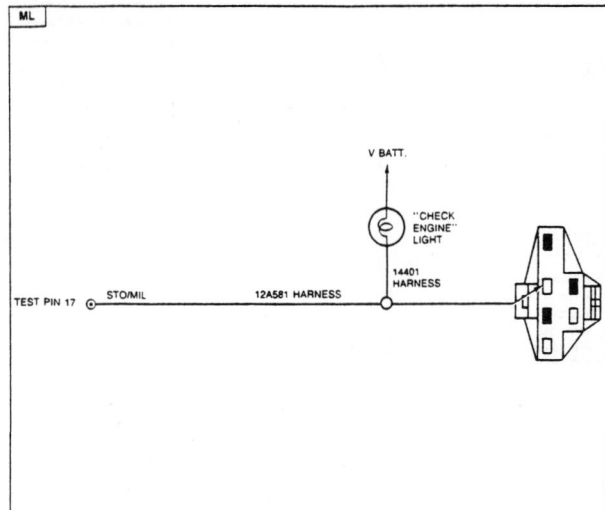

V BATT.

"CHECK ENGINE" LIGHT

TEST PIN 17   STO/MIL   12A581 HARNESS   14401 HARNESS

STOP-WARNING

You should enter this Pinpoint Test only from Diagnostic by Symptom.

To prevent the replacement of good components, be aware that the following non-EEC areas may be at fault:

- Fuse, bulb or socket.

This Pinpoint Test is intended to diagnose only the following:

- STO/MIL circuit.
- Processor assembly.

"CHECK ENGINE" Light (Malfunction Indicator Light)	Pinpoint Test	ML

TEST STEP	RESULT	▶	ACTION TO TAKE
ML1 CHECK FOR SHORT TO GROUND			
NOTE: If vehicle will not start go to Pinpoint Test Step A1.	Yes	▶	SERVICE harness for short to ground (from Pin 17 to Self-Test connector or from Pin 17 to the "CHECK ENGINE" light).
• If any Key On Engine Off service codes are present, repair before proceeding. If no codes are outputted, continue with this Test Step.			
• Key Off.	No	▶	REPLACE processor.
• Disconnect processor.			
• Inspect 60 Pin connector for damaged pins/ corrosion and service as necessary.			
• Install Breakout box. Leave processor disconnected.			
• DVOM on 200 ohm scale.			
• Connect DVOM between test Pin 17 and test Pin 40.			
• Is resistance less than 5 ohms?			
ML5 CONTINUITY CHECK			
NOTE: If vehicle will not start go to Pinpoint Test Step A1.	Yes	▶	GO to Pinpoint Test Step ML6 .
• Key Off.			
• Disconnect processor.	No	▶	SERVICE OPEN in harness.
• Inspect 60 Pin connector for damaged pins/ corrosion and service as necessary.			
• Install Breakout box. Leave processor disconnected.			
• DVOM on 200 ohm scale.			
• Measure resistance between Pin 17 and STO at the Self-Test connector.			
• Measure resistance between Pin 17 and the "CHECK ENGINE" light.			
• Are the resistances less than 5 ohms?			

"CHECK ENGINE" Light (Malfunction Indicator Light)	Pinpoint Test	ML

TEST STEP	RESULT ▶	ACTION TO TAKE
ML6 POWER TO BULB • Check for power to "CHECK ENGINE" light bulb. • Is there power at the light bulb?	Yes No	REPLACE bulb or socket. GO to Pinpoint Test Step ML7. CHECK fuse and input circuit. GO to Pinpoint Test Step ML7.
ML7 CONFIRM CIRCUIT REPAIR • Reconnect processor. • Turn key to run. • Is "CHECK ENGINE" light ON? NOTE: Refer to the appendix for a detailed description of HOW the "CHECK ENGINE" light (malfunction indicator light) operates.	Yes No	System OK. REPLACE processor.

Ignition Diagnostic Monitor (IDM)	Pinpoint Test	N

TEST STEP	RESULT ▶	ACTION TO TAKE
N1 CHECK CONTINUITY OF IDM CIRCUIT • Key Off, wait 10 seconds. • Disconnect E-core ignition connector from coil. • Disconnect processor and inspect both 60 Pin connectors for damaged pins, corrosion, loose wires. Service as necessary. • Connect Breakout box to harness. Leave processor disconnected. • DVOM on 200,000 ohm scale. • Measure resistance between test Pin 4 at the Breakout box and ignition coil harness connector negative terminal. • Is resistance between 20,000 and 24,000 ohms?	Yes No	GO to N2. SERVICE open IDM circuit. RERUN Quick Test. RECONNECT E-core ignition connector to coil.
N2 CHECK FOR SHORT TO GROUND • Key Off, wait 10 seconds. • Leave Breakout box installed and processor disconnected. • DVOM on 200,000 ohm scale. • Measure resistance between test Pin 4 and test Pins 40, 46 and 60 at the Breakout box. • Are all resistances above 10,000 ohms?	Yes No	RECONNECT E-core ignition connector and processor. GO to N3. SERVICE short to ground in IDM circuit. RECONNECT E-core ignition connector to coil. RERUN Quick Test.
N3 CHECK TFI MODULE • Key Off, wait 10 seconds. • Deactivate Self-Test. • Connect VOM or STAR per Quick Test Step 2.0. • Enter Engine Running Continuous Monitor Test (as instructed in Quick Test Step 6.0B). • Observe VOM or STAR LED for indication of a fault while performing the following: • Lightly tap on TFI module (simulate road shock). • Wiggle TFI connector. • Is a fault indicated?	Yes No	DISCONNECT and INSPECT connectors. If connector and terminals are good, GO to Section 15, TFI Ignition Diagnostics. GO to N4.

Ignition Diagnostic Monitor (IDM)	Pinpoint Test	N

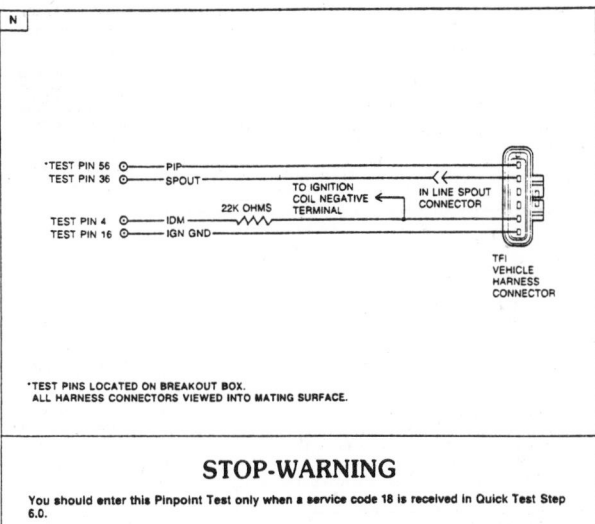

*TEST PIN 56 — PIP
TEST PIN 36 — SPOUT
22K OHMS
TEST PIN 4 — IDM
TEST PIN 16 — IGN GND
TO IGNITION COIL NEGATIVE TERMINAL
IN LINE SPOUT CONNECTOR
TFI VEHICLE HARNESS CONNECTOR

*TEST PINS LOCATED ON BREAKOUT BOX.
ALL HARNESS CONNECTORS VIEWED INTO MATING SURFACE.

STOP-WARNING

You should enter this Pinpoint Test only when a service code 18 is received in Quick Test Step 6.0.

To prevent the replacement of good components, be aware that the following non-EEC areas may be at fault:
• Ignition module.
• Ignition coil.
• Spark plugs and high tension cables.
• Distributor and PIP sensor.

This Pinpoint Test is intended to diagnose only the following:
• Harness circuits: ignition ground, spout, PIP, IDM.

Ignition Diagnostic Monitor (IDM)	Pinpoint Test	N

TEST STEP	RESULT ▶	ACTION TO TAKE
N4 CHECK EEC-IV HARNESS • While still in continuous monitor test from Step N3, observe VOM or STAR LED for a fault indication while performing the following: • While looking for faults listed in the table below, grasp the harness close to the TFI connector. Wiggle, shake or bend a small section of the EEC-IV system harness while working your way to the dash panel. Also wiggle, shake or bend the EEC-IV harness from the dash panel to the processor. Do this test on the circuits listed one at a time if needed to locate a faulty circuit. FAULT BREAKOUT BOX NO. PIP shorted to ground or open Test Pin 56 Spout shorted to ground Test Pin 36 Ign. ground open Test Pin 16 IDM open or shorted to ground, power Test Pin 4 • Is a fault indicated?	Yes No	ISOLATE fault and make necessary repairs. RERUN Quick Test. GO to N5.
N5 CHECK PROCESSOR AND HARNESS CONNECTORS • Key Off, wait 10 seconds. • Disconnect processor 60 Pin connector and inspect for damaged pins, corrosion, loose wires. • Are connectors and terminals OK?	Yes No	REPLACE processor. Start engine and run for about one minute. RERUN Key On Engine Off Self Test observing continuous codes. SERVICE as necessary. RECONNECT processor. RERUN Quick Test.

Spark Timing Check	Pinpoint Test	P

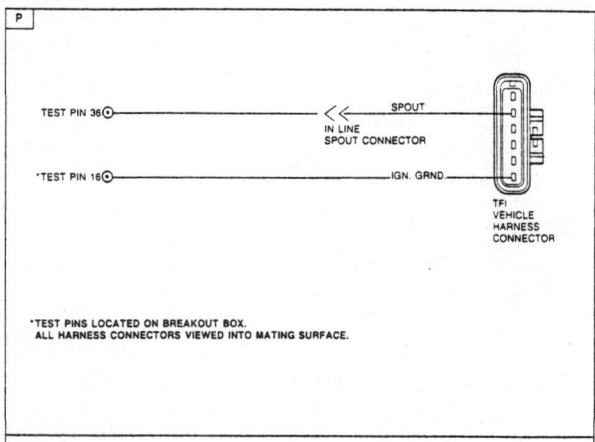

P

TEST PIN 36 ⊙───────────<< ─── SPOUT
IN LINE
SPOUT CONNECTOR

*TEST PIN 16 ⊙───────────── IGN. GRND

TFI VEHICLE HARNESS CONNECTOR

*TEST PINS LOCATED ON BREAKOUT BOX.
ALL HARNESS CONNECTORS VIEWED INTO MATING SURFACE.

STOP-WARNING

You should enter this Pinpoint Test only when directed here from Quick Test Step 4.0 or when a Service Code 18 is received in Quick Test Step 5.0.

To prevent the replacement of good components, be aware that the following non-EEC areas may be at fault:

• Base Engine.
• PIP Sensor.
• TFI Module.

This Pinpoint Test is intended to diagnose only the following:

• Harness Spout Circuit.
• Base Timing.
• Processor Assembly.

Spark Timing Check	Pinpoint Test	P

TEST STEP	RESULT	▶	ACTION TO TAKE
P1 CHECK SPARK TIMING			
• If Quick Test cannot be run, Go to Q1, otherwise continue with Test Step. NOTE: Self-Test locks the timing at 20 degrees plus base during code output and for two minutes after the last service code is outputed. Timing check must be made during this time period. Self-Test timing is base +20 degrees (±3 degrees) BTDC. (See VECI decal for base value.) • Check timing. Record value. • Is timing equal to base plus 20 degrees (±3 degrees)?	Yes	▶	GO to Quick Test Step 5.0 .
	No	▶	GO to P2 .
P2 CHECK SPARK OUTPUT (SPOUT) CIRCUIT TO THE TFI MODULE			
• Locate spout connector and open this connection. • Start engine. • Check base timing. • Is base timing within ±3 degrees of value on VECI decal?	Yes	▶	RECONNECT spout connection. GO to P3 .
	No	▶	Adjust base timing if necessary. REFER to Section 15 for engine timing instructions. After timing is reset, RECONNECT spout and PERFORM Quick Test Step 4.0 .
P3 CHECK FOR POWER TO PROCESSOR			
• Key Off, wait 10 seconds. • Disconnect processor 60 Pin connector and inspect for damaged pins, corrosion, loose wires. Service as necessary. • Install Breakout Box. • Key on, engine off. • DVOM on 20V scale. • Measure voltage between test Pin 37 and test Pin 40 and between test Pin 57 and test Pin 60 at the Breakout Box. • Is voltage less than 10.5 volts?	Yes	▶	GO to Pinpoint Test Step B1 except 2.3L EFI TC, 2.5L HSC CFI and 3.0L EFI passenger car: GO to Pinpoint Test Step X1 .
	No	▶	GO to P4 .

Spark Timing Check	Pinpoint Test	P

TEST STEP	RESULT	▶	ACTION TO TAKE
P4 CHECK HARNESS FOR CONTINUITY			
• Key Off, wait 10 seconds. • DVOM on 200 ohm scale. • Measure resistance between test Pin 36 at the Breakout box and the spout pin at the TFI vehicle harness connector. • Is resistance less than 5 ohms?	Yes	▶	GO to P5 .
	No	▶	SERVICE open circuit CHECK timing per P1 .

TEST PIN 36 ⊙───────<< ─── SPOUT
IN LINE
SPOUT CONNECTOR

TEST PIN 16 ⊙───────── IGN GND

TFI VEHICLE HARNESS CONNECTOR

A9990-A

TEST STEP	RESULT	▶	ACTION TO TAKE
P5 HARNESS CHECK — IGNITION GROUND			
• Breakout box installed. • Key Off. • DVOM on 200 ohm scale • Measure resistance between test Pin 16 at the Breakout box and the ignition ground at the TFI vehicle harness connector. • Is resistance less than 5 ohms?	Yes	▶	REPLACE processor. GO to Pinpoint Test Step A7 .
	No	▶	SERVICE harness as necessary. RERUN Quick Test.

No Codes/Codes Not Listed	Pinpoint Test	Q

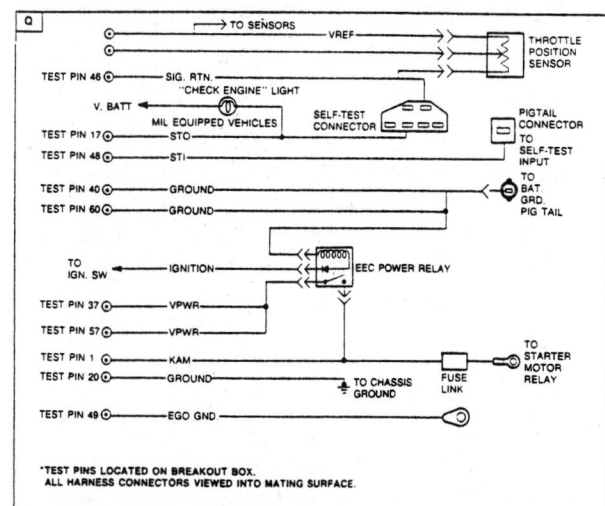

Q

→ TO SENSORS ── VREF ──── THROTTLE POSITION SENSOR

TEST PIN 46 ⊙── SIG. RTN. ──
"CHECK ENGINE" LIGHT
V. BATT
MIL EQUIPPED VEHICLES   SELF-TEST CONNECTOR

PIGTAIL CONNECTOR TO SELF-TEST INPUT

TEST PIN 17 ⊙── STO ──
TEST PIN 48 ⊙── STI ──

TO BAT. GRD. PIG TAIL

TEST PIN 40 ⊙── GROUND ──
TEST PIN 60 ⊙── GROUND ──

TO IGN. SW ←── IGNITION ── EEC POWER RELAY

TEST PIN 37 ⊙── VPWR ──
TEST PIN 57 ⊙── VPWR ──

TO STARTER MOTOR RELAY

TEST PIN 1 ⊙── KAM ──
TEST PIN 20 ⊙── GROUND ── TO CHASSIS GROUND   FUSE LINK

TEST PIN 49 ⊙── EGO GND ──

*TEST PINS LOCATED ON BREAKOUT BOX.
ALL HARNESS CONNECTORS VIEWED INTO MATING SURFACE.

STOP-WARNING

You should enter this Pinpoint Test only when directed here from Quick Test Step 3.0, 5.0 or 6.0 or when directed here from Diagnostics by Symptom in the Engine Supplement Section or from a Pinpoint Test Step.

This Pinpoint Test is intended to diagnose only the following:

• Processor.
• Harness Circuits: Signal Return, STO, STI, Ground, VPWR, KAM, VREF, Ignition, NDS, EEC Power Relay.

No Codes/Codes Not Listed	Pinpoint Test	Q

TEST STEP	RESULT	▶	ACTION TO TAKE
Q1 CHECK FOR VREF AT TP SENSOR			
Refer to illustration Q. • Key Off, wait 10 seconds. • DVOM on 20V scale. • Disconnect TP sensor. • Key on, engine off. • Measure voltage between VREF at the TP harness connector and signal return in Self-Test connector. • Is voltage between 4.0 and 6.0 volts?	Yes No	▶ ▶	RECONNECT TP Sensor. GO to Q2. GO to Pinpoint Test Step C1.
Q2 SELF-TEST INPUT CONTINUITY CHECK			
Refer to illustration Q. • Key Off, wait 10 seconds. • Disconnect processor 60 Pin connector and inspect for damaged pins, corrosion, loose wires. Service as necessary. • Install Breakout box, leave processor disconnected. • Set DVOM to 200 ohm scale. • Measure resistance between Self-Test input at the Self-Test single pin connector and test Pin 48 at the Breakout box. • Is resistance less than 5 ohms?	Yes No	▶ ▶	GO to Q3. CORRECT open in circuit.
Q1 SELF-TEST OUTPUT CIRCUIT CONTINUITY CHECK			
Refer to illustration Q. • Breakout box installed. • DVOM to 200 ohm scale. • Measure resistance between Self-Test output at the Self-Test connector and test Pin 17 at the Breakout box. • Is resistance less than 5 ohms?	Yes No	▶ ▶	GO to Q4. CORRECT open in circuit.

No Codes/Codes Not Listed	Pinpoint Test	Q

TEST STEP	RESULT	▶	ACTION TO TAKE
Q4 EGO SENSOR GROUND CONTINUITY CHECK			
Refer to illustration Q. • Breakout box installed. • Key Off. • DVOM on 200 ohm scale. • Measure resistance between EGO ground on engine and test Pin 49 at the Breakout box. • Is resistance less than 5 ohms?	Yes No	▶ ▶	GO to Q5. SERVICE EGO sensor ground wire or open circuit bad connection.
Q5 STO SHORT TO GROUND			
• Breakout box installed. • DVOM on 200 ohm scale. • Measure resistance between Self-Test output at Self-Test connector and engine block ground. • Is resistance greater than 5 ohms?	No Yes	▶ ▶	REPAIR STO circuit (or "CHECK ENGINE" light circuit on MIL equipped vehicles) for short to ground. RERUN Quick Test. 3.0L EFI passenger car GO to Q7. All others GO to Q6.
Q6 INTERMITTENT NDS			
• Key Off. • Breakout box installed. • Processor connected. • Connect DVOM between test Pin 30 and test Pin 40 or 60 at the Breakout box. • Key On Engine Running Self-Test. • Is voltage greater than 1V? NOTE: Refer to FA for connector orientation.	Yes No	▶ ▶	SERVICE intermittent open in NDS harness, connector or switch. If OK, GO to Quick Test Step 5.0 for appropriate service codes. GO to Q7.

No Codes/Codes Not Listed	Pinpoint Test	Q

TEST STEP	RESULT	▶	ACTION TO TAKE
Q7 POWER RELAY ALWAYS ON			
• Key Off. • Breakout box installed. • Connect DVOM to test Pin 37 or 57 and to test Pin 40 or 60 at the Breakout box. • Turn key on and off. Wait 10 seconds. • Does voltage change from greater than 10.5V to zero volts?	Yes No	▶ ▶	If vehicle is equipped with MIL (malfunction indicator light displayed as "CHECK ENGINE" light) or SIL (shift indicator light) GO to Q9. If not, REPLACE the processor. RERUN Quick Test. GO to Q8.
Q8 VPWR HARNESS SHORT TO POWER			
• Key Off. • Breakout box installed. • EEC Power Relay or Integrated Relay Controller disconnected. • Connect DVOM to test Pin 37 or 57 and to test Pin 40 or 60 at the Breakout box. • Is voltage greater than 10.5V?	Yes No	▶ ▶	REPAIR VPWR harness short to power. RERUN Quick Test. REPLACE EEC Power Relay or Integrated Relay Controller. RERUN Quick Test.
Q9 MIL AND/OR SIL EQUIPPED VEHICLES			
• Are any of these conditions present? • Shift indicator light: — Always ON		▶	GO to KL1.
— Always OFF		▶	GO to KL1.
• Malfunction indicator light: — Always ON		▶	GO to ML1.
— Always OFF		▶	GO to ML5.
• Shift and malfunction indicator lights functioning normally.		▶	REPLACE the processor. RERUN Quick Test.

Continuous Test Code 15	Pinpoint Test	Q

TEST STEP	RESULT	▶	ACTION TO TAKE
Q10 CONDITIONS FOR CONTINUOUS CODE 15			
• Power interruption to Keep Alive Memory (KAM) Pin 1 may result in a service code being outputted.* • Clear continuous memory codes (use procedure described in Quick Test Step 6). • Repeat Quick Test Step 3.0 through Continuous memory code output. • Code 15 present on retest? *NOTE: Anytime power is interrupted to the processor, for example when installing a Breakout box, a code 15 may be outputted the first time Self-Test is run after restoration of power. Repeat Self-Test to ensure correct diagnosis.	Yes No	▶ ▶	GO to Q11. Test complete.
Q11 INSPECT ENGINE COMPARTMENT WIRING FOR PROPER ROUTING			
• Are any EEC components or EEC wiring close to ignition components or wires (High Electrical Energy Sources)? If EEC wiring close, reroute and rerun Quick Test. • Is code 15 still present?	Yes No	▶ ▶	GO to Q12. Test complete.
Q12 CHECK POWER CIRCUIT TO KEEP ALIVE MEMORY			
• Key Off, wait 10 seconds. • Disconnect processor and inspect both 60 Pin connectors. • Connect Breakout box to harness, leave processor disconnected. • DVOM on 20V scale. • Connect positive test lead to test Pin 1 and negative test lead to test Pin 40 or 60 at the Breakout box. • Key On. • Is voltage reading less than 10.5 volts?	Yes No	▶ ▶	SERVICE open to KAM circuit. RERUN Quick Test. REPLACE processor. RERUN Quick Test.

Output State Check Not Functioning | Pinpoint Test | Q

TEST STEP	RESULT	▶	ACTION TO TAKE
Q40 CHECK FOR CODES 23, 53, 63 OR 68			
• Key Off, wait 10 seconds. • Perform Key On Engine Off Self-Test. • Leave Key On to enter Output State Check. • Key On Engine Off. Are codes 23, 53, 63 or 68 present?	Yes	▶	GO to Quick Test Step 3.0B and SERVICE appropriate code as instructed.
	Code 11	▶	GO to Q41.
	No Codes	▶	GO to Q1.
Q41 CHECK THROTTLE LINKAGE			
• Check throttle and throttle linkages for sticking and binding. • Throttle OK?	Yes	▶	REPLACE TP sensor. RERUN Quick Test.
	No	▶	SERVICE as necessary. RERUN Quick Test.

Processor Power Check | Pinpoint Test | Q

TEST STEP	RESULT	▶	ACTION TO TAKE
Q50 CHECK FOR POWER TO PROCESSOR			
• Key Off, wait 10 seconds. • Disconnect processor 60 Pin connector and inspect for damaged pins, corrosion, loose wires. Service as necessary. • Install Breakout box. • Key On Engine Off. • DVOM on 20V scale. • Measure voltage between test Pin 37 and test Pin 40 at the Breakout box and between test Pin 57 and test Pin 60 at the Breakout box. • Is either voltage reading less than 10.5 volts?	Yes	▶	2.3L EFI TC, 2.5L CFI and 3.0L EFI passenger car GO to Pinpoint Test X1. All others GO to Pinpoint Test B1.
	No	▶	REPLACE processor. RERUN Quick Test.

Re-Initialization Check | Pinpoint Test | Q

TEST STEP	RESULT	▶	ACTION TO TAKE
Q60 CHECK FOR EEC IV WIRING POSITION			
• Key Off. • Check that the EEC IV wiring and components are greater than 2 inches from secondary ignition wires and ignition coil. • Check that the EEC IV wiring and components are greater than 4 inches from distributor, coil tower, starter motor and its wiring. • Are all above conditions intact?	Yes	▶	GO to Q61.
	No	▶	SERVICE as necessary. RERUN Quick Test.
Q61 HARNESS CHECK — CASE GROUND			
• Key Off. • Install Breakout box. Leave processor disconnected. • Disconnect processor 60 pin connector. Inspect for damaged pins, corrosion, loose wires, etc. Service as necessary. • DVOM on 200 ohm scale. • Measure resistance between test Pin 20 at the Breakout box and chassis ground. • Is the resistance less than 5 ohms?	Yes	▶	GO to Q62.
	No	▶	SERVICE harness as necessary. RERUN Quick Test.
Q62 DISCONNECT HARNESS — CASE GROUND CHECK			
• Key Off. • Reconnect processor to Breakout box, but disconnect harness from Breakout box. • DVOM on 200 ohm scale. • Measure resistance between test Pin 20 at the Breakout box and metal case of processor. • Is the resistance less than 5 ohms?	Yes	▶	GO to Pinpoint Test Step B10.
	No	▶	REPLACE Processor. RERUN Quick Test.

System Check | Pinpoint Test | S

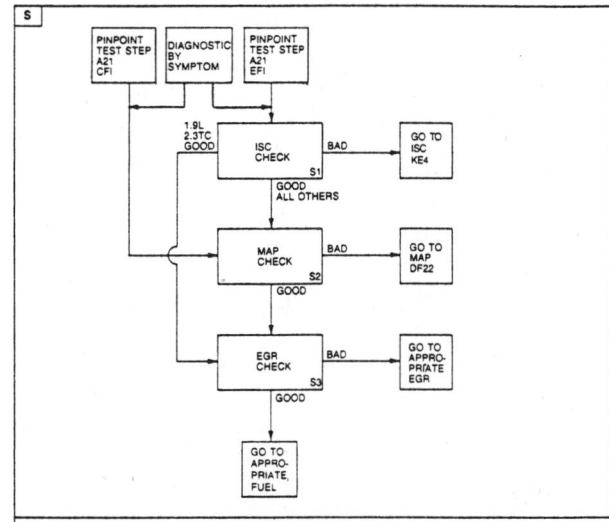

STOP-WARNING

You should enter this Pinpoint Test only after a code 11 is received in Quick Test Step 3.0, and you have been directed here from EEC-IV No-Start Pinpoint Test Step A21 or Diagnostics by symptom.

This Pinpoint Test is intended only as a Quick Check for the basic functioning of the following:

• ISC Bypass Air System
• MAP System
• EGR System

System Check	Pinpoint Test	S

TEST STEP	RESULT ▶	ACTION TO TAKE
S1 ISC-BPA CHECK		
• If you are here for any reason other than stalls or a no start, go to S2. Except 1.9L EFI and 2.3L EFI TC, go to S3. • Attempt to start engine at part throttle. • Will engine run at part throttle?	Yes, but runs rough ▶ Yes, and runs smooth ▶ No ▶	GO to S2 . GO to KE4 . 1.9 EFI and 2.3L EFI TC GO to S3 . All others GO to S2 .
S2 MAP CHECK		

• Key Off.
 • Disconnect the MAP sensor from the vehicle harness.
 • Connect the MAP tester between the vehicle harness and the MAP sensor.
 • Plug MAP tester banana plugs into DVOM.
 • Set DVOM to 20V scale.
 • Key On.
 • Observe DVOM.
 	
 • Approximate Altitude (Ft.) Voltage Output (+/−.04V)
    0   1.59
  1000   1.56
  2000   1.53
  3000   1.50
  4000   1.47
  5000   1.44
  6000   1.41
  7000   1.39
 • If MAP sensor is out of limits (voltage output for altitude) GO to DF21.
 • Crank engine.
 • While cranking, does DVOM reading decrease from the appropriate reading for your altitude listed above?
	Yes ▶
	
	 No ▶
		3.0L EFI Truck, GO to Pinpoint Test Step HG1 .
		
		 all others, GO to S3 .
		
		 GO to DF22 .

System Check	Pinpoint Test	S

TEST STEP	RESULT ▶	ACTION TO TAKE
S3 EGR CHECK		
NOTE: This test step will attempt to determine if the EGR system is the cause of the current symptom and/or no start. • Disconnect and plug vacuum line at EGR valve. • Inspect EGR valve to ensure valve is closed. • Start or attempt to start engine. • Is symptom eliminated or is no start resolved?	Yes ▶ No ▶	For 1.9L EFI & 2.3L EFI TC, GO to KA1 . For 3.8L CFI, 2.3L EFI Car and Truck, GO to DD11 . For 2.3L HSC CFI, 2.5L HSC CFI, 4.9L EFI, 5.0L EFI, 7.5L EFI Truck and 5.0L SEFI, GO to DN60 . For 1.9L CFI, 3.0L EFI Passenger Car, and 2.9L EFI Truck. GO to Section 6, EGR Valve Diagnostics. For 1.9L EFI and 2.3L EFI TC GO to HA1 . For 1.9L CFI, 2.3L HSC CFI and 2.5L HSC CFI, GO to HF1 . For 2.9L EFI, 3.0L EFI, and 4.9L EFI, GO to HG1 . For 3.8L CFI, GO to HD1 . For 5.0L SEFI, GO to HC1 . For 2.3L EFI Car and Truck, GO to HE1 . For 5.0L EFI, 7.5L EFI Truck, GO to HH1 .

CADILLAC DIGITAL ELECTRONIC FUEL INJECTION

All Models Except 1986–88 Eldorado and Seville

GENERAL INFORMATION

The Digital Fuel Injection (DFI) system, is a speed density fuel system that accurately controls the air/fuel mixture into the engine in order to achieve desired performance and emission goals. The manifold absolute pressure sensor (MAP) and the manifold air temperature (MAT), and the barometric pressure sensor (BARO) are used to determine the density (amount) of air entering the engine.

The HEI distributor provides the engine with speed (rpm) information. All of this information is then fed to the Electronic Control Module (ECM) and the ECM performs a high speed digital computations to determine the proper amount of fuel necessary to achieve the desired air/fuel mixture.

Once the ECM has calculated how much fuel to deliver, it signals the fuel injectors to meter the fuel into the throttle body. When the combustion process has been completed, some Hydro Carbons (HC), Carbon Monoxide (CO) and Nitrous Oxides (NOx) result, therefore, each DFI engine has an emission system to reduce the amount of these gases into the exhaust stream.

The dual be catalytic converter coverts these gases into a more inert gases, however, the conversion process is most efficient (lower emission levels) at an air fuel/mixture of 14.7:1.

Once the engine is warmed up, the ECM uses the input from the oxygen sensor to more precisely control the air/fuel mixture to 14.7:1. This correction process is known a s closed loop operation. Because a vehicle is driven under a wide range of operating conditions, the ECM must provide the correct quantity of fuel under all operating conditions.

Therefore, additional sensors and switches are necessary to determine what operating conditions exist so that the ECM can provide an acceptable level of engine control and driveability under all operating conditions. So the closed loop DFI operation provides the acceptable level of driveability and fuel economy while improving emission levels.

The following subsystems combine to form the DFI closed loop system
  a. Fuel Delivery.
  b. Air Induction.
  c. Data Sensors.
  d. Electronic Control Module.
  e. Body Control Module.
  f. Electric Spark Timing.
  g. Idle Speed Control.
  h. Emission Controls.
  i. Closed Loop Fuel Control.
  j. System Diagnosis.
  k. Cruise Control.
  l. Torque Converter Clutch.

The 1985 and later models are also equipped with a Body Control Module (BCM) that is used to control various vehicle body functions based upon data sensors and switch inputs. The ECM and BCM exchange information to maintain efficient operation of all vehicle functions. This transfer of information gives the BCM control over the ECM's self-diagnostic capabilities as well as its own.

Both the ECM and the BCM have the capability to diagnose faults with the various inputs and systems they control. When the ECM recognizes a problem, it lights a "Service Soon" telltale lamp on the instrument panel to alert the driver that a malfunction has occurred.

The digital electronic fuel injection consists of a pair of electronically actuated fuel metering valves, which, when actu-

ated, spray a calculated quantity of fuel into the engine intake manifold. These valves or injectors are mounted on the throttle body above the throttle blades with the metering tip pointed into the throttle throats. The injectors are normally actuated alternately.

Gasoline is supplied to the inlet of the injectors through the fuel lines and is maintained at a constant pressure across the injector inlets. When the solenoid-operated valves are energized, the injector ball valve moves to the full open position. Since the pressure differential across the valve is constant, the fuel quantity is changed by varying the time that the injector is held open.

The amount of air entering the engine is measured by monitoring the intake manifold absolute pressure (MAP), the intake manifold air temperature (MAT) and the engine speed (in rpm). This information allows the computer to compute the flow rate of air being inducted into the engine and, consequently, the flow rate of fuel required to achieve the desired air/fuel mixture for the particular engine operating condition.

FUEL SUPPLY SYSTEM

The fuel supply system components provide fuel at the correct pressure for metering into the throttle bores by the injectors. The pressure regulator controls fuel pressure to a nominal 10.5 psi across the injectors. The fuel supply system is made up a fuel tank mounted electric pump, a full-flow fuel filter mounted on the vehicle frame, a fuel pressure regulator integral with the throttle body, fuel supply and fuel return lines and two fuel injectors. The timing and amount of fuel supplied is controlled by the computer.

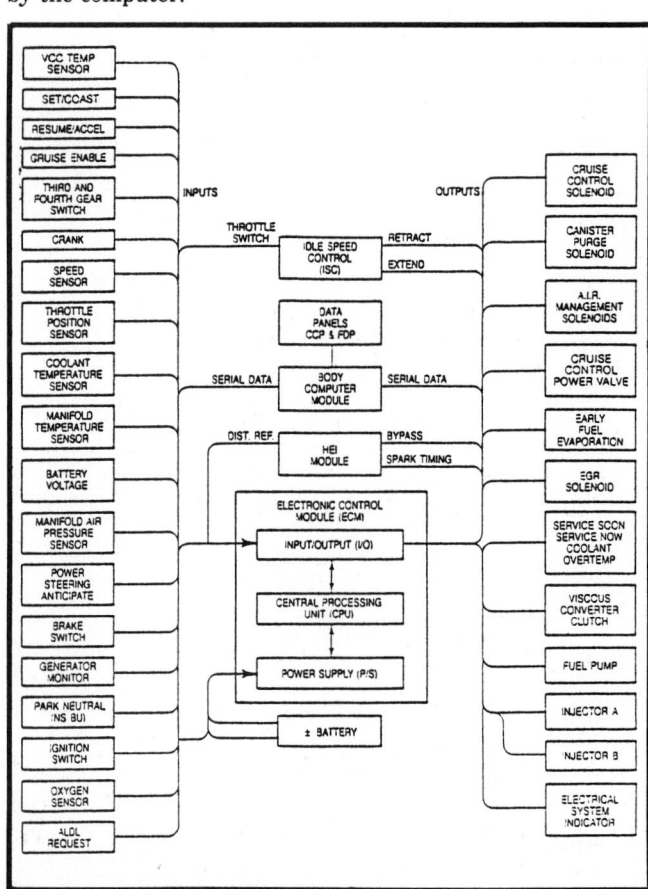

ECM operating conditions sensed and systems controlled—1984 DFI system

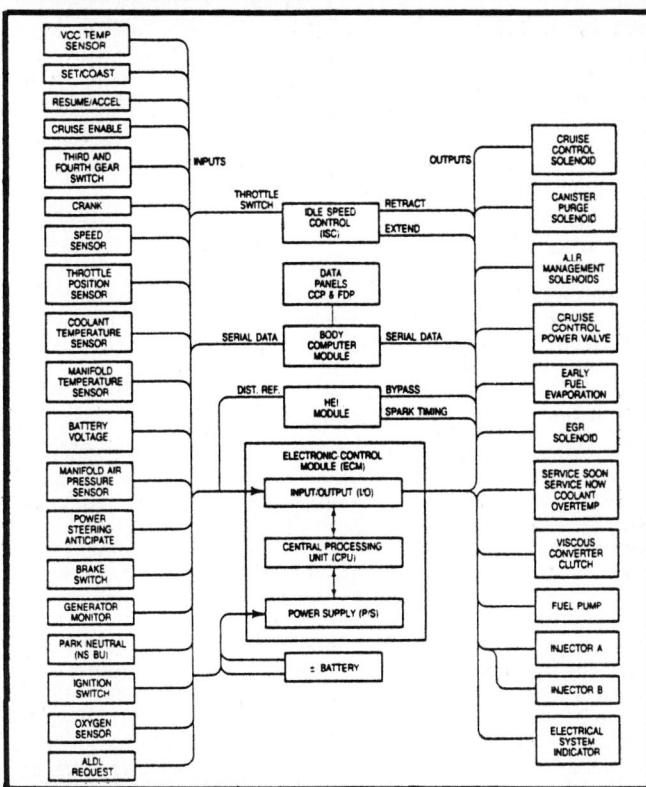

ECM operating conditions sensed and systems controlled – 1985–86 DFI system

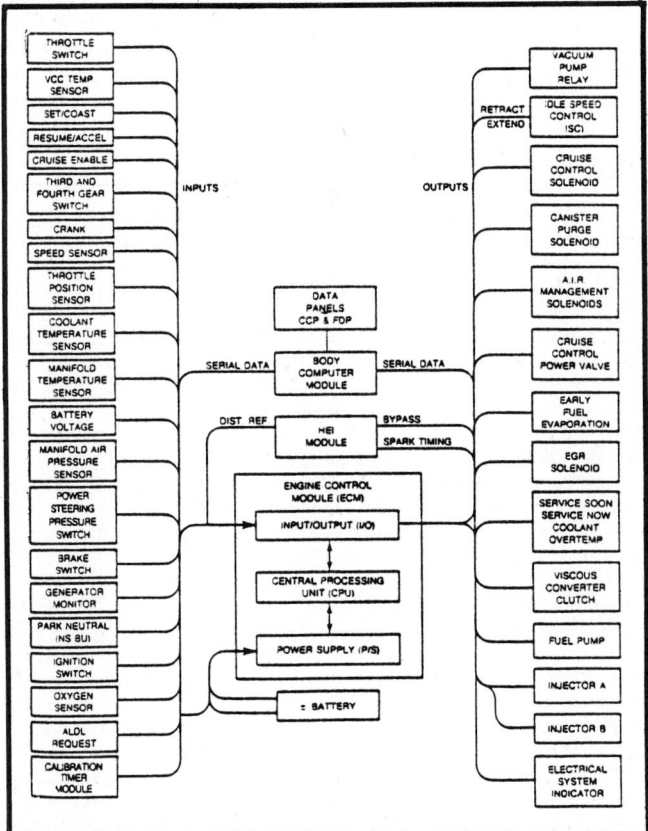

ECM operating conditions sensed and systems controlled – 1987–88 DFI system

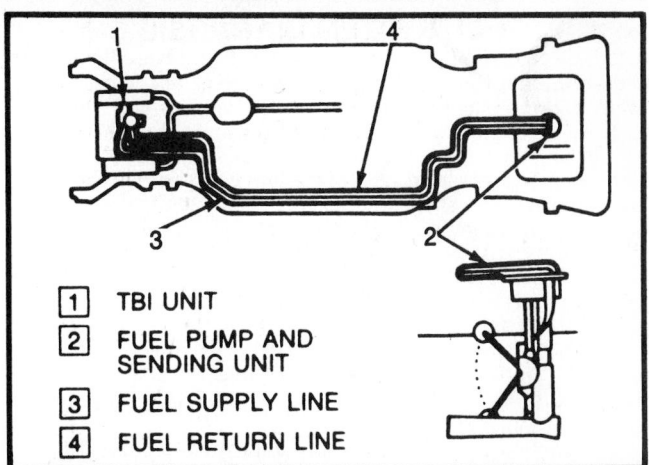

1	TBI UNIT
2	FUEL PUMP AND SENDING UNIT
3	FUEL SUPPLY LINE
4	FUEL RETURN LINE

DFI fuel supply system schematic

An electric motor-driven twin turbine-type pump is integral with the fuel tank float unit. It provides fuel at a positive pressure to the throttle body and fuel pressure regulator. The pump is specific for DEFI application and is not repairable. However, the pump may be serviced separately from the fuel gauge unit.

Fuel pump operation is controlled by the fuel pump relay, located in the relay center. Operation of the relay is controlled by a signal from the computer. The fuel pump circuit is protected by a 10 amp fuse, located in the mini-fuse block. The computer turns the pump on with the ignition "ON" or "START". However, if the engine is not cranked within one second after the ignition is turned on, the computer signal is removed and the pump turns off.

Fuel is pumped from the fuel tank through the supply line and the filter to the throttle body and pressure regulator. The injectors supply fuel to the engine in precisely timed bursts as a result of electrical signals from the computer. Excess fuel is returned to the fuel tank through the fuel return line.

The fuel tank incorporates a reservoir directly below the sending unit-in-tank pump assembly. The "bathtub" shaped reservoir is used to ensure a constant supply of fuel for the in-tank pump even at low fuel level and severe maneuvering conditions.

Fuel Pump Relay

When the key is first turned on (key in the "Run" position with the engine off), the ECM will turn the fuel pump relay on for two seconds. This builds up the fuel pressure for cranking. If the engine is not started within two seconds, the ECM will shut off the fuel pump and wait until the engine starts. As soon as the engine is cranked, the ECM will turn the relay on a run the fuel pump.

Oil Pressure Switch

As a backup system to the fuel pump relay, the fuel pump can also be turned on by the oil presure switch. The oil pressure switch has two circuits internally. One operates the oil pressure indicator lamp while the other is a normally closed open switch which closes when the oil pressure reaches about 4 psi. If the fuel pump relay fails, the oil pressure switch contacts will close and run the fuel pump.

An inoperative fuel pump relay can result in long cranking times, particularly if the engine is cold. The fuel pump relay inoperative will result in a code E20. The oil pressure switch acts as a backup to the relay to turn on the fuel pump as soon as the oil pressure reaches 4 psi.

An inoperative fuel pump would cause a no start condition. A fuel pump which does not provide enough pressure can result in poor performance.

FUEL SYSTEM DIAGNOSIS

1. Low or no fuel pressure diagnosis should begin by trying to determine if the fuel pump is operating or not. This is most easily accomplished by turning the ignition on and listening for the one second "run" of the fuel pump and the associated relay clicks. Since this may not be possible in some shops, the best test is to probe both sides of the fuel pump fuse in the mini-fuse block with a voltmeter. Observe the meter as the ignition is turned on. It should go to battery voltage (12 volts) and then, after one second, to zero volts.

2. If the fuel pump circuit is operating properly, the computer signal and the relay are okay. The last connector in the fuel pump circuit is the six-way connector at the tail panel. The voltage actions seen at the fuse should be repeated. If not, there is an open in the circuit. Check the connectors and repair wiring as required. Individual sections of the wiring can be tested with an ohmmeter.

3. If the fuel pump signal is correct at the tail panel connector, a fuel delivery system situation exists. If the pump cannot be hears to run during the one second on period, the pump should be replaced. This observation is more easily made if helper turns the ignition on as the technician listens at the fuel tank or filler neck area. If the fuel pump can be heard to run, disconnect the fuel return line at the throttle body and install a plug in the throttle body opening. This will effectively "dead head" the fuel pump and eliminate the pressure regulator. If the pump is able to produce above 9 psi under these conditions (with the ignition on), replace the fuel pressure regulator as it is controlling at too low pressure.

4. If the fuel pressure remains below 9 psi with the return line plugged, a restriction in the fuel supply line may exist. A blocked fuel line or fuel filter can be determined by visually inspecting the filter element and the fuel line routing for kinks, damage, etc. If lines and filter are okay, replace fuel pump.

5. If the voltage at the fuel pump fuse does not go to 12 volts, first inspect the fuse. If the fuse is okay, check the contacts at terminals 1 and 3 of the fuel pump relay connecting block. The contacts close when the relay coil is energized by the computer. Remove the relay. Probe the relay center socket, which corresponds to relay terminal 4, with a voltmeter.

6. After ignition has been off for at least 10 seconds, turn the ignition on. If the voltage does not go to 12 volts and back to zero, inspect for opens or shorts to ground. Checking for opens can be done with an ohmmeter connected to both ends of the circuit. If continuity is indicated () ohms), check for a short to ground by jumping one end to ground and probing the opposite end with an ohmmeter to ground. An infinite reading indicates the wire is not grounded and the circuit is okay. Replace the computer. If a short to ground in the circuit is found the computer will be damaged. Replace the computer after repair.

7. If voltage at relay terminal 4 goes to 12 volts and then to zero, the computer is performing properly. Probe the relay center socket which corresponds to relay pin 3 with a voltmeter. Since this circuit comes directly from the battery terminal of the starter solenoid, it should be 12 volts at all times. If voltage is zero, inspect the circuit for open.

8. Twelve volts at pin 3 indicates that most of the relay's requirements are met. However, there are still two wiring circuits which could prevent proper relay operation. The computer signal has been proven okay. However, if the coil ground is open, the coil will not be energized. To check, probe the relay center socket which corresponds to relay pin 5, with an ohmmeter connected to ground. Continuity () ohms) indicates a good circuit. An infinite reading indicates an open. Repair wire as required.

9. The second circuit in which an open could occur, preventing the proper voltage at the fuse, is between the fuel pump relay terminal 1 and the mini-fuse block. This circuit can be checked by probing both ends with an ohmmeter. If the circuit has continuity as indicated by a zero ohms reading, replace fuel pump relay.

10. High fuel pressure is caused by either a malfunction of the pressure regulator or a restriction in the fuel return line. To determine which of these problems exists, disconnect the fuel return line at the throttle body and connect a suitable fitting to the throttle body to accept a length of flexible rubber fuel hose. Insert the open end of the hose into a suitable fuel container. Observe the fuel pressure as the ignition switch is turned on. If the fuel pressure remains above 12 psi, replace the pressure regulator as it is unable to regulate with no return restriction.

11. If the fuel pressure now falls into the correct pressure range of 9–12 psi, the restriction has been eliminated by bypassing the return system. A restricted fuel return line can be located by visually inspecting the line routing for kinks, damage, etc.

Diagnosing Poor Performance

1. Unsatisfactory engine performance complaints which are related to the digital electronic fuel injection system are caused either by improper fuel delivery or improper fuel delivery or improper ignition advance (controlled by the computer). To isolate the problem to one of these systems, remove the air cleaner and observe the injector spray pattern of both injectors at idle. The spray pattern should be compared to a proper injector spray pattern of a known good car.

2. Improper fuel delivery which affects both injectors is most likely a fuel delivery system problem. By switching injector connectors, it can be determined if the problem is the injector assembly or the signal to the injector. If the problem remains with the original injector, it is most likely an injector problem. Replace the injector. If the problem moves with the injector connector, an improper signal circuit is indicated. The injectors are powered through the 3 amp fuses in the mini-fuse block. The fuse block receives battery voltage from the starter solenoid battery terminal when the fuel pump relay is energized by the computer during crank or run. With the relay closed, the circuits apply 12 volts to the injector. The computer provides the ground to energize the solenoid.

— **CAUTION** —

Do not apply direct battery voltage to the injector, 12 volts will destroy the fuel injector coil within ½ second.

3. Check the injector fuses by visually inspecting the fuse filament. If the fuses are okay there is a harness problem in the voltage feed or ground. The troubled circuit should be investigated. Check for opens with an ohmmeter. If harness checks okay, replace computer.

4. A blown injector fuse should be replaced. If it blows again, a short to ground is indicated. To check for this condition, connect ohmmeter between the red or white wire at the injector connector and ground (ignition off and computer disconnected). A low reading indicates a short circuit. Repair as required. If harness is okay, replace the computer.

5. A proper injector spray pattern indicates that improper ignition timing is the main DFI component which can cause poor performance. Ground the "set timing" pigtail and check timing. It should be at the base (or initial) value of 10°BTDC (800 rpm or less). If not, reset to 10°.

6. Once it has been established that the ignition timing is using the proper reference signal, the system's ability to advance the spark must also be determined. Since the actual ignition advance produced is the result of other variables besides engine rpm and manifold vacuum, it is not possible to establish checkpoints. However, if the system does advance, the shape of the advance curve can be assumed to be correct, since it is determined by the electronic circuitry which was able to recognize that some advance was required and did respond to this information. Disconnect the "set timing" jumper and check ignition timing. At normal idle, this should be approximately 20° to 30°BTDC.

7. If the ignition timing does not advance as a result of disconnecting the "set timing" jumper, a problem with the advance system is indicated. Since the computer selects and determines the spark advance curve, it is necessary to determine if the computer is operating properly or not. During cranking, no spark advance is desired. The computer limits the advance to base timing by turning off the voltage signal. The pick-up coil pulse is used directly to turn the HEI module on. When the engine starts, the computer turns on the voltage in the circuit and the pick-up coil pulse is sent to the computer, modified by the computer and sent back to the module. Whether the computer advances the timing or not depends upon whether it applied a voltage to the circuit or not (no voltage = base timing; voltage = electric spark timing). To check the circuit, disconnect the four-way connector at the distributor while the engine is idling. This will stop the engine. Probe the harness side pin C (not distributor side harness) with a voltmeter while the ignition switch remains on. If voltage is greater than 4 volts, refer to HEI diagnosis because the computer has signaled that EST should be used, but timing did not advance when checked.

8. Voltage less than 1 volt indicates that either the computer signal is not being produced or the circuit is open or shorted to the ground. To check for shorts, disconnect the black/green computer connector and probe harness pin D with an ohmmeter to ground (ignition off and distributor connector disconnected). A zero ohm reading indicates a short. Repair as required.

9. If the ohmmeter reads infinity, check for opens by jumping distributor connector pin C to ground. If the ohmmeter reading remains infinite, circuit is open. repair as required. If the ohmmeter reads zero ohms, the circuit is okay. Check MAT and coolant sensor circuits for an open between the splice and the computer. Attention should be focused on the bulk head and computer connectors. If the circuit is okay, substitute a new computer and observe performance.

10. The EGR system utilizes various controls in order to provide EGR gases only when they are needed for emission control. One of these controls is the EGR solenoid, with power feed from the ignition switch through the 20 amp fuse. Ground for the solenoid is provided by the computer. The computer provides this ground whenever the coolant temperature signal from the coolant sensor says the temperature is below 43°C (110°F). This energizes the solenoid and blocks the flow of vacuum to the EGR transducer thus preventing EGR operation at cold engine temperatures. Above 71°C (160°F), the solenoid ground is removed and the solenoid opens, allowing vacuum to the EGR valve. This vacuum signal is a ported vacuum which exists only off idle. This means that even on a warm engine, there is no EGR vacuum signal and no EGR flow at idle.

11. If EGR operation is okay, check to make sure that throttle valves open to wide open throttle when the accelerator pedal is wide open. If this is okay, the performance problem is not related to the DEFI system. If EGR problems are found, check hoses, etc.

NOTE: Some 1984-85 DFI equipped vehicles may experience an intermittent reduction of the power and or the engine stops running due to intermittent injector circuit operation. The following trouble tree charts should be used when attempting to diagnose such a condition. In some cases, it may be necessary to operate the vehicle and record the voltages as outlined, while the performance condition exists.

AIR INDUCTION SYSTEM

The air induction system consists of a throttle body and an intake manifold. Air for the combustion enters the throttle body and is distributed to each cylinder through the intake manifold. The throttle body contains a special distribution skirt below each injector to improve the fuel distribution.

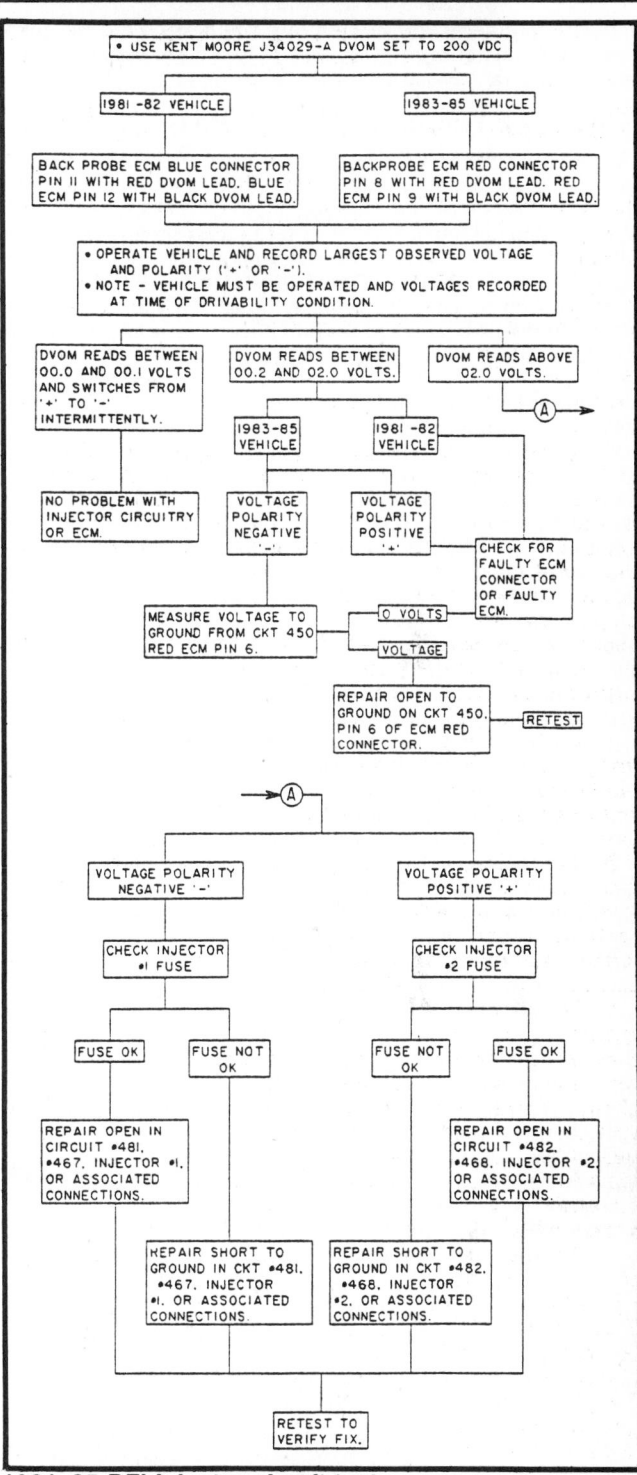

1981–85 DFI injector circuit test

The air flow rate is controlled by the throttle valves, which are connected to the accelerator linkage. The idle speed is determined by the position of the throttle valves and is controlled by the idle speed control (ISC).

DATA SENSORS

The purpose of the sensors is to supply electronic impulses to the ECM. The ECM then computes the spark timing and fuel delivery rate necessary to maintain the desired air/fuel mixture, thus controlling the amount of fuel delivered to the engine. The data sensors are interelated.

Manifold Air Temperature Sensor (MAT)

This sensor measures tethe the temperature of the air/fuel mixture in the intake manifold and provided this infortmation to the ECM. The sensor is a thermistor whose resistance changes as a function of temperature. When the temperature is low the resistance is high. When the temperature is high the resistance is low. This sensor is mounted in the intake manifol directly in fron tof the throttle body on the DeVille and Fleetwood. On the Eldorado and Seville, the sensor is located on the top right side of the engine near the alternator.

Coolant Temperature Sensor

The coolant temperature sensor is similar to the MAT sensor. This sensor provides coolant temperature information to the ECM for fuel enrichment, ignition timing, EGR operation, canister purge control, air management, EFE operation, idle speed control and closed loop fuel control. This sensor is located in the left front corner of the intake manifold on the DeVille and Fleetwood. On the Eldorado and Seville, it is located on the top left side of the engine near the distributor.

Manifold Absolute Pressure Sensor (MAP)

This sensor monitors the changes in the intake manifold pressure which result from engine load and speed changes. These pressure changes are supplied to the ECM in the form of electrical signals. As the intake manifold pressures increases, additional fuel is required. The MAP sensor sends information to the ECM and the ECM increase the injector on time (pulse width). When the manifold presure decrease, the pule width will be shortened.

On the DeVille and Fleetwood, the MAP sensor is mounted near the right rear side of the engine compartment. On the Eldorado and Seville, the MAP sensor is located on the top right side of the engine above the rear valve cover. On some models the MAP sensor may be located under the instrument panel near the right hand A/C outlet and electrically connected to the ECM.

Barometric Pressure Sensor (BARO)

This sensor, senses the ambient or barometric pressure and provides information to the ECM on ambient pressure changesdut ot the altitude and ot the weather. This sensor is usually mounted under the instrument panel near the right hand A/C outlet and sensds and electrical signal to the ECM.

Throttle Position Sensor (TPS)

The TPs sensor is a variable resistor mounted on the throttle body and is connected to the throttle valve shaft. Movement of aceleration causes the throttle shaft to rotate and the throttle shaft rotation opens or closes the throttle blades. The sensor determines the shaft position (throttle angle) and transmits the appropiate electrical signal to the ECM.

The ECM processes these signals and uses the the throttle angle informatio to operate the idle speed control system and to supply fuel enrichment as the throttle blades are opened.

Vehicle Speed Sensor

The vehicle speed sensor informs the ECM as to how fast the vehicle is being driven. The ECM uses this signal for the logic required to operate the fuel economy data panel, the integral Cruise Control and the idle speed control system.

The speed sensor produces a very week signal. So therefore a vehicle speed sensor buffer is placed between the speed sensor and the ECM to amplify the speed signal. Th e speed sensor and the vehicle speed sensor buffer ampilfier are located behind the speedometer cluster.

Oxygen Sensor

The oxygen sensor in the DFI system consists of a closed end Zirconia sensor placed in the engine exhaust gas stream This sensor generates a very weak voltage signal that varies with the oxygen content of the exhaust stream. As the oxygen content of the exhaust stream increases relative to the surrounding atmosphere, a lean fuel mixture is indicated by a low voltage output, as the oxygen content decrease, a rich fuel mixture is indicated by a rising voltage output from the sensor.

When the oxygen sensor is warm 392°F (200°C) The output voltage swings between 200 millivolts (lean mixture) and 800 millivolts (rich mixture). However, when the oxygen sensor is cold (below 392°F). the voltage output drops below this range and the respons time of the sensor is much slower. The sensor cannot react quickly to rich-lean or lean-rich transitions; therefore, the sensor does not supply accurate information to the ECM. The output voltage may be read using a high impedance digital voltmeter.

NOTE: The high impedencae digital voltmeter must a minimum 5 mega-ohm input impedance. Digital voltmeter's with a lower input impedenance may cause an inaccurate reading or force the system to behave incorrectly.

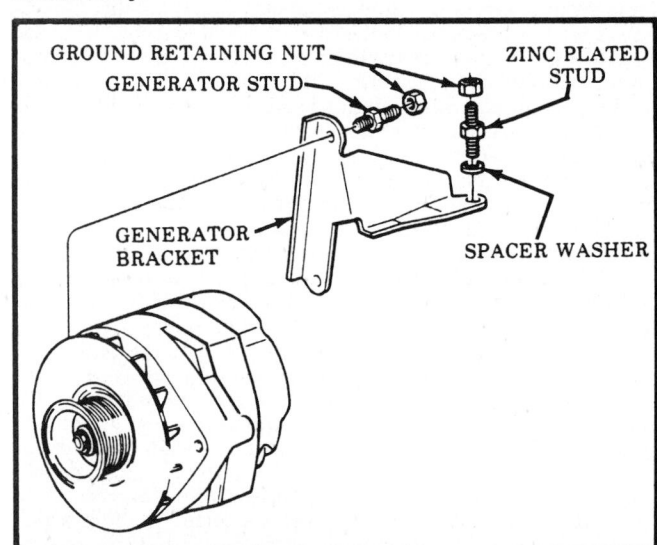

Relocating the oxygen sensor ground

Some 1985 FWD DeVilles and Fleetwoods may experience a lean drivability condition and possibly ECM diagnostic codes 13 and or 45. Symptoms of a lean driveability condition can cause chuggle, surge sag, or reduced engine performance. This condition may be caused by a voltage difference between the oxygen sensor ground (engine block) and the ECM oxygen sensor ground reference, circuit 413, which connects to the generator bracket. Should a poor ground exist, the voltage difference between these two grounds is added to the oxygen sensor signal, falsely indicating a rich (high voltage) oxygen sensor signal to the ECM. The ECM compensates for a high oxygen sensor voltage by commanding a lean mixture.

If the generator stud has a black or brown single wire ring terminal on it, then the ECM oxygen sensor ground must be relocated. If the generator stud does nut have a black or brown single wire ring terminal on it, then the ECM oxygen sensor ground has been relocated. So proceed to the trouble code diagnosis if a code 13 or 45 is present.

Engine Speed Sensor

The engine speed sensor signal comes from the seven terminal

HEI module in the distributor. Pulse from the distributor are sent to the ECM where the time between these pulses is used to calculate engine speed. The ECM adds the spark advance modifications to the signal and sends the signal back to the distributor.

Power Steering Switch

The power steering pressure switch is normally closed and opens with power steering pressure. The power steering pressure switch recieves 12 volts from a the 10 amp solenoid fuse which is located in the relay center.

When high power steering pressures occur, the switch contacts are opened by the power steering oil pressure and the ECM reads 0 volts on the line which goes from the switch to the ECM. The ECM uses the power steering switch input to extend the ISC motor when high power steering loads occur, to help maintain and stable idle. Switch tset code E.7.8 can be used to check the power steering pressure switch for poroper operation.

Park/Neutral Switch

The park/neutral switch is part of the transmission neutral safety-backup switch Pin "A" of the six way weather pack connector on this switch is the park/neutral switch contacts. The park/neutral switch contatcs are closed in park or neutral shorting the neutral safety-backup switch Pin "A" to ground. In any other gear range, pin "A" is open.

The ECM sends 12 volts to pin "A" of the neutral safety-backup switch. When the gear selector is in park or neutral, the 12 volt signal from the ECM is shorted to ground, resulting in 0 volts at the ECM. In reverse or forward gears the switch will be opened, resulting in 12 volts at the ECM.

The switch test code E.7.4 can be used to check the park/neutral switch for proper operation. An inoperative park/neutral switch could cause improper idle speed, cruise control or transmission converter clutch.

Crank Signal

The ECM looks at the starter solenoid to tell when the engine is cranking. It uses this to tell when the car is in the starting mode. If the crank signal is recieved by the ECM, a code 18 will be stored. Under these circumstances the vehicle may be difficult to start.

ELECTRONIC CONTROL MODULE (ECM)

The Electronic Control Module, (ECM) or computer provides all computation and controls for the DEFI system. Sensor inputs are fed into the computer from the various sensors. They are processed to produce the appropriate pulse duration for the injectors, the correct idle speed for the particular operating condition and the proper spark advance. Analog inputs from the sensors are converted to digital signals before processing. The computer assembly is mounted under the instrument panel and consists of various printed circuit boards mounted in a protective metal box. The computer receives power from the vehicle battery. When the ignition is set to the "ON" or "CRANK" position, the following information is received from the sensors:

1. Engine coolant temperature
2. Intake manifold air temperature
3. Intake manifold absolute pressure
4. Barometric pressure
5. Engine speed
6. Throttle position

The following commands are transmitted by the ECM:

1. Electric fuel pump activation
2. Idle speed control
3. Spark advance control
4. Injection valve activation

5. EGR solenoid activation

The desired air/fuel mixture for various driving and atmospheric conditions are programmed into the computer. As signals are received from the sensors, the computer processes the signals and computes the engine's fuel requirements. The computer issues commands to the injection valves to open for a specific time duration. The duration of the command pulses varies as the operating conditions change.

The digital electronic fuel injection system is activated when the ignition switch is turned to the "ON" position. The following events occur at this moment.

1. The computer receives the ignition "ON" signal.
2. The fuel pump is activated by the ECM. The pump will operate for approximately one second only, unless the engine is cranking or funning.
3. All engine sensors are activated and begin transmitting signals to the computer.
4. The EGR solenoid is activated to block the vacuum signal to the EGR valve at coolant temperatures below 110°F.
5. The "CHECK ENGINE" and "COOLANT" lights are illuminated as a functional check of the bulb and circuit.
6. Operation of the fuel economy lamps begins.

The following events occur when the engine is started.

1. The fuel pump is activated for continuous operation.
2. The idle speed control motor will begin controlling idle speed, including fast idle speed, if the throttle switch is closed.
3. The spark advance shifts from base (bypass) timing to the computer programmed spark curve.
4. The fuel pressure regulator maintains the fuel pressure at 9–12 psi by returning excess fuel to the fuel tank.
5. The following sensor signals are continuously received and processed by the computer:
   a. Engine coolant temperature
   b. Intake manifold air temperature
   c. Barometric pressure
   d. Intake manifold absolute air pressure
   e. Engine speed
   f. Throttle position changes
6. The computer alternately grounds each injector, precisely controlling the opening and closing time (pulse width) to deliver fuel to the engine.

Central Processing Unit (CPU)

The digital signals received by the CPU are used to perform all mathematical computations and logic functions necessary to deliver the proper air/fuel mixture. The CPU also calculates the spark timing and idle speed information. The CPU commands the operation of emission controls, closed loop fuel control, cruise control and diagnostic system.

Input and Output Devices

These integral devices of the ECM, convert the electrical signals received by the data sensors and change them over to digital signals for use by the CPU.

Power Supply

The main source of power for the ECM is from the battery, through the number one ignition cicuit.

ECM Memory

There are three types of memory in the ECM and they are as follows:

a. Programmable Read Only Memory (Prom) - The purpose of this memory is to contain the calibration information about each engine, transmission, body and rear axle ratio combination. If the battery voltage is lost for any reason, the PROM information is retained. The PROM chip can be easily changed if necessary.

b. Read Only Memory (ROM) - The read only memory is programmed information that can only be read by the ECM.

The read only memory program cannot be changed. If the battery voltage is lost at any time, the read only memory will be retained.

c. Random Access Memory (RAM) - Random access memory acts as the scratch pad for the CPU. Information can be read into or out of the RAM memory hence it is called the scratch pad memory. The engine sensor information, diagnostic codes, and the results of calculations are temporarily stored here. If the battery voltage is removed, all the information in the RAm memory will be lost (this is similar to a hand held caculator when the switch is turned off).

d. These three memory devices are all removable from the ECM unit.

To demonstrate how the ECM operates, the following is a list of events that will occur when the ignition switch is turned on.

1. The ECM receives the ignition on signal.

2. The fuel pump is activated by the ECM. The pump will operate for approximately one to two seconds only, unless the engine is being cranked or has started.

3. All engine sensors are activated and begin transmitting signals to the ECM.

4. The EGR solenoid is activated to block the vacuum signal to the EGR valve at a temperatures below 175°F.

5. The coolant light will be illuminated as a functional check of the bulb and the circuit.

6. The HEI bypass line is pulled down to 0 volts.

The following events are what occurs when the engine is being cranked.

1. The 12 volt crank signal is sent to the ECM.

2. The fuel pump is operating.

3. After a short series of prime pulses, injectors alternately deliver a fuel pulse on each distributor reference pulse.

4. The engine sensors continue to transmit signals to the ECM.

5. The "Service Soon" and "Service Now" lights are illuminated as a functional check of the bulb and circuit.

6. The other events are similar to the events which occur when the ignition switch is turned on.

The following events are what occurs when the engine is started.

1. The crank signal is removed from the ECM.

2. The injectors deliver fuel pulses alternately for each distributor reference pulse.

3. The HEI bypass line is pulled up to 5 volts and the HEI module receives spark advance signals from the ECM.

4. The ISC motor begins to control the idle speed if the throttle switch is closed.

5. The fuel pump operates continuously.

6. The pressure regulator maintains fuel pressure at 10.5 psi by returning excess fuel to the fuel tank.

7. The other events are similar to the events which occur when the ignition switch is turned on.

BODY CONTROL MODULE (BCM)

The BCM monitors and controls Electronic Climate Controls (ECC), rear defogger, outside temperature display, coling fan control, fuel data display center display information, vacuum flourescent display dimming, self diagnostics and retained accessory power system functions.

The BCM consists of input and output devices, CPU, power supply and memeories that coincide with those of the ECM. The BCM exchanges information with the ECM to provide maximum reliability and improved servicability of the body related systems.

ELECTRONIC SPARK TIMING (EST)

The EST type HEI distributor receives all spark timing information from the computer when the engine is running. The computer provides spark plug firing pulses based upon the var-

BCM/ECM DATA TRANSFER

CIRCUIT 526-ECM TO BCM DATA

- REQUESTED DIAGNOSTIC DATA
- FUEL ECONOMY DATA
- VEHICLE SPEED
- COOLANT TEMPERATURE
- ENGINE RUN STATUS
- WIDE OPEN THROTTLE STATUS

BODY COMPUTER MODULE   ELECTRONIC CONTROL MODULE

CIRCUIT 491-BCM TO ECM DATA

- DIAGNOSTIC ACTION REQUEST
- OUTSIDE AIR TEMPERATURE
- A/C HIGH SIDE TEMPERATURE
- A/C CLUTCH STATUS
- REAR DEFOG STATUS
- HIGH BLOWER STATUS
- HIGH COOLING FANS STATUS

Data transfer from the BCM to the ECM

ious engine operating parameters. The electronic components for the electronic spark control system are integral with the computer. The two basic operating modes are cranking (or bypass) and normal engine operation.

When the engine is in the cranking/bypass mode, ignition timing occurs at a reference setting (distributor timing set point) regardless of other engine operating parameters. Under all other normal operating conditions, basic engine ignition timing is controlled by the computer and modified or added to, depending on particular conditions such as altitude and/or engine loading.

The HEI distributor communicates to the ECM through a four terminal connector which contains four circuits, these four circuits are as follows;

1. The distributor reference circuit.

2. The bypas circuit.

3. The EST circuit.

4. The ground circuit.

Whenever the pickup coil signals the HEI module to open the primary circuit, it also sends the spark timing signals to the ECM through the reference line.

When the voltage on the HEI bypass line is 0 volts (engine cranking), the HEI module is forced into the bypass mode which means that the HEI module provides spark advance at base timing and disregards the spark advance signal from the ECM. If the volatge on the HEI bypass line is 5 volts (engine running), the HEi module accepts the spark timing signal provided by the ECM.

IDLE SPEED CONTROL SYSTEM

The idle speed control system is controlled by the computer. The system acts to control engine idle speed in three ways; as a normal idle (rpm) control, as a fast idle device and as a "dashpot" on decelerations and throttle closing. The normal engine

ECM SWITCH TESTS	
DIAGNOSTIC DISPLAY	CIRCUIT TEST
E.7.1	Brake Switch
E.7.2	Throttle Switch
E.7.4	Park/Neutral Switch
E.7.5	Cruise "ON-OFF"
E.7.6	Cruise "SET/COAST" †
E.7.7	Cruise "RESUME/ACCEL." †
E.7.8	Power Steering Pressure Switch (Engine Running)

† Switch Cruise "ON" Before Testing

ECM OUTPUT CYCLING

"COOLANT TEMP FAN" Light
"SERVICE ELECTRICAL SYSTEM" Light
Air Switch Solenoid
Air Divert Solenoid
ISC Motor
Cruise Vacuum Solenoid & Engage Light*
Cruise Power Solenoid *
Canister Purge Solenoid
EGR Solenoid
VCC Solenoid
EFE Relay

*To Activate These Outputs, The Following Must Occur:

A) Engine Running
B) Cruise Switch "ON"
C) Key OFF And ON Within 2 Seconds Prior To Entering Diagnostics.

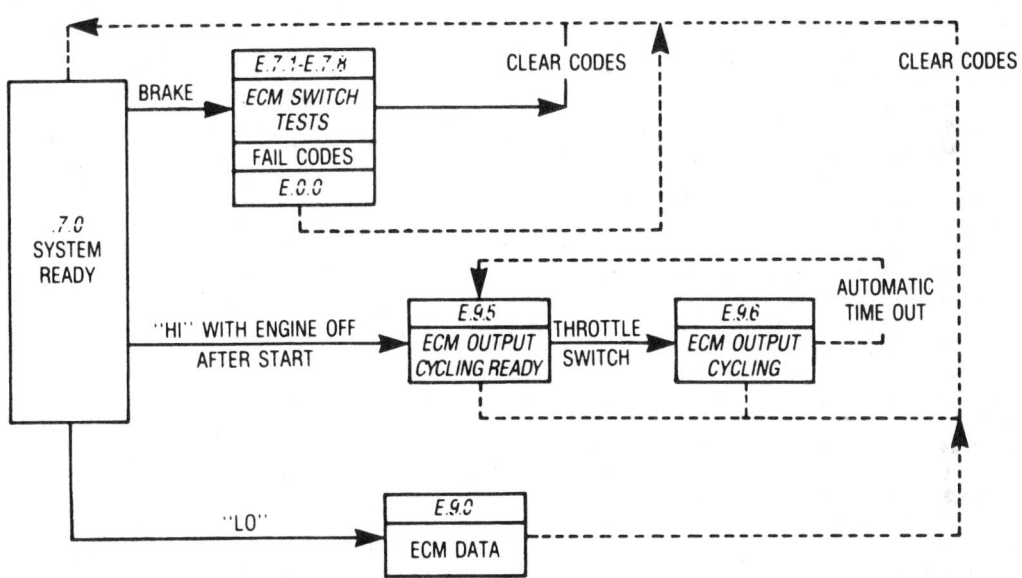

KEY
To Select Another Test Press: "HI" — To Increment "LO" — To Decrement
ECM DATA P.1.6 "LO" ↓↑ "HI" P.0.1

ECM DATA			
PARAMETER NUMBER	PARAMETER	DISPLAY	
		RANGE	UNITS
P.0.1	Throttle Position	− 10.0 - 90.0	Degrees
P.0.2	MAP	14 - 109	kPa
P.0.3	Computed BARO	61 - 103	kPa
P.0.4	Coolant Temperature	− 40 - 151	°C
P.0.5	MAT	− 40 - 151	°C
P.0.6	Injector Pulse Width	0 - 99.9	ms
P.0.7	Oxygen Sensor Voltage	0 - 1.14	Volts
P.0.8	Spark Advance	− 30 - 60	Degrees
P.0.9	Ignition Cycle Counter	0 - 50	Key Cycles
P.1.0	Battery Voltage	0 - 25.5	Volts
P.1.1	Engine RPM	0 - 6370	RPM ÷ 10
P.1.2	Car Speed	0 - 255	MPH
P.1.3	Oxygen Sensor Cross Cts.	0 - 255	Number
P.1.4	Fuel Integrator	0 - 255	Counts
P.1.5	VCC Volts	0 - 5.12	Volts
P.1.6	ECM PROM ID	0 - 999	Code •

FIXED SPARK
Exit Diagnostics And Connect Pins A&B Of ALDL Test Connector. Vehicle Will Be In Fixed Spark Mode If At Curb Idle With Transmission In Park.

• PROM ID

PROM ID Code Number Identifies An Individual Calibration And Is Periodically Updated; Refer To Latest Service Publication For Correct ID Number.

1984–85 Diagnostic flow schematic

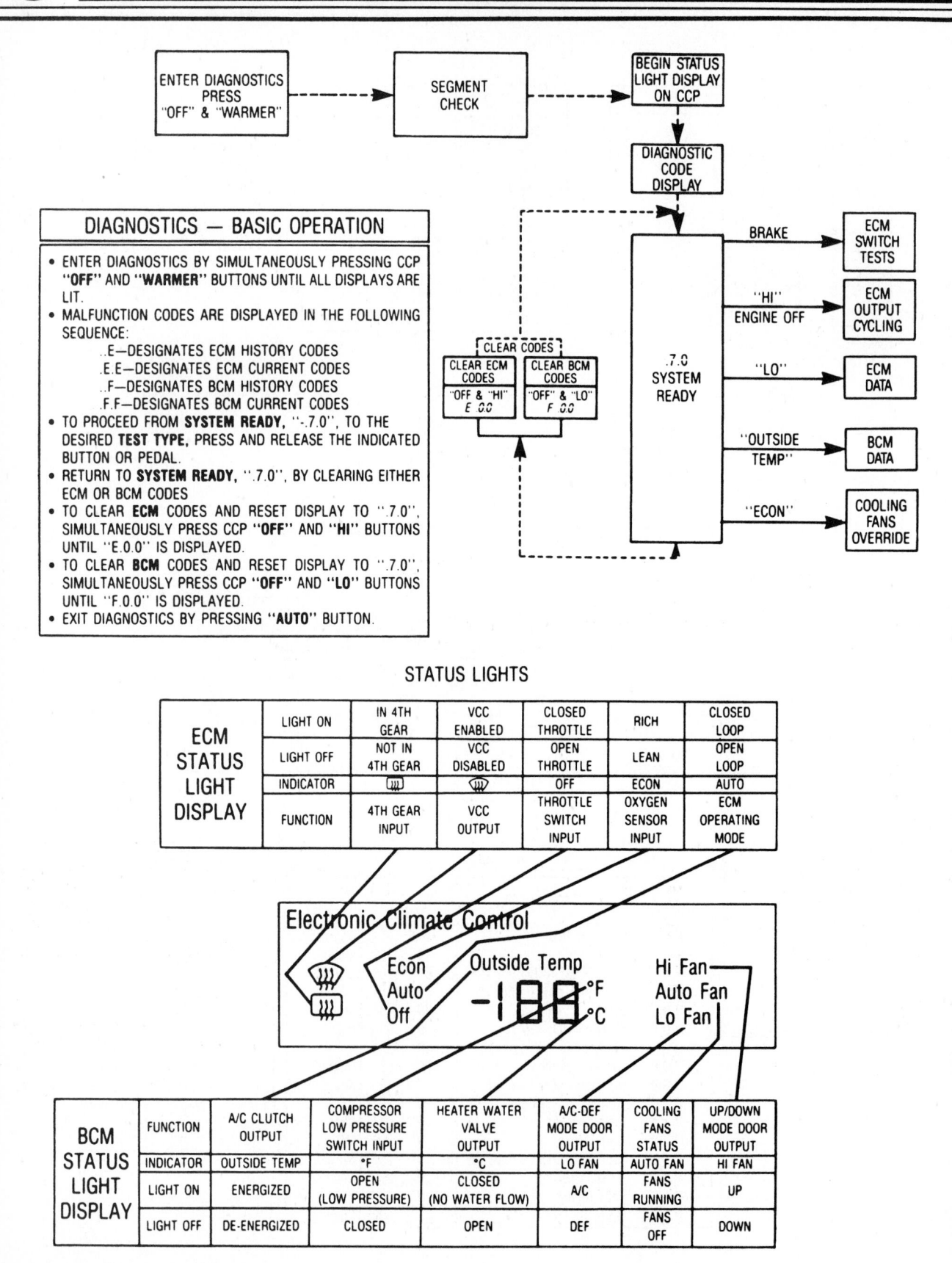

DIAGNOSTICS — BASIC OPERATION

- ENTER DIAGNOSTICS BY SIMULTANEOUSLY PRESSING CCP "OFF" AND "WARMER" BUTTONS UNTIL ALL DISPLAYS ARE LIT.
- MALFUNCTION CODES ARE DISPLAYED IN THE FOLLOWING SEQUENCE:
  - ..E—DESIGNATES ECM HISTORY CODES
  - .E.E—DESIGNATES ECM CURRENT CODES
  - ..F—DESIGNATES BCM HISTORY CODES
  - .F.F—DESIGNATES BCM CURRENT CODES
- TO PROCEED FROM **SYSTEM READY**, "-.7.0", TO THE DESIRED **TEST TYPE**, PRESS AND RELEASE THE INDICATED BUTTON OR PEDAL.
- RETURN TO **SYSTEM READY**, ".7.0", BY CLEARING EITHER ECM OR BCM CODES
- TO CLEAR **ECM** CODES AND RESET DISPLAY TO ".7.0", SIMULTANEOUSLY PRESS CCP "OFF" AND "HI" BUTTONS UNTIL "E.0.0" IS DISPLAYED.
- TO CLEAR **BCM** CODES AND RESET DISPLAY TO ".7.0", SIMULTANEOUSLY PRESS CCP "OFF" AND "LO" BUTTONS UNTIL "F.0.0" IS DISPLAYED.
- EXIT DIAGNOSTICS BY PRESSING "AUTO" BUTTON.

STATUS LIGHTS

ECM STATUS LIGHT DISPLAY	LIGHT ON	IN 4TH GEAR	VCC ENABLED	CLOSED THROTTLE	RICH	CLOSED LOOP
	LIGHT OFF	NOT IN 4TH GEAR	VCC DISABLED	OPEN THROTTLE	LEAN	OPEN LOOP
	INDICATOR			OFF	ECON	AUTO
	FUNCTION	4TH GEAR INPUT	VCC OUTPUT	THROTTLE SWITCH INPUT	OXYGEN SENSOR INPUT	ECM OPERATING MODE

Electronic Climate Control

Econ
Auto
Off

Outside Temp

-188 °F °C

Hi Fan
Auto Fan
Lo Fan

BCM STATUS LIGHT DISPLAY	FUNCTION	A/C CLUTCH OUTPUT	COMPRESSOR LOW PRESSURE SWITCH INPUT	HEATER WATER VALVE OUTPUT	A/C-DEF MODE DOOR OUTPUT	COOLING FANS STATUS	UP/DOWN MODE DOOR OUTPUT
	INDICATOR	OUTSIDE TEMP	°F	°C	LO FAN	AUTO FAN	HI FAN
	LIGHT ON	ENERGIZED	OPEN (LOW PRESSURE)	CLOSED (NO WATER FLOW)	A/C	FANS RUNNING	UP
	LIGHT OFF	DE-ENERGIZED	CLOSED	OPEN	DEF	FANS OFF	DOWN

1986–88 Diagnostic flow schematic

ECM SWITCH TESTS	
DIAGNOSTIC DISPLAY	CIRCUIT TEST
E.7.1	Brake Switch
E.7.2	Throttle Switch
E.7.4	Park/Neutral Switch
E.7.5	Cruise "ON-OFF"
E.7.6	Cruise "SET/COAST" †
E.7.7	Cruise "RESUME/ACCEL." †
E.7.8	Power Steering Pressure Switch (Engine Running)

† Switch Cruise "ON"
Before Testing

ECM OUTPUT CYCLING

"COOLANT TEMP FAN" Light
"SERVICE ELECTRICAL SYSTEM" Light
Air Switch Solenoid
Air Divert Solenoid
ISC Motor
Cruise Vacuum Solenoid & Engage Light *
Cruise Power Solenoid *
Canister Purge Solenoid
EGR Solenoid
VCC Solenoid
EFE Relay

*To Activate These
Outputs, The Following
Must Occur:

A) Engine Running
B) Cruise Switch "ON"
C) Key OFF And ON Within
  2 Seconds Prior To
  Entering Diagnostics.

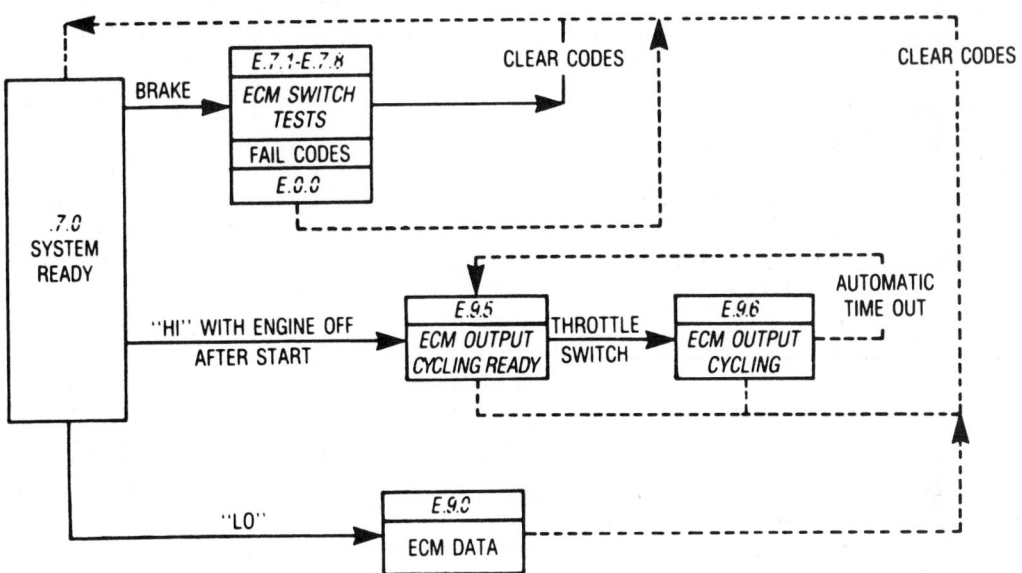

KEY
To Select Another Test Press: "HI" — To Increment "LO" — To Decrement
ECM DATA P.1.6 "LO" ↓↑ "HI" P.0.1

ECM DATA			
PARAMETER NUMBER	PARAMETER	DISPLAY	
		RANGE	UNITS
P.0.1	Throttle Position	− 10.0 - 90.0	Degrees
P.0.2	MAP	14 - 109	kPa
P.0.3	Computed BARO	61 - 103	kPa
P.0.4	Coolant Temperature	− 40 - 151	°C
P.0.5	MAT	− 40 - 151	°C
P.0.6	Injector Pulse Width	0 - 99.9	ms
P.0.7	Oxygen Sensor Voltage	0 - 1.14	Volts
P.0.8	Spark Advance	− 30 - 60	Degrees
P.0.9	Ignition Cycle Counter	0 - 50	Key Cycles
P.1.0	Battery Voltage	0 - 25.5	Volts
P.1.1	Engine RPM	0 - 6370	RPM − 10
P.1.2	Car Speed	0 - 255	MPH
P.1.3	Oxygen Sensor Cross Cts.	0 - 255	Number
P.1.4	Fuel Integrator	0 - 255	Counts
P.1.5	VCC Volts	0 - 5.12	Volts
P.1.6	ECM PROM ID	0 - 999	Code •

FIXED SPARK

Exit Diagnostics And Connect Pins A&B Of ALDL Test Connector. Vehicle Will Be In Fixed Spark Mode If At Curb Idle With Transmission In Park.

• PROM ID

PROM ID Code Number Identifies An Individual Calibration And Is Periodically Updated; Refer To Latest Service Publication For Correct ID Number.

1986–88 Diagnostic flow schematic (cont.)

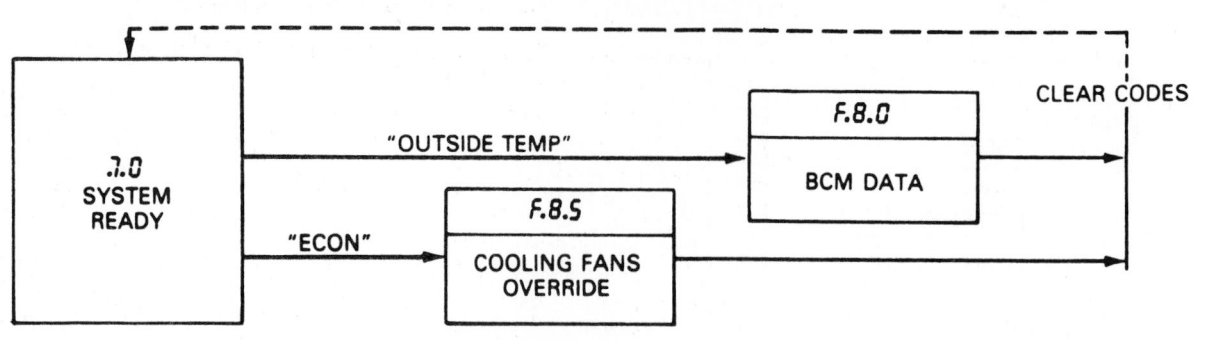

CLEAR CODES

BCM DATA			

<table>
<tr><td rowspan="2">PARAMETER NUMBER*</td><td rowspan="2">PARAMETER</td><td colspan="2">DISPLAY</td></tr>
<tr><td>RANGE</td><td>UNITS</td></tr>
<tr><td>P.2.0</td><td>COMMANDED BLOWER VOLTAGE</td><td>−3.3-18.0</td><td>VOLTS</td></tr>
<tr><td>P.2.1</td><td>COOLANT TEMPERATURE</td><td>−40-151</td><td>°C</td></tr>
<tr><td>P.2.2</td><td>COMMANDED AIR MIX POSITION</td><td>0-100</td><td>%</td></tr>
<tr><td>P.2.3</td><td>ACTUAL AIR MIX DOOR POSITION</td><td>0-100</td><td>%</td></tr>
<tr><td>P.2.4</td><td>AIR DELIVERY MODE</td><td>0-7</td><td>CODE □</td></tr>
<tr><td>P.2.5</td><td>IN-CAR TEMPERATURE</td><td>−40-102</td><td>°C</td></tr>
<tr><td>P.2.6</td><td>ACTUAL OUTSIDE TEMPERATURE</td><td>−40-93</td><td>°C</td></tr>
<tr><td>P.2.7</td><td>HIGH SIDE TEMPERATURE (CONDENSOR OUT)</td><td>−40-215</td><td>°C</td></tr>
<tr><td>P.2.8</td><td>LOW SIDE TEMPERATURE (EVAPORATOR IN)</td><td>−40-93</td><td>°C</td></tr>
<tr><td>P.2.9</td><td>ACTUAL FUEL LEVEL</td><td>0-19</td><td>GALLONS</td></tr>
<tr><td>P.3.0</td><td>IGNITION CYCLE COUNTER</td><td>0-99</td><td>KEY CYCLES</td></tr>
<tr><td>P.3.1</td><td>BCM PROM I.D.</td><td>·0-255</td><td>CODE●</td></tr>
</table>

ECC PROGRAM NUMBER OVERRIDE

ECC PROGRAM NUMBER (0-100) IS DISPLAYED ON CCP DURING F.8.0 SEQUENCE.

0 = MAX A/C   100 = MAX HEAT

TO INCREASE PROGRAM NUMBER, PRESS "WARMER";
TO DECREASE PROGRAM NUMBER, PRESS "COOLER".

*KEY	BCM DATA	●BCM PROM ID
TO SELECT ANOTHER TEST PRESS: "HI" — TO INCREMENT "LO" — TO DECREMENT	P.2.0 "HI" "LO" P.3.1	CODE NUMBER IDENTIFIES AN INDIVIDUAL CALIBRATION AND IS PERIODICALLY UPDATED; REFER TO LATEST SERVICE PUBLICATION FOR CORRECT ID NUMBER.

COOLING FANS OVERRIDE	□ AIR DELIVERY MODE			
PRESS AND HOLD THE FOLLOWING BUTTONS: "LO" — FANS OFF "HI" — HI FANS NONE — NORMAL	BCM AIR DELIVERY MODE IS PARAMETER 24 (P.2.4) OF BCM DATA AND IS DISPLAYED AS A NUMERICAL CODE AS FOLLOWS:			

<table>
<tr><td colspan="2" rowspan="5"></td><td>CODE NO.</td><td>MODE</td><td>CODE NO.</td><td>MODE</td></tr>
<tr><td>0</td><td>MAX. A/C</td><td>4</td><td>OFF</td></tr>
<tr><td>1</td><td>A/C</td><td>5</td><td>NORMAL PURGE</td></tr>
<tr><td>2</td><td>INTERMEDIATE</td><td>6</td><td>COLD PURGE</td></tr>
<tr><td>3</td><td>HEATER</td><td>7</td><td>FRONT DEFOG</td></tr>
</table>

1986–88 Diagnostic flow schematic (cont.)

idle speed is programmed into the computer and no adjustments are possible. Under normal engine operating conditions, idle speed is maintained by monitoring idle speed in a closed loop fashion. To accomplish this loop, the computer periodically senses the engine idle speed and issues commands to the idle speed control to move the throttle stop to maintain the correct speed.

For engine starting, the throttle is either held open by the idle speed control for a longer (cold) or a shorter (hot) period to provide adequate engine warm-up prior to normal operation. When the engine is shut off, the throttle is opened by fully extending the idle speed control actuator to get ready for the next start.

Signal inputs for transmission gear, air conditioning compressor clutch (engaged or not engaged) and throttle (open or closed) are used to either increase or decrease throttle angle in response to these particular engine loadings.

Vehicle idle speed is controlled by an electrically driven actuator (idle speed control) which changes the throttle angle by acting as a movable idle stop. Inputs to the ISC actuator motor come from the ECM and are determined by the idle speed required for the particular operating condition. The electronic components for the ISC system are integral with the ECM. An integral part of the ISC is the throttle switch. The position of the switch determines whether the ISC should control idle speed or not. When the switch is closed, as determined by the throttle lever resting upon the end of the ISC actuator, the ECM will issue the appropriate commands to move the idle speed control to provide the programmed idle speed. When the throttle lever moves off the idle speed control actuator from idle, the throttle switch is opened. The computer than extends the actuator and stops sending idle speed commands and the driver controls the engine speed.

EMISSION CONTROLS

EGR Opertaion

The ECM controls controls the operation of the EGR system. Whenever the EGR solenoid is energized by the ECM, the EGR systenm is disabled (meaning no exhaust gas will be recirculated through the intake manifold). When the EGR solenoid is deenergized, the EGR system is enabled and exhaust gas will be recircultaed through the inatke manifold.

Air Management Operation

The ECM controls the operations of the air management system. The air pump delivers the air to the diveret (control) valve which sends the air to the air cleaner and the air switching valve. The switching valve sends the air either to the catayltic converter or the exhaust ports of the engine

When the switching valve is energized by the ECM, it direct the air to the exhaust ports to aid in quickly heating the oxygen sensor to 600°F. When the eninge is warm or in closed loop operation, the ECM will deenergize the air switching valve and direct the air to the catalytic converter to assist in oxidation of the hydro-carbons (HC) and the carbon monoxide (CO).

If the air control valve detects a rapid increase in intake manifold (deceleration), if certian operating modes exist or if the ECM detects any failure in the system, the air is diverted to the air cleaner or dumped into the atmosphere.

Canister Purge Control Operation

The ECM controls the operations of the canister purge control system. The ECM energizes the canister purge control solenoid by suppling a ground signal to the solenoid. The solenois is energized by the ECM during cold engine operation. When the solenoid is energized, the vacuum to the canister line is blocked.

When the engine is at normal operating temperature the ECM deenergizes the canister purge control solenoid by remov-

ing the ground signal. When the solenoid id deenergized, the vacuum is supplied to the canister.

Early Fuel Evaporation (EFE) Operation

The EFE system is made up of a ceramic electric grid located under the throttle body. The EFE system improves the air/fuel ratio control, improves fuel evaporation during ciold engine operation and improves the idle quality. The ECM activates the EFE relay when the MAT sensor is less than 167°F., coolant temperature is less than 223°F and battery voltage is greater than 10 volts.

If any of these conditions are not met, the EFE relay is deactivated. If the EFE system is off when the vehicle is running, it will be reactivated when all three of the following condtions are met;

a. The MAT sensor is less than 100°F.
b. The coolant temperature is less than 223°F.
c. The battery voltage is greater than 12 volts.

The EFE system is activated for approximately 15 seconds when the TPS position is greater than 30° and the MAT sensor is less than 140°F to prevent icing of the EFE ceramic grid.

NOTE: On some of the earlier Cadillac models, the EFE was located in between the exhaust pipe and the exhaust manifold. This vacuum servo EFE system uses a valve which increase the exhaust gas flow under the itake manifol during cold engine operation. The valve is vacuum operated and is controlled by the thermal vacuum switch which passes vacuum to the EFE valve when the engine collant temperature is below approximately 120°F. The primary function of this EFE system is to provide a source of rapid heat to the engine induction system during cold driveaway.

CLOSED LOOP FUEL CONTROL

The purpose of closed loop fuel control is to precisely maintain an air/fuel mixture 14.7:1. When the air/fuel mixture is main-

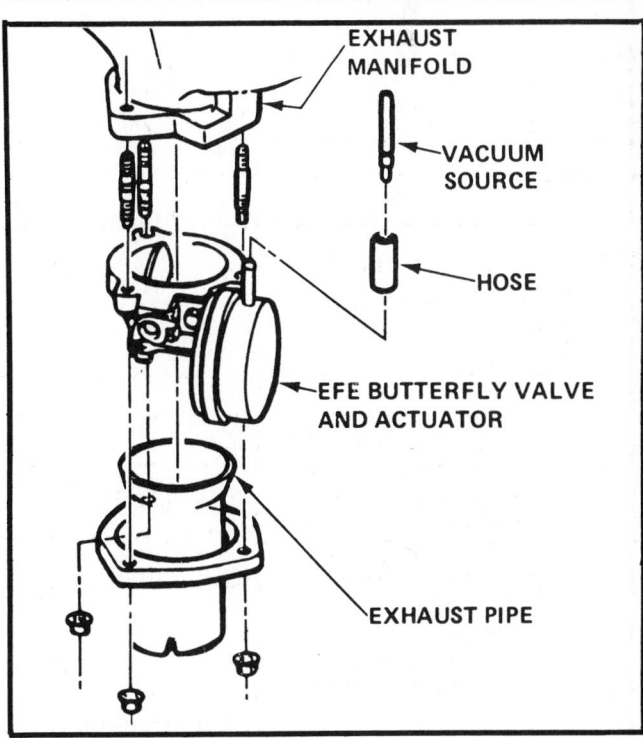

Early model Cadillac EFE valve assembly

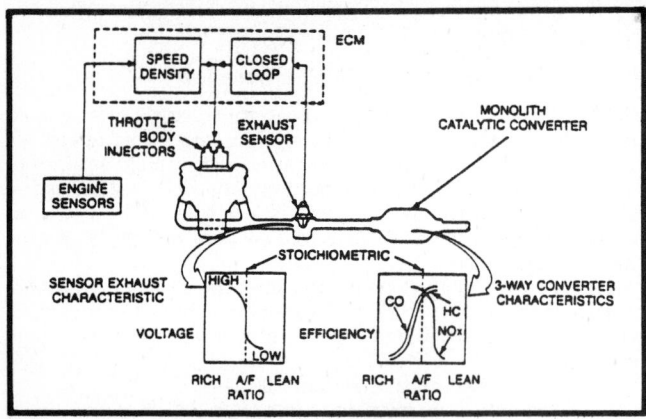

DFI closed loop system schematic

tained at 14.7:1, the catalytic converter is able to operate at maximum efficiency which results in lower emission levels.

Since the ECM controls the air/fuel mixture, it needs to check its ouput and correct the fuel mixture for deviations from the "Ideal" ratio. The oxygen sensor feeds this output information back to the ECM.

A catalytic converter is used on all vehicles to reduce the emissions levels of the three major pollutnats; hrdrocarbons (HC), carbon monoxide (CO) and oxides of nitrogen (NOx). There are two coverter designs being used, a pellet type on all California models and a monolithic honeycomb design on all others.

The converter, whether pellets or ceramic monolith, is coatedwith platinum, palladium and rhodium. When exhaust gases come into contact with these metals, the three pollutants are oxidized (burned off), further reducing the total engine emission levels.

CRUISE CONTROL

The ECM receives input signals from the cruise control engagement switches, instrument panel switch, brake release switch, drive switch and speed sensor. The ECM processes the cruise control inputs together with the DFI engine control inputs and transmits command signals to the vacuum control solenoid valve and power unit solenoid valve to control the vehicle speed.

TORQUE CONVERTER CLUTCH (TCC) CONTROL

The ECM controls an electrical solenoid mounted in the automatic transmission. When the vehicle reaches a specified speed, the ECM energizes the solenoid and allows the torque converter to mechanically couple the engine to the transmission.

When operating conditions indicate the transmission should operate as a normal fluid-coupled transmission (deceleration, passing, etc.) the solenoid is de-energized. The transmission also returns to normal (fluid-coupled) automatic operation when the brake pedal is depressed.

TBI Unit Component Removal

Service Precautions

1. When working around any part of the fuel system, take precautionary steps to prevent fire and/or explosion:

   a. Disconnect negative terminal from battery (except when testing with battery voltage is required).

   b. When ever possible, use a flashlight instead of a drop light.

   c. Keep all open flame and smoking material out of the area.

   d. Use a shop cloth or similar to catch fuel when opening a fuel system.

   e. Relieve fuel system pressure before servicing.

   f. Use eye protection.

   g. Always keep a dry chemical (class B) fire extinguisher near the area.

NOTE: Due to the amount of fuel pressure in the fuel lines, before doing any work to the fuel system, the fuel system should be depressurized. To depressurize the fuel system, disconnect the fuel pump electrical connections at the fuel pump and start the vehicle. Let the vehicle run until it burns up the remaining fuel in the fuel lines. This way there will be no pressure left in the fuel system and the repair work can be performed.

THROTTLE BODY

Removal and Installation

Due to the varied application of throttle body units, a general throttle body unit removal and installation procedure is out-

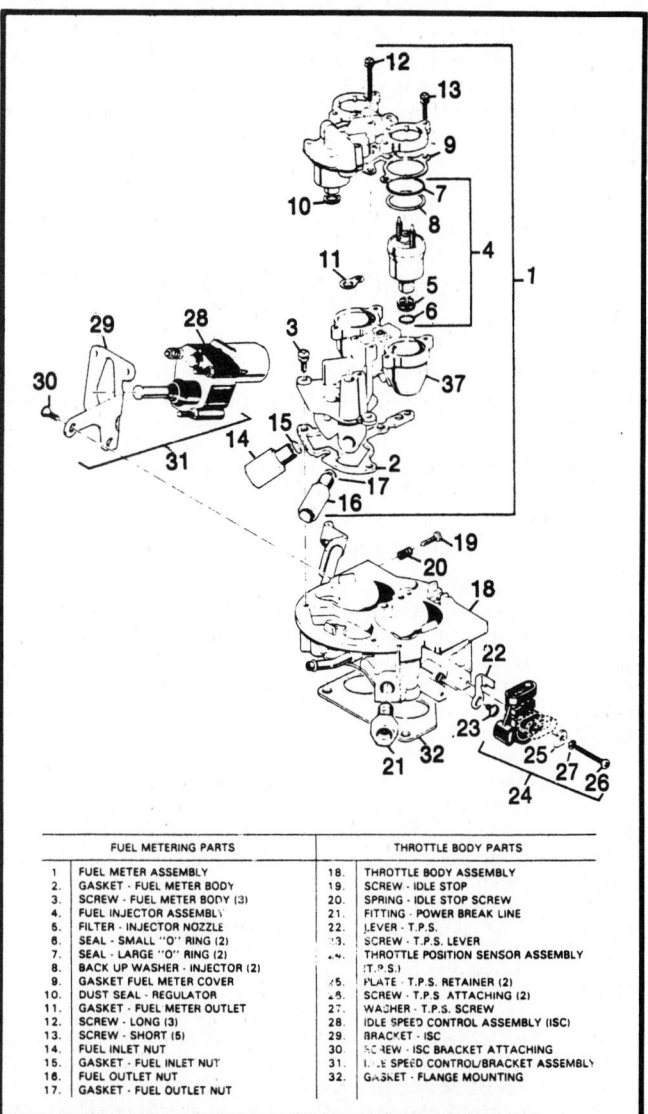

FUEL METERING PARTS		THROTTLE BODY PARTS	
1	FUEL METER ASSEMBLY	18.	THROTTLE BODY ASSEMBLY
2.	GASKET - FUEL METER BODY	19.	SCREW - IDLE STOP
3.	SCREW - FUEL METER BODY (3)	20.	SPRING - IDLE STOP SCREW
4.	FUEL INJECTOR ASSEMBLY	21.	FITTING - POWER BREAK LINE
5.	FILTER - INJECTOR NOZZLE	22.	LEVER - T.P.S.
6.	SEAL - SMALL "O" RING (2)	23.	SCREW - T.P.S. LEVER
7.	SEAL - LARGE "O" RING (2)	24.	THROTTLE POSITION SENSOR ASSEMBLY (T.P.S.)
8.	BACK UP WASHER - INJECTOR (2)		
9.	GASKET FUEL METER COVER	25.	PLATE - T.P.S. RETAINER (2)
10.	DUST SEAL - REGULATOR	26.	SCREW - T.P.S ATTACHING (2)
11.	GASKET - FUEL METER OUTLET	27.	WASHER - T.P.S. SCREW
12.	SCREW - LONG (3)	28.	IDLE SPEED CONTROL ASSEMBLY (ISC)
13.	SCREW - SHORT (5)	29.	BRACKET - ISC
14.	FUEL INLET NUT	30.	SCREW - ISC BRACKET ATTACHING
15.	GASKET - FUEL INLET NUT	31.	IDLE SPEED CONTROL/BRACKET ASSEMBLY
16.	FUEL OUTLET NUT	32.	GASKET - FLANGE MOUNTING
17.	GASKET - FUEL OUTLET NUT		

Exploded view of DFI throttle body assembly

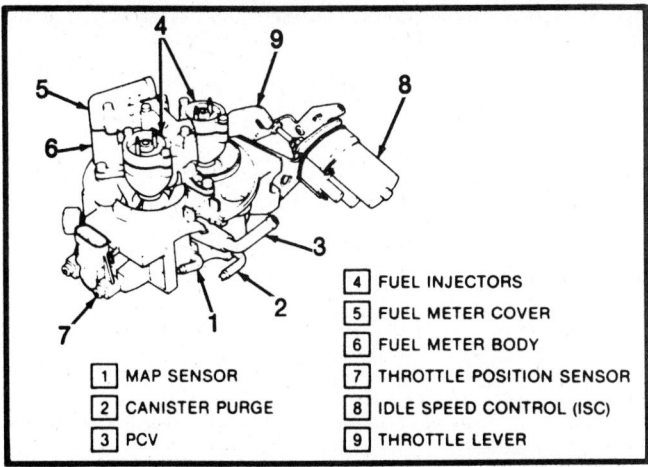

Exploded view of the TBI unit and the vacuum ports—DFI

1	MAP SENSOR	**4**	FUEL INJECTORS
2	CANISTER PURGE	**5**	FUEL METER COVER
3	PCV	**6**	FUEL METER BODY
		7	THROTTLE POSITION SENSOR
		8	IDLE SPEED CONTROL (ISC)
		9	THROTTLE LEVER

lined. The removal steps can be altered as required by the technician.

1. Depressurize the fuel system. Raise the hood, install fender covers and remove the air cleaner assembly. Disconnect the negative battery cable.
2. Disconnect the electrical connectors for the idle speed control motor, the throttle position sensor, both fuel injectors and any other component necessary in order to remove the throttle body.
3. Remove the throttle return spring, cruise control, throttle linkage and downshift cable.
4. Disconnect all necessary vacuum line, the fuel inlet line, fuel return line, brake booster line, MAP sensor hose and the AIR hose. Be sure to use a back-up wrench on all metal lines.
5. Remove the PCV, EVAP and EGR hoses from the front of the throttle body.
6. Remove the three throttle body mounting screws and remove the throttle body and gasket.
7. Installation is the reverse order of the removal procedure. Torque the throttle body retaining screws to 15 ft. lbs.

FUEL METER COVER

Removal and Installation

The fuel meter cover contains the pressure regulator and is only serviced as a complete preset assembly. The fuel pressure regulator is preset and plugged at the factory. DO NOT remove

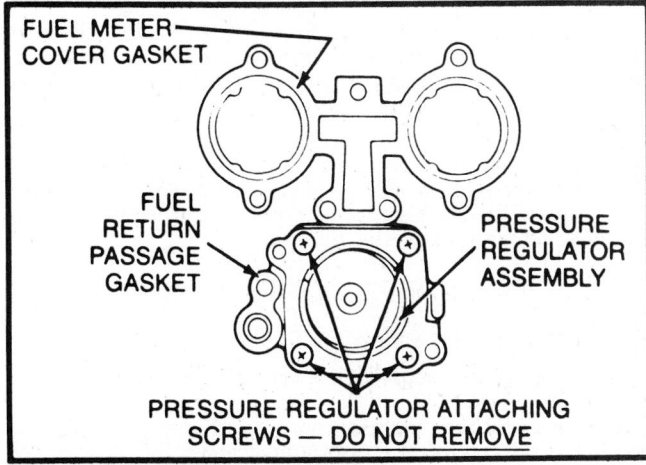

Fuel meter cover installation—DFI

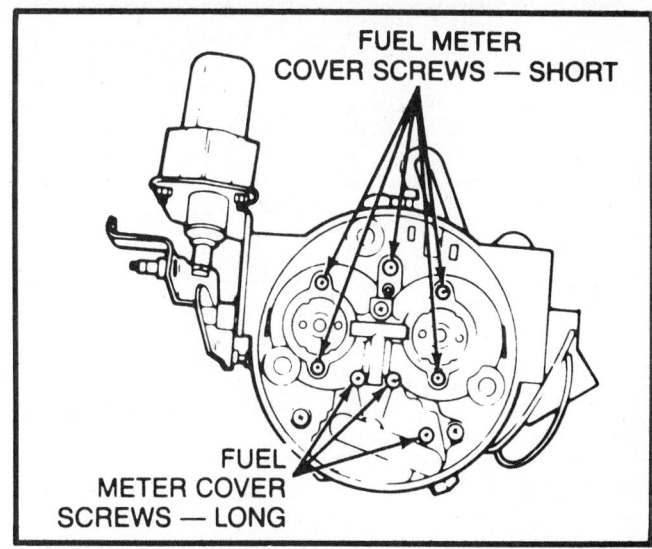

Fuel meter cover removal—DFI

the four screws securing the pressure regulator to the fuel meter cover. The fuel pressure regulator incorporates a large spring under heavy tension which, if accidentally released, could cause personal injury.

1. Depressurize the fuel system. Raise the hood, install fender covers and remove the air cleaner assembly. Disconnect the negative battery cable.
2. Disconnect the electrical connector to the fuel injectors.
3. Remove the eight screws securing the fuel meter cover to the fuel meter body. Be sure to take note of the location of the four short screws.
4. Remove the fuel meter cover from the fuel meter body.

NOTE: DO NOT immerse the fuel meter cover (with pressure regulator) in any type of cleaner. Immersion in cleaner will damage the internal fuel pressure regulator diaphragms and gaskets.

5. Installation is the reverse order of the removal procedure. Be sure to install a new dust seal and all new gaskets.

FUEL INJECTOR

Removal

Use care in removing the injector to prevent damage to the electrical connector pins on top of the injector, the injector fuel filter and the nozzle. The fuel injector is serviced as a complete assembly only. The fuel injector is an electrical component and should not be immersed in any type of cleaner.

1. Depressurize the fuel system. Raise the hood, install fender covers and remove the air cleaner assembly. Disconnect the negative battery cable.
2. Disconnect the injector electrical connector by sqeezing the two tabs together and pulling straight up.
3. Remove the fuel meter cover (refer to the fuel meter cover procedure).
4. With the fuel meter cover gasket in place to prevent damage to the casting, use a suitable dowel rod and lay the dowel rod on top of the fuel meter body.
5. Insert a suitable pry tool into the small lip of the injector and pry against the dowel rod lifting the injector straight up. Tool J-26868 or equivalent can also be used.
6. Remove the injector from the fuel meter body. Remove the small O-ring at the bottom of the injector cavity. Be sure to discard both O-rings.

Fuel injector removal – DFI

Installation

1. Lubricate the new small O-ring with pertroleum jelly or equivalent. Push the new O-ring on the nozzle end of the injector, pressing the O-ring up against the injector fuel filter.

2. Install a new steel backup washer in the recess of the fuel meter body.

3. Lubricate the new large O-ring with pertroleum jelly or equivalent. Install the new O-ring directly above the backup washer, pressing the O-ring down into the cavity recess. The O-ring is installed properly when it is flush with the fuel meter body casting surface.

NOTE: Do not attempt to reverse the installation of the large O-ring procedure. Install the backup washer and O-ring after the injector is located in the cavity. To do so will prevent the seating of the O-ring in the cavity recess.

4. Install the injector by using as pushing and twisting motion to center the nozzle O-ring in the bottom of the injector cavity and aligning the raised lug on the injector base with the notch cast into the fuel meter body.

5. Push down on theinjector making sure it is fully seated in the cavity. The injector is installed correctly when the lug is seated in the notch and the electrical terminals are parallel to the throttle shaft in the throttle body.

6. Install the fuel meter cover. Install the injector electrical connector and all electrical and vacuum lines. Install the air cleaner assembly.

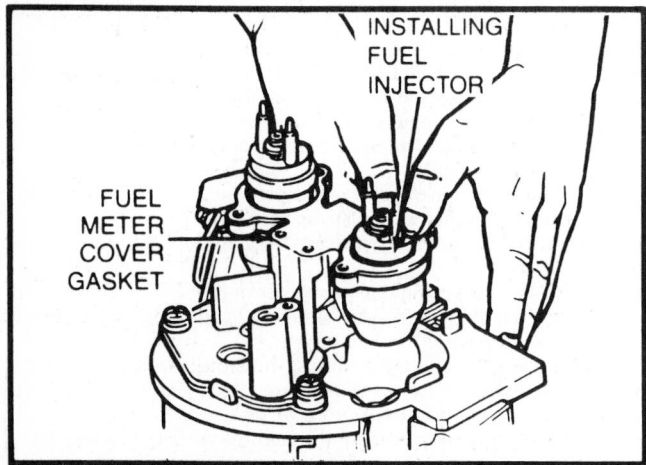

Fuel injector installation – DFI

7. Start the engine and check for leaks and proper injector operation.

FUEL METER BODY

Removal and Installation

1. Depressurize the fuel system. Raise the hood, install fender covers and remove the air cleaner assembly. Disconnect the negative battery cable.

2. Remove the fuel meter cover assembly. Remove the fuel meter cover gasket, fuel meter outlet gasket and pressure regulator seal.

3. Remove the fuel injectors. Remove the fuel inlet and fuel outlet nuts and gaskets from the fuel meter body.

4. Remove the three screws and lockwashers, then remove the fuel meter body from the throttle assembly.

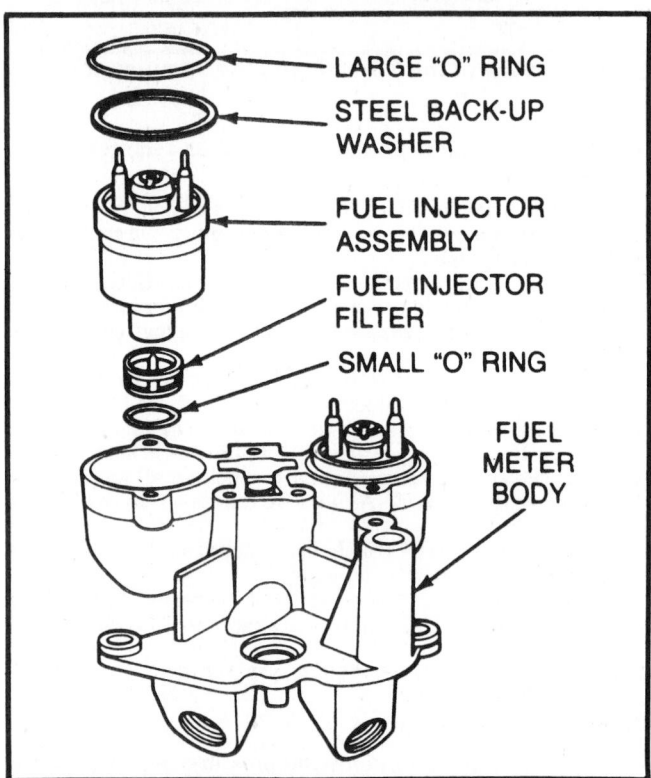

Exploded view of a typical DFI fuel injector

NOTE: Do not remove the center screw and staking at each end holding the fuel distribution skirt in the throttle body. The skirt is an integral part of the throttle body and is not serviced separately.

5. Remove the fuel meter body insulator gasket.

6. Installation is the reverse order of the removal procedure. Be sure to install new gaskets and O-rings whereever necessary. Apply threadlocking compound, Threadlock Sealer 262 or equivalent to the fuel meter retaining screws.

IDLE SPEED CONTROL (ISC)

Removal and Installation

1. Disconnect the negative battery cable and remove the air cleaner assembly.

2. Disconnect the electrical connector. Remove the two idle speed control mounting screws. Remove the ISC motor from the throttle body.

NOTE: The idle speed control motor is calibrated at the factory and NO attempt should be made to disassemble the unit. Do not immerse the ISC in any type of cleaner and always remove before the throttle body cleaning and servicing of components. Immersion in cleaner will damage the ISC unit.

3. To install position the ISC motor to the throttle body and secure it with the retaining screws. Adjust the ISC as necessary. Reconnect the electrical connector and the negative battery cable. Install the air cleaner assembly.

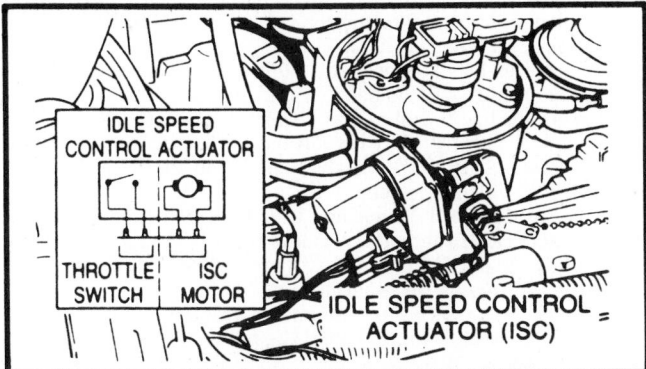

Idle Speed Control (ISC) motor used on DFI system

Idle Speed Control Motor Adjustment

RETRACTING THE ISC PLUNGER

1. Disconnect the ISC connector and connect a jumper harness to the ISC.
2. Connect a jumper wire leading to the ISC terminal "C" to a 12 volt source at the battery or junction block.
3. Apply finger pressure to the ISC plunger (close the throttle switch). Touch the jumper wire connected to the ISC terminal "D" to a ground until the ISC plunger retracts fully and stops. Remove the ground immediately.

NOTE: Do not leave terminal "D" grounded longer than necessary to fully retract the ISC plunger. If the ISC is stalled retracted for prolonged periods of time, damage to the ISC will result. Apply finger pressure to the ISC plunger before connecting terminal "D" to ground. Retracting the ISC plunger without pressure on the plunger may cause the internal gears to clash and bind. Never connect a voltage source to the ISC motor terminals "A" and "B" as damage to the internal throttle switch contacts will result.

EXTENDING THE ISC PLUNGER

1. Connect the ISC terminal "D" to 12 volts at the battery or the junction block.
2. Connect the ISC terminal "C" to a ground until the ISC plunger is partially or fully extended.
3. If the ISC motor fails to extend, disconnect and reconnect terminal "C" to ground to bump the motor from its stalled fully retracted position.

Minimum Idle Speed Check

1. Remove the air cleaner and plug the thermac vacuum tap. Start the engine.
2. Enter diagnostics; select ECM parameter P.O.4, coolant temperature. Operate the engine until the engine coolant temperature is greater than 185°F.
3. Retract the idle speed control motor until the throttle lever is clear of the ISC plunger. Use "Idle Speed Control Motor Tester" tool J-34025 or equivalent or use the jumper harness procedure as outlined in this section.

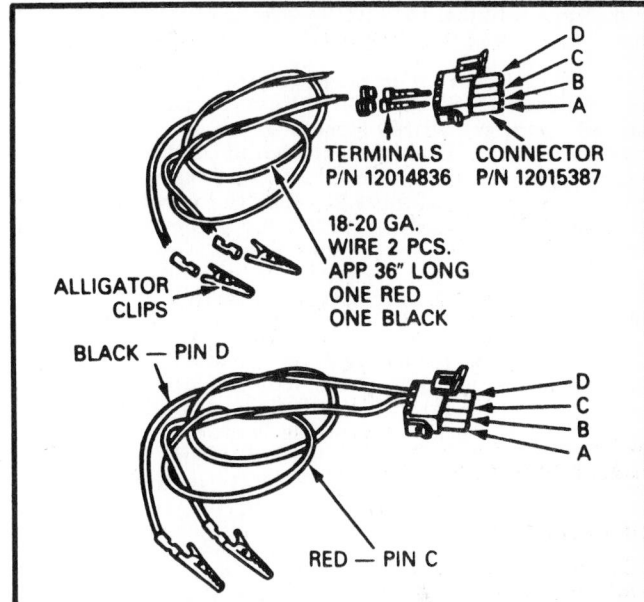

Setting the ISC connector up for testing—DFI

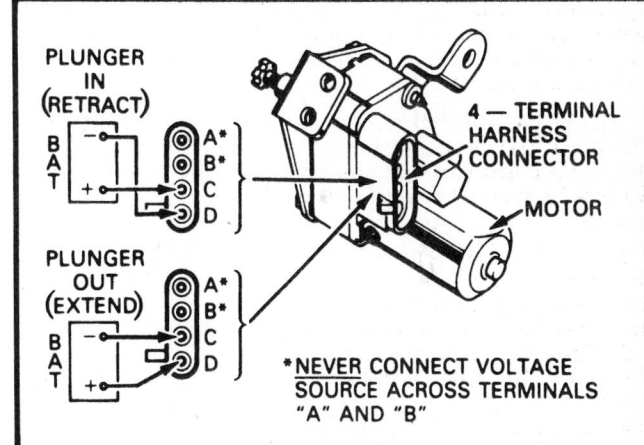

Exploded view of ISC motor—DFI

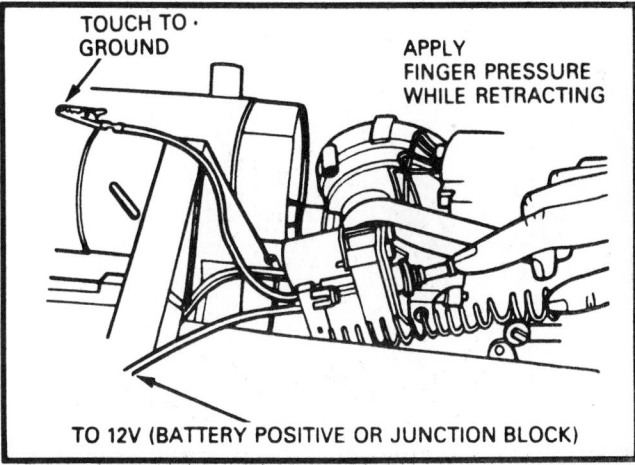

Retracting the ISC plunger—DFI

5–253

4. Make sure that the throttle lever is resting on the minimum air screw.

NOTE: To prevent damage to the ISC. Apply finger pressure to the ISC plunger while retracting. Retracting the ISC plunger without pressure on the plunger may cause the internal gears to clash and bind. Do not leave external power applied to the ISC for longer than necessary to cause the plunger to clear the throttle lever. If the motor is stalled retracted for prolonged periods, damage to the ISC motor may result. Never connect a voltage source to the ISC motor terminals "A" and "B" as damage to the internal throttle switch contacts will result.

5. With the ISC plunger fully retracted the plunger should not be touching the throttle lever. If contact is noted, adjust the ISC plunger (turn in) with a suitable pair of pliers or tool J-29607 so that it is not touching the throttle lever.

6. Make sure that the throttle lever is being bound by the throttle, cruise or T.V. cables. The throttle lever must be resting on the minimum air screw.

7. Disable the alternator by grounding the green test connector under the hood near the alternator. The alternator will turn off and the "No Charge" telltale light will illuminate.

8. Check the minimum idle speed; it should be 475–550 rpm. If the minimum idle speed is outside the limits go on to Step 9. If the minimum idle speed is good, than no further adjustment is necessary.

NOTE: If the engine speed in not within specifications, check for a vacuum leak at the throttle body, intake manifold vacuum fittings, tees and hoses. If the minimum air setting is made with a vacuum leak present, fuel control can be adversely affected throughout the driving range.

9. Make sure that the alternator is disabled; the "No Charge" telltale light will be illuminated.

10. If the minimum idle speed is out of specifications, connect a tachometer to the engine and adjust the minimum idle screw to obtain 525 rpm.

ISC Maximum Extension Check and Adjustment

1. Connect a high impedance digital voltmeter to the TPS test point (outlined in the TPS adjustment). With the key ON and the engine OFF, extend the ISC motor using tool J-34025 or equivalent or as outlined in this section.

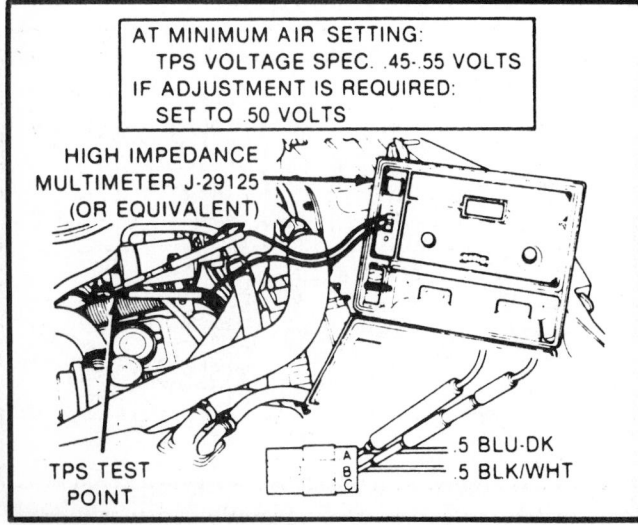

AT MINIMUM AIR SETTING:
TPS VOLTAGE SPEC. .45-.55 VOLTS
IF ADJUSTMENT IS REQUIRED:
SET TO .50 VOLTS

HIGH IMPEDANCE
MULTIMETER J-29125
(OR EQUIVALENT)

.5 BLU-DK
.5 BLK/WHT

TPS TEST
POINT

A
B
C

TPS signal volatge measurement – DFI

2. If the ISC motor is jammed in the fully retracted position, it may be necessary to apply and release the ground several times to bump the ISC from its stalled retracted position.

3. With the ISC fully extended (so that it ratchets) apply and release power to extend the ISC while watching the voltmeter at the TPS test point.

4. Backprobe the TPS test point with the meter positive lead connected to circuit 417 (pin A) dark blue wire, and the negative lead connected to circuit 476 (pin B) black and white wire. Set the meter to the two volt scale.

5. The procedure taht should be used is apply voltage, release voltage, note the voltmeter valvue when the ISC stoped. This should be done multiple times.

6. With the ISC stopped and at full extension, one of two voltmeter values will be seen; a high value at the top of the ratchet and a low value at the bottom of the ratchet.

7. Look for the highest TPS voltage, which will be seen when the ISC stops at the top of its ratchet. Stop the ISC when the highest TPS voltage is seen.

8. If the highest TPS voltage is 1.05–1.10 volts, no adjustment is needed. If the voltage is less than 1.05 or greater than 1.10, adjust the ISC plunger in to lower the voltage or out to raise the voltage as necessary.

9. Recheck the maximum extension voltage by again applying power to extend the ISC until the maximum TPS voltage is seen.

10. Once the adjustment is final, turn off the ignition and remove all test equipment.

Minimum Air, Throttle Position Sensor and ISC Motor Adjustments

1. Enter diagnostic mode and record all trouble codes displayed (numbers displayed between the time "1.8.8" is displayed and ".7.0" is displayed). If no codes are displayed, proceed to step 2.

2. Remove the air cleaner, start the engine, and warm the engine up to normal operating temperature (parameter .0.4 greater than 185°F). Turn A/C off. Check the engine timing and adjust as necessary.

3. Turn off all electric accessories. Place steering wheel in its center position. Place the transmission in Park.

4. Retract the ISC motor plunger using the following procedure:

    a. Unlock the ISC motor connector but do not disconnect it from the motor.

    b. Open the throttle and hold at approximately 1500 rpm. With the same hand close the throttle switch by depressing the ISC plunger.

    c. When the ISC plunger is fully retracted, continue to hold the throttle switch closed while disconnecting the ISC motor connector with the other hand.

NOTE: Do not power the ISC motor in the fully retracted position for more than 4 seconds or ECM damage may occur.

    d. After the connector is removed release the throttle switch and return the throttle to idle.

5. Under these conditions, the ISC plunger should not be touching the throttle lever. If the contact is noted, adjust the ICS plunger (turn in) with pliers or suitable available special tool so that it is not touching the throttle lever.

6. Enter diagnostics and depress the "outside temp." button to turn the "A/C Clutch" status light off. Display engine data parameter .1.1 and observe "engine speed" at minimum air. If the displayed value is "40" to "50" proceed to Step 8.

7. If the "engine speed" value does not fall within the above limits, then connect a tachometer to the engine and adjust the throttle stop screw to obtain 450 rpm. If the engine speed cannot be corrected, check that the throttle is not held off the minimum stop screw because of linkage binding or interference with the ISC motor plunger.

8. With the vehicle at ignition on (engine off), enter diagnostics and display engine data parameter .0.1. Open the throttle and let it snap fully shut against the throttle stop screw. If the displayed "throttle" angle value is "0", procede to Step 10.

9. If the "throttle angle" value is not "0", refer to the TPS adjustment in this section.

10. With the ISC motor fully retracted and the throttle fully shut against the throttle stop screw, turn the ISC motor plunger adjustment screw to obtain a 0.060 in.(1.50mm) gap between ISC motor plunger and the throttle lever.

11. Disconnect all test equipment and reconnect all connections. Turn ignition off for at least 10 seconds. Start engine and check the ISC motor for proper operation.

12. The above procedure may have turned to the check engine light and/or may have set a trouble code. After the system is restored to its normal operation, the check engine light will go out but the trouble code will remain as an "intermittent" problem. Enter diagnostics, clear the stored codes, and turn the ignition off for at least 10 seconds.

THROTTLE POSITION SENSOR (TPS)

Removal and Installation

It may be necessary to remove the throttle body assembly, in order to gain access to the TPS retaining screws.

1. Disconnect the negative battery cable and remove the air cleaner assembly.

2. Disconnect the electrical connector. Remove the two throttle position sensor screws, lockwashers and retainers.

3. Remove the throttle position sensor from the throttle body.

4. Install the TPS with the throttle valve in the normal closed position, install the throttle position sensor on the throttle body assembly, making sure that the TPS pickup lever is located above the tang on the throttle actuator lever.

5. Install the retainers and tew new TPS screws and lockwashers. DO NOT use thread locking compound on the TPS attaching screws. They are aluminumand will break.

6. New screws are supplied with the TPS service kit. DO NOT tighten the screws until the TPS is adjusted.

TPS Adjustment

The throttle position sensor adjustment should be checked after the minimum air adjustment is completed.

1. Remove the air cleaner assembly.

2. Disconnect the TPS harness from the throttle position sensor.

3. Using three suitable jumper wires connect the TPS harness to throttle position sensor.

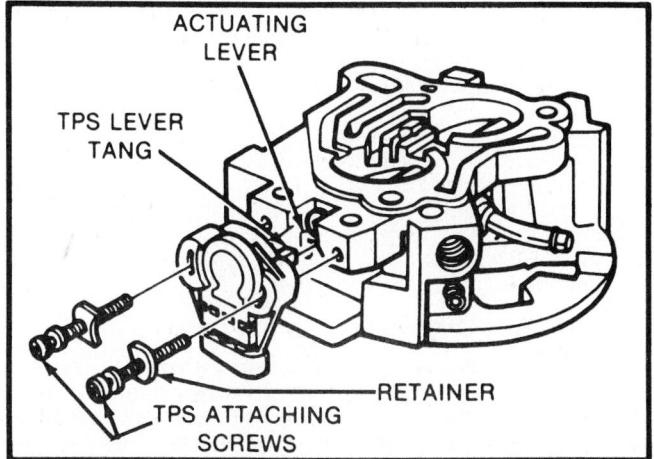

Throttle position sensor removal and installation— DFI

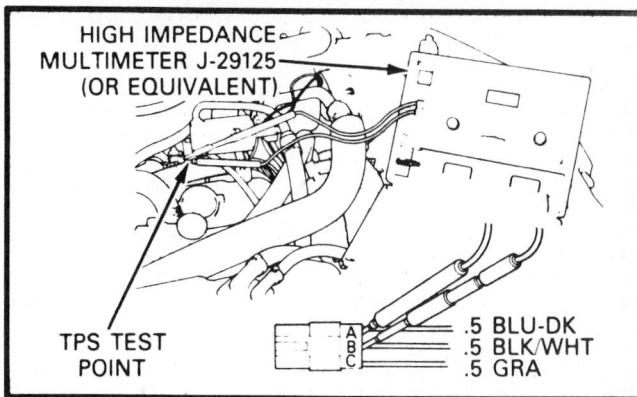

TPS volatge test point location—DFI

4. With the ignition on and the engine off, measure the reference voltage, connect the probe's from a suitable high impedance digital voltmeter to the TPS harness test point which connects to circuit #474 (gray wire) and circuit #476 (black/white wire). The reference should be as follows:

    a. If the reference voltage is less than 4.90 volts - set the TPS voltage to .48 volts.

    b. If the reference voltage is 4.90 to 5.10 volts - set the TPS voltage to .50 volts.

    c. If the reference voltage is 5.11 to 5.30 volts - set the TPS voltage to .52 volts.

    d. If the reference voltage is more than 5.30 volts - set the TPS voltage to .54 volts.

5. After measuring the reference voltage, connect the digital voltmeter positive (+) probe to the TPS harness test point (A) which connects to circuit #417 (dark blue wire).

6. Connect the digital voltmeter negative (-) probe to the TPS harness test point (B) which connects to circuit #476 (black/white wire).

7. Set the digital voltmeter ton the 2 volt DC scale. With the throttle fully shut against the throttle stop screw, check the voltmeter reading.

8. If the TPS voltage is within .05 volts of the specified voltage no adjustment is necessary.

9. If the TPS voltage does not fall within specifications, adjust the TPS as follows:

    a. Loosen the TPS retaining screws just enough to permit rotation of the TPS.

    b. With the throttle fully shut against the throttle stop

IF THE REFERENCE VOLTAGE IS	SET TPS VOLTAGE TO
LESS THAN 4.90 VOLTS	.48 VOLTS
4.90 TO 5.10 VOLTS	.50 VOLTS
5.11 TO 5.30 VOLTS	.52 VOLTS
MORE THAN 5.30 VOLTS	.54 VOLTS

MEASURE REFERENCE VOLTAGE BETWEEN CIRCUITS #474 (GRAY WIRE) AND #476 (BLACK/WHITE WIRE)

TPS TEST POINT

TPS voltage reference point location and TPS voltage settings—DFI

screw, turn the TPS left or right until the voltmeter falls within specifications.

   c. Tighten the TPS mounting screws with the sensor in this position.

10. Recheck the voltmeter reading to make sure that the adjustment remained within .05 volts of the specified voltage.

11. Turn off the ignition, reconnect the TPS harness to the throttle position sensor and remove all test equipment.

NOTE: Some 1981–85 DFI equipped vehicles may experience a high idle or an intermittent code 26, under various operating conditions due to installation of an improper throttle position sensor (TPS) while servicing the vehicle. The 1984–85 TPS is different in appearance than the 1981–83 TPS. As with all electrical and emission related parts, it is essential that the correct service part be used. The part numbers are as follows: Type 1 part number 17067979 with TPS ID number 59085 is used on the 1984 368 cu. in.(V8–6–4) "D" body limousine. Type 3 part number 17110352 with TPS ID number 74958, is used on the 1984–85 HT4100 DW, DM, E, and K body (excluding the limousine).

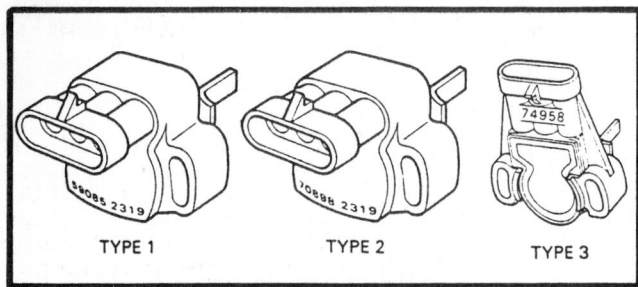

DFI throttle position sensor identification

Diagnostic Procedure

The dash mounted "Service Now" and "Service Soon" telltale lights are used to inform the technician of detected system malfunctions or abnormalities. These malfunctions may be related to the various ECM inputs or controlled functions or to the ECM itself. The service telltale light that was illuminated by the fault occurrence will automatically go out if the fault clears. The fault is logged as an intermittent trouble code by the ECM; the ECM stores the trouble code associated with the detected failure until the diagnostic codes are cleared or until 50 ignition switch (on and off) cycles have occurred without any fault reappearing.

Service Telltale Operation

Proper operation of the service telltale lights are as follows:

   a. Both lights are normally off (engine running or key on, engine nut running).

   b. A bulb check is performed; both bulbs turn on, when the ignition is in the "Crank" position only. When the engine starts, both bulbs should go out.

   c. Depending on the trouble code set, either the "Service Soon" telltale light or the "Service Now" telltale light comes on and stays on while the malfunction (trouble code) is detected.

   d. If the malfunction is intermittent, the "Service light that came on will go out when the malfunction is no longer detected. The light will come on each time the malfunction is again detected; the light may come on and go out again in the same key cycle. When a "Service Soon" malfunction is detected at the same time a "Service Now" malfunction is detected, only the "Service Now" telltale light comes on.

   e. Both service lights stay on when the system is displaying the diagnostic routine.

Intermittent Codes Verus Hard Failures

On the codes E12 through E51, the service telltale light will go out automatically if the malfunction clears. However the ECM stores the trouble associated with the detected failure until the diagnostic codes are cleared or until 50 ignition switch (ON/OFF) cycles have occurred without any fault reappearing. This condition is known as an intermittent failure.

Therefore the ECM may have two types of trouble codes stored in its memory. These two codes type are as follows:

   a. A code for a malfunction which is a hard failure. A hard failure turns on the appropriate service telltale light and keeps it on as long as the malfunction is present.

   b. A code intermittent malfunction which occurred within the last 50 ignition cycles. An intermittent failure will allow the service telltale light to turn off either when the malfunction clears up or when the key is next cycled to the OFF position.

The first pass of diagnostics, prefixed by ".E", will contain all history codes, both hard and intermittent. The second pass contains only the hard codes that are present and will be prefixed by ".E.E".

When trouble code E30 or E48 is set, the "Service Soon" light will illuminate for the entire ignition cycle and system operation is not tested again until the next ignition cycle. This means that an intermittent malfunction will appear as a hard failure during the ignition cycle in which it occurs.

For codes E52 through E67, the service telltale lights will never come on. These codes indicate that a specific condition occurred of which the technician should be aware. Since most of these codes can be operator induced, a judgement must be made whether or not the code requires investigation. These codes will also be stored until the diagnostic system is cleared or until 50 ignition cycles have passed without any fault appearing.

SELF DIAGNOSTIC FEATURES

Trouble Codes

In the process of controlling its various subsystems, the ECM and BCM continually monitor operating conditions for possible system malfunctions. By comparing system conditions against standard operating limits certain circuit and component malfunctions can be detected. A two digit numerical "Trouble Code" is stored in the computer memory when a problem is detected by this diagnostic system. These "Trouble Codes" can later be displayed by the service technician as an aid in the system repair.

The occurance of certain system malfunctions required that the vehicle operator be alerted to the problem so as to avoid prolonged operation of the vehicle under a degraded system operation. The computer controlled service telltale lights will be illuminated under these conditions which indicate that service is required.

If a particular malfunction would result in a unacceptable system operation, the self-diagnostics will attempt to minimize the effect by taking "Failsoft" action. "Failsoft" action refers to any specific attempt by the computer system to compensate for a detected problem. A typical "Failsoft" action would be substitution of a fixed input value when a sensor is detected to be open or shorted.

Trouble Code Diagnosis

The diagnostic charts in this section are used on the basis of trouble codes which can be displayed during a diagnostic readout. The text that accompanies the charts is used as guide to explain what action to take when the code has been set.

When certain circuits need to be check a wiring schematic or diagram is usually included and will make reference to the circuit numbers. The circuit number is usually shown inside the box which represents the connector body in the complete diagram.

ECM/BCM Service Precautions

The ECM and BCM are designed to withstand normal current draws associated with vehicle operation, however care must be taken to avoid overloading any of these circuits. In testing for opens or shorts, do not ground or apply voltage to any of these circuits unless instructed to do so by the diagnostic procedures.

These circuits should be tested using a suitable high impedance multimeter J-34029A or J29125-A) or equivalent, if they remain connected to the ECM or BCM. Power should never be removed or applied to the ECM or BCM with the key in "On " position. Before removing or connecting battery cables, fuses or connectors always turn the ignition switch to the "Off" position.

Entering Diagnostic Mode

To enter the diagnostic mode, proceed as follows:
1. Turn the ignition switch to the "ON" position.
2. Depress the "OFF" and "WARMER" buttons on the climate control panel (CCP) simultaneously and hold until ".." appears. Then "88" will be displayed, which indicates the begining of the diagnostic readout.

NOTE: The purpose of illuminating the two display panels is to check that all segments of the displays are working. Diagnosis should not be attempted unless all segments appear as this could lead to mis-diagnosis (code 31 could be code 34 with two segments inoperative, etc.). If any of the segments are inoperative, the affected display will need to be replaced.

Trouble Code Display

After the displays end the segment check, any "Trouble Codes" stored in computer memory will be displayed. If the "Trouble Code" (other than E51) are present, they will be displayed on the "Fuel Data Center" panel as follows:
1. Display of trouble codes will begin with an "8.8.8" on the "Fuel Data Center" panel approximately one second. Then this "..E" will be displayed which indicates the begining of the ECM stored trouble codes. This first pass of the ECM codes includes all detected malfunctions whether they are currently present or not. If no ECM trouble codes are stored the "..E" display will be bypassed.
2. Following the display of the "..E" the lowest numbered ECM code will be displayed for approximately two seconds. All ECM codes will be prefixed with an "E"(i.e. E12, E13, etc.).
3. Progressively higher number ECM codes. if present will be displayed consecutively for two second intervals until the highest code present has been displayed.
4. The ".E.E" will then be displayed which indicates the begining of the second pass of the ECM trouble codes. On the second pass, only "hard" trouble codes will be displayed. These are the codes which indicate a currently present malfunction. Codes which are displayed during the first pass but not during the second are "Intermittent" the ".E.E" display will be bypassed.
5. When all the ECM codes have been displayed, the BCM codes will then be displayed in a similar fashion. The only exceptions during the BCM code display are:
   a. This "..F" precedes the first pass.
   b. BCM codes are prefixed by an "F".
   c. This ".F.F" precedes the second pass.
6. After all the ECM and BCM codes have been displayed or if no codes are present, code .7.0 will be displayed. Code .7.0 indicates that the system is ready for the next diagnostic feature to be selected.
7. If a code E51 is currently being detected, it will be displayed continuously until the diagnostic mode is exited. Dur-

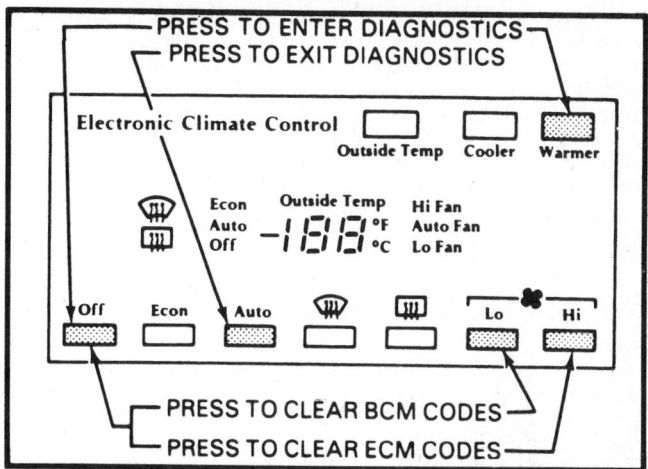

Typical DFI climate control panel (CCP) diplay

ing this display of code E51, none of the other diagnostic features will be possible (i.e. switch tests. output cycling, etc.).

Clearing The Trouble Codes

Trouble codes are stored in the ECM's memory may be cleared (erased) by entering the diagnostic mode and then depressing the "OFF" and "HI" buttons on the climate control panel (CCP) simultaneously. Hold the buttons in until "E.0.0" appears. Trouble codes stored in the BCM's memory may be cleared by depresing the "OFF" and "LO" buttons simultaneously until the "F.0.0" appears. After the "E.0.0 or F.0.0" is displayed, the ".7.0" will appear. With the ".7.0" is displayed turn the ignition off for at least 10 seconds before re-entering the diagnostic mode.

Exiting Diagnostic Mode

To get out of the diagnostic mode, depress the "Auto" button or turn the ignition switch OFF for 10 seconds. Trouble codes are not erased when this is done. The temperature setting will reappear in the display panel.

Climate Control In Diagnostic Mode

Upon entering the diagnostic mode, the ECC will operate in whatever mode was being commanded just prior to depressing the "OFF" and "WARMER" buttons. Even through the display may change to the "OFF" mode just as the buttons are pushed, the prior operating mode is remembered and will resume after diagnostics is entered.

Status Display

While in the diagnostic mode, the mode indicators on the climate control panel (CCP) are used to indicate status of certain system operation modes. The different modes of operation are indicated by the status light either being turned on or turned off. A brief summary of each status light is provided below:
1. The "AUTO" status indicator is turned on whenever the ECM is operating in "Closed Loop" fuel control. This light should come on after the coolant and oxygen sensors have reached normal operating temperature.
2. The "ECON" status indicator is turned on whenever the oxygen sensor signal to the ECM indicates a "RICH" exhaust condition. This light should toggle between "RICH" and "LEAN" (flash on and off) during warm during warm steady throttle operation.
3. The "OFF" status indicator is turned on whenever the ECM senses that the throttle switch is closed. This light should be off whenever the throttle is applied.

4. The "FRONT DEFOG" status indicator is turned on whenever the ECM is commanding the VCC (viscous (torque) converter clutch) to engage. This light indicates whether the VCC is enabled or disabled by the ECM. Actual operation depends on the integrity of the VCC system.

5. The "REAR DEFOG" status indicator is turned on whenever the ECM senses that the 4th gear pressure switch is open. This light should only be on while in 4th gear operation.

6. The "OUTSIDE TEMP" status indicator is turned on whenever the BCM is commanding the ECC (electronic comfort control) compressor clutch to engage. This light only indicates whether the clutch is enabled or disabled by the BCM. Actual operation depends on the integrity of the compressor clutch system.

NOTE: The ECC is inhibited during diagnostic mode.

7. The "AUTO FAN" status indicator is turned on whenever the feedback signal from the colling fan control module to the BCM indicates that the fans are running. This light should be off whenever the fans are off.

NOTE: "Fans Before Idle" is inhibited during the diagnostic mode.

8. The "HI-FAN" status indicator is turned on whenever the BCM is commanding the UP-DOWN mode door to divert air flow up away from the heater outlet. This light will be off whenever the ECC system is in the "HEATER" or "NORMAL PURGE" modes.

9. The "LO-FAN" status indicator is turned on whenever the BCM is commanding the AC−DEF mode to divert air flow from the A/C outlets as in the "A/C" or "NORMAL PURGE" modes. This light will be off whenever the ECC system is in the "HEATER", "INTERMEDIATE", "DEFROST" and "COLD PURGE" modes.

10. The "°F" status indicator is turned on whenever the BCM senses that the refrigerant low pressure switch is open. The light will come on when the ambient temperature falls below approximately -5°F due to pressure temperature relationship of refrigerant -12. This light should remain off under all other conditions if the refrigerant system is fully charged and being controlled properly.

11. The "°C" status indicator is turned on whenever the BCM is commanding the heater water valve to block the coolant flow through the heater core. This light should remain off except when the air mix door is being commanded to the MAX A/C position (0%).

Code .7.0

Code .7.0 is a decision point. When code .7.0 is displayed on the Data Center, the technician may select the diagnostic feature that he wants to display. The following choices are available:

a. ECM switch test.
b. ECM data display.
c. ECM output cycling.
d. BCM dat display.
e. ECC program overide.
f. Cooling fans overide.
g. Exit the diagnostics or clear the codes and exit the diagnostics.

ECM Switch Test Series

The engine must be running and Code .7.0 must be displayed on the Data Center panel before the switch test can begin. To start the switch tests sequence depress and release the brake pedal; the switch test begins as the display switches from Code .7.0 to Code E.7.1.

NOTE: If the display does not advance to Code E.7.1, refer to diagnosis chart E.7.1, because the ECM is not processing the brake signal.

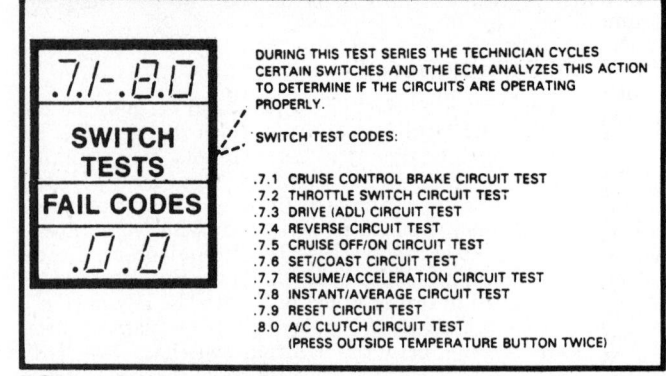

DURING THIS TEST SERIES THE TECHNICIAN CYCLES CERTAIN SWITCHES AND THE ECM ANALYZES THIS ACTION TO DETERMINE IF THE CIRCUITS ARE OPERATING PROPERLY.

SWITCH TEST CODES:

.7.1 CRUISE CONTROL BRAKE CIRCUIT TEST
.7.2 THROTTLE SWITCH CIRCUIT TEST
.7.3 DRIVE (ADL) CIRCUIT TEST
.7.4 REVERSE CIRCUIT TEST
.7.5 CRUISE OFF/ON CIRCUIT TEST
.7.6 SET/COAST CIRCUIT TEST
.7.7 RESUME/ACCELERATION CIRCUIT TEST
.7.8 INSTANT/AVERAGE CIRCUIT TEST
.7.9 RESET CIRCUIT TEST
.8.0 A/C CLUTCH CIRCUIT TEST
(PRESS OUTSIDE TEMPERATURE BUTTON TWICE)

ECM switch test series

ENGINE DATA

PARAMETER NO.	PARAMETER	RANGE	DISPLAY UNITS
.0.1	THROTTLE POSITION	−10 to 90	DEGREES
.0.2	MAP	14 to 108	kPa
.0.3	BARO	14 to 108	kPa
.0.4	COOLANT	−40 to 151	°C
.0.5	MAT	−40 to 151	°C
.0.6	INJECTOR PULSE WIDTH	0 to 19.9	MSEC
.0.7	O_2 SENSOR	0 to 1.99	VOLTS
.0.8	SPARK ADVANCE	0 to 52	DEGREES
.0.9	IGNITION CYCLES	0 to 50	KEY CYCLES
.1.0	BATTERY VOLTAGE	0 to 19.9	VOLTS
.1.1	ENGINE RPM	0 to 1990	RPM ÷ 10
.1.2	VEHICLE SPEED	0 to 199	MPH
.1.3	PROM I.D.	0 to 199	CODE

ECM engine data display

As each code is displayed, the associated switch must be cycled within 10 seconds or the code will be recorded in the ECM's memory as a failure. After the ECM recognizes a test as passing or after 10 seconds time-out elaspes without the proper cycling being recognized, the display automatically advances to the next switch test code. The switch tests sequence is performed as follows:

1. With Code E.7.1 displayed, depress and release the brake pedal again to test the Cruise Control brake circuit.
2. With Code E.7.2 displayed. depress the throttle from the idle position to an open throttle position and then slowly release the throttle. While this action is being performed, the ECM checks the throttle switch for proper operation.
3. With Code E.7.4 displayed and the brakes applied, shift the transmission lever into reverse and then neutral. This action checks the operation of the park neutral switch.

NOTE:On vehicles without cruise control, codes E.7.5, E.7.6 and E.7.7 will be displayed but cannot be performed during the vehcile switch tests. When these codes are displayed during the switch tests, allow each code to reach its 10 second time out. After this time out has elasped, the display will advance to the next code. Allow codes E.7.5, E.7.6 and E.7.7 to time out (30 seconds). Since these codes will be recorded as failures in the switch test sequence, a display E.0.0 will never be observed at the completion of the tests (see Step 9). To confirm proper operation of the remaining switch, Code E.7.8 must be observed as having advanced within 10 second time out. If the code cannot be advanced within its time out, it should be considered a failed test.

4. With Code E.7.5 displayed, switch the Cruise Control instrument panel switch from OFF to ON and back to OFF to check the operation of this switch.

5. With Code E.7.6 displayed and with the cruise instrument panel switch in the on position, depress and release the set coast button to check the operation of this switch.

6. With Code E.7.7 displayed and with the cruise instrument panel switch in the on position, depress and release the resume/acceleration switch to check the operation of this switch.

7. With Code E.7.8 displayed and the engine running, turn the wheels from straight ahead to the full right or left position and then return it to the straight ahead position. While this action is being performed, the ECM checks the power steering pressure switch for proper operation.

8. When the switch test are completed, the ECM will no go back and display the switch codes which did not test properly. Each code which did not pass will be displayed begining with the lowest number. The codes will not disappear until the affected switch circuit has been repaired and retested.

9. After the switch tests are completed and all circuits pass, the "Fuel Data Center" displays "E.0.0" and then returns to code .7.0. The "E.0.0" indicates that all of the switch circuits are operating properly.

ECM DATA DISPLAY

Code .7.0 must be displayed on the "Data Center" panel before the diagnostics can begin to display the ECM data series. To display the ECM data information proceed as follows:

1. Depress the and release the "Lo" button on the climate control panel (CCP). The ECM data series will begin as the display switches from Code .7.0 to Code E.9.0. It is possible to leave the ECM data series at anytime and return to Code .7.0 by clearing the ECM or BCM codes.

2. To advance the display, depress the "Hi" button on the climate control panel (CCP). To return to a lower number parameter or jump directly from E.9.0 to the end of the parameter list (P.1.3). depress the "Lo" button on the CCP.

3. When troubleshooting a malfunction, the ECM data display can be used to compare the vehicle with problems to a vehicle which is functioning properly. A brief summary of each parameter is provided below:

    a. **P.0.1** - The throttle angle is displayed in degrees, the parameter range if from 10.0 to + 90.0. The throttle angle displayed is actual indicated angle, not the throttle angle corrected by the ECM adaptive learning routine. A decimal point will appear before the last digit.

    b. **P.0.2** - The map value is displayed in kilopascals (kPa), the parameter range is from 14 to 109.

    c. **P.0.3** - The computed BARO value is displayed in kilopascals (kPa), the parameter range is from 61 to 103 kPa. BARO is calculated from the MAP reading taken at wide open throttle.

    d. **P.0.4** - The coolant temperature is displayed in degrees celsius (°C), the parameter display range is from –40 to 151°C.

    e. **P.0.5** - The manifold air temperature is displayed in degrees celsius (°C), the parameter display range is from –40 to 151°C.

    f. **P.0.6** - The injector pulse width is displayed in milliseconds. A decimal point will appear before the last digit, the parameter display range is 0 to 99 ms.

    g. **P.0.7** - The oxygen sensor voltage is displayed in volts, the display range is 0 to 1.14 volts. A decimal point will appear before the last two digits.

    h. **P.0.8** - The spark advance value is displayed in degrees. This value will agree with a timing light on the engine (± 2 degrees) if the base timing has been adjusted properly. The parameter display range is from 0 to 52°.

    i. **P.0.9** - The ignition cycle counter value is the number of times that the ignition has been cycled to the off since the ECM trouble code was last detected. After 50 ignition cycles without any malfunctions being detected, all stored ECM codes are cleared and the counter is reset to 0.

    j. **P.1.0** - The battery voltage is read in volts. A decimal point will appear before the last digit. The parameter display range is from 0 to 25.5 volts.

    k. **P.1.1** - The engine speed is displayed in rpm/10 (120 should be read at 1200 rpm). The parameter display range is 0 to 637 rpm; multiply the parameter by 10 to get rpm.

    l. **P.1.2** - The vehicle speed is displayed in miles per hour (MPH). The parameter display range is 0 to 255 MPH.

    m. **P.1.3** - The oxygen sensor cross counts is a counter that is incremented by one (1) each time the oxygen sensor "Crosses" the line from the rich to lean to lean to rich. Cross counts start at 0 increments to 255 where it rolls over and begins to increment again.

    n. **P.1.4** - The fuel integrator is a record of how long the oxygen sensor has spent in the rich or lean voltage regions. The fuel integrator starts at 128 counts and reset to 128 counts on acceleration, deceleration and at heavy engine loads. If the fuel system is running to rich for current conditions, the integrator gets smaller to indicate less fuel is needed. If the fuel system is running too lean for current conditions, the integrator will get larger to indicate more fuel is needed. The parameter display range is from 0 (being a fuel system too rich, a lean command) to 255 (being a fuel system too lean, a rich command).

    o. **P.1.5** - VCC volts is the voltage reading from the VCC temperature thermistor. The parameter display range is 0 volts (hot thermistor or circuit shorted) to 5.1 volts (cold thermistor or circuit open).

    p. **P.1.6** - The ECM prom I.D. is displayed as a number up to three digits long which can be used to verify that the proper PROM was installed in the ECM.

When the ECM data display is initiated, the "Fuel Data Center" will display a parameter identification (i.e. P.0.1 or P.1.3) for one second and then a number will be displayed for nine seconds to indicate the parameter value. The display will continue to repeat this sequence of events until the technician decides to move another parameter.

ECM OUTPUT CYCLING

This mode can be initiated after E.9.5 is displayed on the "Fuel Data Center". The display of the E.9.5 can be reached by depressing the "Hi" button while Code .7.0 is displayed. The ECM output cycling mode, Code E.9.6 turns the ECM's outputs on and off. To enter the output cycling mode, procedd as follows;

    a. The engine must be running.

    b. Turn the cruise instrument panel switch to the on position so that the Cruise Control outputs will cycle.

    c. Turn the engine off and within two seconds, turn the ignition on.

    d. Enter the diagnostics and display Code E.9.5.

    e. Depress the accelerator pedal (throttle switch open) and release it (throttle switch closed). The ECM output cycling mode begins as the display switches from Code E.9.5 to Code E.9.6.

    f. It is possible to leave the ECM output cycling mode at any time and return to .7.0 by clearing the ECM and BCM codes. If the display does not advance to Code E.9.6, refer to Code E.7.2 of the switch test.

    g. The output cycling mode will end automatically after two minutes of cycling and the display will switch from Code E.9.6 to Code E.9.5.

    h. The outputs will cycle on and off every three seconds until the two minute automatic shut off occurs. The only exception to this three second cycle is the cruise control power valve which cycles continuously. If addtional output cycling is desired, recycle the throttle switch.

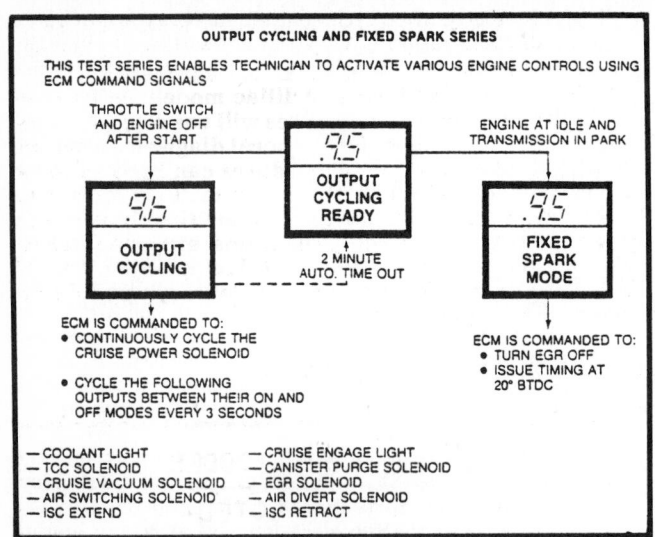

Typical output cycling test and fixed spark mode

NOTE: The ECM has a "learning" capability. If the battery is disconnected the learning process has to begin all over again. A change may be noted in the vehicle's performance. To "teach" the ECM, insure the vehicle is at operating temperature and drive at part throttle, with moderate acceleration and idle conditions, until performance returns.

FIXED SPARK MODE PROCEDURE (SET TIMING)

To verify the proper adjustment of spark timing, the ECM will command a fixed 10° of spark advance and disable the EGR operation whenever the following conditions are met:

a. The engine must be running at warm (parameter P.0.4 greater than 85°C.).

b. The engine speed must be under 900 rpm.

c. The transmission must be in Park.

d. Exist diagnostics (press "Auto") and jumper pins "A" (circuit #150) and "B" (circuit #451) in the ALDL connector. The service soon light may begin to flicker when pins "A" and "B" are jumped together.

BCM DATA DISPLAY

Code .7.0 must be displayed on the "Fuel Data Center" panel before the diagnostics can begin to display the BCM data series. To display the BCM data information proceed as follows:

1. Depress the and release the "Outside Temp" button on the climate control panel (CCP). The BCM data series will begin as the display switches from Code .7.0 to Code F.8.0. It is possible to leave the BCM data series at anytime and return to Code .7.0 by clearing the ECM or BCM codes.

2. To advance the display, depress the "Hi" button on the climate control panel (CCP). To return to a lower number parameter or jump directly from F.8.0 to the end of the parameter list (P.3.1) depress the "Lo" button on the CCP.

3. When troubleshooting a malfunction, the BCM data display can be used to compare the vehicle with problems to a vehicle which is functioning properly. A brief summary of each parameter is provided below:

a. **P.2.0** - The commanded blower voltage is read in volts. A decimal point will appear before the last digit.

b. **P.2.1** - The coolant temperature is displayed in degrees celsius (°C). This value is sent from the ECM to BCM.

c. **P.2.2** - The commanded air mix door position is diplayed in percent (%). A value close to 0% represents a cold air mix and a value close to 100% represents a warm air mix.

d. **P.2.3** - The actual air mix door position is displayed in percent (%). This value should follow the commanded air mix door position (P.2.2) except when the door is commanded beyond its mechanical limits of travel.

e. **P.2.4** - The air delivery mode is displayed as a number from 0 to 7. Each number is a code which represents the following air delivery modes; O = Max A/C , 1 = A/C, 2 = Intermediate, 3 = heater, 4 = Off, 5 = Normal Purge, 6 = Cold Purge and 7 = Defrost.

f. **P.2.5** - The in car temperature is displayed in degrees celsius (°C).

g. **P.2.6** - The actual outside temperature is displayed in degrees celsius (°C). This value represents actual sensor temperature and is not restricted by the features used to minimize engine heat affects on the customer display value.

h. **P.2.7** - The high side temperature (condenser output) is displayed in degrees celsius (°C).

i. **P.2.8** - The low side temperature (evaporator output) is displayed in degrees celsius (°C).

j. **P.2.9** - The actual fuel level is read in gallons. A decimal point will appear before the last digit. The value represents actual sensor position and is not restricted by the features used to eliminate fuel slosh affects on the customer display value.

k. **P.3.0** - The ignition cycle counter value is the number of times that the ignition has been cycled to the off or start since a BCM trouble code was last detected. After 100 ignition cycles without any malfunctions being detected, all BCM codes are cleared and the counter is reset to 0.

l. **P.3.1** - The BCM prom I.D. is displayed as a number up to three digits long which can be used to verify that the proper PROM was installed in the BCM.

When the ECM data display is initiated, the "Fuel Data Center" will display a parameter check (i.e. P.2.0 or P.3.1) for one second and then a number will be displayed for nine seconds to indicate the parameter value. The display will continue to repeat this sequence of events until the technician decides to move another parameter.

Electronic Comfort Control (EEC)

During the display data on the "Fuel Data Center" (see BCM Data Display previously outlined in this section), the climate control panel (CCP) will display a two digit number which represents the ECC program number. This number represents various levels of heating and cooling effort. As F.8.0 first appears on the "Fuel Data Center", the CCP will begin displaying the program number which is currently being used by the ECC system. As operating conditions change, this number will automatically change in response.

The automatic calculation of the program number can be bypassed by a manual override feature using ther "Warmer" and "Cooler" buttons. While in the F.8.0 mode pressing the "Warmer" button will force the program number to increase at a controlled rate until the value of 100 is reached. The 100 represents the "Max Heat" mode of the ECC operation. Pressing the "Cooler" button will force the program number to decrease until the value of 0 is reached which represents the "Max A/C " mode.

This manual override of the automatic program number calculation will continue until the F.8.0 mode is exited. This allows the service technician to control the program number to any number from 0 to 100 and simultaneously observe the reaction of any of the BCM data parameters.

Cooling Fan Override

Code .7.0 must be displayed on the "Fuel Data Center" panel before the cooling fan override feature can be selected. This feature allows the service technician to manually override the BCM's automatic control of the cooling fans speed. To manually command either "high fans" of "fans off", proceed as follows:

1. Depress and release the "Econ" button on the comfort control panel (CCP). The cooling fans override mode begins as the display switches from Code .7.0 to code F.8.5. It is possible to leave the cooling fans override mode at any time and return to .7.0 by clearing the ECM and the BCM codes.

2. To command the "high fans" hold in the "Hi" button on the CCP. Fan speed should increase until the maximum speed is achieved. Releasing the "Hi" button will return the calculation of fan speed to automatic BCM control.

3. To command the "fans off" hold the "Lo" button on the CCP. The fan speed should decrease until the fans and completely stopped. Releasing the "Lo" button will return the calculation of fan speed to automatic BCM control.

NOTE: Due to the varied Cadillac models being covered in this section, some vehicles will use more sensors than others. Also, a complete general diagnostic section is outlined. The steps and procedures can be altered as required (if necessary) by the technician according to the specific model being diagnosed and the sensors it is equipped with. The wiring diagrams and schematics may not coincide with every Cadillac model in use. If this situation should arise, use the wiring diagram or schematic as a general guide.

BCM DIAGNOSTIC CODES	
CODE	CIRCUIT AFFECTED
▼ F10	OUTSIDE TEMP SENSOR CKT
▼ F11	A/C HIGH SIDE TEMP SENSOR CKT
▼ F12	A/C LOW SIDE TEMP SENSOR CKT
▼ F13	IN-CAR TEMP SENSOR CKT
▼ F14	DIESEL COOLANT SENSOR CKT
▼ F30	CCP TO BCM DATA CKT
▼ F31	FDC/DDC TO BCM DATA CKT
▼ F32	ECM-BCM DATA CKT'S
▼ F40	AIR MIX DOOR PROBLEM
▼ F41	COOLING FANS PROBLEM
☑ F46	LOW REFRIGERANT WARNING
☑ F47	LOW REFRIGERANT CONDITION
☑ F48	LOW REFRIGERANT PRESSURE
▼ F49	HIGH TEMP CLUTCH DISENGAGE
▼ F51	BCM PROM ERROR

☑ TURNS ON "SERVICE AIR COND" LIGHT
▼ DOES NOT TURN ON ANY LIGHT

COMMENTS:
F11 TURNS ON COOLING FANS WHEN
    A/C CLUTCH IS ENGAGED
F12 DISENGAGES A/C CLUTCH
F14 & F32 TURN ON COOLING FANS
F30 TURNS ON FT. DEFOG AT 75° F
F41 TURNS ON "COOLANT TEMP/FANS"
    LIGHT WHEN FANS SHOULD BE ON
F47 & F48 SWITCHES FROM "AUTO"
        TO "ECON"

1985 BCM diagnostic codes—DFI

BCM DIAGNOSTIC CODES	
CODE	CIRCUIT AFFECTED
▼ F10	OUTSIDE TEMP SENSOR CKT
▼ F11	A/C HIGH SIDE TEMP SENSOR CKT
▼ F12	A/C LOW SIDE TEMP SENSOR CKT
▼ F13	IN-CAR TEMP SENSOR CKT
▼ F30	CCP TO BCM DATA CKT
▼ F31	FDC TO BCM DATA CKT
▼ F32	ECM-BCM DATA CKT'S
▼ F40	AIR MIX DOOR PROBLEM
▼ F41	COOLING FANS PROBLEM
☑ F46	LOW REFRIGERANT WARNING
☑ F47	LOW REFRIGERANT CONDITION
☑ F48	LOW REFRIGERANT PRESSURE
▼ F49	HIGH TEMP CLUTCH DISENGAGE
▼ F51	BCM PROM ERROR

☑ TURNS ON "SERVICE AIR COND" LIGHT
▼ DOES NOT TURN ON ANY LIGHT

COMMENTS:
F11 TURNS ON COOLING FANS WHEN
    A/C CLUTCH IS ENGAGED
F12 DISENGAGES A/C CLUTCH
F32 TURNS ON COOLING FANS
F30 TURNS ON FT. DEFOG AT 75° F
F41 TURNS ON "COOLANT TEMP/FANS"
    LIGHT WHEN FANS SHOULD BE ON
F47 & F48 SWITCHES FROM "AUTO"
        TO "ECON"

1986–88 BCM diagnostic codes—DFI

CODE	CIRCUIT AFFECTED
■■ 12	NO DISTRIBUTOR (TACH) SIGNAL
□ 13	O₂ SENSOR NOT READY
□ 14	SHORTED COOLANT SENSOR CIRCUIT
□ 15	OPEN COOLANT SENSOR CIRCUIT
■■ 16	GENERATOR VOLTAGE OUT OF RANGE
□ 18	OPEN CRANK SIGNAL CIRCUIT
□ 19	SHORTED FUEL PUMP CIRCUIT
■■ 20	OPEN FUEL PUMP CIRCUIT
□ 21	SHORTED THROTTLE POSITION SENSOR CIRCUIT
□ 22	OPEN THROTTLE POSITION SENSOR CIRCUIT
□ 23	EST/BYPASS CIRCUIT PROBLEM
□ 24	SPEED SENSOR CIRCUIT PROBLEM
□ 26	SHORTED THROTTLE SWITCH CIRCUIT
□ 27	OPEN THROTTLE SWITCH CIRCUIT
□ 28	OPEN FOURTH GEAR CIRCUIT
□ 29	SHORTED FOURTH GEAR CIRCUIT
□ 30	ISC CIRCUIT PROBLEM
■■ 31	SHORTED MAP SENSOR CIRCUIT
■■ 32	OPEN MAP SENSOR CIRCUIT
■■ 33	MAP/BARO SENSOR CORRELATION
■■ 34	MAP SIGNAL TOO HIGH
□ 35	SHORTED BARO SENSOR CIRCUIT
□ 36	OPEN BARO SENSOR CIRCUIT
□ 37	SHORTED MAT SENSOR CIRCUIT
□ 38	OPEN MAT SENSOR CIRCUIT
□ 39	TCC ENGAGEMENT PROBLEM
■■ 44	LEAN EXHAUST SIGNAL
■■ 45	RICH EXHAUST SIGNAL
■■ 51	PROM ERROR INDICATOR
▼ 52	ECM MEMORY RESET INDICATOR
▼ 53	DISTRIBUTOR SIGNAL INTERRUPT
▼ 60	TRANSMISSION NOT IN DRIVE
▼ 63	CAR AND SET SPEED TOLERANCE EXCEEDED
▼ 64	CAR ACCELERATION EXCEEDS MAX. LIMIT
▼ 65	COOLANT TEMPERATURE EXCEEDS MAX. LIMIT
▼ 66	ENGINE RPM EXCEEDS MAXIMUM LIMIT
▼ 67	SHORTED SET OR RESUME CIRCUIT
.7.0	SYSTEM READY FOR FURTHER TESTS
.7.1	CRUISE CONTROL BRAKE CIRCUIT TEST
.7.2	THROTTLE SWITCH CIRCUIT TEST
.7.3	DRIVE (ADL) CIRCUIT TEST
.7.4	REVERSE CIRCUIT TEST
.7.5	CRUISE ON/OFF CIRCUIT TEST
.7.6	"SET/COAST" CIRCUIT TEST
.7.7	"RESUME/ACCELERATION" CIRCUIT TEST
.7.8	"INSTANT/AVERAGE" CIRCUIT TEST
.7.9	"RESET" CIRCUIT TEST
.8.0	A/C CLUTCH CIRCUIT TEST
-1.8.8	DISPLAY CHECK
.9.0	SYSTEM READY TO DISPLAY ENGINE DATA
.9.5	SYSTEM READY FOR OUTPUT CYCLING OR IN FIXED SPARK MODE
.9.6	OUTPUT CYCLING
.0.0	ALL DIANOSTICS COMPLETE
■■	TURNS ON "SERVICE NOW" LIGHT
□	TURNS ON "SERVICE SOON" LIGHT
▼	DOES NOT TURN ON ANY TELLTALE LIGHT

NOTE: CRUISE IS DISENGAGED WITH ANY "SERVICE NOW" LIGHT OR WITH CODES 60-67.

1984 ECM diagnostic codes—DFI

ECM DIAGNOSTIC CODES

CODE	DESCRIPTION	COMMENTS
E12	No Distributor Signal	Ⓐ
E13	Oxygen Sensor Not Ready [AIR, CL & Canister Purge]	Ⓑ
E14	Shorted Coolant Sensor Circuit [AIR]	ⒷⒼ
E15	Open Coolant Sensor Circuit [AIR]	ⒷⒼ
E16	Generator Voltage Out Of Range [All Solenoids]	ⒶⒻ
E18	Open Crank Signal Circuit	Ⓑ
E19	Shorted Fuel Pump Circuit	Ⓑ
E20	Open Fuel Pump Circuit	Ⓐ
E21	Shorted Throttle Position Sensor Circuit	Ⓑ
E22	Open Throttle Position Sensor Circuit	Ⓑ
E23	EST/Bypass Circuit Problem [AIR]	ⒷⒻ
E24	Speed Sensor Circuit Problem [VCC & Cruise]	ⒷⒹⒻ
E26	Shorted Throttle Switch Circuit	Ⓑ
E27	Open Throttle Switch Circuit	Ⓑ
E28	Open Third Or Fourth Gear Circuit	Ⓑ
E30	ISC Circuit Problem	Ⓑ
E31	Shorted MAP Sensor Circuit [AIR]	Ⓐ
E32	Open MAP Sensor Circuit [AIR]	Ⓐ
E34	MAP Sensor Signal Too High [AIR]	Ⓐ
E37	Shorted MAT Sensor Circuit [AIR]	Ⓑ
E38	Open MAT Sensor Circuit [AIR]	Ⓑ
E39	VCC Engagement Problem	Ⓑ
E40	Open Power Steering Pressure Switch Circuit	Ⓑ
E44	Lean Exhaust Signal [AIR, CL & Canister Purge]	Ⓐ
E45	Rich Exhaust Signal [AIR, CL & Canister Purge]	Ⓐ
E47	BCM — ECM Data Problem	Ⓑ
E48	EGR System Fault [EGR]	Ⓑ
E51	ECM PROM Error	Ⓐ
E52	ECM Memory Reset Indicator	Ⓒ
E53	Distributor Signal Interrupt	Ⓒ
E55	TPS Misadjusted	Ⓒ
E59	VCC Temperature Sensor Circuit Problem	Ⓒ
E60	Cruise - Transmission Not In Drive [Cruise]	Ⓒ
E63	Cruise - Car Speed And Set Speed Difference Too High [Cruise]	Ⓒ
E64	Cruise - Car Acceleration Too High [Cruise]	Ⓒ
E65	Cruise - Coolant Temperature Too High [Cruise]	Ⓒ
E66	Cruise - Engine RPM Too High [Cruise]	Ⓒ
E67	Cruise - Cruise Switch Shorted During Enable [Cruise]	ⒸⒹ

DIAGNOSTIC CODE COMMENTS

A	Turns On "SERVICE NOW" Light.
B	Turns On "SERVICE SOON" Light
C	Does Not Turn On Any Telltale Light.
D	Disables Cruise For Entire Ignition Cycle.
E	Causes System To Operate On Bypass Spark.
F	Disengages VCC For Entire Ignition Cycle.
G	Forces Cooling Fans On Full Speed
H	Turns On Cooling Fans Whenever A/C Clutch Is Engaged
I	Displays "c" for Clock Problem Or "d" for Data Problem.
J	Turns On Front Defog At 75°F.
K	Turns On "COOLANT TEMP/FAN" Light Whenever Cooling Fans Should Be Operating
L	Turns On "SERVICE AIR COND" Light For A Period Of Time.
M	Turns On "SERVICE AIR COND" Light For A Period Of Time, & Switches ECC Mode To ECON.
N	Displays "-151" On CCP And Turns On Front Defog.
[ ]	Functions Within Bracket Are Disengaged While Specified Malfunction Remains Current.

1985–88 ECM diagnostic codes—DFI

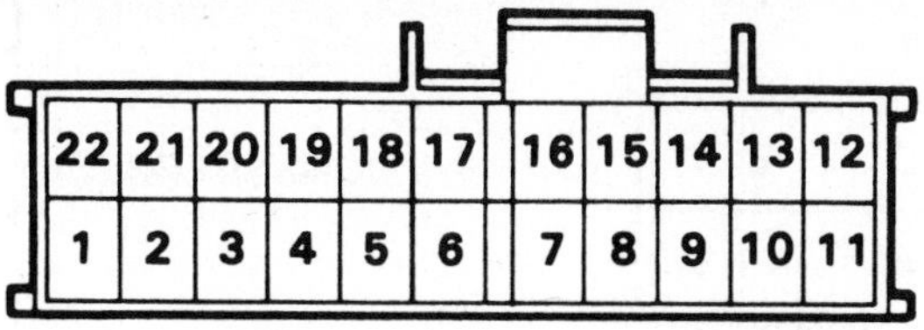

P-1 CONNECTOR (BLU)

```
22 21 20 19 18 17 | 16 15 14 13 12
 1  2  3  4  5  6 |  7  8  9 10 11
```

CAVITY	CIRCUIT #	WIRE COLOR	CIRCUIT
1	6	0.5 PPL	CRANK
2	430	0.8 PPL/WHT	DIST. REF. SIGNAL
3	453	0.8 TAN	DIST. REF. GROUND
4	410	0.35 YEL	COOLANT
5	417	0.35 BLU-DRK	TPS
6	464	0.22 BRN/WHT	DATA RESET
7	—	—	NOT USED
8	412	0.35 PPL	O$_2$ SENSOR SIGNAL
9	428	0.8 GRN-DRK/YEL	CANISTER PURGE
10	462	0.35 PNK/BLK	HEI BYPASS
11	476Y	0.8 BLK/PNK	SENSOR GROUND
12	—	—	NOT USED
13	—	—	NOT USED
14	436	0.8 BRN	AIR SWITCH SOLENOID
15	413	0.35 TAN	O$_2$ SENSOR GROUND
16	429	0.8 BLU/RED	AIR DIVERT SOLENOID
17	—	—	NOT USED
18	—	—	NOT USED
19	423	0.35 WHT	SPARK TIMING
20	432	0.8 BLU-DRK/GRA	MAP
21	472	0.35 TAN	MANIFOLD TEMP.
22	435	0.35 BRN	EGR SOLENOID

1984 ECM P-1 blue connector — all 4.1L DFI engines

P-2 CONNECTOR (RED)

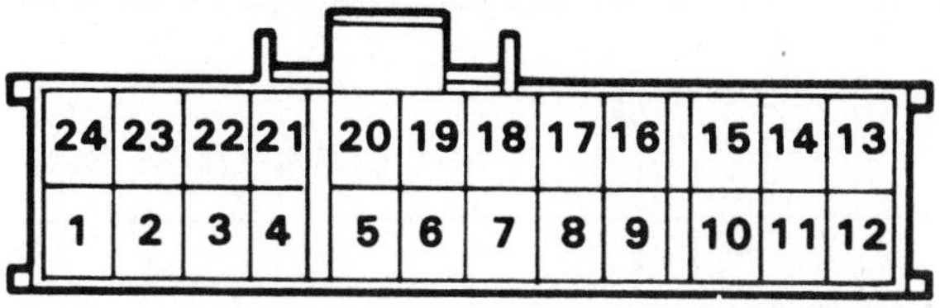

```
24 23 22 21 | 20 19 18 17 16 | 15 14 13
 1  2  3  4 |  5  6  7  8  9 | 10 11 12
```

CAVITY	CIRCUIT #	WIRE COLOR	CIRCUIT
1	—	—	BACKUP FUEL B
2	961	0.5 TAN	SPEED SENSOR
3	451	0.35 BLK/WHT	DIAGNOSTIC REQUEST
4	—	—	NOT USED
5	811	0.5 BLU-LGT	METRIC SELECT
6	450	0.8 BLK/WHT	DUEL INJECTOR SELECT
7	461	0.35 BRN	SERIAL DATA
8	467	0.8 BLU-LGT	INJECTOR #1
9	468	0.8 GRN-LGT	INJECTOR #2
10	480	1.0 ORN	12V BATTERY
11	474	0.8 GRA	5V SENSOR REF.
12	450	1.0 BLK/WHT	GROUND
13	450	1.0 BLK/WHT	GROUND
14	497	0.5 GRN-LGT	RELAY GROUND
15	480	1.0 ORN	12V BATTERY
16	439	0.5 PNK/BLK	12V IGNITION
17	120	0.8 BLU-LGT	FUEL PUMP FEEDBACK
18	465	0.5 GRN-DRK/WHT	RELAY DRIVE
19	422	0.5 TAN/WHT	TCC ENABLE
20	—	—	NOT USED
21	977	0.35 GRA/BLK	ECC COMPRESSOR CLUTCH
22	438	0.5 GRN-DRK/WHT	4TH GEAR
23	477	0.35 BRN	DATA REQUEST
24	—	—	BACKUP FUEL A

1984 ECM P-2 red connector — all 4.1L DFI engines

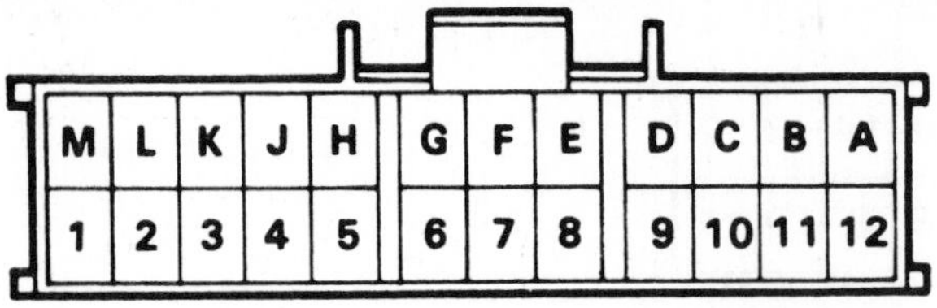

P-3 CONNECTOR (ORN)

```
M L K J H  G F E  D C B A
1 2 3 4 5  6 7 8  9 10 11 12
```

CAVITY	CIRCUIT #	WIRE COLOR	CIRCUIT
1	—		NOT USED
2	425	0.5 BLU-LGT	IDLE SPEED EXTEND
3	403	0.5 BLU-DRK/WHT	CRUISE ENGAGE
4	419	0.35 BRN/WHT	SERVICE NOW
5	426	0.5 BLU-DRK	IDLE SPEED RETRACT
6	243	0.8 BLK/WHT	DRIVE
7	86	0.5 BRN	BRAKE
8	—		NOT USED
9	433	0.8 GRA/BLK	BARO
10	—		NOT USED
11	—		NOT USED
12	910	0.5 GRN-LGT/BLK	OUTSIDE TEMPERATURE
A	402	0.35 GRN-LGT	CRUISE POWER SOLENOID
B	476X	0.8 BLK/WHT	SENSOR GROUND
C	30	0.5 PNK	FUEL SIGNAL
D	427	0.35 PNK	THROTTLE SWITCH
E	87	0.5 GRA/BLK	RESUME/ACCELERATE
F	84	0.5 BLU-DRK	SET/COAST
G	24	0.5 GRN-LGT	REVERSE
H	—		NOT USED
J	903	0.5 BLU-LGT/BLK	CRUISE ENABLE
K	35	0.35 GRN-DRK	COOLANT INDICATOR
L	—		NOT USED
M	499	0.5 GRA/BLK	SERVICE SOON

1984 ECM P-3 orange connector—all 4.1L DFI engines

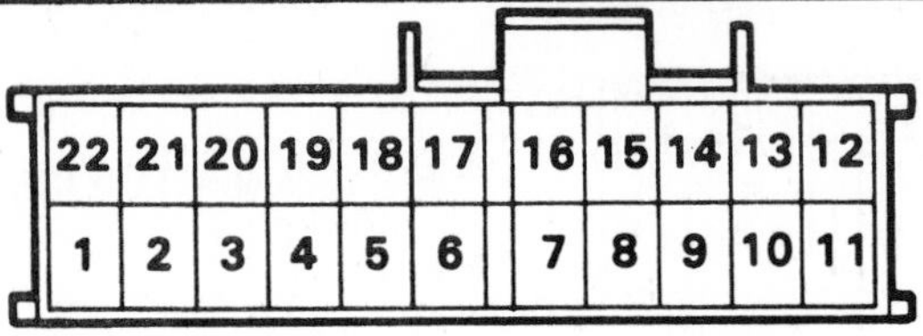

P-1 CONNECTOR (BLU)

```
22 21 20 19 18 17  16 15 14 13 12
1  2  3  4  5  6   7  8  9  10 11
```

CAVITY	CIRCUIT #	WIRE COLOR	CIRCUIT
1	806	0.35 PPL	CRANK
2	430	0.8 PPL/WHT	DIST. REF. SIGNAL
3	453	0.8 TAN	DIST. REF. GROUND
4	410	0.35 YEL	COOLANT
5	417	0.35 BLU-DRK	TPS
6	464	0.22 BRN/WHT	DATA RESET
7	—		NOT USED
8	412	0.35 PPL	O$_2$ SENSOR SIGNAL
9	428	0.8 GRN-DRK/YEL	CANISTER PURGE
10	462	0.35 PNK/BLK	HEI BYPASS
11	476Y	0.35 BLK/PNK	SENSOR GROUND
12	—		NOT USED
13	—		NOT USED
14	436	0.8 BRN	AIR SWITCH SOLENOID
15	413	0.35 TAN	O$_2$ SENSOR GROUND
16	429	0.8 BLK/PNK	AIR DIVERT SOLENOID
17	—		NOT USED
18	—		NOT USED
19	423	0.35 WHT	SPARK TIMING
20	432	0.8 BLU-DRK/GRA	MAP
21	472	0.35 TAN	MANIFOLD TEMP.
22	435	0.35 BRN	EGR SOLENOID

1985 ECM P-1 blue connector—Eldorado, Seville, RWD Brougham

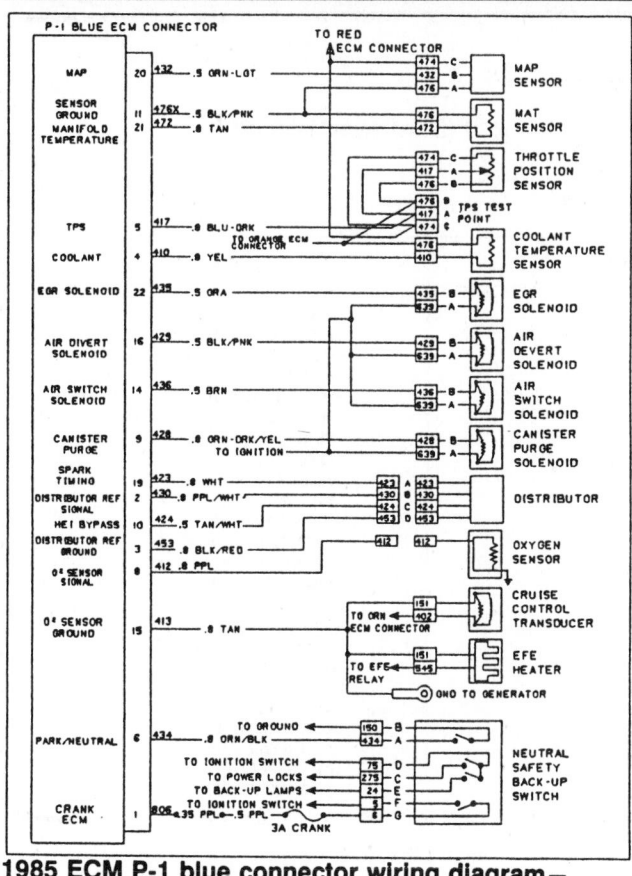

1985 ECM P-1 blue connector wiring diagram—Fleetwoood and DeVille

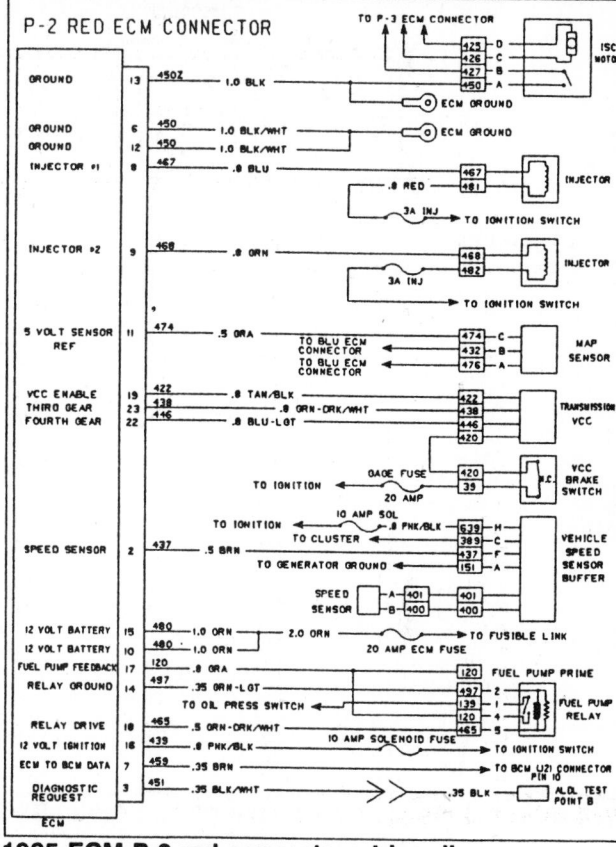

1985 ECM P-2 red connector wiring diagram—Fleetwoood and DeVille

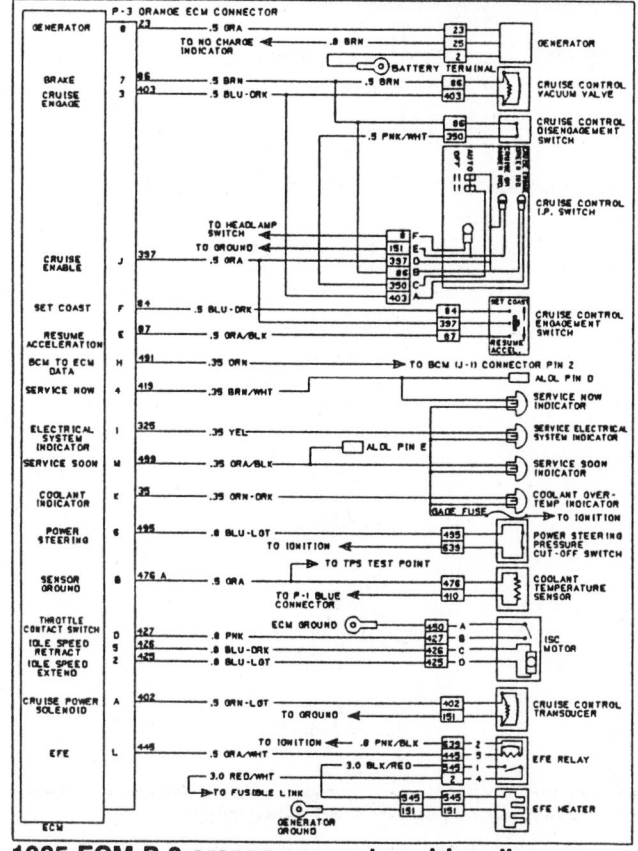

1985 ECM P-3 orange connector wiring diagram—Fleetwood and DeVille

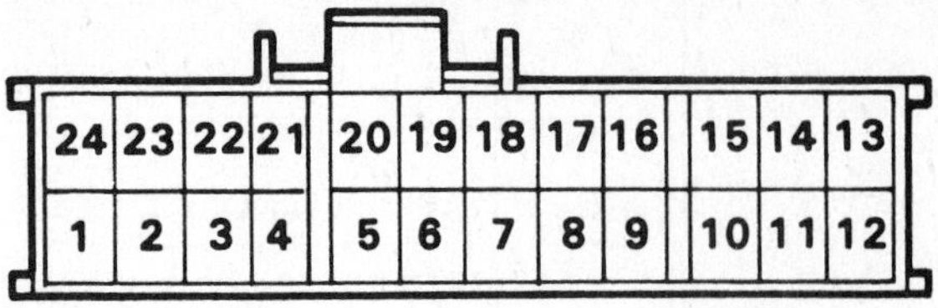

```
    24 23 22 21   20 19 18 17 16   15 14 13
     1  2  3  4    5  6  7  8  9    10 11 12
```

P-2 CONNECTOR (RED)

CAVITY	CIRCUIT #	WIRE COLOR	CIRCUIT
1	988	0.8 WHT	BACKUP FUEL B
2	961	0.5 TAN	SPEED SENSOR
3	451	0.35 BLK/WHT	DIAGNOSTIC REQUEST
4	—	—	NOT USED
5	811	0.5 BLU-LGT	METRIC SELECT
6	450	1.0 BLK/WHT	DUEL INJECTOR SELECT
7	461	0.35 BRN	SERIAL DATA
8	467	0.8 BLU-LGT	INJECTOR #1
9	468	0.8 GRN-LGT	INJECTOR #2
10	480	1.0 ORN	12V BATTERY
11	474	0.35 GRA	5V SENSOR REF.
12	450	1.0 BLK/WHT	GROUND
13	450	1.0 BLK	GROUND
14	497	0.5 GRN-LGT	RELAY GROUND
15	480	1.0 ORN	12V BATTERY
16	439	0.5 PNK/BLK	12V IGNITION
17	120	0.8 BLU-LGT	FUEL PUMP FEEDBACK
18	465	0.5 GRN-DRK/WHT	RELAY DRIVE
19	422	0.5 TAN/WHT	TCC ENABLE
20	—	—	NOT USED
21	977	0.35 GRA/BLK	ECC COMPRESSOR CLUTCH
22	438	0.5 GRN-DRK/WHT	4TH GEAR
23	477	0.35 BRN	DATA REQUEST
24	988	0.8 WHT	BACKUP FUEL A

1985 ECM P-2 red connector—Eldorado, Seville, RWD Brougham

```
    M L K J H   G F E   D C B A
    1 2 3 4 5   6 7 8   9 10 11 12
```

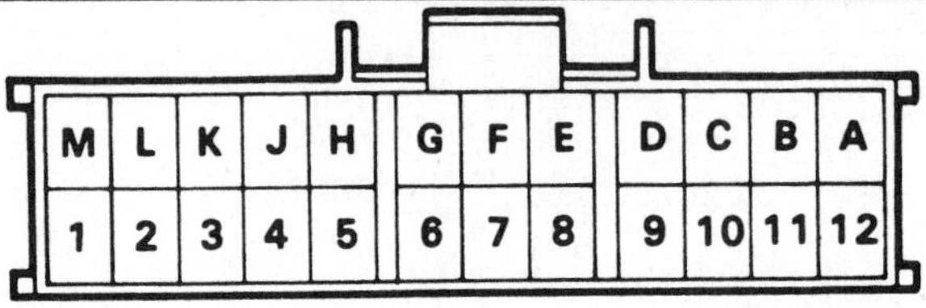

P-3 CONNECTOR (ORN)

CAVITY	CIRCUIT #	WIRE COLOR	CIRCUIT
1	—	—	NOT USED
2	425	0.5 BLU-LGT	IDLE SPEED EXTEND
3	403	0.5 BLU-DRK/WHT	CRUISE ENGAGE
4	419	0.35 BRN/WHT	SERVICE NOW
5	426	0.5 BLU-DRK	IDLE SPEED RETRACT
6	243	0.8 BLK/WHT	DRIVE
7	86	0.5 BRN	BRAKE
8	—	—	NOT USED
9	433	0.8 GRA/BLK	BARO
10	—	—	NOT USED
11	—	—	NOT USED
12	910	0.5 GRN-LGT/BLK	OUTSIDE TEMPERATURE
A	402	0.35 GRN-LGT	CRUISE POWER SOLENOID
B	476X	0.35 BLK/WHT	SENSOR GROUND
C	30	0.35 PNK	FUEL SIGNAL
D	427	0.35 PNK	THROTTLE SWITCH
E	87	0.5 GRA/BLK	RESUME/ACCELERATE
F	84	0.5 BLU-DRK	SET/COAST
G	24	0.5 GRN-LGT	REVERSE
H	—	—	NOT USED
J	397	0.5 GRA	CRUISE ENABLE
K	35	0.35 GRN-DRK	COOLANT INDICATOR
L	—	—	NOT USED
M	499	0.35 GRA/BLK	SERVICE SOON

1985 ECM P-3 orange connector—Eldorado, Seville, RWD Brougham

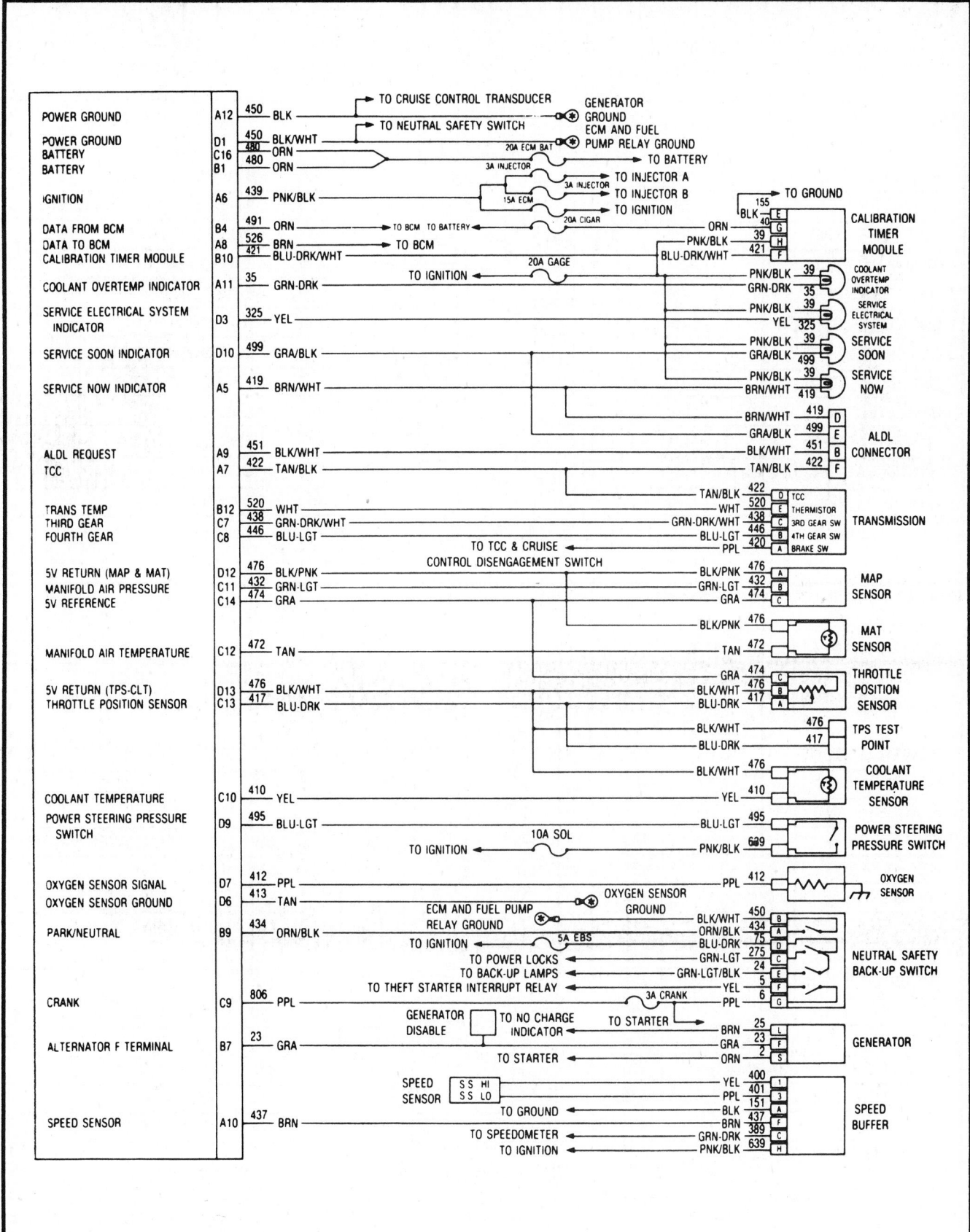

1986–87 ECM wiring diagram A—DeVille

CIRCUIT DESCRIPTION	CIRCUIT NUMBER	ECM J1	CIRCUIT NUMBER	CIRCUIT DESCRIPTION
BATTERY POSITIVE	480		465	FUEL PUMP RELAY
BRAKE SWITCH	86		428	CANISTER PURGE SOLENOID
DIST. REF. LOW	453		403	CRUISE ENGAGE
SERIAL DATA IN	491		435	EGR SOLENOID
DIST. REF. HIGH	430		419	SERVICE NOW
SET/COAST SWITCH	84		439	IGNITION-3
GENERATOR F	23		422	TCC SOLENOID
CRUISE ENABLE	397		526	SERIAL DATA OUT
PARK/NEUTRAL SWITCH	434		451	ALDL REQUEST
TIMER MODULE	421		437	VEHICLE SPEED
RESUME/ACCEL. SWITCH	87		35	COOLANT OVERTEMP. LIGHT
TRANS. TEMP.	520		450	POWER GROUND

1986–87 ECM P-1 A/B connector circuits — DeVille

CIRCUIT DESCRIPTION	CIRCUIT NUMBER	ECM J2	CIRCUIT NUMBER	CIRCUIT DESCRIPTION
POWER GROUND	450		429	AIR DIVERT
EFE RELAY	¾45		436	AIR SWITCHING
ELEC. SYS. INDICATOR	325		—	SPARE
EST.	423		402	CRUISE POWER VALVE
HEI BYPASS	424		425	ISC EXTEND
OXYGEN SENSOR LOW	413		426	ISC RETRACT
OXYGEN SENSOR HIGH	412		438	3RD GEAR SWITCH
SPARE	—		446	4TH GEAR SWITCH
POWER STEERING PRES. SW.	495		806	CRANK
SERVICE SOON	499		410	COOLANT TEMP
FUEL PUMP RELAY FEEDBACK	120		432	MAP SENSOR
5 VOLT RETURN (MAP/MAT)	476		472	MAT SENSOR
5 VOLT RETURN (TPS/COOL)	476		417	TPS SENSOR
INJECTOR B	468		474	5 VOLT REF. (MAP/TPS)
THROTTLE SWITCH	427		—	SPARE
INJECTOR A	467		480	BATTERY POSITIVE

1986–87 ECM P-2 C/D connector circuits — DeVille

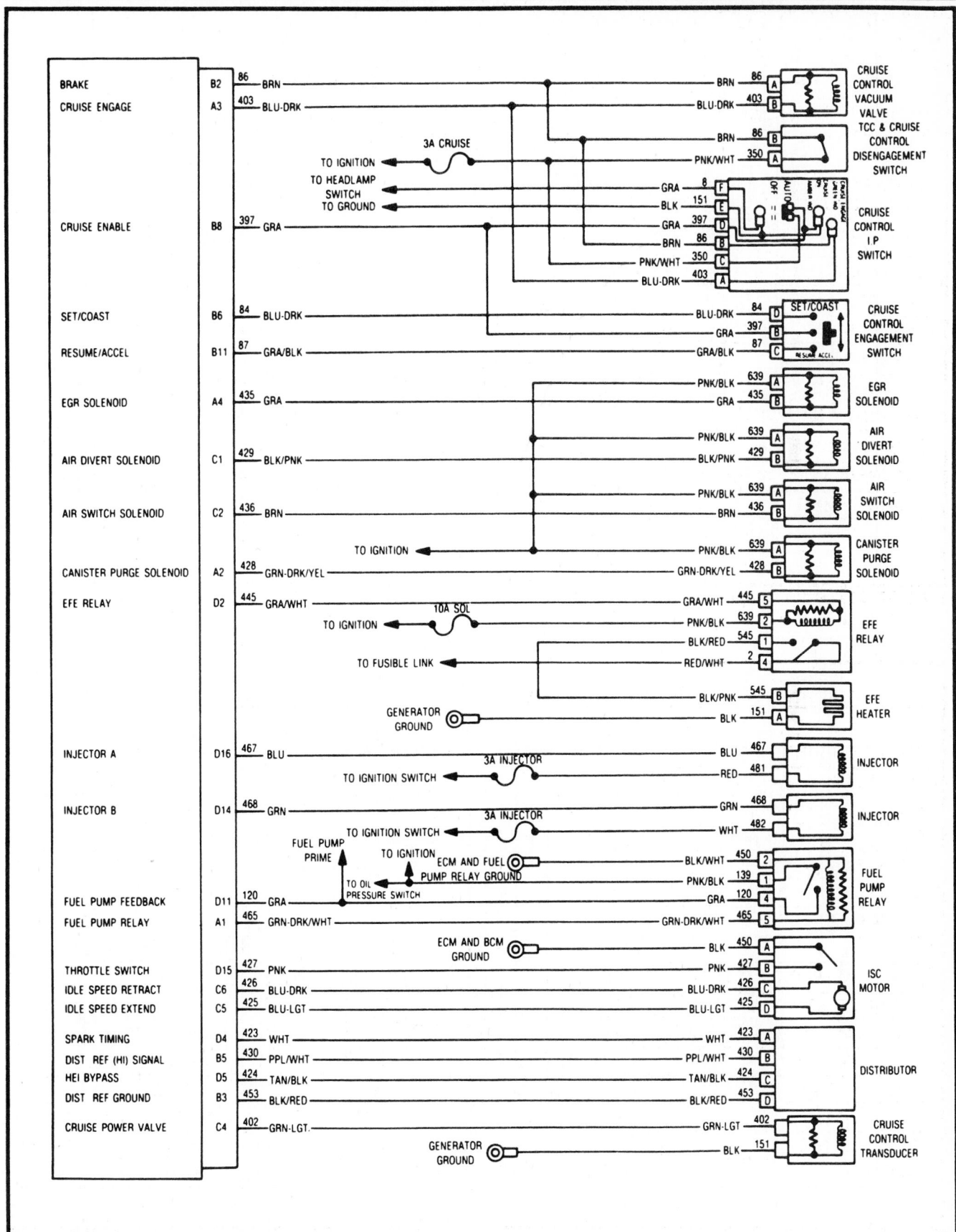

1986–87 ECM wiring diagram B — DeVille

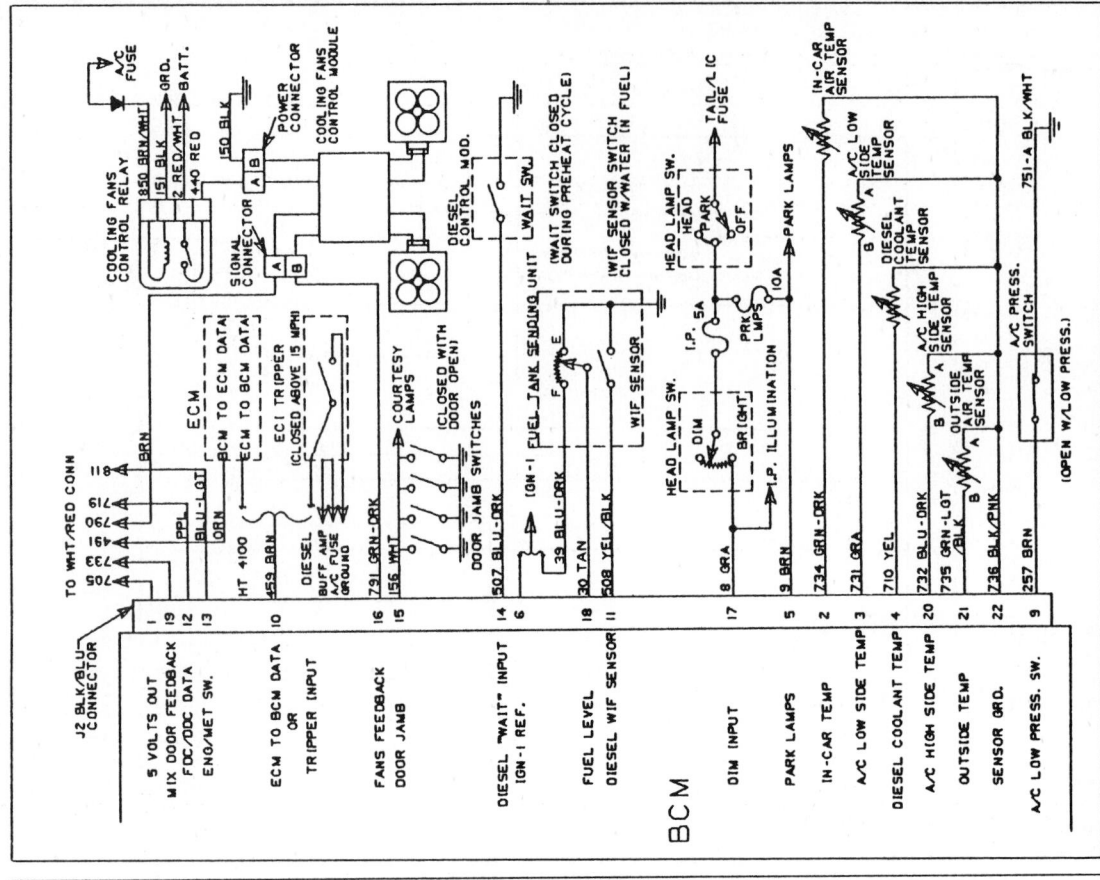

BCM wiring diagram—black/blue J2 connector

BCM wiring diagram—white/red J1 connector

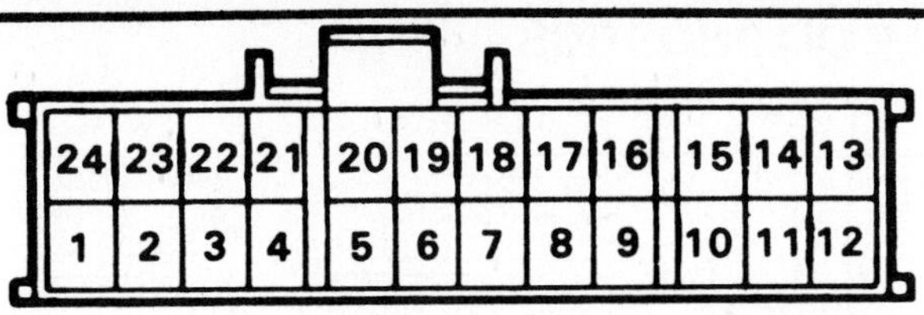

J-1 CONNECTOR (WHT/RED)

( ) = DIESEL ONLY

CAVITY	CIRCUIT #	WIRE COLOR	CIRCUIT
1	751-A	1.0 BLK/WHT	POWER GROUND
2	491	0.5 ORN	BCM TO ECM DATA
3	713	0.35 YEL	CLOCK OUT
4	—	—	NOT USED
5	761	1.0 ORN	BLOWER FEEDBACK
6	721	0.35 WHT	"SERVICE AIR COND"
7	35	0.8 GRN-DRK	("COOLANT TEMP/FAN")
8	790	0.8 BRN	COOLING FANS SIGNAL
9	707	0.8 BLK	R.A.P. RELAY GROUND
10	50	0.8 BRN	12V IGNITION-3
11	43	0.8 YEL/BLK	12V ACC POWER
12	840	1.0 ORN	12V BATTERY
13	840	1.0 ORN	12V BATTERY
14	716	0.8 ORN/BLK	16 VOLTS OUT
15	—	—	NOT USED
16	717	0.35 GRA/WHT	V.F. DIM CONTROL
17	—	—	NOT USED
18	—	—	NOT USED
19	760	0.5 PPL/WHT	BLOWER SIGNAL
20	—	—	NOT USED
21	—	—	NOT USED
22	720	0.35 BLU-LGT	PROGRAMMER DATA
23	718	0.35 BLU-DRK/WHT	CCP DATA
24	751-B	1.0 BLK/YEL	GROUND REF. OUT

Exploded view of the BCM J1 connector

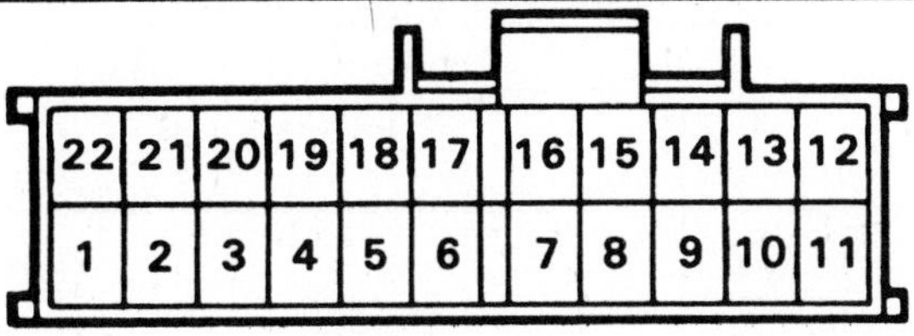

J-2 CONNECTOR (BLK/BLU)

( ) = DIESEL ONLY

CAVITY	CIRCUIT #	WIRE COLOR	CIRCUIT
1	705	0.8 TAN	5 VOLTS OUT
2	734	0.35 GRN-DRK	IN-CAR TEMP
3	731	0.5 GRA	A/C LOW SIDE TEMP
4	710	0.8 YEL	(DIESEL COOLANT TEMP)
5	9	0.5 BRN	PARK LAMPS
6	39(239)	0.8 PNK/BLK	12V IGNITION-1 REF.
7	—	—	NOT USED
8	—	—	NOT USED
9	257	0.8 BRN	A/C LOW PRESSURE
10	459	0.35 BRN	ECM TO BCM DATA (ECI TRIPPER)
11	508	0.8 YEL/BLK	(WIF SENSOR)
12	719	0.35 PPL	FDC DATA (DDC DATA)
13	811	0.5 BLU-LGT	ENG/MET SWITCH
14	507	0.5 BLU-DRK	(WAIT SWITCH)
15	156	0.5 WHT	DOOR JAMB
16	791	0.8 GRN-DRK	FANS FEEDBACK
17	8	0.5 GRA	DIM INPUT
18	30	0.5 TAN	FUEL LEVEL
19	733	0.5 BLU-LGT	MIX DOOR FEEDBACK
20	732	0.5 BLU-DRK	A/C HIGH SIDE TEMP
21	735	0.35 GRN-LGT/BLK	OUTSIDE TEMP
22	736	0.35 BLK/PNK	SENSOR GROUND

Exploded view of the BCM J2 connector

DFI TROUBLE DIAGNOSTICS

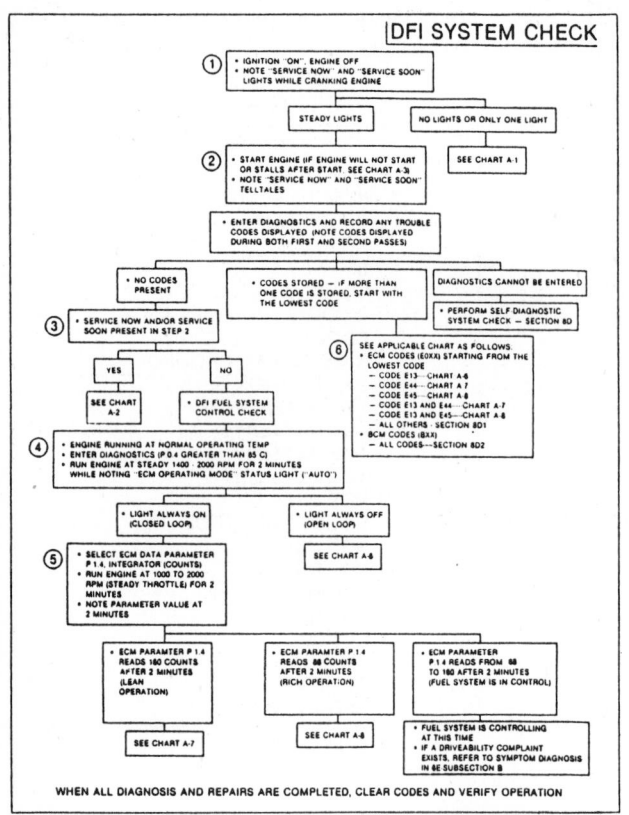

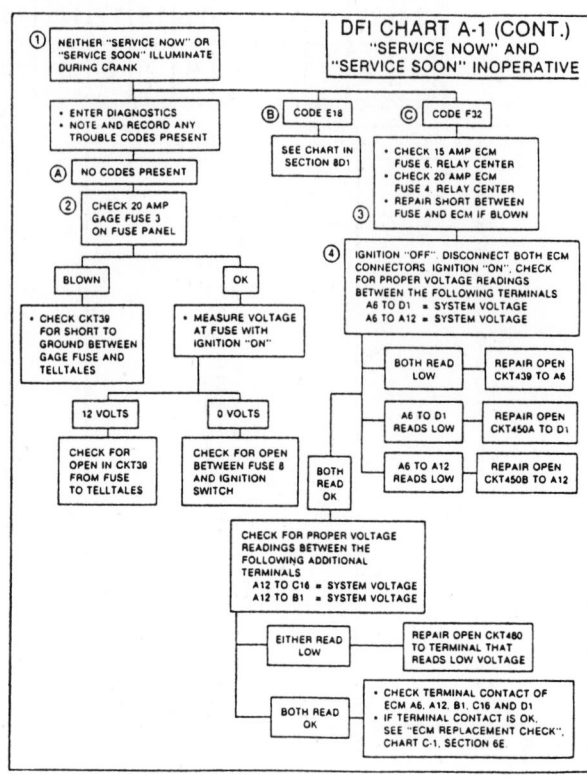

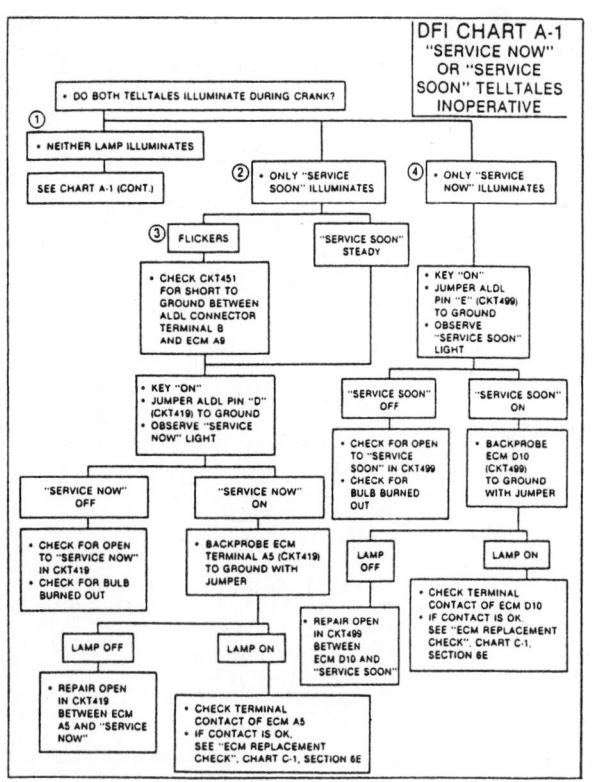

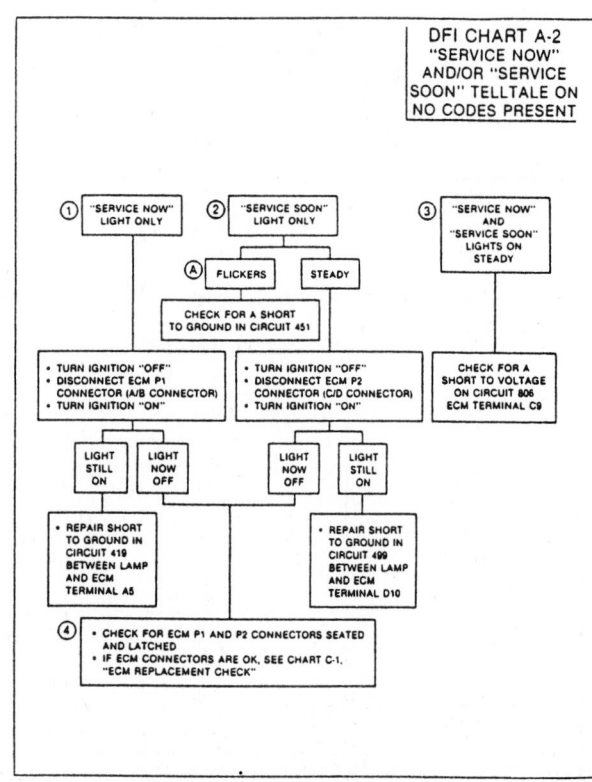

DFI TROUBLE DIAGNOSTICS

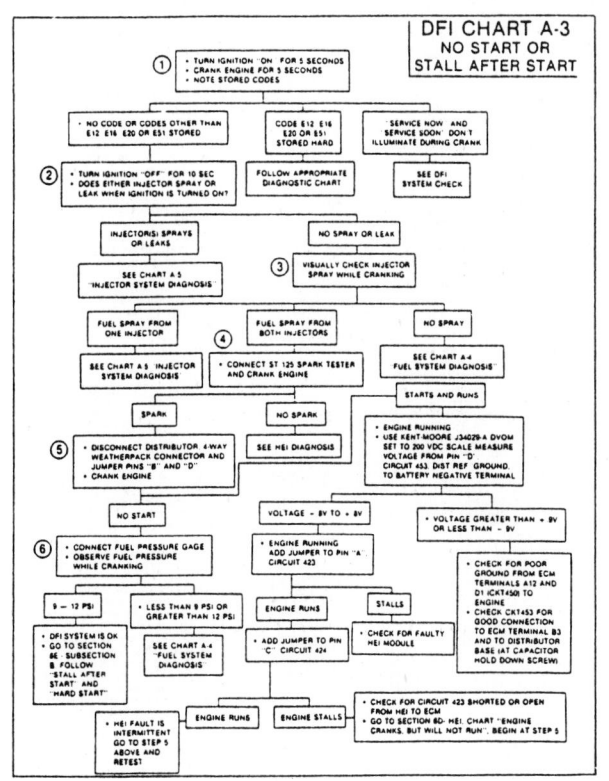

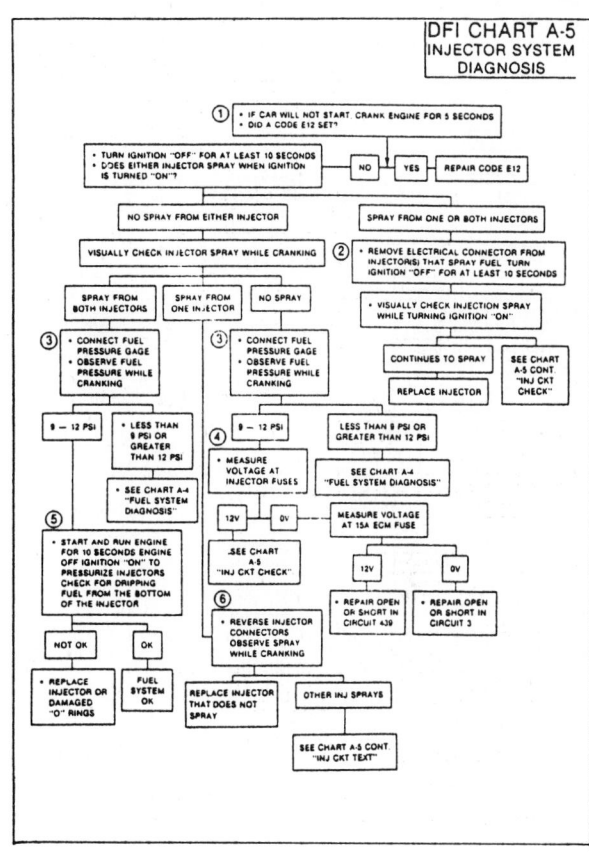

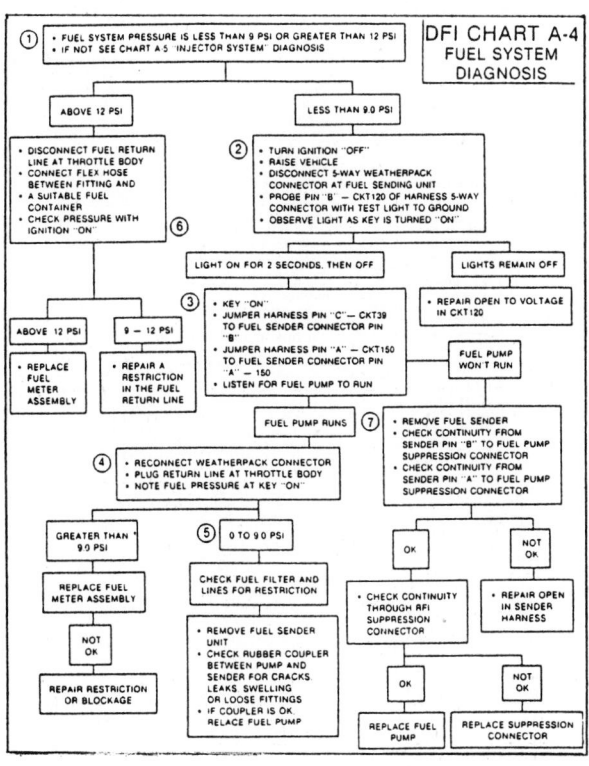

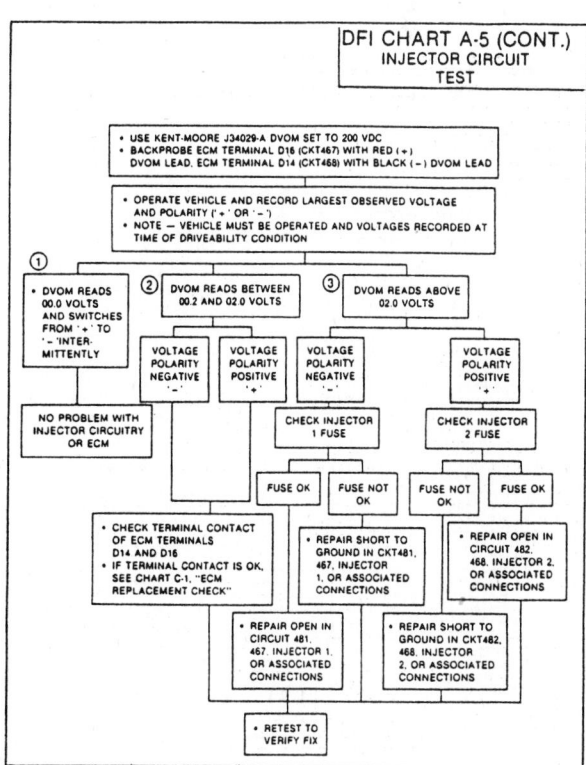

DFI TROUBLE DIAGNOSTICS

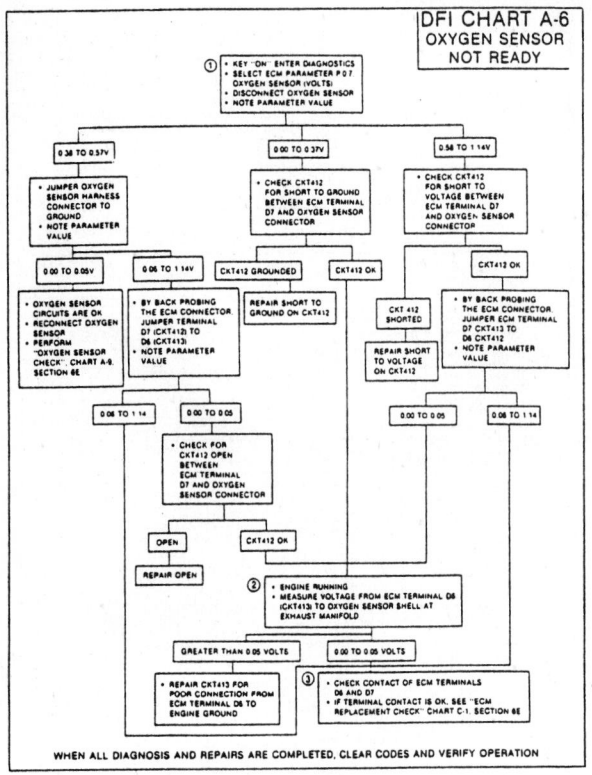

DFI CHART A-6
OXYGEN SENSOR
NOT READY

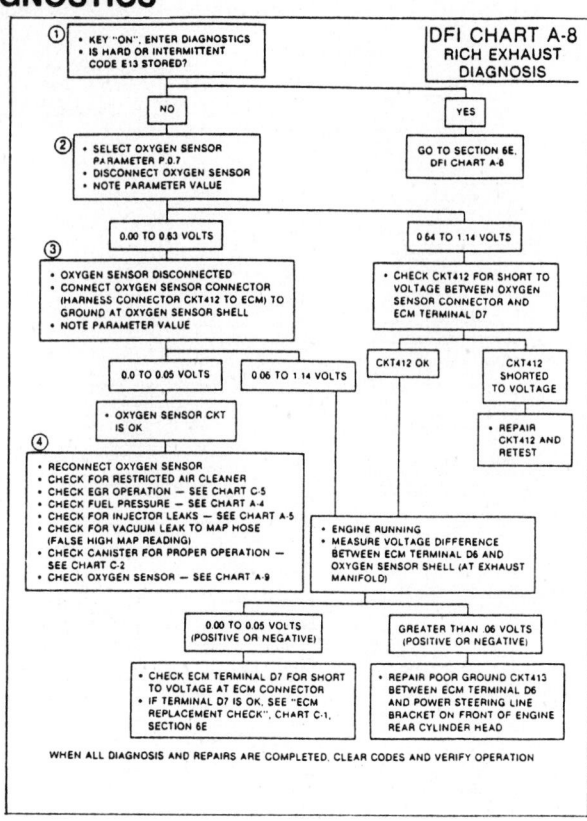

DFI CHART A-8
RICH EXHAUST
DIAGNOSIS

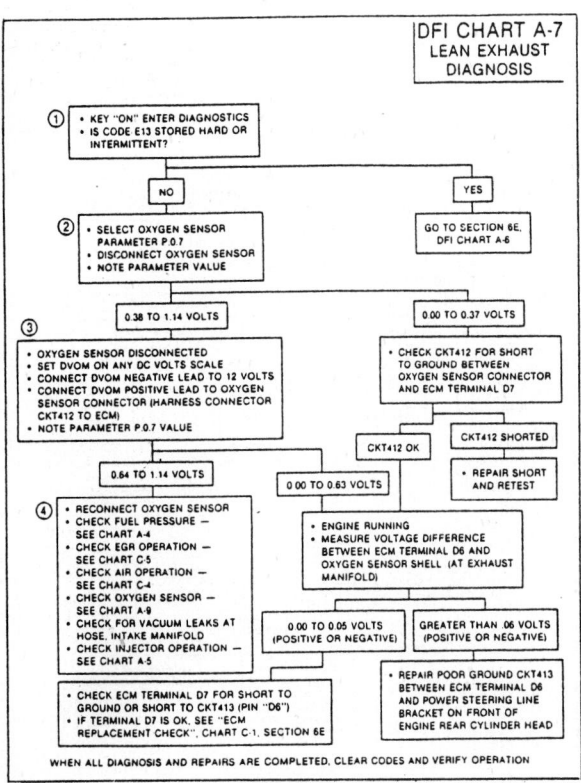

DFI CHART A-7
LEAN EXHAUST
DIAGNOSIS

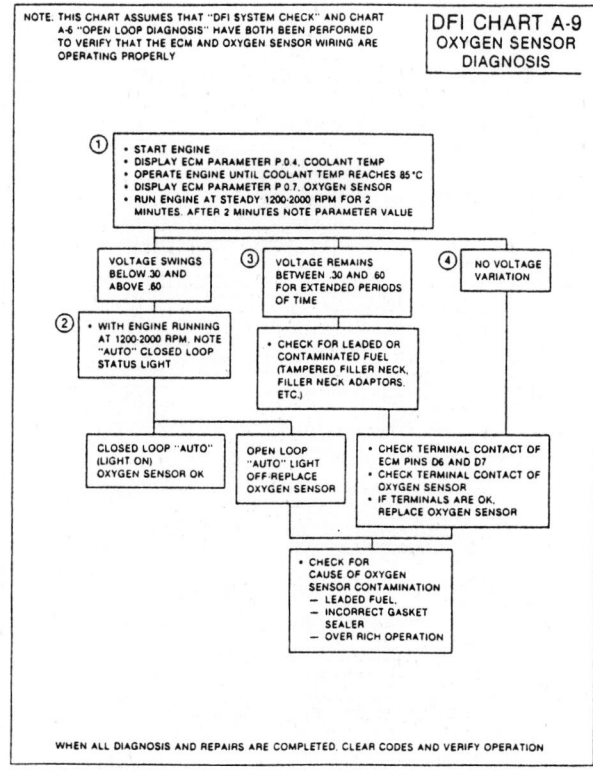

DFI CHART A-9
OXYGEN SENSOR
DIAGNOSIS

DFI TROUBLE DIAGNOSTICS

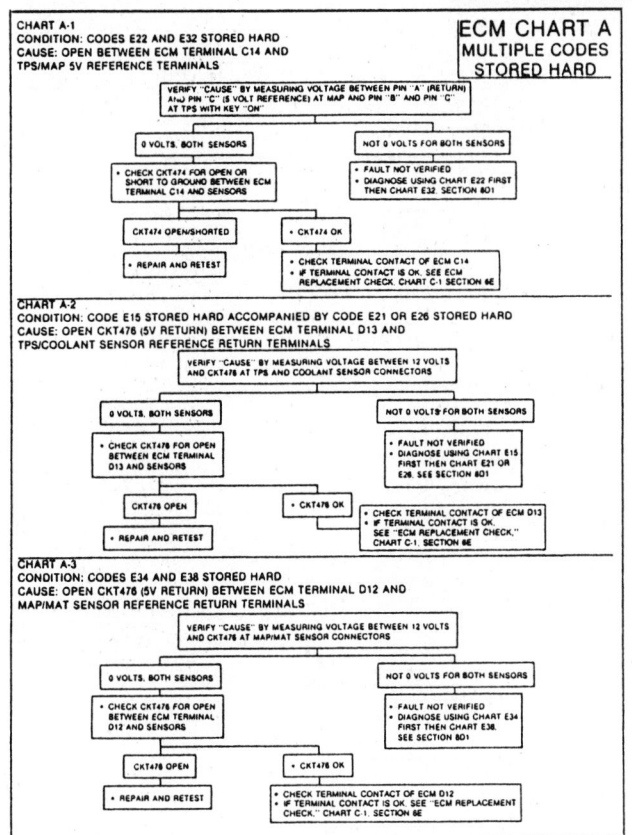

ECM CHART A
MULTIPLE CODES STORED HARD

CHART A-1
CONDITION: CODES E22 AND E32 STORED HARD
CAUSE: OPEN BETWEEN ECM TERMINAL C14 AND TPS/MAP 5V REFERENCE TERMINALS

CHART A-2
CONDITION: CODE E15 STORED HARD ACCOMPANIED BY CODE E21 OR E26 STORED HARD
CAUSE: OPEN CKT476 (5V RETURN) BETWEEN ECM TERMINAL D13 AND TPS/COOLANT SENSOR REFERENCE RETURN TERMINALS

CHART A-3
CONDITION: CODES E34 AND E38 STORED HARD
CAUSE: OPEN CKT476 (5V RETURN) BETWEEN ECM TERMINAL D12 AND MAP/MAT SENSOR REFERENCE RETURN TERMINALS

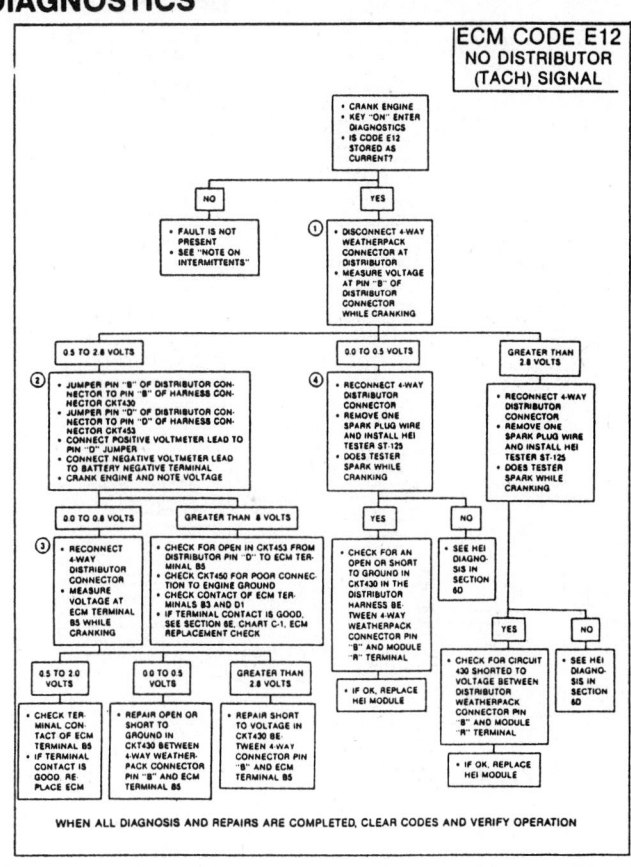

ECM CODE E12
NO DISTRIBUTOR (TACH) SIGNAL

WHEN ALL DIAGNOSIS AND REPAIRS ARE COMPLETED, CLEAR CODES AND VERIFY OPERATION

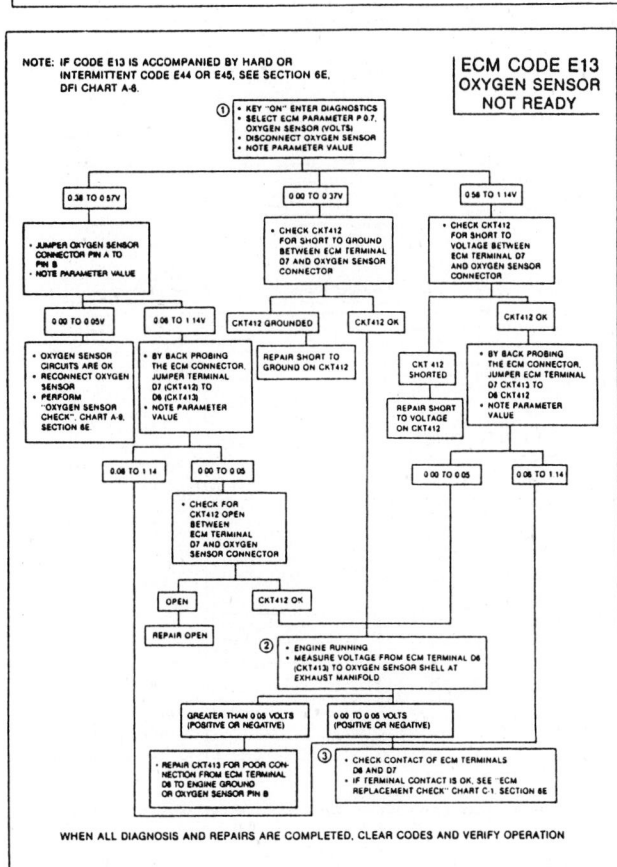

ECM CODE E13
OXYGEN SENSOR NOT READY

NOTE: IF CODE E13 IS ACCOMPANIED BY HARD OR INTERMITTENT CODE E44 OR E45, SEE SECTION 6E, DFI CHART A-6.

WHEN ALL DIAGNOSIS AND REPAIRS ARE COMPLETED, CLEAR CODES AND VERIFY OPERATION

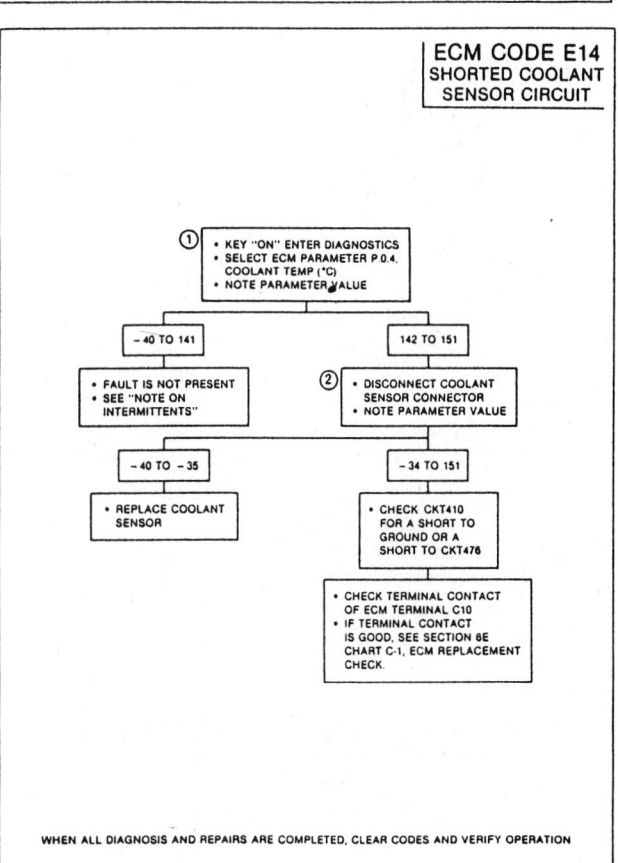

ECM CODE E14
SHORTED COOLANT SENSOR CIRCUIT

WHEN ALL DIAGNOSIS AND REPAIRS ARE COMPLETED, CLEAR CODES AND VERIFY OPERATION

DFI TROUBLE DIAGNOSTICS

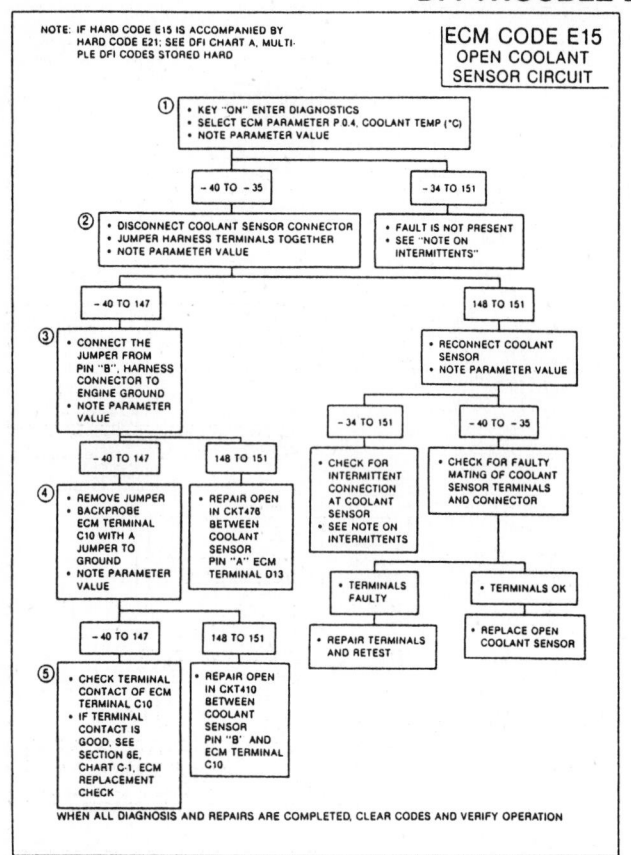

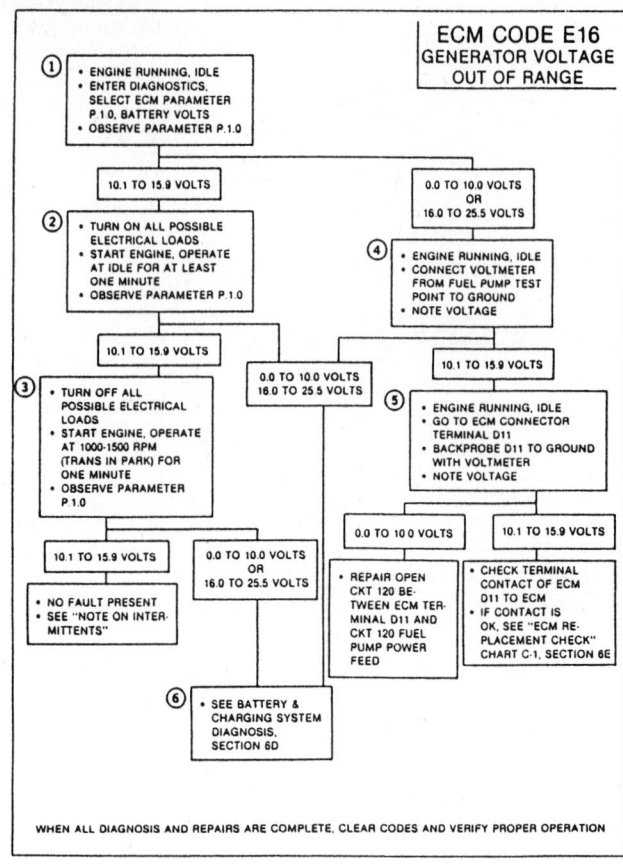

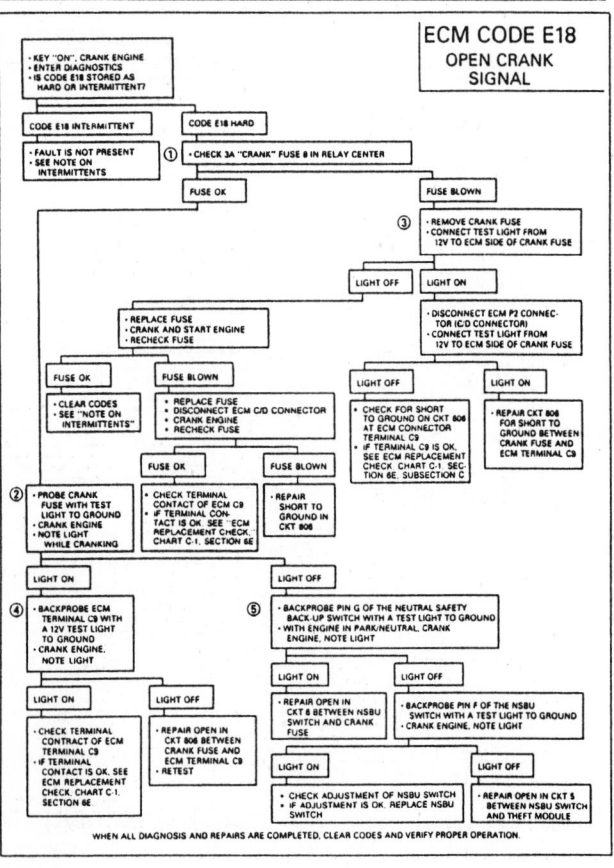

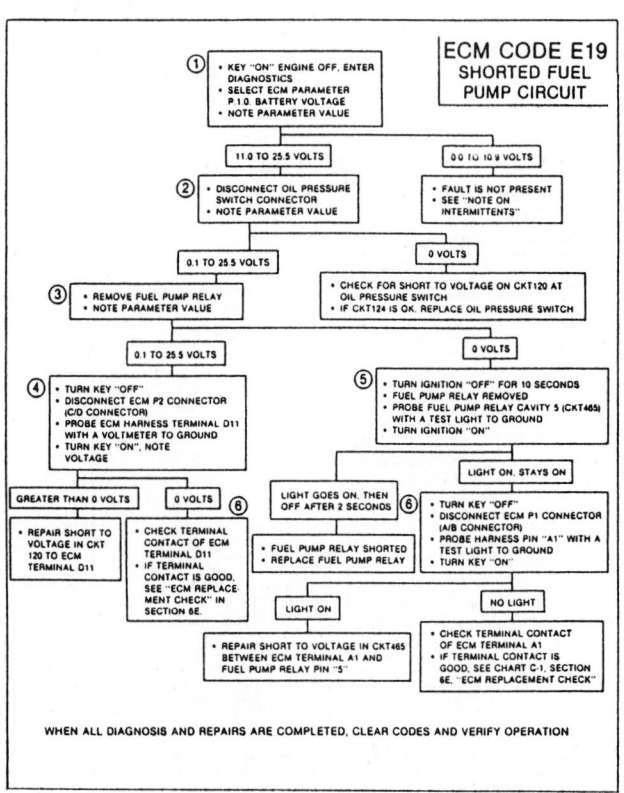

DFI TROUBLE DIAGNOSTICS

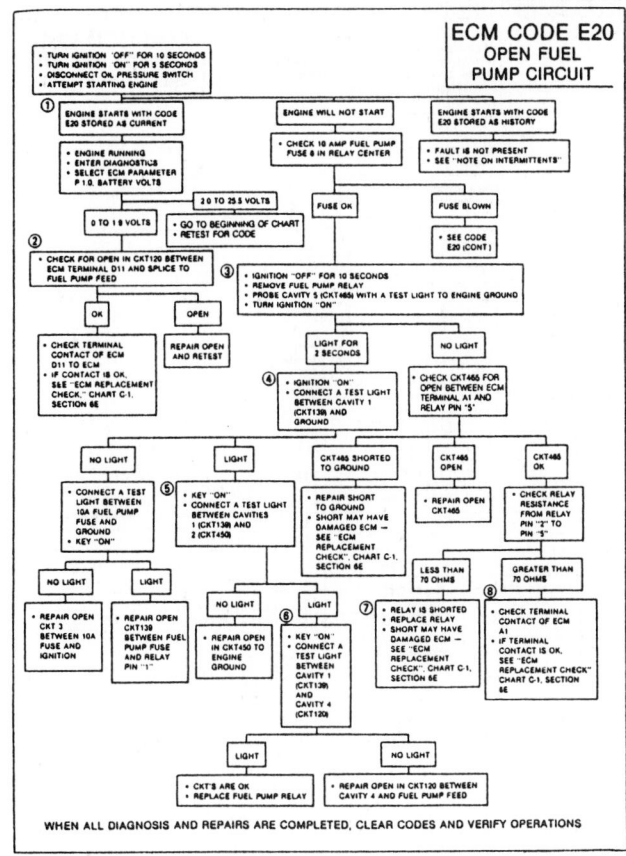

ECM CODE E20
OPEN FUEL
PUMP CIRCUIT

WHEN ALL DIAGNOSIS AND REPAIRS ARE COMPLETED, CLEAR CODES AND VERIFY OPERATIONS

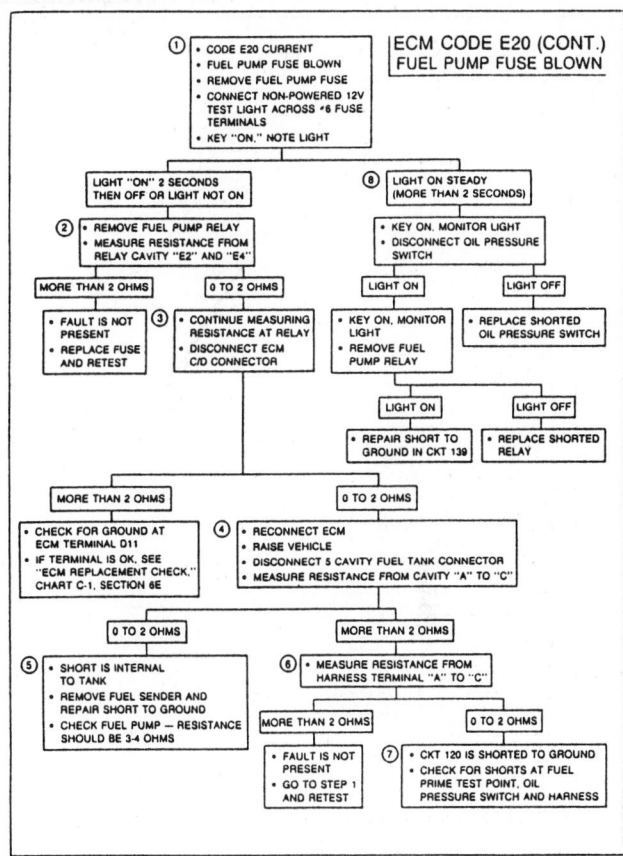

ECM CODE E20 (CONT.)
FUEL PUMP FUSE BLOWN

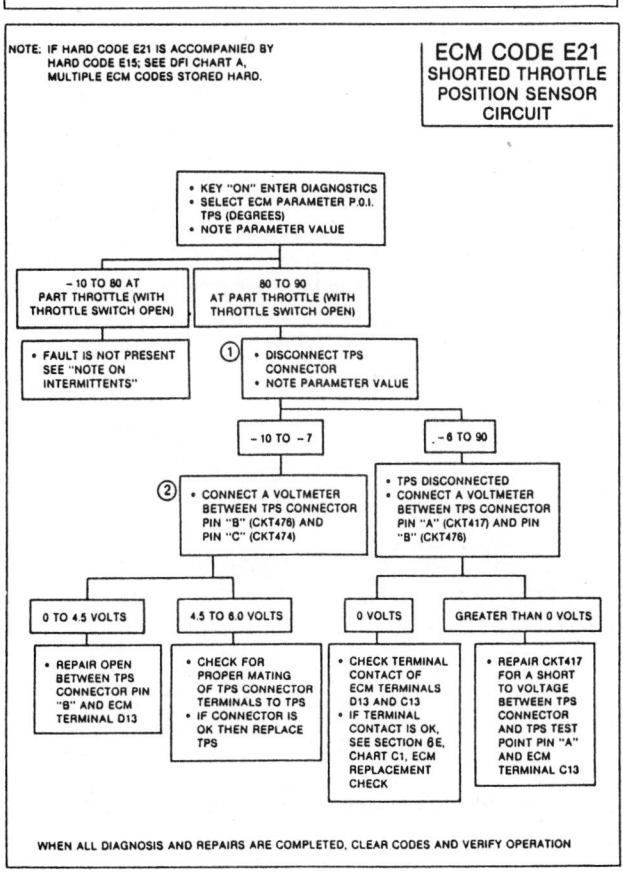

NOTE: IF HARD CODE E21 IS ACCOMPANIED BY
HARD CODE E15; SEE DFI CHART A,
MULTIPLE ECM CODES STORED HARD.

ECM CODE E21
SHORTED THROTTLE
POSITION SENSOR
CIRCUIT

WHEN ALL DIAGNOSIS AND REPAIRS ARE COMPLETED, CLEAR CODES AND VERIFY OPERATION

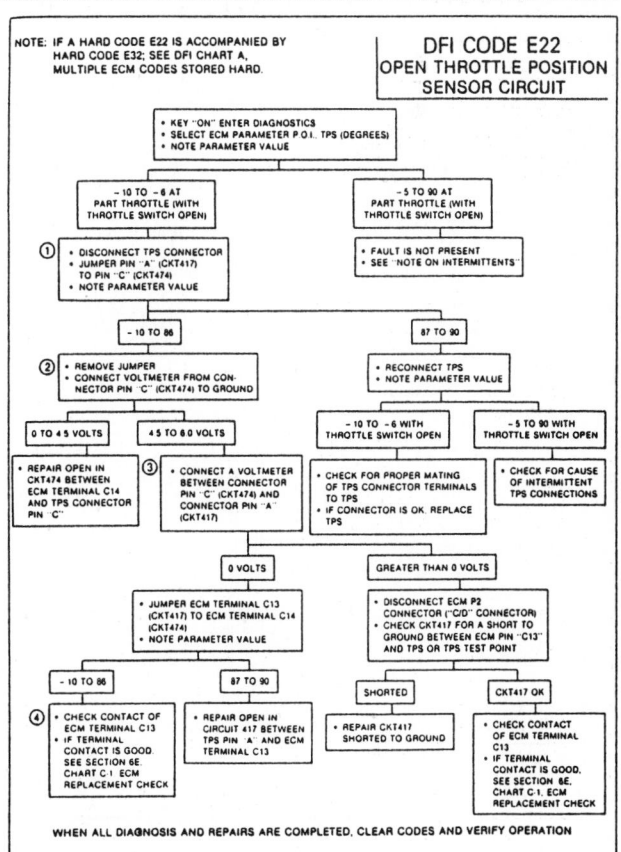

NOTE: IF A HARD CODE E22 IS ACCOMPANIED BY
HARD CODE E32; SEE DFI CHART A,
MULTIPLE ECM CODES STORED HARD.

DFI CODE E22
OPEN THROTTLE POSITION
SENSOR CIRCUIT

WHEN ALL DIAGNOSIS AND REPAIRS ARE COMPLETED, CLEAR CODES AND VERIFY OPERATION

DFI TROUBLE DIAGNOSTICS

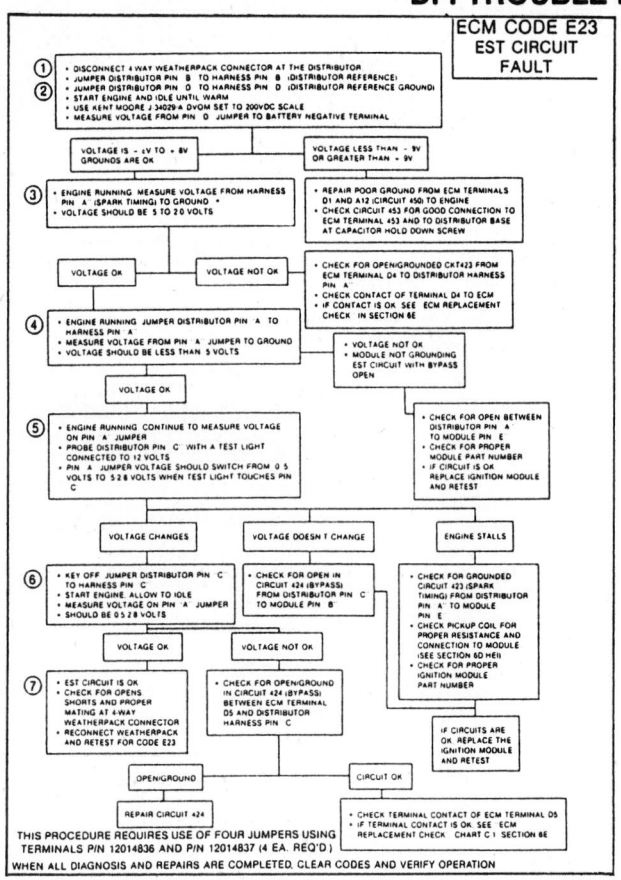

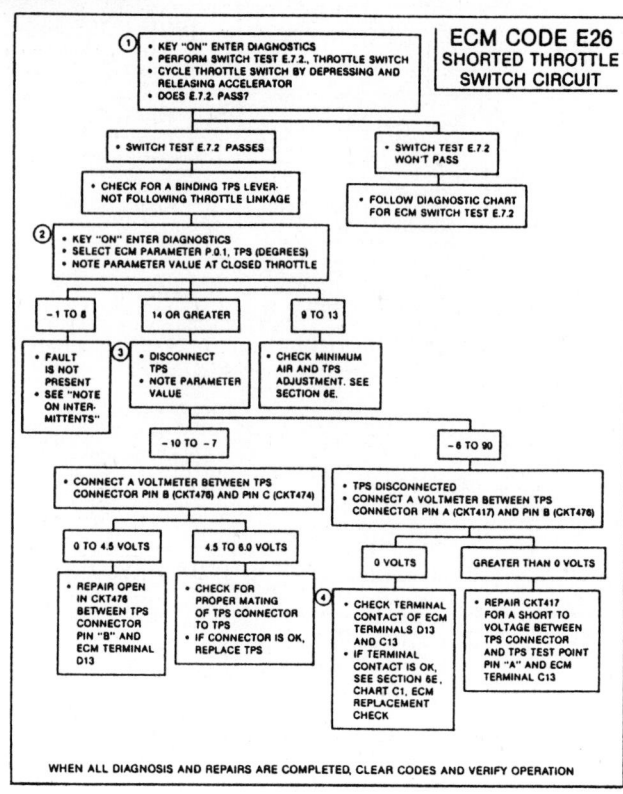

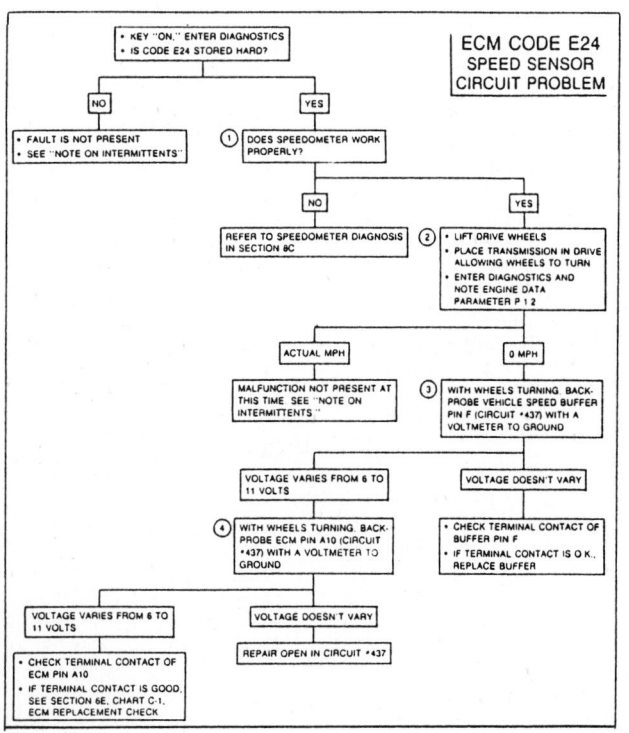

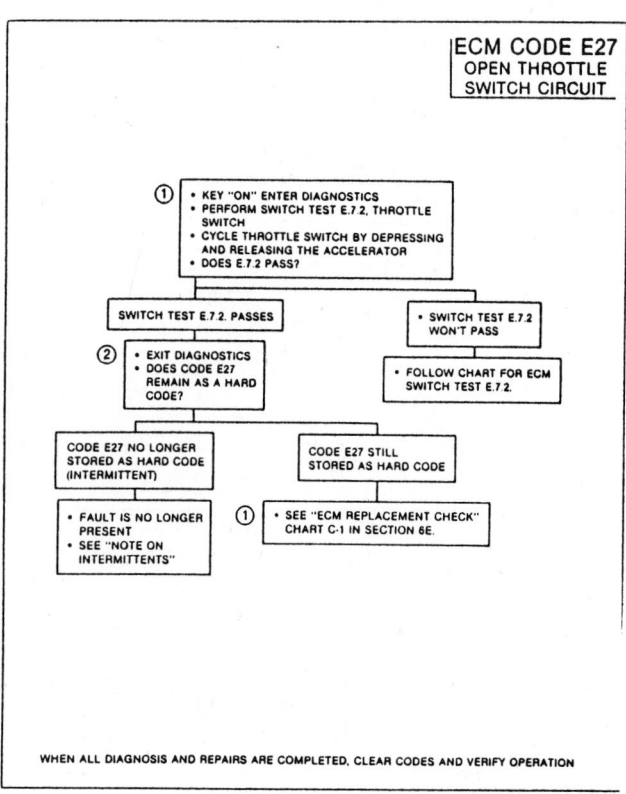

DFI TROUBLE DIAGNOSTICS

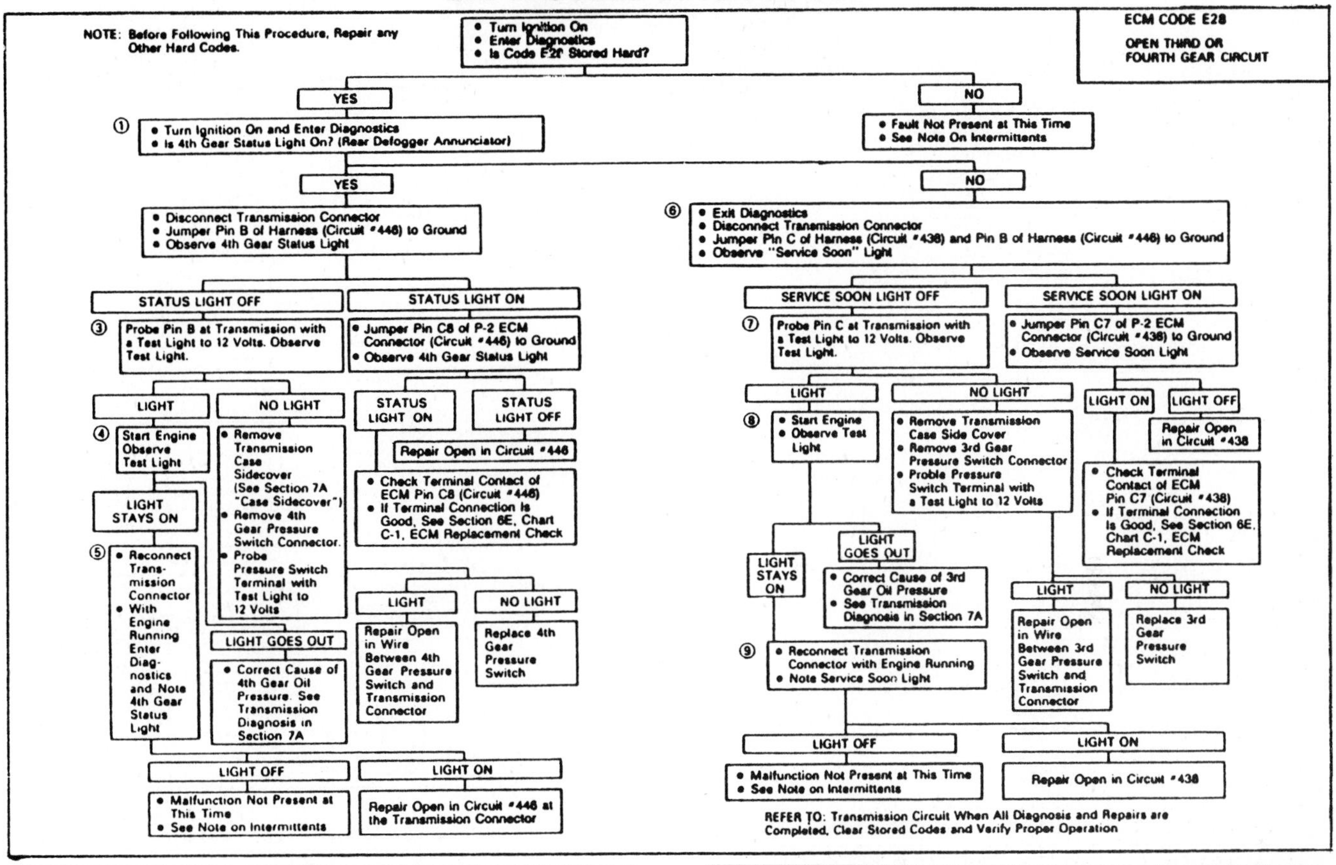

ECM CODE E28 — OPEN THIRD OR FOURTH GEAR CIRCUIT

ECM CODE E28
OPEN THIRD OR FOURTH GEAR CIRCUIT
NOTE: Before Following This Procedure, Repair any Other Hard Codes.
• Turn Ignition On • Enter Diagnostics • Is Code E28 Stored Hard?
YES
NO
① • Turn Ignition On and Enter Diagnostics • Is 4th Gear Status Light On? (Rear Defogger Annunciator)
• Fault Not Present at This Time • See Note On Intermittents
YES
NO
• Disconnect Transmission Connector • Jumper Pin B of Harness (Circuit #446) to Ground • Observe 4th Gear Status Light
⑥ • Exit Diagnostics • Disconnect Transmission Connector • Jumper Pin C of Harness (Circuit #438) and Pin B of Harness (Circuit #446) to Ground • Observe "Service Soon" Light
STATUS LIGHT OFF
STATUS LIGHT ON
③ Probe Pin B at Transmission with a Test Light to 12 Volts. Observe Test Light.
• Jumper Pin C8 of P-2 ECM Connector (Circuit #446) to Ground • Observe 4th Gear Status Light
LIGHT
NO LIGHT
STATUS LIGHT ON
STATUS LIGHT OFF
Repair Open in Circuit #446
④ Start Engine Observe Test Light
• Remove Transmission Case Sidecover (See Section 7A "Case Sidecover") • Remove 4th Gear Pressure Switch Connector. • Probe Pressure Switch Terminal with Test Light to 12 Volts
• Check Terminal Contact of ECM Pin C8 (Circuit #446) • If Terminal Connection Is Good, See Section 6E, Chart C-1, ECM Replacement Check
LIGHT STAYS ON
⑤ • Reconnect Transmission Connector • With Engine Running Enter Diagnostics and Note 4th Gear Status Light
LIGHT
NO LIGHT
LIGHT GOES OUT
Repair Open in Wire Between 4th Gear Pressure Switch and Transmission Connector
Replace 4th Gear Pressure Switch
• Correct Cause of 4th Gear Oil Pressure. See Transmission Diagnosis in Section 7A
LIGHT OFF
LIGHT ON
• Malfunction Not Present at This Time • See Note on Intermittents
Repair Open in Circuit #446 at the Transmission Connector
SERVICE SOON LIGHT OFF
SERVICE SOON LIGHT ON
⑦ Probe Pin C at Transmission with a Test Light to 12 Volts. Observe Test Light.
• Jumper Pin C7 of P-2 ECM Connector (Circuit #438) to Ground • Observe Service Soon Light
LIGHT
NO LIGHT
LIGHT ON
LIGHT OFF
Repair Open in Circuit #438
⑧ • Start Engine • Observe Test Light
• Remove Transmission Case Side Cover • Remove 3rd Gear Pressure Switch Connector • Proble Pressure Switch Terminal with a Test Light to 12 Volts
• Check Terminal Contact of ECM Pin C7 (Circuit #438) • If Terminal Connection Is Good, See Section 6E, Chart C-1, ECM Replacement Check
LIGHT GOES OUT
LIGHT STAYS ON
• Correct Cause of 3rd Gear Oil Pressure • See Transmission Diagnosis in Section 7A
LIGHT
NO LIGHT
⑨ • Reconnect Transmission Connector with Engine Running • Note Service Soon Light
Repair Open in Wire Between 3rd Gear Pressure Switch and Transmission Connector
Replace 3rd Gear Pressure Switch
LIGHT OFF
LIGHT ON
• Malfunction Not Present at This Time • See Note on Intermittents
Repair Open in Circuit #438
REFER TO: Transmission Circuit When All Diagnosis and Repairs are Completed, Clear Stored Codes and Verify Proper Operation

ECM CODE E29 — SHORTED FOURTH GEAR CIRCUIT

ECM CODE E29
SHORTED FOURTH GEAR CIRCUIT
① • DISCONNECT TRANSMISSION CONNECTOR • TURN IGNITION ON AND ENTER DIAGNOSTICS. • OBSERVE 4TH GEAR STATUS LIGHT ABOVE "HI" BUTTON ON ECC CONTROL HEAD.
STATUS LIGHT OFF
STATUS LIGHT ON
CHECK CIRCUIT #438 FOR A SHORT TO GROUND.
CHECK FOR A FAULTY ECM CONNECTOR OR FAULTY ECM.
② • RECONNECT TRANSMISSION CONNECTOR • ROAD TEST TO VERIFY 4TH GEAR OPERATION (COUNT NUMBER OF SHIFTS).
NO 4TH GEAR OPERATION
4TH GEAR OPERATION
CORRECT CAUSE OF NO 4TH GEAR OPERATION. SEE TRANSMISSION DIAGNOSIS IN SECTION 7 OF SERVICE MANUAL.
③ • WHILE IN 4TH GEAR, ENTER DIAGNOSTICS • IS 4TH GEAR STATUS LIGHT NOW ON?
NO
YES
④ • REMOVE TRANSMISSION OIL PAN • REMOVE 4TH GEAR PRESSURE SWITCH CONNECTOR. • TURN IGNITION ON AND ENTER DIAGNOSTICS • OBSERVE 4TH GEAR STATUS LIGHT
MALFUNCTION NOT PRESENT AT THIS TIME. TREAT AS AN INTERMITTENT (SEE "NOTE ON INTERMITTENTS").
STATUS LIGHT ON
STATUS LIGHT OFF
CHECK FOR FAULTY PRESSURE SWITCH CONNECTOR OR FAULTY PRESSURE SWITCH.
REPAIR SHORT TO GROUND IN WIRE BETWEEN 4TH GEAR PRESSURE SWITCH AND TRANSMISSION CONNECTOR.
REFER TO: TRANSMISSION CIRCUIT
WHEN ALL DIAGNOSIS AND REPAIRS ARE COMPLETED, CLEAR STORED CODES AND VERIFY PROPER OPERATION.

ECM CODE E30 — IDLE SPEED CONTROL SYSTEM PROBLEM

ECM CODE E30
IDLE SPEED CONTROL SYSTEM PROBLEM
① • KEY "ON", ENTER DIAGNOSTICS • IS CODE E55 STORED AS HARD OR INTERMITTENT?
NO
YES
② • GO TO E.9.5 • PERFORM SWITCH TEST • DO ALL SWITCH TESTS PASS?
• GO TO DIAGNOSTIC CHART "ECM CODE E55" • REPAIR AND RETEST FOR CODE E30
YES
NO
③ • GO TO E.9.6 OUTPUT CYCLING • DOES ISC MOTOR EXTEND AND RETRACT?
• GO TO DIAGNOSTIC CHART FOR SWITCH TESTS THAT DO NOT PASS • REPAIR AND RETEST FOR CODE E30
YES
NO
④ • KEY OFF FOR TEN SECONDS • START ENGINE, ALLOW TO RETURN TO WARM IDLE • IS IDLE SPEED STEADY?
• CHECK FOR BINDING THROTTLE LINKAGE
YES
NO
BINDING
OK
• ENTER DIAGNOSTICS • IS E30 STORED HARD?
• SEE SECTION 6E SYMPTOM "ROUGH, UNSTABLE, INCORRECT IDLE, STALLING" • IN PARTICULAR, CHECK FOR – CRACKED SPARK PLUGS, HEI ARCING – VACUUM LEAKS (HOSES/MANIFOLD) – DISTRIBUTOR GEAR WORN – VALVE OPERATION FAULTS
• CHECK FOR THROTTLE, CRUISE AND TV CABLES BINDING • CHECK FOR PROPER TPS TO THROTTLE BODY INSTALLATION • CHECK FOR PROPER THROTTLE SPRING • REPAIR AS NECESSARY AND RETEST
• DISCONNECT ISC CONNECTOR • JUMPER ISC CONNECTOR PINS "A" & "B" TOGETHER • GO TO E.9.6 (OUTPUT CYCLING) • CONNECT TEST LIGHT FROM PIN "D" OF ISC CONNECTOR TO GROUND
NO
YES
• FAULT IS NOT PRESENT • SEE "NOTE ON INTERMITTENTS"
NO LIGHT
• LIGHT FLASHES EVERY 3 SECONDS
• GO TO E.9.6 OUTPUT CYCLING • MOVE TEST LIGHT TO PIN "C" OF ISC TO GROUND
⑤ • CHECK MINIMUM AIR, TPS AND ISC ADJUSTMENTS. SEE SECTION 6E
NO LIGHT
• LIGHT FLASHES EVERY 3 SECONDS
ADJUSTMENT REQ'D
ADJUSTMENT OK
• KEY "OFF" • RECONNECT ISC MOTOR, DISCONNECT ECM P2 CONNECTOR (C/D CONNECTOR) • MEASURE RESISTANCE FROM ECM TERMINAL C5 (CKT425) TO C8 (CKT426)
• GO TO E.9.6 OUTPUT CYCLING • CONNECT TEST LIGHT FROM PIN "C" TO PIN "D" OF HARNESS CONNECTOR
• PERFORM ADJUSTMENT AND RETEST FOR CODE E30
4 – 100 OHMS
0 – 3 OHMS
OPEN
• NO LIGHT OR LIGHT FLASHES EVERY 3 SECONDS
• LIGHT FLASHES CONTINUOUSLY
• CHECK CKT425 AND 426 FOR SHORTS TO GROUND BETWEEN ISC CONNECTOR AND ECM
• CHECK FOR CKT425 426 SHORTED TOGETHER OR SHORTED TO GROUND BETWEEN ECM & ISC CONNECTORS
• REPAIR OPEN CKT425 OR 426 BETWEEN ECM CONNECTOR AND ISC
• REPLACE ECM AND RETEST FOR CODE E30 • SEE "ECM REPLACEMENT CHECK", CHART C-1, SECTION 6E
• CHECK ISC CONNECTOR FOR PROPER MATING TO ISC • IF CONNECTOR IS OK, REPLACE ISC MOTOR
OK
SHORTED
OK
• IF IDLE SPEED IS STABLE, REPLACE ECM AND RETEST FOR CODE E30 • SEE "ECM REPLACEMENT CHECK" CHART C-1, SECTION 6E
• REPAIR SHORT • TEST FOR ECM DAMAGED BY SHORT
• REPLACE ISC MOTOR
WHEN ALL DIAGNOSIS AND REPAIRS ARE COMPLETED, CLEAR CODES AND VERIFY OPERATION

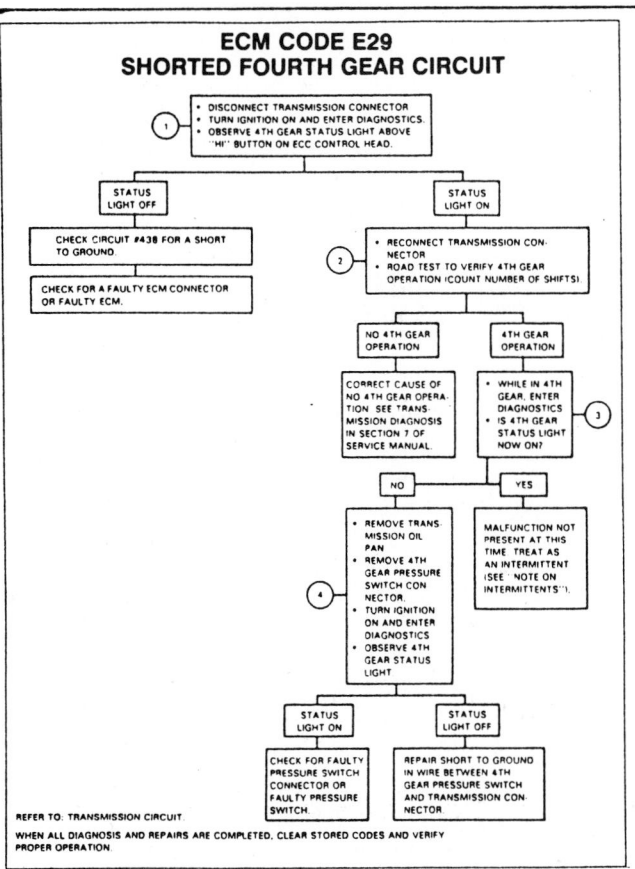

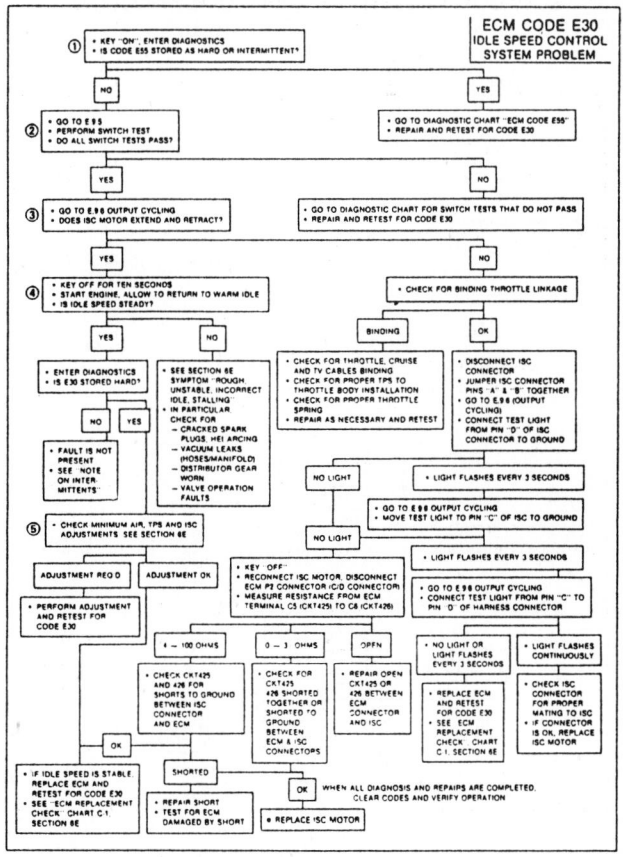

DFI TROUBLE DIAGNOSTICS

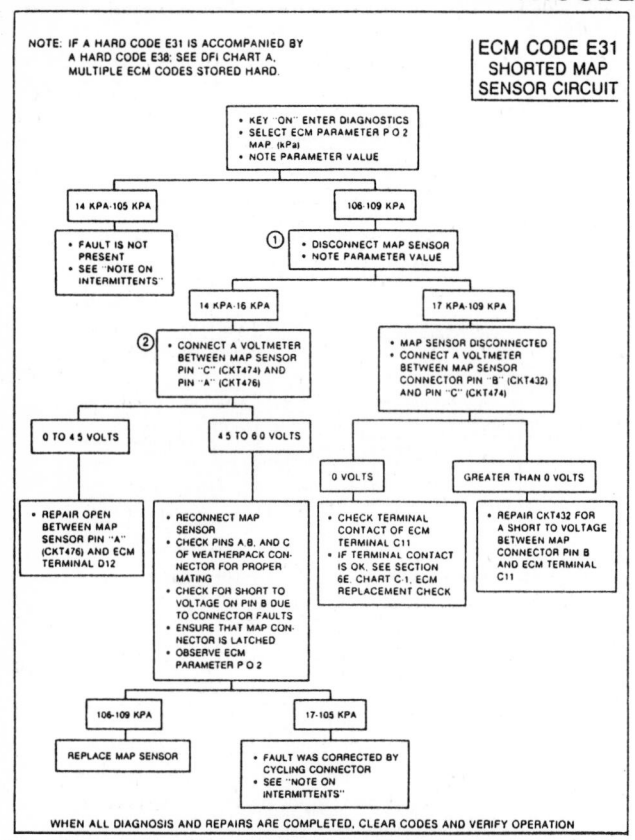

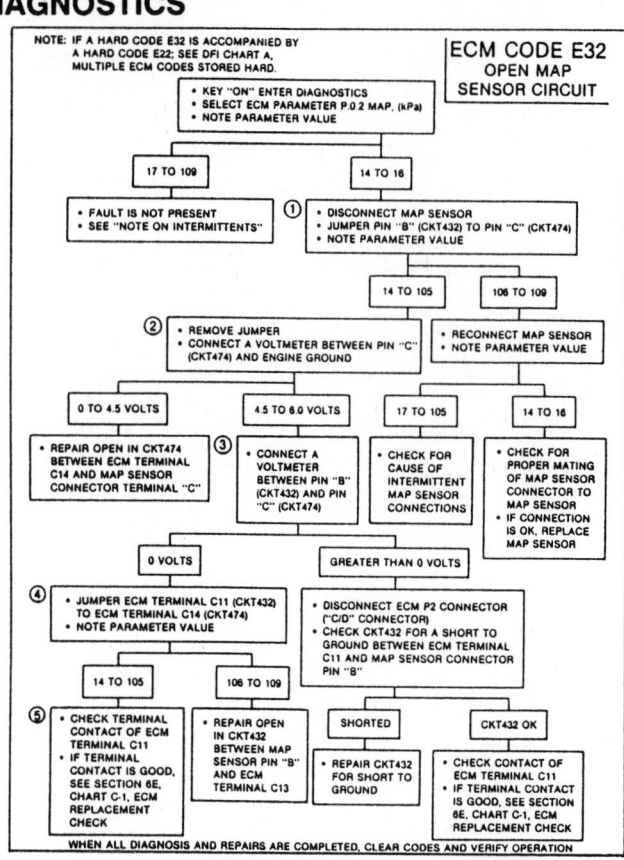

ECM CODE E32, OPEN MANIFOLD ABSOLUTE PRESSURE SENSOR CIRCUIT

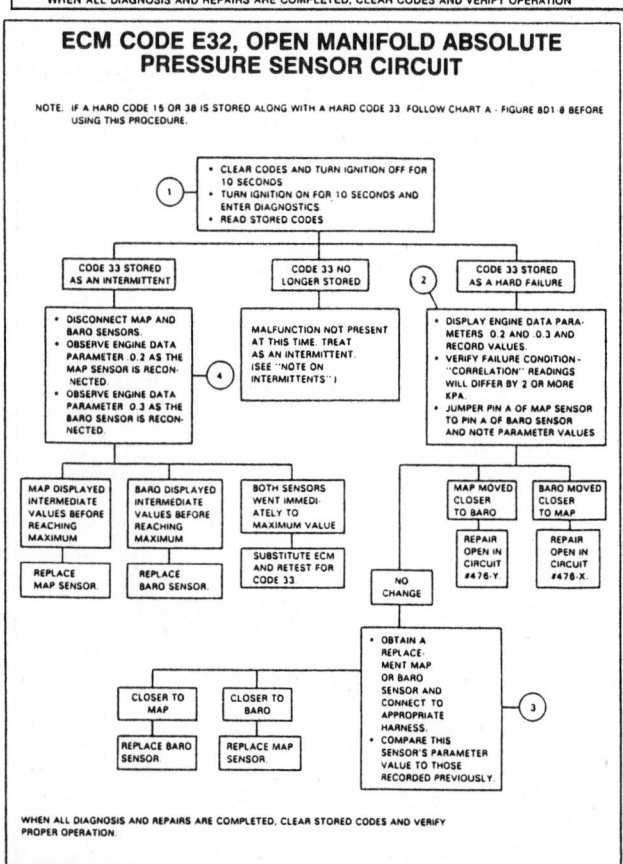

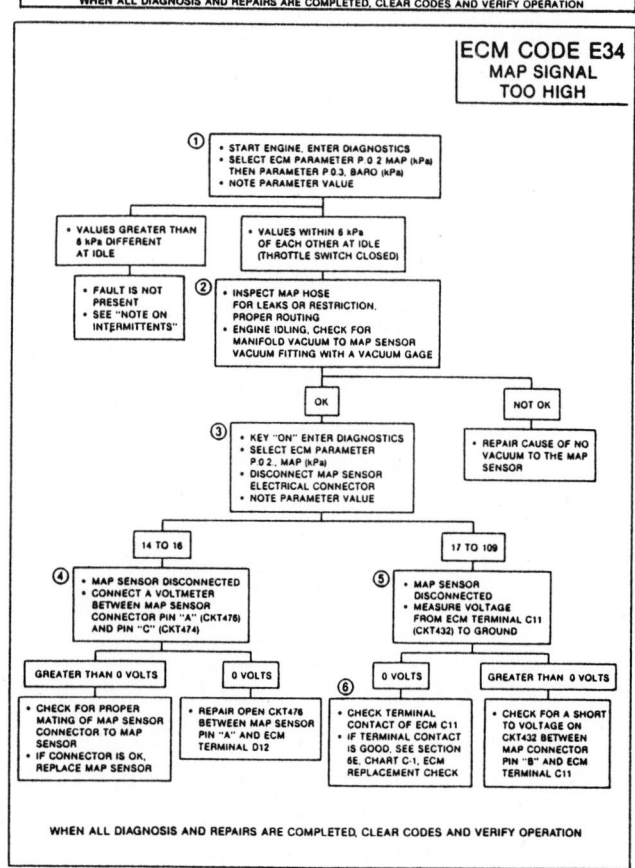

DFI TROUBLE DIAGNOSTICS

ECM CODE E35
SHORTED BAROMETRIC PRESSURE SENSOR CIRCUIT

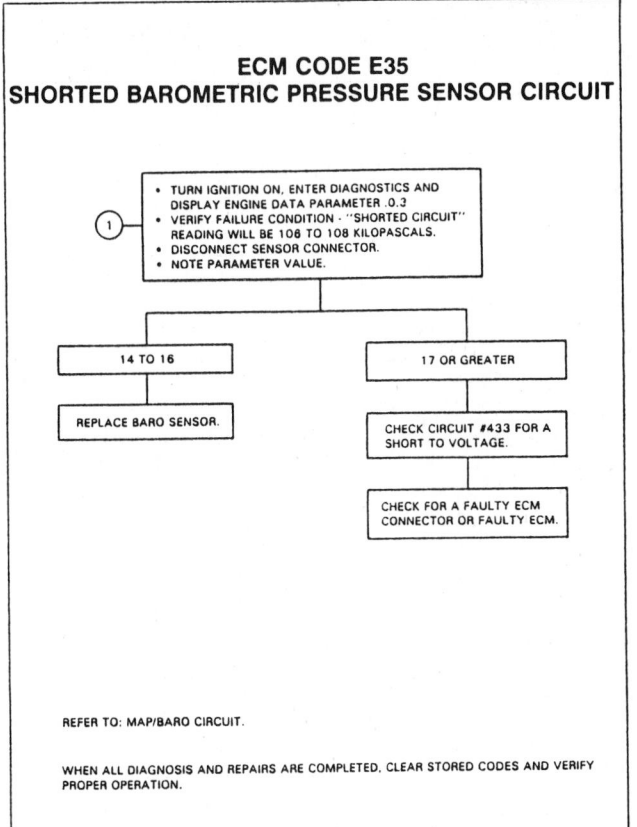

① • TURN IGNITION ON, ENTER DIAGNOSTICS AND DISPLAY ENGINE DATA PARAMETER .0.3
• VERIFY FAILURE CONDITION - "SHORTED CIRCUIT" READING WILL BE 106 TO 108 KILOPASCALS.
• DISCONNECT SENSOR CONNECTOR.
• NOTE PARAMETER VALUE.

14 TO 16 → REPLACE BARO SENSOR.

17 OR GREATER → CHECK CIRCUIT #433 FOR A SHORT TO VOLTAGE. → CHECK FOR A FAULTY ECM CONNECTOR OR FAULTY ECM.

REFER TO: MAP/BARO CIRCUIT.

WHEN ALL DIAGNOSIS AND REPAIRS ARE COMPLETED, CLEAR STORED CODES AND VERIFY PROPER OPERATION.

ECM CODE E36
OPEN BAROMETRIC PRESSURE SENSOR CIRCUIT

NOTE: IF CODES 22 AND 32 ARE STORED HARD ALONG WITH A HARD CODE 36, FOLLOW CHART A -FIGURE 8D1-8 BEFORE USING THIS PROCEDURE.

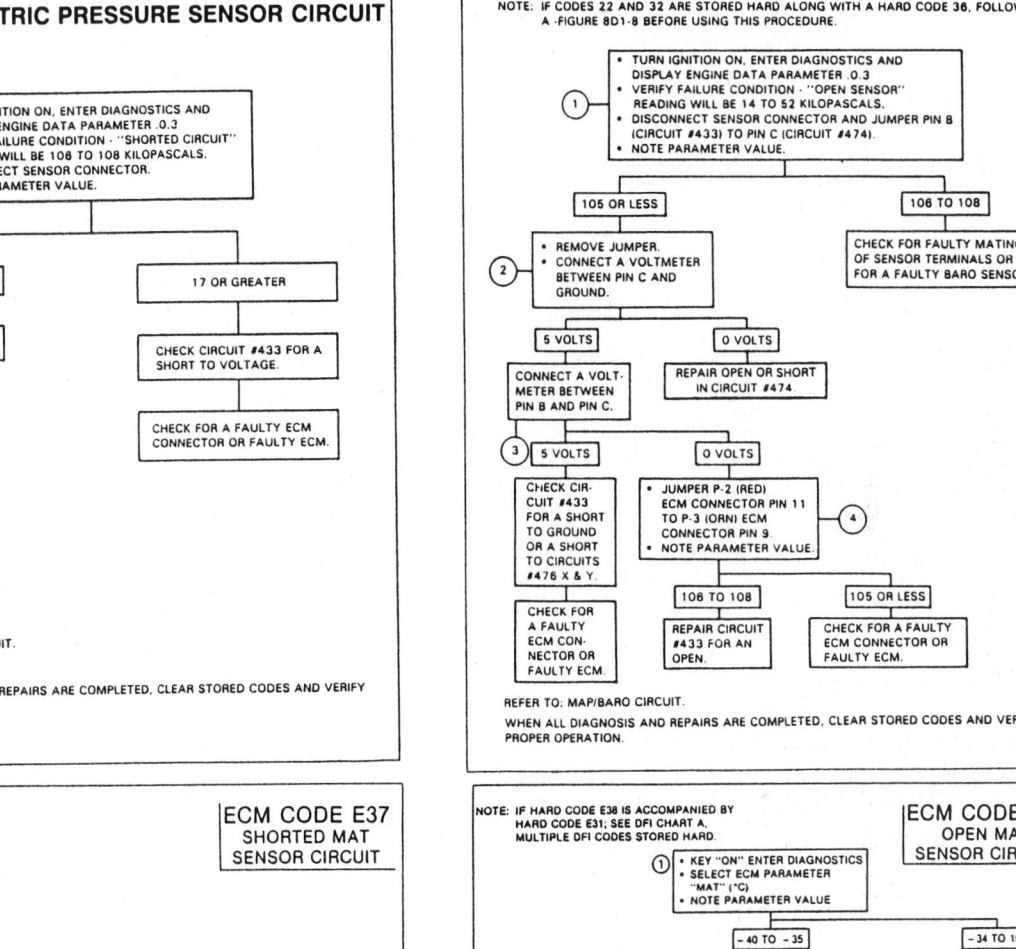

① • TURN IGNITION ON, ENTER DIAGNOSTICS AND DISPLAY ENGINE DATA PARAMETER .0.3
• VERIFY FAILURE CONDITION - "OPEN SENSOR" READING WILL BE 14 TO 52 KILOPASCALS.
• DISCONNECT SENSOR CONNECTOR AND JUMPER PIN B (CIRCUIT #433) TO PIN C (CIRCUIT #474).
• NOTE PARAMETER VALUE.

105 OR LESS → ② • REMOVE JUMPER. • CONNECT A VOLTMETER BETWEEN PIN C AND GROUND.

106 TO 108 → CHECK FOR FAULTY MATING OF SENSOR TERMINALS OR FOR A FAULTY BARO SENSOR.

5 VOLTS → CONNECT A VOLT-METER BETWEEN PIN B AND PIN C.

0 VOLTS → REPAIR OPEN OR SHORT IN CIRCUIT #474.

③ 5 VOLTS → CHECK CIRCUIT #433 FOR A SHORT TO GROUND OR A SHORT TO CIRCUITS #476 X & Y. → CHECK FOR A FAULTY ECM CONNECTOR OR FAULTY ECM.

0 VOLTS → • JUMPER P-2 (RED) ECM CONNECTOR PIN 11 TO P-3 (ORN) ECM CONNECTOR PIN 9. • NOTE PARAMETER VALUE. ④

106 TO 108 → REPAIR CIRCUIT #433 FOR AN OPEN.

105 OR LESS → CHECK FOR A FAULTY ECM CONNECTOR OR FAULTY ECM.

REFER TO: MAP/BARO CIRCUIT.

WHEN ALL DIAGNOSIS AND REPAIRS ARE COMPLETED, CLEAR STORED CODES AND VERIFY PROPER OPERATION.

ECM CODE E37
SHORTED MAT SENSOR CIRCUIT

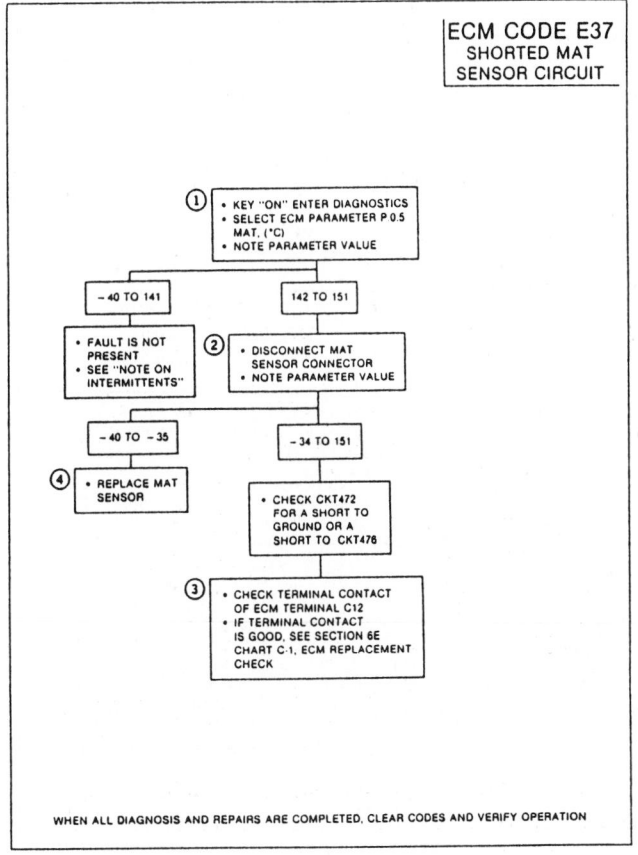

① • KEY "ON" ENTER DIAGNOSTICS
• SELECT ECM PARAMETER P 0.5 MAT. (°C)
• NOTE PARAMETER VALUE

-40 TO 141 → • FAULT IS NOT PRESENT • SEE "NOTE ON INTERMITTENTS"

142 TO 151 → ② • DISCONNECT MAT SENSOR CONNECTOR • NOTE PARAMETER VALUE

-40 TO -35 → ④ • REPLACE MAT SENSOR

-34 TO 151 → • CHECK CKT472 FOR A SHORT TO GROUND OR A SHORT TO CKT476

③ • CHECK TERMINAL CONTACT OF ECM TERMINAL C12
• IF TERMINAL CONTACT IS GOOD, SEE SECTION 6E CHART C-1, ECM REPLACEMENT CHECK

WHEN ALL DIAGNOSIS AND REPAIRS ARE COMPLETED, CLEAR CODES AND VERIFY OPERATION

ECM CODE E38
OPEN MAT SENSOR CIRCUIT

NOTE: IF HARD CODE E38 IS ACCOMPANIED BY HARD CODE E31; SEE DFI CHART A, MULTIPLE DFI CODES STORED HARD.

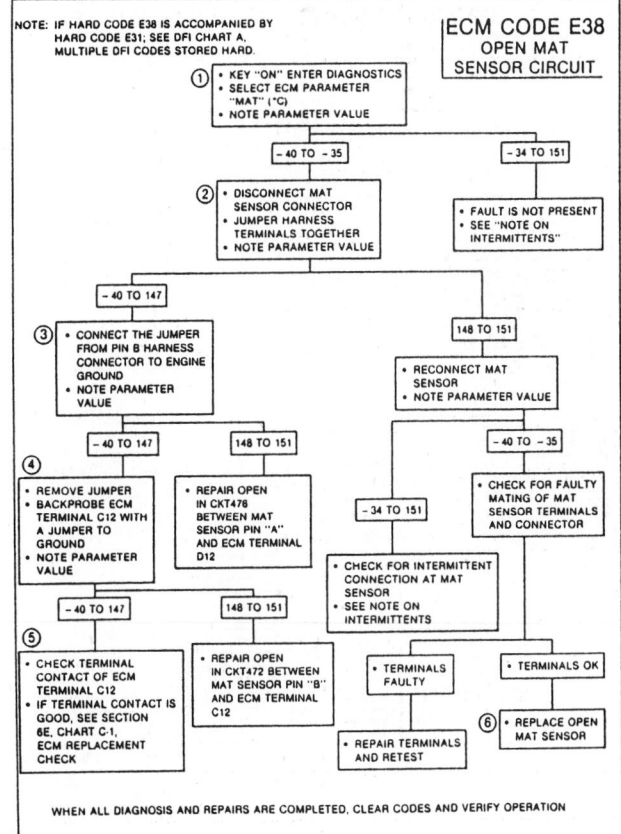

① • KEY "ON" ENTER DIAGNOSTICS
• SELECT ECM PARAMETER "MAT" (°C)
• NOTE PARAMETER VALUE

-40 TO -35 → ② • DISCONNECT MAT SENSOR CONNECTOR • JUMPER HARNESS TERMINALS TOGETHER • NOTE PARAMETER VALUE

-34 TO 151 → • FAULT IS NOT PRESENT • SEE "NOTE ON INTERMITTENTS"

-40 TO 147 → ③ • CONNECT THE JUMPER FROM PIN B HARNESS CONNECTOR TO ENGINE GROUND • NOTE PARAMETER VALUE

148 TO 151 → • RECONNECT MAT SENSOR • NOTE PARAMETER VALUE

-40 TO 147 → ④ • REMOVE JUMPER • BACKPROBE ECM TERMINAL C12 WITH A JUMPER TO GROUND • NOTE PARAMETER VALUE

148 TO 151 → • REPAIR OPEN IN CKT476 BETWEEN MAT SENSOR PIN "A" AND ECM TERMINAL D12

-34 TO 151 → • CHECK FOR INTERMITTENT CONNECTION AT MAT SENSOR • SEE NOTE ON INTERMITTENTS

-40 TO -35 → • CHECK FOR FAULTY MATING OF MAT SENSOR TERMINALS AND CONNECTOR

-40 TO 147 → ⑤ • CHECK TERMINAL CONTACT OF ECM TERMINAL C12 • IF TERMINAL CONTACT IS GOOD, SEE SECTION 6E, CHART C-1, ECM REPLACEMENT CHECK

148 TO 151 → • REPAIR OPEN IN CKT472 BETWEEN MAT SENSOR PIN "B" AND ECM TERMINAL C12

• TERMINALS FAULTY → • REPAIR TERMINALS AND RETEST

• TERMINALS OK → ⑥ • REPLACE OPEN MAT SENSOR

WHEN ALL DIAGNOSIS AND REPAIRS ARE COMPLETED, CLEAR CODES AND VERIFY OPERATION

DFI TROUBLE DIAGNOSTICS

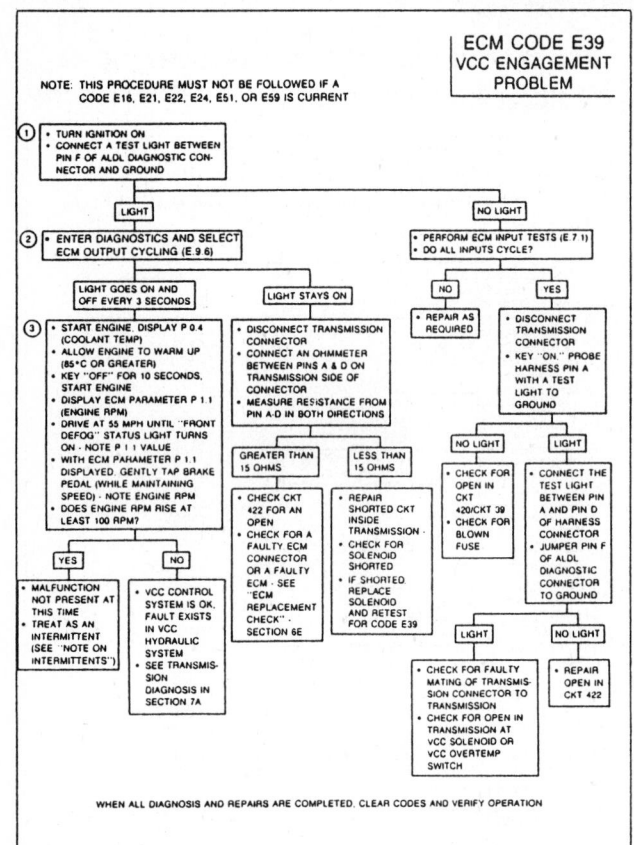

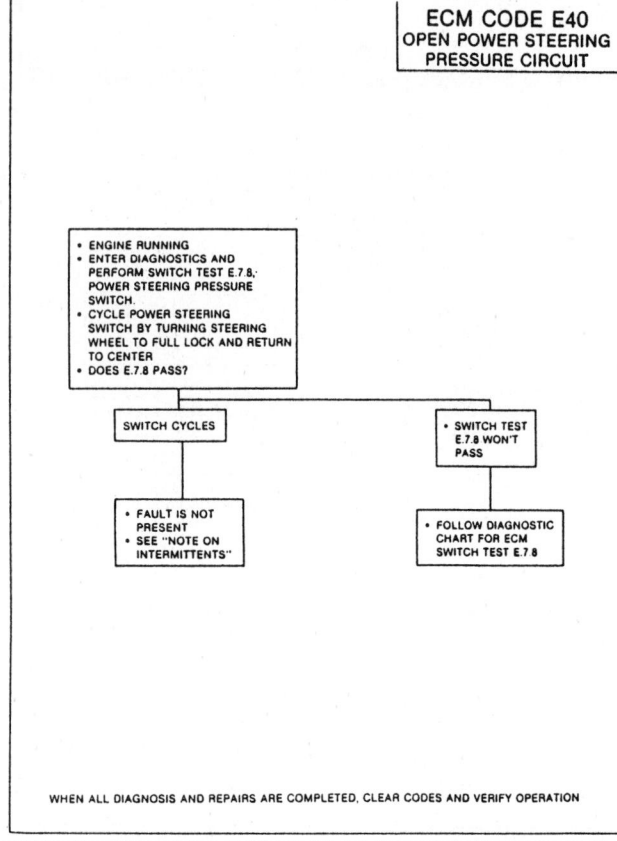

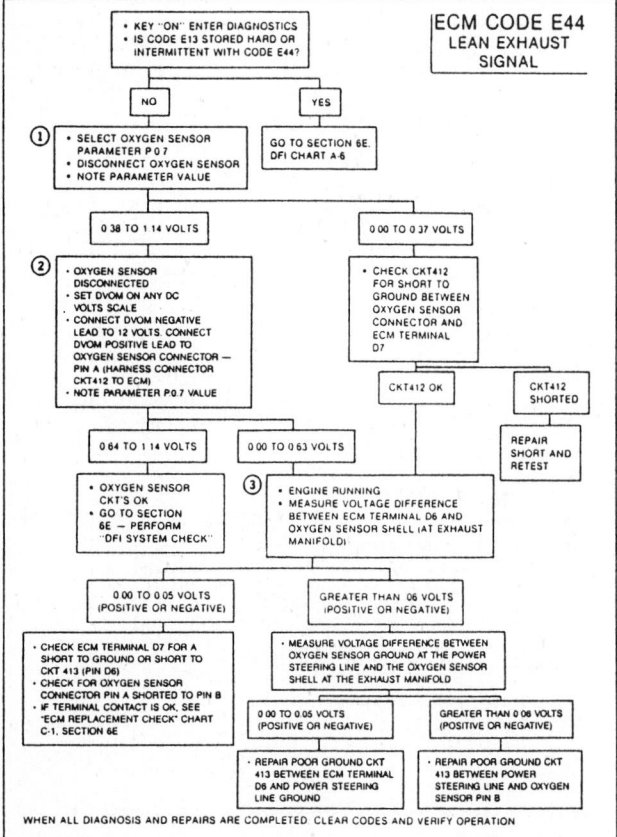

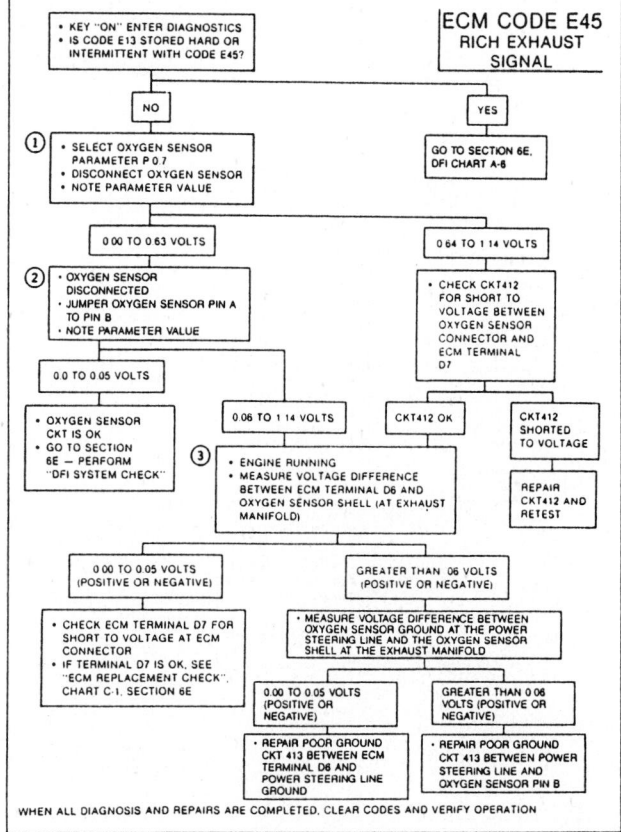

DFI TROUBLE DIAGNOSTICS

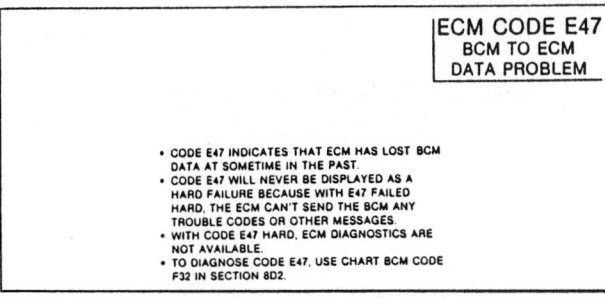

ECM CODE E47
BCM TO ECM DATA PROBLEM

- CODE E47 INDICATES THAT ECM HAS LOST BCM DATA AT SOMETIME IN THE PAST.
- CODE E47 WILL NEVER BE DISPLAYED AS A HARD FAILURE BECAUSE WITH E47 FAILED HARD, THE ECM CAN'T SEND THE BCM ANY TROUBLE CODES OR OTHER MESSAGES.
- WITH CODE E47 HARD, ECM DIAGNOSTICS ARE NOT AVAILABLE.
- TO DIAGNOSE CODE E47, USE CHART BCM CODE F32 IN SECTION 8D2.

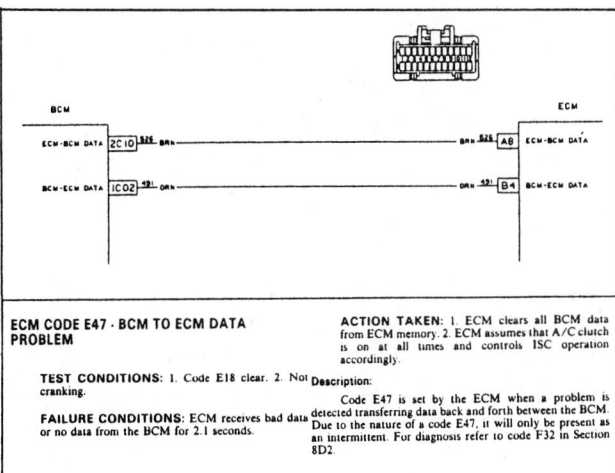

ECM CODE E47 · BCM TO ECM DATA PROBLEM

TEST CONDITIONS: 1. Code E18 clear. 2. Not cranking.

FAILURE CONDITIONS: ECM receives bad data or no data from the BCM for 2.1 seconds.

ACTION TAKEN: 1. ECM clears all BCM data from ECM memory. 2. ECM assumes that A/C clutch is on at all times and controls ISC operation accordingly.

Description:
Code E47 is set by the ECM when a problem is detected transferring data back and forth between the BCM. Due to the nature of a code E47, it will only be present as an intermittent. For diagnosis refer to code F32 in Section 8D2.

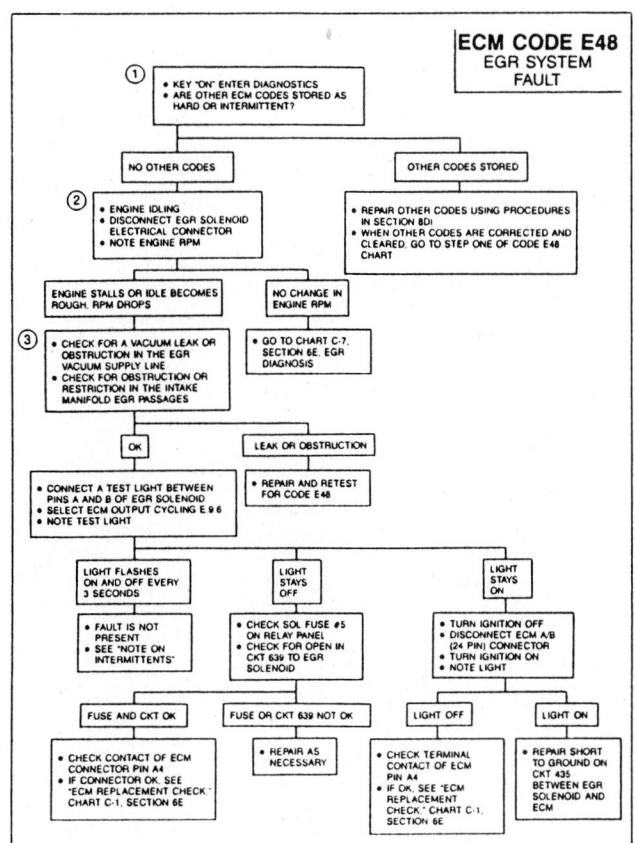

ECM CODE E48
EGR SYSTEM FAULT

① • KEY "ON" ENTER DIAGNOSTICS
• ARE OTHER ECM CODES STORED AS HARD OR INTERMITTENT?

NO OTHER CODES — OTHER CODES STORED

② • ENGINE IDLING
• DISCONNECT EGR SOLENOID ELECTRICAL CONNECTOR
• NOTE ENGINE RPM

• REPAIR OTHER CODES USING PROCEDURES IN SECTION 8D1
• WHEN OTHER CODES ARE CORRECTED AND CLEARED, GO TO STEP ONE OF CODE E48 CHART

ENGINE STALLS OR IDLE BECOMES ROUGH. RPM DROPS — NO CHANGE IN ENGINE RPM

③ • CHECK FOR A VACUUM LEAK OR OBSTRUCTION IN THE EGR VACUUM SUPPLY LINE
• CHECK FOR OBSTRUCTION OR RESTRICTION IN THE INTAKE MANIFOLD EGR PASSAGES

• GO TO CHART C-7, SECTION 6E, EGR DIAGNOSIS

OK — LEAK OR OBSTRUCTION

• CONNECT A TEST LIGHT BETWEEN PINS A AND B OF EGR SOLENOID
• SELECT ECM OUTPUT CYCLING E 9 6
• NOTE TEST LIGHT

• REPAIR AND RETEST FOR CODE E48

LIGHT FLASHES ON AND OFF EVERY 3 SECONDS — LIGHT STAYS OFF — LIGHT STAYS ON

• FAULT IS NOT PRESENT
• SEE "NOTE ON INTERMITTENTS"

• CHECK SOL FUSE #5 ON RELAY PANEL
• CHECK FOR OPEN IN CKT 639 TO EGR SOLENOID

• TURN IGNITION OFF
• DISCONNECT ECM A/B (24 PIN) CONNECTOR
• TURN IGNITION ON
• NOTE LIGHT

FUSE AND CKT OK — FUSE OR CKT 639 NOT OK — LIGHT OFF — LIGHT ON

• CHECK CONTACT OF ECM CONNECTOR PIN A4
• IF CONNECTOR OK, SEE "ECM REPLACEMENT CHECK" CHART C-1, SECTION 6E

• REPAIR AS NECESSARY

• CHECK TERMINAL CONTACT OF ECM PIN A4
• IF OK, SEE "ECM REPLACEMENT CHECK" CHART C-1, SECTION 6E

• REPAIR SHORT TO GROUND ON CKT 435 BETWEEN EGR SOLENOID AND ECM

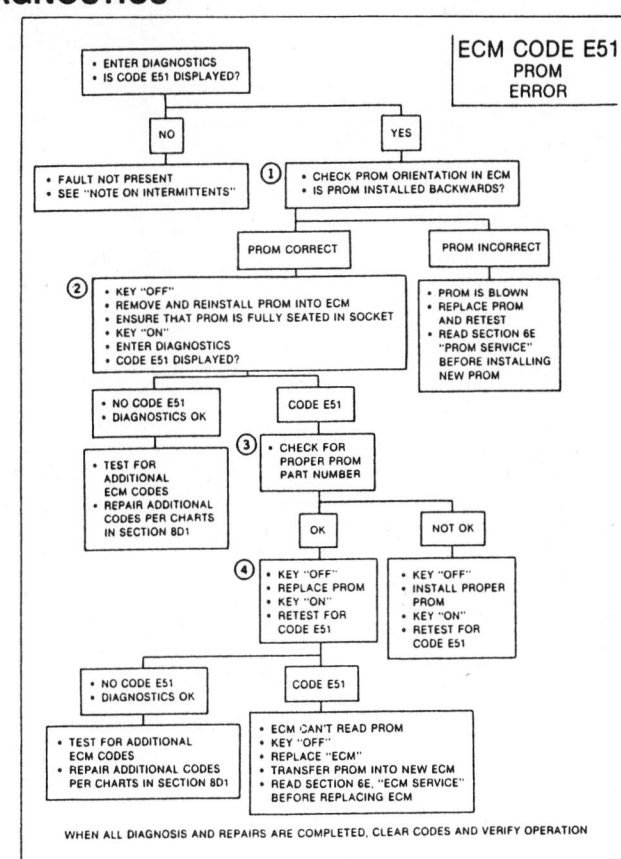

ECM CODE E51
PROM ERROR

• ENTER DIAGNOSTICS
• IS CODE E51 DISPLAYED?

NO — YES

• FAULT NOT PRESENT
• SEE "NOTE ON INTERMITTENTS"

① • CHECK PROM ORIENTATION IN ECM
• IS PROM INSTALLED BACKWARDS?

PROM CORRECT — PROM INCORRECT

② • KEY "OFF"
• REMOVE AND REINSTALL PROM INTO ECM
• ENSURE THAT PROM IS FULLY SEATED IN SOCKET
• KEY "ON"
• ENTER DIAGNOSTICS
• CODE E51 DISPLAYED?

• PROM IS BLOWN
• REPLACE PROM AND RETEST
• READ SECTION 6E "PROM SERVICE" BEFORE INSTALLING NEW PROM

• NO CODE E51
• DIAGNOSTICS OK — CODE E51

• TEST FOR ADDITIONAL ECM CODES
• REPAIR ADDITIONAL CODES PER CHARTS IN SECTION 8D1

③ • CHECK FOR PROPER PROM PART NUMBER

OK — NOT OK

④ • KEY "OFF"
• REPLACE PROM
• KEY "ON"
• RETEST FOR CODE E51

• KEY "OFF"
• INSTALL PROPER PROM
• KEY "ON"
• RETEST FOR CODE E51

• NO CODE E51
• DIAGNOSTICS OK — CODE E51

• TEST FOR ADDITIONAL ECM CODES
• REPAIR ADDITIONAL CODES PER CHARTS IN SECTION 8D1

• ECM CAN'T READ PROM
• KEY "OFF"
• REPLACE "ECM"
• TRANSFER PROM INTO NEW ECM
• READ SECTION 6E, "ECM SERVICE" BEFORE REPLACING ECM

WHEN ALL DIAGNOSIS AND REPAIRS ARE COMPLETED, CLEAR CODES AND VERIFY OPERATION

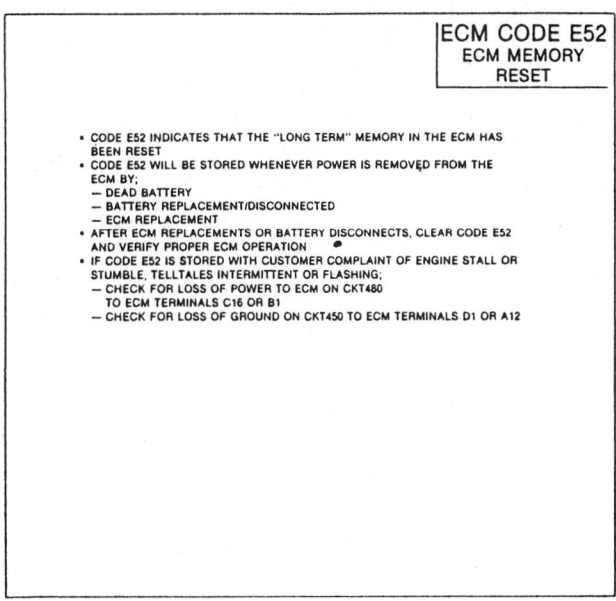

ECM CODE E52
ECM MEMORY RESET

- CODE E52 INDICATES THAT THE "LONG TERM" MEMORY IN THE ECM HAS BEEN RESET
- CODE E52 WILL BE STORED WHENEVER POWER IS REMOVED FROM THE ECM BY;
  — DEAD BATTERY
  — BATTERY REPLACEMENT/DISCONNECTED
  — ECM REPLACEMENT
- AFTER ECM REPLACEMENTS OR BATTERY DISCONNECTS, CLEAR CODE E52 AND VERIFY PROPER ECM OPERATION
- IF CODE E52 IS STORED WITH CUSTOMER COMPLAINT OF ENGINE STALL OR STUMBLE, TELLTALES INTERMITTENT OR FLASHING;
  — CHECK FOR LOSS OF POWER TO ECM ON CKT480 TO ECM TERMINALS C16 OR B1
  — CHECK FOR LOSS OF GROUND ON CKT450 TO ECM TERMINALS D1 OR A12

DFI TROUBLE DIAGNOSTICS

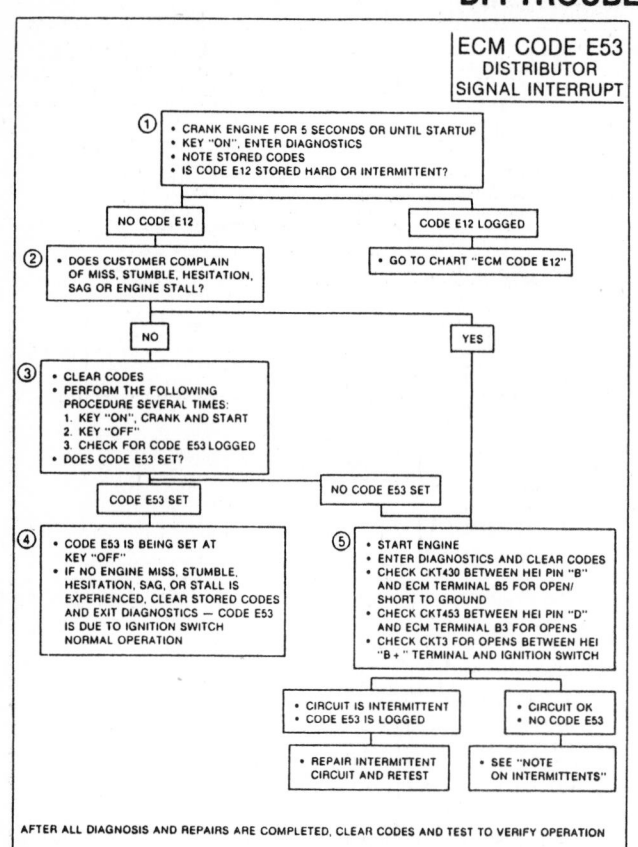

ECM CODE E53
DISTRIBUTOR SIGNAL INTERRUPT

AFTER ALL DIAGNOSIS AND REPAIRS ARE COMPLETED, CLEAR CODES AND TEST TO VERIFY OPERATION

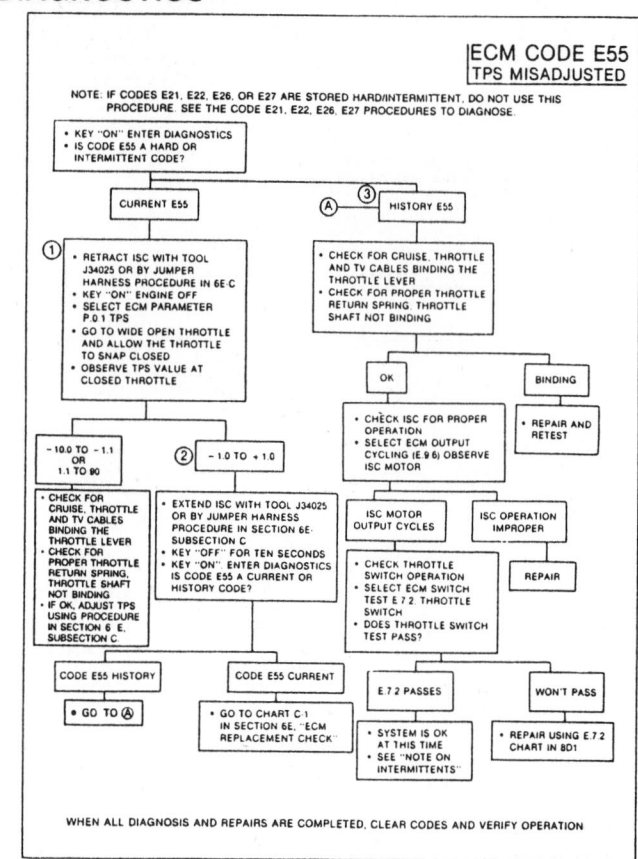

ECM CODE E55
TPS MISADJUSTED

NOTE: IF CODES E21, E22, E26, OR E27 ARE STORED HARD/INTERMITTENT, DO NOT USE THIS PROCEDURE. SEE THE CODE E21, E22, E26, E27 PROCEDURES TO DIAGNOSE.

WHEN ALL DIAGNOSIS AND REPAIRS ARE COMPLETED, CLEAR CODES AND VERIFY OPERATION

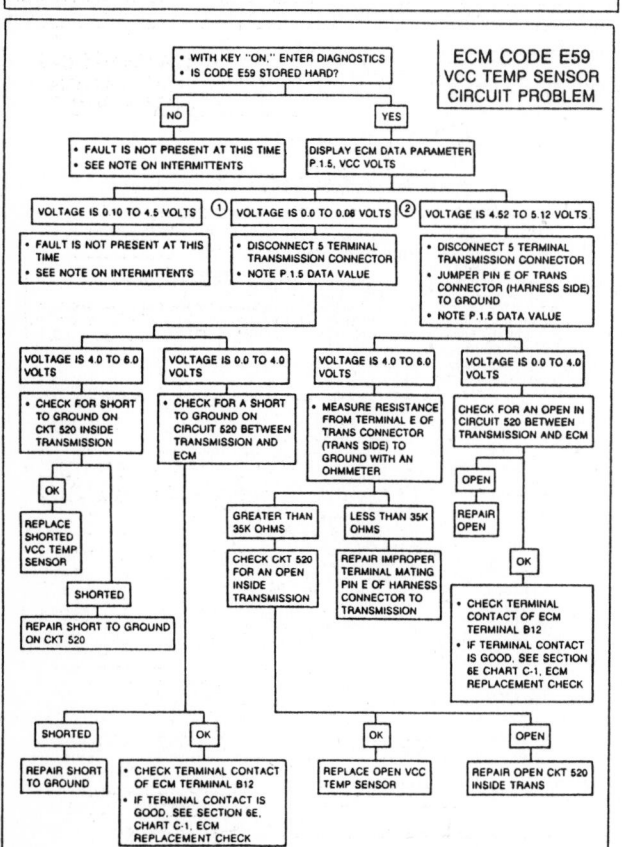

ECM CODE E59
VCC TEMP SENSOR CIRCUIT PROBLEM

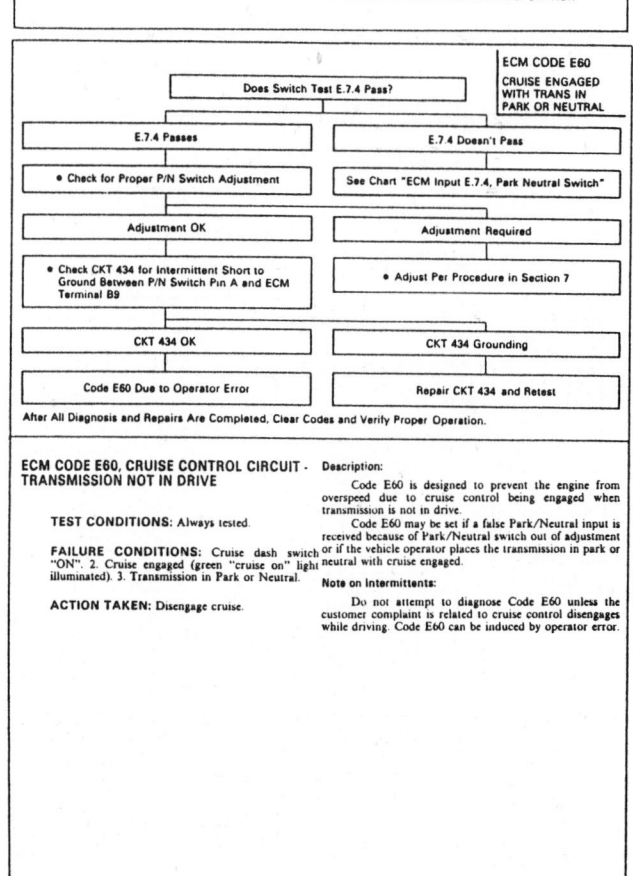

ECM CODE E60
CRUISE ENGAGED WITH TRANS IN PARK OR NEUTRAL

After All Diagnosis and Repairs Are Completed, Clear Codes and Verify Proper Operation.

ECM CODE E60, CRUISE CONTROL CIRCUIT - TRANSMISSION NOT IN DRIVE

TEST CONDITIONS: Always tested.

FAILURE CONDITIONS: Cruise dash switch "ON". 2. Cruise engaged (green "cruise on" light illuminated). 3. Transmission in Park or Neutral.

ACTION TAKEN: Disengage cruise.

Description:
Code E60 is designed to prevent the engine from overspeed due to cruise control being engaged when transmission is not in drive.
Code E60 may be set if a false Park/Neutral input is received because of Park/Neutral switch out of adjustment or if the vehicle operator places the transmission in park or neutral with cruise engaged.

Note on intermittents:
Do not attempt to diagnose Code E60 unless the customer complaint is related to cruise control disengages while driving. Code E60 can be induced by operator error.

DFI TROUBLE DIAGNOSTICS

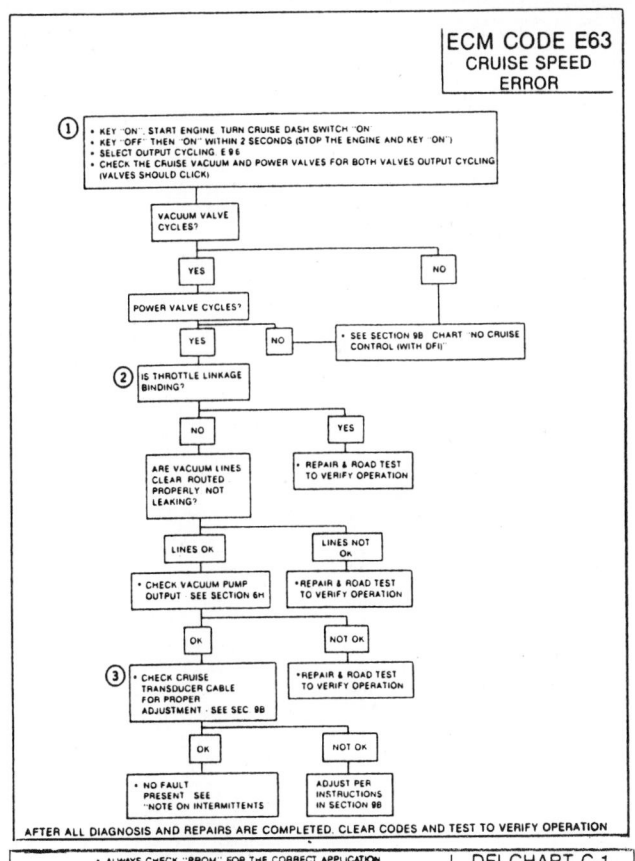

ECM CODE E63
CRUISE SPEED ERROR

① • KEY "ON", START ENGINE, TURN CRUISE DASH SWITCH "ON"
• KEY "OFF" THEN "ON" WITHIN 2 SECONDS (STOP THE ENGINE AND KEY "ON")
• SELECT OUTPUT CYCLING E 9.6
• CHECK THE CRUISE VACUUM AND POWER VALVES FOR BOTH VALVES OUTPUT CYCLING (VALVES SHOULD CLICK)

AFTER ALL DIAGNOSIS AND REPAIRS ARE COMPLETED, CLEAR CODES AND TEST TO VERIFY OPERATION

ECM CODE E64
ACCELERATION TOO HIGH
CRUISE ENGAGED

• CODE E64 SETS WHEN VEHICLE SPEED INCREASES GREATER THAN 16 MPH IN ONE SECOND, CRUISE ENGAGED
• IF CODE E64 IS SET, CRUISE WILL DISENGAGE AND CODE E64 WILL STORE IN MEMORY — NO TELLTALES ARE ILLUMINATED
• MOST OCCURRENCES OF CODE E64 ARE CAUSED BY WHEELSPIN DUE TO ICY OR WET CONDITIONS
• IF CODE E64 IS FOUND AND NO OTHER CRUISE CONTROL FAULTS EXIST, CLEAR CODES AND ROAD TEST. IF CODE E64 SETS WITHOUT WHEELSPIN OCCURRING, SEE "ECM REPLACEMENT CHECK", CHART C-1, SECTION 6E

WHEN ALL DIAGNOSIS AND REPAIRS ARE COMPLETED, CLEAR CODES AND VERIFY OPERATION

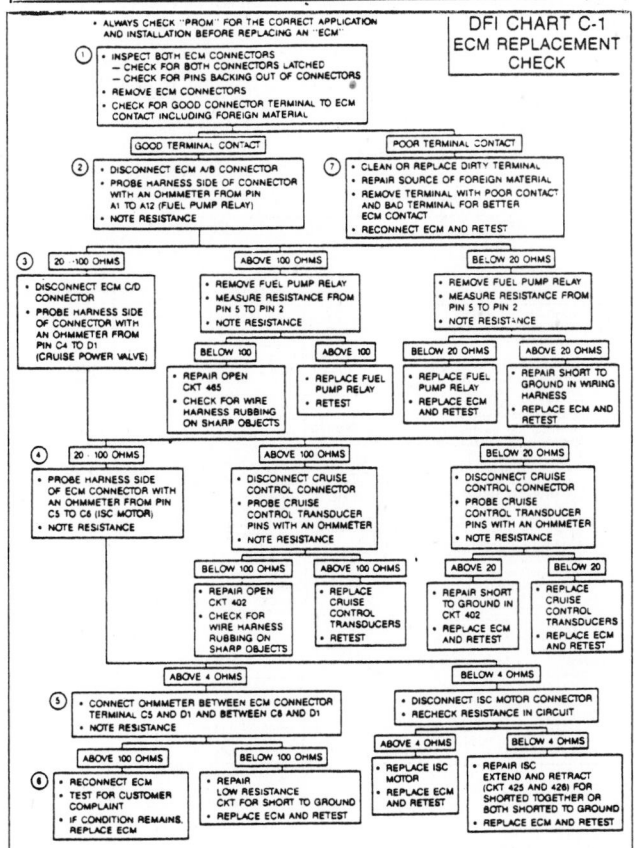

DFI CHART C-1
ECM REPLACEMENT CHECK

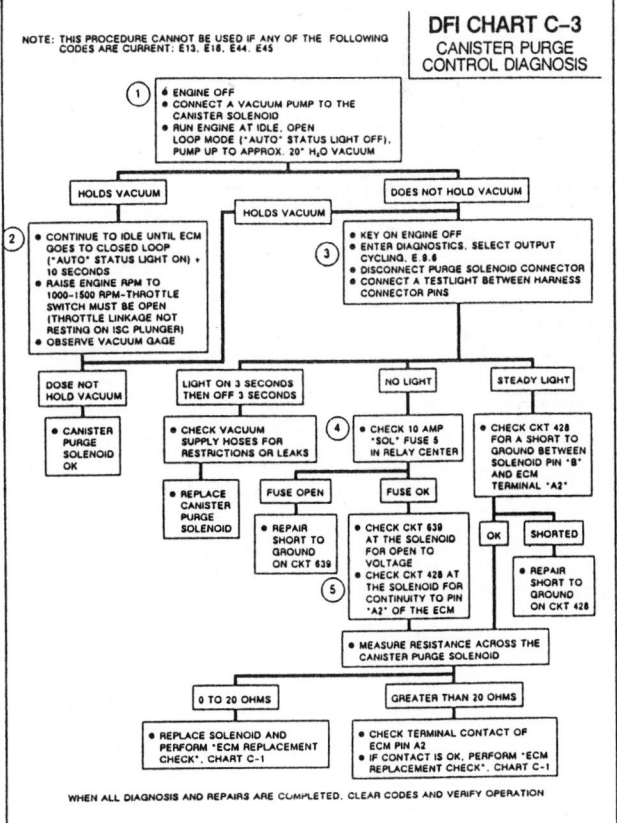

DFI CHART C-3
CANISTER PURGE CONTROL DIAGNOSIS

NOTE: THIS PROCEDURE CANNOT BE USED IF ANY OF THE FOLLOWING CODES ARE CURRENT: E13, E18, E44, E45

WHEN ALL DIAGNOSIS AND REPAIRS ARE COMPLETED, CLEAR CODES AND VERIFY OPERATION

DFI TROUBLE DIAGNOSTICS

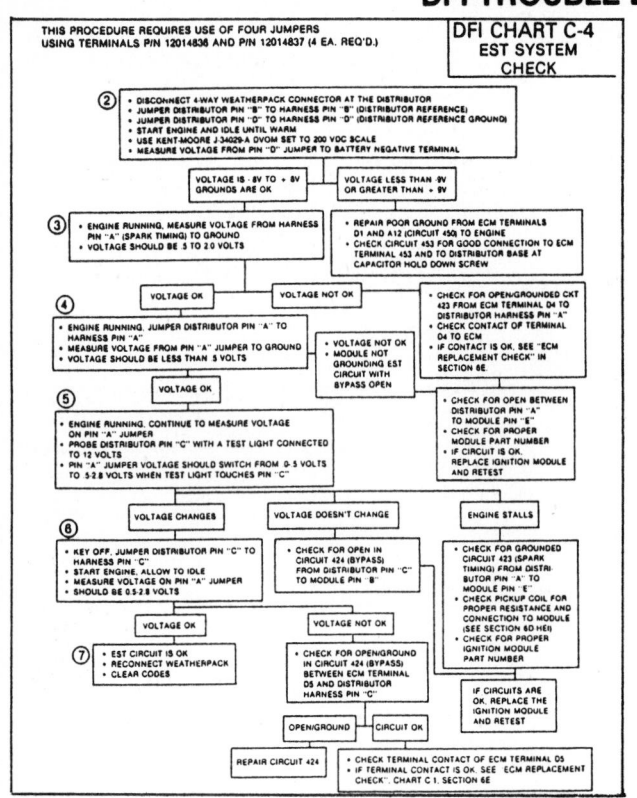

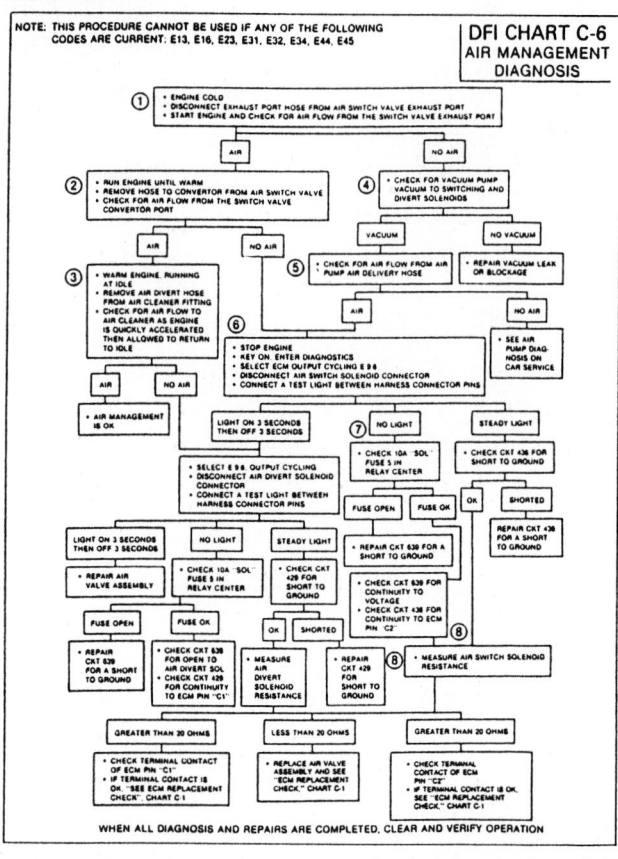

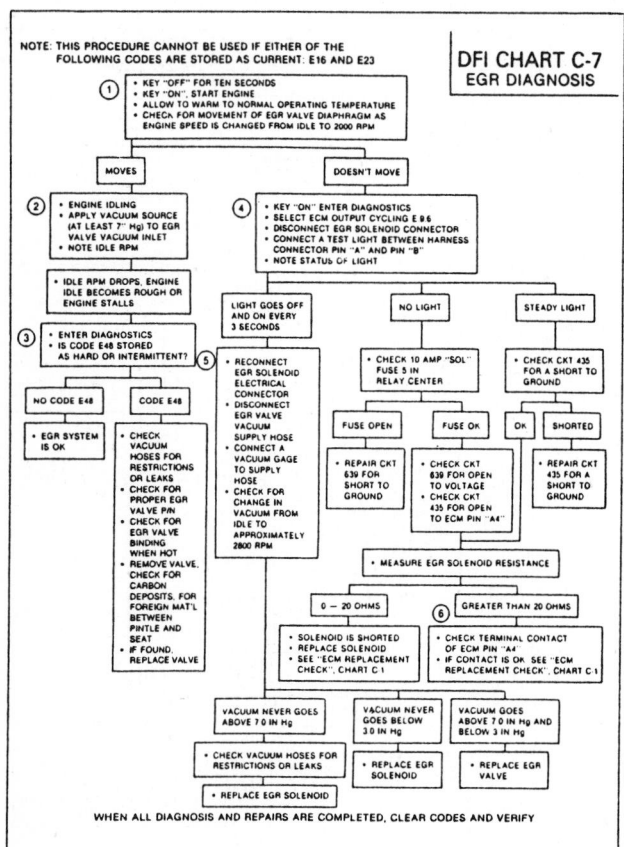

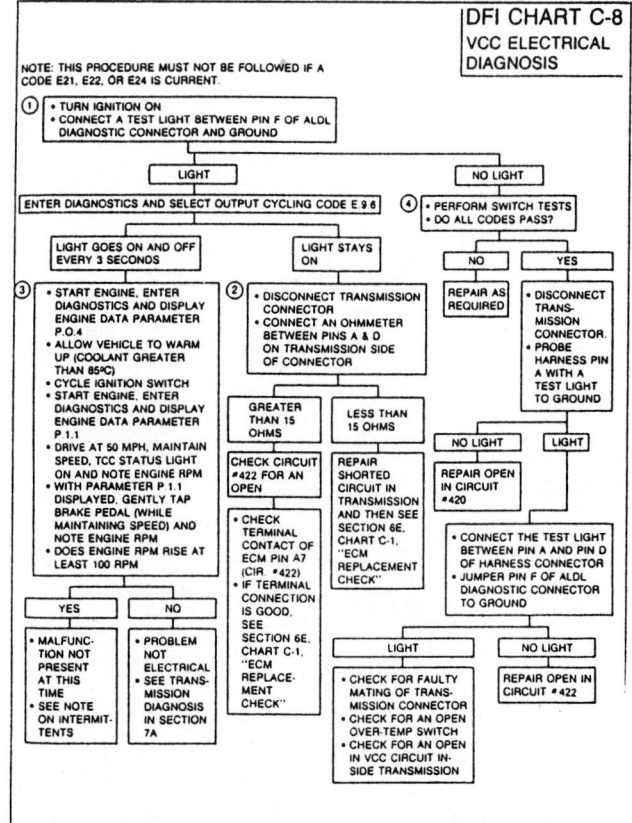

DFI TROUBLE DIAGNOSTICS

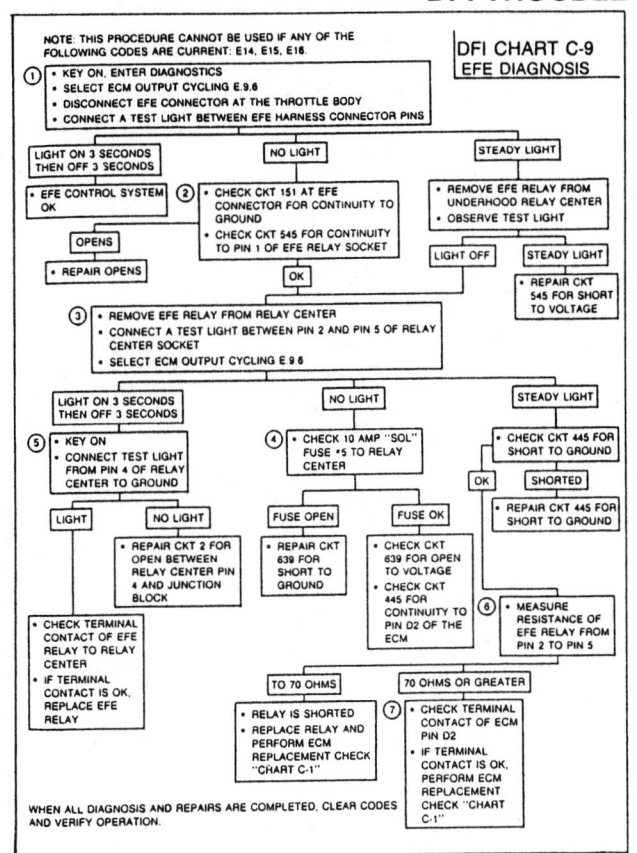

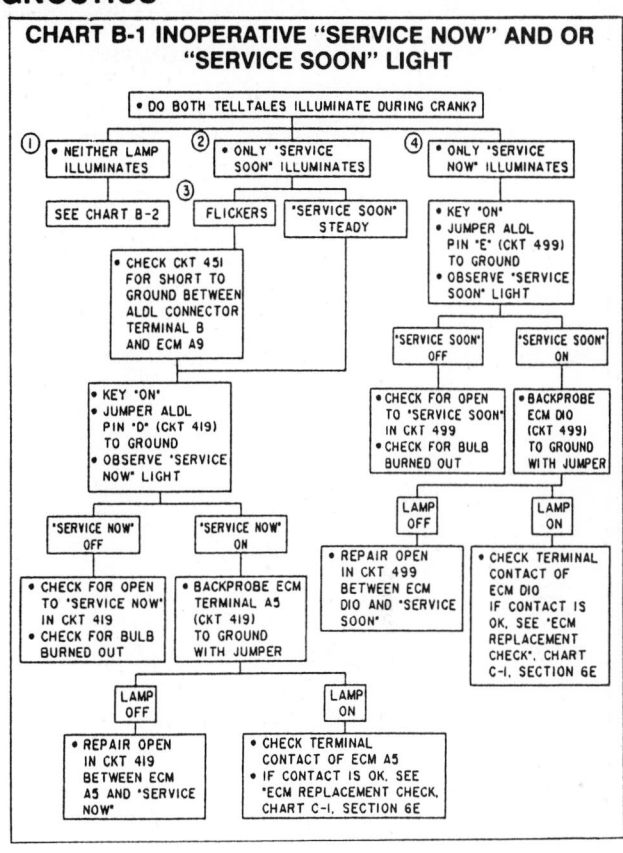

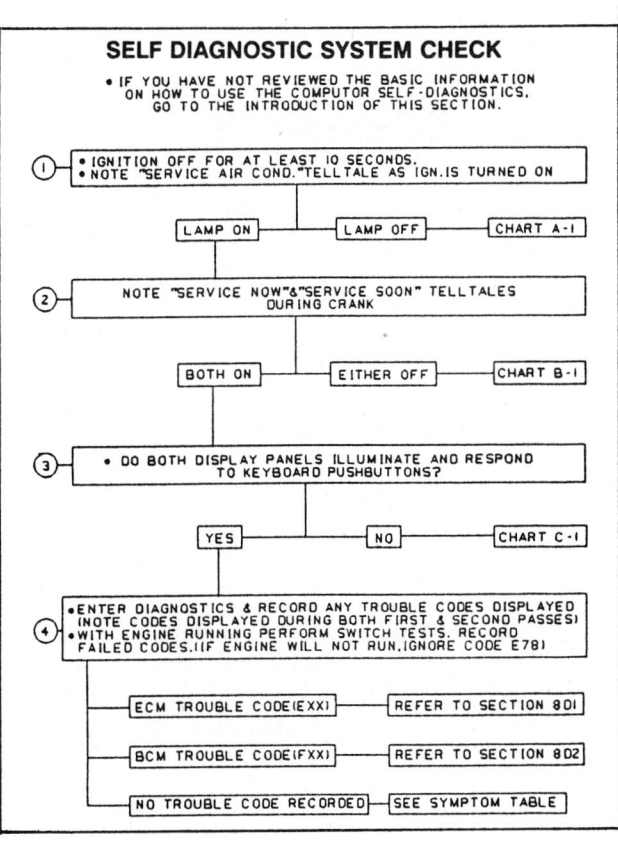

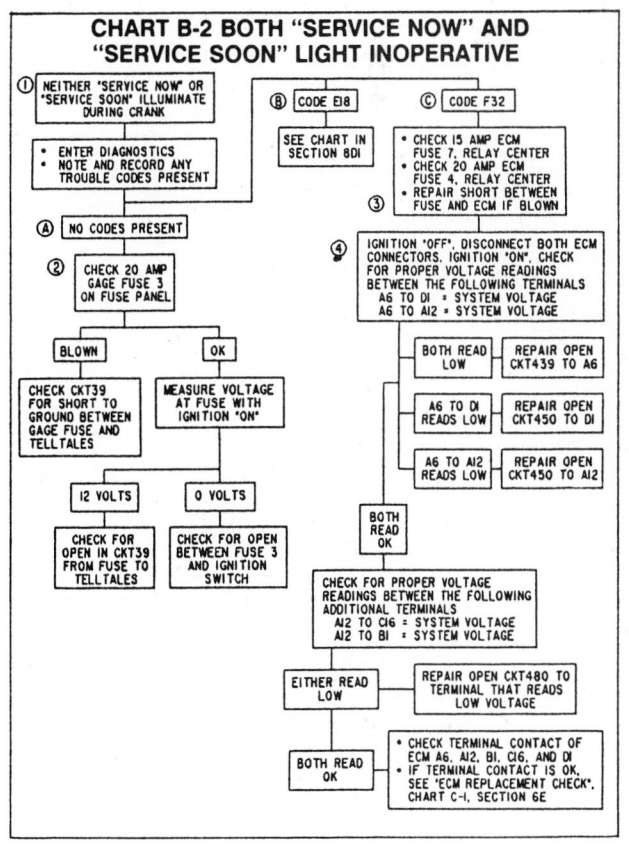

DFI TROUBLE DIAGNOSTICS

CHART C-1 DISPLAY PANEL DIAGNOSIS

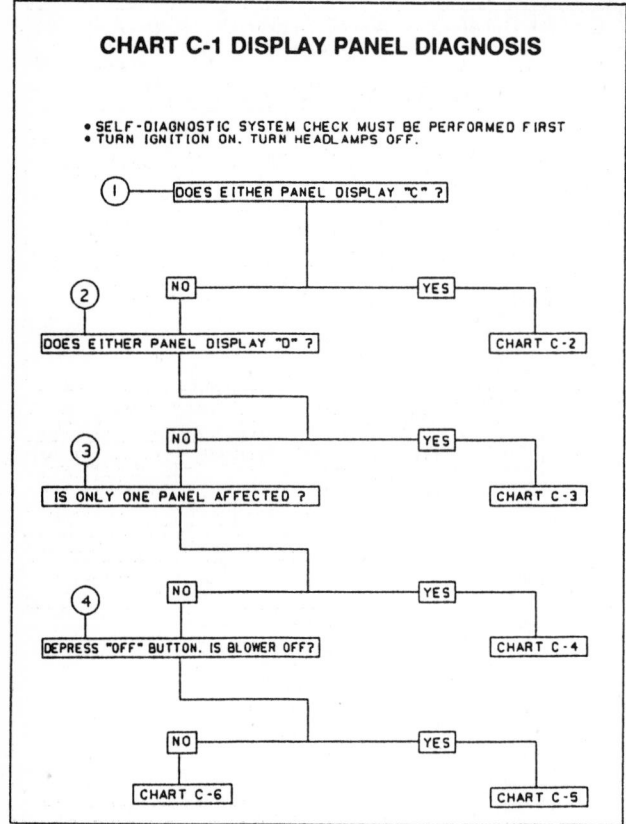

CHART C-3 DISPLAY PANEL DIAGNOSIS

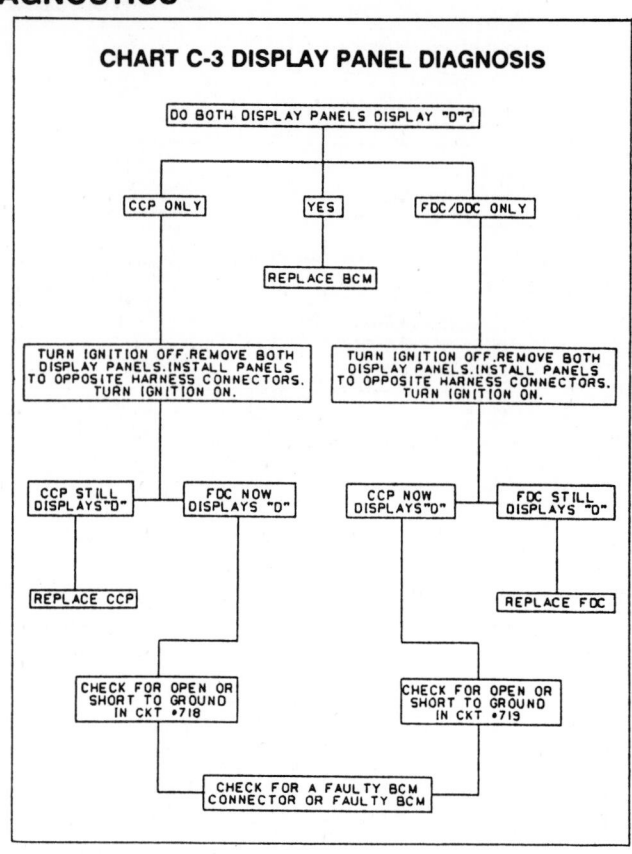

CHART C-2 DISPLAY PANEL DIAGNOSIS

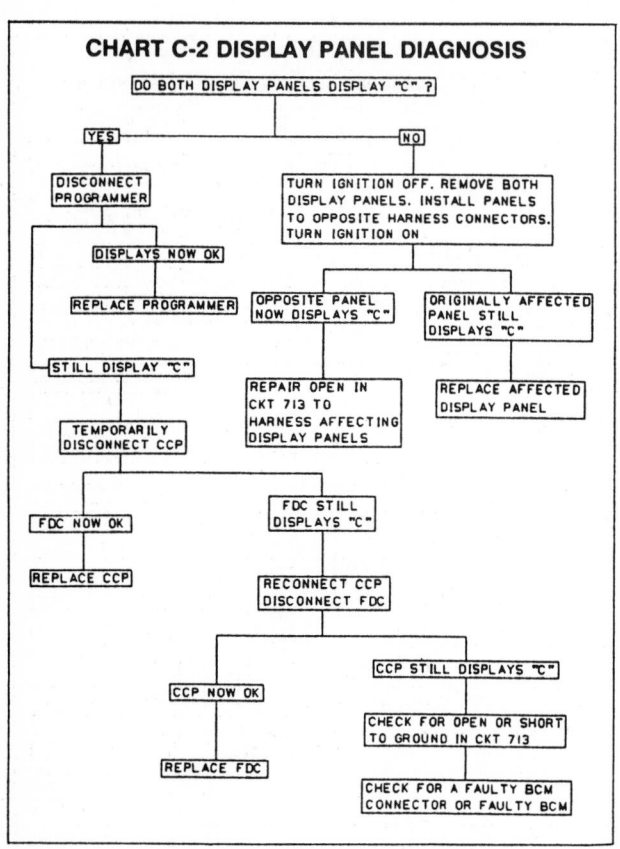

CHART C-4 DISPLAY PANEL DIAGNOSIS

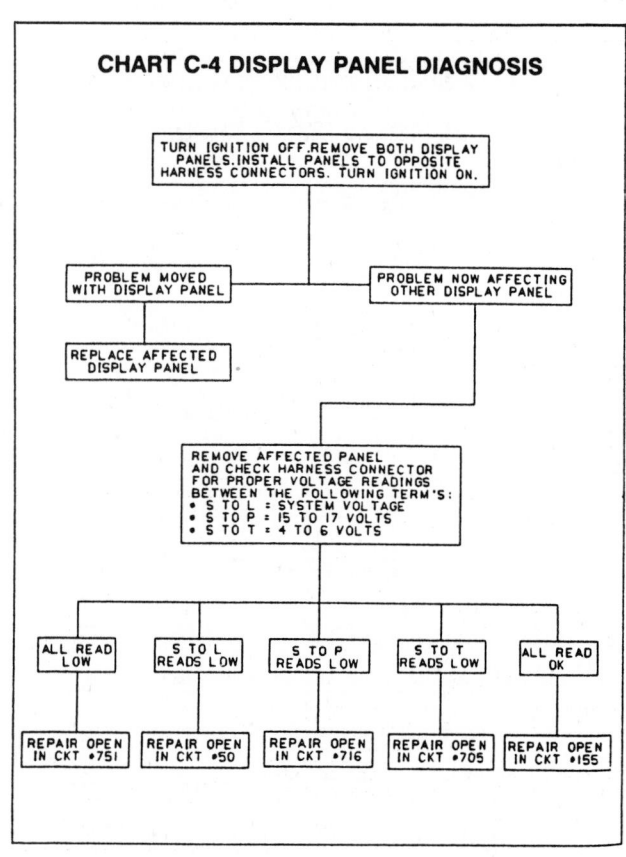

DFI TROUBLE DIAGNOSTICS

CHART C-5 DISPLAY PANEL DIAGNOSIS

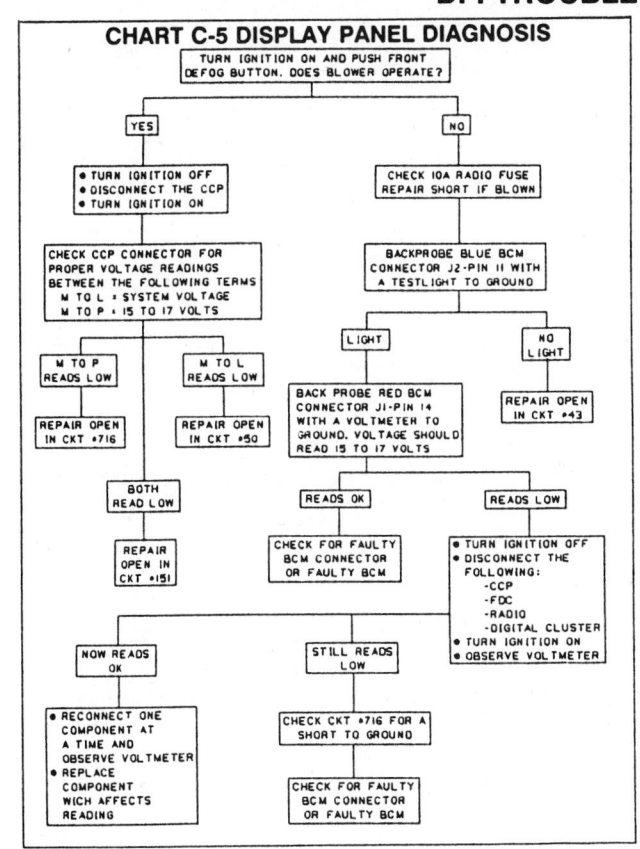

CHART C-6 DISPLAY PANEL DIAGNOSIS

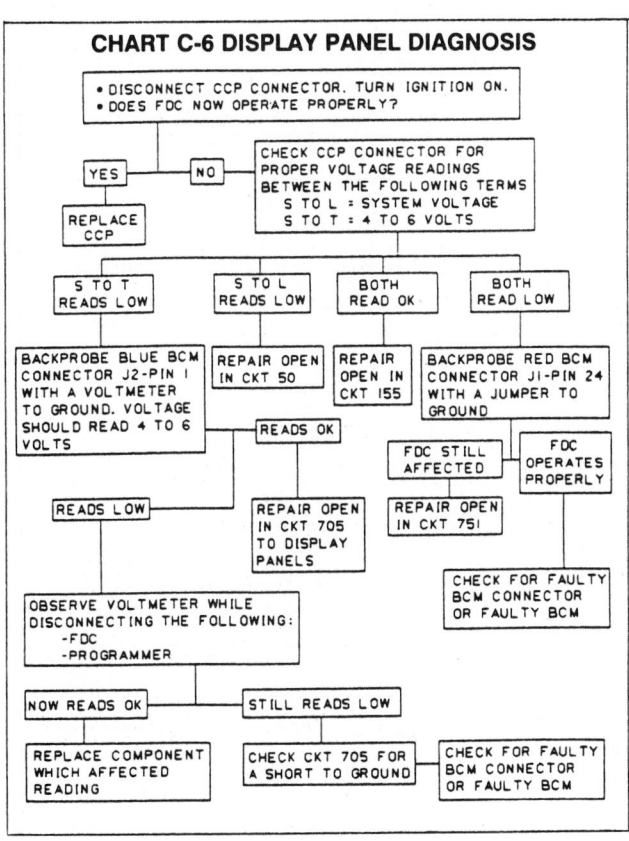

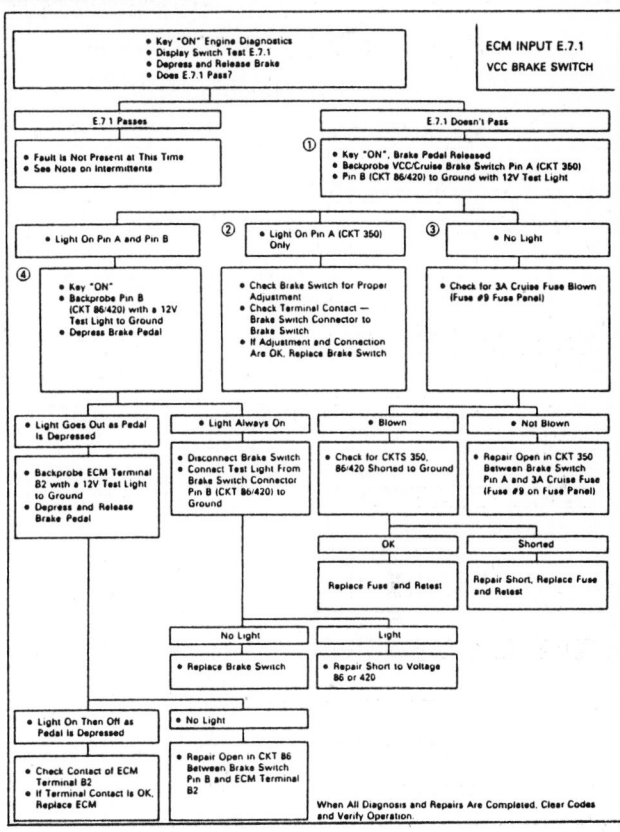

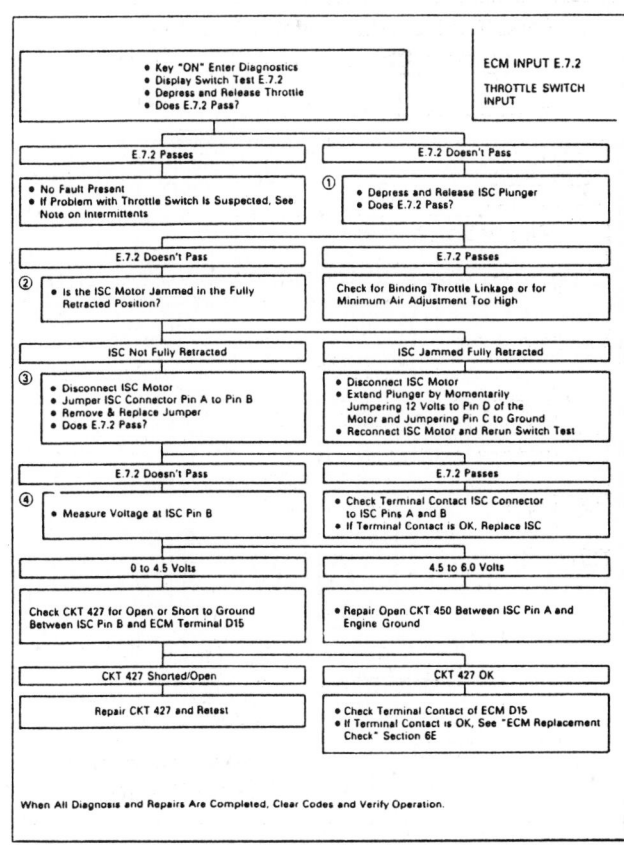

DFI TROUBLE DIAGNOSTICS

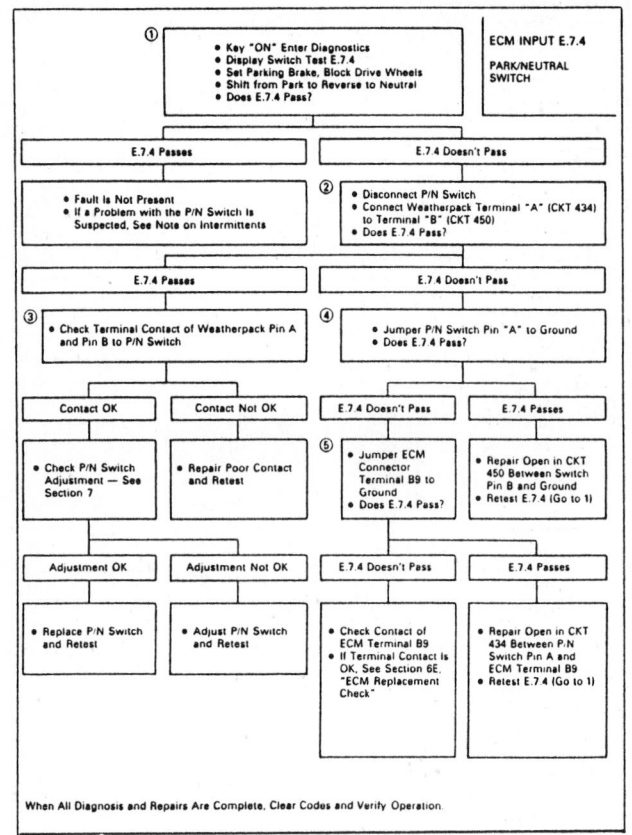

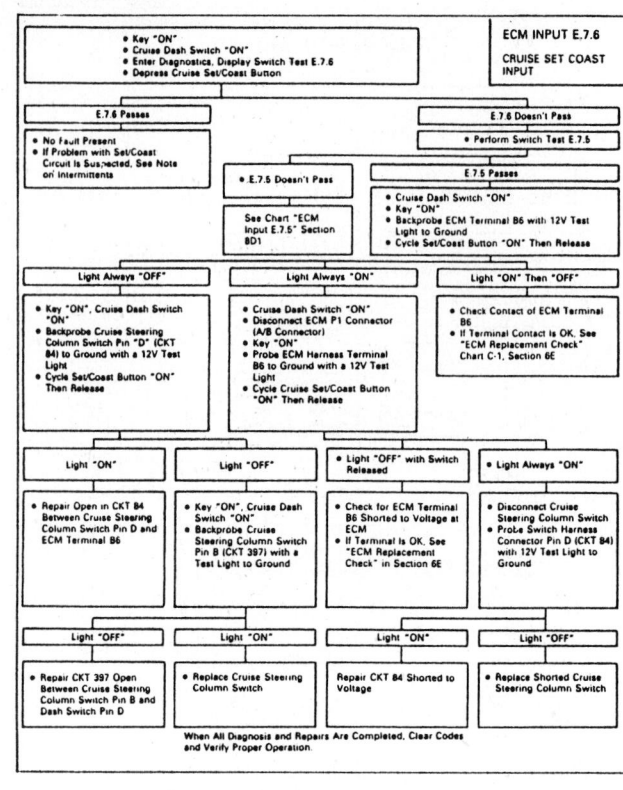

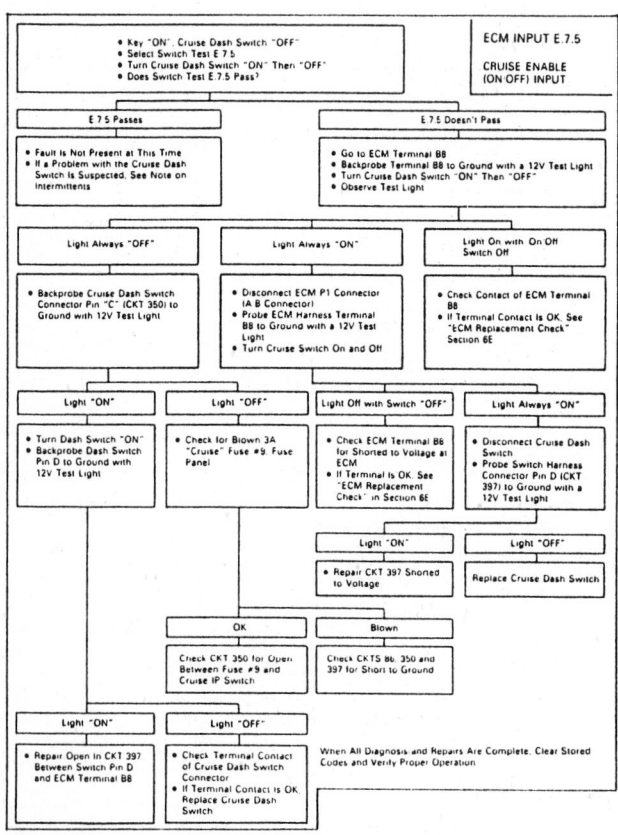

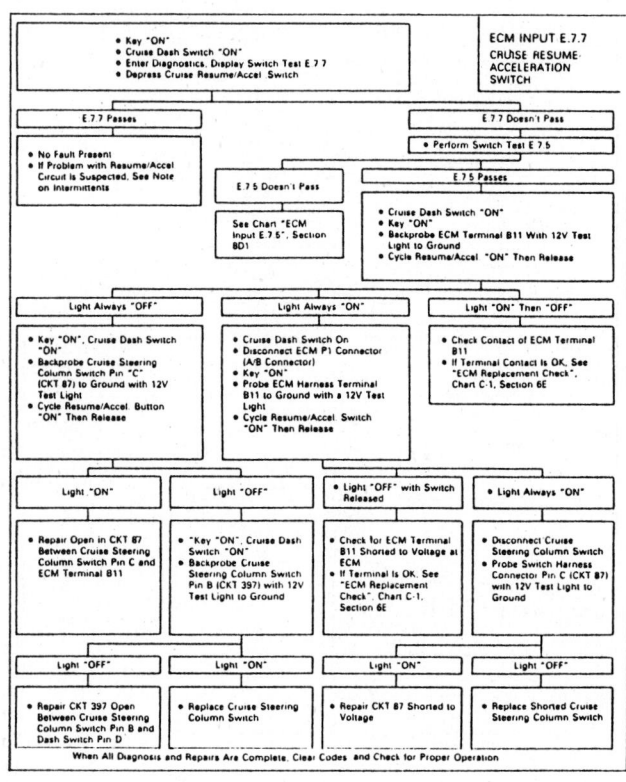

DFI TROUBLE DIAGNOSTICS

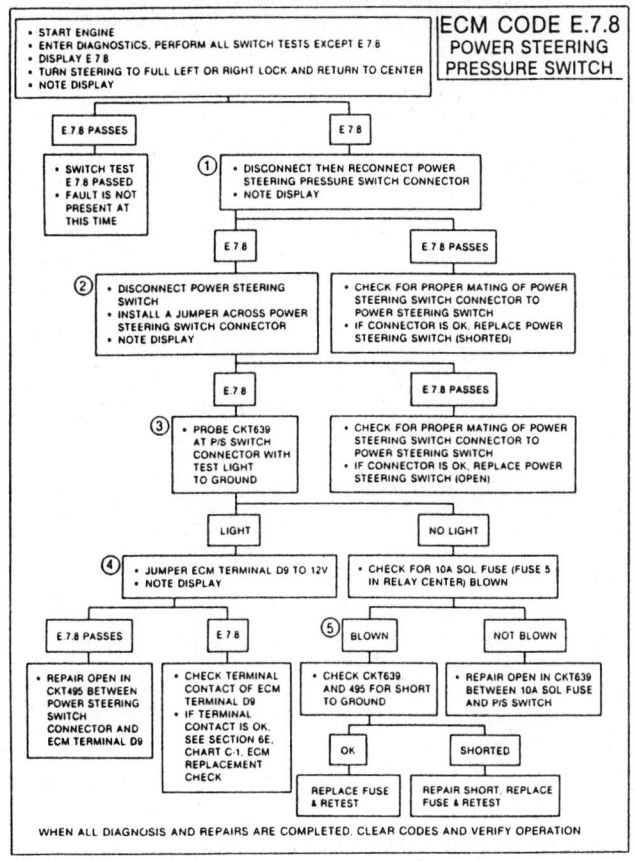

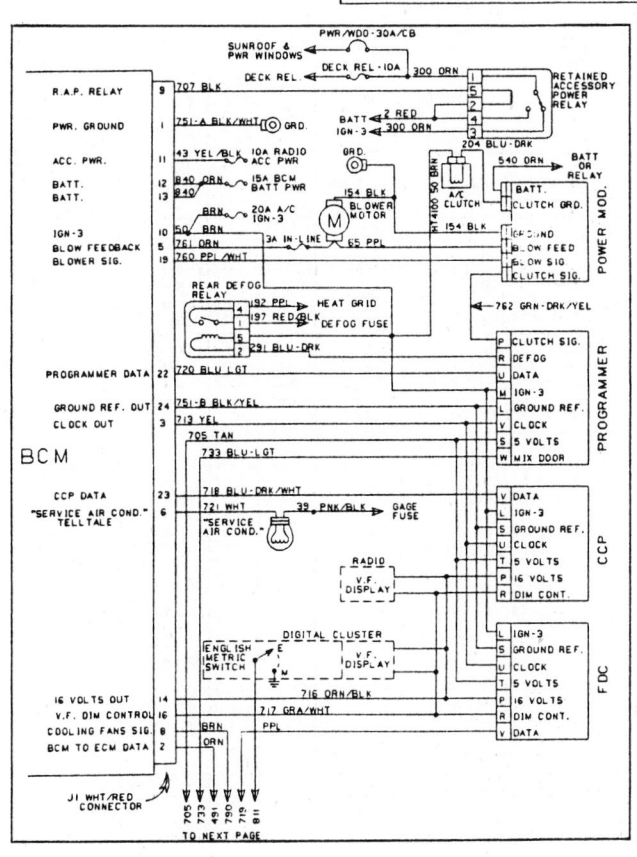

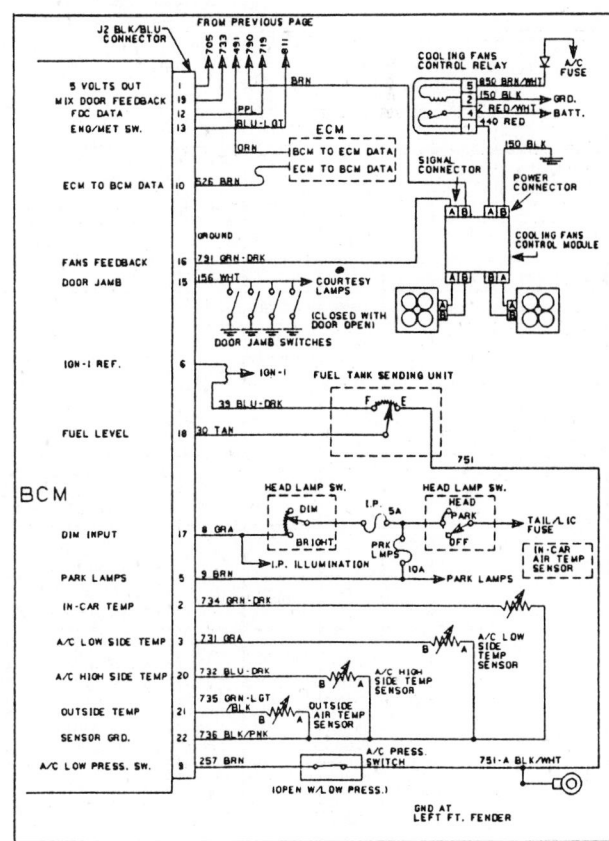

DFI TROUBLE DIAGNOSTICS

TROUBLE CODE	VEHICLE SPEED (MPH)	THROTTLE ANGLE	THROTTLE SWITCH	ENGINE SPEED (RPM)	ADDITIONAL REQUIREMENTS	FAILURE CONDITION	TIME (SEC)	FAIL SOFT ACTION	DISABLED FUNCTIONS
	DFI DIAGNOSTIC TESTING CONDITION (CONT'D)					FAILURE REQUIREMENTS			
51						PROM/CALPAK NOT BEING READ PROPERLY AT KEY 'ON'		9	H
52						FULL TIME MEMORY ERASED/RESET		N	N
53						NO DISTRIBUTOR REFERENCE PULSES	.7	N	N
55						IF TPS CORRECTION ⟨ – 2.9° ⟩ – 10° OR ⟨90° ⟩3°		N	N
60						CRUISE DASH SWITCH 'ON' CRUISE ENGAGED TRANSMISSION IN P/N		N	A
63					CRUISE ENABLED AND ENGAGED NOT IN ''RESUME'' MODE	VEHICLE SPEED AND CRUISE SET SPEED DIFFERENCE ⟩20 MPH		N	A
64					CRUISE ENGAGED	VEHICLE SPEED INCREASE ⟩16 MPH	1.0	N	A
65					CRUISE ENGAGED	COOLANT TEMP ⟩126°C		N	A
66					CRUISE ENGAGED	ENGINE RPM ⟩4800		N	A
67					CRUISE DASH SWITCH 'ON'	''SET/COAST'' OR ''RESUME/ ACCEL'' INPUT TO ECM = 12V		N	A

DFI DIAGNOSTIC TESTING CONDITIONS (Cont'd.)

TROUBLE CODE	VEHICLE SPEED (MPH)	THROTTLE ANGLE	THROTTLE SWITCH	ENGINE SPEED (RPM)	ADDITIONAL REQUIREMENTS	FAILURE CONDITION	TIME (SEC)	FAILSOFT ACTION	DISABLED FUNCTIONS
		TESTING REQUIREMENTS				FAILURE REQUIREMENTS			
28	<4				PARK/NEUTRAL	3RD GEAR SIGNAL = 12 VOLTS OR 4TH GEAR SIGNAL = 12 VOLTS		N	N
30	= 0	>2.5 <9°	CLOSED		NOT A COLD START FUEL PUMP VOLTAGE >11	RPM >152 FROM DESIRED	15	5	N
31						MAP > 105 kPa	.2	6,7	B
32-A		<12°	CLOSED	<700		MAP < 16 kPa		6,7	B
32-B		<9.6°	OPEN			MAP < 16 kPa		6,7	B
34		<12	CLOSED	>400	BARO >75 kPa	MAP < 6 kPa FROM BARO	2.1	6	B
37					COOLANT < 105°C	MANIFOLD AIR >142°C		8	B
38					COOLANT > – 5°C	MANIFOLD AIR < – 35°C		8	B
39			OPEN		CLOSED LOOP, 4TH GEAR BRAKE OFF, DRIVE, STEADY THROTTLE & TCC ENGAGED	TABLE LOOK-UP	30	N	N
40	>40					POWER STEERING SWITCH INPUT	10	N	N
44		>6° <29°	OPEN	>800	CLOSED LOOP & STEADY THROTTLE COOLANT TEMP > 80°C	O₂ VOLTAGE < .47 VOLTS	45	N	B,D,G
45		>6° <29°	OPEN	>800	CLOSED LOOP & STEADY THROTTLE COOLANT TEMP > 80°C	O₂ VOLTAGE > .47 VOLTS	45	N	B,D,G
47						LOSS OF BCM DATA	2.1	N	N
48		>8° <15°		>1450 <1650	COOLANT TEMP > 85° < 110°C CLOSED LOOP	FAILS 3 OUT OF 5 LEANER MIXTURE TESTS		5	C
59						TRANS TEMP INPUT < .1 OR > 4.5 VOLTS		N	N

DFI TROUBLE DIAGNOSTICS

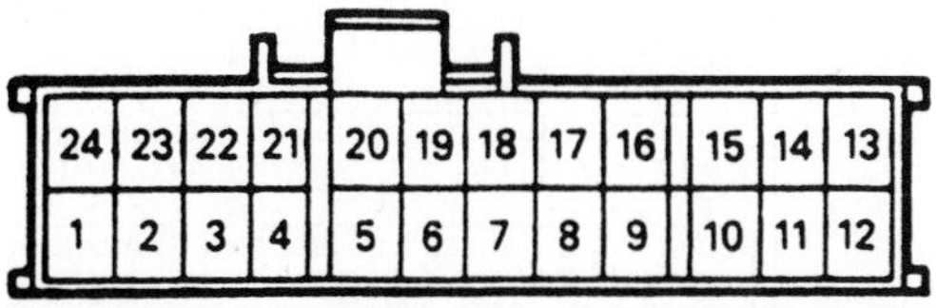

24	23	22	21	20	19	18	17	16	15	14	13
1	2	3	4	5	6	7	8	9	10	11	12

J-1 CONNECTOR (WHT/RED)

CAVITY	CIRCUIT #	WIRE COLOR	CIRCUIT
1	751-A	1.0 BLK/WHT	POWER GROUND
2	491	0.5 ORN	BCM TO ECM DATA
3	713	0.35 YEL	CLOCK OUT
4	—	—	NOT USED
5	761	1.0 ORN	BLOWER FEEDBACK
6	721	0.35 WHT	"SERVICE AIR COND"
7	—	—	NOT USED
8	790	0.8 BRN	COOLING FANS SIGNAL
9	707	0.8 BLK	R.A.P. RELAY GROUND
10	50	0.8 BRN	12V IGNITION-3
11	43	0.8 YEL/BLK	12V ACC POWER
12	840	1.0 ORN	12V BATTERY
13	840	1.0 ORN	12V BATTERY
14	716	0.8 ORN/BLK	16 VOLTS OUT
15	—	—	NOT USED
16	717	0.35 GRA/WHT	V.F. DIM CONTROL
17	—	—	NOT USED
18	—	—	NOT USED
19	760	0.5 PPL/WHT	BLOWER SIGNAL
20	—	—	NOT USED
21	—	—	NOT USED
22	720	0.35 BLU-LGT	PROGRAMMED DATA
23	718	0.35 BLU-DRK/WHT	CCP DATA
24	751-B	1.0 BLK/YEL	GROUND REF. OUT

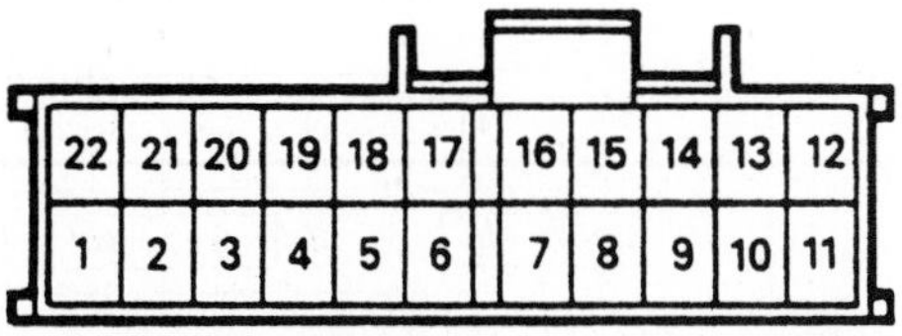

22	21	20	19	18	17	16	15	14	13	12
1	2	3	4	5	6	7	8	9	10	11

J-2 CONNECTOR (BLK/BLU)

CAVITY	CIRCUIT #	WIRE COLOR	CIRCUIT
1	705	0.8 TAN	5 VOLTS OUT
2	734	0.35 GRN-DRK	IN-CAR TEMP
3	731	0.5 GRA	A/C LOW SIDE TEMP
4	—	—	NOT USED
5	9	0.5 BRN	PARK LAMPS
6	39(239)	0.8 PNK/BLK	12V IGNITION-1 REF.
7	—	—	NOT USED
8	—	—	NOT USED
9	257	0.8 BRN	A/C LOW PRESSURE
10	526	0.35 BRN	ECM TO BCM DATA
11	—	—	NOT USED
12	719	0.35 PPL	FDC DATA
13	811	0.5 BLU-LGT	ENG/MET SWITCH
14	—	—	NOT USED
15	156	0.5 WHT	DOOR JAMB
16	791	0.8 GRN-DRK	FANS FEEDBACK
.17	8	0.5 GRA	DIM INPUT
18	30	0.5 TAN	FUEL LEVEL
19	733	0.5 BLU-LGT	MIX DOOR FEEDBACK
20	732	0.5 BLU-DRK	A/C HIGH SIDE TEMP
21	735	0.35 GRN-LGT/BLK	OUTSIDE TEMP
22	736	0.35 BLK/PNK	SENSOR GROUND

DFI TROUBLE DIAGNOSTICS

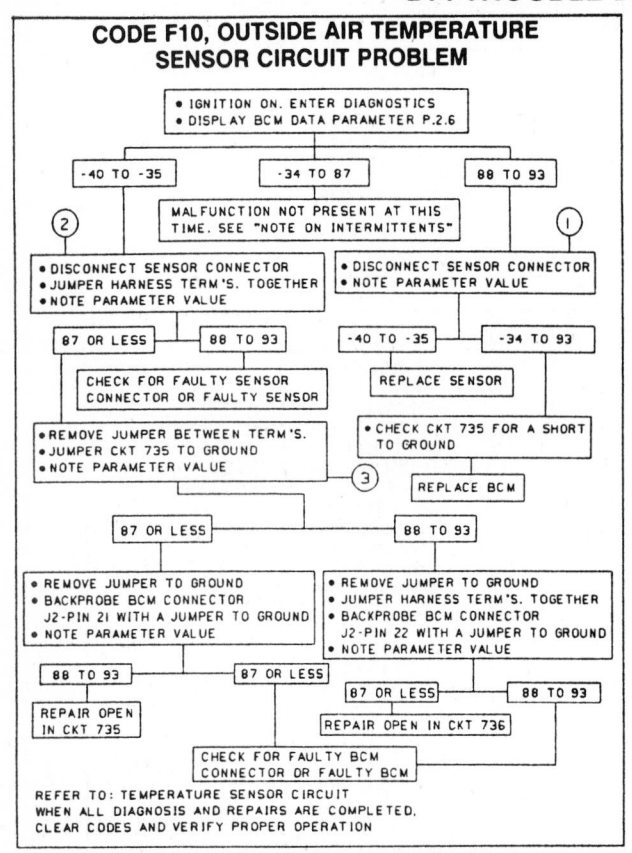

CODE F10, OUTSIDE AIR TEMPERATURE SENSOR CIRCUIT PROBLEM

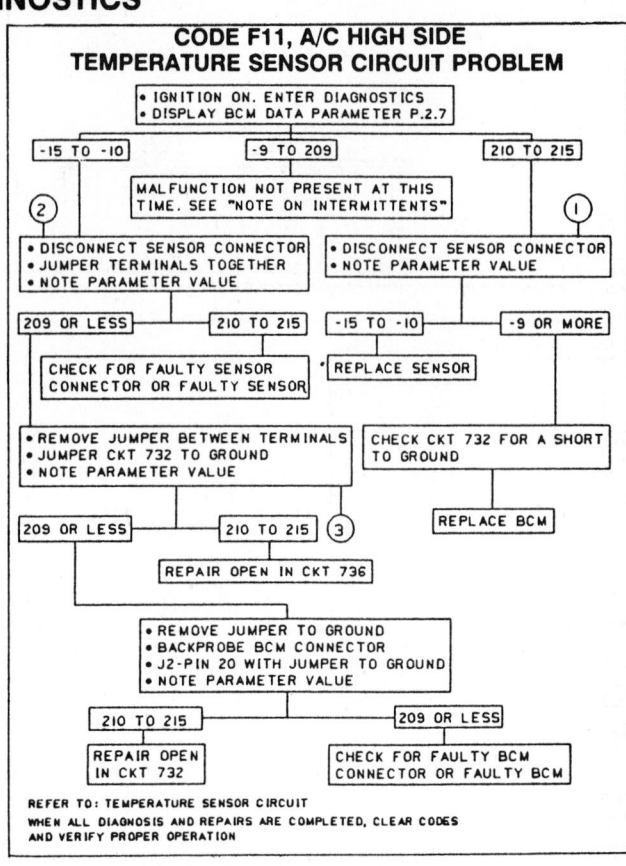

CODE F11, A/C HIGH SIDE TEMPERATURE SENSOR CIRCUIT PROBLEM

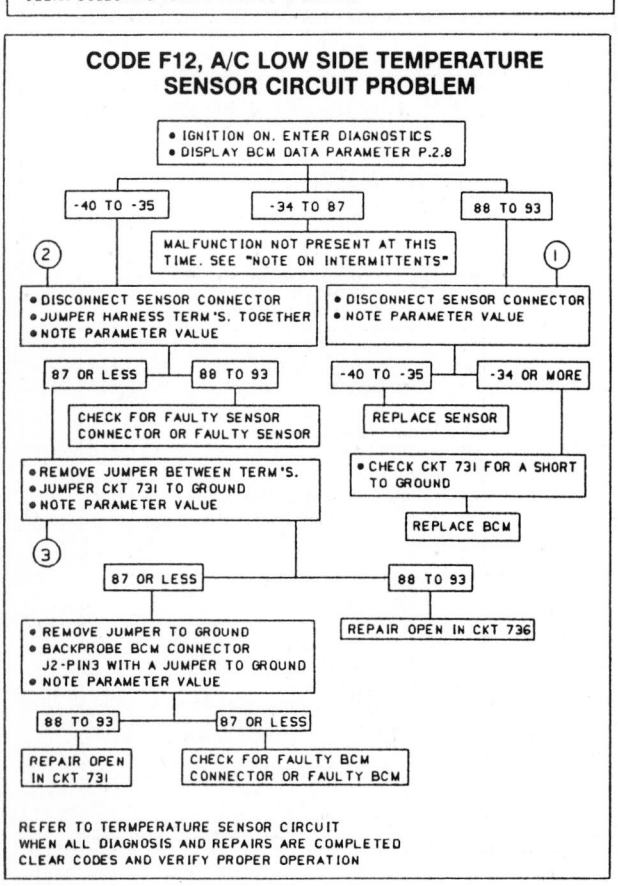

CODE F12, A/C LOW SIDE TEMPERATURE SENSOR CIRCUIT PROBLEM

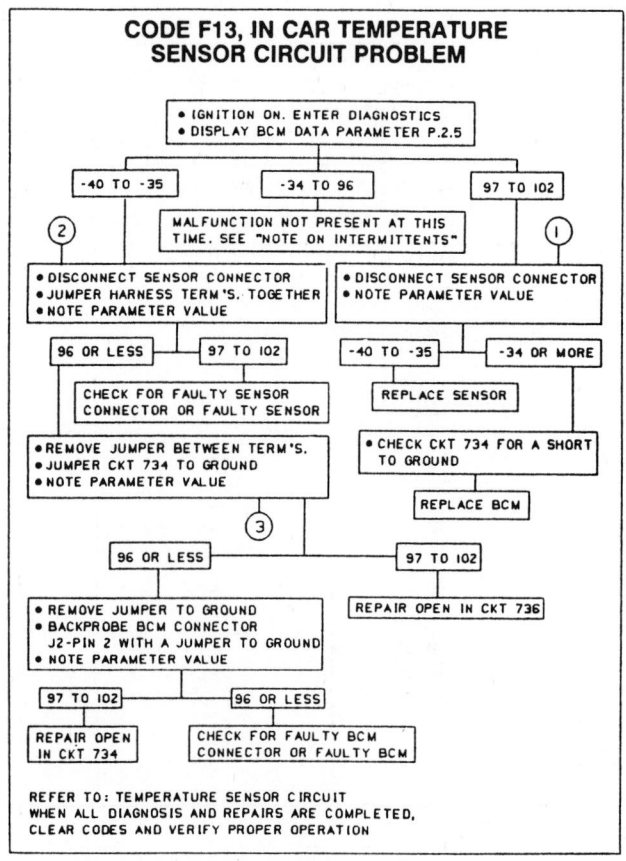

CODE F13, IN CAR TEMPERATURE SENSOR CIRCUIT PROBLEM

DFI TROUBLE DIAGNOSTICS

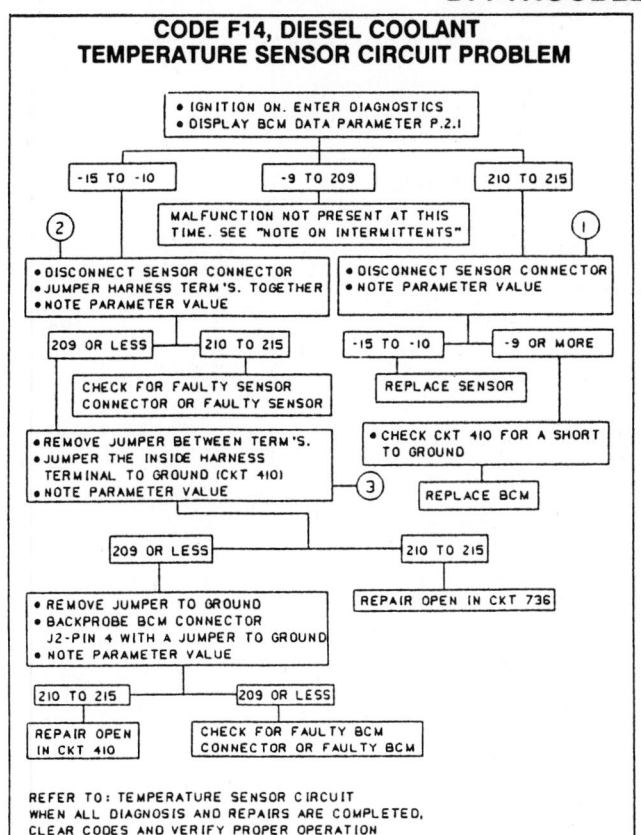

CODE F14, DIESEL COOLANT TEMPERATURE SENSOR CIRCUIT PROBLEM

REFER TO: TEMPERATURE SENSOR CIRCUIT
WHEN ALL DIAGNOSIS AND REPAIRS ARE COMPLETED,
CLEAR CODES AND VERIFY PROPER OPERATION

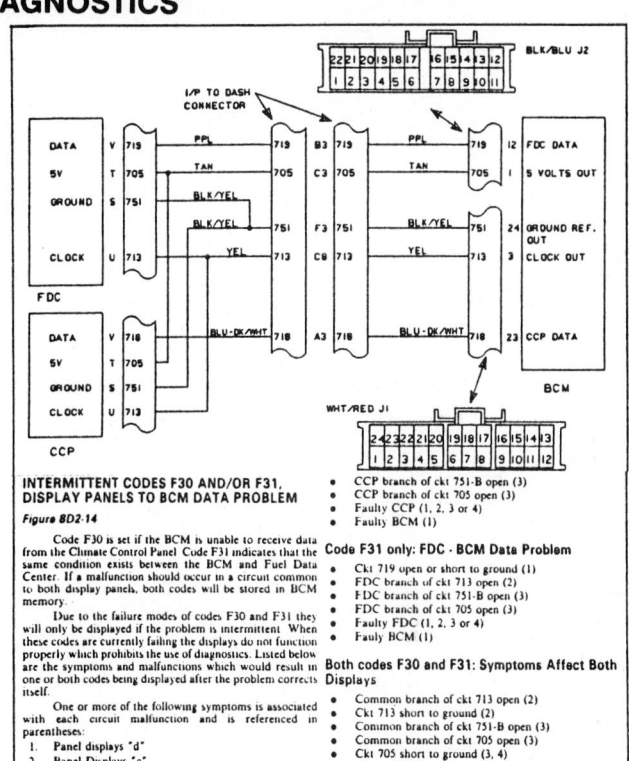

INTERMITTENT CODES F30 AND/OR F31, DISPLAY PANELS TO BCM DATA PROBLEM

Figure 8D2-14

Code F30 is set if the BCM is unable to receive data from the Climate Control Panel. Code F31 indicates that the same condition exists between the BCM and Fuel Data Center. If a malfunction should occur in a circuit common to both display panels, both codes will be stored in BCM memory.

Due to the failure modes of codes F30 and F31 they will only be displayed if the problem is intermittent. When these codes are currently failing the displays do not function properly which prohibits the use of diagnostics. Listed below are the symptoms and malfunctions which would result in one or both codes being displayed after the problem corrects itself.

One or more of the following symptoms is associated with each circuit malfunction and is referenced in parentheses:

1. Panel displays "d"
2. Panel Displays "c"
3. Panel frozen, dim or blank
4. Displays flash on and off

Code F30 only: CCP - BCM Data Problem

- Ckt 718 open or short to ground (1)
- CCP branch of ckt 713 open (2)
- CCP branch of ckt 751-B open (3)
- CCP branch of ckt 705 open (3)
- Faulty CCP (1, 2, 3 or 4)
- Faulty BCM (1)

Code F31 only: FDC - BCM Data Problem

- Ckt 719 open or short to ground (1)
- FDC branch of ckt 713 open (2)
- FDC branch of ckt 751-B open (3)
- FDC branch of ckt 705 open (3)
- Faulty FDC (1, 2, 3 or 4)
- Faulty BCM (1)

Both codes F30 and F31: Symptoms Affect Both Displays

- Common branch of ckt 713 open (2)
- Ckt 713 short to ground (2)
- Common branch of ckt 751-B open (3)
- Common branch of ckt 705 open (3)
- Ckt 705 short to ground (3, 4)
- Faulty BCM (1, 2, 3, 4)

If an intermittent Code F30 and/or F31 is being set, manipulate the related wiring while observing the display panels. If the failure is induced, the associated symptom will appear. This will help to isolate the location of the malfunction. If the failure is induced but cannot be isolated to a given circuit, follow the "Self-Diagnostic System Check" in Section 8D which is designed to locate display malfunctions which are currently failing.

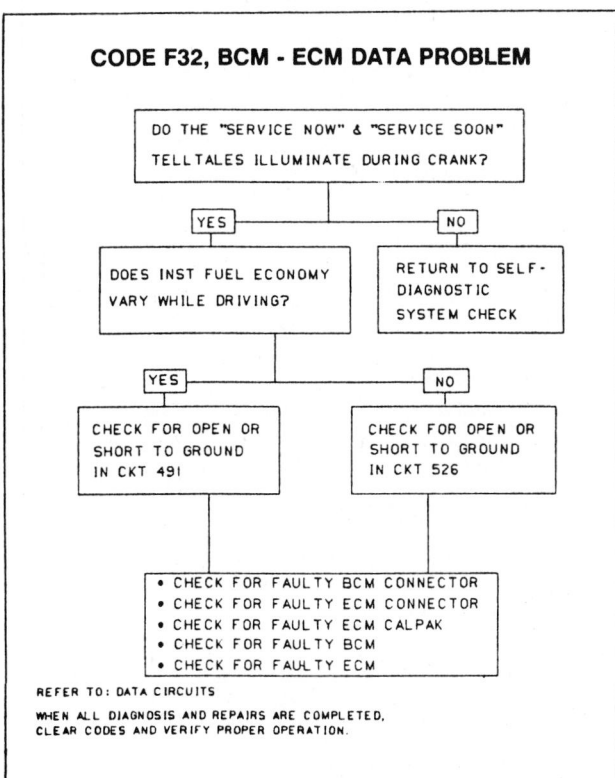

CODE F32, BCM - ECM DATA PROBLEM

REFER TO: DATA CIRCUITS
WHEN ALL DIAGNOSIS AND REPAIRS ARE COMPLETED,
CLEAR CODES AND VERIFY PROPER OPERATION

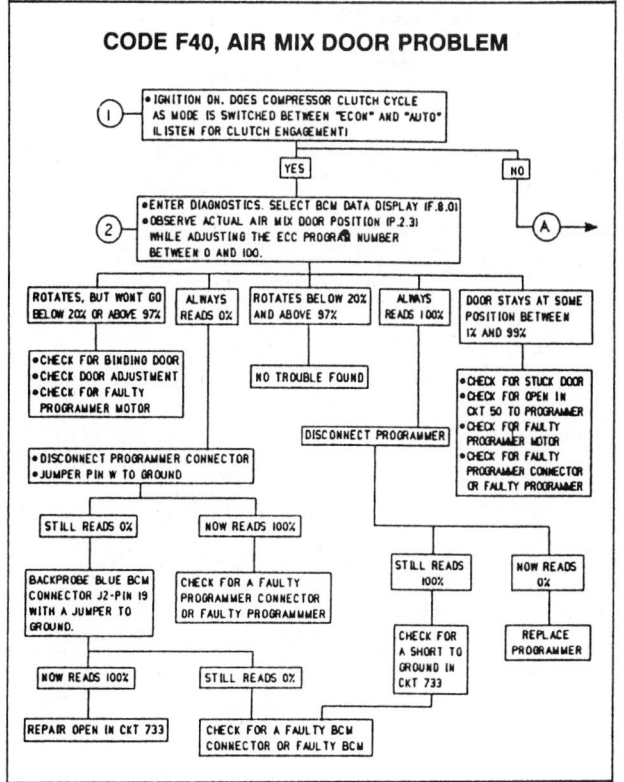

CODE F40, AIR MIX DOOR PROBLEM

DFI TROUBLE DIAGNOSTICS

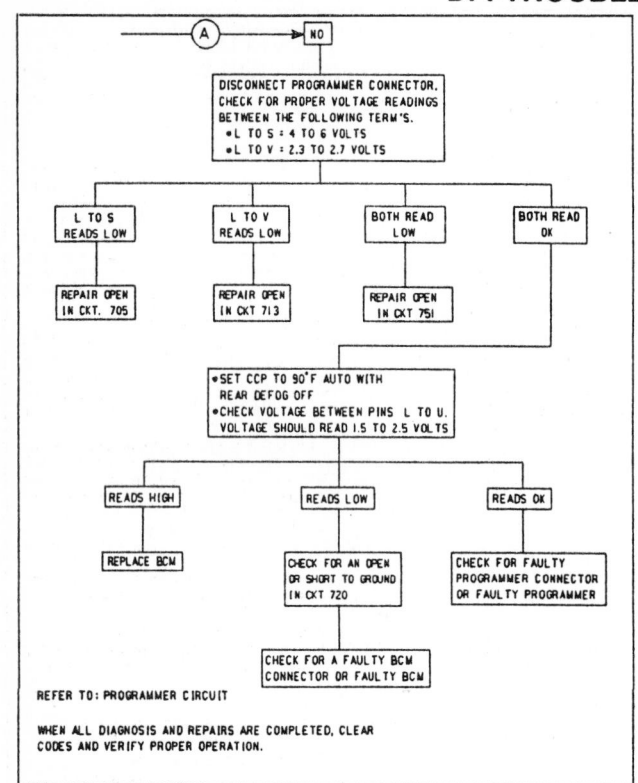

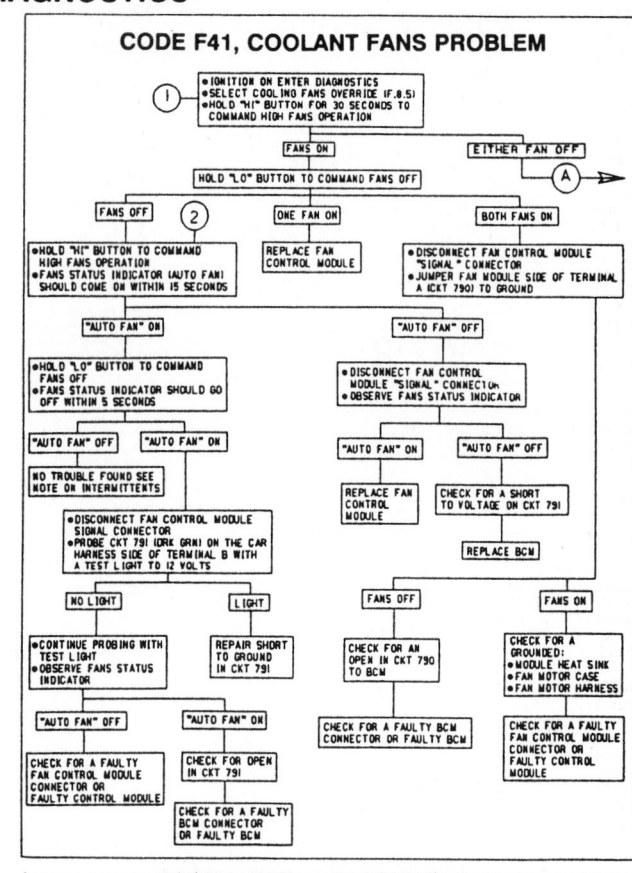

CODE F41, COOLANT FANS PROBLEM

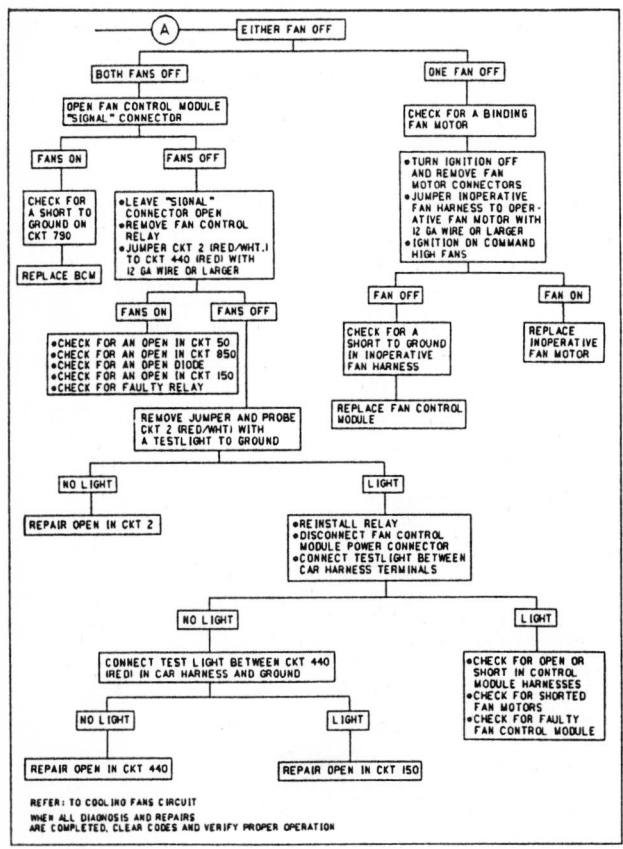

CODES F46, F47, AND/OR F48, REFRIGERANT SYSTEM PROBLEM

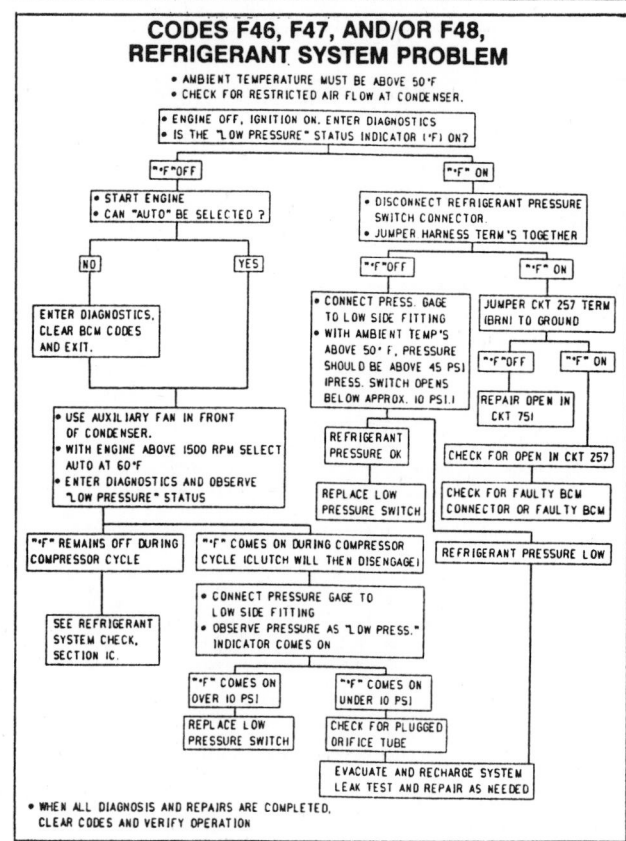

DFI TROUBLE DIAGNOSTICS

CODE F49, HIGH TEMPERATURE CLUTCH DISENGAGE

To protect the vehicles cooling system from overheating, the BCM does not allow the compressor clutch to engage if the coolant exceeds 126°C (259°F). Also, if the A/C high pressure refrigerant temperature exceeds 93°C (200°F) the clutch is turned off to prevent refrigerant "blow-out". The Code F49 is stored by the BCM whenever the clutch is being disengaged due to one of the above conditions. Customer complaints of "insufficient cooling" or "engine overheating" may be associated with this code. If a hard or intermittent Code F49 has been stored, the coolant and refrigerant systems must be investigated for the cause of a high temperature condition. Possible causes would include blockage in coolant flow, blockage in refrigerant flow or insufficient air flow over radiator/condenser.

CODE F51, BCM PROM ERROR INDICATOR

Code F51 indicates that the calibration PROM is not being read properly by the BCM. While the PROM error condition is present a "-151" will be displayed on the CCP and diagnostics cannot be entered. If the problem becomes intermittent, the Code F51 will be displayed during the first pass of BCM codes. A Code E47 may also be stored as an intermittent after the problem is corrected since data is not sent to the ECM while a PROM error condition exists.

A PROM installed backwards or installed with bent pins may cause this code to set. Remove the trap door on the BCM and verify that the calibration PROM is installed properly. Refer to Section 8C for PROM removal and installation procedure.

If the PROM appears to be installed properly, turn the ignition off for 10 seconds and then back on. If "-151" is displayed on the CCP, replace the PROM. Again turn the ignition off for 10 seconds and then back on. If "-151" is again displayed after replacing the PROM, replace the BCM.

ADDITIONAL BCM DIAGNOSTIC INFORMATION

The following chart, **Figure 8D2-27** defines the testing and failure conditions associated with each trouble code. This information is presented here to help explain how the BCM determines that a malfunction has occurred. The information contained in the chart is detailed below:

1. **Trouble Codes** - This is the code which is displayed in diagnostic display if the testing and failure requirements are both met. Codes F32, F40, F41, F47 and F49 have more than one set of requirements which will cause them to set. These different conditions are identified by a letter following the trouble code (i.e. 32-A and 32-B).

2. **Testing Requirements** - These are the conditions which must be met before the BCM will test for the failure requirements.

3. **Failure Requirements** - This is the input which the BCM identifies as abnormal under the conditions of the testing requirements. If a time is included in the requirements, this is how long all of the testing and failure requirements must be present in order to satisfy setting the trouble code.

4. **Failsoft Action** - After the BCM has identified a system malfunction, it may take some action to keep the system operational. The following failsoft actions are taken by the BCM and are identified on the chart:

   N - No Action taken.

   1- Set outside air temperature to 56°F for internal processing. Display outside air temperature sensor value.
   This code is calibrated to eliminate a false failure from excessive engine heat on hot ambients. This code may set under extremely cold ambients (-40°C). If this failure is repaired, the displayed outside air temperature is reset to sensor value.

   2- Turn engine cooling fans on to full speed if the A/C clutch is engaged.

   3- Set A/C low side equal to A/C high side.

   4- Set in-car temperature to 75°F.

   5- Climate control system mode will be set to front defrost and the set temperature will be set to 75°F.

   6- All ECM inputs are cleared, coolant temperature is set to 90°C and the cooling fans are turned on to full speed.

   7- The code is latched for the ignition cycle, the fans will continue to be controlled and the test is no longer performed.

   8- If test is satisfied, an occurrence counter is incremented. A failure is set when the counter reaches 7. Whenever the test is not satisfied, this occurrence counter is decremented. If a code was set, this counter is stored in keep alive memory and is preset to **4 occurrences** at the next key-on and the current code is cleared (history code remains).

   9- If either subtest is satisfied, an occurrence counter is incremented. A failure is set when the counter reaches 7. Whenever neither subtest is satisfied, the occurrence counter is decremented.

   10- The operating mode is set to 75°F front defrost, the blower is set to 9 volts, the air mix door is set to mid-position and the coolant fans are turned on to full speed.

5. **Disabled Functions** - depending on the detected malfunction, certain functions will be disabled. These functions are disabled since their proper operation is dependent upon the input which has malfunctioned. The following functions are disabled and are identified on the chart:

   N- No action taken.

   A- Force the A/C clutch off.

   B- The code renders the diagnostic display inoperative. The communication problem must be repaired to display this code.

   C- Disable extended compressor at idle (ECI).

   D- Fans will be disabled and remain disabled until fan operation is no longer required. Fan operation will be allowed if cooling is once again required. If the fans are commanded on, after being enabled, a retest is initiated.

   E- The A/C clutch is disabled for the entire ignition cycle. If the system is in the AUTO mode, it will change to ECON and AUTO is disabled for the entire ignition cycle. The current code is forced to set for each ignition cycle, until BCM codes are cleared or keep alive memory is reset.

   F- The A/C clutch is disabled for the entire igntion cycle. If the system is in the AUTO mode, it will change to ECON and AUTO is disabled for the entire ignition cycle. At the next key on, the current code is cleared (history code remains) and AUTO can once again be selected.

   G- The PROM is not used, the A/C clutch is disabled, RAP is disabled, rear defrost is disabled, ECM communications are disabled and the heater water valve is disabled (open position).

6. **Lamp/V.F. Indication** - depending on the detected malfunction, certain indicators will be displayed to the driver. The following indicators are displayed and are identified on the chart:

   N- No telltale lamp.

   1- If CCP/FDC are operational, they will display a "d" for loss of data or a "c" for loss of clock.

   2- If the diagnostic display is active:
      (a) Bypass all ECM display modes.
      (b) Clear all ECM status lights.

   3- A fan failure flag is transmitted to the ECM whenever the fans are desired. The ECM turns on the Coolant/Fans telltale.

   4- "Service Air Cond" telltale is turned on for **60 seconds**. At next key-on, the telltale lamp is turned on for the same time period.

ECC DIAGNOSTIC TESTING CONDITIONS

(1) TROUBLE CODE (F/FF)	Rap inactive	Code F10 clear	Outside air temperature > 0°C	ECI inactive	Low side temp at clutch turn on < 14°C	ADDITIONAL REQUIREMENTS	FAILURE CONDITION	TIME (SEC)	(4) FAILSOFT ACTION	(5) DISABLED FUNCTIONS	(6) LAMP/V.F. INDICATION
10	YES						Outside air temperature < -34°C or Outside air temperature > 87°C		1	N	N
11	YES	YES	YES				A/C high side < -9°C or A/C high side > 209°C		2	N	N
12	YES	YES	YES				A/C low side < -34°C or A/C low side > 87°C		3	A	N
13	YES	YES	YES				In-car < -34°C or In-car > 96°C		4	N	N
30	YES						A complete frame of data has not been received from the CCP	2	5	B	1
31	YES						A complete frame of data has not been received from the FDC	2	N	B	1
32-A	YES						A complete frame of data has not been received from the ECM	5	6	C	2
32-B	YES						BCM is not receiving the 8.8.8 or .7.0 upon entering diagnostics		6	C	2
40-A	YES					Mix door position increasing	Feedback < 80% and feedback is not within 2% of commanded	60	N	N	N
40-B	YES					Mix door position decreasing	Feedback > 30% and feedback is not within 2% of commanded	60	N	N	N
41-A						Fans commanded OFF	Feedback low	15	7	N	3
41-B						Fans commanded ON	Feedback high	15	N	D	3
46		YES		YES	YES	A/C clutch was not turned off before MOI has expired	Large difference between the low side temp at clutch turn-on and MOI	> 18	8	N	4
47-A		YES		YES	YES	A/C clutch was not turned off before MOI has expired	Excessive difference between the low side temp at clutch turn-on and MOI	> 18	9	E	5
47-B				YES	YES		Low refrigerant pressure switch opened at or during MOI	> 18	9	E	5
48						All conditions present for the clutch to turn on	Pressure switch is open (low-pressure)	30	N	F	5
49-A	YES						A/C high side temperature > 93°C		N	A	N
49-B	YES						Filtered coolant temperature > 126°C		N	A	N
51						Power-on initialization or a running reset	PROM data values read incorrectly		10	G	6

1986-88 Eldorado and SeVille

GENERAL INFORMATION

Aboard this vehicle are several electronic components which can be controlled by the service technician to provide valuable self-diagnostic information. These components are part of an electrical network, designed to control various engine and body subsystems. A description of each of these subsystems will be found in appropriate places in this section. However, this section will provide a description of the overall electronic network and the on-car diagnostic capabilities which have been designed to aid the service technician in system repair.

At the heart of the computer system is the Body Computer Module (BCM). The BCM is located in the middle of the instrument panel, behind the Driver Information Center display. It has climate control an internal microprocessor which is the center for communication with all the other components in the system. All system sensors and switches are monitored by the BCM or one of the four other major components that complete the computer system. These four components are:

1. Electronic Control Module (ECM).
2. Instrument Panel Cluster (IPC).
3. Programmer - Heating - Ventilation - A/C.
4. Climate Control/Driver Information Center.

A combination of inputs from these major components and the other sensors and switches communicate with the BCM, either as individual inputs, or on the common communications link called the data line. The various input to the BCM combine with program instructions within the system memory to provide accurate control over the many subsystems involved. When a subsystem circuit exceeds pre-programmed limits, a system malfunction is indicated and may provide certain back-up functions. Providing control over the many subsystems from the BCM is done by controlling system outputs. This can be either direct or transmitted along the data line to one of the four other major components. The process of receiving, storing, testing, and controlling information is continuous. The data communication gives the BCM control over the ECM's self-diagnostic capabilities in addition to its own.

Between the BCM and the other four major components of the computer system, a communication process has been incorporated, which allows the devices to share information and thereby provide for additional control capability. In a method similar to that used by a telegraph system, the BCM's internal circuitry rapidly switches a circuit between 0 and 5 volts like a telegraph key. This process is used to convert information into a series of pulses which represents coded data messages understood by the other component. Also, much like a telegraph system, each major component has its own recognition code (address). so when a message is sent out on the data line, only the component or station that matches the assigned recognition code will pay attention, and the rest of the components or stations will ignore it.

Each individual subsystem and its interrelation with the BCM will be covered in a specific section. Below is a list of the subsystems that are controlled by the computer system.

DIAGNOSTIC PROCEDURE

This section can be used to begin diagnosis of any customer complaint which does not directly relate to a specific subsystem or to obtain a detailed understanding of the vehicle self-diagnostic capabilities.

1. Is the "Engine Control System" telltale working? If this telltale fails to illuminate during crank, then the problem could be in the power supply circuits to the computer system. The "Self-Diagnostic Check" will direct you to an appropriate diagnosis chart contained under the "General Diagnosis" portion of this section.

2. Can "Service Mode" be accessed? If the display is not operating, self-diagnostics cannot be used. In this case, the "Self-Diagnostic System Check" will lead you to an appropriate diagnosis chart contained under "General Diagnosis".

3. Is there a Trouble Code displayed? If a trouble code is identified using the self-diagnostics, a problem has been detected by the system which can be corrected following the appropriately numbered code chart. Codes with a prefix of "E" are ECM codes. Codes with a prefix of "B" are BCM codes.

Visual Inspection

One of the most important checks, which must be done before any diagnostic activity, is a careful visual inspection of suspect wiring and components. This can often lead to fixing a problem without further steps. Inspect all vacuum hoses for pinches, cuts or disconnections.

Be sure to inspect hoses that are difficult to see beneath the air cleaner. Inspect all the related wiring for disconnects, for example, burned or chaffed spots, pinched wires, or contact with sharp edges or hot exhaust manifolds. This visual inspection is very important. It must be done carefully and thoroughly.

1. The "Engine Control System" telltale is working.

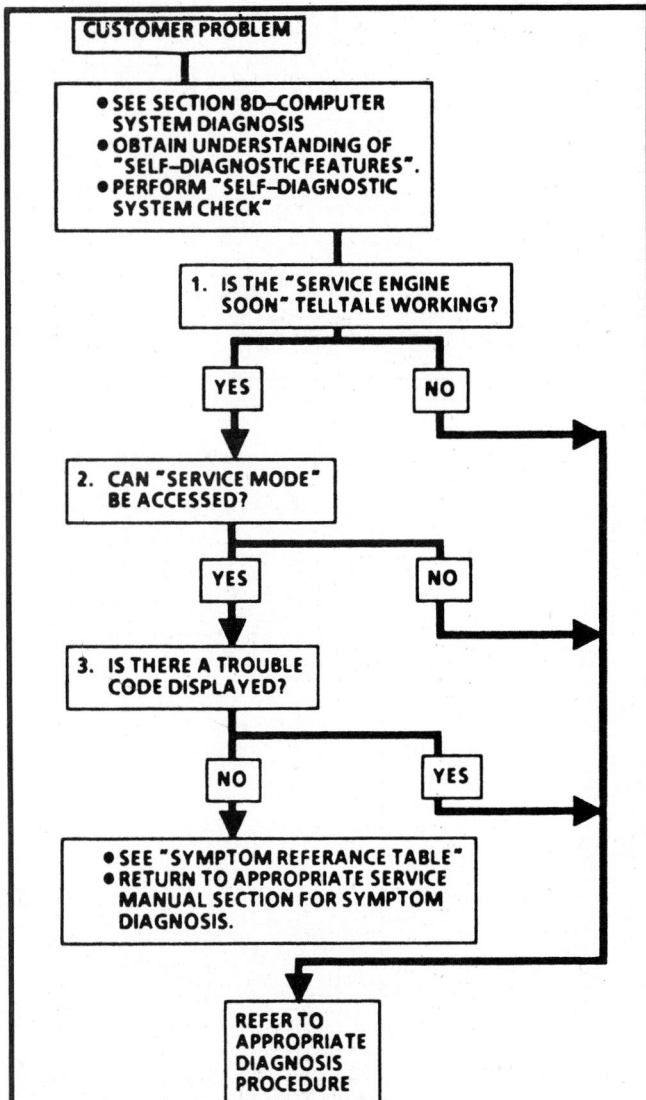

Diagnostic procedure use—Eldorado and Seville

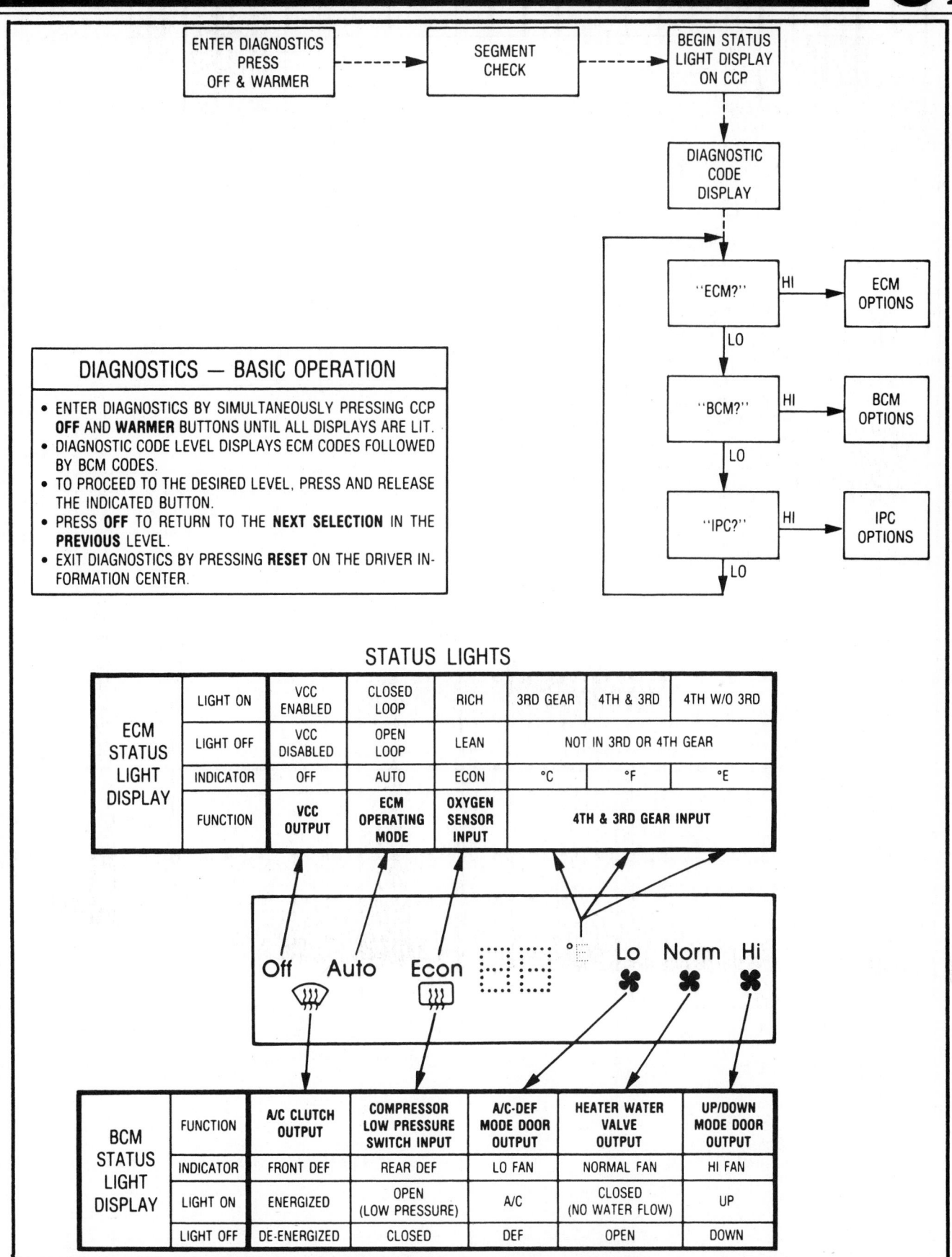

DIAGNOSTICS — BASIC OPERATION

- ENTER DIAGNOSTICS BY SIMULTANEOUSLY PRESSING CCP **OFF** AND **WARMER** BUTTONS UNTIL ALL DISPLAYS ARE LIT.
- DIAGNOSTIC CODE LEVEL DISPLAYS ECM CODES FOLLOWED BY BCM CODES.
- TO PROCEED TO THE DESIRED LEVEL, PRESS AND RELEASE THE INDICATED BUTTON.
- PRESS **OFF** TO RETURN TO THE **NEXT SELECTION** IN THE **PREVIOUS** LEVEL.
- EXIT DIAGNOSTICS BY PRESSING **RESET** ON THE DRIVER IN-FORMATION CENTER.

STATUS LIGHTS

ECM STATUS LIGHT DISPLAY	LIGHT ON	VCC ENABLED	CLOSED LOOP	RICH	3RD GEAR	4TH & 3RD	4TH W/O 3RD
	LIGHT OFF	VCC DISABLED	OPEN LOOP	LEAN	NOT IN 3RD OR 4TH GEAR		
	INDICATOR	OFF	AUTO	ECON	°C	°F	°E
	FUNCTION	**VCC OUTPUT**	**ECM OPERATING MODE**	**OXYGEN SENSOR INPUT**	**4TH & 3RD GEAR INPUT**		

BCM STATUS LIGHT DISPLAY	FUNCTION	A/C CLUTCH OUTPUT	COMPRESSOR LOW PRESSURE SWITCH INPUT	A/C-DEF MODE DOOR OUTPUT	HEATER WATER VALVE OUTPUT	UP/DOWN MODE DOOR OUTPUT
	INDICATOR	FRONT DEF	REAR DEF	LO FAN	NORMAL FAN	HI FAN
	LIGHT ON	ENERGIZED	OPEN (LOW PRESSURE)	A/C	CLOSED (NO WATER FLOW)	UP
	LIGHT OFF	DE-ENERGIZED	CLOSED	DEF	OPEN	DOWN

Basic ECM diagnostics operation and status lights—Eldorado and Seville

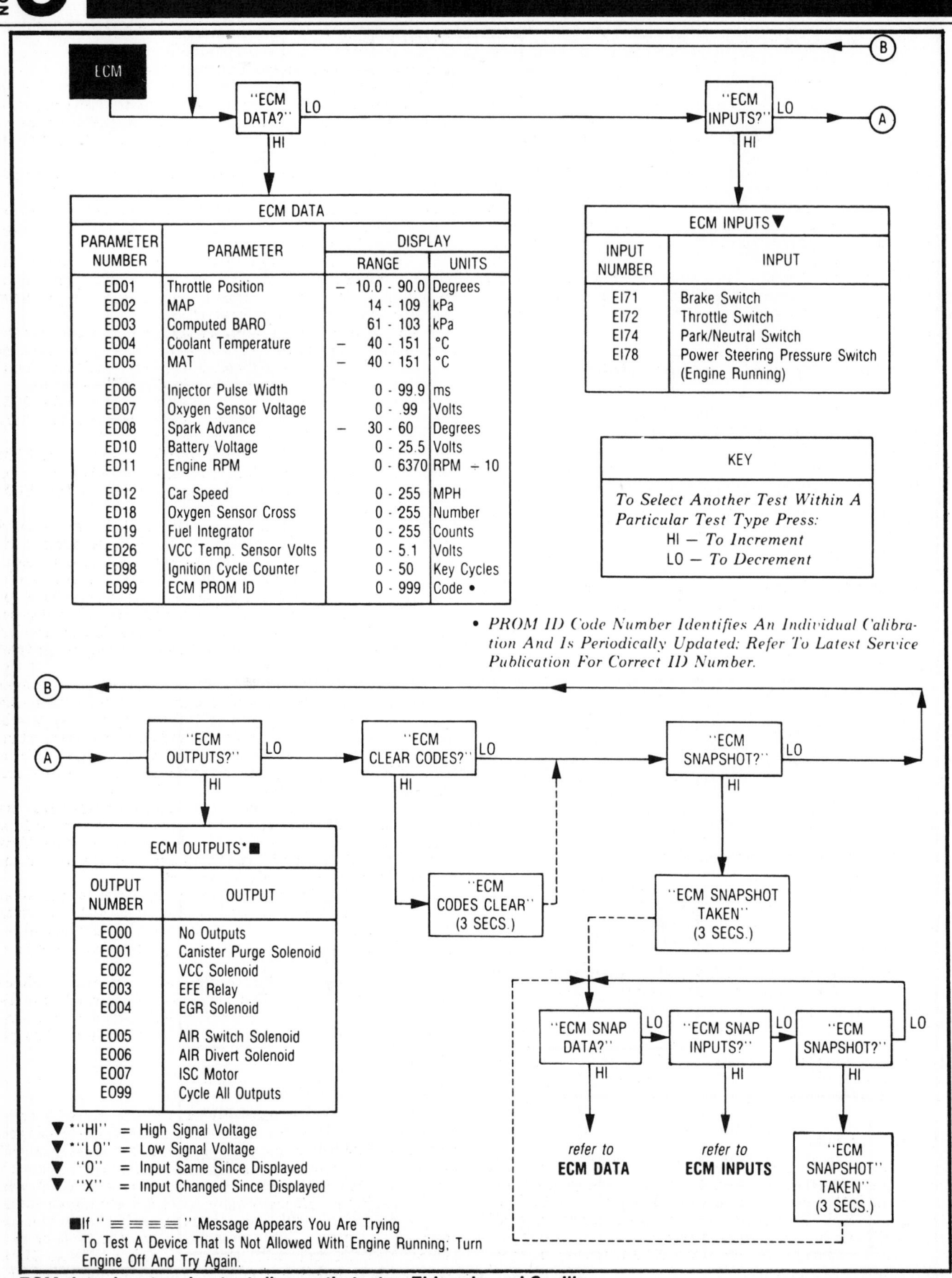

ECM DATA

PARAMETER NUMBER	PARAMETER	DISPLAY	
		RANGE	UNITS
ED01	Throttle Position	− 10.0 - 90.0	Degrees
ED02	MAP	14 - 109	kPa
ED03	Computed BARO	61 - 103	kPa
ED04	Coolant Temperature	− 40 - 151	°C
ED05	MAT	− 40 - 151	°C
ED06	Injector Pulse Width	0 - 99.9	ms
ED07	Oxygen Sensor Voltage	0 - .99	Volts
ED08	Spark Advance	− 30 - 60	Degrees
ED10	Battery Voltage	0 - 25.5	Volts
ED11	Engine RPM	0 - 6370	RPM − 10
ED12	Car Speed	0 - 255	MPH
ED18	Oxygen Sensor Cross	0 - 255	Number
ED19	Fuel Integrator	0 - 255	Counts
ED26	VCC Temp. Sensor Volts	0 - 5.1	Volts
ED98	Ignition Cycle Counter	0 - 50	Key Cycles
ED99	ECM PROM ID	0 - 999	Code •

ECM INPUTS ▼

INPUT NUMBER	INPUT
EI71	Brake Switch
EI72	Throttle Switch
EI74	Park/Neutral Switch
EI78	Power Steering Pressure Switch (Engine Running)

KEY

To Select Another Test Within A Particular Test Type Press:
HI — *To Increment*
LO — *To Decrement*

• *PROM ID Code Number Identifies An Individual Calibration And Is Periodically Updated; Refer To Latest Service Publication For Correct ID Number.*

ECM OUTPUTS •■

OUTPUT NUMBER	OUTPUT
EO000	No Outputs
EO001	Canister Purge Solenoid
EO002	VCC Solenoid
EO003	EFE Relay
EO004	EGR Solenoid
EO005	AIR Switch Solenoid
EO006	AIR Divert Solenoid
EO007	ISC Motor
EO099	Cycle All Outputs

▼ •"HI" = High Signal Voltage
▼ •"LO" = Low Signal Voltage
▼ "O" = Input Same Since Displayed
▼ "X" = Input Changed Since Displayed

■If " ≡ ≡ ≡ ≡ " Message Appears You Are Trying To Test A Device That Is Not Allowed With Engine Running; Turn Engine Off And Try Again.

ECM data, input and output diagnostic tests—Eldorado and Seville

2. "Service Mode" can be accessed.
3. No trouble codes are stored.
4. A careful visual check found no problems.

Computer System Service Precautions

The computer system is designated to withstand normal current draws associated with vehicle operation, however, care must be taken to avoid overloading any of these circuits. In testing for opens or shorts, do not ground or apply voltage to any of the circuits unless instructed to do so by the diagnostic procedures. These circuits should only be tested using the High Impedance Multimeter (J-29125A, J-34029A, or equivalent) if they remain connected to one of the computers. Power should never be removed or applied to one of the computers with the key in the ON position. Before removing or connecting battery cables, fuses or connectors always turn the ignition to the OFF position.

SELF-DIAGNOSTIC FEATURES

Trouble Codes

In the process of controlling the various subsystems, the ECM and BCM continually monitor operating conditions for possible system malfunctions. By comparing system conditions against standard operating limits certain circuit and component malfunctions can be detected. A three digit numerical Trouble Code is stored in computer memory when a problem is detected by this self diagnostic system. These Trouble Codes can later be displayed by the service technician as an aid in system repair.

The occurrence of certain system malfunctions require that the vehicle operator be alerted to the problem so as to avoid prolonged operation of the vehicle under subnormal system operation. Computer controlled diagnostic messages and/or telltales will appear under these conditions which indicate that service is required.

If a particular malfunction would result in unacceptable system operation, the self-diagnostics will attempt to minimize the effect by taking "failsoft" action. "Failsoft" action refers to any specific attempt by the computer system to compensate for the detected problem. A typical failsoft action would be the substitution of a fixed input when a sensor is detected to be open or shorted.

Entering Service Mode

To enter diagnostic mode, proceed as follows:
1. Turn the ignition ON.
2. Push the "OFF" and "WARM" buttons on the Climate Control Panel simultaneously and hold until the segment check appears on the Instrument Panel Cluster (IPC) and Climate Control Driver Information Center (CCDIC).

NOTE: Operating the vehicle in the Service Mode for extended time periods without the engine running or without a battery charger will cause the battery to run down and possibly relate false diagnostic information, or cause a no start condition. To ensure proper operation, attach a batter charger if vehicle is to be operated in Service Mode without engine running for periods longer than $\frac{1}{2}$ hour.

Segment Check

The purpose of illuminating the IPC and CCDIC is to check that all segments of the vacuum flourescent displays are working. On the IPC however, the turn signal indicators do not light during this check. Diagnosis should not be attempted unless all the CCDIC segments appear, as this could lead to misdiagnosis. If any portions or segments of the CCDIC display are inoperative, it must be replaced.

Status Lights

While in the diagnostic service mode, the mode indicators on the Climate Control Panel (CCP) of the CCDIC are used to indicated the status of certain operating modes. The different modes of operation are indicted by the status light being turned on or turned off. A brief summary of each status light is provided below.

1. The "OFF" status indicator is turned on whenever the ECM is commanding the Viscous Converter Clutch (VCC) to engage. The light only indicated whether the VCC is enabled or disabled by the ECM. Actual operation depends on the integrity of the VCC system.
2. The "AUTO" status indicator is turned on whenever the ECM is operating in "closed loop" fuel control. This light should come on after the coolant and oxygen sensors have reached normal operating temperatures.
3. The "ECON" status indicator is turned on whenever the oxygen sensor signal to the ECM indicates a "rich" exhaust condition. This light should switch between "rich" and "lean" (flash on and off) during warm steady throttle operation.
4. The "C" status indicator is turned on whenever the ECM senses that the 3rd gear pressure switch is open. The light should be on while in 3rd gear operation.
5. The "F" status indicator is turned on whenever the ECM senses that the 3rd and 4th gear pressure switches are open. the light should be on while in 4th gear operation and the ECM had received a 3rd gear input signal.
6. The "E" status indicator is turned on whenever the ECM senses that the 4th gear pressure switch is open, but not the 3rd gear switch. The light should be on while in 4th gear operation and the ECM had not received a 3rd gear input signal.
7. The (front defog) status indicator is turned on whenever the BCM is commanding the ECC compressor clutch to engage. The light indicated whether the clutch is enabled or disabled by the BCM and actual operation depends on the integrity of the compressor clutch system.
8. The (rear defog) status indicator is turned on whenever the BCM senses that the low refrigerant pressure switch is open. The light should remain off if the refrigerant system is fully charged and being properly controlled. However, when the ambient temperature drops below approximately -5°F (-21°C), the light will come on due to the pressure-temperature relationship of refrigerant-12.
9. The "LO Fan" status indicator is turned on whenever the BCM is commanding the A/C- DEF mode door to divert air flow to the A/C outlets, as in the A/C or normal purge modes. This light will be off whenever the ECC system is in the heater, intermediate, defrost and cold purge modes.
10. The "NORM Fan Symbol" status indicator is turned on whenever the BCM is commanding the heater water valve to block coolant flow through the heater core. the light should remain off except when the air mix door is being commanded to the max A/C position (0%).
11. The "HI Fan Symbol" status indicator is turned on whenever the BCM is commanding the UP-DOWN mode door to divert air flow up, away from the heater outlet. This light will be off whenever the ECC system is in the heater or normal purge mode.

Trouble Code Display

After Service Mode is entered any trouble codes stored in computer memory will be displayed. ECM codes will be displayed first. If no ECM trouble codes are stored, a "NO ECM CODES" message will be displayed. All ECM codes will be prefixed with a "E" (i.e. EO13, EO14, etc.). The lowest numbered ECM code will be displayed first followed by progressively higher numbered codes present. Following the highest ECM code present or the "NO ECM CODES" message, BCM codes will be displayed. All BCM codes will be prefixed with a "B" (i.e. B110, B111, etc.). If no BCM Trouble Codes are stored "NO BCM

ECM DIAGNOSTIC CODES

CODE	DESCRIPTION	COMMENTS
E012	No Distributor Signal	Ⓐ
E013	Oxygen Sensor Not Ready [AIR, CL & Canister Purge]	Ⓑ
E014	Shorted Coolant Sensor Circuit [AIR]	Ⓑ Ⓕ
E015	Open Coolant Sensor Circuit [AIR]	Ⓑ Ⓕ
E016	Generator Voltage Out Of Range [All Solenoids]	Ⓐ Ⓔ
E018	Open Crank Signal Circuit	Ⓑ
E019	Shorted Fuel Pump Circuit	Ⓑ
E020	Open Fuel Pump Circuit	Ⓐ
E021	Shorted Throttle Position Sensor Circuit	Ⓑ
E022	Open Throttle Position Sensor Circuit	Ⓑ
E023	EST/Bypass Circuit Problem [AIR]	Ⓑ Ⓓ
E024	Speed Sensor Circuit Problem [VCC]	Ⓑ Ⓔ
E026	Shorted Throttle Switch Circuit	Ⓑ
E027	Open Throttle Switch Circuit	Ⓑ
E028	Open Third or Fourth Gear Circuit	Ⓑ
E030	ISC Circuit Problem	Ⓑ
E031	Shorted MAP Sensor Circuit [AIR]	Ⓐ
E032	Open MAP Sensor Circuit [AIR]	Ⓐ
E034	MAP Sensor Signal Too High [AIR]	Ⓐ
E037	Shorted MAT Sensor Circuit [AIR]	Ⓑ
E038	Open MAT Sensor Circuit [AIR]	Ⓑ
E039	VCC Engagement Problem	Ⓑ
E040	Open Power Steering Pressure Switch Circuit	Ⓑ
E044	Lean Exhaust Signal [AIR, CL & Canister Purge]	Ⓐ
E045	Rich Exhaust Signal [AIR, CL & Canister Purge]	Ⓐ
E047	BCM — ECM Data Problem	Ⓑ
E048	EGR System Fault [EGR]	Ⓑ
E051	ECM PROM Error	Ⓐ Ⓕ
E052	ECM Memory Reset Indicator	Ⓒ
E053	Distributor Signal Interrupt	Ⓒ
E055	TPS Misadjusted	Ⓒ
E059	VCC Temperature Sensor Circuit Problem	Ⓒ

DIAGNOSTIC CODE COMMENTS

Ⓐ	Displays "SERVICE NOW" Message And Turns On "ENGINE CONTROL SYSTEM" Light.
Ⓑ	Displays "SERVICE SOON" Message And Turns On "ENGINE CONTROL SYSTEM" Light.
Ⓒ	Does Not Turn On Any Telltale Light Or Display Any Message.
Ⓓ	Causes System To Operate On Bypass Spark.
Ⓔ	Disengages VCC For Entire Ignition Cycle.
Ⓕ	Forces Cooling Fans On Full Speed.
[ ]	Functions Within Bracket Are Disengaged While Specified Malfunction Remains Current.

ECM diagnostic codes — 1986–88 Eldorado and Seville

CODES" message will be displayed. Any BCM and ECM codes displayed will also be accompanied by "Current" or "History". "History" indicated the failure was not present the last time the code was tested and "Current" indicated the fault still exists. At any time during the display of ECM or BCM codes, it

BCM DIAGNOSTIC CODES

Code	Circuit Affected	Code	Circuit Affected
B110	Outside Temp Sensor	B412	Battery High
B111	A/C Hi Side Temp Sensor	B420	Relays
B112	A/C Lo Side Temp Sensor	B440	Air Mix Door
B113	In-Car Temp Sensor	B441	Cooling Fans
B115	Sunload Temp Sensor	B446	Low Refrigerant Warning
B119	Twilight Photocell	B447	Very Low Refrigerant Problem
B120	Twilight Delay Pot	B448	Low Refrigerant Pressure
B121	Twilight Enable Switch	B449	A/C HI Temp
B122	Panel Lamp Dimming Pot	B450	Coolant High Temp – A/C
B123	Courtesy Light Switch	B552	BCM Memory Reset
B124	Vehicle Speed Sensor	B556	EE Prom
B127	PRND321 Sensor	B660	Cruise – Not In Drive
B128	Bulb Reference Circuit	B663	Cruise – Speed Difference
B334	ECM Data	B664	Cruise – Acceleration
B335	CCDIC Data	B665	Cruise – Coolant Temp Too High
B336	IPC Data	B666	Cruise – RPM Too High
B337	Programmer Data	B667	Cruise – Switch Shorted
B410	Regulator	B671	Cruise – Position Sensor
B411	Battery Low	B672	Cruise – Vent Solenoid
		B673	Cruise – Vacuum Solenoid

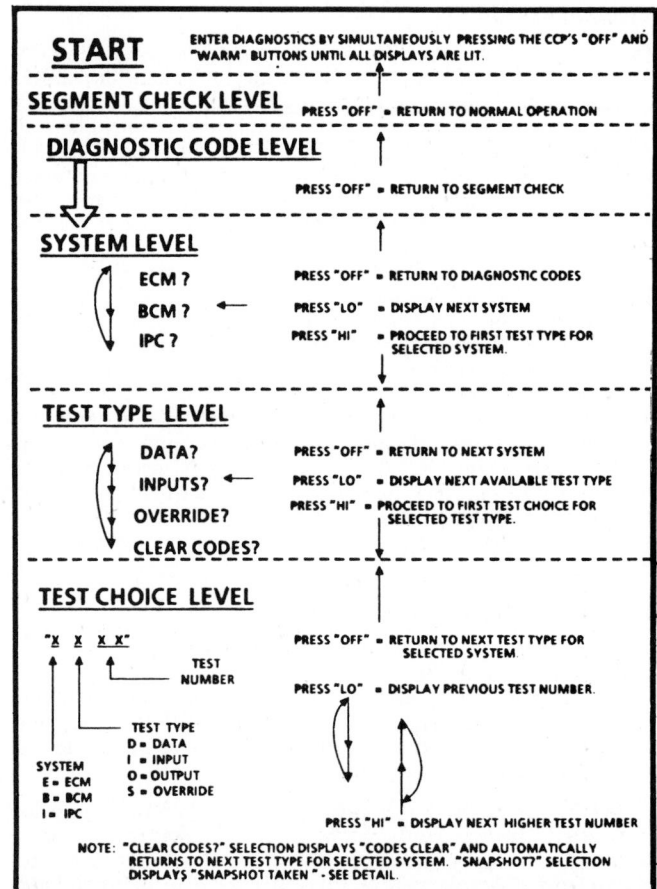

How to operate the SERVICE MODE — Eldorado and Seville

the "LO" button on the CCP is depressed, the display of codes will be bypassed. At anytime during the display of trouble codes, it the "Reset/Recall" button on the Driver Information Center (DIC) is depressed the system will exit Service Mode and go back to normal vehicle operation.

Climate Control in Service Mode

Upon entering the Service Mode, the climate control will operate in whatever mode was being commanded just prior to depressing the "OFF" and "WARM" buttons. Even though the display may change just as the buttons are touched, the prior operating mode is remembered and will resume after "Service Mode" is entered. Extended Compressor at Idle (ECI) is not allowed while in the diagnostic mode. This allows observation of system parameters during normal compressor cycles.

Operating The Service Mode

After trouble codes have been displayed, the Service Mode can be used to perform several tests on different systems one at a time. Upon completion of code display, a specific system may be selected for testing. Following the display of trouble codes, the first available system will be displayed (i.e. ECM?). While selecting a system to test, any of the following actions may be taken to control the display:

1. Depressing the "Off" button the CCP will stop the system selection process and return the display to the beginning of the trouble code sequence.

2. Depressing the "LO" button on the CCP will display the next available system selection. this allows the display to be stepped through all system choices. This list of systems can be repeated following the end of the system list.

3. Depressing the "HI" button on the CCP will select the displayed system for testing.

Selecting the Test Type

Having selected a system, the first available test type will be displayed (i.e. ECM DATA?). While selecting a specific test type, any of the following actions may be taken to control the display:

1. Depressing the "OFF" button on the CCP will stop the test type selection process and return the display the next available system selection.

2. Depressing the "LO" button on the CCP will display the next available test type for the selected system. This allows the display to be stepped through all available test type choices. This list of test types can be repeated following the display of the last test type.

3. Depressing the "HI" button on the CCP will select the displayed test type. At this point the first of several specific tests will appear.

Selecting the Test

Selection of the "DATA?", "INPUTS?", "OUTPUTS?" or "OVERRIDE?" test types will result in the first available test being displayed. If dashes ever appear, this test is not allowed with the engine running. four characters of the display will contain a test code to identify the selection. The first two characters are letters which identify the system and test type (i.e. ED for ECM DATA) and the last two characters numerically identify the test (i.e. ED01 for Throttle Position). While selecting a specific test, any of the following actions may be taken to control the display:

1. Depressing the "OFF" button on the CCP will stop the test selection process and return the display to the next available test type for the selected system.

2. Depressing the "LO" button on the CCP will display the next smaller test number for the selected test type. If this button is pressed with the lowest test number displayed, the highest test number will then appear.

3. Depressing the "HI" button on the CCP will display the next larger test number for the selected test type. If this button is pressed with the highest test number displayed, the lowest test number will then appear.

Selecting "CLEAR CODES?"

Selection of the" CLEAR CODES?" test type will result in the message "CODES CLEAR" being displayed alone with the selected system name. this message will appear for 3 seconds to indicated that all stored trouble codes have been erased from that system's memory. After 3 seconds the display will auto-

matically return to the next available test type for the selected system.

Selecting "SNAPSHOT?"

Selection of the "SNAPSHOT?" test type will result in the message "SNAPSHOT TAKEN" being displayed with the selected system name preceeding it. This message will appear for 3 seconds to indicate that all system data and inputs have been stored in memory. After 3 seconds the display will automatically proceed to the first available snapshot test type (i.e. SNAP DATA). While selecting a snapshot test type, any of the following actions may be taken to control the display.

This ECM snapshot feature is included to assist in diagnosis of intermittent problems. The ECM snapshot selection will store one set of all of the ECM data parameter values and output status indications at the time that the snapshot is requested. To use the snapshot, enter the diagnostics and allow the climate control drive information center (CCDIC) to idle at "ECM SNAPSHOT". When intermittent condition occurs, or when the parameters are to be recorded, press HI and hold until the message "ECM SNAPSHOT TAKEN" appears. The ECM snapshot taken message indicates that the data is now stored for review.

1. Depressing the "OFF" button on the CCP will stop the test type selection process and return the display to the next available system selection.

2. Depressing the "LO" button will display the next available snapshot test type. this allows the display to be stepped through all available choices. This list of snapshot test types can be repeated following the display of the last choice.

3. Depressing the "HI" button with "SNAPDATA?" or "SNAP INPUTS?" displayed will select that test type. At this point the display is controlled as it would be for non-snapshot data and inputs displays, however, all values and status information represents memorized vehicle conditions.

4. Depressing the "HI" button with "SNAPSHOT?" displayed will again display the "SNAPSHOT TAKEN" message to indicate that new information has been stored in memory. Access to this information is obtained the same as previously described.

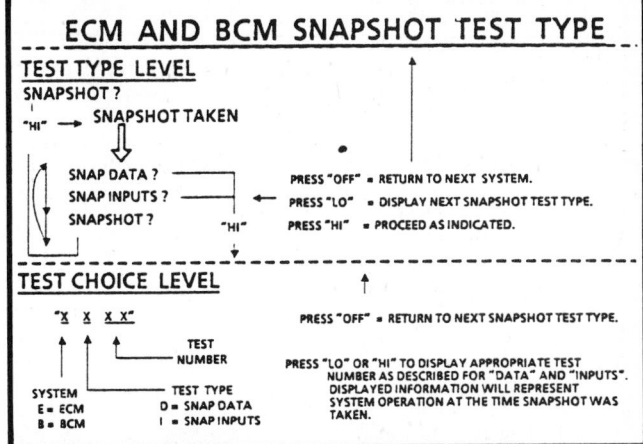

Selecting SNAPSHOT—Eldorado and Seville

Exiting The Service Mode

To get out of the service mode, depress the "Reset/Recall" button on the DIC or turn the ignition switch off. Trouble codes are not erased when this is done.

DATA DISPLAYS

Data displays are operated as defined under "Operating The Service Mode". When troubleshooting a malfunction, the ECM and BCM data displayed can be used to compare the vehicle with problems to a vehicle which is functioning properly. A brief summary of each parameter is provided below:

ECM PARAMETERS

1. **ED01** - The throttle position (TPS) is displayed in degrees from -10 to 90.
2. **ED02** - The manifold air pressure (MAP) is displayed in kilopascals (kPa) from 14 to 109.
3. **ED03** - The computed barometric pressure (BARO) is displayed in kilopascals (kpa) from 61 to 103.
4. **ED04** - The coolant temperature is displayed in degrees Celsius (°C) from -40 to 151.
5. **ED05** - The manifold air temperature (MAT) sensor reading is displayed in degrees Celsius (°C) from –40 to 151.
6. **ED06** - The fuel injector pulse width (ON time) is displayed in milliseconds (ms), from 0 to 99.9.
7. **ED07** - The oxygen sensor voltage is displayed in volts from 0 to 1.14.
8. **ED08** - The amount of spark advance is displayed in degrees, from 0 to 52.
9. **ED10** - The battery voltage is read in volts, from 0 to 25.5.
10. **ED11** - The engine speed is displayed in rpm from 0 to 6370.
11. **ED12** - The vehicle speed is displayed in miles per hour (MPH) from 0 to 159.
12. **ED18** - The oxygen sensor cross count is displayed as the number of times the O_2 sensor crossed the reference line each second.
13. **ED19** - The fuel integrator is displayed in counts, from 88 to 160.
14. **ED26** - The viscous converter clutch (VCC) temperature is displayed as a voltage level at the ECM. The normal range is from 0 to 5.12 volts.
15. **ED98** - The ignition cycle counter valve is the number of times the ignition has been cycled to OFF since an ECM Trouble code was last detected. After 50 ignition cycles without any malfunction being detected, all stored ECM codes are cleared.

BCM PARAMETERS

1. **BD20** - The commanded blower voltage is read in volts from –3.3 to 18.0.
2. **BD21** - The coolant temperature is displayed in degrees Celsius (°C) from .40 to 151. This value is sent from the ECM to the BCM. If this circuit malfunctions as determined by the ECM, the ECM will send the BCM a "Failsoft" value for display.
3. **BD22** - The commanded air mix door position is displayed in percent (%). A value close to 0% represents a cold air mix and a value close to 100% represents a warm air mix.
4. **BD23** - The actual air mix door position is displayed in percent (%). This value should follow the commanded air mix door position (BD22) except when the door is commanded beyond its mechanical limits of travel.
   a. 0 = MAX A/C.
   b. 1 = A/C.
   c. 2 = Intermediate.
   d. 3 = Heater.
   e. 4 = OFF.
   f. 5 = Normal Purge.
   g. 6 = Cold Purge.
   h. 7 = Front Defog.
5. **BD25** - The in-car temperature is displayed in degrees Celsius (°C), from –40 to 102.
6. **BD26** - The actual outside temperature is displayed in degrees Celsius (°C), from –40 to 93. This value represents actual sensor temperature and is not restricted by the features used to minimize engine heat affects on the customer display value.
7. **BD27** - The high side temperature (condenser output) is displayed in degrees Celsius (°C) from –40 to 215.
8. **BD28** - The low side temperature (evaporator input) is displayed in degrees Celsius (°C) from –40 to 93.

9. **BD32** - The sunload temperature sensor is displayed in degrees Celsius (°C) from –40 to 102.
10. **BD40** - The actual fuel level is read in gallons between 0 and 19.0 (the display can read to 25.0). This value represents actual sensor position and is not restricted by the features used to eliminate fuel slosh effects on the customer display value.
11. **BD41** - The PRND 321 display in percent (%). PARKshould display the highest percentage and 1 should display the lowest percentage.
12. **BD42** - The dimming potentiometer is displayed in percent (%). A value close to 0% represents maximum dimming and a value close to 100% represents maximum brightness.
13. **BD43** - The twilight delay potentiometer is displayed in percent (%). A value close to 0% represents minimum delay time and a value close to 100% represents maximum delay time.
14. **BD44** - The twilight photocell is displayed in percent (%). A value close to 0% represents daylight and value close to 100% represents darkness.
15. **BD50** - The battery voltage is read in volts between 0 and 16.3.
16. **BD51** - The generator field is displayed in percent (%). A value close to 0% represents minimum regulator on time and a value close to 100% represents maximum regulator on time.
17. **BD52** - The incandescent bulb reference is displayed in volts. With the parking lamps/headlamps OFF, the value is Zero (0) and with either parking or headlamps ON, the value is battery voltage.
18. **BD60** - The vehicle speed is displayed in miles per hour (MPH) from 0 to 159.
19. **BD61** - The engine speed is displayed in rpm from 0 to 6375.
20. **BD70** - The cruise control servo position is displayed in percent (%) from 0 to 100. A value close to 0% represents at rest position and a value close to 100% represents wide open throttle.
21. **BD98** - The ignition cycle value is the number of times that the BCM has been turned OFF since a BCM trouble code was last detected. After 100 ignition cycles without any malfunction being detected, all BCM codes are cleared.
22. **BD99** - The BCM PROM I.D. is displayed as a number, up to four digits long, which can be used to verify that the proper PROM was installed in the BCM.

INPUT DISPLAYS

Input displays are operated as defined under "Selecting the Test" under the heading "Operating The Service Mode". When troubleshooting a malfunction, the ECM, BCM, or IPC input display can be used to determine it the switch inputs can be properly interpreted. When one of the various input tests is selected, the state of the device is displayed as HI or LO. In general, the HI and LO refer to the input terminal voltage for that circuit. The display also indicates if the input changed state so that the technician can activate or deactivate any listed device and return to the display to see if it changed state. If a change of state occurred, an "X" will only appear once per selected input, although the HI/LO indication will continue to change as the input changes. Some tests are momentary and the "X" can be used as an indication of a change. The following is a list of ECM, BCM and IPC inputs:

ECM INPUT DISPLAYS

1. **EI71** - The brake switch display is "LO" when the brake pedal is depressed.
2. **EI72** - The throttle switch display is "HI" when the accelerator pedal is depressed.
3. **EI74** - The Park/Neutral (P/N) display is "LO" when the vehicle is in Park or Neutral.
4. **EI78** - The power steering pressure switch display is "LO" when power steering pressure (effort) is high, wheel in crimp position.

BCM INPUT DISPLAYS

1. **BI01** - The courtesy lamp panel switch display is "LO" when courtesy lights are on from switch.
2. **BI02** - The park lamp switch display is "LO" when the park lamp switch is in the OFF position.
3. **BI03** - The driver (front) door ajar switch display is "LO" when the driver (front) door is ajar.
4. **BI04** - The passenger (rear) door ajar switch display is "LO" when the passenger's (rear) door is ajar.
5. **BI05** - The door jamb switch display is "LO" when any door is open.
6. **BI06** - The door handle switch display is momentarily "LO" when either front outside door handle button is depressed.
7. **BI07** - The trunk open switch display is "LO" when the truck is open.
8. **BI08** - The low refrigerant pressure switch display is "LO" when the system is low on refrigerant.
9. **BI09** - The washer fluid level switch display is "LO" when the vehicle is low on washer fluid.
10. **BI30** - The TEMP/TIME switch display is "LO" when the button is depressed.
11. **BI41** - The cooling fan feedback display is "LO" when the cooling fans are running.
12. **BI51** - The generator feedback display is "LO" when there is a generator problem (or engine not running).
13. **BI71** - The cruise control brake switch display is "HI" when the cruise ON/OFF switch is ON and the brake pedal is not depressed (free state).
14. **BI75** - The cruise control ON/OFF switch display is "HI" when the switch is ON.
15. **BI76** - The cruise control SET/COAST switch display is "HI" when the cruise ON/OFF switch is ON and the SET/COAST switch is depressed.
16. **BI77** - The cruise control RESUME/ACCEL switch display is "HI" when the cruise ON/OFF switch is ON and the RESUME/ACCEL switch is pushed.

IPC INPUT DISPLAYS

1. **II78** - The headlamp switch display is "HI" whenever the headlamps are ON.
2. **II79** - The high beam switch display is "LO" as long as the lever is pulled in.
3. **II80** - The dimming sentinel switch display is "LO" whenever the system is on.
4. **II81** - The dimming sentinel photosensor display is "HI" whenever it senses light.
5. **II82** - The twilight enable switch display is "LO" whenever the system is ON.

OUTPUT DISPLAYS

Output displays are operated as defined under the heading "Operating The Service Mode". When troubleshooting a malfunction, the ECM and BCM output cycling can be used to determine if the output tests can be actuated regardless of the inputs and normal program instructions. Once a test in outputs has been selected, the test will display HI and LO for three seconds in each state to indicated the command and output terminal voltage. A brief summary of each output is provided below:

ECM OUPUT DISPLAYS

1. **EO00** - This test displays "cycle none" as no outputs are activated at this point.
2. **EO01** - The canister purge solenoid display will be "LO" when the solenoid is on (energized).
3. **EO02** - The viscous converter clutch (VCC) display will be "LO" when the solenoid is energized.
4. **EO03** - The EFE relay display will be "LO" when the relay is energized.

5. **EO04** - The EGR solenoid display will be "LO" when the solenoid is energized.
6. **EO05** - The air switch solenoid display will be "LO" when the solenoid is energized.
7. **EO06** - The air divert solenoid display will be "LO" when the solenoid is energized.
8. **EO07** - The ISC motor display will be "LO" when the plunger is retracting and "HI" during its extension.
9. **EO99** - This test displays "CYCLE ALL" as all outputs are cycled at this point.

BCM OUTPUT DIPLAYS

1. **BO00** - The NO OUTPUTS display will not display "HI" nor "LO" as this is a resting spot where no outputs will be cycled.
2. **BO01** - The cruise control vent solenoid display is "HI" when the vent solenoid is on (energized). The cruise ON/OFF switch must be on and the engine off for this output to cycle.
3. **BO02** - The cruise control vacuum solenoid display is "HI" when the vacuum solenoid is on (energized). The cruise ON/OFF switch must be ON and the engine OFF for this output to cycle.
4. **BO03** - The retained accessory power (RAP) relays display is "LO" when the relays are ON (energized).
5. **BO04** - The courtesy relay display is "LO" when the relay is ON (energized).
6. **BO05** - The twilight relays display is "LO" when the relays are ON (energized) with the lights ON.
7. **BO06** - The HI/LO beam relays display is "LO" when the relays are ON (energized) with the high beams ON.

OVERRIDE DISPLAYS

Override displays are operated as defined under the heading "Operating The Service Mode". When troubleshooting a malfunction, the BCM override feature allows testing of certain system functions regardless of normal program instructions.

Upon selecting a test, that function's current operation will be represented as a percentage of its full range and this value will be displayed on the ECC panel. The display will alternate between "--" for 1 second followed by he normal program value for 10 seconds. This alternating display is a reminder that the function is not currently being overriden.

Touching the "WARM" or "COOL" buttons on the ECC panel begins the override at which time the display will no longer alternate to "--". Touching the "WARM" button increases the value while the "COOL" button decreases the value. Upon release of the button, the display may either remain at the override value or automatically return to normal program control. This depends on which function is being overriden at the time. If the display remains at the override value, normal program control can be resumed in one of three ways:

1. Selection of another override test will cancel the current override.
2. Selection of another system will cancel the current override.
3. Overriding the value beyond either extreme (0 or 99) will display "--" momentarily and then jump to the opposite extreme. If the button is released while "--" is displayed, normal program control will resume and the display will again alternate.

The override test type is unique in that any other test type within the selected system may be active at the same time. After selecting an override test, touching the "OFF" button will allow selection of another test type and test, while at the same time touching the "WARM" or "COOL" button, it is possible to monitor the effect of the override on different vehicle parameters.

1. **BS00** - This test will display "none" as no overrides are active at this point.

2. **BS01** - The program number override can be controlled from "0" (Max A/C) to "99" (Max heat). The display will hold the override value upon release of the buttons.

3. **BS02** - The vacuum fluorescent (VF) dimming override can be controlled from "0" (Max dim) to "99" (Max bright). The display will hold the override value upon release of the buttons.

4. **BS03** - The incandescent bulb-dimming override can be controlled from "0" (Max dim) to "99" (Max bright) if the park lamps have been turned on. The display will hold the override value upon release of the buttons.

5. **BS04** - The cooling fans override will control to "0" (fan OFF) or "99" (MAX fan) as long as the button is held. Normal control will resume upon release of the button.

6. **BS06** - The generator disable override will control to "0" (generator ON) or "99" (generator disabled) as long as the button is held. Normal control will resume upon release of the buttons.

SET TIMING MODE

The set timing mode is used to tell the ECM to control the spark timing to the ten degree BTDC base timing setting, to permit verification and setting of spark timing. The ECM has a SET TIMING request line that goes to the ALDL connector terminal "B". The set timing mode is requested as follows:

1. Place the transmission in the Park (P) position and block the drive wheels. Start the engine and allow it to idle until the coolant temperature reaches 85°C.

2. Verify that the engine is idling at less than 900 rpm. If in the diagnostics mode, exit the diagnostics by pressing "OFF" on the CCDIC until the CCDIC is back in the standard climate control mode.

3. Using a suitable jumper wire, jumper pin **B** of the ALDL to ALDL pin **A** (ground).

    a. The ECM will command the BCM to display a message "SET TIMING" on the CCDIC.

    b. The engine will operate at base timing.

    c. Timing can now be checked with a standard timing light, it should be set to 10 degrees BTDC.

4. To exit the SET TIMING mode, remove the ground from pin **B** of the ALDL connector and verify proper display operation.

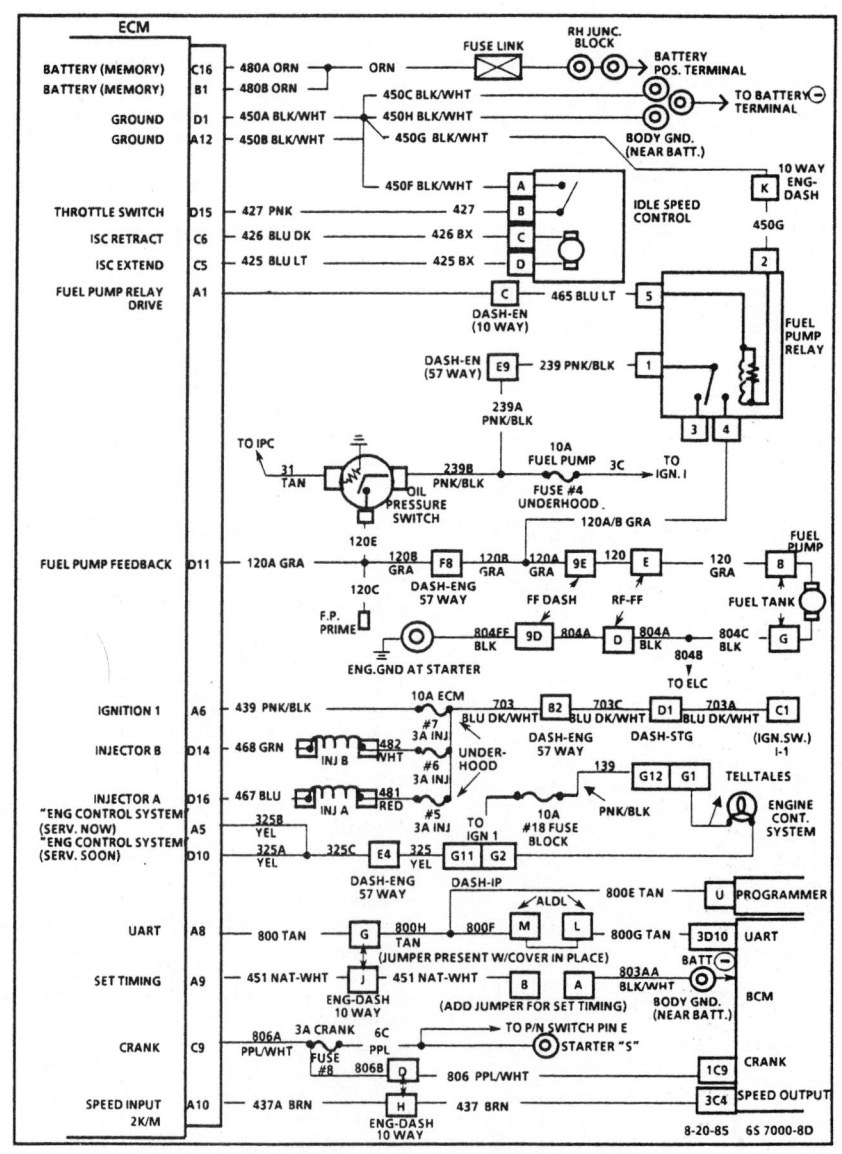

ECM wiring diagram A—Elodorado and Seville

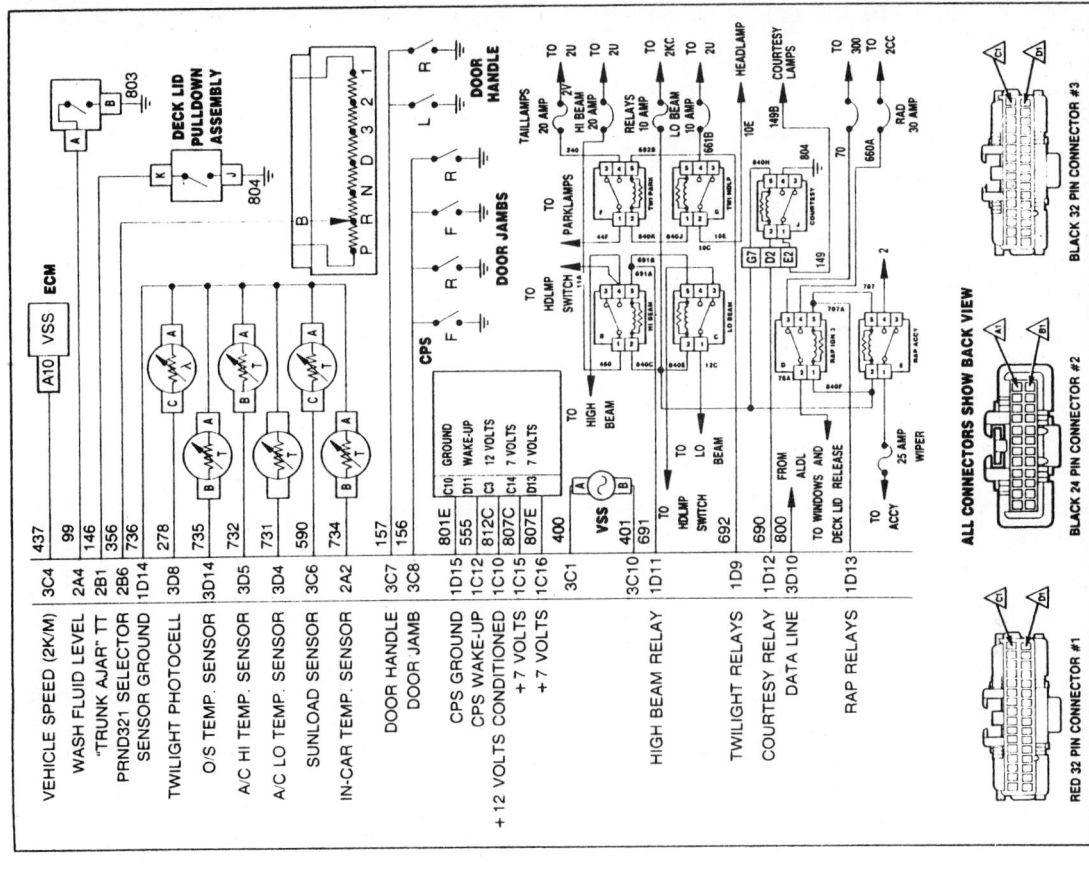

Exploded view of the BCM connector—Eldorado and Seville

ALL CONNECTORS SHOW BACK VIEW

BLACK 32 PIN CONNECTOR #3

BLACK 24 PIN CONNECTOR #2

RED 32 PIN CONNECTOR #1

ECM wiring diagram B—Elodorado and Seville

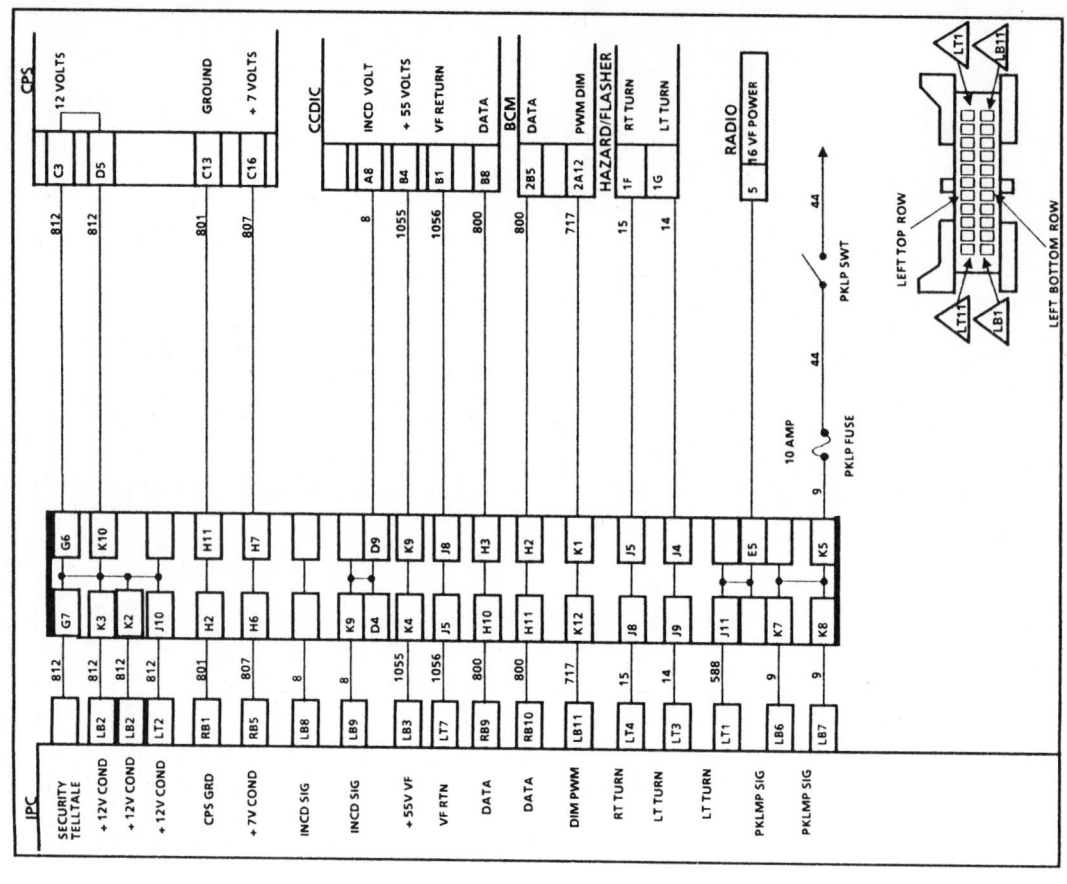

Exploded view of the BCM IPC connector—Eldorado and Seville

Exploded view of the BCM connector—Eldorado and Seville (cont.)

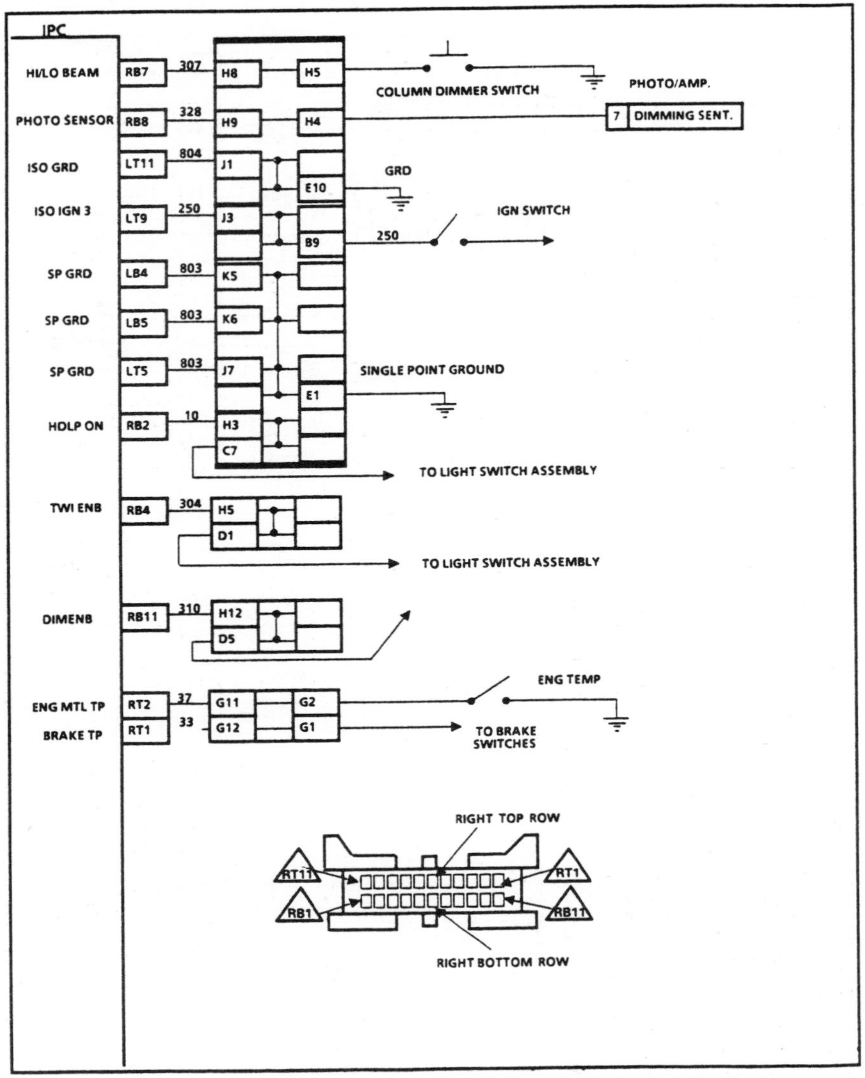

ECM P1 (A/B)

CIRCUIT DESCRIPTION	CIRCUIT NUMBER		CIRCUIT NUMBER	CIRCUIT DESCRIPTION
BATTERY (MEMORY)	480B		465	FUEL PUMP RELAY DRIVE
BRAKE SWITCH	420A		428	CANISTER PURGE SOLENOID
DIST. REF. LOW	453F		—	SPARE
SPARE	—		435	EGR SOLENOID
DIST. REF. HIGH	430BS		325B	ENGINE CONTROL SYS. (SERV. NOW)
SPARE	—		439	IGNITION-1 (CLEAN IGN)
SPARE	—		422A	VCC SOLENOID
SPARE	—		800	UART (DATA LINK)
PARK/NEUTRAL SWITCH	434		451	SET TIMING REQUEST
SPARE	—		437A	VEHICLE SPEED — 2K/MI FROM BCM
SPARE	—		—	SPARE
TRANS. TEMP.	520		450B	POWER GROUND

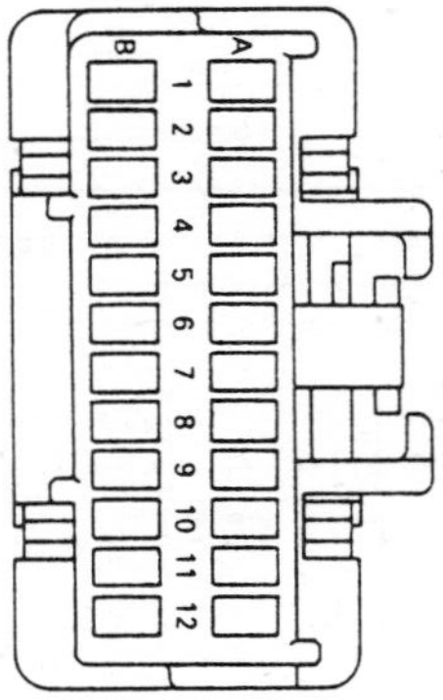

ECM P2 (C/D)

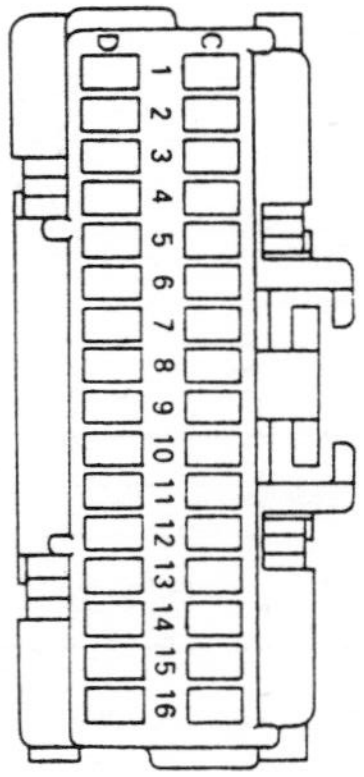

CIRCUIT DESCRIPTION	CIRCUIT NUMBER		CIRCUIT NUMBER	CIRCUIT DESCRIPTION
POWER GROUND	450A		429	AIR DIVERT
EFE RELAY DRIVE	445		436	AIR SWITCH
ELEC. SYS. INDICATOR	325		—	SPARE
EST	423		—	SPARE
HEI BYPASS	424		425BX	ISC EXTEND
OXYGEN SENSOR LOW	413		426BX	ISC RETRACT
OXYGEN SENSOR HIGH	412		438	3RD GEAR SWITCH
SPARE	—		446	4TH GEAR SWITCH
POWER STEERING PRES. SW.	495		806A	CRANK
ENG. CONTROL SYS. (SERV. SOON)	325A		410PC	COOLANT TEMP
FUEL PUMP FEEDBACK	120A		432A	MAP SENSOR
5 VOLT RETURN (MAP/MAT)	476A		472PM	MAT SENSOR
5 VOLT RETURN (TPS/COOL)	476B		417A	TPS SENSOR
INJECTOR B	468		474A	5 VOLT REF. (MAP TPS)
THROTTLE SWITCH	427		—	SPARE
INJECTOR A	467		480A	BATTERY (MEMORY)

Exploded view of the ECM connectors

Exploded view of the BCM IPC connector—Eldorado and Seville

IPC

H/LO BEAM	RB7	307	H5
PHOTO SENSOR	RB8	328	H8 / H9
ISO GRD	LT11	804	H4 / J1
ISO IGN 3	LT9	250	J3
SP GRD	LB4	803	K5
SP GRD	LB5	803	K6
SP GRD	LT5	803	J7
HDLP ON	RB2	10	H3 / C7
TWI ENB	RB4	304	H5 / D1
DIMENB	RB11	310	H12 / D5
ENG MTL TP	RT2	37	G11 / G2
BRAKE TP	RT1	33	G12 / G1

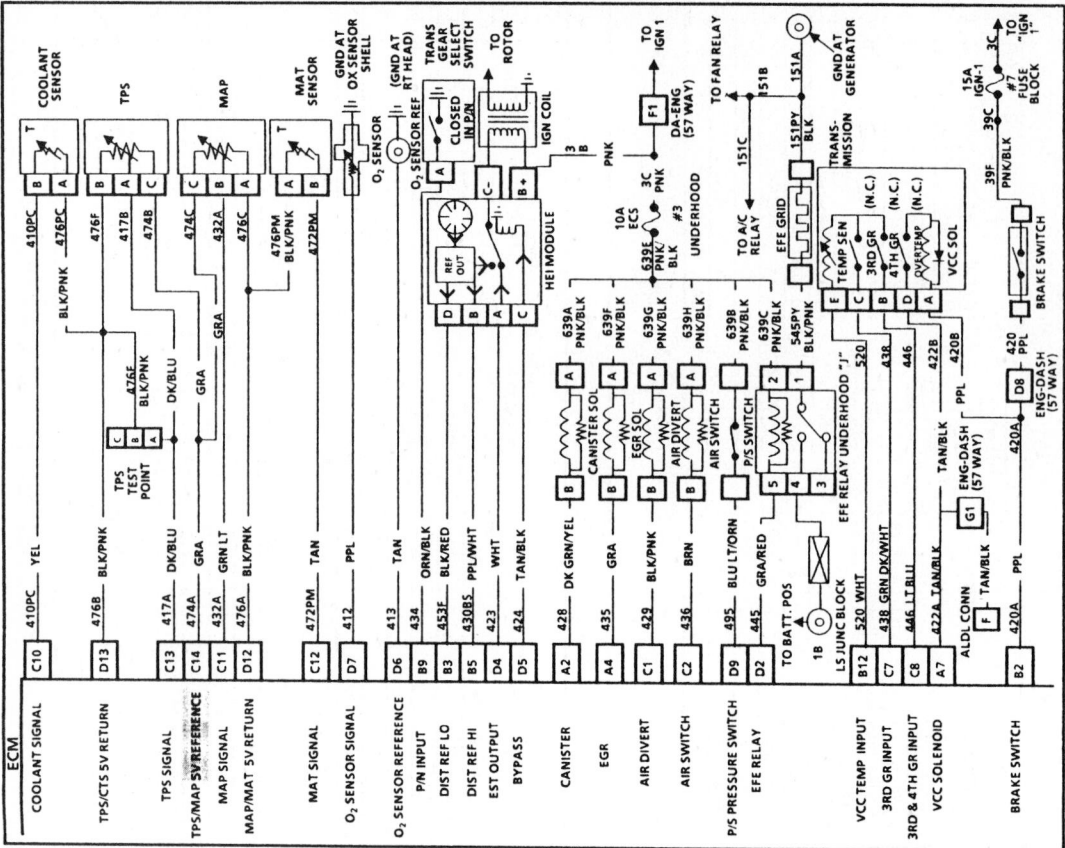

ECM wiring diagram B—Eldorado and Seville

ECM wiring diagram A—Eldorado and Seville

DFI TROUBLE DIAGNOSTICS

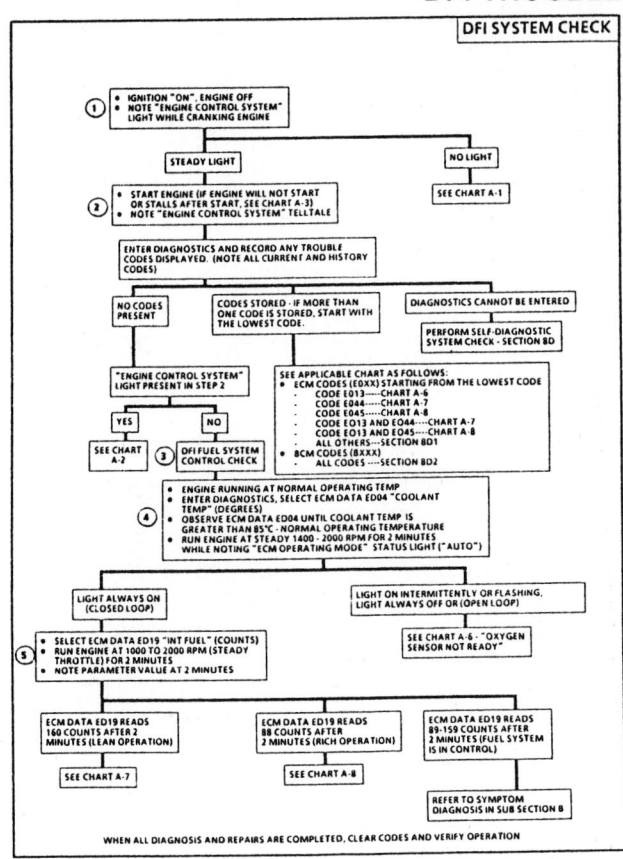

DFI SYSTEM CHECK

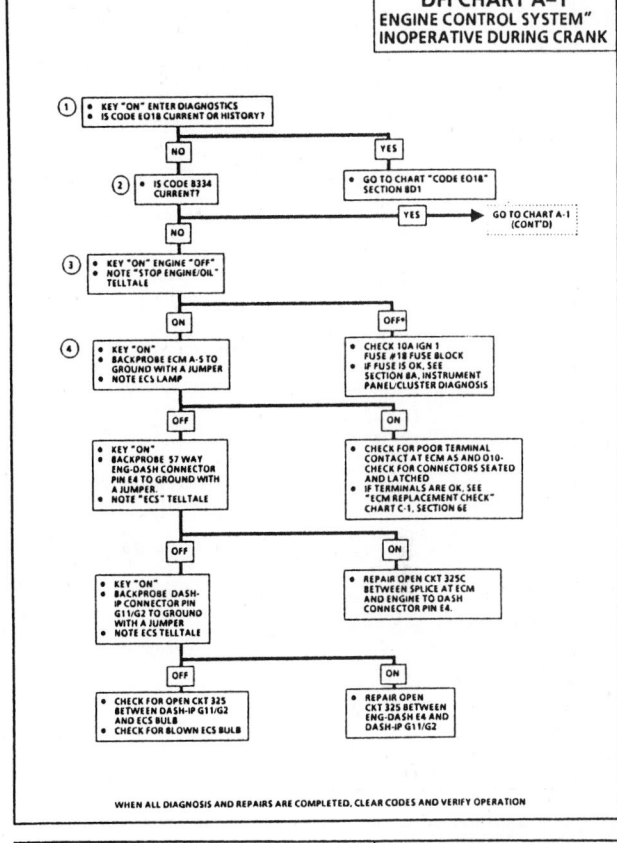

DFI CHART A-1
ENGINE CONTROL SYSTEM"
INOPERATIVE DURING CRANK

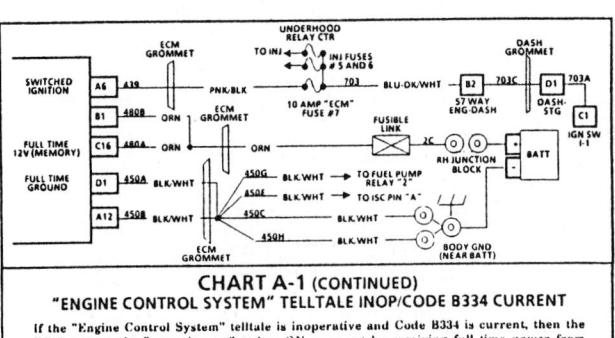

CHART A-1 (CONTINUED)
"ENGINE CONTROL SYSTEM" TELLTALE INOP/CODE B334 CURRENT

If the "Engine Control System" telltale is inoperative and Code B334 is current, then the ECM may not be "powering up" at key ON, may not be receiving full time power from battery or may be damaged due to electrical overload or water intrusion.

Notes on Chart A-1 (Cont):

1. Checking for switched ignition power to ECM.

2. Checking for ground to ECM. Pin A12 and Pin D1 are redundant grounds - if either ground is OK, the ECM should be able to operate normally. If both grounds are open, the ECM will not power up.

3. Checking for full time memory voltage supply to ECM. Pin C16 and B1 are redundant power supplies to the ECM. If either power supply is OK, the ECM can operate normally.

4. If power, grounds and connections are OK then be sure to perform Chart C-1 before replacing ECM. The ECM may have been damaged by electrical overload due to a low resistance component.

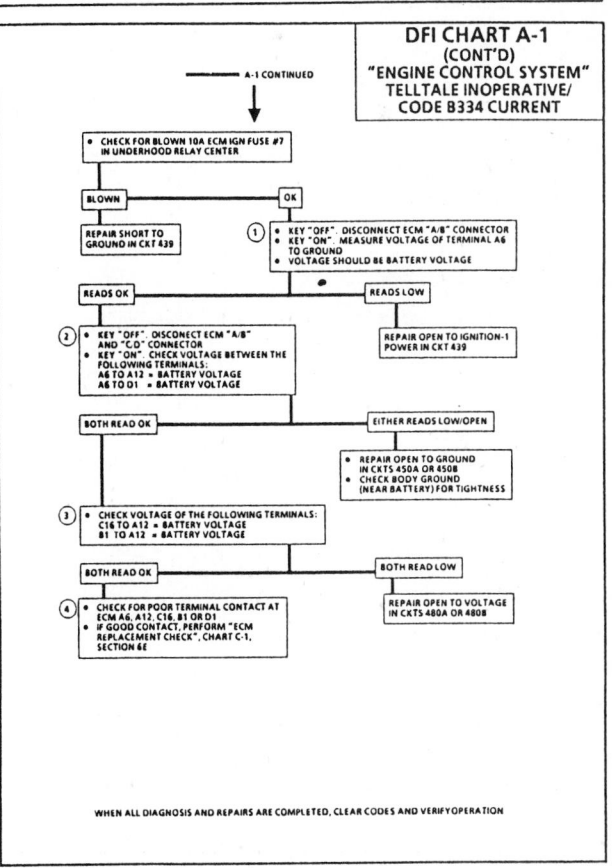

DFI CHART A-1
(CONT'D)
"ENGINE CONTROL SYSTEM"
TELLTALE INOPERATIVE/
CODE B334 CURRENT

DFI TROUBLE DIAGNOSTICS

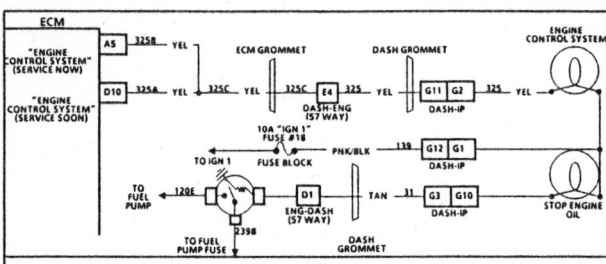

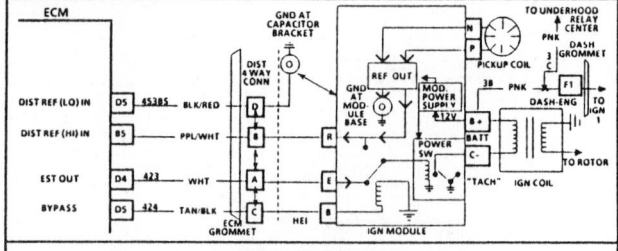

CHART A-2
"ENGINE CONTROL SYSTEM" TELLTALE ON, NO CODES PRESENT

DESCRIPTION:

The "Engine Control System" lamp is powered through the 10 AMP "Ign-1" Fuse 18 in the fuse block and grounded by the ECM Pin "A5" (Service Now) or Pin "D10" (Service Soon) to illuminate. The ECS telltale will bulb check at key on, is illuminated steadily during cranking and is illuminated whenever a trouble code with Service Now or Service Soon message is set.

ECM Pin "A5" is turned on in conjunction with a code with Service Now message. If a Service Now trouble code is set, the ECM will send a Service Now status to the BCM over the UART data link. At the same time, the ECM grounds Pin "A5" to turn on the "ENGINE CONTROL SYSTEM" telltale. ECM Pin "D10" is turned on in conjunction with a code with Service Soon message. If a Service Soon trouble code is set, the ECM will send a Service Soon status to the BCM over the UART data link. At the same time, the ECM grounds pin D10 to turn on the "ENGINE CONTROL SYSTEM" telltale.

The "Engine Control System" telltale will flicker when Pin "A" and Pin "B" of the ALDL connector are jumpered together to enter set timing mode. (In set timing mode the message "Set Timing" will be displayed on the CCDIC.)

Notes on Chart A-2

1. Loose grounds or power connections intermittent can cause the ECM to repeatedly power-up then power-down or to "reset".

2. Checking for bulb grounded by ECM through Pin "A5","D10", or through a circuit fault.

3. Remove and replace both ECM connectors and ensure that they are latched. Check the PROM for proper orientation, pins bent, fully seated in the PROM socket. Substitute a test PROM to see if the PROM is causing the light to flicker. If the test PROM does not correct the condition, replace the ECM. Be sure to perform "ECM Replacement Check", Chart C-1. The ECM may be damaged due to electrical overload from a low resistance component.

DFI CHART A-3
NO START OR STALL AFTER START

All internal combustion engines require spark, fuel, air, and proper timing to operate. DFI is no different. If the battery is at the proper charge level, the first step should be to determine which of these elements is missing.

Notes on Fault Tree:

1. Checking for codes stored and for proper "Engine Control System" lamp operation. Repair stored codes and improper telltale operation before proceeding with Chart A-3.

2. Injectors should spray only when the engine is cranking or running. Look for spray, drips or leaks at key on/engine off.

3. Checking for both injectors to spray fuel while cranking.

4. Fuel is OK, checking for spark. Note: Use an ST 125 to test. A spark plug with a wide gap or allowing a plug wire to arc to ground may not test the HEI for sufficient output and may damage the coil, cap or rotor.

5. This step bypasses the EST system. If the vehicle will start and run with the EST system disabled (Bypass open), then the "No Start" condition may be due to an EST system fault. If the ECM has a poor ground

to the engine or if the distributor has a poor ground connection to the ECM, the distributor may not be able to recognize EST pulses and the engine will stall as the ECM tries to enable EST (use EST to control spark timing).

6. If the vehicle will not start, then the fuel system must be checked next. Connect the J-25400-300 Fuel Pressure gage and observe fuel pressure while cranking. The gage should be installed in the fuel inlet line at the service fitting. A fuel pressure reading of between 9-12 PSI during cranking indicates that the fuel system is operating properly. Improper fuel pressure indicates a fuel problem, refer to Chart A-4 "Fuel System Diagnosis".

Since we now have spark and fuel spray from both injectors at the correct fuel pressure, all DFI functions for starting are operating normally. The cause of the no start condition is a mechanical problem (spark plugs, valves, valve timing, etc.). See also Subsection B, "Hard Start" and "Stall After Start" for diagnosis.

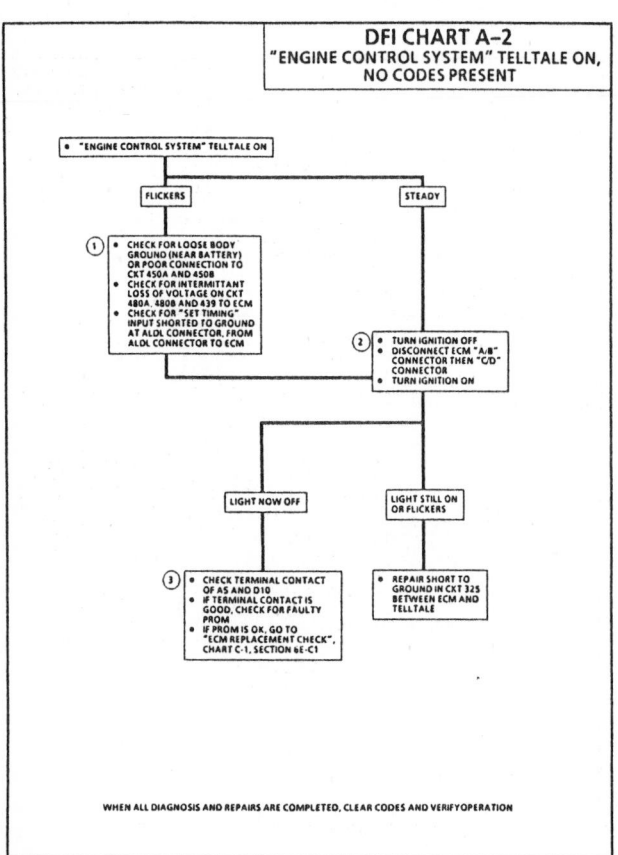

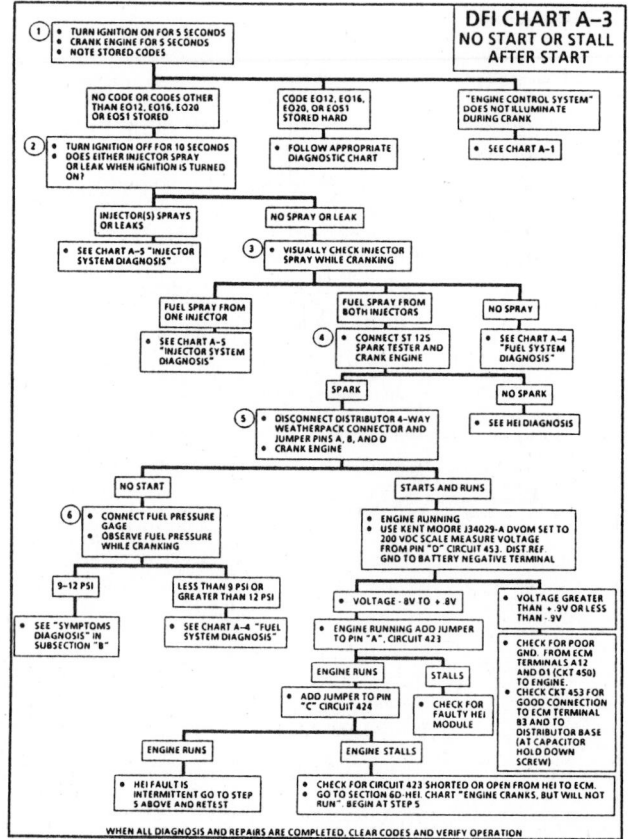

DFI TROUBLE DIAGNOSTICS

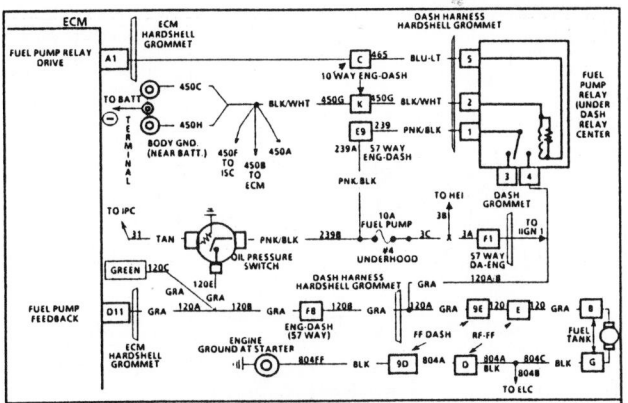

DFI CHART A-4
FUEL SYSTEM DIAGNOSIS

This procedure tests for fuel supply system problems that can cause incorrect fuel pressure or incorrect fuel pump operation.

Notes on Fault Tree:

1. The fuel pressure gage J-25400-300 should be installed at the fuel line service fitting. Measure the fuel pressure while cranking the engine. If the fuel pressure is between 9.0 and 12.0 PSI, then refer to the performance diagnosis chart A-5, "Injector System Diagnosis".

2. If the fuel pump relay or ECM were the cause of a low fuel pressure, there would be an ECM code EO20 set. This step is to check for voltage supply to the fuel tank four-way connector.

3. If the voltage signal to the fuel tank connector is OK, then an open may exist between the four-way fuel tank connector and the fuel pump. If fuel pump runs with an alternative power source connected, the fuel tank unit is OK; check throttle body fuel metering assembly for cause of low pressure.

4. Checking for fuel supply system (tank, filter, pump, sender, supply line) able to deliver at least 9.0 psi pressure or for throttle body fuel pressure regulator fault.

5. If pressure is low with fuel return line plugged, then throttle body fuel metering assembly is not at fault. A restriction or blockage may exist in the fuel supply system. The fuel supply line should be checked visually for kinks, damage, etc.; the fuel filter element can also restrict flow. Check for proper fuel line routing as shown in Section 6C under the heading "Fuel Tank and Fuel Lines". Check sender tubes for restrictions, check for rubber coupler between pump and sender leaking or restricted, check for fuel strainer in tank collapsed, mispositioned or restricted. If all of the above are OK, replace the fuel pump.

6. Fuel pressure above 12.0 psi is caused either by a malfunction of the pressure regulator or by a restriction in the fuel return line. It should be noted that a secondary condition of spark plug fouling, code EO45 or oxygen sensor contamination resulting in Coded EO13 accompanied by EO45 may result from the too rich fuel flow. To isolate the cause of the high fuel pressure, disconnect the return line at the throttle body and connect a suitable fitting to the throttle body which will accept a length of flexible rubber fuel hose. Insert the other end of the hose into a suitable fuel container and observe the fuel pressure as the ignition switch is turned on. If the fuel pressure remains above 12.0 psi, replace the fuel metering assembly -- it is unable to control pressure properly.
If the fuel pressure drops into the correct pressure range of 9.0-12.0 psi, with the fuel return line bypassed, then the fuel return line is restricted. A restricted fuel return line can be diagnosed by visually inspecting the line for kinks, damage, etc. A kink in the Teflon fuel line (braided stainless steel clad) may not be visually obvious.

7. If the fuel pump will not run with externally applied power, the fault is an electrical open in the fuel sender unit wiring to the pump, an open at the RFI suppression connector inside the tank on the pump or a faulty fuel pump. The fuel sending unit must be removed from the vehicle to check.

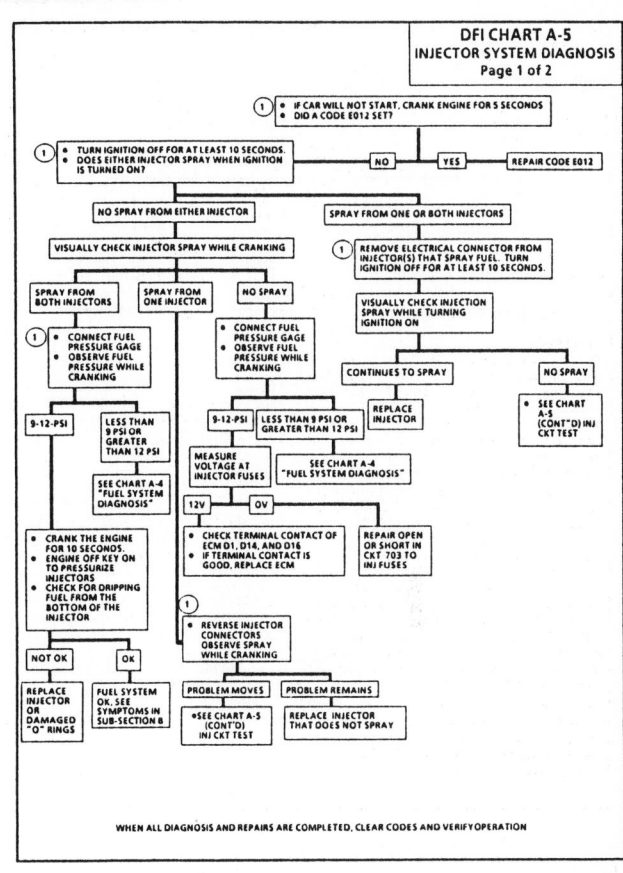

DFI CHART A-5
INJECTOR SYSTEM DIAGNOSIS
Page 1 of 2

WHEN ALL DIAGNOSIS AND REPAIRS ARE COMPLETED, CLEAR CODES AND VERIFY OPERATION

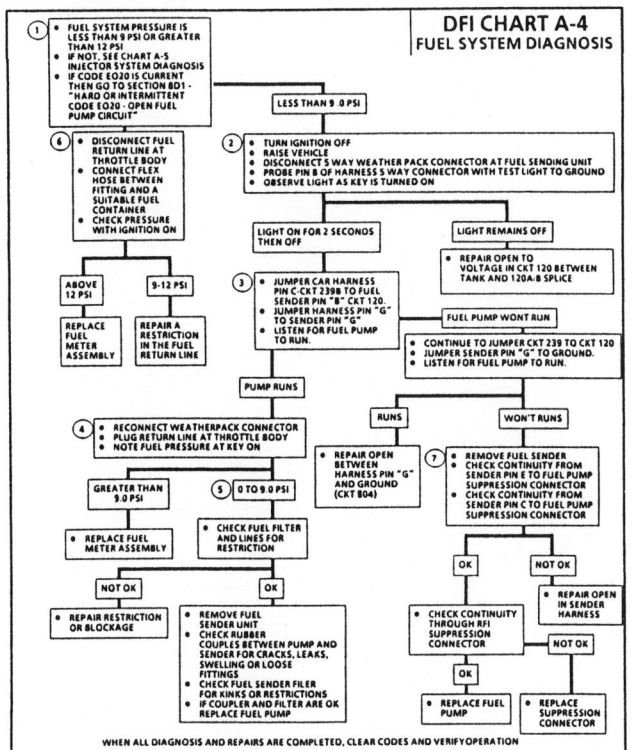

DFI CHART A-4
FUEL SYSTEM DIAGNOSIS

WHEN ALL DIAGNOSIS AND REPAIRS ARE COMPLETED, CLEAR CODES AND VERIFY OPERATION

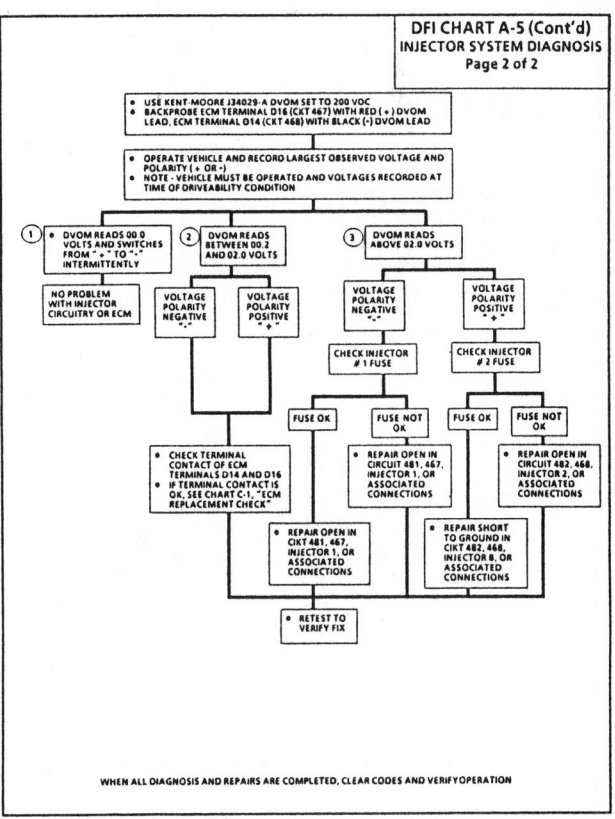

DFI CHART A-5 (Cont'd)
INJECTOR SYSTEM DIAGNOSIS
Page 2 of 2

WHEN ALL DIAGNOSIS AND REPAIRS ARE COMPLETED, CLEAR CODES AND VERIFY OPERATION

DFI TROUBLE DIAGNOSTICS

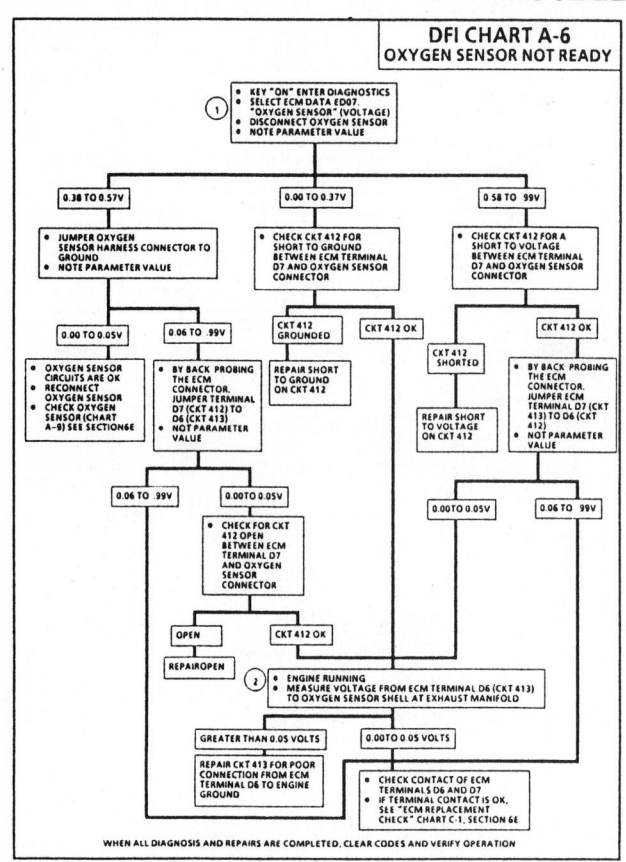

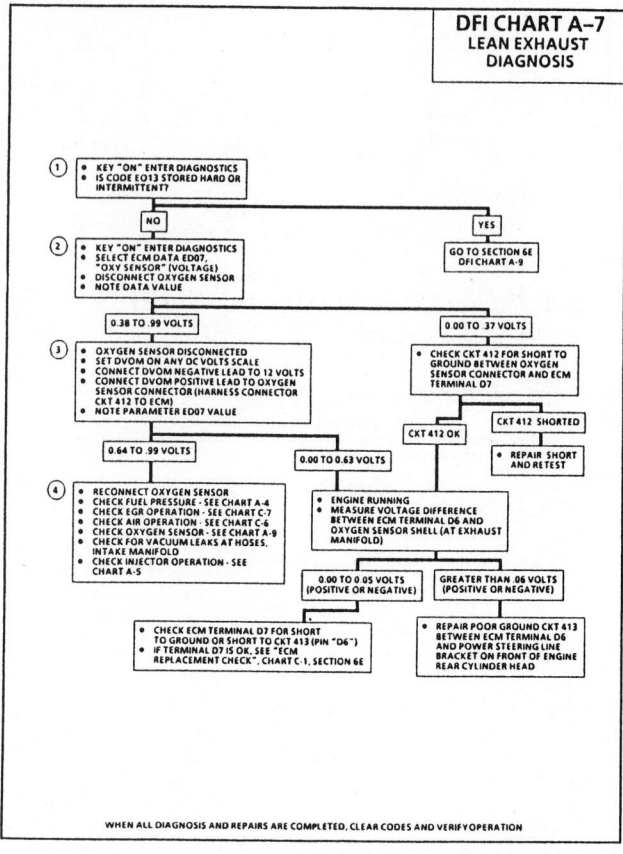

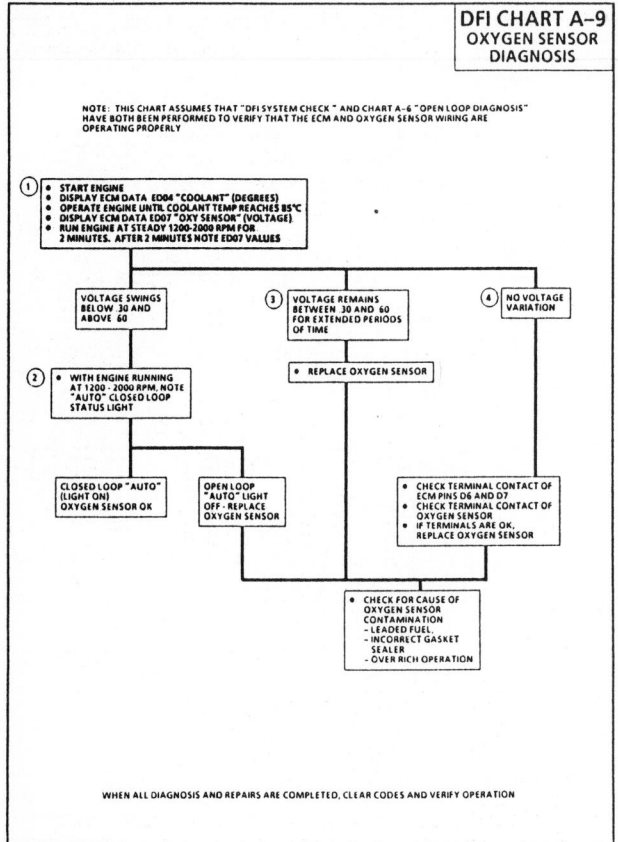

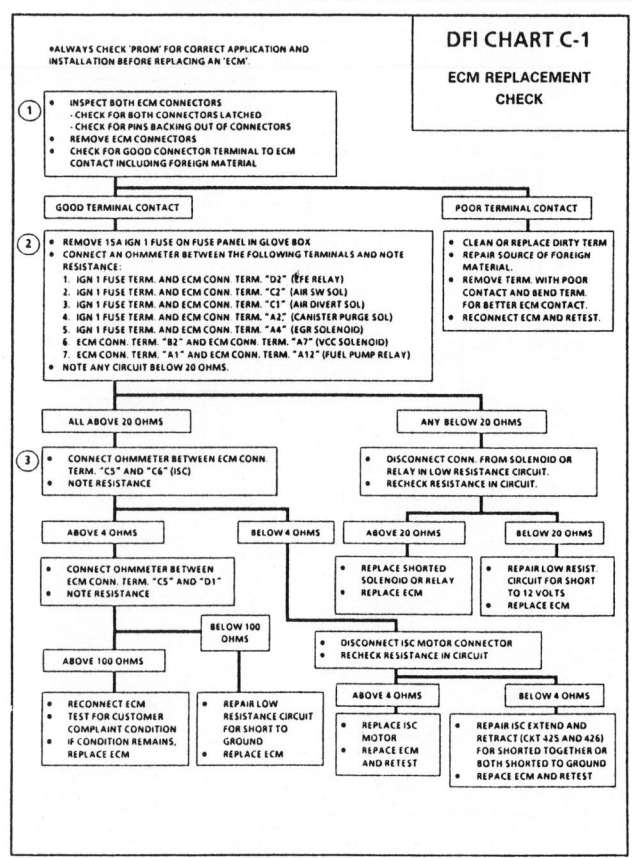

DFI TROUBLE DIAGNOSTICS

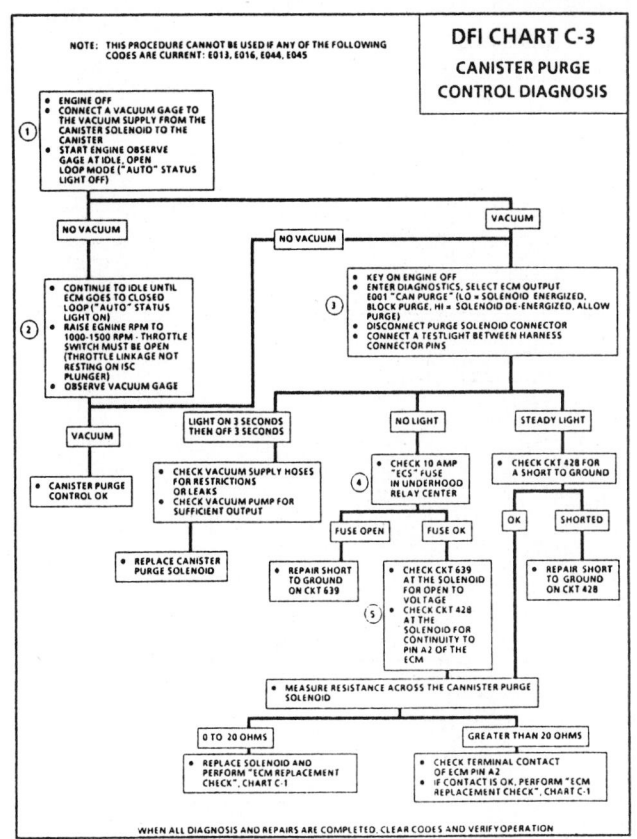

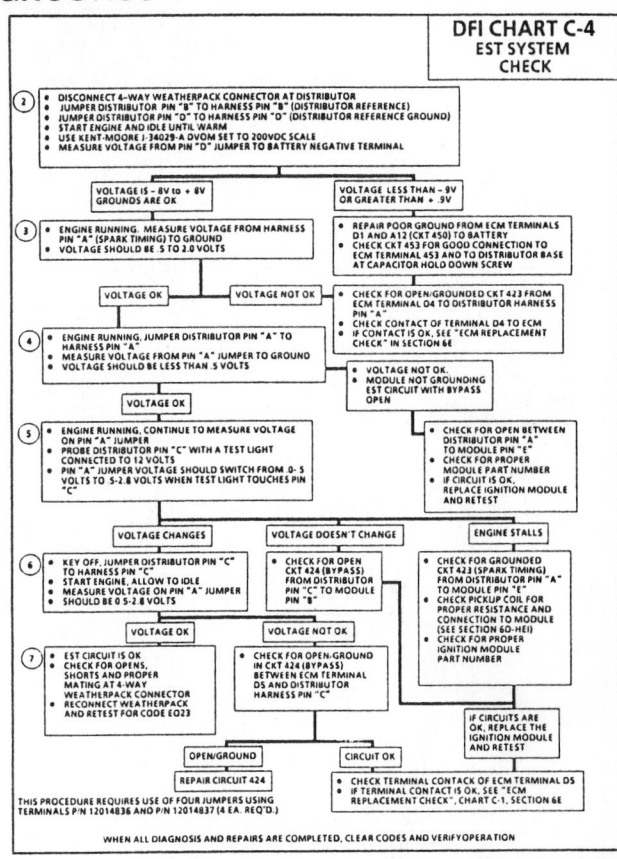

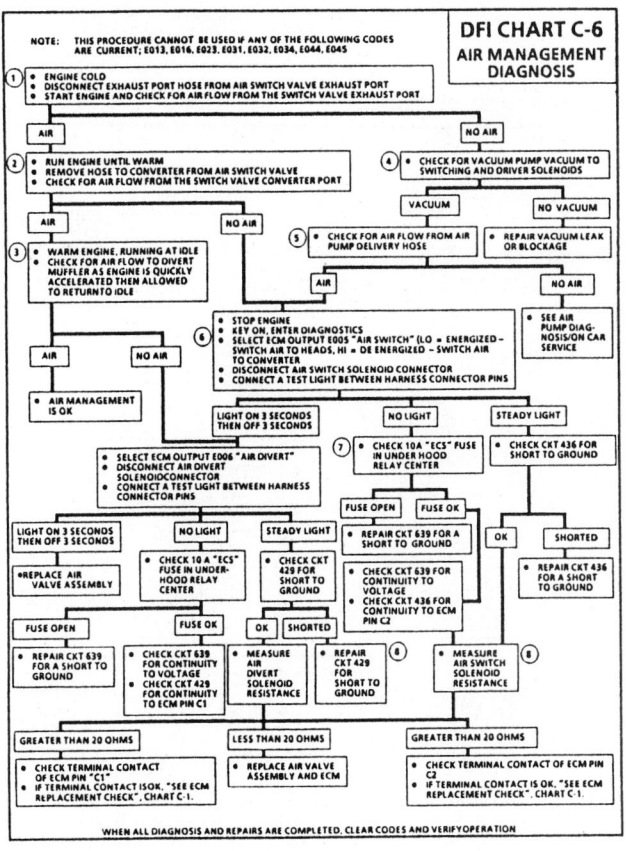

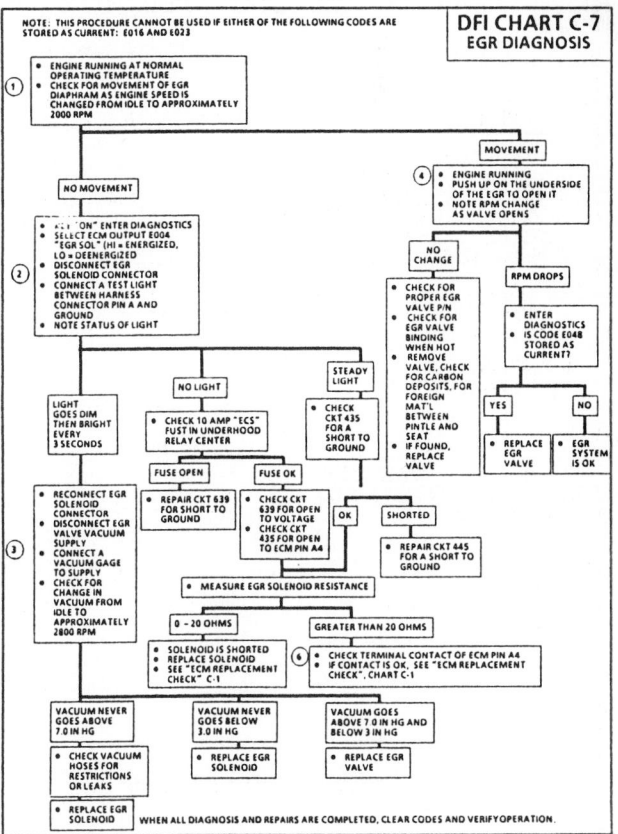

DFI TROUBLE DIAGNOSTICS

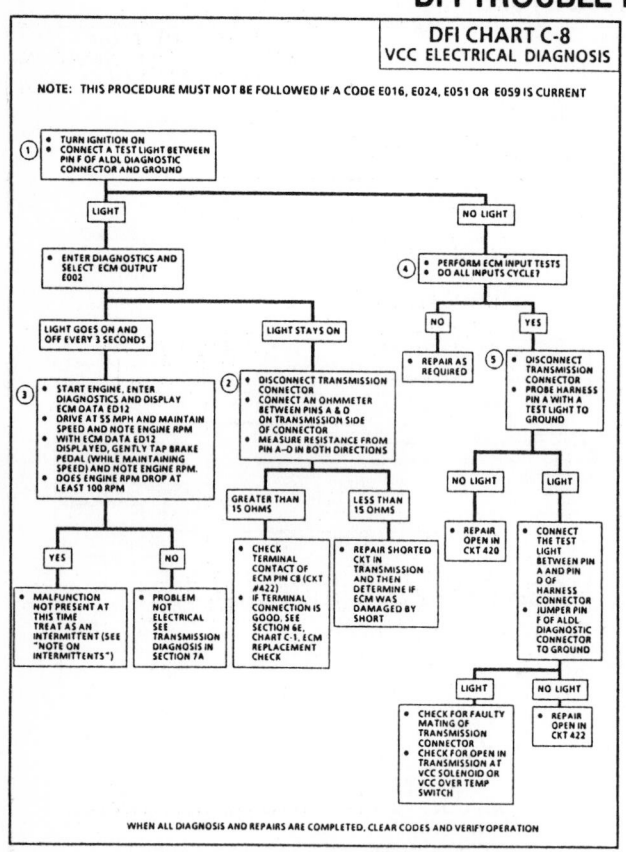

DFI CHART C-8
VCC ELECTRICAL DIAGNOSIS

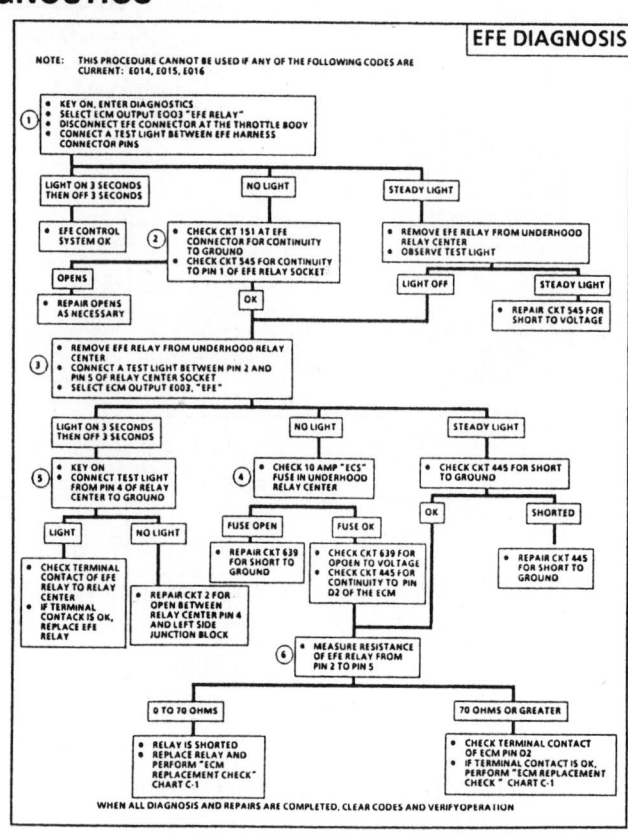

EFE DIAGNOSIS

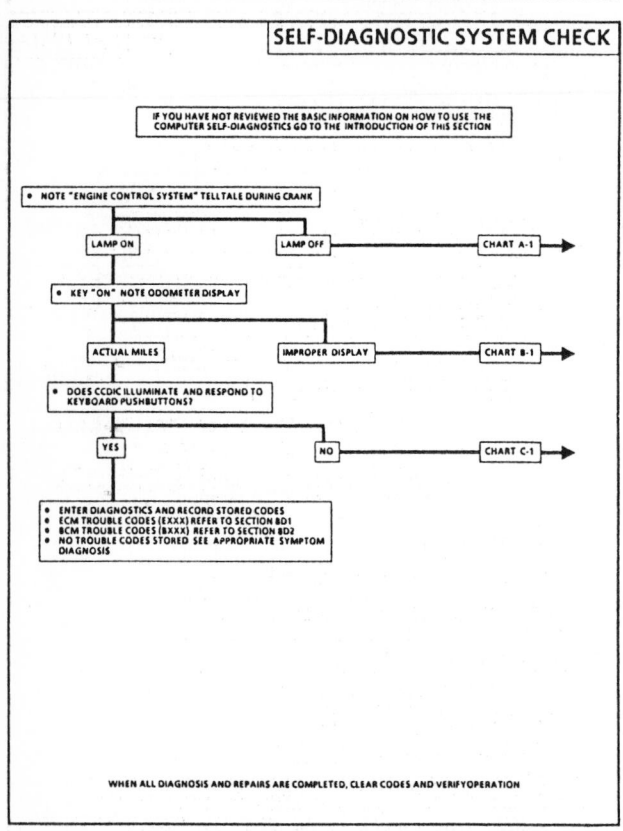

SELF-DIAGNOSTIC SYSTEM CHECK

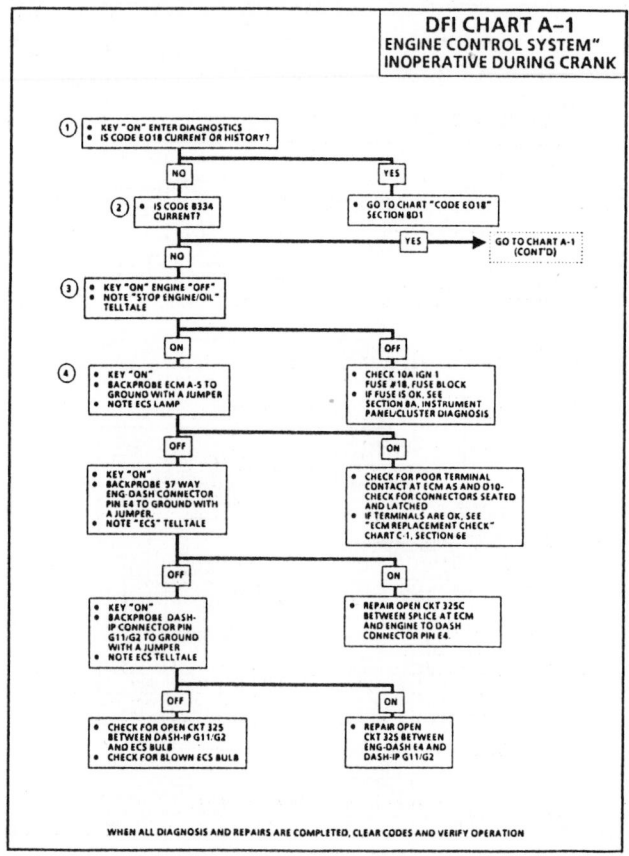

DFI CHART A-1
ENGINE CONTROL SYSTEM
INOPERATIVE DURING CRANK

DFI TROUBLE DIAGNOSTICS

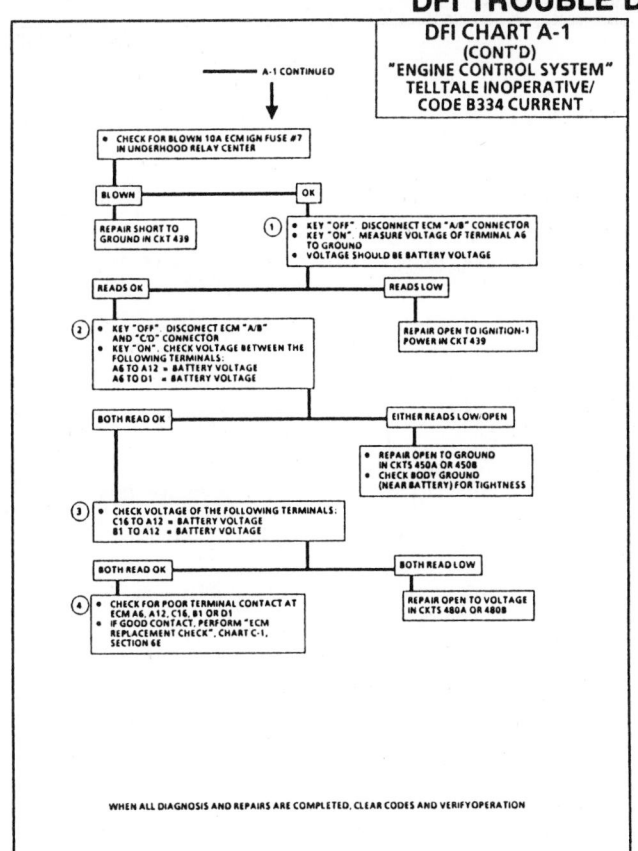

DFI CHART A-1
(CONT'D)
"ENGINE CONTROL SYSTEM"
TELLTALE INOPERATIVE/
CODE B334 CURRENT

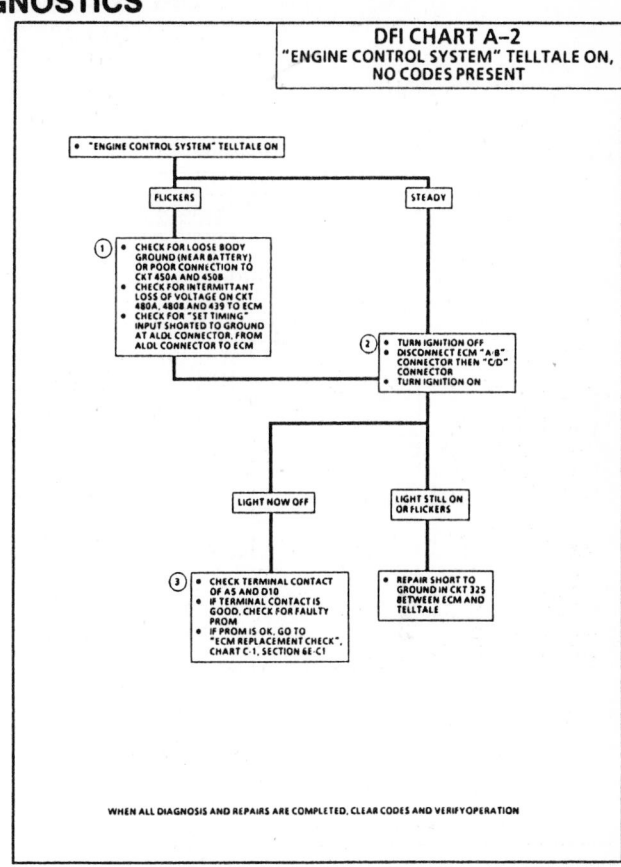

DFI CHART A-2
"ENGINE CONTROL SYSTEM" TELLTALE ON,
NO CODES PRESENT

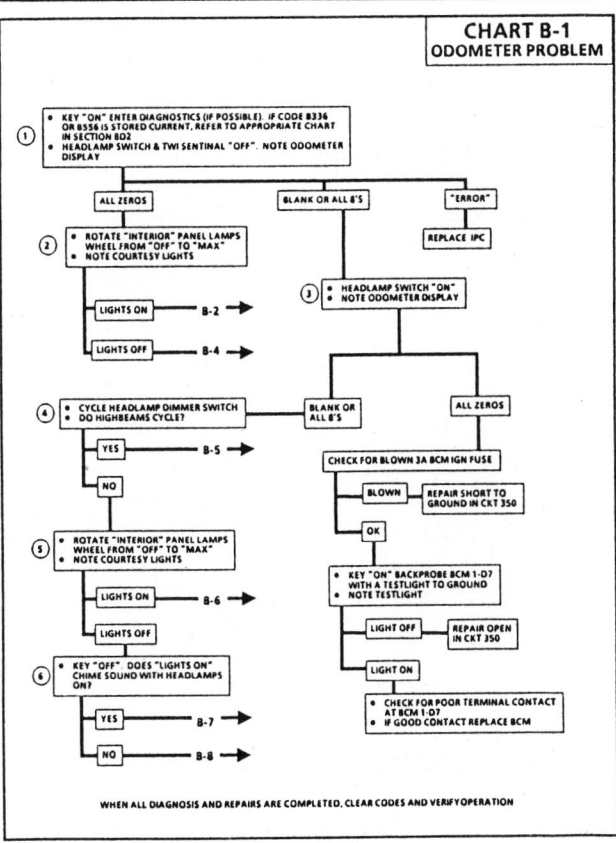

CHART B-1
ODOMETER PROBLEM

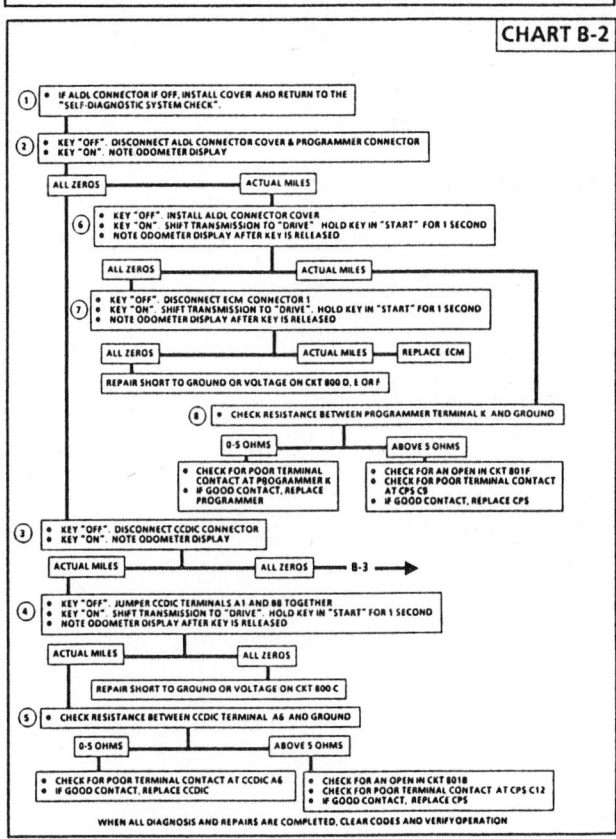

CHART B-2

DFI TROUBLE DIAGNOSTICS

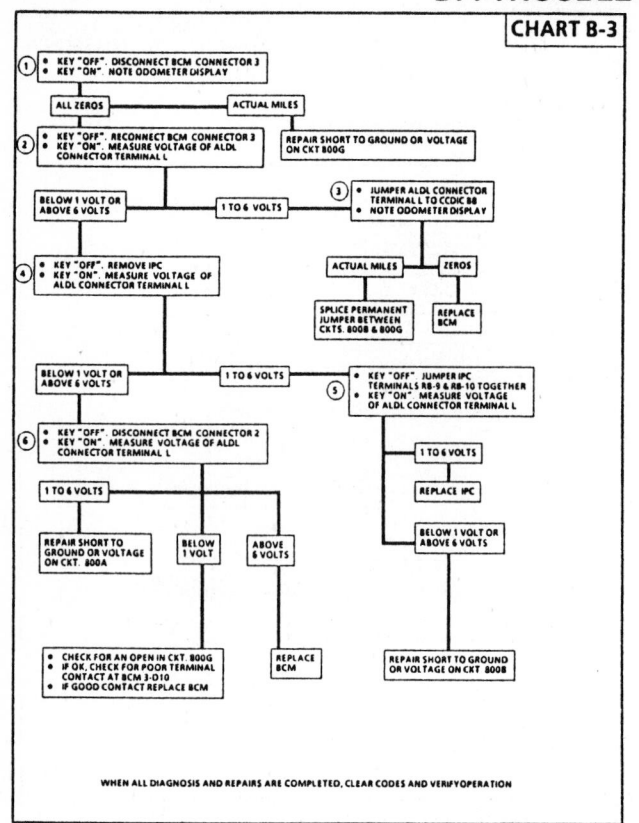

CHART B-3

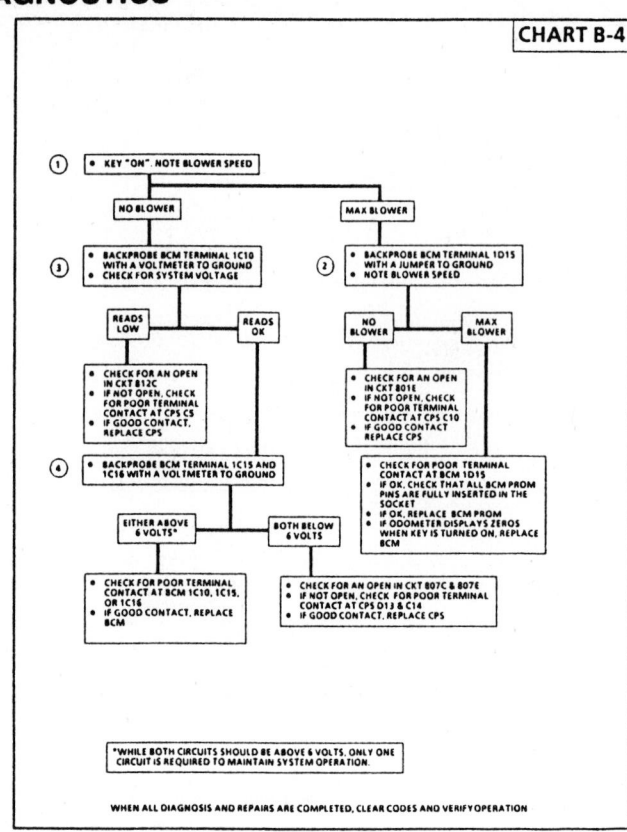

CHART B-4

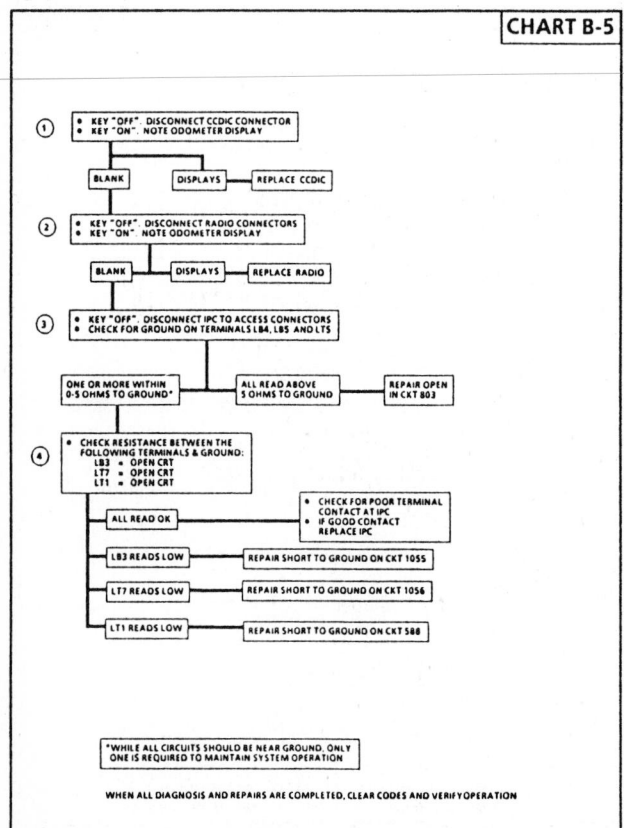

CHART B-5

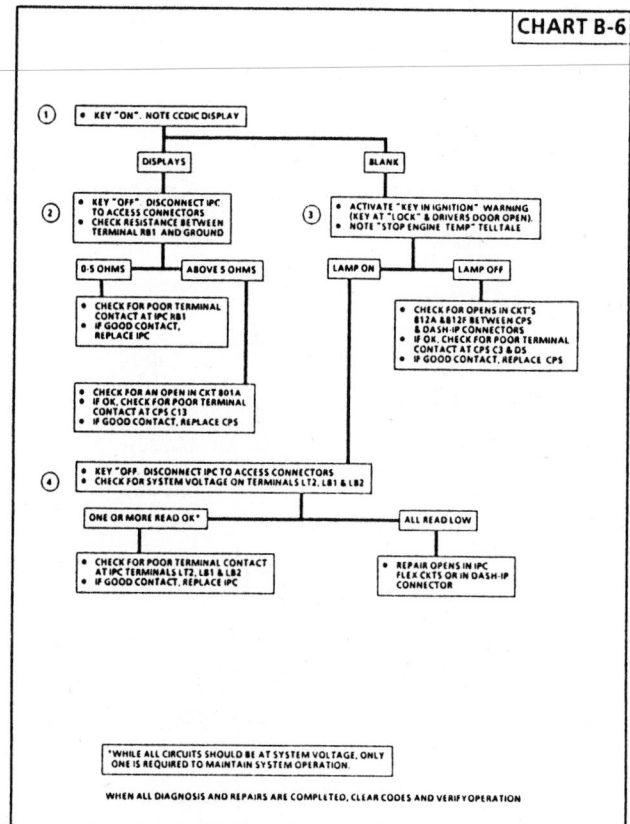

CHART B-6

DFI TROUBLE DIAGNOSTICS

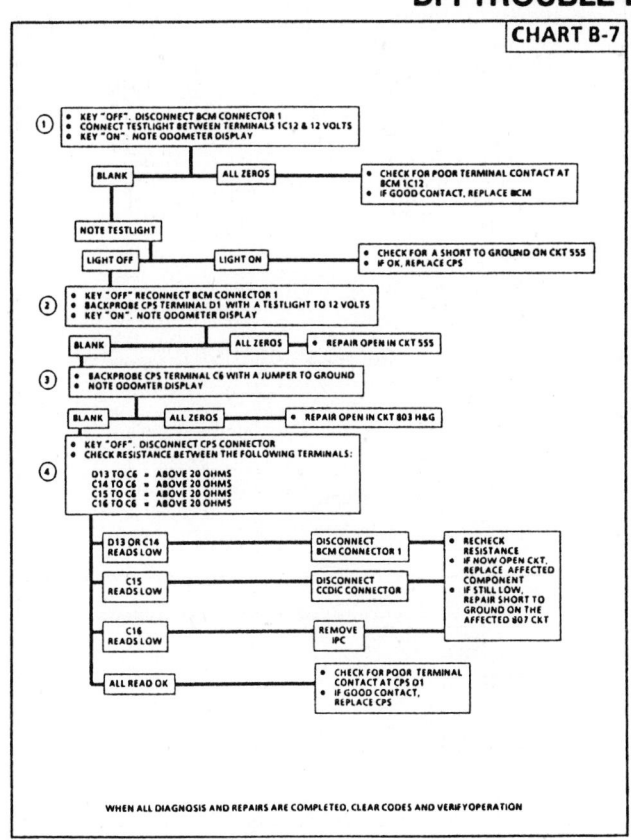

CHART B-7

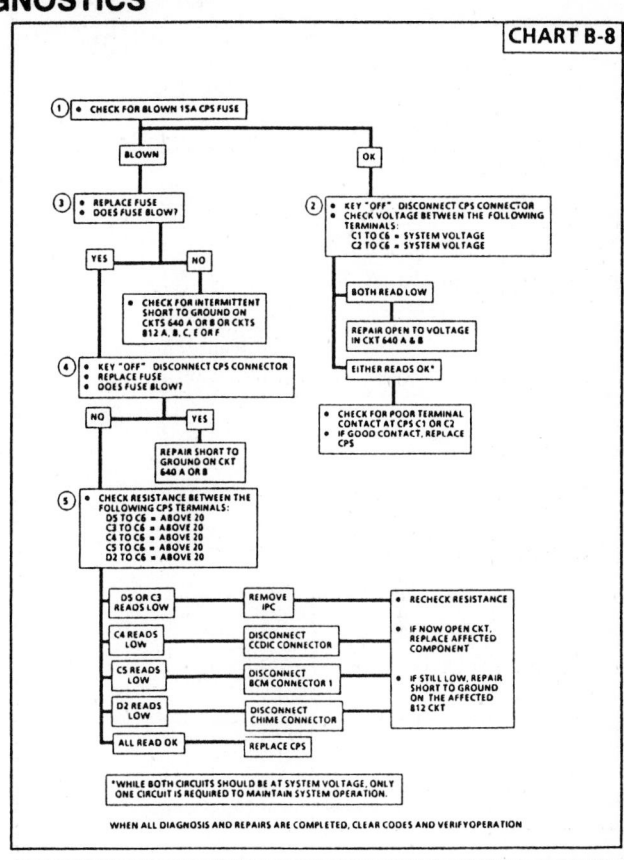

CHART B-8

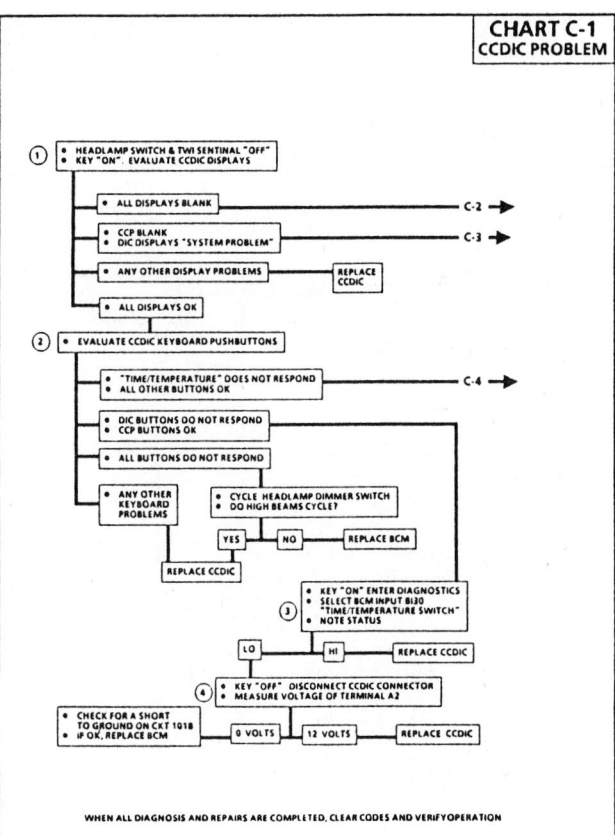

CHART C-1
CCDIC PROBLEM

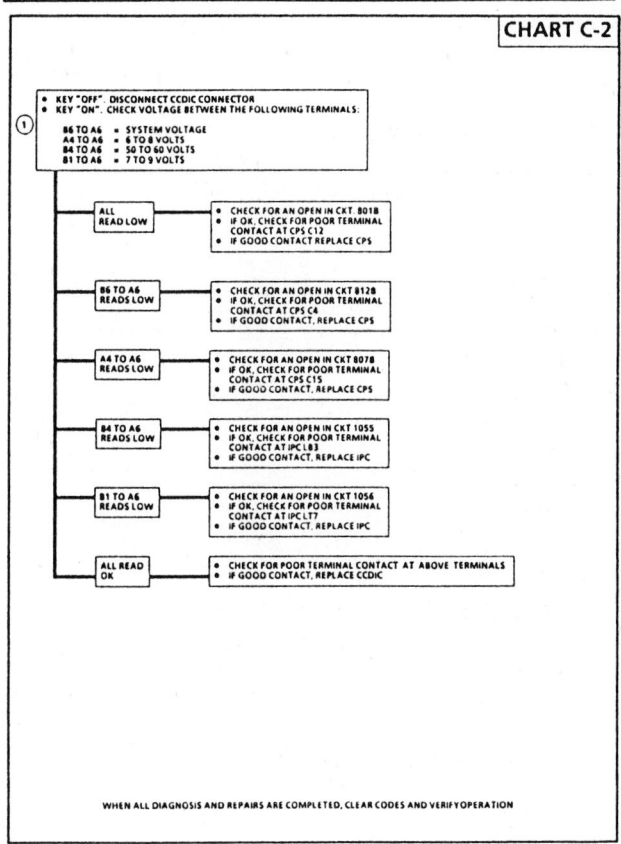

CHART C-2

DFI TROUBLE DIAGNOSTICS

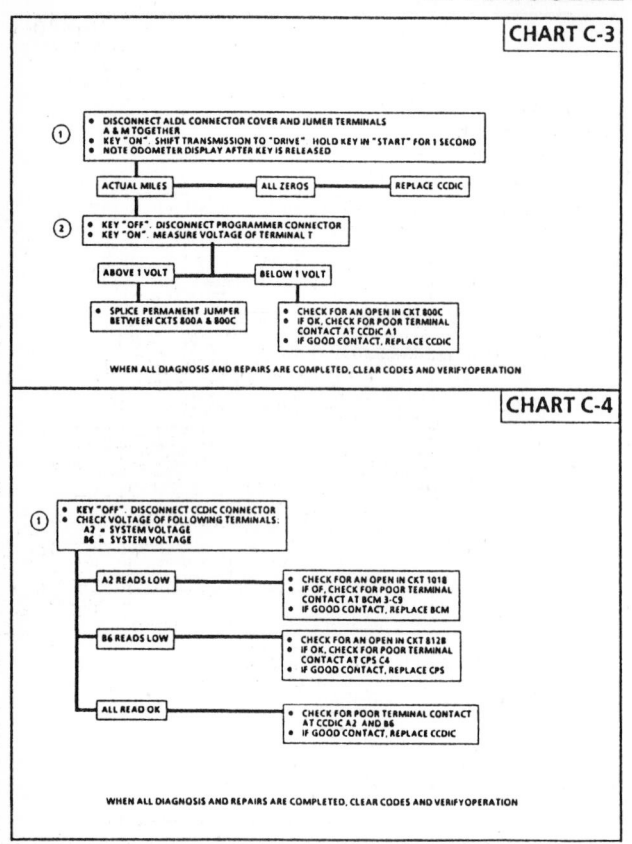

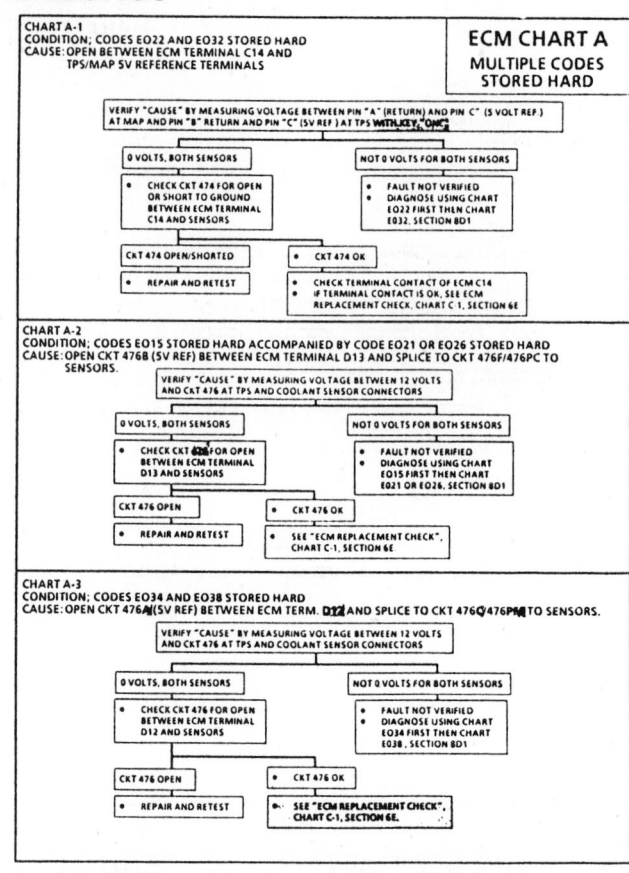

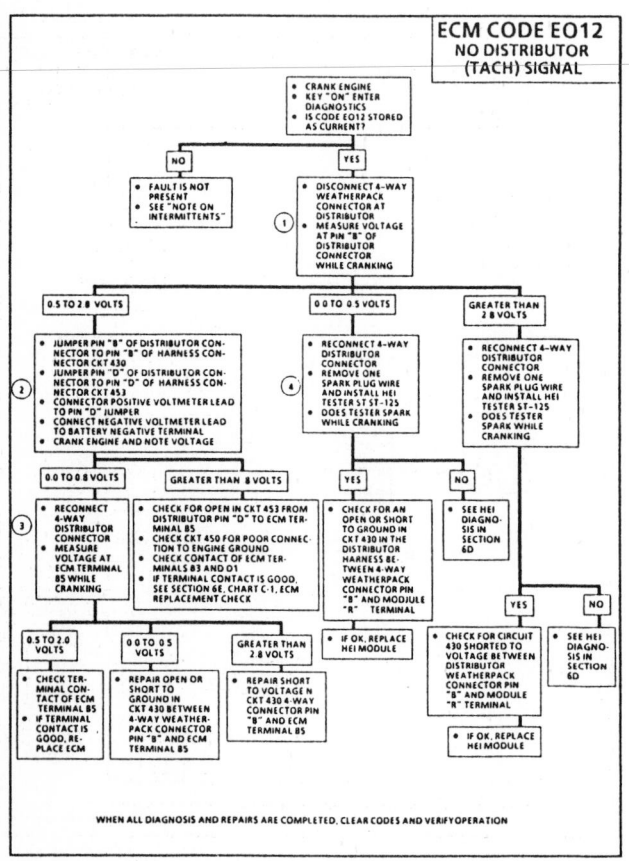

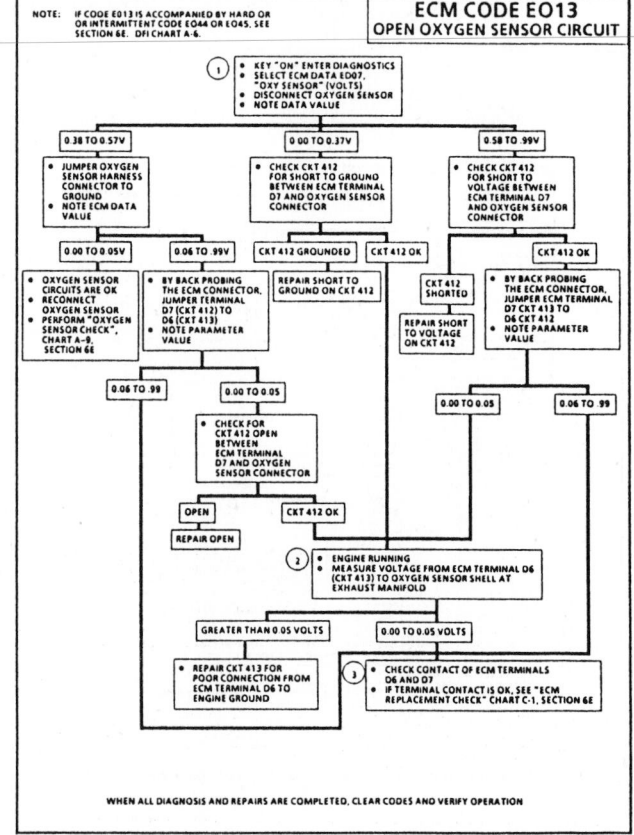

DFI TROUBLE DIAGNOSTICS

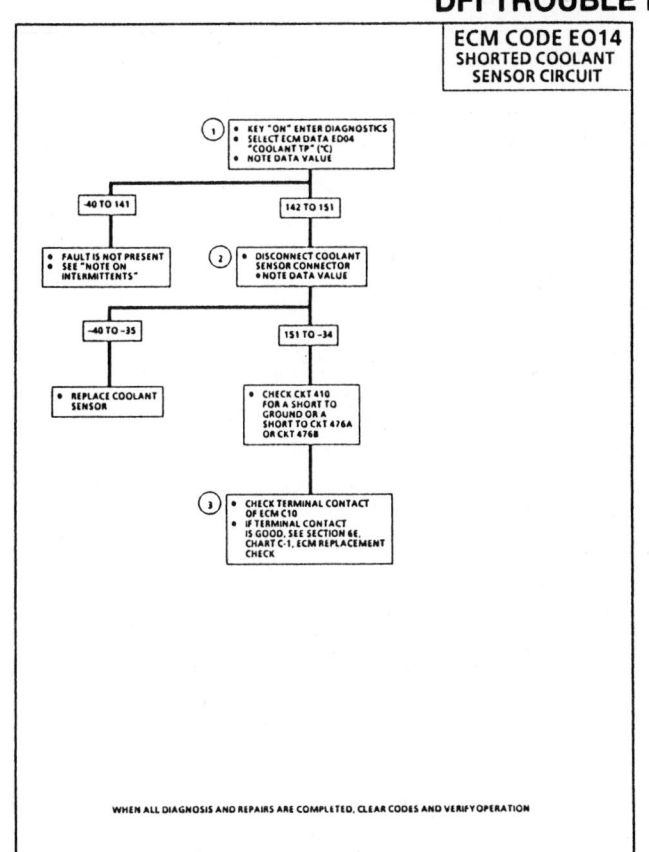

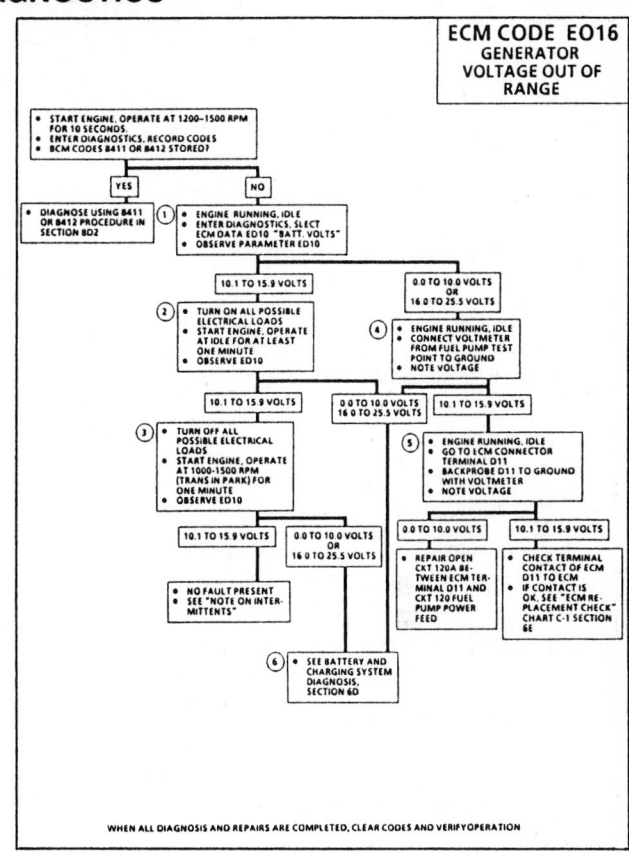

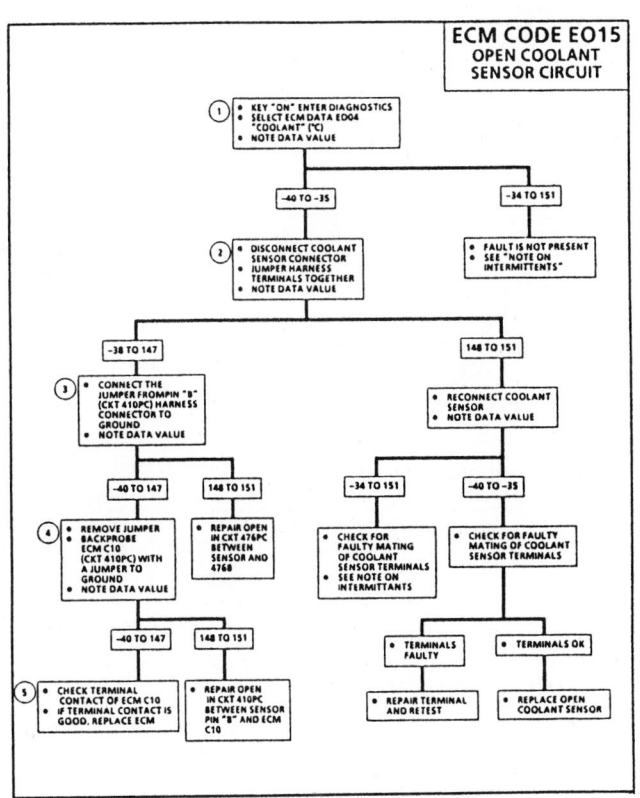

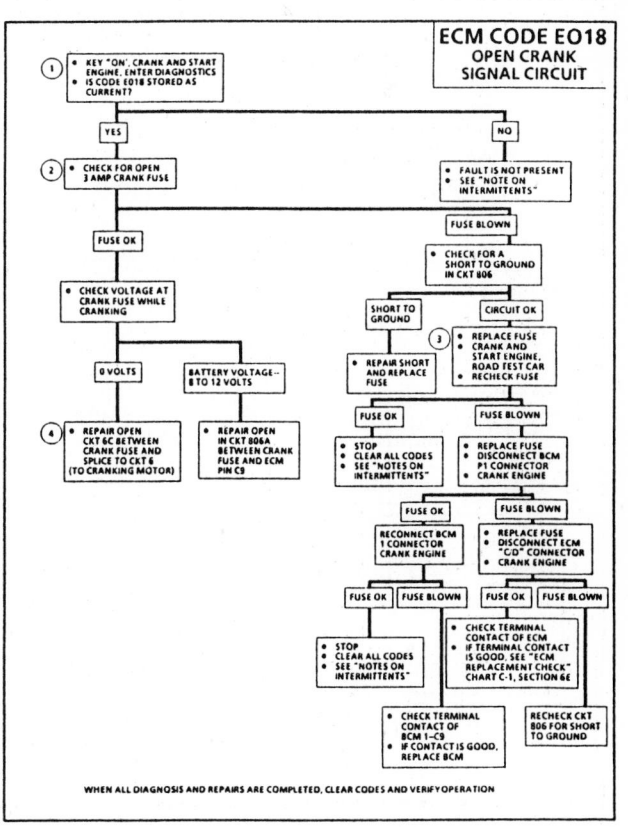

DFI TROUBLE DIAGNOSTICS

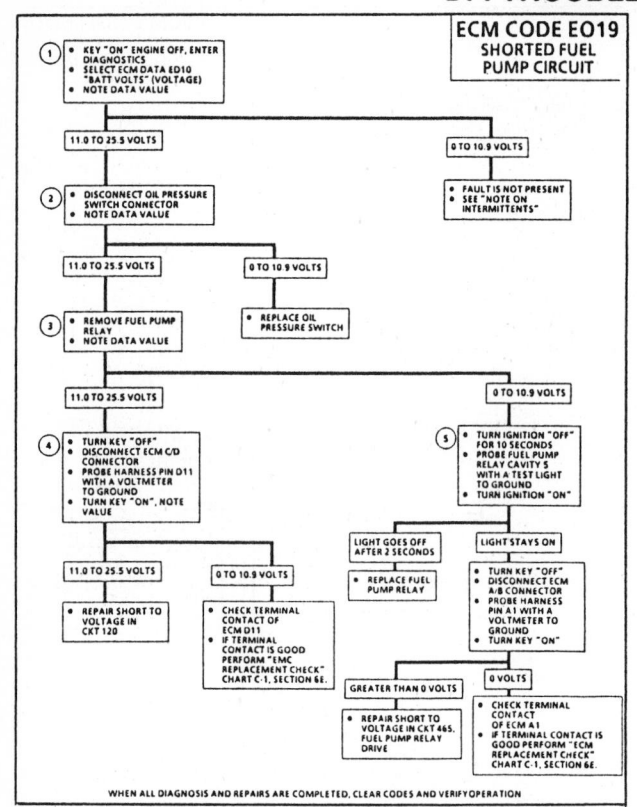

ECM CODE EO19
SHORTED FUEL
PUMP CIRCUIT

WHEN ALL DIAGNOSIS AND REPAIRS ARE COMPLETED, CLEAR CODES AND VERIFY OPERATION

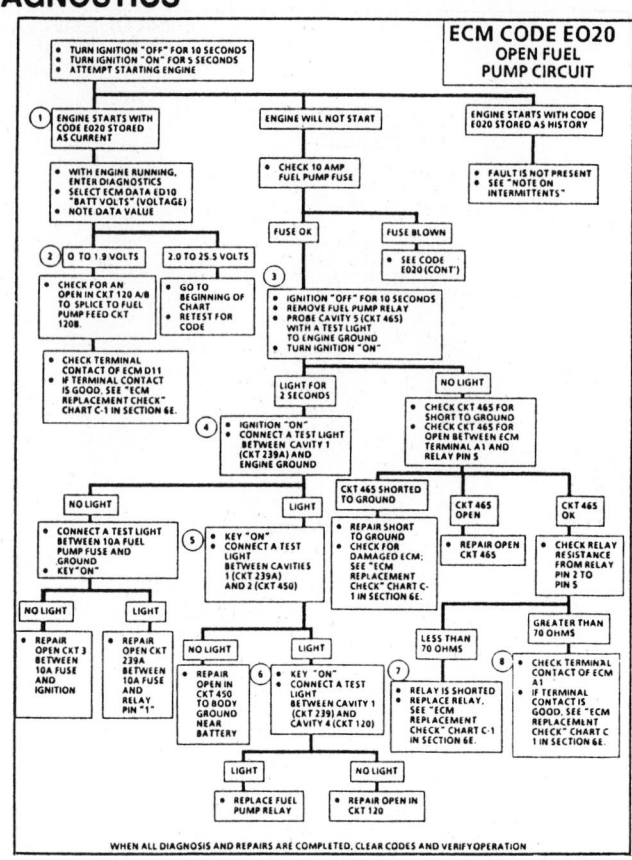

ECM CODE EO20
OPEN FUEL
PUMP CIRCUIT

WHEN ALL DIAGNOSIS AND REPAIRS ARE COMPLETED, CLEAR CODES AND VERIFY OPERATION

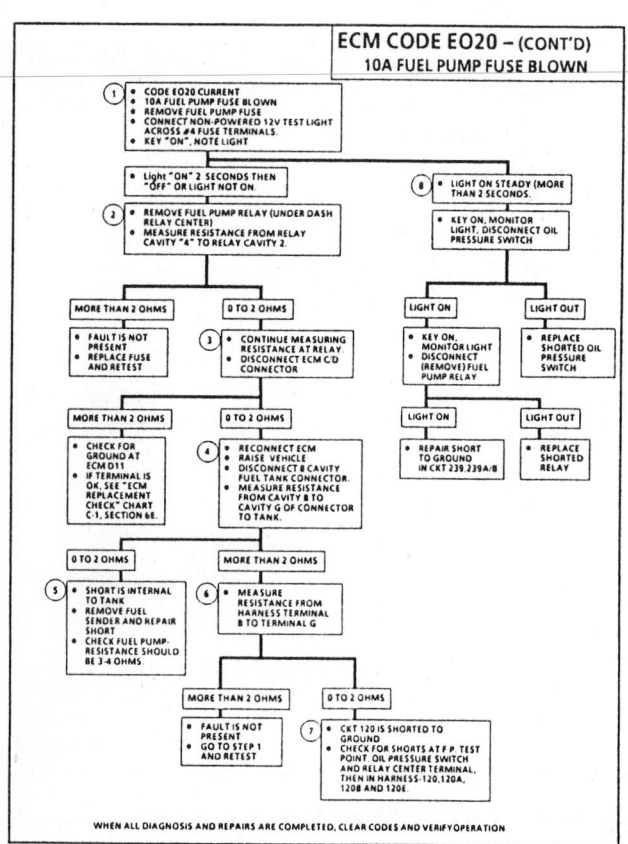

ECM CODE EO20 – (CONT'D)
10A FUEL PUMP FUSE BLOWN

WHEN ALL DIAGNOSIS AND REPAIRS ARE COMPLETED, CLEAR CODES AND VERIFY OPERATION

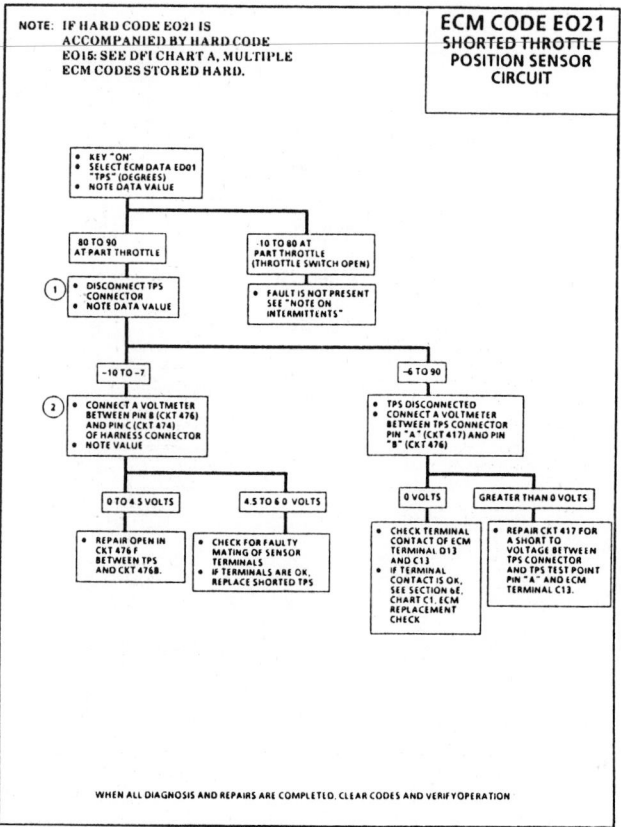

NOTE: IF HARD CODE EO21 IS
ACCOMPANIED BY HARD CODE
EO15: SEE DFI CHART A, MULTIPLE
ECM CODES STORED HARD.

ECM CODE EO21
SHORTED THROTTLE
POSITION SENSOR
CIRCUIT

WHEN ALL DIAGNOSIS AND REPAIRS ARE COMPLETED, CLEAR CODES AND VERIFY OPERATION

DFI TROUBLE DIAGNOSTICS

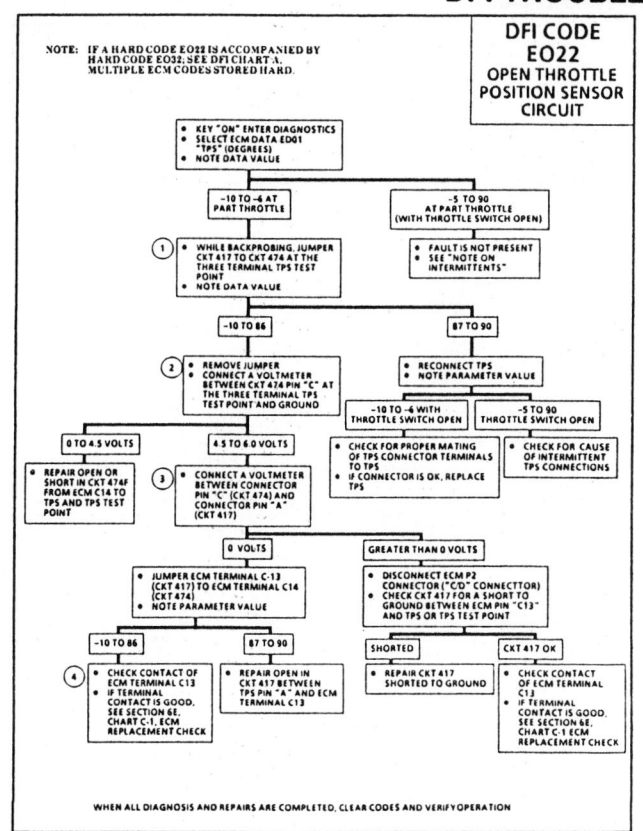

DFI CODE EO22 OPEN THROTTLE POSITION SENSOR CIRCUIT

NOTE: IF A HARD CODE EO22 IS ACCOMPANIED BY HARD CODE EO32, SEE DFI CHART A. MULTIPLE ECM CODES STORED HARD.

WHEN ALL DIAGNOSIS AND REPAIRS ARE COMPLETED, CLEAR CODES AND VERIFY OPERATION

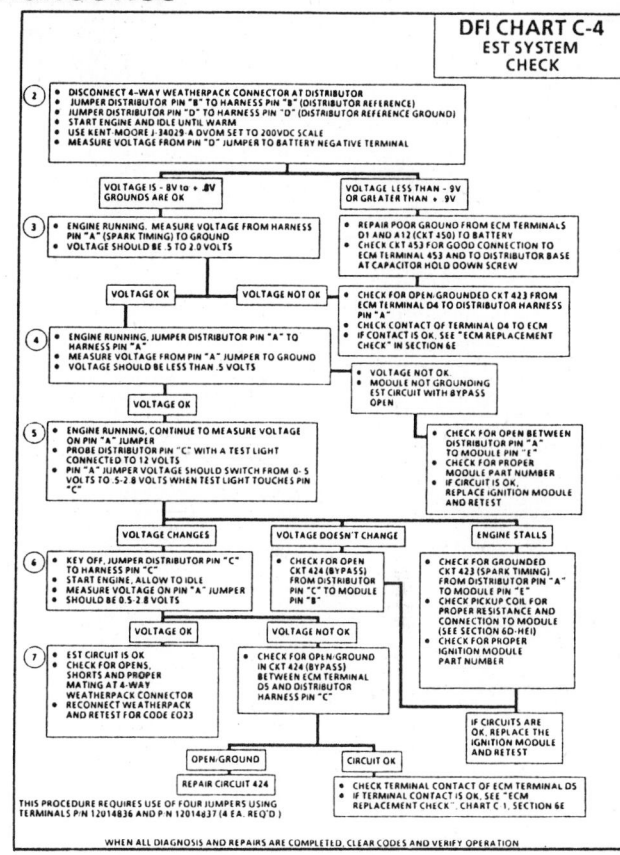

DFI CHART C-4 EST SYSTEM CHECK

WHEN ALL DIAGNOSIS AND REPAIRS ARE COMPLETED, CLEAR CODES AND VERIFY OPERATION

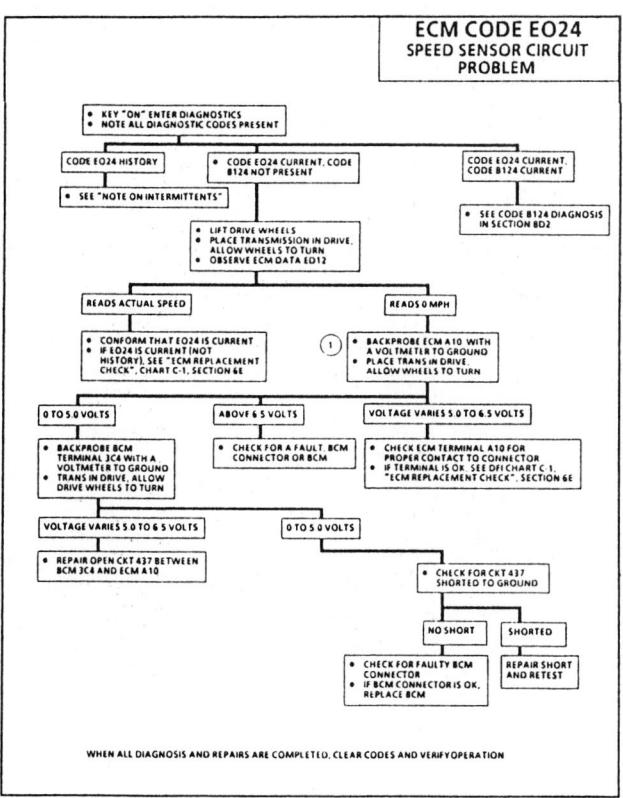

ECM CODE EO24 SPEED SENSOR CIRCUIT PROBLEM

WHEN ALL DIAGNOSIS AND REPAIRS ARE COMPLETED, CLEAR CODES AND VERIFY OPERATION

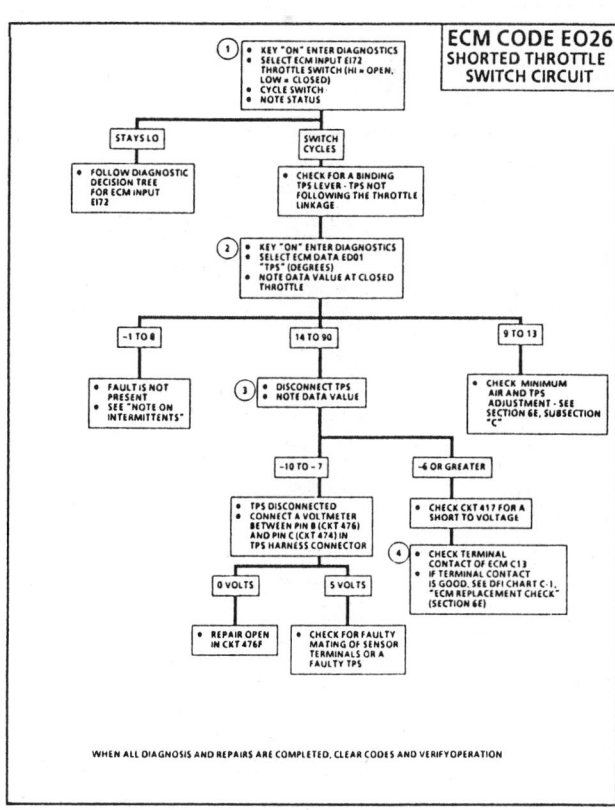

ECM CODE EO26 SHORTED THROTTLE SWITCH CIRCUIT

WHEN ALL DIAGNOSIS AND REPAIRS ARE COMPLETED, CLEAR CODES AND VERIFY OPERATION

DFI TROUBLE DIAGNOSTICS

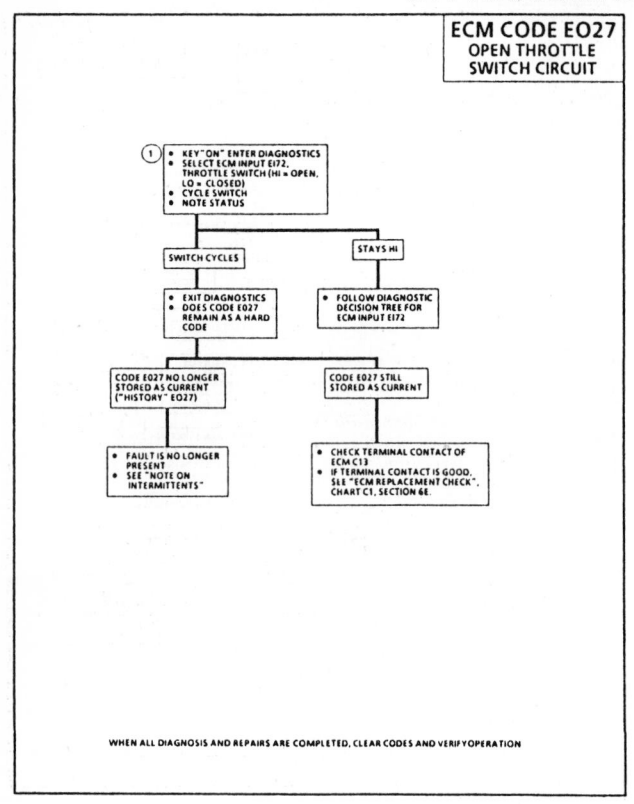

ECM CODE EO27
OPEN THROTTLE SWITCH CIRCUIT

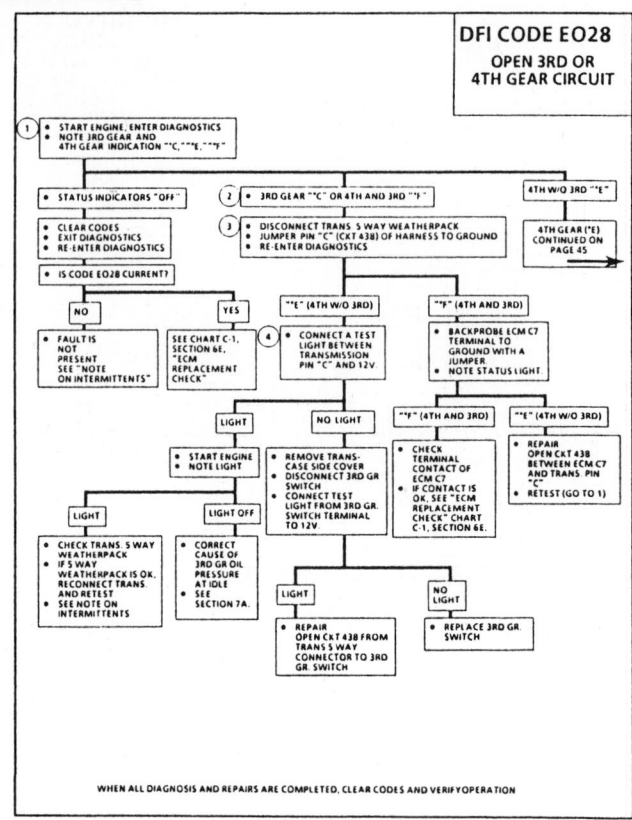

DFI CODE EO28
OPEN 3RD OR 4TH GEAR CIRCUIT

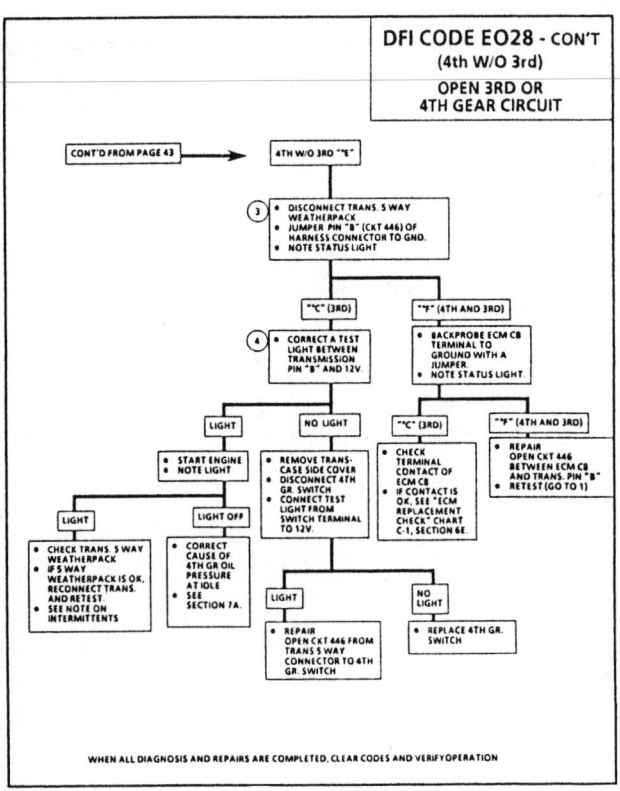

DFI CODE EO28 - CON'T
(4th W/O 3rd)

OPEN 3RD OR 4TH GEAR CIRCUIT

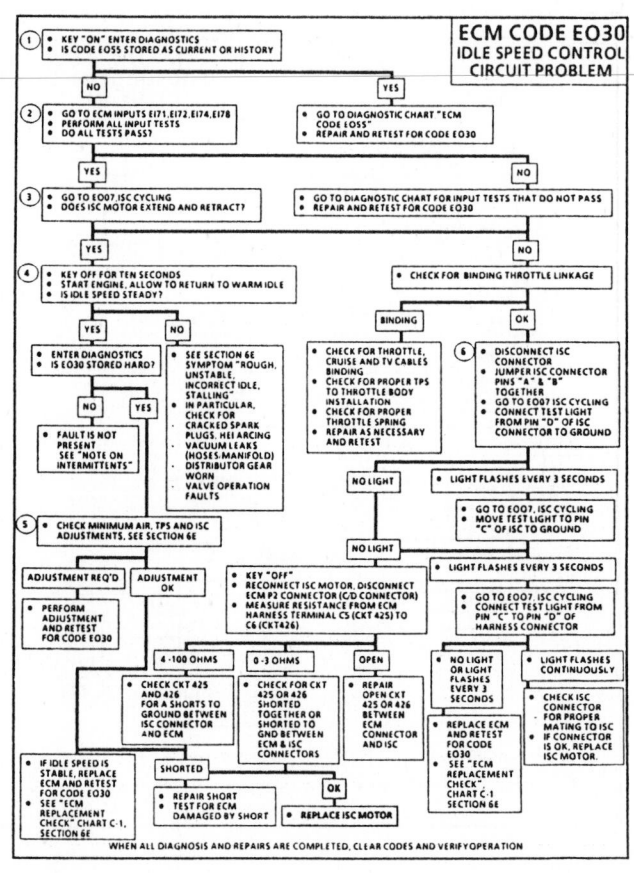

ECM CODE EO30
IDLE SPEED CONTROL CIRCUIT PROBLEM

DFI TROUBLE DIAGNOSTICS

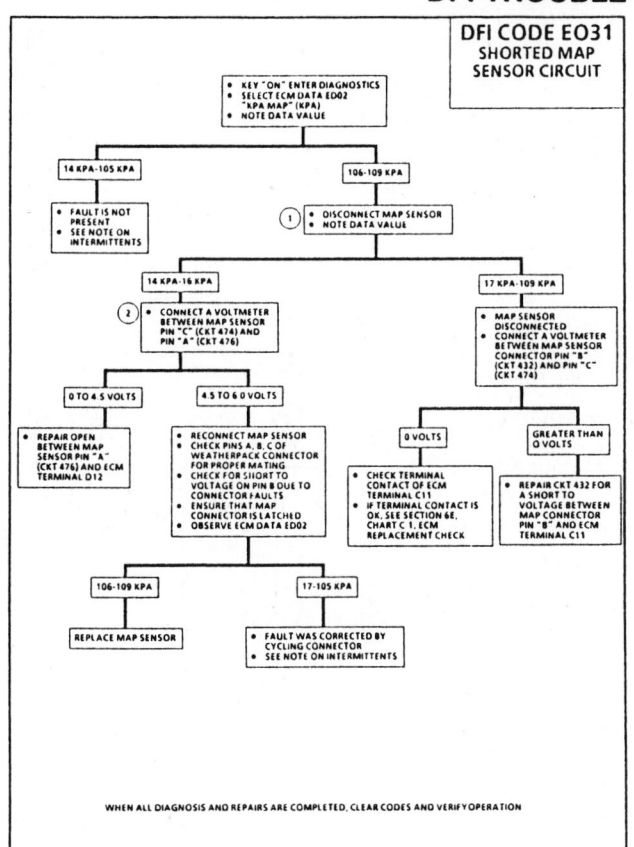

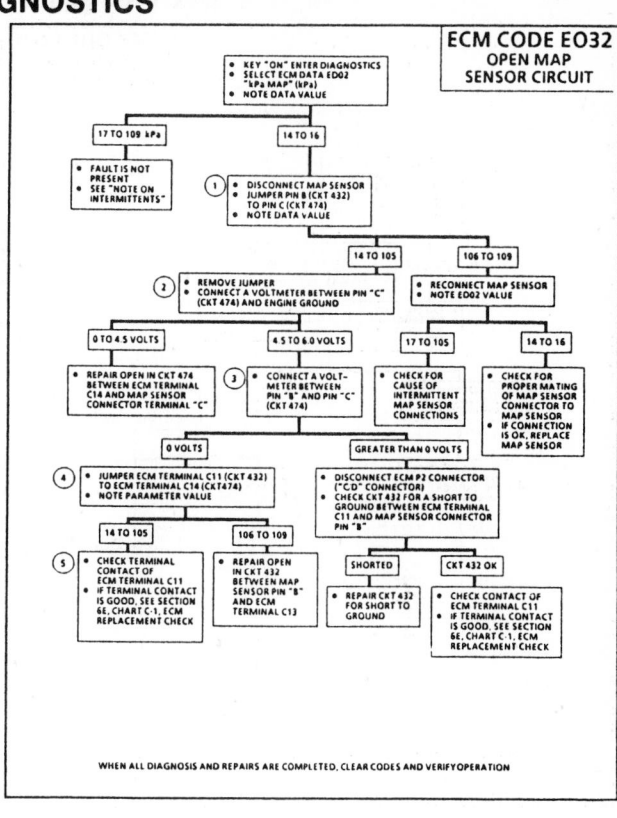

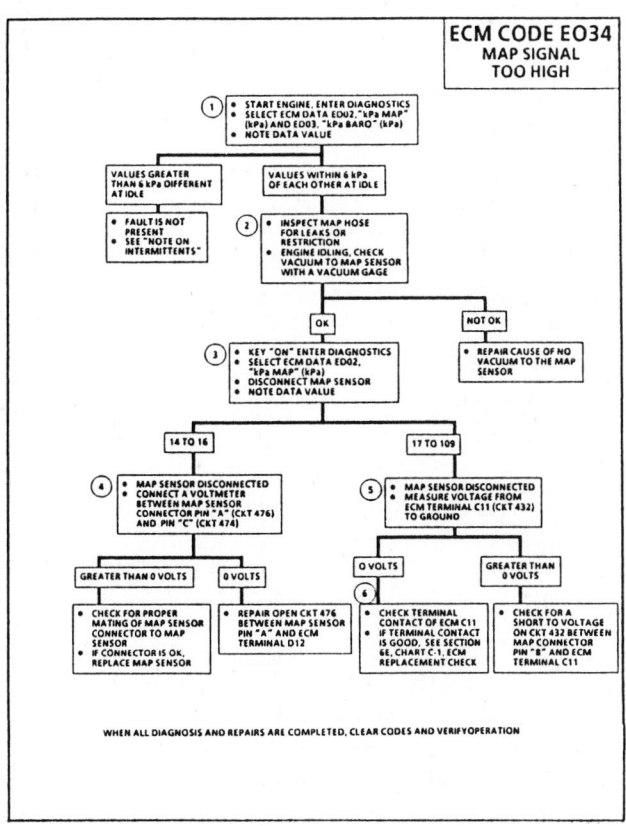

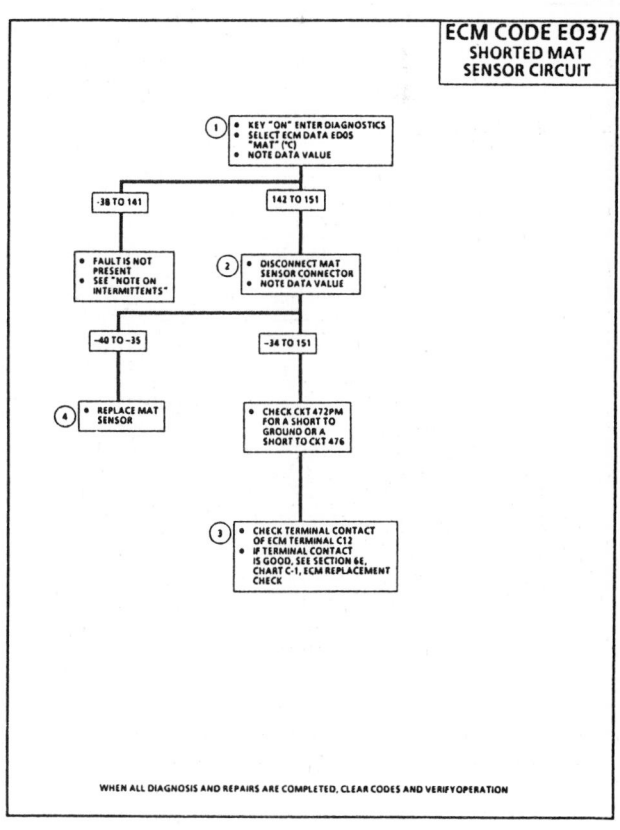

DFI TROUBLE DIAGNOSTICS

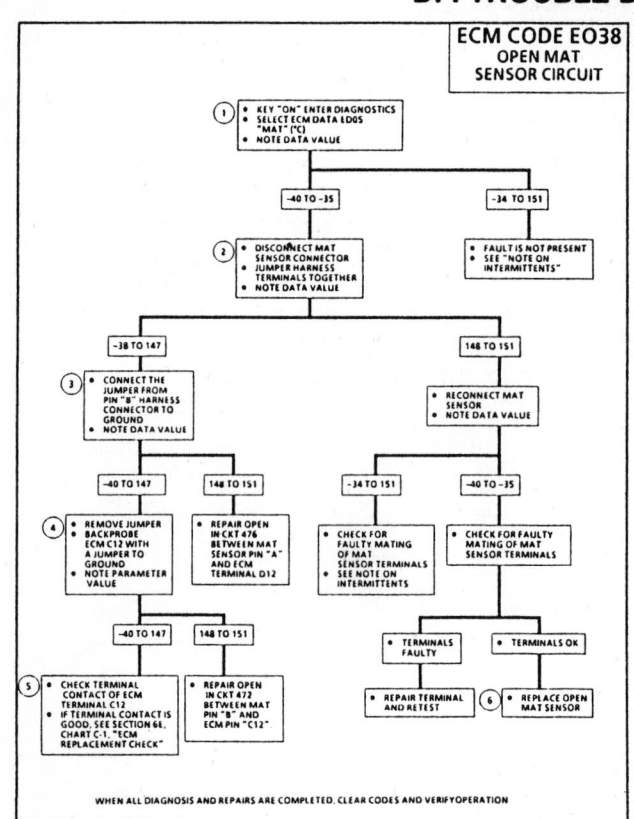

ECM CODE EO38
OPEN MAT SENSOR CIRCUIT

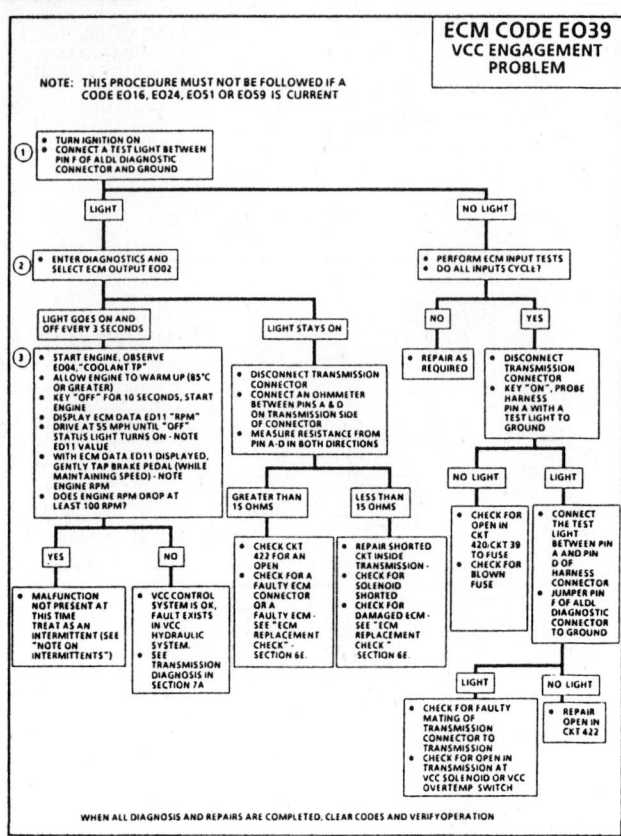

ECM CODE EO39
VCC ENGAGEMENT PROBLEM

NOTE: THIS PROCEDURE MUST NOT BE FOLLOWED IF A CODE EO16, EO24, EO51 OR EO59 IS CURRENT

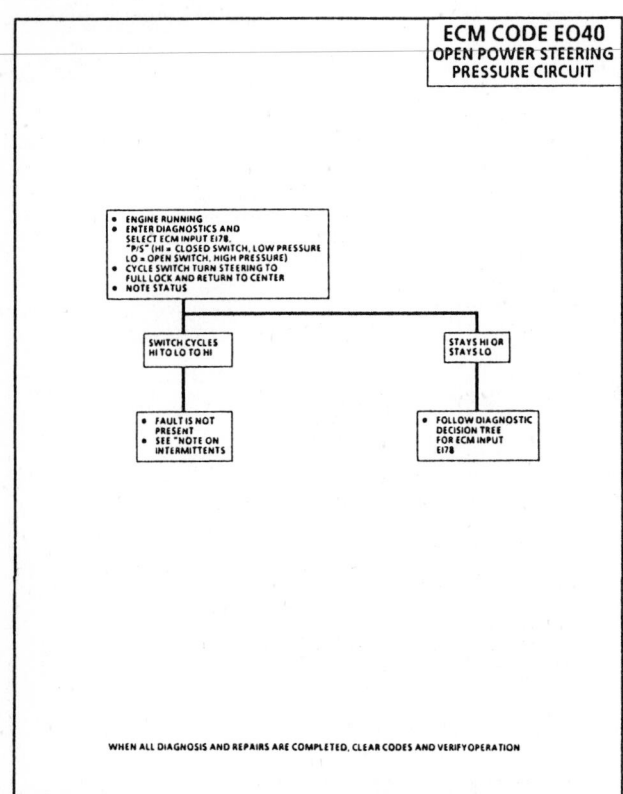

ECM CODE EO40
OPEN POWER STEERING PRESSURE CIRCUIT

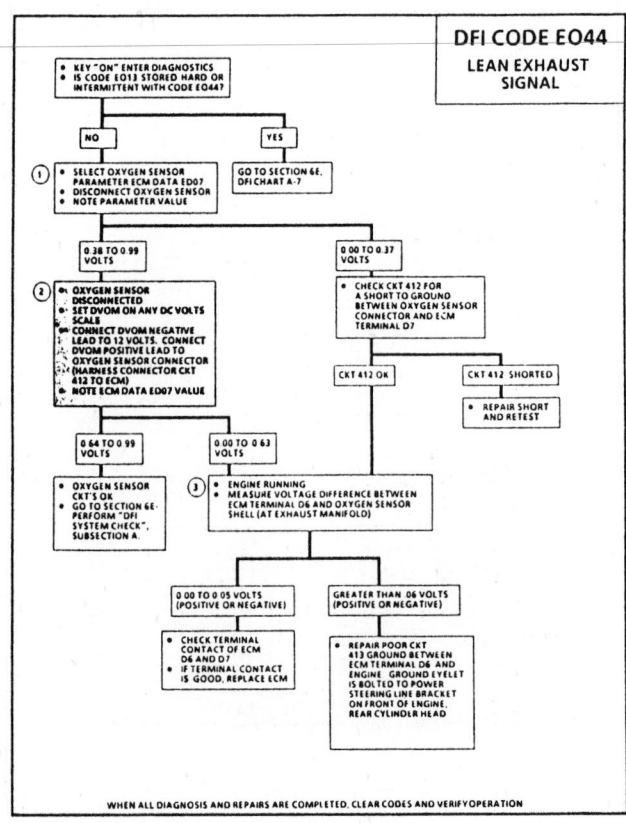

DFI CODE EO44
LEAN EXHAUST SIGNAL

DFI TROUBLE DIAGNOSTICS

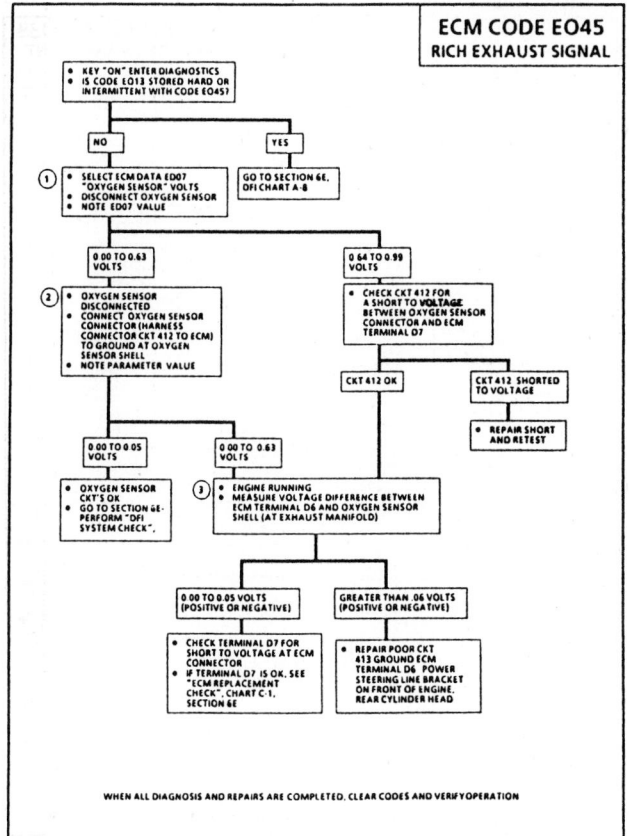

ECM CODE E045
RICH EXHAUST SIGNAL

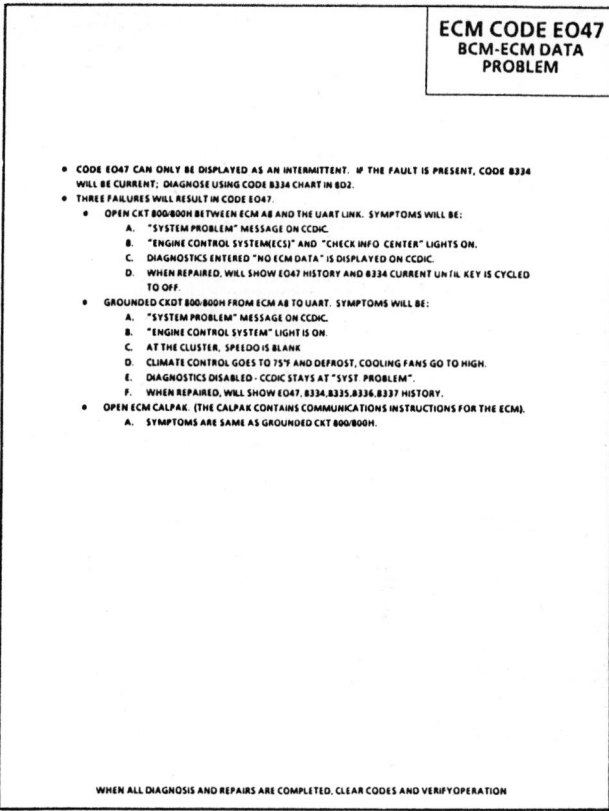

ECM CODE E047
BCM-ECM DATA PROBLEM

- CODE E047 CAN ONLY BE DISPLAYED AS AN INTERMITTENT. IF THE FAULT IS PRESENT, CODE B334 WILL BE CURRENT; DIAGNOSE USING CODE B334 CHART IN BD2.
- THREE FAILURES WILL RESULT IN CODE E047.
  - OPEN CKT 800/800H BETWEEN ECM A8 AND THE UART LINK. SYMPTOMS WILL BE:
    - A. "SYSTEM PROBLEM" MESSAGE ON CCDIC.
    - B. "ENGINE CONTROL SYSTEM(ECS)" AND "CHECK INFO CENTER" LIGHTS ON.
    - C. DIAGNOSTICS ENTERED "NO ECM DATA" IS DISPLAYED ON CCDIC.
    - D. WHEN REPAIRED, WILL SHOW E047 HISTORY AND B334 CURRENT UNTIL KEY IS CYCLED TO OFF.
  - GROUNDED CKDT 800/800H FROM ECM A8 TO UART. SYMPTOMS WILL BE:
    - A. "SYSTEM PROBLEM" MESSAGE ON CCDIC.
    - B. "ENGINE CONTROL SYSTEM" LIGHT IS ON.
    - C. AT THE CLUSTER, SPEEDO IS BLANK
    - D. CLIMATE CONTROL GOES TO 75°F AND DEFROST, COOLING FANS GO TO HIGH.
    - E. DIAGNOSTICS DISABLED - CCDIC STAYS AT "SYST PROBLEM".
    - F. WHEN REPAIRED, WILL SHOW E047, B334,B335,B336,B337 HISTORY.
  - OPEN ECM CALPAK. (THE CALPAK CONTAINS COMMUNICATIONS INSTRUCTIONS FOR THE ECM).
    - A. SYMPTOMS ARE SAME AS GROUNDED CKT 800/800H.

WHEN ALL DIAGNOSIS AND REPAIRS ARE COMPLETED, CLEAR CODES AND VERIFY OPERATION

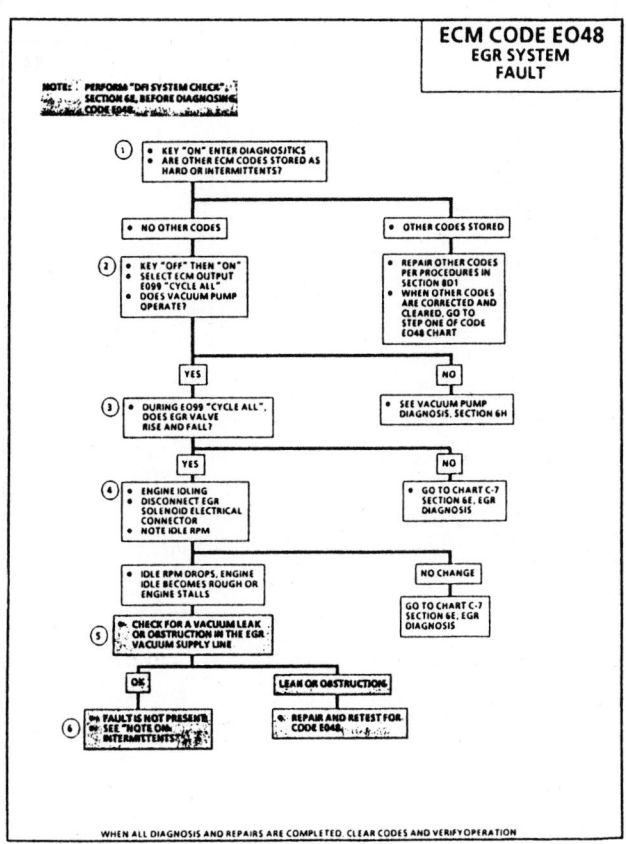

ECM CODE E048
EGR SYSTEM FAULT

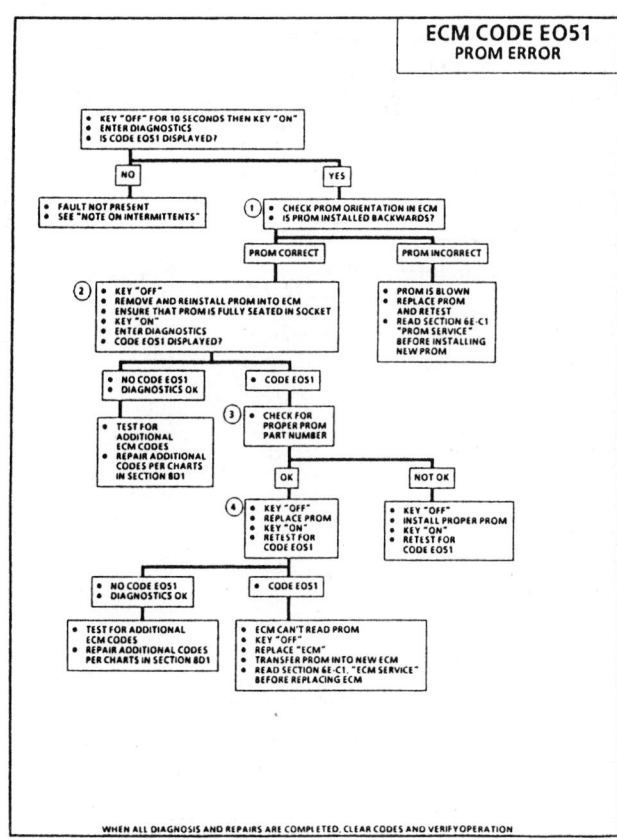

ECM CODE E051
PROM ERROR

WHEN ALL DIAGNOSIS AND REPAIRS ARE COMPLETED, CLEAR CODES AND VERIFY OPERATION

DFI TROUBLE DIAGNOSTICS

ECM CODE E052
ECM MEMORY RESET

Code E052 indicates that the "long term" memory in the ECM has been reset.

This will be the case whenever power is removed from the ECM (i.e., disconnecting battery cables, disconnecting ECM connector, etc.) This code should be "cleared" from memory after restoring the ECM's power supply.

If Code E052 is seen accompanied by complaint of engine quit, stumble, telltale's flashing or other stored codes, check for intermittent loss of power or ground to the ECM on CKT 480 and 150 respectively. Manipulate wiring and connections with engine running. Remove and replace the ECM J1 and J2 connectors and ensure that they are latched.

ECM CODE E055
TPS MISADJUSTED

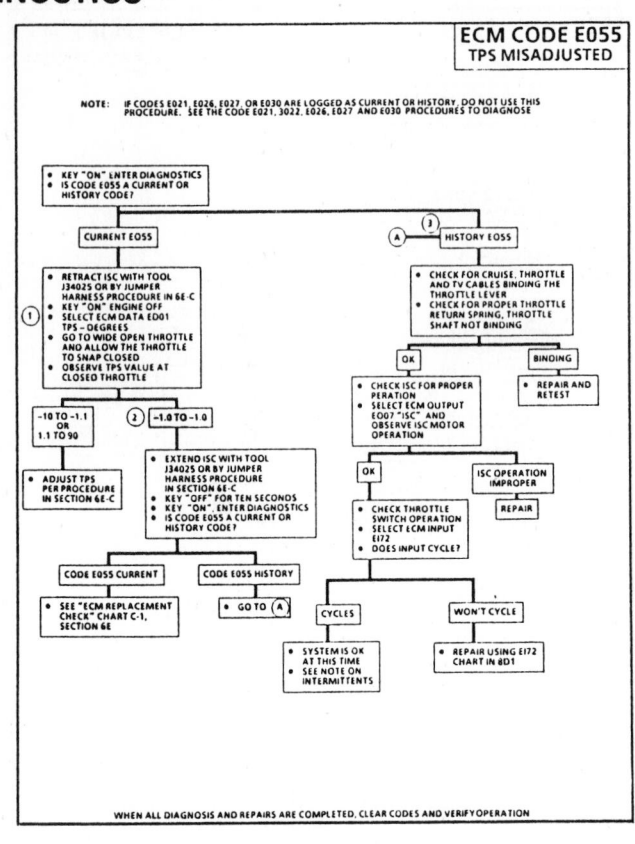

ECM CODE E053
DISTRIBUTOR SIGNAL INTERRUPT

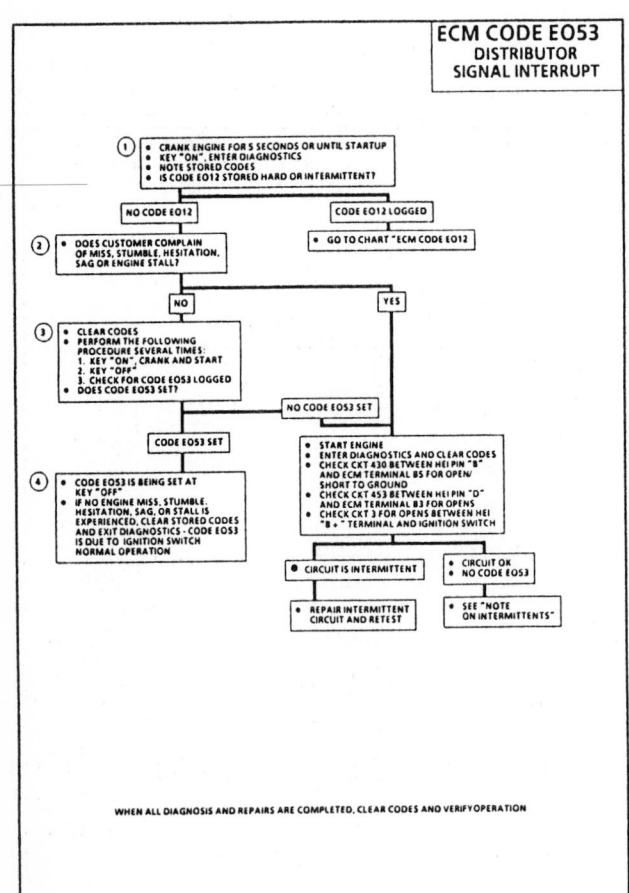

WHEN ALL DIAGNOSIS AND REPAIRS ARE COMPLETED, CLEAR CODES AND VERIFY OPERATION

ECM CODE E059
VCC TEMP SENSOR CIRCUIT

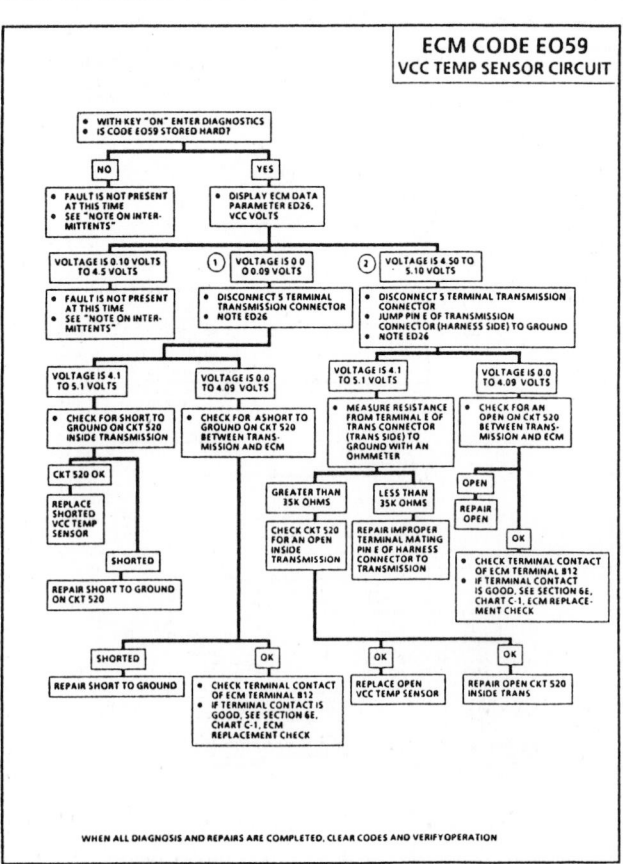

WHEN ALL DIAGNOSIS AND REPAIRS ARE COMPLETED, CLEAR CODES AND VERIFY OPERATION

DFI TROUBLE DIAGNOSTICS

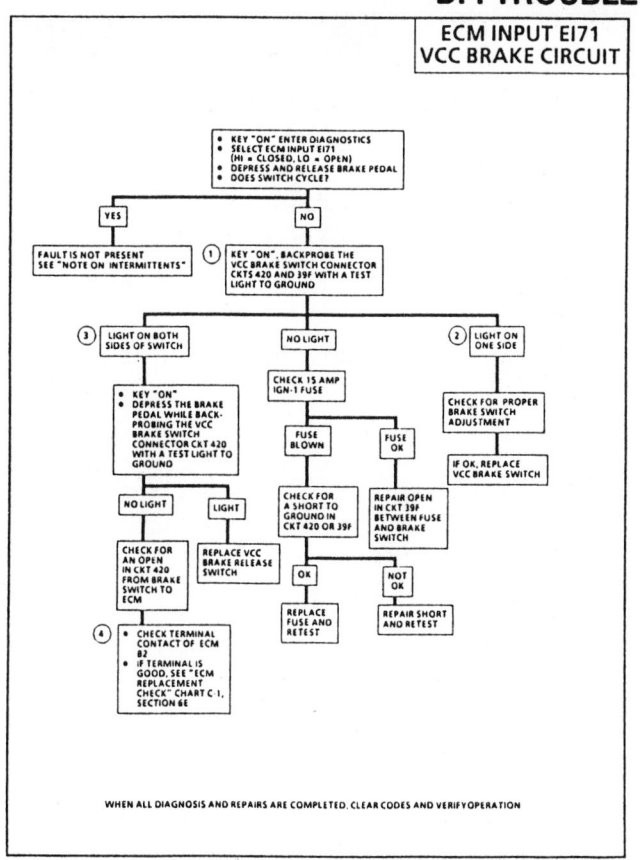

ECM INPUT EI71
VCC BRAKE CIRCUIT

WHEN ALL DIAGNOSIS AND REPAIRS ARE COMPLETED, CLEAR CODES AND VERIFY OPERATION

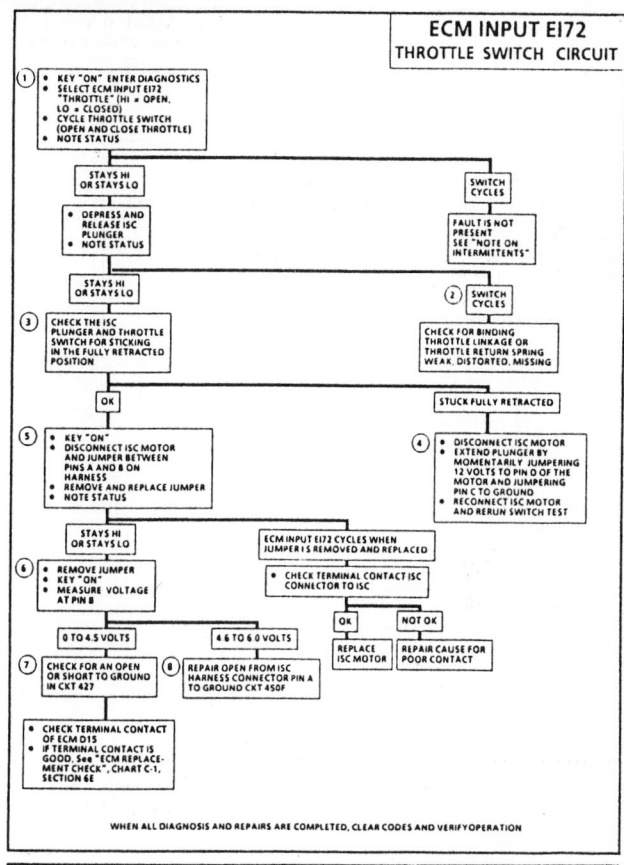

ECM INPUT EI72
THROTTLE SWITCH CIRCUIT

WHEN ALL DIAGNOSIS AND REPAIRS ARE COMPLETED, CLEAR CODES AND VERIFY OPERATION

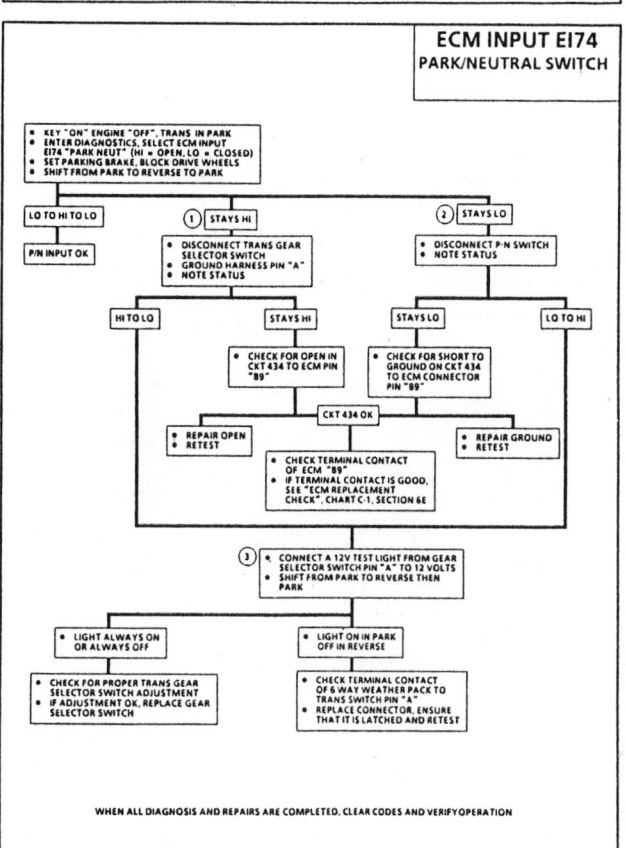

ECM INPUT EI74
PARK/NEUTRAL SWITCH

WHEN ALL DIAGNOSIS AND REPAIRS ARE COMPLETED, CLEAR CODES AND VERIFY OPERATION

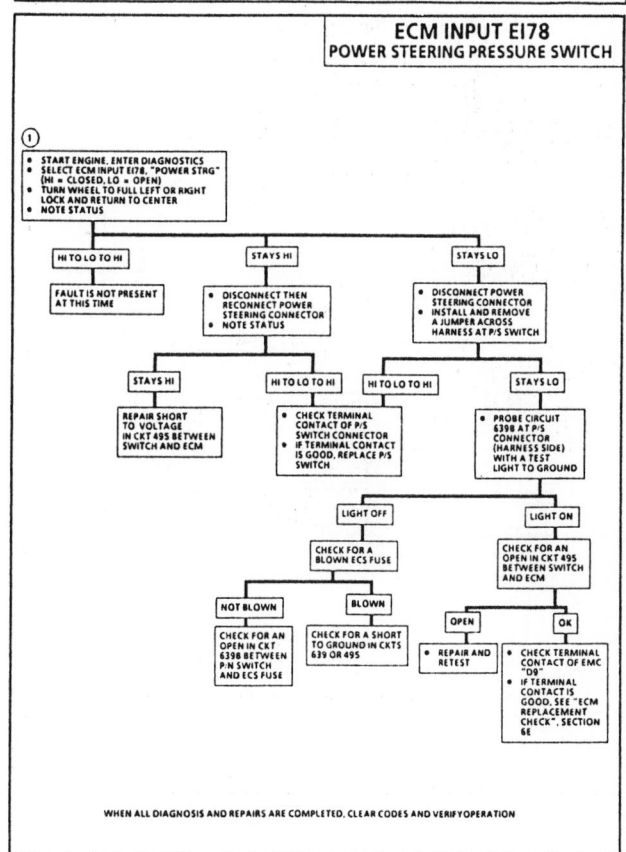

ECM INPUT EI78
POWER STEERING PRESSURE SWITCH

WHEN ALL DIAGNOSIS AND REPAIRS ARE COMPLETED, CLEAR CODES AND VERIFY OPERATION

DFI TROUBLE DIAGNOSTICS

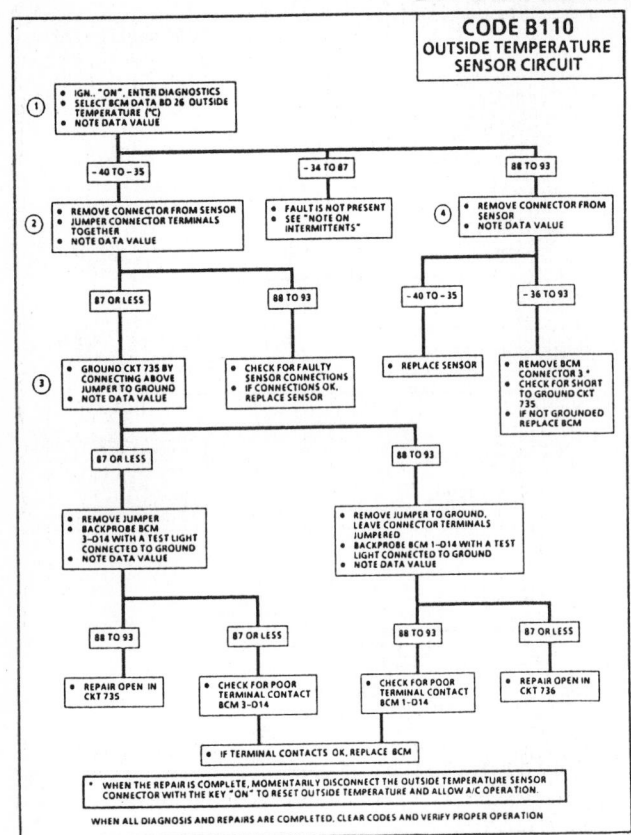

CODE B110
OUTSIDE TEMPERATURE SENSOR CIRCUIT

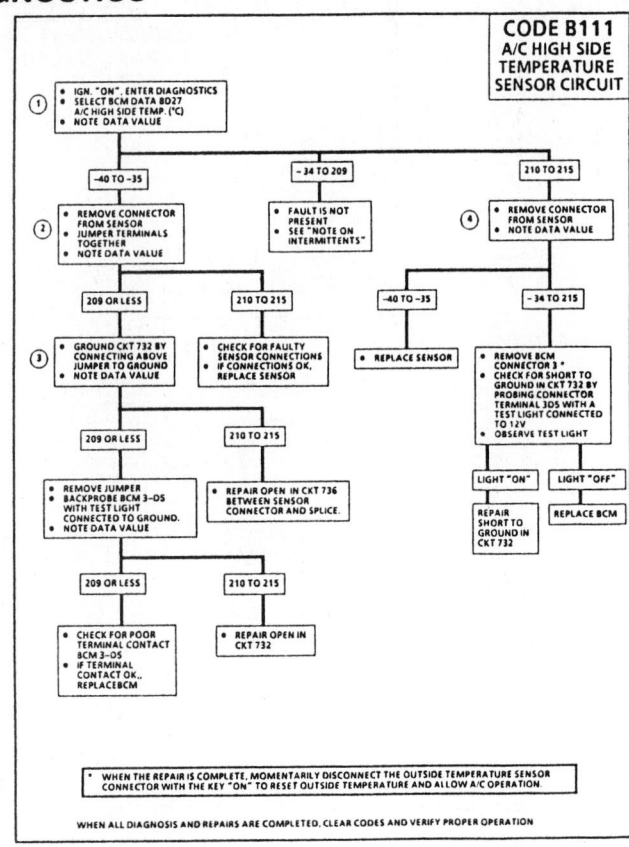

CODE B111
A/C HIGH SIDE TEMPERATURE SENSOR CIRCUIT

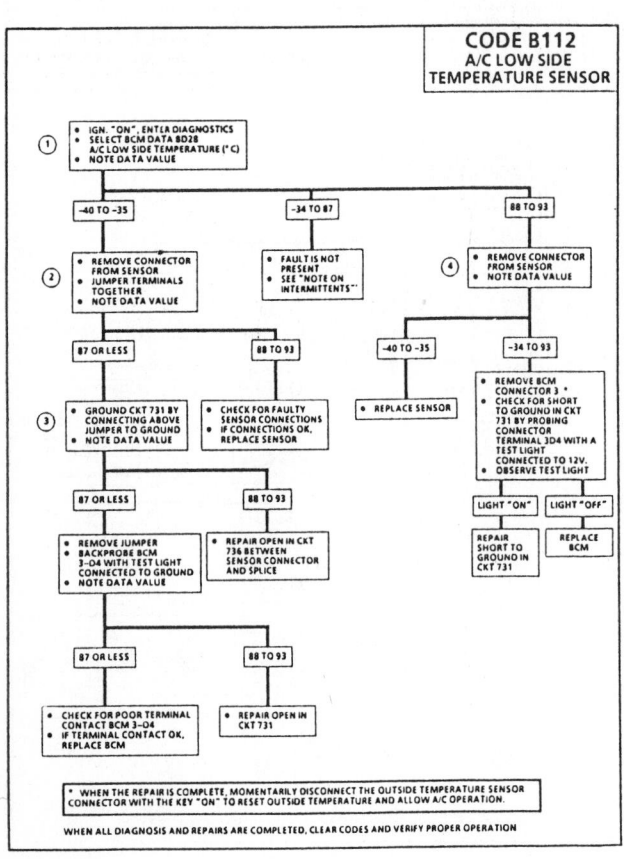

CODE B112
A/C LOW SIDE TEMPERATURE SENSOR

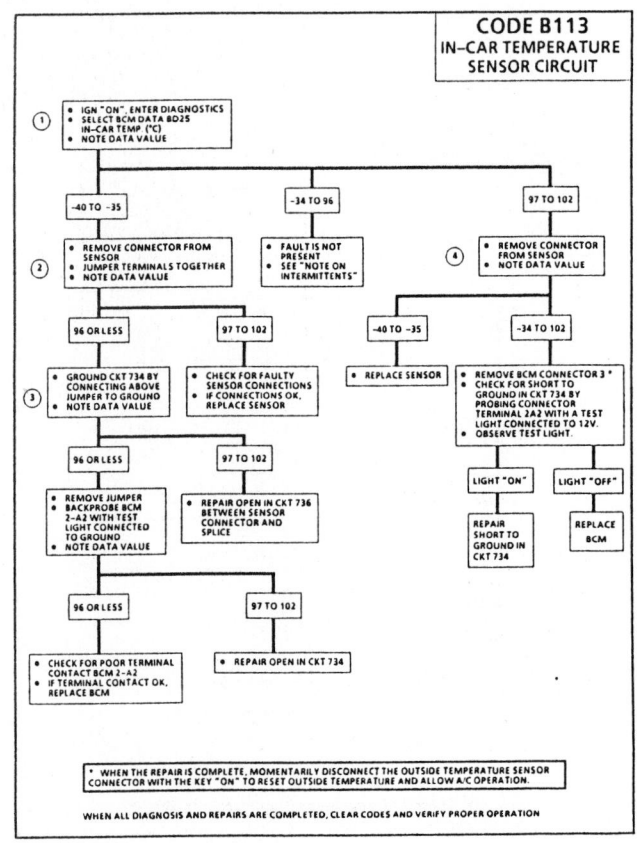

CODE B113
IN–CAR TEMPERATURE SENSOR CIRCUIT

DFI TROUBLE DIAGNOSTICS

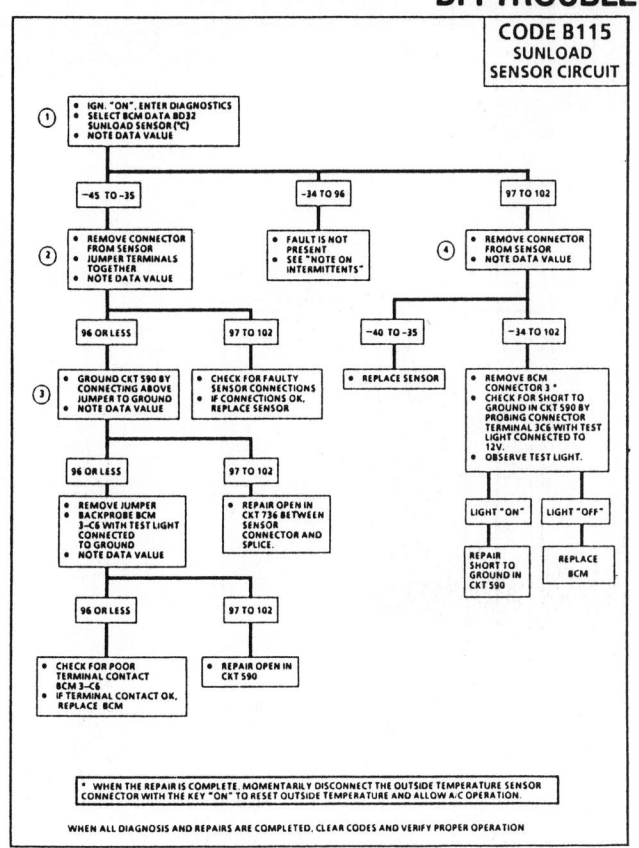

CODE B115
SUNLOAD SENSOR CIRCUIT

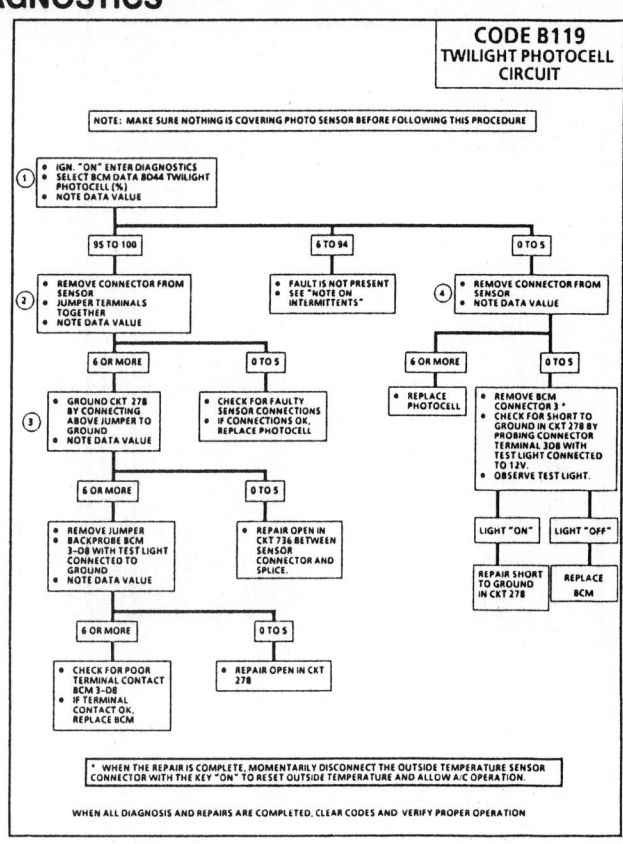

CODE B119
TWILIGHT PHOTOCELL CIRCUIT

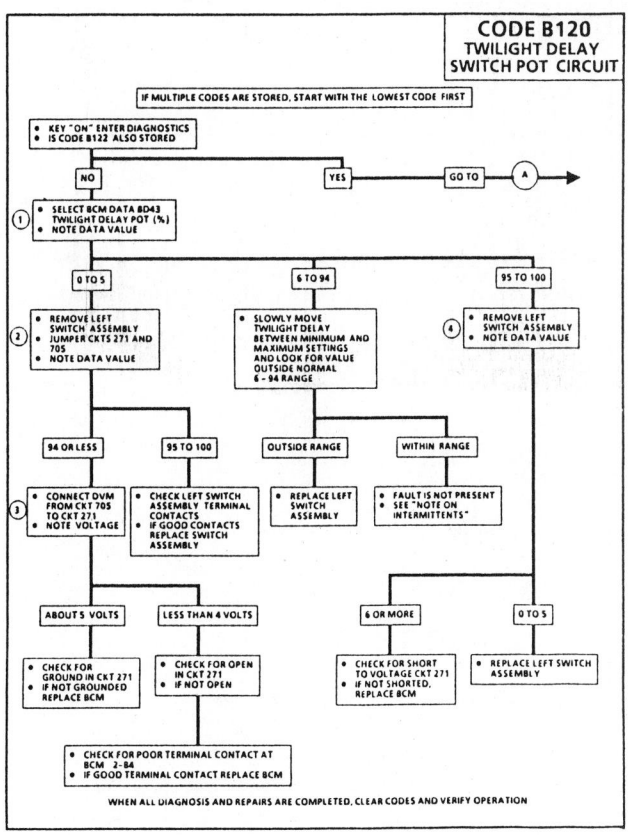

CODE B120
TWILIGHT DELAY SWITCH POT CIRCUIT

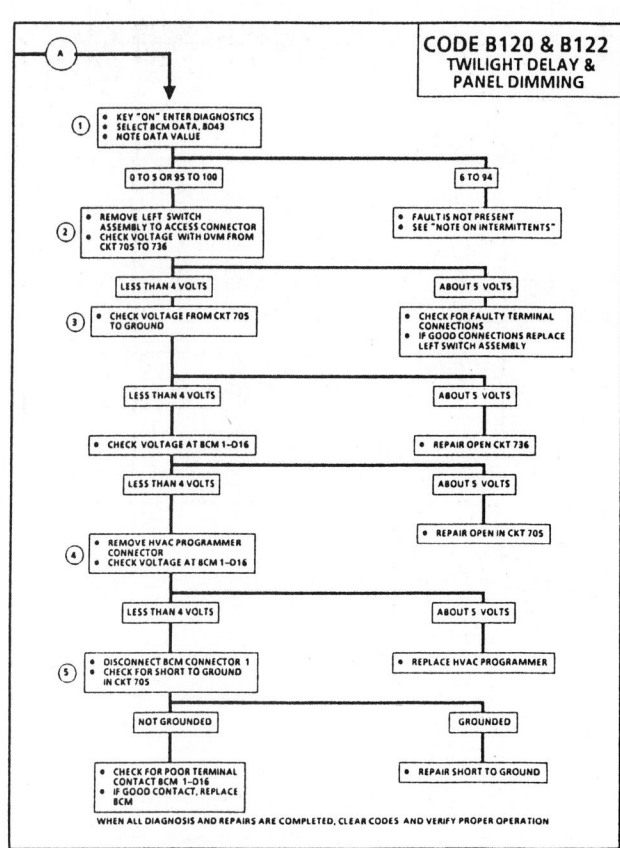

CODE B120 & B122
TWILIGHT DELAY & PANEL DIMMING

DFI TROUBLE DIAGNOSTICS

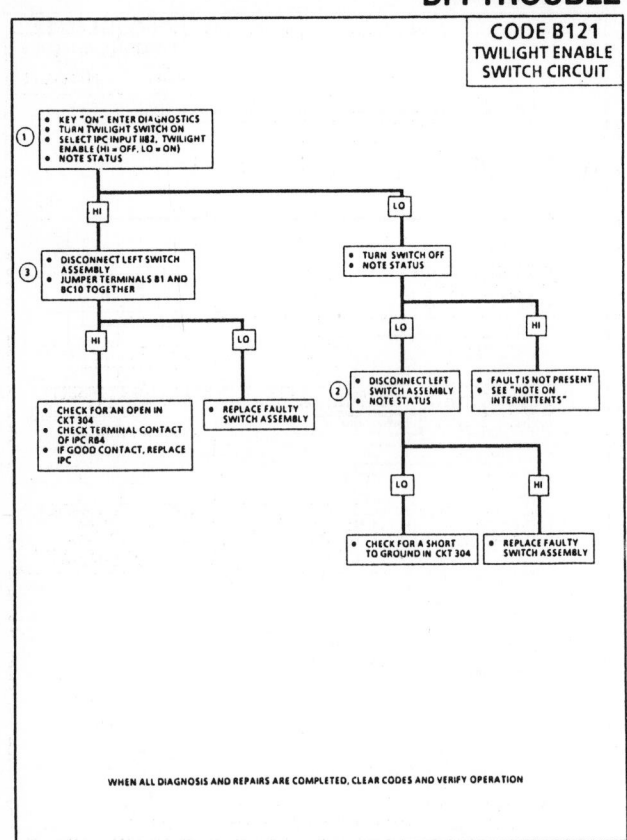

CODE B121
TWILIGHT ENABLE SWITCH CIRCUIT

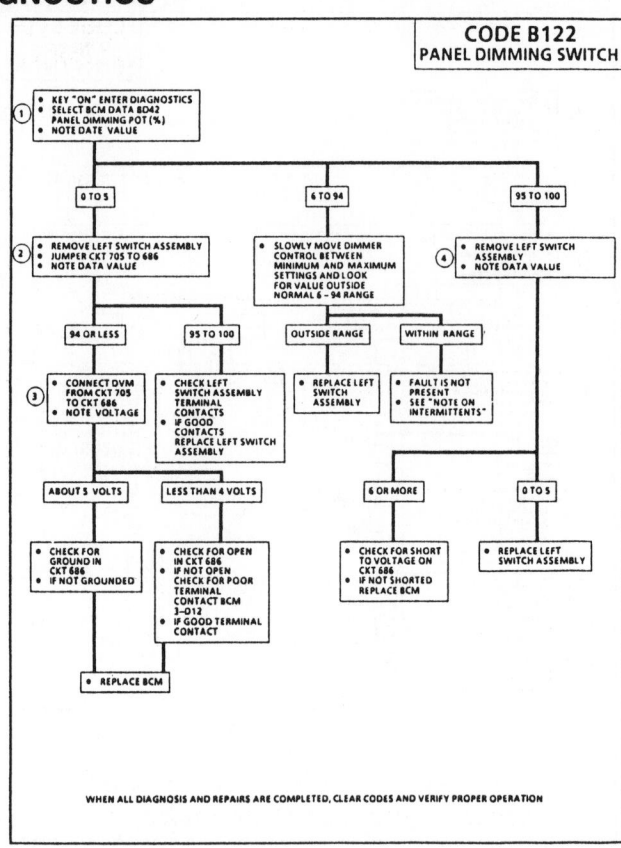

CODE B122
PANEL DIMMING SWITCH

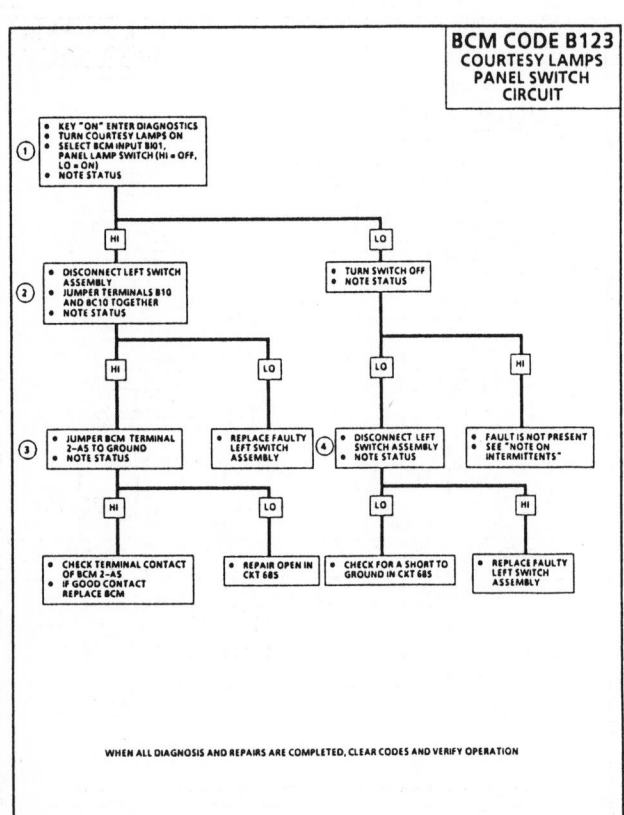

BCM CODE B123
COURTESY LAMPS PANEL SWITCH CIRCUIT

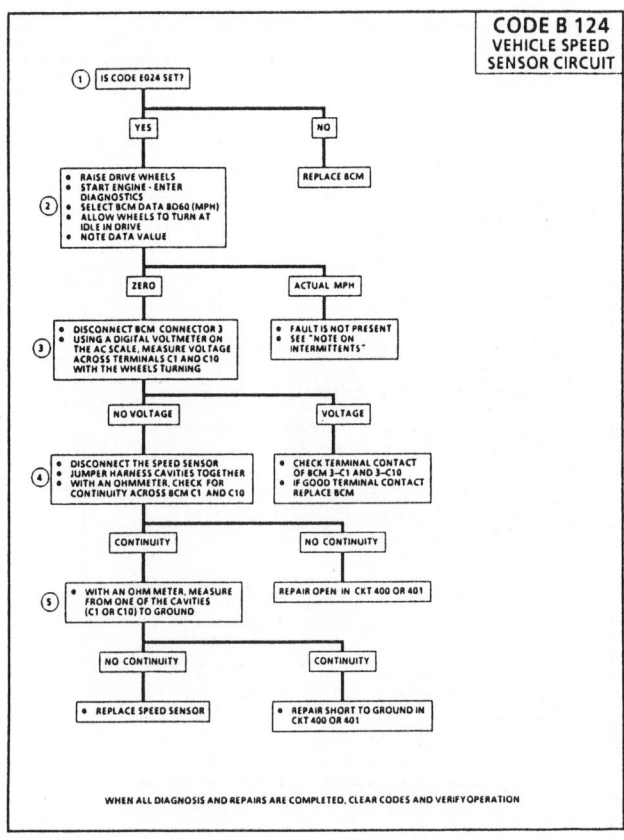

CODE B 124
VEHICLE SPEED SENSOR CIRCUIT

DFI TROUBLE DIAGNOSTICS

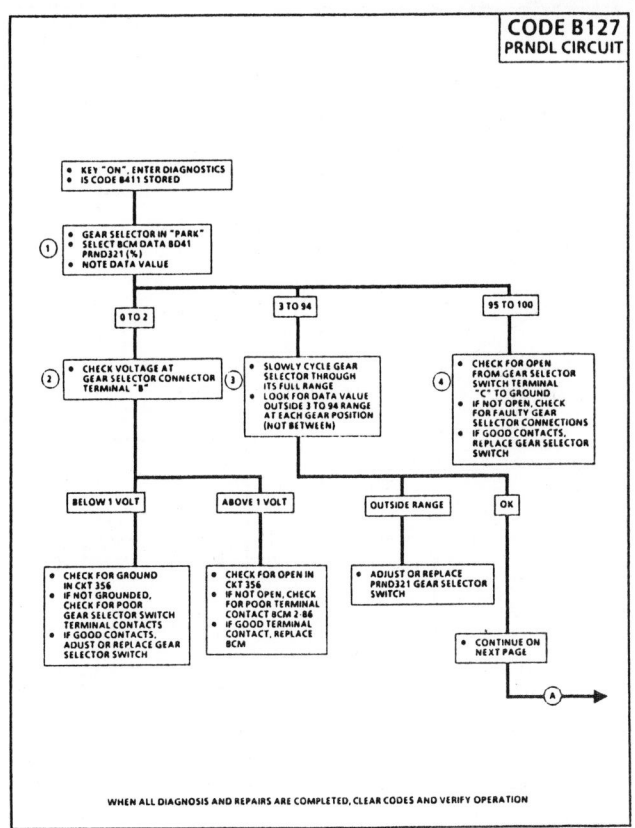

CODE B127
PRNDL CIRCUIT

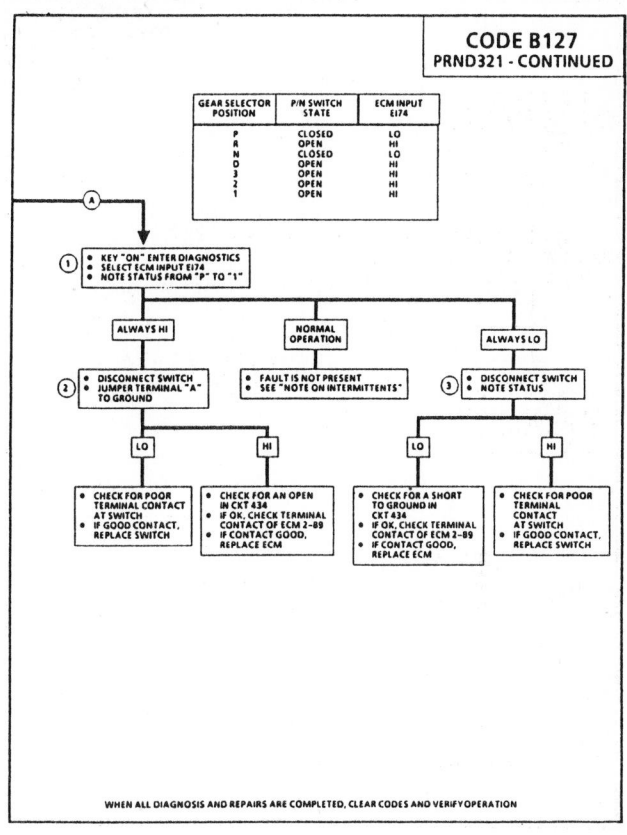

CODE B127
PRND321 - CONTINUED

GEAR SELECTOR POSITION	P/N SWITCH STATE	ECM INPUT E174
P	CLOSED	LO
R	OPEN	HI
N	CLOSED	LO
D	OPEN	HI
3	OPEN	HI
2	OPEN	HI
1	OPEN	HI

WHEN ALL DIAGNOSIS AND REPAIRS ARE COMPLETED, CLEAR CODES AND VERIFY OPERATION

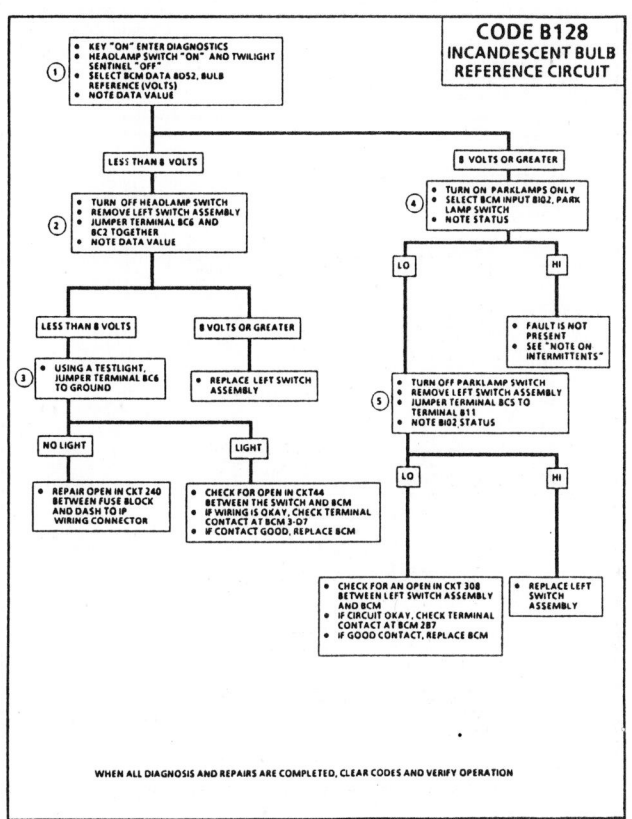

CODE B128
INCANDESCENT BULB
REFERENCE CIRCUIT

WHEN ALL DIAGNOSIS AND REPAIRS ARE COMPLETED, CLEAR CODES AND VERIFY OPERATION

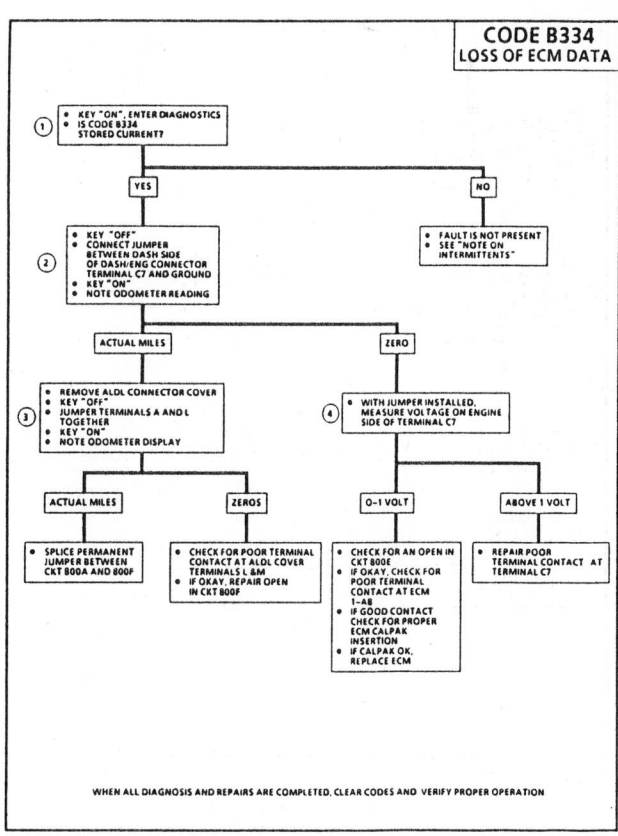

CODE B334
LOSS OF ECM DATA

WHEN ALL DIAGNOSIS AND REPAIRS ARE COMPLETED, CLEAR CODES AND VERIFY PROPER OPERATION

DFI TROUBLE DIAGNOSTICS

CODE B335
LOSS OF CCDIC DATA

BCM CODE B335 INDICATES A LOSS OF DATA COMMUNICTION BETWEEN THE CCDIC AND THE BCM. WHEN THIS EVENT OCCURS, THE CCDIC WILL DISPLAY "SYSTEM PROBLEM" UNTIL THE CONDITION IS CORRECTED. DUE TO THE NATURE OF THIS CODE, IT WILL ONLY BE DISPLAYED AS AN INTERMITTENT.

POSSIBLE CAUSES OF THIS CODE ARE A FAULTY CCDIC PANEL, A LOSS OF 7 VOLTS (CKT 807) OR GROUND (CKT 801) FROM THE CENTRAL POWER SUPPLY, OR THE ACTUAL LOSS OF THE DATA COMMUNICATION CIRCUIT TO THE BCM.

WHEN ALL DIAGNOSIS AND REPAIRS ARE COMPLETED, CLEAR CODES AND VERIFY OPERATION

CODE B336
LOSS OF IPC DATA

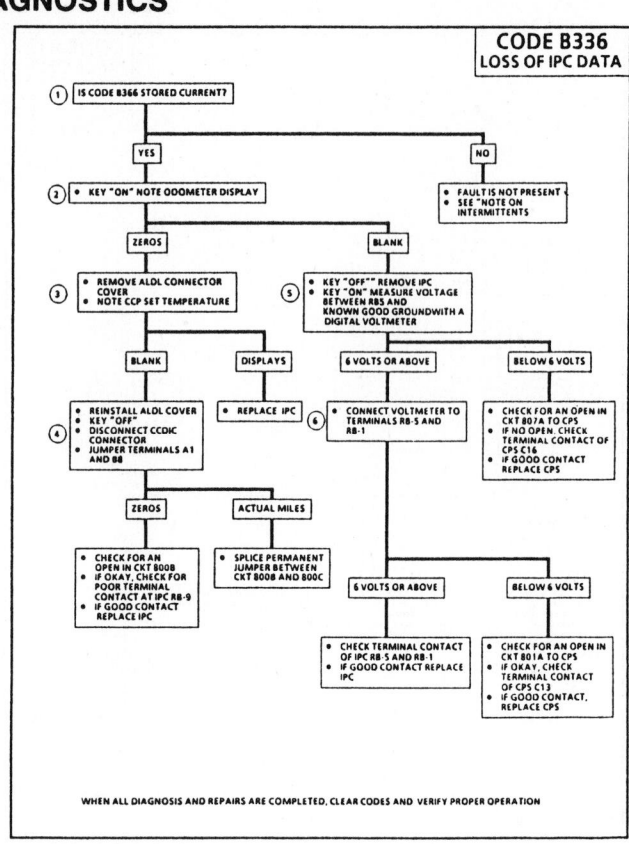

WHEN ALL DIAGNOSIS AND REPAIRS ARE COMPLETED, CLEAR CODES AND VERIFY PROPER OPERATION

CODE B337
LOSS OF HVAC PROGRAMMER DATA

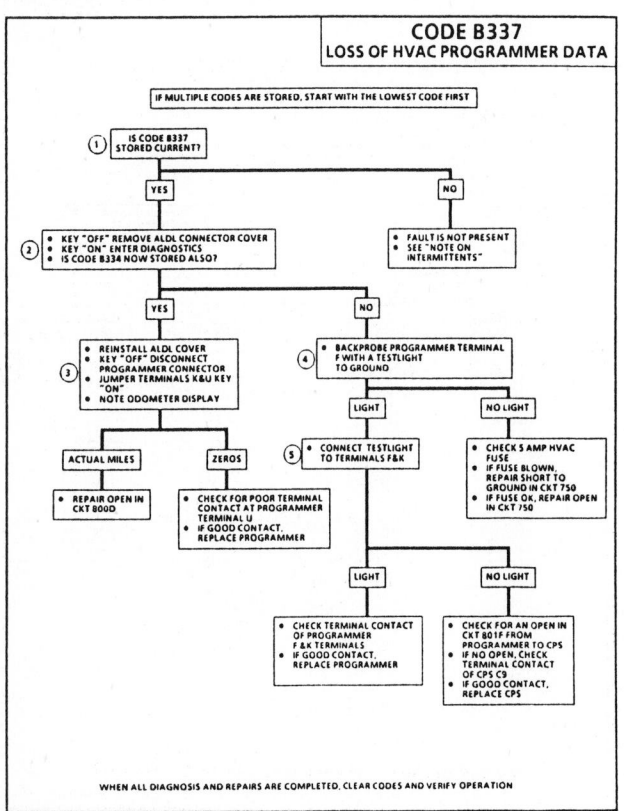

WHEN ALL DIAGNOSIS AND REPAIRS ARE COMPLETED, CLEAR CODES AND VERIFY OPERATION

CODE B410
CHARGING SYSTEM CIRCUIT

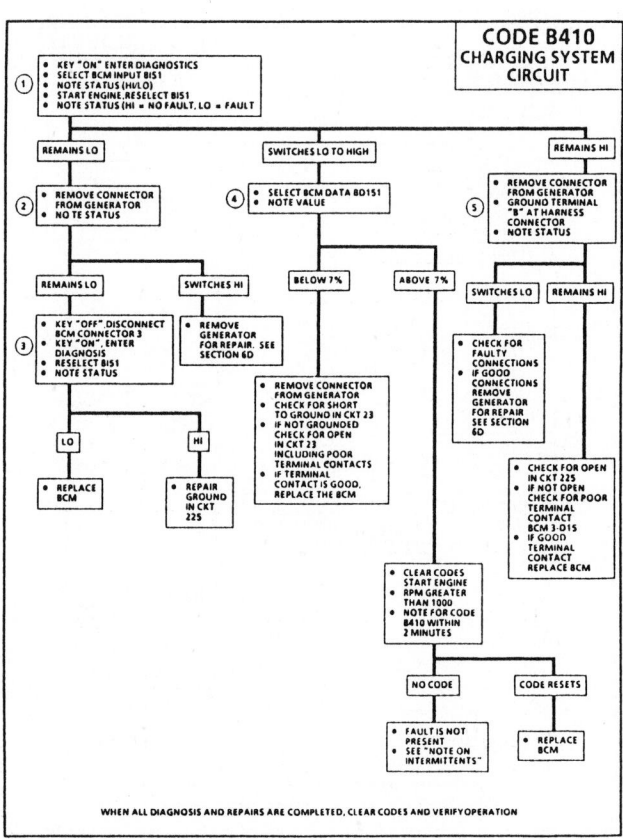

WHEN ALL DIAGNOSIS AND REPAIRS ARE COMPLETED, CLEAR CODES AND VERIFY OPERATION

DFI TROUBLE DIAGNOSTICS

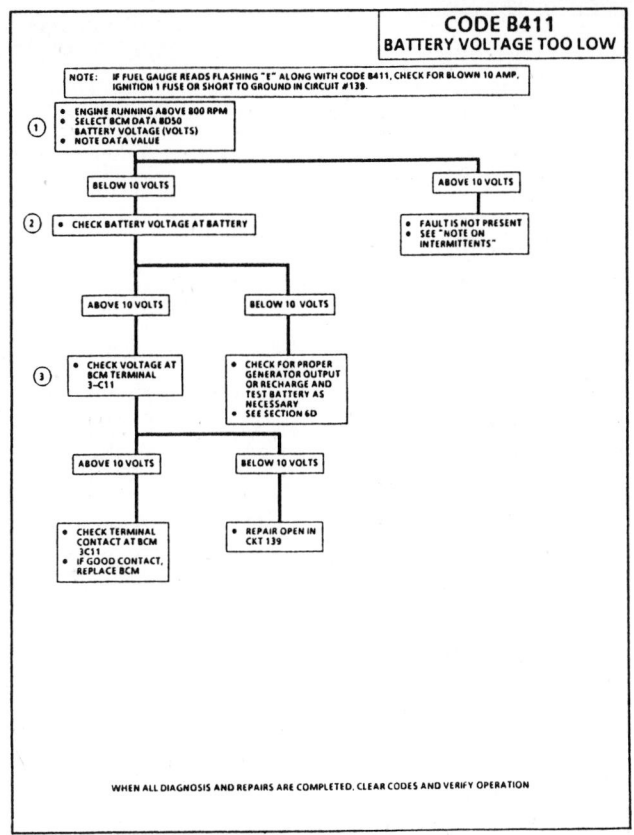

CODE B411
BATTERY VOLTAGE TOO LOW

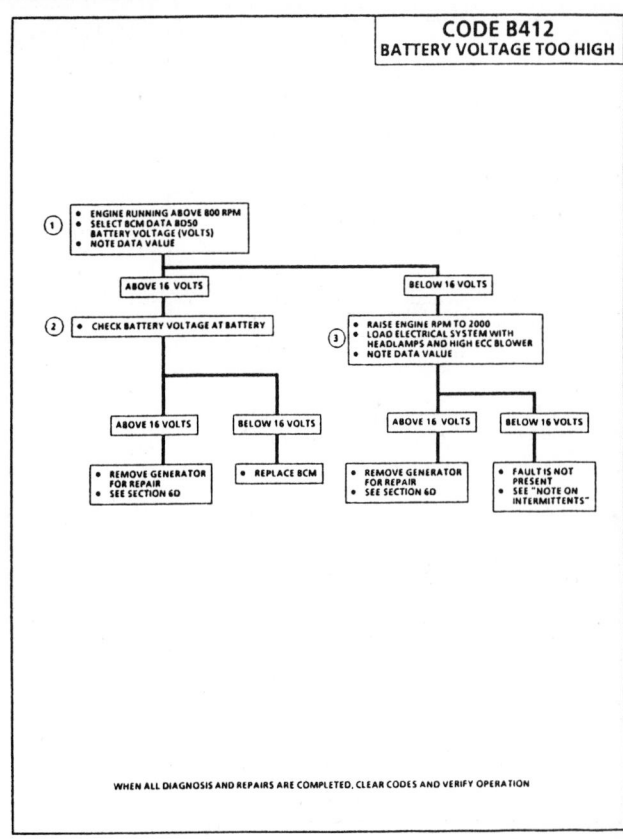

CODE B412
BATTERY VOLTAGE TOO HIGH

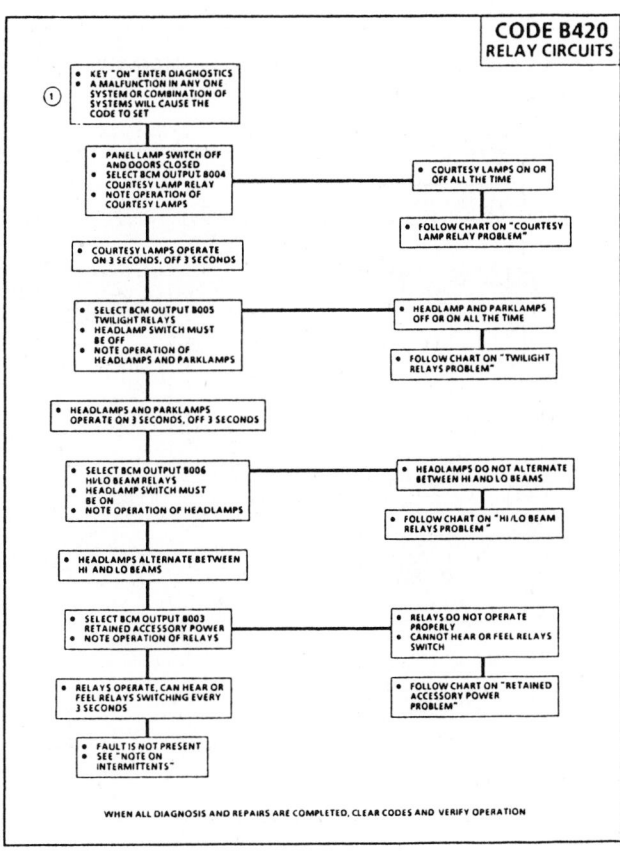

CODE B420
RELAY CIRCUITS

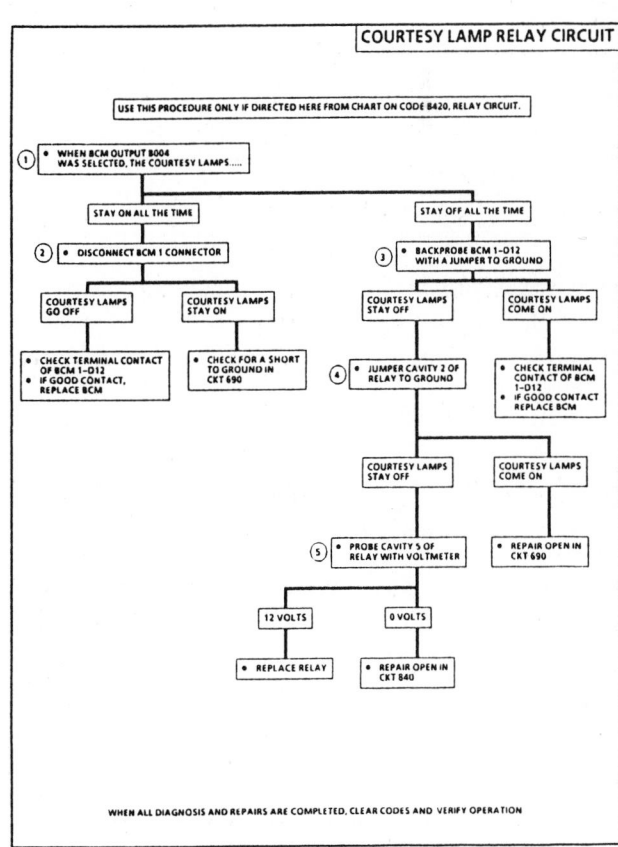

COURTESY LAMP RELAY CIRCUIT

DFI TROUBLE DIAGNOSTICS

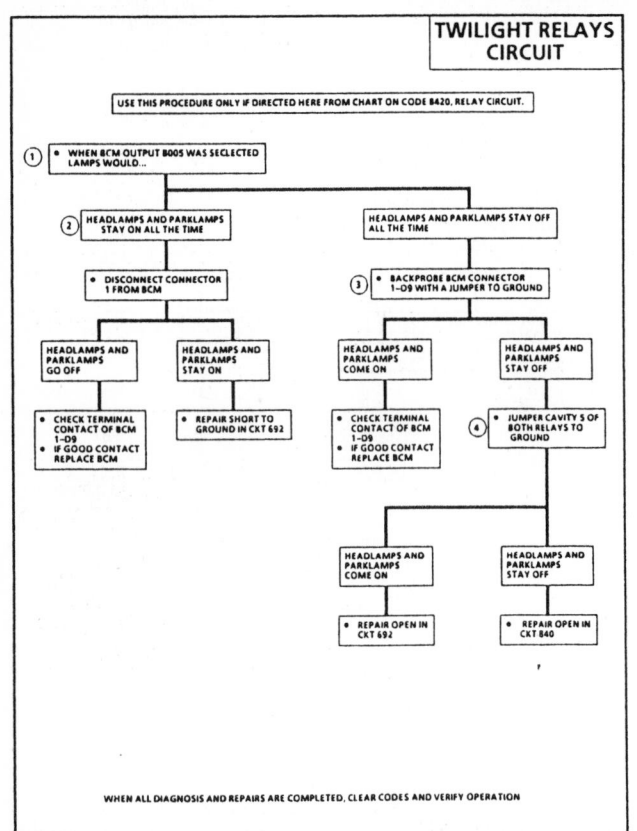

TWILIGHT RELAYS CIRCUIT

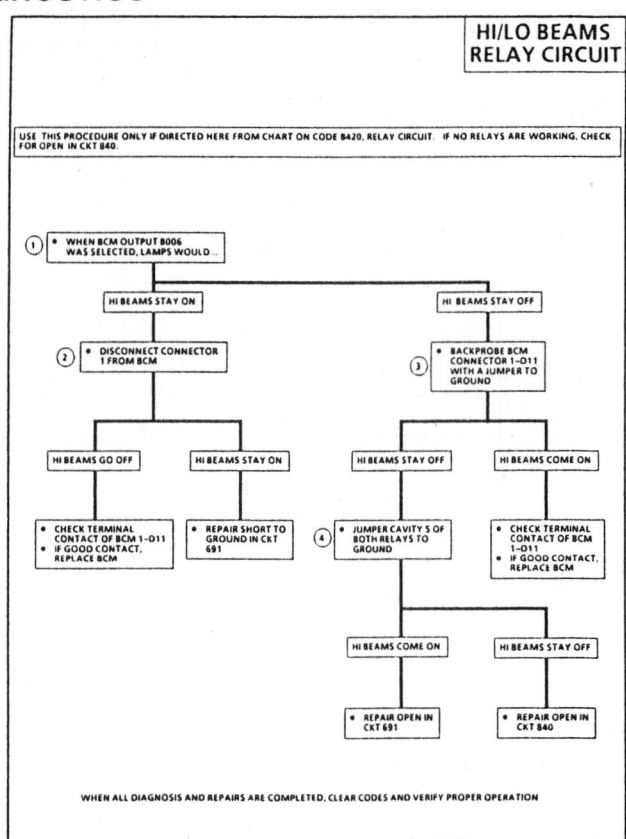

HI/LO BEAMS RELAY CIRCUIT

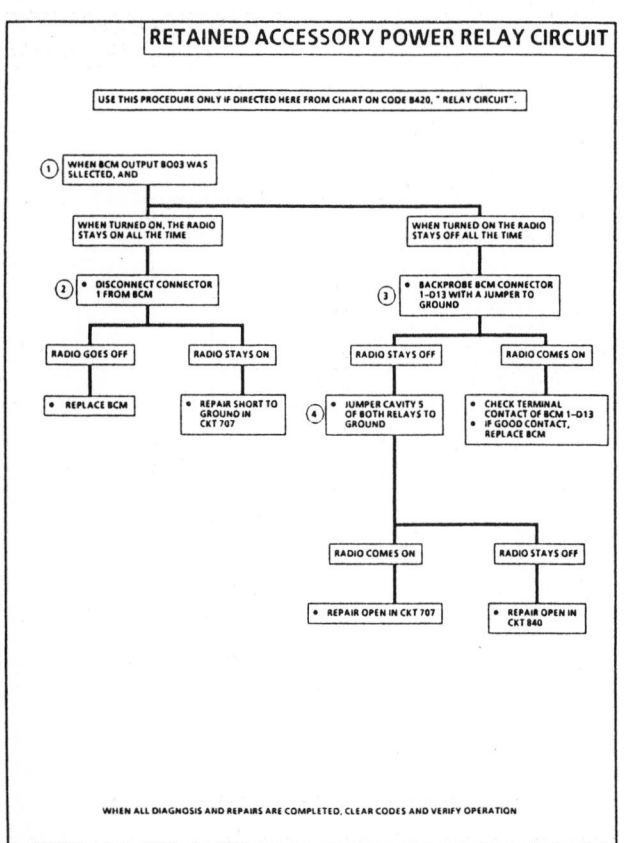

RETAINED ACCESSORY POWER RELAY CIRCUIT

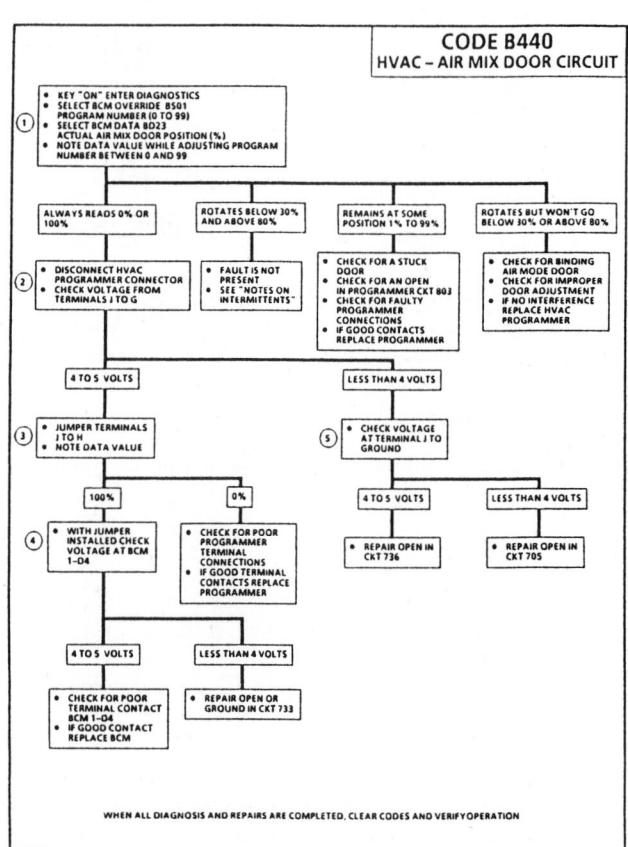

CODE B440
HVAC – AIR MIX DOOR CIRCUIT

DFI TROUBLE DIAGNOSTICS

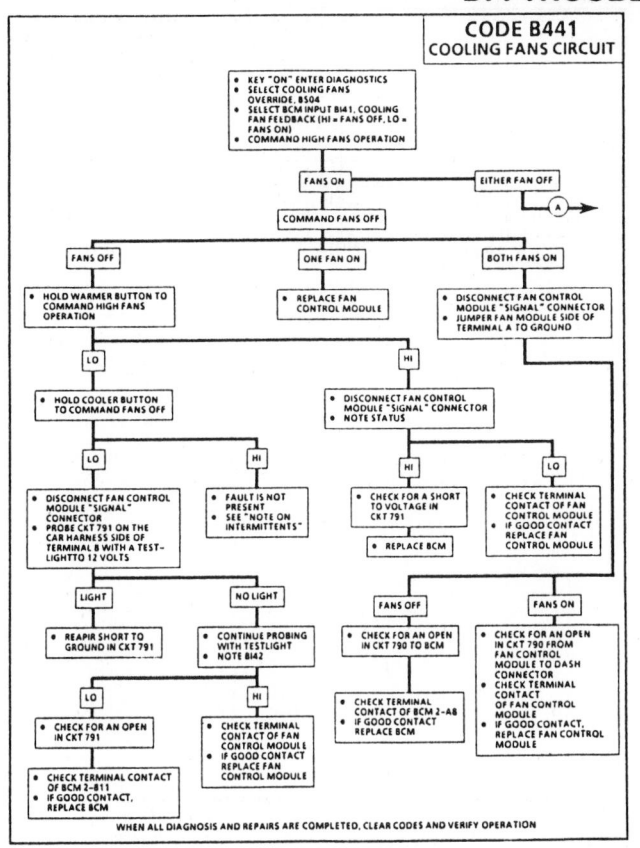

CODE B441
COOLING FANS CIRCUIT

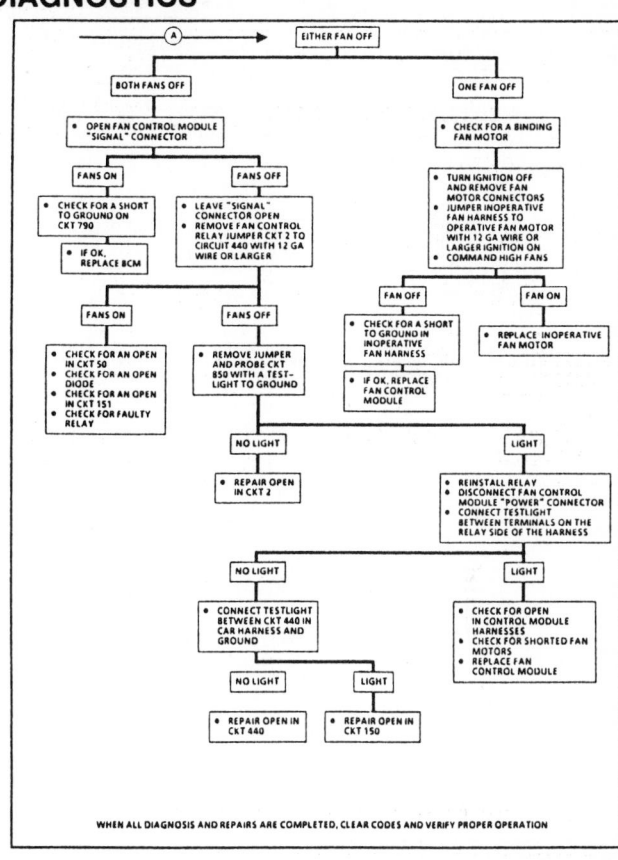

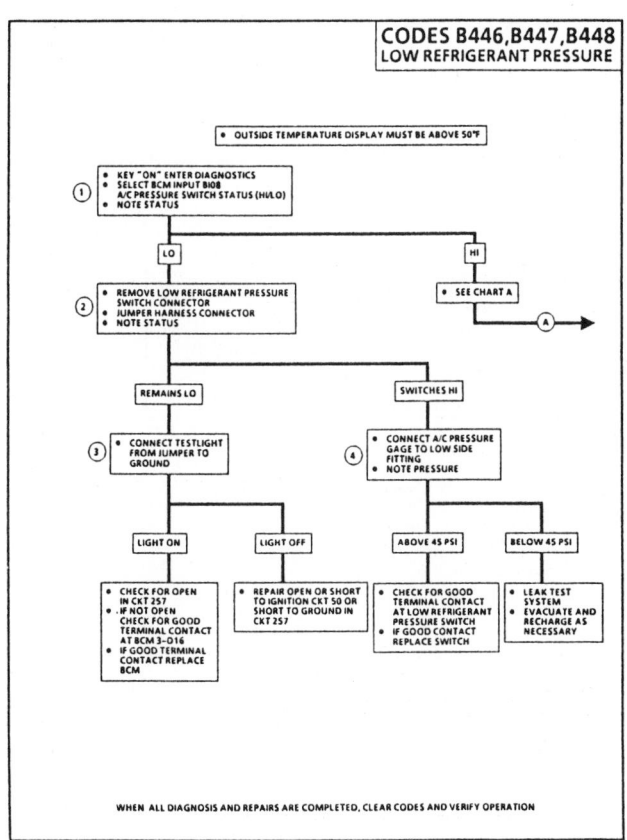

CODES B446, B447, B448
LOW REFRIGERANT PRESSURE

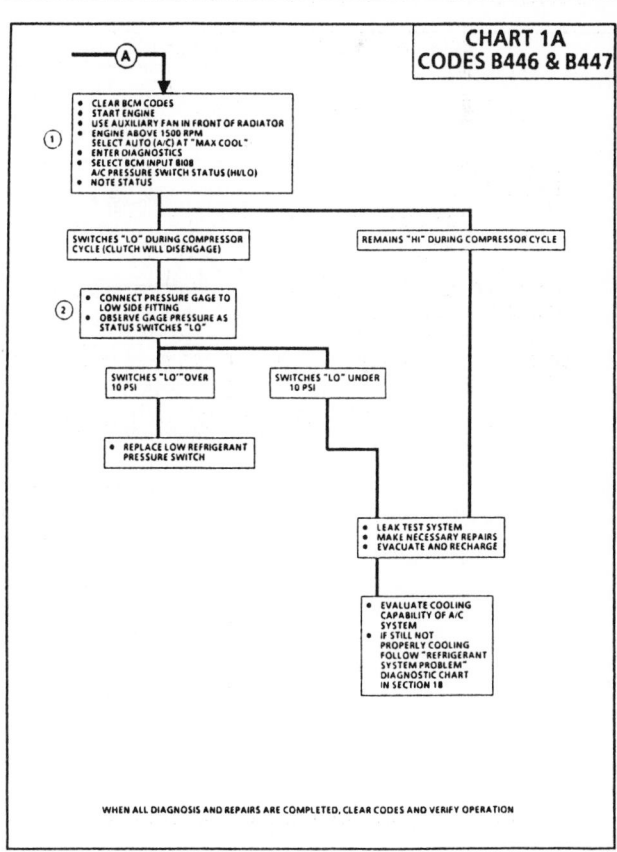

CHART 1A
CODES B446 & B447

DFI TROUBLE DIAGNOSTICS

CODE B449
HVAC – HIGH SIDE TEMPERATURE TOO HIGH

CODE B449 IS DESIGNED TO DISENGAGE THE A/C COMPRESSOR CLUTCH IN THE EVENT THAT HIGH SIDE REFRIGERANT TEMPERATURE EXCEEDS 93°C (199°F). THE A/C COMPRESSOR WILL COME BACK ON ONCE THE HI SIDE TEMPERATURE FALLS BELOW 93°C.

- KEY "ON" ENGINE RUNNING WITH A/C ON
- SELECT BCM DATA BD27
- A/C HIGH SIDE TEMPERATURE (°C)
- NOTE TEMPERATURE DISPLAYED DURING A/C OPERATION

IF THE CODE WAS STORED OR CURRENT TEMPERATURE EXCEEDS 93°C, POSSIBLE CAUSES FOR EXCESSIVE HIGH A/C HEAD PRESSURE MUST BE CHECKED. FOR A REFRIGERANT SYSTEM PERFORMANCE TEST SEE SECTION 1B.

WHEN ALL DIAGNOSIS AND REPAIRS ARE COMPLETED, CLEAR CODES AND VERIFY OPERATION

CODE B552
KEEP ALIVE MEMORY ERROR

CODE B552 INDICATES THAT THE KEEP ALIVE – OR "LONG TERM" – MEMORY IN THE BCM HAS BEEN RESET. THIS WILL BE THE CASE WHENEVER POWER IS REMOVED FROM THE BCM (SUCH AS, DISCONNECTING THE BATTERY CABLES OR DISCONNECTING BCM POWER CONNECTOR). THIS CODE SHOULD BE CLEARED FROM MEMORY AFTER RESTORING THE BCM POWER SUPPLY.

- VEHICLE MUST BE AT NORMAL OPERATING TEMPERATURE
- CHARGING AND STARTER SYSTEM MUST BE IN GOOD OPERATING CONDITION

WHEN ALL DIAGNOSIS AND REPAIRS ARE COMPLETED, CLEAR CODES AND VERIFY OPERATION

CODE B450
HVAC – COOLANT TEMPERATURE TOO HIGH

IF CODE E014 IS ALSO STORED, GO THERE FIRST

CODE B450 IS DESIGNED TO DISENGAGE THE A/C COMPRESSOR CLUTCH IF THE ENGINE COOLANT TEMPERATURE EXCEEDS 126°C (261°F) AND RE-ENGAGE WHEN THE TEMPERATURE FALLS BELOW 120°C.

- ENGINE RUNNING, ENTER DIAGNOSTICS
- SELECT BCM DATA BD21, COOLANT TEMPERATURE (°C)
- NOTE COOLANT TEMPERATURE

ENGINE OVERHEATING MAY ACCOMPANY THIS CODE. IF COOLANT TEMPERATURE EXCEEDS NORMAL OPERATING RANGE CHECK FOR SOURCES OF OVERHEATING (SEE ENGINE COOLING SECTION 6B). CAREFULLY CHECK ALL SOURCES OF INTERMITTENT ENGINE OVERHEATING SUCH AS IMPROPER COOLING FAN OPERATION (SECTION 6), FAULTY BELT OR BELT TENSION, COOLANT LEVEL, AND RESTRICTIONS, FAULTY HOSES, OR ROUTINGS. IF COOLANT TEMPERATURE DISPLAYED EXCEEDS ACTUAL COOLANT TEMPERATURE AS MEASURED WITH A RADIATOR COOLANT TEMPERATURE TESTING DEVICE, THE SENSOR MAY BE FAULTY.

WHEN ALL DIAGNOSIS AND REPAIRS ARE COMPLETED, CLEAR CODES AND VERIFY OPERATION

CODE B556
ODOMETER (EE) PROM ERROR

CODE B556 INDICATES THAT THE EE PROM, WHICH RECORDS ELAPSED ODOMETER MILEAGE IS NOT BEING READ BY THE BCM. USUALLY ALONG WITH CODE B556 "ERROR" WILL BE DISPLAYED IN THE ODOMETER DISPLAY.

- CHECK FOR PROPER EE PROM INSTALLATION
- IF PROM IS PROPERLY INSTALLED, NO BENT PINS, THEN REPLACE EE PROM.

  NOTE: NEW EE PROM WILL HAVE TO BE ADJUSTED TO THE CURRENT MILEAGE AND PROPER VIN AND OPTION CONTENT BY THE AC DELCO REPAIR STATION.

- IF A PROPERLY INSTALLED EE PROM CONTINUES TO SET B556, REPLACE BCM

WHEN ALL DIAGNOSIS AND REPAIRS ARE COMPLETED, CLEAR CODES AND VERIFY OPERATION

DFI TROUBLE DIAGNOSTICS

CODE B660
CRUISE – NOT IN DRIVE

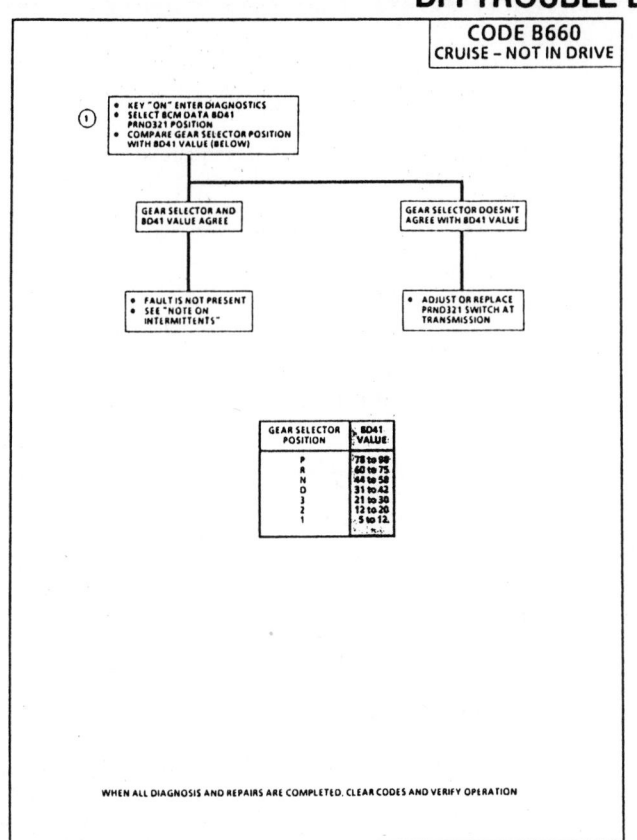

GEAR SELECTOR POSITION	BD41 VALUE
P	78 to 90
R	60 to 75
N	44 to 58
D	31 to 42
3	21 to 30
2	12 to 20
1	5 to 12

WHEN ALL DIAGNOSIS AND REPAIRS ARE COMPLETED, CLEAR CODES AND VERIFY OPERATION

CODE B664
CRUISE - ACCELERATION TOO HIGH

IF ANY CODES HIGHER THAN B664 ARE ALSO SET, GO TO THAT CODE(S) FIRST.

THIS CODE WILL SET AND DISENGAGE THE CRUISE CONTROL IF VEHICLE ACCELERATION EXCEEDS A PRESET RATE CALIBRATED IN THE BCM.

THIS COULD OCCUR ON SLIPPERY PAVEMENT. UNDER THESE CONDITIONS CODE SETTING IS NORMAL.

CLEAR THE CODES AND ROAD TEST VEHICLE TO VERIFY NORMAL OPERATION.

WHEN ALL DIAGNOSIS AND REPAIRS ARE COMPLETED, CLEAR CODES AND VERIFY OPERATION

CODE B663
CRUISE - VEHICLE SPEED TOO HIGH ABOVE SET SPEED

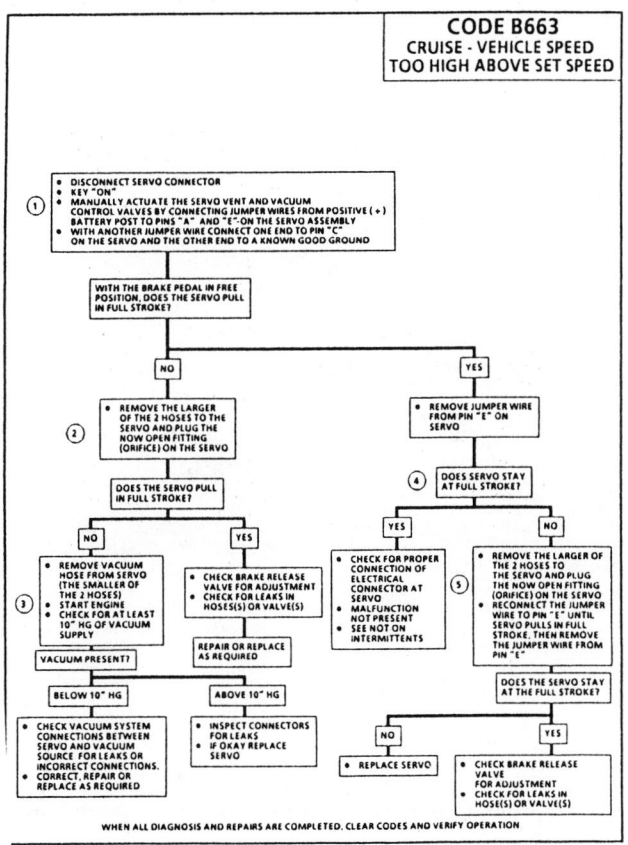

WHEN ALL DIAGNOSIS AND REPAIRS ARE COMPLETED, CLEAR CODES AND VERIFY OPERATION

CODE B666
CRUISE – ENGINE RPM TOO HIGH

IF ANY CODES HIGHER THAN B666 ARE ALSO SET, GO TO THAT CODE(S) FIRST.

THIS CODE WILL SET AND DISENGAGE THE CRUISE CONTROL IF ENGINE EXCEEDS 5000 RPM. THIS COULD OCCUR ON SLIPPERY PAVEMENT, ON EXTENDED WIDE OPEN THROTTLE ACCELERATION, OR FOR SOME MECHANICAL PROBLEMS SUCH AS TRANSMISSION SLIPPAGE. UNDER THESE CONDITIONS CODE SETTING IS NORMAL AND THE DRIVER SHOULD BE ADVISED. CLEAR THE CODE AND ROAD TEST VEHICLE TO VERIFY NORMAL OPERATION.

CODE B667
CRUISE – SET/COAST OR RESUME/ACCEL SWITCH SHORTED

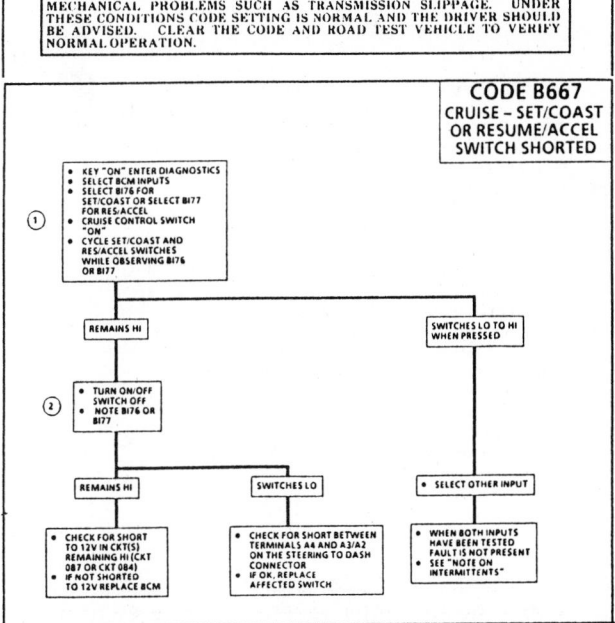

GENERAL MOTORS MULTI-PORT (MPI) AND TUNED PORT INJECTION (TPI)

GENERAL INFORMATION

The multi-port fuel injection system is controlled by an electronic control module (ECM) which monitors engine operations and generates output signals to provide the correct air/fuel mixture, ignition timing and engine idle speed control. Input to the control unit is provided by an oxygen sensor, coolant temperature sensor, detonation sensor, hot file mass sensor and throttle position sensor. The ECM also receives information concerning engine rpm, road speed, transmission gear position, power steering and air conditioning.

The injectors are located, one at each intake port, rather than the single injector found on the earlier throttle body system. The injectors are mounted on a fuel rail and are activated by a signal from the electronic control module. The injector is a solenoid-operated valve which remains open depending on the width of the electronic pulses (length of the signal) from the ECM; the longer the open time, the more fuel is injected. In this manner, the air/fuel mixture can be precisely controlled for maximum performance with minimum emissions.

Fuel is pumped from the tank by a high pressure fuel pump, located inside the fuel tank. It is a positive displacement roller vane pump. The impeller serves as a vapor separator and pre-charges the high pressure assembly. A pressure regulator maintains 28–36 psi (28–50 psi on turbocharged engines) in the fuel line to the injectors and the excess fuel is fed back to the tank. A fuel accumulator is used to dampen the hydraulic line hammer in the system created when all injectors open simultaneously.

The Mass Air Flow Sensor is used to measure the mass of air that is drawn into the engine cylinders. It is located just ahead of the air throttle in the intake system and consists of a heated film which measures the mass of air, rather than just the volume. A resistor is used to measure the temperature of the film at 75 degrees above ambient temperature. As the ambient (outside) air temperature rises, more energy is required to maintain the heated film at the higher temperature and the control unit used this difference in required energy to calculate the mass of the incoming air. The control unit uses this information to determine the duration of fuel injection pulse, timing and EGR.

The throttle body incorporates an idle air control (IAC) that provides for a bypass channel through which air can flow. It consists of an orifice and pintle which is controlled by the ECM through a step motor. The IAC provides air flow for idle and allows additional air during cold start until the engine reaches operating temperature. As the engine temperature rises, the opening through which air passes is slowly closed.

The throttle position sensor (TPS) provides the control unit with information on throttle position, in order to determine injector pulse width and hence correct mixture. The TPS is connected to the throttle shaft on the throttle body and consists of as potentiometer with on end connected to a 5 volt source from the ECM and the other to ground. A third wire is connected to the ECM to measure the voltage output from the TPS which changes as the throttle valve angle is changed (accelerator pedal moves). At the closed throttle position, the output is low (approximately .4 volts); as the throttle valve opens, the output increases to a maximum 5 volts at wide open throttle (WOT). The TPS can be misadjusted open, shorted, or loose and if it is out of adjustment, the idle quality or WOT performance may be poor. A loose TPS can cause intermittent bursts of fuel from the injectors and an unstable idle because the ECM thinks the throttle is moving. This should cause a trouble code to be set. Once a trouble code is set, the ECM will use a preset value for TPS and some vehicle performance may return. A small amount of engine coolant is routed through the throttle assembly to prevent freezing inside the throttle bore during cold operation.

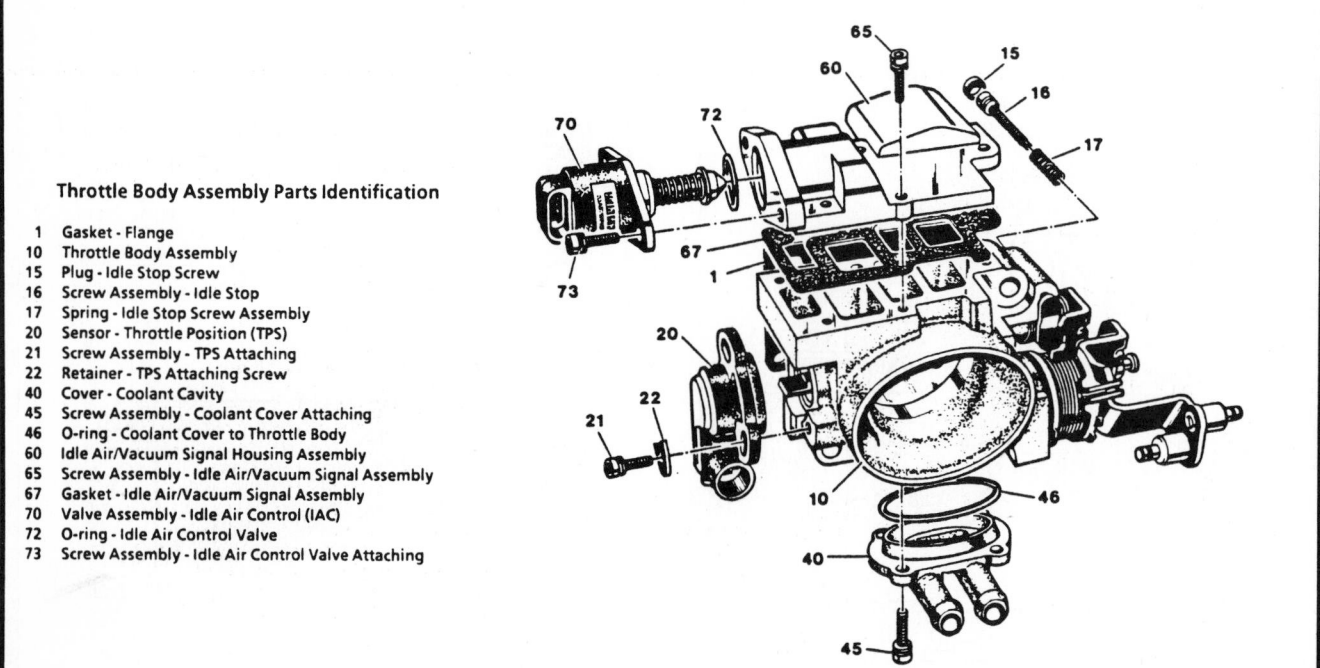

Throttle Body Assembly Parts Identification

1	Gasket - Flange
10	Throttle Body Assembly
15	Plug - Idle Stop Screw
16	Screw Assembly - Idle Stop
17	Spring - Idle Stop Screw Assembly
20	Sensor - Throttle Position (TPS)
21	Screw Assembly - TPS Attaching
22	Retainer - TPS Attaching Screw
40	Cover - Coolant Cavity
45	Screw Assembly - Coolant Cover Attaching
46	O-ring - Coolant Cover to Throttle Body
60	Idle Air/Vacuum Signal Housing Assembly
65	Screw Assembly - Idle Air/Vacuum Signal Assembly
67	Gasket - Idle Air/Vacuum Signal Assembly
70	Valve Assembly - Idle Air Control (IAC)
72	O-ring - Idle Air Control Valve
73	Screw Assembly - Idle Air Control Valve Attaching

T1D Model throttle body assembly—2.8L engine

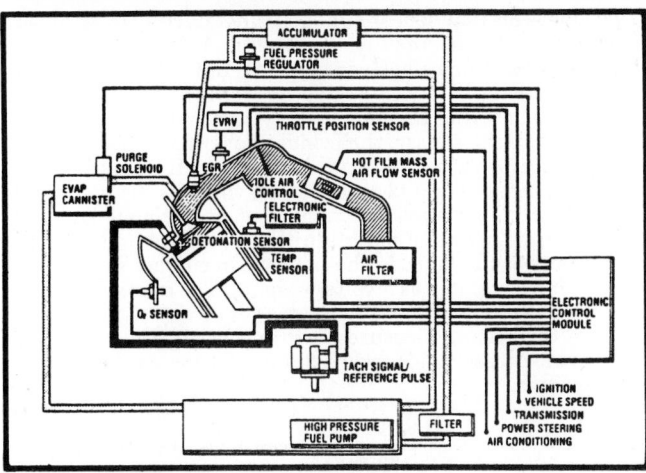

Systems overview—3.8L engine

TUNE PORT INJECTION (TPI)

This system started in 1985 and can be found in the Camaro/Firebird with the 5.0 liter V8 engine and the Corvette with the 5.7 liter V8 engine. The introduction of this TPI system to these engines has improved the torque and power from both engines. The induction system for the TPI is made up of large forward mounted air cleaners, a new mass airflow sensor, a cast aluminum throttle body assembly with dual throttle blades, a large extended cast aluminum plenum, individual aluminum tuned runners and a protruding dual fuel rail assembly with computer controlled injectors. The base plate is cast aluminum and incorporated the crossover portion of the tuned runners. The base plate also serves as a mounting for the fuel injectors. The individual aluminum runners are designed to provide the best tuning or frequency of air pulses within the runners and for the optimum throttle response throughout the driving range, thus the name Tuned Port Injection. The runners are selected by length and size so as to take advantage of the air pulses set up by the opening and closing of the intake valves.

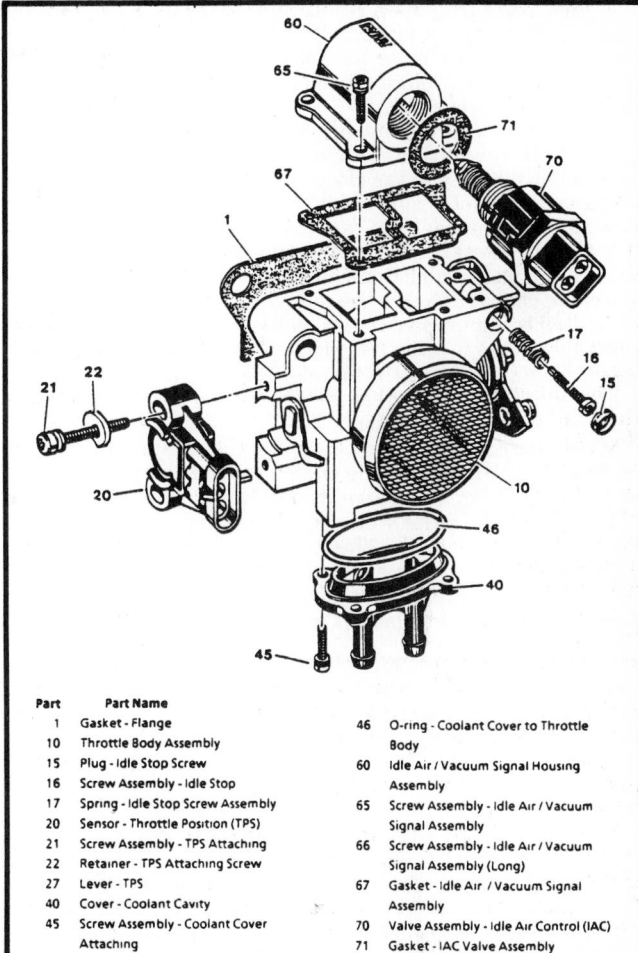

Part	Part Name	Part	Part Name
1	Gasket - Flange	46	O-ring - Coolant Cover to Throttle
10	Throttle Body Assembly		Body
15	Plug - Idle Stop Screw	60	Idle Air / Vacuum Signal Housing
16	Screw Assembly - Idle Stop		Assembly
17	Spring - Idle Stop Screw Assembly	65	Screw Assembly - Idle Air / Vacuum
20	Sensor - Throttle Position (TPS)		Signal Assembly
21	Screw Assembly - TPS Attaching	66	Screw Assembly - Idle Air / Vacuum
22	Retainer - TPS Attaching Screw		Signal Assembly (Long)
27	Lever - TPS	67	Gasket - Idle Air / Vacuum Signal
40	Cover - Coolant Cavity		Assembly
45	Screw Assembly - Coolant Cover	70	Valve Assembly - Idle Air Control (IAC)
	Attaching	71	Gasket - IAC Valve Assembly

Typical throttle body assembly—3.0L and 3.8L engine

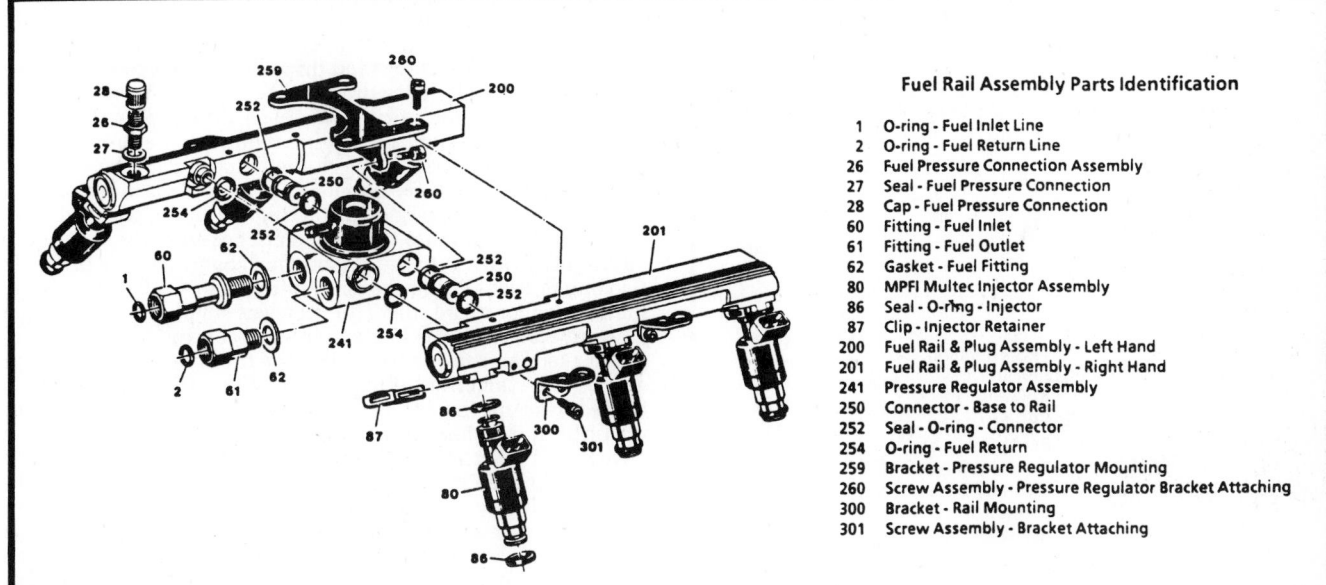

Fuel Rail Assembly Parts Identification

1	O-ring - Fuel Inlet Line
2	O-ring - Fuel Return Line
26	Fuel Pressure Connection Assembly
27	Seal - Fuel Pressure Connection
28	Cap - Fuel Pressure Connection
60	Fitting - Fuel Inlet
61	Fitting - Fuel Outlet
62	Gasket - Fuel Fitting
80	MPFI Multec Injector Assembly
86	Seal - O-ring - Injector
87	Clip - Injector Retainer
200	Fuel Rail & Plug Assembly - Left Hand
201	Fuel Rail & Plug Assembly - Right Hand
241	Pressure Regulator Assembly
250	Connector - Base to Rail
252	Seal - O-ring - Connector
254	O-ring - Fuel Return
259	Bracket - Pressure Regulator Mounting
260	Screw Assembly - Pressure Regulator Bracket Attaching
300	Bracket - Rail Mounting
301	Screw Assembly - Bracket Attaching

F6C Model fuel rail assembly

The high pressure pulses result in denser air at each intake valve, and timing the pressure pulses to occur during the valve open period forces more air into the combustion chamber, which results in a more efficient cylinder charging and improved volumetric efficiency.

The eight fuel injectors fire at the same time, once each crankshaft revolution. During the first injection, fuel is sprayed at the base of the closed intake valve, during the second injection, fuel is sprayed into the air stream entering the combustion chamber. The fuel from the first injection vaporizes from the heat of the intake valve, and the fuel vapors are drawn into the combustion chamber along with the air when the valve opens to charge the cylinder. The regulated pressure of the fuel being injected in the 5.0 liter V8 engine is 44 psi and the 37 psi in the 5.7 liter V8 engine. This fuel pressure is regulated constantly, or, as the manifold vacuum changes, the regulator adjusts the fuel pressure to maintain a constant drop in pressure across the injectors.

When the signals are received by the computer from the mass airflow sensor and the engine coolant temperature sensor, the computer will search its pre-programmed information to determine the pulse width of the fuel injectors required to match the input signals. The computer now, based on the engine rpm, signals the injectors to release the required amount of fuel. The computer makes mass air flow sensor readings and fuel requirement calculations every 12.5 milliseconds.

The mass air flow sensor and the individual fuel injectors are made by Bosch and supplied by General Motors. The mass air flow sensor contains a hot-wire sensing unit, which is make up of an electronic balanced bridge network, and measures the mass of air entering the injections system. When ever current is supplied to the sensor, the bridge is energized and the sensing hot-wire is heated. When the air enters the mass air flow sensor is passes over and cools the hot wire. As the hot wire is cooled down its resistance is changed and additional current is then required, so as to maintain the resistance and keep the bridge network balanced. The increase in current is then supplied to the computer as a voltage signal. The computer inturn coverts the voltage signal into grams per second of air flow and because the system measures in grams of air, the changes in barometric pressure, altitude and humidity are automatically compensated.

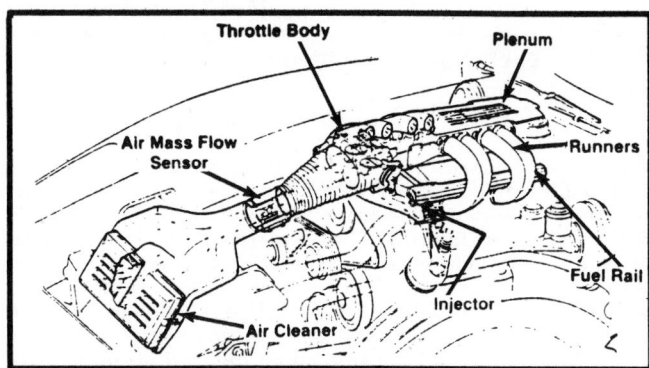

Typical Tuned Port Injection system

The fuel rail assembly is located under the inlet plenum, between the right and left side runners. The fuel injectors (8) mount in the base plate and each injector is sealed with the use of an O-ring. The fuel injectors are mounted approximately 7/16 in. (110mm) from the intake valve and projects a cone-shaped spray with a 20 degree cone angle that is aimed at the base of the valve stem. The injectors are the pintle type, have electromagnetic solenoids, and operate on ignition voltage.

During cold starting, additional fuel is supplied by a cold start valve that is mounted in the left side of the base plate. The additional fuel is injected into a long passage in the base plate and fuel vapors are drawn out at low ambient temperatures (−20°F) through orifices to each intake port. During a cold starting situation, the engine requires an extremely rich air-fuel ratio to provide enough fuel vaporization for combustion. Because of the small amount of air drawn into the combustion chamber during cold starting cranking, the cold start valve supplies fuel into the base plate passage where only the vapors are drawn into the combustion chamber. This prevents flooding or fuel fouling the spark plugs that would occur if the fuel needed for a cold start situation was supplied only from the main injectors. This cold start valve is controlled by a type of coolant temperature sensor called the thermo-time switch, and also by the starter cranking circuit. When the ignition key is turned to crank the engine, the thermal-time switch will heat up until it reaches approximately 95°F at which time the switch will open and de-energize the cold start injector. The maximum time for the cold start injector to be energized is 12 seconds, with an engine temperature of −4°F or below. When the engine starts and the ignition key is released, the circuit is also de-energized. Except for the new mass air flow system, the new tuned runners and longer plenum assembly the rest of this TPI system is very similar to the multi-port fuel injection system.

1. Flange Gasket
2. Throttle Body Assembly
3. Idle Stop Screw Plug
4. Idle Stop Screw Assembly
5. Idle Stop Screw Spring
6. Throttle Position Sensor (TPS)
7. TPS Attaching Screw Assembly
8. TPS Attaching Screw Retainer
9. Clean Air Cover
10. Clean Air Cover Screw Assembly
11. Clean Air Cover Gasket
12. Idle Air Control Valve Coolant Cover Assembly
13. Idle Air Control Valve Screw Assembly
14. Idle Air Control Valve Coolant Cover Gasket to Throttle Body
15. Idle Air Control Valve Assembly
16. Idle Air Control Valve Assembly Gasket

Exploded view of the TPI throttle body

FUEL CONTROL SYSTEM

The basic function of the fuel control system is to control the fuel delivery to the engine. The fuel is delivered to the engine by individual fuel injectors mounted on the intake manifold near each cylinder.

The main control sensor is the oxygen sensor which is located in the exhaust manifold. The oxygen sensor tells the ECM how much oxygen is in the exhaust gas and the ECM changes the air/fuel ratio to the engine by controlling the fuel injectors. The best mixture to minimize exhaust emissions is 14.7:1 which allows the catalytic converter to operate the most efficiently. Because of the constant measuring and adjusting of the air/fuel ratio, the fuel injection system is called a "Closed Loop" system.

Modes Of Operation

The ECM looks at voltage from several sensors to determine how much fuel to give the engine. The fuel is delivered under one of several conditions, called "Modes".

STARTING MODE

When the engine is first turned "ON", the ECM will turn on the fuel pump relay for two seconds and the the fuel pump will build up pressure. The ECM then checks the coolant temperature sensor, throttle position sensor and crank sensor, then the ECM determines the proper air/fuel ratio for starting. This ranges from 1.5:1 at −33°F (−36°C) to 14.7:1 at 201°F (94°C).

The ECM controls the amount of fuel that is delivered in the Starting Mode by changing how long the injectors are turned "ON" and "OFF". This is done by "pulsing" the injectors for very short times.

CLEAR FLOOD MODE

If for some reason the engine should become flooded, provisions have been made to clear this condition. To clear the flood, the driver must depress the accelerator pedal enough to open to wide-open throttle position. The ECM then issues injector pulses at a rate that would be equal to an air/fuel ratio of 20:1. The ECM maintains this injector rate as long as the throttle remains wide open and the engine RPM is below 600. If the throttle position becomes less than 80%, the ECM then would return to the Starting Mode.

RUN MODE

There are two different run modes. When the engine is first started and the RPM is above 400, the system goes into open loop operation. In open loop operation, the ECM will ignore the signal from the oxygen (0_2) sensor and calculate the injector on-time based upon inputs from the coolant and MAP sensors (or MAF sensor).

During open loop operation, the ECM analyzes the following items to determine when the system is ready to go to the closed loop mode.

1. The oxygen sensor varying voltage output. (This is dependent on temperature).
2. The coolant sensor must be above specified temperature.
3. A specific amount of time must elapse after starting the engine. These values are stored in the PROM.

When these conditions have been met, the system goes into closed loop operation In closed loop operation, the ECM will modify the pulse width (injector on-time) based upon the signal from the oxygen sensor. The ECM will decrease the on-time if the air/fuel ratio is too rich, and will increase the on-time if the air/fuel ratio is too lean.

ACCELERATION MODE

When the engine is required to accelerate, the opening of the throttle valve(s) causes a rapid increase in manifold absolute pressure (MAP). This rapid increase in MAP causes fuel to condense on the manifold walls. The ECM senses this increase in throttle angle and MAP, and supplies additional fuel for a short period of time. This prevents the engine from stumbling due to too lean a mixture.

DECELERATION MODE

Upon deceleration, a leaner fuel mixture is required to reduce emission of hydrocarbons (HC) and carbon monoxide (CO). To adjust the injection on-time, the ECM uses the decrease in MAP and the decrease in throttle position to calculate a decrease in pulse width. To maintain an idle fuel ratio of 14.7:1, fuel output is momentarily reduced. This is done because of the fuel remaining in the intake manifold. The ECM can cut off the fuel completely for short periods of time.

BATTERY VOLTAGE CORRECTION MODE

The purpose of battery voltage correction is to compensate for variations in battery voltage to fuel pump and injector response. The ECM modifies the pulse width by a correction factor in the PROM. When battery voltage decreases, pulse width increases.

Battery voltage correction takes place in all operating modes.

When battery voltage is low, the spark delivered by the distributor may be low. To correct this low battery voltage problem, the ECM can do any or all of the following:

a. Increase injector pulse width (increase fuel).
b. Increase idle RPM.
c. Increase ignition dwell time.

FUEL CUT-OFF MODE

When the ignition is off, the ECM will not energize the injector. Fuel will also be cut off if the ECM does not receive a reference pulse from the distributor. To prevent dieseling, fuel delivery is completely stopped as soon as the engine is stopped. The ECM will not allow any fuel supply until it receives distributor reference pulses which prevents flooding.

CONVERTER PROTECTION MODE

In this mode the ECM estimates the temperature of the catalytic converter and then modifies fuel delivery to protect the converter from high temperatures. When the ECM has determined that the converter may overheat, it will cause open loop operation and will enrichen the fuel delivery. A slightly richer mixture will then cause the converter temperature to be reduced.

Fuel Control Systems Components

The fuel control system is made up of the following components:

1. Fuel Supply System.

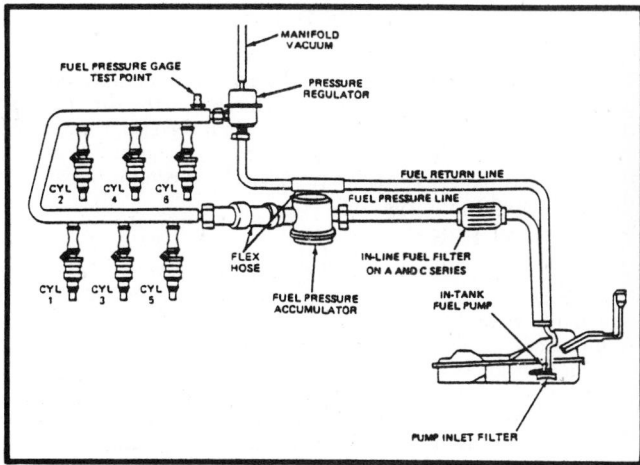

Typical fuel system layout

2. Throttle Body Assembly.
3. Fuel Injectors.
4. Fuel Rail.
5. Fuel Pressure Regulator.
6. Idle Air Control (IAC).
7. Fuel Pump.
8. Fuel Pump Relay.

The fuel control system starts with the fuel in the fuel tank. An electric fuel pump, located in the fuel tank with the fuel gauge sending unit, pumps fuel to the fuel rail through an in-line fuel filter. The pump is designed to provide fuel at a pressure above the pressure needed by the injectors. A pressure regulator in the fuel rail keeps fuel available to the injectors at a constant pressure. Unused fuel is returned to the fuel tank by a separate line.

The injectors are controlled by the ECM. They deliver fuel in one of several modes as previously described. In order to properly control the fuel supply, the fuel pump is operated by the ECM through the fuel pump relay and oil pressure switch.

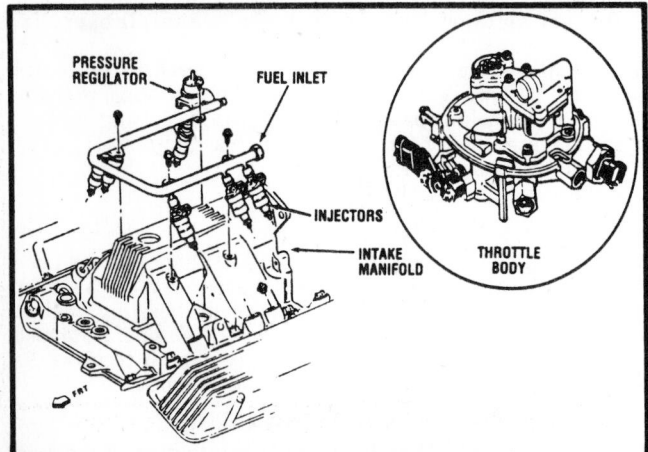

Typical fuel rail and throttle body assemblies

THROTTLE BODY UNIT

The throttle body unit has a throttle valve to control the amount of air delivered to the engine. The TPS and IAC valve are also mounted onto the throttle body. The throttle body contains vacuum ports located at, above or below the throttle valve. These vacuum ports generate the vacuum signals needed by various components.

On some models, the engine coolant is directed through the coolant cavity at the bottom of the throttle body to warm the throttle valve and prevent icing.

FUEL RAIL

The fuel rail is mounted on top of the engine. It distributes fuel to the individual injectors. Fuel is delivered to the input end of the fuel rail by the fuel lines, goes through the rail, then to the fuel pressure regulator. The regulator keeps the fuel pressure to the injectors at a constant pressure. The remaining fuel is then returned to the fuel tank.

FUEL INJECTOR

The fuel injector is a solenoid operated device controlled by the ECM. The ECM turns on the solenoid, which opens the a valve which allows fuel delivery. The fuel, under pressure, is injected in a conical spray pattern at the opening of the intake valve. The fuel, which is not used by the injectors, passes through the pressure regulator before returning to the fuel tank.

An injector that is partly open, will cause loss of fuel pressure after the engine is shut down, so long crank time would be noticed on some engines. Also dieseling could occur because some fuel could be delivered after the ignition is turned "OFF".

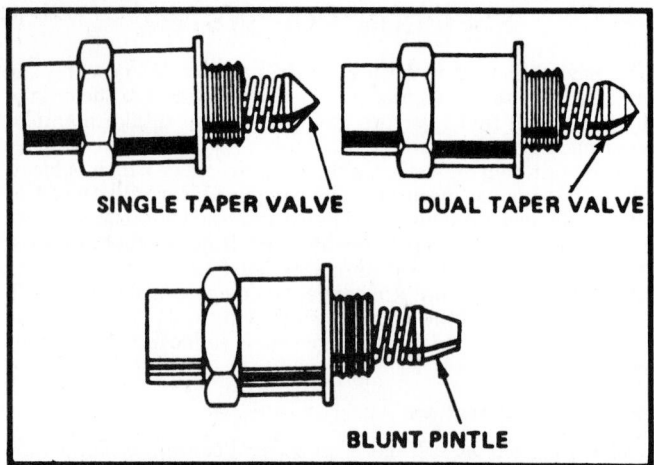

The three different designs of the idle air control valve

PRESSURE REGULATOR

The fuel pressure regulator is a diaphragm operated relief valve with injector pressure on one side and manifold pressure on the other. The function of the regulator is to maintain a constant pressure at the injector at all times. The pressure regulator also compensates for engine load, by increasing fuel pressure when it sees low engine vacuum.

The pressure regulator is mounted on the fuel rail and serviced separately. If the pressure is too low, poor performance could result. If the pressure is too high, excessive odor and a code 45 may result.

IDLE AIR CONTROL (IAC)

The purpose of the idle air control (IAC) system is to control engine idle speeds while preventing stalls due to changes in engine load. The IAC assembly, mounted on the throttle body, controls bypass air around the throttle plate. By extending or retracting a conical valve, a controlled amount of air can move around the throttle plate. If rpm is too low, more air is diverted around the throttle plate to increase rpm.

During idle, the proper position of the IAC valve is calculated by the ECM based on battery voltage, coolant temperature, engine load, and engine RPM. If the rpm drops below a specified rate, the throttle plate is closed. The ECM will then calculate a new valve position.

Three different designs are used for the IAC conical valve. The first design used is single 35 taper while the second design used is a dual taper. The third design is a blunt valve. Care should be taken to insure use of the correct design when service replacement is required.

The IAC motor has 255 different positions or steps. The zero, or reference position, is the fully extended position at which the pintle is seated in the air bypass seat and no air is allowed to bypass the throttle plate. When the motor is fully retracted, maximum air is allowed to bypass the throttle plate. When the motor is fully retracted, maximum air is allowed to bypass the throttle plate.

The ECM always monitors how many steps it has extended or retracted the pintle from the zero or reference position; thus, it always calculates the exact position of the motor. Once the engine has started and the vehicle has reached approximately 40 mph, the ECM will extend the motor 255 steps from whatever position it is in. This will bottom out the pintle against the seat. The ECM will call this position "0" and thus keep its zero reference updated.

The IAC only affects the engine's idle characteristics. If it is stuck fully open, idle speed is too high (too much air enters the throttle bore) If it is stuck closed, idle speed is too low (not enough air entering). If it is stuck somewhere in the middle, idle may be rough, and the engine won't respond to load changes.

FUEL PUMP RELAY CIRCUIT

The fuel pump relay is usually located on the left front inner fender (or shock tower) or on the engine side of the firewall (center cowl). The fuel pump electrical system consists of the fuel pump relay, ignition circuit 3 and the ECM circuits are protected by a 10 amp fuse. The fuel pump relay contact switch is in the normally open (N.O.) position.

When the ignition is turned on the ECM will for two seconds, supply voltage to the fuel pump relay coil, closing the open contact switch. The ignition circuit 3 10 amp fuse can now supply ignition voltage to the circuit which feeds the relay contact switch. With the relay contacts closed, ignition voltage is supplied to the fuel pump. The ECM will continue to supply voltage to the relay coil circuit as long as the ECM receives the rpm reference pulses from the HEI module.

The fuel pump control circuit also includes an engine oil pressure switch with a set of normally open contacts. The switch closes at approximately 4 pounds of oil pressure and provides a secondary battery feed path to the fuel pump. If the relay fails, the pump will continue to run using the battery feed supplied by the closed oil pressure switch. A failed fuel pump relay will result in extended engine crank times in order to build up enough oil pressure to close the switch and turn on the fuel pump.

Fuel System Pressure Test

When the ignition switch is turned ON, the in-tank fuel pump is energized for as long as the engine is cranking or running and the control unit is receiving signals from the HEI distributor. If there are no reference pulses, the control unit will shut off the fuel pump within two seconds. The pump will deliver fuel to the fuel rail and injectors, then the pressure regulator where the system pressure is controlled to maintain 26–46 psi.

1. Connect pressure gauge J-34730-1, or equivalent, to fuel pressure test point on the fuel rail. Wrap a rag around the pressure tap to absorb any leakage that may occur when installing the gauge.

2. Turn the ignition ON and check that pump pressure is 24–40 psi. This pressure is controlled by spring pressure within the regulator assembly.

3. Start the engine and allow it to idle. The fuel pressure should drop to 28–32 psi due to the lower manifold pressure.

NOTE: The idle pressure will vary somewhat depending on barometric pressure. Check for a drop in pressure indicating regulator control, rather than specific values.

4. On turbocharged models, use a low pressure air pump to apply air pressure to the regulator to simulate turbocharger boost pressure. Boost pressure should increase fuel pressure one pound for every pound of boost. Again, look for changes rather than specific pressures. The maximum fuel pressure should not exceed 46 psi.

5. If the fuel pressure drops, check the operation of the check valve, the pump coupling connection, fuel pressure regulator valve and the injectors. A restricted fuel line or filter may also cause a pressure drip. To check the fuel pump output, restrict the fuel return line and run 12 volts to the pump. The fuel pressure should rise to approximately 75 psi with the return line restricted.

—————— **CAUTION** ——————

Before attempting to remove or service any fuel system component, it is necessary to relieve the fuel system pressure.

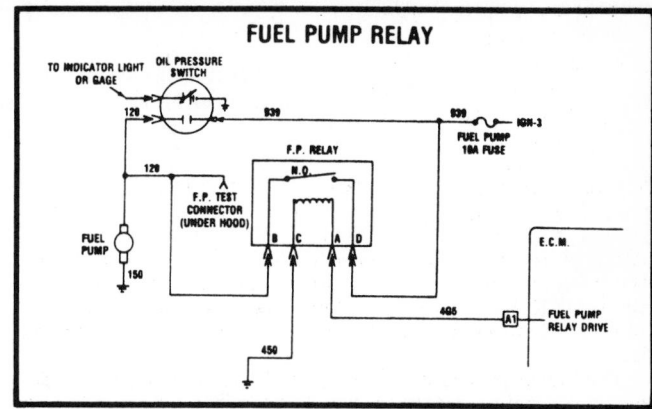

Fuel pump relay schematic in the OFF position

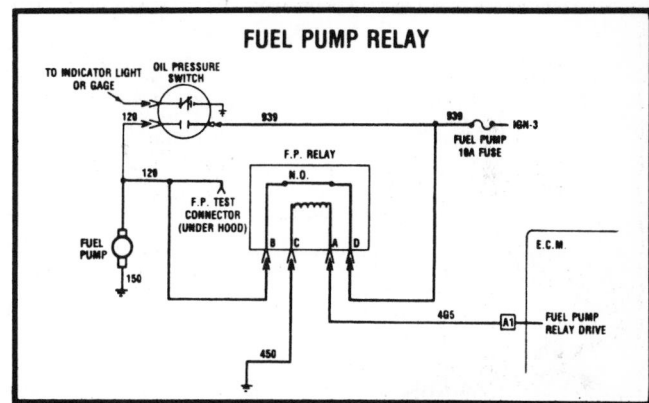

Fuel pump relay schematic in the RUN position

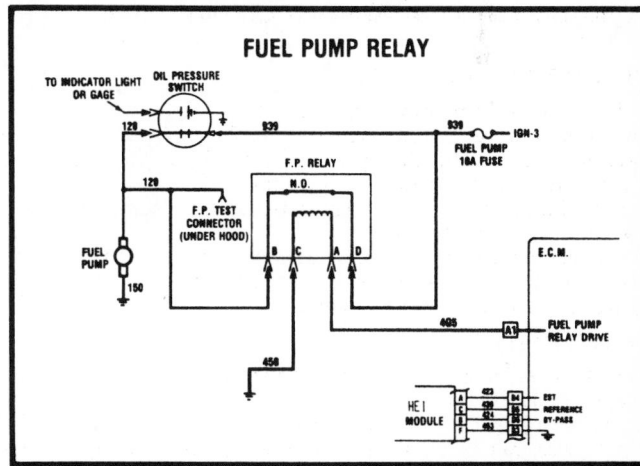

Fuel pump relay schematic in the RUN operation

Relieving Fuel System Pressure

1. Remove the fuel pump fuse from the fuse block.

2. Start the engine. It should run and then stall when the fuel in the lines is exhausted. When the engine stops, crank the starter for about three seconds to make sure all pressure in the fuel lines is released.

3. Replace the fuel pump fuse.

4. On some models a pressure relief valve is located on the fuel rail. Connect fuel gauge J-34730-1, or equivalent, to fuel pressure relief valve on the fuel rail. Wrap a rag around the

PORT FUEL INJECTION–INJECTOR BALANCE TEST
Before performing this test, the items listed below must be done.

- Check spark plugs and wires.
- Check compression.
- Check fuel injection harness for being open or shorted.

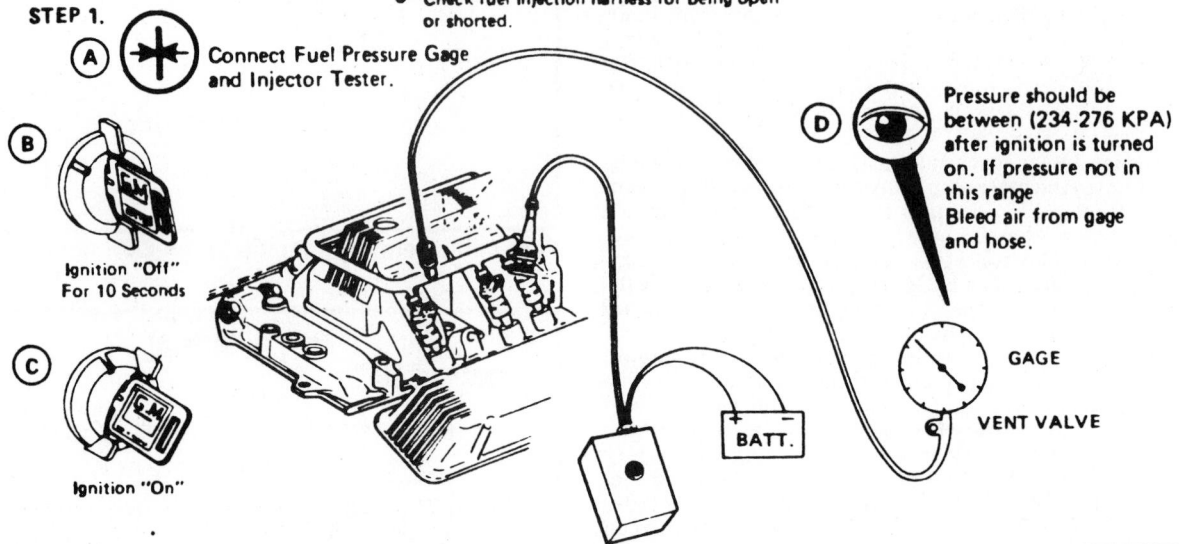

STEP 1.

(A) Connect Fuel Pressure Gage and Injector Tester.

(B) Ignition "Off" For 10 Seconds

(C) Ignition "On"

(D) Pressure should be between (234-276 KPA) after ignition is turned on. If pressure not in this range Bleed air from gage and hose.

BATT.

GAGE

VENT VALVE

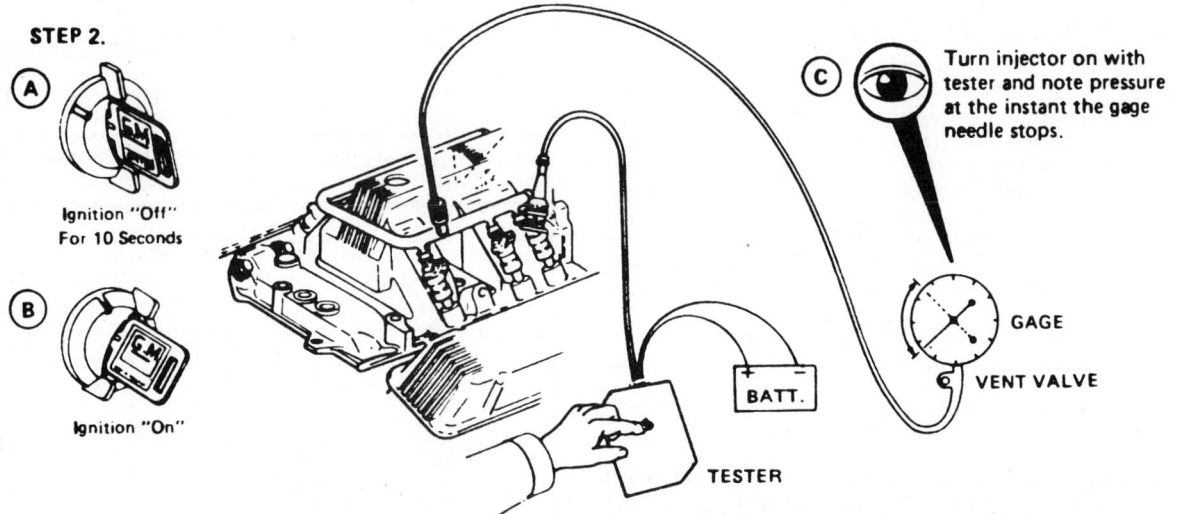

STEP 2.

(A) Ignition "Off" For 10 Seconds

(B) Ignition "On"

(C) Turn injector on with tester and note pressure at the instant the gage needle stops.

BATT.

TESTER

GAGE

VENT VALVE

STEP 3.

Repeat test as in step 2 on all injectors and record pressure drop on each.

Retest injectors that appear faulty. Replace any injectors that have a 10 KPA difference either (more or less) in pressure.

– EXAMPLE –

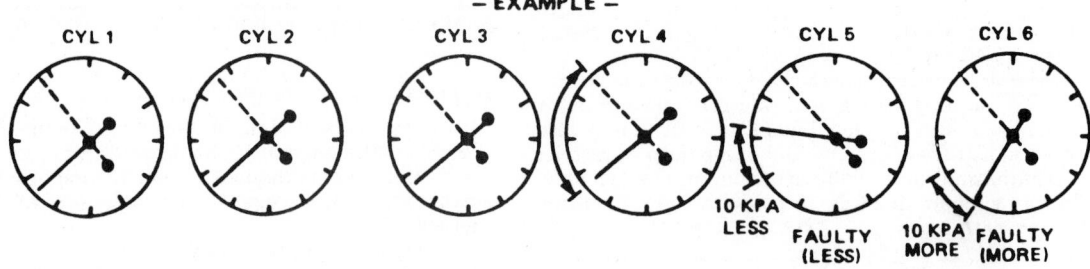

CYL 1	CYL 2	CYL 3	CYL 4	CYL 5	CYL 6

10 KPA LESS — FAULTY (LESS)

10 KPA MORE — FAULTY (MORE)

Fuel Injection balance test

pressure tap to absorb any leakage that may occur when installing the gauge.

5. Install bleed hose into a suitable container and open the the valve to bleed off the fuel pressure in the fuel system.

FUEL INJECTORS

Removal and Installation

Use care in removing the fuel injectors to prevent damage to the electrical connector pins on the injector and the nozzle. The fuel injector is serviced as a complete assembly only and should not be immersed in any kind of cleaner.

NOTE: The most widely used injector for the MPI units are Bosch injectors, but starting in 1987 there will also be a new injector being used. This new injector will be a Multec MPI injector (a Rochester product). It is classified as a top feed design because the fuel enters the top of the injector and then flows through the entire length of the injector. It is designed to operate with the system fuel pressures ranging from 36–51 psi (250–350 kPa), and uses a high impedenace (12.2 ohms) solenoid coil. It is used in the multi-port fuel injection system on some Chevrolet produced 2.8L V6 engines.

1. Relieve fuel system pressure.
2. Remove the injector electrical connections.
3. Remove the fuel rail.

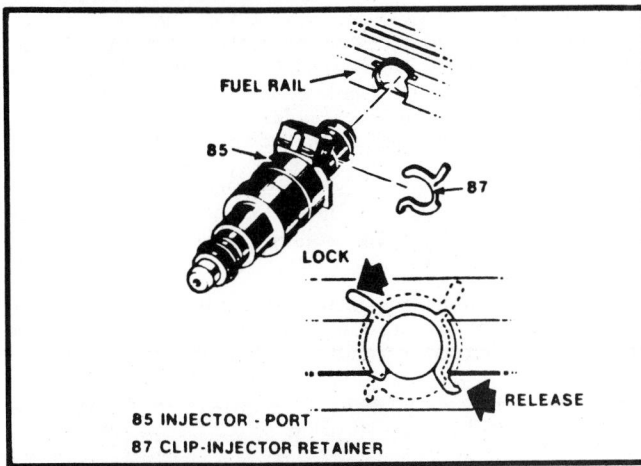

85 INJECTOR - PORT
87 CLIP-INJECTOR RETAINER

Fuel injector removal and installation

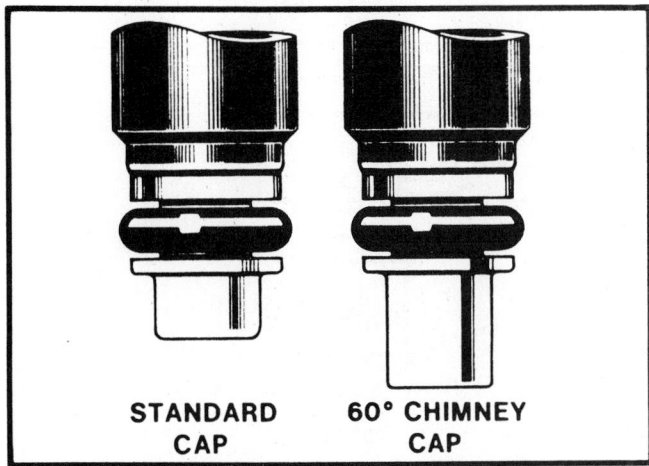

STANDARD CAP **60° CHIMNEY CAP**

Standard and Chimney—Bosch injector caps

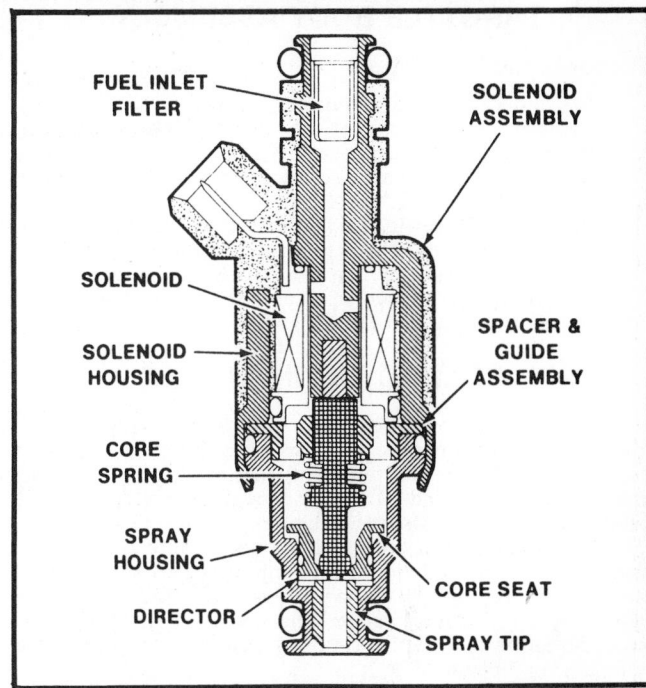

Typical Multec (top feed) injector

4. Remove the injector retaining clip (if used). Separate the injector from the fuel rail.

5. Installation is the reverse of removal. Replace the O-rings when installing injectors into intake manifold.

NOTE: As a running change during the 1987 model year, the model F8A fuel rails, used on the 5.0 and 5.7 liter V8 multi-port fuel injection engines, will be produced with Bosch injectors having aluminum "Chimney Caps" with a 60° taper opening. The chimney cap replaces the plastic protective caps earlier designs, and shrouds the pintle to reduce chance of plugging. Both engines use a new intake manifold to accept the 60° chimney cap injector, so this injector will not fit in the earlier engines.

FUEL PRESSURE REGULATOR

Removal and Installation

EXCEPT 2.8L ENGINE

1. Relieve fuel system pressure.
2. Remove pressure regulator from fuel rail. Place a rag around the base of the regulator to catch any spilled fuel.
3. Installation is the reverse of removal.

2.8L ENGINE WITH FUEL RAIL REMOVED

Be sure to support the fuel rail to avoid damaging components.

1. Remove the fuel inlet fitting and fuel outlet fitting, along with the gaskets from the fuel pressure regulator.
2. Remove the fuel pressure regulator bracket attaching screws and then remove the bracket.
3. Remove the left hand fuel rail assembly and the right hand fuel rail assembly, from the fuel pressure regulator assembly.
4. Remove the base rail connectors from the pressure regulator or rails.
5. Installation is the reverse order of the removal procedure. Be sure to use new O-rings and gaskets.

THROTTLE BODY ASSEMBLY

Removal and Installation

1. Disconnect the negative battery cable.
2. Remove the air inlet duct. The idle air control valve and throttle position sensor connectors.
3. Remove and mark all necessary vacuum lines. Remove and plug the two coolant hoses.
4. Remove the throttle, TV and cruise control cables.
5. Remove the throttle body retaining bolts and then remove the throttle body assembly. Discard the flange gasket.
6. Installation is the reverse order of the removal procedure. Torque the retaining bolts to 11 ft. lbs.

COLD START INJECTOR

The cold start injector is used to provide addtional fuel during the crank mode to improve cold start-ups. This circuit is important when engine coolant temperature is low because the main injectors are not pulsed "ON" long enough to provide the needed amount of fuel to start the engine.

During engine cranking, fuel is injected into the cylinder port through the individual fuel injectors and the required addtional fuel is injected into a passage within the intake manifold by the cold start injector. The cold start injector is controlled by a thermal (Bosch) time switch and operates at engine temperatures below 95°F.

The circuit is activated only in the crank mode. The power is supplied directly from the starter solenoid and is protected by a fusible link. The system is control by a thermal time switch which provides a ground path for the cold start injector during cranking when the engine coolant is below 95°F.

The thermal switch is made of a bimetal material which opens at a specified coolant temperature. The bimetal is also heated by winding in the thermal switch which allows the injector to stay "ON" for eight seconds at 68°F coolant. The time the thermal switch will stay closed varies inversely with the coolant temperature. In other words, as the coolant temperature goes up, the cold start injector "ON" time goes down.

The circuit is protected with a crank fuse. When installing the cold start injector to the fuel line, screw the injector in a clockwise direction until the injector bottoms and then back it out one turn. Bend the locking tab into the lock position.

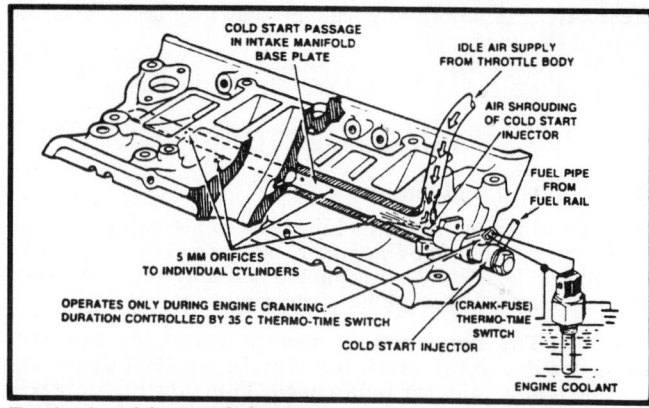

Typical cold start injector

Removal and Installation

1. Relieve fuel system pressure.
2. Provide a clean container to catch any fuel, or wrap some clean rags around the electrical connections.

─────────── **CAUTION** ───────────

Be careful not to let any dirt enter the fuel system and take precautions to avoid the risk of fire.

3. Disconnect the electrical connector from the cold start injector and clean off any dirt or grease from the injector.
4. Remove the fuel line from the injector and be careful because the injector body is plastic. After removing the fuel hose from the injector, inspect the hose from cracks and/or leaks.
5. Remove the two fasteners holding the cold start injector in the base plate, remove the injector and discard the old O-ring or gasket.
6. Installation is the reverse order of the removal procedure. After installation make sure the system is tight and free from leaks and replace the rubber sealing ring, or gasket and hose clamp is necessary.

NOTE: The fuel injections systems are very susceptible to dirt in the system, Be sure that all components are clean and free from dirt and grease before reinstalling them.

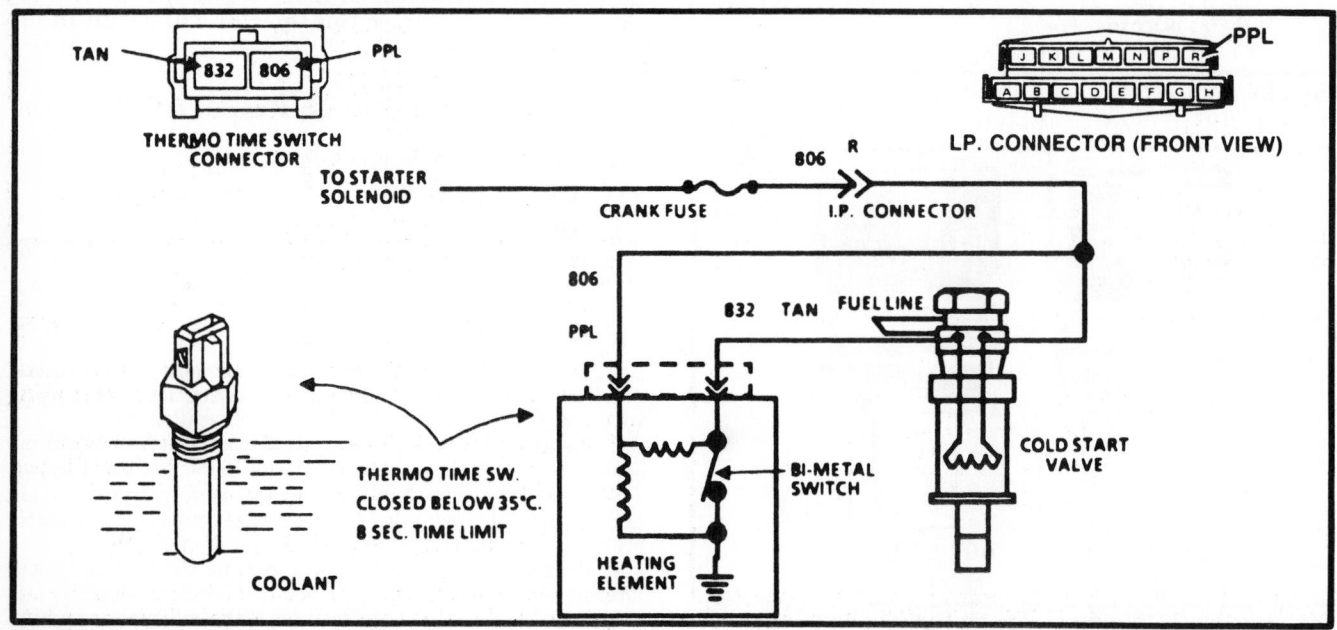

Typical cold start injector circuit

Testing

1. Remove the screws holding the injector in the intake manifold. DO NOT disconnect the fuel lines or electrical connector.
2. Place the cold start injector in a container to catch fuel. Wrap a clean rag around the mouth of the container.
3. Operate the starter and note the injection time. injector should spray fuel for 1–12 seconds if the coolant temperature is lower than approximately 35°C (95°F). Above this temperature, no drip or spray should be noted.
4. If the cold start injector sprays continuously or drips, replace it.
5. If the cold start injector fails to function below 35°C (95°F), replace it.

NOTE: Perform this test as quickly as possible. Avoid energizing the injector for any length of time.

6. Disconnect the cold start injector and hook up a test light across its connector. Ground the No. 1 coil terminal and run the starter. The light should glow for several seconds and then go out. If not, replace the termo-time switch. Measure the resistance of the coils start injector using an ohmmeter. Correct resistance is 3–5 ohms. Check continuity across the cold start injector terminals.

NOTE: No starts or poor cold starting can be caused by a malfunctioning cold start injector. Cranking a cold engine with the coil wire grounded should produce a cone-shaped spray from the cold start injector. Cranking a warm engine should produce no fuel; if the injector dribbles gas, replace it.

IDLE AIR CONTROL VALVE

Removal and Installation

1. Removal electrical connector from idle air control valve.
2. Remove the idle air control valve using a suitable (1¼) wrench.
3. Installation is the reverse of removal. Before installing the idle air control valve, measure the distance that the valve is extended. Measurement should be made from the motor housing to the end of the cone. The distance should not exceed 1⅛ inches, or damage to the valve may occur when installed. Use a new gasket and turn the ignition on then off again to allow the ECM to reset the idle air control valve.

NOTE: Identify replacement IAC valve as being either. Type 1 (with collar at electric terminal end) or Type 2 (without collar). If measuring distance is greater than specified above, proceed as follows:

a. Type 1: Press on valve firmly to retract it.
b. Type 2: Compress retaining spring from valve while turning valve in with a clockwise motion. Return spring to original position with straight portion of spring end aligned with flat surface of valve.

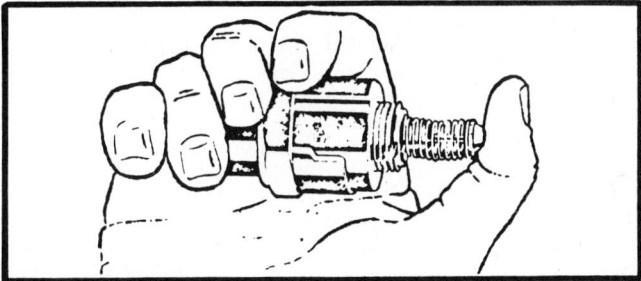

Adjusting the idle air control valve (with a collar at the electrical terminal end)

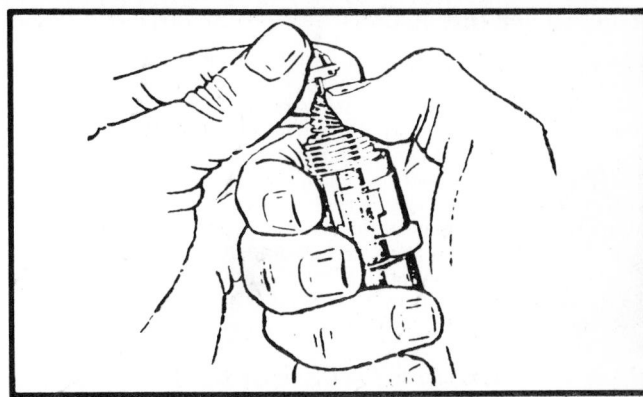

Adjusting the idle air control valve (without a collar at the electrical terminal end)

Minimum Idle Speed Adjustment

The throttle stop screw that is used to adjust the idle speed of the vehicle, is adjusted to specifications at the factory. The throttle stop screw is then covered with a steel plug to prevent the unnecessary readjustment in the field. If it is necessary to gain access to the throttle stop screw, the following procedure will allow access to the throttle stop screw without removing the throttle body unit from the manifold.

1. Apply the parking brake and block the drive wheels. Remove the plug from the idle stop screw by piercing it first with a suitable tool, then applying leverage to the tool to lift the plug out.
2. Leave the idle air control (IAC) valve connected and ground the diagnostic terminal (ALDL connector).
3. Turn the ignition switch to the on position, do not start the engine. Wait for at least 30 seconds (this allows the IAC valve pintle to extend and seat in the throttle body).

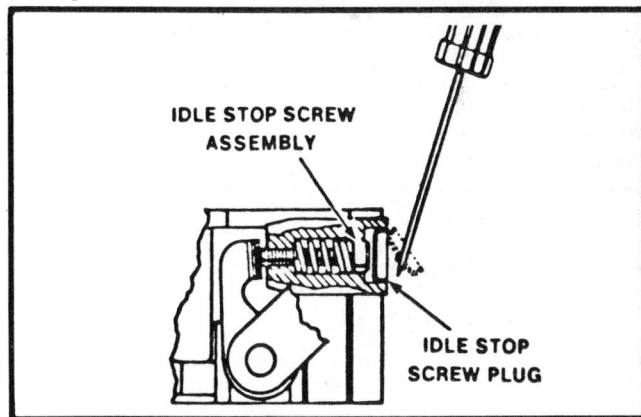

IDLE STOP SCREW ASSEMBLY

IDLE STOP SCREW PLUG

Idle stop screw plug removal

4. With the ignition switch still in the on position, disconnect IAC electrical connector.
5. Remove the ground from the diagnostic terminal and start the engine. Let the engine reach normal operating temperature.
6. Apply the parking brake and block the drive wheels.
7. With the engine in the drive position adjust the idle stop screw to obtain the correct specifications.

THROTTLE POSITION SENSOR

The throttle position sensor on some 1987–88 models are not adjustable. If the sensor is found out of specifications and the sensor is at fault it cannot be adjusted and should be replaced.

Removal and Installation

1. Disconnect the electrical connector from the sensor.
2. Remove the attaching screws, lock washers and retainers.
3. Remove the throttle position sensor. If necessary, remove the screw holding the actuator to the end of the throttle shaft.
4. With the throttle valve in the normal closed idle position, install the throttle position sensor on the throttle body assembly, making sure the sensor pickup lever is located above the tang on the throttle actuator lever.
5. Install the retainers, screws and lock washers using a thread locking compound. DO NOT tighten the screws until the throttle position switch is adjusted.
6. Install three jumper wires between the throttle position sensor and the harness connector.
7. With the ignition switch ON, use a digital voltmeter connected to the correct TPS terminals, (a suitable ALDL scanner can also be used to read the TPS output voltage):
   a. Terminals A and B on all models except the ones listed below.
   b. Terminals C and B on 1985–86 3.8L with MPI/SFI.
8. If the TPS is out of specifications, loosen the two TPS attaching screws and rotate throttle position sensor to obtain a correct voltage reading.
9. Tighten the mounting screws, then recheck the reading to insure that the adjustment hasn't changed.
9. Turn ignition OFF, remove jumper wires, then reconnect harness to throttle position switch.

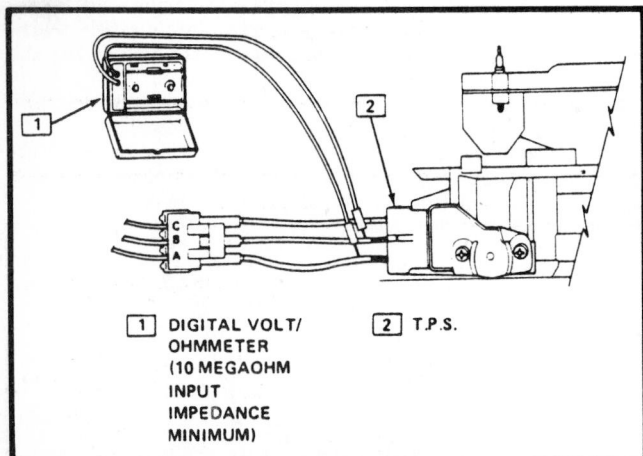

1 DIGITAL VOLT/
OHMMETER
(10 MEGAOHM
INPUT
IMPEDANCE
MINIMUM)

2 T.P.S.

Throttle position sensor adjustment

Non-Adjustable TPS Output Check

This check should only be performed, when the throttle body or the TPS has been replaced or after the minimum idle speed has been adjusted.

1. Remove air cleaner. Disconnect the TPS harness from the TPS.
2. Using suitable jumper wires, connect a digital voltmeter J–29125-A or equivalent to the correct TPS terminals; (a suitable ALDL scanner can also be used to read the TPS output voltage):
   a. Terminals A and B on all models except the ones listed below.
   b. Terminals C and B on 1985–86 3.8L with MPI/SFI.
3. With the ignition ON and the engine running, The TPS voltage should be 0.450–1.25 volts at base idle to approximately 4.5 volts at wide open throttle.
4. If the reading on the TPS is out of specification, check the minimum idle speed before replacing the TPS.
5. If the voltage reading is correct, remove the voltmeter and jumper wires and reconnect the TPS connector to the sensor. Re-install the air cleaner.

OXYGEN SENSOR

Removal and Installation

NOTE: The oxygen sensor uses a permanently attached pigtail and connector. This pigtail should not be removed from the oxygen sensor. Damage or removal of the pigtail or connector could affect proper operation of the oxygen sensor.

The oxygen sensor is installed in the exhaust manifold and is removed in the same manner as a spark plug. The sensor may be difficult to remove when the engine temperature is below 120°F (48°C) (so it may be a good idea to warm the engine up for approximately two minutes before removing the sensor) and excessive force may damage threads in the exhaust manifold or exhaust pipe. Exercise care when handling the oxygen sensor; the electrical connector and louvered end must be kept free of grease, dirt, or other contaminants. Avoid using cleaning solvents of any kind and don't drop or roughly handle the sensor. A special anti-seize compound is used on the oxygen sensor threads when installing and care should be used NOT to get compound on the sensor itself. Disconnect the negative battery cable when servicing the oxygen sensor and torque to 30 ft. lbs. (41 Nm) when installing.

CRANKSHAFT SENSOR OR COMBINATION SENSOR

On the 3.0L engine the crankshaft sensor and camshaft sensor functions are combined into one sensor called the combination sensor which is mounted at the harmonic balancer.

Removal and Installation

NOTE: It is not necessary to remove sensor bracket.

1. Disconnect negative battery cable.
2. Disconnect 3 terminal sensor connector.
3. Raise vehicle and support safely.
4. Position harmonic balancer so slot in disc is lined up with sensor.
5. Loosen sensor retaining bolt.
6. Slide sensor outboard and remove through notch in sensor housing.
7. To install, position sensor in housing.
8. Rotate harmonic balancer so disc is positioned in sensor.
9. Adjust sensor for equal distance on each side of disc. Should be approximately 0.030 in. (0.76 mm) clearance between disc and sensor.
10. Tighten retaining bolt and recheck clearance.

NOTE: This adjustment does not effect engine timing.

11. Complete installation by reversing removal procedure.

CRANKSHAFT SENSOR

Adjustment
1986–88 MODELS

1. Using a 28mm socket and pull handle, rotate the harmonic balancer until the interrupter ring(s) fills the sensor slot(s) and edge of interrupter window is aligned with edge of the deflector on the pedestal.
2. Insert adjustment tool (J–36179 or equivalent) into the gap between sensor and interrupter on each side of interrupter ring. If gauge will not slide past sensor on either side of interrupter ring, the sensor is out of adjustment or interrupter ring is bent. This clearance should be checked at three positions around the outer interrupter ring, approximately 120° apart.

NOTE: If found out of adjustment, the sensor should be removed and inspected for potential damage. A clear-

ance of 0.025 in. of an inch is required on either side of the interrupter ring.

3. Loosen the pinch bolt on sensor pedestal and insert adjustment tool (J–36179 or equivalent) into the gap between sensor and interrupter on each side of interrupter ring.

4. Slide the sensor into contact against gauge (0.025 in.) and interrupter ring.

5. Torque sensor retaining pinch bolt to 30 inch lbs. (3.4 Nm) while maintaining light pressure on sensor against gauge and interrupter ring. This clearance should be checked again, at three positions around the interrupter ring, approximately 120° apart. If interrupter ring contacts sensor at any point during harmonic balancer rotation, the interrupter ring has excessive runout and must be replaced.

ELECTRONIC CONTROL MODULE (ECM)

The electronic control module (ECM), usually located under the instrument panel, is the control center of the fuel injection system. It constantly looks at information from various sensors, and controls the systen that affect vehicle performance.

The ECM also performs the diagnostic function of the system. It can recognize operational problems, alert the driver through the "Service Engine Soon" light and store a code or codes which identify the problem areas to aid the technician in making repairs.

The 1987–88 2.8L engine will use a new type of ECM. For service, this ECM only consists of two parts' a Controller (the ECM without a Mem-Cal) and an assembly called a Mem-Cal (this stands for "Memory and Calibration" unit).

The other MFI vehicles will use the standard ECM for service. The ECM consists of three parts; a Controller (the ECM without a Prom), a Calibrator called a Prom (Programmable read only memory) and a CalPak.

PROM

To allow one model of the ECM to be used for many different vehicles, a device called a Calibrator (or PROM) is used. The prom is located inside the ECM and has information on the vehicle's weight, engine, transmission, axle ratio and other components.

While one ECM part number can be used by many different vehicles, a prom is very specific and must be used for the right vehicle. For this reason, it is very important to check the latest parts book and or service bulletin information for the correct prom part number when replacing the prom.

An ECM used for service (called a controller) comes without a prom. The prom from the old ECM must be carefully removed and installed in the new ECM.

CALPAK

A device called a CALPAK is uded to allow fuel delivery if other parts of the ECM are damaged. It has an access door in the

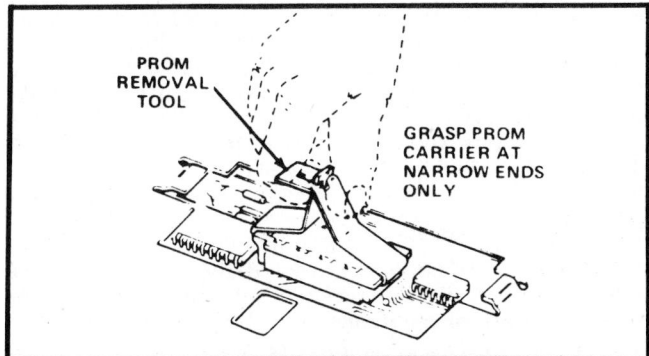

Removing the ECM Prom with a Prom removal tool

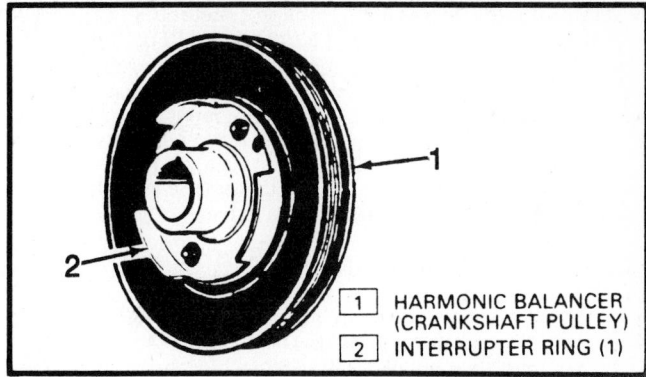

| 1 | HARMONIC BALANCER (CRANKSHAFT PULLEY) |
| 2 | INTERRUPTER RING (1) |

Typical harmonic balancer with interrupter ring

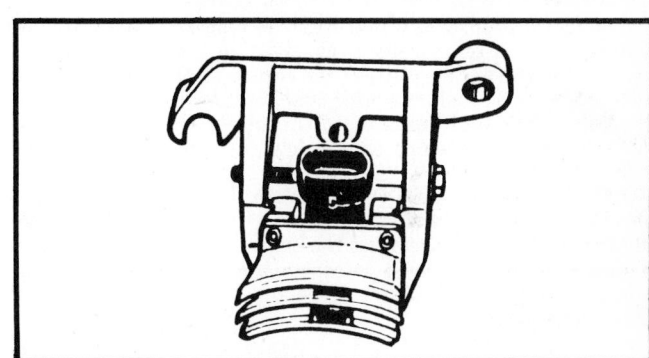

Typical crankshaft sensor

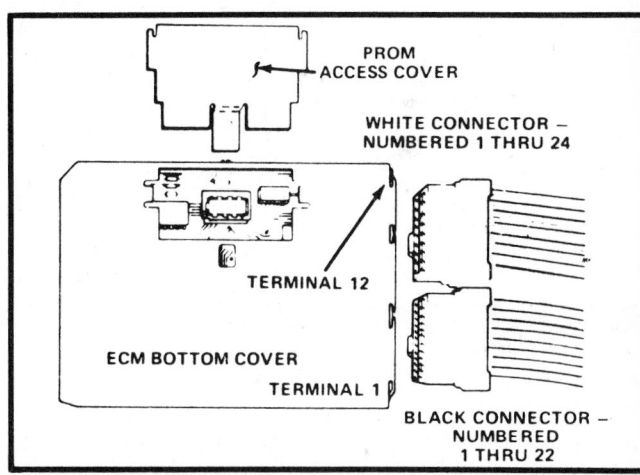

Typical General Motors ECM showing the Prom access cover and harness connectors

ECM, and removal and replacement procedures are the same as with the prom. If the CALPAK is missing, a code 52 will be set.

MEM-CAL (2.8L ENGINE ONLY)

This assembly contains the functions of the prom CALPAK and the ESC module used on other GM applications. Like the prom, it contains the calibrations needed for a specific vehicle as well as the back-up fuel control circuitry required if the rest of the ECM becomes damaged or faulty.

ECM Function

The ECM supplies either 5 or 12 volts to power various sensors and or switches. This is done through resistances in the ECM which are so high in value that a test light will not light when connected to the circuit. In some cases, even an ordinary shop voltmeter will not give an accurate reading because its resistance is too low. Therefore, a 10 meg ohm input impedance digital voltmeter is required to assure accurate voltage readings.

The ECM controls output circuits such as injectors, IAC, cooling fan relay, etc. by controlling the ground circuit through transistors or a device called a quad driver.

INFORMATION DATA SENSOR

A variety of sensors provide information to the ECM regarding engine operating characteristics. These sensors and their functions are described below.

Engine Coolant Temperature

The coolant sensor is a thermister (a resistor which changes value based on temperature) mounted on the engine coolant stream. As the temperature of the engine coolant changes, the resistance of the coolant sensor changes. Low coolant temperature produces a high resistance (100,000 ohms at –40°C/–40°F), while high temperature causes low resistance (70 ohms at 130°C/266°F).

The ECM supplies a 5-volt signal to the coolant sensor and measures the voltage that returns. By measuring the voltage change, the ECM determines the engine coolant temperature. This information is used to control fuel management, IAC, spark timing, EGR, canister purge and other engine operating conditions.

Oxygen Sensor

The exhaust oxygen sensor is mounted in the exhaust system where it can monitor the oxygen content of the exhaust gas stream. The oxygen content in the exhaust reacts with the oxygen sensor to produce a voltage output. This voltage ranges from approximately 100 millivolts (high oxygen – lean mixture) to 900 millivolts (low oxygen – rich mixture).

By monitoring the voltage output of the oxygen sensor, the ECM will determine what fuel mixture command to give to the injector (lean mixture–low voltage–rich command, rich mixture–high voltage lean command).

Remember that oxygen sensor indicates to the ECM what is happening in the exhaust. It does not cause things to happen. It is a type of gauge: high oxygen content = lean mixture; low oxygen content = rich mixture. The ECM adjust fuel to keep the system working.

MAP Sensor

The manifold absolute pressure (MAP) sensor measures the changes in the intake manifold pressure which result from engine load and speed changes. The pressure measured by the MAP sensor is the difference between barometric pressure (outside air) and manifold pressure (vacuum). A closed throttle engine coastdown would produce a relatively low MAP value (approximately 20–35 kPa), while wide-open throttle would produce a high value (100 kPa). This high value is produced when the pressure inside the manifold is the same as outside the manifold, and 100% of outside air (or 100 kPa) is being measured. This MAP output is the opposite of what you would measure on a vacuum gauge. The use of this sensor also allows the ECM to adjust automatically for different altitude.

The ECM sends a 5-volt reference signal to the MAP sensor. As the MAP changes, the electrical resistance of the sensor also changes. By monitoring the sensor output voltage the ECM can determine the manifold pressure. A higher pressure, lower vacuum (high voltage) requires more fuel, while a lower pressure, higher vacuum (low voltage) requires less fuel.

Mass Air Flow Sensor (MAF)

The mass air flow sensor measures the amount of air which passes through it. THe ECM uses this information to determine the operating condition of the engine, to control fuel delivery. A large quantity of air indicates acceleration, while a small quantity indicates deceleration or idle.

This sensor produces a frequency output between 32 and 150 hertz. A "SCAN" tool will display air flow in terms of grams of air per second (gm/sec), with a range from 3gm/sec to 150 gm/sec.

Manifold Air Temperature (MAT) Sensor

The manifold air temperature sensor (is a part of the MAF or MAP sensor) is a thermistor, a resistor, which changes the value based on the temperature of air entering the engine. Low temperature produces a high resistance (100,000 ohms at –40°C/–40°F), while high temperature causes low resistance (70 ohms at 130°C/266°F).

The ECM supplies a 5 volt signal to the sensor thru a resistor in the ECM and measures the voltage. The voltage will be high when the incoming air is cold and low when the air is hot. By measuring the voltage, the ECM calculates the incomming air temperature and uses this signal to compensate the MAF sensor signal based on temperature. The MAT sensor is also used to control spark timing.

Vehicle Speed Sensor (VSS)

NOTE: Vehicle should not be driven without a VSS as idle quality may be affected.

The vehicle speed sensor (VSS) is mounted behind the speedometer in the instrument cluster. It provides electrical pulses to the ECM from the speedometer head. The pulses indicate the road speed. The ECM uses this information to operate the IAC, canister purge, and TCC.

Some vehicles equipped with digital instrument clusters use a permanent magnet (PM) generator to provide the VSS signal. The PM generator is located in the transmission and replaces the speedometer cable. The signal from the PM generator drives a stepper motor which drives the odometer.

Throttle Position Sensor (TPS)

The throttle position sensor (TPS) is connected to the throttle shaft and is controlled by the throttle mechanism. A 5-volt reference signal is sent to the TPS from the ECM. As the throttle valve angle is changed (accelerator pedal moved), the resistance of the TPS also changes. At a closed throttle position, the resistance of the TPS is high, so the output voltage to the ECM will be low (approximately .5 volt). As the throttle plate opens, the resistance decreases so that, at wide open throttle, the output voltage should be approximately 5 volts.

By monitoring the output voltage from the TPS, the ECM can determine fuel delivery based on throttle valve angle (driver demand). The TPS can either be misadjusted, shorted, open or loose. Misadjustment might result in poor idle or poor wide-open throttle performance. An open TPS signals the ECM that the throttle is always closed ... resulting in poor performance. This usually sets a Code 22. A shorted TPS gives the ECM a constant wide-open throttle signal and should set a Code 21. A loose TPS indicates to the ECM that the throttle is moving. This causes intermittent bursts of fuel from the injector and an unstable idle.

Park/Neutral Switch

NOTE: Vehicle should not be driven with the Park/Neutral switch disconnected as idle quality may be affected in Park or Neutral.

This switch indicates to the ECM when the transmission is in Park or Neutral.

A/C Compressor Clutch Engagement. This signal indicates to the ECM that the A/C compressor clutch is engaged.

A/C "Request" Signal

This signal tells the ECM that the A/C selector switch is turned on and that the A/C pressure switches are closed. The ECM uses this to adjust the idle speed before turning on the A/C clutch. If this signal is not available to the ECM, the A/C compressor will be inoperative.

Power Steering Pressure Switch

This switch tells the ECM that the vehicle is in a parking maneuver. The ECM uses this information to compensate for additional engine load by moving the idle air control valve. The ECM will also, turn off the A/C clutch when high pressure is detected.

Crankshaft Sensor

The crankshaft sensor provides a signal, through the ignition module, which the ECM uses as a reference to calculate rpm and crankshaft position. The crankshaft sensor is mounted in a pedestal on the front of the engine near the harmonic balancer. The sensor is a "Hall Effect" switch which depends on a metal interrupter ring, mounted on the balancer to activate it.

Windows in the interrupter activate the hall effect switch as they provide a path for the magnetic field between the switch's transducer and it's magnet. When the hall effect switch is activated, it grounds the signal line to the C³I (or DIS) module, pulling the crank signal line's applied voltage low, which is interpreted as a crank signal.

Because of the way the signal by the crank sensor is created, the signal circuit is always either at high or low voltage (square wave signal) and three signal pulses are created during each crankshaft revolution. The signal issued by the the C³I (or DIS) module to create a "Reference Signal" which is also a square wave signal.

The reference signal is used to calculate the engine rpm and crankshaft position by the ECM. A misadjusted sensor or a bent interrupter ring could cause rubbing of the sensor resulting in potential driveability problems such as rough idle, poor performance and or a no start condition.

NOTE: Failure to have the correct clearance will damage the sensor. The crank sensor is not adjustable for ignition timing but positioning of the interrupter ring is very important. A clearance of 0.025 in. of an inch is required on either side of the interrupter ring.

Camshaft Sensor

The cam sensor sends a signal to the ECM, which uses it as a "sync pulse" to trigger the injectors in proper sequence. The cam sensor is usually located on the timing cover behind the water pump, near the camshaft sprocket. As the camshaft sprocket turns, a magnet mounted on the camshaft sprocket activates the hall effect switch in the cam sensor. When the hall effect switch is activated, it grounds the signal line to the C³I (or DIS) module, pulling the crank signal line's applied voltage low.

This is interpreted as a cam signal ("Synchronization Pulse"). Because of the way the signal is created, by the crank sensor, the signal circuit is always either at a high or low voltage (square wave signal). While the camshaft sprocket continues to turn, the hall effect switch turns off as the magnetic field passes the Cam sensor resulting in one signal each time the camshaft makes one revolution. The cam signal is created as the number one piston and number four piston reach approximately 25° after top dead center.

It is then used by the C³I (or DIS) module to begin the ignition coil firing sequence starting with the number 3/6 coil. The

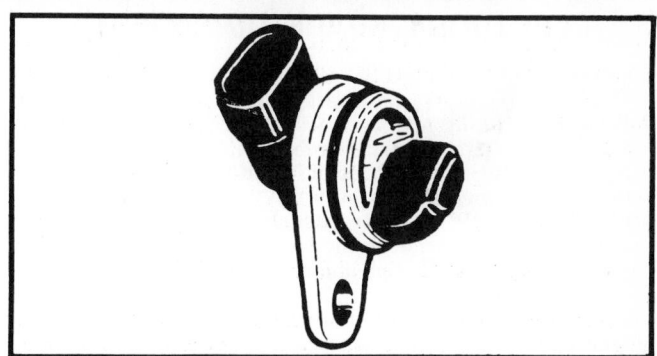

Tyical cam shaft sensor

firing sequence begins with this coil because piston number 6 is now at the correct position in the compression stroke for the spark plugs to be fired. This cam signal, which actually represents the camshaft position due to the sensor's mounting location, is also used by the ECM to properly time its fuel injection operation.

NOTE: On the 3.0L engine the crankshaft sensor and camshaft sensor functions are combined into one sensor called the combination sensor which is mounted at the harmonic balancer.

Combination Sensor

This sensor is used on the 3.0L engine only. Since the 3.0L engine is a simultaneously injected engine, it does not require an actual cam signal. Instead, it utilizes a "Sync-Pulse" signal from its combination sensor at a rate of once per every crankshaft revolution. The combination sensor is activated and controls its signal line(s) in the same way as the crnakshaft sensor does on the 3.8L engine.

The only difference is the "Sync-Pulse" portion of the sensor, which serves the same purpose as the Cam sensor on the 3.8L relative to the ignition operation. That is, it begins the ignition coil firing sequence with the number 3/6 ignition coil.

Detonation (Knock) Sensor

This sensor is a piezoelectric sensor located near the back of the engine (transmission end). It generates electrical impulses which are directly proportional to the frequency of the knock which is detected. A buffer then sorts these signals and eliminates all except for those frequency range of detonation. This information is passed to the ESC module and then to the ECM, so that the ignition timing advance can be retarded until the detonation stops.

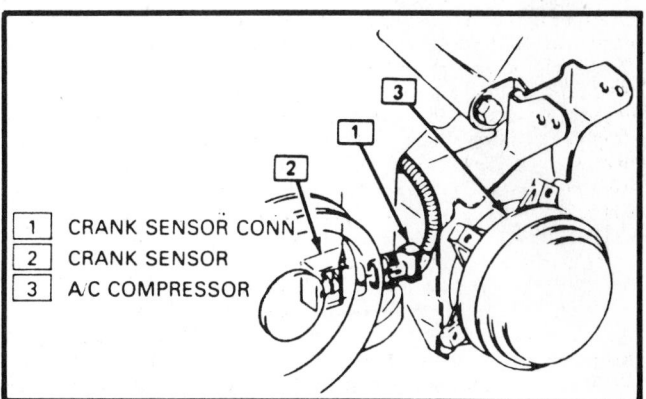

1	CRANK SENSOR CONN.
2	CRANK SENSOR
3	A/C COMPRESSOR

Tyical combination sensor

ELECTRONIC SPARK TIMING (EST)

Electronic spark timing (EST) is used on all engines equipped with HEI distributors and direct ignition systems. The EST distributor contains no vacuum or centrifugal advance and uses a seven-terminal distributor module. It also has four wires going to a four-terminal connector in addition to the connectors normally found on HEI distributors. A reference pulse, indicating both engine RPM and crankshaft position, is sent to the ECM. The ECM determines the proper spark advance for the engine operating conditions and sends an "EST" pulse to the distributor.

The EST system is designed to optimize spark timing for better control of exhaust emissions and for fuel economy improvements. The ECM monitors information from various engine sensors, computes the desired spark timing and changes the timing accordingly. A backup spark advance system is incorporated in the module in case of EST failure.

ELECTRONIC SPARK CONTROL (ESC)

When engines are equipped with ESC in conjunction with EST, ESC is used to reduce spark advance under conditions of detonation. A knock sensor signals a separate ESC controller to retard the timing when it senses knock. The ESC controller signals the ECM which reduces spark advance until no more signals are received from the knock sensor.

COMPUTER CONTROLLED COIL IGNITION SYSTEM (C³I)

The heart of this system is a electronic coil module that replaces the standard distributorand coil. Logic circuits within the module receive and buffer signals from the crankshaft and camshaft and by way of three interconnected coils contained in the cover of the module, distribute high voltage current to spark plugs.

The C³I system eliminates the need for a distributor to control the flow or current between the battery and spark plugs. In its place is an electro magnetic sensor consisting of a hall effect sensor, magnet and interruptor ring. The gear on the shaft of this sensor is connected directly to the camshaft gear.

As the camshaft turns, the interruptor ring, moving at camshaft speed (½ the engine rpm), rotates between the hall sensor and the magnet to produce a signal which is fed to the electronic coil module. This signal provides the exact position of the valves as they open and close. At the same time, the cam sensor is used to drive the engine oil pump.

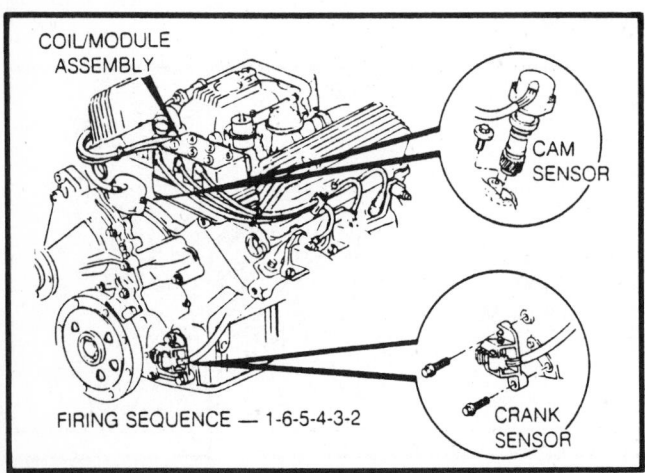

COIL/MODULE ASSEMBLY

CAM SENSOR

CRANK SENSOR

FIRING SEQUENCE — 1-6-5-4-3-2

C³I Components

Another sensor is mounted to the crankshaft. This sensor also consists of a hall sensor, magnet and interrupt ring. As with the cam sensor, the crankshaft causes the interruptor ring to rotate between the hall sensor and magnet to produce a signal which is fed to the electronic module. This signal gives the top center position of each piston.

DIRECT IGNITION SYSTEM

A distributor is not used in a Direct Ignition System or in a Integrated Direct Ignition System. These two systems are basically the same electrically, and where a reference is made only to Direct Ignition System, the content applies to both Direct Ignition System and Integrated Direct Ignition. The components of the direct ignition system are a coil pack, ignition module, crankshaft reluctor ring, magnetic sensor and the ECM. The coil pack consists of two or three separate, interchangeable, ignition coils. These coils operate in the same manner as previous coils. More than one coil is needed because each coil fires for two cylinders. The ignition module is located under the coil pack and is connected to the ECM by a 6 pin connector. The ignition module controls the primary circuits to the coils, turning them on and off and controls spark timing below 400 rpm and if the ECM bypass circuit becomes open or grounded.

The magnetic pickup sensor inserts through the engine block, just above the pan rail in proximity to the crankshaft reluctor ring. Notches in the crankshaft reluctor ring trigger the magnetic pickup sensor to provide timing information to the ECM. The magnetic pickup sensor provides a cam signal to identify correct firing sequence and crank signals to trigger each coil at the proper time.

This system uses EST and control wires from the ECM, as with the distributor systems. The ECM controls the timing using crankshaft position, engine rpm, engine temperature and manifold absolute pressure sensing.

When the engine is running at normal operating speeds, the bypass signal from the ECM to the ignition module will "Effectively" connect the base of the transistor to the EST terminal. The EST sisgnal is determined by not only the kind of reference signal the ECM receives, but also by all of the other engine sensors which at the same time are sending voltage signals to the ECM. Under these conditions, the ECM is controlling the timing and is constantly "Tuning" the engine for control of exhaust emissions and good fuel economy.

Under certian condtions, such as during starting, the crankshaft, reference and bypass signals will be different because the engine rpm will be very low. The transistor base "Effectively" will be connected to the crankshaft input voltage. Thus, the crankshaft sensor will control the timing and duration of the primary current.

This means the engine can start and can run without the ECM if the ECM should not operate properly due to defects in the system. The engine will not run well and a warning light or other signal will tell the driver to obtain service attention at the earliest convenience. This back-up feature allows the operator to continue driving the vehicle until it can be serviced.

In summary, the bypass signal connects the transistor base to the EST signal for complete computer control by the ECM, or to crankshaft sensor for ignition control during cranking and other engine conditions, including some defects. The two ends of the coil secondary are connected internally to the two high voltage towers of each coil. These towers are then connected with high voltage wiring to two spark plugs.

On the four cylinder engines with a firing order of 1–3–4–2, one coil secondary would be connected to cylinders 1 and 4 and the other coil secondary would be connected to cylinders 2 and 3. When high voltage is induced in a secondary, both spark plugs will fire in series. This will occur at the end of the compression stroke on number one cylinder and at the end of the exhaust stroke in the number four cylinder.

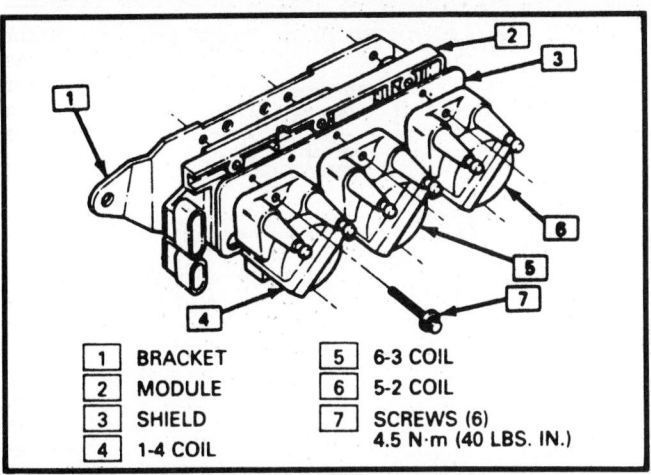

1	BRACKET	5	6-3 COIL
2	MODULE	6	5-2 COIL
3	SHIELD	7	SCREWS (6) 4.5 N·m (40 LBS. IN.)
4	1-4 COIL		

Exploded view of a typical Direct Ignition System

Since the exhaust stroke cylinder is at atmosphere pressure, very little voltage is required to fire this plug, leaving most of the secondary voltage available to fire the plug in the cylinder under compression (the begining of the power stroke). One engine revolution later the same ignition coil will fire number 4 at the end of compression and number one at the end of exhaust. The other ignition coil fires cylinders 2 and 3 in the same manner.

ALDL CONNECTOR

The assembly line diagnostic link (ALDL) (or also known as the assembly line communication link (ALCL)) is a diagnostic connector located in the passenger compartment usually under the instrument panel (except Pontiac Fiero which is located in the console). The assembly plant were the vehicles originate use the connector to check the engine for proper operation before it leaves the plant. Terminal "B" is the diagnostic "Test" terminal (lead) and it can be connected to terminal "A", or ground, to enter the Diagnostic mode or the Field Service Mode.

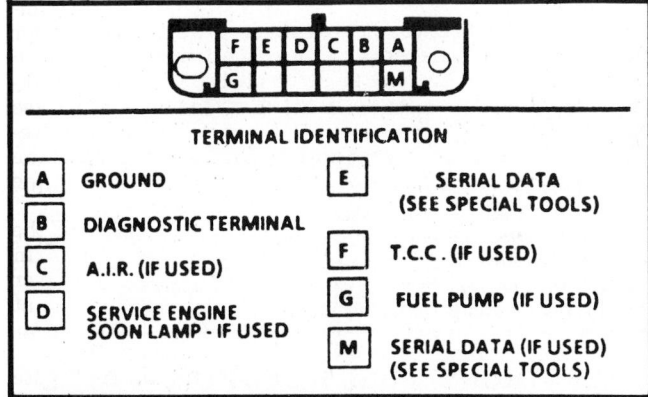

TERMINAL IDENTIFICATION

A	GROUND	E	SERIAL DATA (SEE SPECIAL TOOLS)
B	DIAGNOSTIC TERMINAL	F	T.C.C . (IF USED)
C	A.I.R. (IF USED)	G	FUEL PUMP (IF USED)
D	SERVICE ENGINE SOON LAMP - IF USED	M	SERIAL DATA (IF USED) (SEE SPECIAL TOOLS)

Typical ALDL connector

FIELD SERVICE MODE

If the "Test" terminal is grounded with the engine running, the system will enter the the Field Service mode. In this mode, the "Check Engine Light" will show whether the system is in Open loop or Closed loop. In Open loop the "Check Engine Light" flashes two times and one half times per second. In Closed loop the light flashes once per second. Also in closed loop, the light will stay OUT most of the time if the system is too lean. It will

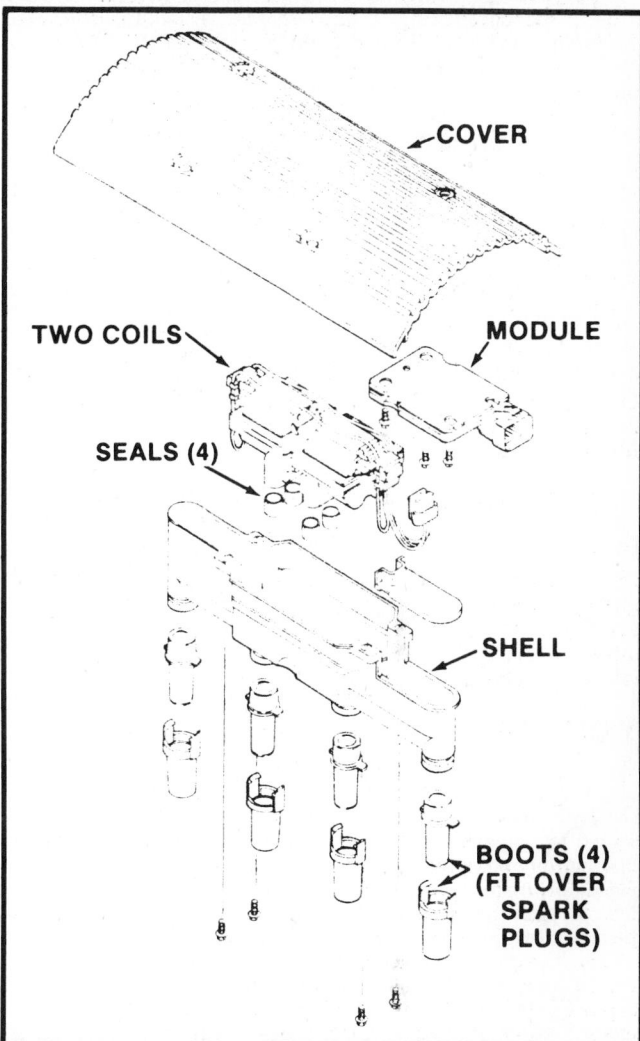

Exploded view of a typical Integrated Direct Ignition System

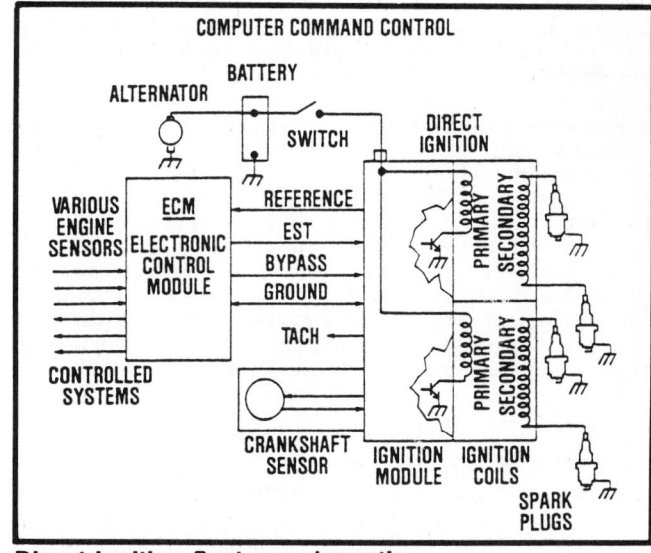

Direct Ignition System schematic

stay ON most of the time if the system is too rich. In either case the Field Service mode check, which is part of the Diagnostic circuit check, will lead the technician into choosing the correct diagnostic chart to refer to.

CLEARING THE TROUBLE CODES

When the ECM finds a problem with the system, the "Check Engine Light" will come ON and a trouble code will be recorded in the ECM memory. If the problem is intermittent, the "Check Engine Light" will go out after 10 seconds, when the fault goes away. However the trouble code will stay in the ECM memory until the battery voltage to the ECM is removed. Removing the battery voltage for 10 seconds will clear all trouble codes. Do this by disconnecting the ECM harness from the positive battery terminal pigtail for 10 seconds with the key in the OFF position, or by removing the ECM fuse for 10 seconds with the key OFF.

CLOSED LOOP FUEL CONTROL

The purpose of closed loop fuel control is to precisely maintain an air/fuel mixture 14.7:1. When the air/fuel mixture is maintained at 14.7:1, the catalytic converter is able to operate at maximum efficiency which results in lower emission levels.

Since the ECM controls the air/fuel mixture, it needs to check its output and correct the fuel mixture for deviations from the "Ideal" ratio. The oxygen sensor feeds this output information back to the ECM.

ECM LEARNING ABILITY

The ECM has a "learning" capability. If the battery is disconnected the "learning" process has to begin all over again. A change may be noted in the vehicle's performance. To "teach" the ECM, insure the vehicle is at operating temperature and drive at part throttle, with moderate acceleration and idle conditions, until performance returns.

Engine Performance Diagnosis
CHECK ENGINE LIGHT

The "check engine" light on the instrument panel is used as a warning lamp to tell the driver that a problem has occurred in the electronic engine control system. When the self-diagnosis mode is activated by grounding the test terminal of the diagnostic connector, the check engine light will flash stored trouble codes to help isolate system problems. The electronic control module (ECM) has a memory that knows what certain engine sensors should be under certain conditions. If a sensor reading is not what the ECM thinks it should be, the control unit will illuminate the check engine light and store a trouble code in its memory. The trouble code indicates what circuit the problem is in, each circuit consisting of a sensor, the wiring harness and connectors to it and the ECM.

The Assembly Line Diagnostic Link (ALDL) (described earlier in this section) can be used as a diagnostic aid. By connecting terminals A and B together with a jumper wire, the diagnostic mode is activated and the control unit will begin to flash trouble codes using the check engine or service engine soon light.

NOTE: Some models have a "Service Engine Soon" light instead of a "Check Engine" display.

When the test terminal is grounded with the key ON and the engine stopped, the ECM will display code 12 to show that the system is working. A code 12 consists of one flash followed by a pause and then two more flashes. The ECM will usually display code 12 three times, then start to display any stored trou-

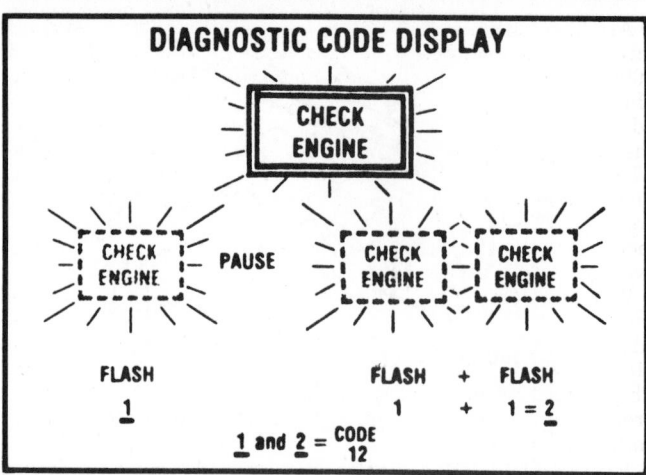

Diagnostic Code 12 display

ble codes. If more than one fault (code) has been detected, the lowest code number will flash three times, followed by the next higher code number (which will flash three times), until all the stored trouble codes have flashed. If there are no trouble codes stored, the ECM will continue to display code 12 until the test terminal is disconnected. Each trouble code will be flashed three times, then code 12 sill display again. The ECM will also energize all controlled relays and solenoids when in the diagnostic mode to check function.

When the test terminal is grounded with the engine running, it will cause the ECM to enter the Field Service Mode. In this mode, the service engine soon light will indicate whether the system is in Open or Closed Loop operation. In open loop, the light will falsh 2½ times per second; in closed loop, the light will flash once per second. In closed loop, the light will stay out most of the time if the system is too lean and will stay on most of the time if the system is too rich.

NOTE: The vehicle may be driven in the Field Service mode and system evaluated at any steady road speed. This mode us useful in diagnosing driveability problems where the system is rich or lean too long.

Trouble codes should be cleared after service is completed. To clear the trouble code memory, disconnect the battery for at least 10 seconds. This may be accomplished by disconnecting the ECM harness from the positive battery pigtail or by removing the ECM fuse.

─────────── CAUTION ───────────

The ignition switch must be OFF when disconnecting or reconnecting power to the ECM. The vehicle should be driven after the ECM memory is cleared to allow the system to readjust itself. The vehicle should be driven at part throttle under moderate acceleration with the engine at normal operating temperature. A change is performance should be noted initially, but normal performance should return quickly.

ELECTRONIC FUEL INJECTION — ALDL TESTER INFORMATION

An ALDL display unit (ALDL tester, scanner, monitor, etc), allows a technician to read the engine control system information from the ALDL connector under the instrument panel. It can provide information faster than a digital voltmeter or ohmmeter can. The scan tool does not diagnose the exact location of the problem. The tool supplies information about the ECM, the information that it is receiving and the commands that it is sending plus special information such as integrator and block learn. To use an ALDL display tool you should understand throughly how an engine control system operates.

An ALDL scanner or monitor puts a fuel injection system into a special test mode. This mode commands an idle speed of 1000 rpm. The idle quality cannot be evaluated with a tester plugged in. Also the test mode commands a fixed spark with no advance. On vehicles with Electronic Spark Control (ESC) there will be a fixed spark, but it will be advanced. On vehicles with ESC there might be a serious spark knock, this spark knock could be bad enough so as not being able to road test the vehicle in the ALDL test mode. Be sure to check the tool manufacturer for instructions on special test modes which should overcome these limitations.

When a tester is used with a fuel injected engine it bypasses the timer that keeps the system in OPEN loop for a certain period of time. When all CLOSED loop conditions are met, the engine will go into CLOSED loop as soon as the vehicle is started. This means that the air management system will not function properly and air may go directly to the converter as soon as the engine is started.

These tools cannot diagnose everything. They do not tell the technician where a problem is located in a circuit. The diagnostic charts to pinpoint the problems must still be used. These tester's do not let a technician know if a solenoid or relay has been turned on. They only tell the technician the ECM command. To find out if a solenoid has been turned on, check it with a suitable test light or digital voltmeter, or see if vacuum through the solenoid changes.

REVISED ECM REPLACEMENT PROCEDURE – CHART C-1

1982 through 1987 ECM Equipped Vehicles

Since 1982, most ECM's have used an integrated circuit (IC) in place of separate transistors to turn ON or OFF different components controlled by the ECM. These IC's are called quad drivers (QDR). Each quad driver has four separate outputs, meaning it can turn ON or OFF four different items independently.

A failed quad driver usually results in an ECM output becoming either shorted to ground or open. Many times all four quad drivers output will be inoperative if just one vehicle circuit is faulty.

This revised diagnosis incorporates new test procedures designed to identify a damaged quad drivers. Once identified, the circuit must be repaired to reduce the incidence of repeat ECM failures.

The following charts are to be used to replace the current service procedure for either:

1. Chart C-1 ECM replacement check.

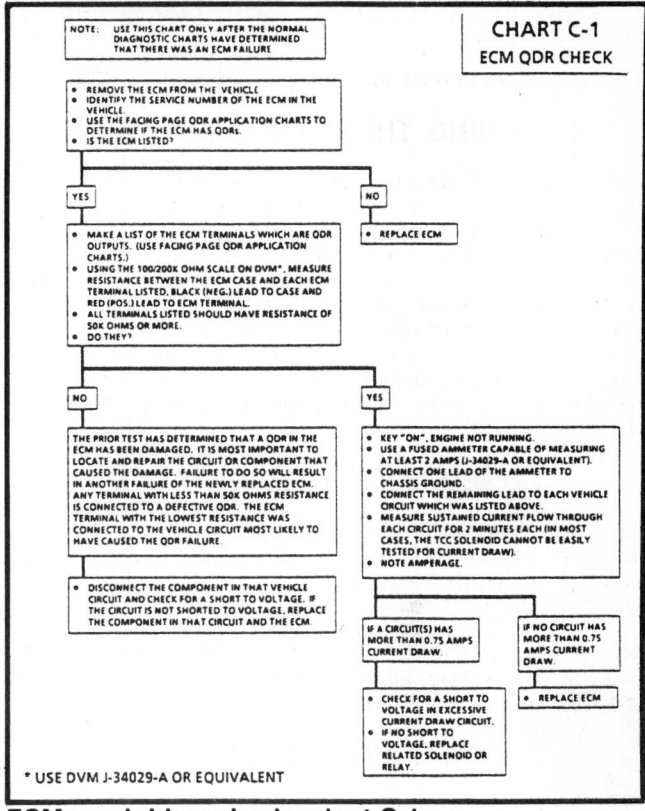

ECM quad driver check – chart C-1

2. Any diagnostic chart where "replace ECM" is the conclusion, especially if a footnote indicates checking certain circuits for less the 20 ohm's resistance.

It is strongly suggested that this chart be used whenever an ECM replacement is indicated for 1982–87 vehicles.

NOTE: Due to the large amount of GM vehicles being covered in this section, some vehicles will use more sensors than others. Also, a complete general diagnostic section is outlined. The steps and procedures can be altered as required (if necessary) by the technician according to the specific model being diagnosed and the sensors it is equipped with. The wiring diagrams and schematics may not coincide with every GM vehicle in use. If this situation should arise, use the wiring diagram or schematic as a general guide.

ECM Service Number	QDR Number	ECM Output Term #1	ECM Output Term #2	ECM Output Term #3	ECM Output Term #4
CCC 83.5-84 S/N 1226153 1226452 1226454 1226455 1226519	1	G	E	6	4
	2	B	19	P	P
	3	18	18	T	T

ECM Service Number	QDR Number	ECM Output Term #1	ECM Output Term #2	ECM Output Term #3	ECM Output Term #4
TBI 82.5-83 S/N 1225610 1226100 1226026 1226430	1	Black 9	Black 14	Black 16	White 20
	2	Black 7	Black 22	White 19	White 19

ECM Service Number	QDR Number	ECM Output Term #1	ECM Output Term #2	ECM Output Term #3	ECM Output Term #4
TBI 83.5-84 S/N 1226156	1	White 20		Black 7	Black 9

ECM Service Number	QDR Number	ECM Output Term #1	ECM Output Term #2	ECM Output Term #3	ECM Output Term #4
DFI 83-86 S/N 1226028 1226462 1226930	1	Blue 9	Blue 14	Blue 16	Red 20
	2	Blue 7	Blue 22	Red 19	Red 19

ECM Service Number	QDR Number	ECM Output Term #1	ECM Output Term #2	ECM Output Term #3	ECM Output Term #4
TBI 84 S/N 1226026 1226430	1	Black 9	Black 14	Black 16	White 20
	2	Black 7	Black 22	White 19	White 19

ECM Service Number	QDR Number	ECM Output Term #1	ECM Output Term #2	ECM Output Term #3	ECM Output Term #4
TBI/PFI 84-85 S/N 1226458 1226460	1	C1	C2	A2	A3
	2	A4	A5	A7	A7

ECM Service Number	QDR Number	ECM Output Term #1	ECM Output Term #2	ECM Output Term #3	ECM Output Term #4
PFI 86-87 S/N 1227165	1	A3	A7	C2	D12
	2	A2	A4	A5	C1

ECM Service Number	QDR Number	ECM Output Term #1	ECM Output Term #2	ECM Output Term #3	ECM Output Term #4
PFI 86-87 S/N 1227153 1227170 1227302	1	A2	A4	A4	A5
	2	A3	A3	D2	D2
	3	A7	A7		C2

ECM Service Number	QDR Number	ECM Output Term #1	ECM Output Term #2	ECM Output Term #3	ECM Output Term #4
TBI 87 S/N 1227748	1	Black 7	Black 7	Black 18	Black 18
	2	Black 3	Black 4	Black 21	Black 22

ECM Service Number	QDR Number	ECM Output Term #1	ECM Output Term #2	ECM Output Term #3	ECM Output Term #4
TBI 85-87 S/N 1226868 1227746 1227747	1	A2	A3	C1	C2
	2	A4	A5	A7	A7

ECM Service Number	QDR Number	ECM Output Term #1	ECM Output Term #2	ECM Output Term #3	ECM Output Term #4
TBI 85-86 S/N 1226864	1	Black 7	Black 9		White 20

ECM Service Number	QDR Number	ECM Output Term #1	ECM Output Term #2	ECM Output Term #3	ECM Output Term #4
TBI 85-86 S/N 1226867	1	A2	A3	A4	C2
	2	C1	A5	A7	A7

ECM Service Number	QDR Number	ECM Output Term #1	ECM Output Term #2	ECM Output Term #3	ECM Output Term #4
PFI 86 S/N 1227151	1	C1	C2	A2	A3
	2	A4	A5	A7	A7

ECM Service Number	QDR Number	ECM Output Term #1	ECM Output Term #2	ECM Output Term #3	ECM Output Term #4
PFI 85-87 S/N 1226869 1226870 1226948 1227065 1227784	1	A2	A4	A4	A5
	2	A3	A3	D2	D2
	3	C2		A7	A7

ECM Service Number	QDR Number	ECM Output Term #1	ECM Output Term #2	ECM Output Term #3	ECM Output Term #4
TBI 86-87 S/N 1227137 1227429	1	A2	A3	C1	C2
	2	A4	A5	A7	A7

ECM Service Number	QDR Number	ECM Output Term #1	ECM Output Term #2	ECM Output Term #3	ECM Output Term #4
TBI 87 S/N 1227749	1	E7	E8	E9	F7
	2	F1	F2	F3	F4

ECM Service Number	QDR Number	ECM Output Term #1	ECM Output Term #2	ECM Output Term #3	ECM Output Term #4
PFI 87 S/N 1227730	1	E7	E8	E9	F7
	2	F1	F2	F3	F4
	3	F5	F5	F6	F8

ECM Service Number	QDR Number	ECM Output Term #1	ECM Output Term #2	ECM Output Term #3	ECM Output Term #4
PFI 87 S/N 1227750	1	2A1	2A8	2A10	2A11
	2	3C7	3C8	3C9	3C10
	3	3D5	3D5	3D6	3C6
	4	3C4	3C4	3C5	3D4

Quad driver application and arrangement chart — 1982-87

ECM Service Number	QDR Number	ECM Output Term #1	ECM Output Term #2	ECM Output Term #3	ECM Output Term #4
PFI 84-85 S.N 1226461	1	A2	A4	A4	A5
	2	A3	A3	D2	D2
	3	A7	A7		C2

ECM Service Number	QDR Number	ECM Output Term #1	ECM Output Term #2	ECM Output Term #3	ECM Output Term #4
PFI (SEQ) 84-85 S.N 1226459	1	A3	A3	D3	D3
	2	A7	A7		D2
	3	A2	A4	A4	A5

ECM Service Number	QDR Number	ECM Output Term #1	ECM Output Term #2	ECM Output Term #3	ECM Output Term #4
CCC 85-87 S.N 1226457 1226519 1226865 1226866 1227076 1227169 1227301 1227855 1228079	1	G	E	4	6
	2	B	19	P	P
	3	18	18	T	T

ECM Service Number	QDR Number	ECM Output Term #1	ECM Output Term #2	ECM Output Term #3	ECM Output Term #4
DFI 86-87 S/N 1227056	1	A7	A7	A11	A11
	2	A2	A5	C3	C3
	3	C1	D2	D3	D10
	4	A3	A3	A4	A4

ECM Service Number	QDR Number	ECM Output Term #1	ECM Output Term #2	ECM Output Term #3	ECM Output Term #4
PFI 86-87 S/N 1227057	1	A3	A7	D2	D3
	2	A4	A5	B2	B9

ECM Service Number	QDR Number	ECM Output Term #1	ECM Output Term #2	ECM Output Term #3	ECM Output Term #4
PFI 86-87 S.N 1227148 1227783 1227886	1	A3	A3	D3	D3
	2	A7	A7	A8	D2
	3	A2	A4	A4	A5

Quad driver application and arrangement chart—1982-87 (cont.)

MPI TROUBLE DIAGNOSTICS

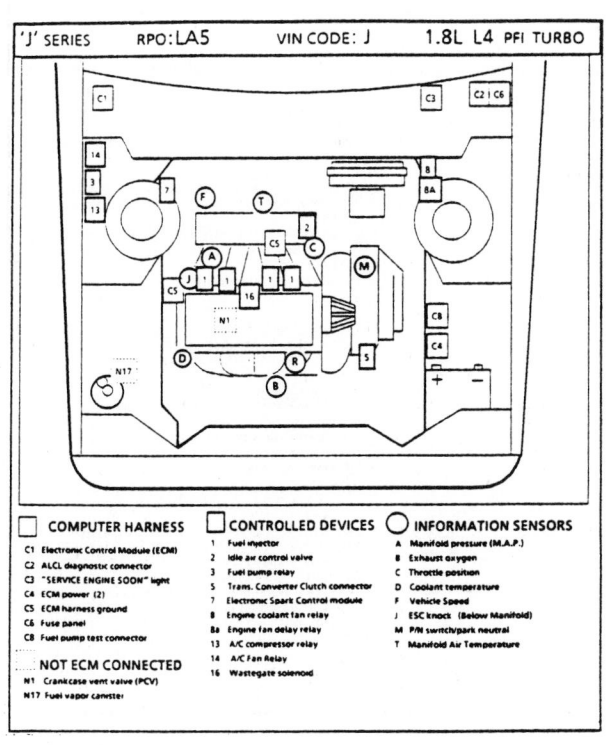

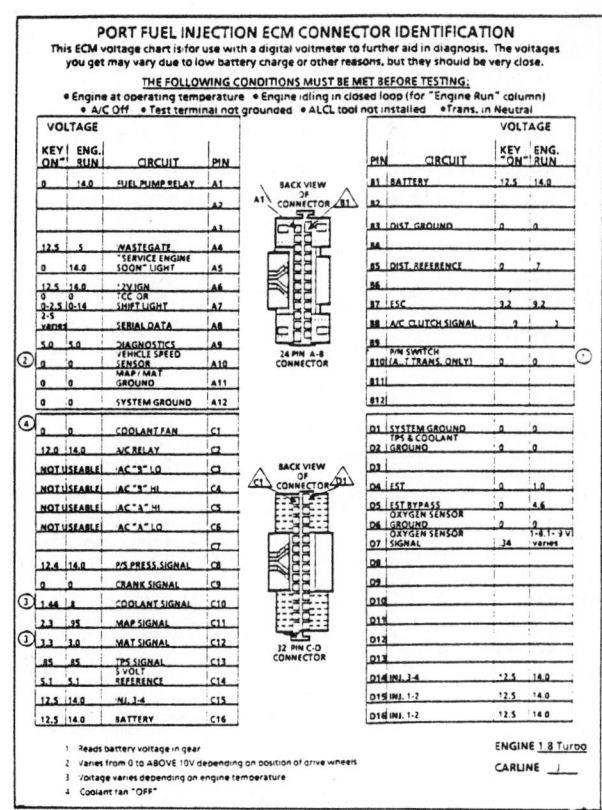

MPI TROUBLE DIAGNOSTICS

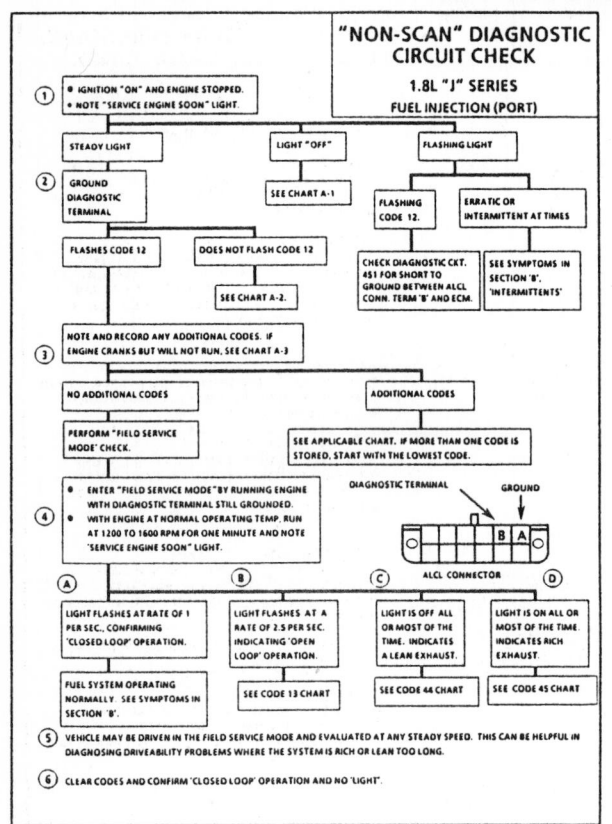

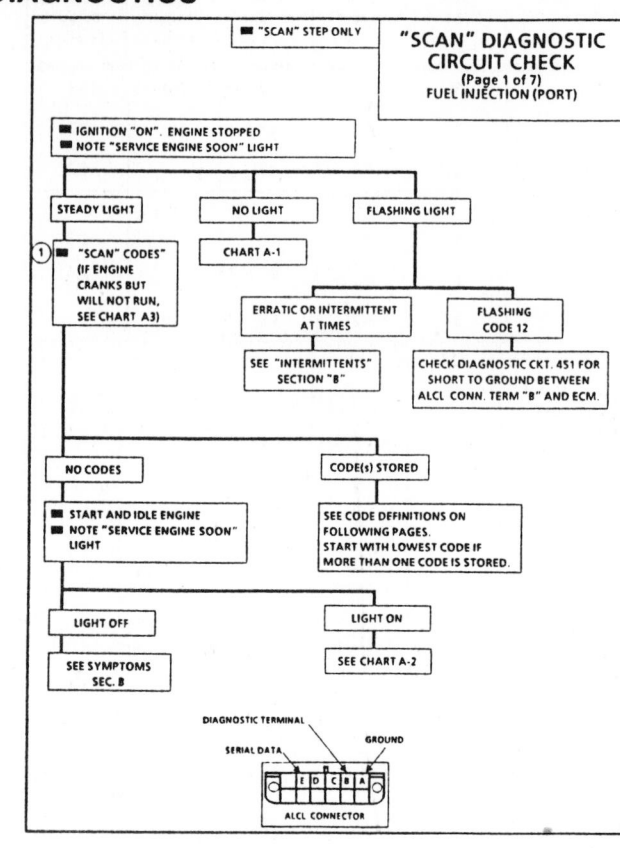

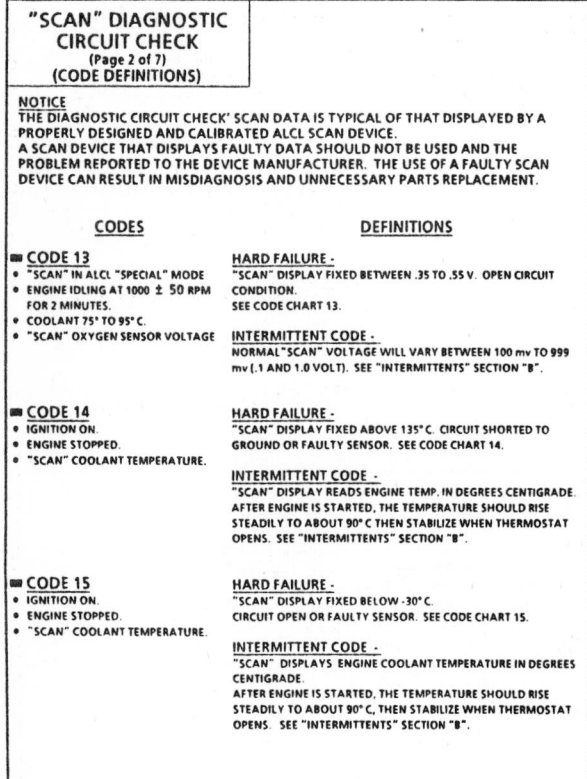

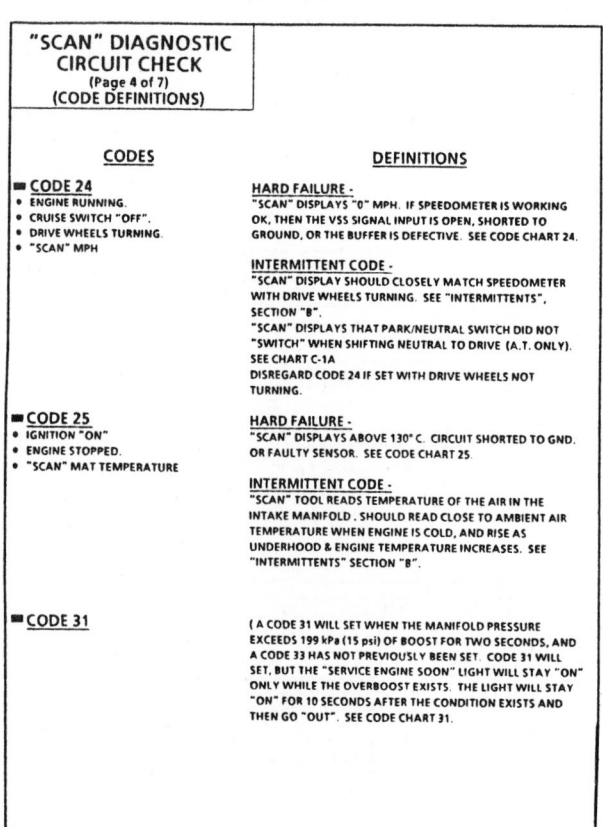

MPI TROUBLE DIAGNOSTICS

"SCAN" DIAGNOSTIC CIRCUIT CHECK
(Page 3 of 7) (CODE DEFINITIONS)

CODES

■ **CODE 21**
- IGNITION "ON".
- THROTTLE CLOSED.
- ENGINE STOPPED.
- "SCAN" TPS

DEFINITIONS

HARD FAILURE -
"SCAN" DISPLAYS A CLOSED THROTTLE VOLTAGE OVER 2.5 VOLTS. SIGNAL VOLTAGE TOO HIGH, GROUND WIRE OPEN, SIGNAL LINE SHORTED TO SENSOR REF. LINE OR FAULTY SENSOR. SEE CODE CHART 21.

INTERMITTENT CODE -
"SCAN" DISPLAYS THROTTLE POSITION IN VOLTS. SHOULD READ BETWEEN 020-125 (200 MV AND 1.25 V). WITH THROTTLE CLOSED AND IGNITION ON OR AT IDLE. VOLTAGE SHOULD INCREASE AT A STEADY RATE AS THROTTLE IS MOVED TOWARD A WIDE OPEN POSITION. SEE "INTERMITTENTS" SECTION "B".

■ **CODE 22**
- IGNITION "ON"
- ENGINE STOPPED.
- THROTTLE CLOSED.
- "SCAN" TPS

HARD FAILURE -
"SCAN" DISPLAYS BELOW 020V (200 mv). OPEN OR SHORT TO GROUND IN 5V REFERENCE OR SIGNAL CIRCUIT, OR FAULTY SENSOR. SEE CODE CHART 22.

INTERMITTENT CODE -
"SCAN" DISPLAYS THROTTLE POSITION IN VOLTS. SHOULD READ BETWEEN 020-125 (200 mv AND 1.25 V). WITH THROTTLE CLOSED AND IGNITION ON OR AT IDLE. VOLTAGE SHOULD INCREASE AT A STEADY RATE AS THROTTLE IS MOVED TOWARD A WIDE OPEN POSITION: SEE "INTERMITTENTS" SECTION "B".

■ **CODE 23**
- IGNITION "ON"
- ENGINE STOPPED.
- "SCAN" MAT TEMPERATURE

HARD FAILURE -
"SCAN" DISPLAYS BELOW -25° C. CIRCUIT OPEN OR FAULTY SENSOR. SEE CODE CHART 23.

INTERMITTENT CODE -
"SCAN" TOOL READS TEMPERATURE OF THE AIR IN THE INTAKE MANIFOLD. SHOULD READ CLOSE TO AMBIENT AIR TEMPERATURE WHEN ENGINE IS COLD, AND RISE AS UNDERHOOD & ENGINE TEMPERATURE INCREASES. SEE "INTERMITTENTS" SECTION "B".

"SCAN" DIAGNOSTIC CIRCUIT CHECK
(Page 5 of 7) (CODE DEFINITIONS)

CODES

■ **CODE 33**
- ENGINE IDLING.
- "SCAN" MAP.

DEFINITIONS

HARD FAILURE -
"SCAN" DISPLAYS ABOVE 2.5 VOLTS. SENSOR GROUND CIRCUIT OPEN, LEAKING VACUUM HOSE OR FAULTY SENSOR. SEE CODE CHART 33.

INTERMITTENT CODE -
"SCAN" DISPLAYS MANIFOLD PRESSURE IN VOLTS. LOW PRESSURE (HIGH VACUUM) READS A LOW VOLTAGE WHILE A HIGH PRESSURE (LOW VACUUM) READS A HIGH VOLTAGE. IF ENGINE IDLE IS LOW AND UNSTABLE IT MAY SET CODE 33. SEE "INTERMITTENTS" SECTION "B".

■ **CODE 34**
- IGNITION "ON"
- SCAN" MAP.

HARD FAILURE -
"SCAN" DISPLAYS BELOW 200 mv (.2 VOLTS). SIGNAL WIRE OR 5V REFERENCE OPEN OR SHORTED TO GROUND OR FAULTY SENSOR. SEE CODE CHART 34.

INTERMITTENT CODE -
"SCAN" DISPLAYS MANIFOLD PRESSURE IN VOLTS. LOW PRESSURE (HIGH VACUUM) READS A LOW VOLTAGE WHILE A HIGH PRESSURE (LOW VACUUM) READS A HIGH VOLTAGE. SEE "INTERMITTENTS" SECTION "B".

■ **CODE 35**
- A/C OFF.
- ENGINE IDLING IN NEUTRAL
- COOLANT TEMP 70° TO 90° C.
- "SCAN" IN "SPECIAL" MODE.
- INCREASE ENGINE RPM TO 2500 TO RESET IAC. CLOSE THROTTLE AND ALLOW IDLE AND IAC COUNTS TO STABILIZE.

HARD FAILURE -
"SCAN" DISPLAYS IDLE SPEED 950 RPM OR ABOVE. IAC COUNTS "0" - THIS CONDITION IS USUALLY CAUSED BY A SMALL VACUUM LEAK SUCH AS CCP OR CRUISE CONTROL HOSE DISCONNECTED.
OR
ENGINE IDLE SPEED 950 PRM OR BELOW. IAC COUNTS ABOVE 80. SEE CODE 35 CHART.

INTERMITTENT CODE -
FOLLOWING AN IAC RESET, RPM SHOULD STABLIZE AT 1000 ± 50 RPM IN "SPECIAL" MODE.
DISCONNECTING "SCAN" TOOL WILL RESTORE NORMAL IDLE.

"SCAN" DIAGNOSTIC CIRCUIT CHECK
(Page 6 of 7) (CODE DEFINITIONS)

CODES

■ **CODE 42**
- CLEAR CODES, START AND IDLE ENGINE FOR 1 MINUTE.

DEFINITIONS

HARD FAILURE -
"SERVICE ENGINE SOON" LIGHT ON AND SCAN DISPLAYS CODE 42.
SEE CODE CHART 42

INTERMITTENT CODE -
THE SCAN TOOL CAN NOT HELP IN THE DIAGNOSIS OF A CODE 42 PROBLEM. IF NO "SERVICE ENGINE SOON "LIGHT, REFER TO INTERMITTENTS IN SECTION "B".

■ **CODE 43**

SEE CODE CHART 43

■ **CODE 44**
- "SCAN" TOOL IN "SPECIAL" MODE.
- COOLANT TEMP 75° to 95° C.
- ENGINE IDLING AT 1000 RPM.

HARD FAILURE -
"SCAN" DISPLAYS O₂ VOLTAGE FIXED BELOW .35V IS CAUSED BY A LEAN EXHAUST OR SIGNAL CIRCUIT SHORTED TO GROUND. SEE CODE CHART 44.

INTERMITTENT CODE -
NORMAL "SCAN" VOLTAGE WILL VARY BETWEEN 100 MV AND 999 mv. (.1 to 1.0V) ALSO SEE CROSSCOUNTS, RICH - LEAN INDICATION, O₂ VOLTAGE. REFER TO "SCAN" INFORMATION IN INTRODUCTION.

■ **CODE 45**
- "SCAN" TOOL IN "SPECIAL" MODE
- ENGINE IDLING AT 1000 RPM
- COOLANT TEMP 75° to 95° C.
- "SCAN" OXYGEN SENSOR VOLTAGE

HARD FAILURE -
"SCAN" O₂ VOLTAGE FIXED ABOVE .65V. RICH EXHAUST CAUSING A HIGH O₂ VOLTAGE. SEE CODE CHART 45.

INTERMITTENT CODE -
NORMAL "SCAN" VOLTAGE WILL VARY BETWEEN 100 MV AND 999 mv. (.1 to 1.0V) ALSO SEE CROSSCOUNTS, RICH - LEAN INDICATION, O₂ VOLTAGE. REFER "SCAN" INFORMATION IN INTRODUCTION.

"SCAN" DIAGNOSTIC CIRCUIT CHECK
(Page 7 of 7) (CODE DEFINITIONS)

CODES

■ **CODE 51**
- CLEAR CODES
- START ENGINE
- CHECK FOR CODE

DEFINITIONS

HARD FAILURE -
CODE 51 RESETS WHICH INDICATES A FAULTY PROM. SEE CODE CHART 51.

■ **CODE 52**
- CLEAR CODES
- START ENGINE
- CHECK FOR CODE

HARD FAILURE -
CODE 52 RESETS WHICH INDICATES FAULTY OR MISSING CALPAK.

■ **CODE 55**
- CLEAR CODES
- START ENGINE
- CHECK FOR CODE

HARD FAILURE -
CODE 55 RESETS WHICH INDICATES THE ECM IS FAULTY. REPLACE ECM.

MPI TROUBLE DIAGNOSTICS

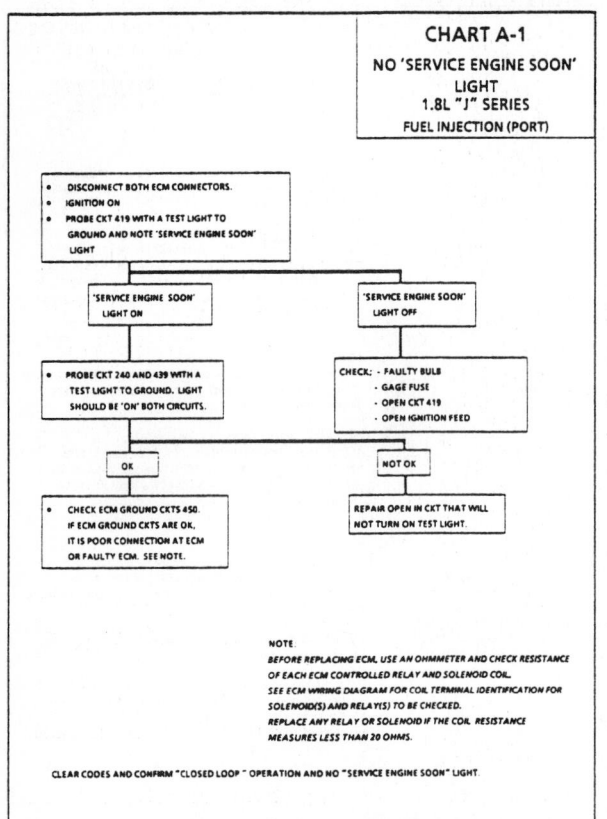

CHART A-1

NO 'SERVICE ENGINE SOON'
LIGHT
1.8L "J" SERIES
FUEL INJECTION (PORT)

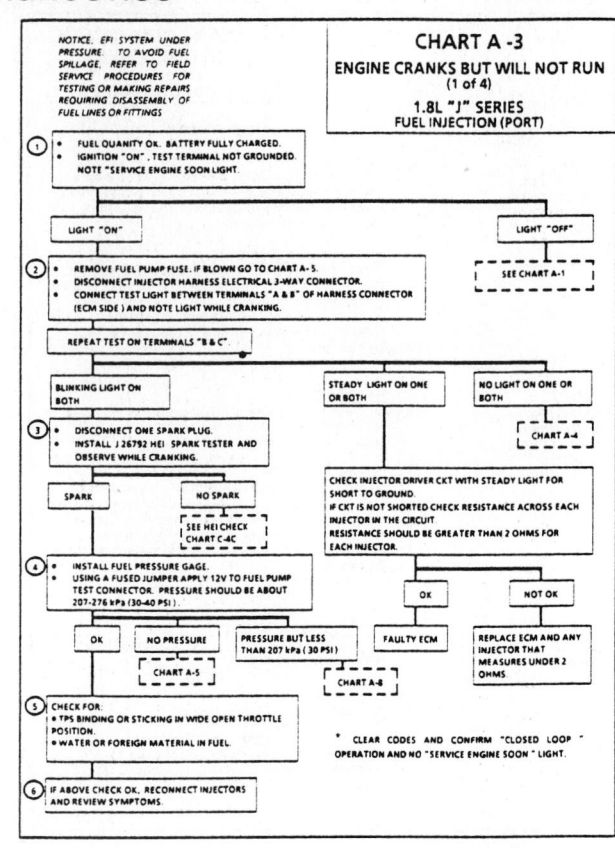

CHART A-3

ENGINE CRANKS BUT WILL NOT RUN
(1 of 4)
1.8L "J" SERIES
FUEL INJECTION (PORT)

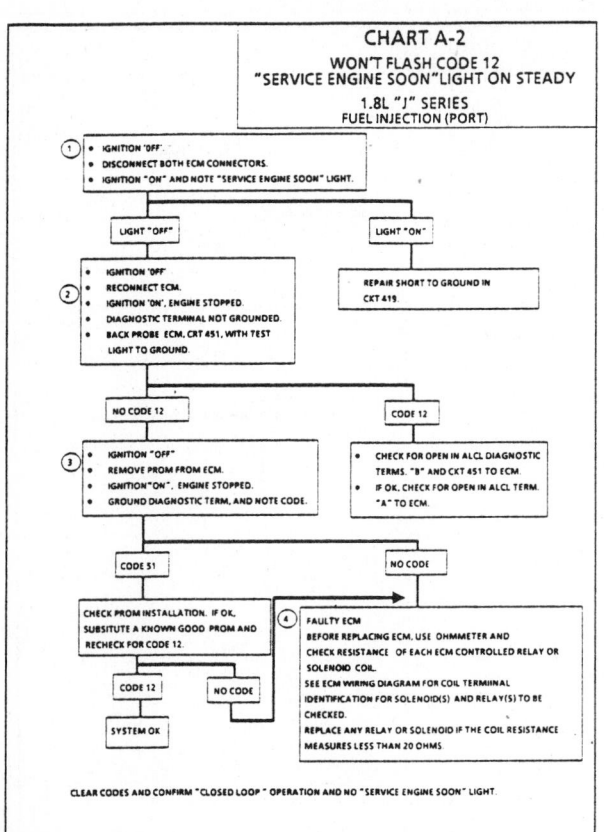

CHART A-2

WON'T FLASH CODE 12
"SERVICE ENGINE SOON"LIGHT ON STEADY
1.8L "J" SERIES
FUEL INJECTION (PORT)

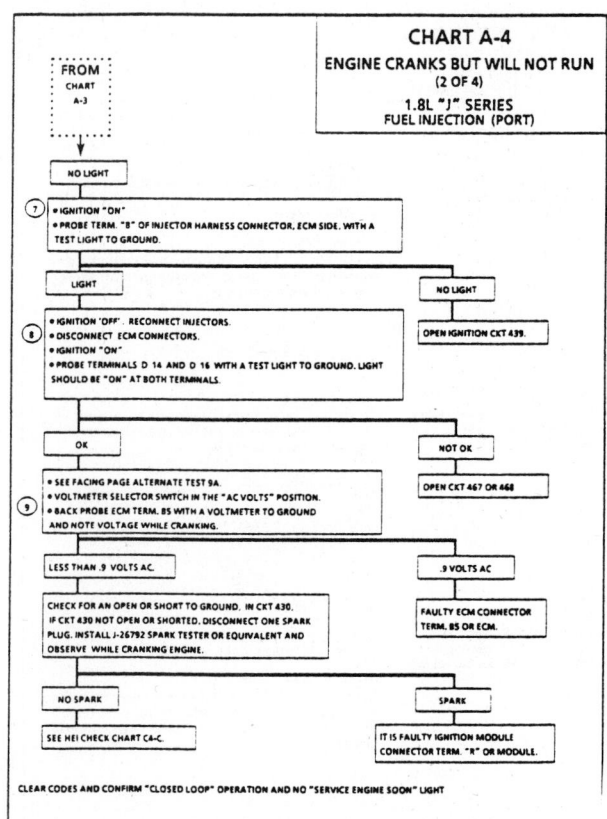

CHART A-4

ENGINE CRANKS BUT WILL NOT RUN
(2 OF 4)
1.8L "J" SERIES
FUEL INJECTION (PORT)

MPI TROUBLE DIAGNOSTICS

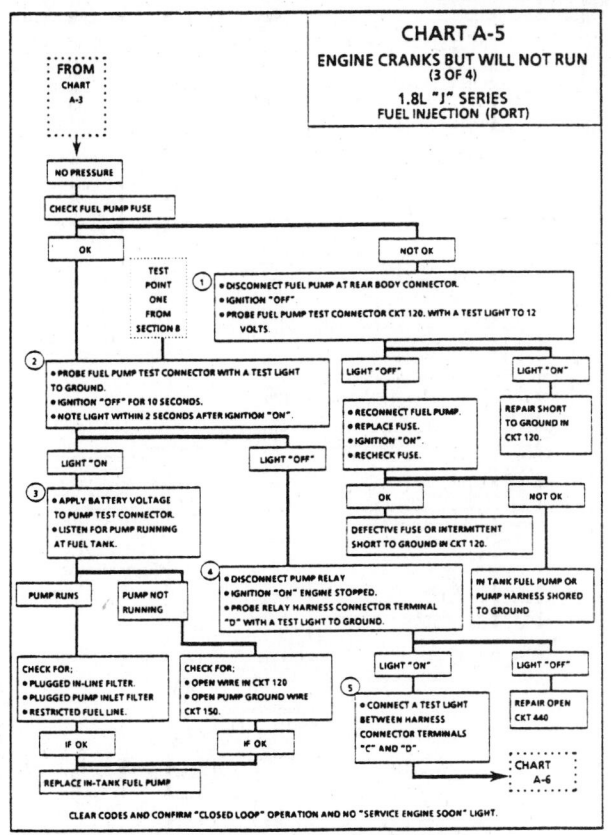

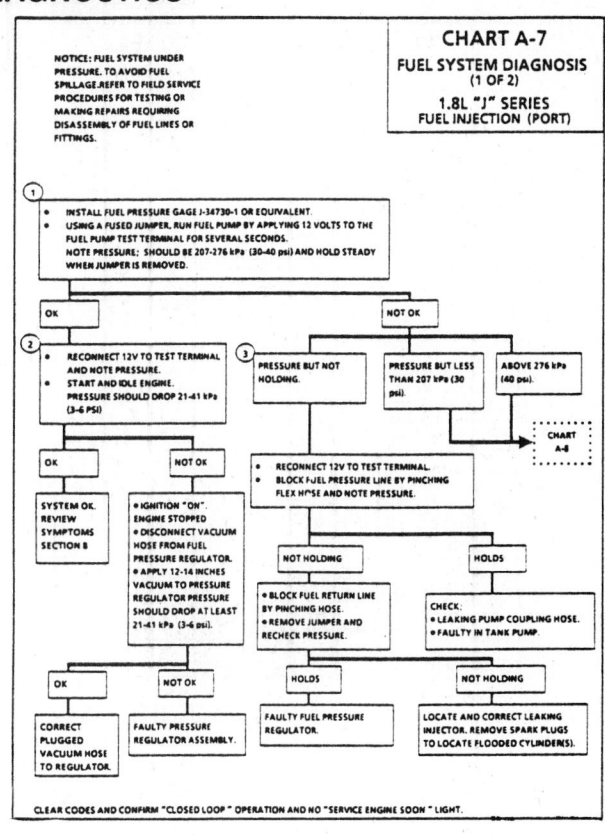

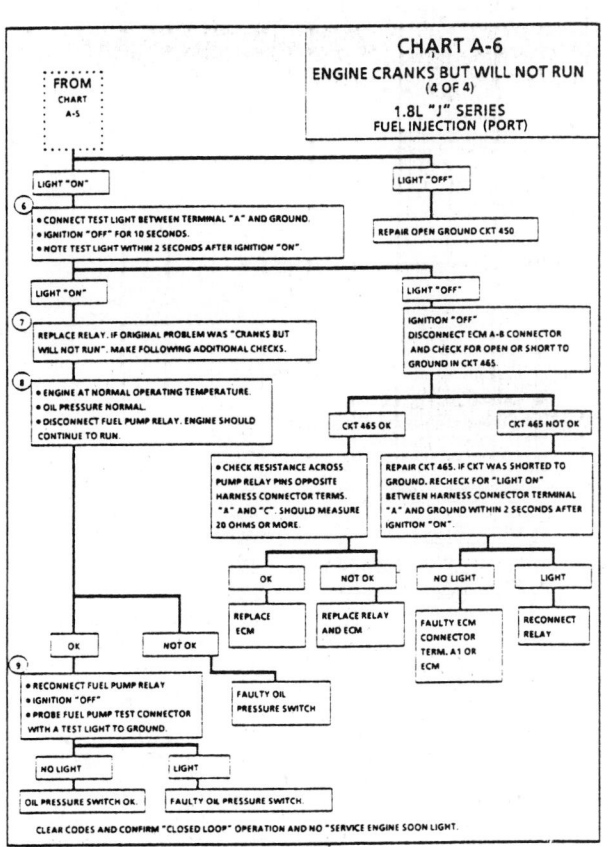

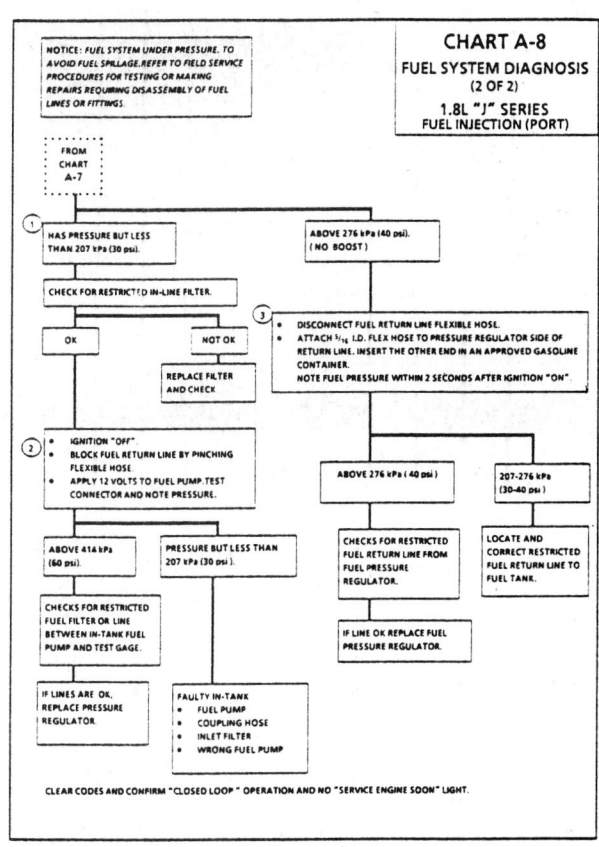

MPI TROUBLE DIAGNOSTICS

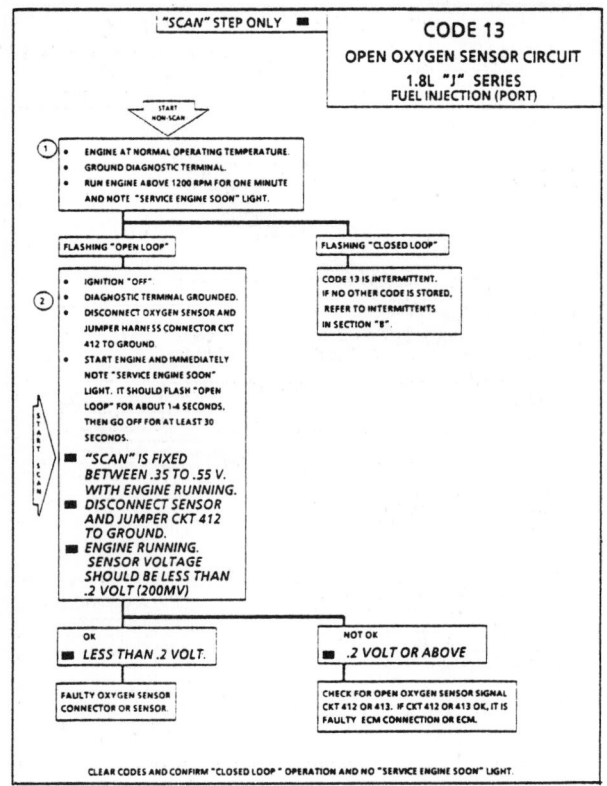

CODE 13
OPEN OXYGEN SENSOR CIRCUIT
1.8L "J" SERIES
FUEL INJECTION (PORT)

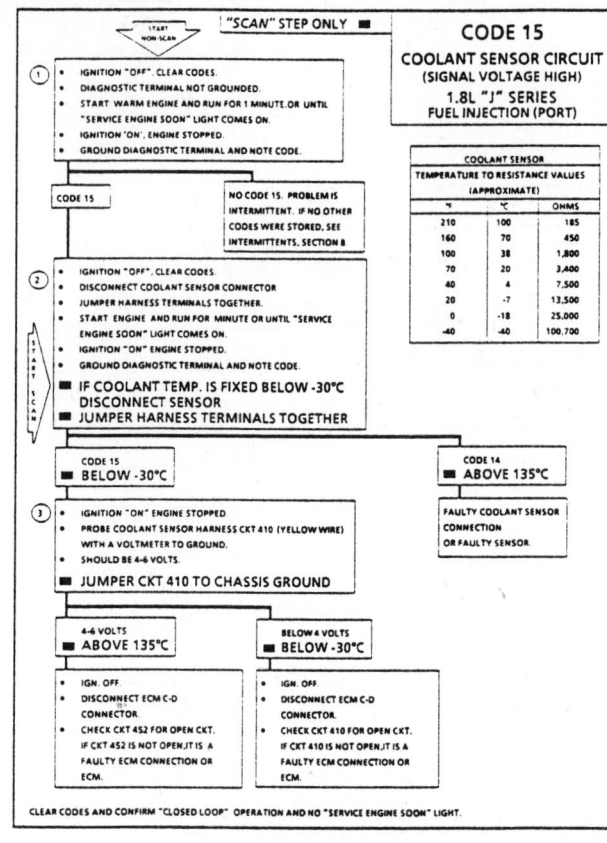

CODE 15
COOLANT SENSOR CIRCUIT
(SIGNAL VOLTAGE HIGH)
1.8L "J" SERIES
FUEL INJECTION (PORT)

COOLANT SENSOR TEMPERATURE TO RESISTANCE VALUES (APPROXIMATE)		
°F	°C	OHMS
210	100	185
160	70	450
100	38	1,800
70	20	3,400
40	4	7,500
20	-7	13,500
0	-18	25,000
-40	-40	100,700

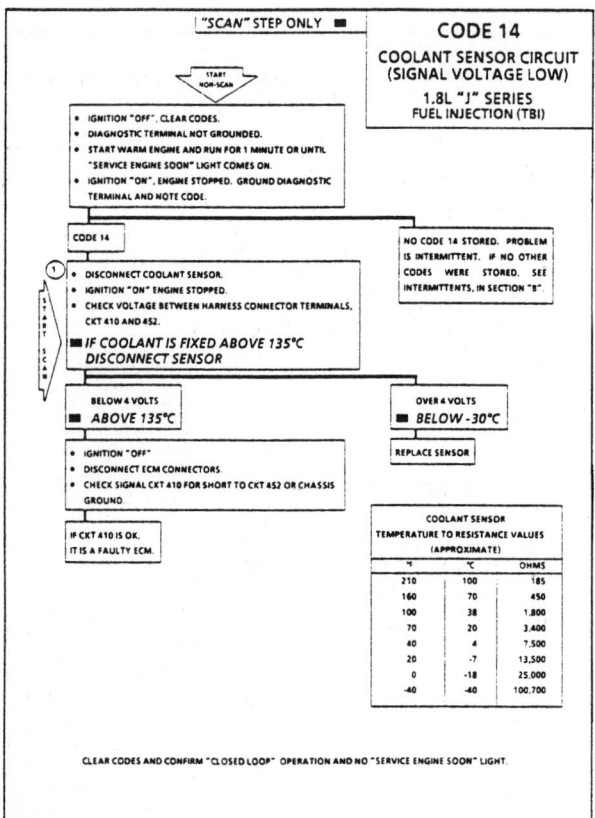

CODE 14
COOLANT SENSOR CIRCUIT
(SIGNAL VOLTAGE LOW)
1.8L "J" SERIES
FUEL INJECTION (TBI)

COOLANT SENSOR TEMPERATURE TO RESISTANCE VALUES (APPROXIMATE)		
°F	°C	OHMS
210	100	185
160	70	450
100	38	1,800
70	20	3,400
40	4	7,500
20	-7	13,500
0	-18	25,000
-40	-40	100,700

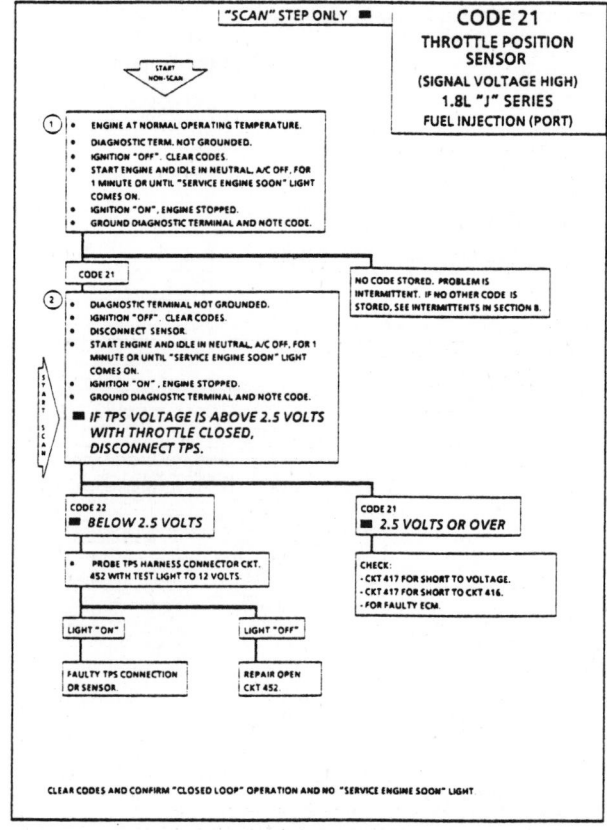

CODE 21
THROTTLE POSITION SENSOR
(SIGNAL VOLTAGE HIGH)
1.8L "J" SERIES
FUEL INJECTION (PORT)

MPI TROUBLE DIAGNOSTICS

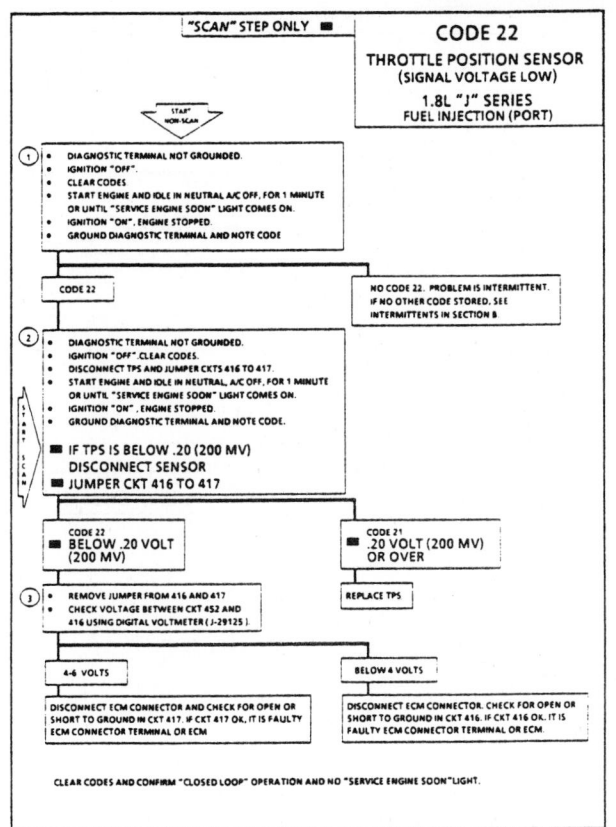

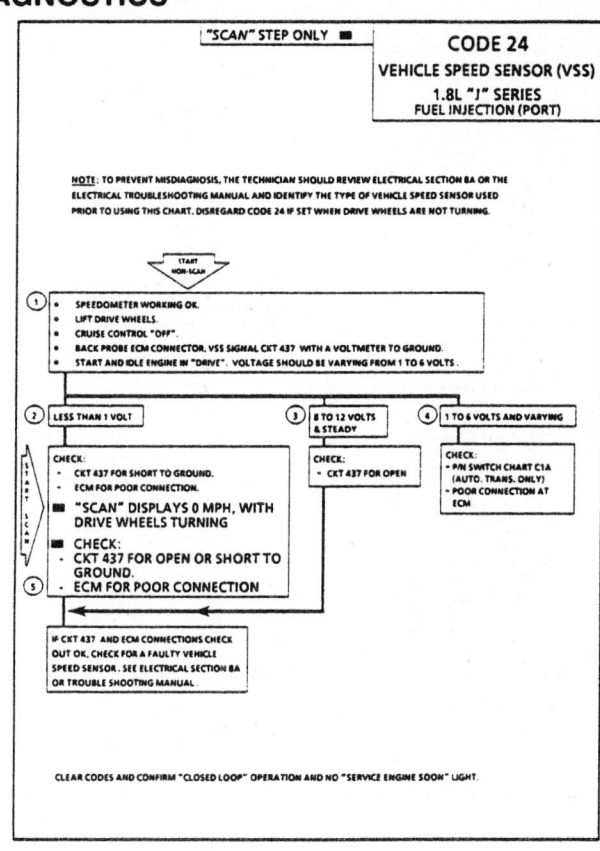

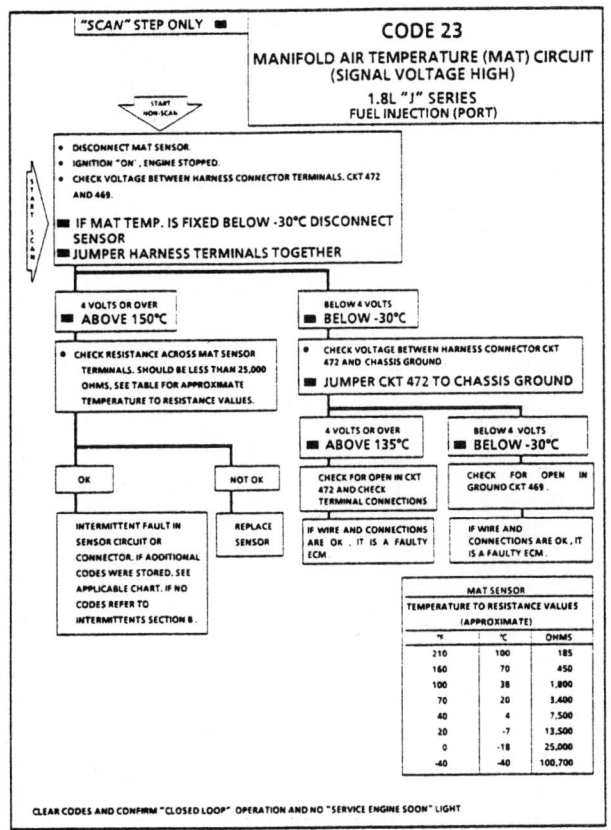

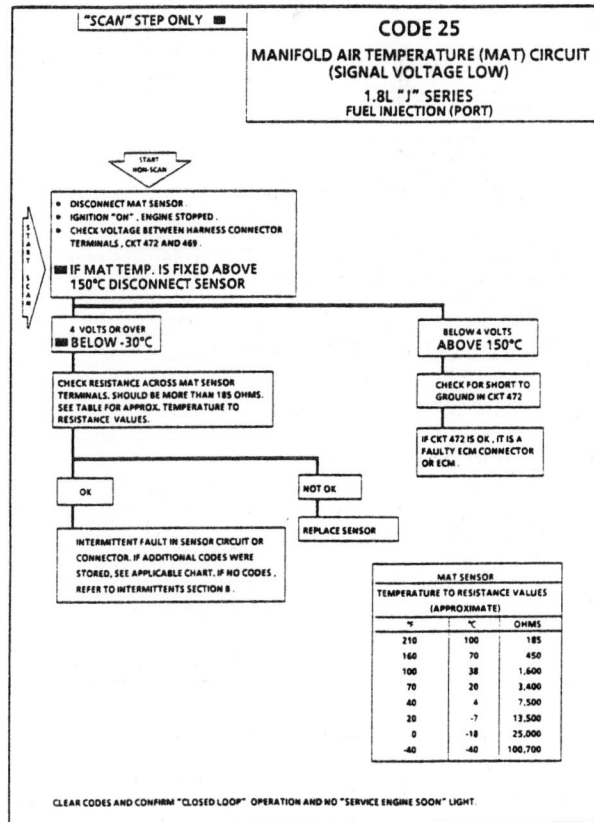

MPI TROUBLE DIAGNOSTICS

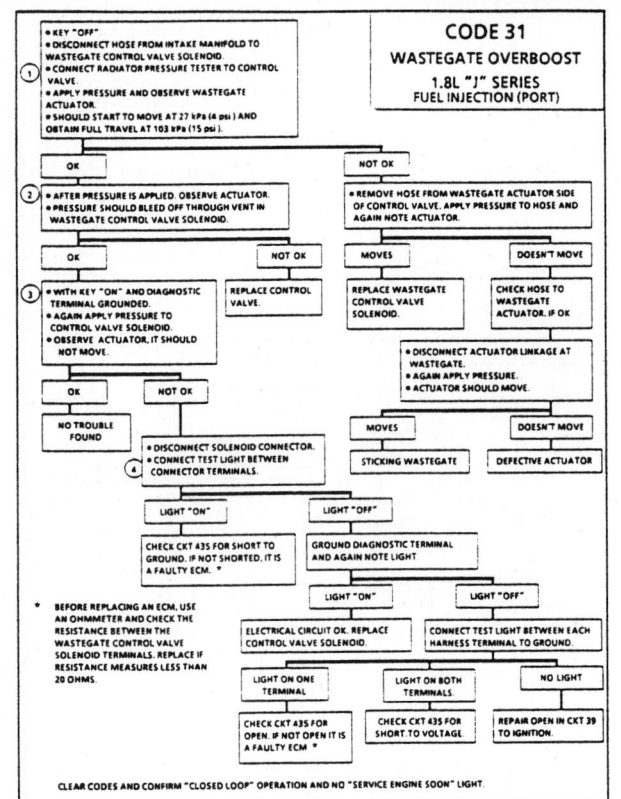

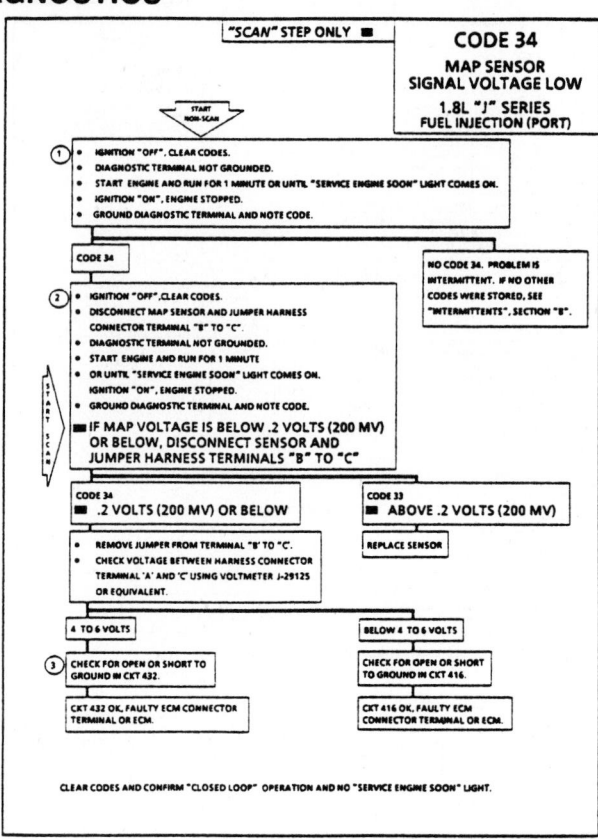

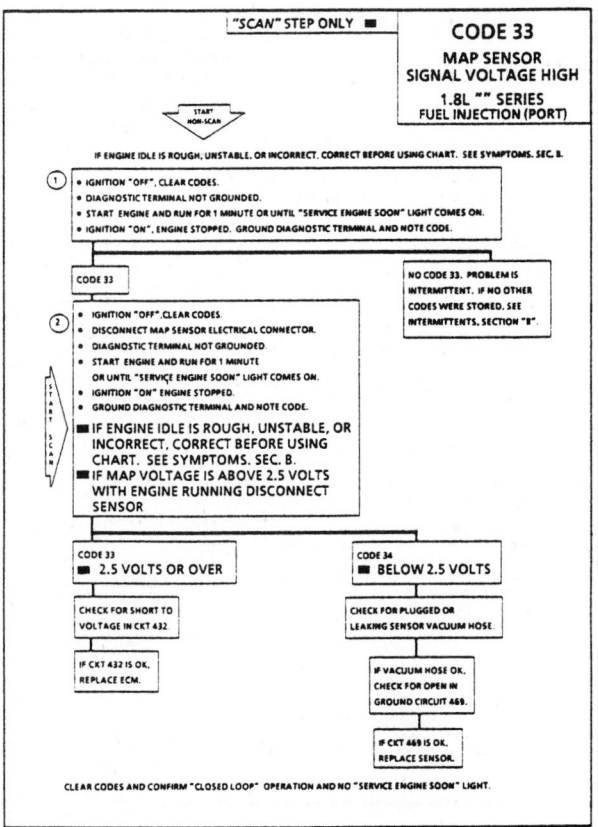

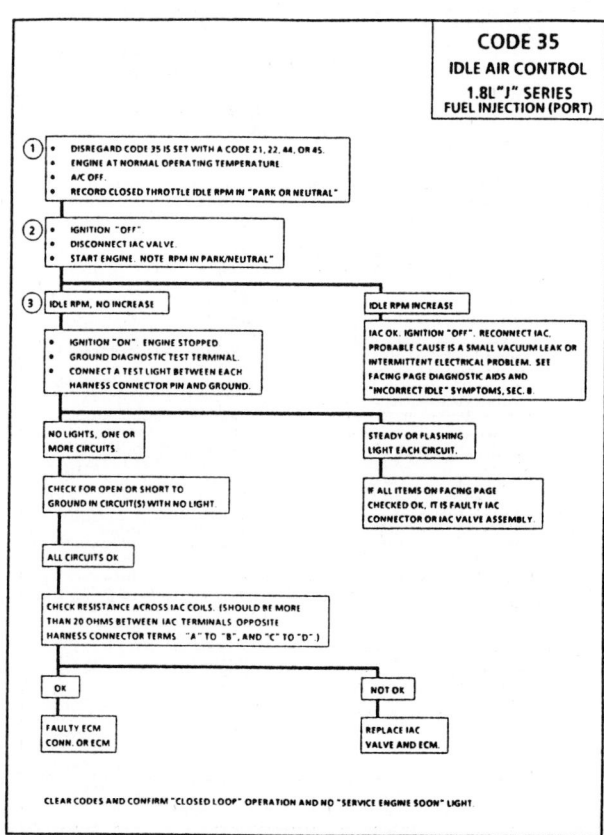

MPI TROUBLE DIAGNOSTICS

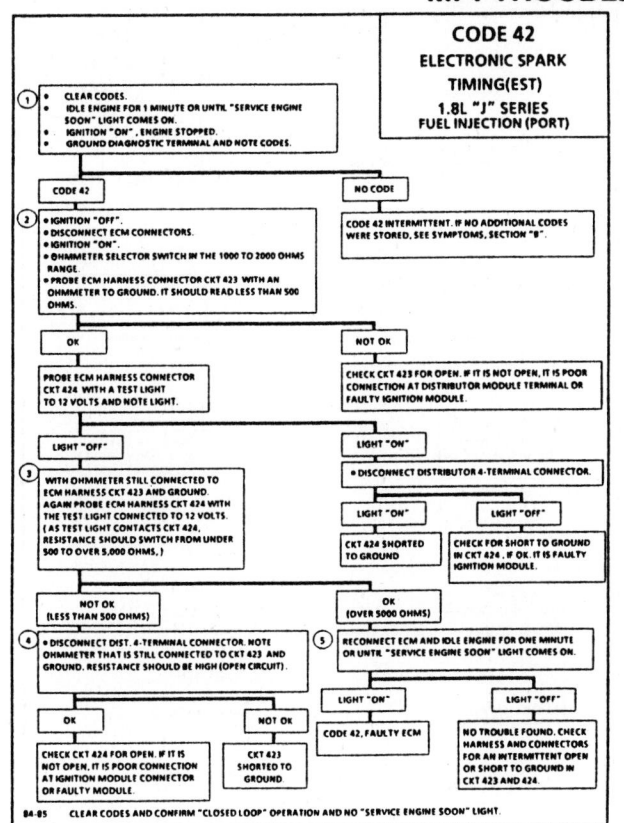

CODE 42
ELECTRONIC SPARK TIMING(EST)
1.8L "J" SERIES
FUEL INJECTION (PORT)

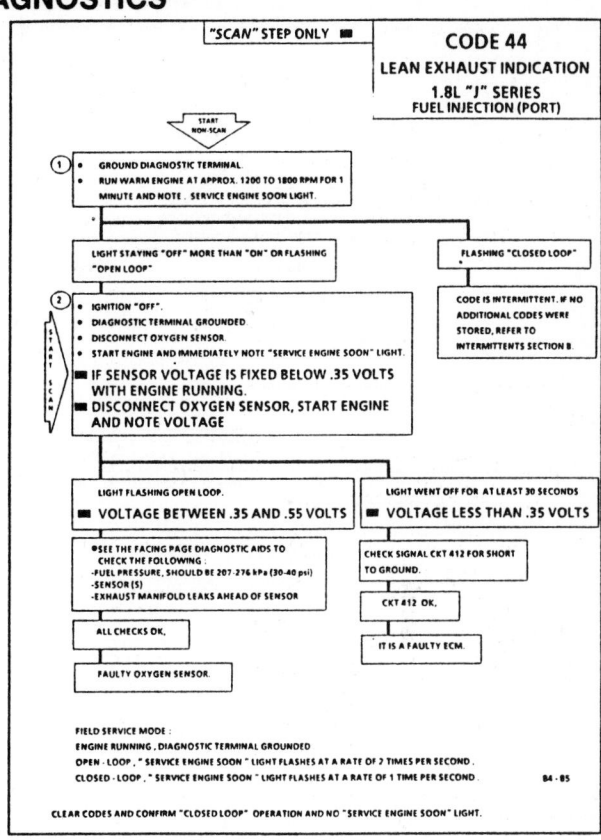

CODE 44
LEAN EXHAUST INDICATION
1.8L "J" SERIES
FUEL INJECTION (PORT)

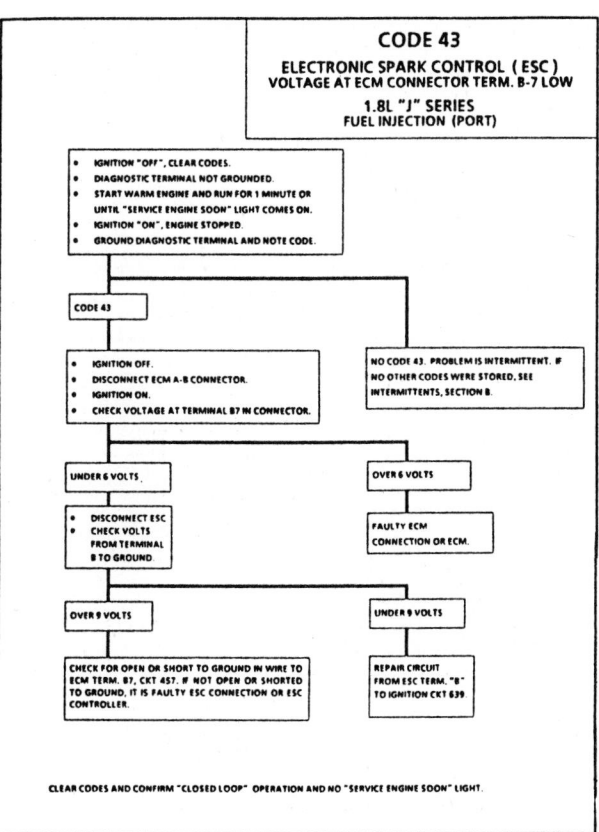

CODE 43
ELECTRONIC SPARK CONTROL (ESC)
VOLTAGE AT ECM CONNECTOR TERM. B-7 LOW
1.8L "J" SERIES
FUEL INJECTION (PORT)

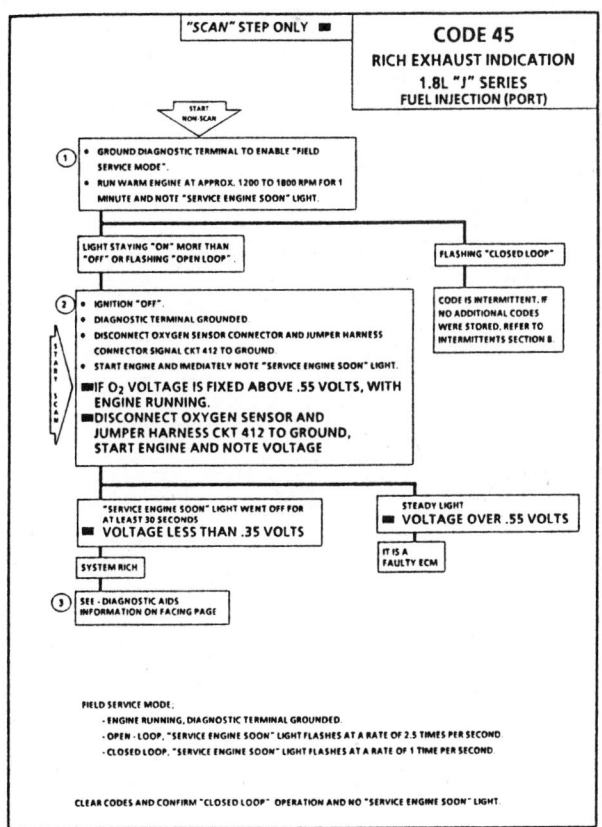

CODE 45
RICH EXHAUST INDICATION
1.8L "J" SERIES
FUEL INJECTION (PORT)

MPI TROUBLE DIAGNOSTICS

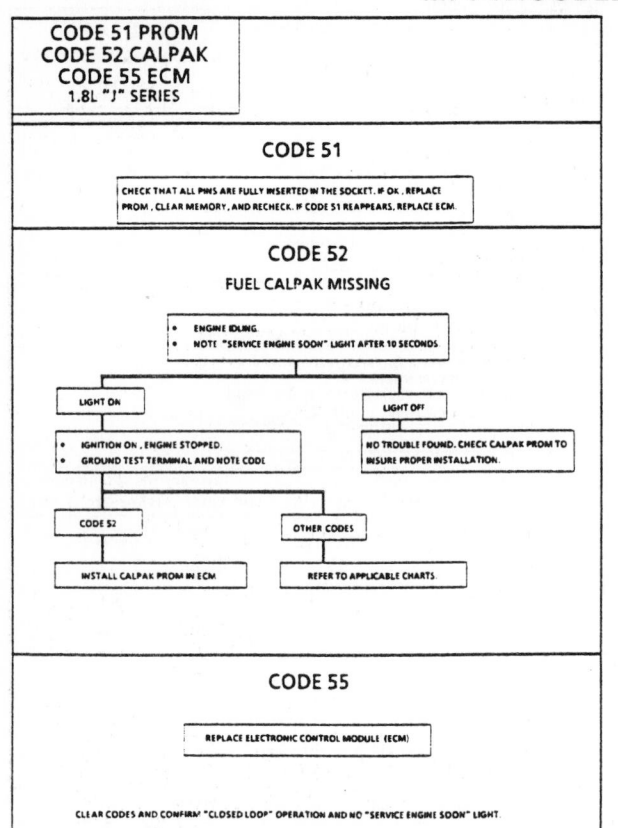

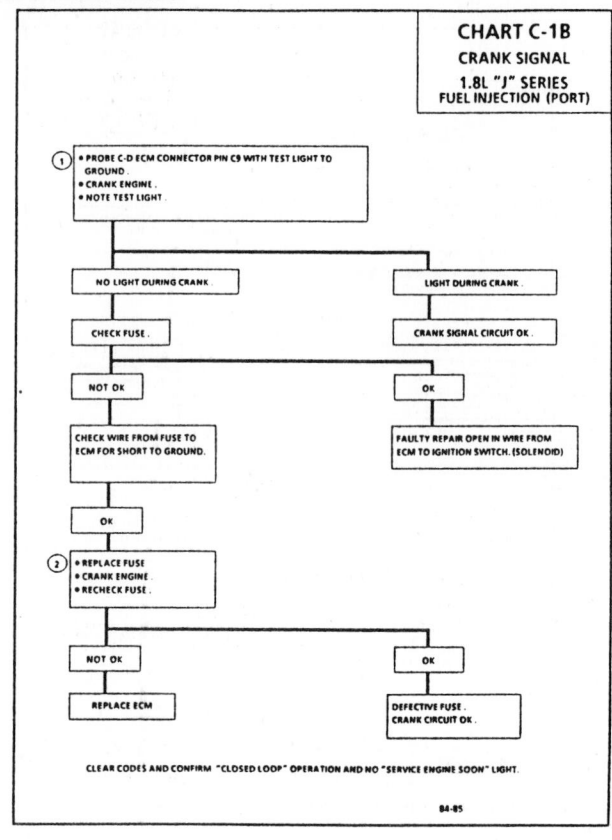

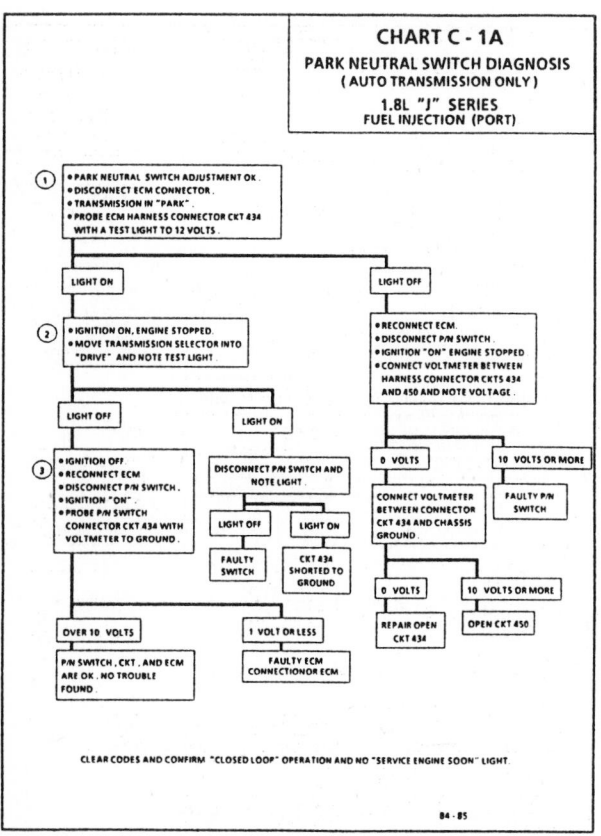

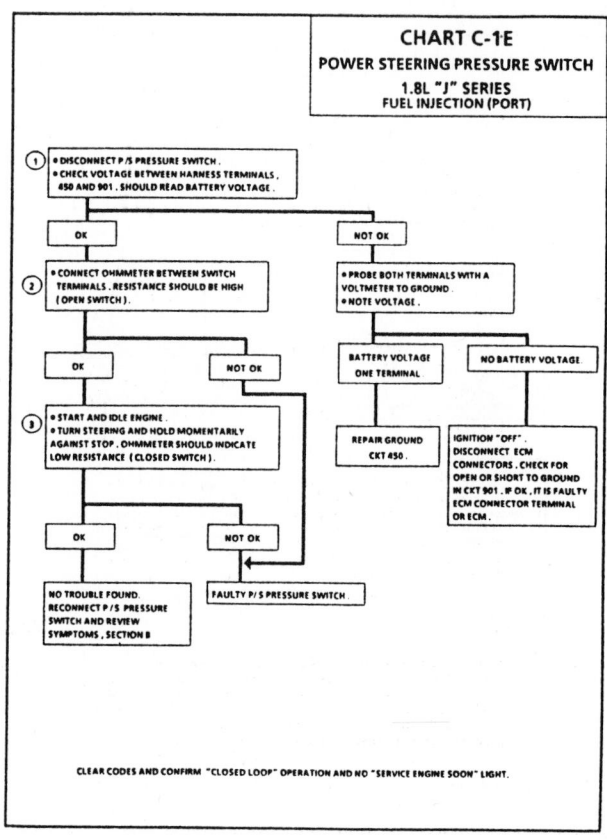

MPI TROUBLE DIAGNOSTICS

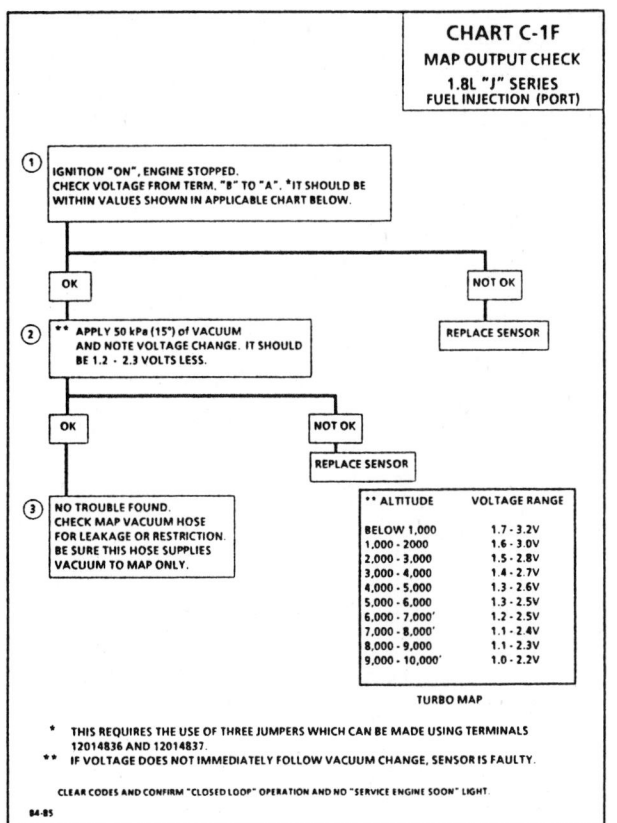

CHART C-1F
MAP OUTPUT CHECK
1.8L "J" SERIES
FUEL INJECTION (PORT)

① IGNITION "ON", engine stopped. CHECK VOLTAGE FROM TERM. "B" TO "A". *IT SHOULD BE WITHIN VALUES SHOWN IN APPLICABLE CHART BELOW.

OK

NOT OK

REPLACE SENSOR

② ** APPLY 50 kPa (15") of VACUUM AND NOTE VOLTAGE CHANGE. IT SHOULD BE 1.2 - 2.3 VOLTS LESS.

OK

NOT OK

REPLACE SENSOR

③ NO TROUBLE FOUND. CHECK MAP VACUUM HOSE FOR LEAKAGE OR RESTRICTION. BE SURE THIS HOSE SUPPLIES VACUUM TO MAP ONLY.

** ALTITUDE	VOLTAGE RANGE
BELOW 1,000	1.7 - 3.2V
1,000 - 2000	1.6 - 3.0V
2,000 - 3.000	1.5 - 2.8V
3,000 - 4.000	1.4 - 2.7V
4,000 - 5.000	1.3 - 2.6V
5,000 - 6.000	1.3 - 2.5V
6,000 - 7,000'	1.2 - 2.5V
7,000 - 8,000'	1.1 - 2.4V
8,000 - 9,000	1.1 - 2.3V
9,000 - 10,000'	1.0 - 2.2V

TURBO MAP

* THIS REQUIRES THE USE OF THREE JUMPERS WHICH CAN BE MADE USING TERMINALS 12014836 AND 12014837.
** IF VOLTAGE DOES NOT IMMEDIATELY FOLLOW VACUUM CHANGE, SENSOR IS FAULTY.

CLEAR CODES AND CONFIRM "CLOSED LOOP" OPERATION AND NO "SERVICE ENGINE SOON" LIGHT.

84-85

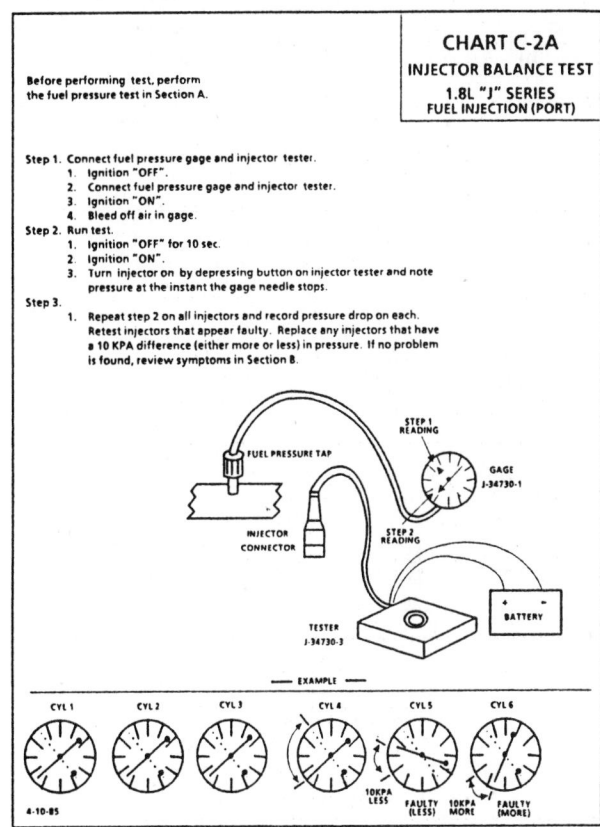

CHART C-2A
INJECTOR BALANCE TEST
1.8L "J" SERIES
FUEL INJECTION (PORT)

Before performing test, perform the fuel pressure test in Section A.

Step 1. Connect fuel pressure gage and injector tester.
 1. Ignition "OFF".
 2. Connect fuel pressure gage and injector tester.
 3. Ignition "ON".
 4. Bleed off air in gage.
Step 2. Run test.
 1. Ignition "OFF" for 10 sec.
 2. Ignition "ON".
 3. Turn injector on by depressing button on injector tester and note pressure at the instant the gage needle stops.
Step 3.
 1. Repeat step 2 on all injectors and record pressure drop on each. Retest injectors that appear faulty. Replace any injectors that have a 10 KPA difference (either more or less) in pressure. If no problem is found, review symptoms in Section B.

4-10-85

CHART C-2A

INJECTOR BALANCE TEST

The injector tester is a timer used to turn each injector on for a precise amount of time. This time allows a measured amount of fuel to be sprayed into the intake manifold thereby reducing the pressure in the fuel rail. All injectors in the engine should measure about the same pressure drop (± 10 kPa).

STEP 1

Connect fuel gage J347301 or equivalent to fuel pressure tap. Wrap a shop towel around fitting while connecting gage to avoid fuel spillage.

Disconnect harness connectors at all injectors, and connect injector tester J-34730-3 or equivalent to one injector. Ignition must be off at least 10 seconds to complete ECM shutdown cycle. Fuel pump should run about 2 seconds after ignition is turned on. At this point, insert clear tubing attached to vent valve into a suitable container and bleed air from gage and hose to insure accurate gage operation.

STEP 2

Turn ignition off for 10 seconds and then on again to get fuel pressure to its maximum. This insures that fuel pressure is precisely the same for each injector tested. Energize tester one time and note pressure drop the instant the gage needle stops. The pressure may increase for a few seconds after the initial pressure drop. This increase should not be considered in the test, because it may vary depending on temperature.

NOTE: *The entire test should not be repeated more than once to prevent flooding.*

STEP 3

This example shows how faulty injectors would appear, as compared to good ones. Usually, good injectors will have virtually the same drop. Retest any injector that has a pressure difference of 10 kPa, either more or less than the average of the other injectors on the engine. Replace any injector that also fails the retest. If the pressure drop of all injectors is within 10 kPa of this average, the injectors appear to be flowing properly. . Reconnect them and review Symptoms, Section B.

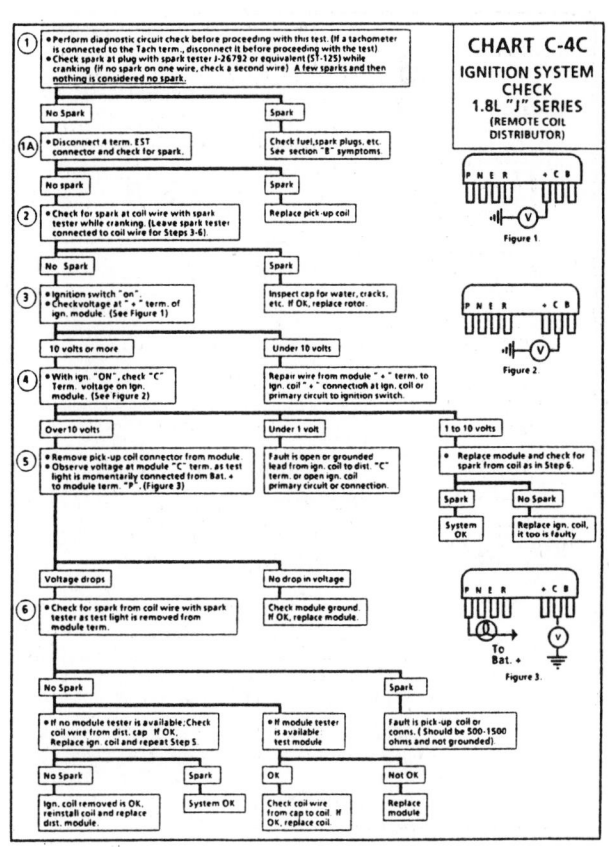

CHART C-4C
IGNITION SYSTEM CHECK
1.8L "J" SERIES
(REMOTE COIL DISTRIBUTOR)

MPI TROUBLE DIAGNOSTICS

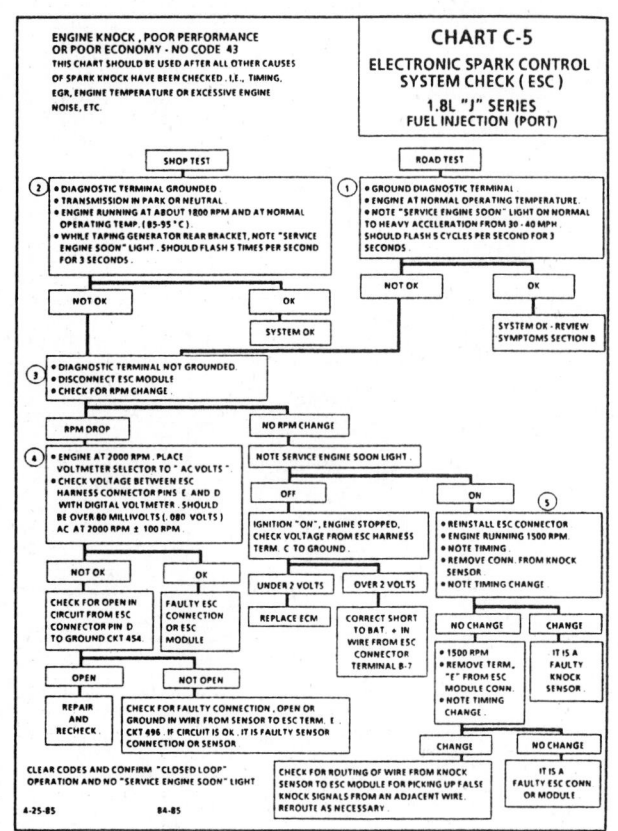

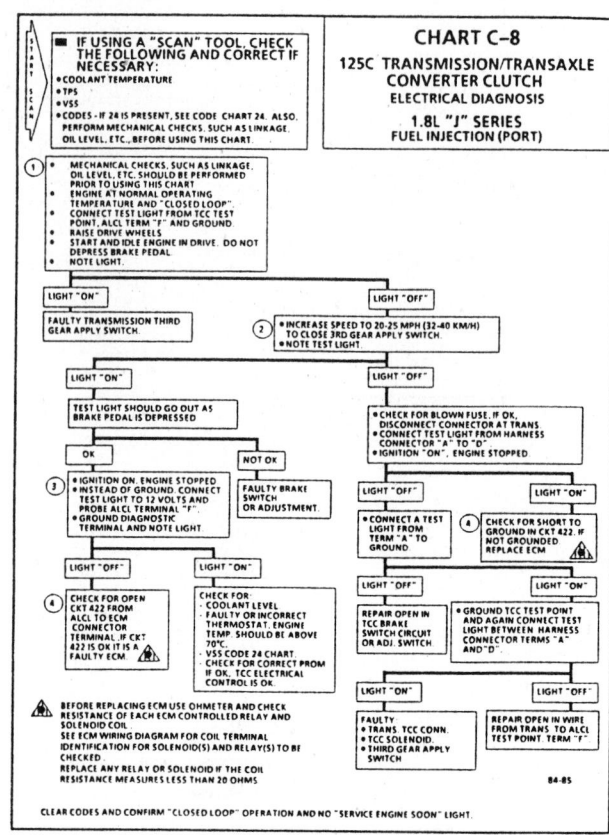

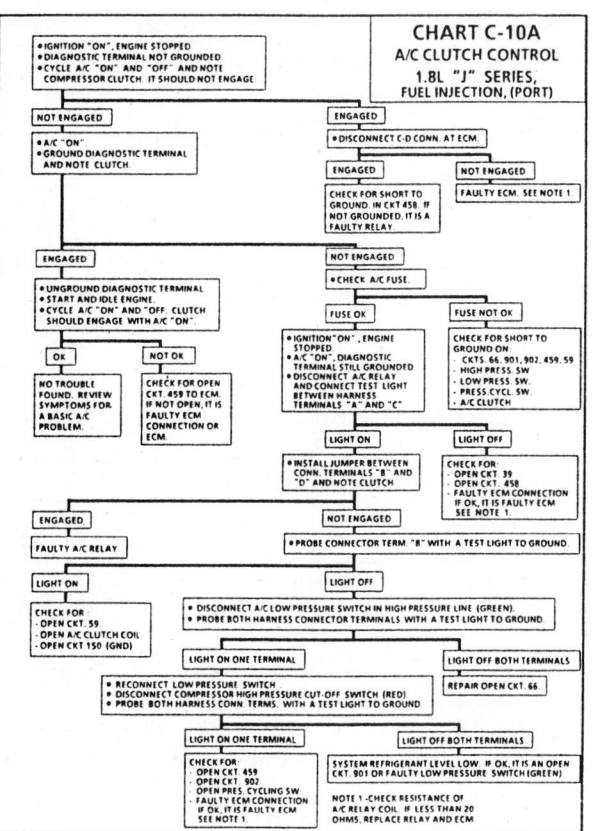

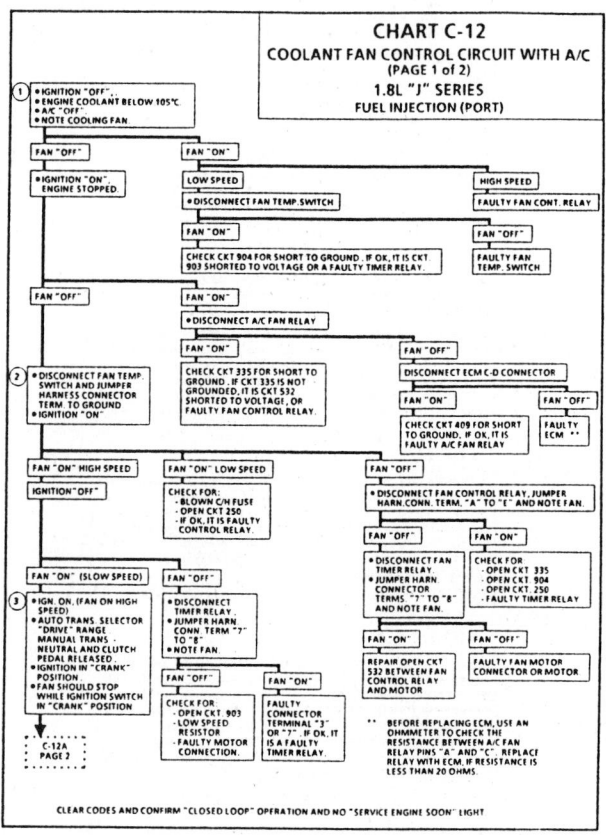

MPI TROUBLE DIAGNOSTICS

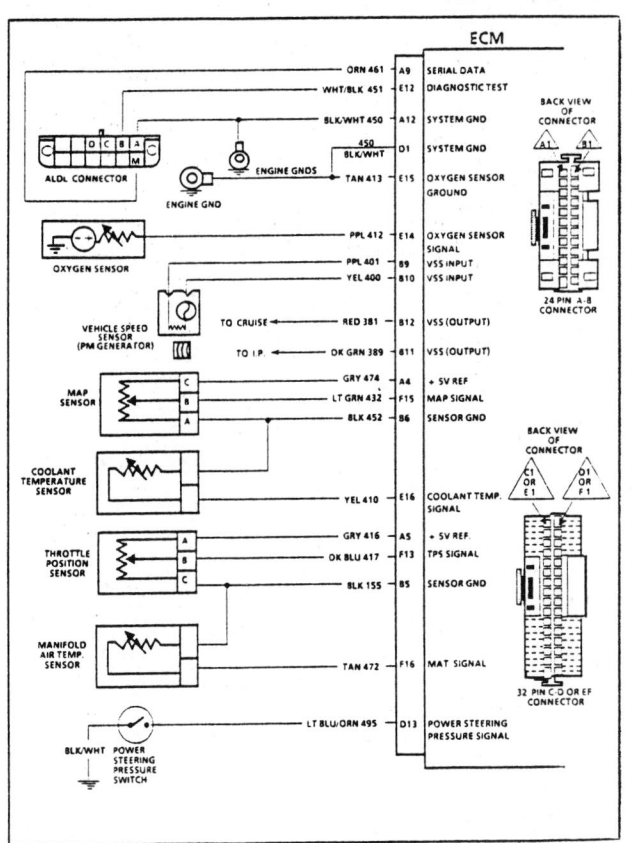

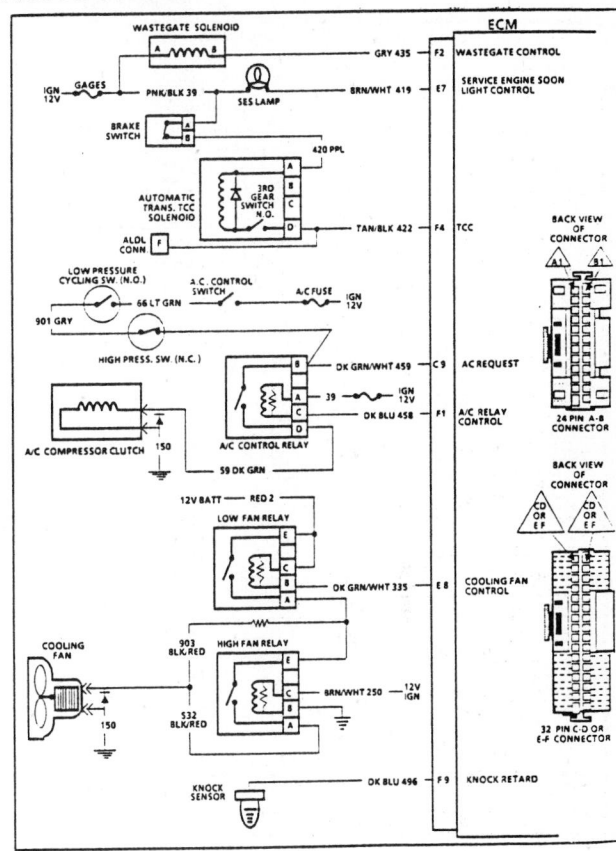

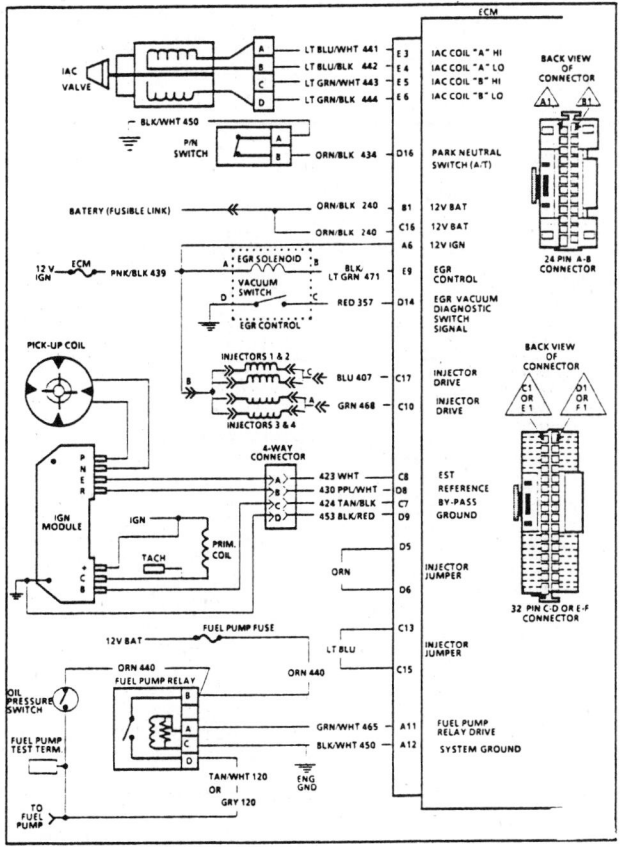

PORT FUEL INJECTION ECM CONNECTOR IDENTIFICATION

This ECM voltage chart is for use with a digital voltmeter to further aid in diagnosis. The voltages you get may vary due to low battery charge or other reasons, but they should be very close.

THE FOLLOWING CONDITIONS MUST BE MET BEFORE TESTING:

• Engine at operating temperature • Engine idling in closed loop (For "Engine Run" column) in park or neutral • Test terminal not grounded • "Scan" tool not installed
• B + indicates battery or charging system voltage

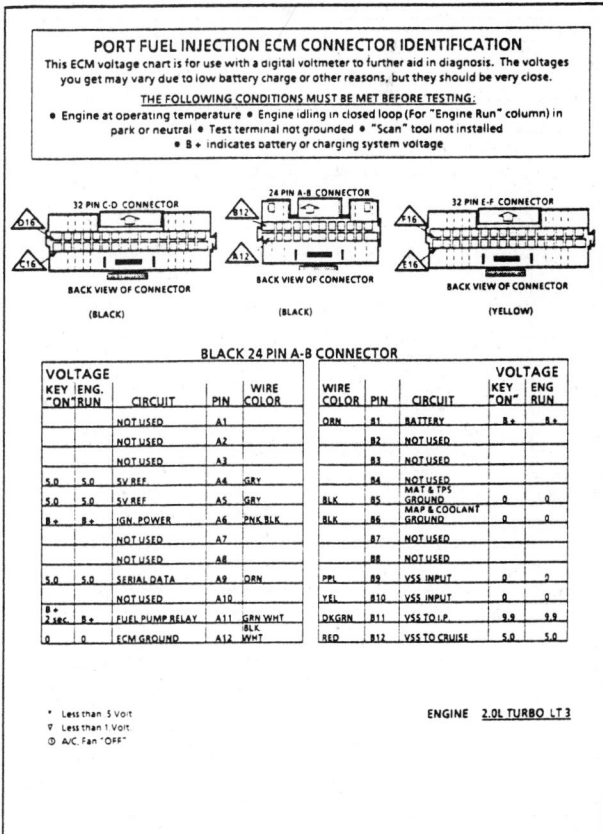

BLACK 24 PIN A-B CONNECTOR

VOLTAGE KEY ENG. "ON" RUN		CIRCUIT	PIN	WIRE COLOR	WIRE COLOR	PIN	CIRCUIT	VOLTAGE KEY "ON"	ENG RUN
		NOT USED	A1		ORN	B1	BATTERY	B+	B+
		NOT USED	A2			B2	NOT USED		
		NOT USED	A3			B3	NOT USED		
5.0	5.0	5V REF.	A4	GRY		B4	NOT USED MAT & TPS		
5.0	5.0	5V REF	A5	GRY	BLK	B5	GROUND	0	0
B+	B+	IGN. POWER	A6	PNK BLK	BLK	B6	MAP & COOLANT GROUND	0	0
		NOT USED	A7			B7	NOT USED		
		NOT USED	A8			B8	NOT USED		
5.0	5.0	SERIAL DATA	A9	ORN	PPL	B9	VSS INPUT	0	0
B+ 2 sec.	B+	FUEL PUMP RELAY	A11	GRN WHT	YEL	B10	VSS INPUT	0	0
0	0	ECM GROUND	A12	BLK WHT	DKGRN	B11	VSS TO I.P.	9.9	9.9
					RED	B12	VSS TO CRUISE	5.0	5.0

* Less than 5 Volt
▼ Less than 1 Volt
⊕ A/C Fan "OFF"

ENGINE **2.0L TURBO LT 3**

MPI TROUBLE DIAGNOSTICS

BLACK 32 PIN C-D CONNECTOR

VOLTAGE KEY ENG. "ON"	RUN	CIRCUIT	PIN	WIRE COLOR	WIRE COLOR	PIN	CIRCUIT	VOLTAGE KEY "ON"	ENG RUN
		NOT USED	C1		BLK/WHT	D1	ECM GROUND	0	0
		NOT USED	C2			D2	NOT USED		
		NOT USED	C3			D3	NOT USED		
		NOT USED	C4			D4	NOT USED		
		NOT USED	C5		ORN	D5	INJ JUMPER	0*	0*
B+	B+	VSS - EXT. (J)	C6	BRN	ORN	D6	INJ JUMPER	0*	0*
0*	1.6	BYPASS	C7	TAN/BLK		D7	NOT USED		
.1	1.2	EST	C8	WHT	PPL/WHT	D8	REFERENCE	0*	varies 1.0
① 0	0	A.C REQUEST	C9	GRN/WHT	BLK/RED	D9	IGN GROUND	0*	0*
B+	B+	INJ DRIVER	C10	LT GRN		D10	NOT USED		
B+	B+	INJ DRIVER	C11	DK BLU		D11	NOT USED	✓	
		NOT USED	C12			D12	NOT USED		
0*	0*	INJ JUMPER	C13	LT BLU	LT BLU/ORN	D13	P.S PRESSURE SW.	B+	B+
		NOT USED	C14		RED	D14	EGR DIAGNOSTIC	B+	B+
0*	2*	INJ JUMPER	C15	LT BLU		D15	NOT USED		
B+	B+	BATTERY	C16	ORN	ORN/BLK	D16	PARK NEUTRAL AUTO TRANS. ONLY	0*	0*

YELLOW 32 PIN E-F CONNECTOR

VOLTAGE KEY ENG. "ON"	RUN	CIRCUIT	PIN	WIRE COLOR	WIRE COLOR	PIN	CIRCUIT	VOLTAGE KEY "ON"	ENG RUN
		NOT USED	E1		DK BLU	F1	A.C CONTROL RELAY	B+	B+ ①
		NOT USED	E2		GRY	F2	WASTE GATE SOL.	B+	0▽
NOT USEABLE		IAC "A" HIGH	E3	LT BLU/WHT	TAN/BLK	F3	NOT USED		
NOT USEABLE		IAC "A" LOW	E4	LT BLU/BLK	TAN/BLK	F4	TCC SOLENOID	0*	0*
NOT USEABLE		IAC "B" HIGH	E5	GRN/WHT		F5	NOT USED		
NOT USEABLE		IAC "B" LOW	E6	GRN/BLK		F6	NOT USED		
.1	13.7	"SES" LAMP	E7	BRN/WHT		F7	NOT USED		
B+	B+	COOLANT FAN RELAY	E8	DK GRN/WHT		F8	NOT USED		
B+	B+	EGR CONTROL	E9	BLK/GRN	DK BLU	F9	ESC SIGNAL	2.0	2.6
		NOT USED	E10			F10	NOT USED		
		NOT USED	E11			F11	NOT USED		
5.1	5.1	ALDL DIAG.	E12	WHT/BLK		F12	NOT USED		
		NOT USED	E13		DK BLU	F13	TPS SIGNAL	.9	.9
3-5	varies 1.9	O² SENSOR SIGNAL	E14	PPL		F14	NOT USED		
0*	0*	O² SENSOR GROUND	E15	TAN	LT GRN	F15	MAP SIGNAL	2.1	varies 2
varies 3.7	varies 1.6	COOLANT SIGNAL	E16	YEL	TAN	F16	MAT SIGNAL	varies 3.0	3.1

* LESS THAN .5 VOLT
▽ LESS THAN 1 VOLT
① A.C. FAN OFF

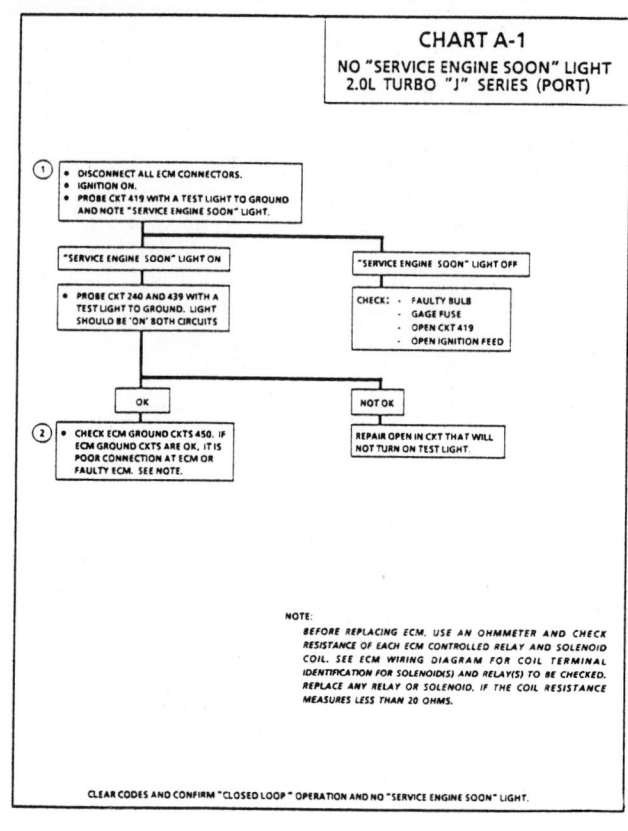

CHART A-1 — NO "SERVICE ENGINE SOON" LIGHT 2.0L TURBO "J" SERIES (PORT)

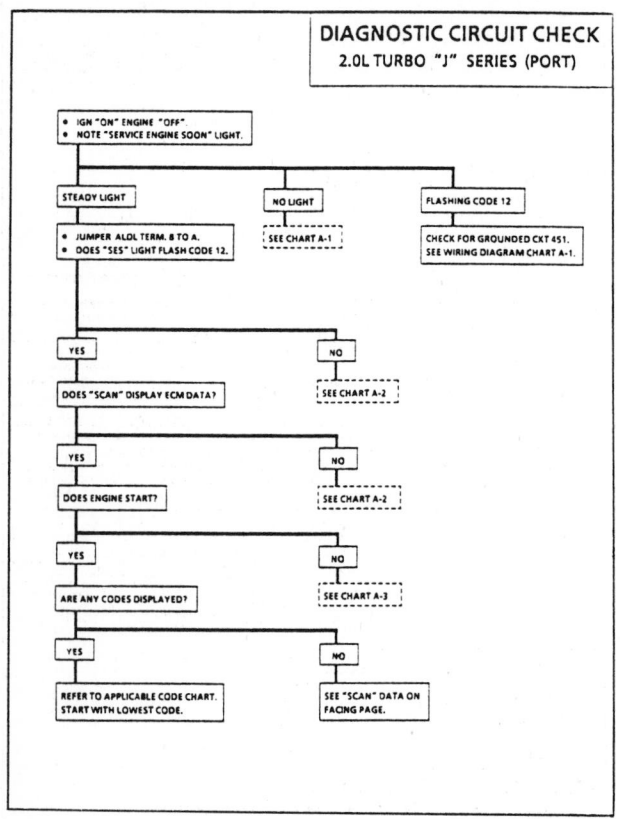

DIAGNOSTIC CIRCUIT CHECK 2.0L TURBO "J" SERIES (PORT)

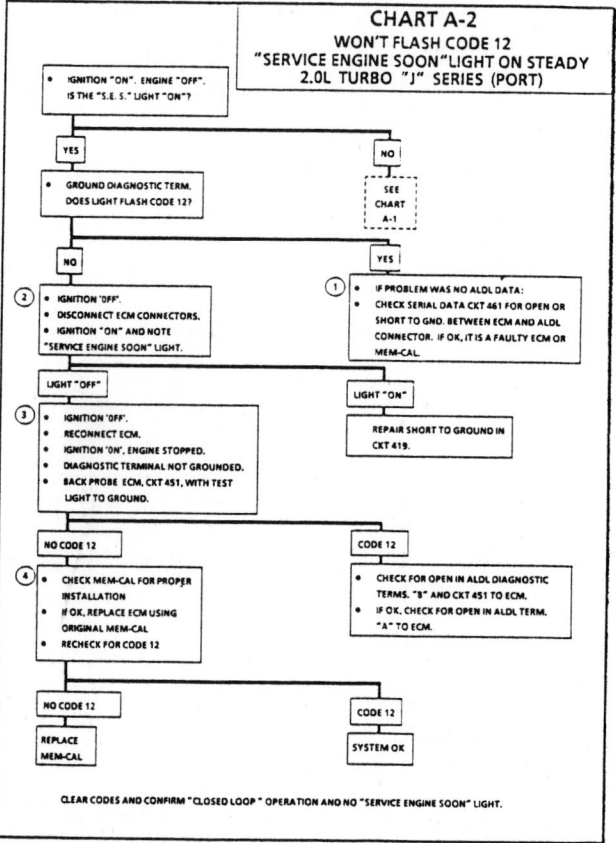

CHART A-2 — WON'T FLASH CODE 12 "SERVICE ENGINE SOON" LIGHT ON STEADY 2.0L TURBO "J" SERIES (PORT)

MPI TROUBLE DIAGNOSTICS

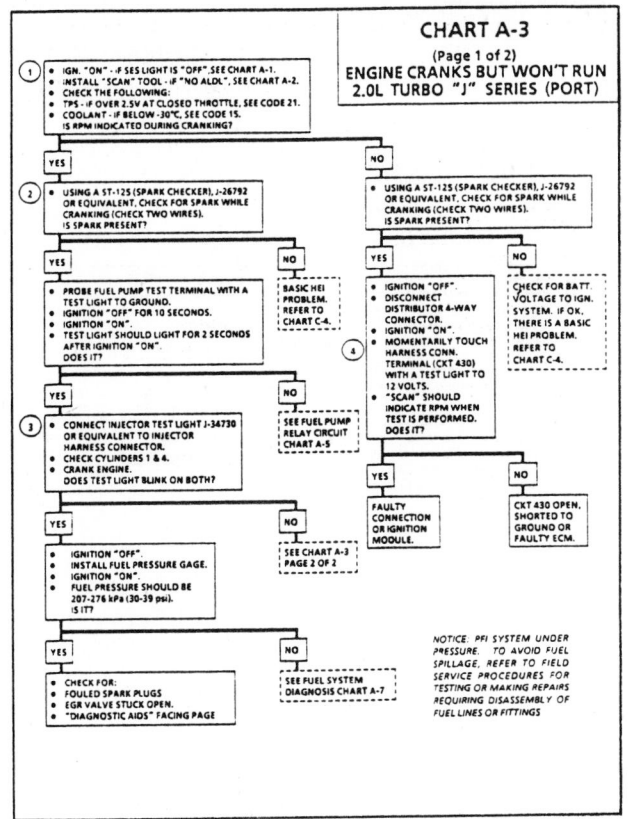

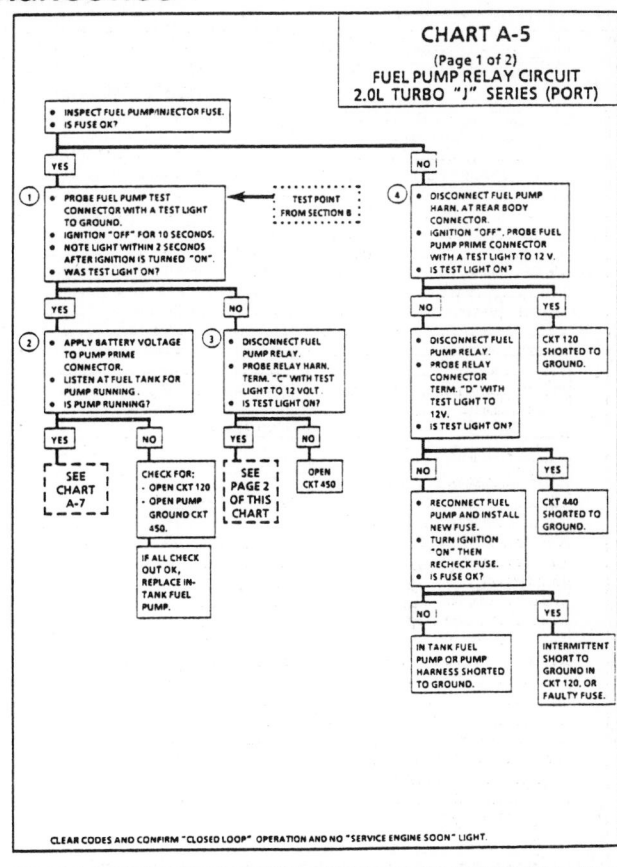

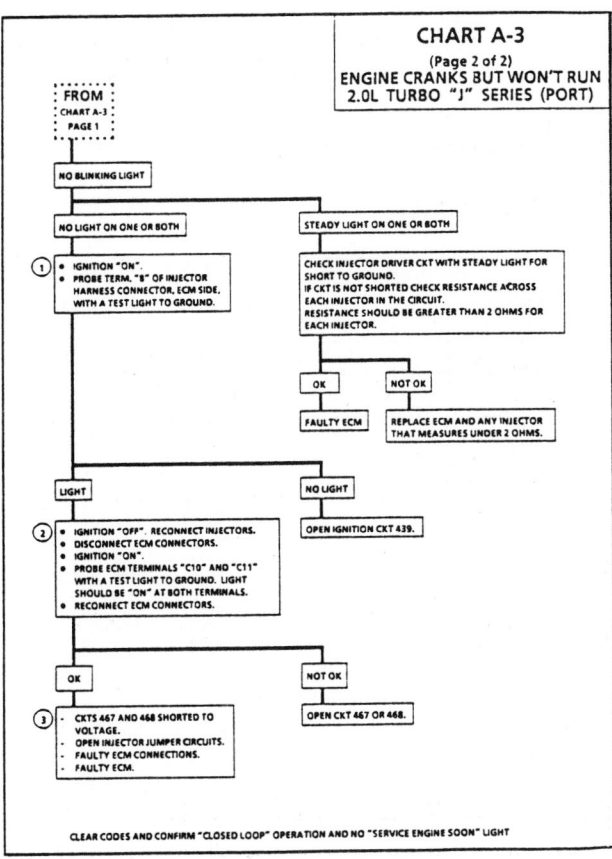

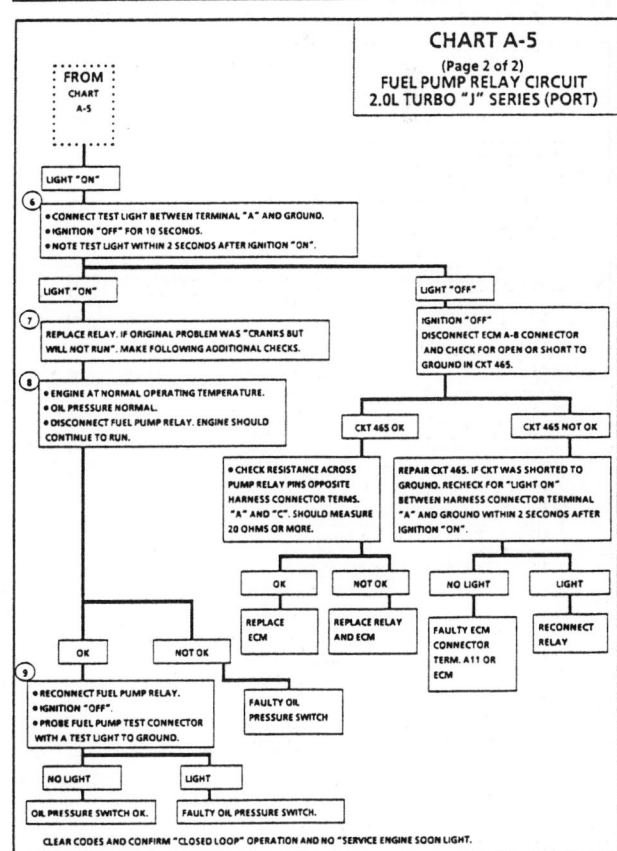

MPI TROUBLE DIAGNOSTICS

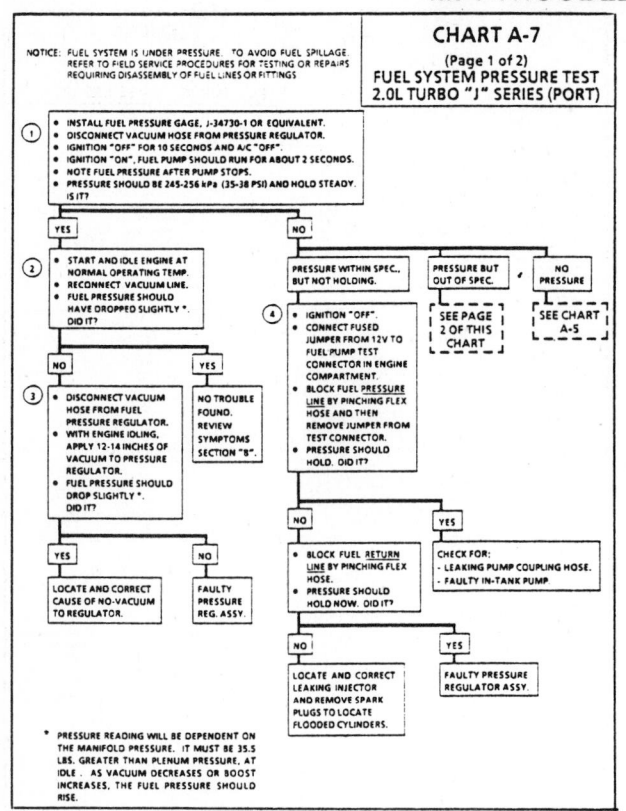

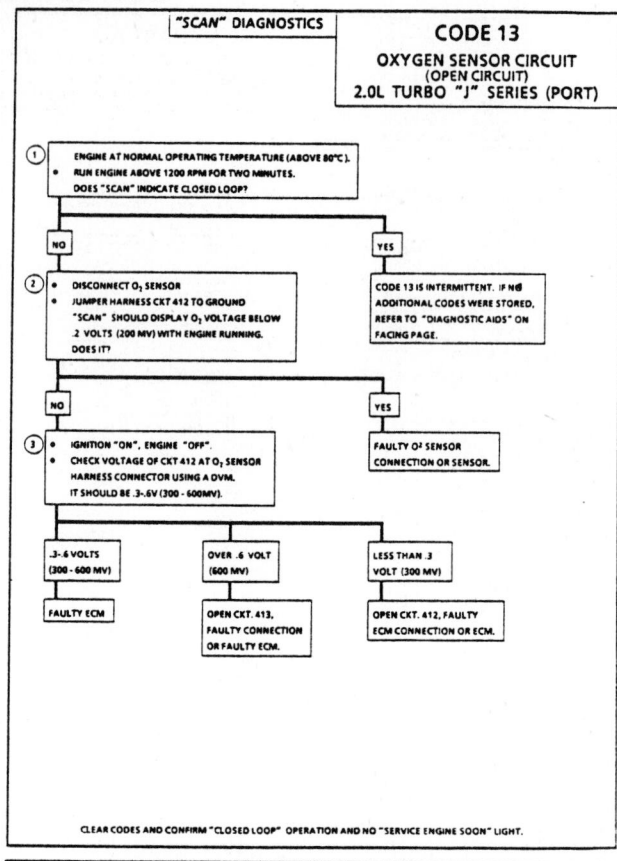

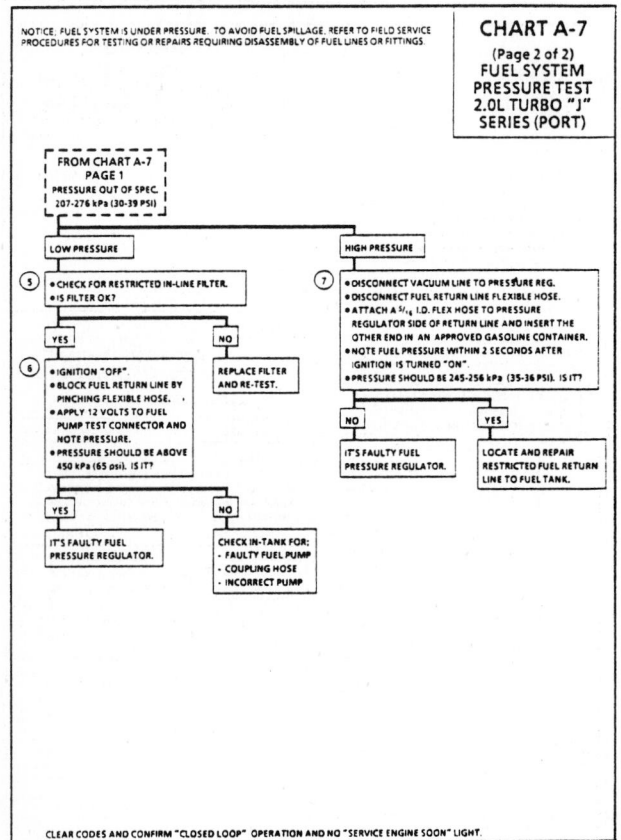

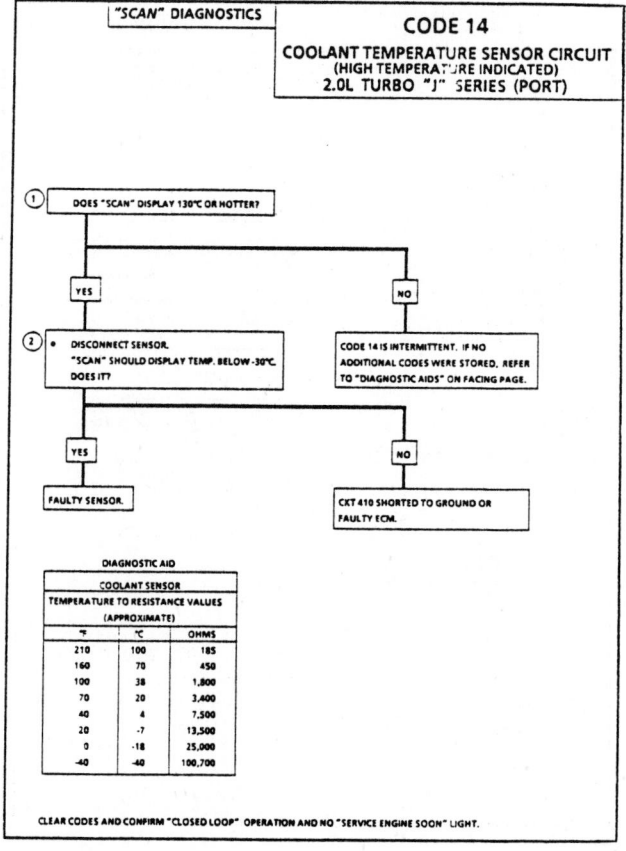

MPI TROUBLE DIAGNOSTICS

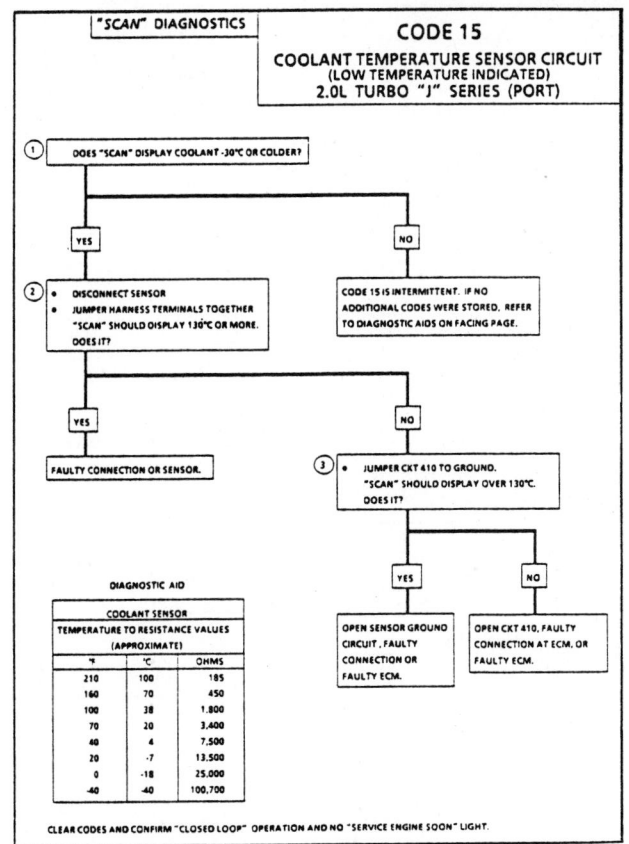

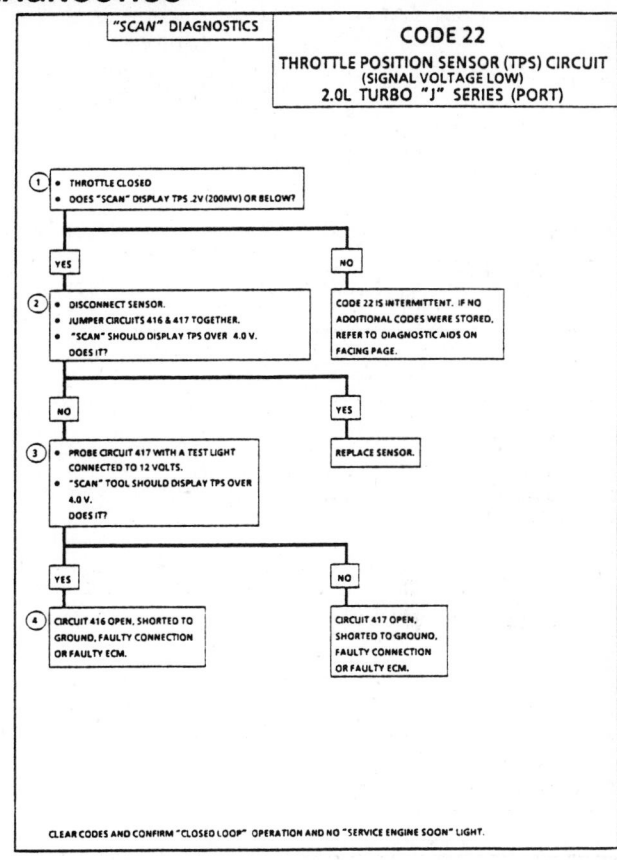

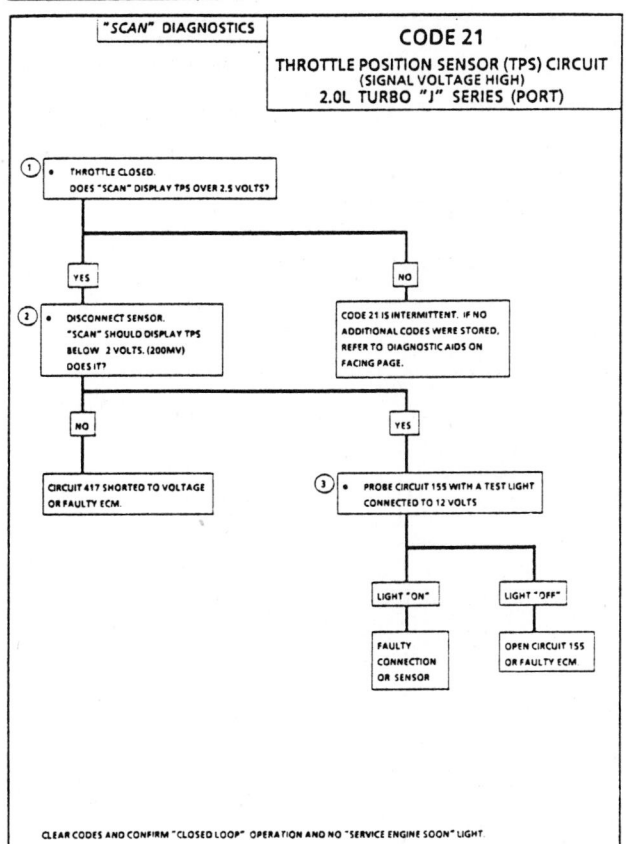

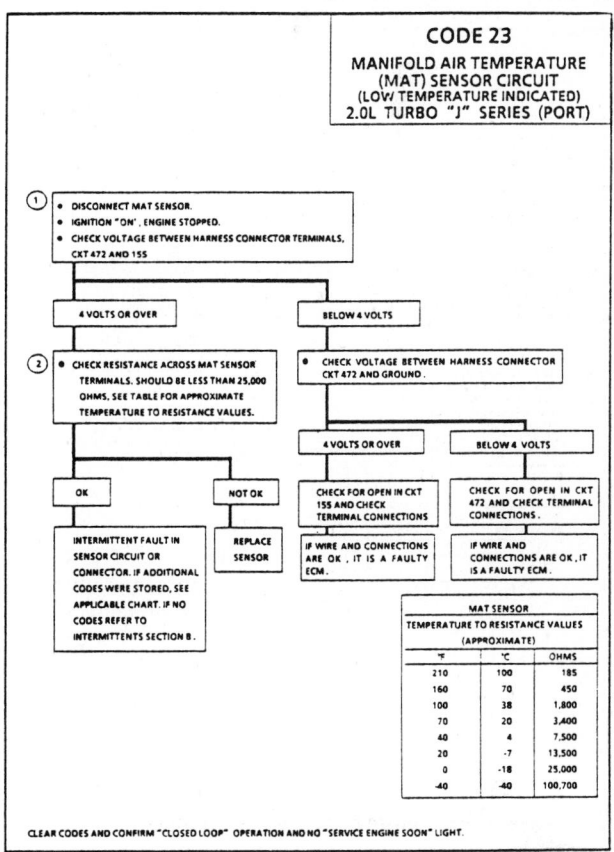

MPI TROUBLE DIAGNOSTICS

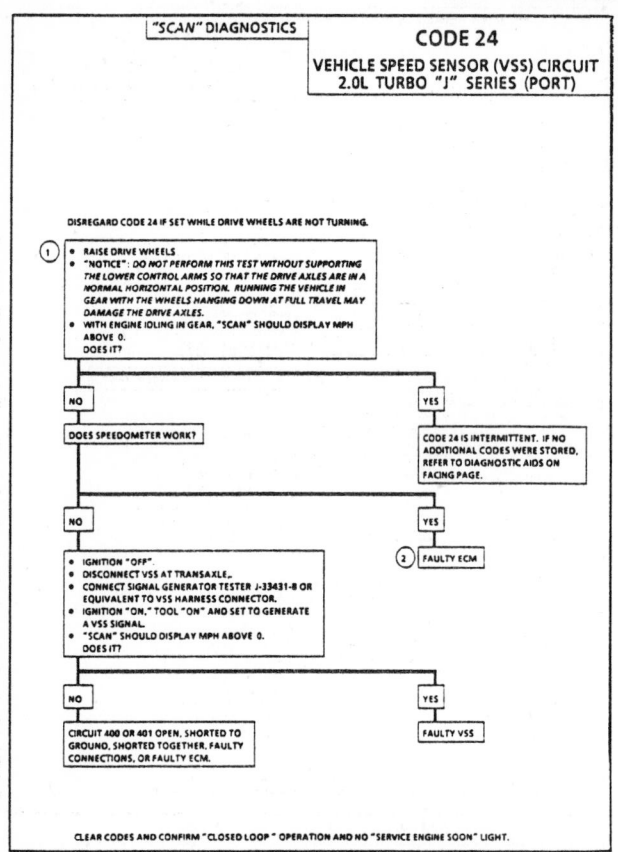

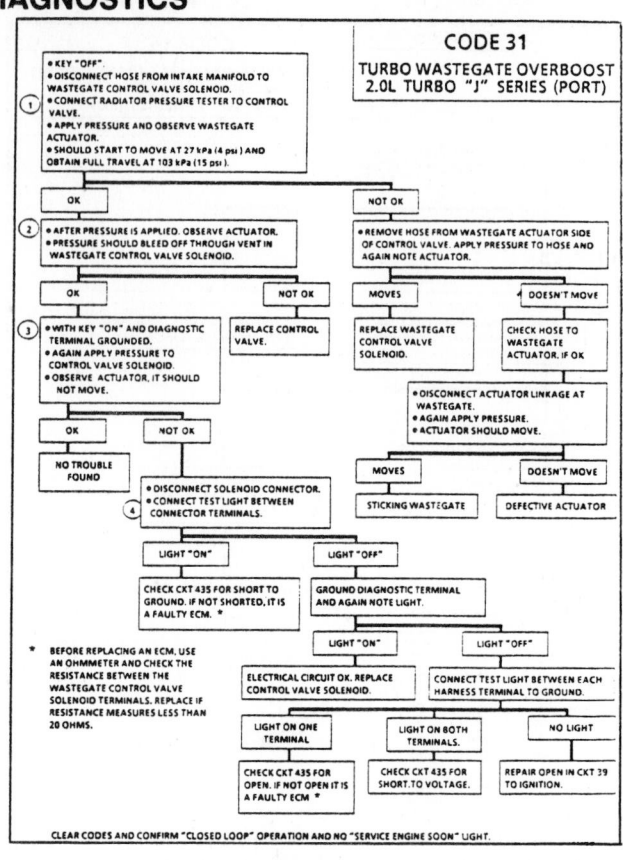

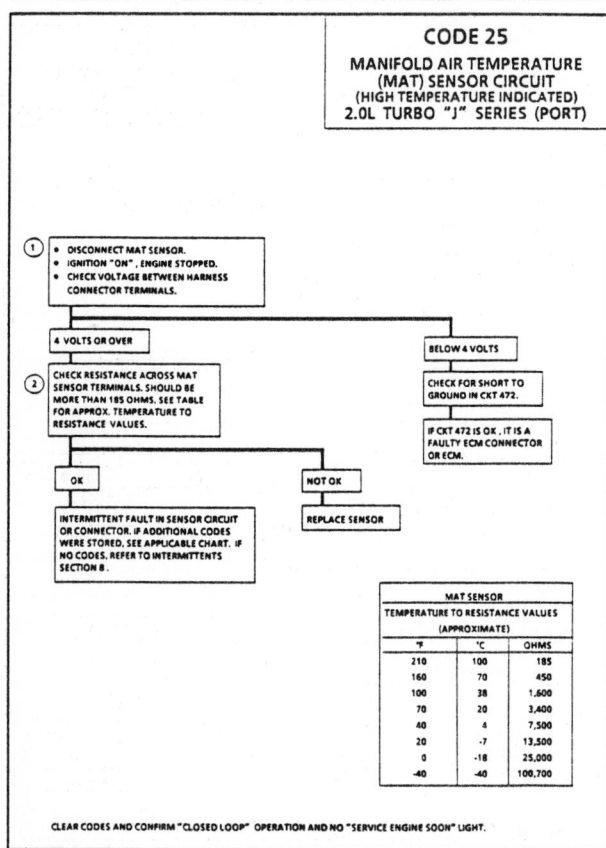

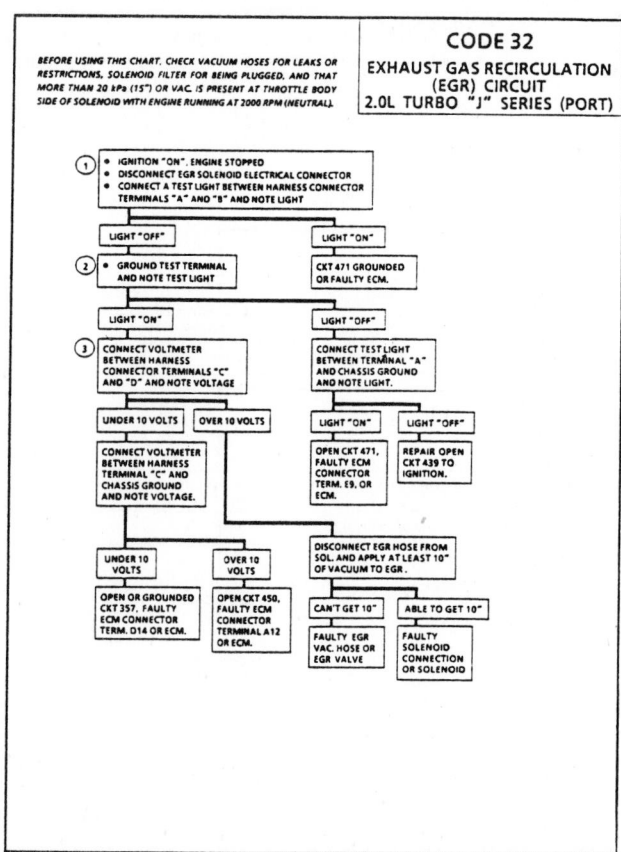

MPI TROUBLE DIAGNOSTICS

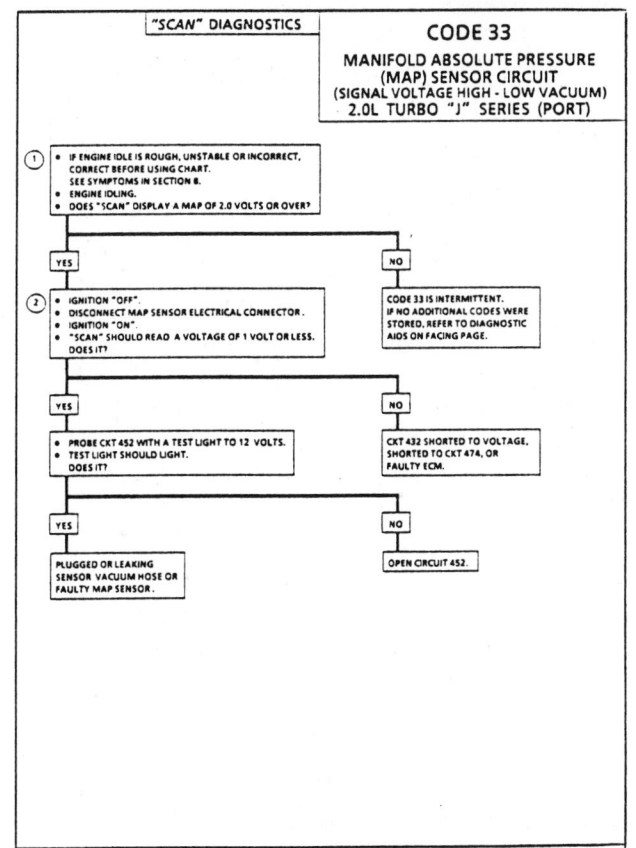

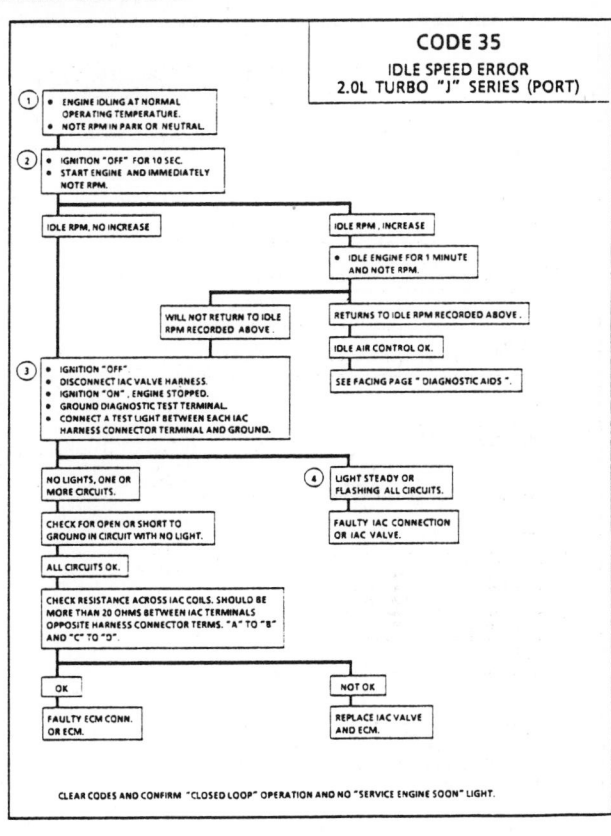

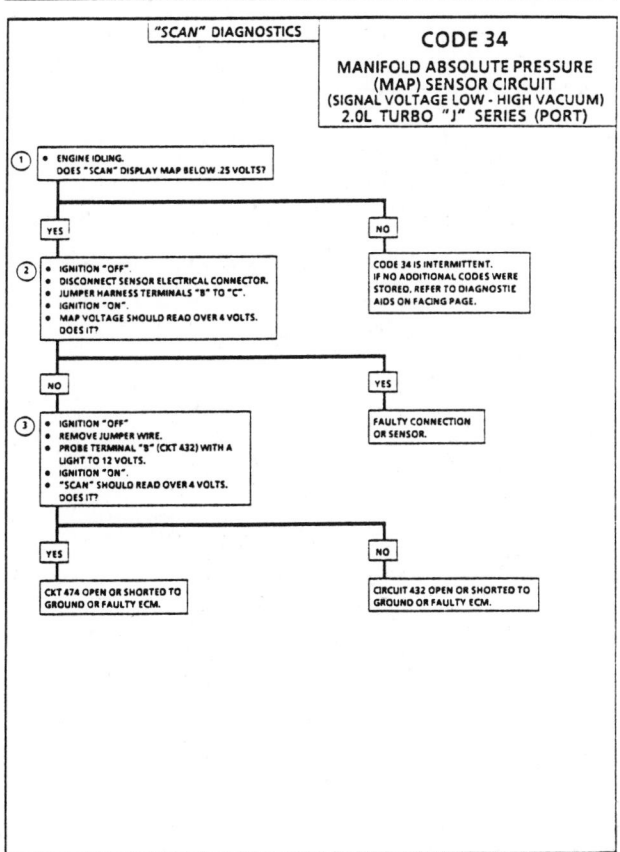

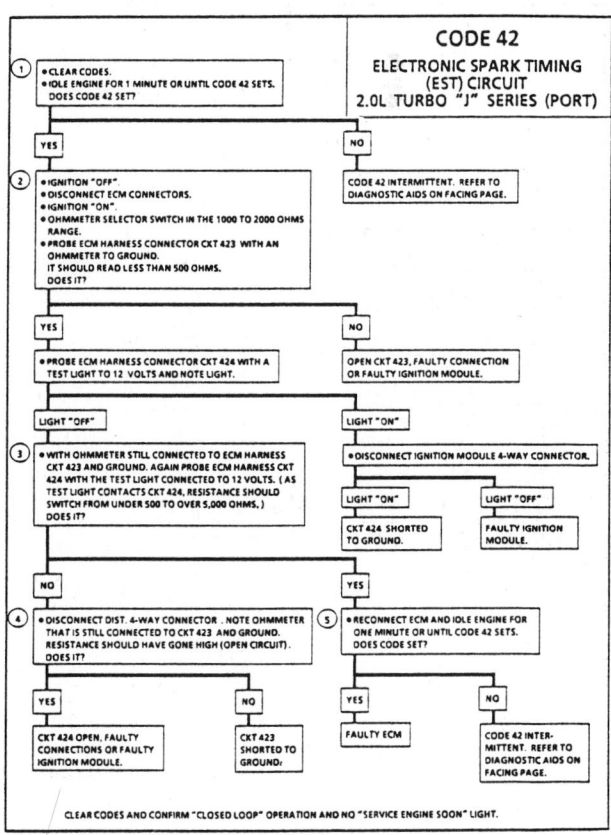

MPI TROUBLE DIAGNOSTICS

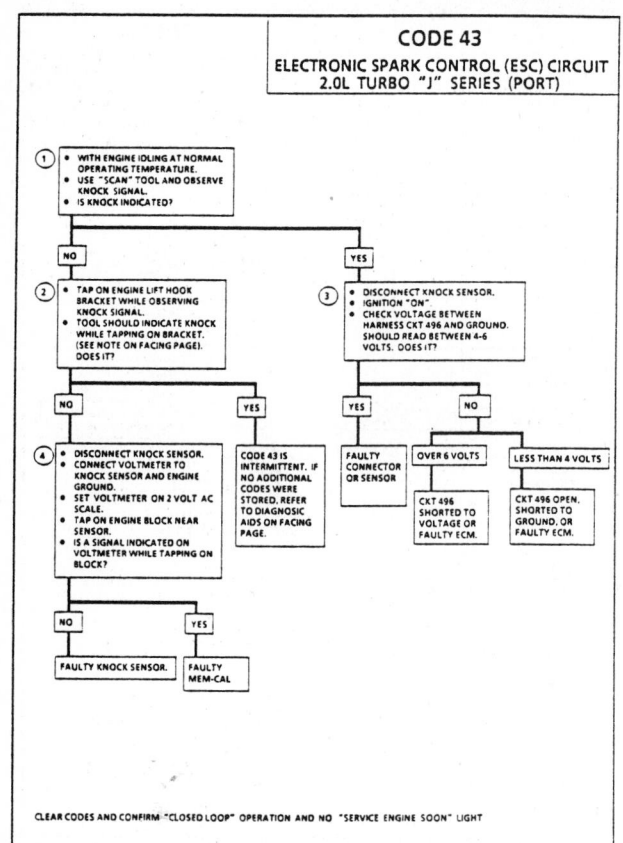

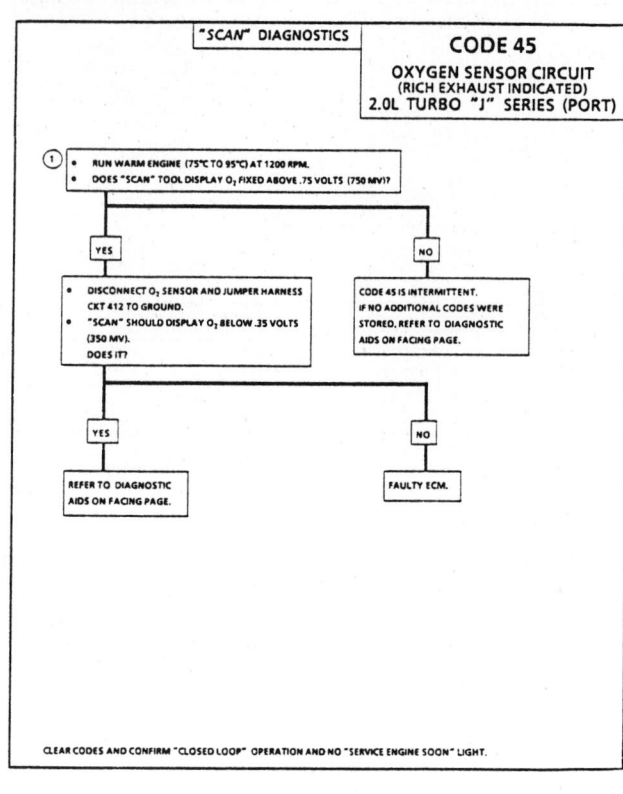

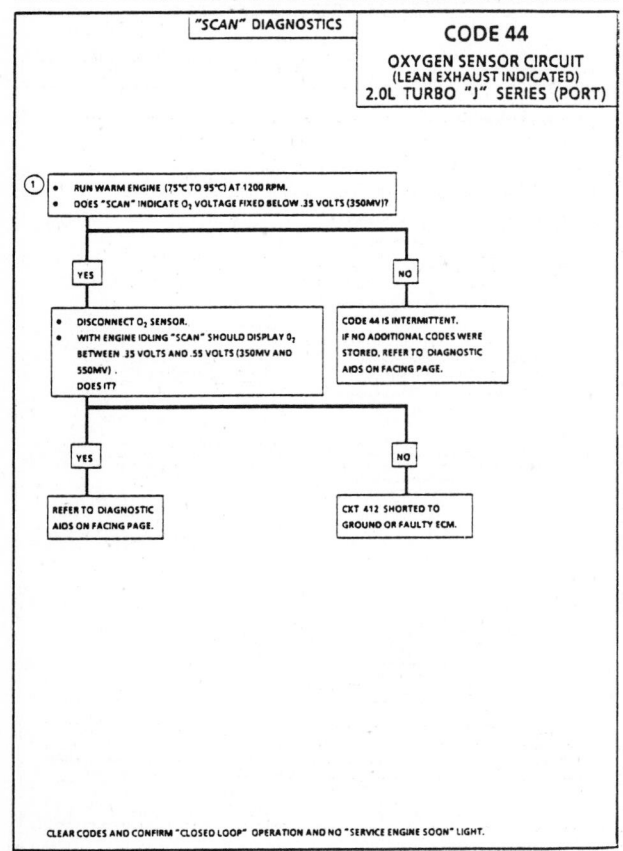

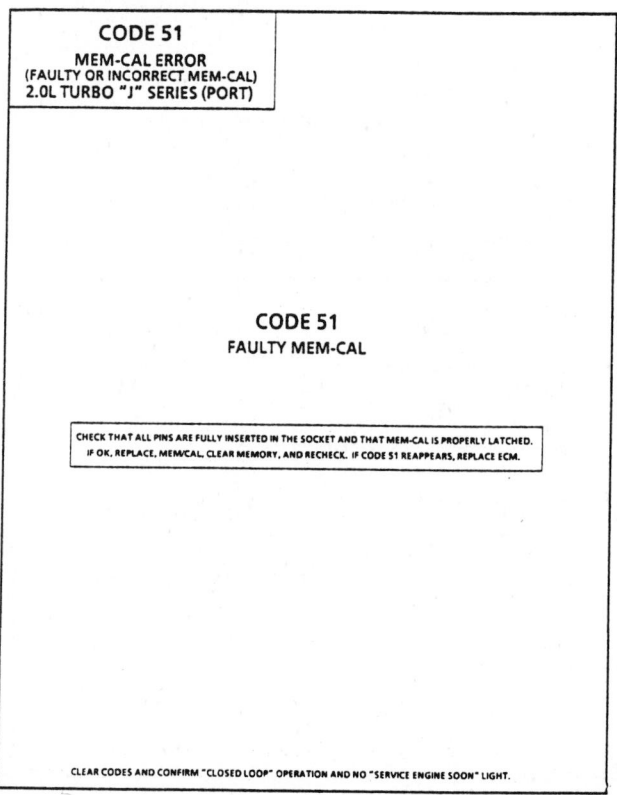

MPI TROUBLE DIAGNOSTICS

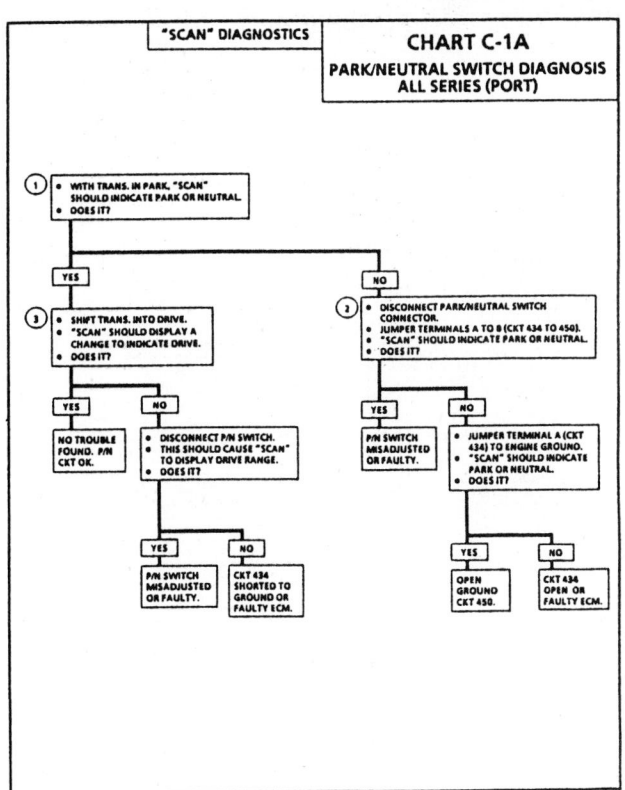

"SCAN" DIAGNOSTICS

CHART C-1A
**PARK/NEUTRAL SWITCH DIAGNOSIS
ALL SERIES (PORT)**

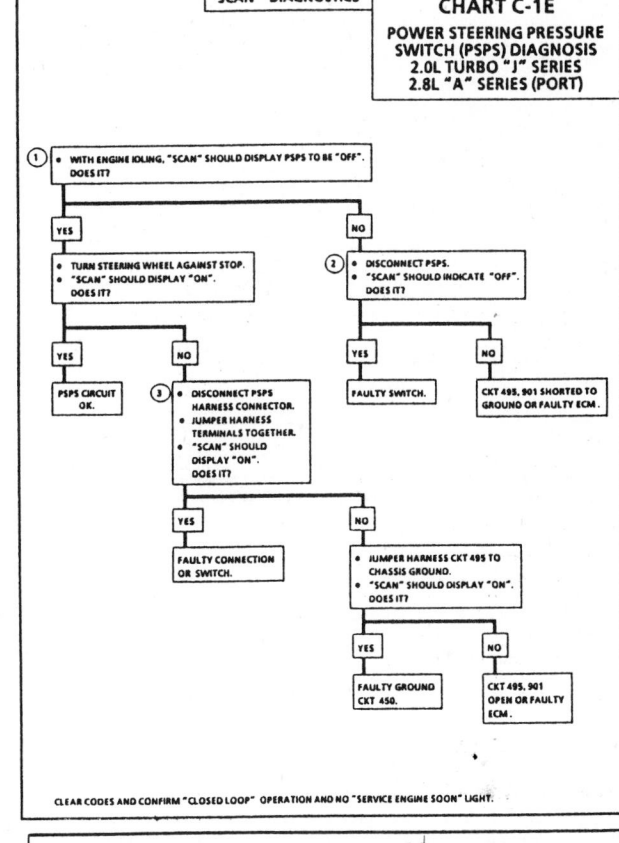

"SCAN" DIAGNOSTICS

CHART C-1E
**POWER STEERING PRESSURE
SWITCH (PSPS) DIAGNOSIS
2.0L TURBO "J" SERIES
2.8L "A" SERIES (PORT)**

CLEAR CODES AND CONFIRM "CLOSED LOOP" OPERATION AND NO "SERVICE ENGINE SOON" LIGHT.

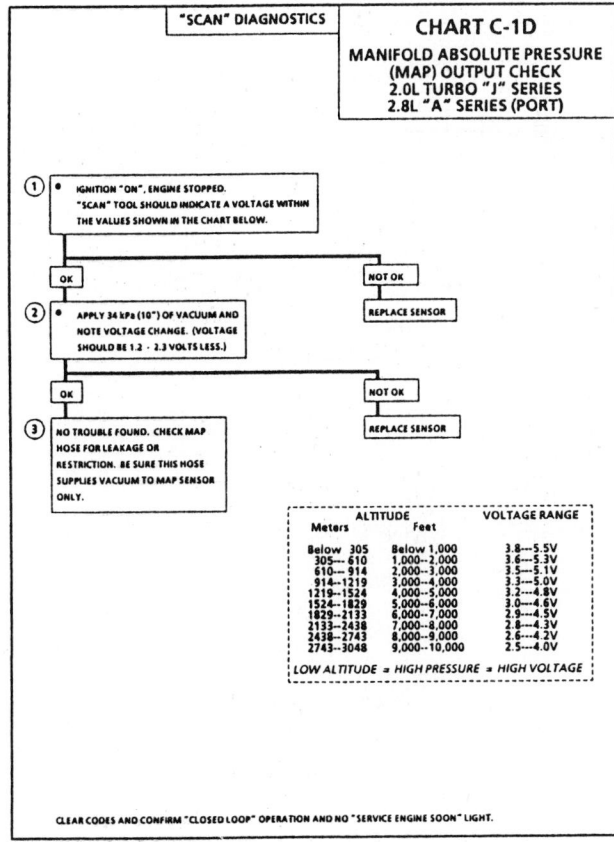

"SCAN" DIAGNOSTICS

CHART C-1D
**MANIFOLD ABSOLUTE PRESSURE
(MAP) OUTPUT CHECK
2.0L TURBO "J" SERIES
2.8L "A" SERIES (PORT)**

ALTITUDE		VOLTAGE RANGE
Meters	Feet	
Below 305	Below 1,000	3.8---5.5V
305--- 610	1,000--2,000	3.6---5.3V
610--- 914	2,000--3,000	3.5---5.1V
914--1219	3,000--4,000	3.3---5.0V
1219--1524	4,000--5,000	3.2---4.8V
1524--1829	5,000--6,000	3.0---4.6V
1829--2133	6,000--7,000	2.9---4.5V
2133--2438	7,000--8,000	2.8---4.3V
2438--2743	8,000--9,000	2.6---4.2V
2743--3048	9,000--10,000	2.5---4.0V

LOW ALTITUDE = HIGH PRESSURE = HIGH VOLTAGE

CLEAR CODES AND CONFIRM "CLOSED LOOP" OPERATION AND NO "SERVICE ENGINE SOON" LIGHT.

NOTE: If injectors are suspected of being dirty, they should be cleaned using an approved tool and procedure prior to performing this test. The fuel pressure test in Section A, Chart A-7, should be completed prior to this test.

CHART C-2A
**INJECTOR BALANCE TEST
(PORT)**

Step 1. If engine is at operating temperature, allow a 10 minute "cool down" period then connect fuel pressure gauge and injector tester.
1. Ignition "OFF".
2. Connect fuel pressure gauge and injector tester.
3. Ignition "ON".
4. Bleed off air in gauge. Repeat until all air is bled from gauge.

Step 2. Run test:
1. Ignition "OFF" for 10 seconds.
2. Ignition "ON". Record gauge pressure. (Pressure must hold steady, if not see the Fuel System diagnosis, Chart A-7, in Section A).
3. Turn injector on, by depressing button on injector tester, and note pressure at the instant the gauge needle stops.

Step 3.
1. Repeat step 2 on all injectors and record pressure drop on each. Retest injectors that appear faulty (Any injectors that have a 10 kPa difference, either more or less, in pressure from the average). If no problem is found, review Symptoms Section B.

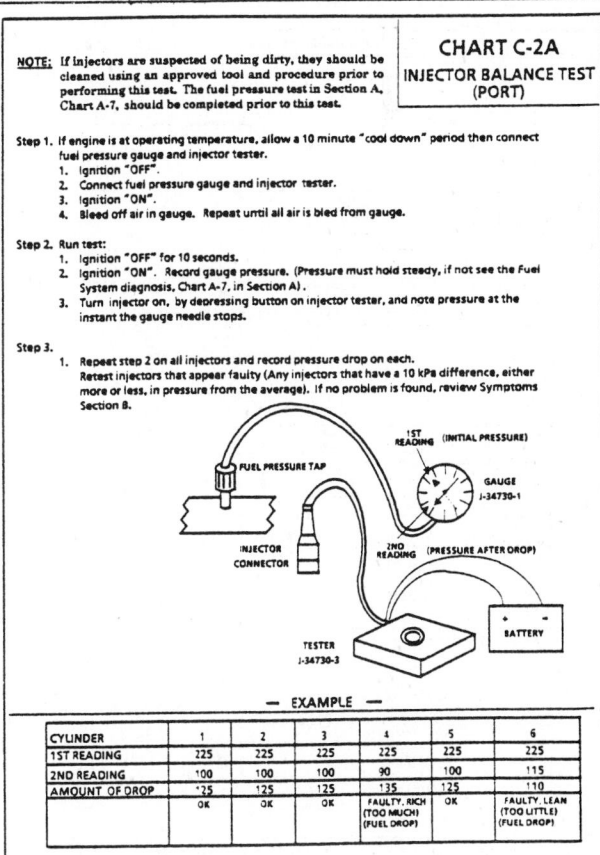

— EXAMPLE —

CYLINDER	1	2	3	4	5	6
1ST READING	225	225	225	225	225	225
2ND READING	100	100	100	90	100	115
AMOUNT OF DROP	*125	125	125	135	125	110
	OK	OK	OK	FAULTY, RICH (TOO MUCH) (FUEL DROP)	OK	FAULTY, LEAN (TOO LITTLE) (FUEL DROP)

MPI TROUBLE DIAGNOSTICS

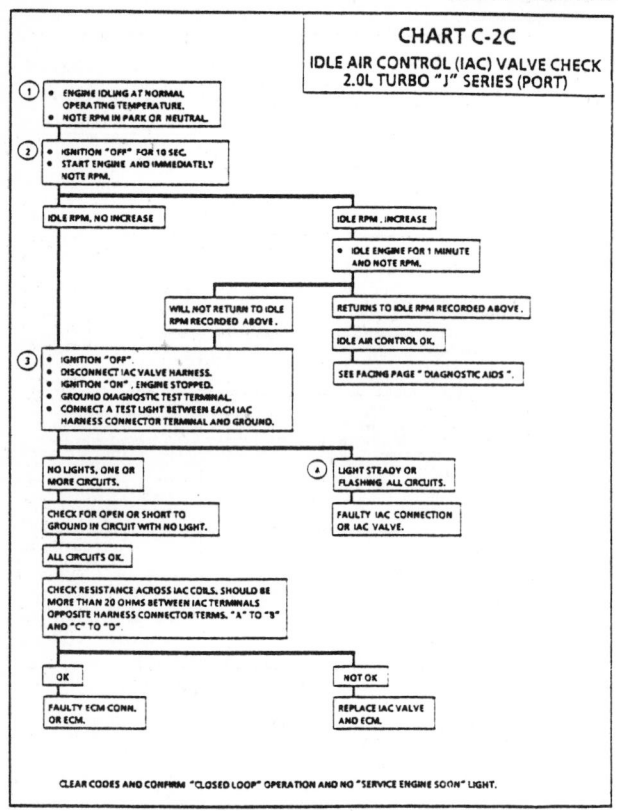

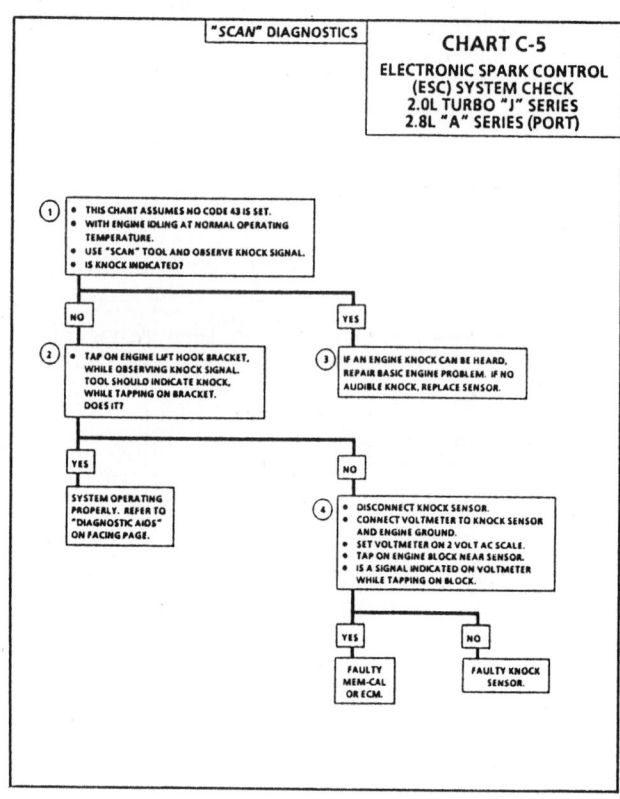

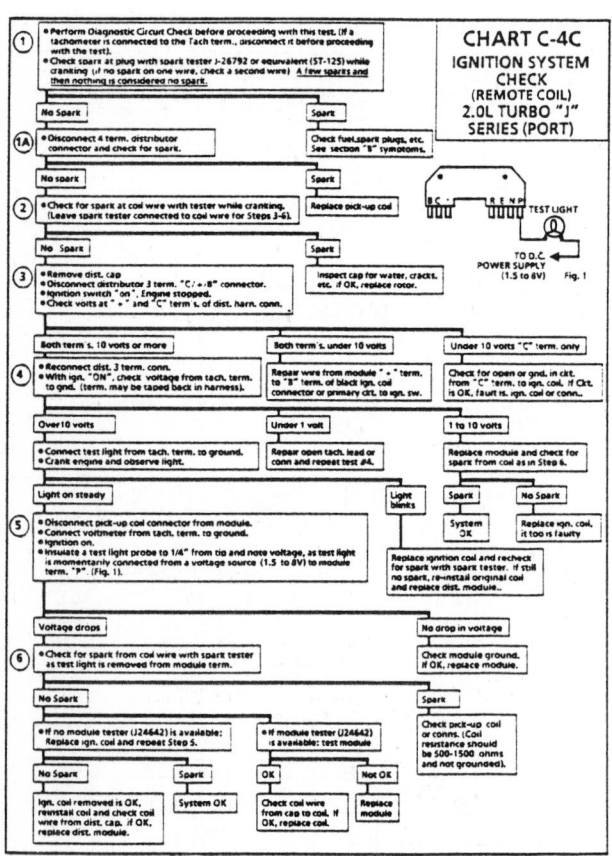

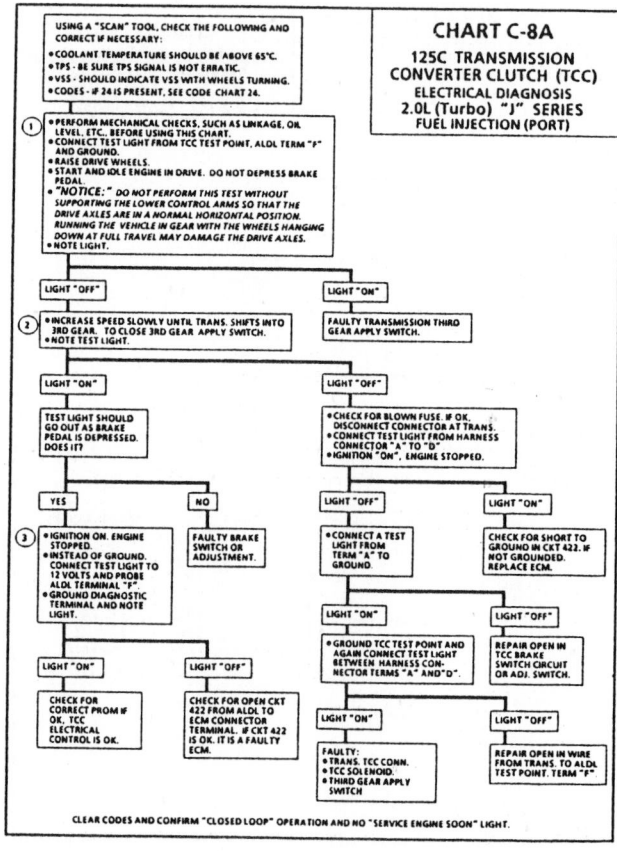

MPI TROUBLE DIAGNOSTICS

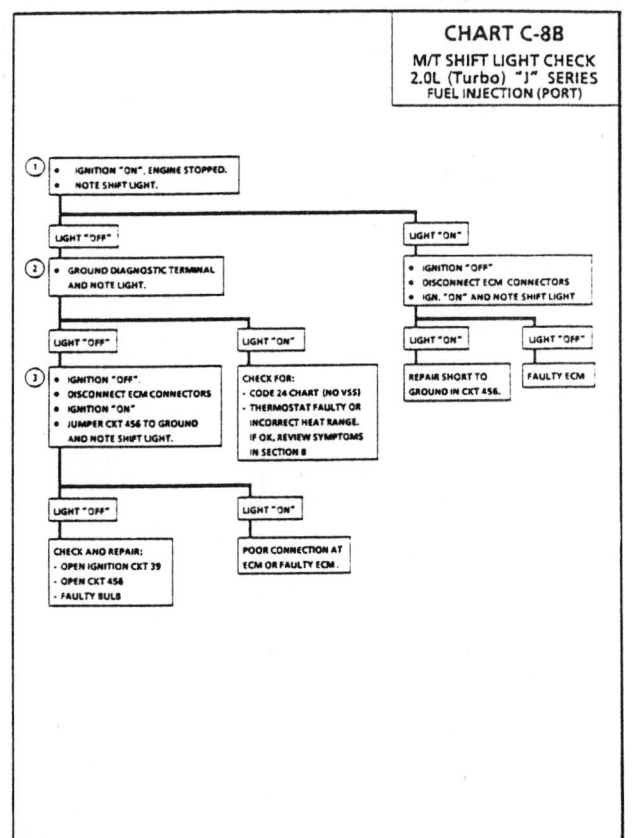

CHART C-8B
M/T SHIFT LIGHT CHECK
2.0L (Turbo) "J" SERIES
FUEL INJECTION (PORT)

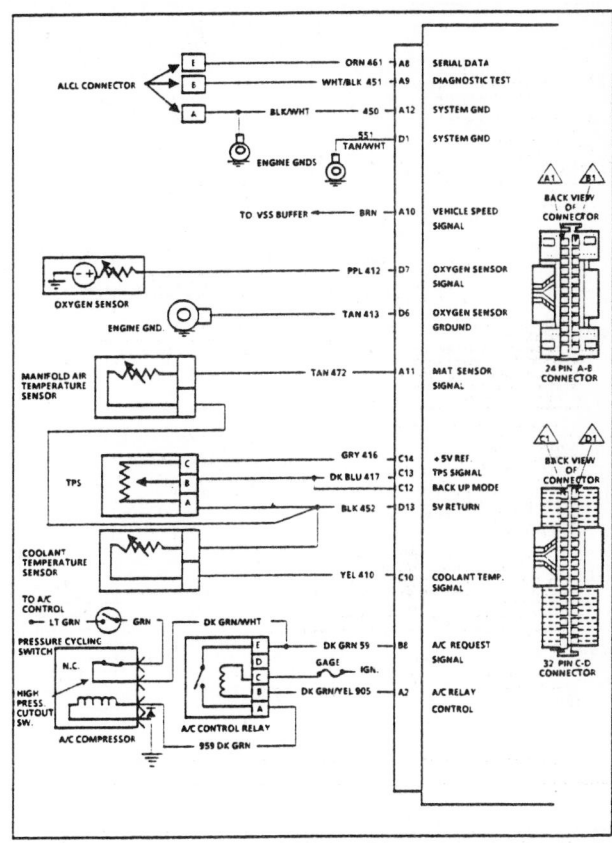

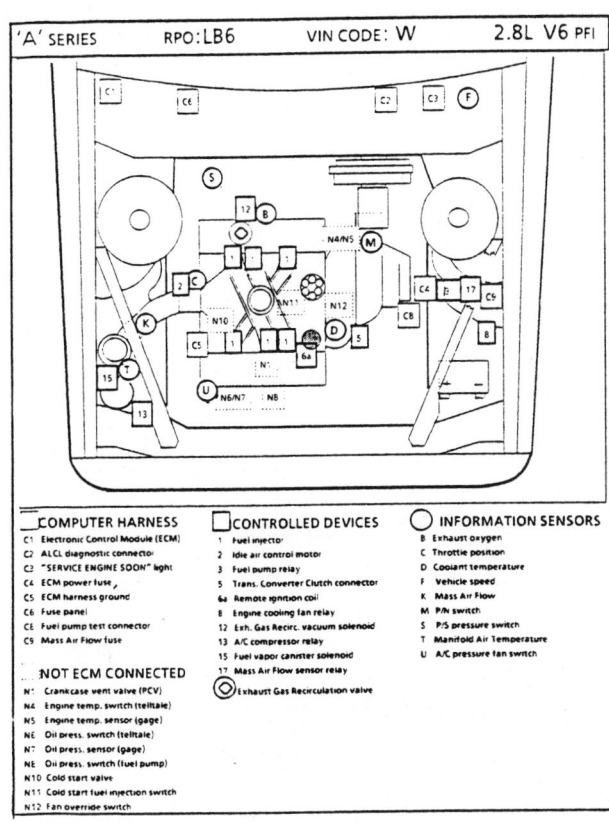

'A' SERIES   RPO: LB6   VIN CODE: W   2.8L V6 PFI

COMPUTER HARNESS
- C1 Electronic Control Module (ECM)
- C2 ALCL diagnostic connector
- C3 "SERVICE ENGINE SOON" light
- C4 ECM power fuse
- C5 ECM harness ground
- C6 Fuse panel
- C8 Fuel pump test connector
- C9 Mass Air Flow fuse

NOT ECM CONNECTED
- N1 Crankcase vent valve (PCV)
- N4 Engine temp. switch (telltale)
- N5 Engine temp. sensor (gage)
- N6 Oil press. switch (telltale)
- N7 Oil press. sensor (gage)
- N8 Oil press. switch (fuel pump)
- N10 Cold start valve
- N11 Cold start fuel injection switch
- N12 Fan override switch

CONTROLLED DEVICES
- 1 Fuel injector
- 2 Idle air control motor
- 3 Fuel pump relay
- 4 Trans. Converter Clutch connector
- 6a Remote ignition coil
- 8 Engine cooling fan relay
- 12 Exh. Gas Recirc. vacuum solenoid
- 13 A/C compressor relay
- 15 Fuel vapor canister solenoid
- 17 Mass Air Flow sensor relay
- Exhaust Gas Recirculation valve

INFORMATION SENSORS
- B Exhaust oxygen
- C Throttle position
- D Coolant temperature
- F Vehicle speed
- K Mass Air Flow
- M P/N switch
- S P/S pressure switch
- T Manifold Air Temperature
- U A/C pressure fan switch

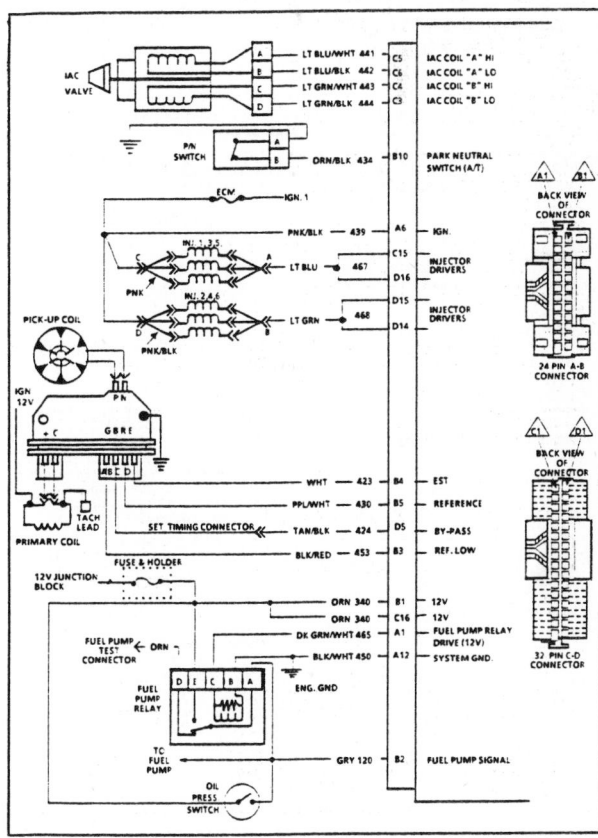

MPI TROUBLE DIAGNOSTICS

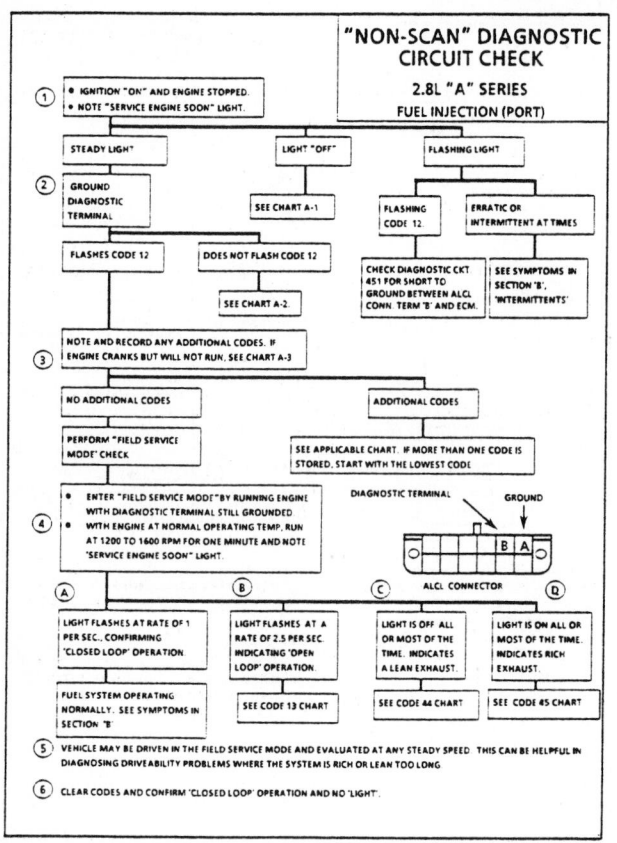

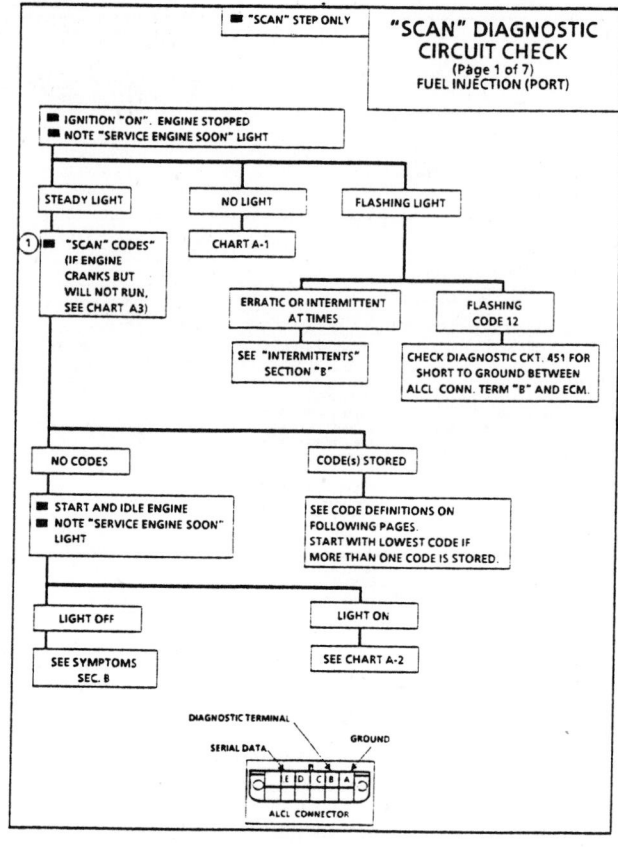

"SCAN" DIAGNOSTIC CIRCUIT CHECK
(Page 2 of 6)
2.8L "A" SERIES - (CODE DEFINITIONS)

THE 'DIAGNOSTIC CIRCUIT CHECK' SCAN DATA IS TYPICAL OF THAT DISPLAYED BY A PROPERLY DESIGNED AND CALIBRATED ALCL SCAN DEVICE.

A SCAN DEVICE THAT DISPLAYS FAULTY DATA SHOULD NOT BE USED AND THE PROBLEM REPORTED TO THE DEVICE MANUFACTURER. THE USE OF A FAULTY SCAN DEVICE CAN RESULT IN MISDIAGNOSIS AND UNNECESSARY PARTS REPLACEMENT.

CODES	DEFINITIONS
CODE 13 • "SCAN" TOOL IN SPECIAL MODE • ENGINE IDLING AT 1000 RPM. • COOLANT 75° TO 95°C. • "SCAN" OXYGEN SENSOR VOLTAGE	**HARD FAILURE -** "SCAN" DISPLAY FIXED BETWEEN .35 TO .55 V. OPEN CIRCUIT CONDITION. SEE CODE CHART 13. **INTERMITTENT CODE -** NORMAL "SCAN" VOLTAGE VARIES BETWEEN 100 MV TO 999 MV (.1 AND 1.0 VOLT). SEE "INTERMITTENTS" IN SECTION B.
CODE 14 • IGNITION ON. • ENGINE STOPPED. • "SCAN" COOLANT TEMPERATURE.	**HARD FAILURE -** "SCAN" TOOL DISPLAY FIXED ABOVE 135°C. CIRCUIT SHORTED TO GROUND OR FAULTY SENSOR. SEE CODE CHART 14. **INTERMITTENT CODE -** "SCAN" TOOL DISPLAYS ENGINE TEMP. IN DEGREES CENTIGRADE. AFTER ENGINE IS STARTED, THE TEMPERATURE SHOULD RISE STEADILY TO ABOUT 90°C THEN STABILIZE WHEN THERMOSTAT OPENS. SEE "INTERMITTENTS" IN SECTION B.
CODE 15 • IGNITION ON. • ENGINE STOPPED. • "SCAN" COOLANT TEMPERATURE.	**HARD FAILURE -** "SCAN" TOOL DISPLAY FIXED BELOW -30°C. CIRCUIT OPEN OR FAULTY SENSOR. SEE CODE CHART 15. **INTERMITTENT CODE -** "SCAN" TOOL DISPLAYS ENGINE COOLANT TEMPERATURE IN DEGREES CENTIGRADE. AFTER ENGINE IS STARTED, THE TEMPERATURE SHOULD RISE STEADILY TO ABOUT 90°C, THEN STABILIZE WHEN THERMOSTAT OPENS. SEE "INTERMITTENTS" IN SECTION B.

"SCAN" DIAGNOSTIC CIRCUIT CHECK
(Page 4 of 6)
2.8L "A" SERIES - (CODE DEFINITIONS)

CODES	DEFINITIONS
CODE 24 • ENGINE RUNNING. • DRIVE WHEELS TURNING. • "SCAN" MPH.	**HARD FAILURE -** "SCAN" TOOL DISPLAYS 0 MPH. IF SPEEDOMETER IS WORKING OK, THEN THE VSS SIGNAL INPUT IS OPEN, SHORTED TO GROUND, OR THE BUFFER IS DEFECTIVE. SEE CODE CHART 24. **INTERMITTENT CODE -** "SCAN" TOOL READING SHOULD CLOSELY MATCH WITH SPEEDOMETER READING WITH DRIVE WHEELS TURNING. USE "SCAN" TOOL AND CHECK PARK/NEUTRAL SWITCH. IF NOT OK, SEE CHART C1-A. IF OK, SEE "INTERMITTENTS" IN SECTION B.
CODE 25 • IGNITION "ON". • ENGINE STOPPED. • "SCAN" MAT TEMPERATURE.	**HARD FAILURE -** "SCAN" TOOL DISPLAY FIXED ABOVE 150°C. CIRCUIT SHORTED TO GROUND OR FAULTY SENSOR. SEE CODE CHART 25. **INTERMITTENT CODE -** "SCAN" TOOL DISPLAYS TEMPERATURE OF THE AIR ENTERING THE ENGINE. SHOULD READ CLOSE TO AMBIENT AIR TEMPERATURE WHEN ENGINE IS COLD, AND RISES AS UNDER HOOD TEMPERATURE INCREASES. SEE "INTERMITTENTS" IN SECTION B.
CODE 32	**HARD FAILURE -** THE "SCAN" TOOL IS NOT USEFUL IN DIAGNOSING CODE 32 PROBLEMS. SEE CODE CHART 32 IF CODE WAS STORED IN MEMORY.

CODE 33 & 34 -
• CLEAR CODES
• START ENGINE AND RECHECK FOR "SERVICE ENGINE SOON" LIGHT.
• LIGHT "ON - CODE 33 OR 34.
• SEE CODE CHART 33 OR 34.
• LIGHT OFF -
   PROBLEM IS INTERMITTENT
   SEE SECTION B "INTERMITTENTS".
	HARD FAILURE -
	"SCAN" TOOL DISPLAYS MAF DEFAULT VALUES BASED ON RPM AND TPS. DIFFICULT TO USE "SCAN" TOOL TO DIAGNOSE.
	
	INTERMITTENT CODE -
	"SCAN" TOOL READS AIR FLOW AND DISPLAYS IN GRAMS PER SECOND. SHOULD READ BETWEEN 5-8 ON A FULLY WARMED UP IDLING ENGINE. VALUES SHOULD CHANGE RATHER QUICKLY ON ACCELERATION, BUT VALUES SHOULD REMAIN FAIRLY STABLE AT ANY GIVEN RPM. SEE "INTERMITTENTS" IN SECTION B.

MPI TROUBLE DIAGNOSTICS

"SCAN" DIAGNOSTIC CIRCUIT CHECK
(Page 3 of 6)
2.8L "A" SERIES - (CODE DEFINITIONS)

CODES	DEFINITIONS
■**CODE 21** • IGNITION "ON". • ENGINE STOPPED. • THROTTLE CLOSED. • "SCAN" TPS. OR • ENGINE IDLING. • THROTTLE CLOSED. • "SCAN" TPS.	**HARD FAILURE -** "SCAN" TOOL DISPLAYS OVER 4.5 VOLTS. GROUND WIRE OPEN, SIGNAL LINE SHORTED TO SENSOR REF. LINE, OR FAULTY SENSOR. SEE CODE CHART 21. OR **HARD FAILURE -** "SCAN" TOOL DISPLAYS OVER 2.5 VOLTS. GROUND WIRE OPEN OR FAULTY SENSOR. SEE CODE CHART 21. **INTERMITTENT CODE -** "SCAN" TOOL DISPLAYS THROTTLE POSITION IN VOLTS. SHOULD READ .55V ± .05V. WITH THROTTLE CLOSED AND IGNITION ON OR AT IDLE. VOLTAGE SHOULD INCREASE AT A STEADY RATE AS THROTTLE IS MOVED TOWARD WOT. SEE "INTERMITTENTS" IN SECTION B.
■**CODE 22** • IGNITION "ON". • ENGINE STOPPED. • "SCAN" TPS.	**HARD FAILURE -** "SCAN" TOOL DISPLAYS BELOW 020V (200 MV) OPEN OR SHORTED TO GROUND CIRCUIT IN 5V REFERENCE, SIGNAL CIRCUIT OR FAULTY SENSOR. SEE CODE CHART 22. **INTERMITTENT CODE -** "SCAN"TOOL DISPLAYS THROTTLE POSITION IN VOLTS. SHOULD READ BETWEEN .55V ± .05V. WITH THROTTLE CLOSED AND IGNITION ON OR AT IDLE. VOLTAGE SHOULD INCREASE AT A STEADY RATE AS THROTTLE IS MOVED TOWARD WOT. SEE "INTERMITTENTS" IN SECTION B.
■**CODE 23** • IGNITION "ON". • ENGINE STOPPED. • "SCAN" MAT TEMPERATURE.	**HARD FAILURE -** "SCAN" TOOL DISPLAY FIXED BELOW -30°C. CIRCUIT OPEN OR FAULTY SENSOR. SEE CODE CHART 23. **INTERMITTENT CODE -** "SCAN"TOOL DISPLAYS TEMPERATURE OF THE AIR ENTERING THE ENGINE. SHOULD READ CLOSE TO AMBIENT AIR TEMPERATURE WHEN ENGINE IS COLD, AND RISE AS UNDERHOOD TEMPERATURE INCREASES. SEE "INTERMITTENTS" IN SECTION B.

"SCAN" DIAGNOSTIC CIRCUIT CHECK
(Page 5 of 6)
2.8L "A" SERIES - (CODE DEFINITIONS)

CODES	DEFINITIONS
■**CODE 41** • CLEAR CODES. START AND IDLE ENGINE FOR 1 MINUTE.	**HARD FAILURE -** "SERVICE ENGINE SOON" LIGHT ON, "SCAN" TOOL DISPLAYS CODE 41. SEE CODE CHART 41.
■**CODE 42** • CLEAR CODES. START AND IDLE ENGINE FOR 1 MINUTE. • IF NO "SERVICE ENGINE SOON" LIGHT, REFER TO INTERMITTENTS IN SECTION "B".	**HARD FAILURE -** "SERVICE ENGINE SOON" ON, SCAN TOOL DISPLAYS CODE 42. SEE CODE CHART 42. **INTERMITTENT CODE -** THE SCAN DOES NOT HAVE THE ABILITY TO HELP DIAGNOSE A CODE 42 PROBLEM. SEE "INTERMITTENTS" IN SECTION B.
■**CODE 44** • "SCAN" TOOL IN SPECIAL MODE. • ENGINE IDLING AT 1000 RPM. • "SCAN" OXYGEN SENSOR VOLTAGE.	**HARD FAILURE -** "SCAN" TOOL DISPLAYS O_2 VOLTAGE CONSISTENTLY BELOW .35V. CAUSED BY A LEAN EXHAUST OR SIGNAL CIRCUIT SHORTED TO GROUND. SEE CODE CHART 44. **INTERMITTENT CODE -** THE "SCAN" TOOL HAS SEVERAL POSITIONS THAT WILL INDICATE THE STATE OF THE EXHAUST GASES. CROSSCOUNTS, RICH-LEAN INDICATION, O_2 VOLTAGE, INTEGRATOR, AND BLOCK LEARN. SEE "SCAN" POSITION INFORMATION IN INTRODUCTION.
■**CODE 45** • "SCAN" TOOL IN "SPECIAL" MODE. • ENGINE IDLING AT 1000 RPM. • "SCAN" OXYGEN SENSOR VOLTAGE.	**HARD FAILURE -** "SCAN" TOOL DISPLAYS O_2 VOLTAGE CONSISTENTLY ABOVE .55V. RICH EXHAUST CAUSES A HIGH O_2 VOLTAGE. SEE CODE CHART 45. **INTERMITTENT CODE -** THE "SCAN" HAS SEVERAL POSITIONS THAT WILL INDICATE THE STATE OF THE EXHAUST GASES. CROSSCOUNTS, RICH-LEAN INDICATION, O_2 VOLTAGE, INTEGRATOR, AND BLOCK LEARN. SEE "SCAN" POSITION INFORMATION IN INTRODUCTION.

"SCAN" DIAGNOSTIC CIRCUIT CHECK
(Page 6 of 6)
2.8L "A" SERIES - (CODE DEFINITIONS)

CODES	DEFINITIONS
■**CODE 51** • CLEAR CODES • START ENGINE • CHECK FOR CODE	**HARD FAILURE -** CODE 51 RESETS WHICH INDICATES A FAULTY PROM. SEE CODE CHART 51.
■**CODE 52** • CLEAR CODES • START ENGINE • CHECK FOR CODE	**HARD FAILURE -** CODE 52 RESETS WHICH INDICATES CALPAK IS MISSING OR FAILED.
■**CODE 53** • CLEAR CODES • START ENGINE • CHECK FOR CODE	**HARD FAILURE -** CODE 53 RESETS WHICH INDICATES GENERATOR VOLTAGE EXCEEDED 17.1 VOLTS REPAIR GENERATOR. **INTERMITTENT CODE-** THE "SCAN" TOOL IS NOT OF MUCH USE IN DIAGNOSING A CODE 53. CHECK FOR ERRATIC GENERATOR OUTPUT OR SEE "INTERMITTENTS" IN SECTION B.
■**CODE 54** • CLEAR CODES • START ENGINE • CHECK FOR CODE	**HARD FAILURE -** CODE 54 RESETS WHICH INDICATES LOW FUEL PUMP VOLTAGE. SEE CODE CHART 54. **INTERMITTENT CODE-** THE "SCAN" TOOL IS NOT OF MUCH USE IN DIAGNOSING A CODE 54 PROBLEM. SEE "INTERMITTENTS" IN SECTION B.
■**CODE 55** • CLEAR CODES • START ENGINE • CHECK FOR CODE	**HARD FAILURE -** CODE 55 RESETS WHICH INDICATES THE ECM IS FAULTY. REPLACE ECM.

CHART A-1
NO "SERVICE ENGINE SOON" LIGHT
2.8L "A" SERIES
FUEL INJECTION (PORT)

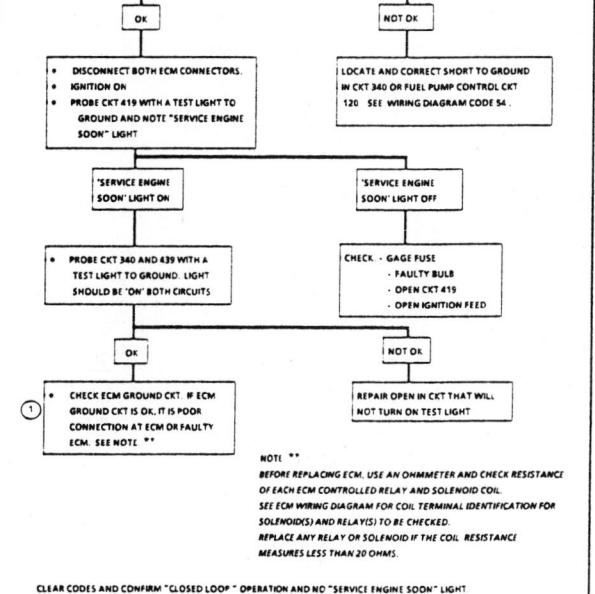

NOTE **
BEFORE REPLACING ECM, USE AN OHMMETER AND CHECK RESISTANCE OF EACH ECM CONTROLLED RELAY AND SOLENOID COIL. SEE ECM WIRING DIAGRAM FOR COIL TERMINAL IDENTIFICATION FOR SOLENOID(S) AND RELAY(S) TO BE CHECKED. REPLACE ANY RELAY OR SOLENOID IF THE COIL RESISTANCE MEASURES LESS THAN 20 OHMS.

CLEAR CODES AND CONFIRM "CLOSED LOOP" OPERATION AND NO "SERVICE ENGINE SOON" LIGHT

MPI TROUBLE DIAGNOSTICS

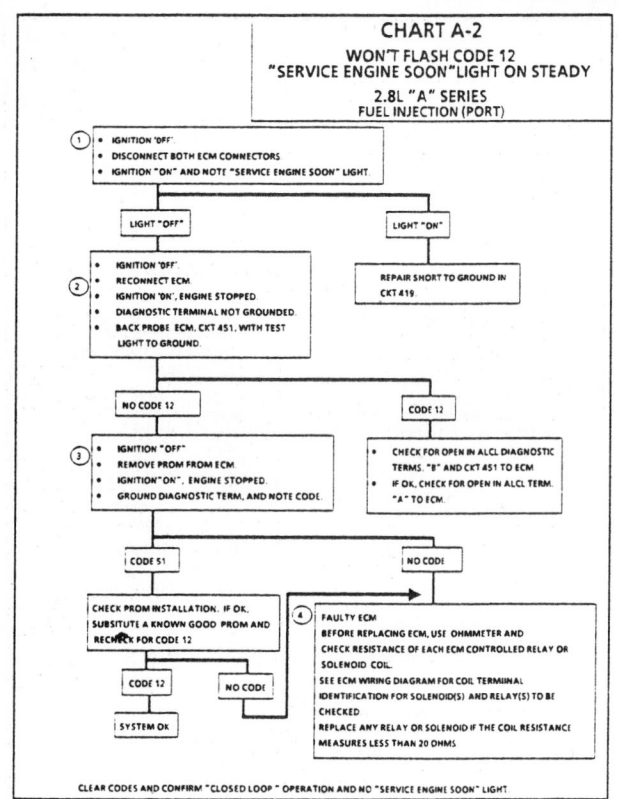

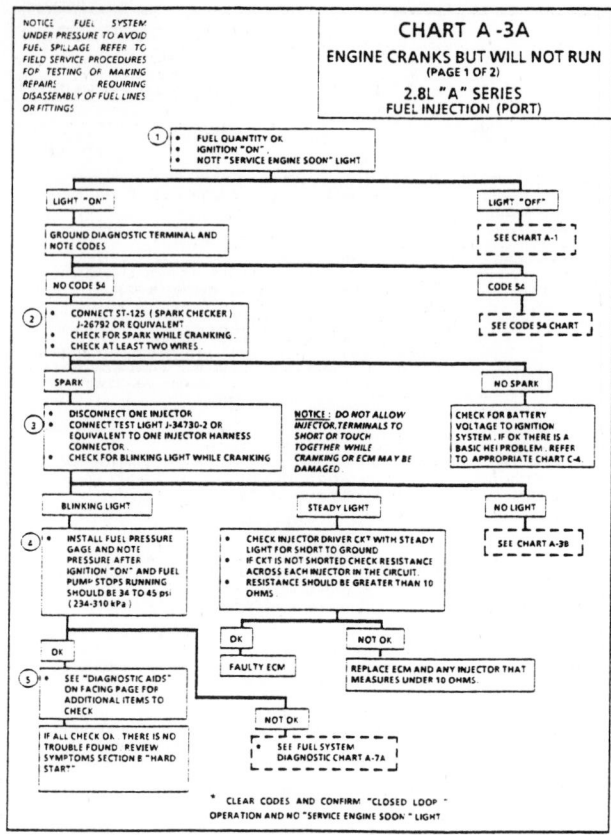

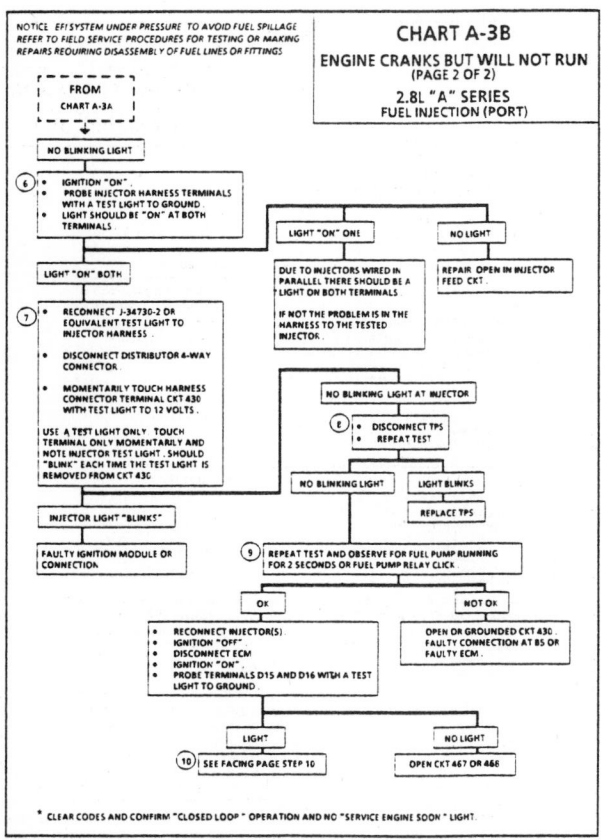

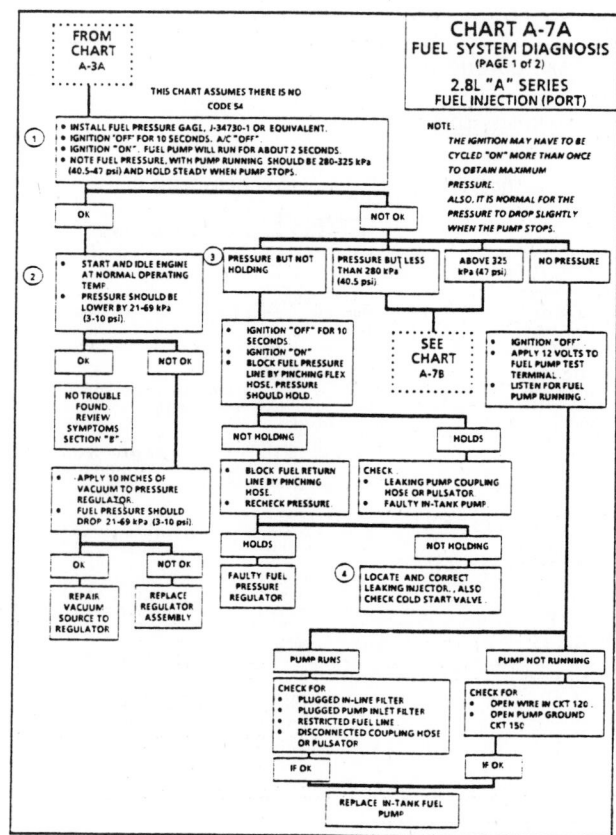

MPI TROUBLE DIAGNOSTICS

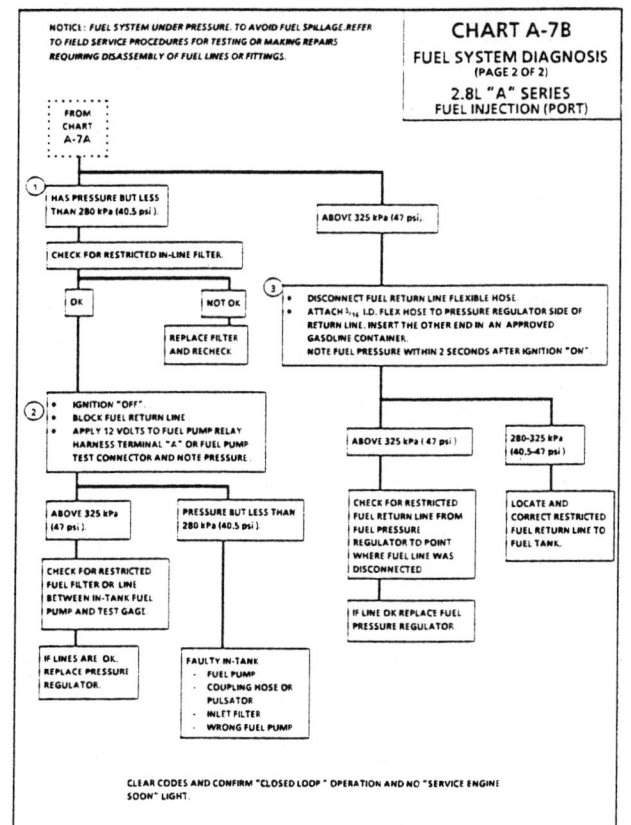

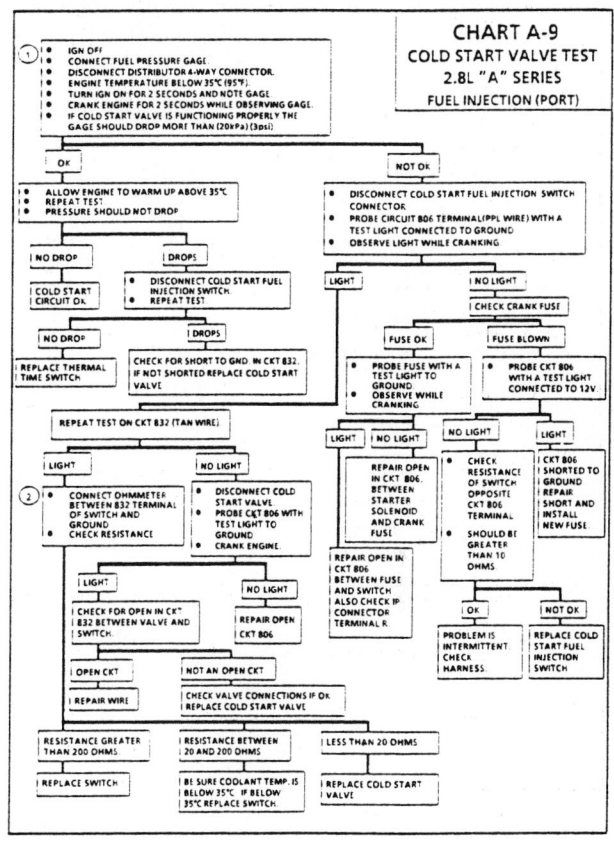

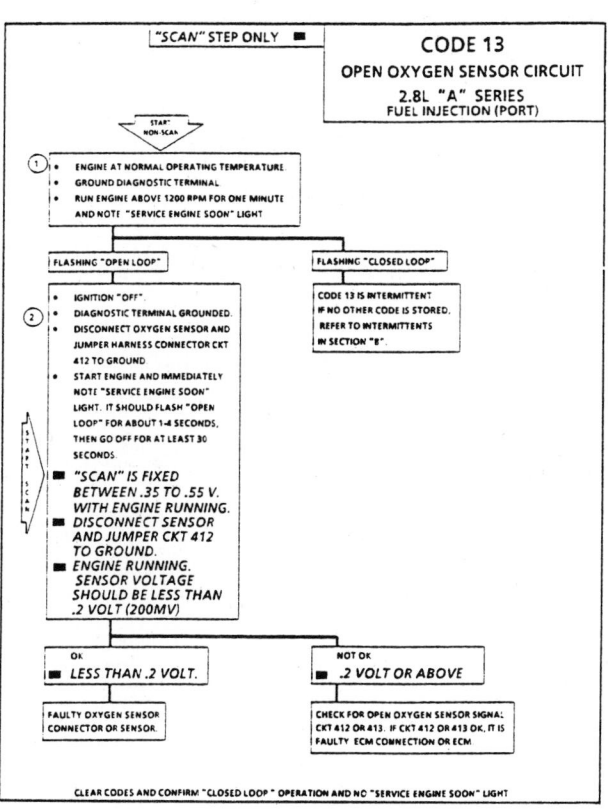

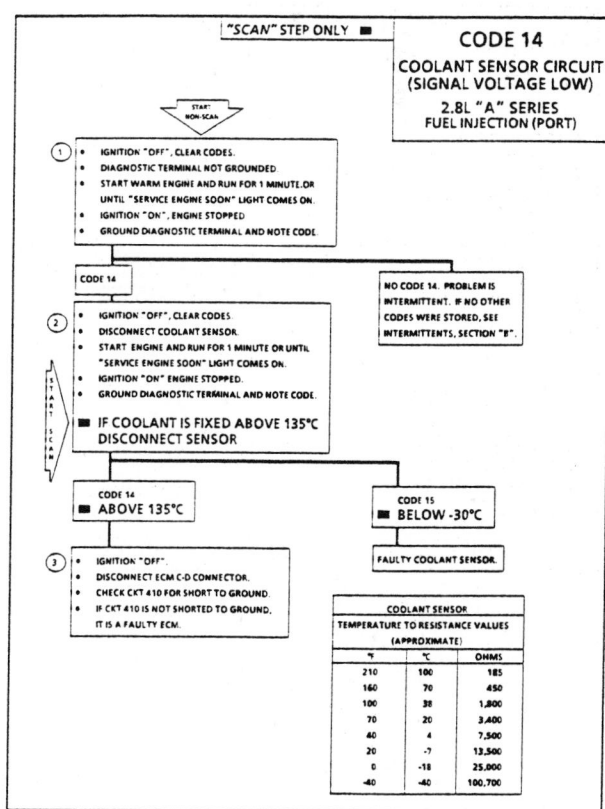

MPI TROUBLE DIAGNOSTICS

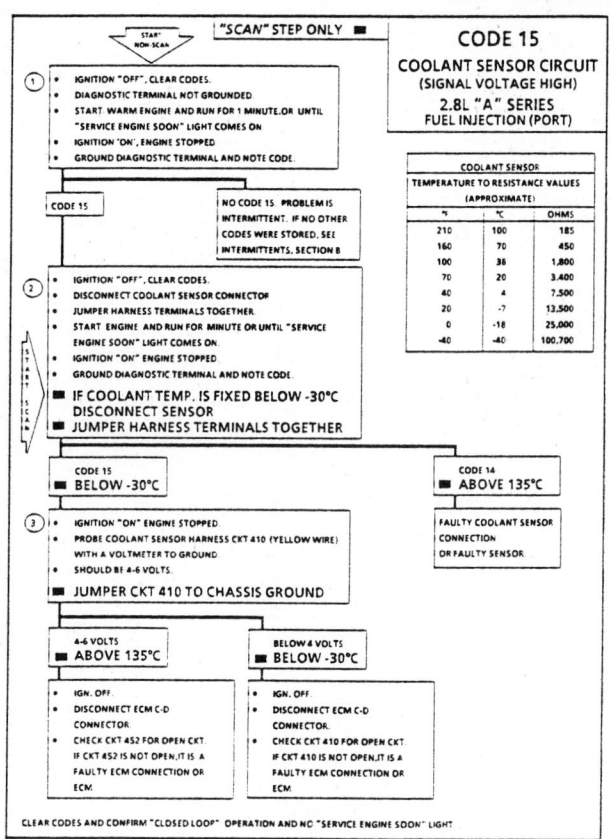

CODE 15
COOLANT SENSOR CIRCUIT
(SIGNAL VOLTAGE HIGH)
2.8L "A" SERIES
FUEL INJECTION (PORT)

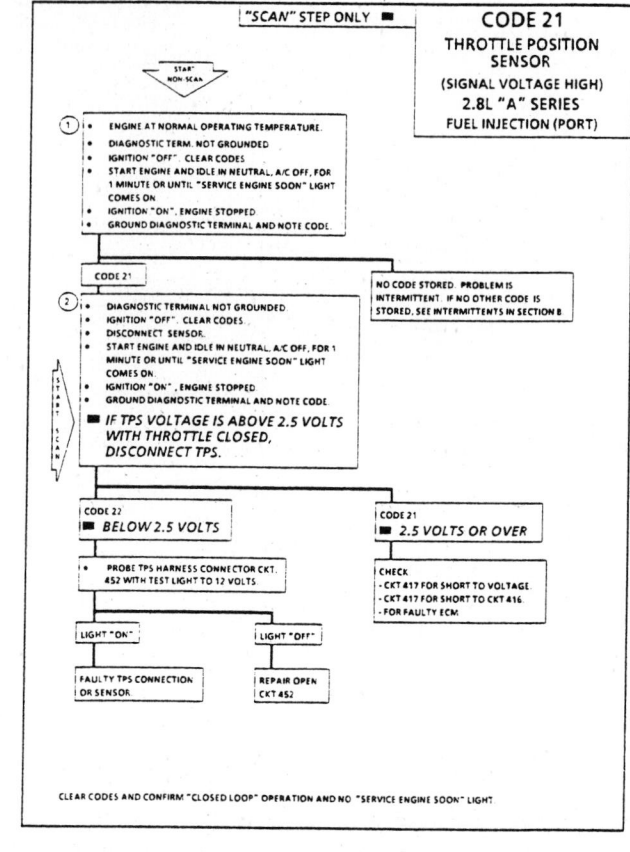

CODE 21
THROTTLE POSITION SENSOR
(SIGNAL VOLTAGE HIGH)
2.8L "A" SERIES
FUEL INJECTION (PORT)

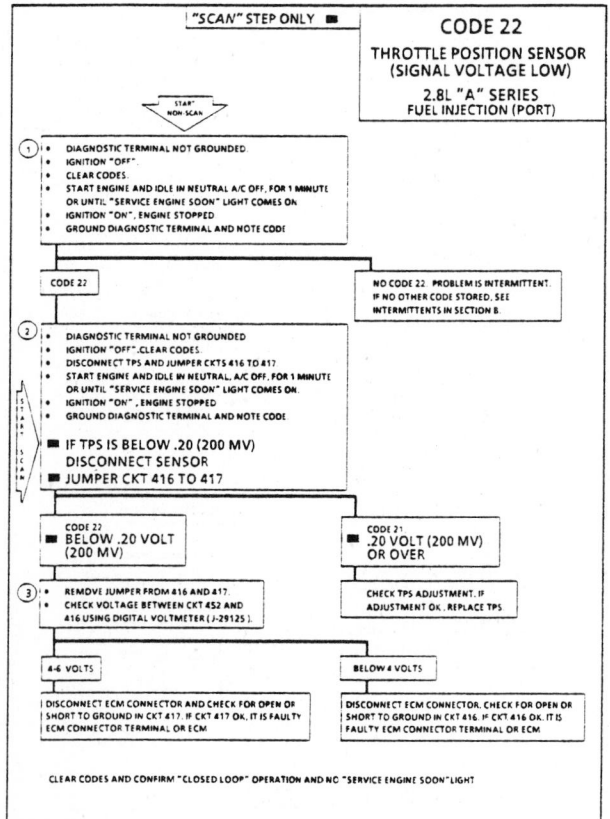

CODE 22
THROTTLE POSITION SENSOR
(SIGNAL VOLTAGE LOW)
2.8L "A" SERIES
FUEL INJECTION (PORT)

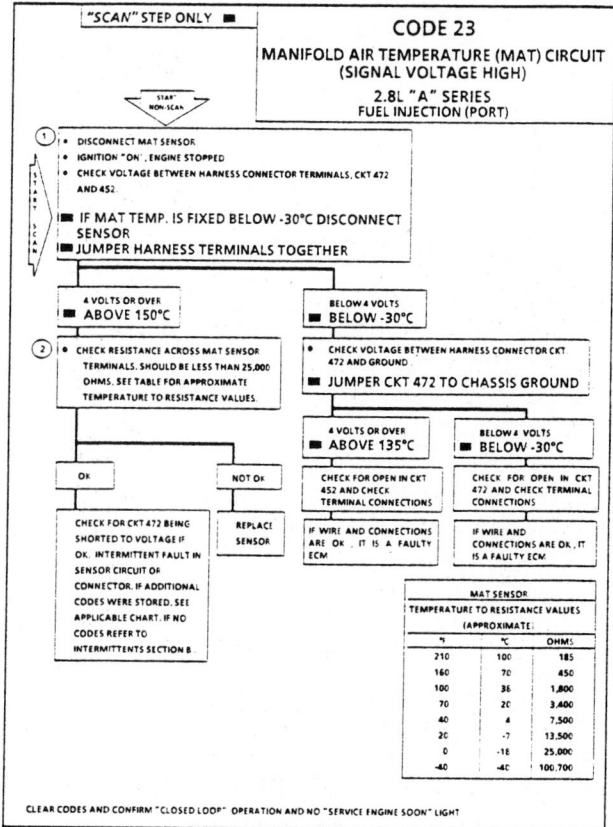

CODE 23
MANIFOLD AIR TEMPERATURE (MAT) CIRCUIT
(SIGNAL VOLTAGE HIGH)
2.8L "A" SERIES
FUEL INJECTION (PORT)

MPI TROUBLE DIAGNOSTICS

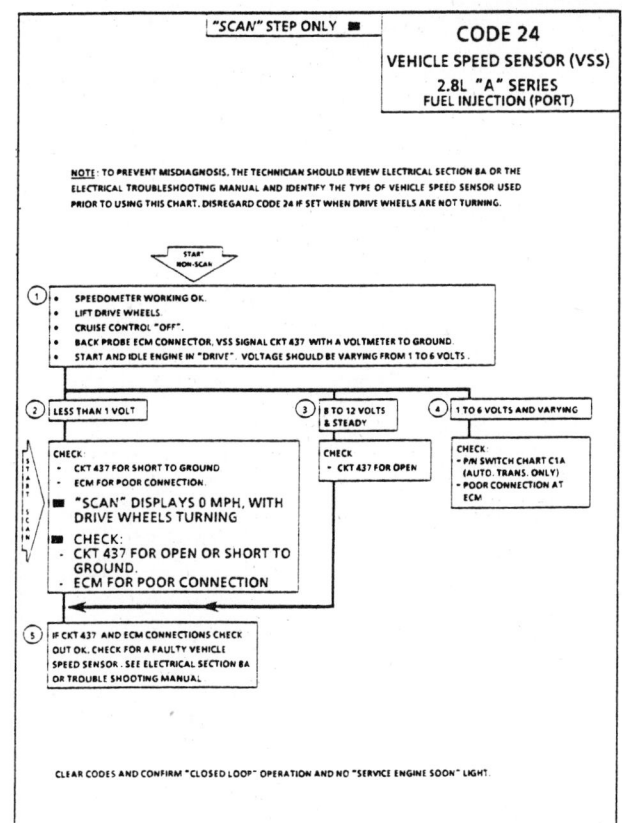

"SCAN" STEP ONLY ■

CODE 24
VEHICLE SPEED SENSOR (VSS)
2.8L "A" SERIES
FUEL INJECTION (PORT)

NOTE: TO PREVENT MISDIAGNOSIS, THE TECHNICIAN SHOULD REVIEW ELECTRICAL SECTION 8A OR THE ELECTRICAL TROUBLESHOOTING MANUAL AND IDENTIFY THE TYPE OF VEHICLE SPEED SENSOR USED PRIOR TO USING THIS CHART. DISREGARD CODE 24 IF SET WHEN DRIVE WHEELS ARE NOT TURNING.

CLEAR CODES AND CONFIRM "CLOSED LOOP" OPERATION AND NO "SERVICE ENGINE SOON" LIGHT.

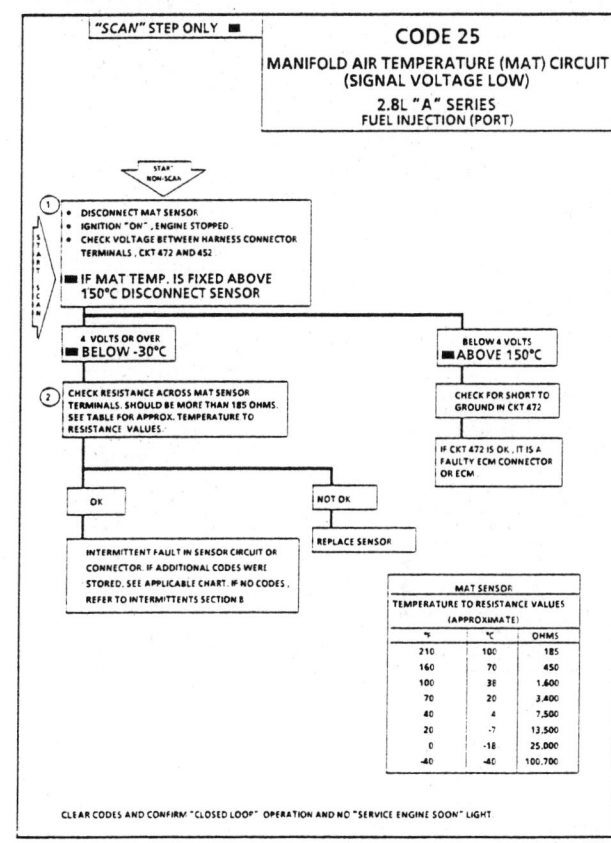

"SCAN" STEP ONLY ■

CODE 25
MANIFOLD AIR TEMPERATURE (MAT) CIRCUIT
(SIGNAL VOLTAGE LOW)
2.8L "A" SERIES
FUEL INJECTION (PORT)

MAT SENSOR		
TEMPERATURE TO RESISTANCE VALUES		
(APPROXIMATE)		
°F	°C	OHMS
210	100	185
160	70	450
100	38	1,600
70	20	3,400
40	4	7,500
20	-7	13,500
0	-18	25,000
-40	-40	100,700

CLEAR CODES AND CONFIRM "CLOSED LOOP" OPERATION AND NO "SERVICE ENGINE SOON" LIGHT.

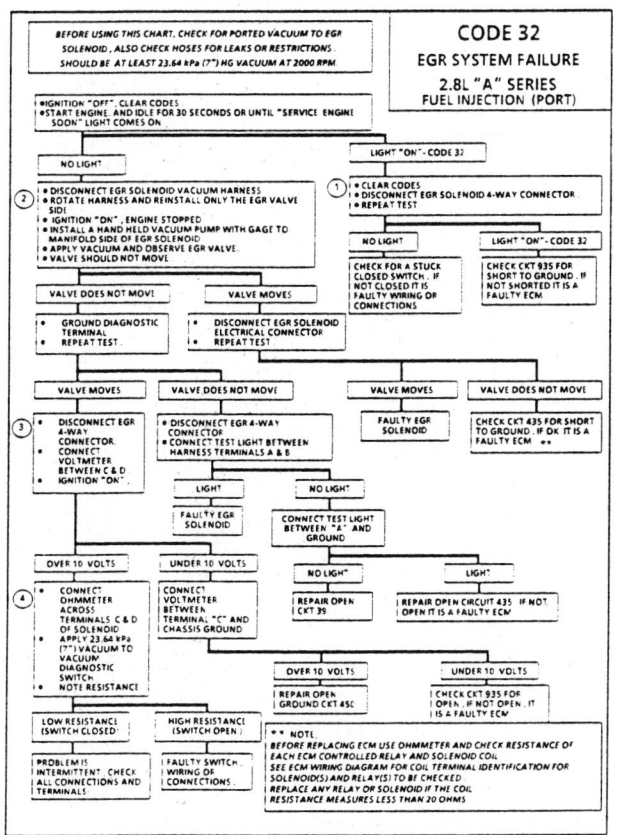

CODE 32
EGR SYSTEM FAILURE
2.8L "A" SERIES
FUEL INJECTION (PORT)

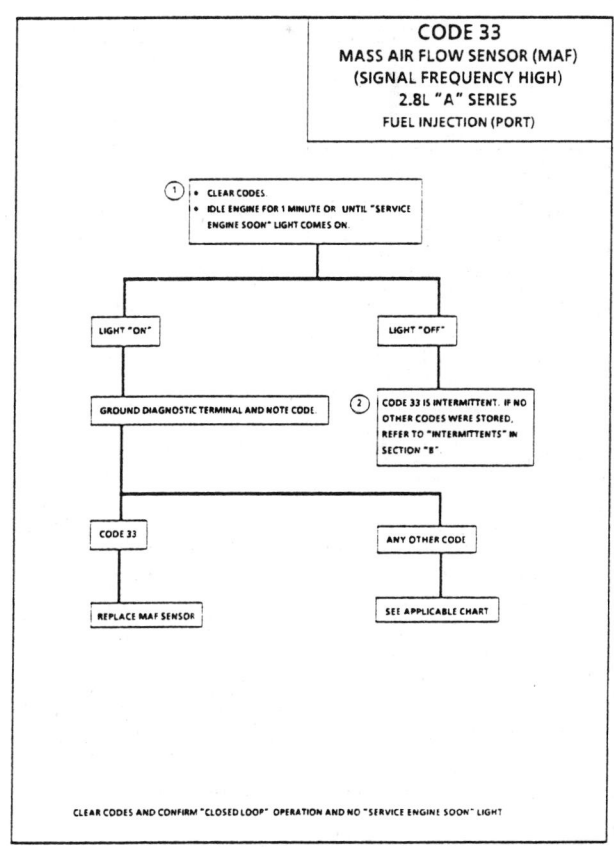

CODE 33
MASS AIR FLOW SENSOR (MAF)
(SIGNAL FREQUENCY HIGH)
2.8L "A" SERIES
FUEL INJECTION (PORT)

CLEAR CODES AND CONFIRM "CLOSED LOOP" OPERATION AND NO "SERVICE ENGINE SOON" LIGHT.

MPI TROUBLE DIAGNOSTICS

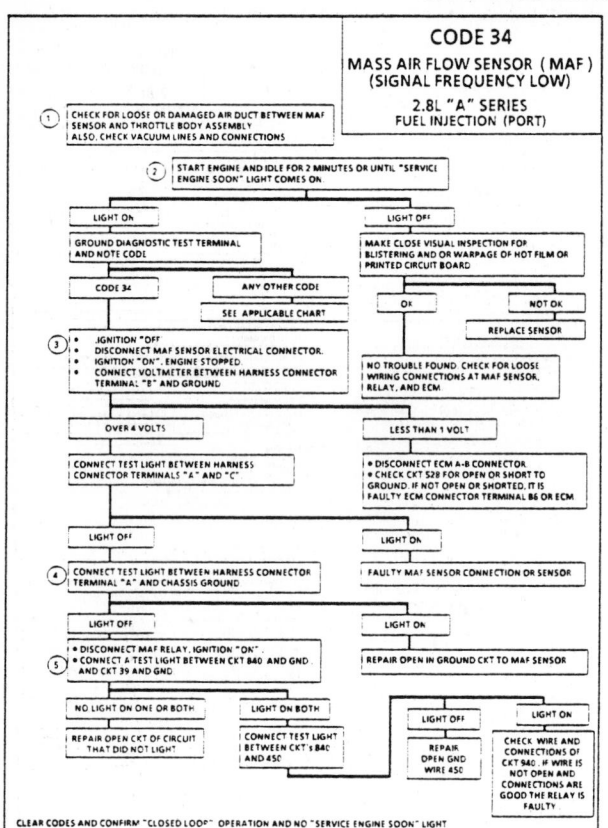

CODE 34
MASS AIR FLOW SENSOR (MAF)
(SIGNAL FREQUENCY LOW)
2.8L "A" SERIES
FUEL INJECTION (PORT)

CLEAR CODES AND CONFIRM "CLOSED LOOP" OPERATION AND NO "SERVICE ENGINE SOON" LIGHT

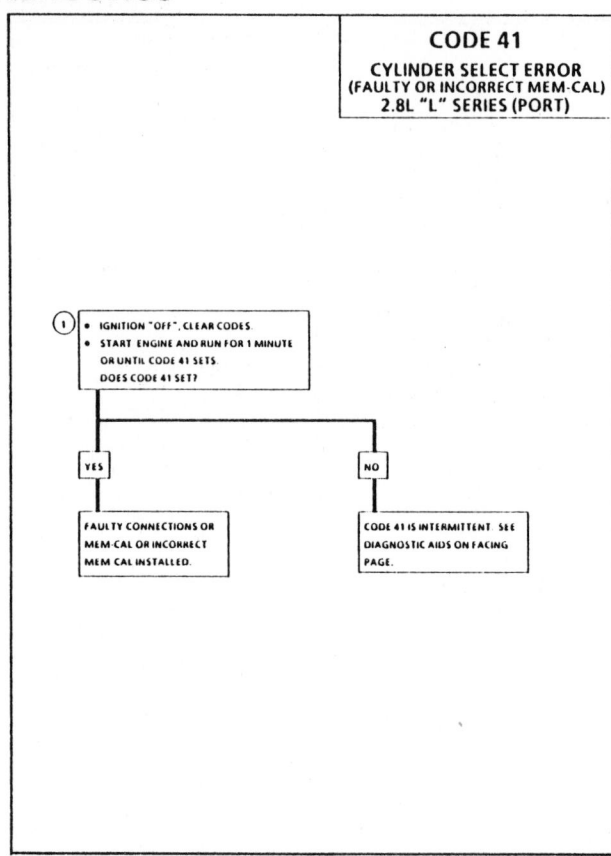

CODE 41
CYLINDER SELECT ERROR
(FAULTY OR INCORRECT MEM-CAL)
2.8L "L" SERIES (PORT)

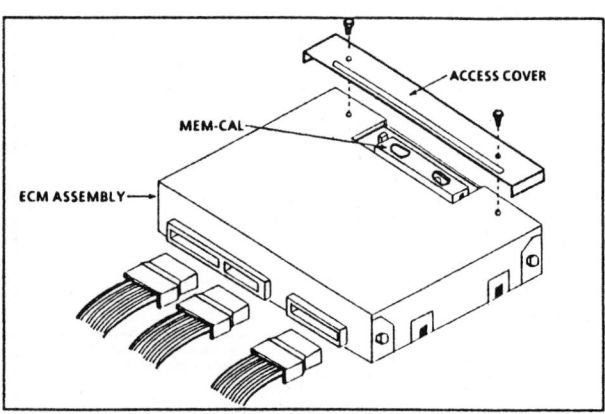

CODE 41
CYLINDER SELECT ERROR
(FAULTY OR INCORRECT MEM-CAL)
2.8L "L" SERIES (PORT)

Test Description: Step numbers refer to step numbers on diagnostic chart.

1 The ECM used for this engine can also be used for other engines, and the difference is in the Mem-Cal. If a Code 41 sets, the incorrect Mem-Cal has been installed or it is faulty and it must be replaced.

Diagnostic Aids:

Check Mem-Cal to be sure locking tabs are secure. Also check the pins on both the Mem-Cal and ECM to assure they are making proper contact. Check the Mem-Cal part number to assure it is the correct part. If the Mem-Cal is faulty it must be replaced. It is also possible that the ECM is faulty, however it should not be replaced until all of the above have been checked. For additional information refer to "Intermittents" on page 6E3-B-2.

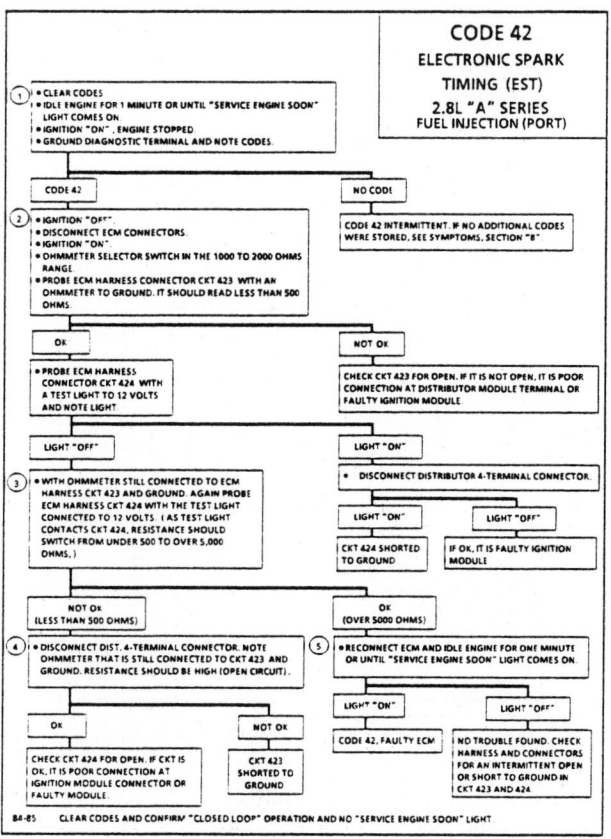

CODE 42
ELECTRONIC SPARK
TIMING (EST)
2.8L "A" SERIES
FUEL INJECTION (PORT)

B4-85   CLEAR CODES AND CONFIRM "CLOSED LOOP" OPERATION AND NO "SERVICE ENGINE SOON" LIGHT.

MPI TROUBLE DIAGNOSTICS

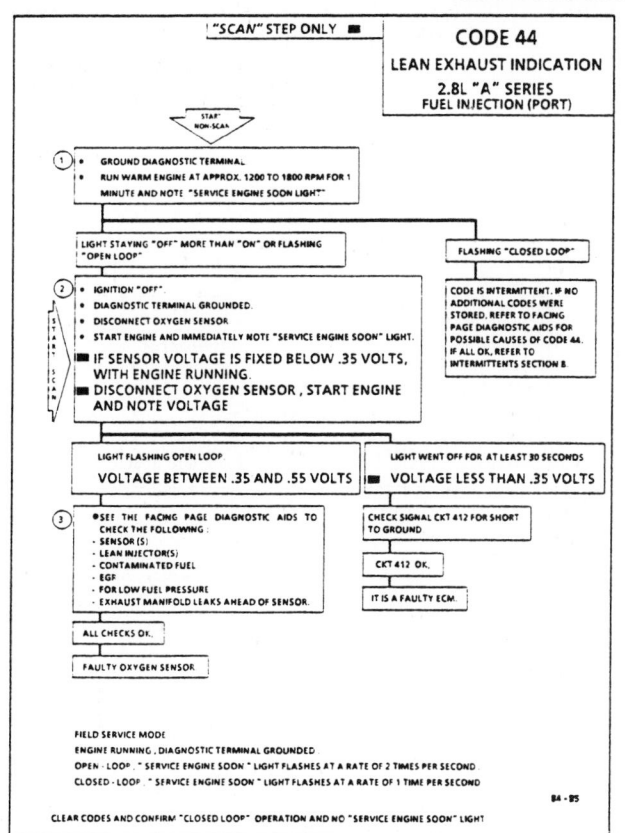

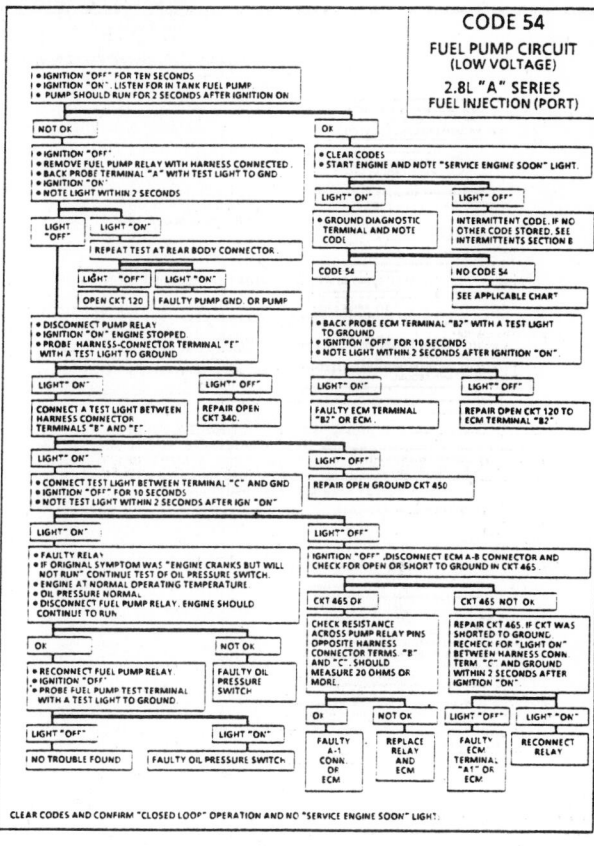

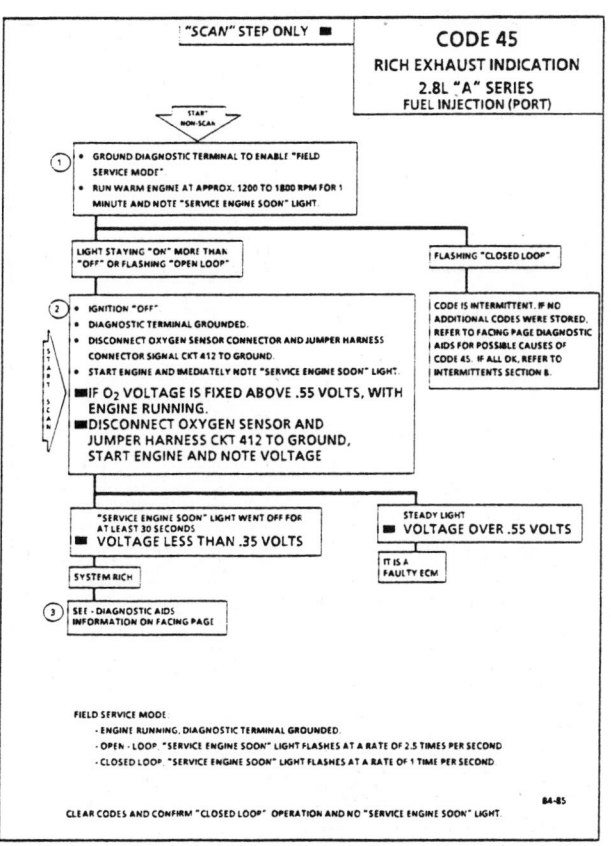

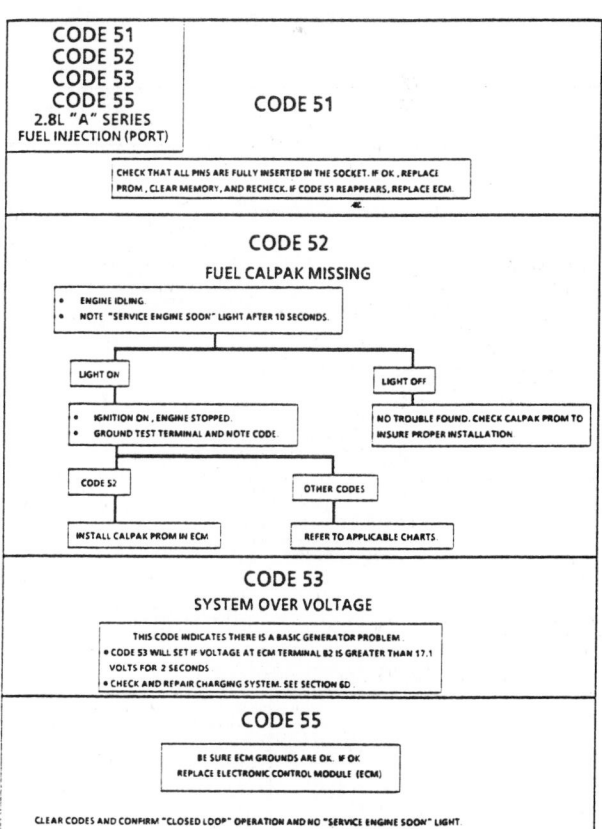

MPI TROUBLE DIAGNOSTICS

CODE 61
DEGRADED OXYGEN SENSOR
2.8L "L" SERIES (PORT)

IF A CODE 61 IS STORED IN MEMORY THE ECM HAS DETERMINED THE OXYGEN SENSOR IS CONTAMINATED OR DEGRADED, BECAUSE THE VOLTAGE CHANGE TIME IS SLOW OR SLUGGISH.

THE ECM PERFORMS THE OXYGEN SENSOR RESPONSE TIME TEST WHEN:

COOLANT TEMPERATURE IS GREATER THAN 85°C.

MAT TEMPERATURE IS GREATER THAN 10°C.

IN CLOSED LOOP.

IN DECEL FUEL CUT-OFF MODE.

IF A CODE 61 IS STORED THE OXYGEN SENSOR SHOULD BE REPLACED. A CONTAMINATED SENSOR CAN BE CAUSED BY FUEL ADDITIVES, SUCH AS SILICON, OR BY USE OF NON-GM APPROVED LUBRICANTS OR SEALANTS. SILICON CONTAMINATION IS USUALLY INDICATED BY A WHITE POWDERY SUBSTANCE ON THE SENSOR FINS.

CLEAR CODES AND CONFIRM "CLOSED LOOP" OPERATION AND NO "SERVICE ENGINE SOON" LIGHT.

"SCAN" DIAGNOSTICS
CODE 63
MANIFOLD ABSOLUTE PRESSURE
(MAP) SENSOR CIRCUIT
(SIGNAL VOLTAGE HIGH - LOW VACUUM)
2.8L "L" SERIES (PORT)

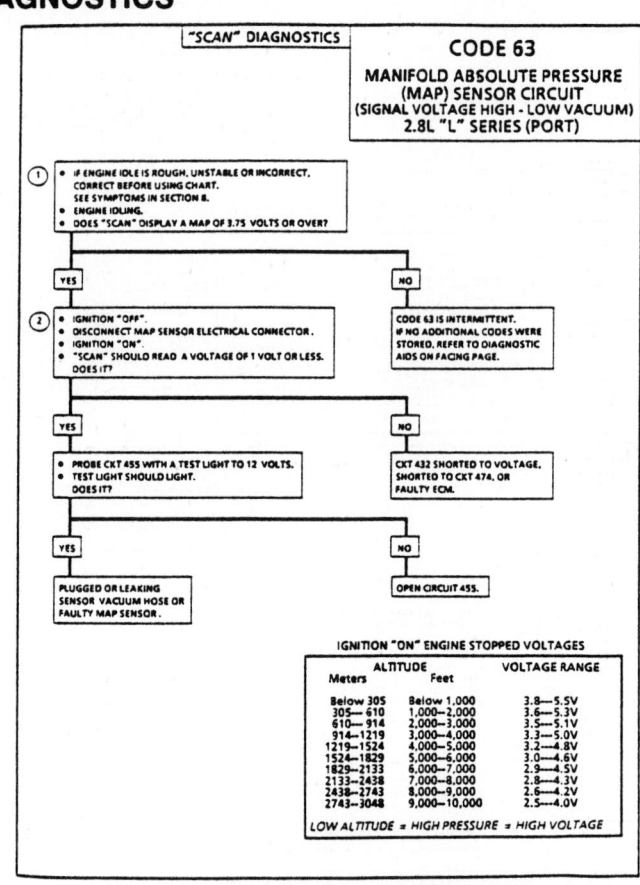

IGNITION "ON" ENGINE STOPPED VOLTAGES

ALTITUDE		VOLTAGE RANGE
Meters	Feet	
Below 305	Below 1,000	3.8—5.5V
305— 610	1,000—2,000	3.6—5.3V
610— 914	2,000—3,000	3.5—5.1V
914—1219	3,000—4,000	3.3—5.0V
1219—1524	4,000—5,000	3.2—4.8V
1524—1829	5,000—6,000	3.0—4.6V
1829—2133	6,000—7,000	2.9—4.5V
2133—2438	7,000—8,000	2.8—4.3V
2438—2743	8,000—9,000	2.6—4.2V
2743—3048	9,000—10,000	2.5—4.0V

LOW ALTITUDE = HIGH PRESSURE = HIGH VOLTAGE

"SCAN" DIAGNOSTICS
CODE 64
MANIFOLD ABSOLUTE PRESSURE
(MAP) SENSOR CIRCUIT
(SIGNAL VOLTAGE LOW - HIGH VACUUM)
2.8L "L" SERIES (PORT)

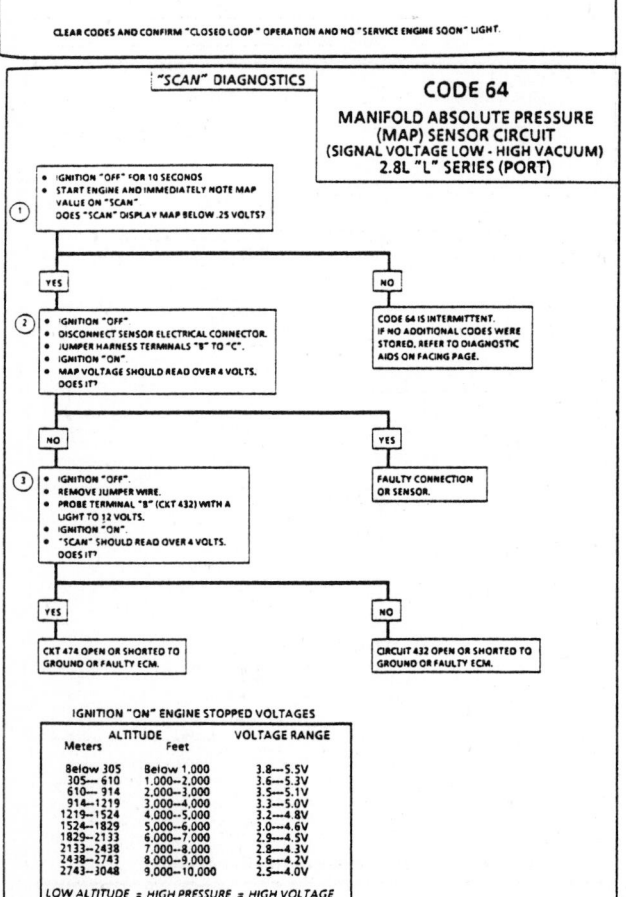

IGNITION "ON" ENGINE STOPPED VOLTAGES

ALTITUDE		VOLTAGE RANGE
Meters	Feet	
Below 305	Below 1,000	3.8—5.5V
305— 610	1,000—2,000	3.6—5.3V
610— 914	2,000—3,000	3.5—5.1V
914—1219	3,000—4,000	3.3—5.0V
1219—1524	4,000—5,000	3.2—4.8V
1524—1829	5,000—6,000	3.0—4.6V
1829—2133	6,000—7,000	2.9—4.5V
2133—2438	7,000—8,000	2.8—4.3V
2438—2743	8,000—9,000	2.6—4.2V
2743—3048	9,000—10,000	2.5—4.0V

LOW ALTITUDE = HIGH PRESSURE = HIGH VOLTAGE

CHART C-1A
PARK NEUTRAL SWITCH DIAGNOSIS
(AUTO TRANSAXLE ONLY)
2.8L "A" SERIES
FUEL INJECTION (PORT)

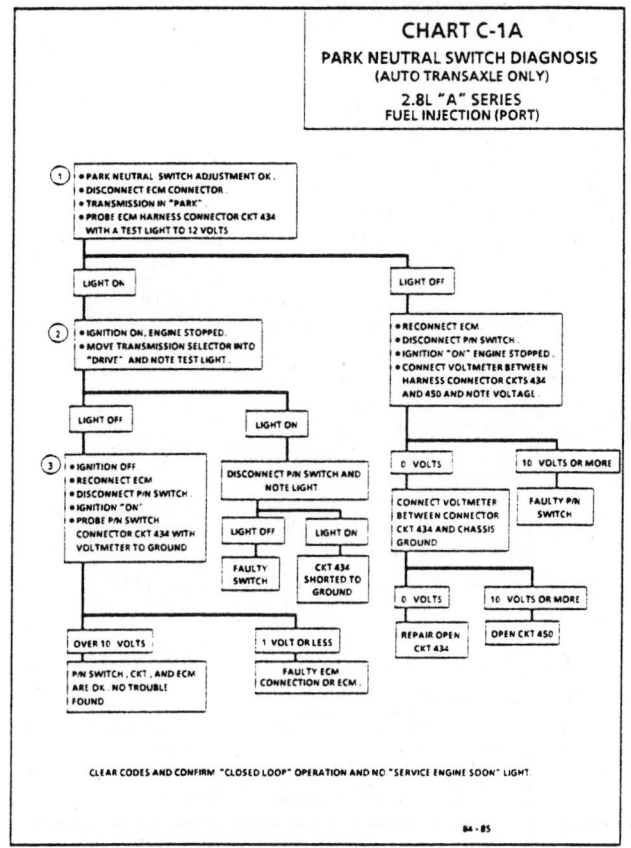

CLEAR CODES AND CONFIRM "CLOSED LOOP" OPERATION AND NO "SERVICE ENGINE SOON" LIGHT.

84 - 85

MPI TROUBLE DIAGNOSTICS

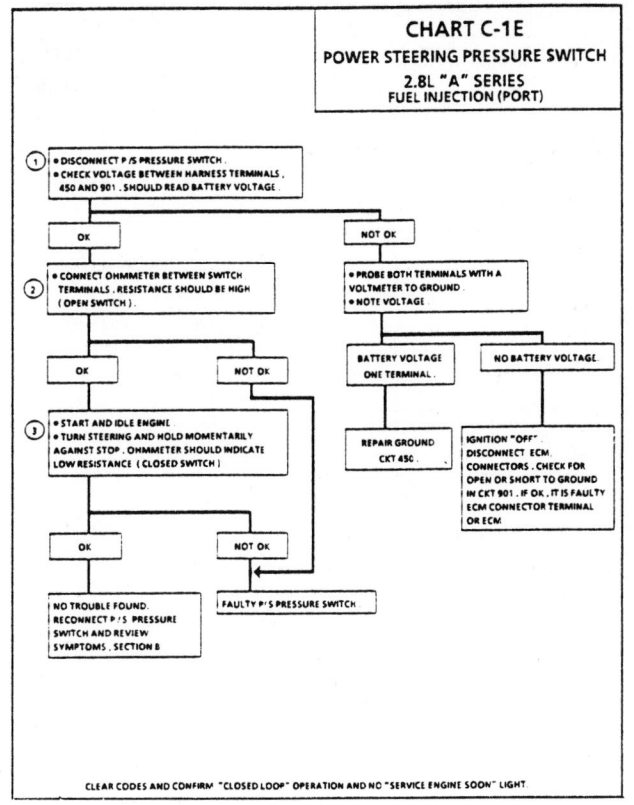

CHART C-1E
POWER STEERING PRESSURE SWITCH
2.8L "A" SERIES
FUEL INJECTION (PORT)

1. • DISCONNECT P/S PRESSURE SWITCH.
   • CHECK VOLTAGE BETWEEN HARNESS TERMINALS, 450 AND 901. SHOULD READ BATTERY VOLTAGE.

OK

2. • CONNECT OHMMETER BETWEEN SWITCH TERMINALS. RESISTANCE SHOULD BE HIGH (OPEN SWITCH).

OK / **NOT OK**

3. • START AND IDLE ENGINE.
   • TURN STEERING AND HOLD MOMENTARILY AGAINST STOP. OHMMETER SHOULD INDICATE LOW RESISTANCE (CLOSED SWITCH).

OK / **NOT OK**

NO TROUBLE FOUND. RECONNECT P/S PRESSURE SWITCH AND REVIEW SYMPTOMS. SECTION B.

FAULTY P/S PRESSURE SWITCH.

NOT OK

• PROBE BOTH TERMINALS WITH A VOLTMETER TO GROUND.
• NOTE VOLTAGE

BATTERY VOLTAGE ONE TERMINAL. / NO BATTERY VOLTAGE.

REPAIR GROUND CKT 450.

IGNITION "OFF". DISCONNECT ECM CONNECTORS. CHECK FOR OPEN OR SHORT TO GROUND IN CKT 901. IF OK, IT IS FAULTY ECM CONNECTOR TERMINAL OR ECM.

CLEAR CODES AND CONFIRM "CLOSED LOOP" OPERATION AND NO "SERVICE ENGINE SOON" LIGHT.

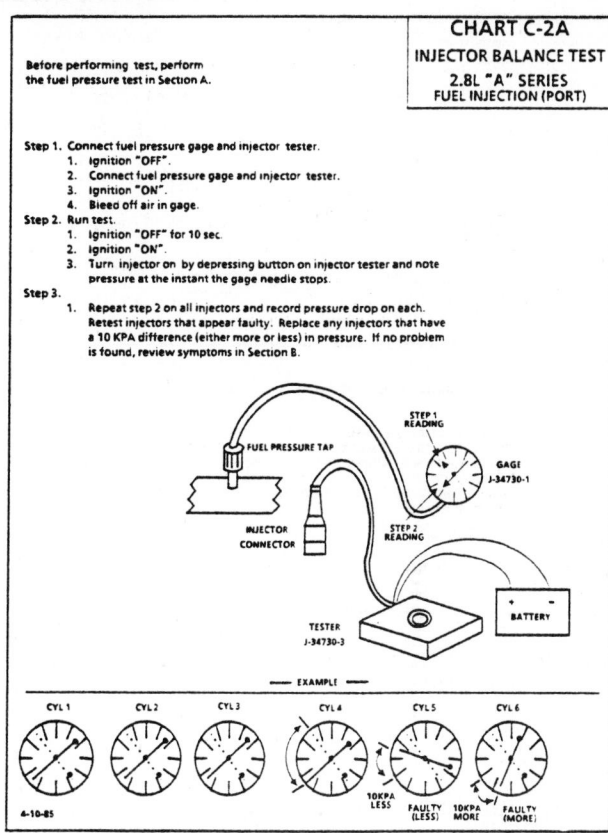

CHART C-2A
INJECTOR BALANCE TEST
2.8L "A" SERIES
FUEL INJECTION (PORT)

Before performing test, perform the fuel pressure test in Section A.

Step 1. Connect fuel pressure gage and injector tester.
   1. Ignition "OFF".
   2. Connect fuel pressure gage and injector tester.
   3. Ignition "ON".
   4. Bleed off air in gage.

Step 2. Run test.
   1. Ignition "OFF" for 10 sec.
   2. Ignition "ON".
   3. Turn injector on by depressing button on injector tester and note pressure at the instant the gage needle stops.

Step 3.
   1. Repeat step 2 on all injectors and record pressure drop on each. Retest injectors that appear faulty. Replace any injectors that have a 10 KPA difference (either more or less) in pressure. If no problem is found, review symptoms in Section B.

EXAMPLE

CYL 1 / CYL 2 / CYL 3 / CYL 4 / CYL 5 / CYL 6

10KPA LESS / FAULTY (LESS) / 10KPA MORE / FAULTY (MORE)

4-10-85

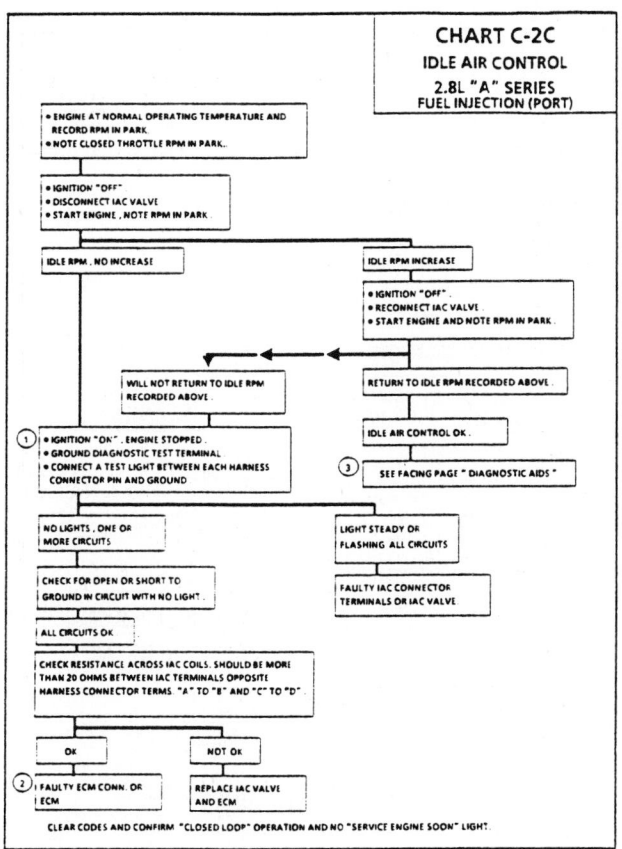

CHART C-2C
IDLE AIR CONTROL
2.8L "A" SERIES
FUEL INJECTION (PORT)

• ENGINE AT NORMAL OPERATING TEMPERATURE AND RECORD RPM IN PARK.
• NOTE CLOSED THROTTLE RPM IN PARK.

• IGNITION "OFF".
• DISCONNECT IAC VALVE.
• START ENGINE, NOTE RPM IN PARK.

IDLE RPM, NO INCREASE / IDLE RPM INCREASE

• IGNITION "OFF".
• RECONNECT IAC VALVE.
• START ENGINE AND NOTE RPM IN PARK.

WILL NOT RETURN TO IDLE RPM RECORDED ABOVE. / RETURN TO IDLE RPM RECORDED ABOVE.

IDLE AIR CONTROL OK.

3. SEE FACING PAGE "DIAGNOSTIC AIDS"

1. • IGNITION "ON", ENGINE STOPPED.
   • GROUND DIAGNOSTIC TEST TERMINAL.
   • CONNECT A TEST LIGHT BETWEEN EACH HARNESS CONNECTOR PIN AND GROUND.

NO LIGHTS, ONE OR MORE CIRCUITS / LIGHT STEADY OR FLASHING ALL CIRCUITS

CHECK FOR OPEN OR SHORT TO GROUND IN CIRCUIT WITH NO LIGHT.

FAULTY IAC CONNECTOR TERMINALS OR IAC VALVE.

ALL CIRCUITS OK.

CHECK RESISTANCE ACROSS IAC COILS. SHOULD BE MORE THAN 20 OHMS BETWEEN IAC TERMINALS OPPOSITE HARNESS CONNECTOR TERMS. "A" TO "B" AND "C" TO "D".

OK / **NOT OK**

2. FAULTY ECM CONN. OR ECM / REPLACE IAC VALVE AND ECM

CLEAR CODES AND CONFIRM "CLOSED LOOP" OPERATION AND NO "SERVICE ENGINE SOON" LIGHT.

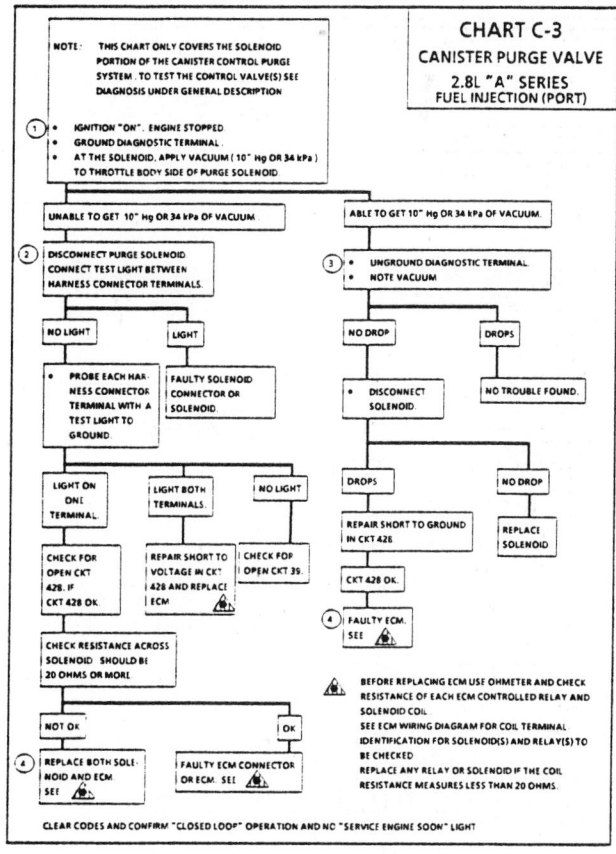

CHART C-3
CANISTER PURGE VALVE
2.8L "A" SERIES
FUEL INJECTION (PORT)

NOTE: THIS CHART ONLY COVERS THE SOLENOID PORTION OF THE CANISTER CONTROL PURGE SYSTEM. TO TEST THE CONTROL VALVE(S) SEE DIAGNOSIS UNDER GENERAL DESCRIPTION.

1. • IGNITION "ON", ENGINE STOPPED.
   • GROUND DIAGNOSTIC TERMINAL.
   • AT THE SOLENOID, APPLY VACUUM (10" Hg OR 34 kPa) TO THROTTLE BODY SIDE OF PURGE SOLENOID.

UNABLE TO GET 10" Hg OR 34 kPa OF VACUUM / ABLE TO GET 10" Hg OR 34 kPa OF VACUUM.

2. DISCONNECT PURGE SOLENOID. CONNECT TEST LIGHT BETWEEN HARNESS CONNECTOR TERMINALS.

NO LIGHT / LIGHT

FAULTY SOLENOID CONNECTOR OR SOLENOID.

• PROBE EACH HARNESS CONNECTOR TERMINAL WITH A TEST LIGHT TO GROUND.

LIGHT ON ONE TERMINAL. / LIGHT BOTH TERMINALS. / NO LIGHT

CHECK FOR OPEN CKT 428. IF CKT 428 OK.

REPAIR SHORT TO VOLTAGE IN CKT 428 AND REPLACE ECM

CHECK FOR OPEN CKT 35.

CHECK RESISTANCE ACROSS SOLENOID SHOULD BE 20 OHMS OR MORE.

NOT OK / **OK**

4. REPLACE BOTH SOLENOID AND ECM. SEE / FAULTY ECM CONNECTOR OR ECM. SEE

3. • UNGROUND DIAGNOSTIC TERMINAL.
   • NOTE VACUUM

NO DROP / DROPS

• DISCONNECT SOLENOID / NO TROUBLE FOUND.

DROPS / NO DROP

REPAIR SHORT TO GROUND IN CKT 428 / REPLACE SOLENOID

CKT 428 OK.

4. FAULTY ECM. SEE

BEFORE REPLACING ECM USE OHMETER AND CHECK RESISTANCE OF EACH ECM CONTROLLED RELAY AND SOLENOID COIL.
SEE ECM WIRING DIAGRAM FOR COIL TERMINAL IDENTIFICATION FOR SOLENOID(S) AND RELAY(S) TO BE CHECKED.
REPLACE ANY RELAY OR SOLENOID IF THE COIL RESISTANCE MEASURES LESS THAN 20 OHMS.

CLEAR CODES AND CONFIRM "CLOSED LOOP" OPERATION AND NO "SERVICE ENGINE SOON" LIGHT.

MPI TROUBLE DIAGNOSTICS

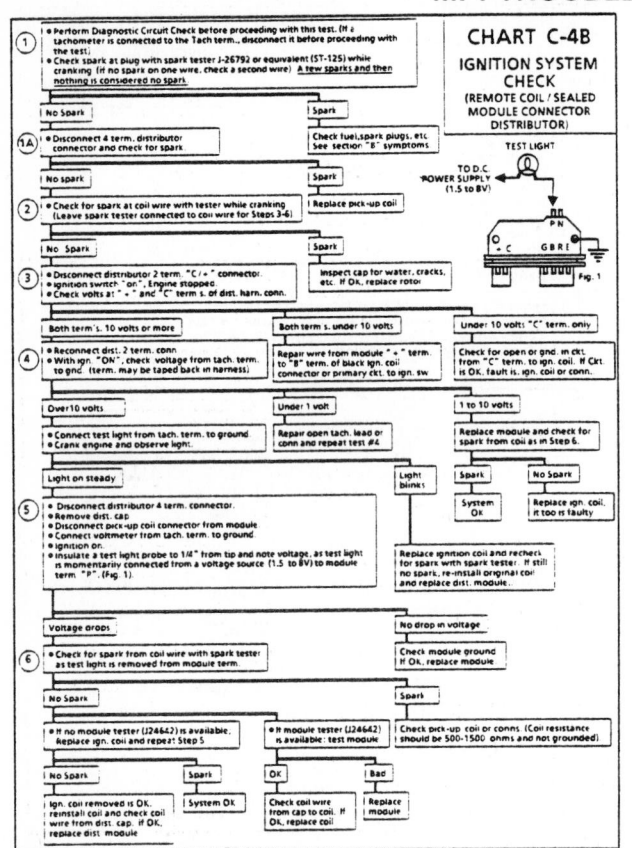

CHART C-4B
IGNITION SYSTEM CHECK
(REMOTE COIL / SEALED MODULE CONNECTOR DISTRIBUTOR)

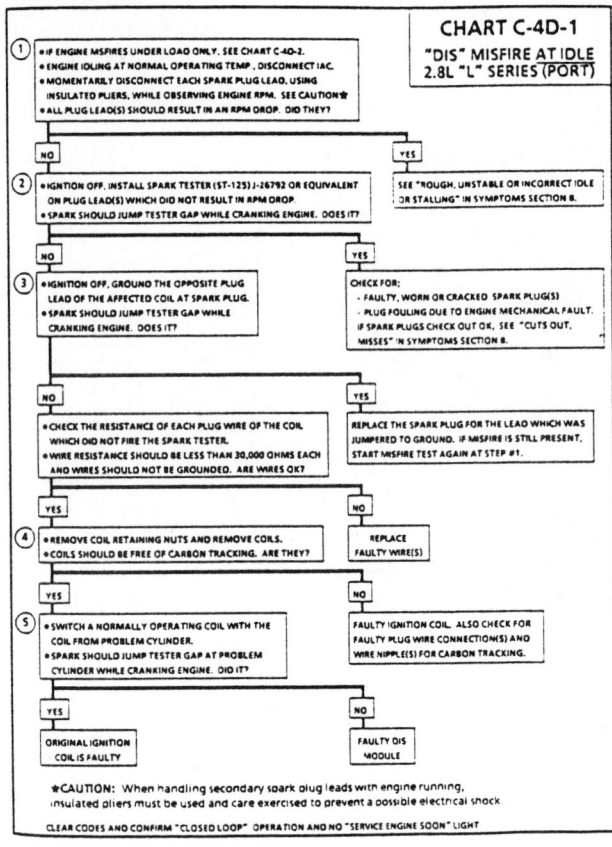

CHART C-4D-1
"DIS" MISFIRE AT IDLE
2.8L "L" SERIES (PORT)

★CAUTION: When handling secondary spark plug leads with engine running, insulated pliers must be used and care exercised to prevent a possible electrical shock.

CLEAR CODES AND CONFIRM "CLOSED LOOP" OPERATION AND NO "SERVICE ENGINE SOON" LIGHT

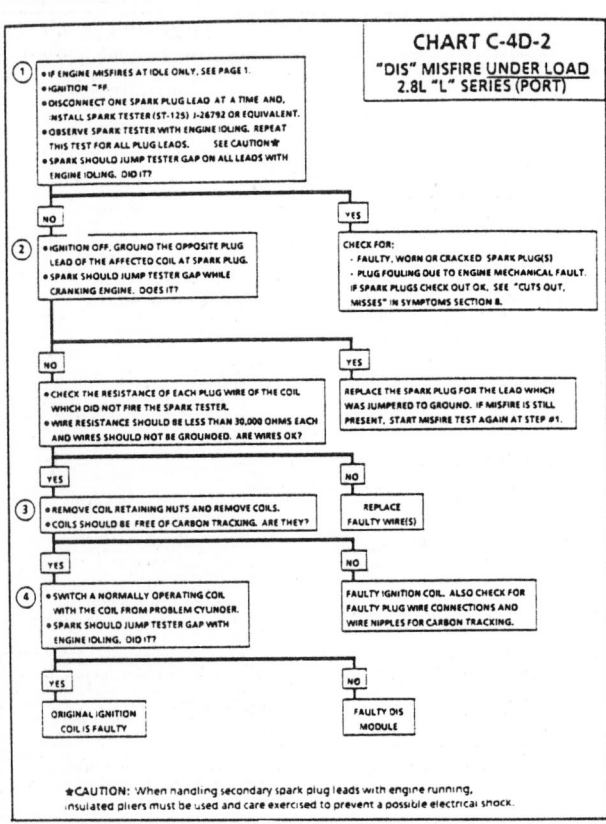

CHART C-4D-2
"DIS" MISFIRE UNDER LOAD
2.8L "L" SERIES (PORT)

★CAUTION: When handling secondary spark plug leads with engine running, insulated pliers must be used and care exercised to prevent a possible electrical shock.

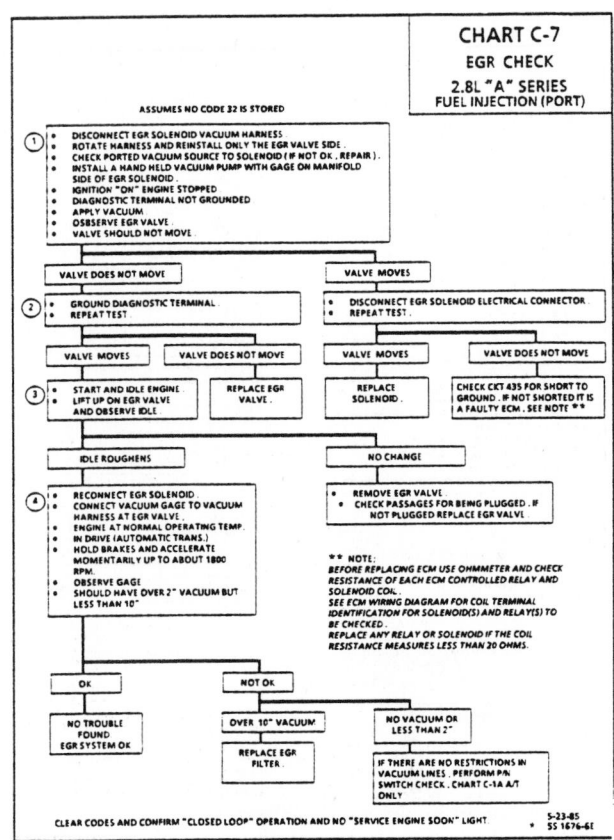

CHART C-7
EGR CHECK
2.8L "A" SERIES
FUEL INJECTION (PORT)

CLEAR CODES AND CONFIRM "CLOSED LOOP" OPERATION AND NO "SERVICE ENGINE SOON" LIGHT.

5-23-85
SS 1676-6E

MPI TROUBLE DIAGNOSTICS

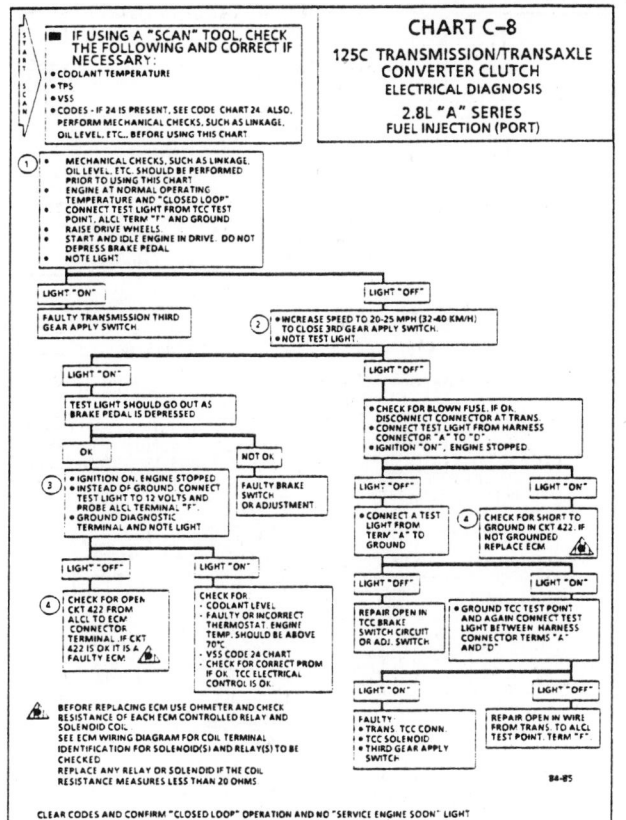

CHART C-8
125C TRANSMISSION/TRANSAXLE
CONVERTER CLUTCH
ELECTRICAL DIAGNOSIS
2.8L "A" SERIES
FUEL INJECTION (PORT)

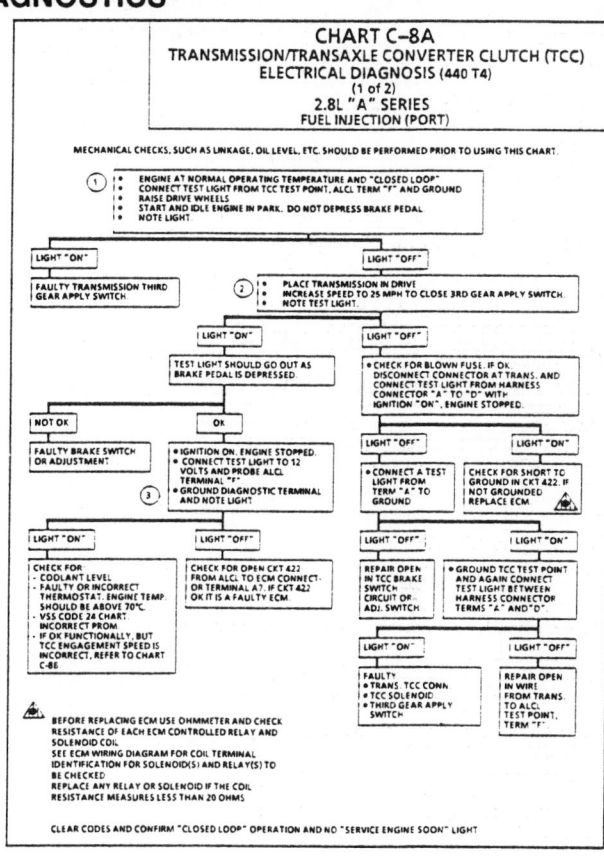

CHART C-8A
TRANSMISSION/TRANSAXLE CONVERTER CLUTCH (TCC)
ELECTRICAL DIAGNOSIS (440 T4)
(1 of 2)
2.8L "A" SERIES
FUEL INJECTION (PORT)

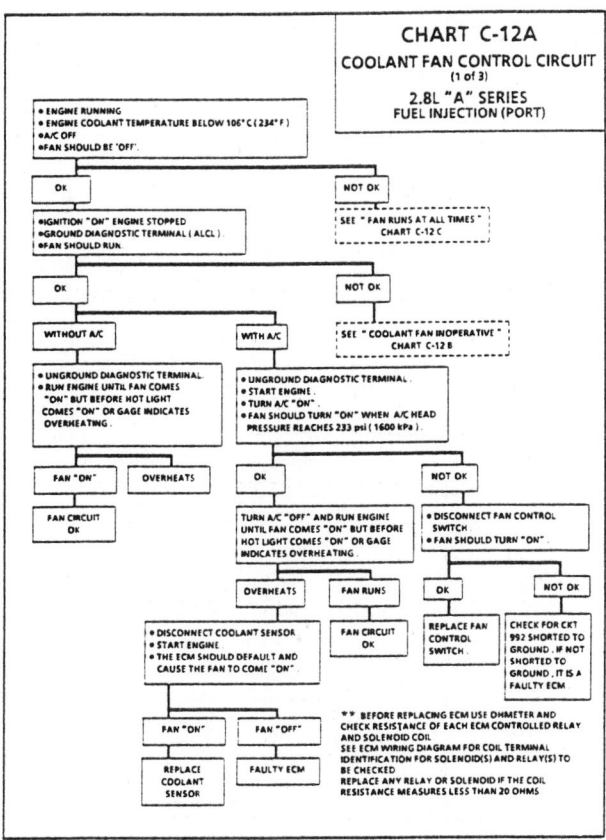

CHART C-12A
COOLANT FAN CONTROL CIRCUIT
(1 of 3)
2.8L "A" SERIES
FUEL INJECTION (PORT)

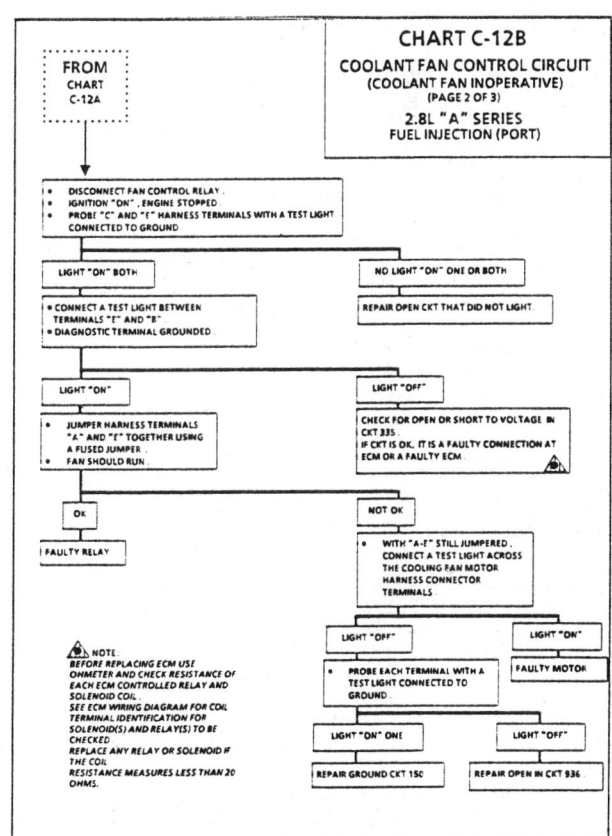

CHART C-12B
COOLANT FAN CONTROL CIRCUIT
(COOLANT FAN INOPERATIVE)
(PAGE 2 OF 3)
2.8L "A" SERIES
FUEL INJECTION (PORT)

MPI TROUBLE DIAGNOSTICS

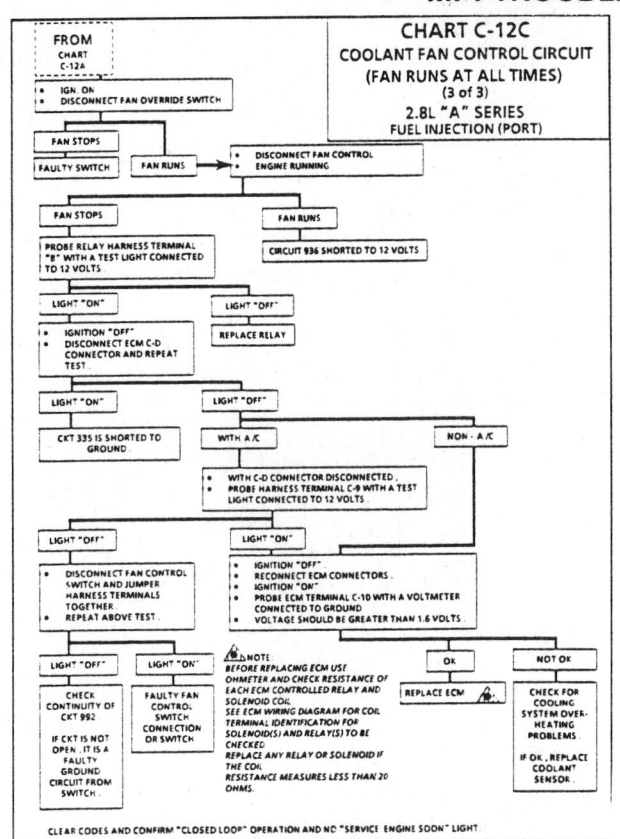

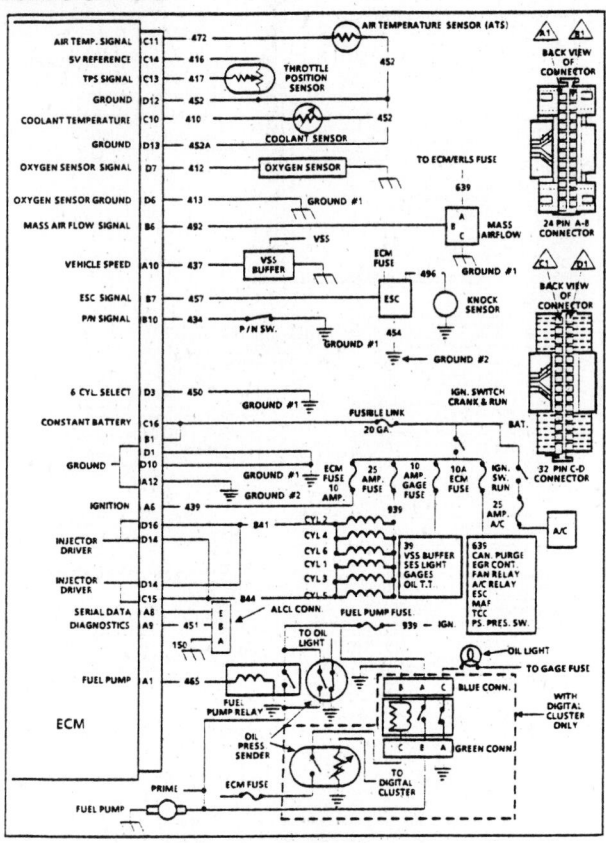

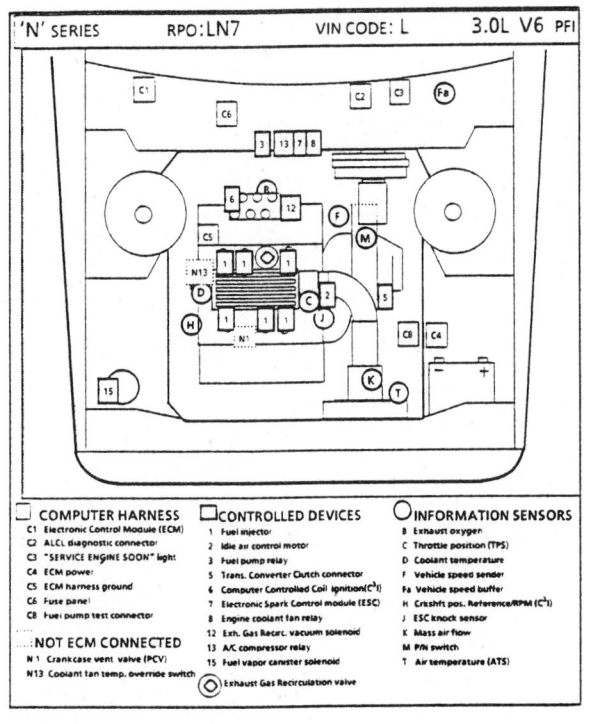

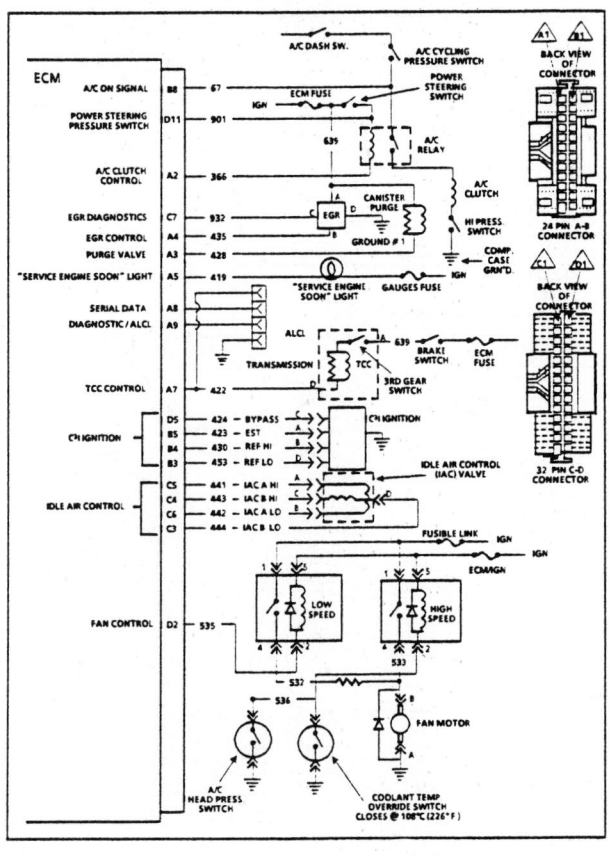

MPI TROUBLE DIAGNOSTICS

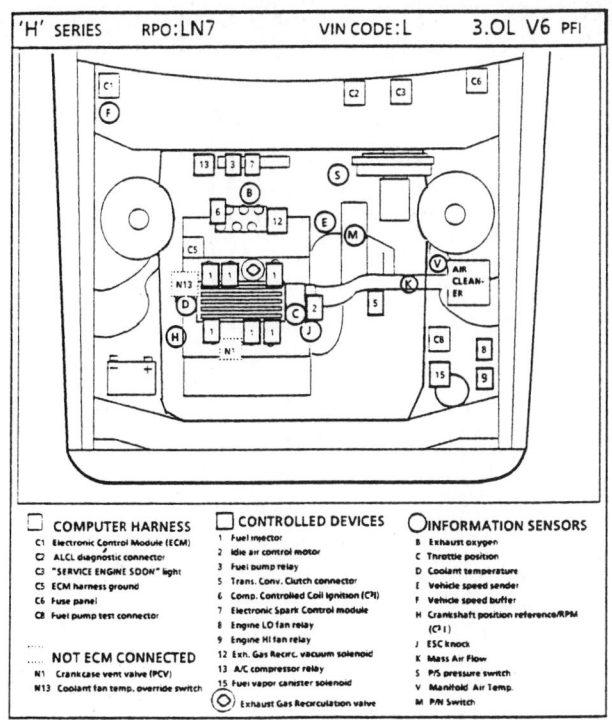

'H' SERIES   RPO: LN7   VIN CODE: L   3.0L V6 PFI

COMPUTER HARNESS
C1 Electronic Control Module (ECM)
C2 ALCL diagnostic connector
C3 "SERVICE ENGINE SOON" light
C5 ECM harness ground
C6 Fuse panel
CB Fuel pump test connector

NOT ECM CONNECTED
N1 Crankcase vent valve (PCV)
N13 Coolant fan temp. override switch

CONTROLLED DEVICES
1 Fuel injector
2 Idle air control motor
3 Fuel pump relay
4 Trans. Conv. Clutch connector
5 Comp. Controlled Coil Ignition (C³I)
7 Electronic Spark Control module
8 Engine LO fan relay
9 Engine HI fan relay
12 Exh. Gas Recrc. vacuum solenoid
13 A/C compressor relay
15 Fuel vapor canister solenoid
Exhaust Gas Recirculation valve

INFORMATION SENSORS
B Exhaust oxygen
C Throttle position
D Coolant temperature
E Vehicle speed sender
F Vehicle speed buffer
H Crankshaft position reference/RPM (C³I)
J ESC knock
K Mass Air Flow
P P/S pressure switch
V Manifold Air Temp.
M P/N Switch

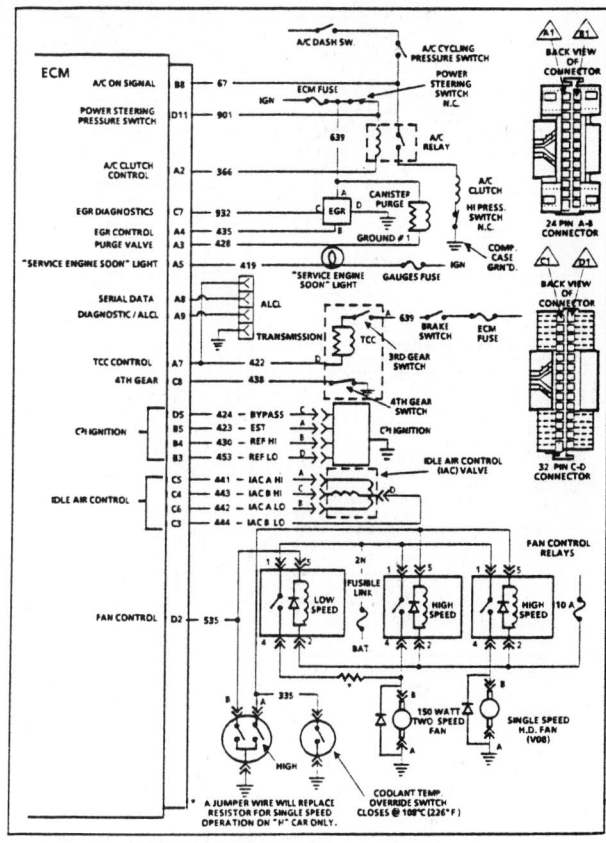

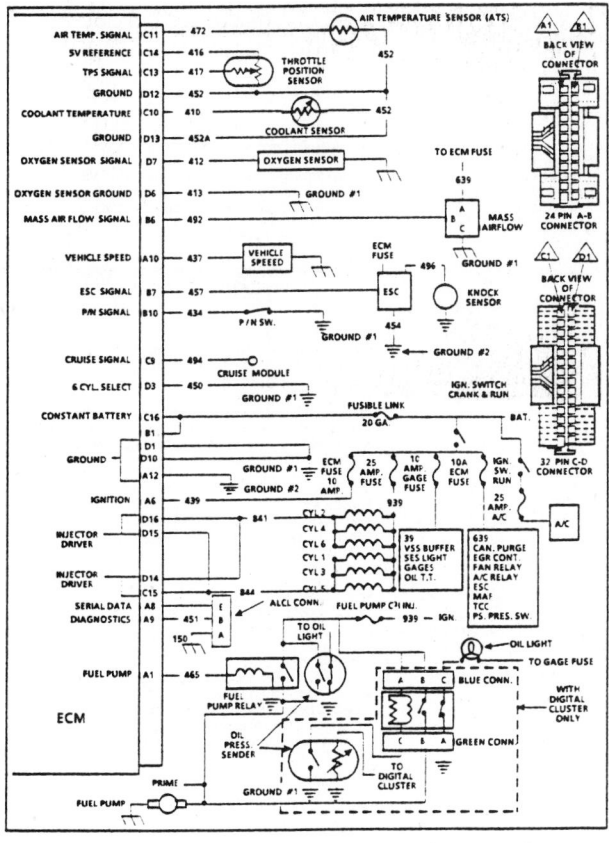

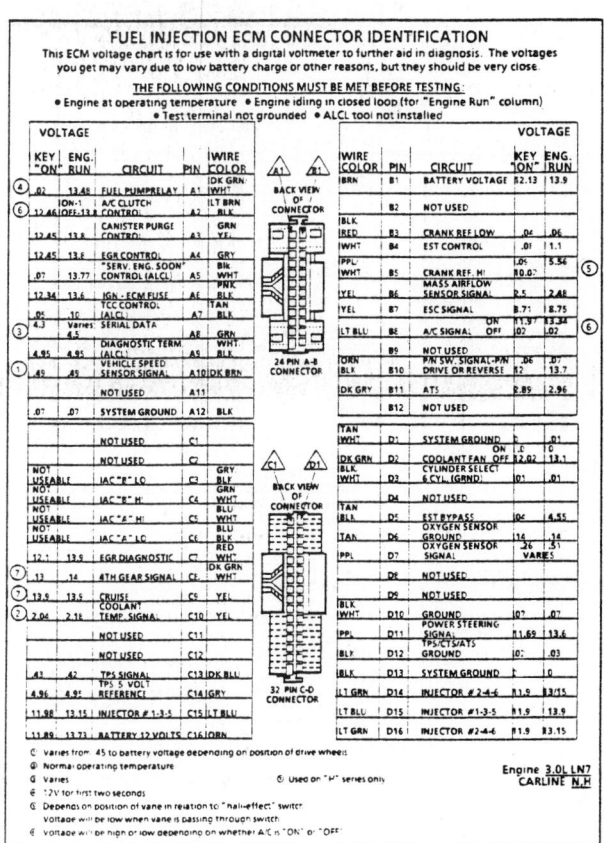

FUEL INJECTION ECM CONNECTOR IDENTIFICATION

This ECM voltage chart is for use with a digital voltmeter to further aid in diagnosis. The voltages you get may vary due to low battery charge or other reasons, but they should be very close.

THE FOLLOWING CONDITIONS MUST BE MET BEFORE TESTING:
• Engine at operating temperature • Engine idling in closed loop (for "Engine Run" column)
• Test terminal not grounded • ALCL tool not installed

Engine 3.0L LN7
CARLINE N,H

MPI TROUBLE DIAGNOSTICS

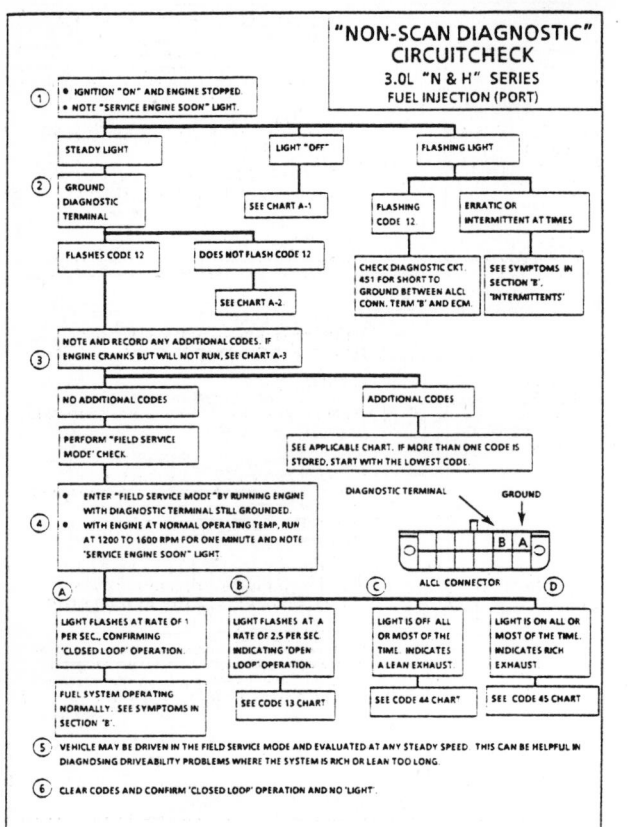

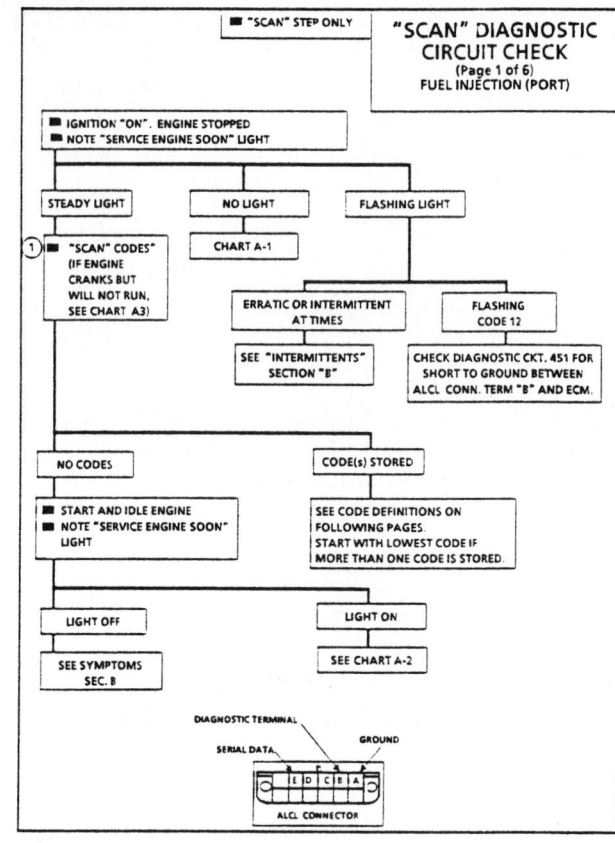

"SCAN" DIAGNOSTIC CIRCUIT CHECK
(Page 2 of 6)
(CODE DEFINITIONS)

THE 'DIAGNOSTIC CIRCUIT CHECK' SCAN DATA IS TYPICAL OF THAT DISPLAYED BY A PROPERLY DESIGNED AND CALIBRATED ALCL SCAN DEVICE.
A SCAN DEVICE THAT DISPLAYS FAULTY DATA SHOULD NOT BE USED AND THE PROBLEM REPORTED TO THE DEVICE MANUFACTURER. THE USE OF A FAULTY SCAN DEVICE CAN RESULT IN MISDIAGNOSIS AND UNNECESSARY PARTS REPLACEMENT.

CODES	DEFINITION
■ **CODE 13** • "SCAN" TOOL IN SPECIAL MODE • ENGINE IDLING AT 1000 RPM. • COOLANT 75° TO 95°C. • "SCAN" OXYGEN SENSOR VOLTAGE.	HARD FAILURE - VOLTAGE FIXED AT .35 TO .55 V. OPEN CIRCUIT CONDITION. SEE CODE CHART 13. INTERMITTENT CODE - NORMAL "SCAN" VOLTAGE VARIES BETWEEN 100MV TO 999 MV (.1 AND 1.0 VOLT). SEE "INTERMITTENTS" SECTION B.
■ **CODE 14** • IGNITION ON. • ENGINE STOPPED. • "SCAN" COOLANT TEMPERATURE.	HARD FAILURE - "SCAN" TOOL READS ABOVE 135°C. CIRCUIT SHORTED TO GROUND OR FAULTY SENSOR. SEE CODE CHART 14. INTERMITTENT CODE - "SCAN" TOOL READS ENGINE TEMP. IN DEGREES CENTIGRADE. AFTER ENGINE IS STARTED, THE TEMPERATURE SHOULD RISE STEADILY TO ABOUT 90°C THEN STABILIZE WHEN THERMOSTAT OPENS. SEE "INTERMITTENTS" SECTION B.
■ **CODE 15** • IGNITION ON. • ENGINE STOPPED. • "SCAN" COOLANT TEMPERATURE.	HARD FAILURE - "SCAN" TOOL READS BELOW -30°C. CIRCUIT OPEN OR FAULTY SENSOR. SEE CODE CHART 15. INTERMITTENT CODE - "SCAN" TOOL READS ENGINE COOLANT TEMPERATURE IN DEGREES CENTIGRADE. AFTER ENGINE IS STARTED, THE TEMPERATURE SHOULD RISE STEADILY TO ABOUT 90°C, THEN STABILIZE WHEN THERMOSTAT OPENS. SEE "INTERMITTENTS" SECTION B.

"SCAN" DIAGNOSTIC CIRCUIT CHECK
(Page 4 of 6)
(CODE DEFINITIONS)

CODES	DEFINITION
■ **CODE 24** • ENGINE RUNNING. • DRIVE WHEELS TURNING. • "SCAN" MPH.	HARD FAILURE - "SCAN" TOOL READS 0 MPH. IF SPEEDOMETER IS WORKING OK, THEN THE VSS SIGNAL INPUT IS OPEN, SHORTED TO GROUND, OR THE BUFFER IS DEFECTIVE. SEE CODE CHART 24. INTERMITTENT CODE - "SCAN" TOOL READING SHOULD CLOSELY MATCH WITH SPEEDOMETER READING WITH DRIVE WHEELS TURNING. SEE 'INTERMITTENTS' SECTION B.
■ **CODE 25** • IGNITION "ON". • ENGINE STOPPED. • "SCAN" MAT TEMPERATURE.	HARD FAILURE - "SCAN" TOOL READS ABOVE 150°C. CIRCUIT SHORTED TO GROUND OR FAULTY SENSOR. SEE CODE CHART 25. INTERMITTENT CODE - "SCAN" TOOL READS TEMPERATURE OF THE AIR ENTERING THE ENGINE. SHOULD READ CLOSE TO AMBIENT AIR TEMPERATURE WHEN ENGINE IS COLD, AND RISE AS TEMPERATURE INCREASES. SEE "INTERMITTENTS" SECTION B.
■ **CODE 32**	HARD FAILURE - THE "SCAN" TOOL IS NOT USEFUL IN DIAGNOSING CODE 32 PROBLEMS. SEE CODE CHART 32 IF CODE WAS STORED IN MEMORY.
■ **CODE 33 & 34** - CLEAR CODES START ENGINE AND RECHECK FOR 'SERVICE ENGINE SOON" LIGHT. LIGHT "ON - CODE 33 OR 34 - SEE CODE CHART 33 OR 34. LIGHT OFF - PROBLEM IS INTERMITTENT SEE SECTION B "INTERMITTENTS".	HARD FAILURE - "SCAN" TOOL READS DEFAULT VALUE BASED ON RPM AND TPS. DIFFICULT TO USE "SCAN" TO DIAGNOSE. INTERMITTENT CODE - "SCAN" TOOL READS AIR FLOW AND DISPLAYS IN GRAMS PER SECOND. SHOULD READ BETWEEN 5-8 ON A FULLY WARMED UP IDLING ENGINE. VALUES SHOULD CHANGE RATHER QUICKLY ON ACCELERATION, BUT VALUES SHOULD REMAIN FAIRLY STABLE AT ANY GIVEN RPM. SEE "INTERMITTENTS" SECTION B.

MPI TROUBLE DIAGNOSTICS

"SCAN" DIAGNOSTIC CIRCUIT CHECK
(Page 3 of 6)
(CODE DEFINITIONS)

DEFINITION

■ CODE 21
- IGNITION "ON".
- ENGINE STOPPED.
- THROTTLE CLOSED.
- "SCAN" TPS.

OR

- ENGINE IDLING.
- THROTTLE CLOSED.
- "SCAN" TPS.

HARD FAILURE -
"SCAN" TOOL READS OVER 4.5 VOLTS. GROUND WIRE OPEN, SIGNAL LINE SHORTED TO SENSOR REF. LINE, OR FAULTY SENSOR
SEE CODE CHART 21.

OR

HARD FAILURE -
"SCAN" TOOL TOOL READS OVER 2.5 VOLTS. GROUND WIRE OPEN OR FAULTY SENSOR. SEE CODE CHART 21.

INTERMITTENT CODE -
"SCAN" TOOL READS THROTTLE POSITION IN VOLTS. SHOULD READ BETWEEN 020-125 (200 MV AND 1.25 V). WITH THROTTLE CLOSED AND IGNITION ON OR AT IDLE. VOLTAGE SHOULD INCREASE AT A STEADY RATE AS THROTTLE IS MOVED TOWARD WOT. SEE "INTERMITTENTS" SECTION B.

■ CODE 22
- IGNITION "ON".
- ENGINE STOPPED.
- "SCAN" TPS.

HARD FAILURE -
"SCAN" TOOL READS BELOW 020V (200 MV) OPEN OR SHORTED TO GROUND CIRCUIT IN 5V REFERENCE, SIGNAL CIRCUIT OR FAULTY SENSOR. SEE CODE CHART 22.

INTERMITTENT CODE -
"SCAN" TOOL READS THROTTLE POSITION IN VOLTS. SHOULD READ BETWEEN 020-125 (200 MV AND 1.25 V). WITH THROTTLE CLOSED AND IGNITION ON OR AT IDLE. VOLTAGE SHOULD INCREASE AT A STEADY RATE AS THROTTLE IS MOVED TOWARD WOT. SEE "INTERMITTENTS" SECTION B.

■ CODE 23
- IGNITION "ON".
- ENGINE STOPPED.
- "SCAN" MAT TEMPERATURE.

HARD FAILURE -
"SCAN" TOOL READS BELOW -30°C. CIRCUIT OPEN OR FAULTY SENSOR. SEE CODE CHART 23.

INTERMITTENT CODE -
"SCAN" TOOL READS TEMPERATURE OF THE AIR ENTERING THE ENGINE. SHOULD READ CLOSE TO AMBIENT AIR TEMPERATURE WHEN ENGINE IS COLD, AND RISE AS TEMPERATURE INCREASES. SEE "INTERMITTENTS" SECTION B.

"SCAN" DIAGNOSTIC CIRCUIT CHECK
(Page 5 of 6)
(CODE DEFINITIONS)

CODES

DEFINITION

■ CODE 42
- CLEAR CODES. START AND IDLE ENGINE FOR 1 MINUTE.
- IF NO "SERVICE ENGINE SOON" LIGHT, REFER TO INTERMITTENTS IN SECTION "B".

HARD FAILURE -
"SERVICE ENGINE SOON" ON, SCAN TOOL INDICATES CODE 42. SEE CODE CHART 42.
INTERMITTENT CODE -
THE SCAN DOES NOT HAVE THE ABILITY TO HELP DIAGNOSE A CODE 42 PROBLEM. SEE "INTERMITTENTS" SECTION B.

■ CODE 43
- "SCAN" TOOL IN SPECIAL MODE.
- ENGINE IDLING AT 1000 RPM.
- "SCAN" KNOCK RETARD OR OLD PA3.

HARD FAILURE -
KNOCK RETARD OR (OLD PA3) WILL DISPLAY NUMBERS THAT ARE CONSTANTLY CHANGING (0TO 255). FAULTY ESC CIRCUIT. SEE CODE CHART 43.

INTERMITTENT CODE -
NUMBERS SHOULD INCREASE WHEN KNOCK IS BEING DETECTED. SEE "INTERMITTENTS" SECTION B.

■ CODE 44
- "SCAN" TOOL IN SPECIAL MODE.
- ENGINE IDLING AT 1000 RPM.
- COOLANT 75° TO 95° C
- "SCAN" OXYGEN SENSOR VOLTAGE.

HARD FAILURE -
"SCAN" TOOL O_2 VOLTAGE CONSISTENTLY BELOW .35V. CAUSED BY A LEAN EXHAUST OR SIGNAL CIRCUIT SHORTED TO GROUND. SEE CODE CHART 44.

INTERMITTENT CODE -
THE "SCAN" TOOL HAS SEVERAL POSITIONS THAT WILL INDICATE THE STATE OF THE EXHAUST GASES. CROSSCOUNTS, RICH-LEAN INDICATION, O_2 VOLTAGE, INTEGRATOR, AND BLOCK LEARN. SEE "SCAN" POSITION INFORMATION IN INTRODUCTION.

■ CODE 45
- "SCAN" TOOL IN "SPECIAL" MODE.
- ENGINE IDLING AT 1000 RPM.
- COOLANT 75° TO 95° C
- "SCAN" OXYGEN SENSOR VOLTAGE.

HARD FAILURE -
"SCAN" O_2 VOLTAGE CONSISTENTLY ABOVE .55V. RICH EXHAUST CAUSES A HIGH O_2 VOLTAGE. SEE CODE CHART 45.

INTERMITTENT CODE -
THE "SCAN" HAS SEVERAL POSITIONS THAT WILL INDICATE THE STATE OF THE EXHAUST GASES. CROSSCOUNTS, RICH-LEAN INDICATION, O_2 VOLTAGE, INTEGRATOR, AND BLOCK LEARN. SEE "SCAN" POSITION INFORMATION IN INTRODUCTION.

"SCAN" DIAGNOSTIC CIRCUIT CHECK
(CODE DEFINITIONS)
(Page 6 of 6)

CODES

DEFINITION

■ CODE 51
- CLEAR CODES
- START ENGINE
- CHECK FOR CODE

HARD FAILURE -
CODE 51 RESETS WHICH INDICATES A FAULTY MEM/CAL. SEE CODE CHART 51.

■ CODE 52
- CLEAR CODES
- START ENGINE
- CHECK FOR CODE

HARD FAILURE -
CODE 52 RESETS WHICH INDICATES CALPAK IS MISSING OR FAILED.

■ CODE 55
- CLEAR CODES
- START ENGINE
- CHECK FOR CODE

HARD FAILURE -
CODE 55 RESETS WHICH INDICATES THE ECM IS FAULTY. REPLACE ECM.

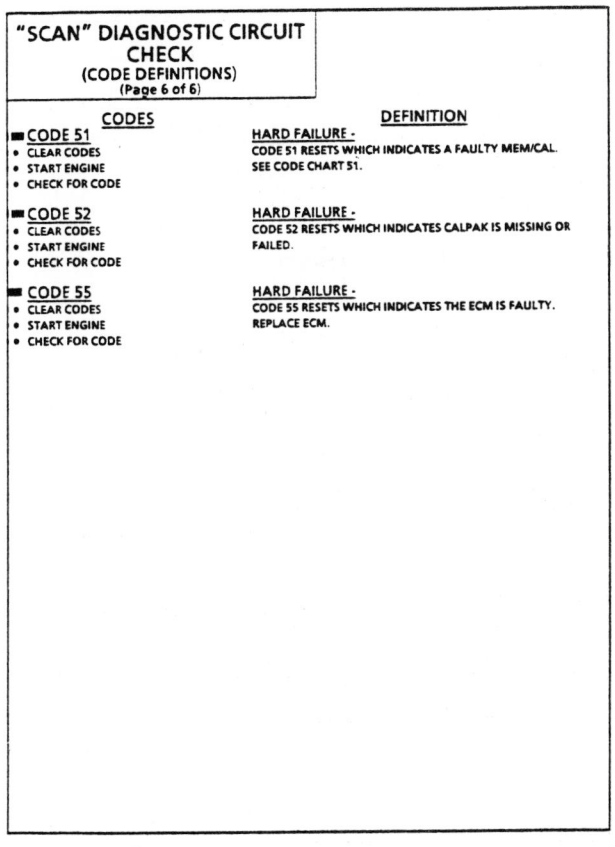

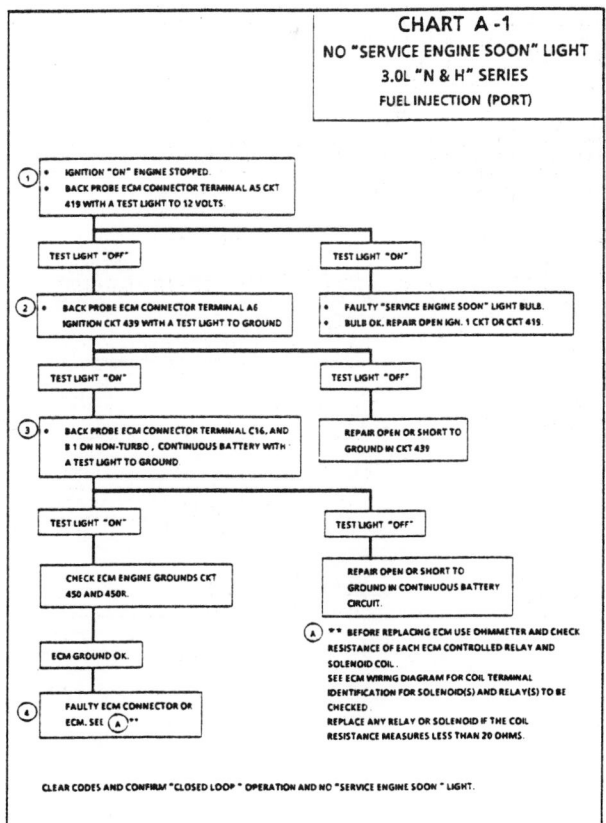

CHART A-1
NO "SERVICE ENGINE SOON" LIGHT
3.0L "N & H" SERIES
FUEL INJECTION (PORT)

MPI TROUBLE DIAGNOSTICS

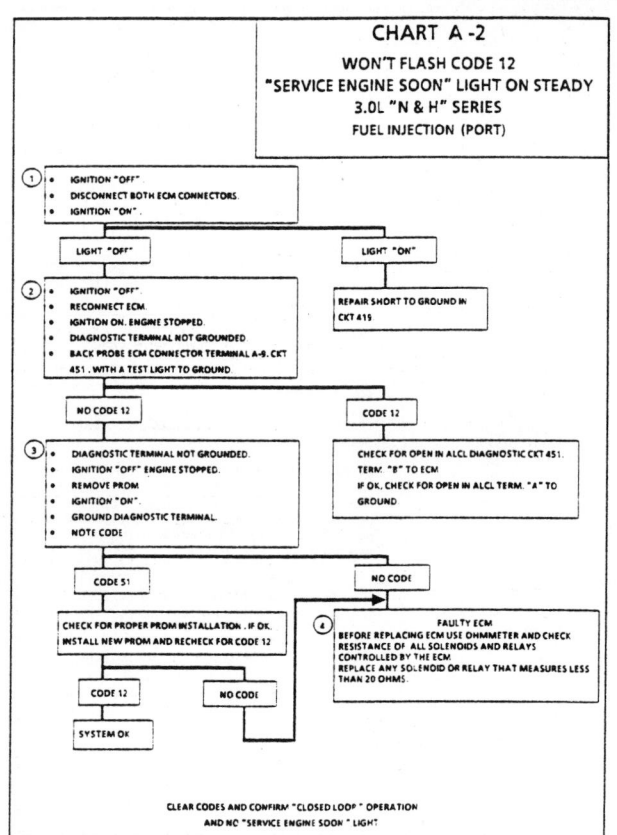

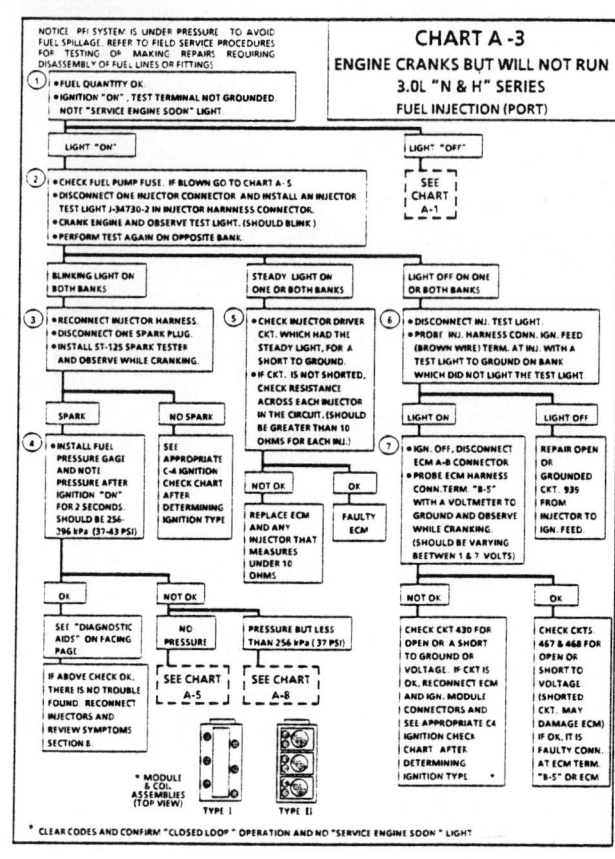

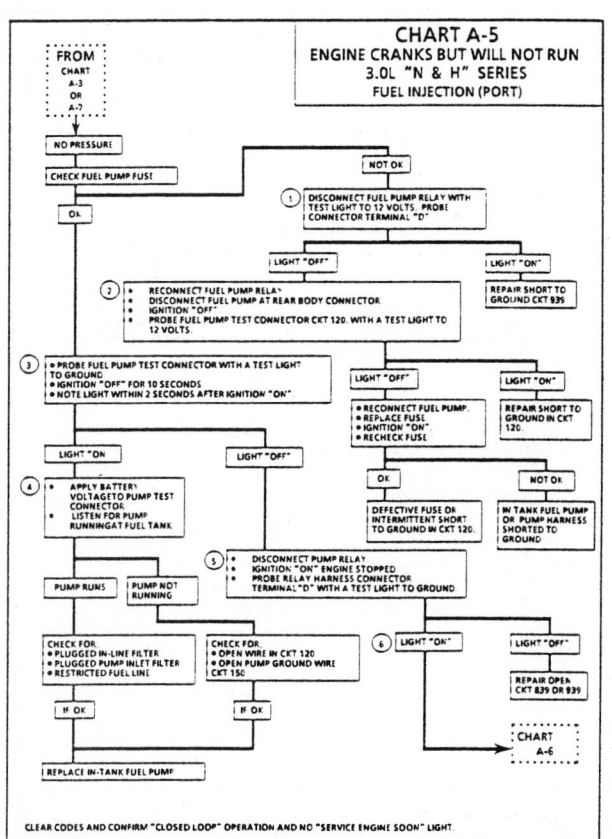

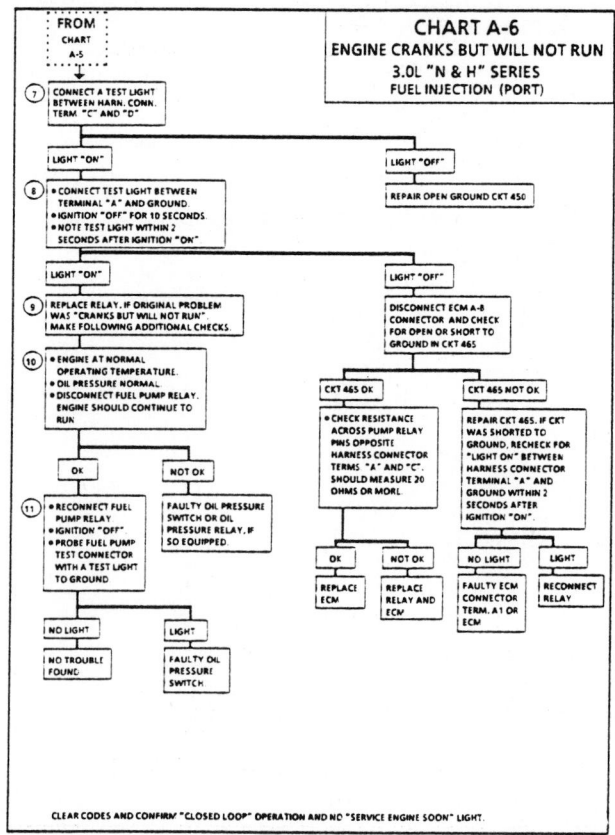

MPI TROUBLE DIAGNOSTICS

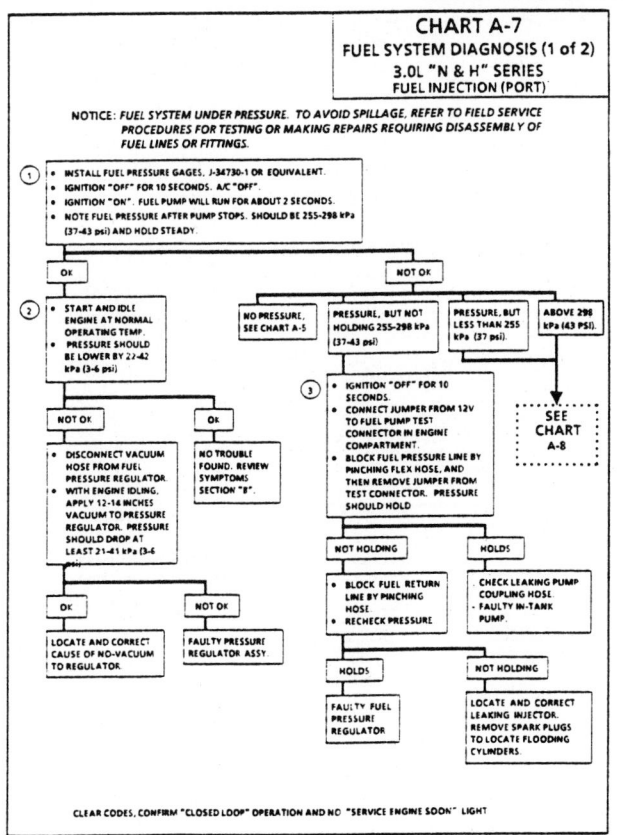

CHART A-7
FUEL SYSTEM DIAGNOSIS (1 of 2)
3.0L "N & H" SERIES
FUEL INJECTION (PORT)

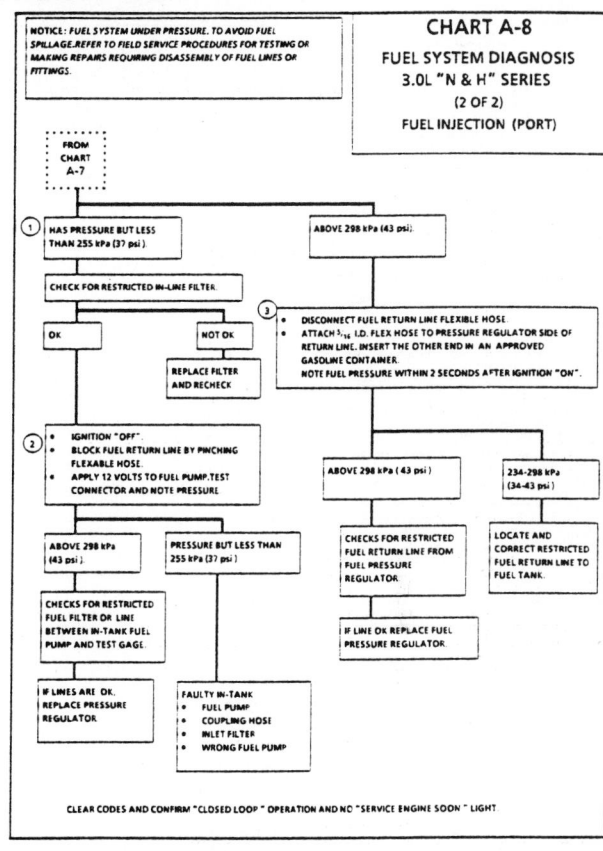

CHART A-8
FUEL SYSTEM DIAGNOSIS
3.0L "N & H" SERIES
(2 of 2)
FUEL INJECTION (PORT)

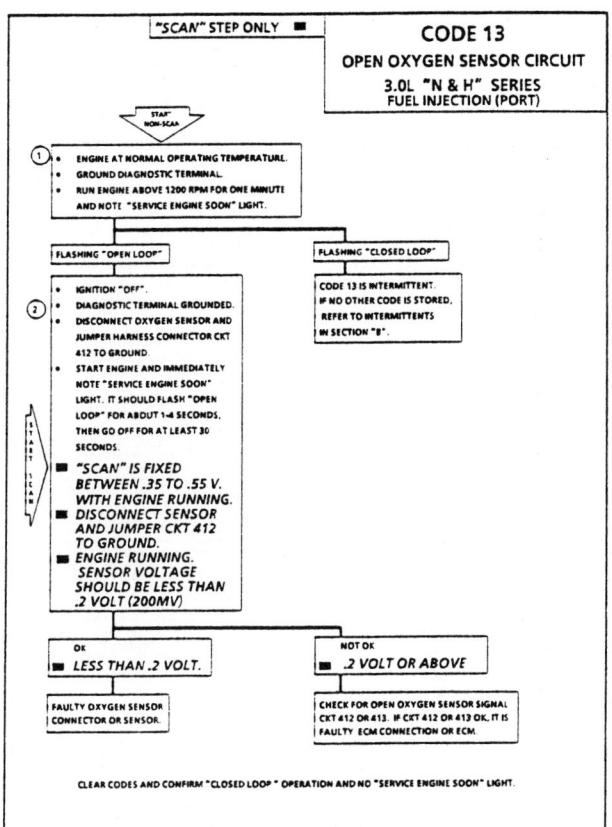

CODE 13
OPEN OXYGEN SENSOR CIRCUIT
3.0L "N & H" SERIES
FUEL INJECTION (PORT)

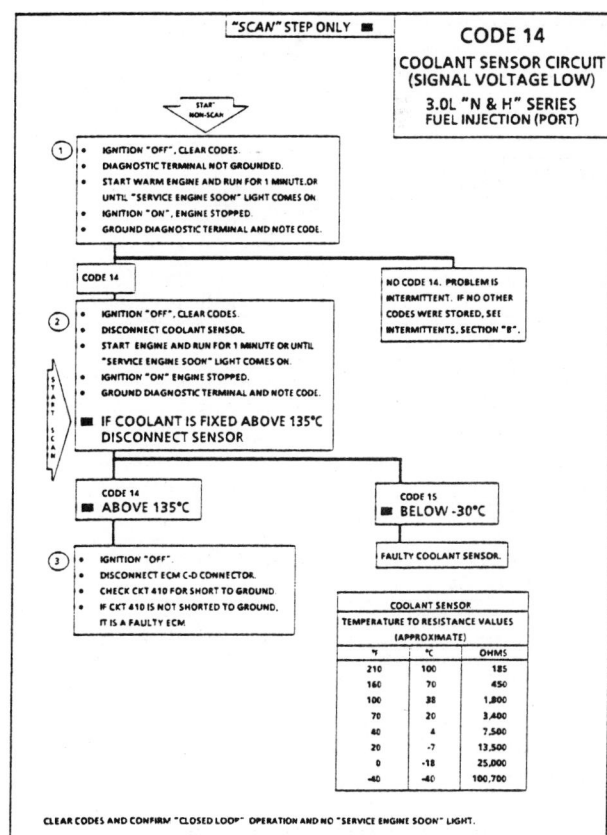

CODE 14
COOLANT SENSOR CIRCUIT
(SIGNAL VOLTAGE LOW)
3.0L "N & H" SERIES
FUEL INJECTION (PORT)

MPI TROUBLE DIAGNOSTICS

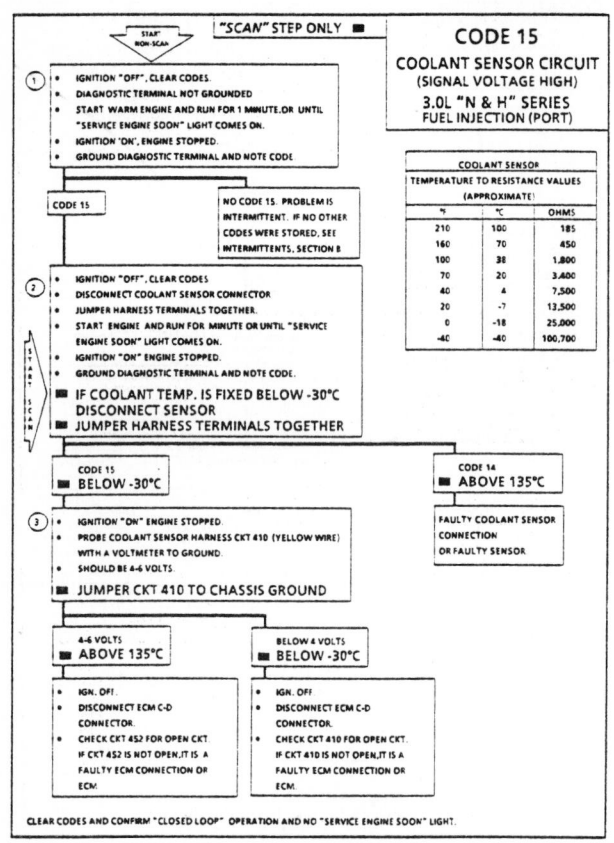

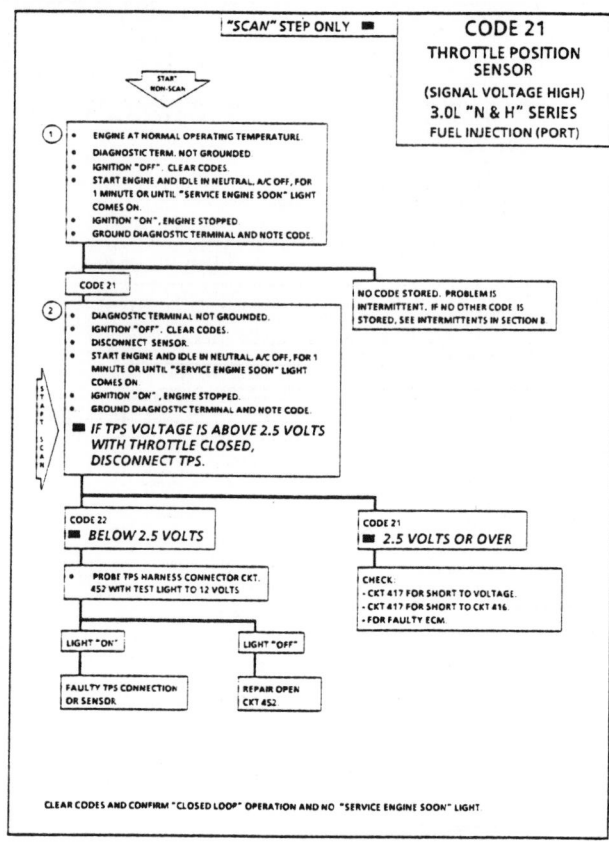

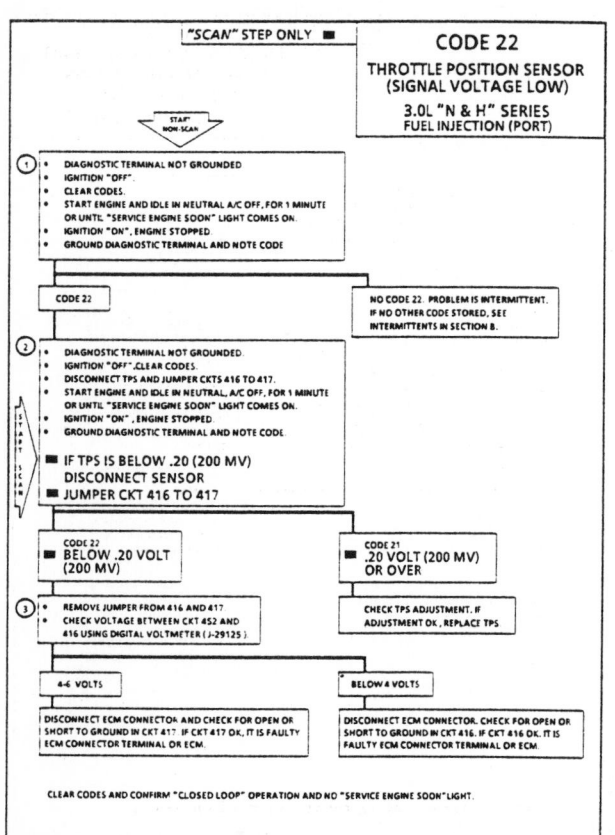

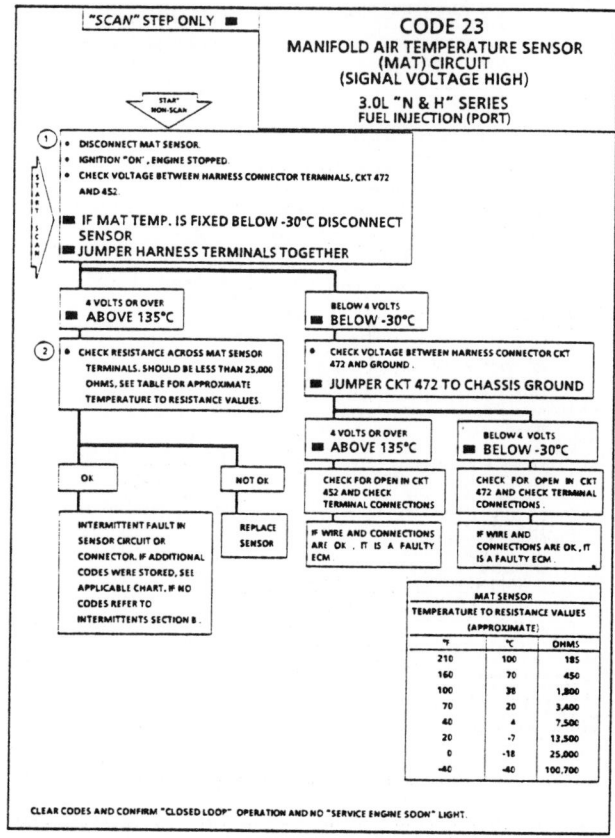

MPI TROUBLE DIAGNOSTICS

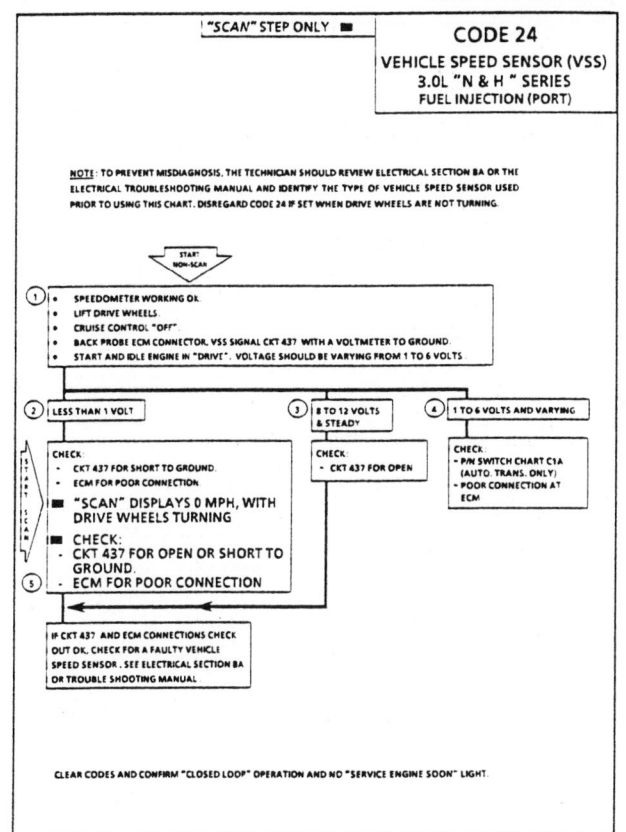

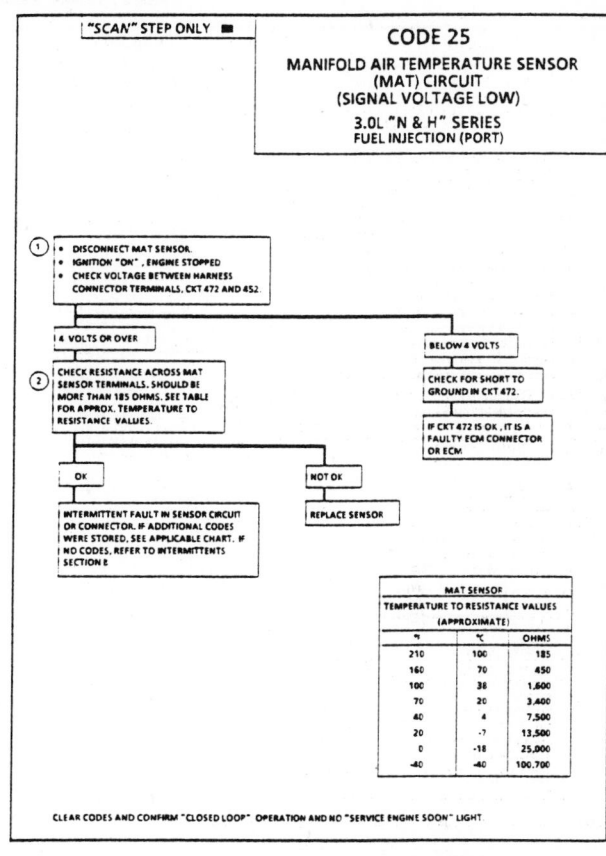

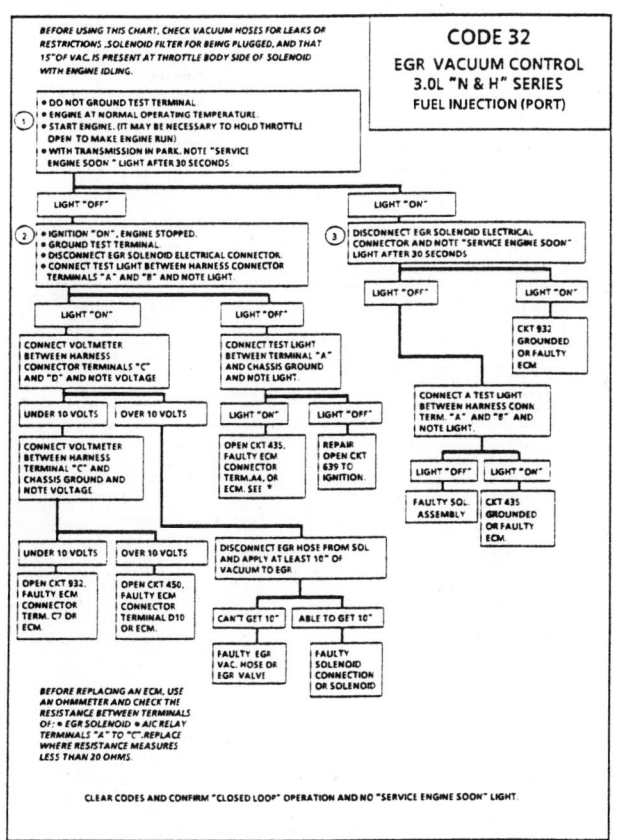

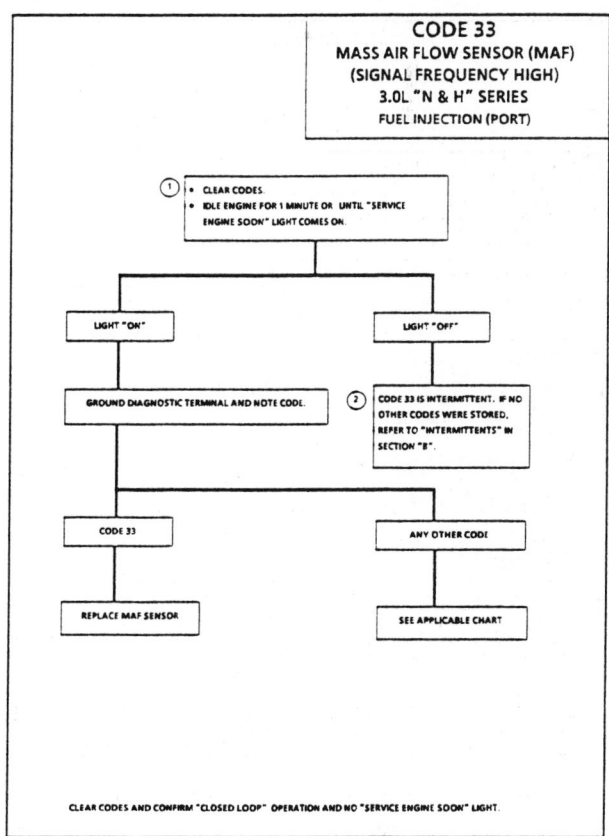

MPI TROUBLE DIAGNOSTICS

CODE 34
MASS AIR FLOW SENSOR (MAF)
(SIGNAL FREQUENCY LOW)
3.0L "N & H" SERIES
FUEL INJECTION (PORT)

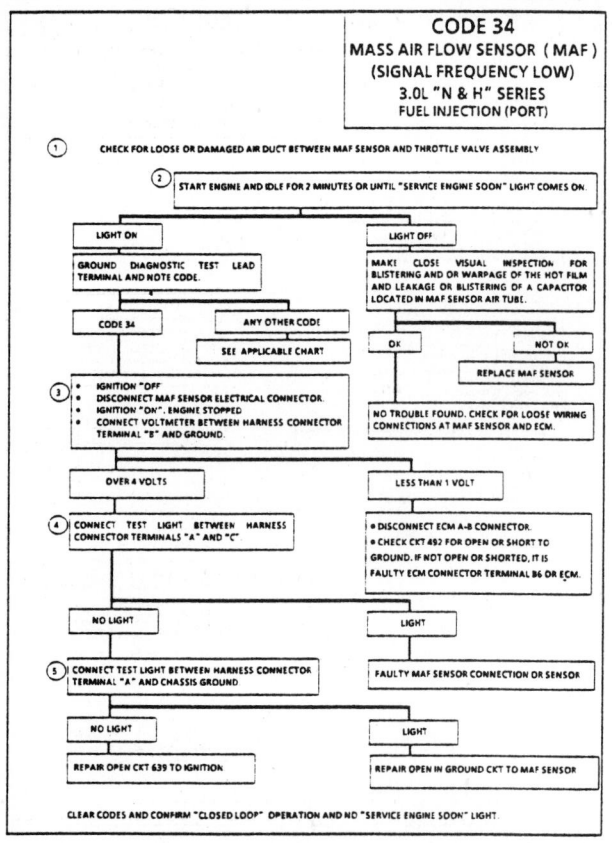

CODE 42
COMPUTER CONTROLLED COIL IGNITION (C 3 1)
3.0L "N & H" SERIES
FUEL INJECTION (PORT)

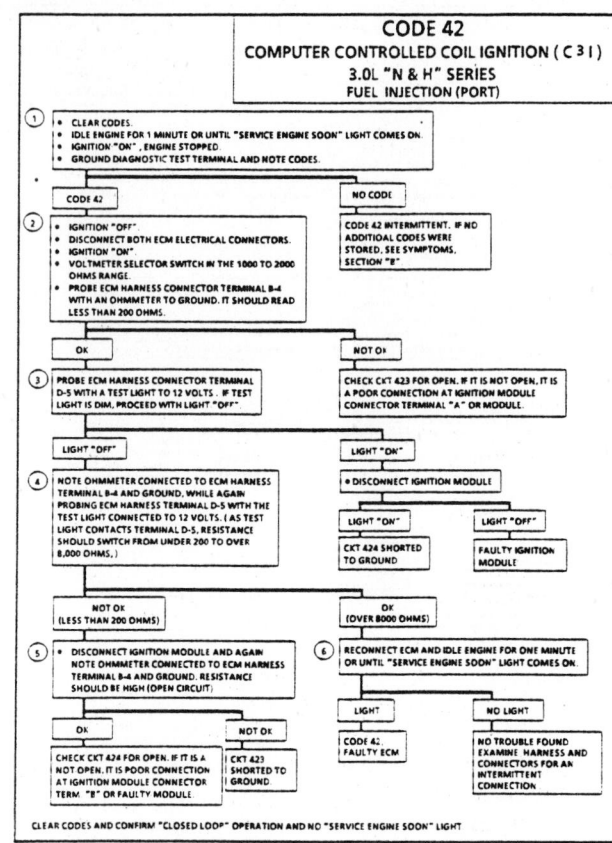

CODE 43
ELECTRONIC SPARK CONTROL (ESC)
3.0L "N & H" SERIES
FUEL INJECTION (PORT)

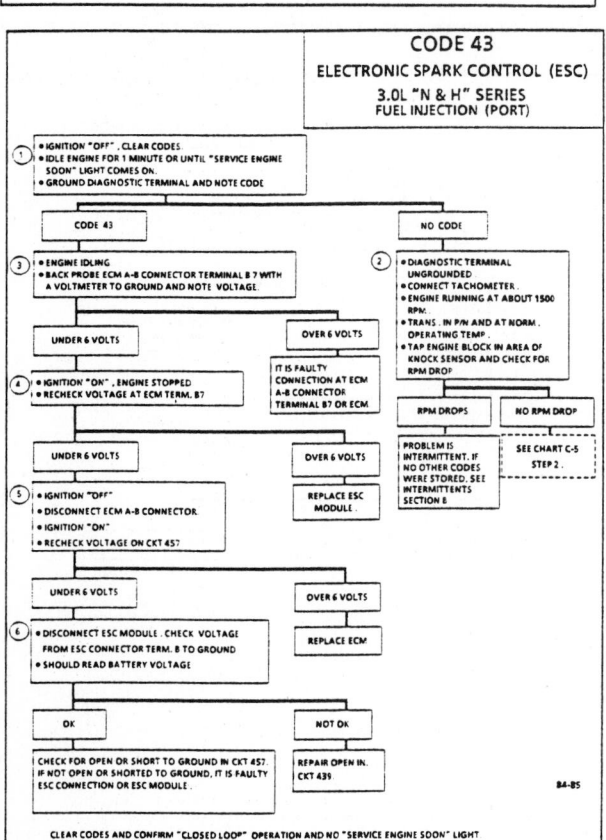

"SCAN" STEP ONLY ■
CODE 44
LEAN EXHAUST INDICATION
3.0L "N & H" SERIES
FUEL INJECTION (PORT)

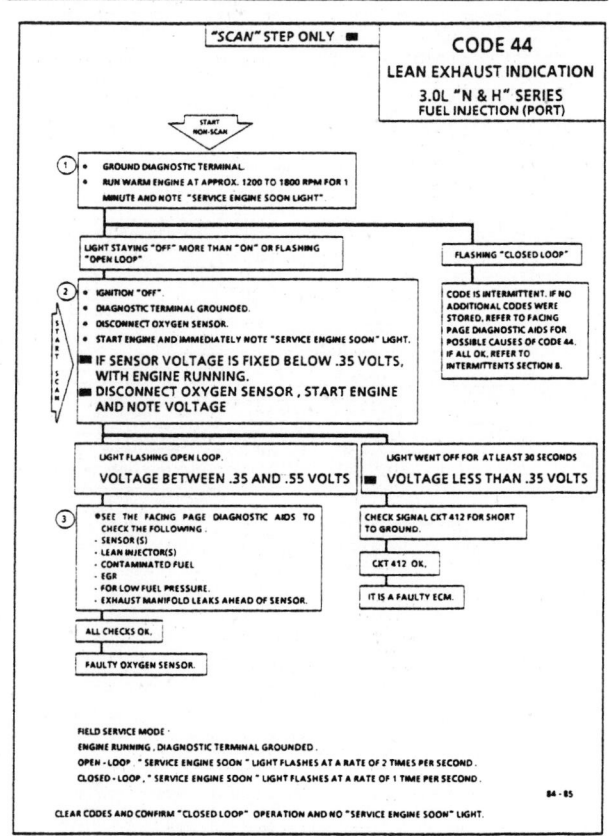

MPI TROUBLE DIAGNOSTICS

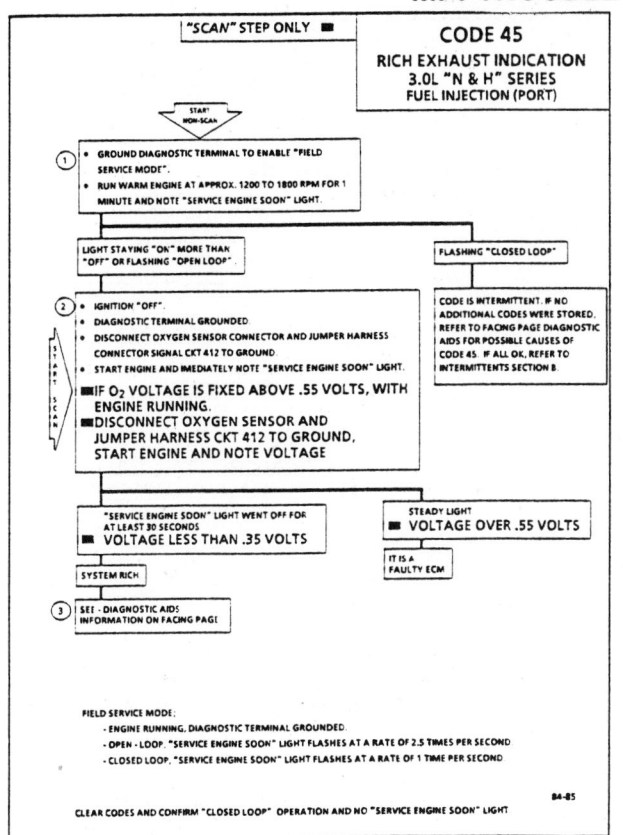

CODE 45
RICH EXHAUST INDICATION
3.0L "N & H" SERIES
FUEL INJECTION (PORT)

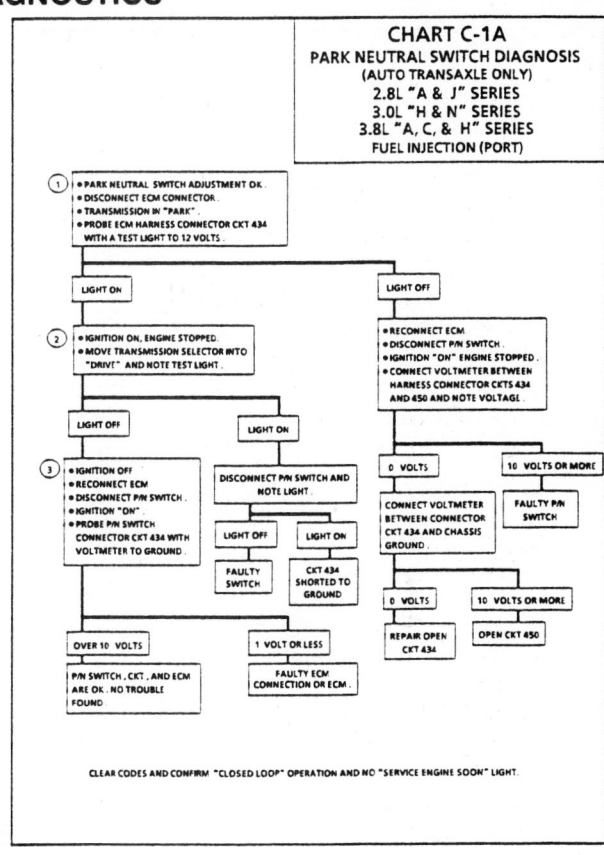

CHART C-1A
PARK NEUTRAL SWITCH DIAGNOSIS
(AUTO TRANSAXLE ONLY)
2.8L "A & J" SERIES
3.0L "H & N" SERIES
3.8L "A, C, & H" SERIES
FUEL INJECTION (PORT)

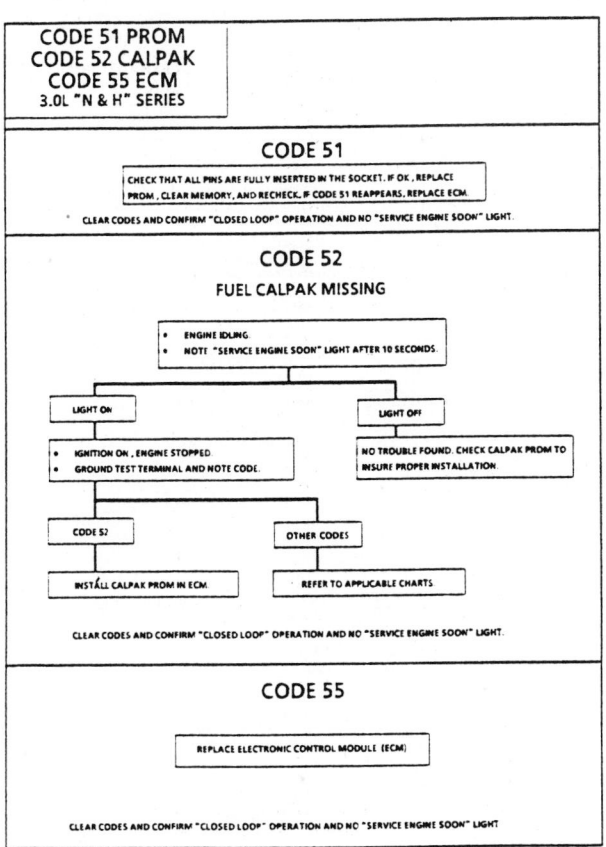

CODE 51 PROM
CODE 52 CALPAK
CODE 55 ECM
3.0L "N & H" SERIES

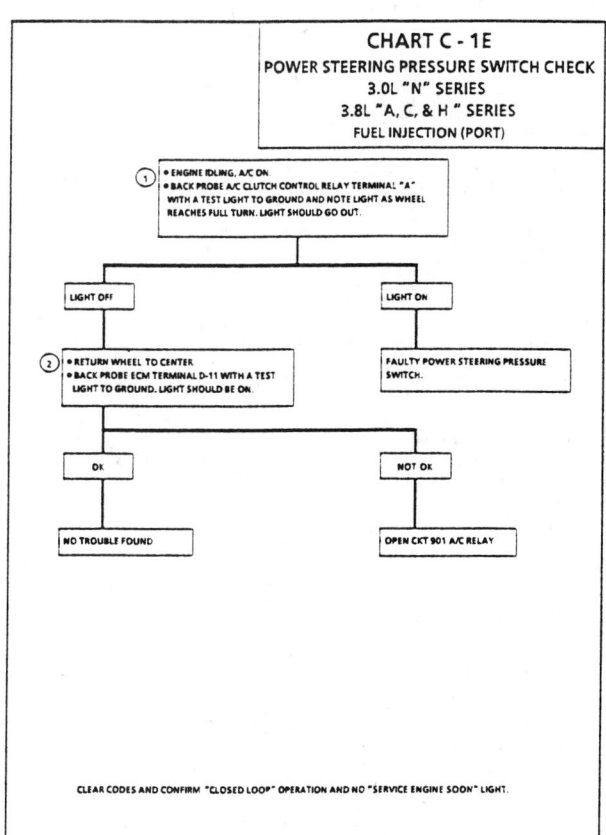

CHART C - 1E
POWER STEERING PRESSURE SWITCH CHECK
3.0L "N" SERIES
3.8L "A, C, & H" SERIES
FUEL INJECTION (PORT)

MPI TROUBLE DIAGNOSTICS

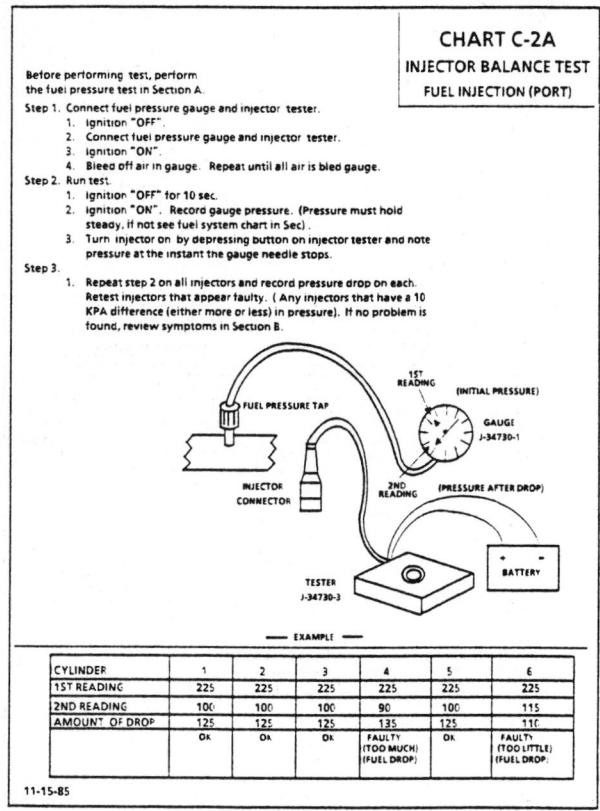

CHART C-2A
INJECTOR BALANCE TEST
FUEL INJECTION (PORT)

Before performing test, perform the fuel pressure test in Section A.

Step 1. Connect fuel pressure gauge and injector tester.
1. Ignition "OFF".
2. Connect fuel pressure gauge and injector tester.
3. Ignition "ON".
4. Bleed off air in gauge. Repeat until all air is bled gauge.

Step 2. Run test.
1. Ignition "OFF" for 10 sec.
2. Ignition "ON". Record gauge pressure. (Pressure must hold steady, if not see fuel system chart in Sec).
3. Turn injector on by depressing button on injector tester and note pressure at the instant the gauge needle stops.

Step 3.
1. Repeat step 2 on all injectors and record pressure drop on each. Retest injectors that appear faulty. (Any injectors that have a 10 KPA difference (either more or less) in pressure). If no problem is found, review symptoms in Section B.

— EXAMPLE —

CYLINDER	1	2	3	4	5	6
1ST READING	225	225	225	225	225	225
2ND READING	100	100	100	90	100	115
AMOUNT OF DROP	125	125	125	135	125	110
	Ok	Ok	Ok	FAULTY (TOO MUCH) (FUEL DROP)	Ok	FAULTY (TOO LITTLE) (FUEL DROP)

11-15-85

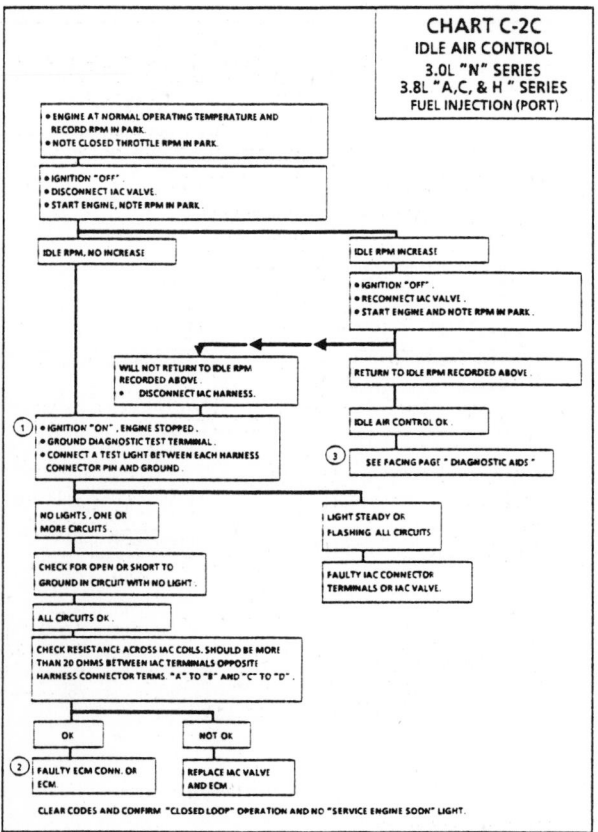

CHART C-2C
IDLE AIR CONTROL
3.0L "N" SERIES
3.8L "A, C, & H" SERIES
FUEL INJECTION (PORT)

CLEAR CODES AND CONFIRM "CLOSED LOOP" OPERATION AND NO "SERVICE ENGINE SOON" LIGHT.

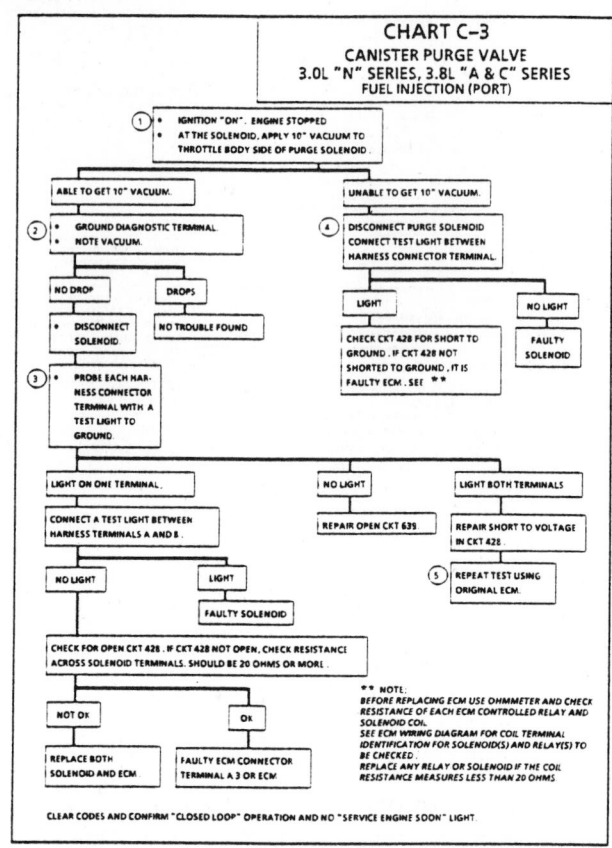

CHART C-3
CANISTER PURGE VALVE
3.0L "N" SERIES, 3.8L "A & C" SERIES
FUEL INJECTION (PORT)

CLEAR CODES AND CONFIRM "CLOSED LOOP" OPERATION AND NO "SERVICE ENGINE SOON" LIGHT.

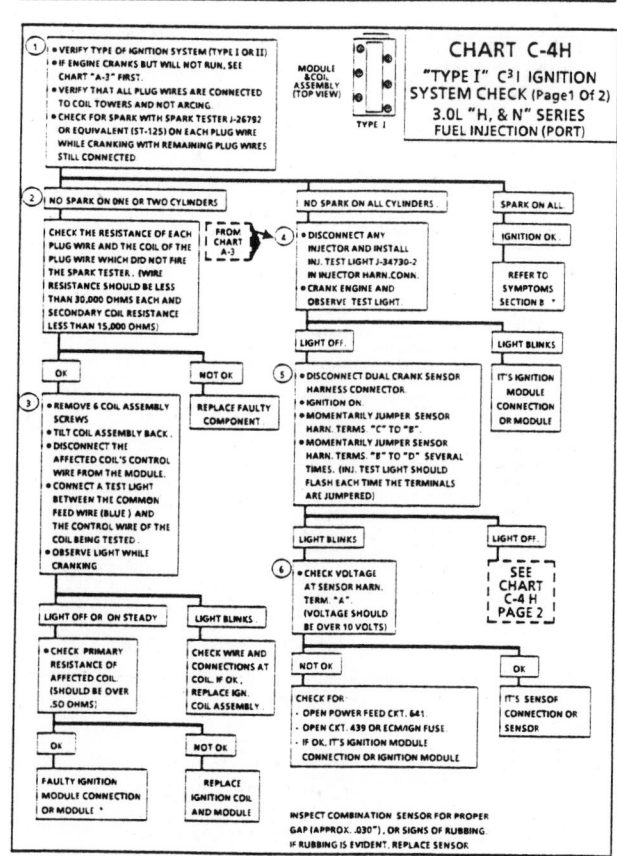

CHART C-4H
"TYPE I" C³I IGNITION
SYSTEM CHECK (Page 1 Of 2)
3.0L "H, & N" SERIES
FUEL INJECTION (PORT)

MPI TROUBLE DIAGNOSTICS

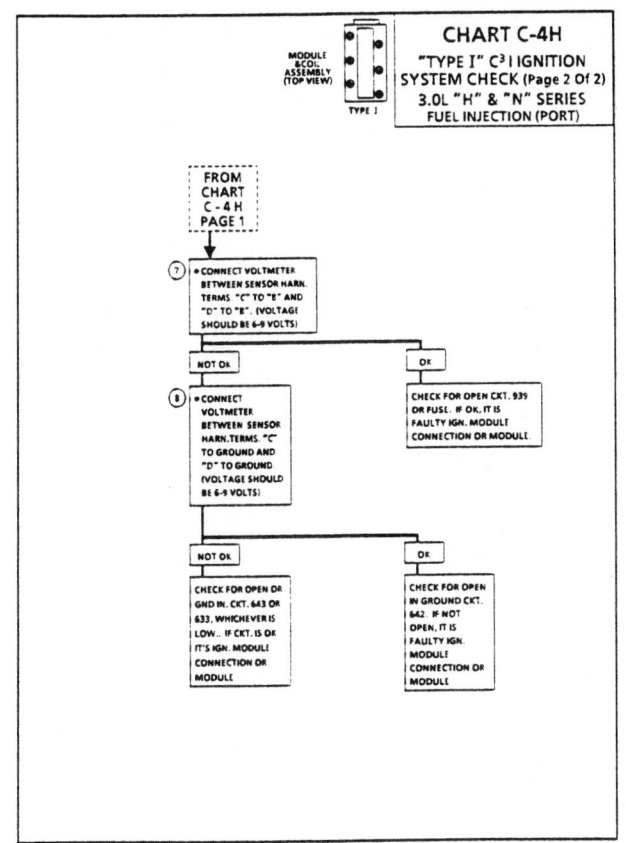

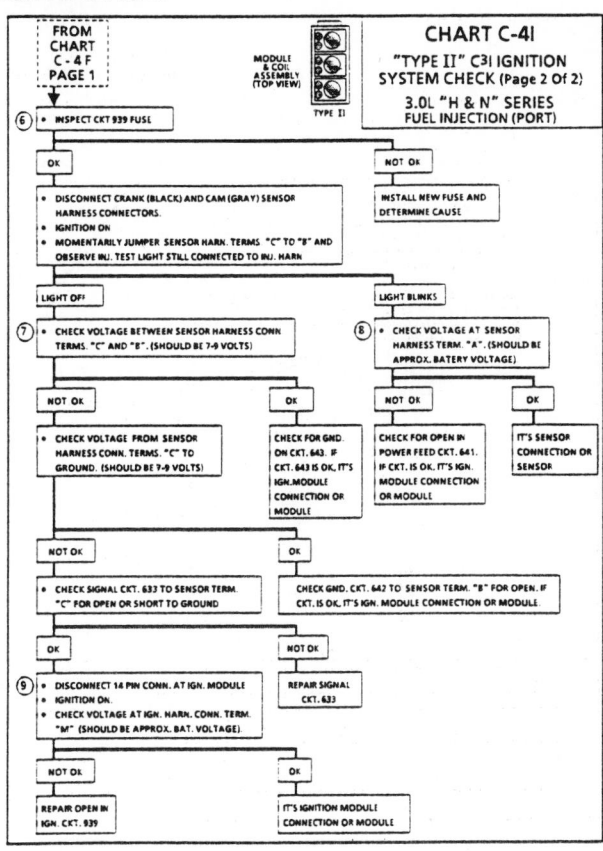

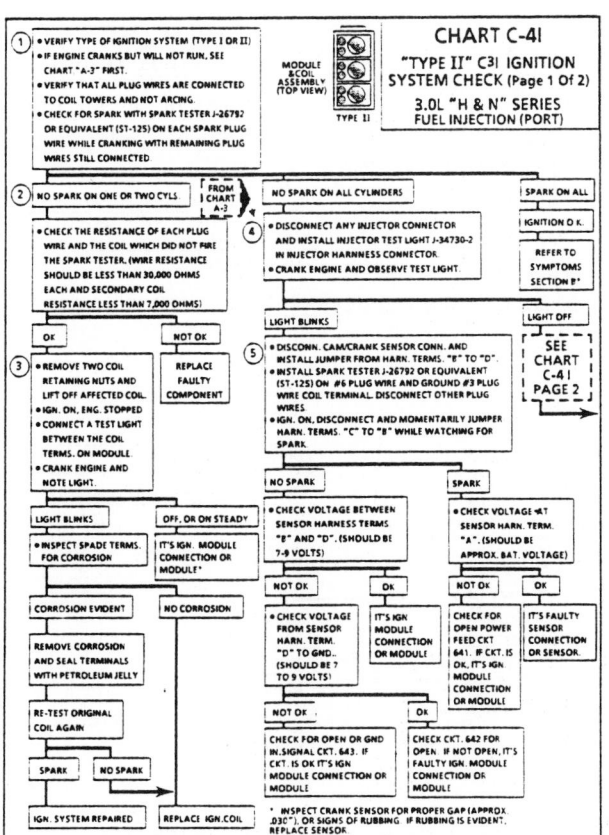

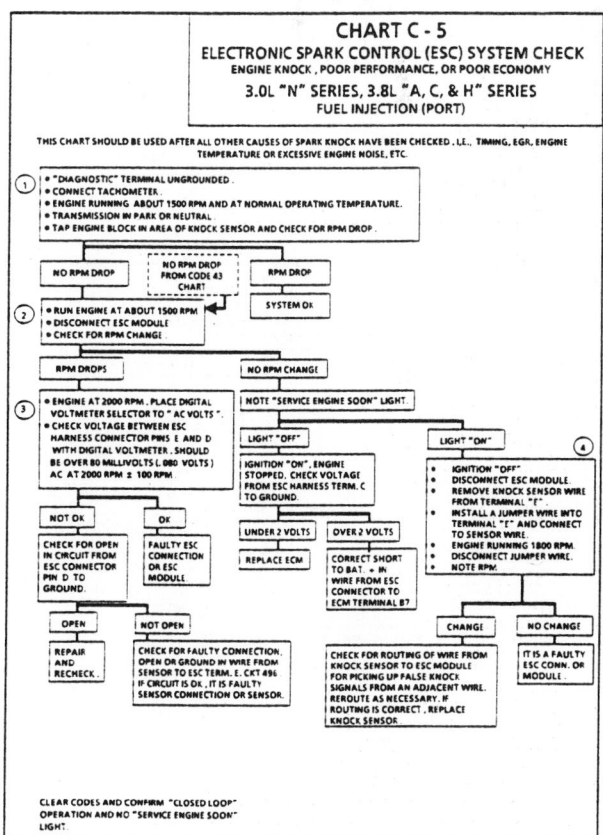

MPI TROUBLE DIAGNOSTICS

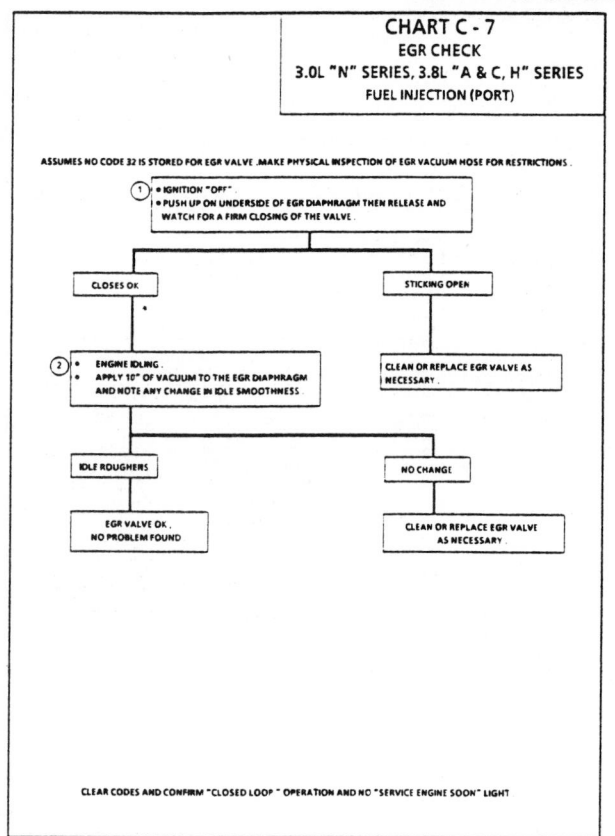

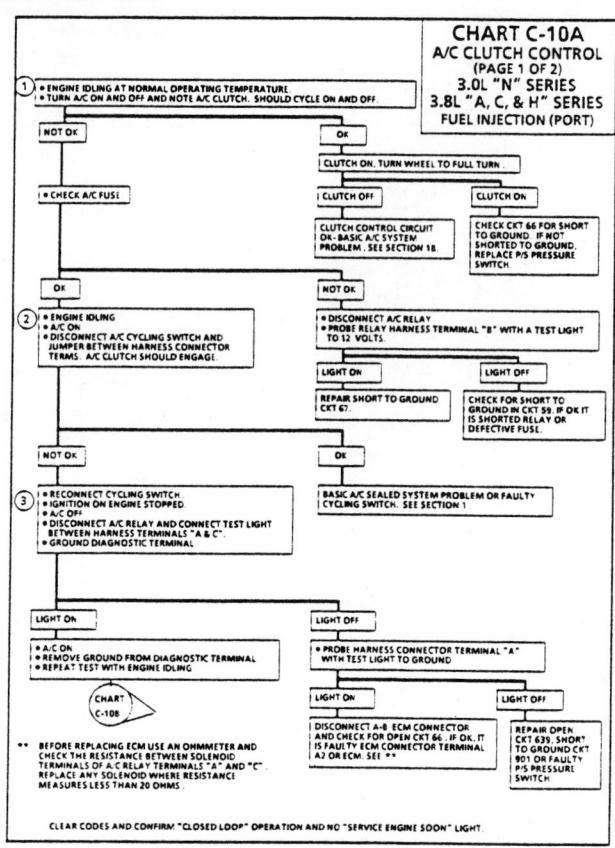

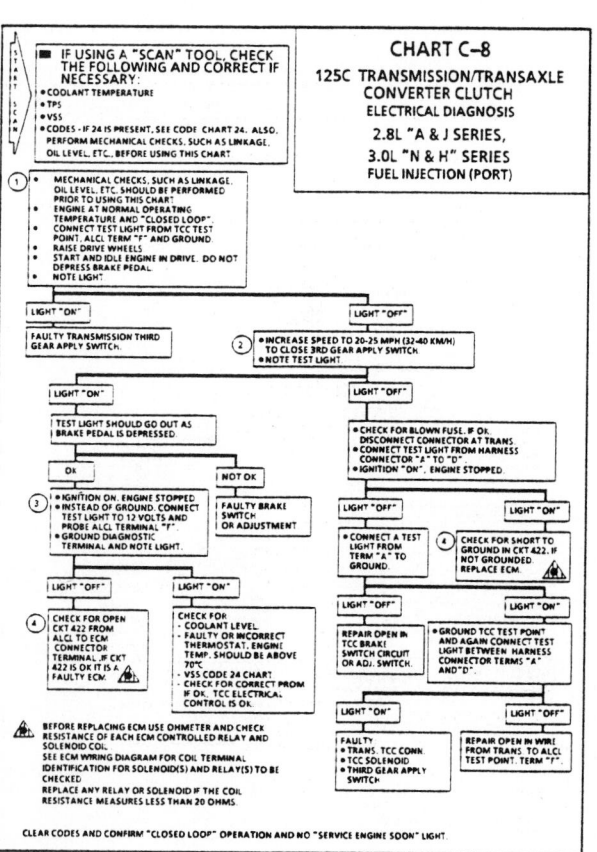

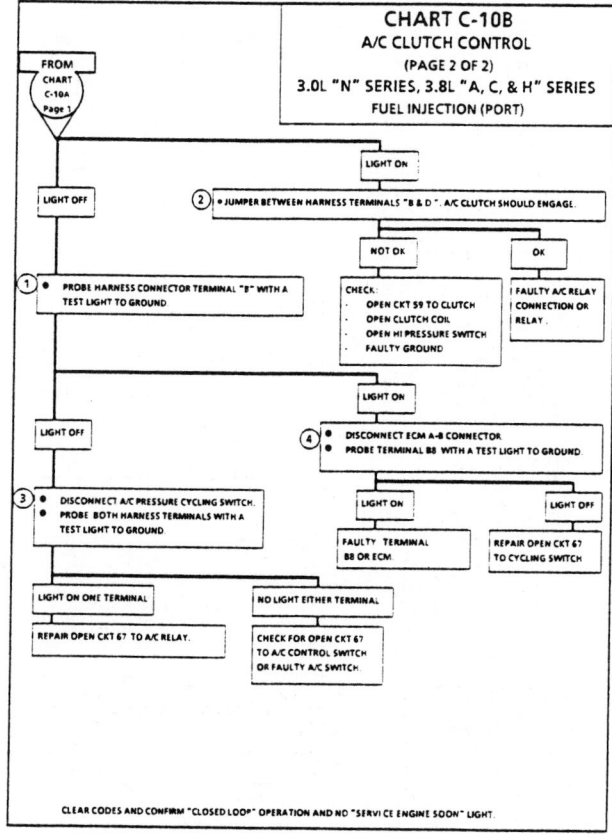

MPI TROUBLE DIAGNOSTICS

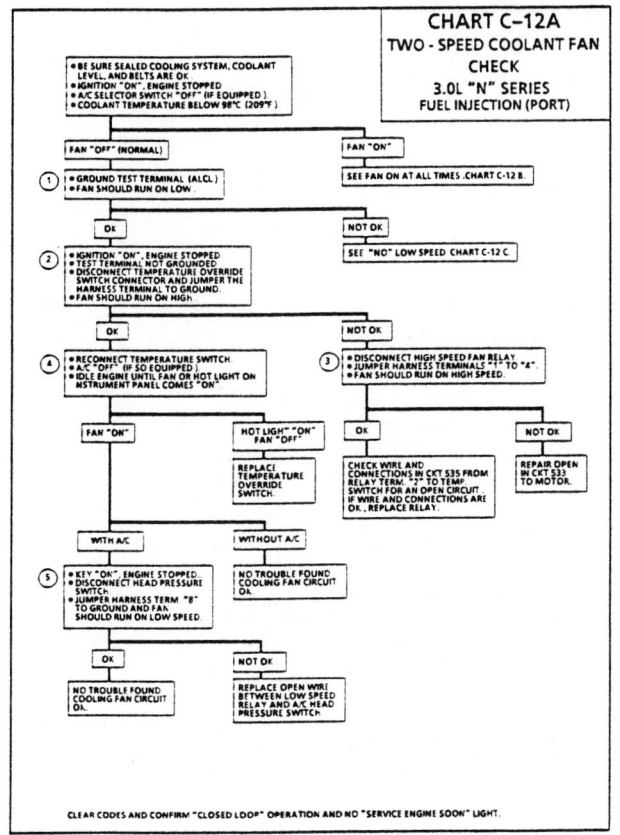

CHART C–12A
TWO - SPEED COOLANT FAN CHECK
3.0L "N" SERIES
FUEL INJECTION (PORT)

CLEAR CODES AND CONFIRM "CLOSED LOOP" OPERATION AND NO "SERVICE ENGINE SOON" LIGHT.

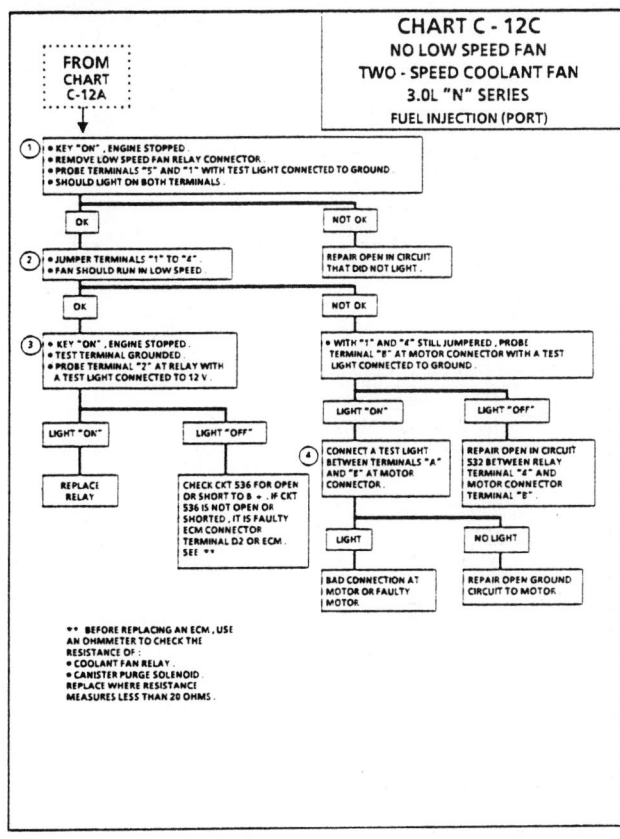

CHART C - 12C
NO LOW SPEED FAN
TWO - SPEED COOLANT FAN
3.0L "N" SERIES
FUEL INJECTION (PORT)

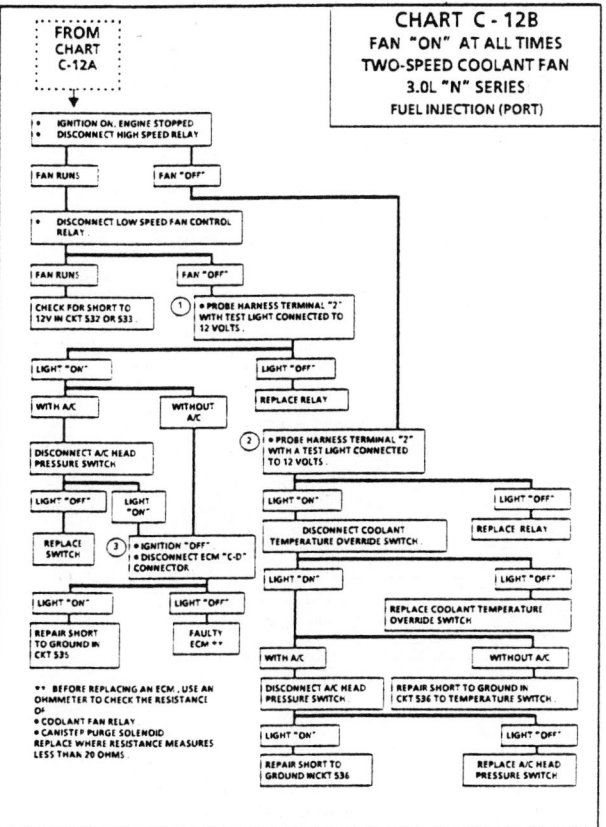

CHART C - 12B
FAN "ON" AT ALL TIMES
TWO-SPEED COOLANT FAN
3.0L "N" SERIES
FUEL INJECTION (PORT)

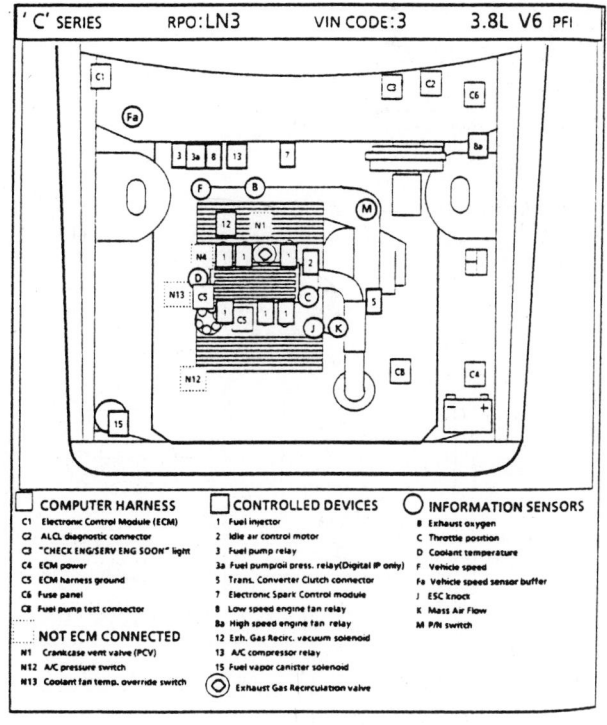

'C' SERIES   RPO: LN3   VIN CODE: 3   3.8L V6 PFI

COMPUTER HARNESS
C1 Electronic Control Module (ECM)
C2 ALCL diagnostic connector
C3 "CHECK ENG/SERV ENG SOON" light
C4 ECM power
C5 ECM harness ground
C6 Fuse panel
C8 Fuel pump test connector

NOT ECM CONNECTED
N1 Crankcase vent valve (PCV)
N12 A/C pressure switch
N13 Coolant fan temp. override switch

CONTROLLED DEVICES
1 Fuel injector
2 Idle air control motor
3 Fuel pump relay
3a Fuel pump/oil press. relay(Digital IP only)
5 Trans. Converter Clutch connector
7 Electronic Spark Control module
8 Low speed engine fan relay
8a High speed engine fan relay
12 Exh. Gas Recirc. vacuum solenoid
13 A/C compressor relay
15 Fuel vapor canister solenoid

INFORMATION SENSORS
B Exhaust oxygen
C Throttle position
D Coolant temperature
F Vehicle speed
Fa Vehicle speed sensor buffer
J ESC knock
K Mass Air Flow
M P/N switch

Exhaust Gas Recirculation valve

MPI TROUBLE DIAGNOSTICS

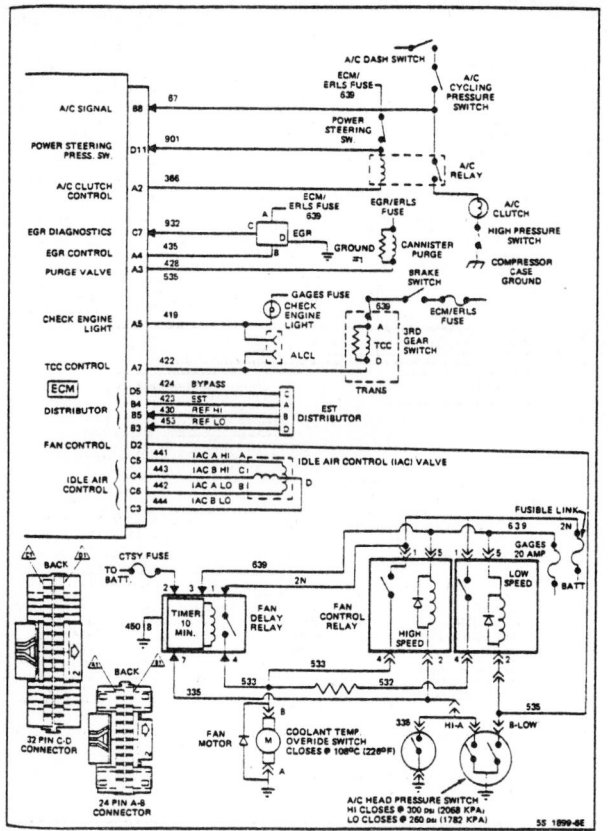

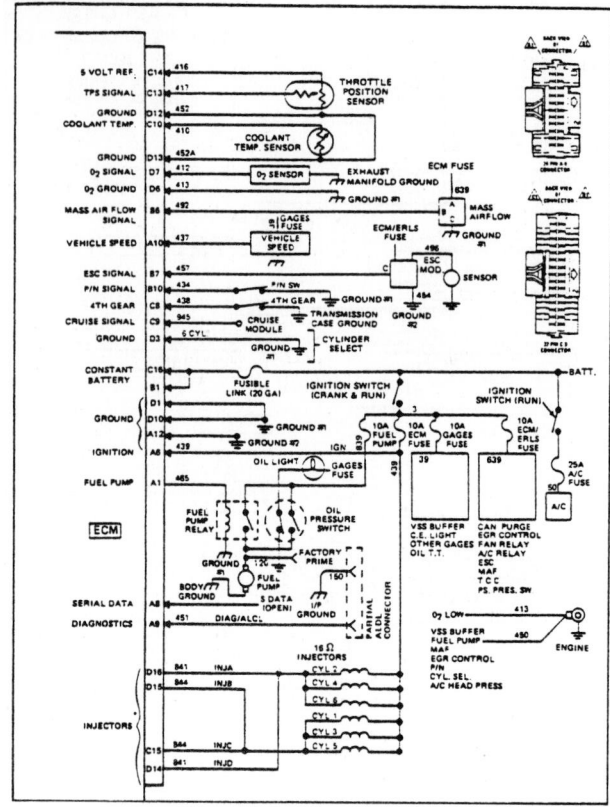

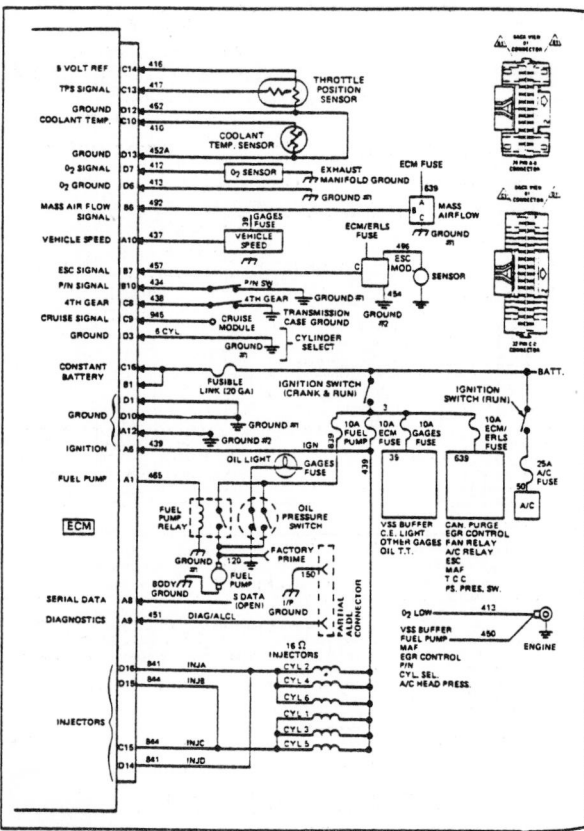

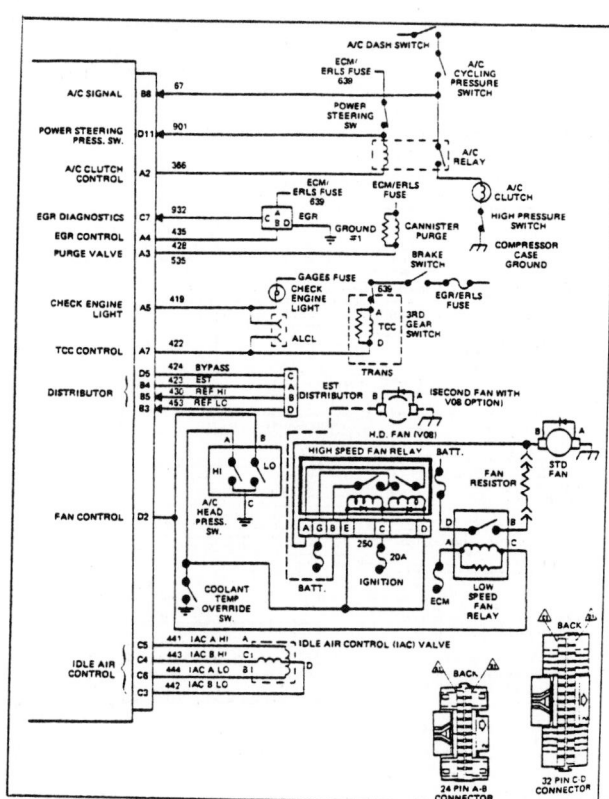

MPI TROUBLE DIAGNOSTICS

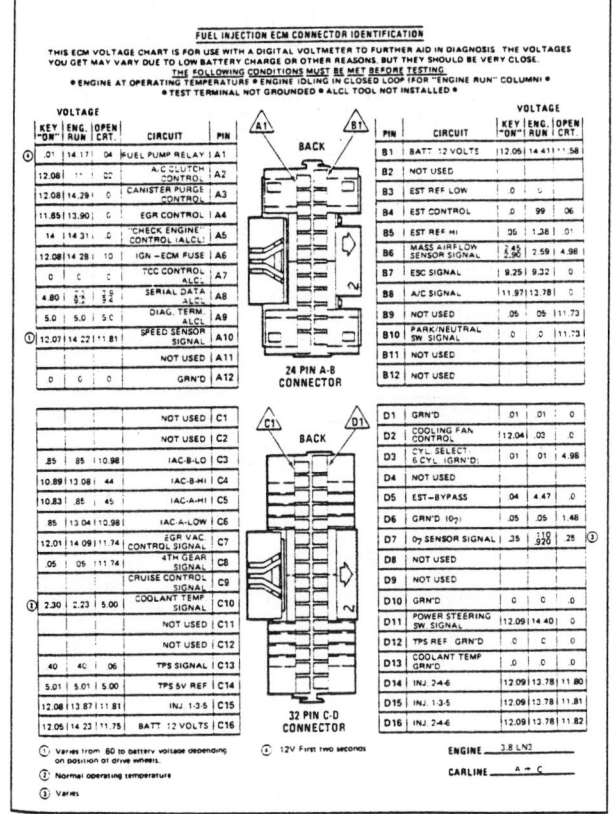

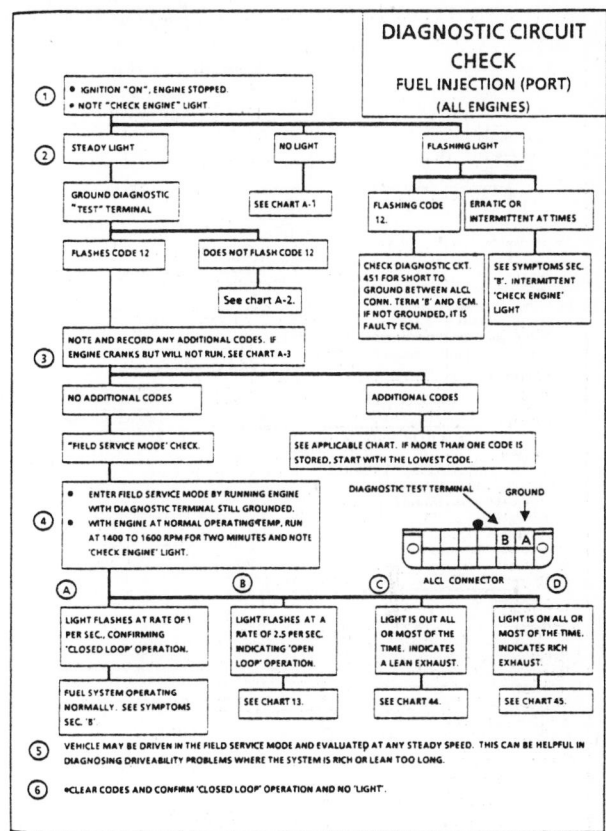

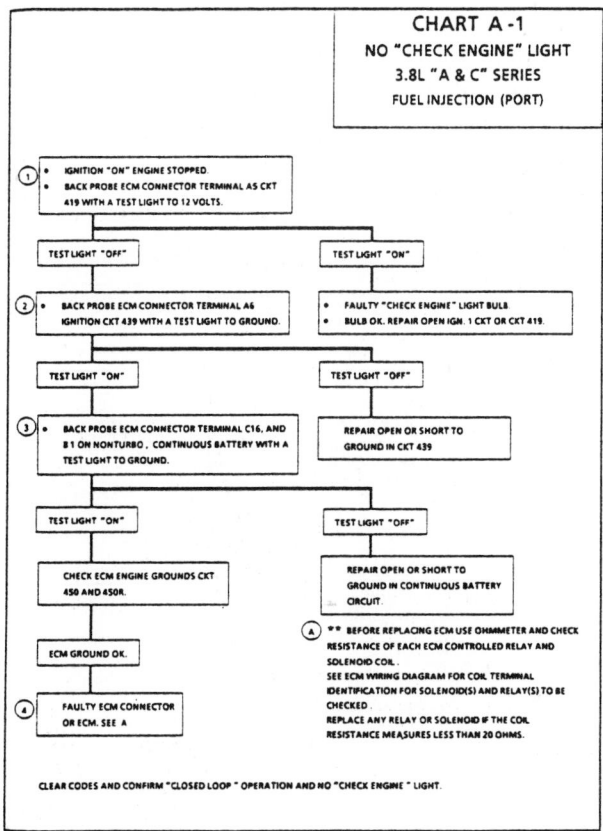

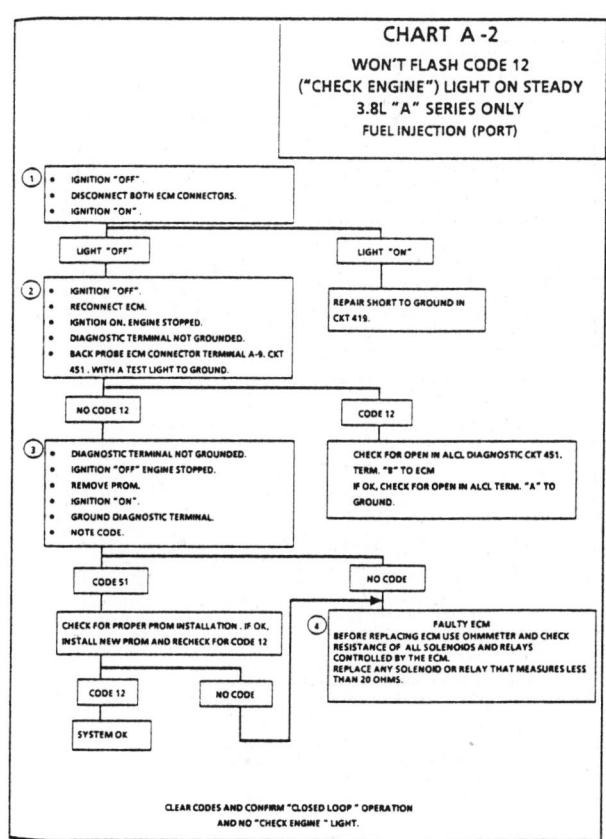

MPI TROUBLE DIAGNOSTICS

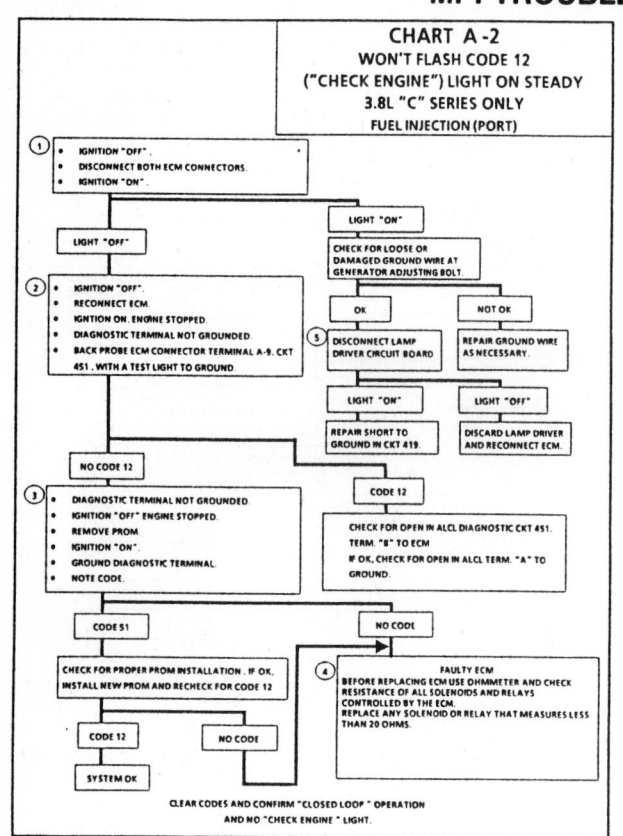

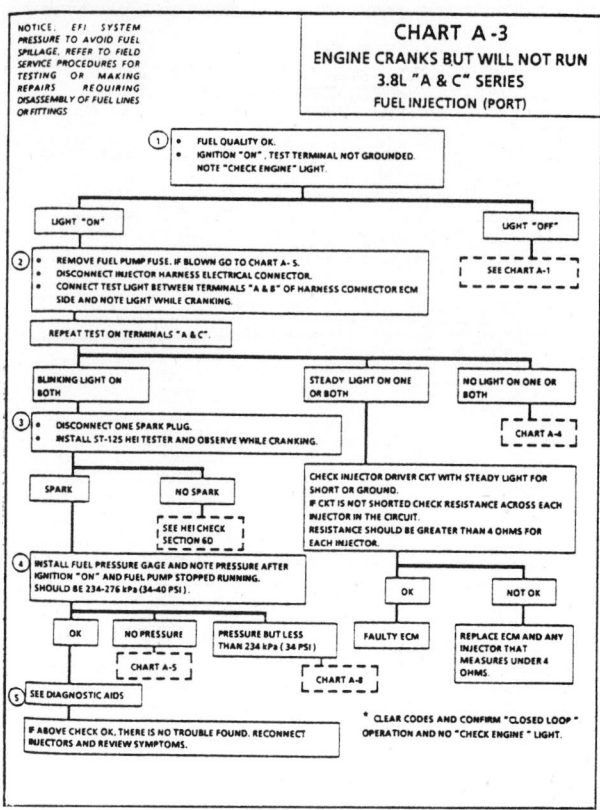

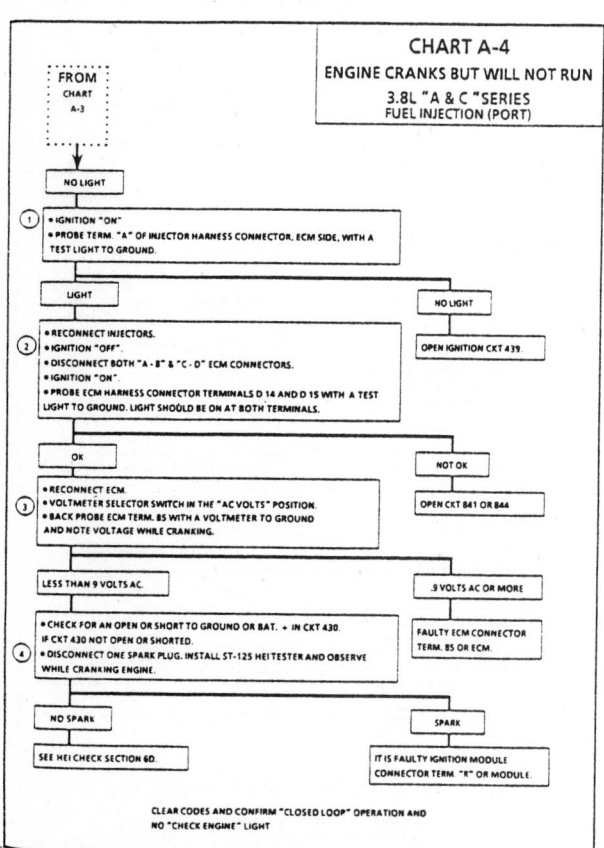

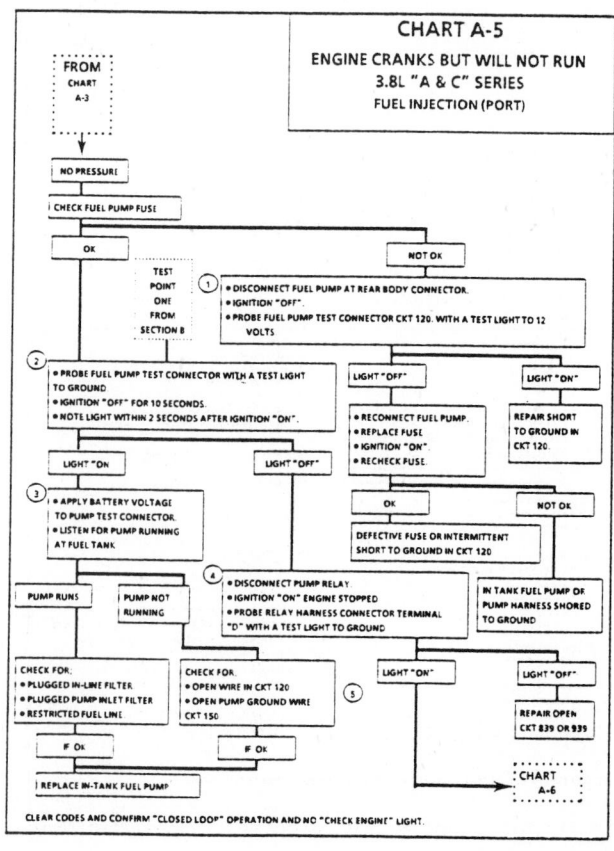

MPI TROUBLE DIAGNOSTICS

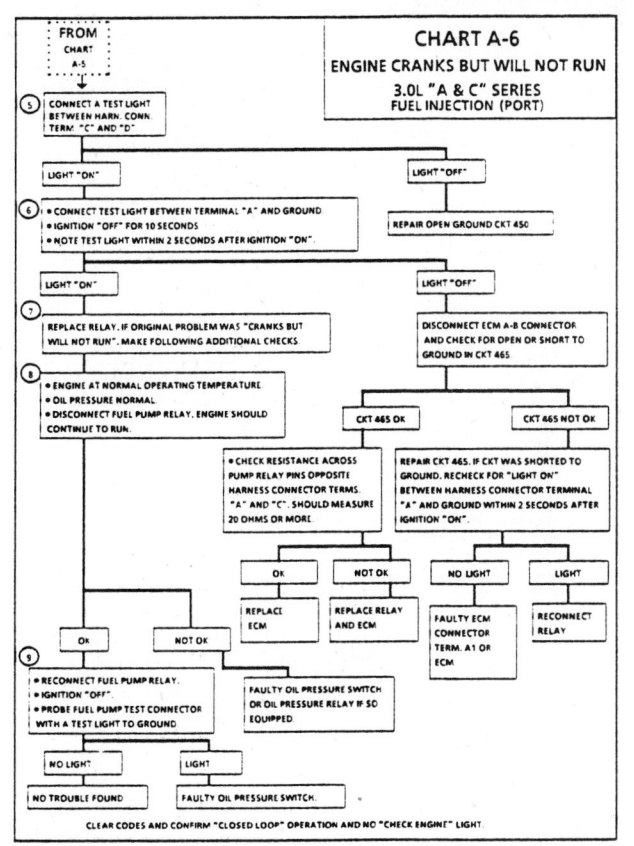

CHART A-6
ENGINE CRANKS BUT WILL NOT RUN
3.0L "A & C" SERIES
FUEL INJECTION (PORT)

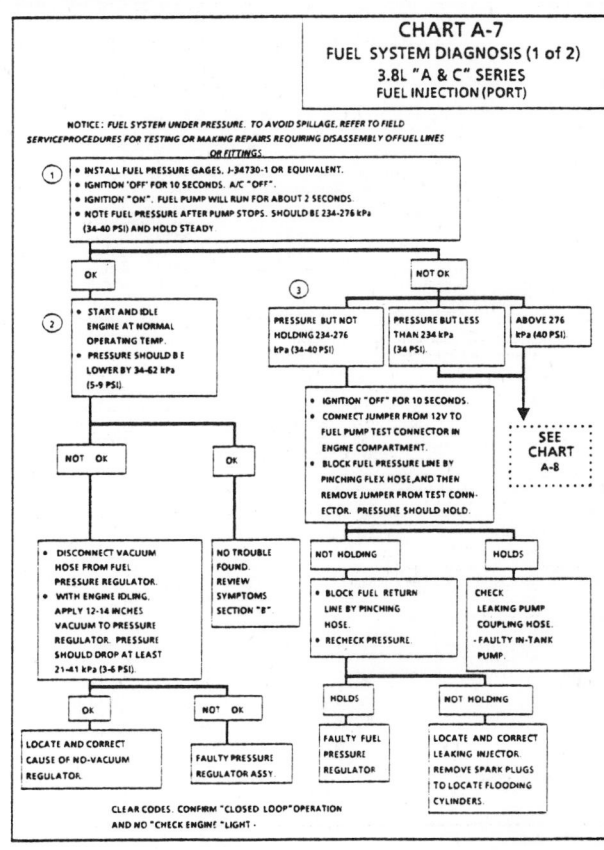

CHART A-7
FUEL SYSTEM DIAGNOSIS (1 of 2)
3.8L "A & C" SERIES
FUEL INJECTION (PORT)

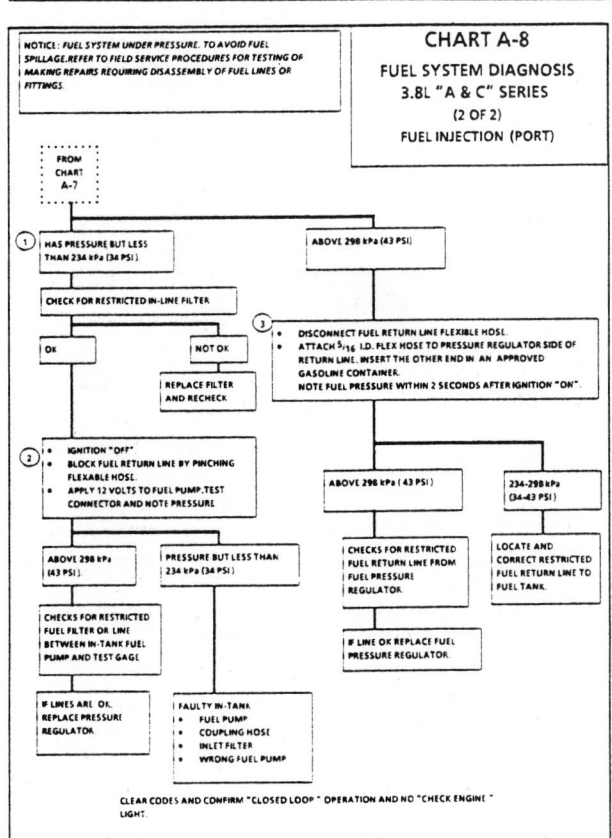

CHART A-8
FUEL SYSTEM DIAGNOSIS
3.8L "A & C" SERIES
(2 OF 2)
FUEL INJECTION (PORT)

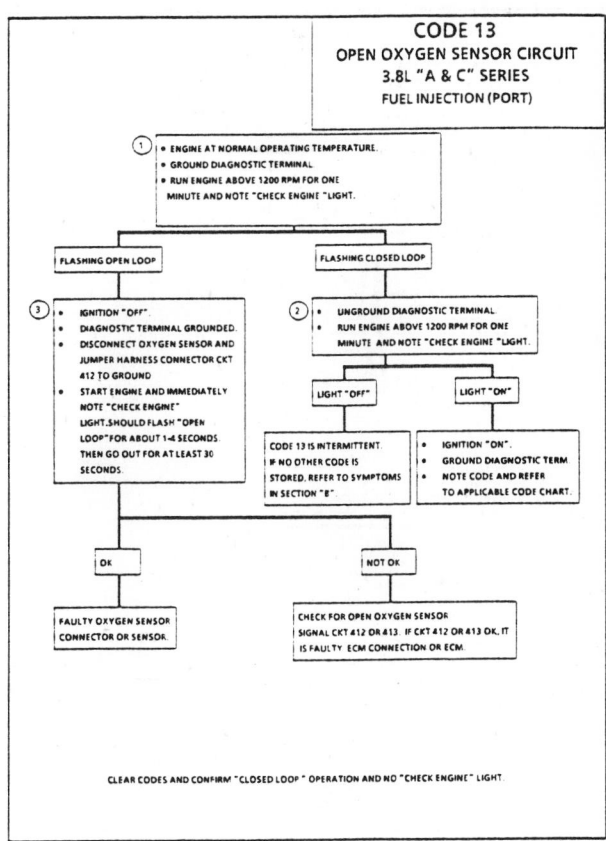

CODE 13
OPEN OXYGEN SENSOR CIRCUIT
3.8L "A & C" SERIES
FUEL INJECTION (PORT)

MPI TROUBLE DIAGNOSTICS

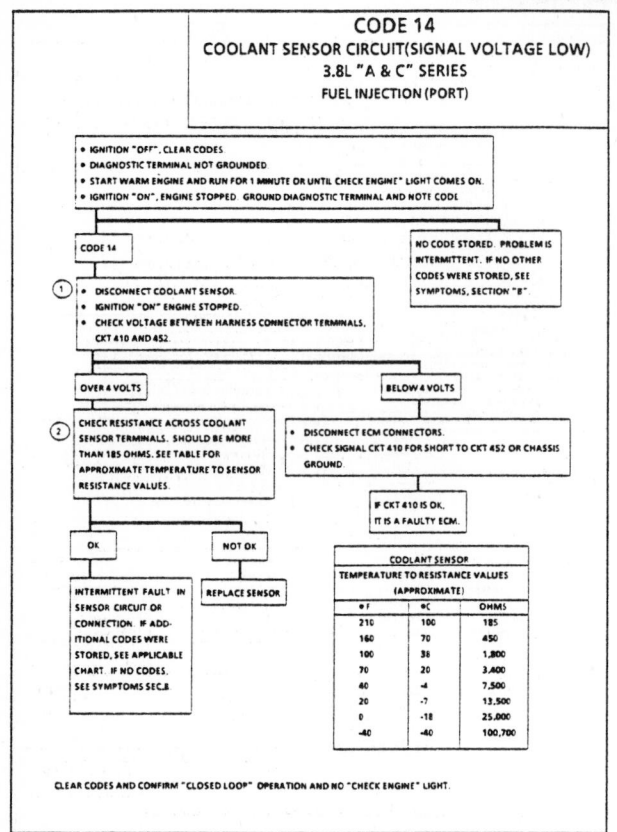

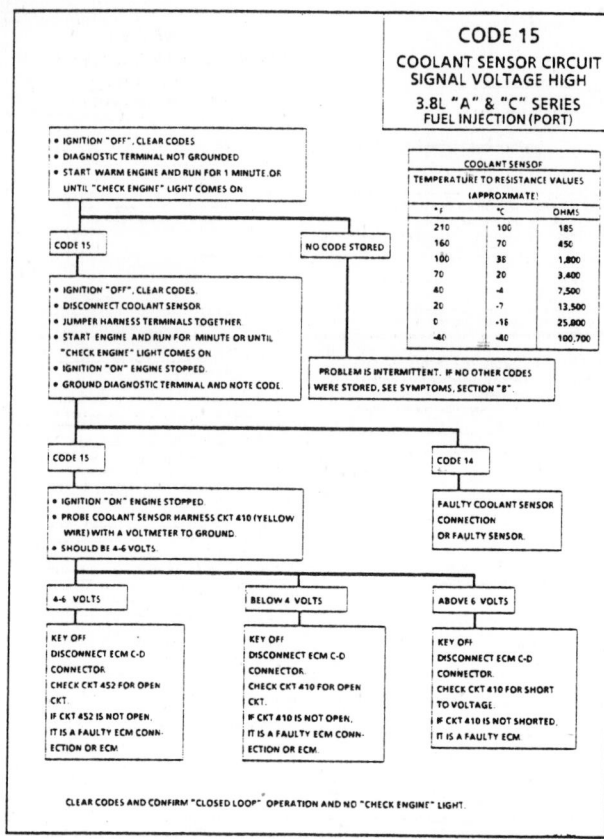

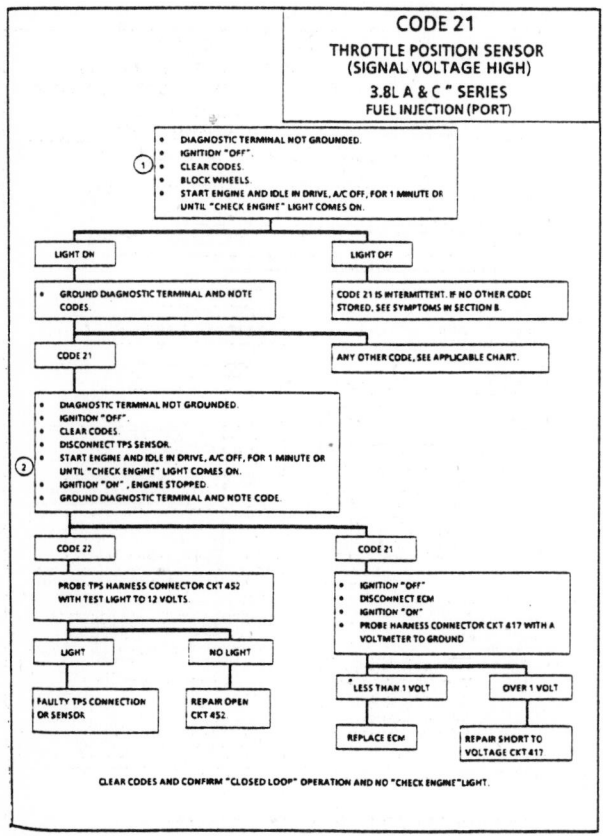

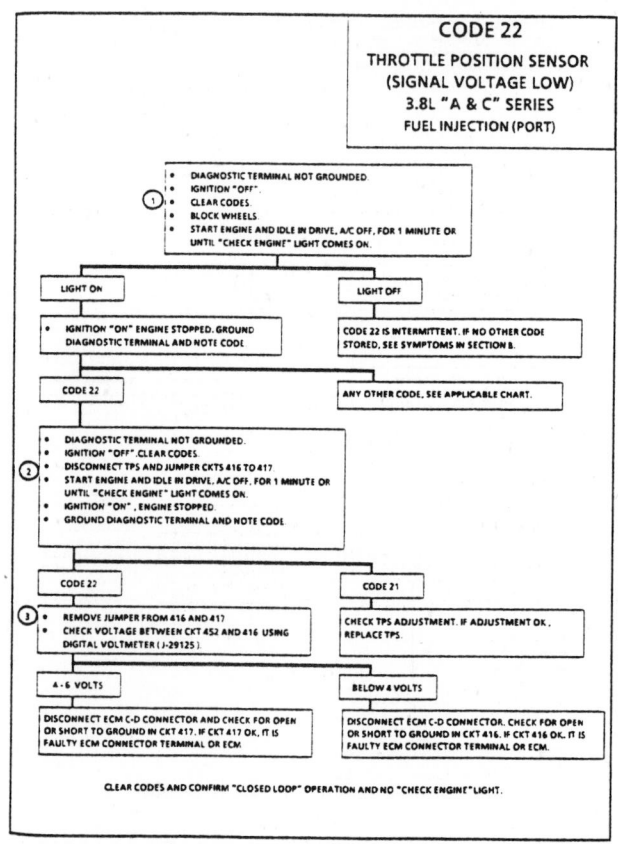

MPI TROUBLE DIAGNOSTICS

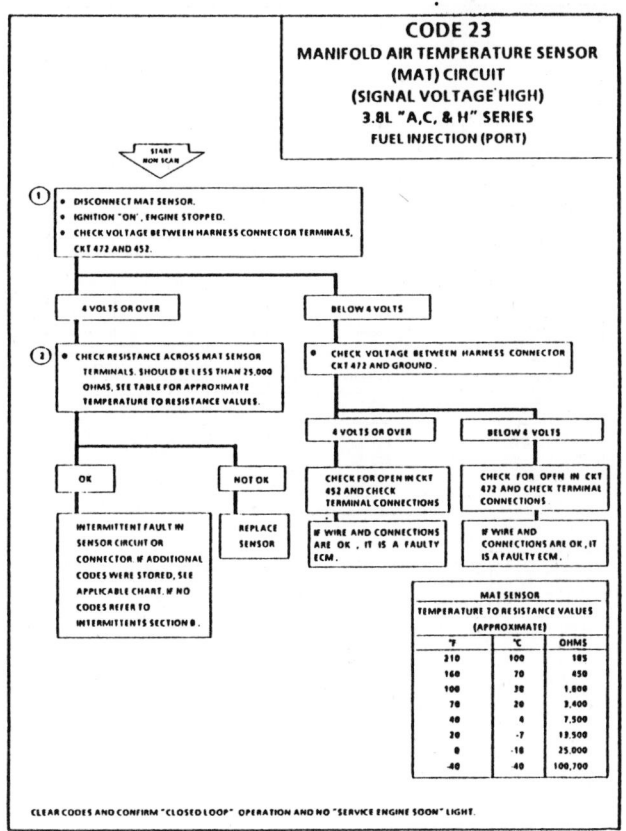

CODE 23
MANIFOLD AIR TEMPERATURE SENSOR (MAT) CIRCUIT (SIGNAL VOLTAGE HIGH) 3.8L "A,C, & H" SERIES FUEL INJECTION (PORT)

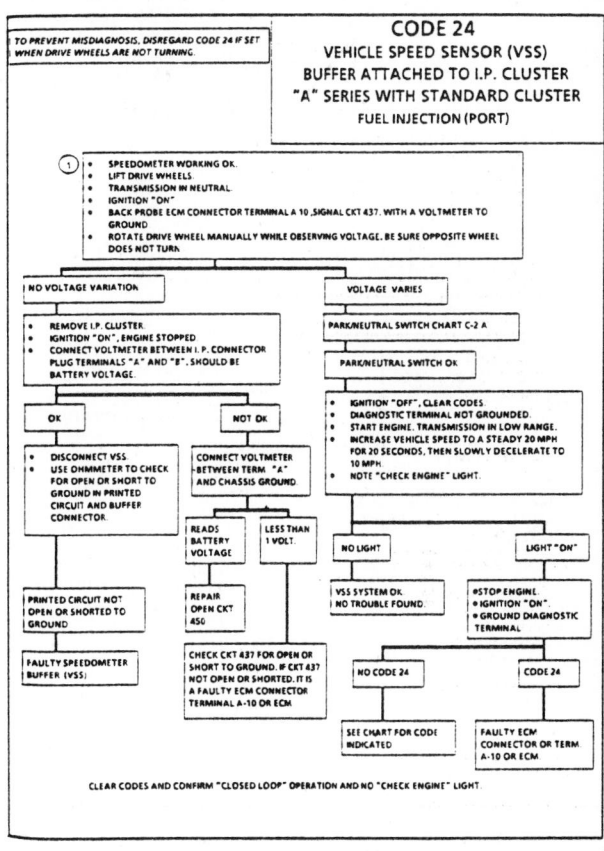

CODE 24
VEHICLE SPEED SENSOR (VSS) BUFFER ATTACHED TO I.P. CLUSTER "A" SERIES WITH STANDARD CLUSTER FUEL INJECTION (PORT)

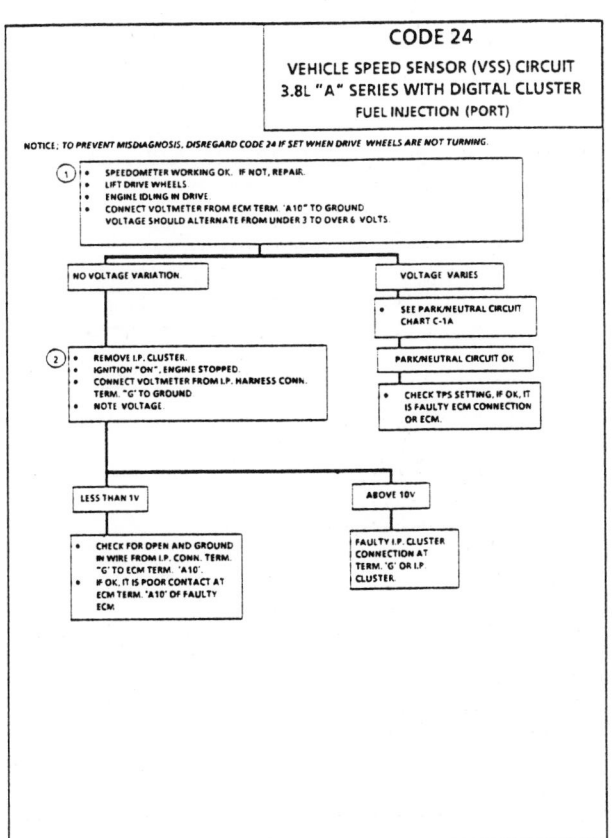

CODE 24
VEHICLE SPEED SENSOR (VSS) CIRCUIT 3.8L "A" SERIES WITH DIGITAL CLUSTER FUEL INJECTION (PORT)

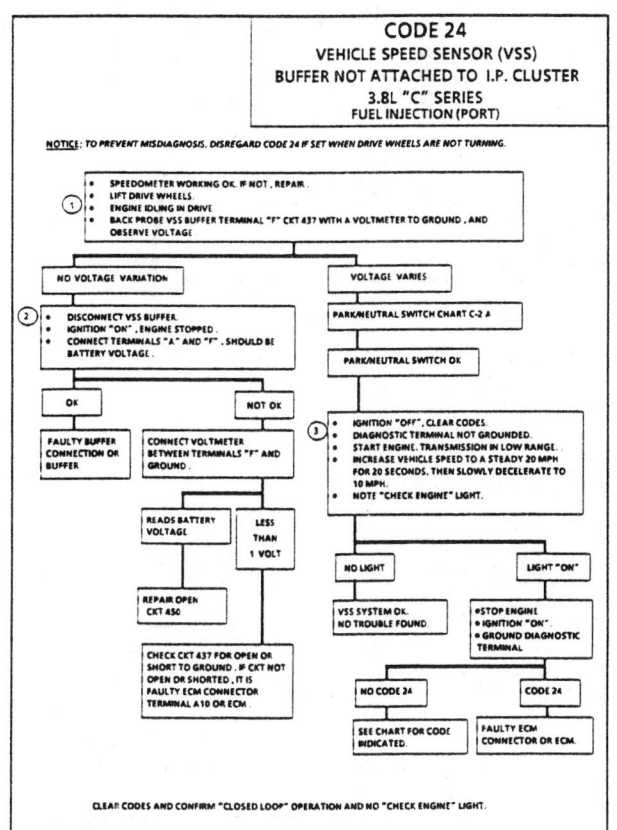

CODE 24
VEHICLE SPEED SENSOR (VSS) BUFFER NOT ATTACHED TO I.P. CLUSTER 3.8L "C" SERIES FUEL INJECTION (PORT)

MPI TROUBLE DIAGNOSTICS

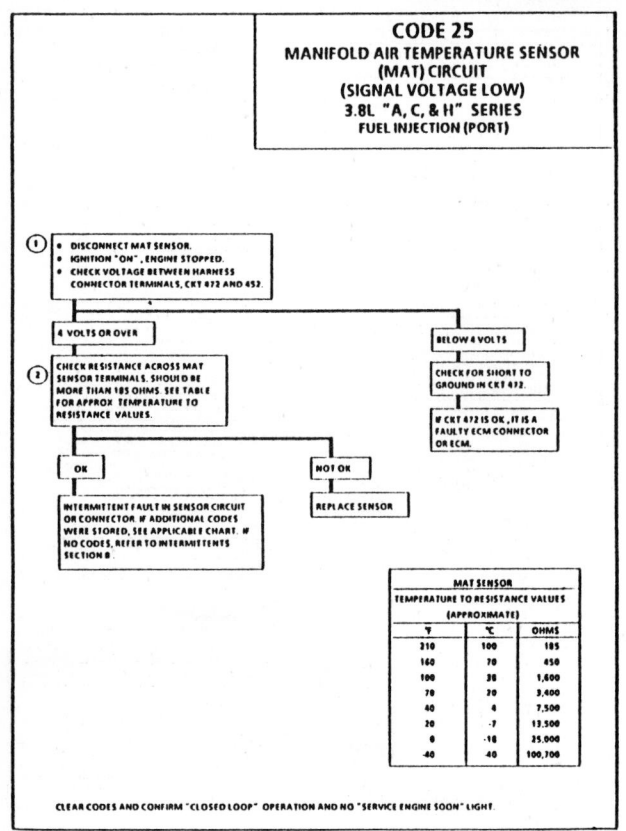

CODE 25
MANIFOLD AIR TEMPERATURE SENSOR (MAT) CIRCUIT
(SIGNAL VOLTAGE LOW)
3.8L "A, C, & H" SERIES
FUEL INJECTION (PORT)

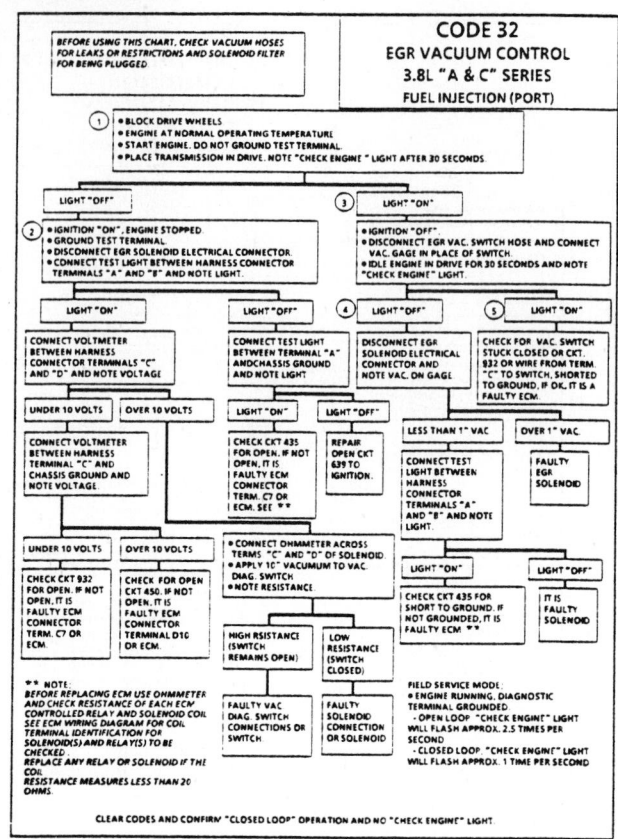

CODE 32
EGR VACUUM CONTROL
3.8L "A & C" SERIES
FUEL INJECTION (PORT)

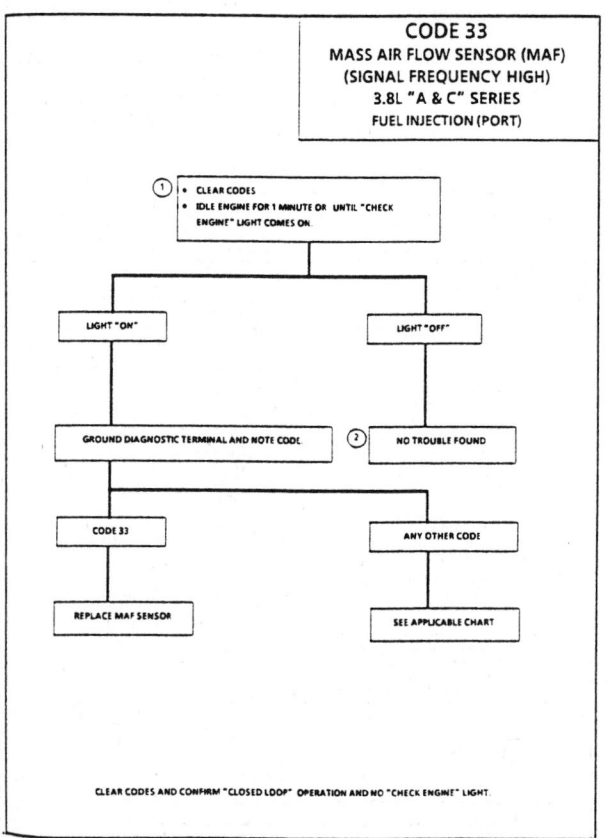

CODE 33
MASS AIR FLOW SENSOR (MAF)
(SIGNAL FREQUENCY HIGH)
3.8L "A & C" SERIES
FUEL INJECTION (PORT)

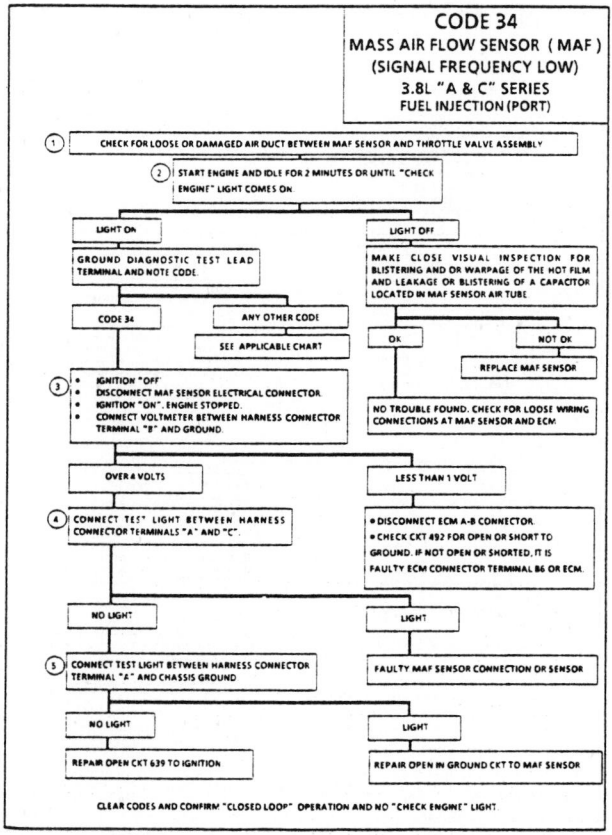

CODE 34
MASS AIR FLOW SENSOR (MAF)
(SIGNAL FREQUENCY LOW)
3.8L "A & C" SERIES
FUEL INJECTION (PORT)

MPI TROUBLE DIAGNOSTICS

CODE 41
COMPUTER CONTROLLED COIL IGNITION (C 31)
CAM SENSOR SIGNAL
3.8L "A, C, & H" SERIES
FUEL INJECTION (PORT)

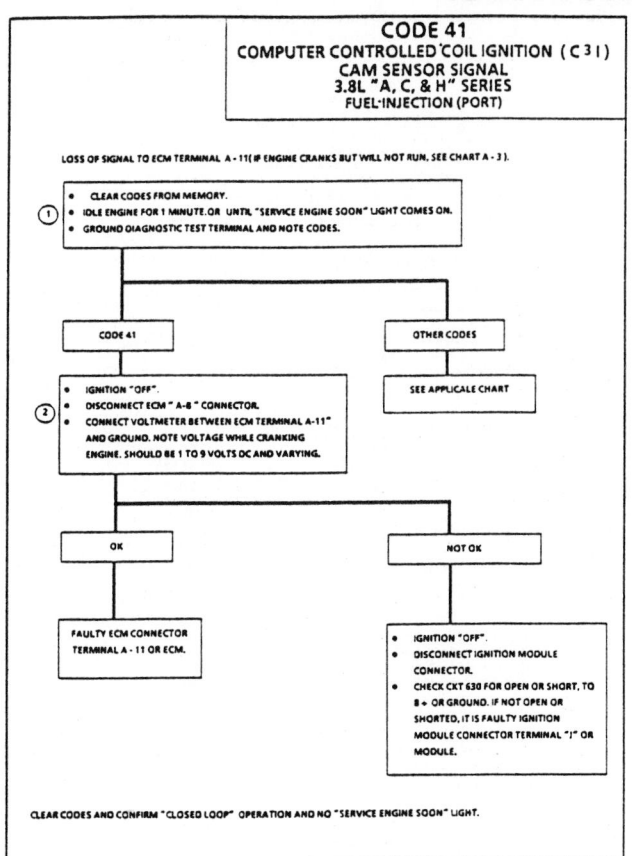

CODE 42
COMPUTER CONTROLLED COIL IGNITION (C 31)
3.8L "A, C & H" SERIES
FUEL INJECTION (PORT)

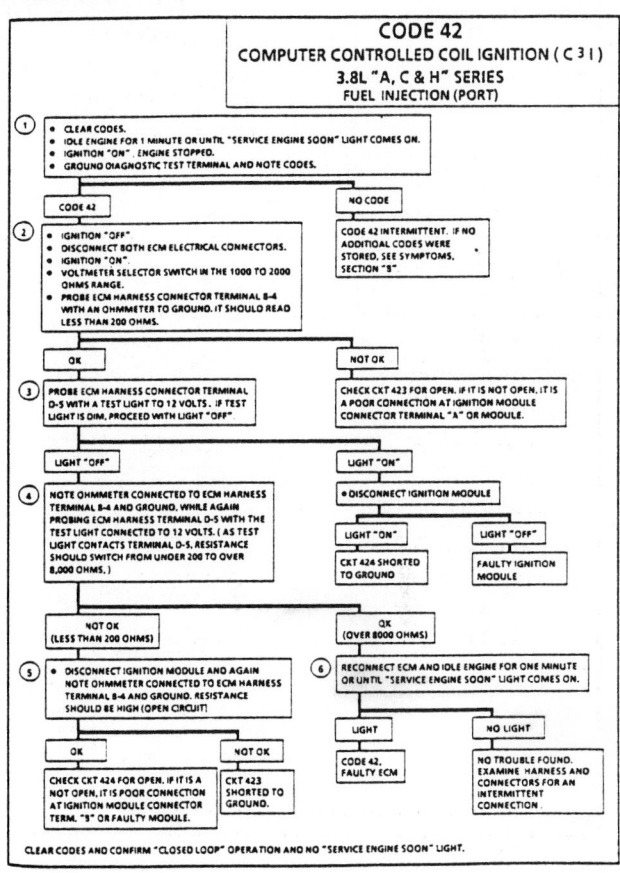

CODE 42
ELECTRONIC SPARK TIMING (EST)
3.8L "A & C" SERIES
FUEL INJECTION (PORT)

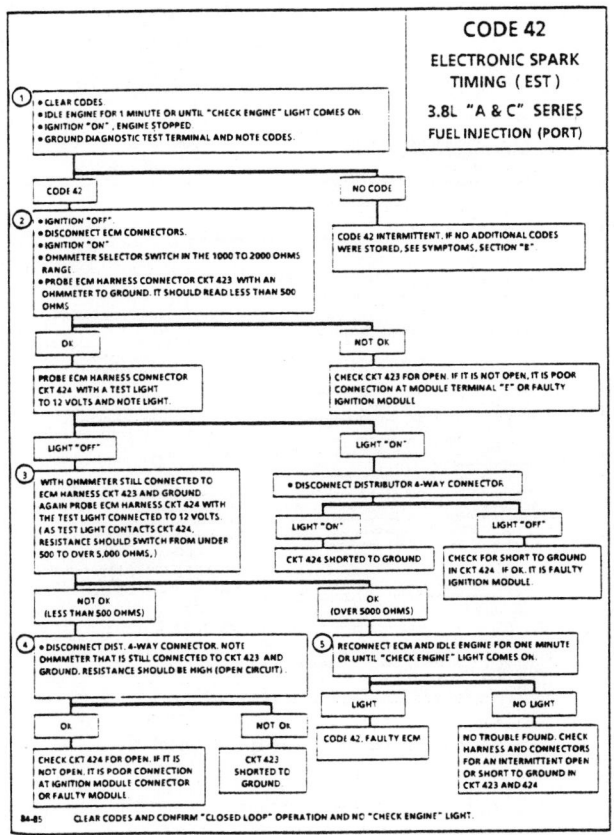

CODE 43
ELECTRONIC SPARK CONTROL (ESC)
3.8L "A & C" SERIES
FUEL INJECTION (PORT)

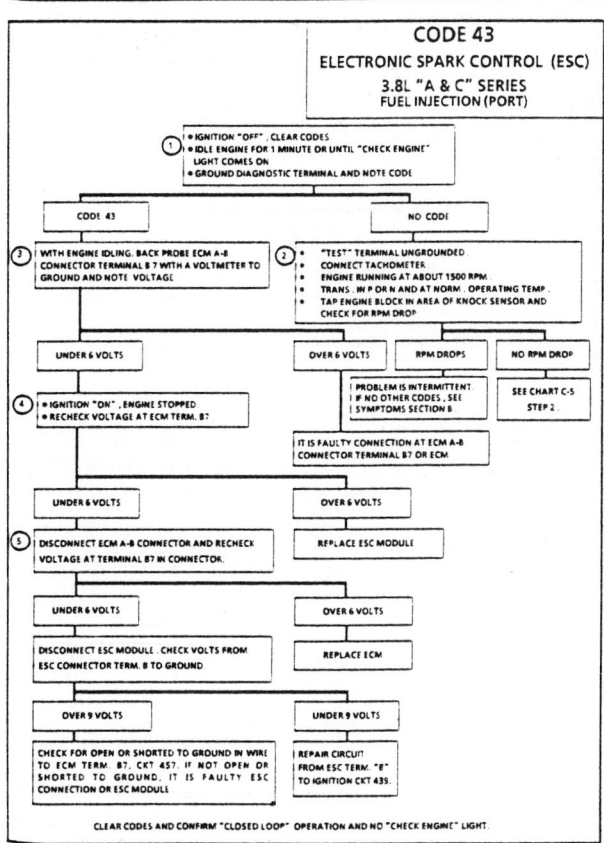

MPI TROUBLE DIAGNOSTICS

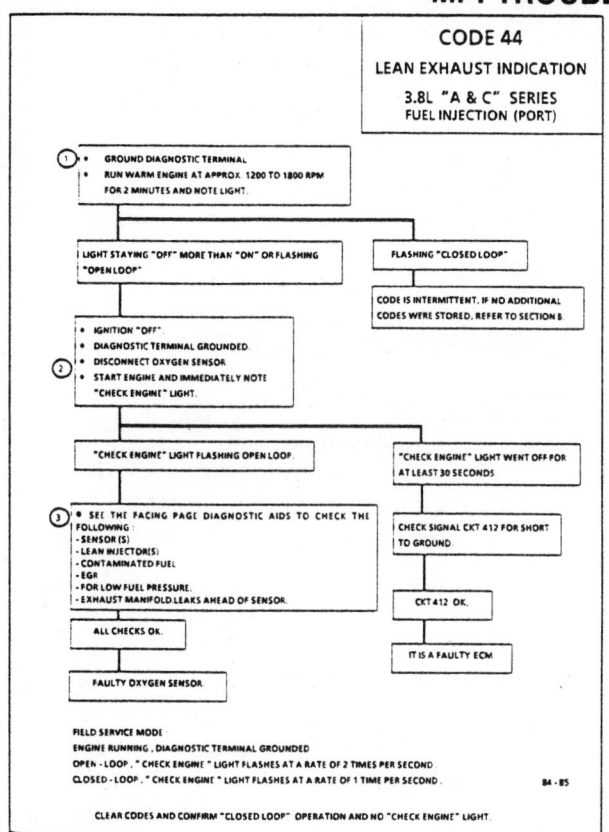

CODE 44
LEAN EXHAUST INDICATION
3.8L "A & C" SERIES
FUEL INJECTION (PORT)

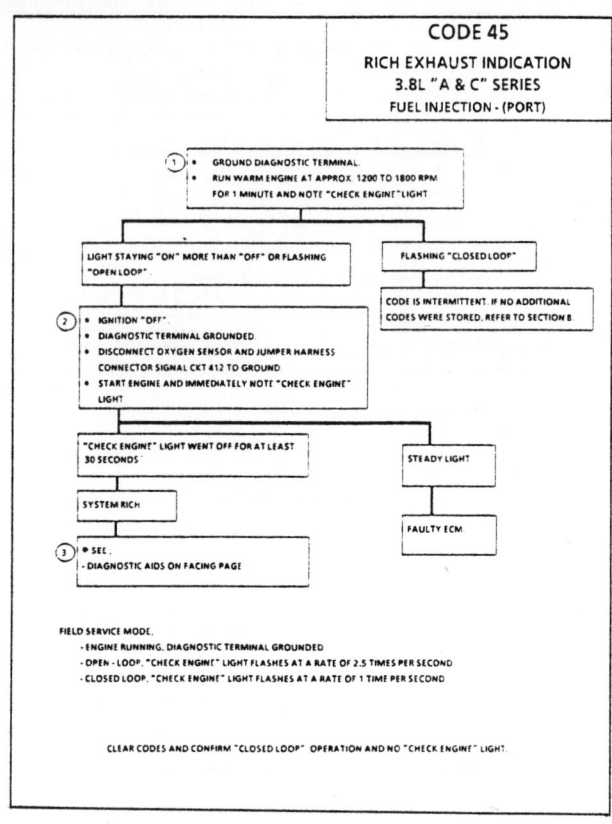

CODE 45
RICH EXHAUST INDICATION
3.8L "A & C" SERIES
FUEL INJECTION - (PORT)

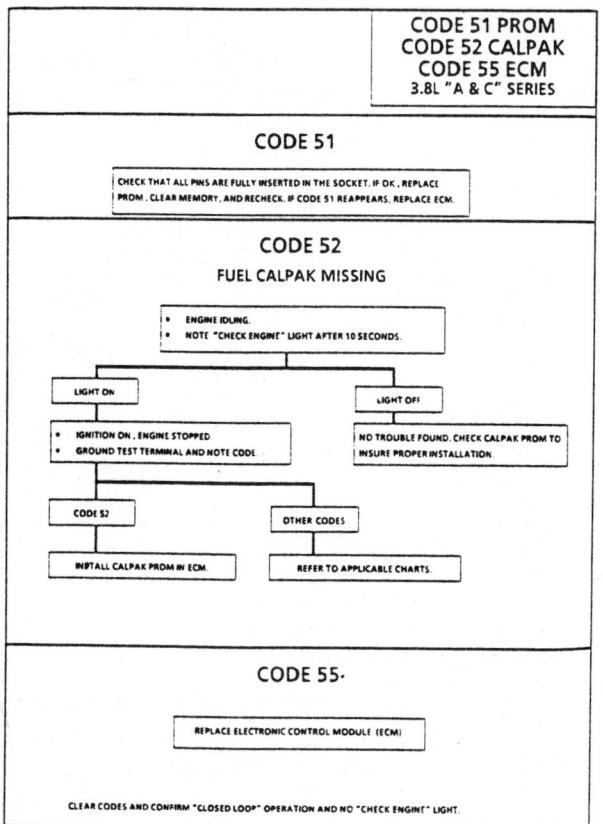

CODE 51 PROM
CODE 52 CALPAK
CODE 55 ECM
3.8L "A & C" SERIES

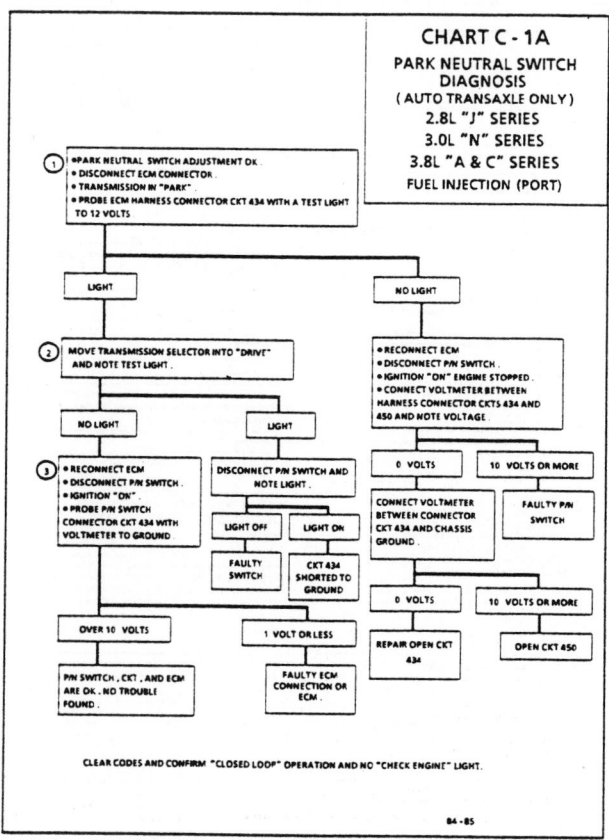

CHART C - 1A
PARK NEUTRAL SWITCH DIAGNOSIS
(AUTO TRANSAXLE ONLY)
2.8L "J" SERIES
3.0L "N" SERIES
3.8L "A & C" SERIES
FUEL INJECTION (PORT)

MPI TROUBLE DIAGNOSTICS

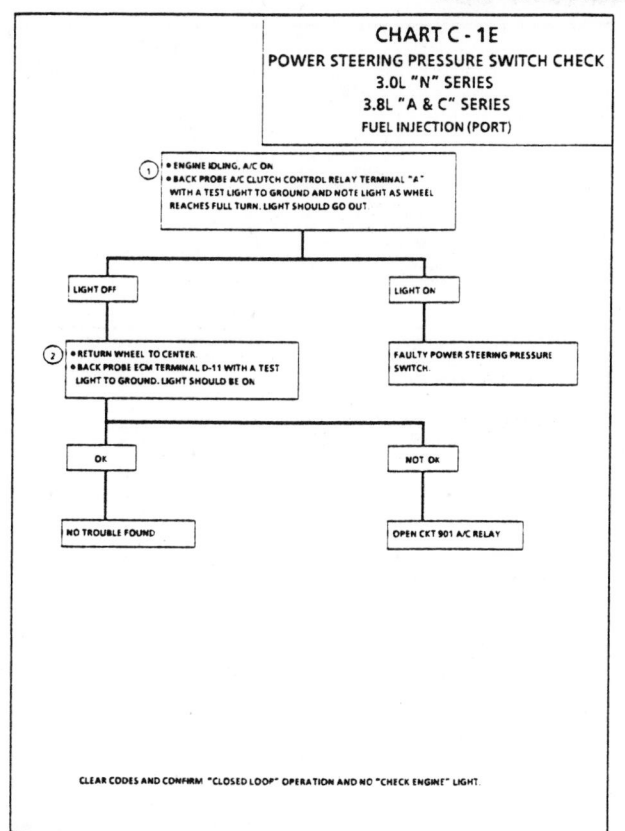

CHART C - 1E
POWER STEERING PRESSURE SWITCH CHECK
3.0L "N" SERIES
3.8L "A & C" SERIES
FUEL INJECTION (PORT)

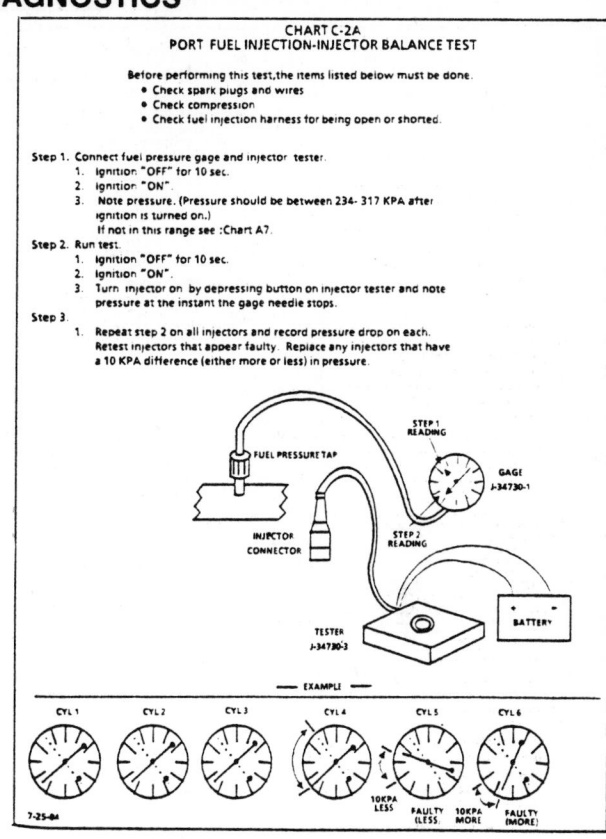

CHART C-2A
PORT FUEL INJECTION-INJECTOR BALANCE TEST

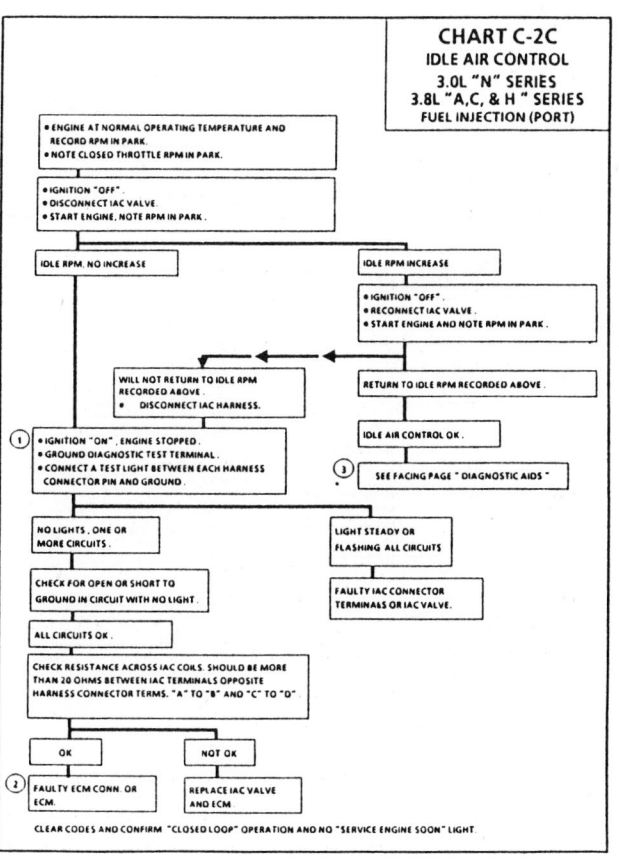

CHART C-2C
IDLE AIR CONTROL
3.0L "N" SERIES
3.8L "A, C, & H " SERIES
FUEL INJECTION (PORT)

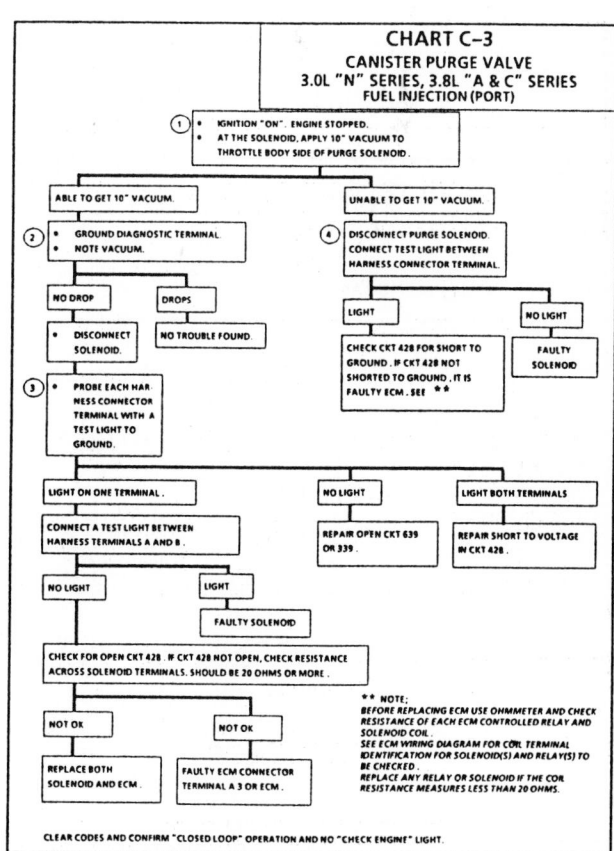

CHART C–3
CANISTER PURGE VALVE
3.0L "N" SERIES, 3.8L "A & C" SERIES
FUEL INJECTION (PORT)

MPI TROUBLE DIAGNOSTICS

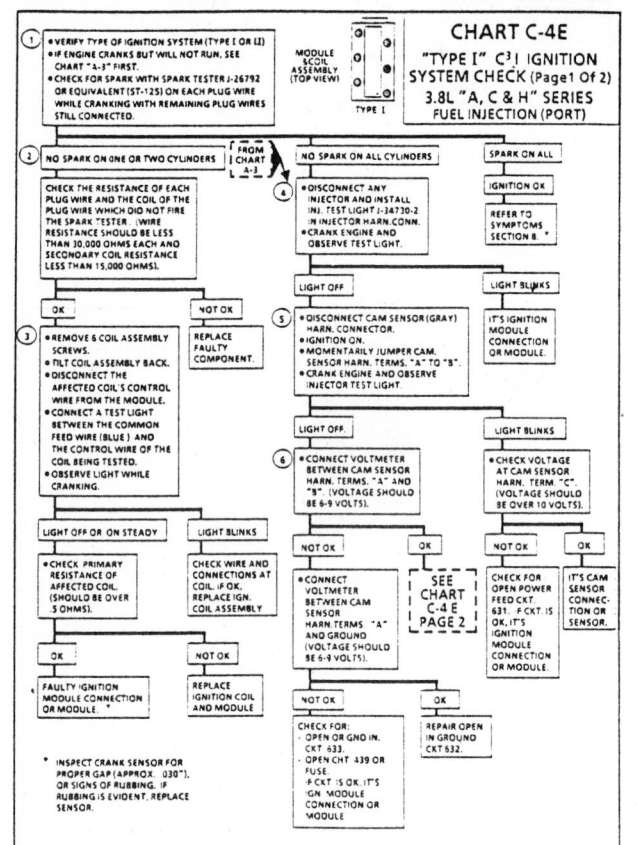

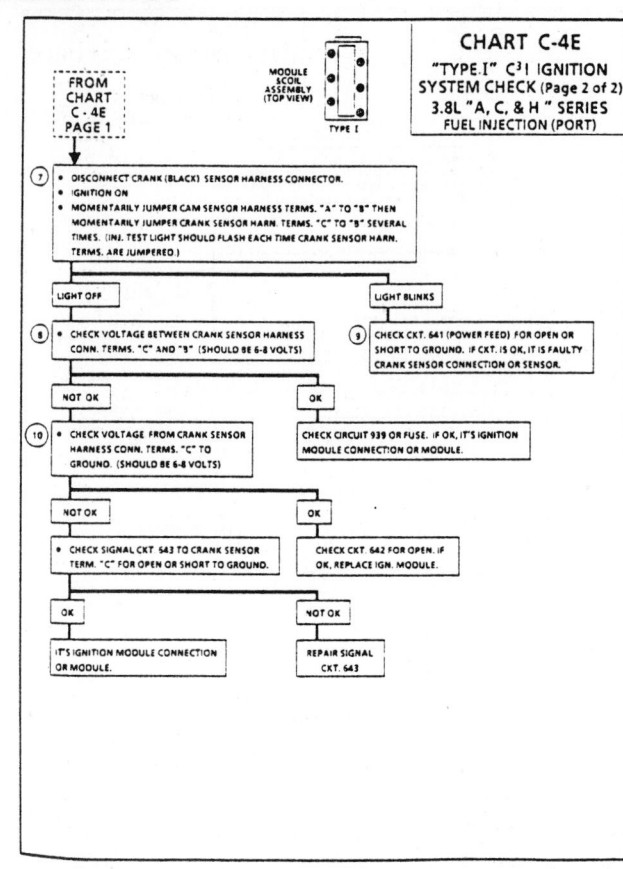

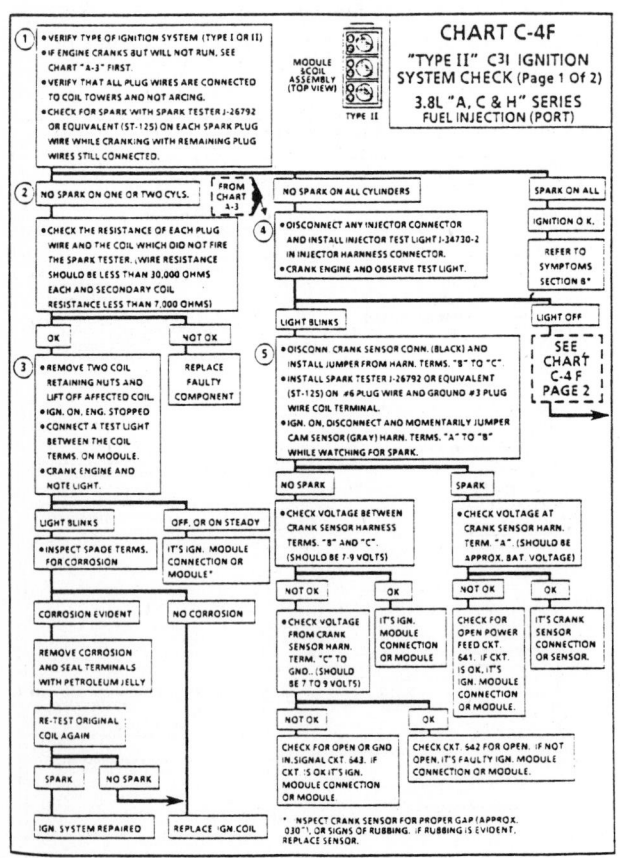

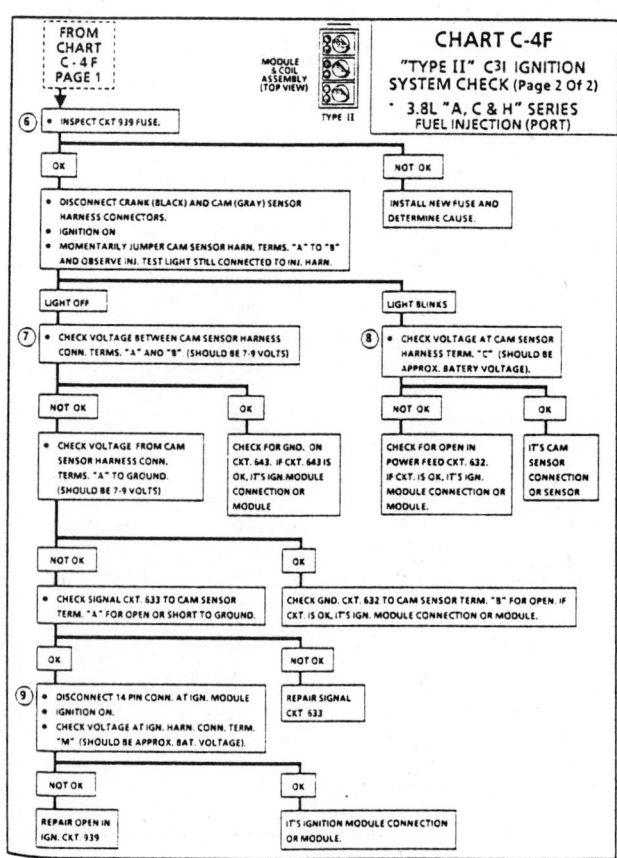

MPI TROUBLE DIAGNOSTICS

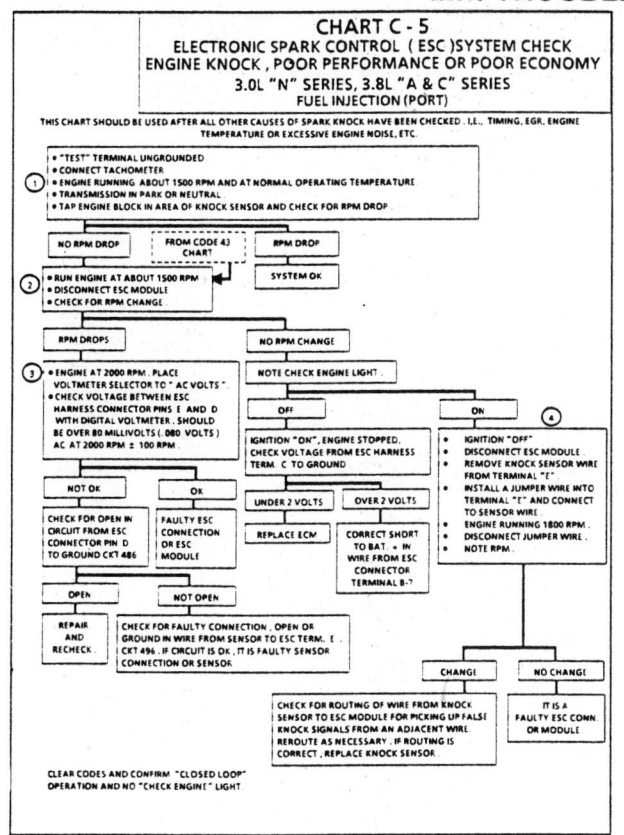

CHART C-5
ELECTRONIC SPARK CONTROL (ESC) SYSTEM CHECK
ENGINE KNOCK, POOR PERFORMANCE OR POOR ECONOMY
3.0L "N" SERIES, 3.8L "A & C" SERIES
FUEL INJECTION (PORT)

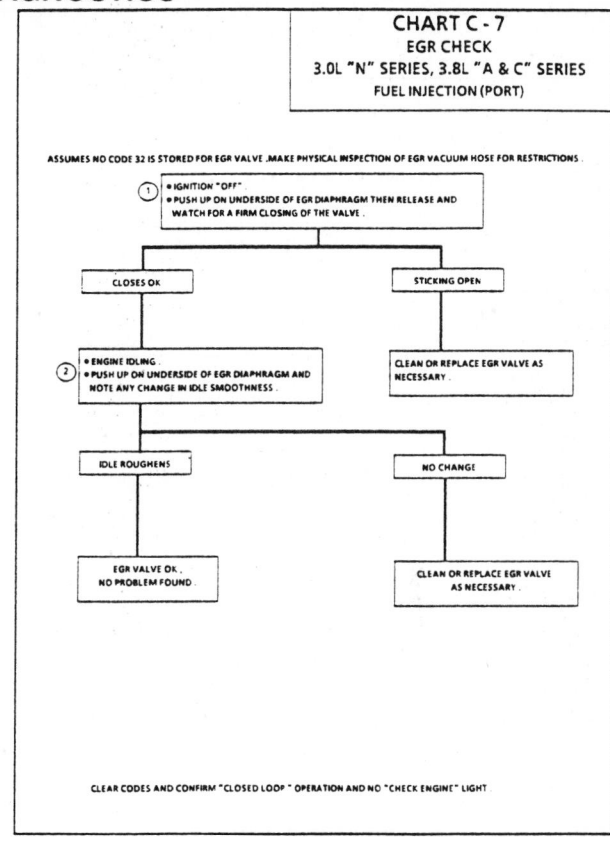

CHART C-7
EGR CHECK
3.0L "N" SERIES, 3.8L "A & C" SERIES
FUEL INJECTION (PORT)

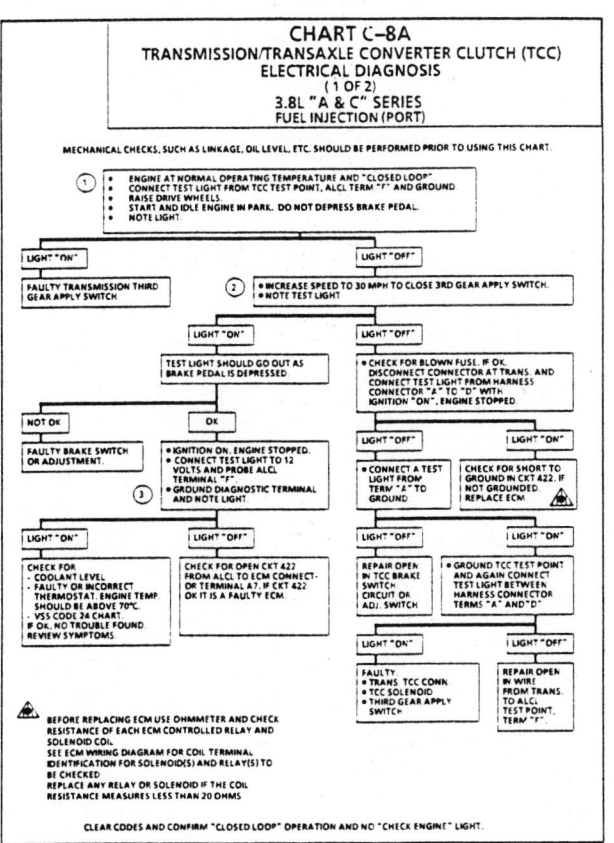

CHART C-8A
TRANSMISSION/TRANSAXLE CONVERTER CLUTCH (TCC)
ELECTRICAL DIAGNOSIS
(1 OF 2)
3.8L "A & C" SERIES
FUEL INJECTION (PORT)

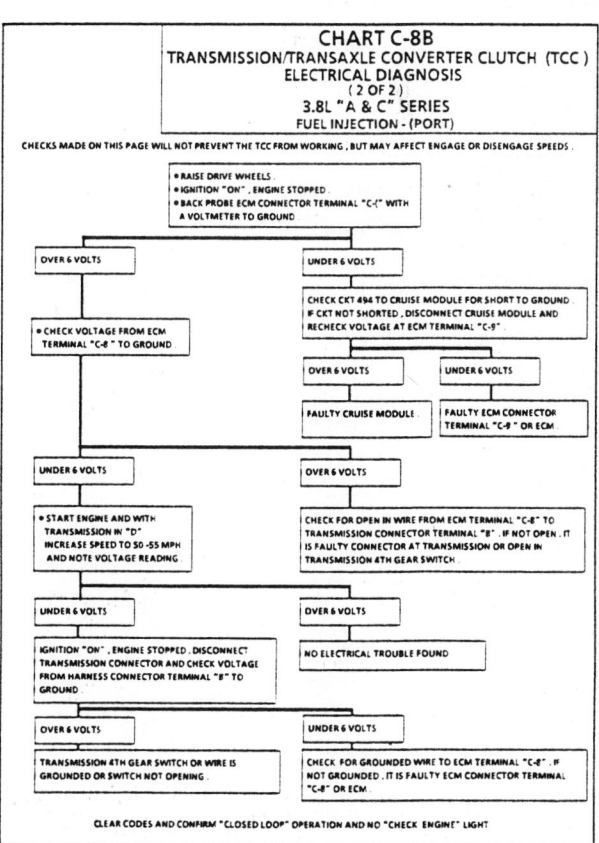

CHART C-8B
TRANSMISSION/TRANSAXLE CONVERTER CLUTCH (TCC)
ELECTRICAL DIAGNOSIS
(2 OF 2)
3.8L "A & C" SERIES
FUEL INJECTION - (PORT)

MPI TROUBLE DIAGNOSTICS

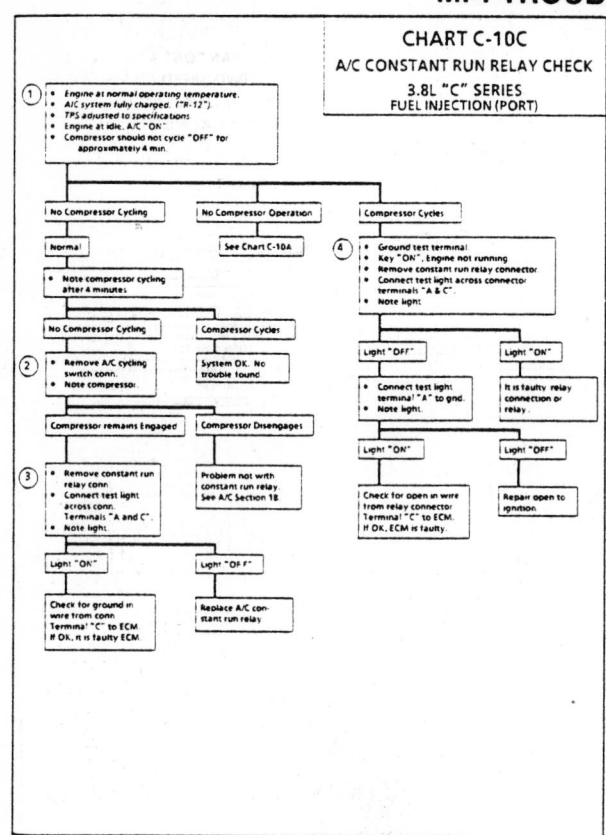

CHART C-10C
A/C CONSTANT RUN RELAY CHECK
3.8L "C" SERIES
FUEL INJECTION (PORT)

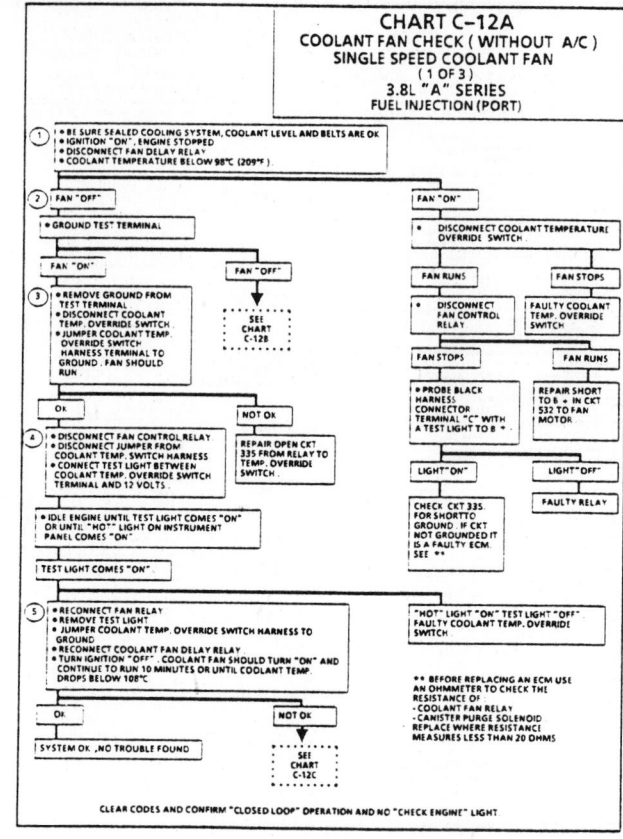

CHART C-12A
COOLANT FAN CHECK (WITHOUT A/C)
SINGLE SPEED COOLANT FAN
(1 OF 3)
3.8L "A" SERIES
FUEL INJECTION (PORT)

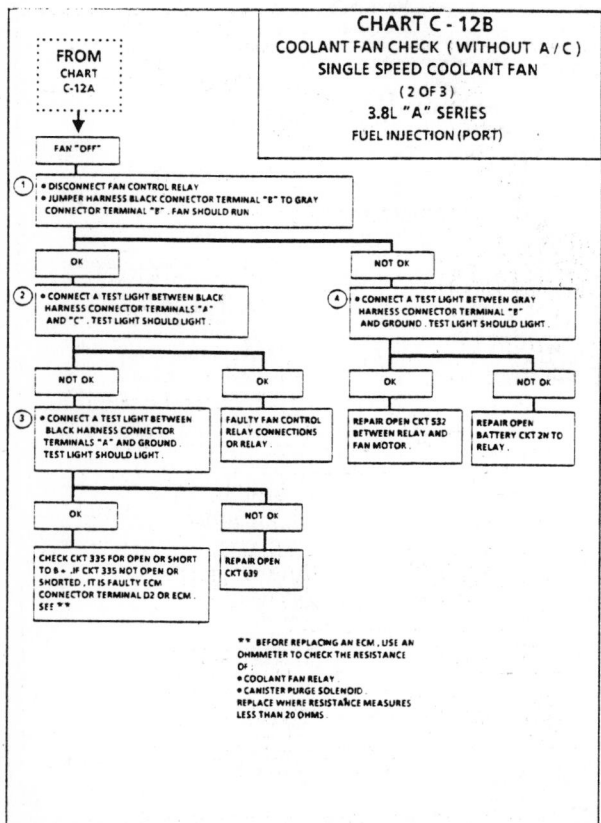

CHART C - 12B
COOLANT FAN CHECK (WITHOUT A/C)
SINGLE SPEED COOLANT FAN
(2 OF 3)
3.8L "A" SERIES
FUEL INJECTION (PORT)

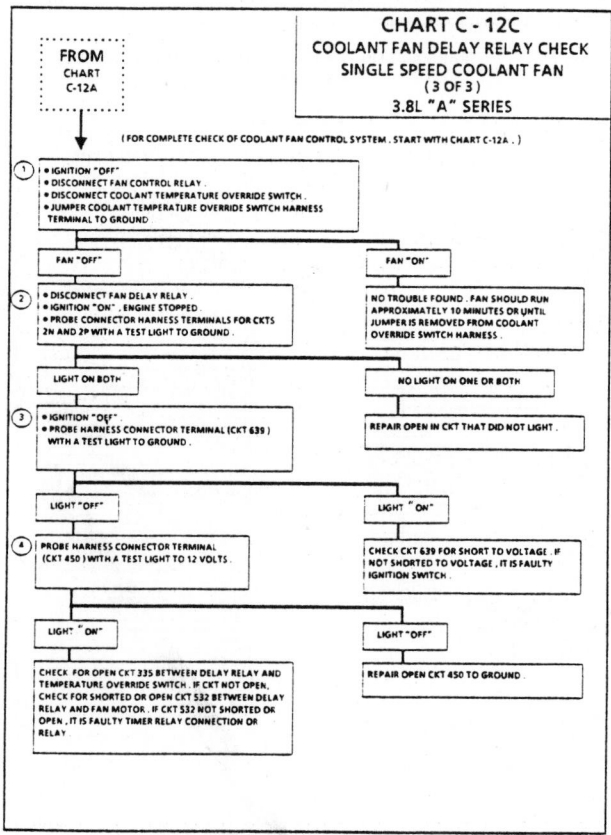

CHART C - 12C
COOLANT FAN DELAY RELAY CHECK
SINGLE SPEED COOLANT FAN
(3 OF 3)
3.8L "A" SERIES

MPI TROUBLE DIAGNOSTICS

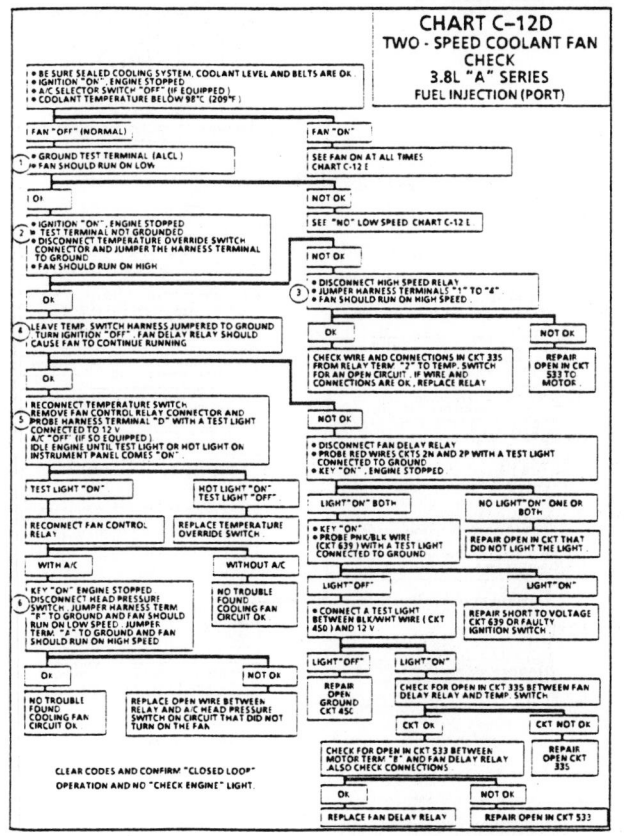

CHART C–12D
TWO - SPEED COOLANT FAN CHECK
3.8L "A" SERIES
FUEL INJECTION (PORT)

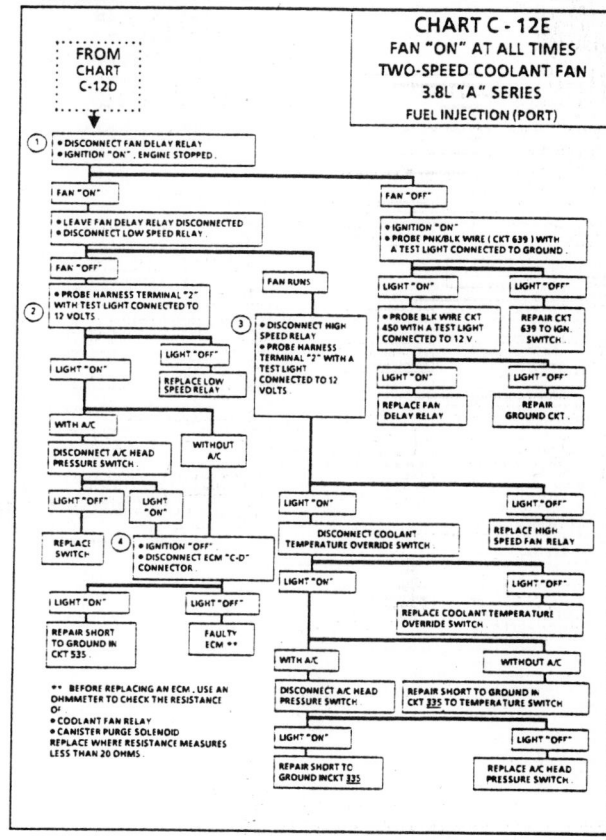

CHART C - 12E
FAN "ON" AT ALL TIMES
TWO-SPEED COOLANT FAN
3.8L "A" SERIES
FUEL INJECTION (PORT)

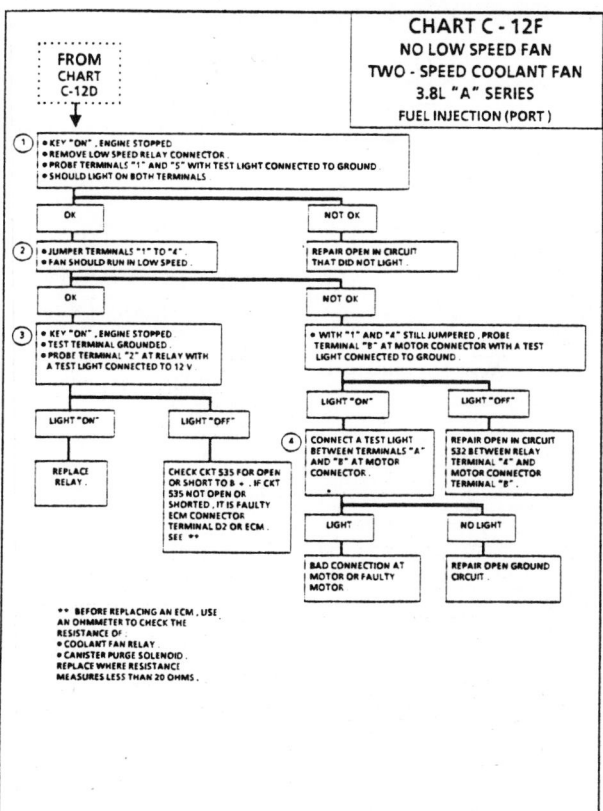

CHART C - 12F
NO LOW SPEED FAN
TWO - SPEED COOLANT FAN
3.8L "A" SERIES
FUEL INJECTION (PORT)

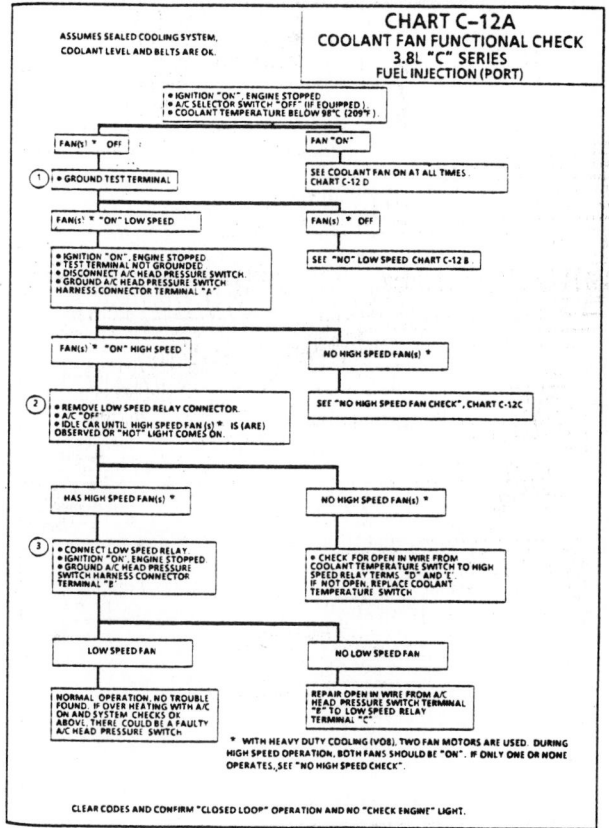

CHART C - 12A
COOLANT FAN FUNCTIONAL CHECK
3.8L "C" SERIES
FUEL INJECTION (PORT)

MPI TROUBLE DIAGNOSTICS

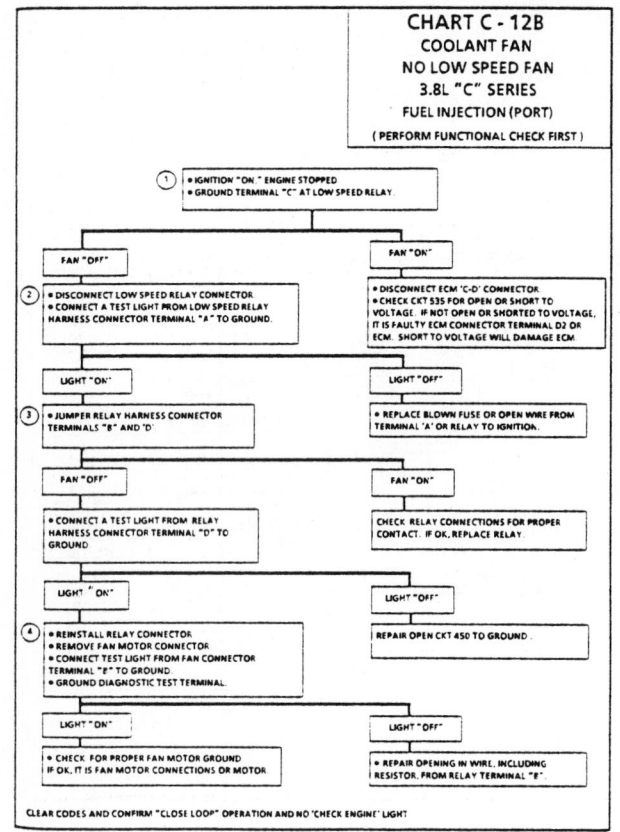

CHART C - 12B
COOLANT FAN
NO LOW SPEED FAN
3.8L "C" SERIES
FUEL INJECTION (PORT)
(PERFORM FUNCTIONAL CHECK FIRST)

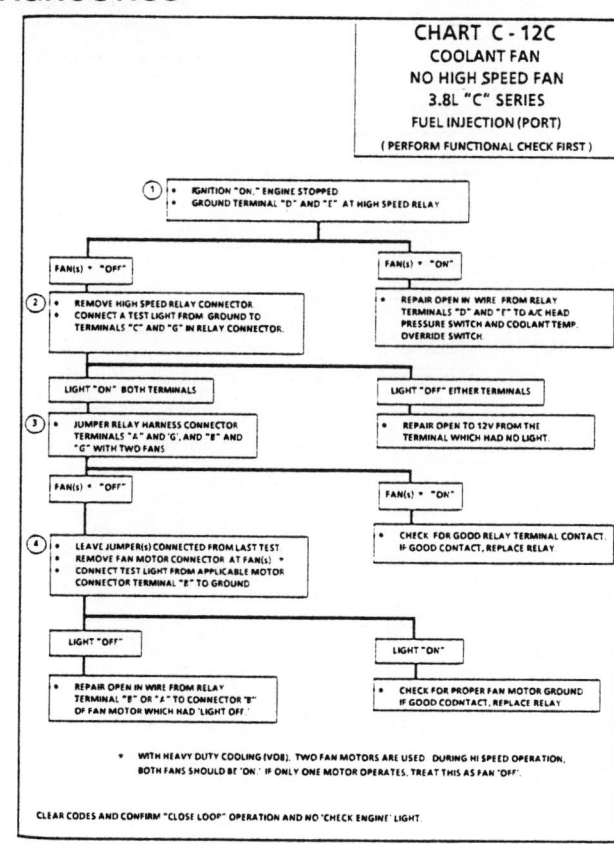

CHART C - 12C
COOLANT FAN
NO HIGH SPEED FAN
3.8L "C" SERIES
FUEL INJECTION (PORT)
(PERFORM FUNCTIONAL CHECK FIRST)

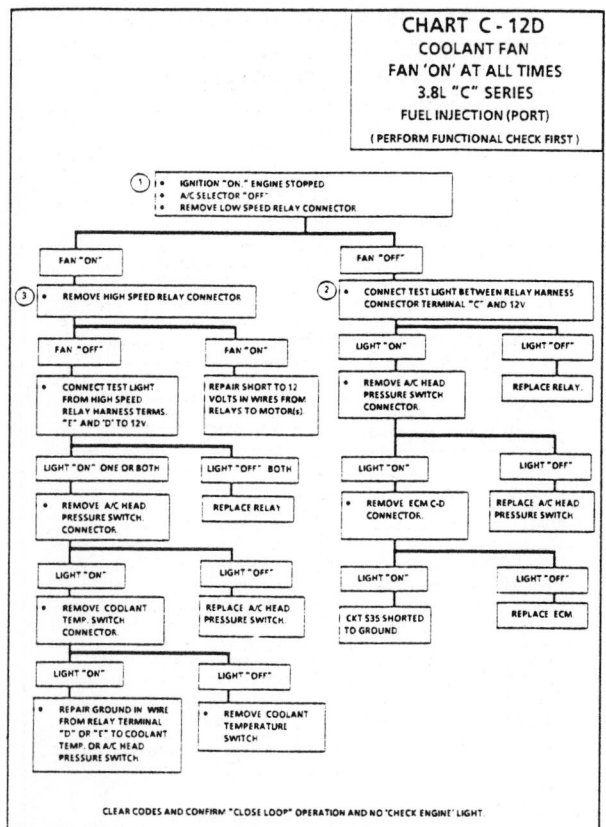

CHART C - 12D
COOLANT FAN
FAN 'ON' AT ALL TIMES
3.8L "C" SERIES
FUEL INJECTION (PORT)
(PERFORM FUNCTIONAL CHECK FIRST)

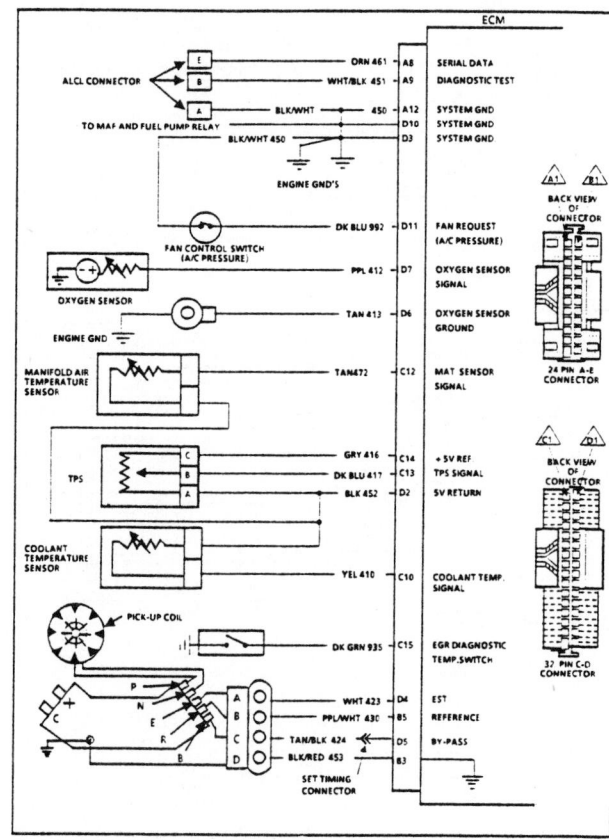

MPI TROUBLE DIAGNOSTICS

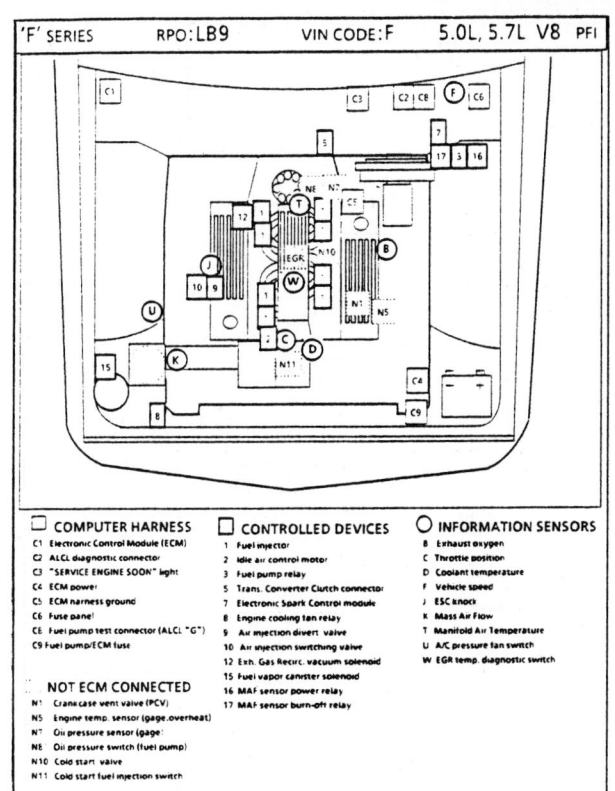

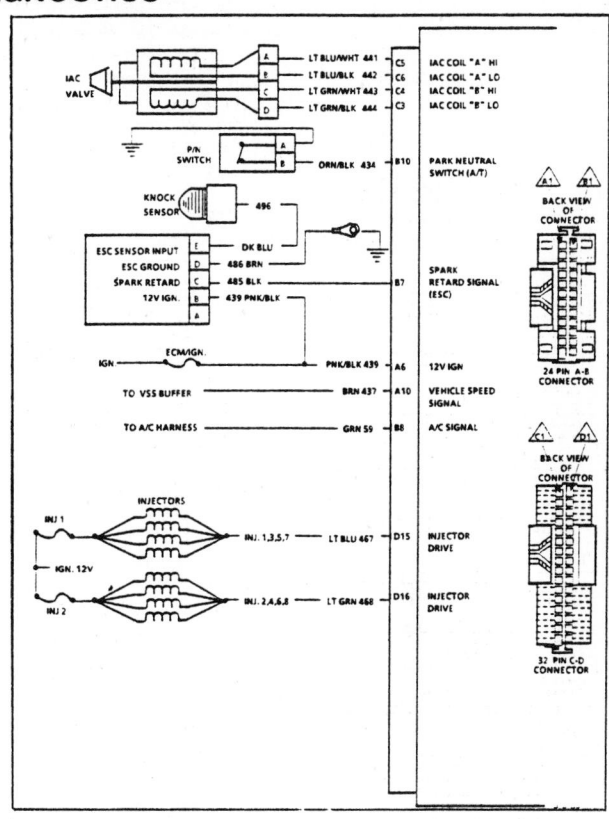

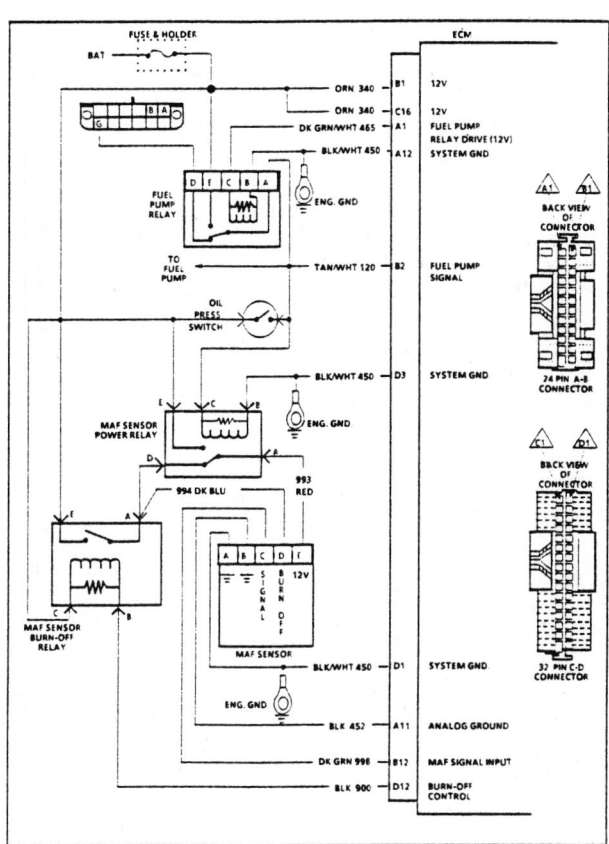

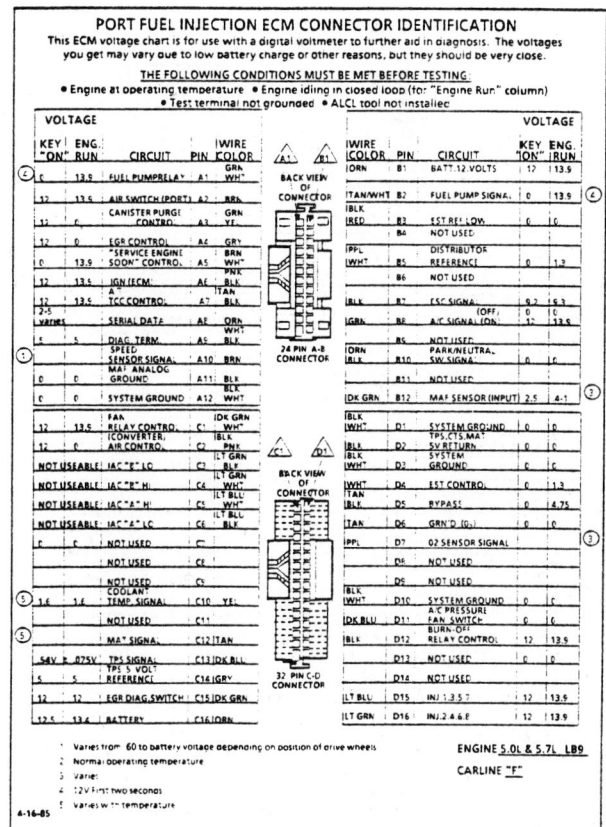

MPI TROUBLE DIAGNOSTICS

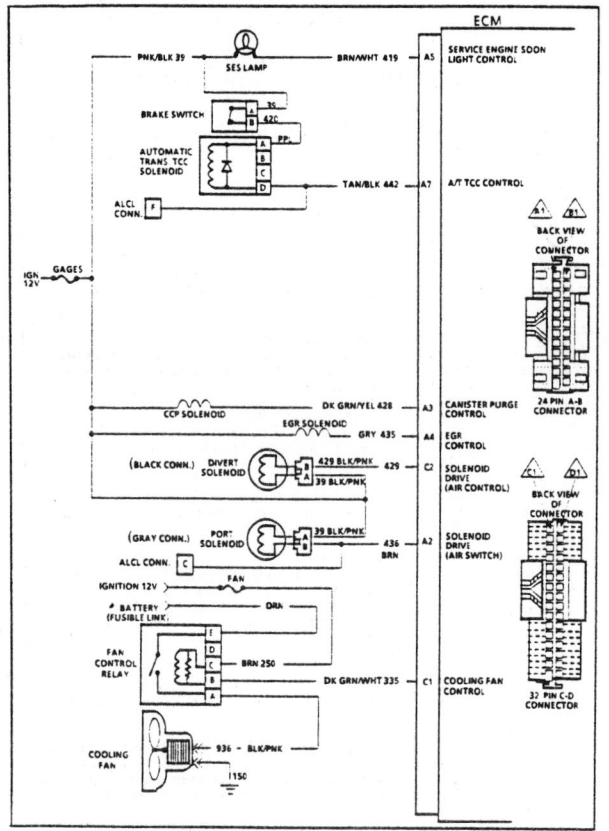

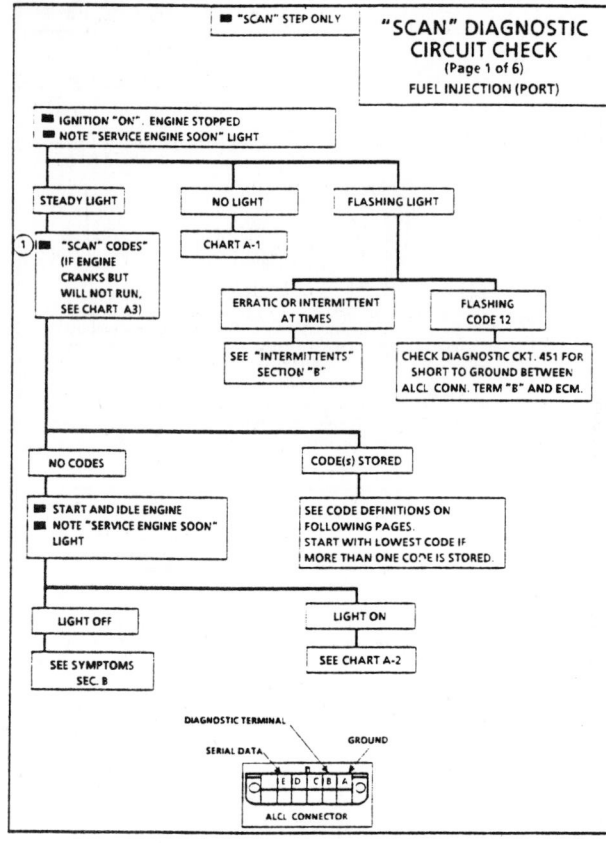

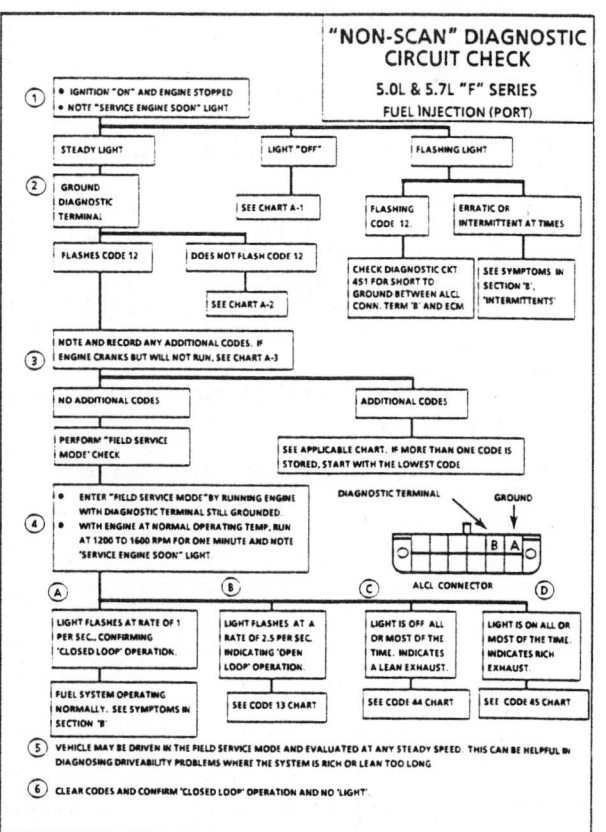

MPI TROUBLE DIAGNOSTICS

"SCAN" DIAGNOSTIC CIRCUIT CHECK
(Page 3 of 6)
5.0L & 5.7L "F" SERIES - (CODE DEFINITIONS)

DEFINITION

CODE 21
- IGNITION "ON".
- ENGINE STOPPED.
- THROTTLE CLOSED.
- "SCAN" TPS.
  OR
- ENGINE IDLING.
- THROTTLE CLOSED.
- "SCAN" TPS.

HARD FAILURE -
"SCAN" TOOL TOOL READS OVER 4.5 VOLTS. GROUND WIRE OPEN, SIGNAL LINE SHORTED TO SENSOR REF. LINE, OR FAULTY SENSOR.
SEE CODE CHART 21.
OR
HARD FAILURE -
"SCAN" TOOL TOOL READS OVER 2.5 VOLTS. GROUND WIRE OPEN OR FAULTY SENSOR. SEE CODE CHART 21.

INTERMITTENT CODE -
"SCAN" TOOL READS THROTTLE POSITION IN VOLTS. SHOULD READ BETWEEN 020-125 (200 MV AND 1.25 V). WITH THROTTLE CLOSED AND IGNITION ON OR AT IDLE. VOLTAGE SHOULD INCREASE AT A STEADY RATE AS THROTTLE IS MOVED TOWARD WOT. SEE "INTERMITTENTS" SECTION B.

CODE 22
- IGNITION "ON".
- ENGINE STOPPED.
- "SCAN" TPS.

HARD FAILURE -
"SCAN" TOOL READS BELOW 020V (200 MV) OPEN OR SHORTED TO GROUND CIRCUIT IN 5V REFERENCE, SIGNAL CIRCUIT OR FAULTY SENSOR. SEE CODE CHART 22.

INTERMITTENT CODE -
"SCAN" TOOL READS THROTTLE POSITION IN VOLTS. SHOULD READ BETWEEN 020-125 (200 MV AND 1.25 V). WITH THROTTLE CLOSED AND IGNITION ON OR AT IDLE. VOLTAGE SHOULD INCREASE AT A STEADY RATE AS THROTTLE IS MOVED TOWARD WOT. SEE "INTERMITTENTS" SECTION B.

CODE 23
- IGNITION "ON".
- ENGINE STOPPED.
- "SCAN" MAT TEMPERATURE.

HARD FAILURE -
"SCAN" TOOL READS BELOW -30°C. CIRCUIT OPEN OR FAULTY SENSOR. SEE CODE CHART 23.

INTERMITTENT CODE -
"SCAN" TOOL READS TEMPERATURE OF THE AIR ENTERING THE ENGINE. SHOULD READ CLOSE TO AMBIENT AIR TEMPERATURE WHEN ENGINE IS COLD, AND RISE AS TEMPERATURE INCREASES. SEE "INTERMITTENTS" SECTION B.

"SCAN" DIAGNOSTIC CIRCUIT CHECK
(Page 5 of 6)
5.0L & 5.7L "F" SERIES - (CODE DEFINITIONS)

CODES — **DEFINITION**

CODE 41
- CLEAR CODES. START AND IDLE ENGINE FOR 1 MINUTE.

HARD FAILURE -
"SERVICE ENGINE SOON" LIGHT ON. "SCAN" TOOL INDICATES CODE 41. SEE CODE CHART 41.

CODE 42
- CLEAR CODES. START AND IDLE ENGINE FOR 1 MINUTE.
- IF NO "SERVICE ENGINE SOON " LIGHT, REFER TO INTERMITTENTS IN SECTION "B".

HARD FAILURE -
"SERVICE ENGINE SOON" ON, SCAN TOOL INDICATES CODE 42. SEE CODE CHART 42.

INTERMITTENT CODE -
THE SCAN DOES NOT HAVE THE ABILITY TO HELP DIAGNOSE A CODE 42 PROBLEM. SEE "INTERMITTENTS" SECTION B.

CODE 43
- "SCAN" TOOL IN SPECIAL MODE.
- ENGINE IDLING AT 1000 RPM.
- "SCAN"KNOCK RETARD OR OLD PA3.

HARD FAILURE -
KNOCK RETARD OR (OLD PA3) WILL DISPLAY NUMBERS THAT ARE CONSTANTLY CHANGING (OTO 255). FAULTY ESC CIRCUIT. SEE CODE CHART 43.

INTERMITTENT CODE -
NUMBERS SHOULD INCREASE WHEN KNOCK IS BEING DETECTED. SEE "INTERMITTENTS" SECTION B.

CODE 44
- "SCAN" TOOL IN SPECIAL MODE.
- ENGINE IDLING AT 1000 RPM.
- COOLANT 75° TO 95° C
- "SCAN" OXYGEN SENSOR VOLTAGE.

HARD FAILURE -
"SCAN" TOOL O_2 VOLTAGE CONSISTENTLY BELOW .35V. CAUSED BY A LEAN EXHAUST OR SIGNAL CIRCUIT SHORTED TO GROUND. SEE CODE CHART 44.

INTERMITTENT CODE -
THE "SCAN" TOOL HAS SEVERAL POSITIONS THAT WILL INDICATE THE STATE OF THE EXHAUST GASES. CROSSCOUNTS, RICH-LEAN INDICATION, O_2 VOLTAGE, INTEGRATOR, AND BLOCK LEARN. SEE "SCAN" POSITION INFORMATION IN INTRODUCTION.

CODE 45
- "SCAN" TOOL IN "SPECIAL" MODE.
- ENGINE IDLING AT 1000 RPM.
- COOLANT 75° TO 95° C
- "SCAN" OXYGEN SENSOR VOLTAGE.

HARD FAILURE -
"SCAN' O_2 VOLTAGE CONSISTENTLY ABOVE .55V. RICH EXHAUST CAUSES A HIGH O_2 VOLTAGE. SEE CODE CHART 45.

INTERMITTENT CODE -
THE "SCAN" HAS SEVERAL POSITIONS THAT WILL INDICATE THE STATE OF THE EXHAUST GASES. CROSSCOUNTS, RICH-LEAN INDICATION, O_2 VOLTAGE, INTEGRATOR, AND BLOCK LEARN. SEE "SCAN" POSITION INFORMATION IN INTRODUCTION.

"SCAN" DIAGNOSTIC CIRCUIT CHECK
(Page 4 of 6)
5.0L & 5.7L "F" SERIES - (CODE DEFINITIONS)

CODES — **DEFINITION**

CODE 24
- ENGINE RUNNING.
- DRIVE WHEELS TURNING.
- "SCAN" MPH.

HARD FAILURE -
"SCAN" TOOL READS 0 MPH. IF SPEEDOMETER IS WORKING OK, THEN THE VSS SIGNAL INPUT IS OPEN, SHORTED TO GROUND, OR THE BUFFER IS DEFECTIVE. SEE CODE CHART 24.

INTERMITTENT CODE -
"SCAN" TOOL READING SHOULD CLOSELY MATCH WITH SPEEDOMETER READING WITH DRIVE WHEELS TURNING. SEE 'INTERMITTENTS' SECTION B.

CODE 25
- IGNITION "ON".
- ENGINE STOPPED.
- "SCAN" MAT TEMPERATURE.

HARD FAILURE -
"SCAN" TOOL READS ABOVE 150°C. CIRCUIT SHORTED TO GROUND OR FAULTY SENSOR. SEE CODE CHART 25.

INTERMITTENT CODE -
"SCAN" TOOL READS TEMPERATURE OF THE AIR ENTERING THE ENGINE. SHOULD READ CLOSE TO AMBIENT AIR TEMPERATURE WHEN ENGINE IS COLD, AND RISE AS TEMPERATURE INCREASES. SEE "INTERMITTENTS" SECTION B.

CODE 32

HARD FAILURE -
THE "SCAN" TOOL IS NOT USEFUL IN DIAGNOSING CODE 32 PROBLEMS. SEE CODE CHART 32 IF CODE WAS STORED IN MEMORY.

CODE 33,& 34 -
- CLEAR CODES
- START ENGINE AND RECHECK FOR "SERVICE ENGINE SOON" LIGHT.
- LIGHT "ON - CODE 33 OR 34 -
- SEE CODE CHART 33 OR 34.
- LIGHT OFF -
  PROBLEM IS INTERMITTENT SEE SECTION B "INTERMITTENTS".

HARD FAILURE -
"SCAN" TOOL READS DEFAULT VALUE BASED ON RPM AND TPS. DIFFICULT TO USE "SCAN" TO DIAGNOSE.

INTERMITTENT CODE -
"SCAN"TOOL READS AIR FLOW AND DISPLAYS IN GRAMS PER SECOND. SHOULD READ BETWEEN 5-8 ON A FULLY WARMED UP IDLING ENGINE. VALUES SHOULD CHANGE RATHER QUICKLY ON ACCELERATION, BUT VALUES SHOULD REMAIN FAIRLY STABLE AT ANY GIVEN RPM. SEE "INTERMITTENTS" SECTION B.

CODE 36

HARD FAILURE -
THE "SCAN" TOOL IS NOT OF MUCH USE IN DIAGNOSING A CODE 32 PROBLEM. SEE CODE CHART 36 IF CODE 36 WAS STORED IN MEMORY.

"SCAN" DIAGNOSTIC CIRCUIT CHECK
(Page 6 of 6)
5.0L & 5.7L "F" SERIES - (CODE DEFINITIONS)

CODES — **DEFINITION**

CODE 51
- CLEAR CODES
- START ENGINE
- CHECK FOR CODE

HARD FAILURE -
CODE 51 RESETS WHICH INDICATES A FAULTY MEM/CAL. SEE CODE CHART 51.

CODE 53
- CLEAR CODES
- START ENGINE
- CHECK FOR CODE

HARD FAILURE -
CODE 53 RESETS WHICH INDICATES GENERATOR VOLTAGE EXCEEDED 17.1 VOLTS REPAIR GENERATOR.

INTERMITTENT CODE -
THE "SCAN" TOOL DOES NOT HAVE THE ABILTIY TO READ BATTERY VOLTAGE. If CODE 53 DID NOT RESET , SEE INTERMITTENTS IN SECTION B.

CODE 54
- CLEAR CODES
- START ENGINE
- CHECK FOR CODE

HARD FAILURE -
CODE 54 RESETS WHICH INDICATES LOW FUEL PUMP VOLTAGE. SEE CODE CHART 54.

CODE 55
- CLEAR CODES
- START ENGINE
- CHECK FOR CODE

HARD FAILURE -
CODE 55 RESETS WHICH INDICATES THE ECM IS FAULTY. REPLACE ECM.

MPI TROUBLE DIAGNOSTICS

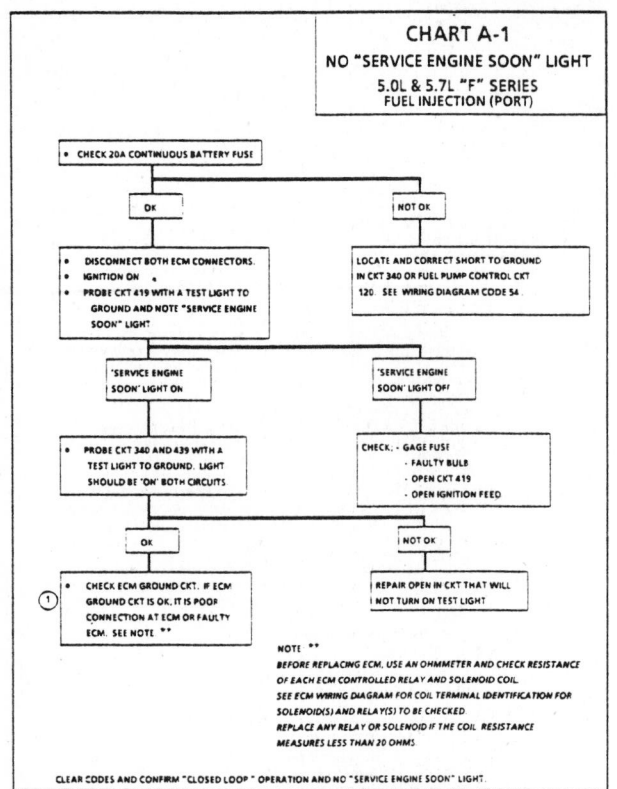

CHART A-1
NO "SERVICE ENGINE SOON" LIGHT

5.0L & 5.7L "F" SERIES
FUEL INJECTION (PORT)

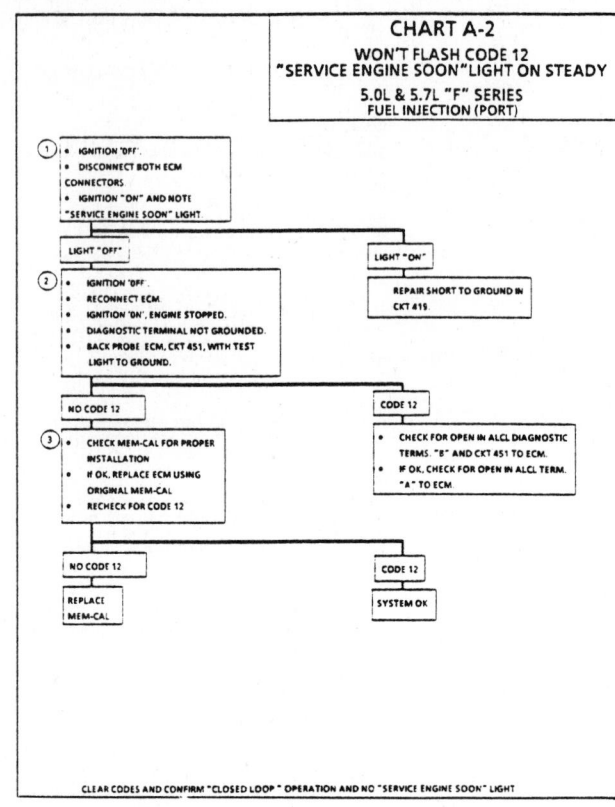

CHART A-2
WON'T FLASH CODE 12
"SERVICE ENGINE SOON" LIGHT ON STEADY

5.0L & 5.7L "F" SERIES
FUEL INJECTION (PORT)

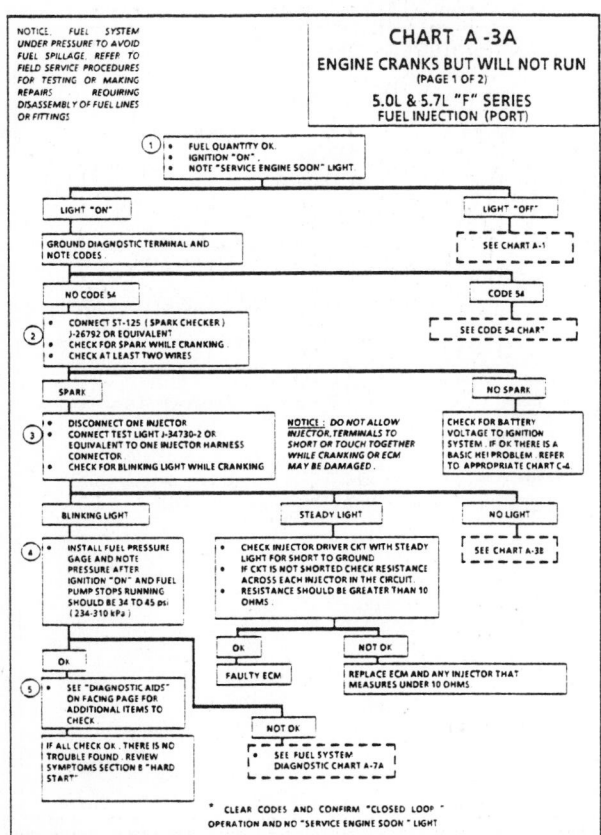

CHART A-3A
ENGINE CRANKS BUT WILL NOT RUN
(PAGE 1 OF 2)

5.0L & 5.7L "F" SERIES
FUEL INJECTION (PORT)

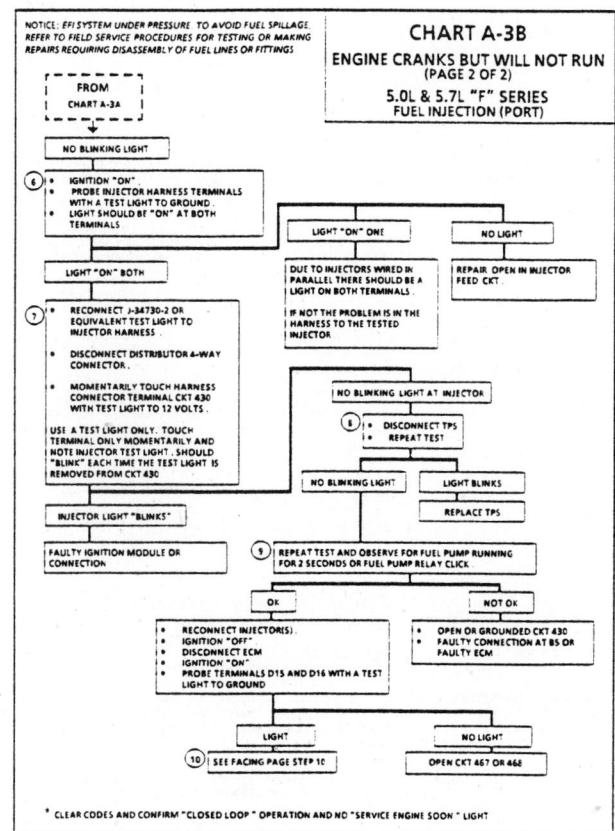

CHART A-3B
ENGINE CRANKS BUT WILL NOT RUN
(PAGE 2 OF 2)

5.0L & 5.7L "F" SERIES
FUEL INJECTION (PORT)

MPI TROUBLE DIAGNOSTICS

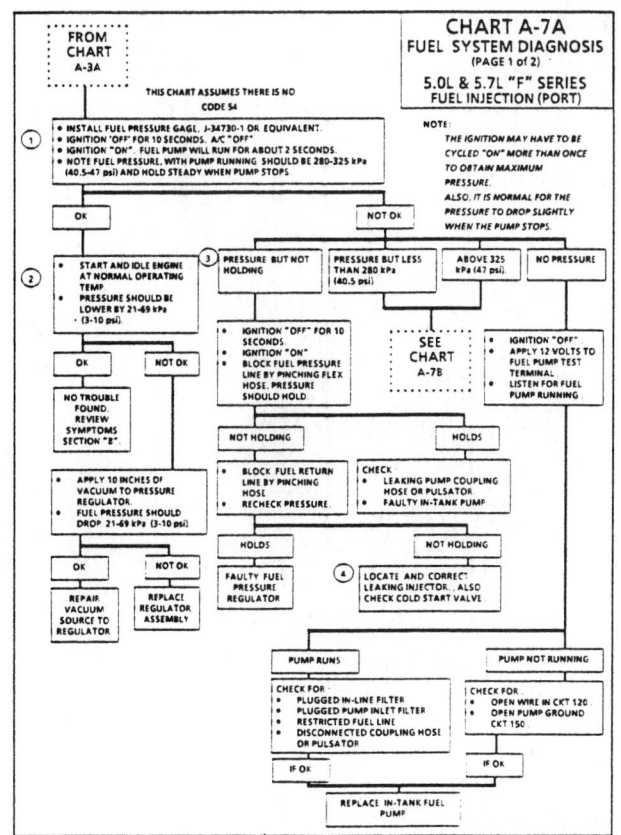

CHART A-7A
FUEL SYSTEM DIAGNOSIS
(PAGE 1 of 2)
5.0L & 5.7L "F" SERIES
FUEL INJECTION (PORT)

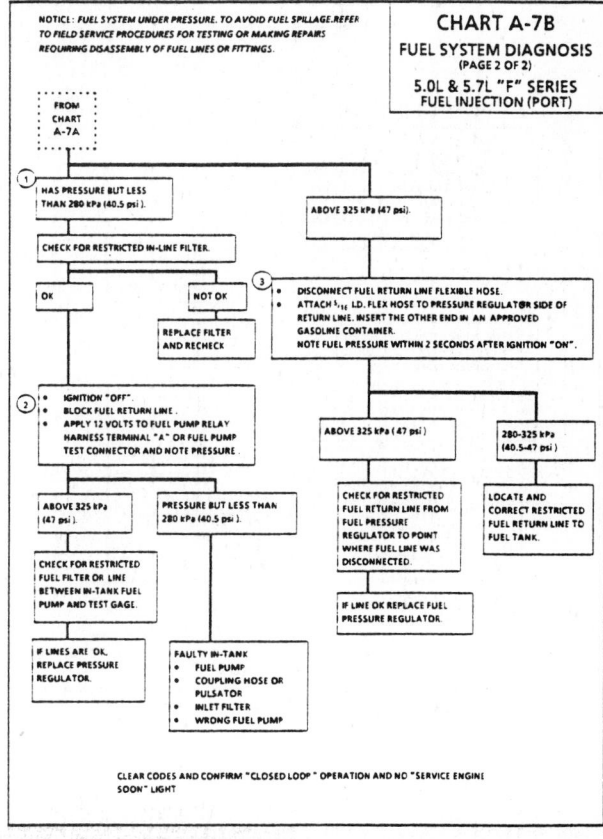

CHART A-7B
FUEL SYSTEM DIAGNOSIS
(PAGE 2 OF 2)
5.0L & 5.7L "F" SERIES
FUEL INJECTION (PORT)

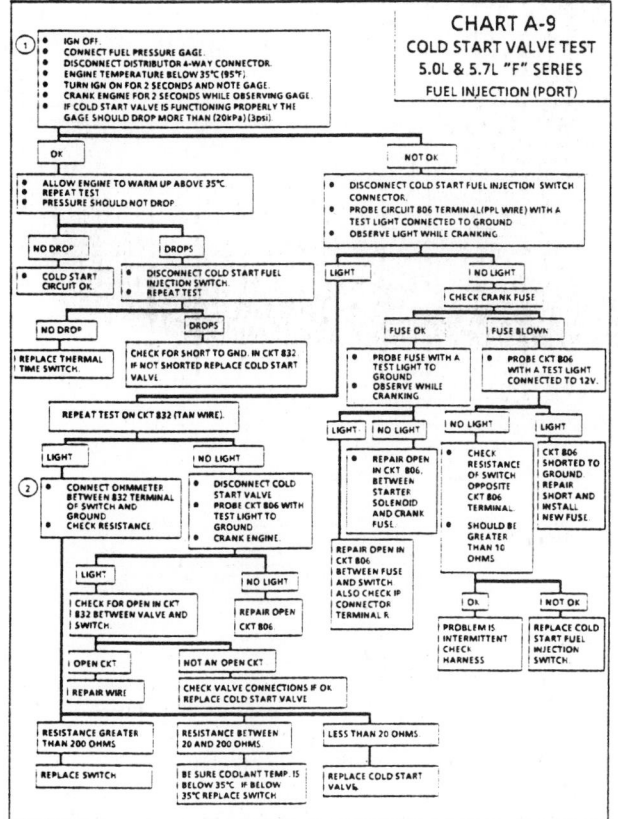

CHART A-9
COLD START VALVE TEST
5.0L & 5.7L "F" SERIES
FUEL INJECTION (PORT)

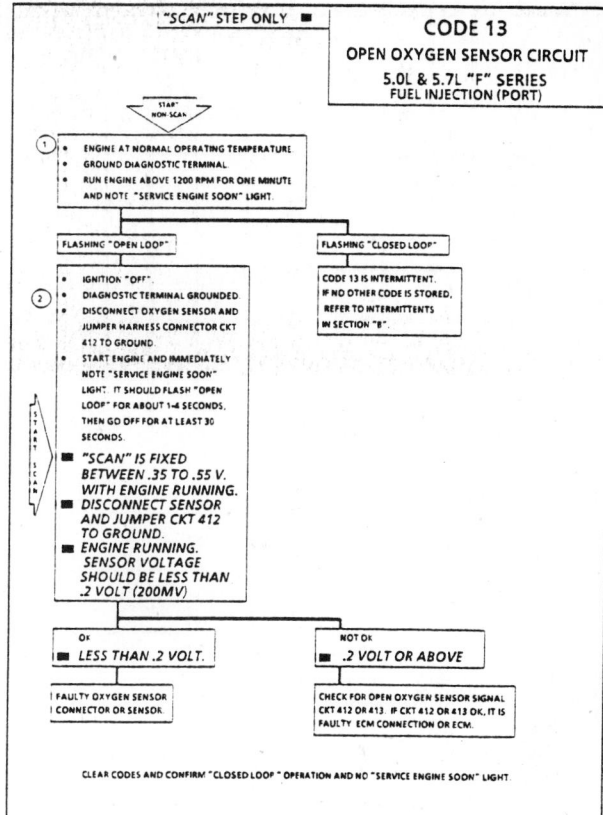

CODE 13
OPEN OXYGEN SENSOR CIRCUIT
5.0L & 5.7L "F" SERIES
FUEL INJECTION (PORT)

FUEL INJECTION SYSTEMS
GENERAL MOTORS CORPORATION

MPI TROUBLE DIAGNOSTICS

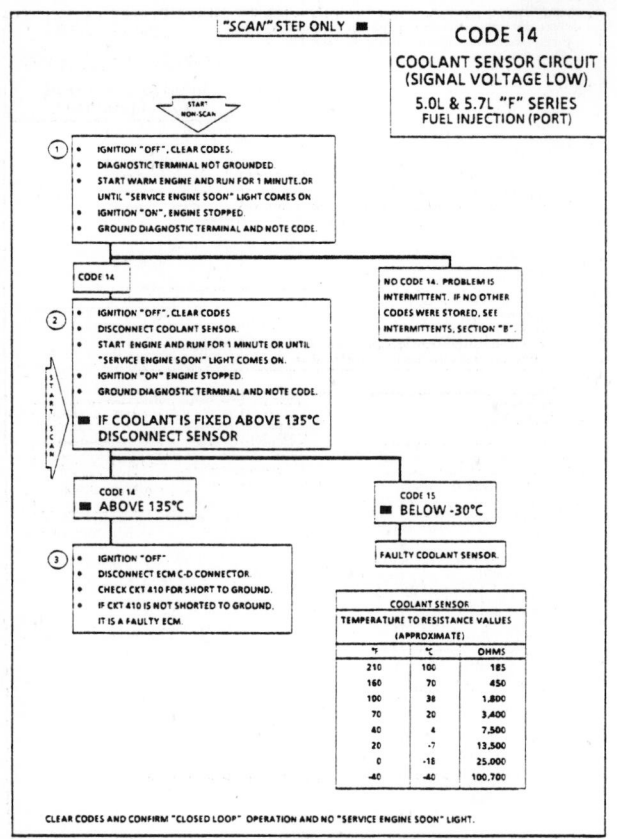

CODE 14
COOLANT SENSOR CIRCUIT
(SIGNAL VOLTAGE LOW)
5.0L & 5.7L "F" SERIES
FUEL INJECTION (PORT)

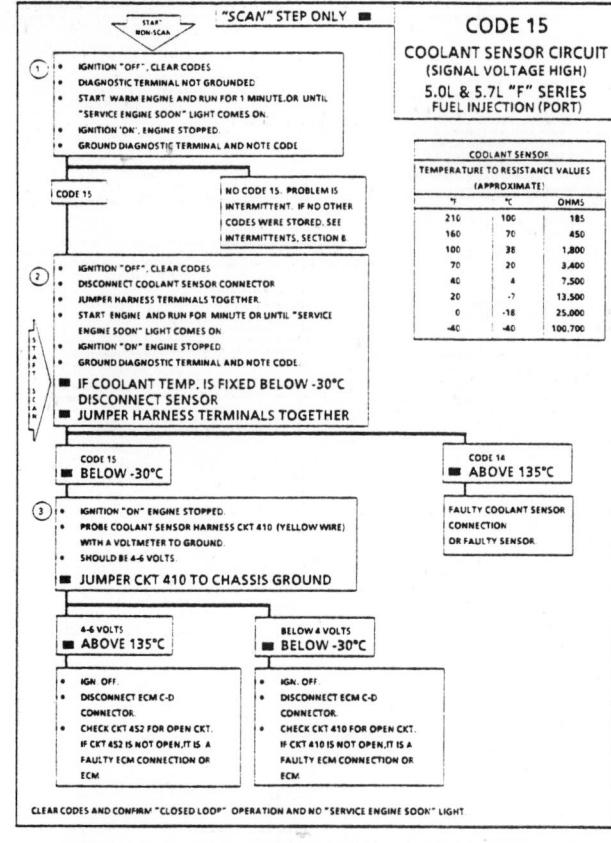

CODE 15
COOLANT SENSOR CIRCUIT
(SIGNAL VOLTAGE HIGH)
5.0L & 5.7L "F" SERIES
FUEL INJECTION (PORT)

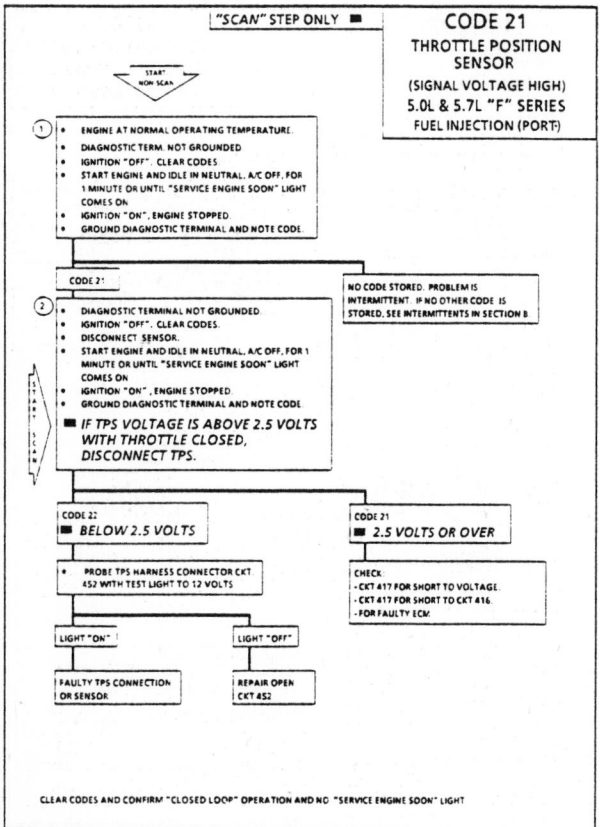

CODE 21
THROTTLE POSITION
SENSOR
(SIGNAL VOLTAGE HIGH)
5.0L & 5.7L "F" SERIES
FUEL INJECTION (PORT)

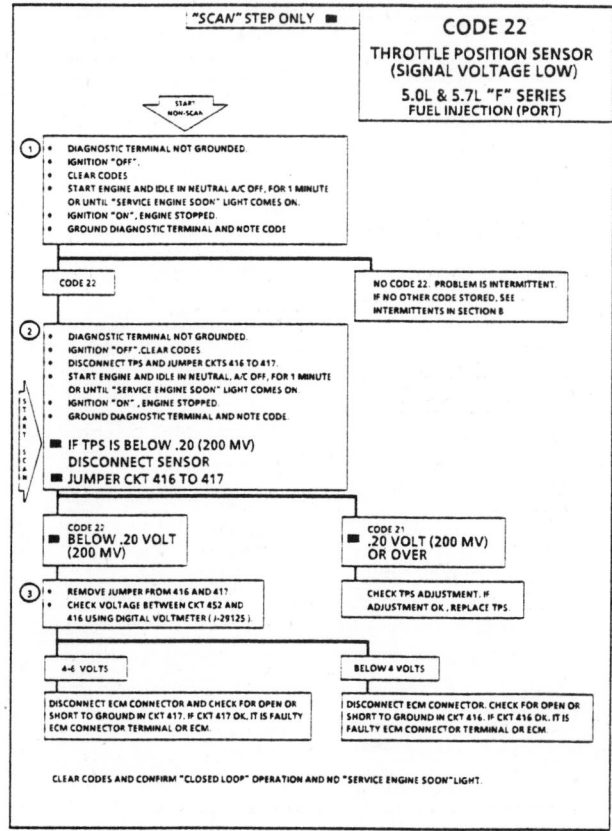

CODE 22
THROTTLE POSITION SENSOR
(SIGNAL VOLTAGE LOW)
5.0L & 5.7L "F" SERIES
FUEL INJECTION (PORT)

MPI TROUBLE DIAGNOSTICS

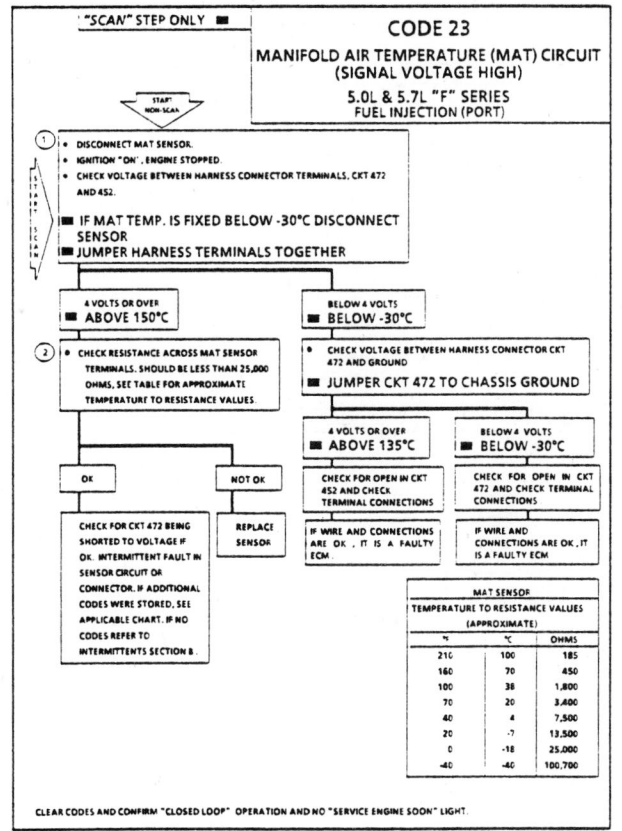

CODE 23

MANIFOLD AIR TEMPERATURE (MAT) CIRCUIT (SIGNAL VOLTAGE HIGH)

5.0L & 5.7L "F" SERIES FUEL INJECTION (PORT)

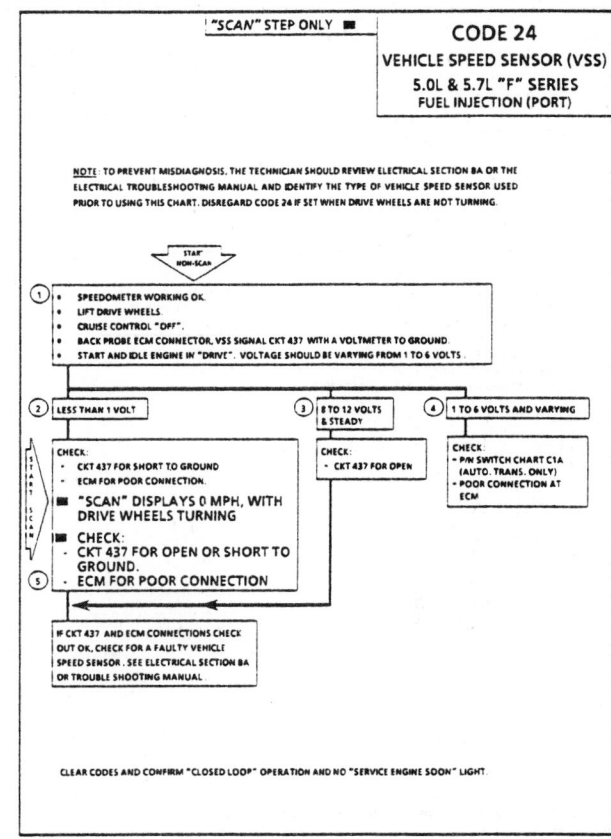

CODE 24

VEHICLE SPEED SENSOR (VSS)

5.0L & 5.7L "F" SERIES FUEL INJECTION (PORT)

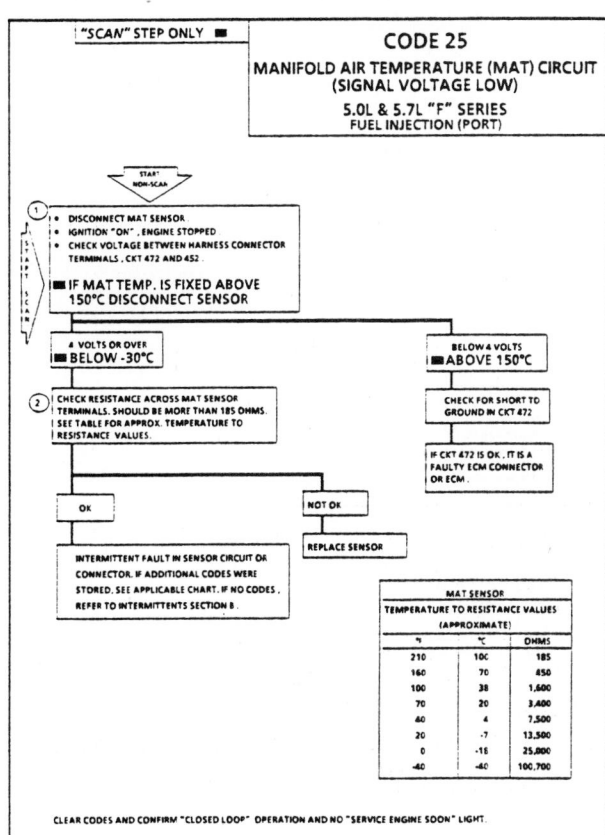

CODE 25

MANIFOLD AIR TEMPERATURE (MAT) CIRCUIT (SIGNAL VOLTAGE LOW)

5.0L & 5.7L "F" SERIES FUEL INJECTION (PORT)

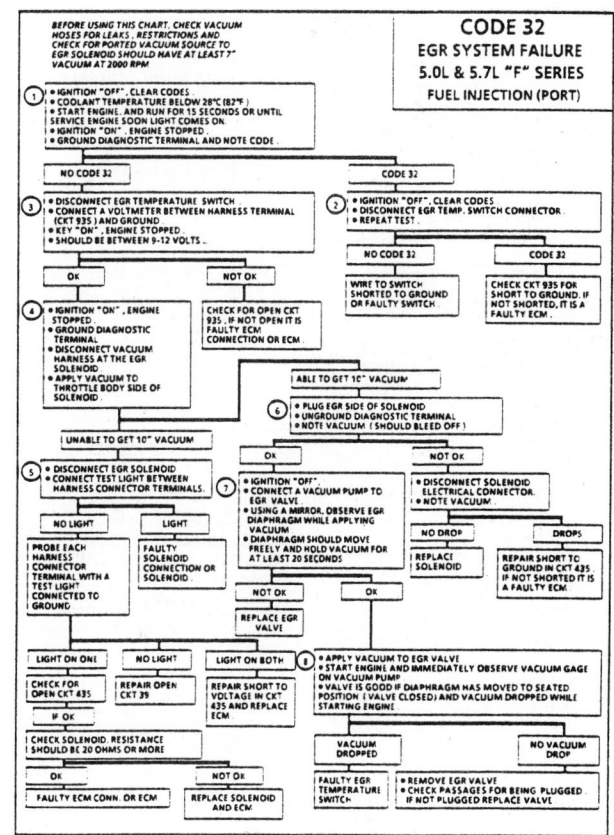

CODE 32

EGR SYSTEM FAILURE

5.0L & 5.7L "F" SERIES FUEL INJECTION (PORT)

MPI TROUBLE DIAGNOSTICS

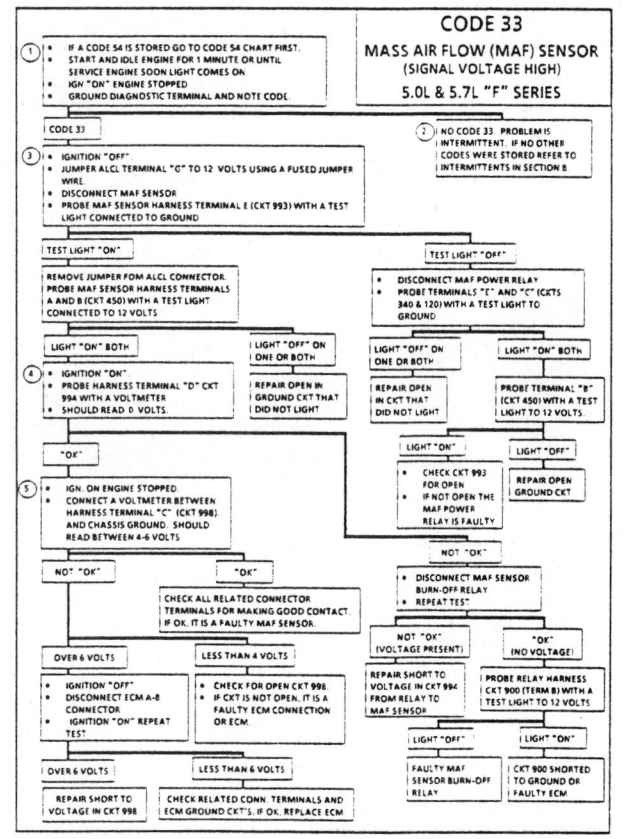

CODE 33

MASS AIR FLOW (MAF) SENSOR
(SIGNAL VOLTAGE HIGH)

5.0L & 5.7L "F" SERIES

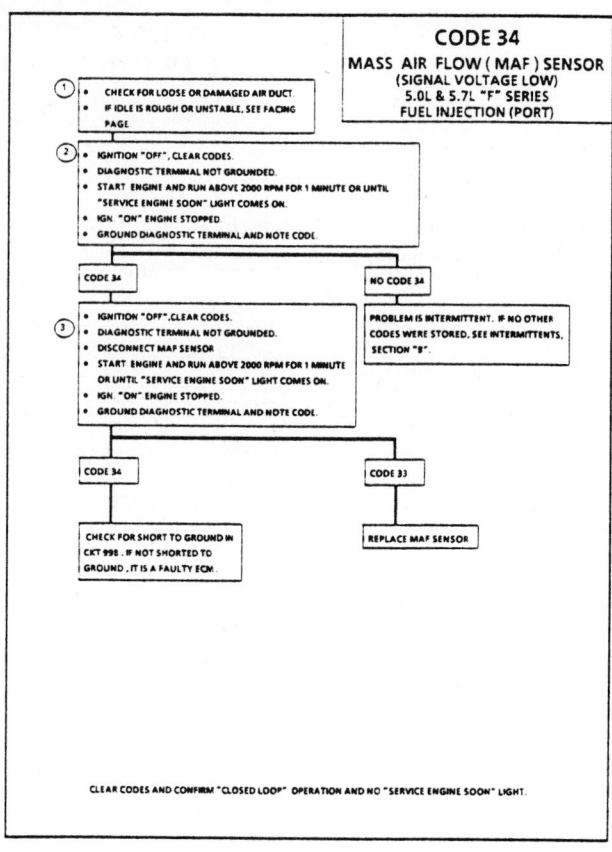

CODE 34

MASS AIR FLOW (MAF) SENSOR
(SIGNAL VOLTAGE LOW)
5.0L & 5.7L "F" SERIES
FUEL INJECTION (PORT)

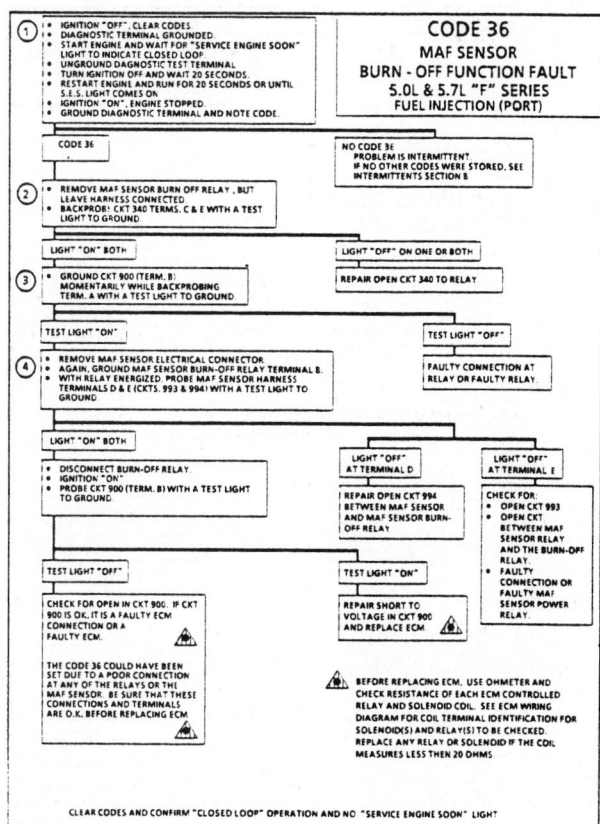

CODE 36

MAF SENSOR
BURN - OFF FUNCTION FAULT
5.0L & 5.7L "F" SERIES
FUEL INJECTION (PORT)

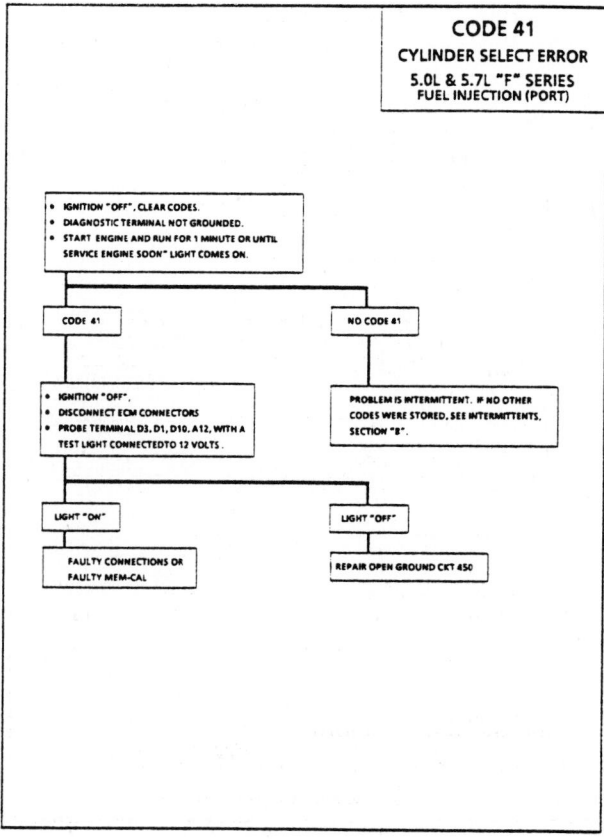

CODE 41

CYLINDER SELECT ERROR

5.0L & 5.7L "F" SERIES
FUEL INJECTION (PORT)

MPI TROUBLE DIAGNOSTICS

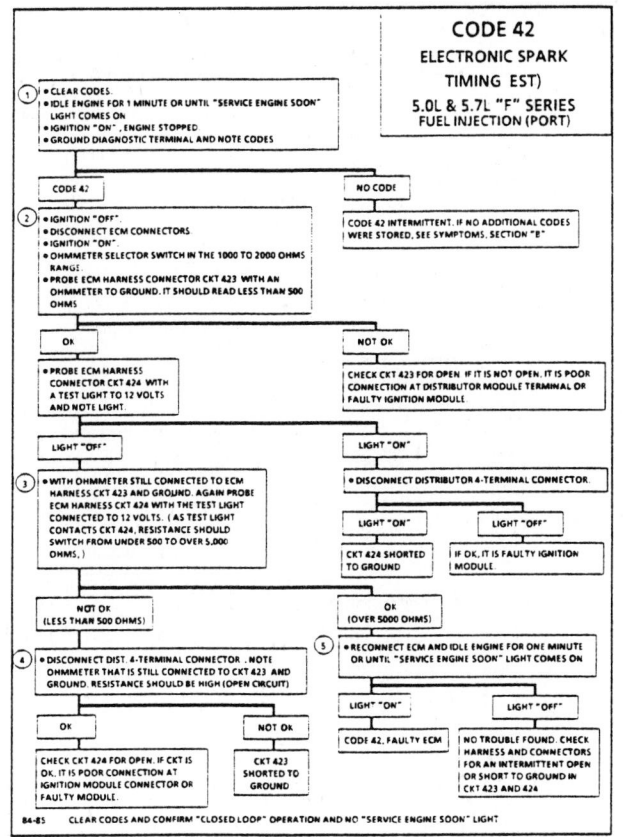

CODE 42

ELECTRONIC SPARK TIMING EST)

5.0L & 5.7L "F" SERIES
FUEL INJECTION (PORT)

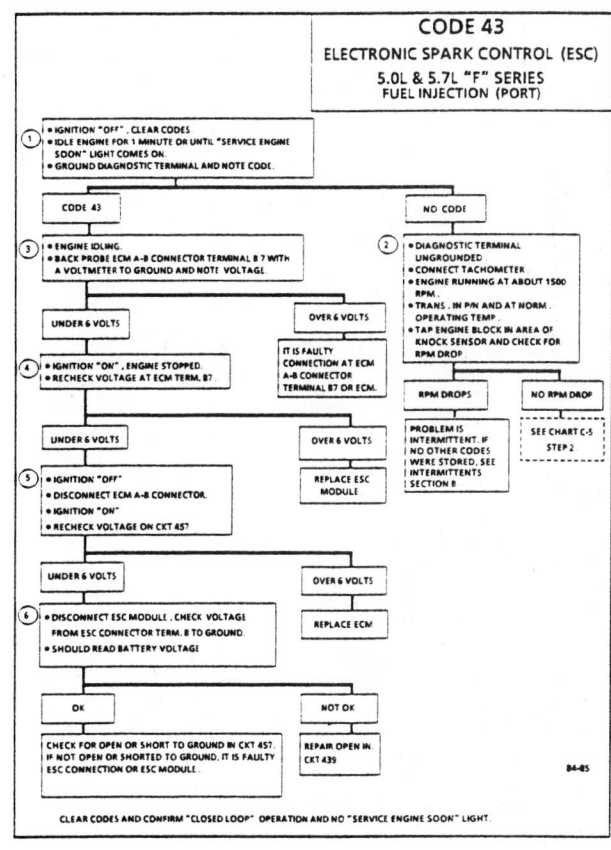

CODE 43

ELECTRONIC SPARK CONTROL (ESC)

5.0L & 5.7L "F" SERIES
FUEL INJECTION (PORT)

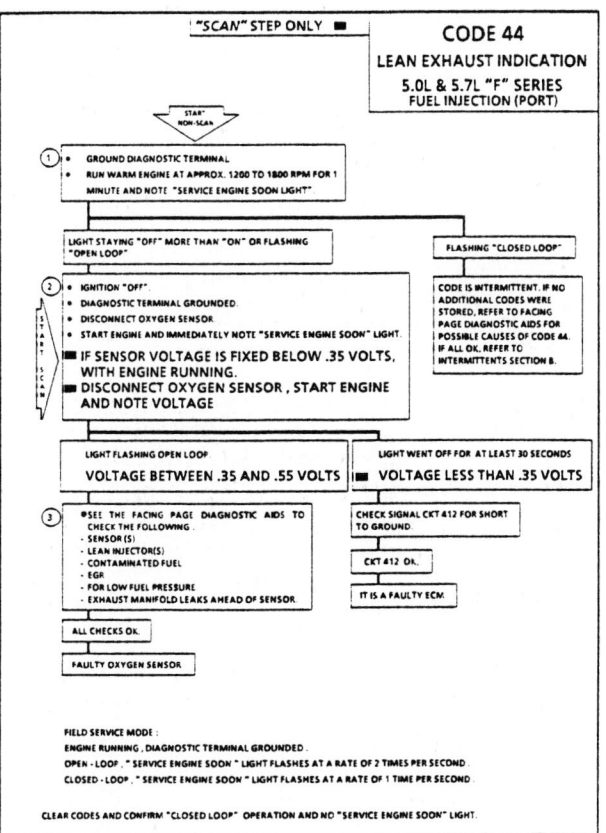

CODE 44

LEAN EXHAUST INDICATION

5.0L & 5.7L "F" SERIES
FUEL INJECTION (PORT)

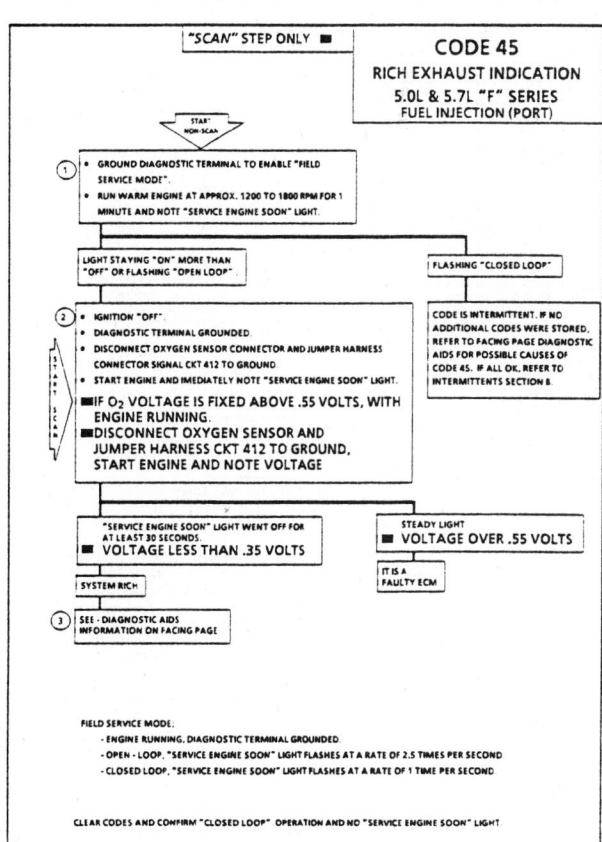

CODE 45

RICH EXHAUST INDICATION

5.0L & 5.7L "F" SERIES
FUEL INJECTION (PORT)

MPI TROUBLE DIAGNOSTICS

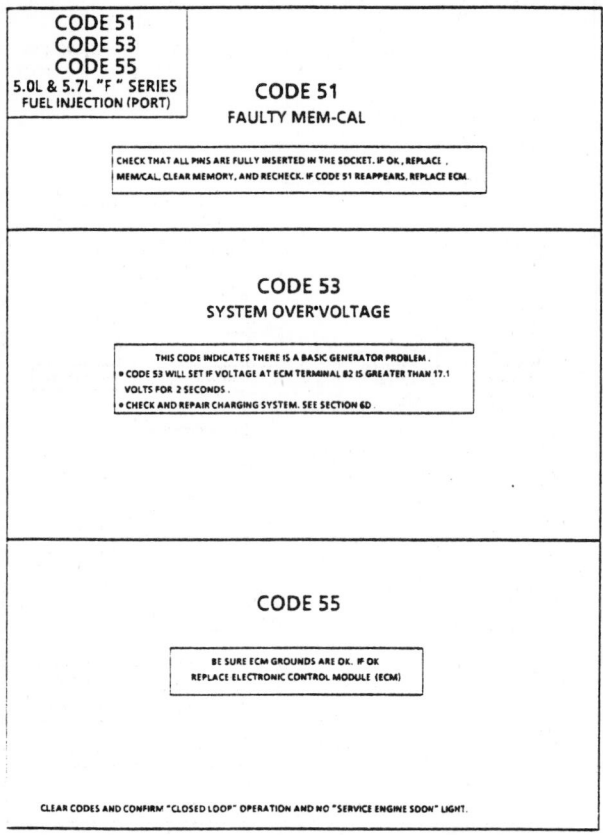

CODE 51
CODE 53
CODE 55
5.0L & 5.7L "F" SERIES
FUEL INJECTION (PORT)

CODE 51
FAULTY MEM-CAL

CHECK THAT ALL PINS ARE FULLY INSERTED IN THE SOCKET. IF OK, REPLACE. MEM/CAL, CLEAR MEMORY, AND RECHECK. IF CODE 51 REAPPEARS, REPLACE ECM.

CODE 53
SYSTEM OVER-VOLTAGE

THIS CODE INDICATES THERE IS A BASIC GENERATOR PROBLEM.
• CODE 53 WILL BE SET IF VOLTAGE AT ECM TERMINAL B2 IS GREATER THAN 17.1 VOLTS FOR 2 SECONDS.
• CHECK AND REPAIR CHARGING SYSTEM. SEE SECTION 6D.

CODE 55

BE SURE ECM GROUNDS ARE OK. IF OK
REPLACE ELECTRONIC CONTROL MODULE (ECM)

CLEAR CODES AND CONFIRM "CLOSED LOOP" OPERATION AND NO "SERVICE ENGINE SOON" LIGHT.

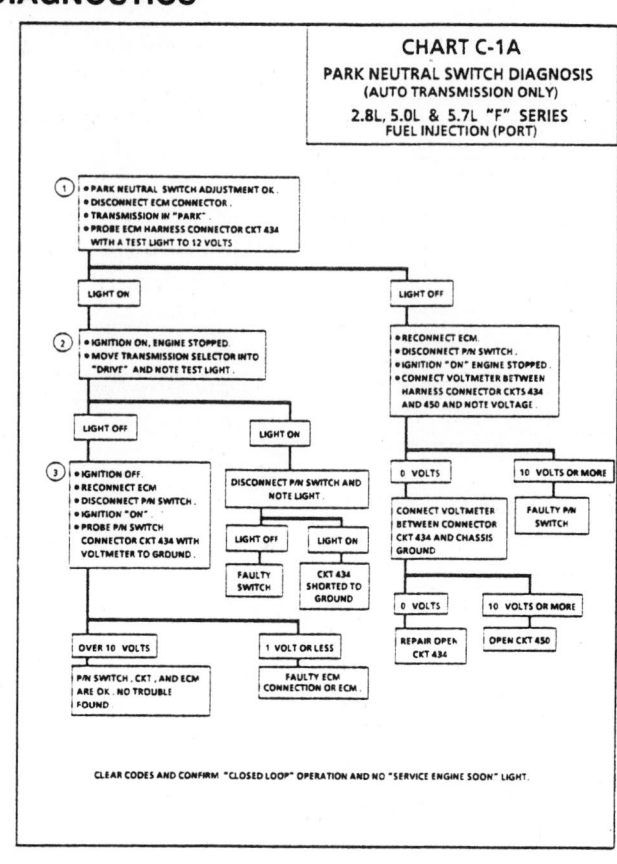

CHART C-1A
PARK NEUTRAL SWITCH DIAGNOSIS
(AUTO TRANSMISSION ONLY)
2.8L, 5.0L & 5.7L "F" SERIES
FUEL INJECTION (PORT)

CLEAR CODES AND CONFIRM "CLOSED LOOP" OPERATION AND NO "SERVICE ENGINE SOON" LIGHT.

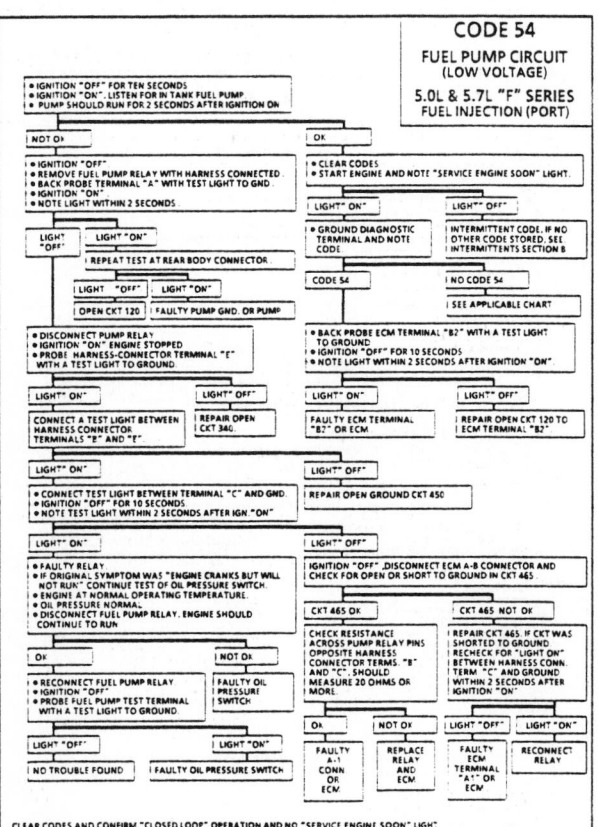

CODE 54
FUEL PUMP CIRCUIT
(LOW VOLTAGE)
5.0L & 5.7L "F" SERIES
FUEL INJECTION (PORT)

CLEAR CODES AND CONFIRM "CLOSED LOOP" OPERATION AND NO "SERVICE ENGINE SOON" LIGHT.

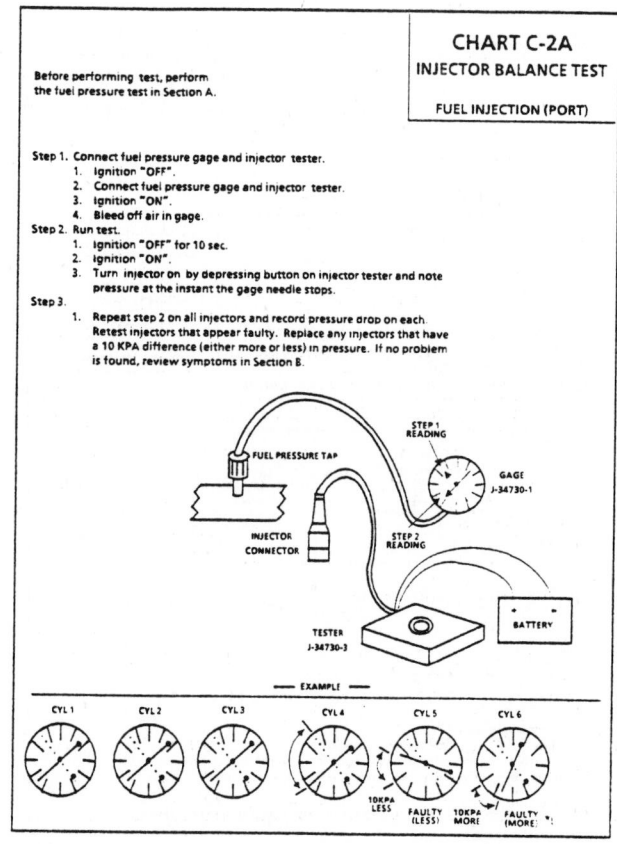

CHART C-2A
INJECTOR BALANCE TEST

FUEL INJECTION (PORT)

Before performing test, perform
the fuel pressure test in Section A.

Step 1. Connect fuel pressure gage and injector tester.
1. Ignition "OFF".
2. Connect fuel pressure gage and injector tester.
3. Ignition "ON".
4. Bleed off air in gage.
Step 2. Run test.
1. Ignition "OFF" for 10 sec.
2. Ignition "ON".
3. Turn injector on by depressing button on injector tester and note pressure at the instant the gage needle stops.
Step 3.
1. Repeat step 2 on all injectors and record pressure drop on each. Retest injectors that appear faulty. Replace any injectors that have a 10 KPA difference (either more or less) in pressure. If no problem is found, review symptoms in Section B.

MPI TROUBLE DIAGNOSTICS

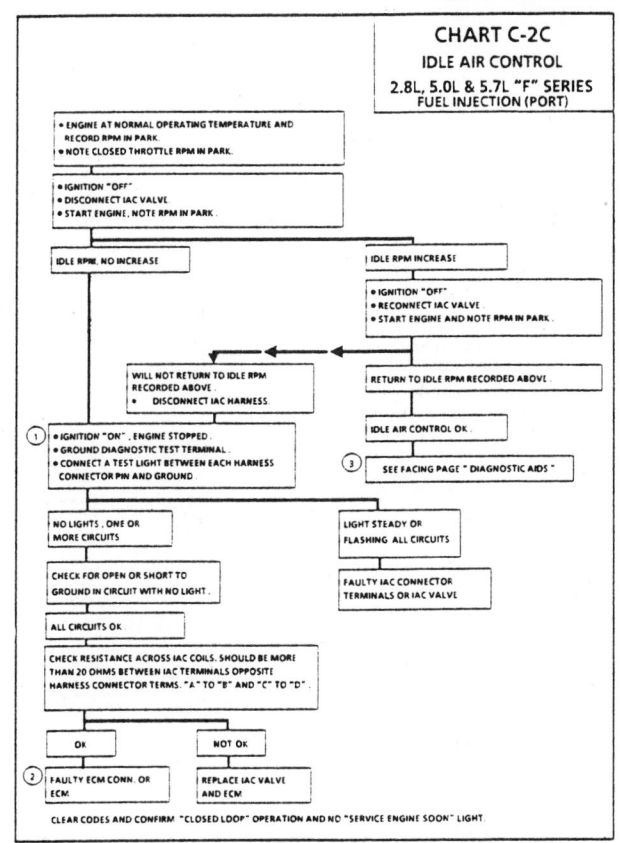

CHART C-2C

IDLE AIR CONTROL

2.8L, 5.0L & 5.7L "F" SERIES
FUEL INJECTION (PORT)

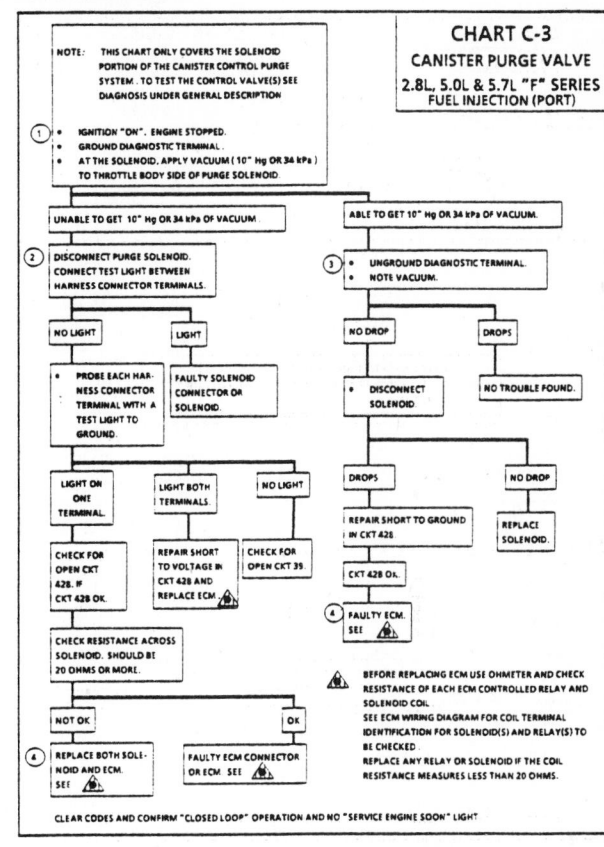

CHART C-3

CANISTER PURGE VALVE

2.8L, 5.0L & 5.7L "F" SERIES
FUEL INJECTION (PORT)

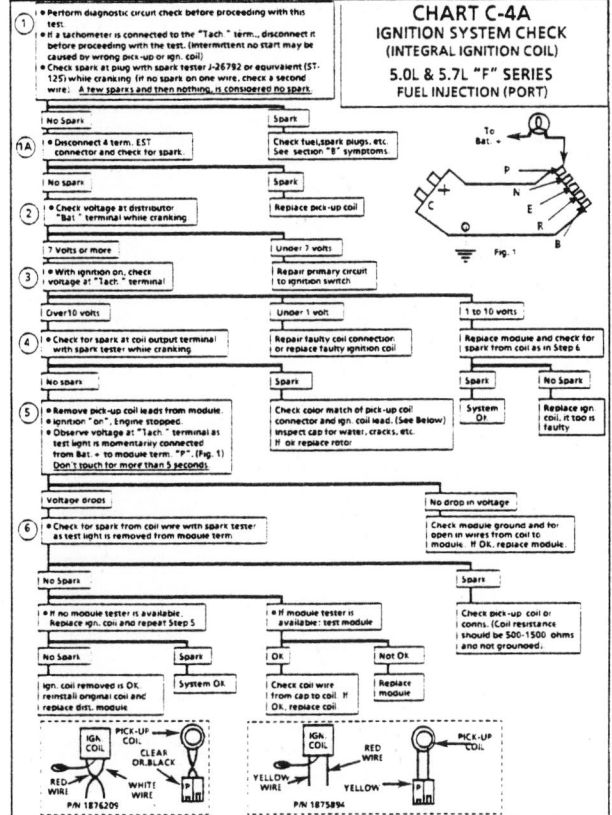

CHART C-4A

IGNITION SYSTEM CHECK
(INTEGRAL IGNITION COIL)

5.0L & 5.7L "F" SERIES
FUEL INJECTION (PORT)

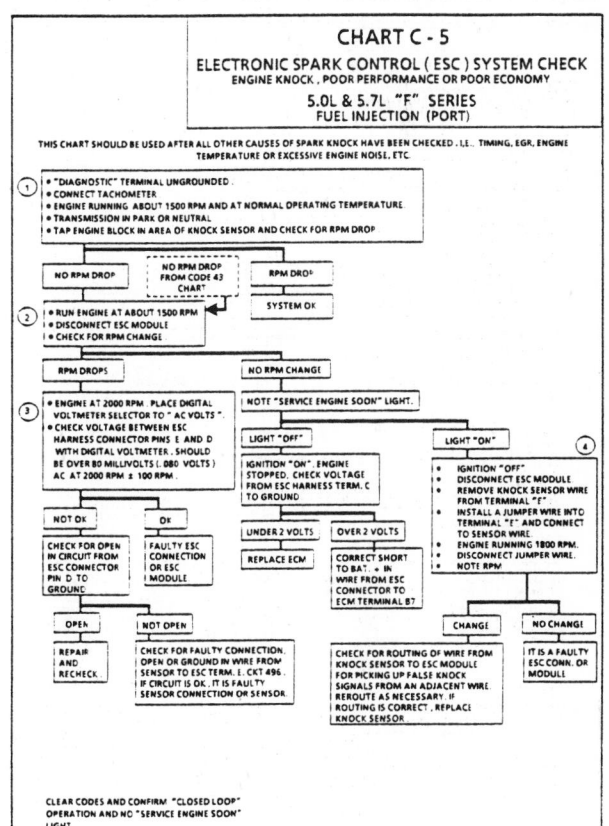

CHART C-5

ELECTRONIC SPARK CONTROL (ESC) SYSTEM CHECK
ENGINE KNOCK , POOR PERFORMANCE OR POOR ECONOMY

5.0L & 5.7L "F" SERIES
FUEL INJECTION (PORT)

MPI TROUBLE DIAGNOSTICS

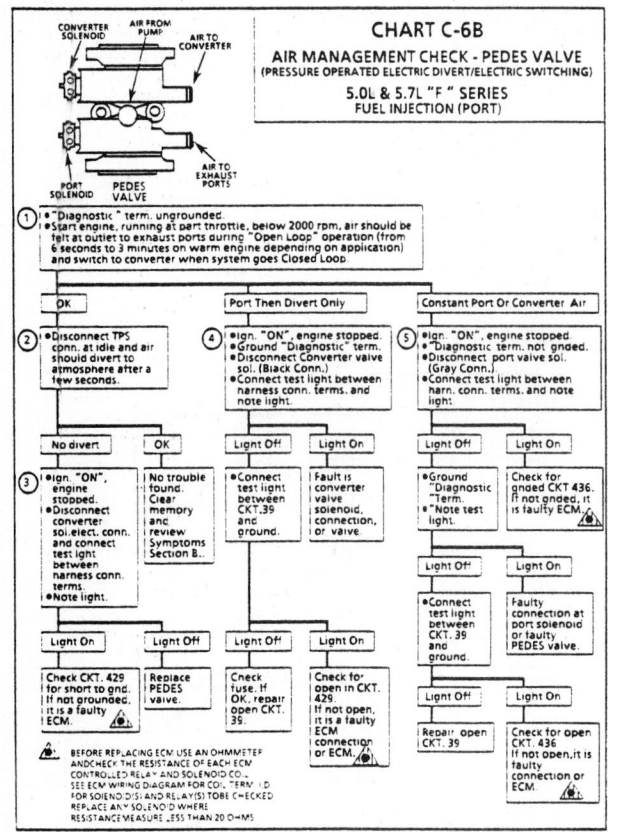

CHART C-6B

AIR MANAGEMENT CHECK - PEDES VALVE
(PRESSURE OPERATED ELECTRIC DIVERT/ELECTRIC SWITCHING)

5.0L & 5.7L "F" SERIES
FUEL INJECTION (PORT)

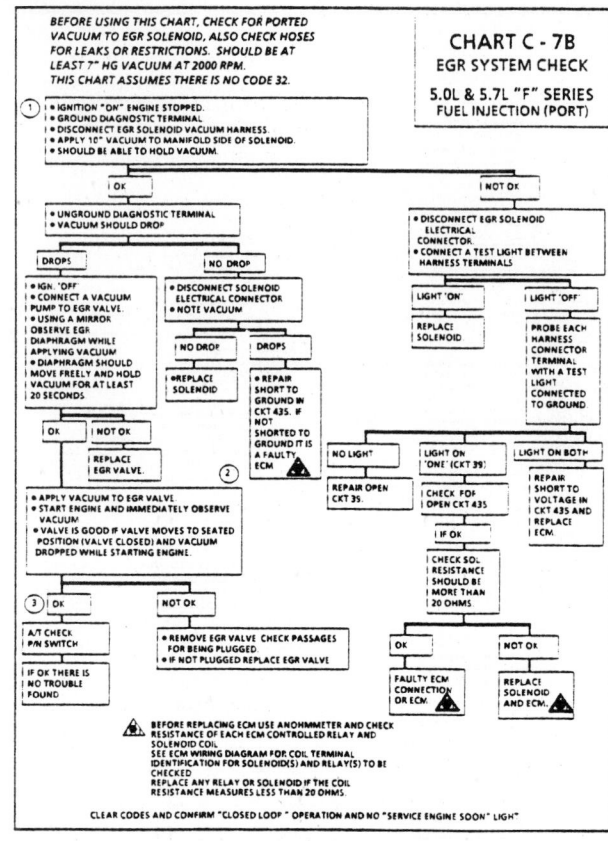

CHART C - 7B

EGR SYSTEM CHECK

5.0L & 5.7L "F" SERIES
FUEL INJECTION (PORT)

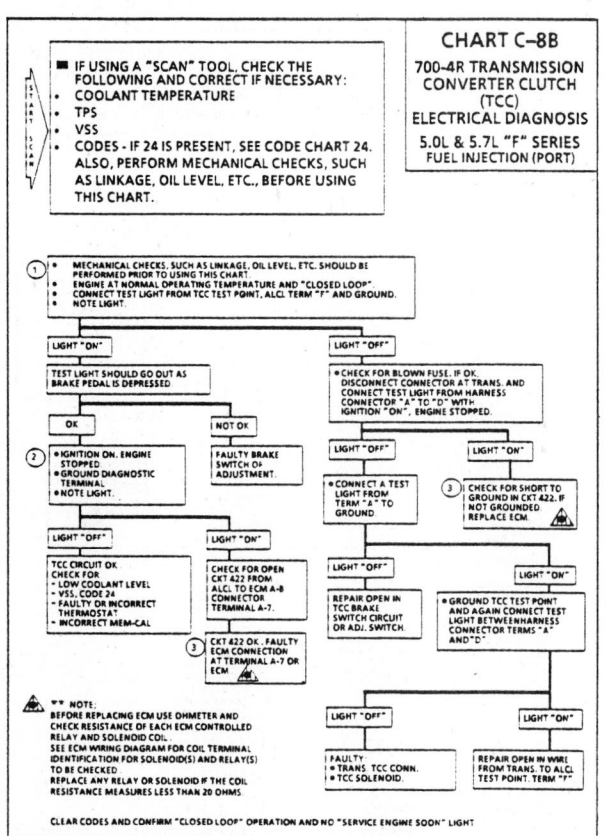

CHART C-8B

700-4R TRANSMISSION
CONVERTER CLUTCH
(TCC)
ELECTRICAL DIAGNOSIS

5.0L & 5.7L "F" SERIES
FUEL INJECTION (PORT)

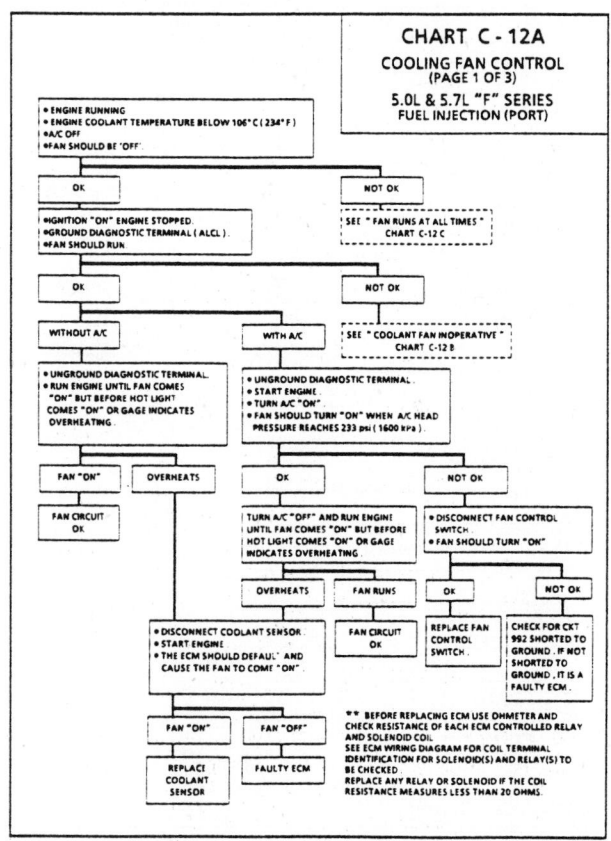

CHART C - 12A

COOLING FAN CONTROL
(PAGE 1 OF 3)

5.0L & 5.7L "F" SERIES
FUEL INJECTION (PORT)

MPI TROUBLE DIAGNOSTICS

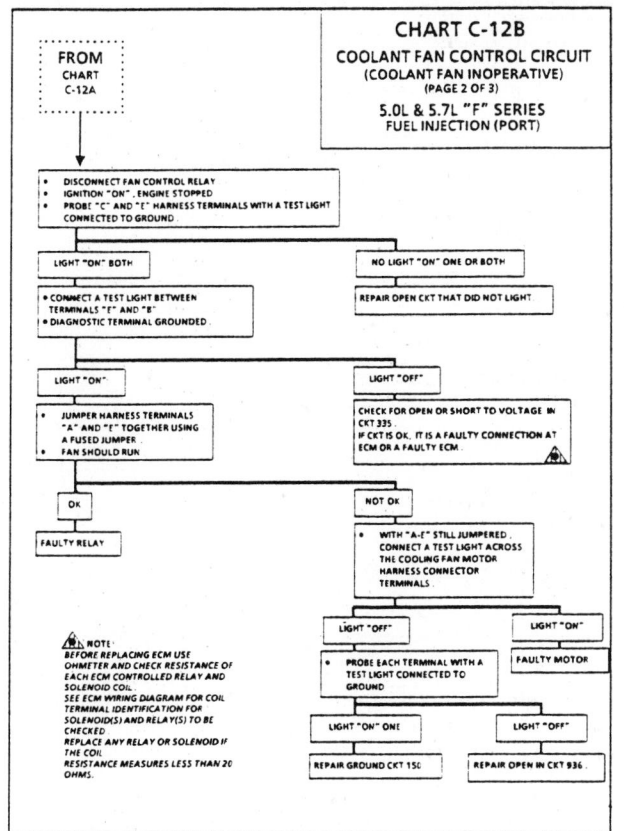

CHART C-12B
COOLANT FAN CONTROL CIRCUIT
(COOLANT FAN INOPERATIVE)
(PAGE 2 OF 3)
5.0L & 5.7L "F" SERIES
FUEL INJECTION (PORT)

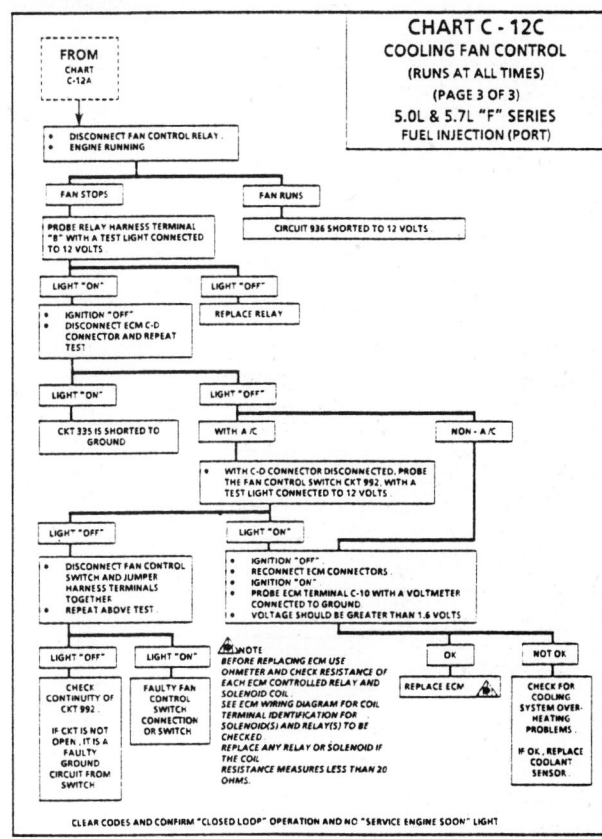

CHART C-12C
COOLING FAN CONTROL
(RUNS AT ALL TIMES)
(PAGE 3 OF 3)
5.0L & 5.7L "F" SERIES
FUEL INJECTION (PORT)

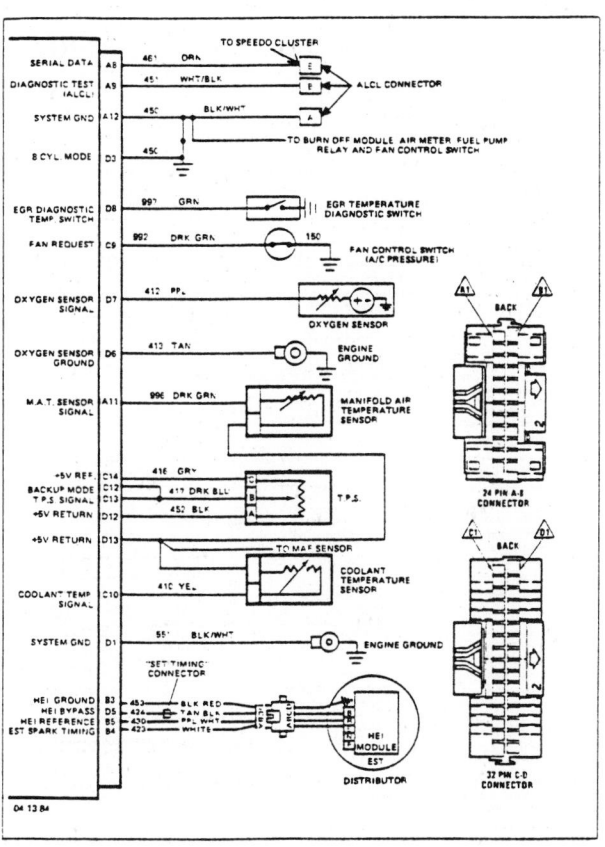

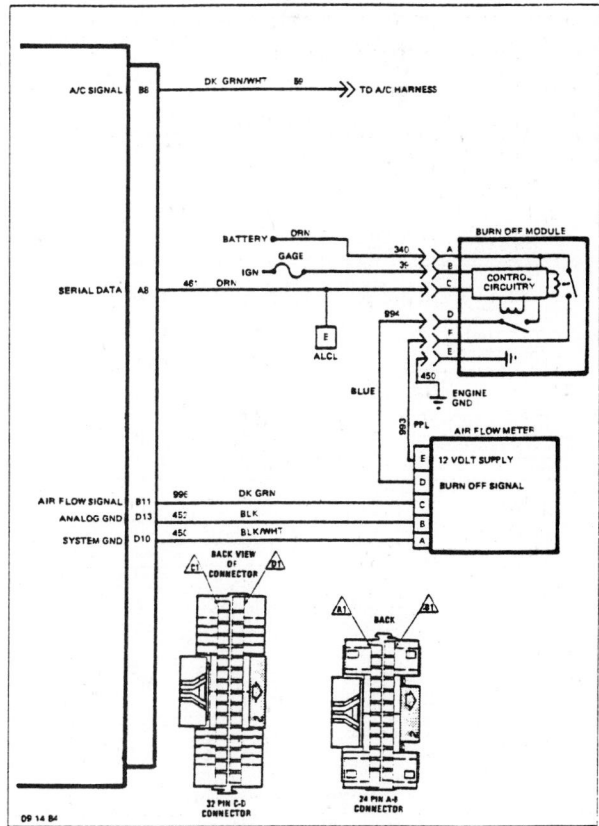

MPI TROUBLE DIAGNOSTICS

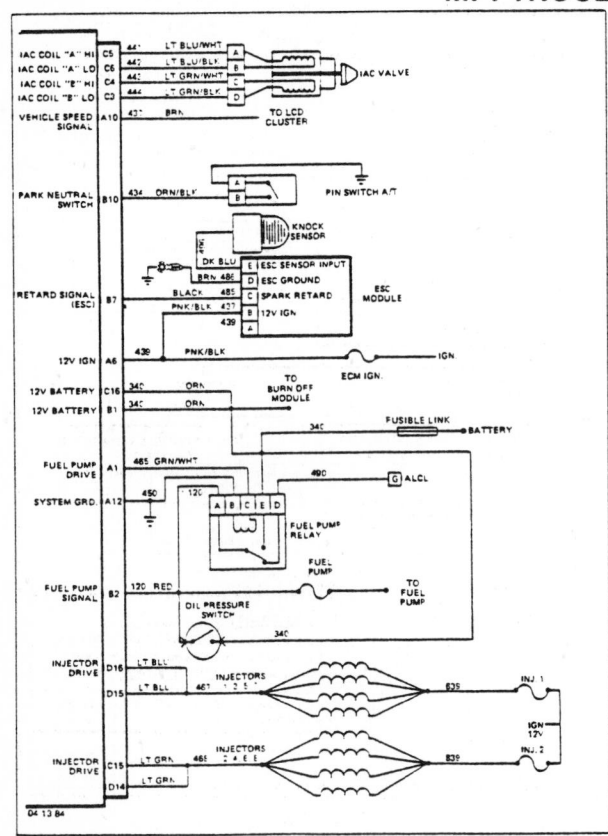

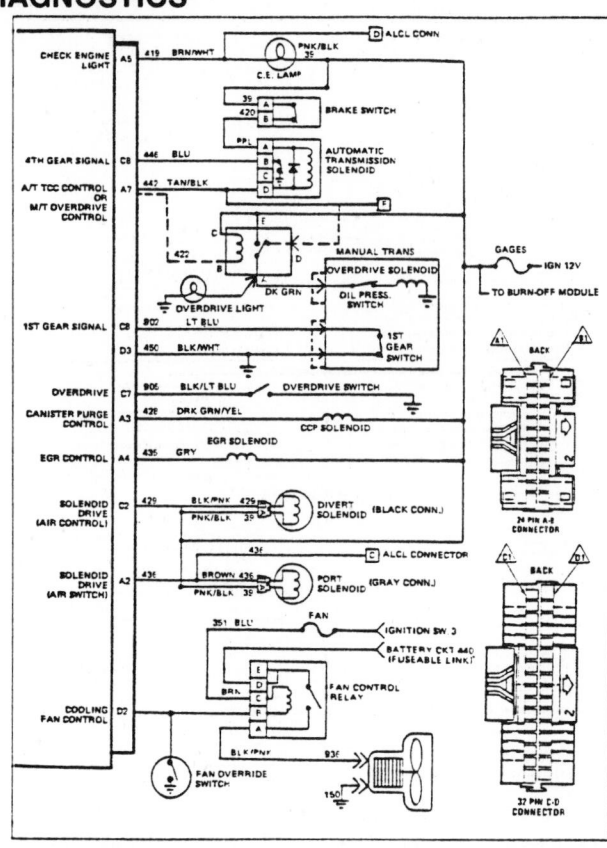

ECM CONNECTOR TERMINAL END VIEW — 5.7L

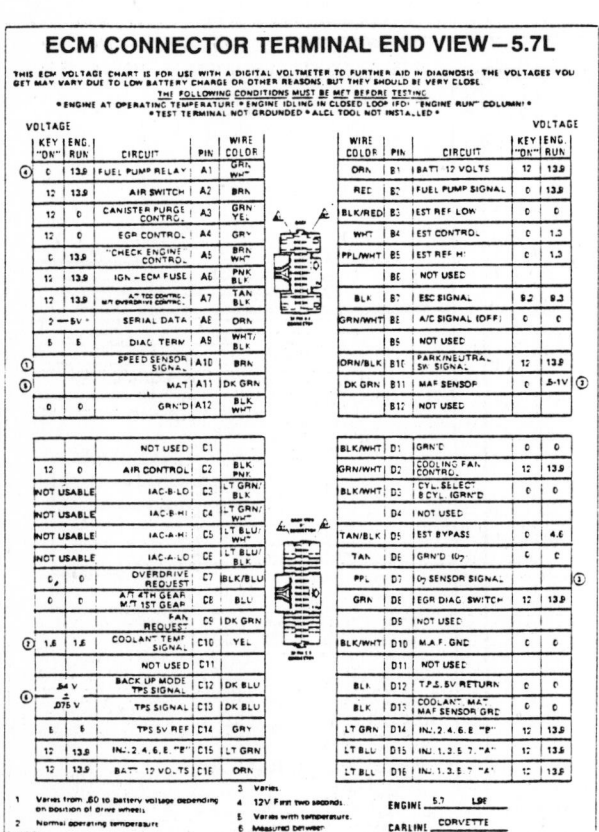

DIAGNOSTIC CIRCUIT CHECK — 5.7L ENGINE (TPI)

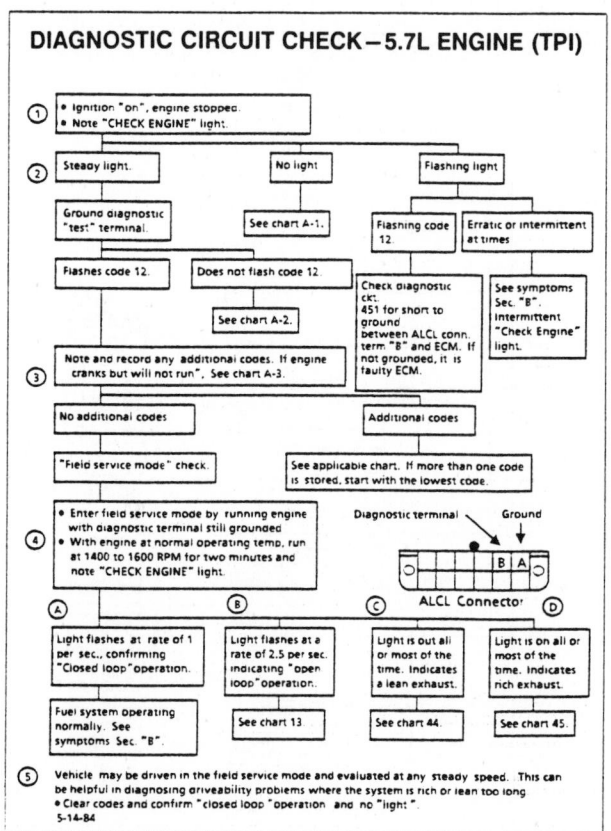

MPI TROUBLE DIAGNOSTICS

CHART A-1 NO CHECK LIGHT — 5.7L ENGINE (TPI)

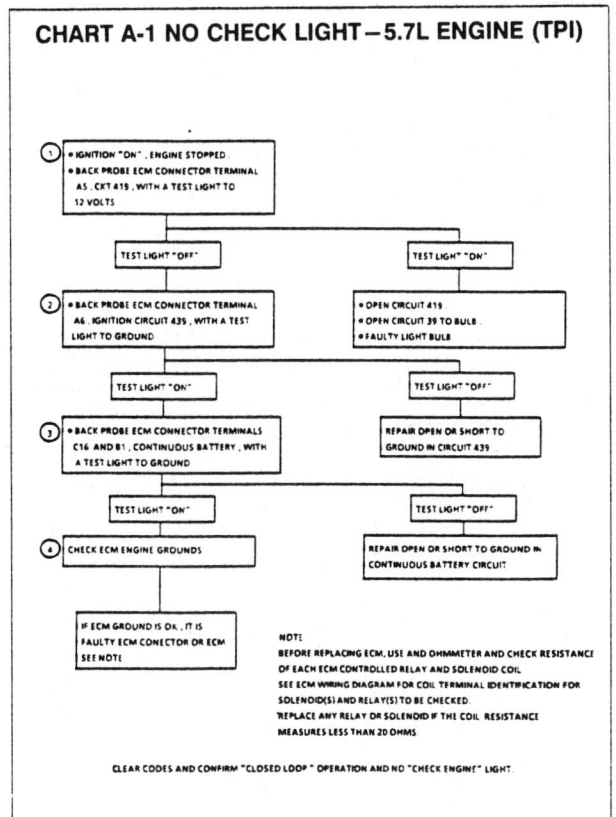

CHART A-2 WON'T FLASH A CODE 12 — 5.7L ENGINE (TPI)

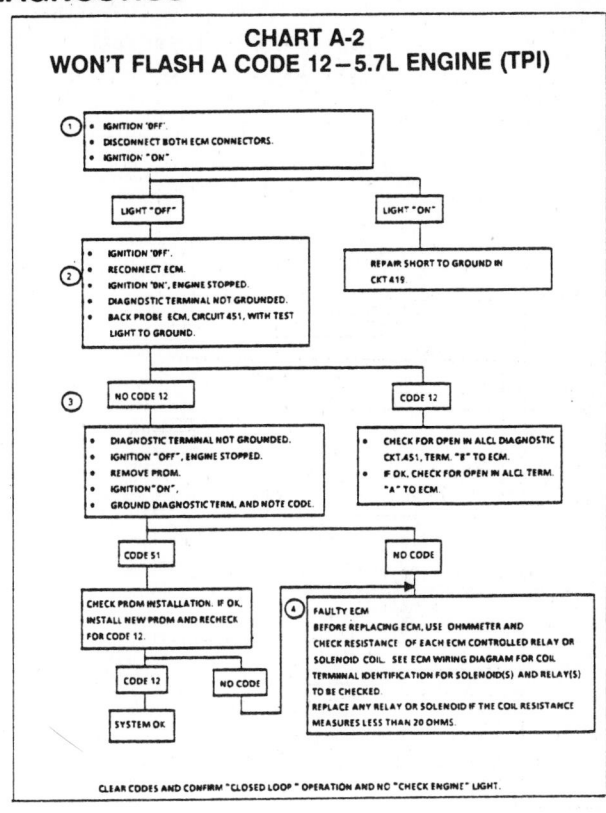

CHART A-3A ENGINE CRANKS BUT WON'T RUN — 5.7L ENGINE (TPI)

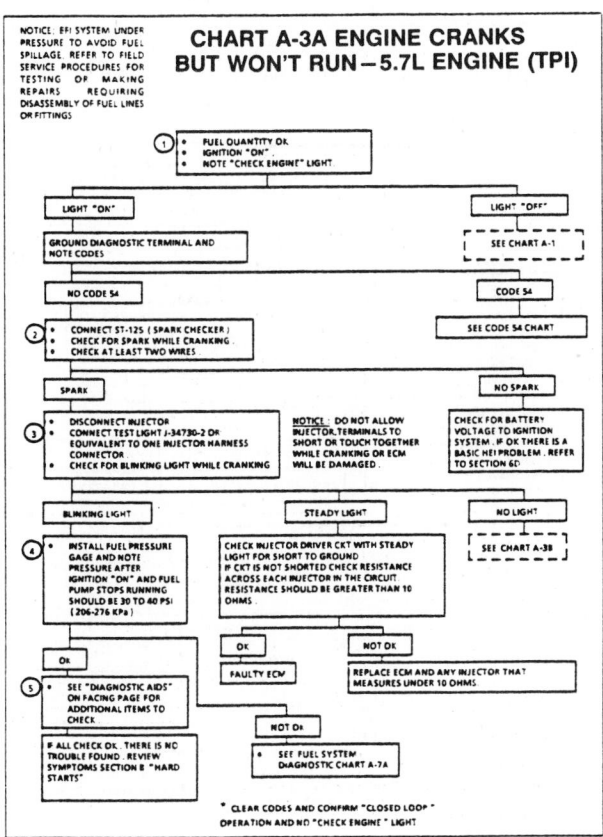

CHART A-3B ENGINE CRANKS BUT WON'T RUN — 5.7L ENGINE (TPI)

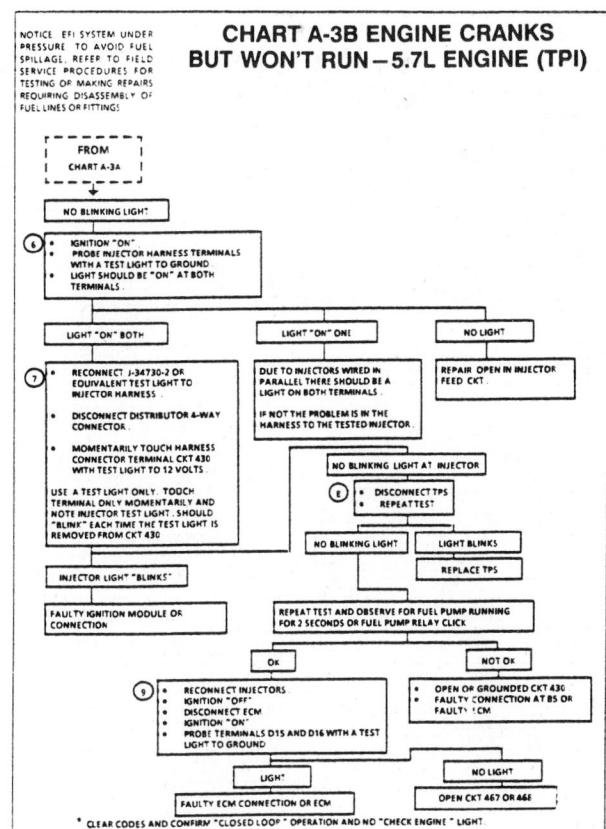

MPI TROUBLE DIAGNOSTICS

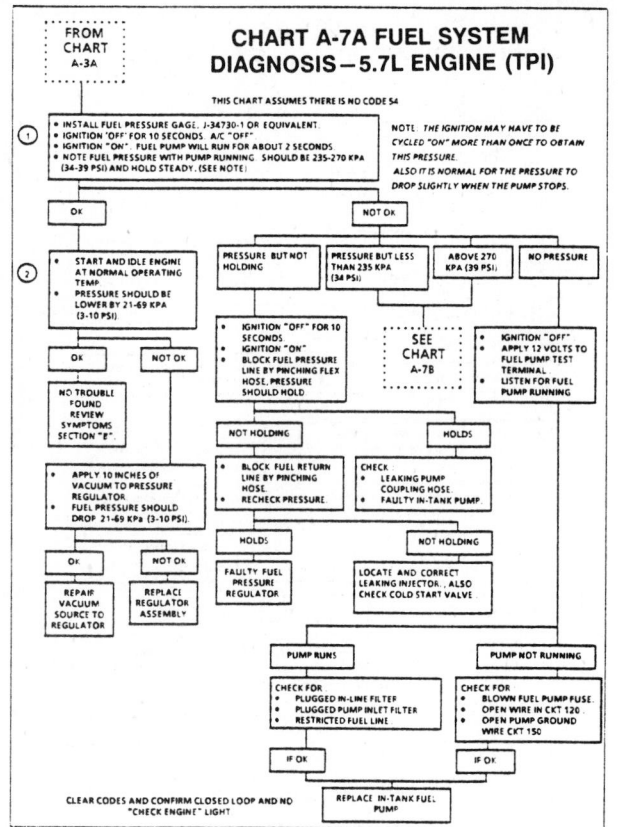

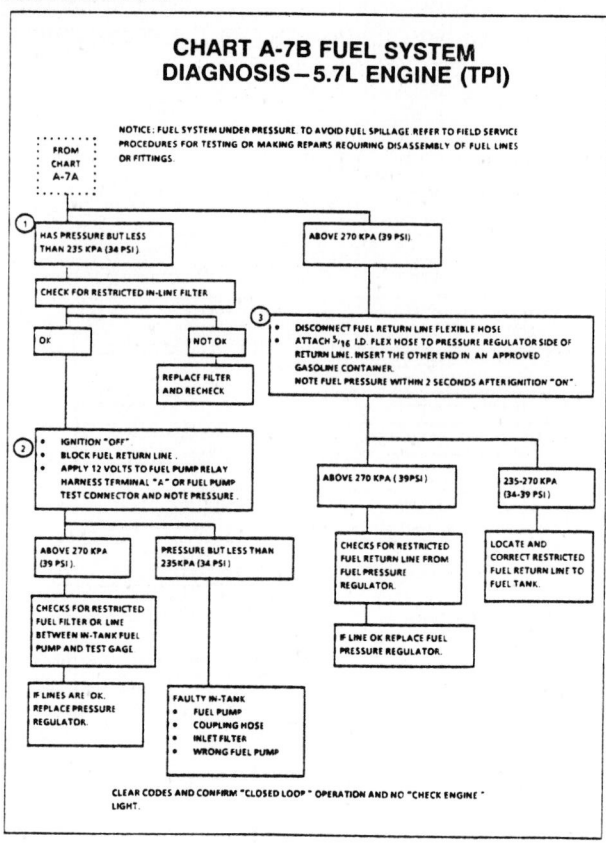

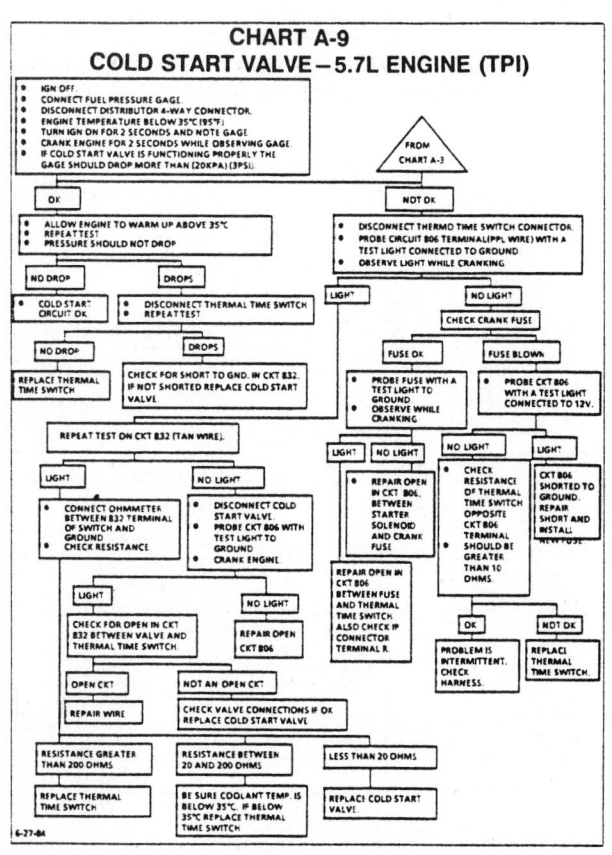

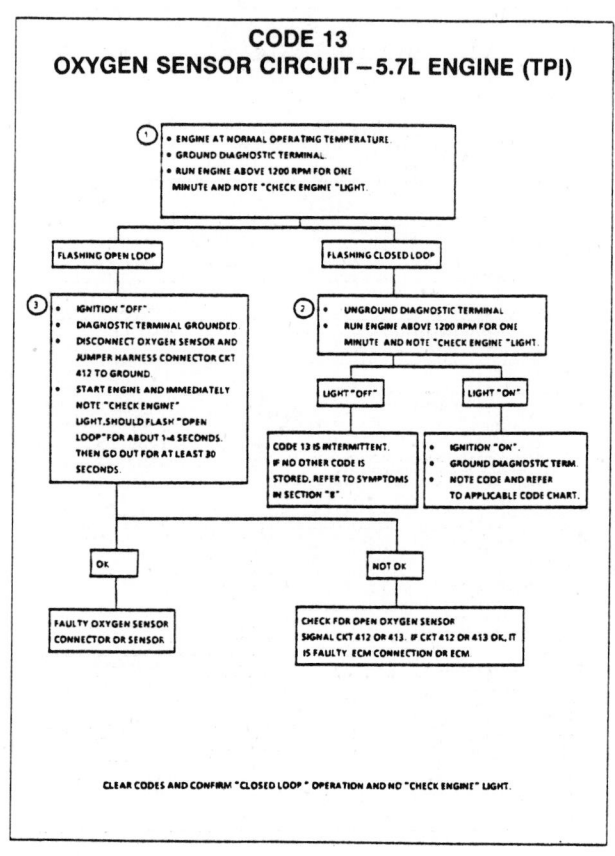

MPI TROUBLE DIAGNOSTICS

CODE 14
COOLANT SENSOR CIRCUIT
VOLTAGE LOW—5.7L ENGINE (TPI)

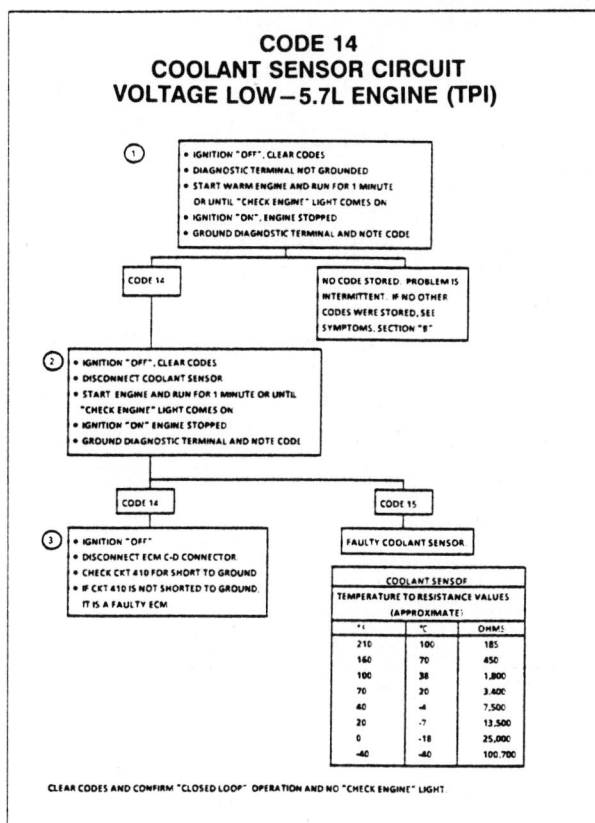

CODE 15
COOLANT SENSOR CIRCUIT
VOLTAGE HIGH—5.7L ENGINE (TPI)

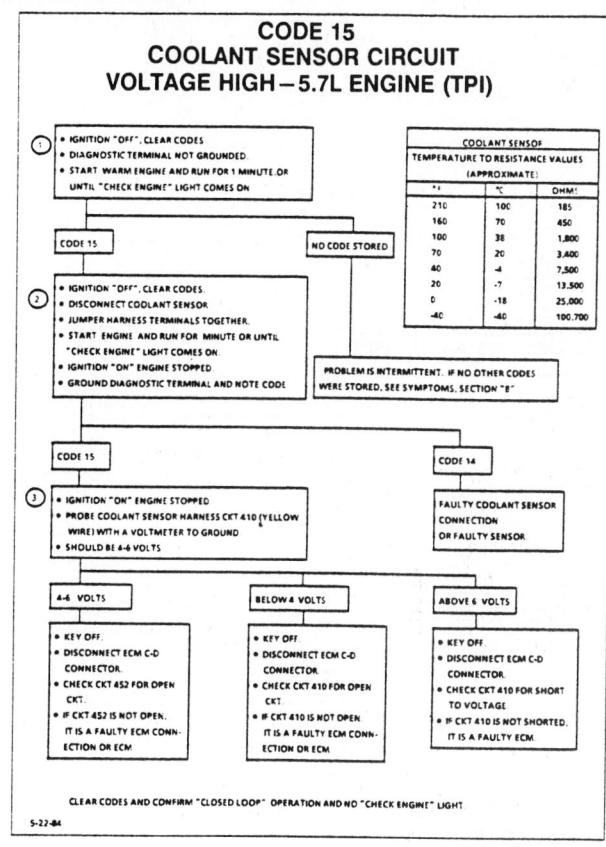

CODE 21
THROTTLE POSITION
SENSOR CIRCUIT—VOLTAGE HIGH
5.7L ENGINE (TPI)

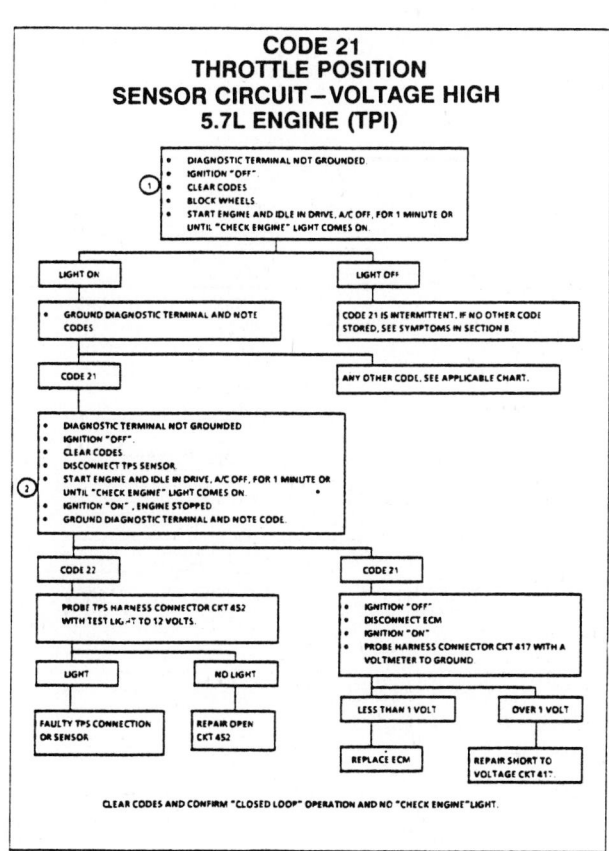

CODE 22
THROTTLE POSITION
SENSOR CIRCUIT—VOLTAGE LOW

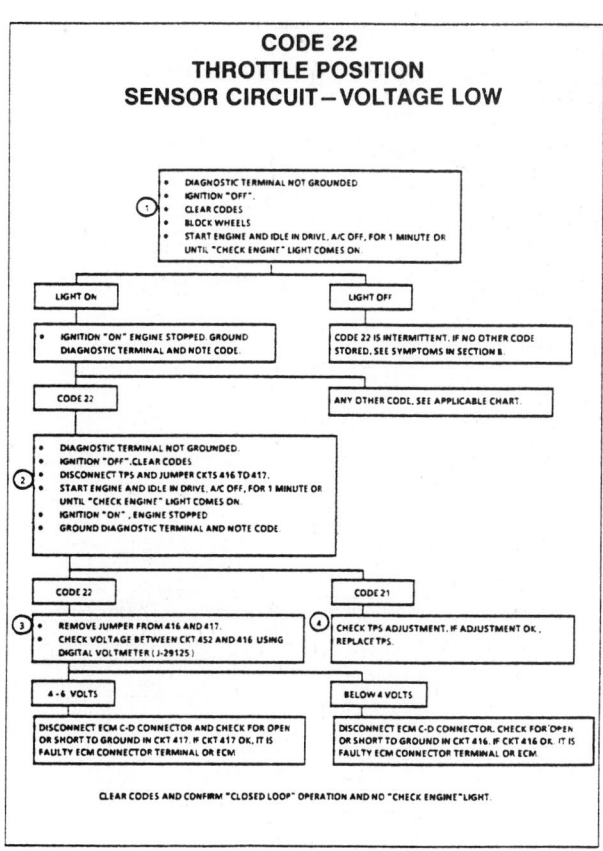

MPI TROUBLE DIAGNOSTICS

CODE 23
MANIFOLD AIR TEMPERATURE
CIRCUIT VOLTAGE HIGH—5.7L ENGINE (TPI)

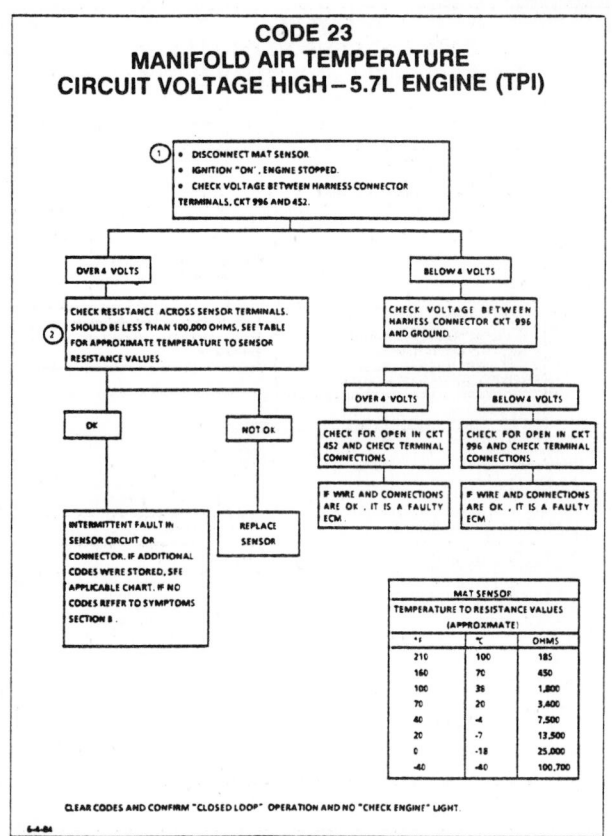

CODE 24
VEHICLE SPEED SENSOR CIRCUIT
5.7L ENGINE (TPI)

BUFFER IS INTERGRAL PART OF I. P. CLUSTER

NOTICE: TO PREVENT MISDIAGNOSIS, DISREGARD CODE 24 IF SET WHEN DRIVE WHEELS ARE NOT TURNING.

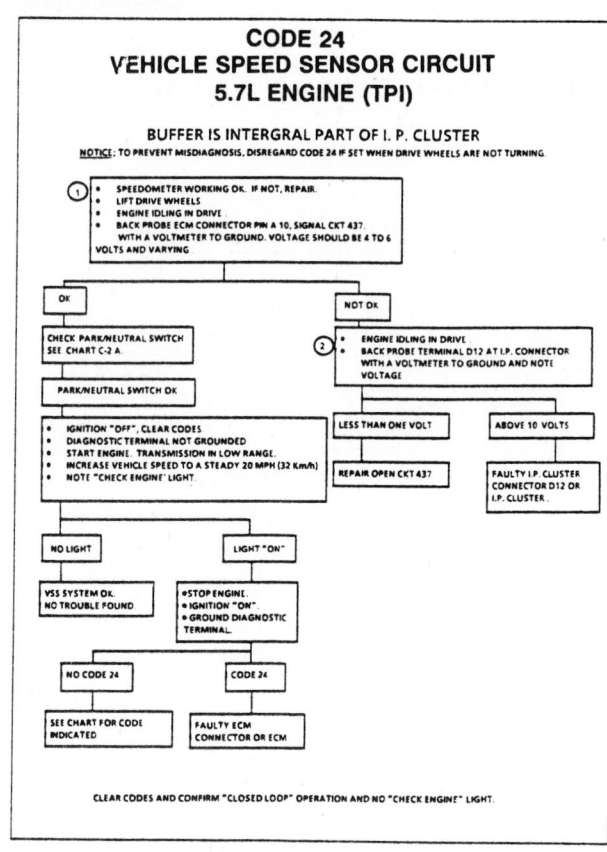

CODE 25
MANIFOLD AIR TEMPERATURE
CIRCUIT VOLTAGE HIGH—5.7L ENGINE (TPI)

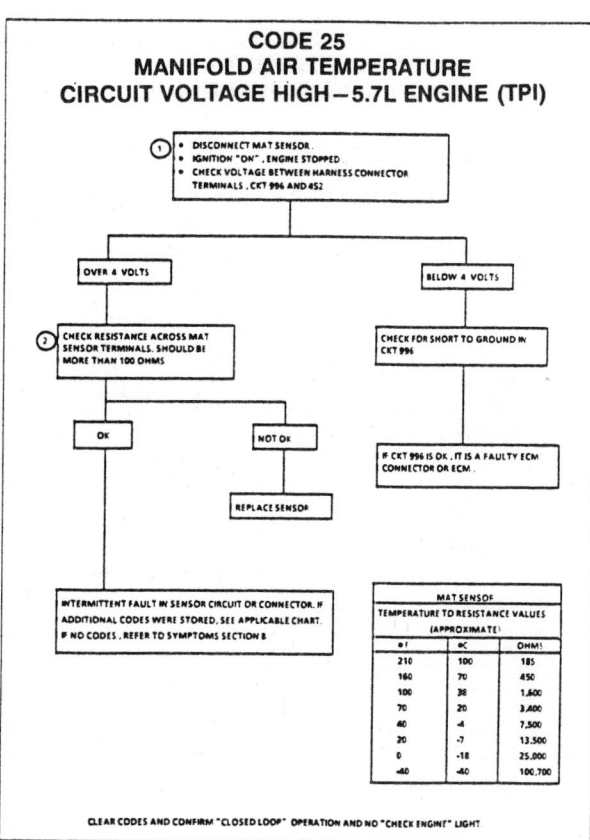

CODE 32
EGR SYSTEM FAILURE—5.7L ENGINE (TPI)

BEFORE USING THIS CHART, CHECK VACUUM HOSES FOR LEAKS, RESTRICTIONS AND CHECK FOR PORTED VACUUM SOURCE TO EGR SOLENOID SHOULD HAVE AT LEAST 7" VACUUM AT 2000 RPM

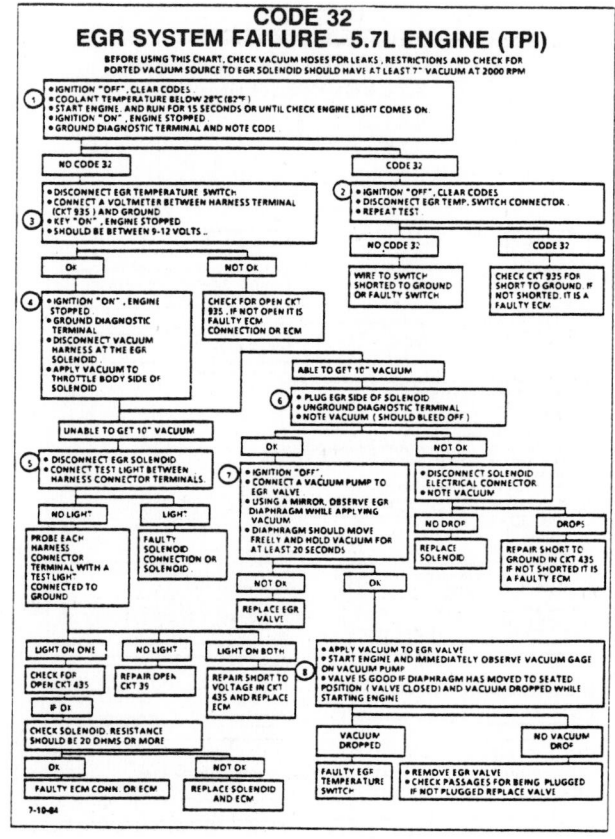

MPI TROUBLE DIAGNOSTICS

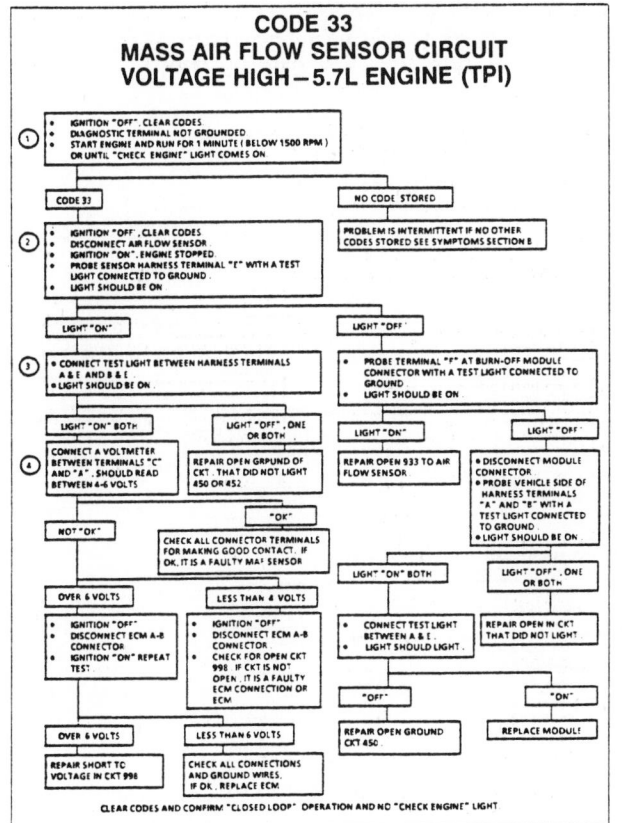

CODE 33
MASS AIR FLOW SENSOR CIRCUIT
VOLTAGE HIGH—5.7L ENGINE (TPI)

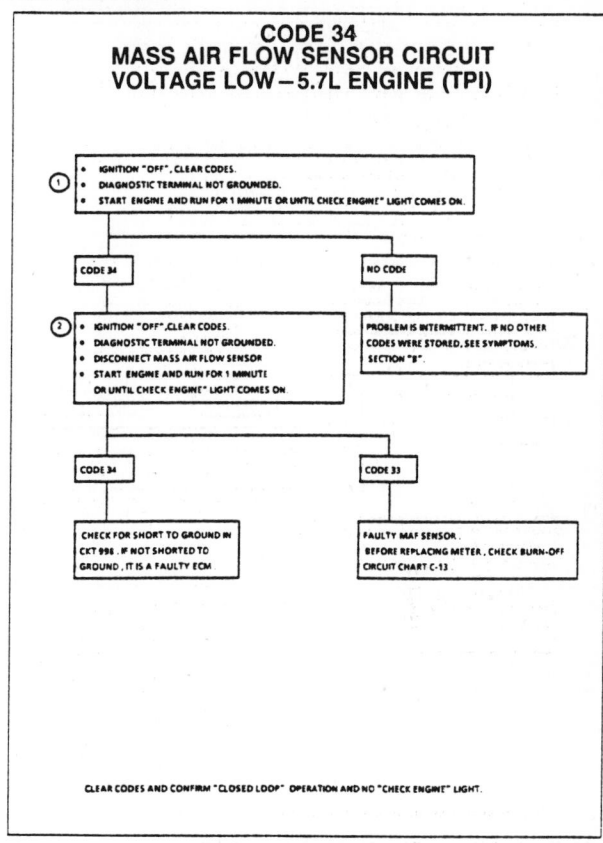

CODE 34
MASS AIR FLOW SENSOR CIRCUIT
VOLTAGE LOW—5.7L ENGINE (TPI)

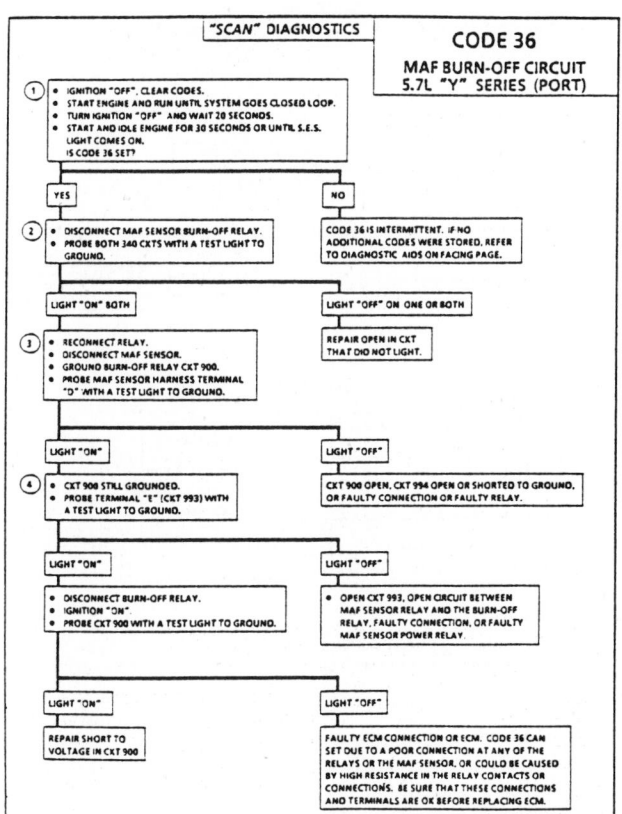

CODE 36
MAF BURN-OFF CIRCUIT
5.7L "Y" SERIES (PORT)

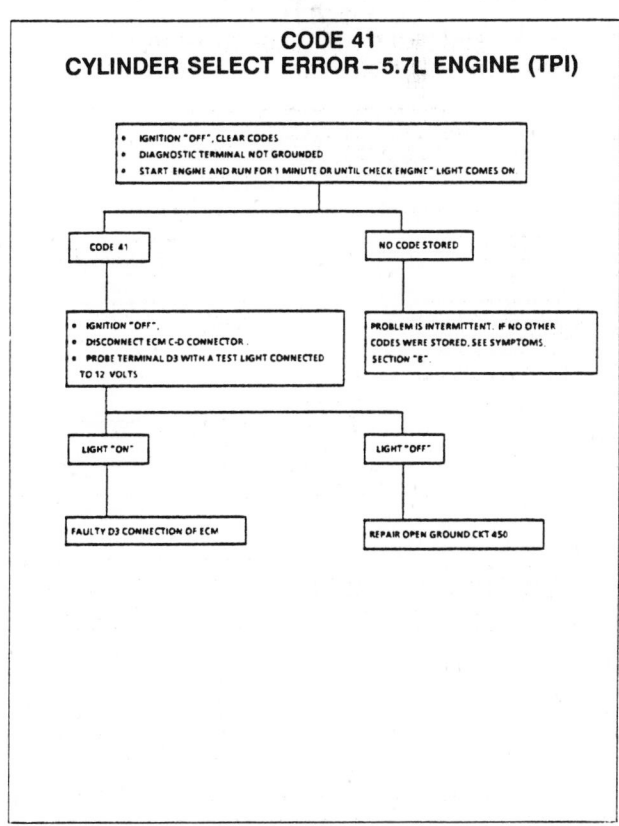

CODE 41
CYLINDER SELECT ERROR—5.7L ENGINE (TPI)

MPI TROUBLE DIAGNOSTICS

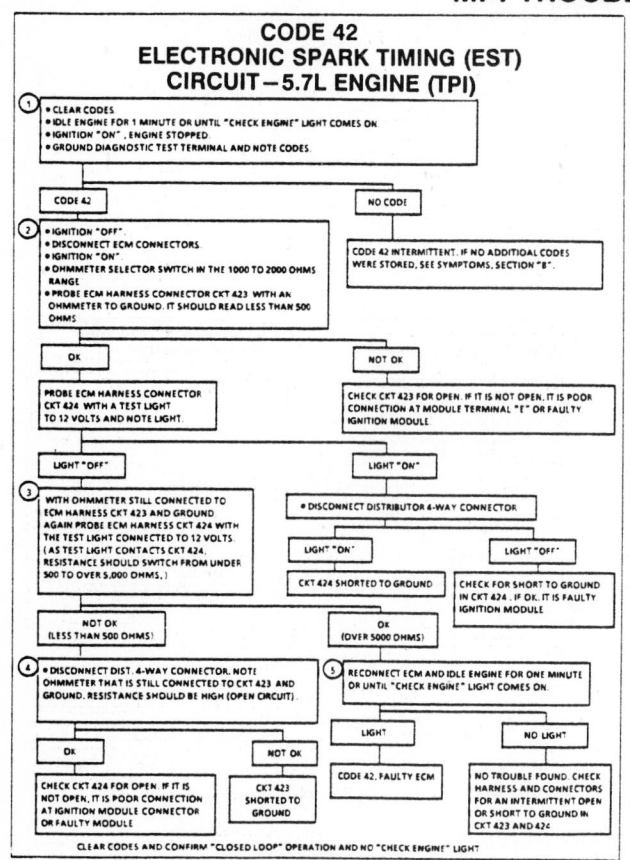

CODE 42
ELECTRONIC SPARK TIMING (EST)
CIRCUIT — 5.7L ENGINE (TPI)

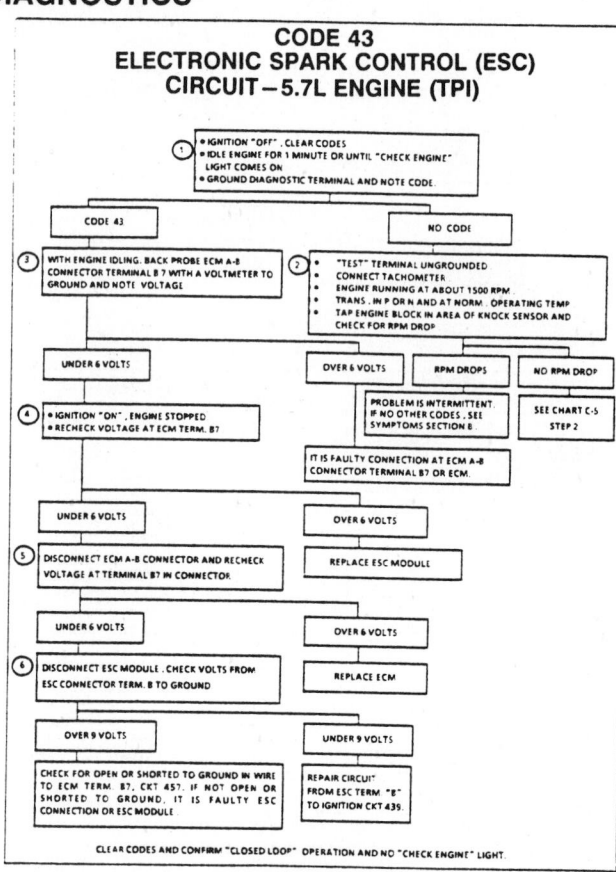

CODE 43
ELECTRONIC SPARK CONTROL (ESC)
CIRCUIT — 5.7L ENGINE (TPI)

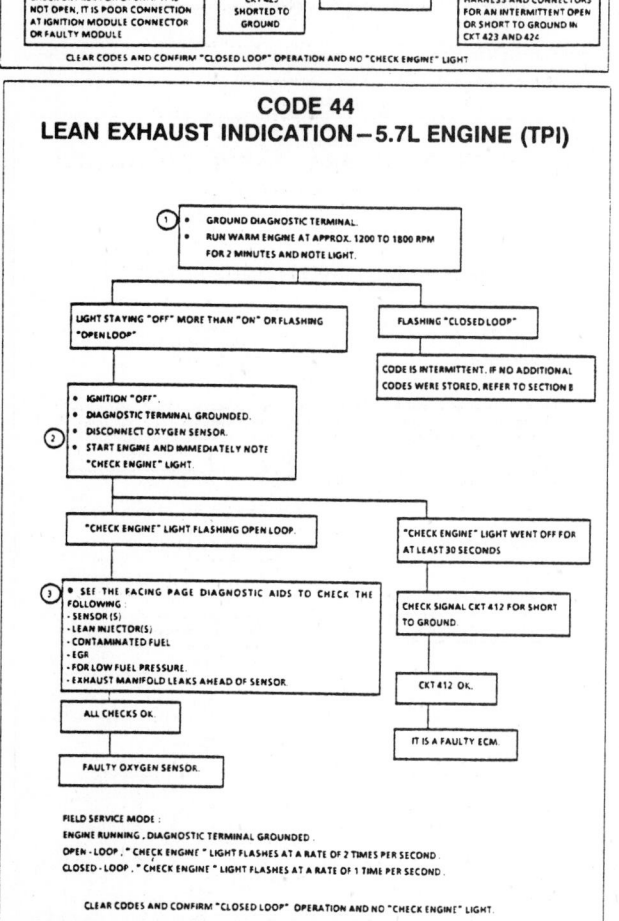

CODE 44
LEAN EXHAUST INDICATION — 5.7L ENGINE (TPI)

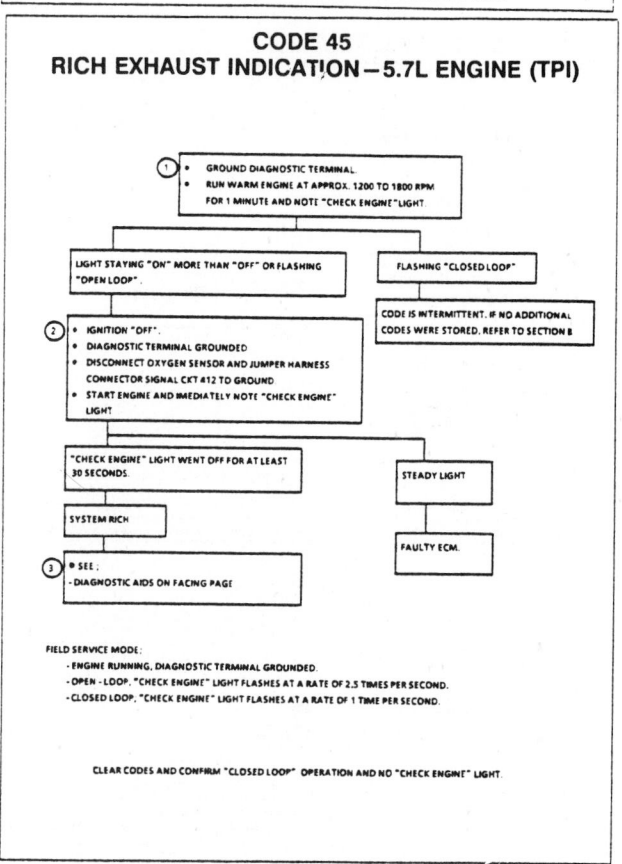

CODE 45
RICH EXHAUST INDICATION — 5.7L ENGINE (TPI)

MPI TROUBLE DIAGNOSTICS

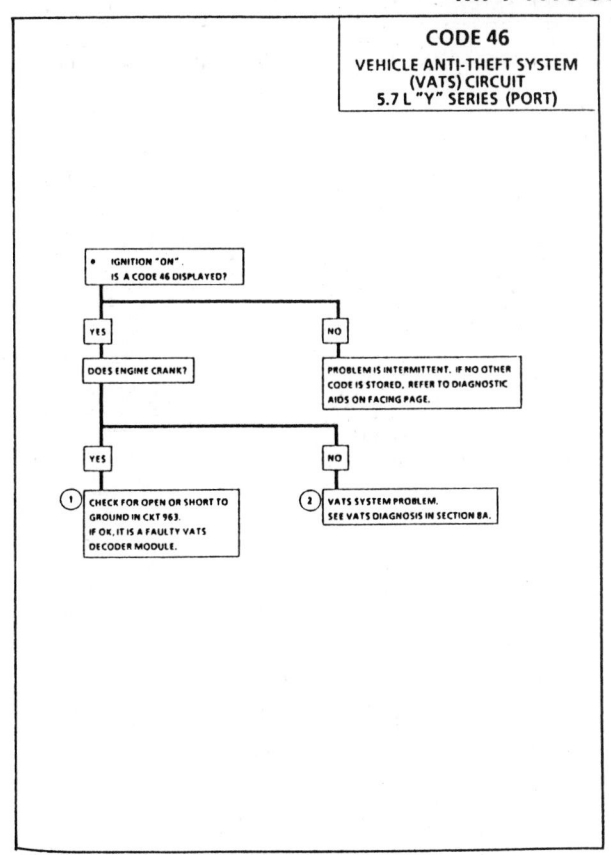

CODE 46
VEHICLE ANTI-THEFT SYSTEM
(VATS) CIRCUIT
5.7 L "Y" SERIES (PORT)

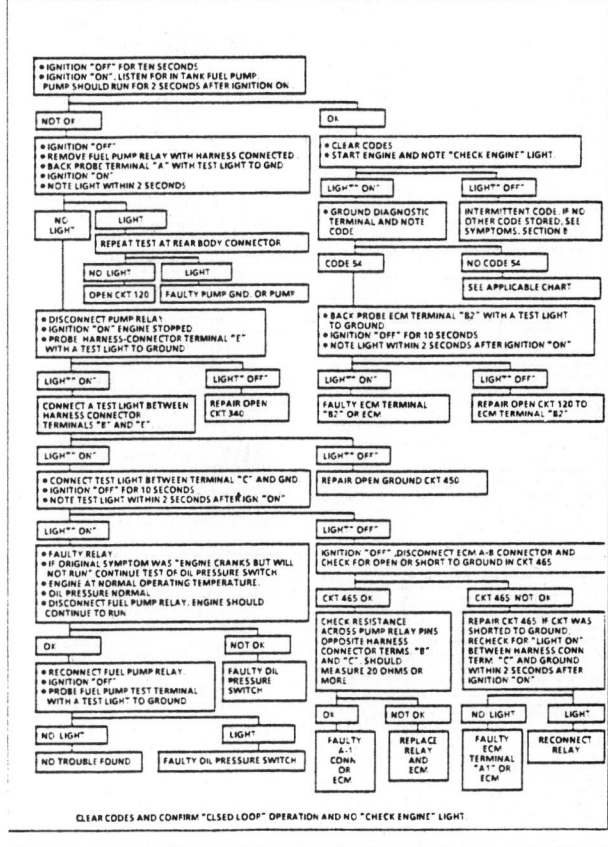

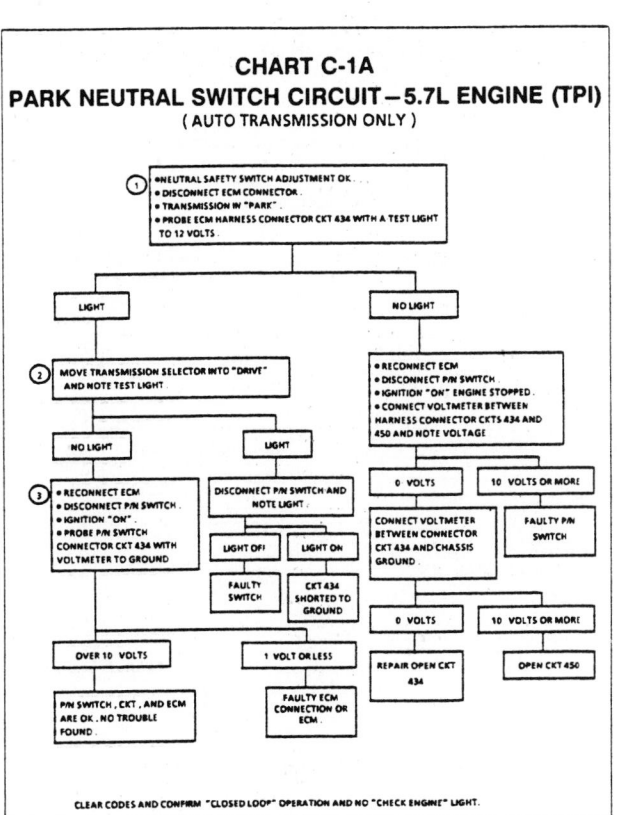

CHART C-1A
PARK NEUTRAL SWITCH CIRCUIT—5.7L ENGINE (TPI)
(AUTO TRANSMISSION ONLY)

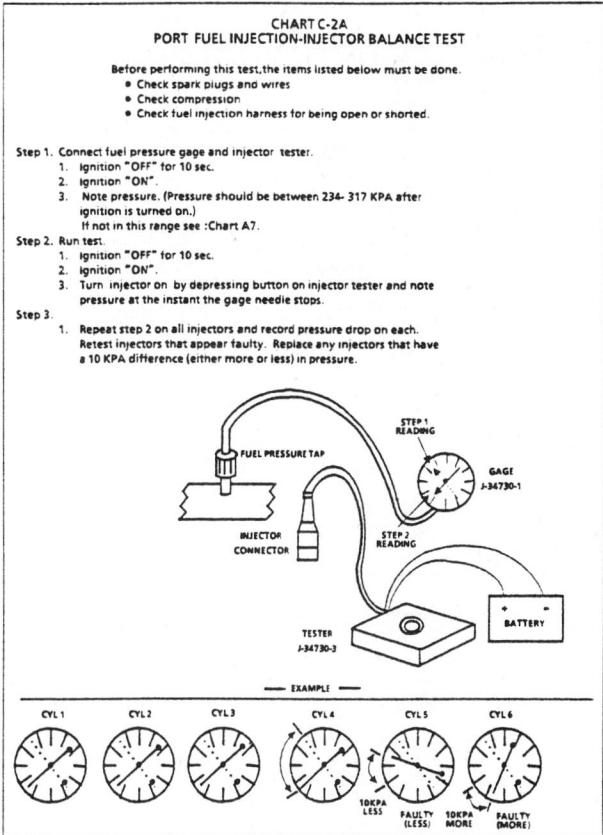

CHART C-2A
PORT FUEL INJECTION-INJECTOR BALANCE TEST

MPI TROUBLE DIAGNOSTICS

CHART C-2C
IDLE AIR CONTROL—5.7L ENGINE (TPI)

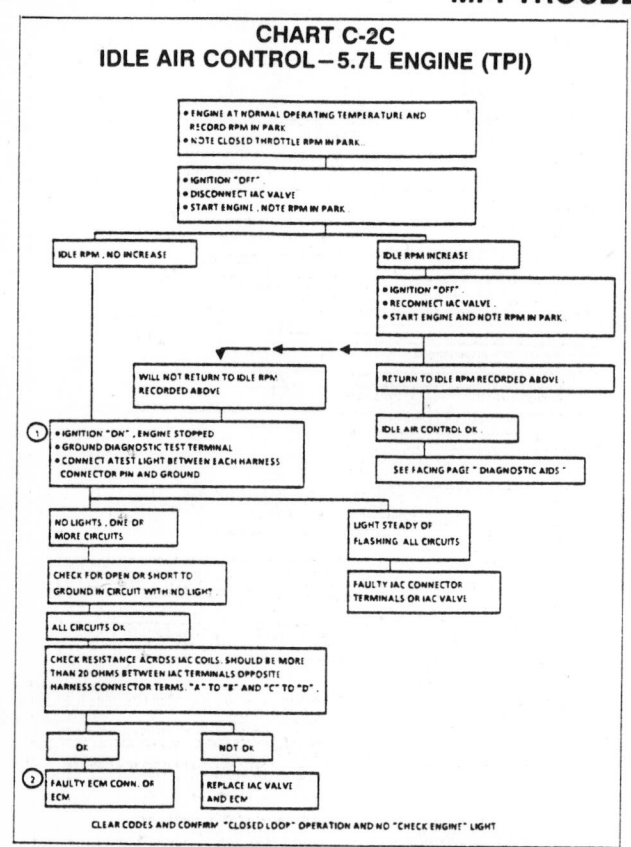

CHART C-3
CANISTER PURGE CHECK—5.7L ENGINE (TPI)

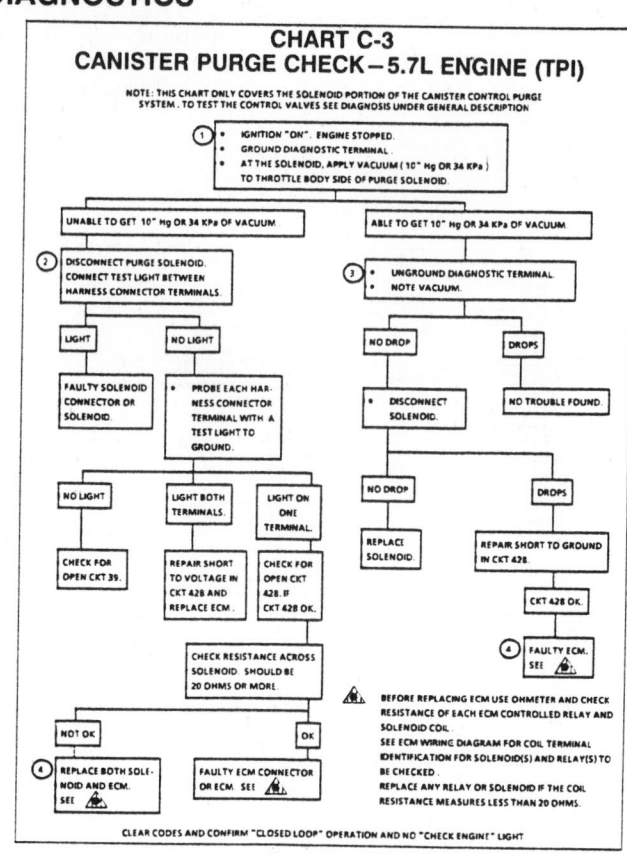

CHART C-4A
IGNITION SYSTEM CHECK
(INTEGRAL COIL)
5.7L "Y" SERIES (PORT)

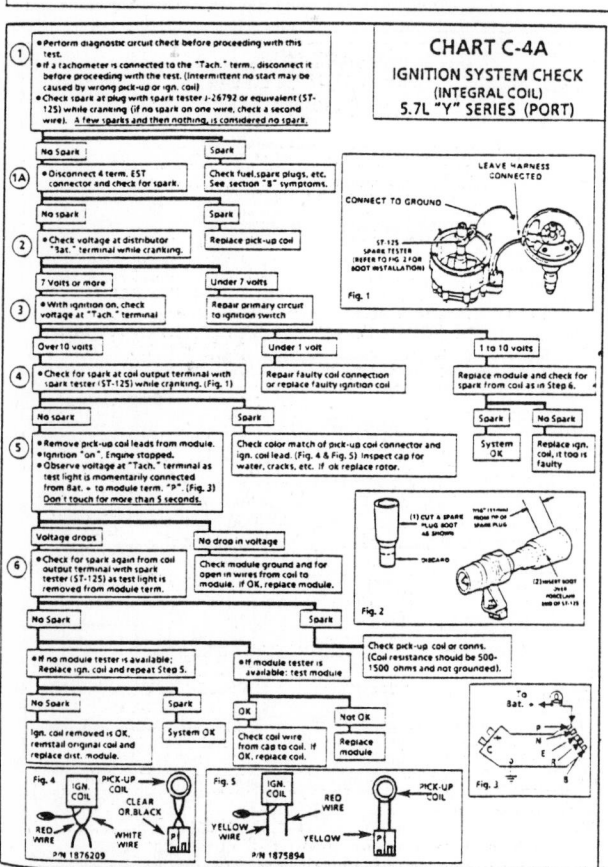

CHART C-5
ELECTRONIC SPARK CONTROL (ESC) CIRCUIT
5.7L ENGINE (TPI)

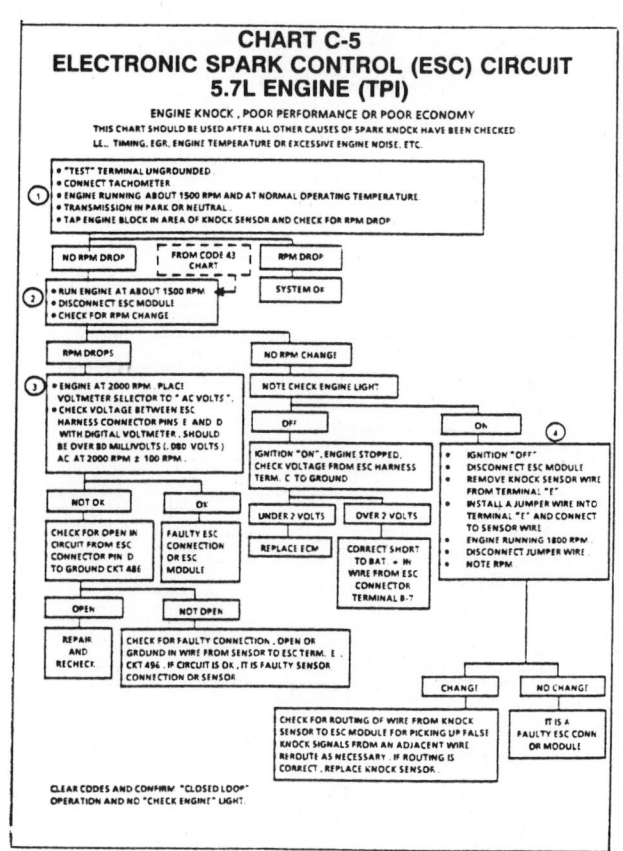

MPI TROUBLE DIAGNOSTICS

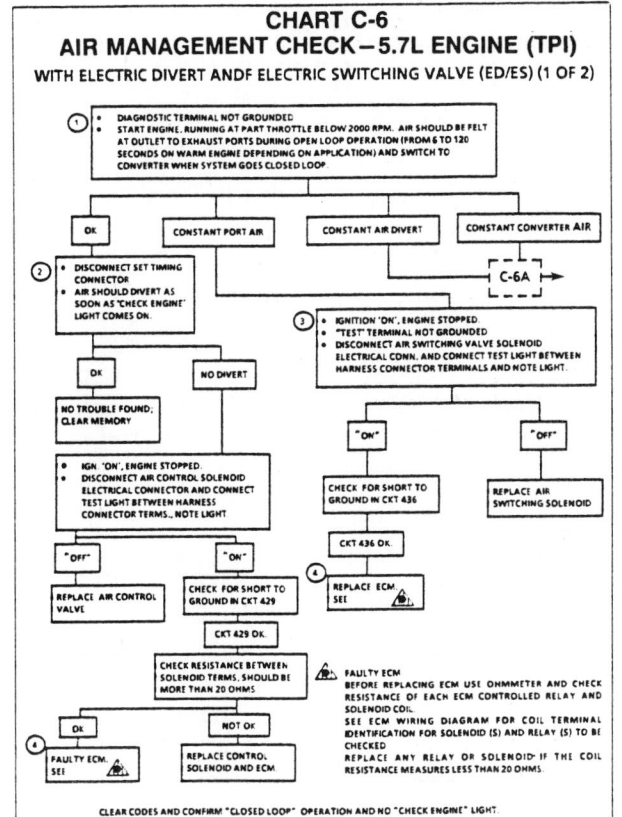

CHART C-6
AIR MANAGEMENT CHECK—5.7L ENGINE (TPI)
WITH ELECTRIC DIVERT AND ELECTRIC SWITCHING VALVE (ED/ES) (1 OF 2)

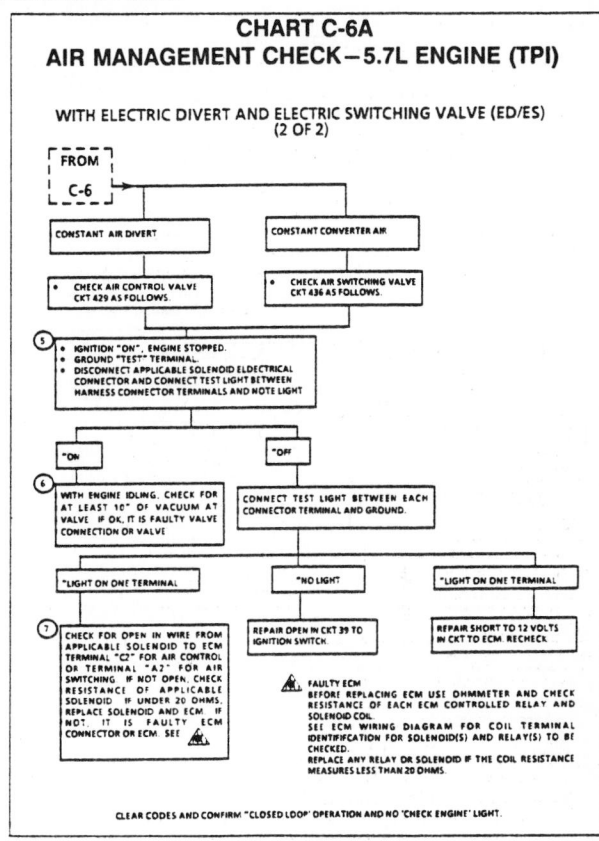

CHART C-6A
AIR MANAGEMENT CHECK—5.7L ENGINE (TPI)
WITH ELECTRIC DIVERT AND ELECTRIC SWITCHING VALVE (ED/ES)
(2 OF 2)

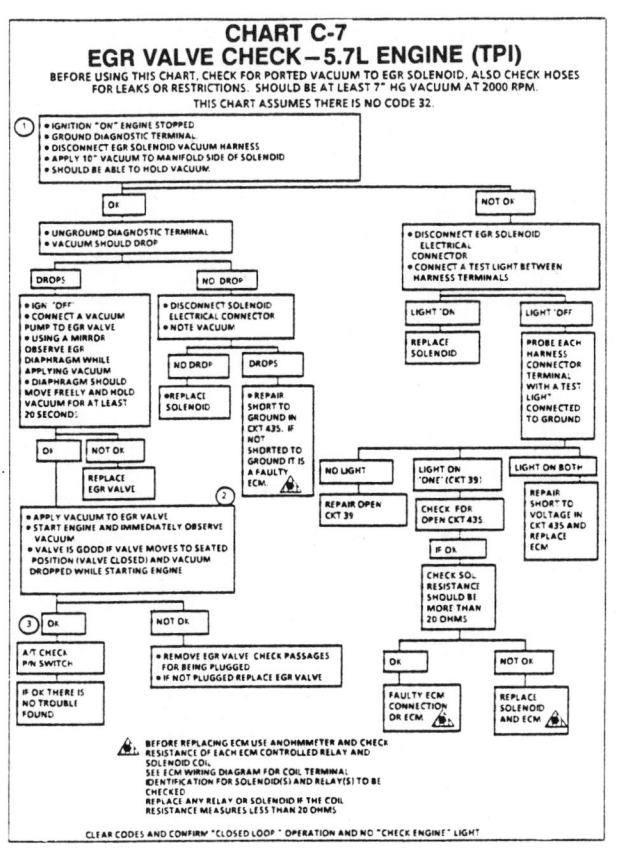

CHART C-7
EGR VALVE CHECK—5.7L ENGINE (TPI)
BEFORE USING THIS CHART, CHECK FOR PORTED VACUUM TO EGR SOLENOID. ALSO CHECK HOSES FOR LEAKS OR RESTRICTIONS. SHOULD BE AT LEAST 7" HG VACUUM AT 2000 RPM. THIS CHART ASSUMES THERE IS NO CODE 32.

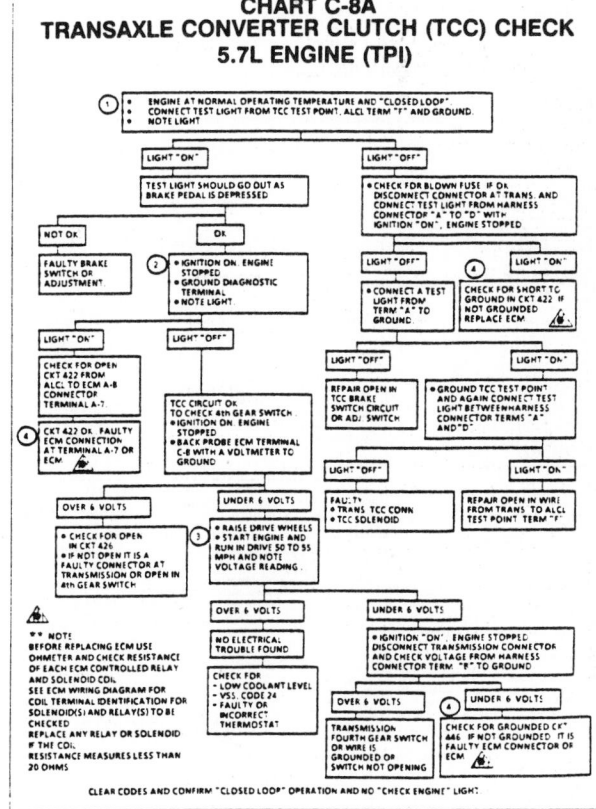

CHART C-8A
TRANSAXLE CONVERTER CLUTCH (TCC) CHECK
5.7L ENGINE (TPI)

MPI TROUBLE DIAGNOSTICS

CHART C-8A
MANUAL TRANSMISSION WITH AUTOMATIC
OVERDRIVE—5.7L ENGINE (TPI)

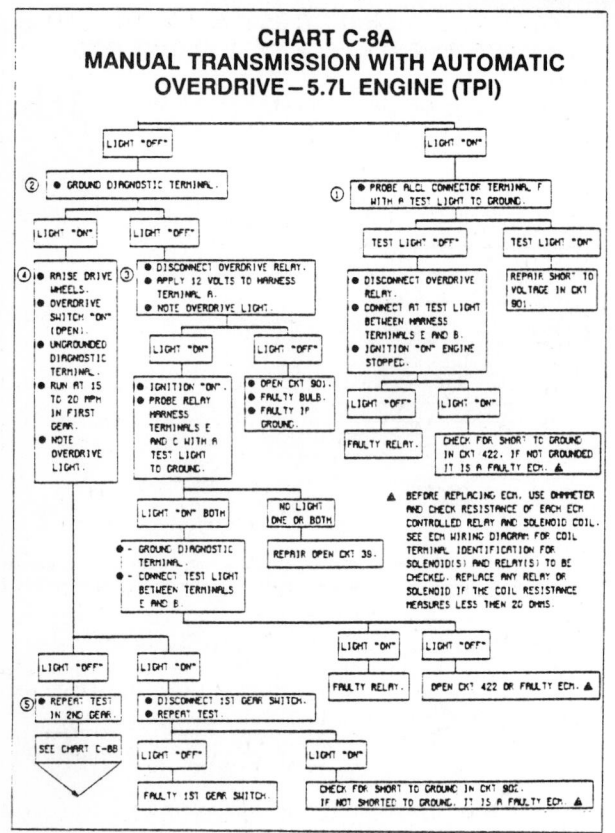

CHART C-8B
MANUAL TRANSMISSION WITH AUTOMATIC
OVERDRIVE—5.7L ENGINE (TPI)

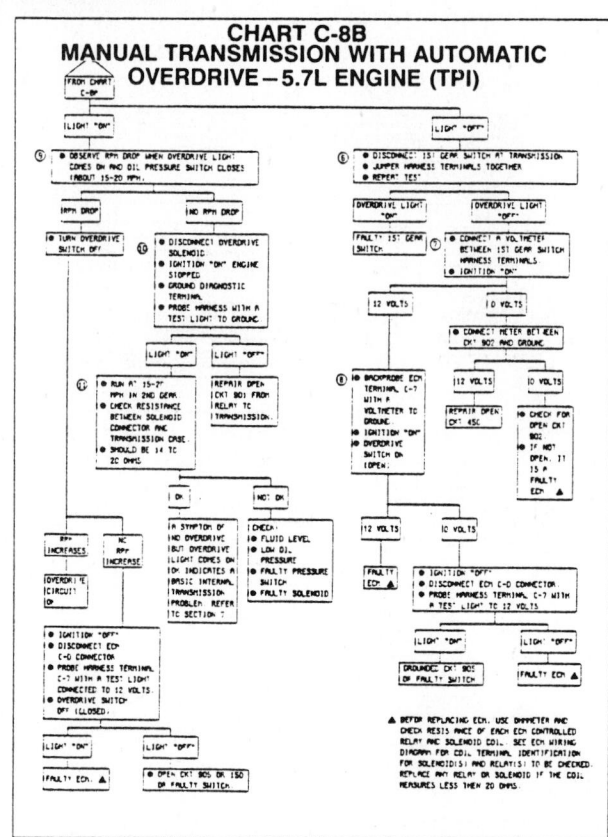

CHART C-12A
COOLANT FAN CONTROL—5.7L ENGINE (TPI)

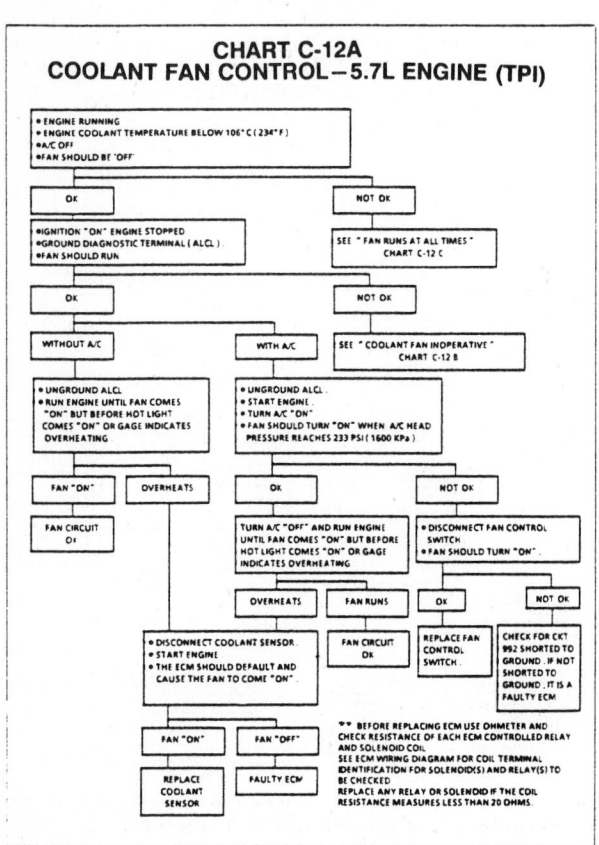

CHART C-12B COOLANT FAN CONTROL
INOPERATIVE—5.7L ENGINE (TPI)

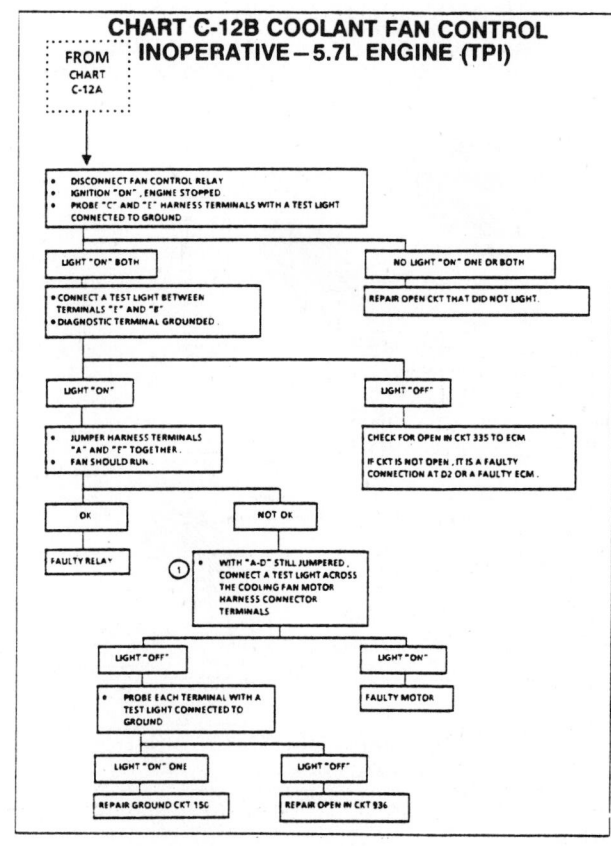

GM THROTTLE BODY INJECTION SYSTEMS

General Information

The electronic fuel injection and crossfire injection systems are fuel metering systems with the amount of fuel delivered by the throttle body injector(s) (TBI) determined by an electronic signal supplied by the Electronic Control Module (ECM). The ECM monitors various engine and vehicle conditions to calculate the fuel delivery time (pulse width) of the injector(s). The fuel pulse may be modified by the ECM to account for special operating conditions, such as cranking, cold starting, altitude, acceleration, and deceleration.

The ECM controls the exhaust emissions by modifying fuel delivery to achieve, as near as possible, and air/fuel ratio of 14.7 to 1. The injector "ON" time is determined by various inputs to the ECM. By increasing the injector pulse, more fuel is delivered, enriching the air/fuel ratio. Decreasing the injector pulse, leans the air/fuel ratio. Pulses are sent to the injector in two different modes: synchronized and nonsynchronized.

Synchronized Mode

In synchronized mode operation, the injector is pulsed once for each distributor reference pulse. In dual throttle body systems, the injectors are pulse alternately.

Nonsynchronized Mode

In nonsynchronized mode operation, the injector is pulsed once every 12.5 milliseconds or 6.25 milliseconds depending on calibration. This pulse time is totally independent of distributor reference pulses.

Nonsynchronized mode results only under the following conditions.

1. The fuel pulse width is too small to be delivered accurately by the injector (approximately 1.5 milliseconds).
2. During the delivery of prime pulses (prime pulses charge the intake manifold with fuel during or just prior to engine starting).
3. During acceleration enrichment.
4. During deceleration leanout.

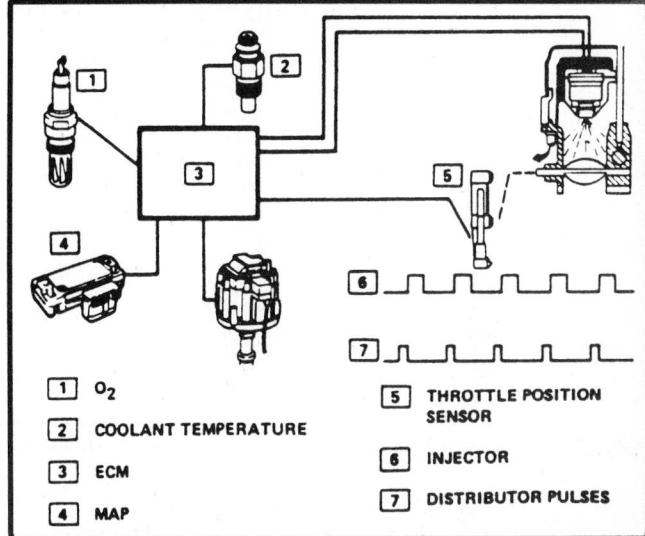

1	O₂	**5**	THROTTLE POSITION SENSOR
2	COOLANT TEMPERATURE	**6**	INJECTOR
3	ECM	**7**	DISTRIBUTOR PULSES
4	MAP		

Typical synchronized mode for single throttle body system

The basic TBI unit is made up of two major casting assemblies: (1) a throttle body with a valve to control airflow and (2) a fuel body assembly with an integral pressure regulator and fuel injector to supply the required fuel. An electronically operated device to control the idle speed and a device to provide information regarding throttle valve position are included as part of the TBI unit.

The fuel injector(s) is a solenoid-operated device controlled by the ECM. The incoming fuel is directed to the lower end of the injector assembly which has a fine screen filter surrounding the injector inlet. The ECM actuates the solenoid, which lifts a normally closed ball valve off a seat. The fuel under pressure is injected in a conical spray pattern at the walls of the throttle body bore above the throttle valve. The excess fuel

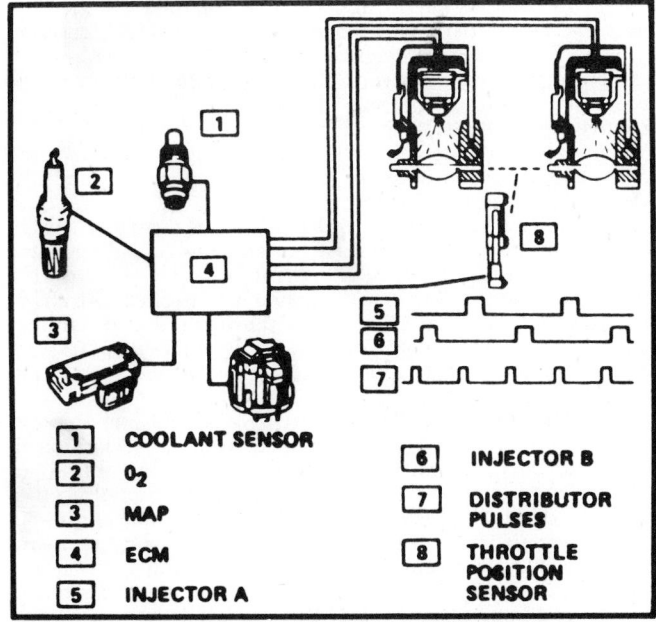

1	COOLANT SENSOR	**6**	INJECTOR B
2	O₂	**7**	DISTRIBUTOR PULSES
3	MAP	**8**	THROTTLE POSITION SENSOR
4	ECM		
5	INJECTOR A		

Typical synchronized mode for dual throttle body system

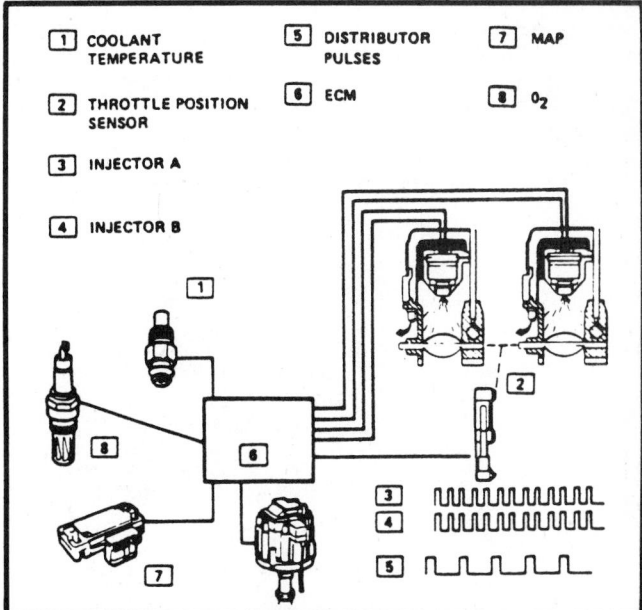

1	COOLANT TEMPERATURE	**5**	DISTRIBUTOR PULSES	**7**	MAP
2	THROTTLE POSITION SENSOR	**6**	ECM	**8**	O₂
3	INJECTOR A				
4	INJECTOR B				

Typical non-synchronized mode for dual throttle body system

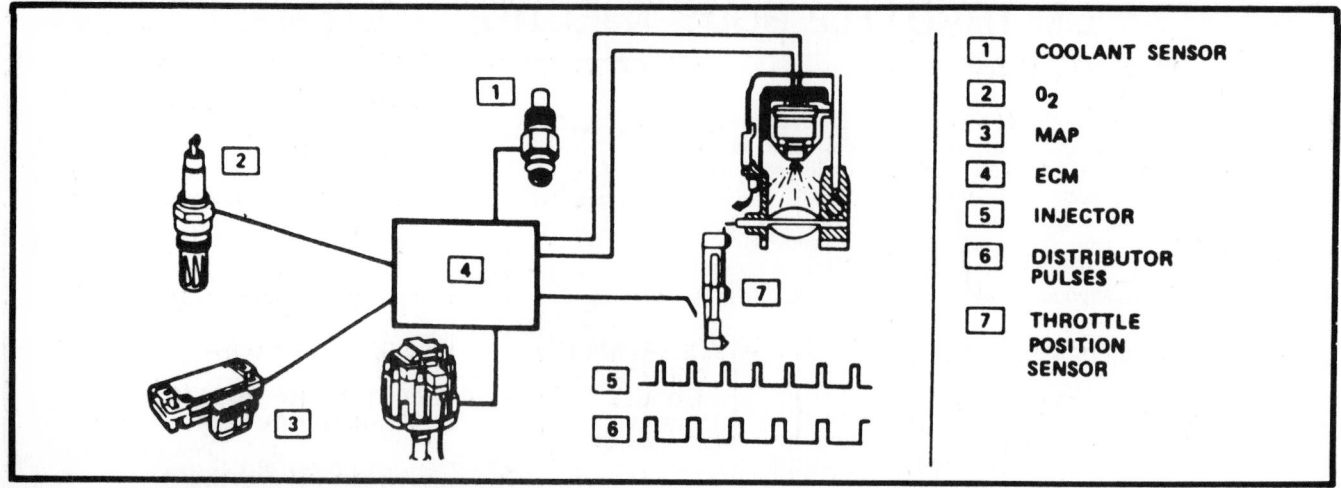

1	COOLANT SENSOR
2	O$_2$
3	MAP
4	ECM
5	INJECTOR
6	DISTRIBUTOR PULSES
7	THROTTLE POSITION SENSOR

Typical non-synchronized mode for single throttle body system

passes through a pressure regulator before being returned to the vehicle fuel tank.

The pressure regulator is a diaphragm-operated relief valve with injector pressure on one side and air cleaner pressure on the other. The function of the regulator is to maintain a constant pressure drop across the injector throughout the operating load and speed range of the engine.

On the dual throttle body system, a fuel pressure compensator is used on the second TBI assembly. The compensator has the same function of maintaining a constant fuel system pressure.

The throttle body portion of the TBI may contain ports located at, above, or below the throttle valve. These ports generate the vacuum signals for the EGR valve, MAP sensor, and the canister purge system.

The throttle position sensor (TPS) is a variable resistor used to convert the degree of throttle plate opening to an electrical signal to the ECM. The ECM uses this signal as a reference point of throttle valve position. In addition, an idle air control assembly (IAC), mounted in the throttle body is used to control idle speeds. A cone-shaped valve in the IAC assembly is located in an air passage in the throttle body that leads from the point beneath the air cleaner to below the throttle valve. The ECM monitors idle speeds and, depending on engine load, moves the IAC cone in the air passage to increase or decrease air bypassing the throttle valve to the intake manifold for control of idle speeds.

COMPONENTS AND OPERATION

The throttle body injection (TBI) and crossfire injection systems provide a means of fuel distribution for controlling exhaust emissions within legislated limits by precisely controlling the air/fuel mixture and under all operating conditions for, as near as possible, complete combustion.

This is accomplished by using an Electronic Control Module (ECM) - a small "on-board" microcomputer - that receives electrical inputs from various sensors about engine operating conditions. An oxygen sensor in the main exhaust stream functions to provide "feedback" information to the ECM as to the oxygen content, lean or rich, in the exhaust. The ECM uses this information from the oxygen sensor, and other sensors, to modify fuel delivery to achieve, as near as possible, an ideal air/fuel ratio of 14.7:1. This air/fuel ratio allows the three-way catalytic converter to be more efficient in the conversion process of reducing exhaust emissions while at the same time providing acceptable levels of driveability and fuel economy.

The ECM program electronically signals the fuel injector in the TBI assembly to provide the correct quantity of fuel for a wide range of operating conditions. Several sensors are used to determine existing operating conditions and the ECM then signals the injector to provide the precise amount of fuel required.

The ECM used on EFI vehicles has a "learning" capability. If the battery is disconnected to clear diagnostic codes, or for repair, the "learning" process has to begin all over again. A change may be noted in vehicle performance. To "teach" the vehicle, make sure the vehicle is at operating temperature and drive at part throttle, under moderate acceleration and idle conditions, until performance returns.

With the EFI system the TBI assembly is centrally located on the intake manifold where air and fuel are distributed through a single bore in the throttle body, similar to a carburated engine. Air for combustion is controlled by a single throttle valve which is connected to the accelerator pedal linkage by a throttle shaft and lever assembly. A special plate is located directly beneath the throttle valve to aid in mixture distribution.

Fuel for combustion is supplied by a single fuel injector, mounted on the TBI assembly, whose metering tip is located directly above the throttle valve. The injector is "pulsed" or "timed" open or closed by an electronic output signal received from the ECM. The ECM receives inputs concerning engine operating conditions from the various sensors (coolant temperature sensor, oxygen sensor, etc.). The ECM, using this information, performs highspeed calculations of engine fuel requirements and "pules" or "times" the injector , open or closed, thereby controlling fuel and air mixtures to achieve, as near as possible, ideal air/fuel mixture ratios.

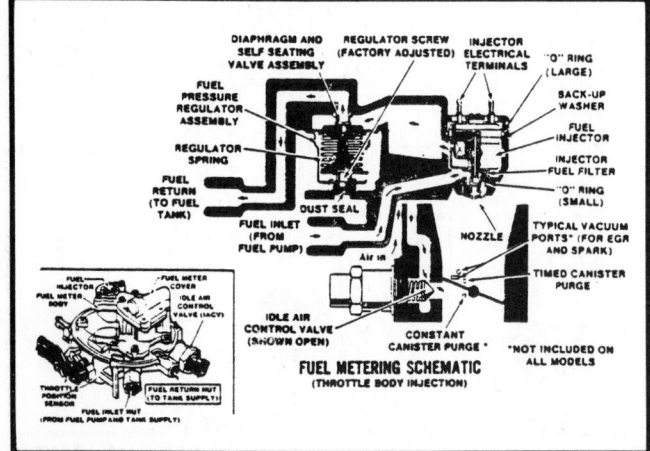

Exploded view of a typical throttle body injector assembly

PARAMETERS SENSED	PARAMETERS CONTROLLED
• A/C SYSTEM ENABLE	• AIR CONTROL VALVE SIGNAL
• BAROMETRIC PRESSURE	• AIR SWITCHING VALVE SIGNAL
• BRAKE PEDAL ENGAGEMENT	• CANISTER PURGE CONTROL SIGNAL
• ENGINE COOLANT TEMPERATURE	• EGR CONTROL SIGNAL·
• ENGINE CRANKSHAFT POSITION	• ELECTRONIC SPARK TIMING SIGNAL
• ENGINE CRANK MODE	• IDLE CONTROL SIGNAL
• ENGINE DETONATION	• THROTTLE BODY INJECTION CONTROL SIGNAL
• EXHAUST OXYGEN CONCENTRATION	• TRANSMISSION TORQUE CONVERTER CLUTCH SIGNAL
• INJECTOR VOLTAGE	• A/C CLUTCH CONTROL SIGNAL
• MANIFOLD ABSOLUTE PRESSURE	• AIR DOOR CONTROL SIGNAL
• PARK/NEUTRAL MODE	• COOLING FAN CONTROL
• THROTTLE POSITION	
• TIME (INTERNALLY GENERATED WITHIN ECM)	
• TRANSMISSION GEAR INDICATION	
• VEHICLE SPEED	

ELECTRONIC CONTROL MODULE (ECM)

*NOT ALL FEATURES ARE USED ON ALL ENGINES.

Engine control systems parameters

The crossfire injection system includes a pair of throttle body injection units - a front and rear unit, each controlled by the ECM. Using two TBI units provides a two-bore induction system whereby single bore units are mounted independently on the intake manifold cover to take advantage of improved manifold design. With this arrangement, each TBI unit supplies the correct air/fuel mixture through long runners in the intake manifold to the bank of cylinders located on the opposite side of the engine, thus the name "crossfire injection." In addition, a special plate is located directly below each throttle valve to aid in mixture distribution.

When the ignition key is turned on, the ECM will initialize (start program running) and energize the fuel pump relay. The fuel pump pressurizes the system to approximately 10 psi. If the ECM does not receive a distributor reference pulse (telling the ECM the engine is turning) within two seconds, the ECM will then de-energize the fuel pump relay, turning off the fuel pump. If a distributor reference pulse is later received, the ECM will turn the fuel pump back on.

Cranking Mode

During engine crank, for each distributor reference pulse the ECM will deliver an injector pulse (synchronized). The crank air/fuel ratio will be used if the throttle position is less than 80% open. Crank air fuel is determined by the ECM and ranges from 1.5:1 at -33°F (-36°C) to 14.7:1 at 201°F (94°C).

The lower the coolant temperature, the longer the pulse width (injector on-time) or richer the air/fuel ratio. The higher the coolant temperature, the less pulse width (injector on-time) or the leaner the air/fuel ratio.

Clear Flood Mode

If for some reason the engine should become flooded, provisions have been made to clear this condition. To clear the flood, the

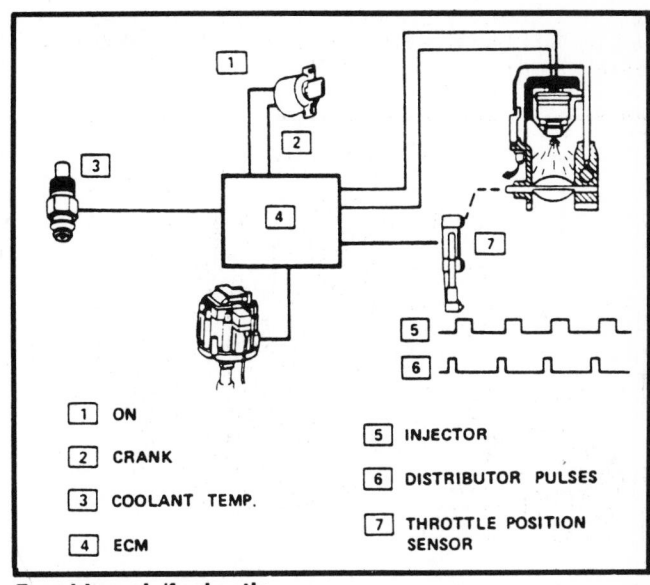

1	ON	5	INJECTOR
2	CRANK	6	DISTRIBUTOR PULSES
3	COOLANT TEMP.	7	THROTTLE POSITION SENSOR
4	ECM		

Cranking air/fuel ratio

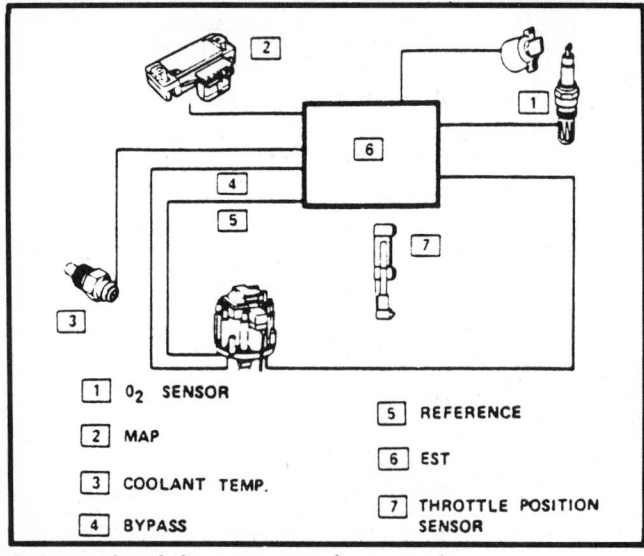

1. O₂ SENSOR
2. MAP
3. COOLANT TEMP.
4. BYPASS
5. REFERENCE
6. EST
7. THROTTLE POSITION SENSOR

Schematic of the run open loop mode

driver must depress the accelerator pedal enough to open to wide-open throttle position. The ECM then issues injector pulses at a rate that would be equal to an air/fuel ratio of 20:1. The ECM maintains this injector rate as long as the throttle remains wide open and the engine RPM is below 600. If the throttle position becomes less than 80%, the ECM then would immediately start issuing crank pulses to the injector calculated by the ECM based on the coolant temperature.

Run Mode
There are two different run modes. When the engine RPM is above 600, the system goes into open loop operation. In open loop operation, the ECM will ignore the signal from the oxygen (O₂) sensor and calculate the injector on-time based upon inputs from the coolant and MAP sensors.

During open loop operation, the ECM analyzes the following items to determine when the system is ready to go to the closed loop mode.

1. The oxygen sensor varying voltage output. (This is dependent on temperature).
2. The coolant sensor must be above specified temperature.
3. A specific amount of time must elapse after starting the engine. These values are stored in the PROM.

When these conditions have been met, the system goes into closed loop operation In closed loop operation, the ECM will modify the pulse width (injector on-time) based upon the signal from the oxygen sensor. The ECM will decrease the on-time if the air/fuel ratio is too rich, and will increase the on-time if the air/fuel ratio is too lean.

The pulse width, thus the amount of enrichment, is determined by manifold pressure change, throttle angle change, and coolant temperature. The higher the manifold pressure and the wider the throttle opening, the wider the pulse width. The acceleration enrichment pulses are delivered nonsynchronized. Any reduction in throttle angle will cancel the enrichment pulses. This way, quick movements of the accelerator will not over-enrich the mixture.

Acceleration Enrichment
When the engine is required to accelerate, the opening of the throttle valve(s) causes a rapid increase in manifold absolute pressure (MAP). This rapid increase in MAP causes fuel to condense on the manifold walls. The ECM senses this increase in throttle angle and MAP, and supplies additional fuel for a short period of time. This prevents the engine from stumbling due to too lean a mixture.

Deceleration Leanout
Upon deceleration, a leaner fuel mixture is required to reduce emission of hydrocarbons (H) and carbon monoxide (CO). To adjust the injection on-time, the ECM uses the decrease in MAP and the decrease in throttle position to calculate a decrease in pulse width. To maintain an idle fuel ratio of 14.7:1, fuel output is momentarily reduced. This is done because of the fuel remaining in the intake manifold.

Deceleration Fuel Cut-Off
The purpose of deceleration fuel cut-off is to remove fuel from the engine during extreme deceleration conditions. Deceleration fuel cut-off is based on values of manifold pressure, throt-

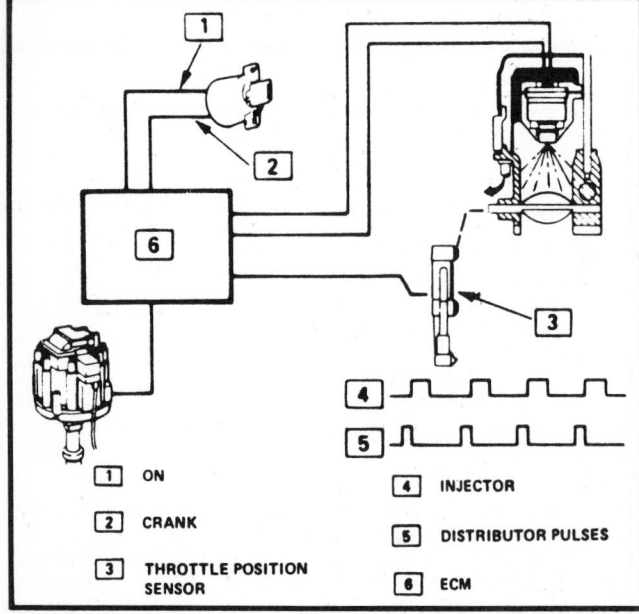

1. ON
2. CRANK
3. THROTTLE POSITION SENSOR
4. INJECTOR
5. DISTRIBUTOR PULSES
6. ECM

Schematic of the clear flood mode (fuel control)

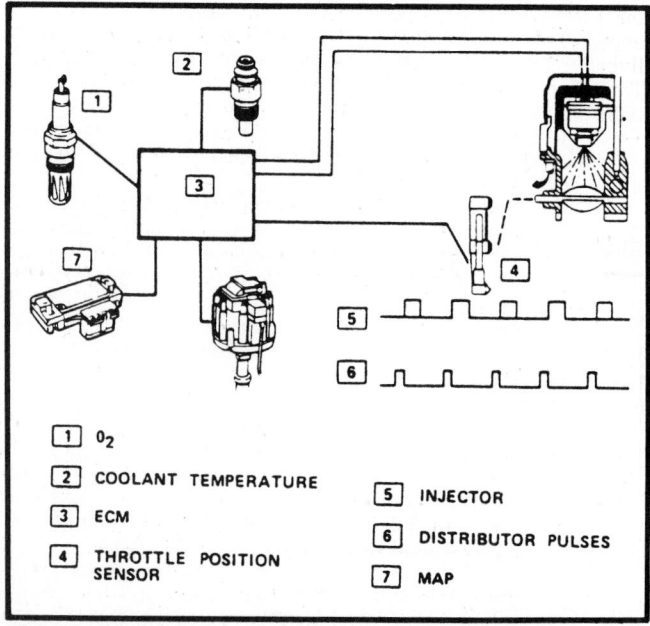

1. O₂
2. COOLANT TEMPERATURE
3. ECM
4. THROTTLE POSITION SENSOR
5. INJECTOR
6. DISTRIBUTOR PULSES
7. MAP

Schematic of the run closed loop mode

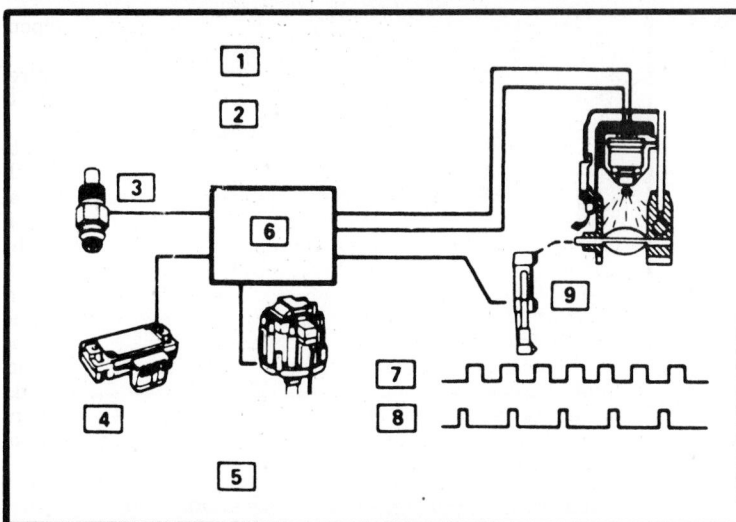

Schematic of the acceleration enrichment

1	A RAPIDLY INCREASING MAP WILL CAUSE FUEL TO CONDENSE ON THE MANIFOLD WALLS.
2	THE ECM WILL INCREASE THE INJECTOR ON TIME TO COMPENSATE.
3	COOLANT SENSOR
4	MAP
5	ACCELERATION ENRICHMENT PULSES ARE DELIVERED ASYCHRONOUSLY BASED UPON MANIFOLD PRESSURE AND THROTTLE ANGLE.
6	ECM
7	INJECTOR
8	DISTRIBUTOR PULSES
9	THROTTLE POSITION SENSOR

tle position, and engine RPM stored in the calibration PROM. Deceleration fuel cut-off overrides the deceleration enleanment mode.

Battery Voltage Correction

The purpose of battery voltage correction is to compensate for variations in battery voltage to fuel pump and injector response. The ECM modifies the pulse width by a correction factor in the PROM. When battery voltage decreases, pulse width increases.

Battery voltage correction takes place in all operating modes. When battery voltage is low, the spark delivered by the distributor may be low. To correct this low battery voltage problem, the ECM can do any or all of the following:
  a. Increase injector pulse width (increase fuel).
  b. Increase idle RPM.
  c. Increase ignition dwell time.

Fuel Cut-Off

When the ignition is off, the ECM will not energize the injector. Fuel will also be cut off if the ECM does not receive a reference pulse from the distributor. To prevent dieseling, fuel delivery is completely stopped as soon as the engine is stopped. The ECM will not allow any fuel supply until it receives distributor reference pulses which prevents flooding.

ELECTRONIC FUEL INJECTION SUBSYSTEMS

Electronic fuel injection (EFI) is the name given to the entire

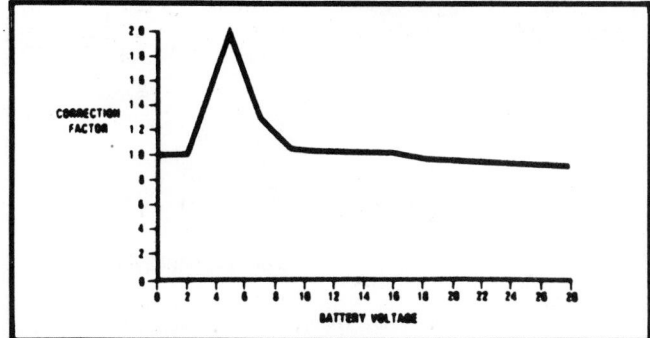

Battery voltage correction graph

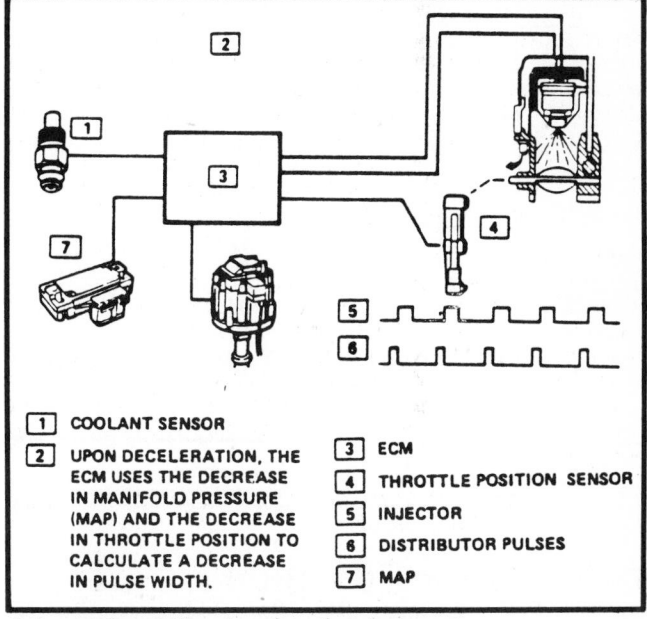

1	COOLANT SENSOR	**3**	ECM
2	UPON DECELERATION, THE ECM USES THE DECREASE IN MANIFOLD PRESSURE (MAP) AND THE DECREASE IN THROTTLE POSITION TO CALCULATE A DECREASE IN PULSE WIDTH.	**4**	THROTTLE POSITION SENSOR
		5	INJECTOR
		6	DISTRIBUTOR PULSES
		7	MAP

Schematic of the deceleration leanout

fuel injection system. Various "subsystems" are combined to form the overall system. These subsystems are:
  1. Fuel Supply System.
  2. Throttle Body Injector Assembly (TBI).
  3. Idle Air Control (IAC).
  4. Electronic Control Module (ECM).
  5. Data Sensors.
  6. Electronic Spark Timing (EST).
  7. Emission Controls.
Each subsystem is described in the following paragraphs.

Fuel Supply System

Fuel, supplied by an electric fuel pump mounted in the fuel tank, passes through an in-line fuel filter to the TBI assembly. To control fuel pump operation, a fuel pump rely is used.

When the ignition switch is turned to the ON position the fuel pump relay activates the electric fuel pump for 1.5–2.0 seconds to prime the injector. If the ECM does not receive reference pulses from the distributor after this time, the ECM signals the relay to turn the fuel pump off. The relay will once again activate the fuel pump when the ECM receives distributor reference pulses.

The oil pressure sender is the backup for the fuel pump relay. The sender has two circuits, one for the instrument cluster light or gauge, the other to activate the fuel pump if the relay fails. If the fuse relay has failed, the sender activates the fuel pump when oil pressure reaches 4 psi. Thus a failed fuel pump relay would cause a longer crank, especially in cold weather. If the fuel pump fails, a no start condition exists.

On the model 300, the fuel feed and return lines are attached with nuts and O-rings. They should be replaced if the lines are disconnected. The Model 500 fuel feed line uses a special banjo bolt for attachment to the fuel meter. The shank of the bolt has a hole drilled through it for fuel passage. It attaches to the fuel meter body fitting with two special O-ring washers. This system design is not interchangeable with any other type of fitting.

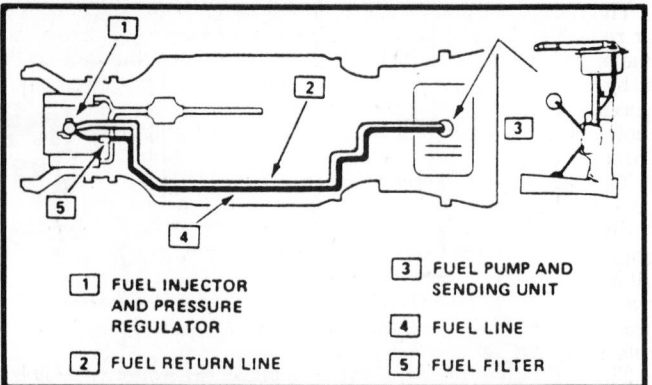

1	FUEL INJECTOR AND PRESSURE REGULATOR	3	FUEL PUMP AND SENDING UNIT
2	FUEL RETURN LINE	4	FUEL LINE
		5	FUEL FILTER

Typical fuel supply system

constant pressure (approximately 11 psi) to the injector throughout the operating loads and speed ranges of the engine. If the regulator pressure is too low, below 9 psi, it can cause poor performance. Too high a pressure could cause detonation and a strong fuel odor.

Idle Air Control (IAC)

The purpose of the idle air control (IAC) system is to control engine idle speeds while preventing stalls due to changes in engine load. The IAC assembly, mounted on the throttle body, controls bypass air around the throttle plate. By extending or retracting a conical valve, a controlled amount of air can move around the throttle plate. If RPM is too low, more air is diverted around the throttle plate to increase RPM.

During idle, the proper position of the IAC valve is calculated by the ECM based on battery voltage, coolant temperature, engine load, and engine RPM. If the RPM drops below a specified rate, the throttle plate is closed. The ECM will then calculate a new valve position.

Three different designs are used for the IAC conical valve. The first design used is single 35 taper while the second design used is a dual taper. The third design is a blunt valve. Care should be taken to insure use of the correct design when service replacement is required.

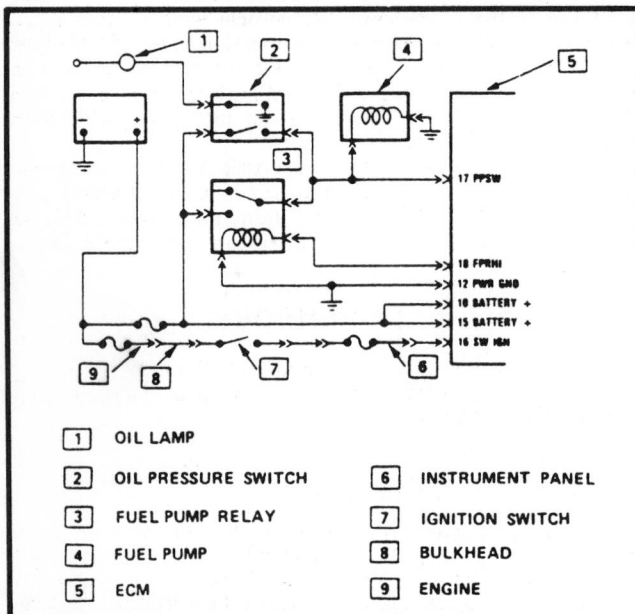

1	OIL LAMP		
2	OIL PRESSURE SWITCH	6	INSTRUMENT PANEL
3	FUEL PUMP RELAY	7	IGNITION SWITCH
4	FUEL PUMP	8	BULKHEAD
5	ECM	9	ENGINE

Typical fuel pump circuit

Throttle Body Injector (TBI) Assembly

The basic TBI unit is made up of two major casting assemblies: (1) a throttle body with a valve to control airflow and (2) a fuel body assembly with an integral pressure regulator and fuel injector to supply the required fuel. A device to control idle speed (IAC) and a device to provide information about throttle valve position (TPS) are included as part of the TBI unit.

The throttle body portion of the TBI unit may contain ports located at, above, or below the throttle valve. These ports generate the vacuum signals for the EGR valve, MAP sensor, and the canister purge system.

The fuel injector is a solenoid-operated device controlled by the ECM. The incoming fuel is directed to the lower end of the injector assembly which has a fine screen filter surrounding the injector inlet. The ECM turns on the solenoid, which lifts a normally closed ball valve off a seat. The fuel, under pressure, is injected in a conical spray pattern at the walls of the throttle body bore above the throttle valve. The excess fuel passes through a pressure regulator before being returned to the vehicle fuel tank.

The pressure regulator is a diaphragm-operated relief valve with the injector pressure on one side, and the air cleaner pressure on the other. The function of the regulator is to maintain

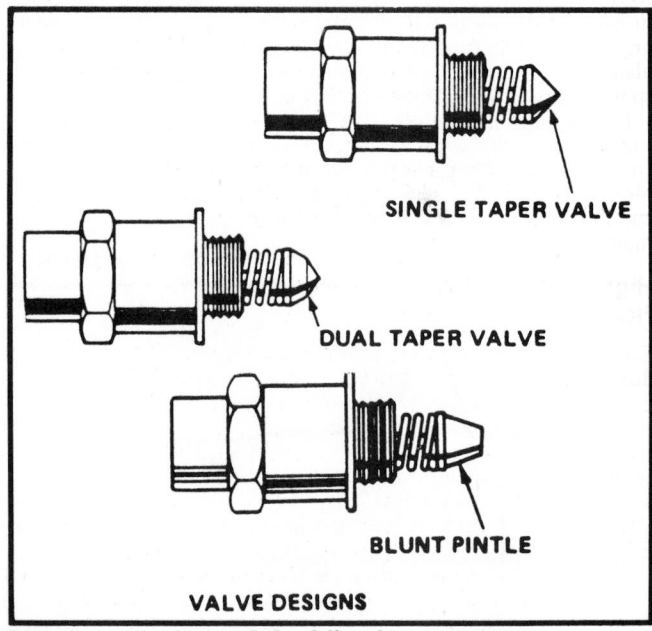

SINGLE TAPER VALVE

DUAL TAPER VALVE

BLUNT PINTLE

VALVE DESIGNS

The three designs of the idle air control valve

The IAC motor has 255 different positions or steps. The zero, or reference position, is the fully extended position at which the pintle is seated in the air bypass seat and no air is allowed to bypass the throttle plate. When the motor is fully retracted, maximum air is allowed to bypass the throttle plate. When the motor is fully retracted, maximum air is allowed to bypass the throttle plate.

The ECM always monitors how many steps it has extended or retracted the pintle from the zero or reference position; thus, it always calculates the exact position of the motor. Once the engine has started and the vehicle has reached approximately 40 MPH, the ECM will extend the motor 255 steps from whatever position it is in. This will bottom out the pintle against the seat. The ECM will call this position "0" and thus keep its zero reference updated.

The IAC only affects the engine's idle characteristics. If it is stuck fully open, idle speed is too high (too much air enters the throttle bore) If it is stuck closed, idle speed is too low (not enough air entering). If it is stuck somewhere in the middle, idle may be rough, and the engine won't respond to load changes.

Idle Speed Control

Incorrect diagnosis and/or misunderstanding of the idle speed control systems used on EFI engines may lead to unnecessary replacement of the IAC valve. Engine idle speed is controlled by the ECM which changes the idle speed by moving the IAC valve. The ECM adjusts idle speed in response to fluctuations in engine load (A/C, power steering, electrical loads, etc.) to maintain acceptable idle quality and proper exhaust emission performance.

The following is provided to assist the technician to better understand the system and correctly respond to the following customer concerns:

1. Rough Idle/Low Idle Speed.
2. High Idle Speed/Warm-up Idle Speed; No "Kickdown".

Rough Idle/Low Idle Speed

The ECM will respond to increases in engine load, which would cause a drop in idle speed, by moving the IAC valve to maintain proper idle speed. After the induced load is removed the ECM will return the idle speed to the proper level.

During A/C compressor operation. (MAX, BI-LEVEL, NORM or DEFROST mode) the ECM will increase idle speed in response to an "A/C-ON" signal, thereby compensating for any drop in idle speed due to compressor load. The ECM will also increase the idle speed on 1984 and 1985 models in response to high power steering loads.

During periods of especially heavy loads (A/C-ON plus parking maneuvers) significant effects on idle quality may be experienced. These effects are more pronounced on 4-cylinder engines. Abnormally low idle, rough idle and idle shake may occur if the ECM does not receive the proper signals from the monitored systems.

High Idle Speed/Warm-Up Idle Speed (No "Kickdown")

Engine idle speeds as high as 2100 RPM may be experienced during cold starts to quickly raise the catalytic converter to operating temperature for proper exhaust emissions performance. The idle speed attained after a cold start is ECM-controlled and will not drop for 45 seconds regardless of diver attempts to "kickdown." On 1984 and 1985 models, after 45 seconds following cold start, depressing the accelerator pedal will rotate the throttle position sensor (TPS), signaling the ECM to reduce the idle speed inprogrammed, fixed steps.

It is important to recognize the EFI engines have no accelerator pump or choke. Idle speed during warm-up is entirely ECM-controlled and cannot be changed by accelerator "kickdown" or "pumping".

DIAGNOSIS

Abnormally low idle speeds are usually caused by an ECM system-controlled or -monitored irregularity, while the most common cause for abnormally high idle speed is an induction (intake air) leak. The idle air control valve may occasionally lose its memory function, and it has an ECM-programmed method of "relearning" the correct idle position. This reset, when required, will occur the next time the car exceeds 35 MPH. At this time the ECM seats the pintle of the IAC valve in the throttle body to determine a reference point. Then it backs out a fixed distance to maintain proper idle speed.

Electronic Control Module (ECM)

The ECM, located in the passenger compartment, is the control center of the fuel injection system. The ECM constantly monitors the input information, processes this information from various sensors, and generates output commands to the various systems that affect vehicle performance.

The ability of the ECM to recognize and adjust for vehicle variations (engine transmission, vehicle weight, axle ratio, etc.) is provided by a removable calibration unit (PROM) that is programmed to tailor the ECM for the particular vehicle. There is a specific ECM/PROM combination for each specific vehicle, and the combinations are not interchangeable with those of other vehicles.

The ECM also performs the diagnostic function of the system. It can recognize operational problems, alert the driver through the "CHECK ENGINE" light, and store a code or codes which identify the problem areas to aid the technician in making repairs.

DATA SENSORS

A variety of sensors provide information to the ECM regarding engine operating characteristics. These sensors and their functions are described below.

Engine Coolant Temperature

The coolant sensor is a thermister (a resistor which changes value based on temperature) mounted on the engine coolant stream. As the temperature of the engine coolant changes, the resistance of the coolant sensor changes. Low coolant temperature produces a high resistance (100,000 ohms at -40°C/-40°F), while high temperature causes low resistance (70 ohms at 130°C/266°F).

The ECM supplies a 5-volt signal to the coolant sensor and measures the voltage that returns. By measuring the voltage change, the ECM determines the engine coolant temperature. This information is used to control fuel management, IAC, spark timing, EGR, canister purge and other engine operating conditions.

Oxygen Sensor

The exhaust oxygen sensor is mounted in the exhaust system where it can monitor the oxygen content of the exhaust gas stream. The oxygen content in the exhaust reacts with the oxygen sensor to produce a voltage output. This voltage ranges from approximately 100 millivolts (high oxygen - lean mixture) to 900 millivolts (low oxygen - rich mixture).

By monitoring the voltage output of the oxygen sensor, the ECM will determine what fuel mixture command to give to the injector (lean mixture-low voltage-rich command, rich mixture-high voltage lean command).

Remember that oxygen sensor indicates to the ECM what is happening in the exhaust. It does not cause things to happen. It is a type of gauge: high oxygen content = lean mixture; low oxygen content = rich mixture. The ECM adjust fuel to keep the system working.

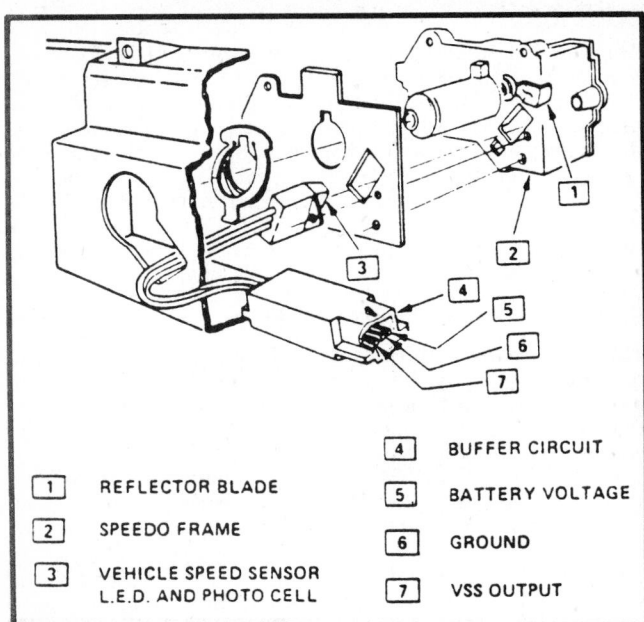

1	REFLECTOR BLADE	4	BUFFER CIRCUIT	
2	SPEEDO FRAME	5	BATTERY VOLTAGE	
3	VEHICLE SPEED SENSOR L.E.D. AND PHOTO CELL	6	GROUND	
		7	VSS OUTPUT	

Typical vehicle speed sensor

MAP Sensor

The manifold absolute pressure (MAP) sensor measures the changes in the intake manifold pressure which result from engine load and speed changes. The pressure measured by the MAP sensor is the difference between barometric pressure (outside air) and manifold pressure (vacuum). A closed throttle engine coastdown would produce a relatively low MAP value (approximately 20-35 kPa), while wide-open throttle would produce a high value (100 kPa). This high value is produced when the pressure inside the manifold is the same as outside the manifold, and 100% of outside air (or 100 kPa) is being measured. This MAP output is the opposite of what you would measure on a vacuum gauge. The use of this sensor also allows the ECM to adjust automatically for different altitude.

The ECM sends a 5-volt reference signal to the MAP sensor. As the MAP changes, the electrical resistance of the sensor also changes. By monitoring the sensor output voltage the ECM can determine the manifold pressure. A higher pressure, lower vacuum (high voltage) requires more fuel, while a lower pressure, higher vacuum (low voltage) requires less fuel.

Vehicle Speed Sensor (VSS)

NOTE: Vehicle should not be driven without a VSS as idle quality may be affected.

The vehicle speed sensor (VSS) is mounted behind the speedometer in the instrument cluster. It provides electrical pulses to the ECM from the speedometer head. The pulses indicate the road speed. The ECM uses this information to operate the IAC, canister purge, and TCC.

Some vehicles equipped with digital instrument clusters use a permanent magnet (PM) generator to provide the VSS signal. The PM generator is located in the transmission and replaces the speedometer cable. The signal from the PM generator drives a stepper motor which drives the odometer.

Throttle Position Sensor (TPS)

The throttle position sensor (TPS) is connected to the throttle shaft and is controlled by the throttle mechanism. A 5-volt reference signal is sent to the TPS from the ECM. As the throttle valve angle is changed (accelerator pedal moved), the resistance of the TPS also changes. At a closed throttle position, the

resistance of the TPS is high, so the output voltage to the ECM will be low (approximately .5 volt). As the throttle plate opens, the resistance decreases so that, at wide open throttle, the output voltage should be approximately 5 volts.

By monitoring the output voltage from the TPS, the ECM can determine fuel delivery based on throttle valve angle (driver demand). The TPS can either be misadjusted, shorted, open or loose. Misadjustment might result in poor idle or poor wide-open throttle performance. An open TPS signals the ECM that the throttle is always closed, resulting in poor performance. This usually sets a Code 22. A shorted TPS gives the ECM a constant wide-open throttle signal and should set a Code 21. A loose TPS indicates to the ECM that the throttle is moving. This causes intermittent bursts of fuel from the injector and an unstable idle.

Hall Effect Unit

This unit is mounted above the pick-up coil in the distributor. It is used in place of the "R" terminal of the conventional HEI module to send engine RPM information to the ECM. The Hall effect switch is only used on 2.5L L4 engines.

Park/Neutral Switch

NOTE: Vehicle should not be driven with the Park/Neutral switch disconnected as idle quality may be affected.

This switch indicates to the ECM when the transmission is in Park or Neutral.
A/C Compressor Clutch Engagement. This signal indicates to the ECM that the A/C compressor clutch is engaged.

ELECTRONIC SPARK TIMING (EST)

Electronic spark timing (EST) is used on all engines. The EST distributor contains no vacuum or centrifugal advance and uses a seven-terminal distributor module. It also has four wires going to a four-terminal connector in addition to the connectors normally found on HEI distributors. A reference pulse, indicating both engine RPM and crankshaft position, is sent to the ECM. The ECM determines the proper spark advance for the engine operating conditions and sends an "EST" pulse to the distributor.

The EST system is designed to optimize spark timing for better control of exhaust emissions and for fuel economy improvements. The ECM monitors information from various engine

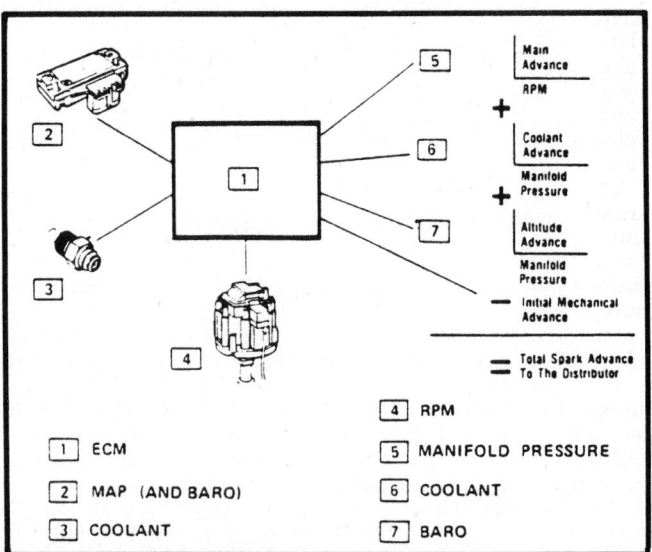

1	ECM	4	RPM
2	MAP (AND BARO)	5	MANIFOLD PRESSURE
3	COOLANT	6	COOLANT
		7	BARO

Schematic of the electronic spark timing

sensors, computes the desired spark timing and changes the timing accordingly. A backup spark advance system is incorporated in the module in case of EST failure.

ELECTRONIC SPARK CONTROL (ESC)

When engines are equipped with ESC in conjunction with EST, ESC is used to reduce spark advance under conditions of detonation. A knock sensor signals a separate ESC controller to retard the timing when it senses knock. The ESC controller signals the ECM which reduces spark advance until no more signals are received from the knock sensor.

DIRECT IGNITION SYSTEM

Components of the direct ignition system are a coil pack, ignition module, crankshaft reluctor ring, magnetic sensor and the ECM. The coil pack consists of two separate, interchangeable, ignition coils. These coils operate in the same manner as previous coils. Two coils are needed because each coil fires for two cylinders. The ignition module is located under the coil pack and is connected to the ECM by a 6 pin connector. The ignition module controls the primary circuits to the coils, turning them on and off and controls spark timing below 400 rpm and if the ECM bypass circuit becomes open or grounded.

The magnetic pickup sensor inserts through the engine block, just above the pan rail in proximity to the crankshaft reluctor ring. Notches in the crankshaft reluctor ring trigger the magnetic pickup sensor to provide timing information to the ECM. The magnetic pickup sensor provides a cam signal to identify correct firing sequence and crank signals to trigger each coil at the proper time.

This system uses EST and control wires from the ECM, as with the distributor systems. The ECM controls the timing using crankshaft position, engine rpm, engine temperature and manifold absolute pressure sensing.

EMISSION CONTROL

Various components are used to control exhaust emissions from a vehicle. These components are controlled by the ECM based on different engine operating conditions. These components are described in the following paragraphs. Not all components are used on all engines.

Exhaust Gas Recirculation (EGR)

EGR is a NOx control which recycles exhaust gases through the combustion cycle by admitting exhaust gases into the intake manifold. The amount of exhaust gas admitted is adjusted by a vacuum controlled valve in response to engine operating conditions. If the valve is open, the recirculated exhaust gas is released into the intake manifold to be drawn into the combustion chamber.

The integral exhaust pressure modulated EGR valve uses a transducer responsive to exhaust pressure to modulate the vacuum signal to the EGR valve. The vacuum signal is provided by an EGR vacuum port in the throttle body valve. Under conditions when exhaust pressure is lower than the control pressure, the EGR signal is reduced by an air bleed within the transducer. Under conditions when exhaust pressure is higher than the control pressure, the air bleed is closed and the EGR valve responds to an unmodified vacuum signal. Physical arrangement of the valve components will vary depending on whether the control pressure is positive or negative.

Positive Crankcase Ventilation (PCV) System

A closed positive crankcase ventilation (PCV) system is used to provide more complete scavenging of crankcase vapors. Fresh air from the air cleaner is supplied to the crankcase, mixed

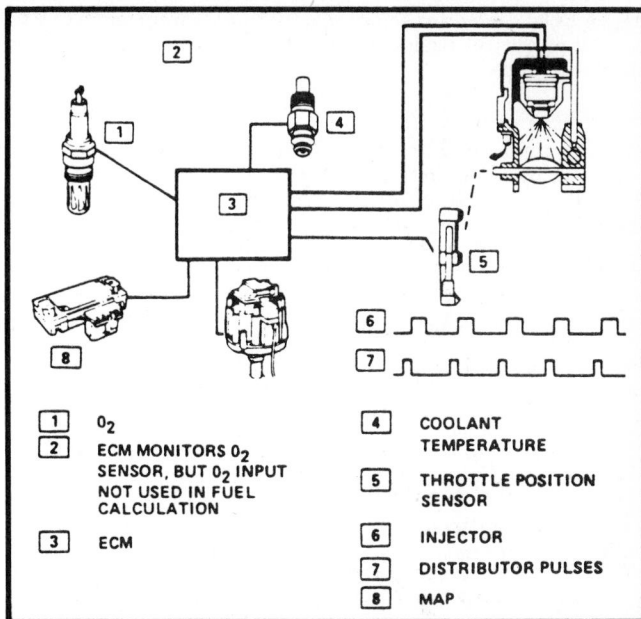

1	O2	4	COOLANT TEMPERATURE
2	ECM MONITORS O2 SENSOR, BUT O2 INPUT NOT USED IN FUEL CALCULATION	5	THROTTLE POSITION SENSOR
3	ECM	6	INJECTOR
		7	DISTRIBUTOR PULSES
		8	MAP

Schematic of the electronic spark timing inputs

with blow-by gases and then passed through a positive crankcase ventilation (PCV) valve into the induction system.

The primary mode of crankcase ventilation control is through the PCV valve which meters the mixture of fresh air and blow-by gases into the induction system at a rate dependent upon manifold vacuum.

To maintain the idle quality, the PCV valve restricts the ventilation system flow whenever intake manifold vacuum is designed to allow excessive amounts of blow-by gases to backflow through the breather assembly into the air cleaner and through the carburetor to be consumed by normal combustion.

Thermostatic Air Cleaner (THERMAC)

To assure optimum driveability under varying climatic conditions, a heated intake air system is used on engines. This system is designed to warm the air entering the TBI to insure uniform inlet air temperatures. Under this condition, the EFI system can be calibrated to efficiently reduce exhaust emission and to eliminate throttle blade icing. The THERMAC system used on vehicles equipped with EFI operates identical to other THERMAC systems.

EVAPORATIVE EMISSION CONTROL (EEC) SYSTEMS

The basic evaporative emission control system used on all vehicles uses the carbon canister storage method. This method transfers fuel vapor to an activated carbon storage device for retention when the vehicle is not operating. A ported vacuum signal is used for purging vapors stored in the canister.

Controlled Canister Purge

The ECM controls a solenoid valve which controls vacuum to the purge valve in the charcoal canister. In open loop, before a specified time has expired and below a specified RPM, the solenoid valve is energized and blocks vacuum to the purge valve. When the system is in closed loop, after a specified time and above a specified RPM, the solenoid valve is de-energized and vacuum can be applied to the purge valve. This releases the collected vapors into the intake manifold. On systems not using an ECM controlled solenoid, a thermo vacuum valve (TVV) is used to control purge. See the appropriate car sections for checking procedures.

Air Management Control

The air management system aids in the reduction of exhaust emissions by supplying air to either the catalytic converter, engine exhaust manifold, or to the air cleaner. The ECM controls the air management system by energizing or denergizing an air switching valve. Operation of the air switching valve is dependent upon such engine operating characteristics as coolant temperature, engine load, and acceleration (or deceleration), all of which are sensed by the ECM.

Pulsair Reactor System

The Pulsair injection reactor (PAIR) system utilizes exhaust pressure pulsations to draw air into the exhaust system. Fresh air from the clean side of the air cleaner supplies filtered air to avoid dirt build-up on the check valve seat. The air cleaner also serves as a muffler for noise reduction.

The internal mechanism of the PULSAIR valve reacts to three distinct conditions.

The firing of the engine creates a pulsating flow of exhaust gases which are of positive (+) or negative (-) pressure. This pressure or vacuum is transmitted through external tubes to the PULSAIR valve.

1. If the pressure is positive, the disc is forced to the closed position and no exhaust gas is allowed to flow past the valve and into the air supply line.

2. If there is a negative pressure (vacuum) in the exhaust system at the valve, the disc will open, allowing fresh air to mix with the exhaust gases.

3. Due to the inertia of the system, the disc ceases to follow the pressure pulsations at high engine RPM. At this point, the disc remains closed, preventing any further fresh air flow.

Catalytic Converter

Of all emission control devices available, the catalytic converter is the most effective in reducing tailpipe emissions. The major tailpipe pollutants are hydrocabons (HC), carbon monoxide (CO), and oxides of nitrogen (NOx).

TBI Unit Component Removal

SERVICE PRECAUTIONS

1. When working around any part of the fuel system, take precautionary steps to prevent fire and/or explosion:

a. Disconnect negative terminal from battery (except when testing with battery voltage is required).

b. When ever possible, use a flashlight instead of a drop light.

c. Keep all open flame and smoking material out of the area.

d. Use a shop cloth or similar to catch fuel when opening a fuel system.

e. Relieve fuel system pressure before servicing.

f. Use eye protection.

g. Always keep a dry chemical (class B) fire extinguisher near the area.

NOTE: Due to the amount of fuel pressure in the fuel lines, before doing any work to the fuel system, the fuel system should be de-pressurized. To de-pressurize the

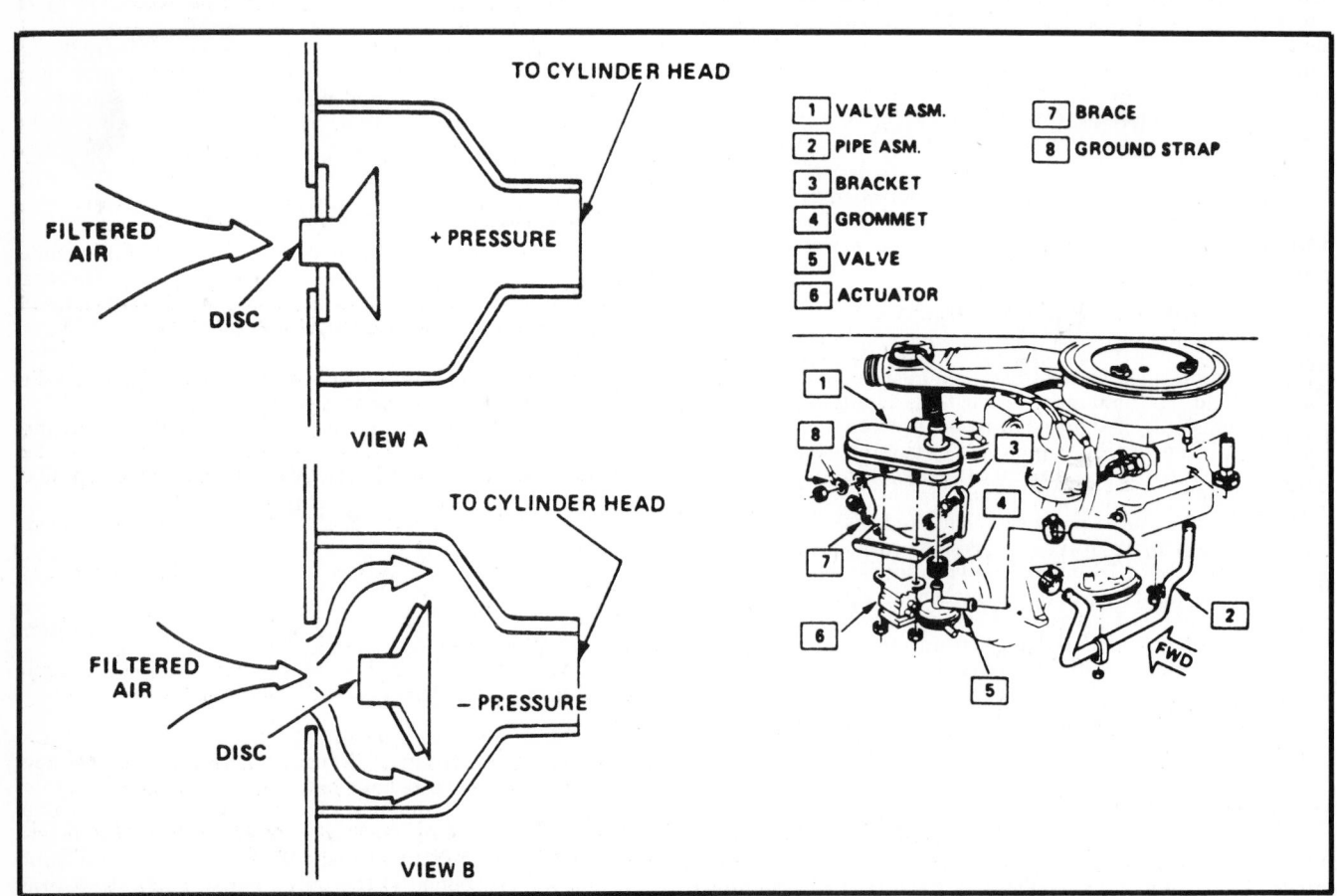

Typical pulsair injection reactor valve

fuel system, remove the fuel pump fuse and disconnect the fuel pump electrical connections at the fuel pump (if necessary) and start the vehicle. Let the vehicle run until it burns up the remaining fuel in the fuel lines. This way there will be no pressure left in the fuel system and the repair work can be performed. Some engines (like the 2.0L engine) may have a bleed valve located in the fuel pressure regulator or on the fuel line, this bleed valve may be used to bleed the fuel pressure from the system instead of using the other method.

THROTTLE BODY

Removal and Installation

SINGLE OR DUAL INJECTOR UNIT

Due to the varied application of throttle body unit's, a general throttle body unit removal and installation procedure is outlined. The removal steps can be altered as required by the technician

1. Depressurize the fuel system. Raise the hood, install fender covers and remove the air cleaner assembly. Disconnect the negative battery cable.
2. Disconnect the electrical connectors for the idle speed control motor, the throttle position sensor, fuel injectors, EFE and any other component necessary in order to remove the throttle body.
3. Remove the throttle return spring, cruise control, throttle linkage and downshift cable.
4. Disconnect all necessary vacuum line, the fuel inlet line, fuel return line, brake booster line, MAP sensor hose and the AIR hose. Be sure to use a back-up wrench on all metal lines.
5. Remove the PCV, EVAP and EGR hoses from the front of the throttle body.
6. Remove the three throttle body mounting screws and remove the throttle body and gasket.
7. Installation is the reverse order of the removal procedure. Torque the throttle body retaining screws to 15 ft. lbs.

CROSSFIRE INJECTION ASSEMBLY

Removal and Installation

FRONT UNIT V8 ENGINE

1. Depressurize the fuel system. Raise the hood, install fender covers and remove the air cleaner assembly, noting the connection points of the vacuum lines. Disconnect the negative battery cable.
2. Disconnect the electrical connectors at the injector and the idle air control motor.
3. Disconnect the vacuum line from the TBI unit, noting the connection points. During installation, refer to the underhood emission control information decal for vacuum line routing information.
4. Disconnect the transmission detent cable from the TBI unit.
5. Disconnect the fuel inlet (feed) and fuel balance line connections at the front TBI unit.
6. Disconnect the throttle control rod between the two TBI units.
7. Unbolt and remove the TBI unit.
8. Installation is the reverse of the previous steps. Torque the TBI bolts to 120-168 in. lbs. during installation.

REAR UNIT V8 ENGINE

1. Depressurize the fuel system. Raise the hood, install fender covers and remove the air cleaner assembly, noting the connection points of the vacuum lines. Disconnect the negative battery cable.

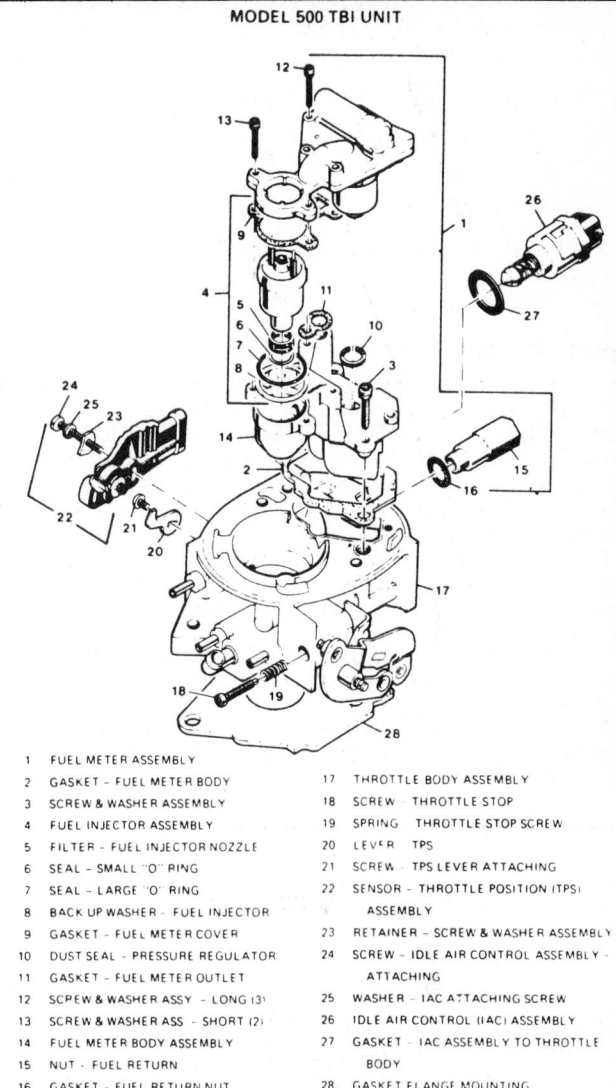

MODEL 500 TBI UNIT

1	FUEL METER ASSEMBLY		
2	GASKET - FUEL METER BODY	17	THROTTLE BODY ASSEMBLY
3	SCREW & WASHER ASSEMBLY	18	SCREW - THROTTLE STOP
4	FUEL INJECTOR ASSEMBLY	19	SPRING - THROTTLE STOP SCREW
5	FILTER - FUEL INJECTOR NOZZLE	20	LEVER - TPS
6	SEAL - SMALL "O" RING	21	SCREW - TPS LEVER ATTACHING
7	SEAL - LARGE "O" RING	22	SENSOR - THROTTLE POSITION (TPS)
8	BACK UP WASHER - FUEL INJECTOR		ASSEMBLY
9	GASKET - FUEL METER COVER	23	RETAINER - SCREW & WASHER ASSEMBLY
10	DUST SEAL - PRESSURE REGULATOR	24	SCREW - IDLE AIR CONTROL ASSEMBLY -
11	GASKET - FUEL METER OUTLET		ATTACHING
12	SCREW & WASHER ASSY - LONG (3)	25	WASHER - IAC ATTACHING SCREW
13	SCREW & WASHER ASS - SHORT (2)	26	IDLE AIR CONTROL (IAC) ASSEMBLY
14	FUEL METER BODY ASSEMBLY	27	GASKET - IAC ASSEMBLY TO THROTTLE
15	NUT - FUEL RETURN		BODY
16	GASKET - FUEL RETURN NUT	28	GASKET FLANGE MOUNTING

Exploded view of the model 500 assembly

2. Disconnect the electrical connectors at the injector, idle air control motor, and throttle position sensor.
3. Disconnect the vacuum lines from the TBI unit, noting the connection points. During installation, refer to the underhood emission control information decal for vacuum line routing information.
4. Disconnect the throttle and cruise control (if so equipped) cables the the TBI unit.
5. Disconnect the fuel return and balance line connections from the rear TBI unit.
6. Disconnect the throttle control rod between the two units.
7. Unbolt and remove the TBI unit.
8. Installation is the reverse of the previous steps. Torque the TBI bolts to 120-168 in. lbs. during installation.

DISASSEMBLY

Use extreme care when handling the TBI unit to avoid damage to the swirl plates located beneath the throttle valve.

NOTE: If both TBI units are to be disassembled, DO NOT mix parts between either unit.

1. Remove the fuel meter cover assembly (five screws). Remove the gaskets after the cover has been removed. The fuel

meter cover assembly is serviced only as a unit. IF necessary, the entire unit must be replaced.

CAUTION

DO NOT remove the four screws which retain the pressure regulator (rear unit) or pressure compensator (front unit). There is a spring beneath the cover which is under great pressure. If the cover is accidentally released, personal injury could result. Do not immerse the fuel meter cover in any type of cleaning solvent.

---

2. Remove the foam dust seal from the meter body of the rear unit.

3. Remove the fuel injector using a pair of small pliers as follows:

    a. Grasp the injector collar between the electrical terminals.

    b. Carefully pull the injector upward in a twisting motion.

    c. If the injectors are to be removed from both TBI units, mark them so that they mat be installed in their original units.

4. Remove the filter from the base of the injector by rotating it back and forth.

5. Remove the O-ring and the steel washer from the top of the fuel meter body, then remove the small O-ring from the bottom of the injector cavity.

6. Remove the fuel inlet and outlet nuts (and gaskets) from the fuel meter body.

7. Remove the fuel meter body assembly and gasket from the throttle body assembly (three screws).

8. For the rear TBI unit only: Remove the throttle position sensor (TPS) front the throttle body (two screws). If necessary, remove the screw which holds the TPS actuator lever to the end of the throttle shaft.

9. Remove the idle air control motor from the throttle body.

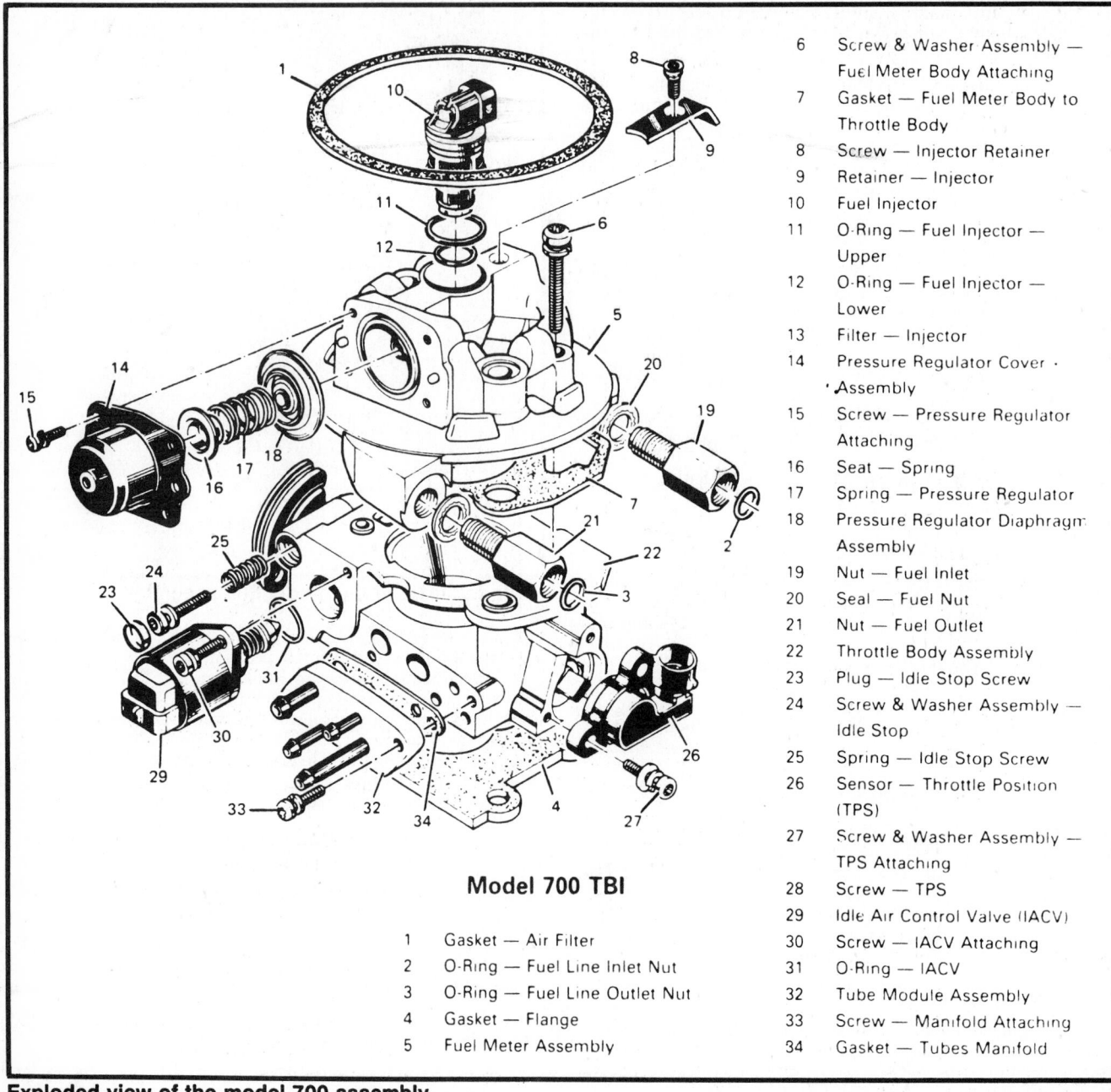

Model 700 TBI

1	Gasket — Air Filter
2	O-Ring — Fuel Line Inlet Nut
3	O-Ring — Fuel Line Outlet Nut
4	Gasket — Flange
5	Fuel Meter Assembly

6	Screw & Washer Assembly — Fuel Meter Body Attaching
7	Gasket — Fuel Meter Body to Throttle Body
8	Screw — Injector Retainer
9	Retainer — Injector
10	Fuel Injector
11	O-Ring — Fuel Injector — Upper
12	O-Ring — Fuel Injector — Lower
13	Filter — Injector
14	Pressure Regulator Cover · Assembly
15	Screw — Pressure Regulator Attaching
16	Seat — Spring
17	Spring — Pressure Regulator
18	Pressure Regulator Diaphragm Assembly
19	Nut — Fuel Inlet
20	Seal — Fuel Nut
21	Nut — Fuel Outlet
22	Throttle Body Assembly
23	Plug — Idle Stop Screw
24	Screw & Washer Assembly — Idle Stop
25	Spring — Idle Stop Screw
26	Sensor — Throttle Position (TPS)
27	Screw & Washer Assembly — TPS Attaching
28	Screw — TPS
29	Idle Air Control Valve (IACV)
30	Screw — IACV Attaching
31	O-Ring — IACV
32	Tube Module Assembly
33	Screw — Manifold Attaching
34	Gasket — Tubes Manifold

Exploded view of the model 700 assembly

— CAUTION —

Because the TPS and idle air control motors are electrical units, they must not be immersed in any type of cleaning solvent.

ASSEMBLY

NOTE: During assembly, replace the gaskets, injector washer, O-rings, and pressure regulator dust seal with new parts.

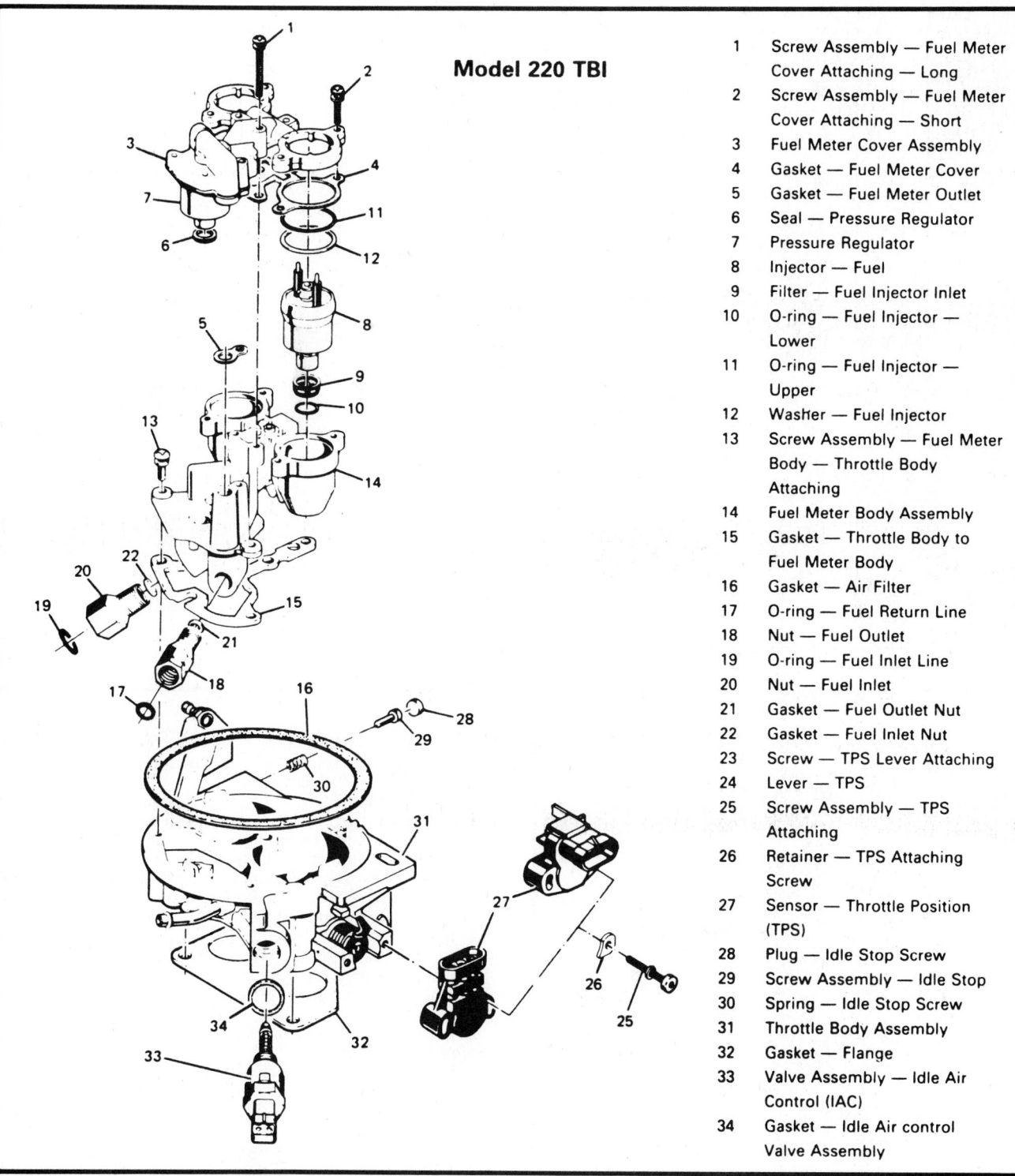

Model 220 TBI

1. Screw Assembly — Fuel Meter Cover Attaching — Long
2. Screw Assembly — Fuel Meter Cover Attaching — Short
3. Fuel Meter Cover Assembly
4. Gasket — Fuel Meter Cover
5. Gasket — Fuel Meter Outlet
6. Seal — Pressure Regulator
7. Pressure Regulator
8. Injector — Fuel
9. Filter — Fuel Injector Inlet
10. O-ring — Fuel Injector — Lower
11. O-ring — Fuel Injector — Upper
12. Washer — Fuel Injector
13. Screw Assembly — Fuel Meter Body — Throttle Body Attaching
14. Fuel Meter Body Assembly
15. Gasket — Throttle Body to Fuel Meter Body
16. Gasket — Air Filter
17. O-ring — Fuel Return Line
18. Nut — Fuel Outlet
19. O-ring — Fuel Inlet Line
20. Nut — Fuel Inlet
21. Gasket — Fuel Outlet Nut
22. Gasket — Fuel Inlet Nut
23. Screw — TPS Lever Attaching
24. Lever — TPS
25. Screw Assembly — TPS Attaching
26. Retainer — TPS Attaching Screw
27. Sensor — Throttle Position (TPS)
28. Plug — Idle Stop Screw
29. Screw Assembly — Idle Stop
30. Spring — Idle Stop Screw
31. Throttle Body Assembly
32. Gasket — Flange
33. Valve Assembly — Idle Air Control (IAC)
34. Gasket — Idle Air control Valve Assembly

Exploded view of the model 220 assembly

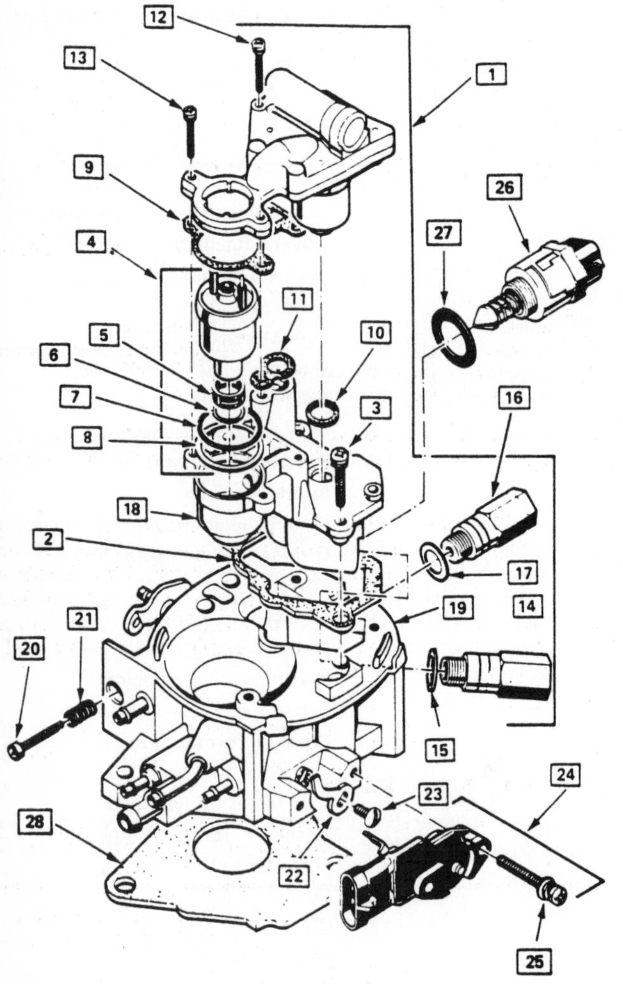

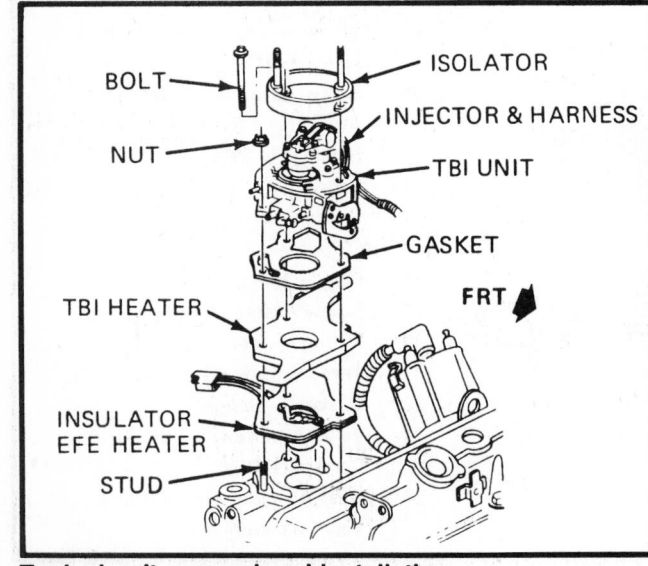

1	FUEL METER ASSEMBLY	**13**	SCREW & WASHER ASSY – SHORT (2)
2	GASKET – FUEL METER BODY	**14**	NUT – FUEL INLET
3	SCREW & WASHER ASSY – ATTACH. (3)	**15**	GASKET – FUEL INLET NUT
4	FUEL INJECTOR KIT	**16**	NUT – FUEL OUTLET
5	FILTER – FUEL INJECTOR NOZZLE	**17**	GASKET – FUEL OUTLET NUT
6	SEAL – SMALL "O" RING	**18**	FUEL METER BODY ASSEMBLY
7	SEAL – LARGE "O" RING	**19**	THROTTLE BODY ASSEMBLY
8	BACK-UP WASHER – FUEL INJECTOR	**20**	SCREW – IDLE STOP
9	GASKET – FUEL METER COVER	**21**	SPRING – IDLE STOP SCREW
10	DUST SEAL – PRESS, REGULATOR	**22**	LEVER – TPS
11	GASKET – FUEL METER OUTLET	**23**	SCREW – TPS LEVER ATTACHING
12	SCREW & WASHER ASSY – LONG (3)	**24**	SENSOR – THROTTLE POSITION KIT
		25	SCREW – TPS ATTACHING (2)
		26	IDLE AIR CONTROL ASSY.
		27	GASKET – CONTROL ASSY. TO T.B.
		28	GASKET – FLANGE MOUNTING

Exploded view of the model 300 assembly

Typical unit removal and installation

1. Install the idle air control motor in the throttle body, using a new gasket. Torque the retaining screws to 13 ft. lbs. DO NOT overtighten the screws.

2. For the rear TBI unit only: If removed, install the TPS actuator lever by aligning the flats of the lever and the shaft. Install and tighten the retaining screw.

3. Install the fuel meter body on the throttle body, using a new gasket. Also, apply thread locking compound to the three fuel meter body screws according to the chemical manufacturers instructions. Torque the screws to 35 in. lbs.

4. Install the fuel inlet and outlet nuts, using new gaskets. Torque the nuts to 260 in. lbs.

5. Carefully twist the fuel filter onto the injector base.

6. Lubricate the new O-rings with pertroleum jelly or equivalent.

7. Install the small O-ring onto the injector, pressing it up against the fuel filter.

8. Install the steel washer into the injector cavity recess of the fuel meter body. Install the large O-ring above the steel washer, in the cavity recess. The O-ring must be flush with the fuel meter body surface.

9. Using a pushing/twisting motion, carefully install the injector. Center the nozzle O-ring in the bottom of the injector cavity and align the raised lug on the injector base with the

notch in the fuel meter body cavity. Make sure the injector is seated fully in the cavity. The electrical connections should be parallel to the throttle shaft of the throttle body.

10. For the rear TBI unit only: Install the new pressure regulator dust seal into the fuel meter body recess.

11. Install the new full meter cover and fuel outlet passage gaskets on the fuel meter cover.

12. Install the fuel meter cover assembly, using thread locking compound on the five retaining screws. Torque the screws to 28 in. lbs. Note that the two short screws must be installed along side the fuel injector (one screw each side).

13. For the rear TBI unit only: With the throttle valve in the closed (idle) position, install the TPS but do not tighten the attaching screws. The TPS lever must be located ABOVE the tang on the throttle actuator lever.

14. Install the TBI unit(s) as previously outlined and adjust the throttle position sensor.

FUEL METER COVER

Removal and Installation

The fuel meter cover contains the pressure regulator and is only serviced as a complete preset assembly. The fuel pressure regulator is preset and plugged at the factory.

1. Depressurize the fuel system. Raise the hood, install fender covers and remove the air cleaner assembly. Disconnect the negative battery cable.

2. Disconnect electrical connector to injector by squeezing on tow tabs and pulling straight up.

3. Remove five screws securing fuel meter cover to fuel meter body. Notice location of two short screws during removal.

------------------ **CAUTION** ------------------

Do not remove the four screws securing the pressure regulator to the fuel meter cover. The fuel pressure regulator includes a large spring under heavy tension which, if accidentally released, could cause personal injury. The fuel meter cover is only serviced as a complete assembly and includes the fuel pressure regulator preset and plugged at the factor.

4. Remove the fuel meter cover assembly from the throttle body.

NOTE: DO NOT immerse the fuel meter cover (with pressure regulator) in any type of cleaner. Immersion of cleaner will damage the internal fuel pressure regulator diaphragms and gaskets.

5. Installation is the reverse order of the removal procedure. Be sure to use new gaskets and torque the fuel meter cover attaching screws to 28 in. lbs.

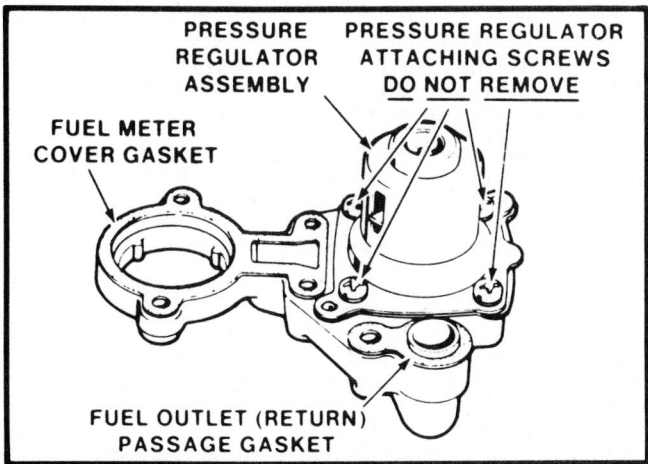

Bottom view of the fuel meter cover

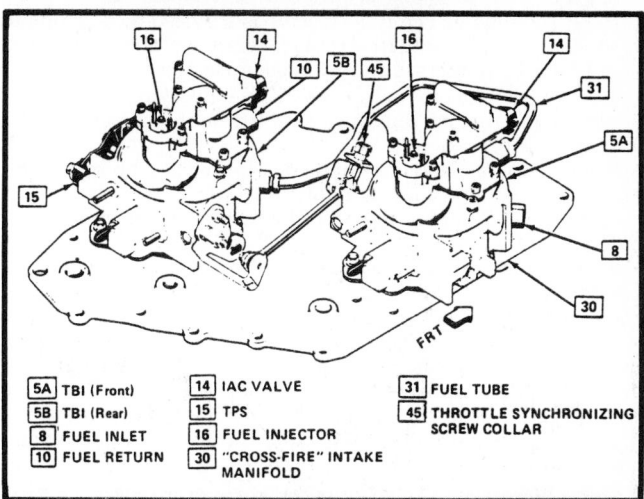

5A TBI (Front)	**14** IAC VALVE	**31** FUEL TUBE
5B TBI (Rear)	**15** TPS	**45** THROTTLE SYNCHRONIZING SCREW COLLAR
8 FUEL INLET	**16** FUEL INJECTOR	
10 FUEL RETURN	**30** "CROSS-FIRE" INTAKE MANIFOLD	

Exploded view of a typical cross fire injection assembly

NOTE: The service kits include a small vial of thread locking compound with directions for use. If the material is not available, use part number 1052624, Loctite® 262, or equivalent. Do not use a higher strength locking compound than recommended, as this may prevent attaching screw removal or breakage of the screwhead if removal is again required.

FUEL INJECTOR

Removal and Installation

Use car in removing the injector to prevent damage to the electrical connector pins on top of the injector, the injector fuel fil-

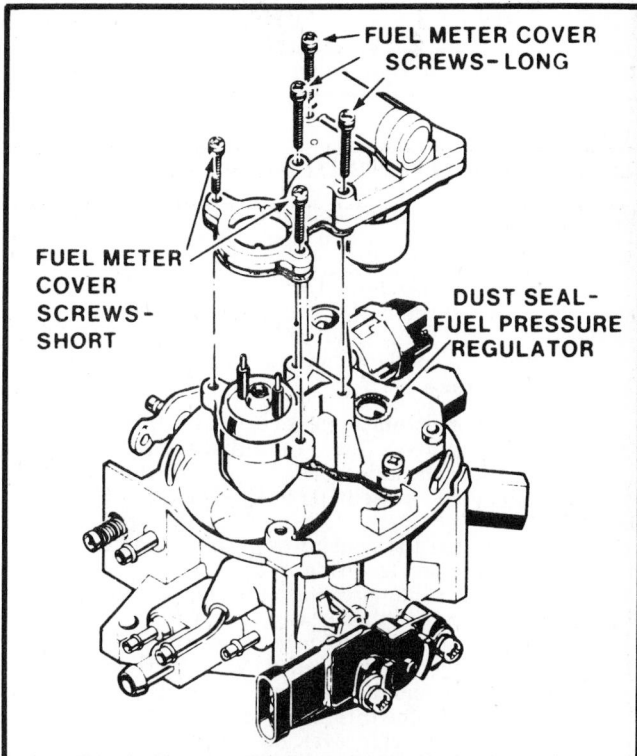

Fuel meter cover removal and installation

ter and the nozzle. The fuel injector is serviced as a complete assembly only. The fuel injector is an electrical component and should not be immersed in any type of cleaner.

1. Depressurize the fuel system. Raise the hood, install fender covers and remove the air cleaner assembly. Disconnect the negative battery cable.

2. Disconnect electrical connector to injector by squeezing on tow tabs and pulling straight up.

3. Remove the fuel meter cover assembly as previously outlined.

4. With the fuel meter cover gasket in place to prevent damage to the casting, use a suitable dowel rod and lay the dowel rod on top of the fuel meter body.

5. Insert a suitable pry tool into the small lip of the injector and pry against the dowel rod lifting the injector straight up. Tool J-26868 or equivalent can also be used.

6. Remove the injector from the fuel meter body. Remove the small O-ring at the bottom of the injector cavity. Be sure to discard both O-rings.

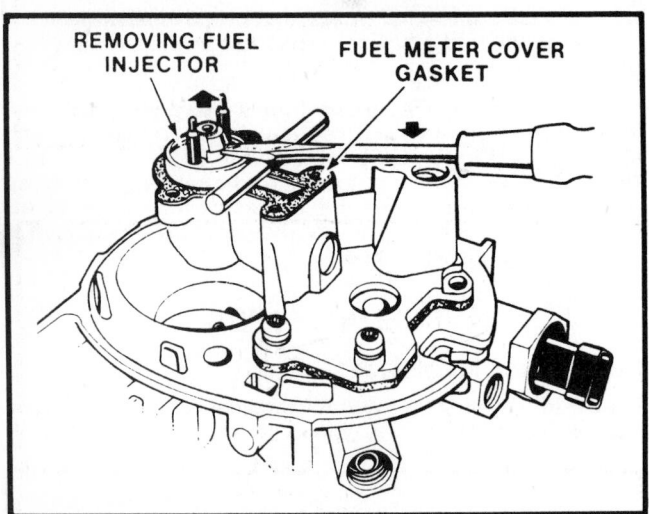

REMOVING FUEL INJECTOR   FUEL METER COVER GASKET

Removing the fuel injector from the throttle body

Installation

1. Lubricate the new small O-ring with petroleum jelly or equivalent. Push the new O-ring on the nozzle end of the injector, pressing the O-ring up against the injector fuel filter.

2. Install a new steel backup washer in the recess of the fuel meter body.

3. Lubricate the new large O-ring with petroleum jelly or equivalent. Install the new O-ring directly above the backup washer, pressing the O-ring down into the cavity recess. The O-ring is installed properly when it is flush with the fuel meter body casting surface.

NOTE: Do not attempt to reverse the installation of the large O-ring procedure. Install the backup washer and O-ring after the injector is located in the cavity. To do so will prevent the seating of the O-ring in the cavity recess.

4. Install the injector by using as pushing and twisting motion to center the nozzle O-ring in the bottom of the injector cavity and aligning the raised lug on the injector base with the notch cast into the fuel meter body.

5. Push down on the injector making sure it is fully seated in the cavity. The injector is installed correctly when the lug is seated in the notch and the electrical terminals are parallel to the throttle shaft in the throttle body.

6. Install the fuel meter cover. Install the injector electrical connector and all electrical and vacuum lines. Install the air cleaner assembly.

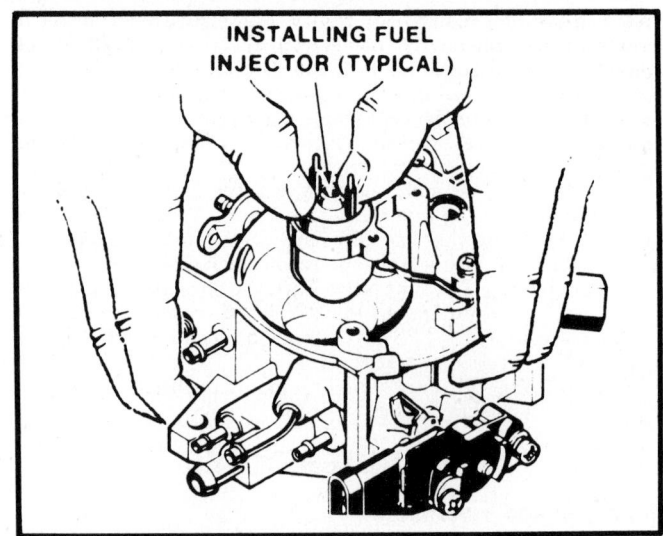

INSTALLING FUEL INJECTOR (TYPICAL)

Installing the fuel injector into the throttle body

7. Start the engine and check for leaks and proper injection operation.

NOTE: The most widely used injector for the TBI unit is a Bosch injector, but starting in 1987 there will also be a new injector being used. This new injector will be a Multec TBI injector (a Rochester product). It is classified as a bottom feed design because the fuel enters the inlet filter near the bottom of the injector. It is designed to operate with the system fuel pressures ranging from 10-29 psi (70-200 kPa) and uses a low impedenace (1.8 ohms) solenoid coil. It is used individually in the new Model 700 TBI units.

FUEL METER BODY
Removal and Installation

1. Depressurize the fuel system. Raise the hood, install fender covers and remove the air cleaner assembly. Disconnect the negative battery cable.

2. Remove the fuel meter cover assembly. Remove the fuel meter cover gasket, fuel meter outlet gasket and pressure regulator seal.

3. Remove the fuel injectors. Remove the fuel inlet and fuel outlet nuts and gaskets from the fuel meter body.

4. Remove the three screws and lockwashers, then remove the fuel meter body from the throttle assembly.

NOTE: DO not remove the center screw and staking at each end holding the fuel distribution skirt in the throttle body. The skirt is an integral part of the throttle body and is not serviced separately.

5. Remove the fuel meter body insulator gasket.

6. Installation is the reverse order of the removal procedure. Be sure to install new gaskets and O-rings where ever necessary. Apply threadlocking compound, Threadlock Sealer 262 or equivalent to the fuel meter retaining screws.

IDLE AIR CONTROL VALVE
Removal and Installation

1. Remove the air cleaner.

2. Disconnect the electrical connection from the idle air control assembly.

3. Using a $1\frac{1}{4}$ in. wrench, remove the idle air control assembly from the throttle body.

NOTE: Before installing a new idle air control valve, measure the distance that the valve is extended. This measurement should be made from motor housing to end of the cone. The distance should be no greater than 1⅛ in. If the cone is extended too far damage to the valve may result.

4. Be sure to identify the replacement idle air control valve as being either Type I (having a collar azt the electric terminal end) or Type II (without a collar). If the measurement dimension is greater than specified, the distance must be reduced as follows:

    a. Type I - Exert firm pressure on the valve to retract it. (A slight side to side movement may be helpful).

    b. Type II - Compress the retaining spring from the valve while turning the valve "in" with a clockwise motion. Return spring to orignial position with the straight portion of the spring enf aligned with the flat surface of the valve.

5. Install the new idle air control valve and torque the valve to 13 ft. lbs.

6. Reconnect all electrical connections. Start th engine and let it reach normal operating temperature. The ECM will reset the idle speed when the vehicle is driven at 30 mph.

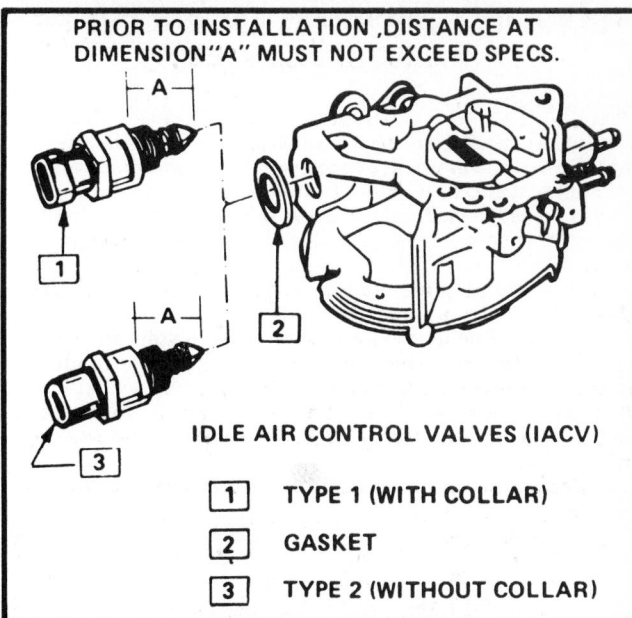

PRIOR TO INSTALLATION ,DISTANCE AT DIMENSION"A" MUST NOT EXCEED SPECS.

IDLE AIR CONTROL VALVES (IACV)

1	TYPE 1 (WITH COLLAR)
2	GASKET
3	TYPE 2 (WITHOUT COLLAR)

Idle air control assembly

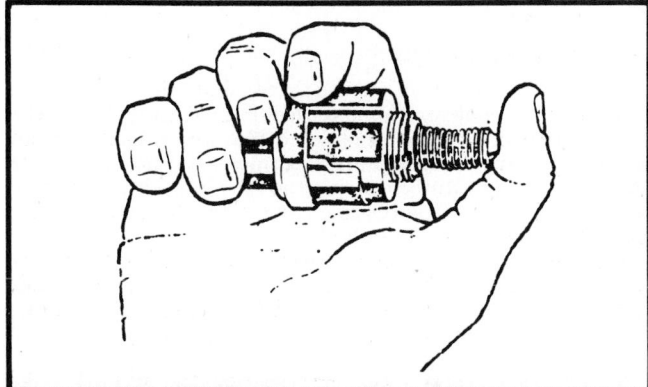

Adjusting the idle air control valve (with a collar at the electrical terminal end)

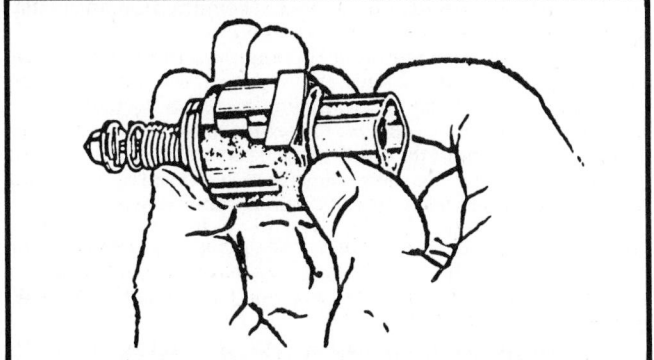

Aligning the spring under the pintle on the idle air control valve

MINIMUM AIR RATE (2.5L ENGINE)

Adjustment

This adjustment should be performed only when the throttle body parts have been replaced or required to do so by the T.P.S. adjustment. Engine should be at normal operating temperature before making adjustment.

1. Remove air cleaner and air cleaner to TBI gasket. Plug vacuum port on TBI unit for THERMAC.

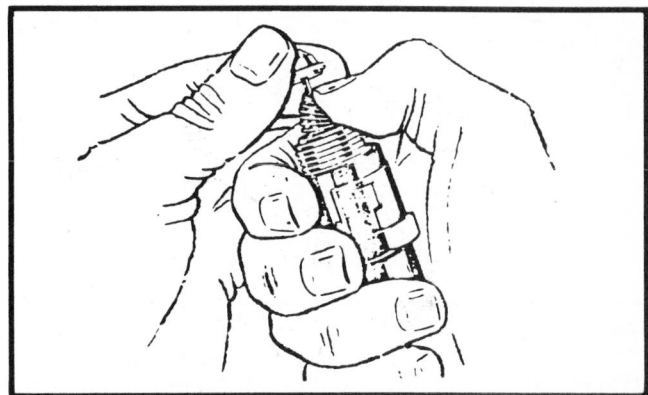

Adjusting the idle air control valve (without a collar at the electrical terminal end)

NOTE: On vehicles equipped with a tamper resistant plug covering the minimum air adjustment screw, the throttle body unit must be removed from the engine to remove the plug.

2. Remove T.V. cable from throttle control bracket to allow access to minimum air adjustment screw.

3. Connect a tachometer to engine.

4. Start engine, transmission in Park (Neutral on a manual transmission) and allow engine RPM to stabilized.

5. Install tool J-33047, or equivalent, and idle air passage of throttle body. Be certain that tool seats fully in passage and no air leaks exist.

6. Using the appropriate tool, turn minimum air screw until engine RPM is 500 ± 25 in neutral with automatic transaxle, and 775 ± 25 in neutral with manual transaxle.

7. Stop engine and remove tool J-33047 from throttle body.

8. Reinstall T.V. cable into throttle control bracket.

9. Use silicone sealant or equivalent to cover minimum air adjustment screw.

10. Install air cleaner gasket and air cleaner to engine.

CURB IDLE AIR RATE (5.0L CROSSFIRE INJECTION SYSTEM)

Adjustment

The throttle position of each throttle body must be balanced so that the throttle plates are synchronized to open simultaneously. This is a checking and adjustment procedure; adjustment should be performed only when a throttle body has been replaced or when checking procedure indicates an adjustment is required.

1. Remove air cleaner and air cleaner to TBI unit for THERMAC.

2. Start engine and allow engine RPM to stabilize.

3. Plug idle air passages of each throttle body with plugs J-33047, or equivalent. Be certain plugs are fully seated in passages and no air leaks exist. Engine RPM should decrease to curb idle air rate. If engine RPM does not decrease, check for vacuum leak.

4. Remove cap from ported tube on rear TBI unit and connect the vacuum gauge.

5. Observe the gauge, reading should be approximately .45 in. Hg. If adjustment is required proceed as follows:

    a. Remove tamper resistant screw covering the minimum air adjustment screw if required.

    b. Adjust minimum air adjustment screw to obtain approximately .45 in Hg.

    c. After adjustment, proceed to front TBI unit.

6. Remove gauge from rear TBI unit and re-install cap on ported tube.

7. Remove cap from ported tube on front TBI unit and connect vacuum gauge. Reading should also be approximately .45 in. Hg. If adjustment is required proceed as follows:

    a. Locate split lever screw on throttle linkage. If screw is welded for tamper resistance, break weld and install new screw with thread locking compound applied.

    b. Adjust split lever screw to obtain approximately .45 in. Hg.

8. Remove gauge from front TBI unit and re-install cap on ported tube.

9. If both readings are approximately .45 in. Hg., no adjustment is required; throttle plates are synchronized.

10. Stop engine and remove idle air passage plugs.

11. Check T.P.S. voltage and adjust if required.

12. Install air cleaner gaskets, connect vacuum line to TBI unit and install air cleaner.

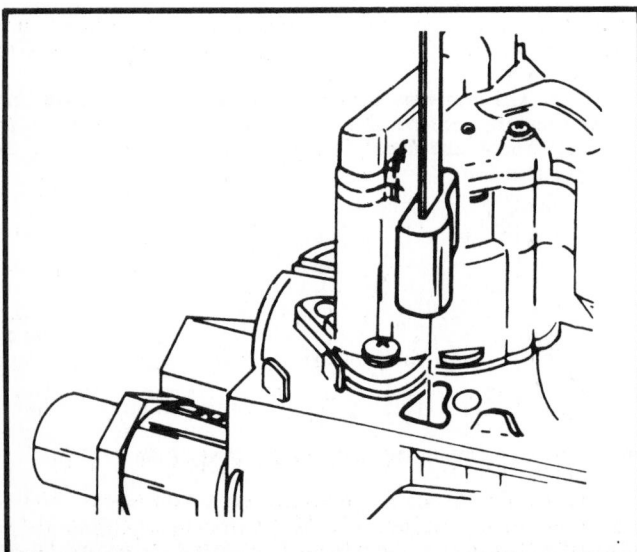

Installing special tool J-33047 or equivalent in the idle air passage of the throttle body

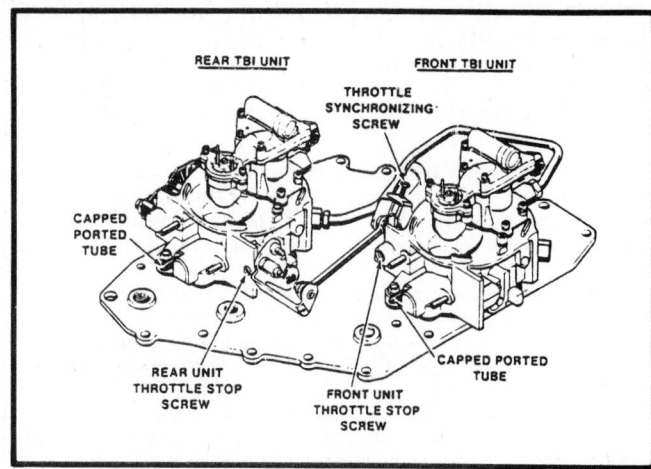

Throttle stop screws and synchronizing screw locations on the crossfire assembly

IDLE SPEED

Adjustment

1.8L and 2.5L ENGINES

The throttle stop screw that is used to adjust the idle speed of the vehicle, is adjusted to specifications at the factory. The throttle stop screw is then covered with a steel plug to prevent the unnecessary readjustment in the field. If it is necessary to gain access to the throttle stop screw, the following procedure will allow access to the throttle stop screw without removing the TBI unit from the manifold.

1. Using a small punch or equivalent mark over the center line of the throttle stop screw. Drill a $\frac{5}{32}$ in. diameter hole through the casting of the hardened steel plug.

2. Using a $\frac{1}{16}$ in. diameter punch or equivalent punch out the steel plug.

3. With the vehicle in the park position, the parking brake applied and the drive wheels blocked, remove the air cleaner and plug the thermac vacuum port.

4. Remove the transmission T.V. cable from the throttle control bracket in order to gain access to the minimum air adjustment screw (automatic transmission only).

5. Connect a tachometer to the engine and disconnect the idle air control motor connector.

6. Start the engine and let the engine reach normal operating temperature and the rpm to stabilize.

7. Install special tool J-33047 or equivalent in the idle air passage of the throttle body. Be sure to seat the tool in the air passage until it is bottomed our and no air leaks exist.

8. Using a #20 torx head bit or equivalent, turn the throttle stop screws until the rpm is 700 ± 25 rpm for the 1.8L and 500 ± 25 rpm for the 2.5L with an automatic transaxle, 800 ± 25 rpm for the 1.8L and 775 ± 25 rpm for the 2.5L with a manual transaxle.

9. Re-install the transmission T.V. cable into the throttle control bracket (automatic transmissions only).

10. Shut down the engine and remove the special tool or equivalent from the throttle body.

11. Reconnect the idle air control motor connector and seal the hole drilled through the throttle body housing with silicone sealant or equivalent.

12. Check the throttle position sensor voltage as outlined in this section and reinstall the air cleaner and thermac vacuum line.

2.0L ENGINE

NOTE: The idle speed adjustment procedure for the 2.0L engine is basically the same as the 1.8L and 2.5L engine, with the exception of the following steps.

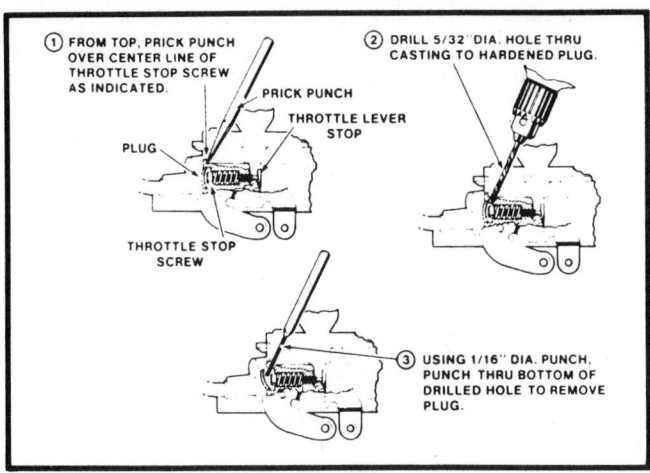

Throttle stop screw plug removal

1. To install special tool J-33047 or equivalent, it may be necessary to remove the air cleaner isolator as follows:
   a. Remove the two isolator attaching bolts and isolator.
   b. Reinstall the bolts with .079 in. (2mm) or thicker washers under each bolt head.
   c. After adjustment has been made, reinstall the isolator without the washers and torque the bolts to 17 ft. lbs. (23 Nm).
2. On vehicles equipped with automatic transaxles, place the selector in the drive position before making adjustment, the idle speed is 650 ± 25 rpm.

4.3L ENGINE

1. Leave the idle air control (IAC) valve connected and ground the diagnostic lead.
2. Turn the ignition switch to the on position, disconnect the engine. Wait for at least 30 seconds.
3. With the ignition switch still in the on position, disconnect IAC electrical connector.
4. Remove the ground from the diagnostic lead and start the engine. Let the engine reach normal operating temperature.
5. Apply the parking brake and block the drive wheels. With the engine in the drive position adjust the idle set screw to obtain 550 ± 50 rpm.
6. Turn the ignition off and reconnect the IAC motor connector.
7. Adjust the throttle position sensor (as outlined in this section) to .525 ± .075 volts.
8. Recheck the adjustment settings, start the engine and check for proper idle operation.

5.7L ENGINE (CFI)

1. Remove the air cleaner and gaskets, plug the thermal vacuum port on there are of the throttle body. Remove the plugs covering both throttle stop screws, one for each throttle body.
2. With a small punch or equivalent mark over the center line of the throttle stop screw. Drill a $^5/_{32}$ in. diameter hole through the casting to the hardened steel plug.
3. Using a $^1/_{16}$ in. diameter punch or equivalent, punch our the steel plug.
4. With the vehicle in the park position, the parking brake applied and the drive wheels blocked, connect a tachometer and disconnect the idle air control (IAC) electrical connectors. Plug the idle air passages of each throttle body.
5. Before starting the engine make sure both throttle valves are slightly opened. Start the engine and let it run till it reaches normal operating temperature.
6. Place the transmission selector in the D position and

check to see if the engine rpm decreases below the curb idle speed. If the rpm does not decrease check for vacuum leaks.
7. Remove the cap from the ported tube on the rear throttle body and connect a water manometer. Adjust the throttle stop screw on the rear throttle body to obtain approximately six inches of water on the manometer.
8. If six inches of water cannot be obtained on the manometer, check the throttle stop screw on the from unit and make sure it is not limiting the throttle rod movement. Remove the manometer and reinstall the cap on the ported tube.
9. Remove the cap from the ported tube on the front throttle body and connect the manometer. The reading on the manometer should be six inches of water. If there is an adjustment required, locate the throttle synchronizing screw on the throttle linkage of the front unit.
10. If the screw is welded in place, grind the weld off of the screw collar and the throttle lever (be sure to block the throttle lever so it cannot move).
11. Remove the screw and collar and install the new screw, being sure to apply thread sealing compound or equivalent to the screw.
12. Adjust the screw to obtain six inches of water on the manometer. Remove the manometer and install the cap on the ported tube.
13. Adjust the throttle stop screw on the rear throttle body to set the idle speed (475 rpm) turn the ignition off and place the transmission selector in the park position.
14. Adjust the from throttle stop screw to obtain .005 in. (.13 mm) between the throttle stop screw and the throttle lever tang. Remove the idle air passage plugs and reconnect the idle air control electrical connectors.
15. Start the engine and wait for the engine rpm to decrease, the rpm will decrease when the idle air control assembly closes the air passages. Check the throttle position sensor voltage.
16. Install the air cleaner gaskets, reconnect the vacuum line to the throttle body and install the air cleaner. Reset the IAC motors by driving the vehicle at 30 mph.

V6 and V8 TRUCK ENGINES

1. Remove the air cleaner, adapter and gaskets. Discard the gaskets. Plug any vacuum line ports, as necessary.
2. Leave the idle air control (IAC) valve connected and ground the diagnostic terminal (ALDL connector).
3. Turn the ignition switch to the on position, do not start the engine. Wait for at least 30 seconds (this allows the IAC valve pintle to extend and seat in the throttle body).
4. With the ignition switch still in the on position, disconnect IAC electrical connector.
5. Remove the ground from the diagnostic terminal and start the engine. Let the engine reach normal operating temperature.
6. Apply the parking brake and block the drive wheels. Remove the plug from the idle stop screw by piercing it first with a suitable tool, then applying leverage to the tool to lift the plug out.
7. With the engine in the drive position adjust the idle stop screw to obtain the following specifications:
   a. 2.8L engine – 700 ± 25 rpm in neutral.
   b. 4.3L and V8 engines – 500–550 rpm in drive on models equipped with automatic transmissions.
   c. 4.3L and V8 engines – 600–650 rpm in neutral on models equipped with manual transmissions.
8. Turn the ignition off and reconnect the IAC valve connector. Unplug any plugged vacuum line ports and install the air cleaner, adapter and new gaskets.

THROTTLE POSITION SENSOR (TPS)

NOTE: The throttle position sensor on some 1987-88 models are not adjustable. If the sensor is found out of specifications and the sensor is at fault it cannot be adjusted and should be replaced.

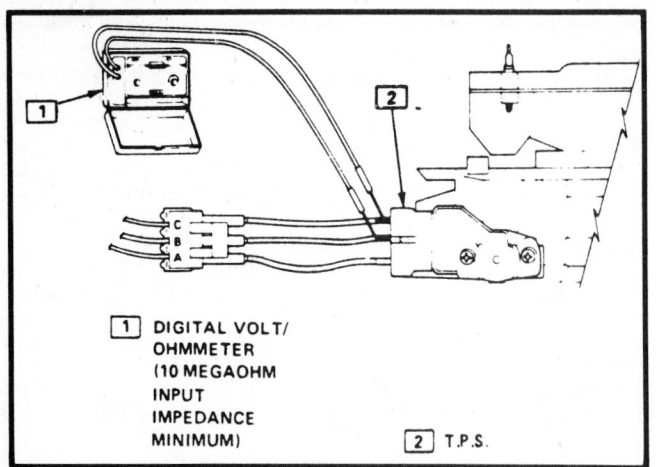

DIGITAL VOLT/
OHMMETER
(10 MEGAOHM
INPUT
IMPEDANCE
MINIMUM)

TPS

TPS voltage check

Removal

The Throttle Position Sensor (TPS) is an electrical unit and must not be immersed in any type of liquid solvent or cleaner. The TPS is factory adjusted and the retaining screws are spot welded in place to retain the critical setting. With these considerations, it is possible to clean the throttle body assembly without removing the TPS if care is used. Should TPS replacement be required however, proceed using the following steps:

NOTE: On some of the earlier models, the TPS retaining screws may be removed from the outside of the throttle body, from the side of the sensor.

1. Remove the throttle body as previously outlined in this section. Invert throttle body and place on a clean, flat surface.
2. Using a $5/16$ in. drill bit, drill completely through two (2) TPS screw access holes in base of throttle body to be sure of removing the spot welds holding TPS screws in place.
3. Remove the two TPS attaching screws, lockwashers, and retainers. Then, remove TPS sensor from throttle body. DISCARD SCREWS. New screws are supplied in service kits.
4. If necessary, remove screw holding Throttle Position Sensor actuator lever to end of throttle shaft.
5. Remove the Idle Air Control assembly and gasket from the throttle body.

NOTE: DO NOT immerse the Idle Air Control motor in any type of cleaner and it should always be removed before throttle body cleaning. Immersion in cleaner will damage the IAC assembly. It is replaced only as a complete assembly. Further disassembly of the throttle body is not required for cleaning purposes. The throttle valve screws are permanently staked in place and should not be removed. The throttle body is serviced as a complete assembly.

Installation

1. Place throttle body assembly on holding fixture to avoid damaging throttle valve.
2. Using a new sealing gasket, install Idle Air Control motor in throttle body. Tighten motor securely. DO NOT overtighten to prevent damage to valve.
3. If removed, install Throttle Position Sensor actuator lever by aligning flats on lever with flats on end of shaft. Install retaining screw and tighten securely.

NOTE: Install Throttle Position Sensor after completion of assembly of the throttle body unit. Use thread locking compound supplied in service kit on attaching screws.

Adjustment

1. After installing TPS to throttle body, install throttle body unit to engine.
2. Remove EGR valve and heat shield from engine.
3. Disconnect the TPS harness from the TPS. Using three six inch jumpers, connect TPS harness to TPS.
4. With ignition ON, engine stopped, use a digital voltmeter to measure voltage between the TPS terminals as follows:
   a. Terminals A and B on all models except the ones listed below.
   b. Terminals C and B on 1.8L and 2.0L engines using the TBI 500 model.
5. Loosen two TPS attaching screws and rotate throttle position sensor to obtain a voltage reading of 0.525 ± 0.75 volts.
6. With ignition OFF, remove jumpers and reconnect TPS harness to TPS.
7. Install EGR valve and heat shield to engine, using new gasket as necessary.
8. Install air cleaner gasket and air cleaner to throttle body unit.

Non-Adjustable TPS Output Check

This check should only be performed, when the throttle body or the TPS has been replaced or after the minimum idle speed has been adjusted.

1. Remove air cleaner. Disconnect the TPS harness from the TPS.
2. Using suitable jumper wires, connect a digital voltmeter J-29125-A or equivalent to the correct TPS terminals; (a suitable ALDL scanner can also be used to read the TPS output voltage):
   a. Terminals A and B on all models except the ones listed below.
   b. Terminals C and B on 1.8L and 2.0L engines using the TBI 500 model.
3. With the ignition ON and the engine running, The TPS voltage should be 0.450–1.25 volts at base idle to approximately 4.5 volts at wide open throttle.
4. If the reading on the TPS is out of specification, check the minimum idle speed before replacing the TPS.
5. If the voltage reading is correct, remove the voltmeter and jumper wires and reconnect the TPS connector to the sensor. Re-install the air cleaner.

Adjustable TPS Output Check
2.8L TRUCK ENGINE

This check should only be performed, when the throttle body or the TPS has been replaced or after the minimum idle speed has been adjusted.

1. Remove air cleaner. Disconnect the TPS harness from the TPS.
2. Using suitable jumper wires, connect a digital voltmeter J-29125-A or equivalent from the TPS connector center terminal "B" to the outside terminal "A". A suitable ALDL scanner can also be used to read the TPS output voltage.
3. With the ignition ON and the engine stopped, The TPS voltage should be between 0.42 and 0.54 volts.
4. If the reading on the TPS is not within the specified range, rotate the the TPS until 0.48 ± .06 volts are obtained. If this specified voltage cannot be obtained, replace the TPS.
5. If the voltage reading is correct, remove the voltmeter and jumper wires and reconnect the TPS connector to the sensor. Re-install the air cleaner.

ALDL CONNECTOR

The assembly line diagnostic link (ALDL) (or also known as the assembly line communication link (ALCL)) is a diagnostic connector located in the passenger compartment usually under

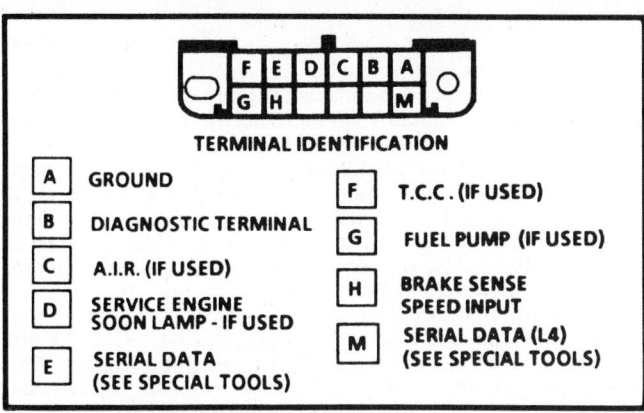

Typical ALDL connector – trucks

the instrument panel (except Pontiac Fiero which is located in the console). The assembly plant were the vehicles originate use the connector to check the engine for proper operation before it leaves the plant. Terminal "B" is the diagnostic "Test" terminal (lead) and it can be connected to terminal "A", or ground, to enter the Diagnostic mode or the Field Service Mode.

FIELD SERVICE MODE

If the "Test" terminal is grounded with the engine running, the system will enter the the Field Service mode. In this mode, the "Check Engine Light" will show whether the system is in Open loop or Closed loop. In Open loop the "Check Engine Light" flashes two times and one half times per second. In Closed loop the light flashes once per second. Also in closed loop, the light will stay OUT most of the time if the system is too lean. It will stay ON most of the time if the system is too rich. In either case the Field Service mode check, which is part of the Diagnostic circuit check, will lead the technician into choosing the correct diagnostic chart to refer to.

CLEARING THE TROUBLE CODES

When the ECM finds a problem with the system, the "Check Engine Light" will come ON and a trouble code will be recorded in the ECM memory. If the problem is intermittent, the "Check Engine Light" will go out after 10 seconds, when the fault goes away. However the trouble code will stay in the ECM memory until the battery voltage to the ECM is removed. Removing the battery voltage for 10 seconds will clear all trouble codes. Do this by disconnecting the ECM harness from the positive battery terminal pigtail for 10 seconds with the key in the OFF position, or by removing the ECM fuse for 10 seconds with the key OFF.

CLOSED LOOP FUEL CONTROL

The purpose of closed loop fuel control is to precisely maintain an air/fuel mixture 14.7:1. When the air/fuel mixture is maintained at 14.7:1, the catalytic converter is able to operate at maximum efficiency which results in lower emission levels.

Since the ECM controls the air/fuel mixture, it needs to check its ouput and correct the fuel mixture for deviations from the "Ideal" ratio. The oxygen sensor feeds this output information back to the ECM.

ECM LEARNING ABILITY

The ECM has a "learning" capability. If the battery is disconnected the "learning" process has to begin all over again. A

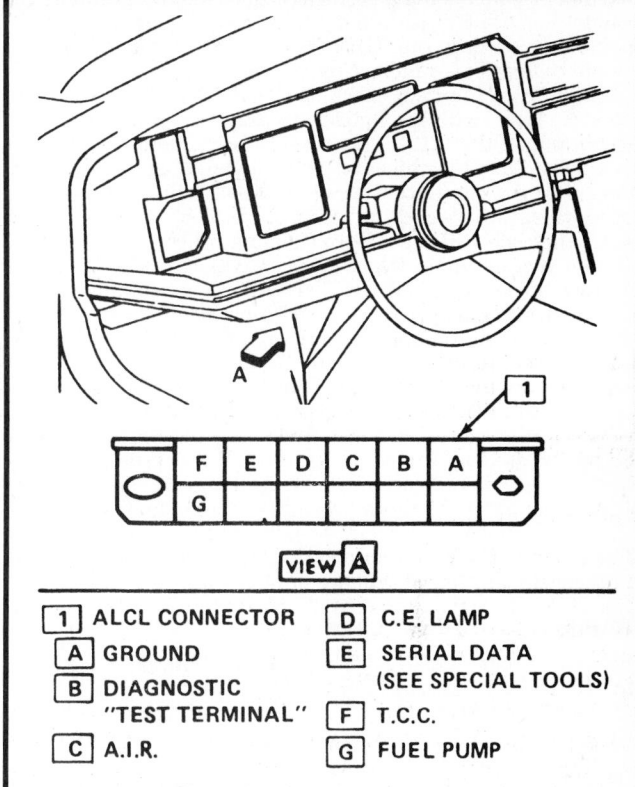

Typical ALDL connector

change may be noted in the vehicle's performance. To "teach" the ECM, insure the vehicle is at operating temperature and drive at part throttle, with moderate acceleration and idle conditions, until performance returns.

ENGINE PERFORMANCE DIAGNOSIS

Engine performance diagnosis procedures are guides that will lead to the most probable causes of engine performance complaints. They consider the components of the fuel, ignition, and mechanical systems that could cause a particular complaint, and then outline repairs in a logical sequence.

It is important to determine if the "CHECK ENGINE" light is "ON" or has come "ON" for a short interval while driving. If the "CHECK ENGINE" light has come "ON", the Computer Command Control System should be checked for stored "Trouble Codes" which may indicate the cause for the performance complaint.

All of the symptoms can be caused by worn out or defective parts such as spark plugs, ignition wiring, etc. If time and/or mileage indicate that parts should be replaced, it is recommended that it be done.

NOTE: Before checking any system controlled by the electric fuel injection (EFI) system, the Diagnostic Circuit Check must be performed or misdiagnosis may occur. If the complaint involves the "CHECK ENGINE" light, go directly to the Diagnostic Circuit Check.

DIAGNOSTIC PROCEDURES

A built-in, self-diagnostic system catches the problems most likely to occur in the Computer Command Control system. The diagnostic system turns on a "CHECK ENGINE" light in the instrument panel when a problem is detected. By grounding a trouble code "TEST" terminal under the dash, (ignition "ON" engine not running) the "CHECK ENGINE" light will flash a trouble code or codes indicating the problem areas.

As a bulb and system check, the "CHECK ENGINE" light will come "ON" with the ignition switch "ON" and the engine not running. If the "TEST" terminal is then grounded, the light will flash a Code 12, which indicates the self-diagnostic system is working. A Code 12 consists of one flash, followed by a short pause, then two flashes in quick succession. After a longer pause, the code will repeat two (2) more times.

When the engine is started, the "CHECK ENGINE" light will turn off. IF the "CHECK ENGINE" light remains on, the self-diagnostic system has detected a problem. If the "TEST" terminal is then grounded with the ignition "ON", engine not running, each trouble code will flash and repeat three (3) times. If more than one problem has been detected, each trouble code will flash three (3) times. Trouble codes will flash in numeric order (lowest number first). The trouble code series will repeat as long as the "TEXT" terminal is grounded.

A trouble code indicates a problem in a given circuit (Code 14, for example, indicates a problem in the coolant sensor circuit; this includes the coolant sensor, connector harness, and ECM). The procedure for pinpointing the problem can be found in diagnosis. Similar charts are provided for each code.

Trouble Code "TEST" Lead

The trouble code "TEST" lead terminal is mounted in a 12-terminal connector located under the dash. Grounding this terminal signals the ECM to flash any trouble codes stored in the memory. This is easily done by jumping to the adjacent ground terminal.

If the TEST terminal is grounded with the ignition "ON" and the engine stopped, the system will enter the diagnostic mode. In the diagnostic mode the ECM will:

1. Flash a Code 12 (indicating system is operating).
2. Energize all ECM-controlled relays.

If the "TEST" terminal is grounded with the engine running, the system will enter the field service mode. In this mode, the "CHECK ENGINE" light will indicate whether the system is in open or closed loop. Open loop is indicated by the "CHECK ENGINE" light flashing approximately twice per second. In closed loop, the light flashes approximately once per second.

Basic Troubleshooting

NOTE: The following explains how to activate the Trouble Code signal light in the instrument cluster and gives an explanation of what each code means. This is not a full CCC System troubleshooting and isolation procedure.

Before suspecting the CCC System or any of its components as faulty, check the ignition system including distributor, timing, spark plugs and wires. Check the engine compression, air cleaner, and emission control components not controlled by the ECM. Also check the intake manifold, vacuum hoses and hose connectors for leaks and the carburetor bolts for tightness.

The following symptoms could indicate a possible problem with the CCC System.
1. Detonation
2. Stalls or rough idle-cold
3. Stalls or rough idle-hot
4. Missing
5. Hesitation
6. Surges
7. Poor gasoline mileage
8. Sluggish or spongy performance
9. Hard starting-cold
10. Objectionable exhaust odors (that "rotten egg" smell)
11. Cuts out

12. Improper idle speed

As a bulb and system check, the CHECK ENGINE light will come on when the ignition switch is turned to the ON position but the engine is not started. The CHECK ENGINE light will also produce the trouble code or codes by a series of flashes which translate as follows. When the diagnostic test terminal under the dash is grounded, with the ignition in the ON position and the engine not running, the CHECK ENGINE light will flash once, pause, then flash twice in rapid succession. This is a code 12, which indicates that the diagnostic system is working. After a long pause, the code 12 will repeat itself two more times. The cycle will then repeat itself until the engine is started or the ignition is turned off.

When the engine is started, the CHECK ENGINE light will remain on for a few seconds, then turn off. If the CHECK ENGINE light remains on, the self-diagnostic system has detected a problem. If the test terminal is then grounded, the trouble code will flash three times. If more than one problem is found, each trouble code will flash three times. Trouble codes will flash in numerical order (lowest code number to highest). The trouble codes series will repeat as long as the test terminal is grounded.

A trouble code indicates a problem with a given circuit. For example, trouble code 14 indicates a problem in the cooling sensor circuit. This includes the coolant sensor, its electrical harness, and the Electronic Control Module (ECM) Since the self-diagnostic system cannot diagnose every possible fault in the system, the absence of a trouble code does not mean the system is trouble-free. To determine problems within the system which do not activate a trouble code, a system performance check must be made.

In the case of an intermittent fault in the system, the CHECK ENGINE light will go out when the fault goes away, but the trouble code will remain in the memory of the ECM. Therefore, it a trouble code can be obtained even though the CHECK ENGINE light is not on, the trouble code must be evaluated. It must be determined if the fault is intermittent or if the engine must be at certain operating conditions (under load, etc.) before the CHECK ENGINE light will come on. Some trouble codes will not be recorded in the ECM until the engine has been operated at part throttle for about 5–18 minutes. On the CCC System, a trouble code will be stored until terminal "R" of the ECM has been disconnected from the battery for 10 seconds.

An easy way to erase the computer memory on the CCC System is to disconnect the battery terminals from the battery. If this method is used, don't forget to reset clocks and electronic pre-programmable radios. Another method is to remove the fuse marked ECM in the fuse panel. Not all models have such a fuse.

CCC SYSTEM CIRCUIT DIAGNOSIS

To diagnosis CCC system circuits, use the same general troubleshooting approach that is used for other automotive electrical systems. Finding the fault in a CCC circuit will require the testing tools described in this section. these tools are used with the diagnostic charts for CCC system troubleshooting. Always use a digital voltmeter for accuracy of readings when using CCC diagnostic charts.

Diagnostic Procedure

The following is a complete diagnosis sequence of the CCC system. In all cases, the sequence is begun with routine engine checks. Then the following:
1. System diagnostic circuit check.
2. Code chart or chart for systems without codes.
3. System performance check. This procedure must be followed each time the CCC system is suspected as the cause of a problem.

Code 13- Oxygen Sensor Circuit
Warm engine running at normal operating temperature for at least 3 minutes at part throttle with Oxygen Sensor signal missing (open) for 60 seconds.

Code 14- Coolant Sensor Circuit Signal Voltage Low
Engine running 10 seconds with no coolant sensor signal voltage.

Code 15- Coolant Sensor Circuit Signal Voltage High
Engine running with coolant sensor signal too high for 60 seconds. If fault occurs with ignition "OFF," engine will crank, but may not start.

Code 21- Throttle Position Sensor Signal Too High
Engine running below 1600 RPM, and TPS is above 50% (2.5 volts) for 2 seconds.

Code 22- Throttle Position Sensor Signal Too Low
Engine running with TPS signal voltage too low.

Code 24- Vehicle Speed Sensor
Vehicle speed about 40-45 MPH steady throttle signal (decelerating on 2.0 and 2.5L) with no VSS for one minute.

Code 33- Manifold Absolute Pressure Signal Too High (LOW VACUUM)
Engine idling and MAP signal is high for 5 seconds.

Code 34- Manifold Absolute Pressure Signal Too Low
Engine running .2 second (200m seconds) with MAP signal voltage too low.

Code 42- Electronic Spark Timing (EST)
Open or grounded EST line, open or grounded bypass line, and engine speed above 500 RPM.

Code 43- Electronic Spark Control - Full Retard
Engine running and ESC signal at ECM is low for 4 seconds.

Code 44- Lean Exhaust System
Engine running in closed loop at normal operating temperature with oxygen sensor signal less than 200mv. for one minute. Forces open loop operation. May require drive position to set on some engines.

Code 45- Rich Exhaust System
Engine idling in closed loop at normal operating temperature with oxygen sensor signal above 750mv. for 20 seconds. Forces open loop operation. May require drive position to set on some engines.

Code 51- Faulty Calibration Unit (PROM) or installation.

Code 55- Replace ECM (faulty)

Basic diagnostic code parameters

Diagnostic Charts

The section contains tree-type charts for locating the source of a fault in the CCC system circuits. When using a tree chart, always start at the first step and follow the sequence from top to bottom. Often there will be two or more branches of the "tree" to follow. Follow the branch that is applicable to the result obtained in that step. Several charts will be used during diagnosis and this procedure will be used in all cases.

NOTE: The CCC system should not be considered as a possible source of poor engine performance, fuel economy, or excessive emissions until you've made all the routine engine checks, such as ignition, plugs, air cleaner, and vacuum hoses.

SYSTEM DIAGNOSTIC CIRCUIT CHECK

Begin the Diagnostic Circuit Check by making sure that the diagnostic system itself is working. Turn the ignition to On with the engine stopped. If the CHECK ENGINE or SERVICE ENGINE SOON light comes on, ground the diagnostic code terminal (test lead) under the dash. If the CHECK ENGINE or SERVICE ENGINE SOON light flashes Code 12, the self-diagnostic system is working and can detect a faulty circuit. If there is no Code 12, see the appropriate chart in this section. If any additional codes flash, record them for later use.

If a Code 51 flashes, use chart 51 to diagnose that condition before proceeding with the Diagnostic Circuit Check. A Code 51 means that the CHECK ENGINE or SERVICE ENGINE SOON light flashes 5 times, pauses, then flashes once. After a longer pause, code 51 will flash again twice in this same way. To find out what diagnostic step to follow, look up the chart for Code 51 in this section. If there is not a Code 51, follow the "No Code 51" branch of the chart.

Clear the ECM memory by disconnecting the voltage lead either at the fuse panel or the ECM letter connector for 10 seconds. This clears any codes remaining from previous repairs, or codes for troubles not present at this time. Remember, even though a code is stored, if the trouble is not present the diagnostic charts cannot be used. The charts are designed only to locate present faults.

NOTE: An easy way to erase the computer memory on the CCC System is to disconnect the battery terminals from the battery. If this method is used, don't forget to reset clocks and electronic pre-programmable radios. Not all models have an ECM fuse.

Next, remove the "Test" terminal ground, set the parking brake and put the transmission in Park. Run the warm engine for two minutes, making sure you run it at the specified curb idle for the two minutes. Then, if the CHECK ENGINE or SERVICE ENGINE SOON light comes on while the engine is idling, ground the "test" lead again and not the flashing trouble code.

If the CHECK ENGINE or SERVICE ENGINE SOON light does not come on, check the codes which were recorded earlier. If there were no additional codes, road test the car for the problem being diagnosed to make sure it still exists.

The purpose of the Diagnostic Circuit check is to make sure the CHECK ENGINE or SERVICE SOON SOON light works, that the ECM is operating and can recognize a fault and to determine if any trouble codes are stored in the ECM memory.

If trouble codes are stored, it also checks to see if they indicate an intermittent problem. This is the starting point of any diagnosis. If there are no codes stored, move on to the System Performance Check.

The codes obtained from the CHECK ENGINE or SERVICE ENGINE SOON light display method indicate which diagnostic charts provide in the section are to be used. For example, code 23 can be diagnosed by following the step-by-step procedures on chart 23.

NOTE: If more than one code is stored in the ECM, the lowest code number must be diagnosed first. then proceed to the next highest code. The only exception is when a 50 series flashes. 50 series code take procedence over all other trouble codes and must be dealt with first, since they point to a fault in the PROM unit or the ECM.

If the diagnostic procedures call for the ECM to be replaced, the calibration unit (PROM) should be checked first to see if it is functioning correctly. If it is correct, the PROM should be removed from the defective ECM and installed in the new service ECM. THE SERVICE ECM WILL NOT CONTAIN A PROM. Trouble Code 51 indicates the PROM is installed improperly or has malfunctioned. When Code 51 is obtained, the PROM installation should be checked for bent pins or pins not fully seated in the socket. If the PROM is installed correctly and Code 51 still shows, the PROM should be replaced.

NOTE: To prevent internal ECM damage, the ignition switch must be in the OFF position when reconnecting power to the ECM (for example, battery positive cable, ECM pigtail, ECM fuse, jumper cables, etc.).

ELECTRONIC FUEL INJECTION — ALDL TESTER INFORMATION

An ALDL display unit (ALDL tester, scanner, monitor, etc), allows a technician to read the engine control system information from the ALDL connector under the instrument panel. It can provide information faster than a digital voltmeter or ohmmeter can. The scan tool does not diagnose the exact location of the problem. The tool supplies information about the ECM, the information that it is receiving and the commands that it is sending plus special information such as integrator and block learn. To use an ALDL display tool you should understand throughly how an engine control system operates.

An ALDL scanner or monitor puts a fuel injection system into a special test mode. This mode commands an idle speed of 1000 rpm. The idle quality cannot be evaluated with a tester plugged in. Also the test mode commands a fixed spark with no advance. On vehicles with Electronic Spark Control (ESC) there will be a fixed spark, but it will be advanced. On vehicles with ESC there might be a serious spark knock, this spark knock could be bad enough so as not being able to road test the vehicle in the ALDL test mode. Be sure to check the tool manufacturer for instructions on special test modes which should overcome these limitations.

When a tester is used with a fuel injected engine it bypasses the timer that keeps the system im OPEN loop for a certain period of time. When all CLOSED loop conditions are met, the engine will go into CLOSED loop as soon as the vehicle is started. This means that the air management system will not function properly and air may go directly to the converter as soon as the engine is started.

These tools cannot diagnose everything. They do not tell the technician where a problem is located in a circuit. The diagnostic charts to pinpoint the problems must still be used. These tester's do not let a technician know if a solenoid or relay has been turned on. They only tell the technician the ECM command. To find out if a soolenoid has been turned on, check it with a suitable test light or digital voltmeter, or see if vacuum through the solenoid changes.

REVISED ECM REPLACEMENT PROCEDURE - CHART C-1

1982 through 1987 ECM Equipped Vehicles

Since 1982, most ECM's have used an intergrated circuit (IC) in place of seperate transistors to turn ON or OFF different components controlled by the ECM. These IC's are called quad drivers (QDR). Each quad driver has four separate outputs, meaning it can turn ON or OFF four different items independently.

A failed quad driver usually results in an ECM output becoming either shorted to ground or open. Many times all four quad drivers output will be inoperative if just one vehicle circuit is faulty.

This revised diagnosis incorporates new test procedures designed to identify a damaged quad drivers. Once identified, the circuit must be repaired to reduce the incidence of repeat ECM failures.

The following charts are to be used to replace the current service procedure for either:

1. Chart C-1 ECM replacement check.
2. Any diagnostic chart where "replace ECM" is the conclusion, especially if a footnote indicates checking certain circuits for less the 20 ohm's resistance.

It is strongly suggested that this chart be used whenever an ECM replacement is indicated for 1982-87 vehicles.

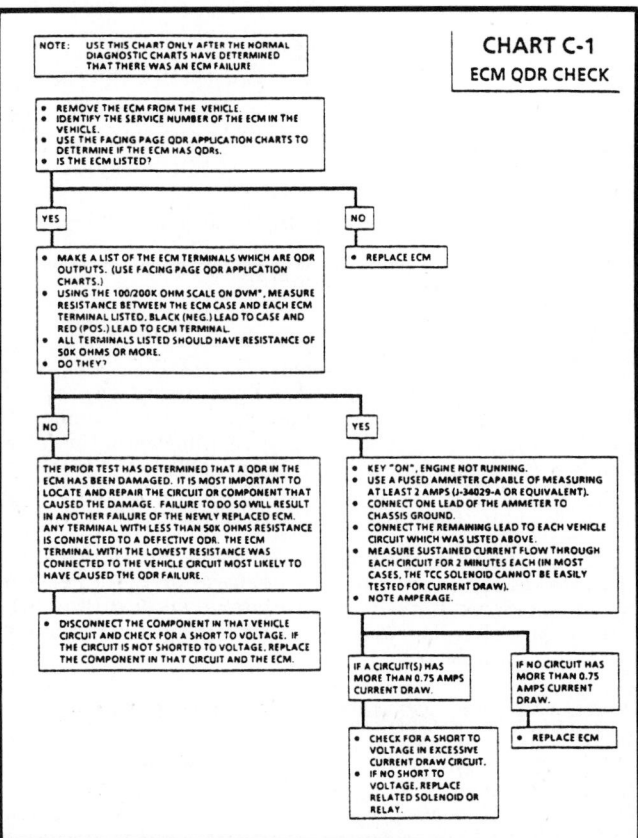

ECM quad driver check—chart C-1

NOTE: Due to the large amount of GM vehicles being covered in this section, some vehicles will use more sensors than others. Also, a complete general diagnostic section is outlined. The steps and procedures can be altered as required (if necessary) by the technician according to the specific model being diagnosed and the sensors it is equipped with. The wiring diagrams and schematics may not coincide with every GM vehicle in use. If this situation should arise, use the wiring diagram or schematic as a general guide.

ECM Service Number	QDR Number	ECM Output Term #1	ECM Output Term #2	ECM Output Term #3	ECM Output Term #4
CCC 83.5-84 S/N 1226153 1226452 1226454 1226455 1226519	1	G	E	6	4
	2	B	19	P	P
	3	18	18	T	T

ECM Service Number	QDR Number	ECM Output Term #1	ECM Output Term #2	ECM Output Term #3	ECM Output Term #4
TBI 82.5-83 S/N 1225610 1226100 1226026 1226430	1	Black 9	Black 14	Black 16	White 20
	2	Black 7	Black 22	White 19	White 19

ECM Service Number	QDR Number	ECM Output Term #1	ECM Output Term #2	ECM Output Term #3	ECM Output Term #4
TBI 83.5-84 S/N 1226156	1	White 20		Black 7	Black 9

ECM Service Number	QDR Number	ECM Output Term #1	ECM Output Term #2	ECM Output Term #3	ECM Output Term #4
DFI 83-86 S/N 1226028 1226462 1226930	1	Blue 9	Blue 14	Blue 16	Red 20
	2	Blue 7	Blue 22	Red 19	Red 19

ECM Service Number	QDR Number	ECM Output Term #1	ECM Output Term #2	ECM Output Term #3	ECM Output Term #4
TBI 84 S/N 1226026 1226430	1	Black 9	Black 14	Black 16	White 20
	2	Black 7	Black 22	White 19	White 19

ECM Service Number	QDR Number	ECM Output Term #1	ECM Output Term #2	ECM Output Term #3	ECM Output Term #4
TBI/PFI 84-85 S/N 1226458 1226460	1	C1	C2	A2	A3
	2	A4	A5	A7	A7

Quad driver application and arrangement chart— 1982-87

ECM Service Number	QDR Number	ECM Output Term #1	ECM Output Term #2	ECM Output Term #3	ECM Output Term #4
TBI 85-87 S/N 1226868 1227746 1227747	1	A2	A3	C1	C2
	2	A4	A5	A7	A7

ECM Service Number	QDR Number	ECM Output Term #1	ECM Output Term #2	ECM Output Term #3	ECM Output Term #4
TBI 85-86 S/N 1226864	1	Black 7	Black 9		White 20

ECM Service Number	QDR Number	ECM Output Term #1	ECM Output Term #2	ECM Output Term #3	ECM Output Term #4
TBI 85-86 S/N 1226867	1	A2	A3	A4	C2
	2	C1	A5	A7	A7

ECM Service Number	QDR Number	ECM Output Term #1	ECM Output Term #2	ECM Output Term #3	ECM Output Term #4
PFI 86 S/N 1227151	1	C1	C2	A2	A3
	2	A4	A5	A7	A7

ECM Service Number	QDR Number	ECM Output Term #1	ECM Output Term #2	ECM Output Term #3	ECM Output Term #4
PFI 85-87 S/N 1226869 1226870 1226948 1227065 1227784	1	A2	A4	A4	A5
	2	A3	A3	D2	D2
	3	C2		A7	A7

ECM Service Number	QDR Number	ECM Output Term #1	ECM Output Term #2	ECM Output Term #3	ECM Output Term #4
TBI 86-87 S/N 1227137 1227429	1	A2	A3	C1	C2
	2	A4	A5	A7	A7

Quad driver application and arrangement chart— 1982-87 (cont.)

ECM Service Number	QDR Number	ECM Output Term #1	ECM Output Term #2	ECM Output Term #3	ECM Output Term #4
PFI 86-87 S/N 1227165	1	A3	A7	C2	D12
	2	A2	A4	A5	C1
PFI 86-87 S/N 1227153 1227170 1227302	1	A2	A4	A4	A5
	2	A3	A3	D2	D2
	3	A7	A7		C2
TBI 87 S/N 1227748	1	Black 7	Black 7	Black 18	Black 18
	2	Black 3	Black 4	Black 21	Black 22
PFI 84-85 S/N 1226461	1	A2	A4	A4	A5
	2	A3	A3	D2	D2
	3	A7	A7		C2
PFI (SEQ) 84-85 S/N 1226459	1	A3	A3	D3	D3
	2	A7	A7		D2
	3	A2	A4	A4	A5
CCC 85-87 S/N 1226457 1226519 1226865 1226866 1227076 1227169 1227301 1227855 1228079	1	G	E	4	6
	2	B	19	P	P
	3	18	18	T	T

ECM Service Number	QDR Number	ECM Output Term #1	ECM Output Term #2	ECM Output Term #3	ECM Output Term #4
TBI 87 S/N 1227749	1	E7	E8	E9	F7
	2	F1	F2	F3	F4
PFI 87 S/N 1227730	1	E7	E8	E9	F7
	2	F1	F2	F3	F4
	3	F5	F5	F6	F8
PFI 87 S/N 1227750	1	2A1	2A8	2A10	2A11
	2	3C7	3C8	3C9	3C10
	3	3D5	3D5	3D6	3C6
	4	3C4	3C4	3C5	3D4
DFI 86-87 S/N 1227056	1	A7	A7	A11	A11
	2	A2	A5	C3	C3
	3	C1	D2	D3	D10
	4	A3	A3	A4	A4
PFI 86-87 S/N 1227057	1	A3	A7	D2	D3
	2	A4	A5	B2	B9
PFI 86-87 S/N 1227148 1227783 1227886	1	A3	A3	D3	D3
	2	A7	A7	A8	D2
	3	A2	A4	A4	A5

TPS MINIMUM IDLE ADJUSTMENT SPECIFICATIONS

Year	Manufacturer	Model	Engine (liters)	VIN	Fuel Injection System	TPS Adjustment Voltage	Minimum Idle (rpm)
1984	Cadillac	Cimarron	2.0	P	TBI	0.525 ±0.075	650 ±25 ②
		DeVille	4.1	8	DFI	0.50 ±0.050	525 ±25 ③
		Eldorado	4.1	8	DFI	0.50 ±0.050	525 ±25 ③
		Seville	4.1	8	DFI	0.50 ±0.050	525 ±25 ③
		Fleetwood	4.1	8	DFI	0.50 ±0.050	525 ±25 ③
	Buick	Century	2.5	R	TBI	NA	500 ±25 ③⑥
		Regal	3.8 T	9	SPI	0.40 ±0.050	500 ±50 ②
		Riviera	3.8 T	9	SPI	0.40 ±0.050	500 ±50 ②

TPS MINIMUM IDLE ADJUSTMENT SPECIFICATIONS

Year	Manufacturer	Model	Engine (liters)	VIN	Fuel Injection System	TPS Adjustment Voltage	Minimum Idle (rpm)
1984		Skyhawk	1.8	0	TBI	NA	700 ±25 ③⑤
			2.0	P	TBI	0.525 ±0.075	650 ±25 ②
			1.8 T	J	MPI	NA	700 ±25 ③⑤
		Skylark	2.5	R	TBI	NA	500 ±25 ③⑥
	Chevrolet	Camaro	2.5	2	TBI	NA	500 ±25 ③⑥
		Cavalier	2.5	2	TBI	NA	500 ±25 ③⑥
		Celebrity	2.5	R	TBI	NA	500 ±25 ③⑥
		Citation	2.5	R	TBI	NA	500 ±25 ③⑥
		Corvette	5.7	8	CFI	.0525 ±0.075	400 ②⑤
	Oldsmobile	Cutlass Ciera	2.5	R	TBI	NA	500 ±25 ③⑥
			3.8	3	MPI	0.40 ±0.050	500 ±50 ②
		Firenza	1.8	0	TBI	NA	700 ±25 ③⑤
			2.0	P	TBI	0.525 ±0.075	650 ±25 ②
		Omega	2.5	R	TBI	NA	500 ±25 ③⑤
		98 Regency	3.8	3	MPI	0.40 ±0.050	500 ±50 ②
	Pontiac	2000 Sunbird	1.8	0	TBI	NA	700 ±25 ③⑤
			2.0	P	TBI	0.525 ±0.075	650 ±25 ②
			1.8 T	J	MPI	NA	700 ±25 ③⑤
		6000	2.5	R	TBI	NA	500 ±25 ③⑥
		Fiero	2.5	R	TBI	NA	500 ±25 ③⑥
		Firebird	2.5	2	TBI	NA	500 ±25 ③⑥
		Phoenix	2.5	R	TBI	NA	500 ±25 ③⑥
1985	Cadillac	Cimarron	2.0	P	TBI	NA	650 ±25 ②
		DeVille	4.1	8	DFI	0.50 ±0.050	525 ±25 ③
		Eldorado	4.1	8	DFI	0.50 ±0.050	525 ±25 ③
		Seville	4.1	8	DFI	0.50 ±0.050	525 ±25 ③
		Fleetwood	4.1	8	DFI	0.50 ±0.050	525 ±25 ③
	Buick	Century	2.5	R	TBI	NA	500 ±25 ③⑥
			3.8	3	MPI	0.40 ±0.050	500 ±50 ②
		Electra	3.8	3	MPI	0.40 ±0.050	500 ±50 ②
		Regal	3.8 T	9	SFI	0.40 ±0.050	500 ±50 ②
		Riviera	3.8 T	9	SFI	0.40 ±0.050	500 ±50 ②
		Skyhawk	1.8	0	TBI	NA	700 ±25 ③⑤
			2.0	P	TBI	NA	650 ±25 ②
			1.8 T	J	MPI	NA	700 ±25 ③⑤
		Skylark	2.8	W	MPI	0.55 ±0.050	600 ±50 ②⑤
			2.5	R	TBI	NA	500 ±25 ③⑥
		Somerset Regal	2.5	U	TBI	NA	500 ±25 ③⑥
			3.0	L	MPI	0.55 ±0.050	500 ±50 ②
	Chevrolet	Camaro	2.5	2	TBI	NA	500 ±25 ③⑥
			2.8	S	MPI	0.55 ±0.050	600 ±50 ②⑤

TPS MINIMUM IDLE ADJUSTMENT SPECIFICATIONS

Year	Manufacturer	Model	Engine (liters)	VIN	Fuel Injection System	TPS Adjustment Voltage	Minimum Idle (rpm)
1985			5.0	F	TPI	0.54 ± 0.075	500 ± 50 ②
		Caprice	4.3	Z	TBI	0.525 ± 0.075	550 ± 50 ②
		Cavalier	2.0	P	TBI	NA	650 ± 25 ②
			2.8	W	MPI	0.55 ± 0.050	600 ± 50 ②⑤
		Celebrity	2.5	R	TBI	NA	500 ± 25 ③⑥
			2.8	W	MPI	0.55 ± 0.050	600 ± 50 ②⑤
		Citation	2.5	R	TBI	NA	500 ± 25 ③⑥
			2.8	W	MPI	0.55 ± 0.050	600 ± 50 ②⑤
		Corvette	5.7	8	TPI	0.54 ± 0.075	400 ②⑤
		El Camino	4.3	Z	MPI	0.525 ± 0.075	550 ± 50 ②
		Monte Carlo	4.3	Z	MPI	0.525 ± 0.075	550 ± 50 ②
	Oldsmobile	Calais	2.5	U	TBI	NA	500 ± 25 ③⑥
			3.0	L	MPI	0.55 ± 0.050	500 ± 50 ②
		Cutlass Ciera	2.5	R	TBI	NA	500 ± 25 ③⑥
			3.8	3	MPI	0.40 ± 0.050	500 ± 50 ②
		Firenza	1.8	0	TBI	NA	700 ± 25 ③⑤
			2.0	P	TBI	NA	650 ± 25 ②
			2.5	U	TBI	NA	500 ± 25 ③⑥
			2.8	W	MPI	0.55 ± 0.050	600 ± 50 ②⑤
			3.0	L	MPI	0.55 ± 0.050	500 ± 50 ②
		98 Regency	3.8	3	MPI	0.40 ± 0.050	500 ± 50 ②
	Pontiac	6000	2.5	R	TBI	NA	500 ± 25 ③⑥
			2.8	W	MPI	0.55 ± 0.050	600 ± 50 ②⑤
		Bonneville	4.3	Z	TBI	0.525 ± 0.075	550 ± 25 ②
		Fiero	2.5	R	TBI	NA	500 ± 25 ③⑥
			2.8	9	MPI	NA	—
		Firebird	2.5	2	TBI	NA	500 ± 25 ③⑥
			2.8	S	MPI	0.55 ± 0.050	600 ± 50 ②⑤
			5.0	F	TPI	0.54 ± 0.075	400 ②
		Grand Am	2.5	U	TBI	NA	500 ± 25 ③⑥
			3.0	L	MPI	0.55 ± 0.050	500 ± 50 ②
		Grand Prix	4.3	Z	TBI	0.525 ± 0.075	550 ± 50 ②
		Parisienne	4.3	Z	TBI	0.525 ± 0.075	550 ± 50 ②
		Sunbird	1.8	0	TBI	NA	700 ± 25 ③⑤
			1.8	J	MPI	NA	700 ± 25 ③⑤
1986	Cadillac	Cimarron	2.0	P	TBI	NA	650 ± 25 ②
			2.8	W	MPI	0.55 ± 0.050	600 ± 50 ②⑤
		De Ville	4.1	8	DFI	0.50 ± 0.050	525 ± 25 ③
		Eldorado	4.1	8	DFI	0.50 ± 0.050	525 ± 25 ③
		Seville	4.1	8	DFI	0.50 ± 0.050	525 ± 25 ③
		Fleetwood	4.1	8	DFI	0.50 ± 0.050	525 ± 25 ③

TPS MINIMUM IDLE ADJUSTMENT SPECIFICATIONS

Year	Manufacturer	Model	Engine (liters)	VIN	Fuel Injection System	TPS Adjustment Voltage	Minimum Idle (rpm)
1986	Buick	Century	2.5	R	TBI	NA	500 ± 25 ③⑥
			3.8	3	SFI	0.40 ± 0.050	500 ± 50 ②
			3.8	B	SFI	0.40 ± 0.050	500 ± 50 ②
		Electra	3.8	B	SFI	0.40 ± 0.050	500 ± 50 ②
		LeSabre	3.0	L	MPI	0.55 ± 0.050	500 ± 50 ②
			3.8	3	SFI	0.40 ± 0.050	500 ± 50 ②
			3.8	B	SFI	0.40 ± 0.050	500 ± 50 ②
		Regal	3.8 T	9	SFI	0.40 ± 0.050	500 ± 50 ②
		Riviera	3.8	B	SFI	0.40 ± 0.050	500 ± 50 ②
		Skyhawk	1.8	0	TBI	NA	700 ± 25 ③⑤
			2.0	P	TBI	NA	650 ± 25 ②
			1.8 T	J	MPI	NA	700 ± 25 ③⑤
		Skylark	2.5	U	TBI	NA	500 ± 25 ③⑥
			3.0	L	MPI	0.55 ± 0.050	500 ± 50 ②
		Somerset Regal	2.5	U	TBI	NA	500 ± 25 ③⑥
			3.0	L	MPI	0.55 ± 0.050	500 ± 50 ②
	Chevrolet	Camaro	2.5	2	TBI	NA	500 ± 25 ③⑥
			2.8	S	MPI	0.55 ± 0.050	600 ± 50 ②⑤
			5.0	F	TPI	0.54 ± 0.075	400 ②
		Caprice	4.3	Z	TBI	NA	425 ± 25 ②
		Cavalier	2.0	P	TBI	NA	650 ± 25 ②
			2.8	W	MPI	0.55 ± 0.050	600 ± 50 ②⑤
		Celebrity	2.5	R	TBI	NA	500 ± 25 ③⑥
			2.8	W	MPI	0.55 ± 0.050	600 ± 50 ②⑤
		Corvette	5.7	Y	TPI	0.54 ± 0.075	400 ②⑥
		El Camino	4.3	Z	TBI	NA	425 ± 25 ②
		Monte Carlo	4.3	Z	TBI	NA	425 ± 25 ②
	Oldsmobile	Calais	2.5	U	TBI	NA	500 ± 25 ③⑥
			3.0	L	MPI	0.55 ± 0.050	500 ± 50 ②
		Cutlass Ciera	2.5	R	TPI	NA	500 ± 25 ③⑥
			2.8	W	MPI	0.55 ± 0.050	600 ± 50 ②⑤
			3.8	B	SFI	0.40 ± 0.050	500 ± 50 ②
			3.8	3	SFI	0.40 ± 0.050	500 ± 50 ②
		Delta 88	3.0	L	MPI	0.55 ± 0.050	500 ± 50 ②
			3.8	B	SFI	0.40 ± 0.050	500 ± 50 ②
			3.8	3	SFI	0.40 ± 0.050	500 ± 50 ②
		Firenza	1.8	0	TBI	NA	700 ± 25 ③⑤
			2.0	P	TBI	NA	650 ± 25 ②
			2.8	W	MPI	0.55 ± 0.050	600 ± 50 ②⑤
		98 Regency	3.8	B	SFI	0.40 ± 0.050	500 ± 50 ②
			3.8	3	SFI	0.40 ± 0.050	500 ± 50 ②

TPS MINIMUM IDLE ADJUSTMENT SPECIFICATIONS

Year	Manufacturer	Model	Engine (liters)	VIN	Fuel Injection System	TPS Adjustment Voltage	Minimum Idle (rpm)
		Toronado	3.8	B	SFI	0.40 ± 0.050	500 ± 50 ②
	Pontiac	6000	2.5	R	TBI	NA	500 ± 25 ③⑥
			2.8	W	MPI	0.55 ± 0.050	600 ± 50 ②⑤
		Bonneville	4.3	Z	TBI	NA	425 ± 25 ②
		Fiero	2.5	R	TBI	NA	500 ± 25 ③⑥
			2.8	9	MPI	—	—
		Firebird	2.5	2	TBI	NA	500 ± 25 ③⑥
			2.8	S	MPI	0.55 ± 0.050	600 ± 50 ②⑤
			5.0	F	TPI	0.54 ± 0.075	400 ②
			5.7	8	MPI	0.54 ± 0.075	400 ②⑤
		Grand Am	2.5	U	TBI	NA	500 ± 25 ③⑥
			3.0	L	MPI	0.55 ± 0.050	500 ± 50 ②
		Grand Prix	4.3	Z	TBI	NA	425 ± 25 ②
		Parisienne	4.3	Z	TBI	NA	425 ± 25 ②
		Sunbird	1.8	0	TBI	NA	700 ± 25 ③⑤
			1.8 T	J	MPI	NA	700 ± 25 ③⑤
1987-88	Cadillac	Cimarron	2.8	W	MPI	0.55 ± 0.075	550 ± 50 ②⑤
		De Ville	4.1	8	DFI	0.50 ± 0.050	500 ± 25 ③
		Eldorado	4.1	8	DFI	0.50 ± 0.050	500 ± 25 ③
		Seville	4.1	8	DFI	0.50 ± 0.050	500 ± 25 ③
		Fleetwood	4.1	8	DFI	0.50 ± 0.050	500 ± 25 ③
	Buick	Century	2.8	W	MPI	0.49–0.61	650 ②⑤
			2.5	R	TBI	NA	600 ± 25 ②
			3.8	3	SFI	0.36–0.44	500 ± 50 ②
		Electra	3.8	3	SFI	0.36–0.44	500 ± 50 ②
		LeSabre	3.8	3	SFI	0.36–0.44	500 ± 50 ②
		Regal	3.8T	7	SFI	0.36–0.44	500 ± 50 ②
		Riviera	3.8	3	SFI	0.36–0.44	500 ± 50 ②
		Skyhawk	2.0	K	TBI	NA	600 ± 20 ②
			2.0 HO	1	TBI	NA	600 ± 25 ②
			2.0	M	MPI	NA	600 ± 25 ②
		Skylark	2.5	U	TBI	NA	600 ± 25 ②
			3.0	L	MPI	0.55 ± 0.050	500 ± 50 ②
		Somerset Regal	2.5	U	TBI	NA	600 ± 25 ②
			3.0	L	MPI	0.55 ± 0.050	500 ± 50 ②
	Chevrolet	Beretta	2.0	1	TBI	NA	600 ± 25 ②
			2.8	W	MPI	0.55 ± 0.10	650 ②⑤
		Camaro	2.8	S	MPI	0.55 ± 0.060	500 ②⑤
			5.0	F	TPI	0.54 ± 0.080	400 ③
			5.7	8	MPI	0.54 ± 0.080	450 ③
		Caprice	4.3	Z	TBI	NA	425 ± 25 ②
		Cavalier	2.0	1	TBI	NA	600 ± 25 ②

TPS MINIMUM IDLE ADJUSTMENT SPECIFICATIONS

Year	Manufacturer	Model	Engine (liters)	VIN	Fuel Injection System	TPS Adjustment Voltage	Minimum Idle (rpm)
1986			2.8	W	MPI	0.55 ±0.10	650 ②⑤
		Celebrity	2.5	R	TBI	NA	600 ±25 ②
			2.8	W	MPI	0.55 ±0.10	650 ②⑤
		Corsica	2.0	1	TBI	NA	600 ±25 ②
			2.8	W	MPI	0.55 ±0.10	650 ②⑤
		Corvette	5.7	8	TPI	0.54 ±0.080	450 ③
		El Camino	4.3	Z	TBI	NA	425 ±25 ②
		Monte Carlo	4.3	Z	TBI	NA	425 ±25 ②
	Oldsmobile	Calais	2.5	U	TBI	NA	600 ±25 ②
			3.0	L	MPI	0.55 ±0.050	500 ±50 ②
		Cutlass Ciera	2.5	R	TBI	NA	600 ±25 ②
			2.8	W	MPI	0.55 ±0.10	650 ②⑤
			3.8	3	MPI	0.36–0.44	500 ±50 ②
		Delta 88	3.8	3	MPI	0.36–0.44	500 ±50 ②
		Firenza	2.0 HO	1	TBI	NA	600 ±25 ②
			2.0	K	TBI	NA	600 ±25 ②
			2.8	W	MPI	0.55 ±0.10	650 ②⑤
		98 Regency	3.8	3	MPI	0.36–0.44	500 ±50 ②
		Toronado	3.8	3	MPI	0.36–0.44	500 ±50 ②
	Pontiac	6000	2.5	R	TBI	NA	600 ±25 ②
			2.8	W	MPI	0.55 ±0.10	650 ②⑤
		Bonneville	3.8	3	MPI	0.36–0.44	500 ±50 ②
		Fiero	2.5	R	TBI	NA	600 ±25 ②
			2.8	9	MPI	—	—
		Firebird	2.8	S	MPI	0.55 ±0.060	600 ±50 ②⑤
			5.0	F	TPI	0.54 ±0.080	400 ③
			5.7	8	MPI	0.54 ±0.080	450 ③
		Grand Am	2.0	M	MPI	NA	600 ±25 ②
			2.5	U	TBI	NA	600 ±25 ②
		Grand Prix	4.3	Z	TBI	NA	425 ±25 ②
		Sunbird	2.0	K	TBI	NA	600 ±25 ②
			2.0 T	M	MPI	NA	600 ±25 ②

T Turbo
HO High Output
SFI Sequential Fuel Injection
TBI Throttle Body Injection
MPI Multi-port Injection
TPI Tuned Port Injection
DFI Digital Fuel Injection
NA Not Adjustable
① Cross Fire Injection – dual TBI units
② Place gear selector in DRIVE for automatic transmission
③ Place gear selector in NEUTRAL for automatic or manual transmission

④ Manual transmission; add 50 rpm
⑤ Manual transmission; add 100 rpm
⑥ Manual transmission; 775 ±25 rpm

TBI TROUBLE DIAGNOSTICS

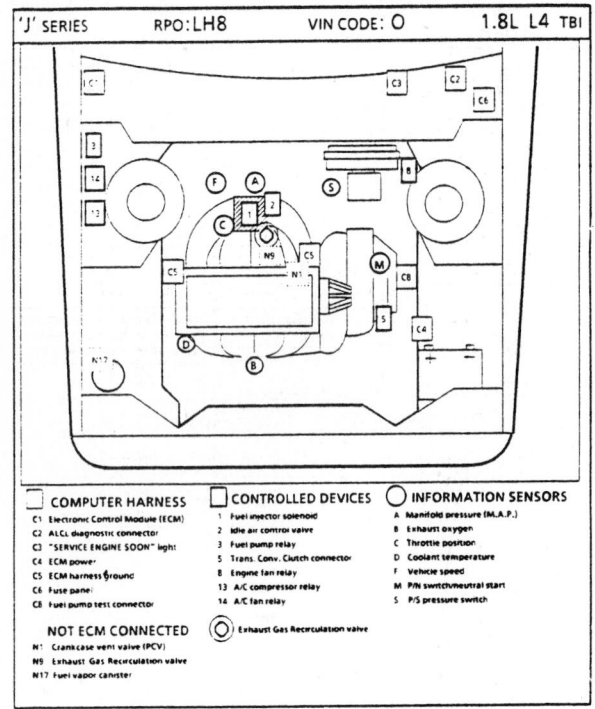

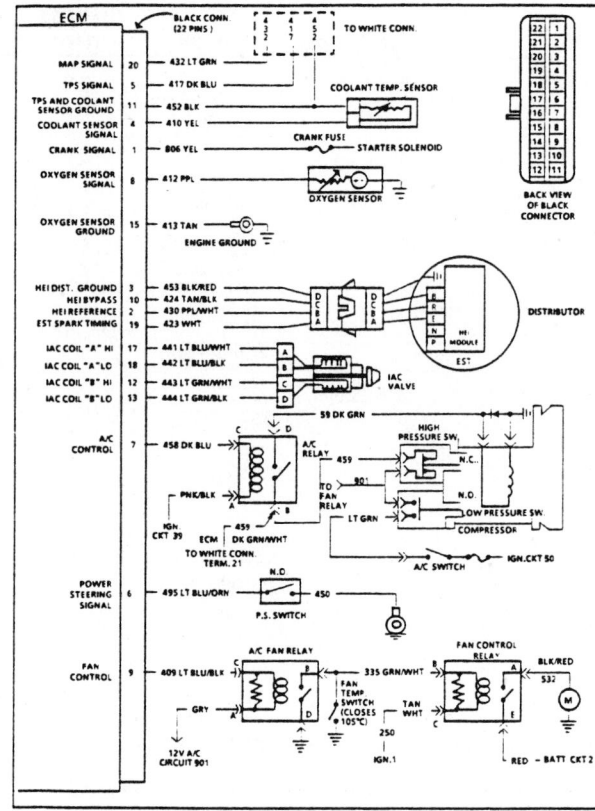

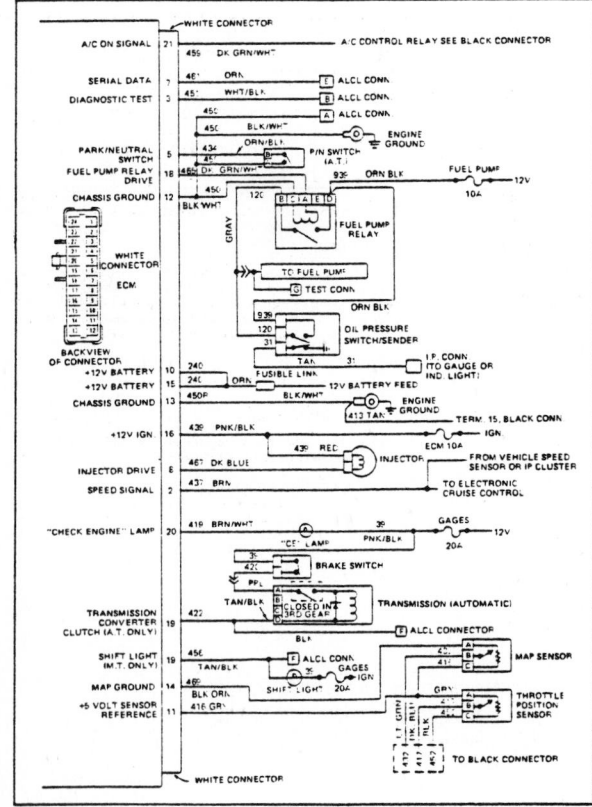

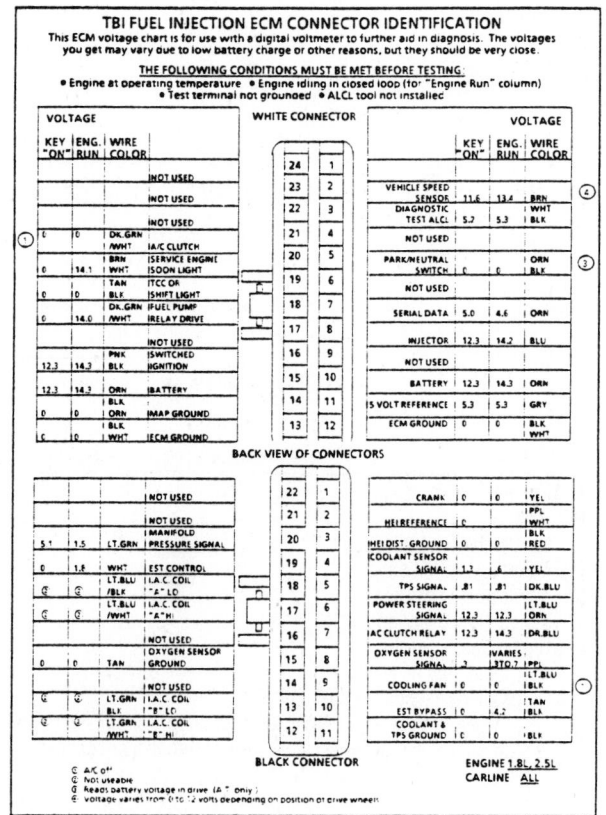

TBI TROUBLE DIAGNOSTICS

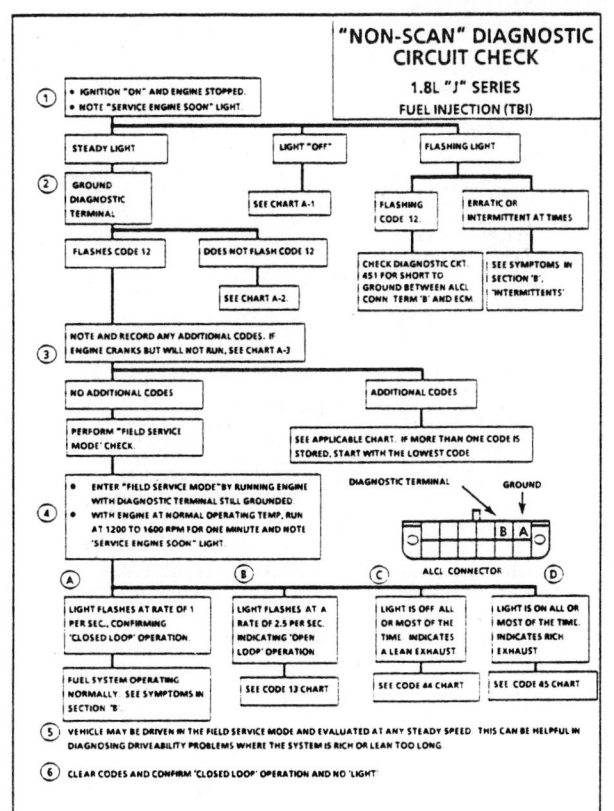

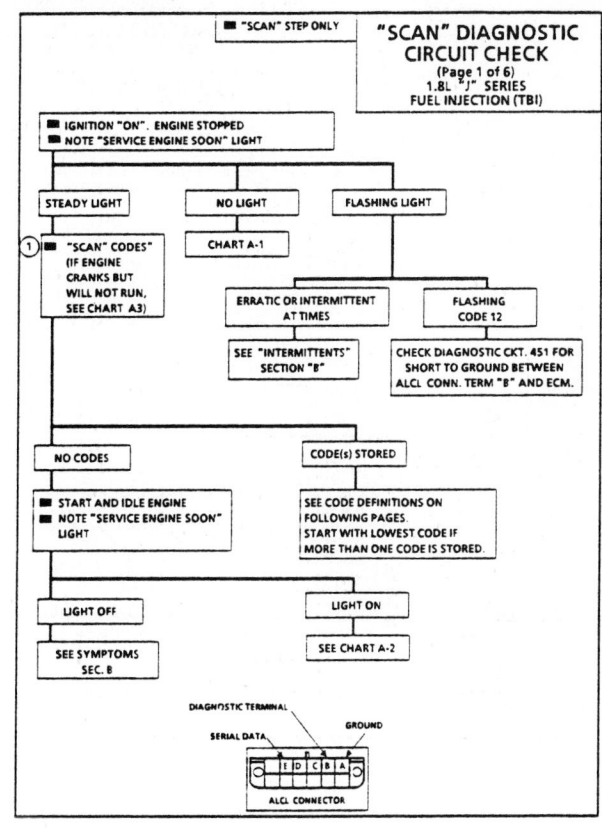

"SCAN" DIAGNOSTIC CIRCUIT CHECK
(Page 2 of 6)
(CODE DEFINITIONS)

NOTICE
THE 'DIAGNOSTIC CIRCUIT CHECK' SCAN DATA IS TYPICAL OF THAT DISPLAYED BY A PROPERLY DESIGNED AND CALIBRATED ALCL SCAN DEVICE.

A SCAN DEVICE THAT DISPLAYS FAULTY DATA SHOULD NOT BE USED AND THE PROBLEM REPORTED TO THE DEVICE MANUFACTURER. THE USE OF A FAULTY SCAN DEVICE CAN RESULT IN MISDIAGNOSIS AND UNNECESSARY PARTS REPLACEMENT.

CODES	DEFINITIONS
■ **CODE 13** • "SCAN" IN ALCL "SPECIAL" MODE • ENGINE IDLING AT 1000 RPM FOR 2 MINUTES. • COOLANT 75° TO 95° C. • "SCAN" OXYGEN SENSOR VOLTAGE	**HARD FAILURE -** "SCAN" DISPLAY FIXED BETWEEN .35 TO .55 V. OPEN CIRCUIT CONDITION. SEE CODE CHART 13 **INTERMITTENT CODE -** NORMAL "SCAN" VOLTAGE WILL VARY BETWEEN 100MV TO 999 MV (.1 AND 1.0 VOLT). SEE "INTERMITTENTS" SECTION B.
■ **CODE 14** • IGNITION ON. • ENGINE STOPPED. • SCAN" COOLANT TEMPERATURE.	**HARD FAILURE -** "SCAN" DISPLAY FIXED ABOVE 135°C. CIRCUIT SHORTED TO GROUND OR FAULTY SENSOR. SEE CODE CHART 14. **INTERMITTENT CODE -** "SCAN" DISPLAY READS ENGINE TEMP. IN DEGREES CENTIGRADE. AFTER ENGINE IS STARTED, THE TEMPERATURE SHOULD RISE STEADILY TO ABOUT 90°C THEN STABILIZE WHEN THERMOSTAT OPENS. SEE "INTERMITTENTS" SECTION B.
■ **CODE 15** • IGNITION ON. • ENGINE STOPPED. • "SCAN" COOLANT TEMPERATURE.	**HARD FAILURE -** "SCAN" DISPLAY FIXED BELOW -30°C. CIRCUIT OPEN OR FAULTY SENSOR. SEE CODE CHART 15. **INTERMITTENT CODE -** "SCAN" TOOL DISPLAYS ENGINE COOLANT TEMPERATURE IN DEGREES CENTIGRADE. AFTER ENGINE IS STARTED, THE TEMPERATURE SHOULD RISE STEADILY TO ABOUT 90°C, THEN STABILIZE WHEN THERMOSTAT OPENS. SEE "INTERMITTENTS" SECTION B.

"SCAN" DIAGNOSTIC CIRCUIT CHECK
(Page 4 of 6)
(CODE DEFINITIONS)

CODES	DEFINITIONS
■ **CODE 33** • ENGINE IDLING. • "SCAN" MAP.	**HARD FAILURE -** "SCAN" TOOL DISPLAYS ABOVE 2.5 VOLTS. SENSOR GROUND CIRCUIT OPEN, LEAKING VACUUM HOSE OR FAULTY SENSOR. SEE CODE CHART 33. **INTERMITTENT CODE -** "SCAN" TOOL DISPLAYS MANIFOLD PRESSURE IN VOLTS. LOW PRESSURE (HIGH VACUUM) DISPLAYS AS A LOW VOLTAGE WHILE A HIGH PRESSURE (LOW VACUUM) DISPLAYS AS A HIGH VOLTAGE. IF ENGINE IDLE IS LOW AND UNSTABLE IT MAY SET CODE 33. SEE "INTERMITTENTS" SECTION B.
■ **CODE 34** • IGNITION "ON" • SCAN" MAP.	**HARD FAILURE -** "SCAN" TOOL DISPLAYS BELOW (200 mv) .2 VOLTS. SIGNAL WIRE OR 5V REFERENCE OPEN OR SHORTED TO GROUND OR FAULTY SENSOR. SEE CODE CHART 34 **INTERMITTENT CODE -** "SCAN" TOOL DISPLAYS MANIFOLD PRESSURE IN VOLTS. LOW PRESSURE (HIGH VACUUM) READS A LOW VOLTAGE, WHILE A HIGH PRESSURE (LOW VACUUM) READS A HIGH VOLTAGE. SEE "INTERMITTENTS" SECTION B.

TBI TROUBLE DIAGNOSTICS

"SCAN" DIAGNOSTIC CIRCUIT CHECK
(Page 3 of 6)
(CODE DEFINITIONS)

CODES	DEFINITIONS
CODE 21 • IGNITION "ON". • THROTTLE CLOSED. • ENGINE STOPPED. • "SCAN" TPS	**HARD FAILURE -** "SCAN" TOOL DISPLAYS A CLOSED THROTTLE VOLTAGE OVER 2.5 VOLTS. SIGNAL VOLTAGE TOO HIGH, GROUND WIRE OPEN, SIGNAL LINE SHORTED TO SENSOR REF. LINE OR FAULTY SENSOR. SEE CODE CHART 21. **INTERMITTENT CODE -** "SCAN" TOOL DISPLAYS THROTTLE POSITION IN VOLTS. SHOULD READ BETWEEN 020-125 (200 mv AND 1.25 V). WITH THROTTLE CLOSED AND IGNITION ON OR AT IDLE, VOLTAGE SHOULD INCREASE AT A STEADY RATE AS THROTTLE IS MOVED TOWARD A WIDE OPEN POSITION. SEE "INTERMITTENTS" SECTION B.
CODE 22 • IGNITION "ON" • ENGINE STOPPED. • THROTTLE CLOSED. • "SCAN" TPS	**HARD FAILURE -** "SCAN" TOOL DISPLAYS BELOW 020V (200 mv). OPEN OR SHORT TO GROUND IN 5V REFERENCE OR SIGNAL CIRCUIT, OR FAULTY SENSOR. SEE CODE CHART 22. **INTERMITTENT CODE -** "SCAN"TOOL DISPLAYS THROTTLE POSITION IN VOLTS. SHOULD READ BETWEEN 020-125 (200 mv AND 1.25 V). WITH THROTTLE CLOSED AND IGNITION ON OR AT IDLE, VOLTAGE SHOULD INCREASE AT A STEADY RATE AS THROTTLE IS MOVED TOWARD A WIDE OPEN POSITION. SEE "INTERMITTENTS" SECTION B.
CODE 24 • ENGINE RUNNING. • DRIVE WHEELS TURNING. • "SCAN" MPH.	**HARD FAILURE -** "SCAN" TOOL DISPLAYS 0 MPH. IF SPEEDOMETER IS WORKING OK, THEN THE VSS SIGNAL INPUT IS OPEN, SHORTED TO GROUND, OR THE BUFFER IS DEFECTIVE. SEE CODE CHART 24. **INTERMITTENT CODE -** "SCAN" TOOL DISPLAY SHOULD CLOSELY MATCH WITH SPEEDOMETER READING WITH DRIVE WHEELS TURNING. SEE 'INTERMITTENTS' SECTION B. "SCAN" DISPLAY INDICATES THAT PARK/NEUTRAL SWITCH DID NOT "SWITCH" WHEN SHIFTING NEUTRAL TO DRIVE (A.T. ONLY). SEE CHART C-1A. DISREGARD CODE 24 IF SET WITH DRIVE WHEELS NOT TURNING.

"SCAN" DIAGNOSTIC CIRCUIT CHECK
(Page 5 of 6)
(CODE DEFINITIONS)

CODES	DEFINITIONS
CODE 35 • A/C OFF. • ENGINE IDLING IN NEUTRAL • COOLANT TEMP 70° TO 90°C • "SCAN" IN "SPECIAL" MODE. • INCREASE ENGINE RPM TO 2500 TO RESET IAC. CLOSE THROTTLE AND ALLOW IDLE AND IAC COUNTS STABILIZE.	**HARD FAILURE -** "SCAN" TOOL DISPLAYS IDLE SPEED 950 RPM OR ABOVE . IAC COUNTS "0". THIS CONDITION IS USUALLY A SMALL VACUUM LEAK SUCH AS THERMAC OR CRUISE CONTROL HOSE DISCONNECTED, OR ENGINE SPEED 950 RPM OR BELOW. IAC COUNTS ABOVE 80. SEE CODE 35 CHART. **INTERMITTENT CODE -** FOLLOWING AN IAC RESET, RPM SHOULD STABLIZE AT 1000 ± 50 RPM IN SPECIAL MODE. DISCONNECTING "SCAN" TOOL WILL RESTORE NORMAL IDLE.
CODE 42 • CLEAR CODES, START AND IDLE ENGINE FOR 1 MINUTE.	**HARD FAILURE -** SERVICE ENGINE SOON" ON, SCAN TOOL DISPLAYS CODE 42. SEE CODE CHART 42. **INTERMITTENT CODE -** THE SCAN TOOL DOES NOT HAVE THE ABILITY TO HELP DIAGNOSE A CODE 42 PROBLEM. IF NO "SERVICE ENGINE SOON "LIGHT, REFER TO INTERMITTENTS IN SECTION "B".
CODE 44 • "SCAN" TOOL IN "SPECIAL" MODE. • COOLANT TEMP 75° to 95° C AND CLOSED LOOP • ENGINE IDLING AT 1000 RPM.	**HARD FAILURE -** "SCAN" TOOL DISPLAYED O₂ VOLTAGE CONSISTENTLY BELOW .35V. CAUSED BY A LEAN EXHAUST OR SIGNAL CIRCUIT SHORTED TO GROUND. SEE CODE CHART 44. **INTERMITTENT CODE -** NORMAL "SCAN" DISPLAY WILL VARY BETWEEN 100 MV AND 999MV. (.1 to 1.0V). ALSO SEE CROSSCOUNTS, RICH - LEAN INDICATION. O₂ VOLTAGE. SEE "SCAN" INFORMATION IN INTRODUCTION.

"SCAN" DIAGNOSTIC CIRCUIT CHECK
(Page 6 of 6)
(CODE DEFINITIONS)

CODES	DEFINITIONS
CODE 45 • "SCAN" TOOL IN "SPECIAL" MODE • ENGINE IDLING AT 1000 RPM • COOLANT TEMP 75° to 95° C AND IN CLOSED LOOP • "SCAN" OXYGEN SENSOR VOLTAGE	**HARD FAILURE -** "SCAN" O₂ VOLTAGE CONSISTENTLY ABOVE .65V. RICH EXHAUST CAUSING A HIGH O₂ VOLTAGE. SEE CODE CHART 45. **INTERMITTENT CODE -** NORMAL "SCAN" VOLTAGE WILL VARY BETWEEN 100 MV AND 999MV. (.1 to 1.0V) ALSO SEE CROSSCOUNTS, RICH - LEAN INDICATION. O₂ VOLTAGE. SEE "SCAN" INFORMATION IN INTRODUCTION.
CODE 51 • CLEAR CODES • START ENGINE • CHECK FOR CODE	**HARD FAILURE -** CODE 51 RESETS WHICH INDICATES A FAULTY PROM. SEE CODE CHART 51.
CODE 55 • CLEAR CODES • START ENGINE • CHECK FOR CODE	**HARD FAILURE -** CODE 55 RESETS WHICH INDICATES THE ECM IS FAULTY. REPLACE ECM.

CHART A-1
NO "SERVICE ENGINE SOON" LIGHT
1.8L "J" SERIES
FUEL INJECTION (TBI)

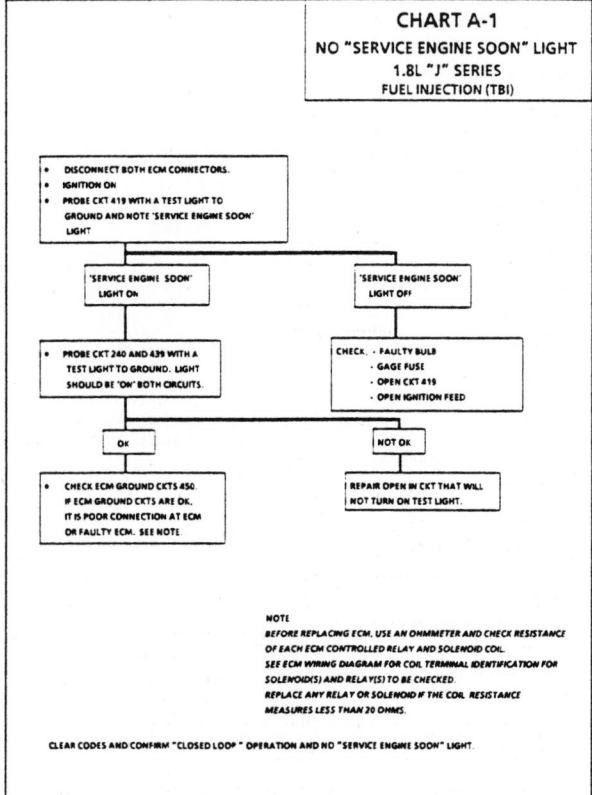

TBI TROUBLE DIAGNOSTICS

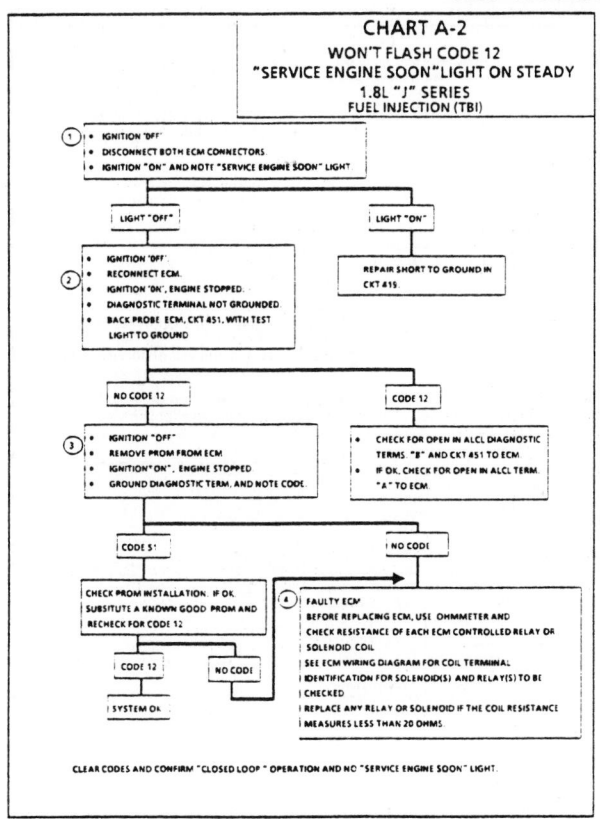

CHART A-2
WON'T FLASH CODE 12
"SERVICE ENGINE SOON" LIGHT ON STEADY
1.8L "J" SERIES
FUEL INJECTION (TBI)

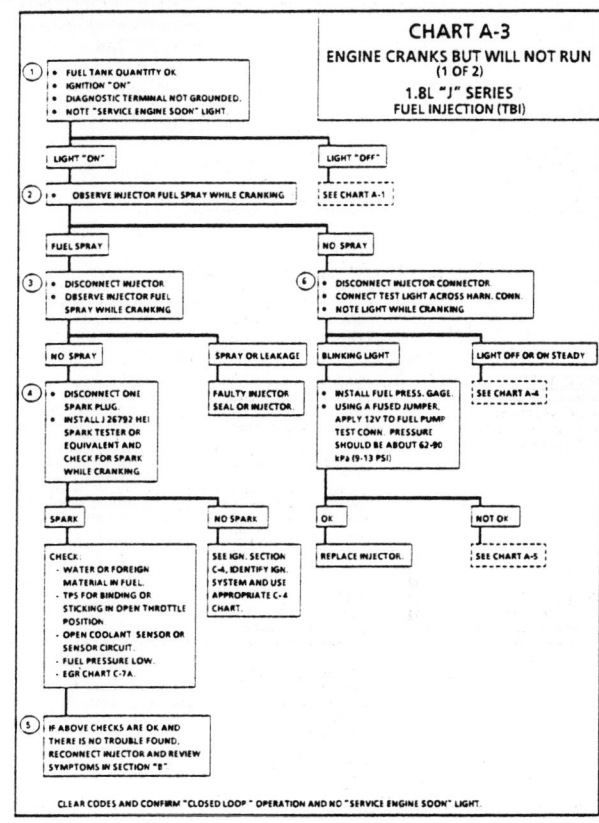

CHART A-3
ENGINE CRANKS BUT WILL NOT RUN
(1 OF 2)
1.8L "J" SERIES
FUEL INJECTION (TBI)

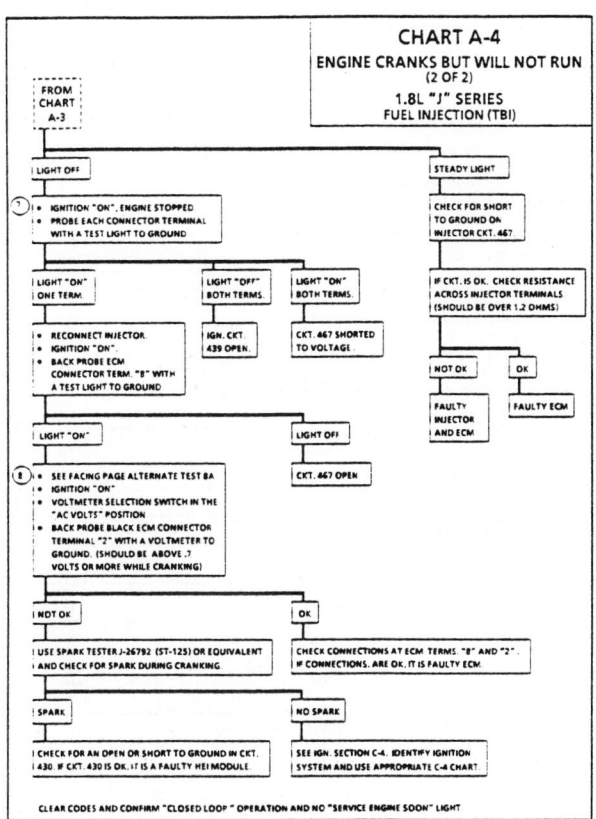

CHART A-4
ENGINE CRANKS BUT WILL NOT RUN
(2 OF 2)
1.8L "J" SERIES
FUEL INJECTION (TBI)

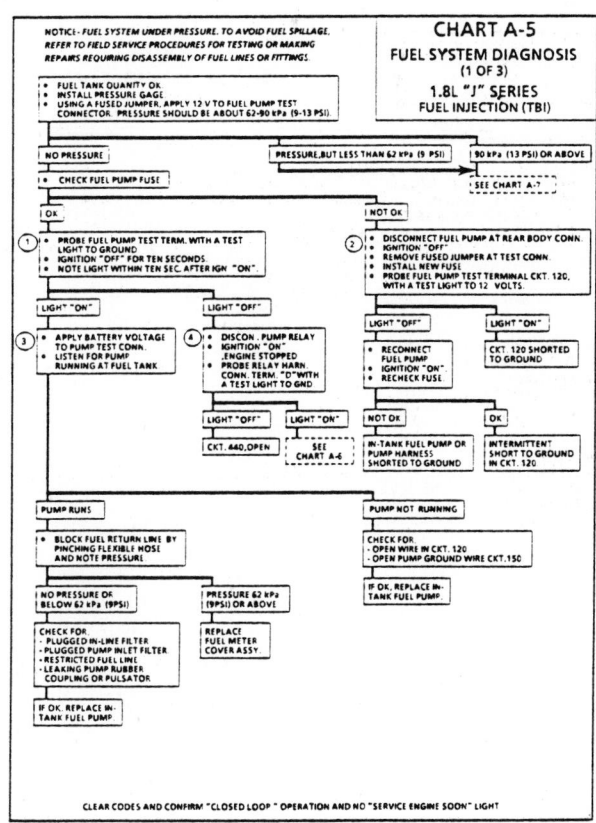

CHART A-5
FUEL SYSTEM DIAGNOSIS
(1 OF 3)
1.8L "J" SERIES
FUEL INJECTION (TBI)

TBI TROUBLE DIAGNOSTICS

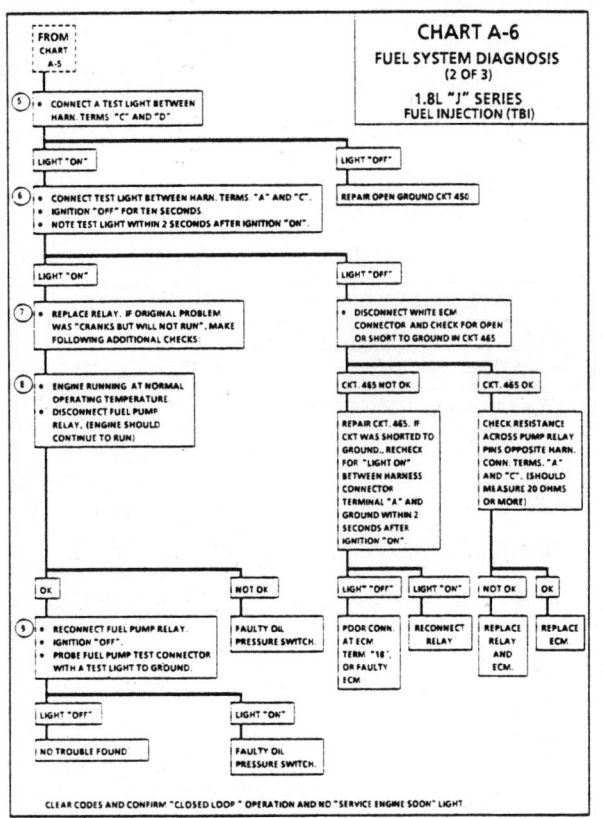

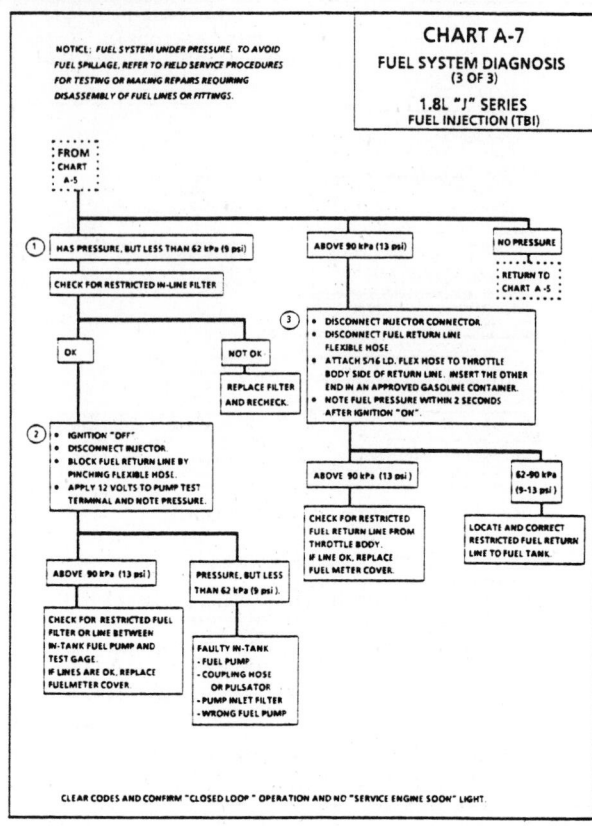

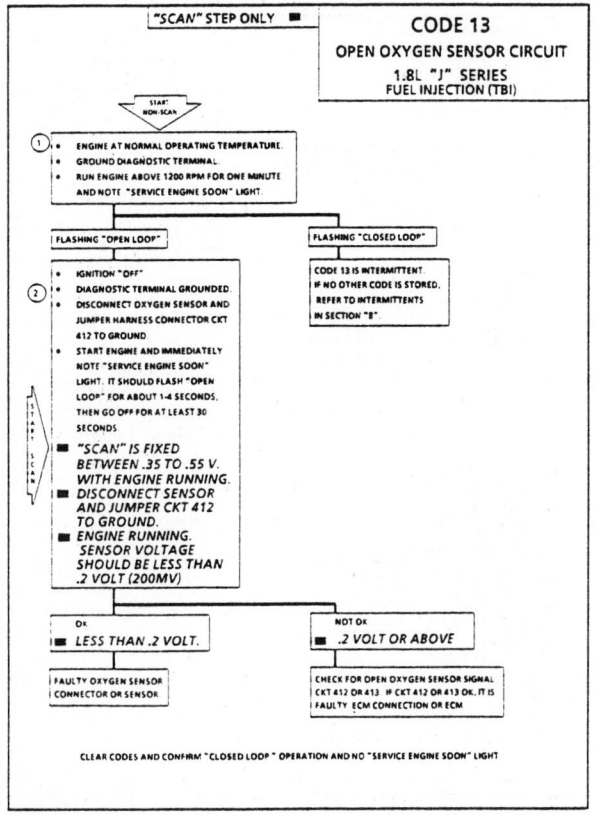

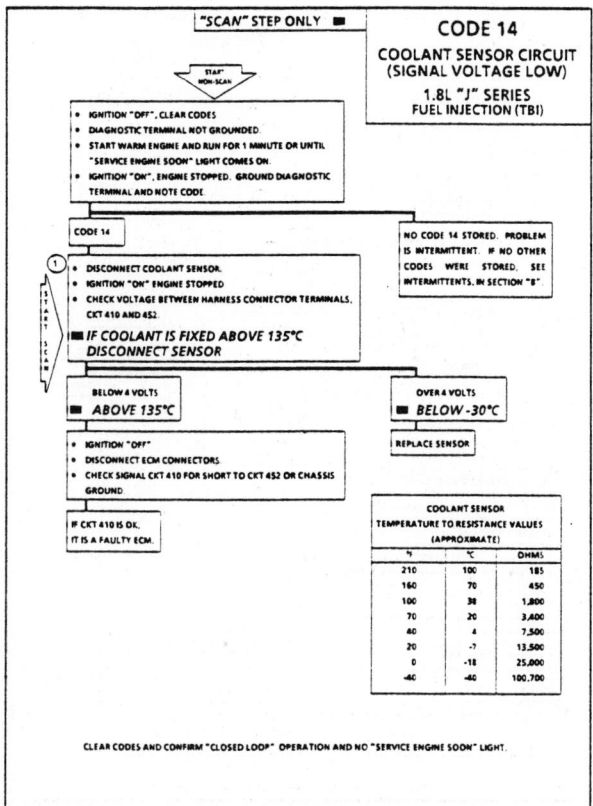

TBI TROUBLE DIAGNOSTICS

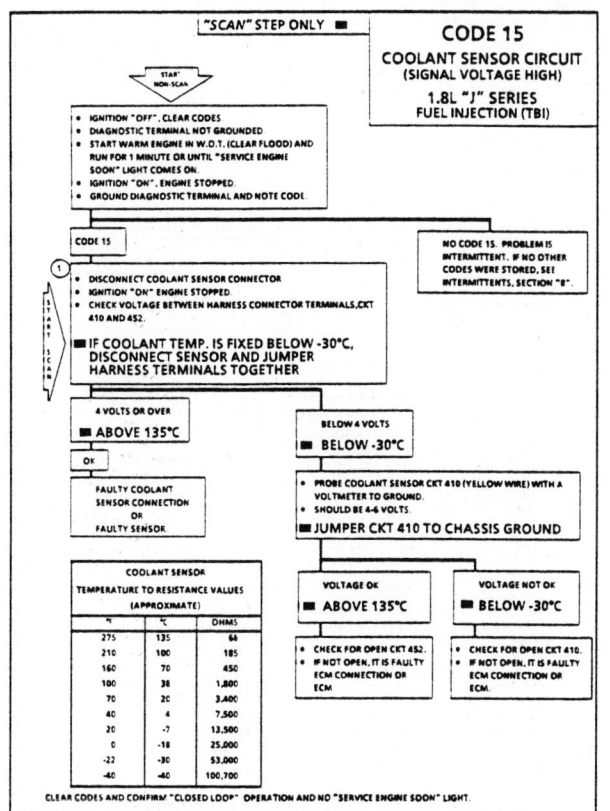

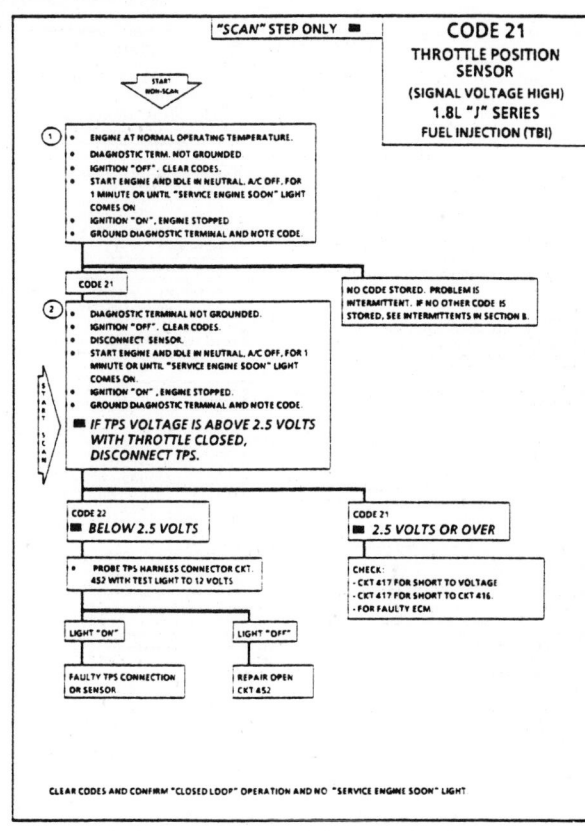

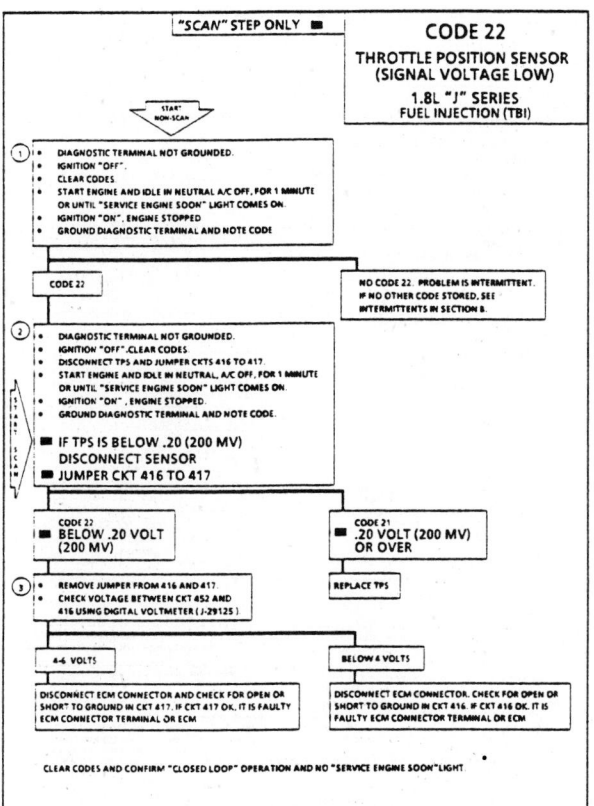

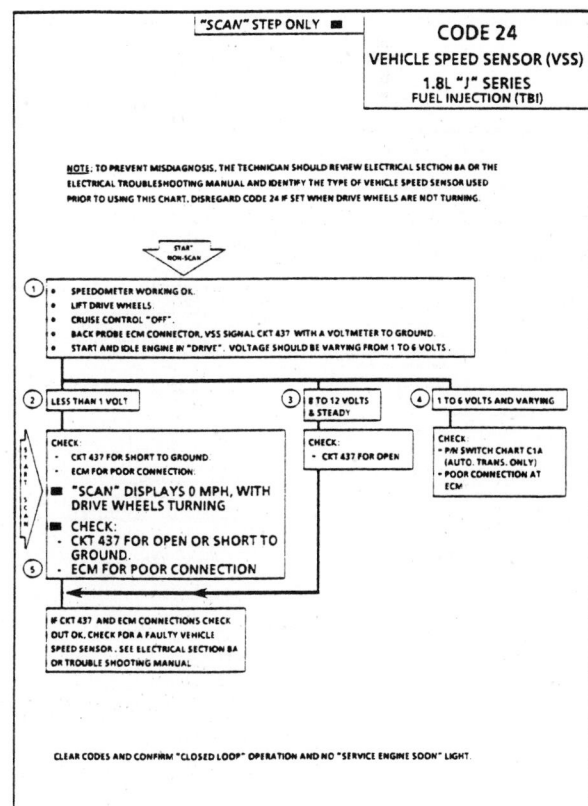

TBI TROUBLE DIAGNOSTICS

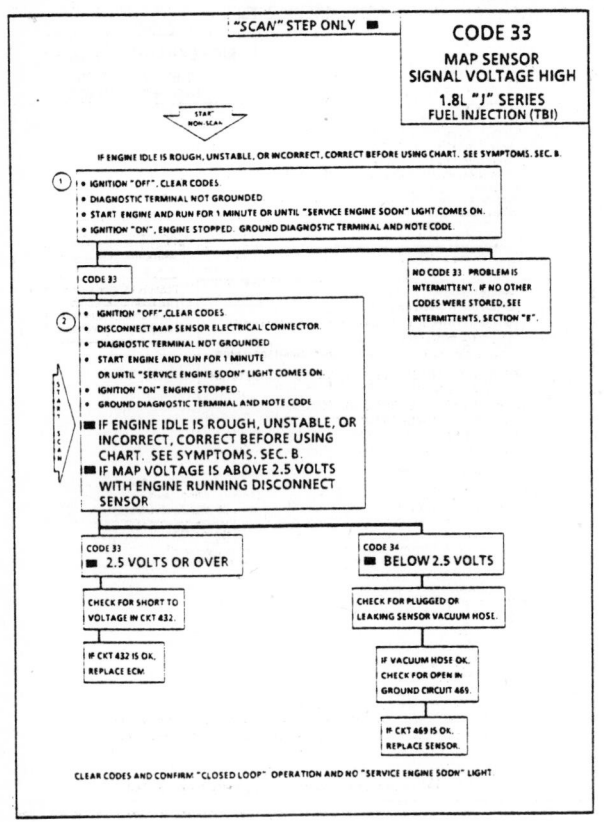

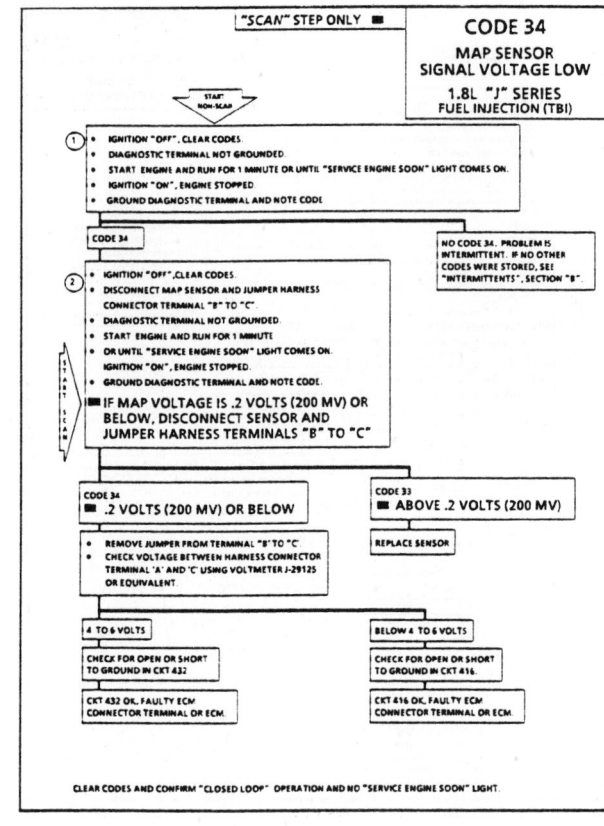

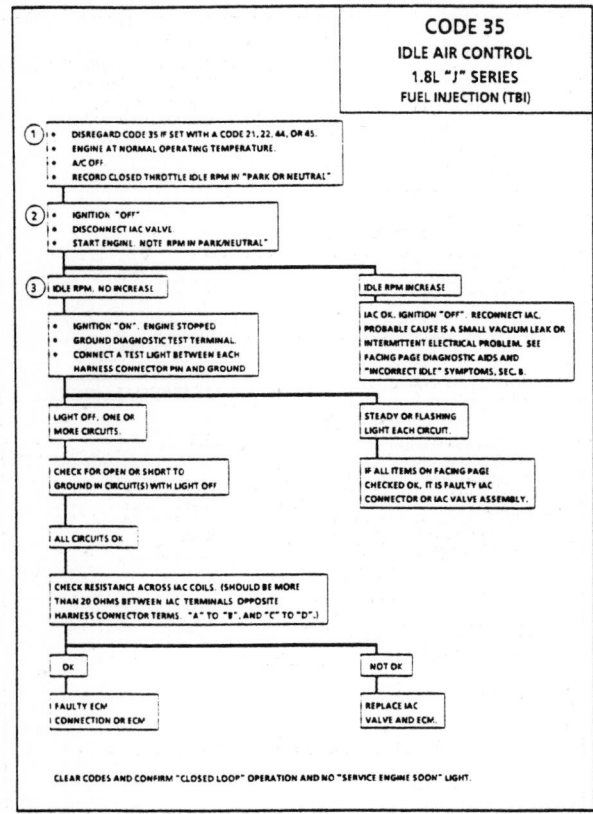

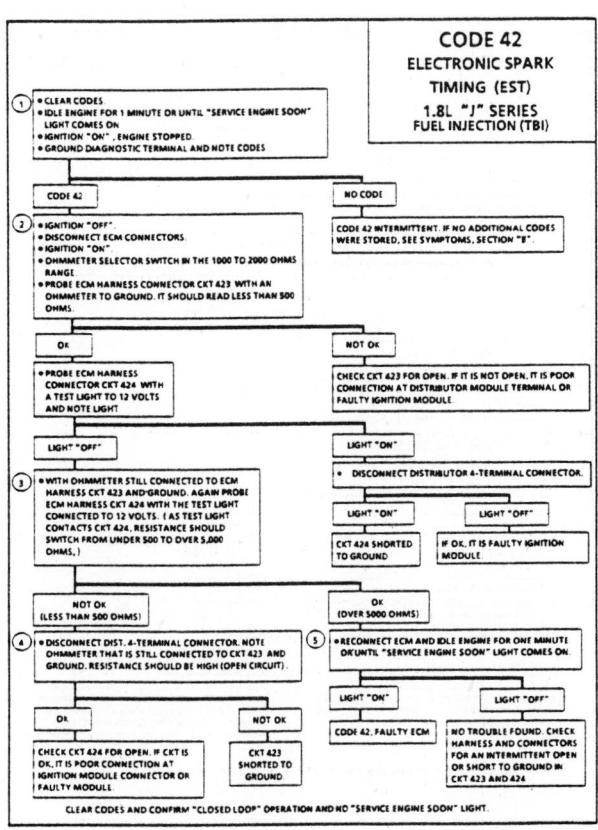

TBI TROUBLE DIAGNOSTICS

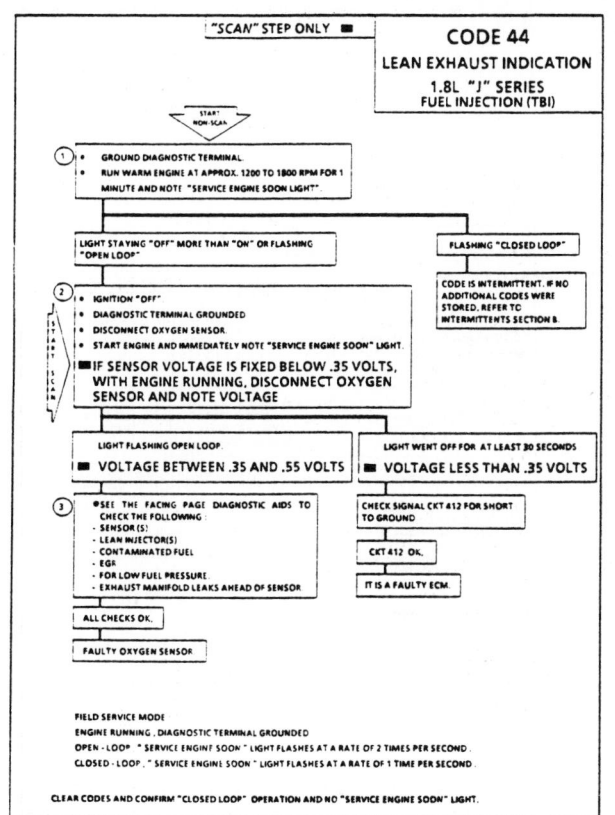

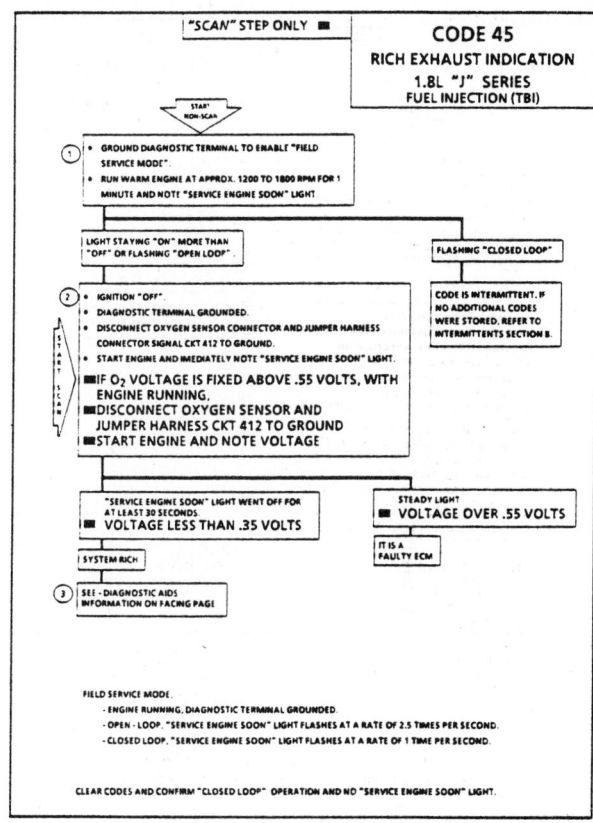

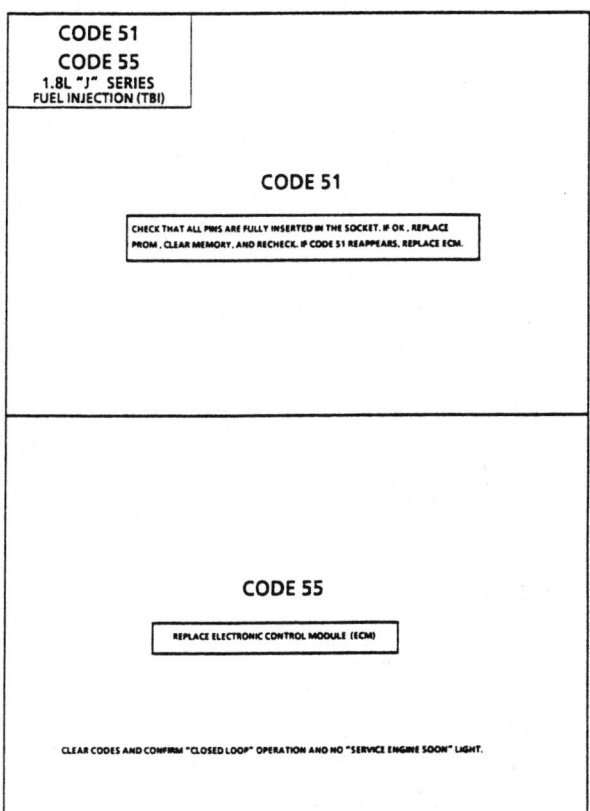

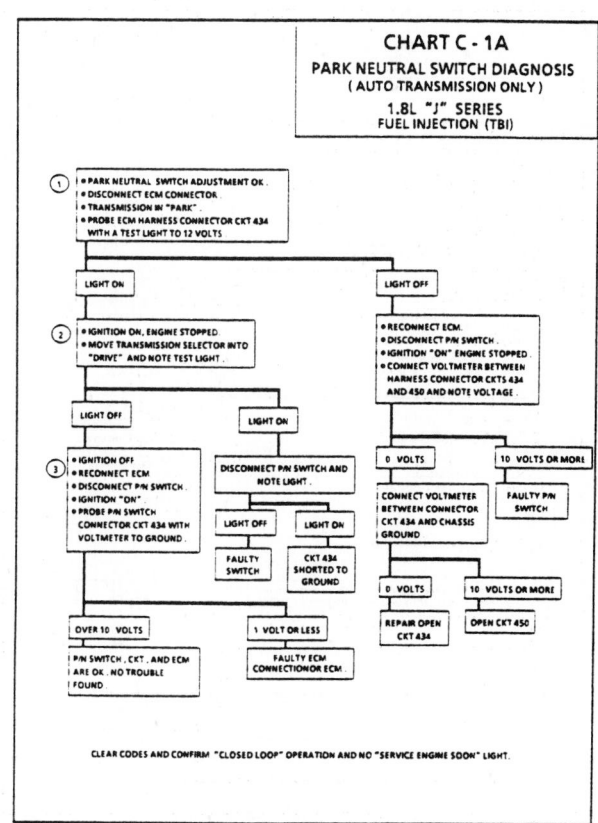

TBI TROUBLE DIAGNOSTICS

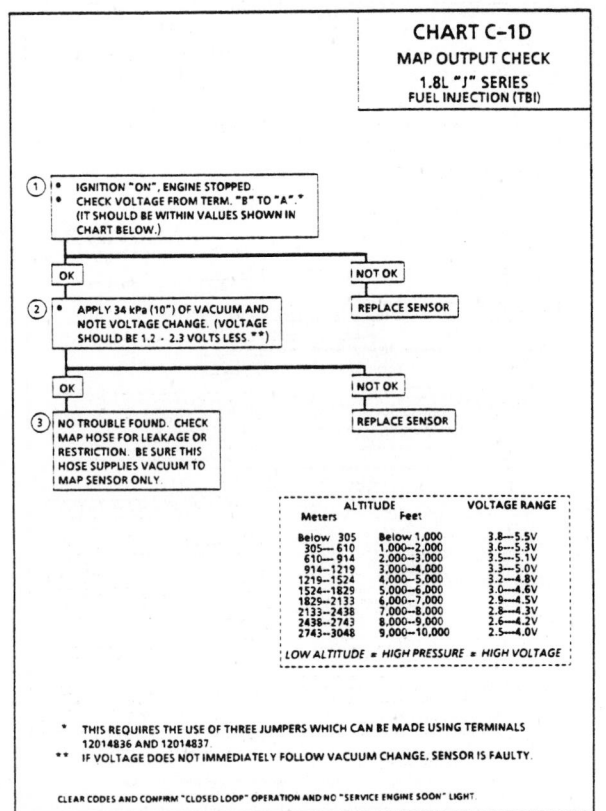

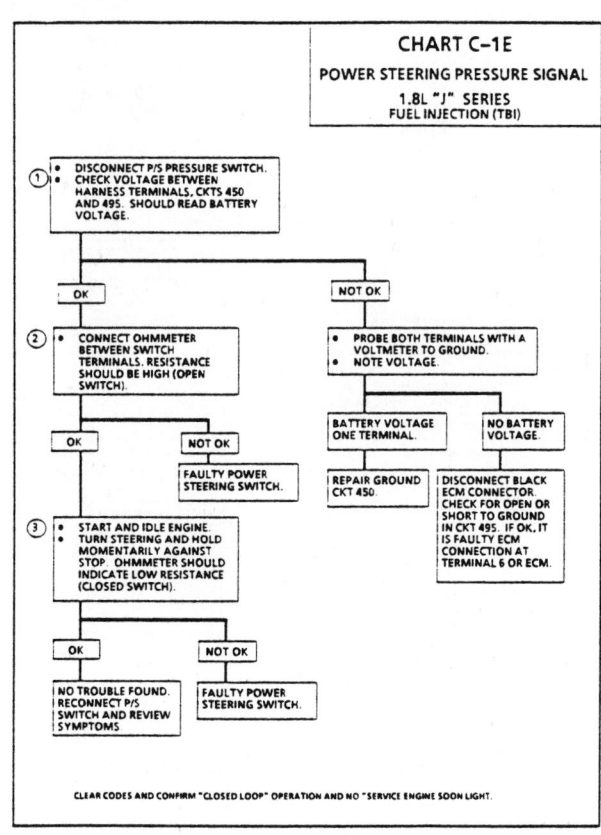

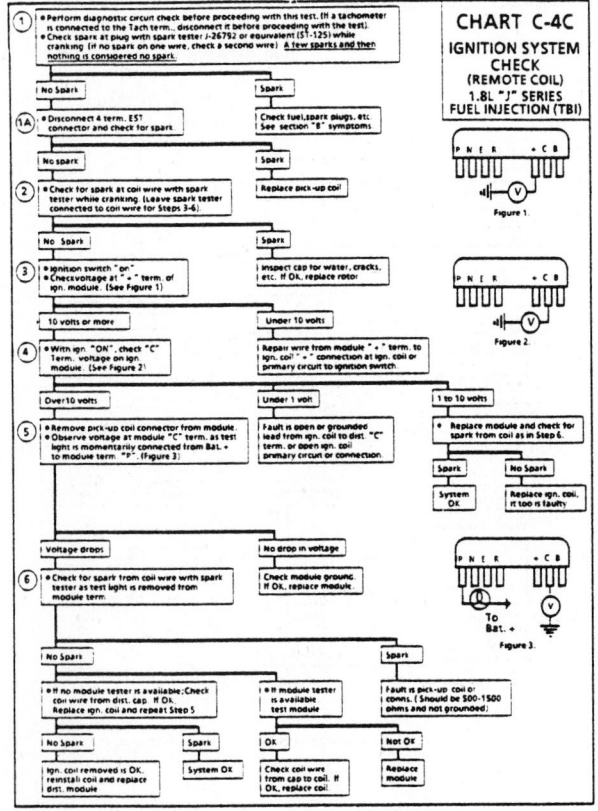

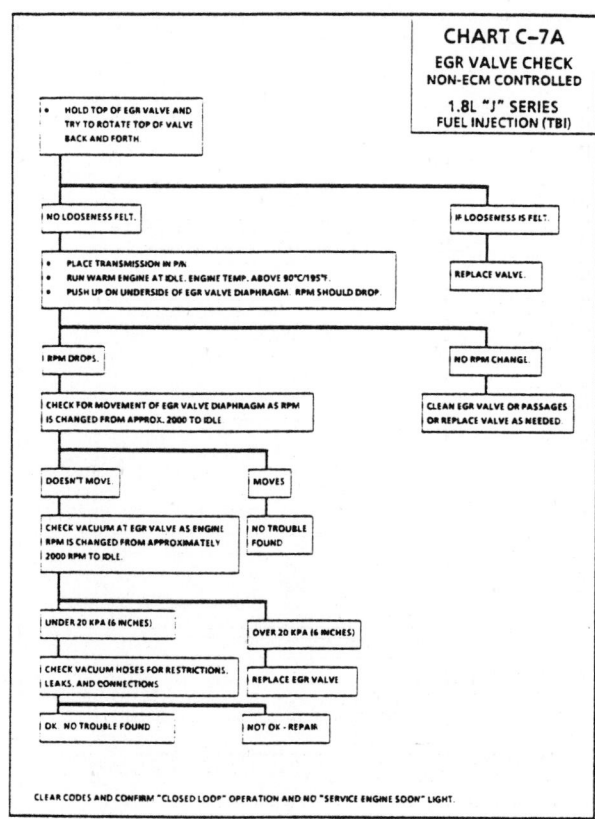

TBI TROUBLE DIAGNOSTICS

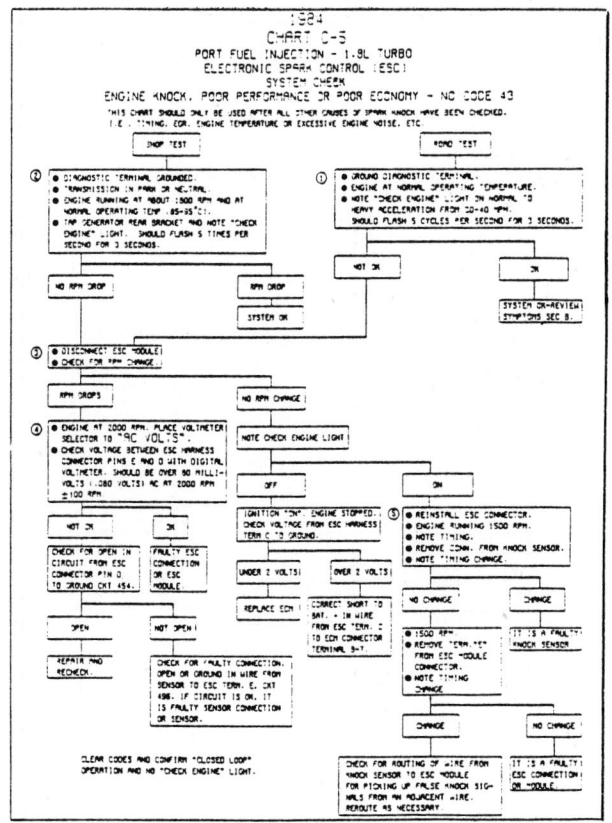

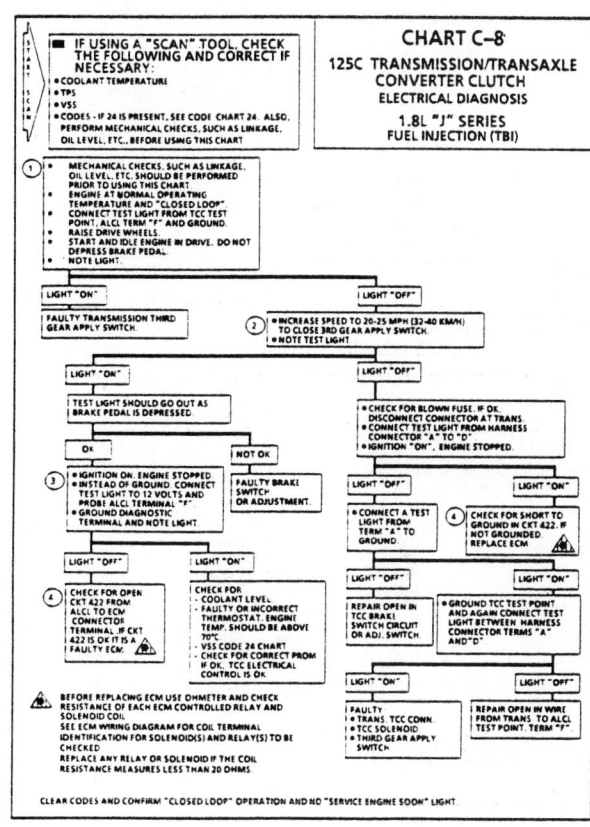

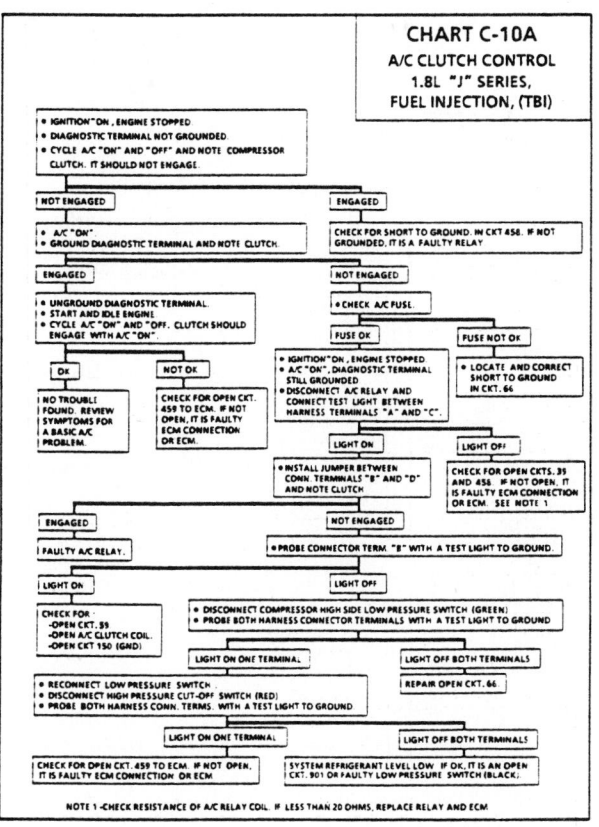

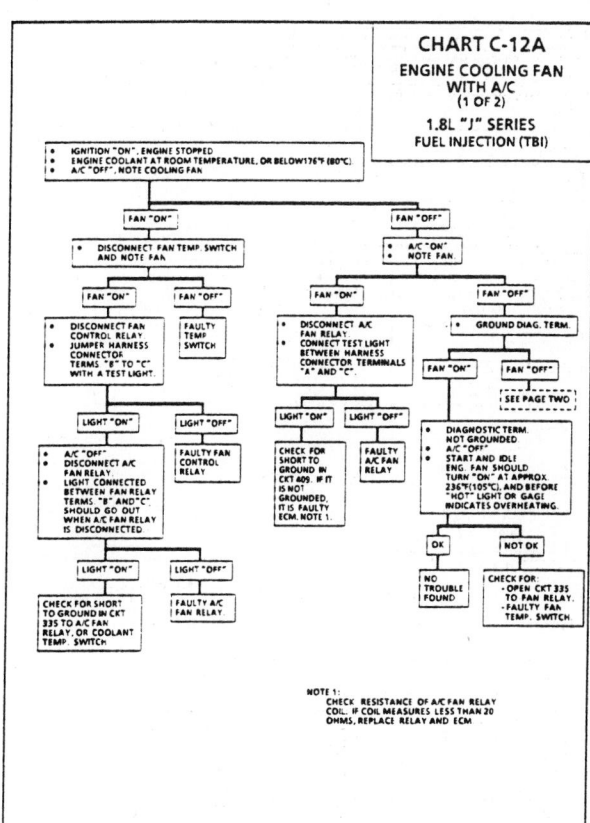

TBI TROUBLE DIAGNOSTICS

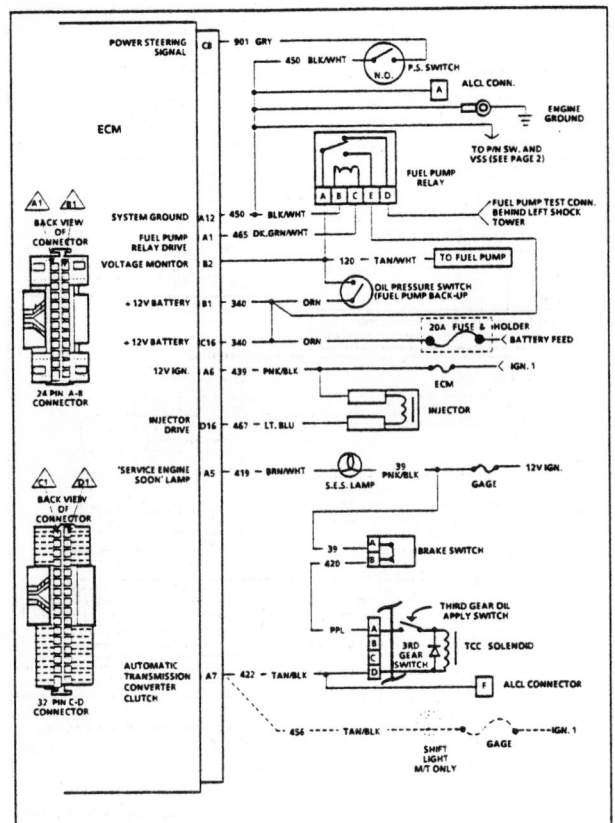

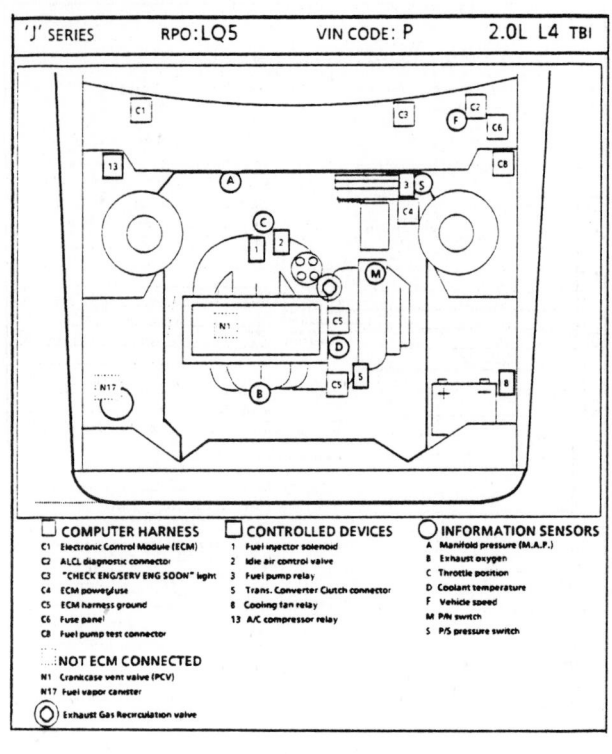

'J' SERIES   RPO: LQ5   VIN CODE: P   2.0L L4 TBI

☐ COMPUTER HARNESS   ☐ CONTROLLED DEVICES   ○ INFORMATION SENSORS

COMPUTER HARNESS	CONTROLLED DEVICES	INFORMATION SENSORS
C1 Electronic Control Module (ECM)	1 Fuel injector solenoid	A Manifold pressure (M.A.P.)
C2 ALCL diagnostic connector	2 Idle air control valve	B Exhaust oxygen
C3 "CHECK ENG/SERV ENG SOON" light	3 Fuel pump relay	C Throttle position
C4 ECM power/fuse	5 Trans. Converter Clutch connector	D Coolant temperature
C5 ECM harness ground	6 Cooling fan relay	F Vehicle speed
C6 Fuse panel	13 A/C compressor relay	M P/N switch
C8 Fuel pump test connector		S P/S pressure switch

☐ NOT ECM CONNECTED

N1 Crankcase vent valve (PCV)
N17 Fuel vapor canister

○ Exhaust Gas Recirculation valve

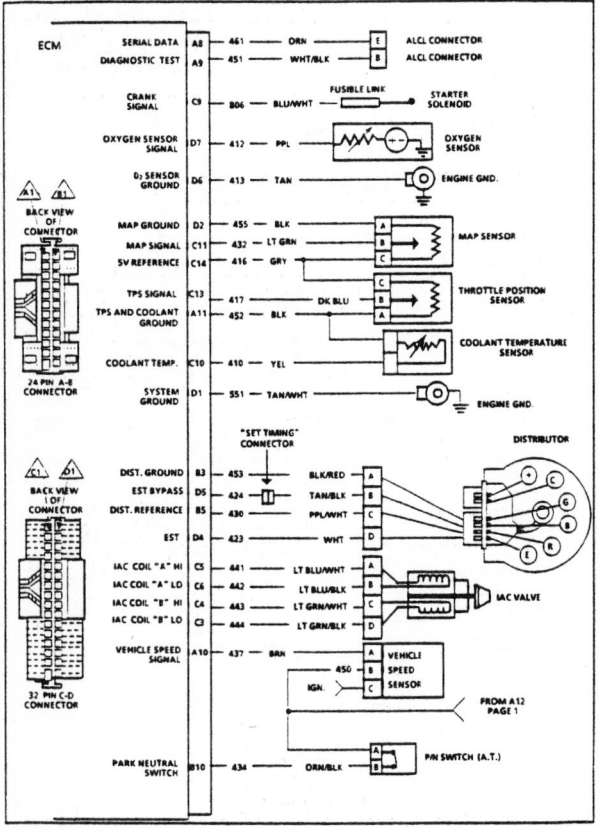

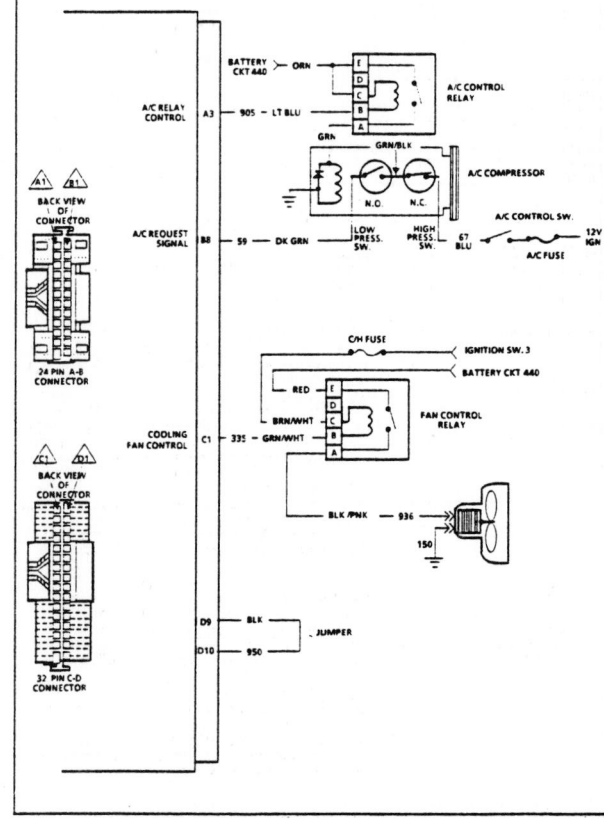

TBI TROUBLE DIAGNOSTICS

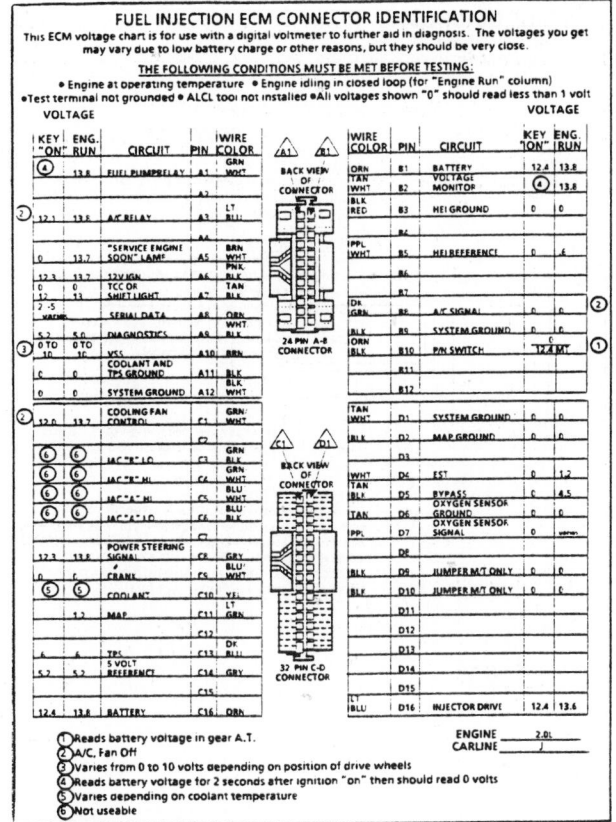

FUEL INJECTION ECM CONNECTOR IDENTIFICATION
This ECM voltage chart is for use with a digital voltmeter to further aid in diagnosis. The voltages you get may vary due to low battery charge or other reasons, but they should be very close.

THE FOLLOWING CONDITIONS MUST BE MET BEFORE TESTING:
- Engine at operating temperature
- Engine idling in closed loop (for "Engine Run" column)
- Test terminal not grounded
- ALCL tool not installed
- All voltages shown "0" should read less than 1 volt

1. Reads battery voltage in gear A.T.
2. A/C, Fan Off
3. Varies from 0 to 10 volts depending on position of drive wheels
4. Reads battery voltage for 2 seconds after ignition "on" then should read 0 volts
5. Varies depending on coolant temperature
6. Not useable

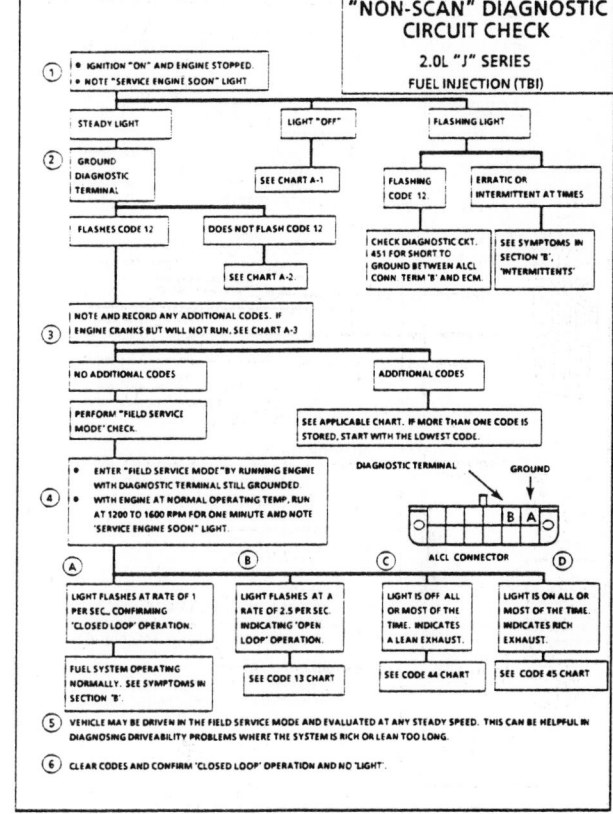

"NON-SCAN" DIAGNOSTIC CIRCUIT CHECK
2.0L "J" SERIES
FUEL INJECTION (TBI)

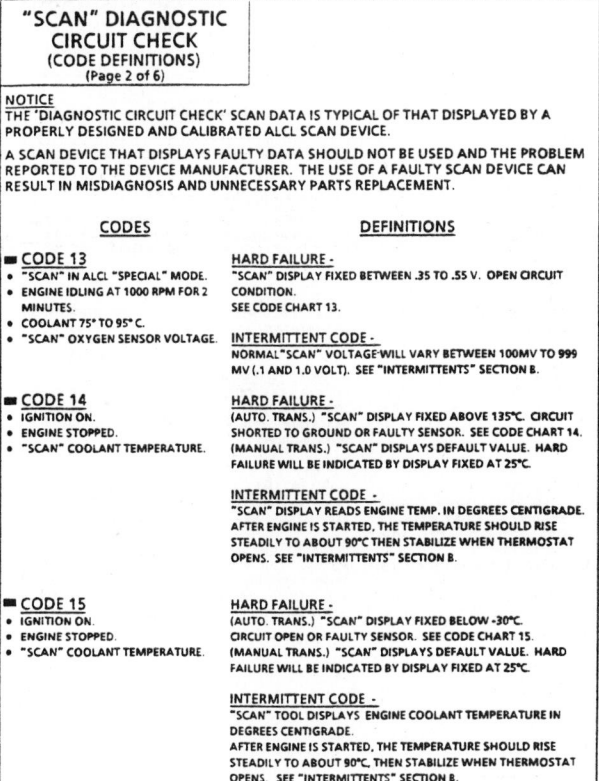

"SCAN" DIAGNOSTIC CIRCUIT CHECK
(CODE DEFINITIONS)
(Page 2 of 6)

NOTICE
THE 'DIAGNOSTIC CIRCUIT CHECK' SCAN DATA IS TYPICAL OF THAT DISPLAYED BY A PROPERLY DESIGNED AND CALIBRATED ALCL SCAN DEVICE.

A SCAN DEVICE THAT DISPLAYS FAULTY DATA SHOULD NOT BE USED AND THE PROBLEM REPORTED TO THE DEVICE MANUFACTURER. THE USE OF A FAULTY SCAN DEVICE CAN RESULT IN MISDIAGNOSIS AND UNNECESSARY PARTS REPLACEMENT.

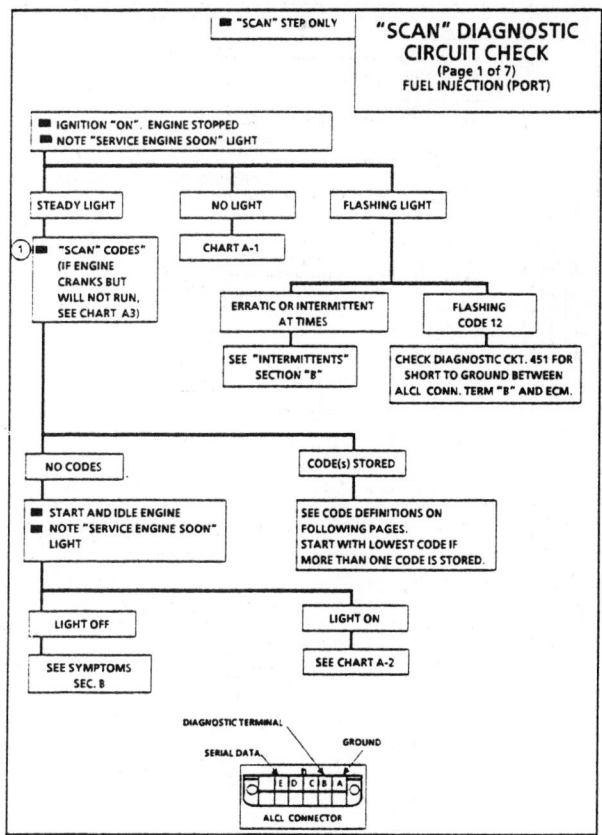

"SCAN" DIAGNOSTIC CIRCUIT CHECK
(Page 1 of 7)
FUEL INJECTION (PORT)

TBI TROUBLE DIAGNOSTICS

"SCAN" DIAGNOSTIC CIRCUIT CHECK (CODE DEFINITIONS) (Page 3 of 6)

CODES

CODE 21
- IGNITION "ON".
- HROTTLE CLOSED.
- ENGINE STOPPED.
- "SCAN" TPS
  OR
- ENGINE IDLING
- THROTTLE CLOSED.
- "SCAN" TPS

CODE 22
- IGNITION "ON"
- ENGINE STOPPED.
- "SCAN" TPS

CODE 24
- ENGINE RUNNING.
- DRIVE WHEELS TURNING.
- "SCAN" MPH.

DEFINITIONS

HARD FAILURE -
"SCAN" TOOL DISPLAYS A CLOSED THROTTLE VOLTAGE OVER 2.5 VOLTS. SIGNAL VOLTAGE TOO HIGH, GROUND WIRE OPEN, SIGNAL LINE SHORTED TO SENSOR REF. LINE OR FAULTY SENSOR. SEE CODE CHART 21.

INTERMITTENT CODE -
"SCAN" TOOL DISPLAYS THROTTLE POSITION IN VOLTS. SHOULD READ BETWEEN 020-125 (200 MV AND 1.25 V). WITH THROTTLE CLOSED AND IGNITION ON OR AT IDLE, VOLTAGE SHOULD INCREASE AT A STEADY RATE AS THROTTLE IS MOVED TOWARD A WIDE OPEN POSITION. SEE "INTERMITTENTS" SECTION B.

HARD FAILURE -
"SCAN" TOOL DISPLAYS BELOW 020V (200 MV). OPEN OR SHORT TO GROUND IN 5V REFERENCE OR SIGNAL CIRCUIT, OR FAULTY SENSOR. SEE CODE CHART 22.

INTERMITTENT CODE -
"SCAN"TOOL DISPLAYS THROTTLE POSITION IN VOLTS. SHOULD READ BETWEEN 020-125 (200 MV AND 1.25 V). WITH THROTTLE CLOSED AND IGNITION ON OR AT IDLE, VOLTAGE SHOULD INCREASE AT A STEADY RATE AS THROTTLE IS MOVED TOWARD A WIDE OPEN POSITION. SEE "INTERMITTENTS" SECTION B.

HARD FAILURE -
"SCAN" TOOL DISPLAYS 0 MPH. IF SPEEDOMETER IS WORKING OK, THEN THE VSS SIGNAL INPUT IS OPEN, SHORTED TO GROUND, OR THE BUFFER IS DEFECTIVE. SEE CODE CHART 24.

INTERMITTENT CODE -
"SCAN" TOOL DISPLAY SHOULD CLOSELY MATCH WITH SPEEDOMETER READING WITH DRIVE WHEELS TURNING. SEE 'INTERMITTENTS' SECTION B.

"SCAN" DIAGNOSTIC CIRCUIT CHECK (CODE DEFINITIONS) (Page 4 of 6)

CODES

CODE 33
- ENGINE IDLING.
- "SCAN" MAP.

CODE 34
- IGNITION "ON"
- "SCAN" MAP.

DEFINITIONS

HARD FAILURE -
"SCAN" TOOL DISPLAYS ABOVE 2.5 VOLTS. SENSOR GROUND CIRCUIT OPEN, LEAKING VACUUM HOSE, OR FAULTY SENSOR. SEE CODE CHART 33.

INTERMITTENT CODE -
"SCAN" TOOL DISPLAYS MANIFOLD PRESSURE IN VOLTS. LOW PRESSURE (HIGH VACUUM) READS A LOW VOLTAGE WHILE A HIGH PRESSURE (LOW VACUUM) READS A HIGH VOLTAGE. QUICK ACCELERATION SHOULD CAUSE A HIGH OUTPUT VOLTAGE WHILE A DECELERATION WILL SHOW A LOW VOLTAGE. IF ENGINE IDLE IS LOW AND UNSTABLE, IT MAY SET CODE 33. SEE "INTERMITTENTS" SECTION B.

HARD FAILURE -
"SCAN" TOOL DISPLAYS BELOW (200 MV) .2 VOLTS. SIGNAL WIRE OR 5V REFERENCE OPEN OR SHORTED TO GROUND OR FAULTY SENSOR. SEE CODE CHART 34.

INTERMITTENT CODE -
"SCAN"TOOL DISPLAYS MANIFOLD PRESSURE IN VOLTS. LOW PRESSURE (HIGH VACUUM) READS A LOW VOLTAGE WHILE A HIGH PRESSURE (LOW VACUUM) READS A HIGH VOLTAGE. QUICK ACCELERATION SHOULD CAUSE A HIGH OUTPUT VOLTAGE, WHILE A DECELERATION WILL SHOW A LOW VOLTAGE. SEE "INTERMITTENTS" SECTION B.

"SCAN" DIAGNOSTIC CIRCUIT CHECK (CODE DEFINITIONS) (Page 6 of 6)

CODES

CODE 51
- CLEAR CODES
- START ENGINE
- CHECK FOR CODE

CODE 52 - (Automatic trans. only)
- CLEAR CODES
- START ENGINE
- CHECK FOR CODE

CODE 54
- CLEAR CODES
- START ENGINE
- CHECK FOR CODE

CODE 55
- CLEAR CODES
- START ENGINE
- CHECK FOR CODE

DEFINITIONS

HARD FAILURE -
CODE 51 RESETS WHICH INDICATES A FAULTY PROM OR MEM/CAL.
SEE CODE CHART 51.

HARD FAILURE -
CODE 52 RESETS WHICH INDICATES CAL PAK IS MISSING OR FAULTY.

HARD FAILURE -
CODE 54 RESETS WHICH INDICATES LOW FUEL PUMP VOLTAGE. SEE CODE CHART 54.

HARD FAILURE -
CODE 55 RESETS WHICH INDICATES THE ECM IS FAULTY. REPLACE ECM.

"SCAN" DIAGNOSTIC CIRCUIT CHECK (CODE DEFINITIONS) (Page 5 of 6)

CODES

CODE 42
- CLEAR CODES, START AND IDLE ENGINE FOR 1 MINUTE.

CODE 44
- "SCAN" TOOL IN "SPECIAL" MODE.
- COOLANT TEMP 75° to 95° C AND CLOSED LOOP.
- ENGINE IDLING AT 1000 RPM.

CODE 45
- "SCAN" TOOL IN "SPECIAL" MODE.
- ENGINE IDLING AT 1000 RPM.
- COOLANT TEMP 75° to 95° C AND IN CLOSED LOOP.
- "SCAN" OXYGEN SENSOR VOLTAGE.

DEFINITIONS

HARD FAILURE -
"SERVICE ENGINE SOON" ON, SCAN TOOL DISPLAYS CODE 42. SEE CODE CHART 42.

INTERMITTENT CODE -
THE "SCAN" TOOL DOES NOT HAVE THE ABILITY TO HELP DIAGNOSE A CODE 42 PROBLEM. IF NO "SERVICE ENGINE SOON" LIGHT, REFER TO INTERMITTENTS IN SECTION "B".

HARD FAILURE -
"SCAN" TOOL DISPLAYED O_2 VOLTAGE CONSISTENTLY BELOW .35°. CAUSED BY A LEAN EXHAUST OR SIGNAL CIRCUIT SHORTED TO GROUND. SEE CODE CHART 44.

INTERMITTENT CODE -
NORMAL "SCAN" DISPLAY WILL VARY BETWEEN 100 MV AND 999MV. (.1 to 1.0V). ALSO SEE CROSSCOUNTS, RICH - LEAN INDICATION, O_2 VOLTAGE. SEE "SCAN" INFORMATION IN INTRODUCTION.

HARD FAILURE -
"SCAN" O_2 VOLTAGE CONSISTENTLY ABOVE .65V. RICH EXHAUST CAUSING A HIGH O_2 VOLTAGE. SEE CODE CHART 45.

INTERMITTENT CODE -
NORMAL "SCAN" VOLTAGE WILL VARY BETWEEN 100 MV AND 999MV. (.1 to 1.0V) ALSO SEE CROSSCOUNTS, RICH - LEAN INDICATION, O_2 VOLTAGE. SEE "SCAN" INFORMATION IN INTRODUCTION.

TBI TROUBLE DIAGNOSTICS

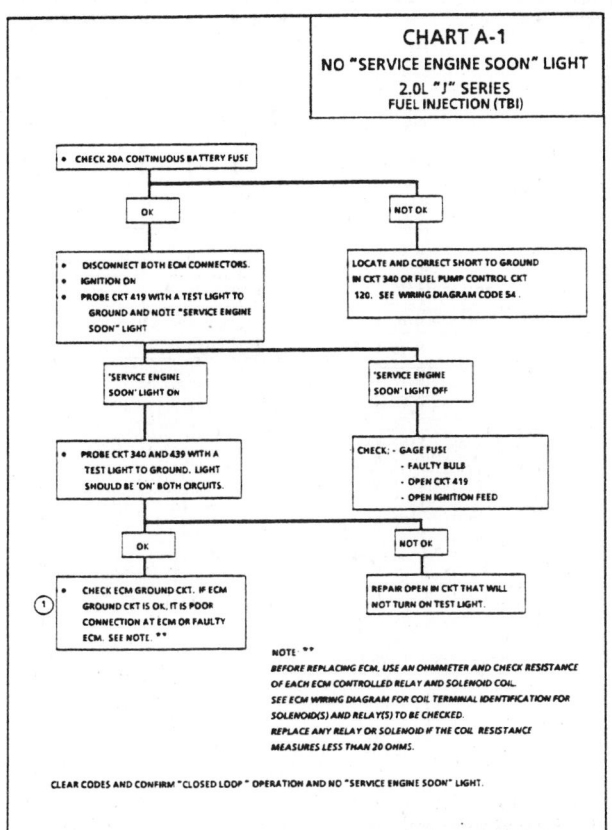

CHART A-1
NO "SERVICE ENGINE SOON" LIGHT
2.0L "J" SERIES
FUEL INJECTION (TBI)

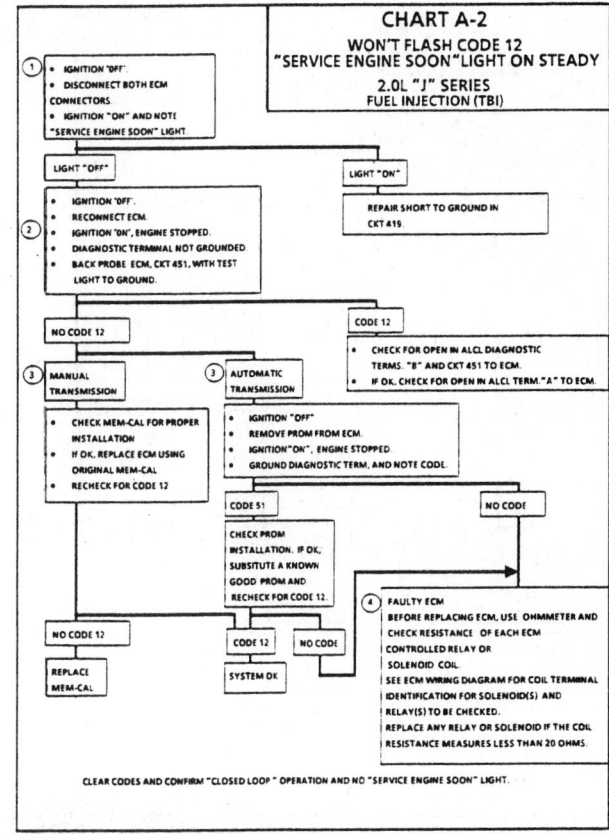

CHART A-2
WON'T FLASH CODE 12
"SERVICE ENGINE SOON" LIGHT ON STEADY
2.0L "J" SERIES
FUEL INJECTION (TBI)

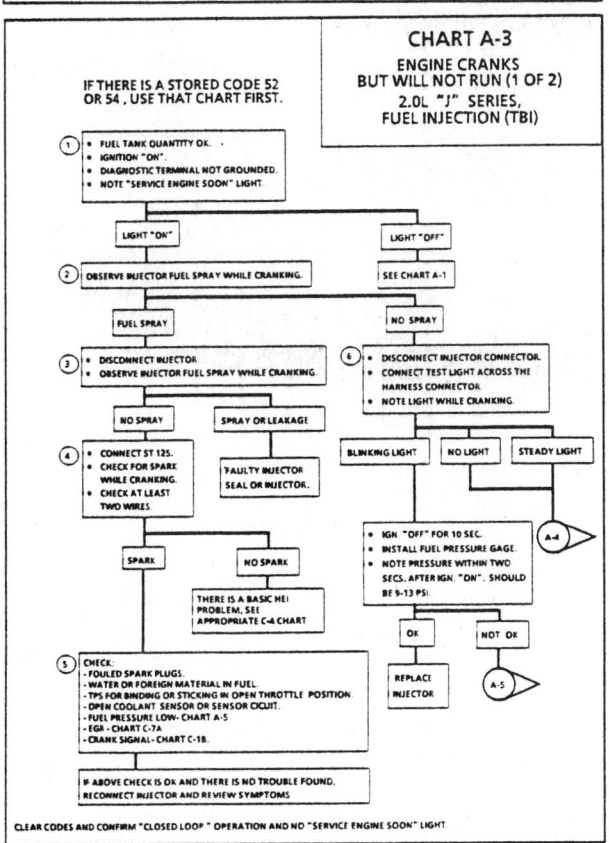

CHART A-3
ENGINE CRANKS
BUT WILL NOT RUN (1 OF 2)
2.0L "J" SERIES,
FUEL INJECTION (TBI)

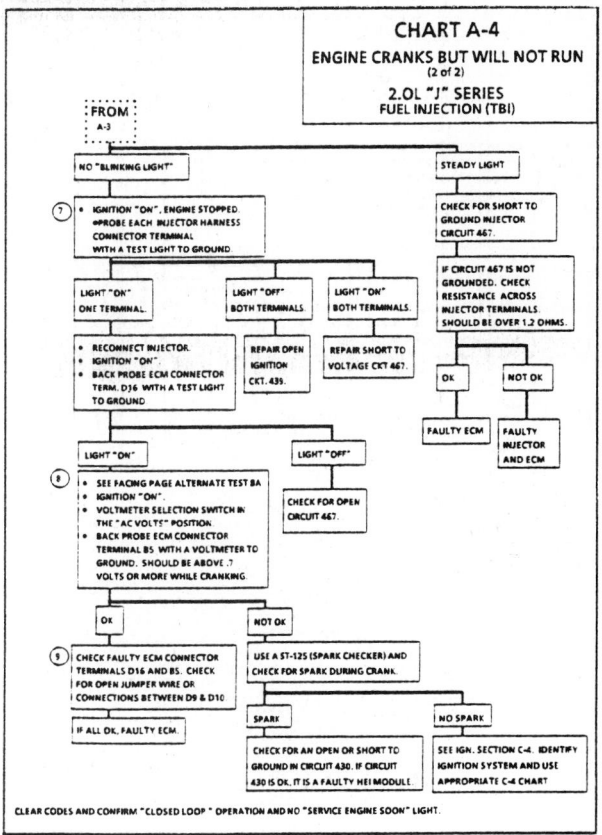

CHART A-4
ENGINE CRANKS BUT WILL NOT RUN
(2 of 2)
2.0L "J" SERIES
FUEL INJECTION (TBI)

TBI TROUBLE DIAGNOSTICS

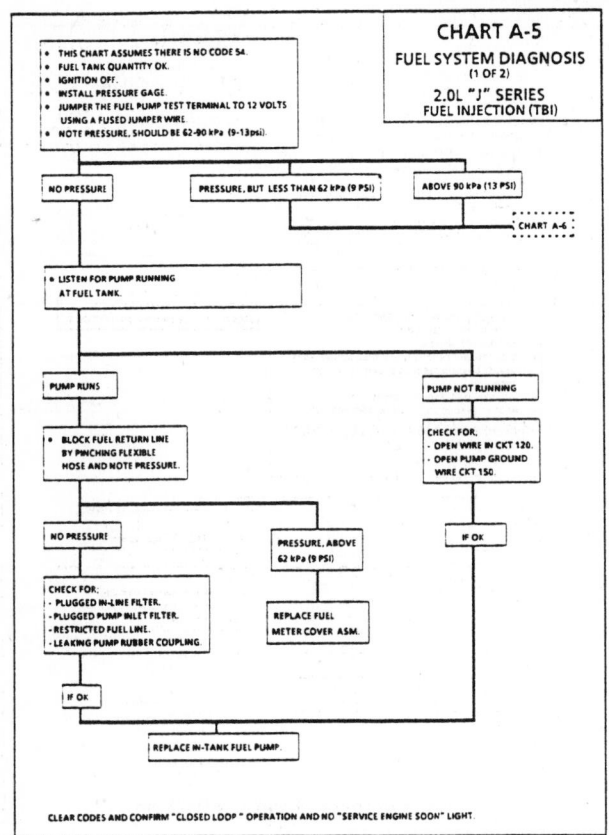

CHART A-5
FUEL SYSTEM DIAGNOSIS
(1 OF 2)

2.0L "J" SERIES
FUEL INJECTION (TBI)

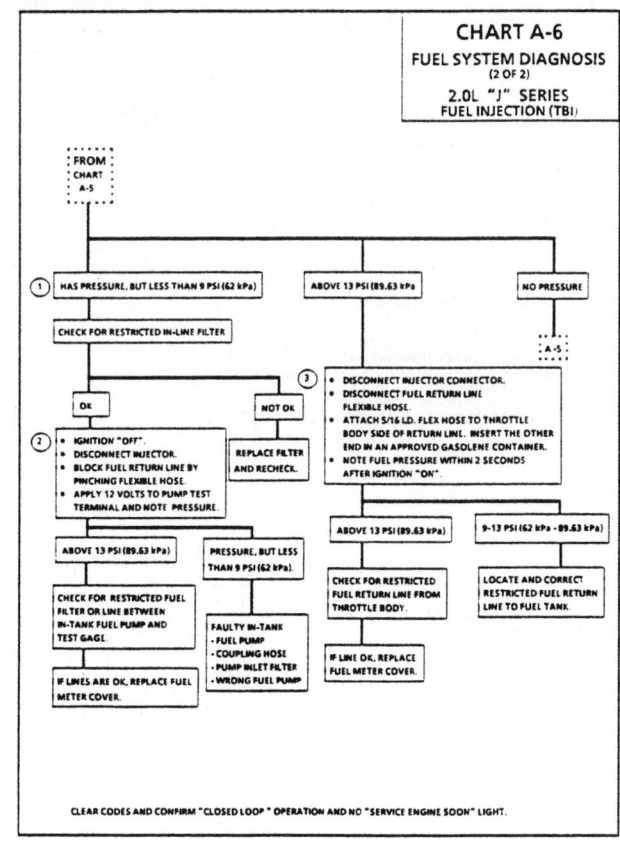

CHART A-6
FUEL SYSTEM DIAGNOSIS
(2 OF 2)

2.0L "J" SERIES
FUEL INJECTION (TBI)

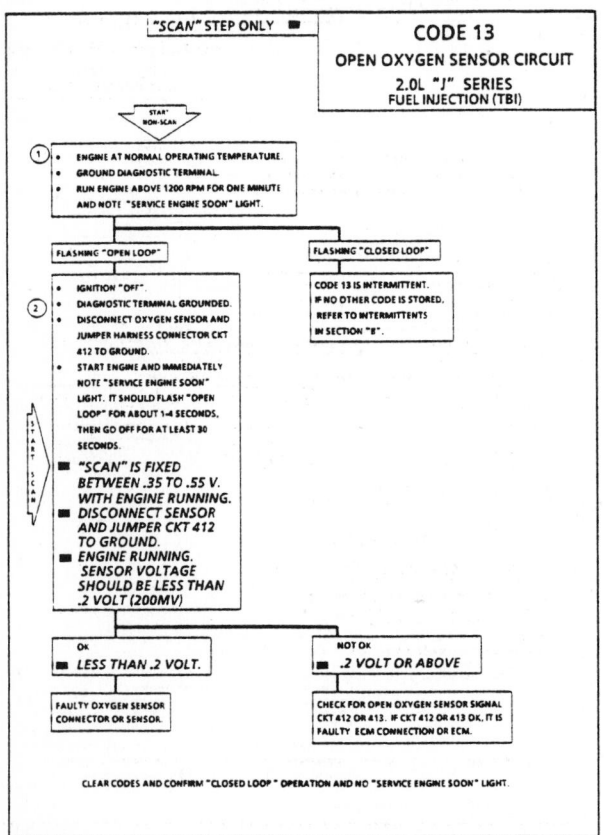

CODE 13
OPEN OXYGEN SENSOR CIRCUIT

2.0L "J" SERIES
FUEL INJECTION (TBI)

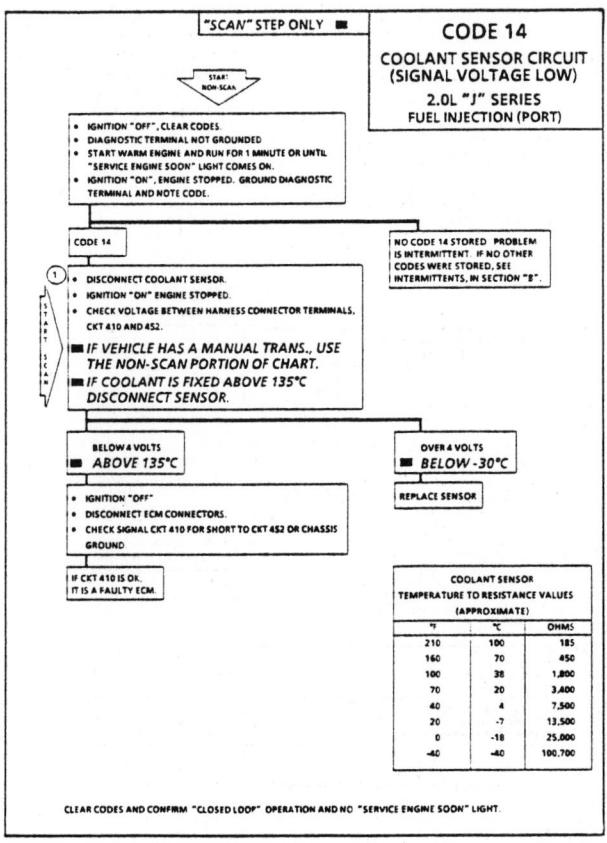

CODE 14
COOLANT SENSOR CIRCUIT
(SIGNAL VOLTAGE LOW)

2.0L "J" SERIES
FUEL INJECTION (PORT)

TBI TROUBLE DIAGNOSTICS

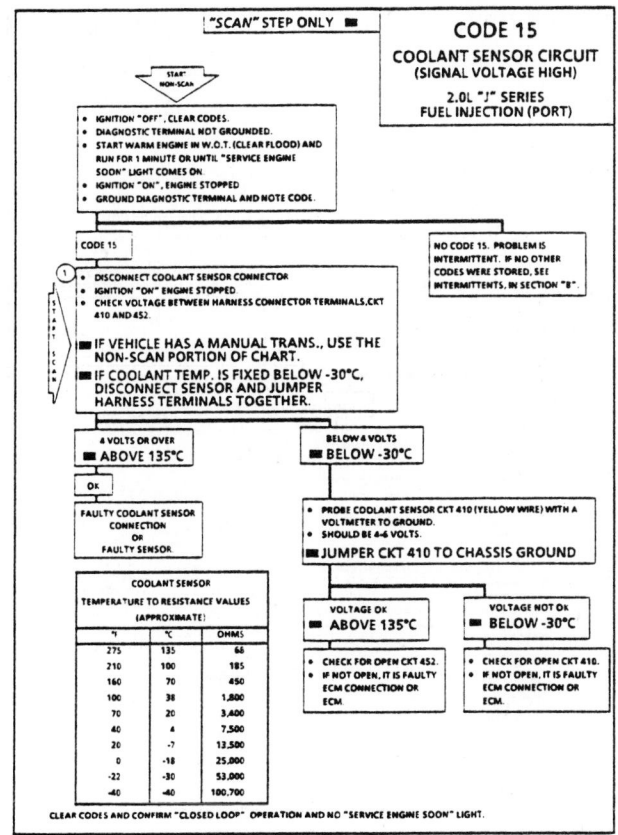

"SCAN" STEP ONLY ■

CODE 15
COOLANT SENSOR CIRCUIT
(SIGNAL VOLTAGE HIGH)

2.0L "J" SERIES
FUEL INJECTION (PORT)

START
NON-SCAN

- IGNITION "OFF". CLEAR CODES.
- DIAGNOSTIC TERMINAL NOT GROUNDED.
- START WARM ENGINE IN W.O.T. (CLEAR FLOOD) AND RUN FOR 1 MINUTE OR UNTIL "SERVICE ENGINE SOON" LIGHT COMES ON.
- IGNITION "ON", ENGINE STOPPED.
- GROUND DIAGNOSTIC TERMINAL AND NOTE CODE.

CODE 15

①
- DISCONNECT COOLANT SENSOR CONNECTOR.
- IGNITION "ON" ENGINE STOPPED.
- CHECK VOLTAGE BETWEEN HARNESS CONNECTOR TERMINALS, CKT 410 AND 452.

■ IF VEHICLE HAS A MANUAL TRANS., USE THE NON-SCAN PORTION OF CHART.
■ IF COOLANT TEMP. IS FIXED BELOW -30°C, DISCONNECT SENSOR AND JUMPER HARNESS TERMINALS TOGETHER.

NO CODE 15. PROBLEM IS INTERMITTENT. IF NO OTHER CODES WERE STORED, SEE INTERMITTENTS IN SECTION "B".

4 VOLTS OR OVER
■ ABOVE 135°C

OK

FAULTY COOLANT SENSOR CONNECTION OR FAULTY SENSOR

BELOW 4 VOLTS
■ BELOW -30°C

- PROBE COOLANT SENSOR CKT 410 (YELLOW WIRE) WITH A VOLTMETER TO GROUND.
- SHOULD BE 4-6 VOLTS.

■ JUMPER CKT 410 TO CHASSIS GROUND

COOLANT SENSOR		
TEMPERATURE TO RESISTANCE VALUES (APPROXIMATE)		
°F	°C	OHMS
275	135	68
210	100	185
160	70	450
100	38	1,800
70	20	3,400
40	4	7,500
20	-7	13,500
0	-18	25,000
-22	-30	53,000
-40	-40	100,700

VOLTAGE OK
■ ABOVE 135°C

- CHECK FOR OPEN CKT 452.
- IF NOT OPEN, IT IS FAULTY ECM CONNECTION OR ECM.

VOLTAGE NOT OK
■ BELOW -30°C

- CHECK FOR OPEN CKT 410.
- IF NOT OPEN, IT IS FAULTY ECM CONNECTION OR ECM.

CLEAR CODES AND CONFIRM "CLOSED LOOP" OPERATION AND NO "SERVICE ENGINE SOON" LIGHT.

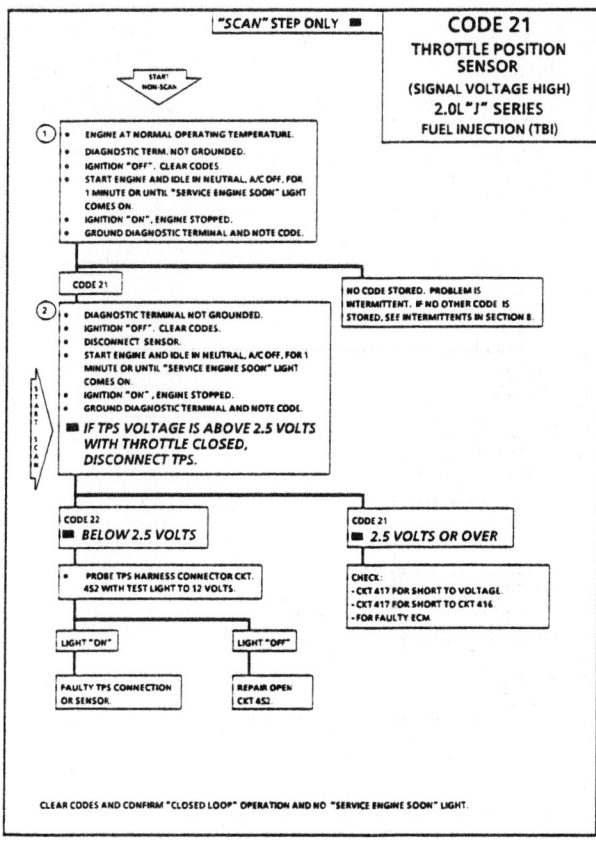

"SCAN" STEP ONLY ■

CODE 21
THROTTLE POSITION SENSOR
(SIGNAL VOLTAGE HIGH)

2.0L "J" SERIES
FUEL INJECTION (TBI)

START
NON-SCAN

①
- ENGINE AT NORMAL OPERATING TEMPERATURE.
- DIAGNOSTIC TERM. NOT GROUNDED.
- IGNITION "OFF". CLEAR CODES.
- START ENGINE AND IDLE IN NEUTRAL, A/C OFF, FOR 1 MINUTE OR UNTIL "SERVICE ENGINE SOON" LIGHT COMES ON.
- IGNITION "ON", ENGINE STOPPED.
- GROUND DIAGNOSTIC TERMINAL AND NOTE CODE.

CODE 21

②
- DIAGNOSTIC TERMINAL NOT GROUNDED.
- IGNITION "OFF". CLEAR CODES.
- DISCONNECT SENSOR.
- START ENGINE AND IDLE IN NEUTRAL, A/C OFF, FOR 1 MINUTE OR UNTIL "SERVICE ENGINE SOON" LIGHT COMES ON.
- IGNITION "ON", ENGINE STOPPED.
- GROUND DIAGNOSTIC TERMINAL AND NOTE CODE.

■ IF TPS VOLTAGE IS ABOVE 2.5 VOLTS WITH THROTTLE CLOSED, DISCONNECT TPS.

NO CODE STORED. PROBLEM IS INTERMITTENT. IF NO OTHER CODE IS STORED, SEE INTERMITTENTS IN SECTION 8.

CODE 22
■ BELOW 2.5 VOLTS

- PROBE TPS HARNESS CONNECTOR CKT. 452 WITH TEST LIGHT TO 12 VOLTS.

CODE 21
■ 2.5 VOLTS OR OVER

CHECK:
- CKT 417 FOR SHORT TO VOLTAGE.
- CKT 417 FOR SHORT TO CKT 416.
- FOR FAULTY ECM.

LIGHT "ON"

FAULTY TPS CONNECTION OR SENSOR

LIGHT "OFF"

REPAIR OPEN CKT 452.

CLEAR CODES AND CONFIRM "CLOSED LOOP" OPERATION AND NO "SERVICE ENGINE SOON" LIGHT.

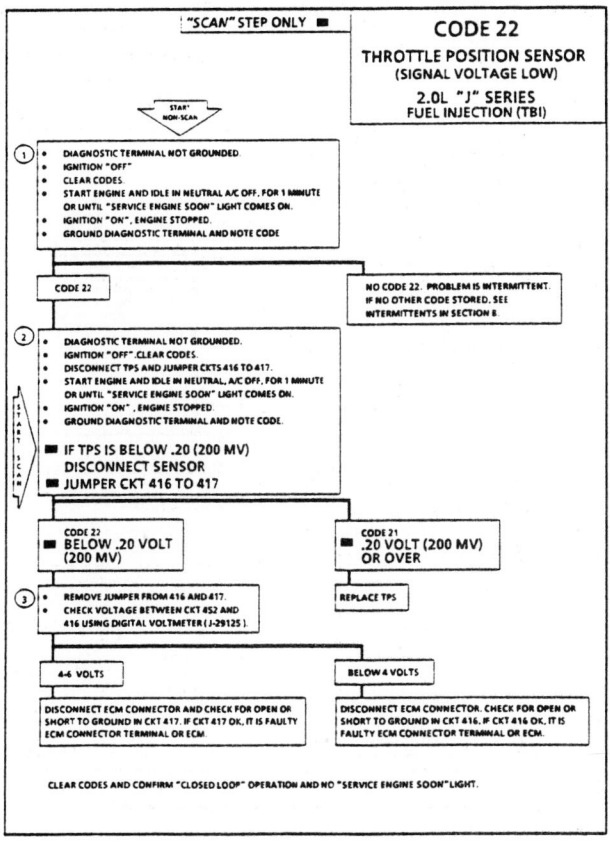

"SCAN" STEP ONLY ■

CODE 22
THROTTLE POSITION SENSOR
(SIGNAL VOLTAGE LOW)

2.0L "J" SERIES
FUEL INJECTION (TBI)

START
NON-SCAN

①
- DIAGNOSTIC TERMINAL NOT GROUNDED.
- IGNITION "OFF"
- CLEAR CODES.
- START ENGINE AND IDLE IN NEUTRAL A/C OFF, FOR 1 MINUTE OR UNTIL "SERVICE ENGINE SOON" LIGHT COMES ON.
- IGNITION "ON", ENGINE STOPPED.
- GROUND DIAGNOSTIC TERMINAL AND NOTE CODE

CODE 22

②
- DIAGNOSTIC TERMINAL NOT GROUNDED.
- IGNITION "OFF". CLEAR CODES.
- DISCONNECT TPS AND JUMPER CKTS 416 TO 417.
- START ENGINE AND IDLE IN NEUTRAL, A/C OFF, FOR 1 MINUTE OR UNTIL "SERVICE ENGINE SOON" LIGHT COMES ON.
- IGNITION "ON", ENGINE STOPPED.
- GROUND DIAGNOSTIC TERMINAL AND NOTE CODE.

■ IF TPS IS BELOW .20 (200 MV) DISCONNECT SENSOR
■ JUMPER CKT 416 TO 417

NO CODE 22. PROBLEM IS INTERMITTENT. IF NO OTHER CODE STORED, SEE INTERMITTENTS IN SECTION 8.

CODE 22
■ BELOW .20 VOLT (200 MV)

CODE 21
■ .20 VOLT (200 MV) OR OVER

③
- REMOVE JUMPER FROM 416 AND 417.
- CHECK VOLTAGE BETWEEN CKT 452 AND 416 USING DIGITAL VOLTMETER (J-29125).

REPLACE TPS

4-6 VOLTS

BELOW 4 VOLTS

DISCONNECT ECM CONNECTOR AND CHECK FOR OPEN OR SHORT TO GROUND IN CKT 417. IF CKT 417 OK, IT IS FAULTY ECM CONNECTOR TERMINAL OR ECM.

DISCONNECT ECM CONNECTOR. CHECK FOR OPEN OR SHORT TO GROUND IN CKT 416. IF CKT 416 OK, IT IS FAULTY ECM CONNECTOR TERMINAL OR ECM.

CLEAR CODES AND CONFIRM "CLOSED LOOP" OPERATION AND NO "SERVICE ENGINE SOON" LIGHT.

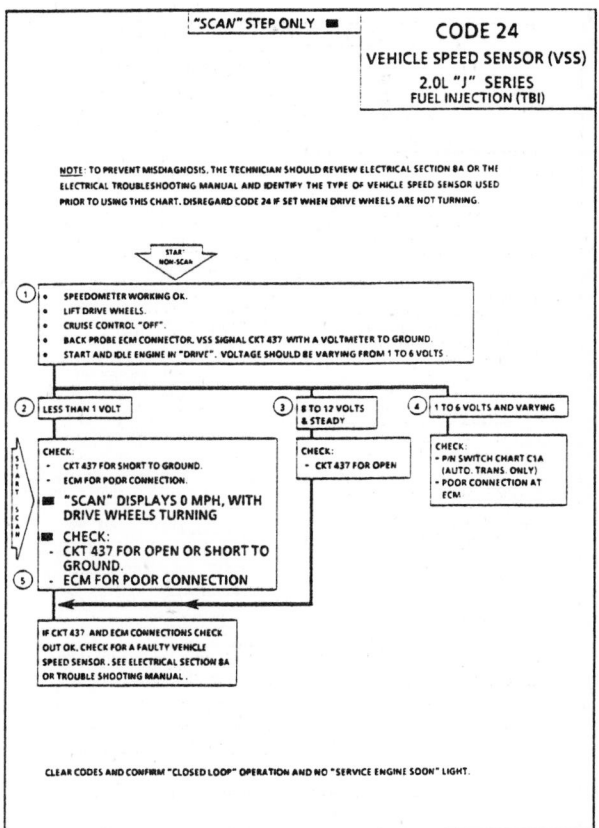

"SCAN" STEP ONLY ■

CODE 24
VEHICLE SPEED SENSOR (VSS)

2.0L "J" SERIES
FUEL INJECTION (TBI)

NOTE: TO PREVENT MISDIAGNOSIS, THE TECHNICIAN SHOULD REVIEW ELECTRICAL SECTION 8A OR THE ELECTRICAL TROUBLESHOOTING MANUAL AND IDENTIFY THE TYPE OF VEHICLE SPEED SENSOR USED PRIOR TO USING THIS CHART. DISREGARD CODE 24 IF SET WHEN DRIVE WHEELS ARE NOT TURNING.

START
NON-SCAN

①
- SPEEDOMETER WORKING OK.
- LIFT DRIVE WHEELS.
- CRUISE CONTROL "OFF".
- BACK PROBE ECM CONNECTOR, VSS SIGNAL CKT 437 WITH A VOLTMETER TO GROUND.
- START AND IDLE ENGINE IN "DRIVE". VOLTAGE SHOULD BE VARYING FROM 1 TO 6 VOLTS.

② LESS THAN 1 VOLT

③ 8 TO 12 VOLTS & STEADY

④ 1 TO 6 VOLTS AND VARYING

CHECK:
- CKT 437 FOR SHORT TO GROUND.
- ECM FOR POOR CONNECTION.

■ "SCAN" DISPLAYS 0 MPH, WITH DRIVE WHEELS TURNING
■ CHECK:
- CKT 437 FOR OPEN OR SHORT TO GROUND.
⑤ - ECM FOR POOR CONNECTION

CHECK:
- CKT 437 FOR OPEN

CHECK:
- PIN SWITCH CHART C1A (AUTO. TRANS. ONLY)
- POOR CONNECTION AT ECM

IF CKT 437 AND ECM CONNECTIONS CHECK OUT OK, CHECK FOR A FAULTY VEHICLE SPEED SENSOR. SEE ELECTRICAL SECTION 8A OR TROUBLE SHOOTING MANUAL.

CLEAR CODES AND CONFIRM "CLOSED LOOP" OPERATION AND NO "SERVICE ENGINE SOON" LIGHT.

TBI TROUBLE DIAGNOSTICS

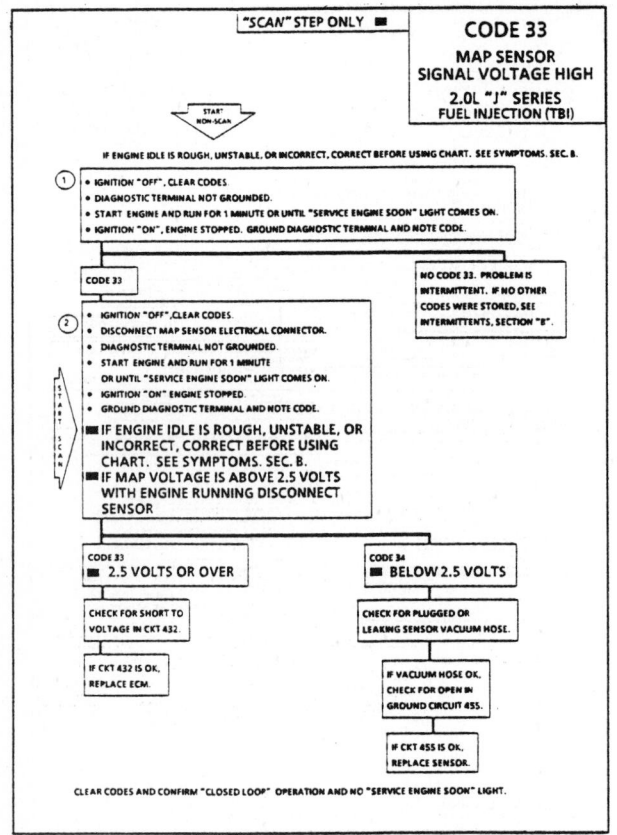

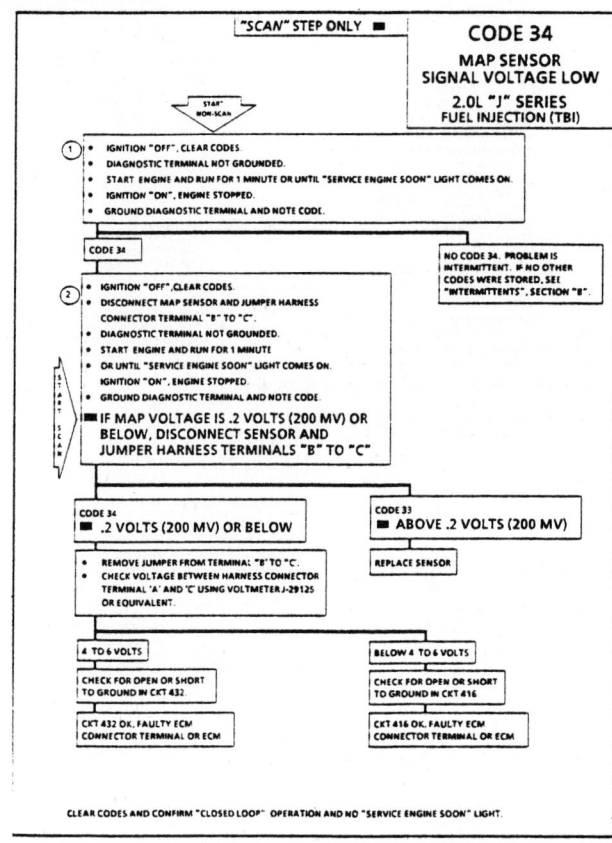

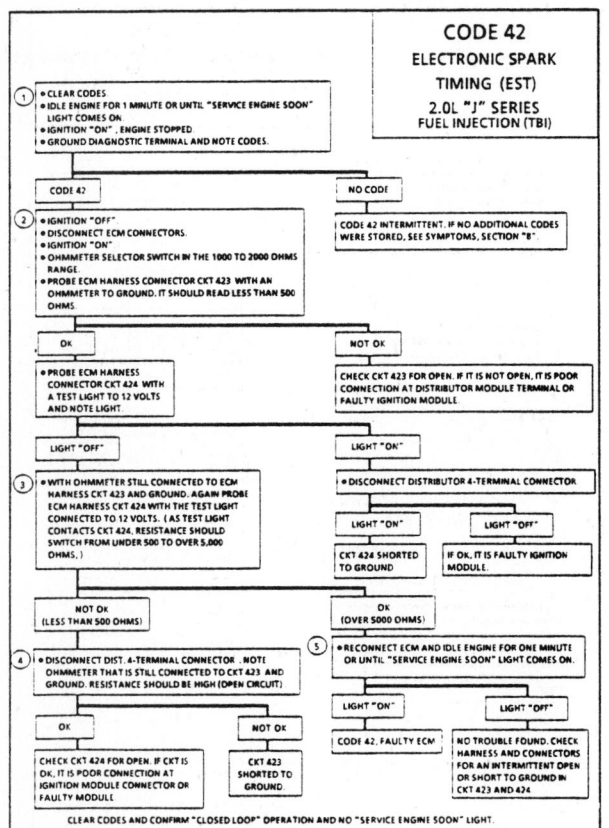

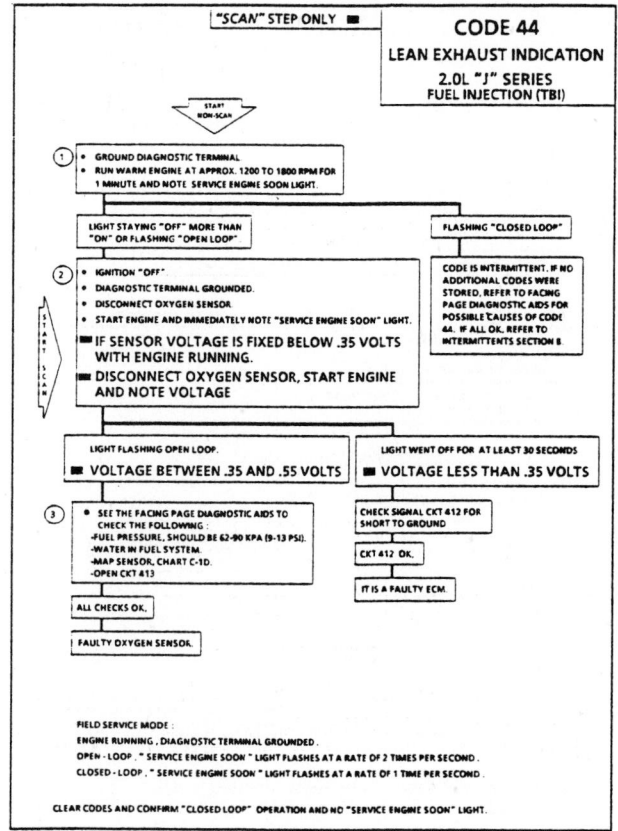

TBI TROUBLE DIAGNOSTICS

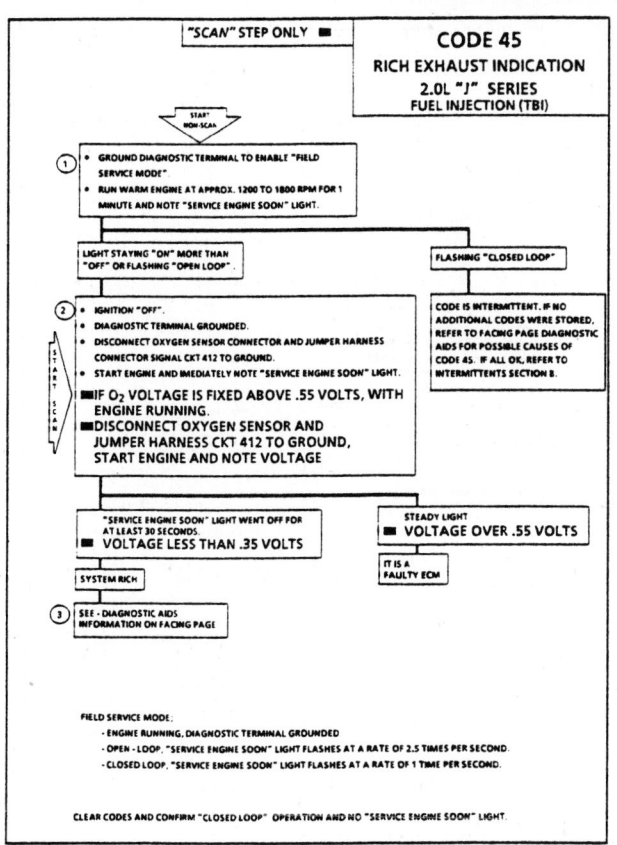

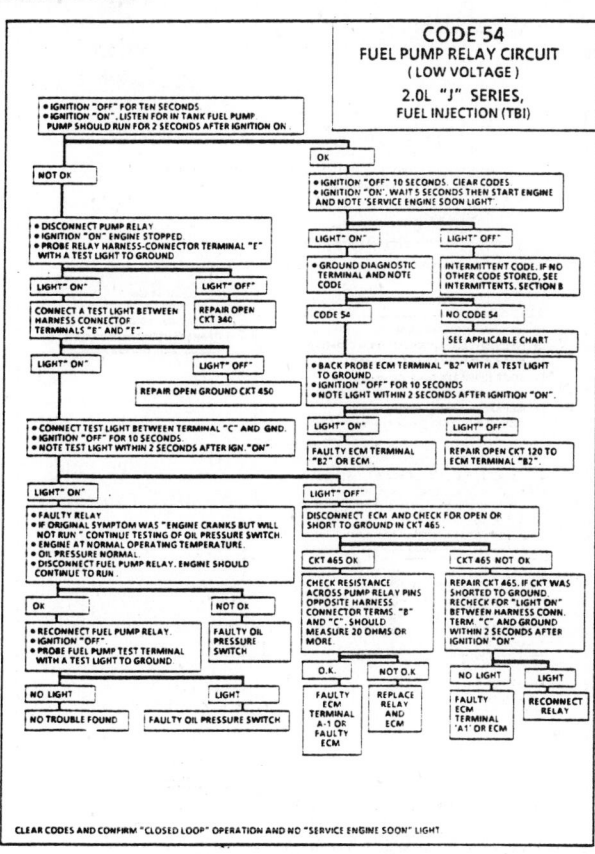

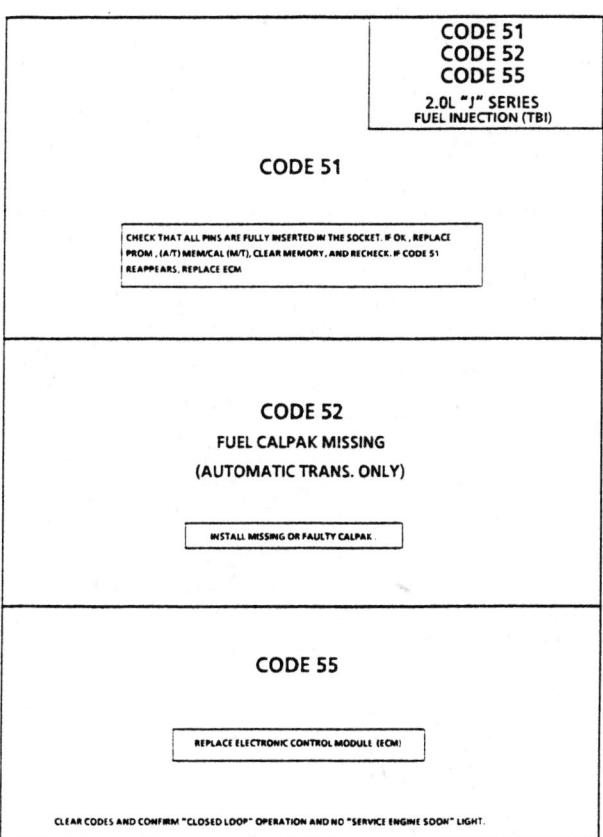

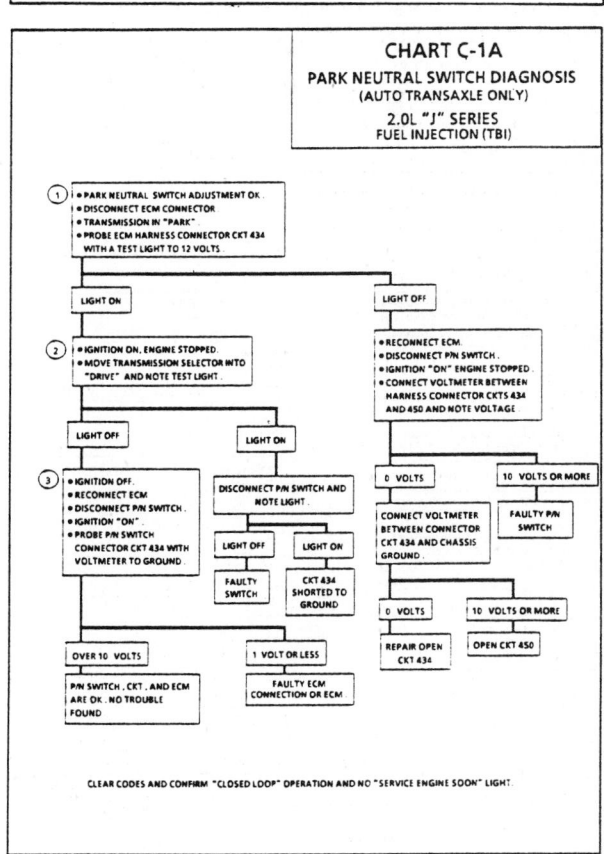

TBI TROUBLE DIAGNOSTICS

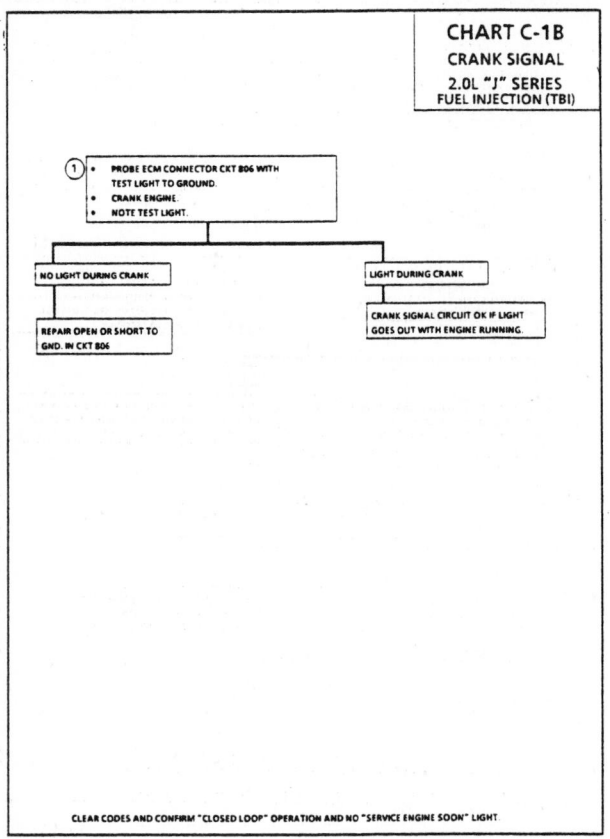

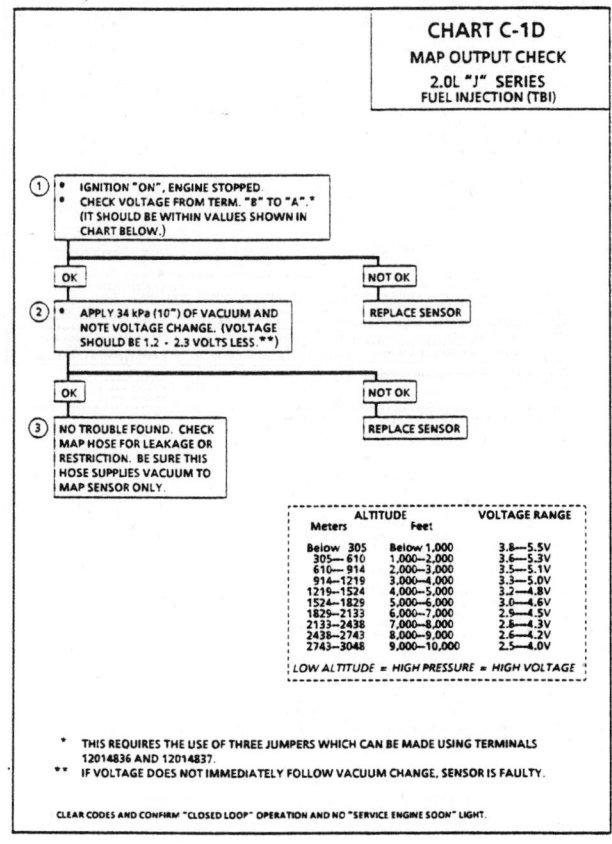

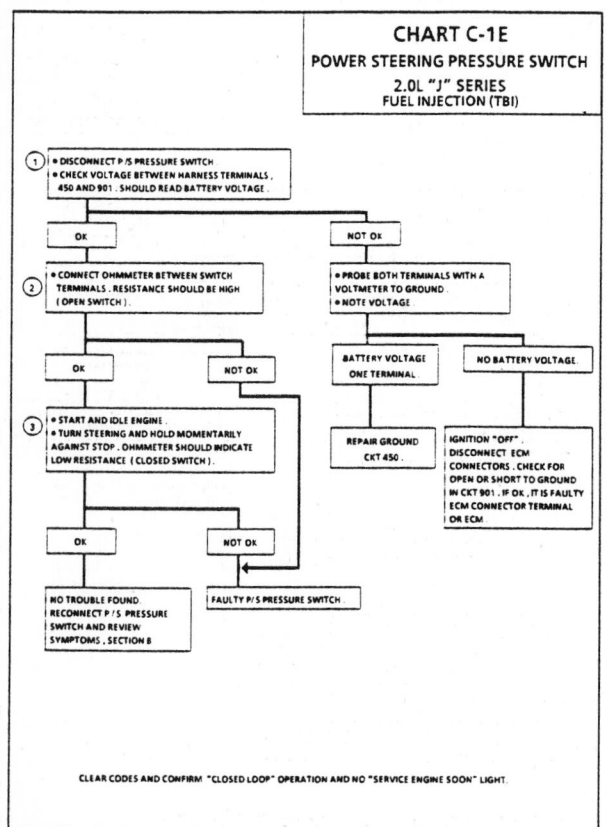

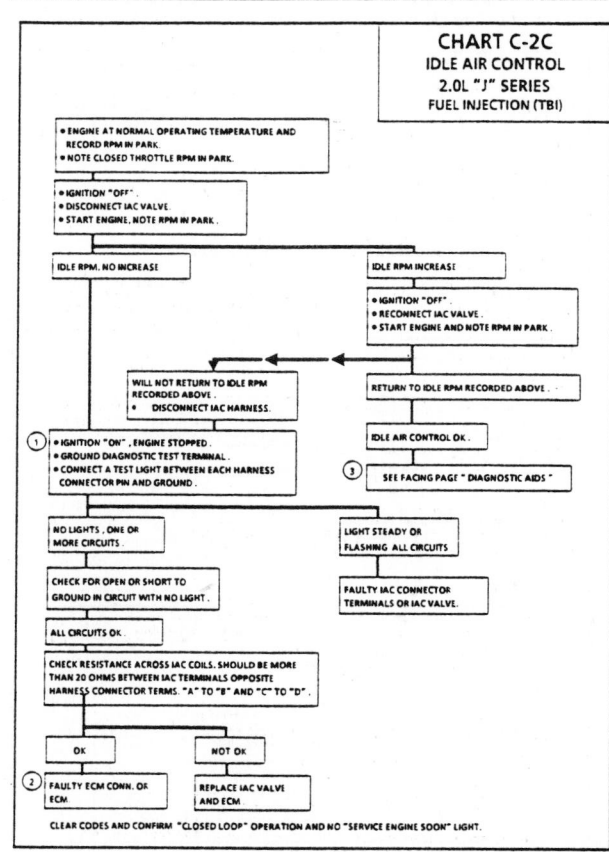

TBI TROUBLE DIAGNOSTICS

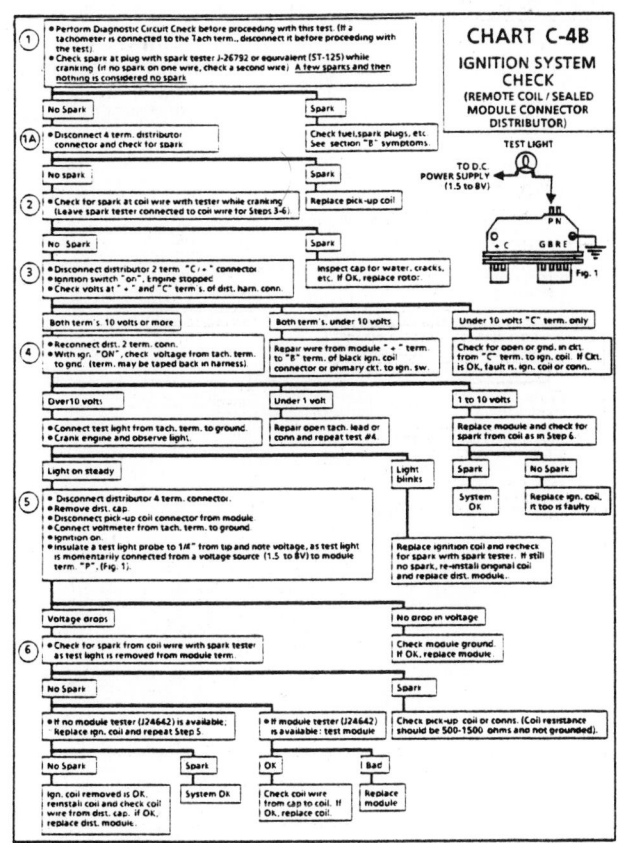

CHART C-4B

IGNITION SYSTEM CHECK
(REMOTE COIL / SEALED MODULE CONNECTOR DISTRIBUTOR)

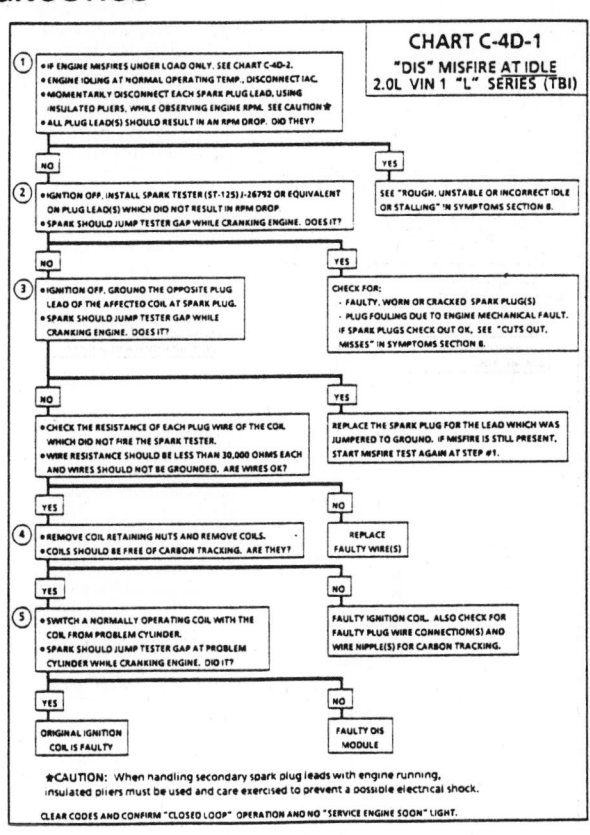

CHART C-4D-1

"DIS" MISFIRE AT IDLE
2.0L VIN 1 "L" SERIES (TBI)

★CAUTION: When handling secondary spark plug leads with engine running, insulated pliers must be used and care exercised to prevent a possible electrical shock.

CLEAR CODES AND CONFIRM "CLOSED LOOP" OPERATION AND NO "SERVICE ENGINE SOON" LIGHT.

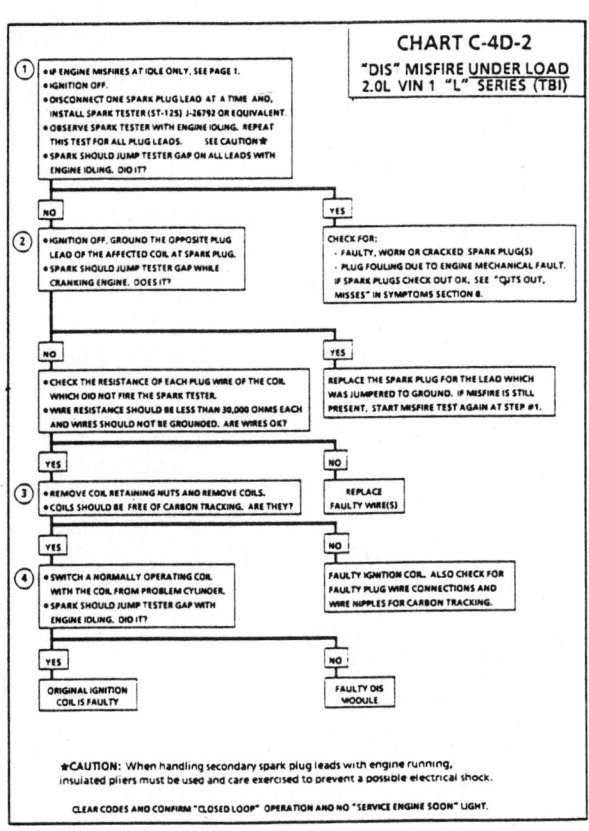

CHART C-4D-2

"DIS" MISFIRE UNDER LOAD
2.0L VIN 1 "L" SERIES (TBI)

★CAUTION: When handling secondary spark plug leads with engine running, insulated pliers must be used and care exercised to prevent a possible electrical shock.

CLEAR CODES AND CONFIRM "CLOSED LOOP" OPERATION AND NO "SERVICE ENGINE SOON" LIGHT.

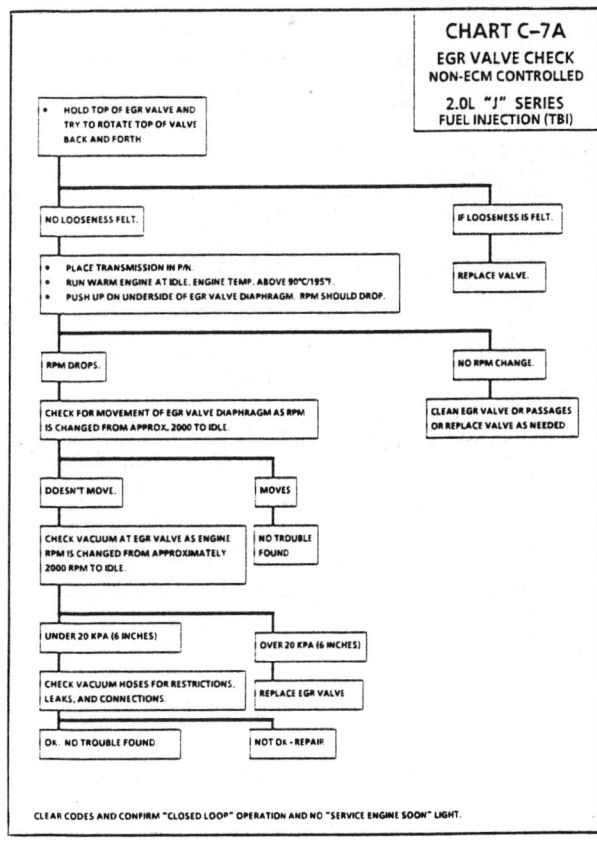

CHART C-7A

EGR VALVE CHECK
NON-ECM CONTROLLED

2.0L "J" SERIES
FUEL INJECTION (TBI)

CLEAR CODES AND CONFIRM "CLOSED LOOP" OPERATION AND NO "SERVICE ENGINE SOON" LIGHT.

TBI TROUBLE DIAGNOSTICS

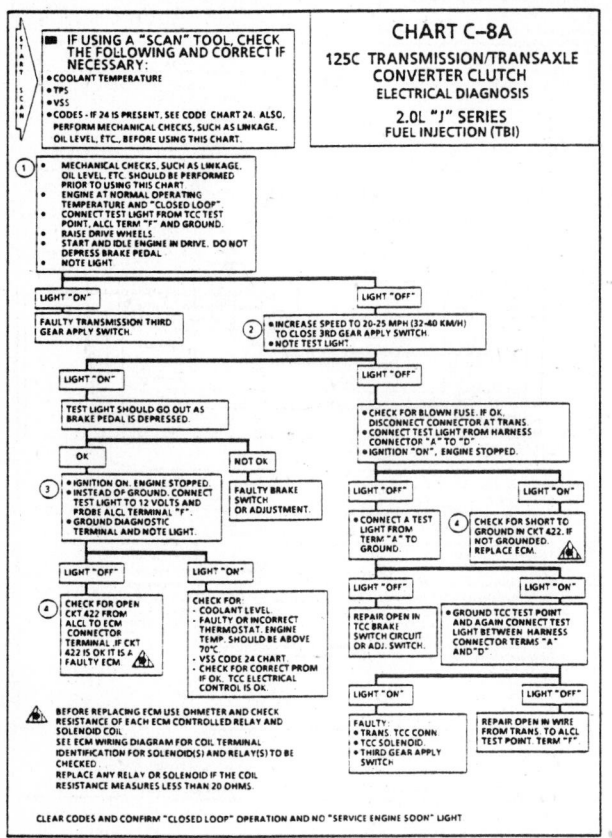

CHART C-8A

125C TRANSMISSION/TRANSAXLE
CONVERTER CLUTCH
ELECTRICAL DIAGNOSIS

2.0L "J" SERIES
FUEL INJECTION (TBI)

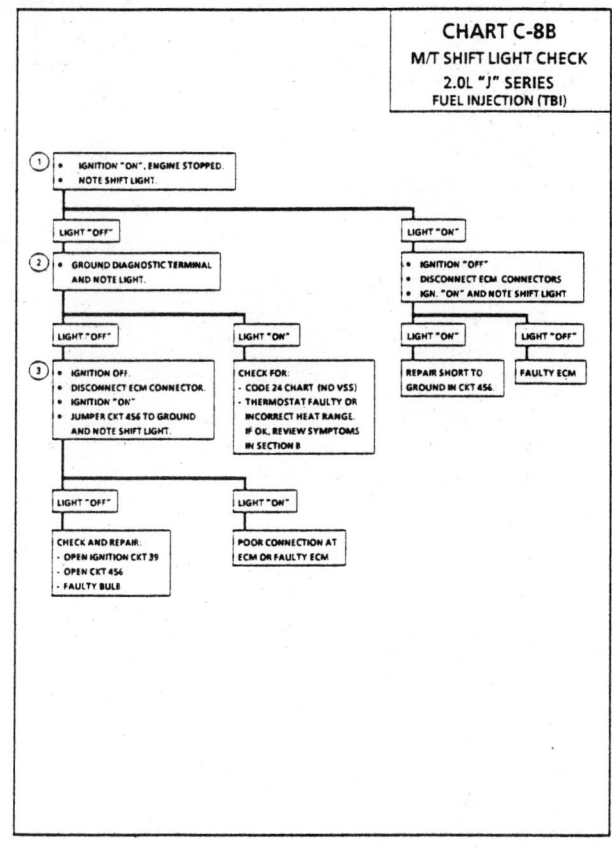

CHART C-8B

M/T SHIFT LIGHT CHECK

2.0L "J" SERIES
FUEL INJECTION (TBI)

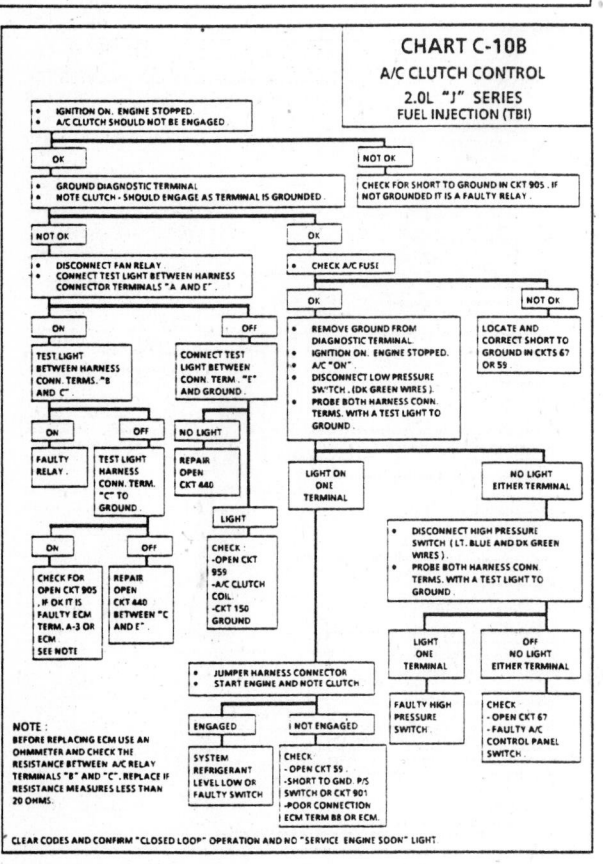

CHART C-10B

A/C CLUTCH CONTROL

2.0L "J" SERIES
FUEL INJECTION (TBI)

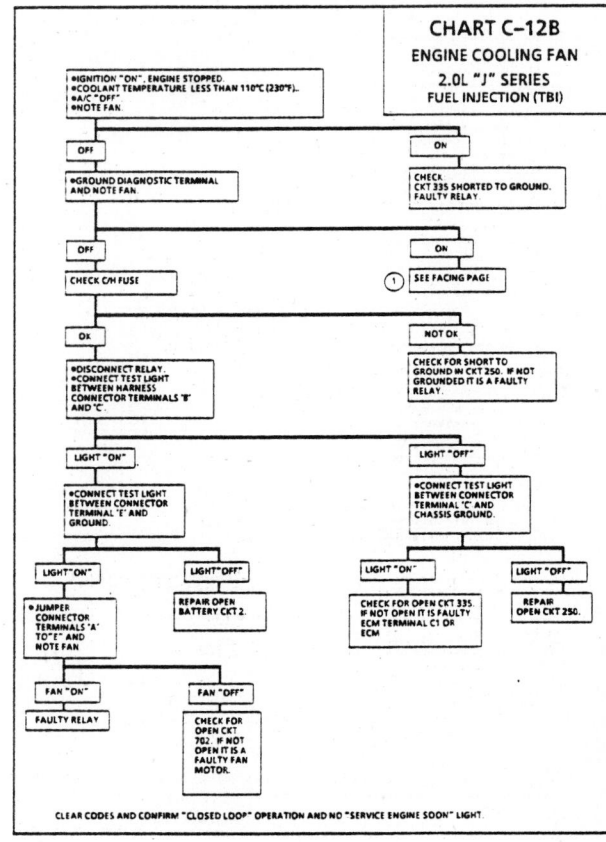

CHART C-12B

ENGINE COOLING FAN

2.0L "J" SERIES
FUEL INJECTION (TBI)

TBI TROUBLE DIAGNOSTICS

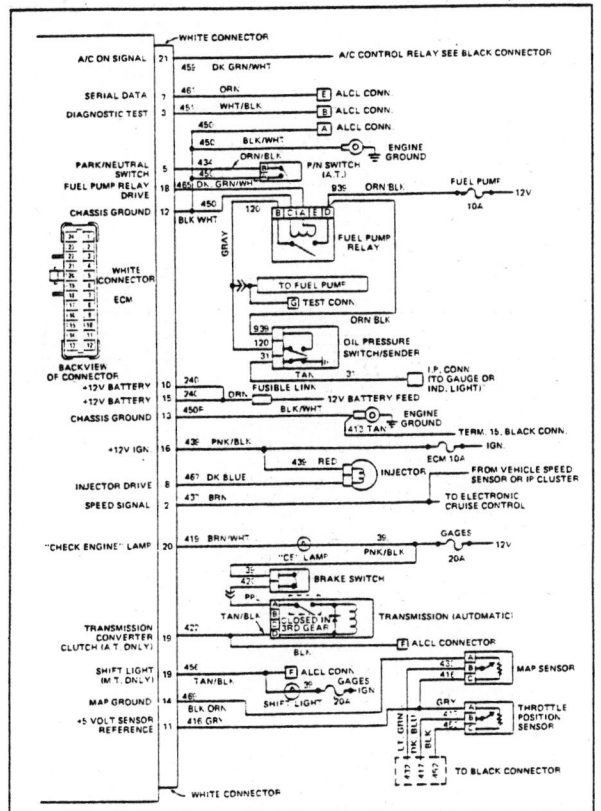

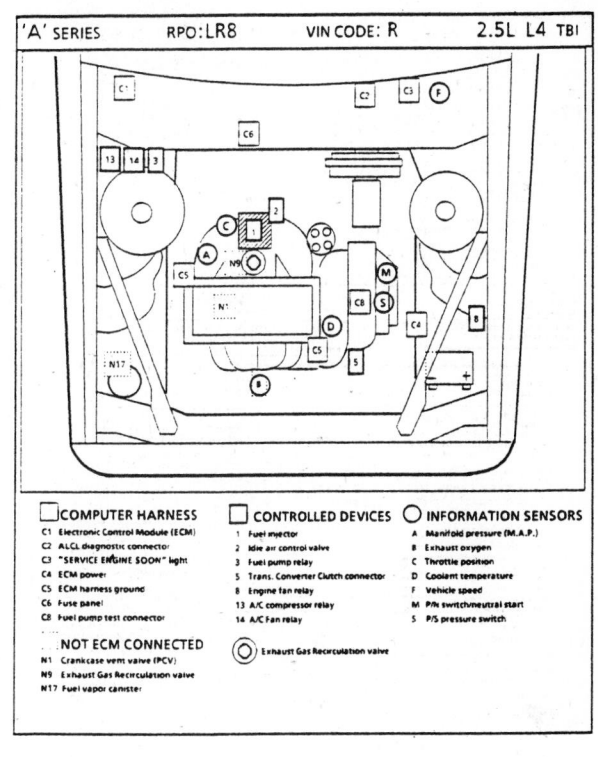

'A' SERIES   RPO: LR8   VIN CODE: R   2.5L L4 TBI

☐ **COMPUTER HARNESS**
- C1 Electronic Control Module (ECM)
- C2 ALCL diagnostic connector
- C3 "SERVICE ENGINE SOON" light
- C4 ECM power
- C5 ECM harness ground
- C6 Fuse panel
- C8 Fuel pump test connector

NOT ECM CONNECTED
- N1 Crankcase vent valve (PCV)
- N9 Exhaust Gas Recirculation valve
- N17 Fuel vapor canister

☐ **CONTROLLED DEVICES**
1. Fuel injector
2. Idle air control valve
3. Fuel pump relay
4. Trans. Converter Clutch connector
5. Trans. Converter Clutch connector
6. Engine fan relay
13. A/C compressor relay
14. A/C Fan relay

○ **INFORMATION SENSORS**
- A Manifold pressure (M.A.P.)
- B Exhaust oxygen
- C Throttle position
- D Coolant temperature
- F Vehicle speed
- M P/N switch/neutral start
- S P/S pressure switch

○ Exhaust Gas Recirculation valve

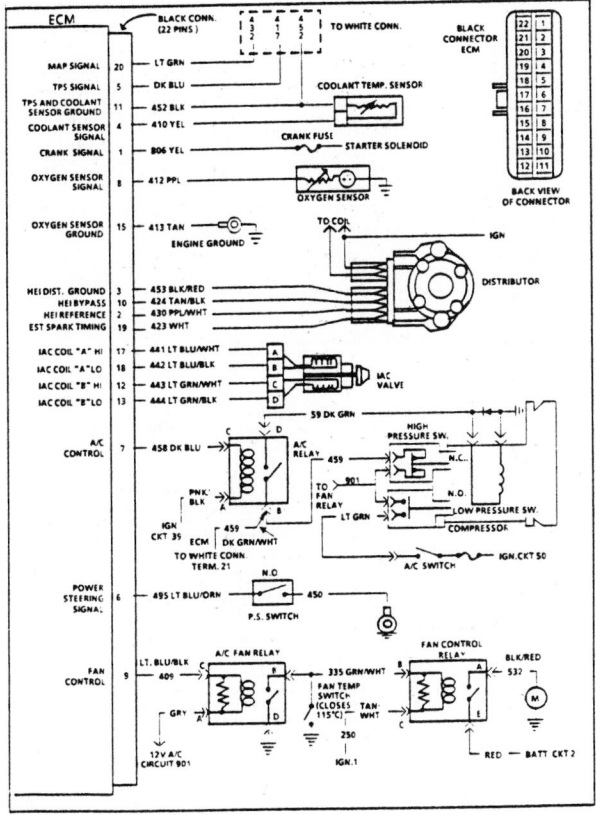

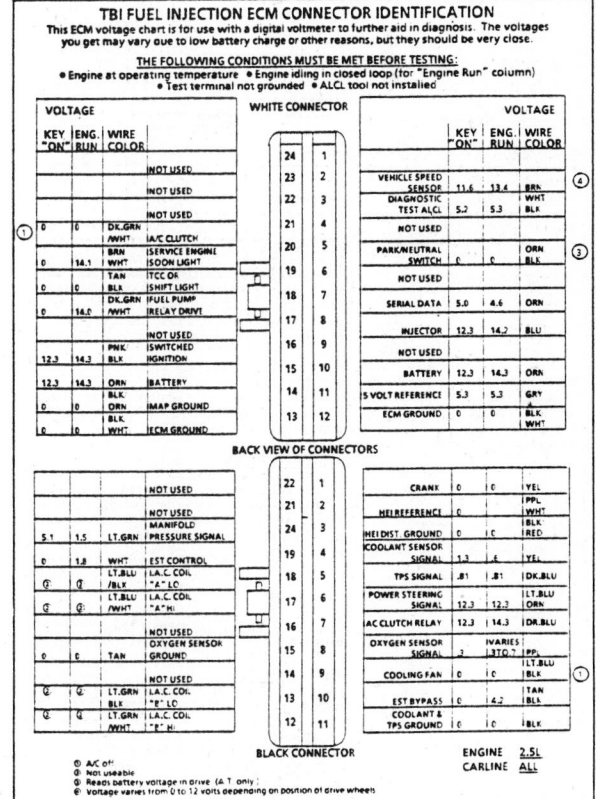

TBI FUEL INJECTION ECM CONNECTOR IDENTIFICATION
This ECM voltage chart is for use with a digital voltmeter to further aid in diagnosis. The voltages you get may vary due to low battery charge or other reasons, but they should be very close.

THE FOLLOWING CONDITIONS MUST BE MET BEFORE TESTING:
- Engine at operating temperature
- Engine idling in closed loop (for "Engine Run" column)
- Test terminal not grounded
- ALCL tool not installed

ENGINE 2.5L
CARLINE ALL

TBI TROUBLE DIAGNOSTICS

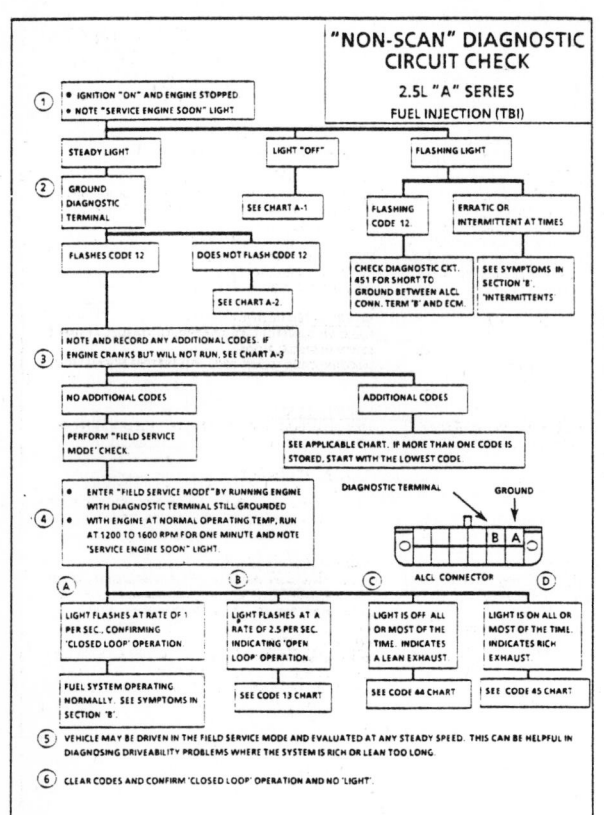

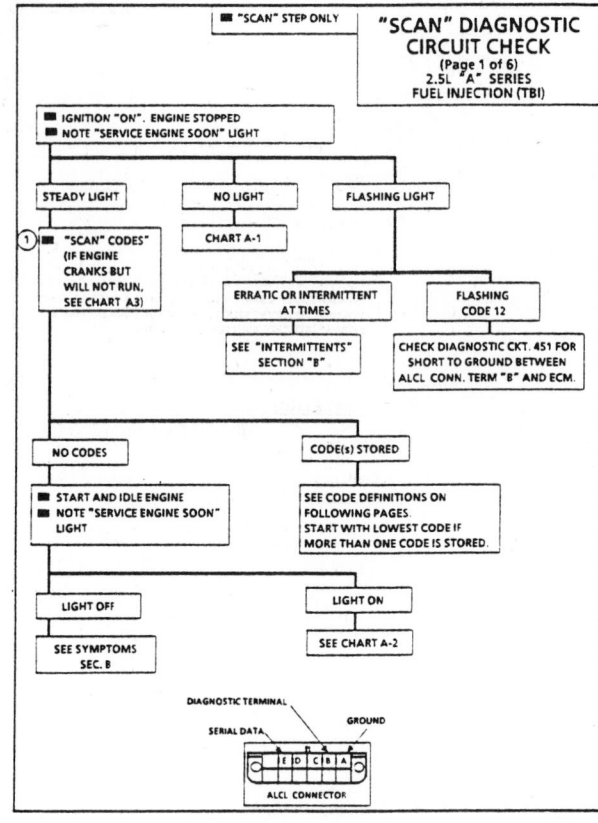

"SCAN" DIAGNOSTIC CIRCUIT CHECK
(Page 3 of 6) (CODE DEFINITIONS)

CODES	DEFINITIONS
CODE 21 • IGNITION "ON". • THROTTLE CLOSED. • ENGINE STOPPED. • "SCAN" TPS	**HARD FAILURE -** "SCAN" TOOL DISPLAYS A CLOSED THROTTLE VOLTAGE OVER 2.5 VOLTS. SIGNAL VOLTAGE TOO HIGH, GROUND WIRE OPEN, SIGNAL LINE SHORTED TO SENSOR REF. LINE OR FAULTY SENSOR. SEE CODE CHART 21. **INTERMITTENT CODE -** "SCAN" TOOL DISPLAYS THROTTLE POSITION IN VOLTS. SHOULD READ BETWEEN 020-125 (200 mv AND 1.25 V). WITH THROTTLE CLOSED AND IGNITION ON OR AT IDLE, VOLTAGE SHOULD INCREASE AT A STEADY RATE AS THROTTLE IS MOVED TOWARD A WIDE OPEN POSITION. SEE "INTERMITTENTS" SECTION B.
CODE 22 • IGNITION "ON" • ENGINE STOPPED. • THROTTLE CLOSED. • "SCAN" TPS	**HARD FAILURE -** "SCAN" TOOL DISPLAYS BELOW 020V (200 MV). OPEN OR SHORT TO GROUND IN 5V REFERENCE OR SIGNAL CIRCUIT, OR FAULTY SENSOR. SEE CODE CHART 22. **INTERMITTENT CODE -** "SCAN"TOOL DISPLAYS THROTTLE POSITION IN VOLTS. SHOULD READ BETWEEN 020-125 (200 mv AND 1.25 V). WITH THROTTLE CLOSED AND IGNITION ON OR AT IDLE, VOLTAGE SHOULD INCREASE AT A STEADY RATE AS THROTTLE IS MOVED TOWARD A WIDE OPEN POSITION. SEE "INTERMITTENTS" SECTION B.
CODE 24 • ENGINE RUNNING. • DRIVE WHEELS TURNING. • "SCAN" MPH.	**HARD FAILURE -** "SCAN" TOOL DISPLAYS 0 MPH. IF SPEEDOMETER IS WORKING OK, THEN THE VSS SIGNAL INPUT IS OPEN, SHORTED TO GROUND, OR THE BUFFER IS DEFECTIVE. SEE CODE CHART 24. **INTERMITTENT CODE -** "SCAN" TOOL DISPLAY SHOULD CLOSELY MATCH WITH SPEEDOMETER READING WITH DRIVE WHEELS TURNING. SEE 'INTERMITTENTS' SECTION B. "SCAN" DISPLAY INDICATES THAT PARK/NEUTRAL SWITCH DID NOT "SWITCH" WHEN SHIFTING NEUTRAL TO DRIVE (A.T. ONLY). SEE CHART C-1A. DISREGARD CODE 24 IF SET WITH DRIVE WHEELS NOT TURNING.

"SCAN" DIAGNOSTIC CIRCUIT CHECK
(Page 2 of 6) (CODE DEFINITIONS)

NOTICE
THE 'DIAGNOSTIC CIRCUIT CHECK' SCAN DATA IS TYPICAL OF THAT DISPLAYED BY A PROPERLY DESIGNED AND CALIBRATED ALCL SCAN DEVICE.

A SCAN DEVICE THAT DISPLAYS FAULTY DATA SHOULD NOT BE USED AND THE PROBLEM REPORTED TO THE DEVICE MANUFACTURER. THE USE OF A FAULTY SCAN DEVICE CAN RESULT IN MISDIAGNOSIS AND UNNECESSARY PARTS REPLACEMENT.

CODES	DEFINITIONS
CODE 13 • "SCAN" IN ALCL "SPECIAL" MODE • ENGINE IDLING AT 1000 RPM FOR 2 MINUTES. • COOLANT 75° TO 95° C. • "SCAN" OXYGEN SENSOR VOLTAGE	**HARD FAILURE -** "SCAN" DISPLAY FIXED BETWEEN .35 TO .55 V. OPEN CIRCUIT CONDITION. SEE CODE CHART 13. **INTERMITTENT CODE -** NORMAL"SCAN" VOLTAGE WILL VARY BETWEEN 100MV TO 999 MV (.1 AND 1.0 VOLT). SEE "INTERMITTENTS" SECTION B.
CODE 14 • IGNITION ON. • ENGINE STOPPED. • SCAN" COOLANT TEMPERATURE.	**HARD FAILURE -** "SCAN" DISPLAY FIXED ABOVE 135°C. CIRCUIT SHORTED TO GROUND OR FAULTY SENSOR. SEE CODE CHART 14. **INTERMITTENT CODE -** "SCAN" DISPLAY READS ENGINE TEMP. IN DEGREES CENTIGRADE. AFTER ENGINE IS STARTED, THE TEMPERATURE SHOULD RISE STEADILY TO ABOUT 90°C THEN STABILIZE WHEN THERMOSTAT OPENS. SEE "INTERMITTENTS" SECTION B.
CODE 15 • IGNITION ON. • ENGINE STOPPED. • "SCAN" COOLANT TEMPERATURE.	**HARD FAILURE -** "SCAN" DISPLAY FIXED BELOW -30°C. CIRCUIT OPEN OR FAULTY SENSOR. SEE CODE CHART 15. **INTERMITTENT CODE -** "SCAN" TOOL DISPLAYS ENGINE COOLANT TEMPERATURE IN DEGREES CENTIGRADE. AFTER ENGINE IS STARTED, THE TEMPERATURE SHOULD RISE STEADILY TO ABOUT 90°C, THEN STABILIZE WHEN THERMOSTAT OPENS. SEE "INTERMITTENTS" SECTION B.

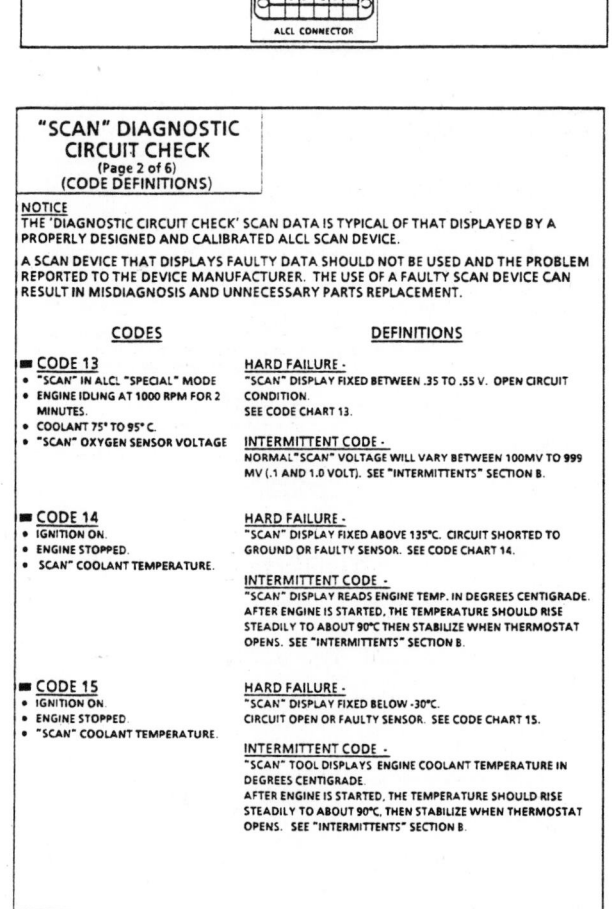

TBI TROUBLE DIAGNOSTICS

"SCAN" DIAGNOSTIC CIRCUIT CHECK
(Page 4 of 6)
(CODE DEFINITIONS)

CODES

■ CODE 33
- ENGINE IDLING.
- "SCAN" MAP.

■ CODE 34
- IGNITION "ON"
- SCAN" MAP.

DEFINITIONS

HARD FAILURE -
"SCAN" TOOL DISPLAYS ABOVE 2.5 VOLTS. SENSOR GROUND CIRCUIT OPEN, LEAKING VACUUM HOSE OR FAULTY SENSOR. SEE CODE CHART 33.

INTERMITTENT CODE -
"SCAN" TOOL DISPLAYS MANIFOLD PRESSURE IN VOLTS. LOW PRESSURE (HIGH VACUUM) DISPLAYS AS A LOW VOLTAGE WHILE A HIGH PRESSURE (LOW VACUUM) DISPLAYS AS A HIGH VOLTAGE. IF ENGINE IDLE IS LOW AND UNSTABLE IT MAY SET CODE 33. SEE "INTERMITTENTS" SECTION B.

HARD FAILURE -
"SCAN" TOOL DISPLAYS BELOW (200 mv) .2 VOLTS. SIGNAL WIRE OR 5V REFERENCE OPEN OR SHORTED TO GROUND OR FAULTY SENSOR. SEE CODE CHART 34.

INTERMITTENT CODE -
"SCAN" TOOL DISPLAYS MANIFOLD PRESSURE IN VOLTS. LOW PRESSURE (HIGH VACUUM) READS A LOW VOLTAGE WHILE A HIGH PRESSURE (LOW VACUUM) READS A HIGH VOLTAGE. SEE "INTERMITTENTS" SECTION B.

"SCAN" DIAGNOSTIC CIRCUIT CHECK
(Page 5 of 6)
(CODE DEFINITIONS)

CODES

■ CODE 35
- A/C OFF.
- ENGINE IDLING IN NEUTRAL
- COOLANT TEMP 70° TO 90°C
- "SCAN" IN "SPECIAL" MODE.
- INCREASE ENGINE RPM TO 2500 TO RESET IAC. CLOSE THROTTLE AND ALLOW IDLE AND IAC COUNTS STABILIZE.

■ CODE 42,
- CLEAR CODES, START AND IDLE ENGINE FOR 1 MINUTE.

■ CODE 44
- "SCAN" TOOL IN "SPECIAL" MODE.
- COOLANT TEMP 75° to 95° C AND CLOSED LOOP
- ENGINE IDLING AT 1000 RPM.

DEFINITIONS

HARD FAILURE -
"SCAN" TOOL DISPLAYS IDLE SPEED 950 RPM OR ABOVE. IAC COUNTS "0". THIS CONDITION IS USUALLY A SMALL VACUUM LEAK SUCH AS THERMAC OR CRUISE CONTROL HOSE DISCONNECTED.
OR
ENGINE SPEED 950 RPM OR BELOW.
IAC COUNTS ABOVE 80.
SEE CODE 35 CHART.

INTERMITTENT CODE -
FOLLOWING AN IAC RESET, RPM SHOULD STABLIZE AT 1000 ± 50 RPM IN SPECIAL MODE.
DISCONNECTING "SCAN" TOOL WILL RESTORE NORMAL IDLE.

HARD FAILURE -
SERVICE ENGINE SOON" ON, SCAN TOOL DISPLAYS CODE 42. SEE CODE CHART 42.

INTERMITTENT CODE -
THE SCAN TOOL DOES NOT HAVE THE ABILITY TO HELP DIAGNOSE A CODE 42 PROBLEM. IF NO "SERVICE ENGINE SOON "LIGHT, REFER TO INTERMITTENTS IN SECTION "B".

HARD FAILURE -
"SCAN" TOOL DISPLAYED O$_2$ VOLTAGE CONSISTENTLY BELOW .35V. CAUSED BY A LEAN EXHAUST OR SIGNAL CIRCUIT SHORTED TO GROUND. SEE CODE CHART 44.

INTERMITTENT CODE -
NORMAL "SCAN" DISPLAY WILL VARY BETWEEN 100 MV AND 999MV. (.1 to 1.0V). ALSO SEE CROSSCOUNTS, RICH - LEAN INDICATION, O$_2$ VOLTAGE. SEE "SCAN" INFORMATION IN INTRODUCTION.

"SCAN" DIAGNOSTIC CIRCUIT CHECK
(Page 6 of 6)
(CODE DEFINITIONS)

CODES

■ CODE 45
- 'SCAN' TOOL IN "SPECIAL" MODE
- ENGINE IDLING AT 1000 RPM
- COOLANT TEMP 75° to 95° C AND IN CLOSED LOOP
- "SCAN" OXYGEN SENSOR VOLTAGE

■ CODE 51
- CLEAR CODES
- START ENGINE
- CHECK FOR CODE

■ CODE 55
- CLEAR CODES
- START ENGINE
- CHECK FOR CODE

DEFINITIONS

HARD FAILURE -
"SCAN" O$_2$ VOLTAGE CONSISTENTLY ABOVE .65V. RICH EXHAUST CAUSING A HIGH O2 VOLTAGE. SEE CODE CHART 45.

INTERMITTENT CODE -
NORMAL "SCAN" VOLTAGE WILL VARY BETWEEN 100 MV AND 999MV. (.1 to 1.0V) ALSO SEE CROSSCOUNTS, RICH - LEAN INDICATION, O$_2$ VOLTAGE. SEE "SCAN" INFORMATION IN INTRODUCTION.

HARD FAILURE -
CODE 51 RESETS WHICH INDICATES A FAULTY PROM. SEE CODE CHART 51.

HARD FAILURE -
CODE 55 RESETS WHICH INDICATES THE ECM IS FAULTY. REPLACE ECM.

CHART A-1
NO 'SERVICE ENGINE SOON' LIGHT
2.5L "A" SERIES
FUEL INJECTION (TBI)

- DISCONNECT BOTH ECM CONNECTORS.
- IGNITION ON
- PROBE CKT 419 WITH A TEST LIGHT TO GROUND AND NOTE 'SERVICE ENGINE SOON' LIGHT

| 'SERVICE ENGINE SOON' LIGHT ON | 'SERVICE ENGINE SOON' LIGHT OFF |

'SERVICE ENGINE SOON' LIGHT ON →
- PROBE CKT 340 AND 439 WITH A TEST LIGHT TO GROUND. LIGHT SHOULD BE "ON" BOTH CIRCUITS.

'SERVICE ENGINE SOON' LIGHT OFF →
CHECK: - FAULTY BULB
- GAGE FUSE
- OPEN CKT 419
- OPEN IGNITION FEED

| OK | NOT OK |

OK →
CHECK ECM GROUND CKTS 450. IF ECM GROUND CKTS ARE OK, IT IS POOR CONNECTION AT ECM OR FAULTY ECM. SEE NOTE.

NOT OK →
REPAIR OPEN IN CKT THAT WILL NOT TURN ON TEST LIGHT.

NOTE:
BEFORE REPLACING ECM, USE AN OHMMETER AND CHECK RESISTANCE OF EACH ECM CONTROLLED RELAY AND SOLENOID COIL.
SEE ECM WIRING DIAGRAM FOR COIL TERMINAL IDENTIFICATION FOR SOLENOID(S) AND RELAY(S) TO BE CHECKED.
REPLACE ANY RELAY OR SOLENOID IF THE COIL RESISTANCE MEASURES LESS THAN 20 OHMS.

CLEAR CODES AND CONFIRM "CLOSED LOOP" OPERATION AND NO "SERVICE ENGINE SOON" LIGHT.

TBI TROUBLE DIAGNOSTICS

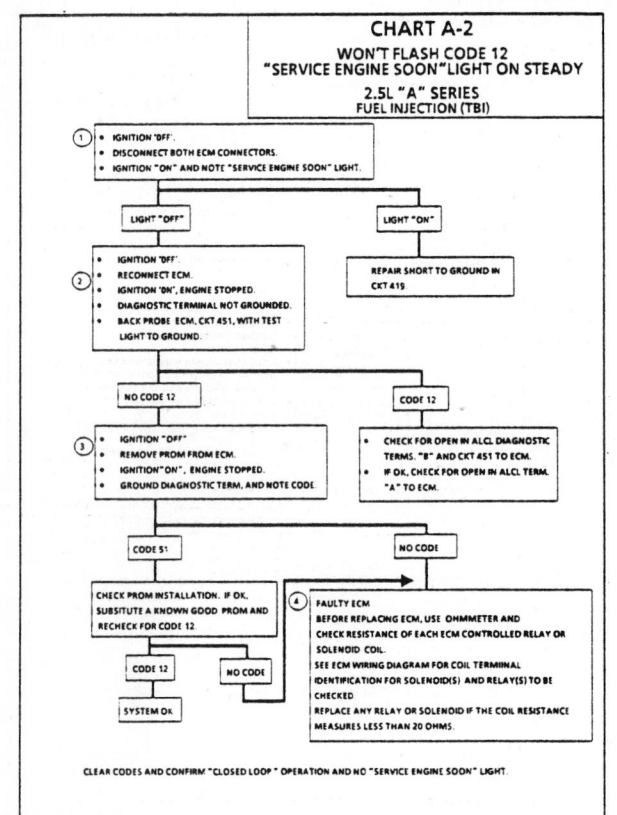

CHART A-2
WON'T FLASH CODE 12
"SERVICE ENGINE SOON" LIGHT ON STEADY
2.5L "A" SERIES
FUEL INJECTION (TBI)

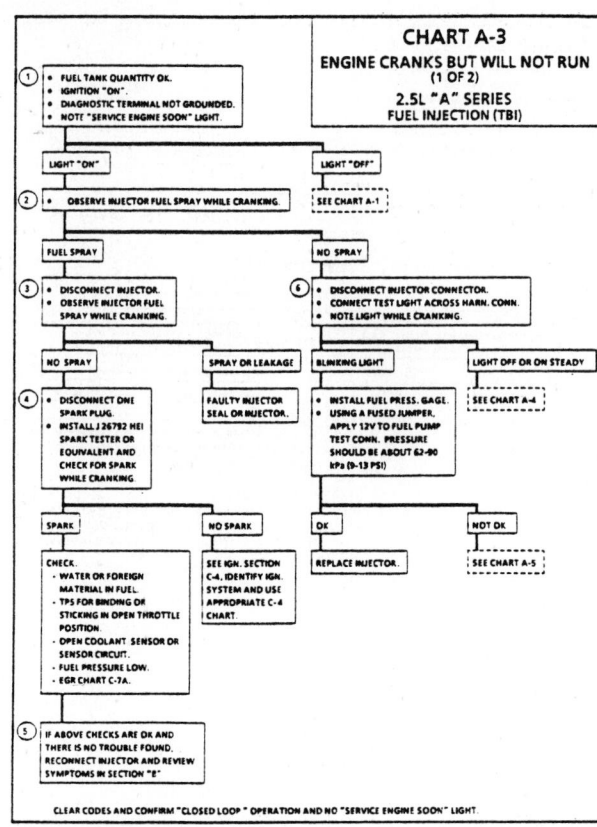

CHART A-3
ENGINE CRANKS BUT WILL NOT RUN
(1 OF 2)
2.5L "A" SERIES
FUEL INJECTION (TBI)

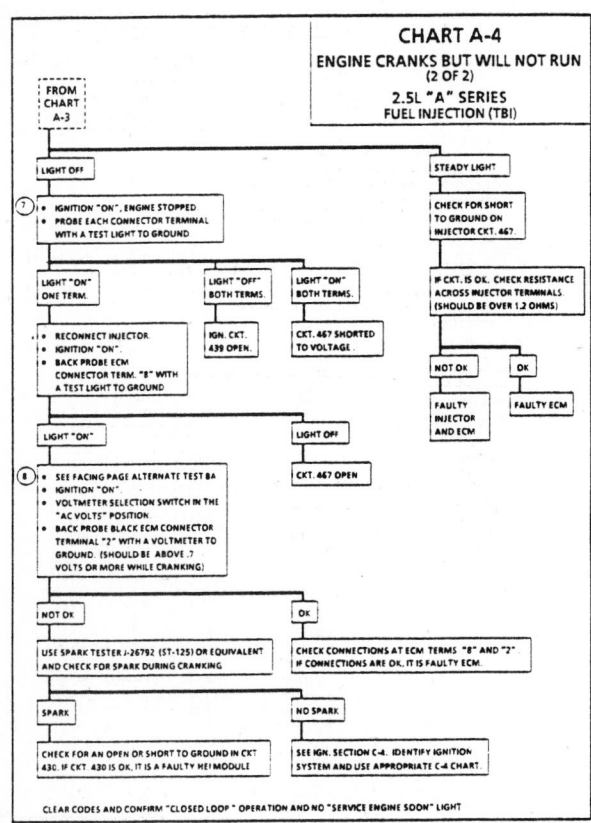

CHART A-4
ENGINE CRANKS BUT WILL NOT RUN
(2 OF 2)
2.5L "A" SERIES
FUEL INJECTION (TBI)

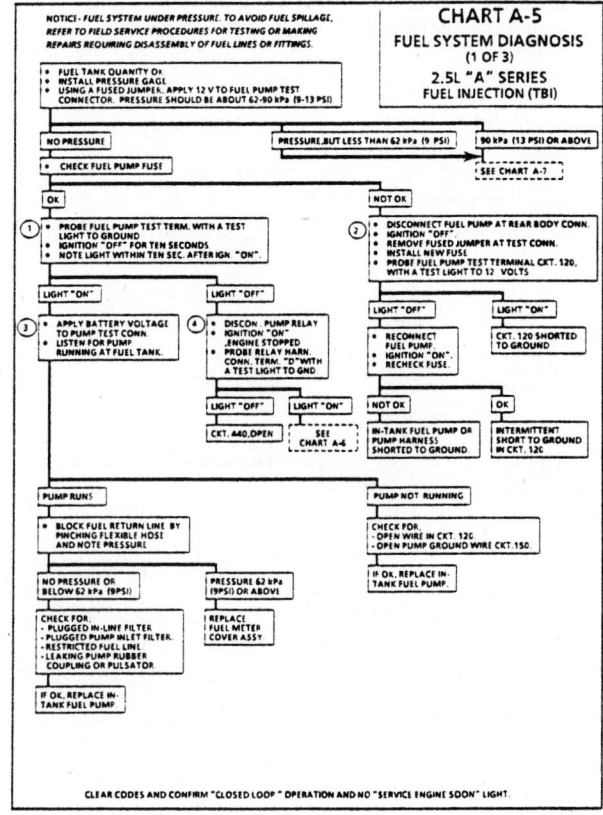

CHART A-5
FUEL SYSTEM DIAGNOSIS
(1 OF 3)
2.5L "A" SERIES
FUEL INJECTION (TBI)

TBI TROUBLE DIAGNOSTICS

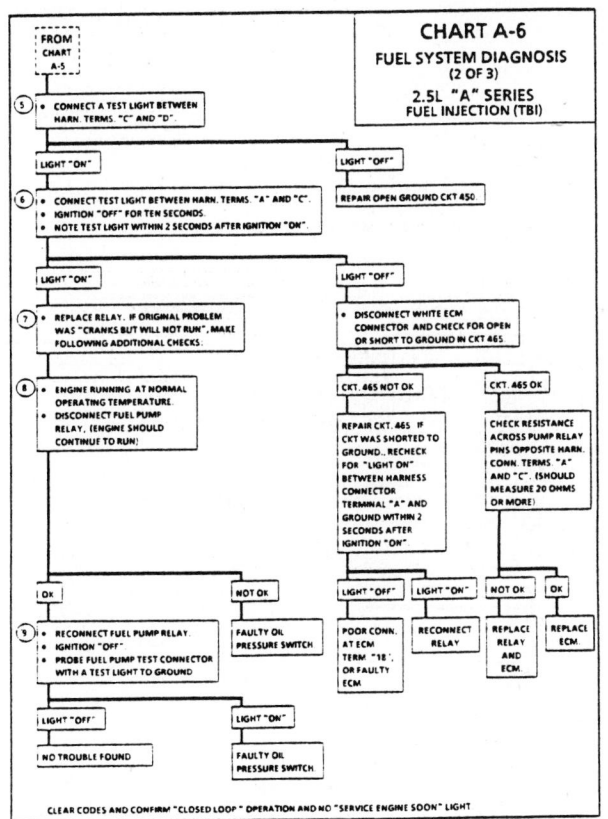

CHART A-6
FUEL SYSTEM DIAGNOSIS (2 OF 3)
2.5L "A" SERIES
FUEL INJECTION (TBI)

FROM CHART A-5

5 • CONNECT A TEST LIGHT BETWEEN HARN. TERMS. "C" AND "D".

LIGHT "ON" / LIGHT "OFF"

6 • CONNECT TEST LIGHT BETWEEN HARN. TERMS. "A" AND "C".
• IGNITION "OFF" FOR TEN SECONDS.
• NOTE TEST LIGHT WITHIN 2 SECONDS AFTER IGNITION "ON".

REPAIR OPEN GROUND CKT 450.

LIGHT "ON" / LIGHT "OFF"

7 • REPLACE RELAY. IF ORIGINAL PROBLEM WAS "CRANKS BUT WILL NOT RUN", MAKE FOLLOWING ADDITIONAL CHECKS.

• DISCONNECT WHITE ECM CONNECTOR AND CHECK FOR OPEN OR SHORT TO GROUND IN CKT 465.

CKT 465 NOT OK / CKT 465 OK

8 • ENGINE RUNNING AT NORMAL OPERATING TEMPERATURE.
• DISCONNECT FUEL PUMP RELAY. (ENGINE SHOULD CONTINUE TO RUN).

REPAIR CKT 465. IF CKT WAS SHORTED TO GROUND, RECHECK FOR "LIGHT ON" BETWEEN HARNESS CONNECTOR TERMINAL "A" AND GROUND WITHIN 2 SECONDS AFTER IGNITION "ON".

CHECK RESISTANCE ACROSS PUMP RELAY PINS OPPOSITE HARN. CONN. TERMS. "A" AND "C". (SHOULD MEASURE 20 OHMS OR MORE).

OK / NOT OK

LIGHT "OFF" / LIGHT "ON" / NOT OK / OK

9 • RECONNECT FUEL PUMP RELAY.
• IGNITION "OFF".
• PROBE FUEL PUMP TEST CONNECTOR WITH A TEST LIGHT TO GROUND.

FAULTY OIL PRESSURE SWITCH

POOR CONN. AT ECM TERM. "1B", OR FAULTY ECM

RECONNECT RELAY

REPLACE RELAY AND ECM.

REPLACE ECM

LIGHT "OFF" / LIGHT "ON"

NO TROUBLE FOUND

FAULTY OIL PRESSURE SWITCH

CLEAR CODES AND CONFIRM "CLOSED LOOP" OPERATION AND NO "SERVICE ENGINE SOON" LIGHT.

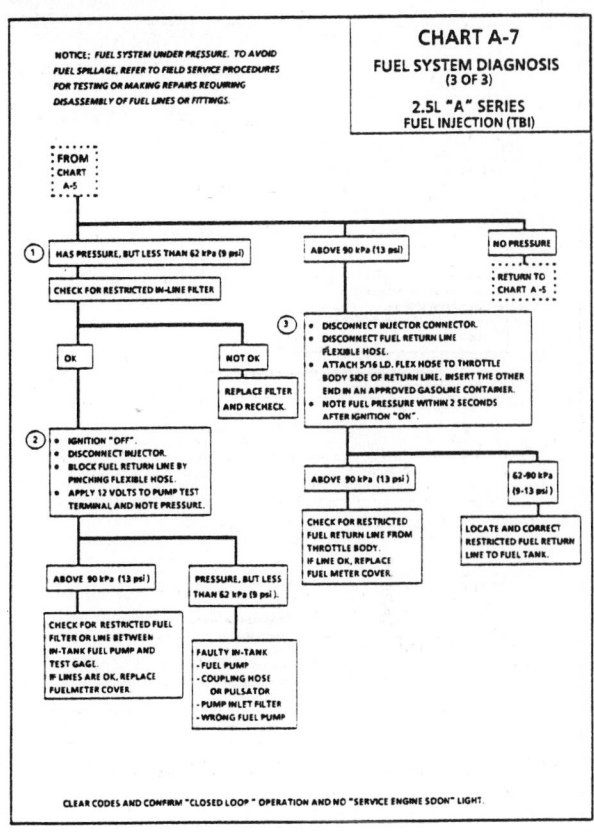

NOTICE: FUEL SYSTEM UNDER PRESSURE. TO AVOID FUEL SPILLAGE, REFER TO FIELD SERVICE PROCEDURES FOR TESTING OR MAKING REPAIRS REQUIRING DISASSEMBLY OF FUEL LINES OR FITTINGS.

CHART A-7
FUEL SYSTEM DIAGNOSIS (3 OF 3)
2.5L "A" SERIES
FUEL INJECTION (TBI)

FROM CHART A-5

1 HAS PRESSURE, BUT LESS THAN 62 kPa (9 psi) / ABOVE 90 kPa (13 psi) / NO PRESSURE

CHECK FOR RESTRICTED IN-LINE FILTER

RETURN TO CHART A-5

OK / NOT OK

REPLACE FILTER AND RECHECK.

3 • DISCONNECT INJECTOR CONNECTOR.
• DISCONNECT FUEL RETURN LINE FLEXIBLE HOSE.
• ATTACH 5/16 I.D. FLEX HOSE TO THROTTLE BODY SIDE OF RETURN LINE. INSERT THE OTHER END IN AN APPROVED GASOLINE CONTAINER.
• NOTE FUEL PRESSURE WITHIN 2 SECONDS AFTER IGNITION "ON".

2 • IGNITION "OFF".
• DISCONNECT INJECTOR.
• BLOCK FUEL RETURN LINE BY PINCHING FLEXIBLE HOSE.
• APPLY 12 VOLTS TO PUMP TEST TERMINAL AND NOTE PRESSURE.

ABOVE 90 kPa (13 psi) / 62-90 kPa (9-13 psi)

CHECK FOR RESTRICTED FUEL RETURN LINE FROM THROTTLE BODY. IF LINE OK, REPLACE FUEL METER COVER.

LOCATE AND CORRECT RESTRICTED FUEL RETURN LINE TO FUEL TANK.

ABOVE 90 kPa (13 psi) / PRESSURE, BUT LESS THAN 62 kPa (9 psi).

CHECK FOR RESTRICTED FUEL FILTER OR LINE BETWEEN IN-TANK FUEL PUMP AND TEST GAGE. IF LINES ARE OK, REPLACE FUELMETER COVER.

FAULTY IN-TANK
- FUEL PUMP
- COUPLING HOSE OR PULSATOR
- PUMP INLET FILTER
- WRONG FUEL PUMP

CLEAR CODES AND CONFIRM "CLOSED LOOP" OPERATION AND NO "SERVICE ENGINE SOON" LIGHT.

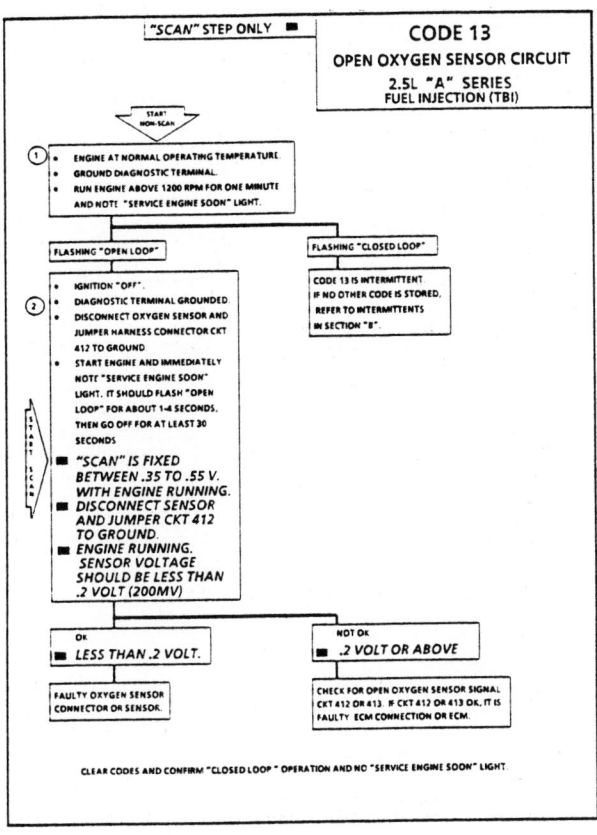

"SCAN" STEP ONLY ■

CODE 13
OPEN OXYGEN SENSOR CIRCUIT
2.5L "A" SERIES
FUEL INJECTION (TBI)

START NON-SCAN

1 • ENGINE AT NORMAL OPERATING TEMPERATURE.
• GROUND DIAGNOSTIC TERMINAL.
• RUN ENGINE ABOVE 1200 RPM FOR ONE MINUTE AND NOTE "SERVICE ENGINE SOON" LIGHT.

FLASHING "OPEN LOOP" / FLASHING "CLOSED LOOP"

CODE 13 IS INTERMITTENT. IF NO OTHER CODE IS STORED, REFER TO INTERMITTENTS IN SECTION "B".

2 • IGNITION "OFF".
• DIAGNOSTIC TERMINAL GROUNDED.
• DISCONNECT OXYGEN SENSOR AND JUMPER HARNESS CONNECTOR CKT 412 TO GROUND.
• START ENGINE AND IMMEDIATELY NOTE "SERVICE ENGINE SOON" LIGHT. IT SHOULD FLASH "OPEN LOOP" FOR ABOUT 1-4 SECONDS, THEN GO OFF FOR AT LEAST 30 SECONDS.

■ "SCAN" IS FIXED BETWEEN .35 TO .55 V. WITH ENGINE RUNNING.
■ DISCONNECT SENSOR AND JUMPER CKT 412 TO GROUND.
■ ENGINE RUNNING. SENSOR VOLTAGE SHOULD BE LESS THAN .2 VOLT (200MV)

OK
■ LESS THAN .2 VOLT.

NOT OK
■ .2 VOLT OR ABOVE

FAULTY OXYGEN SENSOR CONNECTOR OR SENSOR.

CHECK FOR OPEN OXYGEN SENSOR SIGNAL CKT 412 OR 413. IF CKT 412 OR 413 OK, IT IS FAULTY ECM CONNECTION OR ECM.

CLEAR CODES AND CONFIRM "CLOSED LOOP" OPERATION AND NO "SERVICE ENGINE SOON" LIGHT.

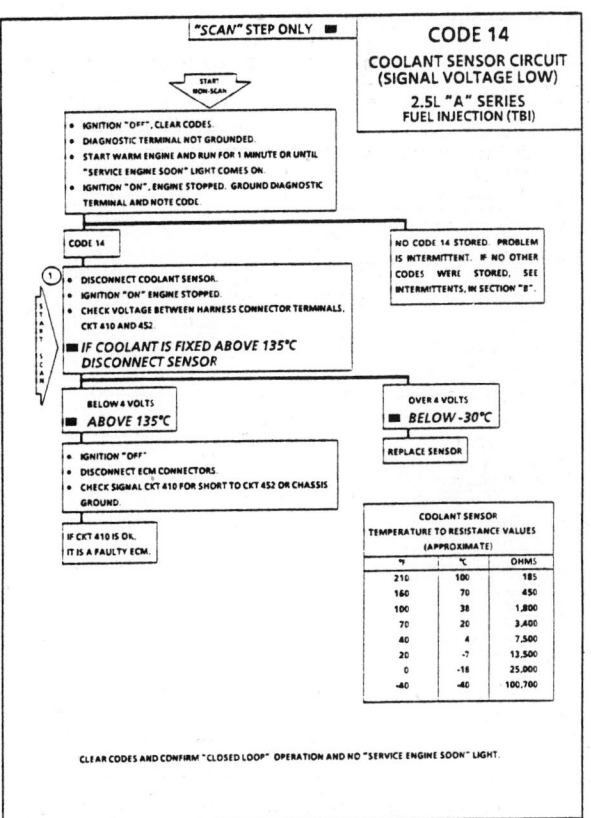

"SCAN" STEP ONLY ■

CODE 14
COOLANT SENSOR CIRCUIT (SIGNAL VOLTAGE LOW)
2.5L "A" SERIES
FUEL INJECTION (TBI)

START NON-SCAN

• IGNITION "OFF", CLEAR CODES.
• DIAGNOSTIC TERMINAL NOT GROUNDED.
• START WARM ENGINE AND RUN FOR 1 MINUTE OR UNTIL "SERVICE ENGINE SOON" LIGHT COMES ON.
• IGNITION "ON", ENGINE STOPPED. GROUND DIAGNOSTIC TERMINAL AND NOTE CODE.

CODE 14

NO CODE 14 STORED. PROBLEM IS INTERMITTENT. IF NO OTHER CODES WERE STORED, SEE INTERMITTENTS, IN SECTION "B".

1 • DISCONNECT COOLANT SENSOR.
• IGNITION "ON" ENGINE STOPPED.
• CHECK VOLTAGE BETWEEN HARNESS CONNECTOR TERMINALS, CKT 410 AND 452.

■ IF COOLANT IS FIXED ABOVE 135°C DISCONNECT SENSOR

BELOW 4 VOLTS
■ ABOVE 135°C

OVER 4 VOLTS
■ BELOW -30°C

REPLACE SENSOR

• IGNITION "OFF".
• DISCONNECT ECM CONNECTORS.
• CHECK SIGNAL CKT 410 FOR SHORT TO CKT 452 OR CHASSIS GROUND.

IF CKT 410 IS OK, IT IS A FAULTY ECM.

COOLANT SENSOR TEMPERATURE TO RESISTANCE VALUES (APPROXIMATE)		
°F	°C	OHMS
210	100	185
160	70	450
100	38	1,800
70	20	3,400
40	4	7,500
20	-7	13,500
0	-18	25,000
-40	-40	100,700

CLEAR CODES AND CONFIRM "CLOSED LOOP" OPERATION AND NO "SERVICE ENGINE SOON" LIGHT.

TBI TROUBLE DIAGNOSTICS

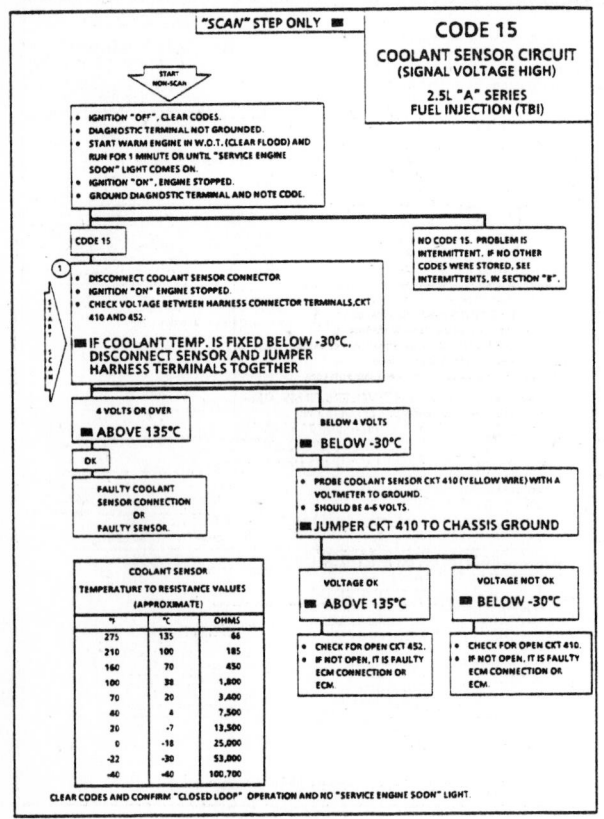

CODE 15
COOLANT SENSOR CIRCUIT
(SIGNAL VOLTAGE HIGH)
2.5L "A" SERIES
FUEL INJECTION (TBI)

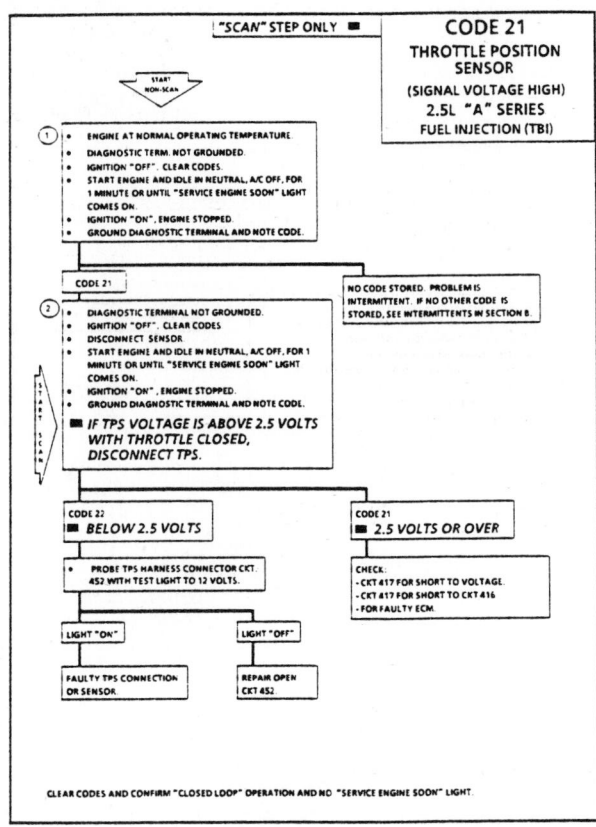

CODE 21
THROTTLE POSITION
SENSOR
(SIGNAL VOLTAGE HIGH)
2.5L "A" SERIES
FUEL INJECTION (TBI)

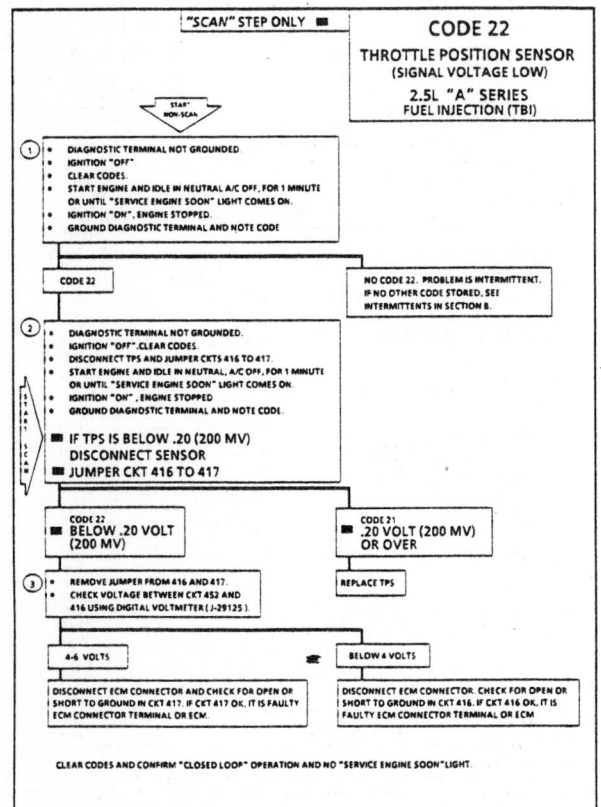

CODE 22
THROTTLE POSITION SENSOR
(SIGNAL VOLTAGE LOW)
2.5L "A" SERIES
FUEL INJECTION (TBI)

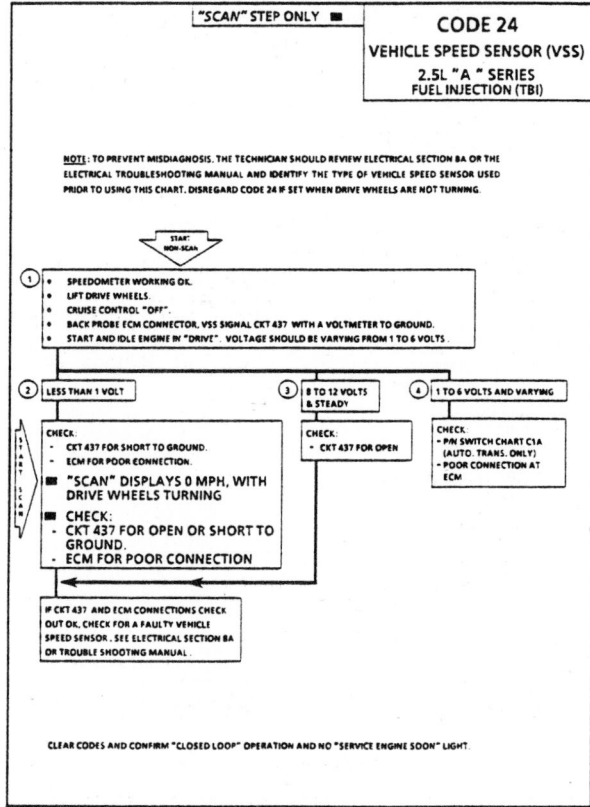

CODE 24
VEHICLE SPEED SENSOR (VSS)
2.5L "A" SERIES
FUEL INJECTION (TBI)

TBI TROUBLE DIAGNOSTICS

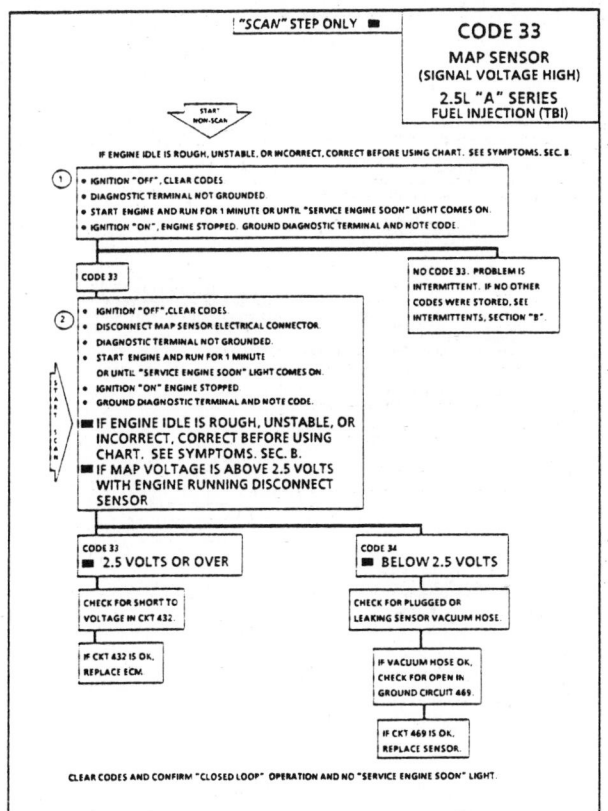

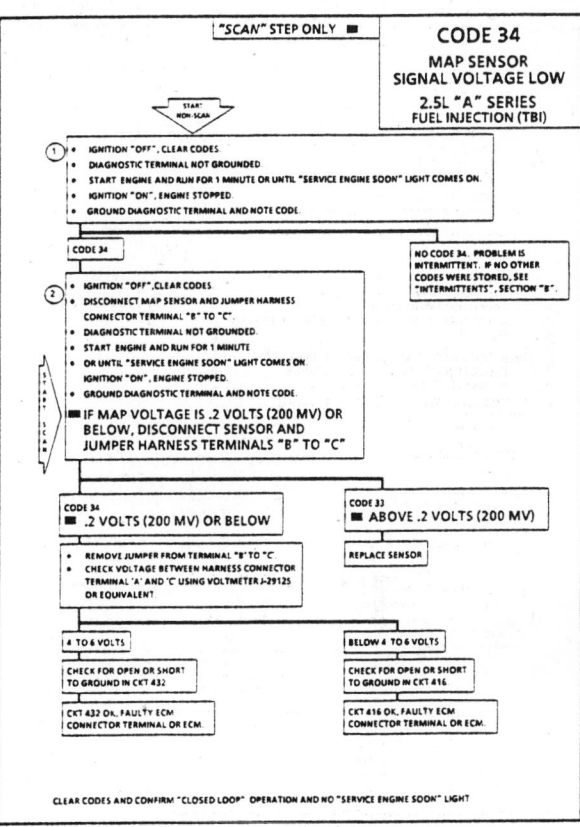

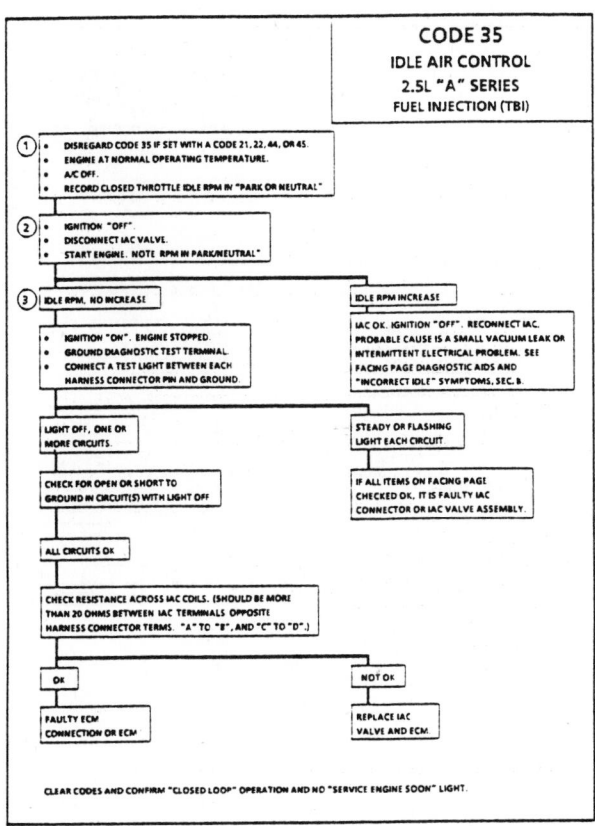

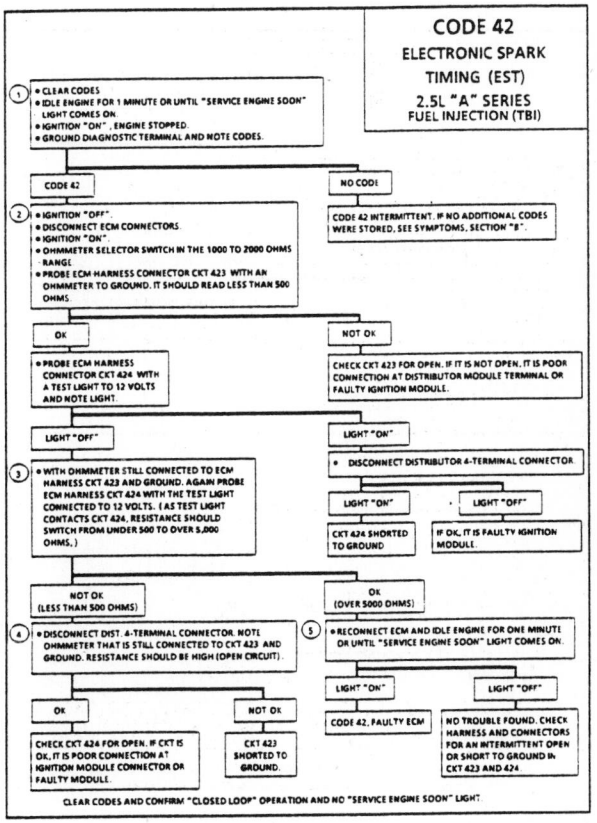

TBI TROUBLE DIAGNOSTICS

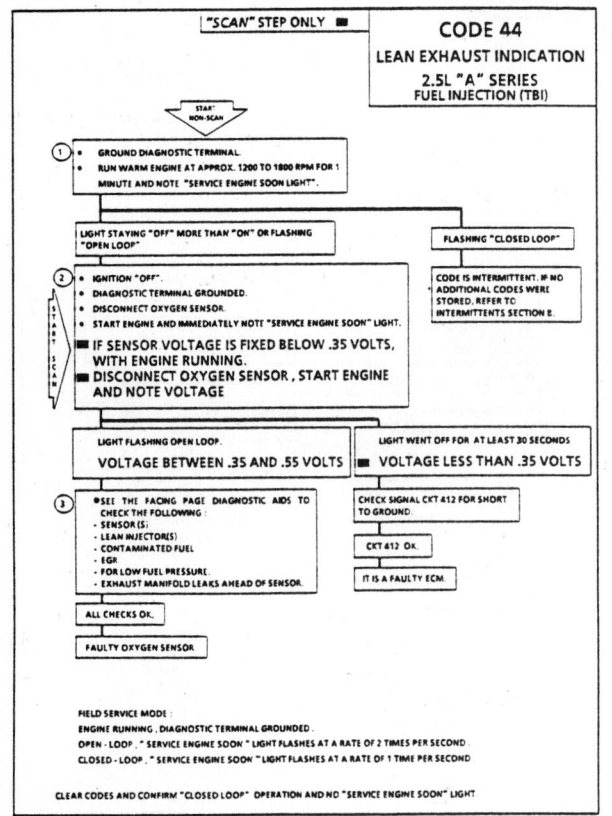

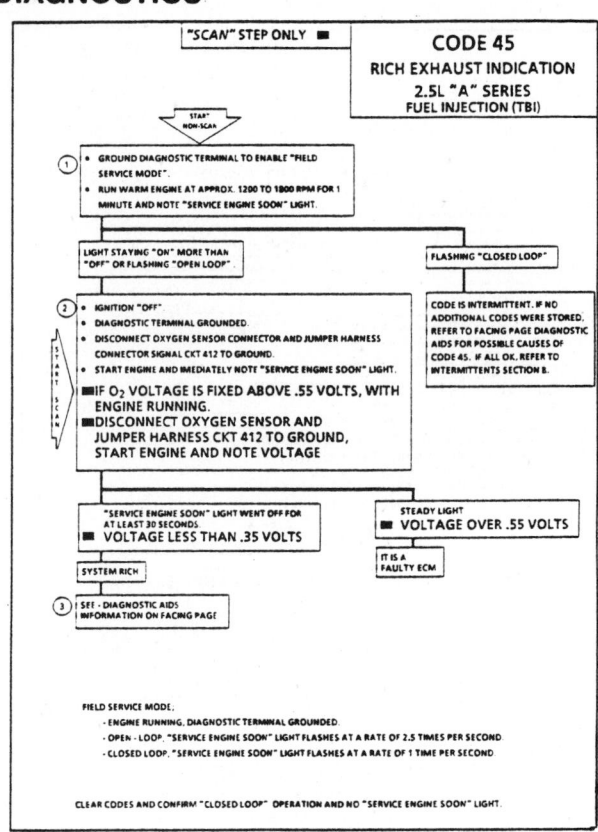

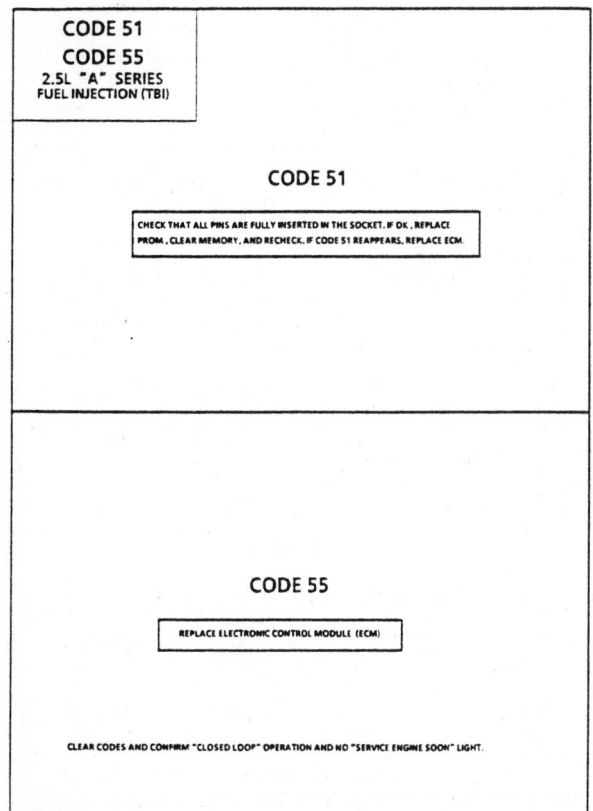

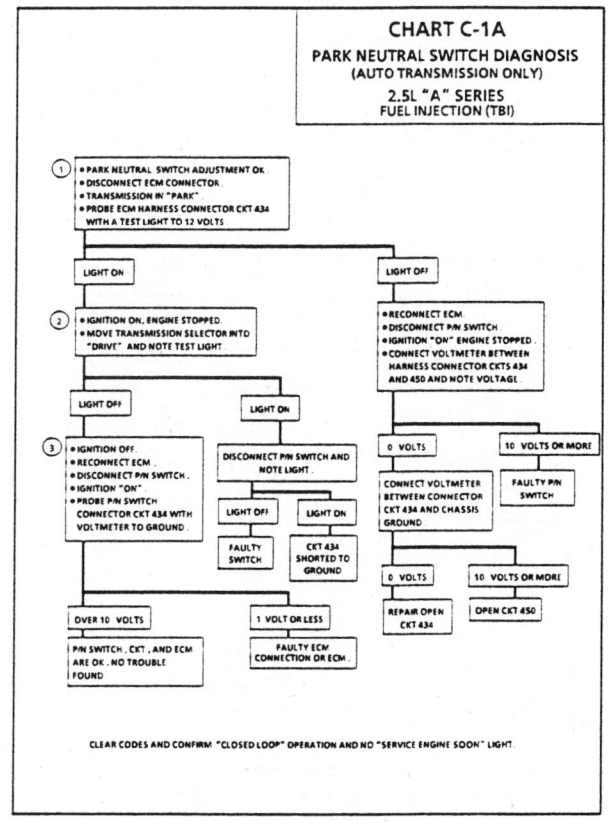

TBI TROUBLE DIAGNOSTICS

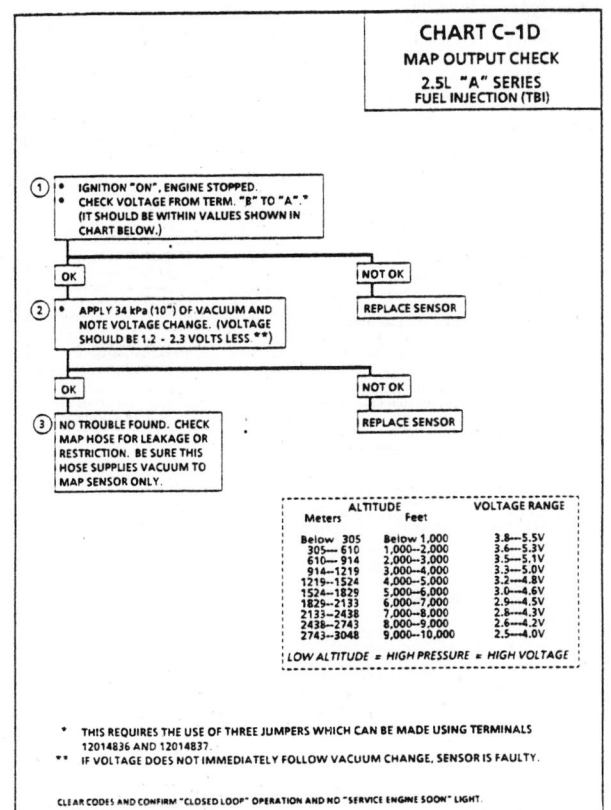

CHART C-1D
MAP OUTPUT CHECK
2.5L "A" SERIES
FUEL INJECTION (TBI)

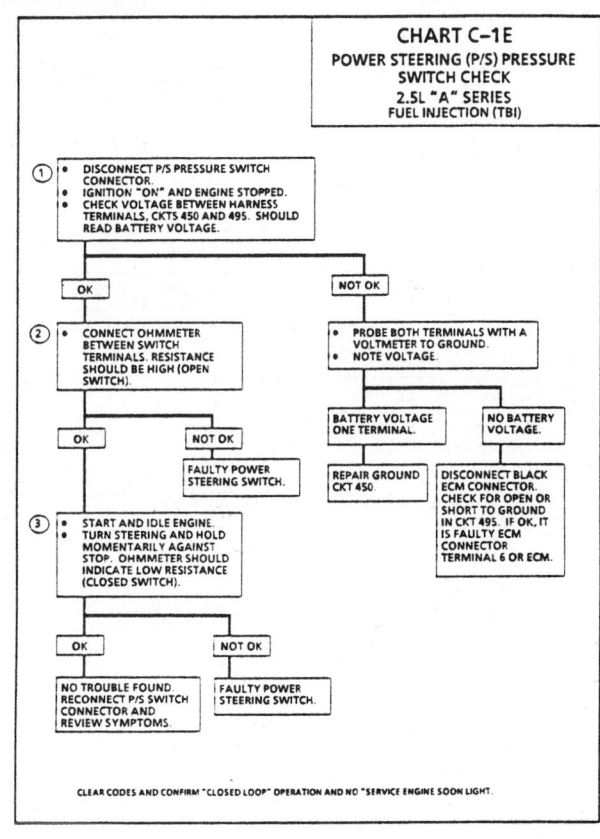

CHART C-1E
POWER STEERING (P/S) PRESSURE SWITCH CHECK
2.5L "A" SERIES
FUEL INJECTION (TBI)

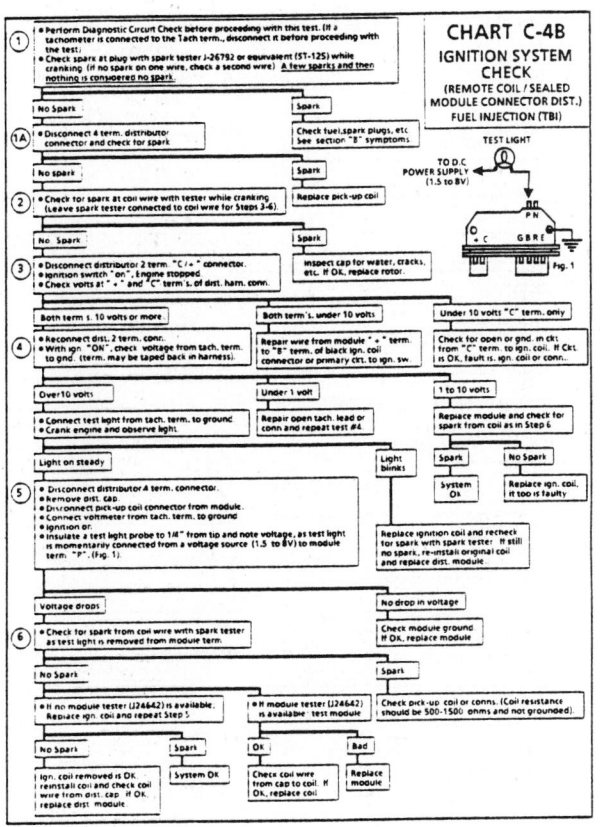

CHART C-4B
IGNITION SYSTEM CHECK
(REMOTE COIL / SEALED MODULE CONNECTOR DIST.)
FUEL INJECTION (TBI)

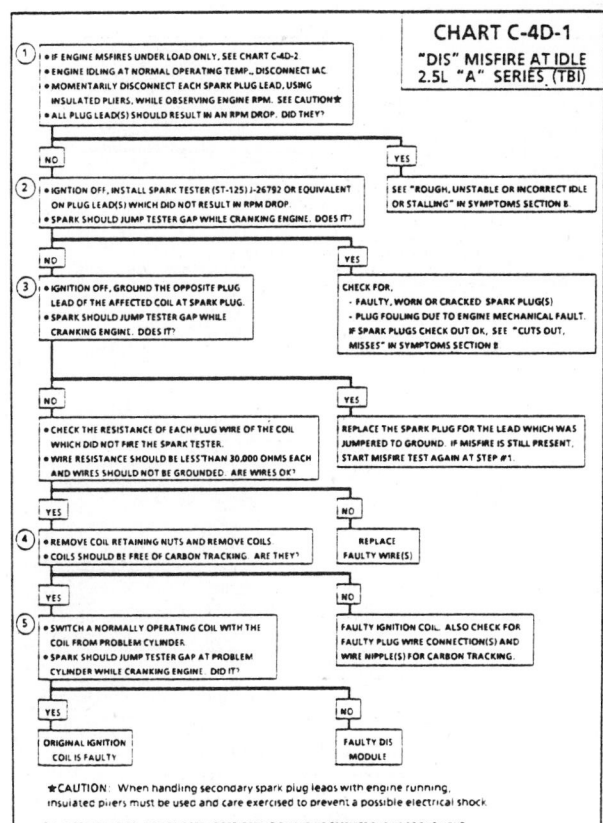

CHART C-4D-1
"DIS" MISFIRE AT IDLE
2.5L "A" SERIES (TBI)

TBI TROUBLE DIAGNOSTICS

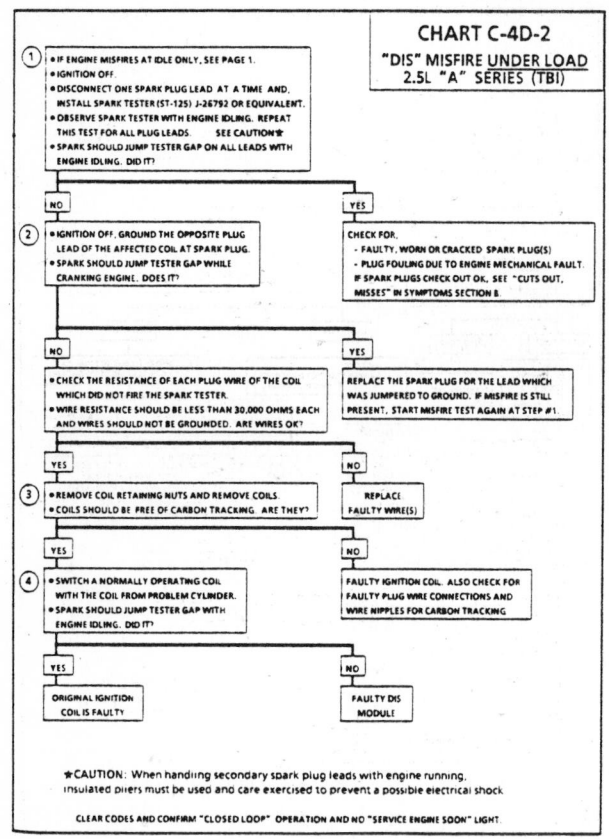

CHART C-4D-2
"DIS" MISFIRE UNDER LOAD
2.5L "A" SERIES (TBI)

★CAUTION: When handling secondary spark plug leads with engine running, insulated pliers must be used and care exercised to prevent a possible electrical shock.

CLEAR CODES AND CONFIRM "CLOSED LOOP" OPERATION AND NO "SERVICE ENGINE SOON" LIGHT.

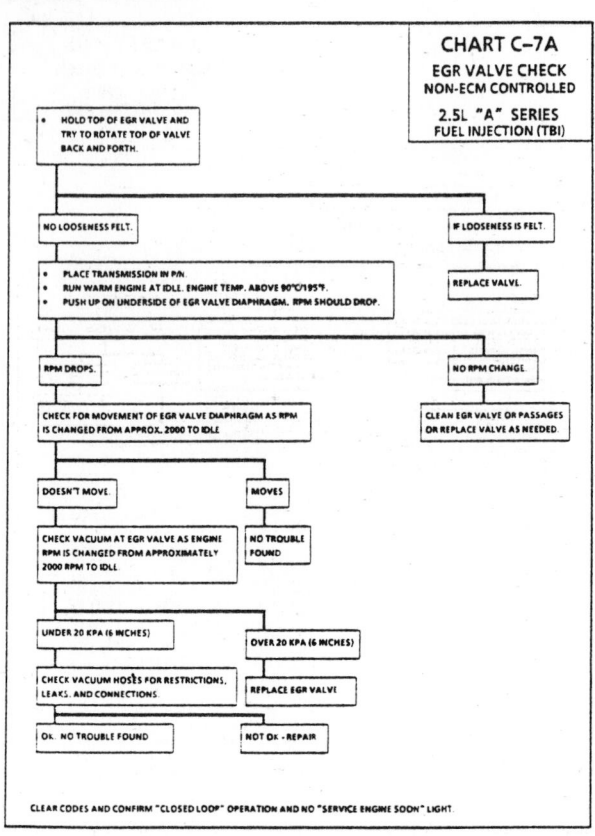

CHART C-7A
EGR VALVE CHECK
NON-ECM CONTROLLED
2.5L "A" SERIES
FUEL INJECTION (TBI)

CLEAR CODES AND CONFIRM "CLOSED LOOP" OPERATION AND NO "SERVICE ENGINE SOON" LIGHT.

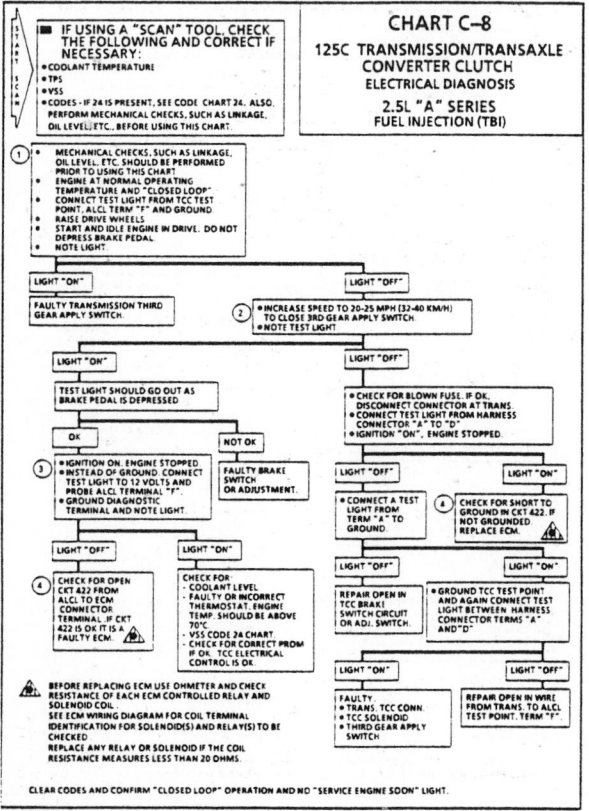

CHART C-8
125C TRANSMISSION/TRANSAXLE
CONVERTER CLUTCH
ELECTRICAL DIAGNOSIS
2.5L "A" SERIES
FUEL INJECTION (TBI)

CLEAR CODES AND CONFIRM "CLOSED LOOP" OPERATION AND NO "SERVICE ENGINE SOON" LIGHT.

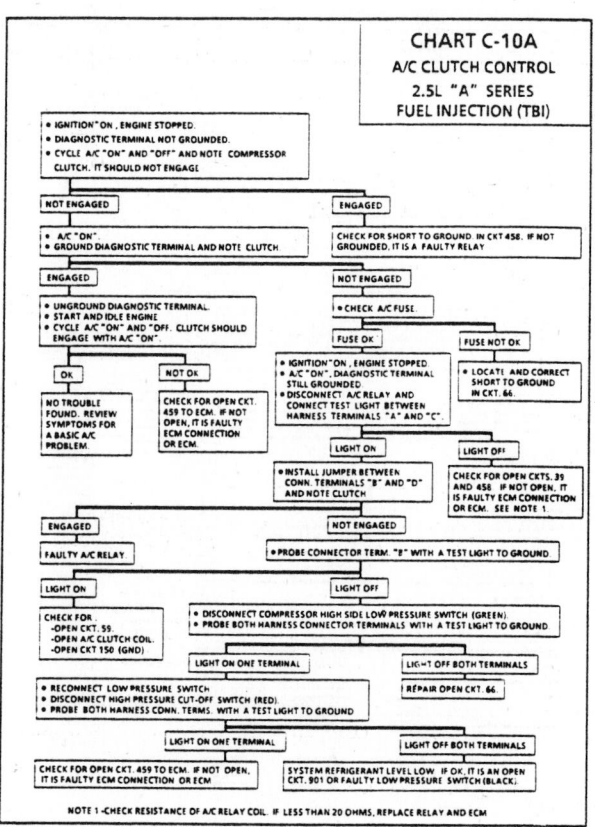

CHART C-10A
A/C CLUTCH CONTROL
2.5L "A" SERIES
FUEL INJECTION (TBI)

NOTE 1-CHECK RESISTANCE OF A/C RELAY COIL. IF LESS THAN 20 OHMS, REPLACE RELAY AND ECM.

TBI TROUBLE DIAGNOSTICS

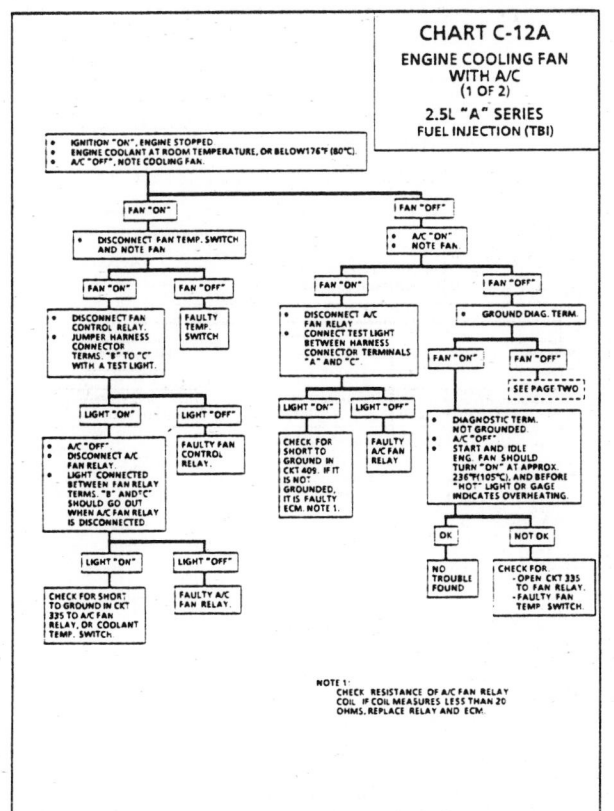

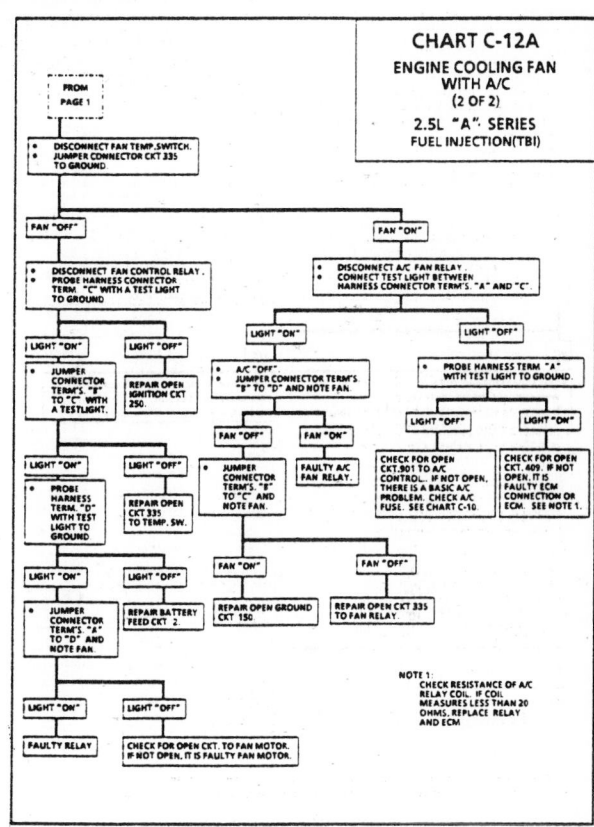

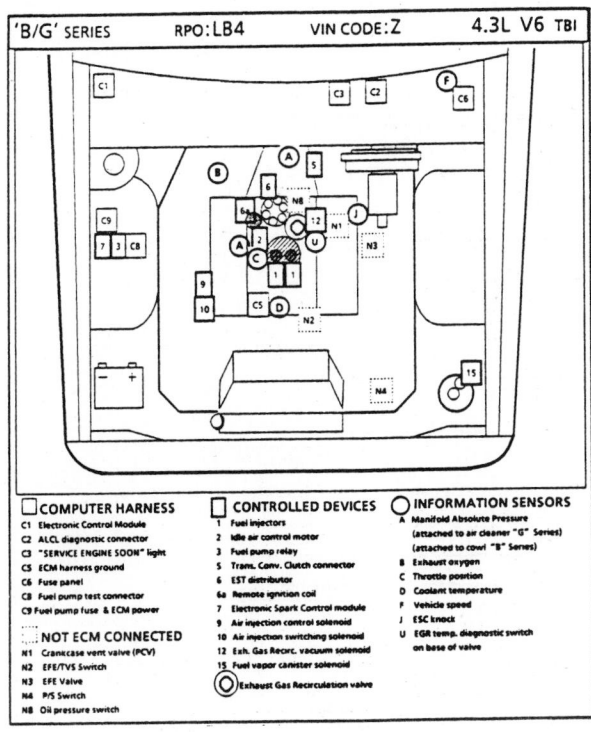

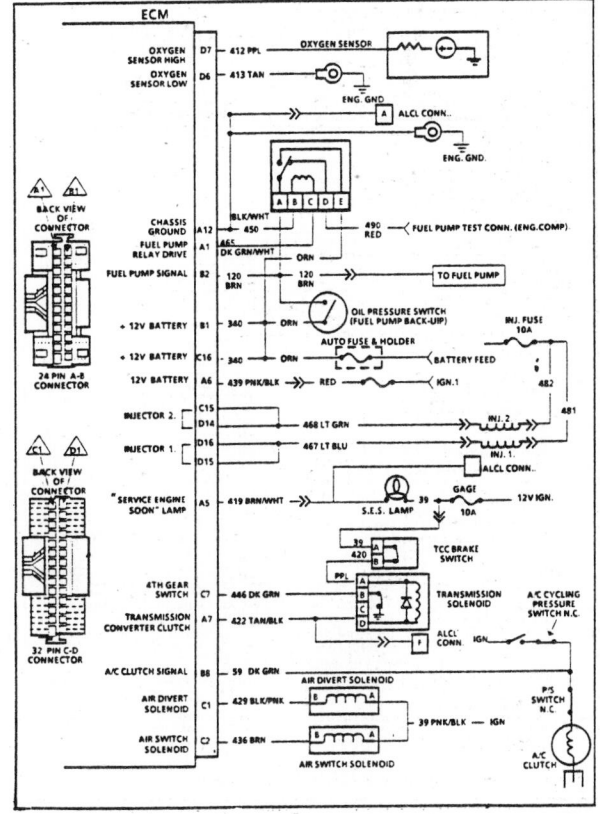

TBI TROUBLE DIAGNOSTICS

FUEL INJECTION ECM CONNECTOR IDENTIFICATION

This ECM voltage chart is for use with a digital voltmeter to further aid in diagnosis. The voltages you get may vary due to low battery charge or other reasons, but they should be very close.

THE FOLLOWING CONDITIONS MUST BE MET BEFORE TESTING:

- Engine at operating temperature • Engine idling in closed loop (for "Engine Run" column)
- Test terminal not grounded • ALCL tool not installed

KEY "ON"	ENG. RUN	CIRCUIT	PIN	WIRE COLOR
0	13.45	FUEL PUMP RELAY CONTROL	A1	GRN/WHT
		NOT USED	A2	
12	3	CANISTER PURGE CONTROL	A3	GRN/YEL
12	12	EGR CONTROL	A4	GRY/RED
0	13.9	"SERVICE ENGINE SOON" CONTROL	A5	BRN/WHT
			A6	PNK/BLK
12	13.9	IGN (ECM)	A6	BLK
12	13.9	TCC CONTROL A/T	A7	TAN/BLK
2-5 VARIES	VARIES	SERIAL DATA	A8	ORN/BLK
5	5	DIAG. TERM	A9	WHT/BLK
0 OR 12	0 OR 12	SPEED SENSOR SIGNAL	A10	BRN
0	0	COOLANT AND TPS GROUND	A11	BLK
0	0	SYSTEM GROUND	A12	WHT
12	12	A.I.R. DIVERT SOLENOID	C1	BLK/PNK
12	12	A.I.R. SWITCH SOLENOID	C2	BRN
NOT USEABLE		IAC "B" LO	C3	LT GRN/BLK
NOT USEABLE		IAC "B" HI	C4	LT GRN/WHT
NOT USEABLE		IAC "A" HI	C5	BLU/WHT
NOT USEABLE		IAC "A" LO	C6	LT BLU/BLK
0	0	4TH GEAR	C7	LT BLU
		NOT USED	C8	
		CRANK DISCRETE	C9	PPL/WHT
1.6	1.6	COOLANT TEMP. SIGNAL	C10	YEL
		MAP	C11	LT GRN
		NOT USED	C12	
5	5	TPS SIGNAL	C13	DK BLU
5	5	TPS 5 VOLT REFERENCE	C14	GRY
12	12	INJECTOR B	C15	LT GRN
12.5	13.4	BATTERY	C16	ORN

BACK VIEW OF CONNECTOR

24 PIN A-B CONNECTOR

△A1 △B1

32 PIN C-D CONNECTOR

VOLTAGE

WIRE COLOR	PIN	CIRCUIT	KEY "ON"	ENG. RUN
ORN	B1	BATT. 12 VOLTS	12	13.9
BRN	B2	FUEL PUMP SIGNAL	0	13.9
BLK/RED	B3	EST REF LOW	0	0
	B4	NOT USED		
PPL/WHT	B5	DISTRIBUTOR REFERENCE	0	1.3
	B6	NOT USED		
BLK	B7	ESC SIGNAL	9.2	9.2
DK GRN	B8	A/C SIGNAL (OFF) (ON)	0 / 12	0 / 12
BLU/ORN	B9	EGR TEMP	12	13.8
ORN/BLK	B10	PARK/NEUTRAL SW SIGNAL (A/T)	0	0
	B11	NOT USED		
	B12	NOT USED		
BLK/WHT	D1	SYSTEM GROUND	0	0
PPL	D2	MAP GROUND	0	0
	D3	NOT USED		
WHT	D4	EST CONTROL	0	1.3
TAN/BLK	D5	BYPASS	0	4.75
TAN	D6	GRN'D (02)	0	0
PPL	D7	02 SENSOR SIGNAL		
	D8	NOT USED		
	D9	NOT USED		
	D10	NOT USED		
	D11	NOT USED		
	D12	NOT USED		
	D13	NOT USED		
LT GRN	D14	INJECTOR B	12	13.9
LT BLU	D15	INJECTOR A	12	13.9
LT BLU	D16	INJECTOR A	12	13.9

BACK VIEW OF CONNECTOR

24 PIN A-B CONNECTOR

△A1 △B1

BACK VIEW OF CONNECTOR

△C1 △D1

32 PIN C-D CONNECTOR

ENGINE 4.3 L

CARLINE B & G

1 Varies from 60 to battery voltage depending on position of drive wheels
2 12 V for first two seconds
3 Varies
4 12 V when fuel pump is running
5 Varies with temperature
6 Reads battery voltage in gear

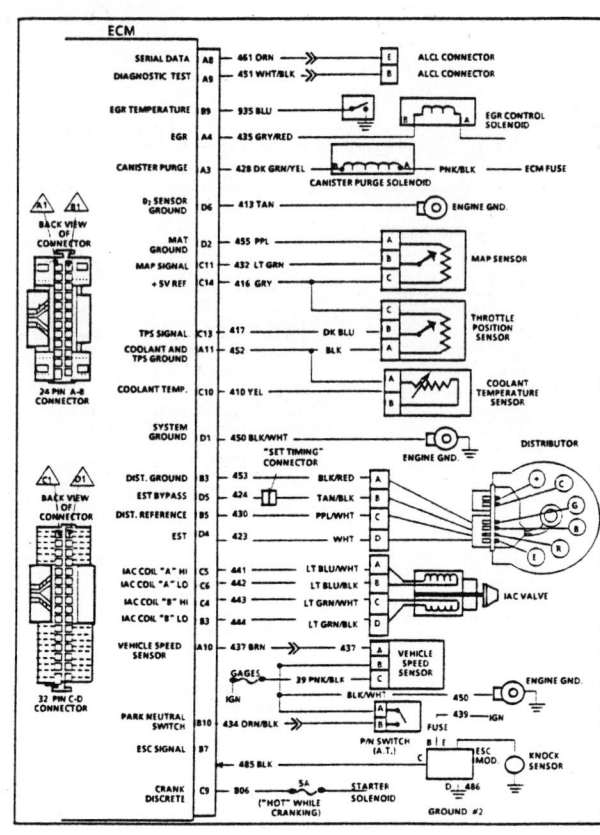

"NON-SCAN" DIAGNOSTIC CIRCUIT CHECK

4.3L "B/G" SERIES FUEL INJECTION (TBI)

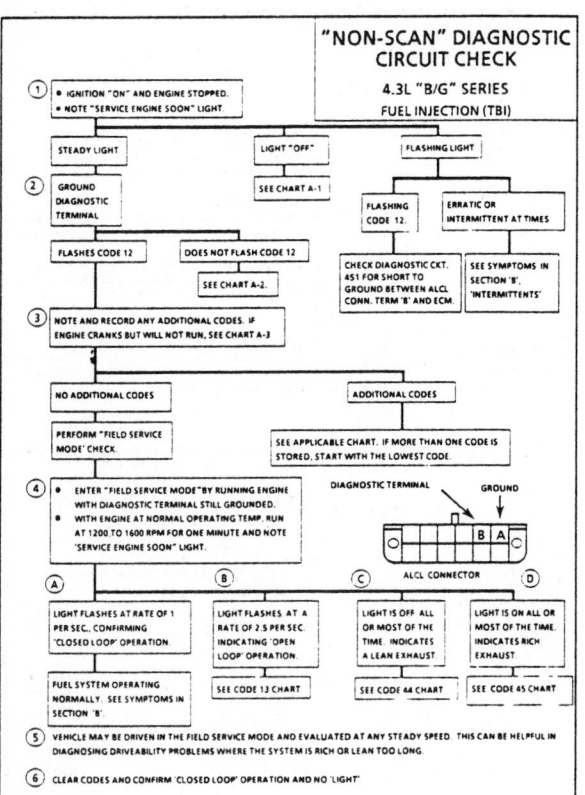

"SCAN" DIAGNOSTIC CIRCUIT CHECK
(Page 1 of 6)
FUEL INJECTION (TBI)

■ "SCAN" STEP ONLY

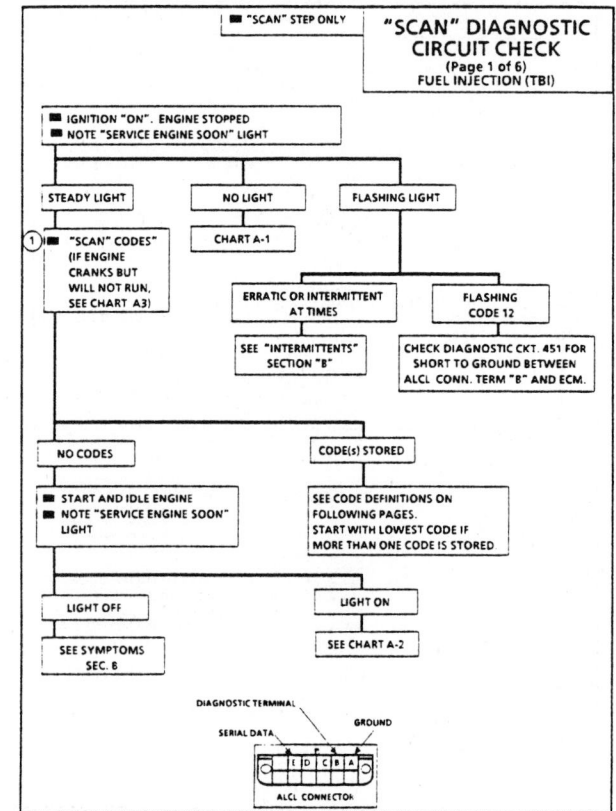

TBI TROUBLE DIAGNOSTICS

"SCAN" DIAGNOSTIC CIRCUIT CHECK
(Page 2 of 6)
4.3L "B/G" SERIES (CODE DEFINITIONS)

THE 'DIAGNOSTIC CIRCUIT CHECK' SCAN DATA IS TYPICAL OF THAT DISPLAYED BY A PROPERLY DESIGNED AND CALIBRATED ALCL SCAN DEVICE.

A SCAN DEVICE THAT DISPLAYS FAULTY DATA SHOULD NOT BE USED AND THE PROBLEM REPORTED TO THE DEVICE MANUFACTURER. THE USE OF A FAULTY SCAN DEVICE CAN RESULT IN MISDIAGNOSIS AND UNNECESSARY PARTS REPLACEMENT.

CODES	DEFINITION
CODE 13 "SCAN" TOOL IN SPECIAL MODE. ENGINE IDLING AT 1000 RPM. MPSI & OTC "SCAN" WILL NOT READ O_2 VOLTS	**HARD FAILURE -** VOLTAGE FIXED BETWEEN .35 TO .55 V. OPEN CIRCUIT CONDITION. SEE CODE CHART 13. **INTERMITTENT CODE -** NORMAL "SCAN" VOLTAGE VARIES BETWEEN 100MV TO 999 MV (.1 AND 1.0 VOLT). SEE "INTERMITTENTS" SECTION B.
CODE 14 IGNITION ON. ENGINE STOPPED. "SCAN" COOLANT TEMPERATURE.	**HARD FAILURE -** "SCAN" TOOL FIXED ABOVE 135°C. CIRCUIT SHORTED TO GROUND OR FAULTY SENSOR. SEE CODE CHART 14. **INTERMITTENT CODE -** "SCAN" TOOL READS ENGINE TEMP. IN DEGREES CENTIGRADE. AFTER ENGINE IS STARTED, THE TEMPERATURE SHOULD RISE STEADILY TO ABOUT 90°C THEN STABILIZE WHEN THERMOSTAT OPENS. SEE "INTERMITTENTS" SECTION B.
CODE 15 IGNITION ON. ENGINE STOPPED. "SCAN" COOLANT TEMPERATURE	**HARD FAILURE -** "SCAN" TOOL FIXED BELOW -30°C. CIRCUIT OPEN OR FAULTY SENSOR. SEE CODE CHART 15. **INTERMITTENT CODE -** "SCAN" TOOL READS ENGINE COOLANT TEMPERATURE IN DEGREES CENTIGRADE. AFTER ENGINE IS STARTED, THE TEMPERATURE SHOULD RISE STEADILY TO ABOUT 90°C, THEN STABILIZE WHEN THERMOSTAT OPENS. SEE "INTERMITTENTS" SECTION B.

"SCAN" DIAGNOSTIC CIRCUIT CHECK
(Page 3 of 6)
4.3L "B/G" SERIES (CODE DEFINITIONS)

CODES	DEFINITION
CODE 21 IGNITION "ON". ENGINE STOPPED. THROTTLE CLOSED "SCAN" TPS OR ENGINE IDLING THROTTLE CLOSED "SCAN" TPS	**HARD FAILURE -** "SCAN" TOOL READS OVER 4.5 VOLTS. GROUND WIRE OPEN, SIGNAL LINE SHORTED TO SENSOR REF. LINE, OR FAULTY SENSOR. SEE CODE CHART 21. OR **HARD FAILURE -** "SCAN" TOOL READS OVER 2.5 VOLTS. GROUND WIRE OPEN OR FAULTY SENSOR. SEE CODE CHART 21. **INTERMITTENT CODE -** "SCAN" TOOL READS THROTTLE POSITION IN VOLTS. SHOULD READ BETWEEN 020-125 (200 MV AND 1.25 V). WITH THROTTLE CLOSED AND IGNITION ON OR AT IDLE. VOLTAGE SHOULD INCREASE AT A STEADY RATE AS THROTTLE IS MOVED TOWARD W.O.T. SEE "INTERMITTENTS" SECTION B.
CODE 22 IGNITION "ON" ENGINE STOPPED. "SCAN" TPS	**HARD FAILURE -** "SCAN" TOOL READS BELOW 020V (200 MV) OPEN OR SHORTED TO GROUND CIRCUIT IN 5V REFERENCE, SIGNAL CIRCUIT OR FAULTY SENSOR. SEE CODE CHART 22. **INTERMITTENT CODE -** "SCAN" TOOL READS THROTTLE POSITION IN VOLTS. SHOULD READ BETWEEN 020-125 (200 MV AND 1.25 V). WITH THROTTLE CLOSED AND IGNITION ON OR AT IDLE. VOLTAGE SHOULD INCREASE AT A STEADY RATE AS THROTTLE IS MOVED TOWARD W.O.T. SEE "INTERMITTENTS" SECTION B.
CODE 24 ENGINE RUNNING. DRIVE WHEELS TURNING. "SCAN" MPH.	**HARD FAILURE -** "SCAN" TOOL READS 0 MPH. IF SPEEDOMETER IS WORKING OK, THEN THE VSS SIGNAL INPUT IS OPEN, SHORTED TO GROUND, OR THE BUFFER IS DEFECTIVE. SEE CODE CHART 24. **INTERMITTENT CODE -** "SCAN" TOOL READING SHOULD CLOSELY MATCH WITH SPEEDOMETER READING WITH DRIVE WHEELS TURNING. SEE "INTERMITTENTS" SECTION B.

"SCAN" DIAGNOSTIC CIRCUIT CHECK
(Page 5 of 6)
4.3L "B/G" SERIES (CODE DEFINITIONS)

CODES	DEFINITION
CODE 43 "SCAN" TOOL IN SPECIAL MODE. ENGINE IDLING AT 1000 RPM. "SCAN" KNOCK RETARD OR OLD PA3	**HARD FAILURE -** KNOCK RETARD OR (OLD PA 3) WILL DISPLAY NUMBERS THAT ARE CONSTANTLY CHANGING (0 TO 255). FAULTY ESC CIRCUIT. SEE CODE CHART 43. **INTERMITTENT CODE -** NUMBERS SHOULD INCREASE WHEN KNOCK IS BEING DETECTED. SEE "INTERMITTENTS" SECTION B.
CODE 44 "SCAN" TOOL IN "SPECIAL" MODE. ENGINE IDLING AT 1000 RPM. "SCAN" OXYGEN SENSOR VOLTAGE	**HARD FAILURE -** "SCAN" TOOL O_2 VOLTAGE CONSISTENTLY BELOW .35V. CAUSED BY A LEAN EXHAUST OR SIGNAL CIRCUIT SHORTED TO GROUND. SEE CODE CHART 44. **INTERMITTENT CODE -** THE "SCAN" TOOL HAS SEVERAL POSITIONS THAT WILL INDICATE THE STATE OF THE EXHAUST GASES. CROSSCOUNTS, RICH - LEAN INDICATION, O_2 VOLTAGE, INTEGRATOR, AND BLOCK LEARN. SEE "SCAN" POSITION INFORMATION IN INTRODUCTION.
CODE 45 "SCAN" TOOL IN "SPECIAL" MODE ENGINE IDLING AT 1000 RPM "SCAN" OXYGEN SENSOR VOLTAGE	**HARD FAILURE -** "SCAN" O_2 VOLTAGE CONSISTENTLY ABOVE .55V. RICH EXHAUST CAUSES A HIGH O_2 VOLTAGE. SEE CODE CHART 45. **INTERMITTENT CODE -** THE "SCAN" HAS SEVERAL POSITIONS THAT WILL INDICATE THE STATE OF THE EXHAUST GASES. CROSSCOUNTS, RICH - LEAN INDICATION, O_2 VOLTAGE, INTEGRATOR, AND BLOCK LEARN. SEE "SCAN" POSITION INFORMATION IN INTRODUCTION.

"SCAN" DIAGNOSTIC CIRCUIT CHECK
(Page 4 of 6)
4.3L "B/G" SERIES (CODE DEFINITIONS)

CODES	DEFINITION
CODE 33 (With MAP Sensor) ENGINE IDLING. "SCAN" MAP.	**HARD FAILURE -** "SCAN" TOOL READS ABOVE 2.5 VOLTS. SENSOR GROUND CIRCUIT OPEN, FAULTY SENSOR, LEAKING VACUUM HOSE OR INSUFFICIENT MANIFOLD VACUUM. SEE CODE CHART 33. **INTERMITTENT CODE -** "SCAN" TOOL READS MANIFOLD PRESSURE IN VOLTS. LOW PRESSURE (HIGH VACUUM) READS A LOW VOLTAGE WHILE A HIGH PRESSURE (LOW VACUUM) READS A HIGH VOLTAGE. QUICK ACCELERATION SHOULD CAUSE A HIGH OUTPUT VOLTAGE WHILE A QUICK DECELERATION WILL SHOW A LOW VOLTAGE. SEE "INTERMITTENTS" SECTION B.
CODE 34 (With MAP Sensor) IGNITION "ON" "SCAN" MAP.	**HARD FAILURE -** "SCAN" TOOL READS BELOW (200 MV) .2 VOLTS. SIGNAL WIRE OR 5V REFERENCE OPEN OR SHORTED TO GROUND OR FAULTY SENSOR. SEE CODE CHART 34. **INTERMITTENT CODE -** "SCAN" TOOL READS MANIFOLD PRESSURE IN VOLTS. LOW PRESSURE (HIGH VACUUM) READS A LOW VOLTAGE WHILE A HIGH PRESSURE (LOW VACUUM) READS A HIGH VOLTAGE. QUICK ACCELERATION SHOULD CAUSE A HIGH OUTPUT VOLTAGE WHILE A QUICK DECELERATION WILL SHOW A LOW VOLTAGE. SEE "INTERMITTENTS" SECTION B.
CODE 42 CLEAR CODES. START AND IDLE ENGINE FOR 1 MINUTE. IF NO "SERVICE ENGINE SOON" LIGHT, REFER TO INTERMITTENTS IN SECTION "B".	**HARD FAILURE -** "SERVICE ENGINE SOON" ON, SCAN TOOL INDICATES CODE 42. SEE CODE CHART 42. **INTERMITTENT CODE -** THE SCAN DOES NOT HAVE THE ABILITY TO HELP DIAGNOSE A CODE 42 PROBLEM. SEE "INTERMITTENTS" SECTION B.

TBI TROUBLE DIAGNOSTICS

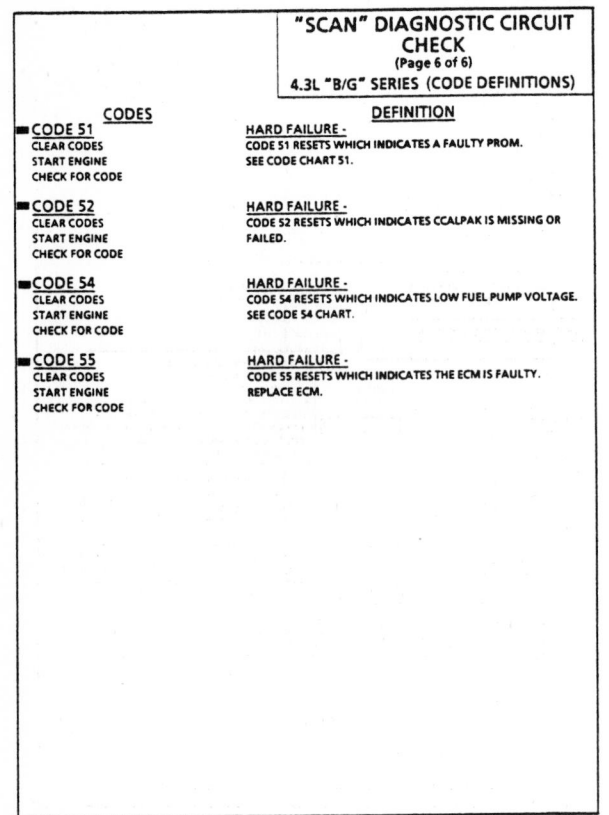

"SCAN" DIAGNOSTIC CIRCUIT CHECK
(Page 6 of 6)
4.3L "B/G" SERIES (CODE DEFINITIONS)

CODES   **DEFINITION**

CODE 51   **HARD FAILURE -**
CLEAR CODES   CODE 51 RESETS WHICH INDICATES A FAULTY PROM.
START ENGINE   SEE CODE CHART 51.
CHECK FOR CODE

CODE 52   **HARD FAILURE -**
CLEAR CODES   CODE 52 RESETS WHICH INDICATES CCALPAK IS MISSING OR
START ENGINE   FAILED.
CHECK FOR CODE

CODE 54   **HARD FAILURE -**
CLEAR CODES   CODE 54 RESETS WHICH INDICATES LOW FUEL PUMP VOLTAGE.
START ENGINE   SEE CODE 54 CHART.
CHECK FOR CODE

CODE 55   **HARD FAILURE -**
CLEAR CODES   CODE 55 RESETS WHICH INDICATES THE ECM IS FAULTY.
START ENGINE   REPLACE ECM.
CHECK FOR CODE

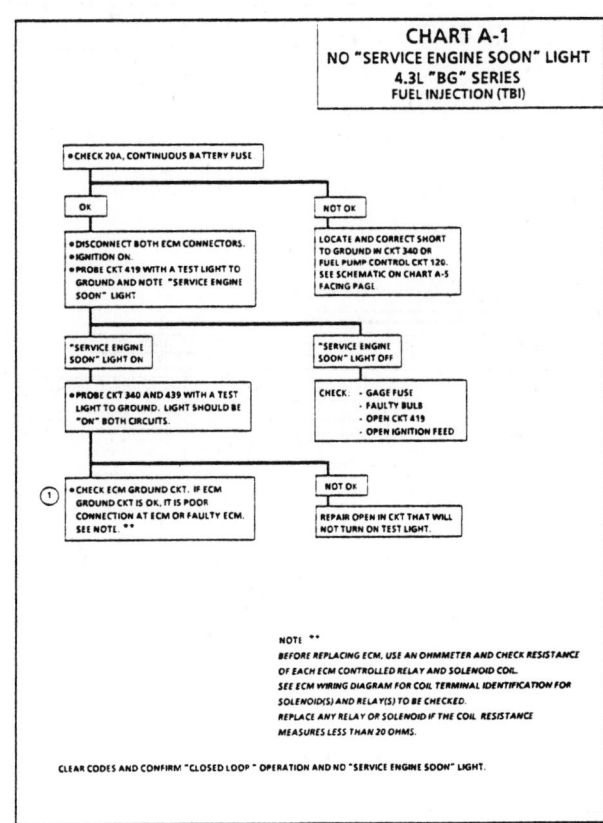

CHART A-1
NO "SERVICE ENGINE SOON" LIGHT
4.3L "BG" SERIES
FUEL INJECTION (TBI)

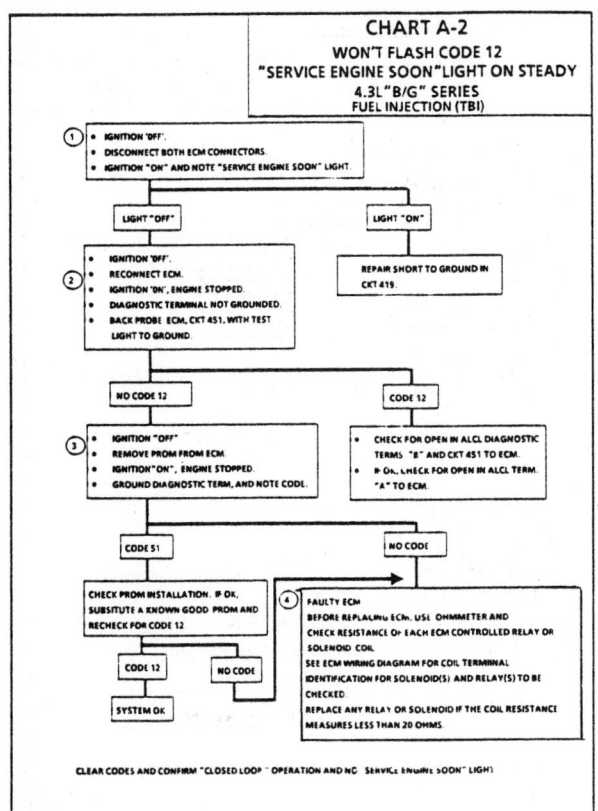

CHART A-2
WON'T FLASH CODE 12
"SERVICE ENGINE SOON" LIGHT ON STEADY
4.3L "B/G" SERIES
FUEL INJECTION (TBI)

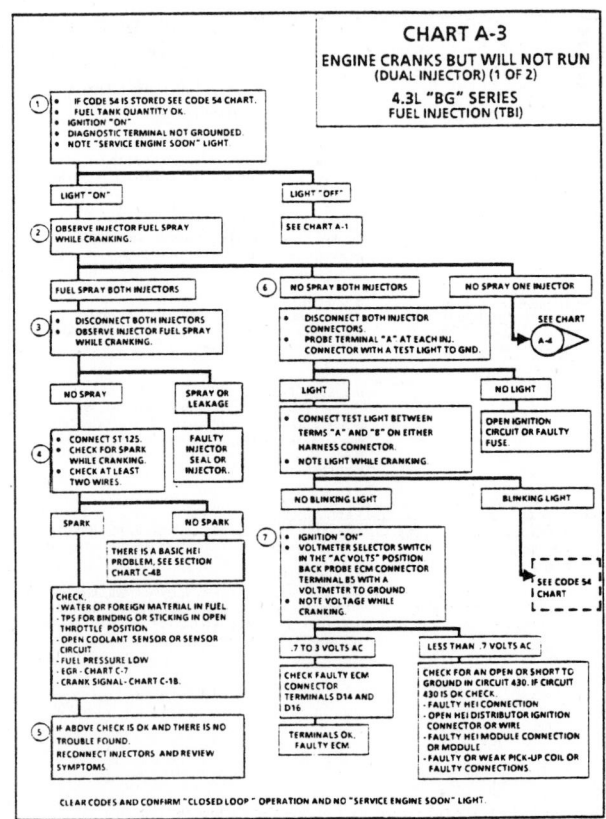

CHART A-3
ENGINE CRANKS BUT WILL NOT RUN
(DUAL INJECTOR) (1 OF 2)
4.3L "BG" SERIES
FUEL INJECTION (TBI)

TBI TROUBLE DIAGNOSTICS

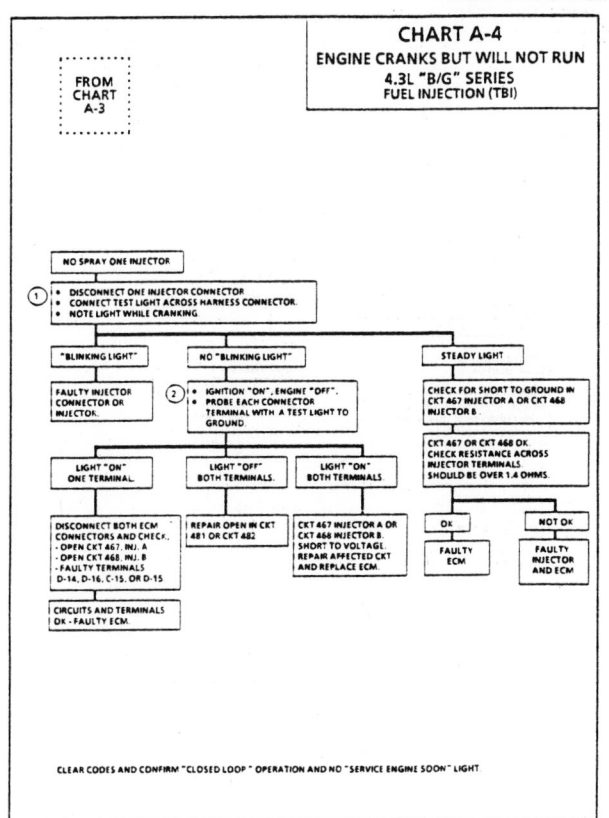

CHART A-4
ENGINE CRANKS BUT WILL NOT RUN
4.3L "B/G" SERIES
FUEL INJECTION (TBI)

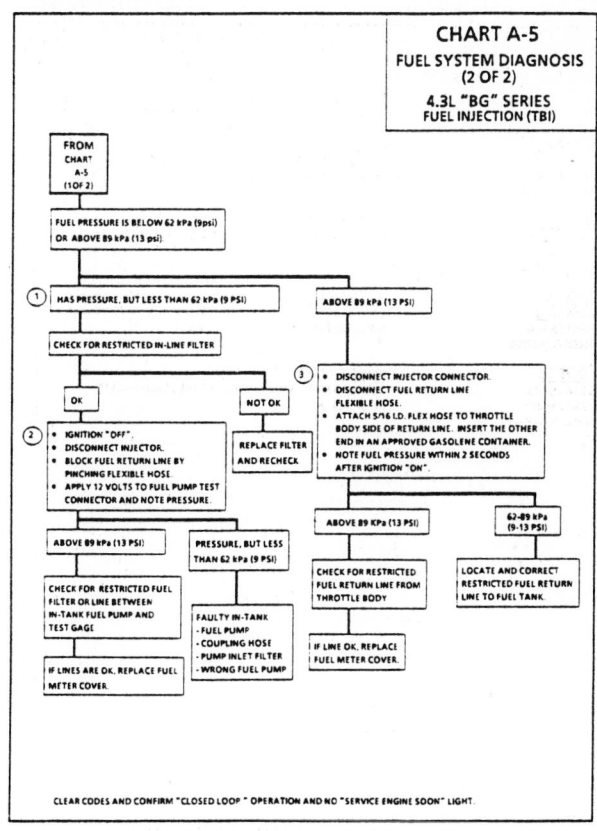

CHART A-5
FUEL SYSTEM DIAGNOSIS
(2 OF 2)
4.3L "BG" SERIES
FUEL INJECTION (TBI)

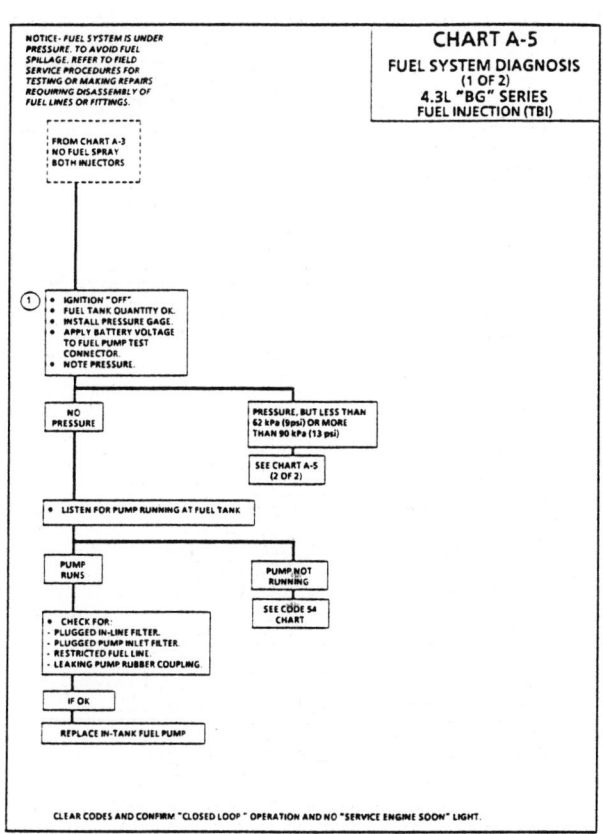

CHART A-5
FUEL SYSTEM DIAGNOSIS
(1 OF 2)
4.3L "BG" SERIES
FUEL INJECTION (TBI)

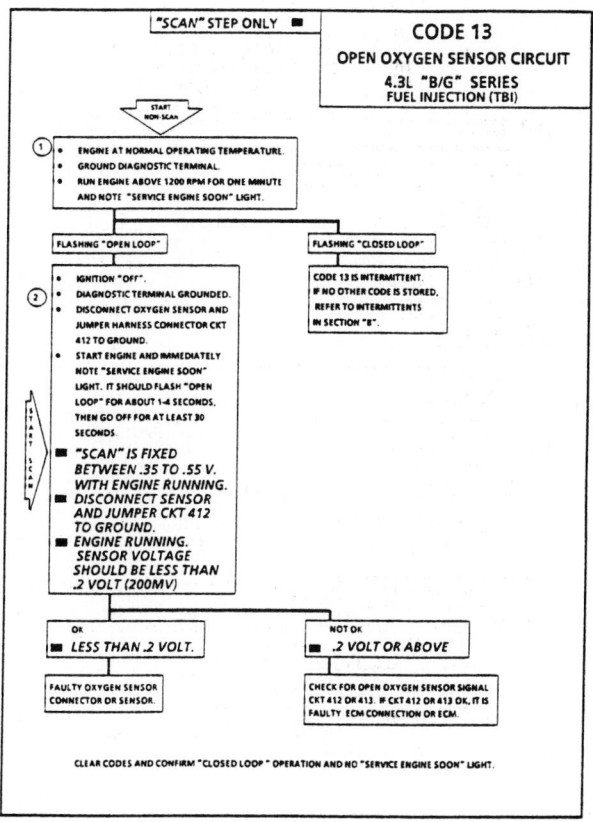

CODE 13
OPEN OXYGEN SENSOR CIRCUIT
4.3L "B/G" SERIES
FUEL INJECTION (TBI)

TBI TROUBLE DIAGNOSTICS

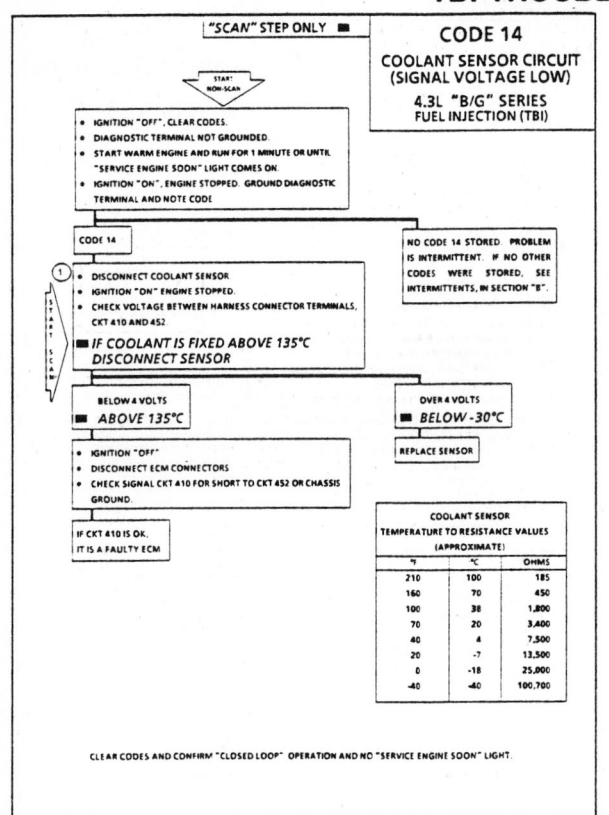

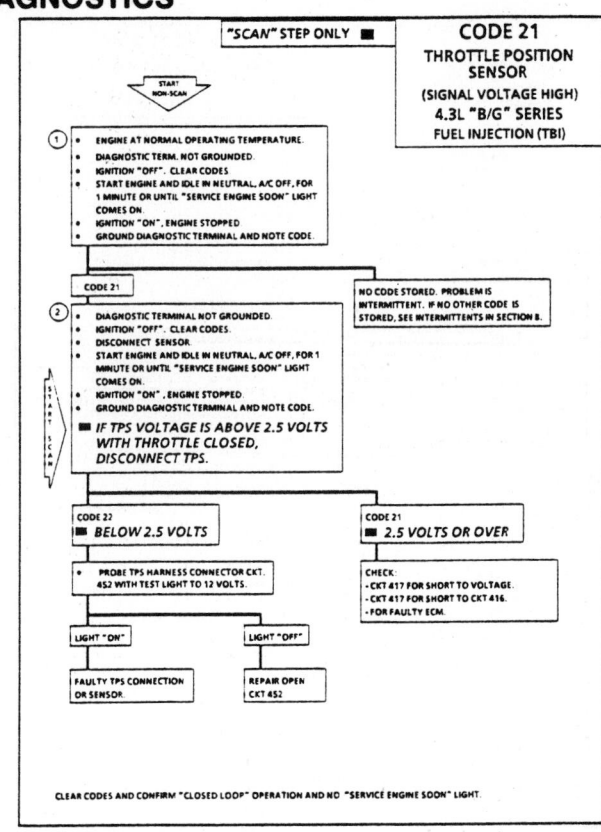

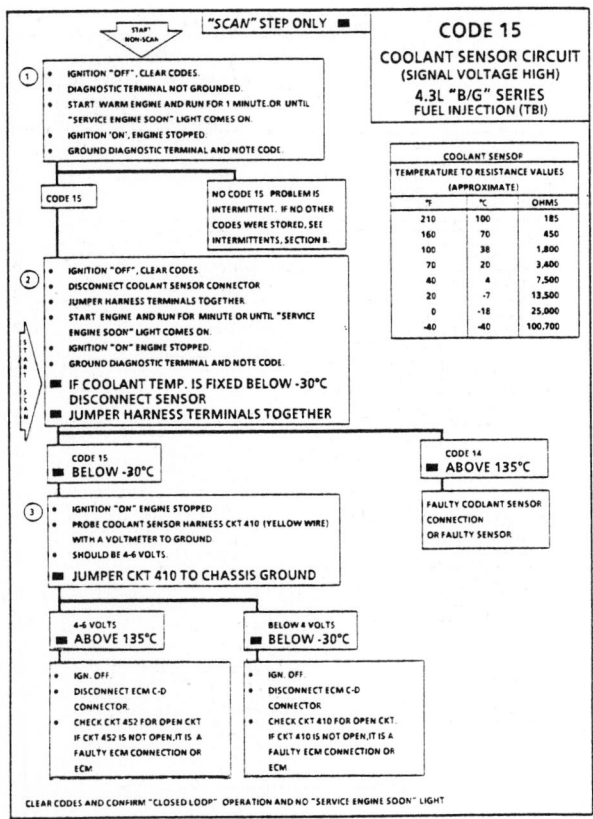

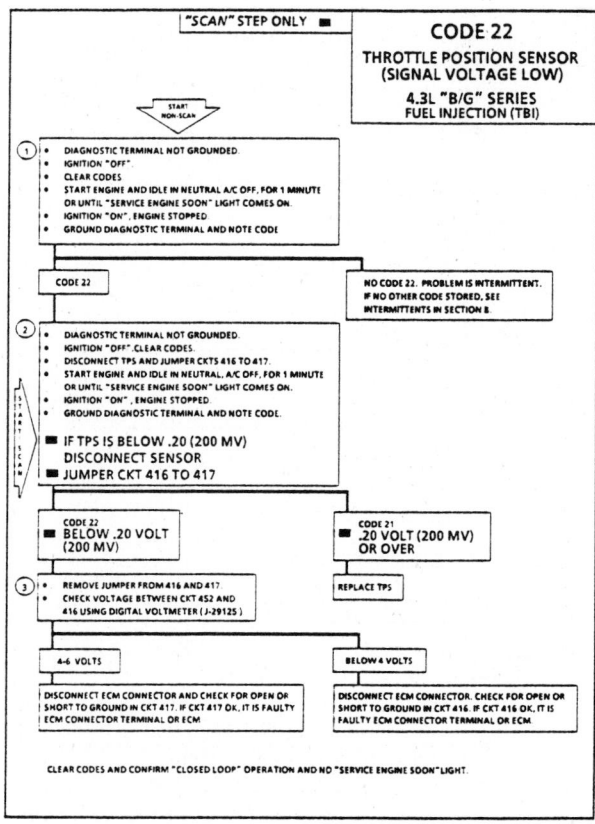

TBI TROUBLE DIAGNOSTICS

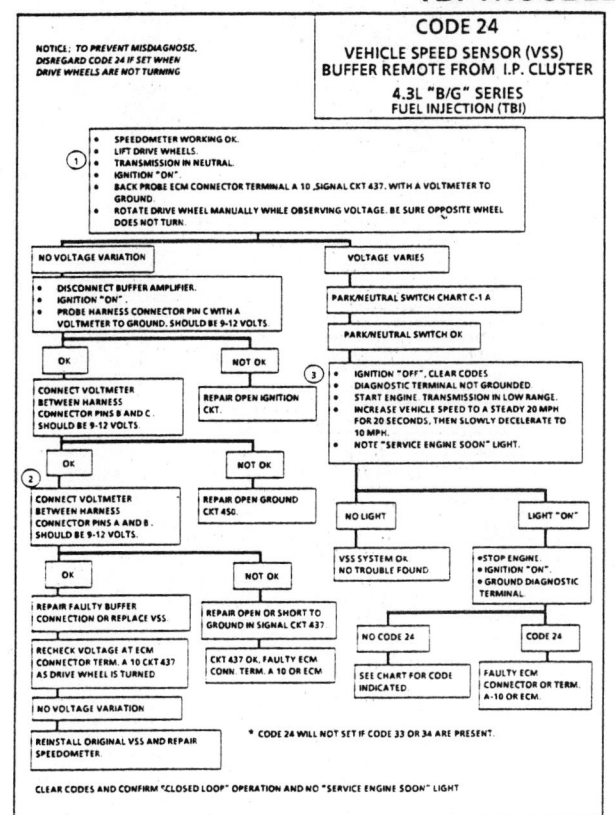

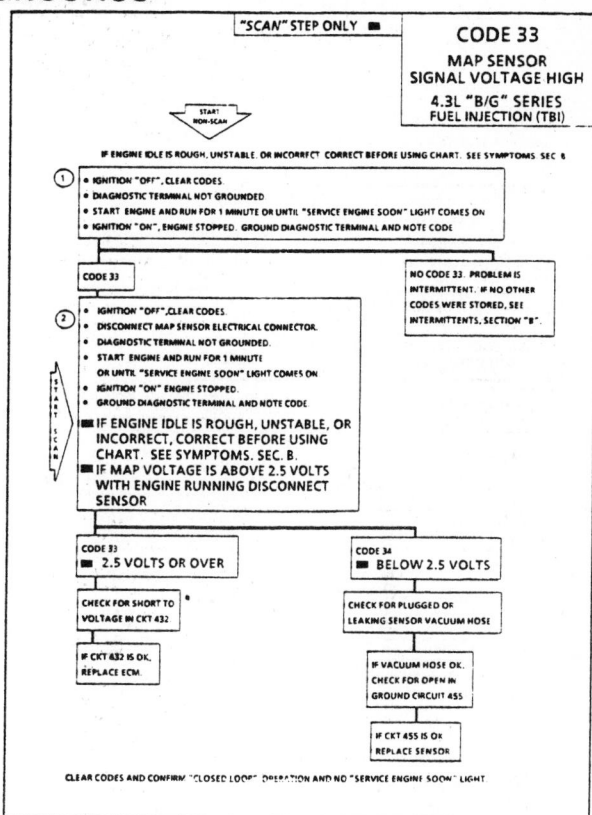

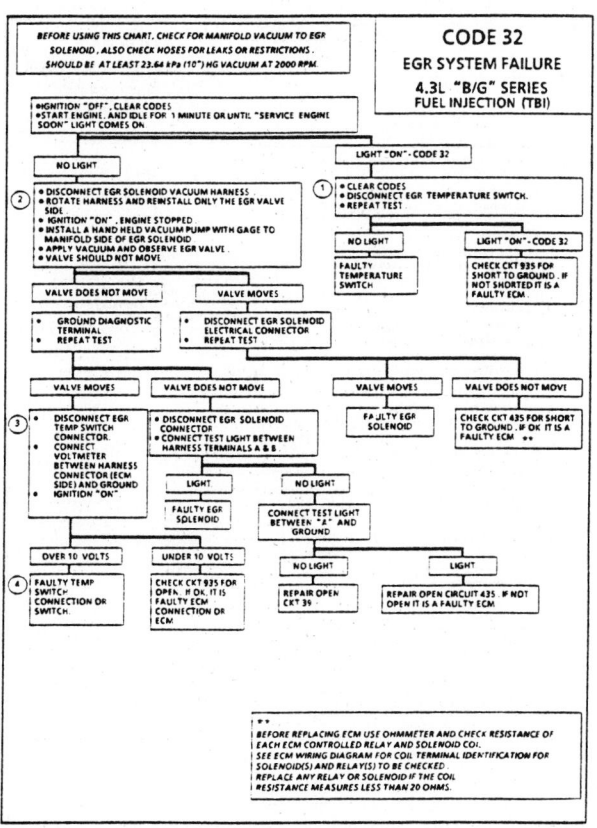

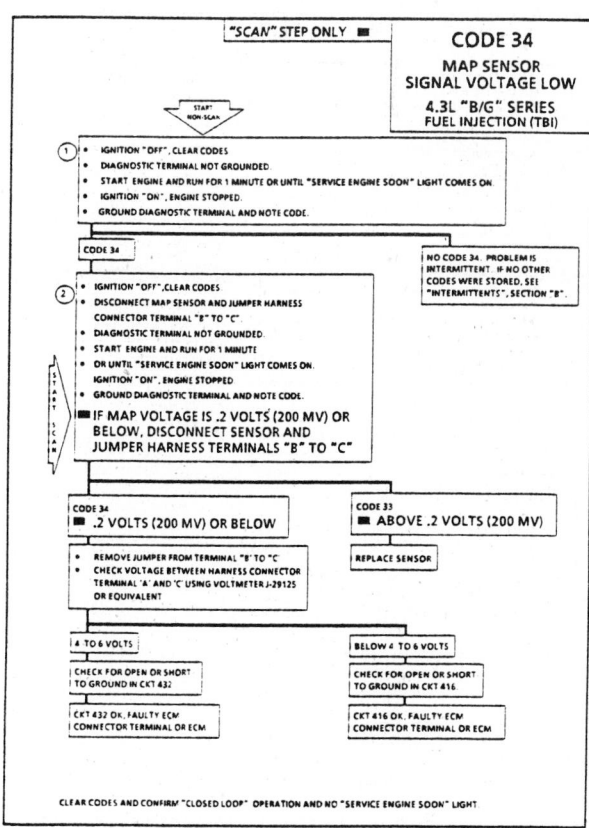

TBI TROUBLE DIAGNOSTICS

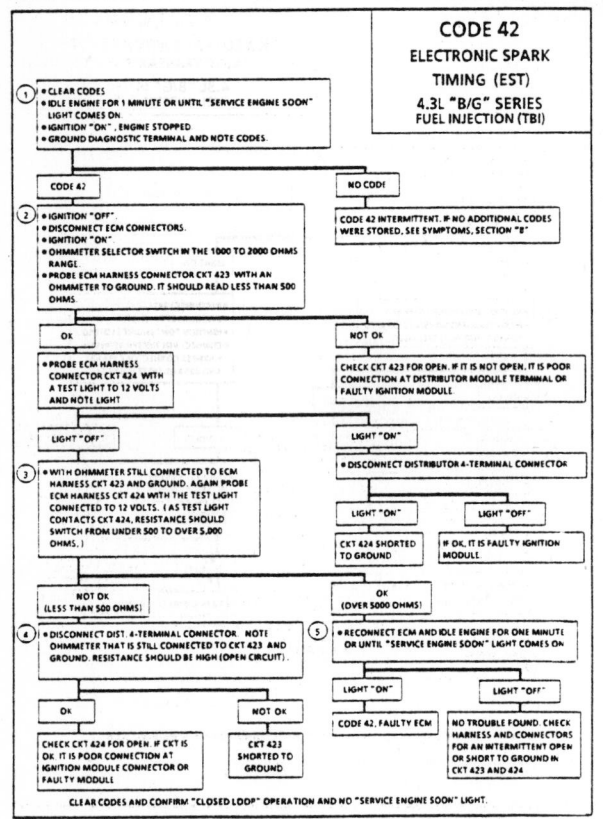

CODE 42
ELECTRONIC SPARK TIMING (EST)
4.3L "B/G" SERIES
FUEL INJECTION (TBI)

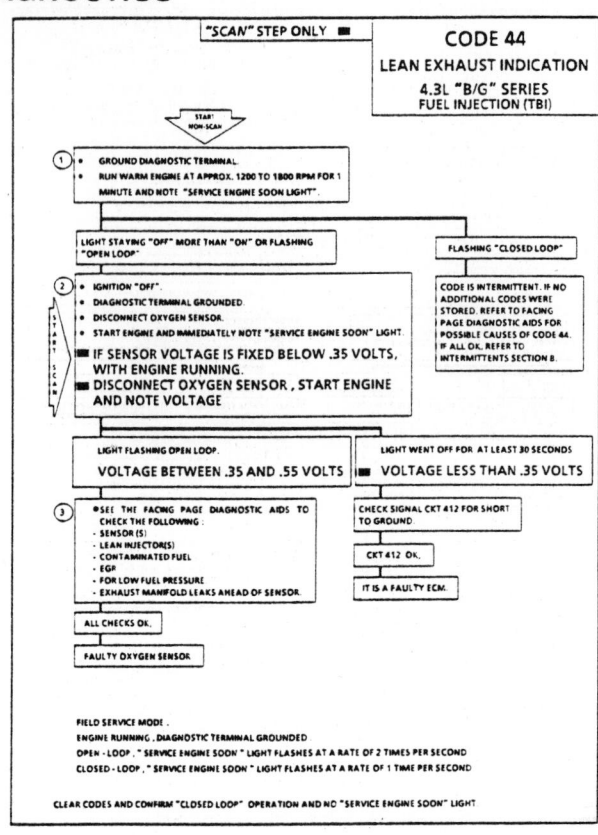

"SCAN" STEP ONLY ■

CODE 44
LEAN EXHAUST INDICATION
4.3L "B/G" SERIES
FUEL INJECTION (TBI)

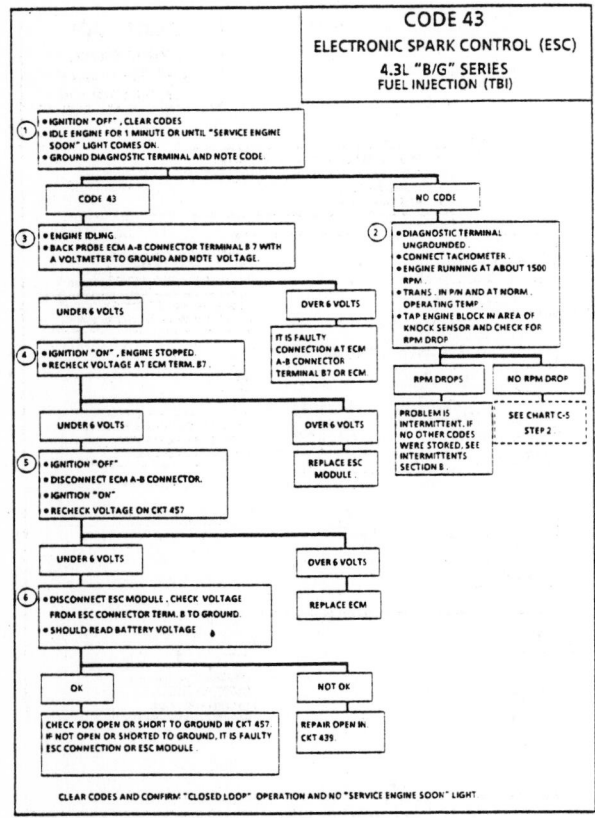

CODE 43
ELECTRONIC SPARK CONTROL (ESC)
4.3L "B/G" SERIES
FUEL INJECTION (TBI)

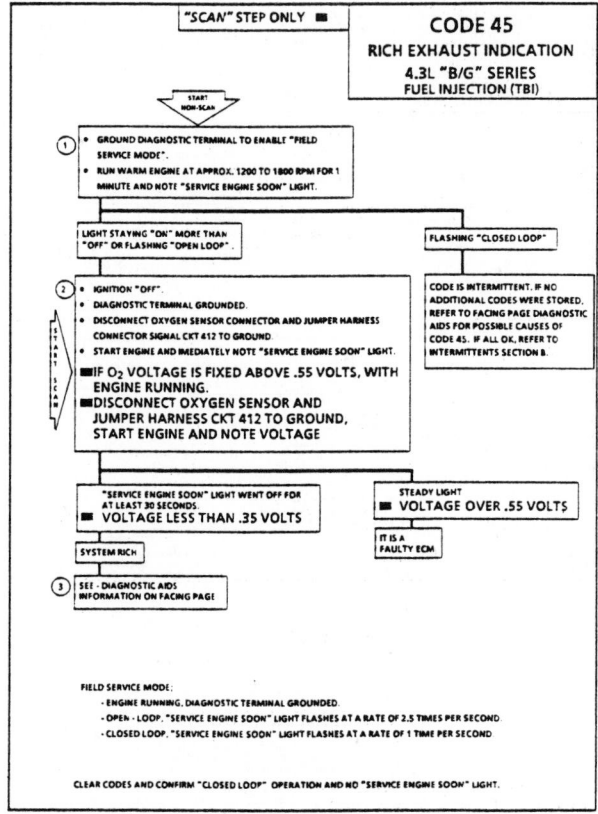

"SCAN" STEP ONLY ■

CODE 45
RICH EXHAUST INDICATION
4.3L "B/G" SERIES
FUEL INJECTION (TBI)

TBI TROUBLE DIAGNOSTICS

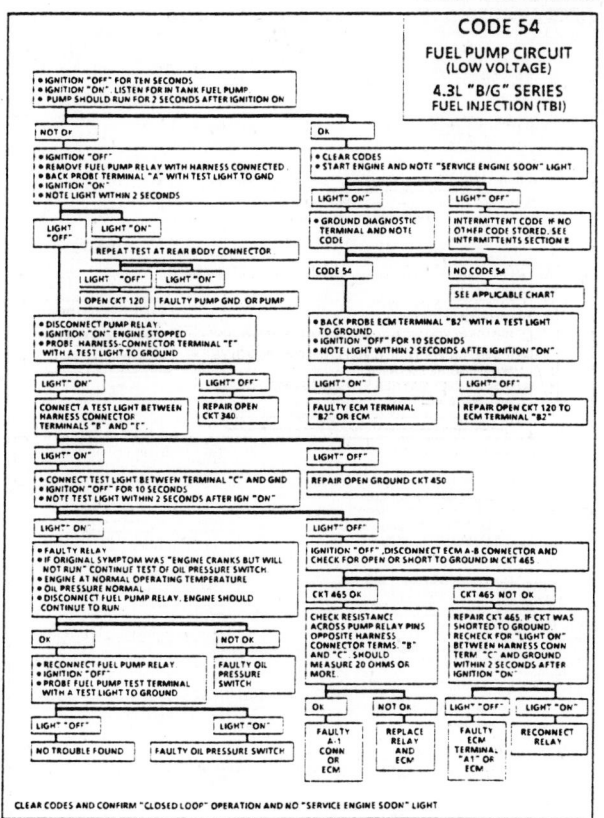

CODE 54

FUEL PUMP CIRCUIT
(LOW VOLTAGE)

4.3L "B/G" SERIES
FUEL INJECTION (TBI)

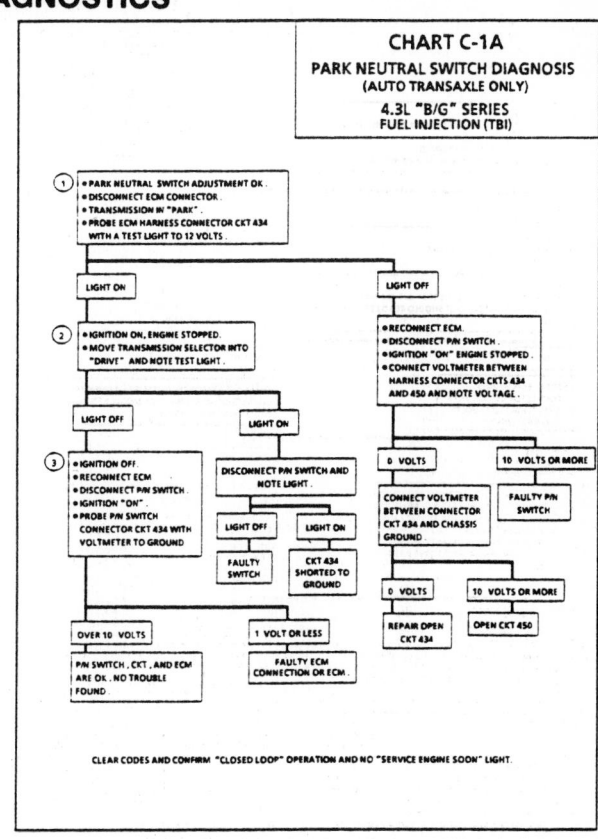

CHART C-1A

PARK NEUTRAL SWITCH DIAGNOSIS
(AUTO TRANSAXLE ONLY)

4.3L "B/G" SERIES
FUEL INJECTION (TBI)

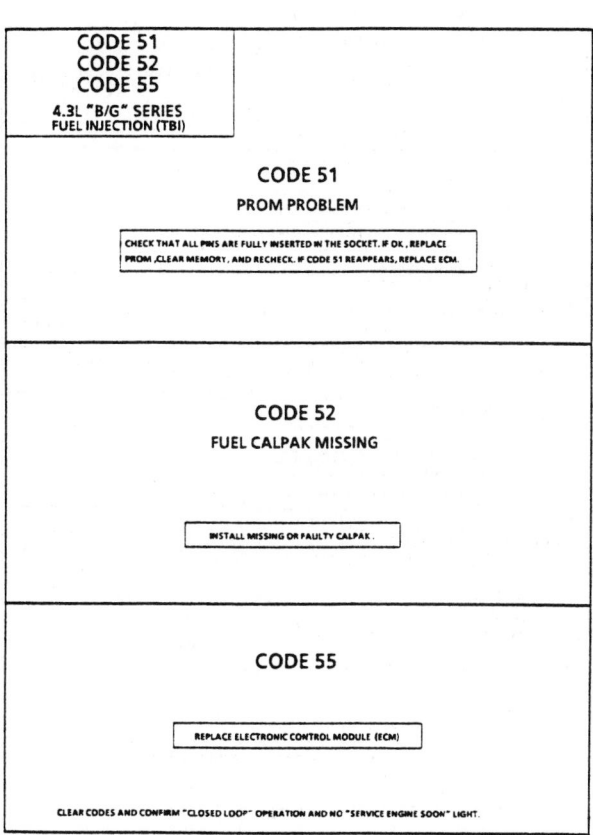

CODE 51
CODE 52
CODE 55

4.3L "B/G" SERIES
FUEL INJECTION (TBI)

CODE 51

PROM PROBLEM

CHECK THAT ALL PINS ARE FULLY INSERTED IN THE SOCKET. IF OK, REPLACE PROM, CLEAR MEMORY, AND RECHECK. IF CODE 51 REAPPEARS, REPLACE ECM.

CODE 52

FUEL CALPAK MISSING

INSTALL MISSING OR FAULTY CALPAK.

CODE 55

REPLACE ELECTRONIC CONTROL MODULE (ECM)

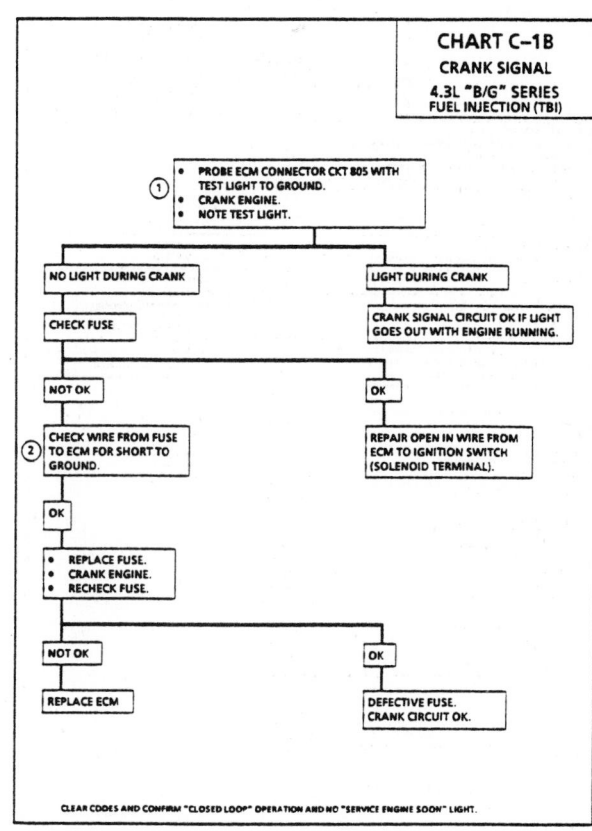

CHART C-1B

CRANK SIGNAL

4.3L "B/G" SERIES
FUEL INJECTION (TBI)

TBI TROUBLE DIAGNOSTICS

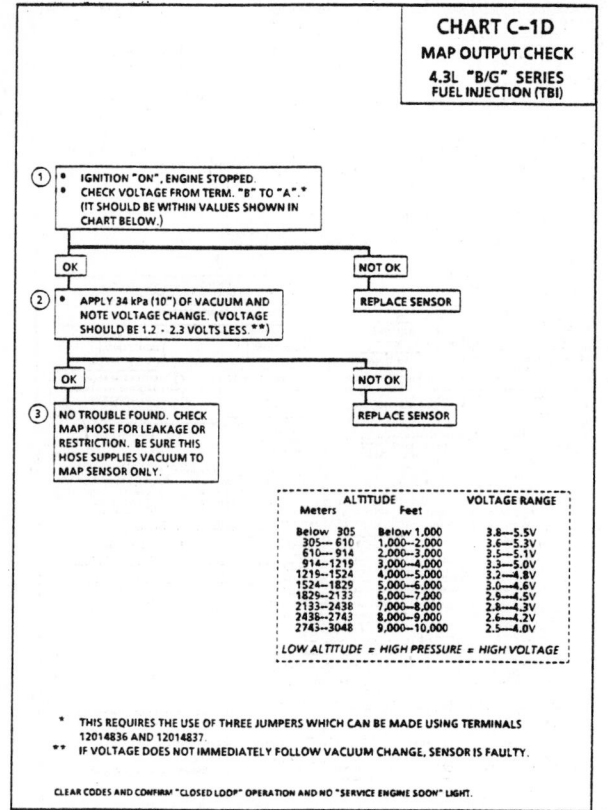

CHART C–1D

MAP OUTPUT CHECK

4.3L "B/G" SERIES
FUEL INJECTION (TBI)

① • IGNITION "ON", ENGINE STOPPED.
   • CHECK VOLTAGE FROM TERM. "B" TO "A".*
     (IT SHOULD BE WITHIN VALUES SHOWN IN CHART BELOW.)

OK → NOT OK → REPLACE SENSOR

② • APPLY 34 kPa (10") OF VACUUM AND NOTE VOLTAGE CHANGE. (VOLTAGE SHOULD BE 1.2 - 2.3 VOLTS LESS.**)

OK → NOT OK → REPLACE SENSOR

③ NO TROUBLE FOUND. CHECK MAP HOSE FOR LEAKAGE OR RESTRICTION. BE SURE THIS HOSE SUPPLIES VACUUM TO MAP SENSOR ONLY.

ALTITUDE		VOLTAGE RANGE
Meters	Feet	
Below 305	Below 1,000	3.8—5.5V
305— 610	1,000—2,000	3.6—5.3V
610— 914	2,000—3,000	3.5—5.1V
914—1219	3,000—4,000	3.3—5.0V
1219—1524	4,000—5,000	3.2—4.8V
1524—1829	5,000—6,000	3.0—4.6V
1829—2133	6,000—7,000	2.9—4.5V
2133—2438	7,000—8,000	2.8—4.3V
2438—2743	8,000—9,000	2.6—4.2V
2743—3048	9,000—10,000	2.5—4.0V

LOW ALTITUDE = HIGH PRESSURE = HIGH VOLTAGE

* THIS REQUIRES THE USE OF THREE JUMPERS WHICH CAN BE MADE USING TERMINALS 12014836 AND 12014837.
** IF VOLTAGE DOES NOT IMMEDIATELY FOLLOW VACUUM CHANGE, SENSOR IS FAULTY.

CLEAR CODES AND CONFIRM "CLOSED LOOP" OPERATION AND NO "SERVICE ENGINE SOON" LIGHT.

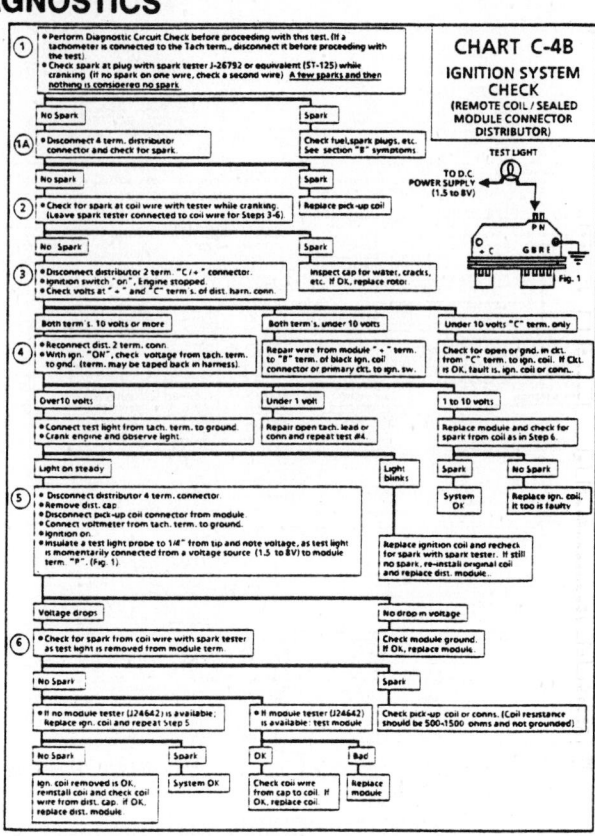

CHART C-4B

IGNITION SYSTEM CHECK
(REMOTE COIL / SEALED MODULE CONNECTOR DISTRIBUTOR)

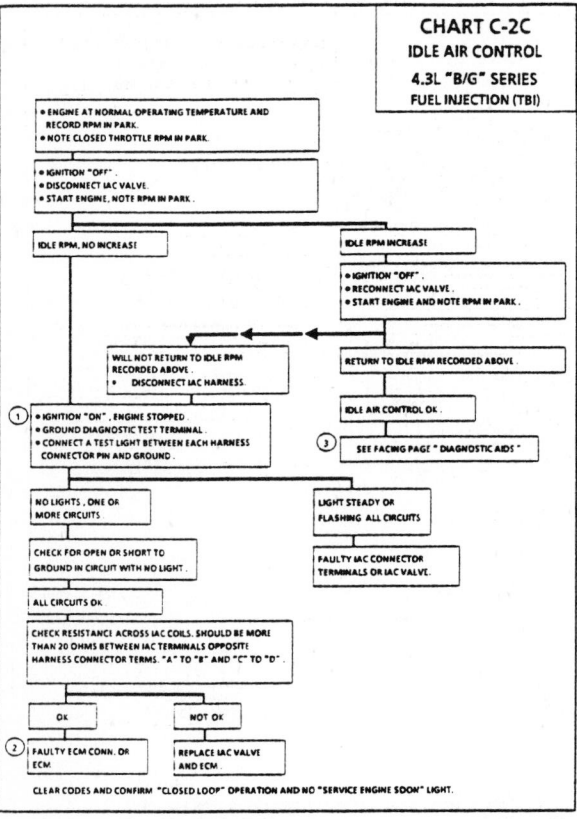

CHART C-2C

IDLE AIR CONTROL

4.3L "B/G" SERIES
FUEL INJECTION (TBI)

CLEAR CODES AND CONFIRM "CLOSED LOOP" OPERATION AND NO "SERVICE ENGINE SOON" LIGHT.

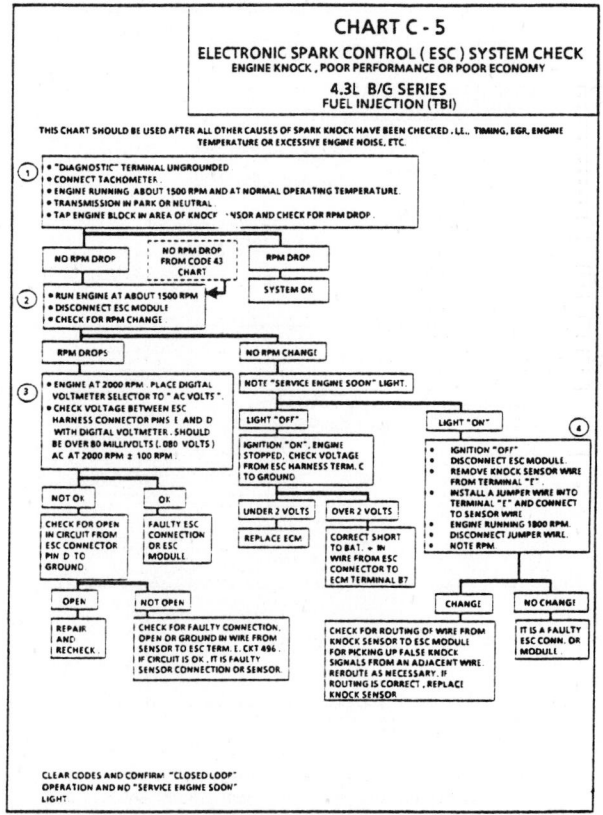

CHART C - 5

ELECTRONIC SPARK CONTROL (ESC) SYSTEM CHECK
ENGINE KNOCK , POOR PERFORMANCE OR POOR ECONOMY

4.3L B/G SERIES
FUEL INJECTION (TBI)

THIS CHART SHOULD BE USED AFTER ALL OTHER CAUSES OF SPARK KNOCK HAVE BEEN CHECKED . i.e. , TIMING, EGR, ENGINE TEMPERATURE OR EXCESSIVE ENGINE NOISE, ETC.

CLEAR CODES AND CONFIRM "CLOSED LOOP"
OPERATION AND NO "SERVICE ENGINE SOON"
LIGHT.

TBI TROUBLE DIAGNOSTICS

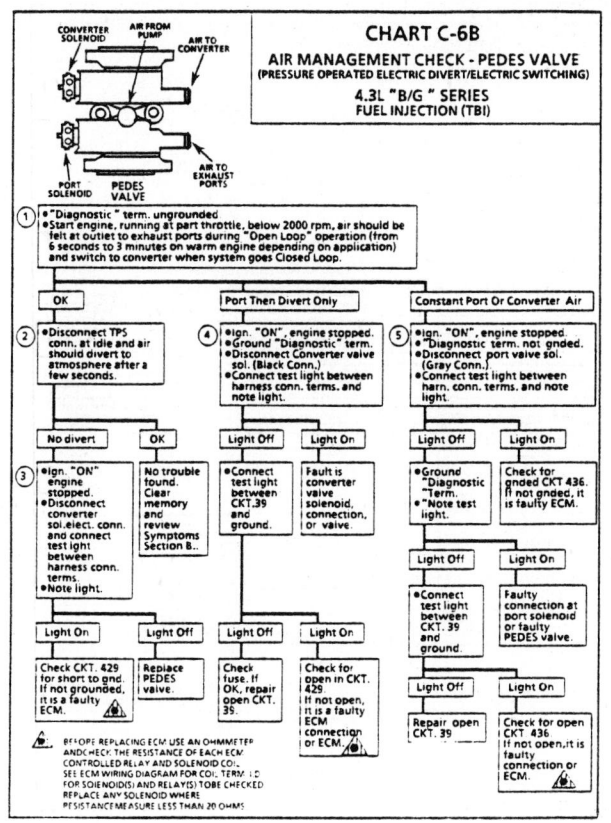

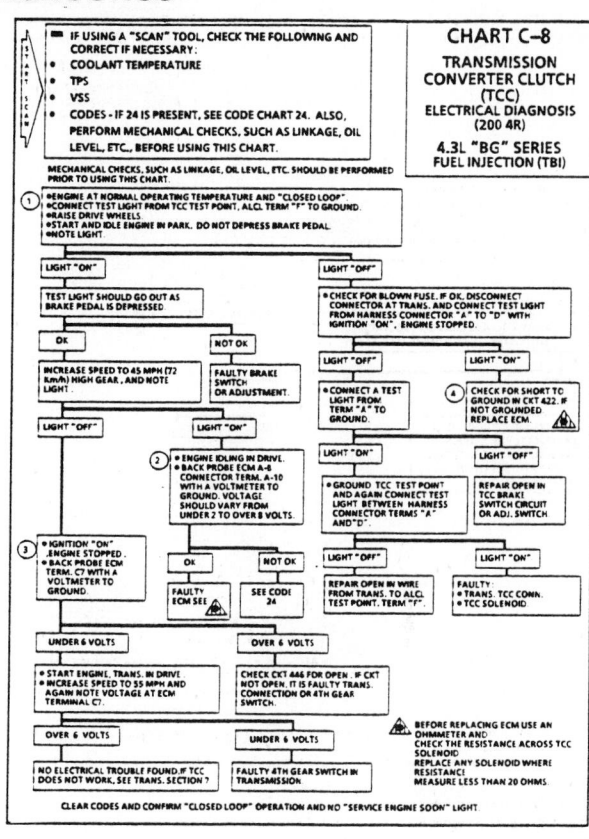

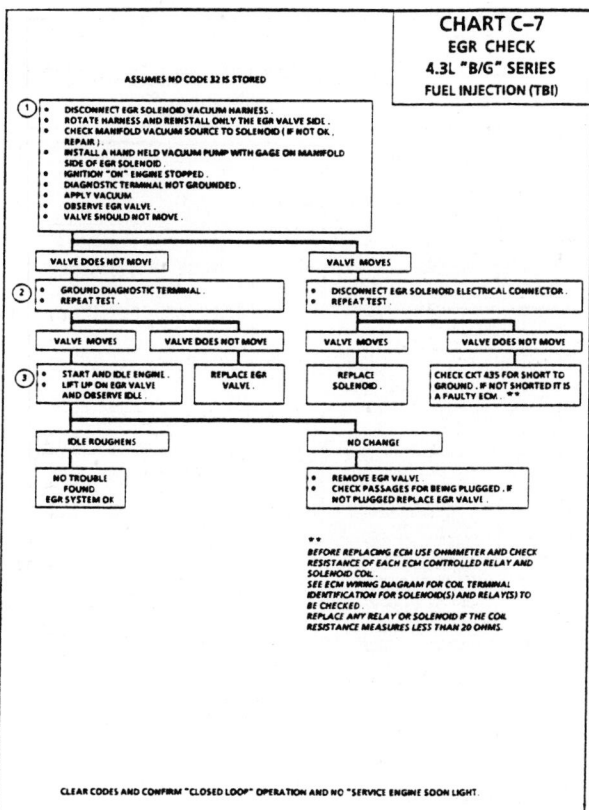

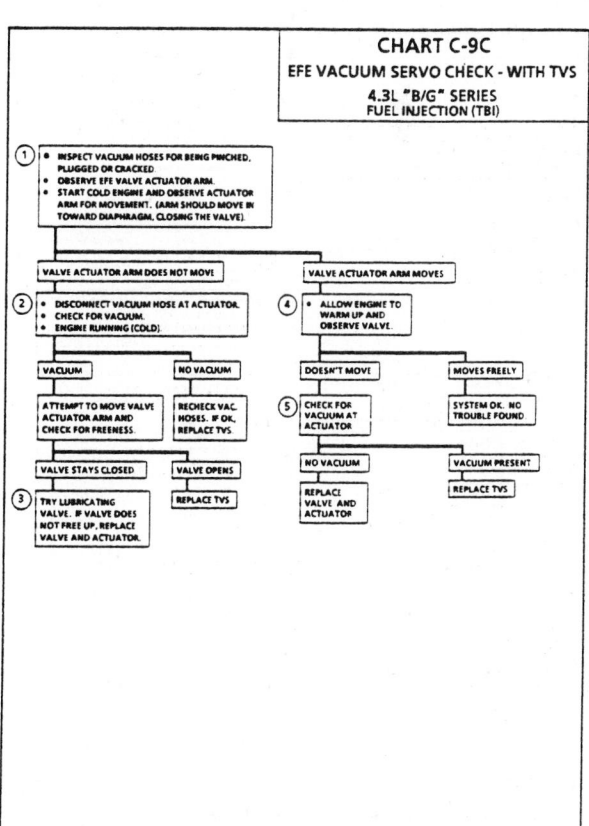

TBI TROUBLE DIAGNOSTICS

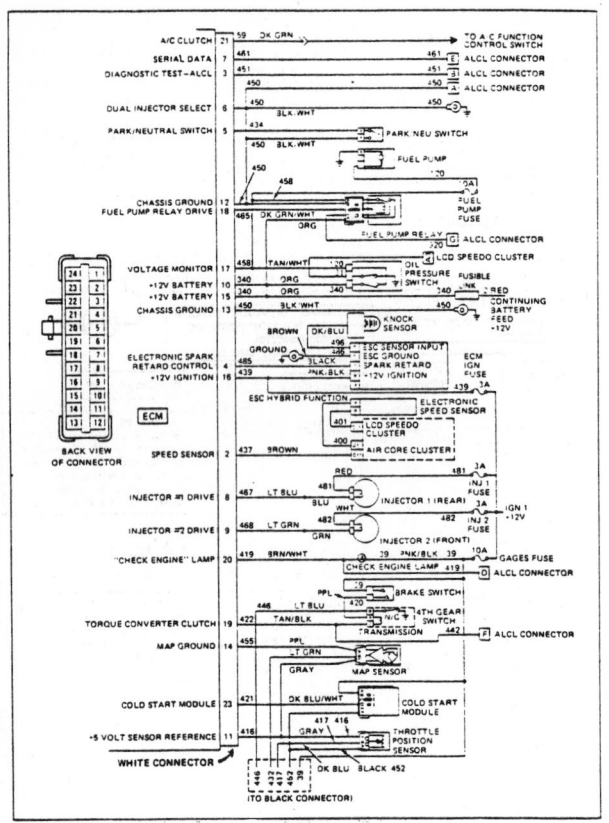

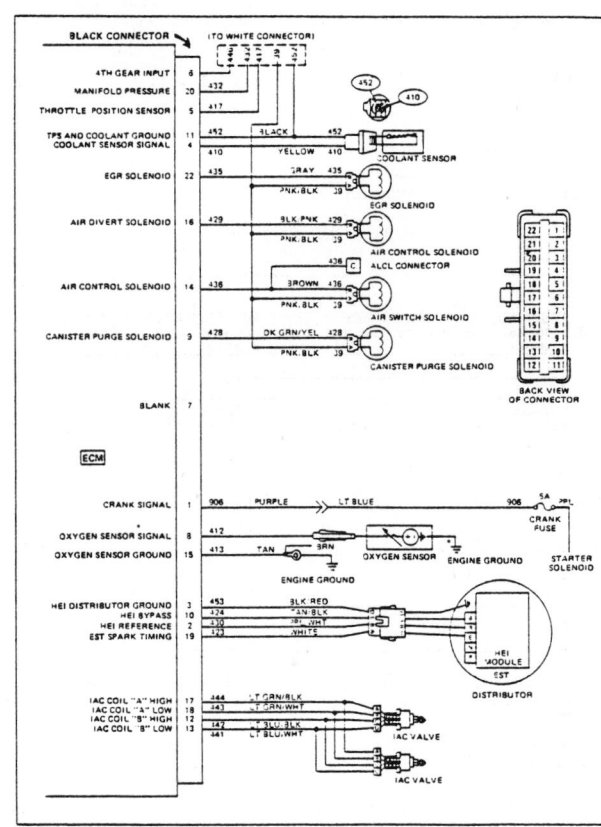

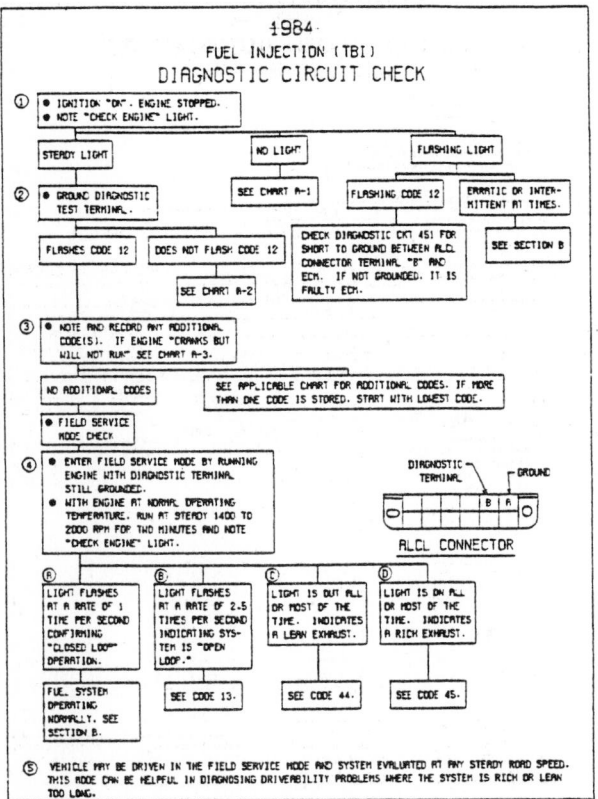

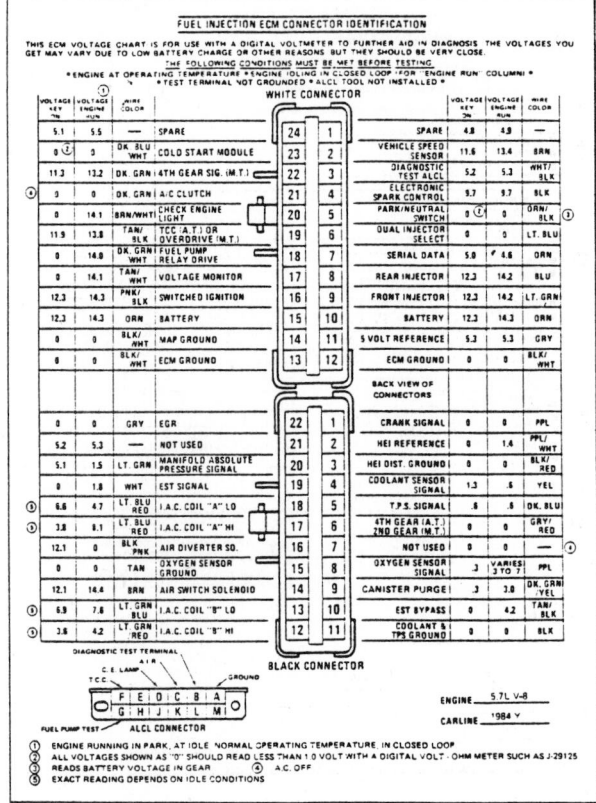

TBI TROUBLE DIAGNOSTICS

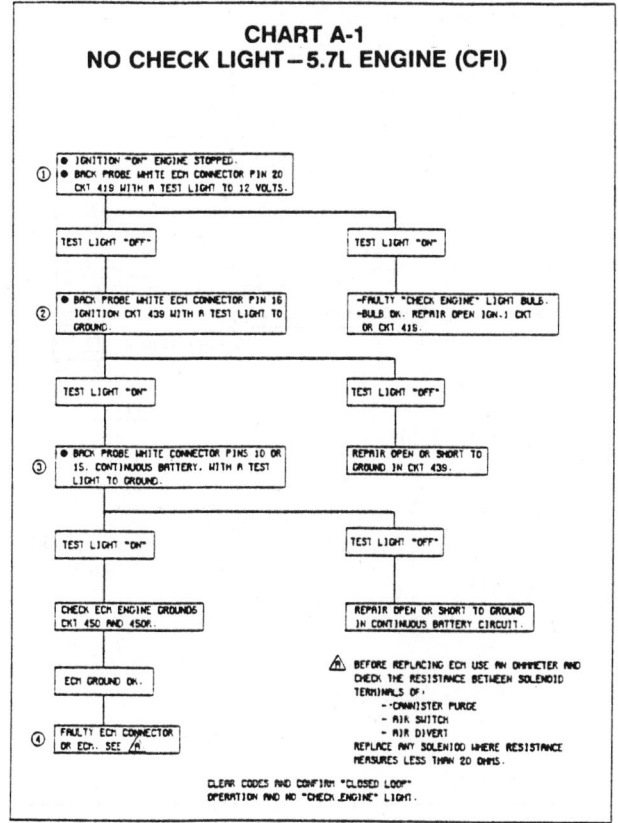

CHART A-1
NO CHECK LIGHT — 5.7L ENGINE (CFI)

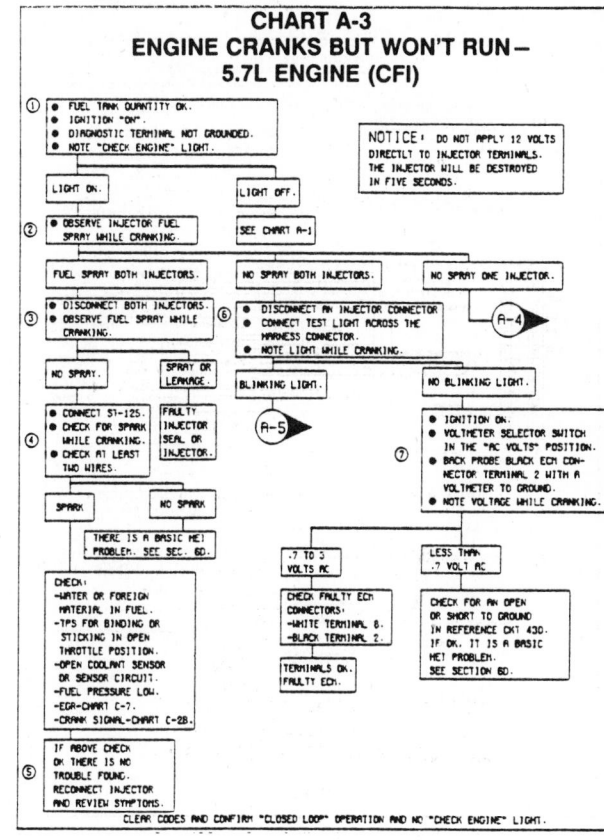

CHART A-3
ENGINE CRANKS BUT WON'T RUN —
5.7L ENGINE (CFI)

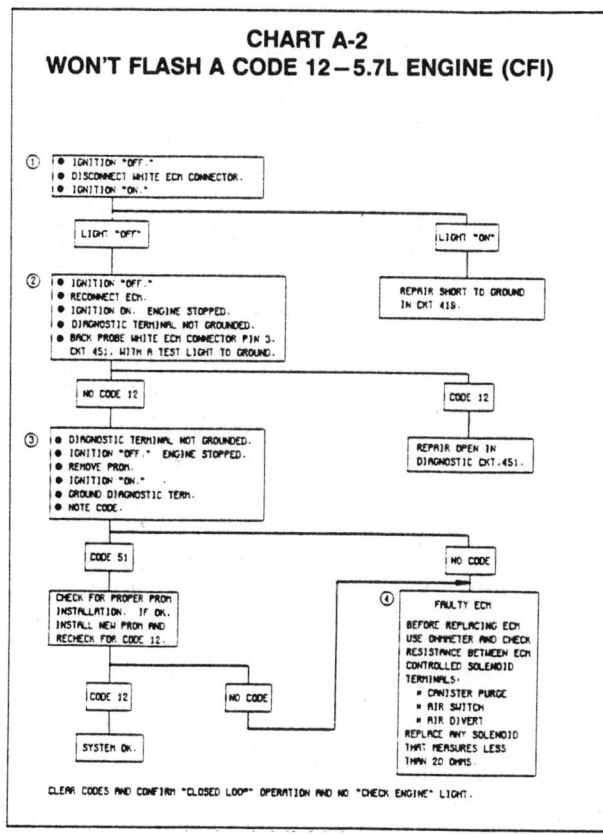

CHART A-2
WON'T FLASH A CODE 12 — 5.7L ENGINE (CFI)

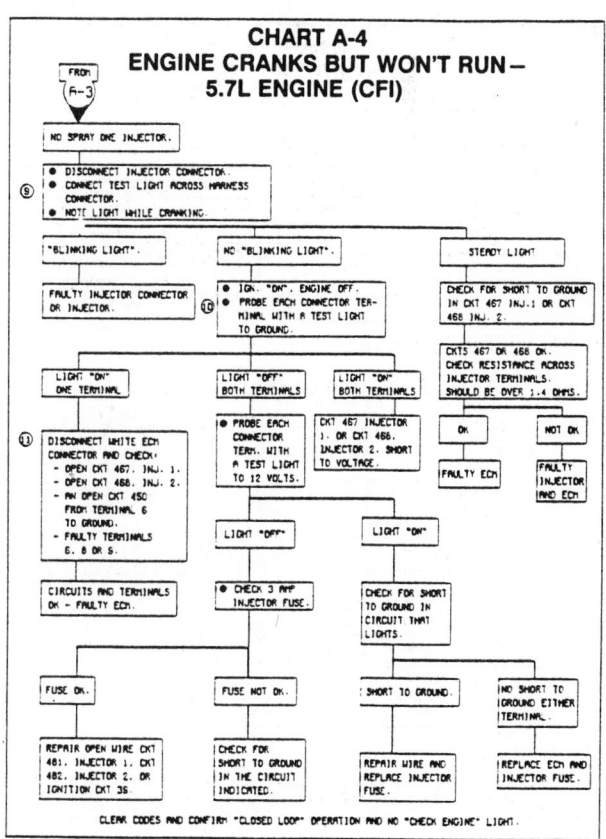

CHART A-4
ENGINE CRANKS BUT WON'T RUN —
5.7L ENGINE (CFI)

TBI TROUBLE DIAGNOSTICS

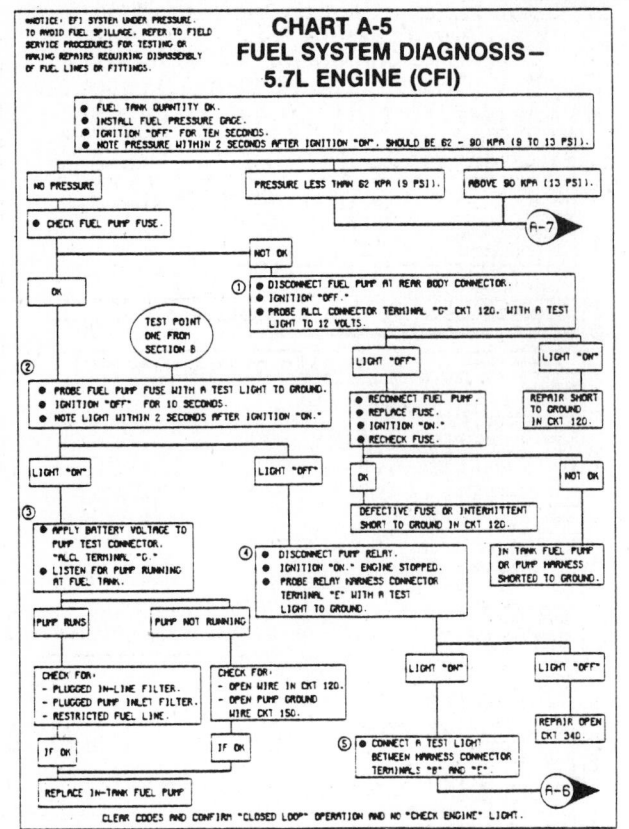

CHART A-5
FUEL SYSTEM DIAGNOSIS—
5.7L ENGINE (CFI)

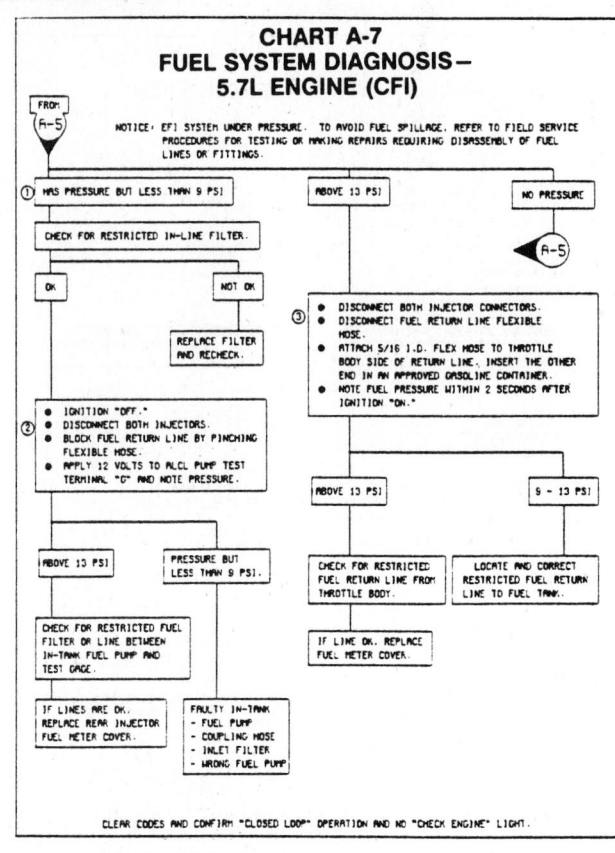

CHART A-7
FUEL SYSTEM DIAGNOSIS—
5.7L ENGINE (CFI)

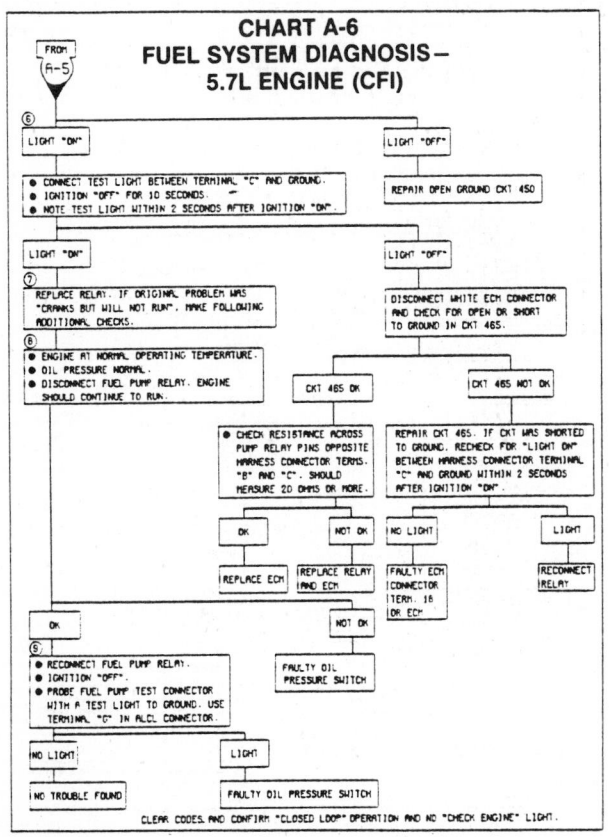

CHART A-6
FUEL SYSTEM DIAGNOSIS—
5.7L ENGINE (CFI)

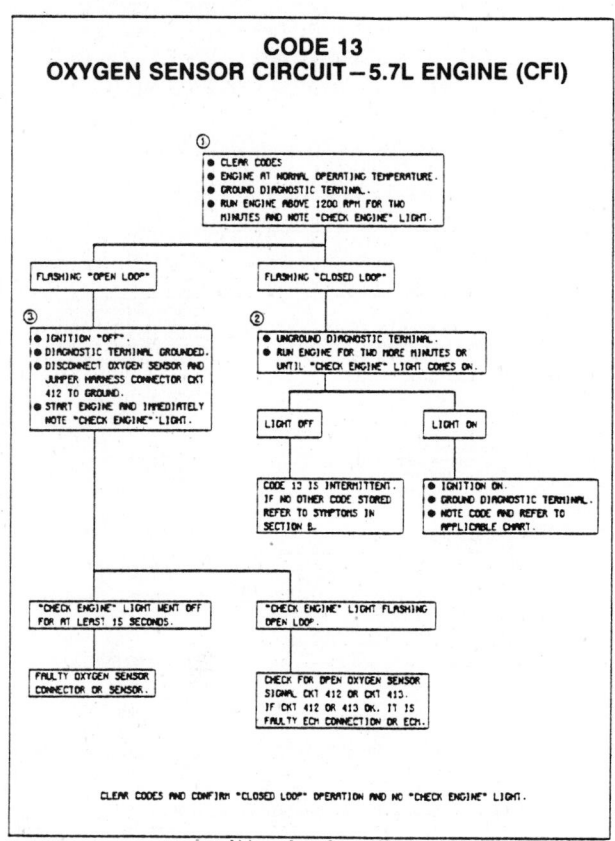

CODE 13
OXYGEN SENSOR CIRCUIT—5.7L ENGINE (CFI)

TBI TROUBLE DIAGNOSTICS

CODE 14
COOLANT SENSOR CIRCUIT — 5.7L ENGINE (CFI)

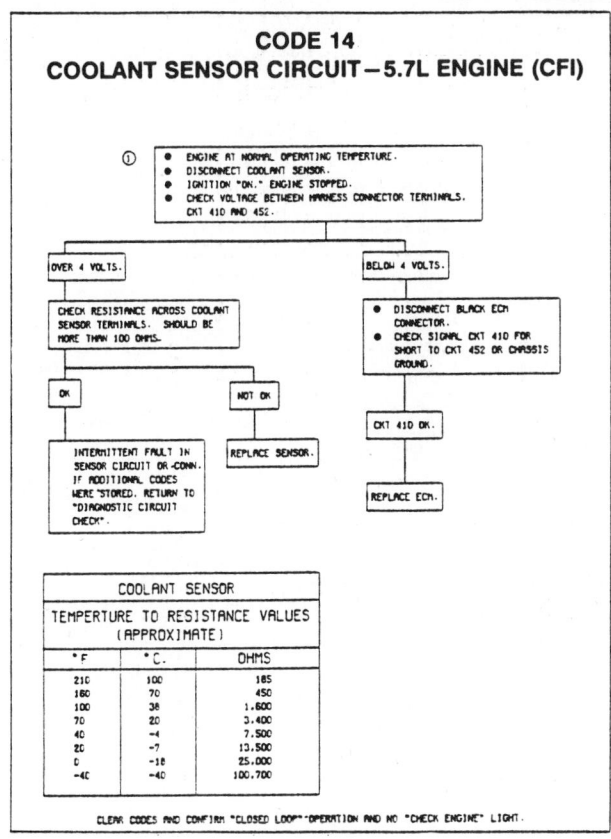

CODE 21
THROTTLE POSITION SENSOR CIRCUIT — 5.7L ENGINE (CFI)

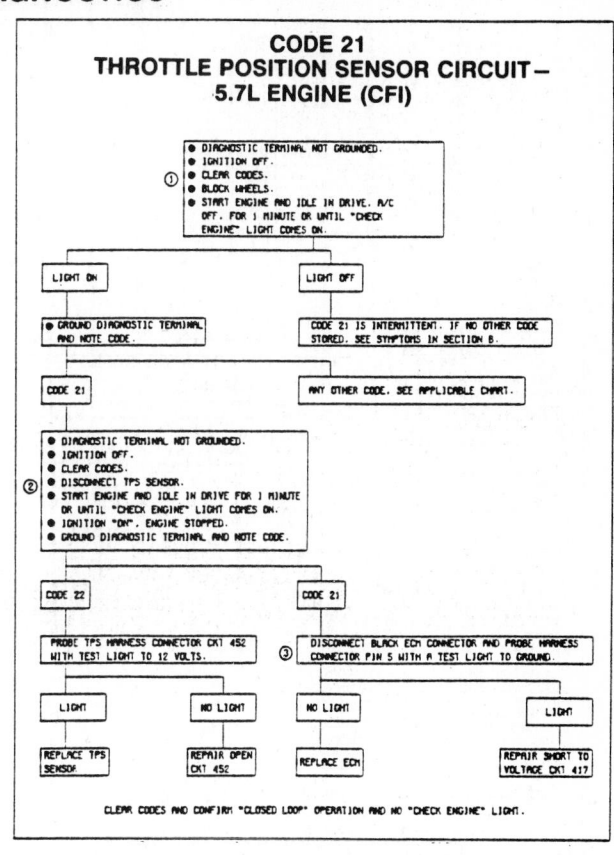

CODE 15
COOLANT SENSOR CIRCUIT — 5.7L ENGINE (CFI)

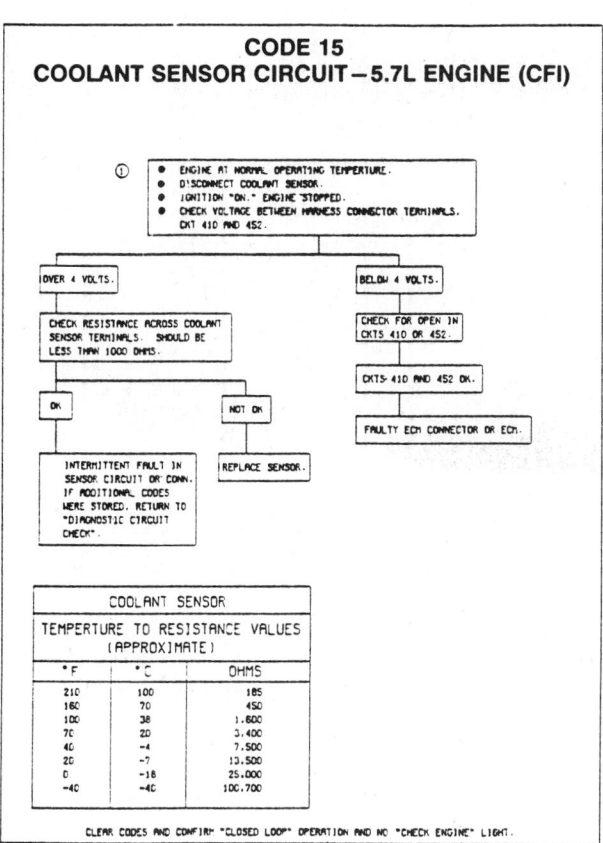

CODE 22
THROTTLE POSITION SENSOR CIRCUIT — 5.7L ENGINE (CFI)

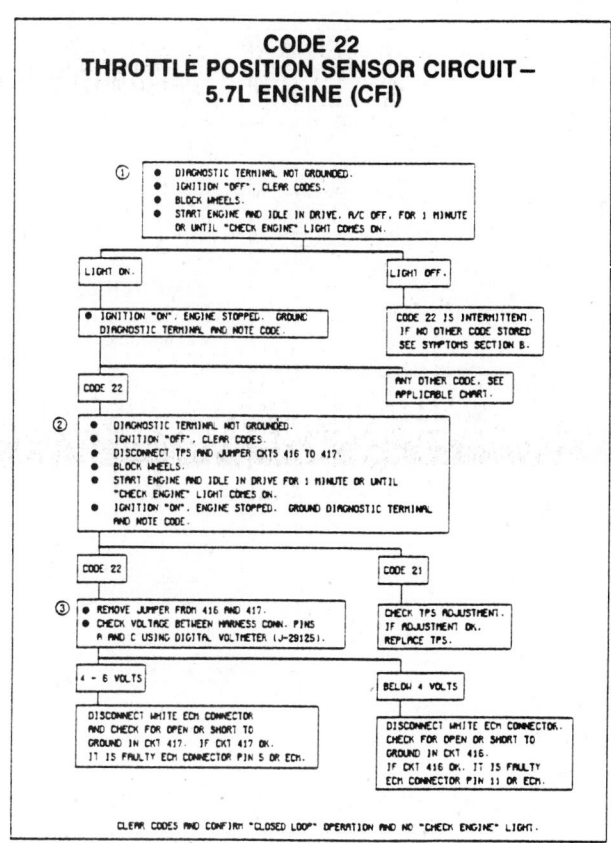

TBI TROUBLE DIAGNOSTICS

CODE 24
VEHICLE SPEED SENSOR CIRCUIT — 5.7L ENGINE (CFI)

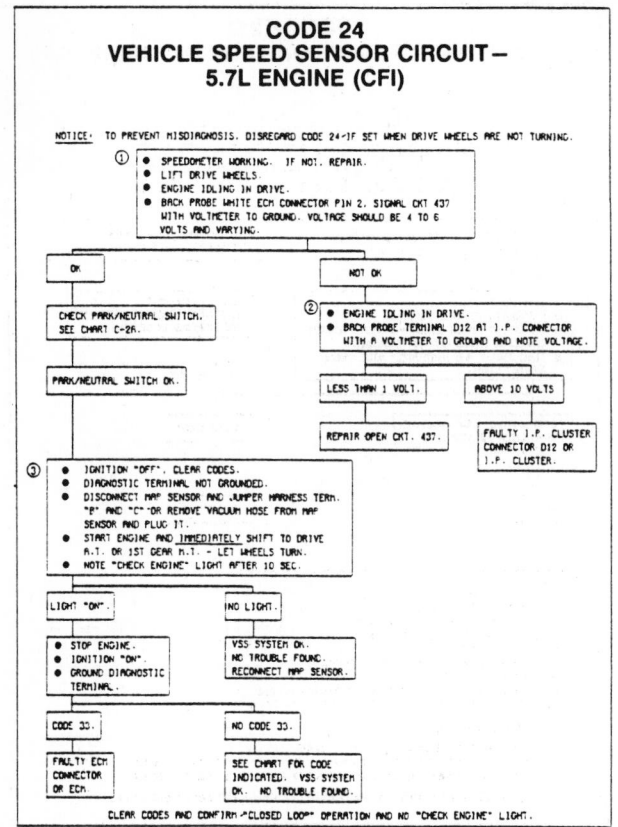

CODE 34
MAP SENSOR CIRCUIT — 5.7L ENGINE (CFI)

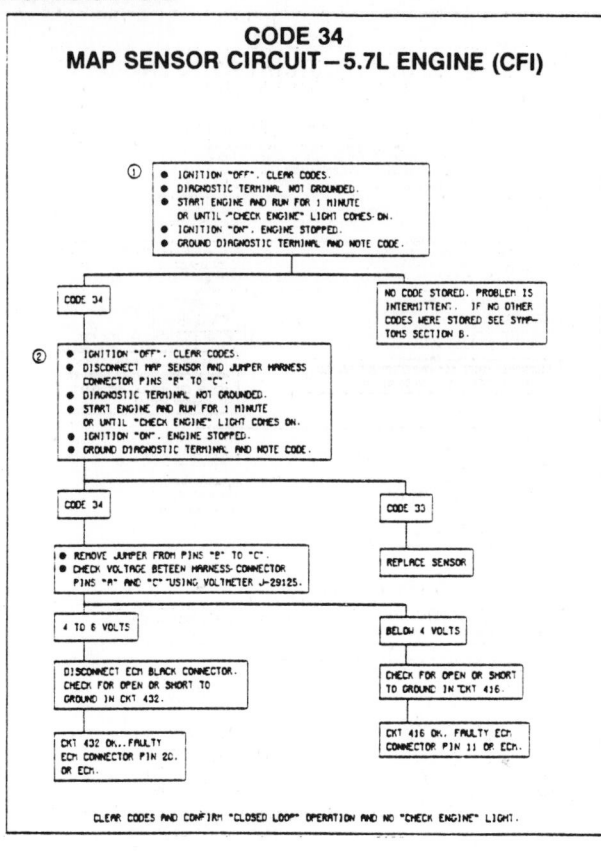

CODE 33
MAP SENSOR CIRCUIT — 5.7L ENGINE (CFI)

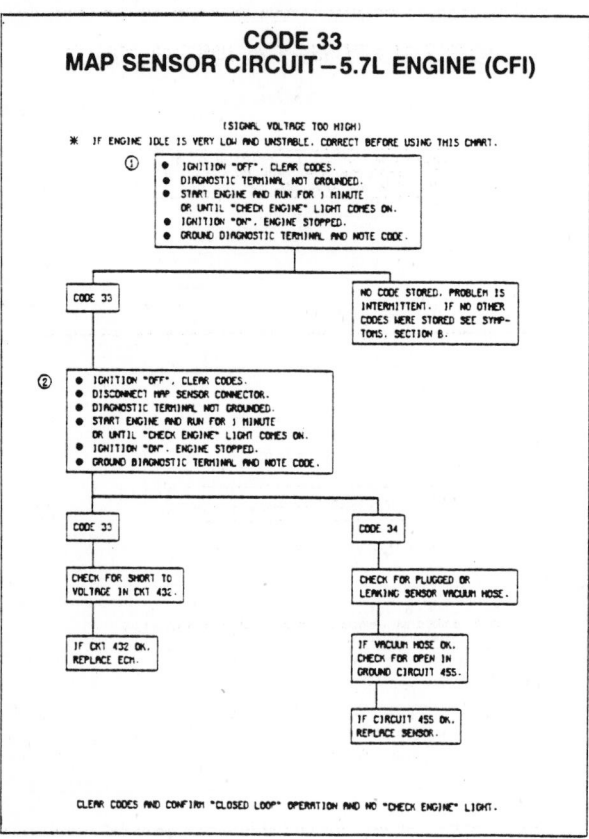

CODE 42
ELECTRONIC SPARK TIMING (EST) CIRCUIT — 5.7L ENGINE (CFI)

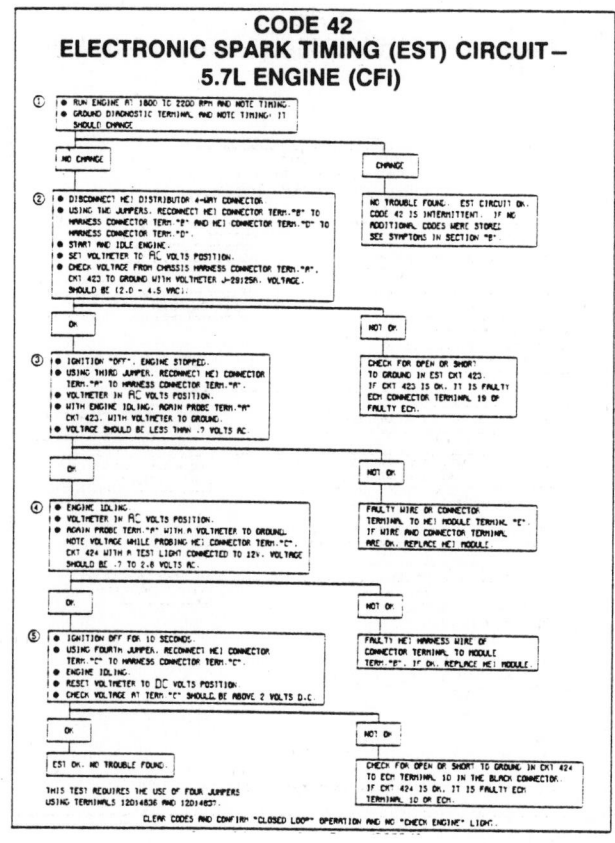

TBI TROUBLE DIAGNOSTICS

CODE 43
ELECTRONIC SPARK CONTROL (ESC) CIRCUIT—5.7L ENGINE (CFI)

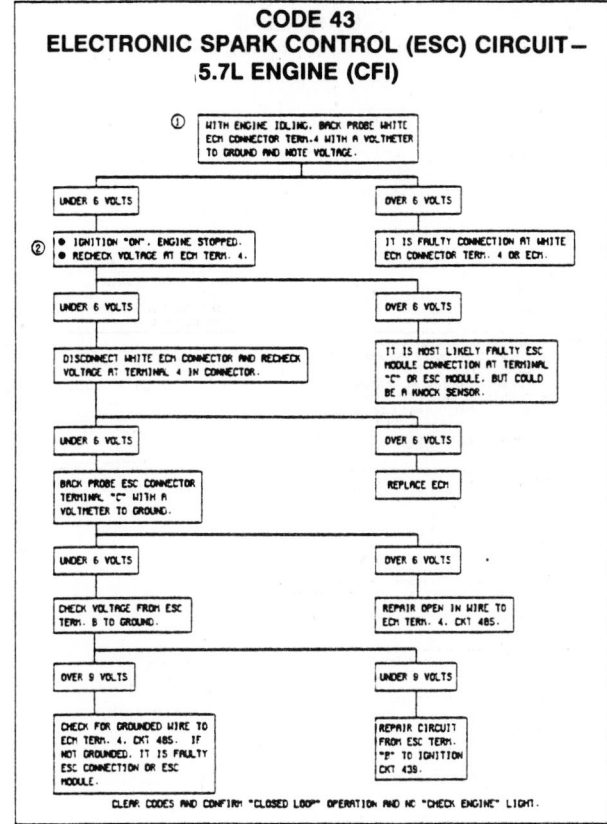

CODE 45
RICH EXHAUST INDICATION—5.7L ENGINE (CFI)

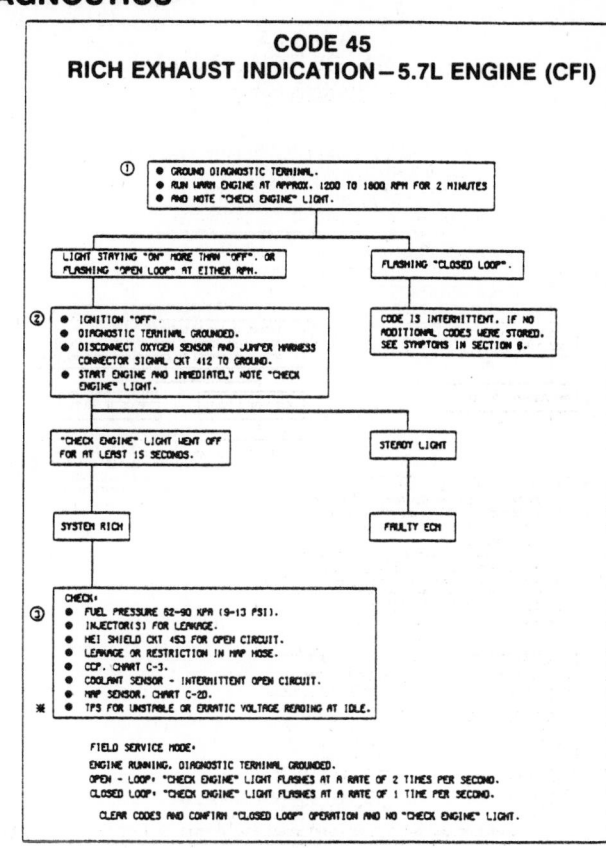

CODE 44
LEAN EXHAUST INDICATION—5.7L ENGINE (CFI)

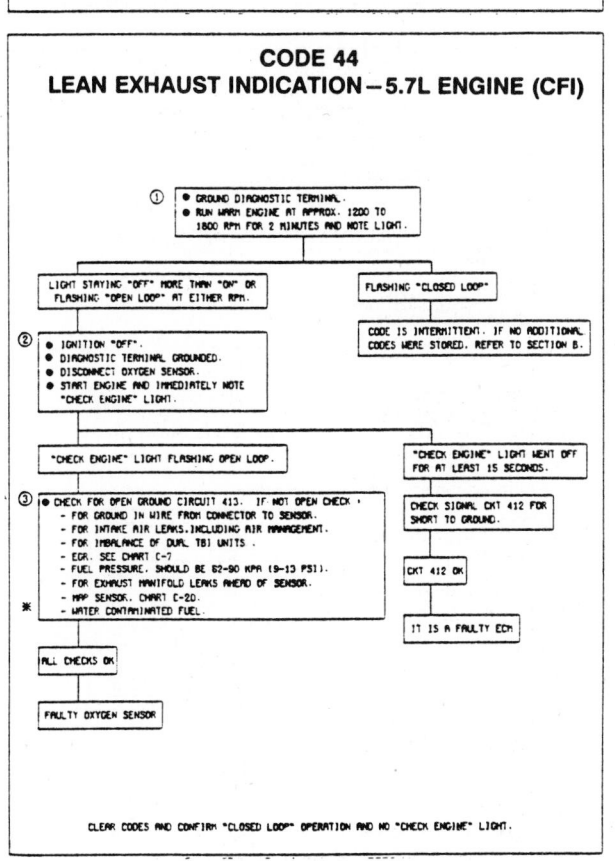

CODES 51 and 55—5.7L ENGINE (CFI)

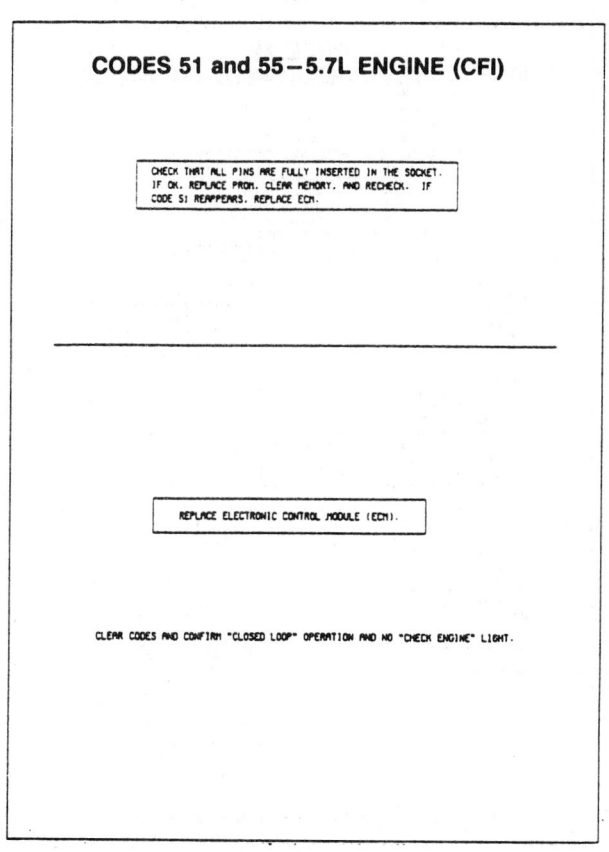

TBI TROUBLE DIAGNOSTICS

CHART C-2A
PARK NEUTRAL SWITCH CIRCUIT— 5.7L ENGINE (CFI)

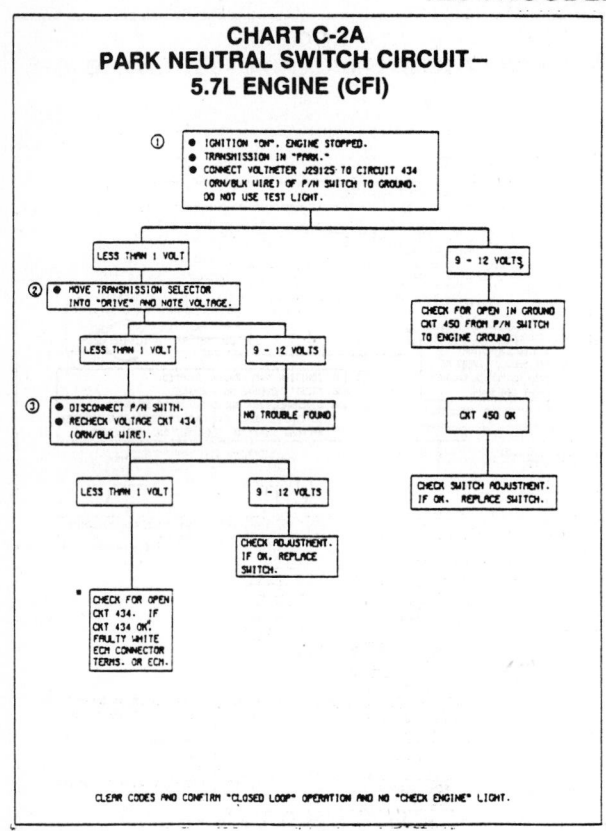

CHART C-2C
IDLE AIR CONTROL—5.7L ENGINE (CFI)

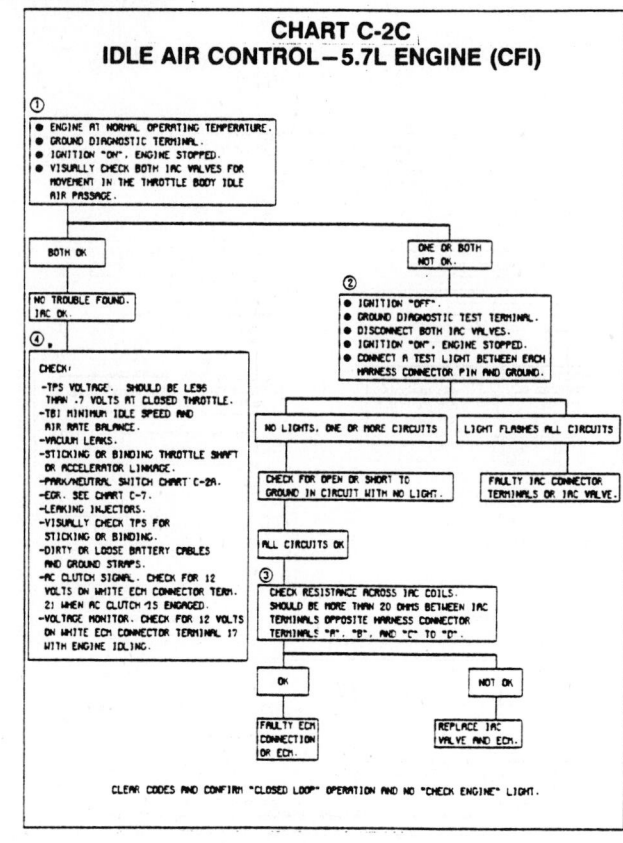

CHART C-2B
CRANK SIGNAL CIRCUIT—5.7L ENGINE (CFI)

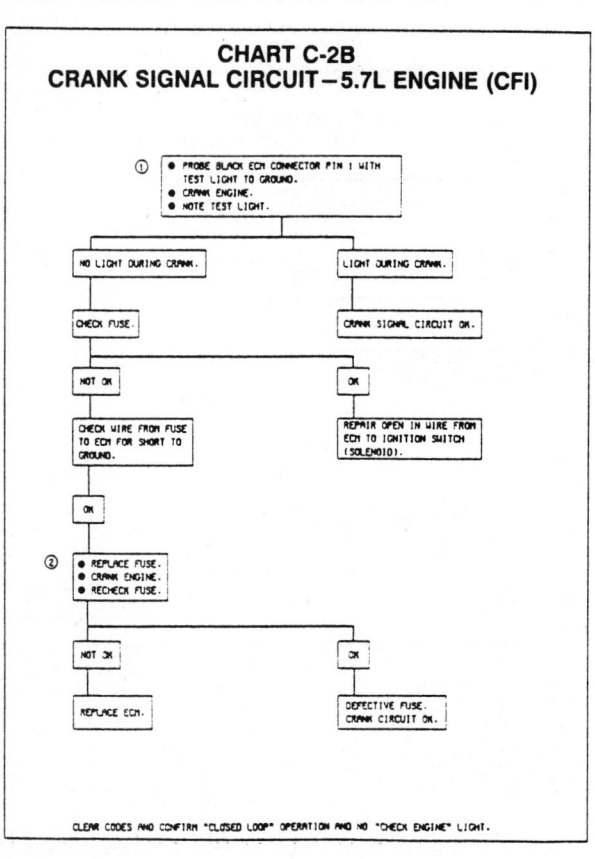

CHART C-2D
MAP OUTPUT CHECK—5.7L ENGINE (CFI)

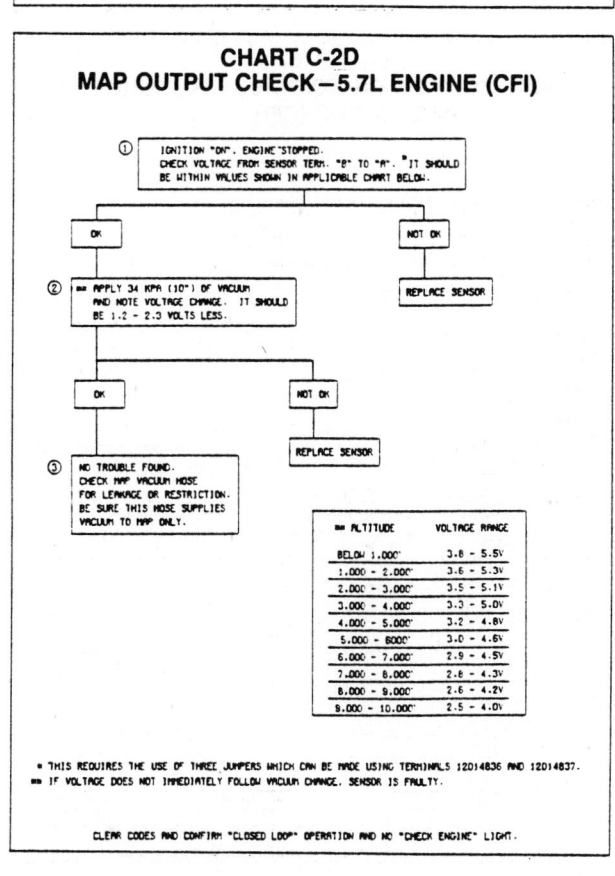

TBI TROUBLE DIAGNOSTICS

CHART C-3
CANISTER PURGE CHECK—5.7L ENGINE (CFI)

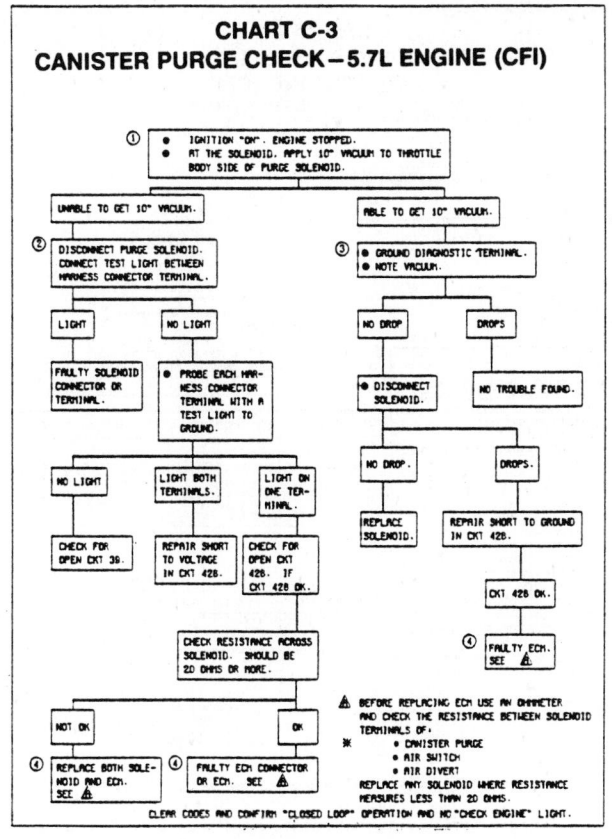

CHART C-6
AIR MANAGEMENT CHECK—5.7L ENGINE (CFI)

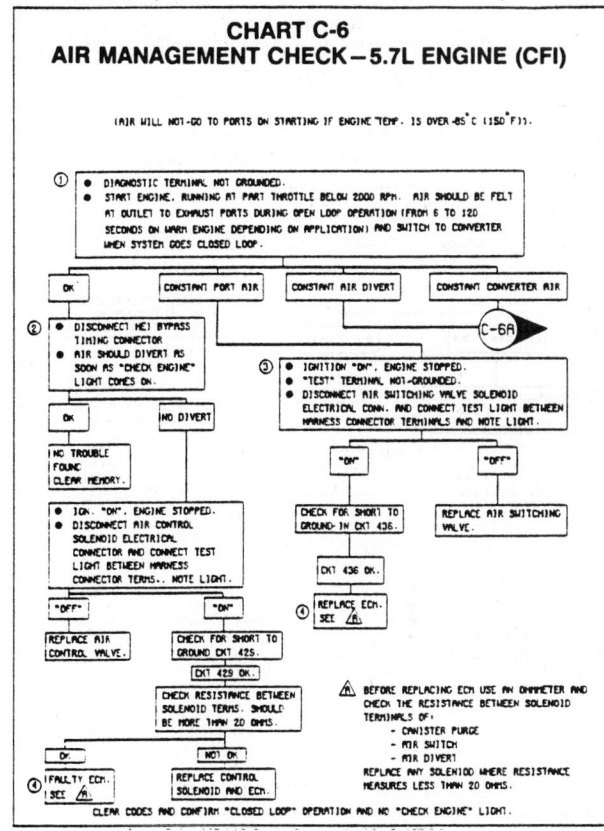

CHART C-5
ELECTRONIC SPARK CONTROL (ESC) CIRCUIT
5.7L ENGINE (CFI)

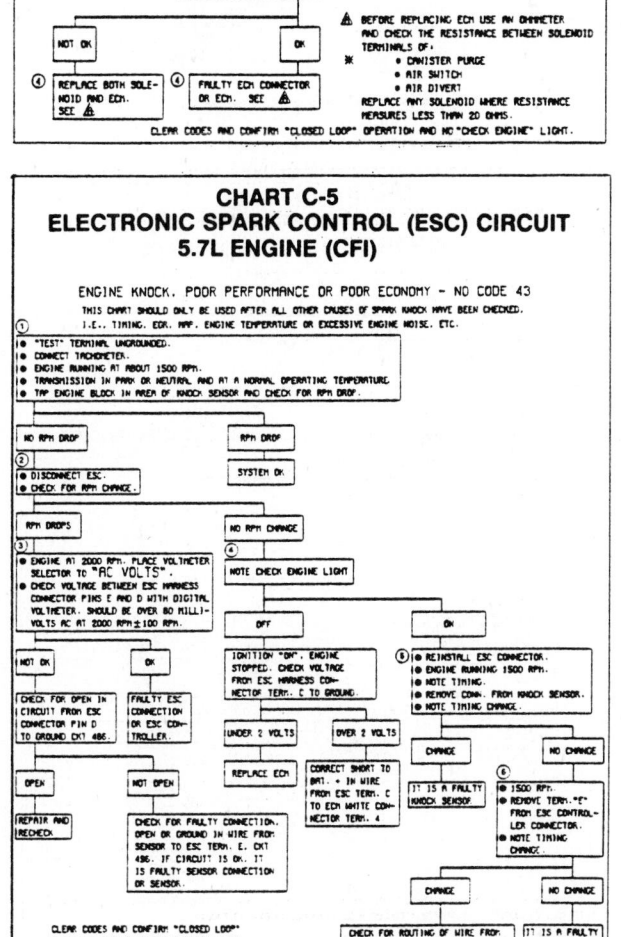

CHART C-6A
AIR MANAGEMENT CHECK—5.7L ENGINE (CFI)

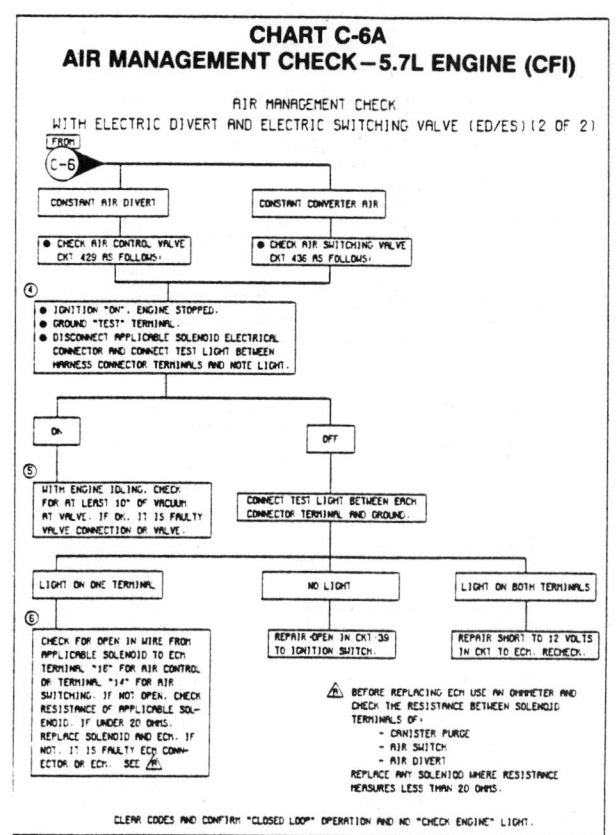

TBI TROUBLE DIAGNOSTICS

CHART C-7
EGR VALVE CHECK—5.7L ENGINE (CFI)

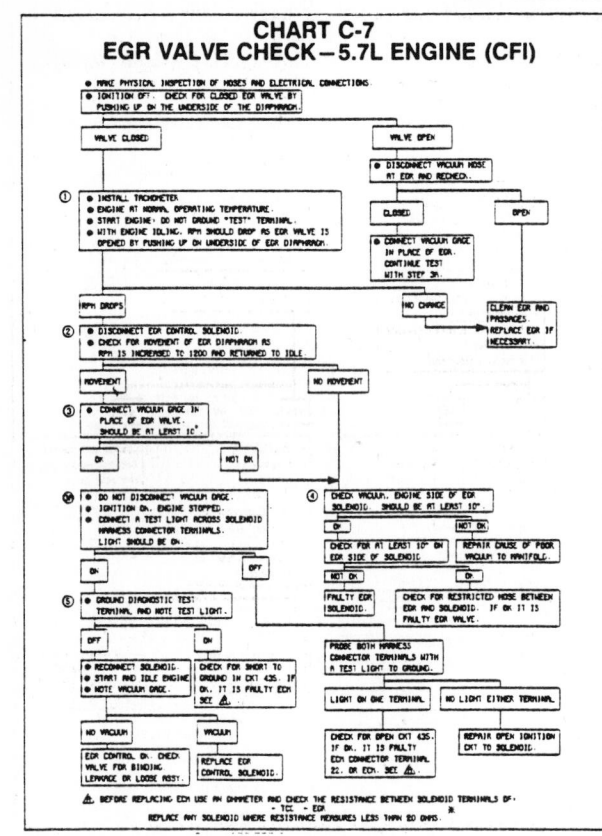

CHART C-8
TRANSAXLE CONVERTER CLUTCH (TCC) CHECK
5.7L ENGINE (CFI)

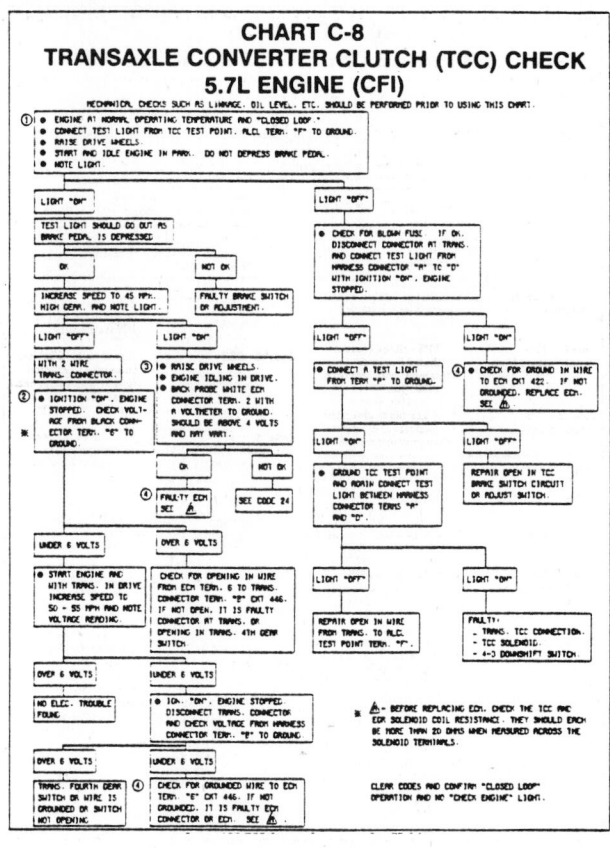

CHART C-8A
MANUAL TRANSMISSION WITH OVERDRIVE—5.7L

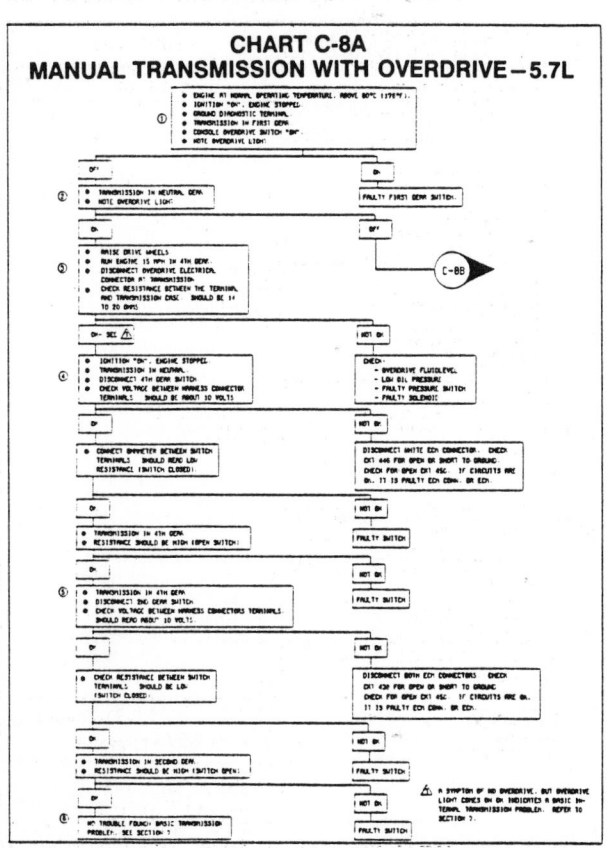

CHART C-8B
MANUAL TRANSMISSION WITH AUTOMATIC
OVERDRIVE—5.7L ENGINE (CFI)

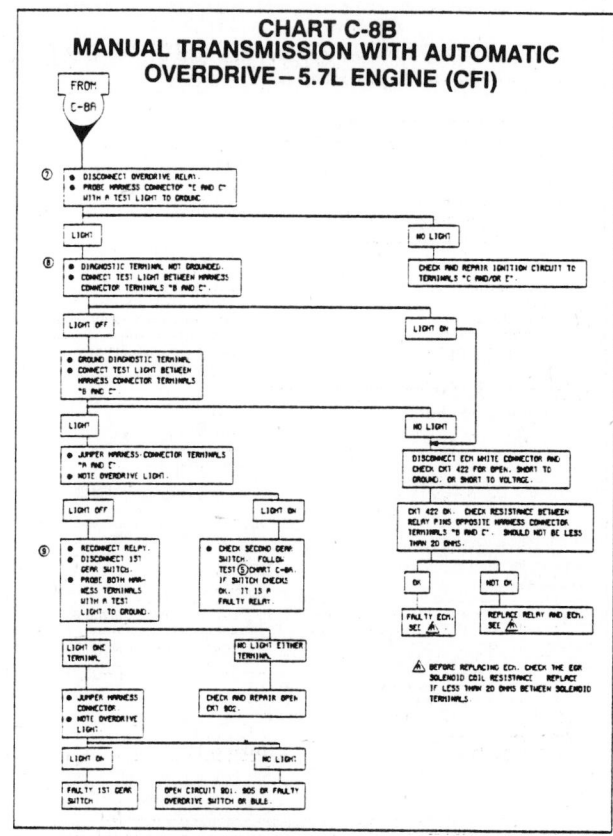

TBI TROUBLE DIAGNOSTICS

CODE IDENTIFICATION

The "Service Engine Soon" light will only be "ON" if the malfunction exists under the conditions listed below. If the malfunction clears, the light will go out and the code will be stored in the ECM. Any codes stored will be erased if no problem reoccurs within 50 engine starts.

CODE AND CIRCUIT	PROBABLE CAUSE	CODE AND CIRCUIT	PROBABLE CAUSE
Code 13 - O_2 Sensor Open Oxygen Sensor Circuit	Indicates that the oxygen sensor circuit or sensor was open for one minute while off idle.	Code 33 - MAP Sensor Low Vacuum	MAP sensor output to high for 5 seconds or an Open signal circuit.
Code 14 - Coolant Sensor High Temperature Indication	Sets if the sensor or signal line becomes grounded for 3 seconds.	Code 34 - MAP Sensor High Vacuum	Low or no output from sensor with engine running.
Code 15 - Coolant Sensor Low Temperature Indication	Sets if the sensor, connections, or wires open for 3 seconds.	Code 35 - IAC	IAC error
		Code 42 - EST	ECM has seen an open or grounded EST or Bypass circuit.
Code 21 - TPS Signal Voltage High	TPS voltage greater than 2.5 volts for 3 seconds with less than 1200 rpm.	Code 43 - ESC	Signal to the ECM has remained low for too long or the system has failed a functional check.
Code 22 - TPS Signal Voltage Low	A shorted to ground or open signal circuit will set code in 3 seconds.	Code 44 Lean Exhaust Indication	Sets if oxygen sensor voltage remains below .2 volts for about 20 seconds.
Code 23 - MAT Low Temperature Indication	Sets if the sensor, connections, or wires open for 3 seconds.	Code 45 Rich Exhaust Indication	Sets if oxygen sensor voltage remains above .7 volts for about 1 minute.
Code 24 - VSS No Vehicle Speed Indication	No vehicle speed present during a road load decel.		
Code 25 - MAT High Temperature Indication	Sets if the sensor or signal line becomes grounded for 3 seconds.	Code 51	Faulty MEM-CAL, Prom, or ECM.
		Code 52	Fuel CALPAK missing or faulty.
Code 32 - EGR	Vacuum switch shorted to ground on start up OR Switch not closed after the ECM has commanded EGR for a specified period of time. OR EGR solenoid circuit open for a specified period of time.	Code 54 - Fuel Pump Low voltage	Sets when the fuel pump voltage is less than 2 volts when reference pulses are being received.
		Code 55	Faulty ECM

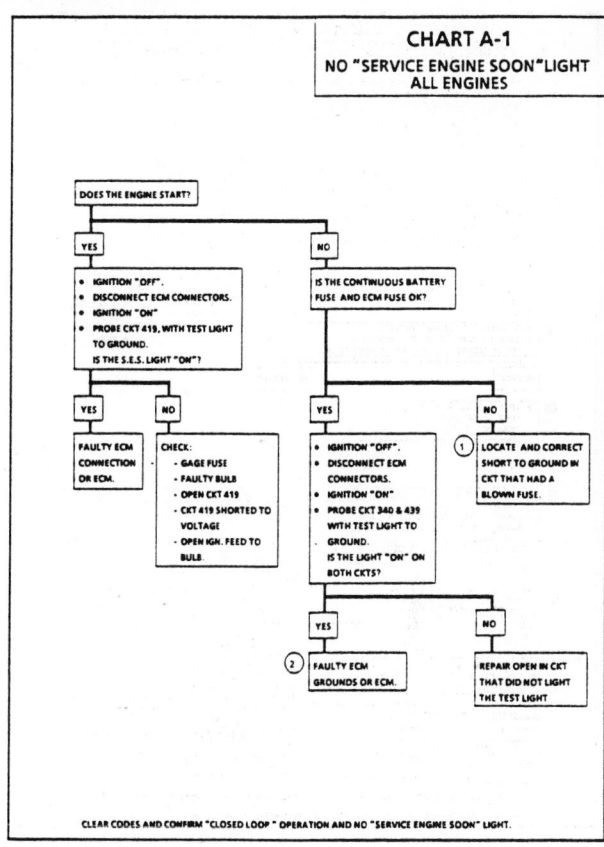

CHART A-1
NO "SERVICE ENGINE SOON" LIGHT ALL ENGINES

CLEAR CODES AND CONFIRM "CLOSED LOOP" OPERATION AND NO "SERVICE ENGINE SOON" LIGHT.

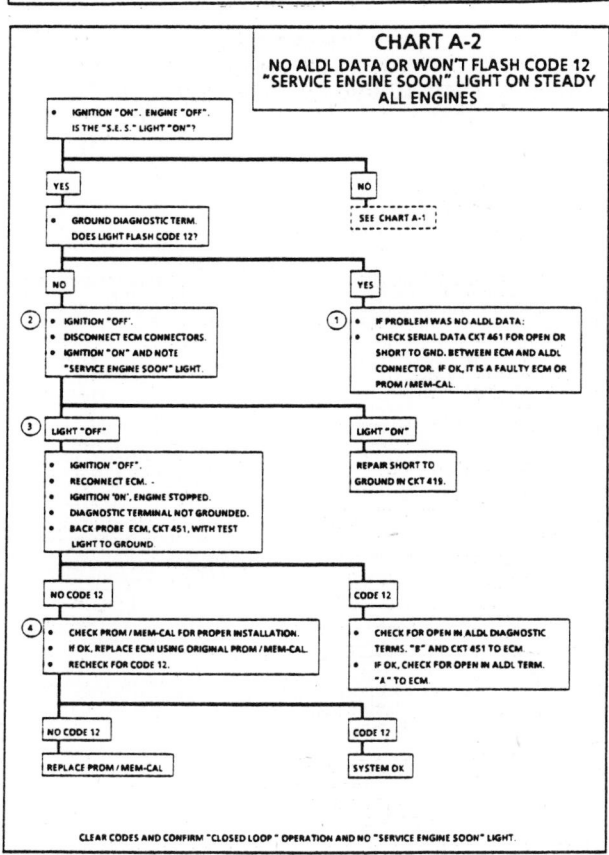

CHART A-2
NO ALDL DATA OR WON'T FLASH CODE 12 "SERVICE ENGINE SOON" LIGHT ON STEADY ALL ENGINES

CLEAR CODES AND CONFIRM "CLOSED LOOP" OPERATION AND NO "SERVICE ENGINE SOON" LIGHT.

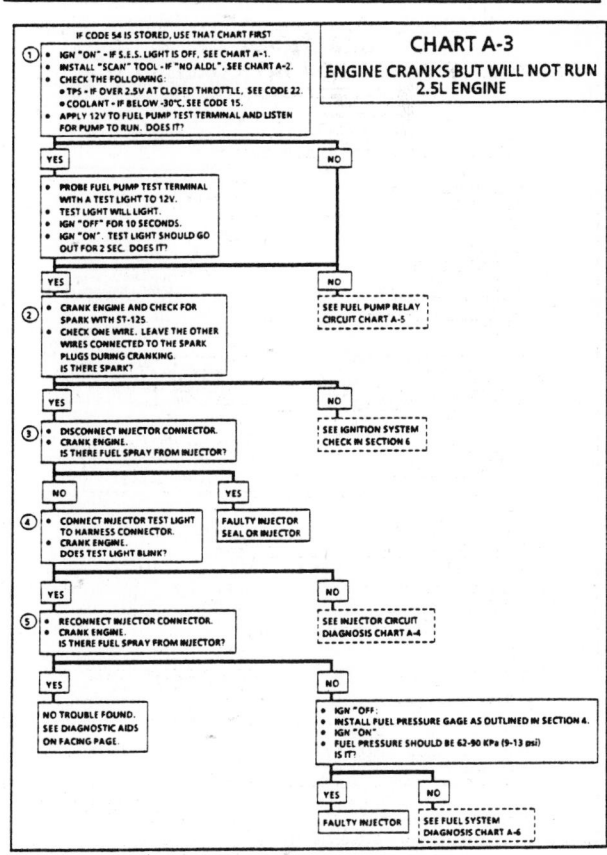

CHART A-3
ENGINE CRANKS BUT WILL NOT RUN 2.5L ENGINE

TBI TROUBLE DIAGNOSTICS

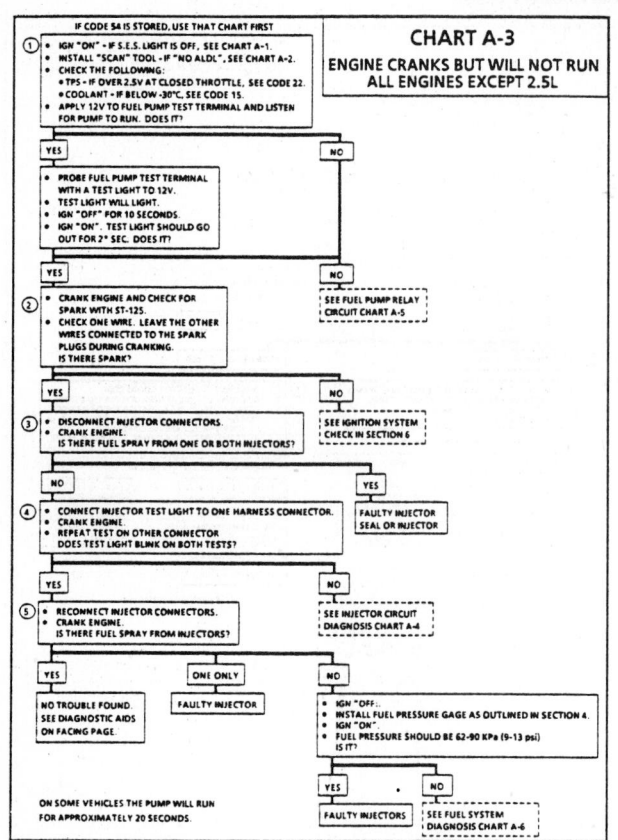

CHART A-3
ENGINE CRANKS BUT WILL NOT RUN
ALL ENGINES EXCEPT 2.5L

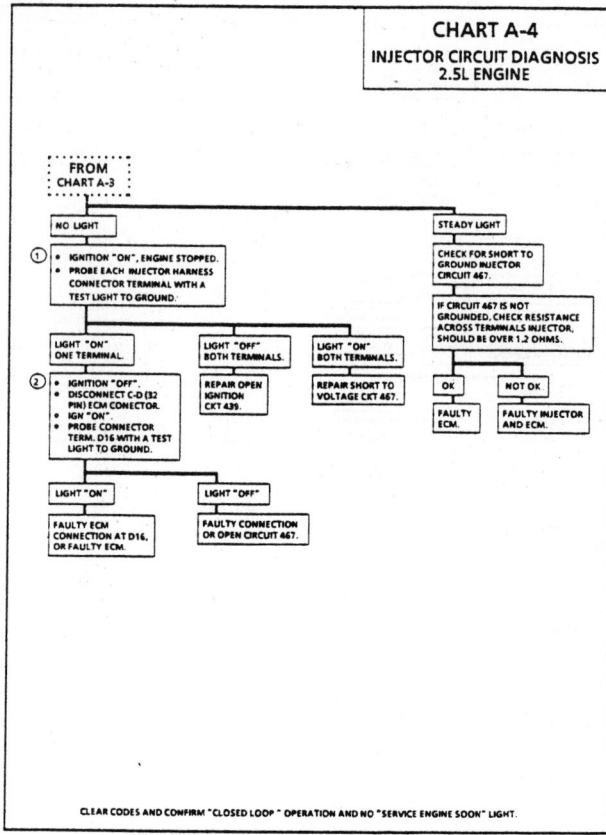

CHART A-4
INJECTOR CIRCUIT DIAGNOSIS
2.5L ENGINE

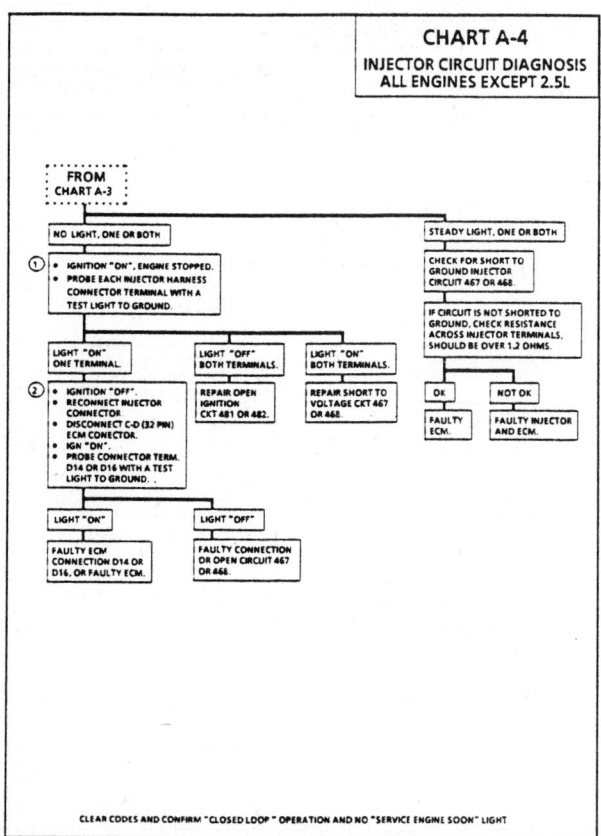

CHART A-4
INJECTOR CIRCUIT DIAGNOSIS
ALL ENGINES EXCEPT 2.5L

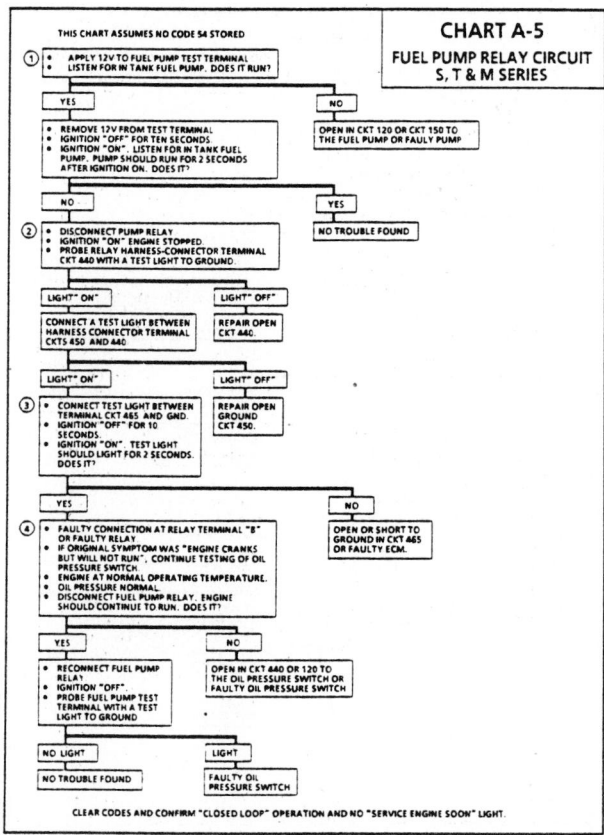

CHART A-5
FUEL PUMP RELAY CIRCUIT
S, T & M SERIES

TBI TROUBLE DIAGNOSTICS

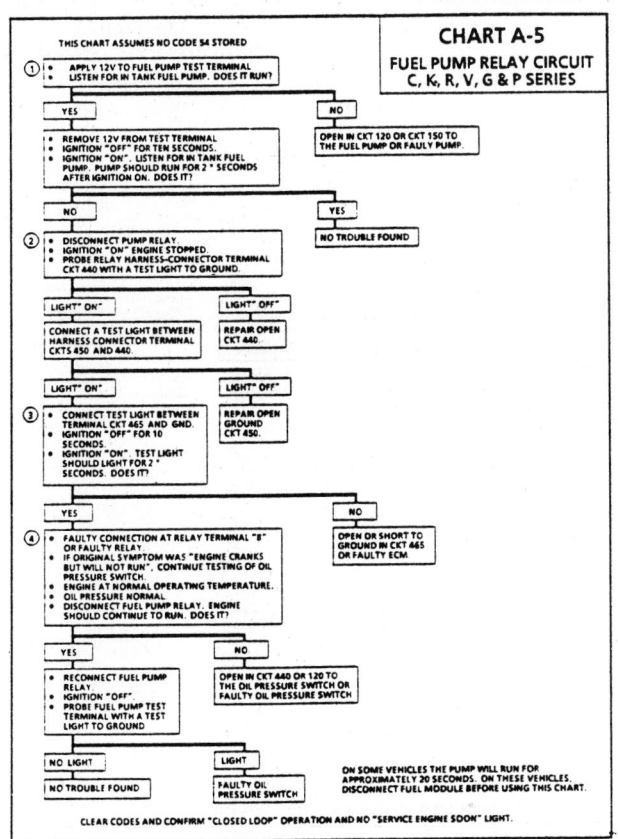

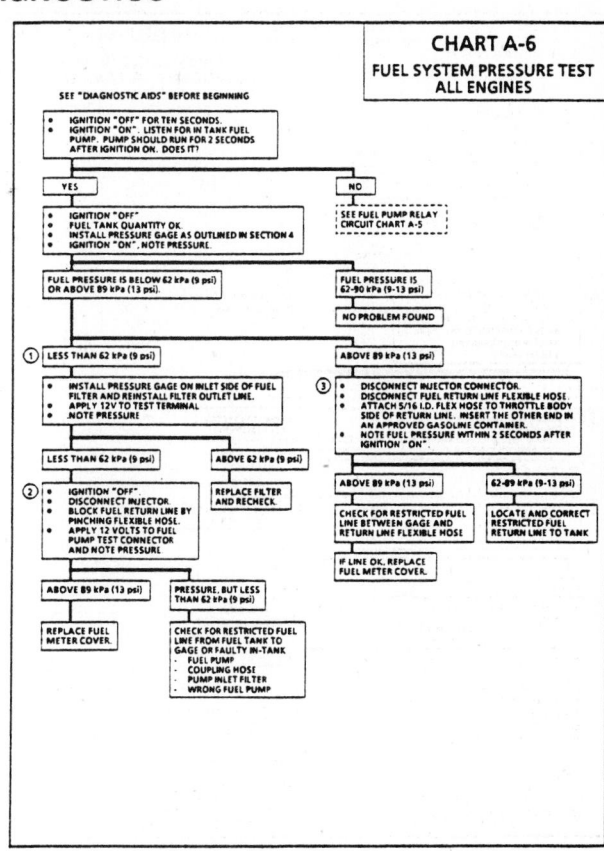

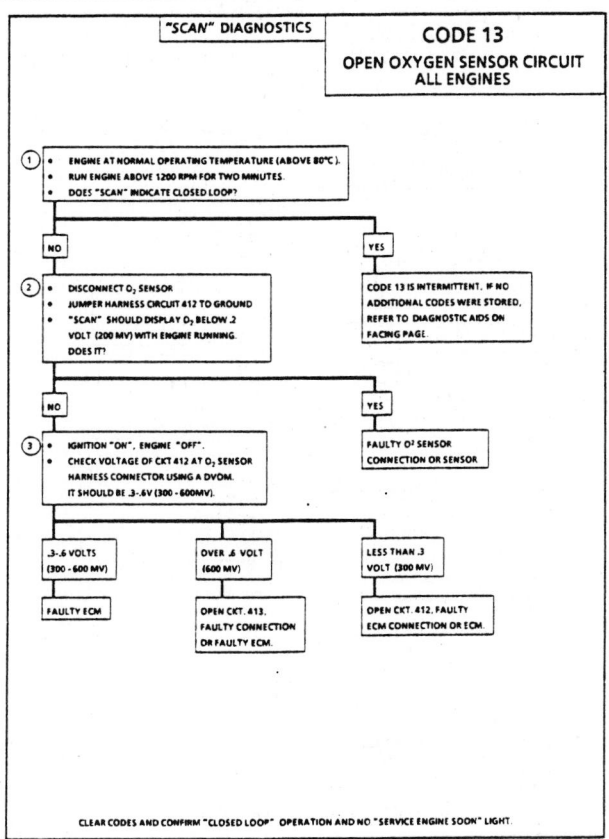

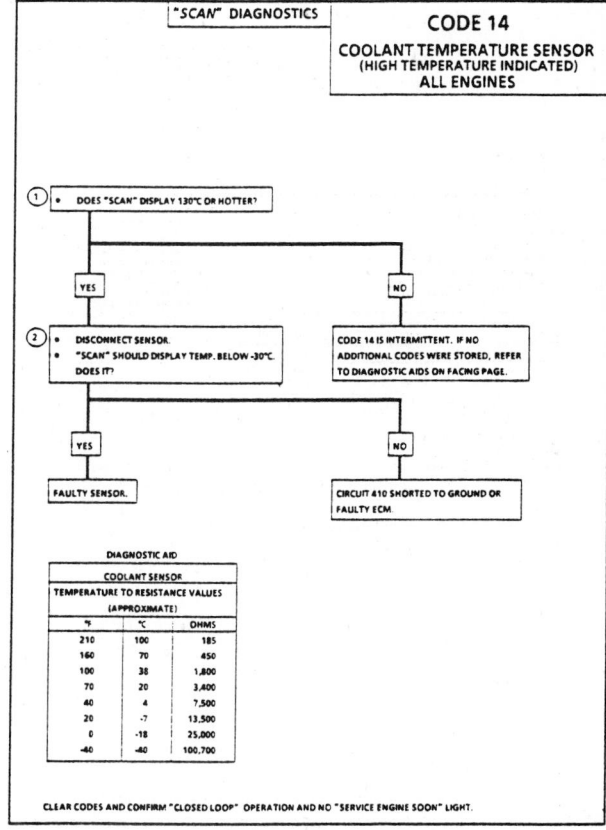

TBI TROUBLE DIAGNOSTICS

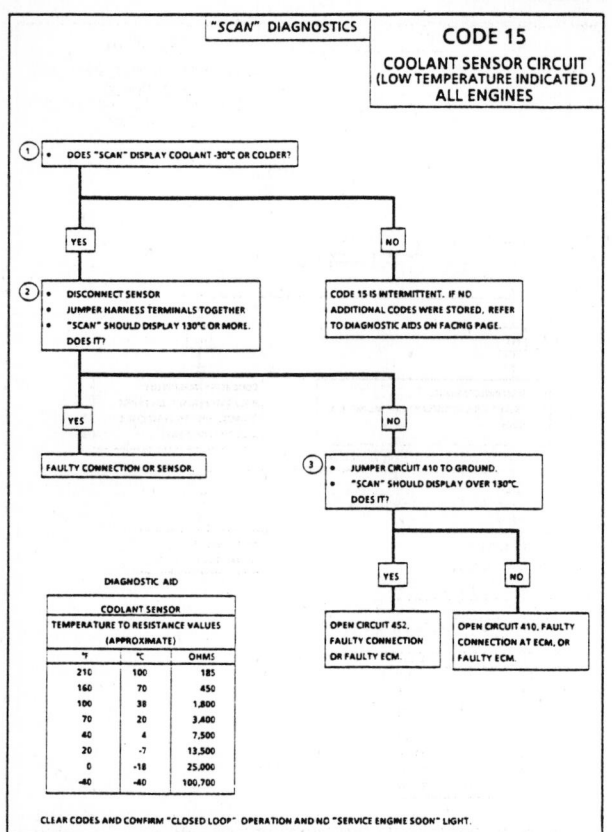

"SCAN" DIAGNOSTICS

CODE 15
COOLANT SENSOR CIRCUIT
(LOW TEMPERATURE INDICATED)
ALL ENGINES

COOLANT SENSOR
TEMPERATURE TO RESISTANCE VALUES
(APPROXIMATE)

°F	°C	OHMS
210	100	185
160	70	450
100	38	1,800
70	20	3,400
40	4	7,500
20	-7	13,500
0	-18	25,000
-40	-40	100,700

CLEAR CODES AND CONFIRM "CLOSED LOOP" OPERATION AND NO "SERVICE ENGINE SOON" LIGHT.

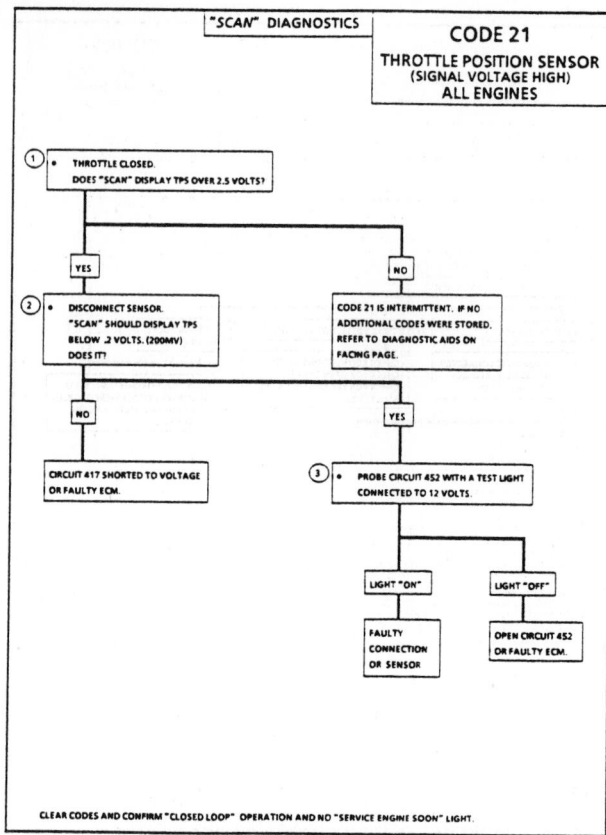

"SCAN" DIAGNOSTICS

CODE 21
THROTTLE POSITION SENSOR
(SIGNAL VOLTAGE HIGH)
ALL ENGINES

CLEAR CODES AND CONFIRM "CLOSED LOOP" OPERATION AND NO "SERVICE ENGINE SOON" LIGHT.

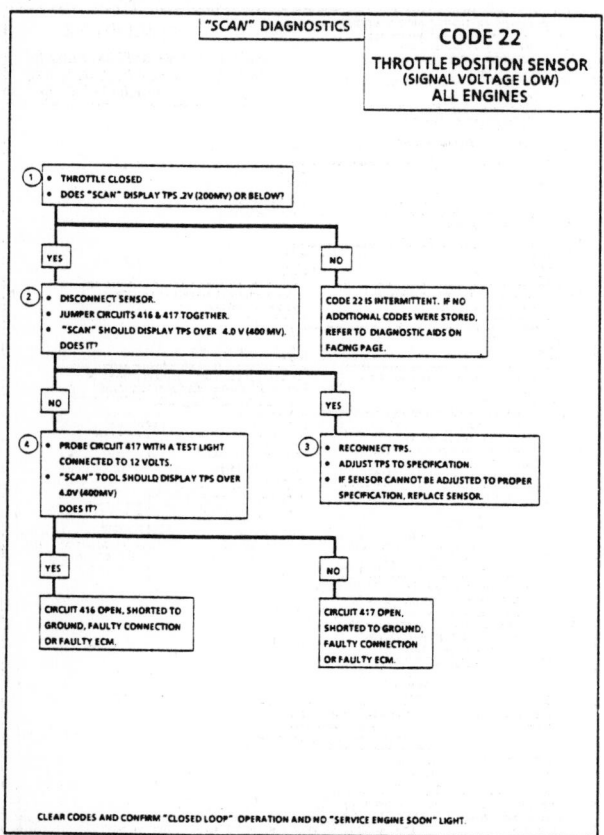

"SCAN" DIAGNOSTICS

CODE 22
THROTTLE POSITION SENSOR
(SIGNAL VOLTAGE LOW)
ALL ENGINES

CLEAR CODES AND CONFIRM "CLOSED LOOP" OPERATION AND NO "SERVICE ENGINE SOON" LIGHT.

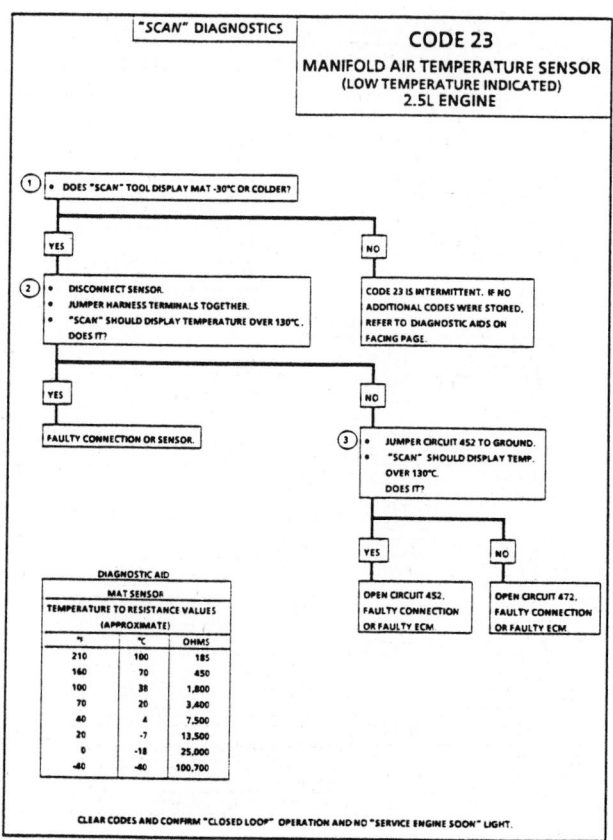

"SCAN" DIAGNOSTICS

CODE 23
MANIFOLD AIR TEMPERATURE SENSOR
(LOW TEMPERATURE INDICATED)
2.5L ENGINE

MAT SENSOR
TEMPERATURE TO RESISTANCE VALUES
(APPROXIMATE)

°F	°C	OHMS
210	100	185
160	70	450
100	38	1,800
70	20	3,400
40	4	7,500
20	-7	13,500
0	-18	25,000
-40	-40	100,700

CLEAR CODES AND CONFIRM "CLOSED LOOP" OPERATION AND NO "SERVICE ENGINE SOON" LIGHT.

TBI TROUBLE DIAGNOSTICS

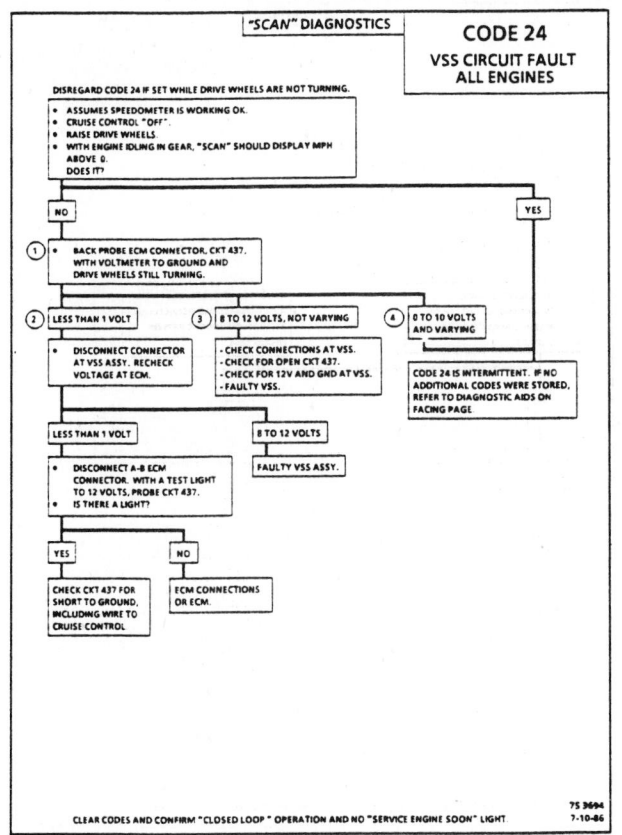

"SCAN" DIAGNOSTICS

CODE 24
VSS CIRCUIT FAULT
ALL ENGINES

CLEAR CODES AND CONFIRM "CLOSED LOOP" OPERATION AND NO "SERVICE ENGINE SOON" LIGHT.

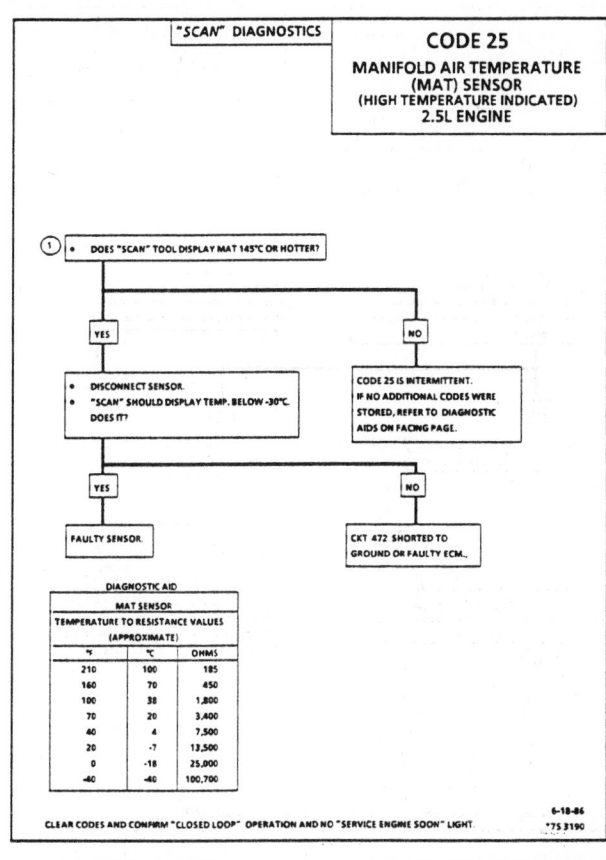

"SCAN" DIAGNOSTICS

CODE 25
MANIFOLD AIR TEMPERATURE (MAT) SENSOR
(HIGH TEMPERATURE INDICATED)
2.5L ENGINE

DIAGNOSTIC AID

| MAT SENSOR |
| TEMPERATURE TO RESISTANCE VALUES |
| (APPROXIMATE) |

°F	°C	OHMS
210	100	185
160	70	450
100	38	1,800
70	20	3,400
40	4	7,500
20	-7	13,500
0	-18	25,000
-40	-40	100,700

CLEAR CODES AND CONFIRM "CLOSED LOOP" OPERATION AND NO "SERVICE ENGINE SOON" LIGHT.

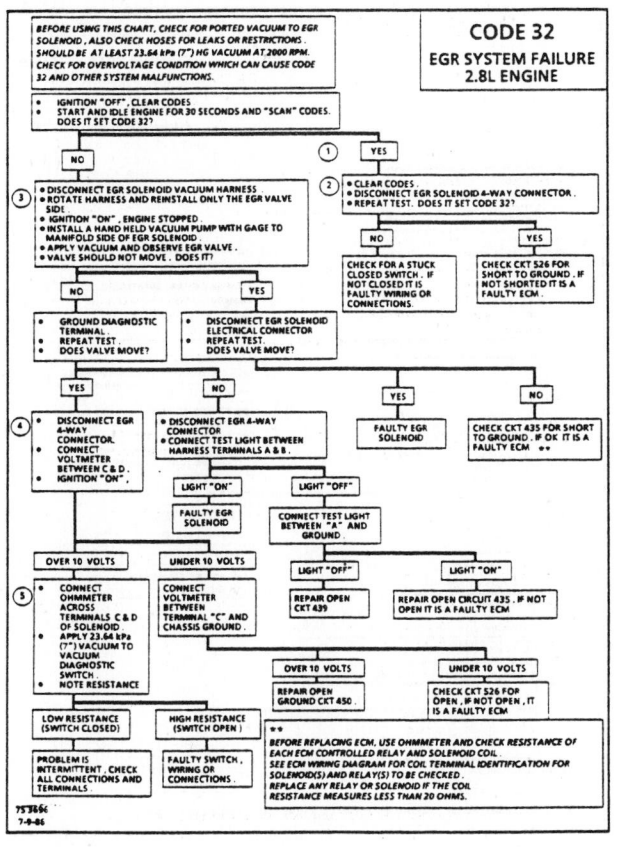

CODE 32
EGR SYSTEM FAILURE
2.8L ENGINE

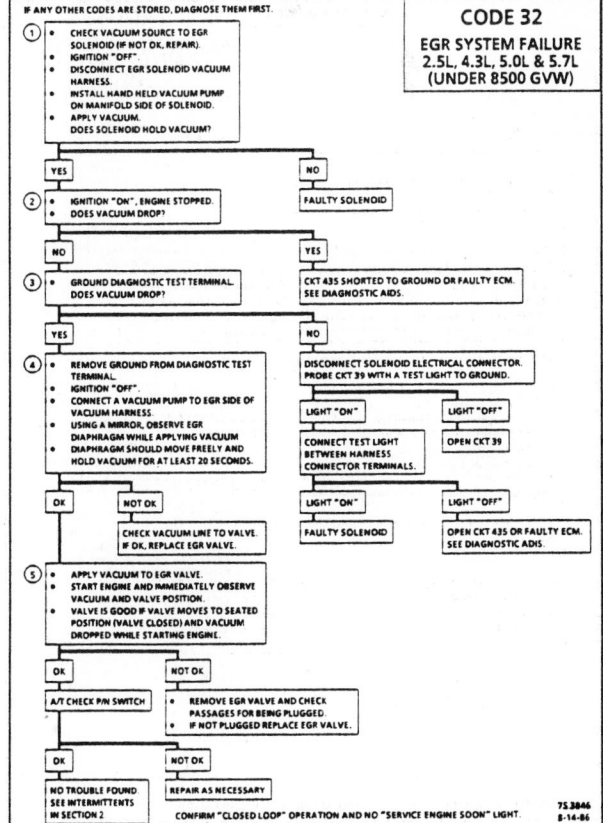

CODE 32
EGR SYSTEM FAILURE
2.5L, 4.3L, 5.0L & 5.7L
(UNDER 8500 GVW)

CONFIRM "CLOSED LOOP" OPERATION AND NO "SERVICE ENGINE SOON" LIGHT.

5-533

TBI TROUBLE DIAGNOSTICS

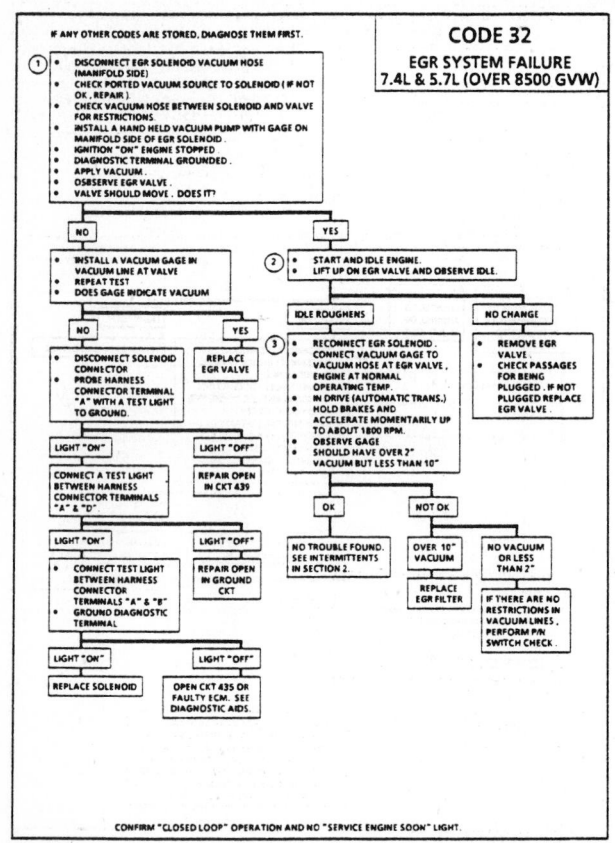

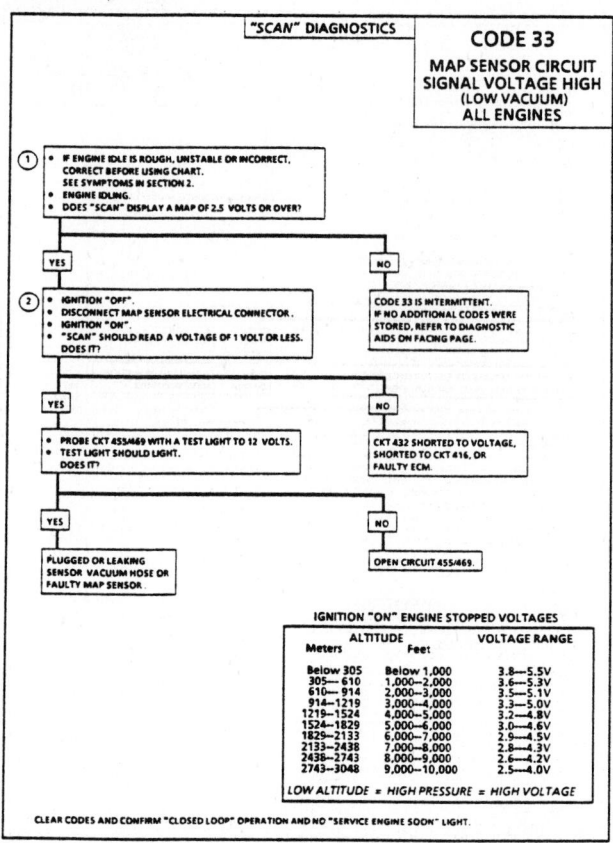

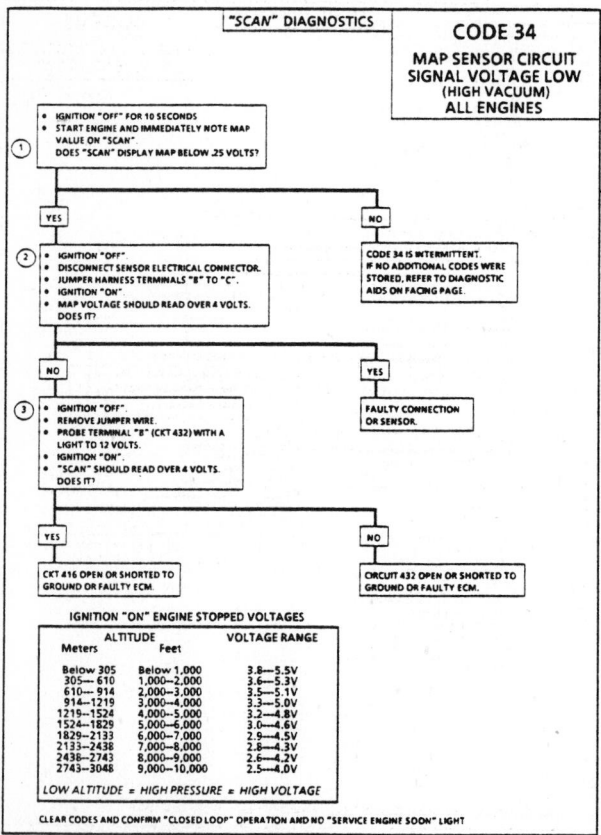

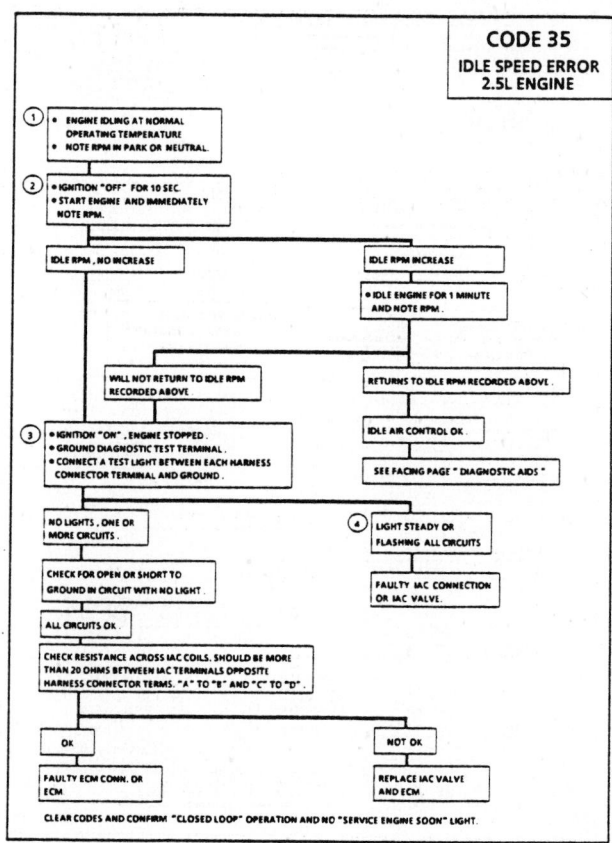

TBI TROUBLE DIAGNOSTICS

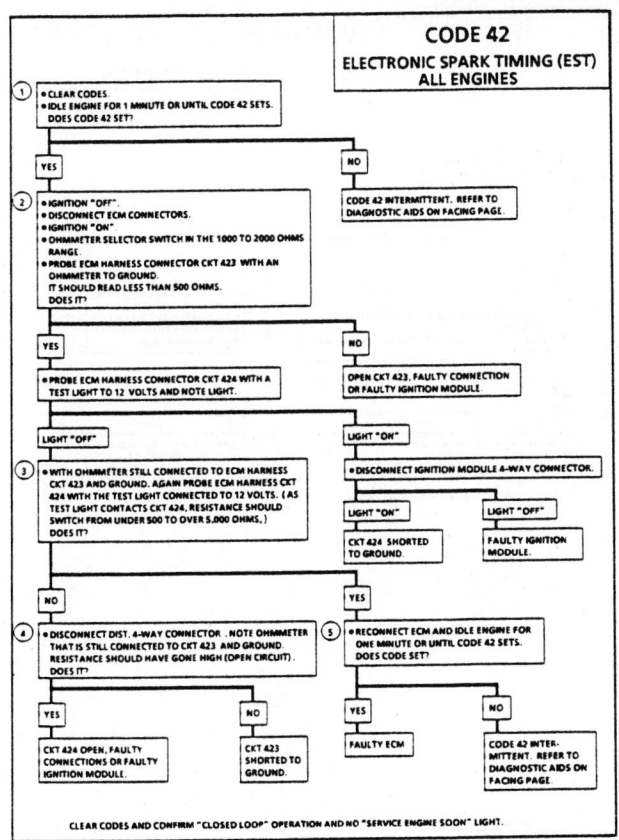

CODE 42
ELECTRONIC SPARK TIMING (EST)
ALL ENGINES

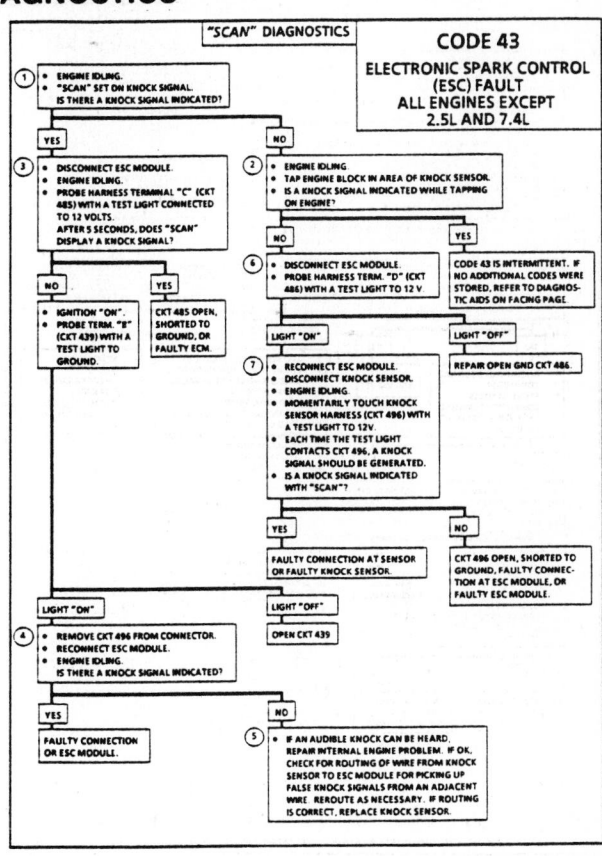

"SCAN" DIAGNOSTICS

CODE 43
ELECTRONIC SPARK CONTROL
(ESC) FAULT
ALL ENGINES EXCEPT
2.5L AND 7.4L

CLEAR CODES AND CONFIRM "CLOSED LOOP" OPERATION AND NO "SERVICE ENGINE SOON" LIGHT.

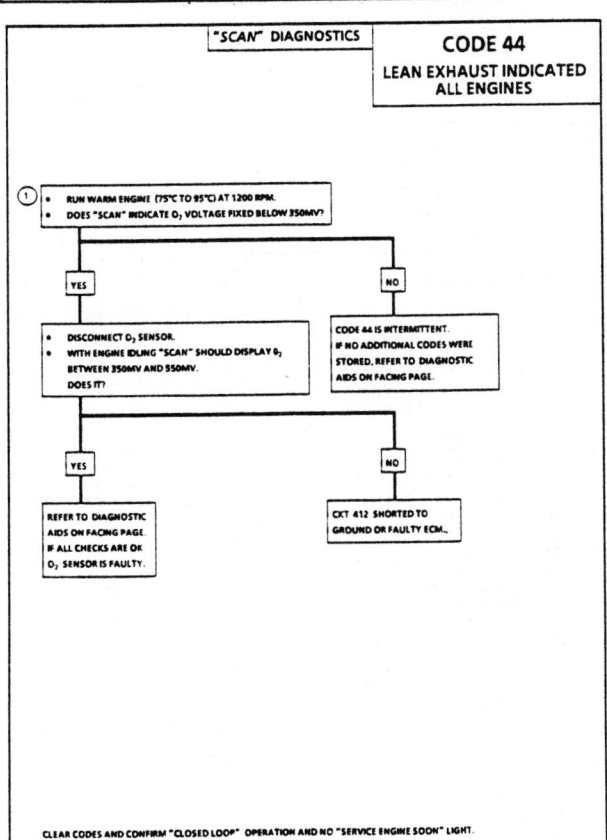

"SCAN" DIAGNOSTICS

CODE 44
LEAN EXHAUST INDICATED
ALL ENGINES

CLEAR CODES AND CONFIRM "CLOSED LOOP" OPERATION AND NO "SERVICE ENGINE SOON" LIGHT.

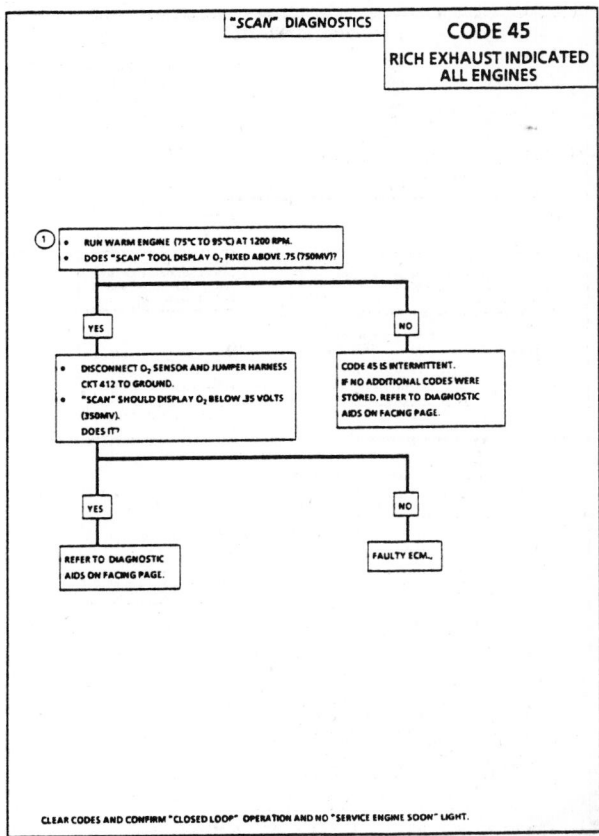

"SCAN" DIAGNOSTICS

CODE 45
RICH EXHAUST INDICATED
ALL ENGINES

CLEAR CODES AND CONFIRM "CLOSED LOOP" OPERATION AND NO "SERVICE ENGINE SOON" LIGHT.

TBI TROUBLE DIAGNOSTICS

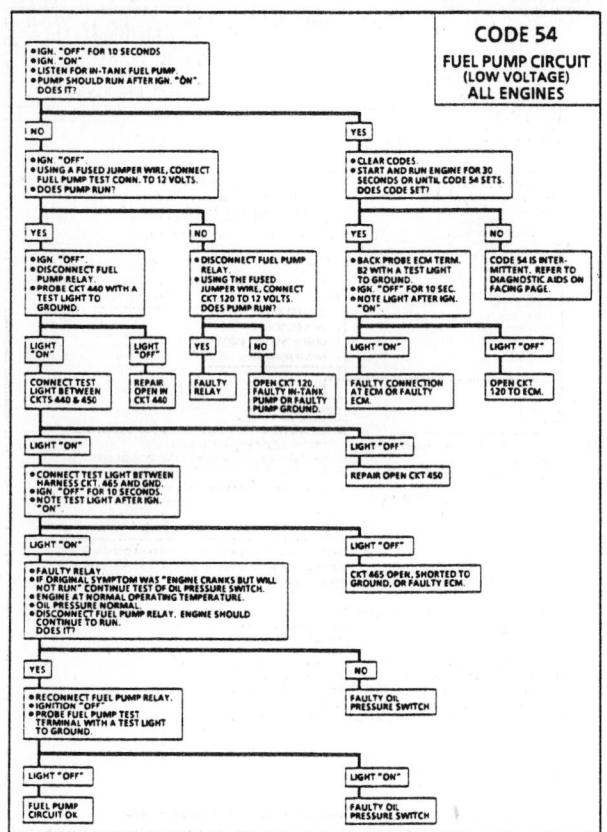

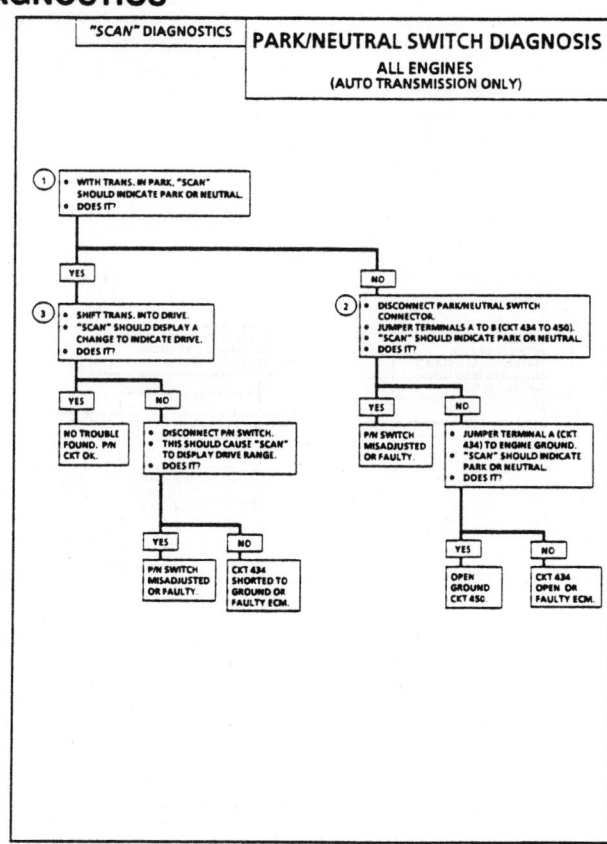

PARK/NEUTRAL SWITCH DIAGNOSIS
ALL ENGINES
(AUTO TRANSMISSION ONLY)

CODE 54
FUEL PUMP CIRCUIT
(LOW VOLTAGE)
ALL ENGINES

CODE 51
CODE 52
CODE 55

CODE 51
FAULTY MEM-CAL
(2.5L ENGINE)

CHECK THAT ALL PINS ARE FULLY INSERTED IN THE SOCKET. IF OK, REPLACE MEM-CAL, CLEAR MEMORY, AND RECHECK. IF CODE 51 REAPPEARS, REPLACE ECM.

CODE 51
PROM PROBLEM
(EXCEPT 2.5L ENGINE)

CHECK THAT ALL PINS ARE FULLY INSERTED IN THE SOCKET. IF OK, REPLACE PROM, CLEAR MEMORY, AND RECHECK. IF CODE 51 REAPPEARS, REPLACE ECM.

CODE 52
FUEL CALPAK MISSING
(EXCEPT 2.5L ENGINE)

INSTALL MISSING OR FAULTY CALPAK.

CODE 55
ALL ENGINES

BE SURE ECM GROUNDS ARE OK AND THAT MEM-CAL IS PROPERLY LATCHED. IF OK REPLACE ELECTRONIC CONTROL MODULE (ECM).

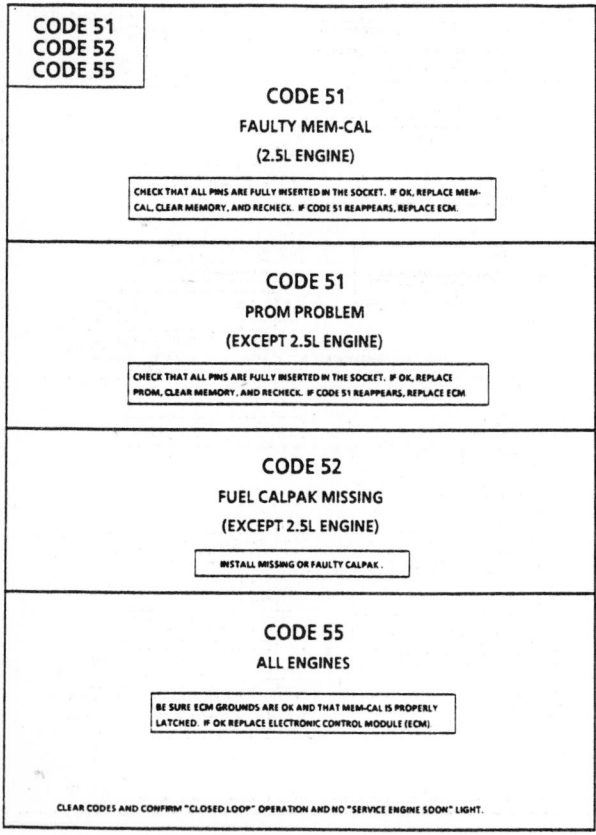

CLEAR CODES AND CONFIRM "CLOSED LOOP" OPERATION AND NO "SERVICE ENGINE SOON" LIGHT.

CRANK SIGNAL DIAGNOSIS
ALL ENGINES

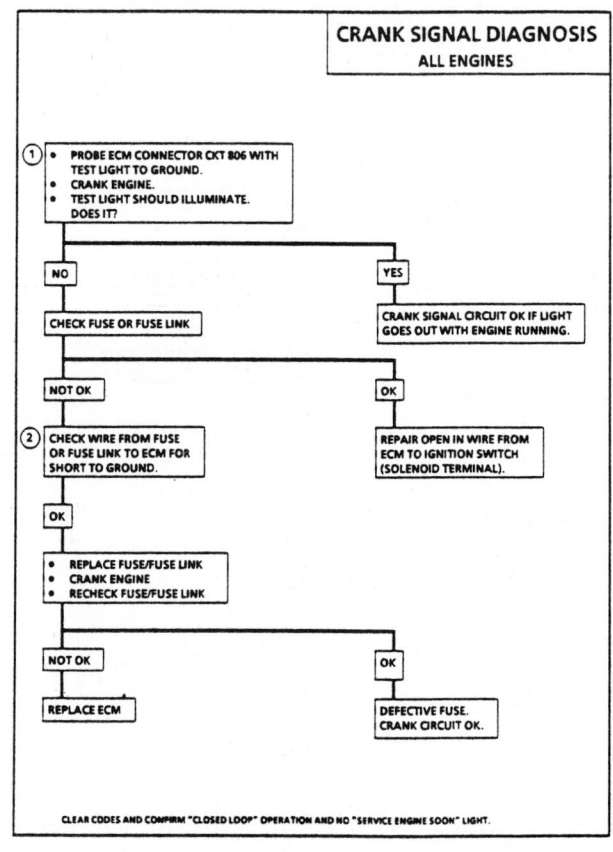

CLEAR CODES AND CONFIRM "CLOSED LOOP" OPERATION AND NO "SERVICE ENGINE SOON" LIGHT.

TBI TROUBLE DIAGNOSTICS

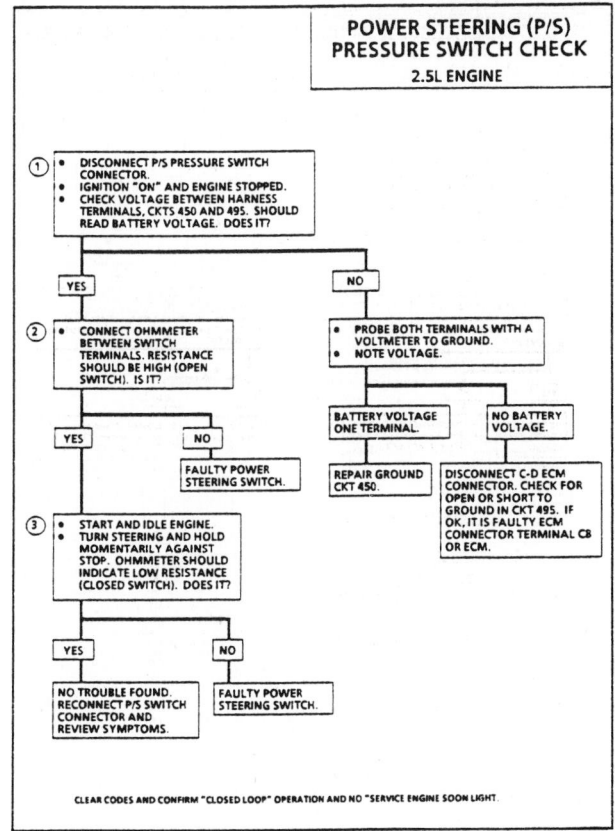

POWER STEERING (P/S) PRESSURE SWITCH CHECK
2.5L ENGINE

① • DISCONNECT P/S PRESSURE SWITCH CONNECTOR.
• IGNITION "ON" AND ENGINE STOPPED.
• CHECK VOLTAGE BETWEEN HARNESS TERMINALS, CKTS 450 AND 495. SHOULD READ BATTERY VOLTAGE. DOES IT?

YES → ② • CONNECT OHMMETER BETWEEN SWITCH TERMINALS. RESISTANCE SHOULD BE HIGH (OPEN SWITCH). IS IT?

NO → • PROBE BOTH TERMINALS WITH A VOLTMETER TO GROUND.
• NOTE VOLTAGE.

BATTERY VOLTAGE ONE TERMINAL.

NO BATTERY VOLTAGE.

REPAIR GROUND CKT 450.

DISCONNECT C-D ECM CONNECTOR. CHECK FOR OPEN OR SHORT TO GROUND IN CKT 495. IF OK, IT IS FAULTY ECM CONNECTOR TERMINAL CB OR ECM.

YES / **NO** → FAULTY POWER STEERING SWITCH.

③ • START AND IDLE ENGINE.
• TURN STEERING AND HOLD MOMENTARILY AGAINST STOP. OHMMETER SHOULD INDICATE LOW RESISTANCE (CLOSED SWITCH). DOES IT?

YES → NO TROUBLE FOUND. RECONNECT P/S SWITCH CONNECTOR AND REVIEW SYMPTOMS.

NO → FAULTY POWER STEERING SWITCH.

CLEAR CODES AND CONFIRM "CLOSED LOOP" OPERATION AND NO "SERVICE ENGINE SOON" LIGHT.

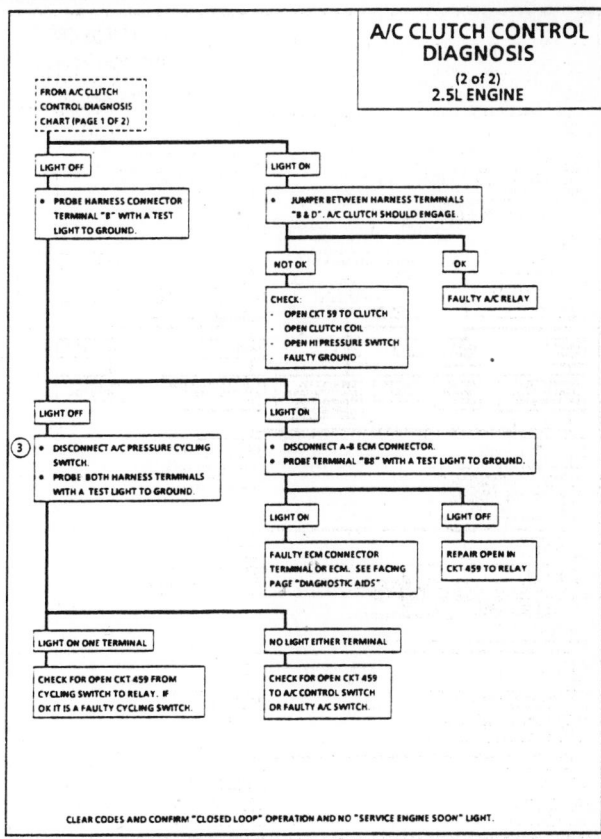

A/C CLUTCH CONTROL DIAGNOSIS
(2 of 2)
2.5L ENGINE

FROM A/C CLUTCH CONTROL DIAGNOSIS CHART (PAGE 1 OF 2)

LIGHT OFF → • PROBE HARNESS CONNECTOR TERMINAL "B" WITH A TEST LIGHT TO GROUND.

LIGHT ON → • JUMPER BETWEEN HARNESS TERMINALS "B & D". A/C CLUTCH SHOULD ENGAGE.

NOT OK → CHECK:
- OPEN CKT 59 TO CLUTCH
- OPEN CLUTCH COIL
- OPEN HI PRESSURE SWITCH
- FAULTY GROUND

OK → FAULTY A/C RELAY

LIGHT OFF → ③ • DISCONNECT A/C PRESSURE CYCLING SWITCH.
• PROBE BOTH HARNESS TERMINALS WITH A TEST LIGHT TO GROUND.

LIGHT ON → • DISCONNECT A-B ECM CONNECTOR.
• PROBE TERMINAL "B8" WITH A TEST LIGHT TO GROUND.

LIGHT ON → FAULTY ECM CONNECTOR TERMINAL OR ECM. SEE FACING PAGE "DIAGNOSTIC AIDS".

LIGHT OFF → REPAIR OPEN IN CKT 459 TO RELAY.

LIGHT ON ONE TERMINAL → CHECK FOR OPEN CKT 459 FROM CYCLING SWITCH TO RELAY. IF OK IT IS A FAULTY CYCLING SWITCH.

NO LIGHT EITHER TERMINAL → CHECK FOR OPEN CKT 459 TO A/C CONTROL SWITCH OR FAULTY A/C SWITCH.

CLEAR CODES AND CONFIRM "CLOSED LOOP" OPERATION AND NO "SERVICE ENGINE SOON" LIGHT.

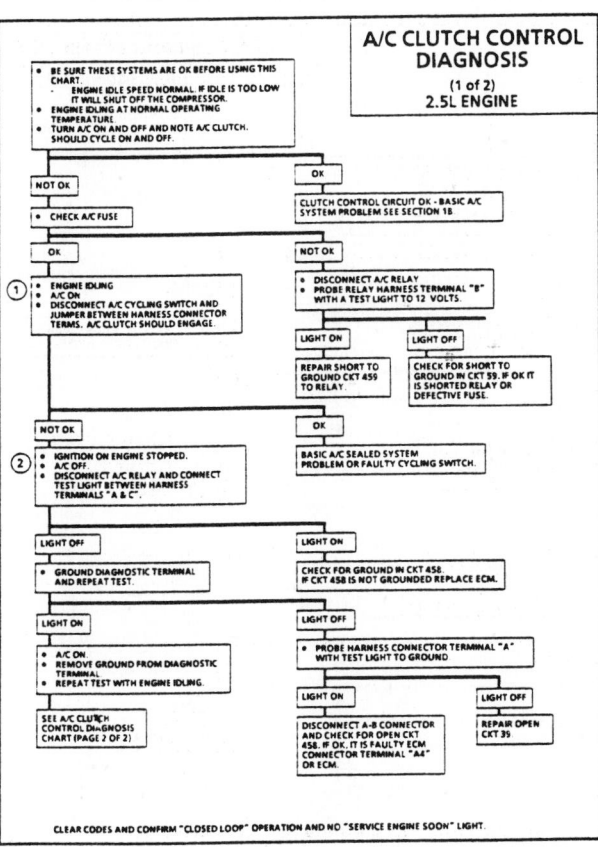

A/C CLUTCH CONTROL DIAGNOSIS
(1 of 2)
2.5L ENGINE

• BE SURE THESE SYSTEMS ARE OK BEFORE USING THIS CHART.
- ENGINE IDLE SPEED NORMAL. IF IDLE IS TOO LOW IT WILL SHUT OFF THE COMPRESSOR.
• ENGINE IDLING AT NORMAL OPERATING TEMPERATURE.
• TURN A/C ON AND OFF AND NOTE A/C CLUTCH. SHOULD CYCLE ON AND OFF.

OK → CLUTCH CONTROL CIRCUIT OK - BASIC A/C SYSTEM PROBLEM SEE SECTION 18.

NOT OK → • CHECK A/C FUSE

OK / NOT OK → • DISCONNECT A/C RELAY
• PROBE RELAY HARNESS TERMINAL "B" WITH A TEST LIGHT TO 12 VOLTS.

① • ENGINE IDLING
• A/C ON
• DISCONNECT A/C CYCLING SWITCH AND JUMPER BETWEEN HARNESS CONNECTOR TERMS. A/C CLUTCH SHOULD ENGAGE.

LIGHT ON → REPAIR SHORT TO GROUND CKT 459 TO RELAY.

LIGHT OFF → CHECK FOR SHORT TO GROUND IN CKT 59. IF OK IT IS SHORTED RELAY OR DEFECTIVE FUSE.

NOT OK → ② • IGNITION ON ENGINE STOPPED.
• A/C OFF.
• DISCONNECT A/C RELAY AND CONNECT TEST LIGHT BETWEEN HARNESS TERMINALS "A & C".

OK → BASIC A/C SEALED SYSTEM PROBLEM OR FAULTY CYCLING SWITCH.

LIGHT OFF → • GROUND DIAGNOSTIC TERMINAL AND REPEAT TEST.

LIGHT ON → CHECK FOR GROUND IN CKT 458. IF CKT 458 IS NOT GROUNDED REPLACE ECM.

LIGHT ON → • A/C ON.
• REMOVE GROUND FROM DIAGNOSTIC TERMINAL.
• REPEAT TEST WITH ENGINE IDLING.

LIGHT OFF → • PROBE HARNESS CONNECTOR TERMINAL "A" WITH TEST LIGHT TO GROUND.

SEE A/C CLUTCH CONTROL DIAGNOSIS CHART (PAGE 2 OF 2)

LIGHT ON → DISCONNECT A-B CONNECTOR AND CHECK FOR OPEN CKT 458. IF OK, IT IS FAULTY ECM CONNECTOR TERMINAL "A4" OR ECM.

LIGHT OFF → REPAIR OPEN CKT 39.

CLEAR CODES AND CONFIRM "CLOSED LOOP" OPERATION AND NO "SERVICE ENGINE SOON" LIGHT.

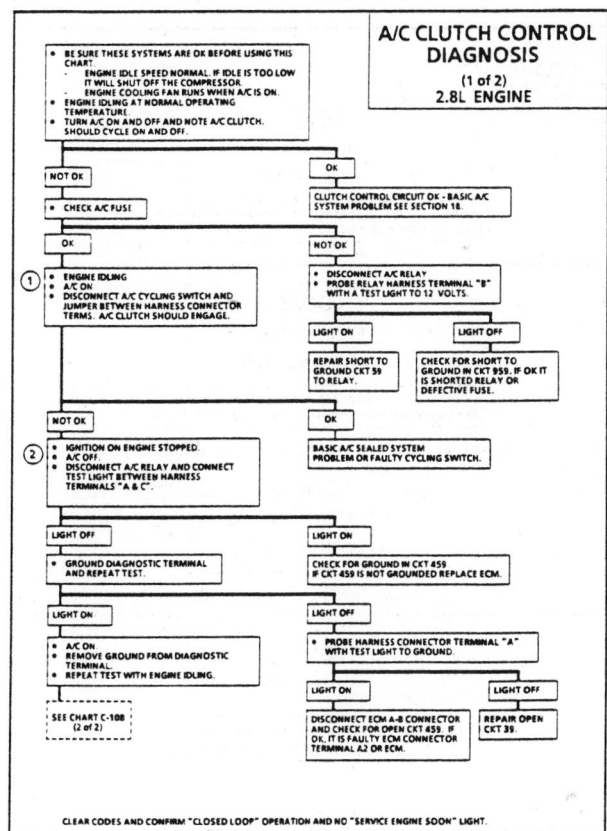

A/C CLUTCH CONTROL DIAGNOSIS
(1 of 2)
2.8L ENGINE

• BE SURE THESE SYSTEMS ARE OK BEFORE USING THIS CHART.
- ENGINE IDLE SPEED NORMAL. IF IDLE IS TOO LOW IT WILL SHUT OFF THE COMPRESSOR.
- ENGINE COOLING FAN RUNS WHEN A/C IS ON.
• ENGINE IDLING AT NORMAL OPERATING TEMPERATURE.
• TURN A/C ON AND OFF AND NOTE A/C CLUTCH. SHOULD CYCLE ON AND OFF.

OK → CLUTCH CONTROL CIRCUIT OK - BASIC A/C SYSTEM PROBLEM SEE SECTION 18.

NOT OK → • CHECK A/C FUSE

OK / NOT OK → • DISCONNECT A/C RELAY
• PROBE RELAY HARNESS TERMINAL "B" WITH A TEST LIGHT TO 12 VOLTS.

① • ENGINE IDLING
• A/C ON
• DISCONNECT A/C CYCLING SWITCH AND JUMPER BETWEEN HARNESS CONNECTOR TERMS. A/C CLUTCH SHOULD ENGAGE.

LIGHT ON → REPAIR SHORT TO GROUND CKT 59 TO RELAY.

LIGHT OFF → CHECK FOR SHORT TO GROUND IN CKT 959. IF OK IT IS SHORTED RELAY OR DEFECTIVE FUSE.

NOT OK → ② • IGNITION ON ENGINE STOPPED.
• A/C OFF.
• DISCONNECT A/C RELAY AND CONNECT TEST LIGHT BETWEEN HARNESS TERMINALS "A & C".

OK → BASIC A/C SEALED SYSTEM PROBLEM OR FAULTY CYCLING SWITCH.

LIGHT OFF → • GROUND DIAGNOSTIC TERMINAL AND REPEAT TEST.

LIGHT ON → CHECK FOR GROUND IN CKT 459. IF CKT 459 IS NOT GROUNDED REPLACE ECM.

LIGHT ON → • A/C ON.
• REMOVE GROUND FROM DIAGNOSTIC TERMINAL.
• REPEAT TEST WITH ENGINE IDLING.

LIGHT OFF → • PROBE HARNESS CONNECTOR TERMINAL "A" WITH TEST LIGHT TO GROUND.

SEE CHART C-10B (2 of 2)

LIGHT ON → DISCONNECT ECM A-B CONNECTOR AND CHECK FOR OPEN CKT 459. IF OK, IT IS FAULTY ECM CONNECTOR TERMINAL A2 OR ECM.

LIGHT OFF → REPAIR OPEN CKT 39.

CLEAR CODES AND CONFIRM "CLOSED LOOP" OPERATION AND NO "SERVICE ENGINE SOON" LIGHT.

TBI TROUBLE DIAGNOSTICS

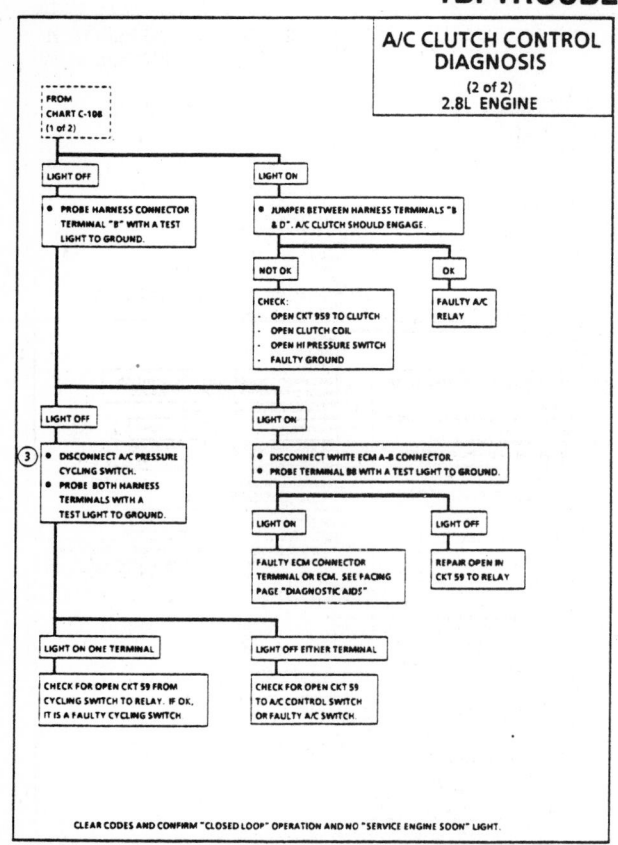

A/C CLUTCH CONTROL DIAGNOSIS
(2 of 2)
2.8L ENGINE

CLEAR CODES AND CONFIRM "CLOSED LOOP" OPERATION AND NO "SERVICE ENGINE SOON" LIGHT.

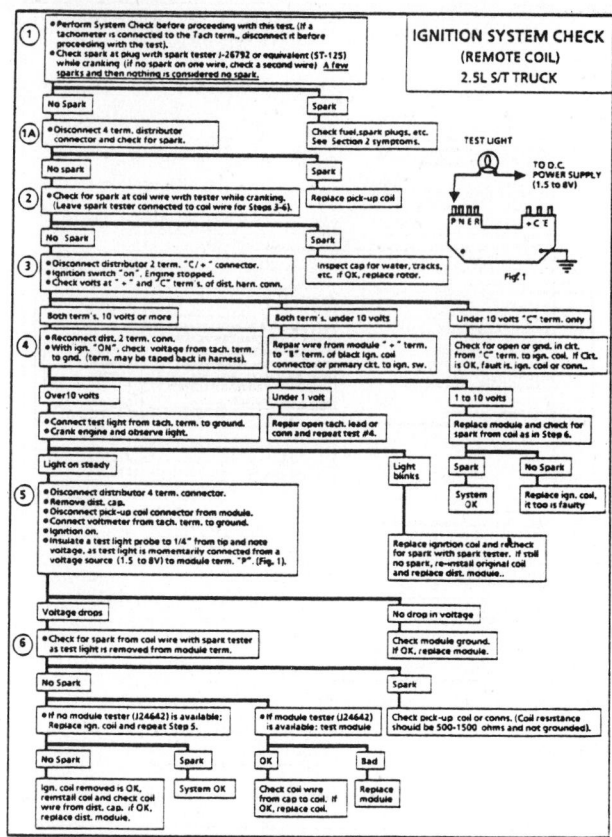

IGNITION SYSTEM CHECK
(REMOTE COIL)
2.5L S/T TRUCK

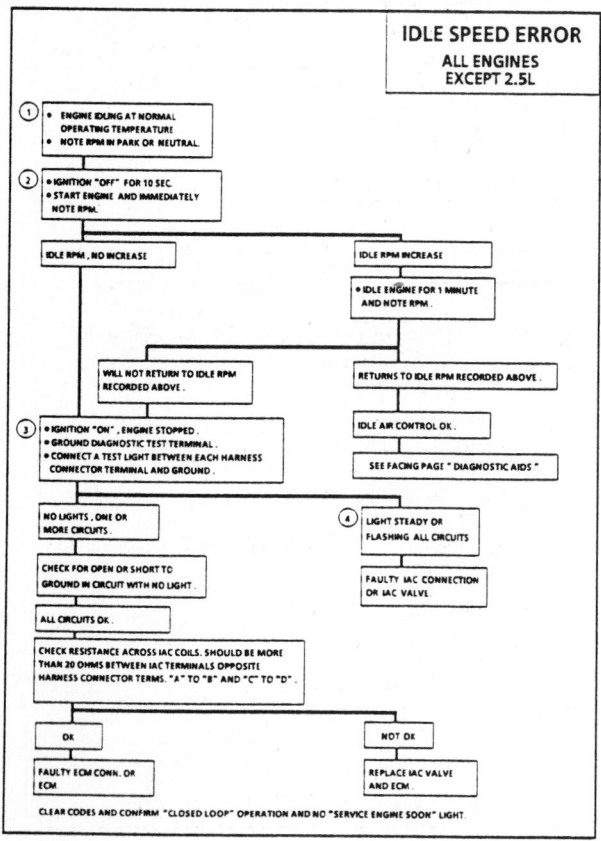

IDLE SPEED ERROR
ALL ENGINES
EXCEPT 2.5L

CLEAR CODES AND CONFIRM "CLOSED LOOP" OPERATION AND NO "SERVICE ENGINE SOON" LIGHT.

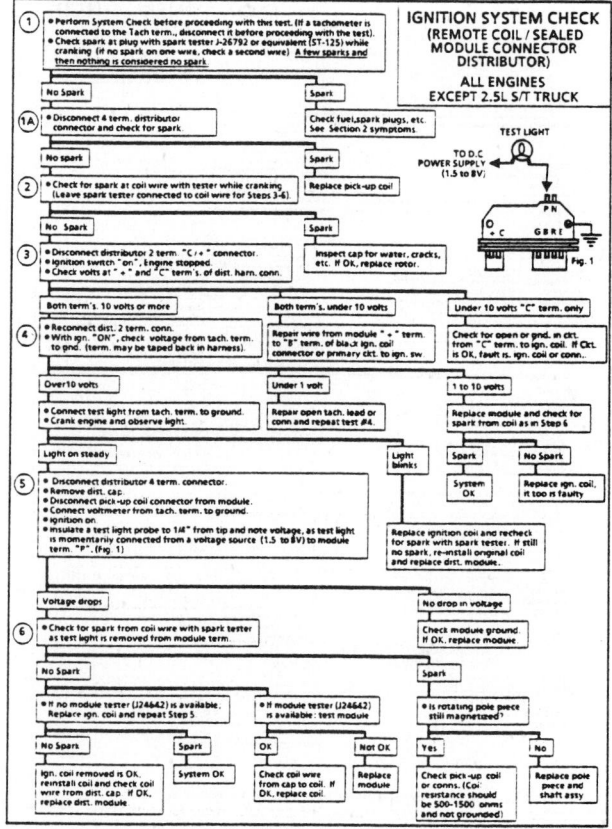

IGNITION SYSTEM CHECK
(REMOTE COIL / SEALED MODULE CONNECTOR DISTRIBUTOR)
ALL ENGINES
EXCEPT 2.5L S/T TRUCK

TBI TROUBLE DIAGNOSTICS

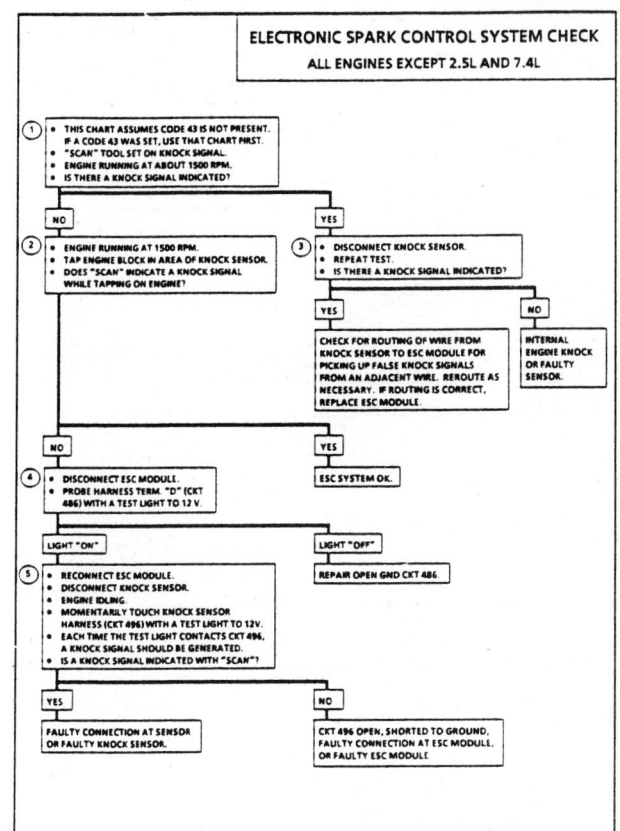

ELECTRONIC SPARK CONTROL SYSTEM CHECK
ALL ENGINES EXCEPT 2.5L AND 7.4L

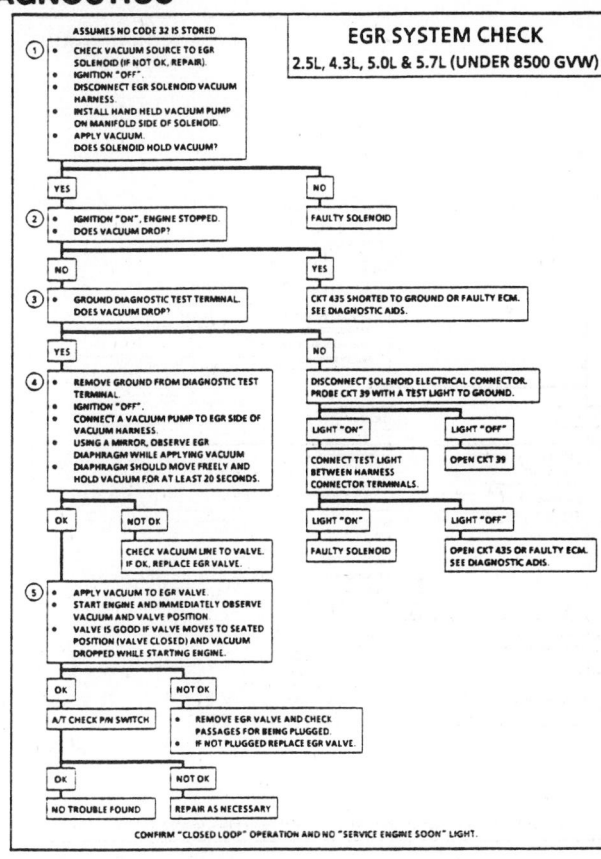

EGR SYSTEM CHECK
2.5L, 4.3L, 5.0L & 5.7L (UNDER 8500 GVW)

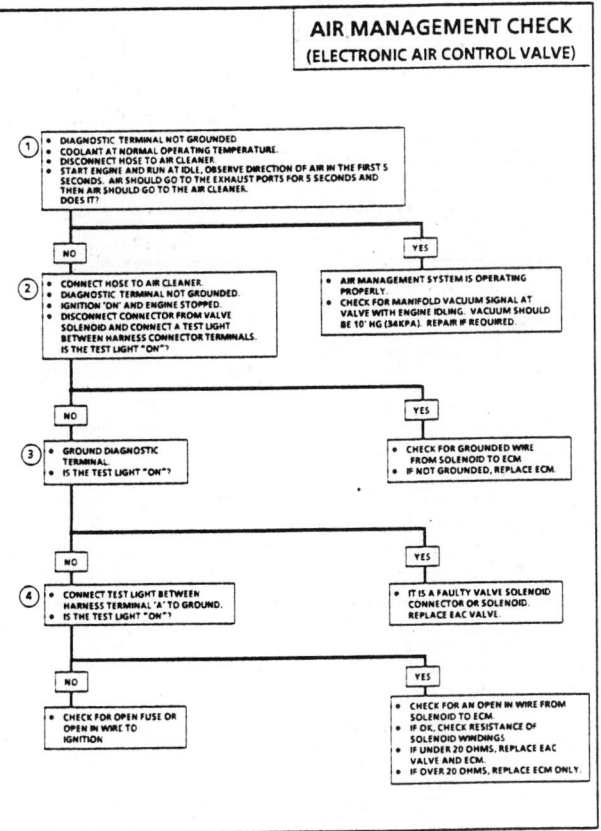

AIR MANAGEMENT CHECK
(ELECTRONIC AIR CONTROL VALVE)

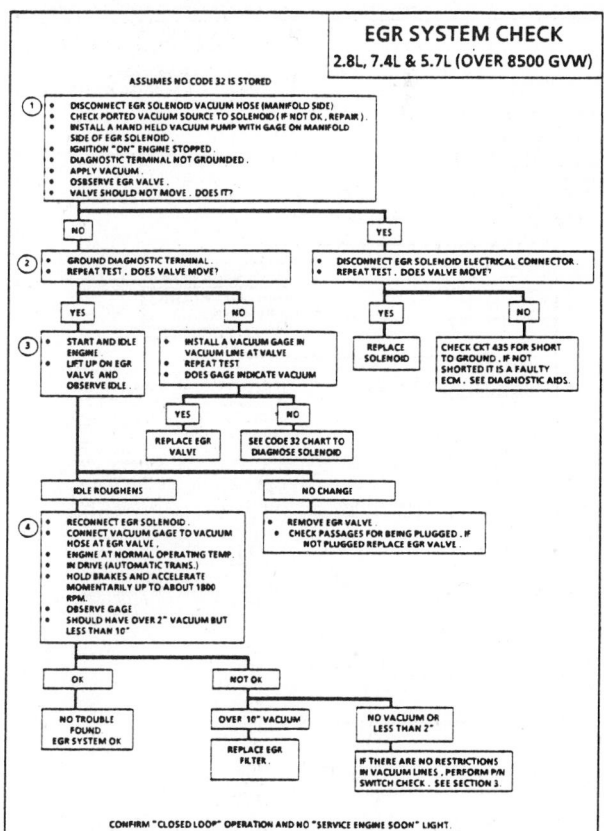

EGR SYSTEM CHECK
2.8L, 7.4L & 5.7L (OVER 8500 GVW)

TBI TROUBLE DIAGNOSTICS

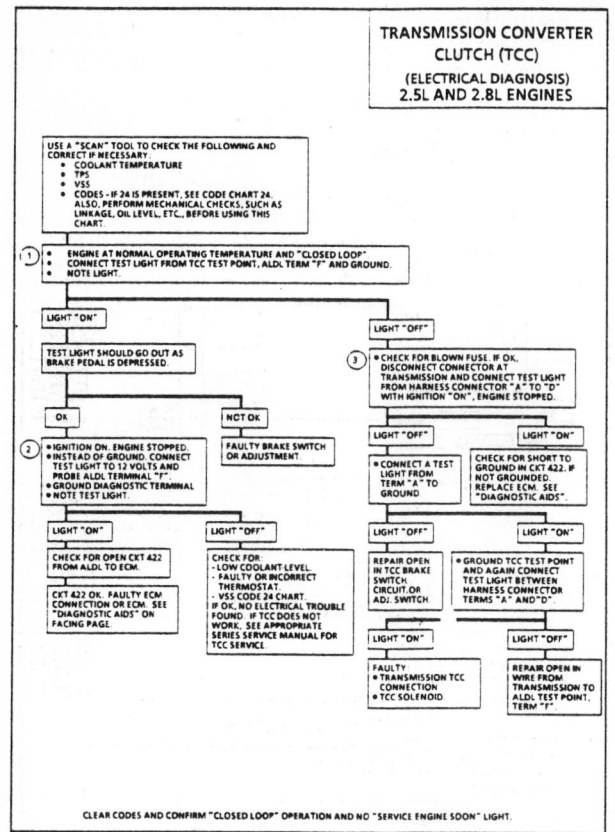

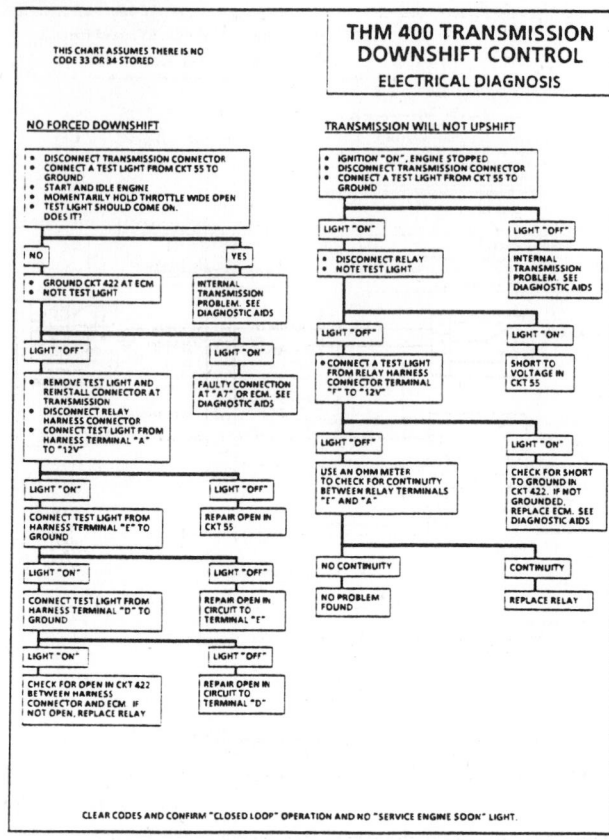

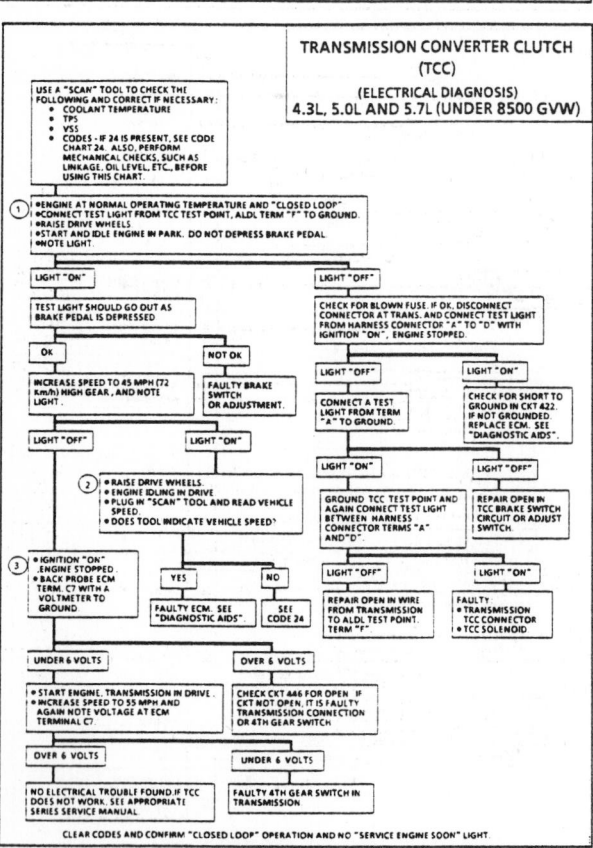

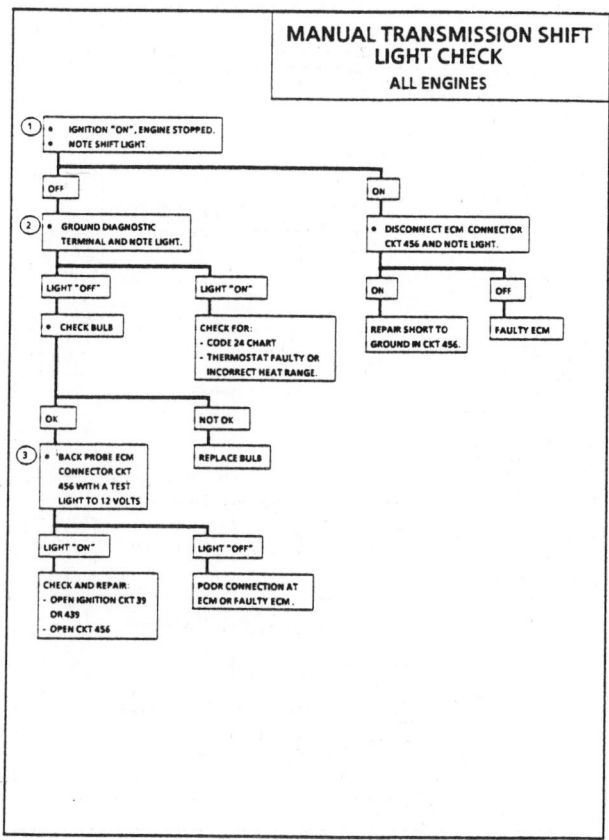

TBI TROUBLE DIAGNOSTICS

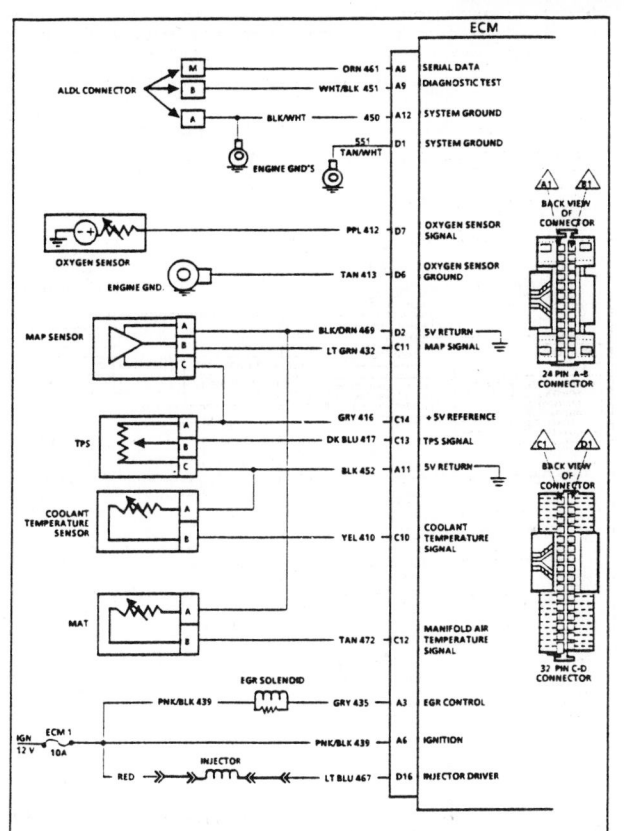

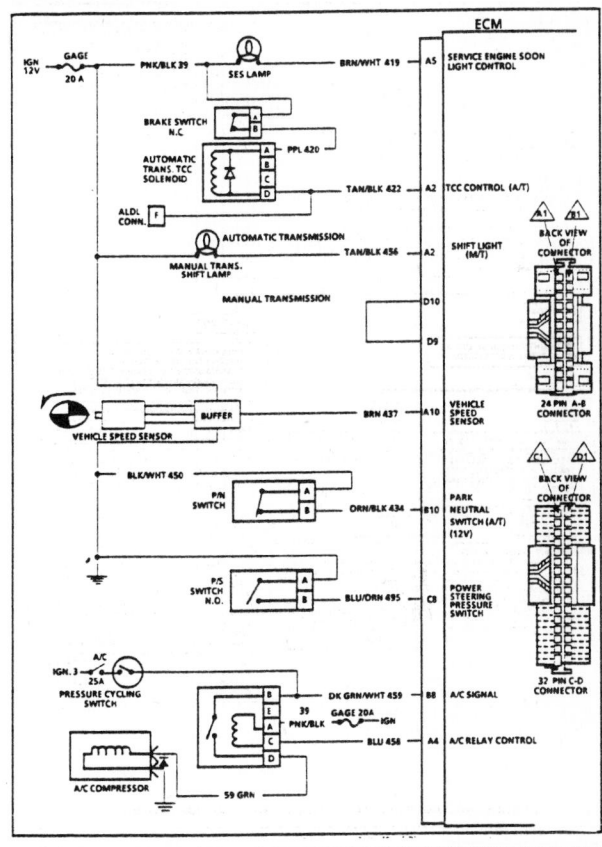

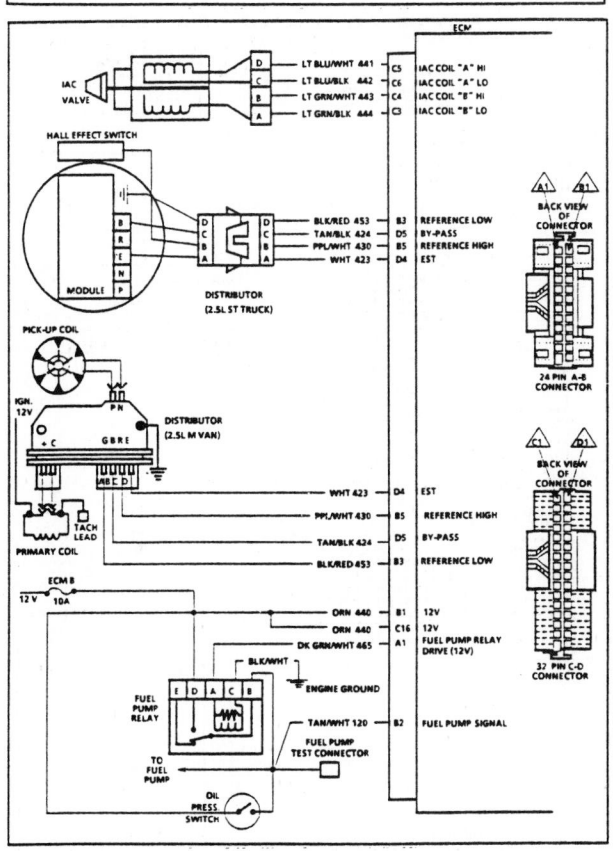

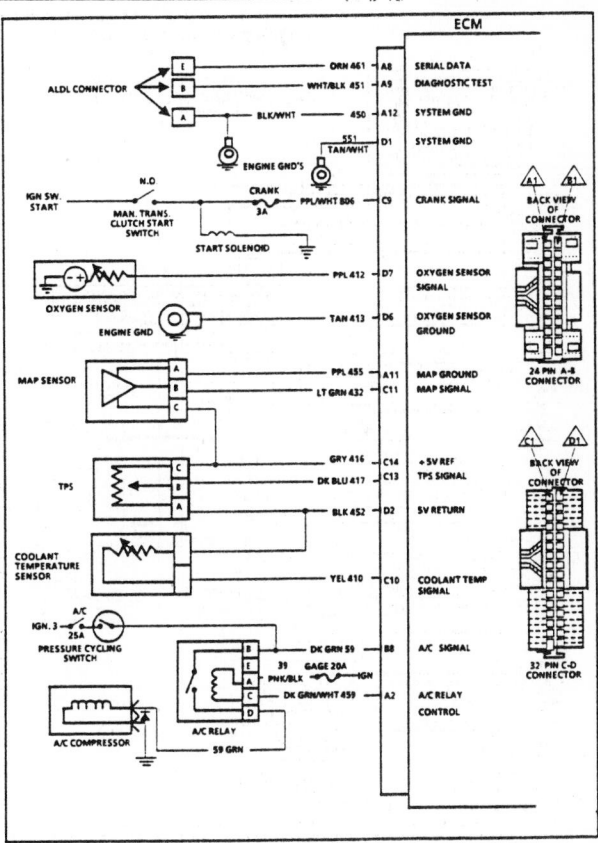

TBI TROUBLE DIAGNOSTICS

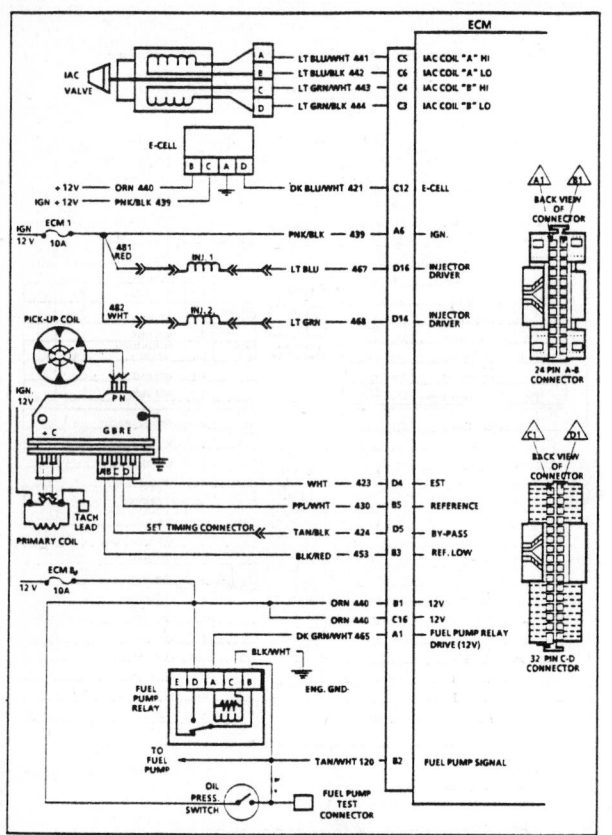

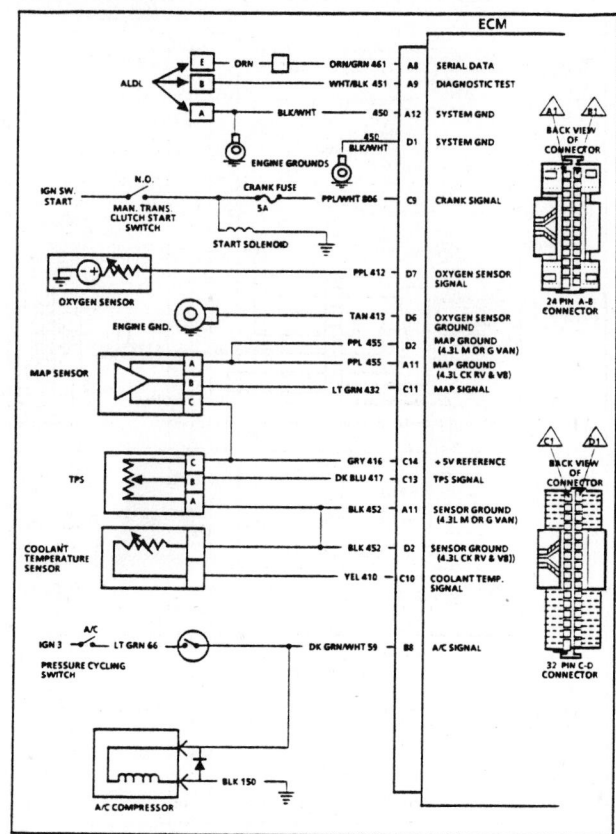

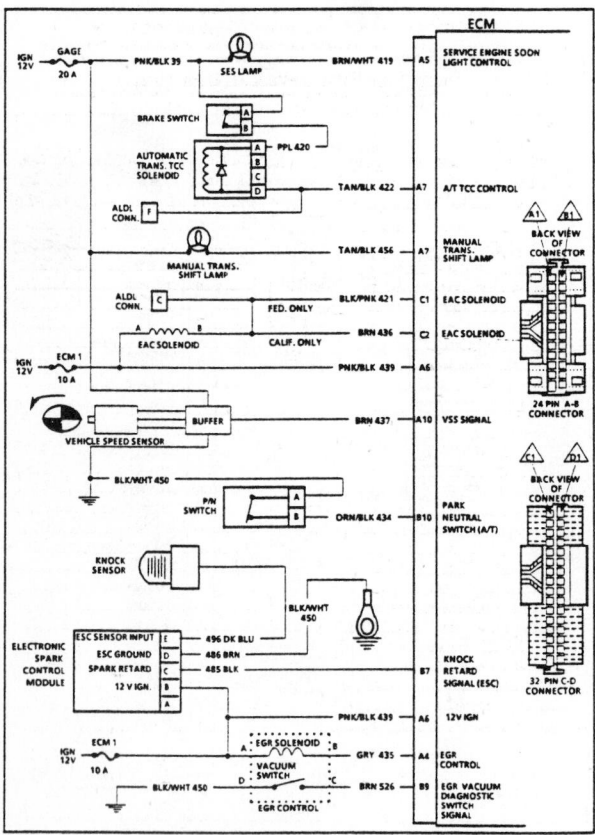

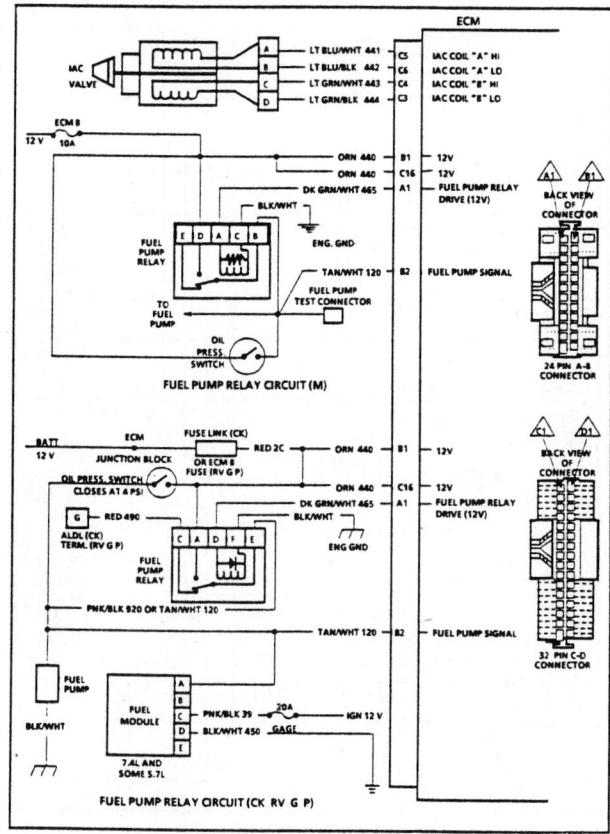

TBI TROUBLE DIAGNOSTICS

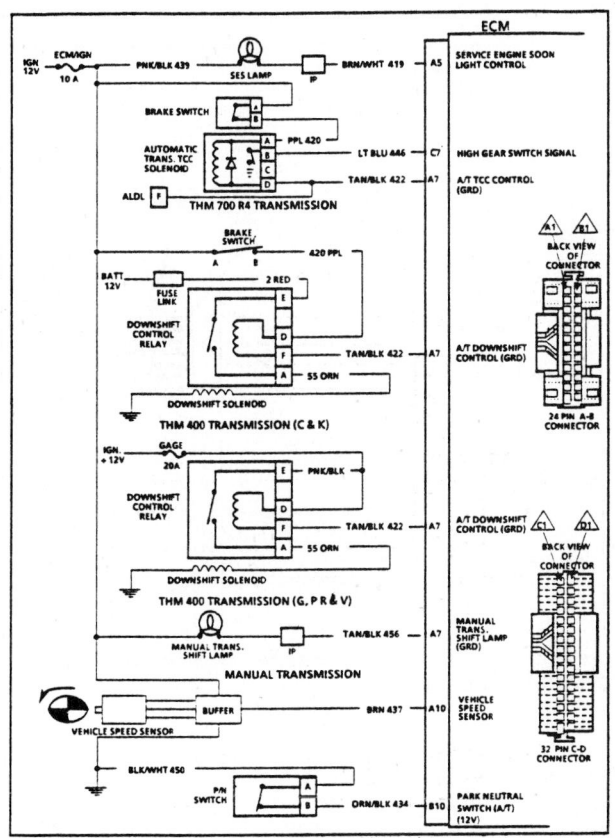

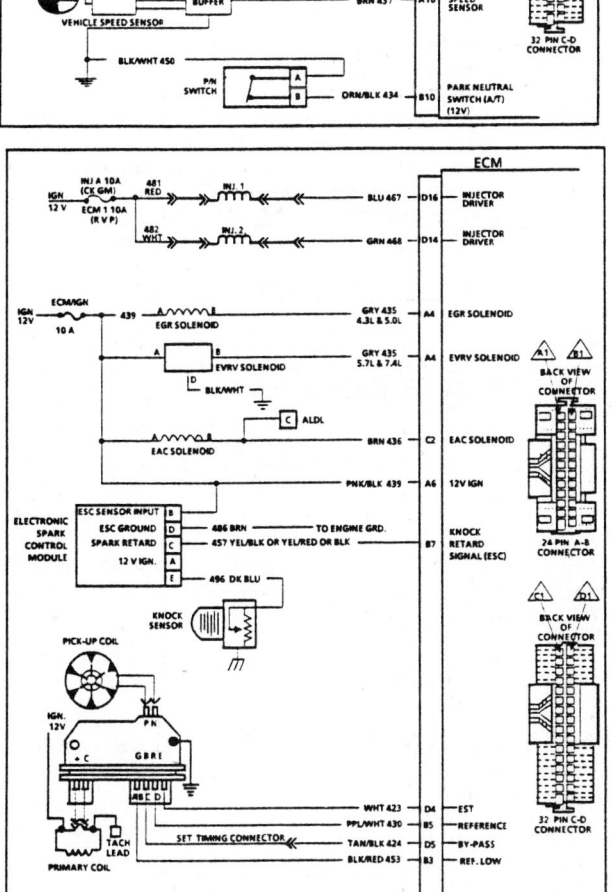

TBI FUEL INJECTION ECM CONNECTOR IDENTIFICATION

This ECM voltage chart is for use with a digital voltmeter to further aid in diagnosis. The voltages you get may vary due to low battery charge or other reasons, but they should be very close.

THE FOLLOWING CONDITIONS MUST BE MET BEFORE TESTING:
- Engine at operating temperature
- Engine idling in closed loop (for "Engine Run" column)
- Diagnostic terminal not grounded
- ALDL tool not installed

VOLTAGE								VOLTAGE	
KEY "ON"	ENG. RUN	CIRCUIT	PIN	WIRE COLOR			WIRE COLOR	PIN	CIRCUIT	KEY "ON"	ENG. RUN
0	14	FUEL PUMP RELAY	A1	DK GRN/WHT			ORN	B1	BATT. 12 VOLTS	12	14
12		SHIFT LIGHT (MT) TCC CONTROL (AT)	A2	TAN/BLK			TAN/WHT	B2	FUEL PUMP SIGNAL	0	14
12	14	EGR SOLENOID	A3	GRY			BLK/RED	B3	EST REF LOW	0	0
12	14	A/C RELAY	A4	BLU				B4	NOT USED		
0	14	"SERVICE ENGINE SOON" CONTROL	A5	BRN/WHT			PPL/WHT	B5	EST REFERENCE HI	0	1.6
12	14	IGN - ECM FUSE	A6	PNK/BLK				B6	NOT USED		
		NOT USED	A7					B7	NOT USED		
2-5	2-5	SERIAL DATA	A8	ORN/WHT			DK GRN/WHT	B8	A/C SIGNAL	0	0
5	5	DIAG. TERM.	A9	BLK				B9	NOT USED		
12		SPEED SENSOR SIGNAL	A10				ORN/BLK	B10	PARK/NEUTRAL SW. SIGNAL	0	0
0	0	MAT & TPS GROUND	A11	BLK				B11	NOT USED		
0	0	SYSTEM GROUND	A12	BLK/WHT				B12	NOT USED		
		NOT USED	C1				TAN/WHT	D1	SYSTEM GROUND	0	0
		NOT USED	C2				BLK/ORN	D2	5V RETURN	0	0
NOT USEABLE		IAC "B" LO	C3	LT GRN/BLK				D3	NOT USED		
NOT USEABLE		IAC "B" HI	C4	LT GRN/WHT			WHT	D4	EST CONTROL	0	1.0
NOT USEABLE		IAC "A" HI	C5	LT BLU/WHT			TAN/BLK	D5	EST BYPASS	0	4.75
NOT USEABLE		IAC "A" LO	C6	LT BLU/BLK			TAN	D6	GRN'D. (O₂)	0	0
		NOT USED	C7				PPL	D7	O₂ SENSOR SIGNAL	0	⑤
12.3	12.3	P/S SWITCH	C8	BLU/YEL				D8	NOT USED		
		NOT USED	C9					D9	NOT USED		
1.9	1.7	COOLANT TEMP. SIGNAL	C10	YEL				D10	NOT USED		
4.7	2.0	MAP SIGNAL	C11	LT GRN				D11	NOT USED		
1.3	1.3	MAT SIGNAL	C12	TAN				D12	NOT USED		
.73 V	.73V	TPS SIGNAL	C13	DK BLU				D13	NOT USED		
5	5	5 VOLT REFERENCE	C14	GRY				D14	NOT USED		
		NOT USED	C15					D15	NOT USED		
12	14	BATTERY 12 VOLTS	C16	ORN			BLU	D16	INJECTOR A	12	14

1. Varies from .60 to battery voltage depending on position of drive wheels
2. Varies with temperature
3. Varies
4. 12V first two seconds
5. Measured between terminals C13 and A11 (± .05V)

ENGINE 2.5L
VEHICLE S/T TRUCK M VAN

TBI FUEL INJECTION ECM CONNECTOR IDENTIFICATION

This ECM voltage chart is for use with a digital voltmeter to further aid in diagnosis. The voltages you get may vary due to low battery charge or other reasons, but they should be very close.

THE FOLLOWING CONDITIONS MUST BE MET BEFORE TESTING:
- Engine at operating temperature
- Engine idling in closed loop (for "Engine Run" column)
- Test terminal not grounded
- ALCL tool not installed

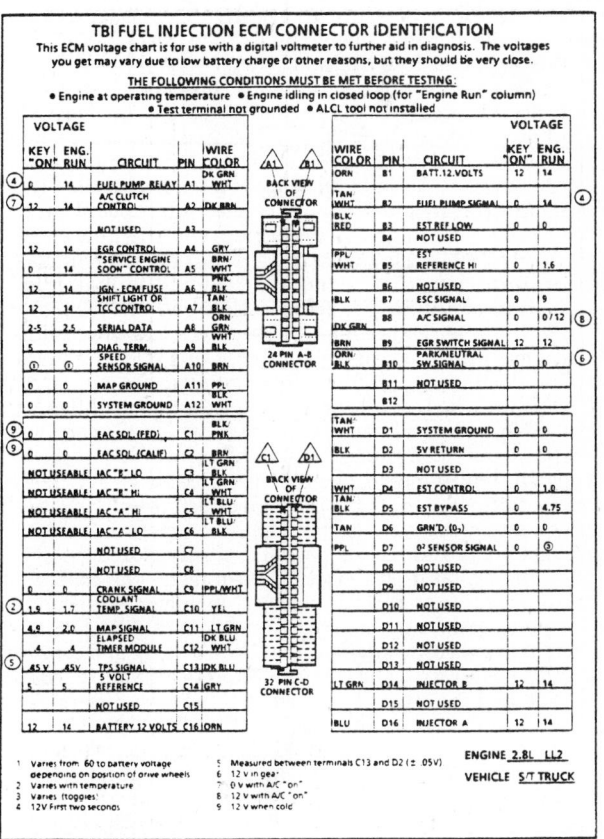

VOLTAGE								VOLTAGE	
KEY "ON"	ENG. RUN	CIRCUIT	PIN	WIRE COLOR		WIRE COLOR	PIN	CIRCUIT	KEY "ON"	ENG. RUN
0	14	FUEL PUMP RELAY	A1	DK GRN/WHT		ORN	B1	BATT. 12 VOLTS	12	14
12	14	A/C CLUTCH CONTROL	A2	DK BRN		TAN/WHT	B2	FUEL PUMP SIGNAL	0	14
		NOT USED	A3			BLK/RED	B3	EST REF LOW	0	0
12	14	EGR CONTROL	A4	GRY			B4	NOT USED		
0	14	"SERVICE ENGINE SOON" CONTROL	A5	BRN/WHT		PPL/WHT	B5	EST REFERENCE HI	0	1.6
12	14	IGN - ECM FUSE	A6	PNK/BLK			B6	NOT USED		
12	14	SHIFT LIGHT OR TCC CONTROL	A7	TAN/BLK		TAN	B7	ESC SIGNAL	9	9
2-5	2.5	SERIAL DATA	A8	ORN/WHT			B8	A/C SIGNAL	0	0/12
5	5	DIAG. TERM.	A9	BLK		BRN	B9	EGR SWITCH SIGNAL	12	12
①	①	SPEED SENSOR SIGNAL	A10			ORN/BLK	B10	PARK/NEUTRAL SW. SIGNAL	0	0
0	0	MAP GROUND	A11	PPL			B11	NOT USED		
0	0	SYSTEM GROUND	A12	BLK/WHT			B12			
0	0	EAC SOL. (FED)	C1	BLK/PNK		TAN/WHT	D1	SYSTEM GROUND	0	0
0	0	EAC SOL. (CALIF)	C2	BRN		BLK	D2	5V RETURN	0	0
NOT USEABLE		IAC "B" LO	C3	LT GRN/BLK			D3	NOT USED		
NOT USEABLE		IAC "B" HI	C4	LT GRN/WHT		WHT	D4	EST CONTROL	0	1.0
NOT USEABLE		IAC "A" HI	C5	LT BLU/WHT		TAN/BLK	D5	EST BYPASS	0	4.75
NOT USEABLE		IAC "A" LO	C6	LT BLU/BLK		TAN	D6	GRN'D. (O₂)	0	0
		NOT USED	C7			PPL	D7	O₂ SENSOR SIGNAL	0	⑤
		NOT USED	C8				D8	NOT USED		
		CRANK SIGNAL	C9	PPL/WHT			D9	NOT USED		
1.9	1.7	COOLANT TEMP. SIGNAL	C10	YEL			D10	NOT USED		
4.9	2.0	MAP SIGNAL	C11	LT GRN			D11	NOT USED		
4	4	ELAPSED TIMER MODULE	C12	DK BLU/WHT			D12	NOT USED		
.45 V	.45V	TPS SIGNAL	C13	DK BLU			D13	NOT USED		
5	5	5 VOLT REFERENCE	C14	GRY		LT GRN	D14	INJECTOR B	12	14
		NOT USED	C15				D15	NOT USED		
12	14	BATTERY 12 VOLTS	C16	ORN		BLU	D16	INJECTOR A	12	14

1. Varies from .60 to battery voltage depending on position of drive wheels
2. Varies with temperature
3. Varies (toggles)
4. 12V first two seconds
5. Measured between terminals C13 and D2 (± .05V)
6. 12 V in gear
7. 0 V with A/C "on"
8. 12 V with A/C "on"
9. 12 V when cold

ENGINE 2.8L LL2
VEHICLE S/T TRUCK

GENERAL MOTORS SEQUENTIAL FUEL INJECTION (SFI) SYSTEM

GENERAL INFORMATION

The sequential fuel injection (SFI) system is controlled by an electronic control module (ECM) which monitors engine operations and generates output signals to provide the correct air/fuel mixture, ignition timing and engine idle speed control. Input to the control unit is provided by an oxygen sensor, coolant temperature sensor, detonation sensor, hot film air mass sensor and throttle position sensor. The ECM also receives information concerning engine rpm, road speed, transmission gear position, power steering and air conditioning.

With SFI, metered fuel is timed and injected sequentially through six injectors into individual cylinder ports. Each cylinder receives one injection per working cycle (every two revolutions), just prior to the opening of the intake valve. In addition, the SFI system incorporates a Computer Controlled Coil Ignition (C^3I) system that uses an electronic coil module that replaced the conventional distributor and coil used on most engines. An electronic spark control (ESC) is used to adjust the spark timing.

The injection system uses solenoid-type fuel injectors, one at each intake port, rather than the single injector found on the earlier throttle body system. The injectors are mounted on a fuel rail and are activated by a signal from the electronic control module. The injector is a solenoid-operated valve which remains open depending on the width of the electronic pulses (length of the open time) from the ECM; the longer the open time, the more fuel is injected. In this manner, the air/fuel mixture can be precisely controlled for maximum performance with minimum emissions.

Fuel is pumped from the tank by a high pressure fuel pump, located inside the fuel tank. It is a positive displacement roller vane pump. The impeller serves as a vapor separator and precharges the high pressure assembly. A pressure regulator maintains 34–40 psi in the fuel line to the injectors and the excess fuel is fed back to the tank.

The Mass Air Flow Sensor is used to measure the mass of air that is drawn into the engine cylinders. It is located just ahead of the air throttle in the intake system and consists of a heated film which measures the mass of air, rather than just the volume. A resistor is used to measure the temperature of the incoming air, the heated film and the electronic module and the MAF sensor maintains the temperature of the film at 75 degrees above ambient temperature. As the ambient (outside) air temperature rises, more energy is required to maintain the heated film at the higher temperature and the control unit uses this difference in required energy to calculate the mass of the incoming air. The control unit uses this information to determine the duration of fuel injection pulse, timing and EGR.

The throttle body incorporates an idle air control (IAC) that provides for a bypass channel through which air can flow. It consists of an orifice and pintle which is controlled by the ECM through a stepper motor. The IAC provides air flow for idle and allows additional air during cold start until the engine reaches operating temperature. As the engine temperature rises, the opening through which air passes is slowly closed.

The throttle position sensor (TPS) provides the control unit with information on throttle position, in order to determine injector pulse width and hence correct mixture. The TPS is connected to the throttle shaft on the throttle body and consists of a potentiometer with one end connected to a 5 volt source from the ECM and the other to ground. A third wire is connected to the ECM to measure the voltage output from the TPS which changes as the throttle valve angle is changed (accelerator pedal moves). At the closed throttle position, the output is low (approximately .4 volts); as the throttle valve opens, the output increases to a maximum 5 volts at wide open throttle (WOT). The

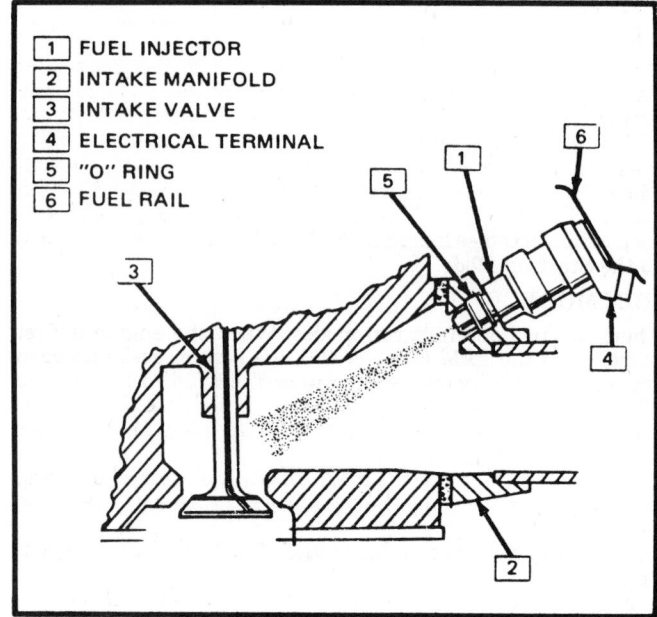

1	FUEL INJECTOR
2	INTAKE MANIFOLD
3	INTAKE VALVE
4	ELECTRICAL TERMINAL
5	"O" RING
6	FUEL RAIL

Port fuel injection

TPS can be misadjusted open, shorted, or loose and if it is out of adjustment, the idle quality of WOT performance may be poor. A loose TPS can cause intermittent bursts of fuel from the injectors and an unstable idle because the ECM thinks the throttle is moving. This should cause a trouble code to be set. Once a trouble code is set, the ECM will use a preset value for TPS and some vehicle performance may return. A small amount of engine coolant is routed through the throttle assembly to prevent freezing inside the throttle bore during cold operation.

FUEL CONTROL SYSTEM

The basic function of the fuel control system is to control the fuel delivery to the engine. The fuel is delivered to the engine by individual fuel injectors mounted on the intake manifold near each cylinder.

The main control sensor is the oxygen sensor which is located in the exhaust manifold. The oxygen sensor tells the ECM how much oxygen is in the exhaust gas and the ECM changes the air/fuel ratio to the engine by controlling the fuel injectors. The best mixture to minimize exhaust emissions is 14.7:1 which allows the catalytic converter to operate the most efficiently. Because of the constant measuring and adjusting of the air/fuel ratio, the fuel injection system is called a "Closed Loop" system.

Modes Of Operation

The ECM looks at voltage from several sensors to determine how much fuel to give the engine. The fuel is delivered under one of several conditions, called "Modes".

STARTING MODE

When the engine is first turned "ON", the ECM will turn on the fuel pump relay for two seconds and the the fuel pump will build up pressure. The ECM then checks the coolant temperature sensor, throttle position sensor and crank sensor, then the ECM determines the proper air/fuel ratio for starting. This ranges from 1.5:1 at -33°F (-36°C) to 14.7:1 at 201°F (94°C).

The ECM controls the amount of fuel that is delivered in the Starting Mode by changing how long the injectors are turned "ON" and "OFF". This is done by "pulsing" the injectors for very short times.

CLEAR FLOOD MODE

If for some reason the engine should become flooded, provisions have been made to clear this condition. To clear the flood, the driver must depress the accelerator pedal enough to open to wide-open throttle position. The ECM then issues injector pulses at a rate that would be equal to an air/fuel ratio of 20:1. The ECM maintains this injector rate as long as the throttle remains wide open and the engine RPM is below 600. If the throttle position becomes less than 80%, the ECM then would return to the Starting Mode.

RUN MODE

There are two different run modes. When the engine is first started and the RPM is above 400, the system goes into open loop operation. In open loop operation, the ECM will ignore the signal from the oxygen (0_2) sensor and calculate the injector on-time based upon inputs from the coolant and MAP sensors (or MAF sensor).

During open loop operation, the ECM analyzes the following items to determine when the system is ready to go to the closed loop mode.

1. The oxygen sensor varying voltage output. (This is dependent on temperature).

2. The coolant sensor must be above specified temperature.

3. A specific amount of time must elapse after starting the engine. These values are stored in the PROM.

When these conditions have been met, the system goes into closed loop operation In closed loop operation, the ECM will modify the pulse width (injector on-time) based upon the signal from the oxygen sensor. The ECM will decrease the on-time if the air/fuel ratio is too rich, and will increase the on-time if the air/fuel ratio is too lean.

ACCELERATION MODE

When the engine is required to accelerate, the opening of the throttle valve(s) causes a rapid increase in manifold absolute pressure (MAP). This rapid increase in MAP causes fuel to condense on the manifold walls. The ECM senses this increase in throttle angle and MAP, and supplies additional fuel for a short period of time. This prevents the engine from stumbling due to too lean a mixture.

DECELERATION MODE

Upon deceleration, a leaner fuel mixture is required to reduce emission of hydrocarbons (H) and carbon monoxide (CO). To adjust the injection on-time, the ECM uses the decrease in MAP and the decrease in throttle position to calculate a decrease in pulse width. To maintain an idle fuel ratio of 14.7:1, fuel output is momentarily reduced. This is done because of the fuel remaining in the intake manifold. The ECM can cut off the fuel completely for short periods of time.

BATTERY VOLTAGE CORRECTION MODE

The purpose of battery voltage correction is to compensate for variations in battery voltage to fuel pump and injector response. The ECM modifies the pulse width by a correction factor in the PROM. When battery voltage decreases, pulse width increases.

Battery voltage correction takes place in all operating modes.

When battery voltage is low, the spark delivered by the distributor may be low. To correct this low battery voltage problem, the ECM can do any or all of the following:

a. Increase injector pulse width (increase fuel).

b. Increase idle RPM.

c. Increase ignition dwell time.

FUEL CUT-OFF MODE

When the ignition is off, the ECM will not energize the injector. Fuel will also be cut off if the ECM does not receive a reference pulse from the distributor. To prevent dieseling, fuel delivery is completely stopped as soon as the engine is stopped. The ECM will not allow any fuel supply until it receives distributor reference pulses which prevents flooding.

CONVERTER PROTECTION MODE

In this mode the ECM estimates the temperature of the catalytic converter and then modifies fuel delivery to protect the converter from high temperatures. When the ECM has determined that the converter may overheat, it will cause open loop operation and will enrichen the fuel delivery. A slightly richer mixture will then cause the converter temperature to be reduced.

Fuel Control System Components

The fuel control system is made up of the following components:

1. Fuel Supply System.
2. Throttle Body Assembly.
3. Fuel Injectors.
4. Fuel Rail.
5. Fuel Pressure Regulator.
6. Idle Air Control (IAC).
7. Fuel Pump.
8. Fuel Pump Relay.

The fuel control system starts with the fuel in the fuel tank. An electric fuel pump, located in the fuel tank with the fuel gauge sending unit, pumps fuel to the fuel rail through an in-line fuel filter. The pump is designed to provide fuel at a pressure above the pressure needed by the injectors. A pressure regulator in the fuel rail keeps fuel available to the injectors at a constant pressure. Unused fuel is returned to the fuel tank by a separate line.

The injectors are controlled by the ECM. They deliver fuel in one of several modes as previously described. In order to properly control the fuel supply, the fuel pump is operated by the ECM through the fuel pump relay and oil pressure switch.

THROTTLE BODY UNIT

The throttle body unit has a throttle valve to control the amount of air delivered to the engine. The TPS and IAC valve are also mounted onto the throttle body. The throttle body contains vacuum ports located at, above or below the throttle valve. These vacuum ports generate the vacuum signals needed by various components.

On some models, the engine coolant is directed through the coolant cavity at the bottom of the throttle body to warm the throttle valve and prevent icing.

FUEL RAIL

The fuel rail is mounted on top of the engine. It distributes fuel to the individual injectors. Fuel is delivered to the input end of the fuel rail by the fuel lines, goes through the rail, then to the fuel pressure regulator. The regulator keeps the fuel pressure to the injectors at a constant pressure. The remaining fuel is then returned to the fuel tank.

FUEL INJECTOR

The fuel injector is a solenoid operated device controlled by the ECM. The ECM turns on the solenoid, which opens the a valve which allows fuel delivery. The fuel, under pressure, is injected in a cone like spray pattern at the opening of the intake valve. The fuel, which is not used by the injectors, passes through the pressure regulator before returning to the fuel tank.

An injector that is partly open, will cause loss of fuel pressure after the engine is shut down, so long crank time would be noticed on some engines. Also dieseling could occur because some fuel could be delivered after the ignition is turned "OFF".

Part	Part Name
1	Gasket - Flange
10	Throttle Body Assembly
15	Plug - Idle Stop Screw
16	Screw Assembly - Idle Stop
17	Spring - Idle Stop Screw Assembly
20	Sensor - Throttle Position (TPS)
21	Screw Assembly - TPS Attaching
22	Retainer - TPS Attaching Screw
27	Lever - TPS
40	Cover - Coolant Cavity
45	Screw Assembly - Coolant Cover Attaching
46	O-ring - Coolant Cover to Throttle Body
60	Idle Air / Vacuum Signal Housing Assembly
65	Screw Assembly - Idle Air / Vacuum Signal Assembly
66	Screw Assembly - Idle Air / Vacuum Signal Assembly (Long)
67	Gasket - Idle Air / Vacuum Signal Assembly
70	Valve Assembly - Idle Air Control (IAC)
71	Gasket - IAC Valve Assembly

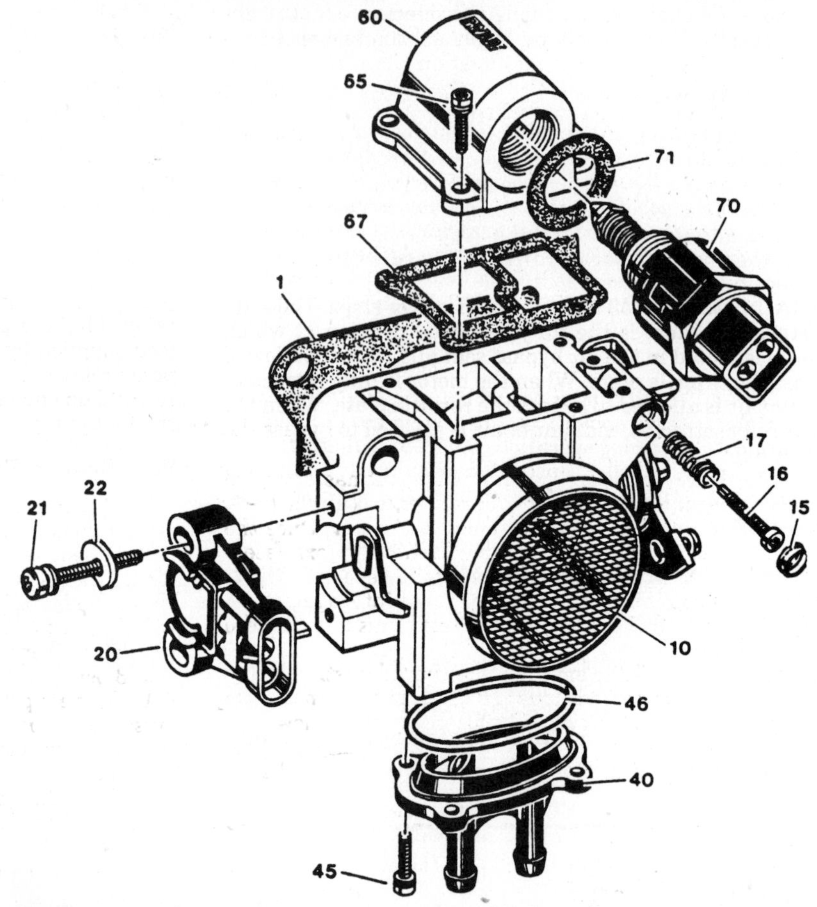

Throttle body assembly

FUEL PRESSURE REGULATOR

The fuel pressure regulator is a diaphragm operated relief valve with injector pressure on one side and manifold pressure on the other. The function of the regulator is to maintain a constant pressure at the injector at all times. The pressure regulator also compensates for engine load, by increasing fuel pressure when it sees low engine vacuum.

The pressure regulator is mounted on the fuel rail and serviced separately. If the pressure is too low, poor performance could result. If the pressure is too high, excessive odor and a code 45 may result.

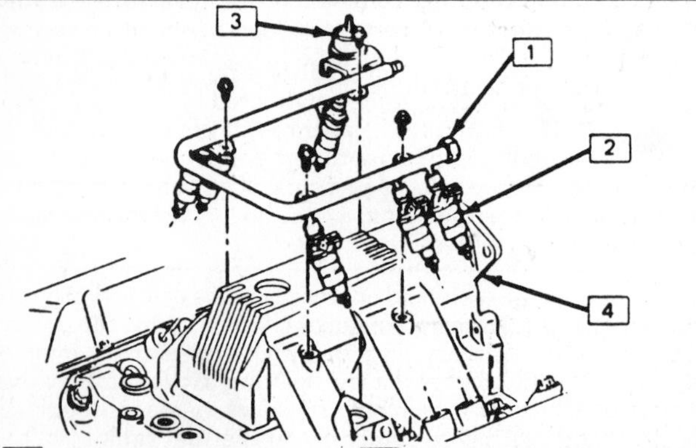

1	FUEL RAIL ASSEMBLY	3	PRESSURE REGULATOR
2	INJECTOR	4	INTAKE MANIFOLD

Fuel rail and injector assembly

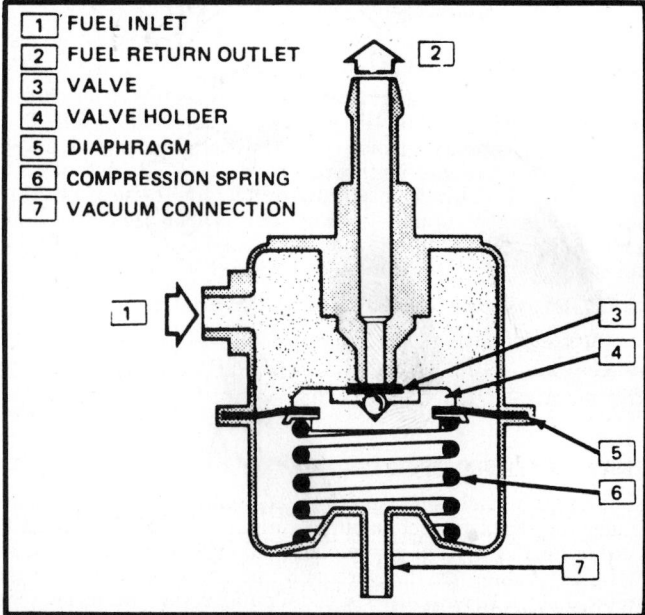

1	FUEL INLET
2	FUEL RETURN OUTLET
3	VALVE
4	VALVE HOLDER
5	DIAPHRAGM
6	COMPRESSION SPRING
7	VACUUM CONNECTION

Fuel pressure regulator

IDLE AIR CONTROL (IAC)

The purpose of the idle air control (IAC) system is to control engine idle speeds while preventing stalls due to changes in engine load. The IAC assembly, mounted on the throttle body, controls bypass air around the throttle plate. By extending or retracting a conical valve, a controlled amount of air can move around the throttle plate. If RPM is too low, more air is diverted around the throttle plate to increase RPM.

During idle, the proper position of the IAC valve is calculated by the ECM based on battery voltage, coolant temperature, engine load, and engine RPM. If the RPM drops below a specified rate, the throttle plate is closed. The ECM will then calculate a new valve position.

The IAC motor has 255 different positions or steps. The zero, or reference position, is the fully extended position at which the pintle is seated in the air bypass seat and no air is allowed to bypass the throttle plate. When the motor is fully retracted, maximum air is allowed to bypass the throttle plate. When the motor is fully retracted, maximum air is allowed to bypass the throttle plate.

The ECM always monitors how many steps it has extended or retracted the pintle from the zero or reference position; thus, it always calculates the exact position of the motor. Once the engine has started and the vehicle has reached approximately 40 MPH, the ECM will extend the motor 255 steps from whatever position it is in. This will bottom out the pintle against the seat. The ECM will call this position "0" and thus keep its zero reference updated.

The IAC only affects the engine's idle characteristics. If it is stuck fully open, idle speed is too high (too much air enters the throttle bore) If it is stuck closed, idle speed is too low (not enough air entering). If it is stuck somewhere in the middle, idle may be rough, and the engine won't respond to load changes.

1. IDLE AIR CONTROL VALVE
A LESS THAN 28mm (1-1/8 IN.)
B TYPE I (WITH COLLAR)
C TYPE II (WITHOUT COLLAR)
D GASKET (PART OF IAC VALVE SERVICE KIT)

Idle air control (IAC) valve assembly

FUEL PUMP RELAY CIRCUIT

The fuel pump relay is usually located on the left front inner fender (or shock tower) or on the engine side of the firewall (center cowl). The fuel pump electrical system consists of the fuel pump relay, ignition circuit 3 and the ECM circuits are protected by a 10 amp fuse. The fuel pump relay contact switch is in the normally open (N.O.) position.

When the ignition is turned on, the ECM will supply voltage to the fuel pump relay coil, closing the open contact switch. The ignition circuit 3 10 amp fuse can now supply ignition voltage to the circuit which feeds the relay contact switch. With the relay contacts closed, ignition voltage is supplied to the fuel pump. If the ECM does not receive a cranking signal within 2 seconds, the ECM will de-energized the fuel pump relay. The ECM will continue to supply voltage to the relay coil circuit as long as the ECM receives the rpm reference pulses from the H.E.I. or C³I module.

The fuel pump control circuit also includes an engine oil pressure switch with a set of normally open contacts. The switch closes at approximately 4 pounds of oil pressure and provides a secondary battery feed path to the fuel pump. If the relay fails, the pump will continue to run using the battery feed supplied by the closed oil pressure switch. A failed fuel pump relay will result in extended engine crank times in order to build up enough oil pressure to close the switch and turn on the fuel pump.

Fuel System Pressure Test

When the ignition switch is turned ON, the in-tank fuel pump is energized for as long as the engine is cranking or running and the control unit is receiving signals from the HEI distributor or C³I module. If there are no reference pulses, the control unit will shut off the fuel pump within two seconds. The pump will deliver fuel to the fuel rail and injectors, then the pressure regulator where the system pressure is controlled to maintain 26–43 psi.

1. Connect pressure gauge J-34730-1, or equivalent, to fuel pressure test point on the fuel rail. Wrap a rag around the pressure tap to absorb any leakage that may occur when installing the gauge.

2. Turn the ignition ON and check that pump pressure is 34–43 psi. This pressure is controlled by spring pressure within the regulator assembly.

3. Start the engine and allow it to idle. The fuel pressure should drop to 29–34 psi due to the lower manifold pressure.

NOTE: The idle pressure will vary somewhat depending on barometric pressure. Check for a drop in pressure indicating regulator control, rather than specific values.

4. On turbocharged models, use a low pressure air pump to apply air pressure to the regulator to simulate turbocharger boost pressure. Boost pressure should increase fuel pressure one pound for every pound of boost. Again, look for changes rather than specific pressures. The maximum fuel pressure should not exceed 46 psi.

5. If the fuel pressure drops, check the operation of the check valve, the pump coupling connection, fuel pressure regulator valve and the injectors. A restricted fuel line or filter may also cause a pressure drip. To check the fuel pump output, restrict the fuel return line and run 12 volts to the pump. The fuel pressure should rise to approximately 75 psi with the return line restricted.

─────── CAUTION ───────

Before attempting to remove or service any fuel system component, it is necessary to relieve the fuel system pressure.

Relieving Fuel System Pressure

1. Remove the fuel pump fuse from the fuse block.
2. Start the engine. It should run and then stall when the fuel in the lines is exhausted. When the engine stops, crank the starter for about three seconds to make sure all pressure in the fuel lines is released.
3. Replace the fuel pump fuse.
4. On some models a pressure relief valve is located on the

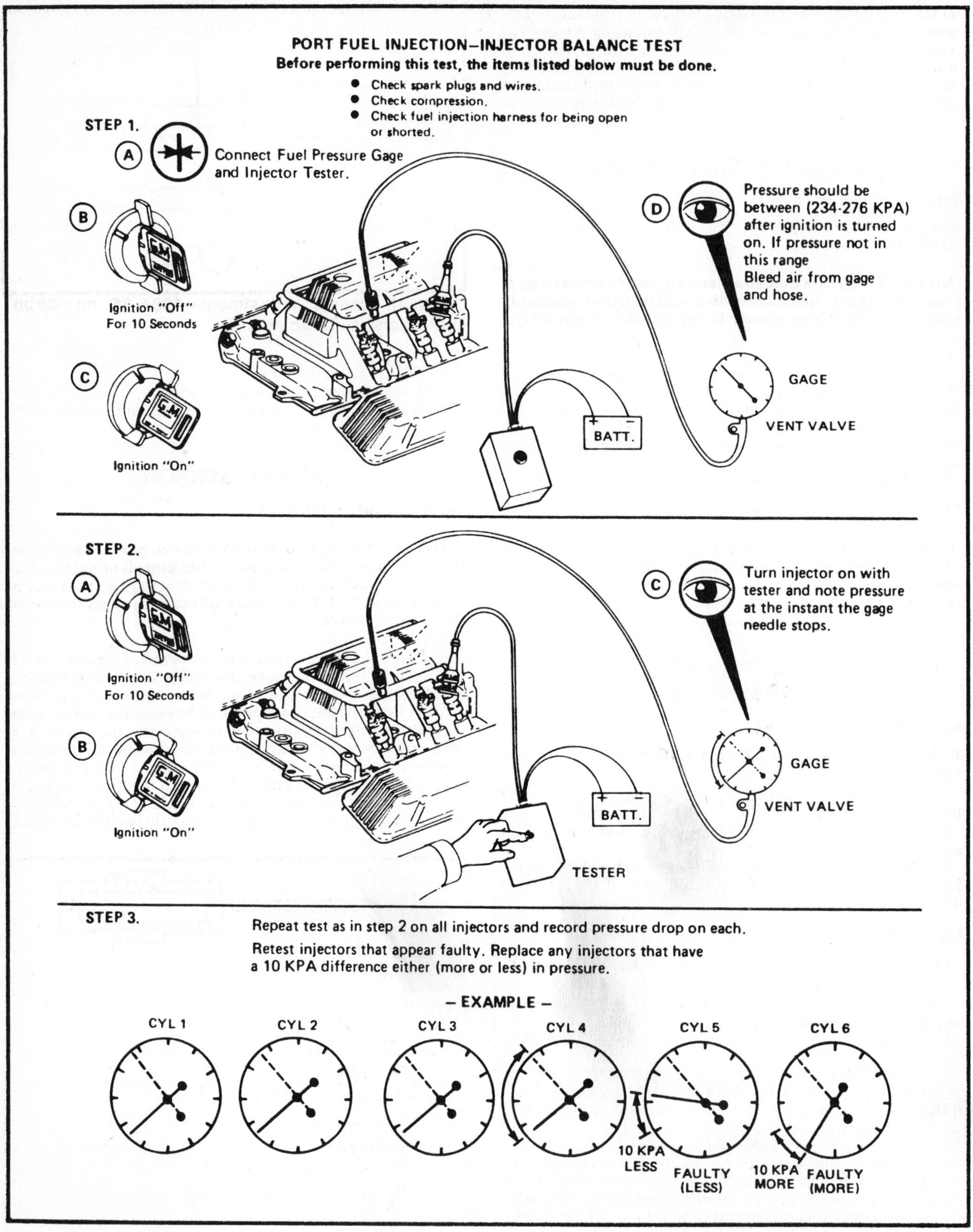

PORT FUEL INJECTION—INJECTOR BALANCE TEST
Before performing this test, the items listed below must be done.

- Check spark plugs and wires.
- Check compression.
- Check fuel injection harness for being open or shorted.

STEP 1.

(A) Connect Fuel Pressure Gage and Injector Tester.

(B) Ignition "Off" For 10 Seconds

(C) Ignition "On"

(D) Pressure should be between (234-276 KPA) after ignition is turned on. If pressure not in this range Bleed air from gage and hose.

GAGE

VENT VALVE

BATT.

STEP 2.

(A) Ignition "Off" For 10 Seconds

(B) Ignition "On"

(C) Turn injector on with tester and note pressure at the instant the gage needle stops.

GAGE

VENT VALVE

BATT.

TESTER

STEP 3.

Repeat test as in step 2 on all injectors and record pressure drop on each.

Retest injectors that appear faulty. Replace any injectors that have a 10 KPA difference either (more or less) in pressure.

— EXAMPLE —

CYL 1	CYL 2	CYL 3	CYL 4	CYL 5	CYL 6

10 KPA LESS   FAULTY (LESS)

10 KPA MORE   FAULTY (MORE)

Fuel injector balance test

fuel rail. Connect fuel gauge J-34730-1, or equivalent, to fuel pressure relief valve on the fuel rail. Wrap a rag around the pressure tap to absorb any leakage that may occur when installing the gauge.

5. Install bleed hose into a suitable container and open the the valve to bleed off the fuel pressure in the fuel system.

CAMSHAFT POSITION SENSOR

Removal and Installation

1984–85 NON-TURBO MODELS AND ALL TURBO MODELS

NOTE: If only the camshaft sensor needs replacing, it is not necessary to remove the entire drive assembly from the engine. The sensor is replaceable separately.

1. Disconnect negative battery cable.
2. Disconnect 14 terminal ignition module connector.
3. Disconnect spark plug wires from coil assembly.
4. Remove ignition module bracket assembly.
5. Disconnect three terminal sensor connector.
6. Remove two attaching screws securing sensor and remove sensor.
7. Installation is the reverse of removal.

1986–88 NON-TURBO MODELS

1. Disconnect negative battery cable.
2. Remove attaching screw securing sensor.
3. Disconnect three terminal sensor connector and remove sensor.
4. Installation is the reverse of removal.

CAMSHAFT POSITION SENSOR DRIVE ASSEMBLY

Removal and Installation

1984–85 NON-TURBO MODELS AND ALL TURBO MODELS

1. Remove camshaft position sensor and note the position of slot in rotating vane.
2. Remove bolt securing drive assembly in engine and remove sensor drive assembly.
3. Install in the reverse order of removal with slot in vane. CAMSHAFT SENSOR MUST BE TIMED TO SPECIFICATIONS.

Adjustment

NOTE: This adjustment does not effect spark timing.

1. Remove #1 spark plug and rotate engine until #1 cylinder comes up on compression stroke.
2. Mark harmonic balancer and rotate engine to 25° after TDC.
3. Remove spark plug wires from coil assembly.
4. Remove terminal "B" of the 3 terminal sensor connector on the ignition module side with a weatherpack removal tool J-28742-A or equivalent.
5. Connect a jumper wire between wire and connect.
6. Connect a voltmeter between jumper and ground.
7. With ignition ON and engine off, rotate camshaft sensor counterclockwise until the sensor switch just closes. This is indicated by the voltage reading going from high 5–12 volts to a low voltage 0–2 volts. The low voltage indicates the switch is closed.

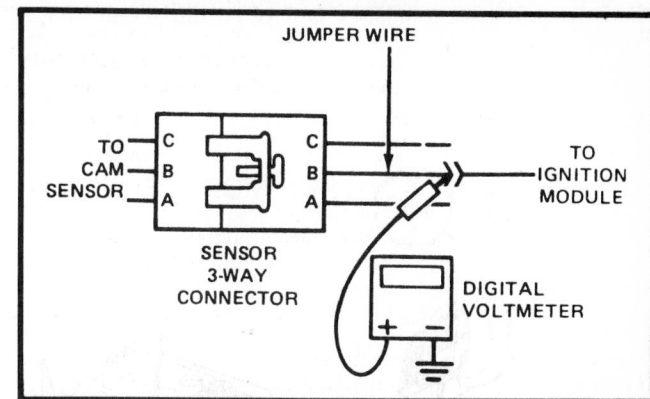

Camshaft sensor adjustment—1984–85 non-turbo models and all turbo models

8. Tighten retaining bolt.
9. Reinstall spark plug and plug wires.
10. Remove jumper wire and reinstall wire into terminal "B". Reconnect connector.

OXYGEN SENSOR

Removal and Installation

NOTE: The oxygen sensor uses a permanently attached pigtail and connector. This pigtail should not be removed from the oxygen sensor. Damage or removal of the pigtail or connector could affect proper operation of the oxygen sensor.

The oxygen sensor is installed in the exhaust manifold and is removed in the same manner as a spark plug. The sensor may be difficult to remove when the engine temperature is below 120°F (48°C) (so it may be a good idea to warm the engine up for approximately two minutes before removing the sensor) and excessive force may damage threads in the exhaust manifold or exhaust pipe. Exercise care when handling the oxygen sensor; the electrical connector and louvered end must be kept free of grease, dirt, or other contaminants. Avoid using cleaning solvents of any kind and don't drop or roughly handle the sensor.

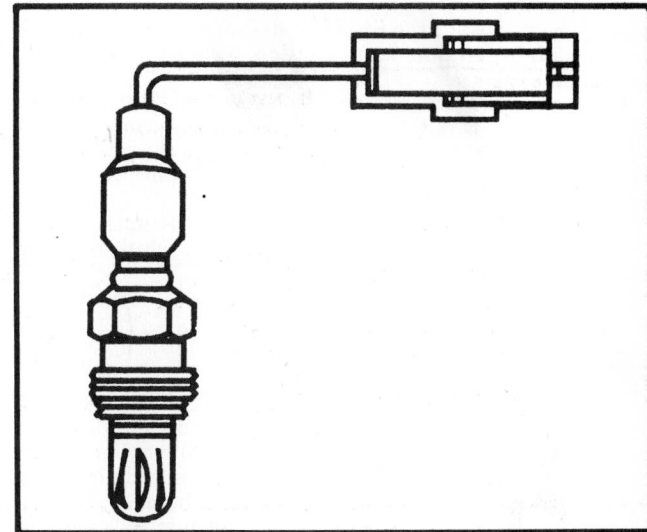

Oxygen (O$_2$) sensor

A special anti-seize compound is used on the oxygen sensor threads when installing and care should be used NOT to get compound on the sensor itself. Disconnect the negative battery cable when servicing the oxygen sensor and torque to 30 ft. lbs. (41 Nm) when installing.

ELECTRONIC CONTROL MODULE (ECM)

The electronic control module (ECM), usually located under the instrument panel, is the control center of the fuel injection system. It constantly looks at information from various sensors, and controls the system that affect vehicle performance.

The ECM also performs the diagnostic function of the system. It can recognize operational problems, alert the driver through the "Service Engine Soon" light and store a code or codes which identify the problem areas to aid the technician in making repairs.

CALPAK

A device called a CALPAK is used to allow fuel delivery if other parts of the ECM are damaged. It has an access door in the ECM, and removal and replacement procedures are the same as with the prom. If the CALPAK is missing, a code 52 will be set.

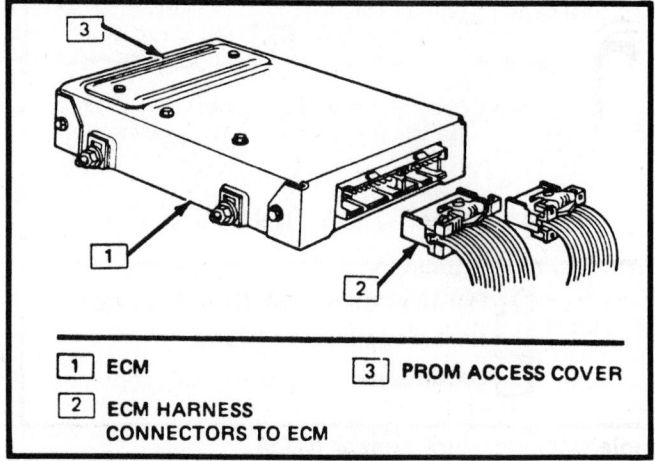

1 ECM		**3**	PROM ACCESS COVER
2 ECM HARNESS CONNECTORS TO ECM			

Electronic control module (ECM)

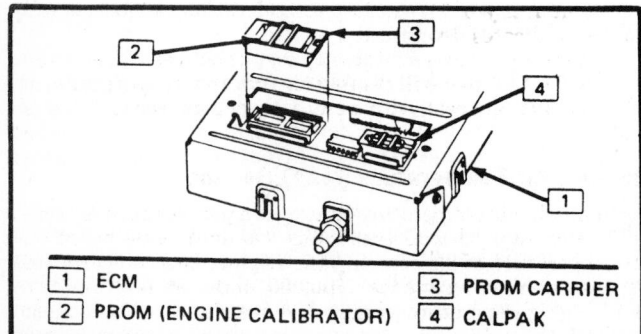

1 ECM	**3**	PROM CARRIER
2 PROM (ENGINE CALIBRATOR)	**4**	CALPAK

ECM prom and calpak locations

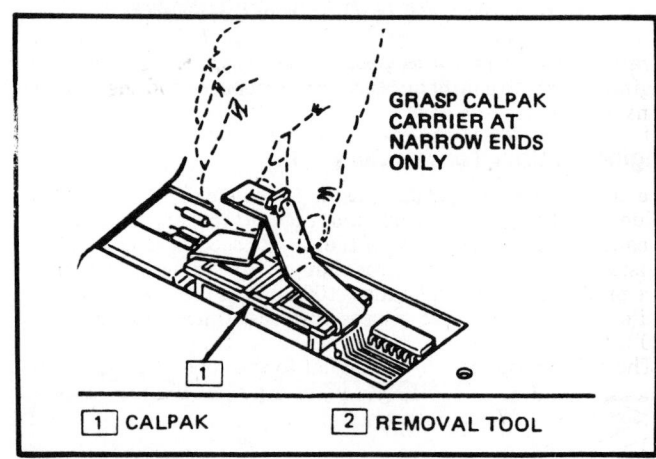

GRASP CALPAK CARRIER AT NARROW ENDS ONLY

1 CALPAK	**2**	REMOVAL TOOL

Calpak removal

PROM

To allow one model of the ECM to be used for many different vehicles, a device called a Calibrator (or PROM) is used. The prom is located inside the ECM and has information on the vehicle's weight, engine, transmission, axle ratio and other components.

While one ECM part number can be used by many different vehicles, a prom is very specific and must be used for the right vehicle. For this reason, it is very important to check the latest parts book and or service bulletin information for the correct prom part number when replacing the prom.

An ECM used for service (called a controller) comes without a prom. The prom from the old ECM must be carefully removed and installed in the new ECM.

ECM Function

The ECM supplies either 5 or 12 volts to power various sensors and or switches. This is done through resistances in the ECM which are so high in value that a test light will not light when connected to the circuit. In some cases, even an ordinary shop voltmeter will not give an accurate reading because its resistance is too low. Therefore, a 10 megohm input impedance digital voltmeter is required to assure accurate voltage readings.

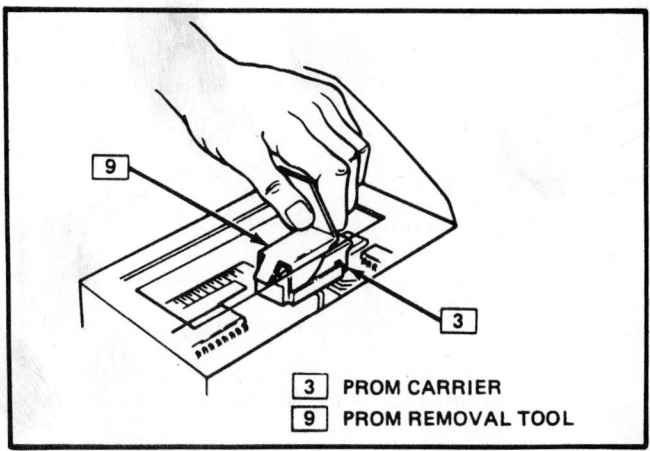

3 PROM CARRIER		
9 PROM REMOVAL TOOL		

Prom removal

The ECM controls output circuits such as injectors, IAC, coolant fan relay, etc. by controlling the ground circuit through transistors or a device called a quad driver.

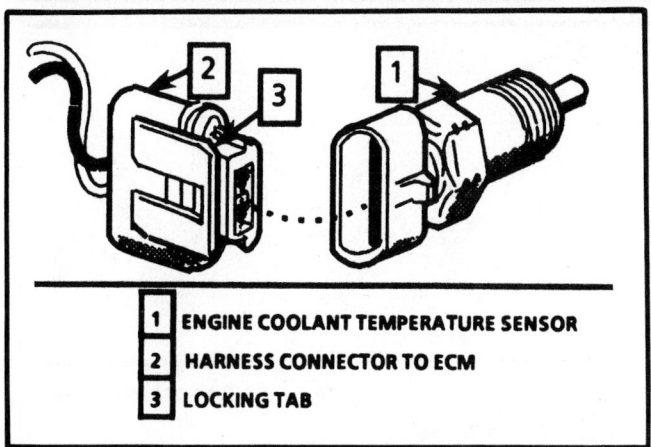

1	**ENGINE COOLANT TEMPERATURE SENSOR**
2	**HARNESS CONNECTOR TO ECM**
3	**LOCKING TAB**

Coolant temperature sensor (CTS)

INFORMATION DATA SENSORS

A variety of sensors provide information to the ECM regarding engine operating characteristics. These sensors and their functions are described below.

Engine Coolant Temperature

The coolant sensor is a thermister (a resistor which changes value based on temperature) mounted on the engine coolant stream. As the temperature of the engine coolant changes, the resistance of the coolant sensor changes. Low coolant temperature produces a high resistance (100,000 ohms at -40°C/-40°F), while high temperature causes low resistance (70 ohms at 130°C/266°F).

The ECM supplies a 5-volt signal to the coolant sensor and

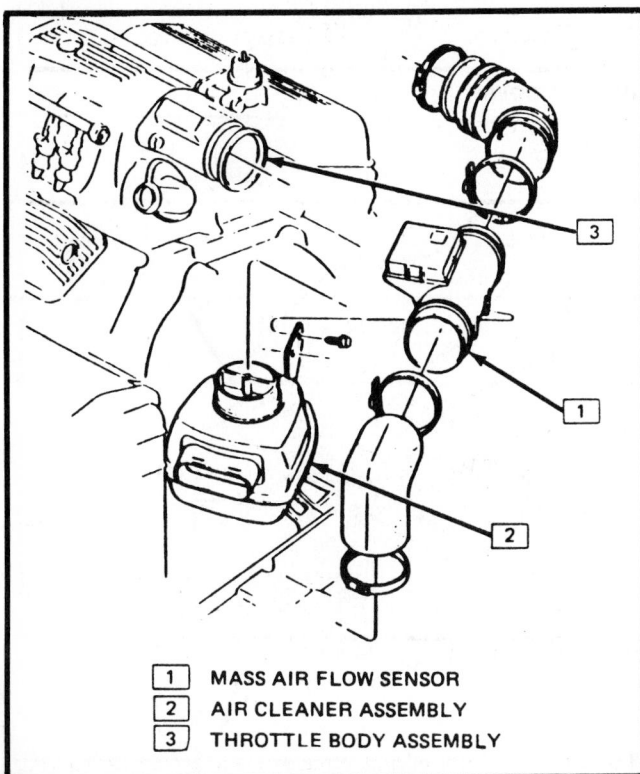

1	**MASS AIR FLOW SENSOR**
2	**AIR CLEANER ASSEMBLY**
3	**THROTTLE BODY ASSEMBLY**

Mass air flow (MAF) sensor location

measures the voltage that returns. By measuring the voltage change, the ECM determines the engine coolant temperature. This information is used to control fuel management, IAC, spark timing, EGR, canister purge and other engine operating conditions.

Oxygen Sensor

The exhaust oxygen sensor is mounted in the exhaust system where it can monitor the oxygen content of the exhaust gas stream. The oxygen content in the exhaust reacts with the oxygen sensor to produce a voltage output. This voltage ranges from approximately 100 millivolts (high oxygen - lean mixture) to 900 millivolts (low oxygen - rich mixture).

By monitoring the voltage output of the oxygen sensor, the ECM will determine what fuel mixture command to give to the injector (lean mixture-low voltage-rich command, rich mixture-high voltage lean command).

Remember that oxygen sensor indicates to the ECM what is happening in the exhaust. It does not cause things to happen. It is a type of gauge: high oxygen content = lean mixture; low oxygen content = rich mixture. The ECM adjust fuel to keep the system working.

Mass Air Flow Sensor (MAF)

The mass air flow sensor measures the amount of air which passes through it. The ECM uses this information to determine the operating condition of the engine, to control fuel delivery. A large quantity of air indicates acceleration, while a small quantity indicates deceleration or idle.

This sensor produces a frequency output between 32 and 150 hertz. A "SCAN" tool will display air flow in terms of grams of air per second (gm/sec), with a range from 3 gm/sec to 150 gm/sec.

Manifold Air Temperature (MAT) Sensor

The manifold air temperature sensor (is a part of the MAF sensor) is a resistor (thermistor), which changes value based on the temperature of air entering the engine. Low temperature produces a high resistance (100,000 ohms at -40°C/-40°F), while high temperature causes low resistance (70 ohms at 130°C/266°F).

The ECM supplies a 5 volt signal to the sensor through a resistor in the ECM and measures the voltage. The voltage will be high when the incoming air is cold and low when the air id hot. By measuring the voltage, the ECM calculates the incoming air temperature and uses this signal to compensate the MAF sensor signal based on temperature. The MAT sensor is also used to control spark timing.

Vehicle Speed Sensor (VSS)

NOTE: Vehicle should not be driven without a VSS as idle quality may be affected.

The vehicle speed sensor (VSS) is mounted behind the speedometer in the instrument cluster. It provides electrical pulses to the ECM from the speedometer head. The pulses indicate the road speed. The ECM uses this information to operate the IAC, canister purge, and TCC.

Some vehicles equipped with digital instrument clusters use a permanent magnet (PM) generator to provide the VSS signal. The PM generator is located in the transmission and replaces the speedometer cable. The signal from the PM generator drives a stepper motor which drives the odometer.

Throttle Position Sensor (TPS)

The throttle position sensor (TPS) is connected to the throttle shaft and is controlled by the throttle mechanism. A 5-volt reference signal is sent to the TPS from the ECM. As the throttle valve angle is changed (accelerator pedal moved), the resistance of the TPS also changes. At a closed throttle position, the resistance of the TPS is high, so the output voltage to the ECM will be low (approximately .5 volt). As the throttle plate opens, the resistance decreases so that, at wide open throttle, the output voltage should be approximately 5 volts.

By monitoring the output voltage from the TPS, the ECM can determine fuel delivery based on throttle valve angle (driver demand). The TPS can either be misadjusted, shorted, open or loose. Misadjustment might result in poor idle or poor wide-open throttle performance. An open TPS signals the ECM that the throttle is always closed, resulting in poor performance. This usually sets a Code 22. A shorted TPS gives the ECM a constant wide-open throttle signal and should set a Code 21. A loose TPS indicates to the ECM that the throttle is moving. This causes intermittent bursts of fuel from the injector and an unstable idle.

Park/Neutral Switch

NOTE: Vehicle should not be driven with the Park/Neutral switch disconnected as idle quality may be affected in Park or Neutral.

This switch indicates to the ECM when the transmission is in Park or Neutral.
A/C Compressor Clutch Engagement. This signal indicates to the ECM that the A/C compressor clutch is engaged.

1 PARK NEUTRAL SWITCH

Park/neutral switch

A/C "Request" Signal

This signal tells the ECM that the A/C selector switch is turned on and that the A/C pressure switches are closed. The ECM uses this to adjust the idle speed before turning on the A/C clutch. If this signal is not available to the ECM, the A/C compressor will be inoperative.

Power Steering Pressure Switch

This switch tells the ECM that the vehicle is in a parking maneuver. The ECM uses this information to compensate for additional engine load by moving the idle air control valve. The ECM will also turn off the A/C clutch when high pressure is detected.

Crankshaft Sensor

The crankshaft sensor provides a signal, through the ignition module, which the ECM uses as a reference to calculate rpm and crankshaft position.

Camshaft Sensor

The cam sensor sends a signal to the ECM, which uses it as a "sync pulse" to trigger the injectors in proper sequence.

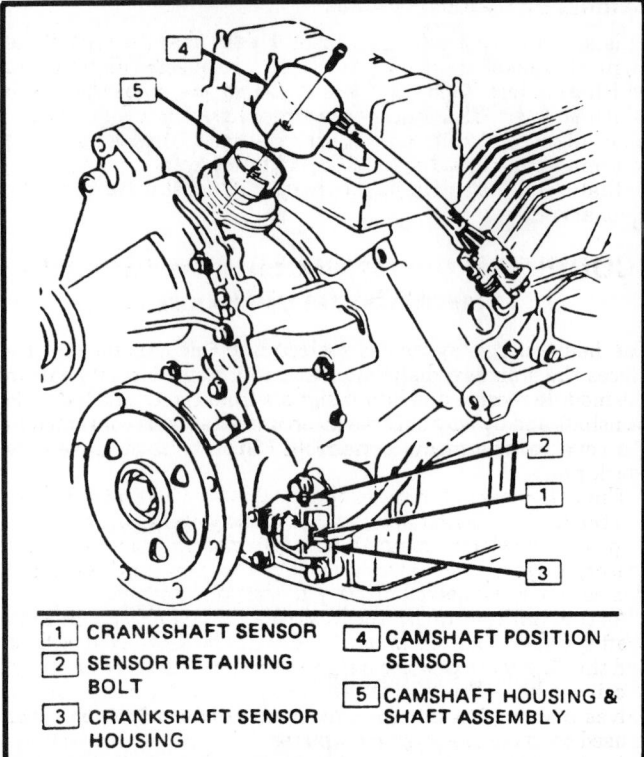

1	CRANKSHAFT SENSOR	4	CAMSHAFT POSITION SENSOR
2	SENSOR RETAINING BOLT	5	CAMSHAFT HOUSING & SHAFT ASSEMBLY
3	CRANKSHAFT SENSOR HOUSING		

Camshaft and crankshaft sensors—1984–85 non-turbo models and all turbo models

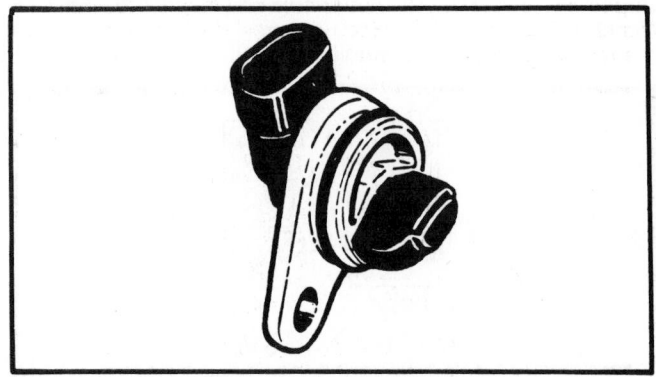

Camshaft position sensor—1986–88 non-turbo models

Crankshaft sensor

Detonation (Knock) Sensor

This sensor is a piezoelectric sensor located near the back of the engine (transmission end). It generates electrical impulses which are directly proportional to the frequency of the knock which is detected. A buffer then sorts these signals and eliminates all except for those frequency range of detonation. This information is passed to the ESC module and then to the ECM, so that the ignition timing advance can be retarded until the detonation stops.

COMPUTER CONTROLLED COIL IGNITION SYSTEM (C³I)

The heart of this system is a electronic coil module that replaces the standard distributor and coil. Logic circuits within the module receive and buffer signals from the crankshaft and camshaft and by way of three interconnected coils contained in the cover of the module, distribute high voltage current to spark plugs.

The C³I system eliminates the need for a distributor to control the flow or current between the battery and spark plugs. In its place is an electro-magnetic sensor consisting of a hall effect sensor, magnet and interruptor ring. The gear on the shaft of this sensor is connected directly to the camshaft gear.

As the camshaft turns, the interruptor ring, moving at camshaft speed (½ the engine rpm), rotates between the hall sensor and the magnet to produce a signal which is fed to the electronic coil module. This signal provides the exact position of the valves as they open and close. At the same time, the cam sensor is used to drive the engine oil pump.

Another sensor is mounted to the crankshaft. This sensor also consists of a hall sensor, magnet and interrupt ring. As with the cam sensor, the crankshaft causes the interruptor ring to rotate between the hall sensor and magnet to produce a signal which is fed to the electronic module. This signal gives the top center position of each piston.

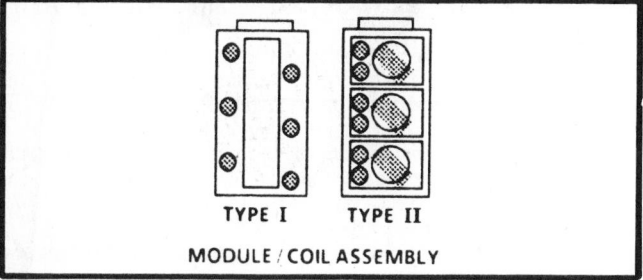

TYPE I   TYPE II

MODULE / COIL ASSEMBLY

ALDL CONNECTOR

The assembly line diagnostic link (ALDL) (or also known as the assembly line communication link (ALCL)) is a diagnostic connector located in the passenger compartment usually under the instrument panel (except Pontiac Fiero which is located in the console). The assembly plant were the vehicles originate use the connector to check the engine for proper operation before it leaves the plant. Terminal "B" is the diagnostic "Test" terminal (lead) and it can be connected to terminal "A", or ground, to enter the Diagnostic mode or the Field Service Mode.

FIELD SERVICE MODE

If the "Test" terminal is grounded with the engine running, the system will enter the the Field Service mode. In this mode, the "Check Engine Light" or "Service Engine Soon Light" will

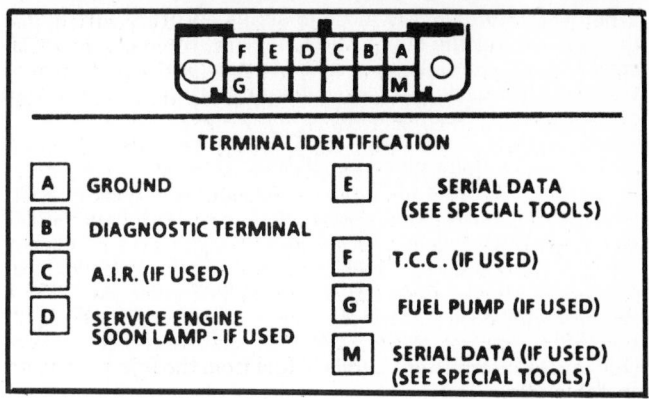

TERMINAL IDENTIFICATION

A	GROUND	**E**	SERIAL DATA (SEE SPECIAL TOOLS)
B	DIAGNOSTIC TERMINAL		
C	A.I.R. (IF USED)	**F**	T.C.C. (IF USED)
D	SERVICE ENGINE SOON LAMP - IF USED	**G**	FUEL PUMP (IF USED)
		M	SERIAL DATA (IF USED) (SEE SPECIAL TOOLS)

show whether the system is in Open loop or Closed loop. In Open loop the light flashes two and one half times per second. In Closed loop the light flashes once per second. Also in closed loop, the light will stay OUT most of the time if the system is too lean. It will stay ON most of the time if the system is too rich. In either case the Field Service mode check, which is part of the Diagnostic circuit check, will lead the technician into choosing the correct diagnostic chart to refer to.

CLEARING THE TROUBLE CODES

When the ECM finds a problem with the system, the "Check Engine Light" or "Service Engine Soon Light" will come ON and a trouble code will be recorded in the ECM memory. If the problem is intermittent, the light will go out after 10 seconds, when the fault goes away. However the trouble code will stay in the ECM memory until the battery voltage to the ECM is removed. Removing the battery voltage for 10 seconds will clear all trouble codes. Do this by disconnecting the ECM harness from the positive battery terminal pigtail for 10 seconds with the key in the OFF position, or by removing the ECM fuse for 10 seconds with the key OFF.

CLOSED LOOP FUEL CONTROL

The purpose of closed loop fuel control is to precisely maintain an air/fuel mixture 14.7:1. When the air/fuel mixture is maintained at 14.7:1, the catalytic converter is able to operate at maximum efficiency which results in lower emission levels.

Since the ECM controls the air/fuel mixture, it needs to check its output and correct the fuel mixture for deviations from the "Ideal" ratio. The oxygen sensor feeds this output information back to the ECM.

ECM LEARNING ABILITY

The ECM has a "learning" capability. If the battery is disconnected the "learning" process has to begin all over again. A change may be noted in the vehicle's performance. To "teach" the ECM, insure the vehicle is at operating temperature and drive at part throttle, with moderate acceleration and idle conditions, until performance returns.

Engine Performance Diagnosis

CHECK ENGINE LIGHT OR SERVICE ENGINE SOON LIGHT

The "Check Engine" or "Service Engine Soon" light on the instrument panel is used as a warning lamp to tell the driver that a problem has occurred in the electronic engine control system.

When the self-diagnosis mode is activated by grounding the test terminal of the diagnostic connector, the light will flash stored trouble codes to help isolate system problems. The electronic control module (ECM) has a memory that knows what certain engine sensors should be under certain conditions. If a sensor reading is not what the ECM thinks it should be, the control unit will illuminate the light and store a trouble code in its memory. The trouble code indicates what circuit the problem is in, each circuit consisting of a sensor, the wiring harness and connectors to it and the ECM.

The Assembly Line Diagnostic Link (ALDL) (described earlier in this section) can be used as a diagnostic aid. By connecting terminals A and B together with a jumper wire, the diagnostic mode is activated and the control unit will begin to flash trouble codes using the "Check Engine" or "Service Engine Soon" light.

When the test terminal is grounded with the key ON and the engine stopped, the ECM will display code 12 to show that the system is working. The ECM will usually display code 12 three times, then start to display any stored trouble codes. If no trouble codes are stored, the ECM will continue to display code 12 until the test terminal is disconnected. Each trouble code will be flashed three times, then code 12 sill display again. The ECM will also energize all controlled relays and solenoids when in the diagnostic mode to check function. When the test terminal is grounded with the engine running, it will cause the ECM to enter the Field Service Mode. In this mode, the service engine soon light will indicate whether the system is in Open or Closed Loop operation. In open loop, the light will flash 2-1/2 times per second; in closed loop, the light will flash once per second. In closed loop, the light will stay out most of the time if the system is too lean and will stay on most of the time if the system is too rich.

NOTE: The vehicle may be driven in the Field Service mode and system evaluated at any steady road speed. This mode us useful in diagnosing driveability problems where the system is rich or lean too long.

Trouble codes should be cleared after service is completed. To clear the trouble code memory, disconnect the battery for at least 10 seconds. This may be accomplished by disconnecting the ECM harness from the positive battery pigtail or by removing the ECM fuse.

─────────── CAUTION ───────────

The ignition switch must be OFF when disconnecting or reconnecting power to the ECM. The vehicle should be driven after the ECM memory is cleared to allow the system to readjust itself. The vehicle should be driven at part throttle under moderate acceleration with the engine at normal operating temperature. A change is performance should be noted initially, but normal performance should return quickly.

ELECTRONIC FUEL INJECTION — ALDL TESTER INFORMATION

An ALDL display unit (ALDL tester, scanner, monitor, etc), allows a technician to read the engine control system information from the ALDL connector under the instrument panel. It can provide information faster than a digital voltmeter or ohmmeter can. The scan tool does not diagnose the exact location of the problem. The tool supplies information about the ECM (and BCM if equipped), the information that it is receiving and the commands that it is sending plus special information such as integrator and block learn. To use an ALDL display tool you should understand throughly how an engine control system operates.

An ALDL scanner or monitor puts a fuel injection system into a special test mode. This mode commands an idle speed of 1000 rpm. The idle quality cannot be evaluated with a tester plugged in. Also the test mode commands a fixed spark with no advance. On vehicles with Electronic Spark Control (ESC) there will be a fixed spark, but it will be advanced. On vehicles with ESC there might be a serious spark knock, this spark knock could be bad enough so as not being able to road test the vehicle in the ALDL test mode. Be sure to check the tool manufacturer for instructions on special test modes which should overcome these limitations.

When a tester is used with a fuel injected engine it by-passes the timer that keeps the system in OPEN loop for a certain period of time. When all CLOSED loop conditions are met, the engine will go into CLOSED loop as soon as the vehicle is started. This means that the air management system will not function properly and air may go directly to the converter as soon as the engine is started.

These tools cannot diagnose everything. They do not tell the technician where a problem is located in a circuit. The diagnostic charts to pinpoint the problems must still be used. These tester's do not let a technician know if a solenoid or relay has been turned on. They only tell the technician the ECM command. To find out if a solenoid has been turned on, check it with a suitable test light or digital voltmeter, or see if vacuum through the solenoid changes.

REVISED ECM REPLACEMENT PROCEDURE - CHART C-1

1982 through 1987 ECM Equipped Vehicles

Since 1982, most ECM's have used an intergrated circuit (IC) in place of separate transistors to turn ON or OFF different components controlled by the ECM. These IC's are called quad drivers (QDR). Each quad driver has four separate outputs, meaning it can turn ON or OFF four different items independently.

A failed quad driver usually results in an ECM output becoming either shorted to ground or open. Many times all four quad drivers output will be inoperative if just one vehicle circuit is faulty.

This revised diagnosis incorporates new test procedures designed to identify a damaged quad drivers. Once identified, the circuit must be repaired to reduce the incidence of repeat ECM failures.

The following charts are to be used to replace the current service procedure for either:

1. Chart C-1 ECM replacement check.
2. Any diagnostic chart where "replace ECM" is the conclusion, especially if a footnote indicates checking certain circuits for less than the 20 ohms resistance.

It is strongly suggested that this chart be used whenever an ECM replacement is indicated for 1982-87 vehicles.

NOTE: For complete system diagnostics, please refer to the diagnostic charts following the Multiport Fuel Injection Section. Due to the large amount of GM vehicles being covered, some will use more sensors than others. The steps and procedures can be altered as required, if necessary, according to the specific model being diagnosed. The wiring diagrams and schematics may not coincide with every GM vehicle in use. If this situation should arise, use the wiring diagram or schematic as a general guide.